# THE 1990 Elias Baseball Analyst

# THE 1990 Elias Baseball Analyst

Seymour Siwoff, Steve Hirdt,
Peter Hirdt & Tom Hirdt

COLLIER BOOKS
Macmillan Publishing Company
New York
COLLIER MACMILLAN PUBLISHERS
London

Collier Books
Macmillan Publishing Company
866 Third Avenue, New York, NY 10022
Collier Macmillan Canada, Inc.

"The Library of Congress has cataloged this serial publication as follows:".

The . . . Elias baseball analyst.—1985– —New York:
Collier Books, c1985–

v.; 28 cm.

Annual.
Re-arrangement of material issued in a series of computerized reports called: The Player analysis.
Produced by the Elias Sports Bureau.
Editors for 1989– by S. Siwoff, S. Hirdt, P. Hirdt, and T. Hirdt.

1. Baseball—United States—Statistics—Periodicals. 2. National League of Professional Baseball Clubs—Statistics—Periodicals. 3. Baseball—Statistics—
1. Baseball—United States—Statistics—Periodicals. 2. National League of Periodicals. 4. Baseball—Miscellanea—Periodicals. I. Siwoff, Seymour. II. Hirdt, Steve. III. Hirdt, Peter. IV. Hirdt, Tom. V. Elias Sports Bureau. VI. Player analysis. VII. Title: Baseball analyst.
GV877.E44 85-643022
796.357'0973—dc19
AACR 2 MARC-S

ISBN 0-02-028712-7

Printed in the United States of America

# Contents

# ACKNOWLEDGEMENTS

In recognition of the invaluable assistance provided by so many, the authors would like to extend their thanks to the following:

The rest of the Elias Sports Bureau staff: Rocky Avakian, Jay Chesler, John Chymczuk, Keung Hui, Frank Labombarda, John Labombarda, Santo Labombarda, Chris Lasch, Bob Rosen, Alex Stern, Christopher Thorn, and Bob Waterman.

Our computer consultants: Warren Bannerman, Carl Friedberg, Larry Meisner, Paul Mort, Bernie Schanker, and Gil Traub.

Our agent, Nat Sobel, and his staff.

Our publicists, Bryan Harris and Tony Signore, of Mike Cohen Communications.

Macmillan Publishing: Andrew Attaway, Jeanine Bucek, Jackie Dickens, David Frost, Peggy Goddard, Paul Heacock, Bob Keefe, Casey Lee, Cheryl Mamaril, Fred Richardson, Bill Rosen, Ken Samelson, and Rick Wolff.

Our families, and those of all the men and women listed above, who sacrificed their own time throughout the year in order to make this book happen.

---

Dedicated to the memory of
A. Bartlett Giamatti

*In a lifetime of baseball,*
*he was our greatest gift.*

---

# THE
# 1990
# Elias Baseball
# Analyst

# I
# Introduction

# INTRODUCTION

Flip through these pages, and you'll see a book of numbers. Read it, and you'll realize that this is really a book of ideas. Our milieu is baseball. Numbers are simply our tools.

Before you get the wrong idea, we're not the kind of fans who can tell you, off the tops of our heads, how many home runs Hank Aaron hit in 1966, or recite the roster of the 1978 Detroit Tigers, or name the players who've won consecutive MVP awards. Unless, of course, we happen to have a copy of *The Baseball Encyclopedia* nearby. And we're *definitely* not the type to foist upon you some arcane mathematical labyrinth that alleges to tell you, under the guise of enlightened truth, how many home runs Honus Wagner would have hit had he played today, or what Wade Boggs would have batted in the 1920s.

But we are the type of baseball fans who are constantly wondering—not about esoteric nonsense, but about the same things you probably discuss over a beer or two while watching the game of the week with your friends. Frankly, that's where most of our ideas are hatched—at the ballpark or in front of the television. Because first and foremost, we like baseball. Not numbers, not jargon. Just baseball, with hot dogs and a cold one.

Since this is our sixth edition, you don't have to take our word for any of this. Let us tell you about some of the ideas we've presented in past years. You be the judge.

Can a starting pitcher contribute as much to a team's performance in just 35 starts as an everyday player does? How many wins does the addition of a star player contribute to a team over the course of a season? How about a top starting pitcher? Or a manager? Are rookie managers with no minor league experience at a disadvantage? Speaking of which, who was the best manager of all time? We tackled that one, too. Not with outrageous opinion, but with cold, hard fact.

Can you handicap a baseball team according to past performances? In other words, what does a baseball team's record over its last few games tell us about its next game? And how about individual players—batters and pitchers—do they really get hot and cold, or is that just an illusion?

Who are baseball's real clutch hitters? Prior to the publication of our first edition in 1985, there was no source for statistics on how batters and pitchers performed with men in scoring position or in the late innings of close games. Now when someone claims that Wade Boggs is a poor clutch hitter, or that Fred Lynn is a good one, you can set them straight. With the help of your *Analyst.*

How should a manager make out his lineup? What's the effect of moving a power hitter to the leadoff spot? Or dropping his best home-run hitter to the sixth or seventh slot? We've not only examined how to construct a batting order, but we've analyzed the value or cost of various changes a manager can make.

We also introduced the first new basis for platooning since Casey Stengel popularized the lefty-righty system. We discovered a few years ago that ground-ball hitters batted much better against fly-ball pitchers than they did against ground-ball pitchers. On the other hand, fly-ball hitters were more effective against ground-ball pitchers. Since then, we've liberally sprinkled our player comments with information on their ground- and fly-ball tendencies.

Does a rotation of alternating junkballers and hard throwers benefit the pitchers? Why does Cal Ripken's iron-man streak hurt the Orioles? Why is the Metrodome's nickname "Homerdome" a misnomer? Does a catcher have an advantage hitting against pitchers for whom he used to call signals? Can a team benefit from taking one of its top starters and using him as its relief stopper? Does good pitching really stop good hitting?

To what extent are southpaws hurt by Fenway Park's Green Monster? What makes Dave Winfield the most underappreciated superstar of the '80s? How many runs does Ozzie Smith save with his glove? What's the best leading indicator of a team ready to improve? Does a late-game, come-from-behind win produce a euphoric carryover effect that helps a team in its next few games as well?

Are there really batters' umpires, with wide strike zones, and pitchers' umpires, with narrow ones? If so, which umpires fall into which categories? Can a manager adjust his pitching rotation to exploit the rotation of the umpires, using his best control pitchers when umpires with smaller zones work the plate? To what extent are players intimidated when they're hit with pitches? Do top hard-throwing relief pitchers really thrive on work? Do veteran players make better pinch hitters than young ones? Can veteran pitchers exploit young hitters?

Was there really a livelier baseball in 1987? Was the fuss over the 40-40 club warranted or overdone? What lesson of life could Alvin Davis learn from Cher? Which was the best young pitching staff in the history of baseball? And if we'd known then what we know today, why would the stunning victory by the 1969 Mets have been far less surprising?

We've examined all those questions and many more in our past five editions. And this year's *Analyst* is loaded with more of the same. For instance: What do spring training statistics tell us about the upcoming season? Who is the best batting coach in baseball, and why? What multi million-dollar free agent may be nothing more than an expensive pinch hitter by the end of the season? What triggered the collapse of the Detroit Tigers? Did Kansas City really need Mark Davis? Who will be the first serious challenger to Pete Rose's hits record? Has the next dynasty finally arrived, in the form of the Oakland A's? Who produced even more talent than the New York Yankees during their glory years? That's only a sample of what's inside.

Maybe you're wondering, What about the player information? Isn't this the book that the announcers always quote from? That's right. You'll find detailed statistics on nearly 600 players, along with a commentary highlighting the most significant, interesting, and sometime humourous facts on each, including opponents that each player loves and hates to face.

Of course, there's lots more, too. A baseball season lasts from spring to autumn, and we've tried to load each edition of the *Analyst* with enough information to keep you reading right through the final postseason contests. And we trust you'll find the 1990 edition to be the best ever.

# II
# Team Section

# *Team Section*

The Team Section consists of comments and statistics for each of the twenty-six major-league teams. The examples here, and in all of the section introductions, just happen to be taken from the 1985 season.

**WON-LOST RECORD BY STARTING POSITION**

| BALTIMORE 83-78 | C | 1B | 2B | 3B | SS | LF | CF | RF | P | DH | Leadoff | Relief | Starts |
|---|---|---|---|---|---|---|---|---|---|---|---|---|---|
| Don Aase | - | - | - | - | - | - | - | - | - | - | - | 26-28 | - |
| Eric Bell | - | - | - | - | - | - | - | - | - | - | - | 0-4 | - |
| Mike Boddicker | - | - | - | - | - | - | - | - | 13-19 | - | - | - | 13-19 |
| Fritz Connally | - | 1-0 | - | 12-15 | - | - | - | - | - | 1-0 | - | - | 14-15 |
| Rich Dauer | - | - | 32-31 | 4-4 | - | - | - | - | - | - | - | - | 36-35 |
| Storm Davis | - | - | - | - | - | - | - | - | 16-12 | - | - | 0-3 | 16-12 |
| Rick Dempsey | 57-56 | - | - | - | - | - | - | - | - | - | - | - | 57-56 |
| Ken Dixon | - | - | - | - | - | - | - | - | 10-8 | - | - | 2-14 | 10-8 |
| Jim Dwyer | - | - | - | - | - | 16-20 | - | 16-9 | - | 0-1 | 9-6 | - | 32-30 |
| Mike Flanagan | - | - | - | - | - | - | - | - | 7-8 | - | - | - | 7-8 |
| Dan Ford | - | - | - | - | - | - | - | - | - | 10-6 | 5-5 | - | 10-6 |
| Wayne Gross | - | 0-5 | - | 30-27 | - | - | - | - | - | 1-3 | - | - | 31-35 |
| John Habyan | - | - | - | - | - | - | - | - | - | - | - | 1-1 | - |
| Brad Havens | - | - | - | - | - | - | - | - | 0-1 | - | - | 2-5 | 0-1 |
| Leo Hernandez | - | - | - | - | - | - | - | - | - | 0-4 | - | - | 0-4 |
| Phil Huffman | - | - | - | - | - | - | - | - | 1-0 | - | - | 0-1 | 1-0 |
| Lee Lacy | - | - | - | - | - | - | - | 51-61 | - | 3-1 | 16-20 | - | 54-62 |
| John Lowenstein | - | - | - | - | - | 1-3 | - | - | - | 2-2 | - | - | 3-5 |

The first table following the team comments is the Won-Lost Record by Starting Position chart. This chart lists, for each player on a team, the team's won-lost record in games started by that player at each position, in the leadoff spot in the lineup, and in games in which a pitcher appeared in relief. (This last is included to give some insight into how the manager chose to use his relief staff.) The players are listed in alphabetical order.

Following this table is a series of eight charts detailing the performance of each player and pitcher on the team who played at least semiregularly. Included are all players who had at least 200 plate appearances in the season, all pitchers who faced at least 200 batters, and selected individuals who did not meet the standard but were still significant enough to merit inclusion.

**Overall Batting Compared to Late Inning Pressure Situations**

| | | BA | Rank | SA | Rank | OBA | Rank | HR % | Rank | BB % | Rank | SO % | Rank | RDI % | Rank |
|---|---|---|---|---|---|---|---|---|---|---|---|---|---|---|---|
| Rich Dauer | Overall | .202 | 155 | .264 | 154 | .275 | 148 | 0.96 | 129 | 8.55 | 73 | 2.99 | 1 | .200 | -- |
| | Pressure | .118 | -- | .118 | -- | .118 | -- | 0.00 | -- | 0.00 | -- | 0.00 | -- | .000 | -- |
| Rick Dempsey | Overall | .254 | 99 | .406 | 88 | .345 | 50 | 3.31 | 61 | 11.90 | 30 | 20.71 | 149 | .318 | 48 |
| | Pressure | .171 | 149 | .293 | 124 | .286 | 118 | 2.44 | 77 | 14.00 | 30 | 24.00 | 146 | .286 | -- |
| Jim Dwyer | Overall | .249 | 106 | .399 | 95 | .353 | 36 | 3.00 | 73 | 13.50 | 16 | 11.31 | 50 | .324 | 43 |
| | Pressure | .344 | 13 | .563 | 10 | .500 | 2 | 3.13 | 56 | 23.81 | 2 | 14.29 | 82 | .455 | 12 |
| Wayne Gross | Overall | .235 | 134 | .424 | 69 | .369 | 17 | 5.07 | 17 | 17.42 | 2 | 18.18 | 133 | .118 | 163 |
| | Pressure | .184 | 143 | .316 | 113 | .225 | 149 | 2.63 | 69 | 5.00 | 124 | 20.00 | 133 | .100 | 155 |
| Lee Lacy | Overall | .293 | 22 | .409 | 82 | .343 | 52 | 1.83 | 105 | 7.22 | 103 | 17.59 | 124 | .262 | 113 |
| | Pressure | .297 | 40 | .453 | 44 | .378 | 33 | 4.69 | 38 | 10.81 | 56 | 16.22 | 100 | .167 | 128 |
| Fred Lynn | Overall | .263 | 78 | .449 | 41 | .339 | 63 | 5.13 | 15 | 10.43 | 40 | 19.69 | 140 | .285 | 88 |
| | Pressure | .231 | 104 | .481 | 34 | .333 | 73 | 7.69 | 11 | 13.33 | 35 | 23.33 | 143 | .214 | 111 |
| Eddie Murray | Overall | .297 | 16 | .523 | 4 | .383 | 6 | 5.32 | 13 | 12.41 | 24 | 10.04 | 42 | .428 | 4 |
| | Pressure | .333 | 15 | .682 | 3 | .400 | 23 | 9.09 | 4 | 10.67 | 57 | 8.00 | 23 | .636 | 1 |
| Floyd Rayford | Overall | .306 | 9 | .521 | 5 | .324 | 84 | 5.01 | 19 | 2.69 | 156 | 18.55 | 136 | .214 | 143 |
| | Pressure | .268 | 64 | .585 | 8 | .333 | 73 | 7.32 | 12 | 8.89 | 79 | 24.44 | 149 | .250 | 87 |
| Cal Ripken | Overall | .282 | 39 | .469 | 25 | .347 | 47 | 4.05 | 44 | 9.33 | 57 | 9.47 | 37 | .378 | 9 |
| | Pressure | .292 | 43 | .528 | 23 | .366 | 41 | 6.94 | 15 | 10.98 | 54 | 9.76 | 37 | .250 | 87 |
| Gary Roenicke | Overall | .218 | 151 | .458 | 30 | .342 | 57 | 6.67 | 4 | 16.06 | 4 | 13.14 | 77 | .364 | 19 |
| | Pressure | .043 | -- | .174 | -- | .185 | -- | 4.35 | -- | 14.81 | -- | 14.81 | -- | .167 | -- |
| Larry Sheets | Overall | .262 | 81 | .442 | 49 | .323 | 90 | 5.18 | 14 | 7.76 | 92 | 14.40 | 98 | .330 | 35 |
| | Pressure | .235 | 102 | .412 | 71 | .291 | 116 | 5.88 | 25 | 7.27 | 101 | 20.00 | 133 | .273 | 78 |
| John Shelby | Overall | .283 | 38 | .434 | 57 | .307 | 121 | 3.41 | 60 | 3.27 | 154 | 20.56 | 147 | .333 | 31 |
| | Pressure | .200 | 130 | .286 | 127 | .222 | 150 | 0.00 | 113 | 2.78 | 143 | 25.00 | 150 | .250 | 87 |
| Alan Wiggins | Overall | .285 | 35 | .349 | 130 | .353 | 38 | 0.00 | 154 | 8.66 | 68 | 4.78 | 2 | .339 | 29 |
| | Pressure | .308 | 32 | .346 | 94 | .438 | 9 | 0.00 | 113 | 18.18 | 7 | 3.03 | 4 | .400 | 22 |
| Mike Young | Overall | .273 | 59 | .513 | 11 | .348 | 43 | 6.22 | 6 | 9.52 | 52 | 20.63 | 148 | .293 | 73 |
| | Pressure | .222 | 114 | .426 | 56 | .311 | 93 | 5.56 | 30 | 11.48 | 52 | 18.03 | 118 | .333 | 55 |

## Column Headings Information

| | |
|---|---|
| BA | Batting Average |
| SA | Slugging Average |
| OBA | On-Base Average |
| HR% | Home Run Percentage (home runs per 100 at bats) |
| BB% | Base-on-Balls Percentage (bases on balls per 100 plate appearances) |
| SO% | Strikeout Percentage (strikeouts per 100 plate appearances) |
| RBI% | Percentage of Runs Batted In (per 100 opportunities) |

Each chart provides a statistical breakdown of player performance in a selected category. For each category, the player's average or percentage is given, along with his ranking within the league. This enables us to see at a glance that while Jim Dwyer ranked 95th in the league in slugging overall in 1985, he ranked tenth in pressure situations (see below). Rankings in each category are listed for the 162 players and 145 pitchers with the most plate appearances or batters faced in the category (plus ties) in the American League, and the top 136 batters and 125 pitchers (plus ties) in the National League. If a player does not qualify under this standard, no ranking is listed. (For a more detailed description of the methods used in determining the number of qualifiers for a given category, see the introduction to the Leaders Section.)

The batter charts list breakdowns against left-handed and right-handed pitching, performance with bases empty and runners on base, and overall performance for the season compared with performance in pressure situations (all at bats occurring in the seventh inning or later with the score tied or the batter's team trailing by one, two, or three runs, or four runs with the bases loaded).

The final batter chart lists miscellaneous comparisons for each player, giving his batting average on grass fields and artificial turf; in home games and in road games; with runners in scoring position and with runners in scoring position and two out; on-base average leading off an inning; and the percentage of runners he drove in from third base with less than two out. (For players who played for more than one team in a league, all totals are combined. The "home" totals for Ken Phelps, for example, include all games played in Oakland when he was with the Athletics, and all games played in New York while he was with the Yankees.)

On each chart, following the individual batter totals, are the team's averages for each category, and the team's ranking within the league. For purposes of comparison, the overall league average is also included.

The pitcher charts list breakdowns against left-handed and right-handed batters, performance with bases empty and runners on base, and overall performance for the season compared with performance in pressure situations (against all batters in the seventh inning or later with the score tied or the pitcher's team leading or trailing by one or two runs).

The final pitcher chart lists miscellaneous comparisons for each pitcher giving his opponents' batting average on grass fields and artificial turf; in home games and in road games; with runners in scoring position and with runners in scoring position and two out; and opponents' on-base average leading off an inning.

On each chart, following the individual pitcher statistics, are the team's averages for each category, and the team's ranking within the league. For purposes of comparison, the overall league average is also included.

For a detailed discussion of the use of opposing batters' records to examine pitching performance, see the introduction to the Pitcher Section.

# American League

# BALTIMORE ORIOLES

- **Spring training results *do* matter!**
- **Tips for fantasy league players.**

For those who think spring training results are meaningless, consider this fact: Last spring, the Baltimore Orioles—less than a year removed from their record 21–game losing streak—identified themselves in Florida as one of the prime turnaround candidates for the 1989 season. But only, of course, to those who knew how to interpret the signal. To refresh your memory, Baltimore compiled a .483 winning percentage (14–15) during the 1989 exhibition season. That might not sound like much, but that's the point. It was 147 points higher than their 1988 regular-season mark. And it's the margin of increase or decrease that's important here. Until now, we've been looking for the wrong signals.

There's a rule for interpreting spring training results that's as simple as it is effective in the determination of a team's direction in the season to follow. Teams that attain a better winning percentage in spring training than in the previous regular season are likely to win more games in the coming regular season than they did the year before. Conversely, teams that perform worse in spring training are unlikely to do so. The following table shows the movement of all teams from 1981 through 1989, improvement or decline from one regular season to the next. The teams are classified according to their spring training records relative to their records in the previous regular season.

| | During Regular Season | |
|---|---|---|
| | Improved | Declined |
| Up in spring training | 78 (69%) | 32 (28%) |
| Down in spring training | 36 (30%) | 79 (66%) |

Simply stated, a team's direction in the regular season usually mirrors the direction taken in the spring. To be more exact, two-thirds of all teams move in the same direction during the regular season that they travelled during the exhibition season. But there's an even stronger relationship if we examine the teams that show the greatest improvement in spring training. Let's divide the "up in spring training" group into teams that show moderate gains, and those that play at least 100 points better in spring training that they did in the previous regular season. Here are those results:

| | During Regular Season | |
|---|---|---|
| | Improved | Declined |
| Up by 100 points or more | 42 (86%) | 7 (14%) |
| Up by less than 100 points | 36 (56%) | 25 (39%) |

Teams that show a 100–point improvement in spring training are almost guaranteed to improve from the previous season to the following one. And the key word there is *almost*, because a 100–point preseason increase is actually Signal Two in a two-step method for identifying teams that are a *dead lock* to improve.

Over the past few seasons, we've written that a team's record in one-run games is the best leading indicator for its direction the following season: A good record in one-run games usually precedes a down season; a poor one generally precedes a year of improvement. (For the details on this technique, see the 1989 *Analyst*, pp. 435–436; 1988, p. 146; 1987, pp. 122–123. For a related technique, see the Toronto essay in this edition, pp. 89–90.) A record at least five games below .500 in one-run games in the year preceding the breakthrough spring training constitutes Signal One. And in this case, One plus Two equals *guaranteed* improvement in the upcoming season.

From 1980 through 1988, 61 teams played at least five games below .500 in one-run contests. Of them, 21 had winning percentages in the following spring training at least 100 points higher than their overall mark the year before. *All 21 of those teams improved their overall records in the season that followed.*

Even more astounding than this seemingly foolproof method for spotting teams on the rise are the margins by which these teams improve. Every one of the 21 teams gained at least five wins; 17 of them improved by the equivalent of 10 wins or more. The average gain was 15 wins. The largest was Baltimore's historic 33–game improvement. But that was hardly the first time during the 1980s that the system correctly identified dark-horse pennant contenders. In fact, over the past eight seasons, it has uncovered three unexpected division winners and five other long shots that stood within five games of a division lead as late as September:

| | | First Season | | Next Season | | Closest Approach |
|---|---|---|---|---|---|---|
| Year | Team | 1-Run | Overall | Spring | Overall | In Sept./Oct. |
| 1981 | Oakland | 16–26 | .512 | .630 | .587 | won division |
| 1982 | San Diego | 12–30 | .372 | .652 | .500 | −4.5, Sept. 9 |

| | | | | | | |
|---|---|---|---|---|---|---|
| 1984 | California | 22–30 | .432 | .591 | .500 | −0.5, Sept. 21 |
| 1986 | Texas | 11–27 | .385 | .536 | .537 | −5.0, Oct. 5 |
| 1987 | Minnesota | 20–27 | .438 | .583 | .525 | won division |
| 1988 | Los Angeles | 19–32 | .450 | .656 | .584 | won division |
| 1989 | Baltimore | 15–24 | .335 | .483 | .537 | −1.0, Sept. 28 |
| 1989 | St. Louis | 24–29 | .469 | .571 | .531 | −0.5, Sept. 8 |

As we went to press, the first spring training games were still six weeks off. So we can't tell you which teams were most improved in Florida or Arizona. But we can tell you which are turnaround contenders based on their records in one-run games last season. The teams that played at least five games below .500 in one-run contests last year, along with their overall winning percentages:

| American | 1-Run | Overall | National | 1-Run | Overall |
|---|---|---|---|---|---|
| Boston | 13–25 | .512 | Atlanta | 24–31 | .394 |
| Chicago | 19–26 | .429 | New York | 22–30 | .537 |
| Detroit | 19–26 | .364 | Pittsburgh | 19–32 | .457 |
| Seattle | 23–28 | .451 | | | |

If you paid no attention to Baltimore's respectable, and auspicious, performance during the 1989 preseason, don't feel bad. Only the most optimistic Orioles fans did. But as that hoary axiom concludes, twice fooled, shame on you. So this spring, keep an eye out for Signal Two. And, in the words of Pete Townshend, don't get fooled again.

Can teams that signal their improvement in March be expected to hit the ground running in April? Looking at Baltimore's month-by-month record last season, you'd think not. The Orioles split 24 games in April, and didn't really get it in gear until May (14–10) and June (17–11). But they were an exception. The composite monthly records of the 21 Signal-Two teams shows that April is their collective best month. And more of those 21 teams had their best month of the season in April than in any other month. In the following table, September includes October games as well:

| | April | May | June | July | August | Sept. |
|---|---|---|---|---|---|---|
| Composite winning pct. | .539 | .462 | .507 | .465 | .479 | .516 |
| Teams with best record | 6 | 3 | 3 | 2 | 2 | 5 |

And now for the question with which every fantasy-league owner wrestles prior to opening day: What is the relationship of spring-training performance to regular-season performance *for individual players?* Until last season, such a question might not have been taken too seriously by anyone *but* fantasy leaguers. Then a journeyman named Kevin Mitchell tore up Arizona. He led the majors with a .455 batting average, and hit seven home runs in 66 at-bats. Three months later, no one was taking his journeyman challenge to Roger Maris's record lightly. (Incidentally, the Rajah's mark has now stood for 29 years, only five less than Ruth's stood. Now back to our show.)

Well, it's true: Last season's spring training results did correspond somewhat to regular-season performance for individual players. Sound the trumpets. But not too loudly, thank you, because the relationship is minimal. There were 120 players with at least 250 at-bats in each of the last two seasons, and 60 or more ABs during the intervening preseason. Those who failed to reach their 1988 batting averages in spring training were far less likely to reach them during the regular season than were those who improved on 1988 in spring training last year:

| | During Regular Season | |
|---|---|---|
| | Improved | Declined |
| Up in spring training | 32 (49%) | 33 (51%) |
| Down in spring training | 16 (29%) | 39 (71%) |

Now for the bad news. Statistically, the preseason increase or decrease was responsible for 11 percent of the fluctuation from one regular season to the next. Want some examples of why that figure is so low? The following table includes the players from the above-mentioned group with the largest increases from 1988 to spring training '89. Note well the randomness of the 1989 regular season figures, as well as the group averages:

| Player | 1988 | Spring | 1989 |
|---|---|---|---|
| Kevin Mitchell | .251 | .455 | .291 |
| Alfredo Griffin | .199 | .366 | .247 |
| Benito Santiago | .248 | .400 | .236 |
| Darnell Coles | .261 | .408 | .252 |
| Dave Henderson | .304 | .448 | .250 |
| Bobby Bonilla | .274 | .407 | .281 |
| Lance Parrish | .215 | .346 | .238 |
| Andres Thomas | .252 | .377 | .213 |
| Mike Scioscia | .257 | .380 | .250 |
| Steve Buechele | .250 | .360 | .235 |
| Averages | .251 | .395 | .249 |

So, fantasy-league owners, *caveat emptor*. And to all you others out there—there *are* still others, aren't there?—rest easy. Mitchell was only an exception. (But what an exception!)

## WON-LOST RECORD BY STARTING POSITION

| BALTIMORE 87-75 | C | 1B | 2B | 3B | SS | LF | CF | RF | P | DH | Leadoff | Relief | Starts |
|---|---|---|---|---|---|---|---|---|---|---|---|---|---|
| Brady Anderson | - | - | - | - | - | - | 34-31 | - | - | - | 34-26 | - | 34-31 |
| Jeff Ballard | - | - | - | - | - | - | - | - | 24-11 | - | - | - | 24-11 |
| Jose Bautista | - | - | - | - | - | - | - | - | 4-6 | - | - | 1-4 | 4-6 |
| Juan Bell | - | - | 1-0 | - | - | - | - | - | - | - | - | - | 1-0 |
| Phil Bradley | - | - | - | - | - | 74-64 | - | - | - | 0-1 | 23-21 | - | 74-65 |
| Butch Davis | - | - | - | - | - | 1-0 | - | - | - | - | - | - | 1-0 |
| Mike Devereaux | - | - | - | - | - | - | 42-29 | 10-16 | - | 1-0 | 25-20 | - | 53-45 |
| Steve Finley | - | - | - | - | - | 2-1 | 6-13 | 20-12 | - | - | 4-5 | - | 28-26 |
| Rene Gonzales | - | - | 18-22 | 7-2 | - | - | - | - | - | - | - | - | 25-24 |
| Pete Harnisch | - | - | - | - | - | - | - | - | 7-10 | - | - | 0-1 | 7-10 |
| Kevin Hickey | - | - | - | - | - | - | - | - | - | - | - | 22-29 | - |
| Chris Hoiles | 1-0 | - | - | - | - | - | - | - | - | 0-1 | - | - | 1-1 |
| Brian Holton | - | - | - | - | - | - | - | - | 9-3 | - | - | 7-20 | 9-3 |
| Mark Huismann | - | - | - | - | - | - | - | - | - | - | - | 6-2 | - |
| Tim Hulett | - | - | 11-10 | 7-2 | - | - | - | - | - | - | - | - | 18-12 |
| Stan Jefferson | - | - | - | - | - | - | 5-2 | 15-10 | - | - | 0-1 | - | 20-12 |
| Dave Johnson | - | - | - | - | - | - | - | - | 5-9 | - | - | - | 5-9 |
| Ben McDonald | - | - | - | - | - | - | - | - | - | - | - | 1-5 | - |
| Francisco Melendez | - | 1-1 | - | - | - | - | - | - | - | - | - | - | 1-1 |
| Bob Melvin | 41-31 | - | - | - | - | - | - | - | - | 2-3 | - | - | 43-34 |
| Bob Milacki | - | - | - | - | - | - | - | - | 19-17 | - | - | 0-1 | 19-17 |
| Randy Milligan | - | 58-48 | - | - | - | - | - | - | - | - | 1-0 | - | 58-48 |
| Keith Moreland | - | - | - | - | - | - | - | - | - | 13-11 | - | - | 13-11 |
| Gregg Olson | - | - | - | - | - | - | - | - | - | - | - | 44-20 | - |
| Joe Orsulak | - | - | - | - | - | 10-10 | - | 42-37 | - | 1-2 | 0-2 | - | 53-49 |
| Jamie Quirk | 9-8 | - | - | - | - | - | - | - | - | - | - | - | 9-8 |
| Billy Ripken | - | - | 57-43 | - | - | - | - | - | - | - | - | - | 57-43 |
| Cal Ripken | - | - | - | - | 87-75 | - | - | - | - | - | - | - | 87-75 |
| Curt Schilling | - | - | - | - | - | - | - | - | 0-1 | - | - | 1-3 | 0-1 |
| Dave Schmidt | - | - | - | - | - | - | - | - | 12-14 | - | - | 2-10 | 12-14 |
| Rick Schu | - | - | - | - | - | - | - | - | - | - | - | - | - |
| Larry Sheets | - | - | - | - | - | - | - | - | - | 44-38 | - | - | 44-38 |
| Mike T. Smith | - | - | - | - | - | - | - | - | 0-1 | - | - | 4-8 | 0-1 |
| Mickey Tettleton | 36-36 | - | - | - | - | - | - | - | - | 23-17 | - | - | 59-53 |
| Mark Thurmond | - | - | - | - | - | - | - | - | 1-1 | - | - | 20-27 | 1-1 |
| Jay Tibbs | - | - | - | - | - | - | - | - | 6-2 | - | - | 0-2 | 6-2 |
| Jim Traber | - | 28-26 | - | - | - | - | - | - | - | 3-2 | - | - | 31-28 |
| Mickey Weston | - | - | - | - | - | - | - | - | - | - | - | 3-4 | - |
| Mark Williamson | - | - | - | - | - | - | - | - | - | - | - | 37-28 | - |
| Craig Worthington | - | - | - | 73 71 | - | - | - | - | - | - | - | - | 73-71 |

## Batting vs. Left and Right Handed Pitchers

| | | BA | Rank | SA | Rank | OBA | Rank | HR % | Rank | BB % | Rank | SO % | Rank |
|---|---|---|---|---|---|---|---|---|---|---|---|---|---|
| Brady Anderson | vs. Lefties | .129 | 173 | .243 | 164 | .265 | 148 | 1.43 | 101 | 15.48 | 7 | 14.29 | 103 |
| | vs. Righties | .235 | 124 | .337 | 115 | .345 | 51 | 1.53 | 101 | 12.88 | 15 | 14.16 | 86 |
| Phil Bradley | vs. Lefties | .297 | 40 | .531 | 9 | .379 | 26 | 4.17 | 28 | 10.96 | 34 | 13.24 | 90 |
| | vs. Righties | .266 | 73 | .354 | 105 | .356 | 38 | 0.85 | 130 | 11.19 | 34 | 18.00 | 125 |
| Mike Devereaux | vs. Lefties | .280 | 65 | .402 | 74 | .351 | 53 | 1.59 | 89 | 9.43 | 54 | 11.32 | 68 |
| | vs. Righties | .252 | 100 | .356 | 103 | .308 | 107 | 2.48 | 62 | 7.21 | 102 | 16.22 | 106 |
| Steve Finley | vs. Lefties | .158 | -- | .263 | -- | .220 | -- | 2.63 | -- | 4.76 | -- | 16.67 | -- |
| | vs. Righties | .268 | 68 | .330 | 125 | .314 | 101 | 0.56 | 145 | 6.53 | 120 | 11.56 | 64 |
| Rene Gonzales | vs. Lefties | .136 | -- | .136 | -- | .224 | -- | 0.00 | -- | 9.80 | -- | 21.57 | -- |
| | vs. Righties | .246 | 108 | .303 | 143 | .285 | 138 | 0.82 | 132 | 5.22 | 147 | 14.18 | 87 |
| Stan Jefferson | vs. Lefties | .210 | 155 | .323 | 139 | .231 | 166 | 1.61 | 88 | 1.54 | 166 | 15.38 | 110 |
| | vs. Righties | .273 | -- | .429 | -- | .296 | -- | 3.90 | -- | 3.70 | -- | 19.75 | -- |
| Bob Melvin | vs. Lefties | .305 | 34 | .397 | 80 | .344 | 67 | 0.66 | 128 | 5.59 | 122 | 13.04 | 88 |
| | vs. Righties | .165 | 169 | .173 | 171 | .201 | 171 | 0.00 | 158 | 4.29 | 156 | 22.86 | 151 |
| Randy Milligan | vs. Lefties | .225 | 144 | .396 | 82 | .351 | 52 | 3.55 | 37 | 16.34 | 5 | 13.86 | 97 |
| | vs. Righties | .306 | 19 | .510 | 6 | .430 | 2 | 3.06 | 48 | 16.94 | 4 | 19.42 | 134 |
| Keith Moreland | vs. Lefties | .288 | 51 | .373 | 99 | .333 | 80 | 1.13 | 115 | 6.35 | 103 | 8.99 | 44 |
| | vs. Righties | .270 | 66 | .363 | 96 | .327 | 79 | 1.61 | 99 | 7.06 | 105 | 10.41 | 49 |
| Joe Orsulak | vs. Lefties | .202 | 159 | .262 | 161 | .244 | 163 | 0.00 | 134 | 5.38 | 128 | 8.60 | 41 |
| | vs. Righties | .307 | 17 | .464 | 29 | .378 | 18 | 2.29 | 71 | 10.20 | 47 | 7.65 | 20 |
| Billy Ripken | vs. Lefties | .272 | 78 | .330 | 135 | .316 | 101 | 0.00 | 134 | 6.72 | 99 | 14.29 | 103 |
| | vs. Righties | .223 | 145 | .293 | 150 | .268 | 153 | 0.93 | 128 | 5.71 | 135 | 14.69 | 94 |
| Cal Ripken | vs. Lefties | .235 | 135 | .372 | 101 | .287 | 138 | 2.55 | 65 | 6.94 | 95 | 9.72 | 54 |
| | vs. Righties | .267 | 71 | .413 | 51 | .331 | 74 | 3.56 | 33 | 8.47 | 74 | 10.28 | 45 |
| Larry Sheets | vs. Lefties | .154 | -- | .179 | -- | .209 | -- | 0.00 | -- | 4.65 | -- | 30.23 | -- |
| | vs. Righties | .257 | 91 | .385 | 76 | .319 | 93 | 2.64 | 58 | 8.14 | 81 | 15.25 | 98 |
| Mickey Tettleton | vs. Lefties | .245 | 123 | .532 | 7 | .346 | 61 | 7.19 | 3 | 13.58 | 15 | 29.01 | 169 |
| | vs. Righties | .265 | 75 | .496 | 14 | .380 | 17 | 5.88 | 7 | 15.60 | 8 | 21.41 | 144 |
| Jim Traber | vs. Lefties | .286 | -- | .429 | -- | .348 | -- | 4.76 | -- | 8.70 | -- | 13.04 | -- |
| | vs. Righties | .202 | 159 | .282 | 156 | .258 | 158 | 1.41 | 106 | 7.26 | 99 | 16.24 | 107 |
| Craig Worthington | vs. Lefties | .258 | 101 | .368 | 105 | .361 | 44 | 2.58 | 61 | 13.26 | 16 | 17.68 | 127 |
| | vs. Righties | .243 | 115 | .392 | 67 | .321 | 89 | 3.22 | 44 | 9.61 | 55 | 21.30 | 143 |
| Team Average | vs. Lefties | .242 | 14 | .376 | 9 | .317 | 11 | 2.39 | 6 | 9.56 | 2 | 15.00 | 10 |
| | vs. Righties | .256 | 9 | .380 | 8 | .331 | 3 | 2.36 | 6 | 9.63 | 3 | 15.74 | 12 |
| League Average | vs. Lefties | .266 | | .391 | | .328 | | 2.18 | | 8.18 | | 13.58 | |
| | vs. Righties | .258 | | .380 | | .325 | | 2.26 | | 8.56 | | 14.57 | |

## Batting with Runners on Base and Bases Empty

| | | BA | Rank | SA | Rank | OBA | Rank | HR % | Rank | BB % | Rank | SO % | Rank |
|---|---|---|---|---|---|---|---|---|---|---|---|---|---|
| Brady Anderson | Runners On | .239 | 133 | .341 | 133 | .417 | 6 | 2.27 | 67 | 21.67 | 4 | 6.67 | 19 |
| | Bases Empty | .191 | 164 | .298 | 152 | .269 | 155 | 1.12 | 116 | 8.63 | 60 | 18.78 | 124 |
| Phil Bradley | Runners On | .264 | 95 | .371 | 93 | .404 | 13 | 1.02 | 121 | 17.32 | 9 | 14.96 | 107 |
| | Bases Empty | .284 | 37 | .443 | 36 | .338 | 48 | 2.59 | 71 | 6.91 | 99 | 17.29 | 112 |
| Mike Devereaux | Runners On | .259 | 99 | .411 | 61 | .341 | 76 | 3.16 | 41 | 10.87 | 43 | 13.04 | 91 |
| | Bases Empty | .270 | 53 | .356 | 102 | .320 | 78 | 1.29 | 112 | 6.40 | 112 | 14.40 | 88 |
| Steve Finley | Runners On | .223 | 157 | .362 | 102 | .279 | 157 | 2.13 | 73 | 6.36 | 122 | 10.00 | 61 |
| | Bases Empty | .268 | 57 | .285 | 157 | .313 | 95 | 0.00 | 153 | 6.11 | 123 | 14.50 | 90 |
| Bob Melvin | Runners On | .311 | 24 | .402 | 72 | .341 | 75 | 0.82 | 131 | 4.41 | 156 | 14.71 | 101 |
| | Bases Empty | .186 | 166 | .212 | 170 | .230 | 170 | 0.00 | 153 | 5.45 | 137 | 20.00 | 134 |
| Randy Milligan | Runners On | .278 | 74 | .469 | 27 | .405 | 12 | 3.70 | 31 | 16.50 | 12 | 15.00 | 109 |
| | Bases Empty | .261 | 77 | .448 | 33 | .385 | 8 | 2.96 | 61 | 16.80 | 4 | 18.44 | 120 |
| Keith Moreland | Runners On | .260 | 97 | .398 | 74 | .330 | 94 | 2.21 | 70 | 8.50 | 86 | 9.00 | 44 |
| | Bases Empty | .291 | 27 | .344 | 111 | .329 | 64 | 0.82 | 131 | 5.43 | 138 | 10.47 | 44 |
| Joe Orsulak | Runners On | .291 | 50 | .412 | 60 | .360 | 52 | 1.10 | 115 | 10.55 | 51 | 7.80 | 28 |
| | Bases Empty | .279 | 43 | .428 | 48 | .342 | 47 | 2.40 | 76 | 7.89 | 77 | 7.89 | 19 |
| Billy Ripken | Runners On | .256 | 108 | .304 | 153 | .269 | 162 | 0.80 | 132 | 2.61 | 167 | 11.76 | 78 |
| | Bases Empty | .228 | 132 | .306 | 146 | .294 | 123 | 0.52 | 146 | 8.53 | 64 | 16.59 | 106 |
| Cal Ripken | Runners On | .277 | 76 | .463 | 30 | .352 | 64 | 4.56 | 22 | 10.40 | 56 | 9.17 | 47 |
| | Bases Empty | .241 | 117 | .352 | 104 | .288 | 131 | 2.22 | 80 | 5.97 | 126 | 10.91 | 50 |
| Larry Sheets | Runners On | .248 | 117 | .346 | 128 | .335 | 85 | 2.26 | 68 | 12.03 | 33 | 15.19 | 111 |
| | Bases Empty | .240 | 119 | .368 | 98 | .278 | 146 | 2.34 | 78 | 3.89 | 158 | 18.89 | 127 |
| Mickey Tettleton | Runners On | .200 | 167 | .394 | 77 | .382 | 29 | 5.29 | 13 | 22.57 | 1 | 22.12 | 150 |
| | Bases Empty | .299 | 20 | .589 | 1 | .357 | 30 | 7.05 | 3 | 8.37 | 68 | 25.48 | 164 |
| Jim Traber | Runners On | .240 | 131 | .337 | 137 | .305 | 125 | 1.92 | 83 | 9.24 | 72 | 12.61 | 90 |
| | Bases Empty | .185 | 167 | .262 | 167 | .232 | 169 | 1.54 | 99 | 5.80 | 130 | 18.84 | 125 |
| Craig Worthington | Runners On | .309 | 28 | .441 | 46 | .381 | 32 | 2.73 | 52 | 9.60 | 66 | 18.80 | 141 |
| | Bases Empty | .199 | 161 | .339 | 115 | .297 | 117 | 3.25 | 50 | 11.71 | 19 | 21.20 | 146 |
| Team Average | Runners On | .265 | 10 | .393 | 7 | .352 | 2 | 2.45 | 3 | 11.63 | 1 | 13.67 | 7 |
| | Bases Empty | .242 | 13 | .369 | 11 | .306 | 11 | 2.32 | 8 | 8.00 | 6 | 16.96 | 13 |
| League Average | Runners On | .268 | | .389 | | .336 | | 2.15 | | 9.17 | | 13.53 | |
| | Bases Empty | .255 | | .380 | | .317 | | 2.29 | | 7.84 | | 14.86 | |

## Overall Batting Compared to Late Inning Pressure Situations

| | | BA | Rank | SA | Rank | OBA | Rank | HR % | Rank | BB % | Rank | SO % | Rank | RDI % | Rank |
|---|---|---|---|---|---|---|---|---|---|---|---|---|---|---|---|
| Brady Anderson | Overall | .207 | 168 | .312 | 153 | .324 | 84 | 1.50 | 106 | 13.56 | 14 | 14.20 | 90 | .182 | 162 |
| | Pressure | .346 | 9 | .462 | 31 | .485 | 2 | 0.00 | 107 | 21.21 | 2 | 15.15 | 71 | .250 | -- |
| Phil Bradley | Overall | .277 | 44 | .417 | 53 | .364 | 25 | 2.02 | 85 | 11.11 | 26 | 16.35 | 109 | .244 | 119 |
| | Pressure | .183 | 148 | .200 | 159 | .310 | 96 | 0.00 | 107 | 15.28 | 14 | 22.22 | 133 | .111 | 151 |
| Mike Devereaux | Overall | .266 | 70 | .379 | 91 | .329 | 74 | 2.05 | 83 | 8.29 | 74 | 13.82 | 87 | .236 | 125 |
| | Pressure | .213 | 117 | .404 | 55 | .255 | 142 | 4.26 | 30 | 5.88 | 127 | 17.65 | 101 | .250 | 87 |
| Steve Finley | Overall | .249 | 116 | .318 | 148 | .298 | 134 | 0.92 | 134 | 6.22 | 127 | 12.45 | 71 | .257 | 98 |
| | Pressure | .367 | 6 | .400 | 57 | .424 | 12 | 0.00 | 107 | 9.09 | 73 | 12.12 | 45 | .417 | 15 |
| Rene Gonzales | Overall | .217 | -- | .259 | -- | .268 | -- | 0.60 | -- | 6.49 | -- | 16.22 | -- | .200 | -- |
| | Pressure | .286 | -- | .286 | -- | .318 | -- | 0.00 | -- | 4.55 | -- | 13.64 | -- | .286 | 68 |
| Bob Melvin | Overall | .241 | 130 | .295 | 162 | .279 | 158 | 0.36 | 156 | 4.98 | 152 | 17.61 | 125 | .278 | 68 |
| | Pressure | .188 | 143 | .188 | 160 | .278 | 129 | 0.00 | 107 | 10.81 | 53 | 16.22 | 87 | .250 | 87 |
| Randy Milligan | Overall | .268 | 64 | .458 | 24 | .394 | 8 | 3.29 | 42 | 16.67 | 3 | 16.89 | 116 | .248 | 116 |
| | Pressure | .348 | 8 | .522 | 13 | .464 | 4 | 4.35 | 29 | 17.86 | 3 | 23.21 | 141 | .500 | 5 |
| Keith Moreland | Overall | .278 | 43 | .367 | 105 | .330 | 71 | 1.41 | 113 | 6.77 | 114 | 9.83 | 46 | .227 | 136 |
| | Pressure | .191 | 141 | .235 | 151 | .267 | 134 | 0.00 | 107 | 8.00 | 95 | 16.00 | 84 | .188 | 119 |
| Joe Orsulak | Overall | .285 | 35 | .421 | 47 | .351 | 41 | 1.79 | 93 | 9.19 | 55 | 7.85 | 20 | .336 | 20 |
| | Pressure | .264 | 73 | .396 | 62 | .381 | 34 | 1.89 | 78 | 14.06 | 22 | 9.38 | 26 | .462 | 8 |
| Billy Ripken | Overall | .239 | 132 | .305 | 157 | .284 | 154 | 0.63 | 144 | 6.04 | 134 | 14.56 | 94 | .220 | 145 |
| | Pressure | .241 | 99 | .276 | 134 | .333 | 72 | 0.00 | 107 | 11.11 | 48 | 13.89 | 58 | .286 | 68 |
| Cal Ripken | Overall | .257 | 91 | .401 | 67 | .317 | 97 | 3.25 | 43 | 8.01 | 87 | 10.11 | 49 | .279 | 67 |
| | Pressure | .247 | 93 | .442 | 38 | .322 | 85 | 3.90 | 36 | 10.34 | 58 | 10.34 | 34 | .160 | 129 |
| Larry Sheets | Overall | .243 | 124 | .359 | 112 | .305 | 121 | 2.30 | 71 | 7.69 | 93 | 17.16 | 119 | .232 | 129 |
| | Pressure | .188 | 143 | .188 | 160 | .220 | 156 | 0.00 | 107 | 4.00 | 151 | 28.00 | 153 | .250 | 87 |
| Mickey Tettleton | Overall | .258 | 87 | .509 | 6 | .369 | 20 | 6.33 | 5 | 14.93 | 7 | 23.93 | 160 | .240 | 120 |
| | Pressure | .263 | 74 | .351 | 97 | .354 | 50 | 1.75 | 81 | 12.31 | 36 | 23.08 | 140 | .200 | 115 |
| Jim Traber | Overall | .209 | 167 | .295 | 163 | .266 | 168 | 1.71 | 97 | 7.39 | 97 | 15.95 | 104 | .239 | 121 |
| | Pressure | .179 | 152 | .256 | 144 | .209 | 161 | 2.56 | 66 | 4.65 | 144 | 18.60 | 109 | .375 | 25 |
| Craig Worthington | Overall | .247 | 120 | .384 | 86 | .334 | 63 | 3.02 | 54 | 10.78 | 31 | 20.14 | 145 | .291 | 53 |
| | Pressure | .155 | 159 | .268 | 139 | .241 | 149 | 2.82 | 59 | 10.00 | 65 | 22.50 | 135 | .200 | 115 |
| Team Average | Overall | .252 | 12 | .379 | 11 | .326 | 8 | 2.37 | 5 | 9.61 | 2 | 15.50 | 12 | .264 | 11 |
| | Pressure | .236 | 11 | .337 | 10 | .318 | 6 | 1.88 | 8 | 10.76 | 2 | 18.10 | 8 | .259 | 7 |
| League Average | Overall | .261 | | .384 | | .326 | | 2.23 | | 8.44 | | 14.26 | | .269 | |
| | Pressure | .247 | | .357 | | .318 | | 2.02 | | 9.02 | | 17.90 | | .254 | |

## Additional Miscellaneous Batting Comparisons

| | Grass Surface BA | Rank | Artificial Surface BA | Rank | Home Games BA | Rank | Road Games BA | Rank | Runners in Scoring Position BA | Rank | Runners in Scoring Pos and Two Outs BA | Rank | Leading Off Inning OBA | Rank | Runners on 3B with less than 2 Outs RDI % | Rank |
|---|---|---|---|---|---|---|---|---|---|---|---|---|---|---|---|---|
| Brady Anderson | .204 | 165 | .217 | 134 | .222 | 145 | .191 | 169 | .200 | 156 | .182 | 136 | .260 | 150 | .250 | -- |
| Phil Bradley | .278 | 50 | .271 | 62 | .286 | 45 | .269 | 67 | .244 | 107 | .264 | 58 | .385 | 18 | .486 | 130 |
| Mike Devereaux | .261 | 82 | .296 | 35 | .246 | 110 | .285 | 42 | .241 | 111 | .230 | 91 | .279 | 137 | .500 | 119 |
| Steve Finley | .251 | 95 | .235 | -- | .219 | 149 | .282 | 48 | .254 | 98 | .250 | 68 | .375 | 25 | .583 | 76 |
| Rene Gonzales | .213 | 161 | .240 | -- | .213 | -- | .220 | -- | .238 | -- | .250 | 68 | .229 | 168 | .444 | -- |
| Stan Jefferson | .242 | -- | .267 | -- | .250 | -- | .240 | -- | .323 | -- | .308 | -- | .286 | -- | .750 | 13 |
| Bob Melvin | .217 | 156 | .448 | -- | .234 | 130 | .250 | 100 | .293 | 42 | .333 | 11 | .243 | 158 | .364 | 158 |
| Randy Milligan | .275 | 54 | .224 | 129 | .287 | 43 | .251 | 98 | .270 | 80 | .344 | 8 | .434 | 6 | .438 | 146 |
| Keith Moreland | .280 | 47 | .264 | 66 | .262 | 78 | .294 | 25 | .205 | 154 | .220 | 103 | .333 | 64 | .455 | 141 |
| Joe Orsulak | .269 | 63 | .373 | 3 | .273 | 60 | .296 | 22 | .272 | 76 | .278 | 38 | .361 | 34 | .615 | 59 |
| Billy Ripken | .245 | 109 | .204 | 141 | .234 | 132 | .245 | 114 | .274 | 73 | .267 | 51 | .276 | 139 | .591 | 72 |
| Cal Ripken | .262 | 80 | .234 | 120 | .247 | 108 | .266 | 73 | .251 | 101 | .224 | 97 | .272 | 143 | .528 | 111 |
| Larry Sheets | .238 | 123 | .262 | 71 | .233 | 133 | .251 | 97 | .234 | 125 | .182 | 136 | .353 | 45 | .529 | 109 |
| Mickey Tettleton | .272 | 58 | .197 | 146 | .310 | 19 | .207 | 164 | .190 | 162 | .122 | 161 | .368 | 29 | .409 | 150 |
| Jim Traber | .226 | 146 | .146 | 166 | .191 | 168 | .226 | 145 | .261 | 94 | .222 | 98 | .169 | 171 | .467 | 137 |
| Craig Worthington | .239 | 122 | .293 | 40 | .262 | 77 | .232 | 139 | .311 | 26 | .254 | 67 | .285 | 127 | .576 | 83 |
| Team Average | .251 | 12 | .255 | 10 | .255 | 9 | .249 | 12 | .260 | 10 | .248 | 3 | .307 | 12 | .520 | 12 |
| League Average | .260 | | .262 | | .262 | | .259 | | .262 | | .232 | | .321 | | .566 | |

## Pitching vs. Left and Right Handed Batters

| | | BA | Rank | SA | Rank | OBA | Rank | HR % | Rank | BB % | Rank | SO % | Rank |
|---|---|---|---|---|---|---|---|---|---|---|---|---|---|
| Jeff Ballard | vs. Lefties | .281 | 95 | .403 | 88 | .331 | 71 | 2.88 | 98 | 6.58 | 34 | 14.47 | 48 |
| | vs. Righties | .288 | 116 | .403 | 92 | .334 | 92 | 1.72 | 50 | 6.18 | 40 | 5.26 | 133 |
| Jose Bautista | vs. Lefties | .280 | 94 | .471 | 115 | .307 | 47 | 3.82 | 116 | 3.66 | 6 | 7.93 | 111 |
| | vs. Righties | .267 | 86 | .513 | 134 | .311 | 51 | 7.33 | 134 | 5.59 | 28 | 10.56 | 112 |
| Pete Harnisch | vs. Lefties | .257 | 63 | .377 | 65 | .390 | 120 | 1.64 | 59 | 16.07 | 128 | 14.73 | 44 |
| | vs. Righties | .242 | 33 | .391 | 82 | .328 | 84 | 3.38 | 117 | 11.48 | 124 | 15.16 | 67 |
| Brian Holton | vs. Lefties | .309 | 115 | .452 | 107 | .359 | 98 | 3.04 | 101 | 7.23 | 43 | 5.22 | 132 |
| | vs. Righties | .291 | 119 | .414 | 98 | .345 | 112 | 1.69 | 46 | 7.92 | 72 | 14.34 | 78 |
| Dave Johnson | vs. Lefties | .303 | 110 | .465 | 110 | .375 | 108 | 2.58 | 89 | 10.73 | 101 | 5.65 | 129 |
| | vs. Righties | .232 | 28 | .389 | 81 | .281 | 19 | 3.78 | 124 | 4.48 | 10 | 7.96 | 127 |
| Bob Milacki | vs. Lefties | .253 | 58 | .371 | 60 | .322 | 60 | 2.15 | 75 | 9.11 | 73 | 11.05 | 77 |
| | vs. Righties | .254 | 61 | .375 | 65 | .315 | 57 | 2.43 | 85 | 8.10 | 77 | 11.07 | 107 |
| Gregg Olson | vs. Lefties | .135 | 1 | .149 | 1 | .247 | 7 | 0.00 | 1 | 12.20 | 111 | 23.78 | 9 |
| | vs. Righties | .233 | 29 | .331 | 30 | .337 | 100 | 0.61 | 6 | 13.54 | 132 | 26.56 | 9 |
| Dave Schmidt | vs. Lefties | .303 | 110 | .471 | 114 | .332 | 72 | 3.87 | 117 | 4.52 | 11 | 8.43 | 105 |
| | vs. Righties | .317 | 132 | .491 | 131 | .358 | 126 | 3.73 | 122 | 5.93 | 33 | 5.08 | 134 |
| Mark Thurmond | vs. Lefties | .284 | 99 | .422 | 94 | .316 | 54 | 0.92 | 23 | 4.39 | 10 | 9.65 | 94 |
| | vs. Righties | .290 | 117 | .400 | 89 | .324 | 74 | 2.04 | 67 | 4.60 | 13 | 8.81 | 125 |
| Jay Tibbs | vs. Lefties | .280 | 97 | .350 | 45 | .356 | 94 | 0.83 | 21 | 10.37 | 95 | 11.85 | 68 |
| | vs. Righties | .292 | -- | .354 | -- | .330 | -- | 1.04 | -- | 5.83 | -- | 13.59 | -- |
| Mark Williamson | vs. Lefties | .260 | 67 | .305 | 26 | .296 | 34 | 0.00 | 1 | 5.18 | 17 | 12.44 | 64 |
| | vs. Righties | .261 | 75 | .376 | 66 | .325 | 76 | 1.77 | 53 | 7.94 | 73 | 12.30 | 93 |
| Team Average | vs. Lefties | .269 | 9 | .390 | 10 | .331 | 7 | 2.20 | 9 | 8.29 | 5 | 10.97 | 13 |
| | vs. Righties | .274 | 14 | .405 | 13 | .331 | 12 | 2.55 | 12 | 7.53 | 5 | 10.89 | 14 |
| League Average | vs. Lefties | .261 | | .382 | | .330 | | 2.16 | | 9.16 | | 13.03 | |
| | vs. Righties | .261 | | .385 | | .323 | | 2.28 | | 7.96 | | 15.09 | |

## Pitching with Runners on Base and Bases Empty

| | | BA | Rank | SA | Rank | OBA | Rank | HR % | Rank | BB % | Rank | SO % | Rank |
|---|---|---|---|---|---|---|---|---|---|---|---|---|---|
| Jeff Ballard | Runners On | .274 | 86 | .428 | 107 | .341 | 81 | 3.24 | 116 | 9.21 | 70 | 8.44 | 117 |
| | Bases Empty | .296 | 120 | .386 | 76 | .328 | 84 | 1.01 | 15 | 4.03 | 8 | 5.57 | 134 |
| Jose Bautista | Runners On | .363 | -- | .745 | -- | .383 | -- | 10.78 | -- | 3.70 | -- | 12.04 | -- |
| | Bases Empty | .229 | 30 | .366 | 59 | .272 | 18 | 2.93 | 93 | 5.07 | 23 | 7.83 | 126 |
| Pete Harnisch | Runners On | .254 | 52 | .376 | 71 | .362 | 110 | 1.73 | 63 | 14.02 | 124 | 15.89 | 41 |
| | Bases Empty | .244 | 52 | .392 | 79 | .354 | 116 | 3.23 | 106 | 13.39 | 131 | 14.17 | 63 |
| Brian Holton | Runners On | .264 | 73 | .373 | 67 | .313 | 43 | 2.27 | 90 | 7.35 | 40 | 9.80 | 103 |
| | Bases Empty | .332 | 134 | .486 | 127 | .387 | 132 | 2.43 | 79 | 7.81 | 75 | 10.04 | 108 |
| Dave Johnson | Runners On | .244 | 37 | .362 | 58 | .327 | 60 | 2.36 | 93 | 10.00 | 84 | 7.33 | 124 |
| | Bases Empty | .277 | 102 | .460 | 117 | .325 | 75 | 3.76 | 122 | 5.70 | 36 | 6.58 | 130 |
| Bob Milacki | Runners On | .261 | 67 | .385 | 79 | .314 | 44 | 2.47 | 96 | 7.60 | 44 | 9.80 | 102 |
| | Bases Empty | .249 | 57 | .366 | 58 | .321 | 71 | 2.16 | 66 | 9.28 | 95 | 11.89 | 88 |
| Gregg Olson | Runners On | .164 | 2 | .200 | 1 | .298 | 20 | 0.00 | 1 | 15.35 | 128 | 23.76 | 8 |
| | Bases Empty | .216 | 19 | .302 | 18 | .292 | 37 | 0.72 | 10 | 9.74 | 104 | 27.27 | 6 |
| Dave Schmidt | Runners On | .327 | 128 | .477 | 129 | .365 | 113 | 3.38 | 119 | 6.29 | 20 | 7.28 | 125 |
| | Bases Empty | .298 | 121 | .484 | 124 | .331 | 87 | 4.10 | 131 | 4.43 | 12 | 6.25 | 131 |
| Mark Thurmond | Runners On | .299 | 118 | .371 | 66 | .344 | 85 | 0.60 | 5 | 6.04 | 15 | 9.34 | 111 |
| | Bases Empty | .278 | 107 | .439 | 111 | .301 | 43 | 2.67 | 85 | 3.11 | 6 | 8.81 | 121 |
| Mark Williamson | Runners On | .290 | 110 | .409 | 98 | .369 | 116 | 2.07 | 79 | 10.92 | 101 | 14.85 | 54 |
| | Bases Empty | .233 | 41 | .286 | 8 | .255 | 7 | 0.00 | 1 | 2.31 | 2 | 9.72 | 111 |
| Team Average | Runners On | .274 | 10 | .404 | 11 | .340 | 9 | 2.69 | 13 | 9.15 | 8 | 11.27 | 14 |
| | Bases Empty | .270 | 12 | .395 | 10 | .323 | 10 | 2.18 | 7 | 6.80 | 4 | 10.64 | 14 |
| League Average | Runners On | .268 | | .389 | | .336 | | 2.15 | | 9.17 | | 13.53 | |
| | Bases Empty | .255 | | .380 | | .317 | | 2.29 | | 7.84 | | 14.86 | |

## Overall Pitching Compared to Late Inning Pressure Situations

| | | BA | Rank | SA | Rank | OBA | Rank | HR % | Rank | BB % | Rank | SO % | Rank |
|---|---|---|---|---|---|---|---|---|---|---|---|---|---|
| Jeff Ballard | Overall | .287 | 113 | .403 | 89 | .334 | 87 | 1.91 | 59 | 6.25 | 28 | 6.80 | 129 |
| | Pressure | .197 | 20 | .197 | 5 | .234 | 5 | 0.00 | 1 | 4.41 | 14 | 7.35 | 121 |
| Jose Bautista | Overall | .274 | 94 | .492 | 133 | .309 | 38 | 5.54 | 134 | 4.62 | 7 | 9.23 | 119 |
| | Pressure | .200 | -- | .667 | -- | .250 | -- | 13.33 | -- | 6.25 | -- | 6.25 | -- |
| Pete Harnisch | Overall | .249 | 49 | .385 | 75 | .358 | 120 | 2.56 | 92 | 13.68 | 132 | 14.96 | 56 |
| | Pressure | .290 | 102 | .484 | 116 | .405 | 115 | 3.23 | 106 | 15.79 | 122 | 5.26 | 125 |
| Kevin Hickey | Overall | .220 | -- | .289 | -- | .315 | -- | 1.73 | -- | 11.56 | -- | 14.07 | -- |
| | Pressure | .250 | 68 | .333 | 57 | .400 | 113 | 1.67 | 59 | 18.18 | 131 | 15.58 | 60 |
| Brian Holton | Overall | .300 | 125 | .433 | 110 | .352 | 109 | 2.36 | 82 | 7.59 | 57 | 9.92 | 109 |
| | Pressure | .383 | 125 | .638 | 131 | .442 | 126 | 4.26 | 120 | 9.26 | 64 | 7.41 | 119 |
| Dave Johnson | Overall | .265 | 76 | .424 | 99 | .325 | 67 | 3.24 | 117 | 7.41 | 53 | 6.88 | 128 |
| | Pressure | .167 | -- | .200 | -- | .242 | -- | 0.00 | -- | 9.09 | -- | 3.03 | -- |
| Bob Milacki | Overall | .254 | 55 | .373 | 62 | .318 | 56 | 2.29 | 77 | 8.61 | 79 | 11.06 | 96 |
| | Pressure | .200 | 25 | .280 | 28 | .310 | 60 | 1.00 | 42 | 12.71 | 106 | 6.78 | 123 |
| Gregg Olson | Overall | .188 | 3 | .247 | 1 | .295 | 26 | 0.33 | 1 | 12.92 | 127 | 25.28 | 7 |
| | Pressure | .199 | 24 | .256 | 20 | .329 | 71 | 0.00 | 1 | 15.42 | 119 | 23.36 | 19 |
| Dave Schmidt | Overall | .310 | 131 | .481 | 132 | .346 | 104 | 3.80 | 129 | 5.25 | 11 | 6.71 | 130 |
| | Pressure | .171 | 10 | .286 | 33 | .237 | 8 | 2.86 | 96 | 7.69 | 49 | 5.13 | 128 |
| Mark Thurmond | Overall | .288 | 114 | .407 | 91 | .322 | 62 | 1.69 | 46 | 4.53 | 6 | 9.07 | 120 |
| | Pressure | .385 | 126 | .615 | 127 | .442 | 125 | 5.13 | 126 | 9.30 | 66 | 0.00 | 133 |
| Mark Williamson | Overall | .261 | 68 | .345 | 39 | .313 | 47 | 0.99 | 11 | 6.74 | 37 | 12.36 | 80 |
| | Pressure | .285 | 96 | .383 | 86 | .354 | 94 | 0.93 | 40 | 8.91 | 57 | 11.74 | 90 |
| Team Average | Overall | .272 | 12 | .399 | 10 | .331 | 10 | 2.40 | 10 | 7.85 | 6 | 10.92 | 14 |
| | Pressure | .247 | 6 | .354 | 6 | .339 | 11 | 1.64 | 4 | 11.50 | 13 | 12.20 | 14 |
| League Average | Overall | .261 | | .384 | | .326 | | 2.23 | | 8.44 | | 14.26 | |
| | Pressure | .250 | | .362 | | .325 | | 2.14 | | 9.50 | | 16.61 | |

## Additional Miscellaneous Pitching Comparisons

| | Grass Surface | | Artificial Surface | | Home Games | | Road Games | | Runners in Scoring Position | | Runners in Scoring Pos and Two Outs | | Leading Off Inning | |
|---|---|---|---|---|---|---|---|---|---|---|---|---|---|---|
| | BA | Rank | BA | Rank | BA | Rank | BA | Rank | BA | Rank | BA | Rank | OBA | Rank |
| Jeff Ballard | .291 | 114 | .270 | 70 | .286 | 111 | .289 | 102 | .238 | 50 | .211 | 52 | .358 | 106 |
| Jose Bautista | .265 | 76 | .344 | -- | .267 | 86 | .284 | 95 | .327 | -- | .320 | -- | .139 | 1 |
| Pete Harnisch | .246 | 46 | .269 | 69 | .228 | 31 | .259 | 66 | .191 | 11 | .104 | 6 | .351 | 102 |
| Kevin Hickey | .222 | 20 | .207 | -- | .247 | -- | .190 | -- | .192 | -- | .333 | -- | .350 | -- |
| Brian Holton | .293 | 116 | .351 | 128 | .309 | 127 | .287 | 99 | .302 | 117 | .217 | 62 | .339 | 87 |
| Dave Johnson | .278 | 100 | .087 | -- | .273 | 96 | .252 | 51 | .208 | 16 | .129 | 11 | .316 | 57 |
| Bob Milacki | .241 | 35 | .318 | 118 | .249 | 64 | .258 | 63 | .251 | 69 | .195 | 45 | .310 | 48 |
| Gregg Olson | .155 | 1 | .308 | 110 | .154 | 1 | .225 | 26 | .162 | 3 | .113 | 7 | .273 | 28 |
| Dave Schmidt | .305 | 125 | .340 | 127 | .339 | 132 | .293 | 109 | .319 | 123 | .253 | 94 | .386 | 121 |
| Mark Thurmond | .297 | 121 | .241 | 41 | .293 | 116 | .283 | 94 | .307 | 120 | .390 | 135 | .337 | 85 |
| Jay Tibbs | .293 | 118 | .250 | -- | .296 | 120 | .270 | -- | .300 | -- | .208 | -- | .316 | 57 |
| Mark Williamson | .267 | 80 | .226 | 24 | .245 | 57 | .278 | 88 | .303 | 118 | .310 | 120 | .258 | 16 |
| Team Average | .270 | 13 | .280 | 12 | .274 | 13 | .269 | 11 | .265 | 9 | .227 | 5 | .319 | 6 |
| League Average | .260 | | .262 | | .259 | | .262 | | .262 | | .232 | | .321 | |

# BOSTON RED SOX

- **What made the '76 Red Sox so special?**
- **A historical perspective on Rice, Lynn, and friends.**

Fifteen years ago, when Boston dropped Game 7 to Cincinnati, the vast majority of Red Sox fans considered the loss merely a repeat of the Great Tease of '67, when the Sox came within one game of erasing half a century of futility. The rare optimists during that long New England winter of 1975 were those with vision enough to identify the Red Sox as a contender for years to come based on an almost unprecedented supply of promising young hitters. Foresight has become hindsight, and the intervening years have proven that the 1976 Red Sox had one of the greatest young lineups in major league history—maybe not equal to those of the first Big Red Machine, that of the late 1960s, or the budding Yankees dynasty of forty years earlier, but about as close as any other team has come to the births of those powerhouses.

Now maybe you don't place Jim Rice and Fred Lynn in that Cooperstown of the mind reserved for Gehrig and Ruth, or for Rose and Bench. But our revisionist spin proposes that the image of the 1975 Red Sox currently suffers from a too-close association with Rice and Lynn. Although they've combined for nearly 700 home runs and driven in more than 2500 runs while batting nearly .300, and each was the dominant hitter in the American League for a time, neither Rice nor Lynn reached the heights in the 1980s that most of us expected during the 1970s. And the image of the 1975 Red Sox is colored as much by their failures as it is by their accomplishments.

But as we cruise into the 1990s, two other members of the Red Sox team that won the 1975 A.L. title remain among the most productive players at their positions in the league: Dwight Evans and Carlton Fisk. And when you consider their accomplishments along with those of Rice and Lynn, adding the not insignificant contributions of Cecil Cooper and Rick Burleson, the conclusion becomes more obvious: Few lineups in baseball history have had as much promise, and realized as much of that potential, as did the Red Sox of the mid–1970s.

Readers of the 1989 *Analyst* will recall that in the retrospective on the 1969 Mets, we designed a system to measure the future potential realized by any team's starting rotation. We've refined that system, and adapted it to batting lineups. The results suggest that only four teams since 1900 have exceeded the '76 Red Sox in terms of what their players went on to accomplish, as measured by the numbers of runs their players, on average, subsequently produced.

We'll explain that more fully in a moment. First, a table of the top 10 teams in modern major league history:

| Year | Team | Runs |
|---|---|---|
| 1968 | Cincinnati Reds | 660 |
| 1926 | New York Yankees | 646 |
| 1954 | Milwaukee Braves | 613 |
| 1949 | Brooklyn Dodgers | 579 |
| 1976 | Boston Red Sox | 576 |
| 1933 | Philadelphia Athletics | 571 |
| 1959 | San Francisco Giants | 554 |
| 1973 | Los Angeles Dodgers | 543 |
| 1968 | Oakland Athletics | 530 |
| 1910 | Boston Red Sox | 527 |

So what does it mean that the 1976 Red Sox ranked fifth with 576 runs? It's fairly simple, really. In 1976, the average player who stepped to the plate for Boston produced 576 runs after that season. How does one produce a run? For every run scored, we assigned one-half to the player who scored, the other half to the player who drove him in. Not exactly a standard of measure we'd use to decide the MVP award, but it is a simple and effective gauge of a player's long-term contribution. Incidentally, pitchers are excluded from consideration, allowing us to place teams that used a designated hitter on a level playing field with the others.

Furthermore, each player contributed to his team's average in proportion to the amount that he batted. For instance, Jim Rice had approximately 10 percent of Boston's plate appearances in 1976, so his 2327 subsequent runs produced had an enormous impact on the team's average. On the other hand, Ernie Whitt, who produced 475 runs from 1977 on, accounted for one-third of 1 percent of Boston's plate appearances in 1976. His effect on the team's average was appropriately negligible.

That feature explains why the Red Sox of 1976, not those of 1975, appear in the table. For each of the teams, only one vintage has been included. Otherwise, you'd have seen a top 10 list that included seven different flavors of the Big Red Machine. Cincinnati's 1968 edition ranked highest, and overlapping Reds teams were discarded. The 1976 Red Sox outranked the previous year's team because, as regular starters, Carlton Fisk and Cecil Cooper accounted for a far greater slice of the pie (17 percent) than they had as part-timers a year earlier (10 percent). Boston also replaced a washed-up 32–year-old third baseman (Rico Petrocelli) with a 24–year-old rookie (Butch Hobson).

With the ground rules established, let's examine the rest of baseball's best examples of offensive potential fulfilled:

- **Cincinnati, 1968**—Johnny Bench joined seven other stars, *all under the age of 30.* Most noteworthy, of course, were Rose and Tony Perez. But Vada Pinson, Lee May, Alex Johnson, Tommy Helms, and Leo Cardenas completed an exceptional lineup clearly destined for greatness.
- **New York, 1926**—Second baseman Tony Lazzeri and shortstop Mark Koenig joined Ruth and Gehrig to lead the team to the first of its three consecutive league titles. Gehrig was a 23–year-old sophomore. Ruth, 31, was the lineup's graybeard, but was on the brink of one of baseball's most legendary achievements. Earl

Combs and Bob Meusel still had several good years ahead of them.

- **Milwaukee, 1954**—Hank Aaron arrived for the team's first season in Wisconsin, one year after Joe Adcock, two years after Eddie Mathews. Young Del Crandall pushed ancient Walker Cooper totally out of the picture. Only one starter was over the age of 30 (Andy Pafko).
- **Brooklyn, 1949**—One lineup change from 1948, but what a change: Duke Snider supplanted Marv Rackley in the outfield, and replaced Gil Hodges as the team's youngest starter. Jackie Robinson reached the big three-oh. Campy was 27, Pee Wee Reese was 31.
- Philadelphia, 1933—Rookies Pinky Higgins and Indian Bob Johnson solidified a lineup that already included a pair of eventual Hall of Famers: Jimmie Foxx (age 25) and Mickey Cochrane (30), and Cooperstown contender Doc Cramer (28).
- **San Francisco, 1959**—Orlando Cepeda's second season was Willie McCovey's first. And the other Willie was only 28. Not much else there —one-third of the Alou brothers and 100 percent of Willie Kirkland—but so what? Had McCovey played a full season (he joined the team in late July), this team would rank among the top three.
- **Los Angeles, 1973**—The arrival of the Infield, although not *in toto*. This was Bill Russell's second season, and the rookie year for Dave Lopes and Ron Cey. Steve Garvey was still a part-timer in search of a glove that fit. Let's not forget the first baseman: 23–year-old Bill Buckner, who'll attain four-decade status should he ever again limp onto the field.
- **Oakland, 1968**—Freshmen Reggie Jackson and Sal Bando joined sophomore Rick Monday for the A's first season in Oakland. Joe Rudi split his time between Charley O. and Uncle Sam. Bert Campaneris was the team's 26–year-old fourth-year shortstop. At 28, Danny Cater was the oldest starter.
- **Boston, 1910**—Rookie Duffy Lewis filled the third spot alongside Tris Speaker and Harry Hooper to form one of the best young outfields of baseball's early days, one that would play together for six years until Speaker was sold to Cleveland during a contract dispute. Larry Gardner, one of the American League's top third basemen for the next decade, was the team's other rookie.

Let's be clear on one point here: We're not presenting these figures as the final word on the matter, right down to the smallest details. We're comfortable with the 1968 Reds and 1926 Yankees standing head-and-shoulders above the rest of the crowd. It would be hard to argue otherwise, whether based on our numbers or any other rationale. But did the 1949 Dodgers truly have a better young lineup than the 1976 Red Sox? Maybe they did, maybe not—but we certainly wouldn't argue that point based on our margin of three more runs produced.

Incidentally, you might be wondering (as we did) about the lowest-ranking teams ever. Five of the bottom 10 teams were from the Federal League, an outlaw major league that lasted only two years (1914 and 1915) and sprinkled its substandard rosters with a smattering of past-prime time players from the American and National Leagues. The bottom rung belongs to the 1915 Baltimore Terrapins, whose players produced an average of six runs thereafter.

Third from the bottom were the 1945 Philadelphia Phillies, whose lineup included the wrong DiMaggio (Vince), and whose bench might have won a pennant 10 years earlier, what with Jimmie Foxx, Gus Mancuso, and Ben Chapman, all in their late 30s. The team merits special mention here because its pitching staff was nearly as void of potential as its lineup. How depressing is that—108 losses, and a team of Senior League impostors.

The most recent team among the bottom 10 was the 1954 Baltimore Orioles, where two notables, Eddie Waitkus and Vern Stephens, crash landed.

Finally, we'd like to update the list of the most promising young pitching staffs from last year's edition for two reasons: (1) to base each pitcher's proportional contribution to the team average on innings rather than starts, thereby factoring a team's relief pitching into the equation; and (2) because the meter is still running on the 1968 Mets, one of the highest-rated teams of all-time. Their average increases every time Nolan Ryan wins another game.

The standard of measure is games won after the season listed. The top 10 teams since 1900:

| Year | Team | Wins |
|---|---|---|
| 1903 | Philadelphia Athletics | 154 |
| 1900 | Pittsburgh Pirates | 148 |
| 1903 | New York Giants | 146 |
| 1912 | Philadelphia Phillies | 128 |
| 1968 | New York Mets | 123 |
| 1910 | Washington Senators | 118 |
| 1919 | Boston Red Sox | 118 |
| 1968 | Chicago Cubs | 114 |
| 1970 | St. Louis Cardinals | 108 |
| 1953 | Milwaukee Braves | 107 |

Some random observations:

Rube Waddell pitched for each of the two top teams (324 innings for the A's at age 26, 209 for the Pirates at 23).

Waddell's rotation-mates at Philadelphia included two other Hall of Famers still in their wonder years: Eddie Plank (27) and Chief Bender (20). At Pittsburgh, he teamed with a 26–year-old Jack Chesbro.

The Phillies staff had a pair of future Famers: rookie Eppa Rixey and Grover Cleveland Alexander in his second season.

The 1919 Red Sox would have ranked among the top three had (1) Babe Ruth pitched another few seasons before his conversion to full-time outfielder; and (2) Waite Hoyt and Carl Mays pitched full seasons with the team. Hoyt was the mid-season replacement for Mays, who was traded to the Yankees.

The 1954 Braves probably were the best young team in major league history. Their batters ranked third for realized potential, and their pitching staff was predictably similar to the one listed tenth above—simply a year older.

## WON-LOST RECORD BY STARTING POSITION

| BOSTON 83-79 | C | 1B | 2B | 3B | SS | LF | CF | RF | P | DH | Leadoff | Relief | Starts |
|---|---|---|---|---|---|---|---|---|---|---|---|---|---|
| Marty Barrett | - | - | 34-43 | - | - | - | - | - | - | 3-1 | - | - | 37-44 |
| Mike Boddicker | - | - | - | - | - | - | - | - | 20-14 | - | - | - | 20-14 |
| Wade Boggs | - | - | - | 77-75 | - | - | - | - | - | 2-1 | 64-59 | - | 79-76 |
| Tom Bolton | - | - | - | - | - | - | - | - | 0-4 | - | - | - | 0-4 |
| Oil Can Boyd | - | - | - | - | - | - | - | - | 5-5 | - | - | - | 5-5 |
| Ellis Burks | - | - | - | - | - | - | 45-51 | - | - | - | 2-3 | - | 45-51 |
| Rick Cerone | 42-43 | - | - | - | - | - | - | - | - | 0-1 | - | - | 42-44 |
| Roger Clemens | - | - | - | - | - | - | - | - | 20-15 | - | - | - | 20-15 |
| John Dopson | - | - | - | - | - | - | - | - | 16-12 | - | - | 1-0 | 16-12 |
| Nick Esasky | - | 79-68 | - | - | - | - | - | - | - | - | - | - | 79-68 |
| Dwight Evans | - | - | - | - | - | - | - | 38-38 | - | 39-30 | - | - | 77-68 |
| Wes Gardner | - | - | - | - | - | - | - | - | 8-8 | - | - | 2-4 | 8-8 |
| Rich Gedman | 39-33 | - | - | - | - | - | - | - | - | - | - | - | 39-33 |
| Mike Greenwell | - | - | - | - | - | 71-68 | - | - | - | 2-3 | - | - | 73-71 |
| Greg A. Harris | - | - | - | - | - | - | - | - | - | - | - | 7-8 | - |
| Danny Heep | - | 4-11 | - | - | - | 8-5 | - | 28-20 | - | 3-6 | - | - | 43-42 |
| Eric Hetzel | - | - | - | - | - | - | - | - | 6-5 | - | - | 0-1 | 6-5 |
| Sam Horn | - | - | - | - | - | - | - | - | - | 5-6 | - | - | 5-6 |
| Randy Kutcher | - | - | - | 3-0 | - | 1-1 | 11-8 | 6-6 | - | - | - | - | 21-15 |
| Dennis Lamp | - | - | - | - | - | - | - | - | - | - | - | 12-30 | - |
| John Marzano | 2-3 | - | - | - | - | - | - | - | - | - | - | - | 2-3 |
| Rob Murphy | - | - | - | - | - | - | - | - | - | - | - | 38-36 | - |
| Joe Price | - | - | - | - | - | - | - | - | 1-4 | - | - | 5-21 | 1-4 |
| Carlos Quintana | - | - | - | - | - | 2-1 | - | 4-8 | - | 2-3 | - | - | 8-12 |
| Jody Reed | - | - | 39-27 | 0-1 | 34-38 | - | - | - | - | - | 17-17 | - | 73-66 |
| Jim Rice | - | - | - | - | - | - | - | - | - | 27-26 | - | - | 27-26 |
| Luis Rivera | - | - | - | - | 47-39 | - | - | - | - | - | - | - | 47-39 |
| Mike Rochford | - | - | - | - | - | - | - | - | - | - | - | 0-4 | - |
| Ed Romero | - | - | 10-9 | 3-3 | 2-2 | - | - | - | - | - | - | - | 15-14 |
| Kevin Romine | - | - | - | - | - | 1-4 | 26-20 | 7-7 | - | 0-1 | - | - | 34-32 |
| Lee Smith | - | - | - | - | - | - | - | - | - | - | - | 44-20 | - |
| Mike Smithson | - | - | - | - | - | - | - | - | 7-12 | - | - | 7-14 | 7-12 |
| Bob Stanley | - | - | - | - | - | - | - | - | - | - | - | 20-23 | - |
| Jeff Stone | - | - | - | - | - | - | 1-0 | - | - | - | - | - | 1-0 |
| Dana Williams | - | - | - | - | - | - | - | - | - | 0-1 | - | - | 0-1 |

## Batting vs. Left and Right Handed Pitchers

| | | BA | Rank | SA | Rank | OBA | Rank | HR % | Rank | BB % | Rank | SO % | Rank |
|---|---|---|---|---|---|---|---|---|---|---|---|---|---|
| Marty Barrett | vs. Lefties | .260 | 97 | .346 | 123 | .325 | 89 | 0.00 | 134 | 8.47 | 65 | 0.00 | 1 |
| | vs. Righties | .254 | 94 | .306 | 139 | .318 | 95 | 0.43 | 148 | 8.09 | 83 | 4.41 | 3 |
| Wade Boggs | vs. Lefties | .295 | 43 | .352 | 113 | .377 | 29 | 0.00 | 134 | 10.46 | 40 | 10.04 | 59 |
| | vs. Righties | .348 | 2 | .499 | 11 | .455 | 1 | 0.73 | 137 | 16.30 | 5 | 5.37 | 6 |
| Ellis Burks | vs. Lefties | .279 | 68 | .413 | 64 | .361 | 43 | 1.92 | 79 | 10.92 | 36 | 8.40 | 38 |
| | vs. Righties | .312 | 14 | .492 | 17 | .366 | 26 | 3.39 | 40 | 7.03 | 106 | 12.84 | 73 |
| Rick Cerone | vs. Lefties | .286 | 55 | .412 | 69 | .373 | 32 | 1.68 | 87 | 12.68 | 24 | 12.68 | 83 |
| | vs. Righties | .215 | 151 | .299 | 144 | .282 | 141 | 1.13 | 126 | 8.04 | 86 | 11.06 | 57 |
| Nick Esasky | vs. Lefties | .250 | 112 | .488 | 24 | .345 | 63 | 6.40 | 6 | 12.69 | 23 | 21.83 | 153 |
| | vs. Righties | .288 | 34 | .505 | 8 | .360 | 35 | 4.85 | 17 | 9.40 | 58 | 16.97 | 117 |
| Dwight Evans | vs. Lefties | .303 | 36 | .452 | 39 | .401 | 14 | 2.58 | 61 | 14.29 | 13 | 14.29 | 103 |
| | vs. Righties | .277 | 51 | .468 | 27 | .396 | 10 | 4.38 | 20 | 16.29 | 6 | 12.95 | 75 |
| Rich Gedman | vs. Lefties | .270 | -- | .405 | -- | .341 | -- | 2.70 | -- | 9.76 | -- | 19.51 | -- |
| | vs. Righties | .202 | 160 | .274 | 157 | .261 | 156 | 1.35 | 116 | 7.66 | 94 | 15.73 | 101 |
| Mike Greenwell | vs. Lefties | .272 | 77 | .332 | 134 | .295 | 133 | 0.99 | 117 | 3.33 | 158 | 7.14 | 25 |
| | vs. Righties | .327 | 6 | .503 | 9 | .406 | 7 | 3.19 | 45 | 11.37 | 29 | 6.73 | 14 |
| Danny Heep | vs. Lefties | .190 | -- | .238 | -- | .217 | -- | 0.00 | -- | 4.35 | -- | 13.04 | -- |
| | vs. Righties | .308 | 16 | .411 | 54 | .366 | 28 | 1.67 | 94 | 8.43 | 75 | 6.93 | 15 |
| Randy Kutcher | vs. Lefties | .215 | 149 | .415 | 61 | .246 | 161 | 3.08 | 53 | 4.35 | 147 | 28.99 | 168 |
| | vs. Righties | .232 | -- | .326 | -- | .291 | -- | 0.00 | -- | 7.55 | -- | 24.53 | -- |
| Jody Reed | vs. Lefties | .321 | 21 | .450 | 40 | .401 | 13 | 0.71 | 125 | 11.98 | 28 | 4.79 | 12 |
| | vs. Righties | .276 | 53 | .372 | 91 | .367 | 25 | 0.52 | 147 | 11.73 | 23 | 7.96 | 23 |
| Jim Rice | vs. Lefties | .254 | 106 | .397 | 81 | .294 | 134 | 1.59 | 89 | 5.88 | 116 | 13.24 | 89 |
| | vs. Righties | .226 | 139 | .322 | 131 | .269 | 152 | 1.37 | 111 | 5.63 | 137 | 18.75 | 132 |
| Luis Rivera | vs. Lefties | .275 | 74 | .402 | 75 | .308 | 110 | 1.96 | 77 | 4.59 | 142 | 16.51 | 119 |
| | vs. Righties | .249 | 107 | .344 | 110 | .298 | 119 | 1.36 | 113 | 6.25 | 125 | 17.50 | 122 |
| Kevin Romine | vs. Lefties | .346 | 7 | .394 | 85 | .386 | 23 | 0.00 | 134 | 6.03 | 112 | 12.93 | 87 |
| | vs. Righties | .229 | 133 | .294 | 148 | .290 | 133 | 0.59 | 143 | 7.49 | 97 | 20.32 | 140 |
| Team Average | vs. Lefties | .279 | 4 | .396 | 5 | .345 | 3 | 1.68 | 13 | 9.14 | 5 | 11.87 | 4 |
| | vs. Righties | .277 | 1 | .405 | 2 | .354 | 1 | 2.00 | 12 | 10.30 | 1 | 11.63 | 1 |
| League Average | vs. Lefties | .266 | | .391 | | .328 | | 2.18 | | 8.18 | | 13.58 | |
| | vs. Righties | .258 | | .380 | | .325 | | 2.26 | | 8.56 | | 14.57 | |

## Batting with Runners on Base and Bases Empty

| | | BA | Rank | SA | Rank | OBA | Rank | HR % | Rank | BB % | Rank | SO % | Rank |
|---|---|---|---|---|---|---|---|---|---|---|---|---|---|
| Marty Barrett | Runners On | .253 | 113 | .305 | 152 | .318 | 109 | 0.00 | 146 | 8.38 | 87 | 3.14 | 2 |
| | Bases Empty | .258 | 79 | .330 | 126 | .322 | 75 | 0.55 | 144 | 8.04 | 73 | 3.02 | 1 |
| Wade Boggs | Runners On | .351 | 2 | .443 | 44 | .469 | 1 | 0.00 | 146 | 17.81 | 7 | 5.82 | 12 |
| | Bases Empty | .318 | 7 | .453 | 30 | .404 | 4 | 0.76 | 132 | 12.22 | 14 | 7.56 | 14 |
| Ellis Burks | Runners On | .315 | 23 | .475 | 23 | .368 | 44 | 3.00 | 49 | 7.56 | 103 | 11.56 | 76 |
| | Bases Empty | .291 | 25 | .467 | 18 | .362 | 23 | 3.02 | 59 | 8.60 | 63 | 11.76 | 58 |
| Rick Cerone | Runners On | .287 | 55 | .420 | 56 | .356 | 57 | 2.00 | 77 | 10.11 | 61 | 10.67 | 65 |
| | Bases Empty | .199 | 160 | .267 | 165 | .282 | 144 | 0.68 | 138 | 9.82 | 35 | 12.88 | 70 |
| Nick Esasky | Runners On | .296 | 41 | .570 | 3 | .390 | 21 | 7.39 | 3 | 13.11 | 24 | 15.85 | 119 |
| | Bases Empty | .257 | 80 | .429 | 46 | .318 | 82 | 3.21 | 51 | 7.54 | 89 | 21.31 | 148 |
| Dwight Evans | Runners On | .284 | 62 | .460 | 32 | .384 | 25 | 3.07 | 45 | 14.56 | 17 | 12.34 | 85 |
| | Bases Empty | .286 | 36 | .467 | 19 | .411 | 2 | 4.63 | 22 | 16.88 | 2 | 14.33 | 87 |
| Rich Gedman | Runners On | .202 | 165 | .266 | 166 | .256 | 166 | 0.92 | 126 | 7.26 | 109 | 15.32 | 114 |
| | Bases Empty | .219 | 141 | .311 | 139 | .285 | 137 | 1.99 | 88 | 8.48 | 65 | 16.97 | 110 |
| Mike Greenwell | Runners On | .301 | 38 | .405 | 68 | .375 | 36 | 1.31 | 107 | 10.60 | 49 | 6.02 | 14 |
| | Bases Empty | .316 | 8 | .485 | 9 | .363 | 21 | 3.68 | 39 | 6.51 | 111 | 7.88 | 17 |
| Danny Heep | Runners On | .344 | 5 | .460 | 31 | .403 | 14 | 1.84 | 87 | 9.63 | 65 | 5.88 | 13 |
| | Bases Empty | .255 | 88 | .338 | 118 | .304 | 105 | 1.27 | 113 | 6.55 | 107 | 8.93 | 28 |
| Jody Reed | Runners On | .304 | 35 | .409 | 65 | .399 | 18 | 0.42 | 145 | 12.50 | 28 | 7.77 | 27 |
| | Bases Empty | .275 | 46 | .380 | 86 | .356 | 31 | 0.70 | 136 | 11.15 | 24 | 6.50 | 9 |
| Jim Rice | Runners On | .226 | 154 | .321 | 146 | .256 | 165 | 1.89 | 85 | 5.13 | 142 | 18.80 | 142 |
| | Bases Empty | .243 | 110 | .369 | 97 | .297 | 118 | 0.97 | 124 | 6.31 | 115 | 15.32 | 95 |
| Luis Rivera | Runners On | .246 | 124 | .380 | 85 | .285 | 150 | 2.11 | 74 | 5.16 | 140 | 18.06 | 136 |
| | Bases Empty | .265 | 64 | .348 | 109 | .314 | 92 | 1.10 | 117 | 6.19 | 121 | 16.49 | 104 |
| Kevin Romine | Runners On | .283 | 64 | .331 | 140 | .324 | 104 | 0.00 | 146 | 6.34 | 123 | 15.49 | 117 |
| | Bases Empty | .265 | 63 | .333 | 121 | .329 | 66 | 0.68 | 139 | 7.45 | 92 | 19.25 | 130 |
| Team Average | Runners On | .285 | 1 | .412 | 1 | .361 | 1 | 1.97 | 11 | 10.61 | 2 | 10.89 | 1 |
| | Bases Empty | .270 | 2 | .394 | 4 | .342 | 1 | 1.85 | 13 | 9.35 | 1 | 12.46 | 2 |
| League Average | Runners On | .268 | | .389 | | .336 | | 2.15 | | 9.17 | | 13.53 | |
| | Bases Empty | .255 | | .380 | | .317 | | 2.29 | | 7.84 | | 14.86 | |

## Overall Batting Compared to Late Inning Pressure Situations

| | | BA | Rank | SA | Rank | OBA | Rank | HR % | Rank | BB % | Rank | SO % | Rank | RDI % | Rank |
|---|---|---|---|---|---|---|---|---|---|---|---|---|---|---|---|
| Marty Barrett | Overall | .256 | 100 | .318 | 146 | .320 | 91 | 0.30 | 159 | 8.21 | 78 | 3.08 | 1 | .226 | 137 |
| | Pressure | .345 | 10 | .382 | 74 | .400 | 20 | 0.00 | 107 | 6.25 | 122 | 6.25 | 12 | .167 | 126 |
| Wade Boggs | Overall | .330 | 3 | .449 | 29 | .430 | 1 | 0.48 | 148 | 14.42 | 9 | 6.87 | 12 | .289 | 55 |
| | Pressure | .234 | 104 | .309 | 115 | .291 | 119 | 0.00 | 107 | 6.80 | 117 | 10.68 | 37 | .138 | 142 |
| Ellis Burks | Overall | .303 | 16 | .471 | 13 | .365 | 24 | 3.01 | 55 | 8.07 | 85 | 11.66 | 63 | .286 | 60 |
| | Pressure | .254 | 86 | .567 | 9 | .306 | 100 | 5.97 | 14 | 5.48 | 137 | 16.44 | 91 | .216 | 109 |
| Rick Cerone | Overall | .243 | 125 | .345 | 123 | .320 | 89 | 1.35 | 115 | 9.97 | 42 | 11.73 | 65 | .384 | 2 |
| | Pressure | .178 | 154 | .222 | 157 | .269 | 133 | 0.00 | 107 | 11.32 | 47 | 9.43 | 27 | .417 | 15 |
| Nick Esasky | Overall | .277 | 45 | .500 | 7 | .355 | 35 | 5.32 | 12 | 10.43 | 37 | 18.48 | 132 | .286 | 59 |
| | Pressure | .308 | 34 | .603 | 4 | .386 | 29 | 6.41 | 10 | 11.36 | 46 | 19.32 | 113 | .214 | 110 |
| Dwight Evans | Overall | .285 | 35 | .463 | 19 | .397 | 6 | 3.85 | 28 | 15.71 | 5 | 13.33 | 79 | .340 | 17 |
| | Pressure | .278 | 58 | .354 | 89 | .341 | 62 | 1.27 | 103 | 7.87 | 101 | 14.61 | 68 | .297 | 65 |
| Rich Gedman | Overall | .212 | 164 | .292 | 165 | .273 | 162 | 1.54 | 104 | 7.96 | 89 | 16.26 | 107 | .139 | 169 |
| | Pressure | .209 | 123 | .279 | 132 | .277 | 130 | 0.00 | 107 | 8.33 | 86 | 16.67 | 93 | .154 | 132 |
| Mike Greenwell | Overall | .308 | 11 | .443 | 32 | .370 | 17 | 2.42 | 68 | 8.74 | 66 | 6.86 | 11 | .321 | 31 |
| | Pressure | .413 | 1 | .600 | 5 | .488 | 1 | 4.00 | 34 | 11.63 | 42 | 6.98 | 13 | .538 | 3 |
| Danny Heep | Overall | .300 | 21 | .400 | 68 | .356 | 32 | 1.56 | 101 | 8.17 | 80 | 7.32 | 15 | .317 | 34 |
| | Pressure | .279 | 56 | .512 | 15 | .392 | 25 | 4.65 | 25 | 13.73 | 27 | 5.88 | 10 | .417 | 15 |
| Sam Horn | Overall | .148 | -- | .185 | -- | .258 | -- | 0.00 | -- | 12.90 | -- | 25.81 | -- | .160 | -- |
| | Pressure | .238 | -- | .238 | -- | .360 | -- | 0.00 | -- | 16.00 | -- | 28.00 | -- | .375 | 25 |
| Randy Kutcher | Overall | .225 | -- | .363 | -- | .273 | -- | 1.25 | -- | 6.29 | -- | 26.29 | -- | .220 | 144 |
| | Pressure | .318 | -- | .636 | -- | .360 | -- | 4.55 | -- | 7.69 | -- | 15.38 | -- | .500 | -- |
| Jody Reed | Overall | .288 | 32 | .393 | 75 | .376 | 15 | 0.57 | 145 | 11.79 | 20 | 7.11 | 13 | .206 | 153 |
| | Pressure | .224 | 112 | .276 | 133 | .299 | 110 | 0.00 | 107 | 8.89 | 79 | 13.33 | 53 | .240 | 100 |
| Jim Rice | Overall | .234 | 144 | .344 | 124 | .276 | 160 | 1.44 | 108 | 5.70 | 139 | 17.11 | 118 | .256 | 99 |
| | Pressure | .174 | -- | .217 | -- | .321 | -- | 0.00 | -- | 17.86 | -- | 25.00 | -- | .000 | 165 |
| Luis Rivera | Overall | .257 | 91 | .362 | 108 | .301 | 126 | 1.55 | 102 | 5.73 | 138 | 17.19 | 120 | .198 | 158 |
| | Pressure | .186 | 145 | .233 | 153 | .222 | 154 | 0.00 | 107 | 4.35 | 147 | 21.74 | 129 | .000 | -- |
| Kevin Romine | Overall | .274 | 51 | .332 | 136 | .327 | 79 | 0.36 | 154 | 6.93 | 110 | 17.49 | 123 | .229 | 134 |
| | Pressure | .278 | 60 | .306 | 117 | .381 | 34 | 0.00 | 107 | 13.95 | 25 | 16.28 | 89 | .083 | 156 |
| Team Average | Overall | .277 | 1 | .403 | 1 | .351 | 1 | 1.91 | 12 | 9.96 | 1 | 11.70 | 1 | .269 | 8 |
| | Pressure | .267 | 3 | .389 | 3 | .341 | 3 | 1.90 | 7 | 9.44 | 6 | 14.32 | 1 | .240 | 11 |
| League Average | Overall | .261 | | .384 | | .326 | | 2.23 | | 8.44 | | 14.26 | | .269 | |
| | Pressure | .247 | | .357 | | .318 | | 2.02 | | 9.02 | | 17.90 | | .254 | |

## Additional Miscellaneous Batting Comparisons

| | Grass Surface | | Artificial Surface | | Home Games | | Road Games | | Runners in Scoring Position | | Runners in Scoring Pos and Two Outs | | Leading Off Inning | | Runners on 3B with less than 2 Outs | |
|---|---|---|---|---|---|---|---|---|---|---|---|---|---|---|---|---|
| | BA | Rank | BA | Rank | BA | Rank | BA | Rank | BA | Rank | BA | Rank | OBA | Rank | RDI % | Rank |
| Marty Barrett | .249 | 100 | .288 | 46 | .263 | 76 | .249 | 107 | .256 | 95 | .180 | 139 | .295 | 116 | .632 | 50 |
| Wade Boggs | .346 | 1 | .252 | 87 | .377 | 2 | .287 | 40 | .336 | 14 | .288 | 33 | .402 | 13 | .679 | 36 |
| Ellis Burks | .296 | 23 | .354 | 8 | .319 | 12 | .287 | 38 | .310 | 27 | .218 | 106 | .443 | 3 | .563 | 92 |
| Rick Cerone | .247 | 104 | .222 | 131 | .303 | 27 | .177 | 171 | .338 | 11 | .368 | 4 | .238 | 162 | .609 | 66 |
| Nick Esasky | .282 | 46 | .250 | 90 | .300 | 28 | .253 | 94 | .304 | 33 | .244 | 78 | .355 | 41 | .571 | 85 |
| Dwight Evans | .289 | 33 | .260 | 76 | .273 | 61 | .295 | 24 | .323 | 20 | .225 | 95 | .406 | 11 | .680 | 33 |
| Rich Gedman | .222 | 152 | .154 | 164 | .222 | 145 | .203 | 166 | .130 | 171 | .154 | 153 | .284 | 129 | .357 | 161 |
| Mike Greenwell | .315 | 6 | .266 | 64 | .325 | 10 | .291 | 28 | .289 | 48 | .200 | 118 | .289 | 122 | .680 | 33 |
| Danny Heep | .306 | 14 | .250 | 90 | .291 | 39 | .309 | 16 | .337 | 13 | .386 | 2 | .308 | 102 | .458 | 140 |
| Randy Kutcher | .240 | -- | .171 | -- | .243 | -- | .211 | -- | .286 | 55 | .233 | 88 | .235 | -- | .571 | -- |
| Jody Reed | .292 | 28 | .264 | 67 | .300 | 29 | .276 | 56 | .244 | 106 | .215 | 109 | .390 | 16 | .438 | 146 |
| Jim Rice | .232 | 136 | .250 | -- | .245 | 111 | .222 | 150 | .242 | 109 | .192 | 126 | .294 | 117 | .647 | 45 |
| Luis Rivera | .263 | 76 | .226 | 127 | .294 | 37 | .219 | 158 | .232 | 127 | .220 | 104 | .279 | 135 | .429 | 148 |
| Kevin Romine | .246 | 106 | .400 | 1 | .260 | 83 | .287 | 39 | .288 | 52 | .324 | 14 | .286 | 124 | .400 | 151 |
| Team Average | .281 | 1 | .260 | 8 | .292 | 1 | .263 | 5 | .281 | 2 | .240 | 6 | .346 | 1 | .573 | 7 |
| League Average | .260 | | .262 | | .262 | | .259 | | .262 | | .232 | | .321 | | .566 | |

## Pitching vs. Left and Right Handed Batters

| | | BA | Rank | SA | Rank | OBA | Rank | HR % | Rank | BB % | Rank | SO % | Rank |
|---|---|---|---|---|---|---|---|---|---|---|---|---|---|
| Mike Boddicker | vs. Lefties | .279 | 90 | .421 | 93 | .333 | 73 | 2.70 | 92 | 7.47 | 48 | 11.72 | 70 |
| | vs. Righties | .252 | 58 | .374 | 62 | .325 | 75 | 1.90 | 60 | 8.15 | 79 | 20.86 | 24 |
| Oil Can Boyd | vs. Lefties | .235 | 39 | .319 | 30 | .300 | 39 | 2.52 | 86 | 8.46 | 62 | 10.77 | 80 |
| | vs. Righties | .274 | -- | .500 | -- | .319 | -- | 4.72 | -- | 6.90 | -- | 10.34 | -- |
| Roger Clemens | vs. Lefties | .243 | 43 | .332 | 38 | .320 | 59 | 1.39 | 46 | 10.00 | 89 | 19.30 | 16 |
| | vs. Righties | .218 | 18 | .345 | 41 | .287 | 27 | 3.05 | 107 | 7.59 | 66 | 25.32 | 13 |
| John Dopson | vs. Lefties | .247 | 49 | .323 | 33 | .315 | 53 | 1.58 | 55 | 9.30 | 77 | 11.55 | 72 |
| | vs. Righties | .266 | 84 | .405 | 94 | .341 | 107 | 2.72 | 96 | 9.68 | 104 | 14.52 | 75 |
| Wes Gardner | vs. Lefties | .313 | 118 | .429 | 97 | .425 | 135 | 1.36 | 44 | 16.76 | 130 | 18.44 | 19 |
| | vs. Righties | .267 | 88 | .461 | 127 | .327 | 81 | 4.19 | 128 | 7.94 | 74 | 22.43 | 20 |
| Eric Hetzel | vs. Lefties | .268 | 82 | .392 | 82 | .374 | 106 | 3.09 | 102 | 14.78 | 119 | 18.26 | 22 |
| | vs. Righties | .321 | -- | .532 | -- | .390 | -- | 3.67 | -- | 8.87 | -- | 9.68 | -- |
| Dennis Lamp | vs. Lefties | .289 | 102 | .350 | 45 | .352 | 89 | 1.11 | 32 | 8.91 | 67 | 7.92 | 112 |
| | vs. Righties | .193 | 6 | .254 | 4 | .220 | 1 | 0.88 | 11 | 3.70 | 4 | 18.52 | 35 |
| Rob Murphy | vs. Lefties | .254 | 59 | .386 | 74 | .280 | 20 | 1.75 | 64 | 3.33 | 4 | 20.83 | 14 |
| | vs. Righties | .250 | 50 | .353 | 49 | .339 | 103 | 1.84 | 59 | 11.64 | 125 | 25.79 | 12 |
| Joe Price | vs. Lefties | .268 | -- | .341 | -- | .295 | -- | 0.00 | -- | 4.55 | -- | 21.59 | -- |
| | vs. Righties | .259 | 74 | .423 | 106 | .347 | 114 | 4.23 | 129 | 11.98 | 126 | 15.21 | 63 |
| Lee Smith | vs. Lefties | .223 | 30 | .364 | 50 | .317 | 55 | 4.13 | 122 | 12.14 | 110 | 32.86 | 1 |
| | vs. Righties | .197 | 7 | .250 | 3 | .282 | 20 | 0.76 | 9 | 10.67 | 115 | 33.33 | 2 |
| Mike Smithson | vs. Lefties | .311 | 116 | .519 | 125 | .358 | 96 | 4.50 | 126 | 5.94 | 26 | 10.00 | 89 |
| | vs. Righties | .282 | 110 | .415 | 100 | .328 | 85 | 2.82 | 102 | 5.13 | 19 | 9.29 | 123 |
| Bob Stanley | vs. Lefties | .348 | 131 | .489 | 123 | .415 | 134 | 1.42 | 48 | 9.94 | 88 | 5.59 | 130 |
| | vs. Righties | .299 | 128 | .373 | 61 | .326 | 78 | 1.13 | 19 | 5.13 | 19 | 11.79 | 97 |
| Team Average | vs. Lefties | .270 | 10 | .387 | 8 | .338 | 10 | 2.17 | 7 | 9.23 | 7 | 14.78 | 3 |
| | vs. Righties | .252 | 4 | .378 | 6 | .318 | 6 | 2.52 | 11 | 8.36 | 11 | 18.75 | 1 |
| League Average | vs. Lefties | .261 | | .382 | | .330 | | 2.16 | | 9.16 | | 13.03 | |
| | vs. Righties | .261 | | .385 | | .323 | | 2.28 | | 7.96 | | 15.09 | |

## Pitching with Runners on Base and Bases Empty

| | | BA | Rank | SA | Rank | OBA | Rank | HR % | Rank | BB % | Rank | SO % | Rank |
|---|---|---|---|---|---|---|---|---|---|---|---|---|---|
| Mike Boddicker | Runners On | .259 | 61 | .354 | 47 | .331 | 66 | 1.49 | 45 | 9.11 | 69 | 14.94 | 53 |
| | Bases Empty | .273 | 93 | .432 | 107 | .329 | 86 | 2.94 | 95 | 6.77 | 55 | 16.63 | 49 |
| Oil Can Boyd | Runners On | .261 | -- | .466 | -- | .302 | -- | 5.68 | -- | 6.25 | -- | 10.42 | -- |
| | Bases Empty | .248 | 56 | .365 | 57 | .313 | 60 | 2.19 | 68 | 8.67 | 89 | 10.67 | 107 |
| Roger Clemens | Runners On | .233 | 28 | .327 | 21 | .331 | 68 | 0.88 | 17 | 11.85 | 109 | 19.51 | 18 |
| | Bases Empty | .231 | 31 | .344 | 40 | .290 | 33 | 2.88 | 92 | 7.04 | 61 | 23.63 | 13 |
| John Dopson | Runners On | .253 | 47 | .368 | 62 | .309 | 34 | 2.11 | 82 | 7.52 | 41 | 10.66 | 93 |
| | Bases Empty | .260 | 71 | .362 | 53 | .343 | 104 | 2.21 | 69 | 11.03 | 117 | 14.95 | 55 |
| Wes Gardner | Runners On | .338 | 132 | .592 | 134 | .420 | 134 | 4.93 | 130 | 12.79 | 119 | 18.02 | 31 |
| | Bases Empty | .250 | 59 | .342 | 39 | .335 | 93 | 1.53 | 35 | 11.31 | 122 | 22.62 | 19 |
| Eric Hetzel | Runners On | .333 | -- | .522 | -- | .404 | -- | 3.33 | -- | 11.43 | -- | 10.48 | -- |
| | Bases Empty | .267 | 84 | .422 | 102 | .366 | 124 | 3.45 | 113 | 11.94 | 127 | 16.42 | 50 |
| Dennis Lamp | Runners On | .263 | 72 | .311 | 15 | .312 | 41 | 1.20 | 28 | 7.33 | 39 | 9.42 | 108 |
| | Bases Empty | .216 | 18 | .286 | 9 | .256 | 9 | 0.83 | 13 | 5.12 | 25 | 16.93 | 46 |
| Rob Murphy | Runners On | .249 | 41 | .355 | 51 | .332 | 70 | 2.03 | 76 | 10.73 | 95 | 27.90 | 4 |
| | Bases Empty | .254 | 63 | .370 | 62 | .312 | 59 | 1.59 | 36 | 7.80 | 74 | 20.49 | 23 |
| Joe Price | Runners On | .255 | 54 | .397 | 89 | .312 | 42 | 2.84 | 108 | 8.23 | 55 | 17.09 | 36 |
| | Bases Empty | .269 | 87 | .400 | 83 | .354 | 114 | 3.08 | 99 | 11.56 | 124 | 17.01 | 45 |
| Lee Smith | Runners On | .233 | 27 | .318 | 19 | .331 | 69 | 1.55 | 49 | 13.07 | 121 | 30.07 | 2 |
| | Bases Empty | .185 | 5 | .290 | 13 | .263 | 12 | 3.23 | 106 | 9.49 | 100 | 36.50 | 1 |
| Mike Smithson | Runners On | .286 | 106 | .440 | 115 | .343 | 84 | 3.63 | 122 | 6.94 | 32 | 8.33 | 118 |
| | Bases Empty | .305 | 125 | .489 | 128 | .343 | 103 | 3.69 | 120 | 4.36 | 11 | 10.76 | 105 |
| Bob Stanley | Runners On | .361 | 133 | .462 | 124 | .401 | 131 | 1.18 | 25 | 8.16 | 53 | 8.67 | 115 |
| | Bases Empty | .275 | 98 | .383 | 74 | .325 | 78 | 1.34 | 24 | 6.25 | 47 | 9.38 | 114 |
| Team Average | Runners On | .274 | 9 | .395 | 7 | .343 | 10 | 2.24 | 9 | 9.57 | 11 | 15.59 | 2 |
| | Bases Empty | .251 | 5 | .373 | 8 | .315 | 9 | 2.45 | 10 | 8.12 | 10 | 17.92 | 2 |
| League Average | Runners On | .268 | | .389 | | .336 | | 2.15 | | 9.17 | | 13.53 | |
| | Bases Empty | .255 | | .380 | | .317 | | 2.29 | | 7.84 | | 14.86 | |

## Overall Pitching Compared to Late Inning Pressure Situations

| | | BA | Rank | SA | Rank | OBA | Rank | HR % | Rank | BB % | Rank | SO % | Rank |
|---|---|---|---|---|---|---|---|---|---|---|---|---|---|
| Mike Boddicker | Overall | .267 | 81 | .400 | 87 | .330 | 76 | 2.34 | 81 | 7.79 | 62 | 15.90 | 47 |
| | Pressure | .169 | 8 | .292 | 36 | .229 | 3 | 3.08 | 103 | 4.29 | 13 | 14.29 | 68 |
| Roger Clemens | Overall | .231 | 24 | .338 | 31 | .305 | 34 | 2.15 | 68 | 8.91 | 84 | 22.03 | 13 |
| | Pressure | .252 | 74 | .423 | 104 | .331 | 74 | 4.50 | 123 | 9.38 | 67 | 21.88 | 24 |
| John Dopson | Overall | .257 | 61 | .365 | 54 | .328 | 74 | 2.16 | 69 | 9.49 | 94 | 13.07 | 72 |
| | Pressure | .250 | 68 | .341 | 63 | .261 | 18 | 2.27 | 82 | 2.08 | 4 | 10.42 | 107 |
| Wes Gardner | Overall | .287 | 112 | .447 | 122 | .372 | 132 | 2.96 | 110 | 11.96 | 122 | 20.61 | 18 |
| | Pressure | .214 | 40 | .286 | 33 | .389 | 111 | 0.00 | 1 | 21.62 | 134 | 13.51 | 72 |
| Greg A. Harris | Overall | .208 | -- | .287 | -- | .308 | -- | 0.99 | -- | 12.71 | -- | 21.19 | -- |
| | Pressure | .225 | 47 | .275 | 26 | .295 | 41 | 0.00 | 1 | 8.89 | 54 | 20.00 | 32 |
| Dennis Lamp | Overall | .235 | 29 | .297 | 8 | .280 | 14 | 0.98 | 9 | 6.07 | 23 | 13.71 | 63 |
| | Pressure | .290 | 102 | .371 | 83 | .328 | 70 | 1.61 | 56 | 5.71 | 26 | 8.57 | 113 |
| Rob Murphy | Overall | .251 | 53 | .363 | 52 | .323 | 63 | 1.81 | 55 | 9.36 | 90 | 24.43 | 9 |
| | Pressure | .290 | 101 | .385 | 87 | .368 | 102 | 1.78 | 64 | 10.77 | 82 | 25.64 | 13 |
| Joe Price | Overall | .262 | 70 | .399 | 85 | .332 | 82 | 2.95 | 109 | 9.84 | 100 | 17.05 | 38 |
| | Pressure | .275 | 93 | .450 | 108 | .341 | 78 | 5.00 | 125 | 8.89 | 54 | 24.44 | 16 |
| Lee Smith | Overall | .209 | 12 | .304 | 13 | .299 | 28 | 2.37 | 83 | 11.38 | 115 | 33.10 | 1 |
| | Pressure | .222 | 45 | .304 | 41 | .298 | 47 | 2.22 | 81 | 9.80 | 74 | 35.95 | 2 |
| Mike Smithson | Overall | .297 | 124 | .468 | 129 | .343 | 98 | 3.66 | 128 | 5.54 | 15 | 9.65 | 113 |
| | Pressure | .391 | 128 | .717 | 132 | .420 | 120 | 8.70 | 132 | 6.00 | 31 | 12.00 | 85 |
| Bob Stanley | Overall | .321 | 133 | .425 | 102 | .366 | 129 | 1.26 | 18 | 7.30 | 50 | 8.99 | 121 |
| | Pressure | .298 | 112 | .426 | 105 | .368 | 101 | 2.13 | 76 | 9.26 | 64 | 7.41 | 119 |
| Team Average | Overall | .261 | 8 | .383 | 8 | .328 | 8 | 2.36 | 9 | 8.77 | 11 | 16.87 | 2 |
| | Pressure | .265 | 11 | .387 | 10 | .335 | 10 | 2.78 | 12 | 9.16 | 6 | 19.86 | 3 |
| League Average | Overall | .261 | | .384 | | .326 | | 2.23 | | 8.44 | | 14.26 | |
| | Pressure | .250 | | .362 | | .325 | | 2.14 | | 9.50 | | 16.61 | |

## Additional Miscellaneous Pitching Comparisons

| | Grass Surface | | Artificial Surface | | Home Games | | Road Games | | Runners in Scoring Position | | Runners in Scoring Pos and Two Outs | | Leading Off Inning | |
|---|---|---|---|---|---|---|---|---|---|---|---|---|---|---|
| | BA | Rank | BA | Rank | BA | Rank | BA | Rank | BA | Rank | BA | Rank | OBA | Rank |
| Mike Boddicker | .273 | 92 | .238 | 37 | .305 | 124 | .227 | 31 | .213 | 18 | .195 | 45 | .348 | 99 |
| Oil Can Boyd | .271 | 87 | .222 | 23 | .321 | -- | .213 | 13 | .302 | -- | .389 | -- | .317 | 60 |
| Roger Clemens | .241 | 34 | .180 | 4 | .248 | 63 | .219 | 18 | .224 | 26 | .250 | 88 | .285 | 32 |
| John Dopson | .260 | 66 | .239 | 38 | .253 | 68 | .263 | 72 | .254 | 73 | .169 | 29 | .333 | 79 |
| Wes Gardner | .285 | 107 | .310 | -- | .227 | 27 | .325 | 129 | .341 | 131 | .351 | 131 | .340 | 89 |
| Eric Hetzel | .295 | 120 | .300 | 105 | .295 | 119 | .300 | -- | .304 | -- | .182 | -- | .345 | 94 |
| Dennis Lamp | .228 | 24 | .333 | -- | .237 | 39 | .232 | 33 | .235 | 40 | .154 | 20 | .260 | 18 |
| Rob Murphy | .245 | 45 | .286 | 89 | .251 | 65 | .251 | 50 | .271 | 88 | .250 | 88 | .273 | 28 |
| Joe Price | .265 | 73 | .143 | -- | .257 | 76 | .267 | 77 | .239 | 51 | .167 | 28 | .391 | 123 |
| Lee Smith | .190 | 7 | .310 | -- | .203 | 11 | .217 | 16 | .220 | 20 | .086 | 3 | .328 | 76 |
| Mike Smithson | .302 | 123 | .234 | 34 | .315 | 129 | .273 | 84 | .321 | 124 | .276 | 106 | .367 | 111 |
| Bob Stanley | .312 | 129 | .381 | -- | .307 | 125 | .335 | 131 | .345 | 132 | .365 | 132 | .366 | 110 |
| Team Average | .263 | 7 | .250 | 3 | .269 | 11 | .252 | 4 | .269 | 11 | .234 | 9 | .325 | 9 |
| League Average | .260 | | .262 | | .259 | | .262 | | .262 | | .232 | | .321 | |

# CALIFORNIA ANGELS

- **And you thought *turnover* applied only to basketball and football.**
- **A heavenly turnaround on the mound.**

Six years ago, Michael Spinks challenged Larry Holmes for the heavyweight title. Most fight fans thought he'd have more luck challenging Gary Kasparov for the world chess title. After all, six other light-heavyweight champs had fought for the heavyweight belt, and the only one to manage even a draw was Philadelphia Jack O'Brien in the early 1900s. Philly Jack actually went 20 rounds on two separate occasions against the heavyweight champ, Tommy Burns, losing the rematch on a decision. But Burns would hardly be mistaken for some of the super–heavies on the current old–timers' tour—he stood five-eight, and weighed only 175 pounds. O'Brien actually had two-and-a-half inches on Burns.

Of the five light-heavyweight champs who challenged heavyweights of more generous proportions for the title, only one was vertical at the final bell: Joey Maxim, who lost a 15–round decision to Ezzard Charles in 1951. John Henry Lewis lasted only one round against Joe Louis. Archie Moore was knocked out by both Rocky Marciano (in the ninth round) and Floyd Patterson (fifth)—on separate occasions, of course. And Bob Foster took a two-round beating from Joe Frazier in 1970 so appalling that for 15 years, no other light-heavy champ dared consider such an act of hubris. Then along came Spinks. Could he be even more daft than his toothless brother?

The answer was obvious when Spinks stepped into the ring that night to face Holmes. Spinks had added 25 pounds since his previous fight just three months earlier. But he wasn't some pencil-necked geek plumped up to face his slaughter like a Thanksgiving turkey. Spinks had lowered his body fat, and added only muscle. He looked as though he'd spent those weeks watching nothing but Cory Everson's "Bodyshaping," and actually paying attention to the *exercises.* (Our apologies to those without cable TV or a libido, who won't understand that reference.) Much to the delight of the Marciano family, and no matter what Larry says, Spinks beat Holmes, proving that sometimes, in sports at least, you can tell a book by its cover.

Actually, horseplayers have always known never to place a serious bet before a trip to the paddock for a firsthand look at the field. Punters who waited for the post parade before betting on the 1982 Kentucky Derby must have stormed the Churchill Downs windows to bet on longshot Gato Del Sol. He pranced onto the track with the squared-shoulders look of a finely chiseled carousel horse: neck arched, and head down—the tell-tale sign of a sharp horse. Gato 's payoff was pretty handsome, too.

Can you handicap baseball teams by changes in appearance as well? Does the degree to which a team alters its makeup from one season to the next tell us anything about its chances for improvement in the upcoming season? And if so, how does one explain the 1989 California Angels, a team that improved by 16 wins over 1988 despite little turnover in personnel, at least in comparison to other teams with losing records?

Teams that make fewer personnel changes coming off losing seasons tend to outperform losing teams that undergo substantial makeovers. With all teams with losing records over the past 50 years classified into four groups, according to the degree to which they changed their personnel in the following seasons, the trend is clear: The greater the turnover, the less likely a team was to improve. Teams with outright makeovers (50 percent or more) showed the smallest average increase: on average, 26 percentage points. Teams with substantial turnover of personnel (40 to 50 percent) improved by an average of 27 points. Those with only moderate turnover (30 to 40 percent) gained an average of 37 points. And teams with only slight change (30 percent or less) gained the most (.043 on average). So it's significant that last season, California changed its personnel by only 36 percent from the previous season, the lowest turnover among the 10 teams that posted losing records in 1988:

| | | | |
|---|---|---|---|
| Philadelphia | 65.9 | Chi. White Sox | 44.6 |
| Texas | 57.6 | Cleveland | 43.8 |
| Atlanta | 53.4 | Chi. Cubs | 41.6 |
| Baltimore | 53.2 | St. Louis | 39.4 |
| Seattle | 47.2 | California | 36.1 |

(For a detailed explanation of how these figures are computed, see the Expos essay, p. 127.)

Since the teams most likely to improve are those coming off losing seasons with little turnover in personnel, it should come as no surprise that winning teams with lots of new faces are most likely to suffer steep declines. And surprisingly, an average of three teams each year change their rosters by at least 50 percent following winning seasons. The 1989 season produced only one such team, but is was an extreme example: the New York Yankees, with a 72 percent turnover despite an 85–76 record in 1988. That marked only the third time in this century that a winning team underwent a change of more than 70 percent. All three instances produced sharp declines:

| | | | Year I | | | Year II | | | |
|---|---|---|---|---|---|---|---|---|---|
| Years | Team | Change | W | L | Pct. | W | L | Pct. | Diff. |
| 1988–89 | New York Yankees | 71.7 | 85 | 76 | .528 | 74 | 87 | .460 | −.068 |
| 1976–77 | Oakland Athletics | 81.8 | 87 | 74 | .540 | 63 | 98 | .391 | −.149 |
| 1945–46 | New York Giants | 81.4 | 78 | 74 | .513 | 61 | 93 | .396 | −.117 |

Getting back to the Angels, all seven players who batted at least 400 times during that losing 1988 season returned to Anaheim in '89. They included Chili Davis, Brian Downing, Jack Howell, Wally Joyner, Johnny Ray, Dick Schofield, and Devon White. All five pitchers who worked at least 100 innings in 1988 returned as well. They were: Chuck Finley, Willie Fraser, Kirk McCaskill, Dan Petry, and Mike Witt. Complacency in the face of defeat is a trait seldom appreciated by local fans or media, and this was no exception. The masses wanted heads to roll. But general manager Mike Port had the conviction to stay with what he perceived as a solid foundation, and merely fill the cracks.

This was no ordinary patchwork job. Port used only quality materials to support his superstructure. The part-timers of '88 were replaced by some masterfully selected veteran free agents in an expensive but successful gambit to improve the team. Out went catchers Bob Boone and Darrell Miller; in came Lance Parrish and Bill Schroeder. George Hendrick departed, and when the Yankees made only a halfhearted attempt to re–sign Claudell Washington, Port got the job done. And after failing to land free agents Nolan Ryan or Bruce Hurst, Port traded for Bert Blyleven, whose injury-induced 10–17 record during 1988 fooled just about everyone else in Anaheim.

Finally, the Angels decided to place rookie Jim Abbott in their starting rotation without ever subjecting him to the standard training techniques designed to develop struggling young prospects into first-rate major leaguers: long bus rides, fast-food meals at 2 a.m., lumpy hotel mattresses, and so forth. For the first two weeks of the season, the press howled at what they perceived as a blatant publicity stunt. Based on a mediocre spring training, many felt Abbott deserved a steady diet of Big Macs for at least a year or two. Some stunt. After losing his first two starts, Abbott won five of his next seven, compiling a 3.22 ERA in 44 innings. But, of course, by that time, the Angels were in first place with twice as many wins as losses, and *all* was forgiven.

In retrospect, the changes to California's lineup were merely cosmetic. Washington, Parrish, and Schroeder looked an awful lot more attractive in victory than Hendrick, Boone, and Miller appeared in defeat. California actually improved its record by 16 games despite a slight decrease in scoring (45 fewer runs last season than in 1988). It was the dramatic improvement in the Angels' pitching rotation that turned the team around. California placed three starters among the American League's top five in ERA: Blyleven and McCaskill, both injury-free; and Finley, who developed a devilish fork ball that made him almost unhittable against left-handed batters. The result: California sliced 25 percent from the generous average of 4.8 runs per game it allowed in 1988, the 10th-largest single-season decrease in league history. The following table shows the runs allowed per game by the A.L.'s all-time top 10. The column labeled "Drop" indicates the percent of decrease; "Change" refers to the turnover in personnel, pitchers only:

| Years | Team | Year 1 | Year 2 | Drop | Change |
|---|---|---|---|---|---|
| 1903–1904 | New York Highlanders | 5.08 | 3.43 | 32.6 | 60.2 |
| 1903–1904 | Chicago White Sox | 4.47 | 3.14 | 29.6 | 45.4 |
| 1942–1943 | Washington Senators | 5.46 | 3.86 | 29.3 | 67.4 |
| 1971–1972 | Cleveland Indians | 4.67 | 3.31 | 29.0 | 65.0 |
| 1970–1971 | Chicago White Sox | 5.17 | 3.71 | 28.4 | 56.5 |
| 1908–1909 | Philadelphia Athletics | 3.67 | 2.65 | 28.0 | 44.6 |
| 1980–1981 | Oakland Athletics | 5.42 | 3.93 | 27.5 | 35.0 |
| 1953–1954 | Detroit Tigers | 5.87 | 4.32 | 26.4 | 34.8 |
| 1911–1912 | Washington Senators | 5.09 | 3.80 | 25.4 | 32.5 |
| 1988–1989 | California Angels | 4.76 | 3.57 | 25.0 | 40.9 |

The changes that California made prior to 1989 were typical of the Port regime. Despite a reputation for upheaval erroneously based on owner Gene Autry's willingness to spend his Rudolph royalties on superstars, Port has overseen a policy of steady but gradual change, on the order of 35 to 40 percent a year (roughly equal to the league average). Considering the narrow margin of error created by a roster that has perennially been among the oldest in major league history, Port's restraint has been noteworthy, his personnel decisions uncannily successful. This past winter, California landed the biggest fish in the ocean when they signed Mark Langston, but once again changed little else. Their other acquisitions—Scott Bailes, Mike Smithson, and Mark Eichhorn—created little excitement, but sustained the team's policy of signing veteran players to fill little cracks before they turn into big ones.

## WON-LOST RECORD BY STARTING POSITION

| CALIFORNIA 91-71 | C | 1B | 2B | 3B | SS | LF | CF | RF | P | DH | Leadoff | Relief | Starts |
|---|---|---|---|---|---|---|---|---|---|---|---|---|---|
| Jim Abbott | - | - | - | - | - | - | - | - | 16-13 | - | - | - | 16-13 |
| Kent Anderson | - | - | 2-1 | 0-3 | 38-27 | - | - | 0-1 | - | 0-1 | 0-1 | - | 40-33 |
| Tony Armas | - | 2-0 | - | - | - | 4-0 | 0-1 | 24-16 | - | 3-1 | - | - | 33-18 |
| Dante Bichette | - | - | - | - | - | 2-6 | 1-5 | 12-10 | - | - | - | - | 15-21 |
| Bert Blyleven | - | - | - | - | - | - | - | - | 23-10 | - | - | - | 23-10 |
| Brian Brady | - | - | - | - | - | - | - | - | - | - | - | - | - |
| Terry Clark | - | - | - | - | - | - | - | - | 0-2 | - | - | 0-2 | 0-2 |
| Sherman Corbett | - | - | - | - | - | - | - | - | - | - | - | 0-4 | - |
| Chili Davis | - | - | - | - | - | 85-61 | - | - | - | 4-2 | - | - | 89-63 |
| Gary Disarcina | - | - | - | - | - | - | - | - | - | - | - | - | - |
| Brian Downing | - | - | - | - | - | - | - | - | - | 78-63 | 30-21 | - | 78-63 |
| Jim Eppard | - | 0-1 | - | - | - | - | - | - | - | - | - | - | 0-1 |
| Mike Fetters | - | - | - | - | - | - | - | - | - | - | - | 0-1 | - |
| Chuck Finley | - | - | - | - | - | - | - | - | 16-13 | - | - | - | 16-13 |
| Willie Fraser | - | - | - | - | - | - | - | - | - | - | - | 11-33 | - |
| Bryan Harvey | - | - | - | - | - | - | - | - | - | - | - | 37-14 | - |
| Glenn Hoffman | - | 0-1 | 0-2 | 7-8 | 4-6 | - | - | - | - | 1-0 | - | - | 12-17 |
| Jack Howell | - | - | - | 79-56 | - | 0-1 | - | 1-0 | - | - | - | - | 80-57 |
| Wally Joyner | - | 86-64 | - | - | - | - | - | - | - | - | - | - | 86-64 |
| Vance Lovelace | - | - | - | - | - | - | - | - | - | - | - | 0-1 | - |
| Kirk McCaskill | - | - | - | - | - | - | - | - | 20-12 | - | - | - | 20-12 |
| Bob McClure | - | - | - | - | - | - | - | - | - | - | - | 21-27 | - |
| Mark McLemore | - | - | 15-10 | - | - | - | - | - | - | - | 0-1 | - | 15-10 |
| Greg Minton | - | - | - | - | - | - | - | - | - | - | - | 38-24 | - |
| Rich Monteleone | - | - | - | - | - | - | - | - | - | - | - | 10-14 | - |
| John Orton | 8-5 | - | - | - | - | - | - | - | - | - | - | - | 8-5 |
| Lance Parrish | 68-50 | - | - | - | - | - | - | - | - | 2-0 | - | - | 70-50 |
| Dan Petry | - | - | - | - | - | - | - | - | 1-3 | - | - | 6-9 | 1-3 |
| Johnny Ray | - | - | 73-57 | - | - | - | - | - | - | - | - | - | 73-57 |
| Bobby Rose | - | - | 1-1 | 5-4 | - | - | - | - | - | - | - | - | 6-5 |
| Dick Schofield | - | - | - | - | 49-38 | - | - | - | - | - | 18-10 | - | 49-38 |
| Bill Schroeder | 15-15 | 3-5 | - | - | - | - | - | - | - | - | - | - | 18-20 |
| Ron Tingley | 0-1 | - | - | - | - | - | - | - | - | - | - | - | 0-1 |
| Max Venable | - | - | - | - | - | 0-3 | 1-0 | 1-6 | - | - | 0-3 | - | 2-9 |
| Claudell Washington | - | - | - | - | - | - | 2-0 | 53-38 | - | 3-4 | 32-20 | - | 58-42 |
| Devon White | - | - | - | - | - | - | 87-65 | - | - | - | 11-15 | - | 87-65 |
| Mike Witt | - | - | - | - | - | - | - | - | 15-18 | - | - | - | 15-18 |

## Batting vs. Left and Right Handed Pitchers

| | | BA | Rank | SA | Rank | OBA | Rank | HR % | Rank | BB % | Rank | SO % | Rank |
|---|---|---|---|---|---|---|---|---|---|---|---|---|---|
| Kent Anderson | vs. Lefties | .275 | 73 | .290 | 155 | .351 | 54 | 0.00 | 134 | 10.26 | 41 | 16.67 | 120 |
| | vs. Righties | .208 | 156 | .253 | 165 | .255 | 162 | 0.00 | 158 | 5.29 | 145 | 17.06 | 118 |
| Tony Armas | vs. Lefties | .235 | 132 | .422 | 56 | .264 | 149 | 4.90 | 18 | 3.77 | 153 | 21.70 | 151 |
| | vs. Righties | .280 | -- | .510 | -- | .295 | -- | 6.00 | -- | 2.86 | -- | 23.81 | -- |
| Dante Bichette | vs. Lefties | .221 | 148 | .395 | 84 | .253 | 156 | 3.49 | 39 | 4.40 | 145 | 18.68 | 133 |
| | vs. Righties | .192 | -- | .212 | -- | .218 | -- | 0.00 | -- | 3.64 | -- | 12.73 | -- |
| Chili Davis | vs. Lefties | .245 | 122 | .415 | 62 | .300 | 123 | 4.00 | 31 | 7.73 | 80 | 20.00 | 138 |
| | vs. Righties | .286 | 37 | .447 | 35 | .361 | 33 | 3.89 | 26 | 10.73 | 41 | 15.85 | 103 |
| Brian Downing | vs. Lefties | .299 | 39 | .476 | 28 | .388 | 20 | 4.28 | 25 | 11.68 | 29 | 13.55 | 91 |
| | vs. Righties | .275 | 58 | .381 | 81 | .336 | 63 | 1.68 | 92 | 7.83 | 89 | 14.65 | 91 |
| Glenn Hoffman | vs. Lefties | .207 | 158 | .276 | 158 | .246 | 162 | 1.72 | 85 | 3.23 | 159 | 9.68 | 52 |
| | vs. Righties | .217 | -- | .261 | -- | .234 | -- | 0.00 | -- | 2.00 | -- | 14.00 | -- |
| Jack Howell | vs. Lefties | .140 | 172 | .235 | 165 | .220 | 170 | 1.47 | 96 | 7.95 | 75 | 29.80 | 170 |
| | vs. Righties | .263 | 77 | .482 | 21 | .342 | 56 | 5.33 | 12 | 10.47 | 46 | 20.94 | 142 |
| Wally Joyner | vs. Lefties | .262 | 91 | .379 | 95 | .305 | 117 | 2.91 | 57 | 4.85 | 140 | 8.81 | 42 |
| | vs. Righties | .292 | 26 | .442 | 38 | .351 | 45 | 2.58 | 60 | 8.20 | 78 | 8.90 | 32 |
| Lance Parrish | vs. Lefties | .236 | 130 | .410 | 70 | .317 | 98 | 4.86 | 20 | 10.91 | 37 | 14.55 | 106 |
| | vs. Righties | .239 | 120 | .377 | 87 | .300 | 118 | 3.46 | 37 | 7.57 | 96 | 25.24 | 163 |
| Johnny Ray | vs. Lefties | .262 | 92 | .318 | 141 | .299 | 125 | 0.51 | 133 | 5.96 | 115 | 5.50 | 15 |
| | vs. Righties | .304 | 20 | .382 | 80 | .343 | 53 | 1.19 | 123 | 6.32 | 124 | 4.95 | 4 |
| Dick Schofield | vs. Lefties | .260 | 96 | .346 | 122 | .304 | 120 | 0.79 | 123 | 5.07 | 137 | 9.42 | 49 |
| | vs. Righties | .206 | 157 | .297 | 146 | .295 | 123 | 1.71 | 90 | 10.10 | 48 | 16.35 | 110 |
| Bill Schroeder | vs. Lefties | .182 | 165 | .364 | 106 | .182 | 173 | 6.06 | 8 | 0.00 | 170 | 36.36 | 172 |
| | vs. Righties | .222 | -- | .333 | -- | .253 | -- | 2.78 | -- | 3.85 | -- | 25.64 | -- |
| Claudell Washington | vs. Lefties | .294 | 45 | .382 | 93 | .333 | 80 | 0.00 | 134 | 5.45 | 126 | 21.82 | 152 |
| | vs. Righties | .266 | 74 | .443 | 37 | .315 | 99 | 4.11 | 23 | 6.16 | 129 | 17.60 | 123 |
| Devon White | vs. Lefties | .248 | 118 | .355 | 111 | .291 | 135 | 0.93 | 120 | 5.58 | 123 | 18.03 | 130 |
| | vs. Righties | .244 | 113 | .379 | 82 | .277 | 145 | 2.37 | 68 | 4.04 | 160 | 19.55 | 135 |
| Team Average | vs. Lefties | .247 | 13 | .370 | 13 | .299 | 14 | 2.49 | 3 | 6.65 | 14 | 16.35 | 13 |
| | vs. Righties | .262 | 4 | .395 | 3 | .317 | 10 | 2.69 | 2 | 7.24 | 14 | 16.69 | 14 |
| League Average | vs. Lefties | .266 | | .391 | | .328 | | 2.18 | | 8.18 | | 13.58 | |
| | vs. Righties | .258 | | .380 | | .325 | | 2.26 | | 8.56 | | 14.57 | |

## Batting with Runners on Base and Bases Empty

| | | BA | Rank | SA | Rank | OBA | Rank | HR % | Rank | BB % | Rank | SO % | Rank |
|---|---|---|---|---|---|---|---|---|---|---|---|---|---|
| Kent Anderson | Runners On | .289 | 52 | .340 | 136 | .314 | 119 | 0.00 | 146 | 3.70 | 165 | 14.81 | 104 |
| | Bases Empty | .183 | 168 | .206 | 171 | .264 | 159 | 0.00 | 153 | 9.29 | 41 | 18.57 | 122 |
| Tony Armas | Runners On | .268 | -- | .415 | -- | .311 | -- | 3.66 | -- | 6.67 | -- | 23.33 | -- |
| | Bases Empty | .250 | 98 | .500 | 8 | .256 | 162 | 6.67 | 5 | 0.83 | 170 | 22.31 | 154 |
| Chili Davis | Runners On | .281 | 67 | .426 | 52 | .360 | 51 | 3.91 | 28 | 11.67 | 36 | 17.67 | 135 |
| | Bases Empty | .263 | 69 | .444 | 35 | .321 | 76 | 3.95 | 32 | 7.88 | 78 | 16.97 | 110 |
| Brian Downing | Runners On | .287 | 54 | .383 | 83 | .368 | 43 | 1.44 | 104 | 11.98 | 34 | 13.64 | 93 |
| | Bases Empty | .281 | 41 | .433 | 42 | .345 | 44 | 3.28 | 49 | 7.34 | 93 | 14.67 | 93 |
| Jack Howell | Runners On | .242 | 129 | .411 | 63 | .333 | 89 | 4.35 | 24 | 10.83 | 44 | 23.33 | 159 |
| | Bases Empty | .217 | 142 | .412 | 56 | .287 | 134 | 4.12 | 29 | 8.87 | 52 | 23.55 | 159 |
| Wally Joyner | Runners On | .297 | 39 | .417 | 58 | .362 | 50 | 1.93 | 82 | 9.03 | 75 | 8.36 | 38 |
| | Bases Empty | .269 | 56 | .422 | 51 | .313 | 96 | 3.29 | 47 | 5.35 | 140 | 9.30 | 31 |
| Lance Parrish | Runners On | .241 | 130 | .377 | 87 | .320 | 107 | 3.02 | 48 | 10.48 | 54 | 22.27 | 152 |
| | Bases Empty | .235 | 123 | .397 | 70 | .292 | 124 | 4.70 | 20 | 7.11 | 97 | 20.95 | 143 |
| Johnny Ray | Runners On | .311 | 26 | .411 | 62 | .337 | 80 | 1.37 | 106 | 6.00 | 129 | 3.60 | 4 |
| | Bases Empty | .273 | 49 | .322 | 133 | .319 | 80 | 0.64 | 141 | 6.33 | 114 | 6.33 | 8 |
| Dick Schofield | Runners On | .198 | 168 | .323 | 144 | .288 | 146 | 1.04 | 117 | 9.02 | 76 | 13.93 | 95 |
| | Bases Empty | .243 | 110 | .316 | 136 | .304 | 105 | 1.46 | 105 | 7.59 | 86 | 13.39 | 78 |
| Claudell Washington | Runners On | .269 | 84 | .353 | 118 | .311 | 122 | 1.28 | 108 | 4.71 | 152 | 18.24 | 139 |
| | Bases Empty | .275 | 47 | .473 | 17 | .324 | 71 | 4.20 | 28 | 6.76 | 104 | 18.86 | 126 |
| Devon White | Runners On | .235 | 138 | .343 | 130 | .281 | 154 | 1.49 | 99 | 5.76 | 132 | 14.58 | 99 |
| | Bases Empty | .253 | 91 | .391 | 74 | .282 | 145 | 2.17 | 81 | 3.66 | 161 | 22.45 | 155 |
| Team Average | Runners On | .267 | 9 | .383 | 11 | .326 | 12 | 2.13 | 8 | 8.00 | 13 | 15.61 | 13 |
| | Bases Empty | .249 | 9 | .388 | 5 | .299 | 14 | 2.96 | 1 | 6.30 | 14 | 17.29 | 14 |
| League Average | Runners On | .268 | | .389 | | .336 | | 2.15 | | 9.17 | | 13.53 | |
| | Bases Empty | .255 | | .380 | | .317 | | 2.29 | | 7.84 | | 14.86 | |

## Overall Batting Compared to Late Inning Pressure Situations

| | | BA | Rank | SA | Rank | OBA | Rank | HR % | Rank | BB % | Rank | SO % | Rank | RDI % | Rank |
|---|---|---|---|---|---|---|---|---|---|---|---|---|---|---|---|
| Kent Anderson | Overall | .229 | 152 | .265 | 167 | .285 | 153 | 0.00 | 166 | 6.85 | 112 | 16.94 | 117 | .194 | 159 |
| | Pressure | .190 | -- | .190 | -- | .292 | -- | 0.00 | -- | 11.54 | -- | 11.54 | -- | .000 | 165 |
| Tony Armas | Overall | .257 | 89 | .465 | 16 | .280 | 157 | 5.45 | 10 | 3.32 | 166 | 22.75 | 154 | .250 | 107 |
| | Pressure | .194 | 138 | .387 | 71 | .194 | 168 | 6.45 | 8 | 0.00 | 171 | 38.71 | 168 | .250 | 87 |
| Chili Davis | Overall | .271 | 60 | .436 | 38 | .340 | 57 | 3.93 | 26 | 9.68 | 49 | 17.30 | 121 | .318 | 33 |
| | Pressure | .227 | 110 | .333 | 103 | .318 | 89 | 2.67 | 65 | 11.49 | 44 | 19.54 | 116 | .067 | 162 |
| Brian Downing | Overall | .283 | 37 | .414 | 57 | .354 | 36 | 2.57 | 64 | 9.18 | 56 | 14.26 | 91 | .277 | 70 |
| | Pressure | .325 | 19 | .506 | 16 | .422 | 13 | 3.90 | 36 | 12.22 | 38 | 12.22 | 46 | .320 | 51 |
| Jack Howell | Overall | .228 | 154 | .411 | 58 | .308 | 111 | 4.22 | 21 | 9.76 | 46 | 23.45 | 157 | .169 | 163 |
| | Pressure | .292 | 46 | .472 | 26 | .370 | 38 | 2.78 | 61 | 10.84 | 51 | 28.92 | 155 | .174 | 125 |
| Wally Joyner | Overall | .282 | 40 | .420 | 49 | .335 | 62 | 2.70 | 60 | 7.03 | 107 | 8.87 | 31 | .297 | 46 |
| | Pressure | .289 | 50 | .410 | 53 | .319 | 88 | 2.41 | 68 | 4.40 | 146 | 8.79 | 22 | .321 | 50 |
| Lance Parrish | Overall | .238 | 134 | .388 | 80 | .306 | 117 | 3.93 | 27 | 8.71 | 67 | 21.58 | 150 | .226 | 138 |
| | Pressure | .194 | 137 | .269 | 138 | .280 | 125 | 1.49 | 94 | 10.53 | 54 | 36.84 | 167 | .056 | 163 |
| Johnny Ray | Overall | .289 | 31 | .358 | 113 | .327 | 77 | 0.94 | 132 | 6.19 | 129 | 5.15 | 7 | .374 | 7 |
| | Pressure | .258 | 82 | .303 | 120 | .307 | 98 | 0.00 | 107 | 7.89 | 97 | 5.26 | 6 | .333 | 42 |
| Dick Schofield | Overall | .228 | 153 | .318 | 149 | .299 | 131 | 1.32 | 118 | 8.09 | 84 | 13.58 | 85 | .237 | 123 |
| | Pressure | .344 | 14 | .406 | 54 | .462 | 5 | 0.00 | 107 | 13.33 | 33 | 15.56 | 76 | .222 | 105 |
| Claudell Washington | Overall | .273 | 55 | .428 | 42 | .319 | 93 | 3.11 | 50 | 5.99 | 136 | 18.63 | 133 | .232 | 128 |
| | Pressure | .260 | 78 | .400 | 57 | .333 | 72 | 2.00 | 75 | 10.34 | 58 | 18.97 | 111 | .250 | 87 |
| Devon White | Overall | .245 | 123 | .371 | 99 | .282 | 155 | 1.89 | 89 | 4.57 | 160 | 19.03 | 137 | .229 | 133 |
| | Pressure | .208 | 126 | .234 | 152 | .265 | 138 | 0.00 | 107 | 7.06 | 111 | 27.06 | 151 | .167 | 126 |
| Team Average | Overall | .256 | 11 | .386 | 6 | .311 | 13 | 2.61 | 1 | 7.03 | 14 | 16.57 | 14 | .261 | 12 |
| | Pressure | .242 | 9 | .336 | 11 | .309 | 9 | 1.74 | 10 | 8.45 | 10 | 21.48 | 14 | .220 | 12 |
| League Average | Overall | .261 | | .384 | | .326 | | 2.23 | | 8.44 | | 14.26 | | .269 | |
| | Pressure | .247 | | .357 | | .318 | | 2.02 | | 9.02 | | 17.90 | | .254 | |

## Additional Miscellaneous Batting Comparisons

| | Grass Surface | | Artificial Surface | | Home Games | | Road Games | | Runners in Scoring Position | | Runners in Scoring Pos and Two Outs | | Leading Off Inning | | Runners on 3B with less than 2 Outs | |
|---|---|---|---|---|---|---|---|---|---|---|---|---|---|---|---|---|
| | BA | Rank | BA | Rank | BA | Rank | BA | Rank | BA | Rank | BA | Rank | OBA | Rank | RDI % | Rank |
| Kent Anderson | .223 | 151 | .250 | 90 | .209 | 155 | .248 | 110 | .262 | 89 | .243 | 79 | .255 | 155 | .500 | -- |
| Tony Armas | .231 | 137 | .357 | 7 | .221 | 147 | .296 | -- | .306 | 31 | .296 | 27 | .250 | 156 | .333 | -- |
| Dante Bichette | .202 | -- | .263 | -- | .206 | -- | .214 | -- | .214 | -- | .154 | -- | .290 | -- | .500 | 119 |
| Chili Davis | .261 | 81 | .320 | 25 | .248 | 106 | .294 | 26 | .320 | 21 | .292 | 30 | .305 | 107 | .585 | 75 |
| Brian Downing | .285 | 38 | .275 | 59 | .296 | 33 | .272 | 62 | .285 | 61 | .246 | 74 | .331 | 69 | .556 | 97 |
| Jack Howell | .228 | 143 | .227 | 125 | .236 | 127 | .221 | 154 | .195 | 158 | .211 | 114 | .310 | 100 | .313 | 167 |
| Wally Joyner | .266 | 69 | .365 | 5 | .273 | 61 | .290 | 31 | .297 | 36 | .233 | 89 | .302 | 111 | .595 | 70 |
| Lance Parrish | .234 | 130 | .261 | 74 | .251 | 97 | .225 | 146 | .210 | 150 | .250 | 68 | .283 | 130 | .385 | 154 |
| Johnny Ray | .291 | 30 | .275 | 57 | .265 | 74 | .313 | 13 | .296 | 37 | .277 | 41 | .320 | 89 | .625 | 52 |
| Dick Schofield | .227 | 145 | .236 | 115 | .203 | 162 | .252 | 96 | .231 | 129 | .265 | 57 | .324 | 80 | .400 | 151 |
| Bill Schroeder | .247 | -- | .111 | 170 | .255 | -- | .169 | -- | .167 | -- | .133 | -- | .333 | -- | .182 | 172 |
| Claudell Washington | .279 | 48 | .237 | 113 | .295 | 35 | .250 | 100 | .261 | 93 | .300 | 24 | .329 | 73 | .500 | 119 |
| Devon White | .250 | 98 | .223 | 130 | .243 | 116 | .248 | 112 | .228 | 135 | .197 | 123 | .329 | 71 | .520 | 115 |
| Team Average | .253 | 10 | .273 | 4 | .253 | 10 | .259 | 7 | .260 | 9 | .253 | 1 | .313 | 11 | .498 | 14 |
| League Average | .260 | | .262 | | .262 | | .259 | | .262 | | .232 | | .321 | | .566 | |

## Pitching vs. Left and Right Handed Batters

| | | BA | Rank | SA | Rank | OBA | Rank | HR % | Rank | BB % | Rank | SO % | Rank |
|---|---|---|---|---|---|---|---|---|---|---|---|---|---|
| Jim Abbott | vs. Lefties | .325 | 125 | .463 | 109 | .388 | 117 | 1.63 | 58 | 10.00 | 89 | 15.71 | 36 |
| | vs. Righties | .263 | 78 | .361 | 55 | .335 | 96 | 1.93 | 61 | 9.26 | 99 | 14.35 | 77 |
| Bert Blyleven | vs. Lefties | .252 | 54 | .318 | 29 | .290 | 29 | 0.82 | 20 | 4.62 | 12 | 14.07 | 50 |
| | vs. Righties | .244 | 38 | .358 | 53 | .283 | 21 | 2.37 | 81 | 4.41 | 9 | 12.78 | 89 |
| Chuck Finley | vs. Lefties | .172 | 8 | .192 | 3 | .252 | 10 | 0.00 | 1 | 8.93 | 68 | 13.39 | 54 |
| | vs. Righties | .243 | 36 | .356 | 51 | .320 | 65 | 2.05 | 69 | 10.07 | 110 | 19.72 | 29 |
| Willie Fraser | vs. Lefties | .246 | 47 | .406 | 89 | .303 | 41 | 2.90 | 99 | 6.49 | 32 | 9.74 | 92 |
| | vs. Righties | .220 | 24 | .297 | 10 | .283 | 23 | 0.99 | 12 | 5.88 | 31 | 14.03 | 80 |
| Bryan Harvey | vs. Lefties | .160 | 5 | .280 | 17 | .303 | 43 | 3.00 | 100 | 17.07 | 132 | 28.46 | 5 |
| | vs. Righties | .206 | -- | .320 | -- | .339 | -- | 3.09 | -- | 16.39 | -- | 35.25 | -- |
| Kirk McCaskill | vs. Lefties | .252 | 56 | .369 | 59 | .297 | 35 | 2.49 | 84 | 6.07 | 27 | 12.15 | 66 |
| | vs. Righties | .256 | 68 | .345 | 42 | .316 | 62 | 1.52 | 39 | 7.57 | 65 | 12.61 | 91 |
| Greg Minton | vs. Lefties | .211 | 20 | .272 | 15 | .282 | 22 | 0.00 | 1 | 9.09 | 71 | 13.33 | 55 |
| | vs. Righties | .245 | 39 | .321 | 25 | .332 | 89 | 2.17 | 73 | 10.58 | 113 | 9.62 | 122 |
| Dan Petry | vs. Lefties | .352 | 132 | .602 | 134 | .404 | 131 | 6.82 | 135 | 9.09 | 71 | 8.08 | 108 |
| | vs. Righties | .210 | -- | .286 | -- | .301 | -- | 1.90 | -- | 11.29 | -- | 10.48 | -- |
| Mike Witt | vs. Lefties | .295 | 105 | .424 | 96 | .326 | 63 | 2.76 | 94 | 5.11 | 15 | 11.49 | 73 |
| | vs. Righties | .288 | 115 | .442 | 119 | .325 | 77 | 3.26 | 110 | 5.14 | 21 | 14.78 | 69 |
| Team Average | vs. Lefties | .257 | 5 | .366 | 5 | .310 | 2 | 2.01 | 5 | 7.12 | 1 | 13.44 | 5 |
| | vs. Righties | .250 | 3 | .355 | 1 | .314 | 4 | 2.10 | 5 | 8.02 | 10 | 15.66 | 6 |
| League Average | vs. Lefties | .261 | | .382 | | .330 | | 2.16 | | 9.16 | | 13.03 | |
| | vs. Righties | .261 | | .385 | | .323 | | 2.28 | | 7.96 | | 15.09 | |

## Pitching with Runners on Base and Bases Empty

| | | BA | Rank | SA | Rank | OBA | Rank | HR % | Rank | BB % | Rank | SO % | Rank |
|---|---|---|---|---|---|---|---|---|---|---|---|---|---|
| Jim Abbott | Runners On | .261 | 66 | .343 | 32 | .336 | 74 | 1.32 | 35 | 10.11 | 87 | 14.61 | 56 |
| | Bases Empty | .284 | 111 | .407 | 91 | .352 | 113 | 2.30 | 73 | 8.80 | 90 | 14.58 | 60 |
| Bert Blyleven | Runners On | .219 | 16 | .296 | 10 | .272 | 9 | 1.14 | 23 | 6.62 | 25 | 13.23 | 67 |
| | Bases Empty | .266 | 80 | .362 | 52 | .297 | 39 | 1.80 | 49 | 3.10 | 5 | 13.62 | 70 |
| Chuck Finley | Runners On | .226 | 21 | .336 | 26 | .298 | 18 | 2.05 | 77 | 8.71 | 60 | 18.92 | 20 |
| | Bases Empty | .238 | 44 | .333 | 34 | .320 | 70 | 1.59 | 36 | 10.73 | 111 | 18.83 | 32 |
| Willie Fraser | Runners On | .282 | 95 | .408 | 97 | .340 | 79 | 1.41 | 40 | 6.75 | 28 | 13.50 | 63 |
| | Bases Empty | .202 | 10 | .293 | 14 | .255 | 8 | 2.02 | 59 | 5.66 | 35 | 11.32 | 97 |
| Bryan Harvey | Runners On | .183 | 4 | .269 | 6 | .351 | 95 | 1.92 | 71 | 20.14 | 134 | 30.94 | 1 |
| | Bases Empty | .183 | -- | .333 | -- | .283 | -- | 4.30 | -- | 12.26 | -- | 33.02 | -- |
| Kirk McCaskill | Runners On | .235 | 31 | .301 | 13 | .291 | 14 | 1.57 | 51 | 7.65 | 46 | 11.61 | 81 |
| | Bases Empty | .267 | 83 | .395 | 81 | .317 | 64 | 2.31 | 74 | 6.26 | 49 | 12.92 | 79 |
| Greg Minton | Runners On | .278 | 90 | .340 | 31 | .359 | 104 | 0.62 | 6 | 10.22 | 89 | 10.75 | 91 |
| | Bases Empty | .183 | 4 | .260 | 4 | .262 | 11 | 1.78 | 47 | 9.63 | 101 | 11.76 | 91 |
| Mike Witt | Runners On | .321 | 126 | .449 | 121 | .347 | 89 | 2.68 | 101 | 4.75 | 8 | 13.46 | 64 |
| | Bases Empty | .273 | 94 | .422 | 101 | .312 | 56 | 3.22 | 105 | 5.38 | 28 | 12.90 | 80 |
| Team Average | Runners On | .251 | 2 | .347 | 2 | .316 | 2 | 1.80 | 5 | 8.59 | 7 | 15.00 | 4 |
| | Bases Empty | .255 | 8 | .369 | 6 | .310 | 5 | 2.25 | 8 | 6.96 | 5 | 14.62 | 7 |
| League Average | Runners On | .268 | | .389 | | .336 | | 2.15 | | 9.17 | | 13.53 | |
| | Bases Empty | .255 | | .380 | | .317 | | 2.29 | | 7.84 | | 14.86 | |

## Overall Pitching Compared to Late Inning Pressure Situations

| | | BA | Rank | SA | Rank | OBA | Rank | HR % | Rank | BB % | Rank | SO % | Rank |
|---|---|---|---|---|---|---|---|---|---|---|---|---|---|
| Jim Abbott | Overall | .274 | 95 | .379 | 68 | .345 | 103 | 1.87 | 57 | 9.39 | 91 | 14.59 | 59 |
| | Pressure | .326 | 118 | .348 | 68 | .404 | 114 | 0.00 | 1 | 11.11 | 87 | 9.26 | 111 |
| Bert Blyleven | Overall | .248 | 46 | .336 | 27 | .287 | 18 | 1.54 | 32 | 4.52 | 5 | 13.46 | 66 |
| | Pressure | .250 | 68 | .315 | 47 | .296 | 42 | 1.09 | 45 | 6.06 | 33 | 17.17 | 48 |
| Chuck Finley | Overall | .233 | 26 | .334 | 24 | .311 | 43 | 1.77 | 52 | 9.92 | 102 | 18.86 | 29 |
| | Pressure | .256 | 77 | .462 | 112 | .341 | 78 | 3.85 | 117 | 11.11 | 87 | 15.56 | 61 |
| Willie Fraser | Overall | .235 | 29 | .341 | 34 | .291 | 21 | 1.76 | 50 | 6.13 | 26 | 12.27 | 81 |
| | Pressure | .248 | 67 | .380 | 85 | .309 | 59 | 2.19 | 80 | 7.74 | 50 | 11.61 | 92 |
| Bryan Harvey | Overall | .183 | -- | .299 | -- | .321 | -- | 3.05 | -- | 16.73 | -- | 31.84 | -- |
| | Pressure | .197 | 22 | .307 | 42 | .350 | 88 | 3.15 | 105 | 18.52 | 132 | 29.01 | 5 |
| Kirk McCaskill | Overall | .254 | 57 | .357 | 48 | .307 | 37 | 2.01 | 63 | 6.83 | 40 | 12.38 | 78 |
| | Pressure | .186 | 14 | .314 | 45 | .240 | 9 | 2.86 | 96 | 6.58 | 37 | 10.53 | 105 |
| Bob McClure | Overall | .212 | -- | .283 | -- | .270 | -- | 1.09 | -- | 7.32 | -- | 17.56 | -- |
| | Pressure | .181 | 12 | .245 | 15 | .233 | 4 | 1.06 | 44 | 6.73 | 40 | 15.38 | 63 |
| Greg Minton | Overall | .230 | 22 | .299 | 10 | .310 | 41 | 1.21 | 17 | 9.92 | 104 | 11.26 | 94 |
| | Pressure | .170 | 9 | .245 | 16 | .285 | 29 | 1.89 | 72 | 13.30 | 110 | 10.64 | 104 |
| Rich Monteleone | Overall | .255 | -- | .359 | -- | .314 | -- | 1.96 | -- | 7.65 | -- | 15.88 | -- |
| | Pressure | .293 | 106 | .415 | 101 | .388 | 110 | 0.00 | 1 | 12.24 | 101 | 16.33 | 53 |
| Mike Witt | Overall | .292 | 119 | .433 | 111 | .326 | 70 | 3.01 | 111 | 5.12 | 9 | 13.13 | 70 |
| | Pressure | .347 | 121 | .413 | 100 | .372 | 104 | 1.33 | 50 | 3.70 | 9 | 17.28 | 47 |
| Team Average | Overall | .253 | 3 | .360 | 3 | .312 | 2 | 2.07 | 5 | 7.66 | 4 | 14.78 | 5 |
| | Pressure | .228 | 3 | .326 | 3 | .312 | 4 | 1.91 | 5 | 10.61 | 11 | 15.87 | 9 |
| League Average | Overall | .261 | | .384 | | .326 | | 2.23 | | 8.44 | | 14.26 | |
| | Pressure | .250 | | .362 | | .325 | | 2.14 | | 9.50 | | 16.61 | |

## Additional Miscellaneous Pitching Comparisons

| | Grass Surface | | Artificial Surface | | Home Games | | Road Games | | Runners in Scoring Position | | Runners in Scoring Pos and Two Outs | | Leading Off Inning | |
|---|---|---|---|---|---|---|---|---|---|---|---|---|---|---|
| | BA | Rank | BA | Rank | BA | Rank | BA | Rank | BA | Rank | BA | Rank | OBA | Rank |
| Jim Abbott | .266 | 77 | .304 | 109 | .294 | 117 | .254 | 59 | .231 | 35 | .250 | 88 | .346 | 96 |
| Bert Blyleven | .264 | 72 | .190 | 7 | .238 | 40 | .258 | 64 | .213 | 17 | .184 | 38 | .309 | 47 |
| Chuck Finley | .235 | 30 | .218 | 21 | .243 | 54 | .220 | 19 | .183 | 6 | .174 | 33 | .271 | 26 |
| Willie Fraser | .223 | 22 | .355 | -- | .232 | 34 | .239 | 38 | .293 | 114 | .244 | 83 | .253 | 11 |
| Bryan Harvey | .178 | 4 | .235 | -- | .190 | 5 | .173 | -- | .147 | 1 | .026 | 1 | .238 | -- |
| Kirk McCaskill | .250 | 53 | .283 | 87 | .246 | 60 | .264 | 74 | .221 | 22 | .171 | 30 | .329 | 77 |
| Bob McClure | .234 | 28 | .077 | -- | .239 | -- | .188 | -- | .217 | -- | .214 | -- | .233 | -- |
| Greg Minton | .229 | 25 | .235 | -- | .242 | 51 | .213 | 13 | .233 | 37 | .119 | 8 | .195 | 3 |
| Dan Petry | .282 | 105 | .250 | -- | .244 | -- | .324 | -- | .209 | -- | .263 | -- | .333 | -- |
| Mike Witt | .287 | 111 | .319 | 119 | .283 | 108 | .300 | 120 | .310 | 122 | .277 | 107 | .322 | 67 |
| Team Average | .253 | 4 | .254 | 6 | .249 | 4 | .257 | 5 | .233 | 2 | .197 | 1 | .302 | 2 |
| League Average | .260 | | .262 | | .259 | | .262 | | .262 | | .232 | | .321 | |

# CHICAGO WHITE SOX

- **H'ray for Hriniak!**
- **God takes a holiday.**

Take a look at these two dissimilar statistical lines, each representing the one-season offense of a particular team. Study the differences between them and then see if you can figure out which teams they represent:

| BA | SA | OBA | AB | R | H | 2B | 3B | HR | BB | SO |
|---|---|---|---|---|---|---|---|---|---|---|
| .244 | .370 | .303 | 5449 | 631 | 1327 | 224 | 35 | 132 | 446 | 908 |
| .271 | .383 | .328 | 5504 | 693 | 1493 | 262 | 36 | 94 | 464 | 873 |

The two lines are quite different. The first is a team with players who produced home runs but not a high batting average; the reverse is true for the second team. If these two are related, it seems, then Danny DeVito and Arnold Schwarzenegger must be twins. But they are and they are! The first line belongs to the Chicago White Sox for the 1988 season. The second is the White Sox' line for 1989. Who could be responsible for such a change?

Hmmm. A big jump in batting average and a big drop in home runs. Inspector, only one man can produce changes like that: put out an APB for Walt Hriniak.

The improvement in Chicago's batting average from .244 to .271 was one of the greatest in recent years. (It looks like a 27–point increase on paper, but actually it's closer to 28 points (27.7) once the vagaries of rounding are taken into account; the increase is actually from .2435 to .2712.)

Just as dramatic was the decrease in home runs. The Sox hit 38 fewer home runs than they had the year before, the largest drop by any team in the majors from 1988 to 1989.

Indeed, both are the handiwork of Hriniak, the former Boston batting coach who changed his Sox after the 1988 season. Hriniak's reputation as a hitting instructor is such that he was hired to coach the 1989 White Sox 11 days before Jeff Torborg was named to manage the team! He inherited an unbalanced offensive team that produced the statistics at the top of the page. Since the adoption of the designated-hitter rule in 1973, only two American League teams (the 1982 A's and the woeful '88 Orioles) had ever produced such a low batting average with so many home runs. And after only a single season, the change he has wrought in Chicago's offense may be dramatic enough to lead us to a new wave of free–agency compensation: would you believe compensation for coaches who move from one team to another?

We have listed here all players with at least 50 at–bats for the Sox in both 1988 and 1989. The most striking changes are seen in the statistics for Boston, Calderon, Karkovice, and Manrique:

| | 1988 Season | | | 1989 Season | | |
|---|---|---|---|---|---|---|
| | BA | AB | HR | BA | AB | HR |
| Harold Baines | .277 | 599 | 13 | .321 | 333 | 13 |
| Daryl Boston | .217 | 281 | 15 | .252 | 218 | 5 |
| Ivan Calderon | .212 | 264 | 14 | .286 | 622 | 14 |
| Carlton Fisk | .277 | 253 | 19 | .293 | 375 | 13 |
| Dave Gallagher | .303 | 347 | 5 | .266 | 601 | 1 |
| Ozzie Guillen | .261 | 566 | 0 | .253 | 597 | 1 |
| Lance Johnson | .185 | 124 | 0 | .300 | 180 | 0 |
| Ron Karkovice | .174 | 115 | 3 | .264 | 182 | 3 |
| Steve Lyons | .269 | 472 | 5 | .264 | 443 | 2 |
| Fred Manrique | .235 | 345 | 5 | .299 | 187 | 2 |
| Carlos Martinez | .164 | 55 | 0 | .300 | 350 | 5 |
| Dan Pasqua | .227 | 422 | 20 | .248 | 246 | 11 |
| Greg Walker | .247 | 377 | 8 | .210 | 233 | 5 |

Those are the players who were with the Sox in both seasons. But even more amazing was the job he did with Ron Kittle, who had played for Cleveland in 1988. That's no typo next to Kittle's name in the official American League averages. He *did* hit .302 in 169 at–bats last season.

The White Sox' one-season batting average jump was not the highest in history. It's not even a club record. Since 1900, the highest one-season jump in the majors was a 57.3 point leap by a White Sox team of an earlier era. They hit .211 in 1910, the year that Comiskey Park opened in midseason, then raised that mark to .269 in the park's first full season of operation. But that 1910–11 surge coincided with a league-wide increase in batting that saw the American League's overall average jump from .243 in 1910 to .273 in 1911. And in looking at the largest one-team single-season increases in batting average, we see that they almost always occur in years in which the overall level of hitting has improved for other teams in the league as well.

This is demonstrated in the following table, which lists the teams with the 10 largest increases since 1900, most of which happened well before your Wonder Years. (In fact, 18 of the 30 largest increases occurred in the period from 1901 to 1921, when livelier baseballs were introduced into the major leagues and hitting styles were altered accordingly.) For each team we list that team's batting average in the two seasons involved, and also the composite batting averages of the other teams in the league for the two seasons:

| | Year 1 Team | Year 2 Team | Diff. Team | Year 1 Others | Year 2 Others | Diff. Others |
|---|---|---|---|---|---|---|
| 1910–11 White Sox | .211 | .269 | +57.3 | .248 | .274 | +25.7 |
| 1920–21 Tigers | .270 | .316 | +45.7 | .285 | .289 | +3.7 |
| 1919–20 Browns | .264 | .308 | +44.0 | .269 | .280 | +11.2 |
| 1928–29 Phillies | .267 | .309 | +42.0 | .283 | .292 | +9.2 |
| 1968–69 Orioles | .225 | .265 | +40.5 | .231 | .244 | +13.5 |
| 1910–11 Indians | .244 | .282 | +37.8 | .243 | .272 | +28.3 |
| * 1972–73 Rangers | .217 | .255 | +37.4 | .241 | .260 | +18.9 |
| * 1972–73 Orioles | .229 | .266 | +36.9 | .240 | .259 | +18.9 |
| 1924–25 Braves | .256 | .292 | +35.6 | .287 | .291 | +4.3 |
| 1981–82 Blue Jays | .226 | .262 | +35.5 | .258 | .264 | +5.9 |

* American League introduced designated-hitter rule in 1973.

What is especially significant about the work that Hriniak did in 1989 is that the Sox raised their team batting average by 27 points in a year in which the collective batting average of the 13 other American League teams actually went down! This is only the third time in this century that a team has had an increase as large as Chicago's against the grain of lower batting averages elsewhere in its league:

| | Year 1 Team | Year 2 Team | Diff. Team | Year 1 Others | Year 2 Others | Diff. Others |
|---|---|---|---|---|---|---|
| 1926–27 Athletics | .269 | .303 | +33.9 | .283 | .282 | −0.1 |
| 1901–02 Reds | .251 | .282 | +31.1 | .269 | .255 | −14.0 |
| 1988–89 White Sox | .244 | .271 | +27.7 | .261 | .260 | −0.6 |

Now, let's consider the decline in home runs. Of the 30 teams in history that had a one-season batting–average increase at least as large as the White Sox had, only four others had suffered any decline in home runs. To those four teams we add the name of the 1989 White Sox:

| | Year 1 BA | Year 2 BA | Diff. BA | Year 1 HR | Year 2 HR | Diff. HR |
|---|---|---|---|---|---|---|
| 1901–02 Reds | .251 | .282 | +31.1 | 38 | 18 | −20 |
| 1908–09 Athletics | .223 | .257 | +33.3 | 21 | 20 | −1 |
| 1926–27 Athletics | .269 | .303 | +33.9 | 61 | 56 | −5 |
| 1947–48 Browns | .241 | .271 | +30.6 | 90 | 63 | −27 |
| 1988–89 White Sox | .244 | .271 | +27.7 | 132 | 94 | −38 |

To summarize, then, only two other major league teams in this century have had as great a one-season batting-average increase as the White Sox in a season in which the combined batting average for the other teams in the league declined. And no team in this century that has had as great a batting-average increase as the White Sox ever had a corresponding decrease of more than 30 home runs.

In last year's *Analyst* (pp. 17–18), we wrote about the Hriniak effect in the makeover of the Red Sox' offense. We found that despite its historic tendency to collect fence-busters, Boston has actually been more successful in seasons in which it has relied on contact hitters. This year, we have expanded on that study and we looked at all teams that have led their league in either batting average or home runs. Given the extent of batting-average-bashing prevalent among some commentators in recent years, the results may surprise you.

We collected the records of all teams in this century that led their league in runs scored. Then we inspected those records to see how many led their league in batting average, and how many led their league in home runs:

| | A.L. | N.L. | Total |
|---|---|---|---|
| Led league in runs scored and batting average | 51 | 53 | 104 |
| Led league in runs scored and home runs | 33 | 33 | 66 |

But those totals include 29 teams that led the league in scoring and also led the league in *both* batting average and home runs. When those teams are taken out of the totals, we are left with these figures:

| | A.L. | N.L. | Total |
|---|---|---|---|
| Led league in runs scored and batting average | 37 | 38 | 75 |
| Led league in runs scored and home runs | 19 | 18 | 37 |

Excluding teams that led the league in both batting average and homers, teams leading in batting average beat teams leading in home runs by better than a two-to-one margin. And if you're thinking that the game has changed and that those figures are weighted heavily by the way the game used to be played, here are the figures since 1969, the first year of divisional play:

| | A.L. | N.L. | Total |
|---|---|---|---|
| Led league in runs scored and batting average | 9 | 8 | 17 |
| Led league in runs scored and home runs | 3 | 6 | 9 |

All of which means that Mr. Hriniak should continue to be a man in demand. Hey, Walt, do coaches have agents? Our number is in the book.

With apologies to Paul Harvey: "Page Two." Last July, unbeknownst to astronomers, the sun began to revolve around the earth. Unknown to geologists, the continents stopped their drift. Unknown to theologians, God took a couple of weeks off.

These cosmic events had a ripple effect down here on earth. Of course, things also went topsy-turvy in major league baseball during this time. From July 13 to July 22, the last-place White Sox won eight games in a row; from July 19 to July 27, the first-place Orioles lost eight games in a row. Then, the craziness ended just as suddenly as it had started, and everything clicked back into place. The White Sox went on to finish in last place; the Orioles took the Blue Jays down to the season's final Saturday before surrendering.

This two-week blip on the baseball landscape whet our curiosity as to what's the longest winning streak in history by a last-place team, and what's the longest losing streak ever by a first-place team. Remember, if a team fell out of first place or emerged from last place at any time during the streak, it no longer is a first-place or last-place team, and the streak (in the sense in which we are considering it here) ends at that point.

| Longest Winning Streak By Last-Place Team | Longest Losing Streak By First-Place Team |
|---|---|
| 9 Cardinals, 1907 | 10 Pirates, 1932 |
| 8 Expos, 1971 | 9 Yankees, 1953 |
| 8 White Sox, 1989 | 9 Twins, 1970 |
| 7 Browns, 1912 | 8 Cardinals, 1973 |
| 7 Phillies, 1933 | 8 Phillies, 1976 |
| 7 Cubs, 1944 | 8 Royals, 1980 |
| 7 Senators, 1963 | 8 Athletics, 1981 |
| 7 Padres, 1980 | 8 Orioles, 1989 |
| 7 Pirates, 1984 | 7 Giants, 1933 |
| 7 Padres, 1987 | 7 Giants, 1971 |
| 7 Pirates, 1987 (twice) | 7 Astros, 1979 |
| | 7 Braves, 1982 |
| | 7 Cardinals, 1987 |

The White Sox' winning streak turned out to be the longest in American League history by a last-place team. Baltimore's losing streak fell one game shy of the American League record for a first-place team.

We offer these tables as a public service. Perhaps the great minds of science can use this information to predict the next time that God will take a holiday.

## WON-LOST RECORD BY STARTING POSITION

| CHICAGO 69-92 | C | 1B | 2B | 3B | SS | LF | CF | RF | P | DH | Leadoff | Relief | Starts |
|---|---|---|---|---|---|---|---|---|---|---|---|---|---|
| Harold Baines | - | - | - | - | - | - | - | 10-14 | - | 27-41 | - | - | 37-55 |
| Jeff Bittiger | - | - | - | - | - | - | - | - | 0-1 | - | - | 0-1 | 0-1 |
| Daryl Boston | - | - | - | - | - | 21-21 | 0-1 | 3-7 | - | 0-1 | 0-1 | - | 24-30 |
| Ivan Calderon | - | 11-9 | - | - | - | 7-9 | - | 31-53 | - | 18-17 | - | - | 67-88 |
| John Davis | - | - | - | - | - | - | - | - | - | - | - | 1-3 | - |
| Richard Dotson | - | - | - | - | - | - | - | - | 8-9 | - | - | - | 8-9 |
| Wayne Edwards | - | - | - | - | - | - | - | - | - | - | - | 3-4 | - |
| Carlton Fisk | 41-44 | - | - | - | - | - | - | - | - | 6-7 | - | - | 47-51 |
| Scott Fletcher | - | - | 23-30 | - | 3-3 | - | - | - | - | - | - | - | 26-33 |
| Dave Gallagher | - | - | - | - | - | 1-0 | 57-75 | 5-8 | - | - | 38-43 | - | 63-83 |
| Ozzie Guillen | - | - | - | - | 66-88 | - | - | - | - | - | 18-29 | - | 66-88 |
| Jerry Hairston | - | - | - | - | - | - | - | - | - | - | - | - | - |
| Jack Hardy | - | - | - | - | - | - | - | - | - | - | - | 0-5 | - |
| Greg Hibbard | - | - | - | - | - | - | - | - | 10-13 | - | - | - | 10-13 |
| Shawn Hillegas | - | - | - | - | - | - | - | - | 6-7 | - | - | 20-17 | 6-7 |
| Lance Johnson | - | - | - | - | - | 16-19 | 1-6 | - | - | - | 13-18 | - | 17-25 |
| Barry Jones | - | - | - | - | - | - | - | - | - | - | - | 6-16 | - |
| Ron Karkovice | 21-34 | - | - | - | - | - | - | - | - | 0-2 | - | - | 21-36 |
| Eric King | - | - | - | - | - | - | - | - | 12-13 | - | - | - | 12-13 |
| Ron Kittle | - | 11-16 | - | - | - | 1-2 | - | - | - | 7-10 | - | - | 19-28 |
| Bill Long | - | - | - | - | - | - | - | - | 3-5 | - | - | 6-16 | 3-5 |
| Steve Lyons | - | 7-12 | 28-32 | 8-10 | - | 3-4 | - | 4-2 | - | - | - | - | 50-60 |
| Fred Manrique | - | - | 18-30 | 1-0 | - | - | - | - | - | - | - | - | 19-30 |
| Carlos Martinez | - | 9-12 | - | 32-34 | - | 2-6 | - | - | - | - | - | - | 43-52 |
| Tom McCarthy | - | - | - | - | - | - | - | - | - | - | - | 6-25 | - |
| Matt Merullo | 7-14 | - | - | - | - | - | - | - | - | - | - | - | 7-14 |
| Russ Morman | - | 10-12 | - | - | - | - | - | - | - | - | - | - | 10-12 |
| Donn Pall | - | - | - | - | - | - | - | - | - | - | - | 19-34 | - |
| Dan Pasqua | - | - | - | - | - | 18-30 | - | 12-5 | - | 2-1 | - | - | 32-36 |
| Ken Patterson | - | - | - | - | - | - | - | - | 0-1 | - | - | 14-35 | 0-1 |
| Melido Perez | - | - | - | - | - | - | - | - | 12-19 | - | - | - | 12-19 |
| Adam Peterson | - | - | - | - | - | - | - | - | 1-1 | - | - | 0-1 | 1-1 |
| Jerry Reuss | - | - | - | - | - | - | - | - | 11-8 | - | - | 0-4 | 11-8 |
| Billy Jo Robidoux | - | 1-7 | - | - | - | - | - | - | - | - | - | - | 1-7 |
| Steve Rosenberg | - | - | - | - | - | - | - | - | 6-15 | - | - | 4-13 | 6-15 |
| Jeff Schaefer | - | - | - | - | 0-1 | - | - | - | - | - | - | - | 0-1 |
| Jose Segura | - | - | - | - | - | - | - | - | - | - | - | 2-5 | - |
| Sammy Sosa | - | - | - | - | - | 0-1 | 11-10 | 4-3 | - | - | 0-1 | - | 15-14 |
| Bobby Thigpen | - | - | - | - | - | - | - | - | - | - | - | 42-19 | - |
| Robin Ventura | - | - | - | 8-7 | - | - | - | - | - | - | - | - | 8-7 |
| Greg Walker | - | 20-24 | - | - | - | - | - | - | - | 9-13 | - | - | 29-37 |
| Eddie Williams | - | - | - | 20-41 | - | - | - | - | - | - | - | - | 20-41 |

## Batting vs. Left and Right Handed Pitchers

| | | BA | Rank | SA | Rank | OBA | Rank | HR % | Rank | BB % | Rank | SO % | Rank |
|---|---|---|---|---|---|---|---|---|---|---|---|---|---|
| Daryl Boston | vs. Lefties | .111 | -- | .185 | -- | .107 | -- | 0.00 | -- | 0.00 | -- | 23.33 | -- |
| | vs. Righties | .272 | 62 | .398 | 62 | .353 | 41 | 2.62 | 59 | 11.06 | 38 | 11.06 | 58 |
| Ivan Calderon | vs. Lefties | .332 | 15 | .495 | 20 | .389 | 19 | 2.17 | 73 | 8.37 | 68 | 8.37 | 37 |
| | vs. Righties | .267 | 69 | .413 | 52 | .308 | 106 | 2.28 | 73 | 5.50 | 140 | 16.28 | 108 |
| Carlton Fisk | vs. Lefties | .325 | 18 | .508 | 13 | .371 | 34 | 3.33 | 45 | 7.58 | 84 | 7.58 | 30 |
| | vs. Righties | .278 | 48 | .459 | 31 | .348 | 46 | 3.53 | 35 | 9.06 | 61 | 17.42 | 121 |
| Scott Fletcher | vs. Lefties | .280 | 64 | .372 | 102 | .359 | 49 | 0.00 | 134 | 10.81 | 38 | 7.57 | 29 |
| | vs. Righties | .241 | 119 | .285 | 154 | .320 | 92 | 0.26 | 153 | 9.91 | 50 | 10.36 | 46 |
| Dave Gallagher | vs. Lefties | .280 | 67 | .335 | 130 | .329 | 86 | 0.00 | 134 | 6.70 | 100 | 9.82 | 57 |
| | vs. Righties | .259 | 87 | .304 | 141 | .315 | 98 | 0.25 | 155 | 7.00 | 107 | 12.87 | 74 |
| Ozzie Guillen | vs. Lefties | .254 | 109 | .292 | 154 | .264 | 149 | 0.00 | 134 | 1.40 | 167 | 9.77 | 56 |
| | vs. Righties | .253 | 99 | .332 | 121 | .273 | 148 | 0.26 | 154 | 2.92 | 166 | 6.57 | 13 |
| Lance Johnson | vs. Lefties | .259 | 99 | .328 | 137 | .306 | 114 | 0.00 | 134 | 6.25 | 106 | 17.19 | 124 |
| | vs. Righties | .320 | 7 | .385 | 74 | .385 | 14 | 0.00 | 158 | 9.63 | 54 | 9.63 | 41 |
| Ron Karkovice | vs. Lefties | .284 | 59 | .398 | 78 | .323 | 94 | 1.14 | 114 | 6.00 | 113 | 22.00 | 154 |
| | vs. Righties | .245 | -- | .372 | -- | .290 | -- | 2.13 | -- | 3.88 | -- | 33.01 | -- |
| Ron Kittle | vs. Lefties | .291 | 49 | .564 | 5 | .403 | 12 | 7.27 | 2 | 16.42 | 4 | 17.91 | 128 |
| | vs. Righties | .307 | 18 | .553 | 2 | .364 | 29 | 6.14 | 6 | 8.53 | 73 | 23.26 | 153 |
| Steve Lyons | vs. Lefties | .213 | 153 | .255 | 162 | .253 | 157 | 0.00 | 134 | 4.76 | 141 | 20.95 | 145 |
| | vs. Righties | .278 | 49 | .361 | 99 | .334 | 66 | 0.57 | 144 | 7.71 | 91 | 11.83 | 68 |
| Carlos Martinez | vs. Lefties | .295 | 42 | .386 | 90 | .316 | 100 | 1.52 | 95 | 2.88 | 163 | 11.51 | 70 |
| | vs. Righties | .303 | 21 | .417 | 50 | .354 | 39 | 1.38 | 110 | 7.08 | 104 | 17.08 | 119 |
| Russ Morman | vs. Lefties | .208 | 157 | .229 | 167 | .250 | 158 | 0.00 | 134 | 5.56 | 124 | 20.37 | 140 |
| | vs. Righties | .300 | -- | .400 | -- | .462 | -- | 0.00 | -- | 23.08 | -- | 38.46 | -- |
| Dan Pasqua | vs. Lefties | .224 | 146 | .355 | 110 | .259 | 153 | 3.95 | 32 | 4.88 | 138 | 19.51 | 137 |
| | vs. Righties | .259 | 88 | .459 | 31 | .338 | 58 | 4.71 | 18 | 10.77 | 40 | 21.54 | 145 |
| Sammy Sosa | vs. Lefties | .346 | 7 | .487 | 25 | .391 | 18 | 2.56 | 63 | 7.95 | 74 | 21.59 | 149 |
| | vs. Righties | .190 | -- | .276 | -- | .234 | -- | 1.90 | -- | 3.48 | -- | 24.35 | -- |
| Greg Walker | vs. Lefties | .188 | -- | .208 | -- | .264 | -- | 0.00 | -- | 7.55 | -- | 20.75 | -- |
| | vs. Righties | .216 | 150 | .368 | 94 | .292 | 129 | 2.70 | 55 | 9.05 | 62 | 18.57 | 130 |
| Eddie Williams | vs. Lefties | .250 | 112 | .300 | 150 | .333 | 80 | 1.25 | 107 | 9.47 | 53 | 12.63 | 82 |
| | vs. Righties | .289 | 32 | .397 | 64 | .346 | 50 | 1.65 | 95 | 6.72 | 112 | 14.18 | 87 |
| Team Average | vs. Lefties | .273 | 5 | .373 | 11 | .326 | 7 | 1.48 | 14 | 7.10 | 12 | 13.85 | 9 |
| | vs. Righties | .270 | 3 | .388 | 5 | .329 | 5 | 1.82 | 14 | 7.78 | 11 | 14.42 | 7 |
| League Average | vs. Lefties | .266 | | .391 | | .328 | | 2.18 | | 8.18 | | 13.58 | |
| | vs. Righties | .258 | | .380 | | .325 | | 2.26 | | 8.56 | | 14.57 | |

## Batting with Runners on Base and Bases Empty

| | | BA | Rank | SA | Rank | OBA | Rank | HR % | Rank | BB % | Rank | SO % | Rank |
|---|---|---|---|---|---|---|---|---|---|---|---|---|---|
| Daryl Boston | Runners On | .247 | 121 | .381 | 84 | .327 | 96 | 3.09 | 44 | 10.53 | 52 | 11.40 | 74 |
| | Bases Empty | .256 | 83 | .364 | 99 | .323 | 72 | 1.65 | 95 | 9.02 | 45 | 13.53 | 81 |
| Ivan Calderon | Runners On | .284 | 61 | .473 | 26 | .343 | 74 | 3.04 | 47 | 8.68 | 81 | 14.97 | 108 |
| | Bases Empty | .288 | 31 | .405 | 64 | .322 | 74 | 1.53 | 100 | 4.09 | 157 | 12.87 | 69 |
| Carlton Fisk | Runners On | .333 | 9 | .519 | 9 | .407 | 10 | 3.28 | 40 | 10.75 | 46 | 11.21 | 69 |
| | Bases Empty | .255 | 86 | .432 | 43 | .302 | 109 | 3.65 | 41 | 6.34 | 113 | 17.56 | 114 |
| Scott Fletcher | Runners On | .246 | 125 | .294 | 157 | .322 | 105 | 0.00 | 146 | 9.88 | 64 | 9.49 | 53 |
| | Bases Empty | .257 | 82 | .322 | 131 | .338 | 48 | 0.30 | 152 | 10.37 | 29 | 9.57 | 34 |
| Dave Gallagher | Runners On | .265 | 94 | .322 | 145 | .324 | 103 | 0.43 | 144 | 7.43 | 104 | 11.90 | 82 |
| | Bases Empty | .267 | 59 | .310 | 140 | .317 | 85 | 0.00 | 153 | 6.53 | 110 | 11.81 | 60 |
| Ozzie Guillen | Runners On | .275 | 78 | .349 | 120 | .290 | 143 | 0.00 | 146 | 2.41 | 168 | 5.17 | 11 |
| | Bases Empty | .235 | 125 | .293 | 154 | .253 | 166 | 0.30 | 151 | 2.38 | 166 | 9.82 | 37 |
| Lance Johnson | Runners On | .364 | -- | .424 | -- | .408 | -- | 0.00 | -- | 6.85 | -- | 9.59 | -- |
| | Bases Empty | .263 | 69 | .333 | 121 | .333 | 53 | 0.00 | 153 | 9.52 | 37 | 13.49 | 79 |
| Ron Karkovice | Runners On | .275 | 79 | .425 | 54 | .310 | 123 | 3.75 | 30 | 4.26 | 157 | 26.60 | 168 |
| | Bases Empty | .255 | -- | .353 | -- | .303 | -- | 0.00 | -- | 5.50 | -- | 28.44 | -- |
| Ron Kittle | Runners On | .338 | 7 | .650 | 1 | .400 | 17 | 7.50 | 2 | 10.53 | 52 | 15.79 | 118 |
| | Bases Empty | .270 | -- | .472 | -- | .356 | -- | 5.62 | -- | 11.88 | -- | 26.73 | -- |
| Steve Lyons | Runners On | .267 | 89 | .348 | 124 | .302 | 129 | 0.95 | 124 | 5.06 | 145 | 11.39 | 73 |
| | Bases Empty | .262 | 76 | .330 | 125 | .331 | 62 | 0.00 | 153 | 8.95 | 49 | 15.95 | 102 |
| Carlos Martinez | Runners On | .278 | 73 | .331 | 139 | .320 | 106 | 0.00 | 146 | 5.88 | 130 | 16.58 | 125 |
| | Bases Empty | .320 | 6 | .475 | 16 | .359 | 27 | 2.76 | 64 | 5.21 | 141 | 13.54 | 82 |
| Dan Pasqua | Runners On | .295 | 43 | .473 | 25 | .346 | 71 | 3.57 | 35 | 8.59 | 83 | 21.88 | 149 |
| | Bases Empty | .209 | 151 | .388 | 78 | .289 | 130 | 5.22 | 14 | 9.40 | 39 | 20.13 | 138 |
| Sammy Sosa | Runners On | .260 | -- | .342 | -- | .309 | -- | 1.37 | -- | 5.81 | -- | 20.93 | -- |
| | Bases Empty | .255 | 89 | .382 | 85 | .299 | 115 | 2.73 | 66 | 5.13 | 142 | 24.79 | 163 |
| Greg Walker | Runners On | .216 | 162 | .284 | 162 | .291 | 142 | 0.00 | 146 | 10.17 | 60 | 15.25 | 113 |
| | Bases Empty | .206 | 156 | .374 | 92 | .283 | 142 | 3.82 | 36 | 7.59 | 87 | 22.07 | 151 |
| Eddie Williams | Runners On | .225 | 156 | .292 | 159 | .301 | 131 | 1.12 | 112 | 10.38 | 57 | 16.04 | 121 |
| | Bases Empty | .313 | 11 | .411 | 57 | .374 | 13 | 1.79 | 92 | 5.69 | 131 | 11.38 | 55 |
| Team Average | Runners On | .282 | 2 | .400 | 3 | .341 | 5 | 1.70 | 14 | 8.22 | 11 | 13.28 | 5 |
| | Bases Empty | .262 | 4 | .369 | 10 | .318 | 8 | 1.71 | 14 | 7.00 | 12 | 15.06 | 7 |
| League Average | Runners On | .268 | | .389 | | .336 | | 2.15 | | 9.17 | | 13.53 | |
| | Bases Empty | .255 | | .380 | | .317 | | 2.29 | | 7.84 | | 14.86 | |

## Overall Batting Compared to Late Inning Pressure Situations

| | | BA | Rank | SA | Rank | OBA | Rank | HR % | Rank | BB % | Rank | SO % | Rank | RDI % | Rank |
|---|---|---|---|---|---|---|---|---|---|---|---|---|---|---|---|
| Daryl Boston | Overall | .252 | 109 | .372 | 95 | .325 | 81 | 2.29 | 72 | 9.72 | 48 | 12.55 | 72 | .224 | 140 |
| | Pressure | .250 | 89 | .425 | 47 | .362 | 45 | 2.50 | 67 | 14.00 | 23 | 16.00 | 84 | .125 | 143 |
| Ivan Calderon | Overall | .286 | 34 | .437 | 36 | .332 | 66 | 2.25 | 73 | 6.36 | 122 | 13.91 | 88 | .309 | 39 |
| | Pressure | .208 | 125 | .317 | 111 | .250 | 143 | 0.99 | 106 | 5.50 | 136 | 22.02 | 132 | .273 | 76 |
| Carlton Fisk | Overall | .293 | 28 | .475 | 12 | .356 | 33 | 3.47 | 36 | 8.59 | 69 | 14.32 | 92 | .323 | 29 |
| | Pressure | .306 | 36 | .500 | 17 | .357 | 47 | 3.23 | 48 | 8.57 | 84 | 21.43 | 127 | .320 | 51 |
| Scott Fletcher | Overall | .253 | 107 | .311 | 154 | .332 | 67 | 0.18 | 163 | 10.17 | 40 | 9.54 | 41 | .248 | 113 |
| | Pressure | .216 | 115 | .243 | 147 | .298 | 111 | 0.00 | 107 | 10.47 | 57 | 13.95 | 59 | .261 | 86 |
| Dave Gallagher | Overall | .266 | 69 | .314 | 152 | .320 | 92 | 0.17 | 165 | 6.90 | 111 | 11.84 | 66 | .227 | 135 |
| | Pressure | .216 | 116 | .239 | 150 | .266 | 137 | 0.00 | 107 | 6.00 | 126 | 9.00 | 24 | .091 | 155 |
| Ozzie Guillen | Overall | .253 | 106 | .318 | 147 | .270 | 164 | 0.17 | 164 | 2.40 | 170 | 7.67 | 18 | .271 | 76 |
| | Pressure | .314 | 28 | .402 | 56 | .324 | 82 | 0.00 | 107 | 1.89 | 168 | 8.49 | 21 | .314 | 55 |
| Lance Johnson | Overall | .300 | -- | .367 | -- | .360 | -- | 0.00 | -- | 8.54 | -- | 12.06 | -- | .283 | 62 |
| | Pressure | .258 | 80 | .290 | 130 | .324 | 83 | 0.00 | 107 | 8.82 | 80 | 23.53 | 142 | .000 | -- |
| Ron Karkovice | Overall | .264 | 75 | .385 | 84 | .306 | 116 | 1.65 | 99 | 4.93 | 154 | 27.59 | 169 | .266 | 81 |
| | Pressure | .125 | 166 | .125 | 169 | .152 | 171 | 0.00 | 107 | 2.94 | 154 | 52.94 | 172 | .000 | 165 |
| Ron Kittle | Overall | .302 | -- | .556 | -- | .378 | -- | 6.51 | -- | 11.22 | -- | 21.43 | -- | .340 | -- |
| | Pressure | .393 | 3 | .571 | 8 | .452 | 6 | 3.57 | 44 | 9.68 | 69 | 19.35 | 115 | .333 | -- |
| Steve Lyons | Overall | .264 | 73 | .339 | 127 | .317 | 96 | 0.45 | 151 | 7.09 | 106 | 13.77 | 86 | .289 | 55 |
| | Pressure | .273 | 62 | .364 | 83 | .317 | 90 | 1.30 | 100 | 5.81 | 130 | 17.44 | 98 | .276 | 75 |
| Carlos Martinez | Overall | .300 | 21 | .406 | 62 | .340 | 56 | 1.43 | 110 | 5.54 | 142 | 15.04 | 97 | .219 | 146 |
| | Pressure | .283 | 55 | .391 | 67 | .340 | 64 | 0.00 | 107 | 5.77 | 131 | 13.46 | 54 | .389 | 23 |
| Dan Pasqua | Overall | .248 | 118 | .427 | 43 | .315 | 101 | 4.47 | 16 | 9.03 | 58 | 20.94 | 149 | .368 | 11 |
| | Pressure | .212 | 119 | .333 | 103 | .297 | 112 | 3.03 | 55 | 7.89 | 97 | 34.21 | 164 | .333 | 42 |
| Sammy Sosa | Overall | .257 | 95 | .366 | 107 | .303 | 124 | 2.19 | 77 | 5.42 | 144 | 23.15 | 156 | .178 | -- |
| | Pressure | .174 | -- | .261 | -- | .240 | -- | 0.00 | -- | 7.69 | -- | 26.92 | -- | .000 | -- |
| Greg Walker | Overall | .210 | 165 | .335 | 130 | .286 | 151 | 2.15 | 81 | 8.75 | 65 | 19.01 | 136 | .247 | 117 |
| | Pressure | .061 | 172 | .061 | 172 | .214 | 158 | 0.00 | 107 | 13.95 | 25 | 13.95 | 59 | .273 | 76 |
| Eddie Williams | Overall | .274 | 52 | .358 | 114 | .341 | 53 | 1.49 | 107 | 7.86 | 90 | 13.54 | 83 | .118 | -- |
| | Pressure | .267 | 69 | .400 | 57 | .333 | 72 | 3.33 | 47 | 9.09 | 73 | 15.15 | 71 | .000 | -- |
| Team Average | Overall | .271 | 3 | .383 | 8 | .328 | 6 | 1.71 | 14 | 7.57 | 12 | 14.24 | 7 | .280 | 5 |
| | Pressure | .253 | 6 | .346 | 8 | .313 | 7 | 1.16 | 14 | 7.81 | 12 | 18.09 | 7 | .244 | 10 |
| League Average | Overall | .261 | | .384 | | .326 | | 2.23 | | 8.44 | | 14.26 | | .269 | |
| | Pressure | .247 | | .357 | | .318 | | 2.02 | | 9.02 | | 17.90 | | .254 | |

## Additional Miscellaneous Batting Comparisons

| | Grass Surface BA | Grass Surface Rank | Artificial Surface BA | Artificial Surface Rank | Home Games BA | Home Games Rank | Road Games BA | Road Games Rank | Runners in Scoring Position BA | Runners in Scoring Position Rank | Runners in Scoring Pos and Two Outs BA | Runners in Scoring Pos and Two Outs Rank | Leading Off Inning OBA | Leading Off Inning Rank | Runners on 3B with less than 2 Outs RDI % | Runners on 3B with less than 2 Outs Rank |
|---|---|---|---|---|---|---|---|---|---|---|---|---|---|---|---|---|
| Daryl Boston | .238 | 124 | .360 | -- | .289 | 40 | .212 | 161 | .277 | 71 | .087 | 169 | .327 | 75 | .800 | 7 |
| Ivan Calderon | .293 | 27 | .252 | 87 | .248 | 105 | .318 | 11 | .270 | 79 | .274 | 45 | .317 | 93 | .526 | 112 |
| Carlton Fisk | .296 | 24 | .281 | 53 | .343 | 6 | .251 | 99 | .352 | 7 | .277 | 41 | .333 | 64 | .818 | 5 |
| Scott Fletcher | .253 | 91 | .250 | 90 | .256 | 91 | .250 | 100 | .236 | 120 | .237 | 84 | .331 | 70 | .529 | 109 |
| Dave Gallagher | .276 | 53 | .215 | 135 | .270 | 66 | .263 | 78 | .255 | 97 | .222 | 98 | .322 | 86 | .444 | 144 |
| Ozzie Guillen | .248 | 103 | .288 | 47 | .240 | 119 | .266 | 75 | .271 | 77 | .239 | 82 | .207 | 169 | .640 | 47 |
| Lance Johnson | .302 | 17 | .293 | 40 | .274 | -- | .323 | -- | .311 | -- | .318 | -- | .368 | 31 | .429 | -- |
| Ron Karkovice | .263 | 74 | .267 | -- | .241 | 117 | .284 | 44 | .280 | 65 | .261 | 61 | .271 | 144 | .471 | 134 |
| Ron Kittle | .313 | 9 | .211 | -- | .271 | -- | .323 | 9 | .342 | -- | .267 | -- | .408 | 9 | .750 | -- |
| Steve Lyons | .265 | 70 | .258 | 79 | .217 | 150 | .305 | 19 | .280 | 65 | .220 | 102 | .308 | 102 | .577 | 81 |
| Carlos Martinez | .291 | 32 | .338 | 14 | .281 | 50 | .318 | 12 | .229 | 134 | .174 | 142 | .382 | 22 | .500 | 119 |
| Dan Pasqua | .245 | 108 | .267 | -- | .257 | 90 | .241 | 123 | .318 | 24 | .280 | 36 | .370 | 28 | .565 | 90 |
| Sammy Sosa | .236 | 126 | .409 | -- | .284 | -- | .241 | 121 | .211 | -- | .000 | -- | .302 | 113 | .300 | 169 |
| Greg Walker | .208 | 164 | .222 | 131 | .165 | 171 | .239 | 125 | .226 | 138 | .148 | 154 | .319 | 91 | .471 | 134 |
| Eddie Williams | .270 | 61 | .304 | -- | .235 | 128 | .311 | 14 | .122 | 172 | .087 | 169 | .364 | 33 | .364 | 158 |
| Team Average | .270 | 3 | .275 | 3 | .258 | 8 | .283 | 1 | .275 | 3 | .232 | 7 | .323 | 6 | .575 | 6 |
| League Average | .260 | | .262 | | .262 | | .259 | | .262 | | .232 | | .321 | | .566 | |

## Pitching vs. Left and Right Handed Batters

| | | BA | Rank | SA | Rank | OBA | Rank | HR % | Rank | BB % | Rank | SO % | Rank |
|---|---|---|---|---|---|---|---|---|---|---|---|---|---|
| Richard Dotson | vs. Lefties | .291 | 103 | .479 | 119 | .342 | 79 | 2.88 | 97 | 7.49 | 50 | 8.93 | 103 |
| | vs. Righties | .298 | 127 | .434 | 113 | .366 | 129 | 2.32 | 77 | 9.47 | 103 | 11.24 | 105 |
| Greg Hibbard | vs. Lefties | .314 | -- | .400 | -- | .390 | -- | 0.00 | -- | 10.84 | -- | 13.25 | -- |
| | vs. Righties | .261 | 77 | .359 | 54 | .310 | 48 | 1.09 | 17 | 6.43 | 46 | 8.84 | 124 |
| Shawn Hillegas | vs. Lefties | .313 | 117 | .449 | 106 | .395 | 128 | 1.76 | 65 | 11.58 | 107 | 10.42 | 86 |
| | vs. Righties | .248 | 47 | .411 | 95 | .310 | 49 | 3.25 | 109 | 7.66 | 67 | 17.88 | 40 |
| Eric King | vs. Lefties | .231 | 36 | .373 | 63 | .312 | 50 | 3.57 | 112 | 10.00 | 89 | 11.71 | 71 |
| | vs. Righties | .258 | 70 | .307 | 15 | .328 | 86 | 0.71 | 8 | 9.18 | 94 | 9.81 | 118 |
| Bill Long | vs. Lefties | .267 | 81 | .432 | 99 | .327 | 64 | 2.27 | 77 | 8.12 | 57 | 10.15 | 87 |
| | vs. Righties | .263 | 80 | .385 | 78 | .336 | 98 | 1.95 | 63 | 8.94 | 91 | 13.19 | 86 |
| Tom McCarthy | vs. Lefties | .292 | 104 | .387 | 75 | .361 | 99 | 0.94 | 25 | 10.08 | 92 | 7.56 | 116 |
| | vs. Righties | .272 | 92 | .450 | 123 | .313 | 56 | 4.64 | 130 | 4.82 | 14 | 10.84 | 109 |
| Donn Pall | vs. Lefties | .255 | 60 | .389 | 79 | .306 | 45 | 2.55 | 88 | 5.78 | 22 | 16.18 | 30 |
| | vs. Righties | .284 | 113 | .432 | 112 | .339 | 101 | 2.84 | 103 | 4.57 | 12 | 15.23 | 62 |
| Ken Patterson | vs. Lefties | .297 | -- | .516 | -- | .395 | -- | 6.25 | -- | 14.47 | -- | 14.47 | -- |
| | vs. Righties | .243 | 37 | .443 | 120 | .309 | 46 | 3.78 | 124 | 8.17 | 80 | 15.38 | 61 |
| Melido Perez | vs. Lefties | .264 | 72 | .445 | 105 | .352 | 88 | 3.23 | 108 | 11.32 | 105 | 16.04 | 31 |
| | vs. Righties | .264 | 82 | .418 | 104 | .344 | 110 | 3.26 | 111 | 10.88 | 122 | 18.91 | 34 |
| Steve Rosenberg | vs. Lefties | .280 | 92 | .390 | 80 | .354 | 92 | 1.00 | 27 | 9.57 | 82 | 13.04 | 58 |
| | vs. Righties | .272 | 93 | .449 | 122 | .337 | 99 | 2.95 | 105 | 9.36 | 100 | 12.35 | 92 |
| Bobby Thigpen | vs. Lefties | .191 | 11 | .338 | 41 | .311 | 49 | 3.68 | 115 | 15.15 | 121 | 10.91 | 79 |
| | vs. Righties | .242 | 34 | .396 | 85 | .311 | 52 | 3.36 | 116 | 8.77 | 89 | 16.96 | 47 |
| Team Average | vs. Lefties | .271 | 11 | .422 | 11 | .347 | 11 | 2.81 | 13 | 9.99 | 11 | 12.41 | 9 |
| | vs. Righties | .267 | 10 | .402 | 11 | .327 | 10 | 2.51 | 10 | 7.93 | 9 | 12.74 | 13 |
| League Average | vs. Lefties | .261 | | .382 | | .330 | | 2.16 | | 9.16 | | 13.03 | |
| | vs. Righties | .261 | | .385 | | .323 | | 2.28 | | 7.96 | | 15.09 | |

## Pitching with Runners on Base and Bases Empty

| | | BA | Rank | SA | Rank | OBA | Rank | HR % | Rank | BB % | Rank | SO % | Rank |
|---|---|---|---|---|---|---|---|---|---|---|---|---|---|
| Richard Dotson | Runners On | .274 | 85 | .413 | 101 | .338 | 75 | 2.14 | 83 | 8.72 | 62 | 9.35 | 110 |
| | Bases Empty | .311 | 129 | .494 | 129 | .368 | 125 | 2.99 | 97 | 8.24 | 81 | 10.71 | 106 |
| Greg Hibbard | Runners On | .258 | 57 | .371 | 65 | .307 | 31 | 1.31 | 34 | 7.03 | 36 | 9.77 | 105 |
| | Bases Empty | .277 | 101 | .360 | 50 | .332 | 92 | 0.67 | 6 | 7.08 | 62 | 9.23 | 117 |
| Shawn Hillegas | Runners On | .284 | 100 | .433 | 112 | .363 | 111 | 2.79 | 107 | 10.44 | 93 | 16.47 | 39 |
| | Bases Empty | .275 | 99 | .426 | 105 | .342 | 100 | 2.33 | 75 | 8.80 | 91 | 12.32 | 84 |
| Eric King | Runners On | .248 | 40 | .298 | 11 | .320 | 52 | 0.84 | 16 | 9.56 | 74 | 10.66 | 92 |
| | Bases Empty | .241 | 48 | .371 | 64 | .320 | 69 | 3.12 | 102 | 9.64 | 102 | 10.91 | 103 |
| Bill Long | Runners On | .253 | 48 | .379 | 73 | .324 | 55 | 2.75 | 105 | 10.28 | 91 | 8.88 | 114 |
| | Bases Empty | .276 | 100 | .432 | 108 | .339 | 98 | 1.51 | 32 | 6.88 | 59 | 14.68 | 57 |
| Tom McCarthy | Runners On | .252 | 46 | .317 | 18 | .312 | 40 | 0.81 | 14 | 7.80 | 49 | 10.64 | 94 |
| | Bases Empty | .306 | 127 | .522 | 134 | .354 | 115 | 5.22 | 134 | 6.25 | 47 | 8.33 | 124 |
| Donn Pall | Runners On | .265 | 74 | .368 | 61 | .299 | 23 | 1.62 | 56 | 3.90 | 3 | 15.61 | 46 |
| | Bases Empty | .277 | 103 | .466 | 121 | .352 | 112 | 4.05 | 130 | 6.67 | 53 | 15.76 | 52 |
| Ken Patterson | Runners On | .232 | 26 | .446 | 119 | .328 | 62 | 5.36 | 132 | 11.85 | 109 | 11.85 | 77 |
| | Bases Empty | .277 | 105 | .474 | 123 | .336 | 94 | 3.65 | 118 | 8.05 | 79 | 18.12 | 35 |
| Melido Perez | Runners On | .286 | 105 | .461 | 123 | .359 | 106 | 3.29 | 118 | 10.00 | 84 | 16.86 | 37 |
| | Bases Empty | .248 | 55 | .411 | 94 | .339 | 97 | 3.22 | 104 | 11.96 | 128 | 17.83 | 37 |
| Steve Rosenberg | Runners On | .282 | 97 | .436 | 113 | .321 | 53 | 1.66 | 60 | 6.55 | 24 | 10.55 | 95 |
| | Bases Empty | .267 | 82 | .440 | 112 | .355 | 119 | 3.33 | 110 | 11.70 | 126 | 14.04 | 65 |
| Bobby Thigpen | Runners On | .204 | 10 | .377 | 72 | .256 | 5 | 4.32 | 126 | 7.03 | 35 | 12.97 | 69 |
| | Bases Empty | .236 | 42 | .358 | 47 | .377 | 128 | 2.44 | 80 | 17.88 | 135 | 15.23 | 53 |
| Team Average | Runners On | .271 | 8 | .397 | 8 | .327 | 5 | 2.17 | 8 | 7.93 | 2 | 12.22 | 12 |
| | Bases Empty | .267 | 11 | .422 | 14 | .342 | 13 | 3.02 | 14 | 9.45 | 13 | 12.96 | 13 |
| League Average | Runners On | .268 | | .389 | | .336 | | 2.15 | | 9.17 | | 13.53 | |
| | Bases Empty | .255 | | .380 | | .317 | | 2.29 | | 7.84 | | 14.86 | |

## Overall Pitching Compared to Late Inning Pressure Situations

| | | BA | Rank | SA | Rank | OBA | Rank | HR % | Rank | BB % | Rank | SO % | Rank |
|---|---|---|---|---|---|---|---|---|---|---|---|---|---|
| Richard Dotson | Overall | .294 | 122 | .457 | 124 | .354 | 113 | 2.60 | 96 | 8.47 | 73 | 10.07 | 105 |
| | Pressure | .182 | 13 | .205 | 7 | .265 | 21 | 0.00 | 1 | 9.62 | 71 | 9.62 | 109 |
| Greg Hibbard | Overall | .268 | 82 | .365 | 55 | .321 | 59 | 0.95 | 8 | 7.06 | 47 | 9.47 | 116 |
| | Pressure | .294 | 108 | .324 | 51 | .351 | 89 | 0.00 | 1 | 5.41 | 23 | 10.81 | 101 |
| Shawn Hillegas | Overall | .279 | 101 | .429 | 103 | .352 | 110 | 2.54 | 88 | 9.57 | 96 | 14.26 | 61 |
| | Pressure | .286 | 97 | .395 | 92 | .368 | 100 | 1.68 | 61 | 10.87 | 83 | 11.59 | 93 |
| Barry Jones | Overall | .208 | -- | .292 | -- | .265 | -- | 1.89 | -- | 6.61 | -- | 14.05 | -- |
| | Pressure | .232 | 54 | .286 | 33 | .295 | 40 | 1.79 | 65 | 6.15 | 34 | 12.31 | 83 |
| Eric King | Overall | .244 | 37 | .342 | 36 | .320 | 58 | 2.20 | 71 | 9.61 | 98 | 10.81 | 98 |
| | Pressure | .246 | 65 | .351 | 71 | .313 | 62 | 1.75 | 63 | 9.23 | 62 | 9.23 | 112 |
| Bill Long | Overall | .265 | 78 | .407 | 92 | .332 | 80 | 2.10 | 66 | 8.56 | 76 | 11.81 | 87 |
| | Pressure | .138 | 3 | .345 | 66 | .286 | 30 | 3.45 | 108 | 17.14 | 128 | 11.43 | 94 |
| Tom McCarthy | Overall | .280 | 103 | .424 | 101 | .333 | 85 | 3.11 | 113 | 7.02 | 45 | 9.47 | 115 |
| | Pressure | .220 | 44 | .480 | 115 | .259 | 15 | 6.00 | 131 | 3.70 | 9 | 3.70 | 130 |
| Donn Pall | Overall | .270 | 87 | .411 | 93 | .323 | 64 | 2.70 | 101 | 5.14 | 10 | 15.68 | 48 |
| | Pressure | .296 | 111 | .444 | 107 | .349 | 86 | 2.96 | 101 | 5.76 | 27 | 13.09 | 76 |
| Ken Patterson | Overall | .257 | 62 | .462 | 127 | .332 | 81 | 4.42 | 132 | 9.86 | 101 | 15.14 | 53 |
| | Pressure | .303 | 115 | .545 | 123 | .382 | 108 | 4.55 | 124 | 11.69 | 96 | 12.99 | 78 |
| Melido Perez | Overall | .264 | 75 | .432 | 109 | .348 | 106 | 3.25 | 118 | 11.11 | 114 | 17.41 | 35 |
| | Pressure | .286 | 97 | .408 | 99 | .327 | 67 | 2.04 | 74 | 5.56 | 25 | 22.22 | 22 |
| Steve Rosenberg | Overall | .274 | 93 | .438 | 116 | .340 | 95 | 2.59 | 95 | 9.40 | 92 | 12.48 | 76 |
| | Pressure | .250 | 68 | .367 | 79 | .357 | 96 | 3.33 | 107 | 14.08 | 116 | 12.68 | 80 |
| Bobby Thigpen | Overall | .218 | 16 | .368 | 58 | .311 | 44 | 3.51 | 126 | 11.90 | 119 | 13.99 | 62 |
| | Pressure | .215 | 41 | .360 | 77 | .312 | 61 | 3.76 | 114 | 11.82 | 99 | 15.00 | 64 |
| Team Average | Overall | .269 | 10 | .410 | 12 | .335 | 12 | 2.63 | 12 | 8.74 | 10 | 12.61 | 13 |
| | Pressure | .259 | 10 | .400 | 13 | .334 | 9 | 3.00 | 14 | 9.29 | 7 | 12.64 | 13 |
| League Average | Overall | .261 | | .384 | | .326 | | 2.23 | | 8.44 | | 14.26 | |
| | Pressure | .250 | | .362 | | .325 | | 2.14 | | 9.50 | | 16.61 | |

## Additional Miscellaneous Pitching Comparisons

| | Grass Surface | | Artificial Surface | | Home Games | | Road Games | | Runners in Scoring Position | | Runners in Scoring Pos and Two Outs | | Leading Off Inning | |
|---|---|---|---|---|---|---|---|---|---|---|---|---|---|---|
| | BA | Rank | BA | Rank | BA | Rank | BA | Rank | BA | Rank | BA | Rank | OBA | Rank |
| Richard Dotson | .292 | 115 | .310 | 114 | .300 | 122 | .289 | 105 | .261 | 81 | .217 | 63 | .329 | 78 |
| Greg Hibbard | .257 | 64 | .317 | 117 | .247 | 62 | .289 | 103 | .244 | 57 | .150 | 18 | .270 | 25 |
| Shawn Hillegas | .269 | 85 | .322 | 121 | .267 | 85 | .291 | 107 | .280 | 101 | .250 | 88 | .322 | 68 |
| Eric King | .242 | 37 | .257 | 52 | .239 | 41 | .251 | 49 | .238 | 49 | .233 | 73 | .335 | 83 |
| Bill Long | .275 | 96 | .233 | 32 | .270 | 94 | .261 | 69 | .248 | 61 | .190 | 42 | .287 | 35 |
| Tom McCarthy | .277 | 98 | .308 | -- | .255 | 72 | .310 | 125 | .222 | 23 | .125 | 10 | .241 | 10 |
| Donn Pall | .268 | 83 | .286 | -- | .261 | 79 | .277 | 87 | .250 | 62 | .286 | 109 | .384 | 120 |
| Ken Patterson | .243 | 41 | .391 | -- | .216 | -- | .293 | 112 | .250 | 62 | .176 | 34 | .361 | 108 |
| Melido Perez | .262 | 68 | .271 | 73 | .276 | 99 | .255 | 61 | .247 | 59 | .229 | 69 | .323 | 70 |
| Steve Rosenberg | .278 | 101 | .247 | 47 | .286 | 111 | .261 | 68 | .293 | 113 | .319 | 125 | .392 | 125 |
| Bobby Thigpen | .208 | 13 | .267 | 67 | .219 | 19 | .216 | 15 | .256 | 75 | .179 | 37 | .344 | 92 |
| Team Average | .266 | 9 | .287 | 13 | .264 | 9 | .274 | 12 | .265 | 10 | .226 | 4 | .333 | 12 |
| League Average | .260 | | .262 | | .259 | | .262 | | .262 | | .232 | | .321 | |

# CLEVELAND INDIANS

- **Can the Tribe come from behind in 1990?**
- **Did Keith Hernandez leave his future in New York?**

Baseball, as Tim McCarver often reminds us, is a game of firsts. The first pitch to each batter, the first batter of each inning, and the first run of each game all set the wheels of strategy spinning. To trace some of those strategic paths to their possible conclusions sometimes requires the foresight and concentration of a chess grand master. But the importance of getting ahead—whether in the count, in the inning, or in the score—is something all of us can understand.

We've written often in the past about the degree to which an inning's leadoff batter affects his team's chances of scoring: 15 percent if he makes out, more than three times that much—50 percent, to be exact—if he reaches base. But did you know that the first run of any game has a comparably significant effect on the outcome? The team that scores the first run wins roughly twice as often as its opponent. For some low-scoring teams, like the 1989 Indians, that ratio can be considerably greater.

Over the past five years, there have been only four teams that, in any one season, were more than three times as likely to win when they scored the first run as when they allowed it. On average, they scored fewer than four runs per game. Those teams are shown in the following table. The Ratio column indicates how many times more likely the team is to win when it scores first than when it doesn't:

| | | Scoring the First Run | | | Allowing the First Run | | | | |
|---|---|---|---|---|---|---|---|---|---|
| Year | Team | W | L | Pct. | W | L | Pct. | Ratio | Avg. Runs |
| 1988 | St. Louis | 57 | 23 | .713 | 19 | 63 | .232 | 3.1 | 3.57 |
| 1989 | Cleveland | 54 | 24 | .692 | 19 | 65 | .226 | 3.1 | 3.73 |
| 1989 | Kansas City | 54 | 27 | .667 | 16 | 65 | .198 | 3.4 | 4.26 |
| 1989 | Philadelphia | 52 | 32 | .619 | 15 | 65 | .198 | 3.2 | 3.86 |

Last season, the Indians tied the White Sox for the fewest come-from-behind wins in the American League (30). But Cleveland had problems coming from behind in 1988 as well, when only the once-lowly Orioles had fewer comeback wins, by a margin of 29 to 26. So it figures that during those two years, no team in the league had a poorer record in games in which they allowed the first run than the Indians did. Teams are listed in order of winning percentage in games in which the opposition scores first. Rankings for games in which the team scores first are shown:

| | Allowing the First Run | | | Scoring the First Run | | | |
|---|---|---|---|---|---|---|---|
| Team | W | L | Pct. | W | L | Pct. | Rank |
| Oakland | 65 | 80 | .448 | 138 | 41 | .771 | 1 |
| Boston | 66 | 85 | .437 | 106 | 67 | .613 | 12 |
| Toronto | 63 | 100 | .387 | 113 | 48 | .702 | 4 |
| Minnesota | 60 | 104 | .366 | 111 | 49 | .694 | 5 |
| New York | 55 | 103 | .348 | 104 | 60 | .634 | 9 |
| California | 54 | 104 | .342 | 112 | 54 | .675 | 6 |
| Milwaukee | 52 | 111 | .319 | 116 | 45 | .720 | 3 |
| Kansas City | 50 | 108 | .316 | 126 | 39 | .764 | 2 |
| Seattle | 57 | 124 | .315 | 84 | 58 | .592 | 14 |
| Detroit | 46 | 114 | .288 | 101 | 63 | .616 | 11 |
| Texas | 46 | 116 | .284 | 107 | 54 | .665 | 7 |
| Chicago | 46 | 121 | .275 | 94 | 61 | .606 | 13 |
| Baltimore | 47 | 124 | .275 | 94 | 58 | .618 | 10 |
| Cleveland | 44 | 119 | .270 | 107 | 54 | .665 | 7 |

The most frustrating aspect of Cleveland's inability to come from behind has been its moderate success after getting out on top. This is a team that knows how to hold a lead, ranking right in the middle of the league with a .665 winning percentage over the past two seasons when scoring first. Perhaps that explains an unusual strategy that the Indians used 11 times last season, tying Chicago for the league lead. We refer to Cleveland's 11 sacrifice bunts in the first inning, including seven by the king of the sacrifice, Felix Fermin. The other 12 A.L. teams averaged only three first-inning sac bunts. But the desperation that Cleveland and Chicago must have felt to strike first in light of the figures above shed a different light on those first-inning bunts.

The Fermin situation is in itself noteworthy. He led the American League with 32 sacrifice bunts, the highest total in the A.L. since Bert Campaneris accumulated 40 for the Texas Rangers in 1977. And there sure wasn't much deception involved. In 38 plate appearances (*a*) with none out, and (*b*) with a runner only on first base, and (*c*) with the Indians no more than one run behind, no more than three runs ahead, Fermin executed 27 successful sacrifice bunts. Assuming that he wasn't even asked to bunt on a few of those other 11 appearances, that would put his success rate somewhere in the neighborhood of 80 percent. Having grown up in New York, we know that Phil Rizzuto has never been one of those broadcasters who spews statistics like a geyser. But given the Scooter's admiration of the few contemporary players who've mastered the art of bunting, those are numbers we're sure even he would appreciate.

Doug Jones has carved himself a nice little niche in the Indians bullpen. He saved 32 games last season, and his total of 69 during two seasons as Cleveland's stopper ranks third in the American League behind guys named Eckersley (78) and Reardon (73). Exactly where he ranks among the league's closers in terms of effectiveness is difficult to say, because last season the best relief pitchers in the A.L. were separated by a very narrow margin. And two of the pitchers mentioned above—Reardon and Jones—actually ranked first and second, respectively, in *failed* save opportunities among pitchers with at least 20 saves.

The following table shows all American League pitchers with 20 or more saves last season, ranked according to save percentage; that is, saves divided by opportunities:

| Pitcher, Team | Opp. | Saves | Pct. |
|---|---|---|---|
| Russell, Tex. | 44 | 38 | 86.4 |
| Henke, Tor. | 24 | 20 | 83.3 |
| Eckersley, Oak. | 40 | 33 | 82.5 |
| Plesac, Mil. | 40 | 33 | 82.5 |
| Schooler, Sea. | 40 | 33 | 82.5 |
| Olson, Balt. | 34 | 27 | 79.4 |
| Thigpen, Chi. | 43 | 34 | 79.1 |
| Harvey, Cal. | 32 | 25 | 78.1 |
| Jones, Clev. | 41 | 32 | 78.0 |
| Reardon, Minn. | 42 | 31 | 73.8 |
| Righetti, N.Y. | 34 | 25 | 73.5 |
| Smith, Bos. | 34 | 25 | 73.5 |

Of course, not all save situations are created equal. Some managers, like Kansas City's John Wathan, rarely ask their closers to enter a game with runners already on base. Oakland manager Tony LaRussa never calls for Eckersley prior to the ninth inning. But in Cleveland, Jones brings a lunch pail to work. No star treatment here: Jones is often called on to put out fires, and to do it as early as the eighth inning if necessary. It may cost him a few more blown save opportunities than the more pampered stoppers on other A.L. teams. But it's a mark of Jones's role that he saved more games last season in which he pitched more than an inning (15) than any other pitcher in the league, except for Bobby Thigpen (18). Following Thigpen and Jones were Henke, Plesac, Schooler, and Russell in a four-way tie for third with 13.

We're often asked why save opportunities aren't part of a relief pitcher's standard record. Although we agree that such a category augments a player's statistical portrait, it is also true that even that figure must be qualified, according to how each individual pitcher is used.

Keith Hernandez has always maintained that he's capable of playing into his 40s, and that his personal goal is to reach the 3000–hit mark. Apparently, Indians management shares Hernandez's generous self-appraisal: They've invited him to pursue his goal at Cleveland Stadium, at least for the next two years. Frankly we agree with Indians general manager Hank Peters, one of the architects of the Orioles' minidynasty of the 1970s. After signing Hernandez to a two-year contract for well over three million dollars, Peters admitted he may have overpaid a tad for a player whose entry into the free-agent market generated little interest.

Hernandez will have to narrow substantially that 844–hit gap that separates him from the 3000 mark to justify Cleveland's investment. But here's the catch: Recent past performances suggest that Hernandez, now 36 years old, might be nothing more than the major leagues' most expensive pinch hitter for the duration of his contract.

On the lookout for the 10 players whose statistical profiles most closely matched Hernandez's—both over his career and in his most recent season—two facts became obvious. First, a majority of past players who reached the crossroads Hernandez now faces at about the same age decided to hang 'em up. Check your *Baseball Encyclopedia:* Felipe Alou (following the 1973 season), Dusty Baker (1986), Cecil Cooper (1987), Joe Cronin (1944), Alvin Dark (1960), Tommy Davis (1976), Pinky Higgins (1946), Gary Matthews (1987), Ken Singleton (1984), Arky Vaughan (1948), Dixie Walker (1949), and Gee Walker (1945). All comparable hitters to Hernandez; all suffered through years like Hernandez had last season; all decided they'd had enough. Of course, no one was waving a seven-figure paycheck at them.

Second, among those who played beyond that point, very few had even a single season of everyday play remaining. Only four of Keith's 10 most comparable stat-twins *who continued beyond that point* had more than 100 hits left in their bats. And of those four, only Enos Slaughter accumulated even one-third the total Hernandez would need from this point to reach the 3000 mark:

| | | | Season Statistics | | | | | | Future | | |
|---|---|---|---|---|---|---|---|---|---|---|---|
| Year | Player | Age | AB | R | H | HR | RBI | BA | AB | H | BA |
| 1942 | Dick Bartell | 34 | 316 | 53 | 77 | 5 | 24 | .244 | 339 | 91 | .268 |
| 1952 | Phil Cavarretta | 36 | 63 | 7 | 15 | 1 | 8 | .238 | 183 | 56 | .306 |
| 1952 | Bob Elliott | 35 | 272 | 33 | 62 | 10 | 35 | .228 | 368 | 94 | .255 |
| 1954 | Enos Slaughter | 38 | 125 | 19 | 31 | 1 | 19 | .248 | 1046 | 288 | .275 |
| 1967 | Ken Boyer | 36 | 346 | 34 | 86 | 7 | 34 | .266 | 279 | 70 | .251 |
| 1975 | Joe Torre | 37 | 361 | 33 | 89 | 6 | 35 | .247 | 361 | 104 | .288 |
| 1983 | Amos Otis | 36 | 356 | 35 | 93 | 4 | 41 | .261 | 97 | 16 | .165 |
| 1984 | Ted Simmons | 35 | 497 | 44 | 110 | 4 | 52 | .221 | 939 | 246 | .262 |
| 1985 | Chris Chambliss | 36 | 170 | 16 | 40 | 3 | 21 | .235 | 123 | 38 | .309 |
| 1985 | George Hendrick | 35 | 297 | 28 | 64 | 4 | 31 | .215 | 613 | 152 | .248 |
| | Averages | 36 | 280 | 30 | 67 | 5 | 30 | .239 | 435 | 116 | .267 |
| 1989 | Keith Hernandez | 35 | 215 | 18 | 50 | 4 | 19 | .233 | | | |

Take a shot at this quiz question. The future track of Hernandez's career will tell us about: (*a*) his determination; (*b*) his aquisitiveness; (*c*) our crystal ball; (*d*) all of the above.

Correct answer: *d*.

## WON-LOST RECORD BY STARTING POSITION

| CLEVELAND 73-89 | C | 1B | 2B | 3B | SS | LF | CF | RF | P | DH | Leadoff | Relief | Starts |
|---|---|---|---|---|---|---|---|---|---|---|---|---|---|
| Luis Aguayo | - | - | 3-6 | 9-3 | 1-3 | - | - | - | - | - | 2-0 | - | 13-12 |
| Andy Allanson | 49-54 | - | - | - | - | - | - | - | - | - | - | - | 49-54 |
| Neil Allen | - | - | - | - | - | - | - | - | - | - | - | 0-3 | - |
| Beau Allred | - | - | - | - | - | 1-1 | - | 1-1 | - | - | - | - | 2-2 |
| Keith Atherton | - | - | - | - | - | - | - | - | - | - | - | 10-22 | - |
| Scott Bailes | - | - | - | - | - | - | - | - | 5-6 | - | - | 6-17 | 5-6 |
| Joey Belle | - | - | - | - | - | 4-9 | - | 16-14 | - | 7-9 | - | - | 27-32 |
| Bud Black | - | - | - | - | - | - | - | - | 12-20 | - | - | 1-0 | 12-20 |
| Jerry Browne | - | - | 67-80 | - | - | - | - | - | - | 0-1 | 47-67 | - | 67-81 |
| Tom Candiotti | - | - | - | - | - | - | - | - | 15-16 | - | - | - | 15-16 |
| Joe Carter | - | 5-6 | - | - | - | 21-21 | 45-56 | - | - | 2-6 | - | - | 73-89 |
| Dave Clark | - | - | - | - | - | 4-4 | - | 4-3 | - | 19-29 | - | - | 27-36 |
| Peter Dalena | - | - | - | - | - | - | - | - | - | 0-1 | - | - | 0-1 |
| Steve Davis | - | - | - | - | - | - | - | - | 1-1 | - | - | 2-8 | 1-1 |
| John Farrell | - | - | - | - | - | - | - | - | 13-18 | - | - | - | 13-18 |
| Felix Fermin | - | - | 1-1 | - | 68-82 | - | - | - | - | - | - | - | 69-83 |
| Denny Gonzalez | - | - | - | - | - | - | - | - | - | 1-3 | - | - | 1-3 |
| Brad Havens | - | - | - | - | - | - | - | - | - | - | - | 2-5 | - |
| Dave Hengel | - | - | - | - | - | 2-5 | - | - | - | - | - | - | 2-5 |
| Mark Higgins | - | 2-1 | - | - | - | - | - | - | - | - | - | - | 2-1 |
| Tommy Hinzo | - | - | 2-2 | - | 0-1 | - | - | - | - | - | 2-2 | - | 2-3 |
| Brook Jacoby | - | - | - | 61-83 | - | - | - | - | - | 2-1 | - | - | 63-84 |
| Dion James | - | - | - | - | - | 11-15 | 0-7 | - | - | 16-10 | 2-1 | - | 27-32 |
| Doug Jones | - | - | - | - | - | - | - | - | - | - | - | 42-17 | - |
| Jeff Kaiser | - | - | - | - | - | - | - | - | - | - | - | 0-6 | - |
| Pat Keedy | - | - | - | 0-1 | - | 2-0 | - | - | - | 1-0 | - | - | 3 1 |
| Brad Komminsk | - | - | - | - | - | - | 28-25 | 0-2 | - | - | - | - | 28-27 |
| Tom Magrann | 1-1 | - | - | - | - | - | - | - | - | - | - | - | 1-1 |
| Oddibe McDowell | - | - | - | - | - | 27-33 | 0-1 | - | - | - | 20-19 | - | 27-34 |
| Luis Medina | - | - | - | - | - | 0-1 | - | 0-1 | - | 13-8 | - | - | 13-10 |
| Rod Nichols | - | - | - | - | - | - | - | - | 6-5 | - | - | 0-4 | 6-5 |
| Pete O'Brien | - | 66-82 | - | - | - | - | - | - | - | - | - | - | 66-82 |
| Steven Olin | - | - | - | - | - | - | - | - | - | - | - | 5-20 | - |
| Jesse Orosco | - | - | - | - | - | - | - | - | - | - | - | 24-45 | - |
| Mark Salas | - | - | - | - | - | - | - | - | - | 10-9 | - | - | 10-9 |
| Rudy Seanez | - | - | - | - | - | - | - | - | - | - | - | 0-5 | - |
| Danny Sheaffer | - | - | - | - | - | 1-0 | - | - | - | 0-3 | - | - | 1-3 |
| Joe Skalski | - | - | - | - | - | - | - | - | 0-1 | - | - | 0-1 | 0-1 |
| Joel Skinner | 23-34 | - | - | - | - | - | - | - | - | - | - | - | 23-34 |
| Cory Snyder | - | - | - | - | 1-1 | - | - | 52-68 | - | - | - | - | 53-69 |
| Tim Stoddard | - | - | - | - | - | - | - | - | - | - | - | 2-12 | - |
| Greg Swindell | - | - | - | - | - | - | - | - | 16-12 | - | - | - | 16-12 |
| Kevin Wickander | - | - | - | - | - | - | - | - | - | - | - | 0-2 | - |
| Ed Wojna | - | - | - | - | - | - | - | - | 0-3 | - | - | 0-6 | 0-3 |
| Rich Yett | - | - | - | - | - | - | - | - | 5-7 | - | - | 2-18 | 5-7 |
| Mike Young | - | - | - | - | - | - | - | - | - | 1-8 | - | - | 1-8 |
| Paul Zuvella | - | - | - | 3-2 | 3-2 | - | - | - | - | 1-1 | - | - | 7-5 |

## Batting vs. Left and Right Handed Pitchers

| | | BA | Rank | SA | Rank | OBA | Rank | HR % | Rank | BB % | Rank | SO % | Rank |
|---|---|---|---|---|---|---|---|---|---|---|---|---|---|
| Andy Allanson | vs. Lefties | .287 | 52 | .351 | 115 | .340 | 73 | 0.00 | 134 | 6.80 | 98 | 9.71 | 53 |
| | vs. Righties | .210 | 155 | .271 | 160 | .268 | 154 | 1.31 | 117 | 6.25 | 125 | 14.45 | 90 |
| Joey Belle | vs. Lefties | .259 | 99 | .448 | 41 | .308 | 111 | 5.17 | 13 | 7.69 | 81 | 20.00 | 138 |
| | vs. Righties | .213 | 154 | .375 | 88 | .254 | 163 | 2.50 | 61 | 4.14 | 159 | 24.85 | 161 |
| Jerry Browne | vs. Lefties | .309 | 30 | .417 | 59 | .349 | 55 | 1.14 | 113 | 6.22 | 107 | 6.74 | 22 |
| | vs. Righties | .296 | 25 | .378 | 85 | .378 | 19 | 0.71 | 138 | 11.38 | 28 | 10.37 | 48 |
| Joe Carter | vs. Lefties | .215 | 150 | .387 | 89 | .267 | 147 | 4.30 | 24 | 6.90 | 96 | 16.26 | 115 |
| | vs. Righties | .254 | 96 | .497 | 13 | .301 | 114 | 5.81 | 8 | 4.98 | 150 | 15.74 | 102 |
| Dave Clark | vs. Lefties | .111 | -- | .111 | -- | .111 | -- | 0.00 | -- | 0.00 | -- | 77.78 | -- |
| | vs. Righties | .242 | 117 | .389 | 71 | .324 | 84 | 3.28 | 42 | 10.87 | 39 | 20.29 | 139 |
| Felix Fermin | vs. Lefties | .246 | 121 | .277 | 157 | .333 | 80 | 0.00 | 134 | 11.04 | 33 | 2.60 | 4 |
| | vs. Righties | .234 | 127 | .254 | 164 | .290 | 135 | 0.00 | 158 | 5.88 | 132 | 5.64 | 8 |
| Brook Jacoby | vs. Lefties | .296 | 41 | .493 | 21 | .363 | 41 | 3.95 | 32 | 9.94 | 47 | 12.87 | 85 |
| | vs. Righties | .262 | 81 | .384 | 78 | .342 | 57 | 1.91 | 83 | 10.69 | 43 | 16.15 | 105 |
| Dion James | vs. Lefties | .259 | -- | .370 | -- | .333 | -- | 0.00 | -- | 9.68 | -- | 9.68 | -- |
| | vs. Righties | .312 | 13 | .404 | 58 | .372 | 23 | 1.83 | 85 | 8.75 | 67 | 9.58 | 39 |
| Brad Komminsk | vs. Lefties | .169 | 169 | .292 | 153 | .233 | 164 | 1.54 | 93 | 6.85 | 97 | 36.99 | 173 |
| | vs. Righties | .271 | 65 | .481 | 22 | .359 | 36 | 5.26 | 13 | 12.34 | 18 | 18.18 | 128 |
| Oddibe McDowell | vs. Lefties | .214 | 151 | .229 | 168 | .304 | 119 | 0.00 | 134 | 10.13 | 43 | 16.46 | 118 |
| | vs. Righties | .225 | 142 | .325 | 129 | .293 | 128 | 1.78 | 87 | 8.90 | 64 | 12.04 | 70 |
| Luis Medina | vs. Lefties | .214 | 151 | .386 | 91 | .276 | 142 | 5.71 | 10 | 7.89 | 76 | 35.53 | 171 |
| | vs. Righties | .154 | -- | .231 | -- | .154 | -- | 0.00 | -- | 0.00 | -- | 61.54 | -- |
| Pete O'Brien | vs. Lefties | .293 | 46 | .425 | 54 | .362 | 42 | 2.40 | 68 | 9.52 | 52 | 9.52 | 50 |
| | vs. Righties | .245 | 111 | .349 | 109 | .353 | 42 | 2.07 | 80 | 14.22 | 10 | 6.56 | 12 |
| Joel Skinner | vs. Lefties | .236 | 129 | .345 | 124 | .263 | 152 | 0.00 | 134 | 3.51 | 156 | 14.04 | 101 |
| | vs. Righties | .228 | 136 | .285 | 155 | .275 | 146 | 0.81 | 133 | 5.30 | 143 | 25.76 | 164 |
| Cory Snyder | vs. Lefties | .250 | 112 | .463 | 36 | .309 | 109 | 6.10 | 7 | 7.73 | 79 | 21.55 | 148 |
| | vs. Righties | .197 | 162 | .308 | 138 | .220 | 170 | 2.46 | 64 | 2.67 | 168 | 28.19 | 168 |
| Team Average | vs. Lefties | .247 | 12 | .370 | 12 | .307 | 13 | 2.39 | 5 | 7.92 | 8 | 15.17 | 11 |
| | vs. Righties | .245 | 13 | .363 | 13 | .312 | 13 | 2.30 | 7 | 8.26 | 9 | 15.33 | 9 |
| League Average | vs. Lefties | .266 | | .391 | | .328 | | 2.18 | | 8.18 | | 13.58 | |
| | vs. Righties | .258 | | .380 | | .325 | | 2.26 | | 8.56 | | 14.57 | |

## Batting with Runners on Base and Bases Empty

| | | BA | Rank | SA | Rank | OBA | Rank | HR % | Rank | BB % | Rank | SO % | Rank |
|---|---|---|---|---|---|---|---|---|---|---|---|---|---|
| Andy Allanson | Runners On | .204 | 164 | .241 | 167 | .282 | 153 | 0.73 | 135 | 7.41 | 105 | 15.43 | 116 |
| | Bases Empty | .253 | 92 | .333 | 121 | .294 | 120 | 1.08 | 119 | 5.58 | 135 | 11.17 | 53 |
| Joey Belle | Runners On | .268 | 87 | .485 | 21 | .291 | 140 | 4.12 | 27 | 2.91 | 166 | 24.27 | 162 |
| | Bases Empty | .190 | 165 | .322 | 132 | .252 | 167 | 2.48 | 74 | 6.87 | 100 | 22.90 | 158 |
| Jerry Browne | Runners On | .293 | 46 | .359 | 111 | .382 | 30 | 0.51 | 142 | 12.15 | 32 | 8.10 | 33 |
| | Bases Empty | .303 | 19 | .405 | 63 | .363 | 21 | 1.00 | 121 | 8.68 | 58 | 10.05 | 38 |
| Joe Carter | Runners On | .252 | 115 | .450 | 40 | .315 | 117 | 4.66 | 21 | 6.65 | 118 | 16.07 | 122 |
| | Bases Empty | .234 | 127 | .480 | 12 | .267 | 157 | 6.08 | 7 | 4.36 | 154 | 15.70 | 100 |
| Dave Clark | Runners On | .248 | 120 | .356 | 114 | .353 | 60 | 1.98 | 79 | 14.17 | 18 | 23.33 | 159 |
| | Bases Empty | .230 | 131 | .395 | 72 | .291 | 125 | 3.95 | 32 | 7.88 | 78 | 21.21 | 147 |
| Felix Fermin | Runners On | .197 | 169 | .213 | 172 | .278 | 158 | 0.00 | 146 | 8.02 | 95 | 5.06 | 10 |
| | Bases Empty | .262 | 73 | .289 | 156 | .317 | 84 | 0.00 | 153 | 6.77 | 103 | 4.62 | 5 |
| Brook Jacoby | Runners On | .291 | 49 | .444 | 43 | .366 | 46 | 3.14 | 42 | 11.07 | 39 | 16.03 | 120 |
| | Bases Empty | .257 | 81 | .395 | 71 | .333 | 53 | 2.03 | 85 | 10.00 | 33 | 14.55 | 91 |
| Dion James | Runners On | .333 | 9 | .459 | 33 | .388 | 22 | 2.70 | 53 | 8.13 | 92 | 9.76 | 57 |
| | Bases Empty | .284 | 39 | .351 | 105 | .351 | 36 | 0.75 | 134 | 9.46 | 38 | 9.46 | 32 |
| Brad Komminsk | Runners On | .232 | 146 | .453 | 37 | .290 | 144 | 6.32 | 6 | 8.33 | 88 | 21.30 | 148 |
| | Bases Empty | .243 | 110 | .388 | 77 | .345 | 46 | 1.94 | 90 | 12.61 | 13 | 26.89 | 166 |
| Oddibe McDowell | Runners On | .194 | 170 | .327 | 142 | .264 | 163 | 3.06 | 46 | 7.96 | 96 | 12.39 | 87 |
| | Bases Empty | .241 | 116 | .277 | 161 | .318 | 81 | 0.00 | 153 | 10.19 | 31 | 14.01 | 86 |
| Pete O'Brien | Runners On | .253 | 112 | .348 | 123 | .384 | 26 | 1.81 | 91 | 17.99 | 5 | 6.83 | 21 |
| | Bases Empty | .264 | 67 | .387 | 79 | .334 | 52 | 2.40 | 77 | 8.97 | 47 | 7.88 | 18 |
| Joel Skinner | Runners On | .203 | -- | .243 | -- | .224 | -- | 0.00 | -- | 2.60 | -- | 23.38 | -- |
| | Bases Empty | .250 | 98 | .346 | 110 | .304 | 105 | 0.96 | 125 | 6.25 | 116 | 21.43 | 149 |
| Cory Snyder | Runners On | .227 | 153 | .361 | 106 | .260 | 164 | 3.70 | 31 | 4.76 | 151 | 24.68 | 163 |
| | Bases Empty | .205 | 157 | .359 | 100 | .244 | 168 | 3.66 | 40 | 4.18 | 155 | 26.83 | 165 |
| Team Average | Runners On | .244 | 14 | .362 | 13 | .317 | 14 | 2.49 | 2 | 9.18 | 6 | 15.29 | 12 |
| | Bases Empty | .246 | 11 | .367 | 12 | .305 | 12 | 2.21 | 10 | 7.38 | 10 | 15.28 | 9 |
| League Average | Runners On | .268 | | .389 | | .336 | | 2.15 | | 9.17 | | 13.53 | |
| | Bases Empty | .255 | | .380 | | .317 | | 2.29 | | 7.84 | | 14.86 | |

## Overall Batting Compared to Late Inning Pressure Situations

| | | BA | Rank | SA | Rank | OBA | Rank | HR % | Rank | BB % | Rank | SO % | Rank | RDI % | Rank |
|---|---|---|---|---|---|---|---|---|---|---|---|---|---|---|---|
| Luis Aguayo | Overall | .175 | -- | .268 | -- | .239 | -- | 1.03 | -- | 6.25 | -- | 16.96 | -- | .148 | -- |
| | Pressure | .067 | -- | .133 | -- | .300 | -- | 0.00 | -- | 14.29 | -- | 23.81 | -- | .143 | 137 |
| Andy Allanson | Overall | .232 | 148 | .294 | 164 | .289 | 149 | 0.93 | 133 | 6.41 | 120 | 13.09 | 78 | .124 | 171 |
| | Pressure | .341 | 15 | .512 | 14 | .357 | 47 | 4.88 | 22 | 2.38 | 161 | 14.29 | 63 | .000 | 165 |
| Joey Belle | Overall | .225 | 156 | .394 | 74 | .269 | 165 | 3.21 | 45 | 5.13 | 150 | 23.50 | 158 | .329 | 24 |
| | Pressure | .242 | 96 | .394 | 63 | .306 | 100 | 3.03 | 55 | 8.33 | 86 | 22.22 | 133 | .889 | 1 |
| Jerry Browne | Overall | .299 | 23 | .390 | 76 | .370 | 18 | 0.84 | 138 | 9.93 | 44 | 9.34 | 38 | .262 | 88 |
| | Pressure | .308 | 34 | .363 | 85 | .394 | 22 | 1.10 | 105 | 12.15 | 40 | 13.08 | 51 | .150 | 135 |
| Joe Carter | Overall | .243 | 127 | .465 | 15 | .292 | 145 | 5.38 | 11 | 5.53 | 143 | 15.89 | 103 | .260 | 93 |
| | Pressure | .149 | 161 | .255 | 145 | .223 | 153 | 3.19 | 51 | 7.77 | 102 | 21.36 | 126 | .114 | 150 |
| Dave Clark | Overall | .237 | 138 | .379 | 90 | .317 | 98 | 3.16 | 48 | 10.53 | 34 | 22.11 | 151 | .230 | 132 |
| | Pressure | .250 | 89 | .393 | 66 | .344 | 57 | 3.57 | 44 | 12.31 | 36 | 18.46 | 106 | .250 | 87 |
| Felix Fermin | Overall | .238 | 135 | .260 | 169 | .302 | 125 | 0.00 | 166 | 7.30 | 100 | 4.80 | 5 | .159 | 165 |
| | Pressure | .273 | 62 | .291 | 129 | .365 | 42 | 0.00 | 107 | 9.33 | 71 | 2.67 | 2 | .200 | 115 |
| Brook Jacoby | Overall | .272 | 59 | .416 | 54 | .348 | 44 | 2.50 | 67 | 10.47 | 35 | 15.20 | 101 | .278 | 69 |
| | Pressure | .229 | 107 | .337 | 102 | .340 | 64 | 2.41 | 68 | 15.00 | 15 | 17.00 | 94 | .296 | 66 |
| Dion James | Overall | .306 | 12 | .400 | 68 | .368 | 22 | 1.63 | 100 | 8.86 | 63 | 9.59 | 42 | .288 | 57 |
| | Pressure | .300 | 38 | .375 | 78 | .404 | 18 | 0.00 | 107 | 14.58 | 18 | 12.50 | 49 | .200 | -- |
| Brad Komminsk | Overall | .237 | 136 | .419 | 51 | .319 | 95 | 4.04 | 24 | 10.57 | 33 | 24.23 | 162 | .280 | 66 |
| | Pressure | .125 | 166 | .375 | 78 | .211 | 159 | 6.25 | 11 | 10.53 | 54 | 39.47 | 170 | .333 | -- |
| Oddibe McDowell | Overall | .222 | 157 | .297 | 160 | .296 | 138 | 1.26 | 121 | 9.26 | 52 | 13.33 | 79 | .221 | 143 |
| | Pressure | .148 | 162 | .259 | 141 | .207 | 162 | 3.70 | 41 | 6.45 | 121 | 12.90 | 50 | .077 | 158 |
| Pete O'Brien | Overall | .260 | 85 | .372 | 94 | .356 | 34 | 2.17 | 80 | 12.85 | 16 | 7.43 | 16 | .253 | 104 |
| | Pressure | .193 | 139 | .265 | 140 | .316 | 92 | 0.00 | 107 | 14.00 | 23 | 11.00 | 39 | .214 | 110 |
| Joel Skinner | Overall | .230 | -- | .303 | -- | .271 | -- | 0.56 | -- | 4.76 | -- | 22.22 | -- | .208 | -- |
| | Pressure | .190 | -- | .238 | -- | .227 | -- | 0.00 | -- | 4.35 | -- | 26.09 | -- | .125 | 143 |
| Cory Snyder | Overall | .215 | 161 | .360 | 110 | .251 | 171 | 3.68 | 30 | 4.44 | 161 | 25.87 | 166 | .231 | 130 |
| | Pressure | .151 | 160 | .172 | 167 | .168 | 170 | 0.00 | 107 | 2.11 | 165 | 26.32 | 149 | .143 | 137 |
| Mike Young | Overall | .186 | -- | .237 | -- | .273 | -- | 1.69 | | 9.09 | -- | 19.70 | -- | .250 | -- |
| | Pressure | .185 | 146 | .185 | 162 | .267 | 134 | 0.00 | 107 | 6.67 | 119 | 30.00 | 157 | .222 | 105 |
| Team Average | Overall | .245 | 13 | .365 | 13 | .310 | 14 | 2.32 | 7 | 8.17 | 9 | 15.28 | 11 | .234 | 14 |
| | Pressure | .214 | 14 | .305 | 13 | .298 | 14 | 1.88 | 9 | 9.97 | 4 | 18.92 | 11 | .200 | 14 |
| League Average | Overall | .261 | | .384 | | .326 | | 2.23 | | 8.44 | | 14.26 | | .269 | |
| | Pressure | .247 | | .357 | | .318 | | 2.02 | | 9.02 | | 17.90 | | .254 | |

## Additional Miscellaneous Batting Comparisons

| | Grass Surface BA | Rank | Artificial Surface BA | Rank | Home Games BA | Rank | Road Games BA | Rank | Runners in Scoring Position BA | Rank | Runners in Scoring Pos and Two Outs BA | Rank | Leading Off Inning OBA | Rank | Runners on 3B with less than 2 Outs RDI % | Rank |
|---|---|---|---|---|---|---|---|---|---|---|---|---|---|---|---|---|
| Andy Allanson | .219 | 155 | .302 | 32 | .208 | 157 | .253 | 93 | .163 | 169 | .130 | 160 | .320 | 89 | .462 | 138 |
| Joey Belle | .213 | 160 | .275 | 57 | .243 | 113 | .204 | 165 | .339 | 10 | .296 | 27 | .327 | 77 | .533 | 107 |
| Jerry Browne | .311 | 10 | .240 | 109 | .332 | 8 | .262 | 80 | .278 | 68 | .109 | 164 | .383 | 21 | .731 | 20 |
| Joe Carter | .243 | 112 | .240 | 109 | .243 | 115 | .242 | 119 | .272 | 75 | .227 | 93 | .302 | 112 | .468 | 136 |
| Dave Clark | .236 | 127 | .250 | -- | .236 | 126 | .238 | 127 | .190 | 160 | .100 | 166 | .241 | 159 | .429 | 148 |
| Felix Fermin | .229 | 141 | .282 | 50 | .226 | 140 | .249 | 105 | .183 | 165 | .111 | 163 | .380 | 23 | .478 | 131 |
| Brook Jacoby | .283 | 41 | .205 | 140 | .266 | 71 | .277 | 53 | .220 | 144 | .250 | 68 | .340 | 56 | .621 | 56 |
| Dion James | .286 | 36 | .377 | 2 | .210 | 154 | .397 | 2 | .262 | 89 | .250 | -- | .313 | 97 | .588 | 74 |
| Brad Komminsk | .230 | 139 | .273 | -- | .270 | 67 | .193 | -- | .262 | 89 | .214 | 110 | .395 | -- | .538 | 104 |
| Oddibe McDowell | .213 | 162 | .281 | -- | .250 | 99 | .203 | 166 | .182 | 166 | .045 | 173 | .307 | 104 | .750 | 13 |
| Pete O'Brien | .263 | 77 | .244 | 105 | .287 | 42 | .235 | 132 | .230 | 133 | .192 | 129 | .387 | 17 | .536 | 106 |
| Joel Skinner | .225 | 147 | .259 | -- | .223 | 143 | .238 | -- | .163 | -- | .200 | -- | .327 | 76 | .167 | -- |
| Cory Snyder | .225 | 148 | .138 | 168 | .207 | 159 | .222 | 150 | .227 | 136 | .189 | 131 | .231 | 165 | .375 | 156 |
| Team Average | .245 | 13 | .245 | 13 | .249 | 13 | .242 | 14 | .227 | 14 | .175 | 14 | .324 | 5 | .510 | 13 |
| League Average | .260 | | .262 | | .262 | | .259 | | .262 | | .232 | | .321 | | .566 | |

## Pitching vs. Left and Right Handed Batters

| | | BA | Rank | SA | Rank | OBA | Rank | HR % | Rank | BB % | Rank | SO % | Rank |
|---|---|---|---|---|---|---|---|---|---|---|---|---|---|
| Scott Bailes | vs. Lefties | .232 | 37 | .280 | 17 | .271 | 16 | 0.80 | 18 | 3.73 | 7 | 10.45 | 85 |
| | vs. Righties | .284 | 114 | .425 | 107 | .334 | 93 | 1.96 | 64 | 7.08 | 55 | 9.73 | 121 |
| Bud Black | vs. Lefties | .158 | 4 | .233 | 8 | .215 | 2 | 1.67 | 61 | 6.87 | 39 | 7.63 | 115 |
| | vs. Righties | .268 | 89 | .384 | 77 | .308 | 45 | 1.66 | 43 | 5.51 | 25 | 9.99 | 116 |
| Tom Candiotti | vs. Lefties | .246 | 45 | .327 | 36 | .306 | 46 | 1.27 | 39 | 7.80 | 54 | 13.30 | 56 |
| | vs. Righties | .238 | 32 | .311 | 16 | .280 | 18 | 1.31 | 26 | 5.11 | 18 | 16.06 | 53 |
| John Farrell | vs. Lefties | .233 | 38 | .333 | 39 | .304 | 44 | 1.43 | 50 | 8.65 | 64 | 12.45 | 63 |
| | vs. Righties | .256 | 66 | .350 | 46 | .315 | 58 | 2.09 | 71 | 7.13 | 57 | 17.34 | 44 |
| Doug Jones | vs. Lefties | .244 | 44 | .369 | 58 | .281 | 21 | 2.50 | 85 | 5.20 | 18 | 15.61 | 39 |
| | vs. Righties | .259 | 73 | .301 | 11 | .276 | 14 | 0.00 | 1 | 2.53 | 1 | 24.05 | 16 |
| Rod Nichols | vs. Lefties | .323 | 123 | .488 | 121 | .386 | 116 | 3.94 | 119 | 8.39 | 61 | 13.99 | 52 |
| | vs. Righties | .255 | 64 | .382 | 75 | .308 | 44 | 2.55 | 89 | 6.98 | 53 | 12.79 | 88 |
| Jesse Orosco | vs. Lefties | .138 | 2 | .184 | 2 | .211 | 1 | 0.00 | 1 | 8.16 | 58 | 30.61 | 2 |
| | vs. Righties | .226 | 23 | .403 | 93 | .297 | 35 | 3.76 | 123 | 8.41 | 83 | 22.90 | 19 |
| Greg Swindell | vs. Lefties | .220 | 25 | .284 | 21 | .265 | 14 | 0.92 | 23 | 5.93 | 25 | 12.71 | 62 |
| | vs. Righties | .251 | 55 | .384 | 76 | .303 | 41 | 2.58 | 91 | 6.97 | 52 | 18.07 | 39 |
| Rich Yett | vs. Lefties | .299 | 108 | .467 | 112 | .381 | 112 | 3.55 | 111 | 11.66 | 108 | 9.42 | 98 |
| | vs. Righties | .267 | 86 | .395 | 83 | .339 | 105 | 1.54 | 40 | 9.42 | 101 | 11.66 | 100 |
| Team Average | vs. Lefties | .247 | 3 | .354 | 4 | .311 | 4 | 1.95 | 4 | 8.27 | 4 | 12.41 | 10 |
| | vs. Righties | .262 | 8 | .380 | 8 | .314 | 3 | 1.92 | 3 | 6.86 | 2 | 14.55 | 7 |
| League Average | vs. Lefties | .261 | | .382 | | .330 | | 2.16 | | 9.16 | | 13.03 | |
| | vs. Righties | .261 | | .385 | | .323 | | 2.28 | | 7.96 | | 15.09 | |

## Pitching with Runners on Base and Bases Empty

| | | BA | Rank | SA | Rank | OBA | Rank | HR % | Rank | BB % | Rank | SO % | Rank |
|---|---|---|---|---|---|---|---|---|---|---|---|---|---|
| Scott Bailes | Runners On | .270 | 81 | .403 | 93 | .324 | 56 | 1.53 | 48 | 7.59 | 43 | 10.27 | 96 |
| | Bases Empty | .268 | 85 | .366 | 60 | .309 | 51 | 1.70 | 44 | 4.82 | 21 | 9.64 | 112 |
| Bud Black | Runners On | .253 | 50 | .351 | 42 | .305 | 28 | 1.58 | 54 | 7.28 | 38 | 11.48 | 84 |
| | Bases Empty | .252 | 60 | .369 | 61 | .288 | 30 | 1.70 | 45 | 4.68 | 16 | 8.47 | 123 |
| Tom Candiotti | Runners On | .259 | 59 | .351 | 41 | .330 | 65 | 1.42 | 41 | 9.26 | 71 | 10.80 | 89 |
| | Bases Empty | .232 | 37 | .300 | 17 | .272 | 16 | 1.21 | 19 | 4.78 | 20 | 17.02 | 44 |
| John Farrell | Runners On | .278 | 91 | .358 | 54 | .342 | 83 | 1.22 | 29 | 8.51 | 59 | 15.43 | 49 |
| | Bases Empty | .221 | 22 | .330 | 32 | .285 | 28 | 2.10 | 64 | 7.51 | 69 | 14.26 | 62 |
| Doug Jones | Runners On | .226 | 22 | .314 | 17 | .250 | 4 | 1.89 | 70 | 3.33 | 1 | 15.56 | 47 |
| | Bases Empty | .278 | 106 | .361 | 51 | .311 | 55 | 0.69 | 9 | 4.64 | 15 | 24.50 | 12 |
| Rod Nichols | Runners On | .280 | 93 | .449 | 120 | .346 | 88 | 3.39 | 120 | 9.56 | 74 | 13.97 | 59 |
| | Bases Empty | .289 | 116 | .416 | 99 | .341 | 99 | 3.01 | 98 | 6.15 | 44 | 12.85 | 81 |
| Jesse Orosco | Runners On | .156 | 1 | .246 | 3 | .215 | 1 | 0.82 | 15 | 6.99 | 34 | 25.87 | 7 |
| | Bases Empty | .232 | 36 | .404 | 86 | .314 | 61 | 3.97 | 128 | 9.47 | 99 | 24.85 | 10 |
| Greg Swindell | Runners On | .247 | 39 | .347 | 36 | .306 | 29 | 1.59 | 55 | 8.16 | 52 | 16.31 | 40 |
| | Bases Empty | .246 | 54 | .380 | 72 | .291 | 35 | 2.73 | 88 | 6.00 | 42 | 17.77 | 40 |
| Rich Yett | Runners On | .277 | 88 | .397 | 87 | .358 | 103 | 1.09 | 21 | 11.21 | 103 | 12.15 | 74 |
| | Bases Empty | .288 | 115 | .462 | 119 | .362 | 123 | 3.85 | 126 | 9.91 | 107 | 9.05 | 119 |
| Team Average | Runners On | .263 | 4 | .373 | 5 | .323 | 4 | 1.63 | 2 | 8.33 | 4 | 13.42 | 7 |
| | Bases Empty | .252 | 6 | .369 | 7 | .305 | 4 | 2.15 | 6 | 6.63 | 1 | 14.05 | 8 |
| League Average | Runners On | .268 | | .389 | | .336 | | 2.15 | | 9.17 | | 13.53 | |
| | Bases Empty | .255 | | .380 | | .317 | | 2.29 | | 7.84 | | 14.86 | |

## Overall Pitching Compared to Late Inning Pressure Situations

| | | BA | Rank | SA | Rank | OBA | Rank | HR % | Rank | BB % | Rank | SO % | Rank |
|---|---|---|---|---|---|---|---|---|---|---|---|---|---|
| Keith Atherton | Overall | .293 | -- | .524 | -- | .345 | -- | 4.27 | -- | 7.30 | -- | 7.30 | -- |
| | Pressure | .289 | 100 | .533 | 122 | .373 | 105 | 4.44 | 122 | 11.76 | 97 | 11.76 | 87 |
| Scott Bailes | Overall | .269 | 83 | .383 | 73 | .316 | 53 | 1.62 | 41 | 6.13 | 25 | 9.94 | 108 |
| | Pressure | .257 | 81 | .343 | 65 | .297 | 45 | 1.43 | 52 | 5.33 | 20 | 9.33 | 110 |
| Bud Black | Overall | .252 | 54 | .363 | 51 | .295 | 25 | 1.66 | 44 | 5.70 | 17 | 9.65 | 114 |
| | Pressure | .269 | 87 | .407 | 98 | .302 | 53 | 1.85 | 71 | 5.00 | 17 | 11.67 | 91 |
| Tom Candiotti | Overall | .242 | 35 | .319 | 20 | .294 | 23 | 1.29 | 19 | 6.49 | 35 | 14.64 | 58 |
| | Pressure | .262 | 82 | .298 | 40 | .337 | 76 | 0.00 | 1 | 10.42 | 77 | 5.21 | 126 |
| John Farrell | Overall | .244 | 38 | .341 | 35 | .309 | 40 | 1.74 | 49 | 7.93 | 64 | 14.75 | 57 |
| | Pressure | .257 | 78 | .405 | 96 | .329 | 72 | 4.05 | 118 | 9.64 | 73 | 14.46 | 67 |
| Doug Jones | Overall | .251 | 52 | .337 | 28 | .279 | 12 | 1.32 | 20 | 3.93 | 2 | 19.64 | 23 |
| | Pressure | .264 | 85 | .366 | 78 | .291 | 36 | 1.63 | 57 | 3.72 | 11 | 18.96 | 37 |
| Rod Nichols | Overall | .285 | 110 | .430 | 104 | .343 | 99 | 3.17 | 114 | 7.62 | 59 | 13.33 | 68 |
| | Pressure | .241 | -- | .448 | -- | .290 | -- | 6.90 | -- | 6.45 | -- | 16.13 | -- |
| Steven Olin | Overall | .255 | -- | .336 | -- | .325 | -- | 0.73 | -- | 9.21 | -- | 15.79 | -- |
| | Pressure | .273 | 91 | .327 | 53 | .355 | 95 | 0.00 | 1 | 11.11 | 87 | 15.87 | 57 |
| Jesse Orosco | Overall | .198 | 6 | .333 | 23 | .270 | 8 | 2.56 | 92 | 8.33 | 70 | 25.32 | 6 |
| | Pressure | .207 | 33 | .337 | 60 | .260 | 17 | 2.72 | 93 | 5.77 | 28 | 26.92 | 10 |
| Greg Swindell | Overall | .246 | 43 | .368 | 57 | .297 | 27 | 2.32 | 79 | 6.81 | 39 | 17.22 | 36 |
| | Pressure | .216 | 43 | .257 | 21 | .256 | 14 | 0.00 | 1 | 5.06 | 19 | 20.25 | 31 |
| Rich Yett | Overall | .283 | 109 | .431 | 107 | .360 | 124 | 2.55 | 90 | 10.54 | 111 | 10.54 | 101 |
| | Pressure | .276 | -- | .414 | -- | .323 | -- | 3.45 | -- | 6.25 | -- | 12.50 | -- |
| Team Average | Overall | .257 | 5 | .371 | 5 | .313 | 3 | 1.93 | 4 | 7.38 | 1 | 13.77 | 8 |
| | Pressure | .254 | 7 | .373 | 9 | .306 | 3 | 2.19 | 8 | 6.84 | 1 | 16.68 | 7 |
| League Average | Overall | .261 | | .384 | | .326 | | 2.23 | | 8.44 | | 14.26 | |
| | Pressure | .250 | | .362 | | .325 | | 2.14 | | 9.50 | | 16.61 | |

## Additional Miscellaneous Pitching Comparisons

| | Grass Surface | | Artificial Surface | | Home Games | | Road Games | | Runners in Scoring Position | | Runners in Scoring Pos and Two Outs | | Leading Off Inning | |
|---|---|---|---|---|---|---|---|---|---|---|---|---|---|---|
| | BA | Rank | BA | Rank | BA | Rank | BA | Rank | BA | Rank | BA | Rank | OBA | Rank |
| Keith Atherton | .298 | -- | .261 | -- | .257 | -- | .319 | -- | .268 | -- | .333 | 128 | .182 | -- |
| Scott Bailes | .266 | 79 | .286 | 89 | .246 | 59 | .296 | 116 | .278 | 98 | .314 | 122 | .393 | 127 |
| Bud Black | .250 | 56 | .259 | 57 | .268 | 87 | .236 | 35 | .227 | 29 | .195 | 44 | .287 | 34 |
| Tom Candiotti | .246 | 47 | .212 | 16 | .255 | 71 | .228 | 32 | .250 | 62 | .241 | 80 | .238 | 8 |
| John Farrell | .252 | 57 | .220 | 22 | .236 | 37 | .253 | 55 | .247 | 60 | .176 | 34 | .301 | 44 |
| Doug Jones | .238 | 33 | .309 | 112 | .240 | 44 | .265 | 76 | .234 | 38 | .196 | 47 | .339 | 86 |
| Rod Nichols | .285 | 109 | .000 | -- | .241 | 49 | .351 | 133 | .340 | -- | .348 | -- | .359 | 107 |
| Jesse Orosco | .183 | 5 | .279 | 81 | .190 | 6 | .206 | 9 | .147 | 1 | .083 | 2 | .368 | 112 |
| Greg Swindell | .252 | 59 | .190 | 8 | .242 | 50 | .251 | 48 | .219 | 19 | .230 | 70 | .266 | 22 |
| Rich Yett | .282 | 106 | .289 | -- | .313 | 128 | .254 | 56 | .283 | 104 | .286 | 109 | .350 | 101 |
| Team Average | .258 | 6 | .248 | 2 | .256 | 6 | .257 | 6 | .255 | 5 | .238 | 11 | .302 | 3 |
| League Average | .260 | | .262 | | .259 | | .262 | | .262 | | .232 | | .321 | |

# DETROIT TIGERS

- **Anatomy of a collapse: Catastrophe Theory 101.**
- **Is there light at the end of the tunnel?**

A few years ago, we stumbled across a branch of mathematics called *catastrophe theory,* dealing with the structure and often hidden causes of chaos. The field was so enticingly named that we hoped eventually to find an application within baseball (probably in the vicinity of Casa Steinbrenner). One concept of catastrophe theory maintains that a system of operation, while appearing to flourish, can silently nurture the seeds of its own destruction. Those seeds mature in obscurity until they destroy the entire operation in a sudden and massive upheaval. That explanation just about exhausts our entire understanding of the theory, but provides an ideal overview of the problems that led to last season's collapse of the Detroit Tigers.

To gain some perspective on Detroit's breakdown, let's go back more than two decades to 1968, when the Tigers won the World Series with a veteran lineup and a young pitching staff. Denny McLain, who won 31 games, was only 24 years old. John Hiller was 25, rookie Pat Dobson and Joe Sparma were 26. Even Mickey Lolich was only 28. But the Detroit lineup was graying: Al Kaline and Norm Cash were 33, Don Wert had just turned 30, and Jim Northrup and Dick McAuliffe weren't far behind. Even more important to the team's future, there were few young prospects who appeared ready to take their places.

In fact, during the seven-year period from 1967 through 1973, only two rookies joined the Tigers who would eventually accumulate as many as 500 games in the majors: Elliott Maddox and Ron Woods. Not what you'd call building-block players. So it's not surprising that in 1973, most of the starters from the 1968 championship team provided the foundation for the oldest team of the 1970s. At the same time, the Detroit system was producing few useful pitchers. No rookie pitcher who joined the team from 1969 through 1973 would win even 40 games in his major league career. The Tigers fell to third place in '73 in their defense of a division title, and to last place a year later. And, of course, the team grew progressively older throughout that post-championship period. The following table shows the team's average age, and their rank within the league:

| | 1968 | 1969 | 1970 | 1971 | 1972 | 1973 | 1974 |
|---|---|---|---|---|---|---|---|
| Batters | 28.8 | 29.7 | 29.8 | 30.5 | 31.6 | 32.3 | 30.7 |
| Pitchers | 27.3 | 28.3 | 27.0 | 27.4 | 28.5 | 30.7 | 29.4 |
| Average | 28.0 | 29.0 | 28.4 | 29.0 | 30.0 | 31.5 | 30.0 |
| A.L. Rank | 8 | 11 | 9 | 11 | 12 | 12 | 12 |

That might seem like a deadly parlay—a collapsing team with few young players. And in most similar cases that's been true (as we will illustrate later). But by the mid–1970s, Detroit was bursting with minor league talent that would stock their major league roster for years thereafter. Over a seven-year period starting in 1974, the following players provided the Tigers with a remarkable stream of rookies: Ron LeFlore (1974); Dan Meyer (1975); Jason Thompson (1976); Steve Kemp (1977); Lance Parrish, Alan Trammell, and Lou Whitaker (1978); Tom Brookens (1979); and Kirk Gibson (1980). In case you didn't notice, those players could form a nine-man lineup, complete with DH. For bench strength, how about Leon Roberts, Tom Veryzer, and John Wockenfuss (1975); Tim Corcoran (1978); and Lynn Jones (1979).

What about pitching, you ask? We were just getting to that. Starting in 1975, Detroit promoted the following starters to the majors, one each season through 1979: Vern Ruhle, Mark Fidrych, Dave Rozema, Jack Morris, and Dan Petry. Rookie relievers didn't match that high standard, but even Ed Glynn (1977) and Dave Tobik and Pat Underwood (1979) could have provided ample support for so talented a rotation, especially if the Bird's wing had remained healthy.

(In order to fulfill our annual obligation to mention our editor's semi-successful baseball career: It was during this wave of player development that current editor-extraordinare and one-time second baseman-ordinaire Rick Wolff flashed across the baseball sky, only to be eclipsed by a guy named Whitaker. *Que sera sera.*)

By 1980, Detroit was clearly positioned as one of baseball's most promising teams for the emerging decade, winning 84 games with the second-youngest team in the American League. The Tigers went on to post the league's second-best record during the 1980s, winning with home-grown talent nearly as many games over those 10 seasons as did the Yankees, the best team money could buy. End of history lesson.

Now notice the uncanny similarity of Detroit's collapse in the 1970s to what transpired last year:

| Year | W–L | Pos. | Year | W–L | Pos. |
|---|---|---|---|---|---|
| 1968 | 103–59 | 1st | 1983 | 92–70 | 2d |
| 1969 | 90–72 | 2d | 1984 | 104–58 | 1st |
| 1970 | 79–83 | 3d | 1985 | 84–77 | 3d |
| 1971 | 91–71 | 2d | 1986 | 87–75 | 3d |
| 1972 | 86–70 | 1st | 1987 | 98–64 | 1st |
| 1973 | 85–77 | 3d | 1988 | 88–74 | 2d |
| 1974 | 72–90 | last | 1989 | 59–103 | last |

It wasn't only the year-by-year pattern of the more recent collapse that resembled the Great Fall of '74. The reasons for Detroit's breakdown in 1989 were strikingly similar to those of 15 years earlier, with its roster a shadow of a championship team from years earlier. The Tigers were already an aging team when they won the World Series in 1984, particularly their pitching staff. Milt Wilcox and Aurelio Lopez were nearing the end of the line when fitted for their World Series rings. Other pitchers, like Morris, Petry, and Willie Hernandez, had hit their peaks. With few first- and second-year players on the roster, and with some of their best young players having fallen into disfavor (Howard Johnson and Barbaro Garbey, for example) the Tigers aged steadily after winning that title, until they'd become the oldest team in the league:

| | 1983 | 1984 | 1985 | 1986 | 1987 | 1988 | 1989 |
|---|---|---|---|---|---|---|---|
| Batters | 28.1 | 28.8 | 29.9 | 30.8 | 31.6 | 32.6 | 31.5 |
| Pitchers | 28.7 | 30.3 | 29.5 | 29.3 | 30.1 | 31.7 | 31.7 |
| Average | 28.4 | 29.5 | 29.7 | 30.1 | 30.9 | 32.1 | 31.6 |
| A.L. Rank | 5 | 10 | 9 | 12 | 13 | 14 | 14 |

As was the case 15 years before, the failure of Detroit's player development system must be held responsible. Only one Tigers rookie during the four-year period from 1983 through 1986 has accumulated the modest total of 250 games in the majors. And even that player, Bob Melvin, started only 25 games in a Tigers uniform (although he was traded as part of a deal that brought Matt Nokes and Eric King to Detroit). Highly touted rookies of that era, like Garbey, Chris Pittaro, Alejandro Sanchez, and Nelson Simmons, lasted about as long as Mike Tyson's last few opponents.

On the pitching side, the developmental process soured earlier, breaking down a few years *before* Detroit wiped out the Royals and Padres in the 1984 postseason. No Tigers rookie pitcher from 1980 until the arrival of King in 1986 had as many as 20 wins in his entire major league career, with the exception of reliever Bob James, who *(a)* compiled a losing career record predominantly in relief (24–26); and *(b)* never won or saved a game for the Tigers. Names you'd remember from those seasons? Only a fanatic would recall even the best (an adjective we use reluctantly): Dave Rucker, Jerry Ujdur, Howard Bailey, Randy O'Neal—stop us if you know of their recent whereabouts. Let's face it, you'd need Robert Stack to track these guys down. (Actually, a new and improved Chuck Cary, Detroit class of '86, did surface last season with the Yankees.)

It's strange but true that even as the champagne flowed in the Tigers locker room in October 1984, the forces that would ultimately lead to collapse were already in motion, though imperceptible. Four more years of apparent prosperity only reinforced the illusion that the Tigers were a healthy organization. But as we said, this is a baseball example of catastrophe theory.

Unfortunately, Detroit's organization continues to flounder, providing little relief for the major league team. For that reason, it's hard to envision a rebound similar to that of 15 years ago, when Detroit's system burped All-Stars at the rate of one or two a year. Last season, six Detroit rookies combined for a .202 batting average in 668 at-bats. Opening-day starter Torey Lovullo and heralded Scott Lusader had only two home runs in 190 at-bats. The composite statistics of the six rookies were nearly identical to the career figures of Bert Adams:

| | AB | H | 2B | 3B | HR | RBI | BA |
|---|---|---|---|---|---|---|---|
| 1989 rookies | 668 | 135 | 19 | 5 | 5 | 47 | .202 |
| Bert Adams | 678 | 137 | 17 | 4 | 2 | 45 | .202 |

You've probably never heard of Adams. He was a seldom-used catcher around the time of the Great War, sort of the Bruce Bochy of your great-grandfather's day. If you've never heard of Bochy, well, that's the point. These Detroit freshmen weren't your typical rookie-of-the-year candidates.

Detroit's seven rookie pitchers combined for a 7–17 record with a 4.70 ERA, and none won more games than he lost. Only Brian Dubois (1.75 ERA in 36 innings) and Kevin Ritz (two home runs allowed in 74 innings) displayed anything approximating major league talent. On the heels of six seasons of austere support from the minor league level, that's bad news.

So much for a fundamental analysis of the situation. But are there any technical signs of life for this struggling team? Once again, the outlook is bleak, based primarily upon the age of the team. Teams that suffer declines similar to that of the 1989 Tigers often rebound more quickly than you might imagine. But the exceptions to that rule are older teams.

Consider the group of teams that, like last season's Tigers, met these two criteria: (1) they lost at least 20 more games than they did a year earlier, (2) crossing the .500–level in the process. We modified point 1 to include teams that fell by the percentage equivalent of 20 losses (.124). There were 50 such teams from 1900 through 1983, a cutoff point that allowed us to track a team's subsequent progress or lack of it.

Six of those 50 teams, like the 1989 Tigers, ranked among their leagues' two oldest teams (or among the three oldest in the era of 12– and 14–team leagues). Of course, six teams doesn't constitute a large enough sample from which to draw any definitive conclusions. But the margin by which those teams underperformed the 44 younger teams provides ample evidence that aging teams don't bounce back from a severe decline with the resiliency of younger clubs. The following table illustrates that rule, showing the average winning percentages in the year preceding the 20–loss increase (Year X–1), the year of the decline (Year X), and the subsequent five seasons:

| | X−1 | X | X+1 | X+2 | X+3 | X+4 | X+5 |
|---|---|---|---|---|---|---|---|
| 44 younger teams | .580 | .411 | .449 | .490 | .513 | .504 | .510 |
| 6 old teams | .572 | .420 | .459 | .452 | .469 | .463 | .486 |

Notice that both groups experienced a technical bounce in the season that immediately followed the steep decline. But while younger teams continued to improve, regaining the .500 mark by the third season after the fall, older teams floundered in subsequent seasons.

Over the past few years, the Tigers have acknowledged the recent failings of their player-development system by adding Joe McDonald as V.P. of Player Procurement and Development. He has overseen an increase not only in the number of scouts (including former major league general managers Joe Klein and Hal Keller) but in minor league teams as well. And according to *Baseball America*, the added emphasis will be paying dividends before too much longer. In particular, catcher Phil Clark, outfielder Milt Cuyler, and pitcher Scott Aldred are rated "legitimate prospects" who should arrive this season or next. But years of negligible productivity have limited Detroit's chances for a quick rebound, a reality underlined this past winter when the Tigers broke their long-standing reluctance to exploit the free-agent market. So at this stage, Detroit, one of the strongest clubs of the past decade, resembles an expansion team.

## WON-LOST RECORD BY STARTING POSITION

| DETROIT 59-103 | C | 1B | 2B | 3B | SS | LF | CF | RF | P | DH | Leadoff | Relief | Starts |
|---|---|---|---|---|---|---|---|---|---|---|---|---|---|
| Doyle Alexander | - | - | - | - | - | - | - | - | 11-22 | - | - | - | 11-22 |
| Bill Bean | - | 0-1 | - | - | - | 0-1 | - | 0-1 | - | - | - | - | 0-3 |
| Dave Beard | - | - | - | - | - | - | - | - | 0-1 | - | - | 0-1 | 0-1 |
| Dave Bergman | - | 37-69 | - | - | - | - | - | - | - | 1-2 | 1-2 | - | 38-71 |
| Randy Bockus | - | - | - | - | - | - | - | - | - | - | - | 0-2 | - |
| Chris Brown | - | - | - | 7-10 | - | - | - | - | - | - | - | - | 7-10 |
| Mike Brumley | - | - | 8-8 | 2-4 | 11-24 | - | - | - | - | 0-1 | - | - | 21-37 |
| Jeff Datz | 0-1 | - | - | - | - | - | - | - | - | 0-1 | - | - | 0-2 |
| Brian Dubois | - | - | - | - | - | - | - | - | 0-5 | - | - | 1-0 | 0-5 |
| Paul Gibson | - | - | - | - | - | - | - | - | 4-9 | - | - | 6-26 | 4-9 |
| Brad Havens | - | - | - | - | - | - | - | - | 0-1 | - | - | 2-10 | 0-1 |
| Mike Heath | 43-64 | - | - | - | - | - | - | - | - | 0-1 | - | - | 43-65 |
| Mike Henneman | - | - | - | - | - | - | - | - | - | - | - | 30-30 | - |
| Willie Hernandez | - | - | - | - | - | - | - | - | - | - | - | 21-11 | - |
| Shawn Holman | - | - | - | - | - | - | - | - | - | - | - | 1-4 | - |
| Charles Hudson | - | - | - | - | - | - | - | - | 2-5 | - | - | 0-11 | 2-5 |
| Tracy Jones | - | - | - | - | - | 10-21 | - | 1-1 | - | 2-3 | 0-2 | - | 13-25 |
| Chet Lemon | - | - | - | - | - | - | - | 39-65 | - | 3-6 | - | - | 42-71 |
| Torey Lovullo | - | 6-10 | - | 3-6 | - | - | - | - | - | - | - | - | 9-16 |
| Scott Lusader | - | - | - | - | - | - | 2-3 | 8-12 | - | - | 2-3 | - | 10-15 |
| Fred Lynn | - | - | - | - | - | 26-37 | - | - | - | 11-23 | - | - | 37-60 |
| Keith Moreland | - | 8-19 | - | 4-5 | - | - | - | - | - | 18-27 | - | - | 30-51 |
| Jack Morris | - | - | - | - | - | - | - | - | 7-17 | - | - | - | 7-17 |
| Matt Nokes | 15-30 | - | - | - | - | - | - | - | - | 9-18 | - | - | 24-48 |
| Randy Nosek | - | - | - | - | - | - | - | - | 0-2 | - | - | - | 0-2 |
| Edwin Nunez | - | - | - | - | - | - | - | - | - | - | - | 7-20 | - |
| David Palmer | - | - | - | - | - | - | - | - | 1-4 | - | - | - | 1-4 |
| Al Pedrique | - | - | 1-4 | 3-4 | 2-6 | - | - | - | - | - | - | - | 6-14 |
| Ramon Pena | - | - | - | - | - | - | - | - | - | - | - | 0-8 | - |
| Gary Pettis | - | - | - | - | - | - | 46-70 | - | - | - | 45-68 | - | 46-70 |
| Rob Richie | - | - | - | - | - | 3-7 | - | 2-0 | - | 1-0 | - | - | 6-7 |
| Kevin Ritz | - | - | - | - | - | - | - | - | 5-7 | - | - | - | 5-7 |
| Jeff M. Robinson | - | - | - | - | - | - | - | - | 9-7 | - | - | - | 9-7 |
| Rick Schu | - | - | - | 20-44 | - | - | - | - | - | 5-2 | - | - | 25-46 |
| Mike Schwabe | - | - | - | - | - | - | - | - | 1-3 | - | - | 2-7 | 1-3 |
| Steve Searcy | - | - | - | - | - | - | - | - | 2-0 | - | - | 0-6 | 2-0 |
| Pat Sheridan | - | - | - | - | - | 3-9 | 3-3 | 1-6 | - | 2-6 | 5-9 | - | 9-24 |
| Matt Sinatro | 1-8 | - | - | - | - | - | - | - | - | - | - | - | 1-8 |
| Doug Strange | - | - | 0-4 | 20-30 | 0-1 | - | - | - | - | 1-0 | - | - | 21-35 |
| Frank Tanana | - | - | - | - | - | - | - | - | 15-18 | - | - | - | 15-18 |
| Alan Trammell | - | - | - | - | 46-72 | - | - | - | - | 0-1 | - | - | 46-73 |
| Mike Trujillo | - | - | - | - | - | - | - | - | 2-2 | - | - | 0-4 | 2-2 |
| Gary Ward | - | 8-4 | - | - | - | 5-17 | 1-2 | 4-6 | - | 5-12 | - | - | 23-41 |
| Lou Whitaker | - | - | 50-87 | - | - | - | - | - | - | 1-0 | - | - | 51-87 |
| Frank Williams | - | - | - | - | - | - | - | - | - | - | - | 12-30 | - |
| Kenny Williams | - | - | - | - | - | 12-11 | 7-25 | 4-12 | - | - | 6-19 | - | 23-48 |

## Batting vs. Left and Right Handed Pitchers

| | | BA | Rank | SA | Rank | OBA | Rank | HR % | Rank | BB % | Rank | SO % | Rank |
|---|---|---|---|---|---|---|---|---|---|---|---|---|---|
| Dave Bergman | vs. Lefties | .200 | 161 | .233 | 166 | .250 | 158 | 0.00 | 134 | 4.41 | 144 | 20.59 | 142 |
| | vs. Righties | .280 | 45 | .385 | 77 | .361 | 32 | 2.15 | 75 | 11.14 | 37 | 8.15 | 25 |
| Mike Brumley | vs. Lefties | .235 | 132 | .309 | 147 | .268 | 146 | 1.47 | 96 | 4.17 | 148 | 13.89 | 98 |
| | vs. Righties | .181 | 168 | .229 | 168 | .244 | 165 | 0.00 | 158 | 6.96 | 109 | 22.15 | 148 |
| Mike Heath | vs. Lefties | .317 | 24 | .472 | 30 | .360 | 47 | 3.11 | 51 | 5.68 | 120 | 6.25 | 19 |
| | vs. Righties | .226 | 141 | .332 | 122 | .273 | 149 | 2.13 | 76 | 5.53 | 139 | 23.72 | 158 |
| Tracy Jones | vs. Lefties | .300 | 38 | .414 | 63 | .366 | 35 | 1.43 | 101 | 9.76 | 49 | 7.32 | 27 |
| | vs. Righties | .227 | -- | .352 | -- | .292 | -- | 2.27 | -- | 8.25 | -- | 10.31 | -- |
| Chet Lemon | vs. Lefties | .275 | 74 | .438 | 46 | .373 | 33 | 3.27 | 48 | 12.99 | 20 | 13.56 | 92 |
| | vs. Righties | .215 | 152 | .287 | 153 | .294 | 125 | 0.77 | 136 | 7.80 | 90 | 15.93 | 104 |
| Fred Lynn | vs. Lefties | .175 | 167 | .190 | 173 | .257 | 154 | 0.00 | 134 | 10.00 | 45 | 22.86 | 158 |
| | vs. Righties | .255 | 92 | .410 | 55 | .342 | 55 | 3.79 | 30 | 11.90 | 22 | 16.37 | 112 |
| Matt Nokes | vs. Lefties | .256 | -- | .442 | -- | .283 | -- | 4.65 | -- | 2.17 | -- | 28.26 | -- |
| | vs. Righties | .249 | 106 | .378 | 86 | .300 | 116 | 3.11 | 47 | 6.56 | 119 | 9.84 | 43 |
| Gary Pettis | vs. Lefties | .263 | 87 | .316 | 142 | .374 | 30 | 0.00 | 134 | 14.92 | 11 | 11.60 | 73 |
| | vs. Righties | .253 | 97 | .305 | 140 | .375 | 21 | 0.34 | 151 | 16.06 | 7 | 23.94 | 160 |
| Rick Schu | vs. Lefties | .261 | 94 | .430 | 49 | .300 | 123 | 3.52 | 38 | 5.33 | 131 | 10.00 | 58 |
| | vs. Righties | .161 | 170 | .226 | 169 | .255 | 160 | 1.61 | 99 | 11.19 | 35 | 15.38 | 99 |
| Pat Sheridan | vs. Lefties | .125 | -- | .125 | -- | .300 | -- | 0.00 | -- | 18.18 | -- | 27.27 | -- |
| | vs. Righties | .250 | 102 | .357 | 102 | .336 | 62 | 2.68 | 57 | 11.72 | 24 | 14.06 | 85 |
| Doug Strange | vs. Lefties | .190 | -- | .214 | -- | .227 | -- | 0.00 | -- | 4.55 | -- | 13.64 | -- |
| | vs. Righties | .221 | 146 | .273 | 158 | .294 | 124 | 0.65 | 142 | 8.62 | 70 | 17.24 | 120 |
| Alan Trammell | vs. Lefties | .286 | 55 | .373 | 100 | .341 | 71 | 0.62 | 130 | 7.26 | 90 | 4.47 | 11 |
| | vs. Righties | .219 | 148 | .313 | 135 | .300 | 117 | 1.39 | 108 | 9.79 | 51 | 11.31 | 61 |
| Gary Ward | vs. Lefties | .278 | 69 | .487 | 26 | .337 | 76 | 4.81 | 21 | 8.29 | 70 | 19.02 | 135 |
| | vs. Righties | .210 | -- | .238 | -- | .252 | -- | 0.00 | -- | 6.03 | -- | 17.24 | -- |
| Lou Whitaker | vs. Lefties | .188 | 164 | .349 | 118 | .305 | 118 | 3.36 | 44 | 12.92 | 21 | 10.11 | 60 |
| | vs. Righties | .278 | 50 | .508 | 7 | .383 | 15 | 6.39 | 5 | 15.24 | 9 | 9.47 | 35 |
| Kenny Williams | vs. Lefties | .225 | 145 | .333 | 131 | .296 | 131 | 2.33 | 70 | 7.75 | 78 | 22.54 | 157 |
| | vs. Righties | .186 | 167 | .271 | 159 | .241 | 167 | 2.33 | 69 | 4.90 | 151 | 21.68 | 147 |
| Team Average | vs. Lefties | .255 | 11 | .375 | 10 | .324 | 8 | 2.22 | 8 | 8.74 | 6 | 12.86 | 8 |
| | vs. Righties | .236 | 14 | .340 | 14 | .315 | 12 | 2.09 | 10 | 9.93 | 2 | 15.54 | 10 |
| League Average | vs. Lefties | .266 | | .391 | | .328 | | 2.18 | | 8.18 | | 13.58 | |
| | vs. Righties | .258 | | .380 | | .325 | | 2.26 | | 8.56 | | 14.57 | |

## Batting with Runners on Base and Bases Empty

| | | BA | Rank | SA | Rank | OBA | Rank | HR % | Rank | BB % | Rank | SO % | Rank |
|---|---|---|---|---|---|---|---|---|---|---|---|---|---|
| Dave Bergman | Runners On | .292 | 48 | .342 | 132 | .388 | 23 | 0.00 | 146 | 12.50 | 28 | 7.29 | 23 |
| | Bases Empty | .250 | 98 | .375 | 91 | .311 | 98 | 3.13 | 54 | 8.20 | 71 | 12.30 | 63 |
| Mike Brumley | Runners On | .177 | 172 | .219 | 171 | .210 | 172 | 1.04 | 117 | 3.88 | 164 | 23.30 | 158 |
| | Bases Empty | .216 | 145 | .284 | 158 | .283 | 139 | 0.00 | 153 | 7.87 | 80 | 16.54 | 105 |
| Mike Heath | Runners On | .231 | 147 | .363 | 100 | .298 | 136 | 2.50 | 60 | 8.24 | 90 | 14.84 | 105 |
| | Bases Empty | .284 | 38 | .407 | 60 | .316 | 88 | 2.54 | 73 | 3.64 | 162 | 17.81 | 117 |
| Chet Lemon | Runners On | .278 | 74 | .439 | 47 | .368 | 41 | 2.78 | 51 | 10.90 | 42 | 14.69 | 100 |
| | Bases Empty | .205 | 157 | .269 | 164 | .287 | 132 | 0.85 | 129 | 8.81 | 54 | 15.33 | 96 |
| Fred Lynn | Runners On | .258 | 103 | .344 | 129 | .338 | 78 | 1.61 | 94 | 11.57 | 38 | 16.67 | 126 |
| | Bases Empty | .222 | 140 | .401 | 68 | .316 | 88 | 4.79 | 18 | 11.58 | 21 | 18.42 | 119 |
| Matt Nokes | Runners On | .282 | 66 | .484 | 22 | .336 | 84 | 5.65 | 11 | 7.25 | 110 | 12.32 | 84 |
| | Bases Empty | .222 | 139 | .306 | 147 | .263 | 160 | 1.39 | 108 | 4.61 | 150 | 13.16 | 74 |
| Gary Pettis | Runners On | .268 | 88 | .294 | 156 | .371 | 39 | 0.00 | 146 | 13.44 | 21 | 15.05 | 110 |
| | Bases Empty | .251 | 97 | .316 | 135 | .377 | 12 | 0.34 | 150 | 16.86 | 3 | 22.29 | 153 |
| Rick Schu | Runners On | .177 | 171 | .234 | 169 | .220 | 171 | 0.00 | 146 | 5.22 | 139 | 11.94 | 83 |
| | Bases Empty | .246 | 108 | .423 | 49 | .327 | 67 | 4.93 | 16 | 10.69 | 28 | 13.21 | 75 |
| Doug Strange | Runners On | .238 | 135 | .275 | 164 | .315 | 118 | 0.00 | 146 | 8.60 | 82 | 11.83 | 79 |
| | Bases Empty | .198 | 162 | .250 | 169 | .256 | 163 | 0.86 | 127 | 7.20 | 96 | 20.00 | 134 |
| Alan Trammell | Runners On | .283 | 65 | .348 | 122 | .344 | 73 | 0.51 | 142 | 8.81 | 77 | 9.69 | 56 |
| | Bases Empty | .211 | 148 | .323 | 130 | .290 | 126 | 1.59 | 97 | 8.96 | 48 | 8.24 | 22 |
| Gary Ward | Runners On | .232 | 143 | .310 | 151 | .298 | 137 | 1.41 | 105 | 9.26 | 71 | 22.84 | 154 |
| | Bases Empty | .273 | 48 | .480 | 13 | .314 | 91 | 4.67 | 21 | 5.66 | 133 | 13.84 | 85 |
| Lou Whitaker | Runners On | .245 | 127 | .455 | 36 | .357 | 56 | 5.45 | 12 | 15.02 | 14 | 8.79 | 42 |
| | Bases Empty | .256 | 85 | .467 | 20 | .364 | 19 | 5.54 | 11 | 14.20 | 9 | 10.36 | 43 |
| Kenny Williams | Runners On | .202 | 165 | .294 | 158 | .246 | 169 | 1.83 | 88 | 5.00 | 148 | 25.00 | 166 |
| | Bases Empty | .208 | 152 | .309 | 144 | .285 | 137 | 2.68 | 70 | 7.27 | 94 | 20.00 | 134 |
| Team Average | Runners On | .246 | 13 | .349 | 14 | .324 | 13 | 1.91 | 12 | 10.04 | 3 | 14.10 | 10 |
| | Bases Empty | .239 | 14 | .353 | 14 | .313 | 10 | 2.31 | 9 | 9.14 | 3 | 15.10 | 8 |
| League Average | Runners On | .268 | | .389 | | .336 | | 2.15 | | 9.17 | | 13.53 | |
| | Bases Empty | .255 | | .380 | | .317 | | 2.29 | | 7.84 | | 14.86 | |

## Overall Batting Compared to Late Inning Pressure Situations

| | | BA | Rank | SA | Rank | OBA | Rank | HR % | Rank | BB % | Rank | SO % | Rank | RDI % | Rank |
|---|---|---|---|---|---|---|---|---|---|---|---|---|---|---|---|
| Dave Bergman | Overall | .268 | 66 | .361 | 109 | .345 | 49 | 1.82 | 92 | 10.09 | 41 | 10.09 | 48 | .248 | 115 |
| | Pressure | .183 | 148 | .183 | 163 | .279 | 128 | 0.00 | 107 | 10.00 | 65 | 17.14 | 96 | .200 | 115 |
| Mike Brumley | Overall | .198 | 170 | .255 | 171 | .251 | 170 | 0.47 | 150 | 6.09 | 133 | 19.57 | 141 | .130 | 170 |
| | Pressure | .172 | 155 | .276 | 134 | .273 | 132 | 0.00 | 107 | 11.43 | 45 | 22.86 | 137 | .000 | 165 |
| Mike Heath | Overall | .263 | 79 | .389 | 78 | .308 | 109 | 2.53 | 65 | 5.59 | 141 | 16.55 | 113 | .250 | 107 |
| | Pressure | .278 | 58 | .443 | 37 | .333 | 72 | 3.80 | 40 | 6.82 | 116 | 19.32 | 113 | .250 | 87 |
| Tracy Jones | Overall | .259 | -- | .380 | -- | .326 | -- | 1.90 | -- | 8.94 | -- | 8.94 | -- | .339 | 18 |
| | Pressure | .273 | 62 | .394 | 63 | .316 | 93 | 3.03 | 55 | 7.89 | 97 | 15.79 | 80 | .333 | 42 |
| Chet Lemon | Overall | .237 | 139 | .343 | 125 | .323 | 85 | 1.69 | 98 | 9.75 | 47 | 15.04 | 98 | .256 | 99 |
| | Pressure | .231 | 105 | .295 | 124 | .294 | 117 | 0.00 | 107 | 8.05 | 94 | 19.54 | 116 | .278 | 74 |
| Fred Lynn | Overall | .241 | 131 | .371 | 98 | .328 | 76 | 3.12 | 49 | 11.58 | 21 | 17.49 | 122 | .252 | 105 |
| | Pressure | .207 | 127 | .293 | 126 | .343 | 59 | 1.72 | 83 | 17.14 | 6 | 18.57 | 108 | .000 | 165 |
| Matt Nokes | Overall | .250 | 115 | .388 | 79 | .298 | 135 | 3.36 | 38 | 5.86 | 137 | 12.76 | 75 | .250 | 107 |
| | Pressure | .217 | 114 | .304 | 119 | .302 | 105 | 2.17 | 72 | 11.11 | 48 | 18.52 | 107 | .333 | 42 |
| Gary Pettis | Overall | .257 | 96 | .309 | 155 | .375 | 16 | 0.23 | 162 | 15.67 | 6 | 19.78 | 142 | .149 | 167 |
| | Pressure | .250 | 89 | .297 | 122 | .422 | 14 | 0.00 | 107 | 22.62 | 1 | 25.00 | 145 | .269 | 81 |
| Rick Schu | Overall | .214 | 162 | .335 | 131 | .278 | 159 | 2.63 | 61 | 8.19 | 79 | 12.63 | 74 | .147 | 168 |
| | Pressure | .179 | 153 | .179 | 164 | .233 | 150 | 0.00 | 107 | 6.56 | 120 | 13.11 | 52 | .000 | 165 |
| Doug Strange | Overall | .214 | 162 | .260 | 170 | .280 | 156 | 0.51 | 147 | 7.80 | 91 | 16.51 | 112 | .212 | -- |
| | Pressure | .200 | 134 | .257 | 142 | .243 | 148 | 0.00 | 107 | 2.63 | 159 | 15.79 | 80 | .111 | 151 |
| Alan Trammell | Overall | .243 | 126 | .334 | 132 | .314 | 104 | 1.11 | 126 | 8.89 | 62 | 8.89 | 32 | .276 | 71 |
| | Pressure | .313 | 29 | .433 | 43 | .439 | 8 | 1.49 | 94 | 15.66 | 12 | 12.05 | 43 | .368 | 31 |
| Gary Ward | Overall | .253 | 103 | .397 | 71 | .306 | 114 | 3.08 | 51 | 7.48 | 96 | 18.38 | 129 | .200 | 154 |
| | Pressure | .211 | 121 | .333 | 103 | .246 | 146 | 1.75 | 81 | 4.84 | 143 | 27.42 | 152 | .150 | 135 |
| Lou Whitaker | Overall | .251 | 111 | .462 | 20 | .361 | 28 | 5.50 | 9 | 14.57 | 8 | 9.66 | 44 | .322 | 30 |
| | Pressure | .229 | 107 | .470 | 29 | .327 | 79 | 7.23 | 5 | 13.27 | 34 | 10.20 | 33 | .346 | 39 |
| Kenny Williams | Overall | .205 | 169 | .302 | 159 | .269 | 166 | 2.33 | 70 | 6.32 | 124 | 22.11 | 151 | .194 | 159 |
| | Pressure | .109 | 171 | .174 | 165 | .146 | 172 | 0.00 | 107 | 4.17 | 149 | 33.33 | 162 | .071 | 160 |
| Team Average | Overall | .242 | 14 | .351 | 14 | .318 | 12 | 2.14 | 10 | 9.54 | 3 | 14.66 | 9 | .236 | 13 |
| | Pressure | .216 | 13 | .302 | 14 | .306 | 12 | 1.50 | 12 | 10.86 | 1 | 18.66 | 10 | .208 | 13 |
| League Average | Overall | .261 | | .384 | | .326 | | 2.23 | | 8.44 | | 14.26 | | .269 | |
| | Pressure | .247 | | .357 | | .318 | | 2.02 | | 9.02 | | 17.90 | | .254 | |

## Additional Miscellaneous Batting Comparisons

| | Grass Surface | | Artificial Surface | | Home Games | | Road Games | | Runners in Scoring Position | | Runners in Scoring Pos and Two Outs | | Leading Off Inning | | Runners on 3B with less than 2 Outs | |
|---|---|---|---|---|---|---|---|---|---|---|---|---|---|---|---|---|
| | BA | Rank | BA | Rank | BA | Rank | BA | Rank | BA | Rank | BA | Rank | OBA | Rank | RDI % | Rank |
| Dave Bergman | .253 | 92 | .344 | 10 | .249 | 103 | .283 | 47 | .303 | 34 | .275 | 44 | .268 | 147 | .632 | 50 |
| Mike Brumley | .214 | 159 | .136 | 169 | .208 | 158 | .189 | 170 | .133 | 170 | .080 | 172 | .236 | 163 | .333 | 163 |
| Mike Heath | .252 | 94 | .327 | 21 | .238 | 122 | .285 | 41 | .230 | 132 | .216 | 107 | .306 | 106 | .579 | 79 |
| Tracy Jones | .248 | 102 | .444 | -- | .253 | -- | .265 | -- | .319 | 22 | .286 | 34 | .371 | -- | .800 | 7 |
| Chet Lemon | .229 | 142 | .275 | 56 | .228 | 136 | .244 | 116 | .288 | 49 | .300 | 24 | .348 | 50 | .520 | 115 |
| Fred Lynn | .233 | 131 | .283 | 49 | .214 | 151 | .267 | 72 | .264 | 85 | .304 | 21 | .341 | 54 | .500 | 119 |
| Matt Nokes | .265 | 71 | .178 | 157 | .268 | 70 | .234 | 136 | .240 | 113 | .186 | 133 | .333 | 64 | .579 | 79 |
| Gary Pettis | .262 | 78 | .227 | 124 | .265 | 73 | .248 | 113 | .190 | 160 | .220 | 104 | .364 | 32 | .083 | 173 |
| Rick Schu | .219 | 154 | .191 | 149 | .192 | 167 | .235 | 133 | .167 | 168 | .091 | 167 | .324 | 81 | .625 | -- |
| Pat Sheridan | .237 | -- | .259 | -- | .241 | -- | .242 | -- | .308 | -- | .278 | 38 | .341 | -- | .857 | -- |
| Doug Strange | .201 | 166 | .281 | -- | .208 | 156 | .220 | 156 | .267 | 83 | .190 | -- | .318 | -- | .286 | -- |
| Alan Trammell | .245 | 110 | .230 | 122 | .250 | 99 | .235 | 135 | .263 | 88 | .229 | 92 | .250 | 156 | .654 | 44 |
| Gary Ward | .241 | 115 | .309 | 29 | .259 | 85 | .248 | 108 | .187 | 164 | .133 | 158 | .281 | 133 | .706 | 22 |
| Lou Whitaker | .252 | 93 | .247 | 102 | .264 | 75 | .241 | 122 | .294 | 40 | .318 | 17 | .352 | 47 | .645 | 46 |
| Kenny Williams | .210 | 163 | .190 | 152 | .202 | 163 | .209 | 163 | .238 | 116 | .273 | 46 | .259 | 152 | .333 | -- |
| Team Average | .241 | 14 | .249 | 11 | .239 | 14 | .245 | 13 | .240 | 13 | .227 | 12 | .313 | 10 | .550 | 9 |
| League Average | .260 | | .262 | | .262 | | .259 | | .262 | | .232 | | .321 | | .566 | |

## Pitching vs. Left and Right Handed Batters

| | | BA | Rank | SA | Rank | OBA | Rank | HR % | Rank | BB % | Rank | SO % | Rank |
|---|---|---|---|---|---|---|---|---|---|---|---|---|---|
| Doyle Alexander | vs. Lefties | .284 | 98 | .437 | 103 | .330 | 68 | 2.86 | 95 | 6.17 | 29 | 7.85 | 113 |
| | vs. Righties | .275 | 97 | .430 | 110 | .345 | 113 | 3.63 | 120 | 9.73 | 106 | 11.99 | 95 |
| Paul Gibson | vs. Lefties | .265 | 76 | .410 | 90 | .341 | 78 | 3.42 | 109 | 10.37 | 95 | 9.63 | 95 |
| | vs. Righties | .257 | 69 | .381 | 71 | .339 | 104 | 1.84 | 58 | 9.82 | 107 | 14.61 | 73 |
| Mike Henneman | vs. Lefties | .266 | 80 | .364 | 50 | .379 | 109 | 0.65 | 13 | 15.22 | 122 | 13.04 | 58 |
| | vs. Righties | .238 | 31 | .315 | 19 | .335 | 94 | 1.66 | 43 | 10.60 | 114 | 20.74 | 25 |
| Charles Hudson | vs. Lefties | .222 | 27 | .385 | 72 | .307 | 48 | 4.44 | 125 | 10.39 | 97 | 4.55 | 134 |
| | vs. Righties | .360 | -- | .632 | -- | .433 | -- | 6.40 | -- | 10.49 | -- | 11.19 | -- |
| Jack Morris | vs. Lefties | .296 | 107 | .479 | 118 | .358 | 97 | 3.58 | 113 | 9.48 | 81 | 15.80 | 34 |
| | vs. Righties | .271 | 91 | .425 | 108 | .322 | 71 | 3.31 | 114 | 6.58 | 47 | 15.19 | 65 |
| Edwin Nunez | vs. Lefties | .270 | 83 | .337 | 40 | .400 | 130 | 1.12 | 34 | 17.86 | 134 | 15.18 | 42 |
| | vs. Righties | .240 | -- | .471 | -- | .336 | -- | 4.81 | -- | 12.70 | -- | 19.05 | -- |
| Kevin Ritz | vs. Lefties | .266 | 79 | .388 | 78 | .381 | 111 | 1.44 | 51 | 15.48 | 124 | 15.48 | 41 |
| | vs. Righties | .264 | 81 | .319 | 23 | .339 | 106 | 0.00 | 1 | 10.84 | 120 | 18.07 | 38 |
| Jeff M. Robinson | vs. Lefties | .265 | 77 | .463 | 108 | .382 | 113 | 4.08 | 121 | 15.56 | 125 | 9.44 | 97 |
| | vs. Righties | .252 | 56 | .374 | 63 | .331 | 88 | 2.72 | 97 | 10.78 | 118 | 13.77 | 83 |
| Mike Schwabe | vs. Lefties | .362 | 134 | .619 | 135 | .395 | 127 | 5.71 | 131 | 6.14 | 28 | 7.02 | 118 |
| | vs. Righties | .241 | -- | .313 | -- | .319 | -- | 0.00 | -- | 9.47 | -- | 5.26 | -- |
| Frank Tanana | vs. Lefties | .304 | 112 | .400 | 85 | .374 | 107 | 1.60 | 57 | 9.29 | 76 | 12.14 | 67 |
| | vs. Righties | .259 | 72 | .376 | 67 | .318 | 64 | 2.60 | 93 | 7.48 | 62 | 15.95 | 55 |
| Frank Williams | vs. Lefties | .260 | 68 | .382 | 68 | .392 | 124 | 2.44 | 82 | 17.65 | 133 | 7.84 | 114 |
| | vs. Righties | .248 | 48 | .320 | 24 | .335 | 95 | 1.31 | 27 | 10.73 | 117 | 11.86 | 96 |
| Team Average | vs. Lefties | .281 | 12 | .430 | 13 | .361 | 13 | 2.75 | 12 | 10.86 | 13 | 11.02 | 12 |
| | vs. Righties | .269 | 12 | .404 | 12 | .346 | 14 | 2.70 | 14 | 9.91 | 13 | 14.54 | 8 |
| League Average | vs. Lefties | .261 | | .382 | | .330 | | 2.16 | | 9.16 | | 13.03 | |
| | vs. Righties | .261 | | .385 | | .323 | | 2.28 | | 7.96 | | 15.09 | |

## Pitching with Runners on Base and Bases Empty

| | | BA | Rank | SA | Rank | OBA | Rank | HR % | Rank | BB % | Rank | SO % | Rank |
|---|---|---|---|---|---|---|---|---|---|---|---|---|---|
| Doyle Alexander | Runners On | .269 | 78 | .404 | 94 | .329 | 63 | 2.39 | 95 | 8.74 | 63 | 11.49 | 82 |
| | Bases Empty | .288 | 113 | .456 | 116 | .343 | 105 | 3.80 | 125 | 7.01 | 60 | 8.30 | 125 |
| Paul Gibson | Runners On | .250 | 43 | .384 | 78 | .347 | 90 | 2.68 | 101 | 11.40 | 105 | 13.24 | 66 |
| | Bases Empty | .266 | 81 | .391 | 78 | .332 | 91 | 1.82 | 50 | 8.64 | 88 | 13.62 | 69 |
| Mike Henneman | Runners On | .277 | 89 | .355 | 49 | .401 | 131 | 0.65 | 7 | 15.58 | 130 | 15.08 | 51 |
| | Bases Empty | .228 | 28 | .322 | 26 | .312 | 57 | 1.67 | 42 | 9.90 | 106 | 19.31 | 30 |
| Charles Hudson | Runners On | .321 | 125 | .587 | 133 | .385 | 122 | 5.50 | 134 | 9.60 | 76 | 5.60 | 133 |
| | Bases Empty | .265 | 77 | .444 | 113 | .355 | 117 | 5.30 | 135 | 11.05 | 118 | 9.30 | 115 |
| Jack Morris | Runners On | .300 | 119 | .401 | 92 | .356 | 100 | 1.08 | 20 | 8.18 | 54 | 14.47 | 58 |
| | Bases Empty | .270 | 90 | .485 | 126 | .327 | 83 | 5.10 | 133 | 7.76 | 73 | 16.24 | 51 |
| Edwin Nunez | Runners On | .219 | 15 | .344 | 34 | .355 | 99 | 2.08 | 81 | 17.32 | 133 | 18.11 | 28 |
| | Bases Empty | .289 | -- | .474 | -- | .378 | -- | 4.12 | -- | 12.61 | -- | 16.22 | -- |
| Kevin Ritz | Runners On | .296 | 114 | .360 | 56 | .400 | 130 | 0.00 | 1 | 15.38 | 129 | 19.23 | 19 |
| | Bases Empty | .241 | 47 | .348 | 43 | .326 | 81 | 1.27 | 22 | 11.24 | 120 | 14.61 | 58 |
| Jeff M. Robinson | Runners On | .257 | 56 | .397 | 88 | .342 | 82 | 2.94 | 112 | 11.18 | 102 | 9.32 | 112 |
| | Bases Empty | .259 | 70 | .437 | 110 | .371 | 126 | 3.80 | 124 | 15.05 | 133 | 13.44 | 73 |
| Frank Tanana | Runners On | .253 | 49 | .369 | 63 | .319 | 51 | 2.84 | 110 | 9.31 | 73 | 13.73 | 61 |
| | Bases Empty | .274 | 96 | .387 | 77 | .331 | 88 | 2.18 | 67 | 6.58 | 51 | 16.64 | 48 |
| Frank Williams | Runners On | .237 | 32 | .329 | 24 | .362 | 109 | 1.97 | 74 | 15.87 | 131 | 8.99 | 113 |
| | Bases Empty | .274 | 97 | .371 | 63 | .362 | 122 | 1.61 | 40 | 11.35 | 123 | 11.35 | 96 |
| Team Average | Runners On | .277 | 12 | .412 | 13 | .361 | 13 | 2.51 | 11 | 11.52 | 14 | 12.92 | 9 |
| | Bases Empty | .272 | 14 | .417 | 12 | .343 | 14 | 2.89 | 13 | 9.19 | 12 | 13.30 | 11 |
| League Average | Runners On | .268 | | .389 | | .336 | | 2.15 | | 9.17 | | 13.53 | |
| | Bases Empty | .255 | | .380 | | .317 | | 2.29 | | 7.84 | | 14.86 | |

## Overall Pitching Compared to Late Inning Pressure Situations

| | | BA | Rank | SA | Rank | OBA | Rank | HR % | Rank | BB % | Rank | SO % | Rank |
|---|---|---|---|---|---|---|---|---|---|---|---|---|---|
| Doyle Alexander | Overall | .280 | 102 | .434 | 112 | .337 | 89 | 3.20 | 115 | 7.78 | 61 | 9.72 | 112 |
| | Pressure | .292 | 105 | .451 | 109 | .350 | 87 | 3.54 | 111 | 8.00 | 52 | 4.00 | 129 |
| Paul Gibson | Overall | .259 | 66 | .388 | 78 | .339 | 93 | 2.21 | 73 | 9.95 | 107 | 13.44 | 67 |
| | Pressure | .253 | 76 | .368 | 81 | .343 | 82 | 2.30 | 84 | 10.68 | 80 | 18.45 | 41 |
| Mike Henneman | Overall | .251 | 51 | .337 | 30 | .355 | 116 | 1.19 | 16 | 12.72 | 126 | 17.21 | 37 |
| | Pressure | .257 | 80 | .346 | 67 | .371 | 103 | 1.40 | 51 | 14.07 | 115 | 15.97 | 55 |
| Willie Hernandez | Overall | .293 | -- | .455 | -- | .379 | -- | 3.25 | -- | 11.35 | -- | 21.28 | -- |
| | Pressure | .288 | 99 | .394 | 91 | .373 | 106 | 1.52 | 53 | 11.84 | 100 | 27.63 | 9 |
| Charles Hudson | Overall | .288 | 116 | .504 | 134 | .367 | 130 | 5.38 | 133 | 10.44 | 110 | 7.74 | 127 |
| | Pressure | .345 | 120 | .552 | 124 | .424 | 122 | 3.45 | 108 | 11.43 | 94 | 8.57 | 113 |
| Jack Morris | Overall | .283 | 106 | .450 | 123 | .339 | 92 | 3.44 | 124 | 7.94 | 65 | 15.48 | 51 |
| | Pressure | .253 | 75 | .354 | 73 | .299 | 49 | 2.02 | 73 | 6.42 | 35 | 18.35 | 42 |
| Edwin Nunez | Overall | .254 | -- | .409 | -- | .366 | -- | 3.11 | -- | 15.13 | -- | 17.23 | -- |
| | Pressure | .197 | 23 | .324 | 52 | .348 | 85 | 2.82 | 95 | 18.09 | 130 | 17.02 | 49 |
| Kevin Ritz | Overall | .265 | 77 | .353 | 45 | .360 | 124 | 0.71 | 3 | 13.17 | 129 | 16.77 | 41 |
| | Pressure | .111 | -- | .148 | -- | .172 | -- | 0.00 | -- | 6.90 | -- | 13.79 | -- |
| Jeff M. Robinson | Overall | .259 | 64 | .418 | 96 | .358 | 119 | 3.40 | 123 | 13.26 | 130 | 11.53 | 91 |
| | Pressure | .000 | -- | .000 | -- | .000 | -- | 0.00 | -- | 0.00 | -- | 66.67 | -- |
| Frank Tanana | Overall | .265 | 79 | .380 | 70 | .326 | 72 | 2.45 | 86 | 7.75 | 60 | 15.39 | 52 |
| | Pressure | .257 | 79 | .422 | 103 | .325 | 65 | 3.67 | 112 | 7.32 | 46 | 20.33 | 30 |
| Frank Williams | Overall | .254 | 56 | .348 | 43 | .362 | 126 | 1.81 | 54 | 13.94 | 133 | 10.00 | 106 |
| | Pressure | .270 | 89 | .405 | 96 | .407 | 116 | 2.70 | 92 | 17.39 | 129 | 13.04 | 77 |
| Team Average | Overall | .274 | 13 | .415 | 13 | .352 | 14 | 2.72 | 13 | 10.29 | 13 | 13.12 | 11 |
| | Pressure | .266 | 12 | .390 | 12 | .358 | 13 | 2.45 | 10 | 11.71 | 14 | 15.77 | 10 |
| League Average | Overall | .261 | | .384 | | .326 | | 2.23 | | 8.44 | | 14.26 | |
| | Pressure | .250 | | .362 | | .325 | | 2.14 | | 9.50 | | 16.61 | |

## Additional Miscellaneous Pitching Comparisons

| | Grass Surface | | Artificial Surface | | Home Games | | Road Games | | Runners in Scoring Position | | Runners in Scoring Pos and Two Outs | | Leading Off Inning | |
|---|---|---|---|---|---|---|---|---|---|---|---|---|---|---|
| | BA | Rank | BA | Rank | BA | Rank | BA | Rank | BA | Rank | BA | Rank | OBA | Rank |
| Doyle Alexander | .272 | 91 | .308 | 110 | .256 | 73 | .305 | 122 | .235 | 39 | .238 | 78 | .314 | 54 |
| Brian Dubois | .221 | -- | .213 | 17 | .219 | -- | .217 | -- | .154 | -- | .267 | -- | .297 | -- |
| Paul Gibson | .252 | 60 | .300 | 105 | .222 | 22 | .297 | 117 | .278 | 96 | .204 | 49 | .371 | 115 |
| Brad Havens | .324 | 133 | .000 | -- | .328 | -- | .321 | -- | .400 | -- | .318 | -- | .294 | -- |
| Mike Henneman | .243 | 38 | .294 | 99 | .221 | 21 | .286 | 96 | .258 | 77 | .265 | 101 | .326 | 72 |
| Charles Hudson | .281 | 104 | .345 | -- | .260 | -- | .299 | 119 | .250 | -- | .143 | -- | .457 | 135 |
| Jack Morris | .268 | 84 | .395 | 134 | .285 | 110 | .280 | 90 | .310 | 121 | .314 | 123 | .339 | 87 |
| Edwin Nunez | .263 | 69 | .182 | -- | .259 | 77 | .247 | -- | .242 | 56 | .154 | 20 | .391 | -- |
| Kevin Ritz | .273 | 93 | .185 | -- | .283 | 106 | .246 | 42 | .286 | 106 | .306 | 118 | .321 | 65 |
| Jeff M. Robinson | .235 | 29 | .373 | 132 | .230 | 32 | .295 | 114 | .274 | 91 | .258 | 97 | .440 | 134 |
| Mike Schwabe | .320 | 132 | .263 | -- | .329 | -- | .292 | 108 | .297 | 116 | .259 | -- | .349 | -- |
| Frank Tanana | .265 | 74 | .264 | 65 | .243 | 53 | .290 | 106 | .285 | 105 | .291 | 113 | .291 | 36 |
| Frank Williams | .244 | 42 | .310 | 113 | .243 | 52 | .264 | 75 | .202 | 15 | .120 | 9 | .323 | 69 |
| Team Average | .269 | 11 | .305 | 14 | .257 | 7 | .292 | 14 | .276 | 13 | .249 | 13 | .347 | 14 |
| League Average | .260 | | .262 | | .259 | | .262 | | .262 | | .232 | | .321 | |

# KANSAS CITY ROYALS

- **If you own a cadillac, do you need a Rolls Royce?**
- **The George Blanda of baseball.**

Easy come, easy go. We spend the entire 1980s drooling in anticipation of the next dynasty. Then along come the Oakland A's, and a month later, the Kansas City Royals spend enough to pay the entire General Assembly of the Show-me State for four years on a couple of pitchers named Davis. The loss of one Davis rips a huge hole in Oakland's starting rotation. The addition of the other supposedly closes one just as big in Kansas City's bullpen. Well, there's always the 1990s.

After all, even the mighty A's won only seven games more than the Davis-less Royals last season. And the 16 million dollars Kansas City spent on Mark Davis alone should be enough to close that gap, shouldn't it? Actually, um, no. The Royals may have signed the Rolls Royce of relievers, but they already had a couple Cadillacs in the garage.

Kansas City started last season with Steve Farr at the top of its bullpen depth chart. Farr had become the Royals' stopper in May 1988, and he finished that season with 20 saves in 25 opportunities. He continued to excel as the successor to Dan Quisenberry early last season, with saves in each of his first 10 opportunities. But he blew four of 10 chances over the next two months, and finished the season 18–for–24, with only five appearances after undergoing knee surgery on August 23. Farr's demotion was expedited by the surprising development of Jeff Montgomery, who saved 17 games in 18 opportunities after the All-Star break, two of them by pitching out of bases-loaded situations. He finished the season with a 1.37 ERA, and 94 strikeouts in 92 innings.

The Royals' bullpen ERA of 3.06 was third-best in the American League. And while no one mistook Farr and Montgomery for Mark Davis, it's a fact the Royals lost very few leads that they should have held, winning 71 of 75 games in which they led after seven innings. Only one team in either league had a better record—and it was Oakland (90–4), not Davis's Padres (69–4)—leaving almost no room for improvement.

So Kansas City could hardly be dissatisfied with the performance of its relief staff last season. And the signings of Storm Davis and Rich Dotson prior to that of Mark Davis indicated that the Royals considered their starting rotation, not the bullpen, to be their most likely source of problems. But given a legitimate chance, what team wouldn't have signed the National League Cy Young Award winner, especially with the singing cowboy crooning a three-million dollar tune on the other line? And so, the deal was done. Whether it will substantially improve the team is debatable.

For the record, let's compare the bullpen performances of the six other teams that, over the past six years, acquired a pitcher coming off a 20–save season. The following table shows the records of those teams in games in which they led after seven innings, the year before and the year after acquiring those pitchers:

| | | | Before | | | After | | |
|---|---|---|---|---|---|---|---|---|
| **Year** | **Team** | **Pitcher** | **W** | **L** | **Pct.** | **W** | **L** | **Pct.** |
| 1984 | Oakland | Bill Caudill | 54 | 10 | .844 | 57 | 4 | .934 |
| 1984 | San Diego | Rich Gossage | 65 | 4 | .942 | 74 | 7 | .914 |
| 1985 | Toronto | Bill Caudill | 61 | 15 | .803 | 82 | 13 | .863 |
| 1985 | Atlanta | Bruce Sutter | 57 | 9 | .864 | 48 | 9 | .842 |
| 1987 | Minnesota | Jeff Reardon | 59 | 7 | .894 | 66 | 4 | .943 |
| 1988 | Boston | Lee Smith | 65 | 6 | .915 | 76 | 6 | .927 |

On average, those teams lost only two fewer games in which they led after seven innings. Obtaining a top-caliber reliever hardly guarantees improvement in that area. As an extreme example, but one that closely parallels Kansas City's acquisition of Mark Davis, consider the 1985 Atlanta Braves. Sutter had just set a National League record with 45 saves and finished third in the Cy Young voting when he signed a megacontract with Atlanta. Not only did the Braves fail to improve upon their mediocre record in games with late leads, they actually declined. For what it's worth, the similarity between Sutter and Davis is striking:

| Year | Pitcher | G | GF | SV | W | L | IP | H | BB | SO | ERA |
|---|---|---|---|---|---|---|---|---|---|---|---|
| 1984 | Sutter | 71 | 63 | 45 | 5 | 7 | 122.2 | 109 | 23 | 77 | 1.54 |
| 1989 | Davis | 70 | 65 | 44 | 4 | 3 | 92.2 | 66 | 31 | 92 | 1.85 |

Of course, that resemblance doesn't make a Sutter-like collapse by Davis any more likely than a Wimbledon victory by Tom Petty on the grounds that he looks like Martina Navratilova. But while it's trite, it's true nonetheless that players come without guarantees for parts or labor. Sutter is only one example of the many players who've signed multi–million-dollar, multiyear contracts and failed to fulfill the lofty and often overly optimistic expectations of fans and management. And unlike Sutter, Davis doesn't enter a can't-lose situation. Kansas City's no-name bullpen simply didn't squander many leads last season. So for more than 16 million dollars, the Royals' state-of-the-art acquisition may amount to little more than an extravagant upgrade.

A legendary old Latin teacher at a private school in New York City used to delight in explaining the following paradox: "A man walks across a room, from one side to the other. But he can never reach the far wall. Why?" he would ask, starting to cross the room himself. "Because to get there, he must reach the halfway point." He walks halfway, stops for emphasis, then proceeds. "From there, he must again halve the remaining distance." Stop. "Over and over again, he advances, each time leaving a smaller slice of the room between him and his destination. But since he always leaves half the remaining space between him and the wall," he says, approaching the wall himself, "he will never reach it." At which point, the professor would slap the wall with tremendous force and conclude with a laugh, "Rubbish!"

We never were sure what that had to do with Cicero, but it reminds us that a few years ago, baseball writers were routinely advancing the notion that aging catchers like Bob Boone, Carlton Fisk, and Jim Sundberg had reached the end of the line. No catchers had ever remained active into their 40s; ergo, they must be washed up. Rubbish! Boone and his colleagues have treated their ongoing careers like the man crossing the room in that variation on Zeno's Paradox—ever diminishing, but oddly enduring. And Boone's career has actually flourished. He's playing more and better in his 40s than he did in his 30s, quashing talk of a genetic limit on games played behind the plate.

Two years ago, Boone was the oldest player in the majors to start at least 100 games, and he established a career high with a .295 batting average, all in his 17th season. Only one player in baseball history had compiled his personal best batting average in a season of 100 or more at-bats later in his career (Tris Speaker, in his 19th season). Last season, Boone batted .274, and—even more impressive—started another 127 games behind the plate. Prior to Boone, no 40–year-old catcher had ever reached the 100–game mark in any season. The major league high was 68, by Chief Zimmer in 1901. Boone has nearly doubled Zimmer's "record" total in each of the past two seasons, with 121 games in 1988 and 129 last year. He's now caught more games after his 40th birthday than any other player in major league history, and by a wide margin. The all-time leaders:

| | | | |
|---|---|---|---|
| Bob Boone | 250 | Deacon McGuire | 52 |
| Chief Zimmer | 144 | Rick Ferrell | 37 |
| Carlton Fisk | 90 | Gabby Hartnett | 34 |
| Wally Schang | 75 | Frank Bowerman | 27 |
| Walker Cooper | 60 | Cap Anson | 21 |

Perhaps the attitude that catchers are washed up at 40 is more understandable when you consider the recent past. Prior to Boone in 1988, and Fisk and Rick Dempsey last season, no player had caught even a single game after his 40th birthday since 1965, when Yogi Berra was the starting catcher for the Mets in the final game of his aborted comeback, just three days after turning 40. Before that, it's back to Walker Cooper, who caught 13 games in 1957 at age 42. Quite simply, 40–year-old catchers had become as rare as 10–year-old thoroughbred champions. (How old was John Henry anyway? Swear he didn't look a day over seven to us.)

It hadn't always been that way. During the first decade of this century, Zimmer, McGuire, and Bowerman all had long careers behind the plate. And again in the 1940s, catcher's careers routinely extended in their late 30s on account of the player shortage during World War II. Some catchers, like Hemsley, Hartnett, Al Todd, Spud Davis, and Clyde Sukeforth (among others) lasted into their forties. But from 1950 until 1988, it was Cooper, Berra, and a 22–year vacuum. Boone and his contemporaries are now undoing 40 years of attitude hardening—a difficult task in any field, nearly impossible in the sometimes Neanderthal world of baseball.

We'll be the first to admit that statistics can be interpreted so as to be misleading. (Of course, *we* never do it. Right?) But, in the sense that statistics are a numerical representation of historical events, all statistics mean *something.* It's the presentation of the numbers that determines whether they're useful, useless, or abused.

The sports media is rife with writers and broadcasters who'll seize particular sets of numbers and twist them to support their own farfetched conclusions. For instance, there was the network play-by-play man who noted a few years back (incorrectly, as it turned out) that after two months of the season, only one regular starting pitcher hadn't allowed a run in the first inning. His conclusion: Starting pitchers no longer know how to warm up prior to a game. Numerical analysis, full of sound and fury, signifying nothing. Never occurred to him (or maybe it didn't suit his agenda) that far more runs are scored in the first inning than in any other. To expect more than one or two pitchers to toss "first-inning shutouts" over as many as 10 starts is foolish.

Anyway, we make no pretense about the following numbers. Don't expect to glean any cosmic truths. We found them interesting, and we think you will, too. But as for any significance, none proffered or implied.

The Royals were shut out 18 times last season, earning a share of the American League lead in that category for the third time in the last six seasons. But five times, Kansas City rebounded to score 10 or more runs in the next game, the highest total in modern major league history. Since 1900, only four teams scored in double figures following shutouts even four times: the 1929 Indians, the 1946 Braves, the 1948 Cubs, and the 1973 Yankees.

Enough said.

## WON-LOST RECORD BY STARTING POSITION

| KANSAS CITY 92-70 | C | 1B | 2B | 3B | SS | LF | CF | RF | P | DH | Leadoff | Relief | Starts |
|---|---|---|---|---|---|---|---|---|---|---|---|---|---|
| Kevin Appier | - | - | - | - | - | - | - | - | 1-4 | - | - | 0-1 | 1-4 |
| Luis Aquino | - | - | - | - | - | - | - | - | 6-10 | - | - | 5-13 | 6-10 |
| Floyd Bannister | - | - | - | - | - | - | - | - | 11-3 | - | - | - | 11-3 |
| Bob Boone | 76-51 | - | - | - | - | - | - | - | - | - | - | - | 76-51 |
| George Brett | - | 61-43 | - | - | - | - | - | - | - | 11-6 | - | - | 72-49 |
| Bob Buchanan | - | - | - | - | - | - | - | - | - | - | - | 1-1 | - |
| Bill Buckner | - | 11-8 | - | - | - | - | - | - | - | 9-8 | - | - | 20-16 |
| Stan Clarke | - | - | - | - | - | - | - | - | 0-2 | - | - | - | 0-2 |
| Steve Crawford | - | - | - | - | - | - | - | - | - | - | - | 10-15 | - |
| Luis de los Santos | - | 11-10 | - | - | - | - | - | - | - | - | - | - | 11-10 |
| Jose DeJesus | - | - | - | - | - | - | - | - | 0-1 | - | - | 0-2 | 0-1 |
| Jim Eisenreich | - | - | - | - | - | 10-9 | 34-23 | 17-17 | - | 5-3 | 12-11 | - | 66-52 |
| Steve Farr | - | - | - | - | - | - | - | - | 1-1 | - | - | 30-19 | 1-1 |
| Jerry Don Gleaton | - | - | - | - | - | - | - | - | - | - | - | 4-11 | - |
| Tom Gordon | - | - | - | - | - | - | - | - | 8-8 | - | - | 19-14 | 8-8 |
| Mark Gubicza | - | - | - | - | - | - | - | - | 21-15 | - | - | - | 21-15 |
| Bo Jackson | - | - | - | - | - | 65-44 | - | - | - | 14-10 | - | - | 79-54 |
| Terry Leach | - | - | - | - | - | - | - | - | 1-2 | - | - | 11-16 | 1-2 |
| Charlie Leibrandt | - | - | - | - | - | - | - | - | 12-15 | - | - | 1-5 | 12 15 |
| Rick Luecken | - | - | - | - | - | - | - | - | - | - | - | 7-12 | - |
| Mike Macfarlane | 16-18 | - | - | - | - | - | - | - | - | 2-1 | - | - | 18-19 |
| Larry McWilliams | - | - | - | - | - | - | - | - | 2-3 | - | - | 1-2 | 2-3 |
| Jeff Montgomery | - | - | - | - | - | - | - | - | - | - | - | 43-20 | - |
| Rey Palacios | 0-1 | 1-3 | - | 0-3 | - | - | - | - | - | - | - | - | 1-7 |
| Bill Pecota | - | - | 4-0 | 1-0 | 8-10 | 2-0 | - | - | - | - | - | - | 15-10 |
| Bret Saberhagen | - | - | - | - | - | - | - | - | 29-6 | - | - | 0-1 | 29-6 |
| Jeff Schulz | - | - | - | - | - | 0-1 | - | - | - | - | - | - | 0-1 |
| Kevin Seitzer | - | - | - | 91-67 | - | 0-1 | - | - | - | - | 21-16 | - | 91-68 |
| Kurt Stillwell | - | - | - | - | 74-50 | - | - | - | - | - | 23-12 | - | 74-50 |
| Pat Tabler | - | 8-6 | - | - | - | 11-12 | - | 15-15 | - | 19-17 | - | - | 53-50 |
| Danny Tartabull | - | - | - | - | - | - | - | 47-24 | - | 30-25 | - | - | 77-49 |
| Gary Thurman | - | - | - | - | - | 4-3 | 7-3 | 1-3 | - | - | 4-2 | - | 12-9 |
| Brad Wellman | - | - | 14-18 | - | 10-10 | - | - | - | - | - | - | - | 24-28 |
| Frank White | - | - | 74-52 | - | - | - | - | - | - | - | - | - | 74-52 |
| Willie Wilson | - | - | - | - | - | - | 51-44 | - | - | - | 32-29 | - | 51-44 |
| Matt Winters | - | - | - | - | - | - | - | 12-11 | - | 2-0 | - | - | 14-11 |

## Batting vs. Left and Right Handed Pitchers

| | | BA | Rank | SA | Rank | OBA | Rank | HR % | Rank | BB % | Rank | SO % | Rank |
|---|---|---|---|---|---|---|---|---|---|---|---|---|---|
| Bob Boone | vs. Lefties | .289 | 50 | .330 | 136 | .408 | 10 | 0.00 | 134 | 15.45 | 8 | 3.25 | 5 |
| | vs. Righties | .269 | 67 | .321 | 132 | .331 | 72 | 0.32 | 152 | 8.67 | 68 | 9.54 | 36 |
| George Brett | vs. Lefties | .222 | 147 | .323 | 138 | .296 | 130 | 1.20 | 111 | 8.99 | 60 | 8.99 | 44 |
| | vs. Righties | .317 | 8 | .493 | 16 | .398 | 8 | 3.45 | 38 | 12.39 | 17 | 8.85 | 31 |
| Bill Buckner | vs. Lefties | .348 | -- | .391 | -- | .375 | -- | 0.00 | -- | 4.17 | -- | 4.17 | -- |
| | vs. Righties | .196 | 163 | .248 | 166 | .220 | 169 | 0.65 | 141 | 3.13 | 165 | 6.25 | 10 |
| Jim Eisenreich | vs. Lefties | .336 | 13 | .430 | 48 | .360 | 46 | 1.87 | 83 | 3.54 | 155 | 8.85 | 43 |
| | vs. Righties | .280 | 46 | .454 | 33 | .336 | 64 | 1.90 | 84 | 8.13 | 82 | 8.37 | 27 |
| Bo Jackson | vs. Lefties | .266 | 84 | .492 | 22 | .365 | 37 | 5.47 | 12 | 12.16 | 27 | 28.38 | 167 |
| | vs. Righties | .253 | 98 | .496 | 15 | .291 | 132 | 6.46 | 4 | 5.08 | 149 | 31.48 | 170 |
| Mike Macfarlane | vs. Lefties | .172 | 168 | .203 | 172 | .197 | 172 | 0.00 | 134 | 3.03 | 160 | 18.18 | 131 |
| | vs. Righties | .258 | -- | .366 | -- | .307 | -- | 2.15 | -- | 4.95 | -- | 14.85 | -- |
| Kevin Seitzer | vs. Lefties | .257 | 103 | .343 | 126 | .387 | 22 | 1.71 | 86 | 16.82 | 3 | 8.41 | 39 |
| | vs. Righties | .291 | 28 | .334 | 118 | .387 | 13 | 0.24 | 157 | 13.17 | 13 | 11.58 | 65 |
| Kurt Stillwell | vs. Lefties | .264 | 85 | .364 | 106 | .336 | 79 | 0.83 | 121 | 8.15 | 71 | 8.15 | 34 |
| | vs. Righties | .260 | 84 | .386 | 73 | .321 | 90 | 1.75 | 88 | 8.14 | 80 | 13.91 | 83 |
| Pat Tabler | vs. Lefties | .350 | 6 | .413 | 65 | .407 | 11 | 1.25 | 107 | 8.38 | 67 | 3.91 | 9 |
| | vs. Righties | .196 | 164 | .235 | 167 | .268 | 155 | 0.00 | 158 | 8.63 | 69 | 13.73 | 80 |
| Danny Tartabull | vs. Lefties | .312 | 26 | .568 | 4 | .420 | 5 | 6.40 | 5 | 15.33 | 9 | 20.67 | 144 |
| | vs. Righties | .250 | 102 | .389 | 72 | .348 | 48 | 3.16 | 46 | 12.60 | 16 | 25.21 | 162 |
| Brad Wellman | vs. Lefties | .281 | 61 | .344 | 125 | .313 | 104 | 1.56 | 91 | 2.94 | 162 | 14.71 | 107 |
| | vs. Righties | .202 | -- | .254 | -- | .235 | -- | 0.88 | -- | 4.13 | -- | 21.49 | -- |
| Frank White | vs. Lefties | .240 | 126 | .296 | 152 | .307 | 112 | 0.00 | 134 | 8.76 | 62 | 5.11 | 14 |
| | vs. Righties | .263 | 79 | .341 | 112 | .307 | 110 | 0.68 | 139 | 5.61 | 138 | 14.02 | 84 |
| Willie Wilson | vs. Lefties | .276 | 72 | .398 | 77 | .306 | 115 | 0.81 | 122 | 5.15 | 135 | 19.12 | 136 |
| | vs. Righties | .242 | 116 | .338 | 114 | .297 | 120 | 0.77 | 135 | 6.97 | 108 | 18.12 | 127 |
| Team Average | vs. Lefties | .273 | 6 | .382 | 8 | .348 | 2 | 1.77 | 12 | 9.84 | 1 | 12.16 | 5 |
| | vs. Righties | .256 | 10 | .369 | 11 | .321 | 9 | 1.88 | 13 | 8.64 | 5 | 15.63 | 11 |
| League Average | vs. Lefties | .266 | | .391 | | .328 | | 2.18 | | 8.18 | | 13.58 | |
| | vs. Righties | .258 | | .380 | | .325 | | 2.26 | | 8.56 | | 14.57 | |

## Batting with Runners on Base and Bases Empty

| | | BA | Rank | SA | Rank | OBA | Rank | HR % | Rank | BB % | Rank | SO % | Rank |
|---|---|---|---|---|---|---|---|---|---|---|---|---|---|
| Bob Boone | Runners On | .307 | 31 | .364 | 98 | .371 | 38 | 0.57 | 140 | 9.52 | 67 | 6.67 | 19 |
| | Bases Empty | .249 | 101 | .293 | 155 | .336 | 50 | 0.00 | 153 | 11.20 | 23 | 8.88 | 27 |
| George Brett | Runners On | .285 | 58 | .413 | 59 | .359 | 54 | 2.48 | 62 | 10.56 | 50 | 9.15 | 46 |
| | Bases Empty | .279 | 42 | .451 | 31 | .365 | 18 | 2.79 | 63 | 11.89 | 17 | 8.61 | 26 |
| Jim Eisenreich | Runners On | .326 | 14 | .492 | 18 | .382 | 28 | 2.59 | 56 | 9.09 | 73 | 8.64 | 41 |
| | Bases Empty | .270 | 55 | .418 | 54 | .311 | 99 | 1.42 | 107 | 5.69 | 132 | 8.36 | 23 |
| Bo Jackson | Runners On | .248 | 118 | .508 | 13 | .318 | 109 | 6.69 | 5 | 8.74 | 79 | 27.62 | 172 |
| | Bases Empty | .264 | 66 | .483 | 11 | .302 | 111 | 5.75 | 9 | 5.09 | 143 | 33.82 | 171 |
| Kevin Seitzer | Runners On | .294 | 45 | .333 | 138 | .416 | 7 | 0.00 | 146 | 17.63 | 8 | 7.46 | 24 |
| | Bases Empty | .273 | 50 | .339 | 116 | .367 | 17 | 1.09 | 118 | 11.90 | 16 | 12.86 | 68 |
| Kurt Stillwell | Runners On | .308 | 29 | .443 | 45 | .355 | 59 | 1.49 | 99 | 7.11 | 112 | 9.33 | 49 |
| | Bases Empty | .225 | 134 | .332 | 124 | .302 | 110 | 1.53 | 101 | 8.93 | 50 | 14.78 | 94 |
| Pat Tabler | Runners On | .270 | 83 | .341 | 134 | .325 | 100 | 1.08 | 116 | 6.80 | 115 | 7.77 | 26 |
| | Bases Empty | .249 | 103 | .278 | 160 | .325 | 69 | 0.00 | 153 | 10.09 | 32 | 11.40 | 56 |
| Danny Tartabull | Runners On | .234 | 142 | .355 | 116 | .352 | 63 | 2.54 | 58 | 15.25 | 13 | 22.88 | 156 |
| | Bases Empty | .295 | 23 | .508 | 7 | .384 | 9 | 5.33 | 13 | 11.83 | 18 | 24.73 | 162 |
| Frank White | Runners On | .281 | 68 | .346 | 127 | .337 | 81 | 0.00 | 146 | 7.62 | 102 | 12.38 | 86 |
| | Bases Empty | .236 | 121 | .313 | 138 | .282 | 143 | 0.86 | 128 | 5.65 | 134 | 10.48 | 45 |
| Willie Wilson | Runners On | .256 | 107 | .359 | 110 | .287 | 148 | 0.64 | 138 | 4.52 | 154 | 16.95 | 131 |
| | Bases Empty | .251 | 95 | .357 | 101 | .309 | 101 | 0.88 | 126 | 7.72 | 84 | 19.51 | 131 |
| Team Average | Runners On | .271 | 6 | .377 | 12 | .342 | 4 | 1.77 | 13 | 9.71 | 4 | 13.34 | 6 |
| | Bases Empty | .253 | 8 | .369 | 9 | .319 | 6 | 1.90 | 12 | 8.41 | 4 | 15.63 | 11 |
| League Average | Runners On | .268 | | .389 | | .336 | | 2.15 | | 9.17 | | 13.53 | |
| | Bases Empty | .255 | | .380 | | .317 | | 2.29 | | 7.84 | | 14.86 | |

## Overall Batting Compared to Late Inning Pressure Situations

| | | BA | Rank | SA | Rank | OBA | Rank | HR % | Rank | BB % | Rank | SO % | Rank | RDI % | Rank |
|---|---|---|---|---|---|---|---|---|---|---|---|---|---|---|---|
| Bob Boone | Overall | .274 | 48 | .323 | 144 | .351 | 40 | 0.25 | 161 | 10.45 | 36 | 7.89 | 21 | .315 | 35 |
| | Pressure | .345 | 10 | .382 | 74 | .403 | 19 | 0.00 | 107 | 7.69 | 103 | 6.15 | 11 | .462 | 8 |
| George Brett | Overall | .282 | 39 | .431 | 41 | .362 | 27 | 2.63 | 62 | 11.17 | 25 | 8.90 | 33 | .352 | 14 |
| | Pressure | .288 | 51 | .390 | 69 | .391 | 26 | 1.69 | 86 | 14.49 | 19 | 10.14 | 32 | .320 | 51 |
| Bill Buckner | Overall | .216 | -- | .267 | -- | .240 | -- | 0.57 | -- | 3.26 | -- | 5.98 | -- | .224 | -- |
| | Pressure | .297 | 41 | .351 | 93 | .325 | 81 | 0.00 | 107 | 5.00 | 142 | 5.00 | 4 | .143 | 137 |
| Jim Eisenreich | Overall | .293 | 29 | .448 | 30 | .341 | 52 | 1.89 | 88 | 7.13 | 104 | 8.48 | 27 | .299 | 44 |
| | Pressure | .207 | 127 | .293 | 126 | .324 | 83 | 1.72 | 83 | 14.71 | 16 | 7.35 | 16 | .286 | 68 |
| Bo Jackson | Overall | .256 | 98 | .495 | 9 | .310 | 108 | 6.21 | 6 | 6.95 | 109 | 30.66 | 171 | .326 | 27 |
| | Pressure | .247 | 94 | .438 | 41 | .304 | 104 | 5.48 | 18 | 7.59 | 106 | 34.18 | 163 | .048 | 164 |
| Mike Macfarlane | Overall | .223 | -- | .299 | -- | .263 | -- | 1.27 | -- | 4.19 | -- | 16.17 | -- | .372 | -- |
| | Pressure | .172 | 155 | .172 | 166 | .200 | 166 | 0.00 | 107 | 3.33 | 152 | 20.00 | 120 | .333 | -- |
| Kevin Seitzer | Overall | .281 | 41 | .337 | 129 | .387 | 10 | 0.67 | 142 | 14.27 | 10 | 10.63 | 55 | .263 | 87 |
| | Pressure | .324 | 20 | .365 | 82 | .432 | 9 | 0.00 | 107 | 14.29 | 20 | 12.09 | 44 | .300 | 63 |
| Kurt Stillwell | Overall | .261 | 82 | .380 | 88 | .325 | 82 | 1.51 | 105 | 8.14 | 82 | 12.40 | 70 | .296 | 47 |
| | Pressure | .207 | 127 | .241 | 149 | .288 | 123 | 0.00 | 107 | 10.29 | 61 | 17.65 | 101 | .154 | 132 |
| Pat Tabler | Overall | .259 | 86 | .308 | 156 | .325 | 83 | 0.51 | 146 | 8.53 | 71 | 9.68 | 45 | .246 | 118 |
| | Pressure | .297 | 42 | .391 | 68 | .338 | 68 | 1.56 | 91 | 5.71 | 132 | 14.29 | 63 | .217 | 108 |
| Danny Tartabull | Overall | .268 | 65 | .440 | 34 | .369 | 19 | 4.08 | 23 | 13.40 | 15 | 23.88 | 159 | .267 | 79 |
| | Pressure | .373 | 5 | .610 | 3 | .479 | 3 | 6.78 | 6 | 15.49 | 13 | 23.94 | 143 | .500 | 5 |
| Frank White | Overall | .256 | 99 | .328 | 140 | .307 | 112 | 0.48 | 149 | 6.55 | 117 | 11.35 | 61 | .281 | 65 |
| | Pressure | .236 | 101 | .327 | 109 | .300 | 107 | 1.82 | 80 | 8.06 | 93 | 11.29 | 41 | .364 | 32 |
| Willie Wilson | Overall | .253 | 105 | .358 | 115 | .300 | 130 | 0.78 | 139 | 6.38 | 121 | 18.44 | 130 | .296 | 48 |
| | Pressure | .208 | 124 | .354 | 90 | .264 | 139 | 2.08 | 73 | 7.02 | 113 | 17.54 | 100 | .313 | 56 |
| Matt Winters | Overall | .234 | -- | .346 | -- | .320 | -- | 1.87 | -- | 11.48 | -- | 18.85 | -- | .189 | -- |
| | Pressure | .150 | -- | .200 | -- | .227 | -- | 0.00 | -- | 9.09 | -- | 31.82 | -- | .125 | 143 |
| Team Average | Overall | .261 | 7 | .373 | 12 | .329 | 5 | 1.84 | 13 | 9.01 | 5 | 14.58 | 8 | .284 | 2 |
| | Pressure | .264 | 4 | .356 | 7 | .341 | 2 | 1.73 | 11 | 10.08 | 3 | 16.69 | 4 | .271 | 5 |
| League Average | Overall | .261 | | .384 | | .326 | | 2.23 | | 8.44 | | 14.26 | | .269 | |
| | Pressure | .247 | | .357 | | .318 | | 2.02 | | 9.02 | | 17.90 | | .254 | |

## Additional Miscellaneous Batting Comparisons

| | Grass Surface BA | Rank | Artificial Surface BA | Rank | Home Games BA | Rank | Road Games BA | Rank | Runners in Scoring Position BA | Rank | Runners in Scoring Pos and Two Outs BA | Rank | Leading Off Inning OBA | Rank | Runners on 3B with less than 2 Outs RDI % | Rank |
|---|---|---|---|---|---|---|---|---|---|---|---|---|---|---|---|---|
| Luis de los Santos | .310 | -- | .200 | 144 | .222 | -- | .275 | -- | .238 | -- | .300 | -- | .333 | -- | .333 | -- |
| Bob Boone | .239 | 120 | .296 | 36 | .317 | 15 | .233 | 137 | .350 | 8 | .300 | 24 | .308 | 101 | .600 | 67 |
| George Brett | .295 | 25 | .274 | 61 | .275 | 57 | .289 | 33 | .293 | 43 | .245 | 76 | .419 | 7 | .703 | 23 |
| Bill Buckner | .238 | -- | .204 | 143 | .190 | -- | .239 | -- | .214 | -- | .188 | -- | .250 | -- | .667 | 39 |
| Jim Eisenreich | .268 | 65 | .311 | 27 | .307 | 22 | .279 | 50 | .319 | 23 | .236 | 86 | .317 | 93 | .583 | 76 |
| Bo Jackson | .277 | 52 | .242 | 106 | .234 | 129 | .277 | 52 | .263 | 87 | .278 | 37 | .353 | 44 | .571 | 85 |
| Mike Macfarlane | .203 | -- | .241 | 108 | .290 | -- | .179 | -- | .306 | -- | .368 | -- | .200 | -- | .750 | -- |
| Bill Pecota | .286 | -- | .146 | 166 | .158 | -- | .244 | -- | .053 | -- | .125 | -- | .316 | -- | .000 | -- |
| Kevin Seitzer | .246 | 106 | .303 | 30 | .311 | 18 | .252 | 95 | .288 | 51 | .264 | 58 | .318 | 92 | .595 | 70 |
| Kurt Stillwell | .270 | 60 | .255 | 82 | .226 | 139 | .293 | 27 | .292 | 45 | .269 | 49 | .352 | 46 | .615 | 59 |
| Pat Tabler | .256 | 87 | .261 | 73 | .271 | 65 | .249 | 106 | .233 | 126 | .207 | 117 | .296 | 115 | .560 | 95 |
| Danny Tartabull | .240 | 117 | .282 | 52 | .280 | 51 | .256 | 87 | .207 | 153 | .105 | 165 | .368 | 29 | .567 | 88 |
| Gary Thurman | .115 | -- | .230 | 122 | .257 | -- | .154 | -- | .136 | -- | .125 | -- | .314 | -- | .286 | -- |
| Brad Wellman | .288 | -- | .190 | 150 | .163 | -- | .293 | -- | .186 | -- | .083 | 171 | .273 | -- | .600 | 67 |
| Frank White | .291 | 29 | .235 | 118 | .238 | 122 | .274 | 59 | .286 | 55 | .156 | 152 | .341 | 55 | .680 | 33 |
| Willie Wilson | .241 | 114 | .260 | 75 | .269 | 69 | .237 | 131 | .264 | 85 | .265 | 55 | .347 | 51 | .625 | 52 |
| Matt Winters | .217 | -- | .246 | 104 | .234 | -- | .233 | -- | .167 | -- | .000 | -- | .357 | -- | .300 | 169 |
| Team Average | .259 | 8 | .262 | 6 | .263 | 5 | .259 | 8 | .267 | 5 | .228 | 9 | .328 | 4 | .590 | 4 |
| League Average | .260 | | .262 | | .262 | | .259 | | .262 | | .232 | | .321 | | .566 | |

## Pitching vs. Left and Right Handed Batters

| | | BA | Rank | SA | Rank | OBA | Rank | HR % | Rank | BB % | Rank | SO % | Rank |
|---|---|---|---|---|---|---|---|---|---|---|---|---|---|
| Luis Aquino | vs. Lefties | .289 | 101 | .375 | 64 | .344 | 83 | 1.19 | 37 | 8.24 | 59 | 8.96 | 101 |
| | vs. Righties | .256 | 67 | .321 | 26 | .294 | 31 | 1.02 | 14 | 3.85 | 6 | 13.78 | 82 |
| Floyd Bannister | vs. Lefties | .354 | -- | .500 | -- | .404 | -- | 2.08 | -- | 7.55 | -- | 11.32 | -- |
| | vs. Righties | .278 | 104 | .417 | 101 | .316 | 61 | 2.78 | 101 | 5.19 | 22 | 10.74 | 110 |
| Steve Crawford | vs. Lefties | .260 | 66 | .365 | 52 | .333 | 73 | 1.92 | 70 | 10.08 | 92 | 9.24 | 99 |
| | vs. Righties | .223 | -- | .255 | -- | .298 | -- | 0.00 | -- | 6.67 | -- | 20.95 | -- |
| Steve Farr | vs. Lefties | .280 | 92 | .352 | 47 | .333 | 73 | 0.00 | 1 | 7.41 | 47 | 17.78 | 25 |
| | vs. Righties | .313 | -- | .508 | -- | .368 | -- | 3.91 | -- | 8.33 | -- | 22.22 | -- |
| Tom Gordon | vs. Lefties | .218 | 23 | .306 | 27 | .322 | 61 | 1.30 | 41 | 13.26 | 116 | 18.23 | 23 |
| | vs. Righties | .200 | 10 | .305 | 14 | .297 | 36 | 2.18 | 74 | 12.06 | 127 | 27.62 | 6 |
| Mark Gubicza | vs. Lefties | .246 | 46 | .320 | 31 | .299 | 38 | 0.78 | 17 | 6.77 | 37 | 14.62 | 46 |
| | vs. Righties | .274 | 96 | .370 | 59 | .312 | 53 | 1.30 | 25 | 5.01 | 16 | 18.24 | 37 |
| Terry Leach | vs. Lefties | .307 | 113 | .423 | 95 | .391 | 122 | 1.46 | 53 | 12.88 | 115 | 6.13 | 124 |
| | vs. Righties | .250 | 50 | .340 | 37 | .323 | 73 | 1.39 | 30 | 9.09 | 92 | 14.55 | 74 |
| Charlie Leibrandt | vs. Lefties | .338 | 130 | .431 | 98 | .365 | 102 | 0.00 | 1 | 3.60 | 5 | 5.04 | 133 |
| | vs. Righties | .296 | 123 | .442 | 118 | .356 | 124 | 2.53 | 86 | 8.55 | 85 | 11.52 | 102 |
| Jeff Montgomery | vs. Lefties | .211 | 18 | .270 | 14 | .264 | 13 | 1.32 | 42 | 6.71 | 35 | 18.29 | 20 |
| | vs. Righties | .187 | 4 | .236 | 1 | .251 | 4 | 0.55 | 4 | 7.04 | 54 | 32.16 | 4 |
| Bret Saberhagen | vs. Lefties | .195 | 14 | .290 | 22 | .236 | 4 | 1.53 | 54 | 5.17 | 16 | 22.28 | 10 |
| | vs. Righties | .245 | 40 | .350 | 47 | .270 | 10 | 1.14 | 22 | 3.04 | 2 | 14.78 | 68 |
| Team Average | vs. Lefties | .249 | 4 | .344 | 3 | .310 | 3 | 1.36 | 1 | 8.19 | 3 | 14.86 | 2 |
| | vs. Righties | .263 | 9 | .373 | 4 | .317 | 5 | 1.72 | 1 | 6.92 | 3 | 17.06 | 3 |
| League Average | vs. Lefties | .261 | | .382 | | .330 | | 2.16 | | 9.16 | | 13.03 | |
| | vs. Righties | .261 | | .385 | | .323 | | 2.28 | | 7.96 | | 15.09 | |

## Pitching with Runners on Base and Bases Empty

| | | BA | Rank | SA | Rank | OBA | Rank | HR % | Rank | BB % | Rank | SO % | Rank |
|---|---|---|---|---|---|---|---|---|---|---|---|---|---|
| Luis Aquino | Runners On | .281 | 94 | .375 | 70 | .324 | 54 | 1.58 | 53 | 5.05 | 9 | 11.19 | 87 |
| | Bases Empty | .263 | 75 | .321 | 25 | .312 | 58 | 0.68 | 8 | 6.69 | 54 | 11.78 | 90 |
| Floyd Bannister | Runners On | .289 | 109 | .421 | 104 | .336 | 73 | 1.75 | 64 | 6.30 | 21 | 10.24 | 97 |
| | Bases Empty | .290 | 118 | .435 | 109 | .327 | 82 | 3.23 | 106 | 5.10 | 24 | 11.22 | 98 |
| Steve Farr | Runners On | .286 | 104 | .393 | 85 | .362 | 108 | 2.68 | 101 | 11.54 | 108 | 20.00 | 15 |
| | Bases Empty | .305 | 126 | .461 | 118 | .342 | 102 | 1.42 | 27 | 4.70 | 17 | 20.13 | 25 |
| Tom Gordon | Runners On | .274 | 84 | .382 | 77 | .381 | 120 | 1.66 | 60 | 14.68 | 125 | 18.77 | 22 |
| | Bases Empty | .164 | 3 | .252 | 3 | .258 | 10 | 1.76 | 46 | 11.20 | 119 | 25.52 | 8 |
| Mark Gubicza | Runners On | .249 | 41 | .338 | 30 | .309 | 35 | 1.27 | 30 | 7.76 | 48 | 15.74 | 45 |
| | Bases Empty | .266 | 79 | .347 | 42 | .302 | 45 | 0.86 | 14 | 4.60 | 14 | 16.75 | 47 |
| Terry Leach | Runners On | .316 | 124 | .426 | 106 | .390 | 123 | 1.47 | 44 | 11.52 | 107 | 6.67 | 130 |
| | Bases Empty | .241 | 49 | .338 | 37 | .325 | 79 | 1.38 | 25 | 10.43 | 110 | 14.11 | 64 |
| Charlie Leibrandt | Runners On | .312 | 123 | .452 | 122 | .355 | 98 | 2.05 | 77 | 6.75 | 28 | 8.59 | 116 |
| | Bases Empty | .298 | 122 | .429 | 106 | .360 | 120 | 1.99 | 57 | 8.29 | 82 | 11.66 | 93 |
| Jeff Montgomery | Runners On | .164 | 3 | .217 | 2 | .220 | 2 | 0.66 | 8 | 6.06 | 16 | 26.06 | 6 |
| | Bases Empty | .225 | 26 | .280 | 7 | .288 | 29 | 1.10 | 17 | 7.58 | 70 | 25.76 | 7 |
| Bret Saberhagen | Runners On | .208 | 12 | .304 | 14 | .259 | 6 | 1.19 | 27 | 6.38 | 22 | 17.29 | 35 |
| | Bases Empty | .222 | 25 | .325 | 28 | .247 | 4 | 1.44 | 30 | 2.95 | 4 | 19.84 | 28 |
| Team Average | Runners On | .266 | 5 | .372 | 4 | .328 | 6 | 1.62 | 1 | 8.40 | 5 | 14.56 | 5 |
| | Bases Empty | .250 | 4 | .351 | 2 | .303 | 2 | 1.52 | 1 | 6.76 | 3 | 17.28 | 3 |
| League Average | Runners On | .268 | | .389 | | .336 | | 2.15 | | 9.17 | | 13.53 | |
| | Bases Empty | .255 | | .380 | | .317 | | 2.29 | | 7.84 | | 14.86 | |

## Overall Pitching Compared to Late Inning Pressure Situations

| | | BA | Rank | SA | Rank | OBA | Rank | HR % | Rank | BB % | Rank | SO % | Rank |
|---|---|---|---|---|---|---|---|---|---|---|---|---|---|
| Luis Aquino | Overall | .271 | 89 | .346 | 42 | .317 | 55 | 1.10 | 13 | 5.92 | 21 | 11.51 | 92 |
| | Pressure | .226 | 48 | .245 | 16 | .293 | 39 | 0.00 | 1 | 8.47 | 53 | 11.86 | 86 |
| Floyd Bannister | Overall | .290 | 117 | .430 | 105 | .330 | 77 | 2.67 | 99 | 5.57 | 16 | 10.84 | 97 |
| | Pressure | .357 | -- | .571 | -- | .412 | -- | 0.00 | -- | 11.76 | -- | 0.00 | -- |
| Steve Crawford | Overall | .242 | -- | .313 | -- | .317 | -- | 1.01 | -- | 8.48 | -- | 14.73 | -- |
| | Pressure | .160 | 4 | .160 | 2 | .236 | 7 | 0.00 | 1 | 7.14 | 44 | 16.07 | 54 |
| Steve Farr | Overall | .296 | 123 | .431 | 106 | .351 | 108 | 1.98 | 62 | 7.89 | 63 | 20.07 | 21 |
| | Pressure | .284 | 95 | .459 | 111 | .331 | 73 | 3.67 | 112 | 6.78 | 41 | 22.88 | 20 |
| Tom Gordon | Overall | .210 | 13 | .306 | 14 | .311 | 42 | 1.72 | 47 | 12.70 | 125 | 22.60 | 10 |
| | Pressure | .188 | 15 | .282 | 31 | .296 | 42 | 1.18 | 46 | 13.00 | 109 | 28.50 | 7 |
| Mark Gubicza | Overall | .259 | 65 | .343 | 38 | .305 | 33 | 1.03 | 12 | 5.94 | 22 | 16.32 | 43 |
| | Pressure | .230 | 51 | .296 | 39 | .262 | 20 | 0.00 | 1 | 4.14 | 12 | 14.48 | 66 |
| Terry Leach | Overall | .278 | 99 | .381 | 72 | .357 | 118 | 1.42 | 27 | 10.98 | 113 | 10.37 | 103 |
| | Pressure | .097 | 1 | .129 | 1 | .317 | 64 | 0.00 | 1 | 20.45 | 133 | 15.91 | 56 |
| Charlie Leibrandt | Overall | .304 | 128 | .439 | 118 | .358 | 121 | 2.02 | 64 | 7.58 | 55 | 10.25 | 104 |
| | Pressure | .271 | 90 | .313 | 43 | .386 | 109 | 0.00 | 1 | 15.52 | 121 | 5.17 | 127 |
| Richard Luecken | Overall | .258 | -- | .416 | -- | .353 | -- | 3.37 | -- | 12.50 | -- | 15.38 | -- |
| | Pressure | .300 | 114 | .400 | 94 | .417 | 119 | 0.00 | 1 | 15.79 | 122 | 10.53 | 105 |
| Jeff Montgomery | Overall | .198 | 5 | .251 | 2 | .257 | 2 | 0.90 | 7 | 6.89 | 42 | 25.90 | 5 |
| | Pressure | .212 | 38 | .280 | 29 | .261 | 19 | 1.06 | 43 | 5.88 | 29 | 28.92 | 6 |
| Bret Saberhagen | Overall | .217 | 15 | .317 | 19 | .251 | 1 | 1.35 | 22 | 4.21 | 4 | 18.90 | 27 |
| | Pressure | .222 | 45 | .356 | 75 | .274 | 24 | 2.96 | 102 | 6.00 | 31 | 10.67 | 103 |
| Team Average | Overall | .257 | 6 | .360 | 4 | .314 | 4 | 1.56 | 1 | 7.48 | 2 | 16.08 | 3 |
| | Pressure | .224 | 2 | .314 | 1 | .296 | 2 | 1.33 | 1 | 8.86 | 5 | 19.26 | 4 |
| League Average | Overall | .261 | | .384 | | .326 | | 2.23 | | 8.44 | | 14.26 | |
| | Pressure | .250 | | .362 | | .325 | | 2.14 | | 9.50 | | 16.61 | |

## Additional Miscellaneous Pitching Comparisons

| | Grass Surface | | Artificial Surface | | Home Games | | Road Games | | Runners in Scoring Position | | Runners in Scoring Pos and Two Outs | | Leading Off Inning | |
|---|---|---|---|---|---|---|---|---|---|---|---|---|---|---|
| | BA | Rank | BA | Rank | BA | Rank | BA | Rank | BA | Rank | BA | Rank | OBA | Rank |
| Luis Aquino | .267 | 81 | .274 | 76 | .253 | 69 | .286 | 96 | .278 | 96 | .300 | 116 | .317 | 59 |
| Floyd Bannister | .281 | -- | .292 | 96 | .280 | 103 | .305 | 121 | .286 | 106 | .273 | 103 | .321 | 66 |
| Steve Crawford | .284 | -- | .218 | 20 | .261 | -- | .226 | 28 | .250 | 62 | .226 | 67 | .292 | -- |
| Steve Farr | .313 | -- | .289 | 94 | .252 | 67 | .351 | 133 | .261 | 80 | .290 | 112 | .286 | 33 |
| Tom Gordon | .244 | 43 | .197 | 11 | .216 | 16 | .201 | 8 | .288 | 108 | .246 | 87 | .264 | 20 |
| Mark Gubicza | .253 | 61 | .262 | 61 | .259 | 78 | .259 | 67 | .223 | 25 | .190 | 43 | .315 | 56 |
| Terry Leach | .311 | -- | .253 | 51 | .252 | 66 | .306 | 123 | .337 | 128 | .275 | 105 | .356 | 105 |
| Charlie Leibrandt | .316 | 131 | .295 | 101 | .297 | 121 | .309 | 124 | .259 | 78 | .200 | 48 | .327 | 75 |
| Richard Luecken | .276 | -- | .250 | 49 | .275 | -- | .245 | -- | .188 | -- | .176 | -- | .333 | -- |
| Larry McWilliams | .263 | -- | .246 | 46 | .246 | -- | .263 | -- | .250 | -- | .250 | -- | .382 | -- |
| Jeff Montgomery | .198 | -- | .197 | 12 | .185 | 2 | .211 | 12 | .163 | 4 | .205 | 50 | .301 | 43 |
| Bret Saberhagen | .220 | 19 | .215 | 18 | .208 | 12 | .227 | 30 | .224 | 26 | .218 | 64 | .264 | 20 |
| Team Average | .266 | 10 | .252 | 5 | .248 | 3 | .266 | 9 | .253 | 3 | .233 | 8 | .313 | 4 |
| League Average | .260 | | .262 | | .259 | | .262 | | .262 | | .232 | | .321 | |

# MILWAUKEE BREWERS

- **The first challenger for Pete Rose's hits record.**
- **Yount a deserving MVP? You bet!**

Of all the lessons that we learn from sports, the primary one should be "Never say never." We have seen Clay whup Liston, the U.S. hockey team beat the Soviets, and the Dodgers defeat the A's. The Jets smothered the Colts, Temperence Hill won the Belmont at 50–1, and Trumbull, Connecticut upset the boys from Taipei. And yet we sports fans fall for it every single time. Here's a typical scenario:

Let's say there's a player, call him Ty Cobb, who holds an all-time record of long standing and significant interest. Call that record "Most Hits, Career." Then let's say that the record is challenged and surpassed by some contemporary player called, oh, Pete Rose (Peter Edward Rose to you, Judge Norbert A. Nadel). All of us will immediately jump to our feet, and after we're through applauding, we'll shout in unison, "Nobody will ever break that baby. That's one record that will stand forever." Happens every time.

Stay tuned to any sports talk show long enough, and you'll hear the question asked, "Which record do you think will never be broken?" The most frequently given answers seem to be Joe DiMaggio's 56–game hitting streak and Lou Gehrig's 2130–game playing streak. And certainly those records have remained intact for a long time. But they are not *unbreakable;* they just haven't been broken. Nothing is so different about the way the game is played today than it was in DiMaggio's or Gehrig's days that would prevent modern-day players from approaching those records. If the same question were asked 50 years ago, the list of responses might have included Babe Ruth's 714 home runs, Cobb's 892 stolen bases or 4191 hits, or Walter Johnson's 3508 strikeouts. Twenty years ago, there were similar noises about Maury Wills's 104 stolen bases in a season and Don Drysdale's 58 consecutive scoreless innings being "unbreakable."

But even though we have seen all of these records broken since 1974, we still don't learn from the experience. Sometimes, the record-challenger is right before our eyes, yet we don't see him. Some didn't take Aaron's pursuit of Ruth's home–run record seriously until he reached six hundred, or even seven hundred. Rose looked like he was on the ropes in the mid-eighties after falling into platoon status with the Phillies and the Expos, but then he became manager of the Reds and as if by wizardry his name appeared on the lineup card every day. Now, even as some are regarding Rose's record of 4256 hits as unassailable, the challenger may be in our midst. His name: Robin Yount.

Yount has had only one 200–hit season in his career, has played in the All-Star Game only three times, and hasn't been named an All-Star in the past six years. But he may not need 200–hit seasons to challenge Rose's record because of his early start in the big leagues. He broke into the majors as Milwaukee's regular shortstop at the age of 18 and played in 243 games as a teenager, the most by anyone in major league history. Yount collected his first major league hit, a single off Dave McNally, on April 12, 1974, four days after Aaron broke Ruth's home–run record. When he stroked his 2500th hit last season, he became the fifth-youngest player in history to reach that milestone:

| | Birthdate | Hit No. 2500 | Yrs, Mos |
|---|---|---|---|
| Ty Cobb | 12/18/1886 | 8/16/18 | 31, 7 |
| Rogers Hornsby | 4/27/1896 | 5/7/29 | 33, 0 |
| Hank Aaron | 2/5/34 | 6/12/67 | 33, 4 |
| Mel Ott | 3/2/09 | 8/30/42 | 33, 5 |
| Robin Yount | 9/16/55 | 7/2/89 | 33, 9 |

As of the start of the 1990 season, Robin owned 2602 hits and one of those new, three-million-per-year contracts, not necessarily in that order. At the age of 34, Yount stands 1,654 hits shy of Rose's mark—a substantial distance, certainly, but not one that can be dismissed out of hand. If conditions are right—freedom from injuries, strikes, and lockouts, continued productivity, the desire or need to play for big bucks at an advanced age, and most importantly, the Rose-like desire to pursue a goal—Yount could approach Rose's "unapproachable" record by the year 2000.

In suggesting that Yount could challenge the record, we are not saying that we think that he'll *set* it. Even Rose himself was not odds-on to break Cobb's record until much later in his career. For years, challengers to Babe Ruth's mark of 60 home runs in a season ran ahead of the Babe's pace of homers, but fell by the wayside during September, when Ruth hit 17 home runs. Rose was able to catch Cobb in career hits precisely because there is no such time limit on career records; he was able to extend the "September" of his career indefinitely until the record was broken. The amazing part of Rose's career is not that he got so many hits; it's that he played in so many games. When someone plays in 250 more games and accumulates nearly 1700 more at–bats than anyone else, should it be a surprise when he also accumulates the most hits?

Perhaps a chart will put things into focus. Cobb was born on December 18, 1886. Rose's birthdate is officially listed as April 14, 1941, and although that date was a source of dispute long before his gambling was, that's the one we'll go with here. Yount was born on September 16, 1955. For each player, we have listed below two figures corresponding to each age. The first is the number of hits that he had that season; the second, in parentheses, is his career total of hits through that season. (Rose's birthday occurs early in the baseball season, and Yount's late, but for clarity we have counted all of each player's hits under whatever age he was for most of that season. For example, Yount had 86 hits in the 1974 season, during which he turned 19 in September.)

| Age | Cobb | Rose | Yount |
|---|---|---|---|
| 18 | 36 (36) | | 86 (86) |
| 19 | 112 (148) | | 149 (235) |
| 20 | 212 (360) | | 161 (396) |
| 21 | 188 (548) | | 174 (570) |
| 22 | 216 (764) | 170 (170) | 147 (717) |
| 23 | 196 (960) | 139 (309) | 154 (871) |
| 24 | 248 (1208) | 209 (518) | 179 (1050) |
| 25 | 227 (1435) | 205 (723) | ** 103 (1153) |
| 26 | 167 (1602) | 176 (899) | 210 (1363) |
| 27 | 127 (1729) | 210 (1109) | 178 (1541) |
| 28 | 208 (1937) | 218 (1327) | 186 (1727) |
| 29 | 201 (2138) | 205 (1532) | 129 (1856) |
| 30 | 225 (2363) | 192 (1724) | 163 (2019) |
| 31 | * 161 (2524) | 198 (1922) | 198 (2217) |
| 32 | 191 (2715) | 230 (2152) | 190 (2407) |
| 33 | 143 (2858) | 185 (2337) | 195 (2602) |
| 34 | 197 (3055) | 210 (2547) | |
| 35 | 211 (3266) | 215 (2762) | |
| 36 | 189 (3455) | 204 (2966) | |
| 37 | 211 (3666) | 198 (3164) | |
| 38 | 157 (3823) | 208 (3372) | |
| 39 | 79 (3902) | 185 (3557) | |
| 40 | 175 (4077) | ** 140 (3697) | |
| 41 | 114 (4191) | 172 (3869) | |
| 42 | | 121 (3990) | |
| 43 | | 107 (4097) | |
| 44 | | 107 (4204) | |
| 45 | | 52 (4256) | |

* 1918 season shortened by war.
** 1981 season interrupted by strike.

Yount started his career with a 570–hit "head start" over Rose. He has used up 305 of those hits, and his current total is still 265 more than Rose had at the same age. But the next six years (playing at ages 34 through 39) is where Rose really kicked into high gear. Batting in the leadoff spot and playing virtually every game, Pete had 1220 hits over those six seasons, an average of 203.3 per year. Yount, who usually hits third or fourth in the Milwaukee lineup, is unlikely to match that pace, but that's no shame. Only one player in history had more hits at the corresponding ages (again using full-season hit totals to roughly correspond with birthdays), and only 10 have even reached 1000:

| | | |
|---|---|---|
| Sam Rice | 1,239 | 1924–29 |
| Pete Rose | 1,220 | 1975–80 |
| Zack Wheat | 1,138 | 1920–25 |
| Bill Terry | 1,078 | 1931–36 |
| Tris Speaker | 1,048 | 1922–27 |
| Doc Cramer | 1,046 | 1940–45 |
| Ty Cobb | 1,044 | 1921–26 |
| Eddie Collins | 1,023 | 1921–26 |
| Cap Anson | 1,019 | 1886–91 |
| Honus Wagner | 1,010 | 1908–13 |

Among players who started their careers after World War II, only one player besides Rose has had as many as 900 hits between ages 34 and 39 (using full-season totals generally corresponding to those birthdays): Jose Cruz had 917.

But Yount is on a roll; he is one of seven players to have batted .300 or higher in each of the past four years. He has had 190 or more hits for three straight seasons, missing only six games over that span. With the right conditions, he could average 175 hits over each of the next four seasons, and maybe 150 for the two after that. That would leave him with 3,602 hits as he heads toward spring training 1996, at the age of 40.

From this point on, it would be a matter of "wanting it." Rose used the carrot-on-a-stick technique very effectively as he climbed up the all-time hits ladder. He focused first on 2000, then 3000, then Stan Musial's National League record of 3,630. He rarely mentioned Cobb during this period, but once past Musial, he bore down on 4191. This single-minded pursuit of an individual record might be the most difficult part of the package for Yount, who, if he possesses any degree of single-mindedness, seems to reserve it for chasing a World Series ring. Rose, on the other hand, often paid an incongruous brand of lip-service to team goals by acknowledging them through the definition of his individual goals. "I can help my team win by leading the league in hits (or runs, or doubles)," he was fond of saying. That was certainly true, but it has a chicken-or-egg quality to it with regard to priorities. One other difference: Yount is a man with stated outside interests (playing golf and racing automobiles come to mind), making him much more of a Renaissance man—in sports terms, anyway—than Rose ever pretended to be.

While Yount may or may not approach Rose's hits record, he has already surpassed Pete in another category: Most Valuable Player Awards. Yount won his second one last season, beating out Ruben Sierra, Cal Ripken, and George Bell in a close decision that was not universally acclaimed. We saw several commentators bemoan the lack of a "true" MVP candidate in the American League last season, while claiming that Yount did not have a good enough season to merit selection from a fourth-place team that finished at 81–81.

Not a good enough season? Yount batted .318 with 101 runs, 195 hits, 21 home runs, 103 RBI, and 19 stolen bases. We decided to look back at the 1980s to see how many other players had a year in which they met Yount's totals in each of those categories. There was one. Then we looked back through all of baseball history to find the same thing. We found three other players, one who did it twice. The complete list:

| | BA | R | H | HR | RBI | SB |
|---|---|---|---|---|---|---|
| Babe Herman, 1929 Dodgers | .381 | 105 | 217 | 21 | 113 | 21 |
| Chuck Klein, 1932 Phillies | .348 | 152 | 226 | 38 | 137 | 20 |
| Hank Aaron, 1961 Braves | .327 | 115 | 197 | 34 | 120 | 21 |
| Hank Aaron, 1963 Braves | .319 | 121 | 201 | 44 | 130 | 31 |
| Alan Trammell, 1987 Tigers | .343 | 109 | 205 | 28 | 105 | 21 |
| Robin Yount, 1989 Brewers | .318 | 101 | 195 | 21 | 103 | 19 |

Just for fun, we checked through baseball history to see how many players enjoyed seasons in which they matched the statistics of Yount's competitors in each of those categories. The answers: 23 matched Sierra; 162 matched Bell; 351 matched Ripken. Case closed on the MVP Award; now on to bigger and better things.

## WON-LOST RECORD BY STARTING POSITION

| MILWAUKEE 81-81 | C | 1B | 2B | 3B | SS | LF | CF | RF | P | DH | Leadoff | Relief | Starts |
|---|---|---|---|---|---|---|---|---|---|---|---|---|---|
| Jay Aldrich | - | - | - | - | - | - | - | - | - | - | - | 7-9 | - |
| Don August | - | - | - | - | - | - | - | - | 11-14 | - | - | 3-3 | 11-14 |
| Billy Bates | - | -- | 1-2 | - | - | - | - | - | - | - | - | - | 1-2 |
| Mike Birkbeck | - | - | - | - | - | - | - | - | 3-6 | - | - | - | 3-6 |
| Chris Bosio | - | - | - | - | - | - | - | - | 18-15 | - | - | - | 18-15 |
| Glenn Braggs | - | - | - | - | - | 60-57 | - | 4-2 | - | 7-6 | - | - | 71-65 |
| Greg Brock | - | 45-48 | - | - | - | - | - | - | - | 4-3 | - | - | 49-51 |
| George Canale | - | 4-3 | - | - | - | - | - | - | - | - | - | - | 4-3 |
| Juan Castillo | - | - | 2-0 | - | - | - | - | - | - | - | - | - | 2-0 |
| Bryan Clutterbuck | - | - | - | - | - | - | - | - | 6-5 | - | - | 0-3 | 6-5 |
| Chuck Crim | - | - | - | - | - | - | - | - | - | - | - | 36-40 | - |
| Rob Deer | - | - | - | - | - | - | - | 58-65 | - | 1-3 | - | - | 59-68 |
| Dave Engle | - | 10-5 | - | - | - | - | - | - | - | 0-2 | - | - | 10-7 |
| Mike Felder | - | - | 4-1 | - | - | 10-13 | 10-9 | 18-10 | - | 1-3 | 15-12 | - | 43-36 |
| Tom Filer | - | - | - | - | - | - | - | - | 8-5 | - | - | - | 8-5 |
| Tony Fossas | - | - | - | - | - | - | - | - | - | - | - | 20-31 | - |
| Terry Francona | - | 13-19 | - | - | - | - | - | 1-4 | - | 10-11 | - | 0-1 | 24-34 |
| Lavel Freeman | - | - | - | - | - | - | - | - | - | 0-1 | - | - | 0-1 |
| Jim Gantner | - | - | 54-55 | - | - | - | - | - | - | 0-2 | 0-1 | - | 54-57 |
| Ted Higuera | - | - | - | - | - | - | - | - | 14-8 | - | - | - | 14-8 |
| Mark Knudson | - | - | - | - | - | - | - | - | 6-1 | - | - | 10-23 | 6-1 |
| Ray Krawczyk | - | - | - | - | - | - | - | - | - | - | - | 0-1 | - |
| Bill Krueger | - | - | - | - | - | - | - | - | 3-2 | - | - | 12-17 | 3-2 |
| Joey Meyer | - | 9-5 | - | - | - | - | - | - | - | 13-17 | - | - | 22-22 |
| Paul Mirabella | - | - | - | - | - | - | - | - | - | - | - | 3-10 | - |
| Paul Molitor | - | - | 7-8 | 59-53 | - | - | - | - | - | 13-15 | 59-60 | - | 79-76 |
| Jaime Navarro | - | - | - | - | - | - | - | - | 6-11 | - | - | 1-1 | 6-11 |
| Charlie O'Brien | 34-27 | - | - | - | - | - | - | - | - | - | - | - | 34-27 |
| Jeff Peterek | - | - | - | - | - | - | - | - | 1-3 | - | - | 0-3 | 1-3 |
| Dan Plesac | - | - | - | - | - | - | - | - | - | - | - | 39-13 | - |
| Gus Polidor | - | - | 10-6 | 7-7 | 8-6 | - | - | - | - | 2-0 | 2-1 | - | 27-19 |
| Jerry Reuss | - | - | - | - | - | - | - | - | 3-4 | - | - | - | 3-4 |
| Ed Romero | - | - | 3-8 | 1-1 | - | - | - | - | - | - | - | - | 4-9 |
| Gary Sheffield | - | - | - | 11-10 | 31-39 | - | - | - | - | 4-0 | - | - | 46-49 |
| Bill Spiers | - | 0-1 | 0-1 | 3-7 | 42-36 | - | - | - | - | 3-1 | 5-7 | - | 48-46 |
| B.J. Surhoff | 47-54 | - | - | 0-3 | - | - | - | - | - | 7-5 | - | - | 54-62 |
| Greg Vaughn | - | - | - | - | - | 11-11 | - | - | - | 8-3 | - | - | 19-14 |
| Randy Veres | - | - | - | - | - | - | - | - | 0-1 | - | - | 0-2 | 0-1 |
| Bill Wegman | - | - | - | - | - | - | - | - | 2-6 | - | - | 0-3 | 2-6 |
| Robin Yount | - | - | - | - | - | - | 71-72 | - | - | 8-9 | - | - | 79-81 |

## Batting vs. Left and Right Handed Pitchers

| | | BA | Rank | SA | Rank | OBA | Rank | HR % | Rank | BB % | Rank | SO % | Rank |
|---|---|---|---|---|---|---|---|---|---|---|---|---|---|
| Glenn Braggs | vs. Lefties | .303 | 37 | .465 | 35 | .365 | 38 | 4.23 | 26 | 9.38 | 55 | 11.25 | 67 |
| | vs. Righties | .226 | 140 | .333 | 119 | .282 | 142 | 2.42 | 67 | 6.59 | 118 | 22.68 | 150 |
| Greg Brock | vs. Lefties | .333 | 14 | .444 | 42 | .388 | 21 | 2.22 | 71 | 6.00 | 113 | 14.00 | 100 |
| | vs. Righties | .244 | 114 | .392 | 66 | .332 | 68 | 3.53 | 34 | 11.49 | 26 | 10.87 | 56 |
| Rob Deer | vs. Lefties | .254 | 108 | .470 | 33 | .340 | 72 | 5.97 | 9 | 11.11 | 31 | 24.18 | 161 |
| | vs. Righties | .193 | 165 | .407 | 56 | .290 | 134 | 5.42 | 11 | 11.35 | 30 | 31.93 | 171 |
| Mike Felder | vs. Lefties | .277 | 71 | .297 | 151 | .336 | 77 | 0.00 | 134 | 8.04 | 72 | 8.04 | 31 |
| | vs. Righties | .224 | 144 | .336 | 116 | .272 | 150 | 1.40 | 107 | 6.01 | 131 | 12.45 | 72 |
| Terry Francona | vs. Lefties | .238 | -- | .333 | -- | .238 | -- | 0.00 | -- | 0.00 | -- | 4.76 | -- |
| | vs. Righties | .231 | 130 | .321 | 133 | .257 | 159 | 1.42 | 105 | 3.59 | 162 | 8.52 | 28 |
| Jim Gantner | vs. Lefties | .274 | 76 | .336 | 129 | .320 | 97 | 0.00 | 134 | 4.88 | 138 | 2.44 | 3 |
| | vs. Righties | .274 | 61 | .331 | 123 | .322 | 87 | 0.00 | 158 | 4.52 | 154 | 9.04 | 34 |
| Joey Meyer | vs. Lefties | .250 | 112 | .389 | 87 | .313 | 106 | 2.78 | 58 | 8.75 | 63 | 13.75 | 95 |
| | vs. Righties | .200 | -- | .427 | -- | .238 | -- | 6.67 | -- | 5.95 | -- | 29.76 | -- |
| Paul Molitor | vs. Lefties | .325 | 19 | .484 | 27 | .413 | 8 | 2.55 | 66 | 13.16 | 18 | 6.84 | 23 |
| | vs. Righties | .312 | 12 | .424 | 46 | .366 | 27 | 1.53 | 102 | 7.71 | 92 | 10.67 | 52 |
| Charlie O'Brien | vs. Lefties | .247 | 120 | .416 | 60 | .337 | 75 | 3.37 | 43 | 7.69 | 81 | 3.85 | 8 |
| | vs. Righties | .222 | -- | .354 | -- | .342 | -- | 3.03 | -- | 10.66 | -- | 5.74 | -- |
| Gus Polidor | vs. Lefties | .176 | 166 | .224 | 170 | .231 | 166 | 0.00 | 134 | 5.38 | 128 | 7.53 | 28 |
| | vs. Righties | .211 | -- | .244 | -- | .228 | -- | 0.00 | -- | 1.08 | -- | 11.83 | -- |
| Ed Romero | vs. Lefties | .167 | -- | .200 | -- | .188 | -- | 0.00 | -- | 2.94 | -- | 2.94 | -- |
| | vs. Righties | .218 | 149 | .263 | 162 | .255 | 160 | 0.00 | 158 | 4.26 | 157 | 11.35 | 62 |
| Gary Sheffield | vs. Lefties | .292 | 48 | .442 | 43 | .336 | 78 | 2.65 | 59 | 6.45 | 102 | 4.84 | 13 |
| | vs. Righties | .227 | 137 | .290 | 151 | .289 | 136 | 0.78 | 134 | 6.76 | 111 | 9.61 | 40 |
| Bill Spiers | vs. Lefties | .271 | 80 | .371 | 103 | .282 | 139 | 1.43 | 101 | 1.37 | 168 | 26.03 | 163 |
| | vs. Righties | .251 | 101 | .324 | 130 | .302 | 113 | 1.09 | 127 | 6.67 | 114 | 14.67 | 92 |
| B.j. Surhoff | vs. Lefties | .310 | 29 | .452 | 38 | .314 | 103 | 2.38 | 69 | 0.00 | 170 | 8.14 | 33 |
| | vs. Righties | .233 | 128 | .313 | 135 | .281 | 143 | 0.85 | 129 | 6.39 | 123 | 5.63 | 7 |
| Robin Yount | vs. Lefties | .341 | 11 | .587 | 3 | .395 | 17 | 3.59 | 36 | 7.49 | 86 | 11.76 | 76 |
| | vs. Righties | .309 | 15 | .483 | 19 | .380 | 16 | 3.36 | 41 | 9.74 | 52 | 9.74 | 42 |
| Team Average | vs. Lefties | .284 | 3 | .424 | 2 | .342 | 4 | 2.57 | 2 | 7.48 | 10 | 10.90 | 1 |
| | vs. Righties | .249 | 12 | .366 | 12 | .309 | 14 | 2.20 | 8 | 7.47 | 13 | 13.81 | 3 |
| League Average | vs. Lefties | .266 | | .391 | | .328 | | 2.18 | | 8.18 | | 13.58 | |
| | vs. Righties | .258 | | .380 | | .325 | | 2.26 | | 8.56 | | 14.57 | |

## Batting with Runners on Base and Bases Empty

| | | BA | Rank | SA | Rank | OBA | Rank | HR % | Rank | BB % | Rank | SO % | Rank |
|---|---|---|---|---|---|---|---|---|---|---|---|---|---|
| Glenn Braggs | Runners On | .274 | 81 | .396 | 75 | .312 | 121 | 2.61 | 55 | 5.86 | 131 | 17.58 | 134 |
| | Bases Empty | .225 | 133 | .349 | 107 | .299 | 113 | 3.17 | 52 | 8.60 | 62 | 21.02 | 144 |
| Greg Brock | Runners On | .290 | 51 | .438 | 49 | .373 | 37 | 3.41 | 38 | 11.82 | 35 | 10.84 | 67 |
| | Bases Empty | .244 | 109 | .376 | 90 | .320 | 79 | 3.05 | 56 | 8.68 | 58 | 12.33 | 64 |
| Rob Deer | Runners On | .228 | 151 | .429 | 50 | .316 | 115 | 5.02 | 17 | 10.40 | 55 | 26.00 | 167 |
| | Bases Empty | .194 | 163 | .421 | 52 | .294 | 121 | 6.07 | 8 | 12.06 | 15 | 32.98 | 170 |
| Mike Felder | Runners On | .269 | 86 | .361 | 105 | .326 | 98 | 0.84 | 130 | 7.35 | 106 | 8.09 | 32 |
| | Bases Empty | .224 | 137 | .301 | 150 | .273 | 153 | 1.02 | 120 | 6.22 | 119 | 12.92 | 71 |
| Terry Francona | Runners On | .265 | 93 | .347 | 125 | .308 | 124 | 1.02 | 120 | 6.48 | 120 | 3.70 | 6 |
| | Bases Empty | .207 | 154 | .304 | 148 | .213 | 171 | 1.48 | 104 | 0.74 | 171 | 11.76 | 58 |
| Jim Gantner | Runners On | .287 | 55 | .347 | 126 | .333 | 89 | 0.00 | 146 | 3.93 | 162 | 7.87 | 30 |
| | Bases Empty | .266 | 61 | .324 | 129 | .314 | 93 | 0.00 | 153 | 5.05 | 144 | 6.86 | 10 |
| Paul Molitor | Runners On | .337 | 8 | .422 | 55 | .397 | 19 | 1.01 | 122 | 10.08 | 62 | 8.40 | 39 |
| | Bases Empty | .305 | 16 | .447 | 34 | .369 | 14 | 2.16 | 82 | 8.73 | 56 | 10.26 | 41 |
| Charlie O'Brien | Runners On | .318 | 21 | .511 | 11 | .412 | 8 | 3.41 | 38 | 10.00 | 63 | 3.64 | 5 |
| | Bases Empty | .160 | 171 | .270 | 163 | .276 | 149 | 3.00 | 60 | 8.62 | 61 | 6.03 | 6 |
| Gary Sheffield | Runners On | .229 | 150 | .282 | 163 | .287 | 147 | 0.59 | 139 | 6.81 | 114 | 7.85 | 29 |
| | Bases Empty | .263 | 71 | .384 | 80 | .318 | 83 | 2.02 | 86 | 6.54 | 109 | 8.41 | 24 |
| Bill Spiers | Runners On | .267 | 89 | .370 | 94 | .303 | 126 | 0.74 | 134 | 5.37 | 135 | 16.78 | 128 |
| | Bases Empty | .248 | 105 | .310 | 142 | .295 | 119 | 1.43 | 106 | 5.80 | 129 | 16.96 | 109 |
| B.j. Surhoff | Runners On | .260 | 97 | .354 | 117 | .284 | 151 | 1.10 | 114 | 3.92 | 163 | 2.94 | 1 |
| | Bases Empty | .239 | 120 | .329 | 127 | .289 | 128 | 1.18 | 115 | 6.23 | 118 | 8.42 | 25 |
| Robin Yount | Runners On | .330 | 11 | .505 | 14 | .402 | 16 | 2.46 | 64 | 10.33 | 58 | 9.42 | 51 |
| | Bases Empty | .307 | 15 | .517 | 6 | .368 | 15 | 4.26 | 27 | 8.03 | 75 | 11.08 | 52 |
| Team Average | Runners On | .280 | 4 | .404 | 2 | .338 | 7 | 2.13 | 7 | 7.79 | 14 | 11.40 | 2 |
| | Bases Empty | .243 | 12 | .367 | 13 | .304 | 13 | 2.42 | 5 | 7.24 | 11 | 14.22 | 5 |
| League Average | Runners On | .268 | | .389 | | .336 | | 2.15 | | 9.17 | | 13.53 | |
| | Bases Empty | .255 | | .380 | | .317 | | 2.29 | | 7.84 | | 14.86 | |

## Overall Batting Compared to Late Inning Pressure Situations

| | | BA | Rank | SA | Rank | OBA | Rank | HR % | Rank | BB % | Rank | SO % | Rank | RDI % | Rank |
|---|---|---|---|---|---|---|---|---|---|---|---|---|---|---|---|
| Glenn Braggs | Overall | .247 | 122 | .370 | 101 | .305 | 119 | 2.92 | 57 | 7.37 | 98 | 19.47 | 139 | .272 | 74 |
| | Pressure | .254 | 86 | .358 | 86 | .315 | 94 | 1.49 | 94 | 6.76 | 118 | 22.97 | 138 | .158 | 131 |
| Greg Brock | Overall | .265 | 71 | .405 | 63 | .345 | 48 | 3.22 | 44 | 10.19 | 39 | 11.61 | 62 | .262 | 90 |
| | Pressure | .159 | 157 | .273 | 136 | .275 | 131 | 2.27 | 71 | 13.73 | 27 | 15.69 | 78 | .357 | 34 |
| Rob Deer | Overall | .210 | 165 | .425 | 45 | .305 | 122 | 5.58 | 8 | 11.28 | 24 | 29.70 | 170 | .211 | 150 |
| | Pressure | .210 | 122 | .532 | 12 | .306 | 100 | 8.06 | 3 | 12.50 | 35 | 44.44 | 171 | .250 | 87 |
| Mike Felder | Overall | .241 | 129 | .324 | 143 | .293 | 144 | 0.95 | 131 | 6.67 | 115 | 11.01 | 58 | .200 | 154 |
| | Pressure | .143 | 164 | .333 | 103 | .280 | 125 | 4.76 | 23 | 16.00 | 8 | 14.00 | 62 | .182 | 121 |
| Terry Francona | Overall | .232 | 149 | .322 | 145 | .255 | 169 | 1.29 | 119 | 3.28 | 167 | 8.20 | 25 | .303 | 41 |
| | Pressure | .184 | 147 | .211 | 158 | .205 | 165 | 0.00 | 107 | 2.56 | 160 | 5.13 | 5 | .125 | 143 |
| Jim Gantner | Overall | .274 | 50 | .333 | 135 | .321 | 88 | 0.00 | 166 | 4.62 | 158 | 7.25 | 14 | .268 | 78 |
| | Pressure | .321 | 25 | .377 | 77 | .345 | 55 | 0.00 | 107 | 3.17 | 153 | 9.52 | 28 | .400 | 19 |
| Paul Molitor | Overall | .315 | 8 | .439 | 35 | .379 | 14 | 1.79 | 95 | 9.20 | 54 | 9.63 | 43 | .312 | 37 |
| | Pressure | .293 | 45 | .397 | 61 | .388 | 28 | 1.72 | 83 | 13.43 | 30 | 8.96 | 23 | .118 | 149 |
| Charlie O'Brien | Overall | .234 | 146 | .383 | 87 | .339 | 58 | 3.19 | 46 | 9.29 | 51 | 4.87 | 6 | .371 | 9 |
| | Pressure | .250 | -- | .333 | -- | .357 | -- | 0.00 | -- | 14.29 | -- | 14.29 | -- | .333 | -- |
| Gus Polidor | Overall | .194 | -- | .234 | -- | .230 | -- | 0.00 | -- | 3.23 | -- | 9.68 | -- | .269 | -- |
| | Pressure | .158 | -- | .158 | -- | .158 | -- | 0.00 | -- | 0.00 | -- | 15.79 | -- | .125 | 143 |
| Gary Sheffield | Overall | .247 | 121 | .337 | 128 | .303 | 123 | 1.36 | 114 | 6.67 | 115 | 8.15 | 24 | .221 | 142 |
| | Pressure | .255 | 85 | .353 | 91 | .291 | 120 | 1.96 | 77 | 5.36 | 138 | 10.71 | 38 | .167 | 126 |
| Bill Spiers | Overall | .255 | 101 | .333 | 133 | .298 | 133 | 1.16 | 124 | 5.63 | 140 | 16.89 | 115 | .270 | 77 |
| | Pressure | .324 | 20 | .351 | 93 | .419 | 15 | 0.00 | 107 | 13.64 | 29 | 13.64 | 57 | .000 | -- |
| B.j. Surhoff | Overall | .248 | 119 | .339 | 126 | .287 | 150 | 1.15 | 125 | 5.24 | 148 | 6.08 | 8 | .344 | 16 |
| | Pressure | .273 | 62 | .364 | 83 | .306 | 100 | 1.52 | 92 | 5.56 | 134 | 8.33 | 20 | .353 | 36 |
| Robin Yount | Overall | .318 | 5 | .511 | 5 | .384 | 12 | 3.42 | 37 | 9.13 | 57 | 10.29 | 50 | .380 | 4 |
| | Pressure | .313 | 29 | .448 | 35 | .373 | 37 | 1.49 | 94 | 9.09 | 73 | 14.29 | 63 | .542 | 2 |
| Team Average | Overall | .259 | 9 | .382 | 9 | .318 | 11 | 2.30 | 8 | 7.48 | 13 | 13.00 | 3 | .288 | 1 |
| | Pressure | .242 | 8 | .357 | 6 | .311 | 8 | 2.11 | 4 | 8.93 | 8 | 17.47 | 6 | .263 | 6 |
| League Average | Overall | .261 | | .384 | | .326 | | 2.23 | | 8.44 | | 14.26 | | .269 | |
| | Pressure | .247 | | .357 | | .318 | | 2.02 | | 9.02 | | 17.90 | | .254 | |

## Additional Miscellaneous Batting Comparisons

| | Grass Surface | | Artificial Surface | | Home Games | | Road Games | | Runners in Scoring Position | | Runners in Scoring Pos and Two Outs | | Leading Off Inning | | Runners on 3B with less than 2 Outs | |
|---|---|---|---|---|---|---|---|---|---|---|---|---|---|---|---|---|
| | BA | Rank | BA | Rank | BA | Rank | BA | Rank | BA | Rank | BA | Rank | OBA | Rank | RDI % | Rank |
| Glenn Braggs | .233 | 132 | .321 | 24 | .211 | 153 | .289 | 35 | .238 | 114 | .133 | 158 | .276 | 141 | .684 | 28 |
| Greg Brock | .268 | 66 | .254 | 84 | .261 | 80 | .269 | 66 | .262 | 92 | .200 | 118 | .303 | 110 | .625 | 52 |
| Rob Deer | .220 | 153 | .167 | 163 | .201 | 164 | .220 | 157 | .234 | 122 | .200 | 118 | .328 | 74 | .333 | 163 |
| Mike Felder | .224 | 149 | .317 | 26 | .180 | 170 | .290 | 32 | .217 | 148 | .182 | 136 | .317 | 95 | .556 | 97 |
| Terry Francona | .227 | 144 | .308 | -- | .227 | 138 | .238 | 128 | .310 | 27 | .267 | 51 | .259 | 153 | .727 | 21 |
| Jim Gantner | .269 | 64 | .302 | 33 | .254 | 93 | .291 | 29 | .308 | 30 | .231 | 90 | .323 | 83 | .733 | 19 |
| Joey Meyer | .220 | -- | .241 | -- | .262 | -- | .198 | -- | .229 | -- | .313 | -- | .294 | -- | .800 | 7 |
| Paul Molitor | .310 | 11 | .343 | 11 | .328 | 9 | .304 | 20 | .331 | 16 | .296 | 27 | .353 | 43 | .739 | 18 |
| Charlie O'Brien | .248 | 101 | .171 | 160 | .244 | 112 | .224 | 147 | .385 | 2 | .333 | 11 | .311 | -- | .615 | 59 |
| Gus Polidor | .196 | 168 | .188 | -- | .259 | -- | .138 | -- | .286 | -- | .273 | -- | .163 | -- | .545 | 103 |
| Ed Romero | .223 | 150 | .152 | -- | .153 | -- | .240 | 124 | .237 | -- | .190 | -- | .261 | 149 | .500 | -- |
| Gary Sheffield | .239 | 121 | .290 | 44 | .258 | 89 | .235 | 133 | .219 | 146 | .244 | 77 | .270 | 145 | .524 | 114 |
| Bill Spiers | .261 | 83 | .214 | 136 | .273 | 59 | .237 | 129 | .277 | 70 | .288 | 32 | .267 | 148 | .600 | 67 |
| B.j. Surhoff | .256 | 88 | .200 | 144 | .239 | 120 | .256 | 86 | .268 | 82 | .277 | 41 | .240 | 161 | .656 | 43 |
| Greg Vaughn | .265 | -- | .267 | -- | .200 | -- | .317 | -- | .462 | -- | .800 | -- | .219 | -- | .667 | 39 |
| Robin Yount | .314 | 8 | .337 | 17 | .307 | 24 | .328 | 6 | .355 | 6 | .266 | 54 | .394 | 14 | .848 | 3 |
| Team Average | .256 | 9 | .270 | 5 | .251 | 11 | .266 | 4 | .283 | 1 | .250 | 2 | .301 | 14 | .639 | 1 |
| League Average | .260 | | .262 | | .262 | | .259 | | .262 | | .232 | | .321 | | .566 | |

## Pitching vs. Left and Right Handed Batters

| | | BA | Rank | SA | Rank | OBA | Rank | HR % | Rank | BB % | Rank | SO % | Rank |
|---|---|---|---|---|---|---|---|---|---|---|---|---|---|
| Don August | vs. Lefties | .300 | 109 | .403 | 87 | .373 | 104 | 2.05 | 72 | 10.54 | 99 | 6.02 | 127 |
| | vs. Righties | .304 | 129 | .462 | 129 | .354 | 123 | 3.85 | 127 | 7.28 | 59 | 9.81 | 118 |
| Mike Birkbeck | vs. Lefties | .307 | 114 | .432 | 99 | .344 | 80 | -1.14 | 35 | 6.19 | 30 | 11.34 | 74 |
| | vs. Righties | .313 | -- | .458 | -- | .422 | -- | 3.13 | -- | 13.68 | -- | 17.09 | -- |
| Chris Bosio | vs. Lefties | .247 | 48 | .325 | 35 | .294 | 31 | 1.75 | 63 | 5.70 | 21 | 14.87 | 43 |
| | vs. Righties | .251 | 53 | .347 | 45 | .285 | 25 | 1.79 | 55 | 4.18 | 8 | 20.92 | 22 |
| Bryan Clutterbuck | vs. Lefties | .259 | 65 | .503 | 124 | .299 | 37 | 6.29 | 134 | 5.84 | 23 | 9.74 | 92 |
| | vs. Righties | .281 | -- | .367 | -- | .314 | -- | 1.56 | -- | 5.11 | -- | 10.22 | -- |
| Chuck Crim | vs. Lefties | .271 | 85 | .367 | 56 | .344 | 83 | 1.81 | 67 | 9.63 | 85 | 11.23 | 76 |
| | vs. Righties | .252 | 57 | .347 | 44 | .295 | 33 | 1.46 | 34 | 6.00 | 35 | 12.67 | 90 |
| Tom Filer | vs. Lefties | .229 | 34 | .340 | 42 | .315 | 51 | 2.08 | 73 | 9.20 | 74 | 6.13 | 124 |
| | vs. Righties | .318 | -- | .434 | -- | .362 | -- | 2.33 | -- | 5.76 | -- | 7.19 | -- |
| Tony Fossas | vs. Lefties | .183 | 10 | .220 | 6 | .253 | 11 | 1.22 | 38 | 7.53 | 51 | 30.11 | 3 |
| | vs. Righties | .298 | 126 | .411 | 96 | .361 | 127 | 1.42 | 31 | 9.20 | 97 | 8.59 | 126 |
| Ted Higuera | vs. Lefties | .215 | 22 | .323 | 32 | .245 | 5 | 2.15 | 76 | 4.00 | 8 | 14.00 | 51 |
| | vs. Righties | .255 | 65 | .350 | 48 | .330 | 87 | 1.70 | 48 | 9.42 | 102 | 16.49 | 52 |
| Mark Knudson | vs. Lefties | .239 | 42 | .373 | 62 | .285 | 24 | 2.49 | 83 | 5.61 | 20 | 7.94 | 110 |
| | vs. Righties | .236 | 30 | .380 | 70 | .286 | 26 | 3.80 | 126 | 5.96 | 34 | 10.53 | 114 |
| Bill Krueger | vs. Lefties | .223 | 31 | .245 | 11 | .298 | 36 | 0.00 | 1 | 9.62 | 83 | 24.04 | 8 |
| | vs. Righties | .278 | 104 | .422 | 105 | .333 | 91 | 3.33 | 115 | 7.69 | 68 | 15.72 | 59 |
| Jaime Navarro | vs. Lefties | .273 | 86 | .356 | 48 | .327 | 65 | 1.03 | 29 | 7.55 | 52 | 12.26 | 65 |
| | vs. Righties | .280 | 109 | .381 | 72 | .327 | 79 | 1.69 | 47 | 6.20 | 41 | 11.63 | 101 |
| Dan Plesac | vs. Lefties | .224 | -- | .306 | -- | .231 | -- | 2.04 | -- | 1.92 | -- | 21.15 | -- |
| | vs. Righties | .209 | 12 | .331 | 31 | .274 | 12 | 2.91 | 104 | 8.42 | 84 | 21.58 | 21 |
| Jerry Reuss | vs. Lefties | .317 | 121 | .535 | 129 | .349 | 87 | 5.94 | 133 | 2.75 | 3 | 5.50 | 131 |
| | vs. Righties | .296 | 125 | .426 | 109 | .339 | 102 | 2.77 | 100 | 6.10 | 37 | 6.69 | 130 |
| Bill Wegman | vs. Lefties | .360 | 133 | .588 | 133 | .394 | 126 | 4.39 | 124 | 7.09 | 41 | 8.66 | 104 |
| | vs. Righties | .277 | -- | .386 | -- | .354 | -- | 0.99 | -- | 10.62 | -- | 14.16 | -- |
| Team Average | vs. Lefties | .259 | 6 | .371 | 6 | .316 | 5 | 2.19 | 8 | 7.43 | 2 | 12.51 | 8 |
| | vs. Righties | .268 | 11 | .386 | 9 | .325 | 8 | 2.44 | 8 | 7.52 | 4 | 13.85 | 12 |
| League Average | vs. Lefties | .261 | | .382 | | .330 | | 2.16 | | 9.16 | | 13.03 | |
| | vs. Righties | .261 | | .385 | | .323 | | 2.28 | | 7.96 | | 15.09 | |

## Pitching with Runners on Base and Bases Empty

| | | BA | Rank | SA | Rank | OBA | Rank | HR % | Rank | BB % | Rank | SO % | Rank |
|---|---|---|---|---|---|---|---|---|---|---|---|---|---|
| Don August | Runners On | .294 | 113 | .465 | 126 | .375 | 118 | 4.49 | 127 | 12.41 | 116 | 6.90 | 128 |
| | Bases Empty | .308 | 128 | .407 | 92 | .355 | 118 | 1.80 | 48 | 6.15 | 44 | 8.66 | 122 |
| Chris Bosio | Runners On | .260 | 62 | .381 | 76 | .310 | 39 | 2.54 | 98 | 5.87 | 13 | 17.86 | 32 |
| | Bases Empty | .241 | 49 | .307 | 19 | .276 | 22 | 1.27 | 23 | 4.33 | 10 | 17.85 | 36 |
| Bryan Clutterbuck | Runners On | .287 | -- | .491 | -- | .308 | -- | 4.63 | -- | 4.27 | -- | 10.26 | -- |
| | Bases Empty | .258 | 69 | .405 | 87 | .305 | 48 | 3.68 | 119 | 6.32 | 50 | 9.77 | 110 |
| Chuck Crim | Runners On | .263 | 71 | .353 | 43 | .329 | 64 | 1.34 | 36 | 9.30 | 72 | 12.40 | 73 |
| | Bases Empty | .255 | 65 | .356 | 46 | .297 | 40 | 1.85 | 53 | 5.24 | 26 | 11.79 | 89 |
| Tom Filer | Runners On | .270 | 80 | .423 | 105 | .325 | 57 | 4.50 | 128 | 5.74 | 12 | 4.92 | 134 |
| | Bases Empty | .272 | 91 | .358 | 48 | .344 | 107 | 0.62 | 4 | 8.89 | 92 | 7.78 | 127 |
| Tony Fossas | Runners On | .283 | 99 | .354 | 46 | .359 | 105 | 1.77 | 66 | 10.87 | 99 | 18.12 | 27 |
| | Bases Empty | .227 | -- | .327 | -- | .280 | -- | 0.91 | -- | 5.93 | -- | 14.41 | -- |
| Ted Higuera | Runners On | .272 | 82 | .359 | 55 | .335 | 71 | 1.46 | 43 | 8.37 | 58 | 11.72 | 79 |
| | Bases Empty | .232 | 35 | .336 | 35 | .302 | 44 | 2.01 | 58 | 8.54 | 86 | 19.21 | 31 |
| Mark Knudson | Runners On | .229 | 25 | .385 | 80 | .276 | 10 | 3.91 | 125 | 6.19 | 18 | 9.79 | 104 |
| | Bases Empty | .242 | 51 | .372 | 66 | .292 | 36 | 2.81 | 91 | 5.57 | 32 | 9.18 | 118 |
| Bill Krueger | Runners On | .275 | 87 | .374 | 68 | .339 | 78 | 1.75 | 64 | 8.76 | 64 | 18.56 | 23 |
| | Bases Empty | .254 | 62 | .378 | 68 | .311 | 54 | 3.11 | 101 | 7.66 | 72 | 17.22 | 42 |
| Jaime Navarro | Runners On | .297 | 116 | .379 | 73 | .340 | 80 | 1.65 | 59 | 5.94 | 14 | 13.37 | 65 |
| | Bases Empty | .262 | 74 | .363 | 54 | .317 | 65 | 1.21 | 19 | 7.46 | 67 | 10.82 | 104 |
| Dan Plesac | Runners On | .205 | 11 | .299 | 12 | .236 | 3 | 2.56 | 99 | 4.72 | 7 | 18.11 | 28 |
| | Bases Empty | .221 | -- | .356 | -- | .296 | -- | 2.88 | -- | 9.57 | -- | 25.22 | -- |
| Jerry Reuss | Runners On | .364 | 134 | .519 | 132 | .392 | 125 | 2.93 | 111 | 5.32 | 10 | 6.84 | 129 |
| | Bases Empty | .254 | 61 | .393 | 80 | .302 | 46 | 3.63 | 117 | 5.65 | 34 | 6.21 | 132 |
| Team Average | Runners On | .274 | 11 | .397 | 9 | .335 | 8 | 2.70 | 14 | 8.50 | 6 | 12.77 | 10 |
| | Bases Empty | .257 | 9 | .366 | 5 | .311 | 6 | 2.05 | 4 | 6.66 | 2 | 13.73 | 10 |
| League Average | Runners On | .268 | | .389 | | .336 | | 2.15 | | 9.17 | | 13.53 | |
| | Bases Empty | .255 | | .380 | | .317 | | 2.29 | | 7.84 | | 14.86 | |

## Overall Pitching Compared to Late Inning Pressure Situations

| | | BA | Rank | SA | Rank | OBA | Rank | HR % | Rank | BB % | Rank | SO % | Rank |
|---|---|---|---|---|---|---|---|---|---|---|---|---|---|
| Don August | Overall | .302 | 127 | .432 | 108 | .364 | 128 | 2.94 | 108 | 8.95 | 86 | 7.87 | 126 |
| | Pressure | .441 | 132 | .765 | 133 | .457 | 129 | 8.82 | 133 | 2.86 | 7 | 2.86 | 131 |
| Chris Bosio | Overall | .249 | 48 | .336 | 26 | .289 | 20 | 1.77 | 51 | 4.95 | 8 | 17.85 | 33 |
| | Pressure | .244 | 62 | .295 | 38 | .289 | 35 | 1.28 | 49 | 5.95 | 30 | 14.29 | 68 |
| Bryan Clutterbuck | Overall | .269 | 84 | .439 | 117 | .306 | 35 | 4.06 | 130 | 5.50 | 13 | 9.97 | 107 |
| | Pressure | .250 | -- | .250 | -- | .250 | -- | 0.00 | -- | 0.00 | -- | 12.50 | -- |
| Chuck Crim | Overall | .259 | 67 | .355 | 46 | .314 | 51 | 1.59 | 37 | 7.39 | 52 | 12.11 | 82 |
| | Pressure | .236 | 57 | .336 | 59 | .306 | 58 | 1.82 | 67 | 9.20 | 61 | 11.20 | 97 |
| Tom Filer | Overall | .271 | 89 | .385 | 75 | .337 | 88 | 2.20 | 70 | 7.62 | 58 | 6.62 | 131 |
| | Pressure | .333 | -- | .500 | -- | .429 | -- | 0.00 | -- | 14.29 | -- | 14.29 | -- |
| Tony Fossas | Overall | .256 | 59 | .341 | 33 | .321 | 60 | 1.35 | 21 | 8.59 | 78 | 16.41 | 42 |
| | Pressure | .298 | 112 | .426 | 105 | .421 | 121 | 2.13 | 76 | 16.13 | 125 | 11.29 | 95 |
| Ted Higuera | Overall | .248 | 45 | .345 | 40 | .316 | 52 | 1.79 | 53 | 8.47 | 72 | 16.05 | 46 |
| | Pressure | .226 | -- | .258 | -- | .250 | -- | 0.00 | -- | 2.94 | -- | 14.71 | -- |
| Mark Knudson | Overall | .237 | 31 | .377 | 66 | .286 | 16 | 3.23 | 116 | 5.81 | 19 | 9.42 | 118 |
| | Pressure | .325 | 117 | .455 | 110 | .354 | 93 | 2.60 | 90 | 3.66 | 8 | 10.98 | 99 |
| Bill Krueger | Overall | .264 | 73 | .376 | 65 | .324 | 65 | 2.47 | 87 | 8.19 | 68 | 17.87 | 32 |
| | Pressure | .238 | 60 | .262 | 23 | .289 | 33 | 0.00 | 1 | 6.67 | 38 | 15.56 | 61 |
| Jaime Navarro | Overall | .277 | 98 | .370 | 59 | .327 | 73 | 1.40 | 25 | 6.81 | 38 | 11.91 | 84 |
| | Pressure | .436 | 131 | .590 | 125 | .436 | 123 | 2.56 | 89 | 0.00 | 1 | 17.95 | 44 |
| Dan Plesac | Overall | .213 | -- | .326 | -- | .264 | -- | 2.71 | -- | 7.02 | -- | 21.49 | -- |
| | Pressure | .190 | 16 | .352 | 72 | .272 | 23 | 4.23 | 119 | 10.49 | 79 | 19.14 | 36 |
| Jerry Reuss | Overall | .300 | 126 | .446 | 121 | .340 | 96 | 3.33 | 120 | 5.51 | 14 | 6.48 | 132 |
| | Pressure | .455 | -- | .818 | -- | .462 | -- | 9.09 | -- | 7.69 | -- | 0.00 | -- |
| Team Average | Overall | .265 | 9 | .379 | 7 | .321 | 6 | 2.33 | 8 | 7.48 | 3 | 13.30 | 10 |
| | Pressure | .267 | 13 | .388 | 11 | .326 | 7 | 2.63 | 11 | 8.07 | 3 | 13.00 | 12 |
| League Average | Overall | .261 | | .384 | | .326 | | 2.23 | | 8.44 | | 14.26 | |
| | Pressure | .250 | | .362 | | .325 | | 2.14 | | 9.50 | | 16.61 | |

## Additional Miscellaneous Pitching Comparisons

| | Grass Surface | | Artificial Surface | | Home Games | | Road Games | | Runners in Scoring Position | | Runners in Scoring Pos and Two Outs | | Leading Off Inning | |
|---|---|---|---|---|---|---|---|---|---|---|---|---|---|---|
| | BA | Rank | BA | Rank | BA | Rank | BA | Rank | BA | Rank | BA | Rank | OBA | Rank |
| Don August | .310 | 127 | .268 | 68 | .340 | 133 | .281 | 91 | .260 | 79 | .274 | 104 | .344 | 93 |
| Mike Birkbeck | .306 | 126 | .320 | 120 | .299 | -- | .320 | -- | .228 | 30 | .185 | 39 | .388 | -- |
| Chris Bosio | .247 | 48 | .261 | 59 | .245 | 58 | .252 | 53 | .239 | 52 | .134 | 12 | .262 | 19 |
| Bryan Clutterbuck | .269 | 86 | .000 | -- | .284 | 109 | .234 | -- | .190 | -- | .241 | -- | .257 | 15 |
| Chuck Crim | .247 | 50 | .324 | 122 | .239 | 43 | .282 | 92 | .235 | 41 | .231 | 71 | .313 | 53 |
| Tom Filer | .281 | 103 | .211 | -- | .346 | -- | .241 | 39 | .276 | -- | .192 | -- | .346 | 97 |
| Tony Fossas | .243 | 39 | .310 | -- | .231 | 33 | .300 | -- | .237 | 46 | .171 | 30 | .365 | -- |
| Ted Higuera | .242 | 36 | .280 | 82 | .217 | 18 | .293 | 110 | .228 | 30 | .259 | 98 | .336 | 84 |
| Mark Knudson | .243 | 40 | .200 | 13 | .254 | 70 | .223 | 23 | .279 | 99 | .293 | 114 | .272 | 27 |
| Bill Krueger | .277 | 97 | .193 | 9 | .261 | 80 | .267 | 77 | .245 | 58 | .224 | 66 | .391 | 124 |
| Jaime Navarro | .272 | 90 | .345 | -- | .264 | 83 | .295 | 115 | .281 | 103 | .216 | 60 | .310 | 48 |
| Dan Plesac | .209 | 15 | .231 | -- | .205 | -- | .221 | 20 | .235 | 42 | .243 | 82 | .348 | -- |
| Jerry Reuss | .295 | 119 | .353 | 130 | .282 | 105 | .320 | 126 | .358 | 135 | .259 | 98 | .320 | 62 |
| Bill Wegman | .340 | 134 | .271 | 72 | .371 | -- | .286 | 96 | .344 | -- | .346 | -- | .333 | -- |
| Team Average | .264 | 8 | .268 | 9 | .263 | 8 | .266 | 8 | .254 | 4 | .227 | 5 | .317 | 5 |
| League Average | .260 | | .262 | | .259 | | .262 | | .262 | | .232 | | .321 | |

# MINNESOTA TWINS

- **Calvin Griffith's legacy: a bumper crop.**
- **The day the "Sweet Music" died.**

During the early 1980s, the Minnesota Twins organization, under difficult circumstances, operated at a level of efficiency rarely attained in organized baseball. Despite the frugal policies of owner Calvin Griffith, Minnesota's player–development system thrived, providing its parent club with a steady stream of prodigious talent. A list of Minnesota's best rookies during a three-year period from 1982 through 1984 is offered as evidence:

- 1982—Tom Brunansky, Gary Gaetti, Kent Hrbek, Tim Laudner, and Frank Viola.
- 1983—Randy Bush and Ray Smith.
- 1984—Jim Eisenreich, Kirby Puckett, and Tim Teufel.

That's a pretty intimidating lineup—minus a shortstop, but complete with an All-Star pitcher, a designated hitter, and an extra catcher thrown into the deal, all produced over a period of just three years. We're not about to track down other teams that were equally productive over a comparable length of time; if any exist at all, there sure can't be many. But two related questions piqued our curiosity. First, was Minnesota's rookie crop of 1982 the greatest ever by one team in a single season? And, second, what went wrong? Why have the Twins so little to show for several consecutive seasons of abundant harvests?

(For purposes of this study, the rookie year for players whose rookie status extended over several seasons is considered to be the season in which that status finally expired. For those who played for more than one team in their rookie seasons, the rookie team is the one with which he started the year.)

Since 1900, less than 700 players reached the majors who eventually attained any of the following plateaus that normally indicate star status: 1500 hits, 150 home runs, 750 RBIs (for batters), or 125 wins (for pitchers). That's fewer than 10 per season. So for a team to produce more than one such rookie in the same season constitutes a windfall. To date, only three teams have produced as many as four in the same season: the 1913 Philadelphia A's (Wally Schang, Herb Pennock, Joe Bush, and Bob Shawkey), the 1933 Detroit Tigers (Pete Fox, Hank Greenberg, Schoolboy Rowe, and Eldon Auker) and the 1978 Tigers (Alan Trammell, Lou Whitaker, Lance Parrish, and Jack Morris). Minnesota's class of '82 will join that elite group as soon as Frank Viola gains eight more wins to reach the 125 mark.

That's pretty heady company. But assuming that Brunansky, Gaetti, Hrbek, and Viola all have productive years ahead of them, it isn't unrealistic to catalog their accomplishments with those of the other players listed above. We used a technique described in detail in the Rangers essay (pp. 83–84) to estimate the final career totals of the three hitters and their classmate Laudner. Simply stated, the estimates are based on the averages of past players whose statistical profiles were most similar:

| Player | G | AB | R | H | 2B | 3B | HR | RBI | BA | SA | OBA |
|---|---|---|---|---|---|---|---|---|---|---|---|
| Brunansky | 1820 | 6301 | 843 | 1632 | 268 | 33 | 260 | 945 | .259 | .435 | .344 |
| Gaetti | 1678 | 5799 | 742 | 1508 | 252 | 26 | 226 | 862 | .260 | .429 | .340 |
| Hrbek | 1985 | 7119 | 1039 | 1997 | 348 | 51 | 318 | 1231 | .281 | .478 | .353 |
| Laudner | 996 | 6301 | 313 | 691 | 117 | 10 | 88 | 365 | .241 | .379 | .321 |

Assuming that those totals are reasonable approximations, the eventual career totals compiled by the position players from Minnesota's class of '82 will exceed those of the 1978 Tigers, not to mention most of the other teams that produced three rookies who met at least one of the batting criteria listed above. Those teams include the 1916 Senators (Sam Rice, Joe Judge, Charlie Jamieson); the 1948 Dodgers (Duke Snider, Gil Hodges, Roy Campanella); the 1958 Giants (Orlando Cepeda, Felipe Alou, and Leon Wagner); the 1959 Dodgers (Ron Fairly, Maury Wills, and Don Demeter); and the 1969 Pirates (Al Oliver, Richie Hebner, and Manny Sanguillen). Remember, Minnesota's projected totals also include the statistics of some lesser retired players, such as Ron Washington and the legendary Boomer Wells. Similarly, totals for the other teams include the career totals of all their rookies. In fact, the dominance of the 1958 Giants in the table below is attributable in part to the depth of its rookie roster, which also included Jim Davenport, Willie Kirkland, Andre Rodgers, and Bob Schmidt. On the other hand, Trammell, Whitaker, and Parrish had only one classmate: Tim Corcoran. Their totals are understandably lower. Teams are listed in order of runs produced (runs plus RBIs):

| Year | Team | G | AB | R | H | 2B | 3B | HR | RBI | BA |
|---|---|---|---|---|---|---|---|---|---|---|
| 1958 | San Francisco | 9769 | 31,589 | 4154 | 8592 | 1405 | 184 | 1105 | 4250 | .272 |
| 1948 | Brooklyn | 8296 | 24,663 | 3711 | 6699 | 1080 | 196 | 1122 | 4128 | .272 |
| 1982 | Minnesota | 6687 | 25,441 | 3308 | 6674 | 1103 | 152 | 935 | 3720 | .263 |
| 1916 | Washington | 6562 | 24,164 | 3804 | 7404 | 1262 | 427 | 124 | 2712 | .306 |
| 1969 | Pittsburgh | 7542 | 23,928 | 3056 | 6817 | 1140 | 208 | 613 | 3312 | .285 |
| 1978 | Detroit | 6624 | 22,666 | 3077 | 6154 | 1074 | 165 | 669 | 3060 | .272 |
| 1959 | Los Angeles | 6035 | 18,658 | 2513 | 5055 | 645 | 124 | 418 | 2113 | .271 |

Whether or not you agree that Minnesota's class of 1982 comprised one of the best single-season harvests in major league history, the addition of Puckett and some other useful players over the next few seasons leads us to an inevitable question: Why have the Twins won only a single division title, albeit one that they parlayed into a World Series victory? The answer is Minnesota failed on two counts.

First, its bounty was predominantly offensive. But only once did the Twins successfully dip into their surplus to acquire a starting pitcher to complement Viola. That was when they traded four prospects (two hitters and two pitchers) for Bert Blyleven in 1985. Other attempts failed, most notably the acquisitions of Mike Smithson and John Butcher for Gary Ward after the 1983 season, and more recently, that of Shane Rawley for Tom Herr. Even when Minnesota won the World Series in 1987, its rotation was suspect, and most post-Series analysis attributed the victory to its reliance on a shallow, top-heavy tandem of Viola and Blyleven, with Les Straker included only out of necessity. (For what it's worth, we revealed in the 1988 *Analyst* (p. 69) that the Twins' rotation wasn't *that* top–heavy, at least by comparison to other championship teams. And, of course, Minnesota's decision to trade Blyleven a year ago now appears shaky as well.

Second, a series of trades parlayed some of Minnesota's best young talent of the decade into nothing more than a group of disappointing minor leaguers and underproductive veterans. The damage done by those transactions more than counteracted the inspired acquisition of Jeff Reardon. Tim Teufel was traded to the Mets for three prospects whose prospects, as it happened, were negligible. Even worse, Minnesota turned Tom Brunansky into Herr, turned Herr into Rawley, and turned Rawley into thin air when he became a free agent following a disastrous 1989 season. That's a disappearing act even Doug Henning couldn't master. Meanwhile, Brunansky continues to hit home runs in underappreciated obscurity for the Cardinals.

No trade since the barter of Rod Carew 10 years earlier generated as much discussion in Minnesota as the swap of Frank Viola to the Mets last July. The Twins swapped their LCS-, Series-, and All-Star-Game-winner for a package of five would-bes: Rick Aguilera, and four others with a total of one major league victory to their credit. As if by reflex, the media labeled the deal a "trade for the future." Sure, it's *possible* that Dave West will become a 200–game winner. Right. And you might hit the lottery. But realistically, what are the chances that all five pitchers combined will win as many games, from this day on as Viola? Actually, let's broaden the topic, and explore the success or failure of these relatively rare trades of a star player for a package of prospects.

We identified 11 other deals in which a single player of star quality fetched at least four players in return. Some involved position players, others involved pitchers. (The actual trades are listed at the end of the essay.) We tracked the performances of the two groups of teams for four seasons after the trade—the group that traded away the star players, and the group that acquired them. Here's how they developed, with Year 1 considered the first complete season after the trade:

| | Year 0 | Year 1 | Year 2 | Year 3 | Year 4 |
|---|---|---|---|---|---|
| Traded star player | .427 | .441 | .423 | .429 | .431 |
| Acquired star player | .540 | .548 | .532 | .537 | .566 |

Both groups varied surprisingly little over the four seasons following the trades. Does such a finding imply that, on the whole, the deals helped (or hurt) both sides equally? Hoo, boy—no way! Poor teams are like hot–air balloons. It takes enormous effort simply to hold them in place, to keep them from rising (although some organizations have mastered the art.) How do teams normally progress from a base of approximately .427, the average winning percentage of the 11 teams before they traded away the star players? From 1900 through 1983, 74 teams had winning percentages between .417 and .437, which is to say, within 10 points of that mark. The following chart contrasts their steady progress with that of the 11 teams under study:

| | Teams | Year 0 | Year 1 | Year 2 | Year 3 | Year 4 |
|---|---|---|---|---|---|---|
| Control group | 74 | .427 | .439 | .461 | .473 | .479 |
| Teams in trades | 11 | .427 | .441 | .423 | .429 | .431 |

The degree to which the teams that traded single players for four- and five-player packages underperformed the group of comparable teams is stunning. Conversely, the teams that acquired those players for multiplayer packages defied baseball gravity by maintaining their high winning percentages over time. The chart below contrasts their buoyancy with the downward trend of teams that started from within 10 points of the same percentage:

| | Teams | Year 0 | Year 1 | Year 2 | Year 3 | Year 4 |
|---|---|---|---|---|---|---|
| Control group | 149 | .540 | .522 | .510 | .515 | .506 |
| Teams in trades | 11 | .540 | .548 | .532 | .537 | .566 |

Data based on as few as 11 test cases rarely provide conclusive evidence of anything, but this comes pretty darn close. Can we say that trading a star player for four or five prospects is generally a losing proposition? Well, each case is different, and there are exceptions to every rule. But it ain't against the law, and, in light of the figures above, we're not about to stop you. Minnesota is already experiencing the downside of such a deal. Within days of the arrival of Aguilera and Co., the Twins were bemoaning the poor mechanics of West, their *sine qua non.* His 6.41 ERA with Minnesota last season doesn't bode well for the Twins, short- or long-term. Whoever it was that said a bird in the hand is worth two in the bush may have actually *under*stated that lonely sparrow's value.

The trades used in the study above include: Art Nehf, Braves to Giants (1919); Rogers Hornsby, Braves to Cubs (1928); Buddy Myer, Red Sox to Senators (1928); Dick Bartell, Phillies to Giants (1934); Jim Bunning, Phillies to Pirates (1967); Jeff Burroughs, Rangers to Braves (1976); Tom Seaver, Reds to Mets (1977); Vida Blue, A's to Giants (1978); Rod Carew, Twins to Angels (1979); Von Hayes, Indians to Phillies (1982); and Kevin McReynolds, Padres to Mets (1986).

## WON-LOST RECORD BY STARTING POSITION

| MINNESOTA 80-82 | C | 1B | 2B | 3B | SS | LF | CF | RF | P | DH | Leadoff | Relief | Starts |
|---|---|---|---|---|---|---|---|---|---|---|---|---|---|
| Rick Aguilera | - | - | - | - | - | - | - | - | 4-7 | - | - | - | 4-7 |
| Allan Anderson | - | - | - | - | - | - | - | - | 20-13 | - | - | - | 20-13 |
| Wally Backman | - | - | 34-45 | - | - | - | - | - | - | - | 11-12 | - | 34-45 |
| Doug Baker | - | - | 4-5 | - | 6-5 | - | - | - | - | - | 0-1 | - | 10-10 |
| Juan Berenguer | - | - | - | - | - | - | - | - | - | - | - | 26-30 | - |
| Greg Booker | - | - | - | - | - | - | - | - | - | - | - | 0-6 | - |
| Randy Bush | - | 12-3 | - | - | - | 11-10 | - | 25-43 | - | 1-1 | 7-3 | - | 49-57 |
| Carmelo Castillo | - | - | - | - | - | 4-3 | - | 28-17 | - | 4-2 | - | - | 36-22 |
| Mike Cook | - | - | - | - | - | - | - | - | - | - | - | 4-11 | - |
| Tim Drummond | - | - | - | - | - | - | - | - | - | - | - | 4-4 | - |
| Jim Dwyer | - | - | - | - | - | - | - | - | - | 27-32 | - | - | 27-32 |
| Mike Dyer | - | - | - | - | - | - | - | - | 6-6 | - | - | 1-3 | 6-6 |
| Gary Gaetti | - | 0-2 | - | 61-62 | - | - | - | - | - | 0-1 | - | - | 61-65 |
| Greg Gagne | - | - | - | - | 67-63 | - | - | - | - | - | 1-0 | - | 67-63 |
| Dan Gladden | - | - | - | - | - | 52-56 | 0-2 | - | - | 1-0 | 18-24 | 0-1 | 53-58 |
| German Gonzalez | - | - | - | - | - | - | - | - | - | - | - | 9-13 | - |
| Mark Guthrie | - | - | - | - | - | - | - | - | 3-5 | - | - | 1-4 | 3-5 |
| Chip Hale | - | - | 7-4 | 0-3 | - | - | - | - | - | 1-1 | 0-1 | - | 8-8 |
| Brian Harper | 47-39 | - | - | - | - | - | - | 0-1 | - | 7-8 | - | - | 54-48 |
| Kent Hrbek | - | 44-42 | - | - | - | - | - | - | - | 7-10 | - | - | 51-52 |
| Terry Jorgensen | - | - | - | 4-4 | - | - | - | - | - | - | - | - | 4-4 |
| Gene Larkin | - | 23-34 | - | - | - | - | - | 15-13 | - | 20-19 | - | - | 58-66 |
| Tim Laudner | 21-36 | - | - | - | - | - | - | - | - | 9-6 | - | - | 30-42 |
| Orlando Mercado | 9-5 | - | - | - | - | - | - | - | - | - | - | - | 9-5 |
| John Moses | - | 0-1 | - | - | - | 11-11 | 3-3 | 12-8 | - | - | 0-2 | 0-1 | 26-23 |
| Al Newman | - | - | 35-28 | 14-12 | 7-14 | 2-2 | - | - | - | - | 43-39 | - | 58-56 |
| Francisco Oliveras | - | - | - | - | - | - | - | - | 4-4 | - | - | 0-4 | 4-4 |
| Greg Olson | - | - | - | - | - | - | - | - | - | - | - | - | - |
| Kirby Puckett | - | - | - | - | - | - | 77-77 | - | - | 0-1 | - | - | 77-78 |
| Shane Rawley | - | - | - | - | - | - | - | - | 9-16 | - | - | 0-2 | 9-16 |
| Jeff Reardon | - | - | - | - | - | - | - | - | - | - | - | 49-16 | - |
| Vic Rodriguez | - | - | - | 1-1 | - | - | - | - | - | - | - | - | 1-1 |
| Steve Shields | - | - | - | - | - | - | - | - | - | - | - | 4-7 | - |
| Roy Smith | - | - | - | - | - | - | - | - | 18-8 | - | - | 1-5 | 18-8 |
| Paul Sorrento | - | 1-0 | - | - | - | - | - | - | - | 3-1 | - | - | 4-1 |
| Randy St. Claire | - | - | - | - | - | - | - | - | - | - | - | 5-9 | - |
| Kevin Tapani | - | - | - | - | - | - | - | - | 2-3 | - | - | - | 2-3 |
| Fred Toliver | - | - | - | - | - | - | - | - | 1-4 | - | - | 1-1 | 1-4 |
| Lee Tunnell | - | - | - | - | - | - | - | - | - | - | - | 4-6 | - |
| Frank Viola | - | - | - | - | - | - | - | - | 10-14 | - | - | - | 10-14 |
| Gary Wayne | - | - | - | - | - | - | - | - | - | - | - | 25-35 | - |
| Lenny Webster | 3-2 | - | - | - | - | - | - | - | - | - | - | - | 3-2 |
| Dave West | - | - | - | - | - | - | - | - | 3-2 | - | - | 1-4 | 3-2 |

## Batting vs. Left and Right Handed Pitchers

| | | BA | Rank | SA | Rank | OBA | Rank | HR % | Rank | BB % | Rank | SO % | Rank |
|---|---|---|---|---|---|---|---|---|---|---|---|---|---|
| Wally Backman | vs. Lefties | .281 | 62 | .351 | 116 | .349 | 55 | 0.00 | 134 | 9.23 | 57 | 9.23 | 47 |
| | vs. Righties | .219 | 147 | .269 | 161 | .296 | 121 | 0.41 | 150 | 9.56 | 56 | 14.34 | 89 |
| Randy Bush | vs. Lefties | .250 | -- | .400 | -- | .250 | -- | 0.00 | -- | 0.00 | -- | 45.00 | -- |
| | vs. Righties | .264 | 76 | .437 | 42 | .351 | 44 | 3.77 | 31 | 11.32 | 31 | 15.09 | 97 |
| Carmen Castillo | vs. Lefties | .316 | 25 | .561 | 6 | .365 | 39 | 5.16 | 14 | 7.51 | 85 | 12.72 | 84 |
| | vs. Righties | .111 | -- | .190 | -- | .152 | -- | 0.00 | -- | 2.99 | -- | 26.87 | -- |
| Jim Dwyer | vs. Lefties | .333 | -- | .333 | -- | .333 | -- | 0.00 | -- | 0.00 | -- | 33.33 | -- |
| | vs. Righties | .315 | 10 | .405 | 57 | .390 | 12 | 1.35 | 115 | 11.16 | 36 | 8.76 | 30 |
| Gary Gaetti | vs. Lefties | .230 | 137 | .368 | 104 | .274 | 143 | 3.29 | 47 | 6.10 | 111 | 11.59 | 72 |
| | vs. Righties | .260 | 85 | .419 | 48 | .291 | 131 | 4.05 | 24 | 4.03 | 161 | 18.28 | 129 |
| Greg Gagne | vs. Lefties | .292 | 47 | .515 | 12 | .320 | 96 | 2.92 | 55 | 3.91 | 152 | 12.29 | 80 |
| | vs. Righties | .260 | 86 | .370 | 92 | .284 | 139 | 1.38 | 109 | 3.21 | 164 | 18.59 | 131 |
| Dan Gladden | vs. Lefties | .306 | 32 | .427 | 52 | .345 | 62 | 1.91 | 80 | 5.33 | 132 | 10.65 | 63 |
| | vs. Righties | .289 | 31 | .401 | 59 | .323 | 85 | 1.64 | 96 | 4.22 | 158 | 10.54 | 51 |
| Brian Harper | vs. Lefties | .310 | 28 | .419 | 57 | .339 | 74 | 1.94 | 78 | 3.61 | 154 | 3.61 | 7 |
| | vs. Righties | .335 | 3 | .470 | 26 | .362 | 31 | 2.17 | 74 | 2.85 | 167 | 4.07 | 2 |
| Kent Hrbek | vs. Lefties | .266 | 82 | .468 | 34 | .374 | 31 | 5.50 | 11 | 14.39 | 12 | 12.88 | 86 |
| | vs. Righties | .274 | 59 | .538 | 3 | .354 | 40 | 7.14 | 3 | 11.26 | 33 | 5.96 | 9 |
| Gene Larkin | vs. Lefties | .365 | 5 | .474 | 29 | .436 | 2 | 0.64 | 129 | 8.70 | 64 | 6.52 | 20 |
| | vs. Righties | .214 | 153 | .310 | 137 | .308 | 105 | 1.72 | 89 | 11.31 | 32 | 13.39 | 78 |
| Tim Laudner | vs. Lefties | .253 | 110 | .429 | 50 | .324 | 91 | 2.20 | 72 | 9.62 | 50 | 25.00 | 162 |
| | vs. Righties | .203 | 158 | .304 | 142 | .274 | 147 | 2.70 | 55 | 9.04 | 63 | 23.49 | 157 |
| John Moses | vs. Lefties | .286 | 55 | .302 | 149 | .343 | 69 | 0.00 | 134 | 8.33 | 69 | 8.33 | 36 |
| | vs. Righties | .279 | 47 | .391 | 69 | .330 | 76 | 0.56 | 145 | 6.67 | 114 | 8.72 | 29 |
| Al Newman | vs. Lefties | .252 | 111 | .319 | 140 | .328 | 87 | 0.00 | 134 | 9.57 | 51 | 11.70 | 75 |
| | vs. Righties | .254 | 93 | .293 | 149 | .348 | 49 | 0.00 | 158 | 12.31 | 20 | 7.21 | 17 |
| Kirby Puckett | vs. Lefties | .304 | 35 | .403 | 73 | .341 | 70 | 0.52 | 132 | 5.85 | 117 | 9.76 | 55 |
| | vs. Righties | .354 | 1 | .491 | 18 | .395 | 11 | 1.80 | 86 | 6.05 | 130 | 8.14 | 24 |
| Team Average | vs. Lefties | .288 | 2 | .422 | 3 | .341 | 5 | 1.98 | 11 | 7.20 | 11 | 11.51 | 2 |
| | vs. Righties | .271 | 2 | .393 | 4 | .331 | 2 | 2.15 | 9 | 7.92 | 10 | 12.17 | 2 |
| League Average | vs. Lefties | .266 | | .391 | | .328 | | 2.18 | | 8.18 | | 13.58 | |
| | vs. Righties | .258 | | .380 | | .325 | | 2.26 | | 8.56 | | 14.57 | |

## Batting with Runners on Base and Bases Empty

| | | BA | Rank | SA | Rank | OBA | Rank | HR % | Rank | BB % | Rank | SO % | Rank |
|---|---|---|---|---|---|---|---|---|---|---|---|---|---|
| Wally Backman | Runners On | .259 | 101 | .319 | 147 | .351 | 65 | 0.00 | 146 | 11.59 | 37 | 15.22 | 112 |
| | Bases Empty | .213 | 146 | .262 | 166 | .276 | 148 | 0.55 | 145 | 8.04 | 73 | 12.06 | 61 |
| Randy Bush | Runners On | .306 | 33 | .519 | 10 | .405 | 11 | 4.38 | 23 | 14.74 | 16 | 14.21 | 98 |
| | Bases Empty | .234 | 129 | .377 | 89 | .303 | 108 | 3.03 | 57 | 7.87 | 80 | 18.11 | 118 |
| Carmen Castillo | Runners On | .279 | 72 | .410 | 64 | .318 | 109 | 2.46 | 63 | 5.15 | 141 | 16.91 | 129 |
| | Bases Empty | .229 | -- | .510 | -- | .288 | -- | 5.21 | -- | 7.69 | -- | 16.35 | -- |
| Jim Dwyer | Runners On | .276 | 77 | .352 | 119 | .364 | 48 | 1.90 | 84 | 12.40 | 31 | 10.74 | 66 |
| | Bases Empty | .350 | 1 | .450 | 32 | .414 | 1 | 0.83 | 130 | 9.77 | 36 | 7.52 | 13 |
| Gary Gaetti | Runners On | .251 | 116 | .427 | 51 | .299 | 134 | 5.02 | 18 | 6.69 | 117 | 14.87 | 106 |
| | Bases Empty | .251 | 96 | .382 | 83 | .273 | 152 | 2.70 | 68 | 2.62 | 165 | 17.60 | 115 |
| Greg Gagne | Runners On | .217 | 161 | .300 | 154 | .255 | 167 | 0.99 | 123 | 5.29 | 138 | 17.18 | 132 |
| | Bases Empty | .315 | 9 | .521 | 4 | .333 | 53 | 2.72 | 67 | 1.89 | 168 | 15.53 | 98 |
| Dan Gladden | Runners On | .279 | 71 | .380 | 86 | .299 | 133 | 1.12 | 113 | 4.02 | 161 | 10.05 | 63 |
| | Bases Empty | .305 | 17 | .429 | 45 | .351 | 37 | 2.13 | 83 | 4.97 | 145 | 10.93 | 51 |
| Brian Harper | Runners On | .310 | 27 | .439 | 48 | .348 | 67 | 2.14 | 72 | 4.81 | 150 | 3.85 | 7 |
| | Bases Empty | .338 | 3 | .460 | 26 | .358 | 29 | 2.02 | 86 | 1.47 | 169 | 3.92 | 2 |
| Kent Hrbek | Runners On | .234 | 141 | .451 | 38 | .335 | 87 | 5.98 | 8 | 13.70 | 20 | 8.22 | 35 |
| | Bases Empty | .309 | 13 | .581 | 2 | .386 | 7 | 7.33 | 2 | 10.70 | 27 | 7.91 | 20 |
| Gene Larkin | Runners On | .269 | 84 | .361 | 107 | .355 | 58 | 1.44 | 103 | 10.80 | 45 | 9.60 | 55 |
| | Bases Empty | .265 | 65 | .374 | 93 | .352 | 33 | 1.26 | 114 | 10.00 | 33 | 12.22 | 62 |
| Tim Laudner | Runners On | .227 | 152 | .364 | 98 | .326 | 98 | 1.82 | 89 | 12.78 | 26 | 27.07 | 170 |
| | Bases Empty | .217 | 143 | .341 | 114 | .263 | 161 | 3.10 | 55 | 5.84 | 128 | 21.17 | 145 |
| John Moses | Runners On | .267 | 89 | .362 | 101 | .331 | 93 | 0.95 | 124 | 8.26 | 89 | 6.61 | 17 |
| | Bases Empty | .292 | 24 | .372 | 95 | .336 | 51 | 0.00 | 153 | 6.16 | 122 | 10.27 | 42 |
| Al Newman | Runners On | .301 | 37 | .349 | 121 | .365 | 47 | 0.00 | 146 | 8.54 | 84 | 6.53 | 16 |
| | Bases Empty | .225 | 135 | .275 | 162 | .326 | 68 | 0.00 | 153 | 13.04 | 12 | 10.25 | 40 |
| Kirby Puckett | Runners On | .343 | 6 | .468 | 28 | .397 | 20 | 1.28 | 108 | 8.05 | 94 | 7.18 | 22 |
| | Bases Empty | .334 | 4 | .461 | 25 | .360 | 26 | 1.55 | 98 | 3.87 | 159 | 10.12 | 39 |
| Team Average | Runners On | .275 | 5 | .397 | 5 | .340 | 6 | 2.11 | 9 | 8.91 | 8 | 11.50 | 3 |
| | Bases Empty | .277 | 1 | .405 | 1 | .330 | 2 | 2.08 | 11 | 6.64 | 13 | 12.38 | 1 |
| League Average | Runners On | .268 | | .389 | | .336 | | 2.15 | | 9.17 | | 13.53 | |
| | Bases Empty | .255 | | .380 | | .317 | | 2.29 | | 7.84 | | 14.86 | |

## Overall Batting Compared to Late Inning Pressure Situations

| | | BA | Rank | SA | Rank | OBA | Rank | HR % | Rank | BB % | Rank | SO % | Rank | RDI % | Rank |
|---|---|---|---|---|---|---|---|---|---|---|---|---|---|---|---|
| Wally Backman | Overall | .231 | 150 | .284 | 166 | .306 | 113 | 0.33 | 157 | 9.50 | 50 | 13.35 | 81 | .259 | 97 |
| | Pressure | .250 | 89 | .306 | 117 | .341 | 61 | 0.00 | 107 | 12.20 | 39 | 17.07 | 95 | .182 | 121 |
| Randy Bush | Overall | .263 | 77 | .435 | 39 | .347 | 46 | 3.58 | 34 | 10.81 | 30 | 16.44 | 111 | .273 | 72 |
| | Pressure | .229 | 106 | .292 | 128 | .321 | 86 | 2.08 | 73 | 8.93 | 78 | 19.64 | 118 | .111 | 151 |
| Carmen Castillo | Overall | .257 | 93 | .454 | 25 | .305 | 120 | 3.67 | 31 | 6.25 | 125 | 16.67 | 114 | .256 | 102 |
| | Pressure | .412 | 2 | .765 | 1 | .429 | 10 | 5.88 | 15 | 2.70 | 157 | 16.22 | 87 | .444 | 12 |
| Jim Dwyer | Overall | .316 | 7 | .404 | 65 | .390 | 9 | 1.33 | 117 | 11.02 | 28 | 9.06 | 36 | .250 | 107 |
| | Pressure | .258 | 80 | .387 | 71 | .368 | 40 | 3.23 | 48 | 15.79 | 9 | 10.53 | 35 | .300 | 63 |
| Gary Gaetti | Overall | .251 | 113 | .404 | 66 | .286 | 152 | 3.82 | 29 | 4.66 | 157 | 16.23 | 106 | .261 | 92 |
| | Pressure | .239 | 100 | .493 | 22 | .280 | 125 | 8.45 | 2 | 5.26 | 139 | 15.79 | 80 | .238 | 101 |
| Greg Gagne | Overall | .272 | 58 | .424 | 46 | .298 | 136 | 1.96 | 86 | 3.46 | 165 | 16.29 | 108 | .237 | 122 |
| | Pressure | .192 | 140 | .288 | 131 | .189 | 169 | 0.00 | 107 | 0.00 | 171 | 29.09 | 156 | .273 | 76 |
| Dan Gladden | Overall | .295 | 26 | .410 | 59 | .331 | 69 | 1.74 | 96 | 4.59 | 159 | 10.58 | 53 | .260 | 95 |
| | Pressure | .333 | 16 | .444 | 36 | .343 | 58 | 1.59 | 90 | 1.43 | 170 | 17.14 | 96 | .375 | 25 |
| Brian Harper | Overall | .325 | 4 | .449 | 28 | .353 | 39 | 2.08 | 82 | 3.16 | 168 | 3.88 | 2 | .336 | 21 |
| | Pressure | .292 | 46 | .500 | 17 | .300 | 107 | 4.17 | 33 | 2.00 | 166 | 4.00 | 3 | .444 | 12 |
| Kent Hrbek | Overall | .272 | 56 | .517 | 4 | .360 | 29 | 6.67 | 3 | 12.21 | 18 | 8.06 | 23 | .354 | 13 |
| | Pressure | .292 | 46 | .667 | 2 | .340 | 66 | 10.42 | 1 | 7.41 | 109 | 14.81 | 70 | .235 | 102 |
| Gene Larkin | Overall | .267 | 67 | .368 | 104 | .353 | 38 | 1.35 | 116 | 10.38 | 38 | 10.96 | 57 | .235 | 127 |
| | Pressure | .258 | 82 | .273 | 136 | .338 | 70 | 0.00 | 107 | 8.00 | 95 | 14.67 | 69 | .231 | 103 |
| Tim Laudner | Overall | .222 | 157 | .351 | 118 | .293 | 142 | 2.51 | 66 | 9.26 | 52 | 24.07 | 161 | .225 | 139 |
| | Pressure | .212 | 119 | .424 | 48 | .257 | 141 | 6.06 | 12 | 5.71 | 132 | 25.71 | 147 | .375 | 25 |
| John Moses | Overall | .281 | 42 | .368 | 103 | .333 | 64 | 0.41 | 153 | 7.12 | 105 | 8.61 | 28 | .351 | 15 |
| | Pressure | .213 | 117 | .255 | 145 | .245 | 147 | 0.00 | 107 | 4.08 | 150 | 16.33 | 90 | .083 | 156 |
| Al Newman | Overall | .253 | 104 | .303 | 158 | .341 | 55 | 0.00 | 166 | 11.32 | 23 | 8.83 | 30 | .260 | 95 |
| | Pressure | .313 | 29 | .358 | 86 | .365 | 43 | 0.00 | 107 | 7.89 | 97 | 7.89 | 19 | .350 | 38 |
| Kirby Puckett | Overall | .339 | 1 | .465 | 18 | .379 | 13 | 1.42 | 112 | 5.99 | 135 | 8.63 | 29 | .335 | 22 |
| | Pressure | .390 | 4 | .597 | 6 | .440 | 7 | 3.90 | 36 | 8.33 | 86 | 11.90 | 42 | .462 | 8 |
| Team Average | Overall | .276 | 2 | .402 | 2 | .334 | 2 | 2.10 | 11 | 7.70 | 11 | 11.97 | 2 | .276 | 6 |
| | Pressure | .281 | 1 | .431 | 1 | .328 | 5 | 3.10 | 2 | 6.22 | 14 | 15.37 | 2 | .297 | 2 |
| League Average | Overall | .261 | | .384 | | .326 | | 2.23 | | 8.44 | | 14.26 | | .269 | |
| | Pressure | .247 | | .357 | | .318 | | 2.02 | | 9.02 | | 17.90 | | .254 | |

## Additional Miscellaneous Batting Comparisons

| | Grass Surface | | Artificial Surface | | Home Games | | Road Games | | Runners in Scoring Position | | Runners in Scoring Pos and Two Outs | | Leading Off Inning | | Runners on 3B with less than 2 Outs | |
|---|---|---|---|---|---|---|---|---|---|---|---|---|---|---|---|---|
| | BA | Rank | BA | Rank | BA | Rank | BA | Rank | BA | Rank | BA | Rank | OBA | Rank | RDI % | Rank |
| Wally Backman | .196 | -- | .250 | 90 | .247 | 109 | .215 | 159 | .246 | 104 | .167 | 144 | .278 | 138 | .500 | 119 |
| Doug Baker | .273 | -- | .324 | 23 | .400 | -- | .245 | -- | .200 | -- | .143 | -- | .385 | -- | 1.000 | -- |
| Randy Bush | .278 | 49 | .253 | 85 | .265 | 72 | .262 | 82 | .295 | 39 | .222 | 98 | .337 | 63 | .563 | 92 |
| Carmen Castillo | .286 | -- | .239 | 112 | .243 | 114 | .271 | 63 | .236 | 119 | .091 | 167 | .306 | -- | .550 | 100 |
| Jim Dwyer | .301 | -- | .326 | 22 | .307 | 22 | .324 | 8 | .226 | 138 | .267 | 51 | .500 | 1 | .286 | -- |
| Gary Gaetti | .257 | 86 | .247 | 103 | .249 | 102 | .253 | 92 | .220 | 145 | .224 | 96 | .279 | 135 | .447 | 143 |
| Greg Gagne | .245 | 111 | .291 | 42 | .298 | 32 | .248 | 109 | .205 | 154 | .164 | 147 | .345 | 53 | .478 | 131 |
| Dan Gladden | .309 | 12 | .287 | 48 | .284 | 46 | .305 | 18 | .238 | 116 | .250 | 68 | .338 | 60 | .550 | 100 |
| Chip Hale | .308 | -- | .185 | 154 | .188 | -- | .229 | -- | .167 | -- | .182 | -- | .176 | -- | .667 | -- |
| Brian Harper | .301 | 18 | .341 | 13 | .304 | 26 | .343 | 5 | .330 | 17 | .259 | 64 | .337 | 62 | .810 | 6 |
| Kent Hrbek | .239 | 119 | .290 | 43 | .283 | 47 | .261 | 83 | .294 | 41 | .188 | 132 | .333 | 64 | .750 | 13 |
| Gene Larkin | .294 | 26 | .251 | 89 | .259 | 84 | .275 | 57 | .231 | 128 | .255 | 66 | .372 | 27 | .500 | 119 |
| Tim Laudner | .213 | -- | .227 | 125 | .220 | 148 | .224 | 149 | .208 | 151 | .160 | 150 | .276 | 140 | .615 | 59 |
| John Moses | .231 | -- | .328 | 20 | .309 | 20 | .262 | 81 | .328 | 19 | .303 | 23 | .293 | 119 | 1.000 | -- |
| Al Newman | .262 | 78 | .248 | 99 | .259 | 86 | .248 | 111 | .248 | 103 | .185 | 135 | .286 | 124 | .842 | 4 |
| Kirby Puckett | .282 | 44 | .372 | 4 | .390 | 1 | .283 | 46 | .330 | 18 | .345 | 7 | .355 | 39 | .681 | 32 |
| Team Average | .267 | 4 | .282 | 2 | .285 | 2 | .268 | 3 | .257 | 12 | .219 | 13 | .322 | 7 | .615 | 2 |
| League Average | .260 | | .262 | | .262 | | .259 | | .262 | | .232 | | .321 | | .566 | |

## Pitching vs. Left and Right Handed Batters

| | | BA | Rank | SA | Rank | OBA | Rank | HR % | Rank | BB % | Rank | SO % | Rank |
|---|---|---|---|---|---|---|---|---|---|---|---|---|---|
| Rick Aguilera | vs. Lefties | .275 | 89 | .437 | 102 | .318 | 56 | 1.41 | 47 | 5.92 | 24 | 15.79 | 35 |
| | vs. Righties | .216 | 16 | .345 | 40 | .261 | 6 | 2.03 | 66 | 5.06 | 17 | 20.89 | 23 |
| Allan Anderson | vs. Lefties | .274 | 88 | .368 | 57 | .348 | 86 | 1.71 | 62 | 10.53 | 98 | 10.53 | 84 |
| | vs. Righties | .276 | 101 | .400 | 89 | .321 | 66 | 1.97 | 65 | 5.47 | 24 | 7.71 | 128 |
| Juan Berenguer | vs. Lefties | .329 | 127 | .524 | 127 | .407 | 132 | 4.27 | 123 | 12.04 | 109 | 17.28 | 27 |
| | vs. Righties | .185 | 3 | .269 | 6 | .266 | 9 | 1.76 | 52 | 9.20 | 96 | 22.99 | 18 |
| Mike Dyer | vs. Lefties | .273 | 87 | .396 | 83 | .386 | 115 | 1.44 | 51 | 14.29 | 118 | 9.52 | 96 |
| | vs. Righties | .273 | 95 | .326 | 29 | .336 | 97 | 0.00 | 1 | 8.72 | 88 | 14.09 | 79 |
| Mark Guthrie | vs. Lefties | .295 | -- | .477 | -- | .333 | -- | 4.55 | -- | 4.17 | -- | 10.42 | -- |
| | vs. Righties | .291 | 120 | .434 | 114 | .351 | 117 | 2.75 | 98 | 9.22 | 98 | 16.02 | 54 |
| Francisco Oliveras | vs. Lefties | .264 | 72 | .472 | 116 | .328 | 67 | 5.66 | 130 | 8.62 | 63 | 6.03 | 126 |
| | vs. Righties | .310 | -- | .422 | -- | .341 | -- | 1.72 | -- | 4.07 | -- | 13.82 | -- |
| Shane Rawley | vs. Lefties | .362 | 135 | .543 | 131 | .393 | 125 | 3.45 | 110 | 4.84 | 14 | 8.06 | 109 |
| | vs. Righties | .276 | 102 | .448 | 121 | .350 | 116 | 3.31 | 113 | 10.51 | 112 | 11.28 | 104 |
| Jeff Reardon | vs. Lefties | .248 | 50 | .434 | 101 | .286 | 25 | 3.88 | 118 | 4.29 | 9 | 12.86 | 61 |
| | vs. Righties | .245 | 41 | .340 | 36 | .276 | 13 | 2.04 | 67 | 3.82 | 5 | 17.83 | 41 |
| Roy Smith | vs. Lefties | .271 | 84 | .382 | 69 | .333 | 73 | 1.59 | 56 | 7.69 | 53 | 14.53 | 47 |
| | vs. Righties | .268 | 90 | .458 | 125 | .317 | 63 | 4.80 | 131 | 6.28 | 43 | 10.73 | 111 |
| Frank Viola | vs. Lefties | .280 | 91 | .475 | 117 | .323 | 62 | 2.54 | 87 | 5.51 | 19 | 11.81 | 69 |
| | vs. Righties | .251 | 54 | .382 | 74 | .303 | 40 | 2.55 | 88 | 6.62 | 49 | 20.36 | 26 |
| Gary Wayne | vs. Lefties | .193 | 12 | .301 | 24 | .280 | 19 | 2.41 | 81 | 9.68 | 86 | 18.28 | 21 |
| | vs. Righties | .222 | 21 | .347 | 43 | .322 | 69 | 1.14 | 20 | 12.92 | 131 | 11.48 | 103 |
| Dave West | vs. Lefties | .227 | -- | .273 | -- | .320 | -- | 0.00 | -- | 8.00 | -- | 24.00 | -- |
| | vs. Righties | .319 | 134 | .496 | 133 | .394 | 134 | 3.70 | 121 | 10.83 | 119 | 15.92 | 56 |
| Team Average | vs. Lefties | .285 | 13 | .428 | 12 | .350 | 12 | 2.42 | 11 | 8.59 | 6 | 12.58 | 7 |
| | vs. Righties | .262 | 7 | .398 | 10 | .322 | 7 | 2.55 | 13 | 7.84 | 8 | 14.38 | 9 |
| League Average | vs. Lefties | .261 | | .382 | | .330 | | 2.16 | | 9.16 | | 13.03 | |
| | vs. Righties | .261 | | .385 | | .323 | | 2.28 | | 7.96 | | 15.09 | |

## Pitching with Runners on Base and Bases Empty

| | | BA | Rank | SA | Rank | OBA | Rank | HR % | Rank | BB % | Rank | SO % | Rank |
|---|---|---|---|---|---|---|---|---|---|---|---|---|---|
| Rick Aguilera | Runners On | .245 | -- | .355 | -- | .303 | -- | 0.91 | -- | 6.61 | -- | 15.70 | -- |
| | Bases Empty | .244 | 53 | .411 | 95 | .280 | 25 | 2.22 | 71 | 4.76 | 19 | 20.11 | 26 |
| Allan Anderson | Runners On | .288 | 107 | .412 | 100 | .326 | 59 | 1.44 | 42 | 5.56 | 11 | 7.14 | 126 |
| | Bases Empty | .265 | 78 | .381 | 73 | .325 | 77 | 2.33 | 75 | 6.84 | 57 | 8.97 | 120 |
| Juan Berenguer | Runners On | .220 | 17 | .349 | 40 | .299 | 22 | 2.69 | 104 | 9.95 | 83 | 18.10 | 30 |
| | Bases Empty | .268 | 86 | .400 | 83 | .351 | 110 | 2.93 | 93 | 10.82 | 114 | 22.94 | 16 |
| Mike Dyer | Runners On | .267 | 77 | .344 | 33 | .364 | 112 | 0.00 | 1 | 12.58 | 118 | 11.95 | 76 |
| | Bases Empty | .279 | 110 | .379 | 69 | .361 | 121 | 1.43 | 28 | 10.76 | 112 | 11.39 | 95 |
| Mark Guthrie | Runners On | .255 | -- | .408 | -- | .304 | -- | 3.06 | -- | 7.08 | -- | 17.70 | -- |
| | Bases Empty | .320 | 131 | .469 | 122 | .383 | 130 | 3.13 | 103 | 9.22 | 94 | 12.77 | 82 |
| Francisco Oliveras | Runners On | .286 | -- | .398 | -- | .324 | -- | 3.06 | -- | 4.76 | -- | 13.33 | -- |
| | Bases Empty | .290 | 118 | .484 | 125 | .343 | 106 | 4.03 | 129 | 7.46 | 67 | 7.46 | 128 |
| Shane Rawley | Runners On | .284 | 102 | .416 | 102 | .336 | 72 | 3.11 | 114 | 7.64 | 45 | 11.46 | 85 |
| | Bases Empty | .301 | 123 | .510 | 133 | .377 | 127 | 3.53 | 116 | 10.86 | 115 | 10.00 | 109 |
| Jeff Reardon | Runners On | .272 | 83 | .441 | 117 | .293 | 15 | 3.68 | 123 | 3.38 | 2 | 11.49 | 83 |
| | Bases Empty | .221 | 24 | .329 | 30 | .268 | 15 | 2.14 | 65 | 4.70 | 17 | 19.46 | 29 |
| Roy Smith | Runners On | .259 | 59 | .418 | 103 | .309 | 36 | 3.19 | 115 | 6.71 | 26 | 13.10 | 68 |
| | Bases Empty | .277 | 104 | .425 | 104 | .336 | 95 | 3.37 | 111 | 7.14 | 63 | 12.14 | 86 |
| Frank Viola | Runners On | .250 | 43 | .381 | 75 | .305 | 27 | 2.24 | 87 | 6.91 | 31 | 20.39 | 13 |
| | Bases Empty | .260 | 72 | .410 | 93 | .307 | 49 | 2.75 | 89 | 6.09 | 43 | 17.80 | 38 |
| Gary Wayne | Runners On | .209 | 13 | .328 | 22 | .299 | 21 | 2.24 | 87 | 10.76 | 97 | 13.92 | 60 |
| | Bases Empty | .216 | 20 | .336 | 36 | .319 | 66 | 0.80 | 12 | 13.19 | 130 | 13.19 | 77 |
| Team Average | Runners On | .267 | 7 | .403 | 10 | .329 | 7 | 2.40 | 10 | 8.15 | 3 | 13.45 | 6 |
| | Bases Empty | .272 | 13 | .412 | 11 | .334 | 12 | 2.59 | 11 | 8.04 | 9 | 14.05 | 9 |
| League Average | Runners On | .268 | | .389 | | .336 | | 2.15 | | 9.17 | | 13.53 | |
| | Bases Empty | .255 | | .380 | | .317 | | 2.29 | | 7.84 | | 14.86 | |

## Overall Pitching Compared to Late Inning Pressure Situations

| | | BA | Rank | SA | Rank | OBA | Rank | HR % | Rank | BB % | Rank | SO % | Rank |
|---|---|---|---|---|---|---|---|---|---|---|---|---|---|
| Rick Aguilera | Overall | .245 | 40 | .390 | 79 | .289 | 19 | 1.72 | 48 | 5.48 | 12 | 18.39 | 30 |
| | Pressure | .148 | -- | .259 | -- | .179 | -- | 0.00 | -- | 3.57 | -- | 14.29 | -- |
| Allan Anderson | Overall | .275 | 96 | .395 | 83 | .325 | 68 | 1.93 | 60 | 6.26 | 29 | 8.16 | 124 |
| | Pressure | .136 | -- | .273 | -- | .136 | -- | 4.55 | -- | 0.00 | -- | 4.55 | -- |
| Juan Berenguer | Overall | .246 | 42 | .376 | 63 | .326 | 71 | 2.81 | 105 | 10.40 | 109 | 20.58 | 19 |
| | Pressure | .214 | 39 | .340 | 62 | .284 | 28 | 3.77 | 115 | 8.89 | 54 | 26.11 | 12 |
| Mike Dyer | Overall | .273 | 92 | .362 | 50 | .362 | 127 | 0.74 | 4 | 11.67 | 117 | 11.67 | 88 |
| | Pressure | .313 | -- | .375 | -- | .353 | -- | 0.00 | -- | 0.00 | -- | 23.53 | -- |
| Mark Guthrie | Overall | .292 | 120 | .442 | 119 | .348 | 106 | 3.10 | 112 | 8.27 | 69 | 14.96 | 55 |
| | Pressure | .529 | -- | .588 | -- | .600 | -- | 0.00 | -- | 10.00 | -- | 0.00 | -- |
| Shane Rawley | Overall | .293 | 121 | .467 | 128 | .359 | 123 | 3.34 | 121 | 9.40 | 93 | 10.66 | 100 |
| | Pressure | .404 | 129 | .532 | 121 | .442 | 126 | 0.00 | 1 | 7.55 | 48 | 1.89 | 132 |
| Jeff Reardon | Overall | .246 | 43 | .384 | 74 | .280 | 15 | 2.90 | 106 | 4.04 | 3 | 15.49 | 50 |
| | Pressure | .229 | 50 | .359 | 76 | .276 | 25 | 2.94 | 100 | 5.38 | 22 | 13.98 | 71 |
| Roy Smith | Overall | .269 | 85 | .422 | 98 | .325 | 66 | 3.29 | 119 | 6.96 | 44 | 12.55 | 75 |
| | Pressure | .167 | 5 | .188 | 3 | .259 | 15 | 0.00 | 1 | 10.71 | 81 | 12.50 | 81 |
| Frank Viola | Overall | .256 | 60 | .398 | 84 | .306 | 36 | 2.54 | 89 | 6.43 | 33 | 18.88 | 28 |
| | Pressure | .206 | 32 | .265 | 24 | .241 | 10 | 0.98 | 41 | 4.55 | 15 | 21.82 | 25 |
| Gary Wayne | Overall | .212 | 14 | .332 | 22 | .309 | 39 | 1.54 | 33 | 11.92 | 120 | 13.58 | 64 |
| | Pressure | .195 | 17 | .232 | 12 | .305 | 56 | 0.00 | 1 | 13.54 | 111 | 14.58 | 65 |
| Team Average | Overall | .269 | 11 | .408 | 11 | .332 | 11 | 2.51 | 11 | 8.09 | 7 | 13.77 | 9 |
| | Pressure | .254 | 8 | .352 | 5 | .313 | 6 | 1.95 | 7 | 7.54 | 2 | 15.91 | 8 |
| League Average | Overall | .261 | | .384 | | .326 | | 2.23 | | 8.44 | | 14.26 | |
| | Pressure | .250 | | .362 | | .325 | | 2.14 | | 9.50 | | 16.61 | |

## Additional Miscellaneous Pitching Comparisons

| | Grass Surface | | Artificial Surface | | Home Games | | Road Games | | Runners in Scoring Position | | Runners in Scoring Pos and Two Outs | | Leading Off Inning | |
|---|---|---|---|---|---|---|---|---|---|---|---|---|---|---|
| | BA | Rank | BA | Rank | BA | Rank | BA | Rank | BA | Rank | BA | Rank | OBA | Rank |
| Rick Aguilera | .253 | -- | .241 | 40 | .239 | 42 | .250 | 46 | .221 | 21 | .303 | 117 | .299 | 42 |
| Allan Anderson | .255 | 62 | .295 | 100 | .317 | 130 | .249 | 45 | .273 | 89 | .244 | 84 | .315 | 55 |
| Juan Berenguer | .282 | -- | .231 | 29 | .227 | 28 | .279 | 89 | .241 | 53 | .164 | 27 | .354 | 104 |
| Mike Cook | .400 | -- | .226 | 24 | .233 | -- | .308 | -- | .400 | -- | .111 | -- | .300 | -- |
| Tim Drummond | .250 | -- | .246 | 45 | .286 | -- | .174 | -- | .167 | -- | .143 | -- | .375 | -- |
| Mike Dyer | .197 | -- | .336 | 126 | .339 | -- | .226 | 28 | .274 | 91 | .212 | 54 | .378 | 119 |
| German Gonzalez | .289 | -- | .264 | 64 | .254 | -- | .296 | -- | .270 | -- | .250 | -- | .379 | -- |
| Mark Guthrie | .327 | -- | .282 | 84 | .270 | 93 | .320 | -- | .269 | -- | .250 | -- | .373 | 117 |
| Francisco Oliveras | .247 | -- | .310 | 115 | .317 | -- | .250 | -- | .293 | -- | .273 | -- | .400 | 130 |
| Shane Rawley | .286 | 110 | .298 | 103 | .307 | 126 | .277 | 86 | .306 | 119 | .250 | 88 | .395 | 128 |
| Jeff Reardon | .235 | -- | .253 | 50 | .240 | 45 | .254 | 57 | .256 | 75 | .214 | 56 | .193 | 2 |
| Steve Shields | .200 | -- | .391 | 133 | .400 | -- | .211 | -- | .417 | -- | .125 | -- | .333 | -- |
| Roy Smith | .279 | 102 | .264 | 63 | .269 | 90 | .270 | 80 | .269 | 86 | .215 | 58 | .335 | 82 |
| Randy St. Claire | .216 | -- | .234 | 34 | .256 | -- | .200 | -- | .172 | -- | .200 | -- | .350 | -- |
| Kevin Tapani | .231 | -- | .275 | 77 | .329 | -- | .182 | -- | .346 | -- | .182 | -- | .229 | -- |
| Fred Toliver | .347 | -- | .271 | 71 | .271 | -- | .347 | -- | .342 | -- | .294 | -- | .355 | -- |
| Lee Tunnell | .500 | -- | .302 | 108 | .333 | -- | .353 | -- | .316 | -- | .273 | -- | .250 | -- |
| Frank Viola | .268 | 82 | .248 | 48 | .227 | 25 | .289 | 103 | .250 | 62 | .267 | 102 | .324 | 71 |
| Gary Wayne | .240 | -- | .194 | 10 | .185 | 3 | .248 | 44 | .230 | 33 | .237 | 77 | .397 | 129 |
| Dave West | .404 | -- | .264 | 62 | .264 | -- | .404 | -- | .341 | -- | .455 | -- | .400 | -- |
| Team Average | .269 | 12 | .270 | 10 | .272 | 12 | .267 | 10 | .273 | 12 | .240 | 12 | .341 | 13 |
| League Average | .260 | | .262 | | .259 | | .262 | | .262 | | .232 | | .321 | |

# NEW YORK YANKEES

- **Best team of the '80s? (This will take some explaining.)**
- **A losing season in '89 could be the start of something big.**

When America's designated New Year's reveller, Dick Clark, rocked in the 1990s, everyone from Pete Rozelle and Paul Tagliabue to Phyllis George and Jayne Kennedy (who *was* she, anyway?) was agreed: The NFL's team of the '80s was the San Francisco 49ers. It mattered little that the 'Niners had the league's best record during that time, a 104–47–1 mark that was seven and a half games better than runner-up Washington's. No, whenever San Francisco was designated the team of the 1980s, faster than you could say *BillWalshisagenius,* its bottom-line credential was cited: The 49ers won three Super Bowls.

Football is defined by the Big Event. Perennial playoff teams like the Browns and the Rams, both with winning percentages above .550 for the decade, are derided as underachievers simply because their seasons routinely end before the last Sunday in January. According to the prevailing attitude, every NFL season produces one winner, one runner-up, and 26 losers. Tough business.

To the extent that football glorifies immediacy and climax, baseball pays homage to its long and winding road. To suggest that division winners like the Cubs or the Blue Jays had disappointing years would be sacrilegious. Baseball's postseason isn't a test to determine the best, it's a month-long celebration of excellence. Everyone invited is a winner. There are no losers.

As a result, selecting baseball's best team of the 1980s isn't as simple as checking a list of World Series winners. For the record, the Dodgers were the only team to win two World Series from 1980 through 1989. Were they better than the Cardinals, the only team to win three league titles? Remember, the Dodgers led the majors with four division championships as well.

Frankly, shouldn't baseball—a pastime that celebrates the macro, not the micro; the journey, not the consummation; it-ain't-over-till-it's-over, not the two-minute drill—shouldn't baseball determine its best team on the basis not of championships, but of games? Before you answer, understand this: The winningest team of the 1980s was the New York Yankees. And if you're not prepared to call the Yankees the team of the 1980s, maybe it's time to admit that the one-winner football mentality has encroached upon your baseball psyche. (And, as we all know, that's a five-yard penalty.) Because not only did New York win more games than any other team last decade, it wasn't even close:

| A.L. East | W | L | GB | A.L. West | W | L | GB |
|---|---|---|---|---|---|---|---|
| New York | 854 | 708 | — | Kansas City | 826 | 734 | — |
| Detroit | 839 | 727 | 17 | Oakland | 803 | 764 | 26.5 |
| Boston | 821 | 742 | 33.5 | California | 783 | 783 | 46 |
| Toronto | 817 | 746 | 37.5 | Chicago | 758 | 802 | 68 |
| Milwaukee | 804 | 760 | 51 | Minnesota | 733 | 833 | 96 |
| Baltimore | 800 | 761 | 53.5 | Texas | 720 | 839 | 105.5 |
| Cleveland | 710 | 849 | 142.5 | Seattle | 673 | 893 | 156 |

| N.L. East | W | L | GB | N.L. West | W | L | GB |
|---|---|---|---|---|---|---|---|
| St. Louis | 825 | 734 | — | Los Angeles | 825 | 741 | — |
| New York | 816 | 743 | 9 | Houston | 819 | 750 | 7.5 |
| Montreal | 811 | 752 | 16 | Cincinnati | 781 | 783 | 43 |
| Philadelphia | 783 | 780 | 44 | San Francisco | 773 | 795 | 53 |
| Chicago | 735 | 821 | 88.5 | San Diego | 762 | 805 | 63.5 |
| Pittsburgh | 732 | 825 | 92 | Atlanta | 712 | 845 | 108.5 |

What makes this a particularly difficult call is the fact that the Yankees won only two division titles and a single league championship during the 1980s, losing to the Dodgers in the 1981 World Series. Only one team ever compiled the best record in the majors over as many as 10 seasons while winning fewer than two titles during that period: the Giants, from 1959 through 1968.

So were the Yankees the team of the decade? We're not about to give thumbs-up or -down. Our books have never sought to tell you all the answers, but rather to supply all the available information, and allow you to decide for yourselves. But the topic is symbolic of the degree to which baseball has developed that most desired football commodity of all—parity. Never before in the history of the major leagues have the teams been so evenly matched that the best over a 10–year period had a winning percentage as low as New York's mark during the 1980s (.547).

From 1928 through 1965, there was always at least one team with a percentage of .600 or better over the previous 10 years. For most of that time, of course, the Yankees were that team. But since then, no team has maintained a .600 mark over a 10–year period. For the past six years, the winning percentage of the best team over 10 years has steadily declined, and the steepness of the decline has accelerated. Simply stated, the best teams aren't nearly as dominant as they once were. Best records over each 10–year period:

| 1974–83 | 1975–84 | 1976–85 | 1977–86 | 1978–87 | 1979–88 | 1980–89 |
|---|---|---|---|---|---|---|
| Orioles | Orioles | Yankees | Yankees | Yankees | Yankees | Yankees |
| .585 | .581 | .578 | .573 | .566 | .557 | .547 |

It's ironic that the growth of parity has coincided with the increased freedom that players have secured in moving from team to team as free agents. When the Yankees made Catfish Hunter baseball's first million-dollar player 15 years ago, reactionary observers despaired that such aggressive spending would destroy what they perceived to be the sport's "competitive balance." Whatever the evils of free agency, it's a fact that the balance of power has never been more evenly distributed than it is today—in part, on account of free agency, not despite it. The richest teams continue to spend exorbitant amounts on desirable players—whatever the market bears. But weaker teams also find a more accessible pool of players to fill their needs at a pace and price they deem appropriate. And above all, the poor investments of the past decade and a half have proven that teams with a shrewd eye for talent can compete on a level playing field with those with bulging wallets.

From a spring of hope to a winter of despair, 1989 was truly a season of both darkness and light for the Yankees. The enlightened hirings and predictable firings of Dallas Green and Syd Thrift were further examples of the unconventional, oddly productive, but ultimately disappointing pattern of comings and goings that have characterized the Yankees during the 1980s. As in each of the previous three seasons, the Yankees challenged for the division lead early, but started to fade by June. Once again, that gradual erosion was a mere prelude to total collapse in August. The return of a hero from the team's most recent glory days—this time, Bucky Dent—created a momentary narcotic like euphoria that yielded to the inevitable sobriety of another September without a pennant race.

But amid the chaos and frustration born of yet another season's opportunities squandered, many detractors failed to notice signs of hope not seen in the Bronx for many years. Sure, the player carousel continued to turn, and the Yankees set a team record by using 49 different players, a major league high for the season that boosted their total for the 1980s to 206, also the most in the majors:

| | | | |
|---|---|---|---|
| New York | 206 | Montreal | 188 |
| Cleveland | 193 | Cincinnati | 186 |
| Chicago | 189 | San Francisco | 181 |
| Texas | 184 | Philadelphia | 179 |
| Oakland | 181 | Pittsburgh | 171 |
| Seattle | 178 | St. Louis | 166 |
| California | 173 | San Diego | 154 |
| Minnesota | 171 | New York | 153 |
| Detroit | 168 | Chicago | 150 |
| Kansas City | 161 | Los Angeles | 144 |
| Baltimore | 156 | Atlanta | 143 |
| Toronto | 146 | Houston | 132 |
| Milwaukee | 136 | | |
| Boston | 125 | | |

But whereas past Yankees teams tossed around their formidable financial prowess to obscure derelict judgment, the 1989 Yankees benefited from sound evaluation of the free-agent market and their own system. No longer stockpiling designated hitters in seeming anticipation of a rule change that would allow them to use nine in the same lineup, New York found everyday starters at key positions: a new second baseman (Steve Sax), a new shortstop (Alvaro Espinoza), and a new center fielder (Roberto Kelly). All were under the age of 30; each played at least 120 games; and none of them played more than 40 games for the Yankees the year before. Together they represented a single-season reconstruction unprecedented in the team's history. In fact, over the past 70 years, only nine other teams filled those three positions in the same season according to the parameters outlined above.

History warns us that such an event is hardly an irrefutable leading indicator of success. Montreal rebuilt in 1985 with Vance Law at second base, Hubie Brooks at shortstop, and Herm Winningham in center, but couldn't withstand the losses of Gary Carter that same season and Andre Dawson two years later. Eight years earlier, the Expos added Dave Cash, Chris Speier, and Dawson (not to mention Warren Cromartie in right field), who formed the nucleus of a team that produced only a single, strike-tainted division title.

Cleveland added Jack Brohamer, Frank Duffy, and Del Unser in 1972, and considered them the solution. But in fact, they were a continuation of the problem. In 1960, the Orioles regarded center fielder Jackie Brandt and their new double-play combo of Marv Breeding and rookie-of-the-year Ron Hansen as the team's foundation for the rest of the decade. Dave Johnson, Mark Belanger, Paul Blair? Who needed 'em, right?

A similar fate may well await the Yankees. After all, Espinoza failed several previous attempts to win a major league position. Both he and Kelly had unsettlingly poor Septembers. On the other hand, the Yankees further helped themselves up the middle by supplementing their battery on both ends. The sudden development of catcher Bob Geren at age 27, after 917 games in the minors, belies the optimistic expectation that he will become an everyday starter. Nevertheless, Geren should provide 60 solid starts a season and adequate accident insurance for years to come at a vital position. And the team's pool of contenders for the starting rotation and long relief was also increased by the unexpected progress of Chuck Cary and Clay Parker, and the acquisition of Eric Plunk and Greg Cadaret. To expect all of them to thrive would be foolish. To expect none of them to contribute would be the same. Sometime within the next few years, after the Yankees finally win another title, they will look back at the reconstruction of 1989 as its foundation.

## WON-LOST RECORD BY STARTING POSITION

| NEW YORK 74-87 | C | 1B | 2B | 3B | SS | LF | CF | RF | P | DH | Leadoff | Relief | Starts |
|---|---|---|---|---|---|---|---|---|---|---|---|---|---|
| Steve Balboni | - | 8-7 | - | - | - | - | - | - | - | 32-30 | - | - | 40-37 |
| Jesse Barfield | - | - | - | - | - | - | 6-6 | 49-65 | - | - | - | - | 55-71 |
| Mike Blowers | - | - | - | 7-4 | - | - | - | - | - | - | - | - | 7-4 |
| Tom Brookens | - | - | 0-1 | 15-21 | 0-1 | - | - | 0-2 | - | 1-1 | - | - | 16-26 |
| Bob Brower | - | - | - | - | - | - | 2-5 | 8-4 | - | - | - | - | 10-9 |
| Greg Cadaret | - | - | - | - | - | - | - | - | 5-8 | - | - | 2-5 | 5-8 |
| John Candelaria | - | - | - | - | - | - | - | - | 4-2 | - | - | 0-4 | 4-2 |
| Chuck Cary | - | - | - | - | - | - | - | - | 6-5 | - | - | 0-11 | 6-5 |
| Bob Davidson | - | - | - | - | - | - | - | - | - | - | - | 0-1 | - |
| Brian Dorsett | 4-2 | - | - | - | - | - | - | - | - | - | - | - | 4-2 |
| Richard Dotson | - | - | - | - | - | - | - | - | 3-6 | - | - | 0-2 | 3-6 |
| David Eiland | - | - | - | - | - | - | - | - | 2-4 | - | - | - | 2-4 |
| Alvaro Espinoza | - | - | - | - | 67-77 | - | - | - | - | - | - | - | 67-77 |
| Bob Geren | 30-26 | - | - | - | - | - | - | - | - | - | - | - | 30-26 |
| Rich Gossage | - | - | - | - | - | - | - | - | - | - | - | 5-6 | - |
| Lee Guetterman | - | - | - | - | - | - | - | - | - | - | - | 30-40 | - |
| Mel Hall | - | - | - | - | - | 18-23 | - | 12-11 | - | 12-16 | - | - | 42-50 |
| Andy Hawkins | - | - | - | - | - | - | - | - | 17-17 | - | - | - | 17-17 |
| Rickey Henderson | - | - | - | - | - | 30-34 | - | - | - | - | 30-34 | - | 30-34 |
| Stan Jefferson | - | - | - | - | - | - | - | 1-1 | - | - | - | - | 1-1 |
| Tommy John | - | - | - | - | - | - | - | - | 3-7 | - | - | - | 3-7 |
| Jimmy Jones | - | - | - | - | - | - | - | - | 4-2 | - | - | 0-5 | 4-2 |
| Roberto Kelly | - | - | - | - | - | - | 59-74 | - | - | - | - | - | 59-74 |
| Steve Kiefer | - | - | - | 1-1 | - | - | - | - | - | - | - | - | 1-1 |
| Dave LaPoint | - | - | - | - | - | - | - | - | 9-11 | - | - | - | 9-11 |
| Marcus Lawton | - | - | - | - | - | 1-2 | - | - | - | - | - | - | 1-2 |
| Al Leiter | - | - | - | - | - | - | - | - | 1-3 | - | - | - | 1-3 |
| Don Mattingly | - | 62-78 | - | - | - | - | - | 0-1 | - | 11-6 | - | - | 73-85 |
| Lance McCullers | - | - | - | - | - | - | - | - | 0-1 | - | - | 17-34 | 0-1 |
| Hensley Meulens | - | - | - | 1-7 | - | - | - | - | - | - | - | - | 1-7 |
| Kevin Mmahat | - | - | - | - | - | - | - | - | 0-2 | - | - | 0-2 | 0-2 |
| Dale Mohorcic | - | - | - | - | - | - | - | - | - | - | - | 12-20 | - |
| Hal Morris | - | 1-0 | - | - | - | - | - | 1-0 | - | 1-0 | - | - | 3-0 |
| Scott Nielsen | - | - | - | - | - | - | - | - | - | - | - | 2-0 | - |
| Mike Pagliarulo | - | - | - | 26-33 | - | - | - | - | - | - | - | - | 26-33 |
| Clay Parker | - | - | - | - | - | - | - | - | 9-8 | - | - | 0-5 | 9-8 |
| Ken Phelps | - | 3-2 | - | - | - | - | - | - | - | 15-26 | - | - | 18-28 |
| Eric Plunk | - | - | - | - | - | - | - | - | 4-3 | - | - | 7-13 | 4-3 |
| Luis Polonia | - | - | - | - | - | 22-28 | - | - | - | 2-6 | 1-3 | - | 24-34 |
| Jamie Quirk | 2-4 | - | - | - | - | - | - | - | - | - | - | - | 2-4 |
| Dave Righetti | - | - | - | - | - | - | - | - | - | - | - | 35-20 | - |
| Deion Sanders | - | - | - | - | - | 3-0 | 7-2 | - | - | - | 3-1 | - | 10-2 |
| Steve Sax | - | - | 73-85 | - | - | - | - | - | - | - | 39-49 | - | 73-85 |
| Don Schulze | - | - | - | - | - | - | - | - | 1-1 | - | - | - | 1-1 |
| Don Slaught | 38-55 | - | - | - | - | - | - | - | - | 0-1 | - | - | 38-56 |
| Walt Terrell | - | - | - | - | - | - | - | - | 6-7 | - | - | - | 6-7 |
| Wayne Tolleson | - | - | 1-1 | 10-10 | 6-6 | - | - | - | - | - | 1-0 | - | 17-17 |
| Randy Velarde | - | - | - | 14-11 | 1-3 | - | - | - | - | - | - | - | 15-14 |
| Gary Ward | - | - | - | - | - | - | - | 3-3 | - | 0-1 | - | - | 3-4 |

## Batting vs. Left and Right Handed Pitchers

| | | BA | Rank | SA | Rank | OBA | Rank | HR % | Rank | BB % | Rank | SO % | Rank |
|---|---|---|---|---|---|---|---|---|---|---|---|---|---|
| Steve Balboni | vs. Lefties | .247 | 119 | .505 | 15 | .296 | 131 | 6.70 | 4 | 6.57 | 101 | 18.31 | 132 |
| | vs. Righties | .217 | -- | .377 | -- | .298 | -- | 3.77 | -- | 9.09 | -- | 23.14 | -- |
| Jesse Barfield | vs. Lefties | .238 | 127 | .419 | 58 | .398 | 16 | 5.00 | 17 | 21.26 | 1 | 21.26 | 147 |
| | vs. Righties | .233 | 129 | .413 | 53 | .319 | 94 | 4.16 | 22 | 10.54 | 44 | 25.98 | 165 |
| Tom Brookens | vs. Lefties | .267 | 81 | .422 | 55 | .312 | 107 | 3.45 | 40 | 6.30 | 105 | 14.17 | 102 |
| | vs. Righties | .135 | -- | .135 | -- | .182 | -- | 0.00 | -- | 5.36 | -- | 16.07 | -- |
| Alvaro Espinoza | vs. Lefties | .383 | 2 | .426 | 53 | .410 | 9 | 0.00 | 134 | 4.42 | 143 | 8.29 | 35 |
| | vs. Righties | .235 | 126 | .287 | 152 | .247 | 164 | 0.00 | 158 | 1.65 | 171 | 12.40 | 71 |
| Bob Geren | vs. Lefties | .284 | 60 | .433 | 47 | .324 | 90 | 2.99 | 54 | 5.41 | 127 | 10.81 | 65 |
| | vs. Righties | .290 | 30 | .464 | 30 | .331 | 73 | 5.07 | 14 | 5.30 | 144 | 23.84 | 159 |
| Mel Hall | vs. Lefties | .159 | 171 | .217 | 171 | .224 | 168 | 1.45 | 98 | 7.79 | 77 | 9.09 | 46 |
| | vs. Righties | .284 | 39 | .476 | 24 | .312 | 102 | 5.48 | 10 | 4.78 | 152 | 9.55 | 37 |
| Roberto Kelly | vs. Lefties | .372 | 4 | .497 | 19 | .424 | 4 | 2.07 | 76 | 7.45 | 88 | 13.66 | 93 |
| | vs. Righties | .267 | 70 | .378 | 84 | .342 | 54 | 2.03 | 82 | 8.61 | 71 | 19.88 | 136 |
| Don Mattingly | vs. Lefties | .338 | 12 | .532 | 8 | .382 | 24 | 3.38 | 42 | 7.25 | 91 | 5.73 | 18 |
| | vs. Righties | .282 | 42 | .444 | 36 | .332 | 70 | 3.81 | 29 | 7.42 | 98 | 3.48 | 1 |
| Mike Pagliarulo | vs. Lefties | .242 | -- | .303 | -- | .306 | -- | 0.00 | -- | 8.33 | -- | 25.00 | -- |
| | vs. Righties | .189 | 166 | .295 | 147 | .260 | 157 | 2.11 | 78 | 7.69 | 93 | 16.35 | 110 |
| Luis Polonia | vs. Lefties | .310 | 27 | .338 | 128 | .347 | 58 | 0.00 | 134 | 4.00 | 150 | 12.00 | 78 |
| | vs. Righties | .298 | 24 | .398 | 63 | .337 | 60 | 0.83 | 131 | 5.63 | 136 | 8.95 | 33 |
| Steve Sax | vs. Lefties | .381 | 3 | .470 | 32 | .427 | 3 | 0.99 | 117 | 7.62 | 83 | 3.59 | 6 |
| | vs. Righties | .285 | 38 | .350 | 108 | .335 | 65 | 0.67 | 140 | 7.09 | 103 | 7.29 | 18 |
| Don Slaught | vs. Lefties | .237 | 128 | .405 | 72 | .301 | 122 | 1.53 | 94 | 8.90 | 61 | 15.75 | 112 |
| | vs. Righties | .260 | 83 | .352 | 107 | .324 | 83 | 1.37 | 111 | 6.91 | 110 | 13.82 | 82 |
| Wayne Tolleson | vs. Lefties | .229 | 139 | .354 | 112 | .315 | 102 | 2.08 | 75 | 11.11 | 31 | 16.67 | 120 |
| | vs. Righties | .130 | -- | .196 | -- | .223 | -- | 0.00 | -- | 9.43 | -- | 13.21 | -- |
| Team Average | vs. Lefties | .298 | 1 | .427 | 1 | .362 | 1 | 2.33 | 7 | 9.18 | 4 | 12.37 | 7 |
| | vs. Righties | .255 | 11 | .373 | 10 | .316 | 11 | 2.41 | 5 | 7.76 | 12 | 14.26 | 6 |
| League Average | vs. Lefties | .266 | | .391 | | .328 | | 2.18 | | 8.18 | | 13.58 | |
| | vs. Righties | .258 | | .380 | | .325 | | 2.26 | | 8.56 | | 14.57 | |

## Batting with Runners on Base and Bases Empty

| | | BA | Rank | SA | Rank | OBA | Rank | HR % | Rank | BB % | Rank | SO % | Rank |
|---|---|---|---|---|---|---|---|---|---|---|---|---|---|
| Steve Balboni | Runners On | .259 | 100 | .500 | 15 | .313 | 120 | 5.88 | 9 | 7.29 | 107 | 16.67 | 126 |
| | Bases Empty | .208 | 153 | .408 | 59 | .275 | 150 | 5.38 | 12 | 7.75 | 83 | 24.65 | 161 |
| Jesse Barfield | Runners On | .226 | 155 | .426 | 53 | .360 | 53 | 5.11 | 15 | 16.90 | 11 | 24.83 | 165 |
| | Bases Empty | .241 | 115 | .406 | 62 | .332 | 59 | 3.85 | 35 | 11.69 | 20 | 24.00 | 160 |
| Tom Brookens | Runners On | .306 | 34 | .400 | 73 | .348 | 68 | 1.18 | 111 | 6.32 | 124 | 9.47 | 52 |
| | Bases Empty | .145 | -- | .265 | -- | .193 | -- | 3.61 | -- | 5.68 | -- | 20.45 | -- |
| Alvaro Espinoza | Runners On | .325 | 15 | .364 | 97 | .336 | 82 | 0.00 | 146 | 1.69 | 171 | 9.28 | 48 |
| | Bases Empty | .253 | 94 | .310 | 141 | .277 | 147 | 0.00 | 153 | 3.26 | 164 | 12.38 | 65 |
| Bob Geren | Runners On | .284 | 60 | .474 | 24 | .303 | 127 | 5.26 | 14 | 1.90 | 170 | 18.10 | 137 |
| | Bases Empty | .291 | 28 | .436 | 39 | .350 | 39 | 3.64 | 42 | 8.33 | 69 | 20.83 | 142 |
| Mel Hall | Runners On | .258 | 104 | .393 | 78 | .291 | 141 | 3.68 | 34 | 6.01 | 128 | 8.20 | 34 |
| | Bases Empty | .263 | 71 | .455 | 29 | .298 | 116 | 5.56 | 10 | 4.81 | 146 | 10.58 | 46 |
| Roberto Kelly | Runners On | .306 | 32 | .392 | 79 | .371 | 40 | 0.54 | 141 | 7.94 | 97 | 15.42 | 115 |
| | Bases Empty | .298 | 22 | .435 | 40 | .367 | 16 | 3.14 | 53 | 8.45 | 67 | 19.72 | 132 |
| Don Mattingly | Runners On | .319 | 20 | .490 | 19 | .379 | 33 | 3.69 | 33 | 10.20 | 59 | 4.66 | 8 |
| | Bases Empty | .288 | 32 | .465 | 22 | .323 | 73 | 3.60 | 43 | 4.57 | 151 | 4.00 | 3 |
| Mike Pagliarulo | Runners On | .231 | 148 | .286 | 161 | .286 | 149 | 0.00 | 146 | 6.12 | 126 | 17.35 | 133 |
| | Bases Empty | .174 | 169 | .303 | 149 | .253 | 165 | 3.03 | 57 | 8.90 | 51 | 17.81 | 116 |
| Luis Polonia | Runners On | .294 | 44 | .394 | 76 | .318 | 112 | 1.67 | 93 | 4.12 | 159 | 9.79 | 58 |
| | Bases Empty | .304 | 18 | .383 | 81 | .353 | 32 | 0.00 | 153 | 6.25 | 116 | 9.19 | 29 |
| Steve Sax | Runners On | .318 | 22 | .376 | 88 | .367 | 45 | 0.78 | 133 | 7.90 | 98 | 6.19 | 15 |
| | Bases Empty | .313 | 10 | .394 | 73 | .362 | 24 | 0.76 | 133 | 6.81 | 102 | 6.10 | 7 |
| Don Slaught | Runners On | .255 | 110 | .324 | 143 | .315 | 116 | 0.00 | 146 | 7.78 | 99 | 11.38 | 72 |
| | Bases Empty | .249 | 103 | .405 | 65 | .316 | 90 | 2.44 | 75 | 7.56 | 88 | 16.89 | 108 |
| Team Average | Runners On | .280 | 3 | .399 | 4 | .343 | 3 | 2.30 | 5 | 8.83 | 9 | 12.43 | 4 |
| | Bases Empty | .261 | 5 | .385 | 6 | .322 | 5 | 2.45 | 4 | 7.75 | 8 | 14.62 | 6 |
| League Average | Runners On | .268 | | .389 | | .336 | | 2.15 | | 9.17 | | 13.53 | |
| | Bases Empty | .255 | | .380 | | .317 | | 2.29 | | 7.84 | | 14.86 | |

## Overall Batting Compared to Late Inning Pressure Situations

| | | BA | Rank | SA | Rank | OBA | Rank | HR % | Rank | BB % | Rank | SO % | Rank | RDI % | Rank |
|---|---|---|---|---|---|---|---|---|---|---|---|---|---|---|---|
| Steve Balboni | Overall | .237 | 140 | .460 | 22 | .296 | 137 | 5.67 | 7 | 7.49 | 95 | 20.06 | 143 | .248 | 114 |
| | Pressure | .300 | 38 | .550 | 11 | .364 | 44 | 7.50 | 4 | 9.09 | 73 | 25.00 | 145 | .143 | 137 |
| Jesse Barfield | Overall | .234 | 145 | .415 | 56 | .345 | 47 | 4.41 | 17 | 14.15 | 11 | 24.39 | 164 | .199 | 157 |
| | Pressure | .141 | 165 | .310 | 113 | .291 | 122 | 4.23 | 31 | 17.44 | 5 | 31.40 | 159 | .273 | 76 |
| Alvaro Espinoza | Overall | .282 | 38 | .332 | 137 | .301 | 127 | 0.00 | 166 | 2.57 | 169 | 11.03 | 59 | .271 | 75 |
| | Pressure | .306 | 36 | .323 | 110 | .328 | 78 | 0.00 | 107 | 2.94 | 154 | 7.35 | 16 | .308 | 58 |
| Bob Geren | Overall | .288 | 33 | .454 | 26 | .329 | 72 | 4.39 | 19 | 5.33 | 147 | 19.56 | 140 | .236 | 124 |
| | Pressure | .265 | 72 | .441 | 39 | .297 | 112 | 5.88 | 15 | 5.26 | 139 | 21.05 | 123 | .182 | 121 |
| Mel Hall | Overall | .260 | 83 | .427 | 44 | .295 | 139 | 4.71 | 13 | 5.37 | 145 | 9.46 | 40 | .321 | 31 |
| | Pressure | .256 | 84 | .419 | 49 | .306 | 99 | 4.65 | 25 | 8.16 | 90 | 12.24 | 47 | .400 | 19 |
| Roberto Kelly | Overall | .302 | 18 | .417 | 52 | .369 | 20 | 2.04 | 84 | 8.23 | 77 | 17.87 | 128 | .282 | 63 |
| | Pressure | .324 | 24 | .437 | 42 | .415 | 16 | 2.82 | 59 | 13.41 | 31 | 21.95 | 130 | .263 | 85 |
| Don Mattingly | Overall | .303 | 17 | .477 | 11 | .351 | 42 | 3.65 | 32 | 7.36 | 99 | 4.33 | 4 | .370 | 10 |
| | Pressure | .313 | 32 | .563 | 10 | .382 | 33 | 5.00 | 21 | 10.11 | 64 | 5.62 | 7 | .538 | 3 |
| Mike Pagliarulo | Overall | .197 | 171 | .296 | 161 | .266 | 167 | 1.79 | 94 | 7.79 | 92 | 17.62 | 126 | .154 | 166 |
| | Pressure | .263 | 74 | .342 | 99 | .333 | 72 | 0.00 | 107 | 9.52 | 70 | 14.29 | 63 | .250 | 87 |
| Luis Polonia | Overall | .300 | 19 | .388 | 80 | .338 | 60 | 0.69 | 141 | 5.36 | 146 | 9.44 | 39 | .264 | 83 |
| | Pressure | .344 | 13 | .475 | 24 | .369 | 39 | 1.64 | 88 | 4.62 | 145 | 15.38 | 73 | .208 | 113 |
| Steve Sax | Overall | .315 | 9 | .387 | 82 | .364 | 26 | 0.77 | 140 | 7.25 | 102 | 6.14 | 9 | .260 | 93 |
| | Pressure | .345 | 12 | .429 | 45 | .356 | 49 | 1.19 | 104 | 2.27 | 163 | 5.68 | 8 | .303 | 62 |
| Don Slaught | Overall | .251 | 112 | .371 | 96 | .315 | 100 | 1.43 | 110 | 7.65 | 94 | 14.54 | 93 | .263 | 86 |
| | Pressure | .295 | 43 | .393 | 65 | .358 | 46 | 0.00 | 107 | 5.88 | 127 | 17.65 | 101 | .346 | 39 |
| Team Average | Overall | .269 | 4 | .391 | 5 | .331 | 3 | 2.38 | 4 | 8.23 | 8 | 13.63 | 4 | .268 | 10 |
| | Pressure | .279 | 2 | .410 | 2 | .343 | 1 | 2.76 | 3 | 8.67 | 9 | 16.63 | 3 | .305 | 1 |
| League Average | Overall | .261 | | .384 | | .326 | | 2.23 | | 8.44 | | 14.26 | | .269 | |
| | Pressure | .247 | | .357 | | .318 | | 2.02 | | 9.02 | | 17.90 | | .254 | |

## Additional Miscellaneous Batting Comparisons

| | Grass Surface | | Artificial Surface | | Home Games | | Road Games | | Runners in Scoring Position | | Runners in Scoring Pos and Two Outs | | Leading Off Inning | | Runners on 3B with less than 2 Outs | |
|---|---|---|---|---|---|---|---|---|---|---|---|---|---|---|---|---|
| | BA | Rank | BA | Rank | BA | Rank | BA | Rank | BA | Rank | BA | Rank | OBA | Rank | RDI % | Rank |
| Steve Balboni | .233 | 134 | .255 | 83 | .236 | 125 | .237 | 129 | .230 | 131 | .216 | 108 | .297 | 114 | .516 | 118 |
| Jesse Barfield | .241 | 113 | .195 | 147 | .241 | 117 | .227 | 143 | .190 | 163 | .171 | 143 | .321 | 88 | .391 | 153 |
| Tom Brookens | .229 | 140 | .208 | -- | .246 | -- | .212 | -- | .190 | -- | .192 | 126 | .176 | -- | .300 | 169 |
| Alvaro Espinoza | .282 | 43 | .282 | 50 | .299 | 31 | .267 | 71 | .318 | 24 | .352 | 6 | .233 | 164 | .519 | 117 |
| Bob Geren | .273 | 56 | .364 | -- | .311 | 17 | .263 | 79 | .277 | 71 | .217 | -- | .333 | 64 | .200 | -- |
| Mel Hall | .263 | 74 | .237 | 114 | .282 | 48 | .233 | 138 | .273 | 74 | .238 | 83 | .207 | 170 | .667 | 39 |
| Roberto Kelly | .289 | 34 | .358 | 6 | .317 | 14 | .288 | 37 | .286 | 55 | .291 | 31 | .355 | 39 | .550 | 100 |
| Don Mattingly | .297 | 21 | .337 | 15 | .334 | 7 | .271 | 64 | .331 | 15 | .260 | 63 | .323 | 84 | .613 | 64 |
| Mike Pagliarulo | .185 | 169 | .265 | -- | .204 | 161 | .191 | 168 | .235 | 121 | .179 | 140 | .230 | 167 | .308 | 168 |
| Luis Polonia | .306 | 15 | .259 | 77 | .372 | 3 | .239 | 126 | .286 | 55 | .340 | 10 | .375 | 25 | .472 | 133 |
| Steve Sax | .316 | 4 | .310 | 28 | .324 | 11 | .306 | 17 | .292 | 44 | .265 | 56 | .356 | 38 | .633 | 49 |
| Don Slaught | .253 | 90 | .241 | 107 | .278 | 55 | .227 | 144 | .281 | 64 | .271 | 48 | .408 | 10 | .684 | 28 |
| Team Average | .266 | 5 | .286 | 1 | .285 | 3 | .254 | 10 | .270 | 4 | .245 | 4 | .320 | 8 | .549 | 10 |
| League Average | .260 | | .262 | | .262 | | .259 | | .262 | | .232 | | .321 | | .566 | |

## Pitching vs. Left and Right Handed Batters

| | | BA | Rank | SA | Rank | OBA | Rank | HR % | Rank | BB % | Rank | SO % | Rank |
|---|---|---|---|---|---|---|---|---|---|---|---|---|---|
| Greg Cadaret | vs. Lefties | .252 | 57 | .325 | 34 | .319 | 58 | 0.81 | 19 | 8.70 | 65 | 15.94 | 33 |
| | vs. Righties | .290 | 118 | .399 | 88 | .372 | 131 | 1.76 | 51 | 11.45 | 123 | 14.76 | 70 |
| John Candelaria | vs. Lefties | .147 | -- | .147 | -- | .194 | -- | 0.00 | -- | 5.56 | -- | 27.78 | -- |
| | vs. Righties | .282 | 111 | .494 | 132 | .321 | 67 | 5.13 | 132 | 5.88 | 31 | 15.88 | 57 |
| Chuck Cary | vs. Lefties | .194 | -- | .343 | -- | .239 | -- | 2.99 | -- | 5.56 | -- | 18.06 | -- |
| | vs. Righties | .212 | 14 | .389 | 80 | .271 | 11 | 3.59 | 119 | 7.53 | 64 | 19.88 | 27 |
| Lee Guetterman | vs. Lefties | .236 | 40 | .283 | 19 | .289 | 27 | 0.94 | 25 | 6.96 | 40 | 15.65 | 38 |
| | vs. Righties | .266 | 85 | .358 | 52 | .310 | 47 | 1.82 | 57 | 6.06 | 36 | 11.11 | 106 |
| Andy Hawkins | vs. Lefties | .323 | 124 | .534 | 128 | .397 | 129 | 3.21 | 107 | 10.69 | 100 | 6.85 | 120 |
| | vs. Righties | .253 | 60 | .375 | 64 | .302 | 38 | 2.34 | 79 | 5.58 | 27 | 15.53 | 60 |
| Tommy John | vs. Lefties | .444 | -- | .611 | -- | .487 | -- | 5.56 | -- | 5.13 | -- | 7.69 | -- |
| | vs. Righties | .318 | 133 | .417 | 102 | .377 | 132 | 1.79 | 56 | 7.97 | 75 | 5.98 | 131 |
| Jimmy Jones | vs. Lefties | .295 | 106 | .466 | 111 | .344 | 80 | 4.55 | 127 | 6.19 | 30 | 8.25 | 106 |
| | vs. Righties | .291 | -- | .437 | -- | .360 | -- | 2.91 | -- | 8.77 | -- | 14.91 | -- |
| Dave LaPoint | vs. Lefties | .326 | 126 | .535 | 130 | .389 | 119 | 4.65 | 128 | 8.25 | 60 | 6.19 | 123 |
| | vs. Righties | .307 | 130 | .469 | 130 | .366 | 130 | 2.08 | 70 | 8.67 | 87 | 10.54 | 113 |
| Lance McCullers | vs. Lefties | .252 | 55 | .392 | 81 | .357 | 95 | 2.10 | 74 | 13.69 | 117 | 16.67 | 28 |
| | vs. Righties | .258 | 71 | .440 | 117 | .312 | 54 | 3.30 | 112 | 6.83 | 50 | 26.34 | 10 |
| Dale Mohorcic | vs. Lefties | .320 | 122 | .520 | 126 | .373 | 104 | 4.00 | 120 | 7.27 | 45 | 6.36 | 121 |
| | vs. Righties | .260 | | .409 | | .336 | -- | 3.15 | -- | 6.94 | -- | 11.81 | -- |
| Clay Parker | vs. Lefties | .281 | 96 | .401 | 86 | .330 | 69 | 1.84 | 69 | 6.75 | 36 | 10.97 | 78 |
| | vs. Righties | .249 | 49 | .382 | 73 | .295 | 32 | 3.21 | 108 | 5.56 | 26 | 10.00 | 115 |
| Eric Plunk | vs. Lefties | .223 | 29 | .380 | 66 | .353 | 90 | 3.61 | 114 | 16.99 | 131 | 21.84 | 11 |
| | vs. Righties | .217 | 17 | .319 | 22 | .315 | 59 | 1.93 | 62 | 12.13 | 128 | 16.74 | 49 |
| Dave Righetti | vs. Lefties | .274 | -- | .355 | -- | .343 | -- | 1.61 | -- | 9.86 | -- | 16.90 | -- |
| | vs. Righties | .277 | 103 | .366 | 57 | .341 | 108 | 0.99 | 12 | 8.30 | 81 | 17.03 | 46 |
| Walt Terrell | vs. Lefties | .333 | 128 | .556 | 132 | .392 | 123 | 4.68 | 129 | 8.99 | 69 | 6.88 | 119 |
| | vs. Righties | .280 | 108 | .379 | 69 | .316 | 60 | 0.62 | 7 | 4.05 | 7 | 9.83 | 117 |
| Team Average | vs. Lefties | .296 | 14 | .463 | 14 | .365 | 14 | 3.14 | 14 | 9.69 | 10 | 10.81 | 14 |
| | vs. Righties | .272 | 13 | .408 | 14 | .332 | 13 | 2.48 | 9 | 7.74 | 7 | 13.86 | 11 |
| League Average | vs. Lefties | .261 | | .382 | | .330 | | 2.16 | | 9.16 | | 13.03 | |
| | vs. Righties | .261 | | .385 | | .323 | | 2.28 | | 7.96 | | 15.09 | |

## Pitching with Runners on Base and Bases Empty

| | | BA | Rank | SA | Rank | OBA | Rank | HR % | Rank | BB % | Rank | SO % | Rank |
|---|---|---|---|---|---|---|---|---|---|---|---|---|---|
| Greg Cadaret | Runners On | .333 | 130 | .432 | 111 | .414 | 133 | 1.35 | 37 | 12.50 | 117 | 15.53 | 48 |
| | Bases Empty | .231 | 34 | .331 | 33 | .303 | 47 | 1.65 | 41 | 8.99 | 93 | 14.61 | 58 |
| Chuck Cary | Runners On | .223 | 20 | .431 | 109 | .301 | 24 | 5.38 | 133 | 10.20 | 88 | 14.97 | 52 |
| | Bases Empty | .202 | 9 | .354 | 45 | .245 | 3 | 2.47 | 81 | 5.45 | 30 | 22.18 | 22 |
| Lee Guetterman | Runners On | .260 | 63 | .349 | 39 | .318 | 48 | 1.56 | 50 | 7.91 | 50 | 11.63 | 80 |
| | Bases Empty | .255 | 68 | .324 | 27 | .289 | 31 | 1.60 | 38 | 4.57 | 13 | 13.20 | 76 |
| Andy Hawkins | Runners On | .322 | 127 | .466 | 127 | .395 | 127 | 2.15 | 85 | 9.92 | 82 | 10.19 | 100 |
| | Bases Empty | .269 | 87 | .455 | 115 | .325 | 80 | 3.24 | 109 | 7.29 | 65 | 11.21 | 99 |
| Tommy John | Runners On | .330 | 129 | .443 | 118 | .397 | 129 | 2.61 | 100 | 9.63 | 78 | 7.41 | 123 |
| | Bases Empty | .340 | 135 | .444 | 114 | .387 | 133 | 2.08 | 61 | 5.81 | 38 | 5.16 | 135 |
| Dave LaPoint | Runners On | .336 | 131 | .464 | 125 | .395 | 128 | 0.95 | 18 | 8.71 | 61 | 8.30 | 119 |
| | Bases Empty | .290 | 117 | .494 | 130 | .350 | 109 | 3.86 | 127 | 8.48 | 85 | 10.95 | 102 |
| Lance McCullers | Runners On | .283 | 98 | .480 | 130 | .367 | 114 | 4.61 | 129 | 11.48 | 106 | 20.77 | 10 |
| | Bases Empty | .231 | 33 | .364 | 56 | .300 | 42 | 1.16 | 18 | 8.42 | 84 | 23.16 | 15 |
| Dale Mohorcic | Runners On | .299 | 117 | .513 | 131 | .391 | 124 | 5.13 | 131 | 10.07 | 86 | 7.91 | 120 |
| | Bases Empty | .273 | -- | .400 | -- | .304 | -- | 1.82 | -- | 3.48 | -- | 11.30 | -- |
| Clay Parker | Runners On | .278 | 92 | .369 | 63 | .338 | 77 | 1.14 | 22 | 7.96 | 51 | 9.45 | 107 |
| | Bases Empty | .255 | 67 | .403 | 85 | .294 | 38 | 3.45 | 113 | 4.90 | 22 | 11.11 | 100 |
| Eric Plunk | Runners On | .212 | 14 | .329 | 25 | .310 | 38 | 2.35 | 92 | 12.32 | 113 | 20.69 | 12 |
| | Bases Empty | .227 | 27 | .360 | 49 | .351 | 111 | 2.96 | 96 | 16.12 | 134 | 17.77 | 41 |
| Dave Righetti | Runners On | .266 | 76 | .345 | 35 | .338 | 75 | 0.72 | 11 | 9.76 | 81 | 15.85 | 43 |
| | Bases Empty | .288 | 113 | .384 | 75 | .346 | 108 | 1.60 | 39 | 7.35 | 66 | 18.38 | 33 |
| Walt Terrell | Runners On | .292 | 112 | .390 | 83 | .319 | 50 | 1.95 | 72 | 4.24 | 5 | 9.70 | 106 |
| | Bases Empty | .320 | 130 | .539 | 135 | .386 | 131 | 3.37 | 112 | 8.63 | 87 | 7.11 | 129 |
| Team Average | Runners On | .300 | 14 | .441 | 14 | .368 | 14 | 2.68 | 12 | 9.56 | 10 | 12.31 | 11 |
| | Bases Empty | .266 | 10 | .417 | 13 | .325 | 11 | 2.75 | 12 | 7.51 | 6 | 13.13 | 12 |
| League Average | Runners On | .268 | | .389 | | .336 | | 2.15 | | 9.17 | | 13.53 | |
| | Bases Empty | .255 | | .380 | | .317 | | 2.29 | | 7.84 | | 14.86 | |

## Overall Pitching Compared to Late Inning Pressure Situations

| | | BA | Rank | SA | Rank | OBA | Rank | HR % | Rank | BB % | Rank | SO % | Rank |
|---|---|---|---|---|---|---|---|---|---|---|---|---|---|
| Greg Cadaret | Overall | .280 | 104 | .379 | 69 | .358 | 121 | 1.51 | 30 | 10.73 | 112 | 15.07 | 54 |
| | Pressure | .389 | 127 | .519 | 120 | .462 | 131 | 0.00 | 1 | 13.85 | 113 | 10.77 | 102 |
| Chuck Cary | Overall | .209 | 11 | .381 | 71 | .266 | 6 | 3.49 | 125 | 7.18 | 49 | 19.55 | 24 |
| | Pressure | .200 | 25 | .250 | 18 | .289 | 33 | 0.00 | 1 | 10.87 | 83 | 21.74 | 26 |
| Lee Guetterman | Overall | .258 | 63 | .337 | 29 | .304 | 32 | 1.58 | 36 | 6.31 | 30 | 12.38 | 79 |
| | Pressure | .263 | 84 | .349 | 69 | .305 | 55 | 2.15 | 78 | 5.53 | 24 | 12.06 | 84 |
| Andy Hawkins | Overall | .290 | 118 | .460 | 126 | .354 | 112 | 2.80 | 104 | 8.37 | 71 | 10.79 | 99 |
| | Pressure | .491 | 133 | .849 | 134 | .550 | 133 | 5.66 | 130 | 11.48 | 95 | 0.00 | 133 |
| Tommy John | Overall | .336 | 134 | .444 | 120 | .392 | 134 | 2.32 | 78 | 7.59 | 56 | 6.21 | 134 |
| | Pressure | .500 | 134 | .625 | 130 | .568 | 134 | 3.13 | 104 | 12.82 | 107 | 12.82 | 79 |
| Dave LaPoint | Overall | .311 | 132 | .481 | 131 | .370 | 131 | 2.55 | 91 | 8.59 | 77 | 9.73 | 111 |
| | Pressure | .500 | -- | .600 | -- | .565 | -- | 0.00 | -- | 8.70 | -- | 17.39 | -- |
| Lance McCullers | Overall | .255 | 58 | .418 | 97 | .332 | 83 | 2.77 | 103 | 9.92 | 104 | 21.98 | 14 |
| | Pressure | .250 | 68 | .404 | 95 | .347 | 84 | 2.88 | 99 | 11.30 | 92 | 26.83 | 11 |
| Dale Mohorcic | Overall | .286 | 111 | .458 | 125 | .352 | 111 | 3.52 | 127 | 7.09 | 48 | 9.45 | 117 |
| | Pressure | .236 | 57 | .327 | 53 | .328 | 69 | 1.82 | 67 | 9.23 | 62 | 7.69 | 118 |
| Clay Parker | Overall | .264 | 74 | .391 | 80 | .311 | 45 | 2.58 | 94 | 6.11 | 24 | 10.45 | 102 |
| | Pressure | .280 | -- | .440 | -- | .333 | -- | 4.00 | -- | 7.14 | -- | 3.57 | -- |
| Eric Plunk | Overall | .220 | 19 | .346 | 41 | .333 | 84 | 2.68 | 100 | 14.38 | 134 | 19.10 | 26 |
| | Pressure | .244 | 64 | .395 | 93 | .347 | 83 | 3.49 | 110 | 13.86 | 114 | 16.83 | 51 |
| Dave Righetti | Overall | .277 | 97 | .364 | 53 | .341 | 97 | 1.14 | 15 | 8.67 | 81 | 17.00 | 40 |
| | Pressure | .270 | 88 | .387 | 90 | .353 | 92 | 1.84 | 70 | 11.40 | 93 | 16.58 | 52 |
| Walt Terrell | Overall | .307 | 130 | .470 | 130 | .356 | 117 | 2.71 | 102 | 6.63 | 36 | 8.29 | 122 |
| | Pressure | .467 | -- | 1.200 | -- | .500 | -- | 20.00 | -- | 6.25 | -- | 0.00 | -- |
| Team Average | Overall | .281 | 14 | .428 | 14 | .344 | 13 | 2.72 | 14 | 8.45 | 8 | 12.76 | 12 |
| | Pressure | .295 | 14 | .438 | 14 | .366 | 14 | 2.79 | 13 | 9.65 | 9 | 14.33 | 11 |
| League Average | Overall | .261 | | .384 | | .326 | | 2.23 | | 8.44 | | 14.26 | |
| | Pressure | .250 | | .362 | | .325 | | 2.14 | | 9.50 | | 16.61 | |

## Additional Miscellaneous Pitching Comparisons

| | Grass Surface | | Artificial Surface | | Home Games | | Road Games | | Runners in Scoring Position | | Runners in Scoring Pos and Two Outs | | Leading Off Inning | |
|---|---|---|---|---|---|---|---|---|---|---|---|---|---|---|
| | BA | Rank | BA | Rank | BA | Rank | BA | Rank | BA | Rank | BA | Rank | OBA | Rank |
| Greg Cadaret | .271 | 88 | .329 | 125 | .263 | 82 | .299 | 118 | .328 | 126 | .323 | 126 | .345 | 94 |
| John Candelaria | .263 | -- | .246 | 43 | .230 | -- | .289 | -- | .324 | -- | .474 | -- | .275 | -- |
| Chuck Cary | .201 | 10 | .333 | -- | .223 | 23 | .186 | 4 | .250 | 62 | .152 | 19 | .220 | 5 |
| Lee Guetterman | .266 | 78 | .190 | -- | .262 | 81 | .253 | 54 | .241 | 55 | .188 | 41 | .313 | 51 |
| Andy Hawkins | .289 | 112 | .298 | 104 | .302 | 123 | .271 | 82 | .351 | 134 | .385 | 134 | .313 | 51 |
| Tommy John | .350 | 135 | .288 | 93 | .352 | -- | .325 | 128 | .339 | 129 | .259 | 100 | .412 | 131 |
| Jimmy Jones | .293 | 117 | .000 | -- | .298 | -- | .286 | -- | .354 | -- | .158 | -- | .333 | -- |
| Dave LaPoint | .313 | 130 | .301 | 107 | .286 | 113 | .327 | 130 | .324 | 125 | .232 | 72 | .387 | 122 |
| Lance McCullers | .249 | 52 | .292 | 95 | .256 | 74 | .254 | 57 | .292 | 112 | .236 | 76 | .342 | 90 |
| Dale Mohorcic | .298 | 122 | .158 | -- | .347 | 134 | .214 | -- | .294 | 115 | .333 | 128 | .347 | -- |
| Clay Parker | .274 | 94 | .185 | 5 | .266 | 84 | .262 | 70 | .266 | 84 | .213 | 55 | .302 | 45 |
| Eric Plunk | .224 | 23 | .186 | 6 | .216 | 17 | .223 | 24 | .231 | 34 | .095 | 5 | .347 | 98 |
| Dave Righetti | .285 | 108 | .222 | -- | .291 | 115 | .263 | 73 | .277 | 94 | .310 | 119 | .293 | 37 |
| Walt Terrell | .311 | 128 | .296 | 102 | .328 | 131 | .294 | 113 | .333 | 127 | .344 | 130 | .326 | 73 |
| Team Average | .282 | 14 | .277 | 11 | .284 | 14 | .278 | 13 | .307 | 14 | .268 | 14 | .327 | 10 |
| League Average | .260 | | .262 | | .259 | | .262 | | .262 | | .232 | | .321 | |

# OAKLAND ATHLETICS

- **Shall we mention the "D" word?**
- **Hot in the playoffs? What about the Series?**

Could this be it? The dynasty that everyone has been waiting for? After a string of unlikely Series winners and unusual paths to the championship, at last we have a world champion that acts the part. This is *not* a Cinderella team, it did *not* eke out a Series win because of a grounder through the first baseman's legs, and it did *not* have a home-run hero who might lose a 40-yard dash to Walter Brennan. If this team were a movie star, it would be Clint Eastwood, not Rick Moranis. If a president, it would be Teddy Roosevelt, not Jimmy Carter. If an archcriminal, it would be Nicholson's Joker, not Cesar Romero's.

The A's looked like the best team in the major leagues in the spring. They looked like the best team in the summer. And they certainly looked like the best team in the fall, with as dominant a World Series victory as has ever been witnessed in nearly a century of Fall Classics.

Oakland's sweep was the 14th in World Series history, although they have become rarer in recent years. It had been 13 years since the last one, when the Reds crushed the Yankees in 1976; in fact, that edition of the Big Red Machine had been the only team to sweep a Series in the past 22 years. But in the case of the A's, it was not only notable *that* they won the Series in four games; it was *how* they won it in four.

The interruption caused by the earthquake will forever mark this Series as unique, but in strictly baseball terms, the Athletics themselves made a pretty good case for uniqueness. The combined score of their four-game sweep of the Giants was 32–14, matching the greatest margin of runs by a team en route to a World Series sweep, a record set by the 1932 Yankees against the Cubs (37–19). Oakland never trailed in any game during the 15-day course of the Series. While two other teams also won Series without ever trailing, those teams (the 1963 Dodgers and the 1966 Orioles) achieved that distinction because their opponents hardly scored at all (the '63 Yankees scored four runs, the '66 Dodgers two). The A's scored more runs while never trailing in 1989 than the '63 Dodgers (12) and the '66 Orioles (13) combined for in their respective sweeps.

But what about 1990? Will the A's be able to fulfill even the minimum criterion for a dynasty, one that has escaped every other champion since 1978—a repeat World Series victory?

History shows us that teams that sweep the Series have a greater tendency to win it again the following year than do teams that win Series of longer duration. In other words, sweepers repeat as Series champs more often than nonsweepers do. Here's the scoreboard (we only considered Series since 1905, when it became an annual event):

| | Series | Repeats | Pct. |
|---|---|---|---|
| Sweepers | 13 | 4 | 30.8% |
| Nonsweepers | 71 | 14 | 19.7% |

The four sweepers that repeated as World Series champions the following year were the Cubs in 1907, and the Yankees in 1927, 1938, and 1950. (Attention, Tony LaRussa: The Yankees teams of 1927–28 and 1938–39 were the only teams in history to sweep two consecutive Series.)

But despite the midseason acquisition of Rickey Henderson, Oakland's sweep didn't exactly come out of left field. The 1989 A's weren't just *any* World Series sweepers; they had also been baseball's dominant team (in terms of winning percentage) during the regular season, winning 99 games in a season in which Jose Canseco, Dennis Eckersley, and Walt Weiss spent a combined 220 days on the disabled list. Let's break down the 13 World Series sweeps to reflect the effect of a dominant regular-season team:

| | Series | Repeats | Pct. |
|---|---|---|---|
| Sweepers Who Had Season's Best Record | 9 | 4 | 44.4% |
| Sweepers Who Did Not Have Best Record | 4 | 0 | 0.0% |

Four out of nine may seem like pretty short odds on a repeat of 1989. But you may be thinking, "So what? What about losing Storm Davis, Tony Phillips, and Dave Parker to free agency? And what about Storm and Mark Davis signing with the Royals, and Mark Langston joining the Angels?"

Well, you're right. Every circumstance is different, and we're the first ones to recognize that while historical information and precedents make the future more interesting, they do not serve as a script. And certainly none of the 13 teams that swept a World Series had to contend with the ravages of free agency that swept through the Athletics last fall. But that doesn't mean that teams that went on to defend a championship successfully did so without any squalls.

For example, just among the four teams discussed earlier, the Cubs' Orval Overall, a 23-game winner in 1907, was reduced to a 15–11 record in 1908 due to a hand injury. The '27 Yankees' two 19–game winners, Wilcy Moore and Herb Pennock, and starting second baseman Tony Lazzeri, all were sidelined for considerable time in 1928. The '38 Yankees lost their captain, Lou Gehrig, to his eventually fatal illness early in the '39 season. And the '50 Yankees saw their leader, Joe DiMaggio, hit only .263 with 12 homers in his final season, 1951.

Personnel shifts will always be a factor in any team's effort to repeat. But beyond that, maybe the Athletics won't be riding the crest of a sweepers' wave after all. None of the last four teams that swept a Series (1954 Giants, 1963 Dodgers, 1966 Orioles, 1976 Reds) has managed even a *return* to the Series the following year, much less a victory, even though two of them (the Orioles and Reds) were also dominant regular-season teams. And this was even before baseball's version of parity (no repeat Series winners of any kind) kicked in following the 1978 season!

The Athletics' domination of postseason play was so thorough that not all of the statistical sidelights have been properly documented. Here's one that slipped through the cracks: Rickey Henderson and Carney Lansford joined a select group of players who have batted .400 or better in both the league Championship Series and the World Series in the same year. Only one other player in the '80s did it, and only once before had it been accomplished by a pair of teammates:

| | League Champ. Series | | | World Series | | |
|---|---|---|---|---|---|---|
| **Player** | **AB** | **H** | **BA** | **AB** | **H** | **BA** |
| Brooks Robinson, 1970 Orioles | 12 | 7 | .583 | 21 | 9 | .429 |
| Thurman Munson, 1976 Yankees | 23 | 10 | .435 | 17 | 9 | .529 |
| Bill Russell, 1978 Dodgers | 17 | 7 | .412 | 26 | 11 | .423 |
| Phil Garner, 1979 Pirates | 12 | 5 | .417 | 24 | 12 | .500 |
| Willie Stargell, 1979 Pirates | 11 | 5 | .455 | 30 | 12 | .400 |
| Graig Nettles, 1981 Yankees | 12 | 6 | .500 | 10 | 4 | .400 |
| Rickey Henderson, 1989 A's | 15 | 6 | .400 | 19 | 9 | .474 |
| Carney Lansford, 1989 A's | 11 | 5 | .455 | 16 | 7 | .438 |

As you might have guessed, we do not offer this chart merely as grist for the mill of the agate-minded, but rather as an introduction into the exploration of a Greater Truth. Actually, the question is a simple one: Do players who are hot in the Championship Series remain hot for the World Series? Or, put another way: which was more unusual, Henderson and Lansford continuing their hot hitting into the World Series, or Will Clark falling from .650 in the playoffs to .250 in the Series?

Including Henderson, Lansford and Clark in 1989, there have been 47 players over the past 21 years who have hit .400 or higher in the playoffs (with a minimum of five hits), and whose team has gone on to play in the World Series. Here is the composite batting line for those 47 players in their hot playoff series:

| BA | AB | H | HR | RBI |
|---|---|---|---|---|
| .449 | 632 | 284 | 31 | 135 |

Now, here is the composite batting line for those same players in the World Series that immediately followed their sizzling Championship Series:

| BA | AB | H | HR | RBI |
|---|---|---|---|---|
| .250 | 910 | 227 | 26 | 100 |

Players who were hot enough, collectively, to hit .449 in early October fell to a .250 average in mid-October. The declines in home runs and RBIs are also steeper than they appear, because of the difference in total at–bats in the two groups (traceable to the best-of-five Championship Series format in use until 1985). On a per-at-bat basis, the decline in home runs from the Championship Series to the World Series is actually 42 percent; in RBI, the decline is 49 percent. For every Brooks Robinson in 1970, there's a Brooks Robinson in 1969. The 1969 model is the leadoff hitter on the list of players who hit over .400 in the playoffs, but less than .100 in the subsequent World Series:

| | League Champ. Series | | | World Series | | |
|---|---|---|---|---|---|---|
| **Player** | **AB** | **H** | **BA** | **AB** | **H** | **BA** |
| Brooks Robinson, 1969 Orioles | 14 | 7 | .500 | 19 | 1 | .053 |
| Frank White, 1980 Royals | 11 | 6 | .545 | 25 | 2 | .080 |
| Mike Schmidt, 1983 Phillies | 15 | 7 | .467 | 20 | 1 | .050 |
| Ozzie Smith, 1985 Cardinals | 23 | 10 | .435 | 23 | 2 | .087 |

These figures are not entirely surprising to us. We have presented in past editions some evidence that in any particular game during the regular season, players who are "hot" based on recent performance hit no better than players who have been "cold" (1988 *Analyst*, p. 113; 1987, pp. 97–99). The statistics presented here corroborate the same finding in a somewhat different setting. Namely, there is not a strong historical carryover effect for a hot hitter from the Championship Series into the World Series.

In short, the fact that Henderson and Lansford hit well throughout both of their team's postseason series is the exception to the rule. Clark's performance, in which he tailed off in the World Series after tearing the Cubs apart in the playoffs, is the norm.

## WON-LOST RECORD BY STARTING POSITION

| OAKLAND 99-63 | C | 1B | 2B | 3B | SS | LF | CF | RF | P | DH | Leadoff | Relief | Starts |
|---|---|---|---|---|---|---|---|---|---|---|---|---|---|
| Larry Arndt | - | 1-0 | - | 1-0 | - | - | - | - | - | - | - | - | 2-0 |
| Chris Bando | - | - | - | - | - | - | - | - | - | - | - | - | - |
| Billy Beane | - | 1-0 | - | - | - | 1-0 | - | 12-6 | - | 0-1 | - | - | 14-7 |
| Lance Blankenship | - | - | 9-5 | - | - | 4-0 | - | 6-7 | - | 3-0 | 2-1 | - | 22-12 |
| Todd Burns | - | - | - | - | - | - | - | - | 1-1 | - | - | 28-20 | 1-1 |
| Greg Cadaret | - | - | - | - | - | - | - | - | - | - | - | 11-15 | - |
| Jose Canseco | - | - | - | - | - | - | - | 36-19 | - | 1-4 | - | - | 37-23 |
| Jim Corsi | - | - | - | - | - | - | - | - | - | - | - | 3-19 | - |
| Storm Davis | - | - | - | - | - | - | - | - | 24-7 | - | - | - | 24-7 |
| Bill Dawley | - | - | - | - | - | - | - | - | - | - | - | 1-3 | - |
| Dennis Eckersley | - | - | - | - | - | - | - | - | - | - | - | 47-4 | - |
| Mike Gallego | - | - | 19-13 | 0-1 | 54-31 | - | - | - | - | - | 1-1 | - | 73-45 |
| Ron Hassey | 40-30 | - | - | - | - | - | - | - | - | 1-1 | - | - | 41-31 |
| Scott Hemond | - | - | - | - | - | - | - | - | - | - | - | - | - |
| Dave Henderson | - | - | - | - | - | - | 90-55 | - | - | 0-2 | - | - | 90-57 |
| Rickey Henderson | - | - | - | - | - | 47-34 | - | - | - | 3-0 | 50-34 | - | 50-34 |
| Rick Honeycutt | - | - | - | - | - | - | - | - | - | - | - | 48-16 | - |
| Dann Howitt | - | - | - | - | - | - | - | - | - | - | - | - | - |
| Glenn Hubbard | - | - | 21-18 | - | - | - | - | - | - | 1-1 | 0-1 | - | 22-19 |
| Stan Javier | - | - | - | - | - | 6-5 | 9-8 | 32-20 | - | - | 3-2 | - | 47-33 |
| Doug Jennings | - | - | - | - | - | 1-0 | - | - | - | - | - | - | 1-0 |
| Felix Jose | - | - | - | - | - | 1-0 | - | 9-4 | - | - | - | - | 10-4 |
| Carney Lansford | - | 9-2 | - | 75-55 | - | - | - | - | - | 1-2 | 0-1 | - | 85-59 |
| Mark McGwire | - | 82-57 | - | - | - | - | - | - | - | 1-0 | - | - | 83-57 |
| Mike Moore | - | - | - | - | - | - | - | - | 21-14 | - | - | - | 21-14 |
| Gene Nelson | - | - | - | - | - | - | - | - | - | - | - | 24-26 | - |
| Dave Otto | - | - | - | - | - | - | - | - | 1-0 | - | - | - | 1-0 |
| Dave Parker | - | - | - | - | - | - | - | 0-1 | - | 84-52 | - | - | 84-53 |
| Ken Phelps | - | 1-0 | - | - | - | - | - | - | - | - | - | - | 1-0 |
| Tony Phillips | - | - | 50-27 | 23-6 | 2-4 | 7-2 | - | 0-3 | - | - | 16-5 | - | 82-42 |
| Eric Plunk | - | - | - | - | - | - | - | - | - | - | - | 13-10 | - |
| Luis Polonia | - | - | - | - | - | 29-19 | - | - | - | - | 27-18 | - | 29-19 |
| Jamie Quirk | - | 1-0 | - | - | - | - | - | - | - | - | - | - | 1-0 |
| Dick Scott | - | - | - | - | - | - | - | - | - | - | - | - | - |
| Brian Snyder | - | - | - | - | - | - | - | - | - | - | - | 0-2 | - |
| Terry Steinbach | 59-33 | 4-4 | - | 0-1 | - | 3-3 | - | 4-3 | - | 4-0 | - | - | 74-44 |
| Dave Stewart | - | - | - | - | - | - | - | - | 25-11 | - | - | - | 25-11 |
| Walt Weiss | - | - | - | - | 43-28 | - | - | - | - | - | - | - | 43-28 |
| Bob Welch | - | - | - | - | - | - | - | - | 19-14 | - | - | - | 19-14 |
| Curt Young | - | - | - | - | - | - | - | - | 8-12 | - | - | 0-5 | 8-12 |
| Matt Young | - | - | - | - | - | - | - | - | 0-4 | - | - | 9-13 | 0-4 |

## Batting vs. Left and Right Handed Pitchers

| | | BA | Rank | SA | Rank | OBA | Rank | HR % | Rank | BB % | Rank | SO % | Rank |
|---|---|---|---|---|---|---|---|---|---|---|---|---|---|
| Billy Beane | vs. Lefties | .226 | 143 | .306 | 148 | .222 | 169 | 0.00 | 134 | 0.00 | 170 | 15.63 | 111 |
| | vs. Righties | .294 | -- | .294 | -- | .294 | -- | 0.00 | -- | 0.00 | -- | 16.67 | -- |
| Jose Canseco | vs. Lefties | .260 | 95 | .700 | 1 | .381 | 25 | 14.00 | 1 | 15.87 | 6 | 20.63 | 143 |
| | vs. Righties | .271 | 64 | .497 | 12 | .318 | 96 | 5.65 | 9 | 6.67 | 114 | 28.72 | 169 |
| Mike Gallego | vs. Lefties | .264 | 86 | .312 | 144 | .333 | 80 | 0.00 | 134 | 9.09 | 59 | 11.19 | 66 |
| | vs. Righties | .246 | 110 | .336 | 117 | .323 | 86 | 1.29 | 118 | 8.27 | 77 | 10.15 | 44 |
| Ron Hassey | vs. Lefties | .235 | -- | .324 | -- | .297 | -- | 2.94 | -- | 7.89 | -- | 2.63 | -- |
| | vs. Righties | .226 | 138 | .329 | 127 | .288 | 137 | 1.71 | 91 | 8.08 | 84 | 16.92 | 116 |
| Dave Henderson | vs. Lefties | .287 | 53 | .427 | 51 | .347 | 57 | 2.92 | 55 | 8.42 | 66 | 13.68 | 94 |
| | vs. Righties | .235 | 122 | .360 | 100 | .301 | 115 | 2.45 | 65 | 8.39 | 76 | 23.18 | 152 |
| Rickey Henderson | vs. Lefties | .277 | 70 | .358 | 109 | .413 | 7 | 0.58 | 131 | 18.78 | 2 | 6.57 | 21 |
| | vs. Righties | .272 | 63 | .418 | 49 | .410 | 6 | 2.99 | 49 | 18.66 | 2 | 11.71 | 67 |
| Glenn Hubbard | vs. Lefties | .228 | 141 | .316 | 142 | .323 | 93 | 1.75 | 84 | 12.31 | 26 | 9.23 | 47 |
| | vs. Righties | .176 | -- | .311 | -- | .276 | -- | 2.70 | -- | 12.50 | -- | 15.91 | -- |
| Stan Javier | vs. Lefties | .230 | 138 | .311 | 145 | .278 | 141 | 1.35 | 104 | 6.17 | 108 | 17.28 | 126 |
| | vs. Righties | .254 | 95 | .318 | 134 | .328 | 78 | 0.00 | 158 | 9.74 | 53 | 11.61 | 66 |
| Carney Lansford | vs. Lefties | .389 | 1 | .503 | 16 | .465 | 1 | 0.67 | 127 | 12.79 | 22 | 1.16 | 2 |
| | vs. Righties | .316 | 9 | .368 | 93 | .372 | 22 | 0.25 | 156 | 6.53 | 121 | 5.18 | 5 |
| Mark McGwire | vs. Lefties | .235 | 134 | .439 | 44 | .344 | 67 | 4.55 | 23 | 15.00 | 10 | 13.75 | 95 |
| | vs. Righties | .229 | 134 | .478 | 23 | .337 | 59 | 7.54 | 2 | 13.82 | 11 | 16.86 | 115 |
| Dave Parker | vs. Lefties | .228 | 140 | .409 | 71 | .233 | 165 | 4.72 | 22 | 0.78 | 169 | 13.95 | 99 |
| | vs. Righties | .275 | 57 | .439 | 40 | .329 | 77 | 3.76 | 32 | 7.86 | 88 | 15.50 | 100 |
| Ken Phelps | vs. Lefties | .182 | -- | .182 | -- | .313 | -- | 0.00 | -- | 18.75 | -- | 25.00 | -- |
| | vs. Righties | .246 | 108 | .383 | 79 | .344 | 52 | 3.83 | 28 | 13.21 | 12 | 20.28 | 138 |
| Tony Phillips | vs. Lefties | .259 | 98 | .360 | 100 | .364 | 40 | 0.00 | 134 | 13.17 | 17 | 11.38 | 69 |
| | vs. Righties | .263 | 78 | .343 | 111 | .336 | 61 | 1.28 | 119 | 10.08 | 49 | 13.17 | 77 |
| Terry Steinbach | vs. Lefties | .258 | 102 | .352 | 114 | .298 | 128 | 1.89 | 81 | 5.36 | 130 | 10.71 | 64 |
| | vs. Righties | .281 | 43 | .353 | 106 | .330 | 75 | 1.36 | 114 | 6.50 | 122 | 14.86 | 96 |
| Walt Weiss | vs. Lefties | .228 | 141 | .281 | 156 | .254 | 155 | 0.00 | 134 | 3.39 | 157 | 15.25 | 109 |
| | vs. Righties | .235 | 125 | .330 | 125 | .312 | 103 | 1.68 | 93 | 9.31 | 59 | 14.71 | 95 |
| Team Average | vs. Lefties | .266 | 7 | .389 | 7 | .335 | 6 | 2.17 | 9 | 9.29 | 3 | 11.74 | 3 |
| | vs. Righties | .259 | 7 | .378 | 9 | .330 | 4 | 2.41 | 4 | 9.16 | 4 | 14.87 | 8 |
| League Average | vs. Lefties | .266 | | .391 | | .328 | | 2.18 | | 8.18 | | 13.58 | |
| | vs. Righties | .258 | | .380 | | .325 | | 2.26 | | 8.56 | | 14.57 | |

## Batting with Runners on Base and Bases Empty

| | | BA | Rank | SA | Rank | OBA | Rank | HR % | Rank | BB % | Rank | SO % | Rank |
|---|---|---|---|---|---|---|---|---|---|---|---|---|---|
| Jose Canseco | Runners On | .322 | 17 | .602 | 2 | .377 | 35 | 7.63 | 1 | 9.42 | 69 | 23.19 | 157 |
| | Bases Empty | .211 | 149 | .477 | 15 | .283 | 141 | 7.34 | 1 | 8.33 | 69 | 30.83 | 169 |
| Mike Gallego | Runners On | .247 | 123 | .318 | 148 | .300 | 132 | 0.65 | 137 | 5.06 | 146 | 7.87 | 30 |
| | Bases Empty | .256 | 84 | .335 | 120 | .346 | 42 | 0.99 | 123 | 11.26 | 22 | 12.55 | 66 |
| Ron Hassey | Runners On | .223 | 158 | .295 | 155 | .289 | 145 | 0.89 | 128 | 9.30 | 70 | 14.73 | 102 |
| | Bases Empty | .231 | 130 | .353 | 103 | .290 | 127 | 2.56 | 72 | 7.10 | 98 | 15.38 | 97 |
| Dave Henderson | Runners On | .255 | 111 | .360 | 108 | .317 | 113 | 1.82 | 89 | 8.71 | 80 | 20.65 | 147 |
| | Bases Empty | .247 | 106 | .398 | 69 | .312 | 97 | 3.29 | 48 | 8.11 | 72 | 20.12 | 137 |
| Rickey Henderson | Runners On | .288 | 53 | .419 | 57 | .449 | 2 | 2.09 | 75 | 22.44 | 2 | 11.42 | 75 |
| | Bases Empty | .266 | 62 | .389 | 76 | .388 | 6 | 2.29 | 79 | 16.43 | 5 | 9.29 | 30 |
| Stan Javier | Runners On | .257 | 106 | .340 | 135 | .335 | 86 | 0.69 | 136 | 10.71 | 47 | 12.50 | 88 |
| | Bases Empty | .241 | 118 | .295 | 153 | .300 | 112 | 0.00 | 153 | 7.22 | 95 | 13.33 | 76 |
| Carney Lansford | Runners On | .321 | 18 | .374 | 90 | .403 | 15 | 0.00 | 146 | 10.92 | 41 | 3.52 | 3 |
| | Bases Empty | .347 | 2 | .429 | 46 | .395 | 5 | 0.65 | 140 | 6.02 | 125 | 4.52 | 4 |
| Mark McGwire | Runners On | .263 | 96 | .522 | 8 | .346 | 72 | 7.14 | 4 | 12.64 | 27 | 16.36 | 124 |
| | Bases Empty | .203 | 159 | .421 | 52 | .333 | 53 | 6.39 | 6 | 15.41 | 7 | 15.72 | 101 |
| Dave Parker | Runners On | .284 | 62 | .464 | 29 | .334 | 88 | 3.83 | 29 | 8.19 | 91 | 11.60 | 77 |
| | Bases Empty | .247 | 107 | .404 | 66 | .283 | 140 | 4.11 | 30 | 4.56 | 152 | 18.57 | 121 |
| Ken Phelps | Runners On | .232 | 144 | .404 | 70 | .325 | 101 | 5.05 | 16 | 12.82 | 25 | 22.22 | 151 |
| | Bases Empty | .253 | 93 | .337 | 119 | .360 | 25 | 2.11 | 84 | 14.41 | 8 | 18.92 | 128 |
| Tony Phillips | Runners On | .286 | 57 | .409 | 66 | .336 | 83 | 1.48 | 102 | 7.69 | 100 | 13.68 | 94 |
| | Bases Empty | .242 | 114 | .298 | 151 | .352 | 34 | 0.40 | 149 | 13.79 | 11 | 11.72 | 57 |
| Terry Steinbach | Runners On | .238 | 134 | .317 | 149 | .283 | 152 | 1.59 | 96 | 5.31 | 137 | 14.01 | 97 |
| | Bases Empty | .298 | 21 | .377 | 88 | .345 | 45 | 1.51 | 103 | 6.69 | 106 | 13.03 | 73 |
| Walt Weiss | Runners On | .232 | 145 | .330 | 141 | .277 | 159 | 2.68 | 54 | 4.84 | 149 | 16.94 | 130 |
| | Bases Empty | .234 | 128 | .306 | 145 | .317 | 86 | 0.00 | 153 | 10.79 | 25 | 12.95 | 72 |
| Team Average | Runners On | .267 | 8 | .390 | 9 | .332 | 8 | 2.35 | 4 | 9.05 | 7 | 14.06 | 9 |
| | Bases Empty | .257 | 7 | .375 | 8 | .330 | 3 | 2.34 | 7 | 9.32 | 2 | 13.94 | 4 |
| League Average | Runners On | .268 | | .389 | | .336 | | 2.15 | | 9.17 | | 13.53 | |
| | Bases Empty | .255 | | .380 | | .317 | | 2.29 | | 7.84 | | 14.86 | |

## Overall Batting Compared to Late Inning Pressure Situations

| | | BA | Rank | SA | Rank | OBA | Rank | HR % | Rank | BB % | Rank | SO % | Rank | RDI % | Rank |
|---|---|---|---|---|---|---|---|---|---|---|---|---|---|---|---|
| Jose Canseco | Overall | .269 | 62 | .542 | 2 | .333 | 64 | 7.49 | 1 | 8.91 | 60 | 26.74 | 167 | .423 | 1 |
| | Pressure | .240 | -- | .520 | -- | .321 | -- | 8.00 | -- | 10.71 | -- | 46.43 | -- | .375 | 25 |
| Mike Gallego | Overall | .252 | 110 | .328 | 141 | .327 | 78 | 0.84 | 136 | 8.56 | 70 | 10.51 | 52 | .223 | 141 |
| | Pressure | .118 | 170 | .118 | 171 | .211 | 159 | 0.00 | 107 | 7.69 | 103 | 15.38 | 73 | .111 | 151 |
| Ron Hassey | Overall | .228 | 155 | .328 | 139 | .290 | 148 | 1.87 | 91 | 8.05 | 86 | 15.10 | 99 | .235 | 126 |
| | Pressure | .243 | 95 | .351 | 93 | .300 | 107 | 2.70 | 63 | 7.50 | 108 | 17.50 | 99 | .333 | 42 |
| Dave Henderson | Overall | .250 | 114 | .380 | 89 | .315 | 103 | 2.59 | 63 | 8.40 | 73 | 20.37 | 147 | .302 | 42 |
| | Pressure | .254 | 86 | .433 | 43 | .311 | 95 | 4.48 | 28 | 8.11 | 92 | 22.97 | 138 | .308 | 58 |
| Rickey Henderson | Overall | .274 | 53 | .399 | 70 | .411 | 3 | 2.22 | 74 | 18.69 | 1 | 10.09 | 47 | .250 | 107 |
| | Pressure | .200 | 134 | .308 | 116 | .342 | 60 | 3.08 | 54 | 17.72 | 4 | 16.46 | 92 | .208 | 113 |
| Stan Javier | Overall | .248 | 117 | .316 | 151 | .317 | 99 | 0.32 | 158 | 8.91 | 61 | 12.93 | 76 | .261 | 91 |
| | Pressure | .277 | 61 | .340 | 100 | .393 | 23 | 0.00 | 107 | 15.79 | 9 | 12.28 | 48 | .313 | 56 |
| Carney Lansford | Overall | .336 | 2 | .405 | 64 | .398 | 5 | 0.36 | 155 | 8.28 | 76 | 4.06 | 3 | .294 | 50 |
| | Pressure | .262 | 76 | .295 | 123 | .338 | 68 | 0.00 | 107 | 10.29 | 61 | 7.35 | 16 | .308 | 58 |
| Mark McGwire | Overall | .231 | 151 | .467 | 14 | .339 | 59 | 6.73 | 2 | 14.14 | 12 | 16.01 | 105 | .329 | 25 |
| | Pressure | .234 | 103 | .344 | 98 | .296 | 114 | 3.13 | 52 | 8.45 | 85 | 22.54 | 136 | .476 | 7 |
| Dave Parker | Overall | .264 | 74 | .432 | 40 | .308 | 110 | 3.98 | 25 | 6.33 | 123 | 15.17 | 100 | .331 | 23 |
| | Pressure | .226 | 111 | .355 | 88 | .294 | 117 | 3.23 | 48 | 8.82 | 80 | 19.12 | 112 | .188 | 119 |
| Ken Phelps | Overall | .242 | 128 | .371 | 97 | .342 | 51 | 3.61 | 33 | 13.60 | 13 | 20.61 | 148 | .311 | 38 |
| | Pressure | .316 | 27 | .500 | 17 | .395 | 21 | 5.26 | 20 | 11.63 | 42 | 18.60 | 109 | .364 | 32 |
| Tony Phillips | Overall | .262 | 81 | .348 | 122 | .345 | 50 | 0.89 | 135 | 11.07 | 27 | 12.60 | 73 | .255 | 103 |
| | Pressure | .242 | 96 | .379 | 76 | .320 | 87 | 1.52 | 92 | 10.53 | 54 | 19.74 | 119 | .286 | 68 |
| Terry Steinbach | Overall | .273 | 54 | .352 | 117 | .319 | 94 | 1.54 | 103 | 6.11 | 132 | 13.44 | 82 | .252 | 106 |
| | Pressure | .259 | 79 | .389 | 70 | .317 | 91 | 3.70 | 41 | 8.20 | 89 | 18.03 | 105 | .273 | 76 |
| Walt Weiss | Overall | .233 | 147 | .318 | 150 | .298 | 132 | 1.27 | 120 | 7.98 | 88 | 14.83 | 95 | .200 | 154 |
| | Pressure | .121 | 169 | .121 | 170 | .216 | 157 | 0.00 | 107 | 10.26 | 63 | 17.95 | 104 | .250 | 87 |
| Team Average | Overall | .261 | 6 | .381 | 10 | .331 | 4 | 2.34 | 6 | 9.20 | 4 | 13.99 | 6 | .282 | 3 |
| | Pressure | .231 | 12 | .334 | 12 | .307 | 10 | 2.09 | 5 | 9.88 | 5 | 18.97 | 12 | .273 | 4 |
| League Average | Overall | .261 | | .384 | | .326 | | 2.23 | | 8.44 | | 14.26 | | .269 | |
| | Pressure | .247 | | .357 | | .318 | | 2.02 | | 9.02 | | 17.90 | | .254 | |

## Additional Miscellaneous Batting Comparisons

| | Grass Surface BA | Grass Surface Rank | Artificial Surface BA | Artificial Surface Rank | Home Games BA | Home Games Rank | Road Games BA | Road Games Rank | Runners in Scoring Position BA | Runners in Scoring Position Rank | Runners in Scoring Pos and Two Outs BA | Runners in Scoring Pos and Two Outs Rank | Leading Off Inning OBA | Leading Off Inning Rank | Runners on 3B with less than 2 Outs RDI % | Runners on 3B with less than 2 Outs Rank |
|---|---|---|---|---|---|---|---|---|---|---|---|---|---|---|---|---|
| Jose Canseco | .299 | 20 | .170 | 162 | .269 | 68 | .268 | 68 | .359 | 5 | .304 | 21 | .302 | -- | .773 | 12 |
| Mike Gallego | .247 | 105 | .279 | 55 | .275 | 56 | .229 | 142 | .217 | 149 | .167 | 144 | .290 | 121 | .538 | 104 |
| Ron Hassey | .235 | 128 | .190 | 150 | .223 | 144 | .231 | 140 | .224 | 141 | .214 | 110 | .339 | 58 | .500 | 119 |
| Dave Henderson | .264 | 72 | .172 | 159 | .280 | 52 | .221 | 155 | .288 | 53 | .208 | 115 | .306 | 105 | .690 | 25 |
| Rickey Henderson | .272 | 57 | .280 | 54 | .289 | 41 | .260 | 84 | .234 | 124 | .250 | 68 | .409 | 8 | .625 | 52 |
| Stan Javier | .238 | 125 | .293 | 39 | .225 | 142 | .267 | 69 | .253 | 99 | .162 | 148 | .310 | 99 | .611 | 65 |
| Carney Lansford | .333 | 3 | .349 | 9 | .309 | 21 | .360 | 3 | .286 | 55 | .278 | 38 | .385 | 19 | .576 | 83 |
| Mark McGwire | .239 | 118 | .184 | 155 | .232 | 134 | .230 | 141 | .269 | 81 | .234 | 87 | .359 | 35 | .581 | 78 |
| Dave Parker | .269 | 62 | .235 | 116 | .279 | 53 | .249 | 104 | .296 | 38 | .241 | 81 | .269 | 146 | .591 | 72 |
| Ken Phelps | .233 | 133 | .290 | -- | .260 | 82 | .222 | -- | .224 | 140 | .143 | 155 | .350 | -- | .750 | 13 |
| Tony Phillips | .261 | 84 | .267 | 63 | .271 | 64 | .253 | 91 | .234 | 123 | .258 | 65 | .339 | 59 | .800 | 7 |
| Terry Steinbach | .282 | 45 | .225 | 128 | .292 | 38 | .256 | 85 | .264 | 84 | .208 | 116 | .357 | 36 | .577 | 81 |
| Walt Weiss | .251 | 96 | .135 | -- | .200 | 165 | .267 | 70 | .231 | 129 | .115 | 162 | .383 | 20 | .444 | 144 |
| Team Average | .266 | 6 | .236 | 14 | .266 | 4 | .256 | 9 | .265 | 7 | .228 | 10 | .335 | 3 | .599 | 3 |
| League Average | .260 | | .262 | | .262 | | .259 | | .262 | | .232 | | .321 | | .566 | |

## Pitching vs. Left and Right Handed Batters

| | | BA | Rank | SA | Rank | OBA | Rank | HR % | Rank | BB % | Rank | SO % | Rank |
|---|---|---|---|---|---|---|---|---|---|---|---|---|---|
| Todd Burns | vs. Lefties | .172 | 7 | .231 | 7 | .250 | 9 | 0.00 | 1 | 9.33 | 79 | 10.00 | 89 |
| | vs. Righties | .212 | 13 | .286 | 9 | .265 | 8 | 1.48 | 37 | 6.25 | 42 | 15.18 | 66 |
| Storm Davis | vs. Lefties | .264 | 74 | .414 | 92 | .353 | 91 | 3.18 | 106 | 12.23 | 112 | 13.04 | 58 |
| | vs. Righties | .310 | 131 | .454 | 124 | .356 | 125 | 2.69 | 95 | 6.30 | 44 | 11.78 | 98 |
| Dennis Eckersley | vs. Lefties | .206 | 16 | .258 | 12 | .218 | 3 | 1.03 | 29 | 0.99 | 1 | 20.79 | 15 |
| | vs. Righties | .119 | | .257 | | .133 | -- | 3.96 | -- | 1.90 | -- | 32.38 | -- |
| Rick Honeycutt | vs. Lefties | .156 | 3 | .200 | 4 | .248 | 8 | 1.11 | 32 | 9.80 | 87 | 15.69 | 37 |
| | vs. Righties | .232 | 27 | .315 | 19 | .291 | 30 | 2.21 | 76 | 7.88 | 70 | 17.73 | 42 |
| Mike Moore | vs. Lefties | .218 | 24 | .277 | 16 | .296 | 33 | 0.70 | 14 | 9.62 | 84 | 17.78 | 24 |
| | vs. Righties | .220 | 19 | .335 | 33 | .277 | 16 | 2.42 | 83 | 7.43 | 61 | 17.47 | 43 |
| Gene Nelson | vs. Lefties | .250 | 53 | .384 | 71 | .331 | 70 | 2.68 | 90 | 10.85 | 103 | 14.73 | 45 |
| | vs. Righties | .174 | 2 | .239 | 2 | .244 | 3 | 1.09 | 16 | 7.77 | 69 | 24.76 | 15 |
| Dave Stewart | vs. Lefties | .264 | 75 | .387 | 77 | .315 | 52 | 2.30 | 78 | 7.33 | 46 | 10.12 | 88 |
| | vs. Righties | .263 | 79 | .403 | 91 | .310 | 50 | 2.37 | 82 | 5.31 | 23 | 19.09 | 32 |
| Bob Welch | vs. Lefties | .211 | 18 | .304 | 25 | .300 | 40 | 0.72 | 16 | 10.74 | 102 | 14.11 | 49 |
| | vs. Righties | .275 | 99 | .417 | 103 | .327 | 80 | 2.67 | 94 | 6.60 | 48 | 17.11 | 45 |
| Curt Young | vs. Lefties | .213 | -- | .250 | -- | .276 | -- | 0.00 | -- | 6.90 | -- | 8.05 | -- |
| | vs. Righties | .275 | 98 | .431 | 111 | .351 | 118 | 2.75 | 98 | 10.05 | 109 | 11.76 | 99 |
| Team Average | vs. Lefties | .226 | 2 | .321 | 1 | .301 | 1 | 1.45 | 2 | 9.48 | 9 | 13.81 | 4 |
| | vs. Righties | .249 | 1 | .370 | 3 | .309 | 2 | 2.28 | 7 | 7.63 | 6 | 16.77 | 4 |
| League Average | vs. Lefties | .261 | | .382 | | .330 | | 2.16 | | 9.16 | | 13.03 | |
| | vs. Righties | .261 | | .385 | | .323 | | 2.28 | | 7.96 | | 15.09 | |

## Pitching with Runners on Base and Bases Empty

| | | BA | Rank | SA | Rank | OBA | Rank | HR % | Rank | BB % | Rank | SO % | Rank |
|---|---|---|---|---|---|---|---|---|---|---|---|---|---|
| Todd Burns | Runners On | .190 | 5 | .246 | 5 | .266 | 7 | 0.70 | 10 | 9.09 | 68 | 12.73 | 71 |
| | Bases Empty | .200 | 8 | .277 | 5 | .254 | 6 | 1.03 | 16 | 6.22 | 46 | 13.40 | 74 |
| Storm Davis | Runners On | .269 | 79 | .364 | 59 | .327 | 61 | 2.02 | 75 | 8.26 | 56 | 13.57 | 62 |
| | Bases Empty | .304 | 124 | .494 | 131 | .378 | 129 | 3.69 | 121 | 10.15 | 108 | 11.42 | 94 |
| Dennis Eckersley | Runners On | .194 | -- | .343 | -- | .194 | -- | 4.48 | -- | 1.39 | -- | 22.22 | -- |
| | Bases Empty | .145 | 1 | .214 | 1 | .164 | 1 | 1.53 | 34 | 1.49 | 1 | 29.10 | 5 |
| Rick Honeycutt | Runners On | .195 | 8 | .276 | 8 | .279 | 11 | 1.63 | 57 | 10.34 | 92 | 15.86 | 42 |
| | Bases Empty | .216 | 21 | .277 | 6 | .275 | 20 | 2.03 | 60 | 6.88 | 58 | 18.13 | 34 |
| Mike Moore | Runners On | .233 | 29 | .337 | 29 | .306 | 30 | 2.15 | 85 | 9.63 | 77 | 17.38 | 34 |
| | Bases Empty | .211 | 12 | .289 | 12 | .274 | 19 | 1.26 | 21 | 7.81 | 76 | 17.77 | 39 |
| Gene Nelson | Runners On | .190 | 6 | .246 | 4 | .293 | 16 | 0.79 | 13 | 13.07 | 121 | 17.65 | 33 |
| | Bases Empty | .212 | 13 | .329 | 31 | .264 | 14 | 2.35 | 77 | 5.49 | 31 | 23.63 | 14 |
| Dave Stewart | Runners On | .243 | 36 | .353 | 44 | .303 | 26 | 1.72 | 62 | 7.69 | 47 | 14.74 | 55 |
| | Bases Empty | .279 | 109 | .424 | 103 | .320 | 68 | 2.77 | 90 | 5.38 | 29 | 14.03 | 66 |
| Bob Welch | Runners On | .221 | 18 | .336 | 27 | .310 | 37 | 1.87 | 69 | 10.51 | 94 | 18.33 | 25 |
| | Bases Empty | .255 | 66 | .372 | 65 | .314 | 62 | 1.49 | 31 | 7.60 | 71 | 13.45 | 72 |
| Curt Young | Runners On | .284 | 103 | .388 | 82 | .361 | 107 | 1.64 | 58 | 9.71 | 79 | 7.77 | 121 |
| | Bases Empty | .249 | 58 | .406 | 90 | .322 | 72 | 2.68 | 86 | 9.34 | 96 | 13.49 | 71 |
| Team Average | Runners On | .234 | 1 | .333 | 1 | .309 | 1 | 1.68 | 4 | 9.54 | 9 | 15.04 | 3 |
| | Bases Empty | .242 | 2 | .359 | 3 | .303 | 1 | 2.08 | 5 | 7.63 | 7 | 15.74 | 4 |
| League Average | Runners On | .268 | | .389 | | .336 | | 2.15 | | 9.17 | | 13.53 | |
| | Bases Empty | .255 | | .380 | | .317 | | 2.29 | | 7.84 | | 14.86 | |

## Overall Pitching Compared to Late Inning Pressure Situations

| | | BA | Rank | SA | Rank | OBA | Rank | HR % | Rank | BB % | Rank | SO % | Rank |
|---|---|---|---|---|---|---|---|---|---|---|---|---|---|
| Todd Burns | Overall | .196 | 4 | .264 | 3 | .259 | 3 | 0.89 | 6 | 7.49 | 54 | 13.10 | 71 |
| | Pressure | .200 | 25 | .283 | 32 | .299 | 50 | 1.67 | 59 | 11.27 | 91 | 13.38 | 73 |
| James Corsi | Overall | .194 | -- | .254 | -- | .252 | -- | 1.49 | -- | 6.71 | -- | 14.09 | -- |
| | Pressure | .195 | 17 | .220 | 10 | .244 | 11 | 0.00 | 1 | 6.67 | 38 | 20.00 | 32 |
| Storm Davis | Overall | .288 | 114 | .435 | 113 | .355 | 115 | 2.93 | 107 | 9.28 | 89 | 12.41 | 77 |
| | Pressure | .278 | 94 | .472 | 114 | .325 | 65 | 5.56 | 129 | 5.00 | 17 | 17.50 | 46 |
| Dennis Eckersley | Overall | .162 | -- | .258 | -- | .175 | -- | 2.53 | -- | 1.46 | -- | 26.70 | -- |
| | Pressure | .130 | 2 | .260 | 22 | .140 | 1 | 3.82 | 116 | 1.47 | 3 | 31.62 | 4 |
| Rick Honeycutt | Overall | .207 | 9 | .277 | 4 | .277 | 10 | 1.85 | 56 | 8.52 | 75 | 17.05 | 38 |
| | Pressure | .210 | 35 | .242 | 14 | .296 | 44 | 0.64 | 37 | 10.87 | 83 | 15.76 | 58 |
| Mike Moore | Overall | .219 | 18 | .307 | 15 | .286 | 17 | 1.59 | 37 | 8.50 | 74 | 17.62 | 34 |
| | Pressure | .228 | 49 | .367 | 80 | .287 | 32 | 1.27 | 48 | 7.78 | 51 | 17.78 | 45 |
| Gene Nelson | Overall | .203 | 7 | .294 | 7 | .277 | 11 | 1.69 | 45 | 8.96 | 87 | 20.90 | 17 |
| | Pressure | .234 | 56 | .315 | 49 | .298 | 46 | 1.80 | 66 | 7.26 | 45 | 16.94 | 50 |
| Dave Stewart | Overall | .264 | 72 | .395 | 81 | .313 | 48 | 2.33 | 80 | 6.38 | 31 | 14.34 | 60 |
| | Pressure | .292 | 104 | .375 | 84 | .340 | 77 | 0.00 | 1 | 6.54 | 36 | 11.21 | 96 |
| Bob Welch | Overall | .241 | 33 | .357 | 49 | .313 | 46 | 1.64 | 42 | 8.82 | 83 | 15.50 | 49 |
| | Pressure | .293 | 107 | .500 | 118 | .379 | 107 | 5.17 | 127 | 11.76 | 97 | 13.24 | 75 |
| Curt Young | Overall | .264 | 71 | .399 | 86 | .338 | 91 | 2.25 | 74 | 9.49 | 95 | 11.11 | 95 |
| | Pressure | .250 | -- | .393 | -- | .364 | -- | 3.57 | -- | 15.15 | -- | 3.03 | -- |
| Team Average | Overall | .239 | 1 | .348 | 1 | .305 | 1 | 1.91 | 3 | 8.46 | 9 | 15.43 | 4 |
| | Pressure | .220 | 1 | .320 | 2 | .289 | 1 | 1.93 | 6 | 8.60 | 4 | 17.39 | 5 |
| League Average | Overall | .261 | | .384 | | .326 | | 2.23 | | 8.44 | | 14.26 | |
| | Pressure | .250 | | .362 | | .325 | | 2.14 | | 9.50 | | 16.61 | |

## Additional Miscellaneous Pitching Comparisons

| | Grass Surface BA | Rank | Artificial Surface BA | Rank | Home Games BA | Rank | Road Games BA | Rank | Runners in Scoring Position BA | Rank | Runners in Scoring Pos and Two Outs BA | Rank | Leading Off Inning OBA | Rank |
|---|---|---|---|---|---|---|---|---|---|---|---|---|---|---|
| Todd Burns | .207 | 12 | .135 | 2 | .195 | 7 | .196 | 6 | .184 | 7 | .156 | 24 | .293 | 38 |
| Storm Davis | .289 | 113 | .281 | 83 | .283 | 107 | .293 | 111 | .269 | 85 | .215 | 58 | .422 | 133 |
| Dennis Eckersley | .170 | 3 | .111 | -- | .176 | -- | .144 | -- | .156 | -- | .118 | -- | .217 | -- |
| Rick Honeycutt | .210 | 16 | .179 | -- | .228 | 30 | .180 | 3 | .268 | -- | .250 | 88 | .254 | 12 |
| Mike Moore | .211 | 17 | .258 | 54 | .202 | 10 | .236 | 36 | .232 | 36 | .235 | 74 | .240 | 9 |
| Gene Nelson | .189 | 6 | .323 | -- | .186 | 4 | .219 | 17 | .178 | 5 | .146 | 17 | .234 | 7 |
| Dave Stewart | .259 | 65 | .288 | 92 | .240 | 46 | .287 | 100 | .222 | 23 | .254 | 95 | .312 | 50 |
| Bob Welch | .236 | 32 | .261 | 60 | .236 | 36 | .247 | 43 | .225 | 28 | .226 | 67 | .269 | 24 |
| Curt Young | .252 | 58 | .328 | 124 | .269 | 91 | .257 | 62 | .264 | 83 | .245 | 85 | .217 | 4 |
| Matt Young | .295 | -- | .257 | -- | .338 | -- | .233 | -- | .254 | 72 | .172 | 32 | .514 | -- |
| Team Average | .236 | 1 | .251 | 4 | .233 | 1 | .244 | 2 | .230 | 1 | .223 | 2 | .294 | 1 |
| League Average | .260 | | .262 | | .259 | | .262 | | .262 | | .232 | | .321 | |

# SEATTLE MARINERS

- **The Kansas City A's are alive and well in Seattle.**
- **Is there life after Langston?**

From 1955 to 1967, there lived a baseball team called the Kansas City Athletics. These were the descendants of the team founded by Connie Mack in Philadelphia in 1901; the team was purchased from Mack by Arnold Johnson and moved to Kansas City in 1955, bringing allegedly major league baseball to what was then its westernmost outpost. But the A's never produced a winning record in their 13 seasons in the Midwest, and under the direction of Charles O. Finley, they set sail for Oakland. It was only after they arrived in the Bay Area in 1968 that they turned things around, winning eight division titles, five Championship Series and four World Series over the past 22 years. During that time, no team has done better in any of those categories.

While they were still in Kansas City, the A's made a series of trades with the New York Yankees that encouraged the media to call the A's the Yankees' "farm team." The reference had some basis in fact: The old Kansas City Blues of the American Association had been a top Yankees' farm team from 1938 through 1954. Mickey Mantle, Phil Rizzuto, Hank Bauer, Bill Skowron, and Billy Martin were some of the blue-chip prospects who played for the Blues en route to New York. But after the Athletics moved there in 1955, the flow of players from Kansas City to New York hardly skipped a beat. Over one four-year span from June 1956 to May 1960, the Yankees and the A's made 14 separate deals that brought the Yankees Roger Maris, Clete Boyer, Ralph Terry, Ryne Duren, and Hector Lopez, among others, for very little in return. In fact, several players (including Terry, Bob Cerv, Enos Slaughter, and Harry "Suitcase" Simpson) shuttled back and forth between the teams, adding to the illusion that Kansas City was still the Yankees' top farm team, and that its players were available to the Bombers as quickly as George Weiss could pick up his telephone.

The Kansas City A's are no more, but the Seattle Mariners are certainly their spiritual successors, in more ways than one. The Mariners have now completed 13 seasons in the American League, and they are the first team since the A's to suffer through 13 consecutive losing seasons. Seattle is now only two years shy of the American League record for consecutive losing seasons; note that counting their last two seasons in Philadelphia, the A's actually share this record with the Red Sox teams of the post-Ruth era:

| | | |
|---|---|---|
| Boston Red Sox | 15 | 1919–33 |
| Phil./K.C. Athletics | 15 | 1953–67 |
| Philadelphia Athletics | 13 | 1934–46 |
| Seattle Mariners | 13 | 1977–89 |

But Seattle's similarity with the A's does not end there. The Mariners also have followed the Kansas City blueprint in terms of trading their young players. Except the Mariners have gone the A's one better. Not content with providing young talent to just *one* major league team, the Mariners have made it their business to spread the best of their young players throughout all of baseball.

Now you might think that all of this is by way of introducing the topic of Mark Langston, who was traded by the Mariners to the Expos last spring. But that trade is probably the *least* damning of their transactions, in our eyes. After all, assuming that Langston was not going to return to the Mariners under any conditions in 1990, Woody Woodward did manage to extract three young pitchers from Montreal (while the Expos received only draft-choice compensation after Langston signed with the Angels following the season). No, the Mariners' reputation for largesse was not built on the Langston deal; a look around the majors reveals the players who spent their rookie seasons with the Mariners but have since moved on.

Oh, one more thing. We're not even going to talk about the ex-Mariners players who are pitchers. The Langston trade stirred up that old litany of Mariners' pitchers who have been traded or who left the team via free agency—you know, Floyd Bannister, Rick Honeycutt, Mike Moore, Shane Rawley, Bud Black. They've taken enough of a beating on that. We'll restrict our discussion to the position players.

Let's see. There's Ivan Calderon with the White Sox and Dave Henderson with the Athletics, Phil Bradley with the Orioles and Danny Tartabull with the Royals, not to mention Spike Owen with the Expos and Kenny Phelps with the Athletics. That's the nucleus of a pretty good team.

We know what you're thinking, "Sure, that list sounds impressive, but perhaps a similar claim could be made for *any* franchise." Frankly, we were struck by the same thought. We've travelled around the country. We know what's in those local sports sections. Who knows how many trees have given their lives for newspaper pages used to chronicle the

"Ones That Got Away" in weekly charts across America?

To find out if the Mariners really have killed themselves with their kindness to others, we tabulated all of the statistics for the 1989 season, assigning each position player's statistics to the organization with which he played his rookie season. (In cases in which someone played for more than one team in his rookie season, or had more than one season qualifying as a rookie with different teams, we assigned his statistics to the last such organization.) Here are the results, with the organizations listed in descending order of at–bats:

| Organization | Players | AB | R | H | HR | RBI | BA |
|---|---|---|---|---|---|---|---|
| Mariners | 31 | 8457 | 1056 | 2170 | 178 | 985 | .257 |
| Mets | 25 | 6422 | 788 | 1640 | 161 | 752 | .255 |
| Blue Jays | 20 | 6269 | 804 | 1621 | 156 | 768 | .259 |
| Cubs | 21 | 6261 | 791 | 1669 | 128 | 730 | .267 |
| White Sox | 24 | 6191 | 753 | 1629 | 91 | 640 | .263 |
| Pirates | 21 | 6010 | 668 | 1540 | 113 | 662 | .256 |
| Reds | 25 | 5825 | 741 | 1538 | 160 | 748 | .264 |
| Red Sox | 19 | 5820 | 783 | 1599 | 106 | 701 | .275 |
| Giants | 24 | 5595 | 760 | 1397 | 160 | 714 | .250 |
| Athletics | 24 | 5477 | 755 | 1413 | 158 | 660 | .258 |
| Brewers | 23 | 5449 | 702 | 1449 | 110 | 627 | .266 |
| Braves | 24 | 5399 | 572 | 1299 | 110 | 551 | .241 |
| Dodgers | 22 | 5359 | 572 | 1415 | 101 | 617 | .264 |
| Twins | 25 | 5347 | 656 | 1415 | 137 | 673 | .265 |
| Rangers | 21 | 5233 | 687 | 1351 | 124 | 563 | .258 |
| Indians | 25 | 5014 | 585 | 1226 | 143 | 610 | .245 |
| Astros | 17 | 4983 | 627 | 1274 | 114 | 612 | .256 |
| Padres | 22 | 4846 | 640 | 1322 | 97 | 544 | .273 |
| Phillies | 23 | 4804 | 550 | 1190 | 104 | 560 | .248 |
| Cardinals | 22 | 4660 | 533 | 1192 | 55 | 416 | .256 |
| Angels | 23 | 4620 | 584 | 1183 | 78 | 463 | .256 |
| Expos | 20 | 4614 | 593 | 1174 | 96 | 510 | .254 |
| Orioles | 17 | 4426 | 520 | 1060 | 98 | 500 | .239 |
| Tigers | 17 | 4077 | 525 | 1005 | 126 | 510 | .247 |
| Royals | 18 | 3745 | 504 | 942 | 75 | 448 | .252 |
| Yankees | 17 | 3673 | 418 | 989 | 86 | 448 | .269 |

The Mariners' organization comes out with a clean sweep with respect to the number of players, total at–bats, runs, hits, home runs, and runs batted in. Twenty-four players who spent their rookie seasons in Seattle had at least 100 major–league at–bats in 1989. Ten had 100 or more hits. Nine reached double figures in home runs.

This tabulation is certainly an indictment of the way business has been conducted in the Kingdome in the past. But the good news for Seattle fans is that under new management, the Mariners may have succeeded in closing the barn door. It's too late to reharness the talents of Henderson, Calderon, Tartabull, and the rest of that group, but it might not be too late to save the current crop of young players. Seattle took a major step in that direction by signing Alvin Davis to a multi year contract last year. Now let's see what happens with Harold Reynolds and Darnell Coles, and eventually with Ken Griffey, Jr., Greg Briley and Jay Buhner.

This latter group is especially interesting because the Mariners gave more playing time to their rookies than did any other team in 1989. That's evident from this chart detailing the offensive totals for last year's rookies (batting by pitchers is not included):

| Team | Rookies | AB | R | H | HR | RBI | BA |
|---|---|---|---|---|---|---|---|
| Mariners | 7 | 1545 | 193 | 380 | 36 | 164 | .245 |
| Cubs | 7 | 1232 | 163 | 343 | 18 | 140 | .278 |
| Orioles | 5 | 1118 | 149 | 282 | 25 | 142 | .252 |
| Brewers | 6 | 869 | 105 | 217 | 15 | 91 | .249 |
| Reds | 6 | 816 | 79 | 193 | 14 | 83 | .236 |
| Mets | 5 | 708 | 101 | 187 | 19 | 75 | .264 |
| Tigers | 7 | 668 | 78 | 135 | 5 | 47 | .202 |
| White Sox | 5 | 585 | 75 | 159 | 9 | 57 | .271 |
| Blue Jays | 7 | 551 | 71 | 136 | 10 | 54 | .246 |
| Rangers | 7 | 483 | 52 | 101 | 10 | 37 | .209 |
| Angels | 7 | 443 | 48 | 97 | 4 | 40 | .218 |
| Braves | 8 | 438 | 30 | 97 | 7 | 39 | .221 |
| Phillies | 6 | 380 | 37 | 96 | 10 | 49 | .252 |
| Yankees | 7 | 372 | 43 | 101 | 11 | 46 | .271 |
| Indians | 7 | 366 | 34 | 77 | 11 | 47 | .210 |
| Dodgers | 6 | 329 | 41 | 78 | 3 | 29 | .237 |
| Pirates | 4 | 287 | 34 | 52 | 6 | 27 | .181 |
| Royals | 4 | 250 | 32 | 57 | 3 | 24 | .228 |
| Astros | 4 | 215 | 31 | 42 | 7 | 28 | .195 |
| A's | 6 | 193 | 28 | 41 | 1 | 10 | .212 |
| Expos | 3 | 189 | 19 | 40 | 1 | 7 | .211 |
| Padres | 5 | 186 | 20 | 41 | 7 | 22 | .220 |
| Giants | 4 | 174 | 20 | 42 | 4 | 19 | .241 |
| Cardinals | 3 | 161 | 19 | 44 | 1 | 16 | .273 |
| Twins | 6 | 144 | 14 | 35 | 0 | 8 | .243 |
| Red Sox | 2 | 82 | 7 | 17 | 0 | 6 | .207 |
| Totals | 144 | 12784 | 1523 | 3090 | 237 | 1307 | .241 |

Once again, the Mariners lead the way in at–bats, runs, hits, home runs, and runs batted in. And for good reason. Of the eight rookies who had the most games, starts, or plate appearances (pick one) in 1989, three were Mariners (Griffey, Briley, and Omar Vizquel). Griffey and Briley were two of the four major league rookies with double-digit home run totals, and Vizquel played in 143 games, two shy of the total of rookie leader Craig Worthington.

What it goes to show is that baseball is a game of redeeming features. Just as a shortstop who throws away a double-play ball or a reliever who gives up a game-winning home run gets an opportunity to redeem himself the next day, so the Mariners have another chance to manage a seemingly talented group of young players. And that talent couldn't have come at a more important time. With the American League West taking on the visage of SuperDivision, the Mariners will need some exceptional performances from their young players if they are to avoid that record of 15 consecutive losing seasons.

## WON-LOST RECORD BY STARTING POSITION

| SEATTLE 73-89 | C | 1B | 2B | 3B | SS | LF | CF | RF | P | DH | Leadoff | Relief | Starts |
|---|---|---|---|---|---|---|---|---|---|---|---|---|---|
| Scott Bankhead | - | - | - | - | - | - | - | - | 18-15 | - | - | - | 18-15 |
| Scott Bradley | 28-33 | 1-1 | - | - | - | 0-1 | - | - | - | 1-3 | - | - | 30-38 |
| Mickey Brantley | - | - | - | - | - | 8-4 | - | 3-7 | - | 4-2 | 1-0 | - | 15-13 |
| Greg Briley | - | - | 5-3 | - | - | 31-48 | - | 5-4 | - | 0-1 | 5-4 | - | 41-56 |
| Jay Buhner | - | - | - | - | - | - | 0-1 | 22-34 | - | - | - | - | 22-35 |
| Mike Campbell | - | - | - | - | - | - | - | - | 2-3 | - | - | - | 2-3 |
| Dave Cochrane | - | 3-3 | 1-0 | 1-5 | 2-2 | 0-2 | - | - | - | - | - | - | 7-12 |
| Darnell Coles | - | 3-8 | - | 12-13 | - | 1-6 | - | 41-38 | - | 4-8 | 0-3 | - | 61-73 |
| Keith Comstock | - | - | - | - | - | - | - | - | - | - | - | 7-24 | - |
| Henry Cotto | - | - | - | - | - | 19-17 | 13-9 | 2-6 | - | - | 2-4 | - | 34-32 |
| Alvin Davis | - | 53-72 | - | - | - | - | - | - | - | 12-2 | - | - | 65-74 |
| Luis DeLeon | - | - | - | - | - | - | - | - | 1-0 | - | - | - | 1-0 |
| Mario Diaz | - | - | 1-4 | - | 11-10 | - | - | - | - | - | - | - | 12-14 |
| Mike Dunne | - | - | - | - | - | - | - | - | 3-12 | - | - | - | 3-12 |
| Bruce Fields | - | - | - | - | - | - | - | - | - | - | - | - | - |
| Ken Griffey Jr. | - | - | - | - | - | - | 54-66 | - | - | - | - | - | 54-66 |
| Erik Hanson | - | - | - | - | - | - | - | - | 11-6 | - | - | - | 11-6 |
| Gene Harris | - | - | - | - | - | - | - | - | 1-5 | - | - | 1-3 | 1-5 |
| Brian Holman | - | - | - | - | - | - | - | - | 9-13 | - | - | 0-1 | 9-13 |
| Mike Jackson | - | - | - | - | - | - | - | - | - | - | - | 25-40 | - |
| Randy D. Johnson | - | - | - | - | - | - | - | - | 10-12 | - | - | - | 10-12 |
| Mike Kingery | - | - | - | - | - | - | 6-13 | - | - | - | - | - | 6-13 |
| Mark Langston | - | - | - | - | - | - | - | - | 5-5 | - | - | - | 5-5 |
| Jeffrey Leonard | - | - | - | - | - | 14-11 | - | - | - | 50-72 | - | - | 64-83 |
| Edgar Martinez | - | - | - | 26-19 | - | - | - | - | - | - | - | - | 26-19 |
| Bill McGuire | 4-6 | - | - | - | - | - | - | - | - | - | - | - | 4-6 |
| Tom Niedenfuer | - | - | - | - | - | - | - | - | - | - | - | 3-22 | - |
| Dennis Powell | - | - | - | - | - | - | - | - | 0-1 | - | - | 17-25 | 0-1 |
| Jim Presley | | 13 5 | - | 34 52 | - | | | | | 1 0 | | | 48 57 |
| Rey Quinones | - | - | - | - | 3-3 | - | - | - | - | - | - | - | 3-3 |
| Jerry Reed | - | - | - | - | - | - | - | - | 0-1 | - | - | 17-34 | 0-1 |
| Harold Reynolds | - | - | 66-82 | - | - | - | - | - | - | 0-1 | 65-78 | - | 66-83 |
| Mike Schooler | - | - | - | - | - | - | - | - | - | - | - | 39-28 | - |
| Julio Solano | - | - | - | - | - | - | - | - | - | - | - | 1-6 | - |
| Bill Swift | - | - | - | - | - | - | - | - | 9-7 | - | - | 5-16 | 9-7 |
| Steve Trout | - | - | - | - | - | - | - | - | 1-2 | - | - | 6-10 | 1-2 |
| Dave Valle | 41-50 | - | - | - | - | - | - | - | - | - | - | - | 41-50 |
| Omar Vizquel | - | - | - | - | 57-74 | - | - | - | - | - | - | - | 57-74 |
| Jim Wilson | - | - | - | - | - | - | - | - | - | 1-0 | - | - | 1-0 |
| Clint Zavaras | - | - | - | - | - | - | - | - | 3-7 | - | - | - | 3-7 |

## Batting vs. Left and Right Handed Pitchers

| | | BA | Rank | SA | Rank | OBA | Rank | HR % | Rank | BB % | Rank | SO % | Rank |
|---|---|---|---|---|---|---|---|---|---|---|---|---|---|
| Scott Bradley | vs. Lefties | .143 | -- | .214 | -- | .250 | -- | 0.00 | -- | 12.50 | -- | 12.50 | -- |
| | vs. Righties | .281 | 44 | .375 | 88 | .326 | 82 | 1.17 | 124 | 6.71 | 113 | 7.42 | 19 |
| Greg Briley | vs. Lefties | .321 | 22 | .472 | 31 | .400 | 15 | 1.89 | 81 | 10.00 | 45 | 21.67 | 150 |
| | vs. Righties | .258 | 89 | .437 | 41 | .326 | 81 | 3.52 | 36 | 8.59 | 72 | 17.97 | 124 |
| Jay Buhner | vs. Lefties | .233 | 136 | .400 | 76 | .299 | 126 | 3.33 | 45 | 7.46 | 87 | 26.87 | 165 |
| | vs. Righties | .292 | 27 | .528 | 4 | .358 | 37 | 4.86 | 16 | 8.81 | 66 | 23.27 | 154 |
| Darnell Coles | vs. Lefties | .242 | 125 | .350 | 117 | .268 | 145 | 1.27 | 106 | 3.03 | 160 | 10.30 | 62 |
| | vs. Righties | .257 | 90 | .362 | 97 | .305 | 111 | 2.12 | 77 | 5.38 | 142 | 10.76 | 54 |
| Henry Cotto | vs. Lefties | .263 | 89 | .413 | 65 | .306 | 116 | 3.13 | 50 | 5.29 | 133 | 12.35 | 81 |
| | vs. Righties | .267 | 71 | .400 | 61 | .293 | 127 | 2.96 | 50 | 2.14 | 169 | 16.43 | 113 |
| Alvin Davis | vs. Lefties | .318 | 23 | .526 | 10 | .416 | 6 | 3.90 | 34 | 12.43 | 25 | 10.27 | 61 |
| | vs. Righties | .299 | 23 | .483 | 20 | .427 | 3 | 4.36 | 21 | 18.31 | 3 | 7.04 | 16 |
| Ken Griffey Jr. | vs. Lefties | .212 | 154 | .339 | 127 | .271 | 144 | 2.54 | 67 | 6.98 | 94 | 24.03 | 160 |
| | vs. Righties | .282 | 41 | .448 | 34 | .348 | 47 | 3.86 | 27 | 9.28 | 60 | 13.79 | 81 |
| Jeffrey Leonard | vs. Lefties | .280 | 66 | .497 | 18 | .326 | 88 | 5.10 | 15 | 5.81 | 118 | 11.63 | 74 |
| | vs. Righties | .244 | 112 | .391 | 68 | .292 | 130 | 3.91 | 25 | 6.24 | 127 | 23.39 | 155 |
| Edgar Martinez | vs. Lefties | .261 | 93 | .348 | 120 | .288 | 137 | 1.45 | 98 | 2.74 | 164 | 9.59 | 51 |
| | vs. Righties | .225 | -- | .275 | -- | .331 | -- | 0.98 | -- | 12.20 | -- | 15.45 | -- |
| Jim Presley | vs. Lefties | .328 | 16 | .491 | 23 | .352 | 51 | 3.45 | 40 | 4.10 | 149 | 20.49 | 141 |
| | vs. Righties | .197 | 161 | .339 | 113 | .243 | 166 | 2.92 | 53 | 5.42 | 141 | 27.80 | 167 |
| Harold Reynolds | vs. Lefties | .324 | 20 | .388 | 88 | .378 | 27 | 0.00 | 134 | 8.02 | 73 | 6.95 | 24 |
| | vs. Righties | .291 | 29 | .361 | 98 | .352 | 43 | 0.00 | 158 | 8.16 | 79 | 6.53 | 11 |
| Dave Valle | vs. Lefties | .236 | 131 | .396 | 83 | .317 | 99 | 3.77 | 35 | 9.92 | 48 | 4.13 | 10 |
| | vs. Righties | .238 | 121 | .333 | 119 | .308 | 107 | 1.43 | 104 | 7.26 | 99 | 11.54 | 63 |
| Omar Vizquel | vs. Lefties | .196 | 162 | .265 | 160 | .212 | 171 | 0.98 | 119 | 1.85 | 165 | 5.56 | 17 |
| | vs. Righties | .228 | 135 | .260 | 163 | .293 | 126 | 0.00 | 158 | 8.05 | 85 | 10.53 | 50 |
| Team Average | vs. Lefties | .259 | 9 | .392 | 6 | .314 | 12 | 2.44 | 4 | 6.78 | 13 | 12.33 | 6 |
| | vs. Righties | .256 | 8 | .380 | 7 | .322 | 8 | 2.43 | 3 | 8.43 | 8 | 14.18 | 5 |
| League Average | vs. Lefties | .266 | | .391 | | .328 | | 2.18 | | 8.18 | | 13.58 | |
| | vs. Righties | .258 | | .380 | | .325 | | 2.26 | | 8.56 | | 14.57 | |

## Batting with Runners on Base and Bases Empty

| | | BA | Rank | SA | Rank | OBA | Rank | HR % | Rank | BB % | Rank | SO % | Rank |
|---|---|---|---|---|---|---|---|---|---|---|---|---|---|
| Scott Bradley | Runners On | .345 | 4 | .487 | 20 | .385 | 24 | 1.77 | 92 | 7.63 | 101 | 7.63 | 25 |
| | Bases Empty | .223 | 138 | .280 | 159 | .274 | 151 | 0.64 | 142 | 6.55 | 107 | 7.74 | 16 |
| Greg Briley | Runners On | .240 | 132 | .389 | 81 | .303 | 127 | 2.29 | 66 | 8.54 | 84 | 20.60 | 146 |
| | Bases Empty | .288 | 34 | .484 | 10 | .363 | 20 | 4.11 | 30 | 8.98 | 46 | 16.73 | 107 |
| Jay Buhner | Runners On | .295 | 42 | .568 | 4 | .351 | 66 | 5.68 | 10 | 7.22 | 111 | 26.80 | 169 |
| | Bases Empty | .259 | 78 | .431 | 44 | .333 | 53 | 3.45 | 44 | 9.30 | 40 | 22.48 | 157 |
| Darnell Coles | Runners On | .230 | 149 | .343 | 131 | .281 | 155 | 2.09 | 76 | 5.32 | 136 | 9.89 | 60 |
| | Bases Empty | .270 | 54 | .372 | 96 | .305 | 104 | 1.69 | 94 | 4.18 | 156 | 11.25 | 54 |
| Henry Cotto | Runners On | .325 | 16 | .496 | 16 | .352 | 61 | 3.42 | 37 | 4.10 | 160 | 14.75 | 103 |
| | Bases Empty | .225 | 136 | .348 | 108 | .266 | 158 | 2.81 | 62 | 3.72 | 160 | 13.83 | 84 |
| Alvin Davis | Runners On | .327 | 13 | .539 | 6 | .445 | 3 | 4.15 | 26 | 17.88 | 6 | 9.12 | 45 |
| | Bases Empty | .288 | 33 | .463 | 24 | .407 | 3 | 4.27 | 26 | 15.43 | 6 | 7.12 | 12 |
| Ken Griffey Jr. | Runners On | .252 | 114 | .361 | 104 | .326 | 97 | 1.98 | 79 | 9.52 | 67 | 18.61 | 140 |
| | Bases Empty | .273 | 51 | .466 | 21 | .331 | 61 | 4.74 | 19 | 8.00 | 76 | 14.55 | 91 |
| Jeffrey Leonard | Runners On | .246 | 126 | .405 | 69 | .292 | 139 | 3.46 | 36 | 6.15 | 125 | 19.69 | 144 |
| | Bases Empty | .264 | 68 | .437 | 38 | .311 | 100 | 5.05 | 15 | 6.08 | 124 | 20.61 | 141 |
| Edgar Martinez | Runners On | .296 | 40 | .358 | 113 | .348 | 68 | 1.23 | 110 | 6.38 | 121 | 9.57 | 54 |
| | Bases Empty | .189 | -- | .256 | -- | .284 | -- | 1.11 | -- | 10.78 | -- | 16.67 | -- |
| Jim Presley | Runners On | .258 | 102 | .388 | 82 | .298 | 135 | 2.25 | 69 | 5.67 | 134 | 24.23 | 161 |
| | Bases Empty | .217 | 144 | .382 | 84 | .256 | 164 | 3.77 | 37 | 4.48 | 153 | 26.91 | 167 |
| Harold Reynolds | Runners On | .320 | 19 | .360 | 109 | .382 | 31 | 0.00 | 146 | 9.09 | 73 | 4.76 | 9 |
| | Bases Empty | .290 | 30 | .373 | 94 | .348 | 41 | 0.00 | 153 | 7.62 | 85 | 7.62 | 15 |
| Dave Valle | Runners On | .271 | 82 | .368 | 96 | .333 | 89 | 1.50 | 98 | 7.28 | 108 | 6.62 | 18 |
| | Bases Empty | .213 | 146 | .344 | 111 | .294 | 122 | 2.73 | 65 | 8.82 | 53 | 10.78 | 48 |
| Omar Vizquel | Runners On | .234 | 140 | .266 | 165 | .273 | 161 | 0.00 | 146 | 5.06 | 146 | 8.99 | 43 |
| | Bases Empty | .210 | 150 | .258 | 168 | .273 | 153 | 0.43 | 148 | 7.51 | 90 | 9.49 | 33 |
| Team Average | Runners On | .269 | 7 | .392 | 8 | .329 | 10 | 2.20 | 6 | 8.12 | 12 | 14.06 | 8 |
| | Bases Empty | .248 | 10 | .377 | 7 | .313 | 9 | 2.61 | 2 | 7.85 | 7 | 13.35 | 3 |
| League Average | Runners On | .268 | | .389 | | .336 | | 2.15 | | 9.17 | | 13.53 | |
| | Bases Empty | .255 | | .380 | | .317 | | 2.29 | | 7.84 | | 14.86 | |

## Overall Batting Compared to Late Inning Pressure Situations

| | | BA | Rank | SA | Rank | OBA | Rank | HR % | Rank | BB % | Rank | SO % | Rank | RDI % | Rank |
|---|---|---|---|---|---|---|---|---|---|---|---|---|---|---|---|
| Scott Bradley | Overall | .274 | 48 | .367 | 106 | .322 | 87 | 1.11 | 127 | 7.02 | 108 | 7.69 | 19 | .337 | 19 |
| | Pressure | .300 | 38 | .460 | 32 | .340 | 66 | 2.00 | 75 | 5.56 | 134 | 11.11 | 40 | .231 | 103 |
| Greg Briley | Overall | .266 | 68 | .442 | 33 | .336 | 61 | 3.30 | 40 | 8.78 | 64 | 18.47 | 131 | .263 | 84 |
| | Pressure | .242 | 96 | .303 | 120 | .296 | 114 | 0.00 | 107 | 7.04 | 112 | 28.17 | 154 | .143 | 137 |
| Jay Buhner | Overall | .275 | 47 | .490 | 10 | .341 | 53 | 4.41 | 18 | 8.41 | 72 | 24.34 | 163 | .293 | 52 |
| | Pressure | .290 | 49 | .484 | 23 | .353 | 51 | 6.45 | 8 | 8.82 | 80 | 35.29 | 166 | .250 | 87 |
| Dave Cochrane | Overall | .235 | -- | .382 | -- | .333 | -- | 2.94 | -- | 11.97 | -- | 23.08 | -- | .138 | -- |
| | Pressure | .207 | 127 | .414 | 52 | .281 | 124 | 3.45 | 46 | 6.25 | 122 | 31.25 | 158 | .250 | 87 |
| Darnell Coles | Overall | .252 | 108 | .359 | 111 | .294 | 140 | 1.87 | 90 | 4.70 | 155 | 10.63 | 54 | .263 | 84 |
| | Pressure | .273 | 62 | .416 | 51 | .337 | 71 | 3.90 | 36 | 6.98 | 114 | 13.95 | 59 | .250 | 87 |
| Henry Cotto | Overall | .264 | 72 | .407 | 61 | .300 | 129 | 3.05 | 53 | 3.87 | 164 | 14.19 | 89 | .267 | 79 |
| | Pressure | .235 | 102 | .353 | 91 | .250 | 143 | 3.92 | 35 | 1.92 | 167 | 21.15 | 124 | .154 | 132 |
| Alvin Davis | Overall | .305 | 14 | .496 | 8 | .424 | 2 | 4.22 | 22 | 16.53 | 4 | 8.02 | 22 | .361 | 12 |
| | Pressure | .222 | 113 | .417 | 50 | .301 | 106 | 5.56 | 17 | 10.84 | 51 | 14.46 | 67 | .346 | 39 |
| Ken Griffey Jr. | Overall | .264 | 75 | .420 | 50 | .329 | 73 | 3.52 | 35 | 8.70 | 68 | 16.40 | 110 | .293 | 51 |
| | Pressure | .267 | 69 | .500 | 17 | .308 | 97 | 6.67 | 7 | 6.06 | 124 | 24.24 | 144 | .267 | 82 |
| Jeffrey Leonard | Overall | .254 | 102 | .420 | 48 | .301 | 128 | 4.24 | 20 | 6.12 | 131 | 20.13 | 144 | .290 | 54 |
| | Pressure | .205 | 132 | .398 | 60 | .230 | 151 | 6.02 | 13 | 2.30 | 162 | 32.18 | 160 | .294 | 67 |
| Jim Presley | Overall | .236 | 142 | .385 | 84 | .275 | 161 | 3.08 | 52 | 5.04 | 151 | 25.66 | 165 | .191 | 161 |
| | Pressure | .196 | 136 | .429 | 45 | .224 | 152 | 5.36 | 19 | 1.64 | 169 | 34.43 | 165 | .333 | 42 |
| Harold Reynolds | Overall | .300 | 20 | .369 | 102 | .359 | 30 | 0.00 | 166 | 8.12 | 83 | 6.65 | 10 | .308 | 40 |
| | Pressure | .324 | 20 | .338 | 101 | .427 | 11 | 0.00 | 107 | 15.73 | 11 | 13.48 | 55 | .267 | 82 |
| Dave Valle | Overall | .237 | 137 | .354 | 116 | .311 | 107 | 2.22 | 75 | 8.17 | 80 | 9.01 | 34 | .219 | 147 |
| | Pressure | .125 | 166 | .167 | 168 | .222 | 154 | 0.00 | 107 | 9.09 | 73 | 9.09 | 25 | .176 | 124 |
| Omar Vizquel | Overall | .220 | 160 | .261 | 168 | .273 | 162 | 0.26 | 160 | 6.50 | 118 | 9.28 | 37 | .165 | 164 |
| | Pressure | .324 | 20 | .351 | 93 | .375 | 36 | 0.00 | 107 | 6.98 | 114 | 0.00 | 1 | .000 | -- |
| Team Average | Overall | .257 | 10 | .384 | 7 | .320 | 10 | 2.43 | 3 | 7.97 | 10 | 13.66 | 5 | .269 | 9 |
| | Pressure | .241 | 10 | .372 | 5 | .299 | 13 | 3.16 | 1 | 6.96 | 13 | 20.64 | 13 | .248 | 9 |
| League Average | Overall | .261 | | .384 | | .326 | | 2.23 | | 8.44 | | 14.26 | | .269 | |
| | Pressure | .247 | | .357 | | .318 | | 2.02 | | 9.02 | | 17.90 | | .254 | |

## Additional Miscellaneous Batting Comparisons

| | Grass Surface BA | Rank | Artificial Surface BA | Rank | Home Games BA | Rank | Road Games BA | Rank | Runners in Scoring Position BA | Rank | Runners in Scoring Pos and Two Outs BA | Rank | Leading Off Inning OBA | Rank | Runners on 3B with less than 2 Outs RDI % | Rank |
|---|---|---|---|---|---|---|---|---|---|---|---|---|---|---|---|---|
| Scott Bradley | .291 | -- | .263 | 68 | .275 | 58 | .273 | 60 | .286 | 55 | .212 | 113 | .240 | 160 | .688 | 26 |
| Mickey Brantley | .192 | -- | .146 | 165 | .171 | -- | .132 | -- | .190 | -- | .200 | -- | .136 | -- | .600 | -- |
| Greg Briley | .278 | 51 | .257 | 81 | .207 | 159 | .309 | 15 | .222 | 143 | .213 | 112 | .356 | 37 | .682 | 31 |
| Jay Buhner | .274 | -- | .275 | 60 | .279 | 54 | .270 | 65 | .300 | 35 | .318 | 17 | .321 | 87 | .455 | 141 |
| Dave Cochrane | .240 | -- | .234 | 119 | .258 | -- | .194 | -- | .154 | -- | .429 | -- | .379 | -- | .333 | -- |
| Darnell Coles | .235 | 128 | .265 | 65 | .286 | 44 | .224 | 147 | .242 | 110 | .197 | 123 | .286 | 124 | .667 | 39 |
| Henry Cotto | .286 | -- | .253 | 86 | .248 | 104 | .281 | 49 | .309 | 29 | .261 | 61 | .231 | 165 | .667 | -- |
| Alvin Davis | .256 | 89 | .333 | 18 | .365 | 4 | .245 | 115 | .362 | 4 | .390 | 1 | .451 | 2 | .500 | 119 |
| Mario Diaz | .206 | -- | .075 | 171 | .069 | -- | .178 | -- | .167 | -- | .083 | -- | .188 | -- | .667 | -- |
| Ken Griffey Jr. | .267 | 68 | .262 | 70 | .261 | 79 | .266 | 74 | .291 | 46 | .268 | 50 | .294 | 118 | .619 | 57 |
| Mike Kingery | .259 | -- | .204 | 141 | .213 | -- | .241 | -- | .267 | -- | .000 | -- | .368 | -- | .750 | -- |
| Jeffrey Leonard | .250 | 98 | .258 | 79 | .260 | 81 | .250 | 100 | .238 | 115 | .197 | 122 | .282 | 132 | .640 | 47 |
| Edgar Martinez | .200 | -- | .261 | 72 | .221 | -- | .255 | 89 | .325 | -- | .368 | -- | .233 | -- | .700 | 24 |
| Jim Presley | .216 | 158 | .250 | 90 | .258 | 88 | .209 | 162 | .227 | 137 | .178 | 141 | .273 | 142 | .381 | 155 |
| Harold Reynolds | .297 | 22 | .302 | 31 | .300 | 30 | .301 | 21 | .283 | 63 | .246 | 74 | .340 | 57 | .560 | 95 |
| Dave Valle | .200 | 167 | .263 | 69 | .252 | 95 | .222 | 150 | .218 | 147 | .186 | 133 | .304 | 109 | .526 | 112 |
| Omar Vizquel | .217 | 157 | .222 | 133 | .228 | 136 | .212 | 160 | .178 | 167 | .190 | 130 | .311 | 98 | .350 | 162 |
| Team Average | .252 | 11 | .261 | 7 | .263 | 6 | .252 | 11 | .258 | 11 | .230 | 8 | .305 | 13 | .563 | 8 |
| League Average | .260 | | .262 | | .262 | | .259 | | .262 | | .232 | | .321 | | .566 | |

## Pitching vs. Left and Right Handed Batters

| | | BA | Rank | SA | Rank | OBA | Rank | HR % | Rank | BB % | Rank | SO % | Rank |
|---|---|---|---|---|---|---|---|---|---|---|---|---|---|
| Scott Bankhead | vs. Lefties | .230 | 35 | .381 | 67 | .284 | 23 | 3.12 | 103 | 7.24 | 44 | 16.01 | 32 |
| | vs. Righties | .248 | 46 | .371 | 60 | .308 | 43 | 1.63 | 42 | 7.39 | 60 | 16.50 | 51 |
| Mike Dunne | vs. Lefties | .333 | 128 | .470 | 113 | .390 | 121 | 1.64 | 59 | 9.22 | 75 | 5.83 | 128 |
| | vs. Righties | .276 | 100 | .397 | 86 | .354 | 122 | 2.56 | 90 | 10.00 | 108 | 14.44 | 76 |
| Erik Hanson | vs. Lefties | .212 | 21 | .283 | 20 | .267 | 15 | 0.88 | 22 | 6.53 | 33 | 15.51 | 40 |
| | vs. Righties | .279 | 107 | .396 | 84 | .344 | 111 | 2.54 | 87 | 7.27 | 58 | 16.82 | 48 |
| Brian Holman | vs. Lefties | .257 | 64 | .366 | 54 | .344 | 85 | 1.37 | 45 | 11.04 | 104 | 8.96 | 102 |
| | vs. Righties | .265 | 83 | .368 | 58 | .323 | 72 | 1.56 | 41 | 7.08 | 56 | 14.73 | 71 |
| Mike Jackson | vs. Lefties | .222 | 26 | .367 | 55 | .344 | 82 | 3.16 | 105 | 15.10 | 120 | 16.67 | 28 |
| | vs. Righties | .224 | 22 | .317 | 21 | .322 | 70 | 1.46 | 35 | 10.46 | 111 | 25.94 | 11 |
| Randy D. Johnson | vs. Lefties | .169 | -- | .271 | -- | .254 | -- | 1.69 | -- | 8.70 | -- | 15.94 | -- |
| | vs. Righties | .255 | 62 | .387 | 79 | .349 | 115 | 2.36 | 80 | 12.72 | 130 | 18.49 | 36 |
| Mark Langston | vs. Lefties | .031 | -- | .094 | -- | .114 | -- | 0.00 | -- | 2.86 | -- | 22.86 | -- |
| | vs. Righties | .247 | 44 | .356 | 50 | .302 | 37 | 1.26 | 24 | 6.87 | 51 | 19.85 | 28 |
| Jerry Reed | vs. Lefties | .257 | 62 | .399 | 84 | .355 | 93 | 2.70 | 92 | 12.72 | 113 | 8.09 | 107 |
| | vs. Righties | .221 | 20 | .364 | 56 | .285 | 24 | 2.60 | 92 | 8.11 | 78 | 13.90 | 81 |
| Mike Schooler | vs. Lefties | .286 | 100 | .386 | 73 | .340 | 77 | 0.71 | 15 | 7.19 | 42 | 17.65 | 26 |
| | vs. Righties | .250 | 50 | .305 | 13 | .289 | 28 | 0.61 | 5 | 4.55 | 11 | 23.86 | 17 |
| Bill Swift | vs. Lefties | .316 | 120 | .411 | 91 | .368 | 103 | 1.30 | 40 | 7.48 | 49 | 6.30 | 122 |
| | vs. Righties | .245 | 42 | .337 | 35 | .296 | 34 | 1.47 | 36 | 6.40 | 45 | 9.76 | 120 |
| Clint Zavaras | vs. Lefties | .262 | 70 | .440 | 104 | .380 | 110 | 2.38 | 79 | 16.00 | 126 | 9.00 | 100 |
| | vs. Righties | .245 | -- | .418 | -- | .339 | -- | 1.82 | -- | 10.69 | -- | 16.79 | -- |
| Team Average | vs. Lefties | .262 | 8 | .388 | 9 | .334 | 8 | 2.13 | 6 | 9.42 | 8 | 11.80 | 11 |
| | vs. Righties | .257 | 6 | .380 | 7 | .327 | 9 | 2.04 | 4 | 8.78 | 12 | 16.51 | 5 |
| League Average | vs. Lefties | .261 | | .382 | | .330 | | 2.16 | | 9.16 | | 13.03 | |
| | vs. Righties | .261 | | .385 | | .323 | | 2.28 | | 7.96 | | 15.09 | |

## Pitching with Runners on Base and Bases Empty

| | | BA | Rank | SA | Rank | OBA | Rank | HR % | Rank | BB % | Rank | SO % | Rank |
|---|---|---|---|---|---|---|---|---|---|---|---|---|---|
| Scott Bankhead | Runners On | .256 | 55 | .430 | 108 | .317 | 47 | 3.41 | 121 | 8.36 | 57 | 18.21 | 26 |
| | Bases Empty | .228 | 29 | .344 | 41 | .281 | 26 | 1.83 | 52 | 6.64 | 52 | 14.99 | 54 |
| Mike Dunne | Runners On | .290 | 111 | .406 | 96 | .354 | 97 | 1.29 | 33 | 8.84 | 65 | 7.73 | 122 |
| | Bases Empty | .321 | 132 | .462 | 120 | .390 | 134 | 2.72 | 87 | 10.24 | 109 | 11.71 | 92 |
| Erik Hanson | Runners On | .282 | 96 | .397 | 90 | .351 | 94 | 1.28 | 31 | 8.99 | 67 | 14.61 | 56 |
| | Bases Empty | .221 | 23 | .300 | 15 | .275 | 21 | 1.87 | 55 | 5.57 | 33 | 17.07 | 43 |
| Brian Holman | Runners On | .258 | 58 | .358 | 53 | .344 | 86 | 1.15 | 24 | 10.23 | 90 | 10.23 | 98 |
| | Bases Empty | .263 | 76 | .374 | 67 | .325 | 76 | 1.70 | 43 | 8.05 | 78 | 13.25 | 75 |
| Mike Jackson | Runners On | .243 | 35 | .337 | 28 | .384 | 121 | 1.18 | 25 | 16.59 | 132 | 20.74 | 11 |
| | Bases Empty | .206 | 11 | .340 | 38 | .280 | 24 | 3.09 | 100 | 8.41 | 83 | 22.90 | 17 |
| Randy D. Johnson | Runners On | .254 | 51 | .386 | 81 | .347 | 91 | 2.54 | 97 | 12.20 | 111 | 15.85 | 43 |
| | Bases Empty | .238 | 43 | .364 | 55 | .331 | 90 | 2.10 | 63 | 12.27 | 129 | 19.94 | 27 |
| Mark Langston | Runners On | .234 | 30 | .360 | 57 | .302 | 25 | 1.80 | 67 | 7.14 | 37 | 16.67 | 38 |
| | Bases Empty | .213 | 14 | .300 | 16 | .263 | 13 | 0.63 | 5 | 5.85 | 39 | 22.81 | 18 |
| Jerry Reed | Runners On | .238 | 34 | .375 | 69 | .353 | 96 | 2.98 | 113 | 14.90 | 127 | 11.06 | 88 |
| | Bases Empty | .232 | 39 | .379 | 71 | .277 | 23 | 2.37 | 78 | 5.36 | 27 | 12.05 | 87 |
| Mike Schooler | Runners On | .262 | 68 | .314 | 16 | .316 | 45 | 0.00 | 1 | 6.84 | 30 | 20.00 | 15 |
| | Bases Empty | .273 | 94 | .379 | 70 | .309 | 52 | 1.52 | 33 | 4.32 | 9 | 22.30 | 21 |
| Bill Swift | Runners On | .305 | 122 | .438 | 114 | .350 | 93 | 2.15 | 84 | 6.98 | 33 | 6.59 | 131 |
| | Bases Empty | .255 | 64 | .314 | 22 | .311 | 53 | 0.74 | 11 | 6.83 | 56 | 9.56 | 113 |
| Team Average | Runners On | .277 | 13 | .409 | 12 | .353 | 12 | 2.16 | 7 | 10.04 | 12 | 13.37 | 8 |
| | Bases Empty | .246 | 3 | .363 | 4 | .311 | 7 | 2.02 | 3 | 8.23 | 11 | 15.44 | 5 |
| League Average | Runners On | .268 | | .389 | | .336 | | 2.15 | | 9.17 | | 13.53 | |
| | Bases Empty | .255 | | .380 | | .317 | | 2.29 | | 7.84 | | 14.86 | |

## Overall Pitching Compared to Late Inning Pressure Situations

| | | BA | Rank | SA | Rank | OBA | Rank | HR % | Rank | BB % | Rank | SO % | Rank |
|---|---|---|---|---|---|---|---|---|---|---|---|---|---|
| Scott Bankhead | Overall | .239 | 32 | .376 | 64 | .295 | 24 | 2.42 | 85 | 7.31 | 51 | 16.24 | 44 |
| | Pressure | .250 | 68 | .350 | 70 | .362 | 99 | 2.50 | 88 | 14.89 | 117 | 21.28 | 27 |
| Keith Comstock | Overall | .268 | -- | .361 | -- | .330 | -- | 2.06 | -- | 9.01 | -- | 19.82 | -- |
| | Pressure | .359 | 124 | .385 | 87 | .413 | 118 | 0.00 | 1 | 10.42 | 77 | 18.75 | 39 |
| Mike Dunne | Overall | .307 | 129 | .437 | 114 | .373 | 133 | 2.06 | 65 | 9.59 | 97 | 9.84 | 110 |
| | Pressure | .235 | -- | .235 | -- | .300 | -- | 0.00 | -- | 10.00 | -- | 5.00 | -- |
| Erik Hanson | Overall | .243 | 36 | .336 | 25 | .304 | 31 | 1.65 | 43 | 6.88 | 41 | 16.13 | 45 |
| | Pressure | .211 | 36 | .237 | 13 | .286 | 30 | 0.00 | 1 | 9.09 | 58 | 22.73 | 21 |
| Brian Holman | Overall | .261 | 69 | .367 | 56 | .333 | 85 | 1.47 | 28 | 9.01 | 88 | 11.92 | 83 |
| | Pressure | .246 | 66 | .328 | 55 | .352 | 91 | 1.64 | 58 | 12.50 | 102 | 9.72 | 108 |
| Mike Jackson | Overall | .223 | 21 | .339 | 32 | .332 | 79 | 2.20 | 72 | 12.53 | 124 | 21.81 | 15 |
| | Pressure | .208 | 34 | .313 | 43 | .343 | 81 | 1.56 | 54 | 15.48 | 120 | 17.99 | 43 |
| Randy D. Johnson | Overall | .244 | 39 | .373 | 61 | .338 | 90 | 2.28 | 76 | 12.24 | 123 | 18.18 | 31 |
| | Pressure | .263 | 83 | .368 | 82 | .293 | 37 | 2.63 | 91 | 4.65 | 16 | 27.91 | 8 |
| Mark Langston | Overall | .221 | 20 | .325 | 21 | .279 | 13 | 1.11 | 14 | 6.40 | 32 | 20.20 | 20 |
| | Pressure | .176 | 11 | .206 | 8 | .194 | 2 | 0.00 | 1 | 2.78 | 5 | 22.22 | 22 |
| Tom Niedenfuer | Overall | .309 | -- | .537 | -- | .371 | -- | 4.70 | -- | 8.77 | -- | 8.77 | -- |
| | Pressure | .351 | 122 | .622 | 129 | .467 | 132 | 5.41 | 128 | 16.67 | 127 | 8.33 | 115 |
| Dennis Powell | Overall | .285 | -- | .436 | -- | .364 | -- | 3.49 | -- | 10.45 | -- | 13.43 | -- |
| | Pressure | .294 | 108 | .471 | 113 | .392 | 112 | 4.41 | 121 | 12.50 | 102 | 12.50 | 81 |
| Jerry Reed | Overall | .235 | 28 | .377 | 67 | .313 | 50 | 2.64 | 97 | 9.95 | 108 | 11.57 | 89 |
| | Pressure | .330 | 119 | .495 | 117 | .440 | 124 | 2.06 | 75 | 15.97 | 124 | 11.76 | 87 |
| Mike Schooler | Overall | .266 | 80 | .342 | 37 | .313 | 49 | 0.66 | 2 | 5.78 | 18 | 20.97 | 16 |
| | Pressure | .264 | 86 | .339 | 61 | .306 | 57 | 0.88 | 39 | 5.35 | 21 | 24.28 | 17 |
| Bill Swift | Overall | .278 | 100 | .371 | 60 | .329 | 75 | 1.39 | 24 | 6.90 | 43 | 8.17 | 123 |
| | Pressure | .167 | 5 | .208 | 9 | .245 | 12 | 0.00 | 1 | 9.09 | 58 | 5.45 | 124 |
| Team Average | Overall | .259 | 7 | .383 | 9 | .330 | 9 | 2.08 | 6 | 9.05 | 12 | 14.50 | 6 |
| | Pressure | .256 | 9 | .355 | 7 | .343 | 12 | 1.64 | 3 | 11.20 | 12 | 17.15 | 6 |
| League Average | Overall | .261 | | .384 | | .326 | | 2.23 | | 8.44 | | 14.26 | |
| | Pressure | .250 | | .362 | | .325 | | 2.14 | | 9.50 | | 16.61 | |

## Additional Miscellaneous Pitching Comparisons

| | Grass Surface | | Artificial Surface | | Home Games | | Road Games | | Runners in Scoring Position | | Runners in Scoring Pos and Two Outs | | Leading Off Inning | |
|---|---|---|---|---|---|---|---|---|---|---|---|---|---|---|
| | BA | Rank | BA | Rank | BA | Rank | BA | Rank | BA | Rank | BA | Rank | OBA | Rank |
| Scott Bankhead | .250 | 54 | .232 | 30 | .244 | 56 | .233 | 34 | .237 | 47 | .208 | 51 | .275 | 30 |
| Mike Campbell | .222 | -- | .351 | 128 | .351 | -- | .222 | -- | .400 | -- | .444 | -- | .375 | -- |
| Keith Comstock | .094 | -- | .354 | 131 | .367 | -- | .108 | -- | .318 | -- | .182 | -- | .143 | -- |
| Mike Dunne | .344 | -- | .293 | 97 | .287 | 114 | .338 | 132 | .281 | 102 | .211 | 52 | .415 | 132 |
| Erik Hanson | .223 | 21 | .258 | 55 | .275 | 98 | .209 | 11 | .229 | 32 | .154 | 20 | .220 | 6 |
| Gene Harris | .484 | -- | .314 | 116 | .313 | -- | .394 | -- | .462 | -- | .467 | -- | .400 | -- |
| Brian Holman | .264 | 71 | .259 | 56 | .273 | 97 | .252 | 52 | .196 | 12 | .141 | 15 | .375 | 118 |
| Mike Jackson | .216 | -- | .227 | 27 | .246 | 61 | .192 | 5 | .256 | 74 | .235 | 74 | .306 | 46 |
| Randy D. Johnson | .232 | 26 | .258 | 53 | .244 | 55 | .245 | 41 | .276 | 93 | .295 | 115 | .371 | 116 |
| Mark Langston | .193 | -- | .241 | 39 | .269 | 89 | .175 | 2 | .250 | 62 | .222 | 65 | .320 | 63 |
| Tom Niedenfuer | .231 | -- | .325 | 123 | .320 | -- | .288 | -- | .326 | -- | .278 | -- | .364 | -- |
| Dennis Powell | .270 | -- | .294 | 98 | .275 | -- | .293 | -- | .279 | -- | .208 | -- | .362 | -- |
| Jerry Reed | .250 | 54 | .226 | 26 | .228 | 29 | .242 | 40 | .188 | 9 | .093 | 4 | .326 | 74 |
| Mike Schooler | .235 | -- | .282 | 86 | .279 | 101 | .250 | 46 | .278 | 95 | .245 | 85 | .349 | 100 |
| Bill Swift | .264 | 70 | .284 | 88 | .295 | 118 | .255 | 60 | .273 | 90 | .310 | 120 | .320 | 64 |
| Steve Trout | .429 | -- | .260 | 58 | .220 | -- | .429 | -- | .370 | -- | .333 | -- | .387 | -- |
| Clint Zavaras | .326 | -- | .232 | 31 | .225 | 24 | .308 | -- | .283 | -- | .182 | -- | .375 | -- |
| Team Average | .255 | 5 | .262 | 8 | .267 | 10 | .251 | 3 | .264 | 8 | .227 | 7 | .330 | 11 |
| League Average | .260 | | .262 | | .259 | | .262 | | .262 | | .232 | | .321 | |

# TEXAS RANGERS

- **Ruben Sierra: the next superstar?**
- **The class of '86: a four-year report card.**

Four years ago, we wrote about the problem of evaluating career potential after only one season: "When two or more teammates develop at the same time, it's not unusual for the public to focus its attention on the wrong [one]. Sometimes, the error is merely in not recognizing a pair as equals. . .In other cases, the more heralded player fizzles as his teammate rises." Among the examples we cited were: Bobby Murcer anointed the Yankees' MVP-in-waiting, when Thurman Munson was really the one; Bob Horner's early publicity obscuring the talents of Dale Murphy; and the greatest example of all—Sonny Jackson likened to Honus Wagner by former Braves general manager Paul Richards, while a prospect named Joe Morgan played alongside him in Houston. In August, it's Morgan, not Jackson, who'll take his place alongside Wagner in Cooperstown.

It's ironic that, as we reflected in the 1986 *Analyst* on our inability to post an accurate morning line on a rookie's potential, baseball was about to raise the curtain on such a promising freshman class. And the subsequent rise of Ruben Sierra, coinciding with declining expectations for teammate Pete Incaviglia (not to mention the elevation of Kevin Mitchell to superstar status alongside Will Clark), has again proven how difficult it is to separate rookies with the potential to be great from those with the potential to be merely good.

Until last season, Sierra was one of baseball's best-kept secrets. His arrival in Arlington in June 1986 was greeted with all the excitement normally reserved for another 90–degree Texas day. But in the grand tradition of Morgan, Munson, and Murphy, Sierra quietly, and over a period of several years, has surpassed the accomplishments not only of Incaviglia, but of most of the other rookies of '86 as well. He leads the group in extra-base hits, and ranks fourth in RBIs (only six short of second place). And it's noteworthy that Sierra is the youngest of them all. In fact, of the 159 players whose rookie status expired in 1986, only one was younger than Sierra: Rangers pitcher Edwin Correa. As we've pointed out in the past, the age at which a player makes his debut is one leading indicator of his potential—the younger the player, the greater his potential. And we expect that ultimately Sierra will rank at or near the head of his class.

One of the most insightful statistical techniques we've discovered in recent years is a method for identifying players throughout baseball history who most closely match a current player's statistical profile. These statistical ancestors can be used to estimate the contemporary player's future performance. That's how weather predictions are made. That's how stock analysis is done. Now baseball players can be evaluated in the same manner. (And if it doesn't work, at least you won't get wet or lose your money!)

The basic structure of the system was published in *The 1986 Bill James Baseball Abstract.* The author developed a series of equations to match rookies to past players with the most similar first-year statistics. Since then, we've tinkered with the formula, and, more importantly, taken the technique into the 21st century with two enhancements.

First, we expanded the scope beyond a player's rookie season, so that stat-clones could be found at any point during a player's career. Sure, finding rookie analogues can be fun. (For example, the most similar partial rookie seasons to Gregg Jefferies's 1988 late–season fragment were Babe Ruth's and Jimmie Foxx's. Made that 10–dollar price for a Jefferies rookie card seem reasonable.) But as we've noted, it's difficult to base any meaningful projections upon a player's first season. Matching at later stages in a player's career allows us to use a larger sample of at-bats and reduces the length of time to be projected. That, of course, makes for a more reliable guide to future performance.

Sometimes the similarity can be uncanny. For example, the player with the most similar career statistics to Sierra's current figures is Johnny Bench, through the 1971 season:

| Player | AB | R | H | 2B | 3B | HR | RBI | BA |
|---|---|---|---|---|---|---|---|---|
| Bench | 2349 | 334 | 636 | 120 | 10 | 114 | 387 | .271 |
| Sierra | 2274 | 325 | 620 | 115 | 30 | 98 | 374 | .273 |

Next, we added a step to select from among those with the most similar *career* profiles players who were coming off *seasons* comparable to those of the player in question. Although Bench's statistics through 1971 were remarkably like Sierra's current career stats, his 1971 season (.238, 27 HR, 61 RBI) was nothing like Sierra's 1989 season. The closest match to Sierra on both counts was Del Ennis through 1949:

| | | Career To Date | | | | | | Most Recent Season | | | | | |
|---|---|---|---|---|---|---|---|---|---|---|---|---|---|
| Year | Player | AB | R | H | HR | RBI | BA | AB | R | H | HR | RBI | BA |
| 1949 | Ennis | 2280 | 319 | 673 | 84 | 359 | .295 | 610 | 92 | 184 | 25 | 110 | .302 |
| 1989 | Sierra | 2274 | 325 | 620 | 98 | 374 | .273 | 634 | 101 | 194 | 29 | 119 | .306 |

To estimate a player's eventual career totals, we determine the 10 players with the most similar profiles to the player in question, based on both their career-to-date totals and their most recent seasons. The average of the final career statistics for those 10 players becomes the contemporary player's projected career totals. That method yielded the following career projections for Sierra, Incaviglia, and some fellow members of the class of '86. Players are ranked by projected runs produced:

| Player | G | AB | R | H | 2B | 3B | HR | RBI | BA | SA | OBA |
|---|---|---|---|---|---|---|---|---|---|---|---|
| Clark | 1939 | 7171 | 1123 | 2074 | 379 | 87 | 270 | 1193 | .289 | .479 | .361 |
| Mitchell | 1893 | 6703 | 1023 | 1824 | 397 | 46 | 368 | 1202 | .272 | .496 | .353 |
| Sierra | 1899 | 6962 | 1054 | 1950 | 338 | 59 | 286 | 1085 | .280 | .469 | .356 |
| Canseco | 1829 | 6394 | 928 | 1729 | 291 | 33 | 337 | 1117 | .270 | .484 | .350 |
| Bonds | 1793 | 6072 | 907 | 1591 | 267 | 44 | 216 | 858 | .262 | .427 | .358 |
| Bonilla | 1691 | 5956 | 866 | 1645 | 283 | 57 | 211 | 865 | .276 | .449 | .350 |
| Galarraga | 1652 | 5593 | 796 | 1544 | 255 | 43 | 204 | 821 | .276 | .446 | .341 |
| Gruber | 1607 | 5544 | 756 | 1520 | 264 | 43 | 208 | 852 | .274 | .450 | .342 |
| Incaviglia | 1523 | 5171 | 687 | 1349 | 206 | 21 | 234 | 809 | .261 | .444 | .342 |
| Joyner | 1495 | 5185 | 715 | 1458 | 246 | 43 | 152 | 751 | .281 | .433 | .345 |
| Tartabull | 1306 | 4459 | 632 | 1217 | 215 | 31 | 212 | 754 | .273 | .478 | .345 |
| Thompson | 1491 | 5047 | 697 | 1345 | 234 | 52 | 111 | 627 | .264 | .397 | .348 |
| Larkin | 1445 | 4958 | 698 | 1397 | 222 | 56 | 87 | 563 | .282 | .402 | .344 |
| Snyder | 1373 | 4656 | 571 | 1192 | 193 | 27 | 157 | 649 | .256 | .410 | .329 |

Sierra's career projections closely resemble the actual totals of Reggie Smith. But remember—that's an average expectation. The range of possibilities extends from Johnny Callison and Harlond Clift on the downside to Billy Williams on the upside. The Incaviglia clones are, for the most part, a list of bashers who burned out early. The best: Boog Powell and Dale Murphy. The worst: Jimmie Hall and Earl Williams. Sadly, we must report that Big Pete's averages are an approximation of the career totals of Big John Mayberry. How the mighty have fallen.

Now if it sounds like we're passing this stuff off as gospel, keep in mind the comparison of Jefferies to Ruth and Foxx. Let's face it, even the weatherman is wrong occasionally.

The rookie crop of 1986 is already regarded as one of the most promising in baseball history. Sierra, Joyner, Canseco, Clark, Mitchell, Bonilla, Thompson, Galarraga, and Barry Larkin have emerged as All-Stars. Canseco and Mitchell have won Most Valuable Player awards, and Sierra was an MVP runner-up. So, four years later, the question arises: Where does the class of '86 rank among baseball's great freshman classes?

Let's state at the outset that we're dealing here only with batters. The class of '86 produced few good starting pitchers, no great ones. For the record, it has produced some fine relievers (Todd Worrell, Dan Plesac, and Mitch Williams), but even the best of its starters (Doug Drabek and Jim Deshaies) are number-two and number-three pitchers.

Of course, it's somewhat unrealistic to evaluate a rookie crop after only four years. So we're obviously not looking to write the final chapter at this time. But it's illuminating to compare the four-year totals of each season's rookies to the corresponding figures for 1986. So far, the class of '86 doesn't rank nearly as high as you might expect. They've produced a total of 16,457 runs to date. (Each time a player scores a run, he is credited with producing half that run. The other half is credited to the player who drives him in.) On a per-team basis (to compare seasons from the pre-expansion era to contemporary season more equitably), that average ranks only 26th among the 87 seasons from 1900 through 1986. The top five since 1900, based on runs produced per team (RP/T):

| Year | RP/T | Leading Run Producers (first four years only) |
|---|---|---|
| 1928 | 466 | Chuck Klein, Red Kress, Pinky Whitney |
| 1909 | 412 | Home Run Baker, Donie Bush, Dick Hoblitzell |
| 1934 | 382 | Zeke Bonura, Harlond Clift, Hal Trosky |
| 1954 | 374 | Hank Aaron, Ernie Banks, Al Kaline |
| 1912 | 368 | Eddie Foster, Del Pratt, Red Smith |

Such a poor showing can be partially explained by lower scoring levels today than in the past. Players just didn't produce as many runs in the 1980s as they did, for instance, in the 1930s. So by selecting runs produced as our standard of measure, we gave the players of 50 years ago an inherent advantage over contemporary rookies. But even two recent seasons (1977 and 1982) spawned rookies who produced more runs in their first four years than the 1986 freshmen did. The best of 1977 were Eddie Murray, Andre Dawson, Jack Clark, and Dale Murphy. Not bad, but the 1982 group was extraordinary. The long and impressive list of its most accomplished members includes: Wade Boggs, Cal Ripken, Tony Gwynn, Ryne Sandberg, Kent Hrbek, Willie McGee, Steve Sax, Gary Gaetti, Tom Brunansky, Von Hayes, Jesse Barfield, Chili Davis, Brett Butler, Dave Henderson, Pat Tabler, and Bob Brenly.

Will the class of '86 eventually produce more All-Stars and more Hall of Famers than any single season's worth of freshmen in baseball history? The potential for greatness is certainly there—in some individual cases, it's already been realized. But other seasons throughout baseball history have produced players who've accomplished even more over their first four years. Simply stated, on the basis of production over their first four years, by the entire group of rookies, not only isn't the 1986 class among the best of the century, it isn't even the best of the decade.

## WON-LOST RECORD BY STARTING POSITION

| TEXAS 83-79 | C | 1B | 2B | 3B | SS | LF | CF | RF | P | DH | Leadoff | Relief | Starts |
|---|---|---|---|---|---|---|---|---|---|---|---|---|---|
| Darrel Akerfelds | - | - | - | - | - | - | - | - | - | - | - | 0-6 | - |
| Wilson Alvarez | - | - | - | - | - | - | - | - | 0-1 | - | - | - | 0-1 |
| Brad Arnsberg | - | - | - | - | - | - | - | - | 0-1 | - | - | 5-10 | 0-1 |
| Harold Baines | - | - | - | - | - | - | - | 0-1 | - | 19-25 | - | - | 19-26 |
| John Barfield | - | - | - | - | - | - | - | - | 0-2 | - | - | 0-2 | 0-2 |
| Buddy Bell | - | 1-0 | - | 4-3 | - | - | - | - | - | 6-8 | - | - | 11-11 |
| Thad Bosley | - | - | - | - | - | 1-1 | - | - | - | 1-0 | - | - | 2-1 |
| Kevin Brown | - | - | - | - | - | - | - | - | 16-12 | - | - | - | 16-12 |
| Steve Buechele | - | - | 3-4 | 66-65 | - | - | - | - | - | 0-1 | - | - | 69-70 |
| Scott Coolbaugh | - | - | - | 9-7 | - | - | - | - | - | 1-1 | - | - | 10-8 |
| Jack Daugherty | - | 9-4 | - | - | - | 0-3 | - | - | - | 3-2 | 1-3 | - | 12-9 |
| Cecil Espy | - | - | - | - | - | 1-0 | 55-53 | - | - | 1-1 | 54-53 | - | 57-54 |
| Scott Fletcher | - | - | - | - | 44-35 | - | - | - | - | 1-0 | 1-1 | - | 45-35 |
| Julio Franco | - | - | 70-69 | - | - | - | - | - | - | 7-3 | 1-0 | - | 77-72 |
| Juan Gonzalez | - | - | - | - | - | - | 9-10 | - | - | - | - | - | 9-10 |
| Cecilio Guante | - | - | - | - | - | - | - | - | - | - | - | 16-34 | - |
| Drew Hall | - | - | - | - | - | - | - | - | - | - | - | 10-28 | - |
| Charlie Hough | - | - | - | - | - | - | - | - | 15-15 | - | - | - | 15-15 |
| Pete Incaviglia | - | - | - | - | - | 58-54 | 2-3 | - | - | 2-1 | - | - | 62-58 |
| Mike Jeffcoat | - | - | - | - | - | - | - | - | 11-11 | - | - | - | 11-11 |
| Chad Kreuter | 29-29 | - | - | - | - | - | - | - | - | - | - | - | 29-29 |
| Jeff Kunkel | - | - | 3-1 | 0-1 | 27-26 | 0-1 | 16-6 | - | - | 1-0 | 12-4 | 0-1 | 47-35 |
| Rick Leach | - | 0-1 | - | - | - | 17-15 | - | - | - | 15-18 | 1-0 | - | 32-34 |
| Fred Manrique | - | - | 7-5 | 3-2 | 12-18 | - | - | - | - | - | 9-12 | - | 22-25 |
| Craig McMurtry | - | - | - | - | - | - | - | - | - | - | - | 5-14 | - |
| Gary Mielke | - | - | - | - | - | - | - | - | - | - | - | 17-26 | - |
| Jamie Moyer | - | - | - | - | - | - | - | - | 6-9 | - | - | - | 6-9 |
| Rafael Palmeiro | - | 71-71 | - | - | - | - | - | - | - | 1-1 | 1-0 | - | 72-72 |
| Dean Palmer | - | - | - | 1-1 | - | - | - | - | - | 1-1 | - | - | 2-2 |
| Geno Petralli | 19-17 | - | - | - | - | - | - | - | - | 7-7 | - | - | 26-24 |
| Kevin Reimer | - | - | - | - | - | - | - | - | - | 1-0 | - | - | 1-0 |
| Kenny Rogers | - | - | - | - | - | - | - | - | - | - | - | 35-38 | - |
| Jeff Russell | - | - | - | - | - | - | - | - | - | - | - | 49-22 | - |
| Nolan Ryan | - | - | - | - | - | - | - | - | 20-12 | - | - | - | 20-12 |
| Ruben Sierra | - | - | - | - | - | - | 0-1 | 83-78 | - | - | - | - | 83-79 |
| Sammy Sosa | - | - | - | - | - | 6-4 | 1-6 | - | - | 2-1 | 3-6 | - | 9-11 |
| Mike Stanley | 9-6 | 2-3 | - | - | - | - | - | - | - | 10-4 | - | - | 21-13 |
| Jeff Stone | - | - | - | - | - | 0-1 | - | - | - | 4-5 | - | - | 4-6 |
| Jim Sundberg | 26-27 | - | - | - | - | - | - | - | - | - | - | - | 26-27 |
| Paul Wilmet | - | - | - | - | - | - | - | - | - | - | - | 0-3 | - |
| Bobby Witt | - | - | - | - | - | - | - | - | 15-16 | - | - | - | 15-16 |

## Batting vs. Left and Right Handed Pitchers

| | | BA | Rank | SA | Rank | OBA | Rank | HR % | Rank | BB % | Rank | SO % | Rank |
|---|---|---|---|---|---|---|---|---|---|---|---|---|---|
| Harold Baines | vs. Lefties | .263 | 88 | .385 | 92 | .347 | 59 | 2.56 | 63 | 11.36 | 30 | 17.05 | 122 |
| | vs. Righties | .330 | 4 | .501 | 10 | .415 | 5 | 3.44 | 39 | 13.02 | 14 | 12.04 | 69 |
| Steve Buechele | vs. Lefties | .257 | 104 | .439 | 45 | .323 | 92 | 4.05 | 29 | 9.15 | 58 | 17.07 | 123 |
| | vs. Righties | .225 | 142 | .364 | 95 | .280 | 144 | 2.96 | 51 | 5.74 | 134 | 21.58 | 146 |
| Cecil Espy | vs. Lefties | .242 | 124 | .347 | 121 | .282 | 140 | 3.16 | 49 | 5.66 | 121 | 18.87 | 134 |
| | vs. Righties | .261 | 82 | .326 | 128 | .321 | 88 | 0.00 | 158 | 7.60 | 95 | 18.76 | 133 |
| Julio Franco | vs. Lefties | .286 | 55 | .453 | 37 | .361 | 45 | 3.11 | 51 | 10.93 | 35 | 12.02 | 79 |
| | vs. Righties | .328 | 5 | .465 | 28 | .397 | 9 | 2.07 | 80 | 10.50 | 45 | 10.73 | 53 |
| Pete Incaviglia | vs. Lefties | .209 | 156 | .412 | 68 | .264 | 151 | 4.05 | 29 | 6.13 | 109 | 28.22 | 166 |
| | vs. Righties | .249 | 105 | .472 | 25 | .307 | 109 | 4.92 | 15 | 6.63 | 117 | 27.11 | 166 |
| Chad Kreuter | vs. Lefties | .229 | -- | .514 | -- | .386 | -- | 8.57 | -- | 19.57 | -- | 15.22 | -- |
| | vs. Righties | .130 | 171 | .195 | 170 | .239 | 168 | 1.63 | 97 | 12.33 | 19 | 22.60 | 149 |
| Jeff Kunkel | vs. Lefties | .307 | 31 | .507 | 14 | .345 | 64 | 2.14 | 74 | 3.97 | 151 | 22.52 | 156 |
| | vs. Righties | .235 | 122 | .373 | 90 | .304 | 112 | 3.27 | 43 | 8.00 | 87 | 23.43 | 156 |
| Rick Leach | vs. Lefties | .143 | -- | .143 | -- | .250 | -- | 0.00 | -- | 12.50 | -- | 37.50 | -- |
| | vs. Righties | .276 | 54 | .358 | 101 | .361 | 34 | 0.43 | 148 | 11.48 | 27 | 11.11 | 60 |
| Fred Manrique | vs. Lefties | .305 | 33 | .390 | 86 | .344 | 65 | 0.71 | 126 | 5.23 | 134 | 16.34 | 116 |
| | vs. Righties | .287 | 35 | .401 | 60 | .315 | 100 | 1.27 | 120 | 3.47 | 163 | 14.67 | 93 |
| Rafael Palmeiro | vs. Lefties | .248 | 117 | .333 | 131 | .298 | 127 | 1.21 | 110 | 6.11 | 110 | 7.22 | 26 |
| | vs. Righties | .287 | 36 | .391 | 70 | .376 | 20 | 1.52 | 103 | 11.50 | 25 | 7.74 | 21 |
| Geno Petralli | vs. Lefties | .111 | -- | .111 | -- | .333 | -- | 0.00 | -- | 25.00 | -- | 33.33 | -- |
| | vs. Righties | .314 | 11 | .423 | 47 | .370 | 24 | 2.29 | 72 | 7.25 | 101 | 10.36 | 47 |
| Ruben Sierra | vs. Lefties | .341 | 10 | .600 | 2 | .378 | 27 | 4.88 | 19 | 6.31 | 104 | 8.11 | 32 |
| | vs. Righties | .289 | 33 | .515 | 5 | .332 | 69 | 4.43 | 19 | 6.21 | 128 | 13.70 | 79 |
| Mike Stanley | vs. Lefties | .256 | 105 | .333 | 131 | .310 | 108 | 1.28 | 105 | 7.14 | 93 | 23.81 | 159 |
| | vs. Righties | .227 | -- | .273 | -- | .346 | -- | 0.00 | -- | 11.32 | -- | 16.98 | -- |
| Jim Sundberg | vs. Lefties | .263 | 89 | .413 | 65 | .366 | 36 | 1.25 | 107 | 13.13 | 19 | 16.16 | 114 |
| | vs. Righties | .119 | -- | .164 | -- | .231 | -- | 1.49 | -- | 12.66 | -- | 26.58 | -- |
| Team Average | vs. Lefties | .266 | 8 | .418 | 4 | .323 | 9 | 2.59 | 1 | 7.63 | 9 | 16.21 | 12 |
| | vs. Righties | .261 | 5 | .384 | 6 | .328 | 6 | 2.08 | 11 | 8.50 | 7 | 16.22 | 13 |
| League Average | vs. Lefties | .266 | | .391 | | .328 | | 2.18 | | 8.18 | | 13.58 | |
| | vs. Righties | .258 | | .380 | | .325 | | 2.26 | | 8.56 | | 14.57 | |

## Batting with Runners on Base and Bases Empty

| | | BA | Rank | SA | Rank | OBA | Rank | HR % | Rank | BB % | Rank | SO % | Rank |
|---|---|---|---|---|---|---|---|---|---|---|---|---|---|
| Harold Baines | Runners On | .311 | 25 | .451 | 39 | .411 | 9 | 2.55 | 57 | 14.89 | 15 | 13.48 | 92 |
| | Bases Empty | .307 | 14 | .478 | 14 | .379 | 11 | 3.70 | 38 | 10.30 | 30 | 13.62 | 83 |
| Steve Buechele | Runners On | .235 | 139 | .362 | 103 | .302 | 130 | 1.88 | 86 | 6.75 | 116 | 20.25 | 145 |
| | Bases Empty | .234 | 126 | .407 | 61 | .287 | 134 | 4.40 | 24 | 6.83 | 101 | 20.14 | 139 |
| Cecil Espy | Runners On | .206 | 163 | .229 | 170 | .246 | 168 | 0.00 | 146 | 5.08 | 144 | 22.84 | 155 |
| | Bases Empty | .287 | 35 | .390 | 75 | .352 | 35 | 1.00 | 121 | 8.48 | 65 | 16.36 | 103 |
| Julio Franco | Runners On | .345 | 3 | .508 | 12 | .428 | 4 | 1.98 | 78 | 13.71 | 19 | 11.37 | 71 |
| | Bases Empty | .291 | 29 | .422 | 50 | .348 | 40 | 2.70 | 68 | 7.76 | 82 | 10.87 | 49 |
| Pete Incaviglia | Runners On | .237 | 137 | .446 | 42 | .277 | 160 | 4.91 | 19 | 4.13 | 158 | 27.27 | 171 |
| | Bases Empty | .236 | 122 | .459 | 27 | .308 | 102 | 4.37 | 25 | 8.70 | 57 | 27.67 | 168 |
| Chad Kreuter | Runners On | .127 | -- | .164 | -- | .210 | -- | 0.00 | -- | 8.82 | -- | 22.06 | -- |
| | Bases Empty | .165 | 170 | .320 | 134 | .306 | 103 | 4.85 | 17 | 16.94 | 1 | 20.16 | 140 |
| Jeff Kunkel | Runners On | .274 | 80 | .407 | 67 | .333 | 89 | 0.88 | 129 | 6.02 | 127 | 24.81 | 164 |
| | Bases Empty | .267 | 60 | .456 | 28 | .316 | 87 | 3.89 | 34 | 6.22 | 120 | 21.76 | 150 |
| Rick Leach | Runners On | .218 | 160 | .238 | 168 | .357 | 55 | 0.00 | 146 | 16.92 | 10 | 10.00 | 61 |
| | Bases Empty | .312 | 12 | .435 | 41 | .358 | 28 | 0.72 | 135 | 6.76 | 105 | 13.51 | 80 |
| Fred Manrique | Runners On | .368 | 1 | .523 | 7 | .383 | 27 | 1.94 | 81 | 2.29 | 169 | 12.57 | 89 |
| | Bases Empty | .242 | 113 | .309 | 143 | .287 | 133 | 0.45 | 147 | 5.49 | 136 | 17.30 | 113 |
| Rafael Palmeiro | Runners On | .292 | 47 | .404 | 71 | .378 | 34 | 1.60 | 95 | 11.03 | 40 | 8.28 | 36 |
| | Bases Empty | .262 | 75 | .350 | 106 | .333 | 53 | 1.29 | 111 | 9.06 | 44 | 7.02 | 11 |
| Geno Petralli | Runners On | .280 | 69 | .390 | 80 | .368 | 41 | 2.44 | 65 | 12.50 | 28 | 9.38 | 50 |
| | Bases Empty | .324 | -- | .422 | -- | .367 | -- | 1.96 | -- | 4.59 | -- | 13.76 | -- |
| Ruben Sierra | Runners On | .329 | 12 | .564 | 5 | .364 | 48 | 4.70 | 20 | 6.53 | 119 | 10.51 | 64 |
| | Bases Empty | .283 | 40 | .521 | 5 | .329 | 65 | 4.44 | 23 | 5.93 | 127 | 13.35 | 77 |
| Team Average | Runners On | .262 | 11 | .389 | 10 | .328 | 11 | 2.02 | 10 | 8.53 | 10 | 16.12 | 14 |
| | Bases Empty | .263 | 3 | .398 | 3 | .325 | 4 | 2.40 | 6 | 8.01 | 5 | 16.30 | 12 |
| League Average | Runners On | .268 | | .389 | | .336 | | 2.15 | | 9.17 | | 13.53 | |
| | Bases Empty | .255 | | .380 | | .317 | | 2.29 | | 7.84 | | 14.86 | |

## Overall Batting Compared to Late Inning Pressure Situations

| | | BA | Rank | SA | Rank | OBA | Rank | HR % | Rank | BB % | Rank | SO % | Rank | RDI % | Rank |
|---|---|---|---|---|---|---|---|---|---|---|---|---|---|---|---|
| Harold Baines | Overall | .309 | 10 | .465 | 16 | .395 | 7 | 3.17 | 47 | 12.52 | 17 | 13.55 | 84 | .313 | 36 |
| | Pressure | .268 | 68 | .451 | 34 | .366 | 41 | 4.23 | 31 | 13.41 | 31 | 15.85 | 83 | .160 | 129 |
| Thad Bosley | Overall | .225 | -- | .350 | -- | .273 | -- | 2.50 | -- | 6.82 | -- | 25.00 | -- | .259 | -- |
| | Pressure | .154 | -- | .154 | -- | .200 | -- | 0.00 | -- | 6.67 | -- | 26.67 | -- | .333 | 42 |
| Steve Buechele | Overall | .235 | 143 | .387 | 83 | .294 | 141 | 3.29 | 41 | 6.79 | 113 | 20.19 | 146 | .218 | 148 |
| | Pressure | .191 | 141 | .294 | 125 | .267 | 134 | 1.47 | 98 | 9.21 | 72 | 26.32 | 149 | .000 | 165 |
| Cecil Espy | Overall | .257 | 94 | .331 | 138 | .313 | 105 | 0.63 | 143 | 7.21 | 103 | 18.79 | 135 | .217 | 149 |
| | Pressure | .311 | 33 | .328 | 108 | .382 | 32 | 0.00 | 107 | 10.00 | 65 | 15.71 | 79 | .211 | 112 |
| Julio Franco | Overall | .316 | 6 | .462 | 21 | .386 | 11 | 2.37 | 69 | 10.63 | 32 | 11.11 | 60 | .384 | 3 |
| | Pressure | .319 | 26 | .472 | 26 | .351 | 53 | 2.78 | 61 | 5.19 | 141 | 15.58 | 77 | .400 | 19 |
| Pete Incaviglia | Overall | .236 | 141 | .453 | 27 | .293 | 143 | 4.64 | 14 | 6.46 | 119 | 27.47 | 168 | .298 | 45 |
| | Pressure | .156 | 158 | .313 | 112 | .206 | 163 | 3.13 | 52 | 5.88 | 127 | 32.35 | 161 | .385 | 24 |
| Jeff Kunkel | Overall | .270 | 61 | .437 | 37 | .323 | 86 | 2.73 | 59 | 6.13 | 130 | 23.01 | 155 | .288 | 57 |
| | Pressure | .182 | 150 | .242 | 148 | .206 | 163 | 0.00 | 107 | 2.86 | 156 | 25.71 | 147 | .000 | -- |
| Rick Leach | Overall | .272 | 57 | .351 | 118 | .358 | 31 | 0.42 | 152 | 11.51 | 22 | 11.87 | 67 | .250 | 107 |
| | Pressure | .262 | 77 | .333 | 103 | .347 | 54 | 0.00 | 107 | 12.00 | 41 | 22.00 | 131 | .333 | 42 |
| Fred Manrique | Overall | .294 | 27 | .397 | 72 | .326 | 80 | 1.06 | 129 | 4.13 | 163 | 15.29 | 102 | .375 | 6 |
| | Pressure | .333 | 16 | .463 | 30 | .390 | 27 | 1.85 | 79 | 7.69 | 103 | 15.38 | 73 | .353 | 36 |
| Rafael Palmeiro | Overall | .275 | 46 | .374 | 93 | .354 | 37 | 1.43 | 109 | 9.97 | 43 | 7.59 | 17 | .324 | 28 |
| | Pressure | .283 | 54 | .383 | 73 | .386 | 30 | 1.67 | 87 | 14.29 | 20 | 7.14 | 14 | .267 | 82 |
| Geno Petralli | Overall | .304 | 15 | .408 | 60 | .368 | 23 | 2.17 | 78 | 8.29 | 75 | 11.71 | 64 | .262 | 89 |
| | Pressure | .211 | -- | .263 | -- | .348 | -- | 0.00 | -- | 17.39 | -- | 21.74 | -- | .286 | 68 |
| Ruben Sierra | Overall | .306 | 13 | .543 | 1 | .347 | 45 | 4.57 | 15 | 6.24 | 126 | 11.90 | 68 | .378 | 5 |
| | Pressure | .284 | 53 | .473 | 25 | .329 | 77 | 2.70 | 63 | 7.32 | 110 | 7.32 | 15 | .400 | 19 |
| Team Average | Overall | .263 | 5 | .394 | 4 | .326 | 7 | 2.24 | 9 | 8.25 | 7 | 16.22 | 13 | .280 | 4 |
| | Pressure | .244 | 7 | .344 | 9 | .306 | 11 | 1.45 | 13 | 8.41 | 11 | 18.24 | 9 | .259 | 7 |
| League Average | Overall | .261 | | .384 | | .326 | | 2.23 | | 8.44 | | 14.26 | | .269 | |
| | Pressure | .247 | | .357 | | .318 | | 2.02 | | 9.02 | | 17.90 | | .254 | |

## Additional Miscellaneous Batting Comparisons

| | Grass Surface | | Artificial Surface | | Home Games | | Road Games | | Runners in Scoring Position | | Runners in Scoring Pos and Two Outs | | Leading Off Inning | | Runners on 3B with less than 2 Outs | |
|---|---|---|---|---|---|---|---|---|---|---|---|---|---|---|---|---|
| | BA | Rank | BA | Rank | BA | Rank | BA | Rank | BA | Rank | BA | Rank | OBA | Rank | RDI % | Rank |
| Harold Baines | .303 | 16 | .342 | 12 | .296 | 34 | .322 | 10 | .270 | 78 | .321 | 16 | .349 | 49 | .531 | 108 |
| Steve Buechele | .232 | 135 | .250 | 90 | .225 | 141 | .243 | 118 | .224 | 142 | .162 | 149 | .292 | 120 | .364 | 158 |
| Jack Daugherty | .319 | -- | .200 | -- | .306 | -- | .295 | -- | .118 | -- | .167 | -- | .448 | -- | .500 | 119 |
| Cecil Espy | .271 | 59 | .182 | 156 | .272 | 63 | .242 | 120 | .208 | 151 | .237 | 84 | .347 | 52 | .375 | 156 |
| Julio Franco | .338 | 2 | .208 | 138 | .356 | 5 | .278 | 51 | .407 | 1 | .343 | 9 | .338 | 60 | .677 | 37 |
| Pete Incaviglia | .251 | 97 | .174 | 158 | .251 | 98 | .222 | 153 | .287 | 54 | .242 | 80 | .325 | 79 | .552 | 99 |
| Chad Kreuter | .148 | 171 | .188 | -- | .176 | -- | .131 | -- | .071 | -- | .000 | -- | .279 | -- | .667 | -- |
| Jeff Kunkel | .267 | 67 | .290 | -- | .255 | 92 | .284 | 45 | .290 | 47 | .308 | 20 | .304 | 108 | .333 | 163 |
| Rick Leach | .240 | 116 | .457 | -- | .214 | 152 | .328 | 7 | .191 | 159 | .158 | 151 | .435 | 4 | .923 | 1 |
| Fred Manrique | .286 | 37 | .329 | 19 | .316 | 16 | .275 | 58 | .384 | 3 | .372 | 3 | .257 | 154 | .684 | 28 |
| Rafael Palmeiro | .263 | 73 | .337 | 16 | .259 | 87 | .291 | 30 | .278 | 69 | .226 | 94 | .260 | 151 | .786 | 11 |
| Geno Petralli | .316 | 4 | .250 | -- | .193 | 166 | .406 | 1 | .241 | 111 | .333 | 11 | .283 | 131 | .500 | -- |
| Ruben Sierra | .308 | 13 | .297 | 34 | .317 | 13 | .295 | 23 | .337 | 12 | .314 | 19 | .329 | 72 | .615 | 59 |
| Jim Sundberg | .157 | 170 | .385 | -- | .108 | -- | .268 | -- | .207 | -- | .455 | -- | .326 | 78 | .200 | -- |
| Team Average | .263 | 7 | .258 | 9 | .263 | 7 | .263 | 6 | .265 | 6 | .244 | 5 | .317 | 9 | .547 | 11 |
| League Average | .260 | | .262 | | .262 | | .259 | | .262 | | .232 | | .321 | | .566 | |

## Pitching vs. Left and Right Handed Batters

| | | BA | Rank | SA | Rank | OBA | Rank | HR % | Rank | BB % | Rank | SO % | Rank |
|---|---|---|---|---|---|---|---|---|---|---|---|---|---|
| Kevin Brown | vs. Lefties | .225 | 32 | .291 | 23 | .294 | 30 | 1.42 | 49 | 9.00 | 70 | 11.31 | 75 |
| | vs. Righties | .242 | 35 | .332 | 32 | .312 | 55 | 1.37 | 28 | 8.56 | 86 | 14.67 | 72 |
| Cecilio Guante | vs. Lefties | .256 | 61 | .488 | 122 | .414 | 133 | 5.81 | 132 | 18.92 | 135 | 13.51 | 53 |
| | vs. Righties | .246 | 43 | .335 | 34 | .303 | 42 | 1.12 | 18 | 7.50 | 63 | 27.00 | 8 |
| Drew Hall | vs. Lefties | .159 | -- | .238 | -- | .260 | -- | 1.59 | -- | 9.46 | -- | 22.97 | -- |
| | vs. Righties | .229 | 25 | .321 | 27 | .353 | 121 | 1.43 | 32 | 15.48 | 134 | 16.67 | 50 |
| Charlie Hough | vs. Lefties | .238 | 41 | .366 | 53 | .327 | 66 | 2.68 | 90 | 11.34 | 106 | 10.57 | 82 |
| | vs. Righties | .252 | 59 | .461 | 128 | .351 | 118 | 5.44 | 133 | 12.53 | 129 | 13.02 | 87 |
| Mike Jeffcoat | vs. Lefties | .263 | 71 | .384 | 70 | .295 | 32 | 1.01 | 28 | 4.72 | 13 | 13.21 | 57 |
| | vs. Righties | .272 | 94 | .398 | 87 | .322 | 68 | 1.45 | 33 | 6.18 | 39 | 11.04 | 108 |
| Gary Mielke | vs. Lefties | .240 | -- | .340 | -- | .345 | -- | 2.00 | -- | 13.79 | -- | 1.72 | -- |
| | vs. Righties | .294 | 121 | .412 | 97 | .378 | 133 | 2.21 | 75 | 10.69 | 116 | 15.72 | 58 |
| Jamie Moyer | vs. Lefties | .214 | -- | .310 | -- | .365 | -- | 2.38 | -- | 15.38 | -- | 11.54 | -- |
| | vs. Righties | .294 | 121 | .459 | 126 | .352 | 120 | 3.53 | 118 | 8.77 | 89 | 13.33 | 84 |
| Kenny Rogers | vs. Lefties | .169 | 6 | .217 | 5 | .303 | 42 | 0.00 | 1 | 12.87 | 114 | 21.78 | 12 |
| | vs. Righties | .261 | 76 | .341 | 38 | .364 | 128 | 1.14 | 20 | 13.62 | 133 | 19.25 | 31 |
| Jeff Russell | vs. Lefties | .205 | 15 | .241 | 10 | .289 | 26 | 0.00 | 1 | 9.38 | 80 | 25.78 | 7 |
| | vs. Righties | .163 | 1 | .311 | 17 | .235 | 2 | 2.96 | 106 | 8.00 | 76 | 29.33 | 5 |
| Nolan Ryan | vs. Lefties | .177 | 9 | .262 | 13 | .261 | 12 | 1.79 | 66 | 10.14 | 94 | 28.63 | 4 |
| | vs. Righties | .197 | 8 | .304 | 12 | .289 | 29 | 2.14 | 72 | 9.69 | 105 | 32.37 | 3 |
| Bobby Witt | vs. Lefties | .249 | 52 | .387 | 76 | .364 | 101 | 2.87 | 96 | 15.46 | 123 | 19.20 | 17 |
| | vs. Righties | .247 | 45 | .326 | 28 | .332 | 90 | 1.04 | 15 | 10.86 | 121 | 19.00 | 33 |
| Team Average | vs. Lefties | .224 | 1 | .333 | 2 | .318 | 6 | 2.22 | 10 | 11.61 | 14 | 17.54 | 1 |
| | vs. Righties | .249 | 2 | .369 | 2 | .328 | 11 | 2.22 | 6 | 9.93 | 14 | 18.40 | 2 |
| League Average | vs. Lefties | .261 | | .382 | | .330 | | 2.16 | | 9.16 | | 13.03 | |
| | vs. Righties | .261 | | .385 | | .323 | | 2.28 | | 7.96 | | 15.09 | |

## Pitching with Runners on Base and Bases Empty

| | | BA | Rank | SA | Rank | OBA | Rank | HR % | Rank | BB % | Rank | SO % | Rank |
|---|---|---|---|---|---|---|---|---|---|---|---|---|---|
| Kevin Brown | Runners On | .237 | 33 | .319 | 20 | .298 | 19 | 1.36 | 38 | 7.53 | 42 | 12.95 | 70 |
| | Bases Empty | .231 | 32 | .307 | 20 | .307 | 50 | 1.43 | 28 | 9.66 | 103 | 13.09 | 78 |
| Cecilio Guante | Runners On | .265 | 75 | .356 | 52 | .369 | 115 | 1.52 | 47 | 14.81 | 126 | 19.75 | 17 |
| | Bases Empty | .233 | 40 | .414 | 97 | .315 | 63 | 3.76 | 123 | 8.05 | 79 | 24.83 | 11 |
| Drew Hall | Runners On | .229 | -- | .253 | -- | .363 | -- | 0.00 | -- | 16.35 | -- | 16.35 | -- |
| | Bases Empty | .192 | 7 | .325 | 29 | .297 | 41 | 2.50 | 82 | 11.59 | 125 | 20.29 | 24 |
| Charlie Hough | Runners On | .255 | 53 | .406 | 95 | .356 | 101 | 3.69 | 124 | 12.88 | 120 | 11.35 | 86 |
| | Bases Empty | .239 | 45 | .420 | 100 | .328 | 85 | 4.35 | 132 | 11.30 | 121 | 12.15 | 85 |
| Mike Jeffcoat | Runners On | .250 | 43 | .391 | 84 | .298 | 17 | 2.27 | 90 | 6.12 | 17 | 10.20 | 99 |
| | Bases Empty | .286 | 112 | .398 | 82 | .331 | 89 | 0.68 | 7 | 5.73 | 37 | 12.42 | 83 |
| Gary Mielke | Runners On | .303 | 121 | .440 | 116 | .394 | 126 | 2.75 | 106 | 12.31 | 112 | 10.00 | 101 |
| | Bases Empty | .247 | -- | .325 | -- | .333 | -- | 1.30 | -- | 10.34 | -- | 14.94 | -- |
| Jamie Moyer | Runners On | .301 | 120 | .472 | 128 | .371 | 117 | 3.25 | 117 | 9.72 | 80 | 11.81 | 78 |
| | Bases Empty | .270 | 89 | .414 | 98 | .342 | 101 | 3.45 | 113 | 9.84 | 105 | 13.99 | 67 |
| Kenny Rogers | Runners On | .263 | 70 | .349 | 38 | .358 | 102 | 0.66 | 8 | 11.35 | 104 | 18.92 | 20 |
| | Bases Empty | .187 | -- | .234 | -- | .326 | -- | 0.93 | -- | 16.28 | -- | 21.71 | -- |
| Jeff Russell | Runners On | .222 | 19 | .365 | 60 | .308 | 32 | 2.38 | 94 | 10.88 | 100 | 23.13 | 9 |
| | Bases Empty | .140 | -- | .190 | -- | .206 | -- | 0.83 | -- | 6.11 | -- | 32.82 | -- |
| Nolan Ryan | Runners On | .261 | 65 | .355 | 50 | .345 | 87 | 1.95 | 73 | 10.74 | 96 | 26.72 | 5 |
| | Bases Empty | .146 | 2 | .243 | 2 | .235 | 2 | 1.96 | 56 | 9.44 | 98 | 32.64 | 3 |
| Bobby Witt | Runners On | .289 | 108 | .410 | 99 | .378 | 119 | 1.51 | 46 | 12.38 | 115 | 15.35 | 50 |
| | Bases Empty | .214 | 15 | .309 | 21 | .323 | 73 | 2.24 | 72 | 13.76 | 132 | 22.37 | 20 |
| Team Average | Runners On | .266 | 6 | .383 | 6 | .350 | 11 | 2.09 | 6 | 11.03 | 13 | 15.69 | 1 |
| | Bases Empty | .217 | 1 | .333 | 1 | .303 | 3 | 2.32 | 9 | 10.28 | 14 | 19.97 | 1 |
| League Average | Runners On | .268 | | .389 | | .336 | | 2.15 | | 9.17 | | 13.53 | |
| | Bases Empty | .255 | | .380 | | .317 | | 2.29 | | 7.84 | | 14.86 | |

## Overall Pitching Compared to Late Inning Pressure Situations

| | | BA | Rank | SA | Rank | OBA | Rank | HR % | Rank | BB % | Rank | SO % | Rank |
|---|---|---|---|---|---|---|---|---|---|---|---|---|---|
| Kevin Brown | Overall | .234 | 27 | .312 | 16 | .303 | 30 | 1.40 | 26 | 8.77 | 82 | 13.03 | 74 |
| | Pressure | .205 | 31 | .315 | 46 | .293 | 37 | 2.74 | 94 | 10.98 | 86 | 10.98 | 99 |
| Cecilio Guante | Overall | .249 | 50 | .385 | 77 | .343 | 100 | 2.64 | 98 | 11.58 | 116 | 22.19 | 11 |
| | Pressure | .241 | 61 | .336 | 58 | .333 | 75 | 1.72 | 62 | 10.29 | 76 | 20.59 | 29 |
| Drew Hall | Overall | .207 | -- | .296 | -- | .325 | -- | 1.48 | -- | 13.64 | -- | 18.60 | -- |
| | Pressure | .233 | 55 | .267 | 25 | .361 | 98 | 0.00 | 1 | 16.22 | 126 | 18.92 | 38 |
| Charlie Hough | Overall | .245 | 41 | .415 | 94 | .340 | 94 | 4.09 | 131 | 11.95 | 121 | 11.82 | 86 |
| | Pressure | .273 | 91 | .621 | 128 | .351 | 89 | 9.09 | 134 | 9.46 | 69 | 8.11 | 116 |
| Mike Jeffcoat | Overall | .270 | 88 | .395 | 82 | .317 | 54 | 1.36 | 23 | 5.90 | 20 | 11.45 | 93 |
| | Pressure | .429 | 130 | .600 | 126 | .444 | 128 | 2.86 | 96 | 2.78 | 5 | 11.11 | 98 |
| Gary Mielke | Overall | .280 | -- | .392 | -- | .369 | -- | 2.15 | -- | 11.52 | -- | 11.98 | -- |
| | Pressure | .357 | 123 | .500 | 118 | .460 | 130 | 2.38 | 85 | 13.73 | 112 | 11.76 | 87 |
| Jamie Moyer | Overall | .283 | 108 | .438 | 115 | .354 | 114 | 3.37 | 122 | 9.79 | 99 | 13.06 | 73 |
| | Pressure | .353 | -- | .588 | -- | .476 | -- | 5.88 | -- | 19.05 | -- | 14.29 | -- |
| Kenny Rogers | Overall | .232 | 25 | .301 | 11 | .344 | 102 | 0.77 | 5 | 13.38 | 131 | 20.06 | 22 |
| | Pressure | .200 | 25 | .250 | 18 | .300 | 51 | 0.83 | 38 | 11.11 | 87 | 19.44 | 35 |
| Jeff Russell | Overall | .182 | 1 | .279 | 5 | .260 | 4 | 1.62 | 40 | 8.63 | 80 | 27.70 | 4 |
| | Pressure | .216 | 42 | .341 | 64 | .298 | 48 | 2.40 | 86 | 9.38 | 67 | 25.52 | 14 |
| Nolan Ryan | Overall | .187 | 2 | .283 | 6 | .275 | 9 | 1.96 | 61 | 9.92 | 103 | 30.47 | 3 |
| | Pressure | .211 | 37 | .321 | 50 | .277 | 26 | 1.83 | 69 | 7.50 | 47 | 35.00 | 3 |
| Bobby Witt | Overall | .248 | 47 | .355 | 47 | .348 | 105 | 1.91 | 58 | 13.12 | 128 | 19.10 | 25 |
| | Pressure | .204 | 30 | .204 | 6 | .328 | 68 | 0.00 | 1 | 15.00 | 118 | 25.00 | 15 |
| Team Average | Overall | .239 | 2 | .355 | 2 | .324 | 7 | 2.22 | 7 | 10.62 | 14 | 18.05 | 1 |
| | Pressure | .243 | 5 | .362 | 8 | .331 | 8 | 2.35 | 9 | 10.55 | 10 | 20.39 | 2 |
| League Average | Overall | .261 | | .384 | | .326 | | 2.23 | | 8.44 | | 14.26 | |
| | Pressure | .250 | | .362 | | .325 | | 2.14 | | 9.50 | | 16.61 | |

## Additional Miscellaneous Pitching Comparisons

| | Grass Surface BA | Rank | Artificial Surface BA | Rank | Home Games BA | Rank | Road Games BA | Rank | Runners in Scoring Position BA | Rank | Runners in Scoring Pos and Two Outs BA | Rank | Leading Off Inning OBA | Rank |
|---|---|---|---|---|---|---|---|---|---|---|---|---|---|---|
| Brad Arnsberg | .247 | 49 | .000 | -- | .267 | -- | .221 | -- | .347 | -- | .222 | -- | .370 | -- |
| Kevin Brown | .233 | 27 | .235 | 36 | .227 | 26 | .238 | 37 | .253 | 71 | .278 | 108 | .294 | 39 |
| Cecilio Guante | .262 | 67 | .143 | -- | .235 | 35 | .267 | 79 | .198 | 13 | .140 | 14 | .333 | 79 |
| Drew Hall | .213 | 18 | .172 | -- | .220 | 20 | .188 | -- | .208 | -- | .154 | -- | .281 | 31 |
| Charlie Hough | .249 | 51 | .234 | 33 | .271 | 95 | .224 | 25 | .190 | 10 | .139 | 13 | .318 | 61 |
| Mike Jeffcoat | .277 | 99 | .243 | 42 | .280 | 102 | .263 | 71 | .291 | 111 | .255 | 96 | .343 | 91 |
| Gary Mielke | .272 | 89 | .385 | -- | .257 | -- | .312 | -- | .347 | 133 | .324 | 127 | .486 | -- |
| Jamie Moyer | .275 | 95 | .375 | -- | .257 | 75 | .322 | 127 | .290 | 110 | .286 | -- | .365 | 109 |
| Kenny Rogers | .236 | 31 | .206 | -- | .241 | 47 | .216 | -- | .253 | 70 | .238 | 79 | .357 | -- |
| Jeff Russell | .156 | 2 | .333 | -- | .140 | -- | .222 | 22 | .235 | 42 | .163 | 26 | .156 | -- |
| Nolan Ryan | .198 | 8 | .128 | 1 | .201 | 9 | .166 | 1 | .236 | 45 | .179 | 36 | .259 | 17 |
| Bobby Witt | .244 | 44 | .276 | 79 | .237 | 38 | .258 | 65 | .289 | 109 | .317 | 124 | .370 | 114 |
| Team Average | .241 | 2 | .227 | 1 | .241 | 2 | .236 | 1 | .260 | 6 | .235 | 10 | .321 | 8 |
| League Average | .260 | | .262 | | .259 | | .262 | | .262 | | .232 | | .321 | |

# TORONTO BLUE JAYS

- **A final coment on Jimy**
- **Cito's turnaround season**

During three-plus seasons as Toronto manager, Jimy Williams was fired on an almost daily basis by the local and national media. Despite a record of 281–241 (only four games worse than Oakland's 284–236 mark, the best in the American League during that period), he was rarely credited with anything other than the team's failure to win even a division title under his aegis. Not that his record was untarnished. There were some noteworthy blots—the most glaring, of course, his bizarre handling of the Blue Jays during the final week of the 1987 season, when they blew a lead of three-and-a-half games to the Tigers. (For our own critique of Williams's, shall we say, *unique* moves during that collapse, see the Toronto essay in the 1988 *Analyst.*)

Still, we've come not to bury Williams—the Jays finally took care of that a year ago. Rather, it's worth noting that he is one of only 33 managers in major league history to compile records at least 10 games above .500 in each of their first three years (seasons of less than 80 games weren't considered)—an enviable mark that was totally ignored during the witch hunt that resulted in one-*M*'s firing last May. And for those who consider Williams's failure to win a title more significant than his overall record, we'd spin this semi-revisionist postscript to his tenure: Of those 33 managers, only seven failed to win a title of some sort during their first three seasons. But among them are two of the top 10 managers of all time when ranked according to winning percentage: Joe McCarthy and Al Lopez. Good company.

All this would be moot were it not for the fact that some overzealous Williams bashers took last season's turnaround, one that produced a spectacular at-the-wire victory in the race for the A.L. East title, as an opportunity to trash Williams anew. Of course, no one can say for sure whether the Jays would have remained in the muck without the cool leadership of Cito Gaston. But one thing is certain: Gaston took over a team that was clearly poised for a dramatic about-face, although few recognized the statistical signposts at the time.

For several seasons, we've written about the use of a team's record in one-run games as a leading indicator of its future direction. Teams that are successful in one-run games tend to fall back in the standings a year later; those that post poor records in games decided by one run generally improve. The basis for the trend is simple, though obscured by the conventional baseball wisdom that falsely attributes intangible but highly desirable traits to good one-run teams. In fact, the smaller the margin of victory in any game, the greater the role of luck in determining its outcome. The results of games decided by a single run are more likely than any others to be determined by luck than by skill. By extension, a team with a good record in one-run games is often the beneficiary of more than its share of luck over a given period, and so is unlikely to maintain such a record in the future, whether that be in the next season or later in the same season.

In the past, we've limited our analysis to identifying teams that are likely to advance or regress in the current season based on their one-run records of a year earlier. (For a new twist on that technique, see the Orioles essay on page 11.) But Toronto's form reversal after the installment of Cito Gaston as manager last season provides an ideal opportunity to illustrate how the trend can be useful for determining likely comeback candidates (as well as contenders unlikely to stay the course) during a season in progress.

During the months of April and May last season, Toronto had a record of 5–12 in one-run games. That margin of seven one-run games below .500 was the poorest in the American League over the first two months of the season. And it was a clear signal that the Jays were a sleeping giant.

From 1900 through 1987, 103 teams stood at least six games below .500 in one-run games at the end of May. Their collective improvement over the remainder of the season was astonishing, especially when contrasted with the declines of teams that posted good one-run records over the first two months.

The table below identifies two groups of teams: those that played at least six games above .500, and those that played at least six games below .500, in one-run games during April and May. The figures indicate the number of teams in each group that improved over the remainder of the season and those that declined, in terms of both overall winning percentage and position in the standings:

| | | Winning Pct. | | Standings | | |
|---|---|---|---|---|---|---|
| | Teams | + | − | + | = | − |
| Above .500 | 99 | 21 | 78 | 17 | 35 | 47 |
| Below .500 | 103 | 83 | 20 | 48 | 48 | 7 |

Stunning results. Among teams that lost at least six more one-run games than they won in April and May, more than 80 percent improved their overall winning percentages by season's end. Of those with six more one-run wins than losses, nearly 80 percent fell. The table doesn't show the margins of increase or decrease, which are equally impressive. The 83 teams that improved after a poor early-season record in one-run games did so by an average of 77 percentage points. The teams whose early-season success in one-run games presaged a decline fell by an average of 76 points.

No question about it, then—the Jays' 5–12 record in one-run games through May 31 indicated that they were primed for a turnaround. But could anyone really have predicted that they might actually rebound to win the division title? On the surface, such a prediction might have seemed like nonsense. After all, the Blue Jays were in seventh place, six-and-a-half games behind. From 1901 through 1988, 323 teams were at least as far behind their league or division leaders on May 31 on both counts, and only one came back to win a title (the 1914 Boston Braves—little wonder they were dubbed the "Miracle Braves"). Nevertheless, Toronto's poor record in one-run games, combined with another key element, made a division title a possibility worth considering.

Among those 103 teams who played at least six games below .500 in one-run games during April and May, there were six whose chances for the ultimate comeback were enhanced by weak front runners, defined as division or league leaders with winning percentages below .550. Two of them, the 1974 Pittsburgh Pirates and the 1984 Kansas City Royals, won division titles, despite ranking last and next-to-last, respectively, in their divisions through May 31. Toronto makes it three-for-seven.

Each team's record in one-run games is now available on at least a weekly basis in *USA Today*. Any time you're wondering what a certain team's chances are to rebound from a slow start, or to maintain an unexpected lead, just check its record in one-run games.

Cito Gaston entered a can't-lose situation. He was named an interim manager after the Blue Jays embarked upon an abortive search for a full-timer, one that resembled nothing as much as George McGovern's hunt for a running mate in 1972 after Tom Eagleton was forced to decline. Gaston replaced a disrespected outgoing manager on a team that had ample reason to play below its potential during the first six weeks. And, of course, there were those technical leading indicators of a pending turnaround.

Still, Gaston closed more ground than any other seventh- or eighth-place team in history had on its way from oblivion on May 31 to a championship, except for those Miracle Braves of 1914. He must've done something right. So let's compare the Blue Jays' performances under Williams and Gaston. We sure won't be able to answer the question of where Toronto would have finished without a change of captains, but you'll have all the necessary data to make your own judgment.

Williams encountered two crippling blows in his final season. On the first Friday of the season, Tony Fernandez suffered a broken cheek bone when struck by a pitch, and missed four weeks. And after earning saves in each of Toronto's first two victories, Tom Henke blew four consecutive save opportunities over the next month. Exactly how many games the absence of Fernandez and the failures of Henke cost Toronto last spring is impossible to determine. But considering that nine of the 24 losses under Williams were by a one-run margin, the total was surely significant. Ironically, it was the absence of Fernandez (with a fractured elbow) and Henke that may have cost Toronto a division title during that final-week collapse in 1987. (Williams, you may recall, had mysteriously reserved Henke for a late-game, lead-saving role that never materialized, while the rest of his bullpen tossed away a pennant.) Similar pairs of events, 20 months apart, cost Williams his job.

But the most glaring deficiency of the Blue Jays early last season was their inability to hold late-game leads. Before Williams was fired, Toronto lost half of the 14 games in which it led after six innings. The rest of the American League compiled an .880 winning percentage when taking a lead to the seventh inning. From the time Gaston took charge, the Blue Jays were 55–6 when leading after six. Only Oakland, Baltimore, and Chicago had better marks. The Jays also improved their record in games *tied* after six innings from 2–5 under Williams to 12–2 under Gaston.

Which leads us to an analysis of players who performed significantly better or worse for Cito than they did for Jimy. And clearly, the major element in Toronto's regained ability to hold leads was the rejuvenation of Henke:

| Manager | W | L | ERA | G | GF | Sv/Opp | IP | H | BB | SO |
|---|---|---|---|---|---|---|---|---|---|---|
| Williams | 1 | 3 | 7.84 | 12 | 11 | 2/5 | 10.1 | 13 | 9 | 8 |
| Gaston | 7 | 0 | 1.14 | 52 | 45 | 18/19 | 78.2 | 53 | 16 | 108 |

Take another look at those numbers. A long look. Do we really need to go any further? Sure George Bell ranked fourth in the A.L. with 87 RBIs while batting .309 after Gaston's arrival. And Lloyd Moseby raised his average from .168 before the change to .239 thereafter. But it was the return of the old Tom Henke, and the departure of his evil twin—a transformation that coincided with the change of managers—that was primarily responsible for the rebirth of the Jays. Henke regained his old form, it seemed, at Cito's push of a button. Did someone mention confidence? Of course, that's a concept tossed about by the baseball media all too freely. But for nearly six weeks after replacing Williams, Gaston never once allowed Henke into a game in a save situation. And freed from the pressure of holding late-game leads, Henke flourished, allowing only 10 hits and four earned runs in 20.1 innings during that time.

It's easy to take a conclusion and make the circumstances fit. But for every George Bell and Lloyd Moseby, there's a Kelly Gruber or an Ernie Whitt, who hit better under Williams than under Gaston. So we won't say that the turnaround of Henke was so immediate, so complete, and so directly proportional to that of the team itself, that it's impossible to deny that Gaston's handling played a major role. Which is not to say that you'd be wrong to conclude just that.

## WON-LOST RECORD BY STARTING POSITION

| TORONTO 89-73 | C | 1B | 2B | 3B | SS | LF | CF | RF | P | DH | Leadoff | Relief | Starts |
|---|---|---|---|---|---|---|---|---|---|---|---|---|---|
| Jim Acker | - | - | - | - | - | - | - | - | - | - | - | 11-3 | - |
| Jesse Barfield | - | - | - | - | - | - | - | 8-12 | - | - | - | - | 8-12 |
| Kevin Batiste | - | - | - | - | - | 1-0 | - | 1-0 | - | - | - | - | 2-0 |
| George Bell | - | - | - | - | - | 74-60 | - | - | - | 13-6 | - | - | 87-66 |
| Pat Borders | 27-17 | - | - | - | - | - | - | - | - | 5-9 | - | - | 32-26 |
| Bob Brenly | 3-4 | 3-0 | - | - | - | - | - | - | - | 8-9 | - | - | 14-13 |
| Dewayne Buice | - | - | - | - | - | - | - | - | - | - | - | 1-6 | - |
| Francisco Cabrera | - | - | - | - | - | - | - | - | - | 2-1 | - | - | 2-1 |
| Tony Castillo | - | - | - | - | - | - | - | - | - | - | - | 3-14 | - |
| John Cerutti | - | - | - | - | - | - | - | - | 16-15 | - | - | 0-2 | 16-15 |
| Steve Cummings | - | - | - | - | - | - | - | - | 2-0 | - | - | 1-2 | 2-0 |
| Rob Ducey | - | - | - | - | - | 2-6 | 0-2 | 4-8 | - | - | - | - | 6-16 |
| Junior Felix | - | - | - | - | - | - | 16-5 | 43-36 | - | 0-1 | 40-32 | - | 59-42 |
| Tony Fernandez | - | - | - | - | 81-59 | - | - | - | - | - | 7-6 | - | 81-59 |
| Mike Flanagan | - | - | - | - | - | - | - | - | 15-15 | - | - | - | 15-15 |
| Mauro Gozzo | - | - | - | - | - | - | - | - | 3-0 | - | - | 2-4 | 3-0 |
| Kelly Gruber | - | - | - | 63-55 | - | 1-1 | - | 9-4 | - | - | - | - | 73-60 |
| Tom Henke | - | - | - | - | - | - | - | - | - | - | - | 47-17 | - |
| Xavier Hernandez | - | - | - | - | - | - | - | - | - | - | - | 3-4 | - |
| Glenallen Hill | - | - | - | - | - | 1-0 | - | 9-3 | - | 0-2 | - | - | 10-5 |
| Alexis Infante | - | - | 0-1 | - | 0-1 | - | - | - | - | - | - | - | 0-2 |
| Jimmy Key | - | - | - | - | - | - | - | - | 15-18 | - | - | - | 15-18 |
| Tom Lawless | - | - | 2-3 | 3-2 | - | 1-1 | - | 4-0 | - | - | 0-2 | - | 10-6 |
| Manny Lee | - | - | 28-11 | 10-6 | 8-13 | - | - | - | - | 1-0 | - | - | 47-30 |
| Al Leiter | - | - | - | - | - | - | - | - | 0-1 | - | - | - | 0-1 |
| Nelson Liriano | - | - | 59-58 | - | - | - | - | - | - | 2-0 | 0-1 | - | 61-58 |
| Lee Mazzilli | - | 1-0 | - | - | - | - | - | 2-0 | - | 9-8 | - | - | 12-8 |
| Fred McGriff | - | 85-72 | - | - | - | - | - | - | - | 1-1 | - | - | 86-73 |
| Lloyd Moseby | - | - | - | - | - | - | 55-63 | - | - | 10-2 | 34-32 | - | 65-65 |
| Rance Mulliniks | - | - | - | 13-10 | - | - | - | - | - | 27-29 | - | - | 40-39 |
| Jeff Musselman | - | - | - | - | - | - | - | - | 1-2 | - | - | 0-2 | 1-2 |
| Greg Myers | 4-4 | - | - | - | - | - | - | - | - | 4-2 | - | - | 8-6 |
| Jose Nunez | - | - | - | - | - | - | - | - | 0-1 | - | - | 1-4 | 0-1 |
| John Olerud | - | 0-1 | - | - | - | - | - | - | - | - | - | - | 0-1 |
| Alex Sanchez | - | - | - | - | - | - | - | - | 2-1 | - | - | 0-1 | 2-1 |
| Dave Stieb | - | - | - | - | - | - | - | - | 21-12 | - | - | - | 21-12 |
| Todd Stottlemyre | - | - | - | - | - | - | - | - | 12-6 | - | - | 1-8 | 12-6 |
| Ozzie Virgil | - | - | - | - | - | - | - | - | - | 3-0 | - | - | 3-0 |
| Duane Ward | - | - | - | - | - | - | - | - | - | - | - | 35-31 | - |
| David Wells | - | - | - | - | - | - | - | - | - | - | - | 29-25 | - |
| Ernie Whitt | 55-48 | - | - | - | - | - | - | - | - | 4-3 | - | - | 59-51 |
| Frank Wills | - | - | - | - | - | - | - | - | 2-2 | - | - | 5-15 | 2-2 |
| Mookie Wilson | - | - | - | - | - | 9-5 | 18-3 | 9-10 | - | - | 8-0 | - | 36-18 |

## Batting vs. Left and Right Handed Pitchers

| | | BA | Rank | SA | Rank | OBA | Rank | HR % | Rank | BB % | Rank | SO % | Rank |
|---|---|---|---|---|---|---|---|---|---|---|---|---|---|
| George Bell | vs. Lefties | .287 | 54 | .517 | 11 | .323 | 94 | 5.06 | 16 | 5.73 | 119 | 11.98 | 77 |
| | vs. Righties | .301 | 22 | .434 | 43 | .333 | 67 | 2.07 | 79 | 4.66 | 153 | 7.84 | 22 |
| Pat Borders | vs. Lefties | .281 | 62 | .374 | 97 | .313 | 105 | 1.17 | 112 | 4.40 | 145 | 15.93 | 113 |
| | vs. Righties | .200 | -- | .286 | -- | .233 | -- | 1.43 | -- | 4.05 | -- | 21.62 | -- |
| Bob Brenly | vs. Lefties | .165 | 170 | .228 | 169 | .250 | 158 | 0.00 | 134 | 10.11 | 44 | 17.98 | 129 |
| | vs. Righties | .222 | -- | .556 | -- | .300 | -- | 11.11 | -- | 10.00 | -- | 10.00 | -- |
| Junior Felix | vs. Lefties | .202 | 160 | .310 | 146 | .291 | 136 | 1.55 | 92 | 10.14 | 42 | 26.35 | 164 |
| | vs. Righties | .283 | 40 | .434 | 44 | .327 | 80 | 2.45 | 66 | 5.88 | 132 | 20.26 | 137 |
| Tony Fernandez | vs. Lefties | .272 | 79 | .380 | 94 | .307 | 113 | 1.09 | 116 | 5.53 | 125 | 5.53 | 16 |
| | vs. Righties | .249 | 104 | .393 | 65 | .284 | 140 | 2.31 | 70 | 4.31 | 155 | 9.57 | 38 |
| Kelly Gruber | vs. Lefties | .325 | 17 | .500 | 17 | .356 | 50 | 4.22 | 27 | 5.08 | 136 | 8.47 | 40 |
| | vs. Righties | .274 | 60 | .425 | 45 | .315 | 97 | 2.90 | 54 | 5.17 | 148 | 11.08 | 59 |
| Tom Lawless | vs. Lefties | .250 | 112 | .250 | 163 | .302 | 121 | 0.00 | 134 | 7.41 | 89 | 14.81 | 108 |
| | vs. Righties | .182 | -- | .227 | -- | .280 | -- | 0.00 | -- | 12.00 | -- | 16.00 | -- |
| Manny Lee | vs. Lefties | .295 | 44 | .374 | 98 | .344 | 65 | 0.72 | 124 | 7.24 | 92 | 16.45 | 117 |
| | vs. Righties | .230 | 132 | .298 | 145 | .271 | 151 | 1.24 | 122 | 5.29 | 145 | 20.59 | 141 |
| Nelson Liriano | vs. Lefties | .266 | 82 | .349 | 119 | .331 | 85 | 0.00 | 134 | 9.38 | 55 | 17.19 | 124 |
| | vs. Righties | .262 | 80 | .385 | 75 | .331 | 71 | 1.62 | 98 | 8.86 | 65 | 8.29 | 26 |
| Fred McGriff | vs. Lefties | .254 | 106 | .376 | 96 | .360 | 47 | 2.65 | 60 | 13.72 | 14 | 22.12 | 155 |
| | vs. Righties | .276 | 52 | .602 | 1 | .419 | 4 | 8.56 | 1 | 19.38 | 1 | 18.06 | 126 |
| Lloyd Moseby | vs. Lefties | .196 | 163 | .268 | 159 | .297 | 129 | 1.45 | 98 | 10.56 | 39 | 21.12 | 146 |
| | vs. Righties | .231 | 131 | .379 | 83 | .310 | 104 | 2.47 | 63 | 9.49 | 57 | 16.30 | 109 |
| Rance Mulliniks | vs. Lefties | .188 | -- | .250 | -- | .316 | -- | 0.00 | -- | 15.79 | -- | 10.53 | -- |
| | vs. Righties | .241 | 118 | .331 | 124 | .321 | 91 | 1.17 | 125 | 10.69 | 42 | 13.10 | 76 |
| Ernie Whitt | vs. Lefties | .159 | -- | .227 | -- | .240 | -- | 2.27 | -- | 10.00 | -- | 22.00 | -- |
| | vs. Righties | .276 | 55 | .440 | 39 | .362 | 30 | 2.93 | 52 | 12.05 | 21 | 10.77 | 55 |
| Mookie Wilson | vs. Lefties | .346 | 7 | .397 | 79 | .346 | 60 | 0.00 | 134 | 0.00 | 170 | 11.54 | 71 |
| | vs. Righties | .275 | 56 | .356 | 104 | .295 | 122 | 1.25 | 121 | 1.78 | 170 | 16.57 | 114 |
| Team Average | vs. Lefties | .257 | 10 | .370 | 14 | .317 | 10 | 2.00 | 10 | 8.00 | 7 | 16.94 | 14 |
| | vs. Righties | .261 | 6 | .411 | 1 | .326 | 7 | 2.80 | 1 | 8.56 | 6 | 13.86 | 4 |
| League Average | vs. Lefties | .266 | | .391 | | .328 | | 2.18 | | 8.18 | | 13.58 | |
| | vs. Righties | .258 | | .380 | | .325 | | 2.26 | | 8.56 | | 14.57 | |

## Batting with Runners on Base and Bases Empty

| | | BA | Rank | SA | Rank | OBA | Rank | HR % | Rank | BB % | Rank | SO % | Rank |
|---|---|---|---|---|---|---|---|---|---|---|---|---|---|
| George Bell | Runners On | .304 | 36 | .450 | 41 | .328 | 95 | 2.50 | 60 | 4.50 | 155 | 8.36 | 37 |
| | Bases Empty | .291 | 26 | .465 | 22 | .331 | 60 | 3.30 | 46 | 5.38 | 139 | 9.63 | 36 |
| Pat Borders | Runners On | .284 | 59 | .376 | 89 | .316 | 114 | 0.92 | 126 | 5.08 | 143 | 11.86 | 81 |
| | Bases Empty | .235 | 124 | .326 | 128 | .268 | 156 | 1.52 | 102 | 3.62 | 163 | 22.46 | 156 |
| Junior Felix | Runners On | .237 | 136 | .373 | 92 | .294 | 138 | 2.96 | 50 | 6.95 | 113 | 22.46 | 153 |
| | Bases Empty | .272 | 52 | .411 | 58 | .330 | 63 | 1.63 | 96 | 7.49 | 91 | 22.10 | 152 |
| Tony Fernandez | Runners On | .248 | 119 | .370 | 95 | .280 | 156 | 2.17 | 71 | 4.69 | 153 | 8.59 | 40 |
| | Bases Empty | .262 | 74 | .402 | 67 | .299 | 114 | 1.75 | 93 | 4.71 | 148 | 8.03 | 21 |
| Kelly Gruber | Runners On | .308 | 30 | .455 | 35 | .347 | 70 | 3.13 | 43 | 5.71 | 133 | 9.80 | 59 |
| | Bases Empty | .277 | 45 | .442 | 37 | .314 | 94 | 3.43 | 45 | 4.73 | 147 | 10.65 | 47 |
| Manny Lee | Runners On | .267 | 89 | .356 | 115 | .324 | 102 | 1.48 | 101 | 8.05 | 93 | 18.12 | 138 |
| | Bases Empty | .255 | 89 | .315 | 137 | .289 | 129 | 0.61 | 143 | 4.62 | 149 | 19.08 | 129 |
| Nelson Liriano | Runners On | .280 | 70 | .373 | 91 | .339 | 77 | 1.04 | 119 | 8.77 | 78 | 11.84 | 80 |
| | Bases Empty | .249 | 102 | .378 | 87 | .324 | 70 | 1.33 | 110 | 9.20 | 42 | 9.60 | 35 |
| Fred McGriff | Runners On | .257 | 105 | .494 | 17 | .420 | 5 | 6.22 | 7 | 21.70 | 3 | 18.87 | 143 |
| | Bases Empty | .277 | 44 | .548 | 3 | .381 | 10 | 6.77 | 4 | 13.81 | 10 | 19.89 | 133 |
| Lloyd Moseby | Runners On | .242 | 128 | .359 | 111 | .338 | 79 | 2.53 | 59 | 10.64 | 48 | 16.17 | 123 |
| | Bases Empty | .207 | 155 | .342 | 113 | .285 | 136 | 1.97 | 89 | 9.20 | 43 | 18.69 | 123 |
| Rance Mulliniks | Runners On | .219 | 159 | .313 | 150 | .320 | 108 | 1.56 | 97 | 13.33 | 22 | 11.33 | 70 |
| | Bases Empty | .255 | 87 | .338 | 117 | .321 | 77 | 0.69 | 137 | 8.81 | 55 | 14.47 | 89 |
| Ernie Whitt | Runners On | .256 | 109 | .458 | 34 | .352 | 62 | 4.17 | 25 | 13.20 | 23 | 11.17 | 68 |
| | Bases Empty | .267 | 58 | .382 | 82 | .346 | 43 | 1.84 | 91 | 10.70 | 26 | 12.76 | 67 |
| Mookie Wilson | Runners On | .247 | 122 | .292 | 159 | .244 | 170 | 0.00 | 146 | 0.00 | 172 | 13.98 | 96 |
| | Bases Empty | .329 | 5 | .416 | 55 | .351 | 38 | 1.34 | 109 | 1.95 | 167 | 15.58 | 99 |
| Team Average | Runners On | .260 | 12 | .394 | 6 | .331 | 9 | 2.67 | 1 | 9.51 | 5 | 14.30 | 11 |
| | Bases Empty | .259 | 6 | .401 | 2 | .318 | 7 | 2.45 | 3 | 7.48 | 9 | 15.28 | 10 |
| League Average | Runners On | .268 | | .389 | | .336 | | 2.15 | | 9.17 | | 13.53 | |
| | Bases Empty | .255 | | .380 | | .317 | | 2.29 | | 7.84 | | 14.86 | |

## Overall Batting Compared to Late Inning Pressure Situations

| | | BA | Rank | SA | Rank | OBA | Rank | HR % | Rank | BB % | Rank | SO % | Rank | RDI % | Rank |
|---|---|---|---|---|---|---|---|---|---|---|---|---|---|---|---|
| George Bell | Overall | .297 | 25 | .458 | 23 | .330 | 70 | 2.94 | 56 | 4.97 | 153 | 9.04 | 35 | .373 | 8 |
| | Pressure | .349 | 7 | .593 | 7 | .383 | 31 | 4.65 | 25 | 4.26 | 148 | 9.57 | 29 | .419 | 14 |
| Pat Borders | Overall | .257 | 90 | .349 | 121 | .290 | 147 | 1.24 | 122 | 4.30 | 162 | 17.58 | 124 | .329 | 25 |
| | Pressure | .279 | 56 | .372 | 80 | .295 | 116 | 2.33 | 70 | 2.27 | 163 | 20.45 | 122 | .455 | 11 |
| Junior Felix | Overall | .258 | 88 | .395 | 73 | .315 | 102 | 2.17 | 79 | 7.27 | 101 | 22.25 | 153 | .256 | 99 |
| | Pressure | .148 | 163 | .230 | 155 | .197 | 167 | 1.64 | 88 | 6.06 | 124 | 39.39 | 169 | .125 | 143 |
| Tony Fernandez | Overall | .257 | 97 | .389 | 77 | .291 | 146 | 1.92 | 87 | 4.70 | 156 | 8.27 | 26 | .284 | 61 |
| | Pressure | .269 | 67 | .372 | 81 | .326 | 80 | 1.28 | 102 | 8.14 | 91 | 5.81 | 9 | .286 | 68 |
| Kelly Gruber | Overall | .290 | 30 | .448 | 31 | .328 | 75 | 3.30 | 39 | 5.15 | 149 | 10.29 | 51 | .272 | 73 |
| | Pressure | .329 | 18 | .471 | 28 | .392 | 24 | 2.86 | 58 | 7.59 | 106 | 10.13 | 31 | .304 | 61 |
| Manny Lee | Overall | .260 | 84 | .333 | 133 | .305 | 118 | 1.00 | 130 | 6.21 | 128 | 18.63 | 134 | .295 | 49 |
| | Pressure | .204 | 133 | .224 | 156 | .291 | 120 | 0.00 | 107 | 10.91 | 50 | 20.00 | 120 | .375 | 25 |
| Nelson Liriano | Overall | .263 | 78 | .376 | 92 | .331 | 68 | 1.20 | 123 | 9.00 | 59 | 10.67 | 56 | .299 | 43 |
| | Pressure | .286 | 52 | .455 | 33 | .345 | 55 | 1.30 | 100 | 8.79 | 83 | 9.89 | 30 | .417 | 15 |
| Fred McGriff | Overall | .269 | 63 | .525 | 3 | .399 | 4 | 6.53 | 4 | 17.50 | 2 | 19.41 | 138 | .282 | 64 |
| | Pressure | .294 | 44 | .494 | 21 | .406 | 17 | 4.71 | 24 | 14.71 | 16 | 21.57 | 128 | .318 | 54 |
| Lloyd Moseby | Overall | .221 | 159 | .349 | 120 | .306 | 115 | 2.19 | 76 | 9.79 | 45 | 17.66 | 127 | .211 | 151 |
| | Pressure | .267 | 69 | .440 | 40 | .353 | 51 | 1.33 | 99 | 10.34 | 58 | 16.09 | 86 | .222 | 105 |
| Rance Mulliniks | Overall | .238 | 133 | .326 | 142 | .320 | 90 | 1.10 | 128 | 11.00 | 29 | 12.94 | 77 | .230 | 131 |
| | Pressure | .205 | 131 | .231 | 154 | .340 | 63 | 0.00 | 107 | 17.02 | 7 | 10.64 | 36 | .077 | 158 |
| Ernie Whitt | Overall | .262 | 80 | .416 | 55 | .349 | 43 | 2.86 | 58 | 11.82 | 19 | 12.05 | 69 | .265 | 82 |
| | Pressure | .182 | 150 | .309 | 114 | .262 | 140 | 3.64 | 43 | 9.84 | 68 | 21.31 | 125 | .357 | 34 |
| Mookie Wilson | Overall | .298 | 24 | .370 | 100 | .311 | 106 | 0.84 | 136 | 1.21 | 171 | 14.98 | 96 | .209 | 152 |
| | Pressure | .229 | 109 | .257 | 142 | .250 | 143 | 0.00 | 107 | 2.70 | 157 | 13.51 | 56 | .071 | 160 |
| Team Average | Overall | .260 | 8 | .398 | 3 | .323 | 9 | 2.54 | 2 | 8.38 | 6 | 14.85 | 10 | .271 | 7 |
| | Pressure | .260 | 5 | .383 | 4 | .333 | 4 | 2.03 | 6 | 9.36 | 7 | 17.14 | 5 | .283 | 3 |
| League Average | Overall | .261 | | .384 | | .326 | | 2.23 | | 8.44 | | 14.26 | | .269 | |
| | Pressure | .247 | | .357 | | .318 | | 2.02 | | 9.02 | | 17.90 | | .254 | |

## Additional Miscellaneous Batting Comparisons

| | Grass Surface BA | Rank | Artificial Surface BA | Rank | Home Games BA | Rank | Road Games BA | Rank | Runners in Scoring Position BA | Rank | Runners in Scoring Pos and Two Outs BA | Rank | Leading Off Inning OBA | Rank | Runners on 3B with less than 2 Outs RDI % | Rank |
|---|---|---|---|---|---|---|---|---|---|---|---|---|---|---|---|---|
| George Bell | .300 | 19 | .295 | 37 | .306 | 25 | .289 | 34 | .343 | 9 | .366 | 5 | .288 | 123 | .674 | 38 |
| Pat Borders | .291 | -- | .232 | 121 | .248 | 107 | .265 | 76 | .288 | 50 | .192 | 126 | .391 | 15 | .688 | 26 |
| Bob Brenly | .143 | -- | .189 | 153 | .178 | -- | .163 | -- | .154 | -- | .091 | -- | .333 | -- | .200 | -- |
| Rob Ducey | .091 | -- | .259 | 77 | .233 | -- | .182 | -- | .316 | -- | .429 | -- | .300 | -- | .400 | -- |
| Junior Felix | .282 | 42 | .239 | 111 | .251 | 96 | .264 | 77 | .243 | 108 | .140 | 156 | .377 | 24 | .565 | 90 |
| Tony Fernandez | .287 | 35 | .235 | 117 | .239 | 121 | .273 | 61 | .252 | 100 | .138 | 157 | .324 | 81 | .900 | 2 |
| Kelly Gruber | .291 | 31 | .289 | 45 | .295 | 36 | .285 | 43 | .279 | 67 | .283 | 35 | .317 | 96 | .561 | 94 |
| Tom Lawless | .192 | -- | .250 | 90 | .281 | -- | .184 | -- | .143 | -- | .167 | -- | .421 | -- | .333 | -- |
| Manny Lee | .314 | 7 | .213 | 137 | .238 | 122 | .276 | 55 | .284 | 62 | .273 | 46 | .280 | 134 | .750 | 13 |
| Nelson Liriano | .284 | 39 | .248 | 100 | .250 | 99 | .276 | 54 | .306 | 32 | .321 | 15 | .323 | 85 | .500 | 119 |
| Lee Mazzilli | .368 | -- | .170 | 161 | .195 | -- | .280 | -- | .214 | -- | .143 | -- | .250 | -- | .600 | -- |
| Fred McGriff | .230 | 138 | .293 | 38 | .282 | 49 | .255 | 88 | .256 | 96 | .197 | 123 | .403 | 12 | .567 | 88 |
| Lloyd Moseby | .259 | 85 | .192 | 148 | .180 | 169 | .254 | 90 | .237 | 118 | .263 | 60 | .284 | 128 | .333 | 163 |
| Rance Mulliniks | .274 | 55 | .208 | 139 | .231 | 135 | .244 | 117 | .195 | 157 | .200 | 118 | .349 | 48 | .619 | 57 |
| Ernie Whitt | .283 | 40 | .248 | 101 | .234 | 131 | .289 | 36 | .250 | 102 | .167 | 144 | .354 | 42 | .571 | 85 |
| Mookie Wilson | .378 | -- | .250 | 90 | .252 | 94 | .351 | 4 | .246 | 105 | .222 | 98 | .435 | 5 | .462 | 138 |
| Team Average | .278 | 2 | .247 | 12 | .250 | 12 | .269 | 2 | .261 | 8 | .228 | 11 | .335 | 2 | .583 | 5 |
| League Average | .260 | | .262 | | .262 | | .259 | | .262 | | .232 | | .321 | | .566 | |

## Pitching vs. Left and Right Handed Batters

| | | BA | Rank | SA | Rank | OBA | Rank | HR % | Rank | BB % | Rank | SO % | Rank |
|---|---|---|---|---|---|---|---|---|---|---|---|---|---|
| John Cerutti | vs. Lefties | .222 | 27 | .341 | 43 | .290 | 28 | 2.38 | 79 | 7.86 | 55 | 10.71 | 81 |
| | vs. Righties | .282 | 112 | .414 | 99 | .328 | 83 | 2.43 | 84 | 5.87 | 30 | 7.54 | 129 |
| Mike Flanagan | vs. Lefties | .208 | 16 | .237 | 9 | .279 | 18 | 0.00 | 1 | 8.11 | 58 | 9.91 | 91 |
| | vs. Righties | .296 | 124 | .435 | 116 | .341 | 109 | 1.78 | 54 | 6.18 | 38 | 5.85 | 132 |
| Tom Henke | vs. Lefties | .195 | 13 | .315 | 28 | .272 | 17 | 2.01 | 71 | 9.30 | 78 | 26.74 | 6 |
| | vs. Righties | .214 | 15 | .312 | 18 | .257 | 5 | 1.16 | 23 | 4.89 | 15 | 38.04 | 1 |
| Jimmy Key | vs. Lefties | .227 | 33 | .327 | 37 | .245 | 6 | 1.33 | 43 | 2.55 | 2 | 19.11 | 18 |
| | vs. Righties | .279 | 106 | .435 | 115 | .302 | 39 | 2.33 | 78 | 3.16 | 3 | 12.07 | 94 |
| Dave Stieb | vs. Lefties | .248 | 50 | .346 | 44 | .319 | 57 | 1.81 | 68 | 8.72 | 66 | 10.55 | 83 |
| | vs. Righties | .188 | 5 | .283 | 8 | .283 | 22 | 1.39 | 29 | 9.18 | 95 | 13.29 | 85 |
| Todd Stottlemyre | vs. Lefties | .314 | 119 | .480 | 120 | .362 | 100 | 3.14 | 104 | 6.83 | 38 | 7.23 | 117 |
| | vs. Righties | .255 | 63 | .376 | 68 | .328 | 82 | 1.52 | 38 | 9.12 | 93 | 15.20 | 64 |
| Duane Ward | vs. Lefties | .262 | 69 | .360 | 49 | .383 | 114 | 1.16 | 36 | 16.06 | 127 | 21.10 | 13 |
| | vs. Righties | .208 | 11 | .263 | 5 | .280 | 17 | 0.85 | 10 | 8.33 | 82 | 27.54 | 7 |
| David Wells | vs. Lefties | .231 | -- | .346 | -- | .294 | -- | 1.28 | -- | 8.14 | -- | 13.95 | -- |
| | vs. Righties | .199 | 9 | .282 | 7 | .261 | 7 | 1.66 | 45 | 7.89 | 71 | 24.81 | 14 |
| Frank Wills | vs. Lefties | .266 | 78 | .372 | 61 | .389 | 118 | 1.06 | 31 | 16.67 | 129 | 3.51 | 135 |
| | vs. Righties | .229 | 25 | .343 | 39 | .277 | 15 | 1.71 | 49 | 5.85 | 29 | 19.68 | 30 |
| Team Average | vs. Lefties | .260 | 7 | .371 | 7 | .337 | 9 | 1.69 | 3 | 10.10 | 12 | 12.73 | 6 |
| | vs. Righties | .253 | 5 | .374 | 5 | .307 | 1 | 1.84 | 2 | 6.66 | 1 | 14.28 | 10 |
| League Average | vs. Lefties | .261 | | .382 | | .330 | | 2.16 | | 9.16 | | 13.03 | |
| | vs. Righties | .261 | | .385 | | .323 | | 2.28 | | 7.96 | | 15.09 | |

## Pitching with Runners on Base and Bases Empty

| | | BA | Rank | SA | Rank | OBA | Rank | HR % | Rank | BB % | Rank | SO % | Rank |
|---|---|---|---|---|---|---|---|---|---|---|---|---|---|
| John Cerutti | Runners On | .263 | 69 | .398 | 91 | .319 | 49 | 2.08 | 80 | 6.73 | 27 | 6.12 | 132 |
| | Bases Empty | .278 | 108 | .405 | 88 | .323 | 74 | 2.62 | 83 | 5.86 | 40 | 9.26 | 116 |
| Mike Flanagan | Runners On | .296 | 115 | .396 | 86 | .326 | 58 | 1.07 | 19 | 4.49 | 6 | 7.05 | 127 |
| | Bases Empty | .272 | 92 | .413 | 96 | .336 | 96 | 1.85 | 53 | 7.97 | 77 | 6.04 | 133 |
| Tom Henke | Runners On | .191 | 7 | .348 | 37 | .282 | 13 | 2.84 | 108 | 10.78 | 98 | 28.74 | 3 |
| | Bases Empty | .215 | 16 | .287 | 10 | .249 | 5 | 0.55 | 3 | 3.70 | 7 | 35.98 | 2 |
| Jimmy Key | Runners On | .284 | 101 | .432 | 110 | .308 | 33 | 2.26 | 89 | 4.08 | 4 | 10.79 | 90 |
| | Bases Empty | .261 | 73 | .405 | 89 | .282 | 27 | 2.08 | 61 | 2.39 | 3 | 14.92 | 56 |
| Dave Stieb | Runners On | .260 | 64 | .354 | 45 | .317 | 46 | 1.29 | 32 | 6.27 | 19 | 9.40 | 109 |
| | Bases Empty | .190 | 6 | .288 | 11 | .291 | 34 | 1.83 | 51 | 10.82 | 113 | 13.63 | 68 |
| Todd Stottlemyre | Runners On | .228 | 23 | .329 | 23 | .282 | 12 | 1.83 | 68 | 6.45 | 23 | 12.10 | 75 |
| | Bases Empty | .326 | 133 | .502 | 132 | .394 | 135 | 2.62 | 84 | 9.43 | 97 | 11.11 | 100 |
| Duane Ward | Runners On | .229 | 24 | .290 | 9 | .331 | 67 | 1.40 | 39 | 12.36 | 114 | 20.36 | 14 |
| | Bases Empty | .232 | 38 | .320 | 24 | .320 | 67 | 0.52 | 2 | 10.96 | 116 | 30.14 | 4 |
| David Wells | Runners On | .196 | 9 | .275 | 7 | .266 | 8 | 0.72 | 12 | 8.92 | 66 | 18.47 | 24 |
| | Bases Empty | .215 | 16 | .315 | 23 | .272 | 17 | 2.21 | 69 | 7.18 | 64 | 25.13 | 9 |
| Frank Wills | Runners On | .244 | 37 | .354 | 48 | .349 | 92 | 1.57 | 52 | 14.00 | 123 | 12.67 | 72 |
| | Bases Empty | .239 | 46 | .352 | 44 | .289 | 32 | 1.41 | 26 | 5.92 | 41 | 14.47 | 61 |
| Team Average | Runners On | .259 | 3 | .370 | 3 | .320 | 3 | 1.64 | 3 | 7.90 | 1 | 12.14 | 13 |
| | Bases Empty | .252 | 7 | .375 | 9 | .314 | 8 | 1.91 | 2 | 7.65 | 8 | 15.09 | 6 |
| League Average | Runners On | .268 | | .389 | | .336 | | 2.15 | | 9.17 | | 13.53 | |
| | Bases Empty | .255 | | .380 | | .317 | | 2.29 | | 7.84 | | 14.86 | |

## Overall Pitching Compared to Late Inning Pressure Situations

| | | BA | Rank | SA | Rank | OBA | Rank | HR % | Rank | BB % | Rank | SO % | Rank |
|---|---|---|---|---|---|---|---|---|---|---|---|---|---|
| Jim Acker | Overall | .235 | -- | .343 | -- | .322 | -- | 0.98 | -- | 10.34 | -- | 20.69 | -- |
| | Pressure | .197 | 20 | .279 | 27 | .300 | 51 | 0.00 | 1 | 12.68 | 105 | 19.72 | 34 |
| John Cerutti | Overall | .273 | 91 | .403 | 88 | .322 | 61 | 2.42 | 84 | 6.19 | 27 | 8.06 | 125 |
| | Pressure | .295 | 110 | .386 | 89 | .361 | 97 | 2.27 | 82 | 9.18 | 60 | 13.27 | 74 |
| Mike Flanagan | Overall | .283 | 107 | .406 | 90 | .331 | 78 | 1.52 | 31 | 6.47 | 34 | 6.47 | 133 |
| | Pressure | .200 | 25 | .222 | 11 | .280 | 27 | 0.00 | 1 | 9.80 | 74 | 15.69 | 59 |
| Tom Henke | Overall | .205 | 8 | .314 | 17 | .264 | 5 | 1.55 | 34 | 7.02 | 46 | 32.58 | 2 |
| | Pressure | .196 | 19 | .315 | 47 | .254 | 13 | 2.17 | 79 | 6.86 | 42 | 36.76 | 1 |
| Jimmy Key | Overall | .270 | 86 | .415 | 95 | .292 | 22 | 2.15 | 67 | 3.05 | 1 | 13.32 | 69 |
| | Pressure | .232 | 53 | .293 | 37 | .235 | 6 | 1.22 | 47 | 1.16 | 2 | 6.98 | 122 |
| Dave Stieb | Overall | .219 | 17 | .316 | 18 | .301 | 29 | 1.60 | 39 | 8.94 | 85 | 11.88 | 85 |
| | Pressure | .167 | 5 | .194 | 4 | .268 | 22 | 0.00 | 1 | 9.52 | 70 | 14.29 | 68 |
| Todd Stottlemyre | Overall | .282 | 105 | .424 | 100 | .343 | 101 | 2.26 | 75 | 8.07 | 67 | 11.56 | 90 |
| | Pressure | .321 | 116 | .415 | 102 | .410 | 117 | 0.00 | 1 | 12.90 | 108 | 8.06 | 117 |
| Duane Ward | Overall | .230 | 23 | .304 | 12 | .326 | 69 | 0.98 | 9 | 11.74 | 118 | 24.70 | 8 |
| | Pressure | .237 | 59 | .329 | 56 | .342 | 80 | 1.61 | 55 | 12.50 | 102 | 23.72 | 18 |
| David Wells | Overall | .207 | 10 | .298 | 9 | .269 | 7 | 1.57 | 35 | 7.95 | 66 | 22.16 | 12 |
| | Pressure | .244 | 63 | .354 | 74 | .315 | 63 | 2.44 | 87 | 9.63 | 72 | 20.86 | 28 |
| Frank Wills | Overall | .242 | 34 | .353 | 44 | .319 | 57 | 1.49 | 29 | 9.93 | 106 | 13.58 | 64 |
| | Pressure | .231 | 52 | .282 | 30 | .302 | 54 | 0.00 | 1 | 6.98 | 43 | 18.60 | 40 |
| Team Average | Overall | .255 | 4 | .373 | 6 | .317 | 5 | 1.80 | 2 | 7.76 | 5 | 13.78 | 7 |
| | Pressure | .238 | 4 | .331 | 4 | .313 | 5 | 1.60 | 2 | 9.30 | 8 | 20.88 | 1 |
| League Average | Overall | .261 | | .384 | | .326 | | 2.23 | | 8.44 | | 14.26 | |
| | Pressure | .250 | | .362 | | .325 | | 2.14 | | 9.50 | | 16.61 | |

## Additional Miscellaneous Pitching Comparisons

| | Grass Surface | | Artificial Surface | | Home Games | | Road Games | | Runners in Scoring Position | | Runners in Scoring Pos and Two Outs | | Leading Off Inning | |
|---|---|---|---|---|---|---|---|---|---|---|---|---|---|---|
| | BA | Rank | BA | Rank | BA | Rank | BA | Rank | BA | Rank | BA | Rank | OBA | Rank |
| Jim Acker | .333 | -- | .175 | 3 | .169 | -- | .326 | -- | .222 | -- | .286 | -- | .259 | -- |
| John Cerutti | .257 | 63 | .282 | 85 | .270 | 92 | .276 | 85 | .262 | 82 | .214 | 56 | .266 | 23 |
| Mike Flanagan | .303 | 124 | .274 | 75 | .277 | 100 | .288 | 101 | .341 | 130 | .373 | 133 | .352 | 103 |
| Mauro Gozzo | .306 | -- | .278 | 80 | .278 | -- | .306 | -- | .265 | -- | .182 | -- | .400 | -- |
| Tom Henke | .200 | 9 | .210 | 14 | .200 | 8 | .208 | 10 | .235 | 42 | .143 | 16 | .256 | 14 |
| Xavier Hernandez | .293 | -- | .265 | 66 | .265 | -- | .293 | -- | .194 | -- | .077 | -- | .364 | -- |
| Jimmy Key | .265 | 75 | .272 | 74 | .268 | 88 | .272 | 83 | .280 | 100 | .289 | 111 | .295 | 40 |
| Al Leiter | .237 | -- | .275 | 77 | .247 | -- | .261 | -- | .286 | -- | .235 | -- | .405 | -- |
| Dave Stieb | .205 | 11 | .230 | 28 | .212 | 13 | .225 | 27 | .271 | 87 | .216 | 61 | .298 | 41 |
| Todd Stottlemyre | .265 | -- | .287 | 91 | .282 | 104 | .282 | 93 | .185 | 8 | .158 | 25 | .392 | 126 |
| Duane Ward | .208 | 13 | .246 | 44 | .241 | 48 | .221 | 21 | .237 | 48 | .155 | 23 | .370 | 113 |
| David Wells | .198 | -- | .212 | 15 | .212 | 14 | .200 | 7 | .200 | 14 | .186 | 40 | .256 | 13 |
| Frank Wills | 277 | -- | 217 | 19 | .213 | 15 | .271 | 81 | .241 | 54 | .242 | 81 | .333 | 79 |
| Team Average | .252 | 3 | .258 | 7 | .249 | 5 | .262 | 7 | .264 | 7 | .223 | 3 | .321 | 7 |
| League Average | .260 | | .262 | | .259 | | .262 | | .262 | | .232 | | .321 | |

# National League

# ATLANTA BRAVES

- **Well armed for the future.**
- **The fat lady sings for Dale Murphy.**

Over the past 30 years, only two kinds of teams have routinely chained together long streaks of sub-.450 seasons. We call one group expansion teams. We call the other the Atlanta Braves. A truly depressed baseball team is one that, over a period of years, fails to reach a level of competence that would label it as simply mediocre, even for a single season. That's pardonable for, maybe even expected of, expansion teams. But look up *depressed* in Roget's special baseball edition and you'll find "See *Noc-A-Homa, Chief.*"

At any given time during the first six decades of this century, there was likely to be at least one team in such a hopeless condition. In fact, from 1924 through 1959, there were only two seasons in which some team didn't wear the scarlet letter *L,* signifying a streak of at least five consecutive losing seasons below the .450 mark. But since the original Washington Senators compiled a six-year streak from 1954 through 1959, only nine teams have posted streaks of five or more seasons below .450.

Six of those recent streaks coincided with the births of new franchises. Actually, only four of baseball's 10 expansion teams managed to play above .450 in any of their first five seasons (Los Angeles Angels, Kansas City Royals, Milwaukee Brewers, and Montreal Expos). But during that same time, only two established teams stooped to the level of those newborns with five-year streaks of their own: the Mets and the Braves. *And the Braves have done it twice in the past 15 years.* The longest streaks of sub-.450 seasons, before and after expansion (asterisks mark expansion teams):

**Longest Pre-Expansion Streaks**

| From To | Team | Years |
|---|---|---|
| 1933–1948 | Phillies | 16 |
| 1922–1933 | Red Sox | 12 |
| 1918–1928 | Phillies | 11 |
| 1930–1940 | Browns | 11 |
| 1946–1956 | Orioles | 11 |
| 1902–1911 | Senators | 10 |
| 1903–1912 | Braves | 10 |
| 1904–1913 | Dodgers | 10 |
| 1935–1943 | Athletics | 9 |
| 1950–1957 | Pirates | 8 |

**Longest Post-Expansion Streaks**

| From To | Team | Years |
|---|---|---|
| *1962–1968 | Astros | 7 |
| *1969–1975 | Padres | 7 |
| 1977–1983 | Mets | 7 |
| *1961–1966 | Senators | 6 |
| *1962–1967 | Mets | 6 |
| 1975–1979 | Braves | 5 |
| *1977–1981 | Mariners | 5 |
| *1977–1981 | Blue Jays | 5 |
| 1985–1989 | Braves | 5 |

The off-season acquisitions of two veterans, catcher Ernie Whitt and pitcher Charlie Leibrandt, are typical of those made by contenders looking for the final pieces to their puzzle. Atlanta's string of poor seasons suggests that the Braves have only a few pieces in place. So it would be as easy as it is wrong to conclude that the Braves don't have a clue about turning their team around. There's reason to believe that things could change quickly.

Bobby Cox was one of baseball's most accomplished managers when he left the Toronto Blue Jays four years ago to become general manager of the Braves. In fact, we ranked him among the 10 best managers in baseball history in the 1988 *Analyst* (pp. 74–76). His work as a general manager has been equally impressive. Cox has overseen the development of one of baseball's most extensive and expensive minor league operations, one that's now bearing fruit. Through a combination of trades and the amateur draft, Atlanta has built one of the youngest starting rotations in major league history, one that rebuts any underestimation of the Braves' player-development system.

The first-round selection of can't-miss Derek Lilliquist in 1987 was a no-brainer. But two other high-round selections, Marty Clary (1983) and Tom Glavine (1984), required and received patient nurturing on their long routes to Atlanta. Pete Smith was a former number-one pick who accompanied Ozzie Virgil from Philadelphia for Steve Bedrosian and Milt Thompson four years ago. John Smoltz, on the other hand, was a 22d-round pick with a career minor-league record of 11–18 when Atlanta nicked the Tigers for his services in 1987. Those pitchers comprised the ninth-youngest starting rotation in modern major league history. The following table lists the youngest staffs since 1900, based on games started:

| Year | Team | Age |
|---|---|---|
| 1967 | Kansas City Athletics | 23.0 |
| 1915 | Philadelphia Athletics | 23.1 |
| 1914 | Washington Senators | 23.3 |
| 1971 | Cincinnati Reds | 23.7 |
| 1966 | Baltimore Orioles | 23.8 |
| 1980 | Chicago White Sox | 23.8 |
| 1960 | Chicago Cubs | 24.0 |
| 1909 | St. Louis Cardinals | 24.1 |
| 1989 | Atlanta Braves | 24.2 |
| 1977 | Milwaukee Brewers | 24.4 |

The wide-ranging fortunes of the teams listed above illustrate that even a rotation of promising 23-year-olds can't guarantee success. Among the 10 teams, the 1914 Washington Senators' rotation, which included a 26–year-old Walter Johnson, proved to have the brightest future. Still, their average starter won less than 100 games after that season (93 to be exact). The 1966 Orioles weren't far behind (88 future wins per starter), but while two of their starters became superstars (first ballot Hall of Famer Jim Palmer, 20, and Dave McNally, 23), two others, Steve Barber and Wally Bunker, had their careers curtailed by injuries.

Lew Krausse, 24, was the oldest member of the 1967 Kansas City rotation, which included Catfish Hunter, Jim Nash (coming off a 12–1 rookie season), Chuck Dobson, and Blue Moon Odom. Dobson and Odom had moderately successful careers. But at the time, few would have expected only Hunter to reach the 100–win mark.

The 1960 Cubs rotation—Glen Hobbie, Bob Anderson, Don Cardwell, and Dick Ellsworth—was an utter disappointment. Ellsworth had one outstanding season (22–10 in 1963) in a mediocre career (115–137). Cardwell, remembered for his work with the 1969 Mets, had only two winning seasons in his 14–year career. Hobbie and Anderson were busts.

Remember the White Sox' promising staff of 1980? You know, um. . . Well, that's our point. LaMarr Hoyt, Britt Burns, and Richard Dotson helped deliver one division title to Chicago's South Side amidst a decade of frustration better symbolized by their rotation-mates, Ross Baumgarten and Steve Trout.

It's apparent that the success rate, even for promising young pitchers, is rather low. The best safeguard, then, against a young staff that might never fulfill its potential would be a matching set of five more prospects to back it up. Dream on, right? Well, actually, Atlanta's stream of promising young starters hasn't nearly run dry. There's another rotation's worth of potential major leaguers in the higher levels of its minor league system. They include two blue-chip prospects, former number-one picks Kent Mercker and Steve Avery. The others are Dennis Burlingame, Ben Rivera, and any one of a number of dark-horse candidates, including Mark Beck, Roger Hailey, and Don Lemon.

Additionally, the Braves have already begun to trade some of their excess for. . . that's right—even more prospects. Zane Smith was shipped to Montreal last July for three minor leaguers. But the acquisitions of Leibrandt as a veteran anchor for the staff and of Whitt to handle it suggest that Atlanta's return to respectability could be closer than most of those outside the organization think. As they say in the *Daily Racing Form,* this is one team it will "pay to follow".

One thing's for sure, though. You can't win a game without scoring a run. And that seemingly simple task has proven increasingly difficult for the Braves. Perhaps playing in one of baseball's best hitter's parks has created the illusion that Atlanta has an adequate attack. Maybe Dale Murphy's reputation lends the Braves' shallow lineup undeserved respect. But whatever the reason, it's a fact the Atlanta has had baseball's worst offense over the last two seasons, and it may get worse before it improves. The Braves will probably have to sacrifice some of its young wings for muscle.

Over the past two seasons, Atlanta has scored an average of 3.55 runs per game, the lowest mark in either league, but not far behind the Dodgers (3.67). Eliminating each team's home games, to discount the inflationary effect of Atlanta Stadium, more than doubles the gap between Atlanta (3.28) and the nearest team, Philadelphia (3.55).

To complicate matters, it's our unhappy duty to report that Dale Murphy's days as a star—be it super-, All-, or otherwise—are over. The fat lady has sung. Stick a fork in him. Like Nora, John, and T.R., he's done. Another good year or two? All right, that's a possibility—albeit an optimistic one, based on the table below. The players included had statistical patterns most like Murphy's at a comparable age, based on career totals at the time ("Past") and their most recent seasons ("Present"). They didn't have much left ("Future"). Listed in order of similarity:

| | | | Past | | | Present | | | Future | | |
|---|---|---|---|---|---|---|---|---|---|---|---|
| **Year** | **Player** | **Age** | **HR** | **RBI** | **BA** | **HR** | **RBI** | **BA** | **HR** | **RBI** | **BA** |
| 1987 | Gary Carter | 33 | 291 | 1082 | .269 | 20 | 83 | .285 | 13 | 61 | .227 |
| 1980 | Johnny Bench | 32 | 356 | 1259 | .267 | 24 | 68 | .250 | 33 | 117 | .267 |
| 1978 | Lee May | 35 | 325 | 1124 | .268 | 25 | 80 | .246 | 29 | 120 | .260 |
| 1971 | Ron Santo | 31 | 300 | 1139 | .279 | 21 | 88 | .267 | 42 | 192 | .266 |
| 1978 | George Scott | 34 | 265 | 1002 | .269 | 12 | 54 | .233 | 6 | 49 | .254 |
| | Averages | 33 | 307 | 1121 | .270 | 20 | 75 | .247 | 25 | 108 | .258 |
| 1989 | Dale Murphy | 33 | 354 | 1088 | .270 | 20 | 84 | .228 | | | |

Unless that pitching staff is ready for prime time *this year*, Murphy should be viewed not as the cornerstone of Atlanta's offense of the early '90s, but rather as a vehicle to procure some young player of promise.

Atlanta's sports fans are the country's most tortured. Among the 13 cities with teams in each of the three major American team sports (we promise to consider hockey's application for reinstatement in the near future), Atlanta is one of two never to win a league championship. At least Houston has reached the NBA's final round—Atlanta hasn't even advanced that far. But things could be changing. The Hawks are now perennial NBA contenders. Even the Falcons have reason for optimism, based on (*a*) a new coach, who actually understands the concept of the blitz, and (*b*) a shot at a franchise-building number-one draft pick who could make that defense *bad* (i.e., good). And the Braves, should they find a way to score some runs, could be among baseball's winners by mid-decade. So the drought in Atlanta may end by the coming millennium. (If not, then by the next one, f'sure.)

## WON-LOST RECORD BY STARTING POSITION

| ATLANTA 63-97 | C | 1B | 2B | 3B | SS | LF | CF | RF | P | Leadoff | Relief | Starts |
|---|---|---|---|---|---|---|---|---|---|---|---|---|
| Jim Acker | - | - | - | - | - | - | - | - | - | - | 15-43 | - |
| Jay Aldrich | - | - | - | - | - | - | - | - | - | - | 2-6 | - |
| Jose Alvarez | - | - | - | - | - | - | - | - | - | - | 7-23 | - |
| Paul Assenmacher | - | - | - | - | - | - | - | - | - | - | 13-35 | - |
| Bruce Benedict | 22-34 | - | - | - | - | - | - | - | - | - | - | 22-34 |
| Geronimo Berroa | - | - | - | - | - | 0-1 | - | 10-14 | - | - | - | 10-15 |
| Jeff Blauser | - | - | 11-14 | 23-42 | 11-11 | - | - | - | - | 1-6 | - | 45-67 |
| Terry Blocker | - | - | - | - | - | - | 0-1 | - | - | - | 0-1 | 0-1 |
| Joe Boever | - | - | - | - | - | - | - | - | - | - | 33-33 | - |
| Francisco Cabrera | 0-1 | 1-1 | - | - | - | - | - | - | - | - | - | 1-2 |
| Tony Castillo | - | - | - | - | - | - | - | - | - | - | 3-9 | - |
| Marty Clary | - | - | - | - | - | - | - | - | 6-11 | - | 0-1 | 6-11 |
| Jody Davis | 24-36 | 0-1 | - | - | - | - | - | - | - | - | - | 24-37 |
| Drew Denson | - | 3-6 | - | - | - | - | - | - | - | - | - | 3-6 |
| Gary Eave | - | - | - | - | - | - | - | - | 2-1 | - | - | 2-1 |
| Mark Eichhorn | - | - | - | - | - | - | - | - | - | - | 13-32 | - |
| Darrell Evans | - | 19-27 | - | 9-15 | - | - | - | - | - | - | - | 28-42 |
| Ron Gant | - | - | - | 22-28 | - | 2-0 | 3-8 | - | - | 13-22 | - | 27-36 |
| Tom Glavine | - | - | - | - | - | - | - | - | 17-12 | - | - | 17-12 |
| Tommy Greene | - | - | - | - | - | - | - | - | 1-3 | - | - | 1-3 |
| Tommy Gregg | - | 9-19 | - | - | - | 0-5 | - | 12-15 | - | 1-0 | - | 21-39 |
| Dwayne Henry | - | - | - | - | - | - | - | - | - | - | 3-9 | - |
| Dion James | - | 3-1 | - | - | - | 7-13 | 1-0 | 7-13 | - | - | - | 18-27 |
| David Justice | - | - | - | - | - | 1-1 | - | 6-6 | - | - | - | 7-7 |
| Mark Lemke | - | - | 5-8 | - | - | - | - | - | - | - | - | 5-8 |
| Derek Lilliquist | - | - | - | - | - | - | - | - | 12-18 | - | 1-1 | 12-18 |
| Kelly Mann | 2-5 | - | - | - | - | - | - | - | - | - | - | 2-5 |
| Oddibe McDowell | - | - | - | - | - | - | 27-39 | - | - | 27-39 | - | 27-39 |
| Kent Mercker | - | - | - | - | - | - | - | - | 1-0 | - | 0-1 | 1-0 |
| John Mizerock | 3-4 | - | - | - | - | - | - | - | - | - | - | 3-4 |
| Dale Murphy | - | - | - | - | - | - | 32-49 | 25-44 | - | - | - | 57-93 |
| Gerald Perry | - | 27-42 | - | - | - | - | - | - | - | 4-6 | - | 27-42 |
| Charlie Puleo | - | - | - | - | - | - | - | - | 0-1 | - | 1-13 | 0-1 |
| Rusty Richards | - | - | - | - | - | - | - | - | 1-1 | - | - | 1-1 |
| Ed Romero | - | - | 1-2 | - | 0-2 | - | - | - | - | - | - | 1-4 |
| John Russell | 12-17 | 1-0 | - | - | - | - | - | 3-4 | - | - | 0-1 | 16-21 |
| Lonnie Smith | - | - | - | - | - | 53-76 | - | - | - | 13-16 | - | 53-76 |
| Pete Smith | - | - | - | - | - | - | - | - | 8-19 | - | 0-1 | 8-19 |
| Zane Smith | - | - | - | - | - | - | - | - | 1-15 | - | - | 1-15 |
| John Smoltz | - | - | - | - | - | - | - | - | 14-15 | - | - | 14-15 |
| Mike Stanton | - | - | - | - | - | - | - | - | - | - | 7-13 | - |
| Andres Thomas | - | - | - | - | 52-84 | - | - | - | - | - | - | 52-84 |
| Jeff Treadway | - | - | 46-73 | 1-1 | - | - | - | - | - | 4-8 | - | 47-74 |
| Sergio Valdez | - | - | - | - | - | - | - | - | 0-1 | - | 3-15 | 0-1 |
| Jeff Wetherby | - | - | - | - | - | 0-1 | - | 0-1 | - | - | - | 0-2 |
| Ed Whited | - | - | - | 8-11 | - | - | - | - | - | - | - | 8-11 |

## Batting vs. Left and Right Handed Pitchers

| | | BA | Rank | SA | Rank | OBA | Rank | HR % | Rank | BB % | Rank | SO % | Rank |
|---|---|---|---|---|---|---|---|---|---|---|---|---|---|
| Geronimo Berroa | vs. Lefties | .278 | 53 | .361 | 76 | .316 | 81 | 1.85 | 66 | 5.26 | 112 | 21.05 | 123 |
| | vs. Righties | .214 | -- | .250 | -- | .241 | -- | 0.00 | -- | 3.45 | -- | 27.59 | -- |
| Jeff Blauser | vs. Lefties | .279 | 51 | .416 | 52 | .342 | 57 | 2.03 | 60 | 8.93 | 60 | 15.63 | 87 |
| | vs. Righties | .263 | 50 | .405 | 43 | .311 | 67 | 3.09 | 34 | 6.36 | 94 | 23.32 | 122 |
| Jody Davis | vs. Lefties | .204 | 117 | .280 | 112 | .286 | 110 | 1.08 | 89 | 10.48 | 39 | 20.95 | 122 |
| | vs. Righties | .145 | 132 | .217 | 132 | .219 | 131 | 2.17 | 60 | 7.89 | 75 | 25.66 | 127 |
| Darrell Evans | vs. Lefties | .247 | 85 | .384 | 63 | .298 | 97 | 2.74 | 42 | 8.33 | 68 | 14.29 | 81 |
| | vs. Righties | .192 | 127 | .345 | 85 | .305 | 75 | 4.43 | 10 | 14.23 | 8 | 14.23 | 66 |
| Ron Gant | vs. Lefties | .114 | 132 | .203 | 130 | .205 | 129 | 1.27 | 84 | 10.11 | 43 | 21.35 | 125 |
| | vs. Righties | .204 | 121 | .392 | 53 | .251 | 127 | 4.42 | 11 | 5.61 | 105 | 22.45 | 120 |
| Tommy Gregg | vs. Lefties | .228 | -- | .246 | -- | .290 | -- | 0.00 | -- | 7.69 | -- | 26.15 | -- |
| | vs. Righties | .247 | 69 | .361 | 76 | .288 | 95 | 2.74 | 39 | 5.58 | 106 | 12.02 | 42 |
| Dion James | vs. Lefties | .160 | -- | .160 | -- | .300 | -- | 0.00 | -- | 16.13 | -- | 6.45 | -- |
| | vs. Righties | .276 | 34 | .345 | 85 | .365 | 23 | 0.69 | 110 | 11.83 | 24 | 12.43 | 48 |
| Oddibe McDowell | vs. Lefties | .230 | 99 | .280 | 111 | .280 | 114 | 0.00 | 112 | 6.54 | 97 | 15.89 | 90 |
| | vs. Righties | .344 | 2 | .578 | 3 | .410 | 5 | 3.89 | 21 | 9.95 | 45 | 9.95 | 28 |
| Dale Murphy | vs. Lefties | .244 | 89 | .355 | 81 | .373 | 25 | 2.91 | 37 | 17.22 | 4 | 16.27 | 94 |
| | vs. Righties | .221 | 103 | .363 | 75 | .274 | 107 | 3.73 | 23 | 6.62 | 90 | 24.66 | 126 |
| Gerald Perry | vs. Lefties | .337 | 8 | .471 | 28 | .386 | 15 | 2.88 | 38 | 6.14 | 107 | 12.28 | 56 |
| | vs. Righties | .198 | 125 | .253 | 129 | .307 | 72 | 0.62 | 114 | 13.23 | 13 | 7.41 | 10 |
| John Russell | vs. Lefties | .118 | 131 | .162 | 132 | .143 | 132 | 1.47 | 78 | 2.86 | 131 | 31.43 | 132 |
| | vs. Righties | .231 | -- | .286 | -- | .283 | -- | 1.10 | -- | 6.06 | -- | 31.31 | -- |
| Lonnie Smith | vs. Lefties | .321 | 12 | .564 | 6 | .429 | 5 | 4.24 | 16 | 14.29 | 13 | 14.29 | 81 |
| | vs. Righties | .312 | 12 | .517 | 8 | .408 | 6 | 4.42 | 12 | 12.57 | 18 | 17.65 | 93 |
| Andres Thomas | vs. Lefties | .208 | 114 | .318 | 101 | .238 | 125 | 2.31 | 55 | 3.87 | 127 | 9.94 | 33 |
| | vs. Righties | .215 | 114 | .315 | 105 | .224 | 130 | 2.36 | 54 | 1.28 | 132 | 11.28 | 38 |
| Jeff Treadway | vs. Lefties | .198 | 118 | .208 | 129 | .254 | 121 | 0.00 | 112 | 6.78 | 95 | 13.56 | 75 |
| | vs. Righties | .300 | 18 | .428 | 27 | .335 | 44 | 2.18 | 59 | 5.56 | 107 | 5.56 | 4 |
| Team Average | vs. Lefties | .231 | 12 | .336 | 11 | .302 | 11 | 1.96 | 8 | 8.91 | 6 | 16.58 | 12 |
| | vs. Righties | .236 | 10 | .356 | 9 | .296 | 12 | 2.53 | 3 | 7.51 | 11 | 16.28 | 9 |
| League Average | vs. Lefties | .251 | | .371 | | .320 | | 2.06 | | 8.85 | | 14.80 | |
| | vs. Righties | .244 | | .362 | | .309 | | 2.08 | | 8.27 | | 15.67 | |

## Batting with Runners on Base and Bases Empty

| | | BA | Rank | SA | Rank | OBA | Rank | HR % | Rank | BB % | Rank | SO % | Rank |
|---|---|---|---|---|---|---|---|---|---|---|---|---|---|
| Bruce Benedict | Runners On | .176 | -- | .196 | -- | .333 | -- | 0.00 | -- | 16.92 | -- | 6.15 | -- |
| | Bases Empty | .202 | 122 | .248 | 124 | .281 | 102 | 0.92 | 102 | 9.92 | 38 | 11.57 | 38 |
| Jeff Blauser | Runners On | .289 | 34 | .376 | 73 | .360 | 42 | 0.67 | 105 | 10.00 | 65 | 20.56 | 121 |
| | Bases Empty | .261 | 58 | .427 | 27 | .306 | 74 | 3.58 | 21 | 6.12 | 85 | 19.57 | 116 |
| Jody Davis | Runners On | .148 | 130 | .250 | 128 | .224 | 129 | 2.27 | 54 | 9.09 | 77 | 23.23 | 130 |
| | Bases Empty | .182 | 128 | .238 | 128 | .259 | 115 | 1.40 | 87 | 8.86 | 49 | 24.05 | 126 |
| Darrell Evans | Runners On | .276 | 48 | .388 | 64 | .362 | 40 | 1.72 | 71 | 13.48 | 28 | 15.60 | 93 |
| | Bases Empty | .156 | 131 | .331 | 98 | .258 | 116 | 5.63 | 7 | 12.09 | 10 | 13.19 | 54 |
| Ron Gant | Runners On | .137 | 131 | .211 | 132 | .168 | 132 | 0.00 | 112 | 3.88 | 127 | 20.39 | 120 |
| | Bases Empty | .200 | 123 | .406 | 43 | .275 | 106 | 5.45 | 9 | 8.79 | 50 | 23.08 | 125 |
| Tommy Gregg | Runners On | .284 | 36 | .388 | 64 | .333 | 72 | 2.59 | 47 | 6.98 | 100 | 11.63 | 52 |
| | Bases Empty | .213 | 109 | .300 | 107 | .254 | 119 | 1.88 | 66 | 5.33 | 99 | 17.75 | 104 |
| Dion James | Runners On | .250 | -- | .297 | -- | .364 | -- | 0.00 | -- | 15.00 | -- | 8.75 | -- |
| | Bases Empty | .264 | 54 | .330 | 100 | .350 | 27 | 0.94 | 99 | 10.83 | 20 | 13.33 | 56 |
| Oddibe McDowell | Runners On | .330 | 9 | .580 | 5 | .404 | 13 | 2.27 | 54 | 11.00 | 54 | 11.00 | 47 |
| | Bases Empty | .292 | 17 | .422 | 30 | .346 | 31 | 2.60 | 41 | 7.69 | 65 | 12.50 | 48 |
| Dale Murphy | Runners On | .249 | 90 | .432 | 35 | .341 | 63 | 5.13 | 10 | 12.50 | 33 | 20.94 | 123 |
| | Bases Empty | .209 | 113 | .296 | 108 | .272 | 108 | 1.99 | 63 | 7.65 | 68 | 22.94 | 124 |
| Gerald Perry | Runners On | .254 | 83 | .365 | 81 | .329 | 77 | 1.59 | 74 | 10.49 | 62 | 10.49 | 40 |
| | Bases Empty | .250 | 66 | .314 | 103 | .344 | 36 | 1.43 | 85 | 10.63 | 28 | 8.13 | 10 |
| Lonnie Smith | Runners On | .407 | 1 | .630 | 2 | .496 | 1 | 3.17 | 27 | 13.92 | 23 | 10.55 | 43 |
| | Bases Empty | .256 | 63 | .471 | 12 | .359 | 19 | 5.12 | 11 | 12.65 | 8 | 20.59 | 121 |
| Andres Thomas | Runners On | .220 | 113 | .314 | 110 | .235 | 127 | 2.45 | 50 | 2.34 | 132 | 10.55 | 42 |
| | Bases Empty | .207 | 116 | .317 | 102 | .222 | 130 | 2.27 | 52 | 1.90 | 130 | 11.11 | 32 |
| Jeff Treadway | Runners On | .267 | 63 | .367 | 80 | .308 | 101 | 1.67 | 73 | 6.37 | 106 | 6.37 | 6 |
| | Bases Empty | .283 | 24 | .386 | 56 | .323 | 50 | 1.71 | 71 | 5.48 | 97 | 8.06 | 9 |
| Team Average | Runners On | .256 | 5 | .376 | 7 | .324 | 10 | 2.08 | 7 | 9.00 | 12 | 14.50 | 6 |
| | Bases Empty | .220 | 12 | .332 | 10 | .280 | 12 | 2.52 | 2 | 7.26 | 8 | 17.71 | 11 |
| League Average | Runners On | .256 | | .379 | | .330 | | 2.13 | | 9.82 | | 14.66 | |
| | Bases Empty | .240 | | .355 | | .299 | | 2.03 | | 7.43 | | 15.93 | |

## Overall Batting Compared to Late Inning Pressure Situations

| | | BA | Rank | SA | Rank | OBA | Rank | HR % | Rank | BB % | Rank | SO % | Rank | RDI % | Rank |
|---|---|---|---|---|---|---|---|---|---|---|---|---|---|---|---|
| Jeff Blauser | Overall | .270 | 44 | .410 | 38 | .325 | 58 | 2.63 | 36 | 7.50 | 85 | 19.92 | 121 | .333 | 9 |
| | Pressure | .233 | 71 | .300 | 89 | .263 | 98 | 0.00 | 81 | 4.17 | 111 | 27.08 | 124 | .318 | 26 |
| Jody Davis | Overall | .169 | 132 | .242 | 130 | .246 | 126 | 1.73 | 71 | 8.95 | 55 | 23.74 | 128 | .211 | 112 |
| | Pressure | .100 | 132 | .100 | 132 | .211 | 126 | 0.00 | 81 | 12.07 | 34 | 34.48 | 131 | .125 | 116 |
| Darrell Evans | Overall | .207 | 123 | .355 | 84 | .303 | 93 | 3.99 | 15 | 12.69 | 14 | 14.24 | 73 | .299 | 29 |
| | Pressure | .203 | 96 | .254 | 105 | .246 | 110 | 1.69 | 64 | 6.15 | 91 | 18.46 | 93 | .111 | 121 |
| Ron Gant | Overall | .177 | 130 | .335 | 102 | .237 | 129 | 3.46 | 24 | 7.02 | 89 | 22.11 | 126 | .171 | 127 |
| | Pressure | .119 | 131 | .190 | 125 | .140 | 132 | 2.38 | 42 | 2.22 | 125 | 28.89 | 127 | .111 | -- |
| Tommy Gregg | Overall | .243 | 87 | .337 | 100 | .288 | 104 | 2.17 | 59 | 6.04 | 105 | 15.10 | 82 | .215 | 106 |
| | Pressure | .222 | 81 | .286 | 93 | .269 | 97 | 1.59 | 66 | 5.88 | 94 | 22.06 | 110 | .222 | 65 |
| Dion James | Overall | .259 | 58 | .318 | 112 | .355 | 30 | 0.59 | 114 | 12.50 | 19 | 11.50 | 40 | .182 | -- |
| | Pressure | .200 | -- | .200 | -- | .294 | -- | 0.00 | -- | 11.76 | -- | 26.47 | -- | .133 | 111 |
| Oddibe McDowell | Overall | .304 | 9 | .471 | 13 | .365 | 25 | 2.50 | 43 | 8.77 | 61 | 12.01 | 43 | .250 | 76 |
| | Pressure | .238 | 65 | .405 | 28 | .333 | 47 | 2.38 | 42 | 12.24 | 28 | 18.37 | 92 | .400 | -- |
| Dale Murphy | Overall | .228 | 109 | .361 | 78 | .306 | 90 | 3.48 | 22 | 10.05 | 47 | 21.95 | 125 | .272 | 56 |
| | Pressure | .287 | 31 | .415 | 26 | .355 | 33 | 3.19 | 24 | 10.28 | 53 | 19.63 | 101 | .481 | 6 |
| Gerald Perry | Overall | .252 | 71 | .338 | 98 | .337 | 46 | 1.50 | 81 | 10.56 | 41 | 9.24 | 20 | .148 | 131 |
| | Pressure | .132 | 130 | .132 | 131 | .327 | 62 | 0.00 | 81 | 18.37 | 5 | 6.12 | 7 | .000 | 131 |
| Lonnie Smith | Overall | .315 | 6 | .533 | 5 | .415 | 1 | 4.36 | 12 | 13.17 | 12 | 16.46 | 98 | .420 | 2 |
| | Pressure | .265 | 45 | .471 | 15 | .378 | 23 | 4.41 | 15 | 13.25 | 23 | 27.71 | 126 | .571 | 2 |
| Andres Thomas | Overall | .213 | 120 | .316 | 113 | .228 | 131 | 2.35 | 48 | 2.10 | 132 | 10.86 | 32 | .234 | 91 |
| | Pressure | .235 | 69 | .357 | 57 | .248 | 109 | 3.06 | 25 | 1.96 | 128 | 10.78 | 27 | .120 | 118 |
| Jeff Treadway | Overall | .277 | 35 | .378 | 62 | .317 | 71 | 1.69 | 74 | 5.84 | 108 | 7.39 | 8 | .265 | 65 |
| | Pressure | .288 | 30 | .363 | 54 | .329 | 56 | 2.50 | 33 | 5.81 | 95 | 12.79 | 40 | .148 | 105 |
| Team Average | Overall | .234 | 12 | .350 | 10 | .298 | 12 | 2.34 | 3 | 7.98 | 11 | 16.38 | 9 | .250 | 8 |
| | Pressure | .214 | 12 | .298 | 11 | .272 | 12 | 1.68 | 6 | 7.06 | 12 | 21.09 | 12 | .233 | 7 |
| League Average | Overall | .246 | | .365 | | .312 | | 2.07 | | 8.47 | | 15.38 | | .253 | |
| | Pressure | .238 | | .337 | | .308 | | 1.73 | | 8.93 | | 16.78 | | .235 | |

## Additional Miscellaneous Batting Comparisons

| | Grass Surface BA | Rank | Artificial Surface BA | Rank | Home Games BA | Rank | Road Games BA | Rank | Runners in Scoring Position BA | Rank | Runners in Scoring Pos and Two Outs BA | Rank | Leading Off Inning OBA | Rank | Runners on 3B with less than 2 Outs RDI % | Rank |
|---|---|---|---|---|---|---|---|---|---|---|---|---|---|---|---|---|
| Bruce Benedict | .189 | 119 | .211 | -- | .202 | 120 | .183 | -- | .158 | -- | .100 | -- | .255 | 107 | .500 | -- |
| Geronimo Berroa | .247 | 67 | .308 | -- | .253 | -- | .279 | -- | .258 | -- | .235 | -- | .364 | -- | .500 | -- |
| Jeff Blauser | .260 | 57 | .295 | 17 | .249 | 81 | .291 | 18 | .321 | 11 | .231 | 60 | .304 | 63 | .706 | 15 |
| Jody Davis | .158 | 131 | .197 | -- | .143 | 132 | .190 | 121 | .191 | 120 | .292 | 22 | .300 | 66 | .222 | 144 |
| Darrell Evans | .197 | 115 | .235 | 101 | .229 | 106 | .182 | 128 | .250 | 75 | .242 | 50 | .284 | 82 | .667 | 25 |
| Ron Gant | .165 | 127 | .208 | -- | .178 | 127 | .176 | 131 | .145 | 132 | .086 | 132 | .280 | 86 | .667 | 25 |
| Tommy Gregg | .234 | 83 | .268 | -- | .293 | 31 | .206 | 114 | .236 | 89 | .111 | 128 | .186 | 131 | .571 | -- |
| Dion James | .270 | 45 | .227 | -- | .235 | -- | .281 | 36 | .176 | -- | .250 | -- | .381 | -- | .429 | -- |
| Oddibe McDowell | .327 | 5 | .232 | -- | .316 | 11 | .292 | 16 | .304 | 21 | .174 | 108 | .378 | 18 | .333 | -- |
| Dale Murphy | .235 | 81 | .210 | 119 | .257 | 67 | .201 | 118 | .283 | 37 | .266 | 34 | .231 | 123 | .576 | 63 |
| Gerald Perry | .286 | 30 | .173 | 130 | .289 | 34 | .210 | 111 | .203 | 112 | .212 | 80 | .262 | 103 | .222 | 144 |
| John Russell | .153 | 132 | .268 | -- | .167 | -- | .195 | -- | .214 | -- | .176 | -- | .109 | -- | .200 | -- |
| Lonnie Smith | .321 | 8 | .299 | 14 | .358 | 3 | .277 | 39 | .414 | 1 | .400 | 3 | .326 | 50 | .556 | 74 |
| Andres Thomas | .211 | 110 | .219 | 115 | .195 | 123 | .228 | 93 | .231 | 91 | .243 | 49 | .242 | 116 | .417 | 127 |
| Jeff Treadway | .264 | 53 | .309 | 8 | .261 | 63 | .293 | 15 | .256 | 71 | .190 | 97 | .333 | 40 | .762 | 8 |
| Team Average | .233 | 9 | .239 | 10 | .242 | 10 | .227 | 12 | .256 | 4 | .233 | 3 | .274 | 12 | .511 | 12 |
| League Average | .244 | | .248 | | .251 | | .242 | | .249 | | .222 | | .302 | | .546 | |

## Pitching vs. Left and Right Handed Batters

| | | BA | Rank | SA | Rank | OBA | Rank | HR % | Rank | BB % | Rank | SO % | Rank |
|---|---|---|---|---|---|---|---|---|---|---|---|---|---|
| Jim Acker | vs. Lefties | .284 | 96 | .383 | 75 | .333 | 71 | 1.64 | 62 | 7.04 | 27 | 9.55 | 97 |
| | vs. Righties | .187 | 10 | .275 | 11 | .217 | 4 | 1.17 | 15 | 3.26 | 2 | 26.63 | 9 |
| Jose Alvarez | vs. Lefties | .236 | 44 | .337 | 45 | .358 | 98 | 1.12 | 38 | 15.74 | 114 | 19.44 | 20 |
| | vs. Righties | .237 | -- | .361 | -- | .292 | -- | 3.09 | -- | 6.42 | -- | 22.02 | -- |
| Joe Boever | vs. Lefties | .251 | 66 | .307 | 32 | .333 | 71 | 0.56 | 17 | 10.84 | 78 | 17.73 | 27 |
| | vs. Righties | .254 | 82 | .423 | 100 | .322 | 85 | 3.85 | 114 | 8.22 | 77 | 21.92 | 27 |
| Marty Clary | vs. Lefties | .239 | 51 | .333 | 43 | .293 | 29 | 1.18 | 41 | 7.19 | 31 | 6.12 | 113 |
| | vs. Righties | .268 | 90 | .382 | 77 | .316 | 81 | 1.91 | 47 | 6.32 | 42 | 7.47 | 116 |
| Mark Eichhorn | vs. Lefties | .350 | 114 | .504 | 113 | .410 | 113 | 1.63 | 61 | 9.15 | 60 | 9.15 | 101 |
| | vs. Righties | .205 | 20 | .318 | 26 | .236 | 7 | 3.03 | 94 | 4.17 | 12 | 25.00 | 15 |
| Tom Glavine | vs. Lefties | .204 | 19 | .269 | 14 | .252 | 9 | 0.00 | 1 | 5.17 | 6 | 22.41 | 10 |
| | vs. Righties | .250 | 75 | .389 | 79 | .289 | 53 | 3.33 | 104 | 5.23 | 23 | 9.85 | 109 |
| Derek Lilliquist | vs. Lefties | .265 | 80 | .412 | 94 | .292 | 28 | 2.94 | 96 | 2.78 | 1 | 17.59 | 28 |
| | vs. Righties | .308 | 111 | .439 | 108 | .343 | 95 | 2.28 | 64 | 5.08 | 22 | 9.84 | 110 |
| Pete Smith | vs. Lefties | .255 | 70 | .355 | 58 | .346 | 91 | 2.18 | 82 | 12.20 | 96 | 13.55 | 59 |
| | vs. Righties | .274 | 96 | .412 | 94 | .306 | 69 | 2.65 | 77 | 4.92 | 21 | 26.64 | 8 |
| John Smoltz | vs. Lefties | .214 | 25 | .317 | 34 | .289 | 25 | 1.32 | 48 | 9.14 | 59 | 15.95 | 41 |
| | vs. Righties | .209 | 23 | .321 | 28 | .266 | 29 | 2.98 | 92 | 7.51 | 69 | 25.83 | 11 |
| Team Average | vs. Lefties | .243 | 3 | .342 | 2 | .317 | 4 | 1.51 | 3 | 9.64 | 8 | 14.94 | 4 |
| | vs. Righties | .256 | 11 | .383 | 11 | .303 | 8 | 2.49 | 9 | 6.28 | 1 | 16.54 | 5 |
| League Average | vs. Lefties | .252 | | .366 | | .325 | | 1.79 | | 9.48 | | 13.93 | |
| | vs. Righties | .242 | | .365 | | .303 | | 2.29 | | 7.70 | | 16.46 | |

## Pitching with Runners on Base and Bases Empty

| | | BA | Rank | SA | Rank | OBA | Rank | HR % | Rank | BB % | Rank | SO % | Rank |
|---|---|---|---|---|---|---|---|---|---|---|---|---|---|
| Jim Acker | Runners On | .233 | 39 | .293 | 13 | .289 | 21 | 0.67 | 7 | 7.60 | 26 | 16.37 | 42 |
| | Bases Empty | .240 | 54 | .358 | 71 | .269 | 23 | 1.96 | 57 | 3.30 | 5 | 18.87 | 36 |
| Joe Boever | Runners On | .228 | 34 | .302 | 16 | .307 | 43 | 1.34 | 33 | 9.36 | 55 | 19.30 | 24 |
| | Bases Empty | .275 | 105 | .406 | 100 | .348 | 110 | 2.50 | 89 | 10.11 | 98 | 19.66 | 31 |
| Marty Clary | Runners On | .254 | 67 | .361 | 59 | .295 | 25 | 2.37 | 77 | 5.35 | 3 | 5.35 | 115 |
| | Bases Empty | .247 | 73 | .346 | 54 | .307 | 69 | 0.82 | 17 | 7.92 | 74 | 7.55 | 116 |
| Mark Eichhorn | Runners On | .306 | 107 | .537 | 116 | .358 | 89 | 4.96 | 115 | 8.33 | 38 | 18.06 | 32 |
| | Bases Empty | .246 | 71 | .291 | 17 | .289 | 46 | 0.00 | 1 | 4.93 | 22 | 16.20 | 44 |
| Tom Glavine | Runners On | .260 | 77 | .409 | 85 | .322 | 61 | 3.72 | 109 | 8.54 | 40 | 9.96 | 100 |
| | Bases Empty | .233 | 42 | .351 | 60 | .262 | 15 | 2.36 | 80 | 3.30 | 4 | 12.78 | 85 |
| Derek Lilliquist | Runners On | .349 | 116 | .471 | 107 | .387 | 110 | 2.30 | 71 | 5.86 | 7 | 8.97 | 107 |
| | Bases Empty | .271 | 100 | .412 | 105 | .301 | 63 | 2.44 | 83 | 3.97 | 12 | 12.38 | 88 |
| Pete Smith | Runners On | .304 | 103 | .435 | 93 | .379 | 107 | 2.42 | 81 | 11.48 | 91 | 15.16 | 49 |
| | Bases Empty | .238 | 51 | .344 | 52 | .298 | 58 | 2.35 | 79 | 7.86 | 73 | 21.14 | 21 |
| John Smoltz | Runners On | .240 | 49 | .357 | 50 | .294 | 24 | 2.33 | 74 | 7.29 | 18 | 18.08 | 31 |
| | Bases Empty | .193 | 10 | .294 | 18 | .270 | 25 | 1.75 | 50 | 9.33 | 92 | 21.03 | 23 |
| Team Average | Runners On | .265 | 10 | .385 | 8 | .330 | 7 | 2.25 | 7 | 8.87 | 2 | 14.71 | 5 |
| | Bases Empty | .240 | 6 | .352 | 6 | .293 | 3 | 1.97 | 5 | 6.78 | 2 | 16.75 | 4 |
| League Average | Runners On | .256 | | .379 | | .330 | | 2.13 | | 9.82 | | 14.66 | |
| | Bases Empty | .240 | | .355 | | .299 | | 2.03 | | 7.43 | | 15.93 | |

## Overall Pitching Compared to Late Inning Pressure Situations

| | | BA | Rank | SA | Rank | OBA | Rank | HR % | Rank | BB % | Rank | SO % | Rank |
|---|---|---|---|---|---|---|---|---|---|---|---|---|---|
| Jim Acker | Overall | .237 | 50 | .331 | 34 | .278 | 20 | 1.41 | 24 | 5.22 | 10 | 17.75 | 39 |
| | Pressure | .267 | 84 | .348 | 69 | .306 | 51 | 0.74 | 30 | 5.41 | 26 | 19.59 | 30 |
| Jose Alvarez | Overall | .257 | -- | .349 | -- | .325 | -- | 2.15 | -- | 11.06 | -- | 20.74 | -- |
| | Pressure | .298 | 101 | .456 | 102 | .310 | 56 | 5.26 | 113 | 1.64 | 3 | 29.51 | 3 |
| Joe Boever | Overall | .252 | 73 | .356 | 62 | .328 | 83 | 1.94 | 54 | 9.74 | 86 | 19.48 | 26 |
| | Pressure | .263 | 81 | .378 | 86 | .345 | 88 | 2.39 | 85 | 10.88 | 82 | 20.50 | 23 |
| Marty Clary | Overall | .250 | 67 | .352 | 59 | .302 | 49 | 1.46 | 25 | 6.86 | 30 | 6.64 | 116 |
| | Pressure | .250 | 70 | .306 | 44 | .349 | 91 | 0.00 | 1 | 13.64 | 103 | 4.55 | 115 |
| Mark Eichhorn | Overall | .275 | 100 | .408 | 97 | .323 | 77 | 2.35 | 83 | 6.64 | 24 | 17.13 | 43 |
| | Pressure | .243 | 64 | .311 | 47 | .298 | 48 | 0.97 | 36 | 7.69 | 48 | 16.24 | 53 |
| Tom Glavine | Overall | .243 | 57 | .371 | 71 | .283 | 28 | 2.82 | 103 | 5.22 | 10 | 11.75 | 94 |
| | Pressure | .186 | 17 | .339 | 64 | .226 | 5 | 5.08 | 112 | 4.76 | 19 | 3.17 | 116 |
| Dwayne Henry | Overall | .250 | -- | .396 | -- | .321 | -- | 4.17 | -- | 9.09 | -- | 29.09 | -- |
| | Pressure | .293 | 97 | .463 | 104 | .370 | 100 | 4.88 | 111 | 10.42 | 79 | 27.08 | 5 |
| Derek Lilliquist | Overall | .301 | 114 | .435 | 113 | .335 | 91 | 2.38 | 86 | 4.74 | 3 | 11.00 | 100 |
| | Pressure | .424 | 116 | .576 | 115 | .429 | 112 | 3.03 | 99 | 2.86 | 7 | 11.43 | 87 |
| Pete Smith | Overall | .263 | 90 | .378 | 73 | .330 | 86 | 2.38 | 85 | 9.30 | 78 | 18.76 | 30 |
| | Pressure | .238 | -- | .286 | -- | .333 | -- | 0.00 | -- | 12.50 | -- | 16.67 | -- |
| John Smoltz | Overall | .212 | 15 | .319 | 23 | .280 | 23 | 1.98 | 57 | 8.50 | 63 | 19.83 | 23 |
| | Pressure | .161 | 6 | .229 | 7 | .231 | 7 | 0.85 | 32 | 7.69 | 48 | 16.92 | 48 |
| Mike Stanton | Overall | .207 | -- | .268 | -- | .278 | -- | 0.00 | -- | 8.51 | -- | 28.72 | -- |
| | Pressure | .226 | 49 | .306 | 45 | .314 | 60 | 0.00 | 1 | 10.96 | 86 | 32.88 | 2 |
| Team Average | Overall | .250 | 10 | .366 | 7 | .309 | 5 | 2.08 | 5 | 7.69 | 1 | 15.87 | 4 |
| | Pressure | .257 | 11 | .362 | 11 | .321 | 10 | 1.86 | 8 | 8.53 | 3 | 18.95 | 3 |
| League Average | Overall | .246 | | .365 | | .312 | | 2.07 | | 8.47 | | 15.38 | |
| | Pressure | .235 | | .336 | | .309 | | 1.77 | | 9.31 | | 16.92 | |

## Additional Miscellaneous Pitching Comparisons

| | Grass Surface | | Artificial Surface | | Home Games | | Road Games | | Runners in Scoring Position | | Runners in Scoring Pos and Two Outs | | Leading Off Inning | |
|---|---|---|---|---|---|---|---|---|---|---|---|---|---|---|
| | BA | Rank | BA | Rank | BA | Rank | BA | Rank | BA | Rank | BA | Rank | OBA | Rank |
| Jim Acker | .235 | 52 | .243 | 53 | .223 | 36 | .250 | 56 | .202 | 24 | .208 | 55 | .287 | 48 |
| Jose Alvarez | .236 | 53 | .237 | -- | .282 | -- | .198 | 12 | .157 | -- | .138 | 12 | .367 | -- |
| Joe Boever | .243 | 61 | .290 | -- | .234 | 49 | .282 | 96 | .253 | 70 | .273 | 93 | .312 | 75 |
| Marty Clary | .273 | 94 | .159 | -- | .263 | 85 | .236 | 39 | .170 | 10 | .104 | 4 | .286 | 45 |
| Gary Eave | .200 | 8 | .000 | -- | .200 | -- | .000 | -- | .091 | -- | .200 | -- | .364 | -- |
| Mark Eichhorn | .277 | 97 | .267 | -- | .292 | 109 | .259 | 77 | .293 | 91 | .333 | 112 | .344 | 97 |
| Tom Glavine | .233 | 50 | .269 | 84 | .238 | 52 | .247 | 54 | .252 | 67 | .208 | 54 | .272 | 35 |
| Derek Lilliquist | .295 | 105 | .330 | 113 | .305 | 113 | .295 | 105 | .324 | 111 | .329 | 111 | .278 | 39 |
| Pete Smith | .248 | 68 | .313 | 109 | .268 | 92 | .258 | 75 | .293 | 91 | .309 | 107 | .276 | 37 |
| John Smoltz | .206 | 16 | .221 | 26 | .189 | 12 | .231 | 36 | .194 | 15 | .135 | 10 | .290 | 50 |
| Sergio Valdez | .275 | 95 | .125 | -- | .206 | -- | .293 | -- | .414 | -- | .357 | -- | .281 | -- |
| Team Average | .247 | 6 | .261 | 12 | .243 | 7 | .258 | 10 | .251 | 7 | .236 | 9 | .305 | 6 |
| League Average | .244 | | .248 | | .242 | | .251 | | .249 | | .222 | | .302 | |

# CHICAGO CUBS

- **Is a walk *really* as good as a hit?**
- **Baseball card collecting, in black and white.**

Once in a while, it's interesting to scrape the crust off some dated axiom, to see whether or not it can withstand the scrutiny of contemporary numerical analysis. Remember that old saw, A walk's as good as a hit? Well, as it happens, the Chicago Cubs have turned venerable Wrigley Field into a modern testing lab for that very subject.

Over the 70 years from 1918 through 1987, only three teams led the National League in batting average while drawing the fewest walks. Then along came the Cubs, who've done it in each of the past two seasons. Call us skeptical, but if a walk is really as good as a hit, how come Chicago ranked fourth in the league in scoring in 1988 and led the league last year? The following table provides a more encompassing look, listing all teams that have ranked first in their leagues in batting average and last in walks since 1900, along with their averages and ranks in scoring (runs per game):

| Year | Team | BA | BB | Runs | League Rank |
|---|---|---|---|---|---|
| 1905 | Cleveland Indians | .255 | 286 | 3.68 | 5th of 8 teams |
| 1914 | Brooklyn Dodgers | .269 | 376 | 4.04 | 4th of 8 teams |
| 1917 | Cincinnati Reds | .264 | 312 | 3.83 | 2d of 8 teams |
| 1925 | Philadelphia A's | .307 | 453 | 5.42 | 4th of 8 teams |
| 1936 | Cleveland Indians | .304 | 514 | 5.87 | 4th of 8 teams |
| 1943 | St. Louis Cardinals | .279 | 428 | 4.32 | 2d of 8 teams |
| 1959 | Cleveland Indians | .263 | 433 | 4.84 | 1st of 8 teams |
| 1972 | Pittsburgh Pirates | .274 | 404 | 4.46 | 3d of 12 teams |
| 1975 | St. Louis Cardinals | .273 | 444 | 4.06 | 7th of 12 teams |
| 1986 | Cleveland Indians | .284 | 456 | 5.10 | 1st of 14 teams |
| 1988 | Chicago Cubs | .261 | 403 | 4.05 | 4th of 12 teams |
| 1989 | Chicago Cubs | .261 | 472 | 4.33 | 1st of 12 teams |

Only two of those 12 teams ranked in the lower halves of their leagues in scoring, and both of them were only one team removed from the top halves. To put a number on their collective ranking, let's score each team on this basis: Assign a win for every team ranked below them, a loss for every one ranked higher. For instance, the 1989 Cubs would be 11–0, having ranked higher in scoring than each of the other 11 N.L. teams. On that basis, the 12 teams above compiled an overall record of 69 wins and 26 losses, for a snazzy .726 winning percentage that says an awful lot about the relative values of hits and walks.

For a point of comparison, let's examine the anti-group—teams that ranked first in walks and last in batting average. Ready or not, here they come:

| Year | Team | BA | BB | Runs | League Rank |
|---|---|---|---|---|---|
| 1906 | Chicago White Sox | .230 | 453 | 3.70 | 4th of 8 teams |
| 1909 | Chicago White Sox | .221 | 441 | 3.09 | 6th of 8 teams |
| 1914 | New York Yankees | .229 | 577 | 3.43 | 5th of 8 teams |
| 1915 | Boston Braves | .240 | 549 | 3.71 | 4th of 8 teams |
| 1916 | Boston Braves | .233 | 437 | 3.43 | 4th of 8 teams |
| 1960 | Detroit Tigers | .239 | 636 | 4.11 | 7th of 8 teams |
| 1962 | New York Mets | .240 | 616 | 3.83 | 9th of 10 teams |
| 1985 | California Angels | .251 | 648 | 4.52 | 7th of 14 teams |

Just as no team in the first group ranked lower than the top of the second division in scoring, none in the group above ranked higher than the lowest rung of the first division. Scored on the same won-lost basis, the high-walk, low-batting average teams had a record of 26 wins and 38 losses (.406). It's obvious that good-hitting teams can thrive without being selective at the plate, while poor-hitting teams won't score much no matter how many free passes they draw.

Another aspect of Chicago's recent disdain for the lowly walk is noteworthy. Ferguson Jenkins spent 10 years pitching in Wrigley Field and another two in Fenway Park, winning an average of 16 games per season during that time. He obviously qualifies as an expert on pitching in good hitters' parks. Jenkins always preached the need to keep bases on balls to a minimum at those stadiums. And Fergy sure practiced what he preached: only seven other pitchers in major league history averaged fewer than two walks per nine innings over a career of more than 4000 innings. But unless the relationship between bases on balls and home-field advantage is far less than Jenkins imagined, the Cubs won a 1989 division title with a team unsuited to their home park.

Over the past 24 years, Chicago has ranked among the top three National League teams in drawing walks seven times (1969, 1972, 1974, 1975, 1978, 1984, and 1985). Their average winning percentage at Wrigley Field during those seasons was 72 points higher than on the road. Consider that margin to be the Cubs' home-field advantage. Their home-field advantage in other seasons during that period, when they didn't draw high totals of walks, was even greater: 100 points. Strike one on Jenkins.

Let's examine the question from the opposite side. Six Cubs teams during that period were among the three National League teams in each season whose pitchers allowed the fewest walks (1970 through 1973, 1982, and 1984). Chicago's home-field advantage in those seasons was 76 points, compared to 98 points in other seasons. Strike two on Jenkins.

We broadened our search to include the performances of two other teams that play in parks similar to Wrigley Field: Fenway Park and Atlanta Stadium. (Incidentally, that's why this study starts in 1966, the year in which the Braves moved to Atlanta.) All three stadiums increase batting averages and home runs, although it should be noted that since the mid–1980s, hitters have chosen to exploit Fenway's characteristics more for batting average and extra–base hits than for home runs. Three teams times 24 seasons produced a sample of 72 team-seasons to study, including 22 that were classified as high-walk teams, ranking among their leagues' top three in drawing BBs. There were 20 classified as low-walk staffs, whose pitchers ranked among the three teams that allowed the fewest bases on balls.

Both groups had home-field advantages slightly greater than expected. The high-walk teams were 93 points better at home than on the road, compared to an 82–point margin for teams that drew fewer walks. The low-walk pitching staffs had a 100–point home-field advantage, a margin 20 points greater than that of teams that issued more bases on balls. That doesn't prove the correctness of Jenkins's viewpoint. The differences simply aren't large enough to warrant such a definitive conclusion.

And even if Jenkins is correct, the 1989 Cubs provided evidence that a team's propensity for drawing walks (or allowing them) is only a small piece of their home-field–advantage puzzle. Players like Shawon Dunston and Andre Dawson more than compensate for their lack of selectivity at the plate with other desirable qualities. Let's not call strike three on Jenkins. But it's clear that he's behind in the count.

Like most other red-blooded children of the '50s, we celebrated our passage into adulthood via the great American ritual of tossing shoe boxes full of baseball cards into the garbage. We're not sure how it happened, but if you haven't heard, those little color photos of Reno Bertoia, Camilo Carreon, and Moe Thacker have become valuable. So valuable, in fact, that mint-condition cards of some Hall of Famers from the 1950s and 1960s regularly trade for more than a thousand dollars.

Whenever we discuss the issue with those who kept their old collections—they occasionally call from the cellular phones in their Maseratis—they make the same recommendation: Invest in mint-condition rookie cards of black Hall of Famers. Many card-collecting insiders apparently feel that because 99 percent of collectors are white, the cards of white superstars are overvalued, and that such a disparity indicates that a boom in the prices of black superstars is around the corner. Only the most avaricious collectors seem intent on exploiting this perceived growth area within the market. But the attitude is so widely acknowledged that virtually no avid collector or dealer to whom we spoke was unaware of it. Many casual collectors were clued in as well.

For one thing, we find the topic morally distasteful. For another, the perceived disparity between the prices of cards of black players and white players simply *does not exist.*

A one–paragraph primer for those without a working knowledge of the basics of investment-level card collecting: The most valuable of any player's cards is his first appearance in the full set of a major manufacturer, known as his "rookie card." For example, the first Ernie Banks card was manufactured by Topps in 1954. It's worth six times as much as his 1955 card. Cards of nondescript players are called "commons," and they form a convenient basis for comparison in the determination of the relative values of rookie cards from different seasons.

The 1954 Banks card, incidentally, is at the center of the black-white question. Al Kaline's rookie card is also from the 1954 set, and it trades for the same price as the Banks rookie card: as much as $600 in near-mint condition. (Prices quoted here are from the January 1990 edition of *Beckett Baseball Card Monthly.*) Kaline was a great player, but would any knowledgeable baseball fan deny that Banks was a superior player? We certainly wouldn't. Assuming that a card's worth is based roughly on the player's accomplishments—actually, it's a popularity vote with collectors' dollars, and popularity itself is based in large part on accomplishment—then why should Kaline's card be worth as much as Banks's?

You'll recall that baseball cards used to be issued in series of roughly one hundred cards per month throughout the season. Since interest was highest on opening day and waned throughout the season, fewer cards were issued in later series to reflect the decrease in demand. The eventual scarcity of those late-series cards increases their value in the current marketplace. In 1954, the Banks card appeared early, from a segment of the set in which commons are worth nine dollars. The Kaline card appeared toward the end of the set, where commons are worth 10 bucks. Which means that the Banks card trades for 67 times the value of a common card ($600 divided by nine), the Kaline card for 60 times common value (600 divided by 10). In other words, the Banks card is judged more valuable.

By ranking the rookie cards of all Hall of Famers from 1950 to the present according to their P/C ratios (price-to-common–value ratios) we can equitably compare the relative values of two cards from different parts of the same set, two cards from different years, or even two cards from different eras:

| Player | Price | Common | P/C | Player | Price | Common | P/C |
|---|---|---|---|---|---|---|---|
| Bench | 350 | 0.50 | 700 | Marichal | 80 | 1.50 | 53 |
| Yastrzemski | 350 | 1.25 | 280 | Brock | 100 | 2.00 | 50 |
| Palmer | 125 | 0.65 | 192 | Killebrew | 250 | 5.50 | 45 |
| Morgan | 90 | 0.50 | 180 | Mays | 1700 | 40.00 | 43 |
| Mantle | 5000 | 40.00 | 125 | F. Robinson | 200 | 5.00 | 40 |
| Koufax | 600 | 5.50 | 109 | Gibson | 300 | 8.50 | 35 |
| Aaron | 1050 | 10.00 | 105 | Drysdale | 165 | 5.00 | 33 |
| McCovey | 135 | 1.50 | 90 | B. Robinson | 350 | 14.00 | 25 |
| Ford | 1200 | 16.00 | 75 | Hunter | 90 | 3.75 | 24 |
| Williams | 75 | 1.10 | 68 | Aparicio | 100 | 7.00 | 14 |
| Banks | 600 | 9.00 | 67 | Mathews | 1500 | 150.00 | 10 |
| Clemente | 900 | 13.50 | 67 | Wilhelm | 500 | 150.00 | 3 |
| Kaline | 600 | 10.00 | 60 | | | | |

If the cards of nonwhite players were truly undervalued, very few would appear in the upper half of the table above. That's not the case. Among those 25 Hall of Famers, the average rank of the white players (12.8) is so close to that of the nonwhite players (13.2) that even random distribution would create so thorough a mix only once in 11 trials. Wouldn't it be something if those "investors" twisted enough to try to exploit this imaginary disparity discover too late that it's nonexistent?

## WON-LOST RECORD BY STARTING POSITION

| CHICAGO 93-69 | C | 1B | 2B | 3B | SS | LF | CF | RF | P | Leadoff | Relief | Starts |
|---|---|---|---|---|---|---|---|---|---|---|---|---|
| Paul Assenmacher | - | - | - | - | - | - | - | - | - | - | 8-6 | - |
| Damon Berryhill | 54-30 | - | - | - | - | - | - | - | - | - | - | 54-30 |
| Mike Bielecki | - | - | - | - | - | - | - | - | 22-11 | - | - | 22-11 |
| Kevin Blankenship | - | - | - | - | - | - | - | - | - | - | 1-1 | - |
| Doug Dascenzo | - | - | - | - | - | - | 19-12 | - | - | 19-11 | - | 19-12 |
| Andre Dawson | - | - | - | - | - | - | - | 66-44 | - | - | - | 66-44 |
| Shawon Dunston | - | - | - | - | 76-60 | - | - | - | - | 1-1 | - | 76-60 |
| Joe Girardi | 24-27 | - | - | - | - | - | - | - | - | - | - | 24-27 |
| Mark Grace | - | 78-59 | - | - | - | - | - | - | - | - | - | 78-59 |
| Darrin Jackson | - | - | - | - | - | 0-2 | 2-0 | 9-4 | - | 1-0 | - | 11-6 |
| Paul Kilgus | - | - | - | - | - | - | - | - | 9-14 | - | 5-7 | 9-14 |
| Joe Kraemer | - | - | - | - | - | - | - | - | 0-1 | - | - | 0-1 |
| Les Lancaster | - | - | - | - | - | - | - | - | - | - | 27-15 | - |
| Vance Law | - | - | - | 67-48 | - | - | - | - | - | - | - | 67-48 |
| Greg Maddux | - | - | - | - | - | - | - | - | 22-13 | - | - | 22-13 |
| Lloyd McClendon | - | 15-10 | - | 1-2 | - | 29-13 | - | - | - | - | - | 45-25 |
| Pat Perry | - | - | - | - | - | - | - | - | - | - | 7-12 | - |
| Jeff Pico | - | - | - | - | - | - | - | - | 1-4 | - | 13-35 | 1-4 |
| Domingo Ramos | - | - | - | 6-6 | 17-9 | - | - | - | - | - | - | 23-15 |
| Luis Salazar | - | - | - | 9-7 | - | 1-1 | - | - | - | - | - | 10-8 |
| Ryne Sandberg | - | - | 89-65 | - | - | - | - | - | - | - | - | 89-65 |
| Scott Sanderson | - | - | - | - | - | - | - | - | 15-8 | - | 3-11 | 15-8 |
| Calvin Schiraldi | - | - | - | - | - | - | - | - | - | - | 27-27 | - |
| Dwight Smith | - | - | - | - | - | 36-27 | - | 10-13 | - | 3-2 | - | 46-40 |
| Greg Smith | - | - | - | - | - | - | - | - | - | - | - | - |
| Phil Stephenson | - | - | - | - | - | 0-3 | - | - | - | - | - | 0-3 |
| Rick Sutcliffe | - | - | - | - | - | - | - | - | 19-15 | - | 1-0 | 19-15 |
| Gary Varsho | - | - | - | - | - | 4-5 | - | 1-1 | - | - | - | 5-6 |
| Jerome Walton | - | - | - | - | - | - | 63-51 | - | - | 63-51 | - | 63-51 |
| Mitch Webster | - | - | - | - | - | 21-17 | 5-4 | 6-6 | - | 0-2 | - | 32-27 |
| Curtis Wilkerson | - | - | 4-4 | 10-6 | - | 1-0 | - | - | - | 2-1 | - | 15-10 |
| Dean Wilkins | - | - | - | - | - | - | - | - | - | - | 4-7 | - |
| Mitch Williams | - | - | - | - | - | - | - | - | - | - | 52-24 | - |
| Steve Wilson | - | - | - | - | - | - | - | - | 5-3 | - | 22-23 | 5-3 |
| Rick Wrona | 15-12 | - | - | - | - | - | - | - | - | - | - | 15-12 |
| Marvell Wynne | - | - | - | - | - | 1-1 | 4-2 | 1-1 | - | 4-1 | - | 6-4 |

## Batting vs. Left and Right Handed Pitchers

| | | BA | Rank | SA | Rank | OBA | Rank | HR % | Rank | BB % | Rank | SO % | Rank |
|---|---|---|---|---|---|---|---|---|---|---|---|---|---|
| Damon Berryhill | vs. Lefties | .340 | 5 | .485 | 22 | .359 | 41 | 3.09 | 33 | 3.88 | 126 | 7.77 | 16 |
| | vs. Righties | .224 | 99 | .283 | 120 | .264 | 120 | 0.84 | 102 | 4.65 | 115 | 17.83 | 96 |
| Andre Dawson | vs. Lefties | .298 | 26 | .579 | 5 | .364 | 35 | 7.02 | 4 | 10.61 | 37 | 10.61 | 41 |
| | vs. Righties | .235 | 82 | .437 | 21 | .284 | 98 | 4.30 | 15 | 6.42 | 93 | 14.68 | 72 |
| Shawon Dunston | vs. Lefties | .338 | 7 | .489 | 18 | .382 | 18 | 1.44 | 79 | 7.19 | 89 | 12.42 | 60 |
| | vs. Righties | .253 | 60 | .367 | 71 | .294 | 88 | 2.11 | 61 | 5.29 | 109 | 18.66 | 102 |
| Mark Grace | vs. Lefties | .264 | 73 | .421 | 49 | .339 | 63 | 2.52 | 50 | 10.06 | 44 | 10.06 | 35 |
| | vs. Righties | .336 | 4 | .473 | 14 | .433 | 1 | 2.56 | 46 | 14.87 | 7 | 5.76 | 6 |
| Vance Law | vs. Lefties | .297 | 29 | .441 | 39 | .363 | 39 | 2.70 | 44 | 9.68 | 52 | 12.90 | 66 |
| | vs. Righties | .212 | 116 | .323 | 100 | .271 | 113 | 1.35 | 85 | 7.88 | 76 | 17.27 | 90 |
| Lloyd McClendon | vs. Lefties | .339 | 6 | .554 | 8 | .432 | 4 | 4.96 | 14 | 15.07 | 9 | 7.53 | 13 |
| | vs. Righties | .239 | 77 | .413 | 38 | .310 | 68 | 4.35 | 14 | 9.43 | 50 | 12.58 | 50 |
| Domingo Ramos | vs. Lefties | .373 | 2 | .441 | 40 | .448 | 3 | 1.69 | 70 | 11.76 | 27 | 11.76 | 48 |
| | vs. Righties | .208 | 117 | .283 | 119 | .275 | 105 | 0.00 | 124 | 6.62 | 91 | 11.03 | 36 |
| Luis Salazar | vs. Lefties | .296 | 31 | .488 | 19 | .338 | 65 | 4.00 | 20 | 5.15 | 113 | 10.29 | 39 |
| | vs. Righties | .274 | 36 | .368 | 70 | .301 | 79 | 1.99 | 67 | 3.76 | 123 | 20.19 | 108 |
| Ryne Sandberg | vs. Lefties | .314 | 19 | .517 | 10 | .414 | 8 | 4.07 | 19 | 14.78 | 10 | 7.39 | 12 |
| | vs. Righties | .281 | 31 | .488 | 11 | .331 | 48 | 5.30 | 8 | 6.18 | 97 | 14.93 | 75 |
| Dwight Smith | vs. Lefties | .241 | -- | .414 | -- | .324 | -- | 3.45 | -- | 11.43 | -- | 22.86 | -- |
| | vs. Righties | .331 | 5 | .500 | 9 | .388 | 13 | 2.55 | 48 | 7.80 | 77 | 12.43 | 49 |
| Jerome Walton | vs. Lefties | .320 | 15 | .438 | 44 | .374 | 22 | 1.56 | 74 | 7.19 | 88 | 17.27 | 103 |
| | vs. Righties | .282 | 30 | .366 | 73 | .321 | 61 | 0.86 | 101 | 4.52 | 116 | 14.10 | 65 |
| Mitch Webster | vs. Lefties | .311 | 20 | .443 | 38 | .364 | 35 | 1.64 | 73 | 7.46 | 83 | 13.43 | 73 |
| | vs. Righties | .242 | 73 | .341 | 88 | .322 | 59 | 0.95 | 97 | 10.37 | 39 | 19.09 | 104 |
| Marvell Wynne | vs. Lefties | .356 | -- | .511 | -- | .370 | -- | 2.22 | -- | 0.00 | -- | 18.37 | -- |
| | vs. Righties | .226 | 97 | .330 | 94 | .260 | 123 | 2.02 | 66 | 4.11 | 120 | 12.34 | 47 |
| Team Average | vs. Lefties | .282 | 1 | .424 | 1 | .346 | 1 | 2.57 | 4 | 9.01 | 5 | 13.23 | 2 |
| | vs. Righties | .252 | 2 | .372 | 4 | .309 | 9 | 2.12 | 7 | 7.14 | 12 | 15.73 | 8 |
| League Average | vs. Lefties | .251 | | .371 | | .320 | | 2.06 | | 8.85 | | 14.80 | |
| | vs. Righties | .244 | | .362 | | .309 | | 2.08 | | 8.27 | | 15.67 | |

## Batting with Runners on Base and Bases Empty

| | | BA | Rank | SA | Rank | OBA | Rank | HR % | Rank | BB % | Rank | SO % | Rank |
|---|---|---|---|---|---|---|---|---|---|---|---|---|---|
| Damon Berryhill | Runners On | .281 | 40 | .329 | 104 | .317 | 92 | 0.68 | 104 | 5.45 | 115 | 12.73 | 62 |
| | Bases Empty | .239 | 78 | .351 | 85 | .270 | 110 | 2.13 | 57 | 3.57 | 120 | 16.84 | 94 |
| Andre Dawson | Runners On | .239 | 99 | .438 | 32 | .325 | 82 | 4.48 | 18 | 11.81 | 44 | 12.66 | 61 |
| | Bases Empty | .265 | 53 | .512 | 7 | .288 | 94 | 5.58 | 8 | 3.15 | 124 | 14.41 | 67 |
| Shawon Dunston | Runners On | .280 | 41 | .417 | 45 | .342 | 60 | 1.90 | 65 | 8.64 | 82 | 16.87 | 97 |
| | Bases Empty | .277 | 31 | .392 | 51 | .301 | 79 | 1.92 | 65 | 3.35 | 122 | 16.73 | 92 |
| Mark Grace | Runners On | .349 | 5 | .500 | 13 | .451 | 3 | 2.94 | 32 | 16.15 | 13 | 5.15 | 4 |
| | Bases Empty | .283 | 25 | .419 | 32 | .361 | 16 | 2.21 | 55 | 10.82 | 22 | 8.85 | 18 |
| Vance Law | Runners On | .209 | 118 | .288 | 122 | .275 | 119 | 0.00 | 112 | 9.13 | 76 | 15.07 | 89 |
| | Bases Empty | .258 | 60 | .415 | 34 | .315 | 60 | 3.23 | 26 | 7.66 | 66 | 17.02 | 96 |
| Lloyd McClendon | Runners On | .260 | 74 | .394 | 58 | .344 | 59 | 2.88 | 34 | 12.40 | 37 | 7.75 | 11 |
| | Bases Empty | .303 | 10 | .535 | 4 | .386 | 8 | 5.81 | 6 | 11.93 | 11 | 11.93 | 43 |
| Domingo Ramos | Runners On | .300 | 26 | .425 | 39 | .364 | 36 | 1.25 | 86 | 8.51 | 84 | 9.57 | 30 |
| | Bases Empty | .232 | -- | .263 | -- | .309 | -- | 0.00 | -- | 8.18 | -- | 12.73 | -- |
| Luis Salazar | Runners On | .308 | 18 | .438 | 31 | .348 | 53 | 3.08 | 30 | 5.52 | 114 | 14.48 | 82 |
| | Bases Empty | .265 | 51 | .398 | 49 | .294 | 89 | 2.55 | 44 | 3.43 | 121 | 17.65 | 102 |
| Ryne Sandberg | Runners On | .262 | 69 | .422 | 42 | .350 | 50 | 3.28 | 25 | 11.39 | 49 | 11.74 | 53 |
| | Bases Empty | .309 | 8 | .547 | 2 | .361 | 17 | 6.08 | 4 | 6.91 | 75 | 13.30 | 55 |
| Dwight Smith | Runners On | .321 | 12 | .500 | 13 | .366 | 34 | 3.09 | 29 | 5.59 | 113 | 14.53 | 83 |
| | Bases Empty | .326 | 5 | .486 | 8 | .396 | 3 | 2.21 | 54 | 10.40 | 30 | 12.38 | 45 |
| Jerome Walton | Runners On | .314 | 15 | .409 | 50 | .340 | 66 | 0.00 | 112 | 4.61 | 124 | 14.47 | 80 |
| | Bases Empty | .284 | 23 | .376 | 66 | .333 | 43 | 1.48 | 82 | 5.51 | 96 | 15.15 | 75 |
| Mitch Webster | Runners On | .269 | 60 | .361 | 86 | .362 | 38 | 1.85 | 68 | 12.31 | 40 | 14.62 | 84 |
| | Bases Empty | .250 | 66 | .366 | 72 | .309 | 71 | 0.61 | 110 | 7.87 | 63 | 20.22 | 120 |
| Marvell Wynne | Runners On | .267 | 63 | .407 | 53 | .306 | 102 | 2.00 | 63 | 5.39 | 117 | 14.97 | 87 |
| | Bases Empty | .224 | 96 | .313 | 104 | .247 | 123 | 2.08 | 59 | 2.02 | 129 | 11.62 | 39 |
| Team Average | Runners On | .267 | 2 | .388 | 3 | .335 | 4 | 1.90 | 9 | 9.19 | 10 | 14.10 | 4 |
| | Bases Empty | .256 | 1 | .387 | 1 | .307 | 2 | 2.50 | 3 | 6.50 | 11 | 15.71 | 7 |
| League Average | Runners On | .256 | | .379 | | .330 | | 2.13 | | 9.82 | | 14.66 | |
| | Bases Empty | .240 | | .355 | | .299 | | 2.03 | | 7.43 | | 15.93 | |

## Overall Batting Compared to Late Inning Pressure Situations

| | | BA | Rank | SA | Rank | OBA | Rank | HR % | Rank | BB % | Rank | SO % | Rank | RDI % | Rank |
|---|---|---|---|---|---|---|---|---|---|---|---|---|---|---|---|
| Damon Berryhill | Overall | .257 | 61 | .341 | 95 | .291 | 103 | 1.50 | 82 | 4.43 | 121 | 14.96 | 81 | .298 | 30 |
| | Pressure | .245 | 57 | .347 | 66 | .269 | 96 | 2.04 | 55 | 3.64 | 121 | 14.55 | 63 | .214 | 68 |
| Andre Dawson | Overall | .252 | 70 | .476 | 12 | .307 | 87 | 5.05 | 8 | 7.63 | 81 | 13.51 | 64 | .308 | 26 |
| | Pressure | .184 | 112 | .367 | 48 | .259 | 103 | 4.08 | 18 | 9.26 | 62 | 11.11 | 28 | .250 | 52 |
| Shawon Dunston | Overall | .278 | 33 | .403 | 44 | .320 | 66 | 1.91 | 66 | 5.86 | 107 | 16.80 | 99 | .298 | 32 |
| | Pressure | .310 | 19 | .328 | 74 | .355 | 34 | 0.00 | 81 | 4.76 | 104 | 20.63 | 107 | .176 | 91 |
| Mark Grace | Overall | .314 | 7 | .457 | 18 | .405 | 5 | 2.55 | 41 | 13.42 | 11 | 7.05 | 6 | .348 | 5 |
| | Pressure | .375 | 1 | .625 | 1 | .481 | 1 | 6.25 | 3 | 16.88 | 8 | 6.49 | 10 | .250 | 52 |
| Vance Law | Overall | .235 | 100 | .355 | 83 | .296 | 101 | 1.72 | 72 | 8.37 | 65 | 16.08 | 94 | .234 | 90 |
| | Pressure | .167 | 116 | .188 | 127 | .196 | 129 | 0.00 | 81 | 3.92 | 117 | 15.69 | 69 | .158 | 102 |
| Lloyd McClendon | Overall | .286 | 24 | .479 | 10 | .368 | 19 | 4.63 | 11 | 12.13 | 23 | 10.16 | 27 | .325 | 14 |
| | Pressure | .195 | 103 | .195 | 124 | .286 | 83 | 0.00 | 81 | 12.24 | 28 | 12.24 | 35 | .273 | 48 |
| Domingo Ramos | Overall | .263 | 53 | .335 | 101 | .333 | 50 | 0.56 | 115 | 8.33 | 66 | 11.27 | 39 | .288 | 38 |
| | Pressure | .162 | 118 | .216 | 121 | .184 | 131 | 0.00 | 81 | 2.33 | 124 | 11.63 | 31 | .143 | -- |
| Luis Salazar | Overall | .282 | 29 | .414 | 36 | .316 | 77 | 2.76 | 33 | 4.30 | 123 | 16.33 | 96 | .209 | 115 |
| | Pressure | .333 | 10 | .456 | 20 | .333 | 47 | 1.75 | 63 | 0.00 | 131 | 14.52 | 61 | .263 | 50 |
| Ryne Sandberg | Overall | .290 | 18 | .497 | 6 | .356 | 28 | 4.95 | 9 | 8.78 | 59 | 12.65 | 56 | .231 | 95 |
| | Pressure | .274 | 40 | .381 | 39 | .315 | 69 | 2.38 | 42 | 5.56 | 97 | 20.00 | 104 | .200 | 74 |
| Dwight Smith | Overall | .324 | 4 | .493 | 7 | .382 | 12 | 2.62 | 38 | 8.14 | 73 | 13.39 | 63 | .324 | 15 |
| | Pressure | .208 | 91 | .354 | 60 | .220 | 125 | 2.08 | 54 | 2.00 | 127 | 16.00 | 70 | .250 | 52 |
| Jerome Walton | Overall | .293 | 15 | .385 | 58 | .335 | 49 | 1.05 | 100 | 5.24 | 115 | 14.95 | 80 | .351 | 4 |
| | Pressure | .222 | 81 | .222 | 118 | .328 | 60 | 0.00 | 81 | 12.31 | 26 | 18.46 | 93 | .385 | 16 |
| Mitch Webster | Overall | .257 | 62 | .364 | 73 | .331 | 51 | 1.10 | 97 | 9.74 | 48 | 17.86 | 104 | .205 | 117 |
| | Pressure | .195 | 103 | .341 | 67 | .327 | 62 | 2.44 | 40 | 15.38 | 12 | 23.08 | 113 | .200 | 74 |
| Marvell Wynne | Overall | .243 | 89 | .354 | 86 | .274 | 120 | 2.05 | 64 | 3.56 | 128 | 13.15 | 59 | .250 | 76 |
| | Pressure | .280 | 35 | .340 | 69 | .294 | 77 | 0.00 | 81 | 1.89 | 129 | 24.53 | 119 | .133 | 111 |
| Team Average | Overall | .261 | 1 | .387 | 2 | .319 | 3 | 2.25 | 6 | 7.69 | 12 | 15.00 | 5 | .271 | 1 |
| | Pressure | .248 | 5 | .344 | 5 | .303 | 9 | 1.64 | 7 | 7.22 | 11 | 16.03 | 8 | .227 | 10 |
| League Average | Overall | .246 | | .365 | | .312 | | 2.07 | | 8.47 | | 15.38 | | .253 | |
| | Pressure | .238 | | .337 | | .308 | | 1.73 | | 8.93 | | 16.78 | | .235 | |

## Additional Miscellaneous Batting Comparisons

| | Grass Surface | | Artificial Surface | | Home Games | | Road Games | | Runners in Scoring Position | | Runners in Scoring Pos and Two Outs | | Leading Off Inning | | Runners on 3B with less than 2 Outs | |
|---|---|---|---|---|---|---|---|---|---|---|---|---|---|---|---|---|
| | BA | Rank | BA | Rank | BA | Rank | BA | Rank | BA | Rank | BA | Rank | OBA | Rank | RDI % | Rank |
| Damon Berryhill | .259 | 58 | .254 | 65 | .311 | 14 | .215 | 103 | .326 | 9 | .240 | 52 | .290 | 72 | .619 | 47 |
| Doug Dascenzo | .165 | 128 | .167 | -- | .176 | -- | .154 | -- | .189 | -- | .048 | -- | .218 | 128 | .800 | 3 |
| Andre Dawson | .258 | 59 | .236 | 100 | .239 | 92 | .268 | 46 | .287 | 33 | .320 | 16 | .232 | 121 | .568 | 68 |
| Shawon Dunston | .274 | 43 | .287 | 27 | .307 | 16 | .252 | 65 | .292 | 30 | .258 | 37 | .310 | 57 | .680 | 24 |
| Joe Girardi | .238 | 77 | .268 | -- | .269 | -- | .228 | -- | .278 | -- | .273 | 31 | .267 | -- | .375 | 136 |
| Mark Grace | .333 | 4 | .262 | 49 | .337 | 5 | .290 | 22 | .311 | 17 | .323 | 14 | .430 | 3 | .765 | 7 |
| Vance Law | .218 | 103 | .267 | 42 | .235 | 94 | .235 | 84 | .197 | 119 | .204 | 86 | .307 | 61 | .552 | 79 |
| Lloyd McClendon | .277 | 42 | .305 | 9 | .301 | 24 | .270 | 43 | .279 | 41 | .156 | 119 | .413 | 7 | .682 | 23 |
| Domingo Ramos | .214 | 105 | .377 | -- | .230 | 105 | .304 | -- | .354 | 6 | .348 | 8 | .348 | -- | .750 | 10 |
| Luis Salazar | .282 | 35 | .282 | 35 | .259 | 66 | .309 | 6 | .276 | 44 | .158 | 117 | .257 | 106 | .750 | 10 |
| Ryne Sandberg | .290 | 25 | .291 | 21 | .297 | 28 | .284 | 31 | .223 | 100 | .208 | 84 | .300 | 66 | .469 | 119 |
| Dwight Smith | .354 | 2 | .265 | 46 | .363 | 2 | .290 | 20 | .297 | 28 | .394 | 5 | .400 | 11 | .571 | 64 |
| Jerome Walton | .302 | 13 | .273 | 39 | .303 | 20 | .283 | 33 | .348 | 7 | .339 | 9 | .377 | 19 | .611 | 52 |
| Mitch Webster | .244 | 74 | .299 | -- | .250 | 79 | .264 | 52 | .210 | 108 | .219 | 72 | .373 | 22 | .286 | 142 |
| Curtis Wilkerson | .267 | 47 | .175 | -- | .284 | -- | .194 | -- | .121 | -- | .154 | -- | .333 | -- | .500 | 98 |
| Marvell Wynne | .265 | 50 | .196 | 126 | .253 | 74 | .234 | 86 | .274 | 49 | .244 | 48 | .278 | 90 | .500 | 98 |
| Team Average | .261 | 2 | .260 | 1 | .272 | 1 | .250 | 3 | .261 | 2 | .252 | 2 | .319 | 2 | .565 | 4 |
| League Average | .244 | | .248 | | .251 | | .242 | | .249 | | .222 | | .302 | | .546 | |

## Pitching vs. Left and Right Handed Batters

| | | BA | Rank | SA | Rank | OBA | Rank | HR % | Rank | BB % | Rank | SO % | Rank |
|---|---|---|---|---|---|---|---|---|---|---|---|---|---|
| Paul Assenmacher | vs. Lefties | .247 | 61 | .271 | 16 | .304 | 41 | 0.00 | 1 | 7.29 | 33 | 31.25 | 2 |
| | vs. Righties | .259 | 87 | .366 | 68 | .326 | 88 | 1.46 | 24 | 8.94 | 88 | 20.85 | 35 |
| Mike Bielecki | vs. Lefties | .252 | 68 | .398 | 86 | .338 | 80 | 2.38 | 88 | 11.53 | 89 | 14.68 | 49 |
| | vs. Righties | .220 | 36 | .322 | 29 | .270 | 30 | 1.63 | 33 | 6.42 | 45 | 19.01 | 44 |
| Paul Kilgus | vs. Lefties | .252 | 67 | .411 | 93 | .344 | 88 | 2.80 | 94 | 9.76 | 69 | 8.94 | 104 |
| | vs. Righties | .290 | 106 | .407 | 90 | .342 | 94 | 1.27 | 17 | 7.13 | 60 | 9.63 | 112 |
| Les Lancaster | vs. Lefties | .203 | 18 | .248 | 7 | .250 | 8 | 0.00 | 1 | 6.16 | 15 | 21.23 | 14 |
| | vs. Righties | .250 | 77 | .326 | 35 | .279 | 44 | 1.52 | 27 | 4.23 | 14 | 17.61 | 52 |
| Greg Maddux | vs. Lefties | .279 | 92 | .366 | 66 | .356 | 95 | 0.81 | 26 | 10.02 | 73 | 11.63 | 79 |
| | vs. Righties | .213 | 29 | .314 | 25 | .262 | 24 | 2.28 | 63 | 5.87 | 32 | 15.80 | 70 |
| Jeff Pico | vs. Lefties | .313 | 112 | .491 | 112 | .381 | 111 | 3.07 | 104 | 9.89 | 71 | 6.04 | 114 |
| | vs. Righties | .249 | 72 | .332 | 41 | .293 | 56 | 1.55 | 30 | 6.13 | 40 | 12.74 | 88 |
| Scott Sanderson | vs. Lefties | .293 | 102 | .422 | 97 | .335 | 75 | 2.35 | 85 | 5.72 | 12 | 12.26 | 74 |
| | vs. Righties | .244 | 65 | .400 | 83 | .277 | 41 | 3.56 | 108 | 4.10 | 11 | 16.80 | 61 |
| Rick Sutcliffe | vs. Lefties | .245 | 55 | .362 | 63 | .305 | 42 | 2.19 | 83 | 8.20 | 50 | 15.69 | 45 |
| | vs. Righties | .233 | 53 | .342 | 49 | .283 | 46 | 2.06 | 53 | 6.10 | 37 | 17.24 | 56 |
| Mitch Williams | vs. Lefties | .254 | -- | .296 | -- | .345 | -- | 0.00 | -- | 11.49 | -- | 29.89 | -- |
| | vs. Righties | .233 | 54 | .357 | 58 | .366 | 106 | 2.64 | 76 | 15.11 | 115 | 14.75 | 75 |
| Steve Wilson | vs. Lefties | .264 | 79 | .396 | 83 | .330 | 66 | 1.10 | 37 | 8.91 | 57 | 15.84 | 42 |
| | vs. Righties | .254 | 83 | .392 | 80 | .317 | 82 | 2.16 | 57 | 8.37 | 79 | 18.63 | 47 |
| Team Average | vs. Lefties | .260 | 10 | .375 | 8 | .333 | 10 | 1.76 | 5 | 9.66 | 9 | 14.06 | 6 |
| | vs. Righties | .241 | 6 | .355 | 5 | .302 | 6 | 2.09 | 4 | 7.72 | 7 | 15.63 | 8 |
| League Average | vs. Lefties | .252 | | .366 | | .325 | | 1.79 | | 9.48 | | 13.93 | |
| | vs. Righties | .242 | | .365 | | .303 | | 2.29 | | 7.70 | | 16.46 | |

## Pitching with Runners on Base and Bases Empty

| | | BA | Rank | SA | Rank | OBA | Rank | HR % | Rank | BB % | Rank | SO % | Rank |
|---|---|---|---|---|---|---|---|---|---|---|---|---|---|
| Paul Assenmacher | Runners On | .239 | 48 | .310 | 22 | .331 | 67 | 0.70 | 8 | 11.43 | 90 | 24.57 | 5 |
| | Bases Empty | .270 | 99 | .365 | 76 | .308 | 71 | 1.35 | 34 | 5.13 | 24 | 23.08 | 12 |
| Mike Bielecki | Runners On | .226 | 29 | .326 | 28 | .318 | 53 | 1.33 | 32 | 11.83 | 97 | 17.46 | 36 |
| | Bases Empty | .244 | 63 | .385 | 90 | .300 | 60 | 2.46 | 84 | 7.40 | 66 | 16.13 | 47 |
| Paul Kilgus | Runners On | .312 | 112 | .478 | 110 | .373 | 102 | 1.98 | 56 | 8.65 | 42 | 9.34 | 104 |
| | Bases Empty | .261 | 90 | .353 | 63 | .317 | 89 | 1.23 | 30 | 6.80 | 58 | 9.63 | 106 |
| Les Lancaster | Runners On | .208 | 12 | .216 | 1 | .243 | 1 | 0.00 | 1 | 5.04 | 2 | 19.42 | 23 |
| | Bases Empty | .243 | 60 | .350 | 57 | .284 | 39 | 1.43 | 39 | 5.37 | 27 | 19.46 | 34 |
| Greg Maddux | Runners On | .248 | 62 | .357 | 49 | .313 | 50 | 1.55 | 36 | 8.22 | 36 | 12.00 | 85 |
| | Bases Empty | .250 | 77 | .332 | 37 | .317 | 87 | 1.39 | 37 | 8.15 | 77 | 14.67 | 65 |
| Jeff Pico | Runners On | .311 | 109 | .488 | 112 | .378 | 106 | 3.05 | 99 | 10.00 | 65 | 7.89 | 111 |
| | Bases Empty | .250 | 76 | .333 | 38 | .294 | 52 | 1.56 | 44 | 5.88 | 37 | 11.27 | 100 |
| Scott Sanderson | Runners On | .301 | 101 | .461 | 104 | .350 | 82 | 2.74 | 90 | 7.23 | 17 | 13.65 | 66 |
| | Bases Empty | .256 | 87 | .383 | 88 | .287 | 43 | 2.88 | 102 | 3.59 | 8 | 14.36 | 70 |
| Rick Sutcliffe | Runners On | .243 | 55 | .353 | 44 | .311 | 46 | 1.94 | 51 | 9.21 | 53 | 17.07 | 39 |
| | Bases Empty | .238 | 52 | .355 | 66 | .286 | 42 | 2.25 | 73 | 6.15 | 44 | 15.82 | 51 |
| Mitch Williams | Runners On | .220 | 22 | .315 | 24 | .358 | 90 | 1.79 | 46 | 16.36 | 115 | 21.50 | 15 |
| | Bases Empty | .262 | 91 | .377 | 83 | .364 | 113 | 2.31 | 75 | 11.26 | 106 | 13.91 | 73 |
| Steve Wilson | Runners On | .236 | 43 | .343 | 39 | .302 | 35 | 0.71 | 9 | 9.15 | 52 | 13.41 | 72 |
| | Bases Empty | .273 | 102 | .432 | 111 | .335 | 103 | 2.73 | 98 | 8.00 | 75 | 21.50 | 18 |
| Team Average | Runners On | .254 | 5 | .373 | 4 | .332 | 8 | 1.89 | 4 | 10.34 | 11 | 14.56 | 6 |
| | Bases Empty | .247 | 11 | .358 | 8 | .305 | 10 | 1.97 | 6 | 7.26 | 5 | 15.16 | 8 |
| League Average | Runners On | .256 | | .379 | | .330 | | 2.13 | | 9.82 | | 14.66 | |
| | Bases Empty | .240 | | .355 | | .299 | | 2.03 | | 7.43 | | 15.93 | |

## Overall Pitching Compared to Late Inning Pressure Situations

| | | BA | Rank | SA | Rank | OBA | Rank | HR % | Rank | BB % | Rank | SO % | Rank |
|---|---|---|---|---|---|---|---|---|---|---|---|---|---|
| Paul Assenmacher | Overall | .255 | 77 | .338 | 40 | .320 | 73 | 1.03 | 13 | 8.46 | 61 | 23.87 | 8 |
| | Pressure | .323 | 108 | .432 | 97 | .378 | 103 | 1.29 | 46 | 7.87 | 50 | 18.54 | 36 |
| Mike Bielecki | Overall | .237 | 48 | .362 | 69 | .307 | 57 | 2.03 | 62 | 9.18 | 76 | 16.67 | 46 |
| | Pressure | .245 | 65 | .388 | 90 | .327 | 77 | 4.08 | 105 | 10.91 | 83 | 23.64 | 12 |
| Paul Kilgus | Overall | .283 | 105 | .408 | 96 | .342 | 101 | 1.55 | 33 | 7.63 | 45 | 9.50 | 110 |
| | Pressure | .348 | 109 | .370 | 81 | .423 | 111 | 0.00 | 1 | 10.91 | 83 | 10.91 | 95 |
| Les Lancaster | Overall | .226 | 34 | .287 | 4 | .264 | 4 | 0.75 | 7 | 5.21 | 9 | 19.44 | 27 |
| | Pressure | .247 | 67 | .327 | 54 | .283 | 39 | 0.67 | 28 | 4.91 | 20 | 20.25 | 25 |
| Greg Maddux | Overall | .249 | 66 | .343 | 45 | .315 | 66 | 1.46 | 26 | 8.18 | 53 | 13.47 | 73 |
| | Pressure | .186 | 16 | .200 | 3 | .260 | 22 | 0.00 | 1 | 8.64 | 58 | 16.05 | 54 |
| Jeff Pico | Overall | .278 | 102 | .404 | 93 | .334 | 89 | 2.25 | 77 | 7.87 | 49 | 9.64 | 109 |
| | Pressure | .203 | 28 | .304 | 41 | .276 | 34 | 1.45 | 53 | 9.21 | 63 | 11.84 | 82 |
| Scott Sanderson | Overall | .274 | 98 | .413 | 103 | .312 | 62 | 2.83 | 104 | 5.07 | 5 | 14.08 | 67 |
| | Pressure | .288 | 95 | .423 | 96 | .383 | 104 | 1.92 | 69 | 12.90 | 99 | 14.52 | 73 |
| Rick Sutcliffe | Overall | .240 | 54 | .354 | 60 | .296 | 42 | 2.14 | 66 | 7.36 | 39 | 16.31 | 52 |
| | Pressure | .322 | 107 | .458 | 103 | .339 | 85 | 3.39 | 103 | 2.99 | 9 | 20.90 | 21 |
| Mitch Williams | Overall | .238 | 51 | .342 | 44 | .361 | 110 | 2.01 | 60 | 14.25 | 115 | 18.36 | 34 |
| | Pressure | .204 | 31 | .311 | 47 | .320 | 68 | 2.43 | 87 | 13.65 | 104 | 19.28 | 34 |
| Steve Wilson | Overall | .257 | 81 | .393 | 86 | .320 | 74 | 1.86 | 50 | 8.52 | 65 | 17.86 | 37 |
| | Pressure | .297 | 99 | .419 | 95 | .386 | 105 | 1.35 | 50 | 13.33 | 101 | 15.56 | 55 |
| Team Average | Overall | .250 | 9 | .364 | 5 | .317 | 10 | 1.93 | 4 | 8.63 | 8 | 14.90 | 8 |
| | Pressure | .239 | 10 | .347 | 10 | .326 | 11 | 2.03 | 10 | 11.11 | 11 | 17.27 | 4 |
| League Average | Overall | .246 | | .365 | | .312 | | 2.07 | | 8.47 | | 15.38 | |
| | Pressure | .235 | | .336 | | .309 | | 1.77 | | 9.31 | | 16.92 | |

## Additional Miscellaneous Pitching Comparisons

| | Grass Surface | | Artificial Surface | | Home Games | | Road Games | | Runners in Scoring Position | | Runners in Scoring Pos and Two Outs | | Leading Off Inning | |
|---|---|---|---|---|---|---|---|---|---|---|---|---|---|---|
| | BA | Rank | BA | Rank | BA | Rank | BA | Rank | BA | Rank | BA | Rank | OBA | Rank |
| Paul Assenmacher | .240 | 57 | .301 | -- | .248 | 65 | .264 | 80 | .253 | 69 | .184 | 33 | .357 | 105 |
| Mike Bielecki | .225 | 36 | .266 | 78 | .218 | 32 | .257 | 73 | .236 | 51 | .225 | 67 | .303 | 63 |
| Paul Kilgus | .270 | 91 | .347 | 114 | .266 | 87 | .307 | 107 | .304 | 101 | .259 | 88 | .314 | 80 |
| Les Lancaster | .242 | 60 | .187 | -- | .283 | 101 | .158 | 1 | .162 | 4 | .111 | 5 | .286 | 45 |
| Greg Maddux | .244 | 64 | .263 | 76 | .243 | 57 | .255 | 68 | .223 | 36 | .194 | 44 | .335 | 95 |
| Pat Perry | .200 | 8 | .152 | -- | .229 | -- | .132 | -- | .235 | -- | .200 | -- | .276 | -- |
| Jeff Pico | .261 | 85 | .320 | 111 | .249 | 66 | .310 | 108 | .270 | 82 | .304 | 104 | .265 | 27 |
| Scott Sanderson | .293 | 104 | .237 | 46 | .284 | 102 | .264 | 81 | .274 | 84 | .167 | 26 | .327 | 91 |
| Rick Sutcliffe | .255 | 76 | .214 | 17 | .260 | 80 | .224 | 28 | .222 | 34 | .203 | 51 | .296 | 54 |
| Mitch Williams | .245 | 65 | .221 | 27 | .280 | 98 | .200 | 13 | .211 | 28 | .200 | 48 | .290 | 51 |
| Steve Wilson | .258 | 81 | .255 | 70 | .263 | 84 | .252 | 61 | .238 | 52 | .244 | 79 | .299 | 57 |
| Team Average | .250 | 9 | .250 | 7 | .252 | 10 | .247 | 5 | .239 | 4 | .214 | 6 | .310 | 10 |
| League Average | .244 | | .248 | | .242 | | .251 | | .249 | | .222 | | .302 | |

# CINCINNATI REDS

- **"Leadoff Batters by Committee".**
- **A first for Eric Davis.**

Question: Which National League team had the most trouble filling the leadoff position in its batting order last season? Answer: the Cincinnati Reds.

Question: Which National League team got the most production out of the leadoff position in its batting order last season? Answer: the Cincinnati Reds.

Although the Giants could lay legitimate claim to being the team whose *pitching staff* was most decimated by injuries in 1989, the Reds saw that dreaded plague affect their entire team. Talk about turmoil; on top of the continued commotion tangential to the Pete Rose investigation, 12 different players went onto the disabled list, two of them twice. And for the most part, the guys who were disabled were the stars rather than the extras.

Consider the Reds' lineup that Rose handed to John Kibler on opening day against the Dodgers: Barry Larkin, ss; Chris Sabo, 3b; Eric Davis, cf; Kal Daniels, lf; Todd Benzinger, 1b; Paul O'Neill, rf; Jeff Reed, c; Ron Oester, 2b; Danny Jackson, p. Seven of those nine players spent time on the disabled list during the 1989 season; only Benzinger and Reed did not (and Reed may not even have been the opening-day starter had Bo Diaz, who had been the regular catcher in 1988, not gone on the disabled list during spring training). Other additions to the Dee-El were starting pitchers Ron Robinson and Jose Rijo, ace relief pitcher Rob Dibble, and outfielder Herm Winningham.

The ebb and flow of personnel was most evident in the number-one spot in the batting order. Eight different players started at least 10 games in the leadoff spot, the highest total by any team in the majors since 1981. Two other players also performed briefly as leadoff starters. Here are the records of all starters in the number-one position for the Reds in 1989, followed by the records of substitutes in that spot:

| | Starts | BA | SA | OBA | AB | R | H | HR | RBI | BB | SO | SB |
|---|---|---|---|---|---|---|---|---|---|---|---|---|
| Sabo | 35 | .297 | .486 | .355 | 138 | 22 | 41 | 5 | 16 | 12 | 12 | 4 |
| Winningham | 34 | .274 | .393 | .342 | 135 | 23 | 37 | 1 | 6 | 14 | 24 | 8 |
| Duncan | 23 | .237 | .392 | .288 | 97 | 18 | 23 | 3 | 9 | 5 | 23 | 4 |
| Harris | 16 | .231 | .246 | .254 | 65 | 4 | 15 | 0 | 1 | 2 | 8 | 2 |
| Larkin | 15 | .279 | .459 | .318 | 61 | 9 | 17 | 2 | 6 | 2 | 6 | 0 |
| Collins | 13 | .300 | .360 | .352 | 50 | 6 | 15 | 0 | 5 | 4 | 5 | 1 |
| Daniels | 12 | .333 | .538 | .519 | 39 | 15 | 13 | 1 | 3 | 15 | 9 | 4 |
| Quinones | 11 | .225 | .575 | .311 | 40 | 7 | 9 | 4 | 7 | 5 | 8 | 0 |
| Roomes | 2 | .125 | .125 | .125 | 8 | 0 | 1 | 0 | 0 | 0 | 1 | 0 |
| Richardson | 1 | .250 | .250 | .250 | 4 | 0 | 1 | 0 | 0 | 1 | 1 | 1 |
| substitutes | 0 | .167 | .300 | .257 | 30 | 2 | 5 | 1 | 6 | 4 | 6 | 0 |
| Totals | 162 | .265 | .412 | .333 | 667 | 106 | 177 | 17 | 59 | 64 | 103 | 24 |

But as we mentioned earlier, the Reds' number-one hitters came through (even though we did not once hear the phrase "Leadoff Batters by Committee") They scored 106 runs and drove in 59. That's a total of 82.5 runs produced (one half-run is credited for each run scored and for each RBI), the highest total from the leadoff spot by any National League team last season:

| | Runs | RBI | RP |
|---|---|---|---|
| Cincinnati | 106 | 59 | 82.5 |
| Atlanta | 106 | 56 | 81.0 |
| Pittsburgh | 107 | 54 | 80.5 |
| Chicago | 94 | 65 | 79.5 |
| San Diego | 107 | 50 | 78.5 |
| New York | 94 | 60 | 77.0 |
| San Francisco | 104 | 43 | 73.5 |
| Houston | 89 | 57 | 73.0 |
| St. Louis | 108 | 37 | 72.5 |
| Montreal | 87 | 57 | 72.0 |
| Philadelphia | 94 | 37 | 65.5 |
| Los Angeles | 83 | 42 | 62.5 |

Of course, you can lead a horse to water, but you cannot make him drink. In baseball terms, that means that while a leadoff batter can get on base and can even get himself into scoring position, he still needs to be driven in. And the Reds had just the man to do that in Eric Davis.

Davis has hit more than 25 home runs in each of his four full seasons in the major leagues. That's a feat impressive enough by itself; only Joe Carter, Glenn Davis, and Darryl Strawberry have matched it over the past four years, and only good friend Darryl (134) has more home runs over than span than Eric (124). But then consider that Davis has had fewer than 475 at–bats in each of those four seasons and the scope of the performance is magnified. No other player in baseball history has ever had *three* consecutive seasons of less than 475 at–bats and more than 25 home runs; Davis has four.

Of course, some players who draw a lot of walks may not reach 475 at–bats in a season even while playing regularly. (Something similar happened to Ted Williams often enough that the qualifier for the batting championship was changed from 400 at–bats to 477 total plate appearances.) In Davis's case, the low at-bat totals are partly traceable to walks, but more so to the amount of time each season that he spends not playing. He's baseball's version of Johnny Carson: makes the big bucks, but oh, that vacation time! In his four years as a "fulltime" player, Davis has started 109, 127, 130, and 123 games. That means that he has *not* started in 159 Reds games over the past four years, virtually an entire season. A few years ago, the Reds even went out and traded for Herm Winningham to play the role of Jay Leno.

All of which makes Davis's statistics all the more remarkable. Despite the limited playing time, he has emerged as a true power-hitting superstar. It's still surprising how some fans, especially older ones, are shy about accepting a home-run hitter with a batting average below .300 as a superstar. But the most legitimate comparisons that can be made are of a player with others in his same era. To trace the evolution of power hitters, we gathered the records of all players who hit 25 or more home runs in a single season, and sorted those records into groups. We then took the average of those numbers to determine the profile of the typical 25–home–run hitter. This chart summarizes the results, with the designation "Early" representing pre–1920 players:

| | Players | AB | R | H | 2B | 3B | HR | RBI | BB | SO | SB | BA | SA |
|---|---|---|---|---|---|---|---|---|---|---|---|---|---|
| Early | 4 | 476 | 100 | 144 | 20 | 14 | 27 | — | 48 | — | — | .303 | .570 |
| 1920s | 43 | 544 | 121 | 186 | 35 | 9 | 36 | 129 | 85 | 59 | 8 | .342 | .636 |
| 1930s | 96 | 560 | 116 | 183 | 34 | 9 | 34 | 128 | 81 | 61 | 6 | .327 | .600 |
| 1940s | 71 | 544 | 102 | 162 | 29 | 6 | 32 | 111 | 86 | 59 | 4 | .298 | .549 |
| 1950s | 184 | 535 | 92 | 157 | 25 | 5 | 32 | 102 | 70 | 70 | 5 | .293 | .537 |
| 1960s | 218 | 546 | 89 | 155 | 24 | 4 | 32 | 98 | 66 | 91 | 6 | .284 | .521 |
| 1970s | 226 | 540 | 86 | 151 | 25 | 3 | 31 | 97 | 69 | 99 | 9 | .280 | .510 |
| 1980s | 249 | 552 | 87 | 153 | 27 | 3 | 31 | 97 | 63 | 103 | 10 | .277 | .504 |

Ever since the 1920s, the composite batting and slugging averages for 25–home–run hitters have been headed downward. Let's compare these figures with Davis's last four seasons:

| | AB | R | H | 2B | 3B | HR | RBI | BB | SO | SB | BA | SA |
|---|---|---|---|---|---|---|---|---|---|---|---|---|
| 1986 | 415 | 97 | 115 | 15 | 3 | 27 | 71 | 68 | 100 | 80 | .277 | .523 |
| 1987 | 474 | 120 | 139 | 23 | 4 | 37 | 100 | 84 | 134 | 50 | .293 | .593 |
| 1988 | 472 | 81 | 129 | 18 | 3 | 26 | 93 | 65 | 124 | 35 | .273 | .489 |
| 1989 | 462 | 74 | 130 | 14 | 2 | 34 | 101 | 68 | 116 | 21 | .281 | .541 |
| Average | 456 | 93 | 128 | 18 | 3 | 31 | 91 | 71 | 119 | 47 | .281 | .537 |

Davis's four-year averages (.281 batting, .537 slugging) are not untypical of sluggers in recent decades. His averages in runs scored, RBIs, and walks compare favorably with contemporary sluggers, especially when it is considered that he is averaging about 90 fewer at–bats in a season that the others. And his RBI total underscores the fact that he has become one of baseball's best clutch hitters. He has a .316 batting average with runners in scoring position over the past two years, and with runners in scoring position *and two outs,* his two-year average is .357. Only Will Clark, Pedro Guerrero, and Milt Thompson have hit higher in those situations.

One-season statistical yardsticks—such as 1000 yards rushing, 20 wins and a .300 batting average—are always subject to eventual erosion as circumstances change. It has happened with 1000 yards rushing as the NFL has expanded its schedule; it has happened with 20 wins as relief pitchers cut deeper and deeper into the middle innings; and it is happening with the .300 batting average. Last year only five qualifying batters hit .300 in the senior circuit (as opposed to the Senior League); the previous year there were only four, the fewest since 1909.

But unless our perceptions change with the conditions, we run the risk of misassessing current players and teams. At least the Reds knew what they had: They signed Davis to a contract in excess of three million dollars per year in January.

Among the Reds who spent a good part of the 1989 season watching other people play his position was 1988 National League Rookie of the Year Chris Sabo. Sabo hyperextended his left knee on June 9, and although he stayed in the lineup for more than two weeks, he eventually went onto the disabled list and didn't play again until September.

On a team with Schottzie as a mascot, it's not surprising that the Reds responded to the absence of "Spuds" like a bunch of dogs. Their record in the games that Sabo started (42–34), projected over a full season, would have earned them a fifth-straight second-place finish in the National League West. But their record when other guys started at third base (33–53), similarly projected, would have left them with the worst record in the National League.

In past editions (1988 *Analyst,* pp. 140–141; 1987, pp. 121–122), we have written about the effect on a team of the absence of a star player. We determined that a missing superstar might cost his team an average of five wins in a season. Don't misunderstand what we're about to say; we still stick by the five-games estimate. But it's interesting that of all the players in the majors last season who started semi regularly (60 to 100 games) either because of injury or platooning, the Reds reacted to Sabo's absence to a greater degree than any other team/player combination in the majors. Here are the figures:

| | In Lineup | | Not In Lineup | | Diff. |
|---|---|---|---|---|---|
| Chris Sabo, Reds | 42–34 | .553 | 33–53 | .384 | .169 |
| Charlie Hayes, Phillies | 38–41 | .481 | 29–54 | .349 | .132 |
| Carlton Fisk, White Sox | 47–51 | .480 | 22–41 | .349 | .131 |
| Barry Larkin, Reds | 43–39 | .524 | 32–48 | .400 | .124 |
| Jeff Kunkel, Rangers | 47–35 | .573 | 36–44 | .450 | .123 |

These differences are much larger than the average of five games produced in our earlier study simply because these are not averages, but rather the largest differences, and because they are taken over the relatively small sample of a single season. (Our earlier study used data amassed over a five-year period, producing greater reliability.) And in the Reds' case, Sabo and Larkin were missing from the lineup concurrently for the greater part of three months. Their combined absence certainly made the Reds a weaker team.

But, hey, if you're Sabo, you can look in the mirror and try to convince yourself that you're the most valuable guy in baseball. OK, it's based on a small sample with other mitigating circumstances, but at least he's got a better case than the players with the largest differences in the other direction:

| | In Lineup | | Not In Lineup | | Diff. |
|---|---|---|---|---|---|
| Eddie Williams, White Sox | 20–41 | .328 | 49–51 | .490 | –.162 |
| Tim Laudner, Twins | 30–42 | .417 | 50–40 | .556 | –.139 |
| Candy Maldonado, Giants | 42–41 | .506 | 50–29 | .633 | –.127 |
| Wally Backman, Twins | 34–45 | .430 | 46–37 | .554 | –.124 |
| Marty Barrett, Red Sox | 37–44 | .457 | 46–35 | .568 | –.111 |

Now there are some guys with some explaining to do.

## WON-LOST RECORD BY STARTING POSITION

| CINCINNATI 75-87 | C | 1B | 2B | 3B | SS | LF | CF | RF | P | Leadoff | Relief | Starts |
|---|---|---|---|---|---|---|---|---|---|---|---|---|
| Jack Armstrong | - | - | - | - | - | - | - | - | 3-5 | - | 0-1 | 3-5 |
| Skeeter Barnes | - | - | - | - | - | - | - | - | - | - | - | - |
| Todd Benzinger | - | 74-84 | - | - | - | - | - | - | - | - | - | 74-84 |
| Tim Birtsas | - | - | - | - | - | - | - | - | 0-1 | - | 8-33 | 0-1 |
| Marty Brown | - | - | - | 2-5 | - | - | - | - | - | - | - | 2-5 |
| Tom Browning | - | - | - | - | - | - | - | - | 20-17 | - | - | 20-17 |
| Norm Charlton | - | - | - | - | - | - | - | - | - | - | 28-41 | - |
| Dave Collins | - | - | - | - | - | 5-8 | - | - | - | 5-8 | - | 5-8 |
| Kal Daniels | - | - | - | - | - | 18-20 | - | - | - | 7-5 | - | 18-20 |
| Eric Davis | - | - | - | - | - | 2-2 | 50-66 | 3-0 | - | - | - | 55-68 |
| Bo Diaz | 17-18 | - | - | - | - | - | - | - | - | - | - | 17-18 |
| Rob Dibble | - | - | - | - | - | - | - | - | - | - | 46-28 | - |
| Mariano Duncan | - | - | 0-2 | - | 18-23 | - | - | - | - | 11-12 | - | 18-25 |
| John Franco | - | - | - | - | - | - | - | - | - | - | 44-16 | - |
| Ken Griffey | - | 1-3 | - | - | - | 29-23 | - | - | - | - | - | 30-26 |
| Mike Griffin | - | - | - | - | - | - | - | - | - | - | 0-3 | - |
| Lenny Harris | - | - | 12-14 | 5-7 | 0-4 | - | - | - | - | 5-11 | - | 17-25 |
| Danny Jackson | - | - | - | - | - | - | - | - | 7-13 | - | - | 7-13 |
| Barry Larkin | - | - | - | - | 43-39 | - | - | - | - | 9-6 | - | 43-39 |
| Tim Leary | - | - | - | - | - | - | - | - | 4-10 | - | - | 4-10 |
| Scotti Madison | - | - | - | 9-12 | - | - | - | - | - | - | - | 9-12 |
| Rick Mahler | - | - | - | - | - | - | - | - | 14-17 | - | 1-8 | 14-17 |
| Terry McGriff | 2-1 | - | - | - | - | - | - | - | - | - | - | 2-1 |
| Paul O'Neill | - | - | - | - | - | - | 3-0 | 47-62 | - | - | - | 50-62 |
| Ron Oester | - | - | 39-46 | - | 1-1 | - | - | - | - | - | - | 40-47 |
| Joe Oliver | 15-22 | - | - | - | - | - | - | - | - | - | - | 15-22 |
| Luis Quinones | - | - | 19-21 | 17-27 | - | - | - | - | - | 2-9 | - | 36-48 |
| Jeff Reed | 41-46 | - | - | - | - | - | - | - | - | - | - | 41-46 |
| Jeff Richardson | - | - | - | 0-2 | 13-20 | - | - | - | - | 0-1 | - | 13-22 |
| Jose Rijo | - | - | - | - | - | - | - | - | 12-7 | - | - | 12-7 |
| Ron Robinson | - | - | - | - | - | - | - | - | 9-6 | - | - | 9-6 |
| Rosario Rodriguez | - | - | - | - | - | - | - | - | - | - | 3-4 | - |
| Mike Roesler | - | - | - | - | - | - | - | - | - | - | 2-15 | - |
| Rolando Roomes | - | - | - | - | - | 9-13 | 8-8 | 17-19 | - | 0-2 | - | 34-40 |
| Chris Sabo | - | - | - | 42-34 | - | - | - | - | - | 19-16 | - | 42-34 |
| Scott Scudder | - | - | - | - | - | - | - | - | 6-11 | - | 1-5 | 6-11 |
| Bob Sebra | - | - | - | - | - | - | - | - | - | - | 3-12 | - |
| Van Snider | - | - | - | - | - | - | - | 0-1 | - | - | - | 0-1 |
| Kent Tekulve | - | - | - | - | - | - | - | - | - | - | 7-30 | - |
| Manny Trillo | - | - | 5-4 | - | - | - | - | - | - | - | - | 5-4 |
| Herm Winningham | - | - | - | - | - | 5-9 | 14-13 | 7-3 | - | 17-17 | - | 26-25 |
| Joel Youngblood | - | - | - | - | - | 7-12 | - | 1-2 | - | - | - | 8-14 |

## Batting vs. Left and Right Handed Pitchers

| | | BA | Rank | SA | Rank | OBA | Rank | HR % | Rank | BB % | Rank | SO % | Rank |
|---|---|---|---|---|---|---|---|---|---|---|---|---|---|
| Todd Benzinger | vs. Lefties | .242 | 90 | .377 | 67 | .283 | 113 | 3.03 | 34 | 5.95 | 108 | 11.90 | 49 |
| | vs. Righties | .247 | 68 | .383 | 57 | .299 | 81 | 2.52 | 50 | 6.68 | 89 | 20.74 | 112 |
| Eric Davis | vs. Lefties | .250 | 82 | .481 | 23 | .369 | 31 | 6.41 | 6 | 16.04 | 6 | 20.32 | 120 |
| | vs. Righties | .297 | 19 | .572 | 4 | .366 | 21 | 7.84 | 1 | 10.70 | 36 | 21.97 | 118 |
| Bo Diaz | vs. Lefties | .215 | 108 | .241 | 122 | .262 | 119 | 0.00 | 112 | 5.95 | 108 | 3.57 | 2 |
| | vs. Righties | .189 | -- | .302 | -- | .204 | -- | 1.89 | -- | 1.85 | -- | 7.41 | -- |
| Mariano Duncan | vs. Lefties | .283 | 45 | .465 | 30 | .324 | 75 | 2.02 | 61 | 2.86 | 131 | 16.19 | 93 |
| | vs. Righties | .226 | 96 | .289 | 118 | .259 | 124 | 0.63 | 113 | 2.98 | 127 | 20.24 | 109 |
| Ken Griffey | vs. Lefties | .313 | -- | .500 | -- | .450 | -- | 0.00 | -- | 15.00 | -- | 20.00 | -- |
| | vs. Righties | .259 | 54 | .418 | 35 | .337 | 42 | 3.64 | 25 | 10.57 | 38 | 15.45 | 83 |
| Barry Larkin | vs. Lefties | .372 | 3 | .488 | 20 | .421 | 7 | 1.65 | 72 | 8.21 | 73 | 2.24 | 1 |
| | vs. Righties | .324 | 7 | .422 | 33 | .347 | 35 | 0.98 | 96 | 4.04 | 122 | 8.97 | 22 |
| Paul O'Neill | vs. Lefties | .178 | 123 | .303 | 106 | .246 | 124 | 2.63 | 46 | 8.38 | 66 | 21.56 | 127 |
| | vs. Righties | .330 | 6 | .525 | 7 | .399 | 8 | 3.99 | 20 | 10.22 | 42 | 8.95 | 21 |
| Ron Oester | vs. Lefties | .175 | 124 | .175 | 131 | .288 | 109 | 0.00 | 112 | 13.70 | 18 | 17.81 | 108 |
| | vs. Righties | .264 | 46 | .339 | 91 | .326 | 54 | 0.41 | 117 | 8.33 | 63 | 12.88 | 55 |
| Joe Oliver | vs. Lefties | .346 | 4 | .449 | 35 | .369 | 30 | 1.28 | 82 | 4.71 | 116 | 20.00 | 119 |
| | vs. Righties | .192 | -- | .315 | -- | .224 | -- | 2.74 | -- | 2.63 | -- | 14.47 | -- |
| Luis Quinones | vs. Lefties | .239 | 94 | .479 | 24 | .297 | 99 | 6.34 | 7 | 6.33 | 102 | 12.03 | 53 |
| | vs. Righties | .247 | 66 | .364 | 74 | .302 | 77 | 1.52 | 77 | 6.82 | 87 | 12.27 | 46 |
| Jeff Reed | vs. Lefties | .171 | -- | .220 | -- | .300 | -- | 0.00 | -- | 11.54 | -- | 17.31 | -- |
| | vs. Righties | .232 | 87 | .305 | 115 | .307 | 73 | 1.22 | 88 | 10.07 | 44 | 13.31 | 60 |
| Rolando Roomes | vs. Lefties | .294 | 33 | .425 | 47 | .314 | 87 | 1.25 | 87 | 2.96 | 130 | 24.26 | 131 |
| | vs. Righties | .232 | 86 | .413 | 39 | .279 | 104 | 3.23 | 30 | 4.85 | 113 | 35.76 | 132 |
| Chris Sabo | vs. Lefties | .290 | 37 | .390 | 59 | .360 | 40 | 0.00 | 112 | 9.82 | 49 | 9.82 | 31 |
| | vs. Righties | .245 | 70 | .397 | 51 | .294 | 87 | 2.94 | 38 | 6.25 | 95 | 9.82 | 27 |
| Herm Winningham | vs. Lefties | .216 | -- | .351 | -- | .256 | -- | 2.70 | -- | 4.88 | -- | 21.95 | -- |
| | vs. Righties | .257 | 56 | .355 | 79 | .326 | 52 | 0.93 | 98 | 9.28 | 51 | 17.30 | 91 |
| Joel Youngblood | vs. Lefties | .247 | 83 | .376 | 69 | .337 | 66 | 2.35 | 53 | 10.20 | 42 | 13.27 | 69 |
| | vs. Righties | .121 | -- | .212 | -- | .194 | -- | 3.03 | -- | 8.33 | -- | 22.22 | -- |
| Team Average | vs. Lefties | .241 | 10 | .364 | 7 | .309 | 10 | 2.32 | 5 | 8.51 | 10 | 16.46 | 11 |
| | vs. Righties | .250 | 4 | .374 | 3 | .310 | 6 | 2.32 | 5 | 7.73 | 10 | 16.82 | 10 |
| League Average | vs. Lefties | .251 | | .371 | | .320 | | 2.06 | | 8.85 | | 14.80 | |
| | vs. Righties | .244 | | .362 | | .309 | | 2.08 | | 8.27 | | 15.67 | |

## Batting with Runners on Base and Bases Empty

| | | BA | Rank | SA | Rank | OBA | Rank | HR % | Rank | BB % | Rank | SO % | Rank |
|---|---|---|---|---|---|---|---|---|---|---|---|---|---|
| Todd Benzinger | Runners On | .208 | 119 | .341 | 96 | .272 | 121 | 2.65 | 44 | 7.95 | 89 | 20.20 | 118 |
| | Bases Empty | .272 | 38 | .409 | 39 | .310 | 70 | 2.75 | 35 | 5.21 | 100 | 15.36 | 80 |
| Eric Davis | Runners On | .304 | 22 | .652 | 1 | .399 | 16 | 10.14 | 1 | 15.12 | 17 | 17.83 | 106 |
| | Bases Empty | .263 | 55 | .451 | 17 | .338 | 40 | 5.10 | 12 | 10.21 | 35 | 24.65 | 127 |
| Mariano Duncan | Runners On | .314 | 14 | .453 | 27 | .344 | 58 | 1.16 | 90 | 3.26 | 128 | 18.48 | 111 |
| | Bases Empty | .215 | 108 | .308 | 106 | .254 | 120 | 1.16 | 94 | 2.76 | 125 | 18.78 | 112 |
| Ken Griffey | Runners On | .220 | 114 | .380 | 70 | .345 | 57 | 4.00 | 20 | 15.13 | 16 | 14.29 | 78 |
| | Bases Empty | .294 | 15 | .456 | 16 | .347 | 30 | 2.94 | 29 | 7.48 | 70 | 17.01 | 95 |
| Barry Larkin | Runners On | .359 | 2 | .470 | 19 | .394 | 20 | 0.85 | 100 | 8.63 | 83 | 8.63 | 21 |
| | Bases Empty | .332 | 2 | .433 | 22 | .362 | 15 | 1.44 | 83 | 3.67 | 118 | 5.05 | 2 |
| Paul O'Neill | Runners On | .323 | 11 | .559 | 7 | .409 | 10 | 4.62 | 15 | 13.04 | 30 | 12.17 | 58 |
| | Bases Empty | .236 | 81 | .352 | 84 | .288 | 95 | 2.58 | 42 | 6.40 | 81 | 14.40 | 66 |
| Ron Oester | Runners On | .304 | 23 | .336 | 98 | .404 | 12 | 0.00 | 112 | 14.38 | 18 | 15.07 | 89 |
| | Bases Empty | .206 | 119 | .283 | 116 | .251 | 122 | 0.56 | 113 | 5.76 | 92 | 13.09 | 53 |
| Luis Quinones | Runners On | .281 | 39 | .400 | 56 | .327 | 81 | 1.48 | 77 | 5.81 | 109 | 8.39 | 19 |
| | Bases Empty | .220 | 104 | .420 | 31 | .283 | 100 | 4.88 | 14 | 7.17 | 73 | 14.80 | 71 |
| Jeff Reed | Runners On | .227 | 109 | .319 | 107 | .314 | 94 | 1.68 | 72 | 11.89 | 43 | 13.29 | 66 |
| | Bases Empty | .220 | 102 | .274 | 120 | .299 | 82 | 0.60 | 111 | 9.09 | 45 | 14.44 | 68 |
| Rolando Roomes | Runners On | .261 | 70 | .485 | 17 | .297 | 108 | 2.99 | 31 | 4.83 | 123 | 30.34 | 132 |
| | Bases Empty | .265 | 52 | .370 | 71 | .296 | 84 | 1.66 | 72 | 3.17 | 123 | 29.63 | 132 |
| Chris Sabo | Runners On | .267 | 63 | .381 | 69 | .352 | 47 | 0.95 | 97 | 11.90 | 42 | 8.73 | 22 |
| | Bases Empty | .256 | 62 | .402 | 46 | .295 | 86 | 2.51 | 46 | 4.76 | 108 | 10.48 | 26 |
| Herm Winningham | Runners On | .256 | 79 | .308 | 115 | .318 | 90 | 1.28 | 82 | 7.95 | 88 | 19.32 | 114 |
| | Bases Empty | .249 | 71 | .376 | 67 | .316 | 58 | 1.16 | 95 | 8.95 | 46 | 17.37 | 100 |
| Team Average | Runners On | .254 | 7 | .394 | 2 | .331 | 7 | 2.71 | 2 | 10.25 | 3 | 16.23 | 11 |
| | Bases Empty | .242 | 6 | .354 | 6 | .294 | 10 | 2.06 | 5 | 6.36 | 12 | 17.03 | 9 |
| League Average | Runners On | .256 | | .379 | | .330 | | 2.13 | | 9.82 | | 14.66 | |
| | Bases Empty | .240 | | .355 | | .299 | | 2.03 | | 7.43 | | 15.93 | |

## Overall Batting Compared to Late Inning Pressure Situations

| | | BA | Rank | SA | Rank | OBA | Rank | HR % | Rank | BB % | Rank | SO % | Rank | RDI % | Rank |
|---|---|---|---|---|---|---|---|---|---|---|---|---|---|---|---|
| Todd Benzinger | Overall | .245 | 83 | .381 | 60 | .293 | 102 | 2.71 | 34 | 6.41 | 102 | 17.49 | 102 | .254 | 73 |
| | Pressure | .159 | 121 | .250 | 107 | .257 | 104 | 2.27 | 48 | 11.54 | 43 | 13.46 | 48 | .214 | 68 |
| Eric Davis | Overall | .281 | 30 | .541 | 4 | .367 | 21 | 7.36 | 2 | 12.55 | 18 | 21.40 | 123 | .345 | 7 |
| | Pressure | .293 | 27 | .585 | 4 | .381 | 19 | 8.54 | 1 | 13.40 | 22 | 17.53 | 85 | .346 | 20 |
| Mariano Duncan | Overall | .248 | 76 | .357 | 81 | .284 | 107 | 1.16 | 93 | 2.93 | 131 | 18.68 | 115 | .231 | 96 |
| | Pressure | .283 | 33 | .377 | 40 | .333 | 47 | 1.89 | 58 | 3.45 | 122 | 24.14 | 118 | .313 | 29 |
| Ken Griffey | Overall | .263 | 52 | .424 | 30 | .346 | 39 | 3.39 | 26 | 10.90 | 36 | 15.79 | 90 | .247 | 79 |
| | Pressure | .289 | 29 | .467 | 17 | .333 | 47 | 2.22 | 50 | 6.25 | 89 | 12.50 | 37 | .313 | 29 |
| Barry Larkin | Overall | .342 | 1 | .446 | 22 | .375 | 15 | 1.23 | 89 | 5.60 | 110 | 6.44 | 4 | .341 | 8 |
| | Pressure | .327 | 12 | .462 | 18 | .390 | 15 | 1.92 | 57 | 8.33 | 74 | 1.67 | 1 | .286 | 43 |
| Paul O'Neill | Overall | .276 | 36 | .446 | 21 | .346 | 40 | 3.50 | 21 | 9.58 | 50 | 13.33 | 62 | .323 | 17 |
| | Pressure | .320 | 15 | .387 | 35 | .378 | 23 | 0.00 | 81 | 8.54 | 69 | 13.41 | 47 | .286 | 43 |
| Ron Oester | Overall | .246 | 80 | .305 | 117 | .318 | 69 | 0.33 | 123 | 9.50 | 52 | 13.95 | 69 | .194 | 122 |
| | Pressure | .241 | 61 | .276 | 99 | .241 | 113 | 0.00 | 81 | 0.00 | 131 | 18.97 | 97 | .375 | -- |
| Luis Quinones | Overall | .244 | 85 | .412 | 37 | .300 | 98 | 3.53 | 20 | 6.61 | 99 | 12.17 | 44 | .213 | 109 |
| | Pressure | .196 | 102 | .304 | 86 | .237 | 114 | 1.79 | 62 | 4.69 | 106 | 9.38 | 20 | .267 | 49 |
| Jeff Reed | Overall | .223 | 111 | .293 | 120 | .306 | 92 | 1.05 | 102 | 10.30 | 44 | 13.94 | 68 | .207 | 116 |
| | Pressure | .150 | 122 | .175 | 128 | .286 | 83 | 0.00 | 81 | 15.69 | 11 | 9.80 | 23 | .182 | 86 |
| Rolando Roomes | Overall | .263 | 51 | .419 | 33 | .296 | 99 | 2.22 | 56 | 3.89 | 126 | 29.94 | 132 | .216 | 105 |
| | Pressure | .318 | 16 | .545 | 6 | .354 | 35 | 2.27 | 48 | 4.17 | 111 | 29.17 | 128 | .400 | 13 |
| Chris Sabo | Overall | .260 | 55 | .395 | 49 | .316 | 75 | 1.97 | 65 | 7.44 | 86 | 9.82 | 23 | .284 | 43 |
| | Pressure | .139 | 127 | .278 | 98 | .256 | 107 | 2.78 | 28 | 11.11 | 44 | 13.33 | 45 | .250 | 52 |
| Herm Winningham | Overall | .251 | 72 | .355 | 85 | .316 | 74 | 1.20 | 91 | 8.63 | 62 | 17.99 | 108 | .161 | 130 |
| | Pressure | .326 | 13 | .442 | 22 | .370 | 27 | 2.33 | 46 | 6.25 | 89 | 16.67 | 74 | .333 | 22 |
| Joel Youngblood | Overall | .212 | -- | .331 | -- | .299 | -- | 2.54 | -- | 9.70 | -- | 15.67 | -- | .250 | -- |
| | Pressure | .094 | -- | .219 | -- | .194 | -- | 3.13 | -- | 11.11 | -- | 19.44 | -- | .300 | 37 |
| Team Average | Overall | .247 | 6 | .370 | 4 | .309 | 9 | 2.32 | 4 | 8.01 | 10 | 16.69 | 11 | .242 | 11 |
| | Pressure | .235 | 8 | .352 | 4 | .307 | 7 | 2.07 | 4 | 9.08 | 6 | 15.34 | 2 | .268 | 1 |
| League Average | Overall | .246 | | .365 | | .312 | | 2.07 | | 8.47 | | 15.38 | | .253 | |
| | Pressure | .238 | | .337 | | .308 | | 1.73 | | 8.93 | | 16.78 | | .235 | |

## Additional Miscellaneous Batting Comparisons

| | Grass Surface BA | Rank | Artificial Surface BA | Rank | Home Games BA | Rank | Road Games BA | Rank | Runners in Scoring Position BA | Rank | Runners in Scoring Pos and Two Outs BA | Rank | Leading Off Inning OBA | Rank | Runners on 3B with less than 2 Outs RDI % | Rank |
|---|---|---|---|---|---|---|---|---|---|---|---|---|---|---|---|---|
| Todd Benzinger | .245 | 70 | .245 | 83 | .278 | 42 | .214 | 106 | .199 | 118 | .133 | 123 | .313 | 56 | .615 | 49 |
| Dave Collins | .313 | -- | .203 | -- | .184 | -- | .281 | -- | .148 | -- | .143 | -- | .429 | -- | .250 | 143 |
| Eric Davis | .258 | 61 | .294 | 18 | .289 | 33 | .275 | 41 | .318 | 12 | .390 | 6 | .313 | 55 | .622 | 46 |
| Bo Diaz | .227 | -- | .193 | 127 | .194 | -- | .215 | -- | .154 | -- | .188 | -- | .212 | -- | .500 | -- |
| Mariano Duncan | .231 | 87 | .262 | 49 | .231 | 102 | .266 | 50 | .300 | 23 | .250 | 42 | .283 | 83 | .462 | 120 |
| Ken Griffey | .282 | -- | .255 | 64 | .267 | 54 | .259 | 57 | .269 | 55 | .182 | 105 | .367 | 26 | .545 | 82 |
| Barry Larkin | .317 | 10 | .353 | 2 | .353 | 4 | .331 | 5 | .299 | 25 | .333 | 10 | .344 | 32 | .762 | 8 |
| Paul O'Neill | .211 | 111 | .299 | 13 | .316 | 12 | .228 | 91 | .312 | 16 | .321 | 15 | .289 | 74 | .591 | 57 |
| Ron Oester | .259 | -- | .241 | 92 | .270 | 51 | .223 | 96 | .310 | 18 | .304 | 19 | .284 | 81 | .357 | 140 |
| Joe Oliver | .341 | -- | .243 | 87 | .278 | -- | .264 | -- | .300 | -- | .227 | -- | .219 | -- | .667 | 25 |
| Luis Quinones | .231 | 87 | .250 | 74 | .241 | 89 | .247 | 72 | .297 | 27 | .233 | 57 | .258 | 105 | .571 | 64 |
| Jeff Reed | .159 | 130 | .251 | 73 | .246 | 86 | .204 | 115 | .239 | 86 | .219 | 72 | .246 | 113 | .643 | 37 |
| Jeff Richardson | .209 | -- | .146 | 132 | .118 | -- | .228 | -- | .167 | -- | .125 | -- | .185 | -- | .625 | 40 |
| Rolando Roomes | .277 | 41 | .255 | 63 | .237 | 93 | .288 | 25 | .230 | 92 | .256 | 39 | .268 | 98 | .400 | 130 |
| Chris Sabo | .278 | 40 | .252 | 70 | .234 | 96 | .288 | 26 | .302 | 22 | .179 | 106 | .361 | 27 | .667 | 25 |
| Herm Winningham | .259 | -- | .249 | 79 | .248 | 82 | .254 | 62 | .191 | 120 | .214 | 77 | .326 | 49 | .250 | -- |
| Joel Youngblood | .143 | -- | .250 | 74 | .250 | -- | .172 | -- | .200 | -- | .267 | -- | .143 | -- | .600 | -- |
| Team Average | .241 | 7 | .249 | 5 | .253 | 5 | .241 | 7 | .247 | 7 | .221 | 6 | .293 | 9 | .546 | 7 |
| League Average | .244 | | .248 | | .251 | | .242 | | .249 | | .222 | | .302 | | .546 | |

## Pitching vs. Left and Right Handed Batters

| | | BA | Rank | SA | Rank | OBA | Rank | HR % | Rank | BB % | Rank | SO % | Rank |
|---|---|---|---|---|---|---|---|---|---|---|---|---|---|
| Jack Armstrong | vs. Lefties | .283 | 94 | .402 | 88 | .368 | 106 | 1.09 | 36 | 12.04 | 94 | 9.28 | 99 |
| | vs. Righties | .197 | -- | .394 | -- | .278 | -- | 5.63 | -- | 10.13 | -- | 16.46 | -- |
| Tim Birtsas | vs. Lefties | .198 | 15 | .346 | 52 | .233 | 4 | 2.47 | 91 | 4.49 | 4 | 20.22 | 17 |
| | vs. Rightics | .289 | 103 | .411 | 93 | .370 | 112 | 1.67 | 37 | 10.90 | 104 | 18.48 | 48 |
| Tom Browning | vs. Lefties | .265 | 82 | .424 | 99 | .327 | 63 | 4.55 | 114 | 8.78 | 56 | 16.22 | 38 |
| | vs. Righties | .253 | 81 | .405 | 87 | .298 | 61 | 3.07 | 95 | 5.78 | 29 | 10.65 | 104 |
| Norm Charlton | vs. Lefties | .148 | 3 | .173 | 2 | .258 | 13 | 0.00 | 1 | 11.11 | 83 | 27.27 | 4 |
| | vs. Righties | .212 | 28 | .324 | 33 | .292 | 55 | 1.93 | 49 | 9.86 | 98 | 24.15 | 18 |
| Rob Dibble | vs. Lefties | .186 | 9 | .256 | 11 | .286 | 23 | 0.58 | 18 | 12.50 | 101 | 36.00 | 1 |
| | vs. Righties | .167 | 4 | .244 | 4 | .236 | 10 | 1.67 | 37 | 6.97 | 57 | 34.33 | 1 |
| John Franco | vs. Lefties | .200 | -- | .240 | -- | .245 | -- | 0.00 | -- | 5.45 | -- | 18.18 | -- |
| | vs. Righties | .269 | 94 | .325 | 34 | .351 | 101 | 1.20 | 16 | 11.38 | 107 | 17.24 | 56 |
| Danny Jackson | vs. Lefties | .269 | -- | .373 | -- | .333 | -- | 1.49 | -- | 9.09 | -- | 27.27 | -- |
| | vs. Righties | .271 | 95 | .398 | 82 | .354 | 102 | 2.34 | 67 | 11.31 | 106 | 11.09 | 100 |
| Tim Leary | vs. Lefties | .300 | 105 | .453 | 106 | .360 | 100 | 2.96 | 97 | 8.39 | 53 | 11.70 | 78 |
| | vs. Righties | .218 | 34 | .308 | 23 | .278 | 43 | 1.32 | 18 | 7.13 | 59 | 16.63 | 62 |
| Rick Mahler | vs. Lefties | .305 | 109 | .451 | 105 | .344 | 86 | 1.64 | 62 | 4.74 | 5 | 9.11 | 102 |
| | vs. Righties | .251 | 78 | .350 | 52 | .307 | 71 | 1.89 | 45 | 6.30 | 41 | 13.08 | 85 |
| Jose Rijo | vs. Lefties | .273 | 89 | .384 | 78 | .372 | 107 | 2.07 | 77 | 13.99 | 107 | 16.43 | 35 |
| | vs. Righties | .215 | 30 | .270 | 9 | .256 | 15 | 0.61 | 7 | 4.49 | 18 | 21.91 | 29 |
| Ron Robinson | vs. Lefties | .274 | 90 | .383 | 76 | .339 | 81 | 1.71 | 68 | 8.29 | 52 | 6.22 | 112 |
| | vs. Righties | .225 | 47 | .387 | 78 | .288 | 52 | 3.52 | 107 | 7.50 | 68 | 15.00 | 72 |
| Scott Scudder | vs. Lefties | .223 | 34 | .340 | 50 | .322 | 58 | 2.03 | 75 | 12.61 | 102 | 13.04 | 67 |
| | vs. Righties | .257 | 86 | .470 | 114 | .369 | 110 | 5.46 | 116 | 14.48 | 114 | 16.29 | 65 |
| Bob Sebra | vs. Lefties | .345 | 113 | .555 | 116 | .452 | 116 | 3.64 | 112 | 12.41 | 100 | 10.22 | 95 |
| | vs. Righties | .245 | -- | .418 | -- | .317 | -- | 3.64 | -- | 8.73 | -- | 16.67 | -- |
| Kent Tekulve | vs. Lefties | .362 | 116 | .543 | 115 | .442 | 115 | 3.81 | 113 | 12.40 | 98 | 5.79 | 115 |
| | vs. Righties | .178 | -- | .248 | -- | .234 | -- | 0.99 | -- | 7.02 | -- | 21.05 | -- |
| Team Average | vs. Lefties | .268 | 12 | .391 | 12 | .341 | 12 | 1.96 | 9 | 9.60 | 7 | 14.85 | 5 |
| | vs. Righties | .244 | 7 | .367 | 7 | .312 | 10 | 2.44 | 7 | 8.49 | 11 | 16.17 | 7 |
| League Average | vs. Lefties | .252 | | .366 | | .325 | | 1.79 | | 9.48 | | 13.93 | |
| | vs. Righties | .242 | | .365 | | .303 | | 2.29 | | 7.70 | | 16.46 | |

## Pitching with Runners on Base and Bases Empty

| | | BA | Rank | SA | Rank | OBA | Rank | HR % | Rank | BB % | Rank | SO % | Rank |
|---|---|---|---|---|---|---|---|---|---|---|---|---|---|
| Tim Birtsas | Runners On | .277 | 87 | .437 | 95 | .343 | 74 | 1.68 | 43 | 10.49 | 72 | 16.08 | 43 |
| | Bases Empty | .246 | 72 | .352 | 61 | .318 | 91 | 2.11 | 64 | 7.64 | 70 | 21.66 | 17 |
| Tom Browning | Runners On | .262 | 79 | .404 | 81 | .310 | 45 | 2.33 | 73 | 6.94 | 15 | 11.31 | 89 |
| | Bases Empty | .251 | 80 | .410 | 104 | .298 | 56 | 3.82 | 114 | 5.76 | 35 | 11.53 | 97 |
| Norm Charlton | Runners On | .217 | 18 | .312 | 23 | .286 | 17 | 2.17 | 68 | 7.98 | 31 | 20.86 | 17 |
| | Bases Empty | .183 | 6 | .272 | 8 | .283 | 36 | 0.99 | 21 | 11.74 | 110 | 27.83 | 5 |
| Rob Dibble | Runners On | .167 | 1 | .230 | 3 | .262 | 6 | 1.15 | 23 | 11.22 | 85 | 31.71 | 1 |
| | Bases Empty | .185 | 7 | .270 | 6 | .260 | 14 | 1.12 | 25 | 8.16 | 78 | 38.78 | 1 |
| John Franco | Runners On | .275 | 86 | .373 | 65 | .361 | 93 | 2.11 | 66 | 12.14 | 102 | 19.65 | 19 |
| | Bases Empty | .242 | 59 | .255 | 2 | .308 | 75 | 0.00 | 1 | 8.72 | 85 | 15.12 | 60 |
| Danny Jackson | Runners On | .312 | 111 | .477 | 109 | .403 | 115 | 3.52 | 104 | 13.22 | 105 | 13.22 | 76 |
| | Bases Empty | .238 | 50 | .329 | 34 | .307 | 70 | 1.19 | 28 | 9.03 | 88 | 13.72 | 74 |
| Tim Leary | Runners On | .244 | 58 | .383 | 73 | .324 | 62 | 1.85 | 48 | 10.50 | 75 | 14.70 | 54 |
| | Bases Empty | .273 | 101 | .383 | 87 | .318 | 90 | 2.38 | 81 | 5.68 | 32 | 13.59 | 77 |
| Rick Mahler | Runners On | .290 | 93 | .420 | 90 | .352 | 86 | 2.32 | 72 | 7.48 | 22 | 10.47 | 95 |
| | Bases Empty | .276 | 107 | .399 | 98 | .310 | 77 | 1.36 | 35 | 3.90 | 11 | 11.13 | 101 |
| Jose Rijo | Runners On | .227 | 30 | .262 | 5 | .305 | 39 | 0.58 | 5 | 9.85 | 63 | 21.67 | 14 |
| | Bases Empty | .266 | 97 | .395 | 95 | .345 | 108 | 2.15 | 68 | 10.73 | 103 | 16.09 | 48 |
| Ron Robinson | Runners On | .252 | 65 | .309 | 21 | .326 | 64 | 0.81 | 14 | 9.79 | 61 | 11.19 | 92 |
| | Bases Empty | .253 | 86 | .433 | 112 | .310 | 76 | 3.61 | 112 | 6.67 | 54 | 9.52 | 107 |
| Scott Scudder | Runners On | .252 | 64 | .454 | 101 | .358 | 88 | 4.91 | 114 | 13.50 | 109 | 13.50 | 70 |
| | Bases Empty | .230 | 38 | .364 | 75 | .335 | 102 | 2.76 | 99 | 13.55 | 112 | 15.54 | 55 |
| Bob Sebra | Runners On | .255 | 68 | .353 | 45 | .352 | 87 | 1.96 | 53 | 11.02 | 82 | 15.75 | 47 |
| | Bases Empty | .331 | 116 | .602 | 116 | .419 | 116 | 5.08 | 116 | 10.29 | 101 | 11.03 | 103 |
| Kent Tekulve | Runners On | .333 | 114 | .465 | 105 | .398 | 113 | 3.03 | 98 | 10.26 | 69 | 13.68 | 65 |
| | Bases Empty | .215 | -- | .336 | -- | .288 | -- | 1.87 | -- | 9.32 | -- | 12.71 | -- |
| Team Average | Runners On | .265 | 9 | .391 | 10 | .339 | 10 | 2.35 | 8 | 9.97 | 8 | 15.48 | 4 |
| | Bases Empty | .245 | 10 | .366 | 10 | .310 | 11 | 2.18 | 9 | 8.10 | 11 | 15.80 | 7 |
| League Average | Runners On | .256 | | .379 | | .330 | | 2.13 | | 9.82 | | 14.66 | |
| | Bases Empty | .240 | | .355 | | .299 | | 2.03 | | 7.43 | | 15.93 | |

## Overall Pitching Compared to Late Inning Pressure Situations

| | | BA | Rank | SA | Rank | OBA | Rank | HR % | Rank | BB % | Rank | SO % | Rank |
|---|---|---|---|---|---|---|---|---|---|---|---|---|---|
| Tim Birtsas | Overall | .261 | 85 | .391 | 84 | .330 | 85 | 1.92 | 53 | 9.00 | 72 | 19.00 | 29 |
| | Pressure | .333 | -- | .417 | -- | .485 | -- | 0.00 | -- | 20.59 | -- | 11.76 | -- |
| Tom Browning | Overall | .255 | 76 | .408 | 98 | .302 | 50 | 3.28 | 111 | 6.21 | 20 | 11.45 | 98 |
| | Pressure | .154 | 3 | .200 | 3 | .225 | 4 | 0.00 | 1 | 6.94 | 36 | 9.72 | 102 |
| Norm Charlton | Overall | .197 | 5 | .288 | 5 | .284 | 29 | 1.47 | 27 | 10.18 | 97 | 24.94 | 4 |
| | Pressure | .184 | 14 | .253 | 11 | .273 | 33 | 0.53 | 25 | 10.31 | 78 | 24.66 | 7 |
| Rob Dibble | Overall | .176 | 1 | .250 | 2 | .261 | 3 | 1.14 | 19 | 9.73 | 85 | 35.16 | 1 |
| | Pressure | .184 | 13 | .261 | 14 | .286 | 43 | 1.28 | 45 | 11.76 | 92 | 33.82 | 1 |
| John Franco | Overall | .258 | 82 | .311 | 16 | .334 | 90 | 1.00 | 12 | 10.43 | 100 | 17.39 | 41 |
| | Pressure | .240 | 62 | .284 | 30 | .320 | 69 | 0.89 | 35 | 10.65 | 80 | 17.87 | 42 |
| Danny Jackson | Overall | .271 | 94 | .395 | 89 | .351 | 106 | 2.22 | 74 | 10.98 | 104 | 13.49 | 72 |
| | Pressure | .174 | -- | .348 | -- | .269 | -- | 4.35 | -- | 11.54 | -- | 11.54 | -- |
| Tim Leary | Overall | .261 | 86 | .383 | 77 | .321 | 76 | 2.16 | 68 | 7.78 | 48 | 14.07 | 68 |
| | Pressure | .293 | 97 | .415 | 94 | .359 | 96 | 1.22 | 43 | 8.42 | 55 | 24.21 | 11 |
| Rick Mahler | Overall | .282 | 103 | .407 | 95 | .328 | 81 | 1.75 | 42 | 5.43 | 13 | 10.85 | 102 |
| | Pressure | .265 | 83 | .449 | 99 | .321 | 70 | 2.04 | 73 | 7.02 | 39 | 17.54 | 44 |
| Jose Rijo | Overall | .249 | 65 | .338 | 41 | .328 | 80 | 1.48 | 28 | 10.34 | 98 | 18.53 | 33 |
| | Pressure | .375 | -- | .458 | -- | .464 | -- | 0.00 | -- | 14.29 | -- | 25.00 | -- |
| Ron Robinson | Overall | .252 | 72 | .385 | 80 | .316 | 69 | 2.52 | 93 | 7.93 | 50 | 10.20 | 106 |
| | Pressure | .333 | -- | .333 | -- | .333 | -- | 0.00 | -- | 0.00 | -- | 11.11 | -- |
| Scott Scudder | Overall | .239 | 53 | .403 | 91 | .345 | 102 | 3.68 | 114 | 13.53 | 114 | 14.63 | 65 |
| | Pressure | .222 | -- | .370 | -- | .276 | -- | 3.70 | -- | 6.90 | -- | 13.79 | -- |
| Bob Sebra | Overall | .295 | 112 | .486 | 116 | .388 | 116 | 3.64 | 113 | 10.65 | 101 | 13.31 | 75 |
| | Pressure | .167 | -- | .278 | -- | .250 | -- | 0.00 | -- | 4.76 | -- | 19.05 | -- |
| Kent Tekulve | Overall | .272 | -- | .398 | -- | .342 | -- | 2.43 | -- | 9.79 | -- | 13.19 | -- |
| | Pressure | .352 | 110 | .389 | 91 | .407 | 108 | 0.00 | 1 | 8.20 | 53 | 14.75 | 69 |
| Team Average | Overall | .253 | 11 | .376 | 11 | .323 | 11 | 2.26 | 10 | 8.92 | 11 | 15.66 | 5 |
| | Pressure | .226 | 3 | .312 | 2 | .313 | 8 | 1.22 | 1 | 10.65 | 10 | 21.82 | 1 |
| League Average | Overall | .246 | | .365 | | .312 | | 2.07 | | 8.47 | | 15.38 | |
| | Pressure | .235 | | .336 | | .309 | | 1.77 | | 9.31 | | 16.92 | |

## Additional Miscellaneous Pitching Comparisons

| | Grass Surface BA | Rank | Artificial Surface BA | Rank | Home Games BA | Rank | Road Games BA | Rank | Runners in Scoring Position BA | Rank | Runners in Scoring Pos and Two Outs BA | Rank | Leading Off Inning OBA | Rank |
|---|---|---|---|---|---|---|---|---|---|---|---|---|---|---|
| Jack Armstrong | .250 | -- | .245 | 56 | .255 | -- | .232 | -- | .294 | -- | .167 | -- | .304 | -- |
| Tim Birtsas | .226 | -- | .271 | 87 | .274 | 95 | .232 | -- | .250 | 62 | .235 | 73 | .297 | 56 |
| Tom Browning | .233 | 46 | .264 | 77 | .281 | 100 | .226 | 30 | .257 | 75 | .195 | 47 | .313 | 78 |
| Norm Charlton | .192 | 5 | .200 | 10 | .165 | 2 | .227 | 32 | .200 | 20 | .143 | 14 | .364 | 107 |
| Rob Dibble | .211 | 25 | .157 | 1 | .151 | 1 | .197 | 11 | .164 | 5 | .113 | 6 | .238 | 12 |
| John Franco | .217 | 31 | .275 | 91 | .257 | 77 | .259 | 76 | .284 | 88 | .282 | 94 | .253 | 18 |
| Danny Jackson | .268 | 90 | .272 | 89 | .264 | 86 | .278 | 92 | .312 | 105 | .263 | 90 | .314 | 79 |
| Tim Leary | .251 | 73 | .268 | 82 | .255 | 76 | .268 | 85 | .200 | 20 | .186 | 37 | .319 | 82 |
| Rick Mahler | .276 | 96 | .283 | 96 | .304 | 112 | .253 | 64 | .309 | 103 | .316 | 110 | .302 | 61 |
| Jose Rijo | .283 | 102 | .232 | 39 | .255 | 74 | .246 | 53 | .238 | 52 | .191 | 41 | .354 | 104 |
| Ron Robinson | .230 | 41 | .267 | 79 | .280 | -- | .240 | 45 | .250 | 62 | .250 | 81 | .299 | 57 |
| Scott Scudder | .230 | 42 | .246 | 57 | .242 | 56 | .237 | 42 | .256 | 73 | .244 | 77 | .264 | 26 |
| Bob Sebra | .350 | -- | .275 | 90 | .239 | 53 | .359 | 116 | .254 | 71 | .229 | 70 | .362 | 106 |
| Kent Tekulve | .215 | -- | .298 | 103 | .288 | 105 | .250 | -- | .313 | 107 | .333 | 112 | .298 | -- |
| Team Average | .244 | 5 | .258 | 11 | .263 | 12 | .243 | 1 | .259 | 10 | .231 | 8 | .305 | 7 |
| League Average | .244 | | .248 | | .242 | | .251 | | .249 | | .222 | | .302 | |

# HOUSTON ASTROS

- **The best in late-inning games in the '80s . . .**
- **. . . with thanks to the middle-relief corps!**

When historians look back on the past 10 years with more than a month or two's worth of perspective, we're sure they'll characterize it as the decade of the short attention span: top–10 lists, sound bites, and—that bane of the waning decade—best-ofs. Best mint-flavored toothpaste of the '80s. Best Gregorian chant of the '80s. Best Scandinavian big-band leader. Best short-haired dog breed. Best child-proofed container. Enough already!

So it's with no small degree of guilt that we acknowledge our role in the festivities. A few pages henceforth, you'll find, under the guise of the Phillies essay, leaders in various categories for every full decade in the history of major league baseball. Between here and there, you'll also encounter a miniversion of that section, pertaining solely to the Dodgers. And now, with solemn face, we nominate the 1989 Astros as the decade's best late-innings team.

Over the past eight years. . . What's that? Oh you're right. Eight years does not a decade make. But we lost a third of the 1981 season to the strike, so let's look at everything since 1982. During that time, only eight teams in either league played .700 or better in games that were tied after the sixth inning. And of those eight teams, only one played better than .200 in games in which it *trailed* after six innings: the '89 'Stros. (For reference, the major league winning percentage for teams trailing after six innings is .139.) Those teams are listed below:

| | | Tied After 6th | | | Trailing After 6th | | |
|---|---|---|---|---|---|---|---|
| **Year** | **Team** | **W** | **L** | **Pct.** | **W** | **L** | **Pct.** |
| 1989 | Astros | 18 | 7 | .720 | 17 | 58 | .227 |
| 1988 | Mets | 20 | 7 | .741 | 11 | 46 | .193 |
| 1985 | Athletics | 10 | 4 | .714 | 14 | 71 | .165 |
| 1983 | Orioles | 17 | 2 | .895 | 10 | 54 | .156 |
| 1989 | Cardinals | 12 | 5 | .706 | 10 | 61 | .141 |
| 1982 | Red Sox | 18 | 7 | .720 | 8 | 55 | .127 |
| 1988 | Dodgers | 21 | 6 | .778 | 6 | 53 | .102 |
| 1987 | Pirates | 20 | 8 | .714 | 5 | 65 | .071 |

Houston's total of 35 wins in games in which it was tied or trailing to start the seventh inning was the highest in the majors during the past eight years. But the Astros' late-inning success can be illustrated in a more straightforward manner by comparing their scoring to that of their opponents on an inning-by-inning basis. Notice in the following table that Houston was outscored in five of the first six innings, for a composite deficit of 61 runs. But the Astros outscored their opponents in each of the final three innings (and overtime as well) for a 39–run surplus from the seventh inning on:

| | 1 | 2 | 3 | 4 | 5 | 6 | 7 | 8 | 9 | Ex. |
|---|---|---|---|---|---|---|---|---|---|---|
| Astros | 83 | 82 | 62 | 67 | 75 | 66 | 84 | 52 | 62 | 14 |
| Opponents | 113 | 53 | 95 | 83 | 77 | 75 | 64 | 44 | 52 | 13 |

To what can the Astros attribute their seventh-inning wake-up calls? Houston stepped up its offense in the late innings, but only slightly. The Astros scored 32.7 percent of their runs from the seventh inning on, compared to a National League average of 30.1 percent. But only 25.9 percent of the runs scored against Houston came after the seventh inning, a far more significant divergence from the league standard, and one that indicates that pitching, not offense, was primarily responsible for the team's comeback potential. So let's narrow our focus to the pitching side of the ledger.

The most outstanding characteristic of Houston's pitchers was their performance in Late-Inning Pressure Situations. Remember that for pitchers, our definition of LIPS is any batter faced in the seventh inning or later while the teams are separated by two runs or fewer. Last season, under those conditions, opposing batters hit .208, and their slugging average of .284 was the third lowest in the past 15 years. And both teams with better marks won world championships: the 1988 Dodgers (.281) and the 1984 Tigers (.283). Plain and simple, Houston's relief staff last season was of championship caliber.

Normally, when a relief staff mounts the stage to accept an award, it's the stopper who steps to the podium for the acceptance speech, while the long- and middle-relief drones smile politely behind him. And Dave Smith surely deserves more notoriety than he's received during his 10 years with Houston that make him the only pitcher to remain with the same National League team for the entire 1980s. You'll note in what we laughingly refer to as the Phillies essay (p. 140) that Smith's 176 saves during that time represent the 10th-highest 10–year total in major league history. But probably even Smith would be the first to acknowledge the support of his advance team, comprised primarily of four veterans with more than 46 years of major league service among them: Juan

Agosto, Larry Andersen, Danny Darwin, and Dan Schatzeder.

Imagine a team that could call on a pitcher like Ron Darling to fill the gap between its starter and its closer every single day of the season. Well, in effect, that's what Houston had last season. The table below compares Darling's statistics for 1989 with the totals of all Astros relievers who entered before the eighth inning:

| | W | L | ERA | IP | H | HR | BB | SO |
|---|---|---|---|---|---|---|---|---|
| Ron Darling | 14 | 14 | 3.52 | 219.2 | 183 | 19 | 70 | 153 |
| Astros relievers | 11 | 5 | 3.53 | 267.1 | 258 | 17 | 96 | 190 |

Those figures are all the more remarkable when you consider the career records of Agosto, Andersen, Darwin, and Schatzeder, the four journeymen who accounted for 76 percent of Houston's long- and middle-relief innings. Their combined career statistics prior to and during the 1989 season ("/9" headings refer to rates per nine innings):

| | W | L | Pct. | IP | ERA | H/9 | BB/9 | SO/9 |
|---|---|---|---|---|---|---|---|---|
| Prior to 1989 | 196 | 202 | .492 | 3759.0 | 3.65 | 8.63 | 3.02 | 5.44 |
| 1989 season | 23 | 14 | .622 | 349.1 | 2.63 | 7.73 | 3.01 | 7.24 |

Never before during the eight previous seasons since Agosto, the youngest of the group, made his major league debut had those four pitchers combined for an ERA below 3.24. Starting with the 1981 season, those figures were: 4.03, 4.95, 3.41, 3.24, 3.85, 3.52, 3.83, and 3.46. Only once during that eight-year period did they win more games than they lost, posting a combined 25–18 record in 1987, compared to 123–149 in the other seven seasons. Mike Scott was voted the most valuable player on the Astros in 1989, and we can't argue with that. But the combined work of Houston's long–and middle–relief pitchers deserves honorable mention.

Trying to determine how a manager could maximize the potential of his relief staff, we discovered that with regard to the lefty-righty platoon advantage, those who wear a path to the mound don't gain a significant advantage over those with a *laissez faire* policy. The following table shows some related figures for all National League teams: the number of pitching changes each team made ("PC"); the average number of batters a relief pitcher faced ("BFP"); the number of times a relief pitcher faced only one batter ("1B"); and the percentage of batters faced in the seventh inning or later that gave the pitcher a platoon advantage—left-hander vs. left-hander or right-hander vs. right-hander ("Pct."):

| Team | PC | BFP | 1B | Pct. |
|---|---|---|---|---|
| Atlanta | 340 | 5.89 | 22 | 35.6 |
| Chicago | 338 | 5.96 | 25 | 36.0 |
| Cincinnati | 339 | 6.00 | 19 | 31.5 |
| Houston | 346 | 6.10 | 19 | 36.2 |
| Los Angeles | 285 | 5.80 | 18 | 40.6 |
| Montreal | 287 | 5.64 | 19 | 37.7 |
| New York | 274 | 6.15 | 18 | 35.2 |
| Philadelphia | 348 | 6.27 | 23 | 37.7 |
| Pittsburgh | 325 | 6.25 | 20 | 38.5 |
| St. Louis | 358 | 5.13 | 39 | 40.4 |
| San Diego | 245 | 6.99 | 9 | 31.4 |
| San Francisco | 318 | 6.58 | 15 | 35.3 |
| N.L. Averages | 317 | 6.04 | 21 | 36.3 |

There's a strong correspondence between the average number of batters a relief pitcher faced and the percentage of late-game batters that gave the pitching team a platoon advantage: The lower the number of batters faced, the greater the advantage. A manager like Jack McKeon—whose stopper, Mark Davis, not only led the majors with 44 saves but also pitched more than one inning in half of them—could afford to sit back and relax. He allowed his relievers to face an average of nearly seven batters per appearance, and accepted the consequence that 69 percent of the batters facing Padres pitchers after the sixth inning had a platoon advantage (righties facing lefties, or vice versa). On the other extreme, Whitey Herzog choreographed a more rapid exchange of pitchers, often making a special trip to the mound for a single batter. The Cardinals predictably gained the advantage on more than 40 percent of the late-game batters that opposed them. But notice that the difference between those teams—on opposite ends of the platoon advantage spectrum—is only nine percent, or one batter in 11.

None of those figures explains the rebirth of Agosto, Andersen, Darwin, and Schatzeder. The statistics label Houston manager Art Howe a typical National League skipper with regard to pitching changes. He made a few more changes than the average manager, but didn't derive any additional platoon advantage from his maneuvers. The renaissance of Houston's veteran relievers appears simply to be one of those baseball events that remains a blissful mystery.

## WON-LOST RECORD BY STARTING POSITION

| HOUSTON 86-76 | C | 1B | 2B | 3B | SS | LF | CF | RF | P | Leadoff | Relief | Starts |
|---|---|---|---|---|---|---|---|---|---|---|---|---|
| Juan Agosto | - | - | - | - | - | - | - | - | - | - | 25-46 | - |
| Larry Andersen | - | - | - | - | - | - | - | - | - | - | 32-28 | - |
| Eric Anthony | - | - | - | - | - | 0-2 | - | 5-9 | - | - | - | 5-11 |
| Alan Ashby | 9-8 | - | - | - | - | - | - | - | - | - | - | 9-8 |
| Kevin Bass | - | - | - | - | - | 14-17 | - | 26-24 | - | - | - | 40-41 |
| Craig Biggio | 63-56 | - | - | - | - | 0-1 | 3-1 | - | - | 6-11 | - | 66-58 |
| Ken Caminiti | - | - | - | 85-74 | - | - | - | - | - | - | - | 85-74 |
| Jose Cano | - | - | - | - | - | - | - | - | 1-2 | - | 1-2 | 1-2 |
| Jim Clancy | - | - | - | - | - | - | - | - | 11-15 | - | 1-6 | 11-15 |
| Danny Darwin | - | - | - | - | - | - | - | - | - | - | 37-31 | - |
| Mark Davidson | - | - | - | - | - | 4-0 | - | 5-6 | - | - | - | 9-6 |
| Glenn Davis | - | 83-70 | - | - | - | - | - | - | - | - | - | 83-70 |
| Jim Deshaies | - | - | - | - | - | - | - | - | 22-12 | - | - | 22-12 |
| Bill Doran | - | - | 68-63 | - | - | - | - | - | - | - | - | 68-63 |
| Bob Forsch | - | - | - | - | - | - | - | - | 8-7 | - | 3-19 | 8-7 |
| Greg Gross | - | 0-3 | - | - | - | 1-2 | - | 3-1 | - | - | 0-1 | 4-6 |
| Billy Hatcher | - | - | - | - | - | 47-36 | 6-4 | - | - | 34-19 | - | 53-40 |
| Bob Knepper | - | - | - | - | - | - | - | - | 9-11 | - | 1-1 | 9-11 |
| Steve Lombardozzi | - | - | 6-4 | - | - | - | - | - | - | - | - | 6-4 |
| Roger Mason | - | - | - | - | - | - | - | - | - | - | 0-2 | - |
| Louie Meadows | - | - | - | - | - | 4-2 | - | - | - | 1-2 | - | 4-2 |
| Brian Meyer | - | - | - | - | - | - | - | - | - | - | 2-10 | - |
| Carl Nichols | 0-2 | - | - | - | - | - | - | - | - | - | - | 0-2 |
| Mark Portugal | - | - | - | - | - | - | - | - | 8-7 | - | 2-3 | 8-7 |
| Terry Puhl | - | - | - | - | - | 16-16 | 2-8 | 34-23 | - | 2-4 | - | 52-47 |
| Rafael Ramirez | - | - | - | - | 72-65 | - | - | - | - | - | - | 72-65 |
| Craig Reynolds | - | 0-1 | 9-6 | 1-2 | 11-8 | - | - | - | - | - | 0-1 | 21-17 |
| Rick Rhoden | - | - | - | - | - | - | - | - | 5-12 | - | 0-3 | 5-12 |
| Dan Schatzeder | - | - | - | - | - | - | - | - | - | - | 16-20 | |
| Mike Scott | - | - | - | - | - | - | - | - | 22-10 | - | 1-0 | 22-10 |
| Dave Smith | - | - | - | - | - | - | - | - | - | - | 39-13 | - |
| Harry Spilman | - | 2-2 | - | - | - | - | - | - | - | - | - | 2-2 |
| Alex Trevino | 14-10 | 1-0 | - | - | - | - | - | - | - | - | - | 15-10 |
| Ron Washington | - | - | - | - | - | - | - | - | - | - | - | - |
| Glenn Wilson | - | - | - | - | - | - | - | 12-13 | - | - | - | 12-13 |
| Eric Yelding | - | - | 3-3 | - | 3-3 | - | 0-2 | 1-0 | - | 6-5 | - | 7-8 |
| Gerald Young | - | - | - | - | - | - | 75-61 | - | - | 37-35 | - | 75-61 |

## Batting vs. Left and Right Handed Pitchers

| | | BA | Rank | SA | Rank | OBA | Rank | HR % | Rank | BB % | Rank | SO % | Rank |
|---|---|---|---|---|---|---|---|---|---|---|---|---|---|
| Kevin Bass | vs. Lefties | .265 | 71 | .434 | 45 | .315 | 83 | 2.41 | 52 | 7.61 | 80 | 18.48 | 114 |
| | vs. Righties | .313 | 10 | .435 | 22 | .373 | 19 | 1.30 | 87 | 8.59 | 59 | 10.55 | 31 |
| Craig Biggio | vs. Lefties | .270 | 62 | .336 | 92 | .352 | 47 | 0.82 | 98 | 9.72 | 50 | 9.03 | 27 |
| | vs. Righties | .252 | 61 | .427 | 28 | .330 | 49 | 3.74 | 22 | 9.59 | 48 | 13.97 | 63 |
| Ken Caminiti | vs. Lefties | .315 | 18 | .473 | 26 | .363 | 38 | 2.42 | 51 | 7.26 | 86 | 12.85 | 65 |
| | vs. Righties | .231 | 88 | .329 | 96 | .297 | 83 | 1.43 | 81 | 8.14 | 70 | 14.99 | 77 |
| Glenn Davis | vs. Lefties | .288 | 39 | .616 | 4 | .392 | 12 | 9.59 | 3 | 14.04 | 16 | 10.53 | 40 |
| | vs. Righties | .262 | 51 | .451 | 18 | .335 | 43 | 4.60 | 9 | 9.15 | 54 | 21.34 | 116 |
| Bill Doran | vs. Lefties | .229 | 101 | .357 | 78 | .316 | 79 | 2.86 | 40 | 11.25 | 33 | 8.75 | 25 |
| | vs. Righties | .215 | 113 | .311 | 109 | .295 | 86 | 1.09 | 93 | 9.90 | 46 | 11.84 | 41 |
| Terry Puhl | vs. Lefties | .246 | -- | .333 | -- | .338 | -- | 0.00 | -- | 10.61 | -- | 12.12 | -- |
| | vs. Righties | .276 | 33 | .370 | 69 | .356 | 28 | 0.00 | 124 | 11.18 | 30 | 9.12 | 24 |
| Rafael Ramirez | vs. Lefties | .269 | 64 | .353 | 85 | .315 | 82 | 1.28 | 82 | 6.55 | 96 | 10.12 | 36 |
| | vs. Righties | .236 | 80 | .312 | 108 | .269 | 114 | 1.05 | 94 | 4.42 | 117 | 11.55 | 39 |
| Craig Reynolds | vs. Lefties | .125 | -- | .125 | -- | .300 | -- | 0.00 | -- | 16.67 | -- | 16.67 | -- |
| | vs. Righties | .204 | 121 | .260 | 127 | .273 | 108 | 1.10 | 92 | 8.46 | 60 | 7.96 | 15 |
| Glenn Wilson | vs. Lefties | .322 | 11 | .517 | 9 | .373 | 23 | 2.80 | 41 | 8.23 | 72 | 8.86 | 26 |
| | vs. Righties | .239 | 78 | .374 | 65 | .296 | 85 | 2.42 | 53 | 7.55 | 80 | 12.26 | 45 |
| Gerald Young | vs. Lefties | .238 | 95 | .265 | 117 | .335 | 67 | 0.00 | 112 | 12.35 | 25 | 10.00 | 34 |
| | vs. Righties | .231 | 89 | .280 | 122 | .322 | 60 | 0.00 | 124 | 11.78 | 26 | 9.56 | 26 |
| Team Average | vs. Lefties | .257 | 4 | .375 | 6 | .327 | 4 | 2.12 | 6 | 9.13 | 4 | 13.07 | 1 |
| | vs. Righties | .232 | 12 | .334 | 12 | .299 | 11 | 1.63 | 10 | 8.34 | 6 | 14.16 | 2 |
| League Average | vs. Lefties | .251 | | .371 | | .320 | | 2.06 | | 8.85 | | 14.80 | |
| | vs. Righties | .244 | | .362 | | .309 | | 2.08 | | 8.27 | | 15.67 | |

## Batting with Runners on Base and Bases Empty

| | | BA | Rank | SA | Rank | OBA | Rank | HR % | Rank | BB % | Rank | SO % | Rank |
|---|---|---|---|---|---|---|---|---|---|---|---|---|---|
| Kevin Bass | Runners On | .341 | 6 | .512 | 11 | .414 | 8 | 1.55 | 76 | 12.42 | 36 | 11.76 | 54 |
| | Bases Empty | .272 | 39 | .380 | 63 | .313 | 65 | 1.63 | 76 | 5.13 | 101 | 13.33 | 56 |
| Craig Biggio | Runners On | .251 | 86 | .387 | 66 | .333 | 72 | 2.62 | 45 | 10.53 | 60 | 10.53 | 41 |
| | Bases Empty | .262 | 56 | .413 | 37 | .338 | 39 | 3.17 | 27 | 8.90 | 47 | 14.23 | 64 |
| Ken Caminiti | Runners On | .277 | 44 | .358 | 89 | .340 | 67 | 1.11 | 91 | 8.17 | 86 | 13.73 | 72 |
| | Bases Empty | .236 | 83 | .379 | 64 | .294 | 89 | 2.23 | 53 | 7.65 | 67 | 15.00 | 74 |
| Glenn Davis | Runners On | .278 | 42 | .512 | 10 | .393 | 21 | 5.24 | 8 | 15.74 | 14 | 17.05 | 100 |
| | Bases Empty | .261 | 57 | .477 | 10 | .313 | 64 | 6.31 | 3 | 5.87 | 91 | 19.83 | 117 |
| Bill Doran | Runners On | .271 | 55 | .414 | 47 | .341 | 64 | 1.97 | 64 | 9.48 | 69 | 8.19 | 17 |
| | Bases Empty | .184 | 127 | .263 | 123 | .275 | 105 | 1.32 | 90 | 10.82 | 23 | 12.87 | 49 |
| Terry Puhl | Runners On | .273 | 51 | .388 | 63 | .356 | 45 | 0.00 | 112 | 11.59 | 46 | 9.15 | 24 |
| | Bases Empty | .270 | 45 | .349 | 89 | .351 | 24 | 0.00 | 122 | 10.74 | 25 | 9.92 | 22 |
| Rafael Ramirez | Runners On | .260 | 72 | .372 | 75 | .306 | 103 | 1.79 | 69 | 6.45 | 105 | 10.89 | 45 |
| | Bases Empty | .236 | 83 | .290 | 113 | .266 | 112 | 0.64 | 107 | 3.98 | 115 | 11.31 | 33 |
| Craig Reynolds | Runners On | .217 | 115 | .277 | 126 | .309 | 100 | 1.20 | 87 | 11.11 | 52 | 8.08 | 16 |
| | Bases Empty | .189 | -- | .236 | -- | .246 | -- | 0.94 | -- | 7.02 | -- | 8.77 | -- |
| Glenn Wilson | Runners On | .282 | 38 | .429 | 37 | .342 | 61 | 2.26 | 56 | 8.91 | 79 | 10.40 | 38 |
| | Bases Empty | .255 | 64 | .416 | 33 | .307 | 73 | 2.75 | 36 | 6.93 | 74 | 11.68 | 41 |
| Gerald Young | Runners On | .300 | 26 | .356 | 90 | .376 | 28 | 0.00 | 112 | 10.65 | 59 | 7.87 | 15 |
| | Bases Empty | .198 | 124 | .235 | 129 | .300 | 81 | 0.00 | 122 | 12.62 | 9 | 10.64 | 28 |
| Team Average | Runners On | .262 | 3 | .376 | 8 | .333 | 5 | 1.70 | 10 | 9.36 | 9 | 12.68 | 1 |
| | Bases Empty | .222 | 11 | .323 | 12 | .287 | 11 | 1.80 | 9 | 7.93 | 3 | 14.78 | 3 |
| League Average | Runners On | .256 | | .379 | | .330 | | 2.13 | | 9.82 | | 14.66 | |
| | Bases Empty | .240 | | .355 | | .299 | | 2.03 | | 7.43 | | 15.93 | |

## Overall Batting Compared to Late Inning Pressure Situations

| | | BA | Rank | SA | Rank | OBA | Rank | HR % | Rank | BB % | Rank | SO % | Rank | RDI % | Rank |
|---|---|---|---|---|---|---|---|---|---|---|---|---|---|---|---|
| Kevin Bass | Overall | .300 | 11 | .435 | 24 | .357 | 27 | 1.60 | 77 | 8.33 | 66 | 12.64 | 55 | .330 | 12 |
| | Pressure | .224 | 79 | .367 | 48 | .345 | 42 | 4.08 | 18 | 15.25 | 14 | 13.56 | 49 | .389 | 15 |
| Craig Biggio | Overall | .257 | 63 | .402 | 45 | .336 | 47 | 2.93 | 31 | 9.63 | 49 | 12.57 | 53 | .269 | 59 |
| | Pressure | .342 | 6 | .589 | 3 | .407 | 8 | 4.11 | 17 | 8.43 | 72 | 9.64 | 21 | .344 | 21 |
| Ken Caminiti | Overall | .255 | 68 | .369 | 69 | .316 | 78 | 1.71 | 73 | 7.89 | 76 | 14.40 | 75 | .293 | 34 |
| | Pressure | .229 | 76 | .330 | 71 | .270 | 95 | 1.83 | 59 | 5.08 | 98 | 18.64 | 95 | .160 | 100 |
| Glenn Davis | Overall | .269 | 45 | .492 | 8 | .350 | 35 | 5.85 | 6 | 10.41 | 43 | 18.55 | 113 | .248 | 78 |
| | Pressure | .230 | 75 | .470 | 16 | .282 | 90 | 7.00 | 2 | 6.36 | 87 | 30.00 | 129 | .222 | 65 |
| Bill Doran | Overall | .219 | 114 | .323 | 111 | .301 | 97 | 1.58 | 78 | 10.28 | 45 | 10.98 | 33 | .281 | 47 |
| | Pressure | .241 | 61 | .368 | 47 | .305 | 73 | 3.45 | 23 | 8.42 | 73 | 12.63 | 39 | .136 | 110 |
| Terry Puhl | Overall | .271 | 41 | .364 | 72 | .353 | 31 | 0.00 | 127 | 11.08 | 32 | 9.61 | 21 | .234 | 92 |
| | Pressure | .250 | 53 | .286 | 93 | .344 | 43 | 0.00 | 81 | 11.94 | 36 | 4.48 | 3 | .143 | 106 |
| Rafael Ramirez | Overall | .246 | 81 | .324 | 109 | .283 | 108 | 1.12 | 96 | 5.04 | 116 | 11.13 | 37 | .234 | 93 |
| | Pressure | .295 | 26 | .375 | 41 | .382 | 18 | 1.14 | 76 | 12.26 | 27 | 13.21 | 43 | .452 | 8 |
| Craig Reynolds | Overall | .201 | 127 | .254 | 128 | .274 | 119 | 1.06 | 99 | 8.92 | 56 | 8.45 | 14 | .212 | 111 |
| | Pressure | .225 | 77 | .350 | 61 | .326 | 64 | 2.50 | 33 | 12.24 | 28 | 6.12 | 7 | .000 | -- |
| Alex Trevino | Overall | .290 | -- | .405 | -- | .329 | -- | 1.53 | -- | 4.96 | -- | 12.77 | -- | .267 | -- |
| | Pressure | .244 | 60 | .390 | 34 | .289 | 78 | 2.44 | 40 | 4.44 | 108 | 22.22 | 111 | .364 | 18 |
| Glenn Wilson | Overall | .266 | 48 | .421 | 32 | .321 | 63 | 2.55 | 42 | 7.77 | 78 | 11.13 | 38 | .318 | 19 |
| | Pressure | .338 | 7 | .500 | 10 | .400 | 9 | 3.75 | 20 | 10.00 | 55 | 15.56 | 68 | .500 | 4 |
| Gerald Young | Overall | .233 | 103 | .276 | 124 | .326 | 56 | 0.00 | 127 | 11.94 | 25 | 9.68 | 22 | .268 | 60 |
| | Pressure | .221 | 84 | .244 | 109 | .316 | 67 | 0.00 | 81 | 11.00 | 47 | 8.00 | 14 | .250 | 52 |
| Team Average | Overall | .239 | 11 | .345 | 11 | .306 | 10 | 1.76 | 9 | 8.55 | 5 | 13.87 | 2 | .253 | 5 |
| | Pressure | .239 | 6 | .353 | 3 | .311 | 6 | 2.41 | 2 | 8.92 | 8 | 15.72 | 5 | .252 | 3 |
| League Average | Overall | .246 | | .365 | | .312 | | 2.07 | | 8.47 | | 15.38 | | .253 | |
| | Pressure | .238 | | .337 | | .308 | | 1.73 | | 8.93 | | 16.78 | | .235 | |

## Additional Miscellaneous Batting Comparisons

| | Grass Surface | | Artificial Surface | | Home Games | | Road Games | | Runners in Scoring Position | | Runners in Scoring Pos and Two Outs | | Leading Off Inning | | Runners on 3B with less than 2 Outs | |
|---|---|---|---|---|---|---|---|---|---|---|---|---|---|---|---|---|
| | BA | Rank | BA | Rank | BA | Rank | BA | Rank | BA | Rank | BA | Rank | OBA | Rank | RDI % | Rank |
| Kevin Bass | .264 | 52 | .314 | 6 | .298 | 27 | .303 | 8 | .324 | 10 | .281 | 27 | .344 | 31 | .522 | 94 |
| Craig Biggio | .231 | 85 | .269 | 40 | .233 | 98 | .281 | 35 | .248 | 81 | .222 | 66 | .250 | 110 | .618 | 48 |
| Ken Caminiti | .227 | 92 | .266 | 45 | .256 | 68 | .253 | 63 | .292 | 29 | .333 | 10 | .314 | 53 | .500 | 98 |
| Glenn Davis | .174 | 124 | .310 | 7 | .317 | 10 | .221 | 98 | .270 | 53 | .175 | 107 | .310 | 59 | .607 | 54 |
| Bill Doran | .174 | 125 | .237 | 97 | .252 | 77 | .187 | 124 | .283 | 36 | .189 | 101 | .263 | 102 | .556 | 74 |
| Terry Puhl | .291 | 21 | .263 | 48 | .254 | 72 | .291 | 17 | .244 | 83 | .233 | 58 | .310 | 57 | .533 | 89 |
| Rafael Ramirez | .266 | 49 | .237 | 95 | .246 | 85 | .245 | 74 | .229 | 93 | .164 | 111 | .277 | 92 | .542 | 85 |
| Craig Reynolds | .138 | -- | .229 | 105 | .196 | 122 | .207 | -- | .152 | 130 | .286 | -- | .318 | -- | .500 | 98 |
| Mike Scott | .148 | -- | .125 | -- | .122 | -- | .147 | -- | .320 | -- | .300 | -- | .125 | -- | .444 | 122 |
| Alex Trevino | .382 | -- | .258 | 58 | .233 | -- | .362 | -- | .229 | -- | .167 | -- | .385 | -- | .571 | -- |
| Glenn Wilson | .298 | 16 | .256 | 61 | .263 | 62 | .269 | 44 | .314 | 15 | .288 | 24 | .243 | 115 | .556 | 74 |
| Gerald Young | .222 | 95 | .237 | 96 | .247 | 84 | .218 | 100 | .290 | 32 | .288 | 24 | .322 | 52 | .522 | 94 |
| Team Average | .217 | 12 | .247 | 6 | .247 | 8 | .231 | 11 | .251 | 6 | .221 | 5 | .288 | 11 | .547 | 6 |
| League Average | .244 | | .248 | | .251 | | .242 | | .249 | | .222 | | .302 | | .546 | |

## Pitching vs. Left and Right Handed Batters

| | | BA | Rank | SA | Rank | OBA | Rank | HR % | Rank | BB % | Rank | SO % | Rank |
|---|---|---|---|---|---|---|---|---|---|---|---|---|---|
| Juan Agosto | vs. Lefties | .220 | 32 | .266 | 13 | .276 | 18 | 0.00 | 1 | 7.94 | 41 | 18.25 | 24 |
| | vs. Righties | .275 | 98 | .362 | 63 | .348 | 96 | 1.45 | 23 | 9.36 | 94 | 9.79 | 111 |
| Larry Andersen | vs. Lefties | .248 | 63 | .304 | 30 | .303 | 40 | 1.24 | 45 | 7.69 | 37 | 18.13 | 25 |
| | vs. Righties | .146 | 2 | .185 | 1 | .195 | 1 | 0.00 | 1 | 5.92 | 33 | 30.77 | 2 |
| Jim Clancy | vs. Lefties | .291 | 100 | .460 | 108 | .377 | 109 | 3.19 | 107 | 12.30 | 97 | 13.39 | 62 |
| | vs. Righties | .243 | 63 | .376 | 76 | .298 | 62 | 1.14 | 13 | 7.27 | 62 | 14.53 | 76 |
| Danny Darwin | vs. Lefties | .246 | 57 | .329 | 41 | .295 | 31 | 1.25 | 46 | 6.49 | 19 | 17.18 | 31 |
| | vs. Righties | .170 | 6 | .268 | 8 | .236 | 9 | 2.58 | 75 | 7.27 | 63 | 26.82 | 7 |
| Jim Deshaies | vs. Lefties | .258 | 74 | .317 | 33 | .361 | 102 | 0.00 | 1 | 14.29 | 108 | 13.61 | 58 |
| | vs. Righties | .210 | 26 | .333 | 42 | .273 | 34 | 2.12 | 55 | 7.43 | 66 | 17.03 | 58 |
| Bob Forsch | vs. Lefties | .304 | 108 | .447 | 104 | .379 | 110 | 2.37 | 87 | 10.96 | 82 | 6.51 | 111 |
| | vs. Righties | .301 | 109 | .419 | 99 | .350 | 98 | 2.15 | 56 | 6.93 | 54 | 10.40 | 105 |
| Mark Portugal | vs. Lefties | .220 | 31 | .321 | 37 | .297 | 34 | 1.44 | 53 | 9.79 | 70 | 17.45 | 29 |
| | vs. Righties | .246 | 67 | .339 | 45 | .305 | 67 | 2.19 | 59 | 6.83 | 53 | 21.95 | 26 |
| Rick Rhoden | vs. Lefties | .271 | 86 | .403 | 89 | .344 | 87 | 1.81 | 69 | 9.09 | 58 | 7.11 | 110 |
| | vs. Righties | .314 | 114 | .431 | 104 | .385 | 114 | 1.96 | 50 | 10.06 | 99 | 12.85 | 87 |
| Dan Schatzeder | vs. Lefties | .288 | 99 | .338 | 46 | .345 | 90 | 0.00 | 1 | 6.82 | 24 | 22.73 | 9 |
| | vs. Righties | .287 | 102 | .448 | 111 | .389 | 115 | 1.40 | 19 | 12.87 | 112 | 15.20 | 71 |
| Mike Scott | vs. Lefties | .247 | 60 | .392 | 81 | .298 | 35 | 2.90 | 95 | 6.86 | 25 | 13.33 | 63 |
| | vs. Righties | .167 | 4 | .281 | 15 | .227 | 6 | 2.46 | 73 | 6.52 | 48 | 25.56 | 13 |
| Dave Smith | vs. Lefties | .237 | 48 | .322 | 40 | .302 | 39 | 0.85 | 29 | 7.58 | 35 | 12.88 | 69 |
| | vs. Righties | .228 | -- | .261 | -- | .294 | -- | 0.00 | -- | 8.41 | -- | 13.08 | -- |
| Team Average | vs. Lefties | .263 | 11 | .381 | 9 | .331 | 9 | 1.87 | 8 | 9.23 | 5 | 13.64 | 7 |
| | vs. Righties | .235 | 5 | .346 | 3 | .303 | 7 | 1.89 | 2 | 8.39 | 10 | 16.69 | 4 |
| League Average | vs. Lefties | .252 | | .366 | | .325 | | 1.79 | | 9.48 | | 13.93 | |
| | vs. Righties | .242 | | .365 | | .303 | | 2.29 | | 7.70 | | 16.46 | |

## Pitching with Runners on Base and Bases Empty

| | | BA | Rank | SA | Rank | OBA | Rank | HR % | Rank | BB % | Rank | SO % | Rank |
|---|---|---|---|---|---|---|---|---|---|---|---|---|---|
| Juan Agosto | Runners On | .237 | 45 | .308 | 19 | .321 | 57 | 1.28 | 29 | 11.11 | 83 | 13.23 | 75 |
| | Bases Empty | .275 | 105 | .350 | 57 | .326 | 96 | 0.63 | 10 | 6.40 | 49 | 12.21 | 92 |
| Larry Andersen | Runners On | .204 | 9 | .219 | 2 | .260 | 4 | 0.00 | 1 | 7.59 | 25 | 19.62 | 20 |
| | Bases Empty | .193 | 11 | .265 | 4 | .244 | 5 | 1.10 | 24 | 6.22 | 46 | 27.98 | 4 |
| Jim Clancy | Runners On | .290 | 94 | .451 | 100 | .375 | 104 | 1.96 | 53 | 12.13 | 101 | 12.46 | 84 |
| | Bases Empty | .252 | 85 | .399 | 97 | .314 | 85 | 2.49 | 88 | 8.29 | 80 | 15.14 | 59 |
| Danny Darwin | Runners On | .212 | 15 | .290 | 11 | .270 | 10 | 1.55 | 37 | 7.62 | 27 | 21.97 | 12 |
| | Bases Empty | .212 | 22 | .311 | 24 | .266 | 19 | 2.07 | 62 | 6.18 | 45 | 21.24 | 20 |
| Jim Deshaies | Runners On | .227 | 32 | .336 | 34 | .299 | 30 | 1.25 | 28 | 9.14 | 51 | 19.09 | 27 |
| | Bases Empty | .211 | 21 | .327 | 32 | .279 | 32 | 2.17 | 70 | 8.09 | 76 | 14.75 | 62 |
| Bob Forsch | Runners On | .306 | 106 | .438 | 102 | .364 | 95 | 3.24 | 103 | 8.94 | 47 | 8.54 | 109 |
| | Bases Empty | .300 | 113 | .413 | 106 | .371 | 114 | 1.35 | 33 | 9.68 | 95 | 7.66 | 115 |
| Mark Portugal | Runners On | .214 | 16 | .318 | 25 | .278 | 13 | 1.95 | 52 | 7.34 | 19 | 19.21 | 25 |
| | Bases Empty | .244 | 62 | .336 | 42 | .316 | 86 | 1.68 | 46 | 9.13 | 90 | 19.77 | 30 |
| Rick Rhoden | Runners On | .297 | 99 | .437 | 94 | .390 | 112 | 2.53 | 84 | 12.12 | 100 | 9.60 | 103 |
| | Bases Empty | .282 | 110 | .398 | 96 | .338 | 105 | 1.39 | 36 | 7.26 | 64 | 9.40 | 109 |
| Dan Schatzeder | Runners On | .333 | 114 | .483 | 111 | .420 | 116 | 0.83 | 15 | 10.49 | 72 | 14.69 | 55 |
| | Bases Empty | .233 | -- | .320 | -- | .319 | -- | 0.97 | -- | 11.21 | -- | 21.55 | -- |
| Mike Scott | Runners On | .217 | 17 | .359 | 55 | .289 | 20 | 2.27 | 70 | 8.78 | 43 | 16.71 | 41 |
| | Bases Empty | .210 | 20 | .336 | 41 | .254 | 10 | 2.97 | 106 | 5.43 | 28 | 19.79 | 29 |
| Team Average | Runners On | .259 | 8 | .381 | 6 | .334 | 9 | 1.88 | 3 | 9.78 | 5 | 14.49 | 7 |
| | Bases Empty | .238 | 5 | .347 | 4 | .301 | 8 | 1.89 | 3 | 7.93 | 10 | 16.04 | 6 |
| League Average | Runners On | .256 | | .379 | | .330 | | 2.13 | | 9.82 | | 14.66 | |
| | Bases Empty | .240 | | .355 | | .299 | | 2.03 | | 7.43 | | 15.93 | |

## Overall Pitching Compared to Late Inning Pressure Situations

| | | BA | Rank | SA | Rank | OBA | Rank | HR % | Rank | BB % | Rank | SO % | Rank |
|---|---|---|---|---|---|---|---|---|---|---|---|---|---|
| Juan Agosto | Overall | .256 | 79 | .329 | 32 | .323 | 79 | 0.95 | 10 | 8.86 | 70 | 12.74 | 83 |
| | Pressure | .274 | 90 | .327 | 55 | .328 | 78 | 0.88 | 34 | 8.53 | 57 | 14.73 | 70 |
| Larry Andersen | Overall | .198 | 7 | .245 | 1 | .251 | 1 | 0.63 | 3 | 6.84 | 28 | 24.22 | 7 |
| | Pressure | .204 | 29 | .253 | 12 | .284 | 41 | 0.62 | 26 | 10.27 | 77 | 20.00 | 26 |
| Jim Clancy | Overall | .269 | 92 | .422 | 105 | .342 | 100 | 2.26 | 78 | 10.08 | 94 | 13.89 | 70 |
| | Pressure | .174 | 10 | .304 | 41 | .240 | 11 | 4.35 | 107 | 8.00 | 52 | 12.00 | 81 |
| Danny Darwin | Overall | .212 | 17 | .302 | 11 | .268 | 9 | 1.84 | 48 | 6.85 | 29 | 21.58 | 15 |
| | Pressure | .204 | 29 | .285 | 31 | .260 | 23 | 1.85 | 67 | 6.95 | 38 | 20.53 | 22 |
| Jim Deshaies | Overall | .217 | 23 | .331 | 35 | .287 | 30 | 1.81 | 45 | 8.51 | 64 | 16.49 | 50 |
| | Pressure | .181 | 11 | .278 | 25 | .234 | 9 | 2.78 | 92 | 6.49 | 33 | 12.99 | 78 |
| Bob Forsch | Overall | .303 | 115 | .435 | 112 | .367 | 113 | 2.28 | 79 | 9.31 | 79 | 8.10 | 115 |
| | Pressure | .195 | 23 | .317 | 52 | .233 | 8 | 2.44 | 88 | 4.65 | 18 | 11.63 | 83 |
| Mark Portugal | Overall | .232 | 39 | .329 | 31 | .301 | 48 | 1.79 | 44 | 8.41 | 60 | 19.55 | 25 |
| | Pressure | .235 | 60 | .265 | 17 | .257 | 21 | 0.00 | 1 | 2.56 | 5 | 17.95 | 40 |
| Rick Rhoden | Overall | .289 | 108 | .414 | 104 | .361 | 111 | 1.87 | 52 | 9.49 | 83 | 9.49 | 111 |
| | Pressure | .333 | -- | .500 | -- | .368 | -- | 5.56 | -- | 5.26 | -- | 5.26 | -- |
| Dan Schatzeder | Overall | .287 | 107 | .408 | 99 | .374 | 114 | 0.90 | 9 | 10.81 | 103 | 17.76 | 38 |
| | Pressure | .143 | 2 | .157 | 1 | .250 | 17 | 0.00 | 1 | 9.88 | 71 | 19.75 | 28 |
| Mike Scott | Overall | .212 | 18 | .344 | 46 | .267 | 6 | 2.71 | 101 | 6.71 | 27 | 18.61 | 32 |
| | Pressure | .185 | 15 | .277 | 24 | .329 | 79 | 1.54 | 58 | 17.28 | 115 | 18.52 | 37 |
| Dave Smith | Overall | .233 | -- | .295 | -- | .299 | -- | 0.48 | -- | 7.95 | -- | 12.97 | -- |
| | Pressure | .201 | 26 | .279 | 27 | .271 | 31 | 0.65 | 27 | 7.87 | 50 | 15.17 | 62 |
| Team Average | Overall | .247 | 6 | .361 | 4 | .315 | 9 | 1.88 | 3 | 8.76 | 10 | 15.34 | 6 |
| | Pressure | .208 | 1 | .284 | 1 | .278 | 1 | 1.51 | 5 | 8.53 | 4 | 17.15 | 6 |
| League Average | Overall | .246 | | .365 | | .312 | | 2.07 | | 8.47 | | 15.38 | |
| | Pressure | .235 | | .336 | | .309 | | 1.77 | | 9.31 | | 16.92 | |

## Additional Miscellaneous Pitching Comparisons

| | Grass Surface | | Artificial Surface | | Home Games | | Road Games | | Runners in Scoring Position | | Runners in Scoring Pos and Two Outs | | Leading Off Inning | |
|---|---|---|---|---|---|---|---|---|---|---|---|---|---|---|
| | BA | Rank | BA | Rank | BA | Rank | BA | Rank | BA | Rank | BA | Rank | OBA | Rank |
| Juan Agosto | .214 | -- | .268 | 83 | .266 | 88 | .245 | 51 | .219 | 33 | .133 | 9 | .333 | 93 |
| Larry Andersen | .218 | 33 | .192 | 6 | .202 | 22 | .192 | 6 | .145 | 2 | .091 | 2 | .231 | 10 |
| Jim Clancy | .215 | 30 | .301 | 107 | .286 | 103 | .256 | 72 | .327 | 112 | .200 | 48 | .368 | 111 |
| Danny Darwin | .239 | 55 | .202 | 14 | .181 | 8 | .254 | 65 | .239 | 55 | .224 | 66 | .267 | 28 |
| Jim Deshaies | .205 | 15 | .221 | 28 | .220 | 33 | .214 | 22 | .210 | 27 | .223 | 64 | .279 | 40 |
| Bob Forsch | .314 | 113 | .300 | 106 | .292 | 110 | .315 | 112 | .336 | 114 | .293 | 97 | .348 | 102 |
| Mark Portugal | .224 | 35 | .236 | 44 | .243 | 58 | .222 | 26 | .169 | 8 | .178 | 31 | .310 | 71 |
| Rick Rhoden | .311 | -- | .284 | 97 | .291 | 107 | .286 | 101 | .283 | 87 | .302 | 100 | .327 | 90 |
| Dan Schatzeder | .347 | -- | .270 | 86 | .254 | 73 | .324 | 114 | .341 | 115 | .250 | 81 | .315 | -- |
| Mike Scott | .203 | 11 | .217 | 21 | .213 | 27 | .211 | 20 | .177 | 11 | .185 | 36 | .273 | 36 |
| Dave Smith | .271 | -- | .219 | 23 | .233 | -- | .234 | 37 | .241 | 58 | .192 | -- | .321 | 84 |
| Team Average | .234 | 2 | .252 | 8 | .246 | 9 | .248 | 6 | .251 | 8 | .211 | 5 | .305 | 5 |
| League Average | .244 | | .248 | | .242 | | .251 | | .249 | | .222 | | .302 | |

# LOS ANGELES DODGERS

- **After 40 years, the talent well runs dry.**
- **100 years of Dodger baseball.**

Remember in *A Streetcar Named Desire* when Blanche told Stanley how she'd always "depended on the kindness of others?" Well, that's how some baseball teams stock their rosters. We chronicled in the Mariners essay the extent to which the Kansas City Athletics became unwitting benefactors to the Yankees during the '50s and '60s. The world champion Athletics were themselves the beneficiaries of the unintended largesse of several philanthropic competitors. Sure, Canseco, McGwire, Steinbach, and the prodigal Rickey Henderson are home-grown. But most of their other everyday starters were produced by other systems, including Dave Henderson (Mariners), Dave Parker (Pirates), Carney Lansford (Angels), and Ron Hassey (Indians). And Oakland's pitching staff is almost entirely store-bought: Dave Stewart and Bob Welch (Dodgers), Mike Moore, Gene Nelson, Rick Honeycutt, and Matt Young (Mariners), Storm Davis (Orioles), and Dennis Eckersley (Indians) represent mercenary baseball raised to its highest degree.

But for most of the last 50 years, the Dodgers have operated according to the contradictory theory that charity begins at home. Since the hiring of Branch Rickey in the 1940s, their organization has been baseball's most self-sufficient, providing the parent club with an abundance of talented homebreds. But as the Dodgers steam ahead into their second century of major league baseball, winds of change are sweeping through Chavez Ravine. And we're not talking about Tommy Lasorda's waistline.

Over the past few years, the Dodgers' lineup has grown increasingly foreign-born, as players developed in their system, like Greg Brock, Pedro Guerrero, Steve Sax, and Mariano Duncan, have been exiled. Last season, Los Angeles could have put a lineup on the field in which all players except for the third baseman were the products of American League teams. The truth is that such a lineup—Eddie Murray, Willie Randolph, and Alfredo Griffin around the infield; Kirk Gibson, John Shelby, and Mike Davis in the outfield; Rick Dempsey behind the plate; and Mike Morgan on the mound —would have differed only slightly from L.A.'s regular set.

The degree of foreign influence on the Dodgers is simple to quantify. Last season, only 2781 of the team's 5465 at-bats (or 51 percent) were attributable to players developed within the Dodgers organization. (Players are considered as having been produced by the teams with which they were rookies. Those whose rookie status extended over two or more seasons are assigned to the teams with which they started the last of those seasons.) The following table shows that 16 of the other 25 teams rated higher on that count than the Dodgers did last season. The percentage of each team's at-bats by players from within their own systems:

| | | | | | |
|---|---|---|---|---|---|
| Blue Jays | 86.4 | Mets | 60.9 | Expos | 47.5 |
| Mariners | 83.0 | Padres | 60.2 | Yankees | 47.1 |
| Brewers | 76.0 | Athletics | 59.7 | Angels | 46.2 |
| White Sox | 68.7 | Rangers | 58.5 | Pirates | 45.8 |
| Red Sox | 68.4 | Twins | 57.1 | Giants | 45.7 |
| Astros | 66.9 | Reds | 55.9 | Phillies | 44.2 |
| Braves | 66.1 | Royals | 53.8 | Cardinals | 36.0 |
| Orioles | 63.0 | Dodgers | 50.9 | Tigers | 34.7 |
| Cubs | 62.1 | Indians | 48.2 | Average | 57.5 |

Of greater significance, the Dodgers' average of only 51 percent represented the team's lowest figure since 1944, when Brooklyn ended a long period of dependence on other teams' players by breaking through the 50–percent barrier from the other side. The following graph traces the Dodgers' progress from dependence to self-sufficiency from the mid–1940s through the mid–1970s, and the erosion of that self-reliance in recent years:

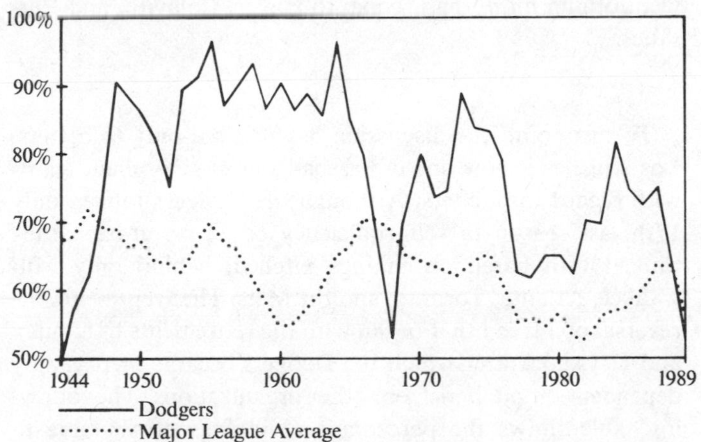


Some essential points can be drawn from that graph. First, for most of the last 50 years, the Dodgers not only exceeded the major league average, but they did it by a remarkable margin. Second, the start of that period corresponds, not coincidentally, to the implementation of programs set in place by Branch Rickey. (For a thorough assessment of Rickey's contributions, see the Cardinals essay.) Third, this is only the second time since the late 1940s that the Dodgers have dipped below the major league average: a two-year period ending in 1968, and the last two seasons. The similarities between those periods aren't compelling, but they are worth noting.

Los Angeles won the National League title three times in four years from 1963 through 1966. But by the end of that period, the Dodgers were an aging team. Their batters ranked eighth among the 10 National League teams with an average age of 29 years, 10 months. Jim Gilliam, Johnny Roseboro, Maury Wills, and Lou Johnson were all nearing the end of the line. The Dodgers responded by opening a halfway house for aging veterans on their way to retirement. Tom Haller,

Paul Popovich, Zoilo Versalles, Bob Bailey, Len Gabrielson, Ken Boyer, and Rocky Colavito all masqueraded as "real" Dodgers in 1968 alone. Luckily, a flow of young talent that included Bill Russell, Ted Sizemore, and Bill Sudakis was just around the corner. A second wave, including Steve Garvey, Bill Buckner, Davey Lopes, Ron Cey, Joe Ferguson, Lee Lacy, and Steve Yeager wasn't far behind.

Last season, in defense of a World Series victory, the Dodgers had the oldest lineup in the National League for only the third time since leaving Ebbets Field in Flatbush. The current team probably won't face the crippling obstacles presented to an earlier generation by the premature retirements of Sandy Koufax and Don Drysdale. (Did someone mention Kirk Gibson?) But neither can they expect lightning to strike again with a team full of emerging All-Stars reaching the major league level over a period of three years. So, the Dodgers have begun to look outside the organization, with mixed results to date. Kirk Gibson was an MVP postseason hero. But Mike Davis was an outright bust. And while Willie Randolph, Eddie Murray, and John Shelby have all provided some temporary relief, 20 years from now, they might seem like nothing more than sequel to Haller, Colavito, and Versalles.

To this point, the discussion has referred only to batters. Los Angeles is now one of baseball's most self-reliant teams with regard to pitchers. Although the Dodgers ranked only 17th last season in self-sufficiency based on at-bats, they ranked fifth based on innings pitched, behind only Milwaukee, Atlanta, Toronto, and the Mets. That represents the reversal of a trend that began with the retirements of Koufax and Drysdale, after which the Dodgers became increasingly dependent on pitchers from other organizations. The following table shows the percentage of innings attributable to pitchers produced by their own organization in each of the past 20 seasons:

| Year | Pct. | Year | Pct. | Year | Pct. | Year | Pct. |
|---|---|---|---|---|---|---|---|
| 1970 | 66.1 | 1975 | 47.2 | 1980 | 56.3 | 1985 | 68.1 |
| 1971 | 52.0 | 1976 | 60.8 | 1981 | 59.5 | 1986 | 76.5 |
| 1972 | 42.8 | 1977 | 59.4 | 1982 | 66.7 | 1987 | 77.9 |
| 1973 | 32.1 | 1978 | 63.0 | 1983 | 66.6 | 1988 | 71.2 |
| 1974 | 46.0 | 1979 | 61.8 | 1984 | 64.6 | 1989 | 71.0 |

Thirty years ago, the Dodgers were a prosperous island, surviving—even thriving—solely on the harvest from its own fields. Every pitcher the Dodgers used in 1960 was developed within their own system. Only three batters from that season were not: regular starter Wally Moon, and two subs who combined for a total of 30 at-bats (Irv Noren and Rip Repulski). Those days are long gone for a variety of reasons, some beyond the control of Dodgers management. It could well be that with the swap of Mike Marshall to the Mets for Juan Samuel, 1990 will be the first season in 47 years in which more than half the team's at-bats are provided by players developed in other systems. That's not a condemnation of either the Dodgers' system or their policy. After all, L.A.'s team of hired guns won a world championship in 1988. Only time will tell whether it's a sound long-term move. But this seems an odd turn of events for a management that stresses team pride in the clubhouse and on the field. Well, as they say, there's no zealot like a convert.

The Dodgers are currently celebrating the 100th anniversary of their franchise. The following lists represent the franchise leaders, decade by decade, in the most important batting and pitching categories. Only statistics compiled while with the Dodgers are included in each player's totals:

Batting average (minimum: 2000 at-bats):1890s, Mike Griffin, .308; 1900s, Jimmy Sheckard, .299; 1910s, Jake Daubert, .305; 1920s, Zach Wheat, .340; 1930s, Johnny Frederick, .302; 1940s, Dixie Walker, .312; 1950s, Jackie Robinson, .311; 1960s, Tommy Davis, .304; 1970s, Steve Garvey, 304; 1980s, Pedro Guerrero, .309.

Home runs: 1890s, Tom Daly, 37; 1900s, Harry Lumley, 38; 1910s, Zack Wheat, 51; 1920s, Jack Fournier, 82; 1930s, Johnny Frederick, 61; 1940s, Dolf Camilli, 89; 1950s, Duke Snider, 326; 1960s, Frank Howard, 121; 1970s, Ron Cey, 163; 1980s, Pedro Guerrero, 169.

Runs batted in: 1890s, Oyster Burns, 483; 1900s, Jimmy Sheckard, 342; 1910s, Zack Wheat, 649; 1920s, Zack Wheat, 570; 1930s, Johnny Frederick, 302; 1940s, Dixie Walker, 687; 1950s, Duke Snider, 1031; 1960s, Willie Davis, 526; 1970s, Steve Garvey, 736; 1980s, Pedro Guerrero, 575.

Stolen bases: 1890s, Mike Griffin, 264; 1900s, Jimmy Sheckard, 199; 1910s, Jake Daubert, 187; 1920s, Jimmy Johnston, 93; 1930s, Danny Taylor, 44; 1940s, Pee Wee Reese, 108; 1950s, Jim Gilliam, 132; 1960s, Maury Wills, 439; 1970s, Davey Lopes, 375; 1980s, Steve Sax, 290.

Earned run average (minimum: 1000 innings; unofficial until 1912): 1890s, Ed Stein, 3.99; 1900s, Harry McIntyre, 3.11; 1910s, Jeff Pfeffer, 2.16; 1920s, Dazzy Vance, 3.10; 1930s, Van Lingle Mungo, 3.42; 1940s, Curt Davis, 3.23; 1950s, Don Newcombe, 3.57; 1960s, Sandy Koufax, 2.36; 1970s, Burt Hooton, 2.87; 1980s, Orel Hershiser, 2.69.

Winning percentage (minimum: 50 wins): 1890s, Tom Lovett, .615; 1900s, Frank Kitson, .596; 1910s, Jeff Pfeffer, .593; 1920s, Dazzy Vance, .620; 1930s, Watty Clark, .550; 1940s, Kirby Higbe, .648; 1950s, Preacher Roe, .742; 1960s, Sandy Koufax, .695; 1970s, Tommy John, .674; 1980s, Orel Hershiser, .605.

Wins: 1890s, Brickyard Kennedy, 151; 1900s, Frank Kitson, 53; 1910s, Jeff Pfeffer, 96; 1920s, Dazzy Vance, 147; 1930s, Van Lingle Mungo, 101; 1940s, Whitlow Wyatt, 72; 1950s, Carl Erskine, 108; 1960s, Don Drysdale, 158; 1970s, Don Sutton, 166; 1980s, Fernando Valenzuela, 128.

Strikeouts: 1890s, Brickyard Kennedy, 646; 1900s, Nap Rucker, 531; 1910s, Nap Rucker, 686; 1920s, Dazzy Vance, 1464; 1930s, Van Lingle Mungo, 1022; 1940s, Ralph Branca, 506; 1950s, Carl Erskine, 903; 1960s, Don Drysdale, 1910; 1970s, Don Sutton, 1767; 1980s, Fernando Valenzuela, 1644.

## WON-LOST RECORD BY STARTING POSITION

| LOS ANGELES 77-83 | C | 1B | 2B | 3B | SS | LF | CF | RF | P | Leadoff | Relief | Starts |
|---|---|---|---|---|---|---|---|---|---|---|---|---|
| Dave Anderson | - | - | 1-3 | 4-0 | 10-12 | - | - | - | - | - | - | 15-15 |
| Bill Bean | - | - | - | - | - | 2-4 | 2-4 | 1-4 | - | 0-1 | - | 5-12 |
| Tim Belcher | - | - | - | - | - | - | - | - | 16-14 | - | 4-5 | 16-14 |
| Tim Crews | - | - | - | - | - | - | - | - | - | - | 5-39 | - |
| Kal Daniels | - | - | - | - | - | 5-6 | - | - | - | - | - | 5-6 |
| Mike Davis | - | - | - | - | - | 4-10 | - | 14-13 | - | - | - | 18-23 |
| Rick Dempsey | 24-14 | - | - | - | - | - | - | - | - | - | - | 24-14 |
| Mariano Duncan | - | - | 1-3 | - | 7-4 | - | - | 1-0 | - | 6-3 | - | 9-7 |
| Jeff Fischer | - | - | - | - | - | - | - | - | - | - | 0-2 | - |
| Darrin Fletcher | 1-0 | - | - | - | - | - | - | - | - | - | - | 1-0 |
| Kirk Gibson | - | - | - | - | - | 20-31 | 9-6 | - | - | 6-4 | - | 29-37 |
| Jose Gonzalez | - | - | - | - | - | 0-1 | 20-24 | 10-7 | - | 6-9 | - | 30-32 |
| Alfredo Griffin | - | - | - | - | 59-67 | - | - | - | - | 32-36 | - | 59-67 |
| Chris Gwynn | - | - | - | - | - | 8-1 | 2-2 | - | - | 5-2 | - | 10-3 |
| Jeff Hamilton | - | - | - | 65-75 | - | - | - | - | - | - | 0-1 | 65-75 |
| Lenny Harris | - | - | 5-6 | 3-0 | - | 8-9 | - | - | - | 3-4 | - | 16-15 |
| Mike Hartley | - | - | - | - | - | - | - | - | - | - | 1-4 | - |
| Mickey Hatcher | - | 1-0 | - | 4-8 | - | 19-11 | - | 2-6 | - | - | 0-1 | 26-25 |
| Orel Hershiser | - | - | - | - | - | - | - | - | 17-16 | - | 0-2 | 17-16 |
| Ricky Horton | - | - | - | - | - | - | - | - | - | - | 5-18 | - |
| Jay Howell | - | - | - | - | - | - | - | - | - | - | 41-15 | - |
| Mike Huff | - | - | - | - | - | 3-3 | 1-0 | 1-0 | - | - | - | 5-3 |
| Tim Leary | - | - | - | - | - | - | - | - | 7-10 | - | 1-1 | 7-10 |
| Mike Marshall | - | - | - | - | - | - | - | 46-52 | - | - | - | 46-52 |
| Ramon Martinez | - | - | - | - | - | - | - | - | 8-7 | - | - | 8-7 |
| Mike Morgan | - | - | - | - | - | - | - | - | 8-11 | - | 6-15 | 8-11 |
| Mike Munoz | - | - | - | - | - | - | - | - | - | - | 1-2 | - |
| Eddie Murray | - | 76-83 | - | - | - | - | - | - | - | - | - | 76-83 |
| Alejandro Pena | - | - | - | - | - | - | - | - | - | - | 21-32 | - |
| Willie Randolph | - | - | 68-71 | - | - | - | - | - | - | 18-24 | - | 68-71 |
| Mike Scioscia | 52-69 | - | - | - | - | - | - | - | - | - | - | 52-69 |
| Ray Searage | - | - | - | - | - | - | - | - | - | - | 12-29 | - |
| Mike Sharperson | - | - | 2-0 | - | - | - | - | - | - | - | - | 2-0 |
| John Shelby | - | - | - | - | - | - | 41-45 | - | - | - | - | 41-45 |
| Franklin Stubbs | - | - | - | - | - | 8-7 | 2-2 | 2-1 | - | - | - | 12-10 |
| John Tudor | - | - | - | - | - | - | - | - | 1-2 | - | 0-3 | 1-2 |
| Fernando Valenzuela | - | - | - | - | - | - | - | - | 16-15 | - | - | 16-15 |
| Jose Vizcaino | - | - | - | - | 1-0 | - | - | - | - | 1-0 | - | 1-0 |
| John Wetteland | - | - | - | - | - | - | - | - | 4-8 | - | 6-13 | 4-8 |
| Tracy Woodson | - | - | - | 1-0 | - | - | - | - | - | - | - | 1-0 |

## Batting vs. Left and Right Handed Pitchers

| | | BA | Rank | SA | Rank | OBA | Rank | HR % | Rank | BB % | Rank | SO % | Rank |
|---|---|---|---|---|---|---|---|---|---|---|---|---|---|
| Dave Anderson | vs. Lefties | .209 | 113 | .209 | 127 | .289 | 107 | 0.00 | 112 | 9.88 | 48 | 12.35 | 58 |
| | vs. Righties | .247 | -- | .315 | -- | .329 | -- | 1.37 | -- | 10.98 | -- | 19.51 | -- |
| Kal Daniels | vs. Lefties | .193 | 121 | .298 | 108 | .373 | 24 | 1.75 | 67 | 22.67 | 2 | 18.67 | 117 |
| | vs. Righties | .272 | 38 | .439 | 20 | .413 | 3 | 2.63 | 45 | 18.18 | 2 | 13.29 | 59 |
| Mike Davis | vs. Lefties | .118 | -- | .118 | -- | .118 | -- | 0.00 | -- | 0.00 | -- | 35.29 | -- |
| | vs. Righties | .263 | 49 | .417 | 37 | .328 | 51 | 3.21 | 31 | 9.20 | 53 | 12.64 | 51 |
| Rick Dempsey | vs. Lefties | .171 | 125 | .239 | 123 | .307 | 92 | 0.85 | 96 | 15.71 | 7 | 18.57 | 116 |
| | vs. Righties | .206 | -- | .529 | -- | .357 | -- | 8.82 | -- | 18.60 | -- | 25.58 | -- |
| Kirk Gibson | vs. Lefties | .126 | 130 | .263 | 119 | .227 | 126 | 4.21 | 17 | 10.91 | 36 | 21.82 | 128 |
| | vs. Righties | .266 | 45 | .430 | 23 | .363 | 24 | 3.16 | 32 | 12.64 | 17 | 17.03 | 89 |
| Jose Gonzalez | vs. Lefties | .306 | 21 | .410 | 53 | .347 | 53 | 1.49 | 77 | 6.25 | 104 | 13.89 | 79 |
| | vs. Righties | .228 | 92 | .307 | 112 | .305 | 76 | 0.79 | 104 | 9.86 | 47 | 23.24 | 121 |
| Alfredo Griffin | vs. Lefties | .282 | 47 | .339 | 90 | .323 | 76 | 0.00 | 112 | 5.64 | 110 | 12.82 | 64 |
| | vs. Righties | .228 | 94 | .292 | 117 | .268 | 116 | 0.00 | 124 | 5.11 | 111 | 9.09 | 23 |
| Jeff Hamilton | vs. Lefties | .210 | 111 | .295 | 109 | .250 | 123 | 0.95 | 92 | 4.42 | 122 | 12.39 | 59 |
| | vs. Righties | .266 | 44 | .429 | 24 | .286 | 96 | 2.96 | 37 | 2.82 | 129 | 12.11 | 44 |
| Lenny Harris | vs. Lefties | .191 | 122 | .221 | 126 | .257 | 120 | 0.00 | 112 | 5.33 | 111 | 12.00 | 52 |
| | vs. Righties | .247 | 67 | .318 | 103 | .290 | 93 | 1.12 | 91 | 5.65 | 103 | 8.48 | 18 |
| Mickey Hatcher | vs. Lefties | .321 | 14 | .443 | 37 | .352 | 47 | 1.53 | 75 | 4.93 | 114 | 5.63 | 6 |
| | vs. Righties | .258 | -- | .290 | -- | .294 | -- | 0.00 | -- | 5.88 | -- | 7.84 | -- |
| Mike Marshall | vs. Lefties | .246 | 87 | .469 | 29 | .340 | 60 | 5.38 | 9 | 11.33 | 31 | 14.67 | 83 |
| | vs. Righties | .267 | 43 | .377 | 61 | .316 | 62 | 1.62 | 72 | 5.95 | 101 | 20.82 | 113 |
| Eddie Murray | vs. Lefties | .210 | 111 | .329 | 95 | .317 | 78 | 1.90 | 65 | 13.01 | 22 | 11.38 | 47 |
| | vs. Righties | .268 | 41 | .440 | 19 | .356 | 29 | 4.17 | 16 | 12.39 | 22 | 12.84 | 53 |
| Willie Randolph | vs. Lefties | .298 | 25 | .356 | 79 | .385 | 16 | 0.52 | 106 | 11.61 | 30 | 5.80 | 7 |
| | vs. Righties | .274 | 35 | .310 | 110 | .355 | 30 | 0.28 | 122 | 11.00 | 32 | 9.29 | 25 |
| Mike Scioscia | vs. Lefties | .230 | 99 | .330 | 94 | .300 | 95 | 3.00 | 36 | 8.77 | 62 | 7.89 | 18 |
| | vs. Righties | .256 | 57 | .373 | 67 | .350 | 33 | 2.27 | 55 | 11.76 | 27 | 5.60 | 5 |
| John Shelby | vs. Lefties | .168 | 126 | .208 | 128 | .206 | 128 | 0.00 | 112 | 4.58 | 119 | 22.14 | 129 |
| | vs. Righties | .191 | 128 | .241 | 130 | .254 | 125 | 0.45 | 116 | 7.92 | 74 | 26.25 | 128 |
| Team Average | vs. Lefties | .234 | 11 | .327 | 12 | .301 | 12 | 1.42 | 10 | 8.23 | 11 | 13.79 | 3 |
| | vs. Righties | .244 | 7 | .346 | 10 | .309 | 8 | 1.74 | 9 | 8.31 | 7 | 14.82 | 3 |
| League Average | vs. Lefties | .251 | | .371 | | .320 | | 2.06 | | 8.85 | | 14.80 | |
| | vs. Righties | .244 | | .362 | | .309 | | 2.08 | | 8.27 | | 15.67 | |

## Batting with Runners on Base and Bases Empty

| | | BA | Rank | SA | Rank | OBA | Rank | HR % | Rank | BB % | Rank | SO % | Rank |
|---|---|---|---|---|---|---|---|---|---|---|---|---|---|
| Kal Daniels | Runners On | .191 | 124 | .294 | 121 | .367 | 33 | 1.47 | 78 | 22.22 | 3 | 14.44 | 79 |
| | Bases Empty | .282 | 28 | .456 | 15 | .422 | 1 | 2.91 | 30 | 17.97 | 2 | 15.63 | 83 |
| Mike Davis | Runners On | .212 | -- | .318 | -- | .239 | -- | 1.52 | -- | 4.23 | -- | 19.72 | -- |
| | Bases Empty | .271 | 41 | .430 | 25 | .350 | 27 | 3.74 | 19 | 10.83 | 20 | 11.67 | 40 |
| Rick Dempsey | Runners On | .200 | 123 | .286 | 123 | .364 | 36 | 1.43 | 79 | 20.22 | 4 | 19.10 | 113 |
| | Bases Empty | .160 | -- | .321 | -- | .277 | -- | 3.70 | -- | 12.77 | -- | 21.28 | -- |
| Kirk Gibson | Runners On | .207 | 122 | .345 | 94 | .319 | 88 | 2.59 | 47 | 13.77 | 25 | 18.12 | 109 |
| | Bases Empty | .219 | 105 | .387 | 55 | .305 | 75 | 4.38 | 17 | 10.39 | 31 | 19.48 | 115 |
| Jose Gonzalez | Runners On | .257 | 77 | .327 | 105 | .321 | 85 | 0.99 | 95 | 8.85 | 81 | 22.12 | 126 |
| | Bases Empty | .275 | 32 | .381 | 62 | .329 | 45 | 1.25 | 92 | 7.51 | 69 | 16.18 | 88 |
| Alfredo Griffin | Runners On | .272 | 53 | .335 | 100 | .294 | 110 | 0.00 | 112 | 3.14 | 130 | 10.99 | 46 |
| | Bases Empty | .234 | 86 | .294 | 110 | .284 | 98 | 0.00 | 122 | 6.46 | 80 | 10.11 | 23 |
| Jeff Hamilton | Runners On | .246 | 92 | .360 | 88 | .290 | 114 | 1.27 | 85 | 6.08 | 107 | 10.65 | 44 |
| | Bases Empty | .244 | 74 | .391 | 54 | .258 | 118 | 2.88 | 31 | 1.26 | 132 | 13.52 | 60 |
| Lenny Harris | Runners On | .236 | 100 | .336 | 99 | .267 | 124 | 2.14 | 59 | 4.08 | 125 | 8.84 | 23 |
| | Bases Empty | .236 | 82 | .272 | 121 | .294 | 91 | 0.00 | 122 | 6.64 | 78 | 9.48 | 21 |
| Mickey Hatcher | Runners On | .255 | 82 | .321 | 106 | .286 | 116 | 0.94 | 99 | 5.88 | 108 | 5.04 | 3 |
| | Bases Empty | .331 | 3 | .432 | 23 | .368 | 13 | 0.85 | 103 | 4.80 | 107 | 8.00 | 8 |
| Mike Marshall | Runners On | .235 | 103 | .419 | 44 | .299 | 105 | 3.91 | 21 | 8.46 | 85 | 20.90 | 122 |
| | Bases Empty | .283 | 26 | .399 | 48 | .349 | 29 | 2.02 | 60 | 7.34 | 71 | 16.51 | 90 |
| Eddie Murray | Runners On | .258 | 75 | .471 | 18 | .361 | 41 | 5.15 | 9 | 14.33 | 19 | 10.03 | 33 |
| | Bases Empty | .238 | 80 | .333 | 95 | .323 | 50 | 1.65 | 73 | 10.85 | 19 | 14.66 | 69 |
| Willie Randolph | Runners On | .301 | 25 | .360 | 87 | .392 | 22 | 0.54 | 107 | 13.27 | 29 | 7.08 | 7 |
| | Bases Empty | .273 | 37 | .309 | 105 | .351 | 23 | 0.28 | 121 | 10.07 | 37 | 8.60 | 14 |
| Mike Scioscia | Runners On | .226 | 110 | .333 | 101 | .321 | 87 | 2.38 | 53 | 12.00 | 41 | 5.50 | 5 |
| | Bases Empty | .267 | 49 | .383 | 58 | .351 | 25 | 2.50 | 47 | 10.33 | 33 | 6.64 | 5 |
| John Shelby | Runners On | .176 | 128 | .250 | 128 | .236 | 126 | 0.74 | 102 | 7.43 | 94 | 23.65 | 131 |
| | Bases Empty | .187 | 126 | .215 | 131 | .238 | 128 | 0.00 | 122 | 6.28 | 84 | 25.56 | 128 |
| Team Average | Runners On | .244 | 12 | .356 | 12 | .316 | 12 | 1.98 | 8 | 9.38 | 8 | 13.68 | 3 |
| | Bases Empty | .237 | 8 | .328 | 11 | .299 | 8 | 1.38 | 11 | 7.44 | 7 | 15.04 | 4 |
| League Average | Runners On | .256 | | .379 | | .330 | | 2.13 | | 9.82 | | 14.66 | |
| | Bases Empty | .240 | | .355 | | .299 | | 2.03 | | 7.43 | | 15.93 | |

## Overall Batting Compared to Late Inning Pressure Situations

| | | BA | Rank | SA | Rank | OBA | Rank | HR % | Rank | BB % | Rank | SO % | Rank | RDI % | Rank |
|---|---|---|---|---|---|---|---|---|---|---|---|---|---|---|---|
| Dave Anderson | Overall | .229 | -- | .264 | -- | .310 | -- | 0.71 | -- | 10.43 | -- | 15.95 | -- | .333 | -- |
| | Pressure | .235 | 68 | .235 | 111 | .333 | 47 | 0.00 | 81 | 11.90 | 37 | 14.29 | 57 | .143 | -- |
| Kal Daniels | Overall | .246 | 82 | .392 | 52 | .399 | 6 | 2.34 | 49 | 19.72 | 2 | 15.14 | 83 | .244 | -- |
| | Pressure | .182 | 113 | .303 | 87 | .333 | 47 | 0.00 | 81 | 19.05 | 3 | 14.29 | 57 | .083 | 127 |
| Mike Davis | Overall | .249 | -- | .387 | -- | .309 | -- | 2.89 | -- | 8.38 | -- | 14.66 | -- | .250 | -- |
| | Pressure | .167 | 116 | .250 | 107 | .286 | 83 | 2.78 | 28 | 14.29 | 19 | 16.67 | 74 | .125 | -- |
| Rick Dempsey | Overall | .179 | -- | .305 | -- | .319 | -- | 2.65 | -- | 16.39 | -- | 20.22 | -- | .234 | -- |
| | Pressure | .190 | 108 | .333 | 70 | .306 | 72 | 4.76 | 12 | 14.00 | 20 | 16.00 | 70 | .211 | 71 |
| Kirk Gibson | Overall | .213 | 119 | .368 | 70 | .312 | 84 | 3.56 | 19 | 11.99 | 24 | 18.84 | 117 | .200 | 119 |
| | Pressure | .136 | 128 | .159 | 129 | .208 | 127 | 0.00 | 81 | 8.33 | 74 | 25.00 | 120 | .167 | 94 |
| Jose Gonzalez | Overall | .268 | 46 | .360 | 80 | .326 | 55 | 1.15 | 94 | 8.04 | 74 | 18.53 | 112 | .212 | 110 |
| | Pressure | .321 | 14 | .396 | 31 | .379 | 20 | 0.00 | 81 | 8.47 | 70 | 15.25 | 66 | .167 | 94 |
| Alfredo Griffin | Overall | .247 | 78 | .308 | 115 | .287 | 105 | 0.00 | 127 | 5.30 | 113 | 10.42 | 29 | .203 | 118 |
| | Pressure | .213 | 89 | .223 | 117 | .253 | 108 | 0.00 | 81 | 4.90 | 103 | 16.67 | 74 | .118 | 119 |
| Jeff Hamilton | Overall | .245 | 84 | .378 | 63 | .272 | 122 | 2.19 | 57 | 3.44 | 129 | 12.22 | 46 | .245 | 82 |
| | Pressure | .248 | 56 | .303 | 88 | .288 | 81 | 0.00 | 81 | 4.96 | 101 | 13.22 | 44 | .250 | 52 |
| Lenny Harris | Overall | .236 | 99 | .299 | 118 | .283 | 109 | 0.90 | 106 | 5.59 | 111 | 9.22 | 19 | .210 | 113 |
| | Pressure | .204 | 95 | .222 | 118 | .271 | 94 | 0.00 | 81 | 8.47 | 70 | 13.56 | 49 | .000 | 131 |
| Mickey Hatcher | Overall | .295 | 14 | .379 | 61 | .328 | 53 | 0.89 | 107 | 5.33 | 112 | 6.56 | 5 | .256 | 71 |
| | Pressure | .264 | 46 | .321 | 81 | .283 | 88 | 0.00 | 81 | 5.00 | 100 | 11.67 | 32 | .238 | 62 |
| Mike Marshall | Overall | .260 | 54 | .408 | 40 | .325 | 59 | 2.92 | 32 | 7.88 | 77 | 18.62 | 114 | .224 | 100 |
| | Pressure | .197 | 101 | .258 | 104 | .284 | 87 | 0.00 | 81 | 9.46 | 60 | 17.57 | 86 | .308 | 35 |
| Eddie Murray | Overall | .247 | 77 | .401 | 46 | .342 | 41 | 3.37 | 27 | 12.61 | 16 | 12.32 | 50 | .282 | 46 |
| | Pressure | .179 | 114 | .321 | 80 | .281 | 91 | 4.46 | 14 | 11.72 | 39 | 14.84 | 65 | .143 | 106 |
| Willie Randolph | Overall | .282 | 28 | .326 | 107 | .366 | 23 | 0.36 | 118 | 11.22 | 31 | 8.06 | 11 | .252 | 75 |
| | Pressure | .245 | 57 | .327 | 76 | .353 | 38 | 1.02 | 80 | 13.68 | 21 | 5.98 | 6 | .200 | 74 |
| Mike Scioscia | Overall | .250 | 73 | .363 | 75 | .338 | 45 | 2.45 | 44 | 11.04 | 34 | 6.16 | 3 | .210 | 114 |
| | Pressure | .224 | 80 | .329 | 72 | .314 | 70 | 1.32 | 73 | 11.11 | 44 | 7.78 | 12 | .111 | 121 |
| John Shelby | Overall | .183 | 129 | .229 | 131 | .237 | 128 | 0.29 | 124 | 6.74 | 96 | 24.80 | 130 | .127 | 132 |
| | Pressure | .149 | 124 | .203 | 123 | .203 | 128 | 1.35 | 72 | 6.33 | 88 | 24.05 | 117 | .000 | 131 |
| Team Average | Overall | .240 | 10 | .339 | 12 | .306 | 11 | 1.63 | 11 | 8.28 | 6 | 14.45 | 3 | .234 | 12 |
| | Pressure | .217 | 11 | .285 | 12 | .288 | 11 | 1.06 | 11 | 8.70 | 9 | 15.78 | 6 | .167 | 12 |
| League Average | Overall | .246 | | .365 | | .312 | | 2.07 | | 8.47 | | 15.38 | | .253 | |
| | Pressure | .238 | | .337 | | .308 | | 1.73 | | 8.93 | | 16.78 | | .235 | |

## Additional Miscellaneous Batting Comparisons

| | Grass Surface | | Artificial Surface | | Home Games | | Road Games | | Runners in Scoring Position | | Runners in Scoring Pos and Two Outs | | Leading Off Inning | | Runners on 3B with less than 2 Outs | |
|---|---|---|---|---|---|---|---|---|---|---|---|---|---|---|---|---|
| | BA | Rank | BA | Rank | BA | Rank | BA | Rank | BA | Rank | BA | Rank | OBA | Rank | RDI % | Rank |
| Dave Anderson | .289 | 27 | .120 | -- | .290 | -- | .179 | -- | .281 | -- | .333 | -- | .205 | -- | .500 | 98 |
| Kal Daniels | .256 | -- | .242 | 89 | .246 | -- | .245 | 75 | .242 | -- | .100 | 130 | .408 | 10 | .667 | -- |
| Mike Davis | .262 | 56 | .216 | -- | .273 | 47 | .224 | -- | .161 | -- | .000 | -- | .255 | 107 | .583 | 61 |
| Rick Dempsey | .178 | 123 | .182 | -- | .181 | -- | .177 | 130 | .222 | -- | .130 | 125 | .171 | -- | .500 | -- |
| Kirk Gibson | .214 | 105 | .211 | -- | .222 | 110 | .203 | 116 | .185 | 123 | .160 | 114 | .232 | 121 | .556 | 74 |
| Jose Gonzalez | .254 | 64 | .300 | 12 | .239 | 91 | .291 | 19 | .207 | 110 | .185 | 103 | .329 | 46 | .400 | 130 |
| Alfredo Griffin | .244 | 73 | .256 | 62 | .252 | 77 | .242 | 78 | .243 | 84 | .200 | 89 | .254 | 109 | .500 | 98 |
| Jeff Hamilton | .244 | 72 | .245 | 84 | .232 | 100 | .256 | 60 | .208 | 109 | .213 | 79 | .275 | 95 | .611 | 52 |
| Lenny Harris | .237 | 78 | .235 | 102 | .255 | 71 | .218 | 99 | .200 | 115 | .314 | 17 | .288 | 75 | .125 | 147 |
| Mickey Hatcher | .296 | 19 | .292 | -- | .284 | 39 | .306 | 7 | .226 | 97 | .273 | 31 | .356 | -- | .529 | 91 |
| Mike Marshall | .279 | 38 | .208 | 122 | .294 | 30 | .230 | 90 | .258 | 67 | .200 | 89 | .409 | 9 | .556 | 74 |
| Eddie Murray | .248 | 66 | .247 | 82 | .253 | 73 | .242 | 80 | .257 | 68 | .218 | 76 | .277 | 91 | .593 | 56 |
| Willie Randolph | .291 | 24 | .260 | 55 | .305 | 18 | .261 | 56 | .260 | 64 | .231 | 60 | .382 | 15 | .650 | 36 |
| Mike Scioscia | .236 | 79 | .284 | 30 | .235 | 95 | .264 | 51 | .204 | 111 | .196 | 94 | .370 | 23 | .500 | 98 |
| John Shelby | .196 | 116 | .129 | -- | .183 | 126 | .182 | 127 | .175 | 127 | .121 | 126 | .226 | 126 | .400 | 130 |
| Team Average | .242 | 6 | .236 | 12 | .241 | 11 | .239 | 9 | .228 | 12 | .207 | 9 | .292 | 10 | .514 | 11 |
| League Average | .244 | | .248 | | .251 | | .242 | | .249 | | .222 | | .302 | | .546 | |

## Pitching vs. Left and Right Handed Batters

| | | BA | Rank | SA | Rank | OBA | Rank | HR % | Rank | BB % | Rank | SO % | Rank |
|---|---|---|---|---|---|---|---|---|---|---|---|---|---|
| Tim Belcher | vs. Lefties | .218 | 29 | .292 | 24 | .298 | 36 | 1.48 | 56 | 9.55 | 66 | 19.48 | 19 |
| | vs. Righties | .216 | 32 | .362 | 62 | .278 | 42 | 3.56 | 109 | 7.20 | 61 | 23.82 | 20 |
| Tim Crews | vs. Lefties | .245 | 56 | .391 | 79 | .341 | 82 | 1.82 | 70 | 12.40 | 99 | 18.60 | 22 |
| | vs. Righties | .316 | 115 | .510 | 116 | .359 | 105 | 0.76 | 112 | 4.79 | 20 | 21.92 | 27 |
| Orel Hershiser | vs. Lefties | .258 | 72 | .339 | 48 | .323 | 59 | 0.96 | 31 | 8.56 | 54 | 13.87 | 55 |
| | vs. Righties | .217 | 33 | .288 | 16 | .265 | 28 | 0.95 | 12 | 5.83 | 30 | 20.95 | 34 |
| Jay Howell | vs. Lefties | .208 | 21 | .270 | 15 | .282 | 21 | 0.63 | 19 | 9.44 | 64 | 17.78 | 26 |
| | vs. Righties | .216 | 31 | .312 | 24 | .244 | 13 | 1.60 | 31 | 3.79 | 7 | 17.42 | 54 |
| Ramon Martinez | vs. Lefties | .246 | 59 | .369 | 67 | .343 | 84 | 2.96 | 97 | 11.44 | 85 | 18.64 | 21 |
| | vs. Righties | .185 | 9 | .318 | 27 | .260 | 19 | 3.18 | 101 | 8.05 | 73 | 25.86 | 10 |
| Mike Morgan | vs. Lefties | .254 | 69 | .355 | 57 | .310 | 50 | 1.67 | 65 | 7.16 | 29 | 12.24 | 75 |
| | vs. Righties | .211 | 27 | .277 | 13 | .236 | 8 | 0.39 | 5 | 3.35 | 3 | 11.52 | 95 |
| Alejandro Pena | vs. Lefties | .232 | 38 | .338 | 47 | .280 | 20 | 2.65 | 92 | 6.17 | 16 | 24.69 | 7 |
| | vs. Righties | .206 | 22 | .305 | 21 | .261 | 21 | 1.53 | 28 | 5.56 | 25 | 24.31 | 17 |
| Fernando Valenzuela | vs. Lefties | .256 | 71 | .352 | 55 | .324 | 60 | 0.80 | 25 | 9.29 | 62 | 15.00 | 47 |
| | vs. Righties | .250 | 76 | .351 | 53 | .340 | 91 | 1.63 | 35 | 11.94 | 108 | 13.34 | 83 |
| John Wetteland | vs. Lefties | .212 | 24 | .295 | 28 | .269 | 15 | 1.55 | 58 | 7.18 | 30 | 21.53 | 11 |
| | vs. Righties | .225 | 45 | .365 | 66 | .296 | 59 | 2.81 | 80 | 9.41 | 95 | 25.25 | 14 |
| Team Average | vs. Lefties | .244 | 4 | .339 | 1 | .315 | 3 | 1.59 | 4 | 9.04 | 4 | 16.63 | 1 |
| | vs. Righties | .231 | 2 | .339 | 1 | .293 | 4 | 1.92 | 3 | 7.71 | 6 | 18.18 | 3 |
| League Average | vs. Lefties | .252 | | .366 | | .325 | | 1.79 | | 9.48 | | 13.93 | |
| | vs. Righties | .242 | | .365 | | .303 | | 2.29 | | 7.70 | | 16.46 | |

## Pitching with Runners on Base and Bases Empty

| | | BA | Rank | SA | Rank | OBA | Rank | HR % | Rank | BB % | Rank | SO % | Rank |
|---|---|---|---|---|---|---|---|---|---|---|---|---|---|
| Tim Belcher | Runners On | .192 | 4 | .295 | 14 | .287 | 19 | 2.24 | 69 | 10.60 | 76 | 23.37 | 7 |
| | Bases Empty | .232 | 40 | .338 | 45 | .290 | 47 | 2.47 | 85 | 7.21 | 63 | 20.04 | 28 |
| Tim Crews | Runners On | .296 | 98 | .500 | 114 | .402 | 114 | 3.70 | 107 | 13.43 | 107 | 18.66 | 29 |
| | Bases Empty | .274 | 104 | .430 | 110 | .305 | 67 | 2.22 | 72 | 3.55 | 7 | 21.99 | 15 |
| Orel Hershiser | Runners On | .227 | 31 | .309 | 20 | .299 | 31 | 1.02 | 21 | 8.91 | 45 | 18.04 | 33 |
| | Bases Empty | .249 | 75 | .322 | 28 | .296 | 54 | 0.91 | 18 | 6.13 | 43 | 16.18 | 45 |
| Jay Howell | Runners On | .188 | 3 | .248 | 4 | .265 | 7 | 0.85 | 16 | 9.56 | 57 | 23.53 | 6 |
| | Bases Empty | .228 | 35 | .317 | 26 | .267 | 20 | 1.20 | 29 | 5.11 | 23 | 13.07 | 82 |
| Ramon Martinez | Runners On | .228 | 33 | .338 | 35 | .304 | 38 | 2.76 | 91 | 7.88 | 30 | 14.55 | 57 |
| | Bases Empty | .214 | 23 | .353 | 64 | .310 | 79 | 3.26 | 108 | 11.43 | 109 | 26.53 | 6 |
| Mike Morgan | Runners On | .236 | 42 | .327 | 30 | .292 | 22 | 0.96 | 19 | 7.05 | 16 | 11.62 | 87 |
| | Bases Empty | .233 | 43 | .314 | 25 | .267 | 21 | 1.15 | 26 | 4.41 | 17 | 12.12 | 93 |
| Alejandro Pena | Runners On | .219 | 21 | .272 | 9 | .268 | 9 | 0.00 | 1 | 5.56 | 5 | 23.02 | 8 |
| | Bases Empty | .220 | 28 | .357 | 70 | .272 | 26 | 3.57 | 110 | 6.11 | 41 | 25.56 | 8 |
| Fernando Valenzuela | Runners On | .263 | 81 | .369 | 63 | .363 | 94 | 1.60 | 40 | 13.98 | 111 | 11.61 | 88 |
| | Bases Empty | .242 | 56 | .338 | 44 | .317 | 88 | 1.41 | 38 | 9.51 | 93 | 15.22 | 58 |
| John Wetteland | Runners On | .232 | 38 | .361 | 60 | .280 | 14 | 2.58 | 85 | 6.40 | 13 | 22.09 | 11 |
| | Bases Empty | .208 | 19 | .306 | 23 | .285 | 41 | 1.85 | 53 | 9.62 | 94 | 24.27 | 10 |
| Team Average | Runners On | .236 | 1 | .340 | 1 | .316 | 2 | 1.64 | 1 | 10.01 | 10 | 16.89 | 3 |
| | Bases Empty | .238 | 4 | .338 | 2 | .295 | 5 | 1.85 | 2 | 7.11 | 4 | 17.85 | 2 |
| League Average | Runners On | .256 | | .379 | | .330 | | 2.13 | | 9.82 | | 14.66 | |
| | Bases Empty | .240 | | .355 | | .299 | | 2.03 | | 7.43 | | 15.93 | |

## Overall Pitching Compared to Late Inning Pressure Situations

| | | BA | Rank | SA | Rank | OBA | Rank | HR % | Rank | BB % | Rank | SO % | Rank |
|---|---|---|---|---|---|---|---|---|---|---|---|---|---|
| Tim Belcher | Overall | .217 | 24 | .322 | 27 | .289 | 34 | 2.39 | 87 | 8.54 | 66 | 21.34 | 16 |
| | Pressure | .189 | 19 | .265 | 19 | .255 | 19 | 1.52 | 56 | 7.43 | 46 | 18.24 | 38 |
| Tim Crews | Overall | .284 | 106 | .461 | 115 | .351 | 105 | 2.88 | 106 | 8.36 | 57 | 20.36 | 20 |
| | Pressure | .301 | 102 | .562 | 114 | .370 | 101 | 4.11 | 106 | 9.64 | 68 | 20.48 | 24 |
| Orel Hershiser | Overall | .240 | 55 | .316 | 21 | .298 | 46 | 0.96 | 11 | 7.35 | 38 | 17.00 | 44 |
| | Pressure | .219 | 41 | .299 | 36 | .323 | 72 | 0.73 | 29 | 12.73 | 97 | 15.15 | 63 |
| Jay Howell | Overall | .211 | 13 | .289 | 6 | .266 | 5 | 1.06 | 15 | 7.05 | 36 | 17.63 | 40 |
| | Pressure | .206 | 32 | .272 | 21 | .262 | 25 | 0.88 | 33 | 7.14 | 40 | 15.48 | 56 |
| Ramon Martinez | Overall | .219 | 27 | .347 | 49 | .308 | 59 | 3.06 | 110 | 10.00 | 91 | 21.71 | 14 |
| | Pressure | .296 | -- | .296 | -- | .387 | -- | 0.00 | -- | 12.50 | -- | 21.88 | -- |
| Mike Morgan | Overall | .234 | 44 | .319 | 24 | .277 | 19 | 1.08 | 17 | 5.46 | 14 | 11.92 | 92 |
| | Pressure | .160 | 5 | .230 | 8 | .190 | 1 | 1.00 | 38 | 3.70 | 12 | 11.11 | 91 |
| Alejandro Pena | Overall | .220 | 28 | .323 | 28 | .271 | 12 | 2.13 | 65 | 5.88 | 18 | 24.51 | 6 |
| | Pressure | .253 | 75 | .390 | 92 | .305 | 50 | 2.75 | 91 | 6.03 | 31 | 22.11 | 19 |
| Ray Searage | Overall | .225 | -- | .287 | -- | .313 | -- | 0.78 | -- | 11.84 | -- | 15.79 | -- |
| | Pressure | .259 | 79 | .370 | 82 | .364 | 97 | 1.85 | 67 | 14.93 | 111 | 14.93 | 67 |
| Fernando Valenzuela | Overall | .251 | 68 | .351 | 55 | .337 | 96 | 1.49 | 29 | 11.50 | 109 | 13.62 | 71 |
| | Pressure | .360 | 112 | .500 | 109 | .407 | 109 | 2.00 | 71 | 7.14 | 40 | 10.71 | 97 |
| John Wetteland | Overall | .218 | 26 | .329 | 30 | .283 | 26 | 2.16 | 67 | 8.27 | 56 | 23.36 | 11 |
| | Pressure | .224 | 47 | .289 | 33 | .280 | 37 | 0.00 | 1 | 7.14 | 40 | 22.62 | 16 |
| Team Average | Overall | .237 | 2 | .339 | 1 | .304 | 2 | 1.76 | 2 | 8.35 | 5 | 17.43 | 2 |
| | Pressure | .236 | 8 | .332 | 7 | .303 | 4 | 1.38 | 2 | 8.51 | 2 | 17.25 | 5 |
| League Average | Overall | .246 | | .365 | | .312 | | 2.07 | | 8.47 | | 15.38 | |
| | Pressure | .235 | | .336 | | .309 | | 1.77 | | 9.31 | | 16.92 | |

## Additional Miscellaneous Pitching Comparisons

| | Grass Surface BA | Rank | Artificial Surface BA | Rank | Home Games BA | Rank | Road Games BA | Rank | Runners in Scoring Position BA | Rank | Runners in Scoring Pos and Two Outs BA | Rank | Leading Off Inning OBA | Rank |
|---|---|---|---|---|---|---|---|---|---|---|---|---|---|---|
| Tim Belcher | .209 | 18 | .235 | 42 | .199 | 18 | .237 | 43 | .189 | 13 | .161 | 20 | .264 | 24 |
| Tim Crews | .282 | 101 | .290 | -- | .277 | 97 | .290 | 104 | .319 | 109 | .357 | 117 | .322 | 87 |
| Orel Hershiser | .248 | 69 | .212 | 16 | .246 | 61 | .234 | 38 | .169 | 9 | .136 | 11 | .322 | 85 |
| Jay Howell | .207 | 17 | .228 | -- | .185 | 11 | .246 | 52 | .197 | 17 | .189 | 39 | .264 | 25 |
| Ramon Martinez | .209 | 19 | .253 | 63 | .182 | 9 | .255 | 69 | .214 | 29 | .143 | 14 | .398 | 116 |
| Mike Morgan | .218 | 32 | .298 | 105 | .215 | 28 | .258 | 74 | .230 | 45 | .231 | 71 | .270 | 31 |
| Alejandro Pena | .228 | 39 | .200 | 10 | .248 | 64 | .193 | 7 | .207 | -- | .250 | 81 | .280 | 42 |
| Ray Searage | .253 | 75 | .180 | -- | .231 | -- | .222 | -- | .326 | -- | .273 | -- | .259 | -- |
| Fernando Valenzuela | .249 | 70 | .256 | 71 | .250 | 69 | .251 | 60 | .240 | 56 | .260 | 89 | .302 | 60 |
| John Wetteland | .227 | 38 | .188 | -- | .228 | 43 | .210 | 19 | .262 | 77 | .231 | 71 | .364 | 110 |
| Team Average | .235 | 3 | .242 | 4 | .228 | 2 | .247 | 4 | .222 | 1 | .208 | 3 | .308 | 9 |
| League Average | .244 | | .248 | | .242 | | .251 | | .249 | | .222 | | .302 | |

# MONTREAL EXPOS

- **Are there any pitchers left in Montreal?**
- **More is less at the top of the Expos' batting order.**

"Scorecard! Scorecard! Get your scorecard. Can't tell the players without a scorecard."

Scorecard sales ought to be as brisk as the weather outside the dome at Olympic Stadium this April, as Expos fans try to familiarize themselves with a cast of characters that's changed as much in the last year as Dallas's (the TV show or the Cowboys, either will do). And wouldn't general manager Dave Dombrowski like to pull a page from one of the Ewings' scripts? Imagine Dombrowski awakening to find that even one of his three departed starters—Bryn Smith, Pascual Perez, or Mark Langston—had returned as a prodigal son, just as Patrick Duffy showed up in Victoria Principal's shower one morning. (Duffy's no dope, eh?) Dream on, Dave.

Over the past few years, Montreal dodged bullets in keeping the foundation of its lineup in Expos *rouge, blanc, et bleu.* On both sides of the border, articles predicting the imminent departure of Tim Raines, or Tim Wallach, or Hubie Brooks traditionally marked the end of the baseball season and the start of hunting season—hunting for Expos, that is. Given the stated reluctance of many players to ply their trade in the provinces, it was natural to expect those already under the maple leaf to plan an escape to the green (as in greenbacks) pastures of the stars and stripes. But the southbound train that carried Gary Carter and Andre Dawson to the States a few years back seemed to solidify the resolve of Expos players and management to bring a pennant to Quebec. And so, over the past three years—even as Carter and Dawson reached the playoffs in successive seasons—only three teams turned their personnel over less than Montreal did.

The process for measuring a team's personnel turnover will be described shortly. But first, a table that illustrates the degree to which the most- and least-stable teams changed their rosters during the three years from 1986 through 1989:

| Most Stable | | Least Stable | |
|---|---|---|---|
| Mets | 51.5% | Orioles | 89.6% |
| Blue Jays | 54.0% | Yankees | 83.8% |
| Astros | 55.3% | White Sox | 80.3% |
| Expos | 62.5% | Braves | 79.7% |
| Indians | 66.1% | Pirates | 78.3% |

If you don't give a Boccabella how to compute a team's personnel turnover, skip two paragraphs ahead. Otherwise, start by considering only its batters—how many plate appearances each player accounted for in season I (1986 in the case above). For instance, three years ago Raines made 664 plate appearances; Mitch Webster, 645; Dawson, 546; Wallach, 539; and so on. The key is to find "matching" plate appearances in season II. For instance, Wallach made 639 PAs last season. But since he batted only 539 times in 1986, only 539 "matches" occurred. Raines had 618 PAs last season, and all qualify as matches since he had an even higher total in 1986. Because neither Dawson nor Webster played for Montreal last season, none of their appearances matched.

All told, there were 2550 matching plate appearances from a possible total of 6174 (the lower of the totals for the seasons marking the start and finish of the range). The difference between those figures (3624) represents the "change" over the period; a percentage is then easily computed. The same computations are performed for pitchers, with innings rather than plate appearances determining each player's contribution to the team pie. And the average of the batting and pitching figures becomes the overall team average.

The implications of personnel turnover will strongly impact Montreal this season according to the following chain of logic: (1) The Expos have finally undergone a major roster overhaul; (2) most of the changes have occurred in their pitching staff; and (3) except for teams with poor staffs to begin with, major changes to a team's roster of pitchers usually portend trouble.

Over the past year, Montreal has added Mark Langston, Zane Smith, Oil Can Boyd, John Candelaria, Dave Schmidt, and One Tough Dominican himself, Joaquin Andujar. Meanwhile, the Expos said *au revoir* to Bryn Smith, Pascual Perez, and Langston, as well as the three young pitchers used to rent Langston for a few months, Randy Johnson, Brian Holman, and Gene Harris. The activity near the door to the Expos' clubhouse has resembled a line change, complete with fresh defensemen, at the Forum. But it's not as though Montreal's pitching staff was in need of overhaul: it ranked seventh among the 12 National League teams in ERA last season. Of course, the losses of Smith, Perez, and Langston were clearly against the hopes, not through the whimsy, of Expos management. Nevertheless, history suggests they will pay a price.

We isolated the 40 teams whose pitching staffs underwent the most drastic single-season turnovers since 1900, and found that slightly more than half (21 of 40) improved their records with the updated rosters. But when we separated the teams with poor staffs prior to the changes (ERAs among the three worst in their leagues) from the other teams, it was obvious that there's truth in the axiom, If it ain't broke, don't fix it. Of the 27 teams with poor staffs, 17 improved, 10 declined. But among the 13 teams that didn't rank among their leagues' three worst in ERA prior to the change, only four improved their overall records after the changes, nine declined.

As recent examples of this trend—both positive and negative—we offer the 1981 Angels and the 1988 White Sox. The '81 Angels turned their staff over by 76 percent from a year earlier, replacing Don Aase, Chris Knapp, Fred Martinez, and Frank Tanana in their rotation with Ken Forsch, Steve Renko, Mike Witt, and Geoff Zahn. They climbed from next-to-last in the league in ERA to eighth. Coupled with an improved offense, California improved its record from 65–95 to 51–59 (an increase of 57 percentage points obscured by the strike of '81). Three years ago, the White Sox ranked fourth in the league in ERA, with a rotation that included Floyd Bannister, Jose DeLeon, and Richard Dotson. None of those pitchers returned in 1988, and Chicago slipped to ninth in ERA, losing five and a half games from their record of 77–85 a year earlier.

Although the losses of three starting pitchers were all via free agency, Montreal's management can't be held entirely blameless. The Expos cried long and loud when Steinbrenner "overpaid" for Perez, and when Whitey "overpaid" for Smith, whose combined total of 19 wins last season understandably placed them somewhere below Koufax and Marichal in Montreal's rating book. The team simply chose not to compete in the megabidding for Langston after a certain threshold was crossed. Although each team draws the salary line at a point on the scale at which it begins to feel uneasy, some teams adjust more slowly than others when the scale itself shifts. (Did Steinbrenner really move the market with his preemptory signing of Perez, or did he simply anticipate the shift?)

On the other hand, Montreal could redeem itself should Boyd, Andujar, or Candelaria replicate the success the Expos have demonstrated in similar reclamation projects. Let's remember that no one was ringing Dennis Martinez's phone off the hook a few years ago, or Perez's either. And Mitch Webster was labelled a career minor leaguer by most other organizations when Montreal fished him from the river bottom at a bargain price. The reborn Webster was eventually swapped for starting center fielder Dave Martinez. So Montreal may be a team in desperate need of magic—someone who can pull a rabbit out of a hat. But necessity being the *mother* of invention, the Expos have a history of doing just that.

As soon as the Expos solve that nasty little problem with their pitchers, they can turn their attention to the top of their batting order. The leadoff position in Montreal's order led that of all other National League teams in on-base average last season. That's good. Nevertheless, Expos batting in the top slot ranked next-to-last in runs, scoring only 87 times. That's bad. The following pair of tables rank the leadoff hitters of each N.L. team in both of those categories (leading off the batting order, not leading off innings):

| Team | OBA | Team | Runs |
|---|---|---|---|
| Montreal | .350 | St. Louis | 108 |
| Pittsburgh | .345 | Pittsburgh | 107 |
| San Diego | .342 | San Diego | 107 |
| Cincinnati | .333 | Atlanta | 106 |
| San Francisco | .332 | Cincinnati | 106 |
| Atlanta | .324 | San Francisco | 104 |
| New York | .322 | Chicago | 94 |
| St. Louis | .318 | New York | 94 |
| Chicago | .314 | Philadelphia | 94 |
| Houston | .310 | Houston | 89 |
| Los Angeles | .293 | Montreal | 87 |
| Philadelphia | .289 | Los Angeles | 83 |

Those lists are almost identical in order, indicating that scoring from the leadoff position is a function of little more than the leadoff batter's ability to reach base. The two-three-four hitters on most teams are so uniformly competent that they drive home leadoff batters who reached base at about the same rate. One of the two exceptions was St. Louis, whose leadoff hitters scored more runs than any other team despite a lower-than-average on-base figure. But then again, its leadoff hitter, Vincent Van Go, turns walks into doubles and triples with the greatest of ease. The other was Montreal.

The Expos had trouble scoring despite a league-leading OBA because their two, three, and four hitters were among the league's least efficient. Montreal produced a .248 batting average from the second and third slots, topped—or bottomed, in this case—only by Houston (.236) and Philadelphia (.242). But those other teams could hardly blame numbers two and three for their lack of production at the top of the order, considering the low on-base averages from their number-one hitters. And despite a cleanup batting average of .277, 11 points above the league average, Montreal failed to generate the power normally expected from the number-four spot: Expos cleanup hitters produced only 18 home runs and a .418 slugging average (compared to league averages of 26 HRs and a .453 SA).

Roll all that together, and despite its many shortcomings, Montreal appears to have fallen only slightly short of the N.L. averages for the second, third, and cleanup slots combined:

| | AB | R | H | 2B | 3B | HR | RBI | BB | BA | SA | OBA |
|---|---|---|---|---|---|---|---|---|---|---|---|
| Montreal | 1936 | 235 | 498 | 97 | 4 | 54 | 228 | 193 | .257 | .395 | .329 |
| N.L. Avg. | 1905 | 261 | 511 | 91 | 13 | 54 | 244 | 207 | .268 | .414 | .340 |

The work we've published in past *Analysts* (1988 edition, pp. 53–55; 1989 edition, pp. 17–18, 139–140) has strongly suggested that the various configurations a lineup can take have little effect on the number of runs a group of players will produce over a period of time. But the data above indicate that the top of Montreal's order failed to create as many runs as it might have not because the individual hitters failed to produce, but because they failed to meld together into a cohesive attack: too low an average in the three slot, too little power in the cleanup hole—or so it appears. Would the Expos have benefited from flip-flopping number-three Andres Galarraga with cleanup hitter Hubie Brooks (or his occasional replacement, Tim Raines)? Based on our past research, we'd guess not. But it's difficult to offer any other solution to the Expos' problem. And with Brooks now gone to L.A., we may never know.

## WON-LOST RECORD BY STARTING POSITION

| MONTREAL 81-81 | C | 1B | 2B | 3B | SS | LF | CF | RF | P | Leadoff | Relief | Starts |
|---|---|---|---|---|---|---|---|---|---|---|---|---|
| Mike Aldrete | - | 3-4 | - | - | - | 6-2 | 0-1 | 5-7 | - | - | - | 14-14 |
| Hubie Brooks | - | - | - | - | - | - | - | 71-68 | - | - | - | 71-68 |
| Tim Burke | - | - | - | - | - | - | - | - | - | - | 51-17 | - |
| John Candelaria | - | - | - | - | - | - | - | - | - | - | 1-11 | - |
| Jim Dwyer | - | - | - | - | - | - | - | - | - | - | - | - |
| Mike R. Fitzgerald | 34-33 | - | - | 2-1 | - | 0-3 | - | - | - | - | - | 36-37 |
| Tom Foley | - | - | 48-43 | 2-4 | 0-2 | - | - | - | - | - | 0-1 | 50-49 |
| Steve Frey | - | - | - | - | - | - | - | - | - | - | 5-15 | - |
| Andres Galarraga | - | 72-70 | - | - | - | - | - | - | - | - | - | 72-70 |
| Damaso Garcia | - | - | 24-22 | - | - | - | - | - | - | - | - | 24-22 |
| Mark Gardner | - | - | - | - | - | - | - | - | 1-3 | - | 0-3 | 1-3 |
| Brett Gideon | - | - | - | - | - | - | - | - | - | - | 1-3 | - |
| Marquis Grissom | - | - | - | - | - | - | 6-13 | - | - | 1-0 | - | 6-13 |
| Kevin Gross | - | - | - | - | - | - | - | - | 16-15 | - | - | 16-15 |
| Gene Harris | - | - | - | - | - | - | - | - | - | - | 3-8 | - |
| Joe Hesketh | - | - | - | - | - | - | - | - | - | - | 16-27 | - |
| Brian Holman | - | - | - | - | - | - | - | - | 1-2 | - | 0-7 | 1-2 |
| Rex Hudler | - | - | 5-5 | - | 3-2 | 10-2 | - | - | - | 2-2 | - | 18-9 |
| Jeff Huson | - | - | 2-5 | 0-1 | 8-5 | - | - | - | - | - | - | 10-11 |
| Randy D. Johnson | - | - | - | - | - | - | - | - | 1-5 | - | 0-1 | 1-5 |
| Wallace Johnson | - | 6-7 | - | - | - | - | - | - | - | - | - | 6-7 |
| Mark Langston | - | - | - | - | - | - | - | - | 14-10 | - | - | 14-10 |
| Urbano Lugo | - | - | - | - | - | - | - | - | - | - | 1-2 | - |
| Dave Martinez | - | - | - | - | - | - | 48-43 | - | - | 28-25 | - | 48-43 |
| Dennis Martinez | - | - | - | - | - | - | - | - | 21-12 | - | 0-1 | 21-12 |
| Andy McGaffigan | - | - | - | - | - | - | - | - | - | - | 20-37 | - |
| Otis Nixon | - | - | - | - | - | 0-1 | 27-24 | - | - | 21-18 | - | 27-25 |
| Junior Noboa | - | - | 2-6 | - | 1-1 | - | - | - | - | - | - | 3-7 |
| Spike Owen | - | - | - | - | 69-71 | - | - | - | - | - | - | 69-71 |
| Pascual Perez | - | - | - | - | - | - | - | - | 12-16 | - | 1-4 | 12-16 |
| Marty Pevey | 6-5 | - | - | - | - | - | - | - | - | - | - | 6-5 |
| Tim Raines | - | - | - | - | - | 65-73 | - | - | - | 29-36 | - | 65-73 |
| Gilberto Reyes | 0-1 | - | - | - | - | - | - | - | - | - | - | 0-1 |
| Nelson Santovenia | 41-42 | - | - | - | - | - | - | - | - | - | - | 41-42 |
| Bryn Smith | - | - | - | - | - | - | - | - | 15-17 | - | 0-1 | 15-17 |
| Zane Smith | - | - | - | - | - | - | - | - | - | - | 15-16 | - |
| Rick Thompson | - | - | - | - | - | - | - | - | 0-1 | - | 2-16 | 0-1 |
| Larry Walker | - | - | - | - | - | - | - | 5-6 | - | - | - | 5-6 |
| Tim Wallach | - | - | - | 77-75 | - | - | - | - | - | - | 0-1 | 77-75 |

## Batting vs. Left and Right Handed Pitchers

| | | BA | Rank | SA | Rank | OBA | Rank | HR % | Rank | BB % | Rank | SO % | Rank |
|---|---|---|---|---|---|---|---|---|---|---|---|---|---|
| Mike Aldrete | vs. Lefties | .235 | -- | .294 | -- | .364 | -- | 0.00 | -- | 18.18 | -- | 18.18 | -- |
| | vs. Righties | .218 | 106 | .319 | 101 | .309 | 69 | 0.84 | 103 | 10.95 | 33 | 18.98 | 103 |
| Hubie Brooks | vs. Lefties | .284 | 44 | .463 | 32 | .352 | 49 | 3.70 | 24 | 8.38 | 67 | 17.32 | 105 |
| | vs. Righties | .261 | 52 | .379 | 59 | .302 | 78 | 2.11 | 62 | 5.80 | 102 | 18.60 | 100 |
| Mike Fitzgerald | vs. Lefties | .267 | 66 | .406 | 55 | .351 | 50 | 1.98 | 64 | 11.30 | 32 | 16.52 | 99 |
| | vs. Righties | .222 | 100 | .376 | 63 | .307 | 71 | 2.65 | 44 | 10.19 | 43 | 19.44 | 106 |
| Tom Foley | vs. Lefties | .261 | -- | .435 | -- | .292 | -- | 0.00 | -- | 3.85 | -- | 15.38 | -- |
| | vs. Righties | .227 | 95 | .341 | 90 | .315 | 65 | 1.99 | 68 | 10.86 | 34 | 12.10 | 43 |
| Andres Galarraga | vs. Lefties | .385 | 1 | .672 | 2 | .449 | 2 | 6.32 | 8 | 9.18 | 58 | 21.43 | 126 |
| | vs. Righties | .201 | 123 | .329 | 95 | .273 | 108 | 3.02 | 35 | 6.82 | 87 | 26.36 | 129 |
| Damaso Garcia | vs. Lefties | .298 | 27 | .427 | 46 | .343 | 55 | 2.29 | 56 | 6.94 | 93 | 9.72 | 30 |
| | vs. Righties | .222 | -- | .264 | -- | .269 | -- | 0.00 | -- | 6.41 | -- | 7.69 | -- |
| Rex Hudler | vs. Lefties | .254 | 80 | .439 | 42 | .286 | 110 | 4.39 | 15 | 3.33 | 129 | 13.33 | 70 |
| | vs. Righties | .220 | -- | .317 | -- | .256 | -- | 2.44 | -- | 4.65 | -- | 16.28 | -- |
| Dave Martinez | vs. Lefties | .133 | -- | .133 | -- | .161 | -- | 0.00 | -- | 3.13 | -- | 31.25 | -- |
| | vs. Righties | .287 | 25 | .405 | 44 | .338 | 41 | 0.91 | 99 | 7.14 | 83 | 12.91 | 56 |
| Otis Nixon | vs. Lefties | .233 | 98 | .273 | 113 | .299 | 96 | 0.00 | 112 | 8.43 | 65 | 12.05 | 54 |
| | vs. Righties | .194 | -- | .241 | -- | .315 | -- | 0.00 | -- | 14.96 | -- | 12.60 | -- |
| Spike Owen | vs. Lefties | .275 | 56 | .374 | 70 | .371 | 28 | 1.53 | 75 | 12.58 | 24 | 11.26 | 46 |
| | vs. Righties | .216 | 112 | .314 | 107 | .340 | 39 | 1.31 | 86 | 15.36 | 6 | 7.28 | 9 |
| Tim Raines | vs. Lefties | .286 | 42 | .406 | 54 | .389 | 14 | 2.26 | 57 | 14.01 | 17 | 7.64 | 14 |
| | vs. Righties | .286 | 26 | .422 | 32 | .397 | 10 | 1.56 | 75 | 15.40 | 5 | 7.81 | 12 |
| Nelson Santovenia | vs. Lefties | .283 | 45 | .394 | 58 | .343 | 56 | 2.02 | 61 | 7.41 | 84 | 6.48 | 10 |
| | vs. Righties | .234 | 84 | .332 | 93 | .291 | 90 | 1.46 | 79 | 6.99 | 84 | 13.10 | 58 |
| Tim Wallach | vs. Lefties | .288 | 40 | .500 | 17 | .358 | 42 | 5.00 | 12 | 10.06 | 44 | 8.38 | 20 |
| | vs. Righties | .274 | 37 | .387 | 54 | .335 | 46 | 1.21 | 90 | 8.70 | 58 | 14.35 | 67 |
| Team Average | vs. Lefties | .272 | 2 | .410 | 2 | .339 | 3 | 2.65 | 2 | 8.74 | 8 | 15.01 | 8 |
| | vs. Righties | .236 | 11 | .341 | 11 | .311 | 3 | 1.48 | 11 | 9.41 | 1 | 15.61 | 7 |
| League Average | vs. Lefties | .251 | | .371 | | .320 | | 2.06 | | 8.85 | | 14.80 | |
| | vs. Righties | .244 | | .362 | | .309 | | 2.08 | | 8.27 | | 15.67 | |

## Batting with Runners on Base and Bases Empty

| | | BA | Rank | SA | Rank | OBA | Rank | HR % | Rank | BB % | Rank | SO % | Rank |
|---|---|---|---|---|---|---|---|---|---|---|---|---|---|
| Hubie Brooks | Runners On | .265 | 66 | .392 | 59 | .321 | 86 | 2.45 | 50 | 7.94 | 90 | 17.69 | 105 |
| | Bases Empty | .269 | 46 | .414 | 35 | .313 | 63 | 2.69 | 38 | 5.38 | 98 | 18.67 | 111 |
| Mike Fitzgerald | Runners On | .255 | 81 | .426 | 38 | .327 | 80 | 2.84 | 35 | 9.32 | 75 | 17.39 | 102 |
| | Bases Empty | .221 | 99 | .349 | 88 | .318 | 56 | 2.01 | 61 | 11.76 | 13 | 19.41 | 114 |
| Tom Foley | Runners On | .242 | 97 | .389 | 62 | .328 | 79 | 2.68 | 43 | 11.24 | 50 | 12.92 | 63 |
| | Bases Empty | .221 | 100 | .319 | 101 | .304 | 76 | 1.33 | 89 | 9.88 | 39 | 11.86 | 42 |
| Andres Galarraga | Runners On | .257 | 78 | .464 | 23 | .346 | 55 | 5.75 | 6 | 9.63 | 68 | 22.92 | 129 |
| | Bases Empty | .257 | 61 | .408 | 40 | .310 | 68 | 2.57 | 43 | 5.67 | 93 | 26.57 | 130 |
| Damaso Garcia | Runners On | .231 | 105 | .282 | 124 | .276 | 118 | 1.28 | 82 | 6.82 | 103 | 10.23 | 36 |
| | Bases Empty | .296 | 13 | .424 | 29 | .343 | 37 | 1.60 | 79 | 6.72 | 77 | 8.21 | 12 |
| Dave Martinez | Runners On | .276 | 46 | .382 | 68 | .333 | 72 | 0.00 | 112 | 7.75 | 92 | 16.90 | 98 |
| | Bases Empty | .273 | 35 | .382 | 61 | .319 | 55 | 1.26 | 91 | 6.30 | 82 | 12.99 | 51 |
| Otis Nixon | Runners On | .211 | 117 | .295 | 120 | .292 | 111 | 0.00 | 112 | 10.19 | 64 | 10.19 | 34 |
| | Bases Empty | .221 | 101 | .239 | 127 | .314 | 62 | 0.00 | 122 | 11.89 | 12 | 13.51 | 59 |
| Spike Owen | Runners On | .271 | 57 | .409 | 49 | .410 | 9 | 2.76 | 40 | 18.97 | 7 | 7.76 | 12 |
| | Bases Empty | .207 | 117 | .277 | 119 | .300 | 80 | 0.39 | 117 | 11.03 | 16 | 8.97 | 19 |
| Tim Raines | Runners On | .306 | 20 | .425 | 40 | .468 | 2 | 1.08 | 93 | 24.21 | 1 | 7.14 | 8 |
| | Bases Empty | .275 | 33 | .414 | 36 | .344 | 35 | 2.11 | 58 | 8.74 | 52 | 8.20 | 11 |
| Nelson Santovenia | Runners On | .270 | 59 | .355 | 91 | .314 | 95 | 1.42 | 80 | 6.96 | 101 | 9.49 | 28 |
| | Bases Empty | .233 | 87 | .350 | 87 | .302 | 78 | 1.84 | 67 | 7.26 | 72 | 12.29 | 44 |
| Tim Wallach | Runners On | .275 | 49 | .439 | 30 | .368 | 31 | 3.14 | 28 | 13.49 | 27 | 11.51 | 50 |
| | Bases Empty | .280 | 29 | .403 | 45 | .316 | 57 | 1.57 | 80 | 5.07 | 103 | 13.73 | 61 |
| Team Average | Runners On | .250 | 9 | .371 | 10 | .336 | 2 | 2.12 | 6 | 11.12 | 1 | 14.94 | 8 |
| | Bases Empty | .244 | 5 | .354 | 7 | .307 | 4 | 1.61 | 10 | 7.70 | 5 | 15.83 | 8 |
| League Average | Runners On | .256 | | .379 | | .330 | | 2.13 | | 9.82 | | 14.66 | |
| | Bases Empty | .240 | | .355 | | .299 | | 2.03 | | 7.43 | | 15.93 | |

## Overall Batting Compared to Late Inning Pressure Situations

| | | BA | Rank | SA | Rank | OBA | Rank | HR % | Rank | BB % | Rank | SO % | Rank | RDI % | Rank |
|---|---|---|---|---|---|---|---|---|---|---|---|---|---|---|---|
| Mike Aldrete | Overall | .221 | -- | .316 | -- | .316 | -- | 0.74 | -- | 11.95 | -- | 18.87 | -- | .209 | -- |
| | Pressure | .162 | 118 | .189 | 126 | .273 | 93 | 0.00 | 81 | 11.11 | 44 | 17.78 | 88 | .250 | 52 |
| Hubie Brooks | Overall | .268 | 47 | .404 | 42 | .317 | 70 | 2.58 | 40 | 6.58 | 101 | 18.21 | 110 | .287 | 40 |
| | Pressure | .350 | 3 | .500 | 10 | .376 | 25 | 2.50 | 33 | 4.71 | 105 | 16.47 | 73 | .409 | 10 |
| Mike Fitzgerald | Overall | .238 | 94 | .386 | 57 | .322 | 62 | 2.41 | 45 | 10.57 | 40 | 18.43 | 111 | .237 | 87 |
| | Pressure | .239 | 64 | .296 | 91 | .333 | 47 | 0.00 | 81 | 12.05 | 35 | 19.28 | 99 | .200 | 74 |
| Tom Foley | Overall | .229 | 108 | .347 | 94 | .314 | 80 | 1.87 | 68 | 10.44 | 42 | 12.30 | 49 | .246 | 81 |
| | Pressure | .255 | 50 | .327 | 75 | .354 | 37 | 0.00 | 81 | 11.76 | 38 | 17.65 | 87 | .188 | 83 |
| Andres Galarraga | Overall | .257 | 64 | .434 | 26 | .327 | 54 | 4.02 | 14 | 7.55 | 83 | 24.84 | 131 | .266 | 64 |
| | Pressure | .232 | 73 | .364 | 50 | .296 | 74 | 3.03 | 26 | 7.41 | 82 | 26.85 | 123 | .219 | 67 |
| Damaso Garcia | Overall | .271 | 42 | .369 | 68 | .317 | 72 | 1.48 | 83 | 6.76 | 95 | 9.01 | 16 | .268 | 61 |
| | Pressure | .278 | -- | .361 | -- | .333 | -- | 2.78 | -- | 7.50 | -- | 7.50 | -- | .400 | 13 |
| Wallace Johnson | Overall | .272 | -- | .368 | -- | .309 | -- | 1.75 | -- | 5.60 | -- | 9.60 | -- | .294 | -- |
| | Pressure | .250 | 53 | .313 | 83 | .288 | 80 | 0.00 | 81 | 5.66 | 96 | 16.98 | 78 | .444 | 9 |
| Dave Martinez | Overall | .274 | 37 | .382 | 59 | .324 | 60 | 0.83 | 109 | 6.82 | 94 | 14.39 | 74 | .275 | 53 |
| | Pressure | .203 | 96 | .271 | 101 | .230 | 121 | 0.00 | 81 | 3.17 | 123 | 23.81 | 116 | .188 | 83 |
| Otis Nixon | Overall | .217 | 118 | .260 | 127 | .306 | 91 | 0.00 | 127 | 11.26 | 30 | 12.29 | 48 | .239 | 85 |
| | Pressure | .262 | 48 | .286 | 93 | .354 | 35 | 0.00 | 81 | 12.24 | 28 | 10.20 | 25 | .300 | 37 |
| Spike Owen | Overall | .233 | 102 | .332 | 106 | .349 | 37 | 1.37 | 85 | 14.56 | 6 | 8.43 | 13 | .270 | 58 |
| | Pressure | .263 | 47 | .375 | 41 | .348 | 41 | 2.50 | 33 | 11.70 | 40 | 8.51 | 18 | .200 | 74 |
| Tim Raines | Overall | .286 | 22 | .418 | 35 | .395 | 7 | 1.74 | 70 | 15.05 | 5 | 7.77 | 10 | .333 | 9 |
| | Pressure | .273 | 41 | .364 | 50 | .379 | 22 | 1.14 | 76 | 14.56 | 17 | 8.74 | 19 | .316 | 28 |
| Nelson Santovenia | Overall | .250 | 73 | .352 | 90 | .307 | 86 | 1.64 | 76 | 7.12 | 88 | 10.98 | 34 | .219 | 102 |
| | Pressure | .296 | 25 | .500 | 10 | .339 | 44 | 3.70 | 21 | 4.92 | 102 | 8.20 | 17 | .313 | 29 |
| Tim Wallach | Overall | .277 | 34 | .419 | 34 | .341 | 42 | 2.27 | 53 | 9.08 | 54 | 12.68 | 57 | .292 | 35 |
| | Pressure | .245 | 59 | .340 | 68 | .351 | 40 | 1.06 | 78 | 14.41 | 18 | 11.71 | 33 | .167 | 94 |
| Team Average | Overall | .247 | 5 | .361 | 8 | .319 | 2 | 1.82 | 8 | 9.22 | 1 | 15.43 | 8 | .250 | 7 |
| | Pressure | .251 | 4 | .342 | 7 | .322 | 4 | 1.37 | 9 | 9.17 | 5 | 15.65 | 3 | .248 | 5 |
| League Average | Overall | .246 | | .365 | | .312 | | 2.07 | | 8.47 | | 15.38 | | .253 | |
| | Pressure | .238 | | .337 | | .308 | | 1.73 | | 8.93 | | 16.78 | | .235 | |

## Additional Miscellaneous Batting Comparisons

| | Grass Surface BA | Rank | Artificial Surface BA | Rank | Home Games BA | Rank | Road Games BA | Rank | Runners in Scoring Position BA | Rank | Runners in Scoring Pos and Two Outs BA | Rank | Leading Off Inning OBA | Rank | Runners on 3B with less than 2 Outs RDI % | Rank |
|---|---|---|---|---|---|---|---|---|---|---|---|---|---|---|---|---|
| Mike Aldrete | .258 | -- | .210 | 120 | .254 | -- | .195 | -- | .171 | -- | .118 | -- | .344 | -- | .500 | 98 |
| Hubie Brooks | .247 | 68 | .276 | 37 | .288 | 35 | .248 | 71 | .283 | 38 | .222 | 66 | .265 | 99 | .625 | 40 |
| Mike Fitzgerald | .181 | 122 | .261 | 52 | .284 | 41 | .195 | 120 | .255 | 73 | .163 | 112 | .279 | 87 | .565 | 70 |
| Tom Foley | .244 | 71 | .225 | 111 | .217 | 113 | .244 | 77 | .248 | 82 | .222 | 66 | .333 | 40 | .600 | 55 |
| Andres Galarraga | .281 | 36 | .248 | 80 | .241 | 88 | .273 | 42 | .217 | 106 | .148 | 120 | .309 | 60 | .548 | 81 |
| Damaso Garcia | .243 | -- | .277 | 36 | .284 | 40 | .255 | 61 | .227 | 95 | .250 | -- | .225 | -- | .692 | 19 |
| Rex Hudler | .206 | -- | .256 | 60 | .258 | -- | .236 | -- | .156 | -- | .167 | -- | .245 | 114 | .500 | -- |
| Wallace Johnson | .227 | -- | .283 | 34 | .250 | -- | .288 | -- | .231 | -- | .118 | -- | .276 | -- | .636 | 38 |
| Dave Martinez | .324 | 7 | .253 | 68 | .208 | 118 | .339 | 3 | .309 | 19 | .400 | 3 | .290 | 73 | .833 | -- |
| Otis Nixon | .220 | -- | .216 | 116 | .212 | 117 | .222 | 97 | .250 | 75 | .200 | 89 | .294 | 69 | .400 | 130 |
| Spike Owen | .167 | 126 | .260 | 53 | .274 | 46 | .199 | 119 | .275 | 47 | .250 | 42 | .345 | 30 | .389 | 135 |
| Tim Raines | .284 | 33 | .287 | 25 | .271 | 49 | .301 | 10 | .330 | 8 | .260 | 36 | .369 | 24 | .700 | 17 |
| Nelson Santovenia | .217 | -- | .260 | 56 | .296 | 29 | .210 | 110 | .241 | 85 | .233 | 58 | .227 | 125 | .727 | 13 |
| Tim Wallach | .225 | 93 | .296 | 16 | .318 | 9 | .237 | 83 | .299 | 24 | .257 | 38 | .331 | 44 | .571 | 64 |
| Team Average | .228 | 11 | .253 | 3 | .257 | 2 | .237 | 10 | .254 | 5 | .220 | 7 | .299 | 7 | .568 | 3 |
| League Average | .244 | | .248 | | .251 | | .242 | | .249 | | .222 | | .302 | | .546 | |

## Pitching vs. Left and Right Handed Batters

| | | BA | Rank | SA | Rank | OBA | Rank | HR % | Rank | BB % | Rank | SO % | Rank |
|---|---|---|---|---|---|---|---|---|---|---|---|---|---|
| Tim Burke | vs. Lefties | .239 | 50 | .371 | 68 | .287 | 24 | 3.14 | 106 | 6.78 | 23 | 12.99 | 68 |
| | vs. Righties | .210 | 25 | .273 | 10 | .258 | 16 | 0.70 | 9 | 6.41 | 44 | 19.87 | 40 |
| Kevin Gross | vs. Lefties | .241 | 53 | .378 | 72 | .337 | 76 | 2.41 | 89 | 11.80 | 91 | 16.36 | 36 |
| | vs. Righties | .255 | 85 | .400 | 83 | .319 | 83 | 2.90 | 88 | 8.07 | 74 | 20.57 | 37 |
| Joe Hesketh | vs. Lefties | .298 | -- | .456 | -- | .412 | -- | 3.51 | -- | 15.71 | -- | 20.00 | -- |
| | vs. Righties | .289 | 104 | .414 | 96 | .359 | 104 | 2.34 | 67 | 10.07 | 100 | 20.13 | 39 |
| Mark Langston | vs. Lefties | .185 | 8 | .247 | 5 | .283 | 22 | 1.23 | 43 | 11.83 | 92 | 25.81 | 6 |
| | vs. Righties | .222 | 40 | .331 | 38 | .321 | 84 | 2.17 | 58 | 12.67 | 111 | 23.34 | 21 |
| Dennis Martinez | vs. Lefties | .285 | 97 | .429 | 101 | .330 | 67 | 2.44 | 90 | 6.21 | 17 | 13.94 | 54 |
| | vs. Righties | .222 | 39 | .342 | 48 | .263 | 25 | 2.30 | 65 | 3.82 | 8 | 16.23 | 66 |
| Andy McGaffigan | vs. Lefties | .229 | 37 | .321 | 39 | .331 | 70 | 0.00 | 1 | 13.33 | 104 | 11.52 | 81 |
| | vs. Righties | .353 | 116 | .460 | 112 | .390 | 116 | 2.00 | 51 | 4.76 | 19 | 12.50 | 91 |
| Pascual Perez | vs. Lefties | .237 | 47 | .362 | 64 | .290 | 26 | 2.17 | 81 | 6.64 | 22 | 17.26 | 30 |
| | vs. Righties | .237 | 56 | .356 | 57 | .273 | 36 | 1.78 | 41 | 4.18 | 13 | 20.61 | 36 |
| Bryn Smith | vs. Lefties | .215 | 28 | .305 | 31 | .265 | 14 | 1.35 | 49 | 5.83 | 13 | 13.33 | 63 |
| | vs. Righties | .233 | 52 | .374 | 75 | .286 | 50 | 2.87 | 86 | 6.77 | 52 | 16.93 | 59 |
| Zane Smith | vs. Lefties | .139 | 2 | .190 | 3 | .196 | 2 | 0.73 | 21 | 6.62 | 21 | 27.15 | 5 |
| | vs. Righties | .289 | 105 | .396 | 81 | .355 | 103 | 1.42 | 21 | 8.70 | 83 | 10.77 | 103 |
| Team Average | vs. Lefties | .243 | 2 | .363 | 5 | .312 | 1 | 2.04 | 10 | 8.74 | 2 | 15.56 | 3 |
| | vs. Righties | .247 | 9 | .370 | 8 | .312 | 11 | 2.32 | 5 | 8.17 | 8 | 18.65 | 2 |
| League Average | vs. Lefties | .252 | | .366 | | .325 | | 1.79 | | 9.48 | | 13.93 | |
| | vs. Righties | .242 | | .365 | | .303 | | 2.29 | | 7.70 | | 16.46 | |

## Pitching with Runners on Base and Bases Empty

| | | BA | Rank | SA | Rank | OBA | Rank | HR % | Rank | BB % | Rank | SO % | Rank |
|---|---|---|---|---|---|---|---|---|---|---|---|---|---|
| Tim Burke | Runners On | .229 | 35 | .305 | 18 | .293 | 23 | 0.76 | 11 | 9.09 | 50 | 18.83 | 28 |
| | Bases Empty | .222 | 30 | .339 | 47 | .257 | 12 | 2.92 | 103 | 4.47 | 18 | 13.97 | 72 |
| Kevin Gross | Runners On | .242 | 53 | .409 | 84 | .342 | 73 | 2.83 | 93 | 12.60 | 103 | 18.11 | 30 |
| | Bases Empty | .251 | 81 | .373 | 81 | .319 | 92 | 2.49 | 87 | 8.23 | 79 | 18.31 | 38 |
| Mark Langston | Runners On | .207 | 11 | .284 | 10 | .300 | 32 | 1.48 | 34 | 11.80 | 96 | 25.47 | 3 |
| | Bases Empty | .226 | 33 | .347 | 55 | .328 | 99 | 2.48 | 86 | 13.16 | 111 | 22.25 | 13 |
| Dennis Martinez | Runners On | .240 | 50 | .360 | 57 | .296 | 26 | 2.10 | 63 | 6.22 | 12 | 14.32 | 60 |
| | Bases Empty | .267 | 98 | .408 | 103 | .303 | 64 | 2.54 | 92 | 4.48 | 19 | 15.34 | 56 |
| Andy McGaffigan | Runners On | .311 | 110 | .430 | 92 | .361 | 92 | 1.32 | 31 | 7.43 | 21 | 14.29 | 61 |
| | Bases Empty | .273 | 103 | .353 | 62 | .361 | 112 | 0.72 | 15 | 10.76 | 104 | 9.49 | 108 |
| Pascual Perez | Runners On | .242 | 52 | .375 | 67 | .308 | 44 | 2.11 | 64 | 8.62 | 41 | 15.69 | 48 |
| | Bases Empty | .234 | 44 | .350 | 56 | .265 | 17 | 1.93 | 56 | 3.50 | 6 | 20.78 | 25 |
| Bryn Smith | Runners On | .234 | 40 | .388 | 77 | .283 | 15 | 2.06 | 60 | 6.46 | 14 | 15.08 | 51 |
| | Bases Empty | .217 | 25 | .304 | 22 | .269 | 24 | 1.99 | 59 | 6.12 | 42 | 14.84 | 61 |
| Zane Smith | Runners On | .239 | 46 | .351 | 43 | .324 | 63 | 1.99 | 57 | 10.49 | 74 | 13.44 | 71 |
| | Bases Empty | .263 | 94 | .341 | 50 | .310 | 78 | 0.65 | 11 | 6.08 | 40 | 15.81 | 52 |
| Team Average | Runners On | .246 | 4 | .371 | 3 | .322 | 4 | 1.99 | 5 | 9.85 | 6 | 16.91 | 2 |
| | Bases Empty | .245 | 9 | .364 | 9 | .304 | 9 | 2.33 | 10 | 7.36 | 7 | 17.44 | 3 |
| League Average | Runners On | .256 | | .379 | | .330 | | 2.13 | | 9.82 | | 14.66 | |
| | Bases Empty | .240 | | .355 | | .299 | | 2.03 | | 7.43 | | 15.93 | |

## Overall Pitching Compared to Late Inning Pressure Situations

| | | BA | Rank | SA | Rank | OBA | Rank | HR % | Rank | BB % | Rank | SO % | Rank |
|---|---|---|---|---|---|---|---|---|---|---|---|---|---|
| Tim Burke | Overall | .225 | 32 | .325 | 29 | .274 | 17 | 1.99 | 58 | 6.61 | 23 | 16.22 | 53 |
| | Pressure | .217 | 40 | .300 | 37 | .262 | 26 | 1.45 | 53 | 5.78 | 30 | 15.11 | 64 |
| John Candelaria | Overall | .283 | -- | .583 | -- | .313 | -- | 5.00 | -- | 5.88 | -- | 20.59 | -- |
| | Pressure | .317 | 105 | .634 | 116 | .341 | 87 | 7.32 | 117 | 4.44 | 15 | 22.22 | 18 |
| Kevin Gross | Overall | .247 | 62 | .388 | 81 | .329 | 84 | 2.63 | 98 | 10.15 | 96 | 18.22 | 35 |
| | Pressure | .298 | 100 | .362 | 76 | .340 | 86 | 2.13 | 75 | 4.00 | 13 | 20.00 | 26 |
| Gene Harris | Overall | .242 | -- | .348 | -- | .338 | -- | 1.52 | -- | 11.90 | -- | 13.10 | -- |
| | Pressure | .478 | 117 | .739 | 117 | .552 | 117 | 4.35 | 107 | 13.89 | 105 | 5.56 | 113 |
| Joe Hesketh | Overall | .292 | -- | .427 | -- | .376 | -- | 2.70 | -- | 11.87 | -- | 20.09 | -- |
| | Pressure | .321 | 106 | .452 | 101 | .408 | 110 | 2.38 | 82 | 12.75 | 98 | 14.71 | 71 |
| Mark Langston | Overall | .218 | 25 | .320 | 25 | .316 | 68 | 2.05 | 64 | 12.57 | 110 | 23.65 | 9 |
| | Pressure | .222 | 43 | .333 | 56 | .355 | 93 | 2.22 | 79 | 16.81 | 114 | 19.47 | 31 |
| Dennis Martinez | Overall | .257 | 80 | .390 | 82 | .300 | 47 | 2.38 | 84 | 5.16 | 7 | 14.95 | 59 |
| | Pressure | .228 | 53 | .337 | 63 | .243 | 14 | 1.98 | 70 | 1.92 | 4 | 16.35 | 51 |
| Andy McGaffigan | Overall | .293 | 110 | .393 | 85 | .361 | 109 | 1.03 | 13 | 9.01 | 73 | 12.01 | 91 |
| | Pressure | .269 | 87 | .336 | 62 | .346 | 89 | 0.75 | 31 | 10.19 | 76 | 10.83 | 96 |
| Pascual Perez | Overall | .237 | 49 | .360 | 64 | .282 | 25 | 2.00 | 59 | 5.55 | 15 | 18.74 | 31 |
| | Pressure | .375 | 113 | .542 | 113 | .439 | 113 | 1.39 | 52 | 9.64 | 68 | 9.64 | 103 |
| Bryn Smith | Overall | .223 | 30 | .335 | 38 | .274 | 18 | 2.02 | 61 | 6.25 | 21 | 14.93 | 60 |
| | Pressure | .274 | 89 | .387 | 89 | .308 | 55 | 3.23 | 101 | 2.99 | 9 | 17.91 | 41 |
| Zane Smith | Overall | .252 | 71 | .345 | 47 | .317 | 71 | 1.25 | 22 | 8.20 | 54 | 14.67 | 64 |
| | Pressure | .248 | 69 | .336 | 61 | .329 | 80 | 1.34 | 49 | 9.94 | 72 | 18.13 | 39 |
| Rick Thompson | Overall | .241 | -- | .313 | -- | .315 | -- | 1.79 | -- | 8.53 | -- | 11.63 | -- |
| | Pressure | .273 | 88 | .273 | 22 | .265 | 27 | 0.00 | 1 | 0.00 | 1 | 8.33 | 106 |
| Team Average | Overall | .245 | 5 | .367 | 8 | .312 | 7 | 2.19 | 8 | 8.44 | 6 | 17.21 | 3 |
| | Pressure | .272 | 12 | .388 | 12 | .340 | 12 | 2.22 | 11 | 8.89 | 5 | 15.35 | 9 |
| League Average | Overall | .246 | | .365 | | .312 | | 2.07 | | 8.47 | | 15.38 | |
| | Pressure | .235 | | .336 | | .309 | | 1.77 | | 9.31 | | 16.92 | |

## Additional Miscellaneous Pitching Comparisons

| | Grass Surface | | Artificial Surface | | Home Games | | Road Games | | Runners in Scoring Position | | Runners in Scoring Pos and Two Outs | | Leading Off Inning | |
|---|---|---|---|---|---|---|---|---|---|---|---|---|---|---|
| | BA | Rank | BA | Rank | BA | Rank | BA | Rank | BA | Rank | BA | Rank | OBA | Rank |
| Tim Burke | .217 | -- | .227 | 34 | .229 | 44 | .220 | 25 | .259 | 76 | .333 | 112 | .239 | 13 |
| Kevin Gross | .233 | 47 | .254 | 67 | .253 | 70 | .243 | 49 | .225 | 38 | .194 | 44 | .351 | 103 |
| Joe Hesketh | .300 | -- | .290 | 99 | .333 | 115 | .234 | -- | .340 | -- | .222 | -- | .354 | -- |
| Brian Holman | .308 | -- | .253 | 63 | .304 | -- | .243 | -- | .262 | -- | .320 | -- | .387 | -- |
| Randy D. Johnson | .235 | -- | .269 | 84 | .146 | -- | .355 | -- | .333 | -- | .235 | -- | .419 | -- |
| Mark Langston | .212 | 28 | .220 | 25 | .227 | 40 | .210 | 18 | .200 | 20 | .154 | 19 | .313 | 77 |
| Dennis Martinez | .271 | 92 | .253 | 62 | .244 | 59 | .269 | 87 | .202 | 25 | .188 | 38 | .305 | 68 |
| Andy McGaffigan | .301 | -- | .290 | 99 | .267 | 90 | .316 | 113 | .319 | 110 | .283 | 95 | .371 | 112 |
| Pascual Perez | .306 | 109 | .226 | 31 | .216 | 29 | .271 | 88 | .229 | 43 | .221 | 61 | .277 | 38 |
| Bryn Smith | .225 | 37 | .222 | 29 | .225 | 37 | .220 | 24 | .196 | 16 | .167 | 26 | .267 | 29 |
| Zane Smith | .247 | 66 | .261 | 75 | .228 | 42 | .279 | 94 | .295 | 94 | .304 | 105 | .345 | 99 |
| Team Average | .256 | 10 | .242 | 2 | .239 | 5 | .252 | 7 | .239 | 3 | .215 | 7 | .315 | 11 |
| League Average | .244 | | .248 | | .242 | | .251 | | .249 | | .222 | | .302 | |

# NEW YORK METS

- **Can the Mets recapture their form of 1986?**
- **Welcome to the Land of Stranded Baserunners.**

Analyzing the Mets is a tricky business, one that has to do with expectations, both realistic and fanciful, and with opportunities, both attained and fumbled. The Mets as we have known them since 1984—Davey Johnson, Strawberry, Hernandez, Gooden, Darling, Carter (since '85), etc.—have defined an era in New York baseball. They have supplanted the Yankees as New York's team, and they have had the best record in the majors over the past six years, 29½ games better than the team with the second-best record, the Toronto Blue Jays. Still, that achievement, legitimate as it is, is muted by their failure to collect anything more than a single division title in the last three seasons, a title that was quickly followed by a disheartening loss to the walking wounded of the Dodgers in the 1988 playoffs.

Some of this bittersweet feeling is the product of the incendiary combination of playing in the New York fishbowl and of following on the heels of the best one-season team of the past decade, the 1986 Mets. Of necessity, such a mixture will produce some high-octane expectations that the Mets would win a World Championship every October.

Were these expectations justified? That 1986 team bullied its way through the regular season, winning two-thirds of its games, before narrowly prevailing over the Astros and the Red Sox in postseason play. Since the World Series became an annual event in 1905, only 18 other teams had won two-thirds of their games en route to winning the Series:

| | | |
|---|---|---|
| 1905 Giants | 1915 Red Sox | 1939 Yankees |
| 1907 Cubs | 1919 Reds | 1942 Cardinals |
| 1909 Pirates | 1927 Yankees | 1944 Cardinals |
| 1910 Athletics | 1929 Athletics | 1961 Yankees |
| 1911 Athletics | 1932 Yankees | 1970 Orioles |
| 1912 Red Sox | 1936 Yankees | 1975 Reds |

Let's look at this list for a minute to determine if the expectations set for the post–1986 Mets were unreasonable. In the fifty years prior to the Mets' championship, only seven teams had dominated a season to the degree that the Mets did in 1986. Five of those seven teams returned to the Series again the next season, and the other two (the 1939 Yankees and the 1944 Cardinals) made it back to the Series (and won it) after a one-year absence.

In fact, on this entire list of 18 teams, only four did not made it back to the World Series within three years of their dominant championship season. They were the 1905 Giants, the 1909 Pirates, the 1919 Reds, and the 1932 Yankees:

- That Giants team, under John McGraw, played .601 ball over the next three years, but fell victim to the great Tinker-Evers-Chance Cubs teams that played .693 ball while winning three consecutive National League pennants. The Giants next won a pennant in 1911.
- The 1909 Pirates went 110–42 to beat out the 104–49 Cubs, but then didn't win again until 1927.
- The 1919 Reds defeated the White Sox in the tainted 1919 World Series, then didn't get into another until 1939. (Incidentally, even though the legend of the Black Sox scandal describes the Sox as heavy favorites in that Series, the Reds weren't chopped liver: they had a regular-season record that was eight games better than the White Sox's.)
- The 1932 team was the last of the pennant-winning Yankees teams to be carried by Babe Ruth, who enjoyed his last 40–home run season that year. The Yankees released him after the '34 season, and they didn't reach the Series again until 1936, Joe DiMaggio's rookie year.

When the Mets regather at an Old–Timers' Day twenty years hence (or in the Senior League five years hence?), how will *they* look back on this time? Will their first thought be of That Championship Season, or of What Might Have Been; of the Ecstasy or the Agony? Because even granting that the expectations that have been set for the Mets may have been unreasonably high, the Mets still cannot be satisfied with the end result of the past three seasons: two second-place finishes and a division title.

And this is where the matter of opportunities comes in. When the Mets and their fans relive the disappointment of this three-year span, they will recall it as the Era of Stranded Baserunners. Over the past three seasons, the Mets have made it a practice to do their worst hitting at the times that are most likely to produce a run: they have hit only .247 with runners in scoring position, compared with .260 at all other times. That's a 13–point dropoff in key situations; only two teams in the major leagues (the Indians and the Cubs) have had larger dropoffs over that span:

| | Other Times | Scoring Pos. | Diff. | | Other Times | Scoring Pos. | Diff. |
|---|---|---|---|---|---|---|---|
| Milwaukee | .256 | .286 | +30 | Atlanta | .242 | .256 | +14 |
| Toronto | .262 | .275 | +13 | Houston | .243 | .251 | +8 |
| Oakland | .259 | .269 | +10 | Montreal | .253 | .260 | +7 |
| Boston | .278 | .284 | +6 | Pittsburgh | .249 | .255 | +6 |
| Texas | .259 | .264 | +5 | San Francisco | .251 | .257 | +6 |
| Kansas City | .260 | .264 | +4 | Cincinnati | .252 | .256 | +4 |
| Chicago | .257 | .259 | +2 | St. Louis | .256 | .259 | +3 |
| New York | .265 | .265 | 0 | Los Angeles | .246 | .247 | +1 |
| Seattle | .262 | .261 | −1 | Philadelphia | .247 | .241 | −6 |
| Detroit | .255 | .253 | −2 | San Diego | .255 | .246 | −9 |
| California | .258 | .254 | −4 | New York | .260 | .247 | −13 |
| Baltimore | .250 | .246 | −4 | Chicago | .267 | .248 | −19 |
| Minnesota | .273 | .263 | −10 | | | | |
| Cleveland | .262 | .240 | −22 | | | | |

In 1989, the Mets added a new wrinkle to this litany of woe. Their .247 batting average with runners in scoring position was no surprise; that's the same average that they showed for the two previous seasons combined. But even *that* modest batting average was deceptively high, inflated by superfluous hits in games in which the Mets were already comfortably in front. How do we know that? Just take a look at this chart, which breaks down all of the Mets' at–bats last season with runners in scoring position, according to what the score was at the time:

| Score | AB | H | Avg. |
|---|---|---|---|
| Mets trailing by 3 runs or more | 163 | 39 | .239 |
| Mets trailing by 1 or 2 runs | 245 | 50 | .204 |
| Score tied | 332 | 78 | .235 |
| Mets leading by 1 or 2 runs | 313 | 82 | .262 |
| Mets leading by 3 runs or more | 320 | 90 | .281 |

Whenever we introduce a new set of figures, we like to compare it to the league average. When we do that in this case, we see that the Mets' tendency to hit poorly at the most important times and best at the least important times is outside the parameters established by the 11 other National League teams last season:

| Score | Mets | Others |
|---|---|---|
| Trailing by 3 runs or more | .239 | .250 |
| Trailing by 1 or 2 runs | .204 | .247 |
| Score tied | .235 | .245 |
| Leading by 1 or 2 runs | .262 | .243 |
| Leading by 3 runs or more | .281 | .261 |

When trailing by a run or two with runners on second or third base—times when a simple single would alter the dynamics of the score—the Mets collectively batted .204, nine points lower than the career batting average of Steve Jeltz. Only the Phillies (.202) and the Dodgers (.201) hit worse in those situations last season. Not surprisingly, the East Division champion Cubs had the league's best such average (.286). And with runners in scoring position and the score tied, the Mets didn't do much better; at those times they hit .235, managing to equal the career batting average of Mariano Duncan.

We don't believe in the innocent being punished along with the guilty, so we'll list the individual figures in those categories. Three sets of figures are indicated, with the Margin heading representing the score of the game from the Mets' vantage point (0 represents a tie score, –1 means that New York trailed by a run, and –2, well, you get the point):

| | Scoring Pos. | | | Scoring Pos. | | | Scoring Pos. | | |
|---|---|---|---|---|---|---|---|---|---|
| Margin: | 0, −1, or −2 | | | −1 or −2 | | | 0 | | |
| | Avg. | AB | H | Avg. | AB | H | Avg. | AB | H |
| Lyons | .355 | 31 | 11 | .353 | 17 | 6 | .357 | 14 | 5 |
| Magadan | .354 | 34 | 12 | .357 | 14 | 5 | .350 | 20 | 7 |
| Johnson | .321 | 56 | 18 | .278 | 18 | 5 | .342 | 38 | 13 |
| Elster | .300 | 50 | 15 | .240 | 25 | 6 | .360 | 25 | 9 |
| Jefferies | .267 | 45 | 12 | .190 | 21 | 4 | .333 | 24 | 8 |
| McReynolds | .226 | 62 | 14 | .087 | 23 | 2 | .308 | 39 | 12 |
| Sasser | .217 | 23 | 5 | .286 | 14 | 4 | .111 | 9 | 1 |
| Strawberry | .169 | 77 | 13 | .125 | 24 | 3 | .189 | 53 | 10 |
| Teufel | .136 | 22 | 3 | .100 | 10 | 1 | .167 | 12 | 2 |
| Samuel | .133 | 30 | 4 | .100 | 10 | 1 | .150 | 20 | 3 |
| Hernandez | .120 | 25 | 3 | .200 | 10 | 2 | .067 | 15 | 1 |
| Wilson | .115 | 26 | 3 | .100 | 10 | 1 | .125 | 16 | 2 |
| Carter | .059 | 17 | 1 | .000 | 8 | 0 | .111 | 9 | 1 |
| Others | | 79 | 14 | | 41 | 10 | | 38 | 4 |
| Team | .222 | 577 | 128 | .204 | 245 | 50 | .235 | 332 | 78 |

It was only a few years ago that "clutch hitting" went either unrecorded or unrespected in evaluating a player's or a team's performance. But for three years now, the Mets' failure to get hits at the most crucial points of a game has been the major blemish on an otherwise admirable record. In two of those three seasons, that failure has led directly to disappointing second-place finishes.

What can they do about it? Short of trading for a bunch of proven clutch hitters (can anyone get Joe McIlvaine the numbers of the Iorg brothers, quick?), the Mets may have to tough it out and hope that their superior pitching staff can offset their offensive problems. It's hard for a leopard to change its spots; to ask an entire *team* of leopards to change its spots may be beyond the possible.

## WON-LOST RECORD BY STARTING POSITION

| NEW YORK 87-75 | C | 1B | 2B | 3B | SS | LF | CF | RF | P | Leadoff | Relief | Starts |
|---|---|---|---|---|---|---|---|---|---|---|---|---|
| Don Aase | - | - | - | - | - | - | - | - | - | - | 19-30 | - |
| Rick Aguilera | - | - | - | - | - | - | - | - | - | - | 16-20 | - |
| Blaine Beatty | - | - | - | - | - | - | - | - | 1-0 | - | 0-1 | 1-0 |
| Mark Carreon | - | - | - | - | - | 6-5 | - | 11-4 | - | 2-0 | - | 17-9 |
| Gary Carter | 22-20 | - | - | - | - | - | - | - | - | - | - | 22-20 |
| David Cone | - | - | - | - | - | - | - | - | 19-14 | - | 0-1 | 19-14 |
| Ron Darling | - | - | - | - | - | - | - | - | 16-17 | - | - | 16-17 |
| Len Dykstra | - | - | - | - | - | - | 21-22 | - | - | 17-20 | - | 21-22 |
| Kevin Elster | - | - | - | - | 71-63 | - | - | - | - | - | - | 71-63 |
| Sid Fernandez | - | - | - | - | - | - | - | - | 20-12 | - | 0-3 | 20-12 |
| Dwight Gooden | - | - | - | - | - | - | - | - | 10-7 | - | 2-0 | 10-7 |
| Keith Hernandez | - | 31-24 | - | - | - | - | - | - | - | - | - | 31-24 |
| Manny Hernandez | - | - | - | - | - | - | - | - | - | - | 0-1 | - |
| Jeff Innis | - | - | - | - | - | - | - | - | - | - | 6-23 | - |
| Gregg Jefferies | - | - | 57-56 | 8-6 | - | - | - | - | - | 18-21 | - | 65-62 |
| Howard Johnson | - | - | - | 69-60 | 11-11 | - | - | - | - | 1-1 | - | 80-71 |
| Terry Leach | - | - | - | - | - | - | - | - | - | - | 0-10 | - |
| Phil Lombardi | 7-4 | - | - | - | - | - | - | - | - | - | - | 7-4 |
| Barry Lyons | 35-26 | - | - | - | - | - | - | - | - | - | - | 35-26 |
| Julio Machado | - | - | - | - | - | - | - | - | - | - | 5-5 | - |
| Dave Magadan | - | 37-37 | - | 10-9 | - | - | - | - | - | - | - | 47-46 |
| Lee Mazzilli | - | 3-2 | - | - | - | 1-0 | - | 2-0 | - | 2-1 | - | 6-2 |
| Roger McDowell | - | - | - | - | - | - | - | - | - | - | 9-16 | - |
| Jeff McKnight | - | - | 1-1 | - | - | - | - | - | - | - | - | 1-1 |
| Kevin McReynolds | - | - | - | - | - | 77-66 | - | - | - | - | - | 77-66 |
| Keith A. Miller | - | - | 11-6 | - | 4-1 | - | 3-4 | 2-1 | - | 13-4 | - | 20-12 |
| John Mitchell | - | - | - | - | - | - | - | - | - | - | 0-2 | - |
| Jeff Musselman | - | - | - | - | - | - | - | - | - | - | 7-13 | - |
| Randy Myers | - | - | - | - | - | - | - | - | - | - | 35 30 | - |
| Tom O'Malley | - | - | - | - | - | - | - | - | - | - | - | - |
| Bob Ojeda | - | - | - | - | - | - | - | - | 16-15 | - | - | 16-15 |
| Juan Samuel | - | - | - | - | - | - | 45-38 | - | - | 16-16 | - | 45-38 |
| Mackey Sasser | 23-25 | - | - | - | - | - | - | - | - | - | - | 23-25 |
| Craig Shipley | - | - | - | - | 1-0 | - | - | - | - | - | - | 1-0 |
| Darryl Strawberry | - | - | - | - | - | - | - | 66-62 | - | - | - | 66-62 |
| Kevin Tapani | - | - | - | - | - | - | - | - | - | - | 0-3 | - |
| Tim Teufel | - | 16-12 | 18-12 | - | - | - | - | - | - | - | - | 34-24 |
| Lou Thornton | - | - | - | - | - | - | - | 2-0 | - | - | - | 2-0 |
| Frank Viola | - | - | - | - | - | - | - | - | 5-7 | - | - | 5-7 |
| Dave West | - | - | - | - | - | - | - | - | 0-2 | - | 3-6 | 0-2 |
| Wally Whitehurst | - | - | - | - | - | - | - | - | 0-1 | - | 3-5 | 0-1 |
| Mookie Wilson | - | - | - | - | - | 3-4 | 18-11 | 4-8 | - | 18-12 | - | 25-23 |

## Batting vs. Left and Right Handed Pitchers

| | | BA | Rank | SA | Rank | OBA | Rank | HR % | Rank | BB % | Rank | SO % | Rank |
|---|---|---|---|---|---|---|---|---|---|---|---|---|---|
| Mark Carreon | vs. Lefties | .276 | 55 | .513 | 11 | .329 | 71 | 6.58 | 5 | 7.23 | 87 | 10.84 | 42 |
| | vs. Righties | .351 | -- | .456 | -- | .422 | -- | 1.75 | -- | 9.38 | -- | 12.50 | -- |
| Gary Carter | vs. Lefties | .167 | 127 | .273 | 114 | .225 | 127 | 3.03 | 34 | 7.04 | 92 | 8.45 | 21 |
| | vs. Righties | .195 | -- | .276 | -- | .253 | -- | 0.00 | -- | 7.37 | -- | 9.47 | -- |
| Kevin Elster | vs. Lefties | .258 | 77 | .365 | 74 | .314 | 86 | 1.26 | 86 | 7.95 | 76 | 10.23 | 37 |
| | vs. Righties | .217 | 108 | .358 | 77 | .266 | 118 | 2.68 | 42 | 6.02 | 99 | 17.77 | 95 |
| Keith Hernandez | vs. Lefties | .291 | 36 | .354 | 82 | .364 | 35 | 1.27 | 84 | 7.95 | 76 | 18.18 | 112 |
| | vs. Righties | .199 | 124 | .309 | 111 | .301 | 80 | 2.21 | 58 | 12.82 | 16 | 14.74 | 73 |
| Gregg Jefferies | vs. Lefties | .253 | 81 | .402 | 57 | .294 | 104 | 2.87 | 39 | 4.26 | 123 | 8.51 | 22 |
| | vs. Righties | .260 | 53 | .386 | 55 | .324 | 56 | 2.10 | 63 | 8.36 | 61 | 8.09 | 16 |
| Howard Johnson | vs. Lefties | .278 | 52 | .464 | 31 | .383 | 17 | 3.61 | 27 | 14.35 | 12 | 21.30 | 124 |
| | vs. Righties | .292 | 23 | .607 | 1 | .362 | 25 | 7.69 | 2 | 10.35 | 40 | 18.12 | 99 |
| Barry Lyons | vs. Lefties | .298 | 28 | .476 | 25 | .341 | 59 | 3.57 | 28 | 6.52 | 98 | 5.43 | 4 |
| | vs. Righties | .219 | 105 | .265 | 126 | .250 | 128 | 0.00 | 124 | 3.13 | 124 | 14.38 | 68 |
| Dave Magadan | vs. Lefties | .261 | 75 | .304 | 105 | .327 | 73 | 0.00 | 112 | 7.92 | 78 | 9.90 | 32 |
| | vs. Righties | .294 | 21 | .422 | 31 | .379 | 18 | 1.42 | 83 | 12.50 | 19 | 8.23 | 17 |
| Kevin McReynolds | vs. Lefties | .296 | 30 | .508 | 14 | .377 | 20 | 5.29 | 10 | 11.63 | 29 | 6.98 | 11 |
| | vs. Righties | .258 | 55 | .419 | 34 | .297 | 84 | 3.37 | 29 | 5.47 | 108 | 15.36 | 82 |
| Juan Samuel | vs. Lefties | .258 | 76 | .384 | 62 | .340 | 62 | 3.16 | 32 | 9.72 | 50 | 17.59 | 106 |
| | vs. Righties | .222 | 100 | .307 | 113 | .282 | 101 | 1.46 | 80 | 5.63 | 104 | 21.98 | 119 |
| Mackey Sasser | vs. Lefties | .208 | -- | .292 | -- | .269 | -- | 0.00 | -- | 7.41 | -- | 22.22 | -- |
| | vs. Righties | .304 | 17 | .424 | 29 | .323 | 57 | 0.63 | 112 | 3.05 | 125 | 5.49 | 3 |
| Darryl Strawberry | vs. Lefties | .219 | 106 | .438 | 43 | .279 | 115 | 5.06 | 11 | 8.12 | 75 | 20.81 | 121 |
| | vs. Righties | .228 | 93 | .483 | 12 | .331 | 47 | 6.71 | 4 | 13.08 | 14 | 18.60 | 101 |
| Tim Teufel | vs. Lefties | .273 | 57 | .333 | 93 | .368 | 32 | 0.76 | 101 | 13.55 | 20 | 18.06 | 111 |
| | vs. Righties | .230 | -- | .333 | -- | .323 | -- | 1.15 | -- | 11.11 | -- | 22.22 | -- |
| Mookie Wilson | vs. Lefties | .164 | 128 | .221 | 125 | .203 | 130 | 0.82 | 98 | 4.69 | 117 | 17.97 | 109 |
| | vs. Righties | .244 | 71 | .354 | 80 | .269 | 115 | 1.57 | 74 | 2.99 | 126 | 17.91 | 97 |
| Team Average | vs. Lefties | .246 | 8 | .377 | 5 | .313 | 9 | 2.64 | 3 | 8.60 | 9 | 15.39 | 9 |
| | vs. Righties | .246 | 5 | .389 | 2 | .310 | 7 | 2.70 | 1 | 8.02 | 8 | 15.15 | 5 |
| League Average | vs. Lefties | .251 | | .371 | | .320 | | 2.06 | | 8.85 | | 14.80 | |
| | vs. Righties | .244 | | .362 | | .309 | | 2.08 | | 8.27 | | 15.67 | |

## Batting with Runners on Base and Bases Empty

| | | BA | Rank | SA | Rank | OBA | Rank | HR % | Rank | BB % | Rank | SO % | Rank |
|---|---|---|---|---|---|---|---|---|---|---|---|---|---|
| Kevin Elster | Runners On | .265 | 66 | .383 | 67 | .330 | 76 | 2.04 | 62 | 9.44 | 72 | 15.02 | 88 |
| | Bases Empty | .206 | 118 | .344 | 94 | .244 | 126 | 2.29 | 51 | 4.36 | 112 | 15.27 | 78 |
| Keith Hernandez | Runners On | .272 | 52 | .370 | 76 | .362 | 39 | 2.17 | 57 | 11.43 | 47 | 15.24 | 91 |
| | Bases Empty | .203 | 120 | .293 | 112 | .295 | 88 | 1.63 | 77 | 10.79 | 24 | 16.55 | 91 |
| Gregg Jefferies | Runners On | .245 | 94 | .365 | 82 | .318 | 89 | 1.56 | 75 | 9.91 | 66 | 7.66 | 10 |
| | Bases Empty | .266 | 50 | .408 | 41 | .312 | 67 | 2.85 | 33 | 5.04 | 104 | 8.61 | 15 |
| Howard Johnson | Runners On | .313 | 16 | .618 | 4 | .403 | 14 | 6.87 | 5 | 13.67 | 26 | 17.99 | 108 |
| | Bases Empty | .269 | 47 | .518 | 5 | .345 | 34 | 5.92 | 5 | 10.34 | 32 | 20.16 | 119 |
| Barry Lyons | Runners On | .243 | 96 | .304 | 116 | .274 | 120 | 0.00 | 112 | 4.00 | 126 | 13.60 | 70 |
| | Bases Empty | .250 | 66 | .375 | 68 | .291 | 92 | 2.50 | 47 | 4.72 | 109 | 8.66 | 16 |
| Dave Magadan | Runners On | .307 | 19 | .405 | 54 | .387 | 24 | 0.61 | 106 | 12.50 | 33 | 7.81 | 14 |
| | Bases Empty | .270 | 44 | .384 | 57 | .350 | 26 | 1.42 | 86 | 10.55 | 29 | 9.28 | 20 |
| Kevin McReynolds | Runners On | .249 | 91 | .415 | 46 | .331 | 75 | 3.23 | 26 | 11.42 | 48 | 11.42 | 49 |
| | Bases Empty | .287 | 21 | .473 | 11 | .322 | 52 | 4.57 | 15 | 4.93 | 106 | 13.04 | 52 |
| Juan Samuel | Runners On | .240 | 98 | .318 | 108 | .298 | 106 | 1.38 | 81 | 5.00 | 120 | 20.00 | 116 |
| | Bases Empty | .232 | 90 | .346 | 91 | .307 | 72 | 2.54 | 45 | 8.60 | 54 | 20.63 | 122 |
| Mackey Sasser | Runners On | .309 | 17 | .420 | 43 | .345 | 56 | 0.00 | 112 | 5.68 | 111 | 10.23 | 36 |
| | Bases Empty | .277 | -- | .396 | -- | .291 | -- | 0.99 | -- | 1.94 | -- | 5.83 | -- |
| Darryl Strawberry | Runners On | .232 | 104 | .464 | 22 | .337 | 70 | 4.91 | 13 | 14.02 | 21 | 21.59 | 125 |
| | Bases Empty | .218 | 106 | .468 | 13 | .289 | 93 | 7.14 | 2 | 8.66 | 53 | 17.33 | 99 |
| Tim Teufel | Runners On | .250 | 88 | .313 | 111 | .386 | 25 | 0.00 | 112 | 17.82 | 8 | 22.77 | 128 |
| | Bases Empty | .259 | 59 | .345 | 92 | .327 | 47 | 1.44 | 84 | 9.15 | 44 | 17.65 | 102 |
| Mookie Wilson | Runners On | .182 | 126 | .222 | 131 | .224 | 130 | 0.00 | 112 | 5.61 | 112 | 19.63 | 115 |
| | Bases Empty | .220 | 103 | .333 | 95 | .245 | 124 | 2.00 | 62 | 2.58 | 127 | 16.77 | 93 |
| Team Average | Runners On | .252 | 8 | .384 | 5 | .327 | 9 | 2.21 | 5 | 9.75 | 7 | 15.39 | 9 |
| | Bases Empty | .242 | 7 | .386 | 2 | .299 | 7 | 3.01 | 1 | 7.06 | 9 | 15.12 | 5 |
| League Average | Runners On | .256 | | .379 | | .330 | | 2.13 | | 9.82 | | 14.66 | |
| | Bases Empty | .240 | | .355 | | .299 | | 2.03 | | 7.43 | | 15.93 | |

## Overall Batting Compared to Late Inning Pressure Situations

| | | BA | Rank | SA | Rank | OBA | Rank | HR % | Rank | BB % | Rank | SO % | Rank | RDI % | Rank |
|---|---|---|---|---|---|---|---|---|---|---|---|---|---|---|---|
| Kevin Elster | Overall | .231 | 106 | .360 | 79 | .283 | 110 | 2.18 | 58 | 6.69 | 97 | 15.16 | 84 | .278 | 50 |
| | Pressure | .250 | 53 | .382 | 38 | .257 | 105 | 1.47 | 71 | 1.39 | 130 | 13.89 | 51 | .188 | 83 |
| Keith Hernandez | Overall | .233 | 104 | .326 | 108 | .324 | 61 | 1.86 | 69 | 11.07 | 33 | 15.98 | 93 | .185 | 124 |
| | Pressure | .225 | 77 | .300 | 89 | .295 | 76 | 0.00 | 81 | 9.09 | 64 | 18.18 | 90 | .286 | -- |
| Gregg Jefferies | Overall | .258 | 60 | .392 | 53 | .314 | 79 | 2.36 | 47 | 6.98 | 91 | 8.23 | 12 | .276 | 52 |
| | Pressure | .213 | 88 | .267 | 102 | .263 | 99 | 0.00 | 81 | 3.70 | 120 | 12.35 | 36 | .235 | 63 |
| Howard Johnson | Overall | .287 | 20 | .559 | 2 | .369 | 18 | 6.30 | 3 | 11.76 | 27 | 19.24 | 118 | .327 | 13 |
| | Pressure | .280 | 35 | .507 | 9 | .419 | 6 | 5.33 | 9 | 18.28 | 6 | 18.28 | 91 | .333 | 22 |
| Barry Lyons | Overall | .247 | 79 | .340 | 96 | .283 | 110 | 1.28 | 88 | 4.37 | 122 | 11.11 | 36 | .288 | 39 |
| | Pressure | .216 | -- | .297 | -- | .237 | -- | 2.70 | -- | 2.63 | -- | 7.89 | -- | .143 | -- |
| Dave Magadan | Overall | .286 | 23 | .393 | 50 | .367 | 22 | 1.07 | 98 | 11.42 | 28 | 8.62 | 15 | .308 | 25 |
| | Pressure | .231 | 74 | .308 | 84 | .296 | 75 | 1.54 | 69 | 6.94 | 85 | 12.50 | 37 | .571 | 2 |
| Kevin McReynolds | Overall | .272 | 39 | .450 | 20 | .326 | 57 | 4.04 | 13 | 7.68 | 80 | 12.35 | 51 | .282 | 44 |
| | Pressure | .298 | 24 | .489 | 13 | .333 | 47 | 5.32 | 10 | 5.05 | 99 | 13.13 | 42 | .167 | 94 |
| Juan Samuel | Overall | .235 | 101 | .335 | 103 | .303 | 94 | 2.07 | 63 | 7.13 | 87 | 20.37 | 122 | .222 | 101 |
| | Pressure | .266 | 43 | .328 | 73 | .338 | 45 | 0.00 | 81 | 8.33 | 74 | 23.61 | 114 | .278 | 46 |
| Mackey Sasser | Overall | .291 | -- | .407 | -- | .316 | -- | 0.55 | -- | 3.66 | -- | 7.85 | -- | .310 | 23 |
| | Pressure | .273 | -- | .333 | -- | .294 | -- | 0.00 | -- | 2.94 | -- | 11.76 | -- | .182 | 86 |
| Darryl Strawberry | Overall | .225 | 110 | .466 | 14 | .312 | 82 | 6.09 | 5 | 11.28 | 29 | 19.41 | 119 | .218 | 103 |
| | Pressure | .160 | 120 | .383 | 37 | .227 | 123 | 6.17 | 4 | 7.95 | 81 | 22.73 | 112 | .115 | 120 |
| Tim Teufel | Overall | .256 | 66 | .333 | 105 | .350 | 34 | 0.91 | 104 | 12.60 | 17 | 19.69 | 120 | .169 | 128 |
| | Pressure | .226 | -- | .387 | -- | .324 | -- | 3.23 | -- | 13.51 | -- | 18.92 | -- | .100 | 124 |
| Mookie Wilson | Overall | .205 | 124 | .289 | 121 | .237 | 130 | 1.20 | 90 | 3.82 | 127 | 17.94 | 105 | .185 | 123 |
| | Pressure | .205 | 94 | .227 | 115 | .229 | 122 | 0.00 | 81 | 4.17 | 111 | 18.75 | 96 | .357 | 19 |
| Team Average | Overall | .246 | 7 | .385 | 3 | .311 | 8 | 2.68 | 1 | 8.22 | 9 | 15.23 | 7 | .251 | 6 |
| | Pressure | .233 | 9 | .367 | 2 | .300 | 10 | 2.85 | 1 | 8.22 | 10 | 16.00 | 7 | .241 | 6 |
| League Average | Overall | .246 | | .365 | | .312 | | 2.07 | | 8.47 | | 15.38 | | .253 | |
| | Pressure | .238 | | .337 | | .308 | | 1.73 | | 8.93 | | 16.78 | | .235 | |

## Additional Miscellaneous Batting Comparisons

| | Grass Surface BA | Rank | Artificial Surface BA | Rank | Home Games BA | Rank | Road Games BA | Rank | Runners in Scoring Position BA | Rank | Runners in Scoring Pos and Two Outs BA | Rank | Leading Off Inning OBA | Rank | Runners on 3B with less than 2 Outs RDI % | Rank |
|---|---|---|---|---|---|---|---|---|---|---|---|---|---|---|---|---|
| Mark Carreon | .299 | -- | .321 | -- | .313 | -- | .304 | -- | .282 | -- | .294 | -- | .323 | -- | .625 | 40 |
| Gary Carter | .188 | 120 | .175 | -- | .143 | -- | .224 | -- | .212 | -- | .286 | -- | .256 | -- | .375 | 136 |
| Kevin Elster | .223 | 94 | .252 | 72 | .226 | 108 | .238 | 82 | .276 | 45 | .226 | 65 | .228 | 124 | .545 | 82 |
| Keith Hernandez | .222 | 95 | .254 | -- | .263 | 60 | .208 | 112 | .183 | 125 | .185 | 103 | .261 | -- | .375 | 136 |
| Gregg Jefferies | .278 | 39 | .207 | 123 | .287 | 37 | .232 | 89 | .256 | 69 | .250 | 42 | .338 | 38 | .552 | 79 |
| Howard Johnson | .286 | 31 | .291 | 23 | .290 | 32 | .285 | 29 | .305 | 20 | .288 | 23 | .380 | 16 | .636 | 38 |
| Barry Lyons | .264 | 54 | .193 | -- | .241 | 90 | .252 | 66 | .273 | 51 | .240 | 52 | .224 | 127 | .529 | 91 |
| Dave Magadan | .305 | 12 | .241 | 90 | .306 | 17 | .267 | 49 | .298 | 26 | .300 | 21 | .348 | 29 | .786 | 4 |
| Kevin McReynolds | .265 | 51 | .288 | 24 | .266 | 56 | .277 | 40 | .273 | 50 | .235 | 56 | .325 | 51 | .500 | 98 |
| Keith A. Miller | .195 | -- | .273 | -- | .207 | -- | .247 | -- | .143 | -- | .188 | -- | .212 | 129 | .667 | -- |
| Juan Samuel | .221 | 98 | .250 | 74 | .230 | 104 | .240 | 81 | .218 | 105 | .250 | 42 | .327 | 47 | .654 | 33 |
| Mackey Sasser | .317 | 9 | .232 | -- | .293 | -- | .289 | -- | .277 | 42 | .194 | 96 | .316 | -- | .857 | -- |
| Darryl Strawberry | .231 | 90 | .209 | 121 | .272 | 48 | .183 | 126 | .224 | 98 | .167 | 110 | .286 | 78 | .433 | 126 |
| Tim Teufel | .257 | 62 | .253 | 67 | .215 | 115 | .295 | 13 | .222 | 101 | .100 | 130 | .314 | 54 | .417 | 127 |
| Mookie Wilson | .192 | 118 | .234 | 103 | .192 | 124 | .217 | 102 | .156 | 129 | .205 | 85 | .250 | 110 | .500 | 98 |
| Team Average | .247 | 5 | .244 | 9 | .249 | 7 | .243 | 4 | .247 | 8 | .226 | 4 | .297 | 8 | .535 | 8 |
| League Average | .244 | | .248 | | .251 | | .242 | | .249 | | .222 | | .302 | | .546 | |

## Pitching vs. Left and Right Handed Batters

| | | BA | Rank | SA | Rank | OBA | Rank | HR % | Rank | BB % | Rank | SO % | Rank |
|---|---|---|---|---|---|---|---|---|---|---|---|---|---|
| Don Aase | vs. Lefties | .272 | 88 | .395 | 82 | .354 | 94 | 0.88 | 30 | 11.45 | 86 | 11.45 | 82 |
| | vs. Righties | .217 | -- | .365 | -- | .287 | -- | 3.48 | -- | 8.46 | -- | 14.62 | -- |
| Rick Aguilera | vs. Lefties | .241 | 52 | .293 | 26 | .301 | 38 | 0.75 | 23 | 8.11 | 47 | 27.70 | 3 |
| | vs. Righties | .221 | 30 | .300 | 20 | .206 | 49 | 1.64 | 36 | 6.62 | 49 | 28.68 | 4 |
| David Cone | vs. Lefties | .234 | 41 | .379 | 73 | .309 | 49 | 2.00 | 73 | 9.36 | 63 | 14.54 | 51 |
| | vs. Righties | .209 | 24 | .335 | 43 | .263 | 26 | 2.95 | 91 | 6.62 | 49 | 28.68 | 4 |
| Ron Darling | vs. Lefties | .283 | 95 | .407 | 91 | .338 | 79 | 1.87 | 71 | 7.68 | 36 | 14.79 | 48 |
| | vs. Righties | .224 | 43 | .353 | 54 | .281 | 45 | 2.87 | 86 | 7.47 | 67 | 19.07 | 43 |
| Sid Fernandez | vs. Lefties | .197 | 14 | .299 | 29 | .258 | 12 | 1.71 | 66 | 6.92 | 26 | 23.08 | 8 |
| | vs. Righties | .198 | 17 | .340 | 46 | .273 | 35 | 2.81 | 79 | 8.76 | 85 | 22.31 | 24 |
| Dwight Gooden | vs. Lefties | .181 | 7 | .259 | 12 | .270 | 16 | 1.29 | 47 | 10.94 | 81 | 21.51 | 12 |
| | vs. Righties | .244 | 64 | .373 | 74 | .309 | 73 | 2.87 | 85 | 7.76 | 70 | 18.97 | 45 |
| Randy Myers | vs. Lefties | .164 | -- | .315 | -- | .244 | -- | 2.74 | -- | 9.64 | -- | 33.73 | -- |
| | vs. Righties | .219 | 35 | .307 | 22 | .314 | 79 | 0.88 | 11 | 12.03 | 109 | 22.56 | 23 |
| Bob Ojeda | vs. Lefties | .236 | 45 | .379 | 74 | .324 | 61 | 3.11 | 105 | 11.41 | 84 | 15.76 | 44 |
| | vs. Righties | .247 | 71 | .354 | 56 | .314 | 80 | 1.93 | 48 | 8.91 | 87 | 10.31 | 106 |
| Frank Viola | vs. Lefties | .241 | -- | .259 | -- | .268 | -- | 0.00 | -- | 3.51 | -- | 15.79 | -- |
| | vs. Righties | .235 | 55 | .330 | 37 | .301 | 64 | 1.89 | 46 | 8.50 | 80 | 21.77 | 31 |
| Team Average | vs. Lefties | .242 | 1 | .359 | 4 | .314 | 2 | 1.76 | 6 | 9.33 | 6 | 16.53 | 2 |
| | vs. Righties | .225 | 1 | .342 | 2 | .292 | 3 | 2.33 | 6 | 8.34 | 9 | 19.20 | 1 |
| League Average | vs. Lefties | .252 | | .366 | | .325 | | 1.79 | | 9.48 | | 13.93 | |
| | vs. Righties | .242 | | .365 | | .303 | | 2.29 | | 7.70 | | 16.46 | |

## Pitching with Runners on Base and Bases Empty

| | | BA | Rank | SA | Rank | OBA | Rank | HR % | Rank | BB % | Rank | SO % | Rank |
|---|---|---|---|---|---|---|---|---|---|---|---|---|---|
| Don Aase | Runners On | .242 | 54 | .343 | 40 | .322 | 60 | 2.02 | 59 | 10.26 | 69 | 17.95 | 34 |
| | Bases Empty | .246 | 70 | .408 | 102 | .319 | 93 | 2.31 | 75 | 9.72 | 96 | 9.03 | 111 |
| Rick Aguilera | Runners On | .275 | 85 | .353 | 45 | .364 | 96 | 1.96 | 53 | 11.38 | 89 | 25.20 | 4 |
| | Bases Empty | .203 | 16 | .261 | 3 | .242 | 3 | 0.65 | 12 | 4.35 | 15 | 30.43 | 2 |
| David Cone | Runners On | .235 | 41 | .382 | 72 | .312 | 49 | 2.61 | 88 | 9.66 | 59 | 19.60 | 21 |
| | Bases Empty | .215 | 24 | .345 | 53 | .274 | 28 | 2.33 | 77 | 7.17 | 61 | 21.68 | 16 |
| Ron Darling | Runners On | .280 | 89 | .419 | 89 | .341 | 72 | 2.80 | 92 | 9.50 | 56 | 17.41 | 38 |
| | Bases Empty | .245 | 66 | .363 | 74 | .295 | 53 | 1.97 | 58 | 6.26 | 48 | 16.02 | 50 |
| Sid Fernandez | Runners On | .230 | 36 | .404 | 80 | .296 | 27 | 3.70 | 107 | 8.20 | 35 | 14.75 | 53 |
| | Bases Empty | .181 | 4 | .298 | 20 | .258 | 13 | 2.10 | 63 | 8.65 | 84 | 26.47 | 7 |
| Dwight Gooden | Runners On | .199 | 6 | .267 | 8 | .287 | 18 | 1.14 | 22 | 10.68 | 77 | 21.84 | 13 |
| | Bases Empty | .219 | 26 | .343 | 51 | .289 | 45 | 2.64 | 94 | 8.59 | 81 | 19.24 | 35 |
| Randy Myers | Runners On | .211 | 13 | .342 | 37 | .303 | 36 | 1.86 | 49 | 11.52 | 92 | 22.51 | 9 |
| | Bases Empty | .200 | 15 | .271 | 7 | .291 | 49 | 0.71 | 14 | 11.39 | 108 | 28.48 | 3 |
| Bob Ojeda | Runners On | .243 | 56 | .342 | 38 | .321 | 58 | 1.64 | 41 | 10.42 | 71 | 11.27 | 90 |
| | Bases Empty | .246 | 69 | .372 | 80 | .313 | 83 | 2.58 | 93 | 8.74 | 86 | 11.73 | 96 |
| Frank Viola | Runners On | .241 | 51 | .372 | 64 | .312 | 47 | 2.92 | 96 | 8.92 | 46 | 22.29 | 10 |
| | Bases Empty | .232 | 41 | .276 | 10 | .284 | 38 | 0.55 | 7 | 6.70 | 56 | 19.59 | 33 |
| Team Average | Runners On | .244 | 2 | .370 | 2 | .320 | 3 | 2.36 | 9 | 9.88 | 7 | 17.32 | 1 |
| | Bases Empty | .223 | 1 | .334 | 1 | .287 | 1 | 1.95 | 4 | 7.88 | 9 | 18.79 | 1 |
| League Average | Runners On | .256 | | .379 | | .330 | | 2.13 | | 9.82 | | 14.66 | |
| | Bases Empty | .240 | | .355 | | .299 | | 2.03 | | 7.43 | | 15.93 | |

## Overall Pitching Compared to Late Inning Pressure Situations

| | | BA | Rank | SA | Rank | OBA | Rank | HR % | Rank | BB % | Rank | SO % | Rank |
|---|---|---|---|---|---|---|---|---|---|---|---|---|---|
| Don Aase | Overall | .245 | 59 | .380 | 76 | .320 | 75 | 2.18 | 69 | 9.96 | 90 | 13.03 | 77 |
| | Pressure | .241 | 63 | .361 | 74 | .331 | 81 | 2.78 | 92 | 11.63 | 91 | 11.63 | 83 |
| Rick Aguilera | Overall | .231 | 37 | .298 | 8 | .294 | 40 | 1.18 | 20 | 7.39 | 40 | 28.17 | 2 |
| | Pressure | .250 | 70 | .341 | 67 | .327 | 76 | 1.52 | 56 | 9.21 | 63 | 28.29 | 4 |
| David Cone | Overall | .223 | 29 | .359 | 63 | .289 | 33 | 2.43 | 88 | 8.13 | 52 | 20.88 | 17 |
| | Pressure | .256 | 76 | .311 | 49 | .306 | 53 | 1.11 | 41 | 7.14 | 40 | 23.47 | 13 |
| Ron Darling | Overall | .258 | 83 | .385 | 79 | .314 | 64 | 2.29 | 81 | 7.59 | 43 | 16.59 | 47 |
| | Pressure | .239 | 61 | .366 | 78 | .267 | 28 | 2.82 | 95 | 2.60 | 6 | 12.99 | 78 |
| Sid Fernandez | Overall | .198 | 6 | .334 | 37 | .271 | 13 | 2.64 | 99 | 8.49 | 62 | 22.42 | 12 |
| | Pressure | .288 | 93 | .500 | 109 | .314 | 60 | 4.55 | 109 | 2.86 | 7 | 24.29 | 9 |
| Dwight Gooden | Overall | .211 | 12 | .313 | 18 | .288 | 31 | 2.04 | 63 | 9.46 | 81 | 20.32 | 21 |
| | Pressure | .213 | 37 | .298 | 35 | .283 | 39 | 2.13 | 75 | 9.43 | 65 | 22.64 | 15 |
| Jeff Musselman | Overall | .267 | -- | .366 | -- | .357 | -- | 0.99 | -- | 11.76 | -- | 9.24 | -- |
| | Pressure | .306 | 103 | .408 | 93 | .358 | 95 | 0.00 | 1 | 7.27 | 45 | 9.09 | 105 |
| Randy Myers | Overall | .206 | 11 | .309 | 14 | .297 | 45 | 1.33 | 23 | 11.46 | 107 | 25.21 | 3 |
| | Pressure | .192 | 22 | .303 | 39 | .296 | 46 | 1.71 | 64 | 12.68 | 95 | 24.28 | 10 |
| Bob Ojeda | Overall | .245 | 60 | .360 | 65 | .317 | 70 | 2.19 | 71 | 9.47 | 82 | 11.53 | 97 |
| | Pressure | .231 | 54 | .333 | 56 | .318 | 65 | 2.56 | 89 | 11.36 | 90 | 11.36 | 89 |
| Frank Viola | Overall | .236 | 46 | .318 | 22 | .296 | 43 | 1.57 | 35 | 7.69 | 46 | 20.80 | 18 |
| | Pressure | .065 | -- | .065 | -- | .121 | -- | 0.00 | -- | 2.94 | -- | 26.47 | -- |
| Team Average | Overall | .231 | 1 | .348 | 2 | .301 | 1 | 2.11 | 6 | 8.72 | 9 | 18.17 | 1 |
| | Pressure | .234 | 7 | .331 | 6 | .307 | 6 | 1.79 | 6 | 9.10 | 7 | 19.77 | 2 |
| League Average | Overall | .246 | | .365 | | .312 | | 2.07 | | 8.47 | | 15.38 | |
| | Pressure | .235 | | .336 | | .309 | | 1.77 | | 9.31 | | 16.92 | |

## Additional Miscellaneous Pitching Comparisons

| | Grass Surface | | Artificial Surface | | Home Games | | Road Games | | Runners in Scoring Position | | Runners in Scoring Pos and Two Outs | | Leading Off Inning | |
|---|---|---|---|---|---|---|---|---|---|---|---|---|---|---|
| | BA | Rank | BA | Rank | BA | Rank | BA | Rank | BA | Rank | BA | Rank | OBA | Rank |
| Don Aase | .241 | 58 | .255 | -- | .200 | 19 | .286 | 101 | .222 | 35 | .194 | 44 | .271 | 34 |
| Rick Aguilera | .203 | 12 | .317 | -- | .173 | 5 | .289 | 103 | .250 | 62 | .306 | 106 | .212 | 4 |
| David Cone | .211 | 26 | .245 | 55 | .202 | 21 | .244 | 50 | .236 | 50 | .220 | 60 | .256 | 20 |
| Ron Darling | .252 | 74 | .276 | 92 | .249 | 68 | .269 | 86 | .249 | 61 | .202 | 50 | .253 | 18 |
| Sid Fernandez | .210 | 23 | .164 | 2 | .203 | 23 | .190 | 5 | .256 | 74 | .238 | 75 | .190 | 3 |
| Dwight Gooden | .213 | 29 | .202 | -- | .190 | 13 | .236 | 40 | .198 | 18 | .148 | 16 | .221 | 9 |
| Jeff Innis | .260 | 84 | .231 | -- | .229 | -- | .288 | -- | .256 | -- | .217 | -- | .286 | -- |
| Randy Myers | .190 | 4 | .242 | 51 | .192 | 15 | .225 | 29 | .167 | 6 | .164 | 23 | .304 | 67 |
| Bob Ojeda | .243 | 62 | .250 | 60 | .236 | 51 | .252 | 62 | .255 | 72 | .203 | 51 | .322 | 86 |
| Frank Viola | .262 | 87 | .188 | 5 | .289 | 106 | .200 | 13 | .271 | 83 | .167 | 26 | .372 | 113 |
| Team Average | .232 | 1 | .230 | 1 | .219 | 1 | .244 | 2 | .236 | 2 | .206 | 2 | .262 | 1 |
| League Average | .244 | | .248 | | .242 | | .251 | | .249 | | .222 | | .302 | |

# PHILADELPHIA PHILLIES

- **Hey, Phillie fans, wait 'til next year.**
- **Baseball history in review, Elias style.**

No pretense here. The authors reserve the right, every couple of years, to replace a team essay with a general–interest piece. Based upon an informal telephone poll of several readers (margin of error: plus or minus a lot), it was determined that the team most of you would least like to read about is the Philadelphia Phillies. Tune in next year, when the Phillies essay will return in its regularly scheduled spot. But now, stay tuned for this special presentation. (And check your local newspapers for information about our special swimsuit edition.)

One thing that distinguished the end of the 1980s from the close of previous decades was the inordinate amount of time and space devoted by the broadcast and print media to retrospectives. Perhaps that was a fitting finale to the "Re Decade". Over the past six months, we've been barraged with requests for lists of leaders for the 1980s, many of which have appeared in a variety of other publications. But, to our knowledge, no reference source has published a list of leaders for each decade. Those batting and pitching lists follow.

Batting average (minimum: 2000 at-bats): 1880s, Dan Brouthers, .348; 1890s, Willie Keeler, .387; 1900s, Honus Wagner, .351; 1910s, Ty Cobb, .387; 1920s, Rogers Hornsby, .382; 1930s, Bill Terry, .352; 1940s, Ted Williams, .356; 1950s, Ted Williams, .336; 1960s, Roberto Clemente, .328; 1970s, Rod Carew, .343; 1980s, Wade Boggs, .352.

Runs: 1880s, Harry Stovey, 1108; 1890s, Billy Hamilton, 1355; 1900s, Honus Wagner, 1013; 1910s, Ty Cobb, 1050; 1920s, Babe Ruth, 1365; 1930s, Lou Gehrig, 1257; 1940s, Ted Williams, 951; 1950s, Mickey Mantle, 994; 1960s, Hank Aaron, 1091; 1970s, Pete Rose, 1068; 1980s, Rickey Henderson, 1122.

Hits: 1880s, Cap Anson, 1518; 1890s, Hugh Duffy, 1880; 1900s, Honus Wagner, 1850; 1910s, Ty Cobb, 1951; 1920s, Rogers Hornsby, 2085; 1930s, Paul Waner, 1959; 1940s, Lou Boudreau, 1578; 1950s, Richie Ashburn, 1875; 1960s, Roberto Clemente, 1877; 1970s, Pete Rose, 2045; 1980s, Robin Yount, 1731.

Home runs: 1880s, Harry Stovey, 90; 1890s, Hugh Duffy, 80; 1900s, Harry Davis, 66; 1910s, Gavvy Cravath, 116; 1920s, Babe Ruth, 467; 1930s, Jimmie Foxx, 415; 1940s, Ted Williams, 234; 1950s, Duke Snider, 326; 1960s, Harmon Killebrew, 393; 1970s, Willie Stargell, 296; 1980s, Mike Schmidt, 313.

Runs batted in (unofficial until 1920): 1880s, Cap Anson, 803; 1890s, Hugh Duffy, 1085; 1900s, Honus Wagner, 956; 1910s, Ty Cobb, 852; 1920s, Babe Ruth, 1330; 1930s, Jimmie Foxx, 1403; 1940s, Bob Elliott, 903; 1950s, Duke Snider, 1031; 1960s, Hank Aaron, 1107; 1970s, Johnny Bench, 1013; 1980s, Eddie Murray, 996.

Pinch hits: 1890s, Duke Farrell, 19; 1900s, Dode Criss, 19; 1910s, Ham Hyatt, 48; 1920s, Bob Fothergill, 47; 1930s, Red Lucas, 86; 1940s, Dom Dallessandro, 45; 1950s, Enos Slaughter, 73; 1960s, Jerry Lynch, 83; 1970s, Manny Mota, 102; 1980s, Greg Gross, 110.

Stolen bases: 1880s, Hugh Nicol, 321; 1890s, Billy Hamilton, 749; 1900s, Honus Wagner, 487; 1910s, Ty Cobb, 577; 1920s, Max Carey, 346; 1930s, Ben Chapman, 269; 1940s, George Case, 285; 1950s, Willie Mays, 179; 1960s, Maury Wills, 535; 1970s, Lou Brock, 551; 1980s, Rickey Henderson, 838.

Earned run average (minimum: 1000 innings; unofficial until 1912): 1880s, Monte Ward, 2.21; 1890s, Amos Rusie, 2.89; 1900s, Three Finger Brown, 1.63; 1910s, Walter Johnson, 1.59; 1920s, Grover Cleveland Alexander, 3.04; 1930s, Carl Hubbell, 2.70; 1940s, Spud Chandler, 2.67; 1950s, Whitey Ford, 2.66; 1960s, Hoyt Wilhelm, 2.16; 1970s, Jim Palmer, 2.58; 1980s, Dwight Gooden, 2.64.

Winning percentage (minimum: 75 wins): 1880s, Bob Caruthers, .732; 1890s, Bill Hoffer, .693; 1900s, Ed Reulbach, .719; 1910s, Smoky Joe Wood, .680; 1920s, Ray Kremer, .660; 1930s, Lefty Grove, .724; 1940s, Spud Chandler, .714; 1950s, Whitey Ford, .708; 1960s, Sandy Koufax, .695; 1970s, Don Gullett, .686; 1980s, Dwight Gooden, .719.

Wins: 1880s, Tim Keefe, 292; 1890s, Kid Nichols, 297; 1900s, Christy Mathewson, 236; 1910s, Walter Johnson, 264; 1920s, Burleigh Grimes, 190; 1930s, Lefty Grove, 199; 1940s, Hal Newhouser, 170; 1950s, Warren Spahn, 202; 1960s, Juan Marichal, 191; 1970s, Jim Palmer, 186; 1980s, Jack Morris, 162.

Losses: 1880s, Pud Galvin, 244; 1890s, Gus Weyhing, 160; 1900s, Vic Willis, 171; 1910s, Walter Johnson, 143; 1920s, Dolf Luque, 146; 1930s, Paul Derringer, 137; 1940s, Dutch Leonard, 123; 1950s, Robin Roberts, 149; 1960s, Jack Fisher, 133; 1970s, Phil Niekro, 151; 1980s, Jim Clancy, 126.

Shutouts: 1880s, Pud Galvin, 48; 1890s, Kid Nichols, 36; 1900s, Christy Mathewson, 62; 1910s, Walter Johnson, 74; 1920s, Walter Johnson, 24; 1930s, Larry French, 32; 1940s, Mort Cooper and Hal Newhouser, 31; 1950s, Billy Pierce and Warren Spahn, 33; 1960s, Juan Marichal, 45; 1970s, Jim Palmer, 44; 1980s, Dave Stieb and Fernando Valenzuela, 27.

Strikeouts: 1880s, Tim Keefe, 2201; 1890s, Amos Rusie, 1838; 1900s, Rube Waddell, 2251; 1910s, Walter Johnson, 2219; 1920s, Dazzy Vance, 1464; 1930s, Lefty Gomez, 1337; 1940s, Hal Newhouser, 1579; 1950s, Early Wynn, 1544; 1960s, Bob Gibson, 2071; 1970s, Nolan Ryan, 2678; 1980s, Nolan Ryan, 2167.

Saves (unofficial until 1969): 1880s, Tony Mullane, 7; 1890s, Kid Nichols, 15; 1900s, Joe McGinnity, 21; 1910s, Slim Sallee, 31; 1920s, Firpo Marberry, 75; 1930s, Johnny Murphy, 54; 1940s, Joe Page, 63; 1950s, Ellis Kinder, 96; 1960s, Hoyt Wilhelm, 152; 1970s, Rollie Fingers, 209; 1980s, Jeff Reardon, 264.

One of the inequities of decade leaders is the bias against players whose parents didn't have the foresight to plan their children on a favorable schedule. Say what you will about the Bambino's mom and dad, they had their timing down pat. Not only did Ruth lead the 1920s in home runs; that was also the highest 10–year total—any 10 years, decade or otherwise —in major league history. On the other hand, Mickey Mantle hit 536 career home runs, almost evenly split between the 1950s and the 1960s. But his best 10–year total, 370 from 1955 through 1964, was among the highest in major league history.

Therefore, what follows are comparable lists of leaders, with *decade* redefined to mean any 10–year period. To qualify for batting average, ERA, or winning percentage, a player must have appeared in the first and last years of the range. For instance, Addie Joss wouldn't qualify because his career lasted only nine seasons. Overlapping totals by the same player have been eliminated.

Highest batting average (minimum: 4000 at–bats): Ty Cobb, .387 (1910–19); Rogers Hornsby, .382 (1920–29); Willie Keeler, .381 (1892–1901); Ed Delahanty, .373 (1893–1902); Jesse Burkett, .372 (1893–1902); Harry Heilmann, .367 (1921–30); Nap Lajoie, .363 (1897–1906); Tris Speaker, .360 (1916–25); Al Simmons, .359 (1925–34); Billy Hamilton, .357 (1891–1900).

Runs: Billy Hamilton, 1436 (1889–98); Lou Gehrig, 1417 (1927–36); Babe Ruth, 1365 (1920–29); Hugh Duffy, 1305 (1889–98); Willie Keeler, 1304 (1894–1903); Jesse Burkett, 1296 (1892–1901); Jimmie Foxx, 1244 (1930–39); Harry Stovey, 1235 (1882–91); Charlie Gehringer, 1224 (1929–38); Ed Delahanty, 1222 (1893–1902).

Hits: Willie Keeler, 2095 (1894–1903); Rogers Hornsby, 2085 (1920–29); Jesse Burkett, 2081 (1893–1902); Paul Waner, 2074 (1927–36); Pete Rose, 2067 (1968–77); Lou Gehrig, 2022 (1927–36); Stan Musial, 2013 (1946–55); Sam Rice, 2010 (1920–29); Al Simmons, 2005 (1925–34); Ty Cobb, 2003 (1908–17).

Home runs: Babe Ruth, 467 (1920–29); Jimmie Foxx, 415 (1930–39); Harmon Killebrew, 403 (1961–70); Lou Gehrig, 390 (1927–36); Willie Mays, 390 (1957–66); Hank Aaron, 386 (1962–71); Eddie Mathews, 374 (1953–62); Mickey Mantle, 370 (1955–64); Mike Schmidt, 370 (1974–83); Ralph Kiner, 369 (1946–55).

Runs batted in: Lou Gehrig, 1527 (1927–36); Jimmie Foxx, 1415 (1929–38); Babe Ruth, 1376 (1923–32); Al Simmons, 1277 (1925–34); Mel Ott, 1206 (1929–38); Hank Aaron, 1165 (1957–66); Rogers Hornsby, 1153 (1920–29); Sam Thompson, 1145 (1887–96); Ed Delahanty, 1144 (1893–1902); Harry Heilmann, 1133 (1921–30).

Stolen bases: Billy Hamilton, 847 (1889–98); Rickey Henderson, 838 (1980–89); Arlie Latham, 678 (1887–96); Lou Brock, 670 (1965–74); Ty Cobb, 625 (1909–18); Tom Brown, 599 (1887–96); Hugh Duffy, 540 (1889–98); Maury Wills, 535 (1960–69); Eddie Collins, 523 (1909–18); Willie Wilson, 521 (1978–87).

Pinch hits: Jose Morales, 117 (1974–83); Greg Gross, 117 (1979–88); Jerry Lynch, 107 (1957–66); Red Lucas, 103 (1928–37); Manny Mota, 102 (1970–79); Smoky Burgess, 98 (1957–66); Steve Braun, 94 (1976–85); Gates Brown, 91 (1965–74); Dave Philley, 89 (1953–62); Terry Crowley, 88 (1974–83).

Earned run average (minimum: 2000 innings): Walter Johnson, 1.59 (1910–19); Ed Walsh, 1.74 (1907–16); Three Finger Brown, 1.82 (1903–12); Christy Mathewson, 1.87 (1904–13); Cy Young, 2.05 (1901–10); Grover Cleveland Alexander, 2.07 (1911–20); Rube Waddell, 2.11 (1901–10); Eddie Plank, 2.15 (1903–12); Chief Bender, 2.17 (1905–14); Doc White, 2.21 (1902–11).

Winning percentage (minimum: 125 wins): Lefty Grove, .724 (1930–39); Christy Mathewson, .718 (1904–13); Whitey Ford, .724 (1949–58); Dwight Gooden, .719 (1980–89); Vic Raschi, .709 (1943–52); Sam Leever, .707 (1901–10); Ron Guidry, .697 (1976–85); Dave Foutz, .690 (1884–93); Red Ruffing, .686 (1936–45); Juan Marichal, .685 (1960–69); Chief Bender, .683 (1905–14); Three Finger Brown, .682 (1906–15).

Wins: John Clarkson, 317 (1884–93); Tim Keefe, 303 (1881–90); Pud Galvin, 302 (1879–88); Kid Nichols, 297 (1890–99); Old Hoss Radbourn, 296 (1881–90); Mickey Welch, 287 (1880–89); Cy Young, 282 (1892–1901); Christy Mathewson, 278 (1903–12); Jim McCormick, 264 (1878–87); Walter Johnson, 264 (1910–19).

Losses: Pud Galvin, 255 (1879–88); Jim McCormick, 214 (1878–87); Jim Whitney, 207 (1881–90); Mickey Welch, 185 (1880–89); Tim Keefe, 185 (1881–90); Old Hoss Radbourn, 180 (1882–91); Gus Weyhing, 178 (1887–96); Chick Fraser, 178 (1896–1905); Pink Hawley, 177 (1892–1901); John Clarkson, 172 (1885–94).

Shutouts: Grover Cleveland Alexander, 77 (1911–20); Walter Johnson, 74 (1910–19); Christy Mathewson, 64 (1901–10); Ed Walsh, 55 (1904–13); Three Finger Brown, 51 (1903–12); Pud Galvin, 50 (1879–88); Eddie Plank, 50 (1904–13); Jim Palmer, 50 (1969–78); Rube Waddell, 49 (1900–09); Bob Gibson, 47 (1962–71).

Strikeouts: Nolan Ryan, 2756 (1972–81); Tom Seaver, 2381 (1969–78); Sandy Koufax, 2336 (1957–66); Bob Gibson, 2295 (1962–71); Sam McDowell, 2253 (1964–73); Rube Waddell, 2251 (1900–09); Tim Keefe, 2246 (1881–90); Mickey Lolich, 2245 (1965–74); Walter Johnson, 2236 (1909–18); Steve Carlton, 2225 (1974–83).

Saves: Bruce Sutter, 283 (1976–85); Jeff Reardon, 264 (1980–89); Rollie Fingers, 249 (1973–82); Rich Gossage, 248 (1977–86); Dan Quisenberry, 239 (1980–89); Lee Smith, 234 (1980–89); Sparky Lyle, 196 (1968–77); Dave Righetti, 188 (1981–89); Mike Marshall, 177 (1970–79); Dave Smith, 176 (1980–89).

That should suffice for another 10 years, when we'll not only update the decade-by-decade leaders, but we'll also close the 1900s with an essay on what promises to be a hot topic—whether the current *millennium* was the best in major league history.

## WON-LOST RECORD BY STARTING POSITION

| PHILADELPHIA 67-95 | C | 1B | 2B | 3B | SS | LF | CF | RF | P | Leadoff | Relief | Starts |
|---|---|---|---|---|---|---|---|---|---|---|---|---|
| Jim Adduci | - | 1-2 | - | - | - | - | - | - | - | - | - | 1-2 |
| Tom Barrett | - | - | 2-5 | - | - | - | - | - | - | - | - | 2-5 |
| Steve Bedrosian | - | - | - | - | - | - | - | - | - | - | 12-15 | - |
| Eric Bullock | - | - | - | - | - | - | - | - | - | - | - | - |
| Don Carman | - | - | - | - | - | - | - | - | 6-14 | - | 8-21 | 6-14 |
| Pat Combs | - | - | - | - | - | - | - | - | 6-0 | - | - | 6-0 |
| Dennis Cook | - | - | - | - | - | - | - | - | 6-10 | - | 2-3 | 6-10 |
| Darren Daulton | 49-57 | - | - | - | - | - | - | - | - | - | - | 49-57 |
| Bob Dernier | - | - | - | - | - | 0-6 | 8-11 | 5-5 | - | 9-18 | - | 13-22 |
| Gordon Dillard | - | - | - | - | - | - | - | - | - | - | 2-3 | - |
| Len Dykstra | - | - | - | - | - | - | 37-48 | - | - | 37-48 | - | 37-48 |
| Curt Ford | - | - | - | - | - | 3-4 | 1-0 | 3-6 | - | 1-1 | - | 7-10 |
| Marvin Freeman | - | - | - | - | - | - | - | - | 1-0 | - | - | 1-0 |
| Todd Frohwirth | - | - | - | - | - | - | - | - | - | - | 11-34 | - |
| Jason Grimsley | - | - | - | - | - | - | - | - | 1-3 | - | - | 1-3 |
| Greg A. Harris | - | - | - | - | - | - | - | - | - | - | 10-34 | - |
| Charlie Hayes | - | - | - | 38-41 | - | - | - | - | - | - | - | 38-41 |
| Von Hayes | - | 10-11 | - | 5-4 | - | - | 4-3 | 42-70 | - | 3-3 | - | 61-88 |
| Tom Herr | - | - | 59-82 | - | - | - | - | - | - | 1-2 | - | 59-82 |
| Ken Howell | - | - | - | - | - | - | - | - | 16-16 | - | 0-1 | 16-16 |
| Chris James | - | - | - | 1-6 | - | 16-21 | - | - | - | - | - | 17-27 |
| Steve Jeltz | - | - | 5-6 | 3-10 | 20-24 | - | - | - | - | 2-3 | - | 28-40 |
| Ron Jones | - | - | - | - | - | - | - | 6-3 | - | - | - | 6-3 |
| Ricky Jordan | - | 55-76 | - | - | - | - | - | - | - | - | - | 55-76 |
| John Kruk | - | 0-5 | - | - | - | 26-32 | - | 6-4 | - | - | - | 32-41 |
| Steve Lake | 14-32 | - | - | - | - | - | - | - | - | - | - | 14-32 |
| Mike Maddux | - | - | - | - | - | - | - | - | 1-3 | - | 3-9 | 1-3 |
| Alex Madrid | - | - | - | - | - | - | - | - | 1-2 | - | 0-3 | 1-2 |
| Roger McDowell | - | - | - | - | - | - | - | - | - | - | 24-20 | - |
| Chuck McElroy | - | - | - | - | - | - | - | - | - | - | 1-10 | - |
| Larry McWilliams | - | - | - | - | - | - | - | - | 5-11 | - | 5-19 | 5-11 |
| N. Keith Miller | - | - | - | - | - | - | 1-0 | - | - | 1-0 | - | 1-0 |
| Terry Mulholland | - | - | - | - | - | - | - | - | 7-10 | - | 1-2 | 7-10 |
| Dwayne Murphy | - | - | - | - | - | 10-14 | - | 5-7 | - | - | - | 15-21 |
| Tom Nieto | 4-6 | - | - | - | - | - | - | - | - | - | - | 4-6 |
| Randy O'Neal | - | - | - | - | - | - | - | - | 1-0 | - | 3-16 | 1-0 |
| Steve Ontiveros | - | - | - | - | - | - | - | - | 2-3 | - | 1-0 | 2-3 |
| Al Pardo | - | - | - | - | - | - | - | - | - | - | - | - |
| Jeff Parrett | - | - | - | - | - | - | - | - | - | - | 30-42 | - |
| Randy Ready | - | - | 1-2 | 4-8 | - | 12-18 | - | - | - | 4-4 | - | 17-28 |
| Bruce Ruffin | - | - | - | - | - | - | - | - | 10-12 | - | 0-1 | 10-12 |
| Mark Ryal | - | 1-1 | - | - | - | - | - | - | - | - | - | 1-1 |
| Juan Samuel | - | - | - | - | - | - | 16-33 | - | - | 9-14 | - | 16-33 |
| Mike Schmidt | - | - | - | 16-26 | - | - | - | - | - | - | - | 16-26 |
| Bob Sebra | - | - | - | - | - | - | - | - | 2-3 | - | 0-1 | 2-3 |
| Steve Stanicek | - | - | - | - | - | - | - | - | - | - | - | - |
| Dickie Thon | - | - | - | - | 47-71 | - | - | - | - | 0-2 | - | 47-71 |
| Floyd Youmans | - | - | - | - | - | - | - | - | 2-8 | - | - | 2-8 |

## Batting vs. Left and Right Handed Pitchers

| | | BA | Rank | SA | Rank | OBA | Rank | HR % | Rank | BB % | Rank | SO % | Rank |
|---|---|---|---|---|---|---|---|---|---|---|---|---|---|
| Darren Daulton | vs. Lefties | .241 | 91 | .328 | 96 | .366 | 34 | 1.72 | 68 | 15.28 | 8 | 12.50 | 62 |
| | vs. Righties | .194 | 126 | .306 | 114 | .290 | 92 | 2.26 | 57 | 11.61 | 28 | 13.88 | 62 |
| Bob Dernier | vs. Lefties | .197 | 119 | .250 | 121 | .253 | 122 | 0.76 | 101 | 7.48 | 82 | 12.24 | 55 |
| | vs. Righties | .109 | -- | .127 | -- | .155 | -- | 0.00 | -- | 5.17 | -- | 17.24 | -- |
| Len Dykstra | vs. Lefties | .222 | 104 | .294 | 110 | .301 | 94 | 0.00 | 112 | 10.23 | 41 | 11.93 | 50 |
| | vs. Righties | .243 | 72 | .383 | 58 | .325 | 55 | 1.96 | 69 | 10.29 | 41 | 7.84 | 13 |
| Curt Ford | vs. Lefties | .267 | -- | .467 | -- | .400 | -- | 0.00 | -- | 15.00 | -- | 15.00 | -- |
| | vs. Righties | .213 | 115 | .268 | 125 | .284 | 100 | 0.79 | 104 | 9.22 | 52 | 21.28 | 114 |
| Charlie Hayes | vs. Lefties | .267 | 68 | .362 | 75 | .295 | 103 | 0.95 | 92 | 4.46 | 121 | 13.39 | 71 |
| | vs. Righties | .251 | 62 | .407 | 42 | .272 | 112 | 3.52 | 27 | 2.88 | 128 | 16.83 | 88 |
| Von Hayes | vs. Lefties | .245 | 88 | .404 | 56 | .356 | 43 | 3.85 | 22 | 14.17 | 15 | 17.00 | 102 |
| | vs. Righties | .268 | 42 | .497 | 10 | .388 | 14 | 5.42 | 7 | 16.30 | 3 | 15.06 | 78 |
| Tom Herr | vs. Lefties | .288 | 38 | .349 | 87 | .353 | 45 | 0.44 | 110 | 9.06 | 59 | 8.66 | 24 |
| | vs. Righties | .286 | 27 | .373 | 66 | .351 | 32 | 0.30 | 120 | 8.31 | 66 | 10.99 | 35 |
| Steve Jeltz | vs. Lefties | .268 | 65 | .366 | 73 | .409 | 9 | 1.41 | 80 | 18.89 | 3 | 5.56 | 5 |
| | vs. Righties | .234 | 83 | .328 | 97 | .335 | 45 | 1.56 | 75 | 12.44 | 21 | 17.33 | 92 |
| Ricky Jordan | vs. Lefties | .333 | 9 | .473 | 27 | .373 | 26 | 1.99 | 63 | 6.36 | 101 | 8.64 | 23 |
| | vs. Righties | .255 | 58 | .366 | 72 | .280 | 102 | 2.48 | 51 | 2.65 | 130 | 12.68 | 52 |
| John Kruk | vs. Lefties | .267 | 66 | .327 | 97 | .315 | 85 | 0.00 | 112 | 6.42 | 100 | 16.51 | 98 |
| | vs. Righties | .313 | 11 | .480 | 13 | .395 | 11 | 3.13 | 33 | 12.46 | 20 | 11.78 | 40 |
| Steve Lake | vs. Lefties | .240 | 93 | .314 | 103 | .290 | 106 | 0.83 | 97 | 6.87 | 94 | 13.74 | 77 |
| | vs. Righties | .294 | -- | .412 | -- | .351 | -- | 2.94 | -- | 7.89 | -- | 5.26 | -- |
| Dwayne Murphy | vs. Lefties | .235 | -- | .471 | -- | .350 | -- | 5.88 | -- | 15.00 | -- | 25.00 | -- |
| | vs. Righties | .216 | 111 | .417 | 36 | .339 | 40 | 5.76 | 6 | 15.76 | 4 | 23.64 | 124 |
| Randy Ready | vs. Lefties | .280 | 48 | .453 | 34 | .375 | 21 | 3.33 | 30 | 13.64 | 19 | 11.93 | 50 |
| | vs. Righties | .240 | -- | .385 | -- | .357 | -- | 2.88 | -- | 14.17 | -- | 12.60 | -- |
| Dickie Thon | vs. Lefties | .273 | 57 | .443 | 36 | .328 | 72 | 3.41 | 29 | 8.21 | 74 | 16.41 | 95 |
| | vs. Righties | .270 | 40 | .429 | 25 | .315 | 63 | 3.47 | 28 | 6.14 | 98 | 17.69 | 94 |
| Team Average | vs. Lefties | .250 | 6 | .359 | 10 | .319 | 7 | 1.92 | 9 | 9.15 | 3 | 14.34 | 6 |
| | vs. Righties | .239 | 8 | .366 | 5 | .311 | 4 | 2.46 | 4 | 9.08 | 2 | 15.58 | 6 |
| League Average | vs. Lefties | .251 | | .371 | | .320 | | 2.06 | | 8.85 | | 14.80 | |
| | vs. Righties | .244 | | .362 | | .309 | | 2.08 | | 8.27 | | 15.67 | |

## Batting with Runners on Base and Bases Empty

| | | BA | Rank | SA | Rank | OBA | Rank | HR % | Rank | BB % | Rank | SO % | Rank |
|---|---|---|---|---|---|---|---|---|---|---|---|---|---|
| Darren Daulton | Runners On | .244 | 95 | .404 | 55 | .353 | 46 | 3.85 | 22 | 13.98 | 22 | 10.22 | 35 |
| | Bases Empty | .170 | 130 | .241 | 125 | .264 | 114 | 0.94 | 99 | 10.88 | 18 | 16.32 | 89 |
| Bob Dernier | Runners On | .213 | -- | .295 | -- | .271 | -- | 1.64 | -- | 8.45 | -- | 14.08 | -- |
| | Bases Empty | .151 | 132 | .175 | 132 | .201 | 132 | 0.00 | 122 | 5.97 | 90 | 13.43 | 58 |
| Len Dykstra | Runners On | .224 | 112 | .350 | 92 | .297 | 107 | 2.10 | 60 | 9.41 | 73 | 11.76 | 54 |
| | Bases Empty | .242 | 75 | .359 | 78 | .326 | 49 | 1.09 | 96 | 10.63 | 27 | 7.97 | 7 |
| Charlie Hayes | Runners On | .296 | 30 | .448 | 28 | .311 | 99 | 2.40 | 52 | 2.99 | 131 | 13.43 | 68 |
| | Bases Empty | .229 | 93 | .352 | 83 | .258 | 117 | 2.79 | 34 | 3.76 | 117 | 17.20 | 98 |
| Von Hayes | Runners On | .283 | 37 | .488 | 16 | .398 | 17 | 5.12 | 11 | 16.56 | 11 | 13.69 | 71 |
| | Bases Empty | .238 | 79 | .437 | 20 | .355 | 20 | 4.55 | 16 | 14.50 | 5 | 17.75 | 104 |
| Tom Herr | Runners On | .296 | 29 | .364 | 84 | .350 | 51 | 0.49 | 110 | 7.33 | 97 | 7.76 | 12 |
| | Bases Empty | .282 | 27 | .363 | 73 | .353 | 22 | 0.28 | 120 | 9.37 | 42 | 11.39 | 34 |
| Steve Jeltz | Runners On | .292 | 32 | .425 | 41 | .385 | 26 | 2.83 | 36 | 12.50 | 33 | 14.06 | 77 |
| | Bases Empty | .210 | 112 | .280 | 117 | .337 | 41 | 0.64 | 107 | 15.51 | 3 | 13.90 | 62 |
| Ricky Jordan | Runners On | .276 | 47 | .407 | 52 | .318 | 91 | 2.61 | 46 | 5.41 | 116 | 11.82 | 56 |
| | Bases Empty | .294 | 15 | .408 | 42 | .316 | 59 | 1.96 | 64 | 2.66 | 126 | 10.27 | 24 |
| John Kruk | Runners On | .276 | 45 | .447 | 29 | .351 | 49 | 2.94 | 32 | 10.71 | 58 | 13.78 | 73 |
| | Bases Empty | .321 | 6 | .428 | 26 | .395 | 4 | 1.60 | 78 | 10.95 | 17 | 12.38 | 46 |
| Dwayne Murphy | Runners On | .184 | 125 | .368 | 78 | .340 | 65 | 5.26 | 7 | 19.15 | 6 | 21.28 | 124 |
| | Bases Empty | .250 | -- | .475 | -- | .341 | -- | 6.25 | -- | 12.09 | -- | 26.37 | -- |
| Randy Ready | Runners On | .215 | 116 | .299 | 117 | .348 | 52 | 1.87 | 66 | 16.91 | 10 | 13.97 | 76 |
| | Bases Empty | .299 | 11 | .517 | 6 | .383 | 10 | 4.08 | 18 | 11.38 | 14 | 10.78 | 30 |
| Mike Schmidt | Runners On | .207 | 121 | .390 | 61 | .299 | 104 | 4.88 | 14 | 12.37 | 38 | 7.22 | 9 |
| | Bases Empty | .197 | -- | .348 | -- | .293 | -- | 3.03 | -- | 12.00 | -- | 13.33 | -- |
| Dickie Thon | Runners On | .316 | 13 | .511 | 12 | .378 | 27 | 4.60 | 16 | 9.64 | 67 | 18.78 | 112 |
| | Bases Empty | .241 | 77 | .383 | 59 | .280 | 103 | 2.68 | 39 | 5.09 | 102 | 16.00 | 86 |
| Team Average | Runners On | .257 | 4 | .386 | 4 | .332 | 6 | 2.62 | 3 | 10.08 | 5 | 14.42 | 5 |
| | Bases Empty | .233 | 10 | .347 | 9 | .300 | 6 | 1.99 | 6 | 8.36 | 1 | 15.64 | 6 |
| League Average | Runners On | .256 | | .379 | | .330 | | 2.13 | | 9.82 | | 14.66 | |
| | Bases Empty | .240 | | .355 | | .299 | | 2.03 | | 7.43 | | 15.93 | |

## Overall Batting Compared to Late Inning Pressure Situations

| | | BA | Rank | SA | Rank | OBA | Rank | HR % | Rank | BB % | Rank | SO % | Rank | RDI % | Rank |
|---|---|---|---|---|---|---|---|---|---|---|---|---|---|---|---|
| Darren Daulton | Overall | .201 | 126 | .310 | 114 | .303 | 95 | 2.17 | 59 | 12.24 | 21 | 13.65 | 65 | .268 | 61 |
| | Pressure | .133 | 129 | .133 | 130 | .235 | 117 | 0.00 | 81 | 11.59 | 42 | 17.39 | 81 | .133 | 111 |
| Bob Dernier | Overall | .171 | 131 | .214 | 132 | .225 | 132 | 0.53 | 116 | 6.83 | 93 | 13.66 | 66 | .183 | 125 |
| | Pressure | .234 | 70 | .319 | 82 | .260 | 102 | 2.13 | 53 | 4.00 | 116 | 12.00 | 34 | .214 | 68 |
| Len Dykstra | Overall | .237 | 96 | .356 | 82 | .318 | 68 | 1.37 | 86 | 10.27 | 46 | 9.08 | 17 | .214 | 108 |
| | Pressure | .278 | 38 | .354 | 59 | .356 | 32 | 0.00 | 81 | 10.87 | 49 | 9.78 | 22 | .143 | 106 |
| Curt Ford | Overall | .218 | -- | .289 | -- | .298 | -- | 0.70 | -- | 9.94 | -- | 20.50 | -- | .256 | -- |
| | Pressure | .222 | 81 | .222 | 118 | .286 | 83 | 0.00 | 81 | 8.16 | 78 | 20.41 | 105 | .143 | 106 |
| Charlie Hayes | Overall | .257 | 65 | .391 | 54 | .280 | 115 | 2.63 | 36 | 3.44 | 130 | 15.63 | 88 | .323 | 16 |
| | Pressure | .238 | 65 | .357 | 57 | .289 | 78 | 2.38 | 42 | 6.52 | 86 | 17.39 | 81 | .222 | -- |
| Von Hayes | Overall | .259 | 57 | .461 | 16 | .376 | 13 | 4.81 | 10 | 15.49 | 4 | 15.80 | 91 | .275 | 55 |
| | Pressure | .238 | 65 | .429 | 25 | .390 | 14 | 4.76 | 12 | 19.05 | 3 | 17.14 | 79 | .160 | 100 |
| Tom Herr | Overall | .287 | 21 | .364 | 74 | .352 | 32 | 0.36 | 119 | 8.61 | 63 | 10.05 | 26 | .260 | 67 |
| | Pressure | .240 | 63 | .323 | 79 | .275 | 92 | 1.04 | 79 | 3.77 | 119 | 11.32 | 29 | .310 | 34 |
| Steve Jeltz | Overall | .243 | 86 | .338 | 97 | .356 | 29 | 1.52 | 79 | 14.29 | 7 | 13.97 | 70 | .247 | 80 |
| | Pressure | .220 | 85 | .288 | 92 | .324 | 66 | 1.69 | 64 | 12.50 | 25 | 13.89 | 51 | .063 | 129 |
| Ricky Jordan | Overall | .285 | 25 | .407 | 41 | .317 | 73 | 2.29 | 52 | 4.11 | 125 | 11.09 | 35 | .295 | 33 |
| | Pressure | .272 | 42 | .370 | 45 | .333 | 47 | 2.47 | 38 | 8.89 | 66 | 7.78 | 12 | .313 | 29 |
| John Kruk | Overall | .300 | 12 | .437 | 23 | .374 | 16 | 2.24 | 55 | 10.84 | 38 | 13.05 | 58 | .242 | 83 |
| | Pressure | .343 | 5 | .571 | 5 | .442 | 2 | 5.71 | 7 | 15.91 | 10 | 11.36 | 30 | .294 | 41 |
| Dwayne Murphy | Overall | .218 | -- | .423 | -- | .341 | -- | 5.77 | -- | 15.68 | -- | 23.78 | -- | .237 | 87 |
| | Pressure | .167 | -- | .200 | -- | .306 | -- | 0.00 | -- | 16.67 | -- | 25.00 | -- | .333 | 22 |
| Randy Ready | Overall | .264 | 50 | .425 | 28 | .368 | 20 | 3.15 | 29 | 13.86 | 8 | 12.21 | 45 | .198 | 121 |
| | Pressure | .282 | 34 | .462 | 18 | .440 | 3 | 2.56 | 32 | 22.00 | 2 | 8.00 | 14 | .313 | 29 |
| Mike Schmidt | Overall | .203 | -- | .372 | -- | .297 | -- | 4.05 | -- | 12.21 | -- | 9.88 | -- | .311 | 22 |
| | Pressure | .238 | -- | .476 | -- | .333 | -- | 4.76 | -- | 12.50 | -- | 20.83 | -- | .000 | -- |
| Dickie Thon | Overall | .271 | 40 | .434 | 25 | .321 | 65 | 3.45 | 25 | 6.99 | 90 | 17.16 | 100 | .279 | 49 |
| | Pressure | .258 | 49 | .409 | 27 | .338 | 46 | 3.03 | 26 | 10.67 | 52 | 17.33 | 80 | .368 | 17 |
| Team Average | Overall | .243 | 8 | .364 | 6 | .314 | 6 | 2.26 | 5 | 9.11 | 2 | 15.11 | 6 | .250 | 9 |
| | Pressure | .237 | 7 | .333 | 9 | .317 | 5 | 1.83 | 5 | 10.14 | 2 | 15.66 | 4 | .225 | 11 |
| League Average | Overall | .246 | | .365 | | .312 | | 2.07 | | 8.47 | | 15.38 | | .253 | |
| | Pressure | .238 | | .337 | | .308 | | 1.73 | | 8.93 | | 16.78 | | .235 | |

## Additional Miscellaneous Batting Comparisons

| | Grass Surface | | Artificial Surface | | Home Games | | Road Games | | Runners in Scoring Position | | Runners in Scoring Pos and Two Outs | | Leading Off Inning | | Runners on 3B with less than 2 Outs | |
|---|---|---|---|---|---|---|---|---|---|---|---|---|---|---|---|---|
| | BA | Rank | BA | Rank | BA | Rank | BA | Rank | BA | Rank | BA | Rank | OBA | Rank | RDI % | Rank |
| Darren Daulton | .212 | 108 | .197 | 125 | .163 | 131 | .235 | 85 | .239 | 88 | .196 | 94 | .250 | 110 | .684 | 22 |
| Bob Dernier | .170 | -- | .171 | 131 | .165 | 129 | .178 | 129 | .175 | -- | .217 | -- | .239 | 119 | .400 | 130 |
| Len Dykstra | .231 | 87 | .241 | 91 | .252 | 76 | .224 | 95 | .203 | 113 | .227 | 63 | .279 | 89 | .474 | 117 |
| Curt Ford | .163 | -- | .242 | 88 | .259 | -- | .190 | -- | .250 | -- | .000 | -- | .240 | 118 | .667 | 25 |
| Charlie Hayes | .275 | -- | .250 | 74 | .231 | 102 | .284 | 32 | .253 | 74 | .114 | 127 | .263 | 101 | .864 | 2 |
| Von Hayes | .297 | 17 | .245 | 85 | .249 | 80 | .269 | 45 | .256 | 70 | .333 | 10 | .377 | 20 | .652 | 35 |
| Tom Herr | .239 | 76 | .303 | 11 | .285 | 38 | .289 | 24 | .261 | 63 | .241 | 51 | .340 | 35 | .588 | 59 |
| Steve Jeltz | .292 | -- | .225 | 109 | .277 | 44 | .211 | 109 | .262 | 62 | .214 | 77 | .338 | 36 | .700 | 17 |
| Ricky Jordan | .291 | 23 | .283 | 33 | .274 | 45 | .296 | 12 | .270 | 53 | .227 | 63 | .301 | 65 | .688 | 20 |
| John Kruk | .273 | 44 | .316 | 5 | .313 | 13 | .285 | 28 | .224 | 98 | .188 | 102 | .455 | 1 | .545 | 82 |
| Steve Lake | .139 | -- | .286 | 28 | .269 | -- | .234 | -- | .216 | -- | .211 | 82 | .364 | -- | .375 | 136 |
| Dwayne Murphy | .195 | -- | .226 | 107 | .270 | -- | .171 | -- | .200 | 115 | .219 | 72 | .395 | -- | .500 | 98 |
| Randy Ready | .282 | -- | .257 | 59 | .263 | 60 | .264 | 52 | .179 | 126 | .162 | 113 | .435 | 2 | .471 | 118 |
| Mike Schmidt | .185 | -- | .213 | 118 | .222 | -- | .188 | 123 | .220 | 103 | .240 | 52 | .293 | -- | .688 | 20 |
| Dickie Thon | .289 | 26 | .264 | 47 | .264 | 58 | .278 | 37 | .356 | 5 | .255 | 40 | .281 | 85 | .536 | 88 |
| Team Average | .237 | 8 | .245 | 7 | .246 | 9 | .240 | 8 | .241 | 10 | .207 | 10 | .304 | 5 | .587 | 1 |
| League Average | .244 | | .248 | | .251 | | .242 | | .249 | | .222 | | .302 | | .546 | |

## Pitching vs. Left and Right Handed Batters

| | | BA | Rank | SA | Rank | OBA | Rank | HR % | Rank | BB % | Rank | SO % | Rank |
|---|---|---|---|---|---|---|---|---|---|---|---|---|---|
| Don Carman | vs. Lefties | .222 | 33 | .435 | 102 | .294 | 30 | 5.56 | 116 | 7.44 | 34 | 11.57 | 80 |
| | vs. Righties | .269 | 92 | .443 | 109 | .369 | 109 | 3.15 | 100 | 13.70 | 113 | 11.92 | 94 |
| Pat Combs | vs. Lefties | .273 | -- | .364 | -- | .333 | -- | 0.00 | -- | 8.33 | -- | 8.33 | -- |
| | vs. Righties | .248 | 69 | .336 | 44 | .273 | 38 | 1.49 | 25 | 3.55 | 5 | 20.57 | 38 |
| Dennis Cook | vs. Lefties | .206 | -- | .429 | -- | .311 | -- | 6.35 | -- | 10.39 | -- | 15.58 | -- |
| | vs. Righties | .249 | 74 | .424 | 101 | .302 | 65 | 3.60 | 110 | 7.11 | 58 | 13.03 | 86 |
| Todd Frohwirth | vs. Lefties | .350 | 115 | .530 | 114 | .409 | 112 | 3.00 | 100 | 8.11 | 47 | 4.50 | 116 |
| | vs. Righties | .159 | 3 | .212 | 2 | .222 | 5 | 0.76 | 10 | 6.12 | 38 | 23.13 | 22 |
| Greg A. Harris | vs. Lefties | .190 | 11 | .281 | 19 | .329 | 65 | 0.83 | 27 | 16.67 | 116 | 13.33 | 63 |
| | vs. Righties | .268 | 91 | .438 | 107 | .349 | 97 | 3.92 | 115 | 10.34 | 102 | 17.82 | 51 |
| Ken Howell | vs. Lefties | .235 | 43 | .341 | 51 | .321 | 57 | 1.45 | 55 | 11.51 | 88 | 16.11 | 39 |
| | vs. Righties | .188 | 11 | .275 | 12 | .264 | 27 | 1.62 | 32 | 8.88 | 86 | 24.93 | 16 |
| Mike Maddux | vs. Lefties | .272 | 87 | .321 | 38 | .333 | 71 | 1.23 | 43 | 7.69 | 37 | 14.29 | 52 |
| | vs. Righties | .333 | -- | .511 | -- | .388 | -- | 2.22 | -- | 7.00 | -- | 13.00 | -- |
| Roger McDowell | vs. Lefties | .265 | 81 | .351 | 54 | .358 | 98 | 1.62 | 60 | 12.15 | 95 | 7.94 | 108 |
| | vs. Righties | .195 | 14 | .247 | 5 | .260 | 20 | 0.00 | 1 | 6.94 | 56 | 17.34 | 55 |
| Larry McWilliams | vs. Lefties | .181 | 6 | .253 | 10 | .277 | 19 | 1.20 | 42 | 11.58 | 90 | 13.68 | 56 |
| | vs. Righties | .283 | 101 | .361 | 61 | .350 | 99 | 0.52 | 6 | 8.72 | 84 | 9.40 | 113 |
| Terry Mulholland | vs. Lefties | .212 | 23 | .282 | 20 | .253 | 10 | 0.00 | 1 | 5.38 | 7 | 20.43 | 15 |
| | vs. Righties | .313 | 113 | .437 | 106 | .371 | 113 | 2.11 | 54 | 7.38 | 65 | 11.19 | 99 |
| Jeff Parrett | vs. Lefties | .218 | 30 | .292 | 25 | .309 | 46 | 0.00 | 1 | 11.49 | 87 | 20.43 | 16 |
| | vs. Righties | .247 | 70 | .435 | 105 | .304 | 66 | 3.23 | 102 | 8.13 | 76 | 23.92 | 19 |
| Bruce Ruffin | vs. Lefties | .281 | -- | .438 | -- | .427 | -- | 1.56 | -- | 19.77 | -- | 9.30 | -- |
| | vs. Righties | .304 | 110 | .431 | 103 | .368 | 108 | 2.04 | 52 | 9.18 | 91 | 12.65 | 89 |
| Floyd Youmans | vs. Lefties | .311 | 111 | .489 | 111 | .411 | 114 | 3.33 | 109 | 14.68 | 110 | 9.17 | 100 |
| | vs. Righties | .286 | -- | .468 | -- | .367 | -- | 5.19 | -- | 9.89 | -- | 10.99 | -- |
| Team Average | vs. Lefties | .249 | 6 | .381 | 10 | .339 | 11 | 2.04 | 11 | 11.50 | 12 | 13.25 | 9 |
| | vs. Righties | .264 | 12 | .400 | 12 | .332 | 12 | 2.49 | 10 | 8.98 | 12 | 15.19 | 10 |
| League Average | vs. Lefties | .252 | | .366 | | .325 | | 1.79 | | 9.48 | | 13.93 | |
| | vs. Righties | .242 | | .365 | | .303 | | 2.29 | | 7.70 | | 16.46 | |

## Pitching with Runners on Base and Bases Empty

| | | BA | Rank | SA | Rank | OBA | Rank | HR % | Rank | BB % | Rank | SO % | Rank |
|---|---|---|---|---|---|---|---|---|---|---|---|---|---|
| Don Carman | Runners On | .257 | 72 | .382 | 71 | .380 | 108 | 2.07 | 62 | 16.89 | 116 | 10.26 | 96 |
| | Bases Empty | .262 | 93 | .484 | 115 | .336 | 104 | 4.66 | 115 | 9.19 | 91 | 13.12 | 81 |
| Dennis Cook | Runners On | .282 | 91 | .490 | 113 | .359 | 91 | 4.70 | 113 | 10.86 | 80 | 12.00 | 85 |
| | Bases Empty | .224 | 32 | .393 | 94 | .275 | 29 | 3.63 | 113 | 5.86 | 36 | 14.20 | 71 |
| Todd Frohwirth | Runners On | .258 | 73 | .381 | 69 | .365 | 97 | 2.06 | 60 | 11.76 | 95 | 17.65 | 35 |
| | Bases Empty | .230 | 37 | .326 | 31 | .252 | 8 | 1.48 | 41 | 2.88 | 2 | 12.95 | 84 |
| Greg A. Harris | Runners On | .246 | 60 | .328 | 31 | .340 | 70 | 1.49 | 35 | 11.95 | 98 | 15.09 | 50 |
| | Bases Empty | .221 | 29 | .407 | 101 | .339 | 106 | 3.57 | 110 | 14.55 | 114 | 16.36 | 43 |
| Ken Howell | Runners On | .226 | 28 | .358 | 52 | .297 | 28 | 2.43 | 82 | 9.76 | 60 | 17.46 | 37 |
| | Bases Empty | .207 | 18 | .283 | 12 | .297 | 55 | 0.92 | 20 | 10.84 | 105 | 21.47 | 19 |
| Roger McDowell | Runners On | .221 | 23 | .291 | 12 | .322 | 59 | 1.16 | 25 | 11.71 | 94 | 13.17 | 77 |
| | Bases Empty | .246 | 67 | .317 | 26 | .308 | 71 | 0.60 | 9 | 7.69 | 71 | 10.99 | 104 |
| Larry McWilliams | Runners On | .303 | 102 | .418 | 88 | .382 | 109 | 1.00 | 20 | 11.16 | 84 | 9.09 | 106 |
| | Bases Empty | .235 | 46 | .284 | 13 | .301 | 62 | 0.38 | 5 | 7.61 | 69 | 11.07 | 102 |
| Terry Mulholland | Runners On | .280 | 90 | .441 | 96 | .352 | 85 | 2.37 | 78 | 9.05 | 49 | 13.58 | 67 |
| | Bases Empty | .307 | 114 | .382 | 85 | .348 | 109 | 1.18 | 27 | 5.19 | 25 | 12.22 | 91 |
| Jeff Parrett | Runners On | .245 | 59 | .368 | 62 | .347 | 79 | 1.84 | 47 | 13.79 | 110 | 20.69 | 18 |
| | Bases Empty | .222 | 30 | .356 | 69 | .274 | 27 | 1.33 | 32 | 6.64 | 52 | 23.24 | 11 |
| Bruce Ruffin | Runners On | .295 | 97 | .398 | 79 | .375 | 105 | 0.80 | 13 | 11.26 | 86 | 9.90 | 101 |
| | Bases Empty | .307 | 114 | .465 | 114 | .378 | 115 | 3.15 | 107 | 10.25 | 100 | 14.49 | 68 |
| Team Average | Runners On | .268 | 12 | .397 | 12 | .358 | 12 | 2.08 | 6 | 11.93 | 12 | 13.70 | 9 |
| | Bases Empty | .251 | 12 | .390 | 12 | .316 | 12 | 2.53 | 12 | 8.17 | 12 | 15.15 | 9 |
| League Average | Runners On | .256 | | .379 | | .330 | | 2.13 | | 9.82 | | 14.66 | |
| | Bases Empty | .240 | | .355 | | .299 | | 2.03 | | 7.43 | | 15.93 | |

## Overall Pitching Compared to Late Inning Pressure Situations

| | | BA | Rank | SA | Rank | OBA | Rank | HR % | Rank | BB % | Rank | SO % | Rank |
|---|---|---|---|---|---|---|---|---|---|---|---|---|---|
| Don Carman | Overall | .260 | 84 | .442 | 114 | .355 | 107 | 3.60 | 112 | 12.59 | 111 | 11.86 | 93 |
| | Pressure | .203 | 27 | .304 | 40 | .337 | 83 | 1.27 | 44 | 14.58 | 108 | 8.33 | 106 |
| Dennis Cook | Overall | .243 | 58 | .425 | 106 | .304 | 54 | 3.98 | 115 | 7.62 | 44 | 13.43 | 74 |
| | Pressure | .171 | 9 | .257 | 13 | .256 | 20 | 2.86 | 96 | 10.00 | 74 | 15.00 | 65 |
| Todd Frohwirth | Overall | .241 | 56 | .349 | 51 | .303 | 53 | 1.72 | 40 | 6.98 | 34 | 15.12 | 58 |
| | Pressure | .233 | 58 | .274 | 23 | .282 | 38 | 0.00 | 1 | 5.06 | 24 | 10.13 | 100 |
| Greg A. Harris | Overall | .234 | 43 | .369 | 70 | .340 | 98 | 2.55 | 94 | 13.27 | 113 | 15.74 | 55 |
| | Pressure | .357 | 111 | .500 | 109 | .460 | 114 | 2.38 | 82 | 14.00 | 106 | 8.00 | 110 |
| Ken Howell | Overall | .215 | 21 | .313 | 19 | .297 | 44 | 1.52 | 31 | 10.40 | 99 | 19.83 | 24 |
| | Pressure | .281 | 92 | .313 | 50 | .352 | 92 | 0.00 | 1 | 9.59 | 66 | 24.66 | 8 |
| Roger McDowell | Overall | .233 | 40 | .304 | 12 | .315 | 65 | 0.88 | 8 | 9.82 | 87 | 12.14 | 87 |
| | Pressure | .223 | 46 | .279 | 26 | .314 | 59 | 1.02 | 39 | 11.01 | 87 | 11.01 | 92 |
| Larry McWilliams | Overall | .265 | 91 | .342 | 43 | .337 | 95 | 0.65 | 4 | 9.23 | 77 | 10.17 | 107 |
| | Pressure | .220 | 42 | .237 | 9 | .324 | 73 | 0.00 | 1 | 13.24 | 100 | 14.71 | 71 |
| Terry Mulholland | Overall | .295 | 111 | .409 | 100 | .350 | 104 | 1.72 | 39 | 7.02 | 35 | 12.87 | 81 |
| | Pressure | .308 | 104 | .333 | 56 | .357 | 94 | 0.00 | 1 | 6.67 | 34 | 6.67 | 111 |
| Jeff Parrett | Overall | .232 | 38 | .361 | 68 | .307 | 56 | 1.55 | 32 | 9.91 | 89 | 22.07 | 13 |
| | Pressure | .211 | 34 | .326 | 53 | .306 | 52 | 1.65 | 62 | 12.20 | 93 | 23.34 | 14 |
| Bruce Ruffin | Overall | .301 | 113 | .432 | 109 | .377 | 115 | 1.98 | 56 | 10.76 | 102 | 12.15 | 86 |
| | Pressure | .190 | -- | .238 | -- | .227 | -- | 0.00 | -- | 4.55 | -- | 4.55 | -- |
| Team Average | Overall | .259 | 12 | .393 | 12 | .335 | 12 | 2.33 | 11 | 9.88 | 12 | 14.49 | 9 |
| | Pressure | .229 | 6 | .331 | 5 | .320 | 9 | 1.80 | 7 | 11.11 | 11 | 15.75 | 8 |
| League Average | Overall | .246 | | .365 | | .312 | | 2.07 | | 8.47 | | 15.38 | |
| | Pressure | .235 | | .336 | | .309 | | 1.77 | | 9.31 | | 16.92 | |

## Additional Miscellaneous Pitching Comparisons

| | Grass Surface | | Artificial Surface | | Home Games | | Road Games | | Runners in Scoring Position | | Runners in Scoring Pos and Two Outs | | Leading Off Inning | |
|---|---|---|---|---|---|---|---|---|---|---|---|---|---|---|
| | BA | Rank | BA | Rank | BA | Rank | BA | Rank | BA | Rank | BA | Rank | OBA | Rank |
| Don Carman | .312 | 111 | .239 | 48 | .249 | 67 | .271 | 89 | .264 | 79 | .164 | 24 | .304 | 65 |
| Pat Combs | .325 | -- | .219 | 24 | .205 | -- | .299 | -- | .219 | -- | .133 | -- | .256 | -- |
| Dennis Cook | .310 | 110 | .228 | 35 | .190 | 14 | .310 | 109 | .297 | 96 | .237 | 74 | .310 | 70 |
| Todd Frohwirth | .265 | -- | .235 | 41 | .233 | 47 | .253 | -- | .303 | 100 | .349 | 116 | .161 | 1 |
| Greg A. Harris | .159 | -- | .248 | 59 | .268 | 91 | .188 | 3 | .269 | 81 | .258 | 87 | .319 | 83 |
| Ken Howell | .203 | 13 | .219 | 22 | .236 | 50 | .193 | 8 | .245 | 60 | .164 | 24 | .329 | 92 |
| Mike Maddux | .185 | -- | .359 | 116 | .369 | -- | .206 | -- | .315 | -- | .320 | -- | .333 | -- |
| Roger McDowell | .236 | 54 | .230 | 37 | .206 | 25 | .253 | 63 | .198 | 18 | .192 | 42 | .308 | 69 |
| Larry McWilliams | .257 | 79 | .267 | 81 | .254 | 71 | .280 | 95 | .296 | 95 | .302 | 100 | .283 | 44 |
| Terry Mulholland | .342 | 115 | .272 | 88 | .240 | 54 | .346 | 115 | .312 | 104 | .310 | 108 | .344 | 97 |
| Randy O'Neal | .302 | 107 | .299 | -- | .328 | -- | .284 | -- | .217 | -- | .182 | -- | .306 | -- |
| Jeff Parrett | .233 | 47 | .232 | 38 | .198 | 17 | .259 | 77 | .277 | 85 | .250 | 81 | .293 | 52 |
| Bruce Ruffin | .235 | 51 | .314 | 110 | .317 | 114 | .276 | 91 | .299 | 98 | .297 | 99 | .435 | 117 |
| Floyd Youmans | .368 | -- | .279 | 94 | .333 | -- | .277 | -- | .292 | -- | .348 | -- | .356 | -- |
| Team Average | .267 | 12 | .256 | 10 | .256 | 11 | .262 | 12 | .271 | 12 | .247 | 12 | .317 | 12 |
| League Average | .244 | | .248 | | .242 | | .251 | | .249 | | .222 | | .302 | |

# PITTSBURGH PIRATES

- **Leadoff sluggers: Rickey Henderson, meet the Bondses.**
- **Andy Van Slyke's worst nightmare.**

The King is dead. And now that Rickey Henderson has played Cromwell to Bobby Bonds's Charles I, deposing him as king of the first-inning leadoff home run, it falls to Barry Bonds to play the avenging son, restoring the family honor by regaining the throne.

This may seem less a crusade than a small brush fire on the baseball landscape, but it was Bobby Bonds who put this particular record in the books. At the time of Daddy Bonds's record-breaking 29th first-inning leadoff home run in 1975, few baseball fans knew whose total he had surpassed. Even today, that player—Eddie Yost—is remembered as the "Walking Man", whose career total of 1614 bases on balls ranks among the 10 highest in major league history. But Yost's 28 home runs leading off the first inning remain merely a footnote to his career. So for those who consider records to be only those events catalogued in a published reference source (a narrow but all too pervasive viewpoint), it's clear that without Bobby Bonds, there would have been no "record" for Henderson to break.

Even *that* wouldn't have been reason enough to commemorate the extinction of Bonds's record here. But the effect that his particular specialty has had on baseball is hardly insignificant. Some teams may still adhere strictly to the classic profile of leadoff hitters, a seldom-found ideal that requires speed, a high batting average, a generous total of bases on balls, but not necessarily power. But over the past 20 years—or since Bonds the Elder redefined the role—many teams have abandoned the notion that power is wasted in the leadoff spot, especially for home-run hitters who otherwise match the standard profile.

It would have required considerable effort not to notice the proliferation of leadoff power hitters since then, with players like Henderson, Juan Samuel, Kirby Puckett, and Kal Daniels—to name just a few—taking at least semi-regular turns in the leadoff spot. But relatively few have noticed that over the past few years, the trend has ebbed. With a perceived scarcity of power hitters, teams have become increasingly reluctant to place their most powerful hitters in a batting-order position that may reduce the number of runners on base when they bat. (Of course, the home-run increases of prior seasons had the opposite effect: They encouraged managers to deploy one of their surplus guns in the leadoff spot, hoping to make a preemptive first-inning strike against the opposition.)

American League hitters batting in the leadoff slot, first inning or otherwise, produced 36 percent fewer home runs last season than in 1986, relative to the league total. The decline hasn't yet become as dramatic in the National League, which appears to have peaked only two years back. But last season's 17 percent drop represents a significant one-year reduction:

| | 1984 | 1985 | 1986 | 1987 | 1988 | 1989 |
|---|---|---|---|---|---|---|
| American League | 98 | 151 | 206 | 219 | 139 | 99 |
| Pct. of all HRs | 4.9 | 6.9 | 9.0 | 8.3 | 7.3 | 5.8 |
| National League | 93 | 118 | 136 | 186 | 131 | 116 |
| Pct. of all HRs | 7.3 | 8.3 | 8.9 | 10.2 | 10.2 | 8.5 |

Should that trend continue, Bonds the Younger, one of the few power hitters still leading off regularly, will become the most likely candidate to dethrone Henderson. During his four seasons, Barry leads the majors with 73 home runs from the leadoff position in the batting order, 11 more than Henderson, and more than double the totals of any other players except Paul Molitor (45) and Lou Whitaker (39). As for leadoff home runs *in the first inning*, Bonds has already hit 19, only three less than what passed for the all-time *career* record until 1959. Meanwhile, with the exception of Henderson, most others with high totals in recent seasons have been dropped in the batting order. The best example is Kal Daniels, who hit eight first-inning leadoff homers in 1987. He batted leadoff in only 41 starts in 1988, 12 last season (and none after joining the Dodgers).

Bonds hasn't been totally immune to batting-order migration. He made 145 starts last season, 39 outside the leadoff spot. On three separate occasions, Jim Leyland temporarily dropped Bonds to fifth in the order, including a stay of nearly a month starting in late August. So it's interesting to consider, with regard both to Pittsburgh's strategy and to Bonds's future: What is the effect of a power hitter batting leadoff?

The best way to answer that question would be to examine the teams that produced more home runs from the first slot than from any other batting-order position. Unfortunately, those cases are too rare to be of much use. It's happened only five times in the last eight years (including the Pirates in 1987 and 1988). Even when the criterion is loosened to include teams whose leadoff slots ranked among their top three positions in home-run production, the list grows only to 18 teams. But that group is large enough to illustrate a surprising conclusion.

Those teams are listed below with three figures: (1) the number of runs they scored; (2) the runs they "should have scored," based on an analysis of their totals in building-block categories (AB, H, 2B, 3B, HR, BB, SB, etc.); and (3) the difference between the first two figures. If a power hitter in the leadoff spot has an impact—either positive or negative—on a team's ability to turn its hits, walks, and so forth into runs, it will show up in the cumulative differences between their actual and expected run totals:

| Year | N.L. Teams | Act. | Exp. | Diff. | Year | A.L. Teams | Act. | Exp. | Diff. |
|---|---|---|---|---|---|---|---|---|---|
| 1983 | Cincinnati | 623 | 615 | +8 | 1982 | Texas | 590 | 587 | +3 |
| 1984 | Atlanta | 632 | 640 | −8 | 1985 | Texas | 617 | 654 | −37 |
| 1984 | Cincinnati | 627 | 644 | −17 | 1986 | Minnesota | 741 | 757 | −16 |
| 1985 | Houston | 706 | 679 | +27 | 1986 | New York | 797 | 837 | −40 |
| 1986 | Cincinnati | 732 | 714 | +18 | 1987 | California | 770 | 761 | +9 |
| 1987 | Cincinnati | 783 | 768 | +15 | 1988 | California | 714 | 693 | +21 |
| 1987 | Philadelphia | 702 | 723 | −21 | | Totals | 4229 | 4289 | −60 |
| 1987 | Pittsburgh | 723 | 733 | −10 | | | | | |
| 1988 | Atlanta | 555 | 538 | +17 | | | | | |
| 1988 | Pittsburgh | 651 | 647 | +4 | | | | | |
| 1989 | Atlanta | 584 | 575 | +9 | | | | | |
| 1989 | Pittsburgh | 637 | 644 | −7 | | | | | |
| | Totals | 7955 | 7920 | +35 | | | | | |

On average, National League teams scored 35 more runs than expected—or a less-than-massive three per season, too small a margin on which to base even a tenuous conclusion. Even the American League average of 10 runs per season less than expected is insignificant for a sample as small as six teams. But the difference *between the two leagues* strongly suggests that leadoff power hitters are more effective in the National League, where they follow the weakest batting-order position on the team, than in the American League, where many teams now stash a so-called "second leadoff hitter" in the ninth spot. Live and learn.

Let's pose a Rod Serling-type scenario. One morning, you awaken to find that the world is a mirror image of itself. Clocks move counterclockwise. Cars travel on the wrong side of the road (except in England). Righty Driesell coaches the men's basketball team at James Madison. And there are twice as many left-handed pitchers as right-handers. This is known as an Andy Van Slyke nightmare.

Van Slyke is a career .267 hitter, with an average of 51 extra-base hits and 72 RBIs over the past five years. Nice numbers, not spectacular. But to speak about averages for Van Slyke is like calling Dr. Jekyll just your average everyday guy—some good points, some bad. Against right-handers, Van Slyke hits like an All-Star. But against southpaws, forget it. His career breakdown:

| | AB | H | 2B | 3B | HR | RBI | BA | SA | OBA |
|---|---|---|---|---|---|---|---|---|---|
| Left-handers | 859 | 185 | 35 | 21 | 10 | 103 | .215 | .340 | .285 |
| Right-handers | 2280 | 654 | 121 | 36 | 86 | 347 | .287 | .485 | .364 |

Nevertheless, Van Slyke is a valuable commodity in a baseball world in which right-handed pitchers outnumber left-handers by a two-to-one margin. Were those figures reversed—if his career figures against left-handers were doubled, and those against right-handers were halved. . .

| Year | AB | H | 2B | 3B | HR | RBI | BA | SA | OBA |
|---|---|---|---|---|---|---|---|---|---|
| 1983 | 232 | 58 | 9 | 4 | 7 | 30 | .250 | .414 | .337 |
| 1984 | 243 | 60 | 11 | 5 | 3 | 38 | .247 | .370 | .347 |
| 1985 | 293 | 64 | 15 | 3 | 6 | 36 | .218 | .352 | .287 |
| 1986 | 383 | 92 | 20 | 9 | 8 | 51 | .240 | .402 | .316 |
| 1987 | 625 | 162 | 33 | 13 | 15 | 81 | .259 | .426 | .320 |
| 1988 | 599 | 143 | 19 | 16 | 17 | 87 | .239 | .409 | .289 |
| 1989 | 481 | 116 | 22 | 9 | 6 | 55 | .241 | .362 | .321 |
| Totals | 2856 | 695 | 129 | 59 | 62 | 378 | .243 | .395 | .317 |

. . .Van Slyke would be little more than a role player, sort of a Mickey Hatcher with a good glove. Van Slyke would be an occasional starter, a frequent pinch-hitter, and a defensive substitute. And in this imaginary mirror-image world, players like Hatcher, Pat Tabler, and Keith Moreland would become stars. Others whose careers ended in obscurity, like Barry Bonnell, Lee Lacy, and Juan Beniquez, would still be signing seven-figure contracts. To fully appreciate the degree to which the lefty-righty imbalance affects baseball, look at the hypothetical year-by-year leaders in batting average during the 1980s, were the ratio of left-and-righthanded pitchers reversed. Actual batting champions are marked with asterisks:

| Year | American League | | National League | |
|---|---|---|---|---|
| 1980 | *George Brett | .351 | Keith Hernandez | .339 |
| 1981 | Kirk Gibson | .350 | Dave Concepcion | .329 |
| 1982 | Eddie Murray | .343 | *Al Oliver | .330 |
| 1983 | Barry Bonnell | .341 | Keith Moreland | .336 |
| 1984 | Chet Lemon | .339 | Jeffrey Leonard | .340 |
| 1985 | *Wade Boggs | .358 | *Willie McGee | .349 |
| 1986 | Don Mattingly | .354 | Ray Knight | .343 |
| 1987 | Alan Trammell | .352 | Tony Gwynn | .365 |
| 1988 | Kirby Puckett | .374 | Barry Larkin | .319 |
| 1989 | Carney Lansford | .359 | Will Clark | .326 |

No longer would there be a preponderance of left-handed batting average leaders. Predictably, the balance would shift in the opposite direction, with right-handed hitters winning a majority of the batting championships. Over the 10–year period, Wade Boggs would still lead the majors in batting average. But his lead would shrink from an actual 20–point margin over Tony Gwynn (.352 to .332) to a mere three-point lead over Kirby Puckett (.333 to .330) in this hypothetical left-skewed world.

Now would someone please wake up Andy Van Slyke. Tell him it's only a dream. A bad one.

## WON-LOST RECORD BY STARTING POSITION

| PITTSBURGH 74-88 | C | 1B | 2B | 3B | SS | LF | CF | RF | P | Leadoff | Relief | Starts |
|---|---|---|---|---|---|---|---|---|---|---|---|---|
| Doug Bair | - | - | - | - | - | - | - | - | - | - | 18-26 | - |
| Stan Belinda | - | - | - | - | - | - | - | - | - | - | 2-6 | - |
| Jay Bell | - | - | - | - | 36-33 | - | - | - | - | - | - | 36-33 |
| Rafael Belliard | - | - | 6-8 | 0-1 | 13-19 | - | - | - | - | 1-0 | - | 19-28 |
| Dann Bilardello | 10-15 | - | - | - | - | - | - | - | - | - | - | 10-15 |
| Barry Bonds | - | - | - | - | - | 68-77 | - | - | - | 48-58 | - | 68-77 |
| Bobby Bonilla | - | 4-4 | - | 70-81 | - | - | - | - | - | - | - | 74-85 |
| Sid Bream | - | 4-9 | - | - | - | - | - | - | - | - | - | 4-9 |
| John Cangelosi | - | - | - | - | - | 3-7 | 3-6 | 0-2 | - | 5-13 | - | 6-15 |
| Steve Carter | - | - | - | - | - | - | - | 2-2 | - | - | - | 2-2 |
| Benny Distefano | - | 13-17 | - | - | - | - | - | 0-1 | - | - | - | 13-18 |
| Doug Drabek | - | - | - | - | - | - | - | - | 16-17 | - | 1-0 | 16-17 |
| Mike Dunne | - | - | - | - | - | - | - | - | 1-2 | - | - | 1-2 |
| Logan Easley | - | - | - | - | - | - | - | - | - | - | 3-7 | - |
| Brian Fisher | - | - | - | - | - | - | - | - | 0-3 | - | 2-4 | 0-3 |
| Miguel Garcia | - | - | - | - | - | - | - | - | - | - | 2-9 | - |
| Jim Gott | - | - | - | - | - | - | - | - | - | - | 0-1 | - |
| Albert Hall | - | - | - | - | - | 1-1 | - | 2-2 | - | 2-3 | - | 3-3 |
| Billy Hatcher | - | - | - | - | - | 1-0 | 4-6 | 4-4 | - | 7-6 | - | 9-10 |
| Neal Heaton | - | - | - | - | - | - | - | - | 5-12 | - | 9-15 | 5-12 |
| Jeff King | - | 18-21 | 2-3 | 4-6 | - | - | - | - | - | - | - | 24-30 |
| Bob Kipper | - | - | - | - | - | - | - | - | - | - | 26-26 | - |
| Randy Kramer | - | - | - | - | - | - | - | - | 6-9 | - | 10-10 | 6-9 |
| Bill Landrum | - | - | - | - | - | - | - | - | - | - | 38-18 | - |
| Mike LaValliere | 30-28 | - | - | - | - | - | - | - | - | - | - | 30-28 |
| Jose Lind | - | - | 66-75 | - | - | - | - | - | - | - | - | 66-75 |
| Scott Little | - | - | - | - | - | - | - | - | - | - | - | - |
| Morris Madden | - | - | - | - | - | - | - | - | 1-2 | - | 1-5 | 1-2 |
| Scott Medvin | - | - | - | - | - | - | - | - | - | - | 2-4 | - |
| Ken Oberkfell | - | 4-5 | 0-2 | - | - | - | - | - | - | - | - | 4-7 |
| Junior Ortiz | 29-35 | - | - | - | - | - | - | - | - | - | - | 29-35 |
| Bob Patterson | - | - | - | - | - | - | - | - | 1-2 | - | 4-5 | 1-2 |
| Tom Prince | 5-10 | - | - | - | - | - | - | - | - | - | - | 5-10 |
| Rey Quinones | - | - | - | - | 25-36 | - | - | - | - | - | - | 25-36 |
| Gary Redus | - | 30-31 | - | - | - | 0-2 | - | 5-3 | - | 6-3 | - | 35-36 |
| Rick Reed | - | - | - | - | - | - | - | - | 2-5 | - | 0-8 | 2-5 |
| R.J. Reynolds | - | - | - | - | - | 1-1 | 10-17 | 25-29 | - | 5-5 | - | 36-47 |
| Jeff D. Robinson | - | - | - | - | - | - | - | - | 11-8 | - | 10-20 | 11-8 |
| Roger Samuels | - | - | - | - | - | - | - | - | - | - | 0-4 | - |
| John Smiley | - | - | - | - | - | - | - | - | 15-13 | - | - | 15-13 |
| Mike M. Smith | - | - | - | - | - | - | - | - | - | - | 2-14 | - |
| Dorn Taylor | - | - | - | - | - | - | - | - | - | - | 2-7 | - |
| Andy Van Slyke | - | - | - | - | - | - | 57-59 | - | - | - | - | 57-59 |
| Bob Walk | - | - | - | - | - | - | - | - | 16-15 | - | 0-2 | 16-15 |
| Glenn Wilson | - | 1-1 | - | - | - | - | - | 36-45 | - | - | - | 37-46 |

## Batting vs. Left and Right Handed Pitchers

| | | BA | Rank | SA | Rank | OBA | Rank | HR % | Rank | BB % | Rank | SO % | Rank |
|---|---|---|---|---|---|---|---|---|---|---|---|---|---|
| Jay Bell | vs. Lefties | .271 | 61 | .355 | 80 | .331 | 69 | 0.93 | 94 | 8.26 | 70 | 16.53 | 100 |
| | vs. Righties | .250 | 63 | .348 | 83 | .291 | 89 | 0.61 | 115 | 4.95 | 112 | 14.84 | 74 |
| Barry Bonds | vs. Lefties | .264 | 74 | .421 | 50 | .371 | 27 | 2.25 | 58 | 14.55 | 11 | 15.49 | 86 |
| | vs. Righties | .241 | 74 | .428 | 26 | .342 | 38 | 3.73 | 23 | 13.30 | 12 | 12.88 | 54 |
| Bobby Bonilla | vs. Lefties | .226 | 102 | .389 | 61 | .310 | 90 | 3.62 | 26 | 11.11 | 35 | 11.11 | 45 |
| | vs. Righties | .311 | 13 | .547 | 6 | .386 | 15 | 4.05 | 18 | 10.76 | 35 | 14.57 | 71 |
| John Cangelosi | vs. Lefties | .207 | 115 | .268 | 116 | .327 | 74 | 0.00 | 112 | 13.27 | 21 | 8.16 | 19 |
| | vs. Righties | .231 | -- | .269 | -- | .402 | -- | 0.00 | -- | 21.36 | -- | 11.65 | -- |
| Benny Distefano | vs. Lefties | .214 | -- | .214 | -- | .421 | -- | 0.00 | -- | 20.00 | -- | 20.00 | -- |
| | vs. Righties | .250 | 63 | .350 | 82 | .323 | 58 | 1.43 | 81 | 8.33 | 63 | 16.67 | 87 |
| Billy Hatcher | vs. Lefties | .269 | 63 | .347 | 88 | .296 | 102 | 1.04 | 90 | 3.94 | 125 | 7.88 | 17 |
| | vs. Righties | .205 | 120 | .281 | 121 | .264 | 119 | 0.69 | 109 | 6.94 | 86 | 14.51 | 70 |
| Jeff King | vs. Lefties | .196 | 120 | .321 | 99 | .279 | 116 | 0.00 | 112 | 9.92 | 46 | 12.98 | 67 |
| | vs. Righties | .194 | -- | .388 | -- | .250 | -- | 4.85 | -- | 6.25 | -- | 15.18 | -- |
| Mike LaValliere | vs. Lefties | .280 | -- | .320 | -- | .379 | -- | 0.00 | -- | 13.33 | -- | 23.33 | -- |
| | vs. Righties | .321 | 8 | .412 | 40 | .411 | 4 | 1.21 | 89 | 12.95 | 15 | 8.81 | 20 |
| Jose Lind | vs. Lefties | .256 | 78 | .318 | 100 | .315 | 84 | 0.51 | 107 | 8.56 | 64 | 9.46 | 29 |
| | vs. Righties | .219 | 104 | .274 | 124 | .262 | 121 | 0.26 | 123 | 4.82 | 114 | 10.36 | 30 |
| Junior Ortiz | vs. Lefties | .216 | 107 | .299 | 107 | .296 | 100 | 1.03 | 91 | 8.26 | 71 | 9.17 | 28 |
| | vs. Righties | .218 | 107 | .241 | 131 | .272 | 111 | 0.00 | 124 | 7.38 | 82 | 6.71 | 8 |
| Rey Quinones | vs. Lefties | .247 | 85 | .384 | 63 | .296 | 100 | 2.74 | 42 | 7.41 | 84 | 17.28 | 104 |
| | vs. Righties | .191 | 129 | .257 | 128 | .232 | 129 | 0.66 | 111 | 5.23 | 110 | 15.12 | 79 |
| Gary Redus | vs. Lefties | .292 | 34 | .558 | 7 | .391 | 13 | 2.65 | 45 | 14.18 | 14 | 16.42 | 96 |
| | vs. Righties | .277 | 32 | .398 | 50 | .358 | 27 | 1.81 | 71 | 11.05 | 31 | 15.26 | 81 |
| R.j. Reynolds | vs. Lefties | .284 | 43 | .336 | 91 | .341 | 58 | 0.86 | 95 | 7.09 | 91 | 16.54 | 101 |
| | vs. Righties | .263 | 48 | .393 | 52 | .326 | 53 | 2.02 | 65 | 9.06 | 55 | 16.30 | 86 |
| Andy Van Slyke | vs. Lefties | .247 | 84 | .358 | 77 | .339 | 64 | 0.62 | 105 | 12.30 | 26 | 17.65 | 107 |
| | vs. Righties | .232 | 85 | .376 | 62 | .291 | 91 | 2.55 | 48 | 6.96 | 85 | 19.42 | 105 |
| Team Average | vs. Lefties | .245 | 9 | .360 | 9 | .319 | 6 | 1.41 | 11 | 9.67 | 2 | 14.12 | 4 |
| | vs. Righties | .239 | 9 | .359 | 8 | .306 | 10 | 1.88 | 8 | 8.63 | 4 | 14.86 | 4 |
| League Average | vs. Lefties | .251 | | .371 | | .320 | | 2.06 | | 8.85 | | 14.80 | |
| | vs. Righties | .244 | | .362 | | .309 | | 2.08 | | 8.27 | | 15.67 | |

## Batting with Runners on Base and Bases Empty

| | | BA | Rank | SA | Rank | OBA | Rank | HR % | Rank | BB % | Rank | SO % | Rank |
|---|---|---|---|---|---|---|---|---|---|---|---|---|---|
| Jay Bell | Runners On | .306 | 21 | .435 | 33 | .325 | 83 | 0.00 | 112 | 3.23 | 129 | 12.10 | 57 |
| | Bases Empty | .227 | 95 | .294 | 109 | .296 | 85 | 1.23 | 93 | 8.38 | 57 | 17.88 | 106 |
| Barry Bonds | Runners On | .251 | 85 | .413 | 48 | .397 | 18 | 2.79 | 38 | 19.57 | 5 | 12.61 | 60 |
| | Bases Empty | .247 | 72 | .431 | 24 | .327 | 46 | 3.49 | 23 | 10.69 | 26 | 14.25 | 65 |
| Bobby Bonilla | Runners On | .270 | 58 | .432 | 36 | .372 | 30 | 2.16 | 58 | 14.20 | 20 | 12.39 | 59 |
| | Bases Empty | .290 | 19 | .538 | 3 | .346 | 32 | 5.33 | 10 | 7.90 | 62 | 14.17 | 63 |
| John Cangelosi | Runners On | .182 | -- | .205 | -- | .377 | -- | 0.00 | -- | 22.58 | -- | 8.06 | -- |
| | Bases Empty | .233 | 89 | .293 | 111 | .360 | 18 | 0.00 | 122 | 15.11 | 4 | 10.79 | 31 |
| Billy Hatcher | Runners On | .261 | 71 | .342 | 95 | .296 | 109 | 1.09 | 92 | 4.95 | 122 | 13.86 | 75 |
| | Bases Empty | .212 | 110 | .286 | 115 | .264 | 113 | 0.67 | 106 | 6.29 | 83 | 10.69 | 29 |
| Jeff King | Runners On | .134 | 132 | .237 | 130 | .200 | 131 | 1.03 | 94 | 8.04 | 87 | 16.96 | 99 |
| | Bases Empty | .246 | 73 | .449 | 19 | .321 | 53 | 3.39 | 24 | 8.40 | 56 | 11.45 | 35 |
| Mike LaValliere | Runners On | .298 | 28 | .369 | 77 | .416 | 7 | 1.19 | 89 | 16.19 | 12 | 13.33 | 67 |
| | Bases Empty | .330 | 4 | .425 | 28 | .398 | 2 | 0.94 | 99 | 10.17 | 36 | 8.47 | 13 |
| Jose Lind | Runners On | .252 | 84 | .311 | 112 | .291 | 113 | 0.00 | 112 | 5.21 | 119 | 9.72 | 31 |
| | Bases Empty | .216 | 107 | .272 | 122 | .272 | 107 | 0.62 | 109 | 6.88 | 76 | 10.32 | 25 |
| Junior Ortiz | Runners On | .229 | 107 | .295 | 119 | .323 | 84 | 0.95 | 97 | 11.81 | 45 | 9.45 | 27 |
| | Bases Empty | .208 | 115 | .240 | 126 | .244 | 125 | 0.00 | 122 | 3.82 | 116 | 6.11 | 4 |
| Rey Quinones | Runners On | .224 | 111 | .318 | 109 | .278 | 117 | 1.87 | 66 | 7.69 | 93 | 13.85 | 74 |
| | Bases Empty | .195 | 125 | .280 | 118 | .228 | 129 | 0.85 | 103 | 4.07 | 114 | 17.89 | 107 |
| Gary Redus | Runners On | .271 | 54 | .458 | 25 | .372 | 29 | 2.80 | 37 | 13.85 | 24 | 15.38 | 92 |
| | Bases Empty | .291 | 18 | .465 | 14 | .371 | 11 | 1.74 | 70 | 11.34 | 15 | 15.98 | 85 |
| R.j. Reynolds | Runners On | .268 | 61 | .391 | 60 | .341 | 62 | 2.79 | 38 | 10.19 | 63 | 17.48 | 103 |
| | Bases Empty | .272 | 39 | .359 | 78 | .320 | 54 | 0.54 | 114 | 6.60 | 79 | 15.23 | 77 |
| Andy Van Slyke | Runners On | .245 | 93 | .399 | 57 | .312 | 98 | 0.96 | 96 | 8.90 | 80 | 17.37 | 101 |
| | Bases Empty | .231 | 92 | .347 | 90 | .304 | 77 | 2.61 | 40 | 8.78 | 51 | 19.93 | 118 |
| Team Average | Runners On | .248 | 11 | .362 | 11 | .328 | 8 | 1.40 | 12 | 10.50 | 2 | 14.51 | 7 |
| | Bases Empty | .236 | 9 | .357 | 5 | .298 | 9 | 1.94 | 8 | 7.83 | 4 | 14.67 | 2 |
| League Average | Runners On | .256 | | .379 | | .330 | | 2.13 | | 9.82 | | 14.66 | |
| | Bases Empty | .240 | | .355 | | .299 | | 2.03 | | 7.43 | | 15.93 | |

## Overall Batting Compared to Late Inning Pressure Situations

| | | BA | Rank | SA | Rank | OBA | Rank | HR % | Rank | BB % | Rank | SO % | Rank | RDI % | Rank |
|---|---|---|---|---|---|---|---|---|---|---|---|---|---|---|---|
| Jay Bell | Overall | .258 | 59 | .351 | 92 | .307 | 88 | 0.74 | 110 | 6.27 | 103 | 15.51 | 87 | .313 | 21 |
| | Pressure | .200 | 98 | .350 | 61 | .233 | 120 | 0.00 | 81 | 2.17 | 126 | 26.09 | 122 | .462 | 7 |
| Barry Bonds | Overall | .248 | 75 | .426 | 27 | .351 | 33 | 3.28 | 28 | 13.70 | 9 | 13.70 | 67 | .267 | 63 |
| | Pressure | .233 | 71 | .400 | 29 | .358 | 30 | 2.22 | 50 | 16.51 | 9 | 17.43 | 84 | .208 | 73 |
| Bobby Bonilla | Overall | .281 | 31 | .490 | 9 | .358 | 26 | 3.90 | 17 | 10.89 | 37 | 13.32 | 61 | .309 | 24 |
| | Pressure | .211 | 90 | .349 | 65 | .306 | 71 | 3.67 | 22 | 12.10 | 33 | 14.52 | 61 | .280 | 45 |
| John Cangelosi | Overall | .219 | 115 | .269 | 125 | .365 | 24 | 0.00 | 127 | 17.41 | 3 | 9.95 | 24 | .216 | -- |
| | Pressure | .200 | 98 | .231 | 114 | .316 | 68 | 0.00 | 81 | 13.16 | 24 | 14.47 | 60 | .071 | 128 |
| Benny Distefano | Overall | .247 | -- | .338 | -- | .333 | -- | 1.30 | -- | 9.66 | -- | 17.05 | -- | .208 | -- |
| | Pressure | .132 | -- | .158 | -- | .175 | -- | 0.00 | -- | 4.88 | -- | 24.39 | -- | .200 | 74 |
| Billy Hatcher | Overall | .231 | 107 | .308 | 116 | .277 | 117 | 0.83 | 108 | 5.77 | 109 | 11.92 | 42 | .285 | 42 |
| | Pressure | .206 | 93 | .286 | 93 | .242 | 112 | 1.59 | 66 | 4.41 | 109 | 20.59 | 106 | .150 | 104 |
| Jeff King | Overall | .195 | 128 | .353 | 89 | .266 | 123 | 2.33 | 50 | 8.23 | 71 | 13.99 | 71 | .214 | 107 |
| | Pressure | .184 | 111 | .368 | 46 | .244 | 111 | 2.63 | 30 | 7.14 | 83 | 4.76 | 4 | .182 | 86 |
| Mike LaValliere | Overall | .316 | 5 | .400 | 48 | .406 | 4 | 1.05 | 100 | 13.00 | 13 | 10.76 | 30 | .333 | 9 |
| | Pressure | .318 | -- | .455 | -- | .375 | -- | 4.55 | -- | 7.69 | -- | 11.54 | -- | .625 | -- |
| Jose Lind | Overall | .232 | 105 | .289 | 122 | .280 | 114 | 0.35 | 121 | 6.12 | 104 | 10.05 | 25 | .241 | 84 |
| | Pressure | .265 | 44 | .306 | 85 | .324 | 65 | 0.00 | 81 | 8.04 | 80 | 10.71 | 26 | .161 | 99 |
| Junior Ortiz | Overall | .217 | 116 | .265 | 126 | .282 | 112 | 0.43 | 117 | 7.75 | 79 | 7.75 | 9 | .260 | 68 |
| | Pressure | .191 | 107 | .213 | 122 | .235 | 117 | 0.00 | 81 | 3.92 | 117 | 9.80 | 23 | .211 | 71 |
| Rey Quinones | Overall | .209 | 122 | .298 | 119 | .253 | 125 | 1.33 | 87 | 5.93 | 106 | 15.81 | 92 | .278 | 50 |
| | Pressure | .140 | 126 | .233 | 113 | .196 | 130 | 2.33 | 46 | 4.08 | 115 | 14.29 | 57 | .125 | 116 |
| Gary Redus | Overall | .283 | 26 | .462 | 15 | .372 | 17 | 2.15 | 61 | 12.35 | 20 | 15.74 | 89 | .275 | 53 |
| | Pressure | .309 | 20 | .473 | 14 | .371 | 26 | 1.82 | 60 | 9.52 | 59 | 25.40 | 121 | .154 | 103 |
| R.j. Reynolds | Overall | .270 | 43 | .375 | 65 | .331 | 52 | 1.65 | 75 | 8.44 | 64 | 16.38 | 97 | .282 | 45 |
| | Pressure | .299 | 23 | .364 | 50 | .365 | 29 | 0.00 | 81 | 9.30 | 61 | 13.95 | 53 | .292 | 42 |
| Andy Van Slyke | Overall | .237 | 95 | .370 | 67 | .308 | 85 | 1.89 | 67 | 8.83 | 58 | 18.80 | 116 | .291 | 36 |
| | Pressure | .150 | 122 | .325 | 78 | .236 | 116 | 2.50 | 33 | 10.11 | 54 | 34.83 | 132 | .130 | 114 |
| Team Average | Overall | .241 | 9 | .359 | 9 | .311 | 7 | 1.72 | 10 | 8.99 | 4 | 14.60 | 4 | .266 | 2 |
| | Pressure | .228 | 10 | .331 | 10 | .305 | 8 | 1.49 | 8 | 9.60 | 4 | 17.33 | 9 | .232 | 8 |
| League Average | Overall | .246 | | .365 | | .312 | | 2.07 | | 8.47 | | 15.38 | | .253 | |
| | Pressure | .238 | | .337 | | .308 | | 1.73 | | 8.93 | | 16.78 | | .235 | |

## Additional Miscellaneous Batting Comparisons

| | Grass Surface BA | Rank | Artificial Surface BA | Rank | Home Games BA | Rank | Road Games BA | Rank | Runners in Scoring Position BA | Rank | Runners in Scoring Pos and Two Outs BA | Rank | Leading Off Inning OBA | Rank | Runners on 3B with less than 2 Outs RDI % | Rank |
|---|---|---|---|---|---|---|---|---|---|---|---|---|---|---|---|---|
| Jay Bell | .244 | -- | .261 | 51 | .255 | 69 | .262 | 55 | .358 | 4 | .310 | 18 | .241 | 117 | .667 | 25 |
| Rafael Belliard | .244 | -- | .204 | 124 | .208 | -- | .220 | -- | .270 | -- | .158 | -- | .094 | -- | .857 | -- |
| Barry Bonds | .258 | 60 | .245 | 86 | .204 | 119 | .290 | 21 | .227 | 96 | .133 | 123 | .329 | 45 | .654 | 33 |
| Bobby Bonilla | .250 | 65 | .292 | 20 | .311 | 14 | .253 | 64 | .287 | 34 | .270 | 33 | .417 | 6 | .581 | 62 |
| John Cangelosi | .206 | -- | .222 | 113 | .269 | 52 | .171 | 132 | .148 | -- | .091 | -- | .333 | 40 | .625 | 40 |
| Benny Distefano | .273 | -- | .232 | 104 | .211 | -- | .277 | -- | .220 | 104 | .412 | -- | .267 | -- | .222 | 144 |
| Billy Hatcher | .212 | 109 | .238 | 93 | .234 | 97 | .228 | 92 | .248 | 80 | .203 | 87 | .259 | 104 | .613 | 50 |
| Jeff King | .250 | -- | .184 | 128 | .185 | 125 | .208 | 112 | .184 | 124 | .150 | -- | .276 | 93 | .533 | 89 |
| Mike LaValliere | .286 | -- | .326 | 3 | .378 | 1 | .250 | 68 | .262 | 60 | .240 | 52 | .548 | -- | .625 | 40 |
| Jose Lind | .219 | 101 | .237 | 98 | .220 | 111 | .245 | 76 | .262 | 61 | .190 | 99 | .297 | 68 | .625 | 40 |
| Junior Ortiz | .192 | -- | .225 | 110 | .248 | 83 | .186 | 125 | .222 | 101 | .160 | 114 | .288 | 75 | .588 | 59 |
| Rey Quinones | .197 | -- | .215 | 117 | .165 | 129 | .242 | 78 | .268 | 56 | .143 | 121 | .185 | 132 | .778 | 5 |
| Gary Redus | .282 | -- | .284 | 31 | .277 | 43 | .289 | 23 | .275 | 46 | .333 | 10 | .427 | 4 | .500 | 98 |
| R.j. Reynolds | .220 | 100 | .287 | 26 | .299 | 25 | .233 | 88 | .264 | 58 | .222 | 66 | .282 | 84 | .567 | 69 |
| Andy Van Slyke | .194 | 117 | .253 | 69 | .213 | 116 | .258 | 59 | .274 | 48 | .220 | 71 | .264 | 100 | .435 | 125 |
| Team Average | .229 | 10 | .245 | 8 | .240 | 12 | .242 | 6 | .257 | 3 | .216 | 8 | .302 | 6 | .571 | 2 |
| League Average | .244 | | .248 | | .251 | | .242 | | .249 | | .222 | | .302 | | .546 | |

## Pitching vs. Left and Right Handed Batters

| | | BA | Rank | SA | Rank | OBA | Rank | HR % | Rank | BB % | Rank | SO % | Rank |
|---|---|---|---|---|---|---|---|---|---|---|---|---|---|
| Doug Bair | vs. Lefties | .193 | 12 | .252 | 8 | .319 | 55 | 0.84 | 28 | 15.60 | 113 | 13.48 | 61 |
| | vs. Righties | .228 | 48 | .346 | 51 | .261 | 23 | 2.36 | 70 | 4.44 | 17 | 27.41 | 6 |
| Doug Drabek | vs. Lefties | .250 | 64 | .339 | 49 | .311 | 51 | 1.42 | 52 | 8.20 | 49 | 9.47 | 98 |
| | vs. Righties | .224 | 44 | .362 | 64 | .270 | 31 | 3.41 | 100 | 5.39 | 24 | 15.96 | 68 |
| Neal Heaton | vs. Lefties | .132 | 1 | .158 | 1 | .194 | 1 | 0.00 | 1 | 5.47 | 10 | 13.28 | 66 |
| | vs. Righties | .260 | 88 | .414 | 95 | .339 | 90 | 2.79 | 78 | 9.76 | 97 | 10.16 | 107 |
| Bob Kipper | vs. Lefties | .170 | 4 | .277 | 17 | .257 | 11 | 0.00 | 1 | 10.19 | 75 | 18.52 | 23 |
| | vs. Righties | .196 | 15 | .342 | 47 | .272 | 33 | 2.51 | 74 | 9.73 | 96 | 16.81 | 60 |
| Randy Kramer | vs. Lefties | .227 | 35 | .373 | 71 | .344 | 85 | 2.73 | 93 | 14.72 | 111 | 8.30 | 107 |
| | vs. Righties | .221 | 37 | .326 | 36 | .322 | 86 | 2.21 | 61 | 10.14 | 101 | 13.82 | 80 |
| Bill Landrum | vs. Lefties | .176 | 5 | .214 | 4 | .241 | 6 | 0.00 | 1 | 8.00 | 43 | 10.86 | 89 |
| | vs. Righties | .241 | 60 | .323 | 31 | .311 | 75 | 1.50 | 26 | 9.33 | 93 | 21.33 | 32 |
| Rick Reed | vs. Lefties | .307 | 110 | .436 | 103 | .363 | 103 | 0.99 | 34 | 7.83 | 40 | 8.70 | 105 |
| | vs. Righties | .274 | -- | .425 | -- | .291 | -- | 3.54 | -- | 1.71 | -- | 20.51 | -- |
| Jeff D. Robinson | vs. Lefties | .258 | 73 | .384 | 77 | .328 | 64 | 1.66 | 64 | 9.71 | 68 | 11.76 | 77 |
| | vs. Righties | .311 | 112 | .476 | 115 | .369 | 111 | 3.37 | 105 | 8.58 | 82 | 18.15 | 50 |
| John Smiley | vs. Lefties | .243 | 54 | .320 | 36 | .291 | 27 | 0.97 | 32 | 5.41 | 9 | 13.51 | 60 |
| | vs. Righties | .223 | 41 | .354 | 55 | .271 | 32 | 3.15 | 99 | 5.94 | 34 | 14.92 | 74 |
| Bob Walk | vs. Lefties | .285 | 98 | .406 | 90 | .343 | 83 | 2.09 | 79 | 8.05 | 45 | 7.20 | 109 |
| | vs. Righties | .252 | 80 | .371 | 70 | .313 | 77 | 1.78 | 41 | 7.28 | 64 | 13.21 | 84 |
| Team Average | vs. Lefties | .247 | 5 | .348 | 3 | .324 | 7 | 1.40 | 2 | 10.06 | 11 | 10.62 | 12 |
| | vs. Righties | .248 | 10 | .382 | 10 | .308 | 9 | 2.69 | 12 | 7.43 | 5 | 14.94 | 11 |
| League Average | vs. Lefties | .252 | | .366 | | .325 | | 1.79 | | 9.48 | | 13.93 | |
| | vs. Righties | .242 | | .365 | | .303 | | 2.29 | | 7.70 | | 16.46 | |

## Pitching with Runners on Base and Bases Empty

| | | BA | Rank | SA | Rank | OBA | Rank | HR % | Rank | BB % | Rank | SO % | Rank |
|---|---|---|---|---|---|---|---|---|---|---|---|---|---|
| Doug Bair | Runners On | .202 | 8 | .266 | 7 | .307 | 42 | 0.92 | 18 | 13.28 | 106 | 19.53 | 22 |
| | Bases Empty | .219 | 27 | .328 | 33 | .277 | 31 | 2.19 | 71 | 7.43 | 67 | 20.95 | 24 |
| Doug Drabek | Runners On | .255 | 69 | .374 | 66 | .319 | 55 | 2.43 | 83 | 8.09 | 33 | 8.88 | 108 |
| | Bases Empty | .229 | 36 | .337 | 43 | .277 | 30 | 2.27 | 74 | 6.22 | 47 | 14.57 | 67 |
| Neal Heaton | Runners On | .243 | 57 | .348 | 42 | .330 | 66 | 1.30 | 30 | 10.87 | 81 | 13.04 | 79 |
| | Bases Empty | .226 | 34 | .369 | 78 | .294 | 51 | 2.87 | 101 | 7.27 | 65 | 9.01 | 112 |
| Bob Kipper | Runners On | .231 | 37 | .359 | 54 | .316 | 52 | 1.71 | 44 | 11.35 | 88 | 19.15 | 26 |
| | Bases Empty | .159 | 1 | .295 | 19 | .233 | 1 | 1.70 | 47 | 8.81 | 87 | 16.06 | 49 |
| Randy Kramer | Runners On | .258 | 74 | .382 | 70 | .346 | 78 | 2.69 | 89 | 10.18 | 66 | 9.29 | 105 |
| | Bases Empty | .195 | 13 | .326 | 30 | .324 | 95 | 2.33 | 77 | 14.84 | 115 | 12.11 | 94 |
| Bill Landrum | Runners On | .222 | 25 | .302 | 15 | .315 | 51 | 1.59 | 39 | 12.08 | 99 | 14.77 | 52 |
| | Bases Empty | .193 | 9 | .235 | 1 | .239 | 2 | 0.00 | 1 | 5.68 | 33 | 16.48 | 42 |
| Rick Reed | Runners On | .367 | -- | .582 | -- | .418 | -- | 3.80 | -- | 7.53 | -- | 10.75 | -- |
| | Bases Empty | .244 | 64 | .341 | 49 | .266 | 18 | 1.48 | 41 | 2.88 | 2 | 17.27 | 41 |
| Jeff D. Robinson | Runners On | .273 | 84 | .390 | 78 | .367 | 100 | 2.41 | 80 | 13.49 | 108 | 14.14 | 62 |
| | Bases Empty | .291 | 111 | .456 | 113 | .330 | 101 | 2.50 | 89 | 5.31 | 26 | 15.34 | 57 |
| John Smiley | Runners On | .211 | 14 | .341 | 36 | .261 | 5 | 3.23 | 102 | 6.09 | 10 | 13.14 | 78 |
| | Bases Empty | .234 | 45 | .354 | 65 | .281 | 35 | 2.65 | 96 | 5.74 | 34 | 15.68 | 54 |
| Bob Walk | Runners On | .308 | 108 | .468 | 106 | .366 | 99 | 2.60 | 86 | 7.87 | 29 | 10.79 | 94 |
| | Bases Empty | .246 | 68 | .339 | 46 | .306 | 68 | 1.52 | 43 | 7.60 | 68 | 9.20 | 110 |
| Team Average | Runners On | .267 | 11 | .395 | 11 | .341 | 11 | 2.40 | 10 | 9.98 | 9 | 12.14 | 12 |
| | Bases Empty | .234 | 3 | .349 | 5 | .294 | 4 | 1.97 | 7 | 7.44 | 8 | 13.85 | 11 |
| League Average | Runners On | .256 | | .379 | | .330 | | 2.13 | | 9.82 | | 14.66 | |
| | Bases Empty | .240 | | .355 | | .299 | | 2.03 | | 7.43 | | 15.93 | |

## Overall Pitching Compared to Late Inning Pressure Situations

| | | BA | Rank | SA | Rank | OBA | Rank | HR % | Rank | BB % | Rank | SO % | Rank |
|---|---|---|---|---|---|---|---|---|---|---|---|---|---|
| Doug Bair | Overall | .211 | 14 | .301 | 10 | .291 | 35 | 1.63 | 37 | 10.14 | 95 | 20.29 | 22 |
| | Pressure | .198 | 25 | .305 | 43 | .269 | 30 | 2.29 | 81 | 8.90 | 59 | 22.60 | 17 |
| Doug Drabek | Overall | .238 | 52 | .350 | 54 | .293 | 37 | 2.33 | 82 | 6.94 | 32 | 12.37 | 85 |
| | Pressure | .212 | 36 | .281 | 28 | .280 | 36 | 1.37 | 51 | 8.48 | 56 | 11.52 | 85 |
| Neal Heaton | Overall | .233 | 42 | .360 | 67 | .309 | 60 | 2.21 | 72 | 8.87 | 71 | 10.81 | 103 |
| | Pressure | .224 | 48 | .313 | 51 | .316 | 62 | 1.49 | 55 | 11.25 | 88 | 10.00 | 101 |
| Bob Kipper | Overall | .188 | 2 | .321 | 26 | .267 | 7 | 1.71 | 38 | 9.88 | 88 | 17.37 | 42 |
| | Pressure | .158 | 4 | .263 | 15 | .243 | 13 | 1.32 | 47 | 9.94 | 72 | 15.20 | 61 |
| Randy Kramer | Overall | .224 | 31 | .352 | 58 | .334 | 88 | 2.49 | 91 | 12.66 | 112 | 10.79 | 104 |
| | Pressure | .267 | 84 | .367 | 79 | .365 | 99 | 2.22 | 79 | 10.09 | 75 | 13.76 | 74 |
| Bill Landrum | Overall | .205 | 10 | .264 | 3 | .273 | 15 | 0.68 | 6 | 8.62 | 68 | 15.69 | 56 |
| | Pressure | .167 | 7 | .200 | 3 | .249 | 16 | 0.00 | 1 | 9.85 | 70 | 14.78 | 68 |
| Jeff D. Robinson | Overall | .283 | 104 | .427 | 107 | .347 | 103 | 2.46 | 89 | 9.18 | 75 | 14.77 | 62 |
| | Pressure | .267 | 84 | .452 | 100 | .346 | 89 | 2.96 | 98 | 10.83 | 81 | 15.29 | 59 |
| John Smiley | Overall | .226 | 33 | .349 | 52 | .273 | 16 | 2.86 | 105 | 5.87 | 17 | 14.73 | 63 |
| | Pressure | .226 | 49 | .441 | 98 | .284 | 42 | 5.38 | 114 | 6.80 | 35 | 19.42 | 32 |
| Bob Walk | Overall | .271 | 96 | .391 | 83 | .330 | 87 | 1.95 | 55 | 7.71 | 47 | 9.85 | 108 |
| | Pressure | .288 | 94 | .475 | 105 | .364 | 97 | 3.39 | 103 | 8.96 | 60 | 1.49 | 117 |
| Team Average | Overall | .248 | 7 | .368 | 9 | .314 | 8 | 2.15 | 7 | 8.54 | 7 | 13.11 | 12 |
| | Pressure | .228 | 4 | .344 | 9 | .304 | 5 | 1.92 | 9 | 9.44 | 9 | 14.71 | 10 |
| League Average | Overall | .246 | | .365 | | .312 | | 2.07 | | 8.47 | | 15.38 | |
| | Pressure | .235 | | .336 | | .309 | | 1.77 | | 9.31 | | 16.92 | |

## Additional Miscellaneous Pitching Comparisons

| | Grass Surface | | Artificial Surface | | Home Games | | Road Games | | Runners in Scoring Position | | Runners in Scoring Pos and Two Outs | | Leading Off Inning | |
|---|---|---|---|---|---|---|---|---|---|---|---|---|---|---|
| | BA | Rank | BA | Rank | BA | Rank | BA | Rank | BA | Rank | BA | Rank | OBA | Rank |
| Doug Bair | .308 | -- | .193 | 8 | .179 | 7 | .255 | 66 | .182 | 12 | .244 | 77 | .217 | 5 |
| Doug Drabek | .296 | 106 | .211 | 15 | .203 | 24 | .279 | 93 | .228 | 41 | .225 | 68 | .296 | 55 |
| Neal Heaton | .229 | 40 | .235 | 40 | .240 | 54 | .227 | 31 | .216 | 30 | .192 | 42 | .311 | 74 |
| Bob Kipper | .162 | 3 | .201 | 13 | .165 | 3 | .208 | 16 | .217 | 31 | .216 | 58 | .263 | 23 |
| Randy Kramer | .209 | 19 | .229 | 36 | .257 | 78 | .196 | 10 | .232 | 49 | .173 | 30 | .342 | 96 |
| Bill Landrum | .113 | 1 | .241 | 50 | .227 | 39 | .189 | 4 | .241 | 57 | .179 | 32 | .236 | 11 |
| Bob Patterson | .167 | -- | .244 | 54 | .257 | -- | .167 | -- | .278 | -- | .182 | -- | .320 | -- |
| Rick Reed | .296 | -- | .289 | 98 | .275 | -- | .309 | -- | .449 | -- | .350 | -- | .333 | 93 |
| Jeff D. Robinson | .257 | 80 | .291 | 101 | .260 | 81 | .301 | 106 | .262 | 78 | .303 | 103 | .326 | 89 |
| John Smiley | .199 | 7 | .236 | 45 | .222 | 34 | .231 | 35 | .226 | 39 | .222 | 62 | .242 | 14 |
| Bob Walk | .305 | 108 | .260 | 74 | .276 | 96 | .266 | 83 | .317 | 108 | .266 | 92 | .271 | 33 |
| Team Average | .257 | 11 | .245 | 5 | .237 | 4 | .259 | 11 | .259 | 9 | .242 | 11 | .295 | 2 |
| League Average | .244 | | .248 | | .242 | | .251 | | .249 | | .222 | | .302 | |

# ST. LOUIS CARDINALS

**• Who built better teams than the Yankees of the '30s, '40s, and '50s? Hats off to the Mahatma.**

Outside Busch Stadium stands a monument dedicated, according to the inscription on its plaque, to baseball's "perfect warrior," Stan Musial. Quite an honor, considering the number of Hall of Famers who spent their summers playing ball for the Cardinals. After all, who could have objected if they'd erected a statue of Rogers Hornsby? Or Dizzy Dean? Or Bob Gibson, Lou Brock, or Frankie Frisch? Joe Medwick, Roger Connor, and Chick Hafey all wore Cardinals uniforms, too, as did Jesse Haines, Red Schoendienst, Enos Slaughter, and Jim Bottomley.

So it's a mark of Musial's greatness (and, to be sure, of his popularity and standing in the community) that, at the time of his retirement, little consideration was given to a monument for any of the other great Cardinals players. When local writers lobbied to immortalize one of their city's baseball heroes—as Philadelphia had honored Connie Mack; and Pittsburgh, Honus Wagner—with a statue outside their new stadium, there was no question as to whose likeness would be cast. It would be the Man's.

Still, the most influential man in the history of St. Louis baseball wasn't Musial. Neither was it Dean or Hornsby, or any of the other great players noted above. In fact, the man with the most lasting effect on St. Louis baseball never even played for the Cardinals. (Actually, he did catch briefly for the St. Louis Browns). The single accomplishment for which he's best known came while he worked for the Dodgers, and his effect on baseball will be more lasting than his work for any one team in particular. But without Branch Rickey, there might not even be a Musial statue in the shadow of the Arch. Because it was Rickey who signed Musial to a Cardinals contract, as he signed many of the Cardinals' other Hall of Famers during his 18 years with St. Louis. Musial may have been the Man, but Rickey was the Mahatma. Without him, the baseball landscape in St. Louis—and everywhere else, for that matter—wouldn't be recognizable.

Most fans know Branch Rickey for his signing of Jackie Robinson, which broke baseball's color barrier in the 1940s. But to define his career by one event—no matter how transcendent—would be like saying "He's the guy who painted the Mona Lisa" of one who gave meaning to the term "Renaissance man." Leonardo did more than paint. Edison invented more than the light bulb. Einstein knew more than *E equals MC squared*. And Branch Rickey was their baseball counterpart. Still, many baseball fans are unaware that he had revolutionized the sport once before. More than 20 years before signing Robinson, Rickey established baseball's first farm system.

The Cardinals soon surpassed all other organizations not only in player procurement, but in development as well, hastening the team's rise to the National League title, and cementing its position as a perennial contender for decades. During subsequent tenures with the Brooklyn Dodgers and Pittsburgh Pirates, Rickey's programs produced similar results. And as you'll soon see, a detailed examination of the players produced by those organizations during his terms at each proves that the Mahatma was baseball's ultimate player-development guru.

But the players were the micro. Let's first examine the macro: wins, losses, and championships. Everyone knows that baseball during the period from the late 1920s to World War II was dominated by the Yankees. But did you know that, to the extent that the Yankees surpassed all other teams during the prewar era, the Cardinals stood above the rest of the pack by a comparable margin? The three best records from 1927 through 1944 follow. (Rickey actually ran the Cardinals from 1925 through 1942. But a two-year shift allows a lag time for the effect of his programs to trickle down to the field.) Notice in particular that New York's margin over St. Louis (42 points) during that 18–year period only slightly exceeded St. Louis's margin over Chicago (39):

| Team | W | L | Pct. | League Titles | Series Wins |
|---|---|---|---|---|---|
| New York Yankees | 1742 | 1014 | .632 | 10 | 9 |
| St. Louis Cardinals | 1631 | 1130 | .590 | 7 | 4 |
| Chicago Cubs | 1525 | 1238 | .551 | 4 | 0 |

Yankees general manager Ed Barrow, relying on scouts like Joe Devine and Bill Essick, compiled an impeccable record of identifying the best talent available: Gehrig, Dickey, Gomez, DiMaggio, Gordon, and so on. The owner, Colonel Jake Ruppert, was the Steinbrenner of his day, an active and competitive owner who spent whatever was required to sign those players and improve his team. But St. Louis battled the Colonel's dollars with Rickey's know-how, and stayed far closer to the Yankees than did any other team over nearly two decades. While the Yankees paid huge sums to sign handpicked minor league stars, the Cardinals signed kids by the hundreds, culled the best, and developed them in their innovative minor league system. Had the Yankees not been first to follow Rickey's lead in establishing a farm system, the gap between the two teams would have been even narrower.

During the period from 1927 through 1944, St. Louis produced 31 rookies who eventually played at least 500 games in the majors, and 16 rookie pitchers who won at least 40 games in their major league careers. That total of 47 players made the Cardinals organization the most productive in baseball during those 18 years. More than half of those rookies—15 position players, nine pitchers—eventually achieved even more impressive totals: 1000 games played or 100 wins, respectively. That total of 24 players was also a major league high. (We'll subsequently refer to those two levels of achievement as Level 1, for the more modest totals, and Level 2, for the higher plateaus.)

For your information, the 24 Level 2 rookies produced by St. Louis from 1927 through 1944 were: Stan Musial, Enos Slaughter, Joe Medwick, Johnny Mize, Marty Marion, Walker Cooper, Gus Mancuso, Spud Davis, Johnny Hopp, Terry Moore, Mickey Owen, Pepper Martin, Don Gutteridge, Ripper Collins, and Dick Siebert; and pitchers Paul Derringer, Murry Dickson, Dizzy Dean, Harry Brecheen, Howie Pollet, Mort Cooper, Max Lanier, Fred Frankhouse, and Tex Carleton.

A more comprehensive way to measure the cumulative accomplishment of players produced by the Cardinals system is to compare the sum of their career statistics to those of other teams' rookies. Each player would be assigned to the team with which he started his rookie season. (Players whose rookie status extended over several seasons are assigned as rookies in the last of those seasons.) As a result, teams would receive full credit for the development of players, whether or not they retained the players throughout their careers. The table below compares the totals of Cardinals rookies from 1927 through 1944 to *(a)*those of the only other teams with 40 or more Level 2 rookies, and *(b)* the major league average for that period. Remember, these are the combined *career* totals for all rookies. *L1* and *L2* indicate Level 1 and Level 2 players. Two different totals of games indicate those played by batters as distinct from those by pitchers:

| Team | L1 | L2 | Games | Runs | Hits | HR | Games | Wins | Saves |
|---|---|---|---|---|---|---|---|---|---|
| Cardinals | 47 | 24 | 45,718 | 18,823 | 38,519 | 2,568 | 7,409 | 1,997 | 435 |
| Yankees | 43 | 22 | 37,957 | 18,204 | 32,311 | 2,324 | 6,011 | 1,735 | 462 |
| Indians | 41 | 18 | 32,772 | 13,491 | 26,669 | 1,705 | 6,884 | 2,127 | 368 |
| Average | 32 | 14 | 31,826 | 12,785 | 25,843 | 1,508 | 5,395 | 1,366 | 270 |

Roughly speaking, the Cardinals system was 50 percent more productive than the major league average over a period of nearly two decades—an awesome achievement, but one merely typical of the performance of the other two organizations that Rickey eventually governed: Brooklyn (1942–1950) and Pittsburgh (1951–1955). From 1944 through 1952 (once again, a two-year lag time to allow his programs to reach fruition), the Dodgers produced 25 Level 1 rookies, the highest total in the majors. Among them were three Hall of Famers and five other Level 2 players (Roy Campanella, Carl Erskine, Carl Furillo, Gil Hodges, Eddie Miksis, Don Newcombe, Jackie Robinson, and Duke Snider). And from 1953 through 1957, the Pirates produced 13 Level 1 rookies, including eight who reached level two (Roberto Clemente, Elroy Face, Gene Freese, Dale Long, Jerry Lynch, Bill Mazeroski, Bob Purkey, and Bob Skinner). Only two teams had higher totals during that period. And guess what? They were the two teams for which Rickey had already put his policies into practice: the Cardinals (20) and Dodgers (14). As Wilfrid Sheed wrote in *Sport Magazine*'s 40th anniversary issue in December 1986: "Even today, the Dodgers system is thought by many to be the best in the business—and the Cardinals still run as if the Mahatma were looking on with a stopwatch in one hand and a contract in the other."

Now let's step back and look at the big picture: the combined career production of rookies produced by Rickey's three organizations during his terms at each:

| Team | L1 | L2 | Games | Runs | Hits | HR | Games | Wins | Saves |
|---|---|---|---|---|---|---|---|---|---|
| Rickey | 85 | 40 | 84,409 | 32,554 | 65,922 | 5,425 | 14,824 | 3,545 | 1049 |
| Yankees | 80 | 39 | 73,692 | 32,466 | 59,996 | 5,378 | 11,137 | 3,001 | 730 |
| Average | 58 | 26 | 59,766 | 22,619 | 45,715 | 3,365 | 10,678 | 2,474 | 629 |

Notice that the cumulative career performance of Rickey's rookies far exceeded that of the average team of that era, and even topped that of the mighty Yankees. That's right—Rickey outproduced the Yankees during his 31 years in player development (1927–1957), a period that coincided with the height of the Yankees dynasty. A quarter-century of worship has been heaped upon that Yankees juggernaut (is Chris Berman editing this?), and appropriately so. They won more championships in a shorter period of time than any team in any sport is likely to accumulate ever again. But considering the data above, it's reasonable to conclude that had Branch Rickey remained with one team for 30 years, that team might now be considered the equal of the Yankees. As it was, Rickey spread his genius around, to the benefit of not only three teams, but all of baseball as well.

## WON-LOST RECORD BY STARTING POSITION

| ST. LOUIS 86-76 | C | 1B | 2B | 3B | SS | LF | CF | RF | P | Leadoff | Relief | Starts |
|---|---|---|---|---|---|---|---|---|---|---|---|---|
| Rod Booker | - | - | 1-0 | - | - | - | - | - | - | - | - | 1-0 |
| Tom Brunansky | - | - | - | - | - | - | - | 79-69 | - | - | - | 79-69 |
| Cris Carpenter | - | - | - | - | - | - | - | - | 2-3 | - | 10-20 | 2-3 |
| Vince Coleman | - | - | - | - | - | 67-66 | - | - | - | 67-66 | - | 67-66 |
| John Costello | - | - | - | - | - | - | - | - | - | - | 25-22 | - |
| Ken Dayley | - | - | - | - | - | - | - | - | - | - | 46-24 | - |
| Jose DeLeon | - | - | - | - | - | - | - | - | 18-17 | - | - | 18-17 |
| Frank DiPino | - | - | - | - | - | - | - | - | - | - | 23-44 | - |
| Leon Durham | - | 1-0 | - | - | - | - | - | - | - | - | - | 1-0 |
| Pedro Guerrero | - | 85-74 | - | - | - | - | - | - | - | - | - | 85-74 |
| Don Heinkel | - | - | - | - | - | - | - | - | 3-2 | - | 1-1 | 3-2 |
| Ken Hill | - | - | - | - | - | - | - | - | 15-18 | - | - | 15-18 |
| Ricky Horton | - | - | - | - | - | - | - | - | 3-5 | - | 0-3 | 3-5 |
| Tim Jones | - | - | 2-6 | 0-1 | 3-2 | - | - | - | - | - | - | 5-9 |
| Matt Kinzer | - | - | - | - | - | - | - | - | 0-1 | - | 2-5 | 0-1 |
| Jim Lindeman | - | - | - | - | - | 0-1 | - | - | - | - | - | 0-1 |
| Joe Magrane | - | - | - | - | - | - | - | - | 22-10 | - | 0-1 | 22-10 |
| Willie McGee | - | - | - | - | - | - | 21-24 | - | - | 14-7 | - | 21-24 |
| John Morris | - | - | - | - | - | 2-2 | - | 6-6 | - | - | - | 8-8 |
| Jose Oquendo | - | - | 83-70 | - | 2-5 | - | - | - | - | - | - | 85-75 |
| Tom Pagnozzi | 8-9 | - | - | - | - | - | - | - | - | - | - | 8-9 |
| Tony Pena | 69-55 | - | - | - | - | - | - | - | - | - | - | 69-55 |
| Terry Pendleton | - | - | - | 85-73 | - | - | - | - | - | - | - | 85-73 |
| Ted Power | - | - | - | - | - | - | - | - | 7-8 | - | 3-5 | 7-8 |
| Dan Quisenberry | - | - | - | - | - | - | - | - | - | - | 22-40 | - |
| Ozzie Smith | - | - | - | - | 81-69 | - | - | - | - | 1-0 | - | 81-69 |
| Scott Terry | - | - | - | - | - | - | - | - | 13-11 | - | 4-3 | 13-11 |
| Bob Tewksbury | - | - | - | - | - | - | - | - | 3-1 | - | 0-3 | 3-1 |
| Milt Thompson | - | - | - | - | - | 15-6 | 65-52 | - | - | 4-3 | | 80-[illegible] |
| Denny Walling | - | 0-2 | - | 1-2 | - | 2-1 | - | 1-1 | - | - | - | 4-6 |
| Craig Wilson | - | - | - | - | - | - | - | - | - | - | - | - |
| Todd Worrell | - | - | - | - | - | - | - | - | - | - | 33-14 | - |
| Todd Zeile | 9-12 | - | - | - | - | - | - | - | - | - | - | 9-12 |

## Batting vs. Left and Right Handed Pitchers

| | | BA | Rank | SA | Rank | OBA | Rank | HR % | Rank | BB % | Rank | SO % | Rank |
|---|---|---|---|---|---|---|---|---|---|---|---|---|---|
| Tom Brunansky | vs. Lefties | .236 | 96 | .423 | 48 | .320 | 77 | 5.00 | 12 | 11.20 | 34 | 13.20 | 68 |
| | vs. Righties | .241 | 75 | .402 | 45 | .306 | 74 | 2.68 | 41 | 8.33 | 63 | 19.89 | 107 |
| Vince Coleman | vs. Lefties | .235 | 97 | .326 | 98 | .285 | 112 | 0.76 | 101 | 6.29 | 103 | 18.53 | 115 |
| | vs. Righties | .271 | 39 | .341 | 89 | .342 | 36 | 0.00 | 124 | 9.47 | 49 | 10.95 | 34 |
| Pedro Guerrero | vs. Lefties | .317 | 17 | .505 | 16 | .402 | 10 | 3.67 | 25 | 12.60 | 23 | 14.96 | 85 |
| | vs. Righties | .307 | 15 | .460 | 17 | .384 | 16 | 2.56 | 47 | 11.44 | 29 | 11.19 | 37 |
| Willie McGee | vs. Lefties | .156 | 129 | .273 | 114 | .195 | 131 | 2.60 | 47 | 4.88 | 115 | 18.29 | 113 |
| | vs. Righties | .287 | -- | .402 | -- | .326 | -- | 0.82 | -- | 4.65 | -- | 14.73 | -- |
| Jose Oquendo | vs. Lefties | .266 | 70 | .354 | 83 | .340 | 61 | 0.00 | 112 | 10.31 | 40 | 11.07 | 44 |
| | vs. Righties | .309 | 14 | .385 | 56 | .398 | 9 | 0.31 | 119 | 13.40 | 11 | 7.73 | 11 |
| Tony Pena | vs. Lefties | .294 | 32 | .371 | 71 | .366 | 33 | 1.18 | 88 | 9.42 | 54 | 4.71 | 3 |
| | vs. Righties | .236 | 80 | .315 | 105 | .284 | 99 | 0.79 | 104 | 6.23 | 96 | 8.79 | 19 |
| Terry Pendleton | vs. Lefties | .279 | 50 | .377 | 68 | .313 | 88 | 0.81 | 100 | 4.63 | 118 | 7.72 | 15 |
| | vs. Righties | .254 | 59 | .399 | 49 | .313 | 66 | 3.01 | 36 | 7.96 | 73 | 15.17 | 80 |
| Ozzie Smith | vs. Lefties | .286 | 41 | .383 | 65 | .346 | 54 | 0.40 | 111 | 8.27 | 69 | 6.12 | 8 |
| | vs. Righties | .264 | 47 | .345 | 84 | .328 | 50 | 0.29 | 121 | 8.29 | 67 | 5.18 | 2 |
| Milt Thompson | vs. Lefties | .267 | 68 | .381 | 66 | .297 | 98 | 0.48 | 109 | 4.05 | 124 | 23.42 | 130 |
| | vs. Righties | .304 | 16 | .400 | 46 | .366 | 22 | 0.90 | 100 | 8.13 | 71 | 10.57 | 33 |
| Team Average | vs. Lefties | .253 | 5 | .361 | 8 | .314 | 8 | 1.37 | 12 | 7.96 | 12 | 14.33 | 5 |
| | vs. Righties | .261 | 1 | .365 | 6 | .326 | 1 | 1.30 | 12 | 8.45 | 5 | 13.47 | 1 |
| League Average | vs. Lefties | .251 | | .371 | | .320 | | 2.06 | | 8.85 | | 14.80 | |
| | vs. Righties | .244 | | .362 | | .309 | | 2.08 | | 8.27 | | 15.67 | |

## Batting with Runners on Base and Bases Empty

| | | BA | Rank | SA | Rank | OBA | Rank | HR % | Rank | BB % | Rank | SO % | Rank |
|---|---|---|---|---|---|---|---|---|---|---|---|---|---|
| Tom Brunansky | Runners On | .258 | 76 | .466 | 20 | .328 | 78 | 4.55 | 17 | 9.36 | 74 | 16.39 | 95 |
| | Bases Empty | .223 | 98 | .360 | 77 | .297 | 83 | 2.74 | 37 | 9.60 | 40 | 17.96 | 108 |
| Vince Coleman | Runners On | .208 | 119 | .280 | 125 | .270 | 122 | 0.00 | 112 | 7.29 | 98 | 13.54 | 69 |
| | Bases Empty | .273 | 34 | .357 | 81 | .336 | 42 | 0.51 | 115 | 8.33 | 58 | 14.81 | 73 |
| Pedro Guerrero | Runners On | .356 | 3 | .551 | 8 | .449 | 4 | 3.75 | 23 | 15.27 | 15 | 10.48 | 39 |
| | Bases Empty | .271 | 42 | .413 | 38 | .332 | 44 | 2.31 | 50 | 8.46 | 55 | 14.80 | 72 |
| Willie McGee | Runners On | .262 | -- | .354 | -- | .290 | -- | 1.54 | -- | 4.35 | -- | 17.39 | -- |
| | Bases Empty | .224 | 97 | .351 | 86 | .268 | 111 | 1.49 | 81 | 4.93 | 105 | 15.49 | 81 |
| Jose Oquendo | Runners On | .285 | 35 | .331 | 102 | .358 | 43 | 0.00 | 112 | 11.19 | 51 | 9.44 | 26 |
| | Bases Empty | .297 | 12 | .404 | 44 | .387 | 6 | 0.32 | 119 | 12.91 | 7 | 8.79 | 17 |
| Tony Pena | Runners On | .271 | 55 | .330 | 103 | .352 | 48 | 0.00 | 112 | 10.78 | 57 | 8.19 | 17 |
| | Bases Empty | .249 | 70 | .344 | 93 | .284 | 97 | 1.81 | 69 | 4.31 | 113 | 6.03 | 3 |
| Terry Pendleton | Runners On | .260 | 73 | .379 | 71 | .313 | 96 | 1.75 | 70 | 7.37 | 95 | 13.14 | 64 |
| | Bases Empty | .268 | 48 | .399 | 47 | .312 | 66 | 2.44 | 49 | 6.02 | 88 | 11.46 | 36 |
| Ozzie Smith | Runners On | .301 | 24 | .368 | 79 | .366 | 35 | 0.00 | 112 | 8.96 | 78 | 3.58 | 1 |
| | Bases Empty | .254 | 65 | .356 | 82 | .314 | 61 | 0.56 | 112 | 7.79 | 64 | 7.01 | 6 |
| Milt Thompson | Runners On | .337 | 8 | .466 | 21 | .391 | 23 | 1.20 | 87 | 7.25 | 99 | 14.86 | 85 |
| | Bases Empty | .250 | 66 | .331 | 99 | .295 | 86 | 0.34 | 118 | 6.03 | 87 | 15.87 | 84 |
| Team Average | Runners On | .272 | 1 | .378 | 6 | .338 | 1 | 1.43 | 11 | 9.04 | 11 | 13.28 | 2 |
| | Bases Empty | .248 | 3 | .352 | 8 | .307 | 3 | 1.25 | 12 | 7.62 | 6 | 14.24 | 1 |
| League Average | Runners On | .256 | | .379 | | .330 | | 2.13 | | 9.82 | | 14.66 | |
| | Bases Empty | .240 | | .355 | | .299 | | 2.03 | | 7.43 | | 15.93 | |

## Overall Batting Compared to Late Inning Pressure Situations

| | | BA | Rank | SA | Rank | OBA | Rank | HR % | Rank | BB % | Rank | SO % | Rank | RDI % | Rank |
|---|---|---|---|---|---|---|---|---|---|---|---|---|---|---|---|
| Tom Brunansky | Overall | .239 | 93 | .410 | 39 | .312 | 83 | 3.60 | 18 | 9.49 | 53 | 17.20 | 101 | .256 | 70 |
| | Pressure | .193 | 106 | .373 | 43 | .287 | 82 | 4.82 | 11 | 11.70 | 40 | 19.15 | 98 | .179 | 90 |
| Vince Coleman | Overall | .254 | 69 | .334 | 104 | .316 | 76 | 0.36 | 120 | 8.01 | 75 | 14.42 | 76 | .177 | 126 |
| | Pressure | .195 | 105 | .234 | 112 | .262 | 100 | 0.00 | 81 | 8.24 | 77 | 15.29 | 67 | .130 | 114 |
| Pedro Guerrero | Overall | .311 | 8 | .477 | 11 | .391 | 9 | 2.98 | 30 | 11.88 | 26 | 12.63 | 54 | .447 | 1 |
| | Pressure | .312 | 18 | .455 | 21 | .368 | 28 | 2.60 | 31 | 9.20 | 63 | 8.05 | 16 | .486 | 5 |
| Willie McGee | Overall | .236 | 97 | .352 | 91 | .275 | 118 | 1.51 | 80 | 4.74 | 119 | 16.11 | 95 | .255 | -- |
| | Pressure | .281 | -- | .281 | -- | .343 | -- | 0.00 | -- | 8.57 | -- | 20.00 | -- | .222 | -- |
| Jose Oquendo | Overall | .291 | 16 | .372 | 66 | .375 | 14 | 0.18 | 126 | 12.15 | 22 | 9.08 | 18 | .253 | 74 |
| | Pressure | .314 | 17 | .372 | 44 | .422 | 5 | 0.00 | 81 | 15.24 | 15 | 13.33 | 45 | .182 | 86 |
| Tony Pena | Overall | .259 | 56 | .337 | 99 | .318 | 67 | 0.94 | 103 | 7.54 | 84 | 7.11 | 7 | .225 | 98 |
| | Pressure | .175 | 115 | .254 | 106 | .224 | 124 | 1.59 | 66 | 5.97 | 92 | 7.46 | 11 | .111 | 121 |
| Terry Pendleton | Overall | .264 | 49 | .390 | 55 | .313 | 81 | 2.12 | 62 | 6.66 | 98 | 12.25 | 47 | .289 | 37 |
| | Pressure | .214 | 87 | .274 | 100 | .283 | 89 | 1.19 | 75 | 8.70 | 67 | 17.39 | 81 | .176 | 91 |
| Ozzie Smith | Overall | .273 | 38 | .361 | 77 | .335 | 48 | 0.34 | 122 | 8.28 | 69 | 5.57 | 2 | .262 | 66 |
| | Pressure | .351 | 2 | .514 | 7 | .430 | 4 | 0.00 | 81 | 12.22 | 32 | 5.56 | 5 | .318 | 26 |
| Milt Thompson | Overall | .290 | 19 | .393 | 51 | .340 | 43 | 0.73 | 111 | 6.60 | 100 | 15.40 | 86 | .318 | 18 |
| | Pressure | .286 | 32 | .364 | 50 | .329 | 56 | 0.00 | 81 | 7.06 | 84 | 21.18 | 108 | .276 | 47 |
| Team Average | Overall | .258 | 2 | .363 | 7 | .321 | 1 | 1.33 | 12 | 8.26 | 8 | 13.81 | 1 | .265 | 3 |
| | Pressure | .252 | 3 | .342 | 6 | .325 | 2 | 1.01 | 12 | 9.71 | 3 | 14.73 | 1 | .251 | 4 |
| League Average | Overall | .246 | | .365 | | .312 | | 2.07 | | 8.47 | | 15.38 | | .253 | |
| | Pressure | .238 | | .337 | | .308 | | 1.73 | | 8.93 | | 16.78 | | .235 | |

## Additional Miscellaneous Batting Comparisons

| | Grass Surface | | Artificial Surface | | Home Games | | Road Games | | Runners in Scoring Position | | Runners in Scoring Pos and Two Outs | | Leading Off Inning | | Runners on 3B with less than 2 Outs | |
|---|---|---|---|---|---|---|---|---|---|---|---|---|---|---|---|---|
| | BA | Rank | BA | Rank | BA | Rank | BA | Rank | BA | Rank | BA | Rank | OBA | Rank | RDI % | Rank |
| Tom Brunansky | .201 | 114 | .254 | 66 | .232 | 100 | .246 | 73 | .259 | 65 | .277 | 29 | .333 | 40 | .500 | 98 |
| Vince Coleman | .221 | 99 | .267 | 44 | .260 | 64 | .248 | 70 | .200 | 115 | .203 | 87 | .336 | 39 | .409 | 129 |
| Pedro Guerrero | .364 | 1 | .291 | 22 | .288 | 36 | .332 | 4 | .405 | 2 | .424 | 2 | .293 | 71 | .660 | 32 |
| Willie McGee | .264 | -- | .226 | 108 | .255 | 70 | .215 | 103 | .268 | -- | .176 | -- | .288 | 77 | .500 | 98 |
| John Morris | .250 | -- | .237 | 99 | .254 | -- | .222 | -- | .320 | -- | .300 | -- | .294 | -- | .667 | -- |
| Jose Oquendo | .309 | 11 | .285 | 29 | .301 | 23 | .282 | 34 | .255 | 72 | .209 | 83 | .368 | 25 | .559 | 73 |
| Tony Pena | .282 | 34 | .250 | 74 | .229 | 107 | .287 | 27 | .229 | 94 | .157 | 118 | .327 | 48 | .522 | 94 |
| Terry Pendleton | .280 | 37 | .258 | 57 | .271 | 50 | .258 | 58 | .265 | 57 | .288 | 26 | .383 | 14 | .438 | 123 |
| Ozzie Smith | .291 | 22 | .267 | 43 | .253 | 75 | .294 | 14 | .292 | 30 | .274 | 30 | .279 | 88 | .515 | 97 |
| Milt Thompson | .284 | 32 | .292 | 19 | .303 | 21 | .277 | 38 | .318 | 14 | .365 | 7 | .273 | 96 | .571 | 64 |
| Team Average | .262 | 1 | .257 | 2 | .256 | 3 | .260 | 1 | .263 | 1 | .259 | 1 | .312 | 3 | .522 | 10 |
| League Average | .244 | | .248 | | .251 | | .242 | | .249 | | .222 | | .302 | | .546 | |

## Pitching vs. Left and Right Handed Batters

| | | BA | Rank | SA | Rank | OBA | Rank | HR % | Rank | BB % | Rank | SO % | Rank |
|---|---|---|---|---|---|---|---|---|---|---|---|---|---|
| Cris Carpenter | vs. Lefties | .277 | 91 | .372 | 70 | .357 | 97 | 0.73 | 21 | 10.90 | 80 | 8.97 | 103 |
| | vs. Righties | .246 | 68 | .415 | 97 | .297 | 60 | 2.31 | 66 | 6.12 | 38 | 14.29 | 77 |
| John Costello | vs. Lefties | .227 | 35 | .318 | 35 | .307 | 44 | 1.14 | 40 | 10.89 | 79 | 15.84 | 42 |
| | vs. Righties | .204 | 19 | .372 | 73 | .258 | 17 | 2.92 | 90 | 5.96 | 35 | 15.89 | 69 |
| Ken Dayley | vs. Lefties | .188 | 10 | .287 | 22 | .248 | 7 | 0.99 | 34 | 7.27 | 32 | 13.64 | 57 |
| | vs. Righties | .251 | 79 | .360 | 60 | .333 | 89 | 1.14 | 14 | 11.00 | 105 | 12.50 | 91 |
| Jose DeLeon | vs. Lefties | .234 | 40 | .360 | 61 | .312 | 53 | 1.96 | 72 | 9.97 | 72 | 15.03 | 46 |
| | vs. Righties | .146 | 1 | .238 | 3 | .204 | 2 | 1.63 | 33 | 5.75 | 28 | 28.75 | 3 |
| Frank DiPino | vs. Lefties | .209 | 22 | .248 | 6 | .241 | 5 | 0.00 | 1 | 4.38 | 3 | 14.60 | 50 |
| | vs. Righties | .240 | 58 | .417 | 98 | .287 | 51 | 3.13 | 97 | 6.67 | 51 | 11.43 | 98 |
| Ken Hill | vs. Lefties | .271 | 85 | .359 | 60 | .372 | 108 | 0.76 | 24 | 13.46 | 105 | 11.32 | 85 |
| | vs. Righties | .230 | 50 | .331 | 40 | .306 | 68 | 1.74 | 39 | 9.14 | 90 | 14.97 | 73 |
| Ricky Horton | vs. Lefties | .343 | -- | .429 | -- | .405 | -- | 0.00 | -- | 7.41 | -- | 7.41 | -- |
| | vs. Righties | .292 | 108 | .407 | 89 | .341 | 92 | 1.44 | 22 | 6.44 | 46 | 8.58 | 114 |
| Joe Magrane | vs. Lefties | .234 | 42 | .289 | 23 | .319 | 56 | 0.00 | 1 | 10.07 | 74 | 16.11 | 40 |
| | vs. Righties | .254 | 84 | .345 | 50 | .309 | 74 | 0.67 | 8 | 6.93 | 55 | 12.53 | 90 |
| Ted Power | vs. Lefties | .280 | 93 | .396 | 84 | .324 | 62 | 1.45 | 54 | 6.25 | 18 | 10.27 | 94 |
| | vs. Righties | .224 | 42 | .371 | 69 | .256 | 14 | 2.35 | 69 | 3.83 | 9 | 10.93 | 101 |
| Dan Quisenberry | vs. Lefties | .238 | 49 | .336 | 44 | .297 | 33 | 1.40 | 51 | 7.69 | 37 | 10.90 | 87 |
| | vs. Righties | .282 | 100 | .365 | 67 | .289 | 54 | 0.00 | 1 | 1.24 | 1 | 12.42 | 93 |
| Scott Terry | vs. Lefties | .261 | 77 | .400 | 87 | .331 | 69 | 2.14 | 80 | 9.58 | 67 | 10.86 | 88 |
| | vs. Righties | .246 | 66 | .409 | 92 | .283 | 47 | 2.85 | 83 | 4.25 | 15 | 11.44 | 97 |
| Todd Worrell | vs. Lefties | .250 | 64 | .455 | 107 | .350 | 93 | 3.41 | 110 | 13.21 | 103 | 19.81 | 18 |
| | vs. Righties | .198 | -- | .287 | -- | .283 | -- | 0.99 | -- | 10.62 | -- | 17.70 | -- |
| Team Average | vs. Lefties | .256 | 8 | .365 | 6 | .330 | 8 | 1.38 | 1 | 9.76 | 10 | 12.61 | 10 |
| | vs. Righties | .233 | 4 | .353 | 4 | .286 | 1 | 1.66 | 1 | 6.44 | 2 | 14.86 | 12 |
| League Average | vs. Lefties | .252 | | .366 | | .325 | | 1.79 | | 9.48 | | 13.93 | |
| | vs. Righties | .242 | | .365 | | .303 | | 2.29 | | 7.70 | | 16.46 | |

## Pitching with Runners on Base and Bases Empty

| | | BA | Rank | SA | Rank | OBA | Rank | HR % | Rank | BB % | Rank | SO % | Rank |
|---|---|---|---|---|---|---|---|---|---|---|---|---|---|
| Cris Carpenter | Runners On | .261 | 78 | .443 | 97 | .346 | 77 | 2.61 | 87 | 10.71 | 79 | 7.86 | 112 |
| | Bases Empty | .263 | 95 | .355 | 68 | .313 | 82 | 0.66 | 13 | 6.75 | 57 | 14.72 | 63 |
| John Costello | Runners On | .253 | -- | .398 | -- | .330 | -- | 2.41 | -- | 10.00 | -- | 16.00 | -- |
| | Bases Empty | .190 | 8 | .324 | 29 | .243 | 4 | 2.11 | 64 | 6.58 | 51 | 15.79 | 53 |
| Ken Dayley | Runners On | .217 | 18 | .304 | 17 | .301 | 34 | 0.72 | 10 | 10.69 | 78 | 12.58 | 83 |
| | Bases Empty | .239 | 53 | .362 | 73 | .305 | 65 | 1.45 | 40 | 8.61 | 82 | 13.25 | 79 |
| Jose DeLeon | Runners On | .248 | 61 | .386 | 76 | .307 | 41 | 1.93 | 50 | 7.49 | 23 | 21.33 | 16 |
| | Bases Empty | .169 | 2 | .266 | 5 | .246 | 7 | 1.76 | 51 | 8.64 | 83 | 20.32 | 27 |
| Frank DiPino | Runners On | .223 | 26 | .367 | 61 | .276 | 12 | 2.16 | 67 | 7.64 | 28 | 13.38 | 73 |
| | Bases Empty | .231 | 39 | .335 | 39 | .263 | 16 | 1.65 | 45 | 4.21 | 14 | 12.11 | 95 |
| Ken Hill | Runners On | .253 | 66 | .354 | 48 | .344 | 75 | 1.19 | 27 | 11.63 | 93 | 13.37 | 74 |
| | Bases Empty | .251 | 78 | .340 | 48 | .341 | 107 | 1.24 | 31 | 11.35 | 107 | 12.66 | 86 |
| Ricky Horton | Runners On | .315 | 113 | .408 | 83 | .388 | 111 | 0.00 | 1 | 8.86 | 44 | 7.59 | 113 |
| | Bases Empty | .295 | 112 | .416 | 108 | .327 | 98 | 2.01 | 61 | 4.49 | 20 | 8.97 | 113 |
| Joe Magrane | Runners On | .265 | 83 | .345 | 41 | .339 | 69 | 0.60 | 6 | 10.25 | 68 | 13.00 | 80 |
| | Bases Empty | .243 | 61 | .331 | 36 | .291 | 48 | 0.56 | 8 | 5.43 | 28 | 13.13 | 80 |
| Ted Power | Runners On | .259 | 76 | .418 | 87 | .306 | 40 | 3.16 | 101 | 6.18 | 11 | 10.11 | 98 |
| | Bases Empty | .251 | 82 | .361 | 72 | .284 | 40 | 0.91 | 19 | 4.37 | 16 | 10.92 | 105 |
| Dan Quisenberry | Runners On | .291 | 95 | .385 | 74 | .349 | 81 | 0.85 | 16 | 8.33 | 38 | 7.58 | 114 |
| | Bases Empty | .242 | 55 | .330 | 35 | .254 | 11 | 0.55 | 6 | 1.62 | 1 | 14.59 | 66 |
| Scott Terry | Runners On | .257 | 71 | .425 | 91 | .312 | 48 | 3.54 | 105 | 7.36 | 20 | 10.85 | 93 |
| | Bases Empty | .251 | 79 | .391 | 91 | .305 | 66 | 1.79 | 52 | 6.65 | 53 | 11.36 | 99 |
| Todd Worrell | Runners On | .221 | 24 | .358 | 53 | .348 | 80 | 2.11 | 64 | 16.10 | 114 | 14.41 | 58 |
| | Bases Empty | .223 | -- | .372 | -- | .277 | -- | 2.13 | -- | 6.93 | -- | 23.76 | -- |
| Team Average | Runners On | .258 | 7 | .384 | 7 | .330 | 6 | 1.78 | 2 | 9.46 | 4 | 13.01 | 10 |
| | Bases Empty | .233 | 2 | .340 | 3 | .288 | 2 | 1.37 | 1 | 6.75 | 1 | 14.50 | 10 |
| League Average | Runners On | .256 | | .379 | | .330 | | 2.13 | | 9.82 | | 14.66 | |
| | Bases Empty | .240 | | .355 | | .299 | | 2.03 | | 7.43 | | 15.93 | |

## Overall Pitching Compared to Late Inning Pressure Situations

| | | BA | Rank | SA | Rank | OBA | Rank | HR % | Rank | BB % | Rank | SO % | Rank |
|---|---|---|---|---|---|---|---|---|---|---|---|---|---|
| Cris Carpenter | Overall | .262 | 89 | .393 | 87 | .328 | 82 | 1.50 | 30 | 8.58 | 67 | 11.55 | 96 |
| | Pressure | .227 | 52 | .333 | 56 | .316 | 64 | 0.00 | 1 | 12.20 | 93 | 10.98 | 94 |
| John Costello | Overall | .213 | 20 | .351 | 56 | .278 | 20 | 2.22 | 75 | 7.94 | 51 | 15.87 | 54 |
| | Pressure | .227 | 51 | .353 | 72 | .290 | 44 | 1.68 | 63 | 8.40 | 54 | 15.27 | 60 |
| Ken Dayley | Overall | .228 | 36 | .333 | 36 | .303 | 52 | 1.09 | 18 | 9.68 | 84 | 12.90 | 80 |
| | Pressure | .232 | 56 | .351 | 71 | .319 | 66 | 1.62 | 61 | 11.27 | 89 | 11.27 | 90 |
| Jose DeLeon | Overall | .197 | 4 | .309 | 13 | .268 | 8 | 1.82 | 47 | 8.23 | 55 | 20.68 | 19 |
| | Pressure | .113 | 1 | .165 | 2 | .211 | 2 | 1.03 | 40 | 10.91 | 83 | 20.91 | 20 |
| Frank DiPino | Overall | .227 | 35 | .349 | 50 | .269 | 10 | 1.87 | 51 | 5.76 | 16 | 12.68 | 84 |
| | Pressure | .263 | 81 | .379 | 87 | .301 | 49 | 2.11 | 74 | 5.77 | 29 | 16.35 | 51 |
| Ken Hill | Overall | .252 | 70 | .346 | 48 | .342 | 99 | 1.22 | 21 | 11.48 | 108 | 12.99 | 78 |
| | Pressure | .404 | 114 | .489 | 107 | .472 | 115 | 2.13 | 75 | 9.09 | 61 | 12.73 | 80 |
| Ricky Horton | Overall | .305 | 116 | .412 | 102 | .357 | 108 | 1.08 | 16 | 6.69 | 26 | 8.28 | 114 |
| | Pressure | .405 | 115 | .541 | 112 | .489 | 116 | 0.00 | 1 | 14.29 | 107 | 8.16 | 109 |
| Joe Magrane | Overall | .251 | 69 | .336 | 39 | .310 | 61 | 0.57 | 2 | 7.42 | 41 | 13.08 | 76 |
| | Pressure | .191 | 21 | .213 | 6 | .242 | 12 | 0.00 | 1 | 5.05 | 23 | 13.13 | 77 |
| Ted Power | Overall | .255 | 75 | .385 | 78 | .294 | 39 | 1.86 | 49 | 5.16 | 8 | 10.57 | 105 |
| | Pressure | .364 | -- | .500 | -- | .375 | -- | 0.00 | -- | 4.17 | -- | 8.33 | -- |
| Dan Quisenberry | Overall | .261 | 87 | .351 | 57 | .293 | 38 | 0.67 | 5 | 4.42 | 1 | 11.67 | 95 |
| | Pressure | .289 | 96 | .367 | 79 | .326 | 75 | 0.00 | 1 | 5.21 | 25 | 11.46 | 86 |
| Scott Terry | Overall | .253 | 74 | .405 | 94 | .308 | 58 | 2.50 | 92 | 6.95 | 33 | 11.15 | 99 |
| | Pressure | .246 | 66 | .351 | 70 | .295 | 45 | 1.75 | 65 | 4.92 | 21 | 16.39 | 50 |
| Todd Worrell | Overall | .222 | -- | .365 | -- | .315 | -- | 2.12 | -- | 11.87 | -- | 18.72 | -- |
| | Pressure | .223 | 45 | .354 | 73 | .338 | 84 | 1.54 | 58 | 14.74 | 110 | 17.31 | 46 |
| Team Average | Overall | .243 | 3 | .358 | 3 | .306 | 4 | 1.54 | 1 | 7.91 | 4 | 13.86 | 10 |
| | Pressure | .236 | 9 | .343 | 8 | .309 | 7 | 1.46 | 4 | 9.37 | 8 | 14.27 | 11 |
| League Average | Overall | .246 | | .365 | | .312 | | 2.07 | | 8.47 | | 15.38 | |
| | Pressure | .235 | | .336 | | .309 | | 1.77 | | 9.31 | | 16.92 | |

## Additional Miscellaneous Pitching Comparisons

| | Grass Surface | | Artificial Surface | | Home Games | | Road Games | | Runners in Scoring Position | | Runners in Scoring Pos and Two Outs | | Leading Off Inning | |
|---|---|---|---|---|---|---|---|---|---|---|---|---|---|---|
| | BA | Rank | BA | Rank | BA | Rank | BA | Rank | BA | Rank | BA | Rank | OBA | Rank |
| Cris Carpenter | .213 | -- | .277 | 93 | .280 | 99 | .239 | 44 | .250 | 62 | .243 | 76 | .300 | 59 |
| John Costello | .328 | -- | .171 | 4 | .157 | -- | .265 | 82 | .259 | -- | .214 | 57 | .217 | 5 |
| Ken Dayley | .194 | -- | .239 | 49 | .261 | 82 | .194 | 9 | .230 | 44 | .184 | 33 | .242 | 15 |
| Jose DeLeon | .209 | 22 | .192 | 7 | .184 | 10 | .212 | 21 | .243 | 59 | .213 | 56 | .263 | 22 |
| Frank DiPino | .194 | -- | .237 | 47 | .201 | 20 | .255 | 67 | .227 | 40 | .122 | 8 | .250 | 17 |
| Don Heinkel | .318 | -- | .355 | 115 | .371 | -- | .311 | -- | .345 | -- | .000 | -- | .367 | -- |
| Ken Hill | .240 | 56 | .256 | 72 | .247 | 63 | .256 | 71 | .251 | 66 | .245 | 80 | .391 | 115 |
| Ricky Horton | .313 | 112 | .298 | 104 | .299 | 111 | .311 | 110 | .313 | 106 | .303 | 102 | .310 | 72 |
| Joe Magrane | .247 | 67 | .253 | 61 | .261 | 83 | .242 | 47 | .266 | 80 | .227 | 69 | .269 | 30 |
| Ted Power | .250 | 71 | .257 | 73 | .260 | 79 | .251 | 58 | .289 | 89 | .190 | 40 | .310 | 73 |
| Dan Quisenberry | .279 | 100 | .254 | 66 | .291 | 108 | .230 | 34 | .309 | 102 | .250 | 81 | .221 | 8 |
| Scott Terry | .289 | 103 | .242 | 52 | .232 | 46 | .282 | 96 | .239 | 54 | .185 | 35 | .346 | 101 |
| Bob Tewksbury | .455 | -- | .200 | 10 | .225 | -- | .225 | -- | .273 | -- | .364 | -- | .375 | -- |
| Todd Worrell | .212 | -- | .226 | 32 | .216 | -- | .228 | -- | .200 | 20 | .121 | 7 | .211 | -- |
| Team Average | .247 | 7 | .242 | 3 | .241 | 6 | .246 | 3 | .260 | 11 | .210 | 4 | .298 | 3 |
| League Average | .244 | | .248 | | .242 | | .251 | | .249 | | .222 | | .302 | |

# SAN DIEGO PADRES

- **Did a late wake-up call cost the Padres a pennant?**
- **Last-chance wins and losses.**

When San Diego defeated Houston, 10–2, on June 5 last season, it marked the first time that the Padres had scored in double figures since September 13, 1987—a streak of 238 games. To put that number in perspective, no American League team ever had a streak that long, and it was the sixth longest in the National League since 1900:

| Years | Team | Games |
|---|---|---|
| 1981–1983 | Houston Astros | 284 |
| 1907–1909 | St. Louis Cardinals | 277 |
| 1967–1968 | Los Angeles Dodgers | 261 |
| 1916–1917 | St. Louis Cardinals | 242 |
| 1962–1963 | Houston Colt .45s | 240 |
| 1987–1989 | San Diego Padres | 238 |

The end of the streak, a footnote at the time, actually marked a significant event: the awakening of San Diego's offense. Based solely on that turnaround, the Padres made a late-season run at the Giants that ultimately fell short only because of their disappointing record prior to the All-Star break (42–46). So remarkable was the rebirth of its attack that, during the second half, San Diego posted a 47–27 record, tying Oakland for the best in the majors, despite a team ERA that was almost exactly the same before the break (3.37) as after it (3.35). The table below illustrates the mid-season turnaround of San Diego's offense:

| | G | HR | Runs | Avg. | Rank |
|---|---|---|---|---|---|
| Before All-Star break | 88 | 46 | 291 | 3.3 | 11th |
| After All-Star break | 74 | 74 | 351 | 4.7 | 1st |

Prior to the All-Star break, only the Dodgers scored fewer runs per game, and by a narrow margin (3.31 to 3.28). After the break, the Padres were the highest-scoring team in the league, an about-face that paralleled the team's increased home- run production: eighth before the break, first thereafter.

Three players alone fueled the turnaround: Roberto Alomar, Jack Clark, and Chris James, who was acquired for John Kruk in June. No other offensive player made a significantly greater contribution in the second half than in the first. Alomar ranked second in the league in batting average after the All-Star break, and Clark ranked fourth in home runs and second in RBIs. It should be noted that although James hit 100 points better in the second half than Kruk hit before the trade, his average was nevertheless 47 points lower than Kruk hit after leaving San Diego for the Phillies. Individual statistics, before and after the break:

| | First Half | | | Second Half | | |
|---|---|---|---|---|---|---|
| Player | BA | HR | RBI | BA | HR | RBI |
| Alomar | .264 | 2 | 21 | .335 | 5 | 35 |
| Clark | .227 | 9 | 40 | .260 | 17 | 54 |
| Kruk/James | .190 | 4 | 14 | .284 | 10 | 38 |
| Others | .248 | 31 | 192 | .242 | 42 | 204 |

Trying to prevent a backslide to their first-half form, San Diego has added Joe Carter to its 1990 lineup. Last season, Carter drove in 105 runs although his Cleveland Indians ranked last in the American League with an average of 3.73 runs per game. Back in the days when a team had to score five runs a game to gain any respect at all, it wasn't too uncommon for players on even the lowest-scoring teams to reach the 100–RBI mark. The Philadelphia A's ranked last in the American League in scoring in 1924 despite two 100–RBI players: Joe Hauser and Al Simmons. They did it again 11 years later, with Jimmie Foxx and Bob Johnson. Johnson hit the 100–RBI mark for three consecutive seasons from 1935 through 1937 playing for Philadelphia, the A.L.'s lowest-scoring team in each of those seasons. The highest total ever by a player on a team that ranked last in its league in runs scored: Wally Berger drove in 130 runs for the 1935 Braves.

That was then, this is now. Carter's 105 RBIs were the most by a player on his league's lowest-scoring team since 1972, when Nate Colbert drove in 111 runs for the Padres. Carter was only the 42d player since 1900 to drive in 100 or more runs for a team that scored less than four runs per game. Roy Sievers is the champ at that—he did it three times. The table below lists those who drove in as many runs as Carter for a team that scored as few runs per game as last season's Indians:

| Year | Player | RBI | Team | Runs |
|---|---|---|---|---|
| 1933 | Wally Berger | 106 | Braves | 3.54 |
| 1958 | Roy Sievers | 108 | Senators | 3.54 |
| 1968 | Frank Howard | 106 | Senators | 3.25 |
| 1968 | Willie McCovey | 105 | Giants | 3.67 |
| 1972 | Dick Allen | 113 | White Sox | 3.68 |
| 1972 | Nate Colbert | 111 | Padres | 3.19 |
| 1984 | Gary Carter | 106 | Expos | 3.68 |
| 1989 | Joe Carter | 105 | Indians | 3.73 |

Don't jump to any conclusions. It might seem that Carter overcame a mighty obstacle in driving in 105 runs for a team with such a poor attack. And that he might have driven in many more runs playing for a higher-scoring team, like Boston or Minnesota. But a closer look reveals that Carter was part of Cleveland's problem. Given the number of runners in scoring position when Carter batted, 105 RBIs hardly represents clutch hitting; only one player in either league had more opportunities last season. and among the 10 players with 200 or more opportunities, only two drove in a lower percentage of those runners than Carter did (and just barely):

| Player | Opp. | RBI | Pct. |
|---|---|---|---|
| George Bell | 209 | 78 | .373 |
| Don Mattingly | 208 | 77 | .370 |
| Dwight Evans | 203 | 70 | .345 |
| Kirby Puckett | 203 | 68 | .335 |
| Mike Greenwell | 218 | 70 | .321 |
| Nick Esasky | 213 | 61 | .286 |
| Cal Ripken | 201 | 55 | .274 |
| Joe Carter | 215 | 56 | .260 |
| Todd Benzinger | 201 | 52 | .259 |
| Steve Sax | 215 | 55 | .256 |

Had Carter driven in even 30 percent of those runners, not an unreasonable expectation for a number-three or cleanup hitter, he would have added another nine RBIs. Had Carter matched Mattingly or Bell, who each drove in 37 percent, he would have reached the 130–RBI mark. Carter's actual 26 percent rate ranked in the lower half of the league. Of course, many of his teammates had far lower averages (see page 38). But there's a saying: If you're not part of the solution, you're part of the problem. Carter, despite 105 RBIs, was part of the problem.

The good news for San Diego is that Carter's 1989 rate was the lowest of his major league career. His lifetime mark, 28.8 percent, isn't great, but it's acceptable considering the number of runners he drives in from first base as well (not to mention from home plate). And it sure won't hurt having Jack Clark in the on-deck circle this season. But another season hitting in the .240s with fewer than 40 walks and 100–plus strikeouts will endear Carter only to members of the Dave Kingman fan club, long in search of a new hero.

Nearly 20 years ago, a network NBA broadcaster offered this opinion: Lakers guard Jerry West makes an average of 10 steals per game. That seemed reasonable, until a few years later when the league began tracking the number of steals made by individual players. The NBA leader in that first season, Larry Steele (we kid you not), made less than three per game. Since then, only 12 different players have made as many as 10 steals in any one game. West may have been the best ball hawk of his era, but an *average* of 10? No way.

Because all sports breed various statistics that are kept only on an informal, unofficial basis, similar misinterpretations occur all the time. Against what standards are we to judge the number of tackles made by Eugene Lockhart of the Dallas Cowboys? The number of jabs landed by Julio Cesar Chavez? The number of triple jumps in Debi Thomas's long program? Statistics presented without a context have no value. But given sports fans' insatiable appetite for numerical analysis, it's inevitable that the domain of sports statistics will expand further. Years from now, we'll have the answers to those questions and many others. (And, yes, fantasy figure-skating leagues will become a reality. Our advice: Take Boitano and that Witt girl. Forget Randy and Tai.)

One of baseball's previously unpublished figures is the number of games a team wins or loses in the final at–bat. Last season the Padres lost nine games in their opponents' last chance to score. Sounds like a typical, close-to-average figure, right? In fact, it was the lowest total in either league. The major-league average in 1989 was 17 such losses. Last-chance wins and losses for the 1989 season:

| Team | W | L | Team | W | L |
|---|---|---|---|---|---|
| Baltimore | 14 | 14 | Atlanta | 10 | 23 |
| Boston | 14 | 15 | Chicago | 17 | 13 |
| California | 20 | 17 | Cincinnati | 21 | 19 |
| Chicago | 12 | 16 | Houston | 19 | 17 |
| Cleveland | 17 | 25 | Los Angeles | 20 | 15 |
| Detroit | 17 | 18 | Montreal | 21 | 16 |
| Kansas City | 22 | 15 | New York | 18 | 20 |
| Milwaukee | 14 | 17 | Philadelphia | 18 | 15 |
| Minnesota | 19 | 12 | Pittsburgh | 14 | 27 |
| New York | 13 | 14 | St. Louis | 18 | 15 |
| Oakland | 16 | 12 | San Diego | 17 | 9 |
| Seattle | 12 | 19 | San Francisco | 13 | 17 |
| Texas | 14 | 17 | | | |
| Toronto | 22 | 15 | | | |

Over the past eight seasons, only one other National League team lost as few as nine games in their opponents' last chance: the 1987 Expos, who lost only eight. Of course, San Diego's exceptional record of slamming the door last season is also one of the best indicators of Mark Davis's value. So this will be a number worth watching during 1990, in order to assess the cost of losing the Cy Young Award winner to Kansas City.

## WON-LOST RECORD BY STARTING POSITION

| SAN DIEGO 89-73 | C | 1B | 2B | 3B | SS | LF | CF | RF | P | Leadoff | Relief | Starts |
|---|---|---|---|---|---|---|---|---|---|---|---|---|
| Shawn Abner | - | - | - | - | - | 2-5 | 14-2 | - | - | 4-5 | - | 16-7 |
| Roberto Alomar | - | - | 86-71 | - | - | - | - | - | - | 21-20 | - | 86-71 |
| Sandy Alomar | 3-1 | - | - | - | - | - | - | - | - | - | - | 3-1 |
| Andy Benes | - | - | - | - | - | - | - | - | 7-3 | - | - | 7-3 |
| Greg Booker | - | - | - | - | - | - | - | - | - | - | 0-11 | - |
| Jack Clark | - | 70-59 | - | - | - | - | - | 6-6 | - | - | - | 76-65 |
| Jerald Clark | - | - | - | - | - | 3-3 | - | 3-1 | - | - | - | 6-4 |
| Pat Clements | - | - | - | - | - | - | - | - | 0-1 | - | 6-16 | 0-1 |
| Joey Cora | - | - | - | - | 2-1 | - | - | - | - | 1-1 | - | 2-1 |
| Mark Davis | - | - | - | - | - | - | - | - | - | - | 55-15 | - |
| Tim Flannery | - | - | - | 9-20 | - | - | - | - | - | - | - | 9-20 |
| Mark Grant | - | - | - | - | - | - | - | - | - | - | 17-33 | - |
| Gary Green | - | - | - | - | 1-5 | - | - | - | - | - | - | 1-5 |
| Tony Gwynn | - | - | - | - | - | - | 41-45 | 45-26 | - | 3-5 | - | 86-71 |
| Greg W. Harris | - | - | - | - | - | - | - | - | 4-4 | - | 25-23 | 4-4 |
| Bruce Hurst | - | - | - | - | - | - | - | - | 19-14 | - | - | 19-14 |
| Darrin Jackson | - | - | - | - | - | - | 16-7 | - | - | - | - | 16-7 |
| Chris James | - | - | - | 1-3 | - | 31-17 | - | 13-13 | - | 1-1 | - | 45-33 |
| John Kruk | - | - | - | - | - | 1-1 | - | 12-10 | - | 2-2 | - | 13-11 |
| Dave Leiper | - | - | - | - | - | - | - | - | - | - | 1-21 | - |
| Carmelo Martinez | - | 4-5 | - | - | - | 28-25 | - | - | - | - | - | 32-30 |
| Dan Murphy | - | - | - | - | - | - | - | - | - | - | 2-5 | - |
| Rob Nelson | - | 13-8 | - | - | - | - | - | - | - | - | - | 13-8 |
| Eric Nolte | - | - | - | - | - | - | - | - | 1-0 | - | 0-2 | 1-0 |
| Mike Pagliarulo | - | - | - | 26-16 | - | - | - | - | - | - | - | 26-16 |
| Mark Parent | 18-18 | - | - | - | - | - | - | - | - | - | - | 18-18 |
| Dennis Rasmussen | - | - | - | - | - | - | - | - | 17-16 | - | - | 17-16 |
| Randy Ready | - | - | - | 9-7 | - | - | - | - | - | 2-0 | - | 9-7 |
| Bip Roberts | - | - | 3-2 | 20-9 | 8-4 | 9-12 | 0-1 | 4-7 | | 44-32 | - | 44-35 |
| Luis Salazar | - | - | - | 24-18 | 2-3 | 1-1 | - | 3-4 | - | 0-2 | - | 30-26 |
| Benito Santiago | 68-54 | - | - | - | - | - | - | - | - | - | - | 68-54 |
| Calvin Schiraldi | - | - | - | - | - | - | - | - | 3-1 | - | 0-1 | 3-1 |
| Don Schulze | - | - | - | - | - | - | - | - | 3-1 | - | 0-3 | 3-1 |
| Eric Show | - | - | - | - | - | - | - | - | 9-7 | - | - | 9-7 |
| Phil Stephenson | - | 2-1 | - | - | - | - | - | - | - | - | - | 2-1 |
| Garry Templeton | - | - | - | - | 76-60 | - | - | - | - | - | - | 76-60 |
| Walt Terrell | - | - | - | - | - | - | - | - | 6-13 | - | - | 6-13 |
| Fred Toliver | - | - | - | - | - | - | - | - | - | - | 0-9 | - |
| Ed Whitson | - | - | - | - | - | - | - | - | 20-13 | - | - | 20-13 |
| Marvell Wynne | - | - | - | - | - | 14-9 | 18-18 | 3-6 | - | 11-5 | - | 35-33 |

## Batting vs. Left and Right Handed Pitchers

| | | BA | Rank | SA | Rank | OBA | Rank | HR % | Rank | BB % | Rank | SO % | Rank |
|---|---|---|---|---|---|---|---|---|---|---|---|---|---|
| Roberto Alomar | vs. Lefties | .256 | 78 | .369 | 72 | .316 | 80 | 2.05 | 59 | 7.66 | 79 | 12.61 | 63 |
| | vs. Righties | .313 | 9 | .379 | 60 | .362 | 26 | 0.70 | 108 | 7.50 | 81 | 10.00 | 29 |
| Jack Clark | vs. Lefties | .272 | 59 | .440 | 41 | .474 | 1 | 3.20 | 31 | 27.75 | 1 | 16.18 | 92 |
| | vs. Righties | .230 | 90 | .467 | 15 | .383 | 17 | 6.67 | 5 | 19.95 | 1 | 27.79 | 131 |
| Tim Flannery | vs. Lefties | .125 | -- | .125 | -- | .300 | -- | 0.00 | -- | 20.00 | -- | 10.00 | -- |
| | vs. Righties | .238 | 79 | .279 | 123 | .299 | 82 | 0.00 | 124 | 8.15 | 69 | 14.07 | 64 |
| Tony Gwynn | vs. Lefties | .305 | 22 | .345 | 89 | .355 | 44 | 0.00 | 112 | 7.17 | 90 | 6.28 | 9 |
| | vs. Righties | .351 | 1 | .463 | 16 | .406 | 7 | 0.99 | 95 | 8.77 | 57 | 3.51 | 1 |
| Darrin Jackson | vs. Lefties | .224 | 103 | .353 | 84 | .292 | 105 | 2.35 | 53 | 9.38 | 55 | 15.63 | 87 |
| | vs. Righties | .212 | -- | .306 | -- | .247 | -- | 2.35 | -- | 4.49 | -- | 21.35 | -- |
| Chris James | vs. Lefties | .292 | 35 | .458 | 33 | .335 | 68 | 4.17 | 18 | 6.52 | 98 | 10.87 | 43 |
| | vs. Righties | .217 | 109 | .318 | 102 | .252 | 126 | 1.91 | 70 | 4.22 | 118 | 14.46 | 69 |
| Carmelo Martinez | vs. Lefties | .271 | 60 | .390 | 60 | .348 | 52 | 1.69 | 70 | 10.61 | 37 | 13.64 | 76 |
| | vs. Righties | .181 | 130 | .315 | 104 | .266 | 117 | 2.68 | 40 | 10.65 | 37 | 21.30 | 115 |
| Mike Pagliarulo | vs. Lefties | .154 | -- | .192 | -- | .185 | -- | 0.00 | -- | 3.57 | -- | 32.14 | -- |
| | vs. Righties | .205 | 119 | .328 | 98 | .307 | 70 | 2.46 | 52 | 12.14 | 23 | 21.43 | 117 |
| Bip Roberts | vs. Lefties | .325 | 10 | .513 | 12 | .397 | 11 | 2.56 | 49 | 9.92 | 46 | 13.74 | 77 |
| | vs. Righties | .288 | 24 | .373 | 68 | .388 | 12 | 0.00 | 124 | 14.06 | 9 | 10.55 | 31 |
| Benito Santiago | vs. Lefties | .222 | 104 | .316 | 102 | .289 | 108 | 1.71 | 69 | 8.59 | 63 | 17.97 | 109 |
| | vs. Righties | .241 | 76 | .412 | 41 | .273 | 108 | 4.06 | 17 | 4.10 | 121 | 18.03 | 98 |
| Garry Templeton | vs. Lefties | .317 | 16 | .421 | 51 | .349 | 51 | 0.69 | 104 | 4.55 | 120 | 12.34 | 57 |
| | vs. Righties | .230 | 91 | .327 | 99 | .261 | 122 | 1.39 | 84 | 4.19 | 119 | 15.97 | 85 |
| Team Average | vs. Lefties | .267 | 3 | .387 | 4 | .340 | 2 | 1.99 | 7 | 9.76 | 1 | 14.67 | 7 |
| | vs. Righties | .244 | 6 | .361 | 7 | .310 | 5 | 2.31 | 6 | 8.70 | 3 | 17.36 | 11 |
| League Average | vs. Lefties | .251 | | .371 | | .320 | | 2.06 | | 8.85 | | 14.80 | |
| | vs. Righties | .244 | | .362 | | .309 | | 2.08 | | 8.27 | | 15.67 | |

## Batting with Runners on Base and Bases Empty

| | | BA | Rank | SA | Rank | OBA | Rank | HR % | Rank | BB % | Rank | SO % | Rank |
|---|---|---|---|---|---|---|---|---|---|---|---|---|---|
| Roberto Alomar | Runners On | .296 | 31 | .364 | 83 | .338 | 68 | 0.81 | 101 | 6.85 | 102 | 9.93 | 32 |
| | Bases Empty | .295 | 14 | .383 | 60 | .354 | 21 | 1.33 | 88 | 8.05 | 60 | 11.46 | 37 |
| Jack Clark | Runners On | .274 | 50 | .543 | 9 | .445 | 5 | 7.83 | 2 | 24.12 | 2 | 22.19 | 127 |
| | Bases Empty | .209 | 114 | .373 | 69 | .371 | 12 | 3.56 | 22 | 20.14 | 1 | 26.86 | 131 |
| Tony Gwynn | Runners On | .327 | 10 | .407 | 51 | .396 | 19 | 0.40 | 111 | 11.04 | 53 | 4.35 | 2 |
| | Bases Empty | .343 | 1 | .435 | 21 | .384 | 9 | 0.84 | 105 | 6.05 | 86 | 4.47 | 1 |
| Chris James | Runners On | .251 | 87 | .372 | 74 | .292 | 112 | 2.51 | 49 | 5.36 | 118 | 11.11 | 48 |
| | Bases Empty | .235 | 85 | .362 | 74 | .271 | 109 | 2.88 | 32 | 4.71 | 110 | 15.29 | 79 |
| Carmelo Martinez | Runners On | .179 | 127 | .338 | 97 | .267 | 125 | 2.76 | 41 | 10.91 | 55 | 17.58 | 104 |
| | Bases Empty | .270 | 43 | .361 | 76 | .346 | 33 | 1.64 | 75 | 10.29 | 34 | 18.38 | 110 |
| Bip Roberts | Runners On | .340 | 7 | .495 | 15 | .400 | 15 | 2.06 | 61 | 9.48 | 69 | 8.62 | 20 |
| | Bases Empty | .284 | 22 | .392 | 52 | .387 | 5 | 0.43 | 116 | 14.02 | 6 | 12.92 | 50 |
| Benito Santiago | Runners On | .230 | 106 | .378 | 72 | .270 | 123 | 3.60 | 24 | 5.00 | 120 | 17.92 | 107 |
| | Bases Empty | .242 | 76 | .396 | 50 | .283 | 99 | 3.33 | 25 | 5.51 | 95 | 18.11 | 109 |
| Garry Templeton | Runners On | .228 | 108 | .297 | 118 | .287 | 115 | 0.50 | 109 | 7.93 | 91 | 13.22 | 65 |
| | Bases Empty | .273 | 36 | .391 | 53 | .285 | 96 | 1.64 | 74 | 1.62 | 131 | 16.18 | 87 |
| Team Average | Runners On | .248 | 10 | .375 | 9 | .322 | 11 | 2.56 | 4 | 9.95 | 6 | 15.50 | 10 |
| | Bases Empty | .253 | 2 | .364 | 4 | .316 | 1 | 1.95 | 7 | 8.26 | 2 | 17.41 | 10 |
| League Average | Runners On | .256 | | .379 | | .330 | | 2.13 | | 9.82 | | 14.66 | |
| | Bases Empty | .240 | | .355 | | .299 | | 2.03 | | 7.43 | | 15.93 | |

## Overall Batting Compared to Late Inning Pressure Situations

| | | BA | Rank | SA | Rank | OBA | Rank | HR % | Rank | BB % | Rank | SO % | Rank | RDI % | Rank |
|---|---|---|---|---|---|---|---|---|---|---|---|---|---|---|---|
| Roberto Alomar | Overall | .295 | 13 | .376 | 64 | .347 | 38 | 1.12 | 95 | 7.55 | 82 | 10.83 | 31 | .270 | 57 |
| | Pressure | .338 | 7 | .363 | 54 | .411 | 7 | 0.00 | 81 | 10.87 | 49 | 14.13 | 56 | .190 | 82 |
| Jack Clark | Overall | .242 | 90 | .459 | 17 | .410 | 2 | 5.71 | 7 | 22.22 | 1 | 24.41 | 129 | .299 | 28 |
| | Pressure | .185 | 110 | .385 | 36 | .379 | 20 | 6.15 | 6 | 24.14 | 1 | 27.59 | 125 | .304 | 36 |
| Tim Flannery | Overall | .231 | -- | .269 | -- | .299 | -- | 0.00 | -- | 8.97 | -- | 13.79 | -- | .194 | -- |
| | Pressure | .370 | -- | .370 | -- | .500 | -- | 0.00 | -- | 20.00 | -- | 5.71 | -- | .200 | 74 |
| Tony Gwynn | Overall | .336 | 2 | .424 | 29 | .389 | 10 | 0.66 | 113 | 8.25 | 70 | 4.42 | 1 | .346 | 6 |
| | Pressure | .338 | 7 | .350 | 61 | .400 | 9 | 0.00 | 81 | 9.68 | 58 | 3.23 | 2 | .409 | 10 |
| Darrin Jackson | Overall | .218 | -- | .329 | -- | .270 | -- | 2.35 | -- | 7.03 | -- | 18.38 | -- | .236 | 89 |
| | Pressure | .172 | -- | .241 | -- | .226 | -- | 0.00 | -- | 6.45 | -- | 25.81 | -- | .250 | -- |
| Chris James | Overall | .243 | 88 | .367 | 71 | .281 | 113 | 2.70 | 35 | 5.04 | 117 | 13.18 | 60 | .259 | 69 |
| | Pressure | .198 | 100 | .284 | 97 | .235 | 117 | 2.47 | 38 | 4.55 | 107 | 14.77 | 64 | .250 | 52 |
| Carmelo Martinez | Overall | .221 | 112 | .348 | 93 | .302 | 96 | 2.25 | 54 | 10.63 | 39 | 17.94 | 106 | .231 | 96 |
| | Pressure | .143 | 125 | .224 | 116 | .236 | 115 | 0.00 | 81 | 10.91 | 48 | 23.64 | 115 | .231 | 64 |
| Bip Roberts | Overall | .301 | 10 | .422 | 31 | .391 | 8 | 0.91 | 105 | 12.66 | 15 | 11.63 | 41 | .286 | 41 |
| | Pressure | .279 | 37 | .349 | 64 | .392 | 12 | 0.00 | 81 | 14.81 | 16 | 12.96 | 41 | .250 | 52 |
| Benito Santiago | Overall | .236 | 98 | .387 | 56 | .277 | 116 | 3.46 | 23 | 5.26 | 114 | 18.02 | 109 | .239 | 86 |
| | Pressure | .303 | 22 | .394 | 33 | .329 | 59 | 1.52 | 70 | 4.17 | 111 | 16.67 | 74 | .300 | 37 |
| Garry Templeton | Overall | .255 | 67 | .354 | 87 | .286 | 106 | 1.19 | 92 | 4.29 | 124 | 14.93 | 79 | .225 | 98 |
| | Pressure | .208 | 92 | .260 | 103 | .256 | 106 | 0.00 | 81 | 5.95 | 93 | 21.43 | 109 | .056 | 130 |
| Team Average | Overall | .251 | 3 | .369 | 5 | .319 | 4 | 2.21 | 7 | 9.02 | 3 | 16.55 | 10 | .245 | 10 |
| | Pressure | .262 | 1 | .336 | 8 | .339 | 1 | 1.07 | 10 | 10.28 | 1 | 18.59 | 10 | .231 | 9 |
| League Average | Overall | .246 | | .365 | | .312 | | 2.07 | | 8.47 | | 15.38 | | .253 | |
| | Pressure | .238 | | .337 | | .308 | | 1.73 | | 8.93 | | 16.78 | | .235 | |

## Additional Miscellaneous Batting Comparisons

| | Grass Surface | | Artificial Surface | | Home Games | | Road Games | | Runners in Scoring Position | | Runners in Scoring Pos and Two Outs | | Leading Off Inning | | Runners on 3B with less than 2 Outs | |
|---|---|---|---|---|---|---|---|---|---|---|---|---|---|---|---|---|
| | BA | Rank | BA | Rank | BA | Rank | BA | Rank | BA | Rank | BA | Rank | OBA | Rank | RDI % | Rank |
| Shawn Abner | .160 | 129 | .375 | -- | .181 | -- | .167 | -- | .200 | -- | .176 | -- | .167 | -- | .875 | 1 |
| Roberto Alomar | .300 | 15 | .283 | 32 | .329 | 6 | .267 | 48 | .250 | 75 | .219 | 72 | .376 | 21 | .613 | 50 |
| Jack Clark | .235 | 82 | .260 | 54 | .232 | 99 | .250 | 68 | .273 | 51 | .222 | 66 | .379 | 17 | .565 | 70 |
| Tim Flannery | .222 | 95 | .250 | -- | .200 | -- | .247 | -- | .242 | -- | .313 | -- | .265 | -- | .400 | -- |
| Tony Gwynn | .325 | 6 | .366 | 1 | .326 | 7 | .345 | 1 | .318 | 12 | .111 | 128 | .419 | 5 | .705 | 16 |
| Darrin Jackson | .209 | 112 | .244 | -- | .193 | -- | .244 | -- | .234 | 90 | .250 | 42 | .279 | -- | .571 | -- |
| Chris James | .246 | 69 | .238 | 94 | .267 | 54 | .224 | 94 | .259 | 66 | .231 | 60 | .275 | 94 | .452 | 121 |
| Carmelo Martinez | .227 | 91 | .203 | -- | .165 | 128 | .267 | 47 | .187 | 122 | .212 | 80 | .343 | 33 | .345 | 141 |
| Mike Pagliarulo | .185 | 121 | .225 | -- | .188 | -- | .203 | -- | .222 | -- | .176 | -- | .375 | -- | .571 | -- |
| Mark Parent | .233 | 84 | .079 | -- | .246 | -- | .139 | -- | .172 | -- | .200 | -- | .455 | -- | .750 | 10 |
| Bip Roberts | .302 | 14 | .298 | 15 | .302 | 22 | .300 | 11 | .281 | 40 | .303 | 20 | .412 | 8 | .500 | 98 |
| Benito Santiago | .243 | 75 | .219 | 114 | .264 | 59 | .212 | 108 | .239 | 86 | .250 | 42 | .302 | 64 | .500 | 98 |
| Garry Templeton | .256 | 63 | .252 | 71 | .259 | 65 | .251 | 67 | .215 | 107 | .170 | 109 | .294 | 69 | .500 | 98 |
| Team Average | .250 | 4 | .252 | 4 | .251 | 6 | .251 | 2 | .230 | 11 | .190 | 12 | .339 | 1 | .557 | 5 |
| League Average | .244 | | .248 | | .251 | | .242 | | .249 | | .222 | | .302 | | .546 | |

## Pitching vs. Left and Right Handed Batters

| | | BA | Rank | SA | Rank | OBA | Rank | HR % | Rank | BB % | Rank | SO % | Rank |
|---|---|---|---|---|---|---|---|---|---|---|---|---|---|
| Andrew Benes | vs. Lefties | .214 | 26 | .359 | 59 | .333 | 71 | 3.05 | 103 | 14.47 | 109 | 21.38 | 13 |
| | vs. Righties | .211 | -- | .339 | -- | .263 | -- | 2.75 | -- | 6.61 | -- | 26.45 | -- |
| Mark Davis | vs. Lefties | .239 | -- | .457 | -- | .321 | -- | 4.35 | -- | 7.41 | -- | 20.37 | -- |
| | vs. Righties | .194 | 12 | .268 | 7 | .261 | 22 | 1.41 | 20 | 8.54 | 81 | 25.63 | 12 |
| Mark Grant | vs. Lefties | .246 | 58 | .347 | 53 | .307 | 45 | 2.01 | 74 | 8.22 | 51 | 12.79 | 70 |
| | vs. Righties | .249 | 73 | .409 | 91 | .300 | 63 | 3.11 | 96 | 5.67 | 27 | 16.60 | 63 |
| Greg W. Harris | vs. Lefties | .196 | 13 | .253 | 9 | .276 | 17 | 0.71 | 20 | 9.49 | 65 | 17.09 | 32 |
| | vs. Righties | .241 | 59 | .358 | 59 | .312 | 76 | 2.83 | 82 | 9.24 | 92 | 21.85 | 30 |
| Bruce Hurst | vs. Lefties | .299 | 103 | .424 | 98 | .357 | 96 | 1.39 | 50 | 8.02 | 44 | 12.35 | 72 |
| | vs. Righties | .225 | 46 | .323 | 30 | .275 | 39 | 1.84 | 43 | 6.40 | 43 | 19.20 | 41 |
| Dennis Rasmussen | vs. Lefties | .248 | 62 | .391 | 80 | .311 | 52 | 3.01 | 102 | 8.72 | 55 | 11.41 | 83 |
| | vs. Righties | .275 | 97 | .406 | 88 | .341 | 93 | 2.45 | 72 | 9.08 | 89 | 10.77 | 102 |
| Calvin Schiraldi | vs. Lefties | .204 | 20 | .294 | 27 | .337 | 78 | 1.49 | 57 | 16.46 | 115 | 12.35 | 72 |
| | vs. Righties | .194 | 13 | .331 | 39 | .293 | 57 | 3.13 | 97 | 12.37 | 110 | 22.04 | 25 |
| Eric Show | vs. Lefties | .269 | 84 | .427 | 100 | .345 | 89 | 1.71 | 66 | 10.23 | 76 | 16.29 | 37 |
| | vs. Righties | .281 | 99 | .444 | 110 | .325 | 87 | 2.81 | 80 | 6.00 | 36 | 11.50 | 96 |
| Walt Terrell | vs. Lefties | .291 | 101 | .398 | 85 | .331 | 68 | 2.05 | 76 | 5.68 | 11 | 10.61 | 91 |
| | vs. Righties | .263 | 89 | .463 | 113 | .294 | 58 | 3.75 | 111 | 4.30 | 16 | 13.67 | 81 |
| Ed Whitson | vs. Lefties | .262 | 78 | .408 | 92 | .305 | 43 | 3.22 | 108 | 6.08 | 14 | 10.50 | 92 |
| | vs. Righties | .198 | 16 | .291 | 17 | .238 | 12 | 1.74 | 39 | 4.04 | 10 | 16.17 | 67 |
| Team Average | vs. Lefties | .253 | 7 | .381 | 11 | .322 | 5 | 2.40 | 12 | 8.92 | 3 | 13.60 | 8 |
| | vs. Righties | .246 | 8 | .373 | 9 | .302 | 5 | 2.45 | 8 | 7.21 | 4 | 16.44 | 6 |
| League Average | vs. Lefties | .252 | | .366 | | .325 | | 1.79 | | 9.48 | | 13.93 | |
| | vs. Righties | .242 | | .365 | | .303 | | 2.29 | | 7.70 | | 16.46 | |

## Pitching with Runners on Base and Bases Empty

| | | BA | Rank | SA | Rank | OBA | Rank | HR % | Rank | BB % | Rank | SO % | Rank |
|---|---|---|---|---|---|---|---|---|---|---|---|---|---|
| Andrew Benes | Runners On | .273 | -- | .455 | -- | .295 | -- | 3.03 | -- | 3.60 | -- | 21.62 | -- |
| | Bases Empty | .170 | 3 | .277 | 11 | .308 | 71 | 2.84 | 100 | 15.98 | 116 | 24.85 | 9 |
| Mark Davis | Runners On | .174 | 2 | .263 | 6 | .248 | 3 | 1.58 | 38 | 9.22 | 54 | 26.73 | 2 |
| | Bases Empty | .236 | 47 | .336 | 40 | .301 | 61 | 2.14 | 66 | 7.19 | 62 | 22.22 | 14 |
| Mark Grant | Runners On | .256 | 70 | .415 | 86 | .318 | 54 | 2.84 | 94 | 8.00 | 32 | 13.00 | 80 |
| | Bases Empty | .242 | 57 | .355 | 67 | .293 | 50 | 2.42 | 82 | 6.02 | 39 | 16.17 | 46 |
| Greg W. Harris | Runners On | .249 | 63 | .324 | 27 | .365 | 98 | 1.16 | 24 | 15.49 | 113 | 15.96 | 44 |
| | Bases Empty | .197 | 14 | .284 | 14 | .246 | 6 | 1.88 | 55 | 5.57 | 31 | 21.11 | 22 |
| Bruce Hurst | Runners On | .236 | 44 | .321 | 26 | .301 | 33 | 1.17 | 26 | 8.31 | 37 | 14.36 | 59 |
| | Bases Empty | .238 | 48 | .350 | 57 | .280 | 33 | 2.14 | 66 | 5.56 | 30 | 20.57 | 26 |
| Dennis Rasmussen | Runners On | .294 | 96 | .446 | 98 | .352 | 84 | 3.63 | 106 | 8.99 | 48 | 10.11 | 98 |
| | Bases Empty | .252 | 83 | .372 | 79 | .323 | 94 | 1.75 | 49 | 9.03 | 89 | 11.51 | 98 |
| Calvin Schiraldi | Runners On | .205 | 10 | .354 | 47 | .326 | 65 | 3.73 | 110 | 14.87 | 112 | 12.82 | 82 |
| | Bases Empty | .195 | 12 | .275 | 9 | .312 | 81 | 1.00 | 22 | 14.53 | 113 | 19.66 | 32 |
| Eric Show | Runners On | .299 | 100 | .500 | 114 | .368 | 101 | 4.27 | 112 | 10.20 | 67 | 15.82 | 45 |
| | Bases Empty | .258 | 88 | .391 | 92 | .313 | 83 | 0.81 | 16 | 7.09 | 60 | 13.06 | 83 |
| Walt Terrell | Runners On | .305 | 104 | .447 | 99 | .320 | 56 | 3.16 | 100 | 2.44 | 1 | 9.76 | 102 |
| | Bases Empty | .259 | 89 | .418 | 109 | .308 | 74 | 2.72 | 97 | 6.67 | 54 | 13.65 | 76 |
| Ed Whitson | Runners On | .219 | 20 | .326 | 28 | .275 | 11 | 1.99 | 58 | 7.49 | 23 | 13.54 | 68 |
| | Bases Empty | .244 | 64 | .380 | 84 | .280 | 34 | 2.96 | 105 | 3.88 | 9 | 12.35 | 89 |
| Team Average | Runners On | .257 | 6 | .388 | 9 | .323 | 5 | 2.50 | 12 | 9.07 | 3 | 14.28 | 8 |
| | Bases Empty | .243 | 8 | .368 | 11 | .300 | 6 | 2.39 | 11 | 7.01 | 3 | 16.08 | 5 |
| League Average | Runners On | .256 | | .379 | | .330 | | 2.13 | | 9.82 | | 14.66 | |
| | Bases Empty | .240 | | .355 | | .299 | | 2.03 | | 7.43 | | 15.93 | |

## Overall Pitching Compared to Late Inning Pressure Situations

| | | BA | Rank | SA | Rank | OBA | Rank | HR % | Rank | BB % | Rank | SO % | Rank |
|---|---|---|---|---|---|---|---|---|---|---|---|---|---|
| Andrew Benes | Overall | .213 | 19 | .350 | 53 | .303 | 51 | 2.92 | 108 | 11.07 | 105 | 23.57 | 10 |
| | Pressure | .294 | -- | .353 | -- | .368 | -- | 0.00 | -- | 9.52 | -- | 14.29 | -- |
| Pat Clements | Overall | .267 | -- | .390 | -- | .333 | -- | 2.74 | -- | 8.98 | -- | 10.78 | -- |
| | Pressure | .279 | 91 | .488 | 106 | .326 | 74 | 6.98 | 116 | 6.12 | 32 | 10.20 | 99 |
| Mark Davis | Overall | .200 | 9 | .294 | 7 | .270 | 11 | 1.82 | 46 | 8.38 | 58 | 24.86 | 5 |
| | Pressure | .189 | 18 | .283 | 29 | .250 | 17 | 2.15 | 78 | 6.95 | 37 | 24.71 | 6 |
| Mark Grant | Overall | .248 | 63 | .380 | 74 | .304 | 55 | 2.59 | 96 | 6.87 | 31 | 14.81 | 61 |
| | Pressure | .248 | 68 | .362 | 77 | .313 | 57 | 2.86 | 96 | 7.56 | 47 | 13.45 | 75 |
| Greg W. Harris | Overall | .215 | 22 | .298 | 9 | .291 | 36 | 1.62 | 36 | 9.39 | 80 | 19.13 | 28 |
| | Pressure | .214 | 38 | .264 | 16 | .296 | 47 | 1.00 | 37 | 9.61 | 67 | 18.78 | 35 |
| Bruce Hurst | Overall | .237 | 47 | .339 | 42 | .288 | 32 | 1.77 | 43 | 6.67 | 25 | 18.08 | 36 |
| | Pressure | .210 | 33 | .306 | 45 | .246 | 15 | 2.42 | 86 | 4.51 | 17 | 16.54 | 49 |
| Dave Leiper | Overall | .333 | -- | .483 | -- | .437 | -- | 1.67 | -- | 13.99 | -- | 4.90 | -- |
| | Pressure | .256 | 77 | .385 | 88 | .396 | 106 | 2.56 | 89 | 14.58 | 108 | 6.25 | 112 |
| Dennis Rasmussen | Overall | .270 | 93 | .403 | 92 | .335 | 92 | 2.56 | 95 | 9.01 | 74 | 10.89 | 101 |
| | Pressure | .250 | 70 | .361 | 74 | .400 | 107 | 2.78 | 92 | 18.75 | 117 | 8.33 | 106 |
| Calvin Schiraldi | Overall | .199 | 8 | .310 | 15 | .319 | 72 | 2.22 | 73 | 14.69 | 116 | 16.55 | 48 |
| | Pressure | .215 | 39 | .376 | 85 | .335 | 82 | 3.36 | 102 | 15.17 | 112 | 17.42 | 45 |
| Eric Show | Overall | .274 | 99 | .434 | 111 | .336 | 93 | 2.18 | 70 | 8.41 | 59 | 14.22 | 66 |
| | Pressure | .222 | 43 | .241 | 10 | .323 | 71 | 0.00 | 1 | 12.70 | 96 | 9.52 | 104 |
| Walt Terrell | Overall | .277 | 101 | .430 | 108 | .313 | 63 | 2.89 | 107 | 5.00 | 4 | 12.12 | 88 |
| | Pressure | .262 | 80 | .492 | 108 | .262 | 24 | 6.15 | 115 | 0.00 | 1 | 15.38 | 58 |
| Ed Whitson | Overall | .235 | 45 | .360 | 66 | .278 | 22 | 2.62 | 97 | 5.25 | 12 | 12.80 | 82 |
| | Pressure | .212 | 35 | .294 | 34 | .239 | 10 | 1.18 | 42 | 3.41 | 11 | 17.05 | 47 |
| Team Average | Overall | .249 | 8 | .376 | 10 | .310 | 6 | 2.43 | 12 | 7.89 | 3 | 15.31 | 7 |
| | Pressure | .224 | 2 | .330 | 4 | .290 | 2 | 2.55 | 12 | 7.80 | 1 | 17.00 | 7 |
| League Average | Overall | .246 | | .365 | | .312 | | 2.07 | | 8.47 | | 15.38 | |
| | Pressure | .235 | | .336 | | .309 | | 1.77 | | 9.31 | | 16.92 | |

### Additional Miscellaneous Pitching Comparisons

| | Grass Surface | | Artificial Surface | | Home Games | | Road Games | | Runners in Scoring Position | | Runners in Scoring Pos and Two Outs | | Leading Off Inning | |
|---|---|---|---|---|---|---|---|---|---|---|---|---|---|---|
| | BA | Rank | BA | Rank | BA | Rank | BA | Rank | BA | Rank | BA | Rank | OBA | Rank |
| Andrew Benes | .220 | 34 | .194 | -- | .232 | 45 | .184 | -- | .283 | -- | .273 | -- | .257 | 21 |
| Pat Clements | .258 | 82 | .308 | -- | .256 | -- | .279 | -- | .290 | -- | .300 | -- | .237 | -- |
| Mark Davis | .202 | 10 | .195 | 9 | .177 | 6 | .223 | 27 | .123 | 1 | .094 | 3 | .364 | 107 |
| Mark Grant | .261 | 85 | .216 | 20 | .254 | 72 | .242 | 48 | .206 | 26 | .205 | 53 | .312 | 76 |
| Greg W. Harris | .204 | 14 | .246 | 58 | .210 | 26 | .219 | 23 | .224 | 37 | .164 | 22 | .180 | 2 |
| Bruce Hurst | .233 | 49 | .254 | 68 | .226 | 38 | .251 | 59 | .253 | 68 | .257 | 86 | .294 | 53 |
| Dave Leiper | .330 | 114 | .353 | -- | .281 | -- | .393 | -- | .250 | -- | .222 | -- | .500 | -- |
| Dennis Rasmussen | .267 | 89 | .281 | 95 | .246 | 62 | .285 | 100 | .282 | 86 | .292 | 96 | .387 | 114 |
| Calvin Schiraldi | .212 | 27 | .165 | 3 | .227 | 41 | .166 | 2 | .169 | 7 | .152 | 18 | .304 | 66 |
| Don Schulze | .352 | 116 | .000 | -- | .351 | -- | .355 | -- | .313 | -- | .231 | -- | .577 | -- |
| Eric Show | .279 | 99 | .267 | 79 | .287 | 104 | .260 | 79 | .298 | 97 | .294 | 98 | .304 | 64 |
| Walt Terrell | .250 | 71 | .324 | 112 | .266 | 89 | .285 | 99 | .333 | 113 | .264 | 91 | .279 | 41 |
| Ed Whitson | .242 | 59 | .215 | 18 | .234 | 48 | .237 | 41 | .231 | 48 | .224 | 65 | .270 | 32 |
| Team Average | .249 | 8 | .247 | 6 | .245 | 8 | .252 | 8 | .249 | 6 | .237 | 10 | .308 | 8 |
| League Average | .244 | | .248 | | .242 | | .251 | | .249 | | .222 | | .302 | |

# SAN FRANCISCO GIANTS

- **The Giants' magic number "15".**
- **Is pitching *really* 75 percent of baseball?**

The Giants' route to the National League West division championship last season may best be described not as a journey but as a survival course. Every team can be expected to encounter injuries during a 162–game season, but the extent to which injuries attacked one portion of the Giants—their pitching staff—was extraordinary for any team. Seven pitchers spent time on the disabled list during the season, with three of them making two separate trips onto the list:

| Pitcher | Dates on Disabled List (injury) |
|---|---|
| Mike Krukow | March 19–April 28 (right shoulder) |
| Karl Best | March 21–end of season (right elbow) |
| Dave Dravecky | March 21–Aug. 10 (left shoulder) |
| Kelly Downs | May 2–Aug. 13 (right shoulder) |
| Krukow | June 5–end of season (right shoulder) |
| Atlee Hammaker | June 19–July 16 (left bicep) |
| Scott Garrelts | June 30–July 15 (left hamstring) |
| Rick Reuschel | July 30–Aug. 16 (right groin) |
| Hammaker | Aug. 3–Sept. 21 (left knee) |
| Dravecky | Aug. 16–end of season (left arm) |

Roger Craig was forced to scramble throughout the season in order to piece together a presentation of healthy starting pitchers. We hesitate to used the word "rotation," since that term implies a regularity that the Giants' sequence of starting pitchers never exhibited.

Throughout baseball history, the number 15 has represented various totals. It has been a league-leading total for triples (such as Andy Van Slyke had in 1988) or for sacrifice bunts (Jim Gilliam in 1962). Tony Lazzeri drove in a record 15 runs in two consecutive games in 1936, and Jim Perry allowed a record 15 home runs *to one team* (the Yankees) in 1960. Shortstop Rick Burleson had 15 assists in an extra-inning game in 1982, and outfielder Happy Felsch started 15 double plays in 1919.

But never before had 15 represented the number of starting pitchers used by a team that won a pennant, or even a division title. Only three other teams used as many starting pitchers in 1989, and none came close to the .500 mark, let alone first place: the Yankees (74–87) used 16, and the Phillies (67–95) and the Tigers (59–103) each used fifteen. In the 1980s, no first-place finisher had even used more than twelve.

The Giants went right to the top not only of the list for the '80s, but of the all-time list of starting pitchers used by a first-place finisher:

| Year | Team | Starters | Starters W–L | Relief W–L |
|---|---|---|---|---|
| 1989 | Giants | 15 | 68–49 | 24–21 |
| 1922 | Giants | 14 | 73–50 | 20–11 |
| 1930 | Cardinals | 14 | 73–45 | 19–17 |
| 1947 | Yankees | 14 | 74–45 | 23–12 |
| 1951 | Yankees | 14 | 80–41 | 18–15 |
| 1952 | Yankees | 14 | 77–44 | 18–15 |
| 1952 | Dodgers | 14 | 58–45 | 38–12 |

The competition looks close in this chart, but that's a deception. In the case of each of the six pennant winners who used 14 different starters, that total was inflated by late-season call-ups and acquistions from other clubs—pitchers who had not started a game before September 1. But not in the Giants' case: They didn't pad their total with rookies in September. When Dave Dravecky made his first start of the season on August 10, he became the 15th and last different starter that Roger Craig used.

With the starting staff in constant disarray, Craig was forced to go to the bullpen early and often. He cajoled 502 1/3 innings out of his relief pitchers last season, a total that was surpassed only by a couple of last-place teams, the Phillies (513) and the White Sox (512). San Francisco's total of relief innings was the fourth-highest in baseball history for a team that won a pennant or division title, and it gave Craig two of the top four positions on that all-time list:

| Year | Team | Starters' Innings | Relievers' Innings |
|---|---|---|---|
| 1982 | Braves | 935.2 | 527.1 |
| 1987 | Giants | 944.1 | 526.2 |
| 1966 | Orioles | 953.1 | 513.0 |
| 1989 | Giants | 954.2 | 502.1 |
| 1984 | Tigers | 964.2 | 499.1 |
| 1987 | Cardinals | 973.1 | 492.2 |
| 1984 | Padres | 980.2 | 479.2 |
| 1979 | Pirates | 1020.1 | 472.1 |
| 1969 | Twins | 1026.2 | 471.0 |
| 1982 | Angels | 999.0 | 465.0 |

The pruning of the pitching staff began in the off-season as Dravecky retired and Bob Knepper and Mike Krukow were permitted to become free agents. Of the 15 pitchers who started for the Giants last year, only nine were listed on the team's 40–player roster as 1990 began. But what happens next is anybody's guess.

*Analyst* fans know by now that a favorite *modus operandi* of ours is to take a set of circumstances that applies to a given player or team, and investigate how players or teams of the past coped in similar situations. When we apply that technique in this case, however, we come away with what can best be described as dueling indicators. Of the six teams that used 14 different starting pitchers, five repeated as pennant winners the following year; but of the nine other teams that finished in first place with high totals of relief innings, only one (the 1969 Twins) repeated the next year. As a public service, we offer both assessments: Just look back to this page in September, and choose the one that applies.

Last season, San Francisco became the 33d team since the turn of the century to play an entire regular season without losing four consecutive games. (Unfortunately, as the Giants found out in the World Series, that charm did not extend beyond the confines of the National League.) Six times the Giants took the field after three straight losses, and six times they left the field with a one-game winning streak.

We're all familiar with the traditional thinking on this topic: Good pitching prevents long losing streaks. To the extent that *(a)* good pitching usually contributes to a winning team, and *(b)* a winning team, by definition, doesn't experience too many long losing streaks, the axiom holds up. The fact that only two National League teams, the Dodgers and the Mets, allowed fewer runs than the Giants did last season seems to support the theory further. But the Giants actually ranked higher in runs scored (second, just three runs behind the Cubs) than in runs allowed. And, as a matter of fact, pitching has no greater an effect on winning streaks than hitting does.

Of the 33 teams not to lose more than three games in a row, 13 ranked higher in their leagues in offense (as measured by runs scored) than in defense (runs allowed); 11 had the same rank in both; only nine ranked higher in pitching. Twelve allowed the fewest runs in their leagues, while 16 led their leagues in runs scored.

It's strange that in a game in which every run that's scored corresponds with a run allowed, pitching has assumed a mythic reputation as the more important element in the offense–defense equation. Granted, an individual pitcher is often many times more important to the outcome of a *particular* game than a typical position player would be. Still, how could anyone suggest that pitching is any more, or less, than 50 percent of the game? This question of streak prevention provides another example that hitting and pitching are, of course, equally important.

For the jingoists, though, pitching is 75 percent of the game. Or is it 90 percent? Or 83.2 percent? With all due respect to Connie Mack, John McGraw, and whoever else might have fathered those estimates, they always were wrong, are wrong now, and will be wrong into the future. Our goal here is a modest one: to eradicate the pitching-is–75–percent-of-the-game mentality that still creeps into too many broadcasts, columns, and discussions about baseball. We would hope for an outright ban on such phrases by the time we move into the next century.

Since civil libertarians are unlikely to allow passage of our proposed constitutional amendment on the subject (something about the First Amendment, they say), we will restrict ourselves to an education campaign for the time being, and hope for voluntary compliance. The little study that we did on avoiding losing streaks is one element in this campaign. Here's another:

We looked at every team since 1901 that either scored the most runs in its league or allowed the fewest runs in its league, and then looked to the final standings each season to see how these teams made out. If baseball were really 75 percent pitching (or more), we could expect to see that teams that allowed the fewest runs in their league would be far more successful over the course of the years than teams that led in runs scored. If that were the case, we could expect three or four times as many first-place finishes from the best-pitching teams than from the best-hitting teams.

The results are summarized here, with the chart indicating the number of teams that finished in first place after leading their league in runs scored or runs allowed:

| | A.L. | N.L. | Total |
|---|---|---|---|
| First-place finishes, most runs scored | 51 | 44 | 95 |
| First-place finishes, fewest runs allowed | 45 | 46 | 91 |

The totals show that for the two leagues combined, 53 percent of the best-hitting teams have finished in first place, compared to 51 percent of the best-pitching teams. In other words, with almost a century's worth of data behind us, teams that have led their league in scoring runs have actually won slightly more pennants and division titles than teams that have led their league in run prevention.

Please keep this fact in mind as we implement Phase I of our 50/50 campaign. We're not yet taking names, but we'll be carefully monitoring the voluntary compliance throughout the 1990 season. If we don't get the cooperation that we're hoping for, then we'll have to get rough in next year's book.

## WON-LOST RECORD BY STARTING POSITION

| SAN FRANCISCO 92-70 | C | 1B | 2B | 3B | SS | LF | CF | RF | P | Leadoff | Relief | Starts |
|---|---|---|---|---|---|---|---|---|---|---|---|---|
| Bill Bathe | - | - | - | - | - | - | - | - | - | - | - | - |
| Steve Bedrosian | - | - | - | - | - | - | - | - | - | - | 26-14 | - |
| Mike Benjamin | - | - | - | - | - | - | - | - | - | - | - | - |
| Jeff Brantley | - | - | - | - | - | - | - | - | 0-1 | - | 29-29 | 0-1 |
| Bob Brenly | 4-2 | - | - | - | - | - | - | - | - | - | - | 4-2 |
| Brett Butler | - | - | - | - | - | - | 87-62 | - | - | 87-62 | - | 87-62 |
| Ernie Camacho | - | - | - | - | - | - | - | - | - | - | 8-5 | - |
| Will Clark | - | 90-67 | - | - | - | - | - | - | - | - | - | 90-67 |
| Dennis Cook | - | - | - | - | - | - | - | - | 1-1 | - | - | 1-1 |
| Kelly Downs | - | - | - | - | - | - | - | - | 5-10 | - | 1-2 | 5-10 |
| Dave Dravecky | - | - | - | - | - | - | - | - | 2-0 | - | - | 2-0 |
| Scott Garrelts | - | - | - | - | - | - | - | - | 19-10 | - | 0-1 | 19-10 |
| Rich Gossage | - | - | - | - | - | - | - | - | - | - | 10-21 | - |
| Atlee Hammaker | - | - | - | - | - | - | - | - | 5-4 | - | 8-11 | 5-4 |
| Charlie Hayes | - | - | - | 0-1 | - | - | - | - | - | - | - | 0-1 |
| Tracy Jones | - | - | - | - | - | 1-2 | 1-3 | 10-3 | - | 1-3 | - | 12-8 |
| Ed Jurak | - | 0-1 | 0-1 | 3-1 | - | - | - | - | - | - | - | 3-3 |
| Terry Kennedy | 54-48 | - | - | - | - | - | - | - | - | - | - | 54-48 |
| Bob Knepper | - | - | - | - | - | - | - | - | 3-3 | - | 2-5 | 3-3 |
| Mike Krukow | - | - | - | - | - | - | - | - | 5-3 | - | - | 5-3 |
| Mike LaCoss | - | - | - | - | - | - | - | - | 10-8 | - | 16-11 | 10-8 |
| Mike Laga | - | 0-1 | - | - | - | - | - | - | - | - | - | 0-1 |
| Craig Lefferts | - | - | - | - | - | - | - | - | - | - | 44-26 | - |
| Greg Litton | - | - | 3-2 | 14-5 | - | 0-1 | - | 0-1 | - | - | - | 17-9 |
| Candy Maldonado | - | - | - | - | - | - | - | 42-41 | - | - | - | 42-41 |
| Kirt Manwaring | 34-20 | - | - | - | - | - | - | - | - | - | - | 34-20 |
| Randy McCament | - | - | - | - | - | - | - | - | - | - | 7-18 | - |
| Kevin Mitchell | - | - | - | 0-1 | - | 85-62 | - | - | - | - | - | 85-63 |
| Terry Mulholland | - | - | - | - | - | - | - | - | 0-1 | - | 3-1 | 0-1 |
| Donell Nixon | - | - | - | - | - | 6-3 | 4-3 | 10-5 | - | 4-3 | - | 20-11 |
| Ken Oberkfell | - | 2-1 | 1-2 | 6-2 | - | - | - | - | - | - | - | 9-5 |
| Joe Price | - | - | - | - | - | - | - | - | 1-0 | - | 2-4 | 1-0 |
| Rick Reuschel | - | - | - | - | - | - | - | - | 21-11 | - | - | 21-11 |
| Ernest Riles | - | - | 3-4 | 36-31 | - | - | - | 0-1 | - | - | - | 39-36 |
| Don Robinson | - | - | - | - | - | - | - | - | 18-14 | - | 0-2 | 18-14 |
| Pat Sheridan | - | - | - | - | - | 0-2 | 0-2 | 28-17 | - | 0-2 | - | 28-21 |
| Chris Speier | - | - | 1-1 | - | 0-2 | - | - | - | - | - | - | 1-3 |
| James Steels | - | - | - | - | - | - | - | - | - | - | - | - |
| Russ Swan | - | - | - | - | - | - | - | - | 0-2 | - | - | 0-2 |
| Stuart Tate | - | - | - | - | - | - | - | - | - | - | 1-1 | - |
| Rob Thompson | - | - | 84-60 | - | - | - | - | - | - | - | - | 84-60 |
| Jose Uribe | - | - | - | - | 85-61 | - | - | - | - | - | - | 85-61 |
| Jim Weaver | - | - | - | - | - | - | - | 2-2 | - | - | - | 2-2 |
| Matt Williams | - | - | - | 33-29 | 7-7 | - | - | - | - | - | - | 40-36 |
| Trevor Wilson | - | - | - | - | - | - | - | - | 2-2 | - | 4-6 | 2-2 |

## Batting vs. Left and Right Handed Pitchers

| | | BA | Rank | SA | Rank | OBA | Rank | HR % | Rank | BB % | Rank | SO % | Rank |
|---|---|---|---|---|---|---|---|---|---|---|---|---|---|
| Brett Butler | vs. Lefties | .280 | 48 | .350 | 86 | .353 | 46 | 0.50 | 108 | 9.61 | 53 | 14.85 | 84 |
| | vs. Righties | .284 | 29 | .355 | 78 | .347 | 34 | 0.76 | 107 | 8.35 | 62 | 7.90 | 14 |
| Will Clark | vs. Lefties | .321 | 13 | .512 | 13 | .371 | 29 | 3.72 | 23 | 6.25 | 104 | 15.83 | 89 |
| | vs. Righties | .340 | 3 | .566 | 5 | .428 | 2 | 4.02 | 19 | 13.56 | 10 | 14.94 | 76 |
| Terry Kennedy | vs. Lefties | .154 | -- | .205 | -- | .233 | -- | 0.00 | -- | 9.09 | -- | 18.18 | -- |
| | vs. Righties | .250 | 63 | .339 | 92 | .315 | 64 | 1.58 | 73 | 8.83 | 56 | 13.68 | 61 |
| Greg Litton | vs. Lefties | .277 | 54 | .485 | 21 | .305 | 93 | 3.96 | 21 | 3.74 | 128 | 18.69 | 118 |
| | vs. Righties | .190 | -- | .238 | -- | .261 | -- | 0.00 | -- | 6.25 | -- | 18.75 | -- |
| Candy Maldonado | vs. Lefties | .211 | 110 | .313 | 104 | .310 | 89 | 1.36 | 81 | 11.70 | 28 | 14.04 | 80 |
| | vs. Righties | .222 | 100 | .399 | 48 | .286 | 97 | 3.54 | 26 | 7.80 | 78 | 20.64 | 110 |
| Kirt Manwaring | vs. Lefties | .205 | 116 | .235 | 124 | .271 | 117 | 0.00 | 112 | 6.16 | 106 | 10.27 | 38 |
| | vs. Righties | .221 | -- | .279 | -- | .250 | -- | 0.00 | -- | 2.60 | -- | 16.88 | -- |
| Kevin Mitchell | vs. Lefties | .304 | 24 | .725 | 1 | .426 | 6 | 11.11 | 1 | 17.22 | 4 | 12.44 | 61 |
| | vs. Righties | .285 | 28 | .594 | 2 | .369 | 20 | 7.53 | 3 | 11.83 | 25 | 20.65 | 111 |
| Donell Nixon | vs. Lefties | .241 | 92 | .265 | 118 | .308 | 91 | 0.00 | 112 | 8.79 | 61 | 16.48 | 97 |
| | vs. Righties | .289 | -- | .325 | -- | .314 | -- | 1.20 | -- | 3.49 | -- | 17.44 | -- |
| Ken Oberkfell | vs. Lefties | .095 | -- | .095 | -- | .136 | -- | 0.00 | -- | 4.55 | -- | 4.55 | -- |
| | vs. Righties | .296 | 20 | .400 | 46 | .342 | 37 | 1.48 | 78 | 5.96 | 100 | 5.96 | 7 |
| Ernest Riles | vs. Lefties | .179 | -- | .282 | -- | .256 | -- | 0.00 | -- | 9.09 | -- | 27.27 | -- |
| | vs. Righties | .293 | 22 | .422 | 30 | .352 | 31 | 2.66 | 43 | 8.19 | 68 | 12.97 | 57 |
| Pat Sheridan | vs. Lefties | .077 | -- | .077 | -- | .077 | -- | 0.00 | -- | 0.00 | -- | 53.85 | -- |
| | vs. Righties | .216 | 110 | .351 | 81 | .280 | 103 | 2.03 | 64 | 8.02 | 72 | 23.46 | 123 |
| Rob Thompson | vs. Lefties | .304 | 23 | .505 | 15 | .378 | 19 | 2.58 | 48 | 9.22 | 57 | 16.13 | 91 |
| | vs. Righties | .207 | 118 | .343 | 87 | .289 | 94 | 2.27 | 56 | 7.69 | 79 | 24.32 | 125 |
| Jose Uribe | vs. Lefties | .213 | 109 | .253 | 120 | .269 | 118 | 0.00 | 112 | 7.60 | 81 | 13.45 | 74 |
| | vs. Righties | .224 | 98 | .294 | 116 | .275 | 106 | 0.33 | 118 | 6.44 | 92 | 15.64 | 84 |
| Matt Williams | vs. Lefties | .264 | 72 | .644 | 3 | .330 | 70 | 10.34 | 2 | 9.28 | 56 | 13.40 | 72 |
| | vs. Righties | .176 | 131 | .376 | 64 | .202 | 132 | 4.39 | 13 | 2.34 | 131 | 27.57 | 130 |
| Team Average | vs. Lefties | .248 | 7 | .391 | 3 | .320 | 5 | 2.65 | 1 | 8.90 | 7 | 16.21 | 10 |
| | vs. Righties | .250 | 3 | .389 | 1 | .314 | 2 | 2.54 | 2 | 7.95 | 9 | 18.08 | 12 |
| League Average | vs. Lefties | .251 | | .371 | | .320 | | 2.06 | | 8.85 | | 14.80 | |
| | vs. Righties | .244 | | .362 | | .309 | | 2.08 | | 8.27 | | 15.67 | |

## Batting with Runners on Base and Bases Empty

| | | BA | Rank | SA | Rank | OBA | Rank | HR % | Rank | BB % | Rank | SO % | Rank |
|---|---|---|---|---|---|---|---|---|---|---|---|---|---|
| Brett Butler | Runners On | .292 | 33 | .345 | 93 | .367 | 32 | 0.00 | 112 | 10.53 | 60 | 9.57 | 29 |
| | Bases Empty | .279 | 30 | .357 | 80 | .341 | 38 | 0.95 | 98 | 7.99 | 61 | 10.58 | 27 |
| Will Clark | Runners On | .355 | 4 | .629 | 3 | .432 | 6 | 5.02 | 12 | 12.99 | 31 | 14.94 | 86 |
| | Bases Empty | .316 | 7 | .480 | 9 | .387 | 7 | 3.04 | 28 | 9.26 | 43 | 15.53 | 82 |
| Terry Kennedy | Runners On | .250 | 88 | .309 | 114 | .346 | 54 | 0.74 | 102 | 12.96 | 32 | 16.67 | 96 |
| | Bases Empty | .233 | 88 | .333 | 95 | .279 | 104 | 1.83 | 68 | 6.01 | 89 | 12.45 | 47 |
| Candy Maldonado | Runners On | .236 | 101 | .363 | 85 | .313 | 97 | 1.27 | 84 | 9.44 | 71 | 16.11 | 94 |
| | Bases Empty | .202 | 121 | .362 | 75 | .282 | 101 | 3.72 | 20 | 9.57 | 41 | 19.14 | 113 |
| Kirt Manwaring | Runners On | .268 | 62 | .310 | 113 | .338 | 69 | 0.00 | 112 | 5.75 | 110 | 9.20 | 25 |
| | Bases Empty | .178 | 129 | .217 | 130 | .221 | 131 | 0.00 | 122 | 4.41 | 111 | 14.71 | 70 |
| Kevin Mitchell | Runners On | .278 | 43 | .573 | 6 | .404 | 11 | 7.64 | 3 | 17.73 | 9 | 18.28 | 110 |
| | Bases Empty | .306 | 9 | .706 | 1 | .366 | 14 | 9.80 | 1 | 8.24 | 59 | 17.56 | 101 |
| Ernest Riles | Runners On | .263 | 68 | .456 | 26 | .358 | 44 | 4.39 | 19 | 12.32 | 39 | 11.59 | 51 |
| | Bases Empty | .287 | 20 | .372 | 70 | .327 | 48 | 1.06 | 97 | 5.53 | 94 | 17.09 | 97 |
| Rob Thompson | Runners On | .256 | 80 | .435 | 34 | .336 | 71 | 2.69 | 42 | 7.34 | 96 | 20.08 | 117 |
| | Bases Empty | .231 | 91 | .377 | 65 | .310 | 69 | 2.16 | 56 | 8.86 | 48 | 22.44 | 123 |
| Jose Uribe | Runners On | .235 | 102 | .267 | 127 | .316 | 93 | 0.53 | 108 | 10.86 | 56 | 14.48 | 81 |
| | Bases Empty | .211 | 111 | .289 | 114 | .239 | 127 | 0.00 | 122 | 3.62 | 119 | 15.22 | 76 |
| Matt Williams | Runners On | .172 | 129 | .463 | 24 | .231 | 128 | 7.46 | 4 | 6.76 | 104 | 20.27 | 119 |
| | Bases Empty | .228 | 94 | .449 | 18 | .252 | 121 | 5.06 | 13 | 2.45 | 128 | 25.77 | 129 |
| Team Average | Runners On | .256 | 6 | .407 | 1 | .335 | 3 | 2.92 | 1 | 10.13 | 4 | 16.75 | 12 |
| | Bases Empty | .245 | 4 | .378 | 3 | .301 | 5 | 2.34 | 4 | 6.84 | 10 | 17.98 | 12 |
| League Average | Runners On | .256 | | .379 | | .330 | | 2.13 | | 9.82 | | 14.66 | |
| | Bases Empty | .240 | | .355 | | .299 | | 2.03 | | 7.43 | | 15.93 | |

## Overall Batting Compared to Late Inning Pressure Situations

| | | BA | Rank | SA | Rank | OBA | Rank | HR % | Rank | BB % | Rank | SO % | Rank | RDI % | Rank |
|---|---|---|---|---|---|---|---|---|---|---|---|---|---|---|---|
| Brett Butler | Overall | .283 | 27 | .354 | 88 | .349 | 36 | 0.67 | 112 | 8.78 | 59 | 10.27 | 28 | .254 | 72 |
| | Pressure | .289 | 28 | .361 | 56 | .352 | 39 | 1.20 | 74 | 8.60 | 68 | 13.98 | 54 | .263 | 50 |
| Will Clark | Overall | .333 | 3 | .546 | 3 | .407 | 3 | 3.91 | 16 | 10.96 | 35 | 15.26 | 85 | .392 | 3 |
| | Pressure | .309 | 21 | .593 | 2 | .387 | 16 | 6.17 | 4 | 10.75 | 51 | 19.35 | 100 | .409 | 10 |
| Terry Kennedy | Overall | .239 | 92 | .324 | 110 | .306 | 89 | 1.41 | 84 | 8.86 | 57 | 14.18 | 72 | .280 | 48 |
| | Pressure | .217 | 86 | .326 | 77 | .357 | 31 | 2.17 | 52 | 17.54 | 7 | 14.04 | 55 | .300 | 37 |
| Candy Maldonado | Overall | .217 | 116 | .362 | 76 | .296 | 100 | 2.61 | 39 | 9.51 | 51 | 17.74 | 103 | .217 | 104 |
| | Pressure | .255 | 50 | .400 | 29 | .328 | 61 | 1.82 | 60 | 9.84 | 57 | 19.67 | 102 | .176 | 91 |
| Kirt Manwaring | Overall | .210 | 121 | .250 | 129 | .264 | 124 | 0.00 | 127 | 4.93 | 118 | 12.56 | 52 | .298 | 30 |
| | Pressure | .091 | -- | .091 | -- | .200 | -- | 0.00 | -- | 11.54 | -- | 7.69 | -- | .000 | -- |
| Kevin Mitchell | Overall | .291 | 17 | .635 | 1 | .388 | 11 | 8.66 | 1 | 13.59 | 10 | 17.97 | 107 | .314 | 20 |
| | Pressure | .274 | 39 | .507 | 8 | .385 | 17 | 5.48 | 8 | 15.38 | 12 | 19.78 | 103 | .583 | 1 |
| Donell Nixon | Overall | .265 | -- | .295 | -- | .311 | -- | 0.60 | -- | 6.21 | -- | 16.95 | -- | .280 | -- |
| | Pressure | .120 | -- | .120 | -- | .120 | -- | 0.00 | -- | 0.00 | -- | 32.00 | -- | .167 | 94 |
| Ken Oberkfell | Overall | .269 | -- | .359 | -- | .316 | -- | 1.28 | -- | 5.78 | -- | 5.78 | -- | .286 | -- |
| | Pressure | .349 | 4 | .395 | 32 | .391 | 13 | 0.00 | 81 | 4.26 | 110 | 6.38 | 9 | .250 | 52 |
| Ernest Riles | Overall | .278 | 32 | .404 | 43 | .339 | 44 | 2.32 | 51 | 8.31 | 68 | 14.84 | 77 | .302 | 27 |
| | Pressure | .333 | 10 | .431 | 24 | .393 | 11 | 1.96 | 56 | 8.93 | 65 | 17.86 | 89 | .333 | 22 |
| Rob Thompson | Overall | .241 | 91 | .400 | 47 | .321 | 64 | 2.38 | 46 | 8.23 | 72 | 21.45 | 124 | .167 | 129 |
| | Pressure | .254 | 52 | .437 | 23 | .329 | 58 | 4.23 | 16 | 10.00 | 55 | 31.25 | 130 | .200 | 74 |
| Jose Uribe | Overall | .221 | 113 | .280 | 123 | .273 | 121 | 0.22 | 125 | 6.84 | 92 | 14.89 | 78 | .231 | 94 |
| | Pressure | .190 | 108 | .238 | 110 | .261 | 101 | 0.00 | 81 | 8.16 | 78 | 16.33 | 72 | .091 | 126 |
| Matt Williams | Overall | .202 | 125 | .455 | 19 | .242 | 127 | 6.16 | 4 | 4.50 | 120 | 23.15 | 127 | .200 | 119 |
| | Pressure | .176 | -- | .235 | -- | .243 | -- | 0.00 | -- | 7.89 | -- | 18.42 | -- | .100 | 124 |
| Team Average | Overall | .250 | 4 | .390 | 1 | .316 | 5 | 2.58 | 2 | 8.27 | 7 | 17.45 | 12 | .254 | 4 |
| | Pressure | .253 | 2 | .378 | 1 | .323 | 3 | 2.34 | 3 | 8.97 | 7 | 19.66 | 11 | .256 | 2 |
| League Average | Overall | .246 | | .365 | | .312 | | 2.07 | | 8.47 | | 15.38 | | .253 | |
| | Pressure | .238 | | .337 | | .308 | | 1.73 | | 8.93 | | 16.78 | | .235 | |

## Additional Miscellaneous Batting Comparisons

| | Grass Surface | | Artificial Surface | | Home Games | | Road Games | | Runners in Scoring Position | | Runners in Scoring Pos and Two Outs | | Leading Off Inning | | Runners on 3B with less than 2 Outs | |
|---|---|---|---|---|---|---|---|---|---|---|---|---|---|---|---|---|
| | BA | Rank | BA | Rank | BA | Rank | BA | Rank | BA | Rank | BA | Rank | OBA | Rank | RDI % | Rank |
| Brett Butler | .288 | 28 | .268 | 41 | .304 | 19 | .262 | 54 | .250 | 75 | .261 | 35 | .338 | 37 | .565 | 70 |
| Will Clark | .339 | 3 | .319 | 4 | .325 | 8 | .341 | 2 | .389 | 3 | .435 | 1 | .395 | 12 | .590 | 58 |
| Terry Kennedy | .236 | 80 | .248 | 81 | .267 | 53 | .213 | 107 | .282 | 39 | .200 | 89 | .286 | 78 | .769 | 6 |
| Greg Litton | .269 | 46 | .200 | -- | .324 | -- | .174 | -- | .293 | -- | .111 | -- | .471 | -- | .429 | -- |
| Candy Maldonado | .215 | 104 | .223 | 112 | .199 | 121 | .233 | 87 | .202 | 114 | .196 | 93 | .286 | 78 | .526 | 93 |
| Kirt Manwaring | .231 | 86 | .125 | -- | .219 | 112 | .202 | 117 | .277 | 42 | .263 | -- | .204 | 130 | .538 | 86 |
| Kevin Mitchell | .297 | 18 | .275 | 38 | .298 | 26 | .285 | 30 | .284 | 35 | .255 | 41 | .349 | 28 | .476 | 116 |
| Donell Nixon | .293 | 20 | .200 | -- | .295 | -- | .239 | -- | .263 | -- | .222 | -- | .222 | -- | .571 | -- |
| Ken Oberkfell | .287 | 29 | .242 | -- | .284 | -- | .258 | -- | .189 | -- | .190 | -- | .341 | -- | .727 | 13 |
| Ernest Riles | .267 | 47 | .304 | 10 | .246 | 86 | .302 | 9 | .263 | 59 | .189 | 100 | .392 | 13 | .500 | 98 |
| Pat Sheridan | .213 | 107 | .179 | -- | .198 | -- | .213 | -- | .195 | -- | .280 | 28 | .304 | 62 | .125 | 147 |
| Rob Thompson | .263 | 55 | .173 | 129 | .266 | 57 | .215 | 105 | .173 | 128 | .159 | 116 | .343 | 34 | .438 | 123 |
| Jose Uribe | .218 | 102 | .228 | 106 | .224 | 109 | .218 | 101 | .250 | 75 | .190 | 97 | .236 | 120 | .538 | 86 |
| Matt Williams | .206 | 113 | .188 | -- | .215 | 114 | .189 | 122 | .150 | 131 | .137 | 122 | .271 | 97 | .667 | 25 |
| Team Average | .254 | 3 | .238 | 11 | .256 | 4 | .243 | 5 | .246 | 9 | .203 | 11 | .311 | 4 | .522 | 9 |
| League Average | .244 | | .248 | | .251 | | .242 | | .249 | | .222 | | .302 | | .546 | |

## Pitching vs. Left and Right Handed Batters

| | | BA | Rank | SA | Rank | OBA | Rank | HR % | Rank | BB % | Rank | SO % | Rank |
|---|---|---|---|---|---|---|---|---|---|---|---|---|---|
| Steve Bedrosian | vs. Lefties | .201 | 17 | .372 | 69 | .314 | 54 | 4.88 | 115 | 13.92 | 106 | 16.49 | 34 |
| | vs. Righties | .173 | 7 | .278 | 14 | .238 | 11 | 3.01 | 93 | 8.11 | 75 | 17.57 | 53 |
| Jeff Brantley | vs. Lefties | .302 | 106 | .422 | 96 | .364 | 105 | 2.08 | 78 | 9.17 | 61 | 11.93 | 76 |
| | vs. Righties | .238 | 57 | .365 | 65 | .308 | 72 | 3.31 | 103 | 8.33 | 78 | 21.08 | 33 |
| Kelly Downs | vs. Lefties | .303 | 107 | .478 | 110 | .349 | 92 | 2.25 | 84 | 7.14 | 28 | 10.20 | 96 |
| | vs. Righties | .206 | 21 | .324 | 32 | .273 | 37 | 2.21 | 60 | 7.84 | 71 | 18.95 | 46 |
| Scott Garrelts | vs. Lefties | .236 | 46 | .353 | 56 | .296 | 32 | 1.59 | 59 | 8.08 | 46 | 12.59 | 71 |
| | vs. Righties | .183 | 8 | .266 | 6 | .211 | 3 | 1.53 | 29 | 3.48 | 4 | 19.13 | 42 |
| Rich Gossage | vs. Lefties | .215 | 27 | .278 | 18 | .337 | 77 | 0.00 | 1 | 15.46 | 112 | 11.34 | 84 |
| | vs. Righties | .208 | -- | .319 | -- | .318 | -- | 2.78 | -- | 14.12 | -- | 15.29 | -- |
| Atlee Hammaker | vs. Lefties | .277 | -- | .292 | -- | .351 | -- | 0.00 | -- | 9.21 | -- | 6.58 | -- |
| | vs. Righties | .269 | 93 | .372 | 72 | .314 | 78 | 2.24 | 62 | 6.50 | 47 | 10.16 | 107 |
| Bob Knepper | vs. Lefties | .300 | 104 | .470 | 109 | .364 | 104 | 3.00 | 100 | 7.96 | 42 | 14.16 | 53 |
| | vs. Righties | .291 | 107 | .426 | 102 | .366 | 107 | 2.37 | 71 | 10.43 | 103 | 7.58 | 115 |
| Mike Krukow | vs. Lefties | .233 | 39 | .360 | 62 | .309 | 48 | 3.49 | 111 | 10.31 | 77 | 10.31 | 93 |
| | vs. Righties | .239 | -- | .380 | -- | .325 | -- | 2.82 | -- | 10.00 | -- | 10.00 | -- |
| Mike LaCoss | vs. Lefties | .266 | 83 | .331 | 42 | .361 | 101 | 0.98 | 33 | 11.83 | 93 | 10.99 | 86 |
| | vs. Righties | .243 | 62 | .298 | 19 | .307 | 70 | 0.00 | 1 | 7.88 | 72 | 13.36 | 82 |
| Craig Lefferts | vs. Lefties | .200 | 16 | .282 | 20 | .227 | 3 | 2.35 | 86 | 3.33 | 2 | 16.67 | 33 |
| | vs. Righties | .242 | 61 | .401 | 86 | .284 | 48 | 2.87 | 84 | 5.59 | 26 | 16.47 | 64 |
| Rick Reuschel | vs. Lefties | .261 | 76 | .364 | 65 | .309 | 47 | 1.12 | 38 | 6.60 | 20 | 8.66 | 106 |
| | vs. Righties | .229 | 49 | .400 | 83 | .275 | 40 | 3.77 | 113 | 5.87 | 31 | 18.40 | 49 |
| Don Robinson | vs. Lefties | .260 | 75 | .412 | 95 | .301 | 37 | 3.00 | 99 | 5.38 | 7 | 10.75 | 90 |
| | vs. Righties | .230 | 51 | .372 | 71 | .258 | 18 | 2.91 | 89 | 3.66 | 6 | 14.02 | 78 |
| Trevor Wilson | vs. Lefties | .222 | -- | .333 | -- | .300 | -- | 0.00 | -- | 6.45 | -- | 9.68 | -- |
| | vs. Righties | .204 | 18 | .296 | 18 | .351 | 100 | 1.85 | 44 | 16.18 | 116 | 13.97 | 79 |
| Team Average | vs. Lefties | .257 | 9 | .372 | 7 | .323 | 6 | 1.85 | 7 | 8.72 | 1 | 11.04 | 11 |
| | vs. Righties | .231 | 3 | .358 | 6 | .287 | 2 | 2.53 | 11 | 6.97 | 3 | 15.26 | 9 |
| League Average | vs. Lefties | .252 | | .366 | | .325 | | 1.79 | | 9.48 | | 13.93 | |
| | vs. Righties | .242 | | .365 | | .303 | | 2.29 | | 7.70 | | 16.46 | |

## Pitching with Runners on Base and Bases Empty

| | | BA | Rank | SA | Rank | OBA | Rank | HR % | Rank | BB % | Rank | SO % | Rank |
|---|---|---|---|---|---|---|---|---|---|---|---|---|---|
| Steve Bedrosian | Runners On | .197 | 5 | .386 | 75 | .298 | 29 | 5.51 | 116 | 13.16 | 104 | 15.79 | 46 |
| | Bases Empty | .182 | 5 | .288 | 16 | .268 | 22 | 2.94 | 104 | 10.00 | 97 | 17.89 | 40 |
| Jeff Brantley | Runners On | .277 | 88 | .405 | 82 | .350 | 83 | 2.89 | 95 | 9.80 | 62 | 13.73 | 64 |
| | Bases Empty | .265 | 96 | .385 | 89 | .326 | 97 | 2.50 | 89 | 7.80 | 72 | 18.81 | 37 |
| Kelly Downs | Runners On | .289 | 92 | .461 | 103 | .340 | 71 | 2.34 | 75 | 8.11 | 34 | 13.51 | 69 |
| | Bases Empty | .242 | 57 | .376 | 82 | .299 | 59 | 2.15 | 69 | 6.97 | 59 | 14.43 | 69 |
| Scott Garrelts | Runners On | .224 | 27 | .360 | 56 | .266 | 8 | 2.40 | 79 | 6.01 | 9 | 16.96 | 40 |
| | Bases Empty | .205 | 17 | .286 | 15 | .253 | 9 | 1.10 | 23 | 6.00 | 38 | 14.70 | 64 |
| Atlee Hammaker | Runners On | .259 | 75 | .336 | 33 | .338 | 68 | 1.72 | 45 | 11.27 | 87 | 4.23 | 116 |
| | Bases Empty | .279 | 108 | .366 | 77 | .311 | 80 | 1.74 | 48 | 3.89 | 10 | 13.33 | 78 |
| Bob Knepper | Runners On | .305 | 105 | .473 | 108 | .374 | 103 | 3.02 | 97 | 9.63 | 58 | 8.22 | 110 |
| | Bases Empty | .282 | 109 | .399 | 99 | .359 | 111 | 1.99 | 60 | 10.43 | 102 | 8.91 | 114 |
| Mike LaCoss | Runners On | .264 | 82 | .331 | 32 | .345 | 76 | 0.79 | 12 | 9.87 | 64 | 10.20 | 97 |
| | Bases Empty | .248 | 74 | .304 | 21 | .329 | 100 | 0.33 | 4 | 10.20 | 99 | 13.70 | 75 |
| Craig Lefferts | Runners On | .200 | 7 | .357 | 51 | .244 | 2 | 3.78 | 111 | 5.37 | 4 | 14.63 | 56 |
| | Bases Empty | .262 | 92 | .393 | 93 | .298 | 57 | 1.87 | 54 | 4.89 | 21 | 18.22 | 39 |
| Rick Reuschel | Runners On | .262 | 80 | .376 | 68 | .304 | 37 | 1.68 | 42 | 6.01 | 8 | 13.81 | 63 |
| | Bases Empty | .238 | 49 | .382 | 86 | .288 | 44 | 2.64 | 95 | 6.45 | 50 | 12.33 | 90 |
| Don Robinson | Runners On | .239 | 47 | .361 | 58 | .284 | 16 | 2.35 | 76 | 5.63 | 6 | 11.27 | 90 |
| | Bases Empty | .252 | 84 | .414 | 107 | .283 | 37 | 3.28 | 109 | 4.13 | 13 | 12.57 | 87 |
| Team Average | Runners On | .245 | 3 | .375 | 5 | .310 | 1 | 2.49 | 11 | 8.45 | 1 | 12.60 | 11 |
| | Bases Empty | .242 | 7 | .358 | 7 | .300 | 7 | 2.02 | 8 | 7.32 | 6 | 13.77 | 12 |
| League Average | Runners On | .256 | | .379 | | .330 | | 2.13 | | 9.82 | | 14.66 | |
| | Bases Empty | .240 | | .355 | | .299 | | 2.03 | | 7.43 | | 15.93 | |

## Overall Pitching Compared to Late Inning Pressure Situations

| | | BA | Rank | SA | Rank | OBA | Rank | HR % | Rank | BB % | Rank | SO % | Rank |
|---|---|---|---|---|---|---|---|---|---|---|---|---|---|
| Steve Bedrosian | Overall | .189 | 3 | .330 | 33 | .282 | 24 | 4.04 | 116 | 11.40 | 106 | 16.96 | 45 |
| | Pressure | .198 | 24 | .374 | 83 | .306 | 54 | 4.81 | 110 | 13.45 | 102 | 19.28 | 33 |
| Jeff Brantley | Overall | .271 | 95 | .394 | 88 | .337 | 97 | 2.68 | 100 | 8.77 | 69 | 16.35 | 51 |
| | Pressure | .259 | 78 | .375 | 84 | .320 | 67 | 1.79 | 66 | 7.20 | 44 | 17.60 | 43 |
| Kelly Downs | Overall | .261 | 88 | .411 | 101 | .316 | 67 | 2.23 | 76 | 7.45 | 42 | 14.04 | 69 |
| | Pressure | .182 | 12 | .333 | 56 | .229 | 6 | 3.03 | 99 | 5.71 | 28 | 11.43 | 87 |
| Scott Garrelts | Overall | .212 | 16 | .313 | 17 | .258 | 2 | 1.56 | 34 | 6.01 | 19 | 15.54 | 57 |
| | Pressure | .232 | 55 | .339 | 65 | .271 | 32 | 0.00 | 1 | 5.00 | 22 | 15.00 | 65 |
| Rich Gossage | Overall | .212 | -- | .298 | -- | .328 | -- | 1.32 | -- | 14.84 | -- | 13.19 | -- |
| | Pressure | .167 | 7 | .286 | 32 | .314 | 58 | 2.38 | 82 | 17.65 | 116 | 19.61 | 29 |
| Atlee Hammaker | Overall | .271 | 96 | .354 | 61 | .323 | 78 | 1.74 | 41 | 7.14 | 37 | 9.32 | 112 |
| | Pressure | .250 | 70 | .265 | 17 | .316 | 62 | 0.00 | 1 | 9.09 | 61 | 5.19 | 114 |
| Bob Knepper | Overall | .293 | 109 | .433 | 110 | .366 | 112 | 2.47 | 90 | 10.05 | 93 | 8.58 | 113 |
| | Pressure | .556 | -- | 1.000 | -- | .636 | -- | 11.11 | -- | 15.38 | -- | 0.00 | -- |
| Mike LaCoss | Overall | .255 | 78 | .316 | 20 | .336 | 94 | 0.54 | 1 | 10.05 | 92 | 12.06 | 90 |
| | Pressure | .250 | 70 | .340 | 66 | .374 | 102 | 2.00 | 71 | 16.00 | 113 | 10.40 | 98 |
| Craig Lefferts | Overall | .233 | 41 | .376 | 72 | .272 | 14 | 2.76 | 102 | 5.12 | 6 | 16.51 | 49 |
| | Pressure | .233 | 59 | .348 | 68 | .279 | 35 | 1.32 | 48 | 5.69 | 27 | 15.45 | 57 |
| Rick Reuschel | Overall | .247 | 61 | .380 | 75 | .294 | 41 | 2.28 | 80 | 6.28 | 22 | 12.91 | 79 |
| | Pressure | .233 | 57 | .302 | 38 | .267 | 28 | 0.00 | 1 | 4.40 | 14 | 10.99 | 93 |
| Don Robinson | Overall | .248 | 64 | .396 | 90 | .283 | 27 | 2.96 | 109 | 4.67 | 2 | 12.11 | 89 |
| | Pressure | .190 | 20 | .270 | 20 | .224 | 3 | 1.59 | 60 | 4.48 | 16 | 13.43 | 76 |
| Team Average | Overall | .243 | 4 | .365 | 6 | .304 | 3 | 2.21 | 9 | 7.80 | 2 | 13.28 | 11 |
| | Pressure | .228 | 5 | .325 | 3 | .299 | 3 | 1.45 | 3 | 9.06 | 6 | 13.91 | 12 |
| League Average | Overall | .246 | | .365 | | .312 | | 2.07 | | 8.47 | | 15.38 | |
| | Pressure | .235 | | .336 | | .309 | | 1.77 | | 9.31 | | 16.92 | |

## Additional Miscellaneous Pitching Comparisons

| | Grass Surface | | Artificial Surface | | Home Games | | Road Games | | Runners in Scoring Position | | Runners in Scoring Pos and Two Outs | | Leading Off Inning | |
|---|---|---|---|---|---|---|---|---|---|---|---|---|---|---|
| | BA | Rank | BA | Rank | BA | Rank | BA | Rank | BA | Rank | BA | Rank | OBA | Rank |
| Steve Bedrosian | .156 | 2 | .226 | 32 | .171 | 4 | .209 | 17 | .228 | 42 | .162 | 21 | .219 | 7 |
| Jeff Brantley | .278 | 98 | .255 | 69 | .270 | 93 | .271 | 90 | .302 | 99 | .311 | 109 | .322 | 88 |
| Kelly Downs | .265 | 88 | .250 | -- | .255 | 75 | .267 | 84 | .344 | 116 | .333 | 112 | .364 | 107 |
| Scott Garrelts | .211 | 24 | .216 | 19 | .196 | 16 | .229 | 33 | .190 | 14 | .138 | 13 | .246 | 16 |
| Rich Gossage | .209 | 19 | .217 | -- | .224 | -- | .206 | 15 | .282 | -- | .211 | -- | .300 | -- |
| Atlee Hammaker | .243 | 63 | .364 | -- | .216 | 30 | .313 | 111 | .291 | 90 | .143 | -- | .346 | 100 |
| Bob Knepper | .271 | 93 | .309 | 108 | .338 | 116 | .256 | 70 | .294 | 93 | .222 | 62 | .316 | 81 |
| Mike Krukow | .233 | 45 | .250 | -- | .238 | -- | .234 | -- | .333 | -- | .333 | -- | .222 | -- |
| Mike LaCoss | .256 | 78 | .253 | 65 | .272 | 94 | .241 | 46 | .231 | 46 | .149 | 17 | .303 | 62 |
| Craig Lefferts | .232 | 44 | .236 | 43 | .216 | 31 | .250 | 56 | .161 | 3 | .089 | 1 | .281 | 43 |
| Randy McCament | .260 | 83 | .172 | -- | .256 | -- | .218 | -- | .213 | -- | .280 | -- | .333 | -- |
| Rick Reuschel | .256 | 77 | .223 | 30 | .246 | 60 | .248 | 55 | .231 | 47 | .167 | 26 | .287 | 47 |
| Don Robinson | .232 | 43 | .294 | 102 | .222 | 35 | .283 | 98 | .218 | 32 | .217 | 59 | .289 | 49 |
| Trevor Wilson | .196 | 6 | .233 | -- | .190 | -- | .222 | -- | .323 | -- | .273 | -- | .415 | -- |
| Team Average | .240 | 4 | .253 | 9 | .234 | 3 | .253 | 9 | .240 | 5 | .197 | 1 | .302 | 4 |
| League Average | .244 | | .248 | | .242 | | .251 | | .249 | | .222 | | .302 | |
| League Average | .244 | | .248 | | .242 | | .251 | | .249 | | .222 | | .302 | |

# III
# Batter Section

# *Batter Section*

The Batter Section is an alphabetical listing of every player who had at least 200 plate appearances in either the American or the National League last season. Players are listed alphabetically within each league, followed by the totals for each team and the league as a whole.

## Column Headings Information

| **Tony Armas**<br>Boston Red Sox | AB | H | 2B | 3B | HR | RBI | BB | SO | BA | SA | Bats Right<br>OBA |
|---|---|---|---|---|---|---|---|---|---|---|---|

| | |
|---|---|
| AB | At Bats |
| H | Hits |
| 2B | Doubles |
| 3B | Triples |
| HR | Home Runs |
| RBI | Runs Batted In |
| BB | Bases on Balls |
| SO | Strikeouts |
| BA | Batting Average |
| SA | Slugging Average |
| OBA | On-Base Average |

For each player, information is provided in eleven offensive categories.

## Season Summary Information

| Season | 493 | 129 | 29 | 1 | 27 | 91 | 38 | 68 | .262 | .489 | .341 |
|---|---|---|---|---|---|---|---|---|---|---|---|
| vs. Left-Handed Pitchers | 188 | 53 | 9 | 0 | 9 | 38 | 18 | 27 | .282 | .473 | .366 |
| vs. Right-Handed Pitchers | 305 | 76 | 20 | 1 | 18 | 53 | 20 | 41 | .249 | .498 | .326 |
| Home | 223 | 55 | 11 | 0 | 10 | 43 | 18 | 38 | .247 | .430 | .325 |
| Road | 270 | 74 | 18 | 1 | 17 | 48 | 20 | 30 | .274 | .537 | .354 |
| Grass | 409 | 106 | 26 | 0 | 21 | 79 | 33 | 57 | .259 | .477 | .336 |
| Artificial Turf | 84 | 23 | 3 | 1 | 6 | 12 | 5 | 11 | .274 | .548 | .365 |
| April | 74 | 16 | 6 | 0 | 3 | 7 | 0 | 9 | .216 | .419 | .244 |
| May | 75 | 21 | 4 | 0 | 6 | 12 | 10 | 12 | .280 | .573 | .386 |
| June | 87 | 23 | 3 | 0 | 7 | 24 | 11 | 9 | .264 | .540 | .360 |
| July | 88 | 22 | 6 | 0 | 3 | 11 | 6 | 10 | .250 | .420 | .316 |
| August | 98 | 25 | 4 | 1 | 5 | 21 | 7 | 14 | .255 | .469 | .333 |
| Sept./Oct. | 71 | 22 | 6 | 0 | 3 | 16 | 4 | 14 | .310 | .521 | .402 |

Each player's seasonal performance is broken down into a variety of special categories. The first line for each player gives his totals for the whole season. This is followed by breakdowns of his performance against left- and right-handed pitchers, in home and road games, on grass fields and on artificial turf, and in each month. (For players who played for more than one team within a league, all totals are combined. The "home" totals for Ken Phelps, for example, include all games he played in Oakland while with the Athletics, and all games played in New York while with the Yankees.)

| Leading Off Inn. | 107 | 25 | 5 | 0 | 6 | 6 | 8 | 16 | .234 | .449 | .311 |
|---|---|---|---|---|---|---|---|---|---|---|---|
| Runners On | 272 | 72 | 18 | 0 | 13 | 77 | 20 | 39 | .265 | .474 | .343 |
| Runners/Scor. Pos. | 140 | 35 | 9 | 0 | 3 | 51 | 13 | 15 | .250 | .379 | .337 |
| Runners On/2 Out | 133 | 29 | 6 | 0 | 5 | 26 | 11 | 19 | .218 | .376 | .325 |
| Scor. Pos./2 Out | 60 | 11 | 2 | 0 | 0 | 12 | 7 | 7 | .183 | .217 | .319 |

Following these breakdowns, each batter's performance is divided into specific game situations. Totals are given for each batter when he led off an inning and when he batted with runners on base. These are followed by his performance with runners in scoring position (on second or third base, or both), with runners on base and two out, and with runners in scoring position and two out.

| Late Inning Pressure | 90 | 23 | 6 | 1 | 3 | 13 | 5 | 13 | .256 | .444 | .299 |
|---|---|---|---|---|---|---|---|---|---|---|---|
| Bases Empty | 42 | 12 | 5 | 1 | 2 | 2 | 1 | 7 | .286 | .595 | .318 |
| Runners On | 48 | 11 | 1 | 0 | 1 | 11 | 4 | 6 | .229 | .313 | .283 |
| Runners/Scor. Pos. | 26 | 7 | 1 | 0 | 1 | 11 | 3 | 2 | .269 | .423 | .333 |

The next group shows the batter's performance in late-inning pressure situations: any plate appearances occurring in the seventh inning or later with the score tied or with the batter's team trailing by one, two, or three runs (or four runs if the bases are loaded).

Each player's totals are listed for all late-inning pressure situations, then broken out for his performance when leading off an inning, with runners on base, and with runners in scoring position.

| RUNS BATTED IN | From 1B | From 2B | From 3B | Scoring Position |
|---|---|---|---|---|
| Total | 6/138 | 14/80 | 21/57 | 35/137 |
| Percentage | 4% | 18% | 37% | 26% |
| Driving In Runners from 3B with Less than Two Out: | | | 15/30 | 50% |

The next section, labeled "Runs Batted In," is a measure of the player's ability to drive in runners from each base. For every base, two numbers are listed: the first is the number of RBIs credited to the batter for bringing home runners from that base; the second is the total number of opportunities the batter faced for that situation. (For example, the notation "14/31" under runners on second would mean that the player batted 31 times with runners on second and drove home 14 of the runners.) Plate appearances that result in a base on balls, hit batsman, sacrifice bunt, or an award of first base through catcher's interference are not treated as "opportunities" if they do not result in a run.

If there is more than one runner on base, there is an "opportunity" to drive in each base runner. A single with the bases loaded that scores only the runner from third is an opportunity and an RBI for the "From 3B" line, but an unsuccessful opportunity for the "From 2B" and "From 1B" lines. (The exception to this is when a base on balls, hit batsman, sacrifice bunt, or award through interference results in a run. A walk with the bases loaded would result in an RBI and an opportunity for the "From 3B" line, but would not be charged as an unsuccessful opportunity for the other two.)

Also given is the percentage of successful opportunities; runners driven in from scoring position (combining the "From 3B" and "From 2B" totals); and a line summarizing the batter's performance driving in runners from third with less than two out.

Following the "Runs Batted In" information are comments for each player. Included are the pitchers each batter loves to face and hates to face. The statistics listed for each individual match-up are from regular season games since 1975.

# American League

## Andy Allanson

Bats Right

| Cleveland Indians | AB | H | 2B | 3B | HR | RBI | BB | SO | BA | SA | OBA |
|---|---|---|---|---|---|---|---|---|---|---|---|
| Season | 323 | 75 | 9 | 1 | 3 | 17 | 23 | 47 | .232 | .294 | .289 |
| vs. Left-Handers | 94 | 27 | 4 | 1 | 0 | 3 | 7 | 10 | .287 | .351 | .340 |
| vs. Right-Handers | 229 | 48 | 5 | 0 | 3 | 14 | 16 | 37 | .210 | .271 | .268 |
| Home | 149 | 31 | 3 | 0 | 1 | 8 | 13 | 22 | .208 | .248 | .279 |
| Road | 174 | 44 | 6 | 1 | 2 | 9 | 10 | 25 | .253 | .333 | .298 |
| Grass | 270 | 59 | 8 | 0 | 3 | 16 | 20 | 41 | .219 | .281 | .280 |
| Artificial Turf | 53 | 16 | 1 | 1 | 0 | 1 | 3 | 6 | .302 | .358 | .333 |
| April | 63 | 14 | 4 | 0 | 0 | 3 | 3 | 9 | .222 | .286 | .258 |
| May | 75 | 16 | 2 | 0 | 0 | 3 | 5 | 10 | .213 | .240 | .272 |
| June | 33 | 5 | 0 | 0 | 1 | 2 | 1 | 4 | .152 | .242 | .222 |
| July | 47 | 11 | 1 | 1 | 1 | 3 | 5 | 9 | .234 | .362 | .315 |
| August | 62 | 17 | 1 | 0 | 0 | 5 | 6 | 12 | .274 | .290 | .329 |
| Sept./Oct. | 43 | 12 | 1 | 0 | 1 | 1 | 3 | 3 | .279 | .372 | .326 |
| Leading Off Inn. | 70 | 19 | 3 | 0 | 2 | 2 | 5 | 7 | .271 | .400 | .320 |
| Runners On | 137 | 28 | 2 | 0 | 1 | 15 | 12 | 25 | .204 | .241 | .282 |
| Runners/Scor. Pos. | 80 | 13 | 0 | 0 | 0 | 12 | 9 | 20 | .163 | .163 | .247 |
| Runners On/2 Out | 73 | 11 | 1 | 0 | 1 | 8 | 6 | 14 | .151 | .205 | .244 |
| Scor. Pos./2 Out | 46 | 6 | 0 | 0 | 0 | 5 | 6 | 12 | .130 | .130 | .231 |
| Late Inning Pressure | 41 | 14 | 1 | 0 | 2 | 3 | 1 | 6 | .341 | .512 | .357 |
| Leading Off | 11 | 5 | 1 | 0 | 1 | 1 | 0 | 2 | .455 | .818 | .455 |
| Runners On | 15 | 5 | 0 | 0 | 1 | 2 | 1 | 3 | .333 | .533 | .375 |
| Runners/Scor. Pos. | 6 | 2 | 0 | 0 | 0 | 0 | 1 | 2 | .333 | .333 | .429 |

| RUNS BATTED IN | From 1B | From 2B | From 3B | Scoring Position |
|---|---|---|---|---|
| Totals | 2/97 | 4/67 | 8/30 | 12/97 |
| Percentage | 2% | 6% | 27% | 12% |
| Driving In Runners from 3B with Less than Two Out: | | | 6/13 | 46% |

Loves to face: Doyle Alexander (.500, 8-for-16, 1 HR)
Hates to face: Mark Gubicza (.154, 2-for-13)
Among players with 350+ plate appearances last season, only John Shelby had fewer RBI. From the same group, only Felix Fermin and Omar Vizquel had fewer extra-base hits. . . . Rate of runners driven in from scoring position (13.4 percent) was 3d-lowest by any player in 1980s (minimum: 75 opportunities). His only RBI over last 22 games came on a solo home run. . . . Stole 10 bases in 11 attempts in 1986 debut, but he's 10-for-24 in three years since. . . . His three home runs last season were all hit off veteran All-Stars: Clemens, Hough, and Morris. All 12 career home runs have been hit against right-handed pitchers. . . . If you don't include anyone who caught Charlie Hough, Allanson tied for A.L. lead in passed balls.

## Brady Anderson

Bats Left

| Baltimore Orioles | AB | H | 2B | 3B | HR | RBI | BB | SO | BA | SA | OBA |
|---|---|---|---|---|---|---|---|---|---|---|---|
| Season | 266 | 55 | 12 | 2 | 4 | 16 | 43 | 45 | .207 | .312 | .324 |
| vs. Left-Handers | 70 | 9 | 1 | 2 | 1 | 2 | 13 | 12 | .129 | .243 | .265 |
| vs. Right-Handers | 196 | 46 | 11 | 0 | 3 | 14 | 30 | 33 | .235 | .337 | .345 |
| Home | 135 | 30 | 7 | 1 | 2 | 8 | 19 | 17 | .222 | .333 | .327 |
| Road | 131 | 25 | 5 | 1 | 2 | 8 | 24 | 28 | .191 | .290 | .321 |
| Grass | 206 | 42 | 9 | 1 | 4 | 14 | 32 | 31 | .204 | .316 | .320 |
| Artificial Turf | 60 | 13 | 3 | 1 | 0 | 2 | 11 | 14 | .217 | .300 | .338 |
| April | 94 | 25 | 9 | 2 | 1 | 6 | 13 | 16 | .266 | .436 | .367 |
| May | 81 | 15 | 2 | 0 | 3 | 9 | 11 | 15 | .185 | .321 | .283 |
| June | 37 | 6 | 1 | 0 | 0 | 0 | 9 | 4 | .162 | .189 | .326 |
| July | 37 | 7 | 0 | 0 | 0 | 1 | 10 | 7 | .189 | .189 | .375 |
| August | 8 | 0 | 0 | 0 | 0 | 0 | 0 | 1 | .000 | .000 | .000 |
| Sept./Oct. | 9 | 2 | 0 | 0 | 0 | 0 | 0 | 2 | .222 | .222 | .222 |
| Leading Off Inn. | 114 | 20 | 7 | 2 | 1 | 1 | 11 | 23 | .175 | .298 | .260 |
| Runners On | 88 | 21 | 3 | 0 | 2 | 14 | 26 | 8 | .239 | .341 | .417 |
| Runners/Scor. Pos. | 50 | 10 | 1 | 0 | 1 | 12 | 18 | 5 | .200 | .280 | .412 |
| Runners On/2 Out | 32 | 9 | 1 | 0 | 1 | 7 | 13 | 4 | .281 | .406 | .500 |
| Scor. Pos./2 Out | 22 | 4 | 0 | 0 | 0 | 5 | 10 | 3 | .182 | .182 | .438 |
| Late Inning Pressure | 26 | 9 | 3 | 0 | 0 | 1 | 7 | 5 | .346 | .462 | .485 |
| Leading Off | 12 | 5 | 2 | 0 | 0 | 0 | 2 | 2 | .417 | .583 | .500 |
| Runners On | 10 | 2 | 0 | 0 | 0 | 1 | 5 | 2 | .200 | .200 | .467 |
| Runners/Scor. Pos. | 4 | 1 | 0 | 0 | 0 | 1 | 2 | 1 | .250 | .250 | .500 |

| RUNS BATTED IN | From 1B | From 2B | From 3B | Scoring Position |
|---|---|---|---|---|
| Totals | 2/57 | 4/38 | 6/17 | 10/55 |
| Percentage | 4% | 11% | 35% | 18% |
| Driving In Runners from 3B with Less than Two Out: | | | 2/8 | 25% |

Loves to face: Mike Witt (.500, 5-for-10)
Hates to face: Mike Moore (.083, 1-for-12)
Started only one of Orioles' last 56 games before elimination, after having started 78 of first 105 games. Drove in only one run in 50 games after May 31. . . . Had two doubles and a single on opening day, but did not have two extra-base hits in any other game, and had only one other three-hit game. . . . Averaged one walk every 13.8 plate appearances in 1988, one walk every 7.4 times up last year. . . . With a .210 average in 591 career at-bats, he's already below the (.215) Mendoza Line and the (.212) Bilardello Line, and he's in danger of falling below the even more dreaded (.207) Nieto Line. But some pretty famous baseball names had a career average of .210, including Joe Altobelli, Rene Lachemann, and Cy Young!

## Kent Anderson

Bats Right

| California Angels | AB | H | 2B | 3B | HR | RBI | BB | SO | BA | SA | OBA |
|---|---|---|---|---|---|---|---|---|---|---|---|
| Season | 223 | 51 | 6 | 1 | 0 | 17 | 17 | 42 | .229 | .265 | .285 |
| vs. Left-Handers | 69 | 19 | 1 | 0 | 0 | 3 | 8 | 13 | .275 | .290 | .351 |
| vs. Right-Handers | 154 | 32 | 5 | 1 | 0 | 14 | 9 | 29 | .208 | .253 | .255 |
| Home | 110 | 23 | 3 | 1 | 0 | 9 | 11 | 16 | .209 | .255 | .281 |
| Road | 113 | 28 | 3 | 0 | 0 | 8 | 6 | 26 | .248 | .274 | .289 |
| Grass | 175 | 39 | 6 | 1 | 0 | 14 | 15 | 33 | .223 | .269 | .286 |
| Artificial Turf | 48 | 12 | 0 | 0 | 0 | 3 | 2 | 9 | .250 | .250 | .280 |
| April | 40 | 11 | 2 | 0 | 0 | 3 | 2 | 7 | .275 | .325 | .302 |
| May | 36 | 9 | 0 | 0 | 0 | 3 | 6 | 6 | .250 | .250 | .357 |
| June | 22 | 2 | 0 | 0 | 0 | 1 | 0 | 5 | .091 | .091 | .091 |
| July | 11 | 1 | 0 | 0 | 0 | 1 | 1 | 4 | .091 | .091 | .167 |
| August | 58 | 15 | 2 | 1 | 0 | 6 | 5 | 10 | .259 | .328 | .317 |
| Sept./Oct. | 56 | 13 | 2 | 0 | 0 | 3 | 3 | 10 | .232 | .268 | .283 |
| Leading Off Inn. | 44 | 9 | 1 | 0 | 0 | 0 | 3 | 11 | .205 | .227 | .255 |
| Runners On | 97 | 28 | 3 | 1 | 0 | 17 | 4 | 16 | .289 | .340 | .314 |
| Runners/Scor. Pos. | 61 | 16 | 1 | 1 | 0 | 16 | 0 | 11 | .262 | .311 | .258 |
| Runners On/2 Out | 51 | 14 | 1 | 1 | 0 | 9 | 2 | 9 | .275 | .333 | .302 |
| Scor. Pos./2 Out | 37 | 9 | 0 | 1 | 0 | 9 | 0 | 8 | .243 | .297 | .243 |
| Late Inning Pressure | 21 | 4 | 0 | 0 | 0 | 0 | 3 | 3 | .190 | .190 | .292 |
| Leading Off | 6 | 1 | 0 | 0 | 0 | 0 | 0 | 0 | .167 | .167 | .167 |
| Runners On | 10 | 1 | 0 | 0 | 0 | 0 | 2 | 2 | .100 | .100 | .250 |
| Runners/Scor. Pos. | 7 | 1 | 0 | 0 | 0 | 0 | 0 | 1 | .143 | .143 | .143 |

| RUNS BATTED IN | From 1B | From 2B | From 3B | Scoring Position |
|---|---|---|---|---|
| Totals | 3/70 | 9/52 | 5/20 | 14/72 |
| Percentage | 4% | 17% | 25% | 19% |
| Driving In Runners from 3B with Less than Two Out: | | | 4/8 | 50% |

Loves to face: Rod Nichols (2-for-2, 1 HBP)
Hates to face: Nolan Ryan (0-for-6, 3 SO)
Made 73 starts in his rookie season, 10th-highest total in A.L.; only nine A.L. rookies and three N.L. rookies started at least half of their team's games in 1989. . . . Angels were 38–27 in Anderson's starts at shortstop, and also played 11 games above .500 (49–38) in Schofield's starts. . . . He's not the guy you pitch around: No walks in 64 plate appearances with runners in scoring position. . . . Batted .257 vs. fly-ball pitchers, .184 vs. ground-ball pitchers. . . . Drove in less than 20 percent of runners from scoring position. Failed to drive in any of nine runners from scoring position in Late-Inning Pressure Situations. . . . Batted five times with the bases loaded, but drove in only one of 15 runners.

## Tony Armas

Bats Right

| California Angels | AB | H | 2B | 3B | HR | RBI | BB | SO | BA | SA | OBA |
|---|---|---|---|---|---|---|---|---|---|---|---|
| Season | 202 | 52 | 7 | 1 | 11 | 30 | 7 | 48 | .257 | .465 | .280 |
| vs. Left-Handers | 102 | 24 | 2 | 1 | 5 | 10 | 4 | 23 | .235 | .422 | .264 |
| vs. Right-Handers | 100 | 28 | 5 | 0 | 6 | 20 | 3 | 25 | .280 | .510 | .295 |
| Home | 104 | 23 | 4 | 0 | 5 | 11 | 5 | 26 | .221 | .404 | .257 |
| Road | 98 | 29 | 3 | 1 | 6 | 19 | 2 | 22 | .296 | .531 | .304 |
| Grass | 160 | 37 | 4 | 0 | 8 | 21 | 6 | 37 | .231 | .406 | .257 |
| Artificial Turf | 42 | 15 | 3 | 1 | 3 | 9 | 1 | 11 | .357 | .690 | .364 |
| April | 9 | 2 | 0 | 0 | 1 | 2 | 0 | 1 | .222 | .556 | .222 |
| May | 1 | 1 | 0 | 0 | 1 | 1 | 1 | 0 | 1.000 | 4.000 | 1.000 |
| June | 27 | 13 | 0 | 0 | 2 | 5 | 0 | 4 | .481 | .704 | .481 |
| July | 65 | 12 | 0 | 0 | 3 | 9 | 2 | 17 | .185 | .323 | .206 |
| August | 70 | 18 | 6 | 1 | 3 | 10 | 3 | 13 | .257 | .500 | .284 |
| Sept./Oct. | 30 | 6 | 1 | 0 | 1 | 3 | 1 | 13 | .200 | .333 | .226 |
| Leading Off Inn. | 48 | 12 | 2 | 0 | 3 | 3 | 0 | 13 | .250 | .479 | .250 |
| Runners On | 82 | 22 | 3 | 0 | 3 | 22 | 6 | 21 | .268 | .415 | .311 |
| Runners/Scor. Pos. | 49 | 15 | 1 | 0 | 3 | 21 | 5 | 12 | .306 | .510 | .357 |
| Runners On/2 Out | 42 | 13 | 2 | 0 | 2 | 12 | 2 | 8 | .310 | .500 | .341 |
| Scor. Pos./2 Out | 27 | 8 | 1 | 0 | 2 | 12 | 2 | 7 | .296 | .556 | .345 |
| Late Inning Pressure | 31 | 6 | 0 | 0 | 2 | 6 | 0 | 12 | .194 | .387 | .194 |
| Leading Off | 6 | 0 | 0 | 0 | 0 | 0 | 0 | 3 | .000 | .000 | .000 |
| Runners On | 16 | 4 | 0 | 0 | 1 | 5 | 0 | 6 | .250 | .438 | .250 |
| Runners/Scor. Pos. | 11 | 3 | 0 | 0 | 1 | 5 | 0 | 3 | .273 | .545 | .273 |

| RUNS BATTED IN | From 1B | From 2B | From 3B | Scoring Position |
|---|---|---|---|---|
| Totals | 4/63 | 7/36 | 8/24 | 15/60 |
| Percentage | 6% | 19% | 33% | 25% |
| Driving In Runners from 3B with Less than Two Out: | | | 3/9 | 33% |

Loves to face: Richard Dotson (.366, 15-for-41, 4 HR)
Hates to face: Mike Smithson (.129, 4-for-31)
Angels' opening-day starter in right field last season. No player has had that job two years in a row since Dan Ford (1979–81). . . . One homer every 18.4 at-bats was his best rate since 1985. . . . Career totals stand at 260 walks, 251 home runs. That ratio (1.04 walks per HR) is lowest among 100-home-run hitters in baseball history. He's followed by Don Demeter (1.10, 180/163), Cory Snyder (1.11, 112/101), Joe Carter (1.12, 169/151), George Bell (1.23, 223/181). . . . What a Difference a Park Makes: In each of three years with Angels, he has hit for higher average in road games than in home games; the opposite was true through his four years with Red Sox.

## Wally Backman

Bats Left and Right

| Minnesota Twins | AB | H | 2B | 3B | HR | RBI | BB | SO | BA | SA | OBA |
|---|---|---|---|---|---|---|---|---|---|---|---|
| Season | 299 | 69 | 9 | 2 | 1 | 26 | 32 | 45 | .231 | .284 | .306 |
| vs. Left-Handers | 57 | 16 | 2 | 1 | 0 | 9 | 6 | 6 | .281 | .351 | .349 |
| vs. Right-Handers | 242 | 53 | 7 | 1 | 1 | 17 | 26 | 39 | .219 | .269 | .296 |
| Home | 150 | 37 | 3 | 2 | 0 | 14 | 21 | 19 | .247 | .293 | .343 |
| Road | 149 | 32 | 6 | 0 | 1 | 12 | 11 | 26 | .215 | .275 | .267 |
| Grass | 107 | 21 | 5 | 0 | 1 | 10 | 9 | 17 | .196 | .271 | .256 |
| Artificial Turf | 192 | 48 | 4 | 2 | 0 | 16 | 23 | 28 | .250 | .292 | .333 |
| April | 84 | 25 | 3 | 1 | 0 | 10 | 5 | 9 | .298 | .357 | .337 |
| May | 32 | 9 | 1 | 0 | 0 | 3 | 4 | 10 | .281 | .313 | .361 |
| June | 68 | 11 | 1 | 0 | 1 | 9 | 9 | 9 | .162 | .221 | .260 |
| July | 25 | 8 | 1 | 0 | 0 | 0 | 2 | 4 | .320 | .360 | .370 |
| August | 42 | 7 | 2 | 0 | 0 | 0 | 8 | 5 | .167 | .214 | .314 |
| Sept./Oct. | 48 | 9 | 1 | 1 | 0 | 4 | 4 | 8 | .188 | .250 | .245 |
| Leading Off Inn. | 90 | 20 | 3 | 0 | 1 | 1 | 7 | 9 | .222 | .289 | .278 |
| Runners On | 116 | 30 | 3 | 2 | 0 | 25 | 16 | 21 | .259 | .319 | .351 |
| Runners/Scor. Pos. | 69 | 17 | 3 | 1 | 0 | 24 | 9 | 15 | .246 | .319 | .329 |
| Runners On/2 Out | 40 | 8 | 1 | 1 | 0 | 8 | 8 | 10 | .200 | .275 | .333 |
| Scor. Pos./2 Out | 30 | 5 | 1 | 0 | 0 | 7 | 6 | 10 | .167 | .200 | .306 |
| Late Inning Pressure | 36 | 9 | 2 | 0 | 0 | 2 | 5 | 7 | .250 | .306 | .341 |
| Leading Off | 10 | 1 | 1 | 0 | 0 | 0 | 3 | 1 | .100 | .200 | .308 |
| Runners On | 14 | 5 | 0 | 0 | 0 | 2 | 1 | 4 | .357 | .357 | .400 |
| Runners/Scor. Pos. | 10 | 2 | 0 | 0 | 0 | 2 | 1 | 4 | .200 | .200 | .273 |

| RUNS BATTED IN | From 1B | From 2B | From 3B | Scoring Position |
|---|---|---|---|---|
| Totals | 3/73 | 12/56 | 10/29 | 22/85 |
| Percentage | 4% | 21% | 34% | 26% |
| Driving In Runners from 3B with Less than Two Out: | | | 8/16 | 50% |

Loves to face: Rick Mahler (.500, 22-for-44)
Hates to face: Fernando Valenzuela (.059, 1-for-17)
Career ratio of 2.46 ground outs for every fly out is highest among players active in A.L. last season. . . . Career batting average breakdown: .295 vs. fly-ball pitchers, .260 vs. ground-ballers. . . . As a right-handed batter exactly half of his fair balls were hit to left field, but batting left-handed he pulled the ball only 34 percent of time. . . . Still owns lowest career batting average (.168) vs. left-handed pitchers among active players (minimum: 400 AB); but he's 25-for-92 (.272) vs. lefties over past two seasons. . . . Stolen-base total has decreased in every year since 1984: 32, 30, 13, 11, 9, 1. . . . Has hit exactly one home run in five of last six seasons; failed to connect in 1988.

## Harold Baines

Bats Left

| White Sox/Rangers | AB | H | 2B | 3B | HR | RBI | BB | SO | BA | SA | OBA |
|---|---|---|---|---|---|---|---|---|---|---|---|
| Season | 505 | 156 | 29 | 1 | 16 | 72 | 73 | 79 | .309 | .465 | .395 |
| vs. Left-Handers | 156 | 41 | 7 | 0 | 4 | 26 | 20 | 30 | .263 | .385 | .347 |
| vs. Right-Handers | 349 | 115 | 22 | 1 | 12 | 46 | 53 | 49 | .330 | .501 | .415 |
| Home | 247 | 73 | 20 | 1 | 5 | 34 | 42 | 40 | .296 | .445 | .395 |
| Road | 258 | 83 | 9 | 0 | 11 | 38 | 31 | 39 | .322 | .484 | .394 |
| Grass | 429 | 130 | 27 | 1 | 13 | 66 | 59 | 66 | .303 | .462 | .386 |
| Artificial Turf | 76 | 26 | 2 | 0 | 3 | 6 | 14 | 13 | .342 | .487 | .440 |
| April | 77 | 25 | 4 | 0 | 2 | 10 | 17 | 7 | .325 | .455 | .447 |
| May | 94 | 34 | 8 | 0 | 1 | 17 | 12 | 14 | .362 | .479 | .426 |
| June | 92 | 24 | 1 | 0 | 7 | 13 | 16 | 16 | .261 | .500 | .376 |
| July | 78 | 27 | 9 | 1 | 3 | 17 | 15 | 16 | .346 | .603 | .447 |
| August | 77 | 21 | 2 | 0 | 2 | 9 | 9 | 10 | .273 | .377 | .345 |
| Sept./Oct. | 87 | 25 | 5 | 0 | 1 | 6 | 4 | 16 | .287 | .379 | .319 |
| Leading Off Inn. | 101 | 30 | 6 | 0 | 4 | 4 | 8 | 15 | .297 | .475 | .349 |
| Runners On | 235 | 73 | 13 | 1 | 6 | 62 | 42 | 38 | .311 | .451 | .411 |
| Runners/Scor. Pos. | 122 | 33 | 3 | 0 | 5 | 55 | 29 | 21 | .270 | .418 | .400 |
| Runners On/2 Out | 81 | 26 | 1 | 1 | 4 | 27 | 13 | 15 | .321 | .506 | .421 |
| Scor. Pos./2 Out | 53 | 17 | 1 | 0 | 3 | 24 | 8 | 8 | .321 | .509 | .410 |
| Late Inning Pressure | 71 | 19 | 4 | 0 | 3 | 8 | 11 | 13 | .268 | .451 | .366 |
| Leading Off | 15 | 5 | 1 | 0 | 1 | 1 | 2 | 3 | .333 | .600 | .412 |
| Runners On | 31 | 5 | 3 | 0 | 1 | 6 | 8 | 8 | .161 | .355 | .333 |
| Runners/Scor. Pos. | 20 | 2 | 1 | 0 | 1 | 6 | 6 | 4 | .100 | .300 | .308 |

| RUNS BATTED IN | From 1B | From 2B | From 3B | Scoring Position |
|---|---|---|---|---|
| Totals | 10/166 | 22/91 | 24/56 | 46/147 |
| Percentage | 6% | 24% | 43% | 31% |
| Driving In Runners from 3B with Less than Two Out: | | | 17/32 | 53% |

Loves to face: Steve Crawford (.692, 9-for-13, 1 HR)
Hates to face: Mark Langston (.139, 5-for-36, 1 HR)
One of three players to bat 100+ points higher in day games (.429) than in night games (.272) last season (minimum: 100 AB each). . . . Failed to reach 600 plate appearances for only second time in last eight years, but still managed to set a career high with 73 walks. . . . Last at-bats of season dropped him five ten-thousandths of a point (.0005) shy of his career-high batting average. . . . Batting average with runners on base has been higher than with bases empty in each of last seven seasons. . . . Has driven in better than 30 percent of runners from scoring position in seven of last eight years. . . . For the '80s, ranked 6th in majors in hits (1547), 7th in total bases (2478), 8th in RBI (835).

## Steve Balboni

Bats Right

| New York Yankees | AB | H | 2B | 3B | HR | RBI | BB | SO | BA | SA | OBA |
|---|---|---|---|---|---|---|---|---|---|---|---|
| Season | 300 | 71 | 12 | 2 | 17 | 60 | 25 | 67 | .237 | .460 | .296 |
| vs. Left-Handers | 194 | 48 | 9 | 1 | 13 | 46 | 14 | 39 | .247 | .505 | .296 |
| vs. Right-Handers | 106 | 23 | 3 | 1 | 4 | 14 | 11 | 28 | .217 | .377 | .298 |
| Home | 127 | 30 | 3 | 0 | 7 | 26 | 10 | 35 | .236 | .425 | .296 |
| Road | 173 | 41 | 9 | 2 | 10 | 34 | 15 | 32 | .237 | .486 | .297 |
| Grass | 245 | 57 | 10 | 1 | 13 | 42 | 22 | 54 | .233 | .441 | .300 |
| Artificial Turf | 55 | 14 | 2 | 1 | 4 | 18 | 3 | 13 | .255 | .545 | .279 |
| April | 52 | 8 | 2 | 1 | 1 | 8 | 2 | 5 | .154 | .288 | .185 |
| May | 46 | 14 | 2 | 0 | 4 | 11 | 4 | 15 | .304 | .609 | .340 |
| June | 53 | 16 | 2 | 0 | 5 | 13 | 6 | 12 | .302 | .623 | .373 |
| July | 47 | 12 | 3 | 0 | 2 | 10 | 2 | 13 | .255 | .447 | .294 |
| August | 40 | 7 | 0 | 0 | 3 | 11 | 4 | 12 | .175 | .400 | .277 |
| Sept./Oct. | 62 | 14 | 3 | 1 | 2 | 7 | 7 | 10 | .226 | .403 | .300 |
| Leading Off Inn. | 56 | 11 | 2 | 0 | 2 | 2 | 7 | 14 | .196 | .339 | .297 |
| Runners On | 170 | 44 | 9 | 1 | 10 | 53 | 14 | 32 | .259 | .500 | .313 |
| Runners/Scor. Pos. | 100 | 23 | 4 | 0 | 3 | 37 | 11 | 23 | .230 | .360 | .297 |
| Runners On/2 Out | 80 | 21 | 5 | 1 | 7 | 27 | 10 | 21 | .263 | .613 | .344 |
| Scor. Pos./2 Out | 51 | 11 | 3 | 0 | 2 | 15 | 8 | 15 | .216 | .392 | .322 |
| Late Inning Pressure | 40 | 12 | 1 | 0 | 3 | 8 | 4 | 11 | .300 | .550 | .364 |
| Leading Off | 5 | 1 | 0 | 0 | 0 | 0 | 1 | 0 | .200 | .200 | .333 |
| Runners On | 26 | 9 | 1 | 0 | 2 | 7 | 3 | 7 | .346 | .615 | .414 |
| Runners/Scor. Pos. | 17 | 3 | 0 | 0 | 0 | 3 | 2 | 7 | .176 | .176 | .263 |

| RUNS BATTED IN | From 1B | From 2B | From 3B | Scoring Position |
|---|---|---|---|---|
| Totals | 12/120 | 11/70 | 20/55 | 31/125 |
| Percentage | 10% | 16% | 36% | 25% |
| Driving In Runners from 3B with Less than Two Out: | | | 16/31 | 52% |

Loves to face: Frank Tanana (.293, 12-for-41, 5 HR)
Hates to face: Willie Fraser (0-for-14)
Led A.L. batters with 13 home runs off left-handed pitchers; No one else had more than 10. In N.L., only Mitchell (19) and Glenn Davis (14) had more. . . . Started 59 of 60 games in which Yankees faced left-handers, 18 of 101 vs. right-handers. . . . Had 0-for-30 streak vs. right-handed pitchers, June 13 to Aug. 28, longest in majors last season and longest on team in past 10 years. . . . Had highest slugging average (.502) among A.L. designated hitters, but batted only .115 in 15 starts at first base. . . . Career home-run rate (one every 17.4 at-bats) is better than rates of Reggie Jackson, Ernie Banks, or Mel Ott; of course, each of those gentlemen saw considerably less platooning than Bye-Bye has.

## Jesse Barfield

Bats Right

| Blue Jays/Yankees | AB | H | 2B | 3B | HR | RBI | BB | SO | BA | SA | OBA |
|---|---|---|---|---|---|---|---|---|---|---|---|
| Season | 521 | 122 | 23 | 1 | 23 | 67 | 87 | 150 | .234 | .415 | .345 |
| vs. Left-Handers | 160 | 38 | 5 | 0 | 8 | 16 | 44 | 44 | .238 | .419 | .398 |
| vs. Right-Handers | 361 | 84 | 18 | 1 | 15 | 51 | 43 | 106 | .233 | .413 | .319 |
| Home | 261 | 63 | 15 | 0 | 7 | 30 | 43 | 78 | .241 | .379 | .352 |
| Road | 260 | 59 | 8 | 1 | 16 | 37 | 44 | 72 | .227 | .450 | .339 |
| Grass | 439 | 106 | 19 | 1 | 20 | 56 | 76 | 125 | .241 | .426 | .355 |
| Artificial Turf | 82 | 16 | 4 | 0 | 3 | 11 | 11 | 25 | .195 | .354 | .290 |
| April | 80 | 16 | 4 | 0 | 5 | 11 | 5 | 28 | .200 | .438 | .256 |
| May | 73 | 12 | 1 | 0 | 3 | 8 | 18 | 22 | .164 | .301 | .323 |
| June | 90 | 27 | 1 | 0 | 3 | 12 | 19 | 17 | .300 | .411 | .422 |
| July | 86 | 25 | 5 | 0 | 6 | 15 | 16 | 25 | .291 | .558 | .398 |
| August | 106 | 24 | 9 | 0 | 4 | 16 | 16 | 33 | .226 | .425 | .333 |
| Sept./Oct. | 86 | 18 | 3 | 1 | 2 | 5 | 13 | 25 | .209 | .337 | .320 |
| Leading Off Inn. | 121 | 30 | 6 | 0 | 7 | 7 | 13 | 33 | .248 | .471 | .321 |
| Runners On | 235 | 53 | 9 | 1 | 12 | 56 | 49 | 72 | .226 | .426 | .360 |
| Runners/Scor. Pos. | 137 | 26 | 4 | 1 | 7 | 46 | 36 | 45 | .190 | .387 | .360 |
| Runners On/2 Out | 113 | 22 | 0 | 1 | 6 | 24 | 25 | 36 | .195 | .372 | .345 |
| Scor. Pos./2 Out | 76 | 13 | 0 | 1 | 4 | 20 | 20 | 28 | .171 | .355 | .351 |
| Late Inning Pressure | 71 | 10 | 3 | 0 | 3 | 11 | 15 | 27 | .141 | .310 | .291 |
| Leading Off | 20 | 2 | 1 | 0 | 1 | 1 | 3 | 5 | .100 | .300 | .217 |
| Runners On | 27 | 4 | 1 | 0 | 2 | 10 | 11 | 13 | .148 | .407 | .395 |
| Runners/Scor. Pos. | 19 | 4 | 1 | 0 | 2 | 10 | 9 | 10 | .211 | .579 | .464 |

| RUNS BATTED IN | From 1B | From 2B | From 3B | Scoring Position |
|---|---|---|---|---|
| Totals | 12/169 | 20/114 | 12/47 | 32/161 |
| Percentage | 7% | 18% | 26% | 20% |
| Driving In Runners from 3B with Less than Two Out: | | | 9/23 | 39% |

Loves to face: Steve Crawford (.333, 5-for-15, 4 HR)
Hates to face: Willie Hernandez (.071, 1-for-14, 9 SO)
Led A.L. outfielders with 20 assists, 19 with Yankees, most by a Yankees' outfielder since Bobby Murcer had 21 in 1974. . . . Has led A.L. outfielders in assists in four of past five years; A.L. record: Yaz led in six years. . . . Only A.L. players to match his totals in both home runs and walks were Fred McGriff and Lou Whitaker. . . . Overall BA has decreased in each of last four seasons, and average with runners in scoring position has followed suit: .276 in 1986, then .235, .211, .190. . . . Set career highs in both walks and strikeouts. . . . Struck out in seven straight times up in July, longest streak on Yankees in 1980s. . . . Has batted below .200 in Late-Inning Pressure Situations in both '88 and '89.

## Marty Barrett

Bats Right

| Boston Red Sox | AB | H | 2B | 3B | HR | RBI | BB | SO | BA | SA | OBA |
|---|---|---|---|---|---|---|---|---|---|---|---|
| Season | 336 | 86 | 18 | 0 | 1 | 27 | 32 | 12 | .256 | .318 | .320 |
| vs. Left-Handers | 104 | 27 | 9 | 0 | 0 | 5 | 10 | 0 | .260 | .346 | .325 |
| vs. Right-Handers | 232 | 59 | 9 | 0 | 1 | 22 | 22 | 12 | .254 | .306 | .318 |
| Home | 167 | 44 | 13 | 0 | 0 | 17 | 18 | 6 | .263 | .341 | .335 |
| Road | 169 | 42 | 5 | 0 | 1 | 10 | 14 | 6 | .249 | .296 | .304 |
| Grass | 277 | 69 | 16 | 0 | 1 | 20 | 26 | 9 | .249 | .318 | .314 |
| Artificial Turf | 59 | 17 | 2 | 0 | 0 | 7 | 6 | 3 | .288 | .322 | .348 |
| April | 78 | 25 | 9 | 0 | 0 | 9 | 8 | 1 | .321 | .436 | .375 |
| May | 100 | 21 | 3 | 0 | 1 | 9 | 11 | 3 | .210 | .270 | .283 |
| June | 9 | 1 | 0 | 0 | 0 | 1 | 1 | 1 | .111 | .111 | .200 |
| July | 0 | 0 | 0 | 0 | 0 | 0 | 0 | 0 | — | — | — |
| August | 85 | 26 | 5 | 0 | 0 | 4 | 7 | 5 | .306 | .365 | .366 |
| Sept./Oct. | 64 | 13 | 1 | 0 | 0 | 4 | 5 | 2 | .203 | .219 | .268 |
| Leading Off Inn. | 57 | 14 | 3 | 0 | 0 | 0 | 3 | 1 | .246 | .298 | .295 |
| Runners On | 154 | 39 | 8 | 0 | 0 | 26 | 16 | 6 | .253 | .305 | .318 |
| Runners/Scor. Pos. | 86 | 22 | 4 | 0 | 0 | 25 | 7 | 4 | .256 | .302 | .296 |
| Runners On/2 Out | 73 | 13 | 2 | 0 | 0 | 11 | 8 | 4 | .178 | .205 | .268 |
| Scor. Pos./2 Out | 50 | 9 | 1 | 0 | 0 | 10 | 4 | 3 | .180 | .200 | .241 |
| Late Inning Pressure | 55 | 19 | 2 | 0 | 0 | 4 | 4 | 4 | .345 | .382 | .400 |
| Leading Off | 14 | 5 | 1 | 0 | 0 | 0 | 1 | 1 | .357 | .429 | .400 |
| Runners On | 26 | 10 | 0 | 0 | 0 | 4 | 2 | 3 | .385 | .385 | .448 |
| Runners/Scor. Pos. | 21 | 7 | 0 | 0 | 0 | 4 | 0 | 3 | .333 | .333 | .333 |

| RUNS BATTED IN | From 1B | From 2B | From 3B | Scoring Position |
|---|---|---|---|---|
| Totals | 2/122 | 5/67 | 19/39 | 24/106 |
| Percentage | 2% | 7% | 49% | 23% |
| Driving In Runners from 3B with Less than Two Out: | | | 12/19 | 63% |

Loves to face: Dave Stewart (.425, 17-for-40, 1 HR)
Hates to face: Jack Morris (.125, 5-for-40)
Red Sox had losing record (34–43) with Barrett starting at second base, but had a winning mark with both Reed (39–27) and Romero (10–9) starting there. . . . His last 192 starts have been from second spot in lineup. . . . Batted .214 in first-inning at-bats, .267 thereafter. . . . Averaged one strikeout every 32.5 plate appearances, best in majors among semi-regulars last season (minimum: 200 PA), and best rate of his career. . . . Batted .310 vs. ground-ball pitchers, .210 vs. fly-ballers. . . . Batted .301 on fair balls to left side, .250 straight away, .215 on fair balls to opposite field. . . . With 846 games at second base, stands third in team history behind Bobby Doerr (1852) and Hobe Ferris (983).

## George Bell

Bats Right

| Toronto Blue Jays | AB | H | 2B | 3B | HR | RBI | BB | SO | BA | SA | OBA |
|---|---|---|---|---|---|---|---|---|---|---|---|
| Season | 613 | 182 | 41 | 2 | 18 | 104 | 33 | 60 | .297 | .458 | .330 |
| vs. Left-Handers | 178 | 51 | 12 | 1 | 9 | 39 | 11 | 23 | .287 | .517 | .323 |
| vs Right-Handers | 435 | 131 | 29 | 1 | 9 | 65 | 22 | 37 | .301 | .434 | .333 |
| Home | 281 | 86 | 17 | 2 | 8 | 47 | 19 | 24 | .306 | .466 | .350 |
| Road | 332 | 96 | 24 | 0 | 10 | 57 | 14 | 36 | .289 | .452 | .312 |
| Grass | 260 | 78 | 18 | 0 | 9 | 49 | 12 | 27 | .300 | .473 | .323 |
| Artificial Turf | 353 | 104 | 23 | 2 | 9 | 55 | 21 | 33 | .295 | .448 | .335 |
| April | 97 | 24 | 6 | 0 | 2 | 12 | 6 | 11 | .247 | .371 | .291 |
| May | 86 | 24 | 4 | 0 | 5 | 17 | 6 | 9 | .279 | .500 | .326 |
| June | 107 | 30 | 7 | 0 | 2 | 19 | 5 | 14 | .280 | .402 | .314 |
| July | 103 | 33 | 9 | 0 | 1 | 12 | 6 | 10 | .320 | .437 | .364 |
| August | 108 | 40 | 10 | 2 | 6 | 26 | 6 | 8 | .370 | .667 | .393 |
| Sept./Oct. | 112 | 31 | 5 | 0 | 2 | 18 | 4 | 8 | .277 | .375 | .289 |
| Leading Off Inn. | 138 | 34 | 7 | 1 | 4 | 4 | 8 | 12 | .246 | .399 | .288 |
| Runners On | 280 | 85 | 18 | 1 | 7 | 93 | 14 | 26 | .304 | .450 | .328 |
| Runners/Scor. Pos. | 169 | 58 | 14 | 1 | 4 | 85 | 10 | 14 | .343 | .509 | .356 |
| Runners On/2 Out | 114 | 36 | 8 | 1 | 1 | 31 | 6 | 10 | .316 | .430 | .350 |
| Scor. Pos./2 Out | 71 | 26 | 6 | 1 | 1 | 30 | 4 | 6 | .366 | .521 | .400 |
| Late Inning Pressure | 86 | 30 | 7 | 1 | 4 | 19 | 4 | 9 | .349 | .593 | .383 |
| Leading Off | 28 | 8 | 1 | 1 | 1 | 1 | 1 | 3 | .286 | .500 | .310 |
| Runners On | 39 | 14 | 4 | 0 | 2 | 17 | 2 | 4 | .359 | .615 | .386 |
| Runners/Scor. Pos. | 25 | 11 | 3 | 0 | 2 | 16 | 1 | 2 | .440 | .800 | .429 |

| RUNS BATTED IN | From 1B | From 2B | From 3B | Scoring Position |
|---|---|---|---|---|
| Totals | 8/177 | 34/130 | 44/79 | 78/209 |
| Percentage | 5% | 26% | 56% | 37% |
| Driving In Runners from 3B with Less than Two Out: | | | 31/46 | 67% |

Loves to face: Scott Bankhead (.481, 13-for-27, 5 HR)
Hates to face: Mike Smithson (.162, 6-for-37)
His .343 batting average with runners in scoring position was 9th highest in A.L. and a career high. Rate of runners driven in from scoring position was also a career high, and it was even better (13-of-31) in Late-Inning Pressure Situations. . . . Homerless streak of 155 at-bats (June 13 to July 28) was longest of career. . . . Only non-Ripken in A.L. to play in 153+ games in each of last six seasons. . . . Hit all 18 home runs to left field. . . . Has 70 career plate appearances with bases loaded; he's batting .361 (22-for-61), with six grand slams and no walks. . . . Led majors with 14 sacrifice flies; this from the man who has never had a sacrifice *bunt* in 4275 plate appearances (2034 of them with runners on base).

## Joey Belle

Bats Right

| Cleveland Indians | AB | H | 2B | 3B | HR | RBI | BB | SO | BA | SA | OBA |
|---|---|---|---|---|---|---|---|---|---|---|---|
| Season | 218 | 49 | 8 | 4 | 7 | 37 | 12 | 55 | .225 | .394 | .269 |
| vs. Left-Handers | 58 | 15 | 2 | 0 | 3 | 11 | 5 | 13 | .259 | .448 | .308 |
| vs. Right-Handers | 160 | 34 | 6 | 4 | 4 | 26 | 7 | 42 | .213 | .375 | .254 |
| Home | 115 | 28 | 6 | 1 | 3 | 25 | 5 | 30 | .243 | .391 | .276 |
| Road | 103 | 21 | 2 | 3 | 4 | 12 | 7 | 25 | .204 | .398 | .261 |
| Grass | 178 | 38 | 7 | 2 | 5 | 30 | 8 | 47 | .213 | .360 | .249 |
| Artificial Turf | 40 | 11 | 1 | 2 | 2 | 7 | 4 | 8 | .275 | .550 | .356 |
| April | 0 | 0 | 0 | 0 | 0 | 0 | 0 | 0 | — | — | — |
| May | 0 | 0 | 0 | 0 | 0 | 0 | 0 | 0 | — | — | — |
| June | 0 | 0 | 0 | 0 | 0 | 0 | 0 | 0 | — | — | — |
| July | 62 | 17 | 3 | 2 | 3 | 16 | 6 | 15 | .274 | .532 | .343 |
| August | 81 | 15 | 3 | 1 | 3 | 11 | 2 | 22 | .185 | .358 | .202 |
| Sept./Oct. | 75 | 17 | 2 | 1 | 1 | 10 | 4 | 18 | .227 | .320 | .275 |
| Leading Off Inn. | 42 | 9 | 0 | 1 | 2 | 2 | 6 | 11 | .214 | .405 | .327 |
| Runners On | 97 | 26 | 5 | 2 | 4 | 34 | 3 | 25 | .268 | .485 | .291 |
| Runners/Scor. Pos. | 59 | 20 | 5 | 2 | 2 | 30 | 1 | 14 | .339 | .593 | .349 |
| Runners On/2 Out | 44 | 10 | 2 | 1 | 1 | 12 | 1 | 10 | .227 | .386 | .244 |
| Scor. Pos./2 Out | 27 | 8 | 2 | 1 | 0 | 10 | 0 | 7 | .296 | .444 | .296 |
| Late Inning Pressure | 33 | 8 | 2 | 0 | 1 | 10 | 3 | 8 | .242 | .394 | .306 |
| Leading Off | 6 | 0 | 0 | 0 | 0 | 0 | 3 | 1 | .000 | .000 | .333 |
| Runners On | 15 | 7 | 2 | 0 | 1 | 10 | 0 | 4 | .467 | .800 | .467 |
| Runners/Scor. Pos. | 8 | 6 | 2 | 0 | 1 | 10 | 0 | 1 | .750 | 1.375 | .750 |

| RUNS BATTED IN | From 1B | From 2B | From 3B | Scoring Position |
|---|---|---|---|---|
| Totals | 5/72 | 13/47 | 12/29 | 25/76 |
| Percentage | 7% | 28% | 41% | 33% |
| Driving In Runners from 3B with Less than Two Out: | | | 8/15 | 53% |

Loves to face: Jeff Ballard (.667, 2-for-3, 2 HR)
Hates to face: Richard Dotson (0-for-6, 4 SO)
Look at the last line on his grid: 6-for-8 in Late-Inning Pressure Situations with runners in scoring position. He drove in eight of the nine runners he found on second or third in LIPS; we know those numbers are small, but that's the best one-season rate by any player in our 15 years compiling the data. (Jim Essian drove in 8-of-10 in his legendary 1982 season.) . . .His overall batting average of .339 with runners in scoring position was 10th in A.L., right after the Bell without an "e." . . . Drove in 15 runs in his first 12 games. . . . Batted .408 on fair balls hit to left side, but only .219 straight away, and .200 to right side. . . . Born Aug. 25, 1966; Indians' starter that night at Baltimore? Gary Bell. Spooky, huh?

## Dave Bergman

Bats Left

| Detroit Tigers | AB | H | 2B | 3B | HR | RBI | BB | SO | BA | SA | OBA |
|---|---|---|---|---|---|---|---|---|---|---|---|
| Season | 385 | 103 | 13 | 1 | 7 | 37 | 44 | 44 | .268 | .361 | .345 |
| vs. Left-Handers | 60 | 12 | 2 | 0 | 0 | 8 | 3 | 14 | .200 | .233 | .250 |
| vs. Right-Handers | 325 | 91 | 11 | 1 | 7 | 29 | 41 | 30 | .280 | .385 | .361 |
| Home | 173 | 43 | 5 | 0 | 6 | 15 | 19 | 26 | .249 | .382 | .325 |
| Road | 212 | 60 | 8 | 1 | 1 | 22 | 25 | 18 | .283 | .344 | .361 |
| Grass | 324 | 82 | 9 | 0 | 6 | 26 | 35 | 38 | .253 | .336 | .329 |
| Artificial Turf | 61 | 21 | 4 | 1 | 1 | 11 | 9 | 6 | .344 | .492 | .429 |
| April | 42 | 10 | 0 | 0 | 1 | 6 | 5 | 6 | .238 | .310 | .319 |
| May | 55 | 15 | 1 | 0 | 0 | 1 | 7 | 11 | .273 | .291 | .355 |
| June | 63 | 18 | 3 | 0 | 1 | 7 | 10 | 6 | .286 | .381 | .378 |
| July | 51 | 13 | 2 | 0 | 2 | 3 | 5 | 2 | .255 | .412 | .321 |
| August | 97 | 23 | 5 | 1 | 2 | 8 | 4 | 8 | .237 | .371 | .275 |
| Sept./Oct. | 77 | 24 | 2 | 0 | 1 | 12 | 13 | 11 | .312 | .377 | .418 |
| Leading Off Inn. | 74 | 14 | 1 | 0 | 2 | 2 | 8 | 9 | .189 | .284 | .268 |
| Runners On | 161 | 47 | 8 | 0 | 0 | 30 | 24 | 14 | .292 | .342 | .388 |
| Runners/Scor. Pos. | 89 | 27 | 6 | 0 | 0 | 29 | 17 | 9 | .303 | .371 | .422 |
| Runners On/2 Out | 65 | 18 | 3 | 0 | 0 | 12 | 14 | 7 | .277 | .323 | .413 |
| Scor. Pos./2 Out | 40 | 11 | 3 | 0 | 0 | 12 | 10 | 4 | .275 | .350 | .431 |
| Late Inning Pressure | 60 | 11 | 0 | 0 | 0 | 4 | 7 | 12 | .183 | .183 | .279 |
| Leading Off | 12 | 1 | 0 | 0 | 0 | 0 | 1 | 1 | .083 | .083 | .154 |
| Runners On | 26 | 5 | 0 | 0 | 0 | 4 | 4 | 5 | .192 | .192 | .323 |
| Runners/Scor. Pos. | 14 | 3 | 0 | 0 | 0 | 4 | 4 | 2 | .214 | .214 | .421 |

| RUNS BATTED IN | From 1B | From 2B | From 3B | Scoring Position |
|---|---|---|---|---|
| Totals | 3/118 | 11/70 | 16/39 | 27/109 |
| Percentage | 3% | 16% | 41% | 25% |
| Driving In Runners from 3B with Less than Two Out: | | | 12/19 | 63% |

Loves to face: Willie Fraser (.462, 6-for-13, 3 HR)
Hates to face: Mike Moore (.133, 4-for-30)
Had career-high totals of starts (106) and at-bats (385). . . . All seven homers were solo shots to right field off right-handed pitchers. Of 44 career homers only two have been off southpaws, none since 1978. . . . One of two players to start at least once in all nine batting-order positions last year. . . . Batted .056 (1-for-18) as a pinch hitter in 1989 after 10 hitless pinch-hit at-bats to end 1988 season. . . . Yearly batting averages with runners in scoring position since 1985: .038, .172, .209, .290, .303. . . . Finished 7th among 10 A.L. qualifiers in fielding at first base. Did you know that in 89 years in A.L., only two Detroit first basemen have led league in fielding (Greenberg in '39, Cash in '64 and '67)?

## Wade Boggs

Bats Left

| Boston Red Sox | AB | H | 2B | 3B | HR | RBI | BB | SO | BA | SA | OBA |
|---|---|---|---|---|---|---|---|---|---|---|---|
| Season | 621 | 205 | 51 | 7 | 3 | 54 | 107 | 51 | .330 | .449 | .430 |
| vs. Left-Handers | 210 | 62 | 10 | 1 | 0 | 17 | 25 | 24 | .295 | .352 | .377 |
| vs. Right-Handers | 411 | 143 | 41 | 6 | 3 | 37 | 82 | 27 | .348 | .499 | .455 |
| Home | 300 | 113 | 37 | 4 | 2 | 27 | 57 | 21 | .377 | .547 | .475 |
| Road | 321 | 92 | 14 | 3 | 1 | 27 | 50 | 30 | .287 | .358 | .386 |
| Grass | 518 | 179 | 47 | 7 | 3 | 42 | 91 | 40 | .346 | .481 | .445 |
| Artificial Turf | 103 | 26 | 4 | 0 | 0 | 12 | 16 | 11 | .252 | .291 | .352 |
| April | 92 | 27 | 6 | 0 | 0 | 6 | 18 | 10 | .293 | .359 | .405 |
| May | 86 | 25 | 8 | 4 | 1 | 13 | 9 | 11 | .291 | .512 | .351 |
| June | 105 | 40 | 8 | 2 | 1 | 14 | 19 | 4 | .381 | .524 | .477 |
| July | 95 | 33 | 11 | 1 | 0 | 7 | 27 | 9 | .347 | .484 | .492 |
| August | 137 | 49 | 10 | 0 | 1 | 5 | 13 | 11 | .358 | .453 | .425 |
| Sept./Oct. | 106 | 31 | 8 | 0 | 0 | 9 | 21 | 6 | .292 | .368 | .411 |
| Leading Off Inn. | 235 | 79 | 18 | 2 | 1 | 1 | 25 | 20 | .336 | .443 | .402 |
| Runners On | 228 | 80 | 17 | 2 | 0 | 51 | 52 | 17 | .351 | .443 | .469 |
| Runners/Scor. Pos. | 125 | 42 | 6 | 1 | 0 | 45 | 39 | 14 | .336 | .400 | .483 |
| Runners On/2 Out | 94 | 29 | 6 | 0 | 0 | 16 | 29 | 5 | .309 | .372 | .476 |
| Scor. Pos./2 Out | 59 | 17 | 4 | 0 | 0 | 15 | 25 | 3 | .288 | .356 | .500 |
| Late Inning Pressure | 94 | 22 | 7 | 0 | 0 | 5 | 7 | 11 | .234 | .309 | .291 |
| Leading Off | 16 | 3 | 2 | 0 | 0 | 0 | 2 | 2 | .188 | .313 | .278 |
| Runners On | 44 | 14 | 4 | 0 | 0 | 5 | 4 | 3 | .318 | .409 | .380 |
| Runners/Scor. Pos. | 24 | 5 | 0 | 0 | 0 | 4 | 4 | 3 | .208 | .208 | .310 |

| RUNS BATTED IN | From 1B | From 2B | From 3B | Scoring Position |
|---|---|---|---|---|
| Totals | 7/175 | 18/98 | 26/54 | 44/152 |
| Percentage | 4% | 18% | 48% | 29% |
| Driving In Runners from 3B with Less than Two Out: | | | 19/28 | 68% |

Loves to face: Bret Saberhagen (.514, 18-for-35, 1 HR)
Hates to face: Bob Welch (0-for-12)
If he gets 200+ hits in 1990, he ties Willie Keeler's record of eight straight years doing that. . . . Led Red Sox in batting for 7th year in a row, breaking Tris Speaker's record of six. . . . Of 570 fair balls, 300 (53%) were hit to opposite field. Batted .445 on balls hit up middle, .373 to left side, but only .241 on balls that he pulled. Hit .150 (6-for-40) on fair balls hit to right side off left-handed pitchers. . . . Career averages: .370 vs. right-handers, .383 at Fenway, .404 vs. right-handers at Fenway. . . . Hit below .300 vs. lefties for first time since 1984. . . . Went 1-for-11 with bases loaded last year. . . . Since 1987, has batted only .248 in Late-Inning Pressure Situations, .368 in other at-bats.

## Bob Boone

Bats Right

| Kansas City Royals | AB | H | 2B | 3B | HR | RBI | BB | SO | BA | SA | OBA |
|---|---|---|---|---|---|---|---|---|---|---|---|
| Season | 405 | 111 | 13 | 2 | 1 | 44 | 49 | 37 | .274 | .323 | .351 |
| vs. Left-Handers | 97 | 28 | 4 | 0 | 0 | 9 | 19 | 4 | .289 | .330 | .408 |
| vs. Right-Handers | 308 | 83 | 9 | 2 | 1 | 35 | 30 | 33 | .269 | .321 | .331 |
| Home | 199 | 63 | 6 | 1 | 1 | 25 | 26 | 11 | .317 | .372 | .392 |
| Road | 206 | 48 | 7 | 1 | 0 | 19 | 23 | 26 | .233 | .277 | .312 |
| Grass | 155 | 37 | 7 | 0 | 0 | 12 | 17 | 21 | .239 | .284 | .316 |
| Artificial Turf | 250 | 74 | 6 | 2 | 1 | 32 | 32 | 16 | .296 | .348 | .373 |
| April | 67 | 20 | 6 | 0 | 0 | 8 | 9 | 3 | .299 | .388 | .390 |
| May | 60 | 12 | 0 | 0 | 0 | 2 | 4 | 11 | .200 | .200 | .262 |
| June | 73 | 27 | 4 | 1 | 1 | 17 | 6 | 5 | .370 | .493 | .413 |
| July | 69 | 18 | 2 | 0 | 0 | 6 | 16 | 7 | .261 | .290 | .395 |
| August | 69 | 14 | 1 | 0 | 0 | 6 | 9 | 4 | .203 | .217 | .288 |
| Sept./Oct. | 67 | 20 | 0 | 1 | 0 | 5 | 5 | 7 | .299 | .328 | .342 |
| Leading Off Inn. | 100 | 26 | 4 | 0 | 0 | 0 | 7 | 9 | .260 | .300 | .308 |
| Runners On | 176 | 54 | 5 | 1 | 1 | 44 | 20 | 14 | .307 | .364 | .371 |
| Runners/Scor. Pos. | 100 | 35 | 3 | 0 | 1 | 42 | 13 | 6 | .350 | .410 | .412 |
| Runners On/2 Out | 67 | 18 | 1 | 0 | 0 | 13 | 9 | 4 | .269 | .284 | .364 |
| Scor. Pos./2 Out | 40 | 12 | 0 | 0 | 0 | 12 | 6 | 1 | .300 | .300 | .404 |
| Late Inning Pressure | 55 | 19 | 2 | 0 | 0 | 6 | 5 | 4 | .345 | .382 | .403 |
| Leading Off | 20 | 10 | 2 | 0 | 0 | 0 | 1 | 2 | .500 | .600 | .524 |
| Runners On | 19 | 7 | 0 | 0 | 0 | 6 | 2 | 0 | .368 | .368 | .409 |
| Runners/Scor. Pos. | 11 | 5 | 0 | 0 | 0 | 6 | 2 | 0 | .455 | .455 | .500 |

| RUNS BATTED IN | From 1B | From 2B | From 3B | Scoring Position |
|---|---|---|---|---|
| Totals | 4/124 | 19/87 | 20/37 | 39/124 |
| Percentage | 3% | 22% | 54% | 31% |
| Driving In Runners from 3B with Less than Two Out: | | | 15/25 | 60% |

Loves to face: Floyd Bannister (.380, 19-for-50, 3 HR)
Hates to face: Dave Stewart (.118, 4-for-34)
Royals had 76–51 record with Boone starting, 16–19 with other catchers. . . . But staff ERA and opponents' stolen-base rate were about the same with Mike Macfarlane as with Boone. . . . Oldest regular catcher in major league history. . . . Has caught all-time record 2185 games; enters 1990 with 257-game lead over Fisk. . . . Last two seasons: .320 on carpets, .259 on grass fields. . . . Has batted .284 over last two years, 2d-highest two-year average of his career. He hit .285 in 1978–79. . . . His first hit in majors came off Jim McAndrew on Sept. 12, 1972, the same pitcher and game that produced Mike Schmidt's first hit. . . . First major league battery-mate was Darrell Brandon; first at-bat: a strikeout vs. Joe Decker.

## Pat Borders

Bats Right

| Toronto Blue Jays | AB | H | 2B | 3B | HR | RBI | BB | SO | BA | SA | OBA |
|---|---|---|---|---|---|---|---|---|---|---|---|
| Season | 241 | 62 | 11 | 1 | 3 | 30 | 11 | 45 | .257 | .349 | .290 |
| vs. Left-Handers | 171 | 48 | 8 | 1 | 2 | 26 | 8 | 29 | .281 | .374 | .313 |
| vs. Right-Handers | 70 | 14 | 3 | 0 | 1 | 4 | 3 | 16 | .200 | .286 | .233 |
| Home | 105 | 26 | 8 | 0 | 1 | 14 | 4 | 18 | .248 | .352 | .279 |
| Road | 136 | 36 | 3 | 1 | 2 | 16 | 7 | 27 | .265 | .346 | .299 |
| Grass | 103 | 30 | 2 | 1 | 1 | 15 | 7 | 19 | .291 | .359 | .333 |
| Artificial Turf | 138 | 32 | 9 | 0 | 2 | 15 | 4 | 26 | .232 | .341 | .257 |
| April | 63 | 16 | 3 | 1 | 1 | 4 | 2 | 15 | .254 | .381 | .277 |
| May | 39 | 6 | 2 | 0 | 0 | 6 | 1 | 11 | .154 | .205 | .175 |
| June | 31 | 12 | 2 | 0 | 0 | 5 | 2 | 4 | .387 | .452 | .441 |
| July | 39 | 13 | 1 | 0 | 1 | 8 | 4 | 4 | .333 | .436 | .386 |
| August | 25 | 6 | 0 | 0 | 1 | 5 | 0 | 3 | .240 | .360 | .231 |
| Sept./Oct. | 44 | 9 | 3 | 0 | 0 | 2 | 2 | 8 | .205 | .273 | .239 |
| Leading Off Inn. | 44 | 16 | 3 | 0 | 1 | 1 | 2 | 9 | .364 | .500 | .391 |
| Runners On | 109 | 31 | 5 | 1 | 1 | 28 | 6 | 14 | .284 | .376 | .316 |
| Runners/Scor. Pos. | 59 | 17 | 3 | 0 | 1 | 26 | 4 | 9 | .288 | .390 | .323 |
| Runners On/2 Out | 39 | 7 | 0 | 0 | 0 | 6 | 1 | 4 | .179 | .179 | .200 |
| Scor. Pos./2 Out | 26 | 5 | 0 | 0 | 0 | 6 | 0 | 2 | .192 | .192 | .192 |
| Late Inning Pressure | 43 | 12 | 1 | 0 | 1 | 7 | 1 | 9 | .279 | .372 | .295 |
| Leading Off | 8 | 2 | 0 | 0 | 0 | 0 | 0 | 3 | .250 | .250 | .250 |
| Runners On | 20 | 6 | 0 | 0 | 1 | 7 | 1 | 0 | .300 | .450 | .333 |
| Runners/Scor. Pos. | 10 | 3 | 0 | 0 | 1 | 7 | 1 | 0 | .300 | .600 | .364 |

| RUNS BATTED IN | From 1B | From 2B | From 3B | Scoring Position |
|---|---|---|---|---|
| Totals | 3/80 | 9/44 | 15/29 | 24/73 |
| Percentage | 4% | 20% | 52% | 33% |
| Driving In Runners from 3B with Less than Two Out: | | | 11/16 | 69% |

Loves to face: Frank Tanana (.467, 7-for-15)
Hates to face: Dave LaPoint (.143, 2-for-14, 1 HR)
Only A.L. catcher to throw out each of the league's top five base stealers (Rickey, Espy, Pettis, Devon White, and Sax). . . . For season, 64 percent of opposing base stealers were successful; with other Jays catching, rate was 70 percent. . . . Jays' staff ERA was lower with Borders catching (3.31) than with any other backstop: Whitt (3.64), Myers (3.75), or Brenly (4.59). Of five pitchers with most starts, only Flanagan had a lower ERA with Whitt catching than with Borders. . . . Had the most hits of any player without a three-hit game. . . . The only player to start all 49 games in which Jays faced left-handed starters, but started only 9 of 113 vs. right-handers. Career averages: .281 vs. lefties, .207 vs. righties.

## Daryl Boston

Bats Left

| Chicago White Sox | AB | H | 2B | 3B | HR | RBI | BB | SO | BA | SA | OBA |
|---|---|---|---|---|---|---|---|---|---|---|---|
| Season | 218 | 55 | 3 | 4 | 5 | 23 | 24 | 31 | .252 | .372 | .325 |
| vs. Left-Handers | 27 | 3 | 0 | 1 | 0 | 2 | 0 | 7 | .111 | .185 | .107 |
| vs. Right-Handers | 191 | 52 | 3 | 3 | 5 | 21 | 24 | 24 | .272 | .398 | .353 |
| Home | 114 | 33 | 1 | 4 | 3 | 12 | 9 | 14 | .289 | .447 | .339 |
| Road | 104 | 22 | 2 | 0 | 2 | 11 | 15 | 17 | .212 | .288 | .311 |
| Grass | 193 | 46 | 2 | 4 | 5 | 21 | 17 | 28 | .238 | .368 | .299 |
| Artificial Turf | 25 | 9 | 1 | 0 | 0 | 2 | 7 | 3 | .360 | .400 | .500 |
| April | 32 | 7 | 0 | 0 | 0 | 2 | 5 | 5 | .219 | .219 | .316 |
| May | 23 | 5 | 0 | 1 | 0 | 0 | 2 | 3 | .217 | .304 | .280 |
| June | 28 | 7 | 0 | 1 | 2 | 9 | 0 | 3 | .250 | .536 | .250 |
| July | 45 | 12 | 3 | 0 | 0 | 2 | 4 | 7 | .267 | .333 | .327 |
| August | 42 | 12 | 0 | 1 | 1 | 2 | 6 | 6 | .286 | .405 | .375 |
| Sept./Oct. | 48 | 12 | 0 | 1 | 2 | 8 | 7 | 7 | .250 | .417 | .345 |
| Leading Off Inn. | 52 | 15 | 0 | 2 | 2 | 2 | 3 | 9 | .288 | .481 | .327 |
| Runners On | 97 | 24 | 2 | 1 | 3 | 21 | 12 | 13 | .247 | .381 | .327 |
| Runners/Scor. Pos. | 47 | 13 | 0 | 1 | 2 | 18 | 10 | 7 | .277 | .447 | .397 |
| Runners On/2 Out | 47 | 9 | 1 | 1 | 1 | 6 | 8 | 7 | .191 | .319 | .309 |
| Scor. Pos./2 Out | 23 | 2 | 0 | 1 | 0 | 4 | 6 | 4 | .087 | .174 | .276 |
| Late Inning Pressure | 40 | 10 | 2 | 1 | 1 | 2 | 7 | 8 | .250 | .425 | .362 |
| Leading Off | 9 | 2 | 0 | 0 | 1 | 1 | 0 | 4 | .222 | .556 | .222 |
| Runners On | 15 | 3 | 1 | 0 | 0 | 1 | 5 | 3 | .200 | .267 | .400 |
| Runners/Scor. Pos. | 6 | 1 | 0 | 0 | 0 | 1 | 5 | 1 | .167 | .167 | .545 |

| RUNS BATTED IN | From 1B | From 2B | From 3B | Scoring Position |
|---|---|---|---|---|
| Totals | 5/79 | 3/38 | 10/20 | 13/58 |
| Percentage | 6% | 8% | 50% | 22% |
| Driving In Runners from 3B with Less than Two Out: | | | 8/10 | 80% |

Loves to face: Charlie Hough (.394, 13-for-33, 2 HR)
Hates to face: Mike Moore (.087, 2-for-23)
Winner of the 1989 Rafael Belliard Award: the only player in majors (minimum: 100 at-bats) with more triples than doubles. . . . Made 54 starts, but only four vs. left-handed pitchers. . . . Of his 38 career homers, 37 have come off right-handers, one off Mark Thurmond. . . . Most career plate appearances (1480) among active A.L. players who have never been hit by a pitch. . . . Batted .364 on fair balls that he pulled, .313 straight away, .194 on balls hit the other way. . . . Grounded into only one double play in 44 DP situations. . . . Has never had a hit with two outs and the bases loaded; he's 0-for-12. Recognizing his limitations, he drew a couple of run-scoring walks in those situations last year!

## Phil Bradley

Bats Right

| Baltimore Orioles | AB | H | 2B | 3B | HR | RBI | BB | SO | BA | SA | OBA |
|---|---|---|---|---|---|---|---|---|---|---|---|
| Season | 545 | 151 | 23 | 10 | 11 | 55 | 70 | 103 | .277 | .417 | .364 |
| vs. Left-Handers | 192 | 57 | 11 | 5 | 8 | 22 | 24 | 29 | .297 | .531 | .379 |
| vs. Right-Handers | 353 | 94 | 12 | 5 | 3 | 33 | 46 | 74 | .266 | .354 | .356 |
| Home | 255 | 73 | 14 | 3 | 3 | 25 | 34 | 42 | .286 | .400 | .378 |
| Road | 290 | 78 | 9 | 7 | 8 | 30 | 36 | 61 | .269 | .431 | .352 |
| Grass | 460 | 128 | 22 | 6 | 7 | 42 | 57 | 86 | .278 | .398 | .363 |
| Artificial Turf | 85 | 23 | 1 | 4 | 4 | 13 | 13 | 17 | .271 | .518 | .370 |
| April | 94 | 24 | 2 | 4 | 3 | 13 | 12 | 26 | .255 | .457 | .336 |
| May | 82 | 26 | 3 | 2 | 0 | 6 | 10 | 13 | .317 | .402 | .404 |
| June | 82 | 22 | 6 | 0 | 1 | 8 | 14 | 10 | .268 | .378 | .375 |
| July | 98 | 33 | 3 | 4 | 3 | 17 | 8 | 13 | .337 | .541 | .394 |
| August | 104 | 21 | 5 | 0 | 2 | 7 | 18 | 26 | .202 | .308 | .325 |
| Sept./Oct. | 85 | 25 | 4 | 0 | 2 | 4 | 8 | 15 | .294 | .412 | .362 |
| Leading Off Inn. | 123 | 40 | 8 | 1 | 3 | 3 | 11 | 19 | .325 | .480 | .385 |
| Runners On | 197 | 52 | 7 | 4 | 2 | 46 | 44 | 38 | .264 | .371 | .404 |
| Runners/Scor. Pos. | 123 | 30 | 4 | 4 | 1 | 43 | 31 | 24 | .244 | .366 | .398 |
| Runners On/2 Out | 81 | 22 | 3 | 2 | 2 | 21 | 21 | 17 | .272 | .432 | .427 |
| Scor. Pos./2 Out | 53 | 14 | 3 | 2 | 1 | 19 | 14 | 12 | .264 | .453 | .418 |
| Late Inning Pressure | 60 | 11 | 1 | 0 | 0 | 3 | 11 | 16 | .183 | .200 | .310 |
| Leading Off | 10 | 1 | 0 | 0 | 0 | 0 | 1 | 2 | .100 | .100 | .182 |
| Runners On | 32 | 6 | 0 | 0 | 0 | 3 | 8 | 6 | .188 | .188 | .350 |
| Runners/Scor. Pos. | 20 | 3 | 0 | 0 | 0 | 3 | 5 | 5 | .150 | .150 | .320 |

| RUNS BATTED IN | From 1B | From 2B | From 3B | Scoring Position |
|---|---|---|---|---|
| Totals | 5/127 | 13/96 | 26/64 | 39/160 |
| Percentage | 4% | 14% | 41% | 24% |
| Driving In Runners from 3B with Less than Two Out: | | | 17/35 | 49% |

Loves to face: Ted Higuera (.424, 14-for-33, 1 HR)
Hates to face: Chuck Cary (0-for-11)

One of six players with five straight seasons of 10+ home runs and 10+ steals; Bradley also has 100+ strikeouts in each of those years. ... Hit six first-inning home runs, second in A.L. to Lou Whitaker's eight. ... Had highest batting average on club, but lowest to lead Orioles since Frank Robinson's .268 in 1968. ... Birds' starting left fielder in 1989 season opener. O's haven't had an opening-day repeater at that position since Gary Roenicke (1978–83). ... Career average is higher vs. right-handers (.292) than vs. left-handers (.287), but has better power vs. lefties. ... Has hit .114 (4-for-35) with bases loaded over last three years. ... Played on a winning team for first time in seven years in majors.

## Scott Bradley

Bats Left

| Seattle Mariners | AB | H | 2B | 3B | HR | RBI | BB | SO | BA | SA | OBA |
|---|---|---|---|---|---|---|---|---|---|---|---|
| Season | 270 | 74 | 16 | 0 | 3 | 38 | 21 | 23 | .274 | .367 | .322 |
| vs. Left-Handers | 14 | 2 | 1 | 0 | 0 | 2 | 2 | 2 | .143 | .214 | .250 |
| vs. Right-Handers | 256 | 72 | 15 | 0 | 3 | 36 | 19 | 21 | .281 | .375 | .326 |
| Home | 131 | 36 | 10 | 0 | 1 | 13 | 11 | 12 | .275 | .374 | .329 |
| Road | 139 | 38 | 6 | 0 | 2 | 25 | 10 | 11 | .273 | .360 | .316 |
| Grass | 103 | 30 | 5 | 0 | 2 | 20 | 7 | 7 | .291 | .398 | .330 |
| Artificial Turf | 167 | 44 | 11 | 0 | 1 | 18 | 14 | 16 | .263 | .347 | .317 |
| April | 27 | 9 | 2 | 0 | 0 | 10 | 3 | 3 | .333 | .407 | .353 |
| May | 48 | 14 | 2 | 0 | 2 | 7 | 1 | 3 | .292 | .458 | .320 |
| June | 68 | 16 | 4 | 0 | 0 | 8 | 4 | 5 | .235 | .294 | .274 |
| July | 41 | 14 | 4 | 0 | 1 | 6 | 6 | 4 | .341 | .512 | .426 |
| August | 48 | 14 | 3 | 0 | 0 | 2 | 4 | 7 | .292 | .354 | .340 |
| Sept./Oct. | 38 | 7 | 1 | 0 | 0 | 5 | 3 | 1 | .184 | .211 | .244 |
| Leading Off Inn. | 73 | 16 | 2 | 0 | 0 | 0 | 2 | 8 | .219 | .247 | .240 |
| Runners On | 113 | 39 | 10 | 0 | 2 | 37 | 10 | 10 | .345 | .487 | .385 |
| Runners/Scor. Pos. | 70 | 20 | 7 | 0 | 2 | 36 | 6 | 6 | .286 | .471 | .325 |
| Runners On/2 Out | 45 | 10 | 4 | 0 | 0 | 13 | 4 | 4 | .222 | .311 | .286 |
| Scor. Pos./2 Out | 33 | 7 | 3 | 0 | 0 | 12 | 2 | 3 | .212 | .303 | .257 |
| Late Inning Pressure | 50 | 15 | 5 | 0 | 1 | 5 | 3 | 6 | .300 | .460 | .340 |
| Leading Off | 15 | 2 | 0 | 0 | 0 | 0 | 0 | 1 | .133 | .133 | .133 |
| Runners On | 23 | 9 | 4 | 0 | 0 | 4 | 2 | 4 | .391 | .565 | .440 |
| Runners/Scor. Pos. | 12 | 3 | 2 | 0 | 0 | 3 | 2 | 3 | .250 | .417 | .357 |

| RUNS BATTED IN | From 1B | From 2B | From 3B | Scoring Position |
|---|---|---|---|---|
| Totals | 3/77 | 14/59 | 18/36 | 32/95 |
| Percentage | 4% | 24% | 50% | 34% |
| Driving In Runners from 3B with Less than Two Out: | | | 11/16 | 69% |

Loves to face: Richard Dotson (.412, 7-for-17, 3 HR)
Hates to face: Roy Smith (0-for-7)

His .345 batting average with runners on base was 4th best in A.L.; hit .397 in those situations after June 15. ... Started 59 percent of games in which Seattle faced right-handed starters, but started only one of 49 games vs. southpaws. Career average of .281 (16 HR) vs. right-handers, only .193 (one HR) vs. lefties. ... Batted .328 vs. ground-ball pitchers, .228 vs. fly-ballers. ... Failed to reach base in 23 consecutive plate appearances leading off innings, July 22–Sept. 22, longest streak in majors in '89 and a team record. ... Owns career rate of one strikeout every 19.1 plate appearances, 2d-best among players active in 1989 (minimum: 1000 plate appearances). Top five: Buckner, Bradley, Gwynn, Mattingly, Ray.

## Glenn Braggs

Bats Right

| Milwaukee Brewers | AB | H | 2B | 3B | HR | RBI | BB | SO | BA | SA | OBA |
|---|---|---|---|---|---|---|---|---|---|---|---|
| Season | 514 | 127 | 12 | 3 | 15 | 66 | 42 | 111 | .247 | .370 | .305 |
| vs. Left-Handers | 142 | 43 | 5 | 0 | 6 | 25 | 15 | 18 | .303 | .465 | .365 |
| vs. Right-Handers | 372 | 84 | 7 | 3 | 9 | 41 | 27 | 93 | .226 | .333 | .282 |
| Home | 275 | 58 | 7 | 3 | 8 | 36 | 24 | 66 | .211 | .345 | .279 |
| Road | 239 | 69 | 5 | 0 | 7 | 30 | 18 | 45 | .289 | .397 | .336 |
| Grass | 433 | 101 | 11 | 3 | 12 | 52 | 35 | 96 | .233 | .356 | .293 |
| Artificial Turf | 81 | 26 | 1 | 0 | 3 | 14 | 7 | 15 | .321 | .444 | .371 |
| April | 82 | 21 | 1 | 1 | 4 | 14 | 8 | 22 | .256 | .439 | .322 |
| May | 103 | 26 | 2 | 1 | 4 | 13 | 7 | 24 | .252 | .408 | .297 |
| June | 109 | 31 | 3 | 1 | 3 | 13 | 5 | 21 | .284 | .413 | .322 |
| July | 73 | 14 | 1 | 0 | 1 | 9 | 9 | 8 | .192 | .247 | .282 |
| August | 93 | 21 | 5 | 0 | 1 | 10 | 6 | 21 | .226 | .312 | .277 |
| Sept./Oct. | 54 | 14 | 0 | 0 | 2 | 7 | 7 | 15 | .259 | .370 | .339 |
| Leading Off Inn. | 114 | 22 | 3 | 0 | 2 | 2 | 11 | 23 | .193 | .272 | .276 |
| Runners On | 230 | 63 | 4 | 3 | 6 | 57 | 15 | 45 | .274 | .396 | .312 |
| Runners/Scor. Pos. | 130 | 31 | 2 | 2 | 1 | 45 | 9 | 26 | .238 | .308 | .279 |
| Runners On/2 Out | 89 | 17 | 0 | 0 | 1 | 10 | 3 | 20 | .191 | .225 | .226 |
| Scor. Pos./2 Out | 60 | 8 | 0 | 0 | 1 | 10 | 2 | 14 | .133 | .183 | .175 |
| Late Inning Pressure | 67 | 17 | 4 | 0 | 1 | 4 | 5 | 17 | .254 | .358 | .315 |
| Leading Off | 24 | 3 | 1 | 0 | 0 | 0 | 0 | 4 | .125 | .167 | .125 |
| Runners On | 24 | 6 | 0 | 0 | 1 | 4 | 3 | 7 | .250 | .375 | .333 |
| Runners/Scor. Pos. | 16 | 3 | 0 | 0 | 1 | 4 | 1 | 5 | .188 | .375 | .235 |

| RUNS BATTED IN | From 1B | From 2B | From 3B | Scoring Position |
|---|---|---|---|---|
| Totals | 7/176 | 15/101 | 29/61 | 44/162 |
| Percentage | 4% | 15% | 48% | 27% |
| Driving In Runners from 3B with Less than Two Out: | | | 26/38 | 68% |

Loves to face: Mike Witt (.423, 11-for-26, 3 HR)
Hates to face: Rich Yett (0-for-7, 4 SO)

Hit 11 of his 15 home runs before the All-Star break. Has hit 22 of his 42 career home runs in April and May, months which have accounted for only 35 percent of his at-bats. ... All 15 home runs were hit to right field. ... Batted over .300 in three of four years in minors, but has not yet reached .270 mark in four seasons in majors. ... Scored from second base on 13 of 13 singles to the outfield last season, but went from first to third on only six of 13 singles to right field. ... A .198 career hitter with two outs and runners in scoring position. ... A total of 106 players active in 1989 have played 300+ major league games in the outfield; 100 of them have higher fielding percentages than Braggs (.963).

## George Brett

Bats Left

| Kansas City Royals | AB | H | 2B | 3B | HR | RBI | BB | SO | BA | SA | OBA |
|---|---|---|---|---|---|---|---|---|---|---|---|
| Season | 457 | 129 | 26 | 3 | 12 | 80 | 59 | 47 | .282 | .431 | .362 |
| vs. Left-Handers | 167 | 37 | 9 | 1 | 2 | 24 | 17 | 17 | .222 | .323 | .296 |
| vs. Right-Handers | 290 | 92 | 17 | 2 | 10 | 56 | 42 | 30 | .317 | .493 | .398 |
| Home | 229 | 63 | 11 | 3 | 3 | 37 | 34 | 21 | .275 | .389 | .363 |
| Road | 228 | 66 | 15 | 0 | 9 | 43 | 25 | 26 | .289 | .474 | .360 |
| Grass | 183 | 54 | 11 | 0 | 8 | 38 | 19 | 22 | .295 | .486 | .362 |
| Artificial Turf | 274 | 75 | 15 | 3 | 4 | 42 | 40 | 25 | .274 | .394 | .361 |
| April | 79 | 20 | 1 | 0 | 2 | 13 | 14 | 9 | .253 | .342 | .358 |
| May | 0 | 0 | 0 | 0 | 0 | 0 | 0 | 0 | — | — | — |
| June | 77 | 16 | 7 | 0 | 1 | 10 | 6 | 11 | .208 | .338 | .259 |
| July | 98 | 27 | 4 | 1 | 4 | 19 | 10 | 6 | .276 | .459 | .342 |
| August | 102 | 33 | 7 | 2 | 2 | 15 | 17 | 8 | .324 | .490 | .418 |
| Sept./Oct. | 101 | 33 | 7 | 0 | 3 | 23 | 12 | 13 | .327 | .485 | .400 |
| Leading Off Inn. | 62 | 19 | 3 | 0 | 2 | 2 | 12 | 8 | .306 | .452 | .419 |
| Runners On | 242 | 69 | 11 | 1 | 6 | 74 | 30 | 26 | .285 | .413 | .359 |
| Runners/Scor. Pos. | 133 | 39 | 6 | 0 | 2 | 63 | 26 | 14 | .293 | .383 | .394 |
| Runners On/2 Out | 78 | 18 | 3 | 1 | 2 | 20 | 14 | 8 | .231 | .372 | .348 |
| Scor. Pos./2 Out | 49 | 12 | 3 | 0 | 1 | 17 | 13 | 6 | .245 | .367 | .403 |
| Late Inning Pressure | 59 | 17 | 3 | 0 | 1 | 9 | 10 | 7 | .288 | .390 | .391 |
| Leading Off | 13 | 4 | 1 | 0 | 0 | 0 | 3 | 4 | .308 | .385 | .438 |
| Runners On | 32 | 8 | 0 | 0 | 0 | 8 | 7 | 2 | .250 | .250 | .385 |
| Runners/Scor. Pos. | 19 | 5 | 0 | 0 | 0 | 8 | 6 | 1 | .263 | .263 | .440 |

| RUNS BATTED IN | From 1B | From 2B | From 3B | Scoring Position |
|---|---|---|---|---|
| Totals | 10/177 | 27/106 | 31/59 | 58/165 |
| Percentage | 6% | 25% | 53% | 35% |
| Driving In Runners from 3B with Less than Two Out: | | | 26/37 | 70% |

Loves to face: Gene Nelson (.417, 10-for-24, 5 HR)
Hates to face: Kevin Hickey (0-for-10)

Only seven other players in history, all Hall of Famers, equal or surpass his career figures in batting average, runs, hits, home runs, and RBI: Foxx, Gehrig, Hornsby, Musial, Ruth, Al Simmons, and Ted Williams. Brett stands alone if you add in stolen bases as an additional category. ... Leads active players with 514 doubles, 901 extra-base hits, and 190 intentional walks. ... Rate of 35 percent of runners driven in from scoring position since 1975 is 2d best among active players; Mattingly has a career rate of 37 percent. George's rate has been above 30 percent (which is about the equivalent of a .290 batting average) in each of last 15 years. ... Had six game-winning RBI last season: one in April, five in September.

## Greg Briley

Bats Left

| Seattle Mariners | AB | H | 2B | 3B | HR | RBI | BB | SO | BA | SA | OBA |
|---|---|---|---|---|---|---|---|---|---|---|---|
| Season | 394 | 105 | 22 | 4 | 13 | 52 | 39 | 82 | .266 | .442 | .336 |
| vs. Left-Handers | 53 | 17 | 3 | 1 | 1 | 7 | 6 | 13 | .321 | .472 | .400 |
| vs. Right-Handers | 341 | 88 | 19 | 3 | 12 | 45 | 33 | 69 | .258 | .437 | .326 |
| Home | 164 | 34 | 7 | 1 | 5 | 23 | 16 | 31 | .207 | .354 | .281 |
| Road | 230 | 71 | 15 | 3 | 8 | 29 | 23 | 51 | .309 | .504 | .376 |
| Grass | 180 | 50 | 7 | 3 | 6 | 19 | 20 | 42 | .278 | .450 | .358 |
| Artificial Turf | 214 | 55 | 15 | 1 | 7 | 33 | 19 | 40 | .257 | .435 | .318 |
| April | 26 | 6 | 4 | 0 | 0 | 4 | 5 | 8 | .231 | .385 | .375 |
| May | 32 | 12 | 2 | 0 | 1 | 4 | 4 | 7 | .375 | .531 | .444 |
| June | 81 | 22 | 5 | 0 | 3 | 12 | 6 | 13 | .272 | .444 | .315 |
| July | 77 | 27 | 5 | 3 | 5 | 16 | 8 | 15 | .351 | .688 | .414 |
| August | 104 | 22 | 3 | 1 | 2 | 9 | 8 | 27 | .212 | .317 | .281 |
| Sept./Oct. | 74 | 16 | 3 | 0 | 2 | 7 | 8 | 12 | .216 | .338 | .293 |
| Leading Off Inn. | 80 | 24 | 5 | 0 | 2 | 2 | 6 | 13 | .300 | .438 | .356 |
| Runners On | 175 | 42 | 10 | 2 | 4 | 43 | 17 | 41 | .240 | .389 | .303 |
| Runners/Scor. Pos. | 90 | 20 | 2 | 2 | 2 | 35 | 10 | 23 | .222 | .356 | .286 |
| Runners On/2 Out | 74 | 17 | 4 | 1 | 2 | 18 | 5 | 19 | .230 | .392 | .278 |
| Scor. Pos./2 Out | 47 | 10 | 2 | 1 | 2 | 16 | 5 | 11 | .213 | .426 | .288 |
| Late Inning Pressure | 66 | 16 | 2 | 1 | 0 | 5 | 5 | 20 | .242 | .303 | .296 |
| Leading Off | 9 | 4 | 0 | 0 | 0 | 0 | 0 | 2 | .444 | .444 | .444 |
| Runners On | 41 | 9 | 2 | 0 | 0 | 5 | 1 | 15 | .220 | .268 | .238 |
| Runners/Scor. Pos. | 23 | 3 | 0 | 0 | 0 | 4 | 1 | 9 | .130 | .130 | .167 |

| RUNS BATTED IN | From 1B | From 2B | From 3B | Scoring Position |
|---|---|---|---|---|
| Totals | 9/120 | 11/65 | 19/49 | 30/114 |
| Percentage | 8% | 17% | 39% | 26% |
| Driving In Runners from 3B with Less than Two Out: | | | 15/22 | 68% |

Loves to face: Dave Stewart (.500, 5-for-10, 1 HR)
Hates to face: Chuck Finley (0-for-4, 4 SO)
Drove in runners from third base with less than two outs in 12 straight opportunities, May 24 to Aug. 7, tying Fisk, Yount, Grace, and Charlie Hayes for longest streak in majors last season. . . . Tied with Ken Griffey for A.L. lead in extra-base hits among rookies. . . . Batted .243 in 68 starts from second spot in batting order, .311 in 29 starts elsewhere in lineup. . . . Season average was over .300 as late as August 9. . . . Stole 11 bases, but none in 40 games after August 12. . . . Including 13 games in 1988, has .318 career average on the road, but he reacts to the Kingdome like Superman to Kryptonite: a .197 mark under the Big Top. How about road domes? He has a .452 average at domes Metro and Sky.

## Greg Brock

Bats Left

| Milwaukee Brewers | AB | H | 2B | 3B | HR | RBI | BB | SO | BA | SA | OBA |
|---|---|---|---|---|---|---|---|---|---|---|---|
| Season | 373 | 99 | 16 | 0 | 12 | 52 | 43 | 49 | .265 | .405 | .345 |
| vs. Left-Handers | 90 | 30 | 4 | 0 | 2 | 20 | 6 | 14 | .333 | .444 | .388 |
| vs. Right-Handers | 283 | 69 | 12 | 0 | 10 | 32 | 37 | 35 | .244 | .392 | .332 |
| Home | 176 | 46 | 4 | 0 | 7 | 28 | 23 | 24 | .261 | .403 | .350 |
| Road | 197 | 53 | 12 | 0 | 5 | 24 | 20 | 25 | .269 | .406 | .341 |
| Grass | 314 | 84 | 14 | 0 | 10 | 39 | 40 | 43 | .268 | .408 | .353 |
| Artificial Turf | 59 | 15 | 2 | 0 | 2 | 13 | 3 | 6 | .254 | .390 | .302 |
| April | 0 | 0 | 0 | 0 | 0 | 0 | 0 | 0 | — | — | — |
| May | 4 | 1 | 0 | 0 | 1 | 3 | 0 | 0 | .250 | 1.000 | .250 |
| June | 90 | 24 | 3 | 0 | 2 | 13 | 12 | 12 | .267 | .367 | .359 |
| July | 95 | 28 | 4 | 0 | 5 | 17 | 10 | 12 | .295 | .495 | .370 |
| August | 101 | 26 | 5 | 0 | 2 | 10 | 15 | 15 | .257 | .366 | .353 |
| Sept./Oct. | 83 | 20 | 4 | 0 | 2 | 9 | 6 | 10 | .241 | .361 | .292 |
| Leading Off Inn. | 89 | 20 | 5 | 0 | 4 | 4 | 8 | 11 | .225 | .416 | .303 |
| Runners On | 176 | 51 | 8 | 0 | 6 | 46 | 24 | 22 | .290 | .438 | .373 |
| Runners/Scor. Pos. | 107 | 28 | 3 | 0 | 3 | 39 | 19 | 16 | .262 | .374 | .370 |
| Runners On/2 Out | 83 | 19 | 3 | 0 | 3 | 18 | 14 | 13 | .229 | .373 | .340 |
| Scor. Pos./2 Out | 50 | 10 | 1 | 0 | 1 | 14 | 12 | 11 | .200 | .280 | .355 |
| Late Inning Pressure | 44 | 7 | 2 | 0 | 1 | 6 | 7 | 8 | .159 | .273 | .275 |
| Leading Off | 12 | 3 | 1 | 0 | 1 | 1 | 2 | 1 | .250 | .583 | .357 |
| Runners On | 17 | 3 | 1 | 0 | 0 | 5 | 4 | 3 | .176 | .235 | .333 |
| Runners/Scor. Pos. | 11 | 2 | 0 | 0 | 0 | 5 | 2 | 2 | .182 | .182 | .308 |

| RUNS BATTED IN | From 1B | From 2B | From 3B | Scoring Position |
|---|---|---|---|---|
| Totals | 7/117 | 14/87 | 19/39 | 33/126 |
| Percentage | 6% | 16% | 49% | 26% |
| Driving In Runners from 3B with Less than Two Out: | | | 15/24 | 63% |

Loves to face: Andy Hawkins (.400, 12-for-30, 2 HR, 8 BB)
Hates to face: Bobby Witt (.063, 1-for-16, 7 SO)
Has hit 102 home runs, including at least one in 22 of 26 current major league stadiums. Still hasn't crossed off Fenway, Kingdome, and Royals Stadium in A.L.; in N.L., he missed Busch. . . . Had .220 career mark vs. left-handed pitchers through 1988, then hit 89 points higher vs. left-handers than vs. right-handers last season. (Yes, he's still a lefty hitter.) . . .Hit .378 vs. left-handers with runners on base. . . . Has hit for higher average with runners on base than with bases empty in each of last five years. Career: .271 with ROB, .227 with bases empty. . . . Has been hit by 12 pitches in three years with Brewers, after being hit only once in five years in L.A.; guess nobody wanted to see him bleed that Dodger Blue.

## Jerry Browne

Bats Left and Right

| Cleveland Indians | AB | H | 2B | 3B | HR | RBI | BB | SO | BA | SA | OBA |
|---|---|---|---|---|---|---|---|---|---|---|---|
| Season | 598 | 179 | 31 | 4 | 5 | 45 | 68 | 64 | .299 | .390 | .370 |
| vs. Left-Handers | 175 | 54 | 9 | 2 | 2 | 17 | 12 | 13 | .309 | .417 | .349 |
| vs. Right-Handers | 423 | 125 | 22 | 2 | 3 | 28 | 56 | 51 | .296 | .378 | .378 |
| Home | 316 | 105 | 18 | 4 | 1 | 24 | 35 | 24 | .332 | .424 | .399 |
| Road | 282 | 74 | 13 | 0 | 4 | 21 | 33 | 40 | .262 | .351 | .336 |
| Grass | 502 | 156 | 25 | 4 | 4 | 37 | 58 | 48 | .311 | .400 | .381 |
| Artificial Turf | 96 | 23 | 6 | 0 | 1 | 8 | 10 | 16 | .240 | .333 | .311 |
| April | 84 | 19 | 0 | 0 | 1 | 7 | 3 | 11 | .226 | .262 | .247 |
| May | 95 | 31 | 9 | 1 | 0 | 17 | 7 | 13 | .326 | .442 | .369 |
| June | 101 | 34 | 5 | 2 | 1 | 6 | 13 | 5 | .337 | .455 | .412 |
| July | 107 | 34 | 8 | 0 | 0 | 2 | 18 | 10 | .318 | .393 | .416 |
| August | 96 | 35 | 3 | 1 | 3 | 10 | 15 | 8 | .365 | .510 | .446 |
| Sept./Oct. | 115 | 26 | 6 | 0 | 0 | 3 | 12 | 17 | .226 | .278 | .305 |
| Leading Off Inn. | 200 | 63 | 15 | 3 | 2 | 2 | 22 | 19 | .315 | .450 | .383 |
| Runners On | 198 | 58 | 8 | 1 | 1 | 41 | 30 | 20 | .293 | .359 | .382 |
| Runners/Scor. Pos. | 115 | 32 | 3 | 1 | 1 | 39 | 25 | 16 | .278 | .348 | .396 |
| Runners On/2 Out | 66 | 12 | 3 | 0 | 0 | 7 | 19 | 12 | .182 | .227 | .365 |
| Scor. Pos./2 Out | 46 | 5 | 1 | 0 | 0 | 7 | 17 | 11 | .109 | .130 | .349 |
| Late Inning Pressure | 91 | 28 | 2 | 0 | 1 | 4 | 13 | 14 | .308 | .363 | .394 |
| Leading Off | 24 | 9 | 0 | 0 | 1 | 1 | 4 | 2 | .375 | .500 | .464 |
| Runners On | 32 | 8 | 0 | 0 | 0 | 3 | 5 | 4 | .250 | .250 | .351 |
| Runners/Scor. Pos. | 19 | 3 | 0 | 0 | 0 | 3 | 4 | 3 | .158 | .158 | .304 |

| RUNS BATTED IN | From 1B | From 2B | From 3B | Scoring Position |
|---|---|---|---|---|
| Totals | 3/141 | 12/93 | 25/48 | 37/141 |
| Percentage | 2% | 13% | 52% | 26% |
| Driving In Runners from 3B with Less than Two Out: | | | 19/26 | 73% |

Loves to face: Mike Witt (.429, 9-for-21, 1 HR)
Hates to face: Chuck Finley (.071, 1-for-14)
Fifth different player in last five years to lead Indians in hits. The other four guys have moved to various points west. . . . Batted leadoff in 107 of 108 starts after May 28. His selectivity improved: 60 walks, 41 strikeouts from leadoff spot after eight walks, 23 strikeouts from other spots. . . . Has batted over .300 in Late-Inning Pressure Situations in each of four years in majors. Carries a .320 career mark in LIPS. . . . Career averages: .326 vs. ground-ball pitchers, .248 vs. fly-ballers. . . . Likes home cookin', be it Texas chili or Cleveland . . .whatever it is they eat there: Has batted 72 points higher at home (.313) than on the road (.241), largest margin of last 10 years.

## Mike Brumley

Bats Left and Right

| Detroit Tigers | AB | H | 2B | 3B | HR | RBI | BB | SO | BA | SA | OBA |
|---|---|---|---|---|---|---|---|---|---|---|---|
| Season | 212 | 42 | 5 | 2 | 1 | 11 | 14 | 45 | .198 | .255 | .251 |
| vs. Left-Handers | 68 | 16 | 2 | 0 | 1 | 5 | 3 | 10 | .235 | .309 | .268 |
| vs. Right-Handers | 144 | 26 | 3 | 2 | 0 | 6 | 11 | 35 | .181 | .229 | .244 |
| Home | 101 | 21 | 4 | 1 | 1 | 9 | 4 | 21 | .208 | .297 | .238 |
| Road | 111 | 21 | 1 | 1 | 0 | 2 | 10 | 24 | .189 | .216 | .262 |
| Grass | 168 | 36 | 5 | 1 | 1 | 11 | 10 | 39 | .214 | .274 | .258 |
| Artificial Turf | 44 | 6 | 0 | 1 | 0 | 0 | 4 | 6 | .136 | .182 | .224 |
| April | 3 | 1 | 0 | 0 | 0 | 0 | 1 | 1 | .333 | .333 | .500 |
| May | 34 | 8 | 0 | 2 | 0 | 2 | 2 | 5 | .235 | .353 | .278 |
| June | 34 | 8 | 1 | 0 | 0 | 2 | 5 | 5 | .235 | .265 | .350 |
| July | 32 | 7 | 2 | 0 | 0 | 0 | 0 | 8 | .219 | .281 | .219 |
| August | 62 | 11 | 2 | 0 | 0 | 1 | 5 | 16 | .177 | .210 | .239 |
| Sept./Oct. | 47 | 7 | 0 | 0 | 1 | 6 | 1 | 10 | .149 | .213 | .167 |
| Leading Off Inn. | 51 | 9 | 3 | 0 | 0 | 0 | 3 | 9 | .176 | .235 | .236 |
| Runners On | 96 | 17 | 1 | 0 | 1 | 11 | 4 | 24 | .177 | .219 | .210 |
| Runners/Scor. Pos. | 60 | 8 | 1 | 0 | 0 | 9 | 3 | 19 | .133 | .150 | .175 |
| Runners On/2 Out | 36 | 5 | 1 | 0 | 0 | 2 | 3 | 8 | .139 | .167 | .205 |
| Scor. Pos./2 Out | 25 | 2 | 1 | 0 | 0 | 2 | 3 | 7 | .080 | .120 | .179 |
| Late Inning Pressure | 29 | 5 | 1 | 1 | 0 | 0 | 4 | 8 | .172 | .276 | .273 |
| Leading Off | 7 | 2 | 1 | 0 | 0 | 0 | 0 | 3 | .286 | .429 | .286 |
| Runners On | 16 | 1 | 0 | 0 | 0 | 0 | 2 | 4 | .063 | .063 | .167 |
| Runners/Scor. Pos. | 8 | 0 | 0 | 0 | 0 | 0 | 2 | 3 | .000 | .000 | .200 |

| RUNS BATTED IN | From 1B | From 2B | From 3B | Scoring Position |
|---|---|---|---|---|
| Totals | 1/62 | 4/44 | 5/25 | 9/69 |
| Percentage | 2% | 9% | 20% | 13% |
| Driving In Runners from 3B with Less than Two Out: | | | 4/12 | 33% |

Loves to face: Bill Long (.667, 2-for-3)
Hates to face: Bret Saberhagen (0-for-6)
Hey, you find a "Loves to face" for a career .199 hitter. . . . Had 230 plate appearances last season, none in the first inning. That's what happens when you never hit higher than 7th for a team with a league-low BA. . . . He and Mike Pagliarulo were the only A.L. players to hit below .200 with 200+ plate appearances. . . . Played 25 percent of Tigers' innings at short: team allowed 5.72 runs per nine innings with Brumley there, 4.84 with Trammell. . . . Yet more evidence of adaptability of humankind through generations: Brumley played only 92 games in 1989, yet played all infield and outfield positions, plus DH; his dad Mike, who played for Senators in mid-60s, played 205 games in the field, all as a catcher!

## Steve Buechele

Texas Rangers — Bats Right

| Texas Rangers | AB | H | 2B | 3B | HR | RBI | BB | SO | BA | SA | OBA |
|---|---|---|---|---|---|---|---|---|---|---|---|
| Season | 486 | 114 | 22 | 2 | 16 | 59 | 36 | 107 | .235 | .387 | .294 |
| vs. Left-Handers | 148 | 38 | 9 | 0 | 6 | 17 | 15 | 28 | .257 | .439 | .323 |
| vs. Right-Handers | 338 | 76 | 13 | 2 | 10 | 42 | 21 | 79 | .225 | .364 | .280 |
| Home | 227 | 51 | 3 | 1 | 7 | 17 | 19 | 54 | .225 | .339 | .296 |
| Road | 259 | 63 | 19 | 1 | 9 | 42 | 17 | 53 | .243 | .429 | .291 |
| Grass | 410 | 95 | 15 | 2 | 15 | 50 | 30 | 92 | .232 | .388 | .291 |
| Artificial Turf | 76 | 19 | 7 | 0 | 1 | 9 | 6 | 15 | .250 | .382 | .305 |
| April | 77 | 20 | 3 | 1 | 2 | 12 | 9 | 22 | .260 | .403 | .345 |
| May | 86 | 24 | 8 | 0 | 2 | 9 | 3 | 18 | .279 | .442 | .311 |
| June | 91 | 17 | 1 | 0 | 0 | 8 | 6 | 16 | .187 | .198 | .242 |
| July | 83 | 24 | 3 | 1 | 5 | 14 | 4 | 16 | .289 | .530 | .330 |
| August | 82 | 18 | 6 | 0 | 5 | 12 | 7 | 19 | .220 | .476 | .281 |
| Sept./Oct. | 67 | 11 | 1 | 0 | 2 | 4 | 7 | 16 | .164 | .269 | .253 |
| Leading Off Inn. | 110 | 25 | 5 | 0 | 6 | 6 | 10 | 23 | .227 | .436 | .292 |
| Runners On | 213 | 50 | 11 | 2 | 4 | 47 | 16 | 48 | .235 | .362 | .302 |
| Runners/Scor. Pos. | 125 | 28 | 7 | 1 | 2 | 39 | 8 | 33 | .224 | .344 | .285 |
| Runners On/2 Out | 102 | 18 | 3 | 0 | 0 | 14 | 4 | 22 | .176 | .206 | .229 |
| Scor. Pos./2 Out | 68 | 11 | 2 | 0 | 0 | 13 | 4 | 15 | .162 | .191 | .230 |
| Late Inning Pressure | 68 | 13 | 4 | 0 | 1 | 1 | 7 | 20 | .191 | .294 | .267 |
| Leading Off | 20 | 3 | 2 | 0 | 0 | 0 | 2 | 5 | .150 | .250 | .227 |
| Runners On | 20 | 1 | 1 | 0 | 0 | 0 | 4 | 8 | .050 | .100 | .208 |
| Runners/Scor. Pos. | 11 | 0 | 0 | 0 | 0 | 0 | 1 | 5 | .000 | .000 | .083 |

| RUNS BATTED IN | From 1B | From 2B | From 3B | Scoring Position |
|---|---|---|---|---|
| Totals | 11/151 | 21/105 | 11/42 | 32/147 |
| Percentage | 7% | 20% | 26% | 22% |
| Driving In Runners from 3B with Less than Two Out: | | | 8/22 | 36% |

Loves to face: Kirk McCaskill (.333, 7-for-21, 4 HR)
Hates to face: Mike Henneman (0-for-11)
Has had between 50 and 59 RBI in each of his four full seasons in majors; he's the only player stuck in the 50s (does he listen to Perry Como?) in each of last four years. Only two players in history have had more consecutive seasons in that RBI range: Muddy Ruel had six (1923–28), Ron Swoboda had five (1965–69). . . . Twelve of 16 homers were solo shots; that rate of 75 percent was 3d highest in A.L. (minimum: 10 HR). Career averages: one HR every 22.5 AB with bases empty, one every 50.5 AB with runners on base. . . . Batting average based on direction of fair balls: .310 (15 HR) to left side, .329 (0 HR) up the middle, .262 (one HR) to right side. . . . One hit in 20 career at-bats with two outs and the bases loaded.

## Jay Buhner

Seattle Mariners — Bats Right

| Seattle Mariners | AB | H | 2B | 3B | HR | RBI | BB | SO | BA | SA | OBA |
|---|---|---|---|---|---|---|---|---|---|---|---|
| Season | 204 | 56 | 15 | 1 | 9 | 33 | 19 | 55 | .275 | .490 | .341 |
| vs. Left-Handers | 60 | 14 | 4 | 0 | 2 | 6 | 5 | 18 | .233 | .400 | .299 |
| vs. Right-Handers | 144 | 42 | 11 | 1 | 7 | 27 | 14 | 37 | .292 | .528 | .358 |
| Home | 104 | 29 | 5 | 0 | 7 | 16 | 10 | 31 | .279 | .529 | .342 |
| Road | 100 | 27 | 10 | 1 | 2 | 17 | 9 | 24 | .270 | .450 | .339 |
| Grass | 62 | 17 | 6 | 0 | 1 | 8 | 5 | 14 | .274 | .419 | .338 |
| Artificial Turf | 142 | 39 | 9 | 1 | 8 | 25 | 14 | 41 | .275 | .521 | .342 |
| April | 0 | 0 | 0 | 0 | 0 | 0 | 0 | 0 | — | — | — |
| May | 0 | 0 | 0 | 0 | 0 | 0 | 0 | 0 | — | — | — |
| June | 79 | 23 | 5 | 1 | 5 | 19 | 8 | 22 | .291 | .570 | .360 |
| July | 0 | 0 | 0 | 0 | 0 | 0 | 0 | 0 | — | — | — |
| August | 45 | 12 | 4 | 0 | 2 | 4 | 3 | 13 | .267 | .489 | .313 |
| Sept./Oct. | 80 | 21 | 6 | 0 | 2 | 10 | 8 | 20 | .263 | .413 | .337 |
| Leading Off Inn. | 51 | 13 | 4 | 0 | 0 | 0 | 4 | 14 | .255 | .333 | .321 |
| Runners On | 88 | 26 | 7 | 1 | 5 | 29 | 7 | 26 | .295 | .568 | .351 |
| Runners/Scor. Pos. | 50 | 15 | 5 | 1 | 1 | 21 | 3 | 18 | .300 | .500 | .333 |
| Runners On/2 Out | 35 | 9 | 3 | 0 | 2 | 11 | 4 | 14 | .257 | .514 | .333 |
| Scor. Pos./2 Out | 22 | 7 | 3 | 0 | 1 | 9 | 3 | 10 | .318 | .591 | .400 |
| Late Inning Pressure | 31 | 9 | 0 | 0 | 2 | 5 | 3 | 12 | .290 | .484 | .353 |
| Leading Off | 8 | 2 | 0 | 0 | 0 | 0 | 1 | 4 | .250 | .250 | .333 |
| Runners On | 16 | 5 | 0 | 0 | 1 | 4 | 1 | 6 | .313 | .500 | .353 |
| Runners/Scor. Pos. | 7 | 4 | 0 | 0 | 0 | 2 | 0 | 2 | .571 | .571 | .571 |

| RUNS BATTED IN | From 1B | From 2B | From 3B | Scoring Position |
|---|---|---|---|---|
| Totals | 7/64 | 10/39 | 7/19 | 17/58 |
| Percentage | 11% | 26% | 37% | 29% |
| Driving In Runners from 3B with Less than Two Out: | | | 5/11 | 45% |

Loves to face: Roy Smith (.667, 4-for-6, 3 2B)
Hates to face: Ted Higuera (0-for-7, 6 SO)
Career numbers look like those of a left-handed hitter: .264 (one HR every 19.9 at-bats) vs. right-handed pitchers, .195 (one HR every 28.1 at-bats) vs. left-handers. Only one right-handed batter over past three years has had a wider difference "the wrong way": K.C. catcher Mike Macfarlane. . . . Batted 46 times last season with a runner on first base and less than two outs, but didn't ground into any double plays. . . . Has played about a full year's worth of games (150) in three partial seasons in majors; has hit .240 with 22 homers, 72 RBI, 154 strikeouts. . . . Yankees fans can forever weigh his 1989 season plus any future accomplishments against Ken Phelps's 17 home runs in two 5th-place seasons in pinstripes.

## Ellis Burks

Boston Red Sox — Bats Right

| Boston Red Sox | AB | H | 2B | 3B | HR | RBI | BB | SO | BA | SA | OBA |
|---|---|---|---|---|---|---|---|---|---|---|---|
| Season | 399 | 121 | 19 | 6 | 12 | 61 | 36 | 52 | .303 | .471 | .365 |
| vs. Left-Handers | 104 | 29 | 6 | 1 | 2 | 12 | 13 | 10 | .279 | .413 | .361 |
| vs. Right-Handers | 295 | 92 | 13 | 5 | 10 | 49 | 23 | 42 | .312 | .492 | .366 |
| Home | 204 | 65 | 9 | 3 | 6 | 29 | 17 | 19 | .319 | .480 | .376 |
| Road | 195 | 56 | 10 | 3 | 6 | 32 | 19 | 33 | .287 | .462 | .353 |
| Grass | 351 | 104 | 17 | 4 | 9 | 50 | 33 | 41 | .296 | .444 | .361 |
| Artificial Turf | 48 | 17 | 2 | 2 | 3 | 11 | 3 | 11 | .354 | .667 | .392 |
| April | 87 | 25 | 3 | 2 | 4 | 14 | 14 | 7 | .287 | .506 | .404 |
| May | 98 | 29 | 6 | 3 | 2 | 10 | 7 | 17 | .296 | .480 | .343 |
| June | 51 | 12 | 6 | 0 | 1 | 8 | 3 | 6 | .235 | .412 | .268 |
| July | 0 | 0 | 0 | 0 | 0 | 0 | 0 | 0 | — | — | — |
| August | 139 | 43 | 2 | 1 | 4 | 23 | 12 | 19 | .309 | .424 | .368 |
| Sept./Oct. | 24 | 12 | 2 | 0 | 1 | 6 | 0 | 3 | .500 | .708 | .500 |
| Leading Off Inn. | 70 | 26 | 3 | 2 | 4 | 4 | 8 | 9 | .371 | .643 | .443 |
| Runners On | 200 | 63 | 10 | 2 | 6 | 55 | 17 | 26 | .315 | .475 | .368 |
| Runners/Scor. Pos. | 116 | 36 | 4 | 1 | 4 | 50 | 14 | 17 | .310 | .466 | .378 |
| Runners On/2 Out | 73 | 14 | 2 | 1 | 2 | 16 | 6 | 13 | .192 | .329 | .253 |
| Scor. Pos./2 Out | 55 | 12 | 2 | 0 | 2 | 15 | 6 | 11 | .218 | .364 | .295 |
| Late Inning Pressure | 67 | 17 | 5 | 2 | 4 | 15 | 4 | 12 | .254 | .567 | .306 |
| Leading Off | 11 | 4 | 0 | 1 | 2 | 2 | 0 | 1 | .364 | 1.091 | .417 |
| Runners On | 38 | 9 | 3 | 1 | 2 | 13 | 3 | 4 | .237 | .526 | .293 |
| Runners/Scor. Pos. | 30 | 6 | 2 | 1 | 1 | 11 | 3 | 4 | .200 | .433 | .273 |

| RUNS BATTED IN | From 1B | From 2B | From 3B | Scoring Position |
|---|---|---|---|---|
| Totals | 7/158 | 21/93 | 21/54 | 42/147 |
| Percentage | 4% | 23% | 39% | 29% |
| Driving In Runners from 3B with Less than Two Out: | | | 18/32 | 56% |

Loves to face: Erik Hanson (6-for-6, 2 HR)
Hates to face: Dennis Eckersley (.091, 1-for-11)
Brings 15-game hitting streak into 1989; season-ending injury came after four consecutive two-hit games that raised his average above .300 for first time since mid-May. . . . Had .443 on-base average leading off innings, 3d-highest mark in A.L. last season. . . . Batting average has increased every season, while his home-run total has declined each year. . . . Takes good advantage of Fenway: .310 career average there, .269 in road games. Has hit at least 30 points higher at home than on road in each of three seasons in majors. . . . Owns .364 career average (16-for-44) with bases loaded. Of his 50 career home runs, five are grand slams; by contrast, Al Kaline had three slams among 399 homers, Duke Snider five among 407.

## Randy Bush

Minnesota Twins — Bats Left

| Minnesota Twins | AB | H | 2B | 3B | HR | RBI | BB | SO | BA | SA | OBA |
|---|---|---|---|---|---|---|---|---|---|---|---|
| Season | 391 | 103 | 17 | 4 | 14 | 54 | 48 | 73 | .263 | .435 | .347 |
| vs. Left-Handers | 20 | 5 | 3 | 0 | 0 | 3 | 0 | 9 | .250 | .400 | .250 |
| vs. Right-Handers | 371 | 98 | 14 | 4 | 14 | 51 | 48 | 64 | .264 | .437 | .351 |
| Home | 181 | 48 | 7 | 3 | 6 | 23 | 27 | 31 | .265 | .436 | .368 |
| Road | 210 | 55 | 10 | 1 | 8 | 31 | 21 | 42 | .262 | .433 | .328 |
| Grass | 158 | 44 | 9 | 1 | 6 | 27 | 19 | 32 | .278 | .462 | .354 |
| Artificial Turf | 233 | 59 | 8 | 3 | 8 | 27 | 29 | 41 | .253 | .416 | .342 |
| April | 45 | 7 | 2 | 1 | 2 | 7 | 4 | 8 | .156 | .378 | .240 |
| May | 63 | 18 | 4 | 0 | 4 | 16 | 11 | 14 | .286 | .540 | .382 |
| June | 62 | 21 | 2 | 2 | 3 | 12 | 7 | 14 | .339 | .581 | .414 |
| July | 87 | 17 | 1 | 0 | 1 | 5 | 8 | 19 | .195 | .241 | .271 |
| August | 64 | 19 | 5 | 1 | 2 | 7 | 11 | 7 | .297 | .500 | .400 |
| Sept./Oct. | 70 | 21 | 3 | 0 | 2 | 7 | 7 | 11 | .300 | .429 | .364 |
| Leading Off Inn. | 85 | 20 | 4 | 0 | 5 | 5 | 13 | 17 | .235 | .459 | .337 |
| Runners On | 160 | 49 | 7 | 3 | 7 | 47 | 28 | 27 | .306 | .519 | .405 |
| Runners/Scor. Pos. | 95 | 28 | 6 | 2 | 4 | 40 | 21 | 18 | .295 | .526 | .415 |
| Runners On/2 Out | 67 | 18 | 3 | 1 | 1 | 17 | 7 | 13 | .269 | .388 | .338 |
| Scor. Pos./2 Out | 45 | 10 | 2 | 0 | 0 | 14 | 7 | 11 | .222 | .267 | .327 |
| Late Inning Pressure | 48 | 11 | 0 | 0 | 1 | 4 | 5 | 11 | .229 | .292 | .321 |
| Leading Off | 7 | 1 | 0 | 0 | 0 | 0 | 0 | 3 | .143 | .143 | .143 |
| Runners On | 24 | 6 | 0 | 0 | 1 | 4 | 4 | 4 | .250 | .375 | .345 |
| Runners/Scor. Pos. | 14 | 1 | 0 | 0 | 0 | 2 | 4 | 3 | .071 | .071 | .263 |

| RUNS BATTED IN | From 1B | From 2B | From 3B | Scoring Position |
|---|---|---|---|---|
| Totals | 10/122 | 17/77 | 13/33 | 30/110 |
| Percentage | 8% | 22% | 39% | 27% |
| Driving In Runners from 3B with Less than Two Out: | | | 9/16 | 56% |

Loves to face: Mike Morgan (.458, 11-for-24, 2 HR)
Hates to face: Storm Davis (.086, 3-for-35)
One of three A.L. players with 10+ starts in both leadoff and cleanup spots. . . . Started 105 of 106 games in which Twins faced right-handed pitchers, but only one of 56 vs. left-handers. Only 102 of 2828 career plate appearances have come vs. lefties; has hit all 82 homers off righties. . . . Averaged 2.64 putouts per nine innings, top rate among right fielders in majors (minimum: 500 innings). . . . A Bush in the White House had no impact on Randy's numbers: .261 with 14 HR in 1988 under Reagan; .263 with 14 HR in 1989 under George. A similar change worked wonders for Gary Carter, who hit .219 with six HR in last year of Ford Administration, then hit .284 with 31 HR in Jimmy's first year in office.

## Ivan Calderon

Bats Right

| Chicago White Sox | AB | H | 2B | 3B | HR | RBI | BB | SO | BA | SA | OBA |
|---|---|---|---|---|---|---|---|---|---|---|---|
| Season | 622 | 178 | 34 | 9 | 14 | 87 | 43 | 94 | .286 | .437 | .332 |
| vs. Left-Handers | 184 | 61 | 10 | 4 | 4 | 29 | 17 | 17 | .332 | .495 | .389 |
| vs. Right-Handers | 438 | 117 | 24 | 5 | 10 | 58 | 26 | 77 | .267 | .413 | .308 |
| Home | 286 | 71 | 13 | 7 | 2 | 34 | 18 | 40 | .248 | .364 | .294 |
| Road | 336 | 107 | 21 | 2 | 12 | 53 | 25 | 54 | .318 | .500 | .364 |
| Grass | 519 | 152 | 26 | 9 | 13 | 76 | 36 | 69 | .293 | .453 | .339 |
| Artificial Turf | 103 | 26 | 8 | 0 | 1 | 11 | 7 | 25 | .252 | .359 | .300 |
| April | 88 | 19 | 4 | 0 | 2 | 11 | 10 | 15 | .216 | .330 | .297 |
| May | 108 | 35 | 8 | 1 | 4 | 16 | 8 | 13 | .324 | .528 | .368 |
| June | 109 | 32 | 4 | 4 | 4 | 17 | 2 | 16 | .294 | .514 | .304 |
| July | 95 | 28 | 4 | 1 | 1 | 14 | 5 | 11 | .295 | .389 | .337 |
| August | 112 | 35 | 9 | 1 | 1 | 14 | 7 | 25 | .313 | .438 | .352 |
| Sept./Oct. | 110 | 29 | 5 | 2 | 2 | 15 | 11 | 14 | .264 | .400 | .331 |
| Leading Off Inn. | 139 | 40 | 8 | 1 | 2 | 2 | 6 | 20 | .288 | .403 | .317 |
| Runners On | 296 | 84 | 17 | 6 | 9 | 82 | 29 | 50 | .284 | .473 | .343 |
| Runners/Scor. Pos. | 163 | 44 | 8 | 3 | 5 | 69 | 19 | 30 | .270 | .448 | .335 |
| Runners On/2 Out | 112 | 28 | 5 | 2 | 2 | 24 | 8 | 17 | .250 | .384 | .300 |
| Scor. Pos./2 Out | 73 | 20 | 4 | 2 | 1 | 22 | 5 | 13 | .274 | .425 | .321 |
| Late Inning Pressure | 101 | 21 | 8 | 0 | 1 | 12 | 6 | 24 | .208 | .317 | .250 |
| Leading Off | 31 | 4 | 1 | 0 | 0 | 0 | 0 | 8 | .129 | .161 | .129 |
| Runners On | 45 | 13 | 6 | 0 | 1 | 12 | 6 | 8 | .289 | .489 | .365 |
| Runners/Scor. Pos. | 25 | 5 | 2 | 0 | 1 | 10 | 5 | 5 | .200 | .400 | .323 |

| RUNS BATTED IN | From 1B | From 2B | From 3B | Scoring Position |
|---|---|---|---|---|
| Totals | 14/218 | 33/123 | 26/68 | 59/191 |
| Percentage | 6% | 27% | 38% | 31% |
| Driving In Runners from 3B with Less than Two Out: | | | 20/38 | 53% |

Loves to face: Chris Bosio (.440, 11-for-25, 2 HR)
Hates to face: Mike Smithson (.040, 1-for-25)
Led White Sox with 14 homers; every other team in majors had a 20-home-run hitter. Last player to lead an A.L. club with fewer than 14 homers? John Castino, who led Twins with 13 in 1980. The last player to lead White Sox with fewer than 14 homers: Steve Souchock, with 7 in 1949. . . . Not exactly a two-out hitter: career batting average is .191 in 314 at-bats with two outs and runners on base. . . . Doesn't leave spring training with guns blazing: .228 career batting average in April, .283 in warmer weather. . . . Hit only two of his 14 home runs at Comiskey Park, lowest percentage hit at home by any of 111 major league players who hit 10+ home runs last season. Patience, Ivan; a new park is on the way.

## Joe Carter

Bats Right

| Cleveland Indians | AB | H | 2B | 3B | HR | RBI | BB | SO | BA | SA | OBA |
|---|---|---|---|---|---|---|---|---|---|---|---|
| Season | 651 | 158 | 32 | 4 | 35 | 105 | 39 | 112 | .243 | .465 | .292 |
| vs. Left-Handers | 186 | 40 | 8 | 0 | 8 | 26 | 14 | 33 | .215 | .387 | .267 |
| vs. Right-Handers | 465 | 118 | 24 | 4 | 27 | 79 | 25 | 79 | .254 | .497 | .301 |
| Home | 329 | 80 | 16 | 3 | 16 | 55 | 19 | 61 | .243 | .456 | .294 |
| Road | 322 | 78 | 16 | 1 | 19 | 50 | 20 | 51 | .242 | .475 | .289 |
| Grass | 555 | 135 | 27 | 4 | 27 | 87 | 32 | 97 | .243 | .452 | .292 |
| Artificial Turf | 96 | 23 | 5 | 0 | 8 | 18 | 7 | 15 | .240 | .542 | .288 |
| April | 92 | 21 | 3 | 0 | 2 | 9 | 4 | 14 | .228 | .326 | .276 |
| May | 113 | 34 | 8 | 2 | 4 | 24 | 9 | 15 | .301 | .513 | .347 |
| June | 106 | 24 | 5 | 1 | 6 | 14 | 6 | 15 | .226 | .462 | .268 |
| July | 111 | 27 | 8 | 1 | 8 | 22 | 7 | 19 | .243 | .550 | .292 |
| August | 113 | 26 | 5 | 0 | 8 | 19 | 5 | 26 | .230 | .487 | .287 |
| Sept./Oct. | 116 | 26 | 3 | 0 | 7 | 17 | 8 | 23 | .224 | .431 | .276 |
| Leading Off Inn. | 123 | 33 | 7 | 0 | 9 | 9 | 6 | 17 | .268 | .545 | .302 |
| Runners On | 322 | 81 | 17 | 1 | 15 | 85 | 24 | 58 | .252 | .450 | .315 |
| Runners/Scor. Pos. | 180 | 49 | 14 | 1 | 6 | 66 | 20 | 38 | .272 | .461 | .352 |
| Runners On/2 Out | 128 | 28 | 6 | 0 | 4 | 25 | 9 | 30 | .219 | .359 | .275 |
| Scor. Pos./2 Out | 75 | 17 | 5 | 0 | 1 | 19 | 8 | 20 | .227 | .333 | .301 |
| Late Inning Pressure | 94 | 14 | 1 | 0 | 3 | 7 | 8 | 22 | .149 | .255 | .223 |
| Leading Off | 20 | 3 | 0 | 0 | 1 | 1 | 0 | 4 | .150 | .300 | .150 |
| Runners On | 49 | 8 | 1 | 0 | 0 | 4 | 7 | 10 | .163 | .184 | .281 |
| Runners/Scor. Pos. | 28 | 5 | 1 | 0 | 0 | 4 | 6 | 6 | .179 | .214 | .343 |

| RUNS BATTED IN | From 1B | From 2B | From 3B | Scoring Position |
|---|---|---|---|---|
| Totals | 14/222 | 25/135 | 31/80 | 56/215 |
| Percentage | 6% | 19% | 39% | 26% |
| Driving In Runners from 3B with Less than Two Out: | | | 22/47 | 47% |

Loves to face: Frank Viola (.357, 15-for-42, 4 HR)
Hates to face: Walt Terrell (.194, 6-for-31, 1 HR)
Has 123 home runs and 430 RBI over past four years; Strawberry and Eric Davis have more homers, Bell and Dwight Evans have more RBI; but no other player is in Carter Country in *both* categories. . . . His 35 homers last year were most by an Indians player since Rocky Colavito hit 42 in 1959. . . . In spite of these and other accomplishments for a team with few other stars, he has never been selected to an All-Star team. . . . Had 0-for-33 streak against left-handed pitchers, June 7 to July 5, longest by any right-handed hitter during the 15 years that we've kept track of it. . . . Remember his previous N.L. experience, with 1983 Cubs? Had 9 hits in 51 at-bats with no home runs and 21 strikeouts.

## Jose Canseco

Bats Right

| Oakland As | AB | H | 2B | 3B | HR | RBI | BB | SO | BA | SA | OBA |
|---|---|---|---|---|---|---|---|---|---|---|---|
| Season | 227 | 61 | 9 | 1 | 17 | 57 | 23 | 69 | .269 | .542 | .333 |
| vs. Left-Handers | 50 | 13 | 1 | 0 | 7 | 18 | 10 | 13 | .260 | .700 | .381 |
| vs. Right-Handers | 177 | 48 | 8 | 1 | 10 | 39 | 13 | 56 | .271 | .497 | .318 |
| Home | 104 | 28 | 2 | 1 | 8 | 23 | 9 | 28 | .269 | .538 | .328 |
| Road | 123 | 33 | 7 | 0 | 9 | 34 | 14 | 41 | .268 | .545 | .338 |
| Grass | 174 | 52 | 7 | 1 | 14 | 46 | 17 | 52 | .299 | .592 | .360 |
| Artificial Turf | 53 | 9 | 2 | 0 | 3 | 11 | 6 | 17 | .170 | .377 | .246 |
| April | 0 | 0 | 0 | 0 | 0 | 0 | 0 | 0 | — | — | — |
| May | 0 | 0 | 0 | 0 | 0 | 0 | 0 | 0 | — | — | — |
| June | 0 | 0 | 0 | 0 | 0 | 0 | 0 | 0 | — | — | — |
| July | 43 | 10 | 0 | 0 | 5 | 9 | 5 | 14 | .233 | .581 | .306 |
| August | 88 | 26 | 5 | 0 | 5 | 25 | 7 | 25 | .295 | .523 | .351 |
| Sept./Oct. | 96 | 25 | 4 | 1 | 7 | 23 | 11 | 30 | .260 | .542 | .330 |
| Leading Off Inn. | 39 | 9 | 2 | 0 | 3 | 3 | 3 | 14 | .231 | .513 | .302 |
| Runners On | 118 | 38 | 6 | 0 | 9 | 49 | 13 | 32 | .322 | .602 | .377 |
| Runners/Scor. Pos. | 64 | 23 | 3 | 0 | 6 | 41 | 9 | 17 | .359 | .688 | .405 |
| Runners On/2 Out | 33 | 12 | 0 | 0 | 3 | 12 | 5 | 8 | .364 | .636 | .447 |
| Scor. Pos./2 Out | 23 | 7 | 0 | 0 | 2 | 10 | 4 | 6 | .304 | .565 | .407 |
| Late Inning Pressure | 25 | 6 | 1 | 0 | 2 | 5 | 3 | 13 | .240 | .520 | .321 |
| Leading Off | 7 | 2 | 1 | 0 | 1 | 1 | 0 | 3 | .286 | .857 | .286 |
| Runners On | 11 | 3 | 0 | 0 | 0 | 3 | 3 | 6 | .273 | .273 | .429 |
| Runners/Scor. Pos. | 8 | 3 | 0 | 0 | 0 | 3 | 1 | 5 | .375 | .375 | .444 |

| RUNS BATTED IN | From 1B | From 2B | From 3B | Scoring Position |
|---|---|---|---|---|
| Totals | 7/89 | 14/47 | 19/31 | 33/78 |
| Percentage | 8% | 30% | 61% | 42% |
| Driving In Runners from 3B with Less than Two Out: | | | 17/22 | 77% |

Loves to face: John Cerutti (.389, 7-for-18, 3 HR)
Hates to face: Mike Witt (.097, 3-for-31, 1 HR, 12 SO)
That .359 batting average with runners in scoring position lifted his career RISP mark to .308. . . . Owns .414 career average in Late-Inning Pressure Situations with runners in scoring position, one point behind Kevin Seitzer, who leads active players. . . . Batted .325 vs. fly-ball pitchers, .209 vs. ground-ballers; difference of 116 points was largest in majors last season (minimum: 100 AB vs. both). . . . Career breakdown: .302 (one home run every 15.1 at-bats) vs. left-handed pitchers, .256 (one every 17.7) vs. right-handers. Career slugging average vs. southpaws (.572) is highest among active players. Scary part for A.L. southpaws is that it has increased every year: .393, .476, .618, .620, .700.

## Carmelo Castillo

Bats Right

| Minnesota Twins | AB | H | 2B | 3B | HR | RBI | BB | SO | BA | SA | OBA |
|---|---|---|---|---|---|---|---|---|---|---|---|
| Season | 218 | 56 | 13 | 3 | 8 | 33 | 15 | 40 | .257 | .454 | .305 |
| vs. Left-Handers | 155 | 49 | 10 | 2 | 8 | 30 | 13 | 22 | .316 | .561 | .365 |
| vs. Right-Handers | 63 | 7 | 3 | 1 | 0 | 3 | 2 | 18 | .111 | .190 | .152 |
| Home | 111 | 27 | 9 | 1 | 2 | 14 | 8 | 20 | .243 | .396 | .292 |
| Road | 107 | 29 | 4 | 2 | 6 | 19 | 7 | 20 | .271 | .514 | .319 |
| Grass | 84 | 24 | 3 | 2 | 5 | 15 | 6 | 14 | .286 | .548 | .341 |
| Artificial Turf | 134 | 32 | 10 | 1 | 3 | 18 | 9 | 26 | .239 | .396 | .283 |
| April | 32 | 13 | 3 | 0 | 1 | 10 | 3 | 3 | .406 | .594 | .444 |
| May | 36 | 9 | 3 | 1 | 1 | 5 | 2 | 6 | .250 | .472 | .289 |
| June | 61 | 17 | 5 | 2 | 3 | 7 | 2 | 14 | .279 | .574 | .302 |
| July | 30 | 5 | 1 | 0 | 0 | 2 | 2 | 10 | .167 | .200 | .242 |
| August | 29 | 5 | 0 | 0 | 0 | 2 | 3 | 5 | .172 | .172 | .250 |
| Sept./Oct. | 30 | 7 | 1 | 0 | 3 | 7 | 3 | 2 | .233 | .567 | .294 |
| Leading Off Inn. | 32 | 7 | 2 | 1 | 2 | 2 | 4 | 5 | .219 | .531 | .306 |
| Runners On | 122 | 34 | 7 | 0 | 3 | 28 | 7 | 23 | .279 | .410 | .318 |
| Runners/Scor. Pos. | 72 | 17 | 4 | 0 | 2 | 26 | 6 | 16 | .236 | .375 | .296 |
| Runners On/2 Out | 54 | 10 | 1 | 0 | 0 | 5 | 5 | 12 | .185 | .204 | .254 |
| Scor. Pos./2 Out | 33 | 3 | 0 | 0 | 0 | 5 | 5 | 10 | .091 | .091 | .211 |
| Late Inning Pressure | 34 | 14 | 4 | 1 | 2 | 7 | 1 | 6 | .412 | .765 | .429 |
| Leading Off | 2 | 0 | 0 | 0 | 0 | 0 | 1 | 0 | .000 | .000 | .333 |
| Runners On | 21 | 11 | 3 | 0 | 1 | 6 | 0 | 4 | .524 | .810 | .524 |
| Runners/Scor. Pos. | 8 | 4 | 3 | 0 | 0 | 4 | 0 | 1 | .500 | .875 | .500 |

| RUNS BATTED IN | From 1B | From 2B | From 3B | Scoring Position |
|---|---|---|---|---|
| Totals | 2/94 | 9/51 | 14/39 | 23/90 |
| Percentage | 2% | 18% | 36% | 26% |
| Driving In Runners from 3B with Less than Two Out: | | | 11/20 | 55% |

Loves to face: Roger Clemens (.375, 9-for-24, 3 HR)
Hates to face: Ted Higuera (.143, 4-for-28, 1 HR, 15 SO)
Batted .412 in Late-Inning Pressure Situations, one point behind major league leader Mike Greenwell. But Castillo led majors with .524 mark in LIPS with runners on base (minimum: 10 hits). . . . Look at that lefty/righty difference: 205 points in batting average, largest in majors last season among players with 50+ at-bats vs. each type. . . . Only player in A.L. to have two multiple-home-run games, but hit fewer than 10 total home runs last season. . . . Tied for A.L. lead with four extra-base hits as a pinch hitter. First pinch-hit appearance of season: grand-slam homer off Willie Hernandez. . . . Started 52 of 56 games in which Twins faced left-handed pitchers, but only six of 106 games vs. right-handers.

## Rick Cerone

| Boston Red Sox | AB | H | 2B | 3B | HR | RBI | BB | SO | BA | SA | OBA |
|---|---|---|---|---|---|---|---|---|---|---|---|
| Season | 296 | 72 | 16 | 1 | 4 | 48 | 34 | 40 | .243 | .345 | .320 |
| vs. Left-Handers | 119 | 34 | 9 | 0 | 2 | 23 | 18 | 18 | .286 | .412 | .373 |
| vs. Right-Handers | 177 | 38 | 7 | 1 | 2 | 25 | 16 | 22 | .215 | .299 | .282 |
| Home | 155 | 47 | 9 | 1 | 2 | 32 | 19 | 18 | .303 | .413 | .376 |
| Road | 141 | 25 | 7 | 0 | 2 | 16 | 15 | 22 | .177 | .270 | .258 |
| Grass | 251 | 62 | 10 | 1 | 4 | 43 | 30 | 34 | .247 | .343 | .326 |
| Artificial Turf | 45 | 10 | 6 | 0 | 0 | 5 | 4 | 6 | .222 | .356 | .288 |
| April | 23 | 8 | 2 | 0 | 0 | 7 | 5 | 5 | .348 | .435 | .448 |
| May | 30 | 7 | 0 | 0 | 1 | 5 | 8 | 5 | .233 | .333 | .395 |
| June | 48 | 13 | 4 | 0 | 0 | 5 | 6 | 5 | .271 | .354 | .352 |
| July | 63 | 16 | 4 | 0 | 0 | 10 | 1 | 9 | .254 | .317 | .269 |
| August | 80 | 19 | 3 | 0 | 2 | 12 | 9 | 10 | .238 | .350 | .311 |
| Sept./Oct. | 52 | 9 | 3 | 1 | 1 | 9 | 5 | 6 | .173 | .327 | .254 |
| Leading Off Inn. | 55 | 7 | 3 | 0 | 1 | 1 | 7 | 11 | .127 | .236 | .238 |
| Runners On | 150 | 43 | 9 | 1 | 3 | 47 | 18 | 19 | .287 | .420 | .356 |
| Runners/Scor. Pos. | 74 | 25 | 6 | 1 | 0 | 39 | 14 | 7 | .338 | .446 | .419 |
| Runners On/2 Out | 72 | 28 | 6 | 1 | 2 | 23 | 6 | 10 | .389 | .583 | .436 |
| Scor. Pos./2 Out | 38 | 14 | 3 | 1 | 0 | 17 | 5 | 5 | .368 | .500 | .442 |
| Late Inning Pressure | 45 | 8 | 2 | 0 | 0 | 5 | 6 | 5 | .178 | .222 | .269 |
| Leading Off | 7 | 1 | 1 | 0 | 0 | 0 | 1 | 2 | .143 | .286 | .250 |
| Runners On | 19 | 3 | 0 | 0 | 0 | 5 | 4 | 2 | .158 | .158 | .292 |
| Runners/Scor. Pos. | 8 | 2 | 0 | 0 | 0 | 5 | 4 | 1 | .250 | .250 | .462 |

Bats Right

| RUNS BATTED IN | From 1B | From 2B | From 3B | Scoring Position |
|---|---|---|---|---|
| Totals | 6/112 | 15/62 | 23/37 | 38/99 |
| Percentage | 5% | 24% | 62% | 38% |
| Driving In Runners from 3B with Less than Two Out: | | | 14/23 | 61% |

Loves to face: Nolan Ryan (.375, 9-for-24, 1 HR)
Hates to face: Jack Morris (.146, 6-for-41)
Returns for third tour of duty at Camp Steinbrenner, scene of best season of his career (14 HR, 85 RBI in 1980). . . . Had there been a *1981 Elias Analyst,* we'd have noted his streak of driving in 19 consecutive runners from third base with less than two outs. It was the longest of the 1980s. . . . Only other player to serve three separate tenures with Yankees: Bob Cerv. . . . Led A.L. with .389 average with two outs and runners on base in 1989, and hit a career-high .338 with runners in scoring position. . . . Set major league mark for catchers with 159 consecutive errorless games. Streak ended on May 9, same day on which Kevin Elster's record 88-game errorless streak at shortstop ended.

## Dave Clark

| Cleveland Indians | AB | H | 2B | 3B | HR | RBI | BB | SO | BA | SA | OBA |
|---|---|---|---|---|---|---|---|---|---|---|---|
| Season | 253 | 60 | 12 | 0 | 8 | 29 | 30 | 63 | .237 | .379 | .317 |
| vs. Left-Handers | 9 | 1 | 0 | 0 | 0 | 0 | 0 | 7 | .111 | .111 | .111 |
| vs. Right-Handers | 244 | 59 | 12 | 0 | 8 | 29 | 30 | 56 | .242 | .389 | .324 |
| Home | 123 | 29 | 8 | 0 | 4 | 15 | 19 | 34 | .236 | .398 | .338 |
| Road | 130 | 31 | 4 | 0 | 4 | 14 | 11 | 29 | .238 | .362 | .296 |
| Grass | 225 | 53 | 12 | 0 | 6 | 25 | 28 | 58 | .236 | .369 | .320 |
| Artificial Turf | 28 | 7 | 0 | 0 | 2 | 4 | 2 | 5 | .250 | .464 | .290 |
| April | 45 | 12 | 3 | 0 | 2 | 4 | 5 | 8 | .267 | .467 | .340 |
| May | 54 | 10 | 0 | 0 | 3 | 7 | 8 | 12 | .185 | .352 | .286 |
| June | 52 | 12 | 2 | 0 | 1 | 4 | 4 | 15 | .231 | .327 | .286 |
| July | 25 | 9 | 4 | 0 | 0 | 4 | 5 | 7 | .360 | .520 | .467 |
| August | 48 | 10 | 2 | 0 | 1 | 6 | 4 | 15 | .208 | .313 | .269 |
| Sept./Oct. | 29 | 7 | 1 | 0 | 1 | 4 | 4 | 6 | .241 | .379 | .333 |
| Leading Off Inn. | 55 | 11 | 3 | 0 | 3 | 3 | 3 | 12 | .200 | .418 | .241 |
| Runners On | 101 | 25 | 5 | 0 | 2 | 23 | 17 | 28 | .248 | .356 | .353 |
| Runners/Scor. Pos. | 63 | 12 | 2 | 0 | 1 | 20 | 16 | 17 | .190 | .270 | .350 |
| Runners On/2 Out | 42 | 9 | 2 | 0 | 0 | 4 | 5 | 11 | .214 | .262 | .298 |
| Scor. Pos./2 Out | 30 | 3 | 2 | 0 | 0 | 4 | 5 | 9 | .100 | .167 | .229 |
| Late Inning Pressure | 56 | 14 | 2 | 0 | 2 | 5 | 8 | 12 | .250 | .393 | .344 |
| Leading Off | 13 | 1 | 0 | 0 | 1 | 1 | 1 | 1 | .077 | .308 | .143 |
| Runners On | 19 | 4 | 1 | 0 | 0 | 3 | 5 | 5 | .211 | .263 | .375 |
| Runners/Scor. Pos. | 11 | 4 | 1 | 0 | 0 | 3 | 5 | 1 | .364 | .455 | .563 |

Bats Left

| RUNS BATTED IN | From 1B | From 2B | From 3B | Scoring Position |
|---|---|---|---|---|
| Totals | 4/69 | 9/56 | 8/18 | 17/74 |
| Percentage | 6% | 16% | 44% | 23% |
| Driving In Runners from 3B with Less than Two Out: | | | 6/14 | 43% |

Loves to face: Walt Terrell (.500, 4-for-8)
Hates to face: Doyle Alexander (.091, 1-for-11)
Started 48 games at DH last season, making him the most frequent among the 14 starting DHs used by Indians last season. . . . Started 123 games for Tribe over last three years, all against right-handers. Last start against a lefty: Sept. 30, 1986. Career averages: .246 (17 HR) vs. right-handers, .207 (no HR) in 29 at-bats vs. lefties. Owns .129 average in 62 career at-bats with two outs and runners in scoring position. . . . Homered in three straight games vs. Twins last May; hit four home runs in 14 at-bats vs. Twins last year, and four in 239 at-bats vs. rest of A.L. . . . Career breakdown: .273 (one HR every 20.5 at-bats) in day games, .226 (one every 49.9 at-bats) at night. Welcome to beautiful Wrigley Field.

## Darnell Coles

| Seattle Mariners | AB | H | 2B | 3B | HR | RBI | BB | SO | BA | SA | OBA |
|---|---|---|---|---|---|---|---|---|---|---|---|
| Season | 535 | 135 | 21 | 3 | 10 | 59 | 27 | 61 | .252 | .359 | .294 |
| vs. Left-Handers | 157 | 38 | 7 | 2 | 2 | 16 | 5 | 17 | .242 | .350 | .268 |
| vs. Right-Handers | 378 | 97 | 14 | 1 | 8 | 43 | 22 | 44 | .257 | .362 | .305 |
| Home | 241 | 69 | 10 | 2 | 4 | 29 | 16 | 21 | .286 | .394 | .337 |
| Road | 294 | 66 | 11 | 1 | 6 | 30 | 11 | 40 | .224 | .330 | .258 |
| Grass | 226 | 53 | 6 | 1 | 5 | 26 | 9 | 32 | .235 | .336 | .268 |
| Artificial Turf | 309 | 82 | 15 | 2 | 5 | 33 | 18 | 29 | .265 | .375 | .313 |
| April | 93 | 23 | 3 | 0 | 1 | 11 | 3 | 6 | .247 | .312 | .271 |
| May | 104 | 22 | 4 | 0 | 1 | 11 | 2 | 12 | .212 | .279 | .236 |
| June | 52 | 19 | 5 | 1 | 1 | 5 | 3 | 9 | .365 | .558 | .400 |
| July | 96 | 27 | 4 | 2 | 3 | 20 | 6 | 9 | .281 | .458 | .327 |
| August | 108 | 24 | 1 | 0 | 3 | 8 | 8 | 15 | .222 | .315 | .288 |
| Sept./Oct. | 82 | 20 | 4 | 0 | 1 | 4 | 5 | 10 | .244 | .329 | .295 |
| Leading Off Inn. | 112 | 27 | 4 | 1 | 1 | 1 | 7 | 11 | .241 | .321 | .286 |
| Runners On | 239 | 55 | 10 | 1 | 5 | 54 | 14 | 26 | .230 | .343 | .281 |
| Runners/Scor. Pos. | 128 | 31 | 5 | 1 | 2 | 46 | 12 | 14 | .242 | .344 | .315 |
| Runners On/2 Out | 103 | 17 | 5 | 0 | 3 | 21 | 8 | 15 | .165 | .301 | .246 |
| Scor. Pos./2 Out | 61 | 12 | 3 | 0 | 1 | 16 | 8 | 10 | .197 | .295 | .310 |
| Late Inning Pressure | 77 | 21 | 2 | 0 | 3 | 10 | 6 | 12 | .273 | .416 | .337 |
| Leading Off | 14 | 4 | 0 | 0 | 1 | 1 | 1 | 1 | .286 | .500 | .333 |
| Runners On | 37 | 9 | 1 | 0 | 2 | 9 | 3 | 6 | .243 | .432 | .310 |
| Runners/Scor. Pos. | 17 | 4 | 0 | 0 | 0 | 5 | 3 | 3 | .235 | .235 | .364 |

Bats Right

| RUNS BATTED IN | From 1B | From 2B | From 3B | Scoring Position |
|---|---|---|---|---|
| Totals | 9/178 | 16/98 | 24/54 | 40/152 |
| Percentage | 5% | 16% | 44% | 26% |
| Driving In Runners from 3B with Less than Two Out: | | | 18/27 | 67% |

Loves to face: Richard Dotson (.417, 10-for-24, 2 HR)
Hates to face: Jimmy Key (.105, 2-for-19)
Drove in 19 runs in 52 at-bats vs. Oakland, no more than 7 vs. any other club. No other player had more than 11 RBI vs. A's in 1989; Giants had only 14 in 134 team at-bats in World Series. . . . Had never had a season average higher than .222 in Late-Inning Pressure Situations before 1989. . . . Hit .292 on fair balls hit to left side, .381 straight away, .201 to opposite field. . . . There were 33 players active in majors in 1989 who have played 250+ games at third base; among those 33, Coles has lowest career fielding percentage (.922). But he started there in 25 of Seattle's last 34 games last season, his first extensive use there since 1986–87 with Tigers, when he regularly endangered fans sitting behind first base.

## Henry Cotto

| Seattle Mariners | AB | H | 2B | 3B | HR | RBI | BB | SO | BA | SA | OBA |
|---|---|---|---|---|---|---|---|---|---|---|---|
| Season | 295 | 78 | 11 | 2 | 9 | 33 | 12 | 44 | .264 | .407 | .300 |
| vs. Left-Handers | 160 | 42 | 5 | 2 | 5 | 19 | 9 | 21 | .263 | .413 | .306 |
| vs. Right-Handers | 135 | 36 | 6 | 0 | 4 | 14 | 3 | 23 | .267 | .400 | .293 |
| Home | 149 | 37 | 4 | 0 | 5 | 16 | 4 | 20 | .248 | .376 | .282 |
| Road | 146 | 41 | 7 | 2 | 4 | 17 | 8 | 24 | .281 | .438 | .318 |
| Grass | 105 | 30 | 4 | 1 | 3 | 10 | 5 | 17 | .286 | .429 | .318 |
| Artificial Turf | 190 | 48 | 7 | 1 | 6 | 23 | 7 | 27 | .253 | .395 | .290 |
| April | 40 | 13 | 1 | 0 | 2 | 6 | 3 | 3 | .325 | .500 | .372 |
| May | 63 | 14 | 2 | 0 | 0 | 4 | 3 | 12 | .222 | .254 | .269 |
| June | 44 | 13 | 1 | 1 | 2 | 6 | 0 | 8 | .295 | .500 | .311 |
| July | 46 | 8 | 1 | 0 | 0 | 5 | 0 | 6 | .174 | .196 | .174 |
| August | 29 | 11 | 0 | 0 | 3 | 4 | 1 | 2 | .379 | .690 | .400 |
| Sept./Oct. | 73 | 19 | 6 | 1 | 2 | 8 | 5 | 13 | .260 | .452 | .316 |
| Leading Off Inn. | 77 | 17 | 1 | 0 | 4 | 4 | 1 | 10 | .221 | .390 | .231 |
| Runners On | 117 | 38 | 4 | 2 | 4 | 28 | 5 | 18 | .325 | .496 | .352 |
| Runners/Scor. Pos. | 55 | 17 | 1 | 1 | 1 | 18 | 5 | 9 | .309 | .418 | .367 |
| Runners On/2 Out | 41 | 13 | 0 | 0 | 1 | 9 | 1 | 6 | .317 | .390 | .333 |
| Scor. Pos./2 Out | 23 | 6 | 0 | 0 | 0 | 7 | 1 | 3 | .261 | .261 | .292 |
| Late Inning Pressure | 51 | 12 | 0 | 0 | 2 | 4 | 1 | 11 | .235 | .353 | .250 |
| Leading Off | 15 | 5 | 0 | 0 | 2 | 2 | 0 | 2 | .333 | .733 | .333 |
| Runners On | 24 | 5 | 0 | 0 | 0 | 2 | 0 | 5 | .208 | .208 | .208 |
| Runners/Scor. Pos. | 12 | 2 | 0 | 0 | 0 | 2 | 0 | 3 | .167 | .167 | .167 |

Bats Right

| RUNS BATTED IN | From 1B | From 2B | From 3B | Scoring Position |
|---|---|---|---|---|
| Totals | 8/91 | 5/41 | 11/19 | 16/60 |
| Percentage | 9% | 12% | 58% | 27% |
| Driving In Runners from 3B with Less than Two Out: | | | 6/9 | 67% |

Loves to face: Curt Young (.500, 6-for-12, 2 HR)
Hates to face: Ted Higuera (.120, 3-for-25)
Hit home runs in three consecutive at-bats in three different games over a 10-day period last August; only one other player in majors hit homers in three consecutive at-bats last season, and that player, Joe Carter, did it twice. . . . Started 44 of 49 games in which Mariners faced a left-handed pitcher, but only 22 of 113 games against right-handers, despite having a higher career average vs. righties (.261) than vs. lefties (.255). . . . Batted .368 (7-for-19, one HR) as a pinch hitter. . . . Stole 27 bases in 30 tries in 1988, but was successful on only 10 of 14 attempts last season. . . . Batted .299 against fly-ball pitchers, .234 vs. ground-ballers. . . . Career breakdown: .283 on grass fields, .227 on artificial turf.

## Alvin Davis

Bats Left

| Seattle Mariners | AB | H | 2B | 3B | HR | RBI | BB | SO | BA | SA | OBA |
|---|---|---|---|---|---|---|---|---|---|---|---|
| Season | 498 | 152 | 30 | 1 | 21 | 95 | 101 | 49 | .305 | .496 | .424 |
| vs. Left-Handers | 154 | 49 | 12 | 1 | 6 | 41 | 23 | 19 | .318 | .526 | .416 |
| vs. Right-Handers | 344 | 103 | 18 | 0 | 15 | 54 | 78 | 30 | .299 | .483 | .427 |
| Home | 249 | 91 | 21 | 1 | 13 | 56 | 42 | 20 | .365 | .614 | .453 |
| Road | 249 | 61 | 9 | 0 | 8 | 39 | 59 | 29 | .245 | .378 | .396 |
| Grass | 180 | 46 | 8 | 0 | 7 | 33 | 45 | 17 | .256 | .417 | .408 |
| Artificial Turf | 318 | 106 | 22 | 1 | 14 | 62 | 56 | 32 | .333 | .541 | .433 |
| April | 84 | 30 | 8 | 0 | 2 | 17 | 14 | 3 | .357 | .524 | .455 |
| May | 59 | 18 | 2 | 0 | 3 | 16 | 9 | 11 | .305 | .492 | .394 |
| June | 71 | 21 | 1 | 0 | 2 | 11 | 15 | 6 | .296 | .394 | .419 |
| July | 84 | 31 | 5 | 1 | 3 | 18 | 27 | 6 | .369 | .560 | .518 |
| August | 106 | 28 | 7 | 0 | 5 | 15 | 19 | 14 | .264 | .472 | .378 |
| Sept./Oct. | 94 | 24 | 7 | 0 | 6 | 18 | 17 | 9 | .255 | .521 | .377 |
| Leading Off Inn. | 82 | 26 | 5 | 0 | 1 | 1 | 18 | 8 | .317 | .415 | .451 |
| Runners On | 217 | 71 | 17 | 1 | 9 | 83 | 49 | 25 | .327 | .539 | .445 |
| Runners/Scor. Pos. | 127 | 46 | 10 | 1 | 6 | 72 | 37 | 16 | .362 | .598 | .491 |
| Runners On/2 Out | 64 | 20 | 3 | 0 | 2 | 23 | 18 | 9 | .313 | .453 | .463 |
| Scor. Pos./2 Out | 41 | 16 | 2 | 0 | 1 | 19 | 14 | 4 | .390 | .512 | .545 |
| Late Inning Pressure | 72 | 16 | 2 | 0 | 4 | 15 | 9 | 12 | .222 | .417 | .301 |
| Leading Off | 17 | 3 | 0 | 0 | 0 | 0 | 5 | 1 | .176 | .176 | .364 |
| Runners On | 35 | 6 | 2 | 0 | 1 | 12 | 4 | 8 | .171 | .314 | .244 |
| Runners/Scor. Pos. | 21 | 6 | 2 | 0 | 1 | 12 | 4 | 3 | .286 | .524 | .370 |

| RUNS BATTED IN | From 1B | From 2B | From 3B | Scoring Position |
|---|---|---|---|---|
| Totals | 17/158 | 33/105 | 24/53 | 57/158 |
| Percentage | 11% | 31% | 45% | 36% |
| Driving In Runners from 3B with Less than Two Out: | | | 19/38 | 50% |

Loves to face: Mike Smithson (.366, 15-for-41, 7 HR)
Hates to face: Bill Wegman (.136, 3-for-22)

One of 38 major league players to hit 20+ home runs last season; the only one of the 38 who had a walk-to-strikeout ratio of two-to-one or better. ... Raised his average above .300 on April 10; it remained there for the rest of the season. ... A .333 career hitter (22-for-66) with the bases loaded, with 6 grand slams and 11 bases-loaded walks. Only A.L. player with a grand slam in each of the last four seasons. With bases loaded and two outs, his career average is .419 (13-for-31). ... Has had both a higher batting average and a higher slugging average vs. left-handers than vs. right-handers in each of the last two seasons (1988 figures: batted .321, slugged .496 vs. lefties, .284 and .449 vs. righties).

## Chili Davis

Bats Left and Right

| California Angels | AB | H | 2B | 3B | HR | RBI | BB | SO | BA | SA | OBA |
|---|---|---|---|---|---|---|---|---|---|---|---|
| Season | 560 | 152 | 24 | 1 | 22 | 90 | 61 | 109 | .271 | .436 | .340 |
| vs. Left-Handers | 200 | 49 | 8 | 1 | 8 | 28 | 17 | 44 | .245 | .415 | .300 |
| vs. Right-Handers | 360 | 103 | 16 | 0 | 14 | 62 | 44 | 65 | .286 | .447 | .361 |
| Home | 274 | 68 | 9 | 1 | 6 | 37 | 37 | 48 | .248 | .354 | .337 |
| Road | 286 | 84 | 15 | 0 | 16 | 53 | 24 | 61 | .294 | .514 | .343 |
| Grass | 463 | 121 | 17 | 1 | 15 | 72 | 54 | 88 | .261 | .400 | .335 |
| Artificial Turf | 97 | 31 | 7 | 0 | 7 | 18 | 7 | 21 | .320 | .608 | .362 |
| April | 81 | 19 | 2 | 0 | 3 | 13 | 7 | 14 | .235 | .370 | .292 |
| May | 89 | 25 | 6 | 0 | 3 | 12 | 9 | 12 | .281 | .449 | .340 |
| June | 85 | 21 | 2 | 0 | 3 | 13 | 8 | 10 | .247 | .376 | .309 |
| July | 90 | 21 | 3 | 0 | 6 | 15 | 11 | 19 | .233 | .467 | .317 |
| August | 104 | 33 | 6 | 0 | 4 | 20 | 12 | 30 | .317 | .490 | .385 |
| Sept./Oct. | 111 | 33 | 5 | 1 | 3 | 17 | 14 | 24 | .297 | .441 | .373 |
| Leading Off Inn. | 124 | 33 | 7 | 0 | 5 | 5 | 7 | 21 | .266 | .444 | .305 |
| Runners On | 256 | 72 | 7 | 0 | 10 | 78 | 35 | 53 | .281 | .426 | .360 |
| Runners/Scor. Pos. | 150 | 48 | 4 | 0 | 8 | 73 | 18 | 32 | .320 | .507 | .379 |
| Runners On/2 Out | 101 | 26 | 4 | 0 | 6 | 36 | 13 | 20 | .257 | .475 | .342 |
| Scor. Pos./2 Out | 65 | 19 | 3 | 0 | 6 | 35 | 11 | 14 | .292 | .615 | .395 |
| Late Inning Pressure | 75 | 17 | 2 | 0 | 2 | 3 | 10 | 17 | .227 | .333 | .318 |
| Leading Off | 20 | 7 | 1 | 0 | 1 | 1 | 0 | 2 | .350 | .550 | .350 |
| Runners On | 28 | 6 | 1 | 0 | 0 | 1 | 9 | 7 | .214 | .250 | .405 |
| Runners/Scor. Pos. | 14 | 3 | 0 | 0 | 0 | 1 | 6 | 3 | .214 | .214 | .450 |

| RUNS BATTED IN | From 1B | From 2B | From 3B | Scoring Position |
|---|---|---|---|---|
| Totals | 11/188 | 23/107 | 34/72 | 57/179 |
| Percentage | 6% | 21% | 47% | 32% |
| Driving In Runners from 3B with Less than Two Out: | | | 24/41 | 59% |

Loves to face: Dave LaPoint (.378, 17-for-45, 2 HR)
Hates to face: Larry McWilliams (.150, 3-for-20)

Has hit home runs in 24 of the 27 major league stadiums in which he has played; he has not connected in Baltimore, Texas, or at Skydome. ... Drove in runner from third base with less than two outs in each of last 11 chances last season. ... Batted .326 (31-for-95, 3 HR) on fair balls hit to the opposite field as a right-handed batter, but only .180 (9-for-50, 2 HR) going the other way as a lefty batter. ... Had a game-winning hit off Dave Dravecky on opening day 1987; since then he's hitless in 26 Late-Inning Pressure at-bats with runners in scoring position and two outs. ... Only player in majors who has batted enough to qualify for batting title in each of last two years without being hit by a pitch in either one.

## Rob Deer

Bats Right

| Milwaukee Brewers | AB | H | 2B | 3B | HR | RBI | BB | SO | BA | SA | OBA |
|---|---|---|---|---|---|---|---|---|---|---|---|
| Season | 466 | 98 | 18 | 2 | 26 | 65 | 60 | 158 | .210 | .425 | .305 |
| vs. Left-Handers | 134 | 34 | 5 | 0 | 8 | 18 | 17 | 37 | .254 | .470 | .340 |
| vs. Right-Handers | 332 | 64 | 13 | 2 | 18 | 47 | 43 | 121 | .193 | .407 | .290 |
| Home | 234 | 47 | 8 | 1 | 15 | 35 | 33 | 81 | .201 | .436 | .310 |
| Road | 232 | 51 | 10 | 1 | 11 | 30 | 27 | 77 | .220 | .414 | .299 |
| Grass | 382 | 84 | 17 | 1 | 22 | 53 | 52 | 134 | .220 | .442 | .320 |
| Artificial Turf | 84 | 14 | 1 | 1 | 4 | 12 | 8 | 24 | .167 | .345 | .234 |
| April | 76 | 18 | 3 | 0 | 5 | 10 | 14 | 24 | .237 | .474 | .370 |
| May | 107 | 23 | 3 | 1 | 7 | 17 | 11 | 35 | .215 | .458 | .286 |
| June | 103 | 24 | 4 | 0 | 9 | 19 | 12 | 30 | .233 | .534 | .322 |
| July | 91 | 22 | 4 | 1 | 4 | 14 | 10 | 34 | .242 | .440 | .317 |
| August | 42 | 4 | 1 | 0 | 0 | 2 | 4 | 14 | .095 | .119 | .174 |
| Sept./Oct. | 47 | 7 | 3 | 0 | 1 | 3 | 9 | 21 | .149 | .277 | .286 |
| Leading Off Inn. | 113 | 29 | 6 | 0 | 9 | 9 | 12 | 38 | .257 | .549 | .328 |
| Runners On | 219 | 50 | 9 | 1 | 11 | 50 | 26 | 65 | .228 | .429 | .316 |
| Runners/Scor. Pos. | 128 | 30 | 4 | 0 | 7 | 41 | 20 | 42 | .234 | .430 | .338 |
| Runners On/2 Out | 90 | 18 | 3 | 1 | 3 | 17 | 10 | 38 | .200 | .356 | .287 |
| Scor. Pos./2 Out | 55 | 11 | 2 | 0 | 2 | 14 | 7 | 26 | .200 | .345 | .290 |
| Late Inning Pressure | 62 | 13 | 5 | 0 | 5 | 10 | 9 | 32 | .210 | .532 | .306 |
| Leading Off | 18 | 3 | 1 | 0 | 2 | 2 | 1 | 10 | .167 | .556 | .211 |
| Runners On | 26 | 7 | 3 | 0 | 2 | 7 | 5 | 11 | .269 | .615 | .375 |
| Runners/Scor. Pos. | 17 | 5 | 1 | 0 | 2 | 7 | 4 | 9 | .294 | .706 | .409 |

| RUNS BATTED IN | From 1B | From 2B | From 3B | Scoring Position |
|---|---|---|---|---|
| Totals | 8/157 | 21/104 | 10/43 | 31/147 |
| Percentage | 5% | 20% | 23% | 21% |
| Driving In Runners from 3B with Less than Two Out: | | | 9/27 | 33% |

Loves to face: Mike Moore (.423, 11-for-26, 4 HR)
Hates to face: Erik Hanson (0-for-10, 5 SO)

His .210 batting average was 2d lowest in history among players with 25+ home runs in a season; Dave Kingman hit 37 home runs and batted .204 in 1982. ... Homered only once in last 97 at-bats after averaging one homer every 15 at-bats before then. ... Led A.L. in home runs in June. ... Struck out at least once in 20 consecutive games (May 13 to June 7). ... Has struck out 676 times since 1986, highest four-year total in major league history. And he hasn't played more than 135 games in any of those seasons! . . .Deer and Jack Clark became 13th and 14th players to hit 100 home runs for other teams after leaving Giants. Top five: Kingman (365), George Foster (344), Hack Wilson (228), Leon Wagner (193), Bill White (179).

## Mike Devereaux

Bats Right

| Baltimore Orioles | AB | H | 2B | 3B | HR | RBI | BB | SO | BA | SA | OBA |
|---|---|---|---|---|---|---|---|---|---|---|---|
| Season | 391 | 104 | 14 | 3 | 8 | 46 | 36 | 60 | .266 | .379 | .329 |
| vs. Left-Handers | 189 | 53 | 10 | 2 | 3 | 16 | 20 | 24 | .280 | .402 | .351 |
| vs. Right-Handers | 202 | 51 | 4 | 1 | 5 | 30 | 16 | 36 | .252 | .356 | .308 |
| Home | 191 | 47 | 7 | 2 | 4 | 19 | 22 | 26 | .246 | .366 | .327 |
| Road | 200 | 57 | 7 | 1 | 4 | 27 | 14 | 34 | .285 | .390 | .330 |
| Grass | 337 | 88 | 10 | 3 | 7 | 33 | 31 | 54 | .261 | .371 | .327 |
| Artificial Turf | 54 | 16 | 4 | 0 | 1 | 13 | 5 | 6 | .296 | .426 | .339 |
| April | 37 | 10 | 2 | 0 | 1 | 8 | 6 | 3 | .270 | .405 | .364 |
| May | 38 | 12 | 3 | 1 | 1 | 4 | 1 | 5 | .316 | .526 | .333 |
| June | 71 | 20 | 1 | 1 | 1 | 5 | 7 | 10 | .282 | .366 | .346 |
| July | 57 | 13 | 1 | 0 | 2 | 8 | 7 | 12 | .228 | .351 | .313 |
| August | 95 | 23 | 1 | 1 | 2 | 9 | 10 | 13 | .242 | .337 | .321 |
| Sept./Oct. | 93 | 26 | 6 | 0 | 1 | 12 | 5 | 17 | .280 | .376 | .316 |
| Leading Off Inn. | 112 | 24 | 4 | 0 | 0 | 0 | 9 | 16 | .214 | .250 | .279 |
| Runners On | 158 | 41 | 5 | 2 | 5 | 43 | 20 | 24 | .259 | .411 | .341 |
| Runners/Scor. Pos. | 108 | 26 | 3 | 2 | 4 | 39 | 14 | 15 | .241 | .417 | .320 |
| Runners On/2 Out | 80 | 18 | 3 | 2 | 1 | 19 | 11 | 15 | .225 | .350 | .319 |
| Scor. Pos./2 Out | 61 | 14 | 3 | 2 | 1 | 19 | 8 | 10 | .230 | .393 | .319 |
| Late Inning Pressure | 47 | 10 | 1 | 1 | 2 | 6 | 3 | 9 | .213 | .404 | .255 |
| Leading Off | 11 | 1 | 0 | 0 | 0 | 0 | 0 | 2 | .091 | .091 | .091 |
| Runners On | 18 | 4 | 0 | 0 | 1 | 5 | 3 | 4 | .222 | .389 | .318 |
| Runners/Scor. Pos. | 9 | 1 | 0 | 0 | 0 | 3 | 3 | 1 | .111 | .111 | .308 |

| RUNS BATTED IN | From 1B | From 2B | From 3B | Scoring Position |
|---|---|---|---|---|
| Totals | 8/101 | 11/75 | 19/52 | 30/127 |
| Percentage | 8% | 15% | 37% | 24% |
| Driving In Runners from 3B with Less than Two Out: | | | 11/22 | 50% |

Loves to face: Greg Swindell (.500, 5-for-10)
Hates to face: Chuck Cary (0-for-11)

Led A.L. rookies with 22 stolen bases. ... Started all 60 games in which Orioles faced left-handed starters, but only 38 of 102 games vs. right-handers. ... Had the lowest fielding percentage (.983) among the six Orioles' outfielders in 20+ games last season; made five errors and had one assist in 112 games; Gary Pettis was only other A.L. outfielder with so many games and so few assists. ... Batted .219 in his first-inning at-bats, .275 subsequently; .322 in day games, .249 at night. ... Hitless in 14 at-bats as a pinch hitter last season; his career average in that role is .038 (1-for-26). His one pinch hit came in May 1988. What did he do to celebrate? He was immediately picked off by Bob Kipper.

## Brian Downing

Bats Right

| California Angels | AB | H | 2B | 3B | HR | RBI | BB | SO | BA | SA | OBA |
|---|---|---|---|---|---|---|---|---|---|---|---|
| Season | 544 | 154 | 25 | 2 | 14 | 60 | 56 | 87 | .283 | .414 | .354 |
| vs. Left-Handers | 187 | 56 | 9 | 0 | 8 | 18 | 25 | 29 | .299 | .476 | .388 |
| vs. Right-Handers | 357 | 98 | 16 | 2 | 6 | 42 | 31 | 58 | .275 | .381 | .336 |
| Home | 250 | 74 | 10 | 1 | 10 | 29 | 29 | 30 | .296 | .464 | .370 |
| Road | 294 | 80 | 15 | 1 | 4 | 31 | 27 | 57 | .272 | .371 | .340 |
| Grass | 453 | 129 | 20 | 2 | 12 | 46 | 49 | 69 | .285 | .417 | .358 |
| Artificial Turf | 91 | 25 | 5 | 0 | 2 | 14 | 7 | 18 | .275 | .396 | .337 |
| April | 83 | 24 | 2 | 0 | 3 | 8 | 9 | 10 | .289 | .422 | .359 |
| May | 100 | 28 | 3 | 1 | 1 | 8 | 12 | 15 | .280 | .360 | .374 |
| June | 101 | 36 | 11 | 1 | 4 | 15 | 9 | 16 | .356 | .604 | .409 |
| July | 96 | 22 | 1 | 0 | 1 | 5 | 17 | 8 | .229 | .271 | .348 |
| August | 56 | 14 | 2 | 0 | 1 | 8 | 5 | 13 | .250 | .339 | .317 |
| Sept./Oct. | 108 | 30 | 6 | 0 | 4 | 16 | 4 | 25 | .278 | .444 | .304 |
| Leading Off Inn. | 162 | 43 | 8 | 0 | 6 | 6 | 14 | 27 | .265 | .426 | .331 |
| Runners On | 209 | 60 | 9 | 1 | 3 | 49 | 29 | 33 | .287 | .383 | .368 |
| Runners/Scor. Pos. | 123 | 35 | 7 | 1 | 0 | 43 | 20 | 21 | .285 | .358 | .374 |
| Runners On/2 Out | 91 | 21 | 5 | 0 | 1 | 21 | 16 | 18 | .231 | .319 | .346 |
| Scor. Pos./2 Out | 61 | 15 | 5 | 0 | 0 | 19 | 13 | 10 | .246 | .328 | .378 |
| Late Inning Pressure | 77 | 25 | 5 | 0 | 3 | 11 | 11 | 11 | .325 | .506 | .422 |
| Leading Off | 20 | 7 | 0 | 0 | 3 | 3 | 2 | 2 | .350 | .800 | .409 |
| Runners On | 30 | 9 | 1 | 0 | 0 | 8 | 7 | 3 | .300 | .333 | .432 |
| Runners/Scor. Pos. | 19 | 6 | 1 | 0 | 0 | 8 | 3 | 1 | .316 | .368 | .409 |

| RUNS BATTED IN | From 1B | From 2B | From 3B | Scoring Position |
|---|---|---|---|---|
| Totals | 5/149 | 18/93 | 23/55 | 41/148 |
| Percentage | 3% | 19% | 42% | 28% |
| Driving In Runners from 3B with Less than Two Out: | | | 15/27 | 56% |

Loves to face: Jose Bautista (.385, 5-for-13, 2 HR)
Hates to face: Don August (0-for-12)

Barring a return by Alan Ashby, Buddy Bell, or Chris Speier, Downing and Frank Tanana are only active 18-year veterans that have never appeared in a World Series game.... Has career fielding percentage of .995 in 777 games in outfield, highest among all players in major league history with 500+ games there. But since the qualifying minimum for the official record is 1000 games and since he hasn't worn a glove (except in winter) since 1987, Terry Puhl's all-time record of .993 is safe.... Played in 141 games in 1989, most among players who did not play in the field.... One of three A.L. players with 10+ starts in both leadoff and cleanup spots.... Had more strikeouts than walks for first time since 1976.

## Jim Dwyer

Bats Left

| Minnesota Twins | AB | H | 2B | 3B | HR | RBI | BB | SO | BA | SA | OBA |
|---|---|---|---|---|---|---|---|---|---|---|---|
| Season | 225 | 71 | 11 | 0 | 3 | 23 | 28 | 23 | .316 | .404 | .390 |
| vs. Left-Handers | 3 | 1 | 0 | 0 | 0 | 0 | 0 | 1 | .333 | .333 | .333 |
| vs. Right-Handers | 222 | 70 | 11 | 0 | 3 | 23 | 28 | 22 | .315 | .405 | .390 |
| Home | 114 | 35 | 8 | 0 | 2 | 13 | 9 | 8 | .307 | .430 | .355 |
| Road | 111 | 36 | 3 | 0 | 1 | 10 | 19 | 15 | .324 | .378 | .423 |
| Grass | 93 | 28 | 3 | 0 | 1 | 8 | 13 | 14 | .301 | .366 | .387 |
| Artificial Turf | 132 | 43 | 8 | 0 | 2 | 15 | 15 | 9 | .326 | .432 | .392 |
| April | 15 | 1 | 0 | 0 | 0 | 0 | 4 | 3 | .067 | .067 | .263 |
| May | 52 | 20 | 1 | 0 | 1 | 8 | 10 | 4 | .385 | .462 | .484 |
| June | 71 | 25 | 3 | 0 | 1 | 9 | 6 | 8 | .352 | .437 | .403 |
| July | 45 | 14 | 5 | 0 | 1 | 5 | 4 | 4 | .311 | .489 | .360 |
| August | 42 | 11 | 2 | 0 | 0 | 1 | 4 | 4 | .262 | .310 | .326 |
| Sept./Oct. | 0 | 0 | 0 | 0 | 0 | 0 | 0 | 0 | — | — | — |
| Leading Off Inn. | 47 | 21 | 3 | 0 | 0 | 0 | 5 | 3 | .447 | .511 | .500 |
| Runners On | 105 | 29 | 2 | 0 | 2 | 22 | 15 | 13 | .276 | .352 | .364 |
| Runners/Scor. Pos. | 62 | 14 | 2 | 0 | 2 | 22 | 8 | 10 | .226 | .355 | .310 |
| Runners On/2 Out | 45 | 14 | 0 | 0 | 1 | 13 | 7 | 5 | .311 | .378 | .404 |
| Scor. Pos./2 Out | 30 | 8 | 0 | 0 | 1 | 13 | 4 | 4 | .267 | .367 | .353 |
| Late Inning Pressure | 31 | 8 | 1 | 0 | 1 | 5 | 6 | 4 | .258 | .387 | .368 |
| Leading Off | 6 | 2 | 0 | 0 | 0 | 0 | 0 | 1 | .333 | .333 | .333 |
| Runners On | 11 | 2 | 0 | 0 | 1 | 5 | 2 | 1 | .182 | .455 | .286 |
| Runners/Scor. Pos. | 7 | 1 | 0 | 0 | 1 | 5 | 1 | 1 | .143 | .571 | .222 |

| RUNS BATTED IN | From 1B | From 2B | From 3B | Scoring Position |
|---|---|---|---|---|
| Totals | 2/76 | 9/50 | 9/22 | 18/72 |
| Percentage | 3% | 18% | 41% | 25% |
| Driving In Runners from 3B with Less than Two Out: | | | 2/7 | 29% |

Loves to face: Mike Smithson (.478, 11-for-23, 3 HR)
Hates to face: Mark Gubicza (0-for-10)

Equalled his career high with 74 hits (he had three with Expos) in his 17th major league season. Excluding pitchers, only one other player in history played as many seasons without ever reaching the 75-hit level: Buck Martinez (17 seasons, career high: 63 hits). Closest contenders: Terry Crowley (15 seasons, 67 hits), Hobie Landrith (14 and 71), J. C. Martin (14 and 63), and Chicken Stanley (14 and 62).... Last 273 starts, since May 1984, have been against right-handed pitchers; he's 8-for-20 vs. lefties over the past three years. ... Reached base on 26 of 52 plate appearances leading off innings last year, best rate in A.L.... Last N.L. home run came off Joaquin Andujar. That was in 1978, not 1989–90 Senior League.

## Jim Eisenreich

Bats Left

| Kansas City Royals | AB | H | 2B | 3B | HR | RBI | BB | SO | BA | SA | OBA |
|---|---|---|---|---|---|---|---|---|---|---|---|
| Season | 475 | 139 | 33 | 7 | 9 | 59 | 37 | 44 | .293 | .448 | .341 |
| vs. Left-Handers | 107 | 36 | 4 | 0 | 2 | 17 | 4 | 10 | .336 | .430 | .360 |
| vs. Right-Handers | 368 | 103 | 29 | 7 | 7 | 42 | 33 | 34 | .280 | .454 | .336 |
| Home | 228 | 70 | 18 | 5 | 4 | 29 | 19 | 21 | .307 | .482 | .359 |
| Road | 247 | 69 | 15 | 2 | 5 | 30 | 18 | 23 | .279 | .417 | .325 |
| Grass | 205 | 55 | 12 | 2 | 2 | 20 | 13 | 21 | .268 | .376 | .309 |
| Artificial Turf | 270 | 84 | 21 | 5 | 7 | 39 | 24 | 23 | .311 | .504 | .365 |
| April | 54 | 18 | 3 | 1 | 2 | 10 | 4 | 4 | .333 | .537 | .373 |
| May | 69 | 22 | 8 | 2 | 0 | 5 | 8 | 10 | .319 | .493 | .385 |
| June | 99 | 26 | 2 | 0 | 1 | 9 | 10 | 4 | .263 | .313 | .324 |
| July | 63 | 14 | 5 | 1 | 0 | 5 | 5 | 8 | .222 | .333 | .279 |
| August | 82 | 33 | 10 | 1 | 3 | 17 | 5 | 6 | .402 | .659 | .437 |
| Sept./Oct. | 108 | 26 | 5 | 2 | 3 | 13 | 5 | 12 | .241 | .407 | .274 |
| Leading Off Inn. | 138 | 39 | 13 | 1 | 2 | 2 | 7 | 14 | .283 | .435 | .317 |
| Runners On | 193 | 63 | 11 | 3 | 5 | 55 | 20 | 19 | .326 | .492 | .382 |
| Runners/Scor. Pos. | 116 | 37 | 8 | 2 | 3 | 50 | 14 | 12 | .319 | .500 | .381 |
| Runners On/2 Out | 78 | 18 | 6 | 0 | 2 | 20 | 12 | 9 | .231 | .385 | .333 |
| Scor. Pos./2 Out | 55 | 13 | 5 | 0 | 2 | 20 | 10 | 6 | .236 | .436 | .354 |
| Late Inning Pressure | 58 | 12 | 2 | 0 | 1 | 6 | 10 | 5 | .207 | .293 | .324 |
| Leading Off | 19 | 3 | 1 | 0 | 0 | 0 | 1 | 1 | .158 | .211 | .200 |
| Runners On | 21 | 7 | 1 | 0 | 1 | 6 | 6 | 3 | .333 | .524 | .481 |
| Runners/Scor. Pos. | 14 | 5 | 1 | 0 | 0 | 4 | 6 | 1 | .357 | .429 | .550 |

| RUNS BATTED IN | From 1B | From 2B | From 3B | Scoring Position |
|---|---|---|---|---|
| Totals | 10/140 | 21/89 | 19/45 | 40/134 |
| Percentage | 7% | 24% | 42% | 30% |
| Driving In Runners from 3B with Less than Two Out: | | | 14/24 | 58% |

Loves to face: Mike Boddicker (.400, 6-for-15, 1 HR)
Hates to face: Bert Blyleven (.050, 1-for-20)

Has .335 career average vs. left-handed pitchers. Granted, he has only 164 career at-bats vs. lefties, but that's the highest lefty-vs.-lefty batting average by any player over past 15 years (minimum: 100 AB).... Had only 61 plate appearances against lefties before 1989 season, then hit .336 against them last year, including 18 hits in his last 47 at-bats.... A .254 career hitter vs. right-handers.... One of four major leaguers to start 15+ games at each outfield position last season. Switched outfield positions within a game 28 times.... Has hit for a higher average at home than on road in each of three years with Royals.... Had 27 steals last season, a career high in either majors or minors.

## Nick Esasky

Bats Right

| Boston Red Sox | AB | H | 2B | 3B | HR | RBI | BB | SO | BA | SA | OBA |
|---|---|---|---|---|---|---|---|---|---|---|---|
| Season | 564 | 156 | 26 | 5 | 30 | 109 | 66 | 117 | .277 | .500 | .355 |
| vs. Left-Handers | 172 | 43 | 6 | 1 | 11 | 31 | 25 | 43 | .250 | .488 | .345 |
| vs. Right-Handers | 392 | 113 | 20 | 4 | 19 | 78 | 41 | 74 | .288 | .505 | .360 |
| Home | 283 | 85 | 13 | 5 | 15 | 62 | 35 | 56 | .300 | .541 | .379 |
| Road | 281 | 71 | 13 | 0 | 15 | 47 | 31 | 61 | .253 | .459 | .331 |
| Grass | 476 | 134 | 21 | 5 | 27 | 99 | 60 | 95 | .282 | .517 | .364 |
| Artificial Turf | 88 | 22 | 5 | 0 | 3 | 10 | 6 | 22 | .250 | .409 | .305 |
| April | 79 | 22 | 7 | 0 | 4 | 13 | 6 | 15 | .278 | .519 | .329 |
| May | 84 | 20 | 3 | 0 | 4 | 15 | 6 | 14 | .238 | .417 | .289 |
| June | 93 | 24 | 2 | 1 | 4 | 16 | 11 | 17 | .258 | .430 | .337 |
| July | 90 | 24 | 5 | 0 | 5 | 17 | 15 | 19 | .267 | .489 | .377 |
| August | 138 | 42 | 4 | 4 | 9 | 36 | 8 | 30 | .304 | .587 | .347 |
| Sept./Oct. | 80 | 24 | 5 | 0 | 4 | 12 | 20 | 22 | .300 | .513 | .446 |
| Leading Off Inn. | 127 | 36 | 6 | 1 | 6 | 6 | 13 | 30 | .283 | .488 | .355 |
| Runners On | 284 | 84 | 11 | 2 | 21 | 100 | 43 | 52 | .296 | .570 | .390 |
| Runners/Scor. Pos. | 181 | 55 | 6 | 2 | 13 | 83 | 30 | 39 | .304 | .575 | .406 |
| Runners On/2 Out | 115 | 27 | 2 | 0 | 9 | 36 | 18 | 26 | .235 | .487 | .343 |
| Scor. Pos./2 Out | 78 | 19 | 1 | 0 | 7 | 32 | 14 | 20 | .244 | .526 | .366 |
| Late Inning Pressure | 78 | 24 | 4 | 2 | 5 | 14 | 10 | 17 | .308 | .603 | .386 |
| Leading Off | 18 | 8 | 3 | 0 | 0 | 0 | 4 | 5 | .444 | .611 | .545 |
| Runners On | 39 | 12 | 0 | 1 | 4 | 13 | 5 | 8 | .308 | .667 | .386 |
| Runners/Scor. Pos. | 25 | 7 | 0 | 1 | 2 | 9 | 5 | 7 | .280 | .600 | .400 |

| RUNS BATTED IN | From 1B | From 2B | From 3B | Scoring Position |
|---|---|---|---|---|
| Totals | 18/202 | 27/137 | 34/76 | 61/213 |
| Percentage | 9% | 20% | 45% | 29% |
| Driving In Runners from 3B with Less than Two Out: | | | 20/35 | 57% |

Loves to face: Steve Bedrosian (.500, 8-for-16, 1 HR)
Hates to face: Ken Dayley (.071, 1-for-14)

Only Red Sox player to start all 47 games against left-handed starting pitchers.... Fourth different player in last four years to lead Red Sox in home runs. Their last streak that long: 1959 through 1963. The leaders: Jackie Jensen, Ted Williams, Gary Geiger, Frank Malzone, and Dick Stuart.... Hit the most homers of any player who didn't homer twice in a game.... First 100-RBI player without a sacrifice fly since 1954, when sac flies regained official status.... Played 154 games. Highest total in six seasons with Cincinnati was 125.... Has hit 14 home runs in 112 at-bats at Atlanta Stadium. Among the 199 players with 100 or more at-bats there over the last 15 years, that is the highest rate (one per 8 AB).

## Alvaro Espinoza

Bats Right

| New York Yankees | AB | H | 2B | 3B | HR | RBI | BB | SO | BA | SA | OBA |
|---|---|---|---|---|---|---|---|---|---|---|---|
| Season | 503 | 142 | 23 | 1 | 0 | 41 | 14 | 60 | .282 | .332 | .301 |
| vs. Left-Handers | 162 | 62 | 7 | 0 | 0 | 12 | 8 | 15 | .383 | .426 | .410 |
| vs. Right-Handers | 341 | 80 | 16 | 1 | 0 | 29 | 6 | 45 | .235 | .287 | .247 |
| Home | 241 | 72 | 12 | 1 | 0 | 22 | 8 | 22 | .299 | .357 | .320 |
| Road | 262 | 70 | 11 | 0 | 0 | 19 | 6 | 38 | .267 | .309 | .284 |
| Grass | 425 | 120 | 21 | 1 | 0 | 36 | 12 | 48 | .282 | .336 | .302 |
| Artificial Turf | 78 | 22 | 2 | 0 | 0 | 5 | 2 | 12 | .282 | .308 | .300 |
| April | 70 | 20 | 1 | 0 | 0 | 7 | 5 | 9 | .286 | .300 | .329 |
| May | 68 | 17 | 1 | 0 | 0 | 5 | 3 | 8 | .250 | .265 | .282 |
| June | 83 | 22 | 5 | 0 | 0 | 6 | 1 | 7 | .265 | .325 | .271 |
| July | 80 | 24 | 4 | 1 | 0 | 7 | 2 | 10 | .300 | .375 | .325 |
| August | 118 | 41 | 3 | 0 | 0 | 9 | 1 | 11 | .347 | .373 | .350 |
| Sept./Oct. | 84 | 18 | 9 | 0 | 0 | 7 | 2 | 15 | .214 | .321 | .233 |
| Leading Off Inn. | 113 | 24 | 5 | 0 | 0 | 0 | 3 | 13 | .212 | .257 | .233 |
| Runners On | 206 | 67 | 8 | 0 | 0 | 41 | 4 | 22 | .325 | .364 | .336 |
| Runners/Scor. Pos. | 110 | 35 | 3 | 0 | 0 | 38 | 3 | 13 | .318 | .345 | .328 |
| Runners On/2 Out | 75 | 23 | 2 | 0 | 0 | 21 | 2 | 8 | .307 | .333 | .333 |
| Scor. Pos./2 Out | 54 | 19 | 1 | 0 | 0 | 20 | 1 | 5 | .352 | .370 | .364 |
| Late Inning Pressure | 62 | 19 | 1 | 0 | 0 | 4 | 2 | 5 | .306 | .323 | .328 |
| Leading Off | 14 | 3 | 0 | 0 | 0 | 0 | 1 | 2 | .214 | .214 | .267 |
| Runners On | 23 | 7 | 0 | 0 | 0 | 4 | 0 | 1 | .304 | .304 | .304 |
| Runners/Scor. Pos. | 11 | 4 | 0 | 0 | 0 | 4 | 0 | 0 | .364 | .364 | .364 |

| RUNS BATTED IN | From 1B | From 2B | From 3B | Scoring Position |
|---|---|---|---|---|
| Totals | 3/149 | 15/90 | 23/50 | 38/140 |
| Percentage | 2% | 17% | 46% | 27% |
| Driving In Runners from 3B with Less than Two Out: | | | 14/27 | 52% |

Loves to face: Ted Higuera (.667, 8-for-12)
Hates to face: Roger Clemens (0-for-12)
One of two active players with 600+ career at-bats but no home runs. . . . Collected 8 doubles vs. Tigers, tying Wade Boggs (vs. Balt.) for the most by any A.L. player against any club last season. . . . Led visiting players with a .462 BA at Cleveland Stadium. . . . How to impress the new manager. Lesson I: Streak of 36 consecutive errorless games was longest by a Yankees shortstop since Bucky Dent's 37-game streak in 1980. . . . How to impress the new manager. Lesson II: Highest batting average by a Yankees shortstop since Tom Tresh batted .286 in 1962. . . . How to impress the new manager. Lesson III: Participated in 114 double plays, most by a Yankees shortstop since Phil Rizzuto in 1952 (116).

## Cecil Espy

Bats Left and Right

| Texas Rangers | AB | H | 2B | 3B | HR | RBI | BB | SO | BA | SA | OBA |
|---|---|---|---|---|---|---|---|---|---|---|---|
| Season | 475 | 122 | 12 | 7 | 3 | 32 | 38 | 99 | .257 | .331 | .313 |
| vs. Left-Handers | 95 | 23 | 1 | 0 | 3 | 10 | 6 | 20 | .242 | .347 | .282 |
| vs. Right-Handers | 380 | 99 | 11 | 7 | 0 | 22 | 32 | 79 | .261 | .326 | .321 |
| Home | 239 | 65 | 6 | 5 | 2 | 15 | 16 | 48 | .272 | .364 | .316 |
| Road | 236 | 57 | 6 | 2 | 1 | 17 | 22 | 51 | .242 | .297 | .310 |
| Grass | 398 | 108 | 9 | 7 | 2 | 27 | 31 | 81 | .271 | .344 | .326 |
| Artificial Turf | 77 | 14 | 3 | 0 | 1 | 5 | 7 | 18 | .182 | .260 | .250 |
| April | 91 | 25 | 2 | 2 | 0 | 6 | 5 | 16 | .275 | .341 | .316 |
| May | 89 | 20 | 2 | 0 | 0 | 1 | 6 | 19 | .225 | .247 | .274 |
| June | 78 | 20 | 2 | 0 | 3 | 11 | 8 | 16 | .256 | .397 | .326 |
| July | 80 | 20 | 1 | 2 | 0 | 8 | 4 | 21 | .250 | .313 | .294 |
| August | 89 | 20 | 3 | 1 | 0 | 5 | 8 | 21 | .225 | .281 | .286 |
| Sept./Oct. | 48 | 17 | 2 | 2 | 0 | 1 | 7 | 6 | .354 | .479 | .436 |
| Leading Off Inn. | 175 | 49 | 4 | 6 | 2 | 2 | 17 | 34 | .280 | .406 | .347 |
| Runners On | 175 | 36 | 4 | 0 | 0 | 29 | 10 | 45 | .206 | .229 | .246 |
| Runners/Scor. Pos. | 106 | 22 | 3 | 0 | 0 | 28 | 5 | 24 | .208 | .236 | .239 |
| Runners On/2 Out | 84 | 19 | 1 | 0 | 0 | 16 | 4 | 20 | .226 | .238 | .261 |
| Scor. Pos./2 Out | 59 | 14 | 1 | 0 | 0 | 16 | 4 | 12 | .237 | .254 | .286 |
| Late Inning Pressure | 61 | 19 | 1 | 0 | 0 | 5 | 7 | 11 | .311 | .328 | .382 |
| Leading Off | 15 | 6 | 0 | 0 | 0 | 0 | 0 | 3 | .400 | .400 | .400 |
| Runners On | 25 | 6 | 0 | 0 | 0 | 5 | 4 | 5 | .240 | .240 | .345 |
| Runners/Scor. Pos. | 17 | 4 | 0 | 0 | 0 | 4 | 2 | 4 | .235 | .235 | .316 |

| RUNS BATTED IN | From 1B | From 2B | From 3B | Scoring Position |
|---|---|---|---|---|
| Totals | 1/112 | 11/84 | 17/45 | 28/129 |
| Percentage | 1% | 13% | 38% | 22% |
| Driving In Runners from 3B with Less than Two Out: | | | 9/24 | 38% |

Loves to face: Don August (.700, 7-for-10)
Hates to face: Willie Fraser (0-for-9)
Needed only an outfielder's mitt last season, after playing every position except third base and pitcher in 1988. . . . Batted .240 as a starter, .500 (15-for-30) off the bench (including 6-for-13 as a pinch hitter). . . . Led Rangers in infield hits (23). . . . Ranked 3d in A.L. with 78 stolen bases over past two seasons, behind Rickey Henderson (170) and Gary Pettis (87). . . . Career batting average is .277 at Arlington Stadium, .227 elsewhere. . . . Career average is .270 (one HR per 41 AB) batting right-handed, .246 (one HR in 678 AB) batting left-handed. . . . Similarity of the statistical profiles indicate that Espy will be to the 1990s what Albie Pearson was to the 1960s. Plus 10 inches.

## Dwight Evans

Bats Right

| Boston Red Sox | AB | H | 2B | 3B | HR | RBI | BB | SO | BA | SA | OBA |
|---|---|---|---|---|---|---|---|---|---|---|---|
| Season | 520 | 148 | 27 | 3 | 20 | 100 | 99 | 84 | .285 | .463 | .397 |
| vs. Left-Handers | 155 | 47 | 9 | 1 | 4 | 22 | 26 | 26 | .303 | .452 | .401 |
| vs. Right-Handers | 365 | 101 | 18 | 2 | 16 | 78 | 73 | 58 | .277 | .468 | .396 |
| Home | 242 | 66 | 12 | 1 | 8 | 46 | 54 | 34 | .273 | .430 | .403 |
| Road | 278 | 82 | 15 | 2 | 12 | 54 | 45 | 50 | .295 | .493 | .392 |
| Grass | 443 | 128 | 20 | 2 | 18 | 87 | 89 | 72 | .289 | .465 | .405 |
| Artificial Turf | 77 | 20 | 7 | 1 | 2 | 13 | 10 | 12 | .260 | .455 | .352 |
| April | 79 | 22 | 3 | 0 | 4 | 13 | 16 | 11 | .278 | .468 | .400 |
| May | 86 | 26 | 5 | 2 | 3 | 16 | 19 | 15 | .302 | .512 | .426 |
| June | 93 | 27 | 5 | 0 | 3 | 19 | 22 | 13 | .290 | .441 | .422 |
| July | 76 | 16 | 4 | 0 | 3 | 10 | 8 | 20 | .211 | .382 | .291 |
| August | 93 | 26 | 5 | 1 | 2 | 14 | 13 | 15 | .280 | .419 | .370 |
| Sept./Oct. | 93 | 31 | 5 | 0 | 5 | 28 | 21 | 10 | .333 | .548 | .448 |
| Leading Off Inn. | 113 | 34 | 6 | 0 | 7 | 7 | 18 | 19 | .301 | .540 | .406 |
| Runners On | 261 | 74 | 16 | 3 | 8 | 88 | 46 | 39 | .284 | .460 | .384 |
| Runners/Scor. Pos. | 161 | 52 | 15 | 3 | 5 | 82 | 35 | 25 | .323 | .547 | .431 |
| Runners On/2 Out | 102 | 22 | 6 | 1 | 1 | 20 | 18 | 16 | .216 | .324 | .339 |
| Scor. Pos./2 Out | 71 | 16 | 5 | 1 | 1 | 20 | 16 | 10 | .225 | .366 | .375 |
| Late Inning Pressure | 79 | 22 | 3 | 0 | 1 | 14 | 7 | 13 | .278 | .354 | .341 |
| Leading Off | 17 | 3 | 0 | 0 | 0 | 0 | 1 | 2 | .176 | .176 | .263 |
| Runners On | 47 | 15 | 3 | 0 | 1 | 14 | 4 | 7 | .319 | .447 | .365 |
| Runners/Scor. Pos. | 29 | 9 | 3 | 0 | 1 | 14 | 4 | 5 | .310 | .517 | .382 |

| RUNS BATTED IN | From 1B | From 2B | From 3B | Scoring Position |
|---|---|---|---|---|
| Totals | 11/189 | 27/121 | 42/82 | 69/203 |
| Percentage | 6% | 22% | 51% | 34% |
| Driving In Runners from 3B with Less than Two Out: | | | 34/50 | 68% |

Loves to face: Dennis Eckersley (.304, 7-for-23, 4 HR)
Hates to face: Dave Righetti (.162, 6-for-37, 1 HR)
Led the majors with 605 extra-base hits during the 1980s. Leaders in past decades: 1880s, Harry Stovey; 1890s, Ed Delahanty; 1900s, Honus Wagner; 1910s, Tris Speaker; 1920s, Babe Ruth; 1930s, Jimmie Foxx; 1940s and 1950s, Stan Musial; 1960s, Hank Aaron; 1970s, Bobby Bonds and Reggie Jackson (tied). . . . Drove in 21 runs in last 15 games to reach the 100 mark for the third straight season. Only three players in team history had longer streaks: Ted Williams (8), Jimmie Foxx (6), and Jim Rice (4). . . . Only 13 of his 100 RBI gave Red Sox a lead, lowest percentage among baseball's top 20 in RBI. . . . None of his 20 home runs were hit to the opposite field (18 to left, 2 to center).

## Mike Felder

Bats Left and Right

| Milwaukee Brewers | AB | H | 2B | 3B | HR | RBI | BB | SO | BA | SA | OBA |
|---|---|---|---|---|---|---|---|---|---|---|---|
| Season | 315 | 76 | 11 | 3 | 3 | 23 | 23 | 38 | .241 | .324 | .293 |
| vs. Left-Handers | 101 | 28 | 2 | 0 | 0 | 6 | 9 | 9 | .277 | .297 | .336 |
| vs. Right-Handers | 214 | 48 | 9 | 3 | 3 | 17 | 14 | 29 | .224 | .336 | .272 |
| Home | 139 | 25 | 2 | 1 | 1 | 8 | 13 | 14 | .180 | .230 | .250 |
| Road | 176 | 51 | 9 | 2 | 2 | 15 | 10 | 24 | .290 | .398 | .328 |
| Grass | 255 | 57 | 8 | 2 | 3 | 19 | 20 | 29 | .224 | .306 | .280 |
| Artificial Turf | 60 | 19 | 3 | 1 | 0 | 4 | 3 | 9 | .317 | .400 | .349 |
| April | 20 | 4 | 0 | 0 | 0 | 0 | 2 | 2 | .200 | .200 | .273 |
| May | 16 | 2 | 0 | 0 | 0 | 0 | 1 | 2 | .125 | .125 | .176 |
| June | 74 | 20 | 4 | 0 | 0 | 5 | 4 | 10 | .270 | .324 | .308 |
| July | 59 | 18 | 3 | 1 | 0 | 6 | 5 | 3 | .305 | .390 | .359 |
| August | 77 | 16 | 3 | 1 | 1 | 4 | 5 | 10 | .208 | .312 | .256 |
| Sept./Oct. | 69 | 16 | 1 | 1 | 2 | 8 | 6 | 11 | .232 | .362 | .293 |
| Leading Off Inn. | 94 | 25 | 3 | 0 | 2 | 2 | 7 | 9 | .266 | .362 | .317 |
| Runners On | 119 | 32 | 6 | 1 | 1 | 21 | 10 | 11 | .269 | .361 | .326 |
| Runners/Scor. Pos. | 69 | 15 | 4 | 0 | 1 | 19 | 8 | 7 | .217 | .319 | .299 |
| Runners On/2 Out | 53 | 11 | 3 | 0 | 1 | 9 | 7 | 9 | .208 | .321 | .300 |
| Scor. Pos./2 Out | 33 | 6 | 1 | 0 | 1 | 8 | 6 | 6 | .182 | .303 | .308 |
| Late Inning Pressure | 42 | 6 | 0 | 1 | 2 | 4 | 8 | 7 | .143 | .333 | .280 |
| Leading Off | 7 | 3 | 0 | 0 | 1 | 1 | 2 | 1 | .429 | .857 | .556 |
| Runners On | 14 | 2 | 0 | 0 | 1 | 3 | 4 | 0 | .143 | .357 | .333 |
| Runners/Scor. Pos. | 9 | 1 | 0 | 0 | 1 | 3 | 3 | 0 | .111 | .444 | .333 |

| RUNS BATTED IN | From 1B | From 2B | From 3B | Scoring Position |
|---|---|---|---|---|
| Totals | 3/82 | 4/56 | 13/29 | 17/85 |
| Percentage | 4% | 7% | 45% | 20% |
| Driving In Runners from 3B with Less than Two Out: | | | 10/18 | 56% |

Loves to face: Tom Candiotti (.462, 6-for-13)
Hates to face: Mike Boddicker (0-for-13)
One of four major leaguers to start 15 or more games at each of the three outfield positions. Also started five at second base. . . . Hit two home runs in a span of eight at-bats in September after hitting only four home runs in his previous 876 at-bats. . . . Average of one walk per 15 plate appearances was an infinite improvement over his rate in 1988, when he batted 85 times without drawing a base on balls. . . . Career stolen-base percentage (.830) ranks second to that of Willie Wilson (.839) among active A.L. players (minimum: 50 SB). . . . Career average of .275 vs. left-handers, .224 vs. right-handers, but all six career home runs have been hit against righties.

## Junior Felix

Bats Left and Right

| Toronto Blue Jays | AB | H | 2B | 3B | HR | RBI | BB | SO | BA | SA | OBA |
|---|---|---|---|---|---|---|---|---|---|---|---|
| Season | 415 | 107 | 14 | 8 | 9 | 46 | 33 | 101 | .258 | .395 | .315 |
| vs. Left-Handers | 129 | 26 | 4 | 2 | 2 | 15 | 15 | 39 | .202 | .310 | .291 |
| vs. Right-Handers | 286 | 81 | 10 | 6 | 7 | 31 | 18 | 62 | .283 | .434 | .327 |
| Home | 199 | 50 | 4 | 6 | 4 | 16 | 20 | 42 | .251 | .392 | .326 |
| Road | 216 | 57 | 10 | 2 | 5 | 30 | 13 | 59 | .264 | .398 | .305 |
| Grass | 177 | 50 | 8 | 1 | 5 | 29 | 11 | 47 | .282 | .424 | .319 |
| Artificial Turf | 238 | 57 | 6 | 7 | 4 | 17 | 22 | 54 | .239 | .374 | .312 |
| April | 0 | 0 | 0 | 0 | 0 | 0 | 0 | 0 | — | — | — |
| May | 94 | 24 | 1 | 3 | 2 | 10 | 5 | 21 | .255 | .394 | .300 |
| June | 115 | 38 | 5 | 0 | 4 | 26 | 11 | 26 | .330 | .478 | .385 |
| July | 102 | 26 | 5 | 2 | 2 | 7 | 10 | 23 | .255 | .402 | .321 |
| August | 64 | 8 | 0 | 1 | 1 | 2 | 4 | 19 | .125 | .203 | .188 |
| Sept./Oct. | 40 | 11 | 3 | 2 | 0 | 1 | 3 | 12 | .275 | .450 | .326 |
| Leading Off Inn. | 142 | 48 | 5 | 6 | 4 | 4 | 9 | 35 | .338 | .542 | .377 |
| Runners On | 169 | 40 | 6 | 1 | 5 | 42 | 13 | 42 | .237 | .373 | .294 |
| Runners/Scor. Pos. | 111 | 27 | 4 | 1 | 3 | 38 | 12 | 29 | .243 | .378 | .315 |
| Runners On/2 Out | 74 | 12 | 3 | 0 | 2 | 13 | 10 | 20 | .162 | .284 | .262 |
| Scor. Pos./2 Out | 50 | 7 | 1 | 0 | 1 | 11 | 10 | 15 | .140 | .220 | .283 |
| Late Inning Pressure | 61 | 9 | 0 | 1 | 1 | 4 | 4 | 26 | .148 | .230 | .197 |
| Leading Off | 12 | 3 | 0 | 1 | 0 | 0 | 0 | 5 | .250 | .417 | .250 |
| Runners On | 29 | 5 | 0 | 0 | 1 | 4 | 1 | 12 | .172 | .276 | .194 |
| Runners/Scor. Pos. | 21 | 2 | 0 | 0 | 1 | 4 | 1 | 9 | .095 | .238 | .130 |

| RUNS BATTED IN | From 1B | From 2B | From 3B | Scoring Position |
|---|---|---|---|---|
| Totals | 4/112 | 16/87 | 17/42 | 33/129 |
| Percentage | 4% | 18% | 40% | 26% |
| Driving In Runners from 3B with Less than Two Out: | | | 13/23 | 57% |

Loves to face: Frank Tanana (.429, 3-for-7, 1 HR)
Hates to face: Melido Perez (.100, 1-for-10)

Led A.L. rookies in runs and triples. . . . Led Blue Jays in infield hits (21). . . . Led major leagues in RBI during June. . . . Batted .278 in 72 starts from the leadoff spot, .204 in 29 starts elsewhere in order. . . . Batted 129 points lower in Late-Inning Pressure Situations than in other at-bats, largest difference in majors (minimum: 50 LIPS AB). . . . Batted .297 vs. ground-ball pitchers, .221 vs. fly-ballers. . . . Only two rookies in team history had more RBI: Doug Ault (64 in 1977) and Jesse Barfield (58 in 1982). . . . Never played above Class A prior to 1989. . . . Comparable rookie seasons: Max Carey (1911), Tito Francona (1956), Lou Brock (1962), Tommy Harper (1963), Jack Clark (1977).

## Tony Fernandez

Bats Left and Right

| Toronto Blue Jays | AB | H | 2B | 3B | HR | RBI | BB | SO | BA | SA | OBA |
|---|---|---|---|---|---|---|---|---|---|---|---|
| Season | 573 | 147 | 25 | 9 | 11 | 65 | 29 | 51 | .257 | .389 | .291 |
| vs. Left-Handers | 184 | 50 | 10 | 2 | 2 | 21 | 11 | 11 | .272 | .380 | .307 |
| vs. Right-Handers | 389 | 97 | 15 | 7 | 9 | 44 | 18 | 40 | .249 | .393 | .284 |
| Home | 276 | 66 | 12 | 5 | 2 | 25 | 20 | 22 | .239 | .341 | .286 |
| Road | 297 | 81 | 13 | 4 | 9 | 40 | 9 | 29 | .273 | .434 | .296 |
| Grass | 237 | 68 | 11 | 4 | 8 | 34 | 7 | 22 | .287 | .468 | .310 |
| Artificial Turf | 336 | 79 | 14 | 5 | 3 | 31 | 22 | 29 | .235 | .333 | .278 |
| April | 16 | 2 | 0 | 0 | 1 | 4 | 0 | 1 | .125 | .313 | .176 |
| May | 110 | 25 | 6 | 0 | 2 | 14 | 5 | 9 | .227 | .336 | .256 |
| June | 122 | 38 | 6 | 0 | 2 | 13 | 8 | 8 | .311 | .410 | .348 |
| July | 111 | 26 | 5 | 1 | 3 | 12 | 3 | 13 | .234 | .378 | .252 |
| August | 112 | 27 | 4 | 5 | 0 | 8 | 5 | 15 | .241 | .366 | .273 |
| Sept./Oct. | 102 | 29 | 4 | 3 | 3 | 14 | 8 | 5 | .284 | .471 | .336 |
| Leading Off Inn. | 128 | 36 | 5 | 3 | 3 | 3 | 8 | 7 | .281 | .438 | .324 |
| Runners On | 230 | 57 | 9 | 2 | 5 | 59 | 12 | 22 | .248 | .370 | .280 |
| Runners/Scor. Pos. | 127 | 32 | 6 | 1 | 2 | 51 | 9 | 15 | .252 | .362 | .291 |
| Runners On/2 Out | 98 | 14 | 0 | 1 | 2 | 15 | 6 | 13 | .143 | .224 | .200 |
| Scor. Pos./2 Out | 65 | 9 | 0 | 0 | 2 | 14 | 5 | 10 | .138 | .231 | .211 |
| Late Inning Pressure | 78 | 21 | 1 | 2 | 1 | 7 | 7 | 5 | .269 | .372 | .326 |
| Leading Off | 23 | 7 | 0 | 2 | 1 | 1 | 3 | 0 | .304 | .609 | .385 |
| Runners On | 28 | 7 | 1 | 0 | 0 | 6 | 2 | 4 | .250 | .286 | .290 |
| Runners/Scor. Pos. | 17 | 3 | 1 | 0 | 0 | 6 | 2 | 4 | .176 | .235 | .250 |

| RUNS BATTED IN | From 1B | From 2B | From 3B | Scoring Position |
|---|---|---|---|---|
| Totals | 8/180 | 16/106 | 30/56 | 46/162 |
| Percentage | 4% | 15% | 54% | 28% |
| Driving In Runners from 3B with Less than Two Out: | | | 27/30 | 90% |

Loves to face: Kirk McCaskill (.514, 18-for-35, 3 HR)
Hates to face: Scott Bankhead (.148, 4-for-27)

Batting average fell from .321 in 1987 to .287 in 1988 to .256 last season. . . . Fernandez and Alan Trammell became 58th and 59th players in major league history to fall 30 points or more in two consecutive seasons of 400+ at-bats each. The good news is that none of the previous 57 scored a hat trick. . . . Drew 11 walks against Detroit pitchers, but no more than two against any other club. What's Sparky scared of? . . . Batting average in Late-Inning Pressure Situations has been higher than his overall average in each of the last six seasons. . . . Percentage of runners driven in from third base with less than two outs was the 2d highest in majors. Previous career average: 55 percent.

## Felix Fermin

Bats Right

| Cleveland Indians | AB | H | 2B | 3B | HR | RBI | BB | SO | BA | SA | OBA |
|---|---|---|---|---|---|---|---|---|---|---|---|
| Season | 484 | 115 | 9 | 1 | 0 | 21 | 41 | 27 | .238 | .260 | .302 |
| vs. Left-Handers | 130 | 32 | 2 | 1 | 0 | 8 | 17 | 4 | .246 | .277 | .333 |
| vs. Right-Handers | 354 | 83 | 7 | 0 | 0 | 13 | 24 | 23 | .234 | .254 | .290 |
| Home | 235 | 53 | 5 | 1 | 0 | 10 | 24 | 11 | .226 | .255 | .304 |
| Road | 249 | 62 | 4 | 0 | 0 | 11 | 17 | 16 | .249 | .265 | .300 |
| Grass | 406 | 93 | 6 | 1 | 0 | 18 | 36 | 21 | .229 | .249 | .298 |
| Artificial Turf | 78 | 22 | 3 | 0 | 0 | 3 | 5 | 6 | .282 | .321 | .325 |
| April | 61 | 15 | 0 | 0 | 0 | 6 | 9 | 3 | .246 | .246 | .343 |
| May | 97 | 26 | 3 | 0 | 0 | 3 | 5 | 3 | .268 | .299 | .304 |
| June | 82 | 20 | 0 | 0 | 0 | 2 | 8 | 6 | .244 | .244 | .311 |
| July | 88 | 17 | 2 | 0 | 0 | 4 | 7 | 7 | .193 | .216 | .260 |
| August | 84 | 23 | 2 | 1 | 0 | 5 | 5 | 1 | .274 | .321 | .326 |
| Sept./Oct. | 72 | 14 | 2 | 0 | 0 | 1 | 7 | 7 | .194 | .222 | .275 |
| Leading Off Inn. | 130 | 42 | 4 | 0 | 0 | 0 | 11 | 2 | .323 | .354 | .380 |
| Runners On | 183 | 36 | 3 | 0 | 0 | 21 | 19 | 12 | .197 | .213 | .278 |
| Runners/Scor. Pos. | 109 | 20 | 2 | 0 | 0 | 21 | 12 | 9 | .183 | .202 | .268 |
| Runners On/2 Out | 69 | 12 | 1 | 0 | 0 | 5 | 8 | 3 | .174 | .188 | .260 |
| Scor. Pos./2 Out | 45 | 5 | 0 | 0 | 0 | 5 | 6 | 3 | .111 | .111 | .216 |
| Late Inning Pressure | 55 | 15 | 1 | 0 | 0 | 2 | 7 | 2 | .273 | .291 | .365 |
| Leading Off | 25 | 9 | 1 | 0 | 0 | 0 | 4 | 0 | .360 | .400 | .467 |
| Runners On | 14 | 3 | 0 | 0 | 0 | 2 | 2 | 2 | .214 | .214 | .313 |
| Runners/Scor. Pos. | 8 | 1 | 0 | 0 | 0 | 2 | 2 | 2 | .125 | .125 | .300 |

| RUNS BATTED IN | From 1B | From 2B | From 3B | Scoring Position |
|---|---|---|---|---|
| Totals | 0/133 | 7/88 | 14/44 | 21/132 |
| Percentage | 0% | 8% | 32% | 16% |
| Driving In Runners from 3B with Less than Two Out: | | | 11/23 | 48% |

Loves to face: Chuck Finley (.667, 4-for-6)
Hates to face: Bob Milacki (.111, 1-for-9)

Led majors with 32 sacrifice bunts, most in A.L. since Bert Campaneris in 1977 (40), and most by a Cleveland player since Joe Sewell in 1929 (41). (See Cleveland essay for more.) . . .Played 156 games, but drove in more than one run only twice. . . . Streak of 99 consecutive plate appearances without striking out was longest in majors. . . . Average of one strikeout every 20.8 plate appearances was 3d best among qualifying A.L. batters, behind Lansford and Mattingly. . . . Went 136 at-bats between extra-base hits, longest streak in A.L. . . . Tied Luis Gomez's A.L. record for fewest extra-base hits in a season of 150+ games. . . . Most career at-bats (639) of any active player who has never hit a home run.

## Steve Finley

Bats Left

| Baltimore Orioles | AB | H | 2B | 3B | HR | RBI | BB | SO | BA | SA | OBA |
|---|---|---|---|---|---|---|---|---|---|---|---|
| Season | 217 | 54 | 5 | 2 | 2 | 25 | 15 | 30 | .249 | .318 | .298 |
| vs. Left-Handers | 38 | 6 | 1 | 0 | 1 | 6 | 2 | 7 | .158 | .263 | .220 |
| vs. Right-Handers | 179 | 48 | 4 | 2 | 1 | 19 | 13 | 23 | .268 | .330 | .314 |
| Home | 114 | 25 | 4 | 0 | 0 | 10 | 9 | 20 | .219 | .254 | .280 |
| Road | 103 | 29 | 1 | 2 | 2 | 15 | 6 | 10 | .282 | .388 | .318 |
| Grass | 183 | 46 | 5 | 2 | 2 | 25 | 10 | 28 | .251 | .333 | .291 |
| Artificial Turf | 34 | 8 | 0 | 0 | 0 | 0 | 5 | 2 | .235 | .235 | .333 |
| April | 23 | 5 | 0 | 0 | 1 | 5 | 1 | 1 | .217 | .348 | .250 |
| May | 46 | 9 | 2 | 1 | 0 | 6 | 3 | 9 | .196 | .283 | .235 |
| June | 44 | 11 | 2 | 0 | 1 | 6 | 5 | 4 | .250 | .364 | .327 |
| July | 54 | 15 | 0 | 0 | 0 | 4 | 4 | 9 | .278 | .278 | .339 |
| August | 0 | 0 | 0 | 0 | 0 | 0 | 0 | 0 | — | — | — |
| Sept./Oct. | 50 | 14 | 1 | 1 | 0 | 4 | 2 | 7 | .280 | .340 | .308 |
| Leading Off Inn. | 45 | 15 | 0 | 0 | 0 | 0 | 3 | 10 | .333 | .333 | .375 |
| Runners On | 94 | 21 | 3 | 2 | 2 | 25 | 7 | 11 | .223 | .362 | .279 |
| Runners/Scor. Pos. | 59 | 15 | 3 | 1 | 2 | 24 | 5 | 9 | .254 | .441 | .313 |
| Runners On/2 Out | 46 | 11 | 1 | 1 | 2 | 14 | 2 | 4 | .239 | .435 | .286 |
| Scor. Pos./2 Out | 32 | 8 | 1 | 1 | 2 | 14 | 2 | 4 | .250 | .531 | .314 |
| Late Inning Pressure | 30 | 11 | 1 | 0 | 0 | 5 | 3 | 4 | .367 | .400 | .424 |
| Leading Off | 5 | 3 | 0 | 0 | 0 | 0 | 0 | 0 | .600 | .600 | .600 |
| Runners On | 15 | 5 | 1 | 0 | 0 | 5 | 3 | 2 | .333 | .400 | .444 |
| Runners/Scor. Pos. | 11 | 5 | 1 | 0 | 0 | 5 | 2 | 2 | .455 | .545 | .538 |

| RUNS BATTED IN | From 1B | From 2B | From 3B | Scoring Position |
|---|---|---|---|---|
| Totals | 4/69 | 8/48 | 11/26 | 19/74 |
| Percentage | 6% | 17% | 42% | 26% |
| Driving In Runners from 3B with Less than Two Out: | | | 7/12 | 58% |

Loves to face: Chuck Finley (.500, 3-for-6)
Hates to face: Bob Welch (0-for-6)

Ranked fifth among major league rookies with 17 stolen bases. . . . Batted 50 points higher vs. ground-ballers (.280) than vs. fly-ballers (.230), but had no extra-base hits in 82 at-bats against the former group. . . . Batted .204 in day games, .262 at night. . . . Batted .286 on fair balls hit to the right side, .471 straight away, and .154 on fair balls hit to the opposite field. . . . Grounded into only three double plays in 41 opportunities. . . . Scored from second base on only four of nine outfield singles. . . . Could this be the start of something big for Steve Allen Finley? Comparable rookie seasons: Bobby LaMotte (1922), Lynn Myers (1938), Al Zarilla (1943), Fred Patek (1968). . . . Guess not.

## Carlton Fisk

Bats Right

| Chicago White Sox | AB | H | 2B | 3B | HR | RBI | BB | SO | BA | SA | OBA |
|---|---|---|---|---|---|---|---|---|---|---|---|
| Season | 375 | 110 | 25 | 2 | 13 | 68 | 36 | 60 | .293 | .475 | .356 |
| vs. Left-Handers | 120 | 39 | 8 | 1 | 4 | 22 | 10 | 10 | .325 | .508 | .371 |
| vs. Right-Handers | 255 | 71 | 17 | 1 | 9 | 46 | 26 | 50 | .278 | .459 | .348 |
| Home | 172 | 59 | 13 | 1 | 4 | 32 | 23 | 24 | .343 | .500 | .417 |
| Road | 203 | 51 | 12 | 1 | 9 | 36 | 13 | 36 | .251 | .453 | .300 |
| Grass | 311 | 92 | 18 | 2 | 10 | 53 | 32 | 46 | .296 | .463 | .360 |
| Artificial Turf | 64 | 18 | 7 | 0 | 3 | 15 | 4 | 14 | .281 | .531 | .333 |
| April | 25 | 6 | 1 | 0 | 2 | 4 | 1 | 7 | .240 | .520 | .269 |
| May | 0 | 0 | 0 | 0 | 0 | 0 | 0 | 0 | — | — | — |
| June | 89 | 29 | 3 | 1 | 2 | 17 | 8 | 19 | .326 | .449 | .379 |
| July | 82 | 22 | 7 | 0 | 3 | 14 | 4 | 11 | .268 | .463 | .299 |
| August | 94 | 29 | 7 | 1 | 3 | 16 | 8 | 13 | .309 | .500 | .363 |
| Sept./Oct. | 85 | 24 | 7 | 0 | 3 | 17 | 15 | 10 | .282 | .471 | .396 |
| Leading Off Inn. | 76 | 22 | 6 | 0 | 2 | 2 | 5 | 13 | .289 | .447 | .333 |
| Runners On | 183 | 61 | 14 | 1 | 6 | 61 | 23 | 24 | .333 | .519 | .407 |
| Runners/Scor. Pos. | 105 | 37 | 4 | 1 | 4 | 49 | 15 | 17 | .352 | .524 | .425 |
| Runners On/2 Out | 79 | 21 | 7 | 0 | 2 | 23 | 11 | 11 | .266 | .430 | .363 |
| Scor. Pos./2 Out | 47 | 13 | 4 | 0 | 1 | 17 | 6 | 9 | .277 | .426 | .358 |
| Late Inning Pressure | 62 | 19 | 6 | 0 | 2 | 14 | 6 | 15 | .306 | .500 | .357 |
| Leading Off | 13 | 5 | 1 | 0 | 1 | 1 | 3 | 2 | .385 | .692 | .500 |
| Runners On | 27 | 10 | 4 | 0 | 1 | 13 | 3 | 6 | .370 | .630 | .406 |
| Runners/Scor. Pos. | 19 | 6 | 1 | 0 | 1 | 10 | 3 | 5 | .316 | .526 | .375 |

| RUNS BATTED IN | From 1B | From 2B | From 3B | Scoring Position |
|---|---|---|---|---|
| Totals | 14/135 | 15/79 | 26/48 | 41/127 |
| Percentage | 10% | 19% | 54% | 32% |
| Driving In Runners from 3B with Less than Two Out: | | | 18/22 | 82% |

Loves to face: Mike Witt (.338, 23-for-68, 3 HR)
Hates to face: Jack Morris (.125, 7-for-56, 1 HR)
With his first game behind the plate in 1990, he will become the first player to catch at least one game in four decades during the 20th century. (Unless Rick Dempsey beats him to it.) . . .Among the seven four-decade players who began their careers in the 1800s, four were catchers: Deacon McGuire, Jack O'Conner, Jim O'Rourke, and John Ryan. . . . Tim McCarver, a four-decade player, didn't appear as a catcher in 1980, his final season. . . . All-time leaders in games behind the plate: Boone, 2185; Fisk, 1928; Sundberg, 1927; Lopez, 1918. . . . Batted .332 vs. fly-ball pitchers, .249 vs. groundballers last season. . . . Batting average in Late-Inning Pressure Situations was his highest of the last 15 years.

## Scott Fletcher

Bats Right

| Rangers/White Sox | AB | H | 2B | 3B | HR | RBI | BB | SO | BA | SA | OBA |
|---|---|---|---|---|---|---|---|---|---|---|---|
| Season | 546 | 138 | 25 | 2 | 1 | 43 | 64 | 60 | .253 | .311 | .332 |
| vs. Left-Handers | 164 | 46 | 13 | 1 | 0 | 10 | 20 | 14 | .280 | .372 | .359 |
| vs. Right-Handers | 382 | 92 | 12 | 1 | 1 | 33 | 44 | 46 | .241 | .285 | .320 |
| Home | 270 | 69 | 11 | 1 | 0 | 21 | 28 | 28 | .256 | .304 | .328 |
| Road | 276 | 69 | 14 | 1 | 1 | 22 | 36 | 32 | .250 | .319 | .335 |
| Grass | 446 | 113 | 21 | 2 | 1 | 33 | 52 | 50 | .253 | .316 | .333 |
| Artificial Turf | 100 | 25 | 4 | 0 | 0 | 10 | 12 | 10 | .250 | .290 | .327 |
| April | 82 | 22 | 3 | 1 | 0 | 9 | 18 | 9 | .268 | .329 | .400 |
| May | 104 | 24 | 2 | 0 | 0 | 4 | 9 | 17 | .231 | .250 | .296 |
| June | 85 | 23 | 8 | 0 | 0 | 7 | 9 | 11 | .271 | .365 | .344 |
| July | 52 | 7 | 1 | 0 | 0 | 3 | 3 | 4 | .135 | .154 | .179 |
| August | 108 | 31 | 7 | 0 | 0 | 10 | 17 | 9 | .287 | .352 | .386 |
| Sept./Oct. | 115 | 31 | 4 | 1 | 1 | 10 | 8 | 10 | .270 | .348 | .315 |
| Leading Off Inn. | 113 | 28 | 5 | 1 | 1 | 1 | 13 | 13 | .248 | .336 | .331 |
| Runners On | 211 | 52 | 10 | 0 | 0 | 42 | 25 | 24 | .246 | .294 | .322 |
| Runners/Scor. Pos. | 140 | 33 | 6 | 0 | 0 | 41 | 17 | 20 | .236 | .279 | .309 |
| Runners On/2 Out | 83 | 20 | 5 | 0 | 0 | 17 | 10 | 12 | .241 | .301 | .323 |
| Scor. Pos./2 Out | 59 | 14 | 4 | 0 | 0 | 16 | 8 | 11 | .237 | .305 | .328 |
| Late Inning Pressure | 74 | 16 | 2 | 0 | 0 | 6 | 9 | 12 | .216 | .243 | .298 |
| Leading Off | 22 | 5 | 1 | 0 | 0 | 0 | 5 | 2 | .227 | .273 | .370 |
| Runners On | 30 | 7 | 1 | 0 | 0 | 6 | 2 | 7 | .233 | .267 | .273 |
| Runners/Scor. Pos. | 20 | 3 | 1 | 0 | 0 | 6 | 1 | 7 | .150 | .200 | .182 |

| RUNS BATTED IN | From 1B | From 2B | From 3B | Scoring Position |
|---|---|---|---|---|
| Totals | 3/119 | 17/102 | 22/55 | 39/157 |
| Percentage | 3% | 17% | 40% | 25% |
| Driving In Runners from 3B with Less than Two Out: | | | 18/34 | 53% |

Loves to face: Frank Tanana (.395, 15-for-38, 2 HR)
Hates to face: Kirk McCaskill (.043, 1-for-23)
Played second base for first time since 1986, and became first player ever to handle more than 200 chances there in a season without committing an error. Fletch was perfect in 269 opportunities. Previous record: 194, Frank Quilici (1968). . . . Streak of 60 consecutive errorless games at second (7 in '86, 53 after joining Sox in July) is 29 short of A.L. record, held by Jerry Adair. . . . Average of 4.15 chances per nine innings was lowest among A.L. shortstops (minimum: 500 innings). . . . Batted above .300 with runners in scoring position in four of the previous five seasons. Career average: .298. . . . Home run off Mickey Weston on Sept. 12 broke streak of 1075 at-bats without one.

## Julio Franco

Bats Right

| Texas Rangers | AB | H | 2B | 3B | HR | RBI | BB | SO | BA | SA | OBA |
|---|---|---|---|---|---|---|---|---|---|---|---|
| Season | 548 | 173 | 31 | 5 | 13 | 92 | 66 | 69 | .316 | .462 | .386 |
| vs. Left-Handers | 161 | 46 | 10 | 1 | 5 | 28 | 20 | 22 | .286 | .453 | .361 |
| vs. Right-Handers | 387 | 127 | 21 | 4 | 8 | 64 | 46 | 47 | .328 | .465 | .397 |
| Home | 267 | 95 | 18 | 4 | 9 | 52 | 37 | 32 | .356 | .554 | .430 |
| Road | 281 | 78 | 13 | 1 | 4 | 40 | 29 | 37 | .278 | .374 | .343 |
| Grass | 452 | 153 | 26 | 5 | 12 | 81 | 56 | 55 | .338 | .498 | .409 |
| Artificial Turf | 96 | 20 | 5 | 0 | 1 | 11 | 10 | 14 | .208 | .292 | .280 |
| April | 82 | 25 | 4 | 0 | 4 | 23 | 9 | 10 | .305 | .500 | .366 |
| May | 98 | 35 | 7 | 0 | 3 | 21 | 15 | 14 | .357 | .520 | .439 |
| June | 106 | 37 | 6 | 2 | 3 | 16 | 12 | 18 | .349 | .528 | .408 |
| July | 94 | 25 | 3 | 1 | 0 | 13 | 8 | 10 | .266 | .319 | .324 |
| August | 101 | 29 | 7 | 1 | 3 | 15 | 12 | 11 | .287 | .465 | .365 |
| Sept./Oct. | 67 | 22 | 4 | 1 | 0 | 4 | 10 | 6 | .328 | .418 | .416 |
| Leading Off Inn. | 126 | 36 | 4 | 1 | 4 | 4 | 10 | 16 | .286 | .429 | .338 |
| Runners On | 252 | 87 | 22 | 2 | 5 | 84 | 41 | 34 | .345 | .508 | .428 |
| Runners/Scor. Pos. | 140 | 57 | 13 | 2 | 3 | 76 | 28 | 20 | .407 | .593 | .489 |
| Runners On/2 Out | 118 | 38 | 9 | 0 | 1 | 31 | 30 | 23 | .322 | .424 | .459 |
| Scor. Pos./2 Out | 70 | 24 | 5 | 0 | 0 | 27 | 21 | 13 | .343 | .414 | .495 |
| Late Inning Pressure | 72 | 23 | 5 | 0 | 2 | 13 | 4 | 12 | .319 | .472 | .351 |
| Leading Off | 18 | 8 | 0 | 0 | 1 | 1 | 1 | 3 | .444 | .611 | .474 |
| Runners On | 38 | 11 | 4 | 0 | 1 | 12 | 2 | 8 | .289 | .474 | .317 |
| Runners/Scor. Pos. | 20 | 7 | 3 | 0 | 1 | 12 | 1 | 4 | .350 | .650 | .364 |

| RUNS BATTED IN | From 1B | From 2B | From 3B | Scoring Position |
|---|---|---|---|---|
| Totals | 13/183 | 33/105 | 33/67 | 66/172 |
| Percentage | 7% | 31% | 49% | 38% |
| Driving In Runners from 3B with Less than Two Out: | | | 21/31 | 68% |

Loves to face: Mike Witt (.378, 17-for-45, 1 HR)
Hates to face: Tom Henke (.071, 1-for-14)
Most hits of any player without a four-hit game last season. . . . Started 133 games from the 5th spot in batting order, most in majors. . . . One of six major leaguers to top the .300 mark in each of last four seasons. Others: Boggs (7 years), Gwynn and Mattingly (6), Puckett and Yount (4). . . . Batted 123 points higher with runners in scoring position than in other at-bats, largest difference in A.L. (minimum: 75 AB with RISP). His RISP average was 3d highest in A.L. during the 1980s, behind .466 by George Brett and .421 by Cecil Cooper, both in 1980. . . . Only player whose name was mispronounced by both Vin Scully and Ronald Reagan on the same telecast.

## Terry Francona

Bats Left

| Milwaukee Brewers | AB | H | 2B | 3B | HR | RBI | BB | SO | BA | SA | OBA |
|---|---|---|---|---|---|---|---|---|---|---|---|
| Season | 233 | 54 | 10 | 1 | 3 | 23 | 8 | 20 | .232 | .322 | .255 |
| vs. Left-Handers | 21 | 5 | 2 | 0 | 0 | 5 | 0 | 1 | .238 | .333 | .238 |
| vs. Right-Handers | 212 | 49 | 8 | 1 | 3 | 18 | 8 | 19 | .231 | .321 | .257 |
| Home | 128 | 29 | 3 | 1 | 1 | 9 | 1 | 12 | .227 | .289 | .231 |
| Road | 105 | 25 | 7 | 0 | 2 | 14 | 7 | 8 | .238 | .362 | .283 |
| Grass | 220 | 50 | 9 | 1 | 2 | 20 | 7 | 18 | .227 | .305 | .250 |
| Artificial Turf | 13 | 4 | 1 | 0 | 1 | 3 | 1 | 2 | .308 | .615 | .333 |
| April | 55 | 10 | 2 | 0 | 0 | 3 | 1 | 9 | .182 | .218 | .196 |
| May | 69 | 19 | 3 | 1 | 1 | 7 | 2 | 5 | .275 | .391 | .292 |
| June | 39 | 9 | 2 | 0 | 1 | 3 | 0 | 1 | .231 | .359 | .231 |
| July | 32 | 7 | 2 | 0 | 1 | 5 | 4 | 1 | .219 | .375 | .306 |
| August | 22 | 4 | 0 | 0 | 0 | 2 | 1 | 3 | .182 | .182 | .217 |
| Sept./Oct. | 16 | 5 | 1 | 0 | 0 | 3 | 0 | 1 | .313 | .375 | .294 |
| Leading Off Inn. | 57 | 14 | 2 | 0 | 1 | 1 | 1 | 6 | .246 | .333 | .259 |
| Runners On | 98 | 26 | 5 | 0 | 1 | 21 | 7 | 4 | .265 | .347 | .308 |
| Runners/Scor. Pos. | 58 | 18 | 5 | 0 | 1 | 21 | 5 | 2 | .310 | .448 | .354 |
| Runners On/2 Out | 46 | 9 | 2 | 0 | 0 | 8 | 3 | 2 | .196 | .239 | .245 |
| Scor. Pos./2 Out | 30 | 8 | 2 | 0 | 0 | 8 | 3 | 1 | .267 | .333 | .333 |
| Late Inning Pressure | 38 | 7 | 1 | 0 | 0 | 1 | 1 | 2 | .184 | .211 | .205 |
| Leading Off | 10 | 3 | 1 | 0 | 0 | 0 | 0 | 0 | .300 | .400 | .300 |
| Runners On | 15 | 2 | 0 | 0 | 0 | 1 | 1 | 0 | .133 | .133 | .188 |
| Runners/Scor. Pos. | 6 | 1 | 0 | 0 | 0 | 1 | 1 | 0 | .167 | .167 | .286 |

| RUNS BATTED IN | From 1B | From 2B | From 3B | Scoring Position |
|---|---|---|---|---|
| Totals | 0/70 | 9/45 | 11/21 | 20/66 |
| Percentage | 0% | 20% | 52% | 30% |
| Driving In Runners from 3B with Less than Two Out: | | | 8/11 | 73% |

Loves to face: Rick Aguilera (.538, 7-for-13)
Hates to face: Dave Stewart (0-for-10)
Must be in the genes: Has played for different teams in each of the last five seasons. Has to make four more stops to match daddy Tito's family record of nine clubs (over 15 years). . . . Trivia: For which team, or teams, did both Tito and Terry play? Answer below. . . . Career batting average dropped to .274, two points higher than Tito's career mark. . . . Was in opening-day lineup against Greg Swindell last season, the first and last start he made against a southpaw. . . . Started at least one game in every batting-order position except the leadoff and cleanup spots. . . . Has struck out only once in 38 career plate appearances with the bases loaded. . . . Answer: Indians and Brewers.

## Gary Gaetti

Bats Right

| Minnesota Twins | AB | H | 2B | 3B | HR | RBI | BB | SO | BA | SA | OBA |
|---|---|---|---|---|---|---|---|---|---|---|---|
| Season | 498 | 125 | 11 | 4 | 19 | 75 | 25 | 87 | .251 | .404 | .286 |
| vs. Left-Handers | 152 | 35 | 2 | 2 | 5 | 24 | 10 | 19 | .230 | .368 | .274 |
| vs. Right-Handers | 346 | 90 | 9 | 2 | 14 | 51 | 15 | 68 | .260 | .419 | .291 |
| Home | 249 | 62 | 5 | 1 | 10 | 40 | 10 | 43 | .249 | .398 | .278 |
| Road | 249 | 63 | 6 | 3 | 9 | 35 | 15 | 44 | .253 | .410 | .294 |
| Grass | 206 | 53 | 6 | 2 | 9 | 30 | 13 | 38 | .257 | .437 | .299 |
| Artificial Turf | 292 | 72 | 5 | 2 | 10 | 45 | 12 | 49 | .247 | .380 | .277 |
| April | 85 | 25 | 2 | 0 | 5 | 18 | 3 | 16 | .294 | .494 | .318 |
| May | 104 | 22 | 3 | 2 | 2 | 13 | 5 | 20 | .212 | .337 | .241 |
| June | 115 | 34 | 2 | 1 | 8 | 23 | 7 | 14 | .296 | .539 | .333 |
| July | 84 | 18 | 2 | 0 | 2 | 9 | 4 | 14 | .214 | .310 | .250 |
| August | 78 | 19 | 2 | 0 | 2 | 9 | 4 | 13 | .244 | .346 | .280 |
| Sept./Oct. | 32 | 7 | 0 | 1 | 0 | 3 | 2 | 10 | .219 | .281 | .286 |
| Leading Off Inn. | 125 | 32 | 2 | 0 | 4 | 4 | 3 | 21 | .256 | .368 | .279 |
| Runners On | 239 | 60 | 2 | 2 | 12 | 68 | 18 | 40 | .251 | .427 | .299 |
| Runners/Scor. Pos. | 132 | 29 | 2 | 0 | 7 | 56 | 13 | 31 | .220 | .394 | .277 |
| Runners On/2 Out | 103 | 27 | 1 | 0 | 5 | 26 | 9 | 15 | .262 | .417 | .321 |
| Scor. Pos./2 Out | 58 | 13 | 1 | 0 | 2 | 20 | 8 | 11 | .224 | .345 | .318 |
| Late Inning Pressure | 71 | 17 | 0 | 0 | 6 | 13 | 4 | 12 | .239 | .493 | .280 |
| Leading Off | 24 | 5 | 0 | 0 | 1 | 1 | 0 | 2 | .208 | .333 | .208 |
| Runners On | 27 | 6 | 0 | 0 | 3 | 10 | 2 | 6 | .222 | .556 | .276 |
| Runners/Scor. Pos. | 17 | 3 | 0 | 0 | 1 | 6 | 2 | 5 | .176 | .353 | .263 |

| RUNS BATTED IN | From 1B | From 2B | From 3B | Scoring Position |
|---|---|---|---|---|
| Totals | 13/184 | 20/96 | 23/69 | 43/165 |
| Percentage | 7% | 21% | 33% | 26% |
| Driving In Runners from 3B with Less than Two Out: | | | 17/38 | 45% |

Loves to face: Dennis Lamp (.378, 14-for-37, 2 HR)
Hates to face: Bobby Witt (0-for-14)
Number of games played has decreased in every season since 1984, when he earned a gold star for perfect attendance: 162, 160, 157, 154, 133, 130. . . . Batting average with runners in scoring position was the lowest of his career. . . . Ended the season with 48 consecutive errorless games at third base. A.L. record is 88, by Don Money (1973–74). . . . One of three players in franchise history with 1000 or more games at third base. The leaders: Eddie Yost (1625), Ossie Bluege (1487), Gaetti (1160). . . . Has hit more home runs on the road (96) than at home (87) since opening of the Metrodome in 1982. . . . Career batting average is .186 with runners in scoring position in LIP Situations.

## Greg Gagne

Bats Right

| Minnesota Twins | AB | H | 2B | 3B | HR | RBI | BB | SO | BA | SA | OBA |
|---|---|---|---|---|---|---|---|---|---|---|---|
| Season | 460 | 125 | 29 | 7 | 9 | 48 | 17 | 80 | .272 | .424 | .298 |
| vs. Left-Handers | 171 | 50 | 13 | 5 | 5 | 16 | 7 | 22 | .292 | .515 | .320 |
| vs. Right-Handers | 289 | 75 | 16 | 2 | 4 | 32 | 10 | 58 | .260 | .370 | .284 |
| Home | 218 | 65 | 20 | 2 | 5 | 25 | 9 | 35 | .298 | .477 | .326 |
| Road | 242 | 60 | 9 | 5 | 4 | 23 | 8 | 45 | .248 | .376 | .272 |
| Grass | 192 | 47 | 8 | 3 | 3 | 15 | 7 | 35 | .245 | .365 | .272 |
| Artificial Turf | 268 | 78 | 21 | 4 | 6 | 33 | 10 | 45 | .291 | .466 | .316 |
| April | 64 | 17 | 4 | 0 | 0 | 4 | 3 | 9 | .266 | .328 | .299 |
| May | 89 | 22 | 4 | 1 | 2 | 11 | 4 | 13 | .247 | .382 | .281 |
| June | 88 | 23 | 6 | 2 | 2 | 11 | 6 | 17 | .261 | .443 | .313 |
| July | 58 | 14 | 3 | 0 | 1 | 4 | 0 | 17 | .241 | .345 | .237 |
| August | 92 | 32 | 8 | 2 | 2 | 7 | 4 | 13 | .348 | .543 | .371 |
| Sept./Oct. | 69 | 17 | 4 | 2 | 2 | 11 | 0 | 11 | .246 | .449 | .246 |
| Leading Off Inn. | 107 | 35 | 12 | 1 | 1 | 1 | 3 | 14 | .327 | .486 | .345 |
| Runners On | 203 | 44 | 7 | 2 | 2 | 41 | 12 | 39 | .217 | .300 | .255 |
| Runners/Scor. Pos. | 112 | 23 | 5 | 2 | 1 | 37 | 10 | 22 | .205 | .313 | .260 |
| Runners On/2 Out | 88 | 18 | 2 | 0 | 0 | 13 | 3 | 20 | .205 | .227 | .231 |
| Scor. Pos./2 Out | 61 | 10 | 1 | 0 | 0 | 12 | 3 | 14 | .164 | .180 | .203 |
| Late Inning Pressure | 52 | 10 | 1 | 2 | 0 | 4 | 0 | 16 | .192 | .288 | .189 |
| Leading Off | 13 | 3 | 0 | 0 | 0 | 0 | 0 | 3 | .231 | .231 | .231 |
| Runners On | 17 | 2 | 0 | 1 | 0 | 4 | 0 | 5 | .118 | .235 | .111 |
| Runners/Scor. Pos. | 9 | 2 | 0 | 1 | 0 | 4 | 0 | 3 | .222 | .444 | .200 |

| RUNS BATTED IN | From 1B | From 2B | From 3B | Scoring Position |
|---|---|---|---|---|
| Totals | 6/146 | 16/91 | 17/48 | 33/139 |
| Percentage | 4% | 18% | 35% | 24% |
| Driving In Runners from 3B with Less than Two Out: | | | 11/23 | 48% |

Loves to face: Tom Candiotti (.414, 12-for-29, 1 HR)
Hates to face: Chuck Finley (.071, 1-for-14)
Batting average was a career high, but rate of one walk per 29 plate appearances was lowest of his career. Walked only once in his last 122 plate appearances. . . . Has batted .320 leading off innings over the last two seasons, but has drawn only three leadoff walks in 210 plate appearances. . . . Yearly batting averages with runners in scoring position over the last five seasons: .303, .267, .238, .210, .205. . . . Batted under .200 with two outs and runners in scoring position in each of the last two. . . . Career batting average is .132 (5-for-38, 1 HR) with the bases loaded. . . . Career mark is .218 in LIP Situations, .253 in other at-bats. . . . Situational hitting isn't exactly his thing.

## Dave Gallagher

Bats Right

| Chicago White Sox | AB | H | 2B | 3B | HR | RBI | BB | SO | BA | SA | OBA |
|---|---|---|---|---|---|---|---|---|---|---|---|
| Season | 601 | 160 | 22 | 2 | 1 | 46 | 46 | 79 | .266 | .314 | .320 |
| vs. Left-Handers | 200 | 56 | 9 | 1 | 0 | 20 | 15 | 22 | .280 | .335 | .329 |
| vs. Right-Handers | 401 | 104 | 13 | 1 | 1 | 26 | 31 | 57 | .259 | .304 | .315 |
| Home | 289 | 78 | 9 | 1 | 1 | 21 | 22 | 29 | .270 | .318 | .322 |
| Road | 312 | 82 | 13 | 1 | 0 | 25 | 24 | 50 | .263 | .311 | .318 |
| Grass | 508 | 140 | 19 | 1 | 1 | 39 | 43 | 61 | .276 | .323 | .333 |
| Artificial Turf | 93 | 20 | 3 | 1 | 0 | 7 | 3 | 18 | .215 | .269 | .245 |
| April | 101 | 27 | 2 | 1 | 1 | 13 | 11 | 8 | .267 | .337 | .336 |
| May | 104 | 35 | 3 | 0 | 0 | 5 | 12 | 11 | .337 | .365 | .405 |
| June | 125 | 38 | 5 | 0 | 0 | 8 | 8 | 15 | .304 | .344 | .346 |
| July | 97 | 26 | 5 | 0 | 0 | 5 | 10 | 22 | .268 | .320 | .343 |
| August | 113 | 20 | 4 | 0 | 0 | 8 | 2 | 16 | .177 | .212 | .197 |
| Sept./Oct. | 61 | 14 | 3 | 1 | 0 | 7 | 3 | 7 | .230 | .311 | .266 |
| Leading Off Inn. | 200 | 55 | 13 | 0 | 0 | 0 | 14 | 25 | .275 | .340 | .322 |
| Runners On | 230 | 61 | 6 | 2 | 1 | 46 | 20 | 32 | .265 | .322 | .324 |
| Runners/Scor. Pos. | 153 | 39 | 5 | 1 | 1 | 45 | 15 | 24 | .255 | .320 | .318 |
| Runners On/2 Out | 113 | 26 | 2 | 1 | 1 | 21 | 12 | 18 | .230 | .292 | .304 |
| Scor. Pos./2 Out | 81 | 18 | 2 | 1 | 1 | 21 | 9 | 14 | .222 | .309 | .300 |
| Late Inning Pressure | 88 | 19 | 2 | 0 | 0 | 3 | 6 | 9 | .216 | .239 | .266 |
| Leading Off | 23 | 7 | 1 | 0 | 0 | 0 | 2 | 2 | .304 | .348 | .360 |
| Runners On | 43 | 8 | 0 | 0 | 0 | 3 | 3 | 5 | .186 | .186 | .239 |
| Runners/Scor. Pos. | 27 | 3 | 0 | 0 | 0 | 3 | 3 | 4 | .111 | .111 | .200 |

| RUNS BATTED IN | From 1B | From 2B | From 3B | Scoring Position |
|---|---|---|---|---|
| Totals | 3/140 | 19/115 | 23/70 | 42/185 |
| Percentage | 2% | 17% | 33% | 23% |
| Driving In Runners from 3B with Less than Two Out: | | | 16/36 | 44% |

Loves to face: Allan Anderson (.400, 6-for-15)
Hates to face: Terry Leach (0-for-9)
First White Sox player to appear in every game of a season since Greg Walker in 1985. . . . Only player on team to start all 53 games in which White Sox faced left-handed pitchers. . . . Iron men have gone the way of undisputed boxing champs and NHL shutouts. Longest current playing streaks: Cal Ripken (1250), Eddie Murray (359), Ruben Sierra (294), and Gallagher (198). . . . Batted 12 times with the bases loaded last season, but drove in only two of 36 runners. . . . Drove in only three of 33 runners from scoring position in Late-Inning Pressure Situations. . . . Has hit half of his six major league home runs in 38 at-bats at Arlington Stadium. Rangers fans probably think he's a slugger.

## Mike Gallego

Bats Right

| Oakland As | AB | H | 2B | 3B | HR | RBI | BB | SO | BA | SA | OBA |
|---|---|---|---|---|---|---|---|---|---|---|---|
| Season | 357 | 90 | 14 | 2 | 3 | 30 | 35 | 43 | .252 | .328 | .327 |
| vs. Left-Handers | 125 | 33 | 6 | 0 | 0 | 9 | 13 | 16 | .264 | .312 | .333 |
| vs. Right-Handers | 232 | 57 | 8 | 2 | 3 | 21 | 22 | 27 | .246 | .336 | .323 |
| Home | 178 | 49 | 5 | 2 | 2 | 17 | 18 | 19 | .275 | .360 | .351 |
| Road | 179 | 41 | 9 | 0 | 1 | 13 | 17 | 24 | .229 | .296 | .302 |
| Grass | 296 | 73 | 10 | 2 | 2 | 24 | 28 | 35 | .247 | .314 | .320 |
| Artificial Turf | 61 | 17 | 4 | 0 | 1 | 6 | 7 | 8 | .279 | .393 | .357 |
| April | 52 | 23 | 6 | 0 | 0 | 7 | 2 | 6 | .442 | .558 | .455 |
| May | 68 | 11 | 2 | 1 | 1 | 4 | 9 | 10 | .162 | .265 | .278 |
| June | 73 | 16 | 0 | 1 | 1 | 9 | 9 | 9 | .219 | .288 | .313 |
| July | 69 | 14 | 2 | 0 | 1 | 7 | 7 | 7 | .203 | .275 | .278 |
| August | 42 | 15 | 3 | 0 | 0 | 2 | 6 | 3 | .357 | .429 | .460 |
| Sept./Oct. | 53 | 11 | 1 | 0 | 0 | 1 | 2 | 8 | .208 | .226 | .236 |
| Leading Off Inn. | 90 | 19 | 3 | 0 | 1 | 1 | 10 | 14 | .211 | .278 | .290 |
| Runners On | 154 | 38 | 4 | 2 | 1 | 28 | 9 | 14 | .247 | .318 | .300 |
| Runners/Scor. Pos. | 83 | 18 | 1 | 1 | 0 | 25 | 4 | 7 | .217 | .253 | .269 |
| Runners On/2 Out | 69 | 16 | 2 | 2 | 1 | 11 | 8 | 7 | .232 | .362 | .329 |
| Scor. Pos./2 Out | 36 | 6 | 1 | 1 | 0 | 8 | 3 | 3 | .167 | .250 | .250 |
| Late Inning Pressure | 34 | 4 | 0 | 0 | 0 | 1 | 3 | 6 | .118 | .118 | .211 |
| Leading Off | 9 | 2 | 0 | 0 | 0 | 0 | 2 | 3 | .222 | .222 | .364 |
| Runners On | 18 | 1 | 0 | 0 | 0 | 1 | 0 | 2 | .056 | .056 | .056 |
| Runners/Scor. Pos. | 8 | 1 | 0 | 0 | 0 | 1 | 0 | 1 | .125 | .125 | .125 |

| RUNS BATTED IN | From 1B | From 2B | From 3B | Scoring Position |
|---|---|---|---|---|
| Totals | 4/113 | 5/58 | 18/45 | 23/103 |
| Percentage | 4% | 9% | 40% | 22% |
| Driving In Runners from 3B with Less than Two Out: | | | 14/26 | 54% |

Loves to face: Scott Bankhead (.667, 6-for-9)
Hates to face: Jeff Ballard (0-for-12)
Has never made an error in 65 games on synthetic turf. . . . Played three games at third base last season, raising career total to 57 games there without an error. The only third baseman with more games and no errors: Bobby Wine (67). . . . Career average of .134 (11-for-82) in Late-Inning Pressure Situations, with only three hits in 36 LIPS at-bats with runners on base. . . . Career average of .244 at the Oakland Coliseum, .185 on other grass fields, .299 on artificial surfaces. . . . Has batted 1005 times in his career, and never received an intentional walk. Won't someone please help? . . . From Seymour's Oddities Dept.: Stole 6 bases in 7 attempts in day games, but was 1-for-5 at night.

## Jim Gantner

Bats Left

| Milwaukee Brewers | AB | H | 2B | 3B | HR | RBI | BB | SO | BA | SA | OBA |
|---|---|---|---|---|---|---|---|---|---|---|---|
| Season | 409 | 112 | 18 | 3 | 0 | 34 | 21 | 33 | .274 | .333 | .321 |
| vs. Left-Handers | 113 | 31 | 5 | 1 | 0 | 10 | 6 | 3 | .274 | .336 | .320 |
| vs. Right-Handers | 296 | 81 | 13 | 2 | 0 | 24 | 15 | 30 | .274 | .331 | .322 |
| Home | 189 | 48 | 9 | 0 | 0 | 14 | 14 | 20 | .254 | .302 | .321 |
| Road | 220 | 64 | 9 | 3 | 0 | 20 | 7 | 13 | .291 | .359 | .322 |
| Grass | 346 | 93 | 14 | 3 | 0 | 28 | 18 | 30 | .269 | .327 | .314 |
| Artificial Turf | 63 | 19 | 4 | 0 | 0 | 6 | 3 | 3 | .302 | .365 | .362 |
| April | 60 | 13 | 1 | 1 | 0 | 5 | 2 | 4 | .217 | .267 | .262 |
| May | 96 | 25 | 5 | 0 | 0 | 9 | 7 | 5 | .260 | .313 | .327 |
| June | 93 | 21 | 5 | 0 | 0 | 6 | 5 | 11 | .226 | .280 | .267 |
| July | 95 | 28 | 2 | 1 | 0 | 13 | 3 | 9 | .295 | .337 | .333 |
| August | 65 | 25 | 5 | 1 | 0 | 1 | 4 | 4 | .385 | .492 | .429 |
| Sept./Oct. | 0 | 0 | 0 | 0 | 0 | 0 | 0 | 0 | — | — | — |
| Leading Off Inn. | 94 | 27 | 5 | 0 | 0 | 0 | 5 | 9 | .287 | .340 | .323 |
| Runners On | 150 | 43 | 7 | 1 | 0 | 34 | 7 | 14 | .287 | .347 | .333 |
| Runners/Scor. Pos. | 91 | 28 | 5 | 1 | 0 | 33 | 6 | 10 | .308 | .385 | .364 |
| Runners On/2 Out | 71 | 15 | 4 | 0 | 0 | 15 | 3 | 9 | .211 | .268 | .273 |
| Scor. Pos./2 Out | 52 | 12 | 4 | 0 | 0 | 15 | 3 | 7 | .231 | .308 | .310 |
| Late Inning Pressure | 53 | 17 | 3 | 0 | 0 | 6 | 2 | 6 | .321 | .377 | .345 |
| Leading Off | 17 | 6 | 2 | 0 | 0 | 0 | 1 | 2 | .353 | .471 | .389 |
| Runners On | 19 | 6 | 1 | 0 | 0 | 6 | 0 | 2 | .316 | .368 | .318 |
| Runners/Scor. Pos. | 11 | 5 | 1 | 0 | 0 | 6 | 0 | 0 | .455 | .545 | .429 |

| RUNS BATTED IN | From 1B | From 2B | From 3B | Scoring Position |
|---|---|---|---|---|
| Totals | 4/99 | 16/74 | 14/38 | 30/112 |
| Percentage | 4% | 22% | 37% | 27% |
| Driving In Runners from 3B with Less than Two Out: | | | 11/15 | 73% |

Loves to face: Jeff Russell (.455, 5-for-11)
Hates to face: Bobby Thigpen (0-for-7)

Two years ago, at age 34, became the fourth-oldest player since 1900 to steal 20 bases for the first time. Only Pete Rose, Joe Kuhel, and Bing Miller first stole 20 or more at a later age. . . . So everyone said, "Gantner, bet you can't do it again." . . . Had already stolen 20 bases on August 15, when Marcus Lawton ended his season with a takeout slide. . . . Resumes a 43-game errorless streak at second base on opening day 1990, almost halfway to A.L. record (89). . . . Hit by 10 pitches, lowest total to lead A.L. since Max Alvis in 1965 (9). . . . Has hit 44 career home runs, but none in 1027 at-bats since June 14, 1987. . . . Has hit better on plastic than *au naturel* in each of last seven seasons.

## Rich Gedman

Bats Left

| Boston Red Sox | AB | H | 2B | 3B | HR | RBI | BB | SO | BA | SA | OBA |
|---|---|---|---|---|---|---|---|---|---|---|---|
| Season | 260 | 55 | 9 | 0 | 4 | 16 | 23 | 47 | .212 | .292 | .273 |
| vs. Left-Handers | 37 | 10 | 2 | 0 | 1 | 4 | 4 | 8 | .270 | .405 | .341 |
| vs. Right-Handers | 223 | 45 | 7 | 0 | 3 | 12 | 19 | 39 | .202 | .274 | .261 |
| Home | 117 | 26 | 3 | 0 | 2 | 9 | 14 | 15 | .222 | .299 | .303 |
| Road | 143 | 29 | 6 | 0 | 2 | 7 | 9 | 32 | .203 | .287 | .247 |
| Grass | 221 | 49 | 8 | 0 | 4 | 13 | 22 | 37 | .222 | .312 | .291 |
| Artificial Turf | 39 | 6 | 1 | 0 | 0 | 3 | 1 | 10 | .154 | .179 | .167 |
| April | 57 | 8 | 2 | 0 | 2 | 5 | 4 | 10 | .140 | .281 | .194 |
| May | 55 | 15 | 2 | 0 | 0 | 3 | 8 | 7 | .273 | .309 | .359 |
| June | 51 | 11 | 1 | 0 | 1 | 3 | 4 | 8 | .216 | .294 | .273 |
| July | 31 | 4 | 1 | 0 | 0 | 0 | 5 | 6 | .129 | .161 | .250 |
| August | 36 | 11 | 2 | 0 | 0 | 4 | 2 | 5 | .306 | .361 | .333 |
| Sept./Oct. | 30 | 6 | 1 | 0 | 1 | 1 | 0 | 11 | .200 | .333 | .200 |
| Leading Off Inn. | 63 | 15 | 2 | 0 | 2 | 2 | 4 | 11 | .238 | .365 | .284 |
| Runners On | 109 | 22 | 4 | 0 | 1 | 13 | 9 | 19 | .202 | .266 | .256 |
| Runners/Scor. Pos. | 69 | 9 | 2 | 0 | 0 | 11 | 4 | 15 | .130 | .159 | .171 |
| Runners On/2 Out | 41 | 11 | 2 | 0 | 0 | 4 | 3 | 7 | .268 | .317 | .318 |
| Scor. Pos./2 Out | 26 | 4 | 1 | 0 | 0 | 4 | 2 | 5 | .154 | .192 | .214 |
| Late Inning Pressure | 43 | 9 | 3 | 0 | 0 | 2 | 4 | 8 | .209 | .279 | .277 |
| Leading Off | 9 | 2 | 0 | 0 | 0 | 0 | 2 | 2 | .222 | .222 | .364 |
| Runners On | 16 | 3 | 2 | 0 | 0 | 2 | 1 | 3 | .188 | .313 | .235 |
| Runners/Scor. Pos. | 10 | 2 | 2 | 0 | 0 | 2 | 0 | 2 | .200 | .400 | .200 |

| RUNS BATTED IN | From 1B | From 2B | From 3B | Scoring Position |
|---|---|---|---|---|
| Totals | 1/75 | 5/58 | 6/21 | 11/79 |
| Percentage | 1% | 9% | 29% | 14% |
| Driving In Runners from 3B with Less than Two Out: | | | 5/14 | 36% |

Loves to face: Bill Swift (.750, 9-for-12)
Hates to face: Mike Witt (.143, 5-for-35, 1 HR)

To whom did Roger prefer to pitch? Opponents stole 12 bases in 17 attempts (71%) against Clemens with Gedman catching, only 7 of 19 (37%) with Cerone. But Clemens's ERA was more than a run per game lower with Rich (2.38) than with Rick (3.74). . . . Staff ERA was 3.67 in front of Gedman, 4.33 with Cerone. . . . Opposing runners were 73-for-97 (75%) vs. Gedman, 88-for-122 (72%) vs. Cerone. . . . Has hit only 13 home runs with 68 RBI over last three seasons, compared to 16 and 65, respectively, in 1986 alone. . . . Losing momentum in drive to become first player to catch 1000 games for Sox. Two others failed after coming within 40: Carlton Fisk (990) and Sammy White (967). Gedman ranks third with 849.

## Bob Geren

Bats Right

| New York Yankees | AB | H | 2B | 3B | HR | RBI | BB | SO | BA | SA | OBA |
|---|---|---|---|---|---|---|---|---|---|---|---|
| Season | 205 | 59 | 5 | 1 | 9 | 27 | 12 | 44 | .288 | .454 | .329 |
| vs. Left-Handers | 67 | 19 | 4 | 0 | 2 | 10 | 4 | 8 | .284 | .433 | .324 |
| vs. Right-Handers | 138 | 40 | 1 | 1 | 7 | 17 | 8 | 36 | .290 | .464 | .331 |
| Home | 106 | 33 | 3 | 0 | 4 | 12 | 5 | 20 | .311 | .453 | .342 |
| Road | 99 | 26 | 2 | 1 | 5 | 15 | 7 | 24 | .263 | .455 | .315 |
| Grass | 172 | 47 | 4 | 1 | 5 | 16 | 8 | 38 | .273 | .395 | .309 |
| Artificial Turf | 33 | 12 | 1 | 0 | 4 | 11 | 4 | 6 | .364 | .758 | .421 |
| April | 0 | 0 | 0 | 0 | 0 | 0 | 0 | 0 | — | — | — |
| May | 14 | 6 | 0 | 0 | 2 | 4 | 0 | 3 | .429 | .857 | .429 |
| June | 21 | 6 | 0 | 0 | 1 | 1 | 1 | 6 | .286 | .429 | .318 |
| July | 36 | 16 | 2 | 0 | 0 | 2 | 2 | 8 | .444 | .500 | .487 |
| August | 86 | 21 | 2 | 1 | 5 | 16 | 6 | 14 | .244 | .465 | .290 |
| Sept./Oct. | 48 | 10 | 1 | 0 | 1 | 4 | 3 | 13 | .208 | .292 | .255 |
| Leading Off Inn. | 47 | 15 | 0 | 1 | 2 | 2 | 1 | 9 | .319 | .489 | .333 |
| Runners On | 95 | 27 | 3 | 0 | 5 | 23 | 2 | 19 | .284 | .474 | .303 |
| Runners/Scor. Pos. | 47 | 13 | 3 | 0 | 1 | 15 | 2 | 9 | .277 | .404 | .300 |
| Runners On/2 Out | 39 | 9 | 1 | 0 | 1 | 8 | 0 | 8 | .231 | .333 | .250 |
| Scor. Pos./2 Out | 23 | 5 | 1 | 0 | 0 | 6 | 0 | 5 | .217 | .261 | .217 |
| Late Inning Pressure | 34 | 9 | 0 | 0 | 2 | 6 | 2 | 8 | .265 | .441 | .297 |
| Leading Off | 9 | 2 | 0 | 0 | 0 | 0 | 0 | 0 | .222 | .222 | .222 |
| Runners On | 17 | 6 | 0 | 0 | 2 | 6 | 1 | 5 | .353 | .706 | .368 |
| Runners/Scor. Pos. | 8 | 2 | 0 | 0 | 0 | 2 | 1 | 1 | .250 | .250 | .300 |

| RUNS BATTED IN | From 1B | From 2B | From 3B | Scoring Position |
|---|---|---|---|---|
| Totals | 5/75 | 10/40 | 3/15 | 13/55 |
| Percentage | 7% | 25% | 20% | 24% |
| Driving In Runners from 3B with Less than Two Out: | | | 1/5 | 20% |

Loves to face: Jimmy Key (2-for-2)
Hates to face: Rob Murphy (0-for-4, 3 SO)

Batting average was 2d highest by a Yankees rookie over the past 30 years (minimum: 200 AB), behind Thurman Munson, who batted .302 in 1970. . . . Rate of one home run per 23 at-bats ranked second among A.L. catchers to Mickey Tettleton. . . . Hit well to all fields: .342 (all 5 HR) on fair balls to the left side, .300 straight away, .367 to the opposite field. . . . One of only three A.L. players with at least 200 at-bats to drive in more base runners from first base than from third. The others: Jack Howell and Rick Schu. Honest. . . . Opposing base stealers were 20-for-34 (59%). A.L. average: 69 percent. . . . Career breakdown: .301 vs. ground-ballers, .262 vs. fly-ballers.

## Dan Gladden

Bats Right

| Minnesota Twins | AB | H | 2B | 3B | HR | RBI | BB | SO | BA | SA | OBA |
|---|---|---|---|---|---|---|---|---|---|---|---|
| Season | 461 | 136 | 23 | 3 | 8 | 46 | 23 | 53 | .295 | .410 | .331 |
| vs. Left-Handers | 157 | 48 | 8 | 1 | 3 | 11 | 9 | 18 | .306 | .427 | .345 |
| vs. Right-Handers | 304 | 88 | 15 | 2 | 5 | 35 | 14 | 35 | .289 | .401 | .323 |
| Home | 222 | 63 | 10 | 1 | 1 | 21 | 13 | 18 | .284 | .351 | .331 |
| Road | 239 | 73 | 13 | 2 | 7 | 25 | 10 | 35 | .305 | .464 | .331 |
| Grass | 175 | 54 | 10 | 1 | 5 | 18 | 8 | 25 | .309 | .463 | .337 |
| Artificial Turf | 286 | 82 | 13 | 2 | 3 | 28 | 15 | 28 | .287 | .378 | .327 |
| April | 77 | 21 | 3 | 0 | 1 | 4 | 3 | 5 | .273 | .351 | .309 |
| May | 111 | 29 | 8 | 0 | 1 | 16 | 4 | 19 | .261 | .360 | .283 |
| June | 75 | 27 | 2 | 1 | 2 | 10 | 8 | 4 | .360 | .493 | .437 |
| July | 11 | 2 | 0 | 0 | 0 | 0 | 1 | 0 | .182 | .182 | .250 |
| August | 73 | 21 | 3 | 0 | 2 | 9 | 3 | 11 | .288 | .411 | .312 |
| Sept./Oct. | 114 | 36 | 7 | 2 | 2 | 7 | 4 | 14 | .316 | .465 | .336 |
| Leading Off Inn. | 127 | 37 | 5 | 1 | 3 | 3 | 5 | 12 | .291 | .417 | .338 |
| Runners On | 179 | 50 | 10 | 1 | 2 | 40 | 8 | 20 | .279 | .380 | .299 |
| Runners/Scor. Pos. | 105 | 25 | 3 | 0 | 1 | 35 | 6 | 13 | .238 | .295 | .263 |
| Runners On/2 Out | 73 | 20 | 3 | 1 | 2 | 19 | 3 | 8 | .274 | .425 | .303 |
| Scor. Pos./2 Out | 48 | 12 | 1 | 0 | 1 | 16 | 3 | 6 | .250 | .333 | .294 |
| Late Inning Pressure | 63 | 21 | 4 | 0 | 1 | 7 | 1 | 12 | .333 | .444 | .343 |
| Leading Off | 18 | 8 | 1 | 0 | 1 | 1 | 0 | 2 | .444 | .667 | .444 |
| Runners On | 24 | 8 | 2 | 0 | 0 | 6 | 1 | 3 | .333 | .417 | .333 |
| Runners/Scor. Pos. | 12 | 3 | 1 | 0 | 0 | 6 | 1 | 3 | .250 | .333 | .267 |

| RUNS BATTED IN | From 1B | From 2B | From 3B | Scoring Position |
|---|---|---|---|---|
| Totals | 5/125 | 17/83 | 16/44 | 33/127 |
| Percentage | 4% | 20% | 36% | 26% |
| Driving In Runners from 3B with Less than Two Out: | | | 11/20 | 55% |

Loves to face: Mike Flanagan (.500, 10-for-20, 1 HR)
Hates to face: Bobby Witt (.095, 2-for-21)

Had hits in eight consecutive at-bats in late September, 3d-longest A.L. streak of the decade. . . . Batted .359 (with all eight HR) on fair balls hit to the left side, .390 straight away, and .236 on fair balls hit to the opposite field. . . . Committed nine errors, equalling his total for the previous three years. . . . Ended the season with 13 consecutive stolen bases, after being caught stealing in 7 of his first 17 attempts. . . . Total of 23 steals was his lowest over the last six seasons. He's one of 11 players to steal 23 or more bases in each season during that period. . . . Has hit better vs. left-handers than right-handers in all seven seasons in majors.

## Mike Greenwell

Bats Left

| Boston Red Sox | AB | H | 2B | 3B | HR | RBI | BB | SO | BA | SA | OBA |
|---|---|---|---|---|---|---|---|---|---|---|---|
| Season | 578 | 178 | 36 | 0 | 14 | 95 | 56 | 44 | .308 | .443 | .370 |
| vs. Left-Handers | 202 | 55 | 6 | 0 | 2 | 28 | 7 | 15 | .272 | .332 | .295 |
| vs. Right-Handers | 376 | 123 | 30 | 0 | 12 | 67 | 49 | 29 | .327 | .503 | .406 |
| Home | 286 | 93 | 22 | 0 | 6 | 54 | 29 | 20 | .325 | .465 | .388 |
| Road | 292 | 85 | 14 | 0 | 8 | 41 | 27 | 24 | .291 | .421 | .352 |
| Grass | 499 | 157 | 34 | 0 | 11 | 85 | 46 | 36 | .315 | .449 | .372 |
| Artificial Turf | 79 | 21 | 2 | 0 | 3 | 10 | 10 | 8 | .266 | .405 | .356 |
| April | 93 | 27 | 2 | 0 | 4 | 12 | 10 | 8 | .290 | .441 | .371 |
| May | 95 | 29 | 7 | 0 | 3 | 18 | 16 | 8 | .305 | .474 | .411 |
| June | 115 | 35 | 6 | 0 | 1 | 20 | 6 | 8 | .304 | .383 | .339 |
| July | 94 | 31 | 6 | 0 | 4 | 15 | 6 | 7 | .330 | .521 | .370 |
| August | 77 | 25 | 9 | 0 | 1 | 14 | 4 | 7 | .325 | .481 | .354 |
| Sept./Oct. | 104 | 31 | 6 | 0 | 1 | 16 | 14 | 6 | .298 | .385 | .372 |
| Leading Off Inn. | 141 | 35 | 7 | 0 | 5 | 5 | 8 | 13 | .248 | .404 | .289 |
| Runners On | 306 | 92 | 20 | 0 | 4 | 85 | 37 | 21 | .301 | .405 | .375 |
| Runners/Scor. Pos. | 173 | 50 | 12 | 0 | 2 | 77 | 28 | 14 | .289 | .393 | .383 |
| Runners On/2 Out | 111 | 23 | 6 | 0 | 0 | 20 | 18 | 12 | .207 | .261 | .323 |
| Scor. Pos./2 Out | 60 | 12 | 2 | 0 | 0 | 18 | 15 | 7 | .200 | .233 | .368 |
| Late Inning Pressure | 75 | 31 | 5 | 0 | 3 | 10 | 10 | 6 | .413 | .600 | .488 |
| Leading Off | 21 | 9 | 1 | 0 | 1 | 1 | 1 | 2 | .429 | .619 | .455 |
| Runners On | 25 | 10 | 3 | 0 | 1 | 8 | 8 | 2 | .400 | .640 | .559 |
| Runners/Scor. Pos. | 12 | 6 | 2 | 0 | 1 | 8 | 7 | 1 | .500 | .917 | .684 |

| RUNS BATTED IN | From 1B | From 2B | From 3B | Scoring Position |
|---|---|---|---|---|
| Totals | 11/238 | 26/135 | 44/83 | 70/218 |
| Percentage | 5% | 19% | 53% | 32% |
| Driving In Runners from 3B with Less than Two Out: | | | 34/50 | 68% |

Loves to face: Jose Bautista (.533, 8-for-15, 3 HR)
Hates to face: Floyd Bannister (.077, 1-for-13)
Tied with Bo Jackson for A.L. lead in assists (11) among left fielders.... Started 144 games, all from the cleanup spot.... Although his 95 RBI ranked third on the club, he led the Red Sox by a wide margin in go-ahead RBI (24).... Has averaged 20.6 RBI per 100 at-bats in his career. He's the only active player above the 20 mark (minimum: 100 games).... Career average of .335 in Late-Inning Pressure Situations is highest of any active A.L. player (minimum: 50 hits). Has career mark of .478 (22-for-46) leading off innings in LIPS, with last season's .429 average in that situation the *lowest* of his career.... Career average of .330 at Fenway Park, .309 on the road.

## Ken Griffey Jr.

Bats Left

| Seattle Mariners | AB | H | 2B | 3B | HR | RBI | BB | SO | BA | SA | OBA |
|---|---|---|---|---|---|---|---|---|---|---|---|
| Season | 455 | 120 | 23 | 0 | 16 | 61 | 44 | 83 | .264 | .420 | .329 |
| vs. Left-Handers | 118 | 25 | 6 | 0 | 3 | 12 | 9 | 31 | .212 | .339 | .271 |
| vs. Right-Handers | 337 | 95 | 17 | 0 | 13 | 49 | 35 | 52 | .282 | .448 | .348 |
| Home | 218 | 57 | 13 | 0 | 10 | 32 | 24 | 36 | .261 | .459 | .335 |
| Road | 237 | 63 | 10 | 0 | 6 | 29 | 20 | 47 | .266 | .384 | .323 |
| Grass | 176 | 47 | 3 | 0 | 5 | 23 | 17 | 35 | .267 | .369 | .332 |
| Artificial Turf | 279 | 73 | 20 | 0 | 11 | 38 | 27 | 48 | .262 | .452 | .327 |
| April | 77 | 25 | 4 | 0 | 3 | 8 | 8 | 11 | .325 | .494 | .388 |
| May | 85 | 24 | 4 | 0 | 6 | 13 | 7 | 21 | .282 | .541 | .337 |
| June | 88 | 22 | 5 | 0 | 2 | 13 | 9 | 13 | .250 | .375 | .320 |
| July | 60 | 18 | 1 | 0 | 2 | 11 | 8 | 11 | .300 | .417 | .375 |
| August | 47 | 13 | 2 | 0 | 2 | 7 | 0 | 11 | .277 | .447 | .277 |
| Sept./Oct. | 98 | 18 | 7 | 0 | 1 | 9 | 12 | 16 | .184 | .286 | .277 |
| Leading Off Inn. | 102 | 25 | 2 | 0 | 5 | 5 | 7 | 14 | .245 | .412 | .294 |
| Runners On | 202 | 51 | 10 | 0 | 4 | 49 | 22 | 43 | .252 | .361 | .326 |
| Runners/Scor. Pos. | 110 | 32 | 7 | 0 | 1 | 42 | 14 | 27 | .291 | .382 | .364 |
| Runners On/2 Out | 92 | 23 | 4 | 0 | 1 | 20 | 15 | 21 | .250 | .326 | .355 |
| Scor. Pos./2 Out | 56 | 15 | 2 | 0 | 1 | 19 | 9 | 14 | .268 | .357 | .369 |
| Late Inning Pressure | 60 | 16 | 2 | 0 | 4 | 10 | 4 | 16 | .267 | .500 | .308 |
| Leading Off | 11 | 2 | 0 | 0 | 0 | 0 | 2 | 0 | .182 | .182 | .308 |
| Runners On | 27 | 7 | 1 | 0 | 2 | 8 | 1 | 6 | .259 | .519 | .276 |
| Runners/Scor. Pos. | 12 | 4 | 1 | 0 | 1 | 6 | 1 | 4 | .333 | .667 | .357 |

| RUNS BATTED IN | From 1B | From 2B | From 3B | Scoring Position |
|---|---|---|---|---|
| Totals | 6/159 | 18/86 | 21/47 | 39/133 |
| Percentage | 4% | 21% | 45% | 29% |
| Driving In Runners from 3B with Less than Two Out: | | | 13/21 | 62% |

Loves to face: Roy Smith (.571, 4-for-7)
Hates to face: Mike Boddicker (0-for-7)
Youngest player on a 1989 opening-day roster.... First player in majors born after an expansion team won a World Series.... With longevity proven to run in family, he's the leading candidate for four-decade status in 2010.... Before anyone could question whether he'd been rushed to the majors, Junior reached base safely in 11 consecutive plate appearances (Apr. 23–27), the 3d-longest A.L. streak of the 1980s.... Most homers of any rookie in majors.... Led center fielders with 10 errors (including 7 in last 46 games).... Most similar rookie seasons: Willie Mays, Gene Freese, and Harold Baines (three guys we always think of together). Not much further down the list: Hank Aaron and Lou Brock.

## Kelly Gruber

Bats Right

| Toronto Blue Jays | AB | H | 2B | 3B | HR | RBI | BB | SO | BA | SA | OBA |
|---|---|---|---|---|---|---|---|---|---|---|---|
| Season | 545 | 158 | 24 | 4 | 18 | 73 | 30 | 60 | .290 | .448 | .328 |
| vs. Left-Handers | 166 | 54 | 8 | 0 | 7 | 23 | 9 | 15 | .325 | .500 | .356 |
| vs. Right-Handers | 379 | 104 | 16 | 4 | 11 | 50 | 21 | 45 | .274 | .425 | .315 |
| Home | 278 | 82 | 16 | 2 | 8 | 34 | 13 | 29 | .295 | .453 | .324 |
| Road | 267 | 76 | 8 | 2 | 10 | 39 | 17 | 31 | .285 | .442 | .331 |
| Grass | 220 | 64 | 8 | 2 | 10 | 37 | 15 | 26 | .291 | .482 | .340 |
| Artificial Turf | 325 | 94 | 16 | 2 | 8 | 36 | 15 | 34 | .289 | .425 | .319 |
| April | 72 | 27 | 1 | 1 | 3 | 16 | 7 | 10 | .375 | .542 | .432 |
| May | 98 | 23 | 5 | 1 | 2 | 10 | 8 | 8 | .235 | .367 | .292 |
| June | 114 | 40 | 6 | 0 | 4 | 17 | 6 | 12 | .351 | .509 | .385 |
| July | 108 | 29 | 4 | 0 | 5 | 9 | 4 | 11 | .269 | .444 | .292 |
| August | 59 | 12 | 5 | 0 | 0 | 6 | 0 | 6 | .203 | .288 | .197 |
| Sept./Oct. | 94 | 27 | 3 | 2 | 4 | 15 | 5 | 13 | .287 | .489 | .330 |
| Leading Off Inn. | 132 | 37 | 6 | 1 | 3 | 3 | 6 | 9 | .280 | .409 | .317 |
| Runners On | 224 | 69 | 8 | 2 | 7 | 62 | 14 | 24 | .308 | .455 | .347 |
| Runners/Scor. Pos. | 140 | 39 | 6 | 2 | 4 | 55 | 8 | 13 | .279 | .436 | .312 |
| Runners On/2 Out | 68 | 21 | 3 | 0 | 3 | 21 | 6 | 6 | .309 | .485 | .365 |
| Scor. Pos./2 Out | 46 | 13 | 3 | 0 | 2 | 19 | 4 | 4 | .283 | .478 | .340 |
| Late Inning Pressure | 70 | 23 | 2 | 1 | 2 | 10 | 6 | 8 | .329 | .471 | .392 |
| Leading Off | 20 | 7 | 1 | 1 | 1 | 1 | 2 | 2 | .350 | .650 | .409 |
| Runners On | 33 | 10 | 1 | 0 | 0 | 8 | 2 | 3 | .303 | .333 | .368 |
| Runners/Scor. Pos. | 16 | 5 | 1 | 0 | 0 | 8 | 2 | 1 | .313 | .375 | .400 |

| RUNS BATTED IN | From 1B | From 2B | From 3B | Scoring Position |
|---|---|---|---|---|
| Totals | 8/145 | 16/107 | 31/66 | 47/173 |
| Percentage | 6% | 15% | 47% | 27% |
| Driving In Runners from 3B with Less than Two Out: | | | 23/41 | 56% |

Loves to face: Doyle Alexander (.556, 10-for-18, 2 HR)
Hates to face: Mark Langston (.059, 1-for-17, 8 SO)
April batting average was 2d highest in A.L.... Rate of one strikeout every 9.7 plate appearances was best of his career, despite establishing a career high for home runs.... Hit 16 home runs to left field, one to center, and one to right.... Average of 3.43 chances per nine innings was highest among A.L. third basemen (minimum: 500 innings).... Also led A.L. third basemen with 22 errors, and had the lowest percentage (.945) among the 10 A.L. qualifiers at that position.... Batted .317 against fly-ball pitchers, .254 vs. ground-ballers.... Has hit better with runners on base than with the bases empty, and better on grass fields than on artificial turf, in each of his six seasons.

## Ozzie Guillen

Bats Left

| Chicago White Sox | AB | H | 2B | 3B | HR | RBI | BB | SO | BA | SA | OBA |
|---|---|---|---|---|---|---|---|---|---|---|---|
| Season | 597 | 151 | 20 | 8 | 1 | 54 | 15 | 48 | .253 | .318 | .270 |
| vs. Left-Handers | 209 | 53 | 4 | 2 | 0 | 17 | 3 | 21 | .254 | .292 | .264 |
| vs. Right-Handers | 388 | 98 | 16 | 6 | 1 | 37 | 12 | 27 | .253 | .332 | .273 |
| Home | 292 | 70 | 7 | 5 | 0 | 23 | 3 | 17 | .240 | .298 | .246 |
| Road | 305 | 81 | 13 | 3 | 1 | 31 | 12 | 31 | .266 | .338 | .292 |
| Grass | 517 | 128 | 18 | 7 | 1 | 43 | 9 | 39 | .248 | .315 | .259 |
| Artificial Turf | 80 | 23 | 2 | 1 | 0 | 11 | 6 | 9 | .288 | .338 | .337 |
| April | 108 | 27 | 3 | 1 | 0 | 7 | 4 | 9 | .250 | .296 | .277 |
| May | 120 | 28 | 3 | 2 | 0 | 6 | 5 | 14 | .233 | .292 | .264 |
| June | 107 | 25 | 3 | 1 | 0 | 11 | 0 | 7 | .234 | .280 | .231 |
| July | 90 | 31 | 5 | 2 | 0 | 11 | 0 | 5 | .344 | .444 | .341 |
| August | 79 | 20 | 3 | 2 | 0 | 10 | 3 | 6 | .253 | .342 | .280 |
| Sept./Oct. | 93 | 20 | 3 | 0 | 1 | 9 | 3 | 7 | .215 | .280 | .237 |
| Leading Off Inn. | 166 | 32 | 5 | 0 | 0 | 0 | 3 | 23 | .193 | .223 | .207 |
| Runners On | 269 | 74 | 10 | 5 | 0 | 53 | 7 | 15 | .275 | .349 | .290 |
| Runners/Scor. Pos. | 155 | 42 | 5 | 3 | 0 | 50 | 6 | 12 | .271 | .342 | .293 |
| Runners On/2 Out | 110 | 33 | 1 | 1 | 0 | 16 | 6 | 8 | .300 | .327 | .336 |
| Scor. Pos./2 Out | 67 | 16 | 0 | 0 | 0 | 15 | 6 | 5 | .239 | .239 | .301 |
| Late Inning Pressure | 102 | 32 | 5 | 2 | 0 | 12 | 2 | 9 | .314 | .402 | .324 |
| Leading Off | 24 | 7 | 1 | 0 | 0 | 0 | 2 | 0 | .292 | .333 | .346 |
| Runners On | 46 | 14 | 3 | 1 | 0 | 12 | 0 | 4 | .304 | .413 | .298 |
| Runners/Scor. Pos. | 27 | 7 | 2 | 0 | 0 | 11 | 0 | 3 | .259 | .333 | .250 |

| RUNS BATTED IN | From 1B | From 2B | From 3B | Scoring Position |
|---|---|---|---|---|
| Totals | 4/196 | 25/129 | 24/52 | 49/181 |
| Percentage | 2% | 19% | 46% | 27% |
| Driving In Runners from 3B with Less than Two Out: | | | 16/25 | 64% |

Loves to face: Ted Higuera (.435, 10-for-23)
Hates to face: Eric Plunk (0-for-9)
Home run off Jack Morris on Sept. 8 broke a streak of 1144 homerless at-bats.... Went 247 consecutive plate appearances between walks, longest one-year streak since Rob Picciolo's 268 in 1980.... Batted .158 (9-for-57) in the first inning.... Scored from second base on 17 of 18 outfield singles.... Led A.L. shortstops with 5.41 chances per nine innings (minimum: 500 innings).... Participated in 499 double plays in first five seasons. Since 1980, the only shortstops to top the 500 mark within four years of their rookie seasons: Cal Ripken (510) and Dick Schofield (507).... Has hit better with runners in scoring position than otherwise in each of five seasons in majors.

## Mel Hall

Bats Left

| New York Yankees | AB | H | 2B | 3B | HR | RBI | BB | SO | BA | SA | OBA |
|---|---|---|---|---|---|---|---|---|---|---|---|
| Season | 361 | 94 | 9 | 0 | 17 | 58 | 21 | 37 | .260 | .427 | .295 |
| vs. Left-Handers | 69 | 11 | 1 | 0 | 1 | 11 | 6 | 7 | .159 | .217 | .224 |
| vs. Right-Handers | 292 | 83 | 8 | 0 | 16 | 47 | 15 | 30 | .284 | .476 | .312 |
| Home | 202 | 57 | 4 | 0 | 11 | 29 | 12 | 10 | .282 | .465 | .317 |
| Road | 159 | 37 | 5 | 0 | 6 | 29 | 9 | 27 | .233 | .377 | .267 |
| Grass | 323 | 85 | 9 | 0 | 15 | 50 | 16 | 29 | .263 | .430 | .291 |
| Artificial Turf | 38 | 9 | 0 | 0 | 2 | 8 | 5 | 8 | .237 | .395 | .326 |
| April | 31 | 8 | 3 | 0 | 0 | 2 | 3 | 3 | .258 | .355 | .324 |
| May | 9 | 2 | 0 | 0 | 0 | 2 | 0 | 0 | .222 | .222 | .200 |
| June | 73 | 21 | 0 | 0 | 5 | 18 | 6 | 5 | .288 | .493 | .333 |
| July | 72 | 20 | 3 | 0 | 4 | 12 | 2 | 9 | .278 | .486 | .293 |
| August | 89 | 24 | 2 | 0 | 1 | 11 | 7 | 14 | .270 | .326 | .313 |
| Sept./Oct. | 87 | 19 | 1 | 0 | 7 | 13 | 3 | 6 | .218 | .471 | .242 |
| Leading Off Inn. | 86 | 17 | 1 | 0 | 3 | 3 | 1 | 10 | .198 | .314 | .207 |
| Runners On | 163 | 42 | 4 | 0 | 6 | 47 | 11 | 15 | .258 | .393 | .291 |
| Runners/Scor. Pos. | 88 | 24 | 3 | 0 | 2 | 39 | 10 | 8 | .273 | .375 | .321 |
| Runners On/2 Out | 72 | 17 | 1 | 0 | 0 | 11 | 3 | 8 | .236 | .250 | .267 |
| Scor. Pos./2 Out | 42 | 10 | 1 | 0 | 0 | 11 | 2 | 3 | .238 | .262 | .273 |
| Late Inning Pressure | 43 | 11 | 1 | 0 | 2 | 7 | 4 | 6 | .256 | .419 | .306 |
| Leading Off | 12 | 2 | 0 | 0 | 1 | 1 | 1 | 2 | .167 | .417 | .231 |
| Runners On | 16 | 5 | 0 | 0 | 1 | 6 | 2 | 2 | .313 | .500 | .350 |
| Runners/Scor. Pos. | 7 | 3 | 0 | 0 | 0 | 4 | 2 | 1 | .429 | .429 | .455 |

| RUNS BATTED IN | From 1B | From 2B | From 3B | Scoring Position |
|---|---|---|---|---|
| Totals | 6/130 | 14/67 | 21/42 | 35/109 |
| Percentage | 5% | 21% | 50% | 32% |
| Driving In Runners from 3B with Less than Two Out: | | | 16/24 | 67% |

Loves to face: Mark Gubicza (.417, 15-for-36, 1 HR)
Hates to face: Scott Sanderson (.100, 1-for-10, 1 HR, 5 SO)
Led the Yankees with 16 home runs against right-handed pitchers. . . . All 17 home runs were hit to right field. . . . Started 14 games vs. left-handed pitchers, or 14 more than he deserved. Career figures vs. right-handers are a carbon copy (a fax, for those with Axl Rose posters on your walls) of Wally Joyner's overall career statistics. Against left-handers, Hall's batting figures bear a strong resemblance to those of Doyle Alexander. . . . Has 65 career plate appearances with the bases loaded, but no walks. Career batting average is .379 (22-for-58) with the bags full. . . . Has driven in over 30 percent of runners from scoring position in each of the last five seasons.

## Brian Harper

Bats Right

| Minnesota Twins | AB | H | 2B | 3B | HR | RBI | BB | SO | BA | SA | OBA |
|---|---|---|---|---|---|---|---|---|---|---|---|
| Season | 385 | 125 | 24 | 0 | 8 | 57 | 13 | 16 | .325 | .449 | .353 |
| vs. Left-Handers | 155 | 48 | 8 | 0 | 3 | 21 | 6 | 6 | .310 | .419 | .339 |
| vs. Right-Handers | 230 | 77 | 16 | 0 | 5 | 36 | 7 | 10 | .335 | .470 | .362 |
| Home | 181 | 55 | 13 | 0 | 4 | 27 | 8 | 6 | .304 | .442 | .333 |
| Road | 204 | 70 | 11 | 0 | 4 | 30 | 5 | 10 | .343 | .456 | .370 |
| Grass | 153 | 46 | 9 | 0 | 3 | 22 | 5 | 9 | .301 | .418 | .331 |
| Artificial Turf | 232 | 79 | 15 | 0 | 5 | 35 | 8 | 7 | .341 | .470 | .367 |
| April | 37 | 12 | 3 | 0 | 2 | 12 | 3 | 1 | .324 | .568 | .395 |
| May | 46 | 9 | 2 | 0 | 2 | 8 | 1 | 0 | .196 | .370 | .235 |
| June | 62 | 20 | 2 | 0 | 0 | 5 | 2 | 5 | .323 | .355 | .344 |
| July | 60 | 21 | 2 | 0 | 0 | 7 | 1 | 2 | .350 | .383 | .355 |
| August | 90 | 33 | 7 | 0 | 2 | 15 | 1 | 3 | .367 | .511 | .374 |
| Sept./Oct. | 90 | 30 | 8 | 0 | 2 | 10 | 5 | 5 | .333 | .489 | .381 |
| Leading Off Inn. | 88 | 27 | 5 | 0 | 2 | 2 | 2 | 1 | .307 | .432 | .337 |
| Runners On | 187 | 58 | 12 | 0 | 4 | 53 | 10 | 8 | .310 | .439 | .348 |
| Runners/Scor. Pos. | 109 | 36 | 7 | 0 | 2 | 49 | 7 | 7 | .330 | .450 | .369 |
| Runners On/2 Out | 89 | 22 | 4 | 0 | 2 | 19 | 3 | 7 | .247 | .360 | .287 |
| Scor. Pos./2 Out | 58 | 15 | 2 | 0 | 2 | 19 | 2 | 6 | .259 | .397 | .295 |
| Late Inning Pressure | 48 | 14 | 4 | 0 | 2 | 10 | 1 | 2 | .292 | .500 | .300 |
| Leading Off | 10 | 3 | 2 | 0 | 1 | 1 | 0 | 0 | .300 | .800 | .300 |
| Runners On | 24 | 8 | 2 | 0 | 0 | 8 | 0 | 1 | .333 | .417 | .320 |
| Runners/Scor. Pos. | 15 | 6 | 1 | 0 | 0 | 8 | 0 | 1 | .400 | .467 | .375 |

| RUNS BATTED IN | From 1B | From 2B | From 3B | Scoring Position |
|---|---|---|---|---|
| Totals | 4/133 | 23/90 | 22/44 | 45/134 |
| Percentage | 3% | 26% | 50% | 34% |
| Driving In Runners from 3B with Less than Two Out: | | | 17/21 | 81% |

Loves to face: Chuck Finley (.429, 6-for-14, 1 HR)
Hates to face: Mark Langston (0-for-8)
This born-and-bred Californian had the highest BA of any visiting player at both Anaheim Stadium (.579) and the Kingdome (.524). . . . Among 123 A.L. players with at least 75 at-bats on the west coast over the last two seasons, Harper's .464 mark (39-for-84) was more than 100 points better than that of runner-up Tony Fernandez (.350). . . . O.K., we'll come clean: He batted .129 (4-for-31) on the west coast during four seasons in the N.L. . . . Made major league debut in 1979 (for perspective, three days after Bill Gullickson), but has played fewer than 400 games. . . . Streak of 86 consecutive plate appearances without a strikeout was 3d longest in majors last season.

## Ron Hassey

Bats Left

| Oakland As | AB | H | 2B | 3B | HR | RBI | BB | SO | BA | SA | OBA |
|---|---|---|---|---|---|---|---|---|---|---|---|
| Season | 268 | 61 | 12 | 0 | 5 | 23 | 24 | 45 | .228 | .328 | .290 |
| vs. Left-Handers | 34 | 8 | 0 | 0 | 1 | 3 | 3 | 1 | .235 | .324 | .297 |
| vs. Right-Handers | 234 | 53 | 12 | 0 | 4 | 20 | 21 | 44 | .226 | .329 | .288 |
| Home | 121 | 27 | 6 | 0 | 3 | 12 | 9 | 24 | .223 | .347 | .276 |
| Road | 147 | 34 | 6 | 0 | 2 | 11 | 15 | 21 | .231 | .313 | .301 |
| Grass | 226 | 53 | 11 | 0 | 5 | 23 | 22 | 38 | .235 | .350 | .300 |
| Artificial Turf | 42 | 8 | 1 | 0 | 0 | 0 | 2 | 7 | .190 | .214 | .227 |
| April | 46 | 9 | 4 | 0 | 0 | 5 | 1 | 6 | .196 | .283 | .204 |
| May | 48 | 11 | 2 | 0 | 2 | 6 | 4 | 8 | .229 | .396 | .278 |
| June | 41 | 13 | 1 | 0 | 2 | 7 | 6 | 6 | .317 | .488 | .404 |
| July | 41 | 10 | 2 | 0 | 1 | 2 | 8 | 8 | .244 | .366 | .367 |
| August | 60 | 12 | 2 | 0 | 0 | 2 | 3 | 10 | .200 | .233 | .250 |
| Sept./Oct. | 32 | 6 | 1 | 0 | 0 | 1 | 2 | 7 | .188 | .219 | .235 |
| Leading Off Inn. | 50 | 13 | 3 | 0 | 2 | 2 | 5 | 9 | .260 | .440 | .339 |
| Runners On | 112 | 25 | 5 | 0 | 1 | 19 | 12 | 19 | .223 | .295 | .289 |
| Runners/Scor. Pos. | 58 | 13 | 3 | 0 | 0 | 16 | 8 | 9 | .224 | .276 | .300 |
| Runners On/2 Out | 53 | 12 | 3 | 0 | 1 | 8 | 5 | 10 | .226 | .340 | .293 |
| Scor. Pos./2 Out | 28 | 6 | 1 | 0 | 0 | 5 | 4 | 3 | .214 | .250 | .313 |
| Late Inning Pressure | 37 | 9 | 1 | 0 | 1 | 4 | 3 | 7 | .243 | .351 | .300 |
| Leading Off | 6 | 1 | 0 | 0 | 1 | 1 | 1 | 1 | .167 | .667 | .286 |
| Runners On | 19 | 3 | 0 | 0 | 0 | 3 | 1 | 4 | .158 | .158 | .200 |
| Runners/Scor. Pos. | 8 | 2 | 0 | 0 | 0 | 3 | 1 | 0 | .250 | .250 | .333 |

| RUNS BATTED IN | From 1B | From 2B | From 3B | Scoring Position |
|---|---|---|---|---|
| Totals | 2/88 | 9/48 | 7/20 | 16/68 |
| Percentage | 2% | 19% | 35% | 24% |
| Driving In Runners from 3B with Less than Two Out: | | | 6/12 | 50% |

Loves to face: Andy Hawkins (5-for-5, 2 2B)
Hates to face: Bret Saberhagen (0-for-13)
Opposing base stealers were successful on 70 percent (51-of-73) of their attempts, compared to 59 percent (38-of-64) against Steinbach. . . . A's pitchers had a 3.46 ERA with Hassey catching, 2.92 with Steinbach. . . . Homered off Mark Thurmond in June, his first against a left-handed pitcher since 1983. . . . Batted .225 on fair balls hit to the opposite field, .469 straight away, .212 on fair balls to the right side. . . . Total of 44 strikeouts vs. right-handers was a career high. Rate of one per 5.9 PA was roughly double his previous career average. . . . Didn't appear in 1989 World Series; originally was scheduled to start the third game until Bob Welch, whom Hassey catches, was passed over in wake of quake.

## Mike Heath

Bats Right

| Detroit Tigers | AB | H | 2B | 3B | HR | RBI | BB | SO | BA | SA | OBA |
|---|---|---|---|---|---|---|---|---|---|---|---|
| Season | 396 | 104 | 16 | 2 | 10 | 43 | 24 | 71 | .263 | .389 | .308 |
| vs. Left-Handers | 161 | 51 | 6 | 2 | 5 | 17 | 10 | 11 | .317 | .472 | .360 |
| vs. Right-Handers | 235 | 53 | 10 | 0 | 5 | 26 | 14 | 60 | .226 | .332 | .273 |
| Home | 189 | 45 | 9 | 0 | 5 | 20 | 11 | 31 | .238 | .365 | .284 |
| Road | 207 | 59 | 7 | 2 | 5 | 23 | 13 | 40 | .285 | .411 | .330 |
| Grass | 341 | 86 | 14 | 1 | 10 | 36 | 15 | 59 | .252 | .387 | .287 |
| Artificial Turf | 55 | 18 | 2 | 1 | 0 | 7 | 9 | 12 | .327 | .400 | .424 |
| April | 14 | 5 | 0 | 0 | 0 | 0 | 1 | 0 | .357 | .357 | .400 |
| May | 41 | 11 | 2 | 0 | 2 | 3 | 2 | 5 | .268 | .463 | .302 |
| June | 71 | 21 | 3 | 0 | 4 | 14 | 10 | 15 | .296 | .507 | .391 |
| July | 70 | 15 | 5 | 1 | 0 | 6 | 3 | 15 | .214 | .314 | .243 |
| August | 105 | 30 | 5 | 1 | 4 | 12 | 3 | 22 | .286 | .467 | .306 |
| Sept./Oct. | 95 | 22 | 1 | 0 | 0 | 8 | 5 | 14 | .232 | .242 | .277 |
| Leading Off Inn. | 107 | 30 | 3 | 0 | 4 | 4 | 4 | 19 | .280 | .421 | .306 |
| Runners On | 160 | 37 | 5 | 2 | 4 | 37 | 15 | 27 | .231 | .363 | .298 |
| Runners/Scor. Pos. | 87 | 20 | 1 | 1 | 3 | 32 | 10 | 20 | .230 | .368 | .304 |
| Runners On/2 Out | 59 | 13 | 2 | 2 | 2 | 14 | 10 | 13 | .220 | .424 | .343 |
| Scor. Pos./2 Out | 37 | 8 | 1 | 1 | 2 | 13 | 6 | 8 | .216 | .459 | .341 |
| Late Inning Pressure | 79 | 22 | 2 | 1 | 3 | 9 | 6 | 17 | .278 | .443 | .333 |
| Leading Off | 23 | 6 | 1 | 0 | 2 | 2 | 1 | 5 | .261 | .565 | .292 |
| Runners On | 32 | 9 | 0 | 1 | 1 | 7 | 5 | 6 | .281 | .438 | .385 |
| Runners/Scor. Pos. | 12 | 3 | 0 | 0 | 1 | 6 | 4 | 4 | .250 | .500 | .412 |

| RUNS BATTED IN | From 1B | From 2B | From 3B | Scoring Position |
|---|---|---|---|---|
| Totals | 6/122 | 12/66 | 15/42 | 27/108 |
| Percentage | 5% | 18% | 36% | 25% |
| Driving In Runners from 3B with Less than Two Out: | | | 11/19 | 58% |

Loves to face: Curt Young (.409, 9-for-22, 3 HR)
Hates to face: Roger Clemens (.056, 1-for-18)
Played 117 games behind the plate (including 107 starts), a career high in his 12th season in majors. . . . Staff ERA was 4.10 with Nokes catching, 4.56 with Heath. . . . Tigers starting catchers combined for 17 home runs. Only the Padres (22), Angels (20), and Orioles (19) had more. . . . Started 49 of 54 games vs. left-handers, 59 of 108 games vs. right-handers. Career BA: .284 vs. lefties, .225 vs. righties. . . . In three-plus seasons with Tigers, he's hit 20 home runs at home, seven on the road. . . . Career average is .218 (17-for-78) with the bases loaded, with only one walk in 87 plate appearances. . . . The prospect Detroit used as bait to acquire him from St. Louis in 1986 was Ken Hill.

## Danny Heep

Bats Left

| Boston Red Sox | AB | H | 2B | 3B | HR | RBI | BB | SO | BA | SA | OBA |
|---|---|---|---|---|---|---|---|---|---|---|---|
| Season | 320 | 96 | 17 | 0 | 5 | 49 | 29 | 26 | .300 | .400 | .356 |
| vs. Left-Handers | 21 | 4 | 1 | 0 | 0 | 1 | 1 | 3 | .190 | .238 | .217 |
| vs. Right-Handers | 299 | 92 | 16 | 0 | 5 | 48 | 28 | 23 | .308 | .411 | .366 |
| Home | 158 | 46 | 9 | 0 | 1 | 22 | 18 | 10 | .291 | .367 | .360 |
| Road | 162 | 50 | 8 | 0 | 4 | 27 | 11 | 16 | .309 | .432 | .352 |
| Grass | 284 | 87 | 15 | 0 | 3 | 42 | 24 | 22 | .306 | .391 | .359 |
| Artificial Turf | 36 | 9 | 2 | 0 | 2 | 7 | 5 | 4 | .250 | .472 | .333 |
| April | 16 | 4 | 0 | 0 | 0 | 1 | 1 | 2 | .250 | .250 | .294 |
| May | 19 | 6 | 1 | 0 | 0 | 2 | 1 | 1 | .316 | .368 | .350 |
| June | 63 | 23 | 3 | 0 | 0 | 9 | 7 | 2 | .365 | .413 | .429 |
| July | 56 | 16 | 3 | 0 | 2 | 13 | 5 | 4 | .286 | .446 | .333 |
| August | 89 | 28 | 6 | 0 | 3 | 13 | 7 | 9 | .315 | .483 | .371 |
| Sept./Oct. | 77 | 19 | 4 | 0 | 0 | 11 | 8 | 8 | .247 | .299 | .310 |
| Leading Off Inn. | 60 | 15 | 3 | 0 | 1 | 1 | 5 | 5 | .250 | .350 | .308 |
| Runners On | 163 | 56 | 10 | 0 | 3 | 47 | 18 | 11 | .344 | .460 | .403 |
| Runners/Scor. Pos. | 101 | 34 | 7 | 0 | 2 | 44 | 10 | 8 | .337 | .465 | .388 |
| Runners On/2 Out | 64 | 24 | 5 | 0 | 3 | 25 | 4 | 4 | .375 | .594 | .412 |
| Scor. Pos./2 Out | 44 | 17 | 3 | 0 | 2 | 23 | 3 | 3 | .386 | .591 | .426 |
| Late Inning Pressure | 43 | 12 | 4 | 0 | 2 | 8 | 7 | 3 | .279 | .512 | .392 |
| Leading Off | 9 | 2 | 2 | 0 | 0 | 0 | 2 | 1 | .222 | .444 | .364 |
| Runners On | 22 | 8 | 2 | 0 | 1 | 7 | 3 | 1 | .364 | .591 | .462 |
| Runners/Scor. Pos. | 11 | 6 | 1 | 0 | 1 | 7 | 3 | 1 | .545 | .909 | .667 |

| RUNS BATTED IN | From 1B | From 2B | From 3B | Scoring Position |
|---|---|---|---|---|
| Totals | 4/125 | 23/81 | 17/45 | 40/126 |
| Percentage | 3% | 28% | 38% | 32% |
| Driving In Runners from 3B with Less than Two Out: | | | 11/24 | 46% |

Loves to face: John Farrell (.667, 4-for-6, 1 HR)
Hates to face: Lance McCullers (0-for-10)
Started 85 games, but only two against left-handed pitchers. . . . Has batted below .200 vs. southpaws in each of the last four seasons. . . . Topped the .300 mark in each of five minor league seasons, but his previous major league–high batting average was .282 (with Mets in 1986). . . . All five home runs were hit to right field, but his average going to the opposite field (.393) was higher than when pulling the ball (.277). . . . Ranked sixth on team with 49 RBI, but second with 17 go-ahead RBI, ahead of both Evans (13) and Esasky (16). . . . Nevertheless, career average is .204 in LIP Situations, .273 in other at-bats, the largest difference over the last 10 years (minimum: 250 LIPS AB).

## Dave Henderson

Bats Right

| Oakland As | AB | H | 2B | 3B | HR | RBI | BB | SO | BA | SA | OBA |
|---|---|---|---|---|---|---|---|---|---|---|---|
| Season | 579 | 145 | 24 | 3 | 15 | 80 | 54 | 131 | .250 | .380 | .315 |
| vs. Left-Handers | 171 | 49 | 9 | 0 | 5 | 27 | 16 | 26 | .287 | .427 | .347 |
| vs. Right-Handers | 408 | 96 | 15 | 3 | 10 | 53 | 38 | 105 | .235 | .360 | .301 |
| Home | 289 | 81 | 12 | 1 | 10 | 45 | 22 | 69 | .280 | .433 | .333 |
| Road | 290 | 64 | 12 | 2 | 5 | 35 | 32 | 62 | .221 | .328 | .297 |
| Grass | 492 | 130 | 20 | 3 | 14 | 72 | 46 | 111 | .264 | .402 | .327 |
| Artificial Turf | 87 | 15 | 4 | 0 | 1 | 8 | 8 | 20 | .172 | .253 | .245 |
| April | 91 | 28 | 2 | 2 | 4 | 13 | 14 | 24 | .308 | .505 | .398 |
| May | 96 | 24 | 3 | 1 | 3 | 16 | 8 | 19 | .250 | .396 | .318 |
| June | 101 | 20 | 4 | 0 | 0 | 10 | 8 | 15 | .198 | .238 | .255 |
| July | 92 | 24 | 3 | 0 | 1 | 10 | 8 | 21 | .261 | .326 | .317 |
| August | 96 | 20 | 8 | 0 | 2 | 13 | 8 | 24 | .208 | .354 | .267 |
| Sept./Oct. | 103 | 29 | 4 | 0 | 5 | 18 | 8 | 28 | .282 | .466 | .333 |
| Leading Off Inn. | 117 | 31 | 9 | 0 | 4 | 4 | 7 | 23 | .265 | .444 | .306 |
| Runners On | 275 | 70 | 10 | 2 | 5 | 70 | 27 | 64 | .255 | .360 | .317 |
| Runners/Scor. Pos. | 153 | 44 | 4 | 1 | 2 | 58 | 17 | 35 | .288 | .366 | .350 |
| Runners On/2 Out | 118 | 26 | 5 | 1 | 0 | 20 | 12 | 26 | .220 | .280 | .292 |
| Scor. Pos./2 Out | 77 | 16 | 2 | 0 | 0 | 16 | 8 | 17 | .208 | .234 | .282 |
| Late Inning Pressure | 67 | 17 | 1 | 1 | 3 | 11 | 6 | 17 | .254 | .433 | .311 |
| Leading Off | 17 | 4 | 1 | 0 | 1 | 1 | 1 | 2 | .235 | .471 | .278 |
| Runners On | 35 | 11 | 0 | 1 | 2 | 10 | 4 | 8 | .314 | .543 | .375 |
| Runners/Scor. Pos. | 21 | 6 | 0 | 1 | 2 | 10 | 2 | 5 | .286 | .667 | .333 |

| RUNS BATTED IN | From 1B | From 2B | From 3B | Scoring Position |
|---|---|---|---|---|
| Totals | 10/201 | 28/118 | 27/64 | 55/182 |
| Percentage | 5% | 24% | 42% | 30% |
| Driving In Runners from 3B with Less than Two Out: | | | 20/29 | 69% |

Loves to face: Mike Flanagan (.351, 13-for-37, 2 HR, 0 SO)
Hates to face: Juan Berenguer (.045, 1-for-22, 9 SO)
Led A.L. in batting average (.448), slugging average (.836), and on-base average (.500) during 1989 spring training. . . . Streak of 198 consecutive at-bats without a home run was longest of his career. . . . One of 20 players with at least seven postseason home runs. Among them, only Gil McDougald (112) had fewer regular-season HR than Hendu's total of 127. . . . Has hit better against left-handers than right-handers in each of his nine seasons in the majors. Career breakdown: .277 vs. LHP, .252 vs. RHP. . . . Career average of .189 (14-for-74, one HR) with the bases loaded. . . . Similar statistical profiles: Willie Upshaw, Jackie Brandt, Johnny Briggs, Dusty Baker.

## Rickey Henderson

Bats Right

| Yankees/As | AB | H | 2B | 3B | HR | RBI | BB | SO | BA | SA | OBA |
|---|---|---|---|---|---|---|---|---|---|---|---|
| Season | 541 | 148 | 26 | 3 | 12 | 58 | 126 | 68 | .274 | .399 | .411 |
| vs. Left-Handers | 173 | 48 | 9 | 1 | 1 | 13 | 40 | 14 | .277 | .358 | .413 |
| vs. Right-Handers | 368 | 100 | 17 | 2 | 11 | 45 | 86 | 54 | .272 | .418 | .410 |
| Home | 253 | 73 | 13 | 2 | 7 | 32 | 70 | 29 | .289 | .439 | .439 |
| Road | 288 | 75 | 13 | 1 | 5 | 26 | 56 | 39 | .260 | .365 | .384 |
| Grass | 441 | 120 | 22 | 3 | 11 | 53 | 103 | 59 | .272 | .410 | .409 |
| Artificial Turf | 100 | 28 | 4 | 0 | 1 | 5 | 23 | 9 | .280 | .350 | .419 |
| April | 93 | 27 | 8 | 1 | 1 | 9 | 17 | 6 | .290 | .430 | .400 |
| May | 91 | 23 | 4 | 0 | 2 | 10 | 24 | 15 | .253 | .363 | .410 |
| June | 83 | 20 | 2 | 0 | 1 | 9 | 22 | 10 | .241 | .301 | .400 |
| July | 86 | 31 | 5 | 1 | 3 | 16 | 22 | 13 | .360 | .547 | .482 |
| August | 100 | 29 | 4 | 0 | 3 | 9 | 17 | 13 | .290 | .420 | .398 |
| Sept./Oct. | 88 | 18 | 3 | 1 | 2 | 5 | 24 | 11 | .205 | .330 | .377 |
| Leading Off Inn. | 235 | 73 | 12 | 2 | 7 | 7 | 39 | 25 | .311 | .468 | .409 |
| Runners On | 191 | 55 | 11 | 1 | 4 | 50 | 57 | 29 | .288 | .419 | .449 |
| Runners/Scor. Pos. | 124 | 29 | 6 | 0 | 2 | 42 | 45 | 22 | .234 | .331 | .434 |
| Runners On/2 Out | 96 | 26 | 6 | 0 | 1 | 28 | 30 | 18 | .271 | .365 | .444 |
| Scor. Pos./2 Out | 72 | 18 | 4 | 0 | 1 | 26 | 27 | 14 | .250 | .347 | .455 |
| Late Inning Pressure | 65 | 13 | 1 | 0 | 2 | 9 | 14 | 13 | .200 | .308 | .342 |
| Leading Off | 15 | 3 | 0 | 0 | 0 | 0 | 2 | 2 | .200 | .200 | .294 |
| Runners On | 34 | 8 | 0 | 0 | 2 | 9 | 8 | 7 | .235 | .412 | .381 |
| Runners/Scor. Pos. | 20 | 4 | 0 | 0 | 1 | 7 | 6 | 3 | .200 | .350 | .385 |

| RUNS BATTED IN | From 1B | From 2B | From 3B | Scoring Position |
|---|---|---|---|---|
| Totals | 8/115 | 17/98 | 21/54 | 38/152 |
| Percentage | 7% | 17% | 39% | 25% |
| Driving In Runners from 3B with Less than Two Out: | | | 10/16 | 63% |

Loves to face: Frank Tanana (.371, 26-for-70, 6 HR)
Hates to face: Bill Swift (.053, 1-for-19)
Most walks by an A.L. batter since Frank Howard in 1970 (132). . . . Career total of 996 walks in 1472 games. Only 11 players reached the 1000 mark in fewer games than Rickey will. The fewest: 1091, by Ted Williams. . . . Scored 16 runs in 11 games vs. Seattle, the most runs by any A.L. player vs. any team. . . . Batting average with runners in scoring position has been lower than his overall average in each of the last six seasons. . . . Career BA is .316 (31-for-98, 14 walks, no HR) with bases loaded. . . . Needs 21 steals to match Ty Cobb's A.L. record (892), 67 to reach Lou Brock's all-time record (938). . . . Has batted leadoff in all but four of his 1434 career starts.

## Jack Howell

Bats Left

| California Angels | AB | H | 2B | 3B | HR | RBI | BB | SO | BA | SA | OBA |
|---|---|---|---|---|---|---|---|---|---|---|---|
| Season | 474 | 108 | 19 | 4 | 20 | 52 | 52 | 125 | .228 | .411 | .308 |
| vs. Left-Handers | 136 | 19 | 5 | 1 | 2 | 9 | 12 | 45 | .140 | .235 | .220 |
| vs. Right-Handers | 338 | 89 | 14 | 3 | 18 | 43 | 40 | 80 | .263 | .482 | .342 |
| Home | 225 | 53 | 10 | 2 | 9 | 25 | 24 | 56 | .236 | .418 | .309 |
| Road | 249 | 55 | 9 | 2 | 11 | 27 | 28 | 69 | .221 | .406 | .306 |
| Grass | 399 | 91 | 14 | 2 | 18 | 45 | 44 | 106 | .228 | .409 | .304 |
| Artificial Turf | 75 | 17 | 5 | 2 | 2 | 7 | 8 | 19 | .227 | .427 | .326 |
| April | 74 | 12 | 3 | 0 | 2 | 7 | 9 | 18 | .162 | .284 | .253 |
| May | 65 | 16 | 4 | 0 | 1 | 4 | 9 | 15 | .246 | .354 | .338 |
| June | 75 | 23 | 1 | 0 | 6 | 12 | 12 | 16 | .307 | .560 | .402 |
| July | 79 | 19 | 2 | 1 | 7 | 16 | 8 | 23 | .241 | .557 | .315 |
| August | 90 | 19 | 4 | 3 | 2 | 5 | 10 | 29 | .211 | .389 | .290 |
| Sept./Oct. | 91 | 19 | 5 | 0 | 2 | 8 | 4 | 24 | .209 | .330 | .258 |
| Leading Off Inn. | 104 | 26 | 6 | 1 | 7 | 7 | 9 | 25 | .250 | .529 | .310 |
| Runners On | 207 | 50 | 6 | 1 | 9 | 41 | 26 | 56 | .242 | .411 | .333 |
| Runners/Scor. Pos. | 113 | 22 | 3 | 0 | 2 | 25 | 20 | 36 | .195 | .274 | .324 |
| Runners On/2 Out | 97 | 23 | 3 | 1 | 4 | 22 | 13 | 22 | .237 | .412 | .333 |
| Scor. Pos./2 Out | 57 | 12 | 2 | 0 | 1 | 14 | 11 | 13 | .211 | .298 | .348 |
| Late Inning Pressure | 72 | 21 | 5 | 1 | 2 | 6 | 9 | 24 | .292 | .472 | .370 |
| Leading Off | 19 | 7 | 2 | 1 | 2 | 2 | 3 | 4 | .368 | .895 | .455 |
| Runners On | 30 | 8 | 1 | 0 | 0 | 4 | 0 | 11 | .267 | .300 | .267 |
| Runners/Scor. Pos. | 22 | 5 | 1 | 0 | 0 | 4 | 0 | 8 | .227 | .273 | .227 |

| RUNS BATTED IN | From 1B | From 2B | From 3B | Scoring Position |
|---|---|---|---|---|
| Totals | 10/169 | 14/86 | 8/44 | 22/130 |
| Percentage | 6% | 16% | 18% | 17% |
| Driving In Runners from 3B with Less than Two Out: | | | 5/16 | 31% |

Loves to face: Dave Stieb (.524, 11-for-21, 3 HR)
Hates to face: Dave Righetti (0-for-10, 9 SO)
Over the past 70 years, there have been 3190 seasons of 20 or more home runs. Only 10 of them produced fewer than 50 RBI. Fewest RBI by a 20-HR hitter: 43, by Carlton Fisk (1984) and Fred McGriff (1987). . . . Only 11 of 52 RBI either tied the score or put California ahead (21%), the 2d-lowest percentage in A.L. (minimum: 50 RBI). . . . Started 105 of 107 games against right-handers, only 32 of 55 against southpaws. . . . One of three active players with career batting averages below .200 vs. left-handers (minimum: 400 AB). Others: Wally Backman and Mike Pagliarulo. . . . Career marks: .262 vs. RHP, .179 vs. LHP. . . . Other career averages: .271 against ground-ball pitchers, .222 vs. fly-ballers.

## Kent Hrbek

Bats Left

| Minnesota Twins | AB | H | 2B | 3B | HR | RBI | BB | SO | BA | SA | OBA |
|---|---|---|---|---|---|---|---|---|---|---|---|
| Season | 375 | 102 | 17 | 0 | 25 | 84 | 53 | 35 | .272 | .517 | .360 |
| vs. Left-Handers | 109 | 29 | 4 | 0 | 6 | 25 | 19 | 17 | .266 | .468 | .374 |
| vs. Right-Handers | 266 | 73 | 13 | 0 | 19 | 59 | 34 | 18 | .274 | .538 | .354 |
| Home | 191 | 54 | 9 | 0 | 17 | 56 | 28 | 13 | .283 | .597 | .371 |
| Road | 184 | 48 | 8 | 0 | 8 | 28 | 25 | 22 | .261 | .435 | .349 |
| Grass | 134 | 32 | 7 | 0 | 5 | 21 | 23 | 15 | .239 | .403 | .350 |
| Artificial Turf | 241 | 70 | 10 | 0 | 20 | 63 | 30 | 20 | .290 | .581 | .366 |
| April | 63 | 17 | 4 | 0 | 4 | 16 | 6 | 6 | .270 | .524 | .338 |
| May | 36 | 13 | 3 | 0 | 3 | 6 | 7 | 3 | .361 | .694 | .465 |
| June | 15 | 3 | 0 | 0 | 0 | 0 | 5 | 0 | .200 | .200 | .400 |
| July | 85 | 23 | 3 | 0 | 7 | 22 | 14 | 10 | .271 | .553 | .374 |
| August | 83 | 19 | 4 | 0 | 6 | 20 | 7 | 9 | .229 | .494 | .286 |
| Sept./Oct. | 93 | 27 | 3 | 0 | 5 | 20 | 14 | 7 | .290 | .484 | .376 |
| Leading Off Inn. | 95 | 25 | 4 | 0 | 6 | 6 | 10 | 10 | .263 | .495 | .333 |
| Runners On | 184 | 43 | 7 | 0 | 11 | 70 | 30 | 18 | .234 | .451 | .335 |
| Runners/Scor. Pos. | 109 | 32 | 7 | 0 | 8 | 64 | 22 | 12 | .294 | .578 | .400 |
| Runners On/2 Out | 74 | 11 | 2 | 0 | 2 | 16 | 16 | 6 | .149 | .257 | .300 |
| Scor. Pos./2 Out | 48 | 9 | 2 | 0 | 1 | 14 | 12 | 3 | .188 | .292 | .350 |
| Late Inning Pressure | 48 | 14 | 3 | 0 | 5 | 11 | 4 | 8 | .292 | .667 | .340 |
| Leading Off | 16 | 5 | 2 | 0 | 1 | 1 | 1 | 2 | .313 | .625 | .353 |
| Runners On | 20 | 4 | 1 | 0 | 2 | 8 | 2 | 4 | .200 | .550 | .261 |
| Runners/Scor. Pos. | 14 | 3 | 1 | 0 | 2 | 8 | 2 | 3 | .214 | .714 | .294 |

| RUNS BATTED IN | From 1B | From 2B | From 3B | Scoring Position |
|---|---|---|---|---|
| Totals | 14/135 | 20/82 | 25/45 | 45/127 |
| Percentage | 10% | 24% | 56% | 35% |
| Driving In Runners from 3B with Less than Two Out: | | | 21/28 | 75% |

Loves to face: Dennis Eckersley (.429, 9-for-21, 2 HR)
Hates to face: Jimmy Key (.133, 2-for-15)
Most RBI by an A.L. player with that few at-bats since Ted Williams drove in 97 runs in 334 AB in 1950. . . . Batted .225 without a home run in 49 first-inning plate appearances. . . . Hasn't had a triple in 1114 at-bats since August 1987. . . . Yearly batting averages with two outs and runners in scoring position since 1985: .211, .188, .177, .215, .188. . . . Career breakdown: .270 (one HR per 29 AB) vs. left-handed pitchers, .299 (one HR per 19 AB) vs. right-handers. . . . Career average of .309 (111 HR) at the Metrodome, .271 (90 HR) elsewhere. . . . During eight full seasons in majors, only one player has surpassed his totals in HR (200) and RBI (717) and his batting average (.290): Eddie Murray.

## Pete Incaviglia

Bats Right

| Texas Rangers | AB | H | 2B | 3B | HR | RBI | BB | SO | BA | SA | OBA |
|---|---|---|---|---|---|---|---|---|---|---|---|
| Season | 453 | 107 | 27 | 4 | 21 | 81 | 32 | 136 | .236 | .453 | .293 |
| vs. Left-Handers | 148 | 31 | 10 | 1 | 6 | 19 | 10 | 46 | .209 | .412 | .264 |
| vs. Right-Handers | 305 | 76 | 17 | 3 | 15 | 62 | 22 | 90 | .249 | .472 | .307 |
| Home | 223 | 56 | 10 | 1 | 13 | 46 | 26 | 60 | .251 | .480 | .327 |
| Road | 230 | 51 | 17 | 3 | 8 | 35 | 6 | 76 | .222 | .426 | .257 |
| Grass | 367 | 92 | 22 | 3 | 21 | 73 | 30 | 105 | .251 | .499 | .311 |
| Artificial Turf | 86 | 15 | 5 | 1 | 0 | 8 | 2 | 31 | .174 | .256 | .211 |
| April | 80 | 20 | 3 | 1 | 3 | 12 | 5 | 27 | .250 | .425 | .307 |
| May | 92 | 19 | 5 | 1 | 3 | 15 | 4 | 24 | .207 | .380 | .235 |
| June | 48 | 8 | 3 | 1 | 0 | 7 | 1 | 12 | .167 | .271 | .200 |
| July | 66 | 19 | 5 | 0 | 7 | 25 | 8 | 19 | .288 | .682 | .373 |
| August | 78 | 13 | 3 | 1 | 3 | 7 | 6 | 29 | .167 | .346 | .235 |
| Sept./Oct. | 89 | 28 | 8 | 0 | 5 | 15 | 8 | 25 | .315 | .573 | .374 |
| Leading Off Inn. | 106 | 29 | 12 | 1 | 5 | 5 | 7 | 36 | .274 | .547 | .325 |
| Runners On | 224 | 53 | 10 | 2 | 11 | 71 | 10 | 66 | .237 | .446 | .277 |
| Runners/Scor. Pos. | 129 | 37 | 9 | 1 | 7 | 61 | 7 | 35 | .287 | .535 | .329 |
| Runners On/2 Out | 89 | 19 | 4 | 0 | 4 | 26 | 3 | 26 | .213 | .393 | .255 |
| Scor. Pos./2 Out | 62 | 15 | 3 | 0 | 3 | 23 | 2 | 17 | .242 | .435 | .277 |
| Late Inning Pressure | 64 | 10 | 4 | 0 | 2 | 7 | 4 | 22 | .156 | .313 | .206 |
| Leading Off | 24 | 3 | 1 | 0 | 1 | 1 | 1 | 12 | .125 | .292 | .160 |
| Runners On | 29 | 5 | 2 | 0 | 1 | 6 | 1 | 5 | .172 | .345 | .200 |
| Runners/Scor. Pos. | 12 | 4 | 2 | 0 | 1 | 6 | 1 | 0 | .333 | .750 | .385 |

| RUNS BATTED IN | From 1B | From 2B | From 3B | Scoring Position |
|---|---|---|---|---|
| Totals | 12/168 | 27/108 | 21/53 | 48/161 |
| Percentage | 7% | 25% | 40% | 30% |
| Driving In Runners from 3B with Less than Two Out: | | | 16/29 | 55% |

Loves to face: Scott Bailes (.615, 8-for-13, 3 HR)
Hates to face: Roger Clemens (0-for-7, 7 SO)
Hit 13 home runs to center or opposite field, third in A.L. to Bo Jackson (26) and Fred McGriff (18). . . . Batted .284 vs. ground-ball pitchers, .196 vs. fly-ballers. . . . Has struck out 642 times over his four-year career. Only Rob Deer has fanned more times during that period (676). . . . Good news: His strikeout total has actually *decreased* in each of the last three seasons (185, 168, 153, 136). Bad news: So has his home-run total (30, 27, 22, 21). . . . One of four active players with 2000 plate appearances and no sacrifice bunts. The others: George Bell, Steve Balboni, and Ron Kittle. . . . Career average is .282 (one HR per 15 AB) vs. left-handers, .238 (one HR per 22 AB) vs. right-handers.

## Bo Jackson

Bats Right

| Kansas City Royals | AB | H | 2B | 3B | HR | RBI | BB | SO | BA | SA | OBA |
|---|---|---|---|---|---|---|---|---|---|---|---|
| Season | 515 | 132 | 15 | 6 | 32 | 105 | 39 | 172 | .256 | .495 | .310 |
| vs. Left-Handers | 128 | 34 | 4 | 2 | 7 | 20 | 18 | 42 | .266 | .492 | .365 |
| vs. Right-Handers | 387 | 98 | 11 | 4 | 25 | 85 | 21 | 130 | .253 | .496 | .291 |
| Home | 248 | 58 | 8 | 4 | 11 | 46 | 21 | 81 | .234 | .431 | .296 |
| Road | 267 | 74 | 7 | 2 | 21 | 59 | 18 | 91 | .277 | .554 | .324 |
| Grass | 213 | 59 | 4 | 1 | 16 | 43 | 15 | 72 | .277 | .531 | .326 |
| Artificial Turf | 302 | 73 | 11 | 5 | 16 | 62 | 24 | 100 | .242 | .470 | .299 |
| April | 85 | 24 | 5 | 1 | 8 | 20 | 7 | 23 | .282 | .647 | .337 |
| May | 98 | 24 | 2 | 2 | 4 | 15 | 5 | 32 | .245 | .429 | .288 |
| June | 97 | 27 | 3 | 1 | 6 | 17 | 4 | 27 | .278 | .515 | .301 |
| July | 54 | 15 | 0 | 0 | 4 | 12 | 6 | 21 | .278 | .500 | .344 |
| August | 81 | 17 | 1 | 1 | 4 | 15 | 7 | 27 | .210 | .395 | .278 |
| Sept./Oct. | 100 | 25 | 4 | 1 | 6 | 26 | 10 | 42 | .250 | .490 | .324 |
| Leading Off Inn. | 125 | 39 | 6 | 1 | 10 | 10 | 8 | 38 | .312 | .616 | .353 |
| Runners On | 254 | 63 | 7 | 4 | 17 | 90 | 25 | 79 | .248 | .508 | .318 |
| Runners/Scor. Pos. | 156 | 41 | 6 | 4 | 13 | 82 | 17 | 51 | .263 | .603 | .328 |
| Runners On/2 Out | 118 | 25 | 3 | 2 | 8 | 39 | 10 | 45 | .212 | .475 | .273 |
| Scor. Pos./2 Out | 79 | 22 | 3 | 2 | 7 | 37 | 7 | 28 | .278 | .633 | .337 |
| Late Inning Pressure | 73 | 18 | 2 | 0 | 4 | 5 | 6 | 27 | .247 | .438 | .304 |
| Leading Off | 20 | 5 | 1 | 0 | 1 | 1 | 1 | 6 | .250 | .450 | .286 |
| Runners On | 28 | 4 | 1 | 0 | 0 | 1 | 5 | 11 | .143 | .179 | .273 |
| Runners/Scor. Pos. | 19 | 1 | 0 | 0 | 0 | 1 | 4 | 9 | .053 | .053 | .217 |

| RUNS BATTED IN | From 1B | From 2B | From 3B | Scoring Position |
|---|---|---|---|---|
| Totals | 12/179 | 30/111 | 31/76 | 61/187 |
| Percentage | 7% | 27% | 41% | 33% |
| Driving In Runners from 3B with Less than Two Out: | | | 20/35 | 57% |

Loves to face: Tom Niedenfuer (.500, 4-for-8, 3 HR)
Hates to face: Mark Langston (.091, 1-for-11, 1 HR, 9 SO)
Increased his batting average and home-run and RBI totals in each of the past three seasons. Only four players have done it four years in a row: Cy Perkins (1918–21), Rogers Hornsby (1919–22), Charlie Gehringer (1926–29), and Rick Cerone (1977–80). . . . Hit 6 home runs to left field, 8 to center field, and 18 to the opposite field. . . . Led A.L. batters in home runs and RBI in road games. . . . Career average is .298 vs. ground-ball pitchers, .204 vs. fly-ballers. Gap of 93 points is largest of last 10 years (minimum: 500 AB both ways). . . . Career batting average is .118 (6-for-51) with runners in scoring position in LIP Situations, the lowest among active A.L. players (minimum: 40 AB).

## Brook Jacoby

Bats Right

| Cleveland Indians | AB | H | 2B | 3B | HR | RBI | BB | SO | BA | SA | OBA |
|---|---|---|---|---|---|---|---|---|---|---|---|
| Season | 519 | 141 | 26 | 5 | 13 | 64 | 62 | 90 | .272 | .416 | .348 |
| vs. Left-Handers | 152 | 45 | 10 | 1 | 6 | 19 | 17 | 22 | .296 | .493 | .363 |
| vs. Right-Handers | 367 | 96 | 16 | 4 | 7 | 45 | 45 | 68 | .262 | .384 | .342 |
| Home | 248 | 66 | 10 | 4 | 7 | 32 | 33 | 37 | .266 | .423 | .353 |
| Road | 271 | 75 | 16 | 1 | 6 | 32 | 29 | 53 | .277 | .410 | .343 |
| Grass | 446 | 126 | 24 | 5 | 12 | 59 | 59 | 70 | .283 | .439 | .364 |
| Artificial Turf | 73 | 15 | 2 | 0 | 1 | 5 | 3 | 20 | .205 | .274 | .237 |
| April | 69 | 20 | 4 | 0 | 1 | 10 | 9 | 16 | .290 | .391 | .361 |
| May | 100 | 29 | 4 | 1 | 8 | 16 | 16 | 23 | .290 | .590 | .388 |
| June | 87 | 18 | 3 | 0 | 0 | 6 | 10 | 11 | .207 | .241 | .283 |
| July | 49 | 15 | 3 | 0 | 0 | 8 | 4 | 6 | .306 | .367 | .358 |
| August | 112 | 37 | 10 | 1 | 2 | 10 | 8 | 16 | .330 | .491 | .375 |
| Sept./Oct. | 102 | 22 | 2 | 3 | 2 | 14 | 15 | 18 | .216 | .353 | .322 |
| Leading Off Inn. | 130 | 35 | 10 | 0 | 3 | 3 | 13 | 22 | .269 | .415 | .340 |
| Runners On | 223 | 65 | 7 | 3 | 7 | 58 | 29 | 42 | .291 | .444 | .366 |
| Runners/Scor. Pos. | 109 | 24 | 4 | 0 | 2 | 43 | 22 | 29 | .220 | .312 | .340 |
| Runners On/2 Out | 102 | 30 | 3 | 1 | 1 | 21 | 13 | 18 | .294 | .373 | .379 |
| Scor. Pos./2 Out | 60 | 15 | 2 | 0 | 1 | 19 | 11 | 14 | .250 | .333 | .375 |
| Late Inning Pressure | 83 | 19 | 3 | 0 | 2 | 12 | 15 | 17 | .229 | .337 | .340 |
| Leading Off | 26 | 7 | 2 | 0 | 1 | 1 | 2 | 5 | .269 | .462 | .321 |
| Runners On | 35 | 11 | 1 | 0 | 1 | 11 | 7 | 6 | .314 | .429 | .409 |
| Runners/Scor. Pos. | 18 | 4 | 0 | 0 | 0 | 8 | 5 | 6 | .222 | .222 | .360 |

| RUNS BATTED IN | From 1B | From 2B | From 3B | Scoring Position |
|---|---|---|---|---|
| Totals | 11/178 | 15/88 | 25/56 | 40/144 |
| Percentage | 6% | 17% | 45% | 28% |
| Driving In Runners from 3B with Less than Two Out: | | | 18/29 | 62% |

Loves to face: Mike Moore (.357, 15-for-42, 2 HR)
Hates to face: Bret Saberhagen (.159, 7-for-44)
A season of weird streaks: Shared A.L. lead in home runs for May, then didn't hit one in June or July. Gap of 163 at-bats between home runs was longest of his career. . . . Had the game-winning RBI in all four games of series against Angels in September. . . . Hit four triples over a 23-game span (Aug. 31–Sept. 23), after hitting only one in his previous 257 games. . . . Stole his customary two bases, for the fifth consecutive season. . . . Has hit better on the road than at home in each of his six seasons with the Indians. . . . Games played has decreased in each of the last four seasons: 161, 158, 155, 152, 147. . . . Career average of .239 in Late-Inning Pressure Situations, .278 in other at-bats.

## Dion James

Bats Left

| Cleveland Indians | AB | H | 2B | 3B | HR | RBI | BB | SO | BA | SA | OBA |
|---|---|---|---|---|---|---|---|---|---|---|---|
| Season | 245 | 75 | 11 | 0 | 4 | 29 | 24 | 26 | .306 | .400 | .368 |
| vs. Left-Handers | 27 | 7 | 3 | 0 | 0 | 2 | 3 | 3 | .259 | .370 | .333 |
| vs. Right-Handers | 218 | 68 | 8 | 0 | 4 | 27 | 21 | 23 | .312 | .404 | .372 |
| Home | 119 | 25 | 3 | 0 | 1 | 11 | 13 | 17 | .210 | .261 | .288 |
| Road | 126 | 50 | 8 | 0 | 3 | 18 | 11 | 9 | .397 | .532 | .445 |
| Grass | 192 | 55 | 7 | 0 | 2 | 18 | 16 | 24 | .286 | .354 | .341 |
| Artificial Turf | 53 | 20 | 4 | 0 | 2 | 11 | 8 | 2 | .377 | .566 | .459 |
| April | 0 | 0 | 0 | 0 | 0 | 0 | 0 | 0 | — | — | — |
| May | 0 | 0 | 0 | 0 | 0 | 0 | 0 | 0 | — | — | — |
| June | 0 | 0 | 0 | 0 | 0 | 0 | 0 | 0 | — | — | — |
| July | 86 | 28 | 7 | 0 | 2 | 12 | 13 | 8 | .326 | .477 | .414 |
| August | 80 | 21 | 3 | 0 | 0 | 4 | 5 | 8 | .263 | .300 | .306 |
| Sept./Oct. | 79 | 26 | 1 | 0 | 2 | 13 | 6 | 10 | .329 | .418 | .376 |
| Leading Off Inn. | 58 | 14 | 2 | 0 | 0 | 0 | 6 | 7 | .241 | .276 | .313 |
| Runners On | 111 | 37 | 5 | 0 | 3 | 28 | 10 | 12 | .333 | .459 | .388 |
| Runners/Scor. Pos. | 61 | 16 | 2 | 0 | 0 | 20 | 9 | 8 | .262 | .295 | .357 |
| Runners On/2 Out | 32 | 12 | 1 | 0 | 0 | 6 | 2 | 4 | .375 | .406 | .412 |
| Scor. Pos./2 Out | 20 | 5 | 0 | 0 | 0 | 5 | 2 | 3 | .250 | .250 | .318 |
| Late Inning Pressure | 40 | 12 | 3 | 0 | 0 | 2 | 7 | 6 | .300 | .375 | .404 |
| Leading Off | 9 | 2 | 0 | 0 | 0 | 0 | 1 | 2 | .222 | .222 | .300 |
| Runners On | 13 | 4 | 1 | 0 | 0 | 2 | 3 | 3 | .308 | .385 | .438 |
| Runners/Scor. Pos. | 5 | 1 | 0 | 0 | 0 | 1 | 3 | 3 | .200 | .200 | .500 |

| RUNS BATTED IN | From 1B | From 2B | From 3B | Scoring Position |
|---|---|---|---|---|
| Totals | 6/73 | 7/43 | 12/23 | 19/66 |
| Percentage | 8% | 16% | 52% | 29% |
| Driving In Runners from 3B with Less than Two Out: | | | 10/17 | 59% |

Loves to face: Storm Davis (.500, 7-for-14)
Hates to face: Nolan Ryan (.067, 1-for-15)
Batted .343 as a designated hitter, and had the highest on-base average (.427) of any DH (minimum: 100 PA).... Three of his four home runs were first-inning shots.... Started 59 games for Cleveland, but only four against left-handers.... Batted .364 in day games, .251 at night. Had hit better in night games than in day games in each of his five previous seasons.... Kills anything that flies. (Remember the pigeon?) Career average of .315 vs. fly-ball pitchers ranks fourth among active players, behind Boggs, Gwynn, and Puckett (minimum: 500 hits).... Career average of .254 vs. ground-ballers provides a difference of 61 points, the largest over the last 10 seasons (minimum: 500 AB both ways).

## Stan Javier

Bats Left and Right

| Oakland As | AB | H | 2B | 3B | HR | RBI | BB | SO | BA | SA | OBA |
|---|---|---|---|---|---|---|---|---|---|---|---|
| Season | 310 | 77 | 12 | 3 | 1 | 28 | 31 | 45 | .248 | .316 | .317 |
| vs. Left-Handers | 74 | 17 | 1 | 1 | 1 | 7 | 5 | 14 | .230 | .311 | .278 |
| vs. Right-Handers | 236 | 60 | 11 | 2 | 0 | 21 | 26 | 31 | .254 | .318 | .328 |
| Home | 138 | 31 | 4 | 1 | 1 | 9 | 19 | 21 | .225 | .290 | .319 |
| Road | 172 | 46 | 8 | 2 | 0 | 19 | 12 | 24 | .267 | .337 | .315 |
| Grass | 252 | 60 | 10 | 3 | 1 | 22 | 28 | 35 | .238 | .313 | .314 |
| Artificial Turf | 58 | 17 | 2 | 0 | 0 | 6 | 3 | 10 | .293 | .328 | .328 |
| April | 56 | 17 | 4 | 1 | 0 | 3 | 9 | 7 | .304 | .411 | .400 |
| May | 72 | 18 | 2 | 2 | 0 | 9 | 6 | 11 | .250 | .333 | .313 |
| June | 83 | 20 | 3 | 0 | 1 | 8 | 7 | 11 | .241 | .313 | .300 |
| July | 40 | 8 | 2 | 0 | 0 | 1 | 3 | 4 | .200 | .250 | .256 |
| August | 43 | 10 | 1 | 0 | 0 | 5 | 3 | 10 | .233 | .256 | .283 |
| Sept./Oct. | 16 | 4 | 0 | 0 | 0 | 2 | 3 | 2 | .250 | .250 | .350 |
| Leading Off Inn. | 81 | 21 | 4 | 2 | 0 | 0 | 6 | 6 | .259 | .358 | .310 |
| Runners On | 144 | 37 | 7 | 1 | 1 | 28 | 18 | 21 | .257 | .340 | .335 |
| Runners/Scor. Pos. | 75 | 19 | 4 | 1 | 0 | 25 | 15 | 10 | .253 | .333 | .370 |
| Runners On/2 Out | 58 | 9 | 1 | 1 | 0 | 7 | 9 | 14 | .155 | .207 | .269 |
| Scor. Pos./2 Out | 37 | 6 | 0 | 1 | 0 | 7 | 7 | 7 | .162 | .216 | .295 |
| Late Inning Pressure | 47 | 13 | 1 | 1 | 0 | 5 | 9 | 7 | .277 | .340 | .393 |
| Leading Off | 13 | 5 | 0 | 1 | 0 | 0 | 4 | 2 | .385 | .538 | .529 |
| Runners On | 23 | 6 | 1 | 0 | 0 | 5 | 4 | 4 | .261 | .304 | .370 |
| Runners/Scor. Pos. | 13 | 4 | 1 | 0 | 0 | 5 | 3 | 1 | .308 | .385 | .438 |

| RUNS BATTED IN | From 1B | From 2B | From 3B | Scoring Position |
|---|---|---|---|---|
| Totals | 3/109 | 10/63 | 14/29 | 24/92 |
| Percentage | 3% | 16% | 48% | 26% |
| Driving In Runners from 3B with Less than Two Out: | | | 11/18 | 61% |

Loves to face: Eric King (.500, 6-for-12)
Hates to face: John Farrell (2-for-13, 6 SO)
One of four A.L. players to start at least 10 games at each of the three outfield positions.... Hitless in seven at-bats as a pinch hitter, but he walked six times in that role.... Highest career stolen base percentage (.878, 43-of-49) among active players with at least 40 steals.... Career average of .159 with two outs and runners in scoring position is the lowest of any active A.L. player (minimum: 100 AB).... Career average with RISP and *less than two outs* is a hardy .310.... Career average of .245 at Oakland Coliseum, .206 on other grass fields, .278 on artificial surfaces.... Has hit for a higher average from the left side of the plate than from the right side in each of his five seasons in majors.

## Wally Joyner

Bats Left

| California Angels | AB | H | 2B | 3B | HR | RBI | BB | SO | BA | SA | OBA |
|---|---|---|---|---|---|---|---|---|---|---|---|
| Season | 593 | 167 | 30 | 2 | 16 | 79 | 46 | 58 | .282 | .420 | .335 |
| vs. Left-Handers | 206 | 54 | 6 | 0 | 6 | 32 | 11 | 20 | .262 | .379 | .305 |
| vs. Right-Handers | 387 | 113 | 24 | 2 | 10 | 47 | 35 | 38 | .292 | .442 | .351 |
| Home | 286 | 78 | 14 | 0 | 8 | 40 | 24 | 29 | .273 | .406 | .332 |
| Road | 307 | 89 | 16 | 2 | 8 | 39 | 22 | 29 | .290 | .433 | .338 |
| Grass | 497 | 132 | 25 | 2 | 12 | 61 | 37 | 50 | .266 | .396 | .318 |
| Artificial Turf | 96 | 35 | 5 | 0 | 4 | 18 | 9 | 8 | .365 | .542 | .425 |
| April | 89 | 19 | 3 | 0 | 1 | 8 | 9 | 12 | .213 | .281 | .283 |
| May | 80 | 23 | 5 | 1 | 0 | 10 | 7 | 3 | .288 | .375 | .330 |
| June | 93 | 33 | 7 | 0 | 1 | 10 | 6 | 8 | .355 | .462 | .400 |
| July | 114 | 38 | 5 | 0 | 5 | 26 | 5 | 14 | .333 | .509 | .371 |
| August | 109 | 25 | 5 | 1 | 5 | 14 | 10 | 11 | .229 | .431 | .303 |
| Sept./Oct. | 108 | 29 | 5 | 0 | 4 | 11 | 9 | 10 | .269 | .426 | .325 |
| Leading Off Inn. | 156 | 43 | 8 | 0 | 4 | 4 | 6 | 16 | .276 | .404 | .302 |
| Runners On | 259 | 77 | 14 | 1 | 5 | 68 | 27 | 25 | .297 | .417 | .362 |
| Runners/Scor. Pos. | 148 | 44 | 7 | 1 | 3 | 61 | 22 | 12 | .297 | .419 | .381 |
| Runners On/2 Out | 124 | 32 | 4 | 0 | 1 | 20 | 13 | 12 | .258 | .315 | .333 |
| Scor. Pos./2 Out | 73 | 17 | 2 | 0 | 1 | 18 | 11 | 8 | .233 | .301 | .341 |
| Late Inning Pressure | 83 | 24 | 2 | 1 | 2 | 12 | 4 | 8 | .289 | .410 | .319 |
| Leading Off | 24 | 8 | 0 | 0 | 0 | 0 | 0 | 2 | .333 | .333 | .333 |
| Runners On | 33 | 9 | 0 | 0 | 1 | 11 | 2 | 4 | .273 | .364 | .308 |
| Runners/Scor. Pos. | 20 | 6 | 0 | 0 | 0 | 9 | 2 | 3 | .300 | .300 | .346 |

| RUNS BATTED IN | From 1B | From 2B | From 3B | Scoring Position |
|---|---|---|---|---|
| Totals | 9/182 | 25/110 | 29/72 | 54/182 |
| Percentage | 5% | 23% | 40% | 30% |
| Driving In Runners from 3B with Less than Two Out: | | | 22/37 | 59% |

Loves to face: Allan Anderson (.476, 10-for-21, 1 HR)
Hates to face: John Cerutti (.067, 1-for-15)
Batted .341 against ground-ball pitchers, .245 vs. fly-ballers.... Batted with bases loaded 14 times, drove in only five of those 42 base runners.... Drove in less than 30 percent of runners from scoring position for first time in career.... Career RBI rate from scoring position (34.1%) still ranks fifth among active players, behind Mattingly, Brett, Boggs, and Guerrero.... Career average of .273 at Anaheim Stadium, .293 on other grass fields, .327 on artificial surfaces.... Only three rookies of the 1980s batted .280 or better in at least 400 at-bats, then repeated that in each of the next three seasons: Willie McGee, Kirby Puckett, and Joyner.

## Ron Karkovice

Bats Right

| Chicago White Sox | AB | H | 2B | 3B | HR | RBI | BB | SO | BA | SA | OBA |
|---|---|---|---|---|---|---|---|---|---|---|---|
| Season | 182 | 48 | 9 | 2 | 3 | 24 | 10 | 56 | .264 | .385 | .306 |
| vs. Left-Handers | 88 | 25 | 5 | 1 | 1 | 13 | 6 | 22 | .284 | .398 | .323 |
| vs. Right-Handers | 94 | 23 | 4 | 1 | 2 | 11 | 4 | 34 | .245 | .372 | .290 |
| Home | 87 | 21 | 6 | 1 | 0 | 8 | 4 | 24 | .241 | .333 | .272 |
| Road | 95 | 27 | 3 | 1 | 3 | 16 | 6 | 32 | .284 | .432 | .337 |
| Grass | 152 | 40 | 7 | 2 | 3 | 22 | 9 | 47 | .263 | .395 | .302 |
| Artificial Turf | 30 | 8 | 2 | 0 | 0 | 2 | 1 | 9 | .267 | .333 | .324 |
| April | 32 | 8 | 0 | 0 | 1 | 4 | 1 | 11 | .250 | .344 | .273 |
| May | 45 | 9 | 1 | 0 | 1 | 7 | 2 | 8 | .200 | .289 | .224 |
| June | 18 | 4 | 2 | 0 | 0 | 1 | 0 | 7 | .222 | .333 | .222 |
| July | 20 | 7 | 2 | 0 | 0 | 1 | 1 | 7 | .350 | .450 | .381 |
| August | 45 | 16 | 4 | 2 | 1 | 9 | 3 | 14 | .356 | .600 | .420 |
| Sept./Oct. | 22 | 4 | 0 | 0 | 0 | 2 | 3 | 9 | .182 | .182 | .280 |
| Leading Off Inn. | 48 | 13 | 6 | 0 | 0 | 0 | 0 | 16 | .271 | .396 | .271 |
| Runners On | 80 | 22 | 1 | 1 | 3 | 24 | 4 | 25 | .275 | .425 | .310 |
| Runners/Scor. Pos. | 50 | 14 | 1 | 0 | 2 | 21 | 4 | 19 | .280 | .420 | .333 |
| Runners On/2 Out | 34 | 11 | 1 | 1 | 2 | 11 | 1 | 13 | .324 | .588 | .361 |
| Scor. Pos./2 Out | 23 | 6 | 1 | 0 | 1 | 8 | 1 | 10 | .261 | .435 | .320 |
| Late Inning Pressure | 32 | 4 | 0 | 0 | 0 | 0 | 1 | 18 | .125 | .125 | .152 |
| Leading Off | 10 | 1 | 0 | 0 | 0 | 0 | 0 | 6 | .100 | .100 | .100 |
| Runners On | 11 | 1 | 0 | 0 | 0 | 0 | 0 | 7 | .091 | .091 | .091 |
| Runners/Scor. Pos. | 7 | 0 | 0 | 0 | 0 | 0 | 0 | 6 | .000 | .000 | .000 |

| RUNS BATTED IN | From 1B | From 2B | From 3B | Scoring Position |
|---|---|---|---|---|
| Totals | 4/50 | 8/38 | 9/26 | 17/64 |
| Percentage | 8% | 21% | 35% | 27% |
| Driving In Runners from 3B with Less than Two Out: | | | 8/17 | 47% |

Loves to face: Curt Young (.571, 4-for-7)
Hates to face: Greg Swindell (0-for-9, 5 SO)
What did White Sox pitchers and opposing base runners have in common? Both preferred Fisk to Karkovice behind the plate.... Sox had a 4.76 ERA with Karkovice catching, 3.82 ERA with Fisk.... Opposing base stealers were 26-for-50 against Karkovice (52%), 58-for-83 against ol' No. 72 (70%).... Batted .466 on fair balls hit to the left side, .308 straight away, .222 on fair balls hit to the opposite field.... Career average is .086 (5-for-58) in Late-Inning Pressure Situations.... Some ghoulish fans may want those 58 AB broken down further. Close your eyes if you're squeamish: 1-for-20 with runners on; 0-for-12 with runners in scoring position.... Hasn't driven in any of 28 base runners in LIPS.

## Roberto Kelly

Bats Right

| New York Yankees | AB | H | 2B | 3B | HR | RBI | BB | SO | BA | SA | OBA |
|---|---|---|---|---|---|---|---|---|---|---|---|
| Season | 441 | 133 | 18 | 3 | 9 | 49 | 41 | 89 | .302 | .417 | .369 |
| vs. Left-Handers | 145 | 54 | 7 | 1 | 3 | 16 | 12 | 22 | .372 | .497 | .424 |
| vs. Right-Handers | 296 | 79 | 11 | 2 | 6 | 33 | 29 | 67 | .267 | .378 | .342 |
| Home | 205 | 65 | 10 | 1 | 2 | 27 | 23 | 32 | .317 | .405 | .397 |
| Road | 236 | 68 | 8 | 2 | 7 | 22 | 18 | 57 | .288 | .428 | .344 |
| Grass | 360 | 104 | 14 | 1 | 7 | 39 | 37 | 73 | .289 | .392 | .365 |
| Artificial Turf | 81 | 29 | 4 | 2 | 2 | 10 | 4 | 16 | .358 | .531 | .388 |
| April | 73 | 24 | 6 | 1 | 1 | 12 | 5 | 20 | .329 | .479 | .380 |
| May | 63 | 16 | 1 | 0 | 1 | 3 | 7 | 14 | .254 | .317 | .329 |
| June | 53 | 18 | 0 | 1 | 2 | 7 | 2 | 5 | .340 | .491 | .375 |
| July | 86 | 30 | 5 | 0 | 2 | 15 | 12 | 16 | .349 | .477 | .434 |
| August | 102 | 33 | 6 | 1 | 0 | 6 | 11 | 22 | .324 | .402 | .400 |
| Sept./Oct. | 64 | 12 | 0 | 0 | 3 | 6 | 4 | 12 | .188 | .328 | .246 |
| Leading Off Inn. | 96 | 27 | 4 | 1 | 2 | 2 | 8 | 19 | .281 | .406 | .355 |
| Runners On | 186 | 57 | 9 | 2 | 1 | 41 | 17 | 33 | .306 | .392 | .371 |
| Runners/Scor. Pos. | 105 | 30 | 5 | 1 | 1 | 39 | 12 | 22 | .286 | .381 | .370 |
| Runners On/2 Out | 85 | 26 | 2 | 1 | 0 | 19 | 9 | 11 | .306 | .353 | .385 |
| Scor. Pos./2 Out | 55 | 16 | 2 | 0 | 0 | 18 | 7 | 8 | .291 | .327 | .391 |
| Late Inning Pressure | 71 | 23 | 2 | 0 | 2 | 8 | 11 | 18 | .324 | .437 | .415 |
| Leading Off | 11 | 2 | 0 | 0 | 0 | 0 | 4 | 5 | .182 | .182 | .400 |
| Runners On | 34 | 9 | 1 | 0 | 0 | 6 | 3 | 8 | .265 | .294 | .324 |
| Runners/Scor. Pos. | 17 | 4 | 1 | 0 | 0 | 6 | 3 | 5 | .235 | .294 | .350 |

| RUNS BATTED IN | From 1B | From 2B | From 3B | Scoring Position |
|---|---|---|---|---|
| Totals | 5/144 | 14/77 | 21/47 | 35/124 |
| Percentage | 3% | 18% | 45% | 28% |
| Driving In Runners from 3B with Less than Two Out: | | | 11/20 | 55% |

Loves to face: Mike Flanagan (.429, 6-for-14)
Hates to face: Mike Witt (0-for-8)
Had four hits on opening day, something no Yankees player had done since 1960, when both Roger Maris (batting *leadoff* in his first game in pinstripes) and Moose Skowron did it. . . . Hit well to all fields: .382 on fair balls to the left side, .415 up the middle, .340 to the right side. But 89 strikeouts dragged his overall average down to .302. . . . Finished season with a streak of 67 consecutive errorless games in outfield. . . . Batted .342 vs. fly-ball pitchers, .259 against ground-ballers. . . . Six A.L. players hit .370 or better vs. left-handers (minimum: 50 hits). Three were Yankees: Kelly, Espinoza, and Sax. . . . Has hit one home run for every 40 at-bats in night games, one in 174 AB in day games.

## Brad Komminsk

Bats Right

| Cleveland Indians | AB | H | 2B | 3B | HR | RBI | BB | SO | BA | SA | OBA |
|---|---|---|---|---|---|---|---|---|---|---|---|
| Season | 198 | 47 | 8 | 2 | 8 | 33 | 24 | 55 | .237 | .419 | .319 |
| vs. Left-Handers | 65 | 11 | 3 | 1 | 1 | 9 | 5 | 27 | .169 | .292 | .233 |
| vs. Right-Handers | 133 | 36 | 5 | 1 | 7 | 24 | 19 | 28 | .271 | .481 | .359 |
| Home | 115 | 31 | 3 | 1 | 6 | 23 | 14 | 29 | .270 | .470 | .348 |
| Road | 83 | 16 | 5 | 1 | 2 | 10 | 10 | 26 | .193 | .349 | .277 |
| Grass | 165 | 38 | 5 | 2 | 7 | 25 | 22 | 48 | .230 | .412 | .321 |
| Artificial Turf | 33 | 9 | 3 | 0 | 1 | 8 | 2 | 7 | .273 | .455 | .306 |
| April | 0 | 0 | 0 | 0 | 0 | 0 | 0 | 0 | — | — | — |
| May | 0 | 0 | 0 | 0 | 0 | 0 | 0 | 0 | — | — | — |
| June | 0 | 0 | 0 | 0 | 0 | 0 | 0 | 0 | — | — | — |
| July | 82 | 24 | 3 | 0 | 5 | 22 | 9 | 16 | .293 | .512 | .362 |
| August | 58 | 18 | 4 | 2 | 2 | 9 | 7 | 19 | .310 | .552 | .379 |
| Sept./Oct. | 58 | 5 | 1 | 0 | 1 | 2 | 8 | 20 | .086 | .155 | .197 |
| Leading Off Inn. | 36 | 10 | 1 | 2 | 0 | 0 | 7 | 8 | .278 | .417 | .395 |
| Runners On | 95 | 22 | 3 | 0 | 6 | 31 | 9 | 23 | .232 | .453 | .290 |
| Runners/Scor. Pos. | 61 | 16 | 3 | 0 | 3 | 25 | 6 | 16 | .262 | .459 | .314 |
| Runners On/2 Out | 36 | 7 | 0 | 0 | 2 | 11 | 2 | 14 | .194 | .361 | .237 |
| Scor. Pos./2 Out | 28 | 6 | 0 | 0 | 2 | 11 | 2 | 11 | .214 | .429 | .267 |
| Late Inning Pressure | 32 | 4 | 2 | 0 | 2 | 5 | 4 | 15 | .125 | .375 | .211 |
| Leading Off | 6 | 0 | 0 | 0 | 0 | 0 | 1 | 1 | .000 | .000 | .143 |
| Runners On | 9 | 1 | 0 | 0 | 1 | 4 | 2 | 4 | .111 | .444 | .231 |
| Runners/Scor. Pos. | 3 | 0 | 0 | 0 | 0 | 2 | 1 | 1 | .000 | .000 | .167 |

| RUNS BATTED IN | From 1B | From 2B | From 3B | Scoring Position |
|---|---|---|---|---|
| Totals | 4/64 | 11/50 | 10/25 | 21/75 |
| Percentage | 6% | 22% | 40% | 28% |
| Driving In Runners from 3B with Less than Two Out: | | | 7/13 | 54% |

Loves to face: Nolan Ryan (.455, 5-for-11)
Hates to face: Rick Honeycutt (0-for-17)
Drove in 22 runs over his first 22 games after Indians brought him up on June 29. . . . Batting average stood at .300 on August 31, then dropped 63 points based on lowest BA in majors during September (minimum: 2 PA per game). . . . Hitless in 13 at-bats when there were runners on base and Indians trailed by one run. No other A.L. player had that large an oh-fer in those situations. . . . Led major league center fielders with 3.15 putouts per nine innings. . . . Committed seven errors in 92 games in the outfield for the Braves in 1986, but only one error in 68 games last season. . . . Career breakdown: .204 with bases empty, .238 with runners on base, .248 with runners in scoring position.

## Jeff Kunkel

Bats Right

| Texas Rangers | AB | H | 2B | 3B | HR | RBI | BB | SO | BA | SA | OBA |
|---|---|---|---|---|---|---|---|---|---|---|---|
| Season | 293 | 79 | 21 | 2 | 8 | 29 | 20 | 75 | .270 | .437 | .323 |
| vs. Left-Handers | 140 | 43 | 15 | 2 | 3 | 16 | 6 | 34 | .307 | .507 | .345 |
| vs. Right-Handers | 153 | 36 | 6 | 0 | 5 | 13 | 14 | 41 | .235 | .373 | .304 |
| Home | 145 | 37 | 8 | 1 | 8 | 17 | 9 | 30 | .255 | .490 | .308 |
| Road | 148 | 42 | 13 | 1 | 0 | 12 | 11 | 45 | .284 | .385 | .338 |
| Grass | 262 | 70 | 17 | 2 | 8 | 26 | 18 | 65 | .267 | .439 | .322 |
| Artificial Turf | 31 | 9 | 4 | 0 | 0 | 3 | 2 | 10 | .290 | .419 | .333 |
| April | 12 | 4 | 1 | 0 | 0 | 2 | 0 | 3 | .333 | .417 | .333 |
| May | 45 | 12 | 4 | 0 | 3 | 6 | 2 | 10 | .267 | .556 | .313 |
| June | 48 | 14 | 5 | 0 | 1 | 7 | 1 | 12 | .292 | .458 | .306 |
| July | 69 | 17 | 4 | 0 | 1 | 5 | 4 | 22 | .246 | .348 | .288 |
| August | 59 | 18 | 4 | 1 | 1 | 3 | 3 | 12 | .305 | .458 | .339 |
| Sept./Oct. | 60 | 14 | 3 | 1 | 2 | 6 | 10 | 16 | .233 | .417 | .361 |
| Leading Off Inn. | 87 | 23 | 4 | 1 | 4 | 4 | 4 | 19 | .264 | .471 | .304 |
| Runners On | 113 | 31 | 12 | 0 | 1 | 22 | 8 | 33 | .274 | .407 | .333 |
| Runners/Scor. Pos. | 62 | 18 | 6 | 0 | 1 | 20 | 6 | 17 | .290 | .435 | .362 |
| Runners On/2 Out | 46 | 16 | 6 | 0 | 1 | 11 | 3 | 9 | .348 | .543 | .400 |
| Scor. Pos./2 Out | 26 | 8 | 3 | 0 | 1 | 10 | 3 | 5 | .308 | .538 | .400 |
| Late Inning Pressure | 33 | 6 | 2 | 0 | 0 | 0 | 1 | 9 | .182 | .242 | .206 |
| Leading Off | 9 | 0 | 0 | 0 | 0 | 0 | 0 | 2 | .000 | .000 | .000 |
| Runners On | 11 | 3 | 0 | 0 | 0 | 0 | 0 | 2 | .273 | .273 | .273 |
| Runners/Scor. Pos. | 6 | 1 | 0 | 0 | 0 | 0 | 0 | 2 | .167 | .167 | .167 |

| RUNS BATTED IN | From 1B | From 2B | From 3B | Scoring Position |
|---|---|---|---|---|
| Totals | 2/72 | 9/45 | 10/21 | 19/66 |
| Percentage | 3% | 20% | 48% | 29% |
| Driving In Runners from 3B with Less than Two Out: | | | 4/12 | 33% |

Loves to face: Chuck Finley (.462, 6-for-13)
Hates to face: Kirk McCaskill (.100, 1-for-10, 1 HR)
One of five A.L. players to start at five different positions (not including DH). . . . Started three straight games in May at three different positions, and from three different batting order slots. . . . Played every position except catcher and first base. Allowed a home run to Randy Bush in his only appearance on the mound. . . . Lowest fielding percentage (.936) of any shortstop in majors (minimum: 50 games). But it *raised* his career figure from .927 to .931. . . . Career batting average prior to 1989: .217 (75-for-345). . . . Career breakdown: .273 vs. left-handers, .213 vs. right-handers. . . . Failed to drive in any of 16 runners (eight from first base, eight from scoring position) in LIPS.

## Carney Lansford

Bats Right

| Oakland As | AB | H | 2B | 3B | HR | RBI | BB | SO | BA | SA | OBA |
|---|---|---|---|---|---|---|---|---|---|---|---|
| Season | 551 | 185 | 28 | 2 | 2 | 53 | 51 | 25 | .336 | .405 | .398 |
| vs. Left-Handers | 149 | 58 | 10 | 2 | 1 | 14 | 22 | 2 | .389 | .503 | .465 |
| vs. Right-Handers | 402 | 127 | 18 | 0 | 1 | 39 | 29 | 23 | .316 | .368 | .372 |
| Home | 259 | 80 | 11 | 0 | 1 | 34 | 22 | 8 | .309 | .363 | .372 |
| Road | 292 | 105 | 17 | 2 | 1 | 19 | 29 | 17 | .360 | .442 | .422 |
| Grass | 468 | 156 | 22 | 1 | 2 | 51 | 38 | 21 | .333 | .397 | .389 |
| Artificial Turf | 83 | 29 | 6 | 1 | 0 | 2 | 13 | 4 | .349 | .446 | .449 |
| April | 92 | 28 | 8 | 1 | 1 | 9 | 6 | 2 | .304 | .446 | .363 |
| May | 96 | 39 | 8 | 0 | 0 | 3 | 12 | 4 | .406 | .490 | .472 |
| June | 65 | 19 | 2 | 0 | 0 | 6 | 8 | 3 | .292 | .323 | .387 |
| July | 84 | 24 | 3 | 0 | 0 | 11 | 13 | 6 | .286 | .321 | .378 |
| August | 113 | 41 | 2 | 1 | 1 | 10 | 7 | 5 | .363 | .425 | .400 |
| Sept./Oct. | 101 | 34 | 5 | 0 | 0 | 14 | 5 | 5 | .337 | .386 | .384 |
| Leading Off Inn. | 120 | 40 | 10 | 0 | 2 | 2 | 8 | 4 | .333 | .467 | .385 |
| Runners On | 243 | 78 | 11 | 1 | 0 | 51 | 31 | 10 | .321 | .374 | .403 |
| Runners/Scor. Pos. | 133 | 38 | 4 | 1 | 0 | 48 | 22 | 6 | .286 | .331 | .385 |
| Runners On/2 Out | 86 | 27 | 3 | 0 | 0 | 20 | 11 | 5 | .314 | .349 | .392 |
| Scor. Pos./2 Out | 54 | 15 | 2 | 0 | 0 | 19 | 8 | 5 | .278 | .315 | .371 |
| Late Inning Pressure | 61 | 16 | 2 | 0 | 0 | 4 | 7 | 5 | .262 | .295 | .338 |
| Leading Off | 18 | 3 | 1 | 0 | 0 | 0 | 3 | 3 | .167 | .222 | .286 |
| Runners On | 19 | 7 | 1 | 0 | 0 | 4 | 3 | 0 | .368 | .421 | .455 |
| Runners/Scor. Pos. | 12 | 3 | 0 | 0 | 0 | 4 | 2 | 0 | .250 | .250 | .357 |

| RUNS BATTED IN | From 1B | From 2B | From 3B | Scoring Position |
|---|---|---|---|---|
| Totals | 3/179 | 23/108 | 25/55 | 48/163 |
| Percentage | 2% | 21% | 45% | 29% |
| Driving In Runners from 3B with Less than Two Out: | | | 19/33 | 58% |

Loves to face: Mike Boddicker (.417, 20-for-48, 4 HR)
Hates to face: Jeff M. Robinson (.143, 3-for-21)
Batting average was just shy of his career high. Led A.L. at .33583 in 1981, eight one-hundred-thousandths of a point higher than his 1989 average. . . . Batted .373 with Oakland trailing by a run. Hit .375 with runners in scoring position and the score tied. . . . Had lowest strikeout rate in majors (one every 25 PA). . . . Average of 2.39 chances per nine innings was lowest among A.L. third basemen (minimum: 500 innings). . . . Ranks third in career games at third base for the Athletics. The top three: Sal Bando, 1446; Frank "Home Run" Baker, 896; Lansford, 845. . . . Batting average in Late-Inning Pressure Situations has been lower than his overall average in each of the last six seasons.

## Gene Larkin

Bats Left and Right

| Minnesota Twins | AB | H | 2B | 3B | HR | RBI | BB | SO | BA | SA | OBA |
|---|---|---|---|---|---|---|---|---|---|---|---|
| Season | 446 | 119 | 25 | 1 | 6 | 46 | 54 | 57 | .267 | .368 | .353 |
| vs. Left-Handers | 156 | 57 | 12 | 1 | 1 | 20 | 16 | 12 | .365 | .474 | .436 |
| vs. Right-Handers | 290 | 62 | 13 | 0 | 5 | 26 | 38 | 45 | .214 | .310 | .308 |
| Home | 239 | 62 | 10 | 0 | 3 | 25 | 25 | 26 | .259 | .339 | .336 |
| Road | 207 | 57 | 15 | 1 | 3 | 21 | 29 | 31 | .275 | .401 | .373 |
| Grass | 163 | 48 | 13 | 0 | 3 | 18 | 24 | 24 | .294 | .429 | .391 |
| Artificial Turf | 283 | 71 | 12 | 1 | 3 | 28 | 30 | 33 | .251 | .332 | .331 |
| April | 73 | 19 | 7 | 0 | 0 | 3 | 6 | 8 | .260 | .356 | .333 |
| May | 76 | 14 | 5 | 0 | 1 | 9 | 14 | 13 | .184 | .289 | .323 |
| June | 66 | 18 | 3 | 0 | 1 | 13 | 12 | 12 | .273 | .364 | .402 |
| July | 79 | 21 | 0 | 0 | 0 | 2 | 10 | 14 | .266 | .266 | .348 |
| August | 62 | 20 | 4 | 0 | 1 | 8 | 3 | 1 | .323 | .435 | .358 |
| Sept./Oct. | 90 | 27 | 6 | 1 | 3 | 11 | 9 | 9 | .300 | .489 | .359 |
| Leading Off Inn. | 100 | 29 | 8 | 1 | 2 | 2 | 12 | 11 | .290 | .450 | .372 |
| Runners On | 208 | 56 | 10 | 0 | 3 | 43 | 27 | 24 | .269 | .361 | .355 |
| Runners/Scor. Pos. | 121 | 28 | 6 | 0 | 2 | 40 | 21 | 20 | .231 | .331 | .340 |
| Runners On/2 Out | 83 | 22 | 5 | 0 | 1 | 17 | 19 | 9 | .265 | .361 | .402 |
| Scor. Pos./2 Out | 55 | 14 | 2 | 0 | 1 | 16 | 14 | 9 | .255 | .345 | .406 |
| Late Inning Pressure | 66 | 17 | 1 | 0 | 0 | 3 | 6 | 11 | .258 | .273 | .338 |
| Leading Off | 17 | 5 | 1 | 0 | 0 | 0 | 1 | 2 | .294 | .353 | .368 |
| Runners On | 27 | 8 | 0 | 0 | 0 | 3 | 5 | 1 | .296 | .296 | .424 |
| Runners/Scor. Pos. | 13 | 4 | 0 | 0 | 0 | 3 | 4 | 1 | .308 | .308 | .471 |

| RUNS BATTED IN | From 1B | From 2B | From 3B | Scoring Position |
|---|---|---|---|---|
| Totals | 5/152 | 18/104 | 17/45 | 35/149 |
| Percentage | 3% | 17% | 38% | 23% |
| Driving In Runners from 3B with Less than Two Out: | | | 13/26 | 50% |

Loves to face: Bud Black (.643, 9-for-14, 1 HR)
Hates to face: Chuck Finley (.077, 1-for-13)
Hit .500 last season (10-for-20) with runners on base and Twins trailing by one run, best mark in A.L. (minimum: 20 AB). . . . Drew walks in five straight plate appearances, something no other Twins player did during 1980s. . . . Career averages are .326 vs. left-handers, .238 vs. right-handers. Last season's breakdown was most lopsided of his career. . . . Career mark is .478 (11-for-23) with two outs and runners in scoring position in LIP Situations, highest over last 15 seasons (minimum: 10 hits). . . . Players with most similar statistical profiles were second basemen: Ron Oester, Tim Teufel, Rob Wilfong, Marty Barrett. Can a first baseman/DH-type survive on that kind of production? Stay tuned.

## Tim Laudner

Bats Right

| Minnesota Twins | AB | H | 2B | 3B | HR | RBI | BB | SO | BA | SA | OBA |
|---|---|---|---|---|---|---|---|---|---|---|---|
| Season | 239 | 53 | 11 | 1 | 6 | 27 | 25 | 65 | .222 | .351 | .293 |
| vs. Left-Handers | 91 | 23 | 8 | 1 | 2 | 12 | 10 | 26 | .253 | .429 | .324 |
| vs. Right-Handers | 148 | 30 | 3 | 0 | 4 | 15 | 15 | 39 | .203 | .304 | .274 |
| Home | 132 | 29 | 5 | 1 | 2 | 12 | 13 | 34 | .220 | .318 | .288 |
| Road | 107 | 24 | 6 | 0 | 4 | 15 | 12 | 31 | .224 | .393 | .300 |
| Grass | 89 | 19 | 5 | 0 | 4 | 13 | 12 | 25 | .213 | .404 | .304 |
| Artificial Turf | 150 | 34 | 6 | 1 | 2 | 14 | 13 | 40 | .227 | .320 | .287 |
| April | 39 | 6 | 1 | 0 | 0 | 2 | 3 | 12 | .154 | .179 | .214 |
| May | 56 | 14 | 3 | 1 | 2 | 6 | 7 | 14 | .250 | .446 | .328 |
| June | 45 | 9 | 1 | 0 | 2 | 8 | 8 | 12 | .200 | .356 | .315 |
| July | 38 | 8 | 1 | 0 | 1 | 7 | 4 | 12 | .211 | .316 | .286 |
| August | 57 | 16 | 5 | 0 | 1 | 4 | 3 | 13 | .281 | .421 | .317 |
| Sept./Oct. | 4 | 0 | 0 | 0 | 0 | 0 | 0 | 2 | .000 | .000 | .000 |
| Leading Off Inn. | 53 | 11 | 1 | 0 | 3 | 3 | 5 | 12 | .208 | .396 | .276 |
| Runners On | 110 | 25 | 7 | 1 | 2 | 23 | 17 | 36 | .227 | .364 | .326 |
| Runners/Scor. Pos. | 53 | 11 | 3 | 1 | 1 | 20 | 11 | 23 | .208 | .358 | .333 |
| Runners On/2 Out | 41 | 9 | 1 | 1 | 0 | 6 | 11 | 14 | .220 | .293 | .385 |
| Scor. Pos./2 Out | 25 | 4 | 1 | 1 | 0 | 6 | 8 | 10 | .160 | .280 | .364 |
| Late Inning Pressure | 33 | 7 | 1 | 0 | 2 | 7 | 2 | 9 | .212 | .424 | .257 |
| Leading Off | 11 | 1 | 0 | 0 | 1 | 1 | 1 | 1 | .091 | .364 | .167 |
| Runners On | 16 | 5 | 1 | 0 | 1 | 6 | 0 | 5 | .313 | .563 | .313 |
| Runners/Scor. Pos. | 7 | 2 | 0 | 0 | 1 | 5 | 0 | 2 | .286 | .714 | .286 |

| RUNS BATTED IN | From 1B | From 2B | From 3B | Scoring Position |
|---|---|---|---|---|
| Totals | 5/81 | 7/47 | 9/24 | 16/71 |
| Percentage | 6% | 15% | 38% | 23% |
| Driving In Runners from 3B with Less than Two Out: | | | 8/13 | 62% |

Loves to face: Gene Nelson (.438, 7-for-16)
Hates to face: Mike Moore (.053, 1-for-19, 8 SO)
One of two visiting players to hit three home runs at Cleveland Stadium last season. Hit three home runs in 13 at-bats there, and another three in 226 at-bats elsewhere. . . . Five hits in 11 at-bats as a pinch hitter. Had gone 7-for-46 prior to 1989. . . . Caught Rawley and Viola for over 90 percent of their innings last season, while catching only two-thirds of an inning, total, for Anderson. . . . Has hit for a higher average against ground-ballers than against fly-ballers in each of the last six seasons. . . . Batted seven times with the bases loaded last season, driving in only two of 21 base runners while going 0-for-6. Career average is .094 (3-for-32) with two outs and bases loaded.

## Rick Leach

Bats Left

| Texas Rangers | AB | H | 2B | 3B | HR | RBI | BB | SO | BA | SA | OBA |
|---|---|---|---|---|---|---|---|---|---|---|---|
| Season | 239 | 65 | 14 | 1 | 1 | 23 | 32 | 33 | .272 | .351 | .358 |
| vs. Left-Handers | 7 | 1 | 0 | 0 | 0 | 0 | 1 | 3 | .143 | .143 | .250 |
| vs. Right-Handers | 232 | 64 | 14 | 1 | 1 | 23 | 31 | 30 | .276 | .358 | .361 |
| Home | 117 | 25 | 6 | 1 | 0 | 8 | 16 | 19 | .214 | .282 | .304 |
| Road | 122 | 40 | 8 | 0 | 1 | 15 | 16 | 14 | .328 | .418 | .410 |
| Grass | 204 | 49 | 11 | 1 | 0 | 21 | 28 | 28 | .240 | .304 | .329 |
| Artificial Turf | 35 | 16 | 3 | 0 | 1 | 2 | 4 | 5 | .457 | .629 | .525 |
| April | 29 | 9 | 3 | 0 | 0 | 5 | 1 | 7 | .310 | .414 | .333 |
| May | 37 | 12 | 2 | 1 | 1 | 6 | 5 | 5 | .324 | .514 | .405 |
| June | 67 | 16 | 2 | 0 | 0 | 9 | 10 | 11 | .239 | .269 | .329 |
| July | 40 | 13 | 4 | 0 | 0 | 1 | 6 | 5 | .325 | .425 | .413 |
| August | 36 | 8 | 3 | 0 | 0 | 1 | 4 | 4 | .222 | .306 | .317 |
| Sept./Oct. | 30 | 7 | 0 | 0 | 0 | 1 | 6 | 1 | .233 | .233 | .361 |
| Leading Off Inn. | 56 | 21 | 7 | 0 | 0 | 0 | 6 | 2 | .375 | .500 | .435 |
| Runners On | 101 | 22 | 2 | 0 | 0 | 22 | 22 | 13 | .218 | .238 | .357 |
| Runners/Scor. Pos. | 68 | 13 | 1 | 0 | 0 | 21 | 17 | 11 | .191 | .206 | .352 |
| Runners On/2 Out | 48 | 8 | 0 | 0 | 0 | 8 | 13 | 10 | .167 | .167 | .344 |
| Scor. Pos./2 Out | 38 | 6 | 0 | 0 | 0 | 8 | 11 | 10 | .158 | .158 | .347 |
| Late Inning Pressure | 42 | 11 | 3 | 0 | 0 | 6 | 6 | 11 | .262 | .333 | .347 |
| Leading Off | 12 | 4 | 1 | 0 | 0 | 0 | 2 | 0 | .333 | .417 | .429 |
| Runners On | 13 | 4 | 1 | 0 | 0 | 6 | 4 | 3 | .308 | .385 | .444 |
| Runners/Scor. Pos. | 10 | 3 | 0 | 0 | 0 | 5 | 3 | 3 | .300 | .300 | .429 |

| RUNS BATTED IN | From 1B | From 2B | From 3B | Scoring Position |
|---|---|---|---|---|
| Totals | 1/70 | 5/53 | 16/31 | 21/84 |
| Percentage | 1% | 9% | 52% | 25% |
| Driving In Runners from 3B with Less than Two Out: | | | 12/13 | 92% |

Loves to face: Bill Swift (.615, 8-for-13)
Hates to face: Kirk McCaskill (.059, 1-for-17)
Batted .310 vs. fly-ball pitchers, .230 vs. ground-ballers. . . . Batted over .340 with runners in scoring position in each of three previous seasons. . . . Started 66 games, all against right-handers. Started only one game against a left-hander in 1988. . . . Only 104 plate appearances against left-handers over nine seasons in majors. Career BA: .196 (0 HR) vs. southpaws, .269 (16 HR) vs. right-handers. . . . Percentage of runners driven in from third base with less than two outs was highest in majors. . . . Addition by subtraction? Spent three years with Tigers, who won everything the year after his release. Then spent five seasons in Toronto, which won division last season, after Leach signed with Rangers.

## Manny Lee

Bats Left and Right

| Toronto Blue Jays | AB | H | 2B | 3B | HR | RBI | BB | SO | BA | SA | OBA |
|---|---|---|---|---|---|---|---|---|---|---|---|
| Season | 300 | 78 | 9 | 2 | 3 | 34 | 20 | 60 | .260 | .333 | .305 |
| vs. Left-Handers | 139 | 41 | 4 | 2 | 1 | 20 | 11 | 25 | .295 | .374 | .344 |
| vs. Right-Handers | 161 | 37 | 5 | 0 | 2 | 14 | 9 | 35 | .230 | .298 | .271 |
| Home | 126 | 30 | 4 | 1 | 1 | 13 | 9 | 23 | .238 | .310 | .289 |
| Road | 174 | 48 | 5 | 1 | 2 | 21 | 11 | 37 | .276 | .351 | .317 |
| Grass | 140 | 44 | 5 | 1 | 2 | 19 | 9 | 31 | .314 | .407 | .353 |
| Artificial Turf | 160 | 34 | 4 | 1 | 1 | 15 | 11 | 29 | .213 | .269 | .263 |
| April | 80 | 19 | 3 | 0 | 0 | 8 | 6 | 15 | .238 | .275 | .291 |
| May | 0 | 0 | 0 | 0 | 0 | 0 | 0 | 0 | — | — | — |
| June | 71 | 25 | 2 | 1 | 0 | 8 | 1 | 8 | .352 | .408 | .361 |
| July | 55 | 12 | 1 | 0 | 1 | 5 | 3 | 17 | .218 | .291 | .254 |
| August | 47 | 11 | 2 | 1 | 2 | 7 | 4 | 10 | .234 | .447 | .294 |
| Sept./Oct. | 47 | 11 | 1 | 0 | 0 | 6 | 6 | 10 | .234 | .255 | .321 |
| Leading Off Inn. | 79 | 20 | 4 | 1 | 1 | 1 | 3 | 20 | .253 | .367 | .280 |
| Runners On | 135 | 36 | 4 | 1 | 2 | 33 | 12 | 27 | .267 | .356 | .324 |
| Runners/Scor. Pos. | 74 | 21 | 3 | 0 | 1 | 29 | 7 | 17 | .284 | .365 | .341 |
| Runners On/2 Out | 53 | 14 | 1 | 0 | 1 | 12 | 3 | 14 | .264 | .340 | .304 |
| Scor. Pos./2 Out | 33 | 9 | 1 | 0 | 1 | 12 | 2 | 10 | .273 | .394 | .314 |
| Late Inning Pressure | 49 | 10 | 1 | 0 | 0 | 6 | 6 | 11 | .204 | .224 | .291 |
| Leading Off | 16 | 3 | 0 | 0 | 0 | 0 | 1 | 5 | .188 | .188 | .235 |
| Runners On | 23 | 5 | 0 | 0 | 0 | 6 | 4 | 6 | .217 | .217 | .333 |
| Runners/Scor. Pos. | 14 | 4 | 0 | 0 | 0 | 6 | 1 | 4 | .286 | .286 | .333 |

| RUNS BATTED IN | From 1B | From 2B | From 3B | Scoring Position |
|---|---|---|---|---|
| Totals | 5/105 | 10/57 | 16/31 | 26/88 |
| Percentage | 5% | 18% | 52% | 30% |
| Driving In Runners from 3B with Less than Two Out: | | | 12/16 | 75% |

Loves to face: Dave Righetti (.533, 8-for-15)
Hates to face: Bret Saberhagen (.133, 2-for-15, 7 SO)
One hit in 13 at-bats as a pinch hitter. Career totals: 4-for-21. . . . Started 39 games at second base, 21 games at shortstop, and 16 games at third base. His last 27 starts were all at second base. . . . Batted .299 against fly-ball pitchers, .217 vs. ground-ballers, roughly his career figures. . . . Only player in majors to hit at least 100 points higher on grass fields than on artificial turf (minimum: 100 AB on each). . . . Career batting averages are .303 vs. left-handers, .242 vs. right-handers. . . . Solution is simple: Play him only on grass fields, against left-handed fly-ball pitchers. Last season, that combination produced a .390 mark (16-for-41). In all other AB, Lee hit .239.

## Chet Lemon

Bats Right

| Detroit Tigers | AB | H | 2B | 3B | HR | RBI | BB | SO | BA | SA | OBA |
|---|---|---|---|---|---|---|---|---|---|---|---|
| Season | 414 | 98 | 19 | 2 | 7 | 47 | 46 | 71 | .237 | .343 | .323 |
| vs. Left-Handers | 153 | 42 | 8 | 1 | 5 | 26 | 23 | 24 | .275 | .438 | .373 |
| vs. Right-Handers | 261 | 56 | 11 | 1 | 2 | 21 | 23 | 47 | .215 | .287 | .294 |
| Home | 189 | 43 | 10 | 2 | 4 | 23 | 25 | 34 | .228 | .365 | .332 |
| Road | 225 | 55 | 9 | 0 | 3 | 24 | 21 | 37 | .244 | .324 | .316 |
| Grass | 345 | 79 | 13 | 2 | 6 | 38 | 37 | 62 | .229 | .330 | .313 |
| Artificial Turf | 69 | 19 | 6 | 0 | 1 | 9 | 9 | 9 | .275 | .406 | .375 |
| April | 60 | 18 | 2 | 0 | 0 | 4 | 14 | 2 | .300 | .333 | .455 |
| May | 90 | 16 | 3 | 1 | 1 | 9 | 9 | 16 | .178 | .267 | .253 |
| June | 51 | 14 | 5 | 0 | 1 | 11 | 5 | 10 | .275 | .431 | .356 |
| July | 90 | 25 | 3 | 0 | 3 | 9 | 8 | 19 | .278 | .411 | .340 |
| August | 91 | 17 | 6 | 0 | 2 | 10 | 8 | 19 | .187 | .319 | .267 |
| Sept./Oct. | 32 | 8 | 0 | 1 | 0 | 4 | 2 | 5 | .250 | .313 | .294 |
| Leading Off Inn. | 100 | 27 | 4 | 0 | 1 | 1 | 10 | 14 | .270 | .340 | .348 |
| Runners On | 180 | 50 | 10 | 2 | 5 | 45 | 23 | 31 | .278 | .439 | .368 |
| Runners/Scor. Pos. | 104 | 30 | 5 | 2 | 1 | 36 | 13 | 10 | .288 | .404 | .361 |
| Runners On/2 Out | 79 | 21 | 4 | 1 | 3 | 21 | 9 | 15 | .266 | .456 | .356 |
| Scor. Pos./2 Out | 50 | 15 | 2 | 1 | 1 | 16 | 7 | 4 | .300 | .440 | .386 |
| Late Inning Pressure | 78 | 18 | 5 | 0 | 0 | 6 | 7 | 17 | .231 | .295 | .294 |
| Leading Off | 24 | 5 | 0 | 0 | 0 | 0 | 3 | 5 | .208 | .208 | .296 |
| Runners On | 32 | 9 | 3 | 0 | 0 | 6 | 2 | 7 | .281 | .375 | .324 |
| Runners/Scor. Pos. | 16 | 5 | 1 | 0 | 0 | 5 | 1 | 2 | .313 | .375 | .353 |

| RUNS BATTED IN | From 1B | From 2B | From 3B | Scoring Position |
|---|---|---|---|---|
| Totals | 7/135 | 14/82 | 19/47 | 33/129 |
| Percentage | 5% | 17% | 40% | 26% |
| Driving In Runners from 3B with Less than Two Out: | | | 13/25 | 52% |

Loves to face: Matt Young (.529, 9-for-17, 4 HR)
Hates to face: Nolan Ryan (.114, 4-for-35, 17 SO)
Has been hit by 147 pitches, most among active players. . . . Lowest batting average of his 15-year career. . . . Started in every batting order position except the leadoff spot and the ninth slot. . . . Reached base 10 times on infield errors, and led the club with 18 infield hits. . . . Has stolen only four bases in 14 attempts over the last five seasons. But in 1989, he scored from second base on all 11 outfield singles. . . . Has batted .272 or higher against left-handed pitchers in eight of the last nine seasons, while reaching that level only once vs. right-handers during that time. . . . Played third base in his first six games in the field in 1975; has played nothing but the outfield in 14 seasons since.

## Nelson Liriano

Bats Left and Right

| Toronto Blue Jays | AB | H | 2B | 3B | HR | RBI | BB | SO | BA | SA | OBA |
|---|---|---|---|---|---|---|---|---|---|---|---|
| Season | 418 | 110 | 26 | 3 | 5 | 53 | 43 | 51 | .263 | .376 | .331 |
| vs. Left-Handers | 109 | 29 | 9 | 0 | 0 | 16 | 12 | 22 | .266 | .349 | .331 |
| vs. Right-Handers | 309 | 81 | 17 | 3 | 5 | 37 | 31 | 29 | .262 | .385 | .331 |
| Home | 208 | 52 | 13 | 2 | 3 | 28 | 25 | 31 | .250 | .375 | .331 |
| Road | 210 | 58 | 13 | 1 | 2 | 25 | 18 | 20 | .276 | .376 | .332 |
| Grass | 176 | 50 | 10 | 1 | 2 | 23 | 14 | 16 | .284 | .386 | .335 |
| Artificial Turf | 242 | 60 | 16 | 2 | 3 | 30 | 29 | 35 | .248 | .368 | .328 |
| April | 68 | 17 | 3 | 1 | 0 | 7 | 5 | 9 | .250 | .324 | .297 |
| May | 82 | 28 | 7 | 2 | 1 | 11 | 6 | 11 | .341 | .512 | .370 |
| June | 95 | 21 | 4 | 0 | 1 | 9 | 6 | 10 | .221 | .295 | .267 |
| July | 56 | 14 | 5 | 0 | 0 | 6 | 12 | 7 | .250 | .339 | .391 |
| August | 54 | 12 | 2 | 0 | 2 | 8 | 6 | 8 | .222 | .370 | .311 |
| Sept./Oct. | 63 | 18 | 5 | 0 | 1 | 12 | 8 | 6 | .286 | .413 | .366 |
| Leading Off Inn. | 83 | 20 | 6 | 0 | 1 | 1 | 9 | 8 | .241 | .349 | .323 |
| Runners On | 193 | 54 | 10 | 1 | 2 | 50 | 20 | 27 | .280 | .373 | .339 |
| Runners/Scor. Pos. | 121 | 37 | 10 | 1 | 1 | 47 | 13 | 19 | .306 | .430 | .360 |
| Runners On/2 Out | 74 | 23 | 5 | 0 | 1 | 26 | 9 | 13 | .311 | .419 | .386 |
| Scor. Pos./2 Out | 56 | 18 | 5 | 0 | 1 | 25 | 7 | 10 | .321 | .464 | .397 |
| Late Inning Pressure | 77 | 22 | 8 | 1 | 1 | 11 | 8 | 9 | .286 | .455 | .345 |
| Leading Off | 20 | 4 | 2 | 0 | 1 | 1 | 2 | 5 | .200 | .450 | .273 |
| Runners On | 31 | 9 | 1 | 1 | 0 | 10 | 3 | 3 | .290 | .387 | .333 |
| Runners/Scor. Pos. | 18 | 6 | 1 | 1 | 0 | 10 | 3 | 3 | .333 | .500 | .391 |

| RUNS BATTED IN | From 1B | From 2B | From 3B | Scoring Position |
|---|---|---|---|---|
| Totals | 4/138 | 21/97 | 23/50 | 44/147 |
| Percentage | 3% | 22% | 46% | 30% |
| Driving In Runners from 3B with Less than Two Out: | | | 13/26 | 50% |

Loves to face: Jack Morris (.385, 5-for-13, 1 HR)
Hates to face: Dave Righetti (0-for-9)
Led visiting players with a .579 BA at Comiskey Park. . . . Reached base nine times on errors by opposing infielders. . . . Reached base safely (on hits, walks, or being hit by pitches) in 22 of last 23 games. . . . Had hits in eight consecutive at-bats vs. right-handed pitchers. . . . Had seven hits in 14 at-bats with bases loaded, after going 0-for-6 in two previous seasons. . . . Career breakdown: .252 with bases empty, .269 with runners on base, .295 with runners in scoring position. . . . Has driven in only 24 of 49 runners from third base with less than two outs. Among the 222 players with at least as many at-bats as Liriano over the last three seasons (852), only 31 were below the 50 percent mark.

## Jeffrey Leonard

Bats Right

| Seattle Mariners | AB | H | 2B | 3B | HR | RBI | BB | SO | BA | SA | OBA |
|---|---|---|---|---|---|---|---|---|---|---|---|
| Season | 566 | 144 | 20 | 1 | 24 | 93 | 38 | 125 | .254 | .420 | .301 |
| vs. Left-Handers | 157 | 44 | 10 | 0 | 8 | 27 | 10 | 20 | .280 | .497 | .326 |
| vs. Right-Handers | 409 | 100 | 10 | 1 | 16 | 66 | 28 | 105 | .244 | .391 | .292 |
| Home | 258 | 67 | 11 | 0 | 9 | 44 | 17 | 59 | .260 | .407 | .307 |
| Road | 308 | 77 | 9 | 1 | 15 | 49 | 21 | 66 | .250 | .432 | .296 |
| Grass | 236 | 59 | 7 | 1 | 14 | 38 | 16 | 49 | .250 | .466 | .297 |
| Artificial Turf | 330 | 85 | 13 | 0 | 10 | 55 | 22 | 76 | .258 | .388 | .304 |
| April | 90 | 26 | 2 | 0 | 7 | 19 | 9 | 19 | .289 | .544 | .350 |
| May | 92 | 24 | 3 | 0 | 4 | 20 | 8 | 28 | .261 | .424 | .317 |
| June | 100 | 26 | 3 | 0 | 4 | 16 | 6 | 17 | .260 | .410 | .303 |
| July | 94 | 22 | 6 | 0 | 0 | 8 | 4 | 20 | .234 | .298 | .280 |
| August | 98 | 23 | 2 | 0 | 6 | 19 | 4 | 21 | .235 | .439 | .252 |
| Sept./Oct. | 92 | 23 | 4 | 1 | 3 | 11 | 7 | 20 | .250 | .413 | .307 |
| Leading Off Inn. | 132 | 30 | 2 | 0 | 6 | 6 | 10 | 23 | .227 | .379 | .282 |
| Runners On | 289 | 71 | 16 | 0 | 10 | 79 | 20 | 64 | .246 | .405 | .292 |
| Runners/Scor. Pos. | 151 | 36 | 5 | 0 | 7 | 71 | 10 | 40 | .238 | .411 | .270 |
| Runners On/2 Out | 130 | 28 | 4 | 0 | 4 | 27 | 12 | 26 | .215 | .338 | .287 |
| Scor. Pos./2 Out | 71 | 14 | 1 | 0 | 3 | 24 | 6 | 18 | .197 | .338 | .260 |
| Late Inning Pressure | 83 | 17 | 1 | 0 | 5 | 11 | 2 | 28 | .205 | .398 | .230 |
| Leading Off | 24 | 6 | 0 | 0 | 2 | 2 | 2 | 5 | .250 | .500 | .308 |
| Runners On | 32 | 6 | 1 | 0 | 1 | 7 | 0 | 12 | .188 | .313 | .206 |
| Runners/Scor. Pos. | 14 | 4 | 0 | 0 | 1 | 7 | 0 | 2 | .286 | .500 | .267 |

| RUNS BATTED IN | From 1B | From 2B | From 3B | Scoring Position |
|---|---|---|---|---|
| Totals | 13/226 | 12/107 | 44/86 | 56/193 |
| Percentage | 6% | 11% | 51% | 29% |
| Driving In Runners from 3B with Less than Two Out: | | | 32/50 | 64% |

Loves to face: Dave Stewart (.440, 11-for-25, 3 HR)
Hates to face: Jeff Reardon (.111, 2-for-18, 8 SO)
Ranked second to Dave Parker in home runs and RBI as a designated hitter, despite playing 26 games in field. . . . Set career highs in games (150), at-bats, home runs, RBI, and strikeouts. . . . Made 134 of 147 starts from the cleanup spot. . . . Had five hits, including two grand slams, in 13 at-bats with the bases loaded. Tenth player ever to hit at least three grand slams in both A.L. and N.L. . . . Has hit better against left-handers than right-handers in each of the last 10 seasons. . . . Wears same uniform number as Jim Otto, and they have an equal number of sacrifice bunts during Leonard's year and a half in the A.L. (That's O.K., Leonard hasn't been called for holding either.)

## Fred Lynn

Bats Left

| Detroit Tigers | AB | H | 2B | 3B | HR | RBI | BB | SO | BA | SA | OBA |
|---|---|---|---|---|---|---|---|---|---|---|---|
| Season | 353 | 85 | 11 | 1 | 11 | 46 | 47 | 71 | .241 | .371 | .328 |
| vs. Left-Handers | 63 | 11 | 1 | 0 | 0 | 1 | 7 | 16 | .175 | .190 | .257 |
| vs. Right-Handers | 290 | 74 | 10 | 1 | 11 | 45 | 40 | 55 | .255 | .410 | .342 |
| Home | 173 | 37 | 4 | 1 | 9 | 29 | 28 | 36 | .214 | .405 | .324 |
| Road | 180 | 48 | 7 | 0 | 2 | 17 | 19 | 35 | .267 | .339 | .332 |
| Grass | 300 | 70 | 7 | 1 | 11 | 42 | 43 | 58 | .233 | .373 | .327 |
| Artificial Turf | 53 | 15 | 4 | 0 | 0 | 4 | 4 | 13 | .283 | .358 | .333 |
| April | 69 | 12 | 0 | 1 | 0 | 2 | 10 | 12 | .174 | .203 | .275 |
| May | 70 | 17 | 4 | 0 | 1 | 10 | 8 | 12 | .243 | .343 | .325 |
| June | 42 | 14 | 2 | 0 | 3 | 9 | 2 | 9 | .333 | .595 | .364 |
| July | 54 | 11 | 1 | 0 | 1 | 7 | 8 | 8 | .204 | .278 | .306 |
| August | 68 | 13 | 1 | 0 | 3 | 5 | 13 | 21 | .191 | .338 | .321 |
| Sept./Oct. | 50 | 18 | 3 | 0 | 3 | 13 | 6 | 9 | .360 | .600 | .407 |
| Leading Off Inn. | 72 | 18 | 3 | 1 | 3 | 3 | 9 | 13 | .250 | .444 | .341 |
| Runners On | 186 | 48 | 7 | 0 | 3 | 38 | 25 | 36 | .258 | .344 | .338 |
| Runners/Scor. Pos. | 91 | 24 | 3 | 0 | 2 | 33 | 18 | 19 | .264 | .363 | .368 |
| Runners On/2 Out | 88 | 27 | 2 | 0 | 2 | 20 | 9 | 16 | .307 | .398 | .371 |
| Scor. Pos./2 Out | 46 | 14 | 1 | 0 | 2 | 19 | 8 | 9 | .304 | .457 | .407 |
| Late Inning Pressure | 58 | 12 | 2 | 0 | 1 | 2 | 12 | 13 | .207 | .293 | .343 |
| Leading Off | 11 | 2 | 1 | 0 | 0 | 0 | 3 | 3 | .182 | .273 | .357 |
| Runners On | 34 | 6 | 1 | 0 | 0 | 1 | 5 | 6 | .176 | .206 | .282 |
| Runners/Scor. Pos. | 14 | 1 | 0 | 0 | 0 | 0 | 3 | 0 | .071 | .071 | .235 |

| RUNS BATTED IN | From 1B | From 2B | From 3B | Scoring Position |
|---|---|---|---|---|
| Totals | 6/146 | 15/74 | 14/41 | 29/115 |
| Percentage | 4% | 20% | 34% | 25% |
| Driving In Runners from 3B with Less than Two Out: | | | 9/18 | 50% |

Loves to face: Walt Terrell (.474, 9-for-19)
Hates to face: Jose Rijo (0-for-8, 5 SO)
Batting average was as low as .210 as late as August 22. . . . Hitless in 25 consecutive at-bats with runners on base, longest Tigers' streak of the 1980s. . . . Didn't drive in any of 17 runners from scoring position in Late-Inning Pressure Situations. . . . Started 97 games, but only eight vs. left-handed pitchers. . . . Only player to hit better against right-handers than left-handers in each of the last 15 seasons. . . . Batting average in Late-Inning Pressure Situations has been lower than his overall average in all but one of his 15 full seasons in majors. . . . RBI totals, year by year since 1984: 79, 68, 67, 60, 56, 46. Last player with a longer streak of declines: Elston Howard (1963 through 1968).

## Steve Lyons

Bats Left

| Chicago White Sox | AB | H | 2B | 3B | HR | RBI | BB | SO | BA | SA | OBA |
|---|---|---|---|---|---|---|---|---|---|---|---|
| Season | 443 | 117 | 21 | 3 | 2 | 51 | 35 | 68 | .264 | .339 | .317 |
| vs. Left-Handers | 94 | 20 | 2 | 1 | 0 | 10 | 5 | 22 | .213 | .255 | .253 |
| vs. Right-Handers | 349 | 97 | 19 | 2 | 2 | 41 | 30 | 46 | .278 | .361 | .334 |
| Home | 207 | 45 | 6 | 3 | 0 | 16 | 10 | 34 | .217 | .275 | .255 |
| Road | 236 | 72 | 15 | 0 | 2 | 35 | 25 | 34 | .305 | .394 | .370 |
| Grass | 377 | 100 | 17 | 3 | 1 | 41 | 27 | 62 | .265 | .334 | .314 |
| Artificial Turf | 66 | 17 | 4 | 0 | 1 | 10 | 8 | 6 | .258 | .364 | .338 |
| April | 83 | 18 | 2 | 0 | 1 | 8 | 8 | 8 | .217 | .277 | .286 |
| May | 73 | 19 | 4 | 0 | 0 | 8 | 8 | 14 | .260 | .315 | .329 |
| June | 69 | 23 | 4 | 0 | 0 | 4 | 4 | 9 | .333 | .391 | .365 |
| July | 76 | 20 | 5 | 1 | 0 | 7 | 4 | 15 | .263 | .355 | .305 |
| August | 77 | 16 | 3 | 1 | 0 | 10 | 6 | 10 | .208 | .273 | .265 |
| Sept./Oct. | 65 | 21 | 3 | 1 | 1 | 14 | 5 | 12 | .323 | .446 | .371 |
| Leading Off Inn. | 84 | 21 | 2 | 0 | 0 | 0 | 7 | 13 | .250 | .274 | .308 |
| Runners On | 210 | 56 | 7 | 2 | 2 | 51 | 12 | 27 | .267 | .348 | .302 |
| Runners/Scor. Pos. | 125 | 35 | 4 | 0 | 2 | 48 | 8 | 22 | .280 | .360 | .316 |
| Runners On/2 Out | 88 | 19 | 2 | 1 | 1 | 21 | 4 | 16 | .216 | .295 | .250 |
| Scor. Pos./2 Out | 59 | 13 | 2 | 0 | 1 | 20 | 3 | 14 | .220 | .305 | .258 |
| Late Inning Pressure | 77 | 21 | 4 | 0 | 1 | 9 | 5 | 15 | .273 | .364 | .317 |
| Leading Off | 17 | 5 | 0 | 0 | 0 | 0 | 1 | 4 | .294 | .294 | .333 |
| Runners On | 36 | 10 | 2 | 0 | 1 | 9 | 1 | 5 | .278 | .417 | .297 |
| Runners/Scor. Pos. | 23 | 9 | 1 | 0 | 1 | 9 | 1 | 5 | .391 | .565 | .417 |

| RUNS BATTED IN | From 1B | From 2B | From 3B | Scoring Position |
|---|---|---|---|---|
| Totals | 5/140 | 22/99 | 22/53 | 44/152 |
| Percentage | 4% | 22% | 42% | 29% |
| Driving In Runners from 3B with Less than Two Out: | | | 15/26 | 58% |

Loves to face: Jeff Russell (.455, 5-for-11)
Hates to face: Dave Stieb (.045, 1-for-22, 7 SO)
Only A.L. player to start at least five games at five different positions (not including DH). Played every position except pitcher. . . . It was second time in last three years he played every infield position. Last White Sox player to do it: Bill Stein (1976). . . . Last White Sox position player to take the mound: Mike Squires (1984). . . . Batted almost everywhere, as well: Started in every batting-order slot except leadoff and cleanup. . . . There were only 12 pinch-hit sacrifice bunts in A.L. last season; Lyons had three. . . . Grounded into only three DP in 100 opportunities. . . . .Batting average with runners in scoring position has been higher than otherwise in each of his five seasons.

## Fred Manrique

Bats Right

| White Sox/Rangers | AB | H | 2B | 3B | HR | RBI | BB | SO | BA | SA | OBA |
|---|---|---|---|---|---|---|---|---|---|---|---|
| Season | 378 | 111 | 25 | 1 | 4 | 52 | 17 | 63 | .294 | .397 | .326 |
| vs. Left-Handers | 141 | 43 | 9 | 0 | 1 | 21 | 8 | 25 | .305 | .390 | .344 |
| vs. Right-Handers | 237 | 68 | 16 | 1 | 3 | 31 | 9 | 38 | .287 | .401 | .315 |
| Home | 174 | 55 | 13 | 1 | 1 | 23 | 12 | 19 | .316 | .420 | .367 |
| Road | 204 | 56 | 12 | 0 | 3 | 29 | 5 | 44 | .275 | .377 | .289 |
| Grass | 308 | 88 | 19 | 1 | 4 | 40 | 17 | 50 | .286 | .393 | .326 |
| Artificial Turf | 70 | 23 | 6 | 0 | 0 | 12 | 0 | 13 | .329 | .414 | .324 |
| April | 11 | 4 | 1 | 0 | 0 | 2 | 0 | 1 | .364 | .455 | .364 |
| May | 52 | 17 | 5 | 0 | 1 | 12 | 4 | 8 | .327 | .481 | .375 |
| June | 80 | 20 | 4 | 0 | 1 | 12 | 2 | 12 | .250 | .338 | .274 |
| July | 47 | 16 | 3 | 1 | 0 | 4 | 3 | 10 | .340 | .447 | .392 |
| August | 90 | 29 | 7 | 0 | 1 | 7 | 5 | 19 | .322 | .433 | .354 |
| Sept./Oct. | 98 | 25 | 5 | 0 | 1 | 15 | 3 | 13 | .255 | .337 | .277 |
| Leading Off Inn. | 98 | 20 | 5 | 1 | 1 | 1 | 7 | 21 | .204 | .306 | .257 |
| Runners On | 155 | 57 | 15 | 0 | 3 | 51 | 4 | 22 | .368 | .523 | .383 |
| Runners/Scor. Pos. | 86 | 33 | 6 | 0 | 1 | 42 | 3 | 8 | .384 | .488 | .402 |
| Runners On/2 Out | 71 | 26 | 7 | 0 | 2 | 24 | 0 | 13 | .366 | .549 | .366 |
| Scor. Pos./2 Out | 43 | 16 | 2 | 0 | 1 | 18 | 0 | 6 | .372 | .488 | .372 |
| Late Inning Pressure | 54 | 18 | 4 | 0 | 1 | 11 | 5 | 10 | .333 | .463 | .390 |
| Leading Off | 11 | 3 | 0 | 0 | 0 | 0 | 1 | 3 | .273 | .273 | .333 |
| Runners On | 28 | 12 | 3 | 0 | 1 | 11 | 1 | 4 | .429 | .643 | .448 |
| Runners/Scor. Pos. | 14 | 7 | 2 | 0 | 0 | 8 | 1 | 1 | .500 | .643 | .533 |

| RUNS BATTED IN | From 1B | From 2B | From 3B | Scoring Position |
|---|---|---|---|---|
| Totals | 9/116 | 19/69 | 20/35 | 39/104 |
| Percentage | 8% | 28% | 57% | 38% |
| Driving In Runners from 3B with Less than Two Out: | | | 13/19 | 68% |

Loves to face: John Cerutti (.364, 8-for-22, 1 HR)
Hates to face: Jaime Navarro (0-for-7)
Lowest fielding percentage (.952) of any second baseman in majors (minimum: 50 games). . . . White Sox allowed 5.68 runs per nine innings with Manrique at second, 4.77 with Lyons, 3.92 with Fletcher. . . . Not as bad at Texas: 4.14 with Manrique, 4.62 with Franco. . . . Favorable difference of 126 points between batting averages with runners on base and bases empty was largest in A.L. (minimum: 100 AB both ways). . . . Career batting average is .321 with runners in scoring position. . . . Rangers were his fifth team in last six years. . . . Made his major league debut in August 1981 (a day before Kent Hrbek). Played 14 games for Blue Jays, then didn't resurface in majors until September 1984.

## Carlos Martinez

Bats Right

| Chicago White Sox | AB | H | 2B | 3B | HR | RBI | BB | SO | BA | SA | OBA |
|---|---|---|---|---|---|---|---|---|---|---|---|
| Season | 350 | 105 | 22 | 0 | 5 | 32 | 21 | 57 | .300 | .406 | .340 |
| vs. Left-Handers | 132 | 39 | 6 | 0 | 2 | 16 | 4 | 16 | .295 | .386 | .316 |
| vs. Right-Handers | 218 | 66 | 16 | 0 | 3 | 16 | 17 | 41 | .303 | .417 | .354 |
| Home | 171 | 48 | 9 | 0 | 2 | 15 | 12 | 27 | .281 | .368 | .328 |
| Road | 179 | 57 | 13 | 0 | 3 | 17 | 9 | 30 | .318 | .441 | .353 |
| Grass | 282 | 82 | 17 | 0 | 4 | 27 | 18 | 40 | .291 | .394 | .332 |
| Artificial Turf | 68 | 23 | 5 | 0 | 1 | 5 | 3 | 17 | .338 | .456 | .375 |
| April | 7 | 1 | 0 | 0 | 0 | 0 | 0 | 2 | .143 | .143 | .143 |
| May | 58 | 15 | 4 | 0 | 1 | 9 | 1 | 10 | .259 | .379 | .283 |
| June | 36 | 9 | 3 | 0 | 0 | 4 | 5 | 6 | .250 | .333 | .341 |
| July | 51 | 16 | 3 | 0 | 3 | 6 | 4 | 4 | .314 | .549 | .364 |
| August | 107 | 36 | 6 | 0 | 0 | 7 | 6 | 22 | .336 | .393 | .372 |
| Sept./Oct. | 91 | 28 | 6 | 0 | 1 | 6 | 5 | 13 | .308 | .407 | .340 |
| Leading Off Inn. | 74 | 27 | 6 | 0 | 3 | 3 | 2 | 7 | .365 | .568 | .382 |
| Runners On | 169 | 47 | 9 | 0 | 0 | 27 | 11 | 31 | .278 | .331 | .320 |
| Runners/Scor. Pos. | 96 | 22 | 6 | 0 | 0 | 26 | 8 | 19 | .229 | .292 | .286 |
| Runners On/2 Out | 74 | 18 | 2 | 0 | 0 | 8 | 4 | 14 | .243 | .270 | .282 |
| Scor. Pos./2 Out | 46 | 8 | 1 | 0 | 0 | 8 | 3 | 10 | .174 | .196 | .224 |
| Late Inning Pressure | 46 | 13 | 5 | 0 | 0 | 8 | 3 | 7 | .283 | .391 | .340 |
| Leading Off | 8 | 2 | 0 | 0 | 0 | 0 | 0 | 0 | .250 | .250 | .250 |
| Runners On | 25 | 10 | 5 | 0 | 0 | 8 | 1 | 5 | .400 | .600 | .423 |
| Runners/Scor. Pos. | 14 | 5 | 3 | 0 | 0 | 7 | 1 | 2 | .357 | .571 | .400 |

| RUNS BATTED IN | From 1B | From 2B | From 3B | Scoring Position |
|---|---|---|---|---|
| Totals | 2/129 | 10/73 | 15/41 | 25/114 |
| Percentage | 2% | 14% | 37% | 22% |
| Driving In Runners from 3B with Less than Two Out: | | | 10/20 | 50% |

Loves to face: Brian Holman (3-for-3, 1 HR)
Hates to face: Allan Anderson (0-for-8, 3 SO)
Only .300 hitter among A.L. rookies with 200 or more plate appearances. . . . Started 72 games, including all but five of Chicago's 73 games after the All-Star break. . . . Scouting report: Hit 67 percent of his ground outs to the left side, but only 23 percent of his fly outs were hit that way. . . . Grounded into 14 double plays in 87 opportunities, or one for every 6.2 chances (43 percent higher than A.L. rate of one per 8.9 chances). . . . Career batting averages: .204 in day games, .312 at night. . . . Players with comparable rookie seasons: Joe Adcock (1950), Billy Sample (1979), and Ethan Allen (1927). Could develop into a home-run hitter, a broadcaster, or a furniture salesman.

## Don Mattingly

Bats Left

| New York Yankees | AB | H | 2B | 3B | HR | RBI | BB | SO | BA | SA | OBA |
|---|---|---|---|---|---|---|---|---|---|---|---|
| Season | 631 | 191 | 37 | 2 | 23 | 113 | 51 | 30 | .303 | .477 | .351 |
| vs. Left-Handers | 237 | 80 | 20 | 1 | 8 | 52 | 19 | 15 | .338 | .532 | .382 |
| vs. Right-Handers | 394 | 111 | 17 | 1 | 15 | 61 | 32 | 15 | .282 | .444 | .332 |
| Home | 317 | 106 | 20 | 0 | 19 | 72 | 26 | 13 | .334 | .577 | .378 |
| Road | 314 | 85 | 17 | 2 | 4 | 41 | 25 | 17 | .271 | .376 | .323 |
| Grass | 545 | 162 | 29 | 0 | 21 | 99 | 45 | 26 | .297 | .466 | .346 |
| Artificial Turf | 86 | 29 | 8 | 2 | 2 | 14 | 6 | 4 | .337 | .547 | .380 |
| April | 77 | 17 | 5 | 0 | 0 | 6 | 14 | 5 | .221 | .286 | .337 |
| May | 111 | 37 | 6 | 0 | 3 | 21 | 4 | 2 | .333 | .468 | .350 |
| June | 109 | 37 | 5 | 1 | 7 | 23 | 10 | 3 | .339 | .596 | .393 |
| July | 109 | 31 | 8 | 0 | 3 | 18 | 5 | 5 | .284 | .440 | .310 |
| August | 127 | 34 | 10 | 1 | 4 | 23 | 7 | 7 | .268 | .457 | .304 |
| Sept./Oct. | 98 | 35 | 3 | 0 | 6 | 22 | 11 | 8 | .357 | .571 | .414 |
| Leading Off Inn. | 125 | 37 | 7 | 1 | 7 | 7 | 4 | 2 | .296 | .536 | .323 |
| Runners On | 298 | 95 | 18 | 0 | 11 | 101 | 35 | 16 | .319 | .490 | .379 |
| Runners/Scor. Pos. | 172 | 57 | 13 | 0 | 5 | 86 | 28 | 9 | .331 | .494 | .405 |
| Runners On/2 Out | 80 | 24 | 2 | 0 | 4 | 24 | 17 | 1 | .300 | .475 | .423 |
| Scor. Pos./2 Out | 50 | 13 | 1 | 0 | 1 | 18 | 14 | 1 | .260 | .340 | .422 |
| Late Inning Pressure | 80 | 25 | 8 | 0 | 4 | 21 | 9 | 5 | .313 | .563 | .382 |
| Leading Off | 16 | 6 | 1 | 0 | 2 | 2 | 1 | 1 | .375 | .813 | .412 |
| Runners On | 40 | 15 | 5 | 0 | 2 | 19 | 8 | 4 | .375 | .650 | .479 |
| Runners/Scor. Pos. | 22 | 13 | 5 | 0 | 1 | 17 | 7 | 3 | .591 | .955 | .690 |

| RUNS BATTED IN | From 1B | From 2B | From 3B | Scoring Position |
|---|---|---|---|---|
| Totals | 13/201 | 30/115 | 47/93 | 77/208 |
| Percentage | 6% | 26% | 51% | 37% |
| Driving In Runners from 3B with Less than Two Out: | | | 38/62 | 61% |

Loves to face: Bert Blyleven (.405, 15-for-37, 3 HR)
Hates to face: Steve Rosenberg (0-for-11)
First Yankees player to hit .300 in six consecutive seasons since Joe DiMaggio (1936–42). . . . One of four .300 hitters with 20+ home runs and 100+ RBI. Others: Will Clark, Ruben Sierra, Robin Yount. . . . Batted .490 (24-for-55) vs. Angels, highest average and most hits by any A.L. player vs. any club. . . . All 23 of his home runs were hit to right field. . . . Has hit 98 home runs at Yankee Stadium, 66 on the road. . . . Career average of .341 on artificial turf is the highest of any active player (minimum: 150 hits). . . . Career average is .275 in April, with four HR in 480 at-bats; .330, one HR per 22 AB thereafter. In other words, he hits like Peanuts (Lowery, that is) in April, Stan Musial afterwards.

## Fred McGriff

Bats Left

| Toronto Blue Jays | AB | H | 2B | 3B | HR | RBI | BB | SO | BA | SA | OBA |
|---|---|---|---|---|---|---|---|---|---|---|---|
| Season | 551 | 148 | 27 | 3 | 36 | 92 | 119 | 132 | .269 | .525 | .399 |
| vs. Left-Handers | 189 | 48 | 4 | 2 | 5 | 23 | 31 | 50 | .254 | .376 | .360 |
| vs. Right-Handers | 362 | 100 | 23 | 1 | 31 | 69 | 88 | 82 | .276 | .602 | .419 |
| Home | 273 | 77 | 15 | 2 | 18 | 48 | 55 | 58 | .282 | .549 | .406 |
| Road | 278 | 71 | 12 | 1 | 18 | 44 | 64 | 74 | .255 | .500 | .393 |
| Grass | 217 | 50 | 9 | 0 | 12 | 28 | 58 | 60 | .230 | .438 | .389 |
| Artificial Turf | 334 | 98 | 18 | 3 | 24 | 64 | 61 | 72 | .293 | .581 | .406 |
| April | 89 | 28 | 5 | 1 | 7 | 17 | 14 | 23 | .315 | .629 | .413 |
| May | 90 | 25 | 8 | 0 | 4 | 14 | 14 | 20 | .278 | .500 | .377 |
| June | 96 | 24 | 4 | 0 | 6 | 14 | 16 | 22 | .250 | .479 | .354 |
| July | 91 | 24 | 3 | 0 | 10 | 22 | 15 | 27 | .264 | .626 | .373 |
| August | 91 | 26 | 5 | 2 | 8 | 13 | 30 | 20 | .286 | .648 | .463 |
| Sept./Oct. | 94 | 21 | 2 | 0 | 1 | 12 | 30 | 20 | .223 | .277 | .408 |
| Leading Off Inn. | 130 | 38 | 8 | 2 | 9 | 9 | 23 | 28 | .292 | .592 | .403 |
| Runners On | 241 | 62 | 10 | 1 | 15 | 71 | 69 | 60 | .257 | .494 | .420 |
| Runners/Scor. Pos. | 133 | 34 | 6 | 0 | 8 | 54 | 45 | 39 | .256 | .481 | .435 |
| Runners On/2 Out | 105 | 21 | 4 | 0 | 6 | 23 | 31 | 29 | .200 | .410 | .382 |
| Scor. Pos./2 Out | 61 | 12 | 2 | 0 | 4 | 18 | 20 | 18 | .197 | .426 | .395 |
| Late Inning Pressure | 85 | 25 | 5 | 0 | 4 | 13 | 15 | 22 | .294 | .494 | .406 |
| Leading Off | 26 | 8 | 2 | 0 | 1 | 1 | 2 | 5 | .308 | .500 | .379 |
| Runners On | 27 | 8 | 3 | 0 | 2 | 11 | 10 | 5 | .296 | .630 | .486 |
| Runners/Scor. Pos. | 18 | 6 | 2 | 0 | 1 | 8 | 6 | 5 | .333 | .611 | .500 |

| RUNS BATTED IN | From 1B | From 2B | From 3B | Scoring Position |
|---|---|---|---|---|
| Totals | 12/161 | 22/97 | 22/59 | 44/156 |
| Percentage | 7% | 23% | 37% | 28% |
| Driving In Runners from 3B with Less than Two Out: | | | 17/30 | 57% |

Loves to face: Mark Gubicza (.474, 9-for-19, 4 HR)
Hates to face: Mike Henneman (0-for-13)
Lowest home-run total to lead A.L. in a full season since Graig Nettles in 1976 (32). . . . Hit as many home runs to center and left fields as he hit to right (18). . . . Had more walks (53) than hits (44) in 54 games from the cleanup spot. . . . Drove in 20 runs against Mariners, the most of any A.L. player vs. any club. . . . Led A.L. first basemen in fielding percentage in 1988, ranked last in '89. . . . Career breakdown: .283 with bases empty, .229 with runners in scoring position, .191 with two outs and RISP. . . . Ranks second to Eric Davis in career slugging average among active players (minimum: 1000 AB). Margin is so narrow that if Davis makes an out in first at-bat of season, McGriff takes the lead.

## Mark McGwire

Bats Right

| Oakland As | AB | H | 2B | 3B | HR | RBI | BB | SO | BA | SA | OBA |
|---|---|---|---|---|---|---|---|---|---|---|---|
| Season | 490 | 113 | 17 | 0 | 33 | 96 | 83 | 94 | .231 | .467 | .339 |
| vs. Left-Handers | 132 | 31 | 9 | 0 | 6 | 25 | 24 | 22 | .235 | .439 | .344 |
| vs. Right-Handers | 358 | 82 | 8 | 0 | 27 | 71 | 59 | 72 | .229 | .478 | .337 |
| Home | 246 | 57 | 12 | 0 | 12 | 46 | 35 | 48 | .232 | .427 | .321 |
| Road | 244 | 56 | 5 | 0 | 21 | 50 | 48 | 46 | .230 | .508 | .357 |
| Grass | 414 | 99 | 15 | 0 | 27 | 81 | 66 | 86 | .239 | .471 | .339 |
| Artificial Turf | 76 | 14 | 2 | 0 | 6 | 15 | 17 | 8 | .184 | .447 | .340 |
| April | 44 | 13 | 2 | 0 | 5 | 13 | 3 | 8 | .295 | .682 | .333 |
| May | 96 | 21 | 3 | 0 | 5 | 16 | 11 | 9 | .219 | .406 | .294 |
| June | 89 | 22 | 4 | 0 | 5 | 19 | 18 | 25 | .247 | .461 | .366 |
| July | 90 | 22 | 2 | 0 | 4 | 18 | 12 | 9 | .244 | .400 | .333 |
| August | 79 | 13 | 1 | 0 | 5 | 11 | 25 | 20 | .165 | .367 | .371 |
| Sept./Oct. | 92 | 22 | 5 | 0 | 9 | 19 | 14 | 23 | .239 | .587 | .333 |
| Leading Off Inn. | 108 | 24 | 6 | 0 | 4 | 4 | 22 | 14 | .222 | .389 | .359 |
| Runners On | 224 | 59 | 10 | 0 | 16 | 79 | 34 | 44 | .263 | .522 | .346 |
| Runners/Scor. Pos. | 119 | 32 | 4 | 0 | 9 | 64 | 25 | 30 | .269 | .529 | .368 |
| Runners On/2 Out | 90 | 22 | 3 | 0 | 6 | 27 | 17 | 23 | .244 | .478 | .364 |
| Scor. Pos./2 Out | 47 | 11 | 1 | 0 | 3 | 20 | 13 | 14 | .234 | .447 | .400 |
| Late Inning Pressure | 64 | 15 | 1 | 0 | 2 | 13 | 6 | 16 | .234 | .344 | .296 |
| Leading Off | 15 | 3 | 0 | 0 | 1 | 1 | 2 | 4 | .200 | .400 | .294 |
| Runners On | 25 | 10 | 1 | 0 | 1 | 12 | 0 | 4 | .400 | .560 | .385 |
| Runners/Scor. Pos. | 17 | 8 | 0 | 0 | 1 | 12 | 0 | 3 | .471 | .647 | .444 |

| RUNS BATTED IN | From 1B | From 2B | From 3B | Scoring Position |
|---|---|---|---|---|
| Totals | 15/176 | 18/90 | 30/56 | 48/146 |
| Percentage | 9% | 20% | 54% | 33% |
| Driving In Runners from 3B with Less than Two Out: | | | 25/43 | 58% |

Loves to face: Mike Boddicker (.333, 7-for-21, 4 HR)
Hates to face: Roger Clemens (0-for-16, 9 SO)
Two years removed from rookie superstardom, has hit 117 home runs, most ever at that stage. Eight others reached the 100 mark within two years of their rookie seasons: Kiner (114), Mathews (112), Canseco (111), DiMaggio (107), Trosky (104), Cash (102), Gentile (101), and Reggie (100). . . . Career average of one HR per 17 AB at home ranks 8th among active players. No one is close to his road-game mark: one per 12.0 AB. . . . Was 7-for-12 with runners in scoring position and A's trailing by a run last season. . . . Batted only .185 (one HR in 54 AB) vs. A.L.'s top 10 strikeout pitchers. . . . Batted .147 (16-for-109) on fair balls hit to the opposite field. But don't let him pull it: .354 (68-for-192).

## Bob Melvin

Bats Right

| Baltimore Orioles | AB | H | 2B | 3B | HR | RBI | BB | SO | BA | SA | OBA |
|---|---|---|---|---|---|---|---|---|---|---|---|
| Season | 278 | 67 | 10 | 1 | 1 | 32 | 15 | 53 | .241 | .295 | .279 |
| vs. Left-Handers | 151 | 46 | 9 | 1 | 1 | 20 | 9 | 21 | .305 | .397 | .344 |
| vs. Right-Handers | 127 | 21 | 1 | 0 | 0 | 12 | 6 | 32 | .165 | .173 | .201 |
| Home | 154 | 36 | 2 | 0 | 0 | 17 | 10 | 34 | .234 | .247 | .279 |
| Road | 124 | 31 | 8 | 1 | 1 | 15 | 5 | 19 | .250 | .355 | .279 |
| Grass | 249 | 54 | 5 | 1 | 1 | 28 | 14 | 51 | .217 | .257 | .258 |
| Artificial Turf | 29 | 13 | 5 | 0 | 0 | 4 | 1 | 2 | .448 | .621 | .467 |
| April | 29 | 10 | 2 | 0 | 0 | 2 | 2 | 7 | .345 | .414 | .387 |
| May | 32 | 7 | 0 | 0 | 0 | 2 | 2 | 3 | .219 | .219 | .265 |
| June | 57 | 15 | 2 | 0 | 0 | 9 | 1 | 10 | .263 | .298 | .276 |
| July | 33 | 8 | 2 | 0 | 0 | 7 | 1 | 5 | .242 | .303 | .265 |
| August | 72 | 18 | 2 | 1 | 1 | 9 | 6 | 14 | .250 | .347 | .304 |
| Sept./Oct. | 55 | 9 | 2 | 0 | 0 | 3 | 3 | 14 | .164 | .200 | .207 |
| Leading Off Inn. | 67 | 14 | 3 | 0 | 0 | 0 | 3 | 9 | .209 | .254 | .243 |
| Runners On | 122 | 38 | 6 | 1 | 1 | 32 | 6 | 20 | .311 | .402 | .341 |
| Runners/Scor. Pos. | 75 | 22 | 4 | 1 | 1 | 31 | 5 | 13 | .293 | .413 | .333 |
| Runners On/2 Out | 61 | 19 | 3 | 1 | 0 | 20 | 2 | 17 | .311 | .393 | .333 |
| Scor. Pos./2 Out | 39 | 13 | 3 | 1 | 0 | 20 | 2 | 10 | .333 | .462 | .366 |
| Late Inning Pressure | 32 | 6 | 0 | 0 | 0 | 3 | 4 | 6 | .188 | .188 | .278 |
| Leading Off | 9 | 3 | 0 | 0 | 0 | 0 | 2 | 0 | .333 | .333 | .455 |
| Runners On | 14 | 2 | 0 | 0 | 0 | 3 | 0 | 3 | .143 | .143 | .143 |
| Runners/Scor. Pos. | 8 | 2 | 0 | 0 | 0 | 3 | 0 | 2 | .250 | .250 | .250 |

| RUNS BATTED IN | From 1B | From 2B | From 3B | Scoring Position |
|---|---|---|---|---|
| Totals | 4/93 | 11/56 | 16/41 | 27/97 |
| Percentage | 4% | 20% | 39% | 28% |
| Driving In Runners from 3B with Less than Two Out: | | | 8/22 | 36% |

Loves to face: Jimmy Key (.500, 4-for-8)
Hates to face: Chuck Finley (0-for-7, 6 SO)
Prior to 1989, his career average was one home run per 33 at-bats. . . . O's staff had a 3.74 ERA with Melvin catching, 4.25 with Tettleton. . . . Opponents' stolen-base rate was virtually the same: 56-for-78 vs. Tettleton (72%), 50-for-70 vs. Melvin (71%). . . . Failed to drive in a runner from third base with less than two outs in eight consecutive opportunities. . . . Career average of .184 vs. right-handed pitchers is the lowest of any active player (minimum: 600 AB). His career mark against southpaws is .283. . . . He's Mr. Turnaround. Giants improved from 62–100 in 1985 to 83–79 in 1986, Melvin's first year with them. Last season, his first with Orioles, Baltimore improved by 32.5 games.

## Randy Milligan

Bats Right

| Baltimore Orioles | AB | H | 2B | 3B | HR | RBI | BB | SO | BA | SA | OBA |
|---|---|---|---|---|---|---|---|---|---|---|---|
| Season | 365 | 98 | 23 | 5 | 12 | 45 | 74 | 75 | .268 | .458 | .394 |
| vs. Left-Handers | 169 | 38 | 9 | 1 | 6 | 22 | 33 | 28 | .225 | .396 | .351 |
| vs. Right-Handers | 196 | 60 | 14 | 4 | 6 | 23 | 41 | 47 | .306 | .510 | .430 |
| Home | 178 | 51 | 9 | 2 | 6 | 19 | 50 | 27 | .287 | .461 | .446 |
| Road | 187 | 47 | 14 | 3 | 6 | 26 | 24 | 48 | .251 | .455 | .338 |
| Grass | 316 | 87 | 20 | 4 | 10 | 37 | 70 | 65 | .275 | .459 | .409 |
| Artificial Turf | 49 | 11 | 3 | 1 | 2 | 8 | 4 | 10 | .224 | .449 | .283 |
| April | 38 | 8 | 3 | 0 | 1 | 5 | 6 | 11 | .211 | .368 | .318 |
| May | 60 | 17 | 6 | 2 | 1 | 5 | 13 | 14 | .283 | .500 | .419 |
| June | 45 | 16 | 3 | 0 | 3 | 10 | 16 | 4 | .356 | .622 | .532 |
| July | 62 | 15 | 1 | 1 | 4 | 8 | 14 | 16 | .242 | .484 | .390 |
| August | 75 | 18 | 4 | 1 | 1 | 8 | 15 | 16 | .240 | .360 | .363 |
| Sept./Oct. | 85 | 24 | 6 | 1 | 2 | 9 | 10 | 14 | .282 | .447 | .354 |
| Leading Off Inn. | 70 | 23 | 7 | 1 | 1 | 1 | 13 | 14 | .329 | .500 | .434 |
| Runners On | 162 | 45 | 11 | 1 | 6 | 39 | 33 | 30 | .278 | .469 | .405 |
| Runners/Scor. Pos. | 89 | 24 | 4 | 0 | 5 | 36 | 22 | 16 | .270 | .483 | .417 |
| Runners On/2 Out | 53 | 16 | 2 | 0 | 3 | 17 | 17 | 9 | .302 | .509 | .471 |
| Scor. Pos./2 Out | 32 | 11 | 1 | 0 | 2 | 15 | 11 | 6 | .344 | .563 | .512 |
| Late Inning Pressure | 46 | 16 | 2 | 0 | 2 | 8 | 10 | 13 | .348 | .522 | .464 |
| Leading Off | 9 | 3 | 0 | 0 | 0 | 0 | 0 | 2 | .333 | .333 | .333 |
| Runners On | 23 | 11 | 2 | 0 | 2 | 8 | 6 | 3 | .478 | .826 | .586 |
| Runners/Scor. Pos. | 6 | 3 | 0 | 0 | 1 | 6 | 5 | 0 | .500 | 1.000 | .727 |

| RUNS BATTED IN | From 1B | From 2B | From 3B | Scoring Position |
|---|---|---|---|---|
| Totals | 7/121 | 13/75 | 13/30 | 26/105 |
| Percentage | 6% | 17% | 43% | 25% |
| Driving In Runners from 3B with Less than Two Out: | | | 7/16 | 44% |

Loves to face: Rob Murphy (3-for-3, 1 HR, 3 BB)
Hates to face: Allan Anderson (0-for-8)
A right-handed hitter who's treated like a right-handed hitter, despite left-handed tendencies. . . . Started all 60 of Baltimore's games vs. left-handers, only 47 of 102 vs. right-handers. . . . Batted .385 when he took right-handers to the opposite field, only .191 going the other way against southpaws. . . . Career batting averages: .217 vs. left-handers, .302 vs. right-handers. . . . Scored from second base on 11 of 12 outfield singles. . . . Career on-base average is .434 leading off innings. . . . Has driven in only 8 of 20 runners from third base with less than two outs (40%). Among the 288 players with 400+ at-bats over the last two seasons, only eight had averages as low as Milligan's.

## Paul Molitor

Bats Right

| Milwaukee Brewers | AB | H | 2B | 3B | HR | RBI | BB | SO | BA | SA | OBA |
|---|---|---|---|---|---|---|---|---|---|---|---|
| Season | 615 | 194 | 35 | 4 | 11 | 56 | 64 | 67 | .315 | .439 | .379 |
| vs. Left-Handers | 157 | 51 | 9 | 2 | 4 | 13 | 25 | 13 | .325 | .484 | .413 |
| vs. Right-Handers | 458 | 143 | 26 | 2 | 7 | 43 | 39 | 54 | .312 | .424 | .366 |
| Home | 296 | 97 | 17 | 1 | 6 | 28 | 37 | 33 | .328 | .453 | .399 |
| Road | 319 | 97 | 18 | 3 | 5 | 28 | 27 | 34 | .304 | .426 | .359 |
| Grass | 513 | 159 | 28 | 3 | 10 | 43 | 54 | 54 | .310 | .435 | .377 |
| Artificial Turf | 102 | 35 | 7 | 1 | 1 | 13 | 10 | 13 | .343 | .461 | .388 |
| April | 60 | 20 | 1 | 0 | 4 | 7 | 6 | 6 | .333 | .550 | .412 |
| May | 112 | 33 | 10 | 0 | 1 | 10 | 10 | 14 | .295 | .411 | .341 |
| June | 115 | 35 | 5 | 3 | 0 | 8 | 16 | 15 | .304 | .400 | .388 |
| July | 101 | 29 | 2 | 1 | 2 | 8 | 15 | 12 | .287 | .386 | .376 |
| August | 120 | 28 | 4 | 0 | 2 | 5 | 12 | 13 | .233 | .317 | .308 |
| Sept./Oct. | 107 | 49 | 13 | 0 | 2 | 18 | 5 | 7 | .458 | .636 | .474 |
| Leading Off Inn. | 232 | 71 | 13 | 3 | 5 | 5 | 16 | 27 | .306 | .453 | .353 |
| Runners On | 199 | 67 | 11 | 0 | 2 | 47 | 24 | 20 | .337 | .422 | .397 |
| Runners/Scor. Pos. | 118 | 39 | 7 | 0 | 2 | 46 | 16 | 13 | .331 | .441 | .393 |
| Runners On/2 Out | 75 | 22 | 3 | 0 | 2 | 16 | 16 | 12 | .293 | .413 | .418 |
| Scor. Pos./2 Out | 54 | 16 | 2 | 0 | 2 | 16 | 10 | 9 | .296 | .444 | .406 |
| Late Inning Pressure | 58 | 17 | 3 | 0 | 1 | 3 | 9 | 6 | .293 | .397 | .388 |
| Leading Off | 13 | 4 | 0 | 0 | 1 | 1 | 1 | 2 | .308 | .538 | .357 |
| Runners On | 27 | 7 | 1 | 0 | 0 | 2 | 5 | 2 | .259 | .296 | .375 |
| Runners/Scor. Pos. | 14 | 3 | 0 | 0 | 0 | 2 | 5 | 0 | .214 | .214 | .421 |

| RUNS BATTED IN | From 1B | From 2B | From 3B | Scoring Position |
|---|---|---|---|---|
| Totals | 1/129 | 24/103 | 20/38 | 44/141 |
| Percentage | 1% | 23% | 53% | 31% |
| Driving In Runners from 3B with Less than Two Out: | | | 17/23 | 74% |

Loves to face: Frank Tanana (.414, 24-for-58, 1 HR)
Hates to face: Mike Moore (.118, 4-for-34, 0 XBH)
Led A.L. with a .354 BA as a designated hitter. Over last four seasons, he's hit .333 as a DH, .309 in other games. . . . Has hit better with runners on base than otherwise in each of last six seasons. During that time: .334 and .293, respectively. . . . Second A.L. player since George Sisler to hit .310 or better and steal 25 or more bases in three consecutive seasons. The other: Rod Carew (1973–76). Record streak: 12, Ty Cobb. . . . Raised career average to .3004, to became one of seven .300-hitters in this century with 100+ home runs and 300+ steals. The other six are Hall of Famers: Ty Cobb, Willie Mays, Tris Speaker, Sisler, Kiki Cuyler, and Frankie Frisch. Tim Raines needs 13 HR to join them.

## Keith Moreland

Bats Right

| Tigers/Orioles | AB | H | 2B | 3B | HR | RBI | BB | SO | BA | SA | OBA |
|---|---|---|---|---|---|---|---|---|---|---|---|
| Season | 425 | 118 | 20 | 0 | 6 | 45 | 31 | 45 | .278 | .367 | .330 |
| vs. Left-Handers | 177 | 51 | 9 | 0 | 2 | 22 | 12 | 17 | .288 | .373 | .333 |
| vs. Right-Handers | 248 | 67 | 11 | 0 | 4 | 23 | 19 | 28 | .270 | .363 | .327 |
| Home | 214 | 56 | 9 | 0 | 2 | 19 | 12 | 22 | .262 | .332 | .304 |
| Road | 211 | 62 | 11 | 0 | 4 | 26 | 19 | 23 | .294 | .403 | .355 |
| Grass | 372 | 104 | 18 | 0 | 6 | 42 | 27 | 38 | .280 | .376 | .330 |
| Artificial Turf | 53 | 14 | 2 | 0 | 0 | 3 | 4 | 7 | .264 | .302 | .328 |
| April | 44 | 12 | 1 | 0 | 0 | 2 | 2 | 0 | .273 | .295 | .304 |
| May | 82 | 31 | 8 | 0 | 3 | 21 | 8 | 9 | .378 | .585 | .433 |
| June | 98 | 25 | 3 | 0 | 2 | 8 | 11 | 11 | .255 | .347 | .342 |
| July | 102 | 28 | 4 | 0 | 1 | 6 | 7 | 14 | .275 | .343 | .321 |
| August | 79 | 20 | 4 | 0 | 0 | 6 | 2 | 9 | .253 | .304 | .272 |
| Sept./Oct. | 20 | 2 | 0 | 0 | 0 | 2 | 1 | 2 | .100 | .100 | .143 |
| Leading Off Inn. | 102 | 30 | 5 | 0 | 0 | 0 | 6 | 11 | .294 | .343 | .333 |
| Runners On | 181 | 47 | 13 | 0 | 4 | 43 | 17 | 18 | .260 | .398 | .330 |
| Runners/Scor. Pos. | 112 | 23 | 5 | 0 | 2 | 34 | 12 | 12 | .205 | .304 | .288 |
| Runners On/2 Out | 77 | 23 | 8 | 0 | 1 | 21 | 8 | 8 | .299 | .442 | .365 |
| Scor. Pos./2 Out | 50 | 11 | 3 | 0 | 0 | 14 | 6 | 6 | .220 | .280 | .304 |
| Late Inning Pressure | 68 | 13 | 3 | 0 | 0 | 3 | 6 | 12 | .191 | .235 | .267 |
| Leading Off | 24 | 4 | 1 | 0 | 0 | 0 | 1 | 3 | .167 | .208 | .200 |
| Runners On | 22 | 5 | 2 | 0 | 0 | 3 | 3 | 6 | .227 | .318 | .346 |
| Runners/Scor. Pos. | 12 | 2 | 1 | 0 | 0 | 3 | 3 | 4 | .167 | .250 | .333 |

| RUNS BATTED IN | From 1B | From 2B | From 3B | Scoring Position |
|---|---|---|---|---|
| Totals | 10/136 | 14/90 | 15/38 | 29/128 |
| Percentage | 7% | 16% | 39% | 23% |
| Driving In Runners from 3B with Less than Two Out: | | | 10/22 | 45% |

Loves to face: Kevin Gross (.380, 19-for-50, 5 HR)
Hates to face: Mike Krukow (.111, 5-for-45)
Played first base (31 games), third base (20), and catcher (1) for Detroit, but didn't play the field in 33 games for Baltimore. . . . Batted .299 in 90 games with the Tigers, but only .215 in 33 games with the Orioles. . . . Batted 98 points lower with runners in scoring position than in other at-bats, the largest margin in the A.L. (minimum: 75 RISP AB). . . . Advanced from first to third on only five of 21 outfield singles. . . . Career average is .300 vs. left-handed pitchers, .271 vs. right-handers. . . . Hasn't had a triple in 1137 at-bats since July 29, 1987. . . . Statistical profile suggests that, if he could field, he'd be Frank Malzone, 25 years later. As it is, he's only Hector Lopez.

## Lloyd Moseby

Bats Left

| Toronto Blue Jays | AB | H | 2B | 3B | HR | RBI | BB | SO | BA | SA | OBA |
|---|---|---|---|---|---|---|---|---|---|---|---|
| Season | 502 | 111 | 25 | 3 | 11 | 45 | 56 | 101 | .221 | .349 | .306 |
| vs. Left-Handers | 138 | 27 | 4 | 0 | 2 | 11 | 17 | 34 | .196 | .268 | .297 |
| vs. Right-Handers | 364 | 84 | 21 | 3 | 9 | 34 | 39 | 67 | .231 | .379 | .310 |
| Home | 222 | 40 | 11 | 1 | 4 | 15 | 32 | 37 | .180 | .293 | .293 |
| Road | 280 | 71 | 14 | 2 | 7 | 30 | 24 | 64 | .254 | .393 | .317 |
| Grass | 216 | 56 | 11 | 1 | 6 | 23 | 20 | 47 | .259 | .403 | .325 |
| Artificial Turf | 286 | 55 | 14 | 2 | 5 | 22 | 36 | 54 | .192 | .308 | .293 |
| April | 89 | 19 | 2 | 1 | 2 | 6 | 15 | 21 | .213 | .326 | .330 |
| May | 86 | 18 | 3 | 0 | 3 | 10 | 6 | 16 | .209 | .349 | .269 |
| June | 58 | 10 | 1 | 0 | 1 | 4 | 7 | 9 | .172 | .241 | .273 |
| July | 80 | 21 | 6 | 2 | 2 | 10 | 7 | 19 | .263 | .463 | .322 |
| August | 93 | 18 | 6 | 0 | 2 | 8 | 6 | 20 | .194 | .323 | .265 |
| Sept./Oct. | 96 | 25 | 7 | 0 | 1 | 7 | 15 | 16 | .260 | .365 | .360 |
| Leading Off Inn. | 159 | 33 | 7 | 1 | 3 | 3 | 16 | 32 | .208 | .321 | .284 |
| Runners On | 198 | 48 | 8 | 0 | 5 | 39 | 25 | 38 | .242 | .359 | .338 |
| Runners/Scor. Pos. | 114 | 27 | 4 | 0 | 2 | 31 | 16 | 29 | .237 | .325 | .343 |
| Runners On/2 Out | 90 | 23 | 4 | 0 | 0 | 16 | 7 | 16 | .256 | .300 | .330 |
| Scor. Pos./2 Out | 57 | 15 | 3 | 0 | 0 | 15 | 5 | 11 | .263 | .316 | .344 |
| Late Inning Pressure | 75 | 20 | 8 | 1 | 1 | 8 | 9 | 14 | .267 | .440 | .353 |
| Leading Off | 12 | 2 | 1 | 0 | 0 | 0 | 3 | 1 | .167 | .250 | .333 |
| Runners On | 36 | 8 | 3 | 0 | 0 | 7 | 4 | 10 | .222 | .306 | .317 |
| Runners/Scor. Pos. | 24 | 5 | 2 | 0 | 0 | 6 | 3 | 8 | .208 | .292 | .321 |

| RUNS BATTED IN | From 1B | From 2B | From 3B | Scoring Position |
|---|---|---|---|---|
| Totals | 6/143 | 12/85 | 16/48 | 28/133 |
| Percentage | 4% | 14% | 33% | 21% |
| Driving In Runners from 3B with Less than Two Out: | | | 8/24 | 33% |

Loves to face: Mike Smithson (.359, 14-for-39, 6 HR)
Hates to face: Tim Leary (.143, 2-for-14)
Lowest home-game batting average in A.L. (minimum: 2 PA per game). . . . Overall batting average was a career low. . . . Hitless in 27 consecutive at-bats, longest streak in A.L. Eleven N.L. players, including only four pitchers, had longer streaks. . . . Drove in less than 20 percent of runners from scoring position in 1988 as well, after two consecutive seasons above the 30 percent mark. . . . Stole 14 bases in 14 attempts at home; 10-for-17 on road. . . . Has played 1349 games in field, all as an outfielder, all with Toronto. . . . One of six players with 100+ games for same team in every season during 1980s. Others: Dwight Evans, Dale Murphy, Alan Trammell, Lou Whitaker, and Willie Wilson.

## John Moses

Bats Left and Right

| Minnesota Twins | AB | H | 2B | 3B | HR | RBI | BB | SO | BA | SA | OBA |
|---|---|---|---|---|---|---|---|---|---|---|---|
| Season | 242 | 68 | 12 | 3 | 1 | 31 | 19 | 23 | .281 | .368 | .333 |
| vs. Left-Handers | 63 | 18 | 1 | 0 | 0 | 9 | 6 | 6 | .286 | .302 | .343 |
| vs. Right-Handers | 179 | 50 | 11 | 3 | 1 | 22 | 13 | 17 | .279 | .391 | .330 |
| Home | 97 | 30 | 9 | 2 | 0 | 19 | 9 | 7 | .309 | .443 | .370 |
| Road | 145 | 38 | 3 | 1 | 1 | 12 | 10 | 16 | .262 | .317 | .308 |
| Grass | 117 | 27 | 2 | 0 | 1 | 9 | 9 | 13 | .231 | .274 | .283 |
| Artificial Turf | 125 | 41 | 10 | 3 | 0 | 22 | 10 | 10 | .328 | .456 | .380 |
| April | 29 | 8 | 1 | 1 | 0 | 1 | 4 | 1 | .276 | .379 | .382 |
| May | 53 | 18 | 1 | 1 | 1 | 11 | 5 | 6 | .340 | .453 | .390 |
| June | 52 | 13 | 2 | 1 | 0 | 9 | 6 | 2 | .250 | .327 | .322 |
| July | 42 | 13 | 3 | 0 | 0 | 0 | 0 | 7 | .310 | .381 | .310 |
| August | 48 | 12 | 4 | 0 | 0 | 9 | 2 | 4 | .250 | .333 | .280 |
| Sept./Oct. | 18 | 4 | 1 | 0 | 0 | 1 | 2 | 3 | .222 | .278 | .300 |
| Leading Off Inn. | 56 | 15 | 2 | 1 | 0 | 0 | 2 | 5 | .268 | .339 | .293 |
| Runners On | 105 | 28 | 5 | 1 | 1 | 31 | 10 | 8 | .267 | .362 | .331 |
| Runners/Scor. Pos. | 61 | 20 | 3 | 1 | 0 | 29 | 5 | 6 | .328 | .410 | .377 |
| Runners On/2 Out | 48 | 13 | 2 | 1 | 1 | 15 | 6 | 1 | .271 | .417 | .352 |
| Scor. Pos./2 Out | 33 | 10 | 1 | 1 | 0 | 13 | 3 | 0 | .303 | .394 | .361 |
| Late Inning Pressure | 47 | 10 | 2 | 0 | 0 | 1 | 2 | 8 | .213 | .255 | .245 |
| Leading Off | 10 | 2 | 0 | 0 | 0 | 0 | 0 | 3 | .200 | .200 | .200 |
| Runners On | 19 | 2 | 0 | 0 | 0 | 1 | 2 | 2 | .105 | .105 | .190 |
| Runners/Scor. Pos. | 11 | 1 | 0 | 0 | 0 | 1 | 1 | 2 | .091 | .091 | .167 |

| RUNS BATTED IN | From 1B | From 2B | From 3B | Scoring Position |
|---|---|---|---|---|
| Totals | 4/81 | 11/50 | 15/24 | 26/74 |
| Percentage | 5% | 22% | 63% | 35% |
| Driving In Runners from 3B with Less than Two Out: | | | 9/9 | 100% |

Loves to face: Dave Stewart (.429, 9-for-21)
Hates to face: Dave Stieb (.087, 2-for-23)
Played 129 games, the highest total of his eight-year career. . . . Led Twins with 33 appearances as a pinch hitter. Batted .267 (8-for-30) with three extra-base hits in that role. . . . Batted .331 vs. fly-ball pitchers, .217 against ground-ballers. . . . No home runs in 226 career at-bats at the *un*-Homerdome. . . . Drove in all nine runners from third base with less than two outs, the "best" perfect mark of the last 15 years. Roger Freed was 8-for-8 in 1978. Tony Solaita (1979) and Del Alston (1980) had 7-for-7 seasons. . . . The most successful left-handed pitcher in history of Fenway Park? He threw a hitless inning in relief there on June 24, and even induced a double-play grounder off the bat of Rick Cerone.

## Rance Mulliniks

Bats Left

| Toronto Blue Jays | AB | H | 2B | 3B | HR | RBI | BB | SO | BA | SA | OBA |
|---|---|---|---|---|---|---|---|---|---|---|---|
| Season | 273 | 65 | 11 | 2 | 3 | 29 | 34 | 40 | .238 | .326 | .320 |
| vs. Left-Handers | 16 | 3 | 1 | 0 | 0 | 2 | 3 | 2 | .188 | .250 | .316 |
| vs. Right-Handers | 257 | 62 | 10 | 2 | 3 | 27 | 31 | 38 | .241 | .331 | .321 |
| Home | 117 | 27 | 6 | 0 | 1 | 14 | 15 | 16 | .231 | .308 | .316 |
| Road | 156 | 38 | 5 | 2 | 2 | 15 | 19 | 24 | .244 | .340 | .324 |
| Grass | 124 | 34 | 3 | 2 | 2 | 14 | 16 | 17 | .274 | .379 | .357 |
| Artificial Turf | 149 | 31 | 8 | 0 | 1 | 15 | 18 | 23 | .208 | .282 | .290 |
| April | 66 | 15 | 1 | 0 | 0 | 6 | 7 | 10 | .227 | .242 | .297 |
| May | 51 | 11 | 0 | 0 | 1 | 5 | 6 | 10 | .216 | .275 | .298 |
| June | 69 | 18 | 4 | 2 | 0 | 5 | 7 | 7 | .261 | .377 | .325 |
| July | 23 | 7 | 2 | 0 | 0 | 3 | 3 | 1 | .304 | .391 | .385 |
| August | 53 | 12 | 3 | 0 | 2 | 9 | 7 | 9 | .226 | .396 | .317 |
| Sept./Oct. | 11 | 2 | 1 | 0 | 0 | 1 | 4 | 3 | .182 | .273 | .400 |
| Leading Off Inn. | 58 | 17 | 4 | 0 | 1 | 1 | 5 | 9 | .293 | .414 | .349 |
| Runners On | 128 | 28 | 4 | 1 | 2 | 28 | 20 | 17 | .219 | .313 | .320 |
| Runners/Scor. Pos. | 82 | 16 | 3 | 0 | 2 | 26 | 18 | 11 | .195 | .305 | .333 |
| Runners On/2 Out | 55 | 11 | 1 | 0 | 1 | 11 | 9 | 7 | .200 | .273 | .313 |
| Scor. Pos./2 Out | 35 | 7 | 0 | 0 | 1 | 10 | 9 | 5 | .200 | .286 | .364 |
| Late Inning Pressure | 39 | 8 | 1 | 0 | 0 | 1 | 8 | 5 | .205 | .231 | .340 |
| Leading Off | 8 | 5 | 1 | 0 | 0 | 0 | 1 | 1 | .625 | .750 | .667 |
| Runners On | 15 | 2 | 0 | 0 | 0 | 1 | 5 | 2 | .133 | .133 | .350 |
| Runners/Scor. Pos. | 12 | 2 | 0 | 0 | 0 | 1 | 5 | 2 | .167 | .167 | .412 |

| RUNS BATTED IN | From 1B | From 2B | From 3B | Scoring Position |
|---|---|---|---|---|
| Totals | 3/90 | 7/64 | 16/36 | 23/100 |
| Percentage | 3% | 11% | 44% | 23% |
| Driving In Runners from 3B with Less than Two Out: | | | 13/21 | 62% |

Loves to face: Mike Moore (.345, 19-for-55, 1 HR)
Hates to face: Dave Stewart (.040, 1-for-25, 7 SO)
May have hit the wall: Fewest games (105), home runs, RBI, and lowest batting average in eight seasons with the Blue Jays. . . . Three hits in 18 at-bats as a pinch hitter, lowering his career mark to .323 (43-for-133). . . . Grounded into 12 double plays in 54 opportunities, worst rate on the Jays. . . . Hasn't started any of the last 110 games in which Toronto faced a left-handed starter. During that time, he's started 205 games vs. right-handers. Career BA: .228 vs. left-handers, .277 vs. right-handers. . . . Batting average with runners in scoring position, year by year since 1984: .372, .381, .310, .284, .232, .195. . . . Most similar career profiles: Johnny Grubb, Ray Knight, Don Hoak, Joel Youngblood.

## Al Newman

Bats Left and Right

| Minnesota Twins | AB | H | 2B | 3B | HR | RBI | BB | SO | BA | SA | OBA |
|---|---|---|---|---|---|---|---|---|---|---|---|
| Season | 446 | 113 | 18 | 2 | 0 | 38 | 59 | 46 | .253 | .303 | .341 |
| vs. Left-Handers | 163 | 41 | 11 | 0 | 0 | 17 | 18 | 22 | .252 | .319 | .328 |
| vs. Right-Handers | 283 | 72 | 7 | 2 | 0 | 21 | 41 | 24 | .254 | .293 | .348 |
| Home | 224 | 58 | 6 | 1 | 0 | 14 | 32 | 20 | .259 | .295 | .351 |
| Road | 222 | 55 | 12 | 1 | 0 | 24 | 27 | 26 | .248 | .311 | .329 |
| Grass | 168 | 44 | 12 | 1 | 0 | 22 | 21 | 23 | .262 | .345 | .344 |
| Artificial Turf | 278 | 69 | 6 | 1 | 0 | 16 | 38 | 23 | .248 | .277 | .339 |
| April | 23 | 6 | 1 | 0 | 0 | 4 | 1 | 4 | .261 | .304 | .292 |
| May | 84 | 21 | 2 | 0 | 0 | 5 | 19 | 12 | .250 | .274 | .385 |
| June | 84 | 21 | 6 | 0 | 0 | 9 | 10 | 7 | .250 | .321 | .326 |
| July | 71 | 12 | 3 | 1 | 0 | 6 | 7 | 7 | .169 | .239 | .250 |
| August | 97 | 32 | 5 | 1 | 0 | 9 | 14 | 7 | .330 | .402 | .411 |
| Sept./Oct. | 87 | 21 | 1 | 0 | 0 | 5 | 8 | 9 | .241 | .253 | .313 |
| Leading Off Inn. | 154 | 29 | 4 | 1 | 0 | 0 | 21 | 18 | .188 | .227 | .286 |
| Runners On | 166 | 50 | 8 | 0 | 0 | 38 | 17 | 13 | .301 | .349 | .365 |
| Runners/Scor. Pos. | 105 | 26 | 4 | 0 | 0 | 35 | 8 | 12 | .248 | .286 | .297 |
| Runners On/2 Out | 82 | 23 | 6 | 0 | 0 | 15 | 4 | 9 | .280 | .354 | .322 |
| Scor. Pos./2 Out | 54 | 10 | 3 | 0 | 0 | 13 | 2 | 8 | .185 | .241 | .228 |
| Late Inning Pressure | 67 | 21 | 3 | 0 | 0 | 8 | 6 | 6 | .313 | .358 | .365 |
| Leading Off | 19 | 3 | 1 | 0 | 0 | 0 | 1 | 3 | .158 | .211 | .200 |
| Runners On | 26 | 13 | 1 | 0 | 0 | 8 | 3 | 1 | .500 | .538 | .533 |
| Runners/Scor. Pos. | 16 | 8 | 1 | 0 | 0 | 8 | 1 | 1 | .500 | .563 | .500 |

| RUNS BATTED IN | From 1B | From 2B | From 3B | Scoring Position |
|---|---|---|---|---|
| Totals | 5/108 | 14/84 | 19/43 | 33/127 |
| Percentage | 5% | 17% | 44% | 26% |
| Driving In Runners from 3B with Less than Two Out: | | | 16/19 | 84% |

Loves to face: Bobby Witt (.429, 9-for-21)
Hates to face: Mark Gubicza (.056, 1-for-18)
Grounded into only three double plays in 67 opportunities, lowest rate on club. . . . Enters 1990 with a streak of 1091 homerless at-bats. Has never homered in 505 Metrodome at-bats, most by anyone without a home run there. . . . Average of 4.58 chances per nine innings was lowest among A.L. second basemen (minimum: 500 innings). . . . A fantasy-league owner's dream come true: Has played at least 20 games at second base, third base, and shortstop in each of the last two seasons. The only other players in franchise history to do that even once: Bill Coughlin (1902) and Jerry Terrell (1974). . . . Career batting average of .187 leading off innings. . . . Other career averages: .263 in day games, .211 at night.

## Matt Nokes

Bats Left

| Detroit Tigers | AB | H | 2B | 3B | HR | RBI | BB | SO | BA | SA | OBA |
|---|---|---|---|---|---|---|---|---|---|---|---|
| Season | 268 | 67 | 10 | 0 | 9 | 39 | 17 | 37 | .250 | .388 | .298 |
| vs. Left-Handers | 43 | 11 | 2 | 0 | 2 | 9 | 1 | 13 | .256 | .442 | .283 |
| vs. Right-Handers | 225 | 56 | 8 | 0 | 7 | 30 | 16 | 24 | .249 | .378 | .300 |
| Home | 127 | 34 | 4 | 0 | 7 | 20 | 8 | 22 | .268 | .465 | .316 |
| Road | 141 | 33 | 6 | 0 | 2 | 19 | 9 | 15 | .234 | .319 | .281 |
| Grass | 223 | 59 | 7 | 0 | 8 | 32 | 14 | 32 | .265 | .404 | .313 |
| Artificial Turf | 45 | 8 | 3 | 0 | 1 | 7 | 3 | 5 | .178 | .311 | .224 |
| April | 67 | 19 | 2 | 0 | 5 | 16 | 7 | 12 | .284 | .537 | .355 |
| May | 66 | 14 | 3 | 0 | 2 | 12 | 3 | 12 | .212 | .348 | .254 |
| June | 33 | 7 | 1 | 0 | 0 | 1 | 1 | 3 | .212 | .242 | .235 |
| July | 0 | 0 | 0 | 0 | 0 | 0 | 0 | 0 | — | — | — |
| August | 62 | 18 | 2 | 0 | 0 | 5 | 2 | 4 | .290 | .323 | .313 |
| Sept./Oct. | 40 | 9 | 2 | 0 | 2 | 5 | 4 | 6 | .225 | .425 | .295 |
| Leading Off Inn. | 52 | 14 | 3 | 0 | 2 | 2 | 4 | 5 | .269 | .442 | .333 |
| Runners On | 124 | 35 | 4 | 0 | 7 | 37 | 10 | 17 | .282 | .484 | .336 |
| Runners/Scor. Pos. | 75 | 18 | 3 | 0 | 2 | 27 | 6 | 11 | .240 | .360 | .298 |
| Runners On/2 Out | 60 | 15 | 0 | 0 | 4 | 16 | 4 | 7 | .250 | .450 | .297 |
| Scor. Pos./2 Out | 43 | 8 | 0 | 0 | 2 | 12 | 2 | 7 | .186 | .326 | .222 |
| Late Inning Pressure | 46 | 10 | 1 | 0 | 1 | 8 | 6 | 10 | .217 | .304 | .302 |
| Leading Off | 11 | 3 | 0 | 0 | 0 | 0 | 2 | 3 | .273 | .273 | .385 |
| Runners On | 23 | 6 | 1 | 0 | 1 | 8 | 4 | 5 | .261 | .435 | .357 |
| Runners/Scor. Pos. | 13 | 4 | 1 | 0 | 0 | 6 | 2 | 3 | .308 | .385 | .375 |

| RUNS BATTED IN | From 1B | From 2B | From 3B | Scoring Position |
|---|---|---|---|---|
| Totals | 7/91 | 8/55 | 15/37 | 23/92 |
| Percentage | 8% | 15% | 41% | 25% |
| Driving In Runners from 3B with Less than Two Out: | | | 11/19 | 58% |

Loves to face: Mike Boddicker (.600, 12-for-20, 2 HR)
Hates to face: Bret Saberhagen (.130, 3-for-23, 5 SO)
Winner of the 1989 A.L. Lummox of the Year Award, for scoring more times on his own home runs (9) than on all other plays combined (6). . . . Why does that make him a lummox? Well, for one thing, the only other A.L. players to do that in 1989 (with at least five HR) were, frankly, lummoxes: Steve Balboni and Joey Meyer. . . . Want more evidence? The most such seasons by one player is 7, by Dave Kingman. Lummox. . . . Two guys have four: Balboni and Harmon Killebrew. Hall of Famer, but a lummox nonetheless. . . . Players with three: Adcock, Kittle, McCovey, Stuart. No question: lummoxes all. . . . Incidentally, you don't have to be famous to be a lummox. Among the two-time recipients: Jesse Gonder.

## Charlie O'Brien

Bats Right

| Milwaukee Brewers | AB | H | 2B | 3B | HR | RBI | BB | SO | BA | SA | OBA |
|---|---|---|---|---|---|---|---|---|---|---|---|
| Season | 188 | 44 | 10 | 0 | 6 | 35 | 21 | 11 | .234 | .383 | .339 |
| vs. Left-Handers | 89 | 22 | 6 | 0 | 3 | 9 | 8 | 4 | .247 | .416 | .337 |
| vs. Right-Handers | 99 | 22 | 4 | 0 | 3 | 26 | 13 | 7 | .222 | .354 | .342 |
| Home | 90 | 22 | 5 | 0 | 4 | 14 | 10 | 4 | .244 | .433 | .327 |
| Road | 98 | 22 | 5 | 0 | 2 | 21 | 11 | 7 | .224 | .337 | .350 |
| Grass | 153 | 38 | 10 | 0 | 5 | 33 | 18 | 9 | .248 | .412 | .350 |
| Artificial Turf | 35 | 6 | 0 | 0 | 1 | 2 | 3 | 2 | .171 | .257 | .293 |
| April | 15 | 3 | 2 | 0 | 0 | 1 | 1 | 0 | .200 | .333 | .333 |
| May | 29 | 7 | 1 | 0 | 1 | 3 | 3 | 2 | .241 | .379 | .333 |
| June | 23 | 4 | 1 | 0 | 1 | 2 | 3 | 0 | .174 | .348 | .269 |
| July | 41 | 10 | 2 | 0 | 1 | 11 | 4 | 1 | .244 | .366 | .340 |
| August | 49 | 12 | 2 | 0 | 1 | 13 | 4 | 4 | .245 | .347 | .327 |
| Sept./Oct. | 31 | 8 | 2 | 0 | 2 | 5 | 6 | 4 | .258 | .516 | .410 |
| Leading Off Inn. | 38 | 7 | 1 | 0 | 3 | 3 | 5 | 1 | .184 | .447 | .311 |
| Runners On | 88 | 28 | 8 | 0 | 3 | 32 | 11 | 4 | .318 | .511 | .412 |
| Runners/Scor. Pos. | 52 | 20 | 5 | 0 | 3 | 31 | 9 | 3 | .385 | .654 | .484 |
| Runners On/2 Out | 33 | 7 | 2 | 0 | 0 | 9 | 6 | 3 | .212 | .273 | .350 |
| Scor. Pos./2 Out | 21 | 7 | 2 | 0 | 0 | 9 | 4 | 3 | .333 | .429 | .440 |
| Late Inning Pressure | 12 | 3 | 1 | 0 | 0 | 1 | 2 | 2 | .250 | .333 | .357 |
| Leading Off | 2 | 0 | 0 | 0 | 0 | 0 | 1 | 1 | .000 | .000 | .333 |
| Runners On | 5 | 2 | 1 | 0 | 0 | 1 | 1 | 0 | .400 | .600 | .500 |
| Runners/Scor. Pos. | 3 | 2 | 1 | 0 | 0 | 1 | 1 | 0 | .667 | 1.000 | .750 |

| RUNS BATTED IN | From 1B | From 2B | From 3B | Scoring Position |
|---|---|---|---|---|
| Totals | 6/60 | 12/39 | 11/23 | 23/62 |
| Percentage | 10% | 31% | 48% | 37% |
| Driving In Runners from 3B with Less than Two Out: | | | 8/13 | 62% |

Loves to face: Greg Cadaret (.750, 3-for-4)
Hates to face: Jeff Ballard (0-for-7)
It was Garry Templeton who said, "If I ain't startin', I ain't departin'." But last season, it was O'Brien who played in only one game in which he wasn't the starting catcher. . . . Brewers had a 34–27 record with O'Brien starting behind the plate, 47–54 with B. J. Surhoff. . . . Why? Team ERA was 3.57 with O'Brien catching, 3.91 with B. J. . . . Opposing base stealers were safe on only 32 of 50 attempts vs. O'Brien (64%), compared to 81-for-109 vs. Surhoff (74%). . . . His streak of 87 consecutive plate appearances without a strikeout, 2d longest in majors, was snapped by Nolan Ryan. . . . Career breakdown: .181 with bases empty, .291 with runners on base, .310 with runners in scoring position.

## Pete O'Brien

Bats Left

| Cleveland Indians | AB | H | 2B | 3B | HR | RBI | BB | SO | BA | SA | OBA |
|---|---|---|---|---|---|---|---|---|---|---|---|
| Season | 554 | 144 | 24 | 1 | 12 | 56 | 83 | 48 | .260 | .372 | .356 |
| vs. Left-Handers | 167 | 49 | 10 | 0 | 4 | 19 | 18 | 18 | .293 | .425 | .362 |
| vs. Right-Handers | 387 | 95 | 14 | 1 | 8 | 37 | 65 | 30 | .245 | .349 | .353 |
| Home | 261 | 75 | 12 | 1 | 5 | 34 | 43 | 18 | .287 | .398 | .386 |
| Road | 293 | 69 | 12 | 0 | 7 | 22 | 40 | 30 | .235 | .348 | .327 |
| Grass | 468 | 123 | 17 | 1 | 11 | 51 | 70 | 42 | .263 | .374 | .358 |
| Artificial Turf | 86 | 21 | 7 | 0 | 1 | 5 | 13 | 6 | .244 | .360 | .340 |
| April | 80 | 32 | 8 | 0 | 2 | 10 | 11 | 4 | .400 | .575 | .462 |
| May | 105 | 23 | 4 | 0 | 5 | 16 | 16 | 6 | .219 | .400 | .317 |
| June | 89 | 23 | 4 | 0 | 3 | 8 | 19 | 10 | .258 | .404 | .396 |
| July | 101 | 28 | 5 | 0 | 0 | 10 | 19 | 7 | .277 | .327 | .392 |
| August | 88 | 18 | 1 | 0 | 1 | 5 | 6 | 10 | .205 | .250 | .255 |
| Sept./Oct. | 91 | 20 | 2 | 1 | 1 | 7 | 12 | 11 | .220 | .297 | .311 |
| Leading Off Inn. | 134 | 42 | 11 | 1 | 3 | 3 | 16 | 9 | .313 | .478 | .387 |
| Runners On | 221 | 56 | 9 | 0 | 4 | 48 | 50 | 19 | .253 | .348 | .384 |
| Runners/Scor. Pos. | 135 | 31 | 7 | 0 | 3 | 45 | 42 | 14 | .230 | .348 | .401 |
| Runners On/2 Out | 114 | 25 | 1 | 0 | 4 | 24 | 29 | 11 | .219 | .333 | .378 |
| Scor. Pos./2 Out | 73 | 14 | 0 | 0 | 3 | 21 | 26 | 9 | .192 | .315 | .404 |
| Late Inning Pressure | 83 | 16 | 4 | 1 | 0 | 6 | 14 | 11 | .193 | .265 | .316 |
| Leading Off | 26 | 9 | 3 | 1 | 0 | 0 | 2 | 1 | .346 | .538 | .393 |
| Runners On | 31 | 5 | 1 | 0 | 0 | 6 | 9 | 4 | .161 | .194 | .350 |
| Runners/Scor. Pos. | 22 | 3 | 1 | 0 | 0 | 6 | 9 | 3 | .136 | .182 | .387 |

| RUNS BATTED IN | From 1B | From 2B | From 3B | Scoring Position |
|---|---|---|---|---|
| Totals | 3/157 | 19/105 | 22/57 | 41/162 |
| Percentage | 2% | 18% | 39% | 25% |
| Driving In Runners from 3B with Less than Two Out: | | | 15/28 | 54% |

Loves to face: Roger Clemens (.455, 15-for-33, 7 BB)
Hates to face: Willie Hernandez (0-for-19, 5 SO)
April BA was highest in majors, but he ended the season 0-for-14. . . . That's the Pete O'Brien signature. Career BA: .299 in April, .247 in September and October. . . . Could be because he's played at least 154 games at first base—a full season's worth prior to expansion—in each of the last five seasons, the longest streak in A.L. history. Even Gehrig had only a four year streak. . . . Career average is .122 (9-for-74) in the Big Kahuna of clutch categories: two outs and runners in scoring position in Late-Inning Pressure Situations. . . . Drove in only 32 of 169 runners from scoring position in LIP Situations (19%), compared to 34 percent at other times.

## Joe Orsulak

Bats Left

| Baltimore Orioles | AB | H | 2B | 3B | HR | RBI | BB | SO | BA | SA | OBA |
|---|---|---|---|---|---|---|---|---|---|---|---|
| Season | 390 | 111 | 22 | 5 | 7 | 55 | 41 | 35 | .285 | .421 | .351 |
| vs. Left-Handers | 84 | 17 | 5 | 0 | 0 | 5 | 5 | 8 | .202 | .262 | .244 |
| vs. Right Handers | 306 | 94 | 17 | 5 | 7 | 50 | 36 | 27 | .307 | .464 | .378 |
| Home | 194 | 53 | 12 | 3 | 0 | 24 | 20 | 18 | .273 | .366 | .339 |
| Road | 196 | 58 | 10 | 2 | 7 | 31 | 21 | 17 | .296 | .474 | .362 |
| Grass | 331 | 89 | 18 | 3 | 6 | 46 | 37 | 30 | .269 | .396 | .340 |
| Artificial Turf | 59 | 22 | 4 | 2 | 1 | 9 | 4 | 5 | .373 | .559 | .413 |
| April | 51 | 15 | 6 | 0 | 1 | 6 | 3 | 7 | .294 | .471 | .333 |
| May | 49 | 15 | 3 | 0 | 0 | 7 | 6 | 6 | .306 | .367 | .382 |
| June | 96 | 27 | 7 | 2 | 1 | 13 | 11 | 4 | .281 | .427 | .352 |
| July | 81 | 20 | 2 | 3 | 1 | 12 | 3 | 7 | .247 | .383 | .267 |
| August | 72 | 23 | 4 | 0 | 3 | 13 | 13 | 9 | .319 | .500 | .422 |
| Sept./Oct. | 41 | 11 | 0 | 0 | 1 | 4 | 5 | 2 | .268 | .341 | .348 |
| Leading Off Inn. | 86 | 24 | 7 | 0 | 3 | 3 | 11 | 7 | .279 | .465 | .361 |
| Runners On | 182 | 53 | 10 | 3 | 2 | 50 | 23 | 17 | .291 | .412 | .360 |
| Runners/Scor. Pos. | 103 | 28 | 6 | 3 | 0 | 44 | 17 | 10 | .272 | .388 | .357 |
| Runners On/2 Out | 79 | 24 | 7 | 0 | 1 | 21 | 11 | 8 | .304 | .430 | .389 |
| Scor. Pos./2 Out | 54 | 15 | 4 | 0 | 0 | 18 | 8 | 5 | .278 | .352 | .371 |
| Late Inning Pressure | 53 | 14 | 2 | 1 | 1 | 8 | 9 | 6 | .264 | .396 | .381 |
| Leading Off | 12 | 1 | 0 | 0 | 0 | 0 | 1 | 1 | .083 | .083 | .154 |
| Runners On | 24 | 7 | 2 | 1 | 1 | 8 | 8 | 4 | .292 | .583 | .469 |
| Runners/Scor. Pos. | 11 | 4 | 1 | 1 | 0 | 6 | 6 | 2 | .364 | .636 | .588 |

| RUNS BATTED IN | From 1B | From 2B | From 3B | Scoring Position |
|---|---|---|---|---|
| Totals | 6/138 | 18/77 | 24/48 | 42/125 |
| Percentage | 4% | 23% | 50% | 34% |
| Driving In Runners from 3B with Less than Two Out: | | | 16/26 | 62% |

Loves to face: Rich Yett (.538, 7-for-13)
Hates to face: Don August (0-for-9)
All seven home runs were hit on the road, all against right-handers (including five off ground-ball pitchers). . . . No home runs in 282 career at-bats vs. left-handers. . . . Batted .351 on fair balls hit to right field, and .371 straight away, but only .215 to the opposite field. . . . One of two players to start at least one game in each of the nine batting-order positions. . . . Only A.L. player in league to "hit for the cycle" as a pinch hitter. Was 6-for-15 with four walks. Previous career pinch hitting: .232 (13-for-56). . . . Career average with runners on base (.245) is 51 points lower than with the bases empty (.296), the largest difference over the last 10 years (minimum: 500 AB each way).

## Mike Pagliarulo

Bats Left

| New York Yankees | AB | H | 2B | 3B | HR | RBI | BB | SO | BA | SA | OBA |
|---|---|---|---|---|---|---|---|---|---|---|---|
| Season | 223 | 44 | 10 | 0 | 4 | 16 | 19 | 43 | .197 | .296 | .266 |
| vs. Left-Handers | 33 | 8 | 2 | 0 | 0 | 4 | 3 | 9 | .242 | .303 | .306 |
| vs. Right-Handers | 190 | 36 | 8 | 0 | 4 | 12 | 16 | 34 | .189 | .295 | .260 |
| Home | 113 | 23 | 4 | 0 | 3 | 9 | 8 | 24 | .204 | .319 | .268 |
| Road | 110 | 21 | 6 | 0 | 1 | 7 | 11 | 19 | .191 | .273 | .264 |
| Grass | 189 | 35 | 7 | 0 | 4 | 11 | 15 | 39 | .185 | .286 | .252 |
| Artificial Turf | 34 | 9 | 3 | 0 | 0 | 5 | 4 | 4 | .265 | .353 | .342 |
| April | 45 | 6 | 1 | 0 | 0 | 1 | 2 | 8 | .133 | .156 | .188 |
| May | 63 | 16 | 5 | 0 | 2 | 9 | 9 | 11 | .254 | .429 | .347 |
| June | 70 | 14 | 3 | 0 | 1 | 3 | 6 | 11 | .200 | .286 | .263 |
| July | 45 | 8 | 1 | 0 | 1 | 3 | 2 | 13 | .178 | .267 | .229 |
| August | 0 | 0 | 0 | 0 | 0 | 0 | 0 | 0 | — | — | — |
| Sept./Oct. | 0 | 0 | 0 | 0 | 0 | 0 | 0 | 0 | — | — | — |
| Leading Off Inn. | 55 | 8 | 1 | 0 | 1 | 1 | 6 | 12 | .145 | .218 | .230 |
| Runners On | 91 | 21 | 5 | 0 | 0 | 12 | 6 | 17 | .231 | .286 | .286 |
| Runners/Scor. Pos. | 51 | 12 | 3 | 0 | 0 | 10 | 3 | 9 | .235 | .294 | .291 |
| Runners On/2 Out | 41 | 10 | 2 | 0 | 0 | 4 | 3 | 7 | .244 | .293 | .311 |
| Scor. Pos./2 Out | 28 | 5 | 1 | 0 | 0 | 3 | 2 | 4 | .179 | .214 | .258 |
| Late Inning Pressure | 38 | 10 | 3 | 0 | 0 | 3 | 4 | 6 | .263 | .342 | .333 |
| Leading Off | 13 | 1 | 0 | 0 | 0 | 0 | 1 | 2 | .077 | .077 | .143 |
| Runners On | 16 | 5 | 1 | 0 | 0 | 3 | 2 | 4 | .313 | .375 | .389 |
| Runners/Scor. Pos. | 9 | 2 | 1 | 0 | 0 | 3 | 1 | 2 | .222 | .333 | .300 |

| RUNS BATTED IN | From 1B | From 2B | From 3B | Scoring Position |
|---|---|---|---|---|
| Totals | 2/72 | 5/40 | 5/25 | 10/65 |
| Percentage | 3% | 13% | 20% | 15% |
| Driving In Runners from 3B with Less than Two Out: | | | 4/13 | 31% |

Loves to face: Dan Quisenberry (.625, 5-for-8)
Hates to face: Charlie Leibrandt (.118, 2-for-17, 6 SO)
Lowest batting average among A.L. players with 200 or more plate appearances, but his average in 50 games with Padres was even worse (.196). . . . Combined-leagues average of .305 (18-for-59) in LIP Situations, .176 in other at-bats. . . . Finished Yankees career with .229 mark, breaking Gene Michael's record (.233) for lowest in team history (minimum: 2000 AB). . . . Lowest career BA (.227) among active players with 2500 PA. . . . Batting averages, year by year since 1985: .239, .238, .234, .216, .197. . . . Many players have had declining averages in four consecutive seasons (184). But Pags is one of only eight, and the first since Phil Roof in the early 1970s, to start from a base below .240.

## Rafael Palmeiro

Bats Left

| Texas Rangers | AB | H | 2B | 3B | HR | RBI | BB | SO | BA | SA | OBA |
|---|---|---|---|---|---|---|---|---|---|---|---|
| Season | 559 | 154 | 23 | 4 | 8 | 64 | 63 | 48 | .275 | .374 | .354 |
| vs. Left-Handers | 165 | 41 | 8 | 0 | 2 | 20 | 11 | 13 | .248 | .333 | .298 |
| vs. Right-Handers | 394 | 113 | 15 | 4 | 6 | 44 | 52 | 35 | .287 | .391 | .376 |
| Home | 263 | 68 | 9 | 2 | 4 | 29 | 35 | 25 | .259 | .354 | .348 |
| Road | 296 | 86 | 14 | 2 | 4 | 35 | 28 | 23 | .291 | .392 | .360 |
| Grass | 467 | 123 | 17 | 3 | 7 | 53 | 52 | 42 | .263 | .358 | .343 |
| Artificial Turf | 92 | 31 | 6 | 1 | 1 | 11 | 11 | 6 | .337 | .457 | .410 |
| April | 83 | 26 | 6 | 0 | 3 | 16 | 13 | 7 | .313 | .494 | .412 |
| May | 109 | 41 | 8 | 1 | 1 | 14 | 5 | 6 | .376 | .495 | .405 |
| June | 110 | 28 | 4 | 0 | 1 | 17 | 10 | 7 | .255 | .318 | .325 |
| July | 87 | 16 | 1 | 0 | 2 | 5 | 10 | 4 | .184 | .264 | .283 |
| August | 94 | 22 | 1 | 2 | 1 | 7 | 10 | 14 | .234 | .319 | .308 |
| Sept./Oct. | 76 | 21 | 3 | 1 | 0 | 5 | 15 | 10 | .276 | .342 | .396 |
| Leading Off Inn. | 92 | 15 | 3 | 0 | 1 | 1 | 11 | 5 | .163 | .228 | .260 |
| Runners On | 250 | 73 | 10 | 3 | 4 | 60 | 32 | 24 | .292 | .404 | .378 |
| Runners/Scor. Pos. | 133 | 37 | 4 | 1 | 1 | 50 | 21 | 15 | .278 | .346 | .384 |
| Runners On/2 Out | 95 | 22 | 7 | 1 | 1 | 19 | 9 | 11 | .232 | .358 | .305 |
| Scor. Pos./2 Out | 62 | 14 | 4 | 1 | 1 | 17 | 5 | 8 | .226 | .371 | .294 |
| Late Inning Pressure | 60 | 17 | 3 | 0 | 1 | 6 | 10 | 5 | .283 | .383 | .386 |
| Leading Off | 14 | 2 | 0 | 0 | 0 | 0 | 1 | 2 | .143 | .143 | .200 |
| Runners On | 25 | 6 | 0 | 0 | 1 | 6 | 5 | 1 | .240 | .360 | .367 |
| Runners/Scor. Pos. | 13 | 4 | 0 | 0 | 0 | 4 | 3 | 1 | .308 | .308 | .438 |

| RUNS BATTED IN | From 1B | From 2B | From 3B | Scoring Position |
|---|---|---|---|---|
| Totals | 8/174 | 21/96 | 27/52 | 48/148 |
| Percentage | 5% | 22% | 52% | 32% |
| Driving In Runners from 3B with Less than Two Out: | | | 22/28 | 79% |

Loves to face: Brian Holman (.667, 6-for-9)
Hates to face: Bob Welch (0-for-9)
Had 47 RBI after his first 76 games, but drove in only 17 more over his remaining 80 games. . . . Of 64 RBI, 26 gave his team a lead (41%), highest rate in majors among players with 40+ RBI. This from the guy who didn't have a game-winning RBI in 152 games with the Cubs in 1988. . . . Batted .224 on fair balls hit to the opposite field, .385 straight away, and .314 to right. . . . Committed 12 errors at first base, only three after All-Star break. Consider first half a grace period after transition from outfield. . . . Career BA of .274 on grass (.300 at Wrigley, .258 on other grass fields), .323 on artificial turf. . . . Batting average with runners on base, year by year: .211, .245, .261, .292.

## Dave Parker

Bats Left

| Oakland As | AB | H | 2B | 3B | HR | RBI | BB | SO | BA | SA | OBA |
|---|---|---|---|---|---|---|---|---|---|---|---|
| Season | 553 | 146 | 27 | 0 | 22 | 97 | 38 | 91 | .264 | .432 | .308 |
| vs. Left-Handers | 127 | 29 | 5 | 0 | 6 | 26 | 1 | 18 | .228 | .409 | .233 |
| vs. Right-Handers | 426 | 117 | 22 | 0 | 16 | 71 | 37 | 73 | .275 | .439 | .329 |
| Home | 272 | 76 | 10 | 0 | 10 | 50 | 24 | 39 | .279 | .426 | .334 |
| Road | 281 | 70 | 17 | 0 | 12 | 47 | 14 | 52 | .249 | .438 | .282 |
| Grass | 468 | 126 | 24 | 0 | 20 | 79 | 32 | 75 | .269 | .449 | .314 |
| Artificial Turf | 85 | 20 | 3 | 0 | 2 | 18 | 6 | 16 | .235 | .341 | .277 |
| April | 93 | 18 | 5 | 0 | 2 | 11 | 4 | 14 | .194 | .312 | .224 |
| May | 94 | 29 | 5 | 0 | 6 | 18 | 8 | 11 | .309 | .553 | .365 |
| June | 88 | 28 | 5 | 0 | 3 | 14 | 3 | 9 | .318 | .477 | .333 |
| July | 87 | 25 | 3 | 0 | 3 | 19 | 10 | 16 | .287 | .425 | .361 |
| August | 82 | 18 | 4 | 0 | 4 | 14 | 3 | 19 | .220 | .415 | .239 |
| Sept./Oct. | 109 | 28 | 5 | 0 | 4 | 21 | 10 | 22 | .257 | .413 | .317 |
| Leading Off Inn. | 124 | 29 | 3 | 0 | 7 | 7 | 6 | 28 | .234 | .427 | .269 |
| Runners On | 261 | 74 | 17 | 0 | 10 | 85 | 24 | 34 | .284 | .464 | .334 |
| Runners/Scor. Pos. | 152 | 45 | 10 | 0 | 6 | 72 | 20 | 23 | .296 | .480 | .361 |
| Runners On/2 Out | 105 | 25 | 5 | 0 | 4 | 27 | 11 | 19 | .238 | .400 | .310 |
| Scor. Pos./2 Out | 58 | 14 | 3 | 0 | 2 | 21 | 9 | 10 | .241 | .397 | .343 |
| Late Inning Pressure | 62 | 14 | 2 | 0 | 2 | 6 | 6 | 13 | .226 | .355 | .294 |
| Leading Off | 16 | 2 | 0 | 0 | 1 | 1 | 1 | 6 | .125 | .313 | .176 |
| Runners On | 29 | 7 | 1 | 0 | 1 | 5 | 5 | 4 | .241 | .379 | .353 |
| Runners/Scor. Pos. | 16 | 5 | 1 | 0 | 0 | 3 | 5 | 3 | .313 | .375 | .476 |

| RUNS BATTED IN | From 1B | From 2B | From 3B | Scoring Position |
|---|---|---|---|---|
| Totals | 16/187 | 29/115 | 30/63 | 59/178 |
| Percentage | 9% | 25% | 48% | 33% |
| Driving In Runners from 3B with Less than Two Out: | | | 26/44 | 59% |

Loves to face: Dennis Eckersley (.348, 8-for-23, 2 HR)
Hates to face: Melido Perez (.111, 2-for-18)
Played only one game in field (April 7). . . . Batted .303 in the first inning, .256 thereafter. . . . Hit 69 percent of his ground outs to the left side, but only 21 percent of his fly outs were hit in that direction. . . . Grounded into 21 DP in 112 opportunities (one per 5.3 chances), compared to 3-for-80 in 1988. . . . Has hit better with runners on base than with the bases empty in each of the last seven seasons. . . . Made major league debut on July 12, 1973, as Pirates leadoff hitter. Only one other player from that game is still active: Dave Winfield. . . . Has played 2159 games since his first and only sacrifice bunt. . . . Let's go to the video tape: Finished a game at second base in 1977.

## Lance Parrish

Bats Right

| California Angels | AB | H | 2B | 3B | HR | RBI | BB | SO | BA | SA | OBA |
|---|---|---|---|---|---|---|---|---|---|---|---|
| Season | 433 | 103 | 12 | 1 | 17 | 50 | 42 | 104 | .238 | .388 | .306 |
| vs. Left-Handers | 144 | 34 | 2 | 1 | 7 | 20 | 18 | 24 | .236 | .410 | .317 |
| vs. Right-Handers | 289 | 69 | 10 | 0 | 10 | 30 | 24 | 80 | .239 | .377 | .300 |
| Home | 215 | 54 | 8 | 0 | 8 | 25 | 17 | 49 | .251 | .400 | .305 |
| Road | 218 | 49 | 4 | 1 | 9 | 25 | 25 | 55 | .225 | .376 | .306 |
| Grass | 364 | 85 | 10 | 1 | 15 | 42 | 35 | 88 | .234 | .390 | .300 |
| Artificial Turf | 69 | 18 | 2 | 0 | 2 | 8 | 7 | 16 | .261 | .377 | .338 |
| April | 74 | 18 | 5 | 1 | 1 | 8 | 8 | 18 | .243 | .378 | .333 |
| May | 76 | 23 | 2 | 0 | 6 | 15 | 13 | 11 | .303 | .566 | .396 |
| June | 71 | 10 | 1 | 0 | 1 | 4 | 2 | 18 | .141 | .197 | .162 |
| July | 80 | 26 | 2 | 0 | 6 | 16 | 10 | 16 | .325 | .575 | .396 |
| August | 68 | 12 | 2 | 0 | 2 | 3 | 3 | 23 | .176 | .294 | .211 |
| Sept./Oct. | 64 | 14 | 0 | 0 | 1 | 4 | 6 | 18 | .219 | .266 | .286 |
| Leading Off Inn. | 100 | 24 | 3 | 0 | 7 | 7 | 6 | 18 | .240 | .480 | .283 |
| Runners On | 199 | 48 | 7 | 1 | 6 | 39 | 24 | 51 | .241 | .377 | .320 |
| Runners/Scor. Pos. | 100 | 21 | 5 | 0 | 4 | 34 | 21 | 27 | .210 | .380 | .341 |
| Runners On/2 Out | 84 | 21 | 4 | 1 | 3 | 18 | 9 | 24 | .250 | .429 | .323 |
| Scor. Pos./2 Out | 44 | 11 | 3 | 0 | 3 | 17 | 8 | 11 | .250 | .523 | .365 |
| Late Inning Pressure | 67 | 13 | 2 | 0 | 1 | 2 | 8 | 28 | .194 | .269 | .280 |
| Leading Off | 17 | 3 | 1 | 0 | 1 | 1 | 2 | 8 | .176 | .412 | .263 |
| Runners On | 26 | 6 | 1 | 0 | 0 | 1 | 5 | 9 | .231 | .269 | .355 |
| Runners/Scor. Pos. | 16 | 2 | 1 | 0 | 0 | 1 | 4 | 8 | .125 | .188 | .300 |

| RUNS BATTED IN | From 1B | From 2B | From 3B | Scoring Position |
|---|---|---|---|---|
| Totals | 5/154 | 14/80 | 14/44 | 28/124 |
| Percentage | 3% | 18% | 32% | 23% |
| Driving In Runners from 3B with Less than Two Out: | | | 10/26 | 38% |

Loves to face: Jamie Moyer (.348, 8-for-23, 4 HR)
Hates to face: Dennis Lamp (.128, 5-for-39, 16 SO)
Hitless in 28 consecutive at-bats with runners on base, longest streak in majors. . . . Opposing base stealers were less successful with Parrish catching (74-for-103, 72%) than with Bill Schroeder (27-for-35, 77%). . . . Only catcher to throw out Rickey Henderson twice. . . . Struck out in eight consecutive at-bats in LIP Situations. . . . Batting average in LIPS has been lower than otherwise in each of the last six seasons. . . . Career batting average of .417, with three home runs in 34 at-bats, on his birthday (June 15). . . . No player had four hits or two home runs on his birthday last season. Birthday-boy totals: .270 (95-for-352), 10 HR, 41 RBI, by players who batted .259 overall.

## Dan Pasqua

Bats Left

| Chicago White Sox | AB | H | 2B | 3B | HR | RBI | BB | SO | BA | SA | OBA |
|---|---|---|---|---|---|---|---|---|---|---|---|
| Season | 246 | 61 | 9 | 1 | 11 | 47 | 25 | 58 | .248 | .427 | .315 |
| vs. Left-Handers | 76 | 17 | 1 | 0 | 3 | 11 | 4 | 16 | .224 | .355 | .259 |
| vs. Right-Handers | 170 | 44 | 8 | 1 | 8 | 36 | 21 | 42 | .259 | .459 | .338 |
| Home | 113 | 29 | 3 | 1 | 5 | 18 | 14 | 30 | .257 | .434 | .336 |
| Road | 133 | 32 | 6 | 0 | 6 | 29 | 11 | 28 | .241 | .421 | .297 |
| Grass | 216 | 53 | 8 | 1 | 11 | 39 | 22 | 49 | .245 | .444 | .314 |
| Artificial Turf | 30 | 8 | 1 | 0 | 0 | 8 | 3 | 9 | .267 | .300 | .324 |
| April | 4 | 2 | 0 | 0 | 0 | 2 | 0 | 0 | .500 | .500 | .333 |
| May | 36 | 9 | 2 | 0 | 2 | 8 | 5 | 12 | .250 | .472 | .333 |
| June | 84 | 20 | 4 | 1 | 4 | 17 | 12 | 16 | .238 | .452 | .340 |
| July | 96 | 25 | 1 | 0 | 3 | 15 | 5 | 23 | .260 | .365 | .294 |
| August | 26 | 5 | 2 | 0 | 2 | 5 | 3 | 7 | .192 | .500 | .276 |
| Sept./Oct. | 0 | 0 | 0 | 0 | 0 | 0 | 0 | 0 | — | — | — |
| Leading Off Inn. | 45 | 11 | 0 | 1 | 5 | 5 | 9 | 11 | .244 | .622 | .370 |
| Runners On | 112 | 33 | 8 | 0 | 4 | 40 | 11 | 28 | .295 | .473 | .346 |
| Runners/Scor. Pos. | 66 | 21 | 6 | 0 | 1 | 34 | 7 | 18 | .318 | .455 | .364 |
| Runners On/2 Out | 44 | 11 | 1 | 0 | 2 | 13 | 6 | 11 | .250 | .409 | .340 |
| Scor. Pos./2 Out | 25 | 7 | 1 | 0 | 1 | 11 | 3 | 7 | .280 | .440 | .357 |
| Late Inning Pressure | 33 | 7 | 1 | 0 | 1 | 7 | 3 | 13 | .212 | .333 | .297 |
| Leading Off | 4 | 2 | 0 | 0 | 0 | 0 | 1 | 0 | .500 | .500 | .600 |
| Runners On | 19 | 4 | 1 | 0 | 1 | 7 | 2 | 9 | .211 | .421 | .286 |
| Runners/Scor. Pos. | 11 | 2 | 1 | 0 | 0 | 5 | 2 | 5 | .182 | .273 | .308 |

| RUNS BATTED IN | From 1B | From 2B | From 3B | Scoring Position |
|---|---|---|---|---|
| Totals | 4/86 | 15/56 | 17/31 | 32/87 |
| Percentage | 5% | 27% | 55% | 37% |
| Driving In Runners from 3B with Less than Two Out: | | | 13/23 | 57% |

Loves to face: Mike Moore (.471, 16-for-34, 2 HR)
Hates to face: Dave Stieb (.103, 3-for-29)
Batted 58 times with a runner on first base and less than two out, but didn't ground into a double play. . . . Drove in only three fewer runs than in 1988, despite playing 56 fewer games, with 176 fewer at-bats, nine fewer home runs, and 43 fewer runners in scoring position. . . . How? He batted 132 points higher with runners in scoring position. . . . Batted .289 against ground-ball pitchers, .203 vs. fly-ballers. . . . Career averages are .211 in LIP Situations, .249 in other at-bats. . . . Other career averages: .176 (6 HR) vs. left-handers, .260 (67 HR) vs. right-handers. . . . Comparable career statistics at same age: Woodie Held, Mike Epstein, Tom Haller, Gene Tenace, Graig Nettles. Not bad.

## Geno Petralli

Bats Left

| Texas Rangers | AB | H | 2B | 3B | HR | RBI | BB | SO | BA | SA | OBA |
|---|---|---|---|---|---|---|---|---|---|---|---|
| Season | 184 | 56 | 7 | 0 | 4 | 23 | 17 | 24 | .304 | .408 | .368 |
| vs. Left-Handers | 9 | 1 | 0 | 0 | 0 | 0 | 3 | 4 | .111 | .111 | .333 |
| vs. Right-Handers | 175 | 55 | 7 | 0 | 4 | 23 | 14 | 20 | .314 | .423 | .370 |
| Home | 88 | 17 | 1 | 0 | 1 | 6 | 7 | 17 | .193 | .239 | .260 |
| Road | 96 | 39 | 6 | 0 | 3 | 17 | 10 | 7 | .406 | .563 | .463 |
| Grass | 152 | 48 | 6 | 0 | 4 | 19 | 11 | 19 | .316 | .434 | .367 |
| Artificial Turf | 32 | 8 | 1 | 0 | 0 | 4 | 6 | 5 | .250 | .281 | .368 |
| April | 52 | 16 | 2 | 0 | 0 | 2 | 5 | 8 | .308 | .346 | .362 |
| May | 52 | 11 | 0 | 0 | 2 | 8 | 6 | 4 | .212 | .327 | .293 |
| June | 32 | 14 | 3 | 0 | 2 | 7 | 1 | 5 | .438 | .719 | .471 |
| July | 0 | 0 | 0 | 0 | 0 | 0 | 0 | 0 | — | — | — |
| August | 24 | 7 | 1 | 0 | 0 | 5 | 3 | 5 | .292 | .333 | .370 |
| Sept./Oct. | 24 | 8 | 1 | 0 | 0 | 1 | 2 | 2 | .333 | .375 | .407 |
| Leading Off Inn. | 43 | 10 | 2 | 0 | 0 | 0 | 3 | 10 | .233 | .279 | .283 |
| Runners On | 82 | 23 | 3 | 0 | 2 | 21 | 12 | 9 | .280 | .390 | .368 |
| Runners/Scor. Pos. | 54 | 13 | 3 | 0 | 1 | 19 | 8 | 7 | .241 | .352 | .333 |
| Runners On/2 Out | 37 | 13 | 2 | 0 | 1 | 14 | 4 | 4 | .351 | .486 | .415 |
| Scor. Pos./2 Out | 27 | 9 | 2 | 0 | 1 | 14 | 4 | 3 | .333 | .519 | .419 |
| Late Inning Pressure | 19 | 4 | 1 | 0 | 0 | 2 | 4 | 5 | .211 | .263 | .348 |
| Leading Off | 7 | 1 | 0 | 0 | 0 | 0 | 1 | 3 | .143 | .143 | .250 |
| Runners On | 11 | 3 | 1 | 0 | 0 | 2 | 3 | 1 | .273 | .364 | .429 |
| Runners/Scor. Pos. | 7 | 2 | 1 | 0 | 0 | 2 | 2 | 1 | .286 | .429 | .444 |

| RUNS BATTED IN | From 1B | From 2B | From 3B | Scoring Position |
|---|---|---|---|---|
| Totals | 3/60 | 8/42 | 8/19 | 16/61 |
| Percentage | 5% | 19% | 42% | 26% |
| Driving In Runners from 3B with Less than Two Out: | | | 4/8 | 50% |

Loves to face: Mike Boddicker (.474, 9-for-19, 2 HR)
Hates to face: Dave Stewart (0-for-15)
Hit three home runs in 20 at-bats at Fenway Park, one in 164 at-bats elsewhere. . . . Staff ERA according to Rangers' catcher: Stanley, 3.43; Kreuter, 3.56; Sundberg, 3.99; Petralli, 4.62. . . . Opposing base stealers: 34-for-55 vs. Sundberg (62%); 33-for-45 vs. Petralli (73%); 9-for-12 vs. Stanley (75%), 64-for-78 vs. Kreuter (82%). . . . Already ranks third in franchise history with 279 games at catcher, behind Sundberg (1495) and Paul ("Blame It On The") Casanova (657). . . . Started 50 games, all against right-handers. Has started 72 games vs. right-handers since his last start against a southpaw. . . . Career batting averages are .184 (no HR) vs. left-handers, .298 (20 HR) vs. right-handers.

## Gary Pettis

Bats Left and Right

| Detroit Tigers | AB | H | 2B | 3B | HR | RBI | BB | SO | BA | SA | OBA |
|---|---|---|---|---|---|---|---|---|---|---|---|
| Season | 444 | 114 | 8 | 6 | 1 | 18 | 84 | 106 | .257 | .309 | .375 |
| vs. Left-Handers | 152 | 40 | 4 | 2 | 0 | 7 | 27 | 21 | .263 | .316 | .374 |
| vs. Right-Handers | 292 | 74 | 4 | 4 | 1 | 11 | 57 | 85 | .253 | .305 | .375 |
| Home | 234 | 62 | 5 | 5 | 1 | 12 | 49 | 53 | .265 | .342 | .392 |
| Road | 210 | 52 | 3 | 1 | 0 | 6 | 35 | 53 | .248 | .271 | .355 |
| Grass | 378 | 99 | 6 | 6 | 1 | 15 | 75 | 87 | .262 | .317 | .384 |
| Artificial Turf | 66 | 15 | 2 | 0 | 0 | 3 | 9 | 19 | .227 | .258 | .320 |
| April | 0 | 0 | 0 | 0 | 0 | 0 | 0 | 0 | — | — | — |
| May | 60 | 13 | 3 | 2 | 0 | 0 | 13 | 15 | .217 | .333 | .356 |
| June | 91 | 23 | 1 | 1 | 1 | 2 | 19 | 21 | .253 | .319 | .382 |
| July | 88 | 25 | 2 | 1 | 0 | 5 | 14 | 16 | .284 | .330 | .382 |
| August | 101 | 24 | 1 | 1 | 0 | 4 | 19 | 33 | .238 | .267 | .358 |
| Sept./Oct. | 104 | 29 | 1 | 1 | 0 | 7 | 19 | 21 | .279 | .308 | .390 |
| Leading Off Inn. | 182 | 46 | 4 | 5 | 1 | 1 | 32 | 45 | .253 | .346 | .364 |
| Runners On | 153 | 41 | 2 | 1 | 0 | 17 | 25 | 28 | .268 | .294 | .371 |
| Runners/Scor. Pos. | 84 | 16 | 0 | 0 | 0 | 15 | 11 | 18 | .190 | .190 | .284 |
| Runners On/2 Out | 63 | 16 | 0 | 0 | 0 | 8 | 10 | 19 | .254 | .254 | .356 |
| Scor. Pos./2 Out | 41 | 9 | 0 | 0 | 0 | 8 | 5 | 15 | .220 | .220 | .304 |
| Late Inning Pressure | 64 | 16 | 1 | 1 | 0 | 8 | 19 | 21 | .250 | .297 | .422 |
| Leading Off | 21 | 4 | 1 | 0 | 0 | 0 | 5 | 8 | .190 | .238 | .346 |
| Runners On | 30 | 10 | 0 | 1 | 0 | 8 | 6 | 8 | .333 | .400 | .444 |
| Runners/Scor. Pos. | 19 | 6 | 0 | 0 | 0 | 7 | 2 | 6 | .316 | .316 | .381 |

| RUNS BATTED IN | From 1B | From 2B | From 3B | Scoring Position |
|---|---|---|---|---|
| Totals | 2/107 | 9/71 | 6/30 | 15/101 |
| Percentage | 2% | 13% | 20% | 15% |
| Driving In Runners from 3B with Less than Two Out: | | | 1/12 | 8% |

Loves to face: Mike Witt (.538, 7-for-13)
Hates to face: Ted Higuera (0-for-22, 7 SO)
Fifth time he's struck out at least 100 times while hitting fewer than 10 home runs. All-time leaders: Omar Moreno (6 times); Pettis (5); Lou Brock and Bobby Knoop (4). . . . Lowest batting average ever to lead the Tigers. . . . Made 113 of his 116 starts from the leadoff spot in batting order. . . . On-base average was highest of his career. Previous career-high in walks: 69. . . . One of three major leaguers with 500 or more plate appearances and no sacrifice flies. . . . Failed to drive in a runner from third base with less than two outs in 11 straight opportunites, matching the longest streak of the 1980s. . . . Played 119 games in the outfield, most of any A.L. player with fewer than two assists.

## Tony Phillips

Bats Left and Right

| Oakland As | AB | H | 2B | 3B | HR | RBI | BB | SO | BA | SA | OBA |
|---|---|---|---|---|---|---|---|---|---|---|---|
| Season | 451 | 118 | 15 | 6 | 4 | 47 | 58 | 66 | .262 | .348 | .345 |
| vs. Left-Handers | 139 | 36 | 6 | 4 | 0 | 10 | 22 | 19 | .259 | .360 | .364 |
| vs. Right-Handers | 312 | 82 | 9 | 2 | 4 | 37 | 36 | 47 | .263 | .343 | .336 |
| Home | 214 | 58 | 6 | 0 | 2 | 23 | 31 | 29 | .271 | .327 | .363 |
| Road | 237 | 60 | 9 | 6 | 2 | 24 | 27 | 37 | .253 | .367 | .328 |
| Grass | 376 | 98 | 10 | 4 | 3 | 41 | 53 | 58 | .261 | .332 | .351 |
| Artificial Turf | 75 | 20 | 5 | 2 | 1 | 6 | 5 | 8 | .267 | .427 | .313 |
| April | 75 | 25 | 5 | 0 | 1 | 6 | 9 | 10 | .333 | .440 | .419 |
| May | 57 | 12 | 2 | 1 | 1 | 6 | 10 | 13 | .211 | .333 | .338 |
| June | 78 | 22 | 4 | 2 | 0 | 9 | 12 | 12 | .282 | .385 | .366 |
| July | 69 | 12 | 1 | 1 | 1 | 5 | 13 | 12 | .174 | .261 | .301 |
| August | 88 | 18 | 1 | 1 | 1 | 10 | 5 | 10 | .205 | .273 | .242 |
| Sept./Oct. | 84 | 29 | 2 | 1 | 0 | 11 | 9 | 9 | .345 | .393 | .404 |
| Leading Off Inn. | 105 | 25 | 3 | 0 | 0 | 0 | 16 | 14 | .238 | .267 | .339 |
| Runners On | 203 | 58 | 10 | 3 | 3 | 46 | 18 | 32 | .286 | .409 | .336 |
| Runners/Scor. Pos. | 111 | 26 | 4 | 2 | 0 | 37 | 11 | 16 | .234 | .306 | .287 |
| Runners On/2 Out | 98 | 28 | 2 | 1 | 2 | 20 | 9 | 15 | .286 | .388 | .352 |
| Scor. Pos./2 Out | 62 | 16 | 2 | 1 | 0 | 16 | 5 | 9 | .258 | .323 | .313 |
| Late Inning Pressure | 66 | 16 | 4 | 1 | 1 | 8 | 8 | 15 | .242 | .379 | .320 |
| Leading Off | 17 | 5 | 1 | 0 | 0 | 0 | 1 | 2 | .294 | .353 | .333 |
| Runners On | 26 | 9 | 3 | 1 | 1 | 8 | 3 | 5 | .346 | .654 | .400 |
| Runners/Scor. Pos. | 12 | 3 | 2 | 0 | 0 | 5 | 2 | 2 | .250 | .417 | .333 |

| RUNS BATTED IN | From 1B | From 2B | From 3B | Scoring Position |
|---|---|---|---|---|
| Totals | 8/149 | 12/91 | 23/46 | 35/137 |
| Percentage | 5% | 13% | 50% | 26% |
| Driving In Runners from 3B with Less than Two Out: | | | 16/20 | 80% |

Loves to face: Mike Witt (.368, 14-for-38, 1 HR)
Hates to face: Mark Gubicza (.083, 2-for-24, 7 SO)
Reached base 11 times on infield errors, fourth in A.L., behind Boggs (13), Molitor (13), and Cal Ripken (12). . . . Hit safely in 10 consecutive at-bats vs. right-handers, tying Ken Singleton for longest streak of the 1980s. . . . One of five A.L. players to start at five fielding positions. . . . First and only player ever to play three positions in a World Series game (2B, 3B, LF). . . . Career fielding average of .944 at shortstop ranks next-to-last among players who played within the last 40 years (minimum: 250 games). Only Derrel Thomas had a lower mark (.937). . . . On same day, Detroit lured Phillips from world champs, and Lloyd Moseby from A.L. East champs. What's the catch—free pepperoni pizza?

## Ken Phelps

Bats Left

| Yankees/As | AB | H | 2B | 3B | HR | RBI | BB | SO | BA | SA | OBA |
|---|---|---|---|---|---|---|---|---|---|---|---|
| Season | 194 | 47 | 4 | 0 | 7 | 29 | 31 | 47 | .242 | .371 | .342 |
| vs. Left-Handers | 11 | 2 | 0 | 0 | 0 | 2 | 3 | 4 | .182 | .182 | .313 |
| vs. Right-Handers | 183 | 45 | 4 | 0 | 7 | 27 | 28 | 43 | .246 | .383 | .344 |
| Home | 104 | 27 | 1 | 0 | 4 | 16 | 17 | 25 | .260 | .385 | .355 |
| Road | 90 | 20 | 3 | 0 | 3 | 13 | 14 | 22 | .222 | .356 | .327 |
| Grass | 163 | 38 | 2 | 0 | 5 | 21 | 30 | 41 | .233 | .337 | .347 |
| Artificial Turf | 31 | 9 | 2 | 0 | 2 | 8 | 1 | 6 | .290 | .548 | .313 |
| April | 43 | 14 | 2 | 0 | 1 | 3 | 6 | 10 | .326 | .442 | .400 |
| May | 43 | 9 | 1 | 0 | 0 | 4 | 11 | 5 | .209 | .233 | .370 |
| June | 38 | 9 | 0 | 0 | 3 | 11 | 3 | 12 | .237 | .474 | .293 |
| July | 22 | 6 | 0 | 0 | 0 | 2 | 1 | 6 | .273 | .273 | .292 |
| August | 39 | 8 | 0 | 0 | 3 | 9 | 6 | 14 | .205 | .436 | .304 |
| Sept./Oct. | 9 | 1 | 1 | 0 | 0 | 0 | 4 | 0 | .111 | .222 | .385 |
| Leading Off Inn. | 37 | 11 | 2 | 0 | 1 | 1 | 3 | 5 | .297 | .432 | .350 |
| Runners On | 99 | 23 | 2 | 0 | 5 | 27 | 15 | 26 | .232 | .404 | .325 |
| Runners/Scor. Pos. | 49 | 11 | 1 | 0 | 3 | 23 | 13 | 16 | .224 | .429 | .369 |
| Runners On/2 Out | 40 | 10 | 1 | 0 | 3 | 9 | 11 | 9 | .250 | .500 | .412 |
| Scor. Pos./2 Out | 21 | 3 | 0 | 0 | 2 | 7 | 9 | 8 | .143 | .429 | .400 |
| Late Inning Pressure | 38 | 12 | 1 | 0 | 2 | 7 | 5 | 8 | .316 | .500 | .395 |
| Leading Off | 7 | 3 | 1 | 0 | 0 | 0 | 0 | 1 | .429 | .571 | .429 |
| Runners On | 20 | 6 | 0 | 0 | 2 | 7 | 2 | 5 | .300 | .600 | .364 |
| Runners/Scor. Pos. | 10 | 3 | 0 | 0 | 1 | 5 | 2 | 3 | .300 | .600 | .417 |

| RUNS BATTED IN | From 1B | From 2B | From 3B | Scoring Position |
|---|---|---|---|---|
| Totals | 3/82 | 7/40 | 12/21 | 19/61 |
| Percentage | 4% | 18% | 57% | 31% |
| Driving In Runners from 3B with Less than Two Out: | | | 9/12 | 75% |

Loves to face: Mark Williamson (.625, 5-for-8, 3 HR, 3 BB)
Hates to face: Jack Morris (,032, 1-for-31, 13 SO)
Led A.L. with three pinch-hit home runs, all with Yankees. Also led A.L. pinch hitters in hits (11), RBI (13), and walks (8). . . . Played only nine games in field last season, all at first base. . . . Career average is .163 with two outs and runners in scoring position. . . . Has hit 122 career HR, only seven against left-handers. . . . Career average of 17.2 walks per 100 plate appearances leads active players (minimum: 1000 PA). . . . Average of 7.04 home runs per 100 at-bats ranks second among that group to Mark McGwire (7.09). . . . Survived challenge of McGwire, and retains major league record of reaching 100 home runs in fewest at-bats (1330). Ralph Kiner ranks second (1351), McGwire third (1400).

## Luis Polonia

Bats Left

| As/Yankees | AB | H | 2B | 3B | HR | RBI | BB | SO | BA | SA | OBA |
|---|---|---|---|---|---|---|---|---|---|---|---|
| Season | 433 | 130 | 17 | 6 | 3 | 46 | 25 | 44 | .300 | .388 | .338 |
| vs. Left-Handers | 71 | 22 | 2 | 0 | 0 | 6 | 3 | 9 | .310 | .338 | .347 |
| vs. Right-Handers | 362 | 108 | 15 | 6 | 3 | 40 | 22 | 35 | .298 | .398 | .337 |
| Home | 199 | 74 | 8 | 3 | 1 | 26 | 12 | 18 | .372 | .457 | .409 |
| Road | 234 | 56 | 9 | 3 | 2 | 20 | 13 | 26 | .239 | .329 | .277 |
| Grass | 379 | 116 | 16 | 5 | 3 | 42 | 22 | 37 | .306 | .398 | .344 |
| Artificial Turf | 54 | 14 | 1 | 1 | 0 | 4 | 3 | 7 | .259 | .315 | .298 |
| April | 60 | 14 | 2 | 2 | 0 | 7 | 3 | 5 | .233 | .333 | .266 |
| May | 86 | 25 | 3 | 2 | 0 | 6 | 4 | 7 | .291 | .372 | .322 |
| June | 83 | 27 | 2 | 0 | 1 | 9 | 4 | 7 | .325 | .386 | .356 |
| July | 93 | 27 | 5 | 0 | 2 | 12 | 8 | 13 | .290 | .409 | .350 |
| August | 65 | 22 | 1 | 2 | 0 | 7 | 4 | 7 | .338 | .415 | .371 |
| Sept./Oct. | 46 | 15 | 4 | 0 | 0 | 5 | 2 | 5 | .326 | .413 | .360 |
| Leading Off Inn. | 104 | 34 | 8 | 1 | 0 | 0 | 8 | 9 | .327 | .423 | .375 |
| Runners On | 180 | 53 | 3 | 3 | 3 | 46 | 8 | 19 | .294 | .394 | .318 |
| Runners/Scor. Pos. | 119 | 34 | 2 | 2 | 1 | 41 | 5 | 15 | .286 | .361 | .305 |
| Runners On/2 Out | 69 | 21 | 0 | 1 | 1 | 18 | 7 | 8 | .304 | .377 | .368 |
| Scor. Pos./2 Out | 53 | 18 | 0 | 1 | 1 | 18 | 5 | 7 | .340 | .434 | .397 |
| Late Inning Pressure | 61 | 21 | 3 | 1 | 1 | 6 | 3 | 10 | .344 | .475 | .369 |
| Leading Off | 13 | 7 | 2 | 1 | 0 | 0 | 0 | 2 | .538 | .846 | .538 |
| Runners On | 27 | 7 | 0 | 0 | 1 | 6 | 2 | 5 | .259 | .370 | .300 |
| Runners/Scor. Pos. | 20 | 4 | 0 | 0 | 1 | 6 | 1 | 5 | .200 | .350 | .227 |

| RUNS BATTED IN | From 1B | From 2B | From 3B | Scoring Position |
|---|---|---|---|---|
| Totals | 4/113 | 15/89 | 24/59 | 39/148 |
| Percentage | 4% | 17% | 41% | 26% |
| Driving In Runners from 3B with Less than Two Out: | | | 17/36 | 47% |

Loves to face: Roy Smith (.667, 6-for-9)
Hates to face: Mark Birkbeck (0-for-7)
Brilliant base runner: Advanced from first base to third on 14 of 21 outfield singles (67%), and scored from second base on 18 of 19 (95%). A.L. averages: 35 percent and 73 percent, respectively. . . . Career batting averages: .300 vs. right-handed pitchers, .258 vs. left-handers (.224 prior to 1989). . . . Three hits, with no walks and no extra-base hits, in 22 career at-bats with the bases loaded. . . . Yankees allowed 5.3 runs per nine innings with Polonia in left field last season, compared to 4.8 with Rickey Henderson there. . . . We defended his fielding in last year's edition, and have come to apologize. He's about the worst we've seen. Ought to call for more fair catches.

## Jim Presley

Bats Right

| Seattle Mariners | AB | H | 2B | 3B | HR | RBI | BB | SO | BA | SA | OBA |
|---|---|---|---|---|---|---|---|---|---|---|---|
| Season | 390 | 92 | 20 | 1 | 12 | 42 | 21 | 107 | .236 | .385 | .275 |
| vs. Left-Handers | 116 | 38 | 5 | 1 | 4 | 11 | 5 | 25 | .328 | .491 | .352 |
| vs. Right-Handers | 274 | 54 | 15 | 0 | 8 | 31 | 16 | 82 | .197 | .339 | .243 |
| Home | 213 | 55 | 12 | 1 | 7 | 23 | 10 | 57 | .258 | .423 | .295 |
| Road | 177 | 37 | 8 | 0 | 5 | 19 | 11 | 50 | .209 | .339 | .253 |
| Grass | 162 | 35 | 8 | 0 | 5 | 18 | 9 | 46 | .216 | .358 | .256 |
| Artificial Turf | 228 | 57 | 12 | 1 | 7 | 24 | 12 | 61 | .250 | .404 | .289 |
| April | 54 | 13 | 3 | 0 | 0 | 5 | 3 | 9 | .241 | .296 | .281 |
| May | 98 | 30 | 7 | 0 | 2 | 9 | 3 | 25 | .306 | .439 | .327 |
| June | 59 | 15 | 2 | 0 | 3 | 6 | 6 | 17 | .254 | .441 | .318 |
| July | 80 | 17 | 3 | 0 | 4 | 14 | 5 | 21 | .213 | .400 | .256 |
| August | 64 | 8 | 1 | 0 | 2 | 7 | 1 | 27 | .125 | .234 | .152 |
| Sept./Oct. | 35 | 9 | 4 | 1 | 1 | 1 | 3 | 8 | .257 | .514 | .316 |
| Leading Off Inn. | 96 | 24 | 4 | 1 | 5 | 5 | 2 | 25 | .250 | .469 | .273 |
| Runners On | 178 | 46 | 11 | 0 | 4 | 34 | 11 | 47 | .258 | .388 | .298 |
| Runners/Scor. Pos. | 97 | 22 | 3 | 0 | 2 | 25 | 9 | 31 | .227 | .320 | .287 |
| Runners On/2 Out | 79 | 17 | 5 | 0 | 1 | 13 | 6 | 23 | .215 | .316 | .271 |
| Scor. Pos./2 Out | 45 | 8 | 2 | 0 | 0 | 8 | 6 | 18 | .178 | .222 | .275 |
| Late Inning Pressure | 56 | 11 | 4 | 0 | 3 | 6 | 1 | 21 | .196 | .429 | .224 |
| Leading Off | 21 | 4 | 2 | 0 | 1 | 1 | 1 | 7 | .190 | .429 | .261 |
| Runners On | 17 | 3 | 1 | 0 | 1 | 4 | 0 | 6 | .176 | .412 | .176 |
| Runners/Scor. Pos. | 8 | 1 | 0 | 0 | 1 | 4 | 0 | 4 | .125 | .500 | .125 |

| RUNS BATTED IN | From 1B | From 2B | From 3B | Scoring Position |
|---|---|---|---|---|
| Totals | 8/133 | 12/78 | 10/37 | 22/115 |
| Percentage | 6% | 15% | 27% | 19% |
| Driving In Runners from 3B with Less than Two Out: | | | 8/21 | 38% |

Loves to face: Mitch Williams (.444, 4-for-9, 1 HR)
Hates to face: Ricky Horton (.091, 1-for-11)
Played only 117 games after four straight seasons of 150 or more. . . . Fielding percentage at third base has decreased in each of the last three seasons, from .965 in 1986 to .924 in 1989. . . . Played 30 games at first base, his first there in his six years in majors. . . . Home runs, year by year since 1985: 28, 27, 24, 14, 12. . . . Struck out in seven consecutive plate appearances, tying Jesse Barfield for the longest streak in A.L. . . . Batted .286 vs. fly-ball pitchers, .201 vs. ground-ballers. . . . Batted .143 in day games, .270 at night, largest difference in majors (minimum: 100 AB each). Ranked among top 10 with a 70-point gap in 1988. . . . Lefty/righty breakdown was the most lopsided of his career.

## Kirby Puckett

Bats Right

| Minnesota Twins | AB | H | 2B | 3B | HR | RBI | BB | SO | BA | SA | OBA |
|---|---|---|---|---|---|---|---|---|---|---|---|
| Season | 635 | 215 | 45 | 4 | 9 | 86 | 41 | 59 | .339 | .465 | .379 |
| vs. Left-Handers | 191 | 58 | 14 | 1 | 1 | 19 | 12 | 20 | .304 | .403 | .341 |
| vs. Right-Handers | 444 | 157 | 31 | 3 | 8 | 67 | 29 | 39 | .354 | .491 | .395 |
| Home | 328 | 128 | 28 | 2 | 7 | 53 | 14 | 26 | .390 | .552 | .412 |
| Road | 307 | 87 | 17 | 2 | 2 | 33 | 27 | 33 | .283 | .371 | .344 |
| Grass | 234 | 66 | 13 | 1 | 2 | 25 | 23 | 28 | .282 | .372 | .347 |
| Artificial Turf | 401 | 149 | 32 | 3 | 7 | 61 | 18 | 31 | .372 | .519 | .398 |
| April | 83 | 28 | 9 | 1 | 3 | 11 | 8 | 8 | .337 | .578 | .391 |
| May | 116 | 40 | 11 | 0 | 0 | 16 | 8 | 8 | .345 | .440 | .392 |
| June | 116 | 37 | 6 | 1 | 2 | 16 | 7 | 18 | .319 | .440 | .360 |
| July | 95 | 36 | 6 | 1 | 2 | 15 | 6 | 7 | .379 | .526 | .412 |
| August | 113 | 37 | 9 | 0 | 0 | 14 | 4 | 9 | .327 | .407 | .347 |
| Sept./Oct. | 112 | 37 | 4 | 1 | 2 | 14 | 8 | 9 | .330 | .438 | .377 |
| Leading Off Inn. | 104 | 35 | 8 | 0 | 2 | 2 | 3 | 8 | .337 | .471 | .355 |
| Runners On | 312 | 107 | 19 | 4 | 4 | 81 | 28 | 25 | .343 | .468 | .397 |
| Runners/Scor. Pos. | 176 | 58 | 10 | 2 | 2 | 71 | 21 | 18 | .330 | .443 | .397 |
| Runners On/2 Out | 86 | 30 | 4 | 1 | 2 | 24 | 13 | 7 | .349 | .488 | .440 |
| Scor. Pos./2 Out | 55 | 19 | 1 | 1 | 1 | 20 | 13 | 4 | .345 | .455 | .471 |
| Late Inning Pressure | 77 | 30 | 7 | 0 | 3 | 17 | 7 | 10 | .390 | .597 | .440 |
| Leading Off | 12 | 4 | 1 | 0 | 1 | 1 | 2 | 2 | .333 | .667 | .429 |
| Runners On | 37 | 14 | 4 | 0 | 0 | 14 | 5 | 2 | .378 | .486 | .452 |
| Runners/Scor. Pos. | 22 | 9 | 1 | 0 | 0 | 12 | 5 | 2 | .409 | .455 | .519 |

| RUNS BATTED IN | From 1B | From 2B | From 3B | Scoring Position |
|---|---|---|---|---|
| Totals | 9/211 | 26/136 | 42/67 | 68/203 |
| Percentage | 4% | 19% | 63% | 33% |
| Driving In Runners from 3B with Less than Two Out: | | | 32/47 | 68% |

Loves to face: Melido Perez (.609, 14-for-23, 1 HR)
Hates to face: Shawn Hillegas (.154, 2-for-13)
What do you think Kirby hit with runners in scoring position and the Twins trailing by one run? How about .619 (13-for-21)—the best in the A.L. . . . Now try this one on for size: Batted .575 (73-for-127) on balls hit up the middle (.306 to the left side, .326 to the right). . . . Hasn't batted leadoff since final game of the 1987 season. . . . Career average vs. left-handers (.339) is highest among active players (minimum: 150 hits). Last season's mark was a career *low*. . . . Career average of .353 at the Metrodome, .293 on the road. . . . Led his league in hits for third consecutive season, tying major league mark shared by Ginger Beaumont (1902–04), Cobb, Hornsby, Frank McCormick, and Tony Oliva.

## Johnny Ray

Bats Left and Right

| California Angels | AB | H | 2B | 3B | HR | RBI | BB | SO | BA | SA | OBA |
|---|---|---|---|---|---|---|---|---|---|---|---|
| Season | 530 | 153 | 16 | 3 | 5 | 62 | 36 | 30 | .289 | .358 | .327 |
| vs. Left-Handers | 195 | 51 | 6 | 1 | 1 | 21 | 13 | 12 | .262 | .318 | .299 |
| vs. Right-Handers | 335 | 102 | 10 | 2 | 4 | 41 | 23 | 18 | .304 | .382 | .343 |
| Home | 268 | 71 | 9 | 1 | 3 | 30 | 14 | 12 | .265 | .340 | .296 |
| Road | 262 | 82 | 7 | 2 | 2 | 32 | 22 | 18 | .313 | .378 | .357 |
| Grass | 450 | 131 | 13 | 3 | 4 | 55 | 29 | 23 | .291 | .360 | .327 |
| Artificial Turf | 80 | 22 | 3 | 0 | 1 | 7 | 7 | 7 | .275 | .350 | .326 |
| April | 41 | 10 | 2 | 0 | 0 | 4 | 0 | 3 | .244 | .293 | .238 |
| May | 102 | 33 | 4 | 1 | 1 | 22 | 8 | 3 | .324 | .412 | .360 |
| June | 99 | 25 | 2 | 2 | 1 | 6 | 3 | 8 | .253 | .343 | .275 |
| July | 108 | 31 | 3 | 0 | 0 | 12 | 11 | 8 | .287 | .315 | .341 |
| August | 103 | 37 | 3 | 0 | 2 | 12 | 11 | 3 | .359 | .447 | .417 |
| Sept./Oct. | 77 | 17 | 2 | 0 | 1 | 6 | 3 | 5 | .221 | .286 | .244 |
| Leading Off Inn. | 95 | 27 | 4 | 0 | 0 | 0 | 5 | 6 | .284 | .326 | .320 |
| Runners On | 219 | 68 | 7 | 3 | 3 | 60 | 15 | 9 | .311 | .411 | .337 |
| Runners/Scor. Pos. | 108 | 32 | 5 | 3 | 1 | 54 | 11 | 4 | .296 | .426 | .328 |
| Runners On/2 Out | 80 | 21 | 3 | 1 | 1 | 20 | 10 | 4 | .263 | .363 | .344 |
| Scor. Pos./2 Out | 47 | 13 | 2 | 1 | 0 | 17 | 7 | 3 | .277 | .362 | .370 |
| Late Inning Pressure | 66 | 17 | 3 | 0 | 0 | 9 | 6 | 4 | .258 | .303 | .307 |
| Leading Off | 15 | 4 | 1 | 0 | 0 | 0 | 0 | 0 | .267 | .333 | .267 |
| Runners On | 29 | 7 | 0 | 0 | 0 | 9 | 6 | 3 | .241 | .241 | .342 |
| Runners/Scor. Pos. | 20 | 7 | 0 | 0 | 0 | 9 | 5 | 2 | .350 | .350 | .429 |

| RUNS BATTED IN | From 1B | From 2B | From 3B | Scoring Position |
|---|---|---|---|---|
| Totals | 5/159 | 22/85 | 30/54 | 52/139 |
| Percentage | 3% | 26% | 56% | 37% |
| Driving In Runners from 3B with Less than Two Out: | | | 25/40 | 63% |

Loves to face: Andy Hawkins (.472, 17-for-36)
Hates to face: Dave Stieb (0-for-12)
Played only 134 games, after topping the 150 mark in each of the previous seven years. . . . Lost a streak of seven straight seasons with 30 or more doubles, dropping from a career high of 42 in 1988. . . . Batted .344 in day games, .271 at night. . . . Turned 98 double plays in only 130 games at second base. He topped that total only once previously: 102 double plays in 1983, with Dale Berra as his middle-infield partner. . . . Fewest games ever by a second baseman with at least 100 DP: 107, by Billy Hitchcock in 1950 (105 DP). . . . One of four player to hit .300 against right-handers in each of the last four seasons (min.: 250 AB). The others: Boggs, Brett, Gwynn, Puckett, Yount. . . . Nice company.

## Jody Reed

Bats Right

| Boston Red Sox | AB | H | 2B | 3B | HR | RBI | BB | SO | BA | SA | OBA |
|---|---|---|---|---|---|---|---|---|---|---|---|
| Season | 524 | 151 | 42 | 2 | 3 | 40 | 73 | 44 | .288 | .393 | .376 |
| vs. Left-Handers | 140 | 45 | 13 | 1 | 1 | 17 | 20 | 8 | .321 | .450 | .401 |
| vs. Right-Handers | 384 | 106 | 29 | 1 | 2 | 23 | 53 | 36 | .276 | .372 | .367 |
| Home | 270 | 81 | 23 | 1 | 2 | 19 | 36 | 26 | .300 | .415 | .384 |
| Road | 254 | 70 | 19 | 1 | 1 | 21 | 37 | 18 | .276 | .370 | .368 |
| Grass | 452 | 132 | 37 | 2 | 3 | 35 | 58 | 40 | .292 | .403 | .373 |
| Artificial Turf | 72 | 19 | 5 | 0 | 0 | 5 | 15 | 4 | .264 | .333 | .398 |
| April | 65 | 14 | 3 | 0 | 0 | 3 | 11 | 9 | .215 | .262 | .329 |
| May | 93 | 31 | 11 | 0 | 0 | 8 | 6 | 7 | .333 | .452 | .370 |
| June | 99 | 24 | 6 | 0 | 0 | 4 | 16 | 11 | .242 | .303 | .353 |
| July | 84 | 21 | 9 | 0 | 0 | 7 | 13 | 5 | .250 | .357 | .356 |
| August | 92 | 32 | 8 | 0 | 2 | 9 | 15 | 5 | .348 | .500 | .436 |
| Sept./Oct. | 91 | 29 | 5 | 2 | 1 | 9 | 12 | 7 | .319 | .451 | .398 |
| Leading Off Inn. | 121 | 38 | 12 | 0 | 1 | 1 | 15 | 8 | .314 | .438 | .390 |
| Runners On | 237 | 72 | 20 | 1 | 1 | 38 | 37 | 23 | .304 | .409 | .399 |
| Runners/Scor. Pos. | 131 | 32 | 9 | 0 | 0 | 35 | 22 | 16 | .244 | .313 | .358 |
| Runners On/2 Out | 112 | 34 | 9 | 1 | 0 | 16 | 16 | 12 | .304 | .402 | .400 |
| Scor. Pos./2 Out | 65 | 14 | 3 | 0 | 0 | 15 | 11 | 9 | .215 | .262 | .346 |
| Late Inning Pressure | 76 | 17 | 4 | 0 | 0 | 6 | 8 | 12 | .224 | .276 | .299 |
| Leading Off | 24 | 4 | 1 | 0 | 0 | 0 | 1 | 4 | .167 | .208 | .200 |
| Runners On | 29 | 7 | 1 | 0 | 0 | 6 | 6 | 4 | .241 | .276 | .368 |
| Runners/Scor. Pos. | 19 | 5 | 1 | 0 | 0 | 6 | 5 | 2 | .263 | .316 | .407 |

| RUNS BATTED IN | From 1B | From 2B | From 3B | Scoring Position |
|---|---|---|---|---|
| Totals | 2/179 | 16/112 | 19/58 | 35/170 |
| Percentage | 1% | 14% | 33% | 21% |
| Driving In Runners from 3B with Less than Two Out: | | | 14/32 | 44% |

Loves to face: Tom Henke (.750, 3-for-4)
Hates to face: Mike Witt (0-for-10)
First Red Sox player, and 7th major leaguer in this century, to play 70 or more games each at second base and shortstop in the same season. . . . Red Sox allowed fewer runs per nine innings with Reed at second base (4.4) than with Barrett there (4.6). . . . Sox had a 39–27 mark with Reed starting at second base, 44–52 record with other starting second basemen. . . . Over last two seasons: 130–105 (.553) with Reed starting at any position, 42–47 (.472) without him. . . . Reached base in leading off nine consecutive innings, longest streak in A.L. last season. . . . One of three active players with 100 games played and more career doubles (66) than strikeouts (65). The others: Bill Buckner and Don Mattingly.

## Harold Reynolds

Bats Left and Right

| Seattle Mariners | AB | H | 2B | 3B | HR | RBI | BB | SO | BA | SA | OBA |
|---|---|---|---|---|---|---|---|---|---|---|---|
| Season | 613 | 184 | 24 | 9 | 0 | 43 | 55 | 45 | .300 | .369 | .359 |
| vs. Left-Handers | 170 | 55 | 9 | 1 | 0 | 14 | 15 | 13 | .324 | .388 | .378 |
| vs. Right-Handers | 443 | 129 | 15 | 8 | 0 | 29 | 40 | 32 | .291 | .361 | .352 |
| Home | 307 | 92 | 13 | 5 | 0 | 27 | 24 | 25 | .300 | .375 | .351 |
| Road | 306 | 92 | 11 | 4 | 0 | 16 | 31 | 20 | .301 | .363 | .367 |
| Grass | 239 | 71 | 7 | 3 | 0 | 15 | 23 | 13 | .297 | .351 | .361 |
| Artificial Turf | 374 | 113 | 17 | 6 | 0 | 28 | 32 | 32 | .302 | .380 | .358 |
| April | 101 | 29 | 1 | 4 | 0 | 11 | 5 | 9 | .287 | .376 | .327 |
| May | 102 | 34 | 8 | 1 | 0 | 9 | 13 | 6 | .333 | .431 | .402 |
| June | 87 | 21 | 2 | 1 | 0 | 5 | 5 | 10 | .241 | .287 | .290 |
| July | 107 | 35 | 1 | 0 | 0 | 9 | 13 | 7 | .327 | .336 | .397 |
| August | 114 | 32 | 7 | 0 | 0 | 4 | 10 | 7 | .281 | .342 | .344 |
| Sept./Oct. | 102 | 33 | 5 | 3 | 0 | 5 | 9 | 6 | .324 | .431 | .378 |
| Leading Off Inn. | 240 | 65 | 8 | 4 | 0 | 0 | 25 | 20 | .271 | .338 | .340 |
| Runners On | 203 | 65 | 8 | 0 | 0 | 43 | 21 | 11 | .320 | .360 | .382 |
| Runners/Scor. Pos. | 113 | 32 | 7 | 0 | 0 | 42 | 18 | 5 | .283 | .345 | .373 |
| Runners On/2 Out | 91 | 24 | 4 | 0 | 0 | 19 | 12 | 5 | .264 | .308 | .356 |
| Scor. Pos./2 Out | 61 | 15 | 3 | 0 | 0 | 18 | 10 | 3 | .246 | .295 | .352 |
| Late Inning Pressure | 74 | 24 | 1 | 0 | 0 | 4 | 14 | 12 | .324 | .338 | .427 |
| Leading Off | 20 | 7 | 0 | 0 | 0 | 0 | 7 | 3 | .350 | .350 | .519 |
| Runners On | 33 | 10 | 0 | 0 | 0 | 4 | 4 | 5 | .303 | .303 | .368 |
| Runners/Scor. Pos. | 12 | 3 | 0 | 0 | 0 | 4 | 3 | 1 | .250 | .250 | .375 |

| RUNS BATTED IN | From 1B | From 2B | From 3B | Scoring Position |
|---|---|---|---|---|
| Totals | 3/151 | 17/72 | 23/58 | 40/130 |
| Percentage | 2% | 24% | 40% | 31% |
| Driving In Runners from 3B with Less than Two Out: | | | 14/25 | 56% |

Loves to face: Jeff Reardon (.833, 5-for-6, 2 2B)
Hates to face: Eric King (0-for-19)
Made 143 of his 149 starts from the leadoff spot. . . . Led the Mariners with 20 infield hits. . . . Career average of .218 with two outs and runners in scoring position. . . . Has never hit a home run in 1192 at-bats outside the Kingdome. . . . Caught stealing 67 times over last three seasons, highest total in majors. Seven players have more steals (120). . . . Has 680 career games at second base, but none at any other position. Only three other Mariners players have even 100 games there: Julio Cruz (720), Jack Perconte (275), and Larry Milbourne (157). . . . Here's what a career in Seattle means: Reynolds has played the most seasons of any active nonpitcher never to play for a team with a winning record (7).

## Jim Rice

Bats Right

| Boston Red Sox | AB | H | 2B | 3B | HR | RBI | BB | SO | BA | SA | OBA |
|---|---|---|---|---|---|---|---|---|---|---|---|
| Season | 209 | 49 | 10 | 2 | 3 | 28 | 13 | 39 | .234 | .344 | .276 |
| vs. Left-Handers | 63 | 16 | 4 | 1 | 1 | 8 | 4 | 9 | .254 | .397 | .294 |
| vs. Right-Handers | 146 | 33 | 6 | 1 | 2 | 20 | 9 | 30 | .226 | .322 | .269 |
| Home | 110 | 27 | 4 | 1 | 1 | 13 | 7 | 21 | .245 | .327 | .283 |
| Road | 99 | 22 | 6 | 1 | 2 | 15 | 6 | 18 | .222 | .364 | .269 |
| Grass | 177 | 41 | 8 | 1 | 2 | 23 | 13 | 31 | .232 | .322 | .281 |
| Artificial Turf | 32 | 8 | 2 | 1 | 1 | 5 | 0 | 8 | .250 | .469 | .250 |
| April | 86 | 25 | 2 | 1 | 3 | 16 | 3 | 14 | .291 | .442 | .309 |
| May | 74 | 13 | 4 | 1 | 0 | 9 | 7 | 18 | .176 | .257 | .244 |
| June | 0 | 0 | 0 | 0 | 0 | 0 | 0 | 0 | — | — | — |
| July | 39 | 9 | 3 | 0 | 0 | 2 | 3 | 7 | .231 | .308 | .286 |
| August | 10 | 2 | 1 | 0 | 0 | 1 | 0 | 0 | .200 | .300 | .200 |
| Sept./Oct. | 0 | 0 | 0 | 0 | 0 | 0 | 0 | 0 | — | — | — |
| Leading Off Inn. | 49 | 13 | 2 | 2 | 1 | 1 | 1 | 10 | .265 | .449 | .294 |
| Runners On | 106 | 24 | 4 | 0 | 2 | 27 | 6 | 22 | .226 | .321 | .256 |
| Runners/Scor. Pos. | 66 | 16 | 2 | 0 | 1 | 23 | 5 | 17 | .242 | .318 | .276 |
| Runners On/2 Out | 41 | 8 | 1 | 0 | 2 | 11 | 6 | 9 | .195 | .366 | .298 |
| Scor. Pos./2 Out | 26 | 5 | 0 | 0 | 1 | 8 | 5 | 7 | .192 | .308 | .323 |
| Late Inning Pressure | 23 | 4 | 1 | 0 | 0 | 0 | 5 | 7 | .174 | .217 | .321 |
| Leading Off | 8 | 1 | 0 | 0 | 0 | 0 | 1 | 3 | .125 | .125 | .222 |
| Runners On | 8 | 1 | 0 | 0 | 0 | 0 | 3 | 4 | .125 | .125 | .364 |
| Runners/Scor. Pos. | 7 | 1 | 0 | 0 | 0 | 0 | 3 | 3 | .143 | .143 | .400 |

| RUNS BATTED IN | From 1B | From 2B | From 3B | Scoring Position |
|---|---|---|---|---|
| Totals | 3/79 | 8/57 | 14/29 | 22/86 |
| Percentage | 4% | 14% | 48% | 26% |
| Driving In Runners from 3B with Less than Two Out: | | | 11/17 | 65% |

Loves to face: Dennis Martinez (.376, 32-for-85, 7 HR)
Hates to face: Danny Darwin (.109, 5-for-46, 12 SO)
Led A.L. players in hits and doubles last spring training. Then hit safely in first 15 games of regular season. . . . Drove in 23 runs in his first 28 games, but five in 28 games thereafter. . . . Should anyone care, still needs nine more double-play ground outs to eclipse Yaz's A.L. record (323), then another five for Aaron's major league mark. . . . Batting average in Late-Inning Pressure Situations has been lower than his overall average in each of the last 11 seasons. . . . Think he won't miss Fenway? Rice has had a higher average in home games than elsewhere in each of his 16 seasons in majors. . . . Career average has dropped to .298. Would need hits in his next 23 consecutive at-bats to regain the .300 mark.

## Billy Ripken

Bats Right

| Baltimore Orioles | AB | H | 2B | 3B | HR | RBI | BB | SO | BA | SA | OBA |
|---|---|---|---|---|---|---|---|---|---|---|---|
| Season | 318 | 76 | 11 | 2 | 2 | 26 | 22 | 53 | .239 | .305 | .284 |
| vs. Left-Handers | 103 | 28 | 4 | 1 | 0 | 9 | 8 | 17 | .272 | .330 | .316 |
| vs. Right-Handers | 215 | 48 | 7 | 1 | 2 | 17 | 14 | 36 | .223 | .293 | .268 |
| Home | 167 | 39 | 5 | 1 | 0 | 12 | 12 | 28 | .234 | .275 | .280 |
| Road | 151 | 37 | 6 | 1 | 2 | 14 | 10 | 25 | .245 | .338 | .288 |
| Grass | 269 | 66 | 10 | 1 | 2 | 20 | 17 | 42 | .245 | .312 | .285 |
| Artificial Turf | 49 | 10 | 1 | 1 | 0 | 6 | 5 | 11 | .204 | .265 | .278 |
| April | 35 | 8 | 0 | 0 | 1 | 4 | 1 | 7 | .229 | .314 | .250 |
| May | 67 | 21 | 4 | 0 | 1 | 6 | 10 | 6 | .313 | .418 | .388 |
| June | 84 | 16 | 4 | 1 | 0 | 9 | 2 | 17 | .190 | .262 | .207 |
| July | 72 | 17 | 2 | 1 | 0 | 5 | 7 | 10 | .236 | .292 | .300 |
| August | 48 | 12 | 0 | 0 | 0 | 2 | 2 | 10 | .250 | .250 | .280 |
| Sept./Oct. | 12 | 2 | 1 | 0 | 0 | 0 | 0 | 3 | .167 | .250 | .167 |
| Leading Off Inn. | 73 | 18 | 3 | 1 | 1 | 1 | 3 | 12 | .247 | .356 | .276 |
| Runners On | 125 | 32 | 3 | 0 | 1 | 25 | 4 | 18 | .256 | .304 | .269 |
| Runners/Scor. Pos. | 73 | 20 | 3 | 0 | 0 | 23 | 3 | 10 | .274 | .315 | .284 |
| Runners On/2 Out | 52 | 14 | 2 | 0 | 0 | 7 | 4 | 9 | .269 | .308 | .321 |
| Scor. Pos./2 Out | 30 | 8 | 2 | 0 | 0 | 7 | 3 | 6 | .267 | .333 | .333 |
| Late Inning Pressure | 29 | 7 | 1 | 0 | 0 | 2 | 4 | 5 | .241 | .276 | .333 |
| Leading Off | 5 | 2 | 0 | 0 | 0 | 0 | 0 | 0 | .400 | .400 | .400 |
| Runners On | 13 | 3 | 1 | 0 | 0 | 2 | 0 | 3 | .231 | .308 | .231 |
| Runners/Scor. Pos. | 7 | 3 | 1 | 0 | 0 | 2 | 0 | 1 | .429 | .571 | .429 |

| RUNS BATTED IN | From 1B | From 2B | From 3B | Scoring Position |
|---|---|---|---|---|
| Totals | 2/94 | 6/61 | 16/39 | 22/100 |
| Percentage | 2% | 10% | 41% | 22% |
| Driving In Runners from 3B with Less than Two Out: | | | 13/22 | 59% |

Loves to face: Chris Bosio (.400, 6-for-15)
Hates to face: Willie Fraser (.077, 1-for-13)
Led major league second basemen with 5.97 chances per nine innings (minimum: 500 innings). . . . Started only four of Baltimore's last 37 games. . . . Ended season with streak of 51 consecutive plate appearances without a walk, and only one extra-base hit in his last 85 at-bats. . . . Advanced from first to third on three of five singles to left field, only two of seven to center and right. . . . Career average of .211 vs. ground-ball pitchers, lowest among active A.L. players (minimum: 400 AB). Career mark is .260 against fly-ballers. . . . Has hit better in night games than in day games in each of his three seasons. Career marks: .255 at night, .179 in daytime (.117 last season).

## Cal Ripken

Bats Right

| Baltimore Orioles | AB | H | 2B | 3B | HR | RBI | BB | SO | BA | SA | OBA |
|---|---|---|---|---|---|---|---|---|---|---|---|
| Season | 646 | 166 | 30 | 0 | 21 | 94 | 57 | 72 | .257 | .401 | .317 |
| vs. Left-Handers | 196 | 46 | 12 | 0 | 5 | 22 | 15 | 21 | .235 | .372 | .287 |
| vs. Right-Handers | 450 | 120 | 18 | 0 | 16 | 72 | 42 | 51 | .267 | .413 | .331 |
| Home | 312 | 77 | 13 | 0 | 13 | 51 | 32 | 41 | .247 | .413 | .317 |
| Road | 334 | 89 | 17 | 0 | 8 | 43 | 25 | 31 | .266 | .389 | .318 |
| Grass | 539 | 141 | 24 | 0 | 18 | 77 | 55 | 64 | .262 | .406 | .329 |
| Artificial Turf | 107 | 25 | 6 | 0 | 3 | 17 | 2 | 8 | .234 | .374 | .255 |
| April | 95 | 27 | 8 | 0 | 2 | 14 | 8 | 6 | .284 | .432 | .349 |
| May | 98 | 29 | 3 | 0 | 1 | 12 | 9 | 10 | .296 | .357 | .355 |
| June | 115 | 31 | 4 | 0 | 5 | 17 | 12 | 11 | .270 | .435 | .341 |
| July | 114 | 28 | 4 | 0 | 5 | 17 | 6 | 12 | .246 | .412 | .281 |
| August | 123 | 31 | 4 | 0 | 5 | 19 | 9 | 16 | .252 | .407 | .301 |
| Sept./Oct. | 101 | 20 | 7 | 0 | 3 | 15 | 13 | 17 | .198 | .356 | .284 |
| Leading Off Inn. | 144 | 34 | 4 | 0 | 4 | 4 | 6 | 17 | .236 | .347 | .272 |
| Runners On | 285 | 79 | 14 | 0 | 13 | 86 | 34 | 30 | .277 | .463 | .352 |
| Runners/Scor. Pos. | 167 | 42 | 5 | 0 | 7 | 66 | 24 | 23 | .251 | .407 | .338 |
| Runners On/2 Out | 108 | 33 | 7 | 0 | 4 | 28 | 13 | 10 | .306 | .481 | .380 |
| Scor. Pos./2 Out | 67 | 15 | 1 | 0 | 1 | 17 | 12 | 8 | .224 | .284 | .342 |
| Late Inning Pressure | 77 | 19 | 6 | 0 | 3 | 11 | 9 | 9 | .247 | .442 | .322 |
| Leading Off | 22 | 5 | 0 | 0 | 0 | 0 | 2 | 4 | .227 | .227 | .292 |
| Runners On | 27 | 6 | 2 | 0 | 2 | 10 | 6 | 4 | .222 | .519 | .353 |
| Runners/Scor. Pos. | 19 | 2 | 0 | 0 | 1 | 6 | 6 | 4 | .105 | .263 | .308 |

| RUNS BATTED IN | From 1B | From 2B | From 3B | Scoring Position |
|---|---|---|---|---|
| Totals | 17/199 | 19/119 | 37/82 | 56/201 |
| Percentage | 9% | 16% | 45% | 28% |
| Driving In Runners from 3B with Less than Two Out: | | | 28/53 | 53% |

Loves to face: Gene Nelson (.360, 9-for-25, 2 HR)
Hates to face: Scott Bailes (0-for-17)
Needs 162 games at shortstop to reach 1400 for his career. . . . All-time franchise leaders in games at shortstop: Mark Belanger (1898), Bobby Wallace (1449), Wally Gerber (1275), Ripken (1238). . . . Has hit at least 21, but no more than 28, home runs for eight consecutive seasons, the longest streak ever in the 20s. Lee May and Fred Lynn each had seven consecutive seasons in the 20s. . . . Led the Orioles with 21 infield hits last season. . . . Batted .310 on fair balls hit to the right side, .330 up the middle, and .217 on balls hit to the opposite field. . . . Had one hit in 14 at-bats with the bases loaded. Career average of only .232 with the bags full. . . . Career BA: .273 on grass, .303 on artificial turf.

## Luis Rivera

Bats Right

| Boston Red Sox | AB | H | 2B | 3B | HR | RBI | BB | SO | BA | SA | OBA |
|---|---|---|---|---|---|---|---|---|---|---|---|
| Season | 323 | 83 | 17 | 1 | 5 | 29 | 20 | 60 | .257 | .362 | .301 |
| vs. Left-Handers | 102 | 28 | 5 | 1 | 2 | 12 | 5 | 18 | .275 | .402 | .308 |
| vs. Right-Handers | 221 | 55 | 12 | 0 | 3 | 17 | 15 | 42 | .249 | .344 | .298 |
| Home | 163 | 48 | 12 | 0 | 4 | 19 | 9 | 27 | .294 | .442 | .333 |
| Road | 160 | 35 | 5 | 1 | 1 | 10 | 11 | 33 | .219 | .281 | .269 |
| Grass | 270 | 71 | 12 | 0 | 5 | 25 | 17 | 53 | .263 | .363 | .308 |
| Artificial Turf | 53 | 12 | 5 | 1 | 0 | 4 | 3 | 7 | .226 | .358 | .268 |
| April | 0 | 0 | 0 | 0 | 0 | 0 | 0 | 0 | — | — | — |
| May | 0 | 0 | 0 | 0 | 0 | 0 | 0 | 0 | — | — | — |
| June | 70 | 20 | 2 | 0 | 1 | 5 | 1 | 11 | .286 | .357 | .296 |
| July | 87 | 24 | 9 | 0 | 1 | 9 | 8 | 16 | .276 | .414 | .337 |
| August | 92 | 26 | 3 | 0 | 2 | 9 | 6 | 18 | .283 | .380 | .330 |
| Sept./Oct. | 74 | 13 | 3 | 1 | 1 | 6 | 5 | 15 | .176 | .284 | .228 |
| Leading Off Inn. | 80 | 18 | 2 | 0 | 0 | 0 | 6 | 15 | .225 | .250 | .279 |
| Runners On | 142 | 35 | 8 | 1 | 3 | 27 | 8 | 28 | .246 | .380 | .285 |
| Runners/Scor. Pos. | 82 | 19 | 5 | 1 | 0 | 20 | 7 | 14 | .232 | .317 | .289 |
| Runners On/2 Out | 66 | 19 | 3 | 1 | 3 | 19 | 4 | 14 | .288 | .500 | .329 |
| Scor. Pos./2 Out | 41 | 9 | 2 | 1 | 0 | 12 | 4 | 8 | .220 | .317 | .289 |
| Late Inning Pressure | 43 | 8 | 2 | 0 | 0 | 0 | 2 | 10 | .186 | .233 | .222 |
| Leading Off | 17 | 2 | 0 | 0 | 0 | 0 | 1 | 2 | .118 | .118 | .167 |
| Runners On | 10 | 1 | 1 | 0 | 0 | 0 | 1 | 4 | .100 | .200 | .182 |
| Runners/Scor. Pos. | 4 | 0 | 0 | 0 | 0 | 0 | 1 | 1 | .000 | .000 | .200 |

| RUNS BATTED IN | From 1B | From 2B | From 3B | Scoring Position |
|---|---|---|---|---|
| Totals | 4/102 | 9/66 | 11/35 | 20/101 |
| Percentage | 4% | 14% | 31% | 20% |
| Driving In Runners from 3B with Less than Two Out: | | | 6/14 | 43% |

Loves to face: Jaime Navarro (.600, 3-for-5, 1 HR)
Hates to face: Jamie Moyer (.056, 1-for-18)
Played 53 percent of Red Sox innings at shortstop. Jody Reed played 44 percent, Ed Romero the rest. . . . Sox allowed 4.3 runs per nine innings with Rivera, 4.9 with Reed. . . . Played second base in his Red Sox debut, the only time in four seasons he's played anywhere but shortstop. . . . Batted .329 vs. ground-ball pitchers, 141 points higher than vs. fly-ballers (.188), largest margin in the majors (minimum: 100 AB vs. both). . . . Batted .371 (with all 5 HR) on fair balls to the left side, .328 straight away, .225 to the opposite field. . . . Has one hit in 19 career at-bats with two outs and runners on base in Late-Inning Pressure Situations. . . . Career average is .294 at Fenway Park, .215 elsewhere.

## Kevin Romine

Bats Right

| Boston Red Sox | AB | H | 2B | 3B | HR | RBI | BB | SO | BA | SA | OBA |
|---|---|---|---|---|---|---|---|---|---|---|---|
| Season | 274 | 75 | 13 | 0 | 1 | 23 | 21 | 53 | .274 | .332 | .327 |
| vs. Left-Handers | 104 | 36 | 5 | 0 | 0 | 10 | 7 | 15 | .346 | .394 | .386 |
| vs. Right-Handers | 170 | 39 | 8 | 0 | 1 | 13 | 14 | 38 | .229 | .294 | .290 |
| Home | 131 | 34 | 5 | 0 | 1 | 18 | 12 | 27 | .260 | .321 | .320 |
| Road | 143 | 41 | 8 | 0 | 0 | 5 | 9 | 26 | .287 | .343 | .333 |
| Grass | 224 | 55 | 7 | 0 | 1 | 22 | 19 | 45 | .246 | .290 | .304 |
| Artificial Turf | 50 | 20 | 6 | 0 | 0 | 1 | 2 | 8 | .400 | .520 | .434 |
| April | 0 | 0 | 0 | 0 | 0 | 0 | 0 | 0 | — | — | — |
| May | 0 | 0 | 0 | 0 | 0 | 0 | 0 | 0 | — | — | — |
| June | 37 | 11 | 0 | 0 | 0 | 3 | 0 | 6 | .297 | .297 | .297 |
| July | 103 | 33 | 9 | 0 | 1 | 11 | 4 | 18 | .320 | .437 | .355 |
| August | 61 | 8 | 1 | 0 | 0 | 3 | 8 | 15 | .131 | .148 | .229 |
| Sept./Oct. | 73 | 23 | 3 | 0 | 0 | 6 | 9 | 14 | .315 | .356 | .386 |
| Leading Off Inn. | 64 | 14 | 2 | 0 | 1 | 1 | 6 | 12 | .219 | .297 | .286 |
| Runners On | 127 | 36 | 6 | 0 | 0 | 22 | 9 | 22 | .283 | .331 | .324 |
| Runners/Scor. Pos. | 73 | 21 | 3 | 0 | 0 | 22 | 7 | 14 | .288 | .329 | .337 |
| Runners On/2 Out | 55 | 18 | 2 | 0 | 0 | 11 | 6 | 6 | .327 | .364 | .393 |
| Scor. Pos./2 Out | 37 | 12 | 2 | 0 | 0 | 11 | 5 | 5 | .324 | .378 | .405 |
| Late Inning Pressure | 36 | 10 | 1 | 0 | 0 | 1 | 6 | 7 | .278 | .306 | .381 |
| Leading Off | 13 | 2 | 0 | 0 | 0 | 0 | 3 | 4 | .154 | .154 | .313 |
| Runners On | 14 | 4 | 0 | 0 | 0 | 1 | 1 | 2 | .286 | .286 | .333 |
| Runners/Scor. Pos. | 7 | 2 | 0 | 0 | 0 | 1 | 1 | 2 | .286 | .286 | .375 |

| RUNS BATTED IN | From 1B | From 2B | From 3B | Scoring Position |
|---|---|---|---|---|
| Totals | 0/90 | 13/62 | 9/34 | 22/96 |
| Percentage | 0% | 21% | 26% | 23% |
| Driving In Runners from 3B with Less than Two Out: | | | 6/15 | 40% |

Loves to face: Jimmy Key (.444, 4-for-9)
Hates to face: Rod Nichols (0-for-7)
Played 41 consecutive games from June 23 through August 6. His longest streak in four previous seasons with Boston: 9 games. . . . Split each of last five seasons between Pawtucket and Boston. . . . No walks in his first 112 plate appearances last season. . . . Grounded into 11 DP in 56 opportunities, worst rate on club. . . . Started in each batting order position except leadoff and cleanup. . . . Hitless in 10 at-bats with bases loaded. . . . Only one RBI in 14 career plate appearances with bases full (on a sac fly in 1989). . . . Hitless in last 21 at-bats against Detroit. . . . Career BA: .343 vs. left-handers, .194 vs. right-handers. But both home runs were hit vs. right-handers (Steve Farr and Tom Gordon).

## Steve Sax

Bats Right

| New York Yankees | AB | H | 2B | 3B | HR | RBI | BB | SO | BA | SA | OBA |
|---|---|---|---|---|---|---|---|---|---|---|---|
| Season | 651 | 205 | 26 | 3 | 5 | 64 | 52 | 44 | .315 | .387 | .364 |
| vs. Left-Handers | 202 | 77 | 10 | 1 | 2 | 17 | 17 | 8 | .381 | .470 | .427 |
| vs. Right-Handers | 449 | 128 | 16 | 2 | 3 | 47 | 35 | 36 | .285 | .350 | .335 |
| Home | 324 | 105 | 17 | 1 | 2 | 38 | 21 | 23 | .324 | .401 | .363 |
| Road | 327 | 100 | 9 | 2 | 3 | 26 | 31 | 21 | .306 | .373 | .365 |
| Grass | 551 | 174 | 22 | 2 | 4 | 53 | 43 | 37 | .316 | .385 | .364 |
| Artificial Turf | 100 | 31 | 4 | 1 | 1 | 11 | 9 | 7 | .310 | .400 | .364 |
| April | 97 | 28 | 4 | 1 | 1 | 14 | 6 | 4 | .289 | .381 | .324 |
| May | 102 | 32 | 4 | 0 | 0 | 3 | 16 | 7 | .314 | .353 | .407 |
| June | 115 | 44 | 4 | 1 | 1 | 12 | 7 | 9 | .383 | .461 | .418 |
| July | 109 | 31 | 4 | 0 | 2 | 14 | 6 | 9 | .284 | .376 | .316 |
| August | 122 | 42 | 6 | 1 | 0 | 11 | 14 | 6 | .344 | .410 | .412 |
| Sept./Oct. | 106 | 28 | 4 | 0 | 1 | 10 | 3 | 9 | .264 | .330 | .288 |
| Leading Off Inn. | 206 | 65 | 7 | 1 | 1 | 1 | 12 | 11 | .316 | .374 | .356 |
| Runners On | 255 | 81 | 5 | 2 | 2 | 61 | 23 | 18 | .318 | .376 | .367 |
| Runners/Scor. Pos. | 171 | 50 | 3 | 1 | 2 | 60 | 16 | 12 | .292 | .357 | .344 |
| Runners On/2 Out | 109 | 30 | 0 | 0 | 1 | 25 | 12 | 10 | .275 | .303 | .347 |
| Scor. Pos./2 Out | 83 | 22 | 0 | 0 | 1 | 25 | 8 | 6 | .265 | .301 | .330 |
| Late Inning Pressure | 84 | 29 | 2 | 1 | 1 | 12 | 2 | 5 | .345 | .429 | .356 |
| Leading Off | 19 | 6 | 0 | 0 | 0 | 0 | 1 | 1 | .316 | .316 | .350 |
| Runners On | 38 | 13 | 1 | 1 | 0 | 11 | 1 | 4 | .342 | .421 | .350 |
| Runners/Scor. Pos. | 27 | 9 | 1 | 1 | 0 | 11 | 1 | 4 | .333 | .444 | .345 |

| RUNS BATTED IN | From 1B | From 2B | From 3B | Scoring Position |
|---|---|---|---|---|
| Totals | 3/162 | 27/149 | 29/66 | 56/215 |
| Percentage | 2% | 18% | 44% | 26% |
| Driving In Runners from 3B with Less than Two Out: | | | 19/30 | 63% |

Loves to face: Scott Sanderson (.436, 17-for-39)
Hates to face: Brian Holman (.067, 1-for-15)
Third second baseman in Yankees' history to accumulate 200 hits in a season. The others: Snuffy Stirnweiss (1944) and Bobby Richardson (1962). . . . Fourth player in last 60 years to lead Yankees in hits in his first season with the club. Others: Joe DiMaggio (1936), Billy Johnson (1943), and Dave Winfield (1981). . . . Led A.L. second basemen in fielding percentage (.987), a feat he never accomplished in N.L. . . . Grounded into 19 double plays in 99 opportunites, a rate nearly 60 percent higher than the league average. . . . Batting average in Late-Inning Pressure Situations has been higher than his overall average in each of the last seven seasons. . . . Has hit .349 in LIPS since 1986.

## Dick Schofield

Bats Right

| California Angels | AB | H | 2B | 3B | HR | RBI | BB | SO | BA | SA | OBA |
|---|---|---|---|---|---|---|---|---|---|---|---|
| Season | 302 | 69 | 11 | 2 | 4 | 26 | 28 | 47 | .228 | .318 | .299 |
| vs. Left-Handers | 127 | 33 | 6 | 1 | 1 | 7 | 7 | 13 | .260 | .346 | .304 |
| vs. Right-Handers | 175 | 36 | 5 | 1 | 3 | 19 | 21 | 34 | .206 | .297 | .295 |
| Home | 143 | 29 | 5 | 1 | 1 | 11 | 14 | 24 | .203 | .273 | .280 |
| Road | 159 | 40 | 6 | 1 | 3 | 15 | 14 | 23 | .252 | .358 | .316 |
| Grass | 247 | 56 | 10 | 2 | 4 | 25 | 24 | 39 | .227 | .332 | .301 |
| Artificial Turf | 55 | 13 | 1 | 0 | 0 | 1 | 4 | 8 | .236 | .255 | .288 |
| April | 25 | 6 | 1 | 0 | 0 | 2 | 0 | 4 | .240 | .280 | .240 |
| May | 48 | 14 | 3 | 1 | 0 | 4 | 3 | 6 | .292 | .396 | .346 |
| June | 83 | 14 | 2 | 0 | 0 | 6 | 5 | 14 | .169 | .193 | .211 |
| July | 98 | 26 | 3 | 1 | 4 | 12 | 14 | 15 | .265 | .439 | .363 |
| August | 31 | 8 | 2 | 0 | 0 | 2 | 1 | 3 | .258 | .323 | .303 |
| Sept./Oct. | 17 | 1 | 0 | 0 | 0 | 0 | 5 | 5 | .059 | .059 | .273 |
| Leading Off Inn. | 104 | 29 | 5 | 0 | 1 | 1 | 6 | 11 | .279 | .356 | .324 |
| Runners On | 96 | 19 | 5 | 2 | 1 | 23 | 11 | 17 | .198 | .323 | .288 |
| Runners/Scor. Pos. | 65 | 15 | 4 | 1 | 1 | 22 | 8 | 13 | .231 | .369 | .316 |
| Runners On/2 Out | 46 | 10 | 2 | 0 | 0 | 11 | 7 | 8 | .217 | .261 | .321 |
| Scor. Pos./2 Out | 34 | 9 | 2 | 0 | 0 | 11 | 6 | 5 | .265 | .324 | .375 |
| Late Inning Pressure | 32 | 11 | 0 | 1 | 0 | 3 | 6 | 7 | .344 | .406 | .462 |
| Leading Off | 4 | 3 | 0 | 0 | 0 | 0 | 1 | 1 | .750 | .750 | .800 |
| Runners On | 14 | 4 | 0 | 1 | 0 | 3 | 4 | 1 | .286 | .429 | .474 |
| Runners/Scor. Pos. | 9 | 2 | 0 | 0 | 0 | 2 | 2 | 0 | .222 | .222 | .417 |

| RUNS BATTED IN | From 1B | From 2B | From 3B | Scoring Position |
|---|---|---|---|---|
| Totals | 4/72 | 11/52 | 7/24 | 18/76 |
| Percentage | 6% | 21% | 29% | 24% |
| Driving In Runners from 3B with Less than Two Out: | | | 4/10 | 40% |

Loves to face: Allan Anderson (.438, 7-for-16)
Hates to face: Mark Gubicza (0-for-25)
Batted .313 vs. ground-ball pitchers, .176 vs. fly-ballers, making it seven times in seven years that he has hit better against ground-ballers than fly-ballers. Career marks: .253 and .215, respectively. . . . Career average of .213 with runners on base is lowest among active players (minimum: 400 AB). Career average is .242 with bases empty. . . . Needs 88 more hits to overtake dad's career total of 699. . . . Schofield the Younger has played his entire career with the Angels. The Elder was born a ramblin' man, relocating eight times in his 19-year career (including three separate tours of duty with the Cardinals). . . . Youngest active player with more than six years of major league service.

## Rick Schu

Bats Right

| Orioles/Tigers | AB | H | 2B | 3B | HR | RBI | BB | SO | BA | SA | OBA |
|---|---|---|---|---|---|---|---|---|---|---|---|
| Season | 266 | 57 | 11 | 0 | 7 | 21 | 24 | 37 | .214 | .335 | .278 |
| vs. Left-Handers | 142 | 37 | 9 | 0 | 5 | 13 | 8 | 15 | .261 | .430 | .300 |
| vs. Right-Handers | 124 | 20 | 2 | 0 | 2 | 8 | 16 | 22 | .161 | .226 | .255 |
| Home | 130 | 25 | 6 | 0 | 3 | 11 | 11 | 18 | .192 | .308 | .255 |
| Road | 136 | 32 | 5 | 0 | 4 | 10 | 13 | 19 | .235 | .360 | .300 |
| Grass | 219 | 48 | 9 | 0 | 7 | 20 | 21 | 27 | .219 | .356 | .286 |
| Artificial Turf | 47 | 9 | 2 | 0 | 0 | 1 | 3 | 10 | .191 | .234 | .240 |
| April | 0 | 0 | 0 | 0 | 0 | 0 | 0 | 0 | — | — | — |
| May | 36 | 11 | 3 | 0 | 1 | 2 | 7 | 3 | .306 | .472 | .419 |
| June | 69 | 10 | 1 | 0 | 0 | 2 | 5 | 12 | .145 | .159 | .203 |
| July | 58 | 15 | 3 | 0 | 3 | 9 | 6 | 6 | .259 | .466 | .323 |
| August | 57 | 11 | 1 | 0 | 3 | 5 | 4 | 9 | .193 | .368 | .246 |
| Sept./Oct. | 46 | 10 | 3 | 0 | 0 | 3 | 2 | 7 | .217 | .283 | .250 |
| Leading Off Inn. | 64 | 18 | 3 | 0 | 2 | 2 | 4 | 12 | .281 | .422 | .324 |
| Runners On | 124 | 22 | 7 | 0 | 0 | 14 | 7 | 16 | .177 | .234 | .220 |
| Runners/Scor. Pos. | 60 | 10 | 1 | 0 | 0 | 11 | 5 | 10 | .167 | .183 | .227 |
| Runners On/2 Out | 55 | 6 | 0 | 0 | 0 | 2 | 4 | 8 | .109 | .109 | .169 |
| Scor. Pos./2 Out | 33 | 3 | 0 | 0 | 0 | 2 | 3 | 6 | .091 | .091 | .167 |
| Late Inning Pressure | 56 | 10 | 0 | 0 | 0 | 0 | 4 | 8 | .179 | .179 | .233 |
| Leading Off | 15 | 5 | 0 | 0 | 0 | 0 | 1 | 3 | .333 | .333 | .375 |
| Runners On | 24 | 2 | 0 | 0 | 0 | 0 | 1 | 1 | .083 | .083 | .120 |
| Runners/Scor. Pos. | 10 | 1 | 0 | 0 | 0 | 0 | 1 | 1 | .100 | .100 | .182 |

| RUNS BATTED IN | From 1B | From 2B | From 3B | Scoring Position |
|---|---|---|---|---|
| Totals | 3/99 | 6/52 | 5/23 | 11/75 |
| Percentage | 3% | 12% | 22% | 15% |
| Driving In Runners from 3B with Less than Two Out: | | | 5/8 | 63% |

Loves to face: Larry McWilliams (.524, 11-for-21, 1 HR)
Hates to face: Andy Hawkins (0-for-14)

Played three full seasons with Phils, 1985–87, during which they finished an average of 21 games behind. Then '88 with Orioles (54–107, 34½ GB) and '89 with Tigers (59–103, 30 GB). Not exactly the Midas touch. . . . Part of the solution or part of the problem? His career batting average is 63 points lower with runners in scoring position (.198) than at other times (.261), the largest difference among active players (minimum: 250 RISP AB). In Late-Inning Pressure Situations: He has driven in only 10 percent of runners from scoring position in his career, again the lowest rate among active players (minimum: 50 opportunities). Didn't drive in any of 19 such runners in 1988–89.

## Kevin Seitzer

Bats Right

| Kansas City Royals | AB | H | 2B | 3B | HR | RBI | BB | SO | BA | SA | OBA |
|---|---|---|---|---|---|---|---|---|---|---|---|
| Season | 597 | 168 | 17 | 2 | 4 | 48 | 102 | 76 | .281 | .337 | .387 |
| vs. Left-Handers | 175 | 45 | 6 | 0 | 3 | 12 | 36 | 18 | .257 | .343 | .387 |
| vs. Right-Handers | 422 | 123 | 11 | 2 | 1 | 36 | 66 | 58 | .291 | .334 | .387 |
| Home | 299 | 93 | 9 | 1 | 2 | 22 | 47 | 34 | .311 | .368 | .405 |
| Road | 298 | 75 | 8 | 1 | 2 | 26 | 55 | 42 | .252 | .305 | .370 |
| Grass | 224 | 55 | 6 | 1 | 1 | 18 | 41 | 30 | .246 | .295 | .369 |
| Artificial Turf | 373 | 113 | 11 | 1 | 3 | 30 | 61 | 46 | .303 | .362 | .398 |
| April | 95 | 27 | 6 | 0 | 1 | 12 | 11 | 12 | .284 | .379 | .358 |
| May | 93 | 29 | 1 | 0 | 2 | 12 | 17 | 12 | .312 | .387 | .429 |
| June | 101 | 27 | 2 | 0 | 0 | 8 | 17 | 11 | .267 | .287 | .370 |
| July | 94 | 26 | 2 | 0 | 0 | 4 | 24 | 12 | .277 | .298 | .420 |
| August | 112 | 30 | 3 | 0 | 0 | 7 | 16 | 17 | .268 | .295 | .351 |
| Sept./Oct. | 102 | 29 | 3 | 2 | 1 | 5 | 17 | 12 | .284 | .382 | .395 |
| Leading Off Inn. | 135 | 30 | 5 | 1 | 0 | 0 | 15 | 18 | .222 | .274 | .318 |
| Runners On | 231 | 68 | 9 | 0 | 0 | 44 | 52 | 22 | .294 | .333 | .416 |
| Runners/Scor. Pos. | 132 | 38 | 4 | 0 | 0 | 42 | 43 | 16 | .288 | .318 | .448 |
| Runners On/2 Out | 74 | 20 | 2 | 0 | 0 | 12 | 22 | 10 | .270 | .297 | .438 |
| Scor. Pos./2 Out | 53 | 14 | 1 | 0 | 0 | 11 | 18 | 8 | .264 | .283 | .451 |
| Late Inning Pressure | 74 | 24 | 3 | 0 | 0 | 6 | 13 | 11 | .324 | .365 | .432 |
| Leading Off | 19 | 5 | 1 | 0 | 0 | 0 | 4 | 3 | .263 | .316 | .391 |
| Runners On | 31 | 11 | 1 | 0 | 0 | 6 | 8 | 3 | .355 | .387 | .500 |
| Runners/Scor. Pos. | 19 | 9 | 1 | 0 | 0 | 6 | 7 | 2 | .474 | .526 | .630 |

| RUNS BATTED IN | From 1B | From 2B | From 3B | Scoring Position |
|---|---|---|---|---|
| Totals | 2/156 | 17/104 | 25/56 | 42/160 |
| Percentage | 1% | 16% | 45% | 26% |
| Driving In Runners from 3B with Less than Two Out: | | | 22/37 | 59% |

Loves to face: Charlie Hough (.370, 10-for-27, 1 HR)
Hates to face: Scott Bankhead (0-for-11)

Has .415 career average (27-for-65) with runners in scoring position in Late-Inning Pressure Situations, highest among active players (minimum: 25 hits). . . . Career on-base average (.394) ranks 4th among active players (minimum: 1000 PA) behind Wade Boggs, Kal Daniels, and Rickey Henderson. . . . Started 111 games from second spot in lineup last season, most of any A.L. player, but was K.C. leadoff man in each of his last 37 games. . . . Did not have more than one RBI any of his last 104 games. . . . Has hit .311 or higher in home games every year in majors; career breakdown: .329 at Royals Stadium, .280 in road games. . . . Batted nine times with the bases loaded in 1989: five hits, two walks, two sacrifice flies.

## Larry Sheets

Bats Left

| Baltimore Orioles | AB | H | 2B | 3B | HR | RBI | BB | SO | BA | SA | OBA |
|---|---|---|---|---|---|---|---|---|---|---|---|
| Season | 304 | 74 | 12 | 1 | 7 | 33 | 26 | 58 | .243 | .359 | .305 |
| vs. Left-Handers | 39 | 6 | 1 | 0 | 0 | 1 | 2 | 13 | .154 | .179 | .209 |
| vs. Right-Handers | 265 | 68 | 11 | 1 | 7 | 32 | 24 | 45 | .257 | .385 | .319 |
| Home | 133 | 31 | 6 | 0 | 1 | 14 | 13 | 26 | .233 | .301 | .302 |
| Road | 171 | 43 | 6 | 1 | 6 | 19 | 13 | 32 | .251 | .404 | .307 |
| Grass | 239 | 57 | 11 | 0 | 7 | 31 | 22 | 44 | .238 | .372 | .306 |
| Artificial Turf | 65 | 17 | 1 | 1 | 0 | 2 | 4 | 14 | .262 | .308 | .300 |
| April | 82 | 18 | 2 | 1 | 1 | 7 | 5 | 13 | .220 | .305 | .258 |
| May | 41 | 11 | 0 | 0 | 3 | 7 | 8 | 11 | .268 | .488 | .392 |
| June | 53 | 13 | 4 | 0 | 2 | 7 | 4 | 6 | .245 | .434 | .293 |
| July | 53 | 11 | 2 | 0 | 0 | 3 | 3 | 12 | .208 | .245 | .246 |
| August | 47 | 14 | 2 | 0 | 1 | 7 | 3 | 10 | .298 | .404 | .353 |
| Sept./Oct. | 28 | 7 | 2 | 0 | 0 | 2 | 3 | 6 | .250 | .321 | .344 |
| Leading Off Inn. | 65 | 21 | 4 | 0 | 2 | 2 | 3 | 12 | .323 | .477 | .353 |
| Runners On | 133 | 33 | 4 | 0 | 3 | 29 | 19 | 24 | .248 | .346 | .335 |
| Runners/Scor. Pos. | 77 | 18 | 1 | 0 | 2 | 25 | 17 | 10 | .234 | .325 | .354 |
| Runners On/2 Out | 61 | 9 | 2 | 0 | 0 | 7 | 9 | 17 | .148 | .180 | .268 |
| Scor. Pos./2 Out | 33 | 6 | 1 | 0 | 0 | 6 | 8 | 5 | .182 | .212 | .341 |
| Late Inning Pressure | 48 | 9 | 0 | 0 | 0 | 2 | 2 | 14 | .188 | .188 | .220 |
| Leading Off | 9 | 1 | 0 | 0 | 0 | 0 | 0 | 2 | .111 | .111 | .111 |
| Runners On | 15 | 3 | 0 | 0 | 0 | 2 | 2 | 5 | .200 | .200 | .294 |
| Runners/Scor. Pos. | 6 | 1 | 0 | 0 | 0 | 2 | 2 | 1 | .167 | .167 | .375 |

| RUNS BATTED IN | From 1B | From 2B | From 3B | Scoring Position |
|---|---|---|---|---|
| Totals | 4/97 | 10/62 | 12/33 | 22/95 |
| Percentage | 4% | 16% | 36% | 23% |
| Driving In Runners from 3B with Less than Two Out: | | | 9/17 | 53% |

Loves to face: Paul Kilgus (.600, 6-for-10, 2 HR)
Hates to face: Paul Gibson (0-for-8)

No Rawlings endorsements in his future: appeared in 102 games last season without ever playing in field. He started 82 games as designated hitter and pinch-hit in 20 games. Played 79 games in field in 1988. . . . Hitless in eight at bats with runners in scoring position and Orioles trailing by one run. . . . A .300 career hitter leading off innings, .259 in other at-bats. . . . Hit 31 home runs in 135 games in 1987, averaging one every 15.1 at-bats. In two subsequent seasons he has 17 homers in 238 games, averaging one every 44.5 at-bats. . . . Batted .303 with 10 home runs vs. left-handers in 1987, but for the rest of his career he has hit .178 in 197 at-bats vs. lefties, with only 2 homers.

## Gary Sheffield

Bats Right

| Milwaukee Brewers | AB | H | 2B | 3B | HR | RBI | BB | SO | BA | SA | OBA |
|---|---|---|---|---|---|---|---|---|---|---|---|
| Season | 368 | 91 | 18 | 0 | 5 | 32 | 27 | 33 | .247 | .337 | .303 |
| vs. Left-Handers | 113 | 33 | 8 | 0 | 3 | 14 | 8 | 6 | .292 | .442 | .336 |
| vs. Right-Handers | 255 | 58 | 10 | 0 | 2 | 18 | 19 | 27 | .227 | .290 | .289 |
| Home | 198 | 51 | 11 | 0 | 2 | 12 | 14 | 24 | .258 | .343 | .307 |
| Road | 170 | 40 | 7 | 0 | 3 | 20 | 13 | 9 | .235 | .329 | .299 |
| Grass | 306 | 73 | 14 | 0 | 4 | 21 | 23 | 31 | .239 | .324 | .296 |
| Artificial Turf | 62 | 18 | 4 | 0 | 1 | 11 | 4 | 2 | .290 | .403 | .343 |
| April | 76 | 18 | 5 | 0 | 3 | 4 | 7 | 4 | .237 | .421 | .310 |
| May | 107 | 27 | 2 | 0 | 1 | 11 | 7 | 12 | .252 | .299 | .311 |
| June | 93 | 27 | 7 | 0 | 0 | 12 | 7 | 7 | .290 | .366 | .337 |
| July | 35 | 5 | 1 | 0 | 0 | 2 | 3 | 3 | .143 | .171 | .211 |
| August | 0 | 0 | 0 | 0 | 0 | 0 | 0 | 0 | — | — | — |
| Sept./Oct. | 57 | 14 | 3 | 0 | 1 | 3 | 3 | 7 | .246 | .351 | .283 |
| Leading Off Inn. | 59 | 13 | 1 | 0 | 0 | 0 | 3 | 6 | .220 | .237 | .270 |
| Runners On | 170 | 39 | 6 | 0 | 1 | 28 | 13 | 15 | .229 | .282 | .287 |
| Runners/Scor. Pos. | 96 | 21 | 4 | 0 | 0 | 26 | 9 | 7 | .219 | .260 | .284 |
| Runners On/2 Out | 70 | 18 | 3 | 0 | 1 | 13 | 4 | 5 | .257 | .343 | .307 |
| Scor. Pos./2 Out | 45 | 11 | 2 | 0 | 0 | 11 | 4 | 3 | .244 | .289 | .320 |
| Late Inning Pressure | 51 | 13 | 2 | 0 | 1 | 4 | 3 | 6 | .255 | .353 | .291 |
| Leading Off | 8 | 3 | 0 | 0 | 0 | 0 | 0 | 2 | .375 | .375 | .375 |
| Runners On | 23 | 2 | 0 | 0 | 0 | 3 | 1 | 3 | .087 | .087 | .120 |
| Runners/Scor. Pos. | 14 | 2 | 0 | 0 | 0 | 3 | 1 | 2 | .143 | .143 | .188 |

| RUNS BATTED IN | From 1B | From 2B | From 3B | Scoring Position |
|---|---|---|---|---|
| Totals | 2/127 | 12/76 | 13/37 | 25/113 |
| Percentage | 2% | 16% | 35% | 22% |
| Driving In Runners from 3B with Less than Two Out: | | | 11/21 | 52% |

Loves to face: Roger Clemens (.714, 5-for-7)
Hates to face: Jerry Reuss (0-for-17)

Played 14 games after his September recall, all at third base. . . . Owns .312 career batting average in four seasons in minors, .246 in 448 major league at-bats. . . . Batted .080 (2-for-25) with runners on base and his team trailing by a run, lowest batting average among the 82 A.L. players with 20+ at-bats in those situations. . . . Interesting breakdown of that .219 average with runners in scoring position: He hit .391 with RISP vs. left-handers, but only .164 with RISP vs. right-handers. . . . Played 94 games of major league shortstop as a teenager, 5th-highest total in history behind Robin Yount (241), Cass Michaels (147), Tommy Brown (102), and Ted Kazanski (95). Michaels and Brown played during World War II.

## Ruben Sierra

Texas Rangers — Bats Left and Right

| | AB | H | 2B | 3B | HR | RBI | BB | SO | BA | SA | OBA |
|---|---|---|---|---|---|---|---|---|---|---|---|
| Season | 634 | 194 | 35 | 14 | 29 | 120 | 43 | 82 | .306 | .543 | .347 |
| vs. Left-Handers | 205 | 70 | 15 | 4 | 10 | 44 | 14 | 18 | .341 | .600 | .378 |
| vs. Right-Handers | 429 | 124 | 20 | 10 | 19 | 76 | 29 | 64 | .289 | .515 | .332 |
| Home | 309 | 98 | 17 | 7 | 21 | 74 | 22 | 51 | .317 | .621 | .356 |
| Road | 325 | 96 | 18 | 7 | 8 | 46 | 21 | 31 | .295 | .468 | .338 |
| Grass | 533 | 164 | 29 | 10 | 26 | 106 | 38 | 73 | .308 | .546 | .350 |
| Artificial Turf | 101 | 30 | 6 | 4 | 3 | 14 | 5 | 9 | .297 | .525 | .330 |
| April | 83 | 26 | 8 | 1 | 4 | 19 | 9 | 14 | .313 | .578 | .365 |
| May | 113 | 35 | 8 | 3 | 1 | 17 | 4 | 15 | .310 | .460 | .339 |
| June | 114 | 43 | 11 | 4 | 7 | 25 | 7 | 13 | .377 | .728 | .418 |
| July | 97 | 29 | 2 | 2 | 6 | 16 | 6 | 13 | .299 | .546 | .340 |
| August | 109 | 27 | 1 | 2 | 4 | 16 | 8 | 18 | .248 | .404 | .292 |
| Sept./Oct. | 118 | 34 | 5 | 2 | 7 | 27 | 9 | 9 | .288 | .542 | .331 |
| Leading Off Inn. | 150 | 44 | 10 | 5 | 10 | 10 | 6 | 17 | .293 | .627 | .329 |
| Runners On | 319 | 105 | 18 | 6 | 15 | 106 | 23 | 37 | .329 | .564 | .364 |
| Runners/Scor. Pos. | 169 | 57 | 7 | 4 | 8 | 87 | 10 | 26 | .337 | .568 | .354 |
| Runners On/2 Out | 145 | 45 | 10 | 3 | 6 | 37 | 10 | 17 | .310 | .545 | .355 |
| Scor. Pos./2 Out | 70 | 22 | 3 | 1 | 2 | 26 | 5 | 11 | .314 | .471 | .360 |
| Late Inning Pressure | 74 | 21 | 4 | 2 | 2 | 13 | 6 | 6 | .284 | .473 | .329 |
| Leading Off | 14 | 3 | 0 | 1 | 0 | 0 | 2 | 2 | .214 | .357 | .313 |
| Runners On | 39 | 12 | 4 | 0 | 2 | 13 | 2 | 2 | .308 | .564 | .326 |
| Runners/Scor. Pos. | 17 | 3 | 1 | 0 | 1 | 9 | 2 | 1 | .176 | .412 | .238 |

| RUNS BATTED IN | From 1B | From 2B | From 3B | Scoring Position |
|---|---|---|---|---|
| Totals | 17/244 | 34/116 | 40/80 | 74/196 |
| Percentage | 7% | 29% | 50% | 38% |
| Driving In Runners from 3B with Less than Two Out: | | | 32/52 | 62% |

Loves to face: Todd Stottlemyre (.500, 5-for-10, 2 HR)
Hates to face: Allan Anderson (0-for-10)
First Rangers player to lead A.L. in slugging average, total bases, or extra-base hits since team moved to Texas in 1972; also led league in RBI, becoming first A.L. player since Jim Rice in 1978 to lead in those four categories.... Has 319 RBI in last three seasons, third in majors behind Bell (335) and Evans (334); has 907 total bases since 1987, fourth in majors behind Puckett (986), Bell (924), and Will Clark (920).... Yearly batting averages with runners in scoring position: .235, .239, .233, .337.... Missed only 22 innings last season. His streak of 294 consecutive games is 2d-longest current streak in A.L.... Started 150 games in cleanup spot, most in league. Other 12 starts were from third slot.

## Don Slaught

New York Yankees — Bats Right

| | AB | H | 2B | 3B | HR | RBI | BB | SO | BA | SA | OBA |
|---|---|---|---|---|---|---|---|---|---|---|---|
| Season | 350 | 88 | 21 | 3 | 5 | 38 | 30 | 57 | .251 | .371 | .315 |
| vs. Left-Handers | 131 | 31 | 10 | 3 | 2 | 13 | 13 | 23 | .237 | .405 | .301 |
| vs. Right-Handers | 219 | 57 | 11 | 0 | 3 | 25 | 17 | 34 | .260 | .352 | .324 |
| Home | 169 | 47 | 13 | 1 | 3 | 24 | 11 | 25 | .278 | .420 | .324 |
| Road | 181 | 41 | 8 | 2 | 2 | 14 | 19 | 32 | .227 | .326 | .307 |
| Grass | 292 | 74 | 18 | 1 | 5 | 34 | 25 | 48 | .253 | .373 | .318 |
| Artificial Turf | 58 | 14 | 3 | 2 | 0 | 4 | 5 | 9 | .241 | .362 | .302 |
| April | 78 | 21 | 6 | 3 | 1 | 14 | 3 | 16 | .269 | .462 | .293 |
| May | 75 | 20 | 5 | 0 | 0 | 4 | 11 | 11 | .267 | .333 | .360 |
| June | 79 | 26 | 5 | 0 | 2 | 8 | 6 | 11 | .329 | .468 | .379 |
| July | 58 | 12 | 2 | 0 | 2 | 7 | 7 | 13 | .207 | .345 | .304 |
| August | 38 | 6 | 3 | 0 | 0 | 2 | 2 | 5 | .158 | .237 | .220 |
| Sept./Oct. | 22 | 3 | 0 | 0 | 0 | 3 | 1 | 1 | .136 | .136 | .200 |
| Leading Off Inn. | 91 | 30 | 7 | 2 | 3 | 3 | 10 | 10 | .330 | .549 | .408 |
| Runners On | 145 | 37 | 10 | 0 | 0 | 33 | 13 | 19 | .255 | .324 | .315 |
| Runners/Scor. Pos. | 89 | 25 | 7 | 0 | 0 | 33 | 11 | 12 | .281 | .360 | .349 |
| Runners On/2 Out | 65 | 18 | 7 | 0 | 0 | 17 | 5 | 9 | .277 | .385 | .338 |
| Scor. Pos./2 Out | 48 | 13 | 6 | 0 | 0 | 17 | 4 | 8 | .271 | .396 | .340 |
| Late Inning Pressure | 61 | 18 | 4 | 1 | 0 | 9 | 4 | 12 | .295 | .393 | .358 |
| Leading Off | 14 | 4 | 1 | 1 | 0 | 0 | 1 | 2 | .286 | .500 | .375 |
| Runners On | 27 | 8 | 2 | 0 | 0 | 9 | 2 | 5 | .296 | .370 | .345 |
| Runners/Scor. Pos. | 19 | 7 | 2 | 0 | 0 | 9 | 2 | 2 | .368 | .474 | .429 |

| RUNS BATTED IN | From 1B | From 2B | From 3B | Scoring Position |
|---|---|---|---|---|
| Totals | 2/107 | 12/77 | 19/41 | 31/118 |
| Percentage | 2% | 16% | 46% | 26% |
| Driving In Runners from 3B with Less than Two Out: | | | 13/19 | 68% |

Loves to face: Jeff Musselman (.714, 5-for-7)
Hates to face: Jim Clancy (.118, 2-for-17)
His .408 on-base average when leading off innings was highest in majors among catchers.... Batting average vs. left-handed pitchers (.237) was lowest of his career, but his career mark of .287 vs. southpaws should complement nicely Mike LaValliere's .283 mark vs. right-handers.... Caught 58 percent of Yankees' innings. Geren played 34 percent, Dorsett 4, and Quirk 3. Yanks' staff had 4.65 ERA with Slaught, 4.63 with Geren.... Back in same division as Oil Can Boyd, who beaned him in 1986. Slaught is 0-for-3 with two strikeouts against Can since then.... Among the 12 N.L. catchers who played majority of innings for their clubs in 1989, only two (Jeff Reed and Terry Kennedy) had previously played in A.L.

## Cory Snyder

Cleveland Indians — Bats Right

| | AB | H | 2B | 3B | HR | RBI | BB | SO | BA | SA | OBA |
|---|---|---|---|---|---|---|---|---|---|---|---|
| Season | 489 | 105 | 17 | 0 | 18 | 59 | 23 | 134 | .215 | .360 | .251 |
| vs. Left-Handers | 164 | 41 | 5 | 0 | 10 | 27 | 14 | 39 | .250 | .463 | .309 |
| vs. Right-Handers | 325 | 64 | 12 | 0 | 8 | 32 | 9 | 95 | .197 | .308 | .220 |
| Home | 246 | 51 | 12 | 0 | 6 | 25 | 11 | 72 | .207 | .329 | .244 |
| Road | 243 | 54 | 5 | 0 | 12 | 34 | 12 | 62 | .222 | .391 | .258 |
| Grass | 431 | 97 | 17 | 0 | 17 | 57 | 20 | 117 | .225 | .383 | .260 |
| Artificial Turf | 58 | 8 | 0 | 0 | 1 | 2 | 3 | 17 | .138 | .190 | .180 |
| April | 86 | 23 | 2 | 0 | 4 | 15 | 4 | 24 | .267 | .430 | .308 |
| May | 96 | 21 | 5 | 0 | 1 | 9 | 4 | 22 | .219 | .302 | .257 |
| June | 103 | 22 | 4 | 0 | 6 | 13 | 3 | 29 | .214 | .427 | .231 |
| July | 34 | 7 | 0 | 0 | 0 | 1 | 1 | 12 | .206 | .206 | .229 |
| August | 80 | 13 | 3 | 0 | 4 | 13 | 5 | 24 | .163 | .350 | .207 |
| Sept./Oct. | 90 | 19 | 3 | 0 | 3 | 8 | 6 | 23 | .211 | .344 | .260 |
| Leading Off Inn. | 125 | 25 | 4 | 0 | 6 | 6 | 4 | 37 | .200 | .376 | .231 |
| Runners On | 216 | 49 | 5 | 0 | 8 | 49 | 11 | 57 | .227 | .361 | .260 |
| Runners/Scor. Pos. | 119 | 27 | 2 | 0 | 3 | 38 | 8 | 36 | .227 | .319 | .267 |
| Runners On/2 Out | 85 | 17 | 2 | 0 | 3 | 19 | 8 | 19 | .200 | .329 | .269 |
| Scor. Pos./2 Out | 53 | 10 | 1 | 0 | 1 | 14 | 7 | 12 | .189 | .264 | .283 |
| Late Inning Pressure | 93 | 14 | 2 | 0 | 0 | 3 | 2 | 25 | .151 | .172 | .168 |
| Leading Off | 25 | 5 | 0 | 0 | 0 | 0 | 0 | 6 | .200 | .200 | .200 |
| Runners On | 36 | 6 | 1 | 0 | 0 | 3 | 0 | 10 | .167 | .194 | .167 |
| Runners/Scor. Pos. | 18 | 5 | 0 | 0 | 0 | 3 | 0 | 6 | .278 | .278 | .278 |

| RUNS BATTED IN | From 1B | From 2B | From 3B | Scoring Position |
|---|---|---|---|---|
| Totals | 8/163 | 10/75 | 23/68 | 33/143 |
| Percentage | 5% | 13% | 34% | 23% |
| Driving In Runners from 3B with Less than Two Out: | | | 15/40 | 38% |

Loves to face: Dan Plesac (.571, 4-for-7, 2 HR)
Hates to face: John Cerutti (.077, 1-for-13, 7 SO)
You may think his .151 batting average in Late-Inning Pressure Situations was the lowest in the league, or something. But three guys had lower averages *just among Indians outfielders:* Komminsk hit .125, McDowell .148, Carter .149.... Lowest on-base average among A.L. players with 200+ plate appearances.... Led A.L. outfielders with .997 fielding percentage.... Has 50 outfield assists, most in majors, over past three seasons.... A .203 career hitter with seven home runs in 241 at-bats with runners in scoring position and two outs.... Career breakdown: .264 in night games, only .209 in day games; 55-point difference is largest in majors over last 10 years (minimum: 500 AB each).

## Sammy Sosa

Rangers/White Sox — Bats Right

| | AB | H | 2B | 3B | HR | RBI | BB | SO | BA | SA | OBA |
|---|---|---|---|---|---|---|---|---|---|---|---|
| Season | 183 | 47 | 8 | 0 | 4 | 13 | 11 | 47 | .257 | .366 | .303 |
| vs. Left-Handers | 78 | 27 | 5 | 0 | 2 | 9 | 7 | 19 | .346 | .487 | .391 |
| vs. Right-Handers | 105 | 20 | 3 | 0 | 2 | 4 | 4 | 28 | .190 | .276 | .234 |
| Home | 67 | 19 | 2 | 0 | 1 | 5 | 7 | 24 | .284 | .358 | .342 |
| Road | 116 | 28 | 6 | 0 | 3 | 8 | 4 | 23 | .241 | .371 | .279 |
| Grass | 161 | 38 | 6 | 0 | 3 | 9 | 9 | 41 | .236 | .329 | .282 |
| Artificial Turf | 22 | 9 | 2 | 0 | 1 | 4 | 2 | 6 | .409 | .636 | .458 |
| April | 0 | 0 | 0 | 0 | 0 | 0 | 0 | 0 | — | — | — |
| May | 0 | 0 | 0 | 0 | 0 | 0 | 0 | 0 | — | — | — |
| June | 52 | 14 | 1 | 0 | 1 | 2 | 0 | 11 | .269 | .346 | .269 |
| July | 32 | 6 | 2 | 0 | 0 | 1 | 0 | 9 | .188 | .250 | .188 |
| August | 31 | 12 | 2 | 0 | 1 | 4 | 2 | 7 | .387 | .548 | .424 |
| Sept./Oct. | 68 | 15 | 3 | 0 | 2 | 6 | 9 | 20 | .221 | .353 | .321 |
| Leading Off Inn. | 50 | 13 | 3 | 0 | 1 | 1 | 2 | 13 | .260 | .380 | .302 |
| Runners On | 73 | 19 | 3 | 0 | 1 | 10 | 5 | 18 | .260 | .342 | .309 |
| Runners/Scor. Pos. | 38 | 8 | 3 | 0 | 0 | 8 | 3 | 9 | .211 | .289 | .273 |
| Runners On/2 Out | 20 | 4 | 0 | 0 | 0 | 0 | 0 | 3 | .200 | .200 | .200 |
| Scor. Pos./2 Out | 10 | 0 | 0 | 0 | 0 | 0 | 0 | 3 | .000 | .000 | .000 |
| Late Inning Pressure | 23 | 4 | 2 | 0 | 0 | 0 | 2 | 7 | .174 | .261 | .240 |
| Leading Off | 9 | 1 | 1 | 0 | 0 | 0 | 0 | 3 | .111 | .222 | .111 |
| Runners On | 6 | 0 | 0 | 0 | 0 | 0 | 0 | 2 | .000 | .000 | .000 |
| Runners/Scor. Pos. | 3 | 0 | 0 | 0 | 0 | 0 | 0 | 0 | .000 | .000 | .000 |

| RUNS BATTED IN | From 1B | From 2B | From 3B | Scoring Position |
|---|---|---|---|---|
| Totals | 1/53 | 5/30 | 3/15 | 8/45 |
| Percentage | 2% | 17% | 20% | 18% |
| Driving In Runners from 3B with Less than Two Out: | | | 3/10 | 30% |

Loves to face: Jeff Ballard (.600, 3-for-5, 1 HR)
Hates to face: Rick Aguilera (0-for-6, 4 SO)
Among all batters in majors last season (minimum: 50 AB vs. both types of pitching), four largest lefty/righty differences were produced by Latin American hitters: Carmelo Castillo (.316 vs. lefties, .111 vs. righties), Andres Galarraga (.385/.201), Domingo Ramos (.373/.208), Sosa (.346/.190).... Batted .238 in 25 games with Texas, .273 in 33 games with White Sox. Had no walks and 20 strikeouts with Texas.... Rate of runners driven in from third base with less than two outs was 3d lowest in A.L. last season.... Only two players younger than Sosa had as many starts (49) as he last season: Ken Griffey, Jr. (120) and Gary Sheffield (95).... Born Nov. 10, 1968, five days after Nixon was elected president.

## Bill Spiers

Bats Left

| Milwaukee Brewers | AB | H | 2B | 3B | HR | RBI | BB | SO | BA | SA | OBA |
|---|---|---|---|---|---|---|---|---|---|---|---|
| Season | 345 | 88 | 9 | 3 | 4 | 33 | 21 | 63 | .255 | .333 | .298 |
| vs. Left-Handers | 70 | 19 | 2 | 1 | 1 | 9 | 1 | 19 | .271 | .371 | .282 |
| vs. Right-Handers | 275 | 69 | 7 | 2 | 3 | 24 | 20 | 44 | .251 | .324 | .302 |
| Home | 172 | 47 | 7 | 1 | 1 | 17 | 7 | 33 | .273 | .343 | .298 |
| Road | 173 | 41 | 2 | 2 | 3 | 16 | 14 | 30 | .237 | .324 | .298 |
| Grass | 303 | 79 | 8 | 3 | 4 | 32 | 16 | 58 | .261 | .347 | .298 |
| Artificial Turf | 42 | 9 | 1 | 0 | 0 | 1 | 5 | 5 | .214 | .238 | .298 |
| April | 26 | 4 | 0 | 0 | 1 | 5 | 4 | 4 | .154 | .269 | .258 |
| May | 54 | 15 | 3 | 0 | 0 | 2 | 6 | 10 | .278 | .333 | .361 |
| June | 25 | 5 | 0 | 0 | 0 | 1 | 2 | 5 | .200 | .200 | .259 |
| July | 44 | 15 | 0 | 0 | 0 | 4 | 0 | 7 | .341 | .341 | .333 |
| August | 89 | 16 | 3 | 0 | 0 | 12 | 6 | 18 | .180 | .213 | .232 |
| Sept./Oct. | 107 | 33 | 3 | 3 | 3 | 9 | 3 | 19 | .308 | .477 | .327 |
| Leading Off Inn. | 92 | 18 | 4 | 0 | 1 | 1 | 8 | 13 | .196 | .272 | .267 |
| Runners On | 135 | 36 | 5 | 3 | 1 | 30 | 8 | 25 | .267 | .370 | .303 |
| Runners/Scor. Pos. | 83 | 23 | 3 | 2 | 1 | 29 | 7 | 17 | .277 | .398 | .326 |
| Runners On/2 Out | 67 | 17 | 3 | 2 | 1 | 20 | 4 | 10 | .254 | .403 | .296 |
| Scor. Pos./2 Out | 52 | 15 | 2 | 2 | 1 | 20 | 4 | 8 | .288 | .462 | .339 |
| Late Inning Pressure | 37 | 12 | 1 | 0 | 0 | 0 | 6 | 6 | .324 | .351 | .419 |
| Leading Off | 13 | 4 | 1 | 0 | 0 | 0 | 1 | 1 | .308 | .385 | .357 |
| Runners On | 12 | 4 | 0 | 0 | 0 | 0 | 2 | 2 | .333 | .333 | .429 |
| Runners/Scor. Pos. | 4 | 1 | 0 | 0 | 0 | 0 | 2 | 1 | .250 | .250 | .500 |

| RUNS BATTED IN | From 1B | From 2B | From 3B | Scoring Position |
|---|---|---|---|---|
| Totals | 2/90 | 12/65 | 15/35 | 27/100 |
| Percentage | 2% | 18% | 43% | 27% |
| Driving In Runners from 3B with Less than Two Out: | | | 6/10 | 60% |

Loves to face: Bob Welch (.500, 4-for-8)
Hates to face: Tom Candiotti (.111, 1-for-9, 5 SO)
Played 49 percent of team's innings at shortstop, compared to 42 percent for Sheffield and 9 percent by others. Team played much better with Spiers at short, allowing 3.92 runs per nine innings with Spiers, 4.91 with Sheffield. Among teams with split-shortstop situations in 1989, that's the largest difference in runs allowed between two shortstops on the same team. . . . One of three A.L. players to start at least one game at each of the four infield positions. . . . Had three hits and a walk in his five pinch-hit appearances. . . . Grounded into only two double plays in 56 double-play situations, best rate on Brewers. . . . Hit a grand-slam home run in his first major league plate appearance with the bases loaded.

## Terry Steinbach

Bats Right

| Oakland As | AB | H | 2B | 3B | HR | RBI | BB | SO | BA | SA | OBA |
|---|---|---|---|---|---|---|---|---|---|---|---|
| Season | 454 | 124 | 13 | 1 | 7 | 42 | 30 | 66 | .273 | .352 | .319 |
| vs. Left-Handers | 159 | 41 | 6 | 0 | 3 | 18 | 9 | 18 | .258 | .352 | .298 |
| vs. Right-Handers | 295 | 83 | 7 | 1 | 4 | 24 | 21 | 48 | .281 | .353 | .330 |
| Home | 216 | 63 | 3 | 1 | 5 | 23 | 12 | 27 | .292 | .384 | .328 |
| Road | 238 | 61 | 10 | 0 | 2 | 19 | 18 | 39 | .256 | .324 | .312 |
| Grass | 383 | 108 | 10 | 1 | 6 | 35 | 26 | 55 | .282 | .360 | .327 |
| Artificial Turf | 71 | 16 | 3 | 0 | 1 | 7 | 4 | 11 | .225 | .310 | .276 |
| April | 73 | 22 | 5 | 0 | 1 | 10 | 9 | 11 | .301 | .411 | .378 |
| May | 78 | 30 | 1 | 1 | 2 | 9 | 5 | 7 | .385 | .500 | .429 |
| June | 89 | 23 | 2 | 0 | 1 | 5 | 2 | 15 | .258 | .315 | .272 |
| July | 65 | 20 | 4 | 0 | 1 | 8 | 2 | 9 | .308 | .415 | .328 |
| August | 75 | 15 | 1 | 0 | 0 | 6 | 3 | 14 | .200 | .213 | .238 |
| Sept./Oct. | 74 | 14 | 0 | 0 | 2 | 4 | 9 | 10 | .189 | .270 | .274 |
| Leading Off Inn. | 104 | 32 | 2 | 0 | 2 | 2 | 8 | 16 | .308 | .385 | .357 |
| Runners On | 189 | 45 | 6 | 0 | 3 | 38 | 11 | 29 | .238 | .317 | .283 |
| Runners/Scor. Pos. | 106 | 28 | 4 | 0 | 2 | 36 | 8 | 15 | .264 | .358 | .314 |
| Runners On/2 Out | 84 | 18 | 1 | 0 | 1 | 10 | 5 | 10 | .214 | .262 | .258 |
| Scor. Pos./2 Out | 53 | 11 | 1 | 0 | 0 | 8 | 3 | 5 | .208 | .226 | .250 |
| Late Inning Pressure | 54 | 14 | 1 | 0 | 2 | 7 | 5 | 11 | .259 | .389 | .317 |
| Leading Off | 16 | 4 | 0 | 0 | 0 | 0 | 2 | 4 | .250 | .250 | .333 |
| Runners On | 18 | 5 | 0 | 0 | 2 | 7 | 0 | 5 | .278 | .611 | .263 |
| Runners/Scor. Pos. | 6 | 2 | 0 | 0 | 1 | 5 | 0 | 2 | .333 | .833 | .286 |

| RUNS BATTED IN | From 1B | From 2B | From 3B | Scoring Position |
|---|---|---|---|---|
| Totals | 3/143 | 13/78 | 19/49 | 32/127 |
| Percentage | 2% | 17% | 39% | 25% |
| Driving In Runners from 3B with Less than Two Out: | | | 15/26 | 58% |

Loves to face: Richard Dotson (.750, 6-for-8)
Hates to face: Clay Parker (0-for-9)
Batted .349 (15-for-43) with Athletics trailing by a run, and hit .455 (10-for-22) with runners in scoring position and the score tied. . . . Batting average vs. left-handed pitchers was a career low. Career breakdown: .296 vs. left-handers, .264 vs. right-handers. . . . Has .394 career mark (13-for-33) with bases loaded; has hit grand slams vs. Toronto in each of last two seasons. . . . One of five A.L. players to start at least one game at five fielding positions last season. Also started four games as DH. . . . Batted .311 on fair balls hit to left side, .418 straight away, .245 to opposite field. . . . Caught majority of innings for Stewart and Moore, while Hassey usually caught Davis and received Welch almost exclusively.

## Kurt Stillwell

Bats Left and Right

| Kansas City Royals | AB | H | 2B | 3B | HR | RBI | BB | SO | BA | SA | OBA |
|---|---|---|---|---|---|---|---|---|---|---|---|
| Season | 463 | 121 | 20 | 7 | 7 | 54 | 42 | 64 | .261 | .380 | .325 |
| vs. Left-Handers | 121 | 32 | 3 | 3 | 1 | 12 | 11 | 11 | .264 | .364 | .336 |
| vs. Right-Handers | 342 | 89 | 17 | 4 | 6 | 42 | 31 | 53 | .260 | .386 | .321 |
| Home | 217 | 49 | 6 | 3 | 2 | 30 | 21 | 34 | .226 | .309 | .293 |
| Road | 246 | 72 | 14 | 4 | 5 | 24 | 21 | 30 | .293 | .443 | .353 |
| Grass | 189 | 51 | 11 | 3 | 2 | 16 | 17 | 22 | .270 | .392 | .333 |
| Artificial Turf | 274 | 70 | 9 | 4 | 5 | 38 | 25 | 42 | .255 | .372 | .319 |
| April | 56 | 10 | 2 | 0 | 0 | 5 | 4 | 7 | .179 | .214 | .230 |
| May | 83 | 25 | 3 | 0 | 3 | 11 | 13 | 13 | .301 | .446 | .396 |
| June | 106 | 28 | 6 | 1 | 0 | 7 | 5 | 11 | .264 | .340 | .304 |
| July | 18 | 6 | 0 | 1 | 0 | 3 | 1 | 1 | .333 | .444 | .368 |
| August | 95 | 30 | 3 | 5 | 3 | 20 | 11 | 14 | .316 | .547 | .389 |
| Sept./Oct. | 105 | 22 | 6 | 0 | 1 | 8 | 8 | 18 | .210 | .295 | .270 |
| Leading Off Inn. | 112 | 31 | 6 | 3 | 3 | 3 | 13 | 15 | .277 | .464 | .352 |
| Runners On | 201 | 62 | 10 | 4 | 3 | 50 | 16 | 21 | .308 | .443 | .355 |
| Runners/Scor. Pos. | 120 | 35 | 6 | 4 | 2 | 46 | 12 | 11 | .292 | .458 | .348 |
| Runners On/2 Out | 77 | 22 | 5 | 2 | 1 | 18 | 8 | 11 | .286 | .442 | .353 |
| Scor. Pos./2 Out | 52 | 14 | 3 | 2 | 1 | 17 | 5 | 5 | .269 | .462 | .333 |
| Late Inning Pressure | 58 | 12 | 2 | 0 | 0 | 2 | 7 | 12 | .207 | .241 | .288 |
| Leading Off | 15 | 5 | 2 | 0 | 0 | 0 | 5 | 1 | .333 | .467 | .500 |
| Runners On | 22 | 5 | 0 | 0 | 0 | 2 | 1 | 5 | .227 | .227 | .250 |
| Runners/Scor. Pos. | 12 | 2 | 0 | 0 | 0 | 2 | 1 | 1 | .167 | .167 | .214 |

| RUNS BATTED IN | From 1B | From 2B | From 3B | Scoring Position |
|---|---|---|---|---|
| Totals | 5/141 | 20/94 | 22/48 | 42/142 |
| Percentage | 4% | 21% | 46% | 30% |
| Driving In Runners from 3B with Less than Two Out: | | | 16/26 | 62% |

Loves to face: Kirk McCaskill (.500, 6-for-12)
Hates to face: Roger Clemens (0-for-13, 6 SO)
Royals had a 74–50 record with Stillwell starting, 18–20 without him; in 1988, they were 66–55 in Still's starts, 18–22 without him. . . . Has 105 RBI as a shortstop over past two years; among A.L. shortstops, only Ripken, Fernandez, and Trammell (who has 106) have more. . . . Grounded into only three double plays in 93 opportunities, best rate by far on team. . . . Career average with runners on base (.296) is 74 points higher than with bases empty (.222), largest difference by any player over last 10 years (minimum: 500 AB each way). . . . Owns .319 career average with runners on base in Late-Inning Pressure Situations. . . . Batted .314 vs. ground-ball pitchers, .214 vs. fly-ball pitchers.

## Doug Strange

Bats Left and Right

| Detroit Tigers | AB | H | 2B | 3B | HR | RBI | BB | SO | BA | SA | OBA |
|---|---|---|---|---|---|---|---|---|---|---|---|
| Season | 196 | 42 | 4 | 1 | 1 | 14 | 17 | 36 | .214 | .260 | .280 |
| vs. Left-Handers | 42 | 8 | 1 | 0 | 0 | 0 | 2 | 6 | .190 | .214 | .227 |
| vs. Right-Handers | 154 | 34 | 3 | 1 | 1 | 14 | 15 | 30 | .221 | .273 | .294 |
| Home | 96 | 20 | 2 | 0 | 1 | 8 | 11 | 19 | .208 | .260 | .296 |
| Road | 100 | 22 | 2 | 1 | 0 | 6 | 6 | 17 | .220 | .260 | .264 |
| Grass | 164 | 33 | 2 | 1 | 1 | 12 | 15 | 32 | .201 | .244 | .272 |
| Artificial Turf | 32 | 9 | 2 | 0 | 0 | 2 | 2 | 4 | .281 | .344 | .324 |
| April | 0 | 0 | 0 | 0 | 0 | 0 | 0 | 0 | — | — | — |
| May | 0 | 0 | 0 | 0 | 0 | 0 | 0 | 0 | — | — | — |
| June | 0 | 0 | 0 | 0 | 0 | 0 | 0 | 0 | — | — | — |
| July | 43 | 9 | 1 | 0 | 0 | 2 | 0 | 8 | .209 | .233 | .209 |
| August | 77 | 16 | 1 | 1 | 0 | 5 | 5 | 14 | .208 | .247 | .256 |
| Sept./Oct. | 76 | 17 | 2 | 0 | 1 | 7 | 12 | 14 | .224 | .289 | .337 |
| Leading Off Inn. | 40 | 10 | 2 | 0 | 0 | 0 | 4 | 7 | .250 | .300 | .318 |
| Runners On | 80 | 19 | 1 | 1 | 0 | 13 | 8 | 11 | .238 | .275 | .315 |
| Runners/Scor. Pos. | 45 | 12 | 1 | 1 | 0 | 13 | 3 | 8 | .267 | .333 | .327 |
| Runners On/2 Out | 37 | 7 | 1 | 1 | 0 | 6 | 6 | 4 | .189 | .270 | .302 |
| Scor. Pos./2 Out | 21 | 4 | 1 | 1 | 0 | 6 | 2 | 3 | .190 | .333 | .261 |
| Late Inning Pressure | 35 | 7 | 0 | 1 | 0 | 3 | 1 | 6 | .200 | .257 | .243 |
| Leading Off | 5 | 3 | 0 | 0 | 0 | 0 | 0 | 0 | .600 | .600 | .600 |
| Runners On | 17 | 2 | 0 | 1 | 0 | 3 | 1 | 3 | .118 | .235 | .211 |
| Runners/Scor. Pos. | 14 | 2 | 0 | 1 | 0 | 3 | 0 | 3 | .143 | .286 | .200 |

| RUNS BATTED IN | From 1B | From 2B | From 3B | Scoring Position |
|---|---|---|---|---|
| Totals | 2/54 | 9/37 | 2/15 | 11/52 |
| Percentage | 4% | 24% | 13% | 21% |
| Driving In Runners from 3B with Less than Two Out: | | | 2/7 | 29% |

Loves to face: Bobby Thigpen (2-for-2, 1 3B)
Hates to face: Bud Black (0-for-6)
Third-lowest fielding percentage (.878) of the past 50 years by a third baseman with at least 50 games; thank God for Dale Sveum (.865 in 1986) and Ray Knight (.868 in 1978). Strange was swimming in Sveumland (.865) as late as Sept. 15, but erred only once in eight games at third after that. . . . Only appearance as DH came on final day of season. . . . Switch-hitter who saw most of his action vs. right-handed pitchers; hit his only home run off Bret Saberhagen, which is something that Mark McGwire, Jim Rice, and Gary Gaetti, among others, have never done. . . . Tigers were 20–30 with Strange starting at third. Hey, that was *good* compared to their 39–73 record with any of six other starting third basemen!

## B. J. Surhoff

Bats Left

| Milwaukee Brewers | AB | H | 2B | 3B | HR | RBI | BB | SO | BA | SA | OBA |
|---|---|---|---|---|---|---|---|---|---|---|---|
| Season | 436 | 108 | 17 | 4 | 5 | 55 | 25 | 29 | .248 | .339 | .287 |
| vs. Left-Handers | 84 | 26 | 6 | 0 | 2 | 17 | 0 | 7 | .310 | .452 | .314 |
| vs. Right-Handers | 352 | 82 | 11 | 4 | 3 | 38 | 25 | 22 | .233 | .313 | .281 |
| Home | 213 | 51 | 9 | 1 | 3 | 29 | 18 | 16 | .239 | .333 | .302 |
| Road | 223 | 57 | 8 | 3 | 2 | 26 | 7 | 13 | .256 | .345 | .272 |
| Grass | 371 | 95 | 15 | 3 | 5 | 48 | 25 | 23 | .256 | .353 | .302 |
| Artificial Turf | 65 | 13 | 2 | 1 | 0 | 7 | 0 | 6 | .200 | .262 | .194 |
| April | 63 | 12 | 1 | 0 | 3 | 10 | 5 | 6 | .190 | .349 | .243 |
| May | 79 | 22 | 3 | 0 | 1 | 6 | 5 | 6 | .278 | .354 | .318 |
| June | 90 | 21 | 3 | 1 | 0 | 15 | 3 | 7 | .233 | .289 | .258 |
| July | 64 | 18 | 1 | 1 | 0 | 7 | 1 | 2 | .281 | .328 | .294 |
| August | 75 | 18 | 4 | 1 | 0 | 8 | 4 | 5 | .240 | .320 | .280 |
| Sept./Oct. | 65 | 17 | 5 | 1 | 1 | 9 | 7 | 3 | .262 | .415 | .329 |
| Leading Off Inn. | 90 | 17 | 5 | 0 | 1 | 1 | 6 | 8 | .189 | .278 | .240 |
| Runners On | 181 | 47 | 5 | 3 | 2 | 52 | 8 | 6 | .260 | .354 | .284 |
| Runners/Scor. Pos. | 97 | 26 | 3 | 1 | 2 | 48 | 8 | 4 | .268 | .381 | .308 |
| Runners On/2 Out | 79 | 18 | 4 | 2 | 1 | 24 | 7 | 3 | .228 | .367 | .299 |
| Scor. Pos./2 Out | 47 | 13 | 3 | 1 | 1 | 22 | 7 | 2 | .277 | .447 | .382 |
| Late Inning Pressure | 66 | 18 | 3 | 0 | 1 | 9 | 4 | 6 | .273 | .364 | .306 |
| Leading Off | 17 | 2 | 0 | 0 | 0 | 0 | 3 | 1 | .118 | .118 | .250 |
| Runners On | 23 | 9 | 3 | 0 | 1 | 9 | 0 | 1 | .391 | .652 | .360 |
| Runners/Scor. Pos. | 14 | 5 | 2 | 0 | 1 | 8 | 0 | 1 | .357 | .714 | .313 |

| RUNS BATTED IN | From 1B | From 2B | From 3B | Scoring Position |
|---|---|---|---|---|
| Totals | 8/144 | 13/71 | 29/51 | 42/122 |
| Percentage | 6% | 18% | 57% | 34% |
| Driving In Runners from 3B with Less than Two Out: | | | 21/32 | 66% |

Loves to face: Dave Righetti (.417, 5-for-12)
Hates to face: Bobby Thigpen (0-for-9)
Turned 25 on Aug. 4; was youngest A.L. catcher to start at least half his team's games in 1989.... Has 10+ steals in three consecutive seasons. Only one other catcher since 1920 had a streak that long: John Wathan, a four-year streak, 1980–83.... Had five hits, including a home run, in eight at-bats with bases loaded. Career bases-loaded numbers: 11-for-30 (including 7-for-16 with two outs).... Owns higher career average vs. left-handers (.264) than vs. right-handers (.262); year-by-year BA vs. lefties: .318, .191, .310.... Career breakdown: .289 with runners on base, .242 with bases empty.... Played at Rye (N.Y.) High School, where he was the shortstop. No, not the Catcher, Mr. Salinger.

## Pat Tabler

Bats Right

| Kansas City Royals | AB | H | 2B | 3B | HR | RBI | BB | SO | BA | SA | OBA |
|---|---|---|---|---|---|---|---|---|---|---|---|
| Season | 390 | 101 | 11 | 1 | 2 | 42 | 37 | 42 | .259 | .308 | .325 |
| vs. Left-Handers | 160 | 56 | 4 | 0 | 2 | 21 | 15 | 7 | .350 | .413 | .407 |
| vs. Right-Handers | 230 | 45 | 7 | 1 | 0 | 21 | 22 | 35 | .196 | .235 | .268 |
| Home | 181 | 49 | 7 | 0 | 2 | 21 | 15 | 17 | .271 | .343 | .327 |
| Road | 209 | 52 | 4 | 1 | 0 | 21 | 22 | 25 | .249 | .278 | .323 |
| Grass | 164 | 42 | 3 | 1 | 0 | 19 | 17 | 15 | .256 | .287 | .330 |
| Artificial Turf | 226 | 59 | 8 | 0 | 2 | 23 | 20 | 27 | .261 | .323 | .321 |
| April | 66 | 17 | 2 | 0 | 0 | 5 | 7 | 6 | .258 | .288 | .329 |
| May | 69 | 19 | 1 | 0 | 0 | 8 | 3 | 7 | .275 | .290 | .301 |
| June | 73 | 20 | 2 | 0 | 0 | 8 | 8 | 6 | .274 | .301 | .354 |
| July | 77 | 20 | 3 | 1 | 1 | 8 | 8 | 9 | .260 | .364 | .329 |
| August | 54 | 13 | 3 | 0 | 0 | 6 | 6 | 7 | .241 | .296 | .323 |
| Sept./Oct. | 51 | 12 | 0 | 0 | 1 | 7 | 5 | 7 | .235 | .294 | .304 |
| Leading Off Inn. | 88 | 19 | 0 | 0 | 0 | 0 | 10 | 10 | .216 | .216 | .296 |
| Runners On | 185 | 50 | 7 | 0 | 2 | 42 | 14 | 16 | .270 | .341 | .325 |
| Runners/Scor. Pos. | 120 | 28 | 3 | 0 | 2 | 39 | 11 | 12 | .233 | .308 | .304 |
| Runners On/2 Out | 88 | 19 | 2 | 0 | 1 | 15 | 9 | 10 | .216 | .273 | .296 |
| Scor. Pos./2 Out | 58 | 12 | 2 | 0 | 1 | 15 | 7 | 6 | .207 | .293 | .303 |
| Late Inning Pressure | 64 | 19 | 3 | 0 | 1 | 7 | 4 | 10 | .297 | .391 | .338 |
| Leading Off | 14 | 2 | 0 | 0 | 0 | 0 | 2 | 4 | .143 | .143 | .250 |
| Runners On | 30 | 9 | 1 | 0 | 1 | 7 | 1 | 2 | .300 | .433 | .323 |
| Runners/Scor. Pos. | 20 | 4 | 0 | 0 | 1 | 6 | 1 | 2 | .200 | .350 | .238 |

| RUNS BATTED IN | From 1B | From 2B | From 3B | Scoring Position |
|---|---|---|---|---|
| Totals | 5/125 | 14/90 | 21/52 | 35/142 |
| Percentage | 4% | 16% | 40% | 25% |
| Driving In Runners from 3B with Less than Two Out: | | | 14/25 | 56% |

Loves to face: Greg A. Harris (.533, 8-for-15, 1 HR)
Hates to face: Steve Crawford (0-for-9)
Closest thing to a platoon player on Royals last season, starting 50 of 55 games vs. left-handers, but only 53 of 107 vs. right-handers. And for good reason: he hit .350 vs. lefties, career-low .196 vs. righties, widest difference in A.L. in 1989 (minimum: 100 at-bats vs. each).... Owns .324 career average with runners in scoring position (second to Boggs's .354 among active A.L. players).... Well, it looks like the pressure finally got to him: he went 1-for-11 with bases loaded in '89 (and finished the year hitless in his last 9 at-bats), dropping career average to .507 (38-for-75). That's still tops in majors since 1975 (minimum: 15 hits); among active players, Denny Walling stands second at .404.

## Danny Tartabull

Bats Right

| Kansas City Royals | AB | H | 2B | 3B | HR | RBI | BB | SO | BA | SA | OBA |
|---|---|---|---|---|---|---|---|---|---|---|---|
| Season | 441 | 118 | 22 | 0 | 18 | 63 | 69 | 123 | .268 | .440 | .369 |
| vs. Left-Handers | 125 | 39 | 8 | 0 | 8 | 22 | 23 | 31 | .312 | .568 | .420 |
| vs. Right-Handers | 316 | 79 | 14 | 0 | 10 | 41 | 46 | 92 | .250 | .389 | .348 |
| Home | 214 | 60 | 12 | 0 | 9 | 32 | 39 | 58 | .280 | .463 | .388 |
| Road | 227 | 58 | 10 | 0 | 9 | 31 | 30 | 65 | .256 | .419 | .350 |
| Grass | 150 | 36 | 7 | 0 | 6 | 19 | 24 | 44 | .240 | .407 | .356 |
| Artificial Turf | 291 | 82 | 15 | 0 | 12 | 44 | 45 | 79 | .282 | .457 | .376 |
| April | 77 | 25 | 4 | 0 | 1 | 12 | 17 | 18 | .325 | .416 | .438 |
| May | 94 | 22 | 5 | 0 | 5 | 15 | 12 | 26 | .234 | .447 | .333 |
| June | 43 | 9 | 0 | 0 | 3 | 5 | 4 | 13 | .209 | .419 | .277 |
| July | 57 | 16 | 3 | 0 | 3 | 12 | 5 | 14 | .281 | .491 | .349 |
| August | 99 | 32 | 7 | 0 | 3 | 10 | 15 | 24 | .323 | .485 | .412 |
| Sept./Oct. | 71 | 14 | 3 | 0 | 3 | 9 | 16 | 28 | .197 | .366 | .345 |
| Leading Off Inn. | 121 | 37 | 8 | 0 | 2 | 2 | 11 | 31 | .306 | .421 | .368 |
| Runners On | 197 | 46 | 9 | 0 | 5 | 50 | 36 | 54 | .234 | .355 | .352 |
| Runners/Scor. Pos. | 116 | 24 | 5 | 0 | 2 | 41 | 28 | 37 | .207 | .302 | .361 |
| Runners On/2 Out | 91 | 14 | 2 | 0 | 4 | 17 | 20 | 34 | .154 | .308 | .306 |
| Scor. Pos./2 Out | 57 | 6 | 0 | 0 | 1 | 9 | 16 | 25 | .105 | .158 | .301 |
| Late Inning Pressure | 59 | 22 | 2 | 0 | 4 | 15 | 11 | 17 | .373 | .610 | .479 |
| Leading Off | 16 | 4 | 0 | 0 | 1 | 1 | 1 | 6 | .250 | .438 | .294 |
| Runners On | 26 | 12 | 1 | 0 | 1 | 12 | 6 | 6 | .462 | .615 | .563 |
| Runners/Scor. Pos. | 14 | 6 | 1 | 0 | 1 | 12 | 5 | 4 | .429 | .714 | .579 |

| RUNS BATTED IN | From 1B | From 2B | From 3B | Scoring Position |
|---|---|---|---|---|
| Totals | 9/140 | 15/81 | 21/54 | 36/135 |
| Percentage | 6% | 19% | 39% | 27% |
| Driving In Runners from 3B with Less than Two Out: | | | 17/30 | 57% |

Loves to face: Roy Smith (.556, 5-for-9, 3 HR)
Hates to face: John Farrell (.071, 1-for-14, 5 SO)
Batting average in Late-Inning Pressure Situations stood over .400 in late August, finally settled at .373, 5th best in A.L. in 1989.... Career slugging average (.529) vs. fly-ball pitchers is best among active A.L. players (minimum: 300 total bases).... Career breakdown with runners in scoring position: .319 with less than two outs, .225 with two outs.... Owns .309 career average (17-for-55) with bases loaded. Included are six grand slams (four with K.C., two shy of Frank White's team mark).... Needs 146 games to match papa Jose's career total. ... Averaged 1.67 putouts per nine innings, lowest rate in majors among right fielders (minimum: 500 innings). Had same distinction among A.L. right fielders in 1988 (1.84).

## Mickey Tettleton

Bats Left and Right

| Baltimore Orioles | AB | H | 2B | 3B | HR | RBI | BB | SO | BA | SA | OBA |
|---|---|---|---|---|---|---|---|---|---|---|---|
| Season | 411 | 106 | 21 | 2 | 26 | 65 | 73 | 117 | .258 | .509 | .369 |
| vs. Left-Handers | 139 | 34 | 10 | 0 | 10 | 20 | 22 | 47 | .245 | .532 | .346 |
| vs. Right-Handers | 272 | 72 | 11 | 2 | 16 | 45 | 51 | 70 | .265 | .496 | .380 |
| Home | 203 | 63 | 12 | 2 | 15 | 41 | 32 | 48 | .310 | .611 | .401 |
| Road | 208 | 43 | 9 | 0 | 11 | 24 | 41 | 69 | .207 | .409 | .339 |
| Grass | 335 | 91 | 18 | 2 | 24 | 59 | 63 | 85 | .272 | .552 | .385 |
| Artificial Turf | 76 | 15 | 3 | 0 | 2 | 6 | 10 | 32 | .197 | .316 | .295 |
| April | 71 | 15 | 3 | 0 | 5 | 11 | 5 | 25 | .211 | .465 | .260 |
| May | 80 | 22 | 3 | 0 | 8 | 16 | 15 | 17 | .275 | .613 | .389 |
| June | 101 | 27 | 8 | 1 | 5 | 18 | 23 | 25 | .267 | .515 | .397 |
| July | 92 | 29 | 6 | 1 | 3 | 10 | 20 | 24 | .315 | .500 | .438 |
| August | 10 | 2 | 0 | 0 | 1 | 1 | 4 | 3 | .200 | .500 | .429 |
| Sept./Oct. | 57 | 11 | 1 | 0 | 4 | 9 | 6 | 23 | .193 | .421 | .281 |
| Leading Off Inn. | 121 | 37 | 8 | 2 | 8 | 8 | 12 | 33 | .306 | .603 | .368 |
| Runners On | 170 | 34 | 6 | 0 | 9 | 48 | 51 | 50 | .200 | .394 | .382 |
| Runners/Scor. Pos. | 100 | 19 | 2 | 0 | 7 | 42 | 33 | 33 | .190 | .420 | .387 |
| Runners On/2 Out | 72 | 10 | 2 | 0 | 1 | 13 | 23 | 21 | .139 | .208 | .347 |
| Scor. Pos./2 Out | 49 | 6 | 0 | 0 | 1 | 12 | 17 | 16 | .122 | .184 | .348 |
| Late Inning Pressure | 57 | 15 | 2 | 0 | 1 | 5 | 8 | 15 | .263 | .351 | .354 |
| Leading Off | 28 | 8 | 1 | 0 | 0 | 0 | 3 | 6 | .286 | .321 | .355 |
| Runners On | 16 | 3 | 1 | 0 | 1 | 5 | 3 | 6 | .188 | .438 | .316 |
| Runners/Scor. Pos. | 10 | 2 | 0 | 0 | 1 | 4 | 2 | 2 | .200 | .500 | .333 |

| RUNS BATTED IN | From 1B | From 2B | From 3B | Scoring Position |
|---|---|---|---|---|
| Totals | 9/130 | 14/72 | 16/53 | 30/125 |
| Percentage | 7% | 19% | 30% | 24% |
| Driving In Runners from 3B with Less than Two Out: | | | 9/22 | 41% |

Loves to face: Frank Tanana (.391, 9-for-23, 3 HR)
Hates to face: Scott Bankhead (0-for-12)
Averaged one home run every 15.8 at-bats in 1989 (Willie McCovey's career rate was 15.7), after averaging one every 30.1 at-bats previously (Ted Lepcio's career rate was 30.3).... Career breakdown: .255 with bases empty, .221 with runners on base, .195 with runners in scoring position.... Lowest batting average in A.L. in road games last season (minimum: 2 PA per game).... One of four A.L. players to hit a home run vs. every opposing club.... Batted .276 with 18 home runs as catcher, .219 with 8 home runs as DH.... Career mark of only .162 with bases loaded, but he has 10 RBI walks in 47 times up with bags full. That's the highest rate of bases-loaded walks in the 15 years that we've been keeping track.

## Jim Traber

Bats Left

| Baltimore Orioles | AB | H | 2B | 3B | HR | RBI | BB | SO | BA | SA | OBA |
|---|---|---|---|---|---|---|---|---|---|---|---|
| Season | 234 | 49 | 8 | 0 | 4 | 26 | 19 | 41 | .209 | .295 | .266 |
| vs. Left-Handers | 21 | 6 | 0 | 0 | 1 | 5 | 2 | 3 | .286 | .429 | .348 |
| vs. Right-Handers | 213 | 43 | 8 | 0 | 3 | 21 | 17 | 38 | .202 | .282 | .258 |
| Home | 110 | 21 | 4 | 0 | 0 | 9 | 6 | 23 | .191 | .227 | .231 |
| Road | 124 | 28 | 4 | 0 | 4 | 17 | 13 | 18 | .226 | .355 | .295 |
| Grass | 186 | 42 | 7 | 0 | 4 | 24 | 16 | 31 | .226 | .328 | .283 |
| Artificial Turf | 48 | 7 | 1 | 0 | 0 | 2 | 3 | 10 | .146 | .167 | .196 |
| April | 51 | 11 | 1 | 0 | 1 | 4 | 6 | 10 | .216 | .294 | .293 |
| May | 33 | 5 | 4 | 0 | 0 | 5 | 2 | 4 | .152 | .273 | .194 |
| June | 55 | 18 | 3 | 0 | 3 | 14 | 3 | 6 | .327 | .545 | .356 |
| July | 47 | 9 | 0 | 0 | 0 | 2 | 2 | 7 | .191 | .191 | .224 |
| August | 35 | 6 | 0 | 0 | 0 | 0 | 6 | 9 | .171 | .171 | .293 |
| Sept./Oct. | 13 | 0 | 0 | 0 | 0 | 1 | 0 | 5 | .000 | .000 | .000 |
| Leading Off Inn. | 56 | 7 | 1 | 0 | 0 | 0 | 3 | 8 | .125 | .143 | .169 |
| Runners On | 104 | 25 | 4 | 0 | 2 | 24 | 11 | 15 | .240 | .337 | .305 |
| Runners/Scor. Pos. | 69 | 18 | 4 | 0 | 2 | 24 | 7 | 11 | .261 | .406 | .316 |
| Runners On/2 Out | 46 | 10 | 2 | 0 | 0 | 8 | 7 | 6 | .217 | .261 | .321 |
| Scor. Pos./2 Out | 36 | 8 | 2 | 0 | 0 | 8 | 4 | 5 | .222 | .278 | .300 |
| Late Inning Pressure | 39 | 7 | 0 | 0 | 1 | 7 | 2 | 8 | .179 | .256 | .209 |
| Leading Off | 9 | 1 | 0 | 0 | 0 | 0 | 1 | 1 | .111 | .111 | .200 |
| Runners On | 15 | 5 | 0 | 0 | 0 | 6 | 0 | 3 | .333 | .333 | .294 |
| Runners/Scor. Pos. | 10 | 4 | 0 | 0 | 0 | 6 | 0 | 3 | .400 | .400 | .333 |

| RUNS BATTED IN | From 1B | From 2B | From 3B | Scoring Position |
|---|---|---|---|---|
| Totals | 0/78 | 11/51 | 11/41 | 22/92 |
| Percentage | 0% | 22% | 27% | 24% |
| Driving In Runners from 3B with Less than Two Out: | | | 7/15 | 47% |

Loves to face: Mike Boddicker (6-for-6)
Hates to face: John Farrell (0-for-12)
A .213 career hitter in Late-Inning Pressure Situations, with one home run in 141 at-bats. That home run won a game for Orioles last June 22 at Anaheim. . . . Finished season with 23 consecutive hitless at-bats to drop his average from .232. Had no extra-base hits in last 106 at-bats. . . . Started 59 games, all vs. right-handed starters. . . . Only A.L. player with 200+ plate appearances and fewer than 15 runs scored last season. . . . Most career at-bats (819) of any active A.L. player who has never hit a triple. . . . Career breakdown: .270 (one HR every 22.4 AB) with runners on base, .190 (one HR every 43.7 AB) with bases empty. . . . One hit in 12 at-bats with bases loaded last year, hitless in 9 bases-loaded at-bats with two outs.

## Alan Trammell

Bats Right

| Detroit Tigers | AB | H | 2B | 3B | HR | RBI | BB | SO | BA | SA | OBA |
|---|---|---|---|---|---|---|---|---|---|---|---|
| Season | 449 | 109 | 20 | 3 | 5 | 43 | 45 | 45 | .243 | .334 | .314 |
| vs. Left-Handers | 161 | 46 | 11 | 0 | 1 | 16 | 13 | 8 | .286 | .373 | .341 |
| vs. Right-Handers | 288 | 63 | 9 | 3 | 4 | 27 | 32 | 37 | .219 | .313 | .300 |
| Home | 236 | 59 | 11 | 2 | 2 | 25 | 25 | 23 | .250 | .339 | .326 |
| Road | 213 | 50 | 9 | 1 | 3 | 18 | 20 | 22 | .235 | .329 | .301 |
| Grass | 388 | 95 | 19 | 3 | 4 | 37 | 38 | 39 | .245 | .340 | .315 |
| Artificial Turf | 61 | 14 | 1 | 0 | 1 | 6 | 7 | 6 | .230 | .295 | .309 |
| April | 85 | 23 | 3 | 0 | 1 | 4 | 10 | 14 | .271 | .341 | .354 |
| May | 80 | 20 | 3 | 0 | 1 | 6 | 12 | 3 | .250 | .325 | .344 |
| June | 39 | 11 | 1 | 0 | 0 | 9 | 5 | 6 | .282 | .308 | .364 |
| July | 91 | 17 | 4 | 2 | 1 | 5 | 6 | 11 | .187 | .308 | .240 |
| August | 88 | 16 | 3 | 1 | 1 | 9 | 6 | 6 | .182 | .273 | .229 |
| Sept./Oct. | 66 | 22 | 6 | 0 | 1 | 10 | 6 | 5 | .333 | .470 | .405 |
| Leading Off Inn. | 92 | 17 | 2 | 0 | 1 | 1 | 8 | 7 | .185 | .239 | .250 |
| Runners On | 198 | 56 | 8 | 1 | 1 | 39 | 20 | 22 | .283 | .348 | .344 |
| Runners/Scor. Pos. | 99 | 26 | 3 | 1 | 0 | 35 | 11 | 10 | .263 | .313 | .322 |
| Runners On/2 Out | 82 | 20 | 1 | 0 | 0 | 10 | 9 | 8 | .244 | .256 | .326 |
| Scor. Pos./2 Out | 48 | 11 | 0 | 0 | 0 | 10 | 6 | 5 | .229 | .229 | .315 |
| Late Inning Pressure | 67 | 21 | 5 | 0 | 1 | 9 | 13 | 10 | .313 | .433 | .439 |
| Leading Off | 18 | 3 | 0 | 0 | 1 | 1 | 2 | 2 | .167 | .333 | .250 |
| Runners On | 30 | 10 | 2 | 0 | 0 | 8 | 7 | 6 | .333 | .400 | .459 |
| Runners/Scor. Pos. | 17 | 7 | 2 | 0 | 0 | 8 | 2 | 2 | .412 | .529 | .474 |

| RUNS BATTED IN | From 1B | From 2B | From 3B | Scoring Position |
|---|---|---|---|---|
| Totals | 4/150 | 12/67 | 22/56 | 34/123 |
| Percentage | 3% | 18% | 39% | 28% |
| Driving In Runners from 3B with Less than Two Out: | | | 17/26 | 65% |

Loves to face: Mark Langston (.372, 16-for-43, 2 HR)
Hates to face: Bob Milacki (.056, 1-for-18)
Even in a year in which his overall batting average (.243) was a career low for a full season, he batted above .300 in Late-Inning Pressure Situations. Only three others have hit that mark in LIPS in each of the last four seasons: Jerry Browne, Tony Gwynn, and Steve Sax. . . . Decrease of 68 points from 1988 batting average was largest decline among players who qualified for batting title in both '88 and '89. . . . Had batted over .300 leading off innings in five of the previous six seasons. . . . Had the highest fielding percentage of his career (.985). . . . Most games at shortstop for Tigers: Donie Bush (1846), Trammell (1649), Billy Rogell (1148), Harvey Kuenn (747), and Dick McAuliffe (663).

## Dave Valle

Bats Right

| Seattle Mariners | AB | H | 2B | 3B | HR | RBI | BB | SO | BA | SA | OBA |
|---|---|---|---|---|---|---|---|---|---|---|---|
| Season | 316 | 75 | 10 | 3 | 7 | 34 | 29 | 32 | .237 | .354 | .311 |
| vs. Left-Handers | 106 | 25 | 3 | 1 | 4 | 10 | 12 | 5 | .236 | .396 | .317 |
| vs. Right-Handers | 210 | 50 | 7 | 2 | 3 | 24 | 17 | 27 | .238 | .333 | .308 |
| Home | 163 | 41 | 5 | 2 | 1 | 17 | 15 | 12 | .252 | .325 | .324 |
| Road | 153 | 34 | 5 | 1 | 6 | 17 | 14 | 20 | .222 | .386 | .297 |
| Grass | 130 | 26 | 3 | 1 | 4 | 14 | 13 | 20 | .200 | .331 | .284 |
| Artificial Turf | 186 | 49 | 7 | 2 | 3 | 20 | 16 | 12 | .263 | .371 | .330 |
| April | 65 | 16 | 3 | 1 | 3 | 13 | 6 | 7 | .246 | .462 | .315 |
| May | 65 | 21 | 2 | 1 | 1 | 2 | 6 | 5 | .323 | .431 | .384 |
| June | 0 | 0 | 0 | 0 | 0 | 0 | 0 | 0 | — | — | — |
| July | 57 | 10 | 1 | 0 | 1 | 5 | 4 | 2 | .175 | .246 | .254 |
| August | 61 | 13 | 2 | 0 | 1 | 5 | 7 | 9 | .213 | .295 | .294 |
| Sept./Oct. | 68 | 15 | 2 | 1 | 1 | 9 | 6 | 9 | .221 | .324 | .299 |
| Leading Off Inn. | 72 | 17 | 2 | 1 | 1 | 1 | 4 | 7 | .236 | .333 | .304 |
| Runners On | 133 | 36 | 5 | 1 | 2 | 29 | 11 | 10 | .271 | .368 | .333 |
| Runners/Scor. Pos. | 78 | 17 | 4 | 1 | 0 | 25 | 7 | 7 | .218 | .295 | .289 |
| Runners On/2 Out | 60 | 14 | 3 | 0 | 1 | 12 | 6 | 7 | .233 | .333 | .333 |
| Scor. Pos./2 Out | 43 | 8 | 3 | 0 | 0 | 10 | 4 | 5 | .186 | .256 | .286 |
| Late Inning Pressure | 48 | 6 | 0 | 1 | 0 | 3 | 5 | 5 | .125 | .167 | .222 |
| Leading Off | 12 | 1 | 0 | 0 | 0 | 0 | 1 | 0 | .083 | .083 | .214 |
| Runners On | 16 | 4 | 0 | 1 | 0 | 3 | 2 | 2 | .250 | .375 | .333 |
| Runners/Scor. Pos. | 11 | 2 | 0 | 1 | 0 | 3 | 1 | 1 | .182 | .364 | .250 |

| RUNS BATTED IN | From 1B | From 2B | From 3B | Scoring Position |
|---|---|---|---|---|
| Totals | 4/90 | 11/68 | 12/37 | 23/105 |
| Percentage | 4% | 16% | 32% | 22% |
| Driving In Runners from 3B with Less than Two Out: | | | 10/19 | 53% |

Loves to face: Tom Candiotti (.455, 5-for-11, 1 HR)
Hates to face: Ted Higuera (.056, 1-for-18)
Only 59 percent of opposing base stealers were successful with Valle catching last season (48-of-82); with Scott Bradley catching, 80.3 percent were successful (61-of-76). . . . Despite .218 mark last season, he owns .300 career batting average with runners in scoring position; has hit .222 in other at-bats. That 78 point difference is the largest by any major leaguer over last 10 years. (minimum: 250 RISP AB). . . . Led Mariners catchers in starts (91) for first time; no Seattle catcher has had 100 starts in a season since Bob Kearney in 1984. . . . Batting average with runners on base has been higher than with bases empty in each of his six seasons in majors. Career averages: .290 with runners on base, .205 with bases empty.

## Omar Vizquel

Bats Left and Right

| Seattle Mariners | AB | H | 2B | 3B | HR | RBI | BB | SO | BA | SA | OBA |
|---|---|---|---|---|---|---|---|---|---|---|---|
| Season | 387 | 85 | 7 | 3 | 1 | 20 | 28 | 40 | .220 | .261 | .273 |
| vs. Left-Handers | 102 | 20 | 4 | 0 | 1 | 6 | 2 | 6 | .196 | .265 | .212 |
| vs. Right-Handers | 285 | 65 | 3 | 3 | 0 | 14 | 26 | 34 | .228 | .260 | .293 |
| Home | 189 | 43 | 6 | 2 | 1 | 12 | 6 | 24 | .228 | .296 | .254 |
| Road | 198 | 42 | 1 | 1 | 0 | 8 | 22 | 16 | .212 | .227 | .290 |
| Grass | 157 | 34 | 1 | 1 | 0 | 5 | 14 | 9 | .217 | .236 | .279 |
| Artificial Turf | 230 | 51 | 6 | 2 | 1 | 15 | 14 | 31 | .222 | .278 | .268 |
| April | 48 | 6 | 0 | 0 | 0 | 0 | 5 | 3 | .125 | .125 | .208 |
| May | 58 | 17 | 1 | 2 | 0 | 7 | 2 | 7 | .293 | .379 | .311 |
| June | 82 | 21 | 2 | 0 | 0 | 4 | 9 | 10 | .256 | .280 | .330 |
| July | 76 | 19 | 3 | 1 | 1 | 5 | 7 | 5 | .250 | .355 | .313 |
| August | 57 | 9 | 1 | 0 | 0 | 1 | 2 | 7 | .158 | .175 | .197 |
| Sept./Oct. | 66 | 13 | 0 | 0 | 0 | 3 | 3 | 8 | .197 | .197 | .232 |
| Leading Off Inn. | 84 | 22 | 1 | 2 | 1 | 1 | 6 | 9 | .262 | .357 | .311 |
| Runners On | 154 | 36 | 3 | 1 | 0 | 19 | 9 | 16 | .234 | .266 | .273 |
| Runners/Scor. Pos. | 90 | 16 | 3 | 1 | 0 | 19 | 6 | 10 | .178 | .233 | .224 |
| Runners On/2 Out | 65 | 13 | 1 | 0 | 0 | 6 | 6 | 7 | .200 | .215 | .268 |
| Scor. Pos./2 Out | 42 | 8 | 1 | 0 | 0 | 6 | 5 | 3 | .190 | .214 | .277 |
| Late Inning Pressure | 37 | 12 | 1 | 0 | 0 | 0 | 3 | 0 | .324 | .351 | .375 |
| Leading Off | 6 | 5 | 0 | 0 | 0 | 0 | 1 | 0 | .833 | .833 | .857 |
| Runners On | 8 | 0 | 0 | 0 | 0 | 0 | 1 | 0 | .000 | .000 | .111 |
| Runners/Scor. Pos. | 4 | 0 | 0 | 0 | 0 | 0 | 1 | 0 | .000 | .000 | .200 |

| RUNS BATTED IN | From 1B | From 2B | From 3B | Scoring Position |
|---|---|---|---|---|
| Totals | 1/109 | 10/73 | 8/36 | 18/109 |
| Percentage | 1% | 14% | 22% | 17% |
| Driving In Runners from 3B with Less than Two Out: | | | 7/20 | 35% |

Loves to face: Bud Black (.500, 4-for-8)
Hates to face: Nolan Ryan (0-for-10)
Made 120 of his 131 starts from 9th spot in lineup, most by any player last season. He moved up one notch in the order for his other 11 starts. . . . How bad a hitter is Mario (.135) Diaz? Vizquel was used as a pinch hitter only three times last year, each time for Not-So-SuperMario. . . . Batted .240 vs. ground-ball pitchers, .198 vs. fly-ballers. . . . Stole 30 bases in 103 games in Double A in 1988, but was 1-for-5 in steal attempts against the big boys last season. . . . Played 143 games in 1989, second among major league rookies, after having A.L.'s lowest batting average in April. How many teams would have had the patience to stick with a rookie after a start like that? (Don't waste time: only consider teams west of the Bronx.)

## Greg Walker

Bats Left

| Chicago White Sox | AB | H | 2B | 3B | HR | RBI | BB | SO | BA | SA | OBA |
|---|---|---|---|---|---|---|---|---|---|---|---|
| Season | 233 | 49 | 14 | 0 | 5 | 26 | 23 | 50 | .210 | .335 | .286 |
| vs. Left-Handers | 48 | 9 | 1 | 0 | 0 | 3 | 4 | 11 | .188 | .208 | .264 |
| vs. Right-Handers | 185 | 40 | 13 | 0 | 5 | 23 | 19 | 39 | .216 | .368 | .292 |
| Home | 91 | 15 | 2 | 0 | 4 | 11 | 10 | 16 | .165 | .319 | .255 |
| Road | 142 | 34 | 12 | 0 | 1 | 15 | 13 | 34 | .239 | .345 | .306 |
| Grass | 197 | 41 | 9 | 0 | 5 | 22 | 17 | 41 | .208 | .330 | .279 |
| Artificial Turf | 36 | 8 | 5 | 0 | 0 | 4 | 6 | 9 | .222 | .361 | .326 |
| April | 44 | 8 | 2 | 0 | 0 | 1 | 2 | 12 | .182 | .227 | .265 |
| May | 27 | 7 | 3 | 0 | 1 | 5 | 1 | 6 | .259 | .481 | .286 |
| June | 70 | 14 | 3 | 0 | 2 | 7 | 10 | 14 | .200 | .329 | .300 |
| July | 41 | 11 | 4 | 0 | 2 | 6 | 3 | 6 | .268 | .512 | .311 |
| August | 42 | 7 | 2 | 0 | 0 | 6 | 7 | 10 | .167 | .214 | .280 |
| Sept./Oct. | 9 | 2 | 0 | 0 | 0 | 1 | 0 | 2 | .222 | .222 | .200 |
| Leading Off Inn. | 63 | 16 | 3 | 0 | 4 | 4 | 6 | 12 | .254 | .492 | .319 |
| Runners On | 102 | 22 | 7 | 0 | 0 | 21 | 12 | 18 | .216 | .284 | .291 |
| Runners/Scor. Pos. | 62 | 14 | 5 | 0 | 0 | 20 | 8 | 14 | .226 | .306 | .301 |
| Runners On/2 Out | 40 | 8 | 2 | 0 | 0 | 5 | 8 | 5 | .200 | .250 | .333 |
| Scor. Pos./2 Out | 27 | 4 | 1 | 0 | 0 | 4 | 5 | 5 | .148 | .185 | .281 |
| Late Inning Pressure | 33 | 2 | 0 | 0 | 0 | 3 | 6 | 6 | .061 | .061 | .214 |
| Leading Off | 10 | 0 | 0 | 0 | 0 | 0 | 2 | 0 | .000 | .000 | .167 |
| Runners On | 11 | 1 | 0 | 0 | 0 | 3 | 3 | 0 | .091 | .091 | .250 |
| Runners/Scor. Pos. | 7 | 1 | 0 | 0 | 0 | 3 | 2 | 0 | .143 | .143 | .273 |

| RUNS BATTED IN | From 1B | From 2B | From 3B | Scoring Position |
|---|---|---|---|---|
| Totals | 2/72 | 9/51 | 10/26 | 19/77 |
| Percentage | 3% | 18% | 38% | 25% |
| Driving In Runners from 3B with Less than Two Out: | | | 8/17 | 47% |

Loves to face: Chris Bosio (.556, 10-for-18, 2 HR)
Hates to face: Bobby Witt (0-for-10)
Now all he needs is a pennant race: Walker has a .312 career batting average in September; he has hit .255 in other months. . . . Hit 27 home runs in 1987, but has only 13 in two years since then. Stands 7th on all-time team list with 113 home runs; team's all-time record is only 186 by Harold Baines. (Among all major league franchises, only 13-year-old Blue Jays and Mariners and 21-year-old Padres have lower career home-run records than 89-year old White Sox). . . . Hitless in nine at-bats as a pinch hitter last season, and 0-for-16 since pinch-hit homer on June 1, 1986. . . . That .061 batting average in Late-Inning Pressure Situations was lowest in majors last season. At least he drove in three runs with those two hits!

## Claudell Washington

Bats Left

| California Angels | AB | H | 2B | 3B | HR | RBI | BB | SO | BA | SA | OBA |
|---|---|---|---|---|---|---|---|---|---|---|---|
| Season | 418 | 114 | 18 | 4 | 13 | 42 | 27 | 84 | .273 | .428 | .319 |
| vs. Left-Handers | 102 | 30 | 9 | 0 | 0 | 5 | 6 | 24 | .294 | .382 | .333 |
| vs. Right-Handers | 316 | 84 | 9 | 4 | 13 | 37 | 21 | 60 | .266 | .443 | .315 |
| Home | 210 | 62 | 11 | 2 | 9 | 25 | 15 | 39 | .295 | .495 | .344 |
| Road | 208 | 52 | 7 | 2 | 4 | 17 | 12 | 45 | .250 | .361 | .294 |
| Grass | 359 | 100 | 17 | 3 | 12 | 36 | 26 | 73 | .279 | .443 | .330 |
| Artificial Turf | 59 | 14 | 1 | 1 | 1 | 6 | 1 | 11 | .237 | .339 | .250 |
| April | 70 | 21 | 2 | 0 | 2 | 10 | 4 | 18 | .300 | .414 | .347 |
| May | 62 | 20 | 4 | 0 | 4 | 11 | 3 | 11 | .323 | .581 | .354 |
| June | 69 | 16 | 2 | 1 | 3 | 3 | 6 | 12 | .232 | .420 | .293 |
| July | 49 | 14 | 2 | 0 | 1 | 3 | 4 | 6 | .286 | .388 | .333 |
| August | 91 | 21 | 3 | 3 | 1 | 8 | 4 | 25 | .231 | .363 | .263 |
| Sept./Oct. | 77 | 22 | 5 | 0 | 2 | 7 | 6 | 12 | .286 | .429 | .345 |
| Leading Off Inn. | 134 | 36 | 6 | 2 | 4 | 4 | 12 | 28 | .269 | .433 | .329 |
| Runners On | 156 | 42 | 7 | 0 | 2 | 31 | 8 | 31 | .269 | .353 | .311 |
| Runners/Scor. Pos. | 88 | 23 | 1 | 0 | 1 | 24 | 4 | 20 | .261 | .307 | .298 |
| Runners On/2 Out | 59 | 18 | 4 | 0 | 1 | 14 | 4 | 12 | .305 | .424 | .359 |
| Scor. Pos./2 Out | 40 | 12 | 1 | 0 | 1 | 11 | 2 | 10 | .300 | .400 | .333 |
| Late Inning Pressure | 50 | 13 | 2 | 1 | 1 | 5 | 6 | 11 | .260 | .400 | .333 |
| Leading Off | 16 | 4 | 0 | 0 | 1 | 1 | 1 | 5 | .250 | .438 | .294 |
| Runners On | 25 | 7 | 1 | 0 | 0 | 4 | 4 | 4 | .280 | .320 | .367 |
| Runners/Scor. Pos. | 14 | 5 | 1 | 0 | 0 | 4 | 3 | 2 | .357 | .429 | .444 |

| RUNS BATTED IN | From 1B | From 2B | From 3B | Scoring Position |
|---|---|---|---|---|
| Totals | 6/107 | 11/67 | 12/32 | 23/99 |
| Percentage | 6% | 16% | 38% | 23% |
| Driving In Runners from 3B with Less than Two Out: | | | 7/14 | 50% |

Loves to face: Mike Smithson (.625, 10-for-16, 2 HR)
Hates to face: Nolan Ryan (.144, 13-for-90, 39 SO)
Has played with seven teams and has hit at least 10 home runs with each of them. That ties Cliff Johnson's major league record of hitting 10+ home runs for the most different teams. . . . Only player in majors with a pinch-hit home run in each of the last five years. . . . Eleven of his 13 home runs were solo shots last season, highest rate among A.L. players with 10+ homers. . . . Last 15 home runs have been hit off right-handers. Career HR totals: 148 vs. RHP; 15 vs. LHP. . . . With the bases loaded, he's 11-for-24 over past three years after hitting .193 from 1975 to 1986. But he's still never hit a grand slam. . . . Stole 13 bases last season at the age of 35. Only one older player stole more: George Brett (14).

## Gary Ward

Bats Right

| Yankees/Tigers | AB | H | 2B | 3B | HR | RBI | BB | SO | BA | SA | OBA |
|---|---|---|---|---|---|---|---|---|---|---|---|
| Season | 292 | 74 | 11 | 2 | 9 | 30 | 24 | 59 | .253 | .397 | .306 |
| vs. Left-Handers | 187 | 52 | 10 | 1 | 9 | 24 | 17 | 39 | .278 | .487 | .337 |
| vs. Right-Handers | 105 | 22 | 1 | 1 | 0 | 6 | 7 | 20 | .210 | .238 | .252 |
| Home | 139 | 36 | 5 | 2 | 6 | 18 | 12 | 23 | .259 | .453 | .314 |
| Road | 153 | 38 | 6 | 0 | 3 | 12 | 12 | 36 | .248 | .346 | .299 |
| Grass | 237 | 57 | 9 | 2 | 8 | 27 | 17 | 47 | .241 | .397 | .287 |
| Artificial Turf | 55 | 17 | 2 | 0 | 1 | 3 | 7 | 12 | .309 | .400 | .387 |
| April | 34 | 8 | 1 | 0 | 0 | 2 | 3 | 8 | .235 | .265 | .297 |
| May | 43 | 12 | 0 | 1 | 1 | 2 | 2 | 6 | .279 | .395 | .311 |
| June | 44 | 12 | 1 | 0 | 2 | 4 | 6 | 9 | .273 | .432 | .360 |
| July | 54 | 10 | 3 | 0 | 3 | 7 | 2 | 12 | .185 | .407 | .207 |
| August | 77 | 23 | 3 | 0 | 3 | 11 | 7 | 16 | .299 | .455 | .349 |
| Sept./Oct. | 40 | 9 | 3 | 1 | 0 | 4 | 4 | 8 | .225 | .350 | .295 |
| Leading Off Inn. | 61 | 15 | 1 | 1 | 3 | 3 | 3 | 6 | .246 | .443 | .281 |
| Runners On | 142 | 33 | 5 | 0 | 2 | 23 | 15 | 37 | .232 | .310 | .298 |
| Runners/Scor. Pos. | 75 | 14 | 2 | 0 | 1 | 21 | 11 | 24 | .187 | .253 | .278 |
| Runners On/2 Out | 66 | 13 | 0 | 0 | 1 | 6 | 8 | 21 | .197 | .242 | .284 |
| Scor. Pos./2 Out | 45 | 6 | 0 | 0 | 1 | 6 | 6 | 18 | .133 | .200 | .235 |
| Late Inning Pressure | 57 | 12 | 4 | 0 | 1 | 4 | 3 | 17 | .211 | .333 | .246 |
| Leading Off | 9 | 3 | 1 | 0 | 0 | 0 | 0 | 0 | .333 | .444 | .333 |
| Runners On | 30 | 6 | 2 | 0 | 0 | 3 | 2 | 11 | .200 | .267 | .242 |
| Runners/Scor. Pos. | 15 | 3 | 0 | 0 | 0 | 3 | 2 | 7 | .200 | .200 | .278 |

| RUNS BATTED IN | From 1B | From 2B | From 3B | Scoring Position |
|---|---|---|---|---|
| Totals | 2/108 | 5/58 | 14/37 | 19/95 |
| Percentage | 2% | 9% | 38% | 20% |
| Driving In Runners from 3B with Less than Two Out: | | | 12/17 | 71% |

Loves to face: Allan Anderson (.615, 8-for-13, 1 HR)
Hates to face: Dennis Eckersley (.100, 2-for-20, 8 SO)
Bases loaded, two outs. Ward has faced that situation 18 times over past three years, and he's a clean 0-for-18: no hits, no walks, no RBI. . . . Started 56 games vs. left-handers last season, only 15 vs. right-handers. . . . Led Tigers with 9 homers vs. left-handers. Last 13 HR have all been off southpaws; last HR off a right-hander: Oct. 1, 1987, vs. Al Nipper. . . . Has batted under .190 with runners in scoring position in each of last two seasons after hitting .319 in those situations over previous three years. . . . Career BA bimonths: April-May, .253; June-July, .270; Aug.-Oct., .306. We could be looking at a surefire candidate for Player of the Month of December in the Senior League!

## Walt Weiss

Bats Left and Right

| Oakland As | AB | H | 2B | 3B | HR | RBI | BB | SO | BA | SA | OBA |
|---|---|---|---|---|---|---|---|---|---|---|---|
| Season | 236 | 55 | 11 | 0 | 3 | 21 | 21 | 39 | .233 | .318 | .298 |
| vs. Left-Handers | 57 | 13 | 3 | 0 | 0 | 4 | 2 | 9 | .228 | .281 | .254 |
| vs. Right-Handers | 179 | 42 | 8 | 0 | 3 | 17 | 19 | 30 | .235 | .330 | .312 |
| Home | 120 | 24 | 4 | 0 | 2 | 10 | 12 | 25 | .200 | .283 | .273 |
| Road | 116 | 31 | 7 | 0 | 1 | 11 | 9 | 14 | .267 | .353 | .325 |
| Grass | 199 | 50 | 9 | 0 | 3 | 20 | 18 | 32 | .251 | .342 | .317 |
| Artificial Turf | 37 | 5 | 2 | 0 | 0 | 1 | 3 | 7 | .135 | .189 | .200 |
| April | 65 | 15 | 4 | 0 | 2 | 6 | 10 | 9 | .231 | .385 | .333 |
| May | 43 | 8 | 1 | 0 | 0 | 5 | 2 | 8 | .186 | .209 | .222 |
| June | 0 | 0 | 0 | 0 | 0 | 0 | 0 | 0 | — | — | — |
| July | 3 | 1 | 0 | 0 | 0 | 0 | 0 | 0 | .333 | .333 | .333 |
| August | 71 | 18 | 5 | 0 | 1 | 5 | 3 | 11 | .254 | .366 | .284 |
| Sept./Oct. | 54 | 13 | 1 | 0 | 0 | 5 | 6 | 11 | .241 | .259 | .328 |
| Leading Off Inn. | 56 | 19 | 5 | 0 | 0 | 0 | 4 | 8 | .339 | .429 | .383 |
| Runners On | 112 | 26 | 2 | 0 | 3 | 21 | 6 | 21 | .232 | .330 | .277 |
| Runners/Scor. Pos. | 65 | 15 | 1 | 0 | 1 | 17 | 5 | 13 | .231 | .292 | .286 |
| Runners On/2 Out | 49 | 11 | 1 | 0 | 2 | 7 | 3 | 12 | .224 | .367 | .269 |
| Scor. Pos./2 Out | 26 | 3 | 0 | 0 | 0 | 3 | 2 | 7 | .115 | .115 | .179 |
| Late Inning Pressure | 33 | 4 | 0 | 0 | 0 | 2 | 4 | 7 | .121 | .121 | .216 |
| Leading Off | 5 | 1 | 0 | 0 | 0 | 0 | 2 | 1 | .200 | .200 | .429 |
| Runners On | 15 | 2 | 0 | 0 | 0 | 2 | 0 | 4 | .133 | .133 | .133 |
| Runners/Scor. Pos. | 8 | 2 | 0 | 0 | 0 | 2 | 0 | 1 | .250 | .250 | .250 |

| RUNS BATTED IN | From 1B | From 2B | From 3B | Scoring Position |
|---|---|---|---|---|
| Totals | 2/81 | 5/47 | 11/33 | 16/80 |
| Percentage | 2% | 11% | 33% | 20% |
| Driving In Runners from 3B with Less than Two Out: | | | 8/18 | 44% |

Loves to face: Bill Long (.625, 5-for-8)
Hates to face: Dave Stieb (.091, 1-for-11)
Lowest batting average by defending A.L. Rookie of the Year (non-pitcher) since Ron Kittle hit .215 in 1984. Fewest games (84) since Joe Charboneau played in only 48 in strike- and injury-interrupted 1981. . . . Batted .264 vs. fly-ball pitchers, .206 vs. ground-ballers; career averages are even more diverse: .306 vs. FBP, .197 vs. GBP. . . . Has .109 career batting average in Late-Inning Pressure Situations. How about another kind of pressure, like the World Series? Three hits in 31 career at-bats. . . . Career breakdown: .262 (and all six home runs) vs. right-handed pitchers, .220 vs. lefties. . . . A's allowed 3.57 runs per nine innings with Weiss at short last year, compared to 3.36 with Mike Gallego there.

## Lou Whitaker

Bats Left

| Detroit Tigers | AB | H | 2B | 3B | HR | RBI | BB | SO | BA | SA | OBA |
|---|---|---|---|---|---|---|---|---|---|---|---|
| Season | 509 | 128 | 21 | 1 | 28 | 85 | 89 | 59 | .251 | .462 | .361 |
| vs. Left-Handers | 149 | 28 | 7 | 1 | 5 | 14 | 23 | 18 | .188 | .349 | .305 |
| vs. Right-Handers | 360 | 100 | 14 | 0 | 23 | 71 | 66 | 41 | .278 | .508 | .383 |
| Home | 235 | 62 | 7 | 1 | 17 | 45 | 42 | 23 | .264 | .519 | .377 |
| Road | 274 | 66 | 14 | 0 | 11 | 40 | 47 | 36 | .241 | .412 | .347 |
| Grass | 424 | 107 | 12 | 1 | 26 | 75 | 77 | 48 | .252 | .469 | .366 |
| Artificial Turf | 85 | 21 | 9 | 0 | 2 | 10 | 12 | 11 | .247 | .424 | .333 |
| April | 75 | 21 | 2 | 0 | 5 | 12 | 15 | 6 | .280 | .507 | .402 |
| May | 96 | 29 | 2 | 1 | 8 | 20 | 16 | 12 | .302 | .594 | .398 |
| June | 90 | 19 | 6 | 0 | 3 | 9 | 14 | 11 | .211 | .378 | .311 |
| July | 80 | 20 | 1 | 0 | 5 | 13 | 10 | 4 | .250 | .450 | .326 |
| August | 89 | 21 | 4 | 0 | 5 | 21 | 20 | 15 | .236 | .449 | .372 |
| Sept./Oct. | 79 | 18 | 6 | 0 | 2 | 10 | 14 | 11 | .228 | .380 | .351 |
| Leading Off Inn. | 113 | 30 | 5 | 1 | 6 | 6 | 15 | 9 | .265 | .487 | .352 |
| Runners On | 220 | 54 | 10 | 0 | 12 | 69 | 41 | 24 | .245 | .455 | .357 |
| Runners/Scor. Pos. | 126 | 37 | 6 | 0 | 6 | 56 | 25 | 13 | .294 | .484 | .391 |
| Runners On/2 Out | 72 | 18 | 3 | 0 | 4 | 26 | 20 | 6 | .250 | .458 | .413 |
| Scor. Pos./2 Out | 44 | 14 | 2 | 0 | 2 | 21 | 14 | 3 | .318 | .500 | .483 |
| Late Inning Pressure | 83 | 19 | 2 | 0 | 6 | 17 | 13 | 10 | .229 | .470 | .327 |
| Leading Off | 19 | 6 | 0 | 0 | 3 | 3 | 3 | 2 | .316 | .789 | .409 |
| Runners On | 40 | 8 | 1 | 0 | 2 | 13 | 4 | 4 | .200 | .375 | .261 |
| Runners/Scor. Pos. | 21 | 5 | 1 | 0 | 0 | 9 | 2 | 2 | .238 | .286 | .280 |

| RUNS BATTED IN | From 1B | From 2B | From 3B | Scoring Position |
|---|---|---|---|---|
| Totals | 10/159 | 23/98 | 24/48 | 47/146 |
| Percentage | 6% | 23% | 50% | 32% |
| Driving In Runners from 3B with Less than Two Out: | | | 20/31 | 65% |

Loves to face: Dave Righetti (.433, 13-for-30, 1 HR)
Hates to face: Tom Henke (0-for-22, 6 SO)
Third player ever to establish career highs in home runs, RBI, and walks in the same season so late in his career (13th year). Others: John Lowenstein and Luke Sewell. . . . Led A.L. with eight first-inning home runs. . . . Batted .122 on balls hit to the opposite field, .229 straight away, and .360 *with all 28 home runs* to right. . . . Led visitors with three home runs at Comiskey Park. Big deal? Ron Kittle led the White Sox with only six there. . . . Batted .300 against ground-ball pitchers, .206 vs. fly-ballers. . . . Of his 85 RBI, 30 put the Tigers ahead (35%), highest rate in majors (minimum: 75 RBI). . . . Percentage of runners driven in from scoring position was highest of career.

## Devon White

Bats Left and Right

| California Angels | AB | H | 2B | 3B | HR | RBI | BB | SO | BA | SA | OBA |
|---|---|---|---|---|---|---|---|---|---|---|---|
| Season | 636 | 156 | 18 | 13 | 12 | 56 | 31 | 129 | .245 | .371 | .282 |
| vs. Left-Handers | 214 | 53 | 9 | 4 | 2 | 17 | 13 | 42 | .248 | .355 | .291 |
| vs. Right-Handers | 422 | 103 | 9 | 9 | 10 | 39 | 18 | 87 | .244 | .379 | .277 |
| Home | 317 | 77 | 5 | 8 | 9 | 26 | 18 | 67 | .243 | .394 | .283 |
| Road | 319 | 79 | 13 | 5 | 3 | 30 | 13 | 62 | .248 | .348 | .281 |
| Grass | 524 | 131 | 15 | 8 | 10 | 41 | 28 | 102 | .250 | .366 | .290 |
| Artificial Turf | 112 | 25 | 3 | 5 | 2 | 15 | 3 | 27 | .223 | .393 | .243 |
| April | 98 | 29 | 6 | 3 | 3 | 14 | 6 | 21 | .296 | .510 | .337 |
| May | 105 | 31 | 4 | 4 | 4 | 16 | 5 | 13 | .295 | .524 | .330 |
| June | 107 | 23 | 3 | 1 | 2 | 5 | 1 | 26 | .215 | .318 | .227 |
| July | 109 | 28 | 1 | 2 | 0 | 8 | 10 | 26 | .257 | .303 | .319 |
| August | 111 | 24 | 1 | 2 | 3 | 9 | 8 | 20 | .216 | .342 | .269 |
| Sept./Oct. | 106 | 21 | 3 | 1 | 0 | 4 | 1 | 23 | .198 | .245 | .206 |
| Leading Off Inn. | 155 | 47 | 3 | 5 | 2 | 2 | 6 | 29 | .303 | .426 | .329 |
| Runners On | 268 | 63 | 9 | 4 | 4 | 48 | 17 | 43 | .235 | .343 | .281 |
| Runners/Scor. Pos. | 136 | 31 | 5 | 1 | 1 | 39 | 10 | 26 | .228 | .301 | .277 |
| Runners On/2 Out | 95 | 20 | 2 | 1 | 1 | 17 | 7 | 11 | .211 | .284 | .272 |
| Scor. Pos./2 Out | 61 | 12 | 2 | 1 | 0 | 15 | 5 | 9 | .197 | .262 | .258 |
| Late Inning Pressure | 77 | 16 | 2 | 0 | 0 | 4 | 6 | 23 | .208 | .234 | .265 |
| Leading Off | 23 | 5 | 0 | 0 | 0 | 0 | 2 | 5 | .217 | .217 | .280 |
| Runners On | 29 | 4 | 0 | 0 | 0 | 4 | 2 | 10 | .138 | .138 | .194 |
| Runners/Scor. Pos. | 20 | 3 | 0 | 0 | 0 | 4 | 2 | 9 | .150 | .150 | .227 |

| RUNS BATTED IN | From 1B | From 2B | From 3B | Scoring Position |
|---|---|---|---|---|
| Totals | 8/192 | 15/102 | 21/55 | 36/157 |
| Percentage | 4% | 15% | 38% | 23% |
| Driving In Runners from 3B with Less than Two Out: | | | 13/25 | 52% |

Loves to face: John Farrell (.400, 6-for-15)
Hates to face: Bret Saberhagen (.100, 3-for-30, 9 SO)
Only A.L. player to start at least 20 games in both the leadoff and cleanup spots. . . . Only one walk in his last 124 plate appearances. . . . Batted .191 during the first inning, .259 thereafter. . . . Tied club record with 13 triples, shared by Jim Fregosi and Mickey Rivers. First Angels player to reach double figures since Jerry Remy in 1977. . . . Advanced from first base to third on 20 of 29 outfield singles (69%; A.L. average: 35%), including 11 of 12 to right field. . . . Batting average with runners in scoring position has been lower than his overall average in each of his five seasons in majors. . . . Career average of .301 leading off innings, .240 in other at-bats.

## Frank White

Bats Right

| Kansas City Royals | AB | H | 2B | 3B | HR | RBI | BB | SO | BA | SA | OBA |
|---|---|---|---|---|---|---|---|---|---|---|---|
| Season | 418 | 107 | 22 | 1 | 2 | 36 | 30 | 52 | .256 | .328 | .307 |
| vs. Left-Handers | 125 | 30 | 7 | 0 | 0 | 10 | 12 | 7 | .240 | .296 | .307 |
| vs. Right-Handers | 293 | 77 | 15 | 1 | 2 | 26 | 18 | 45 | .263 | .341 | .307 |
| Home | 210 | 50 | 13 | 0 | 1 | 20 | 11 | 27 | .238 | .314 | .277 |
| Road | 208 | 57 | 9 | 1 | 1 | 16 | 19 | 25 | .274 | .341 | .336 |
| Grass | 158 | 46 | 5 | 1 | 0 | 12 | 10 | 21 | .291 | .335 | .335 |
| Artificial Turf | 260 | 61 | 17 | 0 | 2 | 24 | 20 | 31 | .235 | .323 | .290 |
| April | 70 | 19 | 7 | 0 | 0 | 8 | 5 | 8 | .271 | .371 | .316 |
| May | 71 | 14 | 1 | 0 | 0 | 3 | 8 | 7 | .197 | .211 | .278 |
| June | 55 | 15 | 3 | 0 | 0 | 5 | 3 | 9 | .273 | .327 | .310 |
| July | 87 | 22 | 4 | 0 | 0 | 9 | 5 | 15 | .253 | .299 | .293 |
| August | 80 | 24 | 4 | 1 | 1 | 8 | 8 | 6 | .300 | .413 | .364 |
| Sept./Oct. | 55 | 13 | 3 | 0 | 1 | 3 | 1 | 7 | .236 | .345 | .263 |
| Leading Off Inn. | 83 | 25 | 4 | 1 | 1 | 1 | 5 | 7 | .301 | .410 | .341 |
| Runners On | 185 | 52 | 12 | 0 | 0 | 34 | 16 | 26 | .281 | .346 | .337 |
| Runners/Scor. Pos. | 98 | 28 | 5 | 0 | 0 | 34 | 12 | 15 | .286 | .337 | .360 |
| Runners On/2 Out | 80 | 15 | 6 | 0 | 0 | 8 | 7 | 14 | .188 | .263 | .253 |
| Scor. Pos./2 Out | 45 | 7 | 4 | 0 | 0 | 8 | 4 | 8 | .156 | .244 | .224 |
| Late Inning Pressure | 55 | 13 | 2 | 0 | 1 | 5 | 5 | 7 | .236 | .327 | .300 |
| Leading Off | 9 | 4 | 2 | 0 | 0 | 0 | 1 | 1 | .444 | .667 | .500 |
| Runners On | 20 | 6 | 0 | 0 | 0 | 4 | 2 | 3 | .300 | .300 | .364 |
| Runners/Scor. Pos. | 8 | 4 | 0 | 0 | 0 | 4 | 0 | 2 | .500 | .500 | .500 |

| RUNS BATTED IN | From 1B | From 2B | From 3B | Scoring Position |
|---|---|---|---|---|
| Totals | 0/138 | 12/73 | 22/48 | 34/121 |
| Percentage | 0% | 16% | 46% | 28% |
| Driving In Runners from 3B with Less than Two Out: | | | 17/25 | 68% |

Loves to face: Shane Rawley (.484, 15-for-31)
Hates to face: Dave Stieb (.169, 10-for-59)
Kansas City's opening-day second baseman in every season since 1976. Could inherit throne from Mike Schmidt, whose streak extended from 1974 to 1989. . . . Needs 135 games at second base to move past Charlie Gehringer into fourth place in major league history. The top five: Eddie Collins, 2650; Joe Morgan, 2527; Nellie Fox, 2295; Gehringer, 2206; White, 2071. . . . Excluding pitchers and catchers, White was oldest everyday player in majors last season. . . . He and Doyle Alexander share the same birthday: Sept. 4, 1950. Other noteworthy players born same day, same year: Carlton Fisk and Chris Chambliss; Jay Johnstone and Rick Monday; Vada Pinson and Frank Howard; Ralph Kiner and Del Rice.

## Ernie Whitt

Bats Left

| Toronto Blue Jays | AB | H | 2B | 3B | HR | RBI | BB | SO | BA | SA | OBA |
|---|---|---|---|---|---|---|---|---|---|---|---|
| Season | 385 | 101 | 24 | 1 | 11 | 53 | 52 | 53 | .262 | .416 | .349 |
| vs. Left-Handers | 44 | 7 | 0 | 0 | 1 | 7 | 5 | 11 | .159 | .227 | .240 |
| vs. Right-Handers | 341 | 94 | 24 | 1 | 10 | 46 | 47 | 42 | .276 | .440 | .362 |
| Home | 184 | 43 | 10 | 0 | 8 | 27 | 32 | 30 | .234 | .418 | .346 |
| Road | 201 | 58 | 14 | 1 | 3 | 26 | 20 | 23 | .289 | .413 | .351 |
| Grass | 159 | 45 | 9 | 0 | 3 | 19 | 18 | 16 | .283 | .396 | .354 |
| Artificial Turf | 226 | 56 | 15 | 1 | 8 | 34 | 34 | 37 | .248 | .429 | .345 |
| April | 52 | 15 | 6 | 1 | 0 | 6 | 6 | 10 | .288 | .442 | .362 |
| May | 59 | 21 | 3 | 0 | 4 | 16 | 11 | 5 | .356 | .610 | .457 |
| June | 77 | 24 | 4 | 0 | 1 | 9 | 11 | 8 | .312 | .403 | .393 |
| July | 53 | 10 | 4 | 0 | 1 | 3 | 11 | 8 | .189 | .321 | .328 |
| August | 83 | 20 | 4 | 0 | 4 | 16 | 8 | 11 | .241 | .434 | .304 |
| Sept./Oct. | 61 | 11 | 3 | 0 | 1 | 3 | 5 | 11 | .180 | .279 | .242 |
| Leading Off Inn. | 90 | 26 | 5 | 0 | 1 | 1 | 9 | 13 | .289 | .378 | .354 |
| Runners On | 168 | 43 | 11 | 1 | 7 | 49 | 26 | 22 | .256 | .458 | .352 |
| Runners/Scor. Pos. | 96 | 24 | 5 | 0 | 5 | 40 | 19 | 15 | .250 | .458 | .368 |
| Runners On/2 Out | 71 | 14 | 1 | 1 | 3 | 14 | 12 | 10 | .197 | .366 | .313 |
| Scor. Pos./2 Out | 42 | 7 | 1 | 0 | 2 | 10 | 8 | 7 | .167 | .333 | .300 |
| Late Inning Pressure | 55 | 10 | 1 | 0 | 2 | 8 | 6 | 13 | .182 | .309 | .262 |
| Leading Off | 10 | 2 | 0 | 0 | 0 | 0 | 0 | 3 | .200 | .200 | .200 |
| Runners On | 22 | 5 | 1 | 0 | 1 | 7 | 4 | 4 | .227 | .409 | .346 |
| Runners/Scor. Pos. | 11 | 3 | 1 | 0 | 1 | 7 | 3 | 2 | .273 | .636 | .429 |

| RUNS BATTED IN | From 1B | From 2B | From 3B | Scoring Position |
|---|---|---|---|---|
| Totals | 12/131 | 12/71 | 18/42 | 30/113 |
| Percentage | 9% | 17% | 43% | 27% |
| Driving In Runners from 3B with Less than Two Out: | | | 16/28 | 57% |

Loves to face: Mike Morgan (.471, 8-for-17, 1 HR)
Hates to face: Jay Howell (.111, 1-for-9)
Hit all 11 of his home runs to right field. . . . Has started 279 games vs. right-handed pitchers since his last start vs. a left-hander, on July 5, 1987. . . . Advanced from first base to third on only 5 of 24 outfield singles (21%). Tried to score from second on eight of nine, but was thrown out as often as he scored. . . . Snapped 0-for-22 streak as a pinch hitter with 3 hits in last 12 at-bats. Career pinch-hitting: .182 (20-for-110). . . . Has hit for a higher average in United States than he has in Canada in each of the last six seasons. . . . Has played 1162 games behind the plate, but no games at any other position. Most games by a catcher who never played elsewhere: 1805, by Rick Ferrell.

## Eddie Williams

Bats Right

| Chicago White Sox | AB | H | 2B | 3B | HR | RBI | BB | SO | BA | SA | OBA |
|---|---|---|---|---|---|---|---|---|---|---|---|
| Season | 201 | 55 | 8 | 0 | 3 | 10 | 18 | 31 | .274 | .358 | .341 |
| vs. Left-Handers | 80 | 20 | 1 | 0 | 1 | 4 | 9 | 12 | .250 | .300 | .333 |
| vs. Right-Handers | 121 | 35 | 7 | 0 | 2 | 6 | 9 | 19 | .289 | .397 | .346 |
| Home | 98 | 23 | 2 | 0 | 2 | 5 | 6 | 14 | .235 | .316 | .283 |
| Road | 103 | 32 | 6 | 0 | 1 | 5 | 12 | 17 | .311 | .398 | .392 |
| Grass | 178 | 48 | 5 | 0 | 2 | 8 | 18 | 29 | .270 | .331 | .345 |
| Artificial Turf | 23 | 7 | 3 | 0 | 1 | 2 | 0 | 2 | .304 | .565 | .304 |
| April | 80 | 27 | 5 | 0 | 2 | 5 | 11 | 12 | .338 | .475 | .424 |
| May | 67 | 16 | 1 | 0 | 0 | 2 | 4 | 9 | .239 | .254 | .297 |
| June | 49 | 12 | 2 | 0 | 1 | 3 | 3 | 8 | .245 | .347 | .291 |
| July | 5 | 0 | 0 | 0 | 0 | 0 | 0 | 2 | .000 | .000 | .000 |
| August | 0 | 0 | 0 | 0 | 0 | 0 | 0 | 0 | — | — | — |
| Sept./Oct. | 0 | 0 | 0 | 0 | 0 | 0 | 0 | 0 | — | — | — |
| Leading Off Inn. | 53 | 18 | 2 | 0 | 2 | 2 | 2 | 9 | .340 | .491 | .364 |
| Runners On | 89 | 20 | 3 | 0 | 1 | 8 | 11 | 17 | .225 | .292 | .301 |
| Runners/Scor. Pos. | 41 | 5 | 0 | 0 | 0 | 6 | 10 | 9 | .122 | .122 | .278 |
| Runners On/2 Out | 37 | 7 | 0 | 0 | 0 | 2 | 7 | 9 | .189 | .189 | .318 |
| Scor. Pos./2 Out | 23 | 2 | 0 | 0 | 0 | 2 | 6 | 5 | .087 | .087 | .276 |
| Late Inning Pressure | 30 | 8 | 1 | 0 | 1 | 1 | 3 | 5 | .267 | .400 | .333 |
| Leading Off | 9 | 4 | 0 | 0 | 1 | 1 | 0 | 1 | .444 | .778 | .444 |
| Runners On | 12 | 3 | 1 | 0 | 0 | 0 | 3 | 3 | .250 | .333 | .400 |
| Runners/Scor. Pos. | 3 | 0 | 0 | 0 | 0 | 0 | 3 | 1 | .000 | .000 | .500 |

| RUNS BATTED IN | From 1B | From 2B | From 3B | Scoring Position |
|---|---|---|---|---|
| Totals | 1/68 | 1/30 | 5/21 | 6/51 |
| Percentage | 1% | 3% | 24% | 12% |
| Driving In Runners from 3B with Less than Two Out: | | | 4/11 | 36% |

Loves to face: Scott Bankhead (.800, 4-for-5)
Hates to face: Roger Clemens (0-for-7)
Fewest RBI of any A.L. player with 200 or more plate appearances. ... Drove in one of 30 runners from second base; 15-year nadir is Bryan Little's 0-for-42 mark in 1984. ... Career BA is .143 (8-for-56) with runners in scoring position, .074 (2-for-27) with two outs and RISP. ... So you're thinking, "Maybe he can field?" Uh-uh. ... Fielding percentage of .909 was lowest by a White Sox third baseman with since 1912 (minimum: 60 games). ... Sox allowed 5.4 runs per nine innings with Williams at third base, compared to 4.4 runs with Carlos Martinez. ... Started at third base in 61 of Chicago's 88 games before the All-Star break. Then sent to Vancouver, and wasn't even recalled in September.

## Kenny Williams

Bats Right

| Detroit Tigers | AB | H | 2B | 3B | HR | RBI | BB | SO | BA | SA | OBA |
|---|---|---|---|---|---|---|---|---|---|---|---|
| Season | 258 | 53 | 5 | 1 | 6 | 23 | 18 | 63 | .205 | .302 | .269 |
| vs. Left-Handers | 129 | 29 | 3 | 1 | 3 | 10 | 11 | 32 | .225 | .333 | .296 |
| vs. Right-Handers | 129 | 24 | 2 | 0 | 3 | 13 | 7 | 31 | .186 | .271 | .241 |
| Home | 119 | 24 | 1 | 1 | 3 | 14 | 11 | 34 | .202 | .303 | .271 |
| Road | 139 | 29 | 4 | 0 | 3 | 9 | 7 | 29 | .209 | .302 | .267 |
| Grass | 200 | 42 | 4 | 1 | 3 | 17 | 16 | 51 | .210 | .285 | .276 |
| Artificial Turf | 58 | 11 | 1 | 0 | 3 | 6 | 2 | 12 | .190 | .362 | .242 |
| April | 78 | 16 | 2 | 0 | 2 | 8 | 3 | 18 | .205 | .308 | .232 |
| May | 55 | 11 | 1 | 0 | 1 | 5 | 1 | 15 | .200 | .273 | .224 |
| June | 16 | 2 | 0 | 0 | 1 | 1 | 1 | 3 | .125 | .313 | .176 |
| July | 3 | 1 | 0 | 0 | 0 | 0 | 1 | 1 | .333 | .333 | .500 |
| August | 73 | 16 | 1 | 0 | 2 | 6 | 7 | 15 | .219 | .315 | .313 |
| Sept./Oct. | 33 | 7 | 1 | 1 | 0 | 3 | 5 | 11 | .212 | .303 | .333 |
| Leading Off Inn. | 74 | 14 | 2 | 0 | 2 | 2 | 7 | 14 | .189 | .297 | .259 |
| Runners On | 109 | 22 | 2 | 1 | 2 | 19 | 6 | 30 | .202 | .294 | .246 |
| Runners/Scor. Pos. | 63 | 15 | 1 | 0 | 1 | 16 | 4 | 19 | .238 | .302 | .275 |
| Runners On/2 Out | 45 | 11 | 0 | 1 | 0 | 8 | 3 | 14 | .244 | .289 | .292 |
| Scor. Pos./2 Out | 33 | 9 | 0 | 0 | 0 | 7 | 3 | 10 | .273 | .273 | .333 |
| Late Inning Pressure | 46 | 5 | 1 | 1 | 0 | 3 | 2 | 16 | .109 | .174 | .146 |
| Leading Off | 7 | 0 | 0 | 0 | 0 | 0 | 2 | 2 | .000 | .000 | .222 |
| Runners On | 25 | 2 | 1 | 1 | 0 | 3 | 0 | 9 | .080 | .200 | .080 |
| Runners/Scor. Pos. | 13 | 1 | 1 | 0 | 0 | 2 | 0 | 5 | .077 | .154 | .077 |

| RUNS BATTED IN | From 1B | From 2B | From 3B | Scoring Position |
|---|---|---|---|---|
| Totals | 3/83 | 8/53 | 6/19 | 14/72 |
| Percentage | 4% | 15% | 32% | 19% |
| Driving In Runners from 3B with Less than Two Out: | | | 3/9 | 33% |

Loves to face: Allan Anderson (.455, 5-for-11)
Hates to face: Greg Cadaret (0-for-7, 6 SO)
One of four major leaguers to start 15 or more games at each of the outfield positions. ... Also started at least one game in every batting-order position except cleanup and 5th slots. ... Had nine hits in 16 at-bats (.563) vs. his old team, the White Sox, but batted only .182 against rest of the league. ... Career batting average of .048 (1-for-21) with two outs and runners in scoring position in Late-Inning Pressure Situations, the lowest of the past 15 years (minimum: 20 AB). ... Has one home run in 136 career at-bats in LIPS, one per 31 at-bats at other times. ... One hit in 15 career at-bats with the bases loaded. ... Career averages are .243 vs. left-handed pitchers, .209 vs. right-handers.

## Mookie Wilson

Bats Left and Right

| Toronto Blue Jays | AB | H | 2B | 3B | HR | RBI | BB | SO | BA | SA | OBA |
|---|---|---|---|---|---|---|---|---|---|---|---|
| Season | 238 | 71 | 9 | 1 | 2 | 17 | 3 | 37 | .298 | .370 | .311 |
| vs. Left-Handers | 78 | 27 | 2 | 1 | 0 | 5 | 0 | 9 | .346 | .397 | .346 |
| vs. Right-Handers | 160 | 44 | 7 | 0 | 2 | 12 | 3 | 28 | .275 | .356 | .295 |
| Home | 127 | 32 | 6 | 0 | 1 | 8 | 1 | 21 | .252 | .323 | .267 |
| Road | 111 | 39 | 3 | 1 | 1 | 9 | 2 | 16 | .351 | .423 | .363 |
| Grass | 90 | 34 | 3 | 1 | 1 | 9 | 2 | 14 | .378 | .467 | .391 |
| Artificial Turf | 148 | 37 | 6 | 0 | 1 | 8 | 1 | 23 | .250 | .311 | .263 |
| April | 0 | 0 | 0 | 0 | 0 | 0 | 0 | 0 | — | — | — |
| May | 0 | 0 | 0 | 0 | 0 | 0 | 0 | 0 | — | — | — |
| June | 0 | 0 | 0 | 0 | 0 | 0 | 0 | 0 | — | — | — |
| July | 0 | 0 | 0 | 0 | 0 | 0 | 0 | 0 | — | — | — |
| August | 118 | 39 | 8 | 1 | 2 | 12 | 1 | 19 | .331 | .466 | .339 |
| Sept./Oct. | 120 | 32 | 1 | 0 | 0 | 5 | 2 | 18 | .267 | .275 | .285 |
| Leading Off Inn. | 46 | 20 | 4 | 0 | 0 | 0 | 0 | 6 | .435 | .522 | .435 |
| Runners On | 89 | 22 | 2 | 1 | 0 | 15 | 0 | 13 | .247 | .292 | .244 |
| Runners/Scor. Pos. | 57 | 14 | 1 | 0 | 0 | 14 | 0 | 9 | .246 | .263 | .241 |
| Runners On/2 Out | 35 | 8 | 0 | 0 | 0 | 6 | 0 | 8 | .229 | .229 | .229 |
| Scor. Pos./2 Out | 27 | 6 | 0 | 0 | 0 | 6 | 0 | 7 | .222 | .222 | .222 |
| Late Inning Pressure | 35 | 8 | 1 | 0 | 0 | 1 | 1 | 5 | .229 | .257 | .250 |
| Leading Off | 11 | 6 | 1 | 0 | 0 | 0 | 0 | 0 | .545 | .636 | .545 |
| Runners On | 19 | 2 | 0 | 0 | 0 | 1 | 0 | 4 | .105 | .105 | .105 |
| Runners/Scor. Pos. | 12 | 1 | 0 | 0 | 0 | 1 | 0 | 2 | .083 | .083 | .083 |

| RUNS BATTED IN | From 1B | From 2B | From 3B | Scoring Position |
|---|---|---|---|---|
| Totals | 1/55 | 5/43 | 9/24 | 14/67 |
| Percentage | 2% | 12% | 38% | 21% |
| Driving In Runners from 3B with Less than Two Out: | | | 6/13 | 46% |

Loves to face: Jamie Moyer (.522, 12-for-23, 1 HR)
Hates to face: Andy Hawkins (.045, 1-for-22, 8 SO)
Overall mark of .251 (including .205 with Mets) snapped a streak of eight consecutive seasons between .270 and .300. ... Combined-leagues breakdown: .297 vs. ground-ball pitchers, .203 vs. fly-ballers. ... Batted 300 times against right-handers (both leagues combined) for first time since 1984. Career BA: .281 vs. right-handers, .270 vs. left-handers. ... Ended season without an extra-base hit in last 118 at-bats. ... Advanced from first base to third on 14 of 18 outfield singles (78%), more than double the major league rate. ... Drew one walk per 82 plate appearances. Theoretically, he would walk once in every 508 PA against Dennis Eckersley, whose average was one walk per 70 batters faced.

## Willie Wilson

Bats Left and Right

| Kansas City Royals | AB | H | 2B | 3B | HR | RBI | BB | SO | BA | SA | OBA |
|---|---|---|---|---|---|---|---|---|---|---|---|
| Season | 383 | 97 | 17 | 7 | 3 | 43 | 27 | 78 | .253 | .358 | .300 |
| vs. Left-Handers | 123 | 34 | 8 | 2 | 1 | 18 | 7 | 26 | .276 | .398 | .306 |
| vs. Right-Handers | 260 | 63 | 9 | 5 | 2 | 25 | 20 | 52 | .242 | .338 | .297 |
| Home | 197 | 53 | 8 | 2 | 1 | 19 | 15 | 39 | .269 | .345 | .318 |
| Road | 186 | 44 | 9 | 5 | 2 | 24 | 12 | 39 | .237 | .371 | .281 |
| Grass | 141 | 34 | 7 | 3 | 1 | 20 | 11 | 30 | .241 | .355 | .295 |
| Artificial Turf | 242 | 63 | 10 | 4 | 2 | 23 | 16 | 48 | .260 | .360 | .303 |
| April | 67 | 13 | 3 | 0 | 0 | 6 | 9 | 13 | .194 | .239 | .278 |
| May | 63 | 12 | 1 | 0 | 1 | 5 | 4 | 12 | .190 | .254 | .239 |
| June | 13 | 3 | 0 | 0 | 0 | 1 | 3 | 4 | .231 | .231 | .375 |
| July | 83 | 30 | 3 | 2 | 1 | 19 | 9 | 17 | .361 | .482 | .415 |
| August | 79 | 19 | 5 | 3 | 1 | 6 | 1 | 13 | .241 | .418 | .247 |
| Sept./Oct. | 78 | 20 | 5 | 2 | 0 | 6 | 1 | 19 | .256 | .372 | .275 |
| Leading Off Inn. | 130 | 36 | 4 | 3 | 0 | 0 | 14 | 21 | .277 | .354 | .347 |
| Runners On | 156 | 40 | 7 | 3 | 1 | 41 | 8 | 30 | .256 | .359 | .287 |
| Runners/Scor. Pos. | 91 | 24 | 4 | 1 | 0 | 36 | 4 | 16 | .264 | .330 | .277 |
| Runners On/2 Out | 69 | 17 | 5 | 1 | 0 | 18 | 2 | 7 | .246 | .348 | .278 |
| Scor. Pos./2 Out | 49 | 13 | 4 | 1 | 0 | 18 | 1 | 3 | .265 | .388 | .280 |
| Late Inning Pressure | 48 | 10 | 4 | 0 | 1 | 7 | 4 | 10 | .208 | .354 | .264 |
| Leading Off | 14 | 4 | 2 | 0 | 0 | 0 | 2 | 2 | .286 | .429 | .375 |
| Runners On | 21 | 5 | 1 | 0 | 1 | 7 | 1 | 3 | .238 | .429 | .261 |
| Runners/Scor. Pos. | 12 | 3 | 1 | 0 | 0 | 5 | 0 | 2 | .250 | .333 | .231 |

| RUNS BATTED IN | From 1B | From 2B | From 3B | Scoring Position |
|---|---|---|---|---|
| Totals | 6/117 | 13/70 | 21/45 | 34/115 |
| Percentage | 5% | 19% | 47% | 30% |
| Driving In Runners from 3B with Less than Two Out: | | | 15/24 | 63% |

Loves to face: Juan Berenguer (.423, 11-for-26, 1 HR)
Hates to face: Chris Bosio (.053, 1-for-19)
Batted .207 before the All-Star break, .288 thereafter. ... Had only six infield hits. No fewer than six teammates had more. ... Scored from second base on 14 of 15 outfield singles (94%, compared to a league average of 73%). ... Stole 24 bases, breaking a streak of 11 straight years with 30 or more. ... Career stolen base percentage (.839) is highest among active A.L. players (minimum: 50 SB). ... Leads active players with 130 career triples. ... Career batting average is .207 (18-for-87, two walks) with the bases loaded. ... Has never drawn as many as 40 walks, driven in as many as 50 runs, or grounded into as many as 10 double plays in a season.

## Craig Worthington

Bats Right

| Baltimore Orioles | AB | H | 2B | 3B | HR | RBI | BB | SO | BA | SA | OBA |
|---|---|---|---|---|---|---|---|---|---|---|---|
| Season | 497 | 123 | 23 | 0 | 15 | 70 | 61 | 114 | .247 | .384 | .334 |
| vs. Left-Handers | 155 | 40 | 5 | 0 | 4 | 19 | 24 | 32 | .258 | .368 | .361 |
| vs. Right-Handers | 342 | 83 | 18 | 0 | 11 | 51 | 37 | 82 | .243 | .392 | .321 |
| Home | 256 | 67 | 7 | 0 | 12 | 42 | 39 | 52 | .262 | .430 | .362 |
| Road | 241 | 56 | 16 | 0 | 3 | 28 | 22 | 62 | .232 | .336 | .302 |
| Grass | 415 | 99 | 17 | 0 | 13 | 54 | 50 | 95 | .239 | .373 | .326 |
| Artificial Turf | 82 | 24 | 6 | 0 | 2 | 16 | 11 | 19 | .293 | .439 | .376 |
| April | 79 | 15 | 4 | 0 | 1 | 10 | 12 | 19 | .190 | .278 | .304 |
| May | 74 | 16 | 3 | 0 | 1 | 13 | 7 | 19 | .216 | .297 | .284 |
| June | 83 | 24 | 7 | 0 | 1 | 10 | 9 | 12 | .289 | .410 | .359 |
| July | 86 | 24 | 2 | 0 | 5 | 18 | 13 | 15 | .279 | .477 | .380 |
| August | 76 | 18 | 5 | 0 | 4 | 12 | 13 | 22 | .237 | .461 | .356 |
| Sept./Oct. | 99 | 26 | 2 | 0 | 3 | 7 | 7 | 27 | .263 | .374 | .315 |
| Leading Off Inn. | 115 | 22 | 6 | 0 | 4 | 4 | 14 | 29 | .191 | .348 | .285 |
| Runners On | 220 | 68 | 11 | 0 | 6 | 61 | 24 | 47 | .309 | .441 | .381 |
| Runners/Scor. Pos. | 135 | 42 | 6 | 0 | 1 | 50 | 13 | 28 | .311 | .378 | .377 |
| Runners On/2 Out | 88 | 20 | 4 | 0 | 2 | 22 | 13 | 26 | .227 | .341 | .327 |
| Scor. Pos./2 Out | 63 | 16 | 3 | 0 | 1 | 20 | 6 | 18 | .254 | .349 | .319 |
| Late Inning Pressure | 71 | 11 | 2 | 0 | 2 | 6 | 8 | 18 | .155 | .268 | .241 |
| Leading Off | 22 | 4 | 1 | 0 | 0 | 0 | 2 | 7 | .182 | .227 | .250 |
| Runners On | 24 | 4 | 0 | 0 | 1 | 5 | 1 | 5 | .167 | .292 | .200 |
| Runners/Scor. Pos. | 13 | 3 | 0 | 0 | 1 | 5 | 1 | 3 | .231 | .462 | .286 |

| RUNS BATTED IN | From 1B | From 2B | From 3B | Scoring Position |
|---|---|---|---|---|
| Totals | 7/161 | 22/104 | 26/61 | 48/165 |
| Percentage | 4% | 21% | 43% | 29% |
| Driving In Runners from 3B with Less than Two Out: | | | 19/33 | 58% |

Loves to face: Chuck Crim (3-for-3, 1 HR)
Hates to face: Eric King (0-for-10, 4 SO)

Led major league rookies in games (145), RBI, walks, and strikeouts. . . . Ended the season with a 20-game errorless streak, his longest of the year. . . . Last Orioles third baseman to start consecutive opening days: Wayne Gross (1984–85). . . . Advanced from first base to third on 9 of 18 singles to center and right fields, but was 0-for-11 on singles to left. . . . Only 1-for-17 with runners in scoring position in 1988. . . . Career batting averages: .262 vs. ground-ball pitchers, .219 vs. fly-ballers. . . . Orioles rookies with as many RBI: Jim Gentile, 98 (1960); Cal Ripken, 93 (1982); Eddie Murray, 88 (1977); Ron Hansen, 86 (1960); Sam Bowens, 71 (1964); and Curt Blefary, 70 (1965).

## Robin Yount

Bats Right

| Milwaukee Brewers | AB | H | 2B | 3B | HR | RBI | BB | SO | BA | SA | OBA |
|---|---|---|---|---|---|---|---|---|---|---|---|
| Season | 614 | 195 | 38 | 9 | 21 | 103 | 63 | 71 | .318 | .511 | .384 |
| vs. Left-Handers | 167 | 57 | 15 | 4 | 6 | 25 | 14 | 22 | .341 | .587 | .395 |
| vs. Right-Handers | 447 | 138 | 23 | 5 | 15 | 78 | 49 | 49 | .309 | .483 | .380 |
| Home | 300 | 92 | 18 | 4 | 14 | 59 | 36 | 43 | .307 | .533 | .383 |
| Road | 314 | 103 | 20 | 5 | 7 | 44 | 27 | 28 | .328 | .490 | .386 |
| Grass | 519 | 163 | 32 | 8 | 20 | 90 | 54 | 66 | .314 | .522 | .381 |
| Artificial Turf | 95 | 32 | 6 | 1 | 1 | 13 | 9 | 5 | .337 | .453 | .402 |
| April | 83 | 22 | 3 | 3 | 0 | 6 | 10 | 11 | .265 | .373 | .351 |
| May | 108 | 35 | 7 | 1 | 5 | 19 | 13 | 10 | .324 | .546 | .407 |
| June | 108 | 33 | 6 | 0 | 3 | 20 | 8 | 10 | .306 | .444 | .350 |
| July | 101 | 40 | 11 | 2 | 5 | 24 | 9 | 8 | .396 | .693 | .455 |
| August | 113 | 34 | 6 | 3 | 3 | 19 | 11 | 15 | .301 | .487 | .359 |
| Sept./Oct. | 101 | 31 | 5 | 0 | 5 | 15 | 12 | 17 | .307 | .505 | .381 |
| Leading Off Inn. | 124 | 44 | 6 | 1 | 7 | 7 | 5 | 11 | .355 | .589 | .394 |
| Runners On | 285 | 94 | 19 | 5 | 7 | 89 | 34 | 31 | .330 | .505 | .402 |
| Runners/Scor. Pos. | 152 | 54 | 9 | 3 | 5 | 78 | 27 | 19 | .355 | .553 | .446 |
| Runners On/2 Out | 118 | 34 | 5 | 2 | 4 | 31 | 14 | 15 | .288 | .466 | .364 |
| Scor. Pos./2 Out | 64 | 17 | 3 | 2 | 2 | 24 | 11 | 10 | .266 | .469 | .373 |
| Late Inning Pressure | 67 | 21 | 4 | 1 | 1 | 16 | 7 | 11 | .313 | .448 | .373 |
| Leading Off | 16 | 5 | 0 | 0 | 0 | 0 | 1 | 1 | .313 | .313 | .353 |
| Runners On | 37 | 13 | 4 | 1 | 0 | 15 | 6 | 7 | .351 | .514 | .432 |
| Runners/Scor. Pos. | 17 | 7 | 3 | 0 | 0 | 14 | 5 | 2 | .412 | .588 | .522 |

| RUNS BATTED IN | From 1B | From 2B | From 3B | Scoring Position |
|---|---|---|---|---|
| Totals | 14/199 | 33/123 | 35/56 | 68/179 |
| Percentage | 7% | 27% | 63% | 38% |
| Driving In Runners from 3B with Less than Two Out: | | | 28/33 | 85% |

Loves to face: Mike Flanagan (.436, 34-for-78, 4 HR)
Hates to face: Mark Langston (.128, 5-for-39, 10 SO)

Only player in majors to hit .300 or better with 20+ homers, 100+ RBI, and 10+ stolen bases. . . . Hit 10 of his 21 homers to the opposite field. . . . First player to hit .350 or better with runners in scoring position in consecutive seasons (minimum: 100 AB) since Larry Parrish (1986–87). . . . Percentage of runners driven in from scoring position was the highest of his career, and was even higher (.542, 13-of-24) in Late-Inning Pressure Situations. . . . First eight seasons: .274, 67 HR, 439 RBI; last eight seasons: .309, 141 HR, 685 RBI. . . . Hitless in seven at-bats in All-Star Games, but he hasn't even appeared in one since 1983, when he was the leading vote-getter. . . . For more, see the Brewers essay.

## Baltimore Orioles

| | AB | H | 2B | 3B | HR | RBI | BB | SO | BA | SA | OBA |
|---|---|---|---|---|---|---|---|---|---|---|---|
| Season | 5440 | 1369 | 238 | 33 | 129 | 660 | 593 | 957 | .252 | .379 | .326 |
| vs. Left-Handers | 1760 | 426 | 85 | 12 | 42 | 195 | 190 | 298 | .242 | .376 | .317 |
| vs. Right-Handers | 3680 | 943 | 153 | 21 | 87 | 465 | 403 | 659 | .256 | .380 | .331 |
| Home | 2654 | 676 | 110 | 14 | 61 | 324 | 311 | 442 | .255 | .376 | .334 |
| Road | 2786 | 693 | 128 | 19 | 68 | 336 | 282 | 515 | .249 | .382 | .318 |
| Grass | 4576 | 1149 | 194 | 23 | 114 | 554 | 509 | 790 | .251 | .378 | .327 |
| Artificial Turf | 864 | 220 | 44 | 10 | 15 | 106 | 84 | 167 | .255 | .381 | .320 |
| April | 825 | 199 | 43 | 7 | 19 | 97 | 85 | 162 | .241 | .379 | .313 |
| May | 795 | 211 | 36 | 6 | 19 | 99 | 98 | 136 | .265 | .397 | .346 |
| June | 958 | 254 | 53 | 5 | 24 | 130 | 119 | 127 | .265 | .406 | .345 |
| July | 910 | 234 | 26 | 10 | 24 | 115 | 99 | 153 | .257 | .387 | .332 |
| August | 1023 | 242 | 35 | 3 | 25 | 117 | 112 | 189 | .237 | .350 | .314 |
| Sept./Oct. | 929 | 229 | 45 | 2 | 18 | 102 | 80 | 190 | .247 | .357 | .307 |
| Leading Off Inn. | 1333 | 329 | 67 | 7 | 29 | 29 | 109 | 231 | .247 | .373 | .307 |
| Runners On | 2290 | 606 | 99 | 13 | 56 | 587 | 318 | 374 | .265 | .393 | .352 |
| Runners/Scor. Pos. | 1376 | 358 | 52 | 11 | 34 | 520 | 219 | 231 | .260 | .388 | .355 |
| Runners On/2 Out | 969 | 244 | 45 | 6 | 17 | 232 | 155 | 182 | .252 | .363 | .357 |
| Scor. Pos./2 Out | 642 | 159 | 28 | 6 | 9 | 206 | 109 | 121 | .248 | .352 | .358 |
| Late Inning Pressure | 692 | 163 | 27 | 2 | 13 | 77 | 85 | 143 | .236 | .337 | .318 |
| Leading Off | 181 | 40 | 4 | 0 | 0 | 0 | 14 | 30 | .221 | .243 | .277 |
| Runners On | 286 | 72 | 13 | 1 | 8 | 72 | 47 | 57 | .252 | .388 | .352 |
| Runners/Scor. Pos. | 160 | 40 | 5 | 1 | 4 | 61 | 35 | 33 | .250 | .369 | .375 |

| RUNS BATTED IN | From 1B | From 2B | From 3B | Scoring Position |
|---|---|---|---|---|
| Totals | 80/1645 | 184/1051 | 267/659 | 451/1710 |
| Percentage | 5% | 18% | 41% | 26% |
| Driving In Runners from 3B with Less than Two Out: | | | 178/342 | 52% |

Love to face: Nolan Ryan (16–5 against him)
Hate to face: Allan Anderson (0–6 against him)
Winning percentage increased 202 points from 1988 to 1989, 6th-largest single-season improvement this century, topped only by that of the 1903 Giants (251 points), 1902 Browns, 1946 Red Sox, 1936 Braves, and 1905 Phillies. . . . Starting second basemen combined for a .229 batting average, lowest in A.L. (league average: .273). . . . Had lowest batting average in A.L. vs. left-handed pitchers. . . . Hit at least one triple in five consecutive games (July 3–7) for the first time since 1954. . . . Haven't been shutout in consecutive games since 1983 (1093 games), longest current streak in the majors, but little more than halfway to the all-time record of 2097 (Detroit, 1976–89).

## Boston Red Sox

| | AB | H | 2B | 3B | HR | RBI | BB | SO | BA | SA | OBA |
|---|---|---|---|---|---|---|---|---|---|---|---|
| Season | 5666 | 1571 | 326 | 30 | 108 | 717 | 643 | 755 | .277 | .403 | .351 |
| vs. Left-Handers | 1663 | 464 | 95 | 8 | 28 | 204 | 171 | 222 | .279 | .396 | .345 |
| vs. Right-Handers | 4003 | 1107 | 231 | 22 | 80 | 513 | 472 | 533 | .277 | .405 | .354 |
| Home | 2767 | 808 | 183 | 18 | 52 | 384 | 337 | 339 | .292 | .428 | .369 |
| Road | 2899 | 763 | 143 | 12 | 56 | 333 | 306 | 416 | .263 | .379 | .335 |
| Grass | 4776 | 1340 | 271 | 24 | 94 | 615 | 553 | 618 | .281 | .406 | .355 |
| Artificial Turf | 890 | 231 | 55 | 6 | 14 | 102 | 90 | 137 | .260 | .382 | .329 |
| April | 788 | 214 | 40 | 3 | 21 | 101 | 101 | 101 | .272 | .410 | .355 |
| May | 887 | 235 | 53 | 10 | 15 | 111 | 102 | 116 | .265 | .398 | .340 |
| June | 956 | 266 | 52 | 3 | 12 | 114 | 107 | 120 | .278 | .377 | .351 |
| July | 892 | 240 | 67 | 2 | 17 | 111 | 101 | 136 | .269 | .406 | .345 |
| August | 1175 | 349 | 61 | 8 | 27 | 154 | 106 | 157 | .297 | .431 | .358 |
| Sept./Oct. | 968 | 267 | 53 | 4 | 16 | 126 | 126 | 125 | .276 | .388 | .357 |
| Leading Off Inn. | 1324 | 369 | 77 | 8 | 31 | 31 | 128 | 181 | .279 | .419 | .346 |
| Runners On | 2686 | 765 | 154 | 14 | 53 | 662 | 334 | 343 | .285 | .412 | .361 |
| Runners/Scor. Pos. | 1571 | 441 | 87 | 11 | 28 | 592 | 231 | 228 | .281 | .404 | .365 |
| Runners On/2 Out | 1117 | 289 | 57 | 6 | 23 | 248 | 150 | 154 | .259 | .382 | .351 |
| Scor. Pos./2 Out | 724 | 174 | 33 | 4 | 14 | 220 | 121 | 109 | .240 | .355 | .353 |
| Late Inning Pressure | 843 | 225 | 47 | 4 | 16 | 94 | 91 | 138 | .267 | .389 | .341 |
| Leading Off | 200 | 52 | 12 | 1 | 3 | 3 | 24 | 34 | .260 | .375 | .345 |
| Runners On | 380 | 108 | 21 | 2 | 9 | 87 | 49 | 54 | .284 | .421 | .367 |
| Runners/Scor. Pos. | 228 | 63 | 12 | 2 | 6 | 80 | 41 | 37 | .276 | .425 | .381 |

| RUNS BATTED IN | From 1B | From 2B | From 3B | Scoring Position |
|---|---|---|---|---|
| Totals | 81/2012 | 229/1261 | 299/704 | 528/1965 |
| Percentage | 4% | 18% | 42% | 27% |
| Driving In Runners from 3B with Less than Two Out: | | | 215/375 | 57% |

Love to face: Steve Farr (4–0)
Hate to face: Tim Leary (0–4)
Led A.L. in doubles for the fifth time in the last seven seasons. . . . Record in one-run games was 11–5 at Fenway, 2–20 on road. (Home teams won 70 percent of A.L. games decided by one run.) . . . Were 8–14 vs. left-handed starters at Fenway, 14–11 vs. southpaw starters on the road. . . . Only three major league teams had losing records despite scoring in first inning: Boston (27–29), Detroit (25–28), and Los Angeles (21–22). . . . Only team in majors not to win a game in which it trailed after eight innings (0–71). . . . Seven-game home-run drought (June 18–24) was their longest since 1974. . . . No opposing pitcher defeated the Red Sox more than twice last season. They are the only major league team that can make that claim.

## California Angels

| | AB | H | 2B | 3B | HR | RBI | BB | SO | BA | SA | OBA |
|---|---|---|---|---|---|---|---|---|---|---|---|
| Season | 5545 | 1422 | 208 | 37 | 145 | 626 | 429 | 1011 | .256 | .386 | .311 |
| vs. Left-Handers | 1971 | 486 | 72 | 12 | 49 | 199 | 144 | 354 | .247 | .370 | .299 |
| vs. Right-Handers | 3574 | 936 | 136 | 25 | 96 | 427 | 285 | 657 | .262 | .395 | .317 |
| Home | 2685 | 680 | 96 | 20 | 73 | 302 | 217 | 464 | .253 | .385 | .309 |
| Road | 2860 | 742 | 112 | 17 | 72 | 324 | 212 | 547 | .259 | .386 | .312 |
| Grass | 4596 | 1163 | 165 | 28 | 119 | 505 | 370 | 834 | .253 | .379 | .309 |
| Artificial Turf | 949 | 259 | 43 | 9 | 26 | 121 | 59 | 177 | .273 | .419 | .319 |
| April | 840 | 211 | 36 | 5 | 20 | 99 | 62 | 150 | .251 | .377 | .305 |
| May | 863 | 245 | 38 | 8 | 25 | 117 | 78 | 118 | .284 | .433 | .342 |
| June | 896 | 229 | 33 | 5 | 23 | 84 | 54 | 150 | .256 | .381 | .297 |
| July | 950 | 254 | 23 | 4 | 33 | 127 | 93 | 170 | .267 | .404 | .333 |
| August | 976 | 241 | 37 | 13 | 25 | 107 | 75 | 205 | .247 | .388 | .303 |
| Sept./Oct. | 1020 | 242 | 41 | 2 | 19 | 92 | 67 | 218 | .237 | .337 | .286 |
| Leading Off Inn. | 1367 | 368 | 60 | 8 | 43 | 43 | 83 | 235 | .269 | .419 | .313 |
| Runners On | 2302 | 614 | 88 | 16 | 49 | 530 | 210 | 410 | .267 | .383 | .326 |
| Runners/Scor. Pos. | 1286 | 335 | 48 | 9 | 26 | 461 | 143 | 248 | .260 | .372 | .328 |
| Runners On/2 Out | 991 | 252 | 38 | 7 | 21 | 229 | 103 | 174 | .254 | .370 | .327 |
| Scor. Pos./2 Out | 616 | 156 | 26 | 4 | 14 | 204 | 79 | 114 | .253 | .377 | .340 |
| Late Inning Pressure | 748 | 181 | 23 | 4 | 13 | 68 | 72 | 183 | .242 | .336 | .309 |
| Leading Off | 195 | 50 | 5 | 1 | 8 | 8 | 14 | 41 | .256 | .415 | .306 |
| Runners On | 306 | 73 | 5 | 1 | 2 | 57 | 41 | 72 | .239 | .281 | .325 |
| Runners/Scor. Pos. | 195 | 48 | 4 | 0 | 1 | 54 | 27 | 46 | .246 | .282 | .332 |

| RUNS BATTED IN | From 1B | From 2B | From 3B | Scoring Position |
|---|---|---|---|---|
| Totals | 78/1699 | 190/985 | 213/558 | 403/1543 |
| Percentage | 5% | 19% | 38% | 26% |
| Driving In Runners from 3B with Less than Two Out: | | | 145/291 | 50% |

Love to face: Shane Rawley (8–3)
Hate to face: Bret Saberhagen (3–9)
Led A.L. in home runs for the first time in club history. . . . Did not hit a home run in Arlington Stadium last season. . . . Haven't won a season series at Memorial Stadium since 1978. . . . The only team in the league without a stolen base by a designated hitter last season. . . . Had a 25–5 record in one-run decisions at home, 8–16 on the road. . . . Had a 34–4 record in home games in which they scored the first run. . . . Starting catchers batted only .229, but led A.L. with 20 home runs. . . . Used only 66 pinch hitters, 2d lowest in majors to Brewers. . . . Were shutout three times in their final six games of the season. . . . Longest losing streak of season coincided with seven-game home-run drought.

## Chicago White Sox

| | AB | H | 2B | 3B | HR | RBI | BB | SO | BA | SA | OBA |
|---|---|---|---|---|---|---|---|---|---|---|---|
| Season | 5504 | 1493 | 262 | 36 | 94 | 662 | 464 | 873 | .271 | .383 | .328 |
| vs. Left-Handers | 1760 | 481 | 73 | 12 | 26 | 215 | 139 | 271 | .273 | .373 | .326 |
| vs. Right-Handers | 3744 | 1012 | 189 | 24 | 68 | 447 | 325 | 602 | .270 | .388 | .329 |
| Home | 2602 | 672 | 107 | 27 | 36 | 289 | 215 | 380 | .258 | .362 | .314 |
| Road | 2902 | 821 | 155 | 9 | 58 | 373 | 249 | 493 | .283 | .402 | .341 |
| Grass | 4651 | 1258 | 205 | 34 | 84 | 556 | 383 | 713 | .270 | .383 | .326 |
| Artificial Turf | 853 | 235 | 57 | 2 | 10 | 106 | 81 | 160 | .275 | .382 | .340 |
| April | 845 | 208 | 32 | 2 | 14 | 80 | 82 | 136 | .246 | .338 | .315 |
| May | 925 | 265 | 46 | 4 | 18 | 125 | 82 | 142 | .286 | .403 | .342 |
| June | 988 | 269 | 40 | 8 | 25 | 128 | 72 | 158 | .272 | .405 | .322 |
| July | 842 | 242 | 50 | 6 | 15 | 103 | 61 | 145 | .287 | .414 | .336 |
| August | 979 | 269 | 53 | 9 | 9 | 115 | 79 | 161 | .275 | .375 | .331 |
| Sept./Oct. | 925 | 240 | 41 | 7 | 13 | 111 | 88 | 131 | .259 | .361 | .323 |
| Leading Off Inn. | 1340 | 369 | 69 | 5 | 28 | 28 | 93 | 217 | .275 | .397 | .323 |
| Runners On | 2465 | 696 | 125 | 20 | 42 | 610 | 234 | 378 | .282 | .400 | .341 |
| Runners/Scor. Pos. | 1423 | 391 | 66 | 9 | 23 | 539 | 162 | 251 | .275 | .382 | .340 |
| Runners On/2 Out | 1025 | 261 | 37 | 8 | 18 | 217 | 102 | 171 | .255 | .359 | .324 |
| Scor. Pos./2 Out | 654 | 152 | 23 | 4 | 10 | 188 | 70 | 124 | .232 | .326 | .309 |
| Late Inning Pressure | 863 | 218 | 45 | 3 | 10 | 89 | 76 | 176 | .253 | .346 | .313 |
| Leading Off | 214 | 53 | 7 | 0 | 4 | 4 | 17 | 40 | .248 | .336 | .303 |
| Runners On | 373 | 101 | 29 | 1 | 5 | 84 | 42 | 72 | .271 | .394 | .339 |
| Runners/Scor. Pos. | 214 | 49 | 13 | 0 | 3 | 72 | 34 | 45 | .229 | .332 | .325 |

| RUNS BATTED IN | From 1B | From 2B | From 3B | Scoring Position |
|---|---|---|---|---|
| Totals | 84/1758 | 224/1112 | 260/615 | 484/1727 |
| Percentage | 5% | 20% | 42% | 28% |
| Driving In Runners from 3B with Less than Two Out: | | | 191/332 | 58% |

Love to face: Chris Bosio (6–1)
Hate to face: Dave Stieb (4–18)
Hit fewest home runs in A.L. for 26th time in league's 89-year history. . . . Have led league in sacrifice bunts for two consecutive seasons, and under different managers. . . . Led majors with a .282 average from pinch hitters. . . . Batted .283 in road games, highest in majors since 1980. . . . Rookies combined for a .271 batting average, highest in the American League. . . . Only A.L. club without an extra-inning home run. Their last overtime dinger was by Dan Pasqua on July 3, 1988. . . . White Sox starting third basemen combined for a .303 average, third-highest in the majors behind Boston (Boggs) and Oakland (Lansford). . . . Homerless in 14 straight games last summer, their longest since 1949.

## Cleveland Indians

| | AB | H | 2B | 3B | HR | RBI | BB | SO | BA | SA | OBA |
|---|---|---|---|---|---|---|---|---|---|---|---|
| Season | 5463 | 1340 | 221 | 26 | 127 | 566 | 499 | 934 | .245 | .365 | .310 |
| vs. Left-Handers | 1589 | 392 | 68 | 7 | 38 | 165 | 140 | 268 | .247 | .370 | .307 |
| vs. Right-Handers | 3874 | 948 | 153 | 19 | 89 | 401 | 359 | 666 | .245 | .363 | .312 |
| Home | 2695 | 671 | 114 | 16 | 56 | 296 | 270 | 445 | .249 | .365 | .321 |
| Road | 2768 | 669 | 107 | 10 | 71 | 270 | 229 | 489 | .242 | .365 | .300 |
| Grass | 4626 | 1135 | 182 | 22 | 104 | 479 | 433 | 785 | .245 | .362 | .312 |
| Artificial Turf | 837 | 205 | 39 | 4 | 23 | 87 | 66 | 149 | .245 | .384 | .300 |
| April | 740 | 188 | 31 | 0 | 15 | 76 | 63 | 127 | .254 | .357 | .314 |
| May | 967 | 241 | 40 | 6 | 25 | 115 | 87 | 149 | .249 | .381 | .311 |
| June | 848 | 199 | 30 | 4 | 21 | 71 | 83 | 131 | .235 | .354 | .305 |
| July | 913 | 241 | 49 | 5 | 21 | 116 | 102 | 147 | .264 | .398 | .339 |
| August | 972 | 243 | 39 | 6 | 24 | 99 | 74 | 180 | .250 | .377 | .305 |
| Sept./Oct. | 1023 | 228 | 32 | 5 | 21 | 89 | 90 | 200 | .223 | .326 | .290 |
| Leading Off Inn. | 1343 | 353 | 70 | 8 | 34 | 34 | 114 | 205 | .263 | .403 | .324 |
| Runners On | 2290 | 558 | 81 | 10 | 57 | 496 | 245 | 408 | .244 | .362 | .317 |
| Runners/Scor. Pos. | 1307 | 297 | 54 | 6 | 23 | 412 | 190 | 275 | .227 | .331 | .321 |
| Runners On/2 Out | 958 | 196 | 25 | 2 | 19 | 164 | 113 | 193 | .205 | .294 | .292 |
| Scor. Pos./2 Out | 605 | 106 | 16 | 1 | 9 | 138 | 98 | 144 | .175 | .250 | .291 |
| Late Inning Pressure | 852 | 182 | 28 | 1 | 16 | 69 | 98 | 186 | .214 | .305 | .298 |
| Leading Off | 224 | 58 | 9 | 1 | 7 | 7 | 20 | 35 | .259 | .402 | .328 |
| Runners On | 334 | 70 | 10 | 0 | 5 | 58 | 53 | 75 | .210 | .284 | .316 |
| Runners/Scor. Pos. | 187 | 39 | 6 | 0 | 2 | 50 | 44 | 46 | .209 | .273 | .356 |

| RUNS BATTED IN | From 1B | From 2B | From 3B | Scoring Position |
|---|---|---|---|---|
| Totals | 70/1650 | 154/1013 | 215/565 | 369/1578 |
| Percentage | 4% | 15% | 38% | 23% |
| Driving In Runners from 3B with Less than Two Out: | | | 155/304 | 51% |

Love to face: Mike Birkbeck (4–1)
Hate to face: Roger Clemens (2–11)
That .214 batting average in Late-Inning Pressure Situations was lowest in majors last season, and 2d lowest over past 15 years. (The Angels hit .202 in LIPS in 1981.) Tribe also had A.L.'s lowest average with runners on base, with runners in scoring position, with two outs and runners on base, and with two outs and runners in scoring position. That last one was the lowest by any team since 1975.... Lost season series to the Tigers in every season during the 1980s. ... pinch hitters came to the plate 149 times last season without grounding into a double play. ... Had a 3–15 record in extra-inning games. Were outscored 22–3 in overtime.... Starting first basemen combined for only 56 RBI, fewest in A.L.

## Kansas City Royals

| | AB | H | 2B | 3B | HR | RBI | BB | SO | BA | SA | OBA |
|---|---|---|---|---|---|---|---|---|---|---|---|
| Season | 5475 | 1428 | 227 | 41 | 101 | 655 | 554 | 897 | .261 | .373 | .329 |
| vs. Left-Handers | 1637 | 447 | 71 | 10 | 29 | 201 | 183 | 226 | .273 | .382 | .348 |
| vs. Right-Handers | 3838 | 981 | 156 | 31 | 72 | 454 | 371 | 671 | .256 | .369 | .321 |
| Home | 2627 | 691 | 116 | 22 | 38 | 315 | 278 | 400 | .263 | .367 | .332 |
| Road | 2848 | 737 | 111 | 19 | 63 | 340 | 276 | 497 | .259 | .377 | .326 |
| Grass | 2180 | 565 | 84 | 13 | 45 | 257 | 209 | 379 | .259 | .372 | .327 |
| Artificial Turf | 3295 | 863 | 143 | 28 | 56 | 398 | 345 | 518 | .262 | .373 | .331 |
| April | 823 | 219 | 44 | 3 | 14 | 111 | 95 | 115 | .266 | .378 | .339 |
| May | 881 | 219 | 26 | 5 | 15 | 91 | 88 | 161 | .249 | .341 | .320 |
| June | 914 | 241 | 38 | 3 | 14 | 105 | 75 | 126 | .264 | .358 | .318 |
| July | 915 | 237 | 32 | 8 | 20 | 115 | 109 | 151 | .259 | .377 | .338 |
| August | 952 | 264 | 45 | 14 | 18 | 119 | 100 | 147 | .277 | .411 | .345 |
| Sept./Oct. | 990 | 248 | 42 | 8 | 20 | 114 | 87 | 197 | .251 | .370 | .315 |
| Leading Off Inn. | 1320 | 349 | 65 | 10 | 22 | 22 | 118 | 208 | .264 | .379 | .328 |
| Runners On | 2430 | 658 | 96 | 16 | 43 | 597 | 273 | 375 | .271 | .377 | .342 |
| Runners/Scor. Pos. | 1412 | 377 | 54 | 11 | 27 | 543 | 203 | 230 | .267 | .378 | .352 |
| Runners On/2 Out | 987 | 222 | 40 | 6 | 20 | 207 | 126 | 182 | .225 | .338 | .315 |
| Scor. Pos./2 Out | 640 | 146 | 28 | 5 | 14 | 187 | 96 | 115 | .228 | .353 | .332 |
| Late Inning Pressure | 751 | 198 | 30 | 0 | 13 | 80 | 87 | 144 | .264 | .356 | .341 |
| Leading Off | 194 | 53 | 13 | 0 | 2 | 2 | 22 | 41 | .273 | .371 | .347 |
| Runners On | 312 | 89 | 8 | 0 | 4 | 71 | 48 | 49 | .285 | .349 | .378 |
| Runners/Scor. Pos. | 185 | 53 | 5 | 0 | 2 | 64 | 38 | 32 | .286 | .346 | .404 |

| RUNS BATTED IN | From 1B | From 2B | From 3B | Scoring Position |
|---|---|---|---|---|
| Totals | 70/1737 | 212/1085 | 272/621 | 484/1706 |
| Percentage | 4% | 20% | 44% | 28% |
| Driving In Runners from 3B with Less than Two Out: | | | 206/349 | 59% |

Love to face: Frank Tanana (21–8)
Hate to face: Roger Clemens (1–9)
Shut out 18 times, the most by an A.L. club since the Blue Jays were blanked in 20 of their 106 games during the 1981 strike season.... Followed five of those shutouts with games in which they scored 10 or more runs.... Haven't lost a season series to the Red Sox since 1979.... Had the best record in the majors (37–13) in games in which they scored in the first inning.... Starting catchers combined for only three home runs, fewest in the majors.... Although their 101 home runs ranked next-to-last in the league, they ranked second in the league with 30 dingers from the cleanup spot.... Batting average with two outs and runners on base was their lowest in the last 15 years.

## Detroit Tigers

| | AB | H | 2B | 3B | HR | RBI | BB | SO | BA | SA | OBA |
|---|---|---|---|---|---|---|---|---|---|---|---|
| Season | 5432 | 1315 | 198 | 24 | 116 | 564 | 585 | 899 | .242 | .351 | .318 |
| vs. Left-Handers | 1799 | 459 | 80 | 8 | 40 | 187 | 176 | 259 | .255 | .375 | .324 |
| vs. Right-Handers | 3633 | 856 | 118 | 16 | 76 | 377 | 409 | 640 | .236 | .340 | .315 |
| Home | 2635 | 629 | 97 | 17 | 74 | 298 | 301 | 436 | .239 | .373 | .319 |
| Road | 2797 | 686 | 101 | 7 | 42 | 266 | 284 | 463 | .245 | .331 | .316 |
| Grass | 4555 | 1097 | 153 | 21 | 105 | 478 | 489 | 755 | .241 | .353 | .316 |
| Artificial Turf | 877 | 218 | 45 | 3 | 11 | 86 | 96 | 144 | .249 | .344 | .326 |
| April | 730 | 170 | 17 | 1 | 16 | 66 | 92 | 121 | .233 | .325 | .322 |
| May | 917 | 226 | 38 | 7 | 23 | 101 | 96 | 140 | .246 | .378 | .318 |
| June | 882 | 228 | 34 | 1 | 20 | 99 | 108 | 141 | .259 | .367 | .342 |
| July | 930 | 215 | 36 | 4 | 19 | 83 | 75 | 140 | .231 | .340 | .288 |
| August | 1088 | 249 | 39 | 5 | 25 | 112 | 110 | 200 | .229 | .343 | .302 |
| Sept./Oct. | 885 | 227 | 34 | 6 | 13 | 103 | 104 | 157 | .256 | .353 | .339 |
| Leading Off Inn. | 1326 | 325 | 49 | 8 | 29 | 29 | 126 | 208 | .245 | .360 | .313 |
| Runners On | 2358 | 580 | 91 | 9 | 45 | 493 | 274 | 385 | .246 | .349 | .324 |
| Runners/Scor. Pos. | 1308 | 314 | 44 | 6 | 21 | 422 | 174 | 233 | .240 | .331 | .324 |
| Runners On/2 Out | 1002 | 237 | 30 | 5 | 19 | 197 | 138 | 179 | .237 | .333 | .332 |
| Scor. Pos./2 Out | 634 | 144 | 19 | 3 | 12 | 173 | 98 | 121 | .227 | .323 | .333 |
| Late Inning Pressure | 931 | 201 | 28 | 5 | 14 | 82 | 117 | 201 | .216 | .302 | .306 |
| Leading Off | 236 | 56 | 7 | 0 | 6 | 6 | 28 | 48 | .237 | .343 | .318 |
| Runners On | 416 | 84 | 11 | 4 | 4 | 72 | 54 | 87 | .202 | .276 | .295 |
| Runners/Scor. Pos. | 211 | 44 | 6 | 1 | 1 | 61 | 32 | 46 | .209 | .261 | .308 |

| RUNS BATTED IN | From 1B | From 2B | From 3B | Scoring Position |
|---|---|---|---|---|
| Totals | 70/1749 | 170/1033 | 208/567 | 378/1600 |
| Percentage | 4% | 16% | 37% | 24% |
| Driving In Runners from 3B with Less than Two Out: | | | 154/280 | 55% |

Love to face: Bobby Thigpen (5–0)
Hate to face: Dennis Lamp (0–11)
Were shut out in consecutive games (July 4–5) for the first time since 1976, breaking the longest streak of games between back-to-back shutouts in this century (2097). Previous record: 1855, Dodgers (1949–61).... Finished last in A.L. in batting average for only 4th time in club history. Other years: 1902, 1960, 1970.... Puckett and Lansford were the first A.L. right-handers to finish one-two in batting average in a full season since Harvey Kuenn and Al Kaline in 1959. ... Used 46 players, 2d-highest total in team history. Record: 53, in 1912, including a lineup of amateurs and retired players who replaced regular starters, who staged a one-day strike in support of suspended teammate, Ty Cobb.

## Milwaukee Brewers

| | AB | H | 2B | 3B | HR | RBI | BB | SO | BA | SA | OBA |
|---|---|---|---|---|---|---|---|---|---|---|---|
| Season | 5473 | 1415 | 235 | 32 | 126 | 660 | 455 | 791 | .259 | .382 | .318 |
| vs. Left-Handers | 1520 | 432 | 80 | 8 | 39 | 212 | 127 | 185 | .284 | .424 | .342 |
| vs. Right-Handers | 3953 | 983 | 155 | 24 | 87 | 448 | 328 | 606 | .249 | .366 | .309 |
| Home | 2673 | 671 | 108 | 13 | 69 | 323 | 246 | 417 | .251 | .379 | .317 |
| Road | 2800 | 744 | 127 | 19 | 57 | 337 | 209 | 374 | .266 | .386 | .319 |
| Grass | 4602 | 1180 | 198 | 27 | 111 | 548 | 391 | 684 | .256 | .384 | .317 |
| Artificial Turf | 871 | 235 | 37 | 5 | 15 | 112 | 64 | 107 | .270 | .375 | .324 |
| April | 720 | 165 | 23 | 5 | 23 | 80 | 64 | 115 | .229 | .371 | .298 |
| May | 949 | 244 | 43 | 4 | 23 | 103 | 79 | 140 | .257 | .384 | .318 |
| June | 1002 | 267 | 45 | 5 | 19 | 126 | 79 | 131 | .266 | .378 | .322 |
| July | 887 | 244 | 34 | 7 | 21 | 124 | 76 | 109 | .275 | .400 | .337 |
| August | 1022 | 243 | 43 | 6 | 13 | 107 | 80 | 150 | .238 | .330 | .296 |
| Sept./Oct. | 893 | 252 | 47 | 5 | 27 | 120 | 77 | 146 | .282 | .437 | .338 |
| Leading Off Inn. | 1332 | 328 | 59 | 4 | 37 | 37 | 92 | 183 | .246 | .380 | .301 |
| Runners On | 2296 | 643 | 103 | 17 | 49 | 583 | 205 | 300 | .280 | .404 | .338 |
| Runners/Scor. Pos. | 1322 | 374 | 60 | 9 | 29 | 521 | 155 | 193 | .283 | .408 | .351 |
| Runners On/2 Out | 980 | 238 | 39 | 7 | 19 | 218 | 97 | 152 | .243 | .355 | .317 |
| Scor. Pos./2 Out | 628 | 157 | 26 | 5 | 13 | 198 | 77 | 108 | .250 | .369 | .338 |
| Late Inning Pressure | 664 | 161 | 30 | 2 | 14 | 69 | 67 | 131 | .242 | .357 | .311 |
| Leading Off | 170 | 40 | 7 | 0 | 5 | 5 | 14 | 31 | .235 | .365 | .293 |
| Runners On | 265 | 68 | 14 | 1 | 6 | 61 | 34 | 46 | .257 | .385 | .336 |
| Runners/Scor. Pos. | 153 | 40 | 8 | 0 | 5 | 57 | 26 | 28 | .261 | .412 | .358 |

| RUNS BATTED IN | From 1B | From 2B | From 3B | Scoring Position |
|---|---|---|---|---|
| Totals | 72/1635 | 204/1060 | 258/544 | 462/1604 |
| Percentage | 4% | 19% | 47% | 29% |
| Driving In Runners from 3B with Less than Two Out: | | | 198/310 | 64% |

Love to face: Charlie Hough (9–1)
Hate to face: Dave Stewart (1–10)
Have led A.L. in stolen bases in all three full seasons under Tom Trebelhorn. Last A.L. club to lead the league in four consecutive seasons: the "Go-Go" White Sox, who led for 11 consecutive seasons from 1951 through 1961.... Brewers, once again, used the fewest pinch hitters (51) of any team in the majors.... Led A.L. in errors (155) for the first time in franchise history.... Used eight different starting second basemen. No other A.L. club used more than five.... Did not hit a home run in seven games at Memorial Stadium (Baltimore) last season.... Seven homers from the third spot in the batting order were the fewest of any A.L. club.

## Minnesota Twins

| | AB | H | 2B | 3B | HR | RBI | BB | SO | BA | SA | OBA |
|---|---|---|---|---|---|---|---|---|---|---|---|
| Season | 5581 | 1542 | 278 | 35 | 117 | 692 | 478 | 743 | .276 | .402 | .334 |
| vs. Left-Handers | 1715 | 494 | 99 | 14 | 34 | 220 | 137 | 219 | .288 | .422 | .341 |
| vs. Right-Handers | 3866 | 1048 | 179 | 21 | 83 | 472 | 341 | 524 | .271 | .393 | .331 |
| Home | 2749 | 783 | 145 | 17 | 59 | 365 | 239 | 320 | .285 | .414 | .343 |
| Road | 2832 | 759 | 133 | 18 | 58 | 327 | 239 | 423 | .268 | .389 | .326 |
| Grass | 2168 | 578 | 112 | 11 | 48 | 258 | 199 | 331 | .267 | .395 | .329 |
| Artificial Turf | 3413 | 964 | 166 | 24 | 69 | 434 | 279 | 412 | .282 | .406 | .338 |
| April | 749 | 205 | 43 | 4 | 18 | 102 | 56 | 93 | .274 | .414 | .329 |
| May | 970 | 262 | 52 | 6 | 20 | 134 | 103 | 145 | .270 | .398 | .339 |
| June | 1009 | 281 | 41 | 10 | 25 | 142 | 97 | 139 | .278 | .413 | .345 |
| July | 859 | 229 | 35 | 3 | 15 | 90 | 68 | 134 | .267 | .367 | .322 |
| August | 998 | 290 | 62 | 4 | 18 | 117 | 73 | 111 | .291 | .415 | .338 |
| Sept./Oct. | 996 | 275 | 45 | 8 | 21 | 107 | 81 | 121 | .276 | .401 | .331 |
| Leading Off Inn. | 1328 | 355 | 67 | 6 | 31 | 31 | 99 | 159 | .267 | .397 | .322 |
| Runners On | 2511 | 691 | 113 | 17 | 53 | 628 | 258 | 333 | .275 | .397 | .340 |
| Runners/Scor. Pos. | 1446 | 372 | 67 | 9 | 32 | 564 | 178 | 235 | .257 | .382 | .331 |
| Runners On/2 Out | 1030 | 261 | 39 | 7 | 17 | 220 | 123 | 145 | .253 | .354 | .335 |
| Scor. Pos./2 Out | 668 | 146 | 20 | 3 | 9 | 194 | 97 | 113 | .219 | .298 | .319 |
| Late Inning Pressure | 743 | 209 | 34 | 4 | 23 | 102 | 51 | 126 | .281 | .431 | .328 |
| Leading Off | 183 | 44 | 10 | 0 | 6 | 6 | 10 | 25 | .240 | .393 | .284 |
| Runners On | 315 | 96 | 14 | 2 | 9 | 88 | 28 | 45 | .305 | .448 | .354 |
| Runners/Scor. Pos. | 181 | 50 | 8 | 1 | 5 | 76 | 23 | 34 | .276 | .414 | .343 |

| RUNS BATTED IN | From 1B | From 2B | From 3B | Scoring Position |
|---|---|---|---|---|
| Totals | 90/1808 | 222/1149 | 263/608 | 485/1757 |
| Percentage | 5% | 19% | 43% | 28% |
| Driving In Runners from 3B with Less than Two Out: | | | 195/317 | 62% |

Love to face: Dave Stewart (10–4)
Hate to face: Roger Clemens (1–10)
Designated hitters led A.L. with .291 average. . . . Batted .281 in Late-Inning Pressure Situations, best in majors. . . . Didn't lose an extra-inning game at home last season (5–0). . . . Won 10 games in which they trailed after seven innings, most of any A.L. club. . . . Scored six or more runs in an inning nine times, most in majors. . . . Started 15 different players in the eighth batting-order position, but got the best production in the majors from that spot. Nineteen different Twins combined for 76 runs and 83 RBI from the eight hole, both figures being major league highs. . . . Twins led the A.L. in singles for the first time in the 1980s. They did it seven times in the 1970s.

## New York Yankees

| | AB | H | 2B | 3B | HR | RBI | BB | SO | BA | SA | OBA |
|---|---|---|---|---|---|---|---|---|---|---|---|
| Season | 5458 | 1470 | 229 | 23 | 130 | 661 | 502 | 831 | .269 | .391 | .331 |
| vs. Left-Handers | 1802 | 537 | 91 | 8 | 42 | 231 | 187 | 252 | .298 | .427 | .362 |
| vs. Right-Handers | 3656 | 933 | 138 | 15 | 88 | 430 | 315 | 579 | .255 | .373 | .316 |
| Home | 2706 | 770 | 120 | 9 | 64 | 354 | 247 | 394 | .285 | .407 | .345 |
| Road | 2752 | 700 | 109 | 14 | 66 | 307 | 255 | 437 | .254 | .376 | .318 |
| Grass | 4621 | 1231 | 190 | 13 | 109 | 545 | 428 | 706 | .266 | .384 | .329 |
| Artificial Turf | 837 | 239 | 39 | 10 | 21 | 116 | 74 | 125 | .286 | .431 | .342 |
| April | 798 | 198 | 42 | 7 | 8 | 83 | 78 | 117 | .248 | .348 | .314 |
| May | 865 | 224 | 34 | 0 | 20 | 95 | 117 | 132 | .259 | .368 | .345 |
| June | 958 | 281 | 31 | 3 | 31 | 129 | 92 | 128 | .293 | .429 | .355 |
| July | 924 | 260 | 43 | 2 | 25 | 123 | 68 | 150 | .281 | .413 | .332 |
| August | 1050 | 283 | 45 | 9 | 21 | 130 | 90 | 171 | .270 | .390 | .329 |
| Sept./Oct. | 863 | 224 | 34 | 2 | 25 | 101 | 57 | 133 | .260 | .390 | .308 |
| Leading Off Inn. | 1314 | 347 | 51 | 9 | 29 | 29 | 100 | 188 | .264 | .383 | .320 |
| Runners On | 2391 | 670 | 102 | 8 | 55 | 586 | 243 | 342 | .280 | .399 | .343 |
| Runners/Scor. Pos. | 1391 | 375 | 59 | 4 | 24 | 508 | 186 | 215 | .270 | .370 | .347 |
| Runners On/2 Out | 999 | 261 | 30 | 4 | 22 | 225 | 129 | 151 | .261 | .365 | .349 |
| Scor. Pos./2 Out | 661 | 162 | 21 | 1 | 10 | 194 | 101 | 107 | .245 | .325 | .349 |
| Late Inning Pressure | 761 | 212 | 31 | 3 | 21 | 110 | 74 | 142 | .279 | .410 | .343 |
| Leading Off | 178 | 41 | 5 | 2 | 4 | 4 | 16 | 31 | .230 | .348 | .301 |
| Runners On | 343 | 102 | 13 | 1 | 13 | 102 | 44 | 71 | .297 | .455 | .373 |
| Runners/Scor. Pos. | 200 | 63 | 11 | 1 | 6 | 88 | 37 | 47 | .315 | .470 | .415 |

| RUNS BATTED IN | From 1B | From 2B | From 3B | Scoring Position |
|---|---|---|---|---|
| Totals | 71/1718 | 198/1080 | 262/638 | 460/1718 |
| Percentage | 4% | 18% | 41% | 27% |
| Driving In Runners from 3B with Less than Two Out: | | | 184/335 | 55% |

Love to face: Bud Black (11–3)
Hate to face: Ted Higuera (2–12)
Their .298 batting average vs. left-handed pitchers is highest by any team in majors over past 15 years. . . . Yanks also led majors with .315 average in Late-Inning Pressure Situations with runners in scoring position. . . . That .286 average on artificial turf was also best in majors in '89. . . . Fewest triples of any major league club for the third straight season. . . . Lost season series at home to Oakland for the first time since 1976. Have lost season series at Milwaukee for nine straight seasons. . . . Designated hitters led A.L. with 27 home runs. . . . Had a 20–6 record in home games in which they scored in the first inning, but only a 11–17 mark in road games in which they scored in the first frame.

## Oakland A's

| | AB | H | 2B | 3B | HR | RBI | BB | SO | BA | SA | OBA |
|---|---|---|---|---|---|---|---|---|---|---|---|
| Season | 5416 | 1414 | 220 | 25 | 127 | 661 | 562 | 855 | .261 | .381 | .331 |
| vs. Left-Handers | 1521 | 405 | 71 | 8 | 33 | 187 | 159 | 201 | .266 | .389 | .335 |
| vs. Right-Handers | 3895 | 1009 | 149 | 17 | 94 | 474 | 403 | 654 | .259 | .378 | .330 |
| Home | 2623 | 698 | 95 | 10 | 65 | 344 | 272 | 415 | .266 | .384 | .335 |
| Road | 2793 | 716 | 125 | 15 | 62 | 317 | 290 | 440 | .256 | .378 | .327 |
| Grass | 4546 | 1209 | 179 | 22 | 111 | 571 | 469 | 718 | .266 | .388 | .335 |
| Artificial Turf | 870 | 205 | 41 | 3 | 16 | 90 | 93 | 137 | .236 | .345 | .312 |
| April | 852 | 234 | 51 | 6 | 19 | 106 | 79 | 124 | .275 | .415 | .337 |
| May | 893 | 243 | 37 | 8 | 21 | 105 | 84 | 116 | .272 | .402 | .337 |
| June | 909 | 238 | 31 | 3 | 15 | 101 | 87 | 134 | .262 | .352 | .325 |
| July | 848 | 215 | 29 | 2 | 21 | 107 | 112 | 135 | .254 | .367 | .338 |
| August | 969 | 242 | 39 | 2 | 22 | 113 | 93 | 169 | .250 | .362 | .318 |
| Sept./Oct. | 945 | 242 | 33 | 4 | 29 | 129 | 107 | 177 | .256 | .392 | .332 |
| Leading Off Inn. | 1304 | 349 | 66 | 5 | 31 | 31 | 127 | 188 | .268 | .397 | .335 |
| Runners On | 2388 | 637 | 102 | 12 | 56 | 590 | 249 | 387 | .267 | .390 | .332 |
| Runners/Scor. Pos. | 1325 | 351 | 50 | 7 | 28 | 506 | 174 | 229 | .265 | .377 | .340 |
| Runners On/2 Out | 997 | 246 | 32 | 6 | 21 | 203 | 115 | 186 | .247 | .354 | .326 |
| Scor. Pos./2 Out | 614 | 140 | 17 | 4 | 8 | 166 | 81 | 116 | .228 | .308 | .319 |
| Late Inning Pressure | 671 | 155 | 19 | 4 | 14 | 72 | 75 | 144 | .231 | .334 | .307 |
| Leading Off | 170 | 42 | 6 | 2 | 5 | 5 | 22 | 40 | .247 | .394 | .333 |
| Runners On | 288 | 73 | 8 | 2 | 8 | 66 | 28 | 59 | .253 | .378 | .315 |
| Runners/Scor. Pos. | 158 | 43 | 4 | 1 | 4 | 57 | 19 | 29 | .272 | .386 | .341 |

| RUNS BATTED IN | From 1B | From 2B | From 3B | Scoring Position |
|---|---|---|---|---|
| Totals | 83/1764 | 192/1016 | 259/585 | 451/1601 |
| Percentage | 5% | 19% | 44% | 28% |
| Driving In Runners from 3B with Less than Two Out: | | | 197/329 | 60% |

Love to face: John Cerutti (6–0)
Hate to face: Charlie Hough (6–15)
Only A.L. club with a winning record (16–10) in day games played on the road. (Home team won 59 percent of A.L. day games in 1989.) . . .Only A.L. club that was winless (0–32) in road games in which they trailed after seven innings. . . . Cleanup hitters batted only .234, 32 points lower than the league average for that spot in the order. . . . Scored 32 runs in the World Series, 2d-highest total ever in a four-game series. The Yanks scored 37 runs in their 1932 sweep of the Cubs. . . . Third team to sweep World Series while never trailing in any game. Others: 1963 Dodgers and 1966 Orioles. . . . Batting average on artificial turf was the lowest in the majors last season.

## Seattle Mariners

| | AB | H | 2B | 3B | HR | RBI | BB | SO | BA | SA | OBA |
|---|---|---|---|---|---|---|---|---|---|---|---|
| Season | 5512 | 1417 | 237 | 29 | 134 | 655 | 489 | 838 | .257 | .384 | .320 |
| vs. Left-Handers | 1558 | 403 | 75 | 9 | 38 | 190 | 116 | 211 | .259 | .392 | .314 |
| vs. Right-Handers | 3954 | 1014 | 162 | 20 | 96 | 465 | 373 | 627 | .256 | .380 | .322 |
| Home | 2714 | 713 | 128 | 15 | 68 | 331 | 226 | 399 | .263 | .396 | .322 |
| Road | 2798 | 704 | 109 | 14 | 66 | 324 | 263 | 439 | .252 | .371 | .318 |
| Grass | 2135 | 537 | 70 | 11 | 55 | 249 | 202 | 326 | .252 | .372 | .318 |
| Artificial Turf | 3377 | 880 | 167 | 18 | 79 | 406 | 287 | 512 | .261 | .391 | .321 |
| April | 854 | 224 | 35 | 5 | 19 | 116 | 77 | 96 | .262 | .382 | .324 |
| May | 919 | 250 | 40 | 5 | 22 | 110 | 67 | 148 | .272 | .398 | .323 |
| June | 906 | 242 | 38 | 4 | 25 | 117 | 82 | 149 | .267 | .401 | .329 |
| July | 888 | 241 | 37 | 7 | 20 | 125 | 95 | 119 | .271 | .396 | .345 |
| August | 975 | 225 | 36 | 1 | 29 | 91 | 77 | 184 | .231 | .359 | .290 |
| Sept./Oct. | 970 | 235 | 51 | 7 | 19 | 96 | 91 | 142 | .242 | .368 | .312 |
| Leading Off Inn. | 1332 | 329 | 43 | 9 | 31 | 31 | 103 | 186 | .247 | .363 | .305 |
| Runners On | 2368 | 636 | 118 | 9 | 52 | 573 | 219 | 379 | .269 | .392 | .329 |
| Runners/Scor. Pos. | 1299 | 335 | 62 | 8 | 25 | 493 | 150 | 230 | .258 | .376 | .328 |
| Runners On/2 Out | 990 | 227 | 43 | 1 | 19 | 208 | 113 | 179 | .229 | .332 | .313 |
| Scor. Pos./2 Out | 609 | 140 | 27 | 1 | 10 | 178 | 83 | 115 | .230 | .327 | .326 |
| Late Inning Pressure | 790 | 190 | 23 | 3 | 25 | 85 | 61 | 181 | .241 | .372 | .299 |
| Leading Off | 189 | 49 | 3 | 0 | 6 | 6 | 22 | 30 | .259 | .370 | .346 |
| Runners On | 341 | 79 | 13 | 1 | 8 | 68 | 20 | 86 | .232 | .346 | .276 |
| Runners/Scor. Pos. | 167 | 40 | 6 | 1 | 4 | 58 | 17 | 41 | .240 | .359 | .307 |

| RUNS BATTED IN | From 1B | From 2B | From 3B | Scoring Position |
|---|---|---|---|---|
| Totals | 93/1762 | 185/1008 | 243/585 | 428/1593 |
| Percentage | 5% | 18% | 42% | 27% |
| Driving In Runners from 3B with Less than Two Out: | | | 175/311 | 56% |

Love to face: Bill Wegman (6–1)
Hate to face: Dave Stewart (2–13)
Rookie batters combined for major league–leading totals in at-bats (1545), runs (193), hits (380), doubles (61), home runs (36), RBI (164), walks (144), strikeouts (267), and stolen bases (26). . . . Hit four extra-inning home runs, tying Pirates and Giants for major league lead. . . Had 19 home runs and 78 RBI from the second spot in the batting order, both league-high figures. . . . Had four rookies in their opening-day lineup last season: Omar Vizquel, Edgar Martinez, Greg Briley, and Ken Griffey, Jr. Last clubs with at least four: Oakland (Tony Armas, Wayne Gross, Rob Picciolo, Rodney Scott, Mark Williams) and Toronto (Doug Ault, Steve Bowling, Rick Aldo Cerone, John Scott, Gary Woods) in 1977.

## Texas Rangers

| | AB | H | 2B | 3B | HR | RBI | BB | SO | BA | SA | OBA |
|---|---|---|---|---|---|---|---|---|---|---|---|
| Season | 5458 | 1433 | 260 | 46 | 122 | 656 | 503 | 989 | .263 | .394 | .326 |
| vs. Left-Handers | 1621 | 431 | 97 | 12 | 42 | 193 | 137 | 291 | .266 | .418 | .323 |
| vs. Right-Handers | 3837 | 1002 | 163 | 34 | 80 | 463 | 366 | 698 | .261 | .384 | .328 |
| Home | 2643 | 694 | 109 | 26 | 75 | 330 | 268 | 487 | .263 | .409 | .331 |
| Road | 2815 | 739 | 151 | 20 | 47 | 326 | 235 | 502 | .263 | .380 | .322 |
| Grass | 4594 | 1210 | 209 | 39 | 111 | 564 | 434 | 836 | .263 | .398 | .329 |
| Artificial Turf | 864 | 223 | 51 | 7 | 11 | 92 | 69 | 153 | .258 | .372 | .315 |
| April | 741 | 202 | 36 | 7 | 17 | 107 | 84 | 144 | .273 | .409 | .347 |
| May | 943 | 255 | 51 | 8 | 17 | 109 | 71 | 149 | .270 | .396 | .324 |
| June | 973 | 262 | 52 | 7 | 19 | 125 | 79 | 161 | .269 | .396 | .327 |
| July | 824 | 202 | 33 | 6 | 21 | 99 | 71 | 155 | .245 | .376 | .308 |
| August | 941 | 238 | 39 | 9 | 23 | 94 | 86 | 186 | .253 | .387 | .315 |
| Sept./Oct. | 1036 | 274 | 49 | 9 | 25 | 122 | 112 | 194 | .264 | .402 | .338 |
| Leading Off Inn. | 1314 | 334 | 65 | 16 | 37 | 37 | 114 | 228 | .254 | .412 | .317 |
| Runners On | 2375 | 623 | 118 | 19 | 48 | 582 | 233 | 440 | .262 | .389 | .328 |
| Runners/Scor. Pos. | 1350 | 358 | 66 | 10 | 26 | 507 | 153 | 265 | .265 | .387 | .336 |
| Runners On/2 Out | 1018 | 251 | 51 | 4 | 16 | 220 | 109 | 192 | .247 | .352 | .324 |
| Scor. Pos./2 Out | 634 | 155 | 28 | 2 | 9 | 193 | 80 | 123 | .244 | .338 | .334 |
| Late Inning Pressure | 689 | 168 | 35 | 2 | 10 | 73 | 65 | 141 | .244 | .344 | .306 |
| Leading Off | 169 | 35 | 4 | 1 | 2 | 2 | 16 | 37 | .207 | .278 | .276 |
| Runners On | 300 | 71 | 18 | 0 | 7 | 70 | 29 | 57 | .237 | .367 | .297 |
| Runners/Scor. Pos. | 169 | 36 | 9 | 0 | 4 | 59 | 17 | 37 | .213 | .337 | .273 |

| RUNS BATTED IN | From 1B | From 2B | From 3B | Scoring Position |
|---|---|---|---|---|
| Totals | 84/1665 | 211/1038 | 239/567 | 450/1605 |
| Percentage | 5% | 20% | 42% | 28% |
| Driving In Runners from 3B with Less than Two Out: | | | 170/311 | 55% |

Love to face: Scott Bailes (6–0)
Hate to face: Storm Davis (3–12)
Became only the third club in last 15 years to lead A.L. in triples while playing their home games on a grass field. The others: Cleveland (1986) and Minnesota (1981). . . . Used pinch hitters 226 times, most in A.L. . . . Six homers by designated hitters were the fewest of any A.L. club. Used 19 starting DHs, a league-high total. . . . Had a record of 17–7 in home games vs. left-handed starters, 11–14 vs. southpaw starters on the road. . . . Starting catchers batted .217, lowest in A.L. . . . Starting first basemen combined for only nine home runs, fewest in A.L. . . . No opposing pitcher threw a complete-game shutout. . . . Had fewest runs scored in majors (83) from first spot in batting order.

## American League

| | AB | H | 2B | 3B | HR | RBI | BB | SO | BA | SA | OBA |
|---|---|---|---|---|---|---|---|---|---|---|---|
| Season | 77004 | 20078 | 3404 | 457 | 1718 | 9124 | 7277 | 12296 | .261 | .384 | .326 |
| vs. Left-Handers | 23714 | 6319 | 1128 | 140 | 516 | 2827 | 2166 | 3596 | .266 | .391 | .328 |
| vs. Right-Handers | 53290 | 13759 | 2276 | 317 | 1202 | 6297 | 5111 | 8700 | .258 | .380 | .325 |
| Home | 37426 | 9818 | 1657 | 245 | 854 | 4566 | 3707 | 5743 | .262 | .388 | .330 |
| Road | 39578 | 10260 | 1747 | 212 | 864 | 4558 | 3570 | 6553 | .259 | .380 | .322 |
| Grass | 54950 | 14298 | 2318 | 302 | 1277 | 6497 | 5276 | 8875 | .260 | .383 | .326 |
| Artificial Turf | 22054 | 5780 | 1086 | 155 | 441 | 2627 | 2001 | 3421 | .262 | .385 | .325 |
| April | 11152 | 2848 | 508 | 61 | 244 | 1322 | 1100 | 1771 | .255 | .378 | .324 |
| May | 12651 | 3344 | 578 | 84 | 287 | 1536 | 1230 | 1931 | .264 | .391 | .330 |
| June | 13188 | 3543 | 563 | 64 | 295 | 1603 | 1217 | 1935 | .269 | .388 | .331 |
| July | 12490 | 3285 | 543 | 71 | 298 | 1539 | 1214 | 2002 | .263 | .389 | .330 |
| August | 14075 | 3620 | 624 | 101 | 312 | 1603 | 1239 | 2368 | .257 | .382 | .319 |
| Sept./Oct. | 13448 | 3438 | 588 | 76 | 282 | 1521 | 1277 | 2289 | .256 | .374 | .322 |
| Leading Off Inn. | 18630 | 4882 | 880 | 118 | 447 | 447 | 1516 | 2829 | .262 | .394 | .321 |
| Runners On | 33543 | 8999 | 1491 | 194 | 722 | 8128 | 3557 | 5248 | .268 | .389 | .336 |
| Runners/Scor. Pos. | 19243 | 5051 | 838 | 117 | 382 | 7120 | 2499 | 3324 | .262 | .378 | .340 |
| Runners On/2 Out | 14032 | 3407 | 537 | 72 | 273 | 2995 | 1682 | 2413 | .243 | .350 | .327 |
| Scor. Pos./2 Out | 8961 | 2081 | 335 | 44 | 157 | 2626 | 1273 | 1652 | .232 | .332 | .331 |
| Late Inning Pressure | 10837 | 2681 | 438 | 44 | 219 | 1171 | 1108 | 2199 | .247 | .357 | .318 |
| Leading Off | 2721 | 677 | 101 | 13 | 63 | 63 | 257 | 501 | .249 | .365 | .316 |
| Runners On | 4617 | 1175 | 193 | 17 | 95 | 1047 | 565 | 900 | .254 | .365 | .333 |
| Runners/Scor. Pos. | 2628 | 665 | 110 | 9 | 53 | 923 | 422 | 550 | .253 | .362 | .349 |

| RUNS BATTED IN | From 1B | From 2B | From 3B | Scoring Position |
|---|---|---|---|---|
| Percentage | 5% | 18% | 42% | 27% |
| Driving In Runners from 3B with Less than Two Out: | | | 2564/4531 | 57% |

## Toronto Blue Jays

| | AB | H | 2B | 3B | HR | RBI | BB | SO | BA | SA | OBA |
|---|---|---|---|---|---|---|---|---|---|---|---|
| Season | 5581 | 1449 | 265 | 40 | 142 | 689 | 521 | 923 | .260 | .398 | .323 |
| vs. Left-Handers | 1798 | 462 | 71 | 12 | 36 | 228 | 160 | 339 | .257 | .370 | .317 |
| vs. Right-Handers | 3783 | 987 | 194 | 28 | 106 | 461 | 361 | 584 | .261 | .411 | .326 |
| Home | 2653 | 662 | 129 | 21 | 64 | 311 | 280 | 405 | .250 | .386 | .323 |
| Road | 2928 | 787 | 136 | 19 | 78 | 378 | 241 | 518 | .269 | .408 | .324 |
| Grass | 2324 | 646 | 106 | 14 | 67 | 318 | 207 | 400 | .278 | .422 | .336 |
| Artificial Turf | 3257 | 803 | 159 | 26 | 75 | 371 | 314 | 523 | .247 | .380 | .315 |
| April | 847 | 211 | 35 | 6 | 21 | 98 | 82 | 170 | .249 | .379 | .318 |
| May | 877 | 224 | 44 | 7 | 24 | 121 | 78 | 139 | .255 | .404 | .316 |
| June | 989 | 286 | 45 | 3 | 22 | 132 | 83 | 140 | .289 | .407 | .344 |
| July | 908 | 231 | 49 | 5 | 26 | 101 | 84 | 158 | .254 | .405 | .318 |
| August | 955 | 242 | 51 | 12 | 33 | 128 | 84 | 158 | .253 | .436 | .315 |
| Sept./Oct. | 1005 | 255 | 41 | 7 | 16 | 109 | 110 | 158 | .254 | .356 | .327 |
| Leading Off Inn. | 1353 | 378 | 72 | 15 | 35 | 35 | 110 | 212 | .279 | .432 | .335 |
| Runners On | 2393 | 622 | 101 | 14 | 64 | 611 | 262 | 394 | .260 | .394 | .331 |
| Runners/Scor. Pos. | 1427 | 373 | 69 | 7 | 36 | 532 | 181 | 261 | .261 | .395 | .338 |
| Runners On/2 Out | 969 | 222 | 31 | 3 | 22 | 207 | 109 | 173 | .229 | .335 | .311 |
| Scor. Pos./2 Out | 632 | 144 | 23 | 1 | 16 | 187 | 83 | 122 | .228 | .343 | .322 |
| Late Inning Pressure | 839 | 218 | 38 | 7 | 17 | 101 | 89 | 163 | .260 | .383 | .333 |
| Leading Off | 218 | 64 | 9 | 5 | 5 | 5 | 18 | 38 | .294 | .450 | .350 |
| Runners On | 358 | 89 | 16 | 1 | 7 | 91 | 48 | 70 | .249 | .358 | .338 |
| Runners/Scor. Pos. | 220 | 57 | 13 | 1 | 6 | 86 | 32 | 49 | .259 | .409 | .349 |

| RUNS BATTED IN | From 1B | From 2B | From 3B | Scoring Position |
|---|---|---|---|---|
| Totals | 82/1673 | 193/1098 | 272/620 | 465/1718 |
| Percentage | 5% | 18% | 44% | 27% |
| Driving In Runners from 3B with Less than Two Out: | | | 201/345 | 58% |

Love to face: Mike Smithson (11–2)
Hate to face: Bud Black (4–10)
Eight different players had a hand in major league–leading total of 16 ninth-inning home runs. . . . Batted .353 (42-for-119) with bases loaded, best in majors. . . . Designated hitters batted .216, lowest in league. . . . Had a 5–13 record in road games played on artificial surfaces. . . . Won all seven extra-inning games after the All-Star break. (And you know what losing any two of them would have meant!) . . .Have won 15 consecutive games at Fenway Park. . . . Ninth spot in the batting order drove in 72 runs last season, most in the A.L. And, of course, in the majors. . . . Highest-scoring position in batting order was fifth slot (101 runs). High scorer on every other A.L. team was among first four slots.

# National League

## Roberto Alomar

Bats Left and Right

| San Diego Padres | AB | H | 2B | 3B | HR | RBI | BB | SO | BA | SA | OBA |
|---|---|---|---|---|---|---|---|---|---|---|---|
| Season | 623 | 184 | 27 | 1 | 7 | 56 | 53 | 76 | .295 | .376 | .347 |
| vs. Left-Handers | 195 | 50 | 10 | 0 | 4 | 20 | 17 | 28 | .256 | .369 | .316 |
| vs. Right-Handers | 428 | 134 | 17 | 1 | 3 | 36 | 36 | 48 | .313 | .379 | .362 |
| Home | 286 | 94 | 9 | 1 | 3 | 34 | 33 | 28 | .329 | .399 | .394 |
| Road | 337 | 90 | 18 | 0 | 4 | 22 | 20 | 48 | .267 | .356 | .306 |
| Grass | 450 | 135 | 16 | 1 | 5 | 46 | 42 | 48 | .300 | .373 | .357 |
| Artificial Turf | 173 | 49 | 11 | 0 | 2 | 10 | 11 | 28 | .283 | .382 | .323 |
| April | 104 | 24 | 3 | 0 | 0 | 4 | 7 | 8 | .231 | .260 | .277 |
| May | 110 | 34 | 3 | 0 | 1 | 7 | 9 | 11 | .309 | .364 | .361 |
| June | 103 | 23 | 3 | 0 | 1 | 9 | 11 | 14 | .223 | .282 | .293 |
| July | 89 | 29 | 7 | 0 | 0 | 6 | 9 | 10 | .326 | .404 | .376 |
| August | 109 | 35 | 5 | 1 | 2 | 14 | 9 | 21 | .321 | .440 | .375 |
| Sept./Oct. | 108 | 39 | 6 | 0 | 3 | 16 | 8 | 12 | .361 | .500 | .402 |
| Leading Off Inn. | 155 | 49 | 12 | 0 | 1 | 1 | 14 | 19 | .316 | .413 | .376 |
| Runners On | 247 | 73 | 9 | 1 | 2 | 51 | 20 | 29 | .296 | .364 | .338 |
| Runners/Scor. Pos. | 128 | 32 | 4 | 0 | 0 | 44 | 11 | 17 | .250 | .281 | .293 |
| Runners On/2 Out | 99 | 21 | 4 | 0 | 1 | 17 | 12 | 13 | .212 | .283 | .297 |
| Scor. Pos./2 Out | 64 | 14 | 3 | 0 | 0 | 14 | 9 | 9 | .219 | .266 | .315 |
| Late Inning Pressure | 80 | 27 | 2 | 0 | 0 | 6 | 10 | 13 | .338 | .363 | .411 |
| Leading Off | 21 | 10 | 0 | 0 | 0 | 0 | 2 | 3 | .476 | .476 | .522 |
| Runners On | 39 | 12 | 2 | 0 | 0 | 6 | 7 | 5 | .308 | .359 | .413 |
| Runners/Scor. Pos. | 19 | 5 | 1 | 0 | 0 | 5 | 4 | 4 | .263 | .316 | .391 |

| RUNS BATTED IN | From 1B | From 2B | From 3B | Scoring Position |
|---|---|---|---|---|
| Totals | 6/164 | 20/104 | 23/55 | 43/159 |
| Percentage | 4% | 19% | 42% | 27% |
| Driving In Runners from 3B with Less than Two Out: | | | 19/31 | 61% |

**Loves to face:** Mike Scott (.389, 7-for-18, 1 HR)
**Hates to face:** Scott Garrelts (.133, 2-for-15)

Committed 28 errors, highest total by a second baseman in majors in past five years. Made 11 of those errors (including 3 in one game) by the end of April. . . . But turnabout is fair play: he reached base on infielders' errors 15 times, the most by any player in majors last season. . . . First San Diego player since Dave Campbell in 1970 to lead N.L. in games at second base (157); he's odds on to become first San Diego second baseman since Juan Bonilla (1981–1983) to start in two consecutive opening-day games. . . . Youngest player on any N.L. opening-day roster last season. . . . Career average of .296 vs. fly-ball pitchers, .266 vs. ground-ballers. . . . Set Padres' record for second baseman with 56 RBI in a season.

## Kevin Bass

Bats Left and Right

| Houston Astros | AB | H | 2B | 3B | HR | RBI | BB | SO | BA | SA | OBA |
|---|---|---|---|---|---|---|---|---|---|---|---|
| Season | 313 | 94 | 19 | 4 | 5 | 44 | 29 | 44 | .300 | .435 | .357 |
| vs. Left-Handers | 83 | 22 | 8 | 0 | 2 | 14 | 7 | 17 | .265 | .434 | .315 |
| vs. Right-Handers | 230 | 72 | 11 | 4 | 3 | 30 | 22 | 27 | .313 | .435 | .373 |
| Home | 168 | 50 | 12 | 1 | 2 | 26 | 13 | 22 | .298 | .417 | .346 |
| Road | 145 | 44 | 7 | 3 | 3 | 18 | 16 | 22 | .303 | .455 | .370 |
| Grass | 87 | 23 | 3 | 1 | 2 | 9 | 11 | 16 | .264 | .391 | .347 |
| Artificial Turf | 226 | 71 | 16 | 3 | 3 | 35 | 18 | 28 | .314 | .451 | .361 |
| April | 84 | 20 | 6 | 1 | 0 | 9 | 12 | 12 | .238 | .333 | .330 |
| May | 78 | 27 | 5 | 2 | 1 | 12 | 7 | 4 | .346 | .500 | .391 |
| June | 0 | 0 | 0 | 0 | 0 | 0 | 0 | 0 | — | — | — |
| July | 0 | 0 | 0 | 0 | 0 | 0 | 0 | 0 | — | — | — |
| August | 74 | 24 | 5 | 0 | 3 | 13 | 5 | 11 | .324 | .514 | .370 |
| Sept./Oct. | 77 | 23 | 3 | 1 | 1 | 10 | 5 | 17 | .299 | .403 | .341 |
| Leading Off Inn. | 54 | 14 | 2 | 0 | 1 | 1 | 7 | 6 | .259 | .352 | .344 |
| Runners On | 129 | 44 | 10 | 3 | 2 | 41 | 19 | 18 | .341 | .512 | .414 |
| Runners/Scor. Pos. | 74 | 24 | 6 | 2 | 2 | 37 | 15 | 11 | .324 | .541 | .419 |
| Runners On/2 Out | 45 | 13 | 1 | 1 | 1 | 13 | 8 | 8 | .289 | .422 | .396 |
| Scor. Pos./2 Out | 32 | 9 | 1 | 0 | 1 | 12 | 8 | 6 | .281 | .406 | .425 |
| Late Inning Pressure | 49 | 11 | 1 | 0 | 2 | 11 | 9 | 8 | .224 | .367 | .345 |
| Leading Off | 11 | 2 | 0 | 0 | 0 | 0 | 3 | 1 | .182 | .182 | .357 |
| Runners On | 20 | 6 | 1 | 0 | 2 | 11 | 5 | 5 | .300 | .650 | .440 |
| Runners/Scor. Pos. | 14 | 5 | 1 | 0 | 2 | 11 | 4 | 2 | .357 | .857 | .500 |

| RUNS BATTED IN | From 1B | From 2B | From 3B | Scoring Position |
|---|---|---|---|---|
| Totals | 7/85 | 16/62 | 16/35 | 32/97 |
| Percentage | 8% | 26% | 46% | 33% |
| Driving In Runners from 3B with Less than Two Out: | | | 12/23 | 52% |

**Loves to face:** Neal Heaton (.471, 8-for-17, 3 HR)
**Hates to face:** Bill Landrum (0-for-9)

Third player in N.L. history to hit grand slams from both sides of plate in one season. Others: George Davis (1896 Giants), and Ted Simmons (1975 Cardinals). It's been done five times in A.L.: thrice by Eddie Murray, once each by Ken Singleton and Bob Stinson. . . . One of four players to switch-hit home runs in same game last season. . . . Has 68 career plate appearances with the bases loaded, but has never drawn a walk. . . . Grounded into only two double plays in 65 opportunities, lowest rate on Astros. . . . Has batted over .300 with runners in scoring position in three of the last four seasons. . . . Signed as free agent by Giants, whose starting right fielders batted only .224 last season, lowest in N.L.

## Jay Bell

Bats Right

| Pittsburgh Pirates | AB | H | 2B | 3B | HR | RBI | BB | SO | BA | SA | OBA |
|---|---|---|---|---|---|---|---|---|---|---|---|
| Season | 271 | 70 | 13 | 3 | 2 | 27 | 19 | 47 | .258 | .351 | .307 |
| vs. Left-Handers | 107 | 29 | 4 | 1 | 1 | 10 | 10 | 20 | .271 | .355 | .331 |
| vs. Right-Handers | 164 | 41 | 9 | 2 | 1 | 17 | 9 | 27 | .250 | .348 | .291 |
| Home | 141 | 36 | 9 | 0 | 1 | 11 | 10 | 29 | .255 | .340 | .303 |
| Road | 130 | 34 | 4 | 3 | 1 | 16 | 9 | 18 | .262 | .362 | .312 |
| Grass | 45 | 11 | 0 | 3 | 0 | 6 | 1 | 9 | .244 | .378 | .261 |
| Artificial Turf | 226 | 59 | 13 | 0 | 2 | 21 | 18 | 38 | .261 | .345 | .316 |
| April | 20 | 1 | 0 | 0 | 0 | 0 | 1 | 5 | .050 | .050 | .095 |
| May | 0 | 0 | 0 | 0 | 0 | 0 | 0 | 0 | — | — | — |
| June | 0 | 0 | 0 | 0 | 0 | 0 | 0 | 0 | — | — | — |
| July | 34 | 5 | 2 | 1 | 0 | 5 | 0 | 4 | .147 | .265 | .147 |
| August | 98 | 27 | 4 | 1 | 1 | 7 | 6 | 20 | .276 | .367 | .324 |
| Sept./Oct. | 119 | 37 | 7 | 1 | 1 | 15 | 12 | 18 | .311 | .412 | .368 |
| Leading Off Inn. | 47 | 6 | 1 | 0 | 0 | 0 | 7 | 15 | .128 | .149 | .241 |
| Runners On | 108 | 33 | 8 | 3 | 0 | 25 | 4 | 15 | .306 | .435 | .325 |
| Runners/Scor. Pos. | 53 | 19 | 4 | 3 | 0 | 23 | 1 | 9 | .358 | .547 | .357 |
| Runners On/2 Out | 39 | 13 | 4 | 3 | 0 | 12 | 2 | 9 | .333 | .590 | .366 |
| Scor. Pos./2 Out | 29 | 9 | 2 | 3 | 0 | 11 | 1 | 7 | .310 | .586 | .333 |
| Late Inning Pressure | 40 | 8 | 2 | 2 | 0 | 7 | 1 | 12 | .200 | .350 | .233 |
| Leading Off | 5 | 1 | 1 | 0 | 0 | 0 | 1 | 3 | .200 | .400 | .333 |
| Runners On | 18 | 5 | 1 | 2 | 0 | 7 | 0 | 3 | .278 | .556 | .263 |
| Runners/Scor. Pos. | 11 | 4 | 1 | 2 | 0 | 7 | 0 | 3 | .364 | .818 | .333 |

| RUNS BATTED IN | From 1B | From 2B | From 3B | Scoring Position |
|---|---|---|---|---|
| Totals | 5/78 | 10/40 | 10/24 | 20/64 |
| Percentage | 6% | 25% | 42% | 31% |
| Driving In Runners from 3B with Less than Two Out: | | | 6/9 | 67% |

**Loves to face:** Mike Bielecki (.833, 5-for-6)
**Hates to face:** Mike Morgan (0-for-10)

Pirates' regular shortstop starting on July 23; for season, he played 44 percent of innings, Rey Quinones played 38 percent, with Rafael Belliard there the rest of the time (O.K., Jeff King played one inning.) Club allowed 3.85 runs per nine innings with Bell, 4.24 with Belliard, and 4.36 with Quinones. . . . Batted .275 after his recall in July, and .356 in his last 20 games. . . . Batted .309 in 48 games from 2d spot in batting order. . . . Batted .361 in first inning, .239 in subsequent at-bats. . . . Career breakdown: .270 with runners on base, .214 with bases empty; .299 vs. left-handers, .211 vs. right-handers; .169 leading off innings. . . . Slow start was nothing new to Bell, who hit .143 for Indians in April 1988.

## Todd Benzinger

Bats Left and Right

| Cincinnati Reds | AB | H | 2B | 3B | HR | RBI | BB | SO | BA | SA | OBA |
|---|---|---|---|---|---|---|---|---|---|---|---|
| Season | 628 | 154 | 28 | 3 | 17 | 76 | 44 | 120 | .245 | .381 | .293 |
| vs. Left-Handers | 231 | 56 | 8 | 1 | 7 | 23 | 15 | 30 | .242 | .377 | .283 |
| vs. Right-Handers | 397 | 98 | 20 | 2 | 10 | 53 | 29 | 90 | .247 | .383 | .299 |
| Home | 306 | 85 | 19 | 3 | 6 | 36 | 23 | 51 | .278 | .418 | .327 |
| Road | 322 | 69 | 9 | 0 | 11 | 40 | 21 | 69 | .214 | .345 | .261 |
| Grass | 196 | 48 | 7 | 0 | 9 | 25 | 16 | 44 | .245 | .418 | .302 |
| Artificial Turf | 432 | 106 | 21 | 3 | 8 | 51 | 28 | 76 | .245 | .363 | .289 |
| April | 80 | 18 | 2 | 1 | 0 | 6 | 4 | 12 | .225 | .275 | .259 |
| May | 99 | 24 | 3 | 0 | 3 | 17 | 12 | 19 | .242 | .364 | .313 |
| June | 114 | 30 | 8 | 0 | 5 | 16 | 9 | 26 | .263 | .465 | .320 |
| July | 100 | 23 | 3 | 0 | 3 | 6 | 5 | 16 | .230 | .350 | .264 |
| August | 118 | 29 | 6 | 2 | 3 | 18 | 5 | 25 | .246 | .407 | .282 |
| Sept./Oct. | 117 | 30 | 6 | 0 | 3 | 13 | 9 | 22 | .256 | .385 | .307 |
| Leading Off Inn. | 133 | 34 | 7 | 0 | 2 | 2 | 11 | 22 | .256 | .353 | .313 |
| Runners On | 264 | 55 | 10 | 2 | 7 | 66 | 24 | 61 | .208 | .341 | .272 |
| Runners/Scor. Pos. | 166 | 33 | 9 | 1 | 6 | 63 | 22 | 46 | .199 | .373 | .288 |
| Runners On/2 Out | 134 | 23 | 2 | 1 | 1 | 14 | 12 | 33 | .172 | .224 | .250 |
| Scor. Pos./2 Out | 90 | 12 | 2 | 0 | 1 | 13 | 12 | 29 | .133 | .189 | .250 |
| Late Inning Pressure | 88 | 14 | 2 | 0 | 2 | 8 | 12 | 14 | .159 | .250 | .257 |
| Leading Off | 25 | 4 | 1 | 0 | 0 | 0 | 3 | 2 | .160 | .200 | .250 |
| Runners On | 31 | 5 | 0 | 0 | 0 | 6 | 8 | 7 | .161 | .161 | .325 |
| Runners/Scor. Pos. | 21 | 4 | 0 | 0 | 0 | 6 | 8 | 6 | .190 | .190 | .400 |

| RUNS BATTED IN | From 1B | From 2B | From 3B | Scoring Position |
|---|---|---|---|---|
| Totals | 8/181 | 25/125 | 26/76 | 51/201 |
| Percentage | 4% | 20% | 34% | 25% |
| Driving In Runners from 3B with Less than Two Out: | | | 24/39 | 62% |

**Loves to face:** Walt Terrell (.455, 5-for-11, 4 HR)
**Hates to face:** Frank Viola (0-for-10)

Alright, who hit the long Vegas odds on this guy leading N.L. in at-bats last year? He started a majority of his games from the 5th spot or lower, becoming first non-leadoff hitter to do it since Bill Buckner in 1982. . . . His 158 games at first base tied Reds' record set not by Rose, Perez, May, Klu, or McCormick, but by Dick Hoblitzell in 1911. . . . Had lowest rate of assists per nine innings (0.46) among the 25 first basemen in majors who played at least 500 innings last season. . . . Reached base on 14 infield errors last season, second most in majors. . . . Career average of .275 with bases empty, but only .229 with runners on base; difference of 46 points is 2d largest by anyone over last 10 years (see Joe Orsulak).

## Damon Berryhill

Bats Left and Right

| Chicago Cubs | AB | H | 2B | 3B | HR | RBI | BB | SO | BA | SA | OBA |
|---|---|---|---|---|---|---|---|---|---|---|---|
| Season | 334 | 86 | 13 | 0 | 5 | 41 | 16 | 54 | .257 | .341 | .291 |
| vs. Left-Handers | 97 | 33 | 5 | 0 | 3 | 13 | 4 | 8 | .340 | .485 | .359 |
| vs. Right-Handers | 237 | 53 | 8 | 0 | 2 | 28 | 12 | 46 | .224 | .283 | .264 |
| Home | 148 | 46 | 9 | 0 | 2 | 22 | 8 | 27 | .311 | .412 | .346 |
| Road | 186 | 40 | 4 | 0 | 3 | 19 | 8 | 27 | .215 | .285 | .247 |
| Grass | 220 | 57 | 10 | 0 | 3 | 32 | 10 | 34 | .259 | .345 | .291 |
| Artificial Turf | 114 | 29 | 3 | 0 | 2 | 9 | 6 | 20 | .254 | .333 | .293 |
| April | 0 | 0 | 0 | 0 | 0 | 0 | 0 | 0 | — | — | — |
| May | 96 | 29 | 7 | 0 | 1 | 14 | 3 | 12 | .302 | .406 | .317 |
| June | 90 | 21 | 4 | 0 | 0 | 13 | 5 | 20 | .233 | .278 | .276 |
| July | 91 | 19 | 1 | 0 | 3 | 11 | 2 | 14 | .209 | .319 | .226 |
| August | 57 | 17 | 1 | 0 | 1 | 3 | 6 | 8 | .298 | .368 | .369 |
| Sept./Oct. | 0 | 0 | 0 | 0 | 0 | 0 | 0 | 0 | — | — | — |
| Leading Off Inn. | 66 | 17 | 6 | 0 | 2 | 2 | 2 | 12 | .258 | .439 | .290 |
| Runners On | 146 | 41 | 4 | 0 | 1 | 37 | 9 | 21 | .281 | .329 | .317 |
| Runners/Scor. Pos. | 92 | 30 | 3 | 0 | 0 | 34 | 7 | 16 | .326 | .359 | .362 |
| Runners On/2 Out | 67 | 14 | 1 | 0 | 1 | 13 | 2 | 9 | .209 | .269 | .243 |
| Scor. Pos./2 Out | 50 | 12 | 1 | 0 | 0 | 11 | 2 | 8 | .240 | .260 | .283 |
| Late Inning Pressure | 49 | 12 | 2 | 0 | 1 | 4 | 2 | 8 | .245 | .347 | .269 |
| Leading Off | 12 | 3 | 1 | 0 | 1 | 1 | 0 | 3 | .250 | .583 | .250 |
| Runners On | 20 | 6 | 0 | 0 | 0 | 3 | 2 | 2 | .300 | .300 | .348 |
| Runners/Scor. Pos. | 12 | 3 | 0 | 0 | 0 | 3 | 2 | 2 | .250 | .250 | .333 |

| RUNS BATTED IN | From 1B | From 2B | From 3B | Scoring Position |
|---|---|---|---|---|
| Totals | 2/116 | 16/70 | 18/44 | 34/114 |
| Percentage | 2% | 23% | 41% | 30% |
| Driving In Runners from 3B with Less than Two Out: | | | 13/21 | 62% |

Loves to face: Rick Mahler (.500, 6-for-12)
Hates to face: Mike Morgan (0-for-7)

Cubs were 54–30 (.643) in games he started; they were 39–39 with other starting catchers. Staff had 2.88 ERA with Berryhill catching, 3.13 with Wrona, 4.45 with Girardi. . . . Opponents stole 36 bases in 65 attempts with Berryhill catching (.554), 5th-lowest rate against any catcher in majors (minimum: 25 attempts) last season. The top four: Steve Lake (.509), Rick Dempsey and Ron Karkovice (.520), John Russell (.553). . . . One of two N.L. players to bat 90 points higher in home games than on road (minimum: 100 AB each). Career averages: .292 at Wrigley Field, .217 on road. . . . Has two years and eight days of major league service and has played in 198 games, but has never played a major league game in April.

## Jeff Blauser

Bats Right

| Atlanta Braves | AB | H | 2B | 3B | HR | RBI | BB | SO | BA | SA | OBA |
|---|---|---|---|---|---|---|---|---|---|---|---|
| Season | 456 | 123 | 24 | 2 | 12 | 46 | 38 | 101 | .270 | .410 | .325 |
| vs. Left-Handers | 197 | 55 | 13 | 1 | 4 | 16 | 20 | 35 | .279 | .416 | .342 |
| vs. Right-Handers | 259 | 68 | 11 | 1 | 8 | 30 | 18 | 66 | .263 | .405 | .311 |
| Home | 229 | 57 | 12 | 1 | 5 | 19 | 19 | 53 | .249 | .376 | .308 |
| Road | 227 | 66 | 12 | 1 | 7 | 27 | 19 | 48 | .291 | .445 | .341 |
| Grass | 327 | 85 | 16 | 1 | 9 | 31 | 28 | 72 | .260 | .398 | .319 |
| Artificial Turf | 129 | 38 | 8 | 1 | 3 | 15 | 10 | 29 | .295 | .442 | .338 |
| April | 66 | 15 | 5 | 0 | 0 | 5 | 2 | 11 | .227 | .303 | .250 |
| May | 40 | 11 | 4 | 1 | 2 | 6 | 1 | 13 | .275 | .575 | .279 |
| June | 66 | 17 | 3 | 1 | 1 | 5 | 6 | 19 | .258 | .379 | .319 |
| July | 86 | 23 | 6 | 0 | 2 | 8 | 9 | 19 | .267 | .407 | .337 |
| August | 103 | 31 | 4 | 0 | 4 | 11 | 10 | 18 | .301 | .456 | .360 |
| Sept./Oct. | 95 | 26 | 2 | 0 | 3 | 11 | 10 | 21 | .274 | .389 | .346 |
| Leading Off Inn. | 119 | 32 | 9 | 1 | 5 | 5 | 6 | 18 | .269 | .487 | .304 |
| Runners On | 149 | 43 | 10 | 0 | 1 | 35 | 18 | 37 | .289 | .376 | .360 |
| Runners/Scor. Pos. | 78 | 25 | 7 | 0 | 0 | 33 | 13 | 20 | .321 | .410 | .400 |
| Runners On/2 Out | 56 | 16 | 6 | 0 | 0 | 12 | 9 | 14 | .286 | .393 | .385 |
| Scor. Pos./2 Out | 39 | 9 | 3 | 0 | 0 | 12 | 6 | 11 | .231 | .308 | .333 |
| Late Inning Pressure | 90 | 21 | 6 | 0 | 0 | 7 | 4 | 26 | .233 | .300 | .263 |
| Leading Off | 28 | 5 | 3 | 0 | 0 | 0 | 1 | 8 | .179 | .286 | .207 |
| Runners On | 27 | 10 | 2 | 0 | 0 | 7 | 1 | 7 | .370 | .444 | .379 |
| Runners/Scor. Pos. | 19 | 7 | 2 | 0 | 0 | 7 | 0 | 6 | .368 | .474 | .350 |

| RUNS BATTED IN | From 1B | From 2B | From 3B | Scoring Position |
|---|---|---|---|---|
| Totals | 2/112 | 14/60 | 18/36 | 32/96 |
| Percentage | 2% | 23% | 50% | 33% |
| Driving In Runners from 3B with Less than Two Out: | | | 12/17 | 71% |

Loves to face: Jim Deshaies (.455, 10-for-22, 2 HR)
Hates to face: Tim Belcher (0-for-8, 3 SO)

Eleven of his 12 homers were solo shots, highest percentage among players with at least 10 home runs last season. . . . Only player to start all 53 games in which the Braves faced a left-handed starter. He started only 60 of 108 games against right-handed starters. . . . Batted .318 vs. ground-ball pitchers, .231 against fly-ballers last season. . . . He and Al Newman were only players in majors with 20+ starts apiece at second, third, and short last season. . . . Batted .321 with runners in scoring position, and hit .346 in those situations against left-handed pitchers. . . . One of two N.L. players to make at least one error against every opposing team in 1989; the other one: first guy on the next page.

## Craig Biggio

Bats Right

| Houston Astros | AB | H | 2B | 3B | HR | RBI | BB | SO | BA | SA | OBA |
|---|---|---|---|---|---|---|---|---|---|---|---|
| Season | 443 | 114 | 21 | 2 | 13 | 60 | 49 | 64 | .257 | .402 | .336 |
| vs. Left-Handers | 122 | 33 | 5 | 0 | 1 | 15 | 14 | 13 | .270 | .336 | .352 |
| vs. Right-Handers | 321 | 81 | 16 | 2 | 12 | 45 | 35 | 51 | .252 | .427 | .330 |
| Home | 219 | 51 | 10 | 2 | 6 | 30 | 28 | 34 | .233 | .379 | .323 |
| Road | 224 | 63 | 11 | 0 | 7 | 30 | 21 | 30 | .281 | .424 | .349 |
| Grass | 134 | 31 | 3 | 0 | 5 | 16 | 13 | 19 | .231 | .366 | .302 |
| Artificial Turf | 309 | 83 | 18 | 2 | 8 | 44 | 36 | 45 | .269 | .417 | .350 |
| April | 29 | 6 | 1 | 0 | 0 | 3 | 4 | 6 | .207 | .241 | .324 |
| May | 74 | 22 | 6 | 1 | 1 | 11 | 5 | 10 | .297 | .446 | .346 |
| June | 86 | 22 | 2 | 0 | 4 | 13 | 7 | 13 | .256 | .419 | .312 |
| July | 72 | 24 | 3 | 0 | 2 | 11 | 6 | 10 | .333 | .458 | .398 |
| August | 89 | 21 | 4 | 1 | 2 | 7 | 18 | 11 | .236 | .371 | .358 |
| Sept./Oct. | 93 | 19 | 5 | 0 | 4 | 15 | 9 | 14 | .204 | .387 | .282 |
| Leading Off Inn. | 109 | 19 | 4 | 1 | 4 | 4 | 11 | 14 | .174 | .339 | .250 |
| Runners On | 191 | 48 | 11 | 0 | 5 | 52 | 24 | 24 | .251 | .387 | .333 |
| Runners/Scor. Pos. | 117 | 29 | 6 | 0 | 4 | 46 | 23 | 19 | .248 | .402 | .363 |
| Runners On/2 Out | 65 | 14 | 3 | 0 | 3 | 18 | 16 | 11 | .215 | .400 | .378 |
| Scor. Pos./2 Out | 45 | 10 | 2 | 0 | 3 | 17 | 16 | 8 | .222 | .467 | .435 |
| Late Inning Pressure | 73 | 25 | 7 | 1 | 3 | 16 | 7 | 8 | .342 | .589 | .407 |
| Leading Off | 13 | 5 | 1 | 1 | 0 | 0 | 0 | 3 | .385 | .615 | .385 |
| Runners On | 31 | 10 | 4 | 0 | 1 | 14 | 7 | 1 | .323 | .548 | .447 |
| Runners/Scor. Pos. | 26 | 9 | 3 | 0 | 1 | 13 | 7 | 1 | .346 | .577 | .485 |

| RUNS BATTED IN | From 1B | From 2B | From 3B | Scoring Position |
|---|---|---|---|---|
| Totals | 8/135 | 12/89 | 27/56 | 39/145 |
| Percentage | 6% | 13% | 48% | 27% |
| Driving In Runners from 3B with Less than Two Out: | | | 21/34 | 62% |

Loves to face: Steve Bedrosian (.667, 4-for-6, 1 HR)
Hates to face: Ed Whitson (0-for-11)

Ranked third in stolen base percentage (.875, 21-of-24) among N.L. players with 10+ steals. He had a better percentage than Coleman (.867), Henderson (.846), or Raines (.820). . . . Led Astros with 26 infield hits, more than twice Gerald Young's total. . . . First catcher to start and bat leadoff since Orioles' Floyd Rayford in 1985. . . . Opponents were successful on 83 percent of steal attempts, highest rate vs. any catcher in majors (minimum: 25 attempts) last year. . . . But Astros' staff had 3.45 ERA with Biggio catching, 3.64 with Ashby, 4.35 with Trevino. . . . Batting average in Late-Inning Pressure Situations was 102 points higher than in other at-bats, largest difference in N.L. last season (minimum: 50 AB in LIPS).

## Barry Bonds

Bats Left

| Pittsburgh Pirates | AB | H | 2B | 3B | HR | RBI | BB | SO | BA | SA | OBA |
|---|---|---|---|---|---|---|---|---|---|---|---|
| Season | 580 | 144 | 34 | 6 | 19 | 58 | 93 | 93 | .248 | .426 | .351 |
| vs. Left-Handers | 178 | 47 | 14 | 1 | 4 | 24 | 31 | 33 | .264 | .421 | .371 |
| vs. Right-Handers | 402 | 97 | 20 | 5 | 15 | 34 | 62 | 60 | .241 | .428 | .342 |
| Home | 280 | 57 | 16 | 1 | 7 | 28 | 43 | 43 | .204 | .343 | .309 |
| Road | 300 | 87 | 18 | 5 | 12 | 30 | 50 | 50 | .290 | .503 | .390 |
| Grass | 159 | 41 | 7 | 2 | 3 | 11 | 24 | 28 | .258 | .384 | .353 |
| Artificial Turf | 421 | 103 | 27 | 4 | 16 | 47 | 69 | 65 | .245 | .442 | .350 |
| April | 98 | 26 | 11 | 1 | 3 | 8 | 8 | 16 | .265 | .490 | .318 |
| May | 98 | 23 | 3 | 1 | 4 | 11 | 19 | 12 | .235 | .408 | .364 |
| June | 96 | 21 | 6 | 1 | 3 | 9 | 21 | 14 | .219 | .396 | .359 |
| July | 92 | 27 | 4 | 1 | 4 | 14 | 17 | 15 | .293 | .489 | .396 |
| August | 94 | 23 | 2 | 0 | 4 | 8 | 20 | 16 | .245 | .394 | .374 |
| Sept./Oct. | 102 | 24 | 8 | 2 | 1 | 8 | 8 | 20 | .235 | .382 | .291 |
| Leading Off Inn. | 230 | 59 | 12 | 4 | 9 | 9 | 25 | 36 | .257 | .461 | .329 |
| Runners On | 179 | 45 | 12 | 1 | 5 | 44 | 45 | 29 | .251 | .413 | .397 |
| Runners/Scor. Pos. | 97 | 22 | 5 | 1 | 3 | 36 | 36 | 16 | .227 | .392 | .428 |
| Runners On/2 Out | 71 | 16 | 4 | 0 | 1 | 9 | 27 | 15 | .225 | .324 | .444 |
| Scor. Pos./2 Out | 45 | 6 | 2 | 0 | 1 | 8 | 21 | 10 | .133 | .244 | .418 |
| Late Inning Pressure | 90 | 21 | 7 | 1 | 2 | 8 | 18 | 19 | .233 | .400 | .358 |
| Leading Off | 22 | 5 | 1 | 0 | 0 | 0 | 2 | 5 | .227 | .273 | .292 |
| Runners On | 35 | 8 | 4 | 0 | 0 | 6 | 13 | 5 | .229 | .343 | .429 |
| Runners/Scor. Pos. | 20 | 4 | 3 | 0 | 0 | 5 | 12 | 4 | .200 | .350 | .485 |

| RUNS BATTED IN | From 1B | From 2B | From 3B | Scoring Position |
|---|---|---|---|---|
| Totals | 8/127 | 12/67 | 19/49 | 31/116 |
| Percentage | 6% | 18% | 39% | 27% |
| Driving In Runners from 3B with Less than Two Out: | | | 17/26 | 65% |

Loves to face: Tom Browning (.455, 10-for-22, 4 HR, 10 BB)
Hates to face: Juan Agosto (0-for-12)

Only N.L. player with 95+ runs scored in each of past three years. In A.L., only Wade Boggs (seven years) has done it. . . . Led major league left fielders with 2.46 putouts per nine innings. . . . Owns career batting average of only .213 with runners in scoring position, .266 in other at-bats. . . . His career average of .103 (8-for-78) with runners in scoring position in Late-Inning Pressure Situations is the lowest by any player since 1975 (minimum: 40 AB). . . . Hit only one home run in his last 111 at-bats. . . . A comparison after four seasons in majors shows dad with an edge over Barry in home runs (100 to 84), stolen bases (135 to 117), runs scored (419 to 364), and batting average (.279 to .256).

## Bobby Bonilla

Bats Left and Right

| Pittsburgh Pirates | AB | H | 2B | 3B | HR | RBI | BB | SO | BA | SA | OBA |
|---|---|---|---|---|---|---|---|---|---|---|---|
| Season | 616 | 173 | 37 | 10 | 24 | 86 | 76 | 93 | .281 | .490 | .358 |
| vs. Left-Handers | 221 | 50 | 10 | 1 | 8 | 30 | 28 | 28 | .226 | .389 | .310 |
| vs. Right-Handers | 395 | 123 | 27 | 9 | 16 | 56 | 48 | 65 | .311 | .547 | .386 |
| Home | 296 | 92 | 20 | 6 | 13 | 42 | 42 | 39 | .311 | .551 | .393 |
| Road | 320 | 81 | 17 | 4 | 11 | 44 | 34 | 54 | .253 | .434 | .325 |
| Grass | 160 | 40 | 4 | 3 | 6 | 21 | 16 | 32 | .250 | .425 | .318 |
| Artificial Turf | 456 | 133 | 33 | 7 | 18 | 65 | 60 | 61 | .292 | .513 | .372 |
| April | 96 | 28 | 5 | 1 | 1 | 12 | 6 | 13 | .292 | .396 | .330 |
| May | 96 | 26 | 6 | 1 | 6 | 12 | 11 | 15 | .271 | .542 | .346 |
| June | 96 | 27 | 6 | 4 | 2 | 16 | 16 | 13 | .281 | .490 | .381 |
| July | 105 | 20 | 5 | 0 | 3 | 11 | 14 | 14 | .190 | .324 | .289 |
| August | 110 | 31 | 6 | 1 | 6 | 19 | 15 | 18 | .282 | .518 | .362 |
| Sept./Oct. | 113 | 41 | 9 | 3 | 6 | 16 | 14 | 20 | .363 | .655 | .433 |
| Leading Off Inn. | 174 | 65 | 15 | 4 | 11 | 11 | 13 | 21 | .374 | .695 | .417 |
| Runners On | 278 | 75 | 17 | 5 | 6 | 68 | 47 | 41 | .270 | .432 | .372 |
| Runners/Scor. Pos. | 143 | 41 | 9 | 4 | 3 | 57 | 42 | 23 | .287 | .469 | .440 |
| Runners On/2 Out | 138 | 37 | 6 | 2 | 2 | 28 | 34 | 23 | .268 | .384 | .413 |
| Scor. Pos./2 Out | 74 | 20 | 2 | 2 | 1 | 23 | 30 | 10 | .270 | .392 | .481 |
| Late Inning Pressure | 109 | 23 | 1 | 1 | 4 | 12 | 15 | 18 | .211 | .349 | .306 |
| Leading Off | 31 | 9 | 1 | 0 | 1 | 1 | 1 | 4 | .290 | .419 | .313 |
| Runners On | 45 | 10 | 0 | 1 | 1 | 9 | 10 | 7 | .222 | .333 | .364 |
| Runners/Scor. Pos. | 23 | 6 | 0 | 1 | 1 | 9 | 10 | 5 | .261 | .478 | .485 |

| RUNS BATTED IN | From 1B | From 2B | From 3B | Scoring Position |
|---|---|---|---|---|
| Totals | 11/190 | 27/103 | 24/62 | 51/165 |
| Percentage | 6% | 26% | 39% | 31% |
| Driving In Runners from 3B with Less than Two Out: | | | 18/31 | 58% |

Loves to face: Ken Howell (.636, 7-for-11, 1 HR)
Hates to face: John Tudor (.091, 2-for-22)
Became only the second Pittsburgh player to start in All-Star Game during 1980s (Parker started twice). Last Pirate to start for N.L. at third base: Frank Thomas in 1958. ... Committed 35 errors last season, most by any third baseman in majors in last five years. ... Started 161 games, all from the cleanup spot. ... Despite 1989 breakdown above, he has career average of .297 on grass fields, .269 on artificial surfaces. ... Batting average with runners in scoring position has increased annually in every season in majors. ... Lefty/righty breakdown above is surprising considering his average vs. southpaws was higher than against right-handers in each of his previous three seasons. Same is true of his home/road breakdown.

## Hubie Brooks

Bats Right

| Montreal Expos | AB | H | 2B | 3B | HR | RBI | BB | SO | BA | SA | OBA |
|---|---|---|---|---|---|---|---|---|---|---|---|
| Season | 542 | 145 | 30 | 1 | 14 | 70 | 39 | 108 | .268 | .404 | .317 |
| vs. Left-Handers | 162 | 46 | 11 | 0 | 6 | 23 | 15 | 31 | .284 | .463 | .352 |
| vs. Right-Handers | 380 | 99 | 19 | 1 | 8 | 47 | 24 | 77 | .261 | .379 | .302 |
| Home | 260 | 75 | 18 | 0 | 7 | 32 | 19 | 55 | .288 | .438 | .339 |
| Road | 282 | 70 | 12 | 1 | 7 | 38 | 20 | 53 | .248 | .372 | .297 |
| Grass | 154 | 38 | 8 | 1 | 3 | 19 | 8 | 30 | .247 | .370 | .285 |
| Artificial Turf | 388 | 107 | 22 | 0 | 11 | 51 | 31 | 78 | .276 | .418 | .329 |
| April | 85 | 24 | 3 | 0 | 3 | 10 | 5 | 19 | .282 | .424 | .309 |
| May | 104 | 26 | 6 | 0 | 1 | 10 | 4 | 20 | .250 | .337 | .282 |
| June | 89 | 27 | 8 | 1 | 1 | 15 | 10 | 13 | .303 | .449 | .370 |
| July | 90 | 16 | 2 | 0 | 3 | 9 | 6 | 20 | .178 | .300 | .235 |
| August | 84 | 17 | 5 | 0 | 1 | 5 | 4 | 16 | .202 | .298 | .236 |
| Sept./Oct. | 90 | 35 | 6 | 0 | 5 | 21 | 10 | 20 | .389 | .622 | .461 |
| Leading Off Inn. | 145 | 34 | 7 | 0 | 4 | 4 | 6 | 27 | .234 | .366 | .265 |
| Runners On | 245 | 65 | 11 | 1 | 6 | 62 | 22 | 49 | .265 | .392 | .321 |
| Runners/Scor. Pos. | 145 | 41 | 9 | 0 | 5 | 58 | 16 | 30 | .283 | .448 | .345 |
| Runners On/2 Out | 105 | 28 | 4 | 0 | 2 | 22 | 9 | 18 | .267 | .362 | .325 |
| Scor. Pos./2 Out | 72 | 16 | 3 | 0 | 2 | 22 | 8 | 15 | .222 | .347 | .300 |
| Late Inning Pressure | 80 | 28 | 4 | 1 | 2 | 12 | 4 | 14 | .350 | .500 | .376 |
| Leading Off | 24 | 7 | 1 | 0 | 0 | 0 | 1 | 3 | .292 | .333 | .320 |
| Runners On | 26 | 10 | 0 | 1 | 0 | 10 | 2 | 5 | .385 | .462 | .414 |
| Runners/Scor. Pos. | 18 | 6 | 0 | 0 | 0 | 9 | 2 | 3 | .333 | .333 | .381 |

| RUNS BATTED IN | From 1B | From 2B | From 3B | Scoring Position |
|---|---|---|---|---|
| Totals | 5/166 | 23/114 | 28/64 | 51/178 |
| Percentage | 3% | 20% | 44% | 29% |
| Driving In Runners from 3B with Less than Two Out: | | | 20/32 | 63% |

Loves to face: Dwight Gooden (.459, 17-for-37, 1 HR)
Hates to face: Todd Worrell (.095, 2-for-21)
Led N.L. with .384 average in September. ... Has six career grand-slam homers, with at least one in each of last five years, longest streak among current players. ... That .284 average vs. left-handed pitchers in '89 was his lowest since 1983. In five seasons with Expos batted .315 vs. lefties, .264 vs. righties. ... He's nothing if not consistent: Brooks and Ryne Sandberg are only N.L. players with 10+ home runs and .260+ batting average in each of last six years. ... Has hit at least .270 with runners in scoring position for seven straight years. ... Has one home run in 140 career at-bats at Dodger Stadium. ... Had lowest rate of putouts per nine innings (1.81) among N.L. right fielders last year (minimum: 500 innings).

## Tom Brunansky

Bats Right

| St. Louis Cardinals | AB | H | 2B | 3B | HR | RBI | BB | SO | BA | SA | OBA |
|---|---|---|---|---|---|---|---|---|---|---|---|
| Season | 556 | 133 | 29 | 3 | 20 | 85 | 59 | 107 | .239 | .410 | .312 |
| vs. Left-Handers | 220 | 52 | 8 | 0 | 11 | 31 | 28 | 33 | .236 | .423 | .320 |
| vs. Right-Handers | 336 | 81 | 21 | 3 | 9 | 54 | 31 | 74 | .241 | .402 | .306 |
| Home | 263 | 61 | 16 | 2 | 4 | 34 | 27 | 49 | .232 | .354 | .300 |
| Road | 293 | 72 | 13 | 1 | 16 | 51 | 32 | 58 | .246 | .461 | .322 |
| Grass | 154 | 31 | 2 | 0 | 8 | 27 | 18 | 30 | .201 | .370 | .287 |
| Artificial Turf | 402 | 102 | 27 | 3 | 12 | 58 | 41 | 77 | .254 | .425 | .321 |
| April | 76 | 16 | 3 | 1 | 3 | 12 | 5 | 12 | .211 | .395 | .256 |
| May | 91 | 22 | 3 | 0 | 2 | 15 | 14 | 12 | .242 | .341 | .343 |
| June | 95 | 26 | 10 | 0 | 4 | 16 | 10 | 18 | .274 | .505 | .340 |
| July | 91 | 23 | 4 | 0 | 5 | 15 | 13 | 25 | .253 | .462 | .346 |
| August | 105 | 26 | 7 | 2 | 4 | 17 | 9 | 22 | .248 | .467 | .313 |
| Sept./Oct. | 98 | 20 | 2 | 0 | 2 | 10 | 8 | 18 | .204 | .286 | .262 |
| Leading Off Inn. | 124 | 32 | 9 | 0 | 3 | 3 | 14 | 23 | .258 | .403 | .333 |
| Runners On | 264 | 68 | 15 | 2 | 12 | 77 | 28 | 49 | .258 | .466 | .328 |
| Runners/Scor. Pos. | 166 | 43 | 10 | 2 | 7 | 64 | 17 | 40 | .259 | .470 | .326 |
| Runners On/2 Out | 114 | 31 | 6 | 1 | 7 | 34 | 11 | 20 | .272 | .526 | .336 |
| Scor. Pos./2 Out | 83 | 23 | 4 | 1 | 5 | 29 | 7 | 18 | .277 | .530 | .333 |
| Late Inning Pressure | 83 | 16 | 3 | 0 | 4 | 12 | 11 | 18 | .193 | .373 | .287 |
| Leading Off | 22 | 3 | 1 | 0 | 0 | 0 | 6 | 7 | .136 | .182 | .321 |
| Runners On | 39 | 9 | 1 | 0 | 3 | 11 | 3 | 5 | .231 | .487 | .286 |
| Runners/Scor. Pos. | 24 | 4 | 0 | 0 | 1 | 6 | 0 | 3 | .167 | .292 | .167 |

| RUNS BATTED IN | From 1B | From 2B | From 3B | Scoring Position |
|---|---|---|---|---|
| Totals | 14/188 | 23/125 | 28/74 | 51/199 |
| Percentage | 7% | 18% | 38% | 26% |
| Driving In Runners from 3B with Less than Two Out: | | | 19/38 | 50% |

Loves to face: Bruce Hurst (.486, 17-for-35, 1 HR)
Hates to face: Sid Fernandez (.063, 1-for-16)
Started 65 games from 6th spot in batting order, most by any N.L. player, but never started more than six straight games from any spot in lineup. ... Batted .071 (1-for-14) with bases loaded; career: .219 with the bags full. ... Has hit 11 homers at home, 31 road homers in N.L. ... One of four players with 20+ homers in each of last eight seasons. Others: Dwight Evans, Murphy, Ripken. ... Has played in 150+ games in each of last seven years. Only Murphy and Ripken (eight each) have active streaks that long. ... One of 154 players in history with 200+ homers; only four of them have lower career averages than Bruno's .247: Gorman Thomas (.225), Dave Kingman (.236), Gene Tenace (.241), Deron Johnson (.244).

## Brett Butler

Bats Left

| San Francisco Giants | AB | H | 2B | 3B | HR | RBI | BB | SO | BA | SA | OBA |
|---|---|---|---|---|---|---|---|---|---|---|---|
| Season | 594 | 168 | 22 | 4 | 4 | 36 | 59 | 69 | .283 | .354 | .349 |
| vs. Left-Handers | 200 | 56 | 7 | 2 | 1 | 15 | 22 | 34 | .280 | .350 | .353 |
| vs. Right-Handers | 394 | 112 | 15 | 2 | 3 | 21 | 37 | 35 | .284 | .355 | .347 |
| Home | 296 | 90 | 13 | 2 | 2 | 21 | 30 | 27 | .304 | .382 | .370 |
| Road | 298 | 78 | 9 | 2 | 2 | 15 | 29 | 42 | .262 | .326 | .328 |
| Grass | 445 | 128 | 19 | 3 | 2 | 25 | 41 | 52 | .288 | .357 | .349 |
| Artificial Turf | 149 | 40 | 3 | 1 | 2 | 11 | 18 | 17 | .268 | .342 | .349 |
| April | 93 | 32 | 6 | 0 | 1 | 6 | 13 | 8 | .344 | .441 | .425 |
| May | 92 | 25 | 3 | 1 | 0 | 7 | 13 | 13 | .272 | .326 | .361 |
| June | 89 | 25 | 3 | 0 | 1 | 6 | 7 | 13 | .281 | .348 | .330 |
| July | 106 | 24 | 2 | 2 | 1 | 5 | 4 | 13 | .226 | .311 | .255 |
| August | 102 | 28 | 4 | 0 | 1 | 7 | 11 | 13 | .275 | .343 | .357 |
| Sept./Oct. | 112 | 34 | 4 | 1 | 0 | 5 | 11 | 9 | .304 | .357 | .366 |
| Leading Off Inn. | 272 | 76 | 12 | 1 | 1 | 1 | 23 | 26 | .279 | .342 | .338 |
| Runners On | 171 | 50 | 5 | 2 | 0 | 32 | 22 | 20 | .292 | .345 | .367 |
| Runners/Scor. Pos. | 100 | 25 | 2 | 2 | 0 | 32 | 15 | 11 | .250 | .310 | .339 |
| Runners On/2 Out | 78 | 25 | 2 | 2 | 0 | 12 | 13 | 7 | .321 | .397 | .418 |
| Scor. Pos./2 Out | 46 | 12 | 0 | 2 | 0 | 12 | 10 | 5 | .261 | .348 | .393 |
| Late Inning Pressure | 83 | 24 | 3 | 0 | 1 | 7 | 8 | 13 | .289 | .361 | .352 |
| Leading Off | 19 | 7 | 0 | 0 | 0 | 0 | 2 | 3 | .368 | .368 | .429 |
| Runners On | 35 | 11 | 1 | 0 | 0 | 6 | 3 | 4 | .314 | .343 | .368 |
| Runners/Scor. Pos. | 17 | 5 | 1 | 0 | 0 | 6 | 3 | 2 | .294 | .353 | .400 |

| RUNS BATTED IN | From 1B | From 2B | From 3B | Scoring Position |
|---|---|---|---|---|
| Totals | 1/113 | 14/81 | 17/41 | 31/122 |
| Percentage | 1% | 17% | 41% | 25% |
| Driving In Runners from 3B with Less than Two Out: | | | 13/23 | 57% |

Loves to face: Jose DeLeon (.368, 7-for-19, 1 HR)
Hates to face: Ramon Martinez (.071, 1-for-14)
Has scored 606 runs in past six years; only Henderson and Boggs have scored more. ... Still has a higher career batting average vs. left-handers (.287) than vs. right-handers (.279), although he has had an advantage vs. right-handers in each of last three seasons. ... Batted .342 (25-for-73) with Giants trailing by one run. ... Had more strikeouts than walks for first time since 1983. Had walked more than 90 times in each of the previous two seasons. ... Has reached base (hit, walk, HBP) 200+ times for seven consecutive seasons; Murray, Ripken, Sandberg, and Boggs are the only other players to have done that (although Boggs, with his seven straight 200-*hit* seasons, can snicker at the others).

## Ken Caminiti

Houston Astros — Bats Left and Right

| Houston Astros | AB | H | 2B | 3B | HR | RBI | BB | SO | BA | SA | OBA |
|---|---|---|---|---|---|---|---|---|---|---|---|
| Season | 585 | 149 | 31 | 3 | 10 | 72 | 51 | 93 | .255 | .369 | .316 |
| vs. Left-Handers | 165 | 52 | 12 | 1 | 4 | 22 | 13 | 23 | .315 | .473 | .363 |
| vs. Right-Handers | 420 | 97 | 19 | 2 | 6 | 50 | 38 | 70 | .231 | .329 | .297 |
| Home | 293 | 75 | 18 | 2 | 3 | 32 | 24 | 47 | .256 | .362 | .313 |
| Road | 292 | 74 | 13 | 1 | 7 | 40 | 27 | 46 | .253 | .377 | .319 |
| Grass | 172 | 39 | 5 | 1 | 5 | 24 | 13 | 27 | .227 | .355 | .280 |
| Artificial Turf | 413 | 110 | 26 | 2 | 5 | 48 | 38 | 66 | .266 | .375 | .330 |
| April | 91 | 25 | 7 | 0 | 2 | 11 | 6 | 14 | .275 | .418 | .323 |
| May | 98 | 24 | 3 | 1 | 2 | 13 | 7 | 11 | .245 | .357 | .292 |
| June | 102 | 24 | 5 | 1 | 1 | 13 | 9 | 19 | .235 | .333 | .295 |
| July | 92 | 24 | 5 | 1 | 1 | 9 | 9 | 11 | .261 | .370 | .333 |
| August | 95 | 22 | 7 | 0 | 1 | 12 | 13 | 21 | .232 | .337 | .327 |
| Sept./Oct. | 107 | 30 | 4 | 0 | 3 | 14 | 7 | 17 | .280 | .402 | .325 |
| Leading Off Inn. | 131 | 35 | 12 | 1 | 3 | 3 | 9 | 19 | .267 | .443 | .314 |
| Runners On | 271 | 75 | 11 | 1 | 3 | 65 | 25 | 42 | .277 | .358 | .340 |
| Runners/Scor. Pos. | 161 | 47 | 7 | 1 | 2 | 62 | 21 | 28 | .292 | .385 | .369 |
| Runners On/2 Out | 119 | 33 | 4 | 0 | 2 | 34 | 14 | 16 | .277 | .361 | .363 |
| Scor. Pos./2 Out | 78 | 26 | 4 | 0 | 2 | 34 | 12 | 11 | .333 | .462 | .422 |
| Late Inning Pressure | 109 | 25 | 3 | 1 | 2 | 7 | 6 | 22 | .229 | .330 | .270 |
| Leading Off | 32 | 8 | 2 | 0 | 1 | 1 | 2 | 7 | .250 | .406 | .294 |
| Runners On | 46 | 10 | 0 | 0 | 1 | 6 | 4 | 9 | .217 | .283 | .280 |
| Runners/Scor. Pos. | 23 | 5 | 0 | 0 | 0 | 4 | 4 | 6 | .217 | .217 | .333 |

| RUNS BATTED IN | From 1B | From 2B | From 3B | Scoring Position |
|---|---|---|---|---|
| Totals | 6/194 | 29/131 | 27/60 | 56/191 |
| Percentage | 3% | 22% | 45% | 29% |
| Driving In Runners from 3B with Less than Two Out: | | | 16/32 | 50% |

Loves to face: Joe Magrane (.462, 6-for-13)
Hates to face: Don Robinson (.083, 2-for-24, 7 SO)
Played 160 games at third base, breaking Bob Aspromonte's club record of 155 that had stood since 1964. . . . In 1989, the average N.L. team received a .250 average, 70 RBI, and 72 runs scored from its starting third baseman. Houston's totals (159 starts by Caminiti, three by Craig Reynolds): .251, 72 RBI, 71 runs scored. . . . Tried to score from second base on 23 of 24 singles to the outfield last season. The only time he stopped at third base was in ninth inning, trailing by two runs. . . . Career averages: batting .298, slugging .439 vs. left-handers; .220 and .304 vs. right-handers. . . . Born April 21, 1963, at Hanford, California; to celebrate, Astros dropped twin-bill at Dodger Stadium that afternoon.

## John Cangelosi

Pittsburgh Pirates — Bats Left and Right

| Pittsburgh Pirates | AB | H | 2B | 3B | HR | RBI | BB | SO | BA | SA | OBA |
|---|---|---|---|---|---|---|---|---|---|---|---|
| Season | 160 | 35 | 4 | 2 | 0 | 9 | 35 | 20 | .219 | .269 | .365 |
| vs. Left-Handers | 82 | 17 | 3 | 1 | 0 | 6 | 13 | 8 | .207 | .268 | .327 |
| vs. Right-Handers | 78 | 18 | 1 | 1 | 0 | 3 | 22 | 12 | .231 | .269 | .402 |
| Home | 78 | 21 | 3 | 1 | 0 | 3 | 20 | 7 | .269 | .333 | .430 |
| Road | 82 | 14 | 1 | 1 | 0 | 6 | 15 | 13 | .171 | .207 | .300 |
| Grass | 34 | 7 | 1 | 0 | 0 | 0 | 7 | 5 | .206 | .235 | .357 |
| Artificial Turf | 126 | 28 | 3 | 2 | 0 | 9 | 28 | 15 | .222 | .278 | .367 |
| April | 27 | 4 | 1 | 0 | 0 | 3 | 8 | 2 | .148 | .185 | .343 |
| May | 17 | 5 | 0 | 0 | 0 | 0 | 2 | 4 | .294 | .294 | .368 |
| June | 25 | 8 | 1 | 1 | 0 | 3 | 6 | 3 | .320 | .440 | .452 |
| July | 36 | 8 | 0 | 0 | 0 | 1 | 10 | 1 | .222 | .222 | .396 |
| August | 29 | 6 | 0 | 1 | 0 | 1 | 3 | 6 | .207 | .276 | .303 |
| Sept./Oct. | 26 | 4 | 2 | 0 | 0 | 1 | 6 | 4 | .154 | .231 | .324 |
| Leading Off Inn. | 77 | 17 | 3 | 2 | 0 | 0 | 12 | 12 | .221 | .312 | .333 |
| Runners On | 44 | 8 | 1 | 0 | 0 | 9 | 14 | 5 | .182 | .205 | .377 |
| Runners/Scor. Pos. | 27 | 4 | 0 | 0 | 0 | 8 | 9 | 4 | .148 | .148 | .359 |
| Runners On/2 Out | 17 | 3 | 1 | 0 | 0 | 3 | 5 | 1 | .176 | .235 | .391 |
| Scor. Pos./2 Out | 11 | 1 | 0 | 0 | 0 | 2 | 4 | 1 | .091 | .091 | .375 |
| Late Inning Pressure | 65 | 13 | 2 | 0 | 0 | 1 | 10 | 11 | .200 | .231 | .316 |
| Leading Off | 33 | 6 | 2 | 0 | 0 | 0 | 3 | 6 | .182 | .242 | .270 |
| Runners On | 16 | 2 | 0 | 0 | 0 | 1 | 5 | 3 | .125 | .125 | .333 |
| Runners/Scor. Pos. | 12 | 1 | 0 | 0 | 0 | 1 | 3 | 2 | .083 | .083 | .267 |

| RUNS BATTED IN | From 1B | From 2B | From 3B | Scoring Position |
|---|---|---|---|---|
| Totals | 1/26 | 2/21 | 6/16 | 8/37 |
| Percentage | 4% | 10% | 38% | 22% |
| Driving In Runners from 3B with Less than Two Out: | | | 5/8 | 63% |

Loves to face: Bruce Ruffin (.286, 6-for-21, 8 BB)
Hates to face: Jeff Parrett (.091, 1-for-11)
Only player in majors last season to have more than 200 plate appearances and fewer than 10 RBI. One reason: 69 percent of his times up came with the bases empty. . . . Pinch-hit in 83 games last season, most in majors and 11 shy of Rusty Staub's major league record. Batted .176 (12-for-68) with 12 walks in that role. . . . Stole 50 bases for White Sox in 1986, when he had 525 plate appearances. Has only 41 thefts and 573 plate appearances in three years with Pirates. . . . Has six career home runs, all against left-handed pitchers; last dinger: Sept. 18, 1987, off John Candelaria. . . . At 5-foot-8, he has been hit by 15 pitches in 1102 plate appearances; at 6-foot-6, Dave Winfield has been hit by 20 in 9466 times up.

## Jack Clark

San Diego Padres — Bats Right

| San Diego Padres | AB | H | 2B | 3B | HR | RBI | BB | SO | BA | SA | OBA |
|---|---|---|---|---|---|---|---|---|---|---|---|
| Season | 455 | 110 | 19 | 1 | 26 | 94 | 132 | 145 | .242 | .459 | .410 |
| vs. Left-Handers | 125 | 34 | 9 | 0 | 4 | 16 | 48 | 28 | .272 | .440 | .474 |
| vs. Right-Handers | 330 | 76 | 10 | 1 | 22 | 78 | 84 | 117 | .230 | .467 | .383 |
| Home | 211 | 49 | 10 | 0 | 11 | 48 | 64 | 63 | .232 | .436 | .406 |
| Road | 244 | 61 | 9 | 1 | 15 | 46 | 68 | 82 | .250 | .480 | .413 |
| Grass | 332 | 78 | 15 | 0 | 19 | 67 | 95 | 107 | .235 | .452 | .402 |
| Artificial Turf | 123 | 32 | 4 | 1 | 7 | 27 | 37 | 38 | .260 | .480 | .429 |
| April | 74 | 17 | 1 | 0 | 4 | 14 | 22 | 29 | .230 | .405 | .398 |
| May | 82 | 17 | 3 | 0 | 2 | 13 | 26 | 31 | .207 | .317 | .394 |
| June | 81 | 18 | 1 | 1 | 3 | 12 | 19 | 30 | .222 | .370 | .370 |
| July | 63 | 19 | 3 | 0 | 3 | 13 | 16 | 17 | .302 | .492 | .438 |
| August | 87 | 21 | 5 | 0 | 8 | 23 | 23 | 19 | .241 | .575 | .396 |
| Sept./Oct. | 68 | 18 | 6 | 0 | 6 | 19 | 26 | 19 | .265 | .618 | .474 |
| Leading Off Inn. | 104 | 22 | 6 | 0 | 3 | 3 | 27 | 40 | .212 | .356 | .379 |
| Runners On | 230 | 63 | 8 | 0 | 18 | 86 | 75 | 69 | .274 | .543 | .445 |
| Runners/Scor. Pos. | 143 | 39 | 4 | 0 | 12 | 72 | 58 | 48 | .273 | .552 | .471 |
| Runners On/2 Out | 84 | 18 | 4 | 0 | 5 | 21 | 36 | 27 | .214 | .440 | .450 |
| Scor. Pos./2 Out | 54 | 12 | 2 | 0 | 5 | 20 | 25 | 19 | .222 | .537 | .468 |
| Late Inning Pressure | 65 | 12 | 1 | 0 | 4 | 13 | 21 | 24 | .185 | .385 | .379 |
| Leading Off | 14 | 1 | 0 | 0 | 1 | 1 | 4 | 10 | .071 | .286 | .278 |
| Runners On | 32 | 5 | 0 | 0 | 2 | 11 | 11 | 8 | .156 | .344 | .364 |
| Runners/Scor. Pos. | 19 | 3 | 0 | 0 | 1 | 9 | 10 | 4 | .158 | .316 | .433 |

| RUNS BATTED IN | From 1B | From 2B | From 3B | Scoring Position |
|---|---|---|---|---|
| Totals | 15/144 | 20/103 | 33/74 | 53/177 |
| Percentage | 10% | 19% | 45% | 30% |
| Driving In Runners from 3B with Less than Two Out: | | | 26/46 | 57% |

Loves to face: Doug Drabek (.417, 5-for-12, 2 HR, 4 BB)
Hates to face: Jose DeLeon (0-for-13, 8 SO)
Has hit 25+ home runs in each of last three seasons, and with a different team each time. Last player to do that: the itinerant Bobby Bonds (Angels in 1977, Rangers in '78, Indians in '79). . . . Flashback to 1988: batted .242, 27 home runs, 93 RBI; in 1989: .242, 26, and 94. . . . First player since Killebrew with 130+ walks in two different seasons. . . . Hit 18 home runs to left field, three to center, five the other way. Overall, he pulled 58 percent of his fair balls last season. . . . Hit below .200 in Late-Inning Pressure Situations in both 1988 and 1989. . . . Career walk/strikeout ratio of 1.52 (414/272) vs. left-handers, 0.69 (592/858) vs. right-handers. . . . Walked intentionally 18 times last season, a career high.

## Will Clark

San Francisco Giants — Bats Left

| San Francisco Giants | AB | H | 2B | 3B | HR | RBI | BB | SO | BA | SA | OBA |
|---|---|---|---|---|---|---|---|---|---|---|---|
| Season | 588 | 196 | 38 | 9 | 23 | 111 | 74 | 103 | .333 | .546 | .407 |
| vs. Left-Handers | 215 | 69 | 11 | 3 | 8 | 54 | 15 | 38 | .321 | .512 | .371 |
| vs. Right-Handers | 373 | 127 | 27 | 6 | 15 | 57 | 59 | 65 | .340 | .566 | .428 |
| Home | 277 | 90 | 20 | 3 | 9 | 57 | 36 | 44 | .325 | .516 | .394 |
| Road | 311 | 106 | 18 | 6 | 14 | 54 | 38 | 59 | .341 | .572 | .420 |
| Grass | 428 | 145 | 29 | 6 | 16 | 85 | 53 | 71 | .339 | .547 | .409 |
| Artificial Turf | 160 | 51 | 9 | 3 | 7 | 26 | 21 | 32 | .319 | .544 | .402 |
| April | 88 | 33 | 6 | 2 | 4 | 18 | 19 | 11 | .375 | .625 | .486 |
| May | 97 | 34 | 7 | 2 | 6 | 24 | 12 | 23 | .351 | .649 | .423 |
| June | 99 | 30 | 5 | 1 | 3 | 16 | 17 | 12 | .303 | .465 | .392 |
| July | 101 | 31 | 5 | 0 | 3 | 17 | 5 | 25 | .307 | .446 | .346 |
| August | 108 | 38 | 9 | 1 | 4 | 21 | 8 | 15 | .352 | .565 | .398 |
| Sept./Oct. | 95 | 30 | 6 | 3 | 3 | 15 | 13 | 17 | .316 | .537 | .400 |
| Leading Off Inn. | 108 | 33 | 2 | 2 | 3 | 3 | 13 | 22 | .306 | .444 | .395 |
| Runners On | 259 | 92 | 20 | 6 | 13 | 101 | 40 | 46 | .355 | .629 | .432 |
| Runners/Scor. Pos. | 144 | 56 | 10 | 3 | 9 | 86 | 32 | 29 | .389 | .688 | .481 |
| Runners On/2 Out | 74 | 30 | 5 | 1 | 6 | 34 | 15 | 6 | .405 | .743 | .506 |
| Scor. Pos./2 Out | 46 | 20 | 3 | 0 | 4 | 28 | 12 | 5 | .435 | .761 | .552 |
| Late Inning Pressure | 81 | 25 | 2 | 3 | 5 | 19 | 10 | 18 | .309 | .593 | .387 |
| Leading Off | 23 | 4 | 1 | 0 | 1 | 1 | 3 | 6 | .174 | .348 | .269 |
| Runners On | 34 | 12 | 0 | 3 | 2 | 16 | 6 | 8 | .353 | .706 | .439 |
| Runners/Scor. Pos. | 18 | 8 | 0 | 2 | 0 | 11 | 6 | 5 | .444 | .667 | .560 |

| RUNS BATTED IN | From 1B | From 2B | From 3B | Scoring Position |
|---|---|---|---|---|
| Totals | 21/183 | 37/111 | 30/60 | 67/171 |
| Percentage | 11% | 33% | 50% | 39% |
| Driving In Runners from 3B with Less than Two Out: | | | 23/39 | 59% |

Loves to face: Ron Robinson (.625, 10-for-16, 1 HR)
Hates to face: Juan Agosto (.071, 1-for-14, 4 SO)
Does good pitching stop good hitting? Not in this case. Will hit .431 (25-for-58) against N.L.'s 10 pitchers with lowest ERA. . . . Batted .450 (27-for-60) vs. left-handers with runners in scoring position. That was during the *regular season*. We all know what he did vs. Mitch Williams in playoffs. . . . He hit .526 (10-for-19) with men in scoring position and his team down a run, and .426 (20-for-47) with men in scoring position and the score tied, and an N.L.-high .435 with runners in scoring position and two outs. . . . Batted .472 in postseason last year; since 1969, only Brooks Robinson (.485 in 1970) and Thurman Munson (.475 in 1976) have had higher postseason averages (minimum: 25 at-bats).

## Vince Coleman

Bats Left and Right

| St. Louis Cardinals | AB | H | 2B | 3B | HR | RBI | BB | SO | BA | SA | OBA |
|---|---|---|---|---|---|---|---|---|---|---|---|
| Season | 563 | 143 | 21 | 9 | 2 | 28 | 50 | 90 | .254 | .334 | .316 |
| vs. Left-Handers | 264 | 62 | 14 | 2 | 2 | 17 | 18 | 53 | .235 | .326 | .285 |
| vs. Right-Handers | 299 | 81 | 7 | 7 | 0 | 11 | 32 | 37 | .271 | .341 | .342 |
| Home | 277 | 72 | 13 | 6 | 1 | 20 | 21 | 35 | .260 | .361 | .316 |
| Road | 286 | 71 | 8 | 3 | 1 | 8 | 29 | 55 | .248 | .308 | .316 |
| Grass | 154 | 34 | 3 | 2 | 1 | 7 | 12 | 27 | .221 | .286 | .275 |
| Artificial Turf | 409 | 109 | 18 | 7 | 1 | 21 | 38 | 63 | .267 | .352 | .331 |
| April | 93 | 31 | 7 | 3 | 0 | 7 | 6 | 16 | .333 | .473 | .370 |
| May | 85 | 22 | 4 | 0 | 0 | 4 | 8 | 12 | .259 | .306 | .330 |
| June | 106 | 22 | 5 | 2 | 0 | 4 | 9 | 14 | .208 | .292 | .267 |
| July | 78 | 20 | 1 | 0 | 0 | 7 | 15 | 12 | .256 | .269 | .376 |
| August | 103 | 30 | 3 | 3 | 1 | 4 | 4 | 14 | .291 | .408 | .324 |
| Sept./Oct. | 98 | 18 | 1 | 1 | 1 | 2 | 8 | 22 | .184 | .245 | .245 |
| Leading Off Inn. | 263 | 73 | 14 | 3 | 1 | 1 | 22 | 44 | .278 | .365 | .336 |
| Runners On | 168 | 35 | 2 | 5 | 0 | 26 | 14 | 26 | .208 | .280 | .270 |
| Runners/Scor. Pos. | 115 | 23 | 2 | 5 | 0 | 26 | 13 | 21 | .200 | .304 | .282 |
| Runners On/2 Out | 77 | 13 | 1 | 2 | 0 | 13 | 11 | 14 | .169 | .234 | .273 |
| Scor. Pos./2 Out | 64 | 13 | 1 | 2 | 0 | 13 | 10 | 13 | .203 | .281 | .311 |
| Late Inning Pressure | 77 | 15 | 3 | 0 | 0 | 3 | 7 | 13 | .195 | .234 | .262 |
| Leading Off | 23 | 7 | 3 | 0 | 0 | 0 | 3 | 4 | .304 | .435 | .385 |
| Runners On | 32 | 5 | 0 | 0 | 0 | 3 | 0 | 6 | .156 | .156 | .156 |
| Runners/Scor. Pos. | 19 | 3 | 0 | 0 | 0 | 3 | 0 | 5 | .158 | .158 | .158 |

| RUNS BATTED IN | From 1B | From 2B | From 3B | Scoring Position |
|---|---|---|---|---|
| Totals | 1/104 | 9/95 | 16/46 | 25/141 |
| Percentage | 1% | 9% | 35% | 18% |
| Driving In Runners from 3B with Less than Two Out: | | | 9/22 | 41% |

Loves to face: Scott Garrelts (.421, 8-for-19)
Hates to face: Derek Lilliquist (0-for-9)
Has 53 career stolen bases in 53 attempts vs. Mets. His 14 steals vs. New York in 1989 were the most by any player vs. any club in majors last year. . . . Has led league in steals in each of last five years; N.L. record: six straight by Maury Wills (1960–65). . . . Had 44 consecutive steals to start season; stole 21 of 31 after that. . . . Had averaged 14 assists per year previously, but had only five last season. . . . Batting average at year's end was at its lowest point of the season. . . . Career breakdowns: .277 at home, .244 on road; .271 before All-Star Game, .249 after. . . . Had 0-for-27 streak with runners in scoring position in August and September, longest such streak in majors since his own streak of 28 in 1988.

## Kal Daniels

Bats Left

| Reds/Dodgers | AB | H | 2B | 3B | HR | RBI | BB | SO | BA | SA | OBA |
|---|---|---|---|---|---|---|---|---|---|---|---|
| Season | 171 | 42 | 13 | 0 | 4 | 17 | 43 | 33 | .246 | .392 | .399 |
| vs. Left-Handers | 57 | 11 | 3 | 0 | 1 | 5 | 17 | 14 | .193 | .298 | .373 |
| vs. Right-Handers | 114 | 31 | 10 | 0 | 3 | 12 | 26 | 19 | .272 | .439 | .413 |
| Home | 69 | 17 | 8 | 0 | 2 | 5 | 19 | 19 | .246 | .449 | .418 |
| Road | 102 | 25 | 5 | 0 | 2 | 12 | 24 | 14 | .245 | .353 | .386 |
| Grass | 43 | 11 | 3 | 0 | 1 | 5 | 12 | 9 | .256 | .395 | .411 |
| Artificial Turf | 128 | 31 | 10 | 0 | 3 | 12 | 31 | 24 | .242 | .391 | .395 |
| April | 71 | 17 | 6 | 0 | 1 | 6 | 19 | 9 | .239 | .366 | .402 |
| May | 16 | 3 | 2 | 0 | 0 | 0 | 9 | 3 | .188 | .313 | .480 |
| June | 9 | 2 | 1 | 0 | 0 | 0 | 0 | 2 | .222 | .333 | .300 |
| July | 72 | 18 | 4 | 0 | 2 | 10 | 14 | 18 | .250 | .389 | .368 |
| August | 3 | 2 | 0 | 0 | 1 | 1 | 1 | 1 | .667 | 1.667 | .750 |
| Sept./Oct. | 0 | 0 | 0 | 0 | 0 | 0 | 0 | 0 | — | — | — |
| Leading Off Inn. | 43 | 14 | 4 | 0 | 3 | 3 | 6 | 4 | .326 | .628 | .408 |
| Runners On | 68 | 13 | 4 | 0 | 1 | 14 | 20 | 13 | .191 | .294 | .367 |
| Runners/Scor. Pos. | 33 | 8 | 1 | 0 | 1 | 13 | 11 | 10 | .242 | .364 | .413 |
| Runners On/2 Out | 33 | 3 | 1 | 0 | 0 | 4 | 11 | 10 | .091 | .121 | .318 |
| Scor. Pos./2 Out | 20 | 2 | 1 | 0 | 0 | 4 | 5 | 7 | .100 | .150 | .280 |
| Late Inning Pressure | 33 | 6 | 4 | 0 | 0 | 1 | 8 | 6 | .182 | .303 | .333 |
| Leading Off | 6 | 2 | 2 | 0 | 0 | 0 | 1 | 0 | .333 | .667 | .429 |
| Runners On | 12 | 1 | 1 | 0 | 0 | 1 | 5 | 3 | .083 | .167 | .333 |
| Runners/Scor. Pos. | 7 | 0 | 0 | 0 | 0 | 1 | 5 | 3 | .000 | .000 | .385 |

| RUNS BATTED IN | From 1B | From 2B | From 3B | Scoring Position |
|---|---|---|---|---|
| Totals | 2/49 | 6/29 | 5/16 | 11/45 |
| Percentage | 4% | 21% | 31% | 24% |
| Driving In Runners from 3B with Less than Two Out: | | | 4/6 | 67% |

Loves to face: Danny Darwin (.526, 10-for-19, 3 HR)
Hates to face: Bob Kipper (.091, 1-for-11)
He and Tim Raines were only N.L. players to start 10+ games in both leadoff and cleanup spots in lineup. . . . Batted a major league low .091 with runners on base and two outs. . . . Career batting breakdown: .323 vs. ground-ball pitchers, .279 vs. fly-ballers; .327 vs. right-handers, .227 vs. left-handers. . . . Career slugging percentage (.570) vs. right-handers is second to Fred McGriff (.591) among active players. . . . Career on-base average (.409) when leading off innings is 4th-best among active players. . . . Career batting averages: .286 from April 1 to May 31, .289 from June 1 to July 31, .332 thereafter. . . . Owns .300+ career average at nine of 12 N.L. parks; exceptions: Olympic, Jack Murphy, Candlestick.

## Darren Daulton

Bats Left

| Philadelphia Phillies | AB | H | 2B | 3B | HR | RBI | BB | SO | BA | SA | OBA |
|---|---|---|---|---|---|---|---|---|---|---|---|
| Season | 368 | 74 | 12 | 2 | 8 | 44 | 52 | 58 | .201 | .310 | .303 |
| vs. Left-Handers | 58 | 14 | 0 | 1 | 1 | 9 | 11 | 9 | .241 | .328 | .366 |
| vs. Right-Handers | 310 | 60 | 12 | 1 | 7 | 35 | 41 | 49 | .194 | .306 | .290 |
| Home | 172 | 28 | 7 | 1 | 2 | 20 | 31 | 28 | .163 | .250 | .291 |
| Road | 196 | 46 | 5 | 1 | 6 | 24 | 21 | 30 | .235 | .362 | .314 |
| Grass | 99 | 21 | 2 | 1 | 4 | 15 | 12 | 19 | .212 | .374 | .310 |
| Artificial Turf | 269 | 53 | 10 | 1 | 4 | 29 | 40 | 39 | .197 | .286 | .300 |
| April | 50 | 14 | 0 | 0 | 5 | 13 | 7 | 7 | .280 | .580 | .379 |
| May | 58 | 7 | 2 | 1 | 1 | 5 | 4 | 8 | .121 | .241 | .177 |
| June | 43 | 6 | 2 | 0 | 0 | 7 | 16 | 5 | .140 | .186 | .367 |
| July | 76 | 15 | 2 | 0 | 1 | 5 | 10 | 10 | .197 | .263 | .291 |
| August | 73 | 14 | 3 | 0 | 1 | 6 | 5 | 14 | .192 | .274 | .253 |
| Sept./Oct. | 68 | 18 | 3 | 1 | 0 | 8 | 10 | 14 | .265 | .338 | .359 |
| Leading Off Inn. | 91 | 16 | 3 | 0 | 1 | 1 | 9 | 16 | .176 | .242 | .250 |
| Runners On | 156 | 38 | 5 | 1 | 6 | 42 | 26 | 19 | .244 | .404 | .353 |
| Runners/Scor. Pos. | 92 | 22 | 3 | 0 | 3 | 35 | 19 | 11 | .239 | .370 | .372 |
| Runners On/2 Out | 71 | 13 | 0 | 0 | 3 | 16 | 18 | 9 | .183 | .310 | .348 |
| Scor. Pos./2 Out | 46 | 9 | 0 | 0 | 2 | 14 | 15 | 6 | .196 | .326 | .393 |
| Late Inning Pressure | 60 | 8 | 0 | 0 | 0 | 2 | 8 | 12 | .133 | .133 | .235 |
| Leading Off | 18 | 2 | 0 | 0 | 0 | 0 | 3 | 3 | .111 | .111 | .238 |
| Runners On | 25 | 3 | 0 | 0 | 0 | 2 | 2 | 4 | .120 | .120 | .185 |
| Runners/Scor. Pos. | 12 | 1 | 0 | 0 | 0 | 2 | 1 | 2 | .083 | .083 | .154 |

| RUNS BATTED IN | From 1B | From 2B | From 3B | Scoring Position |
|---|---|---|---|---|
| Totals | 6/111 | 12/71 | 18/41 | 30/112 |
| Percentage | 5% | 17% | 44% | 27% |
| Driving In Runners from 3B with Less than Two Out: | | | 13/19 | 68% |

Loves to face: Andy McGaffigan (.385, 5-for-13, 1 HR)
Hates to face: John Smoltz (0-for-15)
Started 100 games vs. right-handers, but only six games against lefties. . . . Had the lowest home-game batting average of any major leaguer last season (minimum: two PA per game). . . . Batted .253 vs. ground-ball pitchers, .158 vs. fly-ballers. Career average of .173 vs. fly-ballers is lowest of any active nonpitcher (minimum: 400 AB). . . . Has seven career home runs at the Vet, 17 on the road. . . . Home run off of Bob Knepper in July is only one of his career off a left-handed pitcher. . . . Only three of his 44 RBI were in situations that either tied the game or put the Phillies in the lead. . . . Opponents stole 78 bases in 117 attempts (.667), as opposed to 27 steals in 53 attempts (.509) against teammate Steve Lake.

## Eric Davis

Bats Right

| Cincinnati Reds | AB | H | 2B | 3B | HR | RBI | BB | SO | BA | SA | OBA |
|---|---|---|---|---|---|---|---|---|---|---|---|
| Season | 462 | 130 | 14 | 2 | 34 | 101 | 68 | 116 | .281 | .541 | .367 |
| vs. Left-Handers | 156 | 39 | 4 | 1 | 10 | 26 | 30 | 38 | .250 | .481 | .369 |
| vs. Right-Handers | 306 | 91 | 10 | 1 | 24 | 75 | 38 | 78 | .297 | .572 | .366 |
| Home | 204 | 59 | 5 | 1 | 15 | 51 | 33 | 50 | .289 | .544 | .380 |
| Road | 258 | 71 | 9 | 1 | 19 | 50 | 35 | 66 | .275 | .539 | .357 |
| Grass | 163 | 42 | 5 | 1 | 12 | 31 | 21 | 41 | .258 | .521 | .344 |
| Artificial Turf | 299 | 88 | 9 | 1 | 22 | 70 | 47 | 75 | .294 | .552 | .379 |
| April | 79 | 19 | 2 | 0 | 6 | 16 | 11 | 18 | .241 | .494 | .323 |
| May | 48 | 16 | 4 | 0 | 1 | 12 | 2 | 11 | .333 | .479 | .340 |
| June | 64 | 21 | 1 | 1 | 7 | 21 | 10 | 11 | .328 | .703 | .419 |
| July | 82 | 18 | 1 | 0 | 5 | 8 | 16 | 25 | .220 | .415 | .347 |
| August | 107 | 29 | 2 | 1 | 9 | 24 | 15 | 31 | .271 | .561 | .360 |
| Sept./Oct. | 82 | 27 | 4 | 0 | 6 | 20 | 14 | 20 | .329 | .598 | .414 |
| Leading Off Inn. | 93 | 25 | 3 | 0 | 4 | 4 | 6 | 22 | .269 | .430 | .313 |
| Runners On | 207 | 63 | 5 | 2 | 21 | 88 | 39 | 46 | .304 | .652 | .399 |
| Runners/Scor. Pos. | 110 | 35 | 4 | 0 | 11 | 66 | 31 | 25 | .318 | .655 | .438 |
| Runners On/2 Out | 73 | 23 | 4 | 1 | 8 | 33 | 17 | 16 | .315 | .726 | .444 |
| Scor. Pos./2 Out | 41 | 16 | 4 | 0 | 6 | 28 | 13 | 5 | .390 | .927 | .537 |
| Late Inning Pressure | 82 | 24 | 3 | 0 | 7 | 21 | 13 | 17 | .293 | .585 | .381 |
| Leading Off | 24 | 9 | 0 | 0 | 0 | 0 | 2 | 5 | .375 | .375 | .423 |
| Runners On | 33 | 11 | 2 | 0 | 7 | 21 | 9 | 4 | .333 | 1.030 | .455 |
| Runners/Scor. Pos. | 20 | 7 | 2 | 0 | 4 | 15 | 7 | 3 | .350 | 1.050 | .483 |

| RUNS BATTED IN | From 1B | From 2B | From 3B | Scoring Position |
|---|---|---|---|---|
| Totals | 19/152 | 17/78 | 31/61 | 48/139 |
| Percentage | 13% | 22% | 51% | 35% |
| Driving In Runners from 3B with Less than Two Out: | | | 23/37 | 62% |

Loves to face: Rick Rhoden (.471, 8-for-17, 5 HR)
Hates to face: Rick Reuschel (.050, 1-for-20, 6 SO)
Career home-run rate vs. left-handed pitchers (one every 12.7 at-bats) is highest among active players (minimum: 20 HR); last season, his home-run rate vs. *right*-handers (one every 12.8 at-bats) was best in N.L. . . . Owns career stolen base percentage of .869 in 244 attempts. All-time record, with 300-attempt minimum, is .867 by Tim Raines. . . . Davis's totals of steals and attempts have fallen every year since 1986: 80-of-91, 50-of-56, 35-of-38, 21-of-28. . . . Over last four years, only Strawberry (134) has hit more home runs than Davis (124); only Coleman, Henderson, and Raines have more steals. . . . Only player in history with four consecutive seasons of less than 475 at-bats and more than 25 home runs.

## Glenn Davis

Bats Right

| Houston Astros | AB | H | 2B | 3B | HR | RBI | BB | SO | BA | SA | OBA |
|---|---|---|---|---|---|---|---|---|---|---|---|
| Season | 581 | 156 | 26 | 1 | 34 | 90 | 69 | 123 | .269 | .492 | .350 |
| vs. Left-Handers | 146 | 42 | 6 | 0 | 14 | 27 | 24 | 18 | .288 | .616 | .392 |
| vs. Right-Handers | 435 | 114 | 20 | 1 | 20 | 63 | 45 | 105 | .262 | .451 | .335 |
| Home | 287 | 91 | 20 | 1 | 15 | 43 | 39 | 57 | .317 | .551 | .402 |
| Road | 294 | 65 | 6 | 0 | 19 | 47 | 30 | 66 | .221 | .435 | .297 |
| Grass | 178 | 31 | 1 | 0 | 9 | 21 | 14 | 43 | .174 | .331 | .232 |
| Artificial Turf | 403 | 125 | 25 | 1 | 25 | 69 | 55 | 80 | .310 | .563 | .399 |
| April | 94 | 28 | 5 | 0 | 7 | 17 | 9 | 22 | .298 | .574 | .362 |
| May | 97 | 23 | 3 | 0 | 5 | 17 | 10 | 25 | .237 | .423 | .313 |
| June | 110 | 26 | 4 | 1 | 4 | 13 | 13 | 25 | .236 | .400 | .315 |
| July | 83 | 23 | 6 | 0 | 6 | 15 | 11 | 13 | .277 | .566 | .371 |
| August | 95 | 28 | 3 | 0 | 9 | 17 | 14 | 20 | .295 | .611 | .385 |
| Sept./Oct. | 102 | 28 | 5 | 0 | 3 | 11 | 12 | 18 | .275 | .412 | .362 |
| Leading Off Inn. | 175 | 46 | 7 | 0 | 11 | 11 | 9 | 38 | .263 | .491 | .310 |
| Runners On | 248 | 69 | 17 | 1 | 13 | 69 | 48 | 52 | .278 | .512 | .393 |
| Runners/Scor. Pos. | 137 | 37 | 10 | 1 | 5 | 48 | 36 | 31 | .270 | .467 | .411 |
| Runners On/2 Out | 126 | 32 | 7 | 1 | 8 | 29 | 30 | 30 | .254 | .516 | .401 |
| Scor. Pos./2 Out | 63 | 11 | 3 | 1 | 2 | 14 | 20 | 18 | .175 | .349 | .381 |
| Late Inning Pressure | 100 | 23 | 3 | 0 | 7 | 16 | 7 | 33 | .230 | .470 | .282 |
| Leading Off | 25 | 6 | 1 | 0 | 2 | 2 | 2 | 10 | .240 | .520 | .321 |
| Runners On | 38 | 9 | 1 | 0 | 3 | 12 | 5 | 13 | .237 | .500 | .311 |
| Runners/Scor. Pos. | 22 | 4 | 1 | 0 | 1 | 7 | 3 | 10 | .182 | .364 | .259 |

| RUNS BATTED IN | From 1B | From 2B | From 3B | Scoring Position |
|---|---|---|---|---|
| Totals | 16/172 | 20/104 | 20/57 | 40/161 |
| Percentage | 9% | 19% | 35% | 25% |
| Driving In Runners from 3B with Less than Two Out: | | | 17/28 | 61% |

Loves to face: Tom Browning (.360, 18-for-50, 5 2B, 6 HR)
Hates to face: Mike Bielecki (0-for-12)
Batted 96 points higher at dome than on road last season, largest such difference by any N.L. player (minimum: 100 at-bats each).... Career averages: .292 at Astrodome, .270 on foreign rugs, .212 on grass fields.... Homered in his first game at five different parks last year (Astrodome, Dodger, the Vet, Three Rivers, and Jack Murphy).... Had 21 RBI vs. Padres, most by any player vs. any club in majors.... Made 153 starts, all in cleanup spot.... Has a career rate of one home run every 18.8 at-bats, but has not had a slam in 44 bases-loaded at-bats.... Career average of .218 with two outs and runners in scoring position. ... Leads N.L. with 1102 total bases over past four years, one ahead of Will Clark.

## Jody Davis

Bats Right

| Atlanta Braves | AB | H | 2B | 3B | HR | RBI | BB | SO | BA | SA | OBA |
|---|---|---|---|---|---|---|---|---|---|---|---|
| Season | 231 | 39 | 5 | 0 | 4 | 19 | 23 | 61 | .169 | .242 | .246 |
| vs. Left-Handers | 93 | 19 | 4 | 0 | 1 | 10 | 11 | 22 | .204 | .280 | .286 |
| vs. Right-Handers | 138 | 20 | 1 | 0 | 3 | 9 | 12 | 39 | .145 | .217 | .219 |
| Home | 105 | 15 | 3 | 0 | 1 | 10 | 11 | 23 | .143 | .200 | .224 |
| Road | 126 | 24 | 2 | 0 | 3 | 9 | 12 | 38 | .190 | .278 | .264 |
| Grass | 165 | 26 | 3 | 0 | 2 | 11 | 18 | 43 | .158 | .212 | .245 |
| Artificial Turf | 66 | 13 | 2 | 0 | 2 | 8 | 5 | 18 | .197 | .318 | .250 |
| April | 76 | 12 | 2 | 0 | 1 | 6 | 5 | 24 | .158 | .224 | .220 |
| May | 61 | 11 | 1 | 0 | 1 | 7 | 5 | 14 | .180 | .246 | .242 |
| June | 31 | 5 | 1 | 0 | 0 | 0 | 5 | 7 | .161 | .194 | .278 |
| July | 25 | 2 | 0 | 0 | 1 | 2 | 4 | 8 | .080 | .200 | .207 |
| August | 21 | 4 | 1 | 0 | 0 | 1 | 2 | 6 | .190 | .238 | .261 |
| Sept./Oct. | 17 | 5 | 0 | 0 | 1 | 3 | 2 | 2 | .294 | .471 | .350 |
| Leading Off Inn. | 61 | 12 | 1 | 0 | 2 | 2 | 8 | 17 | .197 | .311 | .300 |
| Runners On | 88 | 13 | 3 | 0 | 2 | 17 | 9 | 23 | .148 | .250 | .224 |
| Runners/Scor. Pos. | 47 | 9 | 2 | 0 | 0 | 12 | 8 | 14 | .191 | .234 | .304 |
| Runners On/2 Out | 40 | 8 | 3 | 0 | 0 | 11 | 6 | 11 | .200 | .275 | .304 |
| Scor. Pos./2 Out | 24 | 7 | 2 | 0 | 0 | 10 | 5 | 7 | .292 | .375 | .414 |
| Late Inning Pressure | 50 | 5 | 0 | 0 | 0 | 2 | 7 | 20 | .100 | .100 | .211 |
| Leading Off | 11 | 2 | 0 | 0 | 0 | 0 | 4 | 4 | .182 | .182 | .400 |
| Runners On | 23 | 2 | 0 | 0 | 0 | 2 | 2 | 11 | .087 | .087 | .160 |
| Runners/Scor. Pos. | 14 | 2 | 0 | 0 | 0 | 2 | 2 | 8 | .143 | .143 | .250 |

| RUNS BATTED IN | From 1B | From 2B | From 3B | Scoring Position |
|---|---|---|---|---|
| Totals | 3/65 | 6/37 | 6/20 | 12/57 |
| Percentage | 5% | 16% | 30% | 21% |
| Driving In Runners from 3B with Less than Two Out: | | | 2/9 | 22% |

Loves to face: Juan Agosto (4-for-4, 2 HR)
Hates to face: Ron Robinson (0-for-16, 5 SO)
Update on Davis Home Run Race: Glenn and Chili are tied for lead (144), Eric (142) and Alvin (131) are climbing, Jody (127) and Mike (91) are fading.... Had lowest BA in majors last season (minimum: 200 AB); home-game average was lowest in N.L. (minimum: 100 AB) since Bud Harrelson hit .142 at Shea in 1977. ... In 113 previous seasons, no Braves player with 200+ AB hit less than .180; in 1989 there were two: Jody and Ron Gant. Only two other teams since 1900 have had such a pair: 1910 White Sox and 1968 Tigers, who overcame Dick Tracewski (.156) and Ray Oyler (.135) to win World Series.... In a season of career lows, his batting average with two outs and runners in scoring position was a career high!

## Andre Dawson

Bats Right

| Chicago Cubs | AB | H | 2B | 3B | HR | RBI | BB | SO | BA | SA | OBA |
|---|---|---|---|---|---|---|---|---|---|---|---|
| Season | 416 | 105 | 18 | 6 | 21 | 77 | 35 | 62 | .252 | .476 | .307 |
| vs. Left-Handers | 114 | 34 | 8 | 0 | 8 | 28 | 14 | 14 | .298 | .579 | .364 |
| vs. Right-Handers | 302 | 71 | 10 | 6 | 13 | 49 | 21 | 48 | .235 | .437 | .284 |
| Home | 218 | 52 | 12 | 1 | 6 | 35 | 18 | 29 | .239 | .385 | .293 |
| Road | 198 | 53 | 6 | 5 | 15 | 42 | 17 | 33 | .268 | .576 | .323 |
| Grass | 306 | 79 | 14 | 4 | 13 | 56 | 23 | 45 | .258 | .458 | .306 |
| Artificial Turf | 110 | 26 | 4 | 2 | 8 | 21 | 12 | 17 | .236 | .527 | .311 |
| April | 79 | 20 | 5 | 1 | 2 | 14 | 8 | 4 | .253 | .418 | .318 |
| May | 26 | 12 | 0 | 3 | 3 | 5 | 0 | 4 | .462 | 1.038 | .462 |
| June | 51 | 8 | 2 | 0 | 2 | 8 | 4 | 7 | .157 | .314 | .207 |
| July | 75 | 19 | 3 | 1 | 3 | 13 | 9 | 12 | .253 | .440 | .330 |
| August | 90 | 22 | 5 | 0 | 4 | 17 | 7 | 15 | .244 | .433 | .299 |
| Sept./Oct. | 95 | 24 | 3 | 1 | 7 | 20 | 7 | 20 | .253 | .526 | .304 |
| Leading Off Inn. | 109 | 23 | 6 | 1 | 5 | 5 | 3 | 18 | .211 | .422 | .232 |
| Runners On | 201 | 48 | 7 | 3 | 9 | 65 | 28 | 30 | .239 | .438 | .325 |
| Runners/Scor. Pos. | 115 | 33 | 7 | 1 | 6 | 57 | 27 | 19 | .287 | .522 | .407 |
| Runners On/2 Out | 89 | 23 | 3 | 2 | 5 | 28 | 15 | 15 | .258 | .506 | .371 |
| Scor. Pos./2 Out | 50 | 16 | 3 | 0 | 4 | 24 | 15 | 6 | .320 | .620 | .485 |
| Late Inning Pressure | 49 | 9 | 1 | 1 | 2 | 7 | 5 | 6 | .184 | .367 | .259 |
| Leading Off | 13 | 2 | 0 | 0 | 0 | 0 | 0 | 1 | .154 | .154 | .154 |
| Runners On | 24 | 3 | 1 | 0 | 1 | 6 | 3 | 4 | .125 | .292 | .222 |
| Runners/Scor. Pos. | 14 | 3 | 1 | 0 | 1 | 6 | 3 | 2 | .214 | .500 | .353 |

| RUNS BATTED IN | From 1B | From 2B | From 3B | Scoring Position |
|---|---|---|---|---|
| Totals | 11/150 | 17/87 | 28/59 | 45/146 |
| Percentage | 7% | 20% | 47% | 31% |
| Driving In Runners from 3B with Less than Two Out: | | | 21/37 | 57% |

Loves to face: John Smiley (.565, 13-for-23, 4 HR)
Hates to face: Bob Kipper (0-for-12)
Batting average decline from .303 in 1988 was traceable to drop of 71 points (.306 to .235) vs. right-handed pitchers; he actually improved his mark vs. lefties from .296 to .298.... Had eight straight hits in May, tying for longest N.L. streak in 1980s. Others: Art Howe (1980), Marvell Wynne (1984), Steve Nicosia (1984), Keith Hernandez (1985), and Dawson himself (he did it for Expos in 1983).... Dawson also had a streak of 28 hitless at-bats last season. ... Career breakdowns paint a picture of a most consistent hitter: .281 with bases empty, .281 with runners on base, .279 with runners in scoring position, .279 vs. ground-ballers, .282 vs. fly-ballers. One notable exception: .303 in day games, .264 at night.

## Bob Dernier

Bats Right

| Philadelphia Phillies | AB | H | 2B | 3B | HR | RBI | BB | SO | BA | SA | OBA |
|---|---|---|---|---|---|---|---|---|---|---|---|
| Season | 187 | 32 | 5 | 0 | 1 | 14 | 14 | 28 | .171 | .214 | .225 |
| vs. Left-Handers | 132 | 26 | 4 | 0 | 1 | 11 | 11 | 18 | .197 | .250 | .253 |
| vs. Right-Handers | 55 | 6 | 1 | 0 | 0 | 3 | 3 | 10 | .109 | .127 | .155 |
| Home | 97 | 16 | 1 | 0 | 1 | 7 | 6 | 18 | .165 | .206 | .210 |
| Road | 90 | 16 | 4 | 0 | 0 | 7 | 8 | 10 | .178 | .222 | .242 |
| Grass | 47 | 8 | 1 | 0 | 0 | 3 | 5 | 4 | .170 | .191 | .250 |
| Artificial Turf | 140 | 24 | 4 | 0 | 1 | 11 | 9 | 24 | .171 | .221 | .217 |
| April | 46 | 13 | 2 | 0 | 0 | 3 | 5 | 5 | .283 | .326 | .353 |
| May | 43 | 5 | 0 | 0 | 1 | 4 | 1 | 6 | .116 | .186 | .133 |
| June | 33 | 3 | 1 | 0 | 0 | 3 | 5 | 6 | .091 | .121 | .211 |
| July | 20 | 6 | 2 | 0 | 0 | 1 | 2 | 4 | .300 | .400 | .348 |
| August | 24 | 3 | 0 | 0 | 0 | 2 | 0 | 4 | .125 | .125 | .125 |
| Sept./Oct. | 21 | 2 | 0 | 0 | 0 | 1 | 1 | 3 | .095 | .095 | .130 |
| Leading Off Inn. | 65 | 14 | 2 | 0 | 0 | 0 | 2 | 10 | .215 | .246 | .239 |
| Runners On | 61 | 13 | 2 | 0 | 1 | 14 | 6 | 10 | .213 | .295 | .271 |
| Runners/Scor. Pos. | 40 | 7 | 0 | 0 | 1 | 13 | 3 | 6 | .175 | .250 | .217 |
| Runners On/2 Out | 29 | 7 | 0 | 0 | 1 | 9 | 0 | 3 | .241 | .345 | .241 |
| Scor. Pos./2 Out | 23 | 5 | 0 | 0 | 1 | 9 | 0 | 2 | .217 | .348 | .217 |
| Late Inning Pressure | 47 | 11 | 1 | 0 | 1 | 5 | 2 | 6 | .234 | .319 | .260 |
| Leading Off | 12 | 4 | 1 | 0 | 0 | 0 | 0 | 3 | .333 | .417 | .333 |
| Runners On | 19 | 5 | 0 | 0 | 1 | 5 | 2 | 2 | .263 | .421 | .318 |
| Runners/Scor. Pos. | 10 | 2 | 0 | 0 | 1 | 5 | 2 | 1 | .200 | .500 | .308 |

| RUNS BATTED IN | From 1B | From 2B | From 3B | Scoring Position |
|---|---|---|---|---|
| Totals | 2/43 | 3/36 | 8/24 | 11/60 |
| Percentage | 5% | 8% | 33% | 18% |
| Driving In Runners from 3B with Less than Two Out: | | | 4/10 | 40% |

Loves to face: John Franco (.538, 7-for-13, 1 HR)
Hates to face: Bryn Smith (.115, 3-for-26)
Lowest on-base average last season among players with 200+ plate appearances.... Batted .098 (4-for-41) as a pinch hitter. Only three other pinch hitters in history had a sub-.100 batting average in a season with 40+ at-bats: Joe (Not Smokin') Frazier was 4-for-45 for '55 Cardinals, Ted Uhlaender went 3-for-41 for '72 Reds, and Danny Heep went 4-for-44 for Dodgers in '88.... Batted .169 on fair balls hit to the opposite field. ... Had batted over .300 vs. left-handers in each of the previous three seasons; including '89, has now hit below .200 vs. right-handers three times in past four years. ... A .267 career hitter from April to July, but has hit only .233 from August 1 on.

## Bill Doran

Bats Left and Right

| Houston Astros | AB | H | 2B | 3B | HR | RBI | BB | SO | BA | SA | OBA |
|---|---|---|---|---|---|---|---|---|---|---|---|
| Season | 507 | 111 | 25 | 2 | 8 | 59 | 59 | 63 | .219 | .323 | .301 |
| vs. Left-Handers | 140 | 32 | 6 | 0 | 4 | 18 | 18 | 14 | .229 | .357 | .316 |
| vs. Right-Handers | 367 | 79 | 19 | 2 | 4 | 41 | 41 | 49 | .215 | .311 | .295 |
| Home | 250 | 63 | 14 | 2 | 3 | 37 | 31 | 29 | .252 | .360 | .332 |
| Road | 257 | 48 | 11 | 0 | 5 | 22 | 28 | 34 | .187 | .288 | .271 |
| Grass | 144 | 25 | 4 | 0 | 2 | 10 | 15 | 18 | .174 | .243 | .255 |
| Artificial Turf | 363 | 86 | 21 | 2 | 6 | 49 | 44 | 45 | .237 | .355 | .320 |
| April | 92 | 23 | 9 | 1 | 1 | 11 | 9 | 12 | .250 | .402 | .317 |
| May | 102 | 32 | 4 | 1 | 3 | 18 | 10 | 12 | .314 | .461 | .377 |
| June | 108 | 27 | 3 | 0 | 4 | 18 | 12 | 9 | .250 | .389 | .325 |
| July | 81 | 12 | 2 | 0 | 0 | 9 | 10 | 18 | .148 | .173 | .245 |
| August | 82 | 10 | 5 | 0 | 0 | 3 | 12 | 9 | .122 | .183 | .234 |
| Sept./Oct. | 42 | 7 | 2 | 0 | 0 | 0 | 6 | 3 | .167 | .214 | .271 |
| Leading Off Inn. | 107 | 20 | 5 | 0 | 2 | 2 | 11 | 17 | .187 | .290 | .263 |
| Runners On | 203 | 55 | 15 | 1 | 4 | 55 | 22 | 19 | .271 | .414 | .341 |
| Runners/Scor. Pos. | 120 | 34 | 7 | 1 | 2 | 46 | 20 | 11 | .283 | .408 | .378 |
| Runners On/2 Out | 68 | 13 | 3 | 1 | 0 | 11 | 6 | 8 | .191 | .265 | .267 |
| Scor. Pos./2 Out | 53 | 10 | 1 | 1 | 0 | 10 | 4 | 8 | .189 | .245 | .246 |
| Late Inning Pressure | 87 | 21 | 2 | 0 | 3 | 8 | 8 | 12 | .241 | .368 | .305 |
| Leading Off | 26 | 6 | 1 | 0 | 1 | 1 | 1 | 3 | .231 | .385 | .259 |
| Runners On | 35 | 6 | 1 | 0 | 1 | 6 | 4 | 5 | .171 | .286 | .256 |
| Runners/Scor. Pos. | 17 | 1 | 0 | 0 | 0 | 3 | 4 | 3 | .059 | .059 | .238 |

| RUNS BATTED IN | From 1B | From 2B | From 3B | Scoring Position |
|---|---|---|---|---|
| Totals | 10/136 | 19/89 | 22/57 | 41/146 |
| Percentage | 7% | 21% | 39% | 28% |
| Driving In Runners from 3B with Less than Two Out: | | | 20/36 | 56% |

Loves to face: Tom Glavine (.615, 8-for-13, 4 BB)
Hates to face: Bob Ojeda (.083, 1-for-12)
Batting average has fallen from .283 (in 1987) to .248 to .219 in successive seasons. Only one other N.L. player suffered declines of 25+ points in each of past two years (minimum: 400 at-bats each year): former teammate Billy Hatcher. . . . August batting average was lowest in majors last season (minimum: two PA per game). . . . Stole 22 bases in 25 tries, best success rate of his career. . . . Passed Joe Morgan as Houston's all-time leader in games at second base. . . . Of his 58 RBI, 28 (or 48 percent) either tied the score or put his team in lead, 2d-best rate among N.L. players with 50+ RBI. . . . Had 12 game-winning RBI to lead Astros; for those of you who just started following baseball in 1989, ask a friend what that means.

## Mariano Duncan

Bats Right

| Dodgers/Reds | AB | H | 2B | 3B | HR | RBI | BB | SO | BA | SA | OBA |
|---|---|---|---|---|---|---|---|---|---|---|---|
| Season | 258 | 64 | 15 | 2 | 3 | 21 | 8 | 51 | .248 | .357 | .284 |
| vs. Left-Handers | 99 | 28 | 8 | 2 | 2 | 14 | 3 | 17 | .283 | .465 | .324 |
| vs. Right-Handers | 159 | 36 | 7 | 0 | 1 | 7 | 5 | 34 | .226 | .289 | .259 |
| Home | 130 | 30 | 8 | 1 | 2 | 11 | 4 | 29 | .231 | .354 | .270 |
| Road | 128 | 34 | 7 | 1 | 1 | 10 | 4 | 22 | .266 | .359 | .299 |
| Grass | 117 | 27 | 7 | 1 | 1 | 12 | 2 | 21 | .231 | .333 | .262 |
| Artificial Turf | 141 | 37 | 8 | 1 | 2 | 9 | 6 | 30 | .262 | .376 | .302 |
| April | 23 | 8 | 2 | 0 | 0 | 0 | 0 | 3 | .348 | .435 | .348 |
| May | 39 | 6 | 2 | 0 | 0 | 5 | 0 | 6 | .154 | .205 | .175 |
| June | 21 | 7 | 1 | 1 | 0 | 3 | 0 | 6 | .333 | .476 | .364 |
| July | 52 | 12 | 3 | 0 | 0 | 2 | 1 | 13 | .231 | .288 | .259 |
| August | 55 | 17 | 2 | 0 | 3 | 6 | 5 | 9 | .309 | .509 | .377 |
| Sept./Oct. | 68 | 14 | 5 | 1 | 0 | 5 | 2 | 14 | .206 | .309 | .239 |
| Leading Off Inn. | 87 | 21 | 5 | 0 | 2 | 2 | 2 | 18 | .241 | .368 | .283 |
| Runners On | 86 | 27 | 7 | 1 | 1 | 19 | 3 | 17 | .314 | .453 | .344 |
| Runners/Scor. Pos. | 60 | 18 | 5 | 1 | 1 | 19 | 2 | 15 | .300 | .467 | .333 |
| Runners On/2 Out | 43 | 12 | 4 | 0 | 1 | 12 | 2 | 9 | .279 | .442 | .326 |
| Scor. Pos./2 Out | 36 | 9 | 3 | 0 | 1 | 12 | 1 | 9 | .250 | .417 | .289 |
| Late Inning Pressure | 53 | 15 | 2 | 0 | 1 | 6 | 2 | 14 | .283 | .377 | .333 |
| Leading Off | 10 | 3 | 0 | 0 | 1 | 1 | 1 | 1 | .300 | .600 | .417 |
| Runners On | 19 | 7 | 0 | 0 | 0 | 5 | 0 | 4 | .368 | .368 | .368 |
| Runners/Scor. Pos. | 11 | 4 | 0 | 0 | 0 | 5 | 0 | 3 | .364 | .364 | .364 |

| RUNS BATTED IN | From 1B | From 2B | From 3B | Scoring Position |
|---|---|---|---|---|
| Totals | 0/54 | 6/49 | 12/29 | 18/78 |
| Percentage | 0% | 12% | 41% | 23% |
| Driving In Runners from 3B with Less than Two Out: | | | 6/13 | 46% |

Loves to face: Bob Kipper (.438, 7-for-16, 2 HR)
Hates to face: Rick Sutcliffe (0-for-11, 4 SO)
Ranks last in fielding percentage (.949) among the 29 players who have played 300+ games at shortstop over the past five years. . . . Did not participate in a double play in any of his last 16 starts at shortstop (Reds finished with only 108 DP, fewest in majors). . . . Hit all three home runs in span of 15 at-bats in August. . . . Batted .389 (7-for-18) as a pinch hitter. . . . Acquired from Dodgers three games into first of Reds' two 10-game losing streaks last season. . . . Career average of .275 (one HR every 39 at-bats) vs. left-handers, .212 (one every 105) vs. right-handers. . . . Career average of .281 in Late-Inning Pressure Situations, .228 at other times. . . . Stole nine bases last season, six vs. Houston.

## Shawon Dunston

Bats Right

| Chicago Cubs | AB | H | 2B | 3B | HR | RBI | BB | SO | BA | SA | OBA |
|---|---|---|---|---|---|---|---|---|---|---|---|
| Season | 471 | 131 | 20 | 6 | 9 | 60 | 30 | 86 | .278 | .403 | .320 |
| vs. Left-Handers | 139 | 47 | 7 | 4 | 2 | 26 | 11 | 19 | .338 | .489 | .382 |
| vs. Right-Handers | 332 | 84 | 13 | 2 | 7 | 34 | 19 | 67 | .253 | .367 | .294 |
| Home | 225 | 69 | 11 | 1 | 3 | 32 | 15 | 33 | .307 | .404 | .347 |
| Road | 246 | 62 | 9 | 5 | 6 | 28 | 15 | 53 | .252 | .402 | .295 |
| Grass | 328 | 90 | 18 | 2 | 4 | 38 | 21 | 57 | .274 | .378 | .316 |
| Artificial Turf | 143 | 41 | 2 | 4 | 5 | 22 | 9 | 29 | .287 | .462 | .329 |
| April | 50 | 8 | 2 | 1 | 0 | 1 | 7 | 9 | .160 | .240 | .259 |
| May | 76 | 15 | 5 | 0 | 1 | 8 | 10 | 14 | .197 | .303 | .291 |
| June | 61 | 19 | 3 | 3 | 3 | 13 | 1 | 14 | .311 | .607 | .333 |
| July | 90 | 32 | 3 | 0 | 3 | 9 | 5 | 18 | .356 | .489 | .385 |
| August | 109 | 32 | 3 | 1 | 1 | 16 | 5 | 16 | .294 | .367 | .325 |
| Sept./Oct. | 85 | 25 | 4 | 1 | 1 | 13 | 2 | 15 | .294 | .400 | .303 |
| Leading Off Inn. | 111 | 31 | 4 | 1 | 3 | 3 | 5 | 19 | .279 | .414 | .310 |
| Runners On | 211 | 59 | 9 | 4 | 4 | 55 | 21 | 41 | .280 | .417 | .342 |
| Runners/Scor. Pos. | 120 | 35 | 4 | 3 | 3 | 52 | 18 | 26 | .292 | .450 | .378 |
| Runners On/2 Out | 100 | 28 | 2 | 0 | 2 | 20 | 14 | 19 | .280 | .360 | .368 |
| Scor. Pos./2 Out | 62 | 16 | 2 | 0 | 1 | 18 | 14 | 15 | .258 | .339 | .395 |
| Late Inning Pressure | 58 | 18 | 1 | 0 | 0 | 4 | 3 | 13 | .310 | .328 | .355 |
| Leading Off | 15 | 5 | 0 | 0 | 0 | 0 | 1 | 2 | .333 | .333 | .375 |
| Runners On | 23 | 6 | 1 | 0 | 0 | 4 | 1 | 6 | .261 | .304 | .320 |
| Runners/Scor. Pos. | 14 | 3 | 1 | 0 | 0 | 4 | 1 | 5 | .214 | .286 | .313 |

| RUNS BATTED IN | From 1B | From 2B | From 3B | Scoring Position |
|---|---|---|---|---|
| Totals | 6/153 | 22/94 | 23/57 | 45/151 |
| Percentage | 4% | 23% | 40% | 30% |
| Driving In Runners from 3B with Less than Two Out: | | | 17/25 | 68% |

Loves to face: John Smiley (.429, 6-for-14, 2 HR)
Hates to face: Eric Show (.067, 1-for-15, 7 SO)
Batted .238 before All-Star Game, .311 in second half, reversing trend of previous years. . . . Had nine hits (most in majors) in 16 at-bats with bases loaded last season. . . . Batted .313 vs. Eastern Division teams. . . . First two years in majors: one error every 4.5 games; last three years: one every 7.5 games. . . . Advanced from first to third 13 times on 13 outfield singles. . . . Career averages: .273 at Wrigley, .239 on road. . . . Owns .256 career mark against both left- and right-handed pitchers. . . . His yearly batting in Late-Inning Pressure Situations has been feast or famine: .217, .215, .313, .173, .310. . . . Half of career-high season total of 30 walks were intentional; one-third of career total of 96 are intentional.

## Len Dykstra

Bats Left

| Mets/Phillies | AB | H | 2B | 3B | HR | RBI | BB | SO | BA | SA | OBA |
|---|---|---|---|---|---|---|---|---|---|---|---|
| Season | 511 | 121 | 32 | 4 | 7 | 33 | 60 | 53 | .237 | .356 | .318 |
| vs. Left-Handers | 153 | 34 | 5 | 3 | 0 | 8 | 18 | 21 | .222 | .294 | .301 |
| vs. Right-Handers | 358 | 87 | 27 | 1 | 7 | 25 | 42 | 32 | .243 | .383 | .325 |
| Home | 234 | 59 | 15 | 2 | 5 | 14 | 34 | 23 | .252 | .397 | .344 |
| Road | 277 | 62 | 17 | 2 | 2 | 19 | 26 | 30 | .224 | .321 | .294 |
| Grass | 208 | 48 | 10 | 3 | 3 | 16 | 25 | 26 | .231 | .351 | .315 |
| Artificial Turf | 303 | 73 | 22 | 1 | 4 | 17 | 35 | 27 | .241 | .360 | .320 |
| April | 56 | 21 | 8 | 1 | 0 | 6 | 9 | 1 | .375 | .554 | .456 |
| May | 67 | 13 | 2 | 0 | 1 | 3 | 10 | 10 | .194 | .269 | .304 |
| June | 73 | 21 | 7 | 1 | 3 | 7 | 9 | 5 | .288 | .534 | .369 |
| July | 119 | 31 | 6 | 1 | 0 | 10 | 13 | 10 | .261 | .328 | .333 |
| August | 106 | 18 | 6 | 1 | 2 | 4 | 7 | 13 | .170 | .302 | .219 |
| Sept./Oct. | 90 | 17 | 3 | 0 | 1 | 3 | 12 | 14 | .189 | .256 | .284 |
| Leading Off Inn. | 242 | 48 | 13 | 3 | 2 | 2 | 26 | 17 | .198 | .302 | .279 |
| Runners On | 143 | 32 | 7 | 1 | 3 | 29 | 16 | 20 | .224 | .350 | .297 |
| Runners/Scor. Pos. | 79 | 16 | 3 | 1 | 0 | 22 | 10 | 11 | .203 | .266 | .284 |
| Runners On/2 Out | 69 | 16 | 5 | 0 | 1 | 14 | 5 | 11 | .232 | .348 | .284 |
| Scor. Pos./2 Out | 44 | 10 | 2 | 0 | 0 | 11 | 5 | 6 | .227 | .273 | .306 |
| Late Inning Pressure | 79 | 22 | 6 | 0 | 0 | 3 | 10 | 9 | .278 | .354 | .356 |
| Leading Off | 19 | 4 | 1 | 0 | 0 | 0 | 5 | 0 | .211 | .263 | .375 |
| Runners On | 38 | 8 | 2 | 0 | 0 | 3 | 2 | 5 | .211 | .263 | .244 |
| Runners/Scor. Pos. | 17 | 3 | 1 | 0 | 0 | 3 | 1 | 3 | .176 | .235 | .211 |

| RUNS BATTED IN | From 1B | From 2B | From 3B | Scoring Position |
|---|---|---|---|---|
| Totals | 4/91 | 8/64 | 14/39 | 22/103 |
| Percentage | 4% | 13% | 36% | 21% |
| Driving In Runners from 3B with Less than Two Out: | | | 9/19 | 47% |

Loves to face: Mike Bielecki (.357, 10-for-28, 2 HR)
Hates to face: Joe Magrane (.053, 1-for-19)
Had more walks than strikeouts for first time since hitting those key postseason home runs in 1986. . . . Started only four of 22 games vs. left-handed starters for Mets, but 21 of 30 games for Phillies. . . . Had topped 100 plate appearances vs. left-handed pitchers only once (121 in 1986) before last season. . . . Had hits in seven consecutive at-bats with runners in scoring position in July, matching Lonnie Smith for longest streak of season in majors. . . . Stole 19 bases in first 20 tries (including 13-of-14 for Mets), but was only 11-for-22 thereafter. . . . Has made only 12 errors in five seasons; his .991 fielding percentage over that span ranks second to Brett Butler among 49 players with 500+ games in outfield.

## Kevin Elster

Bats Right

| New York Mets | AB | H | 2B | 3B | HR | RBI | BB | SO | BA | SA | OBA |
|---|---|---|---|---|---|---|---|---|---|---|---|
| Season | 458 | 106 | 25 | 2 | 10 | 55 | 34 | 77 | .231 | .360 | .283 |
| vs. Left-Handers | 159 | 41 | 11 | 0 | 2 | 13 | 14 | 18 | .258 | .365 | .314 |
| vs. Right-Handers | 299 | 65 | 14 | 2 | 8 | 42 | 20 | 59 | .217 | .358 | .266 |
| Home | 235 | 53 | 11 | 1 | 5 | 30 | 18 | 44 | .226 | .345 | .281 |
| Road | 223 | 53 | 14 | 1 | 5 | 25 | 16 | 33 | .238 | .377 | .285 |
| Grass | 327 | 73 | 17 | 1 | 8 | 41 | 21 | 56 | .223 | .355 | .268 |
| Artificial Turf | 131 | 33 | 8 | 1 | 2 | 14 | 13 | 21 | .252 | .374 | .319 |
| April | 66 | 16 | 6 | 1 | 0 | 6 | 5 | 9 | .242 | .364 | .296 |
| May | 70 | 14 | 2 | 0 | 0 | 4 | 7 | 14 | .200 | .229 | .269 |
| June | 66 | 13 | 1 | 0 | 2 | 8 | 4 | 14 | .197 | .303 | .250 |
| July | 69 | 19 | 6 | 0 | 2 | 14 | 3 | 12 | .275 | .449 | .293 |
| August | 98 | 26 | 6 | 0 | 3 | 12 | 8 | 16 | .265 | .418 | .315 |
| Sept./Oct. | 89 | 18 | 4 | 1 | 3 | 11 | 7 | 12 | .202 | .371 | .265 |
| Leading Off Inn. | 110 | 22 | 4 | 1 | 4 | 4 | 4 | 20 | .200 | .364 | .228 |
| Runners On | 196 | 52 | 9 | 1 | 4 | 49 | 22 | 35 | .265 | .383 | .330 |
| Runners/Scor. Pos. | 116 | 32 | 4 | 1 | 3 | 45 | 18 | 29 | .276 | .405 | .352 |
| Runners On/2 Out | 84 | 23 | 5 | 0 | 1 | 16 | 13 | 15 | .274 | .369 | .371 |
| Scor. Pos./2 Out | 53 | 12 | 0 | 0 | 0 | 12 | 13 | 15 | .226 | .226 | .379 |
| Late Inning Pressure | 68 | 17 | 6 | 0 | 1 | 5 | 1 | 10 | .250 | .382 | .257 |
| Leading Off | 17 | 4 | 1 | 0 | 1 | 1 | 1 | 4 | .235 | .471 | .278 |
| Runners On | 25 | 7 | 3 | 0 | 0 | 4 | 0 | 5 | .280 | .400 | .269 |
| Runners/Scor. Pos. | 13 | 3 | 1 | 0 | 0 | 3 | 0 | 5 | .231 | .308 | .214 |

| RUNS BATTED IN | From 1B | From 2B | From 3B | Scoring Position |
|---|---|---|---|---|
| Totals | 5/144 | 16/86 | 24/58 | 40/144 |
| Percentage | 3% | 19% | 41% | 28% |
| Driving In Runners from 3B with Less than Two Out: | | | 18/33 | 55% |

Loves to face: Zane Smith (.500, 7-for-14)
Hates to face: Bryn Smith (.067, 1-for-15)
Started 134 games, all from 8th spot in batting order.... Avoided platoon status with July/August offensive surge.... Of his 55 RBI, 26 (47 percent) either tied score or put Mets in front, 4th best rate in majors (minimum: 50 RBI).... Hit .173 on fair balls to opposite field, .294 on balls hit straight away, .344 when he pulled ball.... Career figures: .247 vs. left-handers, .211 vs. right-handers; .256 with runners on base, .199 with bases empty.... Set record with 88-game errorless streak at shortstop; made 10 errors over next 88 games.... Ranks fifth on Mets' all-time honor (?) roll of games at short: Bud Harrelson (1281), Rafael Santana (478), Frank Taveras (372), Roy McMillan (335), Elster (320).

## Darrell Evans

Bats Left

| Atlanta Braves | AB | H | 2B | 3B | HR | RBI | BB | SO | BA | SA | OBA |
|---|---|---|---|---|---|---|---|---|---|---|---|
| Season | 276 | 57 | 6 | 1 | 11 | 39 | 41 | 46 | .207 | .355 | .303 |
| vs. Left-Handers | 73 | 18 | 4 | 0 | 2 | 17 | 7 | 12 | .247 | .384 | .298 |
| vs. Right-Handers | 203 | 39 | 2 | 1 | 9 | 22 | 34 | 34 | .192 | .345 | .305 |
| Home | 144 | 33 | 5 | 1 | 5 | 22 | 17 | 22 | .229 | .382 | .309 |
| Road | 132 | 24 | 1 | 0 | 6 | 17 | 24 | 24 | .182 | .326 | .298 |
| Grass | 208 | 41 | 5 | 1 | 8 | 29 | 28 | 38 | .197 | .346 | .289 |
| Artificial Turf | 68 | 16 | 1 | 0 | 3 | 10 | 13 | 8 | .235 | .382 | .345 |
| April | 27 | 6 | 0 | 0 | 3 | 3 | 5 | 5 | .222 | .556 | .344 |
| May | 33 | 5 | 0 | 1 | 0 | 4 | 6 | 5 | .152 | .212 | .275 |
| June | 44 | 7 | 0 | 0 | 1 | 5 | 6 | 10 | .159 | .227 | .255 |
| July | 67 | 12 | 2 | 0 | 3 | 7 | 9 | 10 | .179 | .343 | .269 |
| August | 58 | 17 | 2 | 0 | 4 | 10 | 11 | 6 | .293 | .534 | .400 |
| Sept./Oct. | 47 | 10 | 2 | 0 | 0 | 10 | 4 | 10 | .213 | .255 | .269 |
| Leading Off Inn. | 63 | 10 | 0 | 0 | 1 | 1 | 11 | 7 | .159 | .206 | .284 |
| Runners On | 116 | 32 | 5 | 1 | 2 | 30 | 19 | 22 | .276 | .388 | .362 |
| Runners/Scor. Pos. | 64 | 16 | 2 | 1 | 1 | 26 | 15 | 13 | .250 | .359 | .365 |
| Runners On/2 Out | 54 | 13 | 3 | 1 | 1 | 14 | 12 | 11 | .241 | .389 | .379 |
| Scor. Pos./2 Out | 33 | 8 | 1 | 1 | 1 | 12 | 11 | 8 | .242 | .424 | .432 |
| Late Inning Pressure | 59 | 12 | 0 | 0 | 1 | 3 | 4 | 12 | .203 | .254 | .246 |
| Leading Off | 9 | 4 | 0 | 0 | 0 | 0 | 1 | 1 | .444 | .444 | .500 |
| Runners On | 28 | 5 | 0 | 0 | 0 | 2 | 3 | 7 | .179 | .179 | .242 |
| Runners/Scor. Pos. | 15 | 1 | 0 | 0 | 0 | 2 | 2 | 5 | .067 | .067 | .158 |

| RUNS BATTED IN | From 1B | From 2B | From 3B | Scoring Position |
|---|---|---|---|---|
| Totals | 5/106 | 11/49 | 12/28 | 23/77 |
| Percentage | 5% | 22% | 43% | 30% |
| Driving In Runners from 3B with Less than Two Out: | | | 10/15 | 67% |

Loves to face: Rick Mahler (.438, 7-for-16, 3 HR)
Hates to face: Rick Sutcliffe (.091, 2-for-22)
He and Dave Kingman are the only 400-home-run hitters with a career batting average below .250.... Batting averages with runners on base and with runners in scoring position have been higher than his overall average in each of last six seasons.... Grounded into only one DP in 61 opportunities last season.... Has played for some poor teams, but none as bad as '89 (63–97) Braves.... Leads players active in 1989 with 2687 games.... First major league game: April 20, 1969, at Crosley Field; he pinch-hit for Braves' Claude Raymond vs. Reds' Jim Maloney. How long ago was that? "Aquarius/Let the Sunshine In" by the Fifth Dimension had just taken over Billboard's top spot from "Dizzy" by Tommy Roe.

## Mike Fitzgerald

Bats Right

| Montreal Expos | AB | H | 2B | 3B | HR | RBI | BB | SO | BA | SA | OBA |
|---|---|---|---|---|---|---|---|---|---|---|---|
| Season | 290 | 69 | 18 | 2 | 7 | 43 | 35 | 61 | .238 | .386 | .322 |
| vs. Left-Handers | 101 | 27 | 4 | 2 | 2 | 12 | 13 | 19 | .267 | .406 | .351 |
| vs. Right-Handers | 189 | 42 | 14 | 0 | 5 | 31 | 22 | 42 | .222 | .376 | .307 |
| Home | 141 | 40 | 9 | 2 | 3 | 23 | 13 | 29 | .284 | .440 | .353 |
| Road | 149 | 29 | 9 | 0 | 4 | 20 | 22 | 32 | .195 | .336 | .295 |
| Grass | 83 | 15 | 5 | 0 | 1 | 8 | 11 | 12 | .181 | .277 | .271 |
| Artificial Turf | 207 | 54 | 13 | 2 | 6 | 35 | 24 | 49 | .261 | .430 | .343 |
| April | 27 | 4 | 0 | 0 | 2 | 3 | 6 | 7 | .148 | .370 | .303 |
| May | 59 | 14 | 3 | 0 | 0 | 9 | 10 | 8 | .237 | .288 | .361 |
| June | 43 | 14 | 8 | 1 | 0 | 9 | 5 | 10 | .326 | .558 | .396 |
| July | 49 | 14 | 2 | 1 | 2 | 9 | 4 | 12 | .286 | .490 | .340 |
| August | 60 | 12 | 2 | 0 | 1 | 7 | 4 | 13 | .200 | .283 | .246 |
| Sept./Oct. | 52 | 11 | 3 | 0 | 2 | 6 | 6 | 11 | .212 | .385 | .293 |
| Leading Off Inn. | 59 | 10 | 0 | 1 | 2 | 2 | 9 | 12 | .169 | .305 | .279 |
| Runners On | 141 | 36 | 10 | 1 | 4 | 40 | 15 | 28 | .255 | .426 | .327 |
| Runners/Scor. Pos. | 98 | 25 | 6 | 1 | 2 | 33 | 12 | 23 | .255 | .398 | .330 |
| Runners On/2 Out | 65 | 15 | 6 | 0 | 1 | 14 | 8 | 18 | .231 | .369 | .315 |
| Scor. Pos./2 Out | 43 | 7 | 2 | 0 | 0 | 9 | 7 | 16 | .163 | .209 | .280 |
| Late Inning Pressure | 71 | 17 | 4 | 0 | 0 | 6 | 10 | 16 | .239 | .296 | .333 |
| Leading Off | 10 | 1 | 0 | 0 | 0 | 0 | 2 | 2 | .100 | .100 | .250 |
| Runners On | 33 | 8 | 3 | 0 | 0 | 6 | 6 | 8 | .242 | .333 | .359 |
| Runners/Scor. Pos. | 23 | 6 | 2 | 0 | 0 | 6 | 6 | 5 | .261 | .348 | .414 |

| RUNS BATTED IN | From 1B | From 2B | From 3B | Scoring Position |
|---|---|---|---|---|
| Totals | 8/92 | 14/73 | 14/45 | 28/118 |
| Percentage | 9% | 19% | 31% | 24% |
| Driving In Runners from 3B with Less than Two Out: | | | 13/23 | 57% |

Loves to face: Sid Fernandez (.500, 5-for-10, 2 2B, 1 HR)
Hates to face: Steve Bedrosian (0-for-17)
Had extra-base hits in five consecutive at-bats in June. Only one other major league player did that during the 1980s (Tim Teufel, 1987).... Has a career mark of .319 with bases loaded, and has hit a grand slam in each of last three seasons.... Set modest career highs in doubles, triples, home runs, and RBI.... Career mark of .265 in day games, .229 at night.... Has batted below .200 leading off innings in each of last two years.... Advanced from first to third on only one of 11 outfield singles.... Opponents succeeded on 74-of-100 stolen base attempts with Fitzgerald catching; success rate was 65 percent vs. Santovenia.... Loss of Bryn Smith may spell less time for Fitz, who caught 86 percent of Smith's innings.

## Tom Foley

Bats Left

| Montreal Expos | AB | H | 2B | 3B | HR | RBI | BB | SO | BA | SA | OBA |
|---|---|---|---|---|---|---|---|---|---|---|---|
| Season | 375 | 86 | 19 | 2 | 7 | 39 | 45 | 53 | .229 | .347 | .314 |
| vs. Left-Handers | 23 | 6 | 2 | 1 | 0 | 2 | 1 | 4 | .261 | .435 | .292 |
| vs. Right-Handers | 352 | 80 | 17 | 1 | 7 | 37 | 44 | 49 | .227 | .341 | .315 |
| Home | 203 | 44 | 8 | 1 | 4 | 19 | 16 | 29 | .217 | .325 | .281 |
| Road | 172 | 42 | 11 | 1 | 3 | 20 | 29 | 24 | .244 | .372 | .350 |
| Grass | 90 | 22 | 5 | 1 | 2 | 9 | 16 | 13 | .244 | .389 | .358 |
| Artificial Turf | 285 | 64 | 14 | 1 | 5 | 30 | 29 | 40 | .225 | .333 | .299 |
| April | 62 | 13 | 4 | 0 | 2 | 9 | 7 | 8 | .210 | .371 | .286 |
| May | 84 | 21 | 5 | 1 | 0 | 6 | 9 | 10 | .250 | .333 | .326 |
| June | 62 | 10 | 3 | 0 | 1 | 3 | 13 | 11 | .161 | .258 | .307 |
| July | 57 | 18 | 4 | 1 | 2 | 9 | 1 | 12 | .316 | .526 | .344 |
| August | 55 | 9 | 1 | 0 | 1 | 7 | 8 | 6 | .164 | .236 | .270 |
| Sept./Oct. | 55 | 15 | 2 | 0 | 1 | 5 | 7 | 6 | .273 | .364 | .349 |
| Leading Off Inn. | 70 | 18 | 1 | 1 | 1 | 1 | 6 | 9 | .257 | .343 | .333 |
| Runners On | 149 | 36 | 8 | 1 | 4 | 36 | 20 | 23 | .242 | .389 | .328 |
| Runners/Scor. Pos. | 101 | 25 | 6 | 1 | 4 | 36 | 14 | 18 | .248 | .446 | .333 |
| Runners On/2 Out | 48 | 10 | 2 | 0 | 2 | 12 | 13 | 7 | .208 | .375 | .377 |
| Scor. Pos./2 Out | 36 | 8 | 2 | 0 | 2 | 12 | 9 | 6 | .222 | .444 | .378 |
| Late Inning Pressure | 55 | 14 | 4 | 0 | 0 | 3 | 8 | 12 | .255 | .327 | .354 |
| Leading Off | 16 | 6 | 0 | 0 | 0 | 0 | 1 | 4 | .375 | .375 | .444 |
| Runners On | 21 | 3 | 1 | 0 | 0 | 3 | 4 | 5 | .143 | .190 | .269 |
| Runners/Scor. Pos. | 13 | 2 | 1 | 0 | 0 | 3 | 3 | 3 | .154 | .231 | .294 |

| RUNS BATTED IN | From 1B | From 2B | From 3B | Scoring Position |
|---|---|---|---|---|
| Totals | 3/91 | 11/79 | 18/39 | 29/118 |
| Percentage | 3% | 14% | 46% | 25% |
| Driving In Runners from 3B with Less than Two Out: | | | 15/25 | 60% |

Loves to face: Jim Clancy (5-for-5, 2 2B, 1 HR)
Hates to face: Scott Garrelts (0-for-12, 5 SO)
Averaged 5.53 chances per nine innings to rank second among N.L. second basemen (minimum: 500 inn.).... Has not started against a left-handed pitcher since July 27, 1988. His last 144 starts, including 99 last year, have all been vs. right-handers.... Has hit 26 home runs in his career, all against right-handed pitchers.... Expos won all seven games in which he homered; he has hit more home runs at the Big O than on the road in each of four years with Expos.... Batted .079 (5-for-63) on fair balls hit to the opposite field, .308 hitting straight away, and .315 on fair balls to the right side.... Has hit for a higher average vs. fly-ball pitchers than he has vs. groundballers in each of last six seasons.

## Andres Galarraga

Bats Right

| Montreal Expos | AB | H | 2B | 3B | HR | RBI | BB | SO | BA | SA | OBA |
|---|---|---|---|---|---|---|---|---|---|---|---|
| Season | 572 | 147 | 30 | 1 | 23 | 85 | 48 | 158 | .257 | .434 | .327 |
| vs. Left-Handers | 174 | 67 | 17 | 0 | 11 | 37 | 18 | 42 | .385 | .672 | .449 |
| vs. Right-Handers | 398 | 80 | 13 | 1 | 12 | 48 | 30 | 116 | .201 | .329 | .273 |
| Home | 286 | 69 | 18 | 1 | 13 | 50 | 29 | 76 | .241 | .448 | .324 |
| Road | 286 | 78 | 12 | 0 | 10 | 35 | 19 | 82 | .273 | .420 | .330 |
| Grass | 153 | 43 | 5 | 0 | 6 | 20 | 12 | 45 | .281 | .431 | .335 |
| Artificial Turf | 419 | 104 | 25 | 1 | 17 | 65 | 36 | 113 | .248 | .434 | .324 |
| April | 87 | 20 | 3 | 0 | 3 | 18 | 5 | 27 | .230 | .368 | .306 |
| May | 83 | 20 | 3 | 0 | 4 | 14 | 7 | 20 | .241 | .422 | .304 |
| June | 101 | 30 | 8 | 0 | 5 | 15 | 12 | 24 | .297 | .525 | .383 |
| July | 98 | 25 | 5 | 0 | 4 | 14 | 11 | 32 | .255 | .429 | .333 |
| August | 103 | 25 | 3 | 0 | 4 | 11 | 9 | 26 | .243 | .388 | .316 |
| Sept./Oct. | 100 | 27 | 8 | 1 | 3 | 13 | 4 | 29 | .270 | .460 | .311 |
| Leading Off Inn. | 100 | 24 | 5 | 1 | 3 | 3 | 8 | 23 | .240 | .400 | .309 |
| Runners On | 261 | 67 | 9 | 0 | 15 | 77 | 29 | 69 | .257 | .464 | .346 |
| Runners/Scor. Pos. | 143 | 31 | 5 | 0 | 5 | 54 | 23 | 42 | .217 | .357 | .335 |
| Runners On/2 Out | 93 | 18 | 2 | 0 | 3 | 18 | 13 | 34 | .194 | .312 | .299 |
| Scor. Pos./2 Out | 61 | 9 | 2 | 0 | 2 | 16 | 11 | 25 | .148 | .279 | .278 |
| Late Inning Pressure | 99 | 23 | 4 | 0 | 3 | 12 | 8 | 29 | .232 | .364 | .296 |
| Leading Off | 25 | 5 | 0 | 0 | 2 | 2 | 2 | 6 | .200 | .440 | .259 |
| Runners On | 45 | 10 | 1 | 0 | 1 | 10 | 5 | 12 | .222 | .311 | .314 |
| Runners/Scor. Pos. | 26 | 4 | 0 | 0 | 0 | 7 | 5 | 7 | .154 | .154 | .313 |

| RUNS BATTED IN | From 1B | From 2B | From 3B | Scoring Position |
|---|---|---|---|---|
| Totals | 15/176 | 16/102 | 31/75 | 47/177 |
| Percentage | 9% | 16% | 41% | 27% |
| Driving In Runners from 3B with Less than Two Out: | | | 23/42 | 55% |

Loves to face: Rick Sutcliffe (.417, 15-for-36, 2 HR)
Hates to face: Jose DeLeon (0-for-14, 6 SO)
Led majors with 9 first-inning home runs last season. . . . Batted 184 points higher vs. left-handers than vs. right-handers last season, largest such difference in majors (minimum: 100 AB vs. each). Career marks: .322 vs. lefties, .263 vs. righties. That .322 mark vs. southpaws is tops among active N.L. players. . . . He's a career .268 hitter in Late-Inning Pressure Situations, but has hit .196 in LIPS with runners in scoring position. . . . Hit by 33 pitches over last three seasons, most in N.L. . . . Even with lowest full-season batting average of his career, his totals for last three seasons show .288 average, 65 home runs, 267 RBI. Will Clark is the only N.L. player to beat him in all three categories.

## Ron Gant

Bats Right

| Atlanta Braves | AB | H | 2B | 3B | HR | RBI | BB | SO | BA | SA | OBA |
|---|---|---|---|---|---|---|---|---|---|---|---|
| Season | 260 | 46 | 8 | 3 | 9 | 25 | 20 | 63 | .177 | .335 | .237 |
| vs. Left-Handers | 79 | 9 | 4 | 0 | 1 | 6 | 9 | 19 | .114 | .203 | .205 |
| vs. Right-Handers | 181 | 37 | 4 | 3 | 8 | 19 | 11 | 44 | .204 | .392 | .251 |
| Home | 135 | 24 | 3 | 2 | 5 | 13 | 11 | 33 | .178 | .341 | .240 |
| Road | 125 | 22 | 5 | 1 | 4 | 12 | 9 | 30 | .176 | .328 | .234 |
| Grass | 188 | 31 | 4 | 3 | 7 | 16 | 16 | 47 | .165 | .330 | .233 |
| Artificial Turf | 72 | 15 | 4 | 0 | 2 | 9 | 4 | 16 | .208 | .347 | .247 |
| April | 75 | 13 | 1 | 2 | 3 | 6 | 10 | 24 | .173 | .360 | .271 |
| May | 100 | 18 | 4 | 0 | 2 | 12 | 3 | 19 | .180 | .280 | .202 |
| June | 29 | 4 | 1 | 0 | 1 | 3 | 3 | 8 | .138 | .276 | .235 |
| July | 0 | 0 | 0 | 0 | 0 | 0 | 0 | 0 | — | — | — |
| August | 0 | 0 | 0 | 0 | 0 | 0 | 0 | 0 | — | — | — |
| Sept./Oct. | 56 | 11 | 2 | 1 | 3 | 4 | 4 | 12 | .196 | .429 | .250 |
| Leading Off Inn. | 87 | 20 | 1 | 0 | 6 | 6 | 6 | 22 | .230 | .448 | .280 |
| Runners On | 95 | 13 | 5 | 1 | 0 | 16 | 4 | 21 | .137 | .211 | .168 |
| Runners/Scor. Pos. | 55 | 8 | 2 | 1 | 0 | 13 | 1 | 14 | .145 | .218 | .155 |
| Runners On/2 Out | 48 | 5 | 1 | 1 | 0 | 5 | 1 | 11 | .104 | .167 | .122 |
| Scor. Pos./2 Out | 35 | 3 | 0 | 1 | 0 | 4 | 0 | 10 | .086 | .143 | .086 |
| Late Inning Pressure | 42 | 5 | 0 | 0 | 1 | 2 | 1 | 13 | .119 | .190 | .140 |
| Leading Off | 12 | 2 | 0 | 0 | 0 | 0 | 0 | 5 | .167 | .167 | .167 |
| Runners On | 16 | 2 | 0 | 0 | 0 | 1 | 0 | 3 | .125 | .125 | .125 |
| Runners/Scor. Pos. | 8 | 1 | 0 | 0 | 0 | 1 | 0 | 1 | .125 | .125 | .125 |

| RUNS BATTED IN | From 1B | From 2B | From 3B | Scoring Position |
|---|---|---|---|---|
| Totals | 4/70 | 5/46 | 7/24 | 12/70 |
| Percentage | 6% | 11% | 29% | 17% |
| Driving In Runners from 3B with Less than Two Out: | | | 6/9 | 67% |

Loves to face: Rick Reuschel (.364, 4-for-11, 2 HR)
Hates to face: Bryn Smith (0-for-15)
Hit opening-day homer off Mike Scott, then went 0-for-29 before ending streak with hit off Dave Smith. That wasn't even the longest hitless streak on the team last year; Gerald Perry went 0-for-35. . . . Homered off some quality pitchers last year, including Scott (twice), Browning, Cone, Gooden, and Reuschel. . . . Had 43 plate appearances with a runner on first and less than two outs, but did not ground into a double play. . . . Made major league outfield debut by started 13 games there after September recall. . . . His .114 batting average vs. left-handers was the lowest by any N.L. player in 1980s. The A.L. low belongs to Carl Yastrzemski (.111 in 1981), who reached Cooperstown by the end of the '80s.

## Damaso Garcia

Bats Right

| Montreal Expos | AB | H | 2B | 3B | HR | RBI | BB | SO | BA | SA | OBA |
|---|---|---|---|---|---|---|---|---|---|---|---|
| Season | 203 | 55 | 9 | 1 | 3 | 18 | 15 | 20 | .271 | .369 | .317 |
| vs. Left-Handers | 131 | 39 | 8 | 0 | 3 | 10 | 10 | 14 | .298 | .427 | .343 |
| vs. Right-Handers | 72 | 16 | 1 | 1 | 0 | 8 | 5 | 6 | .222 | .264 | .269 |
| Home | 109 | 31 | 5 | 0 | 3 | 10 | 6 | 14 | .284 | .413 | .322 |
| Road | 94 | 24 | 4 | 1 | 0 | 8 | 9 | 6 | .255 | .319 | .311 |
| Grass | 37 | 9 | 2 | 0 | 0 | 4 | 3 | 3 | .243 | .297 | .286 |
| Artificial Turf | 166 | 46 | 7 | 1 | 3 | 14 | 12 | 17 | .277 | .386 | .324 |
| April | 51 | 13 | 2 | 1 | 0 | 6 | 5 | 3 | .255 | .333 | .321 |
| May | 17 | 3 | 0 | 0 | 0 | 1 | 0 | 3 | .176 | .176 | .167 |
| June | 37 | 8 | 1 | 0 | 0 | 3 | 3 | 3 | .216 | .243 | .275 |
| July | 50 | 18 | 5 | 0 | 2 | 4 | 3 | 8 | .360 | .580 | .389 |
| August | 34 | 10 | 1 | 0 | 1 | 2 | 2 | 1 | .294 | .412 | .333 |
| Sept./Oct. | 14 | 3 | 0 | 0 | 0 | 2 | 2 | 2 | .214 | .214 | .294 |
| Leading Off Inn. | 37 | 6 | 0 | 0 | 2 | 2 | 3 | 5 | .162 | .324 | .225 |
| Runners On | 78 | 18 | 1 | 0 | 1 | 16 | 6 | 9 | .231 | .282 | .276 |
| Runners/Scor. Pos. | 44 | 10 | 0 | 0 | 1 | 16 | 4 | 6 | .227 | .295 | .275 |
| Runners On/2 Out | 33 | 7 | 1 | 0 | 0 | 5 | 2 | 4 | .212 | .242 | .257 |
| Scor. Pos./2 Out | 20 | 5 | 0 | 0 | 0 | 5 | 2 | 2 | .250 | .250 | .318 |
| Late Inning Pressure | 36 | 10 | 0 | 0 | 1 | 5 | 3 | 3 | .278 | .361 | .333 |
| Leading Off | 7 | 0 | 0 | 0 | 0 | 0 | 2 | 1 | .000 | .000 | .222 |
| Runners On | 14 | 6 | 0 | 0 | 1 | 5 | 1 | 0 | .429 | .643 | .467 |
| Runners/Scor. Pos. | 8 | 4 | 0 | 0 | 1 | 5 | 1 | 0 | .500 | .875 | .556 |

| RUNS BATTED IN | From 1B | From 2B | From 3B | Scoring Position |
|---|---|---|---|---|
| Totals | 0/61 | 4/32 | 11/24 | 15/56 |
| Percentage | 0% | 13% | 46% | 27% |
| Driving In Runners from 3B with Less than Two Out: | | | 9/13 | 69% |

Loves to face: Ted Higuera (.400, 6-for-15, 1 HR)
Hates to face: Dennis Lamp (.091, 1-for-11)
Has 130 walks in 1032 games; Jack Clark had 132 in 142 last season. . . . Has walked once for every 31.7 plate appearances, lowest rate among active players with 4000+ times up (Rafael Ramirez ranks 2d, one per 22.2). Garcia's 1989 rate of a walk every 14.8 times up is the highest single-season rate of his career. . . . Batted .385 in day games last season. Career: .297 in daylight, .275 at night. . . . Yankees sent him to Toronto after '79 season, signed him as free agent last winter. What did Garcia miss? Twelve Yankees managerial changes, a Mets World Series, and a Giants Super Bowl; there's a new mayor and transit tokens are $1.15. What's the same? Yankees' last world championship is still 1978.

## Kirk Gibson

Bats Left

| Los Angeles Dodgers | AB | H | 2B | 3B | HR | RBI | BB | SO | BA | SA | OBA |
|---|---|---|---|---|---|---|---|---|---|---|---|
| Season | 253 | 54 | 8 | 2 | 9 | 28 | 35 | 55 | .213 | .368 | .312 |
| vs. Left-Handers | 95 | 12 | 1 | 0 | 4 | 10 | 12 | 24 | .126 | .263 | .227 |
| vs. Right-Handers | 158 | 42 | 7 | 2 | 5 | 18 | 23 | 31 | .266 | .430 | .363 |
| Home | 135 | 30 | 5 | 2 | 4 | 10 | 19 | 31 | .222 | .378 | .318 |
| Road | 118 | 24 | 3 | 0 | 5 | 18 | 16 | 24 | .203 | .356 | .304 |
| Grass | 196 | 42 | 8 | 2 | 6 | 18 | 27 | 42 | .214 | .367 | .313 |
| Artificial Turf | 57 | 12 | 0 | 0 | 3 | 10 | 8 | 13 | .211 | .368 | .309 |
| April | 50 | 14 | 3 | 0 | 2 | 8 | 8 | 11 | .280 | .460 | .393 |
| May | 33 | 10 | 1 | 1 | 1 | 3 | 3 | 4 | .303 | .485 | .361 |
| June | 110 | 22 | 2 | 1 | 5 | 12 | 16 | 24 | .200 | .373 | .302 |
| July | 60 | 8 | 2 | 0 | 1 | 5 | 8 | 16 | .133 | .217 | .232 |
| August | 0 | 0 | 0 | 0 | 0 | 0 | 0 | 0 | — | — | — |
| Sept./Oct. | 0 | 0 | 0 | 0 | 0 | 0 | 0 | 0 | — | — | — |
| Leading Off Inn. | 51 | 8 | 0 | 1 | 2 | 2 | 4 | 7 | .157 | .314 | .232 |
| Runners On | 116 | 24 | 5 | 1 | 3 | 22 | 19 | 25 | .207 | .345 | .319 |
| Runners/Scor. Pos. | 54 | 10 | 1 | 1 | 0 | 13 | 15 | 12 | .185 | .241 | .361 |
| Runners On/2 Out | 42 | 8 | 3 | 0 | 1 | 9 | 8 | 14 | .190 | .333 | .320 |
| Scor. Pos./2 Out | 25 | 4 | 1 | 0 | 0 | 5 | 7 | 8 | .160 | .200 | .344 |
| Late Inning Pressure | 44 | 6 | 1 | 0 | 0 | 3 | 4 | 12 | .136 | .159 | .208 |
| Leading Off | 13 | 0 | 0 | 0 | 0 | 0 | 1 | 3 | .000 | .000 | .071 |
| Runners On | 19 | 3 | 1 | 0 | 0 | 3 | 2 | 7 | .158 | .211 | .238 |
| Runners/Scor. Pos. | 10 | 2 | 0 | 0 | 0 | 2 | 2 | 1 | .200 | .200 | .333 |

| RUNS BATTED IN | From 1B | From 2B | From 3B | Scoring Position |
|---|---|---|---|---|
| Totals | 6/89 | 6/46 | 7/19 | 13/65 |
| Percentage | 7% | 13% | 37% | 20% |
| Driving In Runners from 3B with Less than Two Out: | | | 5/9 | 56% |

Loves to face: Charlie Leibrandt (.500, 6-for-12, 1 HR)
Hates to face: Ed Whitson (0-for-12)
Batted .213 the year after MVP season, lowest year-after batting average by any N.L. MVP since '63 winner Sandy Koufax hit .095 in 1964. (Last pitcher to win N.L. MVP, Bob Gibson in 1968, hit .246 the next year!) . . .July batting average was lowest in majors last season (minimum: two PA per game). . . . Batting average vs. lefties (.126) was 3d-lowest in N.L. . . . Has batted 89 times with the bases loaded, but he's still slamless. . . . Needs 16 home runs to join Dawson and Yount as the only active players with 200 homers and 200 steals. . . . Has 30 assists in 980 career games in outfield; rate of one every 32.7 games is lowest among active players (minimum: 500 games). Magic Johnson he ain't.

## Jose Gonzalez

Bats Right

| Los Angeles Dodgers | AB | H | 2B | 3B | HR | RBI | BB | SO | BA | SA | OBA |
|---|---|---|---|---|---|---|---|---|---|---|---|
| Season | 261 | 70 | 11 | 2 | 3 | 18 | 23 | 53 | .268 | .360 | .326 |
| vs. Left-Handers | 134 | 41 | 6 | 1 | 2 | 10 | 9 | 20 | .306 | .410 | .347 |
| vs. Right-Handers | 127 | 29 | 5 | 1 | 1 | 8 | 14 | 33 | .228 | .307 | .305 |
| Home | 113 | 27 | 5 | 0 | 2 | 10 | 11 | 28 | .239 | .336 | .304 |
| Road | 148 | 43 | 6 | 2 | 1 | 8 | 12 | 25 | .291 | .378 | .344 |
| Grass | 181 | 46 | 9 | 1 | 3 | 15 | 18 | 38 | .254 | .365 | .320 |
| Artificial Turf | 80 | 24 | 2 | 1 | 0 | 3 | 5 | 15 | .300 | .350 | .341 |
| April | 0 | 0 | 0 | 0 | 0 | 0 | 0 | 0 | — | — | — |
| May | 0 | 0 | 0 | 0 | 0 | 0 | 0 | 0 | — | — | — |
| June | 58 | 21 | 1 | 1 | 0 | 2 | 7 | 6 | .362 | .414 | .424 |
| July | 74 | 15 | 3 | 0 | 1 | 6 | 5 | 13 | .203 | .284 | .253 |
| August | 85 | 20 | 3 | 1 | 1 | 5 | 8 | 20 | .235 | .329 | .301 |
| Sept./Oct. | 44 | 14 | 4 | 0 | 1 | 5 | 3 | 14 | .318 | .477 | .362 |
| Leading Off Inn. | 78 | 23 | 3 | 0 | 1 | 1 | 4 | 12 | .295 | .372 | .329 |
| Runners On | 101 | 26 | 4 | 0 | 1 | 16 | 10 | 25 | .257 | .327 | .321 |
| Runners/Scor. Pos. | 58 | 12 | 3 | 0 | 0 | 14 | 8 | 16 | .207 | .259 | .299 |
| Runners On/2 Out | 39 | 8 | 2 | 0 | 0 | 6 | 5 | 15 | .205 | .256 | .295 |
| Scor. Pos./2 Out | 27 | 5 | 2 | 0 | 0 | 6 | 4 | 9 | .185 | .259 | .290 |
| Late Inning Pressure | 53 | 17 | 2 | 1 | 0 | 2 | 5 | 9 | .321 | .396 | .379 |
| Leading Off | 15 | 3 | 1 | 0 | 0 | 0 | 1 | 2 | .200 | .267 | .250 |
| Runners On | 23 | 9 | 0 | 0 | 0 | 2 | 1 | 6 | .391 | .391 | .417 |
| Runners/Scor. Pos. | 11 | 2 | 0 | 0 | 0 | 2 | 1 | 3 | .182 | .182 | .250 |

| RUNS BATTED IN | From 1B | From 2B | From 3B | Scoring Position |
|---|---|---|---|---|
| Totals | 1/75 | 8/45 | 6/21 | 14/66 |
| Percentage | 1% | 18% | 29% | 21% |
| Driving In Runners from 3B with Less than Two Out: | | | 4/10 | 40% |

Loves to face: John Franco (.750, 3-for-4)
Hates to face: Larry Andersen (0-for-6, 3 SO)
Career average is .279 vs. left-handers, .197 vs. right-handers. Round tripper off Bucs' Doug Drabek last July is his only circuit smash against a portsider. (There it is, *Analyst* fans, our annual salute to the glory of 1940s sportswriting.) . . .Grounded into only two double plays in 48 opportunities. . . . With 13 errors in 310 chances, his .958 career fielding percentage is the lowest among active N.L. outfielders (minimum: 200 games). . . . Dodgers' seven starting center fielders (principally John Shelby and Gonzalez) batted a combined .214 last season, with 55 runs scored and 28 RBI. Each of those figures repesents the lowest totals by starting center fielders on any major league team in '89.

## Mark Grace

Bats Left

| Chicago Cubs | AB | H | 2B | 3B | HR | RBI | BB | SO | BA | SA | OBA |
|---|---|---|---|---|---|---|---|---|---|---|---|
| Season | 510 | 160 | 28 | 3 | 13 | 80 | 80 | 42 | .314 | .457 | .405 |
| vs. Left-Handers | 159 | 42 | 9 | 2 | 4 | 25 | 18 | 18 | .264 | .421 | .339 |
| vs. Right-Handers | 351 | 118 | 19 | 1 | 9 | 55 | 62 | 24 | .336 | .473 | .433 |
| Home | 258 | 87 | 15 | 2 | 8 | 45 | 48 | 21 | .337 | .504 | .440 |
| Road | 252 | 73 | 13 | 1 | 5 | 35 | 32 | 21 | .290 | .409 | .367 |
| Grass | 369 | 123 | 22 | 3 | 9 | 69 | 59 | 28 | .333 | .482 | .422 |
| Artificial Turf | 141 | 37 | 6 | 0 | 4 | 11 | 21 | 14 | .262 | .390 | .358 |
| April | 81 | 26 | 6 | 0 | 2 | 11 | 13 | 5 | .321 | .469 | .415 |
| May | 98 | 30 | 2 | 0 | 0 | 15 | 10 | 13 | .306 | .327 | .367 |
| June | 33 | 11 | 2 | 0 | 0 | 1 | 7 | 1 | .333 | .394 | .450 |
| July | 98 | 34 | 10 | 0 | 5 | 24 | 12 | 4 | .347 | .602 | .411 |
| August | 109 | 31 | 4 | 2 | 6 | 16 | 20 | 9 | .284 | .523 | .395 |
| Sept./Oct. | 91 | 28 | 4 | 1 | 0 | 13 | 18 | 10 | .308 | .374 | .422 |
| Leading Off Inn. | 110 | 41 | 9 | 0 | 5 | 5 | 11 | 6 | .373 | .591 | .430 |
| Runners On | 238 | 83 | 13 | 1 | 7 | 74 | 47 | 15 | .349 | .500 | .451 |
| Runners/Scor. Pos. | 135 | 42 | 7 | 1 | 2 | 60 | 36 | 9 | .311 | .422 | .448 |
| Runners On/2 Out | 104 | 35 | 3 | 0 | 4 | 27 | 25 | 6 | .337 | .481 | .465 |
| Scor. Pos./2 Out | 65 | 21 | 1 | 0 | 1 | 20 | 20 | 3 | .323 | .385 | .482 |
| Late Inning Pressure | 64 | 24 | 4 | 0 | 4 | 10 | 13 | 5 | .375 | .625 | .481 |
| Leading Off | 17 | 6 | 1 | 0 | 2 | 2 | 2 | 1 | .353 | .765 | .421 |
| Runners On | 26 | 11 | 1 | 0 | 2 | 8 | 6 | 2 | .423 | .692 | .531 |
| Runners/Scor. Pos. | 18 | 6 | 1 | 0 | 1 | 6 | 3 | 2 | .333 | .556 | .429 |

| RUNS BATTED IN | From 1B | From 2B | From 3B | Scoring Position |
|---|---|---|---|---|
| Totals | 12/170 | 23/98 | 32/60 | 55/158 |
| Percentage | 7% | 23% | 53% | 35% |
| Driving In Runners from 3B with Less than Two Out: | | | 26/34 | 76% |

Loves to face: Scott Garrelts (.700, 7-for-10, 1 HR)
Hates to face: Ron Darling (.083, 1-for-12)
Also went 4-for-5 with a triple and a homer vs. Garrelts in N.L. Championship Series. . . . Led N.L. in RBI in July. . . . Hit .375 (best in N.L.) in Late-Inning Pressure Situations. Has .350 career average in LIPS, and owns .600 career average (9-for-15) with bases loaded. . . . Has driven in 72 percent of runners from third base with less than two outs in his career, top rate among active players. . . . Cut his error count from 17 in 1988 to 6 last season. . . . Led N.L. first basemen with 0.91 assists per nine innings. . . . Owns career on-base average of .410 leading off innings, 3d best among active players. . . . Night games at Wrigley? It's no *tsimmis* to Grace, who has .305 career average under both sun and moon.

## Tommy Gregg

Bats Left

| Atlanta Braves | AB | H | 2B | 3B | HR | RBI | BB | SO | BA | SA | OBA |
|---|---|---|---|---|---|---|---|---|---|---|---|
| Season | 276 | 67 | 8 | 0 | 6 | 23 | 18 | 45 | .243 | .337 | .288 |
| vs. Left-Handers | 57 | 13 | 1 | 0 | 0 | 2 | 5 | 17 | .228 | .246 | .290 |
| vs. Right-Handers | 219 | 54 | 7 | 0 | 6 | 21 | 13 | 28 | .247 | .361 | .288 |
| Home | 116 | 34 | 5 | 0 | 2 | 10 | 10 | 14 | .293 | .388 | .349 |
| Road | 160 | 33 | 3 | 0 | 4 | 13 | 8 | 31 | .206 | .300 | .243 |
| Grass | 205 | 48 | 6 | 0 | 3 | 16 | 14 | 32 | .234 | .307 | .282 |
| Artificial Turf | 71 | 19 | 2 | 0 | 3 | 7 | 4 | 13 | .268 | .423 | .307 |
| April | 36 | 14 | 4 | 0 | 1 | 8 | 3 | 4 | .389 | .583 | .425 |
| May | 0 | 0 | 0 | 0 | 0 | 0 | 0 | 0 | — | — | — |
| June | 86 | 24 | 3 | 0 | 0 | 5 | 6 | 8 | .279 | .314 | .326 |
| July | 57 | 9 | 0 | 0 | 1 | 4 | 4 | 12 | .158 | .211 | .213 |
| August | 63 | 14 | 1 | 0 | 3 | 4 | 1 | 11 | .222 | .381 | .234 |
| Sept./Oct. | 34 | 6 | 0 | 0 | 1 | 2 | 4 | 10 | .176 | .265 | .263 |
| Leading Off Inn. | 59 | 11 | 2 | 0 | 1 | 1 | 0 | 13 | .186 | .271 | .186 |
| Runners On | 116 | 33 | 3 | 0 | 3 | 20 | 9 | 15 | .284 | .388 | .333 |
| Runners/Scor. Pos. | 55 | 13 | 2 | 0 | 1 | 15 | 6 | 9 | .236 | .327 | .306 |
| Runners On/2 Out | 47 | 10 | 2 | 0 | 0 | 5 | 7 | 9 | .213 | .255 | .315 |
| Scor. Pos./2 Out | 27 | 3 | 1 | 0 | 0 | 4 | 5 | 8 | .111 | .148 | .250 |
| Late Inning Pressure | 63 | 14 | 1 | 0 | 1 | 5 | 4 | 15 | .222 | .286 | .269 |
| Leading Off | 20 | 3 | 1 | 0 | 0 | 0 | 0 | 7 | .150 | .200 | .150 |
| Runners On | 24 | 8 | 0 | 0 | 1 | 5 | 3 | 2 | .333 | .458 | .407 |
| Runners/Scor. Pos. | 14 | 4 | 0 | 0 | 1 | 5 | 2 | 2 | .286 | .500 | .375 |

| RUNS BATTED IN | From 1B | From 2B | From 3B | Scoring Position |
|---|---|---|---|---|
| Totals | 3/93 | 9/49 | 5/16 | 14/65 |
| Percentage | 3% | 18% | 31% | 22% |
| Driving In Runners from 3B with Less than Two Out: | | | 4/7 | 57% |

Loves to face: Rick Rhoden (3-for-3, 2 2B)
Hates to face: Scott Scudder (.083, 1-for-12)
Had a home run and a double in season opener, then went 5-for-5 on April 18, the first five-hit game by an Atlanta rookie since Barry Bonnell had one in May 1977. . . . Those were the only games all season in which Gregg had more than one extra-base hit. . . . Apparently benefits from opposing teams holding runners on first base: he batted .304 when first base was occupied, .158 when first base was empty. . . . Hit two pinch-hit home runs last season; Braves tied for major league lead with five pinch homers. . . . Career average of .275 vs. ground-ball pitchers, .232 vs. fly-ballers. . . . Had one hit in 23 at-bats vs. New York last season, and went 1-for-24 against San Diego, the only hit being a home run off Don Schulze.

## Ken Griffey, Sr.

Bats Left

| Cincinnati Reds | AB | H | 2B | 3B | HR | RBI | BB | SO | BA | SA | OBA |
|---|---|---|---|---|---|---|---|---|---|---|---|
| Season | 236 | 62 | 8 | 3 | 8 | 30 | 29 | 42 | .263 | .424 | .346 |
| vs. Left-Handers | 16 | 5 | 1 | 1 | 0 | 0 | 3 | 4 | .313 | .500 | .450 |
| vs. Right-Handers | 220 | 57 | 7 | 2 | 8 | 30 | 26 | 38 | .259 | .418 | .337 |
| Home | 120 | 32 | 5 | 1 | 2 | 11 | 16 | 26 | .267 | .375 | .353 |
| Road | 116 | 30 | 3 | 2 | 6 | 19 | 13 | 16 | .259 | .474 | .338 |
| Grass | 71 | 20 | 3 | 1 | 2 | 9 | 7 | 12 | .282 | .437 | .354 |
| Artificial Turf | 165 | 42 | 5 | 2 | 6 | 21 | 22 | 30 | .255 | .418 | .342 |
| April | 9 | 1 | 0 | 0 | 1 | 2 | 1 | 1 | .111 | .444 | .200 |
| May | 48 | 15 | 2 | 0 | 1 | 6 | 8 | 8 | .313 | .417 | .411 |
| June | 51 | 13 | 1 | 0 | 2 | 5 | 2 | 9 | .255 | .392 | .296 |
| July | 46 | 13 | 2 | 2 | 2 | 7 | 5 | 7 | .283 | .543 | .353 |
| August | 62 | 13 | 1 | 0 | 1 | 5 | 12 | 12 | .210 | .274 | .338 |
| Sept./Oct. | 20 | 7 | 2 | 1 | 1 | 5 | 1 | 5 | .350 | .700 | .381 |
| Leading Off Inn. | 44 | 13 | 2 | 1 | 1 | 1 | 5 | 5 | .295 | .455 | .367 |
| Runners On | 100 | 22 | 2 | 1 | 4 | 26 | 18 | 17 | .220 | .380 | .345 |
| Runners/Scor. Pos. | 67 | 18 | 2 | 1 | 4 | 26 | 16 | 13 | .269 | .507 | .410 |
| Runners On/2 Out | 49 | 7 | 1 | 0 | 2 | 9 | 10 | 7 | .143 | .286 | .300 |
| Scor. Pos./2 Out | 33 | 6 | 1 | 0 | 2 | 9 | 9 | 5 | .182 | .394 | .357 |
| Late Inning Pressure | 45 | 13 | 5 | 0 | 1 | 6 | 3 | 6 | .289 | .467 | .333 |
| Leading Off | 5 | 2 | 1 | 0 | 0 | 0 | 2 | 0 | .400 | .600 | .571 |
| Runners On | 20 | 4 | 0 | 0 | 0 | 5 | 1 | 0 | .200 | .200 | .238 |
| Runners/Scor. Pos. | 13 | 4 | 0 | 0 | 0 | 5 | 1 | 0 | .308 | .308 | .357 |

| RUNS BATTED IN | From 1B | From 2B | From 3B | Scoring Position |
|---|---|---|---|---|
| Totals | 3/63 | 9/48 | 10/29 | 19/77 |
| Percentage | 5% | 19% | 34% | 25% |
| Driving In Runners from 3B with Less than Two Out: | | | 6/11 | 55% |

Loves to face: Kevin Gross (.500, 7-for-14, 3 HR)
Hates to face: Neal Heaton (0-for-16)
The Final Jeopardy! category is "The Griffeys." The wagers are in place and the answer is: "The only two pitchers who have allowed home runs to both Ken Sr. and Ken Jr." Good luck. . . . Started 56 games, all against right-handed pitchers. Has not started against a lefty since July 31, 1987. . . . Oldest player to start 50+ games in outfield last season. The next oldest: Dwight Evans and Fred Lynn. . . . Pinch-hitting numbers over past two years are poor (13-for-73), dropping career pinch-hit average from .338 to .284. . . . The last time that he started a season playing for Lou Piniella (New York, 1986), he was traded to Atlanta at the end of June. . . . Final Jeopardy! Question: Who are Charlie Hough and Doyle Alexander?

## Alfredo Griffin

Bats Left and Right

| Los Angeles Dodgers | AB | H | 2B | 3B | HR | RBI | BB | SO | BA | SA | OBA |
|---|---|---|---|---|---|---|---|---|---|---|---|
| Season | 506 | 125 | 27 | 2 | 0 | 29 | 29 | 57 | .247 | .308 | .287 |
| vs. Left-Handers | 177 | 50 | 8 | 1 | 0 | 10 | 11 | 25 | .282 | .339 | .323 |
| vs. Right-Handers | 329 | 75 | 19 | 1 | 0 | 19 | 18 | 32 | .228 | .292 | .268 |
| Home | 250 | 63 | 13 | 1 | 0 | 8 | 13 | 24 | .252 | .312 | .289 |
| Road | 256 | 62 | 14 | 1 | 0 | 21 | 16 | 33 | .242 | .305 | .286 |
| Grass | 377 | 92 | 19 | 1 | 0 | 19 | 20 | 45 | .244 | .300 | .281 |
| Artificial Turf | 129 | 33 | 8 | 1 | 0 | 10 | 9 | 12 | .256 | .333 | .304 |
| April | 82 | 16 | 8 | 0 | 0 | 5 | 2 | 8 | .195 | .293 | .214 |
| May | 17 | 3 | 0 | 0 | 0 | 0 | 2 | 2 | .176 | .176 | .263 |
| June | 107 | 38 | 7 | 1 | 0 | 5 | 6 | 14 | .355 | .439 | .389 |
| July | 94 | 23 | 5 | 0 | 0 | 6 | 8 | 3 | .245 | .298 | .304 |
| August | 111 | 27 | 5 | 0 | 0 | 8 | 9 | 15 | .243 | .288 | .300 |
| Sept./Oct. | 95 | 18 | 2 | 1 | 0 | 5 | 2 | 15 | .189 | .232 | .204 |
| Leading Off Inn. | 168 | 33 | 5 | 2 | 0 | 0 | 13 | 19 | .196 | .250 | .254 |
| Runners On | 173 | 47 | 11 | 0 | 0 | 29 | 6 | 21 | .272 | .335 | .294 |
| Runners/Scor. Pos. | 107 | 26 | 8 | 0 | 0 | 29 | 4 | 17 | .243 | .318 | .268 |
| Runners On/2 Out | 82 | 20 | 5 | 0 | 0 | 14 | 2 | 8 | .244 | .305 | .262 |
| Scor. Pos./2 Out | 55 | 11 | 4 | 0 | 0 | 14 | 2 | 7 | .200 | .273 | .228 |
| Late Inning Pressure | 94 | 20 | 1 | 0 | 0 | 4 | 5 | 17 | .213 | .223 | .253 |
| Leading Off | 24 | 1 | 0 | 0 | 0 | 0 | 2 | 5 | .042 | .042 | .115 |
| Runners On | 49 | 15 | 1 | 0 | 0 | 4 | 0 | 8 | .306 | .327 | .306 |
| Runners/Scor. Pos. | 30 | 5 | 0 | 0 | 0 | 4 | 0 | 6 | .167 | .167 | .167 |

| RUNS BATTED IN | From 1B | From 2B | From 3B | Scoring Position |
|---|---|---|---|---|
| Totals | 3/113 | 13/91 | 13/37 | 26/128 |
| Percentage | 3% | 14% | 35% | 20% |
| Driving In Runners from 3B with Less than Two Out: | | | 8/16 | 50% |

Loves to face: Ken Hill (.556, 5-for-9)
Hates to face: Randy O'Neal (0-for-11)
Hit 10 of his career-high 27 doubles vs. Cincinnati, the most by any player in majors against any team last season. . . . Batted .309 vs. ground-ball pitchers, .175 vs. fly-ballers. . . . Has six hits, all for extra bases, in 16 bases-loaded at-bats in N.L.: three triples in '88, three doubles in '89. . . . Has sub-.200 BA leading off innings in each of last three years. . . . Had exactly 100 sacrifice bunts during the '80s; only Ozzie Smith (110) and Bob Boone (104) had more. . . . Last year's .975 fielding percentage was the highest of his 14-year career. . . . Among active shortstops only Garry Templeton (352) has made more errors than Griffin (287); Griffin's ranking is residue of four straight years leading A.L. shortsops in errors.

## Pedro Guerrero

Bats Right

| St. Louis Cardinals | AB | H | 2B | 3B | HR | RBI | BB | SO | BA | SA | OBA |
|---|---|---|---|---|---|---|---|---|---|---|---|
| Season | 570 | 177 | 42 | 1 | 17 | 117 | 79 | 84 | .311 | .477 | .391 |
| vs. Left-Handers | 218 | 69 | 17 | 0 | 8 | 41 | 32 | 38 | .317 | .505 | .402 |
| vs. Right-Handers | 352 | 108 | 25 | 1 | 9 | 76 | 47 | 46 | .307 | .460 | .384 |
| Home | 281 | 81 | 25 | 0 | 3 | 49 | 40 | 43 | .288 | .409 | .372 |
| Road | 289 | 96 | 17 | 1 | 14 | 68 | 39 | 41 | .332 | .543 | .410 |
| Grass | 151 | 55 | 11 | 0 | 9 | 39 | 17 | 21 | .364 | .616 | .427 |
| Artificial Turf | 419 | 122 | 31 | 1 | 8 | 78 | 62 | 63 | .291 | .427 | .379 |
| April | 80 | 22 | 8 | 0 | 3 | 19 | 11 | 11 | .275 | .488 | .362 |
| May | 96 | 32 | 8 | 0 | 3 | 17 | 8 | 11 | .333 | .510 | .374 |
| June | 86 | 25 | 6 | 1 | 0 | 13 | 15 | 11 | .291 | .384 | .398 |
| July | 89 | 26 | 7 | 0 | 2 | 16 | 15 | 14 | .292 | .438 | .398 |
| August | 113 | 41 | 6 | 0 | 4 | 26 | 12 | 16 | .363 | .522 | .421 |
| Sept./Oct. | 106 | 31 | 7 | 0 | 5 | 26 | 18 | 21 | .292 | .500 | .386 |
| Leading Off Inn. | 142 | 36 | 9 | 0 | 2 | 2 | 8 | 18 | .254 | .359 | .293 |
| Runners On | 267 | 95 | 20 | 1 | 10 | 110 | 51 | 35 | .356 | .551 | .449 |
| Runners/Scor. Pos. | 168 | 68 | 16 | 1 | 6 | 100 | 41 | 25 | .405 | .619 | .495 |
| Runners On/2 Out | 128 | 47 | 11 | 0 | 6 | 48 | 29 | 20 | .367 | .594 | .491 |
| Scor. Pos./2 Out | 85 | 36 | 9 | 0 | 5 | 45 | 25 | 13 | .424 | .706 | .559 |
| Late Inning Pressure | 77 | 24 | 5 | 0 | 2 | 21 | 8 | 7 | .312 | .455 | .368 |
| Leading Off | 19 | 5 | 1 | 0 | 1 | 1 | 0 | 1 | .263 | .474 | .263 |
| Runners On | 40 | 14 | 1 | 0 | 1 | 20 | 6 | 0 | .350 | .450 | .417 |
| Runners/Scor. Pos. | 30 | 12 | 1 | 0 | 1 | 20 | 6 | 0 | .400 | .533 | .474 |

| RUNS BATTED IN | From 1B | From 2B | From 3B | Scoring Position |
|---|---|---|---|---|
| Totals | 11/169 | 36/111 | 53/88 | 89/199 |
| Percentage | 7% | 32% | 60% | 45% |
| Driving In Runners from 3B with Less than Two Out: | | | 33/50 | 66% |

Loves to face: Dennis Rasmussen (.750, 9-for-12)
Hates to face: Orel Hershiser (0-for-7)
Unusual combination: 17 home runs, 117 RBI; that's the most RBI by a player with so few home runs since Jackie Robinson had 16 homers and 124 RBI in 1949. . . . One reason that Pedro drove in so many runs: he batted 134 points higher with runners in scoring position than in other at-bats, largest such difference in majors last season (minimum: 75 AB with RISP). . . . One of two N.L. players in 1980s to reach .400 mark with runners in scoring position; Tony Gwynn hit .418 in 1984. . . . Guerrero's scoring-position batting averages were .344 and .371 in 1987 and 1988. . . . Led majors with 40 go-ahead RBI, one more than Will Clark, four more than Kevin Mitchell. . . . Also led majors with .364 average on grass fields.

## Tony Gwynn

Bats Left

| San Diego Padres | AB | H | 2B | 3B | HR | RBI | BB | SO | BA | SA | OBA |
|---|---|---|---|---|---|---|---|---|---|---|---|
| Season | 604 | 203 | 27 | 7 | 4 | 62 | 56 | 30 | .336 | .424 | .389 |
| vs. Left-Handers | 200 | 61 | 4 | 2 | 0 | 23 | 16 | 14 | .305 | .345 | .355 |
| vs. Right-Handers | 404 | 142 | 23 | 5 | 4 | 39 | 40 | 16 | .351 | .463 | .406 |
| Home | 288 | 94 | 12 | 4 | 3 | 29 | 29 | 13 | .326 | .427 | .384 |
| Road | 316 | 109 | 15 | 3 | 1 | 33 | 27 | 17 | .345 | .421 | .394 |
| Grass | 443 | 144 | 18 | 4 | 3 | 39 | 44 | 19 | .325 | .404 | .383 |
| Artificial Turf | 161 | 59 | 9 | 3 | 1 | 23 | 12 | 11 | .366 | .478 | .407 |
| April | 101 | 33 | 3 | 2 | 2 | 9 | 8 | 4 | .327 | .455 | .376 |
| May | 110 | 34 | 6 | 3 | 0 | 9 | 10 | 3 | .309 | .418 | .369 |
| June | 105 | 47 | 7 | 0 | 2 | 16 | 9 | 8 | .448 | .571 | .483 |
| July | 91 | 22 | 2 | 1 | 0 | 4 | 12 | 5 | .242 | .286 | .327 |
| August | 105 | 40 | 3 | 1 | 0 | 12 | 9 | 7 | .381 | .429 | .426 |
| Sept./Oct. | 92 | 27 | 6 | 0 | 0 | 12 | 8 | 3 | .293 | .359 | .343 |
| Leading Off Inn. | 132 | 53 | 0 | 3 | 1 | 1 | 3 | 3 | .402 | .470 | .419 |
| Runners On | 248 | 81 | 13 | 2 | 1 | 59 | 33 | 13 | .327 | .407 | .396 |
| Runners/Scor. Pos. | 132 | 42 | 5 | 2 | 1 | 55 | 30 | 10 | .318 | .409 | .426 |
| Runners On/2 Out | 53 | 11 | 1 | 0 | 0 | 5 | 7 | 3 | .208 | .226 | .300 |
| Scor. Pos./2 Out | 27 | 3 | 0 | 0 | 0 | 4 | 7 | 2 | .111 | .111 | .294 |
| Late Inning Pressure | 80 | 27 | 1 | 0 | 0 | 9 | 9 | 3 | .338 | .350 | .400 |
| Leading Off | 30 | 9 | 0 | 0 | 0 | 0 | 1 | 1 | .300 | .300 | .323 |
| Runners On | 33 | 11 | 0 | 0 | 0 | 9 | 5 | 2 | .333 | .333 | .410 |
| Runners/Scor. Pos. | 18 | 6 | 0 | 0 | 0 | 9 | 4 | 1 | .333 | .333 | .435 |

| RUNS BATTED IN | From 1B | From 2B | From 3B | Scoring Position |
|---|---|---|---|---|
| Totals | 5/168 | 20/95 | 33/58 | 53/153 |
| Percentage | 3% | 21% | 57% | 35% |
| Driving In Runners from 3B with Less than Two Out: | | | 31/44 | 70% |

Loves to face: Ron Darling (.500, 24-for-48)
Hates to face: Frank DiPino (.063, 1-for-16)
Third consecutive N.L. batting title puts him in company with Stan Musial. Rogers Hornsby, the last to win four straight, won six straight N.L. titles in 1920s. . . . While driving toward batting title, he finished season without a strikeout in his last 86 plate appearances, longest N.L. streak of the year. . . . Only player in majors to collect 30 hits vs. any club last season. He did it against both Astros (31) and Giants (30). . . . Faced N.L.'s top 10 strikeout leaders 72 times, fanned only once. Woof! . . .Exactly half of his RBI either knotted a game or put his club in lead, highest rate by any N.L. player with 50+ RBI. . . . Shock stat of the year: Gwynn hit .111 (3-for-27) with two outs and runners in scoring position.

## Jeff Hamilton

Bats Right

| Los Angeles Dodgers | AB | H | 2B | 3B | HR | RBI | BB | SO | BA | SA | OBA |
|---|---|---|---|---|---|---|---|---|---|---|---|
| Season | 548 | 134 | 35 | 1 | 12 | 56 | 20 | 71 | .245 | .378 | .272 |
| vs. Left-Handers | 210 | 44 | 12 | 0 | 2 | 16 | 10 | 28 | .210 | .295 | .250 |
| vs. Right-Handers | 338 | 90 | 23 | 1 | 10 | 40 | 10 | 43 | .266 | .429 | .286 |
| Home | 263 | 61 | 16 | 1 | 8 | 28 | 8 | 32 | .232 | .392 | .259 |
| Road | 285 | 73 | 19 | 0 | 4 | 28 | 12 | 39 | .256 | .365 | .284 |
| Grass | 393 | 96 | 24 | 1 | 10 | 38 | 13 | 47 | .244 | .387 | .271 |
| Artificial Turf | 155 | 38 | 11 | 0 | 2 | 18 | 7 | 24 | .245 | .355 | .274 |
| April | 62 | 14 | 5 | 0 | 0 | 5 | 1 | 9 | .226 | .306 | .238 |
| May | 78 | 19 | 4 | 0 | 5 | 10 | 5 | 8 | .244 | .487 | .306 |
| June | 112 | 26 | 8 | 0 | 2 | 11 | 6 | 18 | .232 | .357 | .269 |
| July | 92 | 24 | 8 | 1 | 1 | 13 | 3 | 17 | .261 | .402 | .276 |
| August | 103 | 26 | 4 | 0 | 4 | 9 | 4 | 10 | .252 | .408 | .287 |
| Sept./Oct. | 101 | 25 | 6 | 0 | 0 | 8 | 1 | 9 | .248 | .307 | .250 |
| Leading Off Inn. | 128 | 33 | 6 | 0 | 6 | 6 | 2 | 18 | .258 | .445 | .275 |
| Runners On | 236 | 58 | 16 | 1 | 3 | 47 | 16 | 28 | .246 | .360 | .290 |
| Runners/Scor. Pos. | 125 | 26 | 8 | 1 | 1 | 40 | 14 | 14 | .208 | .312 | .276 |
| Runners On/2 Out | 96 | 24 | 8 | 0 | 3 | 23 | 8 | 12 | .250 | .427 | .308 |
| Scor. Pos./2 Out | 61 | 13 | 3 | 0 | 1 | 18 | 7 | 6 | .213 | .311 | .294 |
| Late Inning Pressure | 109 | 27 | 6 | 0 | 0 | 5 | 6 | 16 | .248 | .303 | .288 |
| Leading Off | 27 | 9 | 1 | 0 | 0 | 0 | 0 | 2 | .333 | .370 | .333 |
| Runners On | 35 | 8 | 1 | 0 | 0 | 5 | 5 | 7 | .229 | .257 | .310 |
| Runners/Scor. Pos. | 15 | 1 | 1 | 0 | 0 | 5 | 4 | 3 | .067 | .133 | .238 |

| RUNS BATTED IN | From 1B | From 2B | From 3B | Scoring Position |
|---|---|---|---|---|
| Totals | 7/173 | 18/104 | 19/47 | 37/151 |
| Percentage | 4% | 17% | 40% | 25% |
| Driving In Runners from 3B with Less than Two Out: | | | 11/18 | 61% |

Loves to face: Sid Fernandez (.462, 6-for-13, 1 HR)
Hates to face: Bruce Hurst (0-for-14, 5 SO)
Drove in 56 runs, but only 12 of them either tied a game or put his club in lead, the lowest rate of "lead-changing" RBI by any N.L. player with 50+ RBI. . . . Hit all 12 of his homers to left field. Batted .324 on fair balls hit to the left side, .318 straight away, .168 to the opposite field. . . . Losing pitcher in 22-inning game at Houston, June 3, despite striking out two (Billy Hatcher and Ken Caminiti) of the eight batters he faced. . . . That leads us into all-time list of Dodgers with most career plate appearances and no stolen bases: Don Drysdale (1309), Hamilton (1150), Sandy Koufax (858), Fernando Valenzuela (821). . . . Hamilton is only active player with 1000+ trips to plate who has never stolen a base.

## Lenny Harris

Bats Left

| Reds/Dodgers | AB | H | 2B | 3B | HR | RBI | BB | SO | BA | SA | OBA |
|---|---|---|---|---|---|---|---|---|---|---|---|
| Season | 335 | 79 | 10 | 1 | 3 | 26 | 20 | 33 | .236 | .299 | .283 |
| vs. Left-Handers | 68 | 13 | 2 | 0 | 0 | 3 | 4 | 9 | .191 | .221 | .257 |
| vs. Right-Handers | 267 | 66 | 8 | 1 | 3 | 23 | 16 | 24 | .247 | .318 | .290 |
| Home | 161 | 41 | 5 | 1 | 1 | 13 | 7 | 13 | .255 | .317 | .290 |
| Road | 174 | 38 | 5 | 0 | 2 | 13 | 13 | 20 | .218 | .282 | .277 |
| Grass | 173 | 41 | 6 | 1 | 3 | 18 | 10 | 19 | .237 | .335 | .279 |
| Artificial Turf | 162 | 38 | 4 | 0 | 0 | 8 | 10 | 14 | .235 | .259 | .287 |
| April | 16 | 4 | 0 | 0 | 0 | 0 | 0 | 1 | .250 | .250 | .250 |
| May | 36 | 6 | 2 | 0 | 0 | 1 | 6 | 7 | .167 | .222 | .302 |
| June | 90 | 24 | 2 | 0 | 1 | 7 | 2 | 8 | .267 | .322 | .283 |
| July | 72 | 15 | 4 | 0 | 1 | 9 | 3 | 4 | .208 | .306 | .250 |
| August | 43 | 12 | 0 | 0 | 0 | 3 | 3 | 4 | .279 | .279 | .326 |
| Sept./Oct. | 78 | 18 | 2 | 1 | 1 | 6 | 6 | 9 | .231 | .321 | .286 |
| Leading Off Inn. | 96 | 22 | 2 | 0 | 0 | 0 | 8 | 8 | .229 | .250 | .288 |
| Runners On | 140 | 33 | 5 | 0 | 3 | 26 | 6 | 13 | .236 | .336 | .267 |
| Runners/Scor. Pos. | 70 | 14 | 1 | 0 | 1 | 20 | 4 | 7 | .200 | .257 | .243 |
| Runners On/2 Out | 57 | 16 | 1 | 0 | 2 | 18 | 0 | 6 | .281 | .404 | .281 |
| Scor. Pos./2 Out | 35 | 11 | 1 | 0 | 1 | 16 | 0 | 2 | .314 | .429 | .314 |
| Late Inning Pressure | 54 | 11 | 1 | 0 | 0 | 0 | 5 | 8 | .204 | .222 | .271 |
| Leading Off | 16 | 5 | 1 | 0 | 0 | 0 | 2 | 0 | .313 | .375 | .389 |
| Runners On | 19 | 1 | 0 | 0 | 0 | 0 | 2 | 5 | .053 | .053 | .143 |
| Runners/Scor. Pos. | 11 | 0 | 0 | 0 | 0 | 0 | 2 | 3 | .000 | .000 | .154 |

| RUNS BATTED IN | From 1B | From 2B | From 3B | Scoring Position |
|---|---|---|---|---|
| Totals | 6/107 | 9/53 | 8/28 | 17/81 |
| Percentage | 6% | 17% | 29% | 21% |
| Driving In Runners from 3B with Less than Two Out: | | | 1/8 | 13% |

Loves to face: Mike LaCoss (.364, 4-for-11)
Hates to face: Bryn Smith (.125, 1-for-8)
Alright, we'll give you some notes on Lenny Harris, but we warn you, it isn't going to be pretty. Unsupervised young children should read no farther.... Grounded into 14 double plays in 64 DP situations, 2d highest rate of any N.L. player last season (minimum: 40 opportunities).... Drove in only one of eight runners from third base with less than two outs, tying Pat Sheridan for lowest rate in N.L.... Batted with 13 runners in scoring position in Late-Inning Pressure Situations, but did not drive in any of them.... Batted .268 vs. fly-ball pitchers, .208 against ground-ballers.... His three home runs were hit against Orel Hershiser, David Cone, and ... Tommy Greene. Well, two out of three ain't bad.

## Mickey Hatcher

Bats Right

| Los Angeles Dodgers | AB | H | 2B | 3B | HR | RBI | BB | SO | BA | SA | OBA |
|---|---|---|---|---|---|---|---|---|---|---|---|
| Season | 224 | 66 | 9 | 2 | 2 | 25 | 13 | 16 | .295 | .379 | .328 |
| vs. Left-Handers | 131 | 42 | 6 | 2 | 2 | 17 | 7 | 8 | .321 | .443 | .352 |
| vs. Right-Handers | 93 | 24 | 3 | 0 | 0 | 8 | 6 | 8 | .258 | .290 | .294 |
| Home | 116 | 33 | 7 | 1 | 0 | 12 | 8 | 3 | .284 | .362 | .323 |
| Road | 108 | 33 | 2 | 1 | 2 | 13 | 5 | 13 | .306 | .398 | .333 |
| Grass | 159 | 47 | 8 | 1 | 2 | 17 | 11 | 9 | .296 | .396 | .333 |
| Artificial Turf | 65 | 19 | 1 | 1 | 0 | 8 | 2 | 7 | .292 | .338 | .314 |
| April | 54 | 14 | 1 | 1 | 0 | 5 | 3 | 4 | .259 | .315 | .283 |
| May | 35 | 11 | 5 | 0 | 0 | 4 | 1 | 1 | .314 | .457 | .324 |
| June | 25 | 10 | 0 | 0 | 0 | 3 | 0 | 3 | .400 | .400 | .400 |
| July | 42 | 16 | 2 | 1 | 1 | 5 | 0 | 2 | .381 | .548 | .381 |
| August | 44 | 8 | 1 | 0 | 0 | 4 | 3 | 4 | .182 | .205 | .224 |
| Sept./Oct. | 24 | 7 | 0 | 0 | 1 | 4 | 6 | 2 | .292 | .417 | .452 |
| Leading Off Inn. | 43 | 14 | 1 | 0 | 0 | 0 | 1 | 5 | .326 | .349 | .356 |
| Runners On | 106 | 27 | 4 | 0 | 1 | 24 | 7 | 6 | .255 | .321 | .286 |
| Runners/Scor. Pos. | 62 | 14 | 2 | 0 | 1 | 23 | 4 | 5 | .226 | .306 | .250 |
| Runners On/2 Out | 44 | 13 | 2 | 0 | 0 | 10 | 2 | 1 | .295 | .341 | .326 |
| Scor. Pos./2 Out | 33 | 9 | 1 | 0 | 0 | 10 | 1 | 1 | .273 | .303 | .294 |
| Late Inning Pressure | 53 | 14 | 3 | 0 | 0 | 6 | 3 | 7 | .264 | .321 | .283 |
| Leading Off | 12 | 5 | 0 | 0 | 0 | 0 | 0 | 2 | .417 | .417 | .417 |
| Runners On | 26 | 5 | 2 | 0 | 0 | 6 | 3 | 4 | .192 | .269 | .242 |
| Runners/Scor. Pos. | 13 | 1 | 1 | 0 | 0 | 5 | 2 | 4 | .077 | .154 | .158 |

| RUNS BATTED IN | From 1B | From 2B | From 3B | Scoring Position |
|---|---|---|---|---|
| Totals | 2/74 | 10/56 | 11/26 | 21/82 |
| Percentage | 3% | 18% | 42% | 26% |
| Driving In Runners from 3B with Less than Two Out: | | | 9/17 | 53% |

Loves to face: Bruce Hurst (.447, 17-for-38, 1 HR)
Hates to face: Jim Clancy (.182, 4-for-22)
How many guys have hit .275 or higher in each of last seven years? Mickey and the Mag Seven: Baines, Boggs, Brett, Gwynn, Lansford, Mattingly, Yount. Those seven have accounted for 28 All-Star selections over that span; Hatch is still waiting for Invitation One.... Batted .176 (6-for-34) as a pinch hitter last season, but tied Mike Aldrete for N.L. lead in pinch RBIs (10).... Started 34 of 58 games in which a left-hander faced Dodgers, but only 17 of 102 games vs. right-handers.... Batted .226 with runners in scoring position, his lowest mark since 1980.... Career averages: .306 on carpets, .263 on grass fields; .305 in day games, .272 at night. Has hit .300+ in day games in five of last six years.

## Billy Hatcher

Bats Right

| Astros/Pirates | AB | H | 2B | 3B | HR | RBI | BB | SO | BA | SA | OBA |
|---|---|---|---|---|---|---|---|---|---|---|---|
| Season | 481 | 111 | 19 | 3 | 4 | 51 | 30 | 62 | .231 | .308 | .277 |
| vs. Left-Handers | 193 | 52 | 7 | 1 | 2 | 20 | 8 | 16 | .269 | .347 | .296 |
| vs. Right-Handers | 288 | 59 | 12 | 2 | 2 | 31 | 22 | 46 | .205 | .281 | .264 |
| Home | 231 | 54 | 9 | 3 | 0 | 23 | 20 | 35 | .234 | .299 | .292 |
| Road | 250 | 57 | 10 | 0 | 4 | 28 | 10 | 27 | .228 | .316 | .261 |
| Grass | 137 | 29 | 5 | 0 | 3 | 14 | 6 | 19 | .212 | .314 | .247 |
| Artificial Turf | 344 | 82 | 14 | 3 | 1 | 37 | 24 | 43 | .238 | .305 | .288 |
| April | 94 | 24 | 4 | 0 | 1 | 13 | 3 | 13 | .255 | .330 | .276 |
| May | 74 | 13 | 2 | 0 | 0 | 7 | 9 | 12 | .176 | .203 | .262 |
| June | 105 | 26 | 6 | 3 | 2 | 13 | 4 | 15 | .248 | .419 | .279 |
| July | 82 | 21 | 2 | 0 | 0 | 8 | 13 | 11 | .256 | .280 | .354 |
| August | 71 | 13 | 2 | 0 | 1 | 5 | 1 | 6 | .183 | .254 | .205 |
| Sept./Oct. | 55 | 14 | 3 | 0 | 0 | 5 | 0 | 5 | .255 | .309 | .255 |
| Leading Off Inn. | 163 | 34 | 4 | 2 | 1 | 1 | 11 | 19 | .209 | .276 | .259 |
| Runners On | 184 | 48 | 9 | 0 | 2 | 49 | 10 | 28 | .261 | .342 | .296 |
| Runners/Scor. Pos. | 129 | 32 | 5 | 0 | 1 | 47 | 9 | 23 | .248 | .310 | .294 |
| Runners On/2 Out | 84 | 17 | 3 | 0 | 0 | 16 | 5 | 17 | .202 | .238 | .256 |
| Scor. Pos./2 Out | 64 | 13 | 2 | 0 | 0 | 16 | 4 | 13 | .203 | .234 | .261 |
| Late Inning Pressure | 63 | 13 | 2 | 0 | 1 | 5 | 3 | 14 | .206 | .286 | .242 |
| Leading Off | 13 | 1 | 0 | 0 | 0 | 0 | 0 | 4 | .077 | .077 | .077 |
| Runners On | 27 | 6 | 2 | 0 | 1 | 5 | 2 | 7 | .222 | .407 | .276 |
| Runners/Scor. Pos. | 18 | 2 | 0 | 0 | 0 | 3 | 1 | 5 | .111 | .111 | .158 |

| RUNS BATTED IN | From 1B | From 2B | From 3B | Scoring Position |
|---|---|---|---|---|
| Totals | 2/111 | 18/96 | 27/62 | 45/158 |
| Percentage | 2% | 19% | 44% | 28% |
| Driving In Runners from 3B with Less than Two Out: | | | 19/31 | 61% |

Loves to face: Tom Glavine (.407, 11-for-27, 1 HR)
Hates to face: Dennis Martinez (.067, 1-for-15)
Batted .296 in year of the corked bat, but has hit .268 and .231 in two full seasons since the discovery. Bill Doran is only other N.L. player with 400+ at-bats in each of last three seasons and batting-average decline of 25+ points in each of last two.... Hatcher's career breakdown: .278 (one HR per 56.4 at-bats) pre-cork, .247 (one per 99.5 AB) post-cork.... Batting average vs. left-handers has been fairly consistent from year to year, but vs. right-handers he has dropped from .307 (1987) to .259 (1988) to .205.... Traded by Houston to Pittsburgh on Aug. 18; in 27 subsequent games with Pirates, he did not draw a single walk.... Had only one assist in 124 outfield games last season; had 16 in 1987 and 7 in 1988.

## Charlie Hayes

Bats Right

| Giants/Phillies | AB | H | 2B | 3B | HR | RBI | BB | SO | BA | SA | OBA |
|---|---|---|---|---|---|---|---|---|---|---|---|
| Season | 304 | 78 | 15 | 1 | 8 | 43 | 11 | 50 | .257 | .391 | .280 |
| vs. Left-Handers | 105 | 28 | 7 | 0 | 1 | 14 | 5 | 15 | .267 | .362 | .295 |
| vs. Right-Handers | 199 | 50 | 8 | 1 | 7 | 29 | 6 | 35 | .251 | .407 | .272 |
| Home | 156 | 36 | 9 | 1 | 3 | 24 | 7 | 31 | .231 | .359 | .262 |
| Road | 148 | 42 | 6 | 0 | 5 | 19 | 4 | 19 | .284 | .426 | .299 |
| Grass | 80 | 22 | 3 | 0 | 4 | 11 | 2 | 11 | .275 | .463 | .289 |
| Artificial Turf | 224 | 56 | 12 | 1 | 4 | 32 | 9 | 39 | .250 | .366 | .277 |
| April | 0 | 0 | 0 | 0 | 0 | 0 | 0 | 0 | — | — | — |
| May | 5 | 1 | 0 | 0 | 0 | 0 | 0 | 1 | .200 | .200 | .200 |
| June | 7 | 2 | 1 | 0 | 0 | 0 | 1 | 3 | .286 | .429 | .375 |
| July | 99 | 24 | 5 | 0 | 4 | 17 | 7 | 19 | .242 | .414 | .290 |
| August | 103 | 28 | 7 | 0 | 3 | 17 | 0 | 12 | .272 | .427 | .269 |
| Sept./Oct. | 90 | 23 | 2 | 1 | 1 | 9 | 3 | 15 | .256 | .333 | .277 |
| Leading Off Inn. | 76 | 20 | 4 | 0 | 4 | 4 | 0 | 9 | .263 | .474 | .263 |
| Runners On | 125 | 37 | 8 | 1 | 3 | 38 | 4 | 18 | .296 | .448 | .311 |
| Runners/Scor. Pos. | 83 | 21 | 6 | 1 | 2 | 36 | 4 | 17 | .253 | .422 | .278 |
| Runners On/2 Out | 52 | 10 | 2 | 0 | 0 | 6 | 2 | 10 | .192 | .231 | .222 |
| Scor. Pos./2 Out | 35 | 4 | 2 | 0 | 0 | 6 | 2 | 9 | .114 | .171 | .162 |
| Late Inning Pressure | 42 | 10 | 2 | 0 | 1 | 3 | 3 | 8 | .238 | .357 | .289 |
| Leading Off | 14 | 4 | 0 | 0 | 1 | 1 | 0 | 2 | .286 | .500 | .286 |
| Runners On | 15 | 4 | 1 | 0 | 0 | 2 | 1 | 3 | .267 | .333 | .313 |
| Runners/Scor. Pos. | 8 | 2 | 1 | 0 | 0 | 2 | 1 | 3 | .250 | .375 | .333 |

| RUNS BATTED IN | From 1B | From 2B | From 3B | Scoring Position |
|---|---|---|---|---|
| Totals | 3/88 | 11/69 | 21/30 | 32/99 |
| Percentage | 3% | 16% | 70% | 32% |
| Driving In Runners from 3B with Less than Two Out: | | | 19/22 | 86% |

Loves to face: Kevin Gross (.667, 4-for-6, 1 HR)
Hates to face: Greg Maddux (.100, 1-for-10)
Last player to lead off as many innings in a season without drawing a leadoff walk was Ray Knight (82 innings) in 1984. Hayes also led off five innings without a walk in 1988.... Had a streak of 175 total trips to the plate without a walk in August and September, an N.L. high for the season.... Ranked second among N.L. third basemen (minimum: 500 inn.) with 2.23 assists per nine innings.... Had most errors (22) by any N.L. rookie last year.... Drove in runners from third base with less than two outs in 12 straight opportunities, tying him with Mark Grace and three A.L. players for top streak in majors.... Who was Phils' last opening-day starting third baseman before Mike Schmidt? How about Jose Pagan in 1973?

## Von Hayes

Bats Left

| Philadelphia Phillies | AB | H | 2B | 3B | HR | RBI | BB | SO | BA | SA | OBA |
|---|---|---|---|---|---|---|---|---|---|---|---|
| Season | 540 | 140 | 27 | 2 | 26 | 78 | 101 | 103 | .259 | .461 | .376 |
| vs. Left-Handers | 208 | 51 | 9 | 0 | 8 | 29 | 35 | 42 | .245 | .404 | .356 |
| vs. Right-Handers | 332 | 89 | 18 | 2 | 18 | 49 | 66 | 61 | .268 | .497 | .388 |
| Home | 257 | 64 | 12 | 1 | 15 | 40 | 54 | 51 | .249 | .479 | .377 |
| Road | 283 | 76 | 15 | 1 | 11 | 38 | 47 | 52 | .269 | .445 | .375 |
| Grass | 148 | 44 | 7 | 0 | 8 | 25 | 21 | 31 | .297 | .507 | .386 |
| Artificial Turf | 392 | 96 | 20 | 2 | 18 | 53 | 80 | 72 | .245 | .444 | .372 |
| April | 76 | 29 | 7 | 1 | 7 | 22 | 21 | 16 | .382 | .776 | .505 |
| May | 79 | 20 | 2 | 0 | 1 | 8 | 20 | 21 | .253 | .316 | .396 |
| June | 104 | 21 | 5 | 1 | 5 | 15 | 17 | 16 | .202 | .413 | .314 |
| July | 102 | 29 | 3 | 0 | 2 | 8 | 16 | 13 | .284 | .373 | .378 |
| August | 92 | 20 | 7 | 0 | 6 | 13 | 14 | 16 | .217 | .489 | .330 |
| Sept./Oct. | 87 | 21 | 3 | 0 | 5 | 12 | 13 | 21 | .241 | .448 | .350 |
| Leading Off Inn. | 104 | 28 | 9 | 0 | 7 | 7 | 17 | 19 | .269 | .558 | .377 |
| Runners On | 254 | 72 | 11 | 1 | 13 | 65 | 52 | 43 | .283 | .488 | .398 |
| Runners/Scor. Pos. | 133 | 34 | 7 | 1 | 8 | 55 | 34 | 24 | .256 | .504 | .394 |
| Runners On/2 Out | 84 | 26 | 4 | 1 | 6 | 29 | 19 | 16 | .310 | .595 | .437 |
| Scor. Pos./2 Out | 48 | 16 | 3 | 1 | 5 | 27 | 13 | 13 | .333 | .750 | .475 |
| Late Inning Pressure | 84 | 20 | 4 | 0 | 4 | 8 | 20 | 18 | .238 | .429 | .390 |
| Leading Off | 19 | 7 | 1 | 0 | 3 | 3 | 3 | 4 | .368 | .895 | .478 |
| Runners On | 39 | 8 | 1 | 0 | 1 | 5 | 12 | 10 | .205 | .308 | .392 |
| Runners/Scor. Pos. | 22 | 4 | 0 | 0 | 1 | 5 | 10 | 6 | .182 | .318 | .438 |

| RUNS BATTED IN | From 1B | From 2B | From 3B | Scoring Position |
|---|---|---|---|---|
| Totals | 10/183 | 18/109 | 24/44 | 42/153 |
| Percentage | 5% | 17% | 55% | 27% |
| Driving In Runners from 3B with Less than Two Out: | | | 15/23 | 65% |

Loves to face: Rick Sutcliffe (.456, 26-for-57, 5 HR)
Hates to face: Dave Smith (0-for-11)

Four home runs in his first eight games last season matched his total of April homers accumulated in 112 games over seven previous years. His '89 April batting average was highest in N.L. . . . Has seven hits (including five doubles) in 12 at-bats with the bases loaded over last two seasons. . . . Has hit for a higher average with runners on base than with the bases empty in each of the last five seasons. . . . Career breakdown: batting .291, slugging .466, one home run every 31 at-bats vs. right-handers; .230, .346, one every 47 at-bats vs. left-handers. The former statistics approximate the numbers generated by Yankees great Tony Lazzeri; the latter ones suggest another infielder, Dick Schofield, Sr.

## Keith Hernandez

Bats Left

| New York Mets | AB | H | 2B | 3B | HR | RBI | BB | SO | BA | SA | OBA |
|---|---|---|---|---|---|---|---|---|---|---|---|
| Season | 215 | 50 | 8 | 0 | 4 | 19 | 27 | 39 | .233 | .326 | .324 |
| vs. Left-Handers | 79 | 23 | 2 | 0 | 1 | 8 | 7 | 16 | .291 | .354 | .364 |
| vs. Right-Handers | 136 | 27 | 6 | 0 | 3 | 11 | 20 | 23 | .199 | .309 | .301 |
| Home | 95 | 25 | 3 | 0 | 2 | 4 | 13 | 16 | .263 | .358 | .358 |
| Road | 120 | 25 | 5 | 0 | 2 | 15 | 14 | 23 | .208 | .300 | .296 |
| Grass | 144 | 32 | 3 | 0 | 2 | 8 | 17 | 26 | .222 | .285 | .309 |
| Artificial Turf | 71 | 18 | 5 | 0 | 2 | 11 | 10 | 13 | .254 | .408 | .354 |
| April | 72 | 17 | 3 | 0 | 3 | 8 | 8 | 9 | .236 | .403 | .313 |
| May | 45 | 16 | 3 | 0 | 0 | 4 | 6 | 14 | .356 | .422 | .442 |
| June | 0 | 0 | 0 | 0 | 0 | 0 | 0 | 0 | — | — | — |
| July | 23 | 5 | 0 | 0 | 0 | 3 | 1 | 1 | .217 | .217 | .250 |
| August | 33 | 5 | 1 | 0 | 0 | 1 | 6 | 5 | .152 | .182 | .300 |
| Sept./Oct. | 42 | 7 | 1 | 0 | 1 | 3 | 6 | 10 | .167 | .262 | .271 |
| Leading Off Inn. | 42 | 8 | 1 | 0 | 1 | 1 | 3 | 6 | .190 | .286 | .261 |
| Runners On | 92 | 25 | 3 | 0 | 2 | 17 | 12 | 16 | .272 | .370 | .362 |
| Runners/Scor. Pos. | 60 | 11 | 0 | 0 | 1 | 14 | 8 | 12 | .183 | .233 | .279 |
| Runners On/2 Out | 37 | 8 | 0 | 0 | 0 | 7 | 3 | 8 | .216 | .216 | .275 |
| Scor. Pos./2 Out | 27 | 5 | 0 | 0 | 0 | 7 | 3 | 6 | .185 | .185 | .267 |
| Late Inning Pressure | 40 | 9 | 3 | 0 | 0 | 2 | 4 | 8 | .225 | .300 | .295 |
| Leading Off | 13 | 2 | 0 | 0 | 0 | 0 | 0 | 4 | .154 | .154 | .154 |
| Runners On | 14 | 4 | 1 | 0 | 0 | 2 | 2 | 0 | .286 | .357 | .375 |
| Runners/Scor. Pos. | 6 | 1 | 0 | 0 | 0 | 2 | 1 | 0 | .167 | .167 | .286 |

| RUNS BATTED IN | From 1B | From 2B | From 3B | Scoring Position |
|---|---|---|---|---|
| Totals | 3/56 | 5/45 | 7/20 | 12/65 |
| Percentage | 5% | 11% | 35% | 18% |
| Driving In Runners from 3B with Less than Two Out: | | | 3/8 | 38% |

Loves to face: Jeff D. Robinson (.455, 5-for-11)
Hates to face: Bob McClure (.118, 2-for-17)

Needs 73 games at first base to crash all-time top 10 in that category, and needs only 112 to jump into 5th place on list. . . . Batting average with runners on base has been higher than with bases empty in each of the last 12 seasons. Last year, he hit .438 (14-for-32) with a runner on first base only, but .183 with runners in scoring position (1 for 15 with RISP and the score tied). . . . Batted .118 (2-for-17) as a pinch hitter. . . . Started in his accustomed 3d spot in Mets' lineup only three times after All-Star break. . . . After reinjuring his knee on an awkward tag play at home plate in July, Keith should consider enrolling in the Pedro Guerrero School of Base Running: Just Say No . . . to sliding.

## Tom Herr

Bats Left and Right

| Philadelphia Phillies | AB | H | 2B | 3B | HR | RBI | BB | SO | BA | SA | OBA |
|---|---|---|---|---|---|---|---|---|---|---|---|
| Season | 561 | 161 | 25 | 6 | 2 | 37 | 54 | 63 | .287 | .364 | .352 |
| vs. Left-Handers | 229 | 66 | 9 | 1 | 1 | 14 | 23 | 22 | .288 | .349 | .353 |
| vs. Right-Handers | 332 | 95 | 16 | 5 | 1 | 23 | 31 | 41 | .286 | .373 | .351 |
| Home | 270 | 77 | 16 | 3 | 0 | 16 | 29 | 27 | .285 | .367 | .360 |
| Road | 291 | 84 | 9 | 3 | 2 | 21 | 25 | 36 | .289 | .361 | .344 |
| Grass | 138 | 33 | 2 | 0 | 1 | 7 | 17 | 23 | .239 | .275 | .321 |
| Artificial Turf | 423 | 128 | 23 | 6 | 1 | 30 | 37 | 40 | .303 | .392 | .362 |
| April | 93 | 33 | 4 | 1 | 0 | 8 | 8 | 9 | .355 | .419 | .412 |
| May | 85 | 20 | 3 | 2 | 0 | 5 | 5 | 15 | .235 | .318 | .286 |
| June | 97 | 25 | 7 | 0 | 1 | 6 | 12 | 9 | .258 | .361 | .345 |
| July | 104 | 27 | 4 | 1 | 0 | 8 | 14 | 10 | .260 | .317 | .347 |
| August | 97 | 27 | 3 | 1 | 0 | 3 | 8 | 7 | .278 | .330 | .330 |
| Sept./Oct. | 85 | 29 | 4 | 1 | 1 | 7 | 7 | 13 | .341 | .447 | .387 |
| Leading Off Inn. | 94 | 26 | 2 | 2 | 0 | 0 | 9 | 14 | .277 | .340 | .340 |
| Runners On | 206 | 61 | 7 | 2 | 1 | 36 | 17 | 18 | .296 | .364 | .350 |
| Runners/Scor. Pos. | 111 | 29 | 4 | 2 | 0 | 33 | 12 | 12 | .261 | .333 | .333 |
| Runners On/2 Out | 80 | 24 | 2 | 0 | 1 | 14 | 6 | 5 | .300 | .363 | .349 |
| Scor. Pos./2 Out | 54 | 13 | 1 | 0 | 0 | 11 | 5 | 4 | .241 | .259 | .305 |
| Late Inning Pressure | 96 | 23 | 1 | 2 | 1 | 11 | 4 | 12 | .240 | .323 | .275 |
| Leading Off | 24 | 6 | 0 | 1 | 0 | 0 | 1 | 2 | .250 | .333 | .280 |
| Runners On | 46 | 13 | 0 | 1 | 1 | 11 | 1 | 5 | .283 | .391 | .292 |
| Runners/Scor. Pos. | 26 | 9 | 0 | 1 | 0 | 9 | 1 | 4 | .346 | .423 | .357 |

| RUNS BATTED IN | From 1B | From 2B | From 3B | Scoring Position |
|---|---|---|---|---|
| Totals | 2/140 | 20/89 | 13/38 | 33/127 |
| Percentage | 1% | 22% | 34% | 26% |
| Driving In Runners from 3B with Less than Two Out: | | | 10/17 | 59% |

Loves to face: Mike Scott (.388, 19-for-49, 7 BB)
Hates to face: Scott Garrelts (.056, 1-for-18)

Of his 37 RBI, 17 (46 percent) gave Phillies a lead, the best rate of "go-ahead" RBI in majors last season (minimum: 20 RBI). . . . If you ask, "Didn't this guy once drive in 110 runs in a season?" remember this: In 1985 he batted with 232 men in scoring position, and drove in over 40 percent of them. In 1989, he drove in 26 percent of 127 runners in scoring position. . . . Batted .341 in first inning, .271 thereafter. . . . Career breakdown: .292 with runners on base, .263 with bases empty. . . . Ranks second in baseball history in fielding percentage among second basemen (minimum: 1000 games). Top four all played in 1989: Sandberg (.9891), Herr (.9886), Gantner (.9850), White (.9842).

## Chris James

Bats Right

| Phillies/Padres | AB | H | 2B | 3B | HR | RBI | BB | SO | BA | SA | OBA |
|---|---|---|---|---|---|---|---|---|---|---|---|
| Season | 482 | 117 | 17 | 2 | 13 | 65 | 26 | 68 | .243 | .367 | .281 |
| vs. Left-Handers | 168 | 49 | 5 | 1 | 7 | 33 | 12 | 20 | .292 | .458 | .335 |
| vs. Right-Handers | 314 | 68 | 12 | 1 | 6 | 32 | 14 | 48 | .217 | .318 | .252 |
| Home | 210 | 56 | 9 | 0 | 7 | 36 | 13 | 25 | .267 | .410 | .310 |
| Road | 272 | 61 | 8 | 2 | 6 | 29 | 13 | 43 | .224 | .335 | .259 |
| Grass | 276 | 68 | 8 | 2 | 10 | 45 | 17 | 43 | .246 | .399 | .290 |
| Artificial Turf | 206 | 49 | 9 | 0 | 3 | 20 | 9 | 25 | .238 | .325 | .270 |
| April | 96 | 29 | 4 | 0 | 2 | 15 | 1 | 11 | .302 | .406 | .306 |
| May | 78 | 8 | 0 | 0 | 0 | 4 | 3 | 12 | .103 | .103 | .136 |
| June | 60 | 10 | 2 | 0 | 0 | 7 | 4 | 8 | .167 | .200 | .219 |
| July | 81 | 26 | 3 | 0 | 5 | 15 | 5 | 9 | .321 | .543 | .368 |
| August | 90 | 30 | 7 | 0 | 5 | 18 | 3 | 13 | .333 | .578 | .351 |
| Sept./Oct. | 77 | 14 | 1 | 2 | 1 | 6 | 10 | 15 | .182 | .286 | .273 |
| Leading Off Inn. | 105 | 26 | 2 | 0 | 4 | 4 | 4 | 19 | .248 | .381 | .275 |
| Runners On | 239 | 60 | 9 | 1 | 6 | 58 | 14 | 29 | .251 | .372 | .292 |
| Runners/Scor. Pos. | 147 | 38 | 7 | 1 | 4 | 53 | 9 | 21 | .259 | .401 | .300 |
| Runners On/2 Out | 106 | 26 | 3 | 1 | 4 | 28 | 8 | 16 | .245 | .406 | .304 |
| Scor. Pos./2 Out | 78 | 18 | 3 | 1 | 2 | 24 | 6 | 11 | .231 | .372 | .294 |
| Late Inning Pressure | 81 | 16 | 1 | 0 | 2 | 11 | 4 | 13 | .198 | .284 | .235 |
| Leading Off | 21 | 2 | 0 | 0 | 0 | 0 | 0 | 2 | .095 | .095 | .095 |
| Runners On | 38 | 8 | 1 | 0 | 1 | 10 | 4 | 7 | .211 | .316 | .286 |
| Runners/Scor. Pos. | 23 | 4 | 0 | 0 | 0 | 7 | 2 | 4 | .174 | .174 | .240 |

| RUNS BATTED IN | From 1B | From 2B | From 3B | Scoring Position |
|---|---|---|---|---|
| Totals | 7/181 | 22/112 | 23/62 | 45/174 |
| Percentage | 4% | 20% | 37% | 26% |
| Driving In Runners from 3B with Less than Two Out: | | | 14/31 | 45% |

Loves to face: Pascual Perez (.417, 5-for-12, 2 HR)
Hates to face: Jeff D. Robinson (0-for-10)

Made at least one start in each of first eight batting-order positions, the only N.L. player to do so last season. This year with Indians, he'll have a chance to bat ninth. . . . Hitless streak of 38 at-bats in May and June equalled the longest of '80s by an N.L. nonpitcher; Vince Coleman went 0-for-38 in 1986. Longest streak by a pitcher: 45 by Mike Torrez in 1983. . . . Hit five home runs off left-handers while with Padres, highest total on the team. . . . Owns .229 career average (8-for-35) with the bases loaded, but hit one grand slam in '88 and two last season. . . . Became 4th player in history to hit slams for two clubs in same season; others: Don Lenhardt (1952), Ray Boone (1953), and Joe Pepitone (1970).

## Gregg Jefferies

Bats Left and Right

| New York Mets | AB | H | 2B | 3B | HR | RBI | BB | SO | BA | SA | OBA |
|---|---|---|---|---|---|---|---|---|---|---|---|
| Season | 508 | 131 | 28 | 2 | 12 | 56 | 39 | 46 | .258 | .392 | .314 |
| vs. Left-Handers | 174 | 44 | 11 | 0 | 5 | 24 | 8 | 16 | .253 | .402 | .294 |
| vs. Right-Handers | 334 | 87 | 17 | 2 | 7 | 32 | 31 | 30 | .260 | .386 | .324 |
| Home | 237 | 68 | 17 | 2 | 7 | 27 | 24 | 22 | .287 | .464 | .357 |
| Road | 271 | 63 | 11 | 0 | 5 | 29 | 15 | 24 | .232 | .328 | .274 |
| Grass | 363 | 101 | 23 | 2 | 9 | 38 | 27 | 31 | .278 | .427 | .333 |
| Artificial Turf | 145 | 30 | 5 | 0 | 3 | 18 | 12 | 15 | .207 | .303 | .268 |
| April | 68 | 12 | 5 | 0 | 0 | 9 | 1 | 6 | .176 | .250 | .200 |
| May | 82 | 16 | 6 | 0 | 0 | 6 | 3 | 9 | .195 | .268 | .224 |
| June | 81 | 23 | 6 | 1 | 1 | 8 | 11 | 5 | .284 | .420 | .383 |
| July | 89 | 22 | 3 | 1 | 3 | 13 | 7 | 9 | .247 | .404 | .300 |
| August | 68 | 22 | 4 | 0 | 0 | 3 | 5 | 9 | .324 | .382 | .378 |
| Sept./Oct. | 120 | 36 | 4 | 0 | 8 | 17 | 12 | 8 | .300 | .533 | .358 |
| Leading Off Inn. | 143 | 43 | 9 | 0 | 7 | 7 | 7 | 15 | .301 | .510 | .338 |
| Runners On | 192 | 47 | 12 | 1 | 3 | 47 | 22 | 17 | .245 | .365 | .318 |
| Runners/Scor. Pos. | 117 | 30 | 7 | 0 | 3 | 45 | 17 | 15 | .256 | .393 | .343 |
| Runners On/2 Out | 71 | 16 | 4 | 0 | 1 | 18 | 11 | 9 | .225 | .324 | .329 |
| Scor. Pos./2 Out | 52 | 13 | 3 | 0 | 1 | 17 | 8 | 9 | .250 | .365 | .350 |
| Late Inning Pressure | 75 | 16 | 4 | 0 | 0 | 4 | 3 | 10 | .213 | .267 | .263 |
| Leading Off | 18 | 6 | 1 | 0 | 0 | 0 | 0 | 2 | .333 | .389 | .333 |
| Runners On | 28 | 3 | 1 | 0 | 0 | 4 | 3 | 3 | .107 | .143 | .194 |
| Runners/Scor. Pos. | 16 | 3 | 1 | 0 | 0 | 4 | 2 | 3 | .188 | .250 | .278 |

| RUNS BATTED IN | From 1B | From 2B | From 3B | Scoring Position |
|---|---|---|---|---|
| Totals | 4/126 | 17/91 | 23/54 | 40/145 |
| Percentage | 3% | 19% | 43% | 28% |
| Driving In Runners from 3B with Less than Two Out: | | | 16/29 | 55% |

Loves to face: Dennis Martinez (.500, 4-for-8)
Hates to face: Jose DeLeon (0-for-9)
Tied Mark McGwire for the major league home-run lead in September. . . . Late-season offensive surge coincided with elevation to leadoff spot Aug. 17. In 39 games there, Jefferies batted .339 and slugged .533 with 30 runs scored, 20 RBI, 8 doubles, 8 homers, and 7 steals. He walked only 12 times in those 39 games. . . . Averaged one strikeout every 12.2 times up, 7th best in N.L. . . . Averaged 4.37 chances per nine innings, lowest rate in majors among 29 second basemen with 500+ innings. . . . Led major league rookies in at-bats, runs, doubles, extra-base hits, and total bases; led N.L. rookies in games (141), homers, hits, and walks. Don't deal that Jefferies card for a Jerome Walton yet.

## Steve Jeltz

Bats Left and Right

| Philadelphia Phillies | AB | H | 2B | 3B | HR | RBI | BB | SO | BA | SA | OBA |
|---|---|---|---|---|---|---|---|---|---|---|---|
| Season | 263 | 64 | 7 | 3 | 4 | 25 | 45 | 44 | .243 | .338 | .356 |
| vs. Left-Handers | 71 | 19 | 2 | 1 | 1 | 9 | 17 | 5 | .268 | .366 | .409 |
| vs. Right-Handers | 192 | 45 | 5 | 2 | 3 | 16 | 28 | 39 | .234 | .328 | .335 |
| Home | 130 | 36 | 5 | 1 | 3 | 17 | 21 | 28 | .277 | .400 | .377 |
| Road | 133 | 28 | 2 | 2 | 1 | 8 | 24 | 16 | .211 | .278 | .335 |
| Grass | 72 | 21 | 2 | 1 | 1 | 4 | 15 | 11 | .292 | .389 | .414 |
| Artificial Turf | 191 | 43 | 5 | 2 | 3 | 21 | 30 | 33 | .225 | .319 | .333 |
| April | 18 | 5 | 2 | 0 | 0 | 1 | 4 | 3 | .278 | .389 | .409 |
| May | 45 | 12 | 2 | 0 | 1 | 5 | 9 | 7 | .267 | .378 | .389 |
| June | 55 | 18 | 0 | 1 | 2 | 11 | 14 | 9 | .327 | .473 | .471 |
| July | 56 | 9 | 0 | 0 | 0 | 3 | 8 | 10 | .161 | .161 | .266 |
| August | 45 | 13 | 3 | 0 | 1 | 3 | 6 | 6 | .289 | .422 | .373 |
| Sept./Oct. | 44 | 7 | 0 | 2 | 0 | 2 | 4 | 9 | .159 | .250 | .229 |
| Leading Off Inn. | 57 | 12 | 0 | 1 | 0 | 0 | 11 | 6 | .211 | .246 | .338 |
| Runners On | 106 | 31 | 1 | 2 | 3 | 24 | 16 | 18 | .292 | .425 | .385 |
| Runners/Scor. Pos. | 65 | 17 | 0 | 2 | 1 | 20 | 12 | 9 | .262 | .369 | .377 |
| Runners On/2 Out | 43 | 13 | 1 | 1 | 1 | 6 | 8 | 8 | .302 | .442 | .412 |
| Scor. Pos./2 Out | 28 | 6 | 0 | 1 | 0 | 4 | 7 | 4 | .214 | .286 | .371 |
| Late Inning Pressure | 59 | 13 | 1 | 0 | 1 | 3 | 9 | 10 | .220 | .288 | .324 |
| Leading Off | 11 | 2 | 0 | 0 | 0 | 0 | 2 | 2 | .182 | .182 | .308 |
| Runners On | 23 | 5 | 0 | 0 | 1 | 3 | 4 | 4 | .217 | .348 | .333 |
| Runners/Scor. Pos. | 15 | 2 | 0 | 0 | 0 | 1 | 2 | 2 | .133 | .133 | .235 |

| RUNS BATTED IN | From 1B | From 2B | From 3B | Scoring Position |
|---|---|---|---|---|
| Totals | 3/75 | 11/54 | 7/19 | 18/73 |
| Percentage | 4% | 20% | 37% | 25% |
| Driving In Runners from 3B with Less than Two Out: | | | 7/10 | 70% |

Loves to face: Kelly Downs (.462, 6-for-13)
Hates to face: Bob Forsch (.042, 1-for-24)
Reached base safely in nine consecutive plate appearances in June. Based on his career .314 on-base average, the odds on reaching base safely in nine straight plate appearances at some point in his career were 25 to one. Against. . . . Give the man credit: his .243 average was a career high. Not high enough to avoid having the worst batting average of the '80s (.213) among players with 1000+ at-bats, but at least he made it close (Steve Yeager hit .216). . . . Breathes there a switch-hitter less likely to hit home runs from both sides of the plate in the same game? How about in a game in which he didn't even start? When Jeltz did it on June 8 he had hit only two career home runs in 581 previous games.

## Howard Johnson

Bats Left and Right

| New York Mets | AB | H | 2B | 3B | HR | RBI | BB | SO | BA | SA | OBA |
|---|---|---|---|---|---|---|---|---|---|---|---|
| Season | 571 | 164 | 41 | 3 | 36 | 101 | 77 | 126 | .287 | .559 | .369 |
| vs. Left-Handers | 194 | 54 | 13 | 1 | 7 | 25 | 33 | 49 | .278 | .464 | .383 |
| vs. Right-Handers | 377 | 110 | 28 | 2 | 29 | 76 | 44 | 77 | .292 | .607 | .362 |
| Home | 276 | 80 | 19 | 1 | 19 | 47 | 38 | 53 | .290 | .572 | .371 |
| Road | 295 | 84 | 22 | 2 | 17 | 54 | 39 | 73 | .285 | .546 | .368 |
| Grass | 406 | 116 | 32 | 2 | 26 | 67 | 50 | 84 | .286 | .567 | .362 |
| Artificial Turf | 165 | 48 | 9 | 1 | 10 | 34 | 27 | 42 | .291 | .539 | .387 |
| April | 60 | 20 | 2 | 0 | 4 | 12 | 8 | 13 | .333 | .567 | .406 |
| May | 102 | 22 | 6 | 1 | 6 | 15 | 15 | 25 | .216 | .471 | .316 |
| June | 100 | 34 | 8 | 1 | 11 | 24 | 9 | 24 | .340 | .770 | .387 |
| July | 95 | 28 | 12 | 0 | 5 | 15 | 20 | 15 | .295 | .579 | .410 |
| August | 95 | 30 | 8 | 1 | 5 | 17 | 13 | 19 | .316 | .579 | .394 |
| Sept./Oct. | 119 | 30 | 5 | 0 | 5 | 18 | 12 | 30 | .252 | .420 | .326 |
| Leading Off Inn. | 129 | 44 | 8 | 2 | 9 | 9 | 8 | 22 | .341 | .643 | .380 |
| Runners On | 233 | 73 | 23 | 0 | 16 | 81 | 38 | 50 | .313 | .618 | .403 |
| Runners/Scor. Pos. | 128 | 39 | 11 | 0 | 9 | 64 | 30 | 31 | .305 | .602 | .424 |
| Runners On/2 Out | 72 | 21 | 6 | 0 | 5 | 23 | 19 | 17 | .292 | .583 | .446 |
| Scor. Pos./2 Out | 52 | 15 | 4 | 0 | 5 | 22 | 17 | 12 | .288 | .654 | .471 |
| Late Inning Pressure | 75 | 21 | 3 | 1 | 4 | 11 | 17 | 17 | .280 | .507 | .419 |
| Leading Off | 24 | 6 | 0 | 0 | 1 | 1 | 2 | 6 | .250 | .375 | .308 |
| Runners On | 23 | 7 | 1 | 0 | 2 | 9 | 11 | 3 | .304 | .609 | .543 |
| Runners/Scor. Pos. | 11 | 3 | 0 | 0 | 0 | 5 | 11 | 2 | .273 | .273 | .652 |

| RUNS BATTED IN | From 1B | From 2B | From 3B | Scoring Position |
|---|---|---|---|---|
| Totals | 13/159 | 29/104 | 23/55 | 52/159 |
| Percentage | 8% | 28% | 42% | 33% |
| Driving In Runners from 3B with Less than Two Out: | | | 21/33 | 64% |

Loves to face: Todd Worrell (.556, 5-for-9, 4 HR, 6 BB)
Hates to face: Jim Deshaies (0-for-16, 8 SO)
Slugging average vs. right-handed pitchers (.607) was best in majors. . . . Boosted his RBI total from 68 (in 1988) to 101, but don't assume that the jump was due to increased opportunities from the No. 3 spot in lineup. The difference was in execution, not chances: in 1988, HoJo drove in 25 percent of 154 mates in scoring position; in 1989, 33 percent of 159. . . . Led N.L. with 12 stolen bases in July. . . . Career ratio of 0.61 ground outs for every out in air is lowest among all players over last 15 years. Kept true to form in 1989 by batting .336 vs. ground-ball pitchers, .232 against fly-ballers. . . . Grounded into only four double plays in 125 opportunities, lowest rate in N.L. (minimum: 75 opporunities).

## Ricky Jordan

Bats Right

| Philadelphia Phillies | AB | H | 2B | 3B | HR | RBI | BB | SO | BA | SA | OBA |
|---|---|---|---|---|---|---|---|---|---|---|---|
| Season | 523 | 149 | 22 | 3 | 12 | 75 | 23 | 62 | .285 | .407 | .317 |
| vs. Left-Handers | 201 | 67 | 12 | 2 | 4 | 29 | 14 | 19 | .333 | .473 | .373 |
| vs. Right-Handers | 322 | 82 | 10 | 1 | 8 | 46 | 9 | 43 | .255 | .366 | .280 |
| Home | 266 | 73 | 10 | 1 | 7 | 37 | 7 | 31 | .274 | .398 | .294 |
| Road | 257 | 76 | 12 | 2 | 5 | 38 | 16 | 31 | .296 | .416 | .339 |
| Grass | 141 | 41 | 5 | 1 | 2 | 20 | 6 | 13 | .291 | .383 | .316 |
| Artificial Turf | 382 | 108 | 17 | 2 | 10 | 55 | 17 | 49 | .283 | .416 | .317 |
| April | 68 | 17 | 2 | 0 | 1 | 10 | 3 | 12 | .250 | .324 | .278 |
| May | 67 | 16 | 0 | 0 | 0 | 2 | 3 | 6 | .239 | .239 | .271 |
| June | 76 | 22 | 4 | 0 | 3 | 11 | 5 | 9 | .289 | .461 | .333 |
| July | 92 | 27 | 4 | 0 | 1 | 13 | 2 | 9 | .293 | .370 | .316 |
| August | 113 | 36 | 7 | 2 | 5 | 28 | 4 | 8 | .319 | .549 | .350 |
| Sept./Oct. | 107 | 31 | 5 | 1 | 2 | 11 | 6 | 18 | .290 | .411 | .322 |
| Leading Off Inn. | 130 | 37 | 5 | 0 | 3 | 3 | 3 | 9 | .285 | .392 | .301 |
| Runners On | 268 | 74 | 10 | 2 | 7 | 70 | 16 | 35 | .276 | .407 | .318 |
| Runners/Scor. Pos. | 137 | 37 | 3 | 2 | 1 | 53 | 12 | 22 | .270 | .343 | .329 |
| Runners On/2 Out | 115 | 33 | 5 | 2 | 1 | 23 | 6 | 13 | .287 | .391 | .333 |
| Scor. Pos./2 Out | 66 | 15 | 1 | 2 | 1 | 21 | 5 | 10 | .227 | .348 | .301 |
| Late Inning Pressure | 81 | 22 | 2 | 0 | 2 | 13 | 8 | 7 | .272 | .370 | .333 |
| Leading Off | 15 | 5 | 1 | 0 | 2 | 2 | 1 | 1 | .333 | .800 | .375 |
| Runners On | 44 | 11 | 1 | 0 | 0 | 11 | 6 | 3 | .250 | .273 | .333 |
| Runners/Scor. Pos. | 26 | 8 | 0 | 0 | 0 | 10 | 4 | 1 | .308 | .308 | .387 |

| RUNS BATTED IN | From 1B | From 2B | From 3B | Scoring Position |
|---|---|---|---|---|
| Totals | 14/208 | 18/103 | 31/63 | 49/166 |
| Percentage | 7% | 17% | 49% | 30% |
| Driving In Runners from 3B with Less than Two Out: | | | 22/32 | 69% |

Loves to face: Jose DeLeon (.500, 7-for-14, 2 2B, 2 HR)
Hates to face: Mike Scott (0-for-10)
Led N.L. with 28 RBI in August, the highest total by any N.L. player in any month last season. . . . Batted cleanup in each of his last 34 starts. . . . Led Phillies with 20 "go-ahead" RBI. . . . Career batting: .261 from April to June, then .303 in July, .314 in August, .307 in September. . . . Career breakdown: .326, 19 walks, 30 strikeouts vs. left-handed pitchers; .274, 11 walks, 71 whiffs vs. right-handers. . . . Reached base on an infield error 13 times last season, 4th-highest total in majors. . . . Grounded into 19 double plays (10 more than anyone else on team) in 132 opportunities last season. . . . Batted .297 on fair balls hit to the right side, .467 straight away, and .255 to the opposite field.

## Terry Kennedy

Bats Left

| San Francisco Giants | AB | H | 2B | 3B | HR | RBI | BB | SO | BA | SA | OBA |
|---|---|---|---|---|---|---|---|---|---|---|---|
| Season | 355 | 85 | 15 | 0 | 5 | 34 | 35 | 56 | .239 | .324 | .306 |
| vs. Left-Handers | 39 | 6 | 2 | 0 | 0 | 3 | 4 | 8 | .154 | .205 | .233 |
| vs. Right-Handers | 316 | 79 | 13 | 0 | 5 | 31 | 31 | 48 | .250 | .339 | .315 |
| Home | 172 | 46 | 7 | 0 | 1 | 16 | 17 | 24 | .267 | .326 | .332 |
| Road | 183 | 39 | 8 | 0 | 4 | 18 | 18 | 32 | .213 | .322 | .282 |
| Grass | 246 | 58 | 9 | 0 | 2 | 26 | 24 | 39 | .236 | .297 | .303 |
| Artificial Turf | 109 | 27 | 6 | 0 | 3 | 8 | 11 | 17 | .248 | .385 | .314 |
| April | 51 | 14 | 3 | 0 | 2 | 10 | 5 | 6 | .275 | .451 | .333 |
| May | 70 | 16 | 4 | 0 | 1 | 7 | 7 | 11 | .229 | .329 | .299 |
| June | 46 | 12 | 2 | 0 | 1 | 4 | 11 | 9 | .261 | .370 | .397 |
| July | 63 | 9 | 2 | 0 | 0 | 3 | 3 | 11 | .143 | .175 | .182 |
| August | 55 | 17 | 2 | 0 | 0 | 7 | 6 | 6 | .309 | .345 | .377 |
| Sept./Oct. | 70 | 17 | 2 | 0 | 1 | 3 | 3 | 13 | .243 | .314 | .274 |
| Leading Off Inn. | 85 | 20 | 3 | 0 | 1 | 1 | 6 | 17 | .235 | .306 | .286 |
| Runners On | 136 | 34 | 5 | 0 | 1 | 30 | 21 | 27 | .250 | .309 | .346 |
| Runners/Scor. Pos. | 78 | 22 | 4 | 0 | 0 | 27 | 18 | 15 | .282 | .333 | .408 |
| Runners On/2 Out | 58 | 11 | 2 | 0 | 1 | 12 | 9 | 14 | .190 | .276 | .299 |
| Scor. Pos./2 Out | 40 | 8 | 1 | 0 | 0 | 9 | 8 | 10 | .200 | .225 | .333 |
| Late Inning Pressure | 46 | 10 | 2 | 0 | 1 | 4 | 10 | 8 | .217 | .326 | .357 |
| Leading Off | 16 | 4 | 1 | 0 | 0 | 0 | 2 | 2 | .250 | .313 | .333 |
| Runners On | 20 | 4 | 1 | 0 | 0 | 3 | 7 | 6 | .200 | .250 | .407 |
| Runners/Scor. Pos. | 10 | 3 | 1 | 0 | 0 | 3 | 6 | 3 | .300 | .400 | .563 |

| RUNS BATTED IN | From 1B | From 2B | From 3B | Scoring Position |
|---|---|---|---|---|
| Totals | 3/91 | 12/62 | 14/31 | 26/93 |
| Percentage | 3% | 19% | 45% | 28% |
| Driving In Runners from 3B with Less than Two Out: | | | 10/13 | 77% |

Loves to face: Rick Mahler (.385, 20-for-52, 2 HR)
Hates to face: Jose DeLeon (.069, 2-for-29, 1 HR)
Overall offensive statistics for 1989 are virtually identical to the man for whom he was traded, Bob Melvin.... Batted .293 vs. ground-ball pitchers, .194 against fly-ballers.... Had a higher batting average (.318) on fair balls hit to the opposite field than on balls he hit straight away (.242), or on balls that he pulled (.284).... Batted .154 vs. left-handers: 3-for-10 with runners in scoring position, 3-for-29 at other times.... Although the rest of the staff had a lower ERA with Kirt Manwaring behind the plate than with Kennedy, ace Scott Garrelts had a lower mark with the veteran (1.89 to 3.24).... Has a record of 1–8 in World Series games; might be 0–8 if not for Kurt Bevacqua.

## Jeff King

Bats Right

| Pittsburgh Pirates | AB | H | 2B | 3B | HR | RBI | BB | SO | BA | SA | OBA |
|---|---|---|---|---|---|---|---|---|---|---|---|
| Season | 215 | 42 | 13 | 3 | 5 | 19 | 20 | 34 | .195 | .353 | .266 |
| vs. Left-Handers | 112 | 22 | 8 | 3 | 0 | 8 | 13 | 17 | .196 | .321 | .279 |
| vs. Right-Handers | 103 | 20 | 5 | 0 | 5 | 11 | 7 | 17 | .194 | .388 | .250 |
| Home | 119 | 22 | 6 | 2 | 3 | 10 | 11 | 15 | .185 | .345 | .252 |
| Road | 96 | 20 | 7 | 1 | 2 | 9 | 9 | 19 | .208 | .365 | .282 |
| Grass | 36 | 9 | 4 | 0 | 1 | 2 | 6 | 6 | .250 | .444 | .372 |
| Artificial Turf | 179 | 33 | 9 | 3 | 4 | 17 | 14 | 28 | .184 | .335 | .242 |
| April | 0 | 0 | 0 | 0 | 0 | 0 | 0 | 0 | — | — | — |
| May | 0 | 0 | 0 | 0 | 0 | 0 | 0 | 0 | — | — | — |
| June | 26 | 5 | 2 | 2 | 0 | 2 | 4 | 3 | .192 | .423 | .300 |
| July | 37 | 7 | 3 | 0 | 1 | 2 | 6 | 5 | .189 | .351 | .318 |
| August | 73 | 14 | 3 | 0 | 3 | 7 | 6 | 11 | .192 | .356 | .256 |
| Sept./Oct. | 79 | 16 | 5 | 1 | 1 | 8 | 4 | 15 | .203 | .329 | .235 |
| Leading Off Inn. | 55 | 13 | 5 | 0 | 2 | 2 | 3 | 4 | .236 | .436 | .276 |
| Runners On | 97 | 13 | 3 | 2 | 1 | 15 | 9 | 19 | .134 | .237 | .200 |
| Runners/Scor. Pos. | 49 | 9 | 2 | 2 | 0 | 12 | 4 | 8 | .184 | .306 | .228 |
| Runners On/2 Out | 39 | 5 | 1 | 0 | 1 | 5 | 4 | 11 | .128 | .231 | .209 |
| Scor. Pos./2 Out | 20 | 3 | 1 | 0 | 0 | 3 | 1 | 4 | .150 | .200 | .190 |
| Late Inning Pressure | 38 | 7 | 2 | 1 | 1 | 3 | 3 | 2 | .184 | .368 | .244 |
| Leading Off | 14 | 3 | 2 | 0 | 1 | 1 | 0 | 0 | .214 | .571 | .214 |
| Runners On | 17 | 3 | 0 | 1 | 0 | 2 | 2 | 2 | .176 | .294 | .263 |
| Runners/Scor. Pos. | 10 | 3 | 0 | 1 | 0 | 2 | 1 | 0 | .300 | .500 | .364 |

| RUNS BATTED IN | From 1B | From 2B | From 3B | Scoring Position |
|---|---|---|---|---|
| Totals | 2/64 | 3/34 | 9/22 | 12/56 |
| Percentage | 3% | 9% | 41% | 21% |
| Driving In Runners from 3B with Less than Two Out: | | | 8/15 | 53% |

Loves to face: Joe Magrane (.417, 5-for-12)
Hates to face: Jim Deshaies (0-for-7)
That .134 batting average with runners on base was the lowest in the majors last season. In our 15 years of compiling situational statistics, only three players had lower one-season, runners-on-base batting averages (minimum: 100 plate appearances with ROB): Andres Mora, .110 for 1978 Orioles; Roger Metzger, .122 for 1977 Astros; and Rick Dempsey, .122 with 1986 Orioles.... King hit .195 for season, but other Pirates' rookies hit a combined .139—and we didn't even include rookie pitchers' at-bats in that average! Pittsburgh's .181 batting average from their nonpitcher rookies was lowest among the 26 major league teams last season. (Houston's rookies hit .195, the only other team below .200.)

## John Kruk

Bats Left

| Padres/Phillies | AB | H | 2B | 3B | HR | RBI | BB | SO | BA | SA | OBA |
|---|---|---|---|---|---|---|---|---|---|---|---|
| Season | 357 | 107 | 13 | 6 | 8 | 45 | 44 | 53 | .300 | .437 | .374 |
| vs. Left-Handers | 101 | 27 | 4 | 1 | 0 | 8 | 7 | 18 | .267 | .327 | .315 |
| vs. Right-Handers | 256 | 80 | 9 | 5 | 8 | 37 | 37 | 35 | .313 | .480 | .395 |
| Home | 192 | 60 | 8 | 5 | 6 | 31 | 23 | 27 | .313 | .500 | .384 |
| Road | 165 | 47 | 5 | 1 | 2 | 14 | 21 | 26 | .285 | .364 | .362 |
| Grass | 132 | 36 | 2 | 1 | 4 | 11 | 24 | 25 | .273 | .394 | .385 |
| Artificial Turf | 225 | 71 | 11 | 5 | 4 | 34 | 20 | 28 | .316 | .462 | .367 |
| April | 49 | 7 | 0 | 0 | 1 | 3 | 11 | 5 | .143 | .204 | .300 |
| May | 27 | 7 | 0 | 0 | 2 | 3 | 5 | 9 | .259 | .481 | .375 |
| June | 86 | 27 | 4 | 2 | 0 | 14 | 7 | 12 | .314 | .407 | .362 |
| July | 19 | 9 | 2 | 1 | 2 | 7 | 1 | 1 | .474 | 1.000 | .500 |
| August | 87 | 30 | 3 | 1 | 1 | 6 | 16 | 9 | .345 | .437 | .442 |
| Sept./Oct. | 89 | 27 | 4 | 2 | 2 | 12 | 4 | 17 | .303 | .461 | .330 |
| Leading Off Inn. | 78 | 30 | 5 | 0 | 2 | 2 | 10 | 9 | .385 | .526 | .455 |
| Runners On | 170 | 47 | 4 | 5 | 5 | 42 | 21 | 27 | .276 | .447 | .351 |
| Runners/Scor. Pos. | 98 | 22 | 2 | 2 | 1 | 31 | 14 | 21 | .224 | .316 | .313 |
| Runners On/2 Out | 78 | 21 | 3 | 1 | 2 | 16 | 8 | 14 | .269 | .410 | .337 |
| Scor. Pos./2 Out | 48 | 9 | 2 | 0 | 1 | 13 | 5 | 12 | .188 | .292 | .264 |
| Late Inning Pressure | 35 | 12 | 2 | 0 | 2 | 9 | 7 | 5 | .343 | .571 | .442 |
| Leading Off | 10 | 4 | 1 | 0 | 0 | 0 | 3 | 1 | .400 | .500 | .538 |
| Runners On | 16 | 5 | 0 | 0 | 2 | 9 | 4 | 3 | .313 | .688 | .429 |
| Runners/Scor. Pos. | 11 | 3 | 0 | 0 | 1 | 7 | 4 | 2 | .273 | .545 | .438 |

| RUNS BATTED IN | From 1B | From 2B | From 3B | Scoring Position |
|---|---|---|---|---|
| Totals | 8/122 | 12/75 | 17/45 | 29/120 |
| Percentage | 7% | 16% | 38% | 24% |
| Driving In Runners from 3B with Less than Two Out: | | | 12/22 | 55% |

Loves to face: Ted Power (.625, 10-for-16)
Hates to face: Zane Smith (0-for-11, 5 SO)
One of those "phony" .300 hitters (actually .29972; see Gerald Perry comments in 1989 *Analyst*, p. 246).... Batted .184 in 31 games for San Diego, .331 in 81 games for Philadelphia.... Led N.L. with .455 on-base average when leading off innings.... Batted .325 with runners in scoring position in first two years in majors; has hit .226 in those situations over last two years. In 1989, Kruk was only player in majors to hit 100 points lower with runners in scoring position than in other at-bats (minimum: 75 AB with RISP).... Despite 1989 showing, his .321 career average with two outs and runners in scoring position ranks second to Boggs (.328) among active players (minimum: 50 hits).

## Barry Larkin

Bats Right

| Cincinnati Reds | AB | H | 2B | 3B | HR | RBI | BB | SO | BA | SA | OBA |
|---|---|---|---|---|---|---|---|---|---|---|---|
| Season | 325 | 111 | 14 | 4 | 4 | 36 | 20 | 23 | .342 | .446 | .375 |
| vs. Left-Handers | 121 | 45 | 4 | 2 | 2 | 16 | 11 | 3 | .372 | .488 | .421 |
| vs. Right-Handers | 204 | 66 | 10 | 2 | 2 | 20 | 9 | 20 | .324 | .422 | .347 |
| Home | 156 | 55 | 7 | 3 | 1 | 21 | 9 | 11 | .353 | .455 | .376 |
| Road | 169 | 56 | 7 | 1 | 3 | 15 | 11 | 12 | .331 | .438 | .373 |
| Grass | 101 | 32 | 6 | 1 | 3 | 10 | 6 | 9 | .317 | .485 | .360 |
| Artificial Turf | 224 | 79 | 8 | 3 | 1 | 26 | 14 | 14 | .353 | .429 | .381 |
| April | 76 | 22 | 3 | 1 | 2 | 8 | 3 | 7 | .289 | .434 | .325 |
| May | 95 | 35 | 3 | 3 | 0 | 12 | 7 | 6 | .368 | .463 | .400 |
| June | 112 | 44 | 7 | 0 | 1 | 11 | 5 | 8 | .393 | .482 | .412 |
| July | 32 | 6 | 0 | 0 | 1 | 1 | 1 | 2 | .188 | .281 | .212 |
| August | 0 | 0 | 0 | 0 | 0 | 0 | 0 | 0 | — | — | — |
| Sept./Oct. | 10 | 4 | 1 | 0 | 0 | 4 | 4 | 0 | .400 | .500 | .533 |
| Leading Off Inn. | 87 | 26 | 6 | 0 | 0 | 0 | 4 | 7 | .299 | .368 | .344 |
| Runners On | 117 | 42 | 4 | 3 | 1 | 33 | 12 | 12 | .359 | .470 | .394 |
| Runners/Scor. Pos. | 67 | 20 | 1 | 2 | 1 | 31 | 12 | 9 | .299 | .418 | .368 |
| Runners On/2 Out | 40 | 16 | 1 | 2 | 1 | 12 | 4 | 3 | .400 | .600 | .455 |
| Scor. Pos./2 Out | 27 | 9 | 0 | 2 | 1 | 11 | 4 | 3 | .333 | .593 | .419 |
| Late Inning Pressure | 52 | 17 | 4 | 0 | 1 | 6 | 5 | 1 | .327 | .462 | .390 |
| Leading Off | 17 | 7 | 2 | 0 | 0 | 0 | 2 | 0 | .412 | .529 | .500 |
| Runners On | 17 | 6 | 2 | 0 | 0 | 5 | 3 | 1 | .353 | .471 | .429 |
| Runners/Scor. Pos. | 11 | 3 | 0 | 0 | 0 | 4 | 3 | 1 | .273 | .273 | .400 |

| RUNS BATTED IN | From 1B | From 2B | From 3B | Scoring Position |
|---|---|---|---|---|
| Totals | 3/76 | 11/58 | 18/27 | 29/85 |
| Percentage | 4% | 19% | 67% | 34% |
| Driving In Runners from 3B with Less than Two Out: | | | 16/21 | 76% |

Loves to face: Greg Maddux (.471, 8-for-17, 1 HR)
Hates to face: David Cone (.071, 1-for-14)
May batting average was N.L.'s highest.... Has hit for higher average with runners on base than with bases empty in each of four seasons in majors. Career averages: .322 with ROB, .271 with bases empty.... Batted .359 with runners on base, 2d in N.L. behind Lonnie Smith.... Led major league shortstops with 5.47 chances per nine innings.... Ranked third in N.L. in batting at time of his injury, but took lead while on DL and held it until Aug. 7, when he no longer qualified.... Injured during a throwing competition the day before the All-Star Game; returned to pinch hit in September, but did not play the field. Unlikely to challenge Larry Bird in Long-Distance Shootout on NBA All-Star Saturday.

## Mike LaValliere

Bats Left

| Pittsburgh Pirates | AB | H | 2B | 3B | HR | RBI | BB | SO | BA | SA | OBA |
|---|---|---|---|---|---|---|---|---|---|---|---|
| Season | 190 | 60 | 10 | 0 | 2 | 24 | 29 | 24 | .316 | .400 | .406 |
| vs. Left-Handers | 25 | 7 | 1 | 0 | 0 | 2 | 4 | 7 | .280 | .320 | .379 |
| vs. Right-Handers | 165 | 53 | 9 | 0 | 2 | 22 | 25 | 17 | .321 | .412 | .411 |
| Home | 98 | 37 | 5 | 0 | 2 | 17 | 21 | 13 | .378 | .490 | .487 |
| Road | 92 | 23 | 5 | 0 | 0 | 7 | 8 | 11 | .250 | .304 | .310 |
| Grass | 49 | 14 | 3 | 0 | 0 | 4 | 2 | 4 | .286 | .347 | .314 |
| Artificial Turf | 141 | 46 | 7 | 0 | 2 | 20 | 27 | 20 | .326 | .418 | .435 |
| April | 25 | 7 | 0 | 0 | 0 | 6 | 2 | 2 | .280 | .280 | .333 |
| May | 0 | 0 | 0 | 0 | 0 | 0 | 0 | 0 | — | — | — |
| June | 0 | 0 | 0 | 0 | 0 | 0 | 0 | 0 | — | — | — |
| July | 51 | 20 | 2 | 0 | 0 | 5 | 7 | 5 | .392 | .431 | .466 |
| August | 64 | 19 | 4 | 0 | 0 | 4 | 11 | 11 | .297 | .359 | .400 |
| Sept./Oct. | 50 | 14 | 4 | 0 | 2 | 9 | 9 | 6 | .280 | .480 | .390 |
| Leading Off Inn. | 37 | 18 | 3 | 0 | 0 | 0 | 5 | 1 | .486 | .568 | .548 |
| Runners On | 84 | 25 | 3 | 0 | 1 | 23 | 17 | 14 | .298 | .369 | .416 |
| Runners/Scor. Pos. | 61 | 16 | 3 | 0 | 1 | 23 | 12 | 11 | .262 | .361 | .384 |
| Runners On/2 Out | 35 | 9 | 1 | 0 | 0 | 6 | 10 | 6 | .257 | .286 | .422 |
| Scor. Pos./2 Out | 25 | 6 | 1 | 0 | 0 | 6 | 8 | 5 | .240 | .280 | .424 |
| Late Inning Pressure | 22 | 7 | 0 | 0 | 1 | 6 | 2 | 3 | .318 | .455 | .375 |
| Leading Off | 4 | 2 | 0 | 0 | 0 | 0 | 2 | 0 | .500 | .500 | .667 |
| Runners On | 10 | 4 | 0 | 0 | 1 | 6 | 0 | 0 | .400 | .700 | .400 |
| Runners/Scor. Pos. | 7 | 2 | 0 | 0 | 1 | 6 | 0 | 0 | .286 | .714 | .286 |

| RUNS BATTED IN | From 1B | From 2B | From 3B | Scoring Position |
|---|---|---|---|---|
| Totals | 0/51 | 10/39 | 12/27 | 22/66 |
| Percentage | 0% | 26% | 44% | 33% |
| Driving In Runners from 3B with Less than Two Out: | | | 10/16 | 63% |

Loves to face: Kelly Downs (.500, 10-for-20)
Hates to face: Frank DiPino (.125, 2-for-16)
Batted .378 at Three Rivers Stadium last season; no N.L. player with as many at-bats hit better in his own home park. . . . Started 56 games vs. right-handed pitchers, three vs. lefties; batted .326 in 59 starts. . . . Did not attempt to score from second base on any of seven singles to outfield. . . . Opponents succeeded on 82 percent of stolen base attempts, 2d-highest rate among major league catchers (minimum: 25 attempts) last season. . . . Pirates' staff had 3.22 ERA with Spanky catching, 3.87 with others in mask; that showed up in won-lost records: 30–28–1 in LaV's starts, 44–60–1 in other games. . . . In each of LaV's three years with team, Bucs have been above .500 in his starts, below .500 with others starting.

## Vance Law

Bats Right

| Chicago Cubs | AB | H | 2B | 3B | HR | RBI | BB | SO | BA | SA | OBA |
|---|---|---|---|---|---|---|---|---|---|---|---|
| Season | 408 | 96 | 22 | 3 | 7 | 42 | 38 | 73 | .235 | .355 | .296 |
| vs. Left-Handers | 111 | 33 | 7 | 0 | 3 | 14 | 12 | 16 | .297 | .441 | .363 |
| vs. Right-Handers | 297 | 63 | 15 | 3 | 4 | 28 | 26 | 57 | .212 | .323 | .271 |
| Home | 187 | 44 | 8 | 2 | 4 | 22 | 20 | 35 | .235 | .364 | .303 |
| Road | 221 | 52 | 14 | 1 | 3 | 20 | 18 | 38 | .235 | .348 | .289 |
| Grass | 262 | 57 | 12 | 3 | 5 | 25 | 25 | 51 | .218 | .344 | .281 |
| Artificial Turf | 146 | 39 | 10 | 0 | 2 | 17 | 13 | 22 | .267 | .377 | .323 |
| April | 58 | 10 | 2 | 0 | 0 | 5 | 4 | 11 | .172 | .207 | .222 |
| May | 89 | 23 | 5 | 0 | 1 | 10 | 3 | 15 | .258 | .348 | .280 |
| June | 84 | 21 | 4 | 1 | 2 | 11 | 9 | 13 | .250 | .393 | .319 |
| July | 70 | 16 | 5 | 1 | 2 | 5 | 7 | 10 | .229 | .414 | .295 |
| August | 68 | 18 | 6 | 0 | 1 | 8 | 6 | 18 | .265 | .397 | .316 |
| Sept./Oct. | 39 | 8 | 0 | 1 | 1 | 3 | 9 | 6 | .205 | .333 | .347 |
| Leading Off Inn. | 82 | 21 | 5 | 0 | 4 | 4 | 6 | 15 | .256 | .463 | .307 |
| Runners On | 191 | 40 | 13 | 1 | 0 | 35 | 20 | 33 | .209 | .288 | .275 |
| Runners/Scor. Pos. | 117 | 23 | 7 | 1 | 0 | 35 | 13 | 22 | .197 | .274 | .263 |
| Runners On/2 Out | 81 | 16 | 6 | 0 | 0 | 13 | 10 | 15 | .198 | .272 | .286 |
| Scor. Pos./2 Out | 54 | 11 | 4 | 0 | 0 | 13 | 9 | 10 | .204 | .278 | .317 |
| Late Inning Pressure | 48 | 8 | 1 | 0 | 0 | 3 | 2 | 8 | .167 | .188 | .196 |
| Leading Off | 10 | 2 | 0 | 0 | 0 | 0 | 0 | 2 | .200 | .200 | .200 |
| Runners On | 22 | 2 | 1 | 0 | 0 | 3 | 1 | 4 | .091 | .136 | .125 |
| Runners/Scor. Pos. | 16 | 2 | 1 | 0 | 0 | 3 | 0 | 4 | .125 | .188 | .118 |

| RUNS BATTED IN | From 1B | From 2B | From 3B | Scoring Position |
|---|---|---|---|---|
| Totals | 1/133 | 14/91 | 20/54 | 34/145 |
| Percentage | 1% | 15% | 37% | 23% |
| Driving In Runners from 3B with Less than Two Out: | | | 16/29 | 55% |

Loves to face: Jim Deshaies (.538, 7-for-13)
Hates to face: Ron Darling (.147, 5-for-34, 10 SO)
Overall average dipped 58 points from .293 mark in 1988, but average vs. left-handers has risen in each of last five years: .241, .245, .252, .288, .291, .297. Batting average vs. right-handers fell 82 points from career-high .294 in 1988. . . . Career batting average: .2574 in N.L., .2572 in A.L. . . . All of his home runs last season were solo shots; in 1988, 8 of his 11 homers came with runners on base. . . . Hitless in 10 at-bats as a pinch hitter last season, and 0-for-13 in that role since Aug. 1987 pinch single off Scott Garrelts. . . . Became first player in history to appear in postseason play for both White Sox and Cubs; celebrated by striking out in all three at-bats in Championship Series.

## Jose Lind

Bats Right

| Pittsburgh Pirates | AB | H | 2B | 3B | HR | RBI | BB | SO | BA | SA | OBA |
|---|---|---|---|---|---|---|---|---|---|---|---|
| Season | 578 | 134 | 21 | 3 | 2 | 49 | 39 | 64 | .232 | .289 | .280 |
| vs. Left-Handers | 195 | 50 | 7 | 1 | 1 | 21 | 19 | 21 | .256 | .318 | .315 |
| vs. Right-Handers | 383 | 84 | 14 | 2 | 1 | 28 | 20 | 43 | .219 | .274 | .262 |
| Home | 296 | 65 | 9 | 1 | 2 | 25 | 23 | 25 | .220 | .277 | .273 |
| Road | 282 | 69 | 12 | 2 | 0 | 24 | 16 | 39 | .245 | .301 | .288 |
| Grass | 160 | 35 | 7 | 0 | 0 | 8 | 7 | 19 | .219 | .263 | .256 |
| Artificial Turf | 418 | 99 | 14 | 3 | 2 | 41 | 32 | 45 | .237 | .299 | .289 |
| April | 91 | 20 | 2 | 0 | 1 | 7 | 8 | 11 | .220 | .275 | .277 |
| May | 90 | 21 | 7 | 0 | 0 | 9 | 4 | 11 | .233 | .311 | .281 |
| June | 108 | 28 | 3 | 1 | 1 | 11 | 7 | 9 | .259 | .333 | .302 |
| July | 111 | 26 | 2 | 2 | 0 | 8 | 7 | 13 | .234 | .288 | .280 |
| August | 83 | 11 | 3 | 0 | 0 | 4 | 8 | 11 | .133 | .169 | .207 |
| Sept./Oct. | 95 | 28 | 4 | 0 | 0 | 10 | 5 | 9 | .295 | .337 | .327 |
| Leading Off Inn. | 83 | 19 | 2 | 0 | 1 | 1 | 8 | 9 | .229 | .289 | .297 |
| Runners On | 254 | 64 | 11 | 2 | 0 | 47 | 15 | 28 | .252 | .311 | .291 |
| Runners/Scor. Pos. | 149 | 39 | 8 | 2 | 0 | 46 | 12 | 16 | .262 | .342 | .311 |
| Runners On/2 Out | 107 | 21 | 3 | 1 | 0 | 18 | 11 | 13 | .196 | .243 | .271 |
| Scor. Pos./2 Out | 79 | 15 | 3 | 1 | 0 | 18 | 10 | 10 | .190 | .253 | .281 |
| Late Inning Pressure | 98 | 26 | 4 | 0 | 0 | 5 | 9 | 12 | .265 | .306 | .324 |
| Leading Off | 19 | 6 | 1 | 0 | 0 | 0 | 2 | 3 | .316 | .368 | .381 |
| Runners On | 41 | 9 | 1 | 0 | 0 | 5 | 5 | 6 | .220 | .244 | .298 |
| Runners/Scor. Pos. | 27 | 3 | 1 | 0 | 0 | 5 | 4 | 4 | .111 | .148 | .219 |

| RUNS BATTED IN | From 1B | From 2B | From 3B | Scoring Position |
|---|---|---|---|---|
| Totals | 5/183 | 21/112 | 21/62 | 42/174 |
| Percentage | 3% | 19% | 34% | 24% |
| Driving In Runners from 3B with Less than Two Out: | | | 15/24 | 63% |

Loves to face: Don Carman (.533, 8-for-15, 1 HR)
Hates to face: Ed Whitson (.067, 1-for-15)
Committed 18 errors last season; had more errors at Wrigley Field (four) than Ryne Sandberg (three) did. . . . Had 15 steals in 16 attempts, best rate (.938) in N.L. (minimum: 10 SB). . . . Suffered through 0-for-27 slump with runners on base in August, longest such streak of N.L. season. . . . Hit both home runs vs. Phillies at Three Rivers. . . . Hitless in 11 at-bats with bases loaded, biggest such oh-fer in majors. But it's not as bad as it sounds: Bucs went 7–3–1 in those games. . . . Pirates' starting second basemen (Lind 143 starts, others 21) batted .221, slugged .279, and on-based .268 last year; batting average was 2d lowest in majors (to Houston's .218); slugging and on-base averages were lows in majors.

## Barry Lyons

Bats Right

| New York Mets | AB | H | 2B | 3B | HR | RBI | BB | SO | BA | SA | OBA |
|---|---|---|---|---|---|---|---|---|---|---|---|
| Season | 235 | 58 | 13 | 0 | 3 | 27 | 11 | 28 | .247 | .340 | .283 |
| vs. Left-Handers | 84 | 25 | 6 | 0 | 3 | 10 | 6 | 5 | .298 | .476 | .341 |
| vs. Right-Handers | 151 | 33 | 7 | 0 | 0 | 17 | 5 | 23 | .219 | .265 | .250 |
| Home | 108 | 26 | 8 | 0 | 1 | 13 | 5 | 12 | .241 | .343 | .276 |
| Road | 127 | 32 | 5 | 0 | 2 | 14 | 6 | 16 | .252 | .339 | .289 |
| Grass | 178 | 47 | 9 | 0 | 1 | 23 | 6 | 21 | .264 | .331 | .287 |
| Artificial Turf | 57 | 11 | 4 | 0 | 2 | 4 | 5 | 7 | .193 | .368 | .270 |
| April | 12 | 2 | 1 | 0 | 0 | 0 | 3 | 1 | .167 | .250 | .333 |
| May | 62 | 22 | 2 | 0 | 2 | 6 | 2 | 9 | .355 | .484 | .375 |
| June | 52 | 6 | 3 | 0 | 0 | 9 | 3 | 4 | .115 | .173 | .158 |
| July | 3 | 1 | 0 | 0 | 0 | 0 | 0 | 0 | .333 | .333 | .333 |
| August | 60 | 16 | 3 | 0 | 1 | 6 | 2 | 9 | .267 | .367 | .286 |
| Sept./Oct. | 46 | 11 | 4 | 0 | 0 | 6 | 1 | 5 | .239 | .326 | .286 |
| Leading Off Inn. | 48 | 10 | 3 | 0 | 0 | 0 | 1 | 4 | .208 | .271 | .224 |
| Runners On | 115 | 28 | 7 | 0 | 0 | 24 | 5 | 17 | .243 | .304 | .274 |
| Runners/Scor. Pos. | 66 | 18 | 5 | 0 | 0 | 24 | 4 | 10 | .273 | .348 | .311 |
| Runners On/2 Out | 45 | 10 | 1 | 0 | 0 | 8 | 3 | 6 | .222 | .244 | .271 |
| Scor. Pos./2 Out | 25 | 6 | 1 | 0 | 0 | 8 | 2 | 3 | .240 | .280 | .296 |
| Late Inning Pressure | 37 | 8 | 0 | 0 | 1 | 2 | 1 | 3 | .216 | .297 | .237 |
| Leading Off | 6 | 1 | 0 | 0 | 0 | 0 | 0 | 1 | .167 | .167 | .167 |
| Runners On | 19 | 4 | 0 | 0 | 0 | 1 | 0 | 1 | .211 | .211 | .211 |
| Runners/Scor. Pos. | 6 | 1 | 0 | 0 | 0 | 1 | 0 | 1 | .167 | .167 | .167 |

| RUNS BATTED IN | From 1B | From 2B | From 3B | Scoring Position |
|---|---|---|---|---|
| Totals | 1/88 | 12/51 | 11/29 | 23/80 |
| Percentage | 1% | 24% | 38% | 29% |
| Driving In Runners from 3B with Less than Two Out: | | | 9/17 | 53% |

Loves to face: Craig Lefferts (.571, 4-for-7)
Hates to face: Don Carman (.111, 1-for-9)
June batting average was lowest in majors (minimum: two PA per game). Lowest average in April belonged to Gary Carter. . . . Batted .295 vs. fly-ball pitchers, .203 vs. ground-ballers. . . . Has led off 90 innings in his career, getting only 16 hits and only one walk. . . . Batted .273 with runners in scoring position, but hit team-high .355 in those situations when game was tied or Mets were trailing by one or two runs. . . . Caught 38 percent of Mets' innings last year; Sasser had 29 percent, Carter 25 percent, Phil Lombardi, 8 percent. Team went 35–26 with Lyons starting, 23–25 with Sasser, 22–20 with Carter, 7–4 with Lombardi. . . . Born the same day and year as Steve Lyons of White Sox. They're not brothers.

## Dave Magadan

Bats Left

| New York Mets | AB | H | 2B | 3B | HR | RBI | BB | SO | BA | SA | OBA |
|---|---|---|---|---|---|---|---|---|---|---|---|
| Season | 374 | 107 | 22 | 3 | 4 | 42 | 49 | 37 | .286 | .393 | .367 |
| vs. Left-Handers | 92 | 24 | 4 | 0 | 0 | 8 | 8 | 10 | .261 | .304 | .327 |
| vs. Right-Handers | 282 | 83 | 18 | 3 | 4 | 34 | 41 | 27 | .294 | .422 | .379 |
| Home | 183 | 56 | 7 | 2 | 3 | 23 | 23 | 18 | .306 | .415 | .378 |
| Road | 191 | 51 | 15 | 1 | 1 | 19 | 26 | 19 | .267 | .372 | .356 |
| Grass | 262 | 80 | 14 | 2 | 3 | 24 | 30 | 26 | .305 | .408 | .375 |
| Artificial Turf | 112 | 27 | 8 | 1 | 1 | 18 | 19 | 11 | .241 | .357 | .348 |
| April | 29 | 7 | 1 | 1 | 0 | 2 | 5 | 4 | .241 | .345 | .343 |
| May | 58 | 19 | 1 | 1 | 1 | 5 | 2 | 9 | .328 | .431 | .350 |
| June | 94 | 30 | 7 | 0 | 3 | 15 | 14 | 6 | .319 | .489 | .407 |
| July | 80 | 20 | 5 | 0 | 0 | 4 | 10 | 4 | .250 | .313 | .330 |
| August | 58 | 15 | 5 | 0 | 0 | 10 | 9 | 6 | .259 | .345 | .362 |
| Sept./Oct. | 55 | 16 | 3 | 1 | 0 | 6 | 9 | 8 | .291 | .382 | .385 |
| Leading Off Inn. | 82 | 22 | 3 | 0 | 2 | 2 | 9 | 7 | .268 | .378 | .348 |
| Runners On | 163 | 50 | 13 | 0 | 1 | 39 | 24 | 15 | .307 | .405 | .387 |
| Runners/Scor. Pos. | 94 | 28 | 6 | 0 | 1 | 36 | 20 | 7 | .298 | .394 | .407 |
| Runners On/2 Out | 66 | 17 | 3 | 0 | 0 | 14 | 8 | 3 | .258 | .303 | .338 |
| Scor. Pos./2 Out | 40 | 12 | 2 | 0 | 0 | 13 | 7 | 1 | .300 | .350 | .404 |
| Late Inning Pressure | 65 | 15 | 2 | 0 | 1 | 9 | 5 | 9 | .231 | .308 | .296 |
| Leading Off | 26 | 4 | 1 | 0 | 0 | 0 | 1 | 4 | .154 | .192 | .214 |
| Runners On | 22 | 8 | 1 | 0 | 1 | 9 | 4 | 3 | .364 | .545 | .462 |
| Runners/Scor. Pos. | 11 | 6 | 1 | 0 | 1 | 9 | 4 | 1 | .545 | .909 | .667 |

| RUNS BATTED IN | From 1B | From 2B | From 3B | Scoring Position |
|---|---|---|---|---|
| Totals | 5/104 | 16/80 | 17/27 | 33/107 |
| Percentage | 5% | 20% | 63% | 31% |
| Driving In Runners from 3B with Less than Two Out: | | | 11/14 | 79% |

Loves to face: Paul Assenmacher (.857, 6-for-7)
Hates to face: Orel Hershiser (0-for-11)
Started 75 percent of games in which Mets faced a right-hander, but only 11 of 53 games vs. southpaws. . . . Among left-handed batters over the past 15 years with at least as many at-bats vs. southpaws as Magadan (229), only four big boys have higher batting averages than Mag's .301: Gwynn (.316), Boggs (.314), Mattingly (.313), and Carew (.310). . . . Has batted over .300 at home and below .300 on road in each of four seasons in majors. Career: .325 at home, .260 abroad. . . . First steal of career came in 331st game, Sept. 27, on back end of double steal. That ties him in steals with teammate Sid Fernandez, but he's still one shy of Willie Hernandez, two shy of Nolan Ryan, three back of Rick Sutcliffe.

## Candy Maldonado

Bats Right

| San Francisco Giants | AB | H | 2B | 3B | HR | RBI | BB | SO | BA | SA | OBA |
|---|---|---|---|---|---|---|---|---|---|---|---|
| Season | 345 | 75 | 23 | 0 | 9 | 41 | 37 | 69 | .217 | .362 | .296 |
| vs. Left-Handers | 147 | 31 | 9 | 0 | 2 | 9 | 20 | 24 | .211 | .313 | .310 |
| vs. Right-Handers | 198 | 44 | 14 | 0 | 7 | 32 | 17 | 45 | .222 | .399 | .286 |
| Home | 156 | 31 | 8 | 0 | 1 | 14 | 10 | 33 | .199 | .269 | .256 |
| Road | 189 | 44 | 15 | 0 | 8 | 27 | 27 | 36 | .233 | .439 | .329 |
| Grass | 251 | 54 | 16 | 0 | 4 | 27 | 22 | 55 | .215 | .327 | .283 |
| Artificial Turf | 94 | 21 | 7 | 0 | 5 | 14 | 15 | 14 | .223 | .457 | .330 |
| April | 79 | 18 | 6 | 0 | 0 | 9 | 12 | 12 | .228 | .304 | .323 |
| May | 62 | 8 | 1 | 0 | 2 | 5 | 5 | 9 | .129 | .242 | .206 |
| June | 62 | 17 | 5 | 0 | 3 | 11 | 9 | 12 | .274 | .500 | .375 |
| July | 69 | 20 | 8 | 0 | 2 | 9 | 2 | 10 | .290 | .493 | .319 |
| August | 50 | 9 | 2 | 0 | 2 | 4 | 5 | 15 | .180 | .340 | .250 |
| Sept./Oct. | 23 | 3 | 1 | 0 | 0 | 3 | 4 | 11 | .130 | .174 | .259 |
| Leading Off Inn. | 82 | 17 | 5 | 0 | 4 | 4 | 9 | 13 | .207 | .415 | .286 |
| Runners On | 157 | 37 | 14 | 0 | 2 | 34 | 17 | 29 | .236 | .363 | .313 |
| Runners/Scor. Pos. | 99 | 20 | 9 | 0 | 1 | 28 | 11 | 20 | .202 | .323 | .281 |
| Runners On/2 Out | 68 | 14 | 5 | 0 | 0 | 12 | 11 | 15 | .206 | .279 | .325 |
| Scor. Pos./2 Out | 51 | 10 | 4 | 0 | 0 | 12 | 8 | 12 | .196 | .275 | .317 |
| Late Inning Pressure | 55 | 14 | 5 | 0 | 1 | 4 | 6 | 12 | .255 | .400 | .328 |
| Leading Off | 13 | 2 | 0 | 0 | 1 | 1 | 2 | 0 | .154 | .385 | .267 |
| Runners On | 25 | 5 | 2 | 0 | 0 | 3 | 3 | 9 | .200 | .280 | .286 |
| Runners/Scor. Pos. | 17 | 4 | 1 | 0 | 0 | 3 | 2 | 5 | .235 | .294 | .316 |

| RUNS BATTED IN | From 1B | From 2B | From 3B | Scoring Position |
|---|---|---|---|---|
| Totals | 6/107 | 12/79 | 14/41 | 26/120 |
| Percentage | 6% | 15% | 34% | 22% |
| Driving In Runners from 3B with Less than Two Out: | | | 10/19 | 53% |

Loves to face: Bob McClure (.800, 4-for-5, 1 HR)
Hates to face: Tim Leary (0-for-17)
Batted .128 vs. left-handed pitchers with runners in scoring position, damning for a right-handed platoon player. . . . Some career averages: .235 with bases empty, .270 with runners on base, .353 with bases loaded. . . . Had .969 fielding percentage over past three years, 2d-lowest in N.L. (minimum: 300 games) since 1987, ahead of only Vince Coleman (.967). . . . Has hit for higher average on road than at home for six years in a row. Has had misfortune to play home games at Dodger Stadium and Candlestick, two of worst parks in majors for hitting. Result: .227 career average at home, .275 on road. Cleveland Stadium is very marginally a hitters' park, but to Candy it'll seem like Wrigley with the wind blowing out.

## Kirt Manwaring

Bats Right

| San Francisco Giants | AB | H | 2B | 3B | HR | RBI | BB | SO | BA | SA | OBA |
|---|---|---|---|---|---|---|---|---|---|---|---|
| Season | 200 | 42 | 4 | 2 | 0 | 18 | 11 | 28 | .210 | .250 | .264 |
| vs. Left-Handers | 132 | 27 | 2 | 1 | 0 | 8 | 9 | 15 | .205 | .235 | .271 |
| vs. Right-Handers | 68 | 15 | 2 | 1 | 0 | 10 | 2 | 13 | .221 | .279 | .250 |
| Home | 96 | 21 | 1 | 1 | 0 | 13 | 2 | 14 | .219 | .250 | .265 |
| Road | 104 | 21 | 3 | 1 | 0 | 5 | 9 | 14 | .202 | .250 | .263 |
| Grass | 160 | 37 | 3 | 1 | 0 | 15 | 5 | 25 | .231 | .263 | .272 |
| Artificial Turf | 40 | 5 | 1 | 1 | 0 | 3 | 6 | 3 | .125 | .200 | .234 |
| April | 37 | 8 | 1 | 1 | 0 | 2 | 2 | 5 | .216 | .297 | .293 |
| May | 30 | 8 | 1 | 0 | 0 | 3 | 1 | 7 | .267 | .300 | .290 |
| June | 48 | 11 | 1 | 0 | 0 | 5 | 4 | 4 | .229 | .250 | .288 |
| July | 34 | 6 | 0 | 1 | 0 | 5 | 2 | 4 | .176 | .235 | .222 |
| August | 42 | 7 | 1 | 0 | 0 | 3 | 2 | 6 | .167 | .190 | .234 |
| Sept./Oct. | 9 | 2 | 0 | 0 | 0 | 0 | 0 | 2 | .222 | .222 | .222 |
| Leading Off Inn. | 46 | 7 | 0 | 0 | 0 | 0 | 2 | 2 | .152 | .152 | .204 |
| Runners On | 71 | 19 | 1 | 1 | 0 | 18 | 5 | 8 | .268 | .310 | .338 |
| Runners/Scor. Pos. | 47 | 13 | 1 | 1 | 0 | 18 | 4 | 5 | .277 | .340 | .352 |
| Runners On/2 Out | 32 | 6 | 1 | 1 | 0 | 8 | 4 | 4 | .188 | .281 | .278 |
| Scor. Pos./2 Out | 19 | 5 | 1 | 1 | 0 | 8 | 3 | 1 | .263 | .421 | .364 |
| Late Inning Pressure | 22 | 2 | 0 | 0 | 0 | 0 | 3 | 2 | .091 | .091 | .200 |
| Leading Off | 6 | 1 | 0 | 0 | 0 | 0 | 0 | 0 | .167 | .167 | .167 |
| Runners On | 7 | 0 | 0 | 0 | 0 | 0 | 2 | 2 | .000 | .000 | .222 |
| Runners/Scor. Pos. | 4 | 0 | 0 | 0 | 0 | 0 | 1 | 1 | .000 | .000 | .200 |

| RUNS BATTED IN | From 1B | From 2B | From 3B | Scoring Position |
|---|---|---|---|---|
| Totals | 1/46 | 6/37 | 11/20 | 17/57 |
| Percentage | 2% | 16% | 55% | 30% |
| Driving In Runners from 3B with Less than Two Out: | | | 7/13 | 54% |

Loves to face: Rick Mahler (.625, 5-for-8, 1 HR)
Hates to face: Zane Smith (0-for-8)
Giants' staff had 3.19 ERA with Manwaring behind the plate, 3.44 with Terry Kennedy. . . . Started only two games after Sept. 1, none in postseason play. . . . Had the fewest extra-base hits among players who came to bat as many times as he did. . . . Eight of 18 RBI came in bases-loaded situations, when he had three hits in seven at-bats. . . . Career averages: .287 with runners on base, .184 with bases empty. . . . San Francisco's second pick in the 1986 amateur draft; Matt Williams was number one. . . . Only two Giants' catchers have ever started All-Star Game: Walker Cooper (1946–47–48) and Ed Bailey (1963). . . . Lives in Horseheads, New York; how do you suppose *The Godfather* went over in *that* town?

## Mike Marshall

Bats Right

| Los Angeles Dodgers | AB | H | 2B | 3B | HR | RBI | BB | SO | BA | SA | OBA |
|---|---|---|---|---|---|---|---|---|---|---|---|
| Season | 377 | 98 | 21 | 1 | 11 | 42 | 33 | 78 | .260 | .408 | .325 |
| vs. Left-Handers | 130 | 32 | 6 | 1 | 7 | 17 | 17 | 22 | .246 | .469 | .340 |
| vs. Right-Handers | 247 | 66 | 15 | 0 | 4 | 25 | 16 | 56 | .267 | .377 | .316 |
| Home | 177 | 52 | 13 | 1 | 6 | 22 | 14 | 32 | .294 | .480 | .352 |
| Road | 200 | 46 | 8 | 0 | 5 | 20 | 19 | 46 | .230 | .345 | .300 |
| Grass | 276 | 77 | 17 | 1 | 7 | 27 | 24 | 51 | .279 | .424 | .341 |
| Artificial Turf | 101 | 21 | 4 | 0 | 4 | 15 | 9 | 27 | .208 | .366 | .281 |
| April | 76 | 18 | 1 | 0 | 4 | 10 | 11 | 17 | .237 | .408 | .337 |
| May | 73 | 18 | 4 | 0 | 0 | 3 | 4 | 21 | .247 | .301 | .295 |
| June | 0 | 0 | 0 | 0 | 0 | 0 | 0 | 0 | — | — | — |
| July | 96 | 28 | 4 | 0 | 2 | 7 | 6 | 16 | .292 | .396 | .346 |
| August | 81 | 23 | 7 | 1 | 5 | 14 | 7 | 16 | .284 | .580 | .341 |
| Sept./Oct. | 51 | 11 | 5 | 0 | 0 | 8 | 5 | 8 | .216 | .314 | .281 |
| Leading Off Inn. | 80 | 25 | 5 | 0 | 3 | 3 | 10 | 12 | .313 | .488 | .409 |
| Runners On | 179 | 42 | 12 | 0 | 7 | 38 | 17 | 42 | .235 | .419 | .299 |
| Runners/Scor. Pos. | 93 | 24 | 8 | 0 | 3 | 28 | 8 | 21 | .258 | .441 | .305 |
| Runners On/2 Out | 82 | 18 | 4 | 0 | 1 | 8 | 8 | 21 | .220 | .305 | .289 |
| Scor. Pos./2 Out | 45 | 9 | 2 | 0 | 0 | 5 | 5 | 13 | .200 | .244 | .280 |
| Late Inning Pressure | 66 | 13 | 2 | 1 | 0 | 4 | 7 | 13 | .197 | .258 | .284 |
| Leading Off | 14 | 2 | 0 | 0 | 0 | 0 | 2 | 3 | .143 | .143 | .294 |
| Runners On | 22 | 5 | 2 | 0 | 0 | 4 | 5 | 4 | .227 | .318 | .370 |
| Runners/Scor. Pos. | 11 | 2 | 2 | 0 | 0 | 4 | 2 | 2 | .182 | .364 | .308 |

| RUNS BATTED IN | From 1B | From 2B | From 3B | Scoring Position |
|---|---|---|---|---|
| Totals | 7/138 | 12/76 | 12/31 | 24/107 |
| Percentage | 5% | 16% | 39% | 22% |
| Driving In Runners from 3B with Less than Two Out: | | | 10/18 | 56% |

Loves to face: Scott Garrelts (.452, 14-for-31, 4 HR)
Hates to face: Roger McDowell (.143, 2-for-14)
Moving from the stadium that had the 2d-largest negative impact on offense over past five years (Dodger Stadium) to the one with the largest negative impact (Shea). . . . Highest batting average in seven seasons in majors: .294 in 1987; lowest batting average in five seasons in minors: .321 in 1980 at San Antonio. . . . Batted .333 in the first inning last season, .251 thereafter. . . . When he hit ball, batting average was well-balanced: .333 on fair balls to left side, .324 straight away, .323 to the opposite field. . . . Since 1983, has had season totals of 103, 104, and 105 games in years in which he played outfield exclusively; in years in which he saw some duty at first base, he played in 140, 134, 135, and 144 games.

## Carmelo Martinez

Bats Right

| San Diego Padres | AB | H | 2B | 3B | HR | RBI | BB | SO | BA | SA | OBA |
|---|---|---|---|---|---|---|---|---|---|---|---|
| Season | 267 | 59 | 12 | 2 | 6 | 40 | 32 | 54 | .221 | .348 | .302 |
| vs. Left-Handers | 118 | 32 | 6 | 1 | 2 | 23 | 14 | 18 | .271 | .390 | .348 |
| vs. Right-Handers | 149 | 27 | 6 | 1 | 4 | 17 | 18 | 36 | .181 | .315 | .266 |
| Home | 121 | 20 | 4 | 0 | 2 | 13 | 15 | 28 | .165 | .248 | .257 |
| Road | 146 | 39 | 8 | 2 | 4 | 27 | 17 | 26 | .267 | .432 | .339 |
| Grass | 198 | 45 | 8 | 1 | 4 | 23 | 21 | 40 | .227 | .338 | .299 |
| Artificial Turf | 69 | 14 | 4 | 1 | 2 | 17 | 11 | 14 | .203 | .377 | .313 |
| April | 81 | 14 | 4 | 0 | 3 | 10 | 8 | 15 | .173 | .333 | .244 |
| May | 51 | 13 | 5 | 1 | 0 | 9 | 10 | 11 | .255 | .392 | .377 |
| June | 41 | 11 | 0 | 0 | 0 | 5 | 4 | 9 | .268 | .268 | .333 |
| July | 21 | 2 | 0 | 0 | 1 | 4 | 0 | 7 | .095 | .238 | .091 |
| August | 56 | 16 | 3 | 1 | 2 | 8 | 7 | 9 | .286 | .482 | .365 |
| Sept./Oct. | 17 | 3 | 0 | 0 | 0 | 4 | 3 | 3 | .176 | .176 | .300 |
| Leading Off Inn. | 58 | 14 | 3 | 0 | 0 | 0 | 9 | 10 | .241 | .293 | .343 |
| Runners On | 145 | 26 | 7 | 2 | 4 | 38 | 18 | 29 | .179 | .338 | .267 |
| Runners/Scor. Pos. | 91 | 17 | 4 | 2 | 3 | 36 | 16 | 24 | .187 | .374 | .303 |
| Runners On/2 Out | 55 | 9 | 1 | 1 | 0 | 11 | 11 | 7 | .164 | .218 | .303 |
| Scor. Pos./2 Out | 33 | 7 | 1 | 1 | 0 | 11 | 9 | 7 | .212 | .303 | .381 |
| Late Inning Pressure | 49 | 7 | 2 | 1 | 0 | 7 | 6 | 13 | .143 | .224 | .236 |
| Leading Off | 8 | 2 | 0 | 0 | 0 | 0 | 0 | 2 | .250 | .250 | .250 |
| Runners On | 30 | 4 | 2 | 1 | 0 | 7 | 6 | 7 | .133 | .267 | .278 |
| Runners/Scor. Pos. | 19 | 3 | 2 | 1 | 0 | 7 | 5 | 6 | .158 | .368 | .333 |

| RUNS BATTED IN | From 1B | From 2B | From 3B | Scoring Position |
|---|---|---|---|---|
| Totals | 7/112 | 11/72 | 16/45 | 27/117 |
| Percentage | 6% | 15% | 36% | 23% |
| Driving In Runners from 3B with Less than Two Out: | | | 10/29 | 34% |

**Loves to face:** Atlee Hammaker (.444, 8-for-18, 4 HR)
**Hates to face:** Danny Jackson (.190, 4-for-21)

Has set new career-low batting average in each of last two years.... Batted 91 points lower with runners on base than with bases empty, largest difference among N.L. players last season (minimum: 100 AB each way).... Hitless in first 10 and in last 7 pinch-hit at-bats, but had seven pinch hits in 15 at-bats in between. One of three players to "hit for the cycle" as a pinch hitter last year.... Had one hit (a triple) in 15 at-bats with bases full last season.... Had only three starts after Sept. 1.... Found new home in Philadelphia after season in which he was one of two N.L. players to bat 100+ points lower at home than on road (minimum: 100 AB each way). The other shares the same surname. Read on....

## Dave Martinez

Bats Left

| Montreal Expos | AB | H | 2B | 3B | HR | RBI | BB | SO | BA | SA | OBA |
|---|---|---|---|---|---|---|---|---|---|---|---|
| Season | 361 | 99 | 16 | 7 | 3 | 27 | 27 | 57 | .274 | .382 | .324 |
| vs. Left-Handers | 30 | 4 | 0 | 0 | 0 | 1 | 1 | 10 | .133 | .133 | .161 |
| vs. Right-Handers | 331 | 95 | 16 | 7 | 3 | 26 | 26 | 47 | .287 | .405 | .338 |
| Home | 178 | 37 | 3 | 2 | 1 | 7 | 12 | 27 | .208 | .264 | .258 |
| Road | 183 | 62 | 13 | 5 | 2 | 20 | 15 | 30 | .339 | .497 | .387 |
| Grass | 108 | 35 | 5 | 4 | 2 | 14 | 9 | 18 | .324 | .500 | .373 |
| Artificial Turf | 253 | 64 | 11 | 3 | 1 | 13 | 18 | 39 | .253 | .332 | .303 |
| April | 45 | 9 | 2 | 0 | 0 | 2 | 3 | 1 | .200 | .244 | .250 |
| May | 68 | 19 | 3 | 3 | 0 | 6 | 8 | 17 | .279 | .412 | .355 |
| June | 52 | 17 | 1 | 1 | 3 | 7 | 2 | 13 | .327 | .558 | .352 |
| July | 66 | 19 | 4 | 1 | 0 | 2 | 3 | 12 | .288 | .379 | .319 |
| August | 94 | 27 | 5 | 2 | 0 | 7 | 9 | 11 | .287 | .383 | .346 |
| Sept./Oct. | 36 | 8 | 1 | 0 | 0 | 3 | 2 | 3 | .222 | .250 | .263 |
| Leading Off Inn. | 136 | 33 | 5 | 1 | 2 | 2 | 9 | 22 | .243 | .338 | .290 |
| Runners On | 123 | 34 | 7 | 3 | 0 | 24 | 11 | 24 | .276 | .382 | .333 |
| Runners/Scor. Pos. | 68 | 21 | 4 | 2 | 0 | 23 | 5 | 12 | .309 | .426 | .351 |
| Runners On/2 Out | 58 | 18 | 3 | 1 | 0 | 16 | 5 | 12 | .310 | .397 | .365 |
| Scor. Pos./2 Out | 40 | 16 | 3 | 1 | 0 | 16 | 3 | 6 | .400 | .525 | .442 |
| Late Inning Pressure | 59 | 12 | 2 | 1 | 0 | 3 | 2 | 15 | .203 | .271 | .230 |
| Leading Off | 22 | 7 | 1 | 0 | 0 | 0 | 0 | 5 | .318 | .364 | .318 |
| Runners On | 26 | 2 | 0 | 0 | 0 | 3 | 1 | 7 | .077 | .077 | .111 |
| Runners/Scor. Pos. | 15 | 1 | 0 | 0 | 0 | 3 | 1 | 3 | .067 | .067 | .125 |

| RUNS BATTED IN | From 1B | From 2B | From 3B | Scoring Position |
|---|---|---|---|---|
| Totals | 2/78 | 14/62 | 8/18 | 22/80 |
| Percentage | 3% | 23% | 44% | 28% |
| Driving In Runners from 3B with Less than Two Out: | | | 5/6 | 83% |

**Loves to face:** Mike Bielecki (.429, 6-for-14, 2 HR)
**Hates to face:** Doug Drabek (.108, 4-for-37, 9 SO)

Batted 131 points higher on the road than he did in home games, largest difference for player in majors last season (minimum: 100 AB each way).... Averaged 2.15 putouts per nine innings last season, lowest in majors among 30 center fielders who played 500+ innings.... Started 91 games, all vs. right-handed pitchers. Since joining Expos, has started only one of 68 games in which club faced a lefty starter. Career average vs. southpaws: .193.... Grounded into only one double play in 52 DP situations, best rate on Expos last year.... Started year going 0-for-25 in Late-Inning Pressure Situations (2d-longest such streak in majors last season), finished year with hits in his last three at-bats in LIPS.

## Lloyd McClendon

Bats Right

| Chicago Cubs | AB | H | 2B | 3B | HR | RBI | BB | SO | BA | SA | OBA |
|---|---|---|---|---|---|---|---|---|---|---|---|
| Season | 259 | 74 | 12 | 1 | 12 | 40 | 37 | 31 | .286 | .479 | .368 |
| vs. Left-Handers | 121 | 41 | 8 | 0 | 6 | 22 | 22 | 11 | .339 | .554 | .432 |
| vs. Right-Handers | 138 | 33 | 4 | 1 | 6 | 18 | 15 | 20 | .239 | .413 | .310 |
| Home | 133 | 40 | 6 | 0 | 9 | 25 | 12 | 14 | .301 | .549 | .358 |
| Road | 126 | 34 | 6 | 1 | 3 | 15 | 25 | 17 | .270 | .405 | .378 |
| Grass | 177 | 49 | 9 | 1 | 10 | 31 | 19 | 18 | .277 | .508 | .342 |
| Artificial Turf | 82 | 25 | 3 | 0 | 2 | 9 | 18 | 13 | .305 | .415 | .422 |
| April | 0 | 0 | 0 | 0 | 0 | 0 | 0 | 0 | — | — | — |
| May | 25 | 7 | 0 | 0 | 2 | 7 | 5 | 3 | .280 | .520 | .387 |
| June | 84 | 26 | 2 | 0 | 4 | 13 | 10 | 12 | .310 | .476 | .375 |
| July | 49 | 13 | 3 | 1 | 3 | 8 | 10 | 6 | .265 | .551 | .377 |
| August | 50 | 15 | 5 | 0 | 2 | 7 | 6 | 5 | .300 | .520 | .386 |
| Sept./Oct. | 51 | 13 | 2 | 0 | 1 | 5 | 6 | 5 | .255 | .353 | .322 |
| Leading Off Inn. | 65 | 21 | 3 | 0 | 5 | 5 | 10 | 11 | .323 | .600 | .413 |
| Runners On | 104 | 27 | 5 | 0 | 3 | 31 | 16 | 10 | .260 | .394 | .344 |
| Runners/Scor. Pos. | 61 | 17 | 4 | 0 | 1 | 27 | 11 | 6 | .279 | .393 | .354 |
| Runners On/2 Out | 46 | 6 | 0 | 0 | 0 | 4 | 6 | 4 | .130 | .130 | .231 |
| Scor. Pos./2 Out | 32 | 5 | 0 | 0 | 0 | 4 | 4 | 3 | .156 | .156 | .250 |
| Late Inning Pressure | 41 | 8 | 0 | 0 | 0 | 3 | 6 | 6 | .195 | .195 | .286 |
| Leading Off | 10 | 2 | 0 | 0 | 0 | 0 | 3 | 1 | .200 | .200 | .385 |
| Runners On | 13 | 2 | 0 | 0 | 0 | 3 | 2 | 2 | .154 | .154 | .235 |
| Runners/Scor. Pos. | 9 | 2 | 0 | 0 | 0 | 3 | 2 | 2 | .222 | .222 | .308 |

| RUNS BATTED IN | From 1B | From 2B | From 3B | Scoring Position |
|---|---|---|---|---|
| Totals | 3/73 | 7/39 | 18/38 | 25/77 |
| Percentage | 4% | 18% | 47% | 32% |
| Driving In Runners from 3B with Less than Two Out: | | | 15/22 | 68% |

**Loves to face:** Joe Magrane (.583, 7-for-12)
**Hates to face:** Zane Smith (.100, 1-for-10)

Started 45 of 53 games in which Cubs faced a left-handed starter, but started only 25 of 109 games vs. right-handers.... Breakdown of batting average with runners on base: .387 with none out, .333 with one out, .130 with two outs.... Batted .321 in day games, .244 at night. Career marks: .293 and .220.... Hit six home runs in his first 60 at-bats, six more in next 199 at-bats.... Batted .313 (5-for-16) as a pinch hitter.... Not your classic game-breaking threat: Mac owns a .177 career batting average in Late-Inning Pressure Situations, with no home runs in 96 at-bats.... Had no home runs in 99 at-bats at Riverfront Stadium while wearing Reds' uniform (1987–88), but homered there in second game as visitor.

## Oddibe McDowell

Bats Left

| Atlanta Braves | AB | H | 2B | 3B | HR | RBI | BB | SO | BA | SA | OBA |
|---|---|---|---|---|---|---|---|---|---|---|---|
| Season | 280 | 85 | 18 | 4 | 7 | 24 | 27 | 37 | .304 | .471 | .365 |
| vs. Left-Handers | 100 | 23 | 3 | 1 | 0 | 7 | 7 | 17 | .230 | .280 | .280 |
| vs. Right-Handers | 180 | 62 | 15 | 3 | 7 | 17 | 20 | 20 | .344 | .578 | .410 |
| Home | 136 | 43 | 10 | 1 | 2 | 12 | 14 | 17 | .316 | .449 | .380 |
| Road | 144 | 42 | 8 | 3 | 5 | 12 | 13 | 20 | .292 | .493 | .350 |
| Grass | 211 | 69 | 16 | 3 | 4 | 17 | 19 | 27 | .327 | .488 | .383 |
| Artificial Turf | 69 | 16 | 2 | 1 | 3 | 7 | 8 | 10 | .232 | .420 | .312 |
| April | 0 | 0 | 0 | 0 | 0 | 0 | 0 | 0 | — | — | — |
| May | 0 | 0 | 0 | 0 | 0 | 0 | 0 | 0 | — | — | — |
| June | 0 | 0 | 0 | 0 | 0 | 0 | 0 | 0 | — | — | — |
| July | 94 | 28 | 4 | 1 | 0 | 6 | 10 | 19 | .298 | .362 | .365 |
| August | 121 | 32 | 5 | 1 | 5 | 13 | 9 | 9 | .264 | .446 | .315 |
| Sept./Oct. | 65 | 25 | 9 | 2 | 2 | 5 | 8 | 9 | .385 | .677 | .452 |
| Leading Off Inn. | 111 | 37 | 6 | 1 | 3 | 3 | 8 | 12 | .333 | .486 | .378 |
| Runners On | 88 | 29 | 10 | 3 | 2 | 19 | 11 | 11 | .330 | .580 | .404 |
| Runners/Scor. Pos. | 46 | 14 | 2 | 3 | 1 | 15 | 11 | 6 | .304 | .543 | .439 |
| Runners On/2 Out | 42 | 10 | 3 | 1 | 1 | 8 | 9 | 6 | .238 | .429 | .373 |
| Scor. Pos./2 Out | 23 | 4 | 0 | 1 | 0 | 5 | 9 | 2 | .174 | .261 | .406 |
| Late Inning Pressure | 42 | 10 | 2 | 1 | 1 | 3 | 6 | 9 | .238 | .405 | .333 |
| Leading Off | 9 | 3 | 1 | 0 | 1 | 1 | 0 | 1 | .333 | .778 | .333 |
| Runners On | 13 | 4 | 1 | 1 | 0 | 2 | 2 | 2 | .308 | .538 | .400 |
| Runners/Scor. Pos. | 5 | 3 | 0 | 1 | 0 | 2 | 2 | 1 | .600 | 1.000 | .714 |

| RUNS BATTED IN | From 1B | From 2B | From 3B | Scoring Position |
|---|---|---|---|---|
| Totals | 4/64 | 9/37 | 4/15 | 13/52 |
| Percentage | 6% | 24% | 27% | 25% |
| Driving In Runners from 3B with Less than Two Out: | | | 2/6 | 33% |

**Loves to face:** Mike Morgan (.444, 8-for-18, 1 HR)
**Hates to face:** Walt Terrell (.074, 2-for-27)

A .330 batting average with runners on base put him among top 10 in N.L. in that category; had hit .194 in those situations with Indians.... Started 67 games for Atlanta, all in leadoff spot; Braves' leadoff hitters had composite .413 slugging average, best by any team in majors.... Highest average vs. left-handers in five years in majors: .244 in 1985, his rookie year.... Had at least one hit against 24 different teams last season, the only player to do that.... Pinch-hit a home run in each league last season; Lee Mazzilli was the only other player to do that in '89.... Last man to play for Indians and Braves in same year? Phil Niekro in 1987. Oddibe must have spent off-season rooting for Redskins and Blackhawks.

## Willie McGee

Bats Left and Right

| St. Louis Cardinals | AB | H | 2B | 3B | HR | RBI | BB | SO | BA | SA | OBA |
|---|---|---|---|---|---|---|---|---|---|---|---|
| Season | 199 | 47 | 10 | 2 | 3 | 17 | 10 | 34 | .236 | .352 | .275 |
| vs. Left-Handers | 77 | 12 | 1 | 1 | 2 | 10 | 4 | 15 | .156 | .273 | .195 |
| vs. Right-Handers | 122 | 35 | 9 | 1 | 1 | 7 | 6 | 19 | .287 | .402 | .326 |
| Home | 106 | 27 | 5 | 1 | 1 | 6 | 5 | 17 | .255 | .349 | .292 |
| Road | 93 | 20 | 5 | 1 | 2 | 11 | 5 | 17 | .215 | .355 | .255 |
| Grass | 53 | 14 | 3 | 1 | 1 | 7 | 3 | 10 | .264 | .415 | .304 |
| Artificial Turf | 146 | 33 | 7 | 1 | 2 | 10 | 7 | 24 | .226 | .329 | .265 |
| April | 12 | 4 | 0 | 0 | 1 | 3 | 1 | 1 | .333 | .583 | .385 |
| May | 79 | 17 | 4 | 1 | 1 | 7 | 6 | 13 | .215 | .329 | .271 |
| June | 9 | 1 | 1 | 0 | 0 | 0 | 0 | 1 | .111 | .222 | .111 |
| July | 29 | 7 | 2 | 0 | 0 | 4 | 3 | 5 | .241 | .310 | .303 |
| August | 36 | 9 | 2 | 0 | 1 | 2 | 0 | 9 | .250 | .389 | .270 |
| Sept./Oct. | 34 | 9 | 1 | 1 | 0 | 1 | 0 | 5 | .265 | .353 | .265 |
| Leading Off Inn. | 69 | 17 | 3 | 1 | 1 | 1 | 4 | 8 | .246 | .362 | .288 |
| Runners On | 65 | 17 | 3 | 0 | 1 | 15 | 3 | 12 | .262 | .354 | .290 |
| Runners/Scor. Pos. | 41 | 11 | 3 | 0 | 0 | 13 | 2 | 7 | .268 | .341 | .295 |
| Runners On/2 Out | 27 | 6 | 1 | 0 | 1 | 6 | 1 | 5 | .222 | .370 | .250 |
| Scor. Pos./2 Out | 17 | 3 | 1 | 0 | 0 | 4 | 1 | 3 | .176 | .235 | .222 |
| Late Inning Pressure | 32 | 9 | 0 | 0 | 0 | 2 | 3 | 7 | .281 | .281 | .343 |
| Leading Off | 11 | 4 | 0 | 0 | 0 | 0 | 1 | 1 | .364 | .364 | .417 |
| Runners On | 13 | 4 | 0 | 0 | 0 | 2 | 1 | 2 | .308 | .308 | .357 |
| Runners/Scor. Pos. | 9 | 3 | 0 | 0 | 0 | 2 | 0 | 1 | .333 | .333 | .333 |

| RUNS BATTED IN | From 1B | From 2B | From 3B | Scoring Position |
|---|---|---|---|---|
| Totals | 2/40 | 6/34 | 6/13 | 12/47 |
| Percentage | 5% | 18% | 46% | 26% |
| Driving In Runners from 3B with Less than Two Out: | | | 4/8 | 50% |

Loves to face: David Cone (.500, 11-for-22)
Hates to face: Walt Terrell (.105, 2-for-19)
Despite career-low overall average (previous low was .256 in 1986), his average with runners in scoring position was his highest since his 1985 MVP season. . . . Batted .353 overall in that MVP season, but hasn't hit .300 in any other season. Norm Cash is only other player in major league history to hit .350 or higher in a 450-at-bat season and never reach .300 in any other season; Cash hit .361 for '61 Tigers. . . . Difference of 131 points between right- and left-handed batting is surprising considering that in each of the previous two years, those averages were not separated by more than five points. . . . Had more home runs than triples for the first time in his career. Career totals: 71 triples, 49 homers.

## Kevin Mitchell

Bats Right

| San Francisco Giants | AB | H | 2B | 3B | HR | RBI | BB | SO | BA | SA | OBA |
|---|---|---|---|---|---|---|---|---|---|---|---|
| Season | 543 | 158 | 34 | 6 | 47 | 125 | 87 | 115 | .291 | .635 | .388 |
| vs. Left-Handers | 171 | 52 | 11 | 2 | 19 | 40 | 36 | 26 | .304 | .725 | .426 |
| vs. Right-Handers | 372 | 106 | 23 | 4 | 28 | 85 | 51 | 89 | .285 | .594 | .369 |
| Home | 255 | 76 | 17 | 5 | 22 | 66 | 47 | 47 | .298 | .663 | .403 |
| Road | 288 | 82 | 17 | 1 | 25 | 59 | 40 | 68 | .285 | .611 | .373 |
| Grass | 401 | 119 | 23 | 5 | 35 | 99 | 61 | 85 | .297 | .641 | .386 |
| Artificial Turf | 142 | 39 | 11 | 1 | 12 | 26 | 26 | 30 | .275 | .620 | .392 |
| April | 96 | 28 | 11 | 2 | 6 | 25 | 10 | 26 | .292 | .635 | .355 |
| May | 98 | 29 | 7 | 1 | 9 | 23 | 12 | 15 | .296 | .663 | .369 |
| June | 89 | 25 | 2 | 1 | 10 | 24 | 18 | 13 | .281 | .663 | .394 |
| July | 71 | 22 | 5 | 0 | 8 | 17 | 15 | 15 | .310 | .718 | .438 |
| August | 95 | 26 | 5 | 2 | 7 | 21 | 16 | 29 | .274 | .589 | .381 |
| Sept./Oct. | 94 | 28 | 4 | 0 | 7 | 15 | 16 | 17 | .298 | .564 | .396 |
| Leading Off Inn. | 119 | 37 | 8 | 3 | 12 | 12 | 6 | 24 | .311 | .731 | .349 |
| Runners On | 288 | 80 | 17 | 1 | 22 | 100 | 64 | 66 | .278 | .573 | .404 |
| Runners/Scor. Pos. | 141 | 40 | 8 | 1 | 12 | 74 | 49 | 30 | .284 | .610 | .457 |
| Runners On/2 Out | 121 | 34 | 7 | 1 | 7 | 32 | 36 | 30 | .281 | .529 | .449 |
| Scor. Pos./2 Out | 51 | 13 | 1 | 1 | 3 | 21 | 29 | 13 | .255 | .490 | .531 |
| Late Inning Pressure | 73 | 20 | 5 | 0 | 4 | 13 | 14 | 18 | .274 | .507 | .385 |
| Leading Off | 20 | 4 | 1 | 0 | 2 | 2 | 0 | 4 | .200 | .550 | .200 |
| Runners On | 28 | 8 | 1 | 0 | 1 | 10 | 9 | 8 | .286 | .429 | .439 |
| Runners/Scor. Pos. | 7 | 3 | 0 | 0 | 0 | 7 | 8 | 1 | .429 | .429 | .632 |

| RUNS BATTED IN | From 1B | From 2B | From 3B | Scoring Position |
|---|---|---|---|---|
| Totals | 25/221 | 26/105 | 27/64 | 53/169 |
| Percentage | 11% | 25% | 42% | 31% |
| Driving In Runners from 3B with Less than Two Out: | | | 20/42 | 48% |

Loves to face: Rick Mahler (.429, 12-for-28, 3 HR)
Hates to face: Pete Smith (.133, 2-for-15)
First N.L. slugging average leader out of Candlestick since McCovey, three years in a row (1968–70). Last major leaguer with more extra-base hits in a season: Willie Stargell (90) in 1973. . . . Batted .362 (nine HR in 69 at-bats) with Giants down by a run. . . . With runners in scoring position, he hit .366 with the score tied and .438 with Giants trailing by a run. . . . Hit eight home runs in 53 at-bats vs. N.L.'s top 10 ERA pitchers. . . . Bounced into only six double plays in 141 DP situations to tie for lowest rate on team. . . . Led majors in all five major power categories (home runs, RBI, slugging average, total bases, extra-base hits). Became 8th man to do that in one season; by contrast, 12 men have walked on the moon.

## Kevin McReynolds

Bats Right

| New York Mets | AB | H | 2B | 3B | HR | RBI | BB | SO | BA | SA | OBA |
|---|---|---|---|---|---|---|---|---|---|---|---|
| Season | 545 | 148 | 25 | 3 | 22 | 85 | 46 | 74 | .272 | .450 | .326 |
| vs. Left-Handers | 189 | 56 | 6 | 2 | 10 | 32 | 25 | 15 | .296 | .508 | .377 |
| vs. Right-Handers | 356 | 92 | 19 | 1 | 12 | 53 | 21 | 59 | .258 | .419 | .297 |
| Home | 274 | 73 | 11 | 1 | 12 | 40 | 27 | 33 | .266 | .445 | .330 |
| Road | 271 | 75 | 14 | 2 | 10 | 45 | 19 | 41 | .277 | .454 | .321 |
| Grass | 389 | 103 | 18 | 1 | 18 | 55 | 32 | 51 | .265 | .455 | .319 |
| Artificial Turf | 156 | 45 | 7 | 2 | 4 | 30 | 14 | 23 | .288 | .436 | .343 |
| April | 77 | 23 | 3 | 0 | 3 | 11 | 10 | 12 | .299 | .455 | .375 |
| May | 95 | 25 | 4 | 0 | 2 | 7 | 7 | 12 | .263 | .368 | .311 |
| June | 82 | 24 | 4 | 0 | 2 | 15 | 10 | 12 | .293 | .415 | .366 |
| July | 102 | 26 | 8 | 0 | 2 | 14 | 6 | 16 | .255 | .392 | .291 |
| August | 99 | 28 | 3 | 2 | 9 | 24 | 7 | 10 | .283 | .626 | .327 |
| Sept./Oct. | 90 | 22 | 3 | 1 | 4 | 14 | 6 | 12 | .244 | .433 | .296 |
| Leading Off Inn. | 142 | 40 | 8 | 0 | 7 | 7 | 9 | 20 | .282 | .486 | .325 |
| Runners On | 217 | 54 | 13 | 1 | 7 | 70 | 29 | 29 | .249 | .415 | .331 |
| Runners/Scor. Pos. | 139 | 38 | 7 | 1 | 5 | 62 | 26 | 19 | .273 | .446 | .376 |
| Runners On/2 Out | 98 | 20 | 4 | 0 | 2 | 25 | 15 | 12 | .204 | .306 | .310 |
| Scor. Pos./2 Out | 68 | 16 | 2 | 0 | 2 | 23 | 12 | 6 | .235 | .353 | .350 |
| Late Inning Pressure | 94 | 28 | 3 | 0 | 5 | 9 | 5 | 13 | .298 | .489 | .333 |
| Leading Off | 29 | 11 | 1 | 0 | 2 | 2 | 0 | 2 | .379 | .621 | .379 |
| Runners On | 33 | 7 | 0 | 0 | 1 | 5 | 3 | 4 | .212 | .303 | .278 |
| Runners/Scor. Pos. | 15 | 4 | 0 | 0 | 0 | 3 | 3 | 3 | .267 | .267 | .389 |

| RUNS BATTED IN | From 1B | From 2B | From 3B | Scoring Position |
|---|---|---|---|---|
| Totals | 13/150 | 26/112 | 24/65 | 50/177 |
| Percentage | 9% | 23% | 37% | 28% |
| Driving In Runners from 3B with Less than Two Out: | | | 18/36 | 50% |

Loves to face: Jeff Parrett (.533, 8-for-15, 3 HR)
Hates to face: Danny Jackson (.067, 1-for-15)
Has 20+ home runs and 85+ RBI in each of last four years; Joe Carter, Glenn Davis, and Dwight Evans are only other players with that notation on their resumes. . . . Committed 10 errors, tied for most among N.L. outfielders; had total of only eight errors in two prior seasons with Mets. . . . Led visiting players with .450 average at Astrodome last season. . . . Has hit for a higher average on artificial turf than on grass fields in each of last five years. . . . Batted .401 (21 HR) on fair balls to left side, .339 (one HR) straight away, .154 (no HR) to opposite field. . . . Batted .471 (8-for-17) with bases loaded with nary a walk or strikeout; he and Dwight Smith were only players in majors to hit for cycle with bases loaded.

## Dale Murphy

Bats Right

| Atlanta Braves | AB | H | 2B | 3B | HR | RBI | BB | SO | BA | SA | OBA |
|---|---|---|---|---|---|---|---|---|---|---|---|
| Season | 574 | 131 | 16 | 0 | 20 | 84 | 65 | 142 | .228 | .361 | .306 |
| vs. Left-Handers | 172 | 42 | 4 | 0 | 5 | 19 | 36 | 34 | .244 | .355 | .373 |
| vs. Right-Handers | 402 | 89 | 12 | 0 | 15 | 65 | 29 | 108 | .221 | .363 | .274 |
| Home | 276 | 71 | 7 | 0 | 9 | 47 | 31 | 62 | .257 | .380 | .329 |
| Road | 298 | 60 | 9 | 0 | 11 | 37 | 34 | 80 | .201 | .342 | .285 |
| Grass | 412 | 97 | 10 | 0 | 17 | 71 | 50 | 99 | .235 | .383 | .316 |
| Artificial Turf | 162 | 34 | 6 | 0 | 3 | 13 | 15 | 43 | .210 | .302 | .281 |
| April | 98 | 20 | 3 | 0 | 4 | 17 | 7 | 33 | .204 | .357 | .257 |
| May | 99 | 28 | 6 | 0 | 1 | 8 | 11 | 21 | .283 | .374 | .351 |
| June | 104 | 27 | 4 | 0 | 1 | 12 | 6 | 24 | .260 | .327 | .304 |
| July | 94 | 18 | 0 | 0 | 5 | 18 | 15 | 18 | .191 | .351 | .297 |
| August | 98 | 16 | 0 | 0 | 7 | 17 | 14 | 27 | .163 | .378 | .270 |
| Sept./Oct. | 81 | 22 | 3 | 0 | 2 | 12 | 12 | 19 | .272 | .383 | .366 |
| Leading Off Inn. | 147 | 27 | 5 | 0 | 2 | 2 | 9 | 38 | .184 | .259 | .231 |
| Runners On | 273 | 68 | 8 | 0 | 14 | 78 | 40 | 67 | .249 | .432 | .341 |
| Runners/Scor. Pos. | 152 | 43 | 4 | 0 | 9 | 67 | 32 | 45 | .283 | .487 | .395 |
| Runners On/2 Out | 129 | 32 | 5 | 0 | 7 | 33 | 23 | 30 | .248 | .450 | .366 |
| Scor. Pos./2 Out | 79 | 21 | 3 | 0 | 6 | 30 | 19 | 21 | .266 | .532 | .408 |
| Late Inning Pressure | 94 | 27 | 3 | 0 | 3 | 18 | 11 | 21 | .287 | .415 | .355 |
| Leading Off | 25 | 6 | 1 | 0 | 0 | 0 | 1 | 4 | .240 | .280 | .269 |
| Runners On | 33 | 13 | 1 | 0 | 2 | 17 | 6 | 8 | .394 | .606 | .463 |
| Runners/Scor. Pos. | 20 | 9 | 1 | 0 | 2 | 17 | 6 | 7 | .450 | .800 | .536 |

| RUNS BATTED IN | From 1B | From 2B | From 3B | Scoring Position |
|---|---|---|---|---|
| Totals | 14/202 | 19/121 | 31/63 | 50/184 |
| Percentage | 7% | 16% | 49% | 27% |
| Driving In Runners from 3B with Less than Two Out: | | | 19/33 | 58% |

Loves to face: Ron Robinson (.375, 9-for-24, 5 HR)
Hates to face: Bill Landrum (0-for-9, 5 SO)
Only batting-average qualifier (502 plate appearances) with sub-.230 average in both 1988 and 1989. . . . Homerless streak of 43 games in May and June; after hitting one, he then went into another 20-game drought. . . . Hit 14 of 20 home runs with someone on base, evening his career ratio: 177 with runners on, 177 with bases empty. . . . Has hit 197 HR at Atlanta Stadium, breaking Hank Aaron's record (190). Among players active at end of year, only Jim Rice (208 at Fenway) had hit 200 at one park. . . . Totals for '80s: 308 home runs, 929 RBI, 596 extra-base hits, 2796 total bases. Finished second in HR (Schmidt, 313), RBI (Murray, 996), and extra-base hits (Dwight Evans, 605); led majors in total bases.

## Eddie Murray

Bats Left and Right

| Los Angeles Dodgers | AB | H | 2B | 3B | HR | RBI | BB | SO | BA | SA | OBA |
|---|---|---|---|---|---|---|---|---|---|---|---|
| Season | 594 | 147 | 29 | 1 | 20 | 88 | 87 | 85 | .247 | .401 | .342 |
| vs. Left-Handers | 210 | 44 | 11 | 1 | 4 | 21 | 32 | 28 | .210 | .329 | .317 |
| vs. Right-Handers | 384 | 103 | 18 | 0 | 16 | 67 | 55 | 57 | .268 | .440 | .356 |
| Home | 292 | 74 | 13 | 1 | 4 | 40 | 40 | 47 | .253 | .346 | .342 |
| Road | 302 | 73 | 16 | 0 | 16 | 48 | 47 | 38 | .242 | .454 | .342 |
| Grass | 428 | 106 | 19 | 1 | 15 | 67 | 63 | 69 | .248 | .402 | .341 |
| Artificial Turf | 166 | 41 | 10 | 0 | 5 | 21 | 24 | 16 | .247 | .398 | .344 |
| April | 92 | 26 | 8 | 0 | 4 | 18 | 9 | 12 | .283 | .500 | .333 |
| May | 85 | 20 | 7 | 0 | 2 | 15 | 21 | 16 | .235 | .388 | .389 |
| June | 110 | 22 | 5 | 0 | 1 | 10 | 20 | 21 | .200 | .273 | .326 |
| July | 105 | 25 | 3 | 0 | 5 | 16 | 10 | 14 | .238 | .410 | .304 |
| August | 101 | 29 | 3 | 1 | 3 | 15 | 18 | 11 | .287 | .426 | .395 |
| Sept./Oct. | 101 | 25 | 3 | 0 | 5 | 14 | 9 | 11 | .248 | .426 | .306 |
| Leading Off Inn. | 146 | 34 | 6 | 0 | 1 | 1 | 8 | 21 | .233 | .295 | .277 |
| Runners On | 291 | 75 | 15 | 1 | 15 | 83 | 50 | 35 | .258 | .471 | .361 |
| Runners/Scor. Pos. | 148 | 38 | 7 | 1 | 9 | 68 | 41 | 22 | .257 | .500 | .406 |
| Runners On/2 Out | 150 | 33 | 7 | 0 | 6 | 31 | 25 | 15 | .220 | .387 | .335 |
| Scor. Pos./2 Out | 78 | 17 | 4 | 0 | 4 | 25 | 21 | 10 | .218 | .423 | .390 |
| Late Inning Pressure | 112 | 20 | 1 | 0 | 5 | 11 | 15 | 19 | .179 | .321 | .281 |
| Leading Off | 27 | 4 | 0 | 0 | 1 | 1 | 1 | 3 | .148 | .259 | .179 |
| Runners On | 44 | 7 | 0 | 0 | 3 | 9 | 10 | 8 | .159 | .364 | .327 |
| Runners/Scor. Pos. | 17 | 2 | 0 | 0 | 2 | 7 | 9 | 5 | .118 | .471 | .444 |

| RUNS BATTED IN | From 1B | From 2B | From 3B | Scoring Position |
|---|---|---|---|---|
| Totals | 19/225 | 26/109 | 23/65 | 49/174 |
| Percentage | 8% | 24% | 35% | 28% |
| Driving In Runners from 3B with Less than Two Out: | | | 16/27 | 59% |

Loves to face: Ed Whitson (.421, 8-for-19, 2 HR)
Hates to face: Rick Rhoden (.100, 2-for-20, 1 HR)
Led majors with 996 RBI in 1980s. . . . Liked what he saw in first year visiting Wrigley Field; hit .474 there, high among visitors. . . . Hit as many home runs at Jack Murphy Stadium as at Dodger Stadium. . . . Yearly averages batting right-handed since 1986: .306, .271, .230, .210. . . . Consecutive-game streak stands at 359, second to Ripken's among current streaks. . . . Led N.L. first basemen in fielding percentage, ending year with streak of 111 errorless games; he ranked last in A.L. in 1988. . . . OK, we'll note that he's the first first baseman since Earl Sheely in '20s to lead both N.L. and A.L. in fielding (he led A.L. in 1981–82), if you promise *not* to mention it among his legit credentials at Hall of Fame time.

## Otis Nixon

Bats Left and Right

| Montreal Expos | AB | H | 2B | 3B | HR | RBI | BB | SO | BA | SA | OBA |
|---|---|---|---|---|---|---|---|---|---|---|---|
| Season | 258 | 56 | 7 | 2 | 0 | 21 | 33 | 36 | .217 | .260 | .306 |
| vs. Left-Handers | 150 | 35 | 4 | 1 | 0 | 12 | 14 | 20 | .233 | .273 | .299 |
| vs. Right-Handers | 108 | 21 | 3 | 1 | 0 | 9 | 19 | 16 | .194 | .241 | .315 |
| Home | 132 | 28 | 4 | 2 | 0 | 12 | 17 | 20 | .212 | .273 | .302 |
| Road | 126 | 28 | 3 | 0 | 0 | 9 | 16 | 16 | .222 | .246 | .310 |
| Grass | 50 | 11 | 0 | 0 | 0 | 4 | 7 | 9 | .220 | .220 | .316 |
| Artificial Turf | 208 | 45 | 7 | 2 | 0 | 17 | 26 | 27 | .216 | .269 | .303 |
| April | 48 | 11 | 2 | 1 | 0 | 7 | 6 | 6 | .229 | .313 | .315 |
| May | 45 | 11 | 0 | 0 | 0 | 2 | 5 | 11 | .244 | .244 | .320 |
| June | 68 | 15 | 2 | 1 | 0 | 9 | 13 | 8 | .221 | .279 | .346 |
| July | 65 | 15 | 3 | 0 | 0 | 2 | 4 | 5 | .231 | .277 | .275 |
| August | 24 | 3 | 0 | 0 | 0 | 0 | 4 | 6 | .125 | .125 | .250 |
| Sept./Oct. | 8 | 1 | 0 | 0 | 0 | 1 | 1 | 0 | .125 | .125 | .222 |
| Leading Off Inn. | 88 | 16 | 2 | 0 | 0 | 0 | 14 | 15 | .182 | .205 | .294 |
| Runners On | 95 | 20 | 4 | 2 | 0 | 21 | 11 | 11 | .211 | .295 | .292 |
| Runners/Scor. Pos. | 56 | 14 | 4 | 1 | 0 | 20 | 9 | 7 | .250 | .357 | .354 |
| Runners On/2 Out | 50 | 8 | 3 | 1 | 0 | 13 | 5 | 5 | .160 | .260 | .236 |
| Scor. Pos./2 Out | 35 | 7 | 3 | 1 | 0 | 13 | 4 | 4 | .200 | .343 | .282 |
| Late Inning Pressure | 42 | 11 | 1 | 0 | 0 | 3 | 6 | 5 | .262 | .286 | .354 |
| Leading Off | 9 | 3 | 0 | 0 | 0 | 0 | 2 | 0 | .333 | .333 | .455 |
| Runners On | 17 | 5 | 1 | 0 | 0 | 3 | 3 | 3 | .294 | .353 | .400 |
| Runners/Scor. Pos. | 8 | 4 | 1 | 0 | 0 | 3 | 1 | 2 | .500 | .625 | .556 |

| RUNS BATTED IN | From 1B | From 2B | From 3B | Scoring Position |
|---|---|---|---|---|
| Totals | 4/65 | 10/49 | 7/22 | 17/71 |
| Percentage | 6% | 20% | 32% | 24% |
| Driving In Runners from 3B with Less than Two Out: | | | 4/10 | 40% |

Loves to face: John Smiley (.357, 5-for-14)
Hates to face: Bob Ojeda (.077, 1-for-13)
Led Expos with 17 infield hits. . . . Career batting average of .194 vs. ground-ball pitchers is 4th-lowest among all players (minimum: 400 AB) over past 15 years. Who's lower? Bob Knepper, .133; Phil Niekro, .165; and Rick Reuschel, .175. Closest active nonpitcher is Steve Jeltz at .209. . . . N.L. stolen base leaders over last two seasons: Coleman (146), Young (99), Ozzie (86), and Otis (83). . . . Hit three home runs over span of 90 at-bats for Indians in 1985, but has no homers in 818 other at-bats, before and since. . . . Brother Donnell's lone 1989 home run gave him a career lead of 4–3 over Otis; next home run by either will pull Nixons into a tie with the Niekros (Phil hit seven, Joe hit one—off Phil).

## Ron Oester

Bats Left and Right

| Cincinnati Reds | AB | H | 2B | 3B | HR | RBI | BB | SO | BA | SA | OBA |
|---|---|---|---|---|---|---|---|---|---|---|---|
| Season | 305 | 75 | 15 | 0 | 1 | 14 | 32 | 47 | .246 | .305 | .318 |
| vs. Left-Handers | 63 | 11 | 0 | 0 | 0 | 1 | 10 | 13 | .175 | .175 | .288 |
| vs. Right-Handers | 242 | 64 | 15 | 0 | 1 | 13 | 22 | 34 | .264 | .339 | .326 |
| Home | 148 | 40 | 10 | 0 | 1 | 8 | 17 | 24 | .270 | .358 | .345 |
| Road | 157 | 35 | 5 | 0 | 0 | 6 | 15 | 23 | .223 | .255 | .291 |
| Grass | 85 | 22 | 3 | 0 | 0 | 3 | 4 | 13 | .259 | .294 | .292 |
| Artificial Turf | 220 | 53 | 12 | 0 | 1 | 11 | 28 | 34 | .241 | .309 | .327 |
| April | 67 | 12 | 2 | 0 | 0 | 2 | 10 | 8 | .179 | .209 | .286 |
| May | 62 | 12 | 3 | 0 | 1 | 4 | 2 | 11 | .194 | .290 | .219 |
| June | 13 | 3 | 0 | 0 | 0 | 1 | 0 | 1 | .231 | .231 | .231 |
| July | 30 | 7 | 0 | 0 | 0 | 1 | 4 | 5 | .233 | .233 | .324 |
| August | 79 | 25 | 6 | 0 | 0 | 5 | 9 | 12 | .316 | .392 | .386 |
| Sept./Oct. | 54 | 16 | 4 | 0 | 0 | 1 | 7 | 10 | .296 | .370 | .377 |
| Leading Off Inn. | 75 | 17 | 6 | 0 | 0 | 0 | 6 | 10 | .227 | .307 | .284 |
| Runners On | 125 | 38 | 4 | 0 | 0 | 13 | 21 | 22 | .304 | .336 | .404 |
| Runners/Scor. Pos. | 58 | 18 | 1 | 0 | 0 | 13 | 18 | 15 | .310 | .328 | .474 |
| Runners On/2 Out | 51 | 17 | 1 | 0 | 0 | 6 | 13 | 7 | .333 | .353 | .469 |
| Scor. Pos./2 Out | 23 | 7 | 0 | 0 | 0 | 6 | 11 | 4 | .304 | .304 | .529 |
| Late Inning Pressure | 58 | 14 | 2 | 0 | 0 | 3 | 0 | 11 | .241 | .276 | .241 |
| Leading Off | 13 | 5 | 1 | 0 | 0 | 0 | 0 | 2 | .385 | .462 | .385 |
| Runners On | 18 | 6 | 1 | 0 | 0 | 3 | 0 | 3 | .333 | .389 | .333 |
| Runners/Scor. Pos. | 6 | 3 | 0 | 0 | 0 | 3 | 0 | 2 | .500 | .500 | .500 |

| RUNS BATTED IN | From 1B | From 2B | From 3B | Scoring Position |
|---|---|---|---|---|
| Totals | 0/102 | 6/44 | 7/23 | 13/67 |
| Percentage | 0% | 14% | 30% | 19% |
| Driving In Runners from 3B with Less than Two Out: | | | 5/14 | 36% |

Loves to face: Kevin Gross (.500, 12-for-24)
Hates to face: Bob Ojeda (0-for-10)
Batting average at year's end was at its highest point of season. . . . Batting average with runners in scoring position was a career-high, but rate of runners driven in from scoring position was a career-low. Why? None of his last five hits in those situations brought home a runner from second base. Since only 15 percent of hits with runners in scoring position fail to produce an RBI, chances of five such hits in a row are more than 11,600 to one. . . . Passed Joe Morgan into 2d place on Reds' list of games at second base: Bid McPhee, 1216; Oester, 1121; Morgan, 1116. McPhee, who retired in 1899, played an additional 909 games at second for the Reds team in the American Assn. before Reds switched into N.L. in 1890.

## Paul O'Neill

Bats Left

| Cincinnati Reds | AB | H | 2B | 3B | HR | RBI | BB | SO | BA | SA | OBA |
|---|---|---|---|---|---|---|---|---|---|---|---|
| Season | 428 | 118 | 24 | 2 | 15 | 74 | 46 | 64 | .276 | .446 | .346 |
| vs. Left-Handers | 152 | 27 | 5 | 1 | 4 | 25 | 14 | 36 | .178 | .303 | .246 |
| vs. Right-Handers | 276 | 91 | 19 | 1 | 11 | 49 | 32 | 28 | .330 | .525 | .399 |
| Home | 231 | 73 | 18 | 1 | 11 | 45 | 21 | 28 | .316 | .545 | .373 |
| Road | 197 | 45 | 6 | 1 | 4 | 29 | 25 | 36 | .228 | .330 | .316 |
| Grass | 114 | 24 | 3 | 1 | 2 | 12 | 16 | 25 | .211 | .307 | .308 |
| Artificial Turf | 314 | 94 | 21 | 1 | 13 | 62 | 30 | 39 | .299 | .497 | .360 |
| April | 75 | 23 | 5 | 0 | 3 | 17 | 4 | 11 | .307 | .493 | .333 |
| May | 97 | 24 | 4 | 0 | 3 | 16 | 12 | 14 | .247 | .381 | .336 |
| June | 106 | 31 | 6 | 0 | 6 | 19 | 11 | 10 | .292 | .519 | .361 |
| July | 56 | 18 | 4 | 0 | 2 | 10 | 7 | 9 | .321 | .500 | .397 |
| August | 0 | 0 | 0 | 0 | 0 | 0 | 0 | 0 | — | — | — |
| Sept./Oct. | 94 | 22 | 5 | 2 | 1 | 12 | 12 | 20 | .234 | .362 | .318 |
| Leading Off Inn. | 106 | 25 | 3 | 0 | 6 | 6 | 7 | 15 | .236 | .434 | .289 |
| Runners On | 195 | 63 | 15 | 2 | 9 | 68 | 30 | 28 | .323 | .559 | .409 |
| Runners/Scor. Pos. | 109 | 34 | 11 | 1 | 6 | 58 | 24 | 16 | .312 | .596 | .428 |
| Runners On/2 Out | 90 | 32 | 8 | 2 | 3 | 31 | 15 | 11 | .356 | .589 | .448 |
| Scor. Pos./2 Out | 53 | 17 | 5 | 1 | 3 | 28 | 13 | 5 | .321 | .623 | .455 |
| Late Inning Pressure | 75 | 24 | 3 | 1 | 0 | 8 | 7 | 11 | .320 | .387 | .378 |
| Leading Off | 18 | 4 | 1 | 0 | 0 | 0 | 0 | 1 | .222 | .278 | .222 |
| Runners On | 33 | 10 | 1 | 1 | 0 | 8 | 6 | 7 | .303 | .394 | .410 |
| Runners/Scor. Pos. | 18 | 6 | 1 | 1 | 0 | 8 | 6 | 4 | .333 | .500 | .500 |

| RUNS BATTED IN | From 1B | From 2B | From 3B | Scoring Position |
|---|---|---|---|---|
| Totals | 18/142 | 23/90 | 18/37 | 41/127 |
| Percentage | 13% | 26% | 49% | 32% |
| Driving In Runners from 3B with Less than Two Out: | | | 13/22 | 59% |

Loves to face: Ron Darling (.500, 7-for-14, 2 HR)
Hates to face: Tom Glavine (.091, 1-for-11)
Had 57 fewer at-bats in 1989 than in 1988, and finished with one fewer single, one fewer double, one fewer triple, and one fewer home run. . . . Only major leaguer to hit 150 points higher vs. right-handers (.330) than vs. left-handers (.178) last season (minimum: 100 AB vs. each). That's a Stan Musialish average vs. righties, a Mudcat Grantish one vs. lefties. . .First Reds' player with a four-hit opening day since Jim Greengrass hit four doubles in '54 opener. . . . Stole 20 bases last year, after total of 10 in 237 previous games in majors. . . . With Bengals' punter Lee Johnson ranking last in NFL in net average, Sam Wyche should review hang time and accuracy of O'Neill's punt to first baseman Todd Benzinger last July.

## Jose Oquendo

Bats Left and Right

| St. Louis Cardinals | AB | H | 2B | 3B | HR | RBI | BB | SO | BA | SA | OBA |
|---|---|---|---|---|---|---|---|---|---|---|---|
| Season | 556 | 162 | 28 | 7 | 1 | 48 | 79 | 59 | .291 | .372 | .375 |
| vs. Left-Handers | 229 | 61 | 14 | 3 | 0 | 14 | 27 | 29 | .266 | .354 | .340 |
| vs. Right-Handers | 327 | 101 | 14 | 4 | 1 | 34 | 52 | 30 | .309 | .385 | .398 |
| Home | 269 | 81 | 15 | 7 | 0 | 26 | 40 | 26 | .301 | .409 | .387 |
| Road | 287 | 81 | 13 | 0 | 1 | 22 | 39 | 33 | .282 | .338 | .364 |
| Grass | 152 | 47 | 4 | 0 | 0 | 9 | 17 | 21 | .309 | .336 | .372 |
| Artificial Turf | 404 | 115 | 24 | 7 | 1 | 39 | 62 | 38 | .285 | .386 | .376 |
| April | 76 | 18 | 3 | 1 | 0 | 8 | 11 | 13 | .237 | .303 | .330 |
| May | 96 | 26 | 4 | 0 | 0 | 3 | 9 | 10 | .271 | .313 | .333 |
| June | 86 | 21 | 3 | 1 | 0 | 5 | 11 | 9 | .244 | .302 | .327 |
| July | 97 | 40 | 6 | 3 | 0 | 16 | 8 | 9 | .412 | .536 | .444 |
| August | 108 | 31 | 9 | 0 | 0 | 8 | 18 | 5 | .287 | .370 | .386 |
| Sept./Oct. | 93 | 26 | 3 | 2 | 1 | 8 | 22 | 13 | .280 | .387 | .410 |
| Leading Off Inn. | 129 | 38 | 8 | 2 | 0 | 0 | 15 | 13 | .295 | .388 | .368 |
| Runners On | 239 | 68 | 7 | 2 | 0 | 47 | 32 | 27 | .285 | .331 | .358 |
| Runners/Scor. Pos. | 141 | 36 | 7 | 2 | 0 | 47 | 23 | 18 | .255 | .333 | .343 |
| Runners On/2 Out | 102 | 24 | 3 | 2 | 0 | 19 | 19 | 16 | .235 | .304 | .355 |
| Scor. Pos./2 Out | 67 | 14 | 3 | 2 | 0 | 19 | 15 | 11 | .209 | .313 | .354 |
| Late Inning Pressure | 86 | 27 | 3 | 1 | 0 | 4 | 16 | 14 | .314 | .372 | .422 |
| Leading Off | 20 | 7 | 2 | 1 | 0 | 0 | 3 | 4 | .350 | .550 | .435 |
| Runners On | 41 | 12 | 0 | 0 | 0 | 4 | 9 | 7 | .293 | .293 | .420 |
| Runners/Scor. Pos. | 20 | 6 | 0 | 0 | 0 | 4 | 5 | 5 | .300 | .300 | .440 |

| RUNS BATTED IN | From 1B | From 2B | From 3B | Scoring Position |
|---|---|---|---|---|
| Totals | 4/171 | 19/110 | 24/60 | 43/170 |
| Percentage | 2% | 17% | 40% | 25% |
| Driving In Runners from 3B with Less than Two Out: | | | 19/34 | 56% |

Loves to face: Pete Smith (5-for-5, 4 BB)
Hates to face: Rick Mahler (.120, 3-for-25, 0 BB)
First N.L. second basemen to lead the league in fielding percentage, putouts, assists, and double plays since Bill Mazeroski in 1966. . . . Also led N.L. second basemen with 5.63 chances per nine innings. . . . Only N.L. player to have a higher average at home than on the road in each of the last six seasons. . . . Batted .465 vs. Dodgers, highest average by any N.L. player vs. any club last season. . . . July batting average was highest in majors. His 23-game hitting streak (June 28 to July 25) was 2d-longest in majors last season. . . . Played "only" three positions last season: second base (156 games), shortstop (seven games), and first base (one inning), after playing all nine in 1988.

## Junior Ortiz

Bats Right

| Pittsburgh Pirates | AB | H | 2B | 3B | HR | RBI | BB | SO | BA | SA | OBA |
|---|---|---|---|---|---|---|---|---|---|---|---|
| Season | 230 | 50 | 6 | 1 | 1 | 23 | 20 | 20 | .217 | .265 | .282 |
| vs. Left-Handers | 97 | 21 | 3 | 1 | 1 | 8 | 9 | 10 | .216 | .299 | .296 |
| vs. Right-Handers | 133 | 29 | 3 | 0 | 0 | 15 | 11 | 10 | .218 | .241 | .272 |
| Home | 117 | 29 | 3 | 1 | 0 | 17 | 16 | 7 | .248 | .291 | .336 |
| Road | 113 | 21 | 3 | 0 | 1 | 6 | 4 | 13 | .186 | .239 | .220 |
| Grass | 52 | 10 | 2 | 0 | 0 | 1 | 1 | 3 | .192 | .231 | .208 |
| Artificial Turf | 178 | 40 | 4 | 1 | 1 | 22 | 19 | 17 | .225 | .275 | .302 |
| April | 41 | 10 | 0 | 0 | 0 | 6 | 3 | 1 | .244 | .244 | .283 |
| May | 57 | 11 | 1 | 0 | 0 | 5 | 5 | 5 | .193 | .211 | .270 |
| June | 55 | 13 | 2 | 1 | 0 | 5 | 4 | 5 | .236 | .309 | .283 |
| July | 42 | 13 | 3 | 0 | 1 | 6 | 3 | 4 | .310 | .452 | .356 |
| August | 32 | 3 | 0 | 0 | 0 | 1 | 3 | 4 | .094 | .094 | .194 |
| Sept./Oct. | 3 | 0 | 0 | 0 | 0 | 0 | 2 | 1 | .000 | .000 | .400 |
| Leading Off Inn. | 50 | 13 | 1 | 0 | 0 | 0 | 2 | 4 | .260 | .280 | .288 |
| Runners On | 105 | 24 | 2 | 1 | 1 | 23 | 15 | 12 | .229 | .295 | .323 |
| Runners/Scor. Pos. | 63 | 14 | 1 | 0 | 1 | 21 | 11 | 11 | .222 | .286 | .325 |
| Runners On/2 Out | 44 | 7 | 2 | 0 | 0 | 6 | 11 | 6 | .159 | .205 | .339 |
| Scor. Pos./2 Out | 25 | 4 | 1 | 0 | 0 | 5 | 9 | 5 | .160 | .200 | .382 |
| Late Inning Pressure | 47 | 9 | 1 | 0 | 0 | 5 | 2 | 5 | .191 | .213 | .235 |
| Leading Off | 9 | 1 | 0 | 0 | 0 | 0 | 1 | 1 | .111 | .111 | .200 |
| Runners On | 22 | 6 | 1 | 0 | 0 | 5 | 1 | 3 | .273 | .318 | .320 |
| Runners/Scor. Pos. | 14 | 1 | 0 | 0 | 0 | 4 | 0 | 3 | .071 | .071 | .067 |

| RUNS BATTED IN | From 1B | From 2B | From 3B | Scoring Position |
|---|---|---|---|---|
| Totals | 2/71 | 8/50 | 12/27 | 20/77 |
| Percentage | 3% | 16% | 44% | 26% |
| Driving In Runners from 3B with Less than Two Out: | | | 10/17 | 59% |

Loves to face: Zane Smith (.563, 9-for-16)
Hates to face: Orel Hershiser (0-for-11)
Started 65 games and accumulated 230 at-bats last season, both career highs, but finished with his lowest batting average since 1984. . . . Started only six games after that date. Did somebody say "Don Slaught"? . . . Opponents stole 73 bases in 96 attempts, 3d-highest rate against any N.L. catcher (minimum: 50 attempts); teammate Mike LaValliere stood second on that list. . . . Career average of .290 with runners on base, .233 with bases empty. . . . Finished season with a hitless streak of 23 at-bats, dating back to August 11. Some others might have sought to challenge the team high for the year, John Smiley's 0-for-29 streak, but Junior's a team guy who doesn't go for that individual-achievement stuff.

## Spike Owen

Bats Left and Right

| Montreal Expos | AB | H | 2B | 3B | HR | RBI | BB | SO | BA | SA | OBA |
|---|---|---|---|---|---|---|---|---|---|---|---|
| Season | 437 | 102 | 17 | 4 | 6 | 41 | 76 | 44 | .233 | .332 | .349 |
| vs. Left-Handers | 131 | 36 | 7 | 0 | 2 | 14 | 19 | 17 | .275 | .374 | .371 |
| vs. Right-Handers | 306 | 66 | 10 | 4 | 4 | 27 | 57 | 27 | .216 | .314 | .340 |
| Home | 201 | 55 | 8 | 2 | 5 | 27 | 36 | 22 | .274 | .408 | .383 |
| Road | 236 | 47 | 9 | 2 | 1 | 14 | 40 | 22 | .199 | .267 | .319 |
| Grass | 126 | 21 | 3 | 0 | 0 | 4 | 20 | 11 | .167 | .190 | .284 |
| Artificial Turf | 311 | 81 | 14 | 4 | 6 | 37 | 56 | 33 | .260 | .389 | .375 |
| April | 61 | 17 | 3 | 2 | 1 | 10 | 10 | 7 | .279 | .443 | .375 |
| May | 82 | 15 | 4 | 0 | 2 | 7 | 22 | 5 | .183 | .305 | .352 |
| June | 84 | 22 | 6 | 0 | 1 | 6 | 21 | 7 | .262 | .369 | .410 |
| July | 37 | 10 | 1 | 1 | 0 | 4 | 6 | 3 | .270 | .351 | .400 |
| August | 89 | 19 | 2 | 1 | 2 | 9 | 15 | 10 | .213 | .326 | .330 |
| Sept./Oct. | 84 | 19 | 1 | 0 | 0 | 5 | 2 | 12 | .226 | .238 | .244 |
| Leading Off Inn. | 103 | 25 | 4 | 3 | 0 | 0 | 14 | 11 | .243 | .340 | .345 |
| Runners On | 181 | 49 | 8 | 1 | 5 | 40 | 44 | 18 | .271 | .409 | .410 |
| Runners/Scor. Pos. | 102 | 28 | 4 | 1 | 2 | 34 | 38 | 9 | .275 | .392 | .465 |
| Runners On/2 Out | 74 | 19 | 2 | 0 | 3 | 18 | 29 | 8 | .257 | .405 | .466 |
| Scor. Pos./2 Out | 52 | 13 | 1 | 0 | 1 | 14 | 25 | 3 | .250 | .327 | .494 |
| Late Inning Pressure | 80 | 21 | 1 | 1 | 2 | 8 | 11 | 8 | .263 | .375 | .348 |
| Leading Off | 20 | 5 | 0 | 1 | 0 | 0 | 5 | 2 | .250 | .350 | .400 |
| Runners On | 30 | 9 | 0 | 0 | 2 | 8 | 4 | 3 | .300 | .500 | .371 |
| Runners/Scor. Pos. | 16 | 5 | 0 | 0 | 0 | 4 | 3 | 2 | .313 | .313 | .400 |

| RUNS BATTED IN | From 1B | From 2B | From 3B | Scoring Position |
|---|---|---|---|---|
| Totals | 4/136 | 20/79 | 11/36 | 31/115 |
| Percentage | 3% | 25% | 31% | 27% |
| Driving In Runners from 3B with Less than Two Out: | | | 7/18 | 39% |

Loves to face: Juan Agosto (.625, 5-for-8, 1 HR)
Hates to face: Dennis Rasmussen (.080, 2-for-25)
Baseball is a Funny Game: Owen left the Kingdome and Fenway Park for cavernous Olympic Stadium, and matched his career high of six home runs. . . . Has hit for a higher average on artificial surfaces than he has on grass fields in each of last five seasons. . . . Still needs 150 games at short to reach the 1000-game qualifier, but his career fielding percentage (.975) is on target for placement in the all-time top ten. . . . Started 140 games last season, all from the 8th spot in batting order. . . . After being walked intentionally only three times in 2715 plate appearances in A.L., he found out what batting 8th in N.L. is all about: 25 IBB, finishing second in majors behind Kevin Mitchell's 32.

## Tony Pena

Bats Right

| St. Louis Cardinals | AB | H | 2B | 3B | HR | RBI | BB | SO | BA | SA | OBA |
|---|---|---|---|---|---|---|---|---|---|---|---|
| Season | 424 | 110 | 17 | 2 | 4 | 37 | 35 | 33 | .259 | .337 | .318 |
| vs. Left-Handers | 170 | 50 | 5 | 1 | 2 | 17 | 18 | 9 | .294 | .371 | .366 |
| vs. Right-Handers | 254 | 60 | 12 | 1 | 2 | 20 | 17 | 24 | .236 | .315 | .284 |
| Home | 201 | 46 | 6 | 1 | 3 | 15 | 21 | 15 | .229 | .313 | .304 |
| Road | 223 | 64 | 11 | 1 | 1 | 22 | 14 | 18 | .287 | .359 | .332 |
| Grass | 124 | 35 | 6 | 1 | 0 | 16 | 11 | 14 | .282 | .347 | .341 |
| Artificial Turf | 300 | 75 | 11 | 1 | 4 | 21 | 24 | 19 | .250 | .333 | .309 |
| April | 75 | 20 | 4 | 0 | 1 | 4 | 2 | 6 | .267 | .360 | .282 |
| May | 77 | 17 | 4 | 0 | 1 | 5 | 4 | 7 | .221 | .312 | .268 |
| June | 71 | 21 | 2 | 2 | 1 | 13 | 4 | 2 | .296 | .423 | .333 |
| July | 75 | 20 | 3 | 0 | 0 | 5 | 15 | 6 | .267 | .307 | .396 |
| August | 71 | 16 | 1 | 0 | 0 | 6 | 6 | 9 | .225 | .239 | .286 |
| Sept./Oct. | 55 | 16 | 3 | 0 | 1 | 4 | 4 | 3 | .291 | .400 | .339 |
| Leading Off Inn. | 91 | 25 | 3 | 1 | 2 | 2 | 6 | 5 | .275 | .396 | .327 |
| Runners On | 203 | 55 | 10 | 1 | 0 | 33 | 25 | 19 | .271 | .330 | .352 |
| Runners/Scor. Pos. | 118 | 27 | 5 | 0 | 0 | 30 | 25 | 11 | .229 | .271 | .361 |
| Runners On/2 Out | 80 | 18 | 5 | 1 | 0 | 13 | 18 | 6 | .225 | .313 | .367 |
| Scor. Pos./2 Out | 51 | 8 | 2 | 0 | 0 | 11 | 18 | 5 | .157 | .196 | .377 |
| Late Inning Pressure | 63 | 11 | 0 | 1 | 1 | 4 | 4 | 5 | .175 | .254 | .224 |
| Leading Off | 9 | 1 | 0 | 0 | 0 | 0 | 1 | 1 | .111 | .111 | .200 |
| Runners On | 30 | 4 | 0 | 1 | 0 | 3 | 2 | 4 | .133 | .200 | .188 |
| Runners/Scor. Pos. | 16 | 1 | 0 | 0 | 0 | 2 | 2 | 2 | .063 | .063 | .167 |

| RUNS BATTED IN | From 1B | From 2B | From 3B | Scoring Position |
|---|---|---|---|---|
| Totals | 4/156 | 11/85 | 18/44 | 29/129 |
| Percentage | 3% | 13% | 41% | 22% |
| Driving In Runners from 3B with Less than Two Out: | | | 12/23 | 52% |

Loves to face: Dave LaPoint (.344, 11-for-32)
Hates to face: Nolan Ryan (.182, 4-for-22, 5 SO)
Led major league catchers in fielding percentage (.997) and double plays (13). First catcher to lead N.L. in fielding for two straight years since Johnny Edwards (1969–1971). Made only two errors, eight fewer than either Gedman or Cerone. . . . Will Green Monster make him adjust his swing? Only 29 percent of fair balls to outfield last season were pulled (37 percent to center, 34 percent to right). . . . He'll experience Spike Owen Syndrome in reverse: 108 of his 125 starts last season were from 8th spot in lineup, and 19 of his 35 walks were intentional. That'll change in A.L. . . . Bounced into 19 double plays in 94 DP situations last season, 3d highest rate in N.L. (minimum: 40 opp.). The replacement for Jim Rice?

## Terry Pendleton

Bats Left and Right

| St. Louis Cardinals | AB | H | 2B | 3B | HR | RBI | BB | SO | BA | SA | OBA |
|---|---|---|---|---|---|---|---|---|---|---|---|
| Season | 613 | 162 | 28 | 5 | 13 | 74 | 44 | 81 | .264 | .390 | .313 |
| vs. Left-Handers | 247 | 69 | 14 | 2 | 2 | 20 | 12 | 20 | .279 | .377 | .313 |
| vs. Right-Handers | 366 | 93 | 14 | 3 | 11 | 54 | 32 | 61 | .254 | .399 | .313 |
| Home | 295 | 80 | 15 | 5 | 8 | 42 | 24 | 33 | .271 | .437 | .324 |
| Road | 318 | 82 | 13 | 0 | 5 | 32 | 20 | 48 | .258 | .346 | .302 |
| Grass | 164 | 46 | 7 | 0 | 2 | 11 | 12 | 25 | .280 | .360 | .330 |
| Artificial Turf | 449 | 116 | 21 | 5 | 11 | 63 | 32 | 56 | .258 | .401 | .306 |
| April | 85 | 21 | 4 | 0 | 0 | 13 | 10 | 14 | .247 | .294 | .326 |
| May | 106 | 24 | 2 | 1 | 1 | 7 | 7 | 12 | .226 | .292 | .274 |
| June | 99 | 22 | 3 | 0 | 3 | 13 | 7 | 10 | .222 | .343 | .271 |
| July | 100 | 32 | 8 | 2 | 2 | 14 | 4 | 14 | .320 | .500 | .346 |
| August | 116 | 29 | 8 | 0 | 5 | 13 | 7 | 16 | .250 | .448 | .293 |
| Sept./Oct. | 107 | 34 | 3 | 2 | 2 | 14 | 9 | 15 | .318 | .439 | .368 |
| Leading Off Inn. | 128 | 46 | 8 | 1 | 2 | 2 | 5 | 12 | .359 | .484 | .383 |
| Runners On | 285 | 74 | 15 | 2 | 5 | 66 | 23 | 41 | .260 | .379 | .313 |
| Runners/Scor. Pos. | 155 | 41 | 11 | 2 | 3 | 60 | 13 | 31 | .265 | .419 | .318 |
| Runners On/2 Out | 111 | 34 | 6 | 1 | 1 | 27 | 7 | 17 | .306 | .405 | .347 |
| Scor. Pos./2 Out | 73 | 21 | 5 | 1 | 1 | 27 | 5 | 14 | .288 | .425 | .333 |
| Late Inning Pressure | 84 | 18 | 2 | 0 | 1 | 4 | 8 | 16 | .214 | .274 | .283 |
| Leading Off | 20 | 6 | 1 | 0 | 0 | 0 | 0 | 3 | .300 | .350 | .300 |
| Runners On | 31 | 4 | 0 | 0 | 0 | 3 | 5 | 5 | .129 | .129 | .250 |
| Runners/Scor. Pos. | 16 | 3 | 0 | 0 | 0 | 3 | 4 | 4 | .188 | .188 | .350 |

| RUNS BATTED IN | From 1B | From 2B | From 3B | Scoring Position |
|---|---|---|---|---|
| Totals | 9/208 | 25/116 | 27/64 | 52/180 |
| Percentage | 4% | 22% | 42% | 29% |
| Driving In Runners from 3B with Less than Two Out: | | | 14/32 | 44% |

Loves to face: Zane Smith (.500, 17-for-34)
Hates to face: Dennis Martinez (.135, 5-for-37)
Has led major league third basemen in assists in three of last four years; previously, no Cardinals' third baseman had even led N.L. once since Ken Boyer in 1961. Pendleton's average of 2.54 assists per nine innings in '89 also led majors. . . . Had highest fielding percentage (.971) of his career. . . . Led Cardinals with 11 home runs off right-handed pitchers, two more than Guerrero or Brunansky. . . . Has 19 career homers at Busch Stadium, 19 on the road. . . . Batted .155 in first inning, .279 subsequently. . . . Set career highs in home runs, walks, and strikeouts. . . . Has batted .333 or higher with the bases loaded in each of last five seasons. Career average: .346 (27-for-78, two HR) with the bags bulging.

## Gerald Perry

Bats Left

| Atlanta Braves | AB | H | 2B | 3B | HR | RBI | BB | SO | BA | SA | OBA |
|---|---|---|---|---|---|---|---|---|---|---|---|
| Season | 266 | 67 | 11 | 0 | 4 | 21 | 32 | 28 | .252 | .338 | .337 |
| vs. Left-Handers | 104 | 35 | 5 | 0 | 3 | 10 | 7 | 14 | .337 | .471 | .386 |
| vs. Right-Handers | 162 | 32 | 6 | 0 | 1 | 11 | 25 | 14 | .198 | .253 | .307 |
| Home | 142 | 41 | 7 | 0 | 2 | 12 | 18 | 13 | .289 | .380 | .368 |
| Road | 124 | 26 | 4 | 0 | 2 | 9 | 14 | 15 | .210 | .290 | .300 |
| Grass | 185 | 53 | 8 | 0 | 4 | 18 | 24 | 20 | .286 | .395 | .371 |
| Artificial Turf | 81 | 14 | 3 | 0 | 0 | 3 | 8 | 8 | .173 | .210 | .256 |
| April | 86 | 27 | 5 | 0 | 3 | 15 | 19 | 6 | .314 | .477 | .444 |
| May | 94 | 16 | 3 | 0 | 0 | 0 | 10 | 14 | .170 | .202 | .257 |
| June | 60 | 16 | 2 | 0 | 0 | 1 | 2 | 6 | .267 | .300 | .290 |
| July | 26 | 8 | 1 | 0 | 1 | 5 | 1 | 2 | .308 | .462 | .321 |
| August | 0 | 0 | 0 | 0 | 0 | 0 | 0 | 0 | — | — | — |
| Sept./Oct. | 0 | 0 | 0 | 0 | 0 | 0 | 0 | 0 | — | — | — |
| Leading Off Inn. | 57 | 12 | 1 | 0 | 1 | 1 | 4 | 5 | .211 | .281 | .262 |
| Runners On | 126 | 32 | 8 | 0 | 2 | 19 | 15 | 15 | .254 | .365 | .329 |
| Runners/Scor. Pos. | 69 | 14 | 6 | 0 | 1 | 15 | 14 | 12 | .203 | .333 | .329 |
| Runners On/2 Out | 47 | 11 | 4 | 0 | 1 | 10 | 9 | 7 | .234 | .383 | .357 |
| Scor. Pos./2 Out | 33 | 7 | 4 | 0 | 1 | 10 | 8 | 7 | .212 | .424 | .366 |
| Late Inning Pressure | 38 | 5 | 0 | 0 | 0 | 0 | 9 | 3 | .132 | .132 | .327 |
| Leading Off | 8 | 2 | 0 | 0 | 0 | 0 | 0 | 1 | .250 | .250 | .250 |
| Runners On | 15 | 1 | 0 | 0 | 0 | 0 | 4 | 2 | .067 | .067 | .263 |
| Runners/Scor. Pos. | 11 | 1 | 0 | 0 | 0 | 0 | 3 | 1 | .091 | .091 | .286 |

| RUNS BATTED IN | From 1B | From 2B | From 3B | Scoring Position |
|---|---|---|---|---|
| Totals | 5/85 | 6/57 | 6/24 | 12/81 |
| Percentage | 6% | 11% | 25% | 15% |
| Driving In Runners from 3B with Less than Two Out: | | | 2/9 | 22% |

Loves to face: Jeff D. Robinson (.476, 10-for-21)
Hates to face: Scott Sanderson (.115, 3-for-26)
That .132 batting average in Late-Inning Pressure Situations was 3d lowest in N.L.; Braves swept gold, silver, and bronze in that category, with Jody Davis (.100) and Ron Gant (.119) the other medalists. . . . Batted .312 on fair balls hit to opposite field, .455 on balls hit straight away, only .178 on fair balls that he pulled. . . . Went 44 games without an RBI, April 24 to June 28; streak of 35 hitless at-bats in May matched Rick Camp's 1982 streak for longest on team in '80s. . . . Comparison to 1988 shows 67-point increase vs. left-handers, but 120-point drop vs. right-handers. . . . Career average of .091 (2-for-22) with bases loaded and two outs. . . . K.C.-bound, but hit .173 (3d lowest in N.L.) on carpets last year.

## Terry Puhl

Bats Left

| Houston Astros | AB | H | 2B | 3B | HR | RBI | BB | SO | BA | SA | OBA |
|---|---|---|---|---|---|---|---|---|---|---|---|
| Season | 354 | 96 | 25 | 4 | 0 | 27 | 45 | 39 | .271 | .364 | .353 |
| vs. Left-Handers | 57 | 14 | 5 | 0 | 0 | 5 | 7 | 8 | .246 | .333 | .338 |
| vs. Right-Handers | 297 | 82 | 20 | 4 | 0 | 22 | 38 | 31 | .276 | .370 | .356 |
| Home | 189 | 48 | 10 | 3 | 0 | 18 | 22 | 23 | .254 | .339 | .330 |
| Road | 165 | 48 | 15 | 1 | 0 | 9 | 23 | 16 | .291 | .394 | .379 |
| Grass | 103 | 30 | 9 | 0 | 0 | 4 | 15 | 9 | .291 | .379 | .381 |
| Artificial Turf | 251 | 66 | 16 | 4 | 0 | 23 | 30 | 30 | .263 | .359 | .342 |
| April | 32 | 10 | 3 | 1 | 0 | 5 | 4 | 3 | .313 | .469 | .378 |
| May | 53 | 14 | 4 | 0 | 0 | 2 | 5 | 7 | .264 | .340 | .339 |
| June | 98 | 29 | 9 | 1 | 0 | 10 | 11 | 11 | .296 | .408 | .364 |
| July | 66 | 13 | 3 | 1 | 0 | 4 | 7 | 12 | .197 | .273 | .274 |
| August | 59 | 15 | 1 | 1 | 0 | 5 | 7 | 1 | .254 | .305 | .333 |
| Sept./Oct. | 46 | 15 | 5 | 0 | 0 | 1 | 11 | 5 | .326 | .435 | .456 |
| Leading Off Inn. | 80 | 20 | 10 | 0 | 0 | 0 | 7 | 9 | .250 | .375 | .310 |
| Runners On | 139 | 38 | 8 | 4 | 0 | 27 | 19 | 15 | .273 | .388 | .356 |
| Runners/Scor. Pos. | 78 | 19 | 4 | 3 | 0 | 24 | 11 | 14 | .244 | .372 | .330 |
| Runners On/2 Out | 63 | 15 | 2 | 2 | 0 | 12 | 10 | 9 | .238 | .333 | .342 |
| Scor. Pos./2 Out | 43 | 10 | 1 | 1 | 0 | 10 | 5 | 8 | .233 | .302 | .313 |
| Late Inning Pressure | 56 | 14 | 2 | 0 | 0 | 2 | 8 | 3 | .250 | .286 | .344 |
| Leading Off | 15 | 5 | 2 | 0 | 0 | 0 | 1 | 0 | .333 | .467 | .375 |
| Runners On | 19 | 3 | 0 | 0 | 0 | 2 | 5 | 2 | .158 | .158 | .333 |
| Runners/Scor. Pos. | 12 | 2 | 0 | 0 | 0 | 2 | 2 | 2 | .167 | .167 | .286 |

| RUNS BATTED IN | From 1B | From 2B | From 3B | Scoring Position |
|---|---|---|---|---|
| Totals | 5/94 | 8/58 | 14/36 | 22/94 |
| Percentage | 5% | 14% | 39% | 23% |
| Driving In Runners from 3B with Less than Two Out: | | | 8/15 | 53% |

Loves to face: Rick Reuschel (.394, 28-for-71)
Hates to face: Bryn Smith (.136, 3-for-22, 1 HR)
Due to Kevin Bass's injury, Puhl started more games last June than he had in any month since August 1984. . . . Career averages: .295 vs. right-handers, .240 vs. left-handers. . . . One of three N.L. players with at least 10 starts at all three outfield spots last year. . . . Played errorless ball last season, but was five games shy of 108-game qualifier for league leadership. However, he raised his career fielding percentage to .993, a major league record for outfielders. His closest competitor among active players: Brett Butler (.991); but because percentages, unlike career totals, can fall lower, Puhl's actual closest competitor may be an inactive player. In fact, a *very* inactive player: Pete Rose (.991).

## Luis Quinones

Bats Left and Right

| Cincinnati Reds | AB | H | 2B | 3B | HR | RBI | BB | SO | BA | SA | OBA |
|---|---|---|---|---|---|---|---|---|---|---|---|
| Season | 340 | 83 | 13 | 4 | 12 | 34 | 25 | 46 | .244 | .412 | .300 |
| vs. Left-Handers | 142 | 34 | 3 | 2 | 9 | 20 | 10 | 19 | .239 | .479 | .297 |
| vs. Right-Handers | 198 | 49 | 10 | 2 | 3 | 14 | 15 | 27 | .247 | .364 | .302 |
| Home | 170 | 41 | 6 | 1 | 5 | 13 | 8 | 20 | .241 | .376 | .278 |
| Road | 170 | 42 | 7 | 3 | 7 | 21 | 17 | 26 | .247 | .447 | .321 |
| Grass | 104 | 24 | 4 | 2 | 5 | 16 | 12 | 15 | .231 | .452 | .308 |
| Artificial Turf | 236 | 59 | 9 | 2 | 7 | 18 | 13 | 31 | .250 | .394 | .296 |
| April | 0 | 0 | 0 | 0 | 0 | 0 | 0 | 0 | — | — | — |
| May | 6 | 2 | 0 | 0 | 1 | 1 | 1 | 0 | .333 | .833 | .429 |
| June | 39 | 7 | 3 | 0 | 2 | 2 | 2 | 5 | .179 | .410 | .220 |
| July | 68 | 12 | 2 | 0 | 3 | 5 | 7 | 11 | .176 | .338 | .263 |
| August | 115 | 36 | 5 | 2 | 3 | 12 | 6 | 17 | .313 | .470 | .358 |
| Sept./Oct. | 112 | 26 | 3 | 2 | 3 | 14 | 9 | 13 | .232 | .375 | .285 |
| Leading Off Inn. | 80 | 14 | 3 | 0 | 3 | 3 | 8 | 10 | .175 | .325 | .258 |
| Runners On | 135 | 38 | 6 | 2 | 2 | 24 | 9 | 13 | .281 | .400 | .327 |
| Runners/Scor. Pos. | 74 | 22 | 4 | 2 | 1 | 22 | 5 | 9 | .297 | .446 | .333 |
| Runners On/2 Out | 49 | 13 | 3 | 1 | 1 | 10 | 4 | 6 | .265 | .429 | .321 |
| Scor. Pos./2 Out | 30 | 7 | 2 | 1 | 1 | 10 | 3 | 5 | .233 | .467 | .303 |
| Late Inning Pressure | 56 | 11 | 3 | 0 | 1 | 5 | 3 | 6 | .196 | .304 | .237 |
| Leading Off | 16 | 2 | 0 | 0 | 0 | 0 | 0 | 1 | .125 | .125 | .125 |
| Runners On | 21 | 5 | 2 | 0 | 1 | 5 | 1 | 1 | .238 | .476 | .273 |
| Runners/Scor. Pos. | 13 | 4 | 1 | 0 | 1 | 5 | 0 | 1 | .308 | .615 | .308 |

| RUNS BATTED IN | From 1B | From 2B | From 3B | Scoring Position |
|---|---|---|---|---|
| Totals | 3/91 | 7/58 | 12/31 | 19/89 |
| Percentage | 3% | 12% | 39% | 21% |
| Driving In Runners from 3B with Less than Two Out: | | | 8/14 | 57% |

Loves to face: Dwight Gooden (.667, 4-for-6, 3 2B)
Hates to face: Jim Deshaies (0-for-14)
Career breakdown shows that he gets his hits at the right times: .291 with runners in scoring position, .265 with runners on base, .194 with bases empty. . . . Raised his average to .280 with an 18-game hitting streak in early September, 3d longest streak in N.L. last season. Then had only 8 hits in last 72 at-bats, including streak of 28 hitless at-bats vs. right-handed pitchers, the longest streak by any N.L. player (including pitchers) last year. . . . Hit 17 home runs in minors in 1982, but won 1989 Wally Moses Award for sudden double-digit home-run outburst. . . . Avenged Pirates' midseason release of *Rey* (no relation) Quinones by hitting .536 and slugging .929 in 33 at-bats vs. Bucs last year.

## Rey Quinones

Bats Right

| Pittsburgh Pirates | AB | H | 2B | 3B | HR | RBI | BB | SO | BA | SA | OBA |
|---|---|---|---|---|---|---|---|---|---|---|---|
| Season | 225 | 47 | 11 | 0 | 3 | 29 | 15 | 40 | .209 | .298 | .253 |
| vs. Left-Handers | 73 | 18 | 4 | 0 | 2 | 13 | 6 | 14 | .247 | .384 | .296 |
| vs. Right-Handers | 152 | 29 | 7 | 0 | 1 | 16 | 9 | 26 | .191 | .257 | .232 |
| Home | 97 | 16 | 6 | 0 | 1 | 8 | 13 | 18 | .165 | .258 | .261 |
| Road | 128 | 31 | 5 | 0 | 2 | 21 | 2 | 22 | .242 | .328 | .246 |
| Grass | 76 | 15 | 2 | 0 | 1 | 11 | 2 | 13 | .197 | .263 | .210 |
| Artificial Turf | 149 | 32 | 9 | 0 | 2 | 18 | 13 | 27 | .215 | .315 | .274 |
| April | 23 | 1 | 0 | 0 | 0 | 2 | 2 | 3 | .043 | .043 | .115 |
| May | 88 | 23 | 5 | 0 | 2 | 19 | 4 | 14 | .261 | .386 | .283 |
| June | 78 | 17 | 4 | 0 | 1 | 6 | 3 | 14 | .218 | .308 | .244 |
| July | 36 | 6 | 2 | 0 | 0 | 2 | 6 | 9 | .167 | .222 | .286 |
| August | 0 | 0 | 0 | 0 | 0 | 0 | 0 | 0 | — | — | — |
| Sept./Oct. | 0 | 0 | 0 | 0 | 0 | 0 | 0 | 0 | — | — | — |
| Leading Off Inn. | 54 | 10 | 2 | 0 | 0 | 0 | 0 | 12 | .185 | .222 | .185 |
| Runners On | 107 | 24 | 4 | 0 | 2 | 28 | 10 | 18 | .224 | .318 | .278 |
| Runners/Scor. Pos. | 71 | 19 | 3 | 0 | 2 | 28 | 9 | 10 | .268 | .394 | .318 |
| Runners On/2 Out | 49 | 8 | 1 | 0 | 0 | 5 | 5 | 9 | .163 | .184 | .241 |
| Scor. Pos./2 Out | 35 | 5 | 1 | 0 | 0 | 5 | 4 | 7 | .143 | .171 | .231 |
| Late Inning Pressure | 43 | 6 | 1 | 0 | 1 | 3 | 2 | 7 | .140 | .233 | .196 |
| Leading Off | 11 | 1 | 1 | 0 | 0 | 0 | 0 | 1 | .091 | .182 | .091 |
| Runners On | 20 | 3 | 0 | 0 | 1 | 3 | 2 | 4 | .150 | .300 | .261 |
| Runners/Scor. Pos. | 15 | 3 | 0 | 0 | 1 | 3 | 1 | 4 | .200 | .400 | .250 |

| RUNS BATTED IN | From 1B | From 2B | From 3B | Scoring Position |
|---|---|---|---|---|
| Totals | 1/76 | 9/56 | 16/34 | 25/90 |
| Percentage | 1% | 16% | 47% | 28% |
| Driving In Runners from 3B with Less than Two Out: | | | 14/18 | 78% |

Loves to face: Oil Can Boyd (.625, 5-for-8, 1 HR)
Hates to face: Walt Terrell (.111, 2-for-18)

Committed errors in four of first seven games with Pirates, then things tailed off from there. . . . Pirates traded Mike Dunne to Seattle for Quinones on April 20, then released him outright on July 22. Regardless, the Tony Pena trade *still* looks good for Pittsburgh. . . . His last home run was a 9th-inning game-winner off Randy Myers. . . . Including his time with Seattle last season, he led off 59 innings without drawing a walk; his .185 on-base average when leading off innings was lowest in N.L. last year. . . . Has five career stolen bases in 16 attempts. . . . Chosen by the Elias staff as the player least likely to appear in *The 1991 Elias Baseball Analyst*; no, we didn't give Jim Leyland a vote!

## Tim Raines

Bats Left and Right

| Montreal Expos | AB | H | 2B | 3B | HR | RBI | BB | SO | BA | SA | OBA |
|---|---|---|---|---|---|---|---|---|---|---|---|
| Season | 517 | 148 | 29 | 6 | 9 | 60 | 93 | 48 | .286 | .418 | .395 |
| vs. Left-Handers | 133 | 38 | 7 | 0 | 3 | 14 | 22 | 12 | .286 | .406 | .389 |
| vs. Right-Handers | 384 | 110 | 22 | 6 | 6 | 46 | 71 | 36 | .286 | .422 | .397 |
| Home | 258 | 70 | 14 | 3 | 6 | 30 | 44 | 24 | .271 | .419 | .375 |
| Road | 259 | 78 | 15 | 3 | 3 | 30 | 49 | 24 | .301 | .417 | .415 |
| Grass | 134 | 38 | 6 | 1 | 2 | 14 | 25 | 14 | .284 | .388 | .400 |
| Artificial Turf | 383 | 110 | 23 | 5 | 7 | 46 | 68 | 34 | .287 | .428 | .393 |
| April | 82 | 23 | 6 | 4 | 0 | 17 | 20 | 6 | .280 | .451 | .415 |
| May | 94 | 28 | 8 | 1 | 4 | 11 | 19 | 9 | .298 | .532 | .421 |
| June | 77 | 23 | 7 | 0 | 0 | 14 | 16 | 7 | .299 | .390 | .415 |
| July | 57 | 19 | 0 | 0 | 2 | 7 | 9 | 8 | .333 | .439 | .424 |
| August | 106 | 28 | 4 | 1 | 3 | 9 | 18 | 12 | .264 | .406 | .368 |
| Sept./Oct. | 101 | 27 | 4 | 0 | 0 | 2 | 11 | 6 | .267 | .307 | .345 |
| Leading Off Inn. | 185 | 55 | 9 | 4 | 3 | 3 | 18 | 17 | .297 | .438 | .369 |
| Runners On | 186 | 57 | 12 | 2 | 2 | 53 | 61 | 18 | .306 | .425 | .468 |
| Runners/Scor. Pos. | 103 | 34 | 8 | 2 | 1 | 48 | 49 | 8 | .330 | .476 | .529 |
| Runners On/2 Out | 94 | 28 | 6 | 0 | 0 | 22 | 29 | 9 | .298 | .362 | .463 |
| Scor. Pos./2 Out | 50 | 13 | 4 | 0 | 0 | 19 | 25 | 4 | .260 | .340 | .507 |
| Late Inning Pressure | 88 | 24 | 5 | 0 | 1 | 11 | 15 | 9 | .273 | .364 | .379 |
| Leading Off | 27 | 5 | 0 | 0 | 1 | 1 | 1 | 4 | .185 | .296 | .214 |
| Runners On | 31 | 14 | 4 | 0 | 0 | 10 | 13 | 1 | .452 | .581 | .614 |
| Runners/Scor. Pos. | 16 | 8 | 1 | 0 | 0 | 8 | 12 | 1 | .500 | .563 | .714 |

| RUNS BATTED IN | From 1B | From 2B | From 3B | Scoring Position |
|---|---|---|---|---|
| Totals | 10/138 | 18/80 | 23/43 | 41/123 |
| Percentage | 7% | 23% | 53% | 33% |
| Driving In Runners from 3B with Less than Two Out: | | | 14/20 | 70% |

Loves to face: Ken Hill (.818, 9-for-11, 6 BB)
Hates to face: John Smiley (.174, 4-for-23)

His .343 career batting average in Late-Inning Pressure Situations is second over past 15 years to Tony Gwynn's .344. . . . In LIPS with two outs and runners on base, he's a .414 career hitter, including 31-for-62 performance over past five years. . . . Has hit .325 or higher with runners in scoring position in each of last five years. . . . Expos' leadoff hitter in April, May, and September, cleanup hitter from June to August. . . . Needs 109 hits to break Andre Dawson's team record; already owns club marks for stolen bases, batting average, runs, and triples. . . . Next steal will be No. 586 to tie Maury Wills for 5th spot in N.L. history. . . . Only player in majors with 300+ extra-base hits and 300+ steals over past six years.

## Rafael Ramirez

Bats Right

| Houston Astros | AB | H | 2B | 3B | HR | RBI | BB | SO | BA | SA | OBA |
|---|---|---|---|---|---|---|---|---|---|---|---|
| Season | 537 | 132 | 20 | 2 | 6 | 54 | 29 | 64 | .246 | .324 | .283 |
| vs. Left-Handers | 156 | 42 | 5 | 1 | 2 | 18 | 11 | 17 | .269 | .353 | .315 |
| vs. Right-Handers | 381 | 90 | 15 | 1 | 4 | 36 | 18 | 47 | .236 | .312 | .269 |
| Home | 268 | 66 | 11 | 1 | 3 | 31 | 18 | 33 | .246 | .328 | .291 |
| Road | 269 | 66 | 9 | 1 | 3 | 23 | 11 | 31 | .245 | .320 | .275 |
| Grass | 158 | 42 | 6 | 0 | 3 | 15 | 4 | 19 | .266 | .361 | .284 |
| Artificial Turf | 379 | 90 | 14 | 2 | 3 | 39 | 25 | 45 | .237 | .309 | .283 |
| April | 95 | 25 | 1 | 1 | 1 | 5 | 3 | 11 | .263 | .326 | .286 |
| May | 91 | 23 | 4 | 0 | 1 | 7 | 2 | 10 | .253 | .330 | .266 |
| June | 93 | 24 | 2 | 0 | 0 | 8 | 6 | 11 | .258 | .280 | .303 |
| July | 88 | 22 | 8 | 0 | 1 | 13 | 4 | 6 | .250 | .375 | .283 |
| August | 90 | 24 | 4 | 1 | 2 | 15 | 11 | 9 | .267 | .400 | .340 |
| Sept./Oct. | 80 | 14 | 1 | 0 | 1 | 6 | 3 | 17 | .175 | .225 | .205 |
| Leading Off Inn. | 114 | 28 | 4 | 0 | 0 | 0 | 5 | 19 | .246 | .281 | .277 |
| Runners On | 223 | 58 | 11 | 1 | 4 | 52 | 16 | 27 | .260 | .372 | .306 |
| Runners/Scor. Pos. | 144 | 33 | 6 | 0 | 1 | 43 | 14 | 22 | .229 | .292 | .292 |
| Runners On/2 Out | 102 | 22 | 4 | 1 | 2 | 24 | 10 | 15 | .216 | .333 | .286 |
| Scor. Pos./2 Out | 73 | 12 | 1 | 0 | 1 | 19 | 9 | 15 | .164 | .219 | .256 |
| Late Inning Pressure | 88 | 26 | 4 | 0 | 1 | 15 | 13 | 14 | .295 | .375 | .382 |
| Leading Off | 23 | 7 | 3 | 0 | 0 | 0 | 4 | 6 | .304 | .435 | .407 |
| Runners On | 36 | 12 | 1 | 0 | 0 | 14 | 6 | 4 | .333 | .361 | .419 |
| Runners/Scor. Pos. | 22 | 9 | 1 | 0 | 0 | 14 | 6 | 3 | .409 | .455 | .517 |

| RUNS BATTED IN | From 1B | From 2B | From 3B | Scoring Position |
|---|---|---|---|---|
| Totals | 8/146 | 20/112 | 20/59 | 40/171 |
| Percentage | 5% | 18% | 34% | 23% |
| Driving In Runners from 3B with Less than Two Out: | | | 13/24 | 54% |

Loves to face: Don Robinson (.306, 11-for-36, 3 HR)
Hates to face: David Cone (.067, 1-for-15)

Led N.L. shortstops in errors (30) for 6th time, tying Dick Groat's record. . . . He can't use the Atlanta–Fulton County Stadium infield as an excuse anymore, nor can he claim a high total of chances handled: of 31 major league shortstops who played at least 500 innings last season, Ramirez was the only one who averaged fewer than four total chances per nine innings. . . . Only one other shortstop in postwar era has had six 30-error seasons: Zoilo Versalles. . . . Has had more errors than walks in each of his 10 years in majors. . . . Made at least one error vs. every N.L. opponent except St. Louis; he was perfect with Ozzie watching. . . . A .286 career hitter in day games, not a very useful talent in the Dome.

## Domingo Ramos

Bats Right

| Chicago Cubs | AB | H | 2B | 3B | HR | RBI | BB | SO | BA | SA | OBA |
|---|---|---|---|---|---|---|---|---|---|---|---|
| Season | 179 | 47 | 6 | 2 | 1 | 19 | 17 | 23 | .263 | .335 | .333 |
| vs. Left-Handers | 59 | 22 | 1 | 0 | 1 | 8 | 8 | 8 | .373 | .441 | .448 |
| vs. Right-Handers | 120 | 25 | 5 | 2 | 0 | 11 | 9 | 15 | .208 | .283 | .275 |
| Home | 100 | 23 | 2 | 2 | 1 | 11 | 11 | 17 | .230 | .320 | .313 |
| Road | 79 | 24 | 4 | 0 | 0 | 8 | 6 | 6 | .304 | .354 | .360 |
| Grass | 126 | 27 | 4 | 2 | 1 | 13 | 11 | 22 | .214 | .302 | .283 |
| Artificial Turf | 53 | 20 | 2 | 0 | 0 | 6 | 6 | 1 | .377 | .415 | .450 |
| April | 29 | 8 | 2 | 0 | 1 | 7 | 1 | 5 | .276 | .448 | .300 |
| May | 20 | 5 | 0 | 0 | 0 | 1 | 1 | 2 | .250 | .250 | .286 |
| June | 48 | 13 | 1 | 1 | 0 | 4 | 5 | 5 | .271 | .333 | .352 |
| July | 16 | 6 | 1 | 0 | 0 | 1 | 1 | 2 | .375 | .438 | .412 |
| August | 41 | 9 | 1 | 0 | 0 | 4 | 7 | 6 | .220 | .244 | .333 |
| Sept./Oct. | 25 | 6 | 1 | 1 | 0 | 2 | 2 | 3 | .240 | .360 | .321 |
| Leading Off Inn. | 42 | 12 | 0 | 0 | 0 | 0 | 4 | 6 | .286 | .286 | .348 |
| Runners On | 80 | 24 | 5 | 1 | 1 | 19 | 8 | 9 | .300 | .425 | .364 |
| Runners/Scor. Pos. | 48 | 17 | 5 | 0 | 0 | 16 | 6 | 6 | .354 | .458 | .426 |
| Runners On/2 Out | 35 | 11 | 3 | 1 | 1 | 10 | 4 | 6 | .314 | .543 | .385 |
| Scor. Pos./2 Out | 23 | 8 | 3 | 0 | 0 | 7 | 3 | 4 | .348 | .478 | .423 |
| Late Inning Pressure | 37 | 6 | 2 | 0 | 0 | 1 | 1 | 5 | .162 | .216 | .184 |
| Leading Off | 14 | 2 | 0 | 0 | 0 | 0 | 0 | 2 | .143 | .143 | .143 |
| Runners On | 13 | 3 | 1 | 0 | 0 | 1 | 0 | 2 | .231 | .308 | .231 |
| Runners/Scor. Pos. | 6 | 2 | 1 | 0 | 0 | 1 | 0 | 2 | .333 | .500 | .333 |

| RUNS BATTED IN | From 1B | From 2B | From 3B | Scoring Position |
|---|---|---|---|---|
| Totals | 3/56 | 8/38 | 7/14 | 15/52 |
| Percentage | 5% | 21% | 50% | 29% |
| Driving In Runners from 3B with Less than Two Out: | | | 6/8 | 75% |

Loves to face: Don Carman (.800, 4-for-5)
Hates to face: Charlie Leibrandt (.167, 2-for-12)

Here's a man who can savor the Cubs' thrill of victory: Ramos made his major league debut playing one game for 1978 Yankees, who won World Series. But from 1979 to 1988 he played for losing teams in Toronto, Seattle, Cleveland, and California. . . . His .373 batting average vs. left-handers included hits in eight consecutive at-bats vs. lefties in July and August, longest streak in majors last season and longest by a Cubs' hitter in 1980s. . . . With runners in scoring position vs. lefties, he had seven hits in 13 at-bats. . . . Batted .290 in 38 starts, and hit .429 (6-for-14) as a pinch hitter. . . . Grounded into 10 double plays in 40 DP situations, highest rate in majors (minimum: 40 opportunities).

## Willie Randolph

Bats Right

| Los Angeles Dodgers | AB | H | 2B | 3B | HR | RBI | BB | SO | BA | SA | OBA |
|---|---|---|---|---|---|---|---|---|---|---|---|
| Season | 549 | 155 | 18 | 0 | 2 | 36 | 71 | 51 | .282 | .326 | .366 |
| vs. Left-Handers | 191 | 57 | 8 | 0 | 1 | 13 | 26 | 13 | .298 | .356 | .385 |
| vs. Right-Handers | 358 | 98 | 10 | 0 | 1 | 23 | 45 | 38 | .274 | .310 | .355 |
| Home | 266 | 81 | 9 | 0 | 0 | 17 | 39 | 23 | .305 | .338 | .393 |
| Road | 283 | 74 | 9 | 0 | 2 | 19 | 32 | 28 | .261 | .314 | .340 |
| Grass | 399 | 116 | 14 | 0 | 1 | 29 | 52 | 36 | .291 | .333 | .373 |
| Artificial Turf | 150 | 39 | 4 | 0 | 1 | 7 | 19 | 15 | .260 | .307 | .347 |
| April | 91 | 20 | 1 | 0 | 0 | 3 | 15 | 9 | .220 | .231 | .333 |
| May | 96 | 32 | 3 | 0 | 0 | 8 | 13 | 7 | .333 | .365 | .414 |
| June | 96 | 32 | 4 | 0 | 0 | 9 | 13 | 6 | .333 | .375 | .414 |
| July | 85 | 20 | 4 | 0 | 0 | 3 | 13 | 9 | .235 | .282 | .337 |
| August | 100 | 21 | 4 | 0 | 1 | 9 | 10 | 10 | .210 | .280 | .277 |
| Sept./Oct. | 81 | 30 | 2 | 0 | 1 | 4 | 7 | 10 | .370 | .432 | .427 |
| Leading Off Inn. | 149 | 47 | 5 | 0 | 0 | 0 | 16 | 10 | .315 | .349 | .382 |
| Runners On | 186 | 56 | 8 | 0 | 1 | 35 | 30 | 16 | .301 | .360 | .392 |
| Runners/Scor. Pos. | 96 | 25 | 5 | 0 | 1 | 34 | 24 | 8 | .260 | .344 | .392 |
| Runners On/2 Out | 89 | 26 | 1 | 0 | 1 | 13 | 19 | 7 | .292 | .337 | .417 |
| Scor. Pos./2 Out | 52 | 12 | 1 | 0 | 1 | 13 | 16 | 5 | .231 | .308 | .412 |
| Late Inning Pressure | 98 | 24 | 5 | 0 | 1 | 9 | 16 | 7 | .245 | .327 | .353 |
| Leading Off | 22 | 7 | 1 | 0 | 0 | 0 | 1 | 0 | .318 | .364 | .348 |
| Runners On | 48 | 12 | 3 | 0 | 1 | 9 | 11 | 5 | .250 | .375 | .383 |
| Runners/Scor. Pos. | 22 | 5 | 2 | 0 | 1 | 8 | 10 | 2 | .227 | .455 | .455 |

| RUNS BATTED IN | From 1B | From 2B | From 3B | Scoring Position |
|---|---|---|---|---|
| Totals | 4/129 | 10/73 | 20/46 | 30/119 |
| Percentage | 3% | 14% | 43% | 25% |
| Driving In Runners from 3B with Less than Two Out: | | | 13/20 | 65% |

Loves to face: Tom Browning (.533, 8-for-15, 1 HR)
Hates to face: Mike Scott (0-for-14)
With 1842 games at second base, has moved ahead of Red Schoendienst into top ten in major league history. Only eight second basemen have reached 2000-game mark. . . . Frank White has played 229 more games there than Randolph, but it's notable that White has been involved in only four more double plays than Willie. All-time Gold Glove standings: White eight, Randolph zero. . . . Did not make an error in 38 day games last season. . . . Led Dodgers with 25 infield singles. . . . Yearly averages vs. left-handed pitchers since 1984: .333, .315, .311, .331, *.208*, .298. . . . That Late-Inning Pressure home run was a three-run, two-out, 9th-inning game-winner off Don Aase, turning point in Mets' season.

## Randy Ready

Bats Right

| Padres/Phillies | AB | H | 2B | 3B | HR | RBI | BB | SO | BA | SA | OBA |
|---|---|---|---|---|---|---|---|---|---|---|---|
| Season | 254 | 67 | 13 | 2 | 8 | 26 | 42 | 37 | .264 | .425 | .368 |
| vs. Left-Handers | 150 | 42 | 7 | 2 | 5 | 14 | 24 | 21 | .280 | .453 | .375 |
| vs. Right-Handers | 104 | 25 | 6 | 0 | 3 | 12 | 18 | 16 | .240 | .385 | .357 |
| Home | 114 | 30 | 7 | 1 | 3 | 9 | 22 | 16 | .263 | .421 | .386 |
| Road | 140 | 37 | 6 | 1 | 5 | 17 | 20 | 21 | .264 | .429 | .352 |
| Grass | 71 | 20 | 3 | 0 | 2 | 7 | 12 | 11 | .282 | .408 | .381 |
| Artificial Turf | 183 | 47 | 10 | 2 | 6 | 19 | 30 | 26 | .257 | .432 | .362 |
| April | 49 | 14 | 2 | 0 | 0 | 5 | 6 | 4 | .286 | .327 | .357 |
| May | 17 | 3 | 0 | 1 | 0 | 0 | 5 | 2 | .176 | .294 | .364 |
| June | 76 | 20 | 6 | 0 | 2 | 6 | 12 | 14 | .263 | .421 | .378 |
| July | 40 | 11 | 1 | 0 | 3 | 9 | 10 | 5 | .275 | .525 | .412 |
| August | 31 | 8 | 0 | 1 | 1 | 2 | 3 | 4 | .258 | .419 | .324 |
| Sept./Oct. | 41 | 11 | 4 | 0 | 2 | 4 | 6 | 8 | .268 | .512 | .347 |
| Leading Off Inn. | 52 | 17 | 3 | 1 | 3 | 3 | 9 | 5 | .327 | .596 | .435 |
| Runners On | 107 | 23 | 3 | 0 | 2 | 20 | 23 | 19 | .215 | .299 | .348 |
| Runners/Scor. Pos. | 67 | 12 | 2 | 0 | 1 | 18 | 14 | 11 | .179 | .254 | .306 |
| Runners On/2 Out | 49 | 9 | 1 | 0 | 1 | 8 | 10 | 8 | .184 | .265 | .322 |
| Scor. Pos./2 Out | 37 | 6 | 1 | 0 | 1 | 8 | 6 | 5 | .162 | .270 | .279 |
| Late Inning Pressure | 39 | 11 | 4 | 0 | 1 | 6 | 11 | 4 | .282 | .462 | .440 |
| Leading Off | 4 | 1 | 0 | 0 | 0 | 0 | 3 | 0 | .250 | .250 | .571 |
| Runners On | 19 | 4 | 1 | 0 | 0 | 5 | 4 | 2 | .211 | .263 | .348 |
| Runners/Scor. Pos. | 13 | 4 | 1 | 0 | 0 | 5 | 3 | 1 | .308 | .385 | .438 |

| RUNS BATTED IN | From 1B | From 2B | From 3B | Scoring Position |
|---|---|---|---|---|
| Totals | 2/75 | 6/48 | 10/33 | 16/81 |
| Percentage | 3% | 13% | 30% | 20% |
| Driving In Runners from 3B with Less than Two Out: | | | 8/17 | 47% |

Loves to face: Dwight Gooden (.545, 6-for-11)
Hates to face: Orel Hershiser (0-for-11)
Attention, Jim Frey! Has a career average of .242 in night games, but his career mark of .326 in day games is 4th highest among active players, behind Boggs, Mattingly, and Gwynn. Over past three years, his day-game batting average is an astounding .377. . . . One hit in 15 career at-bats (.067) with two outs and the bases loaded. . . . Career average of .291 against ground-ball pitchers, .247 vs. fly-ballers. . . . Last June, he reached base safely in nine consecutive plate appearances when leading off an inning, longest such streak of season in N.L. . . . For season, his .435 on-base average when leading off innings was 2d highest in N.L.; highest? John Kruk (.455), his Padres-to-Phillies trademate.

## Gary Redus

Bats Right

| Pittsburgh Pirates | AB | H | 2B | 3B | HR | RBI | BB | SO | BA | SA | OBA |
|---|---|---|---|---|---|---|---|---|---|---|---|
| Season | 279 | 79 | 18 | 7 | 6 | 34 | 40 | 51 | .283 | .462 | .372 |
| vs. Left-Handers | 113 | 33 | 9 | 6 | 3 | 16 | 19 | 22 | .292 | .558 | .391 |
| vs. Right-Handers | 166 | 46 | 9 | 1 | 3 | 18 | 21 | 29 | .277 | .398 | .358 |
| Home | 137 | 38 | 10 | 2 | 3 | 17 | 21 | 28 | .277 | .445 | .373 |
| Road | 142 | 41 | 8 | 5 | 3 | 17 | 19 | 23 | .289 | .479 | .370 |
| Grass | 71 | 20 | 2 | 3 | 1 | 5 | 9 | 12 | .282 | .437 | .358 |
| Artificial Turf | 208 | 59 | 16 | 4 | 5 | 29 | 31 | 39 | .284 | .471 | .376 |
| April | 22 | 7 | 2 | 0 | 0 | 2 | 6 | 4 | .318 | .409 | .448 |
| May | 38 | 10 | 4 | 1 | 0 | 3 | 3 | 9 | .263 | .421 | .317 |
| June | 73 | 20 | 4 | 1 | 2 | 12 | 13 | 7 | .274 | .438 | .375 |
| July | 56 | 16 | 1 | 2 | 1 | 1 | 5 | 16 | .286 | .429 | .355 |
| August | 35 | 13 | 3 | 1 | 1 | 6 | 4 | 8 | .371 | .600 | .436 |
| Sept./Oct. | 55 | 13 | 4 | 2 | 2 | 10 | 9 | 7 | .236 | .491 | .344 |
| Leading Off Inn. | 68 | 21 | 5 | 2 | 1 | 1 | 14 | 10 | .309 | .485 | .427 |
| Runners On | 107 | 29 | 3 | 4 | 3 | 31 | 18 | 20 | .271 | .458 | .372 |
| Runners/Scor. Pos. | 69 | 19 | 1 | 2 | 3 | 28 | 13 | 14 | .275 | .478 | .384 |
| Runners On/2 Out | 48 | 15 | 1 | 3 | 2 | 19 | 7 | 10 | .313 | .583 | .411 |
| Scor. Pos./2 Out | 36 | 12 | 0 | 2 | 2 | 17 | 5 | 8 | .333 | .611 | .429 |
| Late Inning Pressure | 55 | 17 | 6 | 0 | 1 | 3 | 6 | 16 | .309 | .473 | .371 |
| Leading Off | 19 | 9 | 3 | 0 | 1 | 1 | 3 | 2 | .474 | .789 | .545 |
| Runners On | 18 | 2 | 1 | 0 | 0 | 2 | 3 | 7 | .111 | .167 | .227 |
| Runners/Scor. Pos. | 11 | 1 | 0 | 0 | 0 | 2 | 3 | 5 | .091 | .091 | .267 |

| RUNS BATTED IN | From 1B | From 2B | From 3B | Scoring Position |
|---|---|---|---|---|
| Totals | 6/78 | 11/53 | 11/27 | 22/80 |
| Percentage | 8% | 21% | 41% | 28% |
| Driving In Runners from 3B with Less than Two Out: | | | 6/12 | 50% |

Loves to face: Rick Mahler (.435, 10-for-23, 3 HR)
Hates to face: Alejandro Pena (.063, 1-for-16)
Pronounced fly-ball hitter whose career breakdown manifests the tendency of such hitters: .271 vs. ground-ball pitchers, .224 vs. fly-ball pitchers. Over last two seasons, the difference is even more apparent: .313 vs. .215. . . . Hit 63 percent of his ground outs, but only 21 percent of his air outs to the left side of the field. To the opposite field, he hit only 25 percent of his ground outs, but 55 percent of his air outs. . . . Batting average with runners on base has been lower than with bases empty in each of last five seasons. . . . Career-high averages vs. both right- and left-handed pitchers. . . . One of six players with 25+ steals in each of last seven seasons; others: Butler, Henderson, Raines, Sax, Ozzie Smith.

## Jeff Reed

Bats Left

| Cincinnati Reds | AB | H | 2B | 3B | HR | RBI | BB | SO | BA | SA | OBA |
|---|---|---|---|---|---|---|---|---|---|---|---|
| Season | 287 | 64 | 11 | 0 | 3 | 23 | 34 | 46 | .223 | .293 | .306 |
| vs. Left-Handers | 41 | 7 | 2 | 0 | 0 | 6 | 6 | 9 | .171 | .220 | .300 |
| vs. Right-Handers | 246 | 57 | 9 | 0 | 3 | 17 | 28 | 37 | .232 | .305 | .307 |
| Home | 130 | 32 | 5 | 0 | 1 | 11 | 16 | 21 | .246 | .308 | .327 |
| Road | 157 | 32 | 6 | 0 | 2 | 12 | 18 | 25 | .204 | .280 | .288 |
| Grass | 88 | 14 | 1 | 0 | 1 | 5 | 11 | 16 | .159 | .205 | .260 |
| Artificial Turf | 199 | 50 | 10 | 0 | 2 | 18 | 23 | 30 | .251 | .332 | .326 |
| April | 60 | 17 | 5 | 0 | 1 | 7 | 3 | 10 | .283 | .417 | .317 |
| May | 61 | 13 | 2 | 0 | 1 | 5 | 7 | 12 | .213 | .295 | .300 |
| June | 39 | 6 | 0 | 0 | 0 | 1 | 2 | 4 | .154 | .154 | .195 |
| July | 49 | 11 | 3 | 0 | 0 | 2 | 7 | 9 | .224 | .286 | .333 |
| August | 50 | 15 | 1 | 0 | 1 | 7 | 4 | 8 | .300 | .380 | .339 |
| Sept./Oct. | 28 | 2 | 0 | 0 | 0 | 1 | 11 | 3 | .071 | .071 | .325 |
| Leading Off Inn. | 63 | 11 | 1 | 0 | 0 | 0 | 6 | 8 | .175 | .190 | .246 |
| Runners On | 119 | 27 | 5 | 0 | 2 | 22 | 17 | 19 | .227 | .319 | .314 |
| Runners/Scor. Pos. | 71 | 17 | 3 | 0 | 1 | 20 | 15 | 14 | .239 | .324 | .356 |
| Runners On/2 Out | 47 | 9 | 1 | 0 | 1 | 8 | 11 | 12 | .191 | .277 | .345 |
| Scor. Pos./2 Out | 32 | 7 | 1 | 0 | 1 | 8 | 10 | 9 | .219 | .344 | .405 |
| Late Inning Pressure | 40 | 6 | 1 | 0 | 0 | 2 | 8 | 5 | .150 | .175 | .286 |
| Leading Off | 14 | 1 | 0 | 0 | 0 | 0 | 2 | 2 | .071 | .071 | .188 |
| Runners On | 13 | 2 | 1 | 0 | 0 | 2 | 4 | 2 | .154 | .231 | .333 |
| Runners/Scor. Pos. | 8 | 0 | 0 | 0 | 0 | 2 | 3 | 1 | .000 | .000 | .250 |

| RUNS BATTED IN | From 1B | From 2B | From 3B | Scoring Position |
|---|---|---|---|---|
| Totals | 2/84 | 7/62 | 11/25 | 18/87 |
| Percentage | 2% | 11% | 44% | 21% |
| Driving In Runners from 3B with Less than Two Out: | | | 9/14 | 64% |

Loves to face: Orel Hershiser (.304, 7-for-23)
Hates to face: Dwight Gooden (.083, 1-for-12)
Opponents stole 84 bases in 129 attempts (.651), compared to a .753 percentage (58-of-77) vs. other Reds' catchers. . . . Started 80 games vs. right-handed pitchers, but only seven vs. lefties. . . . Owns .254 career average vs. ground-ball pitchers, .186 vs. fly-ball pitchers. . . . Had four multiple-hit games before the season was a week old, but had only eight more for the rest of the season. . . . Reds' starting catchers batted .238 last season, one point above overall N.L. average, after hitting .216 (25th in majors) the previous year. That improvement is not thanks to Reed (.226 in '88, .223 in '89), but to Joe Oliver, rookie who hit .272 overall and .300 with runners in scoring position in 49 games.

## Craig Reynolds

Bats Left

| Houston Astros | AB | H | 2B | 3B | HR | RBI | BB | SO | BA | SA | OBA |
|---|---|---|---|---|---|---|---|---|---|---|---|
| Season | 189 | 38 | 4 | 0 | 2 | 14 | 19 | 18 | .201 | .254 | .274 |
| vs. Left-Handers | 8 | 1 | 0 | 0 | 0 | 0 | 2 | 2 | .125 | .125 | .300 |
| vs. Right-Handers | 181 | 37 | 4 | 0 | 2 | 14 | 17 | 16 | .204 | .260 | .273 |
| Home | 102 | 20 | 1 | 0 | 0 | 8 | 12 | 9 | .196 | .206 | .281 |
| Road | 87 | 18 | 3 | 0 | 2 | 6 | 7 | 9 | .207 | .310 | .266 |
| Grass | 58 | 8 | 1 | 0 | 0 | 3 | 6 | 7 | .138 | .155 | .219 |
| Artificial Turf | 131 | 30 | 3 | 0 | 2 | 11 | 13 | 11 | .229 | .298 | .299 |
| April | 25 | 4 | 0 | 0 | 1 | 5 | 3 | 5 | .160 | .280 | .250 |
| May | 33 | 6 | 1 | 0 | 0 | 1 | 3 | 4 | .182 | .212 | .250 |
| June | 28 | 7 | 0 | 0 | 0 | 1 | 3 | 2 | .250 | .250 | .323 |
| July | 30 | 7 | 1 | 0 | 0 | 0 | 0 | 2 | .233 | .267 | .233 |
| August | 36 | 8 | 1 | 0 | 0 | 4 | 6 | 1 | .222 | .250 | .333 |
| Sept./Oct. | 37 | 6 | 1 | 0 | 1 | 3 | 4 | 4 | .162 | .270 | .244 |
| Leading Off Inn. | 42 | 12 | 0 | 0 | 1 | 1 | 2 | 1 | .286 | .357 | .318 |
| Runners On | 83 | 18 | 2 | 0 | 1 | 13 | 11 | 8 | .217 | .277 | .309 |
| Runners/Scor. Pos. | 46 | 7 | 0 | 0 | 0 | 11 | 8 | 5 | .152 | .152 | .278 |
| Runners On/2 Out | 25 | 7 | 0 | 0 | 0 | 5 | 6 | 3 | .280 | .280 | .419 |
| Scor. Pos./2 Out | 14 | 4 | 0 | 0 | 0 | 5 | 6 | 2 | .286 | .286 | .500 |
| Late Inning Pressure | 40 | 9 | 2 | 0 | 1 | 1 | 6 | 3 | .225 | .350 | .326 |
| Leading Off | 8 | 5 | 0 | 0 | 1 | 1 | 0 | 0 | .625 | 1.000 | .625 |
| Runners On | 16 | 1 | 1 | 0 | 0 | 0 | 5 | 2 | .063 | .125 | .286 |
| Runners/Scor. Pos. | 8 | 0 | 0 | 0 | 0 | 0 | 3 | 0 | .000 | .000 | .273 |

| RUNS BATTED IN | From 1B | From 2B | From 3B | Scoring Position |
|---|---|---|---|---|
| Totals | 1/57 | 6/41 | 5/11 | 11/52 |
| Percentage | 2% | 15% | 45% | 21% |
| Driving In Runners from 3B with Less than Two Out: | | | 4/8 | 50% |

Loves to face: Pascual Perez (.440, 11-for-25, 3 HR)
Hates to face: Mark Davis (0-for-13)
One of four players to remain active or disabled on the same N.L. club throughout the 1980s. The others: teammates Terry Puhl and Dave Smith, and Atlanta's Dale Murphy. . . . Only three active players have more career sacrifice bunts than Reynolds (124): Ozzie Smith (160), Bob Boone (140), and Rick Reuschel (132). His total of 34 sacrifices in 1979 is N.L.'s highest since Harry Walker had 36 in 1943. . . . Only N.L. player last season to start at least once at each of the four infield positions. . . . Hit .315 in 101 plate appearances with bases loaded, with more grand slams (3) than strikeouts (2). . . . Made two of those position-player-masquerading-as-pitcher appearances in his career; once struck out Howard Johnson.

## R. J. Reynolds

Bats Left and Right

| Pittsburgh Pirates | AB | H | 2B | 3B | HR | RBI | BB | SO | BA | SA | OBA |
|---|---|---|---|---|---|---|---|---|---|---|---|
| Season | 363 | 98 | 16 | 2 | 6 | 48 | 34 | 66 | .270 | .375 | .331 |
| vs. Left-Handers | 116 | 33 | 3 | 0 | 1 | 11 | 9 | 21 | .284 | .336 | .341 |
| vs. Right-Handers | 247 | 65 | 13 | 2 | 5 | 37 | 25 | 45 | .263 | .393 | .326 |
| Home | 204 | 61 | 13 | 2 | 3 | 27 | 18 | 35 | .299 | .426 | .354 |
| Road | 159 | 37 | 3 | 0 | 3 | 21 | 16 | 31 | .233 | .308 | .301 |
| Grass | 91 | 20 | 3 | 0 | 3 | 13 | 9 | 20 | .220 | .352 | .290 |
| Artificial Turf | 272 | 78 | 13 | 2 | 3 | 35 | 25 | 46 | .287 | .382 | .344 |
| April | 65 | 21 | 5 | 0 | 1 | 7 | 3 | 10 | .323 | .446 | .353 |
| May | 65 | 15 | 4 | 0 | 1 | 3 | 7 | 13 | .231 | .338 | .311 |
| June | 36 | 16 | 1 | 0 | 1 | 10 | 8 | 6 | .444 | .556 | .522 |
| July | 63 | 15 | 4 | 0 | 2 | 18 | 3 | 14 | .238 | .397 | .269 |
| August | 63 | 16 | 0 | 0 | 0 | 4 | 6 | 7 | .254 | .254 | .319 |
| Sept./Oct. | 71 | 15 | 2 | 2 | 1 | 6 | 7 | 16 | .211 | .338 | .282 |
| Leading Off Inn. | 74 | 18 | 5 | 1 | 1 | 1 | 4 | 13 | .243 | .378 | .282 |
| Runners On | 179 | 48 | 7 | 0 | 5 | 47 | 21 | 36 | .268 | .391 | .341 |
| Runners/Scor. Pos. | 106 | 28 | 5 | 0 | 1 | 38 | 17 | 22 | .264 | .340 | .354 |
| Runners On/2 Out | 67 | 15 | 2 | 0 | 2 | 15 | 11 | 14 | .224 | .343 | .333 |
| Scor. Pos./2 Out | 45 | 10 | 2 | 0 | 0 | 11 | 10 | 10 | .222 | .267 | .364 |
| Late Inning Pressure | 77 | 23 | 5 | 0 | 0 | 7 | 8 | 12 | .299 | .364 | .365 |
| Leading Off | 13 | 5 | 1 | 0 | 0 | 0 | 0 | 3 | .385 | .462 | .385 |
| Runners On | 37 | 13 | 3 | 0 | 0 | 7 | 7 | 6 | .351 | .432 | .455 |
| Runners/Scor. Pos. | 19 | 5 | 2 | 0 | 0 | 7 | 5 | 6 | .263 | .368 | .417 |

| RUNS BATTED IN | From 1B | From 2B | From 3B | Scoring Position |
|---|---|---|---|---|
| Totals | 7/129 | 15/74 | 20/50 | 35/124 |
| Percentage | 5% | 20% | 40% | 28% |
| Driving In Runners from 3B with Less than Two Out: | | | 17/30 | 57% |

Loves to face: Craig Lefferts (.727, 8-for-11)
Hates to face: Danny Darwin (0-for-15, 7 SO)
Has landed between 48 and 51 RBI in each of last four years; no one else has stayed in that narrow range for more than last two years. . . . Career batting average is higher from right side (.281) than from left (.258), but his power is from left side: .391 slugging average and one home run every 50 at-bats batting left-handed, .369 and one every 112 at-bats from right side. . . . Has hit for higher average in home games than in road games in four of five seasons with Bucs. . . . Stole career-high 22 bases in 1989. Over past three years, has stolen 51 bases in 59 attempts, a rate of 86.4 percent; among players with 30+ steals, only Stan Javier (87.5) and Eric Davis (86.9) have higher rates over that span.

## Ernest Riles

Bats Left

| San Francisco Giants | AB | H | 2B | 3B | HR | RBI | BB | SO | BA | SA | OBA |
|---|---|---|---|---|---|---|---|---|---|---|---|
| Season | 302 | 84 | 13 | 2 | 7 | 40 | 28 | 50 | .278 | .404 | .339 |
| vs. Left-Handers | 39 | 7 | 2 | 1 | 0 | 2 | 4 | 12 | .179 | .282 | .256 |
| vs. Right-Handers | 263 | 77 | 11 | 1 | 7 | 38 | 24 | 38 | .293 | .422 | .352 |
| Home | 130 | 32 | 6 | 2 | 5 | 17 | 19 | 15 | .246 | .438 | .346 |
| Road | 172 | 52 | 7 | 0 | 2 | 23 | 9 | 35 | .302 | .378 | .333 |
| Grass | 210 | 56 | 7 | 2 | 6 | 25 | 26 | 32 | .267 | .405 | .350 |
| Artificial Turf | 92 | 28 | 6 | 0 | 1 | 15 | 2 | 18 | .304 | .402 | .313 |
| April | 38 | 11 | 2 | 0 | 1 | 3 | 5 | 7 | .289 | .421 | .364 |
| May | 72 | 22 | 3 | 2 | 3 | 12 | 9 | 9 | .306 | .528 | .386 |
| June | 65 | 16 | 5 | 0 | 0 | 8 | 3 | 14 | .246 | .323 | .286 |
| July | 46 | 12 | 1 | 0 | 1 | 5 | 4 | 7 | .261 | .348 | .320 |
| August | 25 | 5 | 0 | 0 | 1 | 6 | 1 | 6 | .200 | .320 | .222 |
| Sept./Oct. | 56 | 18 | 2 | 0 | 1 | 6 | 6 | 7 | .321 | .411 | .387 |
| Leading Off Inn. | 72 | 27 | 2 | 2 | 2 | 2 | 2 | 8 | .375 | .542 | .392 |
| Runners On | 114 | 30 | 7 | 0 | 5 | 38 | 17 | 16 | .263 | .456 | .358 |
| Runners/Scor. Pos. | 76 | 20 | 6 | 0 | 4 | 36 | 13 | 13 | .263 | .500 | .368 |
| Runners On/2 Out | 51 | 12 | 3 | 0 | 4 | 17 | 12 | 7 | .235 | .529 | .391 |
| Scor. Pos./2 Out | 37 | 7 | 2 | 0 | 3 | 15 | 9 | 5 | .189 | .486 | .362 |
| Late Inning Pressure | 51 | 17 | 2 | 0 | 1 | 7 | 5 | 10 | .333 | .431 | .393 |
| Leading Off | 9 | 4 | 0 | 0 | 0 | 0 | 1 | 1 | .444 | .444 | .500 |
| Runners On | 20 | 4 | 0 | 0 | 1 | 7 | 3 | 5 | .200 | .350 | .304 |
| Runners/Scor. Pos. | 13 | 4 | 0 | 0 | 1 | 7 | 0 | 3 | .308 | .538 | .308 |

| RUNS BATTED IN | From 1B | From 2B | From 3B | Scoring Position |
|---|---|---|---|---|
| Totals | 4/82 | 17/56 | 12/40 | 29/96 |
| Percentage | 5% | 30% | 30% | 30% |
| Driving In Runners from 3B with Less than Two Out: | | | 9/18 | 50% |

Loves to face: Dave Schmidt (.714, 5-for-7, 1 HR)
Hates to face: Mitch Williams (0-for-5, 3 SO)
Batted .313 (15-for-48) with Giants trailing by one run. . . . Hit .432 (16-for-37) vs. N.L.'s top 10 pitchers in strikeouts, best by any N.L. batter with at least 30 at-bats against them; this group of pitchers held opponents to a composite average of .217. . . . Started 71 games vs. right-handers, but only four vs. lefties; that reflects career .284 batting average vs. righties, .217 vs. lefties. . . . Batted .345 leading off innings, .248 in other at-bats. . . . Batted .237 (9-for-38) pinch hitting. . . . Has two home runs in five career plate appearances against Roger McDowell, who has allowed a career average of one home run every 91 batters faced. Only four other players have hit two homers off McDowell.

## Bip Roberts

Bats Left and Right

| San Diego Padres | AB | H | 2B | 3B | HR | RBI | BB | SO | BA | SA | OBA |
|---|---|---|---|---|---|---|---|---|---|---|---|
| Season | 329 | 99 | 15 | 8 | 3 | 25 | 49 | 45 | .301 | .422 | .391 |
| vs. Left-Handers | 117 | 38 | 5 | 4 | 3 | 13 | 13 | 18 | .325 | .513 | .397 |
| vs. Right-Handers | 212 | 61 | 10 | 4 | 0 | 12 | 36 | 27 | .288 | .373 | .388 |
| Home | 159 | 48 | 7 | 4 | 2 | 15 | 21 | 26 | .302 | .434 | .385 |
| Road | 170 | 51 | 8 | 4 | 1 | 10 | 28 | 19 | .300 | .412 | .397 |
| Grass | 245 | 74 | 11 | 4 | 2 | 16 | 37 | 36 | .302 | .404 | .394 |
| Artificial Turf | 84 | 25 | 4 | 4 | 1 | 9 | 12 | 9 | .298 | .476 | .381 |
| April | 13 | 2 | 0 | 1 | 0 | 0 | 2 | 2 | .154 | .308 | .267 |
| May | 26 | 10 | 0 | 3 | 0 | 2 | 6 | 5 | .385 | .615 | .500 |
| June | 54 | 16 | 2 | 2 | 0 | 2 | 6 | 8 | .296 | .407 | .367 |
| July | 59 | 17 | 2 | 1 | 0 | 5 | 8 | 8 | .288 | .356 | .373 |
| August | 92 | 26 | 5 | 1 | 3 | 9 | 11 | 13 | .283 | .457 | .358 |
| Sept./Oct. | 85 | 28 | 6 | 0 | 0 | 7 | 16 | 9 | .329 | .400 | .436 |
| Leading Off Inn. | 147 | 47 | 11 | 3 | 1 | 1 | 22 | 26 | .320 | .456 | .412 |
| Runners On | 97 | 33 | 3 | 3 | 2 | 24 | 11 | 10 | .340 | .495 | .400 |
| Runners/Scor. Pos. | 57 | 16 | 3 | 1 | 2 | 22 | 6 | 5 | .281 | .474 | .338 |
| Runners On/2 Out | 41 | 14 | 2 | 0 | 1 | 12 | 2 | 4 | .341 | .463 | .372 |
| Scor. Pos./2 Out | 33 | 10 | 2 | 0 | 1 | 12 | 1 | 2 | .303 | .455 | .324 |
| Late Inning Pressure | 43 | 12 | 1 | 1 | 0 | 4 | 8 | 7 | .279 | .349 | .392 |
| Leading Off | 13 | 3 | 0 | 0 | 0 | 0 | 1 | 3 | .231 | .231 | .286 |
| Runners On | 15 | 3 | 1 | 1 | 0 | 4 | 4 | 2 | .200 | .400 | .368 |
| Runners/Scor. Pos. | 10 | 1 | 1 | 0 | 0 | 3 | 2 | 1 | .100 | .200 | .250 |

| RUNS BATTED IN | From 1B | From 2B | From 3B | Scoring Position |
|---|---|---|---|---|
| Totals | 2/64 | 13/45 | 7/25 | 20/70 |
| Percentage | 3% | 29% | 28% | 29% |
| Driving In Runners from 3B with Less than Two Out: | | | 6/12 | 50% |

Loves to face: Derek Lilliquist (.800, 4-for-5, 1 HR)
Hates to face: Fernando Valenzuela (.158, 3-for-19, 5 SO)
Only major leaguer to start at six different positions last season (not including DH). . . . Batted .353 (6-for-17) as a pinch hitter; San Diego's other pinch hitters combined to hit .205. . . . After playing in 101 games for Padres in 1986, he spent 1987 and 1988 in minors, hitting to a .329 tune. . . . In favor of starting season on May 1; he's 2-for-33 in two major league Aprils. . . . Batting average of .3009 topped the career high of the other Leon Roberts, who hit .3008 for Seattle in 1978. You don't remember Leon the First? Odds are he played in a theater near you, having made stops in Detroit, Houston, Seattle, Texas, Toronto, and Kansas City during 11-year (1974–84) career in majors.

## Rolando Roomes

Bats Right

| Cincinnati Reds | AB | H | 2B | 3B | HR | RBI | BB | SO | BA | SA | OBA |
|---|---|---|---|---|---|---|---|---|---|---|---|
| Season | 315 | 83 | 18 | 5 | 7 | 34 | 13 | 100 | .263 | .419 | .296 |
| vs. Left-Handers | 160 | 47 | 11 | 2 | 2 | 16 | 5 | 41 | .294 | .425 | .314 |
| vs. Right-Handers | 155 | 36 | 7 | 3 | 5 | 18 | 8 | 59 | .232 | .413 | .279 |
| Home | 152 | 36 | 11 | 1 | 5 | 15 | 7 | 49 | .237 | .421 | .278 |
| Road | 163 | 47 | 7 | 4 | 2 | 19 | 6 | 51 | .288 | .417 | .314 |
| Grass | 119 | 33 | 6 | 2 | 2 | 13 | 6 | 39 | .277 | .412 | .313 |
| Artificial Turf | 196 | 50 | 12 | 3 | 5 | 21 | 7 | 61 | .255 | .423 | .286 |
| April | 0 | 0 | 0 | 0 | 0 | 0 | 0 | 0 | — | — | — |
| May | 47 | 17 | 4 | 1 | 2 | 6 | 1 | 6 | .362 | .617 | .375 |
| June | 69 | 15 | 4 | 0 | 1 | 4 | 4 | 25 | .217 | .319 | .260 |
| July | 60 | 20 | 2 | 1 | 3 | 11 | 1 | 23 | .333 | .550 | .344 |
| August | 95 | 20 | 2 | 3 | 1 | 10 | 1 | 30 | .211 | .326 | .216 |
| Sept./Oct. | 44 | 11 | 6 | 0 | 0 | 3 | 6 | 16 | .250 | .386 | .365 |
| Leading Off Inn. | 69 | 17 | 2 | 1 | 1 | 1 | 1 | 21 | .246 | .348 | .268 |
| Runners On | 134 | 35 | 10 | 4 | 4 | 31 | 7 | 44 | .261 | .485 | .297 |
| Runners/Scor. Pos. | 74 | 17 | 3 | 3 | 1 | 22 | 4 | 27 | .230 | .392 | .268 |
| Runners On/2 Out | 64 | 19 | 5 | 1 | 2 | 15 | 3 | 16 | .297 | .500 | .328 |
| Scor. Pos./2 Out | 39 | 10 | 2 | 1 | 1 | 11 | 3 | 12 | .256 | .436 | .310 |
| Late Inning Pressure | 44 | 14 | 5 | 1 | 1 | 8 | 2 | 14 | .318 | .545 | .354 |
| Leading Off | 6 | 4 | 0 | 0 | 0 | 0 | 0 | 1 | .667 | .667 | .667 |
| Runners On | 16 | 7 | 3 | 1 | 1 | 8 | 1 | 6 | .438 | .938 | .444 |
| Runners/Scor. Pos. | 6 | 3 | 1 | 1 | 0 | 5 | 1 | 2 | .500 | 1.000 | .500 |

| RUNS BATTED IN | From 1B | From 2B | From 3B | Scoring Position |
|---|---|---|---|---|
| Totals | 8/101 | 8/50 | 11/38 | 19/88 |
| Percentage | 8% | 16% | 29% | 22% |
| Driving In Runners from 3B with Less than Two Out: | | | 8/20 | 40% |

Loves to face: Derek Lilliquist (.500, 6-for-12, 3 2B)
Hates to face: Greg Maddux (.167, 1-for-6, 5 SO)
Tied major league record for fewest walks by a player with 100+ strikeouts; John Bateman had 13 walks, 103 strikeouts with Astros in 1963. . . . Only N.L. rookie to whiff 100 times last season. . . . Only N.L. player to start 15+ games at each outfield position. . . . Batted N.L.-high .402 in day games, .192 at night. Difference of 210 points was by far the largest in majors last season (minimum: 100 AB each way). . . . Drove in as many runners from first base as he did from second (eight). . . . Grounded into only two double plays in 59 opportunities, the lowest rate on the team last season. . . . In case you missed the fine print, take a look at that breakdown of at-bats and hits in Late-Inning Pressure Situations.

## Chris Sabo

Bats Right

| Cincinnati Reds | AB | H | 2B | 3B | HR | RBI | BB | SO | BA | SA | OBA |
|---|---|---|---|---|---|---|---|---|---|---|---|
| Season | 304 | 79 | 21 | 1 | 6 | 29 | 25 | 33 | .260 | .395 | .316 |
| vs. Left-Handers | 100 | 29 | 8 | 1 | 0 | 6 | 11 | 11 | .290 | .390 | .360 |
| vs. Right-Handers | 204 | 50 | 13 | 0 | 6 | 23 | 14 | 22 | .245 | .397 | .294 |
| Home | 158 | 37 | 13 | 1 | 3 | 14 | 15 | 12 | .234 | .386 | .303 |
| Road | 146 | 42 | 8 | 0 | 3 | 15 | 10 | 21 | .288 | .404 | .331 |
| Grass | 90 | 25 | 5 | 0 | 2 | 8 | 7 | 15 | .278 | .400 | .327 |
| Artificial Turf | 214 | 54 | 16 | 1 | 4 | 21 | 18 | 18 | .252 | .393 | .312 |
| April | 91 | 21 | 8 | 0 | 0 | 3 | 6 | 8 | .231 | .319 | .278 |
| May | 90 | 21 | 5 | 0 | 4 | 16 | 9 | 12 | .233 | .422 | .304 |
| June | 92 | 29 | 6 | 1 | 1 | 5 | 7 | 9 | .315 | .435 | .364 |
| July | 0 | 0 | 0 | 0 | 0 | 0 | 0 | 0 | — | — | — |
| August | 0 | 0 | 0 | 0 | 0 | 0 | 0 | 0 | — | — | — |
| Sept./Oct. | 31 | 8 | 2 | 0 | 1 | 5 | 3 | 4 | .258 | .419 | .324 |
| Leading Off Inn. | 89 | 27 | 4 | 0 | 3 | 3 | 7 | 7 | .303 | .449 | .361 |
| Runners On | 105 | 28 | 9 | 0 | 1 | 24 | 15 | 11 | .267 | .381 | .352 |
| Runners/Scor. Pos. | 63 | 19 | 6 | 0 | 1 | 22 | 13 | 8 | .302 | .444 | .410 |
| Runners On/2 Out | 41 | 7 | 3 | 0 | 1 | 7 | 12 | 2 | .171 | .317 | .358 |
| Scor. Pos./2 Out | 28 | 5 | 1 | 0 | 1 | 6 | 12 | 2 | .179 | .321 | .425 |
| Late Inning Pressure | 36 | 5 | 2 | 0 | 1 | 4 | 5 | 6 | .139 | .278 | .256 |
| Leading Off | 8 | 1 | 0 | 0 | 1 | 1 | 0 | 2 | .125 | .500 | .222 |
| Runners On | 14 | 2 | 1 | 0 | 0 | 3 | 4 | 2 | .143 | .214 | .316 |
| Runners/Scor. Pos. | 9 | 2 | 1 | 0 | 0 | 3 | 4 | 2 | .222 | .333 | .429 |

| RUNS BATTED IN | From 1B | From 2B | From 3B | Scoring Position |
|---|---|---|---|---|
| Totals | 2/63 | 13/54 | 8/20 | 21/74 |
| Percentage | 3% | 24% | 40% | 28% |
| Driving In Runners from 3B with Less than Two Out: | | | 6/9 | 67% |

Loves to face: Kelly Downs (.714, 5-for-7, 3 2B, 1 HR)
Hates to face: Greg Maddux (.091, 1-for-11)
The winners of 1988's MVP and Rookie Awards (Gibson, Canseco, Sabo, and Weiss) played an average of 148 games en route to those awards; last season, they averaged only 75 games, with all four spending large portions of 1989 on the disabled list. . . . Reds had 42–34 (.553) record with Sabo starting, 33–53 (.384) mark with others starting at third base. . . . Committed 10 errors over his first 41 games at third base, but only one in 35 games after that. . . . Missed 59 games due to knee injury before returning on Sept. 1. . . . Two-year totals: .288, 15 home runs, 59 RBI before All-Star Game; .221, 2, and 14, after All-Star Game. . . . Career breakdown for the Party Animal: .287 in night games, .223 in day games.

## Luis Salazar

Bats Right

| Padres/Cubs | AB | H | 2B | 3B | HR | RBI | BB | SO | BA | SA | OBA |
|---|---|---|---|---|---|---|---|---|---|---|---|
| Season | 326 | 92 | 12 | 2 | 9 | 34 | 15 | 57 | .282 | .414 | .316 |
| vs. Left-Handers | 125 | 37 | 5 | 2 | 5 | 22 | 7 | 14 | .296 | .488 | .338 |
| vs. Right-Handers | 201 | 55 | 7 | 0 | 4 | 12 | 8 | 43 | .274 | .368 | .301 |
| Home | 174 | 45 | 6 | 2 | 6 | 18 | 9 | 32 | .259 | .420 | .299 |
| Road | 152 | 47 | 6 | 0 | 3 | 16 | 6 | 25 | .309 | .408 | .335 |
| Grass | 241 | 68 | 10 | 2 | 7 | 25 | 11 | 40 | .282 | .427 | .316 |
| Artificial Turf | 85 | 24 | 2 | 0 | 2 | 9 | 4 | 17 | .282 | .376 | .315 |
| April | 54 | 15 | 0 | 0 | 2 | 3 | 0 | 10 | .278 | .389 | .278 |
| May | 76 | 18 | 3 | 0 | 1 | 2 | 3 | 16 | .237 | .316 | .275 |
| June | 57 | 14 | 3 | 1 | 1 | 2 | 4 | 8 | .246 | .386 | .295 |
| July | 29 | 10 | 0 | 1 | 2 | 5 | 3 | 4 | .345 | .621 | .406 |
| August | 30 | 9 | 1 | 0 | 2 | 10 | 1 | 6 | .300 | .533 | .323 |
| Sept./Oct. | 80 | 26 | 5 | 0 | 1 | 12 | 4 | 13 | .325 | .425 | .357 |
| Leading Off Inn. | 69 | 17 | 2 | 1 | 2 | 2 | 1 | 11 | .246 | .391 | .257 |
| Runners On | 130 | 40 | 5 | 0 | 4 | 29 | 8 | 21 | .308 | .438 | .348 |
| Runners/Scor. Pos. | 76 | 21 | 2 | 0 | 1 | 21 | 5 | 13 | .276 | .342 | .321 |
| Runners On/2 Out | 51 | 9 | 1 | 0 | 1 | 8 | 4 | 12 | .176 | .255 | .236 |
| Scor. Pos./2 Out | 38 | 6 | 1 | 0 | 0 | 6 | 4 | 9 | .158 | .184 | .238 |
| Late Inning Pressure | 57 | 19 | 4 | 0 | 1 | 7 | 0 | 9 | .333 | .456 | .333 |
| Leading Off | 12 | 3 | 0 | 0 | 0 | 0 | 0 | 2 | .250 | .250 | .250 |
| Runners On | 29 | 12 | 1 | 0 | 0 | 6 | 0 | 5 | .414 | .448 | .414 |
| Runners/Scor. Pos. | 16 | 8 | 0 | 0 | 0 | 5 | 0 | 3 | .500 | .500 | .500 |

| RUNS BATTED IN | From 1B | From 2B | From 3B | Scoring Position |
|---|---|---|---|---|
| Totals | 6/88 | 3/56 | 16/35 | 19/91 |
| Percentage | 7% | 5% | 46% | 21% |
| Driving In Runners from 3B with Less than Two Out: | | | 12/16 | 75% |

Loves to face: Oil Can Boyd (.545, 6-for-11, 1 HR)
Hates to face: Fernando Valenzuela (.119, 7-for-59, 1 HR, 12 SO)
The Dennis Rodman of baseball hit .257 in 74 starts, but .435 (20-for-46) in 47 games off the bench, with a 6-for-15 pinch-hitting mark. . . . Drove in runners from third base with less than two outs in 10 straight opportunities last year, two shy of majors' longest streak of year. . . . Hit .325 in 26 games with Cubs, after batting .268 in 95 games with San Diego. . . . Played every nonbattery position except second base last year. . . . Owns .353 career batting average in Late-Inning Pressure Situations with runners in scoring position. . . . Had three tours of duty with Padres during 1980s, moving from Padres to White Sox to Padres to Tigers to Padres to Cubs. In the old days, a padre could be excommunicated for less.

## Juan Samuel

Bats Right

| Phillies/Mets | AB | H | 2B | 3B | HR | RBI | BB | SO | BA | SA | OBA |
|---|---|---|---|---|---|---|---|---|---|---|---|
| Season | 532 | 125 | 16 | 2 | 11 | 50 | 42 | 120 | .235 | .335 | .303 |
| vs. Left-Handers | 190 | 49 | 4 | 1 | 6 | 23 | 21 | 38 | .258 | .384 | .340 |
| vs. Right-Handers | 342 | 76 | 12 | 1 | 5 | 27 | 21 | 82 | .222 | .307 | .282 |
| Home | 269 | 62 | 7 | 1 | 5 | 27 | 21 | 55 | .230 | .320 | .296 |
| Road | 263 | 63 | 9 | 1 | 6 | 23 | 21 | 65 | .240 | .350 | .311 |
| Grass | 276 | 61 | 7 | 0 | 3 | 21 | 21 | 60 | .221 | .279 | .282 |
| Artificial Turf | 256 | 64 | 9 | 2 | 8 | 29 | 21 | 60 | .250 | .395 | .325 |
| April | 43 | 10 | 1 | 0 | 1 | 2 | 2 | 4 | .233 | .326 | .267 |
| May | 98 | 20 | 2 | 0 | 4 | 8 | 8 | 23 | .204 | .347 | .269 |
| June | 84 | 25 | 0 | 2 | 3 | 13 | 13 | 24 | .298 | .452 | .392 |
| July | 101 | 25 | 4 | 0 | 1 | 8 | 4 | 17 | .248 | .317 | .290 |
| August | 110 | 26 | 5 | 0 | 2 | 10 | 8 | 25 | .236 | .336 | .306 |
| Sept./Oct. | 96 | 19 | 4 | 0 | 0 | 9 | 7 | 27 | .198 | .240 | .284 |
| Leading Off Inn. | 152 | 41 | 8 | 1 | 6 | 6 | 12 | 33 | .270 | .454 | .327 |
| Runners On | 217 | 52 | 6 | 1 | 3 | 42 | 12 | 48 | .240 | .318 | .298 |
| Runners/Scor. Pos. | 133 | 29 | 1 | 1 | 1 | 37 | 6 | 34 | .218 | .263 | .269 |
| Runners On/2 Out | 98 | 24 | 2 | 1 | 2 | 20 | 7 | 24 | .245 | .347 | .321 |
| Scor. Pos./2 Out | 72 | 18 | 1 | 1 | 1 | 18 | 4 | 18 | .250 | .333 | .299 |
| Late Inning Pressure | 64 | 17 | 2 | 1 | 0 | 5 | 6 | 17 | .266 | .328 | .338 |
| Leading Off | 14 | 3 | 0 | 0 | 0 | 0 | 1 | 5 | .214 | .214 | .267 |
| Runners On | 31 | 11 | 1 | 1 | 0 | 5 | 3 | 7 | .355 | .452 | .429 |
| Runners/Scor. Pos. | 16 | 6 | 1 | 1 | 0 | 5 | 1 | 4 | .375 | .563 | .444 |

| RUNS BATTED IN | From 1B | From 2B | From 3B | Scoring Position |
|---|---|---|---|---|
| Totals | 3/134 | 10/106 | 26/56 | 36/162 |
| Percentage | 2% | 9% | 46% | 22% |
| Driving In Runners from 3B with Less than Two Out: | | | 17/26 | 65% |

Loves to face: Randy Myers (.625, 5-for-8, 3 XBH)
Hates to face: Craig Lefferts (.063, 1-for-16)
Batted .246 in 51 games with Phillies, .228 in 86 games with Mets. . . . Two disappointing years at-bat stem from trouble with right-handed pitchers. Yearly averages vs. lefties have been consistent, but average and home run output vs. right-handers have fallen since 1987: .281 (19 HR), .243 (10 HR), .222 (5 HR). . . . Had batted over .300 with runners in scoring position in each of two previous seasons. . . . One of four players with 30+ steals in each of last six years; others: Henderson, Raines, Butler. . . . Are there auditions for "Mr. October"? Sammy has hit .397 (25-for-63) in the scattering of *regular-season* games played in that month, but has just one postseason at-bat in his career (1983 Phils).

## Ryne Sandberg

Bats Right

| Chicago Cubs | AB | H | 2B | 3B | HR | RBI | BB | SO | BA | SA | OBA |
|---|---|---|---|---|---|---|---|---|---|---|---|
| Season | 606 | 176 | 25 | 5 | 30 | 76 | 59 | 85 | .290 | .497 | .356 |
| vs. Left-Handers | 172 | 54 | 10 | 2 | 7 | 20 | 30 | 15 | .314 | .517 | .414 |
| vs. Right-Handers | 434 | 122 | 15 | 3 | 23 | 56 | 29 | 70 | .281 | .488 | .331 |
| Home | 303 | 90 | 9 | 3 | 16 | 50 | 23 | 41 | .297 | .505 | .351 |
| Road | 303 | 86 | 16 | 2 | 14 | 26 | 36 | 44 | .284 | .488 | .362 |
| Grass | 431 | 125 | 14 | 3 | 21 | 59 | 32 | 60 | .290 | .483 | .343 |
| Artificial Turf | 175 | 51 | 11 | 2 | 9 | 17 | 27 | 25 | .291 | .531 | .387 |
| April | 92 | 25 | 3 | 0 | 2 | 12 | 6 | 14 | .272 | .370 | .313 |
| May | 97 | 31 | 3 | 1 | 2 | 5 | 7 | 9 | .320 | .433 | .377 |
| June | 91 | 19 | 4 | 1 | 6 | 16 | 11 | 13 | .209 | .473 | .308 |
| July | 110 | 29 | 4 | 1 | 5 | 10 | 7 | 17 | .264 | .455 | .305 |
| August | 111 | 37 | 6 | 1 | 11 | 21 | 17 | 18 | .333 | .703 | .422 |
| Sept./Oct. | 105 | 35 | 5 | 1 | 4 | 12 | 11 | 14 | .333 | .514 | .397 |
| Leading Off Inn. | 124 | 33 | 4 | 1 | 8 | 8 | 6 | 16 | .266 | .508 | .300 |
| Runners On | 244 | 64 | 9 | 3 | 8 | 54 | 32 | 33 | .262 | .422 | .350 |
| Runners/Scor. Pos. | 130 | 29 | 6 | 2 | 0 | 36 | 21 | 21 | .223 | .300 | .331 |
| Runners On/2 Out | 73 | 19 | 5 | 1 | 2 | 17 | 11 | 9 | .260 | .438 | .357 |
| Scor. Pos./2 Out | 48 | 10 | 3 | 1 | 0 | 12 | 9 | 8 | .208 | .313 | .333 |
| Late Inning Pressure | 84 | 23 | 3 | 0 | 2 | 7 | 5 | 18 | .274 | .381 | .315 |
| Leading Off | 23 | 7 | 1 | 0 | 1 | 1 | 1 | 4 | .304 | .478 | .333 |
| Runners On | 33 | 7 | 0 | 0 | 0 | 5 | 2 | 8 | .212 | .212 | .257 |
| Runners/Scor. Pos. | 21 | 5 | 0 | 0 | 0 | 5 | 2 | 5 | .238 | .238 | .304 |

| RUNS BATTED IN | From 1B | From 2B | From 3B | Scoring Position |
|---|---|---|---|---|
| Totals | 12/163 | 14/94 | 20/53 | 34/147 |
| Percentage | 7% | 15% | 38% | 23% |
| Driving In Runners from 3B with Less than Two Out: | | | 15/32 | 47% |

Loves to face: Bob Ojeda (.478, 11-for-23, 3 HR)
Hates to face: Larry Andersen (.100, 3-for-30, 8 SO)
Tied Will Clark and Howard Johnson for lead in runs scored (104), lowest total to lead N.L. in a full season since 1968. . . . Hit eight first-inning homers last season; Galarraga led majors with nine. . . . Had 0-for-25 streak in Late-Inning Pressure Situations, May 31 to July 26, 2d-longest streak in majors last year. At one point during that span, his overall batting average was .165 over a 29-game period. . . . Has 1394 hits in eight years with Cubs, most in N.L. over that time. . . . Ended regular season with 90-game errorless streak at second base (including token appearances in last four games), a one-season major league mark. Needs two more errorless games to top Joe Morgan's *all-time* record of 91 games.

## Benito Santiago

Bats Right

| San Diego Padres | AB | H | 2B | 3B | HR | RBI | BB | SO | BA | SA | OBA |
|---|---|---|---|---|---|---|---|---|---|---|---|
| Season | 462 | 109 | 16 | 3 | 16 | 63 | 26 | 89 | .236 | .387 | .277 |
| vs. Left-Handers | 117 | 26 | 3 | 1 | 2 | 12 | 11 | 23 | .222 | .316 | .289 |
| vs. Right-Handers | 345 | 83 | 13 | 2 | 14 | 51 | 15 | 66 | .241 | .412 | .273 |
| Home | 212 | 56 | 8 | 2 | 8 | 31 | 12 | 43 | .264 | .434 | .302 |
| Road | 250 | 53 | 8 | 1 | 8 | 32 | 14 | 46 | .212 | .348 | .256 |
| Grass | 334 | 81 | 11 | 2 | 13 | 48 | 23 | 72 | .243 | .404 | .290 |
| Artificial Turf | 128 | 28 | 5 | 1 | 3 | 15 | 3 | 17 | .219 | .344 | .242 |
| April | 82 | 17 | 3 | 0 | 3 | 12 | 4 | 12 | .207 | .354 | .244 |
| May | 80 | 21 | 4 | 1 | 0 | 12 | 2 | 14 | .263 | .338 | .280 |
| June | 77 | 21 | 2 | 1 | 2 | 7 | 2 | 16 | .273 | .403 | .291 |
| July | 56 | 14 | 1 | 1 | 1 | 9 | 5 | 13 | .250 | .357 | .323 |
| August | 78 | 17 | 4 | 0 | 3 | 7 | 8 | 13 | .218 | .385 | .287 |
| Sept./Oct. | 89 | 19 | 2 | 0 | 7 | 16 | 5 | 21 | .213 | .472 | .253 |
| Leading Off Inn. | 98 | 24 | 5 | 0 | 4 | 4 | 8 | 20 | .245 | .418 | .302 |
| Runners On | 222 | 51 | 5 | 2 | 8 | 55 | 12 | 43 | .230 | .378 | .270 |
| Runners/Scor. Pos. | 142 | 34 | 3 | 2 | 5 | 48 | 11 | 31 | .239 | .394 | .295 |
| Runners On/2 Out | 101 | 25 | 2 | 1 | 3 | 26 | 4 | 23 | .248 | .376 | .283 |
| Scor. Pos./2 Out | 76 | 19 | 1 | 1 | 3 | 25 | 4 | 19 | .250 | .408 | .296 |
| Late Inning Pressure | 66 | 20 | 3 | 0 | 1 | 11 | 3 | 12 | .303 | .394 | .329 |
| Leading Off | 19 | 4 | 2 | 0 | 0 | 0 | 0 | 6 | .211 | .316 | .211 |
| Runners On | 32 | 11 | 1 | 0 | 1 | 11 | 3 | 6 | .344 | .469 | .389 |
| Runners/Scor. Pos. | 24 | 9 | 1 | 0 | 0 | 9 | 3 | 6 | .375 | .417 | .429 |

| RUNS BATTED IN | From 1B | From 2B | From 3B | Scoring Position |
|---|---|---|---|---|
| Totals | 8/158 | 21/107 | 18/56 | 39/163 |
| Percentage | 5% | 20% | 32% | 24% |
| Driving In Runners from 3B with Less than Two Out: | | | 11/22 | 50% |

Loves to face: Scott Garrelts (.389, 7-for-18, 1 HR)
Hates to face: Jim Clancy (0-for-13)
First catcher in history to lead majors in errors three years in a row, but repeated as Gold Glove winner anyway. The '80s cliche that the toughest achievement in sports is for a champion to repeat doesn't apply to Gold Glove Awards, where 63 percent of winners in '80s were repeaters (repeater rate was 62 percent in '70s and 62 percent in '60s). . . . Hit 10 home runs in his last 33 games. . . . Has only three hits in 22 at-bats with the bases loaded over the last two seasons, but two of those three hits were grand slams. . . . Career breakdown: .306 in Late-Inning Pressure Situations, .256 in other at-bats. That 50-point difference is largest among N.L. players over last 10 years (minimum: 250 AB in LIPS).

## Nelson Santovenia

Bats Right

| Montreal Expos | AB | H | 2B | 3B | HR | RBI | BB | SO | BA | SA | OBA |
|---|---|---|---|---|---|---|---|---|---|---|---|
| Season | 304 | 76 | 14 | 1 | 5 | 31 | 24 | 37 | .250 | .352 | .307 |
| vs. Left-Handers | 99 | 28 | 5 | 0 | 2 | 9 | 8 | 7 | .283 | .394 | .343 |
| vs. Right-Handers | 205 | 48 | 9 | 1 | 3 | 22 | 16 | 30 | .234 | .332 | .291 |
| Home | 142 | 42 | 7 | 0 | 4 | 18 | 13 | 19 | .296 | .430 | .350 |
| Road | 162 | 34 | 7 | 1 | 1 | 13 | 11 | 18 | .210 | .284 | .269 |
| Grass | 69 | 15 | 2 | 0 | 0 | 2 | 3 | 12 | .217 | .246 | .250 |
| Artificial Turf | 235 | 61 | 12 | 1 | 5 | 29 | 21 | 25 | .260 | .383 | .323 |
| April | 61 | 16 | 3 | 0 | 2 | 8 | 8 | 6 | .262 | .410 | .361 |
| May | 27 | 9 | 1 | 0 | 0 | 1 | 4 | 6 | .333 | .370 | .438 |
| June | 40 | 9 | 4 | 0 | 0 | 1 | 1 | 11 | .225 | .325 | .244 |
| July | 59 | 17 | 3 | 1 | 3 | 11 | 4 | 3 | .288 | .525 | .333 |
| August | 54 | 12 | 2 | 0 | 0 | 3 | 4 | 6 | .222 | .259 | .271 |
| Sept./Oct. | 63 | 13 | 1 | 0 | 0 | 7 | 3 | 5 | .206 | .222 | .235 |
| Leading Off Inn. | 68 | 10 | 2 | 0 | 2 | 2 | 6 | 13 | .147 | .265 | .227 |
| Runners On | 141 | 38 | 6 | 0 | 2 | 28 | 11 | 15 | .270 | .355 | .314 |
| Runners/Scor. Pos. | 79 | 19 | 3 | 0 | 0 | 22 | 9 | 10 | .241 | .278 | .304 |
| Runners On/2 Out | 61 | 17 | 3 | 0 | 1 | 13 | 5 | 10 | .279 | .377 | .333 |
| Scor. Pos./2 Out | 43 | 10 | 2 | 0 | 0 | 11 | 4 | 7 | .233 | .279 | .298 |
| Late Inning Pressure | 54 | 16 | 5 | 0 | 2 | 9 | 3 | 5 | .296 | .500 | .339 |
| Leading Off | 15 | 5 | 1 | 0 | 1 | 1 | 1 | 3 | .333 | .600 | .375 |
| Runners On | 23 | 6 | 1 | 0 | 1 | 8 | 1 | 2 | .261 | .435 | .280 |
| Runners/Scor. Pos. | 13 | 4 | 1 | 0 | 0 | 6 | 1 | 0 | .308 | .385 | .333 |

| RUNS BATTED IN | From 1B | From 2B | From 3B | Scoring Position |
|---|---|---|---|---|
| Totals | 5/101 | 7/67 | 14/29 | 21/96 |
| Percentage | 5% | 10% | 48% | 22% |
| Driving In Runners from 3B with Less than Two Out: | | | 8/11 | 73% |

Loves to face: Joe Magrane (.500, 6-for-12)
Hates to face: Jose DeLeon (.083, 1-for-12, 5 SO)
One of three N.L. players who hit over .300 vs. ground-ball pitchers but below .200 vs. fly-ball pitchers in 1989 (minimum: 100 at-bats vs. each); others: Mitch Webster and Alfredo Griffin. Memo to Buck: How about giving him his days off against the likes of Tim Belcher, John Smoltz, David Cone, etc., especially since his career batting average vs. *all* right-handed pitchers is only .228? . . . Career average of .279 with runners on base, .213 with bases empty. . . . Averaged one strikeout every 9.1 plate appearances last season, more than halving his 1988 rate of one every 4.4 times up. . . . Expos' opponents were successful in 65 percent of their attempts with Santovenia catching, 75 percent with others catching.

## Mike Scioscia

Bats Left

| Los Angeles Dodgers | AB | H | 2B | 3B | HR | RBI | BB | SO | BA | SA | OBA |
|---|---|---|---|---|---|---|---|---|---|---|---|
| Season | 408 | 102 | 16 | 0 | 10 | 44 | 52 | 29 | .250 | .363 | .338 |
| vs. Left-Handers | 100 | 23 | 1 | 0 | 3 | 8 | 10 | 9 | .230 | .330 | .300 |
| vs. Right-Handers | 308 | 79 | 15 | 0 | 7 | 36 | 42 | 20 | .256 | .373 | .350 |
| Home | 200 | 47 | 8 | 0 | 4 | 21 | 25 | 15 | .235 | .335 | .329 |
| Road | 208 | 55 | 8 | 0 | 6 | 23 | 27 | 14 | .264 | .389 | .347 |
| Grass | 292 | 69 | 12 | 0 | 5 | 25 | 36 | 25 | .236 | .329 | .325 |
| Artificial Turf | 116 | 33 | 4 | 0 | 5 | 19 | 16 | 4 | .284 | .448 | .371 |
| April | 68 | 18 | 7 | 0 | 0 | 5 | 7 | 4 | .265 | .368 | .342 |
| May | 73 | 19 | 1 | 0 | 2 | 7 | 9 | 7 | .260 | .356 | .349 |
| June | 80 | 17 | 1 | 0 | 1 | 7 | 11 | 6 | .213 | .263 | .308 |
| July | 72 | 18 | 3 | 0 | 1 | 5 | 11 | 6 | .250 | .333 | .357 |
| August | 65 | 17 | 2 | 0 | 2 | 9 | 4 | 4 | .262 | .385 | .304 |
| Sept./Oct. | 50 | 13 | 2 | 0 | 4 | 11 | 10 | 2 | .260 | .540 | .377 |
| Leading Off Inn. | 109 | 29 | 8 | 0 | 2 | 2 | 17 | 10 | .266 | .394 | .370 |
| Runners On | 168 | 38 | 6 | 0 | 4 | 38 | 24 | 11 | .226 | .333 | .321 |
| Runners/Scor. Pos. | 98 | 20 | 2 | 0 | 3 | 32 | 21 | 8 | .204 | .316 | .342 |
| Runners On/2 Out | 81 | 18 | 3 | 0 | 1 | 13 | 12 | 7 | .222 | .296 | .323 |
| Scor. Pos./2 Out | 46 | 9 | 1 | 0 | 1 | 11 | 11 | 5 | .196 | .283 | .351 |
| Late Inning Pressure | 76 | 17 | 5 | 0 | 1 | 4 | 10 | 7 | .224 | .329 | .314 |
| Leading Off | 22 | 7 | 2 | 0 | 0 | 0 | 5 | 2 | .318 | .409 | .444 |
| Runners On | 27 | 5 | 2 | 0 | 0 | 3 | 5 | 3 | .185 | .259 | .313 |
| Runners/Scor. Pos. | 15 | 3 | 1 | 0 | 0 | 2 | 5 | 1 | .200 | .267 | .400 |

| RUNS BATTED IN | From 1B | From 2B | From 3B | Scoring Position |
|---|---|---|---|---|
| Totals | 8/127 | 10/78 | 16/46 | 26/124 |
| Percentage | 6% | 13% | 35% | 21% |
| Driving In Runners from 3B with Less than Two Out: | | | 12/24 | 50% |

Loves to face: Don Robinson (.344, 11-for-32, 2 HR)
Hates to face: Larry Andersen (0-for-12, 12 ground outs).
Fourth man to catch 1000 games in Dodger Blue: Roseboro (1218), Campanella (1183), Yeager (1181), Scioscia (1040). . . . Started 99 of 102 games in which Dodgers faced right-handed pitchers, but vs. lefties Rick Dempsey started 36 times, Scioscia 22. . . . Caught 73 percent of L.A.'s innings last year; Dempsey caught 26 percent. But staff ERA was lower with Dempsey (2.28 to 3.20), and opponents' stolen-base rate was also lower with Dempsey (.520 to .603). . . . One of five players with more walks than strikeouts in every year of the '80s; others: Brett, Greg Gross, Randolph, and Ozzie Smith. . . . Had two hits in 16 bases-loaded at-bats in '89, but those two were the only grand slams of his career.

## John Shelby

Bats Left and Right

| Los Angeles Dodgers | AB | H | 2B | 3B | HR | RBI | BB | SO | BA | SA | OBA |
|---|---|---|---|---|---|---|---|---|---|---|---|
| Season | 345 | 63 | 11 | 1 | 1 | 12 | 25 | 92 | .183 | .229 | .237 |
| vs. Left-Handers | 125 | 21 | 5 | 0 | 0 | 4 | 6 | 29 | .168 | .208 | .206 |
| vs. Right-Handers | 220 | 42 | 6 | 1 | 1 | 8 | 19 | 63 | .191 | .241 | .254 |
| Home | 186 | 34 | 4 | 1 | 0 | 5 | 9 | 52 | .183 | .215 | .221 |
| Road | 159 | 29 | 7 | 0 | 1 | 7 | 16 | 40 | .182 | .245 | .256 |
| Grass | 275 | 54 | 10 | 1 | 1 | 10 | 16 | 72 | .196 | .251 | .240 |
| Artificial Turf | 70 | 9 | 1 | 0 | 0 | 2 | 9 | 20 | .129 | .143 | .228 |
| April | 86 | 16 | 2 | 0 | 0 | 2 | 11 | 18 | .186 | .209 | .278 |
| May | 63 | 9 | 2 | 0 | 0 | 2 | 7 | 21 | .143 | .175 | .229 |
| June | 89 | 13 | 2 | 0 | 1 | 3 | 4 | 25 | .146 | .202 | .183 |
| July | 6 | 0 | 0 | 0 | 0 | 0 | 0 | 2 | .000 | .000 | .000 |
| August | 14 | 2 | 1 | 0 | 0 | 1 | 0 | 3 | .143 | .214 | .143 |
| Sept./Oct. | 87 | 23 | 4 | 1 | 0 | 4 | 3 | 23 | .264 | .333 | .286 |
| Leading Off Inn. | 81 | 16 | 3 | 0 | 0 | 0 | 3 | 22 | .198 | .235 | .226 |
| Runners On | 136 | 24 | 5 | 1 | 1 | 12 | 11 | 35 | .176 | .250 | .236 |
| Runners/Scor. Pos. | 63 | 11 | 2 | 1 | 0 | 10 | 8 | 18 | .175 | .238 | .264 |
| Runners On/2 Out | 64 | 10 | 1 | 1 | 0 | 4 | 6 | 17 | .156 | .203 | .229 |
| Scor. Pos./2 Out | 33 | 4 | 0 | 1 | 0 | 4 | 6 | 11 | .121 | .182 | .256 |
| Late Inning Pressure | 74 | 11 | 1 | 0 | 1 | 2 | 5 | 19 | .149 | .203 | .203 |
| Leading Off | 25 | 3 | 0 | 0 | 0 | 0 | 1 | 8 | .120 | .120 | .154 |
| Runners On | 24 | 6 | 1 | 0 | 1 | 2 | 1 | 5 | .250 | .417 | .280 |
| Runners/Scor. Pos. | 9 | 1 | 0 | 0 | 0 | 0 | 1 | 3 | .111 | .111 | .200 |

| RUNS BATTED IN | From 1B | From 2B | From 3B | Scoring Position |
|---|---|---|---|---|
| Totals | 1/108 | 5/54 | 5/25 | 10/79 |
| Percentage | 1% | 9% | 20% | 13% |
| Driving In Runners from 3B with Less than Two Out: | | | 4/10 | 40% |

Loves to face: Ron Robinson (.409, 9-for-22)
Hates to face: Mike Scott (.067, 2-for-30, 1 HR, 12 SO)
His .183 batting average was lowest by any Dodgers' player in a 300-at-bat season since Mickey Doolan hit .179 in 1918. . . . Slugging average was lowest in majors last year (minimum: 200 PA), as was road-game batting average (minimum: two PA per game). . . . It gets worse: His 13 percent rate of runners driven in from scoring position is worst one-year rate in N.L. over last 15 years (minimum: 75 opportunities). Drove in none of 12 men in scoring position in Late-Inning Pressure Situations. . . . Hitless in 27 consecutive at-bats vs. left-handed pitchers in May and June, longest streak in N.L. in '89 and longest on club over past 15 years. . . . Annual rate of at-bats per home run since 1987: 23.1, 49.4, 345.0.

## Dwight Smith

Bats Left

| Chicago Cubs | AB | H | 2B | 3B | HR | RBI | BB | SO | BA | SA | OBA |
|---|---|---|---|---|---|---|---|---|---|---|---|
| Season | 343 | 111 | 19 | 6 | 9 | 52 | 31 | 51 | .324 | .493 | .382 |
| vs. Left-Handers | 29 | 7 | 0 | 1 | 1 | 5 | 4 | 8 | .241 | .414 | .324 |
| vs. Right-Handers | 314 | 104 | 19 | 5 | 8 | 47 | 27 | 43 | .331 | .500 | .388 |
| Home | 157 | 57 | 9 | 2 | 5 | 28 | 15 | 17 | .363 | .541 | .423 |
| Road | 186 | 54 | 10 | 4 | 4 | 24 | 16 | 34 | .290 | .452 | .347 |
| Grass | 226 | 80 | 13 | 3 | 6 | 30 | 18 | 26 | .354 | .518 | .405 |
| Artificial Turf | 117 | 31 | 6 | 3 | 3 | 22 | 13 | 25 | .265 | .444 | .338 |
| April | 0 | 0 | 0 | 0 | 0 | 0 | 0 | 0 | — | — | — |
| May | 55 | 18 | 4 | 2 | 0 | 8 | 3 | 8 | .327 | .473 | .362 |
| June | 87 | 29 | 6 | 1 | 2 | 13 | 12 | 11 | .333 | .494 | .420 |
| July | 58 | 21 | 9 | 0 | 3 | 11 | 5 | 7 | .362 | .672 | .422 |
| August | 77 | 14 | 0 | 0 | 3 | 12 | 1 | 18 | .182 | .299 | .190 |
| Sept./Oct. | 66 | 29 | 0 | 3 | 1 | 8 | 10 | 7 | .439 | .576 | .513 |
| Leading Off Inn. | 58 | 19 | 4 | 0 | 0 | 0 | 7 | 7 | .328 | .397 | .400 |
| Runners On | 162 | 52 | 10 | 2 | 5 | 48 | 10 | 26 | .321 | .500 | .366 |
| Runners/Scor. Pos. | 91 | 27 | 5 | 1 | 2 | 39 | 8 | 18 | .297 | .440 | .356 |
| Runners On/2 Out | 54 | 22 | 5 | 1 | 2 | 20 | 3 | 9 | .407 | .648 | .439 |
| Scor. Pos./2 Out | 33 | 13 | 3 | 1 | 1 | 17 | 3 | 7 | .394 | .636 | .444 |
| Late Inning Pressure | 48 | 10 | 2 | 1 | 1 | 6 | 1 | 8 | .208 | .354 | .220 |
| Leading Off | 10 | 1 | 0 | 0 | 0 | 0 | 0 | 2 | .100 | .100 | .100 |
| Runners On | 21 | 6 | 1 | 0 | 1 | 6 | 0 | 4 | .286 | .476 | .273 |
| Runners/Scor. Pos. | 13 | 3 | 1 | 0 | 0 | 4 | 0 | 2 | .231 | .308 | .214 |

| RUNS BATTED IN | From 1B | From 2B | From 3B | Scoring Position |
|---|---|---|---|---|
| Totals | 10/110 | 13/64 | 20/38 | 33/102 |
| Percentage | 9% | 20% | 53% | 32% |
| Driving In Runners from 3B with Less than Two Out: | | | 12/21 | 57% |

Loves to face: Walt Terrell (.600, 6-for-10, 1 HR)
Hates to face: Scott Garrelts (.100, 1-for-10)
Led major league rookies in batting, slugging, and on-base averages (minimum: 350 PA), but wasn't even Rookie of the Year in his own clubhouse. . . . Out-hit Walton .348 to .263 after Aug. 10. . . . Had top batting average in majors (.364) vs. ground-ball pitchers (minimum: 60 hits); batted .269 vs. fly-ballers. . . . Batted .533 (8-for-15) as a pinch hitter, best in majors in 1989 among players with 15+ pinch hit at-bats, and 12th on all-time list (same minimum). All-time leaders: Pedro Guerrero (11-for-17 in 1980); Ken Griffey (11-for-18 in 1987); Rich McKinney (11-for-19 in 1971); and Bruce Boisclair (12-for-21 in 1976). . . . One of three players to "hit for the cycle" as a pinch hitter last season.

## Lonnie Smith

Bats Right

| Atlanta Braves | AB | H | 2B | 3B | HR | RBI | BB | SO | BA | SA | OBA |
|---|---|---|---|---|---|---|---|---|---|---|---|
| Season | 482 | 152 | 34 | 4 | 21 | 79 | 76 | 95 | .315 | .533 | .415 |
| vs. Left-Handers | 165 | 53 | 13 | 3 | 7 | 28 | 29 | 29 | .321 | .564 | .429 |
| vs. Right-Handers | 317 | 99 | 21 | 1 | 14 | 51 | 47 | 66 | .312 | .517 | .408 |
| Home | 226 | 81 | 18 | 3 | 10 | 46 | 35 | 43 | .358 | .597 | .442 |
| Road | 256 | 71 | 16 | 1 | 11 | 33 | 41 | 52 | .277 | .477 | .392 |
| Grass | 355 | 114 | 23 | 3 | 18 | 61 | 57 | 67 | .321 | .555 | .418 |
| Artificial Turf | 127 | 38 | 11 | 1 | 3 | 18 | 19 | 28 | .299 | .472 | .405 |
| April | 92 | 30 | 5 | 1 | 3 | 10 | 18 | 18 | .326 | .500 | .451 |
| May | 53 | 17 | 6 | 1 | 3 | 8 | 13 | 7 | .321 | .642 | .463 |
| June | 58 | 19 | 3 | 1 | 4 | 10 | 4 | 6 | .328 | .621 | .388 |
| July | 96 | 33 | 4 | 1 | 6 | 19 | 18 | 20 | .344 | .594 | .448 |
| August | 105 | 32 | 12 | 0 | 3 | 17 | 12 | 19 | .305 | .505 | .378 |
| Sept./Oct. | 78 | 21 | 4 | 0 | 2 | 15 | 11 | 25 | .269 | .397 | .362 |
| Leading Off Inn. | 115 | 26 | 2 | 1 | 6 | 6 | 15 | 29 | .226 | .417 | .326 |
| Runners On | 189 | 77 | 20 | 2 | 6 | 64 | 33 | 25 | .407 | .630 | .496 |
| Runners/Scor. Pos. | 99 | 41 | 7 | 1 | 4 | 54 | 18 | 18 | .414 | .626 | .500 |
| Runners On/2 Out | 70 | 30 | 7 | 1 | 2 | 25 | 14 | 10 | .429 | .643 | .545 |
| Scor. Pos./2 Out | 40 | 16 | 3 | 1 | 0 | 18 | 6 | 8 | .400 | .525 | .510 |
| Late Inning Pressure | 68 | 18 | 3 | 1 | 3 | 11 | 11 | 23 | .265 | .471 | .378 |
| Leading Off | 16 | 3 | 0 | 1 | 1 | 1 | 4 | 11 | .188 | .500 | .381 |
| Runners On | 26 | 11 | 1 | 0 | 1 | 9 | 4 | 5 | .423 | .577 | .500 |
| Runners/Scor. Pos. | 12 | 6 | 1 | 0 | 1 | 9 | 2 | 2 | .500 | .833 | .563 |

| RUNS BATTED IN | From 1B | From 2B | From 3B | Scoring Position |
|---|---|---|---|---|
| Totals | 8/135 | 29/77 | 21/42 | 50/119 |
| Percentage | 6% | 38% | 50% | 42% |
| Driving In Runners from 3B with Less than Two Out: | | | 15/27 | 56% |

Loves to face: Dennis Cook (.667, 6-for-9, 3 HR)
Hates to face: Jose Rijo (0-for-10, 5 SO)
Second-highest one-year batting average with runners on base over past 15 years (minimum: 75 hits). Highest: Carew's .422 in 1977. Batted 151 points higher with runners on base than with bases empty, largest difference in majors in '89 (minimum: 100 AB each way). . . . Average with runners in scoring position (.414) also led majors. . . . Had best home-game batting average in N.L.; top five players in that category all played home games on grass fields. Also stood second to Mitchell in home *slugging* average. . . . Had highest average by any visitor at three parks last season: the Vet (.524), the Big O (.429), and Candlestick (.406); his .574 on-base average vs. Expos was N.L. high by any player vs. any team.

## Ozzie Smith

Bats Left and Right

| St. Louis Cardinals | AB | H | 2B | 3B | HR | RBI | BB | SO | BA | SA | OBA |
|---|---|---|---|---|---|---|---|---|---|---|---|
| Season | 593 | 162 | 30 | 8 | 2 | 50 | 55 | 37 | .273 | .361 | .335 |
| vs. Left-Handers | 248 | 71 | 17 | 2 | 1 | 16 | 23 | 17 | .286 | .383 | .346 |
| vs. Right-Handers | 345 | 91 | 13 | 6 | 1 | 34 | 32 | 20 | .264 | .345 | .328 |
| Home | 297 | 75 | 10 | 5 | 1 | 29 | 30 | 21 | .253 | .330 | .323 |
| Road | 296 | 87 | 20 | 3 | 1 | 21 | 25 | 16 | .294 | .392 | .348 |
| Grass | 158 | 46 | 11 | 3 | 0 | 11 | 9 | 11 | .291 | .399 | .327 |
| Artificial Turf | 435 | 116 | 19 | 5 | 2 | 39 | 46 | 26 | .267 | .347 | .338 |
| April | 54 | 16 | 1 | 0 | 1 | 10 | 7 | 4 | .296 | .370 | .371 |
| May | 108 | 27 | 5 | 2 | 0 | 7 | 9 | 7 | .250 | .333 | .317 |
| June | 100 | 33 | 8 | 2 | 0 | 13 | 14 | 4 | .330 | .450 | .412 |
| July | 100 | 31 | 7 | 1 | 0 | 9 | 8 | 8 | .310 | .400 | .358 |
| August | 113 | 25 | 5 | 0 | 0 | 6 | 8 | 6 | .221 | .265 | .273 |
| Sept./Oct. | 118 | 30 | 4 | 3 | 1 | 5 | 9 | 8 | .254 | .364 | .307 |
| Leading Off Inn. | 98 | 18 | 5 | 2 | 0 | 0 | 12 | 8 | .184 | .276 | .279 |
| Runners On | 239 | 72 | 14 | 1 | 0 | 48 | 25 | 10 | .301 | .368 | .366 |
| Runners/Scor. Pos. | 144 | 42 | 8 | 0 | 0 | 43 | 20 | 7 | .292 | .347 | .375 |
| Runners On/2 Out | 90 | 27 | 5 | 0 | 0 | 19 | 9 | 5 | .300 | .356 | .364 |
| Scor. Pos./2 Out | 62 | 17 | 3 | 0 | 0 | 17 | 8 | 5 | .274 | .323 | .357 |
| Late Inning Pressure | 74 | 26 | 6 | 3 | 0 | 7 | 11 | 5 | .351 | .514 | .430 |
| Leading Off | 18 | 6 | 2 | 2 | 0 | 0 | 4 | 2 | .333 | .667 | .455 |
| Runners On | 31 | 13 | 2 | 0 | 0 | 7 | 5 | 1 | .419 | .484 | .486 |
| Runners/Scor. Pos. | 18 | 8 | 2 | 0 | 0 | 7 | 4 | 1 | .444 | .556 | .522 |

| RUNS BATTED IN | From 1B | From 2B | From 3B | Scoring Position |
|---|---|---|---|---|
| Totals | 5/148 | 16/98 | 27/66 | 43/164 |
| Percentage | 3% | 16% | 41% | 26% |
| Driving In Runners from 3B with Less than Two Out: | | | 17/33 | 52% |

Loves to face: Dan Schatzeder (.429, 12-for-28, 2 HR, 10 BB)
Hates to face: Walt Terrell (0-for-15, 0 BB)
Batting average with runners on base has been higher than with bases empty in each of last seven seasons. . . . Batted .263 in 105 starts from second spot in lineup, .293 in 53 starts from other spots. Could that be the result of taking pitches for Coleman? . . . Needs 308 games at shortstop to equal Marty Marion's team record. . . . His most amazing fielding number may not be a very familiar one: his career rate of 3.49 assists per nine innings stands 7th all-time among shortstops in 1000 or more games. But you have to go down to the 20th spot on that list to find the next guy (Luke Appling) who played a single inning of shortstop in postwar era. Rick Burleson is nearest contemporary player, with 3.24 average.

## Darryl Strawberry

Bats Left

| New York Mets | AB | H | 2B | 3B | HR | RBI | BB | SO | BA | SA | OBA |
|---|---|---|---|---|---|---|---|---|---|---|---|
| Season | 476 | 107 | 26 | 1 | 29 | 77 | 61 | 105 | .225 | .466 | .312 |
| vs. Left-Handers | 178 | 39 | 12 | 0 | 9 | 33 | 16 | 41 | .219 | .438 | .279 |
| vs. Right-Handers | 298 | 68 | 14 | 1 | 20 | 44 | 45 | 64 | .228 | .483 | .331 |
| Home | 224 | 61 | 15 | 1 | 15 | 41 | 29 | 51 | .272 | .549 | .355 |
| Road | 252 | 46 | 11 | 0 | 14 | 36 | 32 | 54 | .183 | .393 | .274 |
| Grass | 347 | 80 | 21 | 1 | 21 | 56 | 42 | 78 | .231 | .478 | .314 |
| Artificial Turf | 129 | 27 | 5 | 0 | 8 | 21 | 19 | 27 | .209 | .434 | .309 |
| April | 66 | 19 | 6 | 0 | 5 | 8 | 9 | 17 | .288 | .606 | .373 |
| May | 104 | 20 | 5 | 0 | 6 | 16 | 10 | 29 | .192 | .413 | .261 |
| June | 53 | 11 | 1 | 0 | 5 | 12 | 9 | 9 | .208 | .509 | .333 |
| July | 81 | 18 | 5 | 0 | 6 | 16 | 8 | 22 | .222 | .506 | .292 |
| August | 103 | 24 | 7 | 1 | 5 | 17 | 16 | 11 | .233 | .466 | .333 |
| Sept./Oct. | 69 | 15 | 2 | 0 | 2 | 8 | 9 | 17 | .217 | .333 | .304 |
| Leading Off Inn. | 111 | 26 | 4 | 0 | 6 | 6 | 8 | 23 | .234 | .432 | .286 |
| Runners On | 224 | 52 | 17 | 1 | 11 | 59 | 37 | 57 | .232 | .464 | .337 |
| Runners/Scor. Pos. | 147 | 33 | 11 | 1 | 6 | 45 | 26 | 40 | .224 | .435 | .335 |
| Runners On/2 Out | 111 | 18 | 5 | 0 | 5 | 20 | 24 | 32 | .162 | .342 | .311 |
| Scor. Pos./2 Out | 72 | 12 | 3 | 0 | 4 | 17 | 16 | 19 | .167 | .375 | .318 |
| Late Inning Pressure | 81 | 13 | 3 | 0 | 5 | 10 | 7 | 20 | .160 | .383 | .227 |
| Leading Off | 15 | 6 | 1 | 0 | 2 | 2 | 1 | 2 | .400 | .867 | .438 |
| Runners On | 30 | 2 | 1 | 0 | 1 | 6 | 5 | 8 | .067 | .200 | .200 |
| Runners/Scor. Pos. | 19 | 1 | 0 | 0 | 1 | 5 | 4 | 4 | .053 | .211 | .217 |

| RUNS BATTED IN | From 1B | From 2B | From 3B | Scoring Position |
|---|---|---|---|---|
| Totals | 11/139 | 18/104 | 19/66 | 37/170 |
| Percentage | 8% | 17% | 29% | 22% |
| Driving In Runners from 3B with Less than Two Out: | | | 13/30 | 43% |

Loves to face: Les Lancaster (.500, 7-for-14, 2 HR)
Hates to face: Calvin Schiraldi (0-for-13, 5 SO)
Hit 200th home run in 3079th at-bat. Nine got there quicker: Kiner (2537), Ruth (2580), Killebrew (2584), Mathews (2811), Colavito (2884), McCovey (2963), Kingman (2976), Mays (3043), Foxx (3049). . . . Had only five game-winning RBI, with only one coming after the 4th inning. . . . From Aug. 28 to Sept. 24, went 0-for-18 with runners in scoring position and score tied or Mets trailing. . . . A .178 career hitter (4 HR in 118 AB) in Late-Inning Pressure Situations with runners in scoring position, 10th-lowest average since 1975 (minimum: 100 such AB). . . . Led N.L. right fielders with 2.23 putouts per nine innings in '89, but remember: Mets' staff (lowest ground outs-to-air outs ratio in N.L.) induces fly balls.

## Garry Templeton

Bats Left and Right

| San Diego Padres | AB | H | 2B | 3B | HR | RBI | BB | SO | BA | SA | OBA |
|---|---|---|---|---|---|---|---|---|---|---|---|
| Season | 506 | 129 | 26 | 3 | 6 | 40 | 23 | 80 | .255 | .354 | .286 |
| vs. Left-Handers | 145 | 46 | 8 | 2 | 1 | 18 | 7 | 19 | .317 | .421 | .349 |
| vs. Right-Handers | 361 | 83 | 18 | 1 | 5 | 22 | 16 | 61 | .230 | .327 | .261 |
| Home | 255 | 66 | 15 | 1 | 5 | 20 | 12 | 42 | .259 | .384 | .292 |
| Road | 251 | 63 | 11 | 2 | 1 | 20 | 11 | 38 | .251 | .323 | .279 |
| Grass | 383 | 98 | 20 | 1 | 5 | 28 | 15 | 65 | .256 | .352 | .283 |
| Artificial Turf | 123 | 31 | 6 | 2 | 1 | 12 | 8 | 15 | .252 | .358 | .293 |
| April | 85 | 20 | 4 | 0 | 1 | 3 | 1 | 16 | .235 | .318 | .244 |
| May | 73 | 16 | 2 | 1 | 1 | 6 | 5 | 13 | .219 | .315 | .269 |
| June | 90 | 27 | 7 | 1 | 0 | 8 | 5 | 13 | .300 | .400 | .330 |
| July | 74 | 20 | 3 | 0 | 1 | 7 | 3 | 5 | .270 | .351 | .299 |
| August | 89 | 26 | 6 | 1 | 1 | 6 | 3 | 11 | .292 | .416 | .315 |
| Sept./Oct. | 95 | 20 | 4 | 0 | 2 | 10 | 6 | 22 | .211 | .316 | .255 |
| Leading Off Inn. | 134 | 38 | 6 | 1 | 1 | 1 | 2 | 22 | .284 | .366 | .294 |
| Runners On | 202 | 46 | 7 | 2 | 1 | 35 | 18 | 30 | .228 | .297 | .287 |
| Runners/Scor. Pos. | 107 | 23 | 5 | 1 | 1 | 32 | 16 | 17 | .215 | .308 | .310 |
| Runners On/2 Out | 69 | 13 | 3 | 1 | 0 | 8 | 14 | 16 | .188 | .261 | .325 |
| Scor. Pos./2 Out | 47 | 8 | 3 | 0 | 0 | 7 | 14 | 11 | .170 | .234 | .361 |
| Late Inning Pressure | 77 | 16 | 2 | 1 | 0 | 2 | 5 | 18 | .208 | .260 | .256 |
| Leading Off | 21 | 5 | 0 | 0 | 0 | 0 | 1 | 6 | .238 | .238 | .273 |
| Runners On | 29 | 5 | 0 | 1 | 0 | 2 | 4 | 6 | .172 | .241 | .273 |
| Runners/Scor. Pos. | 14 | 1 | 0 | 0 | 0 | 1 | 4 | 5 | .071 | .071 | .278 |

| RUNS BATTED IN | From 1B | From 2B | From 3B | Scoring Position |
|---|---|---|---|---|
| Totals | 5/146 | 14/82 | 15/47 | 29/129 |
| Percentage | 3% | 17% | 32% | 22% |
| Driving In Runners from 3B with Less than Two Out: | | | 14/28 | 50% |

Loves to face: Danny Darwin (.571, 8-for-14, 2 HR)
Hates to face: Dennis Martinez (.056, 1-for-18)
His 20 errors last season boosted career total to 352; among shortstops who played their entire careers in postwar era, only Dick Groat (374) made more errors. . . . Batting average vs. left-handers was his highest since 1980 (.321) with St. Louis. . . . Twelve of his 23 walks were intentional; perennial 8th-spot hitter has accumulated 134 IBB in his career (39 percent of his total walks). . . . Among players active at the end of 1989, only three have played more seasons than Templeton (14) without ever venturing into A.L.: Greg Gross (17 years), Gary Carter (16), and Cleveland-bound Keith Hernandez (16). Andre Dawson, Dale Murphy, and Joel Youngblood are even with Tempy at 14.

## Tim Teufel

Bats Right

| New York Mets | AB | H | 2B | 3B | HR | RBI | BB | SO | BA | SA | OBA |
|---|---|---|---|---|---|---|---|---|---|---|---|
| Season | 219 | 56 | 7 | 2 | 2 | 15 | 32 | 50 | .256 | .333 | .350 |
| vs. Left-Handers | 132 | 36 | 3 | 1 | 1 | 9 | 21 | 28 | .273 | .333 | .368 |
| vs. Right-Handers | 87 | 20 | 4 | 1 | 1 | 6 | 11 | 22 | .230 | .333 | .323 |
| Home | 107 | 23 | 1 | 0 | 1 | 7 | 16 | 20 | .215 | .252 | .320 |
| Road | 112 | 33 | 6 | 2 | 1 | 8 | 16 | 30 | .295 | .411 | .380 |
| Grass | 136 | 35 | 3 | 0 | 1 | 9 | 23 | 26 | .257 | .301 | .364 |
| Artificial Turf | 83 | 21 | 4 | 2 | 1 | 6 | 9 | 24 | .253 | .386 | .326 |
| April | 33 | 9 | 0 | 1 | 0 | 3 | 4 | 6 | .273 | .333 | .351 |
| May | 47 | 12 | 2 | 0 | 0 | 2 | 12 | 12 | .255 | .298 | .407 |
| June | 18 | 3 | 0 | 0 | 0 | 1 | 1 | 5 | .167 | .167 | .211 |
| July | 46 | 14 | 1 | 0 | 1 | 3 | 5 | 13 | .304 | .391 | .377 |
| August | 38 | 6 | 3 | 0 | 0 | 3 | 4 | 5 | .158 | .237 | .233 |
| Sept./Oct. | 37 | 12 | 1 | 1 | 1 | 3 | 6 | 9 | .324 | .486 | .419 |
| Leading Off Inn. | 46 | 11 | 0 | 0 | 2 | 2 | 5 | 9 | .239 | .370 | .314 |
| Runners On | 80 | 20 | 3 | 1 | 0 | 13 | 18 | 23 | .250 | .313 | .386 |
| Runners/Scor. Pos. | 54 | 12 | 1 | 0 | 0 | 11 | 12 | 17 | .222 | .241 | .353 |
| Runners On/2 Out | 28 | 5 | 1 | 0 | 0 | 2 | 8 | 10 | .179 | .214 | .378 |
| Scor. Pos./2 Out | 20 | 2 | 1 | 0 | 0 | 2 | 5 | 9 | .100 | .150 | .280 |
| Late Inning Pressure | 31 | 7 | 2 | 0 | 1 | 2 | 5 | 7 | .226 | .387 | .324 |
| Leading Off | 9 | 2 | 0 | 0 | 1 | 1 | 2 | 1 | .222 | .556 | .364 |
| Runners On | 13 | 2 | 1 | 0 | 0 | 1 | 1 | 4 | .154 | .231 | .200 |
| Runners/Scor. Pos. | 7 | 0 | 0 | 0 | 0 | 1 | 0 | 2 | .000 | .000 | .000 |

| RUNS BATTED IN | From 1B | From 2B | From 3B | Scoring Position |
|---|---|---|---|---|
| Totals | 2/44 | 4/42 | 7/23 | 11/65 |
| Percentage | 5% | 10% | 30% | 17% |
| Driving In Runners from 3B with Less than Two Out: | | | 5/12 | 42% |

Loves to face: Tom Browning (.519, 14-for-27, 3 HR)
Hates to face: any pitcher named Smith (.114, 5-for-44, 15 SO)
Every year, it seems Tuff might get more at-bats than the year before; but for each of four years with Mets, he has landed somewhere in 200s. Only two other players, Rick Cerone and Bob Melvin, have been there with him in every year since 1986. . . . Started 42 of 53 games in which Mets faced a left-handed starter, but only 16 of 109 games vs. right-handers. . . . Career batting: .268 vs. lefties, .260 vs. righties; career slugging: .408 vs. each type. . . . Has hit for higher average vs. fly-ball pitchers than vs. ground-ballers in each of last five seasons. . . . In four years in N.L., has hit .248 (8 HR) at Shea, .276 (16 HR) on road. . . . Has hit .175 with runners in scoring position over past two years.

## Andres Thomas

Bats Right

| Atlanta Braves | AB | H | 2B | 3B | HR | RBI | BB | SO | BA | SA | OBA |
|---|---|---|---|---|---|---|---|---|---|---|---|
| Season | 554 | 118 | 18 | 0 | 13 | 57 | 12 | 62 | .213 | .316 | .228 |
| vs. Left-Handers | 173 | 36 | 7 | 0 | 4 | 18 | 7 | 18 | .208 | .318 | .238 |
| vs. Right-Handers | 381 | 82 | 11 | 0 | 9 | 39 | 5 | 44 | .215 | .315 | .224 |
| Home | 251 | 49 | 8 | 0 | 5 | 26 | 6 | 24 | .195 | .287 | .212 |
| Road | 303 | 69 | 10 | 0 | 8 | 31 | 6 | 38 | .228 | .340 | .242 |
| Grass | 403 | 85 | 12 | 0 | 10 | 39 | 7 | 50 | .211 | .315 | .223 |
| Artificial Turf | 151 | 33 | 6 | 0 | 3 | 18 | 5 | 12 | .219 | .318 | .242 |
| April | 73 | 19 | 0 | 0 | 2 | 7 | 3 | 12 | .260 | .342 | .289 |
| May | 113 | 26 | 6 | 0 | 4 | 18 | 2 | 8 | .230 | .389 | .243 |
| June | 107 | 26 | 4 | 0 | 4 | 16 | 1 | 8 | .243 | .393 | .243 |
| July | 88 | 18 | 5 | 0 | 0 | 5 | 2 | 10 | .205 | .261 | .222 |
| August | 98 | 16 | 3 | 0 | 1 | 7 | 2 | 12 | .163 | .224 | .178 |
| Sept./Oct. | 75 | 13 | 0 | 0 | 2 | 4 | 2 | 12 | .173 | .253 | .195 |
| Leading Off Inn. | 116 | 25 | 7 | 0 | 1 | 1 | 4 | 12 | .216 | .302 | .242 |
| Runners On | 245 | 54 | 5 | 0 | 6 | 50 | 6 | 27 | .220 | .314 | .235 |
| Runners/Scor. Pos. | 134 | 31 | 5 | 0 | 1 | 40 | 5 | 13 | .231 | .291 | .252 |
| Runners On/2 Out | 122 | 27 | 2 | 0 | 1 | 22 | 4 | 12 | .221 | .262 | .246 |
| Scor. Pos./2 Out | 74 | 18 | 2 | 0 | 0 | 20 | 3 | 7 | .243 | .270 | .273 |
| Late Inning Pressure | 98 | 23 | 3 | 0 | 3 | 8 | 2 | 11 | .235 | .357 | .248 |
| Leading Off | 25 | 7 | 2 | 0 | 1 | 1 | 0 | 4 | .280 | .480 | .280 |
| Runners On | 39 | 10 | 0 | 0 | 2 | 7 | 1 | 5 | .256 | .410 | .268 |
| Runners/Scor. Pos. | 21 | 3 | 0 | 0 | 0 | 3 | 0 | 3 | .143 | .143 | .136 |

| RUNS BATTED IN | From 1B | From 2B | From 3B | Scoring Position |
|---|---|---|---|---|
| Totals | 7/184 | 17/106 | 20/52 | 37/158 |
| Percentage | 4% | 16% | 38% | 23% |
| Driving In Runners from 3B with Less than Two Out: | | | 10/24 | 42% |

Loves to face: John Franco (.467, 7-for-15, 1 HR)
Hates to face: Joe Magrane (.067, 1-for-15)
Toughest N.L. batter to walk last season: one walk every 47.6 plate appearances. Three of his 12 walks were intentional. . . . Only player in majors with 350+ plate appearances and more home runs than walks. . . . September batting average (.173) was lowest in N.L. (minimum: two PA per game). His career batting average from August 1 to end of season is .199. . . . His 29 errors were 2d most among major league shortstops (Ramirez had 30), with 22 coming in 65 home games, and only seven in 76 games on road. Most errors in home games last season: Thomas (22), Bonilla (19), Guillen (16), HoJo (15). Is that a lousy infield or an unforgiving official scorer?

## Milt Thompson

Bats Left

| St. Louis Cardinals | AB | H | 2B | 3B | HR | RBI | BB | SO | BA | SA | OBA |
|---|---|---|---|---|---|---|---|---|---|---|---|
| Season | 545 | 158 | 28 | 8 | 4 | 68 | 39 | 91 | .290 | .393 | .340 |
| vs. Left-Handers | 210 | 56 | 15 | 3 | 1 | 28 | 9 | 52 | .267 | .381 | .297 |
| vs. Right-Handers | 335 | 102 | 13 | 5 | 3 | 40 | 30 | 39 | .304 | .400 | .366 |
| Home | 271 | 82 | 17 | 6 | 2 | 39 | 14 | 36 | .303 | .432 | .336 |
| Road | 274 | 76 | 11 | 2 | 2 | 29 | 25 | 55 | .277 | .354 | .344 |
| Grass | 141 | 40 | 6 | 2 | 1 | 12 | 14 | 26 | .284 | .376 | .357 |
| Artificial Turf | 404 | 118 | 22 | 6 | 3 | 56 | 25 | 65 | .292 | .399 | .334 |
| April | 75 | 25 | 6 | 1 | 0 | 5 | 6 | 11 | .333 | .440 | .383 |
| May | 48 | 12 | 2 | 1 | 1 | 8 | 10 | 4 | .250 | .396 | .379 |
| June | 98 | 28 | 5 | 1 | 1 | 15 | 10 | 19 | .286 | .388 | .349 |
| July | 99 | 25 | 3 | 2 | 0 | 9 | 3 | 19 | .253 | .323 | .282 |
| August | 113 | 34 | 3 | 2 | 2 | 16 | 8 | 19 | .301 | .416 | .352 |
| Sept./Oct. | 112 | 34 | 9 | 1 | 0 | 15 | 2 | 19 | .304 | .402 | .322 |
| Leading Off Inn. | 112 | 24 | 2 | 2 | 0 | 0 | 9 | 22 | .214 | .268 | .273 |
| Runners On | 249 | 84 | 15 | 4 | 3 | 67 | 20 | 41 | .337 | .466 | .391 |
| Runners/Scor. Pos. | 151 | 48 | 8 | 3 | 3 | 64 | 16 | 28 | .318 | .470 | .384 |
| Runners On/2 Out | 96 | 35 | 5 | 1 | 0 | 26 | 9 | 17 | .365 | .438 | .425 |
| Scor. Pos./2 Out | 63 | 23 | 3 | 1 | 0 | 25 | 6 | 11 | .365 | .444 | .429 |
| Late Inning Pressure | 77 | 22 | 4 | 1 | 0 | 8 | 6 | 18 | .286 | .364 | .329 |
| Leading Off | 19 | 5 | 1 | 0 | 0 | 0 | 1 | 4 | .263 | .316 | .300 |
| Runners On | 38 | 11 | 2 | 0 | 0 | 8 | 3 | 9 | .289 | .342 | .326 |
| Runners/Scor. Pos. | 25 | 8 | 2 | 0 | 0 | 8 | 3 | 8 | .320 | .400 | .367 |

| RUNS BATTED IN | From 1B | From 2B | From 3B | Scoring Position |
|---|---|---|---|---|
| Totals | 7/168 | 27/120 | 30/59 | 57/179 |
| Percentage | 4% | 23% | 51% | 32% |
| Driving In Runners from 3B with Less than Two Out: | | | 20/35 | 57% |

Loves to face: David Cone (.571, 12-for-21, 1 HR)
Hates to face: Pete Smith (0-for-12)
Career ratio of 2.48 ground outs to every out made in air is highest by any player in majors over last 15 years. Ran contrary to usual tendencies of ground-ball hitters last season, batting .333 vs. ground-ball pitchers, .248 vs. fly-ballers. . . . His .331 career average with two outs and runners on base is second to Boggs (.332) among active players (minimum: 75 hits). . . . His .325 career average in Late-Inning Pressure Situations ranks third among active N.L. players, behind Gwynn (.344) and Raines (.343) (minimum: 50 hits). . . . No steals in three attempts vs. Giants last season, 27-for-32 vs. other N.L. teams. . . . Had more plate appearances vs. left-handed pitchers last year than in five previous seasons combined.

## Rob Thompson

Bats Right

| San Francisco Giants | AB | H | 2B | 3B | HR | RBI | BB | SO | BA | SA | OBA |
|---|---|---|---|---|---|---|---|---|---|---|---|
| Season | 547 | 132 | 26 | 11 | 13 | 50 | 51 | 133 | .241 | .400 | .321 |
| vs. Left-Handers | 194 | 59 | 12 | 6 | 5 | 17 | 20 | 35 | .304 | .505 | .378 |
| vs. Right-Handers | 353 | 73 | 14 | 5 | 8 | 33 | 31 | 98 | .207 | .343 | .289 |
| Home | 286 | 76 | 17 | 5 | 7 | 29 | 23 | 64 | .266 | .434 | .333 |
| Road | 261 | 56 | 9 | 6 | 6 | 21 | 28 | 69 | .215 | .364 | .307 |
| Grass | 414 | 109 | 23 | 9 | 11 | 43 | 35 | 96 | .263 | .442 | .333 |
| Artificial Turf | 133 | 23 | 3 | 2 | 2 | 7 | 16 | 37 | .173 | .271 | .286 |
| April | 91 | 22 | 4 | 1 | 1 | 4 | 10 | 21 | .242 | .341 | .317 |
| May | 87 | 27 | 6 | 3 | 4 | 11 | 9 | 18 | .310 | .586 | .381 |
| June | 106 | 29 | 6 | 4 | 4 | 12 | 13 | 24 | .274 | .519 | .364 |
| July | 89 | 16 | 5 | 1 | 2 | 8 | 5 | 20 | .180 | .326 | .277 |
| August | 82 | 20 | 1 | 1 | 0 | 4 | 8 | 21 | .244 | .280 | .326 |
| Sept./Oct. | 92 | 18 | 4 | 1 | 2 | 11 | 6 | 29 | .196 | .326 | .253 |
| Leading Off Inn. | 96 | 27 | 6 | 1 | 2 | 2 | 9 | 23 | .281 | .427 | .343 |
| Runners On | 223 | 57 | 12 | 5 | 6 | 43 | 19 | 52 | .256 | .435 | .336 |
| Runners/Scor. Pos. | 127 | 22 | 6 | 1 | 4 | 31 | 12 | 40 | .173 | .331 | .271 |
| Runners On/2 Out | 91 | 17 | 5 | 2 | 3 | 20 | 8 | 29 | .187 | .385 | .267 |
| Scor. Pos./2 Out | 69 | 11 | 3 | 0 | 3 | 16 | 6 | 26 | .159 | .333 | .247 |
| Late Inning Pressure | 71 | 18 | 2 | 1 | 3 | 9 | 8 | 25 | .254 | .437 | .329 |
| Leading Off | 15 | 3 | 0 | 0 | 0 | 0 | 2 | 5 | .200 | .200 | .294 |
| Runners On | 34 | 10 | 2 | 1 | 2 | 8 | 2 | 16 | .294 | .588 | .333 |
| Runners/Scor. Pos. | 22 | 5 | 2 | 0 | 2 | 7 | 1 | 12 | .227 | .591 | .261 |

| RUNS BATTED IN | From 1B | From 2B | From 3B | Scoring Position |
|---|---|---|---|---|
| Totals | 13/144 | 14/104 | 10/40 | 24/144 |
| Percentage | 9% | 13% | 25% | 17% |
| Driving In Runners from 3B with Less than Two Out: | | | 7/16 | 44% |

Loves to face: Paul Assenmacher (.857, 6-for-7, 2 2B)
Hates to face: Mike Scott (.108, 4-for-37, 16 SO)
Only N.L. player last year, and first Giants player since Maddox and Matthews in 1973, with 10+ doubles, triples, homers, and steals. . . . Batted .320 with Giants trailing by a run; was 6-for-17 in those situations with runners in scoring position. But he has hit below .190 with runners on base and two outs in each of past two years. . . . Has batted over .300 vs. left-handed pitchers in each of last three years. Career: .305 vs. lefties, .237 vs. righties. . . . Started 133 games from 2d spot in lineup, most in majors. . . . Scored from second base 12 times on 12 outfield singles. . . . Stolen-base rate has improved each year in majors: .444 (12-of-27) in '86, then .593 (16-of-27), .737 (14-of-19), .857 (12-of-14).

## Dickie Thon

Bats Right

| Philadelphia Phillies | AB | H | 2B | 3B | HR | RBI | BB | SO | BA | SA | OBA |
|---|---|---|---|---|---|---|---|---|---|---|---|
| Season | 435 | 118 | 18 | 4 | 15 | 60 | 33 | 81 | .271 | .434 | .321 |
| vs. Left-Handers | 176 | 48 | 6 | 3 | 6 | 22 | 16 | 32 | .273 | .443 | .328 |
| vs. Right-Handers | 259 | 70 | 12 | 1 | 9 | 38 | 17 | 49 | .270 | .429 | .315 |
| Home | 208 | 55 | 6 | 2 | 8 | 29 | 8 | 37 | .264 | .428 | .292 |
| Road | 227 | 63 | 12 | 2 | 7 | 31 | 25 | 44 | .278 | .441 | .345 |
| Grass | 121 | 35 | 7 | 0 | 3 | 15 | 17 | 24 | .289 | .421 | .374 |
| Artificial Turf | 314 | 83 | 11 | 4 | 12 | 45 | 16 | 57 | .264 | .439 | .298 |
| April | 65 | 13 | 1 | 0 | 0 | 5 | 7 | 12 | .200 | .215 | .274 |
| May | 63 | 18 | 2 | 1 | 2 | 9 | 5 | 9 | .286 | .444 | .338 |
| June | 66 | 13 | 2 | 0 | 4 | 13 | 6 | 15 | .197 | .409 | .260 |
| July | 63 | 19 | 4 | 1 | 1 | 4 | 3 | 16 | .302 | .444 | .333 |
| August | 76 | 18 | 4 | 1 | 2 | 7 | 6 | 15 | .237 | .395 | .289 |
| Sept./Oct. | 102 | 37 | 5 | 1 | 6 | 22 | 6 | 14 | .363 | .608 | .398 |
| Leading Off Inn. | 107 | 25 | 5 | 1 | 2 | 2 | 7 | 15 | .234 | .355 | .281 |
| Runners On | 174 | 55 | 6 | 2 | 8 | 53 | 19 | 37 | .316 | .511 | .378 |
| Runners/Scor. Pos. | 104 | 37 | 5 | 1 | 6 | 47 | 13 | 24 | .356 | .596 | .417 |
| Runners On/2 Out | 76 | 21 | 2 | 1 | 2 | 14 | 10 | 15 | .276 | .408 | .360 |
| Scor. Pos./2 Out | 47 | 12 | 2 | 0 | 0 | 9 | 9 | 11 | .255 | .298 | .375 |
| Late Inning Pressure | 66 | 17 | 4 | 0 | 2 | 10 | 8 | 13 | .258 | .409 | .338 |
| Leading Off | 20 | 5 | 3 | 0 | 0 | 0 | 1 | 1 | .250 | .400 | .286 |
| Runners On | 23 | 6 | 0 | 0 | 1 | 9 | 4 | 6 | .261 | .391 | .370 |
| Runners/Scor. Pos. | 14 | 5 | 0 | 0 | 1 | 9 | 2 | 4 | .357 | .571 | .438 |

| RUNS BATTED IN | From 1B | From 2B | From 3B | Scoring Position |
|---|---|---|---|---|
| Totals | 9/127 | 19/83 | 17/46 | 36/129 |
| Percentage | 7% | 23% | 37% | 28% |
| Driving In Runners from 3B with Less than Two Out: | | | 15/28 | 54% |

Loves to face: Bob Forsch (.462, 12-for-26, 2 HR)
Hates to face: Andy McGaffigan (0-for-9)
Hit 15 home runs, more than his combined total for five prior seasons; his 60 RBI tied Shawon Dunston for high among regular N.L. shortstops. . . . Batting average with runners in scoring position was a career high. . . . Had six hits in 15 at-bats with men in scoring position and Phils down by a run. . . . Has been hit by only one pitch in 1432 plate appearances since Mike Torrez incident. . . . Has higher career batting average vs. left-handers (.279) than vs. right-handers (.262), but career slugging average is higher vs. righties (.393 to .382). . . . Owns .345 career batting average in Late-Inning Pressure Situations with runners in scoring position (5th highest among active N.L. players with 25+ such hits).

## Jeff Treadway

Bats Left

| Atlanta Braves | AB | H | 2B | 3B | HR | RBI | BB | SO | BA | SA | OBA |
|---|---|---|---|---|---|---|---|---|---|---|---|
| Season | 473 | 131 | 18 | 3 | 8 | 40 | 30 | 38 | .277 | .378 | .317 |
| vs. Left-Handers | 106 | 21 | 1 | 0 | 0 | 10 | 8 | 16 | .198 | .208 | .254 |
| vs. Right-Handers | 367 | 110 | 17 | 3 | 8 | 30 | 22 | 22 | .300 | .428 | .335 |
| Home | 234 | 61 | 8 | 2 | 2 | 22 | 19 | 14 | .261 | .338 | .313 |
| Road | 239 | 70 | 10 | 1 | 6 | 18 | 11 | 24 | .293 | .418 | .321 |
| Grass | 337 | 89 | 11 | 2 | 5 | 30 | 26 | 26 | .264 | .353 | .313 |
| Artificial Turf | 136 | 42 | 7 | 1 | 3 | 10 | 4 | 12 | .309 | .441 | .326 |
| April | 61 | 14 | 1 | 1 | 1 | 5 | 1 | 4 | .230 | .328 | .242 |
| May | 72 | 25 | 4 | 1 | 0 | 3 | 6 | 5 | .347 | .431 | .392 |
| June | 103 | 30 | 4 | 0 | 2 | 5 | 4 | 9 | .291 | .388 | .318 |
| July | 82 | 20 | 2 | 0 | 1 | 7 | 6 | 9 | .244 | .305 | .295 |
| August | 94 | 28 | 4 | 1 | 3 | 8 | 7 | 8 | .298 | .457 | .343 |
| Sept./Oct. | 61 | 14 | 3 | 0 | 1 | 12 | 6 | 3 | .230 | .328 | .286 |
| Leading Off Inn. | 112 | 34 | 7 | 1 | 1 | 1 | 5 | 10 | .304 | .411 | .333 |
| Runners On | 180 | 48 | 7 | 1 | 3 | 35 | 13 | 13 | .267 | .367 | .308 |
| Runners/Scor. Pos. | 90 | 23 | 3 | 1 | 1 | 31 | 12 | 7 | .256 | .344 | .327 |
| Runners On/2 Out | 78 | 17 | 4 | 0 | 3 | 14 | 6 | 6 | .218 | .385 | .274 |
| Scor. Pos./2 Out | 42 | 8 | 2 | 0 | 1 | 10 | 6 | 4 | .190 | .310 | .292 |
| Late Inning Pressure | 80 | 23 | 0 | 0 | 2 | 7 | 5 | 11 | .288 | .363 | .329 |
| Leading Off | 13 | 5 | 0 | 0 | 0 | 0 | 1 | 1 | .385 | .385 | .429 |
| Runners On | 38 | 10 | 0 | 0 | 1 | 6 | 3 | 3 | .263 | .342 | .317 |
| Runners/Scor. Pos. | 22 | 3 | 0 | 0 | 0 | 4 | 2 | 3 | .136 | .136 | .208 |

| RUNS BATTED IN | From 1B | From 2B | From 3B | Scoring Position |
|---|---|---|---|---|
| Totals | 2/137 | 11/72 | 19/41 | 30/113 |
| Percentage | 1% | 15% | 46% | 27% |
| Driving In Runners from 3B with Less than Two Out: | | | 16/21 | 76% |

Loves to face: Rick Reuschel (.381, 8-for-21, 1 HR)
Hates to face: Mike LaCoss (.077, 1-for-13)
Batted .429 (24-for-56) in first innings, highest in majors last year (minimum: 50 AB); Ellis Burks (.403) was only other player above .400 mark. . . . Started 98 of 108 games in which Braves faced a right-handed pitcher, but started only 23 of 53 games vs. southpaws. . . . Has some pop vs. right-handers: career averages (.288 batting, .410 slugging) are approximations of career rates of Bill Buckner or Barry Larkin. . . . Owns .205 career mark vs. left-handers, with only three extra-base hits in 146 at-bats. . . . Drove in runners from third base with less than two outs in each of his last 10 opportunities. But he did not drive in any of 16 runners from scoring position with two out in Late-Inning Pressure Situations.

## Jose Uribe

Bats Left and Right

| San Francisco Giants | AB | H | 2B | 3B | HR | RBI | BB | SO | BA | SA | OBA |
|---|---|---|---|---|---|---|---|---|---|---|---|
| Season | 453 | 100 | 12 | 6 | 1 | 30 | 34 | 74 | .221 | .280 | .273 |
| vs. Left-Handers | 150 | 32 | 2 | 2 | 0 | 13 | 13 | 23 | .213 | .253 | .269 |
| vs. Right-Handers | 303 | 68 | 10 | 4 | 1 | 17 | 21 | 51 | .224 | .294 | .275 |
| Home | 214 | 48 | 7 | 3 | 0 | 13 | 20 | 38 | .224 | .285 | .287 |
| Road | 239 | 52 | 5 | 3 | 1 | 17 | 14 | 36 | .218 | .276 | .260 |
| Grass | 317 | 69 | 10 | 3 | 0 | 23 | 24 | 56 | .218 | .268 | .270 |
| Artificial Turf | 136 | 31 | 2 | 3 | 1 | 7 | 10 | 18 | .228 | .309 | .281 |
| April | 78 | 19 | 2 | 2 | 0 | 6 | 6 | 17 | .244 | .321 | .294 |
| May | 89 | 21 | 3 | 1 | 0 | 5 | 7 | 18 | .236 | .292 | .289 |
| June | 87 | 20 | 3 | 1 | 1 | 6 | 9 | 13 | .230 | .322 | .299 |
| July | 82 | 19 | 3 | 2 | 0 | 7 | 5 | 10 | .232 | .317 | .273 |
| August | 73 | 10 | 0 | 0 | 0 | 4 | 4 | 10 | .137 | .137 | .182 |
| Sept./Oct. | 44 | 11 | 1 | 0 | 0 | 2 | 3 | 6 | .250 | .273 | .298 |
| Leading Off Inn. | 109 | 25 | 4 | 2 | 0 | 0 | 1 | 19 | .229 | .303 | .236 |
| Runners On | 187 | 44 | 1 | 1 | 1 | 30 | 24 | 32 | .235 | .267 | .316 |
| Runners/Scor. Pos. | 100 | 25 | 1 | 1 | 1 | 30 | 17 | 19 | .250 | .310 | .347 |
| Runners On/2 Out | 74 | 11 | 0 | 1 | 0 | 9 | 18 | 14 | .149 | .176 | .315 |
| Scor. Pos./2 Out | 42 | 8 | 0 | 1 | 0 | 9 | 13 | 7 | .190 | .238 | .382 |
| Late Inning Pressure | 42 | 8 | 2 | 0 | 0 | 1 | 4 | 8 | .190 | .238 | .261 |
| Leading Off | 9 | 2 | 1 | 0 | 0 | 0 | 0 | 1 | .222 | .333 | .222 |
| Runners On | 16 | 2 | 0 | 0 | 0 | 1 | 1 | 4 | .125 | .125 | .176 |
| Runners/Scor. Pos. | 8 | 1 | 0 | 0 | 0 | 1 | 1 | 1 | .125 | .125 | .222 |

| RUNS BATTED IN | From 1B | From 2B | From 3B | Scoring Position |
|---|---|---|---|---|
| Totals | 1/139 | 9/72 | 19/49 | 28/121 |
| Percentage | 1% | 13% | 39% | 23% |
| Driving In Runners from 3B with Less than Two Out: | | | 14/26 | 54% |

Loves to face: Rick Mahler (.471, 16-for-34)
Hates to face: Ed Whitson (.091, 2-for-22)
Led N.L. shortstops in double plays (85), first member of Giants to do that since Alvin Dark in New York in 1952. . . . Averaged 5.04 chances per nine innings, second among N.L. shortstops (minimum: 500 inn.). . . . Batted .435 (10-for-23) with runners in scoring position and the score tied in 1989, but has hit below .200 with two outs and runners in scoring position in each of last three years. . . . Started 146 games, all from 8th spot in lineup, most by any player in majors last season. . . . Double in his last game of regular season ended streak of 140 at-bats without an extra-base hit, longest such streak in majors last season and longest single-season streak by any Giants hitter over past 15 years.

## Tim Wallach

Bats Right

| Montreal Expos | AB | H | 2B | 3B | HR | RBI | BB | SO | BA | SA | OBA |
|---|---|---|---|---|---|---|---|---|---|---|---|
| Season | 573 | 159 | 42 | 0 | 13 | 77 | 58 | 81 | .277 | .419 | .341 |
| vs. Left-Handers | 160 | 46 | 10 | 0 | 8 | 25 | 18 | 15 | .288 | .500 | .358 |
| vs. Right-Handers | 413 | 113 | 32 | 0 | 5 | 52 | 40 | 66 | .274 | .387 | .335 |
| Home | 286 | 91 | 28 | 0 | 6 | 42 | 31 | 42 | .318 | .479 | .386 |
| Road | 287 | 68 | 14 | 0 | 7 | 35 | 27 | 39 | .237 | .359 | .297 |
| Grass | 151 | 34 | 7 | 0 | 3 | 19 | 12 | 20 | .225 | .331 | .275 |
| Artificial Turf | 422 | 125 | 35 | 0 | 10 | 58 | 46 | 61 | .296 | .450 | .364 |
| April | 78 | 25 | 7 | 0 | 2 | 9 | 7 | 11 | .321 | .487 | .372 |
| May | 108 | 26 | 7 | 0 | 1 | 14 | 4 | 19 | .241 | .333 | .261 |
| June | 95 | 23 | 9 | 0 | 0 | 12 | 18 | 16 | .242 | .337 | .360 |
| July | 102 | 35 | 9 | 0 | 5 | 19 | 10 | 16 | .343 | .578 | .402 |
| August | 110 | 30 | 4 | 0 | 3 | 11 | 12 | 10 | .273 | .391 | .339 |
| Sept./Oct. | 80 | 20 | 6 | 0 | 2 | 12 | 7 | 9 | .250 | .400 | .318 |
| Leading Off Inn. | 123 | 38 | 12 | 0 | 2 | 2 | 4 | 16 | .309 | .455 | .331 |
| Runners On | 255 | 70 | 18 | 0 | 8 | 72 | 41 | 35 | .275 | .439 | .368 |
| Runners/Scor. Pos. | 147 | 44 | 13 | 0 | 3 | 58 | 35 | 22 | .299 | .449 | .418 |
| Runners On/2 Out | 97 | 23 | 7 | 0 | 1 | 20 | 23 | 14 | .237 | .340 | .383 |
| Scor. Pos./2 Out | 70 | 18 | 6 | 0 | 1 | 19 | 20 | 12 | .257 | .386 | .422 |
| Late Inning Pressure | 94 | 23 | 6 | 0 | 1 | 8 | 16 | 13 | .245 | .340 | .351 |
| Leading Off | 16 | 5 | 3 | 0 | 0 | 0 | 0 | 2 | .313 | .500 | .313 |
| Runners On | 43 | 9 | 2 | 0 | 1 | 8 | 13 | 5 | .209 | .326 | .386 |
| Runners/Scor. Pos. | 26 | 5 | 1 | 0 | 0 | 6 | 12 | 3 | .192 | .231 | .436 |

| RUNS BATTED IN | From 1B | From 2B | From 3B | Scoring Position |
|---|---|---|---|---|
| Totals | 12/195 | 25/113 | 27/65 | 52/178 |
| Percentage | 6% | 22% | 42% | 29% |
| Driving In Runners from 3B with Less than Two Out: | | | 20/35 | 57% |

Loves to face: Bruce Ruffin (.500, 9-for-18, 2 HR)
Hates to face: John Smiley (.150, 3-for-20)
Leads majors with 263 doubles over last eight seasons; only Dale Murphy has been in more N.L. games than Wallach's 1229 over that span. . . . Grounded into 21 double plays, most in N.L. last season. No player has led N.L. in consecutive seasons since Willie Montanez (1975–76). . . . Career batting breakdown: .270 from April to August, .230 from Sept. 1 to end of season. . . . Career BA is .300 leading off innings. . . . Doesn't make much difference to him who's on the mound. Career breakdown: .268 (one HR every 29.1 AB) vs. left-handers, .261 (one HR every 30.2 AB) vs. right-handers. . . . But it matters where the game is played: has hit 99 of his 161 HR away from Olympic Stadium.

## Andy Van Slyke

Bats Left

| Pittsburgh Pirates | AB | H | 2B | 3B | HR | RBI | BB | SO | BA | SA | OBA |
|---|---|---|---|---|---|---|---|---|---|---|---|
| Season | 476 | 113 | 18 | 9 | 9 | 53 | 47 | 100 | .237 | .370 | .308 |
| vs. Left-Handers | 162 | 40 | 9 | 3 | 1 | 19 | 23 | 33 | .247 | .358 | .339 |
| vs. Right-Handers | 314 | 73 | 9 | 6 | 8 | 34 | 24 | 67 | .232 | .376 | .291 |
| Home | 216 | 46 | 5 | 6 | 4 | 22 | 27 | 45 | .213 | .347 | .304 |
| Road | 260 | 67 | 13 | 3 | 5 | 31 | 20 | 55 | .258 | .388 | .311 |
| Grass | 124 | 24 | 2 | 3 | 1 | 10 | 10 | 27 | .194 | .282 | .250 |
| Artificial Turf | 352 | 89 | 16 | 6 | 8 | 43 | 37 | 73 | .253 | .401 | .327 |
| April | 28 | 7 | 3 | 0 | 0 | 2 | 2 | 5 | .250 | .357 | .290 |
| May | 62 | 15 | 2 | 1 | 1 | 8 | 7 | 17 | .242 | .355 | .314 |
| June | 102 | 31 | 4 | 4 | 1 | 11 | 11 | 16 | .304 | .451 | .383 |
| July | 98 | 16 | 1 | 2 | 1 | 6 | 8 | 17 | .163 | .245 | .229 |
| August | 94 | 22 | 5 | 0 | 4 | 17 | 6 | 19 | .234 | .415 | .280 |
| Sept./Oct. | 92 | 22 | 3 | 2 | 2 | 9 | 13 | 26 | .239 | .380 | .333 |
| Leading Off Inn. | 100 | 19 | 1 | 0 | 1 | 1 | 10 | 19 | .190 | .230 | .264 |
| Runners On | 208 | 51 | 12 | 7 | 2 | 46 | 21 | 41 | .245 | .399 | .312 |
| Runners/Scor. Pos. | 113 | 31 | 7 | 6 | 1 | 40 | 17 | 20 | .274 | .469 | .363 |
| Runners On/2 Out | 66 | 15 | 5 | 1 | 1 | 14 | 10 | 13 | .227 | .379 | .338 |
| Scor. Pos./2 Out | 41 | 9 | 3 | 1 | 0 | 11 | 8 | 6 | .220 | .341 | .360 |
| Late Inning Pressure | 80 | 12 | 0 | 4 | 2 | 6 | 9 | 31 | .150 | .325 | .236 |
| Leading Off | 25 | 3 | 0 | 0 | 0 | 0 | 3 | 11 | .120 | .120 | .214 |
| Runners On | 36 | 5 | 0 | 2 | 0 | 4 | 2 | 10 | .139 | .250 | .184 |
| Runners/Scor. Pos. | 19 | 3 | 0 | 2 | 0 | 4 | 2 | 6 | .158 | .368 | .238 |

| RUNS BATTED IN | From 1B | From 2B | From 3B | Scoring Position |
|---|---|---|---|---|
| Totals | 7/143 | 25/89 | 12/38 | 37/127 |
| Percentage | 5% | 28% | 32% | 29% |
| Driving In Runners from 3B with Less than Two Out: | | | 10/23 | 43% |

Loves to face: Rick Mahler (.524, 22-for-42, 3 HR)
Hates to face: Randy Myers (.095, 2-for-21, 10 SO)
Batted 105 points lower in Late-Inning Pressure Situations than in other at-bats, top drop among N.L. players in '89 (minimum: 50 LIPS AB). . . . Overall batting average was a career low. . . . You wouldn't know it looking at '89 numbers, but he'd hit .313 vs. right-handers, .202 vs. lefties from 1985 to 1988. . . . Hit .312 vs. left-handers over first three months, but had 0-for-26 streak vs. lefties, July 7 to Aug. 7, 2d-longest streak in N.L. last year. . . . Started five double plays to tie Gerald Young for N.L. outfielders' lead. That's 3d time Van has led N.L., one shy of Mays's record. . . . Attention, catchers: play him deep and away. He has reached base 11 times on catcher's interference, most by any active batter.

## Jerome Walton

Bats Right

| Chicago Cubs | AB | H | 2B | 3B | HR | RBI | BB | SO | BA | SA | OBA |
|---|---|---|---|---|---|---|---|---|---|---|---|
| Season | 475 | 139 | 23 | 3 | 5 | 46 | 27 | 77 | .293 | .385 | .335 |
| vs. Left-Handers | 128 | 41 | 5 | 2 | 2 | 19 | 10 | 24 | .320 | .438 | .374 |
| vs. Right-Handers | 347 | 98 | 18 | 1 | 3 | 27 | 17 | 53 | .282 | .366 | .321 |
| Home | 231 | 70 | 10 | 2 | 3 | 24 | 14 | 31 | .303 | .403 | .345 |
| Road | 244 | 69 | 13 | 1 | 2 | 22 | 13 | 46 | .283 | .369 | .326 |
| Grass | 321 | 97 | 18 | 2 | 3 | 27 | 21 | 47 | .302 | .399 | .352 |
| Artificial Turf | 154 | 42 | 5 | 1 | 2 | 19 | 6 | 30 | .273 | .357 | .299 |
| April | 76 | 19 | 6 | 1 | 2 | 7 | 6 | 10 | .250 | .434 | .318 |
| May | 10 | 2 | 0 | 0 | 0 | 0 | 1 | 2 | .200 | .200 | .273 |
| June | 79 | 26 | 6 | 0 | 1 | 6 | 7 | 16 | .329 | .443 | .386 |
| July | 113 | 35 | 7 | 0 | 1 | 13 | 2 | 18 | .310 | .398 | .322 |
| August | 120 | 39 | 3 | 2 | 1 | 14 | 10 | 12 | .325 | .408 | .383 |
| Sept./Oct. | 77 | 18 | 1 | 0 | 0 | 6 | 1 | 19 | .234 | .247 | .244 |
| Leading Off Inn. | 207 | 65 | 9 | 1 | 4 | 4 | 16 | 33 | .314 | .425 | .377 |
| Runners On | 137 | 43 | 9 | 2 | 0 | 41 | 7 | 22 | .314 | .409 | .340 |
| Runners/Scor. Pos. | 92 | 32 | 7 | 2 | 0 | 41 | 4 | 17 | .348 | .467 | .363 |
| Runners On/2 Out | 71 | 22 | 5 | 1 | 0 | 23 | 2 | 11 | .310 | .408 | .338 |
| Scor. Pos./2 Out | 59 | 20 | 5 | 1 | 0 | 23 | 2 | 10 | .339 | .458 | .371 |
| Late Inning Pressure | 54 | 12 | 0 | 0 | 0 | 5 | 8 | 12 | .222 | .222 | .328 |
| Leading Off | 13 | 2 | 0 | 0 | 0 | 0 | 4 | 4 | .154 | .154 | .389 |
| Runners On | 18 | 5 | 0 | 0 | 0 | 5 | 3 | 6 | .278 | .278 | .364 |
| Runners/Scor. Pos. | 10 | 3 | 0 | 0 | 0 | 5 | 2 | 4 | .300 | .300 | .385 |

| RUNS BATTED IN | From 1B | From 2B | From 3B | Scoring Position |
|---|---|---|---|---|
| Totals | 1/78 | 19/71 | 21/43 | 40/114 |
| Percentage | 1% | 27% | 49% | 35% |
| Driving In Runners from 3B with Less than Two Out: | | | 11/18 | 61% |

Loves to face: Jose DeLeon (.357, 5-for-14, 1 HR)
Hates to face: Walt Terrell (0-for-8)
Full name: Jerome O'Terrell Walton, so it's only natural that he's never had a hit o'Terrell. . . . Led Cubs with 31 infield hits, and twice extended his long hitting streak (eventually 30 games) on infield hits. . . . Started 114 games, all from the leadoff spot. . . . Led N.L. rookies in hits and stolen bases (24). . . . Don't be fooled by modest RBI total (46); he drove in 35 percent of runners who were in scoring position, 4th-highest rate in league. . . . Batting average with runners in scoring position was 7th best in N.L. (.387); he hit .382 with RISP from June through September, and he batted .455 (10-for-22) with runners in scoring position with the score tied or the Cubs trailing by one run.

## Mitch Webster

Bats Left and Right

| Chicago Cubs | AB | H | 2B | 3B | HR | RBI | BB | SO | BA | SA | OBA |
|---|---|---|---|---|---|---|---|---|---|---|---|
| Season | 272 | 70 | 12 | 4 | 3 | 19 | 30 | 55 | .257 | .364 | .331 |
| vs. Left-Handers | 61 | 19 | 3 | 1 | 1 | 2 | 5 | 9 | .311 | .443 | .364 |
| vs. Right-Handers | 211 | 51 | 9 | 3 | 2 | 17 | 25 | 46 | .242 | .341 | .322 |
| Home | 132 | 33 | 5 | 2 | 1 | 9 | 13 | 25 | .250 | .341 | .315 |
| Road | 140 | 37 | 7 | 2 | 2 | 10 | 17 | 30 | .264 | .386 | .346 |
| Grass | 205 | 50 | 8 | 3 | 1 | 11 | 20 | 38 | .244 | .327 | .313 |
| Artificial Turf | 67 | 20 | 4 | 1 | 2 | 8 | 10 | 17 | .299 | .478 | .385 |
| April | 90 | 26 | 4 | 1 | 0 | 6 | 10 | 17 | .289 | .356 | .360 |
| May | 43 | 7 | 0 | 0 | 0 | 0 | 0 | 4 | .163 | .163 | .163 |
| June | 60 | 17 | 3 | 1 | 3 | 8 | 10 | 12 | .283 | .517 | .389 |
| July | 37 | 10 | 3 | 1 | 0 | 3 | 4 | 10 | .270 | .405 | .341 |
| August | 27 | 4 | 1 | 0 | 0 | 1 | 4 | 8 | .148 | .185 | .250 |
| Sept./Oct. | 15 | 6 | 1 | 1 | 0 | 1 | 2 | 4 | .400 | .600 | .471 |
| Leading Off Inn. | 62 | 20 | 4 | 2 | 0 | 0 | 5 | 13 | .323 | .452 | .373 |
| Runners On | 108 | 29 | 4 | 0 | 2 | 18 | 16 | 19 | .269 | .361 | .362 |
| Runners/Scor. Pos. | 62 | 13 | 1 | 0 | 1 | 16 | 12 | 14 | .210 | .274 | .338 |
| Runners On/2 Out | 48 | 12 | 1 | 0 | 0 | 6 | 6 | 10 | .250 | .271 | .345 |
| Scor. Pos./2 Out | 32 | 7 | 0 | 0 | 0 | 6 | 6 | 6 | .219 | .219 | .359 |
| Late Inning Pressure | 41 | 8 | 1 | 1 | 1 | 3 | 8 | 12 | .195 | .341 | .327 |
| Leading Off | 7 | 2 | 0 | 1 | 0 | 0 | 1 | 3 | .286 | .571 | .375 |
| Runners On | 13 | 4 | 1 | 0 | 0 | 2 | 4 | 3 | .308 | .385 | .471 |
| Runners/Scor. Pos. | 8 | 2 | 0 | 0 | 0 | 2 | 4 | 2 | .250 | .250 | .500 |

| RUNS BATTED IN | From 1B | From 2B | From 3B | Scoring Position |
|---|---|---|---|---|
| Totals | 1/75 | 10/49 | 5/24 | 15/73 |
| Percentage | 1% | 20% | 21% | 21% |
| Driving In Runners from 3B with Less than Two Out: | | | 4/14 | 29% |

Loves to face: Rick Honeycutt (.455, 5-for-11)
Hates to face: Nolan Ryan (0-for-16, 11 SO)
Batted .317 vs. ground-ball pitchers, .189 vs. fly-ball pitchers last season; one of three N.L. players who hit above .300 vs. groundballers but below .200 vs. fly-ballers. A tip for Pinky: Webster has hit for higher average vs. ground-ballers than vs. fly-ballers in each of seven years in majors. . . . Went 27 consecutive plate appearances without reaching base in April, longest streak by any nonpitcher last season. . . . His three home runs came in consecutive games in June over a span of seven at-bats. . . . Batted .133 (4-for-30) as a pinch hitter. . . . Batted .313 vs. N.L. East teams, .179 vs. N.L. West teams; we'll see if he can transfer that geographic dominance to the American League in 1990.

## Matt Williams

Bats Right

| San Francisco Giants | AB | H | 2B | 3B | HR | RBI | BB | SO | BA | SA | OBA |
|---|---|---|---|---|---|---|---|---|---|---|---|
| Season | 292 | 59 | 18 | 1 | 18 | 50 | 14 | 72 | .202 | .455 | .242 |
| vs. Left-Handers | 87 | 23 | 6 | 0 | 9 | 21 | 9 | 13 | .264 | .644 | .330 |
| vs. Right-Handers | 205 | 36 | 12 | 1 | 9 | 29 | 5 | 59 | .176 | .376 | .202 |
| Home | 144 | 31 | 11 | 1 | 10 | 33 | 7 | 40 | .215 | .514 | .248 |
| Road | 148 | 28 | 7 | 0 | 8 | 17 | 7 | 32 | .189 | .399 | .236 |
| Grass | 223 | 46 | 16 | 1 | 14 | 40 | 11 | 56 | .206 | .475 | .245 |
| Artificial Turf | 69 | 13 | 2 | 0 | 4 | 10 | 3 | 16 | .188 | .391 | .233 |
| April | 53 | 7 | 1 | 0 | 2 | 5 | 2 | 17 | .132 | .264 | .179 |
| May | 1 | 0 | 0 | 0 | 0 | 0 | 0 | 1 | .000 | .000 | .000 |
| June | 0 | 0 | 0 | 0 | 0 | 0 | 0 | 0 | — | — | — |
| July | 23 | 6 | 1 | 0 | 0 | 1 | 3 | 4 | .261 | .304 | .346 |
| August | 111 | 28 | 8 | 1 | 11 | 22 | 2 | 23 | .252 | .640 | .263 |
| Sept./Oct. | 104 | 18 | 8 | 0 | 5 | 22 | 7 | 27 | .173 | .394 | .230 |
| Leading Off Inn. | 68 | 17 | 3 | 1 | 6 | 6 | 2 | 17 | .250 | .588 | .271 |
| Runners On | 134 | 23 | 9 | 0 | 10 | 42 | 10 | 30 | .172 | .463 | .231 |
| Runners/Scor. Pos. | 80 | 12 | 5 | 0 | 5 | 29 | 8 | 18 | .150 | .400 | .231 |
| Runners On/2 Out | 73 | 9 | 5 | 0 | 2 | 16 | 4 | 20 | .123 | .274 | .179 |
| Scor. Pos./2 Out | 51 | 7 | 3 | 0 | 2 | 14 | 3 | 14 | .137 | .314 | .200 |
| Late Inning Pressure | 34 | 6 | 2 | 0 | 0 | 2 | 3 | 7 | .176 | .235 | .243 |
| Leading Off | 4 | 2 | 1 | 0 | 0 | 0 | 1 | 0 | .500 | .750 | .600 |
| Runners On | 18 | 1 | 1 | 0 | 0 | 2 | 1 | 3 | .056 | .111 | .105 |
| Runners/Scor. Pos. | 9 | 0 | 0 | 0 | 0 | 1 | 1 | 0 | .000 | .000 | .100 |

| RUNS BATTED IN | From 1B | From 2B | From 3B | Scoring Position |
|---|---|---|---|---|
| Totals | 14/99 | 9/61 | 9/29 | 18/90 |
| Percentage | 14% | 15% | 31% | 20% |
| Driving In Runners from 3B with Less than Two Out: | | | 6/9 | 67% |

Loves to face: Dennis Rasmussen (.500, 4-for-8, 1 HR)
Hates to face: Orel Hershiser (.125, 2-for-16, 6 SO)
Led majors with 20 extra-base hits in August; that tied Howard Johnson's June tally for highest monthly total in N.L. in 1989. . . . Has three home runs in 12 career bases-loaded at-bats. . . . His .134 career average with two outs and runners on base is lowest among active nonpitchers (minimum: 100 AB); same goes for .143 average with two outs and runners in scoring position. . . . After pieces of three years in majors, his homer rate (one every 20.4 at-bats) equals Jack Clark's; his batting average (.198) is one point below Herman Franks's. Which Hall of Famer will he chase in team record book: Most Career Home Runs (646 by Mays), or Lowest Career Batting Average (with a minimum of 1000 at-bats, .166 by Marichal)?

## Glenn Wilson

Bats Right

| Pirates/Astros | AB | H | 2B | 3B | HR | RBI | BB | SO | BA | SA | OBA |
|---|---|---|---|---|---|---|---|---|---|---|---|
| Season | 432 | 115 | 26 | 4 | 11 | 65 | 37 | 53 | .266 | .421 | .321 |
| vs. Left-Handers | 143 | 46 | 14 | 1 | 4 | 25 | 13 | 14 | .322 | .517 | .373 |
| vs. Right-Handers | 289 | 69 | 12 | 3 | 7 | 40 | 24 | 39 | .239 | .374 | .296 |
| Home | 198 | 52 | 13 | 1 | 4 | 32 | 21 | 23 | .263 | .399 | .332 |
| Road | 234 | 63 | 13 | 3 | 7 | 33 | 16 | 30 | .269 | .440 | .312 |
| Grass | 104 | 31 | 7 | 0 | 7 | 20 | 9 | 14 | .298 | .567 | .348 |
| Artificial Turf | 328 | 84 | 19 | 4 | 4 | 45 | 28 | 39 | .256 | .375 | .313 |
| April | 65 | 13 | 2 | 0 | 3 | 13 | 9 | 11 | .200 | .369 | .299 |
| May | 82 | 30 | 7 | 1 | 4 | 14 | 7 | 10 | .366 | .622 | .411 |
| June | 48 | 11 | 1 | 1 | 0 | 4 | 2 | 5 | .229 | .292 | .260 |
| July | 74 | 18 | 7 | 0 | 2 | 12 | 11 | 10 | .243 | .419 | .333 |
| August | 106 | 31 | 6 | 2 | 1 | 14 | 5 | 8 | .292 | .415 | .321 |
| Sept./Oct. | 57 | 12 | 3 | 0 | 1 | 8 | 3 | 9 | .211 | .316 | .250 |
| Leading Off Inn. | 104 | 20 | 5 | 0 | 2 | 2 | 7 | 13 | .192 | .298 | .243 |
| Runners On | 177 | 50 | 12 | 1 | 4 | 58 | 18 | 21 | .282 | .429 | .342 |
| Runners/Scor. Pos. | 118 | 37 | 10 | 1 | 2 | 53 | 15 | 15 | .314 | .466 | .379 |
| Runners On/2 Out | 84 | 24 | 5 | 1 | 3 | 26 | 6 | 7 | .286 | .476 | .341 |
| Scor. Pos./2 Out | 59 | 17 | 4 | 1 | 1 | 22 | 5 | 5 | .288 | .441 | .354 |
| Late Inning Pressure | 80 | 27 | 4 | 0 | 3 | 14 | 9 | 14 | .338 | .500 | .400 |
| Leading Off | 19 | 6 | 0 | 0 | 1 | 1 | 1 | 2 | .316 | .474 | .350 |
| Runners On | 23 | 10 | 2 | 0 | 0 | 11 | 5 | 5 | .435 | .522 | .517 |
| Runners/Scor. Pos. | 15 | 8 | 2 | 0 | 0 | 11 | 4 | 3 | .533 | .667 | .600 |

| RUNS BATTED IN | From 1B | From 2B | From 3B | Scoring Position |
|---|---|---|---|---|
| Totals | 7/120 | 19/86 | 28/62 | 47/148 |
| Percentage | 6% | 22% | 45% | 32% |
| Driving In Runners from 3B with Less than Two Out: | | | 20/36 | 56% |

Loves to face: Ken Howell (.429, 6-for-14, 2 HR)
Hates to face: Frank Viola (0-for-12)
Starting opening-day right fielder for Pittsburgh last season, a job that no player has had for two consecutive years since the Dave Parker days. Starters since 1983: Parker, Doug Frobel, George Hendrick, Joe Orsulak, Andy Van Slyke, Darnell Coles, and Wilson. There's one streak bound to continue into 1990. . . . Batted .282 in 100 games for Pittsburgh, .225 in 28 games for Houston. . . . His 71 assists over the last five seasons rank second among outfielders to Jesse Barfield (91). . . . One of the fastest-growing clubs in baseball is the group of players for whom Wilson has been traded. Members in good standing: Darnell Coles, Billy Hatcher, Dave Bergman, Willie Hernandez, Phil Bradley, and Tim Fortugno.

## Herm Winningham

Bats Left

| Cincinnati Reds | AB | H | 2B | 3B | HR | RBI | BB | SO | BA | SA | OBA |
|---|---|---|---|---|---|---|---|---|---|---|---|
| Season | 251 | 63 | 11 | 3 | 3 | 13 | 24 | 50 | .251 | .355 | .316 |
| vs. Left-Handers | 37 | 8 | 2 | 0 | 1 | 1 | 2 | 9 | .216 | .351 | .256 |
| vs. Right-Handers | 214 | 55 | 9 | 3 | 2 | 12 | 22 | 41 | .257 | .355 | .326 |
| Home | 133 | 33 | 6 | 2 | 1 | 6 | 16 | 28 | .248 | .346 | .329 |
| Road | 118 | 30 | 5 | 1 | 2 | 7 | 8 | 22 | .254 | .364 | .302 |
| Grass | 58 | 15 | 3 | 0 | 2 | 6 | 7 | 10 | .259 | .414 | .338 |
| Artificial Turf | 193 | 48 | 8 | 3 | 1 | 7 | 17 | 40 | .249 | .337 | .310 |
| April | 16 | 4 | 0 | 0 | 2 | 3 | 0 | 5 | .250 | .625 | .250 |
| May | 50 | 13 | 1 | 0 | 0 | 3 | 5 | 11 | .260 | .280 | .327 |
| June | 22 | 5 | 1 | 0 | 0 | 0 | 2 | 4 | .227 | .273 | .292 |
| July | 30 | 6 | 0 | 0 | 0 | 1 | 4 | 9 | .200 | .200 | .294 |
| August | 54 | 16 | 2 | 1 | 0 | 2 | 5 | 6 | .296 | .370 | .356 |
| Sept./Oct. | 79 | 19 | 7 | 2 | 1 | 4 | 8 | 15 | .241 | .418 | .310 |
| Leading Off Inn. | 83 | 19 | 2 | 3 | 0 | 0 | 12 | 14 | .229 | .325 | .326 |
| Runners On | 78 | 20 | 1 | 0 | 1 | 11 | 7 | 17 | .256 | .308 | .318 |
| Runners/Scor. Pos. | 47 | 9 | 1 | 0 | 0 | 9 | 7 | 13 | .191 | .213 | .296 |
| Runners On/2 Out | 39 | 10 | 0 | 0 | 1 | 9 | 3 | 10 | .256 | .333 | .310 |
| Scor. Pos./2 Out | 28 | 6 | 0 | 0 | 0 | 7 | 3 | 8 | .214 | .214 | .290 |
| Late Inning Pressure | 43 | 14 | 2 | 0 | 1 | 5 | 3 | 8 | .326 | .442 | .370 |
| Leading Off | 16 | 5 | 0 | 0 | 0 | 0 | 2 | 1 | .313 | .313 | .389 |
| Runners On | 11 | 4 | 0 | 0 | 0 | 4 | 1 | 3 | .364 | .364 | .417 |
| Runners/Scor. Pos. | 9 | 3 | 0 | 0 | 0 | 4 | 1 | 2 | .333 | .333 | .400 |

| RUNS BATTED IN | From 1B | From 2B | From 3B | Scoring Position |
|---|---|---|---|---|
| Totals | 1/53 | 7/40 | 2/16 | 9/56 |
| Percentage | 2% | 18% | 13% | 16% |
| Driving In Runners from 3B with Less than Two Out: | | | 1/4 | 25% |

Loves to face: Doug Drabek (.385, 5-for-13, 3 2B)
Hates to face: Danny Darwin (.071, 1-for-14)
A mild-mannered .240 career hitter who has a .333 career mark in 75 at-bats in Late-Inning Pressure Situations with runners on base. He's 11-for-24 in those situations over last two seasons. . . . Left-handed batter who has a higher career batting average vs. left-handed pitchers (.264 in 178 at-bats) than he has against right-handers (.236). Still, 48 of his 51 starts last season came in games in which Reds faced a right-handed starter. . . . Has never been hit by a pitch in 1466 plate appearances in majors; among active players, only John Kruk (1726) and Daryl Boston (1480) have more trips to the plate without being plunked. . . . One of three N.L. players to start 10+ games at each outfield position in 1989.

## Marvell Wynne

Bats Left

| Padres/Cubs | AB | H | 2B | 3B | HR | RBI | BB | SO | BA | SA | OBA |
|---|---|---|---|---|---|---|---|---|---|---|---|
| Season | 342 | 83 | 13 | 2 | 7 | 39 | 13 | 48 | .243 | .354 | .274 |
| vs. Left-Handers | 45 | 16 | 4 | 0 | 1 | 7 | 0 | 9 | .356 | .511 | .370 |
| vs. Right-Handers | 297 | 67 | 9 | 2 | 6 | 32 | 13 | 39 | .226 | .330 | .260 |
| Home | 150 | 38 | 7 | 0 | 3 | 12 | 7 | 16 | .253 | .360 | .289 |
| Road | 192 | 45 | 6 | 2 | 4 | 27 | 6 | 32 | .234 | .349 | .261 |
| Grass | 230 | 61 | 10 | 0 | 5 | 23 | 7 | 33 | .265 | .374 | .292 |
| Artificial Turf | 112 | 22 | 3 | 2 | 2 | 16 | 6 | 15 | .196 | .313 | .237 |
| April | 41 | 12 | 2 | 0 | 2 | 6 | 1 | 4 | .293 | .488 | .310 |
| May | 66 | 18 | 5 | 1 | 1 | 9 | 2 | 9 | .273 | .424 | .294 |
| June | 63 | 14 | 1 | 0 | 0 | 4 | 3 | 13 | .222 | .238 | .269 |
| July | 87 | 23 | 3 | 0 | 1 | 9 | 4 | 10 | .264 | .333 | .297 |
| August | 37 | 7 | 0 | 0 | 2 | 7 | 2 | 5 | .189 | .351 | .225 |
| Sept./Oct. | 48 | 9 | 2 | 1 | 1 | 4 | 1 | 7 | .188 | .333 | .220 |
| Leading Off Inn. | 94 | 24 | 4 | 0 | 3 | 3 | 3 | 11 | .255 | .394 | .278 |
| Runners On | 150 | 40 | 8 | 2 | 3 | 35 | 9 | 25 | .267 | .407 | .306 |
| Runners/Scor. Pos. | 84 | 23 | 2 | 2 | 3 | 31 | 7 | 14 | .274 | .452 | .326 |
| Runners On/2 Out | 69 | 16 | 3 | 2 | 2 | 17 | 6 | 12 | .232 | .420 | .293 |
| Scor. Pos./2 Out | 45 | 11 | 0 | 2 | 2 | 16 | 5 | 8 | .244 | .467 | .320 |
| Late Inning Pressure | 50 | 14 | 3 | 0 | 0 | 4 | 1 | 13 | .280 | .340 | .294 |
| Leading Off | 10 | 2 | 0 | 0 | 0 | 0 | 0 | 4 | .200 | .200 | .200 |
| Runners On | 24 | 8 | 3 | 0 | 0 | 4 | 0 | 6 | .333 | .458 | .333 |
| Runners/Scor. Pos. | 14 | 3 | 0 | 0 | 0 | 2 | 0 | 4 | .214 | .214 | .214 |

| RUNS BATTED IN | From 1B | From 2B | From 3B | Scoring Position |
|---|---|---|---|---|
| Totals | 8/107 | 13/65 | 11/31 | 24/96 |
| Percentage | 7% | 20% | 35% | 25% |
| Driving In Runners from 3B with Less than Two Out: | | | 7/14 | 50% |

Loves to face: Orel Hershiser (.343, 12-for-35)
Hates to face: Dwight Gooden (.042, 1-for-24, 7 SO)

He certainly got traded to the right place: Wynne has a .324 career batting average at Wrigley Field, compared to .245 elsewhere in the majors. He hasn't even hit .270 at any other park. . . . Batted .118 (2-for-17) as a pinch hitter, lowering his career pinch-hit batting average to .151 (13-for-86). . . . Started 68 games for Padres, all against right-handed pitchers. Made one of his ten starts for Cubs against a lefty. . . . Yearly batting average breakdown since 1986 shows a couple of lines moving in opposite directions. Against left-handed pitchers: .186, .231, .327, .356. Against right-handers: .289, .255, .252, .226. Plot those on your trusty X and Y axes and you'll get a major league "X."

## Gerald Young

Bats Left and Right

| Houston Astros | AB | H | 2B | 3B | HR | RBI | BB | SO | BA | SA | OBA |
|---|---|---|---|---|---|---|---|---|---|---|---|
| Season | 533 | 124 | 17 | 3 | 0 | 38 | 74 | 60 | .233 | .276 | .326 |
| vs. Left-Handers | 147 | 35 | 4 | 0 | 0 | 11 | 21 | 17 | .238 | .265 | .335 |
| vs. Right-Handers | 386 | 89 | 13 | 3 | 0 | 27 | 53 | 43 | .231 | .280 | .322 |
| Home | 267 | 66 | 10 | 1 | 0 | 19 | 36 | 23 | .247 | .292 | .336 |
| Road | 266 | 58 | 7 | 2 | 0 | 19 | 38 | 37 | .218 | .259 | .316 |
| Grass | 162 | 36 | 5 | 0 | 0 | 16 | 22 | 24 | .222 | .253 | .312 |
| Artificial Turf | 371 | 88 | 12 | 3 | 0 | 22 | 52 | 36 | .237 | .286 | .332 |
| April | 93 | 18 | 2 | 0 | 0 | 1 | 12 | 11 | .194 | .215 | .283 |
| May | 84 | 17 | 2 | 1 | 0 | 7 | 21 | 8 | .202 | .250 | .364 |
| June | 103 | 29 | 6 | 0 | 0 | 11 | 14 | 15 | .282 | .340 | .358 |
| July | 92 | 21 | 2 | 1 | 0 | 8 | 11 | 13 | .228 | .272 | .311 |
| August | 75 | 22 | 2 | 1 | 0 | 4 | 6 | 5 | .293 | .347 | .354 |
| Sept./Oct. | 86 | 17 | 3 | 0 | 0 | 7 | 10 | 8 | .198 | .233 | .281 |
| Leading Off Inn. | 172 | 37 | 7 | 1 | 0 | 0 | 27 | 20 | .215 | .267 | .322 |
| Runners On | 180 | 54 | 6 | 2 | 0 | 38 | 23 | 17 | .300 | .356 | .376 |
| Runners/Scor. Pos. | 107 | 31 | 4 | 2 | 0 | 38 | 18 | 14 | .290 | .364 | .386 |
| Runners On/2 Out | 86 | 25 | 4 | 2 | 0 | 20 | 11 | 10 | .291 | .384 | .371 |
| Scor. Pos./2 Out | 59 | 17 | 3 | 2 | 0 | 20 | 9 | 9 | .288 | .407 | .382 |
| Late Inning Pressure | 86 | 19 | 2 | 0 | 0 | 4 | 11 | 8 | .221 | .244 | .316 |
| Leading Off | 25 | 5 | 0 | 0 | 0 | 0 | 6 | 1 | .200 | .200 | .355 |
| Runners On | 27 | 6 | 0 | 0 | 0 | 4 | 4 | 3 | .222 | .222 | .344 |
| Runners/Scor. Pos. | 14 | 3 | 0 | 0 | 0 | 4 | 3 | 3 | .214 | .214 | .389 |

| RUNS BATTED IN | From 1B | From 2B | From 3B | Scoring Position |
|---|---|---|---|---|
| Totals | 1/117 | 19/88 | 18/50 | 37/138 |
| Percentage | 1% | 22% | 36% | 27% |
| Driving In Runners from 3B with Less than Two Out: | | | 12/23 | 52% |

Loves to face: Pete Smith (.409, 9-for-22)
Hates to face: John Smiley (.056, 1-for-18)

First outfielder since Farmer Weaver (Earl's great-grampa?) in 1891 to lead league in fielding percentage, putouts, and assists in same season (Weaver did it with Louisville in American Assn.'s final year as a major league). Two other outfielders did it before Weaver: Jim Fogarty in '89, Tom Dolan in '83. . . . Also led N.L. center fielders with 2.96 putouts per nine innings. . . . Reached base on 14 infield errors last season, 2d highest total in majors. . . . Career breakdown: .317 batting average with runners in scoring position, .247 in other at-bats. . . . Enters 1990 season with 1146 at-bats since his last, and only, home run. . . . Stole 33 bases in his first 49 attempts, but was thrown out in 9 of last 10 tries.

## Atlanta Braves

| | AB | H | 2B | 3B | HR | RBI | BB | SO | BA | SA | OBA |
|---|---|---|---|---|---|---|---|---|---|---|---|
| Season | 5463 | 1281 | 201 | 22 | 128 | 546 | 485 | 996 | .234 | .350 | .298 |
| vs. Left-Handers | 1787 | 413 | 66 | 8 | 35 | 176 | 180 | 335 | .231 | .336 | .302 |
| vs. Right-Handers | 3676 | 868 | 135 | 14 | 93 | 370 | 305 | 661 | .236 | .356 | .296 |
| Home | 2698 | 654 | 109 | 12 | 55 | 291 | 241 | 457 | .242 | .353 | .304 |
| Road | 2765 | 627 | 92 | 10 | 73 | 255 | 244 | 539 | .227 | .346 | .292 |
| Grass | 3986 | 928 | 141 | 16 | 96 | 402 | 354 | 736 | .233 | .348 | .296 |
| Artificial Turf | 1477 | 353 | 60 | 6 | 32 | 144 | 131 | 260 | .239 | .353 | .303 |
| April | 843 | 197 | 29 | 5 | 21 | 88 | 85 | 174 | .234 | .355 | .308 |
| May | 923 | 217 | 40 | 5 | 14 | 83 | 90 | 150 | .235 | .335 | .303 |
| June | 903 | 220 | 32 | 3 | 18 | 76 | 58 | 141 | .244 | .346 | .290 |
| July | 919 | 208 | 29 | 2 | 21 | 93 | 92 | 173 | .226 | .331 | .297 |
| August | 948 | 228 | 36 | 3 | 32 | 103 | 82 | 162 | .241 | .386 | .300 |
| Sept./Oct. | 927 | 211 | 35 | 4 | 22 | 103 | 78 | 196 | .228 | .345 | .288 |
| Leading Off Inn. | 1376 | 309 | 49 | 5 | 34 | 34 | 90 | 256 | .225 | .342 | .274 |
| Runners On | 2166 | 555 | 100 | 12 | 45 | 463 | 226 | 364 | .256 | .376 | .324 |
| Runners/Scor. Pos. | 1154 | 295 | 49 | 10 | 21 | 392 | 174 | 219 | .256 | .370 | .346 |
| Runners On/2 Out | 974 | 236 | 45 | 8 | 19 | 207 | 129 | 172 | .242 | .363 | .334 |
| Scor. Pos./2 Out | 584 | 136 | 24 | 7 | 10 | 176 | 101 | 120 | .233 | .349 | .349 |
| Late Inning Pressure | 950 | 203 | 28 | 2 | 16 | 82 | 74 | 221 | .214 | .298 | .272 |
| Leading Off | 243 | 53 | 11 | 1 | 3 | 3 | 14 | 70 | .218 | .309 | .264 |
| Runners On | 362 | 93 | 9 | 1 | 8 | 74 | 32 | 71 | .257 | .354 | .315 |
| Runners/Scor. Pos. | 208 | 52 | 6 | 1 | 5 | 67 | 22 | 48 | .250 | .361 | .318 |

| RUNS BATTED IN | From 1B | From 2B | From 3B | Scoring Position |
|---|---|---|---|---|
| Totals | 69/1642 | 163/923 | 186/472 | 349/1395 |
| Percentage | 4% | 18% | 39% | 25% |
| Driving In Runners from 3B with Less than Two Out: | | | 115/225 | 51% |

Love to face: Rick Sutcliffe (7–1 against him)
Hate to face: Eric Show (3–16 against him)
Batting average is 2d lowest by any team in majors over past 16 years; only '85 Giants (.233) had lower average. Ranked last in N.L. in batting average for only the second time since moving from Milwaukee; N.L. teams with worst yearly batting averages from 1985 through 1987 (Giants, Cardinals, and Dodgers) all made playoff appearances within two seasons. . . . Two N.L. teams with fewest runners left on base were Cubs (1093), who scored the most runs in N.L., and Braves (1096), who scored the fewest. . . . Used six starting catchers (most in majors) for a combined .191 average (lowest in majors). Also last in batting average of starting first basemen (.230), third basemen (.213), and shortstops (.222).

## Chicago Cubs

| | AB | H | 2B | 3B | HR | RBI | BB | SO | BA | SA | OBA |
|---|---|---|---|---|---|---|---|---|---|---|---|
| Season | 5513 | 1438 | 235 | 45 | 124 | 654 | 472 | 921 | .261 | .387 | .319 |
| vs. Left-Handers | 1593 | 449 | 79 | 12 | 41 | 218 | 162 | 238 | .282 | .424 | .346 |
| vs. Right-Handers | 3920 | 989 | 156 | 33 | 83 | 436 | 310 | 683 | .252 | .372 | .309 |
| Home | 2698 | 734 | 113 | 19 | 61 | 352 | 237 | 421 | .272 | .396 | .331 |
| Road | 2815 | 704 | 122 | 26 | 63 | 302 | 235 | 500 | .250 | .379 | .309 |
| Grass | 3809 | 995 | 165 | 28 | 81 | 461 | 311 | 618 | .261 | .383 | .317 |
| Artificial Turf | 1704 | 443 | 70 | 17 | 43 | 193 | 161 | 303 | .260 | .397 | .325 |
| April | 760 | 187 | 34 | 6 | 10 | 77 | 61 | 110 | .246 | .346 | .302 |
| May | 914 | 223 | 32 | 7 | 11 | 87 | 57 | 145 | .244 | .330 | .288 |
| June | 946 | 240 | 40 | 9 | 24 | 116 | 97 | 160 | .254 | .391 | .325 |
| July | 914 | 251 | 55 | 5 | 28 | 123 | 72 | 145 | .275 | .438 | .325 |
| August | 989 | 260 | 38 | 6 | 30 | 127 | 99 | 178 | .263 | .404 | .330 |
| Sept./Oct. | 990 | 277 | 36 | 12 | 21 | 124 | 86 | 183 | .280 | .404 | .339 |
| Leading Off Inn. | 1355 | 366 | 62 | 7 | 40 | 40 | 90 | 215 | .270 | .415 | .319 |
| Runners On | 2319 | 620 | 106 | 21 | 44 | 574 | 249 | 382 | .267 | .388 | .335 |
| Runners/Scor. Pos. | 1374 | 359 | 65 | 13 | 17 | 495 | 191 | 254 | .261 | .365 | .344 |
| Runners On/2 Out | 998 | 257 | 44 | 9 | 20 | 229 | 120 | 169 | .258 | .380 | .341 |
| Scor. Pos./2 Out | 674 | 170 | 31 | 4 | 9 | 195 | 106 | 120 | .252 | .350 | .358 |
| Late Inning Pressure | 730 | 181 | 28 | 3 | 12 | 66 | 59 | 131 | .248 | .344 | .303 |
| Leading Off | 192 | 46 | 8 | 1 | 5 | 5 | 12 | 33 | .240 | .370 | .288 |
| Runners On | 286 | 74 | 10 | 0 | 4 | 58 | 28 | 54 | .259 | .336 | .320 |
| Runners/Scor. Pos. | 180 | 46 | 7 | 0 | 2 | 52 | 23 | 40 | .256 | .328 | .332 |

| RUNS BATTED IN | From 1B | From 2B | From 3B | Scoring Position |
|---|---|---|---|---|
| Totals | 81/1615 | 188/1017 | 261/640 | 449/1657 |
| Percentage | 5% | 18% | 41% | 27% |
| Driving In Runners from 3B with Less than Two Out: | | | 188/333 | 56% |

Love to face: Floyd Youmans (7–1)
Hate to face: Dwight Gooden (3–18)
Scored 702 runs, lowest total to lead N.L. (excluding '81 strike season) since 1968 Reds (690); also led league in batting average (.2608) with lowest N.L.-leading average since 1915 Cards hit .254. . . . Have led N.L. in batting average while drawing the league's fewest walks for two straight seasons. . . . That .282 mark vs. left-handed pitchers was also an N.L. high. . . . Rookie batters combined for 1232 at-bats, 163 runs, 343 hits, 10 triples, and 140 RBI, all league highs. . . . Batted N.L.-high .340 in 100 at-bats with bases loaded; but that was a comedown from their .351 average with bags full in 1988. . . . First team to hit into two triple plays since 1982 Cubs. Last team to hit into three: 1979 Rangers.

## Cincinnati Reds

| | AB | H | 2B | 3B | HR | RBI | BB | SO | BA | SA | OBA |
|---|---|---|---|---|---|---|---|---|---|---|---|
| Season | 5520 | 1362 | 243 | 28 | 128 | 588 | 493 | 1028 | .247 | .370 | .309 |
| vs. Left-Handers | 1936 | 466 | 80 | 12 | 45 | 201 | 185 | 358 | .241 | .364 | .309 |
| vs. Right-Handers | 3584 | 896 | 163 | 16 | 83 | 387 | 308 | 670 | .250 | .374 | .310 |
| Home | 2686 | 680 | 133 | 14 | 59 | 292 | 241 | 475 | .253 | .379 | .316 |
| Road | 2834 | 682 | 110 | 14 | 69 | 296 | 252 | 553 | .241 | .362 | .303 |
| Grass | 1719 | 415 | 72 | 8 | 47 | 185 | 152 | 345 | .241 | .375 | .305 |
| Artificial Turf | 3801 | 947 | 171 | 20 | 81 | 403 | 341 | 683 | .249 | .369 | .311 |
| April | 736 | 171 | 35 | 2 | 16 | 70 | 65 | 118 | .232 | .351 | .295 |
| May | 910 | 233 | 38 | 4 | 18 | 108 | 92 | 153 | .256 | .366 | .323 |
| June | 991 | 270 | 45 | 2 | 28 | 107 | 67 | 158 | .272 | .407 | .320 |
| July | 891 | 201 | 29 | 3 | 22 | 76 | 83 | 197 | .226 | .339 | .294 |
| August | 997 | 252 | 40 | 9 | 26 | 117 | 84 | 202 | .253 | .389 | .314 |
| Sept./Oct. | 995 | 235 | 56 | 8 | 18 | 110 | 102 | 200 | .236 | .363 | .307 |
| Leading Off Inn. | 1367 | 324 | 52 | 5 | 27 | 27 | 100 | 223 | .237 | .342 | .293 |
| Runners On | 2211 | 562 | 98 | 16 | 60 | 520 | 267 | 423 | .254 | .394 | .331 |
| Runners/Scor. Pos. | 1273 | 315 | 61 | 10 | 36 | 453 | 214 | 283 | .247 | .396 | .348 |
| Runners On/2 Out | 981 | 235 | 41 | 8 | 25 | 206 | 142 | 194 | .240 | .374 | .338 |
| Scor. Pos./2 Out | 630 | 139 | 27 | 5 | 20 | 186 | 117 | 137 | .221 | .375 | .345 |
| Late Inning Pressure | 869 | 204 | 44 | 2 | 18 | 96 | 90 | 152 | .235 | .352 | .307 |
| Leading Off | 225 | 57 | 10 | 0 | 2 | 2 | 18 | 24 | .253 | .324 | .314 |
| Runners On | 327 | 81 | 17 | 2 | 10 | 88 | 56 | 63 | .248 | .404 | .351 |
| Runners/Scor. Pos. | 186 | 49 | 8 | 2 | 5 | 75 | 49 | 39 | .263 | .409 | .404 |

| RUNS BATTED IN | From 1B | From 2B | From 3B | Scoring Position |
|---|---|---|---|---|
| Totals | 83/1547 | 169/1002 | 208/556 | 377/1558 |
| Percentage | 5% | 17% | 37% | 24% |
| Driving In Runners from 3B with Less than Two Out: | | | 153/280 | 55% |

Love to face: Alejandro Pena (7–2)
Hate to face: Rick Sutcliffe (3–12)
Led N.L. in 9th-inning runs (64), extra-inning runs (20), and runs scored from 7th inning on (221) last season. Also led N.L. in 9th-inning *home runs* (14), half of them coming off bat of Eric Davis. . . . Finished season tied for third in N.L. with 128 home runs. A little history: in 100 years that current Reds team has been in N.L. (1890–1989), Reds have led league in home runs only four times: 1956, 1969–70, and 1976. . . . Six starting right fielders combined for 100 RBI, tying Cubs for N.L. lead. . . . Had a losing record in one-run decisions (21–24) for the first time since 1982. . . . Ah, the Early Opener: Reds won their 7th straight season opener, giving them 14 opening-day wins in the last 16 years.

## Houston Astros

| | AB | H | 2B | 3B | HR | RBI | BB | SO | BA | SA | OBA |
|---|---|---|---|---|---|---|---|---|---|---|---|
| Season | 5516 | 1316 | 239 | 28 | 97 | 601 | 530 | 860 | .239 | .345 | .306 |
| vs. Left-Handers | 1460 | 375 | 69 | 5 | 31 | 177 | 151 | 216 | .257 | .375 | .327 |
| vs. Right-Handers | 4056 | 941 | 170 | 23 | 66 | 424 | 379 | 644 | .232 | .334 | .299 |
| Home | 2753 | 679 | 137 | 17 | 42 | 320 | 278 | 420 | .247 | .355 | .315 |
| Road | 2763 | 637 | 102 | 11 | 55 | 281 | 252 | 440 | .231 | .335 | .297 |
| Grass | 1608 | 349 | 47 | 2 | 33 | 152 | 144 | 262 | .217 | .310 | .282 |
| Artificial Turf | 3908 | 967 | 192 | 26 | 64 | 449 | 386 | 598 | .247 | .359 | .316 |
| April | 862 | 205 | 39 | 5 | 13 | 87 | 76 | 131 | .238 | .340 | .301 |
| May | 908 | 221 | 37 | 6 | 13 | 101 | 91 | 129 | .243 | .340 | .313 |
| June | 979 | 242 | 41 | 6 | 17 | 115 | 84 | 161 | .247 | .353 | .305 |
| July | 852 | 205 | 41 | 4 | 15 | 102 | 81 | 141 | .241 | .351 | .309 |
| August | 955 | 221 | 39 | 4 | 19 | 99 | 108 | 132 | .231 | .340 | .310 |
| Sept./Oct. | 960 | 222 | 42 | 3 | 20 | 97 | 90 | 166 | .231 | .344 | .299 |
| Leading Off Inn. | 1358 | 304 | 63 | 5 | 25 | 25 | 118 | 211 | .224 | .333 | .288 |
| Runners On | 2290 | 600 | 113 | 15 | 39 | 543 | 251 | 340 | .262 | .376 | .333 |
| Runners/Scor. Pos. | 1385 | 347 | 60 | 11 | 20 | 474 | 202 | 245 | .251 | .353 | .339 |
| Runners On/2 Out | 1003 | 233 | 37 | 8 | 16 | 211 | 134 | 170 | .232 | .333 | .327 |
| Scor. Pos./2 Out | 670 | 148 | 21 | 5 | 9 | 183 | 108 | 132 | .221 | .307 | .332 |
| Late Inning Pressure | 912 | 218 | 34 | 2 | 22 | 101 | 93 | 164 | .239 | .353 | .311 |
| Leading Off | 232 | 61 | 11 | 1 | 6 | 6 | 24 | 44 | .263 | .397 | .340 |
| Runners On | 362 | 83 | 15 | 0 | 9 | 88 | 53 | 64 | .229 | .345 | .324 |
| Runners/Scor. Pos. | 211 | 47 | 8 | 0 | 4 | 73 | 42 | 41 | .223 | .318 | .345 |

| RUNS BATTED IN | From 1B | From 2B | From 3B | Scoring Position |
|---|---|---|---|---|
| Totals | 77/1560 | 193/1095 | 234/593 | 427/1688 |
| Percentage | 5% | 18% | 39% | 25% |
| Driving In Runners from 3B with Less than Two Out: | | | 168/307 | 55% |

Love to face: Danny Jackson (4–0)
Hate to face: Sid Fernandez (2–9)
Led majors in games won when trailing after six innings (17), after seven innings (12), and after eight innings (6). . . . Lowest team batting average and fewest walks since 1968; in one stretch in June, Astros drew no walks in three straight games. . . . Had lowest average in majors vs. right-handed pitchers (.232), lowest average on grass fields (.217), and hit only .2239 when leading off inning, lowest in N.L. since 1976 Expos hit .2238. . . . Pinch hitters batted only .185, lowest in N.L. . . . Stole only four bases in their last 18 games, after averaging about one per game until then. . . . With Dome as home, Astros may never lead league in home runs, but they did lead in grand-slam home runs in 1989, with six.

## Los Angeles Dodgers

| | AB | H | 2B | 3B | HR | RBI | BB | SO | BA | SA | OBA |
|---|---|---|---|---|---|---|---|---|---|---|---|
| Season | 5465 | 1313 | 241 | 17 | 89 | 513 | 507 | 885 | .240 | .339 | .306 |
| vs. Left-Handers | 1967 | 460 | 83 | 8 | 28 | 173 | 182 | 305 | .234 | .327 | .301 |
| vs. Right-Handers | 3498 | 853 | 158 | 9 | 61 | 340 | 325 | 580 | .244 | .346 | .309 |
| Home | 2659 | 641 | 111 | 12 | 37 | 233 | 244 | 428 | .241 | .334 | .306 |
| Road | 2806 | 672 | 130 | 5 | 52 | 280 | 263 | 457 | .239 | .345 | .305 |
| Grass | 3954 | 956 | 175 | 13 | 65 | 365 | 370 | 643 | .242 | .342 | .307 |
| Artificial Turf | 1511 | 357 | 66 | 4 | 24 | 148 | 137 | 242 | .236 | .333 | .302 |
| April | 817 | 186 | 40 | 2 | 10 | 70 | 73 | 130 | .228 | .318 | .292 |
| May | 823 | 198 | 45 | 2 | 12 | 79 | 91 | 137 | .241 | .344 | .321 |
| June | 1047 | 247 | 35 | 5 | 16 | 87 | 101 | 187 | .236 | .325 | .303 |
| July | 931 | 224 | 45 | 2 | 15 | 90 | 83 | 134 | .241 | .342 | .305 |
| August | 949 | 230 | 40 | 3 | 20 | 97 | 92 | 145 | .242 | .354 | .309 |
| Sept./Oct. | 898 | 228 | 36 | 3 | 16 | 90 | 67 | 152 | .254 | .354 | .306 |
| Leading Off Inn. | 1365 | 322 | 54 | 4 | 20 | 20 | 97 | 196 | .236 | .325 | .292 |
| Runners On | 2273 | 555 | 109 | 5 | 45 | 469 | 249 | 363 | .244 | .356 | .316 |
| Runners/Scor. Pos. | 1229 | 280 | 57 | 5 | 24 | 403 | 190 | 214 | .228 | .341 | .323 |
| Runners On/2 Out | 1025 | 234 | 45 | 1 | 18 | 187 | 119 | 180 | .228 | .327 | .310 |
| Scor. Pos./2 Out | 617 | 128 | 24 | 1 | 11 | 161 | 97 | 115 | .207 | .303 | .317 |
| Late Inning Pressure | 1036 | 225 | 31 | 3 | 11 | 65 | 102 | 185 | .217 | .285 | .288 |
| Leading Off | 268 | 56 | 7 | 0 | 4 | 4 | 23 | 42 | .209 | .280 | .276 |
| Runners On | 415 | 88 | 13 | 0 | 5 | 59 | 57 | 82 | .212 | .280 | .303 |
| Runners/Scor. Pos. | 210 | 29 | 7 | 0 | 3 | 51 | 45 | 48 | .138 | .214 | .283 |

| RUNS BATTED IN | From 1B | From 2B | From 3B | Scoring Position |
|---|---|---|---|---|
| Totals | 72/1675 | 160/977 | 192/530 | 352/1507 |
| Percentage | 4% | 16% | 36% | 23% |
| Driving In Runners from 3B with Less than Two Out: | | | 130/253 | 51% |

Love to face: Frank DiPino (6–0)
Hate to face: Craig Lefferts (0–8)
Opposing starters completed 25 games, the most CG against any N.L. club. . . . Batted .217 in Late-Inning Pressure Situations, 2d-lowest mark in N.L. over past 15 years. The lowest also came out of last year's N.L. West: Atlanta hit .214 in LIPS. . . . But no N.L. team out-lowed the Dodgers in batting average with runners on base (.244) or with runners in scoring position (.228). . . . Oh yes, the Big One: L.A. hit .138 (29-for-210) in Late-Inning Pressure Situations with runners in scoring position, and they hit .099 (10-for-101) in those situations with two outs. Both of those figures are the lowest N.L. averages we've seen in those categories in our 15 years of tracking them.

## Montreal Expos

| | AB | H | 2B | 3B | HR | RBI | BB | SO | BA | SA | OBA |
|---|---|---|---|---|---|---|---|---|---|---|---|
| Season | 5482 | 1353 | 267 | 30 | 100 | 589 | 572 | 958 | .247 | .361 | .319 |
| vs. Left-Handers | 1623 | 442 | 87 | 4 | 43 | 194 | 159 | 273 | .272 | .410 | .339 |
| vs. Right-Handers | 3859 | 911 | 180 | 26 | 57 | 395 | 413 | 685 | .236 | .341 | .311 |
| Home | 2711 | 696 | 142 | 15 | 55 | 314 | 282 | 482 | .257 | .381 | .329 |
| Road | 2771 | 657 | 125 | 15 | 45 | 275 | 290 | 476 | .237 | .342 | .310 |
| Grass | 1397 | 318 | 53 | 8 | 23 | 131 | 142 | 257 | .228 | .326 | .298 |
| Artificial Turf | 4085 | 1035 | 214 | 22 | 77 | 458 | 430 | 701 | .253 | .373 | .327 |
| April | 774 | 190 | 38 | 8 | 15 | 105 | 89 | 127 | .245 | .373 | .325 |
| May | 931 | 223 | 42 | 5 | 14 | 96 | 107 | 159 | .240 | .340 | .319 |
| June | 919 | 234 | 64 | 5 | 13 | 108 | 116 | 165 | .255 | .378 | .338 |
| July | 923 | 251 | 49 | 5 | 27 | 111 | 79 | 173 | .272 | .424 | .332 |
| August | 976 | 220 | 33 | 5 | 17 | 82 | 105 | 161 | .225 | .322 | .301 |
| Sept./Oct. | 959 | 235 | 41 | 2 | 14 | 87 | 76 | 173 | .245 | .336 | .303 |
| Leading Off Inn. | 1349 | 316 | 54 | 11 | 24 | 24 | 114 | 219 | .234 | .344 | .299 |
| Runners On | 2312 | 579 | 106 | 13 | 49 | 538 | 306 | 411 | .250 | .371 | .336 |
| Runners/Scor. Pos. | 1364 | 346 | 72 | 9 | 24 | 468 | 240 | 263 | .254 | .372 | .359 |
| Runners On/2 Out | 999 | 237 | 46 | 3 | 13 | 198 | 160 | 193 | .237 | .328 | .344 |
| Scor. Pos./2 Out | 672 | 148 | 33 | 3 | 8 | 181 | 133 | 140 | .220 | .314 | .350 |
| Late Inning Pressure | 950 | 238 | 38 | 5 | 13 | 97 | 99 | 169 | .251 | .342 | .322 |
| Leading Off | 245 | 62 | 6 | 1 | 4 | 4 | 18 | 43 | .253 | .335 | .307 |
| Runners On | 382 | 98 | 14 | 2 | 7 | 91 | 59 | 69 | .257 | .359 | .353 |
| Runners/Scor. Pos. | 224 | 61 | 8 | 0 | 2 | 76 | 51 | 41 | .272 | .335 | .401 |

| RUNS BATTED IN | From 1B | From 2B | From 3B | Scoring Position |
|---|---|---|---|---|
| Totals | 77/1613 | 186/1083 | 226/562 | 412/1645 |
| Percentage | 5% | 17% | 40% | 25% |
| Driving In Runners from 3B with Less than Two Out: | | | 163/287 | 57% |

Love to face: Tom Glavine (4–0)
Hate to face: Doug Drabek (1–6)
Led N.L. with 160 stolen bases, breaking Cardinals' seven-year reign. Last club to lead N.L. with so few steals (we are officially tired of writing "except 1981"): 1973 Reds (148). . . . Leadoff hitters in batting order had on-base average of .350, best in league. There was no payoff, however: their leadoff hitters scored only 87 runs, second-lowest total in N.L. . . . Third team in history to finish at .500 for two years in a row; others: 1972–73 Twins, 1982–83 Padres. Expos scored only two more runs than they allowed; of 42 teams in history that finished season at .500, there have been two that were the ultimate .500 teams, scoring and allowing equal amounts of runs: 1922 White Sox and 1983 Padres.

## New York Mets

| | AB | H | 2B | 3B | HR | RBI | BB | SO | BA | SA | OBA |
|---|---|---|---|---|---|---|---|---|---|---|---|
| Season | 5489 | 1351 | 280 | 21 | 147 | 634 | 504 | 934 | .246 | .385 | .311 |
| vs. Left-Handers | 1929 | 475 | 88 | 6 | 51 | 219 | 186 | 333 | .246 | .377 | .313 |
| vs. Right-Handers | 3560 | 876 | 192 | 15 | 96 | 415 | 318 | 601 | .246 | .389 | .310 |
| Home | 2649 | 660 | 129 | 10 | 78 | 307 | 252 | 441 | .249 | .394 | .315 |
| Road | 2840 | 691 | 151 | 11 | 69 | 327 | 252 | 493 | .243 | .377 | .307 |
| Grass | 3795 | 937 | 188 | 12 | 106 | 419 | 328 | 634 | .247 | .387 | .308 |
| Artificial Turf | 1694 | 414 | 92 | 9 | 41 | 215 | 176 | 300 | .244 | .382 | .318 |
| April | 722 | 176 | 40 | 5 | 19 | 80 | 73 | 109 | .244 | .392 | .312 |
| May | 929 | 211 | 40 | 2 | 20 | 80 | 87 | 185 | .227 | .339 | .294 |
| June | 893 | 225 | 47 | 3 | 32 | 118 | 91 | 147 | .252 | .419 | .323 |
| July | 924 | 231 | 57 | 2 | 22 | 114 | 80 | 153 | .250 | .387 | .310 |
| August | 966 | 244 | 54 | 5 | 25 | 113 | 82 | 150 | .253 | .396 | .312 |
| Sept./Oct. | 1055 | 264 | 42 | 4 | 29 | 129 | 91 | 190 | .250 | .380 | .314 |
| Leading Off Inn. | 1363 | 341 | 63 | 5 | 45 | 45 | 84 | 219 | .250 | .403 | .297 |
| Runners On | 2266 | 572 | 134 | 7 | 50 | 537 | 258 | 407 | .252 | .384 | .327 |
| Runners/Scor. Pos. | 1373 | 339 | 68 | 5 | 31 | 474 | 196 | 272 | .247 | .371 | .335 |
| Runners On/2 Out | 984 | 220 | 47 | 0 | 17 | 198 | 128 | 185 | .224 | .323 | .317 |
| Scor. Pos./2 Out | 656 | 148 | 27 | 0 | 14 | 182 | 99 | 130 | .226 | .331 | .330 |
| Late Inning Pressure | 806 | 188 | 37 | 1 | 23 | 78 | 74 | 144 | .233 | .367 | .300 |
| Leading Off | 215 | 54 | 6 | 0 | 10 | 10 | 14 | 39 | .251 | .419 | .300 |
| Runners On | 309 | 67 | 15 | 0 | 6 | 61 | 38 | 52 | .217 | .324 | .302 |
| Runners/Scor. Pos. | 156 | 34 | 7 | 0 | 3 | 53 | 29 | 31 | .218 | .321 | .339 |

| RUNS BATTED IN | From 1B | From 2B | From 3B | Scoring Position |
|---|---|---|---|---|
| Totals | 70/1520 | 192/1077 | 225/585 | 417/1662 |
| Percentage | 5% | 18% | 38% | 25% |
| Driving In Runners from 3B with Less than Two Out: | | | 161/301 | 53% |

Love to face: Craig Lefferts (7–0)
Hate to face: John Smiley (1–7)
Despite hitting only one home run in first seven games, became first N.L. team to lead majors in home runs since Big Red Machine of 1976. . . . Led N.L. in doubles for first time; when Cubs led in 1988, they were first natural-turf team to lead N.L. in doubles since 1970. . . . With all that power, they finished last in N.L. in li'l ol' singles. Despite what you may think, leading league in most home runs and fewest singles in same year is not a common occurrance; no N.L. team had done it since 1967 Braves. . . . Starting first basemen batted .285, 4th highest in N.L., but slugging average (.384) ranked 11th. Mets' starting first basemen combined for fewest home runs (7) and RBI (55) in majors.

## Phila. Phillies

| | AB | H | 2B | 3B | HR | RBI | BB | SO | BA | SA | OBA |
|---|---|---|---|---|---|---|---|---|---|---|---|
| Season | 5447 | 1324 | 215 | 36 | 123 | 600 | 558 | 926 | .243 | .364 | .314 |
| vs. Left-Handers | 2036 | 508 | 74 | 16 | 39 | 217 | 210 | 329 | .250 | .359 | .319 |
| vs. Right-Handers | 3411 | 816 | 141 | 20 | 84 | 383 | 348 | 597 | .239 | .366 | .311 |
| Home | 2644 | 650 | 112 | 22 | 61 | 308 | 279 | 449 | .246 | .374 | .319 |
| Road | 2803 | 674 | 103 | 14 | 62 | 292 | 279 | 477 | .240 | .354 | .309 |
| Grass | 1425 | 338 | 41 | 6 | 38 | 151 | 148 | 256 | .237 | .354 | .309 |
| Artificial Turf | 4022 | 986 | 174 | 30 | 85 | 449 | 410 | 670 | .245 | .367 | .315 |
| April | 781 | 210 | 31 | 2 | 23 | 109 | 83 | 119 | .269 | .402 | .339 |
| May | 837 | 170 | 19 | 4 | 14 | 72 | 78 | 148 | .203 | .286 | .271 |
| June | 909 | 223 | 43 | 7 | 23 | 116 | 121 | 161 | .245 | .384 | .336 |
| July | 981 | 241 | 39 | 6 | 17 | 104 | 106 | 165 | .246 | .350 | .318 |
| August | 962 | 231 | 45 | 8 | 24 | 99 | 77 | 134 | .240 | .378 | .298 |
| Sept./Oct. | 977 | 249 | 38 | 9 | 22 | 100 | 93 | 199 | .255 | .380 | .319 |
| Leading Off Inn. | 1342 | 329 | 56 | 6 | 35 | 35 | 111 | 194 | .245 | .374 | .304 |
| Runners On | 2289 | 588 | 76 | 20 | 60 | 537 | 269 | 385 | .257 | .386 | .332 |
| Runners/Scor. Pos. | 1338 | 323 | 45 | 14 | 30 | 461 | 188 | 255 | .241 | .363 | .329 |
| Runners On/2 Out | 999 | 234 | 29 | 7 | 25 | 202 | 127 | 178 | .234 | .352 | .322 |
| Scor. Pos./2 Out | 651 | 135 | 17 | 5 | 15 | 175 | 101 | 130 | .207 | .318 | .316 |
| Late Inning Pressure | 872 | 207 | 29 | 3 | 16 | 87 | 101 | 156 | .237 | .333 | .317 |
| Leading Off | 215 | 56 | 8 | 1 | 7 | 7 | 22 | 32 | .260 | .405 | .332 |
| Runners On | 390 | 90 | 6 | 2 | 7 | 78 | 51 | 77 | .231 | .310 | .318 |
| Runners/Scor. Pos. | 232 | 56 | 4 | 2 | 4 | 71 | 38 | 51 | .241 | .328 | .343 |

| RUNS BATTED IN | From 1B | From 2B | From 3B | Scoring Position |
|---|---|---|---|---|
| Totals | 72/1636 | 168/1051 | 237/570 | 405/1621 |
| Percentage | 4% | 16% | 42% | 25% |
| Driving In Runners from 3B with Less than Two Out: | | | 169/288 | 59% |

Love to face: Bob Kipper (5–0)
Hate to face: John Tudor (4–12)
N.L.'s highest April batting average, and May's lowest. . . . Started 10 different players in the leadoff spot, tying Reds and Padres for most in majors; Phils had a winning record with only one of those 10 players: 1–0 with Keith Miller. . . . Had an 11-game streak without a home run, June 25 to July 5, their longest since 12 games in August 1960. (Did someone say "Mike Schmidt"?). . . . Only team that did not win a home game in which they trailed going into the 9th inning; they didn't win any such games in 1988, either, and bring a streak of 75 losses in home games of this type into '90s. . . . Let's finish on an upbeat note, just as Phils did: They ended season with four wins, their longest winning streak of 1989.

## Pittsburgh Pirates

| | AB | H | 2B | 3B | HR | RBI | BB | SO | BA | SA | OBA |
|---|---|---|---|---|---|---|---|---|---|---|---|
| Season | 5539 | 1334 | 263 | 53 | 95 | 589 | 563 | 914 | .241 | .359 | .311 |
| vs. Left-Handers | 1913 | 469 | 100 | 19 | 27 | 209 | 211 | 308 | .245 | .360 | .319 |
| vs. Right-Handers | 3626 | 865 | 163 | 34 | 68 | 380 | 352 | 606 | .239 | .359 | .306 |
| Home | 2678 | 642 | 129 | 24 | 45 | 280 | 316 | 420 | .240 | .356 | .319 |
| Road | 2861 | 692 | 134 | 29 | 50 | 309 | 247 | 494 | .242 | .361 | .303 |
| Grass | 1438 | 329 | 54 | 14 | 25 | 132 | 116 | 259 | .229 | .338 | .288 |
| Artificial Turf | 4101 | 1005 | 209 | 39 | 70 | 457 | 447 | 655 | .245 | .366 | .319 |
| April | 791 | 183 | 39 | 3 | 10 | 85 | 72 | 114 | .231 | .326 | .292 |
| May | 869 | 210 | 47 | 5 | 18 | 102 | 95 | 148 | .242 | .369 | .319 |
| June | 881 | 217 | 38 | 16 | 11 | 97 | 101 | 128 | .246 | .363 | .323 |
| July | 979 | 225 | 41 | 8 | 15 | 99 | 105 | 163 | .230 | .334 | .306 |
| August | 985 | 235 | 39 | 7 | 21 | 96 | 95 | 172 | .239 | .356 | .308 |
| Sept./Oct. | 1034 | 264 | 59 | 14 | 20 | 110 | 95 | 189 | .255 | .397 | .317 |
| Leading Off Inn. | 1374 | 329 | 65 | 13 | 30 | 30 | 122 | 210 | .239 | .371 | .302 |
| Runners On | 2290 | 567 | 112 | 27 | 32 | 526 | 286 | 395 | .248 | .362 | .328 |
| Runners/Scor. Pos. | 1330 | 342 | 66 | 21 | 17 | 462 | 222 | 236 | .257 | .377 | .355 |
| Runners On/2 Out | 984 | 225 | 43 | 12 | 14 | 198 | 155 | 202 | .229 | .339 | .338 |
| Scor. Pos./2 Out | 643 | 139 | 25 | 10 | 6 | 167 | 125 | 132 | .216 | .314 | .349 |
| Late Inning Pressure | 940 | 214 | 37 | 9 | 14 | 83 | 103 | 186 | .228 | .331 | .305 |
| Leading Off | 244 | 57 | 13 | 0 | 4 | 4 | 23 | 46 | .234 | .336 | .302 |
| Runners On | 375 | 85 | 14 | 6 | 3 | 72 | 58 | 71 | .227 | .320 | .329 |
| Runners/Scor. Pos. | 228 | 47 | 10 | 6 | 3 | 70 | 47 | 53 | .206 | .342 | .335 |

| RUNS BATTED IN | From 1B | From 2B | From 3B | Scoring Position |
|---|---|---|---|---|
| Totals | 75/1584 | 187/974 | 232/603 | 419/1577 |
| Percentage | 5% | 19% | 38% | 27% |
| Driving In Runners from 3B with Less than Two Out: | | | 177/310 | 57% |

Love to face: Greg Maddux (7–2)
Hate to face: Bob Ojeda (3–10)

Led N.L. in triples for 39th time this century, but for first time since 1978. . . . N.L. pinch hitters had only 27 sacrifices last season, but Leyland wasn't shy about doing it: Pittsburgh accounted for 7 of those 27 (or 27 percent). . . . Maybe he just got tired of seeing pinch hitters ground into double plays; Bucs and Cards shared N.L. lead in that category (10). . . . One of three major league clubs with a losing record in one-run decisions at home: Pirates, 11–15; Braves, 11–12; Expos, 16–17. . . . Batted .240 in home games, lowest such average by any N.L. team. . . . Third-place hitters in lineup batted a major league–low .242; we don't want to mention any names, but do the initials "A.V.S." mean anything to you?

## St. Louis Cardinals

| | AB | H | 2B | 3B | HR | RBI | BB | SO | BA | SA | OBA |
|---|---|---|---|---|---|---|---|---|---|---|---|
| Season | 5492 | 1418 | 263 | 47 | 73 | 588 | 507 | 848 | .258 | .363 | .321 |
| vs. Left-Handers | 2184 | 553 | 117 | 14 | 30 | 217 | 194 | 349 | .253 | .361 | .314 |
| vs. Right-Handers | 3308 | 865 | 146 | 33 | 43 | 371 | 313 | 499 | .261 | .365 | .326 |
| Home | 2675 | 686 | 142 | 34 | 27 | 302 | 251 | 391 | .256 | .365 | .320 |
| Road | 2817 | 732 | 121 | 13 | 46 | 286 | 256 | 457 | .260 | .361 | .322 |
| Grass | 1461 | 383 | 60 | 9 | 22 | 143 | 123 | 240 | .262 | .361 | .320 |
| Artificial Turf | 4031 | 1035 | 203 | 38 | 51 | 445 | 384 | 608 | .257 | .364 | .321 |
| April | 738 | 198 | 41 | 7 | 11 | 92 | 65 | 111 | .268 | .388 | .326 |
| May | 911 | 221 | 42 | 5 | 9 | 78 | 84 | 118 | .243 | .329 | .309 |
| June | 898 | 220 | 49 | 9 | 10 | 101 | 94 | 129 | .245 | .353 | .316 |
| July | 859 | 242 | 46 | 8 | 9 | 101 | 87 | 151 | .282 | .385 | .348 |
| August | 1058 | 278 | 46 | 8 | 20 | 115 | 85 | 160 | .263 | .378 | .319 |
| Sept./Oct. | 1028 | 259 | 39 | 10 | 14 | 101 | 92 | 179 | .252 | .350 | .312 |
| Leading Off Inn. | 1351 | 347 | 74 | 12 | 13 | 13 | 102 | 208 | .257 | .358 | .312 |
| Runners On | 2372 | 644 | 112 | 19 | 34 | 549 | 249 | 366 | .272 | .378 | .338 |
| Runners/Scor. Pos. | 1443 | 379 | 77 | 16 | 20 | 502 | 190 | 261 | .263 | .380 | .342 |
| Runners On/2 Out | 1032 | 276 | 47 | 9 | 16 | 236 | 126 | 175 | .267 | .377 | .349 |
| Scor. Pos./2 Out | 704 | 182 | 34 | 8 | 12 | 221 | 104 | 133 | .259 | .381 | .356 |
| Late Inning Pressure | 789 | 199 | 35 | 6 | 8 | 78 | 87 | 132 | .252 | .342 | .325 |
| Leading Off | 196 | 52 | 15 | 3 | 1 | 1 | 21 | 33 | .265 | .388 | .339 |
| Runners On | 361 | 93 | 9 | 1 | 4 | 74 | 40 | 54 | .258 | .321 | .326 |
| Runners/Scor. Pos. | 216 | 55 | 6 | 0 | 2 | 68 | 29 | 40 | .255 | .310 | .333 |

| RUNS BATTED IN | From 1B | From 2B | From 3B | Scoring Position |
|---|---|---|---|---|
| Totals | 62/1634 | 186/1077 | 266/626 | 452/1703 |
| Percentage | 4% | 17% | 42% | 27% |
| Driving In Runners from 3B with Less than Two Out: | | | 169/324 | 52% |

Love to face: Kevin Gross (14–3)
Hate to face: Steve Bedrosian (2–9)

Scored only 50 unearned runs, fewest in majors. . . . Only team in majors without a pinch-hit home run in both '88 and '89. Last one: Jose Oquendo, July 25, 1987. . . . Have not suffered consecutive shutouts since Aug. 1, 1988, longest streak by any N.L. club. . . . Started season with home runs in each of first seven games, a feat aided by a six-game road trip. Cards didn't hit home runs in more than two straight games at Busch all year. . . . Batted .324 with the bases loaded, second-best to Cubs in N.L.; but Cards' .351 mark (20-for-57) with bases loaded and two outs was best in majors. . . . Had N.L.'s best record (54–41–1) vs. right-handed starters, but were only N.L. team to see fewer than 100 of them.

## San Diego Padres

| | AB | H | 2B | 3B | HR | RBI | BB | SO | BA | SA | OBA |
|---|---|---|---|---|---|---|---|---|---|---|---|
| Season | 5422 | 1360 | 215 | 32 | 120 | 600 | 552 | 1013 | .251 | .369 | .319 |
| vs. Left-Handers | 1606 | 428 | 67 | 15 | 32 | 199 | 179 | 269 | .267 | .387 | .340 |
| vs. Right-Handers | 3816 | 932 | 148 | 17 | 88 | 401 | 373 | 744 | .244 | .361 | .310 |
| Home | 2592 | 650 | 101 | 15 | 66 | 305 | 279 | 485 | .251 | .378 | .323 |
| Road | 2830 | 710 | 114 | 17 | 54 | 295 | 273 | 528 | .251 | .360 | .315 |
| Grass | 3981 | 997 | 154 | 18 | 93 | 434 | 414 | 755 | .250 | .368 | .320 |
| Artificial Turf | 1441 | 363 | 61 | 14 | 27 | 166 | 138 | 258 | .252 | .370 | .316 |
| April | 854 | 198 | 28 | 3 | 20 | 76 | 81 | 149 | .232 | .342 | .297 |
| May | 921 | 222 | 36 | 11 | 10 | 85 | 97 | 191 | .241 | .337 | .313 |
| June | 917 | 242 | 34 | 7 | 13 | 86 | 85 | 181 | .264 | .359 | .325 |
| July | 811 | 200 | 27 | 4 | 16 | 90 | 83 | 133 | .247 | .349 | .315 |
| August | 978 | 265 | 49 | 5 | 31 | 135 | 95 | 182 | .271 | .426 | .334 |
| Sept./Oct. | 941 | 233 | 41 | 2 | 30 | 128 | 111 | 177 | .248 | .391 | .326 |
| Leading Off Inn. | 1314 | 355 | 58 | 9 | 29 | 29 | 131 | 261 | .270 | .394 | .339 |
| Runners On | 2341 | 581 | 89 | 14 | 60 | 540 | 274 | 427 | .248 | .375 | .322 |
| Runners/Scor. Pos. | 1367 | 315 | 50 | 10 | 40 | 478 | 209 | 285 | .230 | .369 | .325 |
| Runners On/2 Out | 955 | 195 | 31 | 5 | 20 | 171 | 140 | 210 | .204 | .310 | .307 |
| Scor. Pos./2 Out | 642 | 122 | 21 | 4 | 16 | 155 | 111 | 155 | .190 | .310 | .311 |
| Late Inning Pressure | 748 | 196 | 25 | 3 | 8 | 75 | 89 | 161 | .262 | .336 | .339 |
| Leading Off | 190 | 51 | 5 | 0 | 1 | 1 | 19 | 46 | .268 | .311 | .335 |
| Runners On | 338 | 84 | 12 | 3 | 4 | 71 | 47 | 62 | .249 | .337 | .338 |
| Runners/Scor. Pos. | 199 | 43 | 6 | 1 | 1 | 59 | 36 | 44 | .216 | .271 | .332 |

| RUNS BATTED IN | From 1B | From 2B | From 3B | Scoring Position |
|---|---|---|---|---|
| Totals | 79/1633 | 177/1047 | 224/590 | 401/1637 |
| Percentage | 5% | 17% | 38% | 24% |
| Driving In Runners from 3B with Less than Two Out: | | | 177/318 | 56% |

Love to face: Jim Deshaies (7–2)
Hate to face: John Franco (2–7)

Batted a major league–low .181 with bases loaded last season; with two outs and the bags full, they hit .091 (5-for-55). . . . Batting average with two outs and runners on base (.204) was lowest in N.L. since '75 Dodgers hit .203; with two outs and runners in scoring position, Padres hit .190, lowest by any N.L. team in the 15 years that we go back. . . . Batters were hit by only nine pitches, tying 1939 Phillies' N.L. record for fewest. . . . Scored 95 unearned runs, most by any team in majors. . . . Led N.L. in sacrifice bunts for 7th time in last 15 years. . . . Started eight different players in cleanup spot, tying Twins for most in majors. . . . Not shut out in last 65 games, longest streak any team takes into '90s.

## San Francisco Giants

| | AB | H | 2B | 3B | HR | RBI | BB | SO | BA | SA | OBA |
|---|---|---|---|---|---|---|---|---|---|---|---|
| Season | 5469 | 1365 | 241 | 52 | 141 | 647 | 508 | 1071 | .250 | .390 | .316 |
| vs. Left-Handers | 1846 | 458 | 75 | 21 | 49 | 227 | 186 | 339 | .248 | .391 | .320 |
| vs. Right-Handers | 3623 | 907 | 166 | 31 | 92 | 420 | 322 | 732 | .250 | .389 | .314 |
| Home | 2652 | 680 | 126 | 30 | 63 | 343 | 252 | 494 | .256 | .398 | .323 |
| Road | 2817 | 685 | 115 | 22 | 78 | 304 | 256 | 577 | .243 | .383 | .310 |
| Grass | 4011 | 1018 | 179 | 40 | 101 | 491 | 359 | 794 | .254 | .394 | .317 |
| Artificial Turf | 1458 | 347 | 62 | 12 | 40 | 156 | 149 | 277 | .238 | .379 | .313 |
| April | 820 | 208 | 43 | 9 | 17 | 89 | 93 | 157 | .254 | .390 | .330 |
| May | 917 | 229 | 40 | 10 | 26 | 109 | 87 | 179 | .250 | .400 | .317 |
| June | 937 | 255 | 40 | 13 | 26 | 129 | 107 | 157 | .272 | .426 | .346 |
| July | 883 | 210 | 35 | 8 | 21 | 95 | 60 | 165 | .238 | .367 | .295 |
| August | 925 | 220 | 38 | 7 | 29 | 105 | 83 | 195 | .238 | .388 | .305 |
| Sept./Oct. | 987 | 243 | 45 | 5 | 22 | 120 | 78 | 218 | .246 | .369 | .302 |
| Leading Off Inn. | 1345 | 349 | 55 | 16 | 33 | 33 | 94 | 244 | .259 | .398 | .311 |
| Runners On | 2264 | 579 | 106 | 19 | 66 | 572 | 271 | 448 | .256 | .407 | .335 |
| Runners/Scor. Pos. | 1326 | 326 | 64 | 11 | 40 | 489 | 206 | 283 | .246 | .401 | .344 |
| Runners On/2 Out | 965 | 205 | 40 | 8 | 27 | 218 | 148 | 208 | .212 | .354 | .321 |
| Scor. Pos./2 Out | 626 | 127 | 23 | 5 | 17 | 186 | 117 | 142 | .203 | .337 | .334 |
| Late Inning Pressure | 770 | 195 | 32 | 5 | 18 | 86 | 78 | 171 | .253 | .378 | .323 |
| Leading Off | 193 | 49 | 7 | 0 | 6 | 6 | 13 | 34 | .254 | .383 | .301 |
| Runners On | 328 | 81 | 13 | 4 | 6 | 74 | 43 | 87 | .247 | .366 | .332 |
| Runners/Scor. Pos. | 184 | 48 | 8 | 2 | 3 | 64 | 34 | 48 | .261 | .375 | .372 |

| RUNS BATTED IN | From 1B | From 2B | From 3B | Scoring Position |
|---|---|---|---|---|
| Totals | 102/1583 | 194/1025 | 210/564 | 404/1589 |
| Percentage | 6% | 19% | 37% | 25% |
| Driving In Runners from 3B with Less than Two Out: | | | 152/291 | 52% |

Love to face: Bruce Ruffin (6–2)
Hate to face: Orel Hershiser (5–15)

Batted .314 in 153 at-bats with runners in scoring position when trailing by one run, best such average in N.L. . . . Only team in N.L. to get 90+ RBI each from third, fourth, and fifth spots in batting order; they also led N.L. in batting average from third (.336) and fourth (.292) spots, but their .217 average from five-hole was worst in majors. . . . Lost only six shutouts last season, fewest in N.L.; last five teams to suffer fewest shutouts in N.L. have all won division title that season. . . . Scored at least one run in 77 games in a row (May 26 to Aug. 18), longest streak in majors last season. Streak started right after Expos shut them out in consecutive games. . . . Used 342 pinch hitters last season, most in majors.

## National League

| | AB | H | 2B | 3B | HR | RBI | BB | SO | BA | SA | OBA |
|---|---|---|---|---|---|---|---|---|---|---|---|
| Season | 65817 | 16215 | 2903 | 411 | 1365 | 7149 | 6251 | 11354 | .246 | .365 | .312 |
| vs. Left-Handers | 21880 | 5496 | 985 | 140 | 451 | 2427 | 2185 | 3652 | .251 | .371 | .320 |
| vs. Right-Handers | 43937 | 10719 | 1918 | 271 | 914 | 4722 | 4066 | 7702 | .244 | .362 | .309 |
| Home | 32095 | 8052 | 1484 | 224 | 649 | 3647 | 3152 | 5363 | .251 | .372 | .318 |
| Road | 33722 | 8163 | 1419 | 187 | 716 | 3502 | 3099 | 5991 | .242 | .359 | .307 |
| Grass | 32584 | 7963 | 1329 | 174 | 730 | 3466 | 2961 | 5799 | .244 | .363 | .308 |
| Artificial Turf | 33233 | 8252 | 1574 | 237 | 635 | 3683 | 3290 | 5555 | .248 | .367 | .317 |
| April | 9498 | 2309 | 437 | 57 | 185 | 1028 | 916 | 1549 | .243 | .360 | .310 |
| May | 10793 | 2578 | 458 | 66 | 179 | 1080 | 1056 | 1842 | .239 | .343 | .308 |
| June | 11220 | 2835 | 508 | 85 | 231 | 1256 | 1122 | 1875 | .253 | .375 | .321 |
| July | 10867 | 2689 | 493 | 57 | 228 | 1198 | 1011 | 1893 | .247 | .366 | .313 |
| August | 11688 | 2884 | 497 | 70 | 294 | 1288 | 1087 | 1973 | .247 | .377 | .312 |
| Sept./Oct. | 11751 | 2920 | 510 | 76 | 248 | 1299 | 1059 | 2222 | .248 | .368 | .311 |
| Leading Off Inn. | 16259 | 3991 | 705 | 98 | 355 | 355 | 1253 | 2656 | .245 | .366 | .302 |
| Runners On | 27393 | 7002 | 1261 | 188 | 584 | 6368 | 3155 | 4711 | .256 | .379 | .330 |
| Runners/Scor. Pos. | 15956 | 3966 | 734 | 135 | 320 | 5551 | 2422 | 3070 | .249 | .372 | .341 |
| Runners On/2 Out | 11899 | 2787 | 495 | 78 | 230 | 2461 | 1628 | 2236 | .234 | .347 | .329 |
| Scor. Pos./2 Out | 7769 | 1722 | 307 | 57 | 147 | 2168 | 1319 | 1586 | .222 | .333 | .337 |
| Late Inning Pressure | 10372 | 2468 | 398 | 44 | 179 | 994 | 1049 | 1972 | .238 | .337 | .308 |
| Leading Off | 2658 | 654 | 107 | 8 | 53 | 53 | 221 | 486 | .246 | .352 | .307 |
| Runners On | 4235 | 1017 | 147 | 21 | 73 | 888 | 562 | 806 | .240 | .336 | .326 |
| Runners/Scor. Pos. | 2434 | 567 | 85 | 14 | 37 | 779 | 445 | 524 | .233 | .325 | .345 |

| RUNS BATTED IN | From 1B | From 2B | From 3B | Scoring Position |
|---|---|---|---|---|
| Percentage | 5% | 18% | 39% | 25% |
| Driving In Runners from 3B with Less than Two Out: | | | 1922/3517 | 55% |

# IV
# Pitcher Section

# *Pitcher Section*

The Pitcher Section is an alphabetical listing of every pitcher who faced at least 300 batters in either the American or the National League last season. Also included are all those who finished at least 20 games in relief. Pitchers are listed alphabetically within each league, followed by the totals of each team and the league as a whole.

## Column Headings Information

**Don Aase**

| Baltimore Orioles | W-L | ERA | AB | H | HR | BB | SO | BA | SA | OBA |
|---|---|---|---|---|---|---|---|---|---|---|

- W-L Won-Lost Record
- ERA Earned-Run Average
- AB At Bats
- H Hits
- HR Home Runs
- BB Bases on Balls
- SO Strikeouts
- BA Batting Average
- SA Slugging Average
- OBA On-Base Average

**In addition to the expected categories for pitchers (won-lost record, ERA, walks, and strikeouts), this book includes a unique perspective on each pitcher's season: the batting performance of the league against him. While this method may be unfamiliar at first, it enables us to look at the pitcher and his abilities in fascinating detail.**

**By compiling pitching statistics in this way, we can examine a pitcher's performance in the same "within the game" contexts we've used to look at batters. To take one example, we're all familiar with platoon differentials for batters; we know that some right-handed batters are far more effective against left-handed pitchers than they are against righties. The same must be true of pitchers, but because the specific information was never available before, who knew how big those differences were? Well,** we know now, and the differences can be huge.

Moreover, by looking at the opponents' batting figures with runners on base or in scoring position, we can show conclusively who are those underrated pitchers who may give up a lot of hits or home runs, but rarely give them up with men on or in clutch situations. And we can also see those pitchers who (whisper the word, please) fold under the same pressure. (Bear in mind that overall batting averages increase with men on base. This makes any pitcher who holds opponents to a lower average with runners on all the more impressive.)

## Season Summary Information

| | | | | | | | | | | |
|---|---|---|---|---|---|---|---|---|---|---|
| Season | 19-7 | 2.87 | 910 | 204 | 19 | 74 | 170 | .224 | .330 | .285 |
| vs. Left-Handed Batters | | | 475 | 95 | 7 | 42 | 93 | .200 | .282 | .269 |
| vs. Right-Handed Batters | | | 435 | 109 | 12 | 32 | 77 | .251 | .382 | .302 |
| Home | 10-2 | 3.23 | 468 | 118 | 10 | 30 | 86 | .252 | .357 | .297 |
| Road | 9-5 | 2.50 | 442 | 86 | 9 | 44 | 84 | .195 | .301 | .272 |
| Grass | 14-6 | 3.06 | 702 | 163 | 16 | 59 | 128 | .232 | .343 | .291 |
| Artificial Turf | 5-1 | 2.22 | 208 | 41 | 3 | 15 | 42 | .197 | .284 | .264 |
| April | 3-1 | 3.00 | 132 | 32 | 2 | 11 | 31 | .242 | .364 | .301 |
| May | 1-1 | 4.26 | 103 | 29 | 1 | 13 | 20 | .282 | .379 | .356 |
| June | 2-1 | 3.26 | 114 | 25 | 4 | 10 | 15 | .219 | .342 | .291 |
| July | 4-1 | 2.93 | 163 | 32 | 7 | 16 | 30 | .196 | .337 | .269 |
| August | 5-1 | 2.51 | 173 | 38 | 2 | 14 | 27 | .220 | .277 | .282 |
| Sept./Oct. | 4-2 | 2.23 | 225 | 48 | 3 | 10 | 47 | .213 | .316 | .249 |

Each pitcher's seasonal performance is broken down into a variety of special categories. The first line for each pitcher gives his totals for the whole season. This is followed by breakdowns of his performance against left- and right-handed hitters, in home and road games, on grass fields and on artificial turf, and by month. (For pitchers who pitched for more than one team within a league, all totals are combined. The "home" totals for Steve Bedrosian, for example, include all games he pitched in Philadelphia while with the Phillies, and all games he pitched in San Francisco while with the Giants.)

| | | | | | | | |
|---|---|---|---|---|---|---|---|
| Leading Off Inn. | 240 | 59 | 6 | 14 | 37 | .246 | .367 | .287 |
| Runners On | 350 | 79 | 8 | 32 | 63 | .226 | .343 | .290 |
| Runners/Scor. Pos. | 178 | 40 | 4 | 21 | 41 | .225 | .343 | .301 |
| Runners On/2 Out | 152 | 30 | 3 | 14 | 31 | .197 | .309 | .278 |
| Scor. Pos./2 Out | 89 | 20 | 2 | 9 | 20 | .225 | .371 | .310 |

Following these breakdowns, each pitcher's performance is divided into specific game situations.

Totals are given for each pitcher against batters who led off an inning, and against players batting with runners on base. These are followed by his performance with runners in scoring position (on second or third base, or both), with runners on base and two out, and with runners in scoring position and two out.

| | | | | | | | | |
|---|---|---|---|---|---|---|---|---|
| Late Inning Pressure | 79 | 19 | 2 | 11 | 19 | .241 | .342 | .333 |
| Leading Off | 24 | 7 | 1 | 3 | 5 | .292 | .458 | .370 |
| Runners On | 26 | 7 | 1 | 3 | 4 | .269 | .385 | .345 |
| Runners/Scor. Pos. | 10 | 1 | 0 | 3 | 2 | .100 | .100 | .308 |

The next group shows the pitcher's performance in late-inning pressure situations, which are defined a little differently for pitchers than they are for batters. For pitchers, late-inning pressure is defined as any situation occurring in the seventh inning or later with the score tied, or with his team leading or trailing by one or two runs.

| | | | | | | | | |
|---|---|---|---|---|---|---|---|---|
| First 9 Batters | 240 | 50 | 2 | 27 | 44 | .208 | .288 | .288 |
| Second 9 Batters | 362 | 81 | 8 | 23 | 75 | .224 | .340 | .272 |
| All Batters Thereafter | 308 | 73 | 9 | 24 | 51 | .237 | .351 | .297 |

Each pitcher's totals are listed for all late-inning pressure situations, then broken out for his performance when facing a leadoff batter, with runners on base, and with runners in scoring position.

The last set of breakdowns tracks a pitcher's performance throughout each appearance by listing the opponents' batting record according to the number of batters he has faced, regardless of when he entered the game. This allows us to spotlight those pitchers who get stronger as the game progresses, and to pick out those who can breeze through the order once, but falter the second or third time around.

Following the statistics for each pitcher are a series of comments, beginning with the batter each pitcher loves to face and hates to face. The statistics listed for each individual match-up are from regular season games since 1975. Contained within the comments for each pitcher is his "Ground outs-to-air outs" ratio, which consists of his total of ground outs divided by outs on balls hit in the air. (Also included are plays in which the batter reaches base on an error.) An average figure is roughly 1.15. Pitchers with ratios below 0.75 have their games charted by NASA; those above 1.50 receive hate mail from burrowing animals.

# American League

## Jim Abbott

Throws Left

| California Angels | W–L | ERA | AB | H | HR | BB | SO | BA | SA | OBA |
|---|---|---|---|---|---|---|---|---|---|---|
| Season | 12-12 | 3.92 | 694 | 190 | 13 | 74 | 115 | .274 | .379 | .345 |
| vs. Left-Handers | | | 123 | 40 | 2 | 14 | 22 | .325 | .463 | .388 |
| vs. Right-Handers | | | 571 | 150 | 11 | 60 | 93 | .263 | .361 | .335 |
| Home | 5-5 | 4.84 | 344 | 101 | 9 | 35 | 61 | .294 | .430 | .358 |
| Road | 7-7 | 3.06 | 350 | 89 | 4 | 39 | 54 | .254 | .329 | .332 |
| Grass | 10-8 | 3.73 | 546 | 145 | 12 | 56 | 96 | .266 | .379 | .336 |
| Artificial Turf | 2-4 | 4.66 | 148 | 45 | 1 | 18 | 19 | .304 | .378 | .380 |
| April | 1-2 | 3.65 | 97 | 28 | 2 | 8 | 14 | .289 | .402 | .336 |
| May | 4-1 | 3.23 | 108 | 26 | 2 | 15 | 21 | .241 | .306 | .333 |
| June | 1-2 | 4.88 | 91 | 22 | 3 | 11 | 10 | .242 | .363 | .330 |
| July | 3-1 | 2.36 | 135 | 39 | 1 | 6 | 24 | .289 | .348 | .322 |
| August | 2-3 | 5.51 | 134 | 40 | 2 | 21 | 27 | .299 | .455 | .394 |
| Sept./Oct. | 1-3 | 4.11 | 129 | 35 | 3 | 13 | 19 | .271 | .388 | .343 |
| Leading Off Inn. | | | 176 | 51 | 2 | 13 | 24 | .290 | .375 | .346 |
| Runners On | | | 303 | 79 | 4 | 36 | 52 | .261 | .343 | .336 |
| Runners/Scor. Pos. | | | 173 | 40 | 2 | 26 | 32 | .231 | .301 | .327 |
| Runners On/2 Out | | | 125 | 35 | 1 | 12 | 22 | .280 | .360 | .348 |
| Scor. Pos./2 Out | | | 84 | 21 | 1 | 8 | 17 | .250 | .333 | .323 |
| Late Inning Pressure | | | 46 | 15 | 0 | 6 | 5 | .326 | .348 | .404 |
| Leading Off | | | 13 | 4 | 0 | 0 | 0 | .308 | .308 | .308 |
| Runners On | | | 21 | 6 | 0 | 5 | 2 | .286 | .286 | .423 |
| Runners/Scor. Pos. | | | 15 | 3 | 0 | 3 | 1 | .200 | .200 | .333 |
| First 9 Batters | | | 230 | 64 | 6 | 25 | 39 | .278 | .400 | .350 |
| Second 9 Batters | | | 227 | 56 | 3 | 23 | 43 | .247 | .330 | .320 |
| All Batters Thereafter | | | 237 | 70 | 4 | 26 | 33 | .295 | .405 | .364 |

Loves to face: Fred McGriff (.125, 1-for-8, 6 SO)
Hates to face: George Bell (.750, 6-for-8)
Ground outs-to-air outs ratio: 1.74 last season, his first in majors. . . . Additional statistics: 23 double-play ground outs in 156 opportunities, 26 doubles, 4 triples in 181.1 innings last season. . . . Allowed 15 first-inning runs in 29 starts. . . . Batting support: 4.14 runs per start. . . . Faced the league's top 10 home-run hitters for 49 at-bats, the most among pitchers who didn't allow that group any HR. . . . Fell two wins short of team record for rookies, co-held by Dean Chance (1962), Marcelino Lopez (1965), and Frank Tanana (1974). . . . Made 26 assists, or one per 7.0 innings. League average for pitchers is one per 6.3 innings. Other pitchers with G/A ratios between 1.5 and 2.0 made one assist per 5.9 innings.

## Rick Aguilera

Throws Right

| Minnesota Twins | W–L | ERA | AB | H | HR | BB | SO | BA | SA | OBA |
|---|---|---|---|---|---|---|---|---|---|---|
| Season | 3-5 | 3.21 | 290 | 71 | 5 | 17 | 57 | .245 | .390 | .289 |
| vs. Left-Handers | | | 142 | 39 | 2 | 9 | 24 | .275 | .437 | .318 |
| vs. Right-Handers | | | 148 | 32 | 3 | 8 | 33 | .216 | .345 | .261 |
| Home | 1-2 | 3.53 | 138 | 33 | 2 | 9 | 27 | .239 | .391 | .291 |
| Road | 2-3 | 2.93 | 152 | 38 | 3 | 8 | 30 | .250 | .388 | .288 |
| Grass | 1-2 | 3.60 | 95 | 24 | 3 | 5 | 18 | .253 | .421 | .290 |
| Artificial Turf | 2-3 | 3.02 | 195 | 47 | 2 | 12 | 39 | .241 | .374 | .288 |
| April | | | 0 | 0 | 0 | 0 | 0 | — | — | — |
| May | | | 0 | 0 | 0 | 0 | 0 | — | — | — |
| June | | | 0 | 0 | 0 | 0 | 0 | — | — | — |
| July | | | 0 | 0 | 0 | 0 | 0 | — | — | — |
| August | 0-3 | 4.42 | 148 | 42 | 4 | 8 | 28 | .284 | .486 | .325 |
| Sept./Oct. | 3-2 | 2.08 | 142 | 29 | 1 | 9 | 29 | .204 | .289 | .252 |
| Leading Off Inn. | | | 70 | 16 | 2 | 7 | 13 | .229 | .400 | .299 |
| Runners On | | | 110 | 27 | 1 | 8 | 19 | .245 | .355 | .303 |
| Runners/Scor. Pos. | | | 68 | 15 | 1 | 7 | 15 | .221 | .338 | .303 |
| Runners On/2 Out | | | 52 | 16 | 1 | 5 | 9 | .308 | .404 | .379 |
| Scor. Pos./2 Out | | | 33 | 10 | 1 | 5 | 7 | .303 | .455 | .410 |
| Late Inning Pressure | | | 27 | 4 | 0 | 1 | 4 | .148 | .259 | .179 |
| Leading Off | | | 7 | 0 | 0 | 1 | 1 | .000 | .000 | .125 |
| Runners On | | | 6 | 1 | 0 | 0 | 1 | .167 | .167 | .167 |
| Runners/Scor. Pos. | | | 3 | 1 | 0 | 0 | 1 | .333 | .333 | .333 |
| First 9 Batters | | | 94 | 27 | 1 | 5 | 20 | .287 | .426 | .323 |
| Second 9 Batters | | | 90 | 22 | 2 | 6 | 18 | .244 | .389 | .299 |
| All Batters Thereafter | | | 106 | 22 | 2 | 6 | 19 | .208 | .358 | .250 |

Loves to face: Jose Canseco (0-for-7)
Hates to face: Johnny Ray (.417, 5-for-12, 2 HR, 6 BB)
Ground outs-to-air outs ratio: 1.28 last season, 1.22 for career. . . . Additional statistics: 5 double-play ground outs in 37 opportunities, 17 doubles, 5 triples in 75.2 innings last season. . . . Allowed 9 first-inning runs in 11 starts. . . . Batting support: 4.27 runs per start. . . . Combined-leagues total of 145 innings was his career high. . . . Inherited 19 runners, stranded only nine (47%) in 36 relief appearances, all with the Mets. . . . Career breakdown: 32–23, 3.75 ERA as a starter; 8–9, 2.64 in relief. Strikeouts per nine innings: 6.06 as a starter; 9.25 in relief. . . . Career record of 19–10 at Shea Stadium, 21–22 elsewhere. . . . Career record of 13–14 (3.95 ERA) before the All-Star break, 27–18 (3.23) after the break.

## Doyle Alexander

Throws Right

| Detroit Tigers | W–L | ERA | AB | H | HR | BB | SO | BA | SA | OBA |
|---|---|---|---|---|---|---|---|---|---|---|
| Season | 6-18 | 4.44 | 876 | 245 | 28 | 76 | 95 | .280 | .434 | .337 |
| vs. Left-Handers | | | 490 | 139 | 14 | 33 | 42 | .284 | .437 | .330 |
| vs. Right-Handers | | | 386 | 106 | 14 | 43 | 53 | .275 | .430 | .345 |
| Home | 3-9 | 4.44 | 457 | 117 | 15 | 49 | 50 | .256 | .403 | .327 |
| Road | 3-9 | 4.44 | 419 | 128 | 13 | 27 | 45 | .305 | .468 | .347 |
| Grass | 5-15 | 4.35 | 694 | 189 | 22 | 66 | 83 | .272 | .419 | .334 |
| Artificial Turf | 1-3 | 4.80 | 182 | 56 | 6 | 10 | 12 | .308 | .489 | .349 |
| April | 3-1 | 2.29 | 143 | 34 | 3 | 10 | 12 | .238 | .378 | .286 |
| May | 1-3 | 3.29 | 141 | 32 | 1 | 9 | 20 | .227 | .305 | .270 |
| June | 0-3 | 4.57 | 178 | 51 | 7 | 15 | 14 | .287 | .449 | .344 |
| July | 1-4 | 7.15 | 136 | 43 | 7 | 16 | 17 | .316 | .507 | .386 |
| August | 0-5 | 5.35 | 143 | 47 | 7 | 13 | 18 | .329 | .545 | .384 |
| Sept./Oct. | 1-2 | 4.46 | 135 | 38 | 3 | 13 | 14 | .281 | .415 | .347 |
| Leading Off Inn. | | | 211 | 54 | 8 | 16 | 23 | .256 | .431 | .314 |
| Runners On | | | 376 | 101 | 9 | 38 | 50 | .269 | .404 | .329 |
| Runners/Scor. Pos. | | | 196 | 46 | 4 | 31 | 33 | .235 | .352 | .326 |
| Runners On/2 Out | | | 166 | 43 | 6 | 23 | 24 | .259 | .428 | .349 |
| Scor. Pos./2 Out | | | 101 | 24 | 2 | 18 | 17 | .238 | .366 | .353 |
| Late Inning Pressure | | | 113 | 33 | 4 | 10 | 5 | .292 | .451 | .350 |
| Leading Off | | | 30 | 6 | 1 | 2 | 2 | .200 | .367 | .250 |
| Runners On | | | 44 | 10 | 2 | 4 | 2 | .227 | .432 | .292 |
| Runners/Scor. Pos. | | | 16 | 4 | 1 | 3 | 2 | .250 | .438 | .368 |
| First 9 Batters | | | 264 | 67 | 6 | 29 | 31 | .254 | .390 | .331 |
| Second 9 Batters | | | 260 | 78 | 6 | 24 | 32 | .300 | .412 | .354 |
| All Batters Thereafter | | | 352 | 100 | 16 | 23 | 32 | .284 | .483 | .328 |

Loves to face: Brian Downing (.157, 8-for-51)
Hates to face: Kelly Gruber (.556, 10-for-18, 2 HR)
Ground outs-to-air outs ratio: 0.88 last season, 0.91 for career. . . . Additional statistics: 15 double-play ground outs in 184 opportunities, 33 doubles, 9 triples in 223.0 innings last season. . . . Allowed 20 first-inning runs in 33 starts. . . . Batting support: 3.27 runs per start, lowest in A.L. (minimum: 15 GS). . . . First Tigers pitcher to lead A.L. in losses since Mickey Lolich (1974). . . . Lost six starts in a row for the first time in his 20-year career. . . . Most wins for other teams after leaving Dodgers: Newsom, 200; McGinnity, 190; Alexander, 188; Leonard, 173; Billingham, 142; Donovan, 141; Hough, 127; Howell, 123; John, 117; Sutcliffe, 111; Rhoden, 109; Grimes, 107; Zahn, 107; Norman, 102.

## Allan Anderson

Throws Left

| Minnesota Twins | W–L | ERA | AB | H | HR | BB | SO | BA | SA | OBA |
|---|---|---|---|---|---|---|---|---|---|---|
| Season | 17-10 | 3.80 | 777 | 214 | 15 | 53 | 69 | .275 | .395 | .325 |
| vs. Left-Handers | | | 117 | 32 | 2 | 14 | 14 | .274 | .368 | .348 |
| vs. Right-Handers | | | 660 | 182 | 13 | 39 | 55 | .276 | .400 | .321 |
| Home | 6-5 | 6.47 | 300 | 95 | 7 | 20 | 28 | .317 | .470 | .359 |
| Road | 11-5 | 2.24 | 477 | 119 | 8 | 33 | 41 | .249 | .348 | .304 |
| Grass | 9-4 | 2.18 | 373 | 95 | 7 | 29 | 26 | .255 | .351 | .314 |
| Artificial Turf | 8-6 | 5.44 | 404 | 119 | 8 | 24 | 43 | .295 | .436 | .336 |
| April | 4-1 | 2.03 | 116 | 29 | 2 | 9 | 6 | .250 | .336 | .310 |
| May | 1-2 | 6.75 | 129 | 37 | 6 | 10 | 18 | .287 | .519 | .333 |
| June | 4-2 | 2.68 | 171 | 45 | 1 | 11 | 10 | .263 | .327 | .311 |
| July | 2-4 | 5.40 | 141 | 42 | 5 | 10 | 18 | .298 | .489 | .350 |
| August | 3-1 | 1.71 | 117 | 29 | 0 | 6 | 9 | .248 | .274 | .285 |
| Sept./Oct. | 3-0 | 4.63 | 103 | 32 | 1 | 7 | 8 | .311 | .427 | .366 |
| Leading Off Inn. | | | 190 | 51 | 2 | 12 | 19 | .268 | .358 | .315 |
| Runners On | | | 347 | 100 | 5 | 21 | 27 | .288 | .412 | .326 |
| Runners/Scor. Pos. | | | 183 | 50 | 1 | 13 | 14 | .273 | .377 | .313 |
| Runners On/2 Out | | | 145 | 39 | 2 | 11 | 11 | .269 | .345 | .325 |
| Scor. Pos./2 Out | | | 86 | 21 | 1 | 9 | 6 | .244 | .302 | .316 |
| Late Inning Pressure | | | 22 | 3 | 1 | 0 | 1 | .136 | .273 | .136 |
| Leading Off | | | 7 | 1 | 0 | 0 | 1 | .143 | .143 | .143 |
| Runners On | | | 2 | 1 | 0 | 0 | 0 | .500 | .500 | .500 |
| Runners/Scor. Pos. | | | 0 | 0 | 0 | 0 | 0 | — | — | — |
| First 9 Batters | | | 269 | 88 | 7 | 18 | 32 | .327 | .483 | .374 |
| Second 9 Batters | | | 245 | 70 | 3 | 19 | 21 | .286 | .380 | .336 |
| All Batters Thereafter | | | 263 | 56 | 5 | 16 | 16 | .213 | .319 | .265 |

Loves to face: Mark McGwire (.063, 1-for-16)
Hates to face: Wally Joyner (.476, 10-for-21, 1 HR)
Ground outs-to-air outs ratio: 1.27 last season, 1.14 for career. . . . Additional statistics: 21 double-play ground outs in 160 opportunities, 40 doubles, 4 triples in 196.2 innings last season. . . . Allowed 27 first-inning runs (2d most in A.L.) in 33 starts. . . . Batting support: 5.73 runs per start, 3d highest in A.L. (minimum: 15 GS). . . . Led A.L. in road-game ERA, and ranked second in road wins to Saberhagen (12). . . . Opposing batters have hit 40 points better at home (.301) than on the road (.261), 3d-largest difference over the last 10 seasons. . . . Career records of 5–1 in April, 7–1 in September, 25–22 in between . . . . Opponents' career average is .143 (3-for-21) with the bases loaded.

## Luis Aquino

Throws Right

| Kansas City Royals | W–L | ERA | AB | H | HR | BB | SO | BA | SA | OBA |
|---|---|---|---|---|---|---|---|---|---|---|
| Season | 6-8 | 3.50 | 546 | 148 | 6 | 35 | 68 | .271 | .346 | .317 |
| vs. Left-Handers | | | 253 | 73 | 3 | 23 | 25 | .289 | .375 | .344 |
| vs. Right-Handers | | | 293 | 75 | 3 | 12 | 43 | .256 | .321 | .294 |
| Home | 4-3 | 3.03 | 245 | 62 | 3 | 14 | 30 | .253 | .339 | .299 |
| Road | 2-5 | 3.91 | 301 | 86 | 3 | 21 | 38 | .286 | .352 | .332 |
| Grass | 1-4 | 3.48 | 243 | 65 | 1 | 16 | 35 | .267 | .321 | .315 |
| Artificial Turf | 5-4 | 3.52 | 303 | 83 | 5 | 19 | 33 | .274 | .366 | .319 |
| April | 2-0 | 0.75 | 40 | 8 | 0 | 5 | 5 | .200 | .200 | .289 |
| May | 1-1 | 3.91 | 87 | 22 | 0 | 6 | 16 | .253 | .253 | .316 |
| June | 0-1 | 3.57 | 68 | 17 | 2 | 4 | 10 | .250 | .353 | .288 |
| July | 3-2 | 2.36 | 154 | 35 | 0 | 9 | 14 | .227 | .286 | .270 |
| August | 0-4 | 6.39 | 138 | 51 | 4 | 8 | 17 | .370 | .536 | .404 |
| Sept./Oct. | 0-0 | 2.30 | 59 | 15 | 0 | 3 | 6 | .254 | .288 | .290 |
| Leading Off Inn. | | | 128 | 33 | 1 | 11 | 16 | .258 | .297 | .317 |
| Runners On | | | 253 | 71 | 4 | 14 | 31 | .281 | .375 | .324 |
| Runners/Scor. Pos. | | | 133 | 37 | 2 | 12 | 19 | .278 | .383 | .333 |
| Runners On/2 Out | | | 106 | 34 | 2 | 7 | 10 | .321 | .425 | .368 |
| Scor. Pos./2 Out | | | 70 | 21 | 1 | 6 | 7 | .300 | .400 | .355 |
| Late Inning Pressure | | | 53 | 12 | 0 | 5 | 7 | .226 | .245 | .293 |
| Leading Off | | | 13 | 2 | 0 | 3 | 4 | .154 | .154 | .313 |
| Runners On | | | 22 | 6 | 0 | 1 | 0 | .273 | .318 | .304 |
| Runners/Scor. Pos. | | | 8 | 4 | 0 | 0 | 0 | .500 | .625 | .500 |
| First 9 Batters | | | 240 | 68 | 0 | 16 | 39 | .283 | .321 | .332 |
| Second 9 Batters | | | 178 | 46 | 2 | 13 | 16 | .258 | .348 | .307 |
| All Batters Thereafter | | | 128 | 34 | 4 | 6 | 13 | .266 | .391 | .304 |

Loves to face: Cory Snyder (0-for-5, 3 SO)
Hates to face: Darnell Coles (.571, 4-for-7, 1 HR)
Ground outs-to-air outs ratio: 0.98 last season, 0.97 for career. . . . Additional statistics: 12 double-play ground outs in 131 opportunities, 21 doubles, 1 triple in 141.1 innings last season. . . . Allowed 7 first-inning runs in 16 starts. . . . Didn't allow a home run during the first two innings of any of his starts. . . . Batting support: 4.25 runs per start. . . . Record of 4–8 (4.26 ERA) as a starter, 2–0 (1.94 ERA, no saves) in 18 relief appearances. . . . Had a 2.49 ERA in 50.2 innings with Mike Macfarlane catching, 4.26 ERA in 86.2 innings with Bob Boone. . . . Opponents' career average of .215 in day games, .303 at night; .299 by left-handed batters, .253 by right-handers.

## Don August

Throws Right

| Milwaukee Brewers | W–L | ERA | AB | H | HR | BB | SO | BA | SA | OBA |
|---|---|---|---|---|---|---|---|---|---|---|
| Season | 12-12 | 5.31 | 579 | 175 | 17 | 58 | 51 | .302 | .432 | .364 |
| vs. Left-Handers | | | 293 | 88 | 6 | 35 | 20 | .300 | .403 | .373 |
| vs. Right-Handers | | | 286 | 87 | 11 | 23 | 31 | .304 | .462 | .354 |
| Home | 5-5 | 5.54 | 212 | 72 | 6 | 23 | 18 | .340 | .458 | .402 |
| Road | 7-7 | 5.18 | 367 | 103 | 11 | 35 | 33 | .281 | .417 | .342 |
| Grass | 10-11 | 5.43 | 467 | 145 | 14 | 46 | 40 | .310 | .441 | .370 |
| Artificial Turf | 2-1 | 4.85 | 112 | 30 | 3 | 12 | 11 | .268 | .393 | .339 |
| April | 1-4 | 3.79 | 142 | 42 | 4 | 14 | 16 | .296 | .430 | .352 |
| May | 3-2 | 5.93 | 114 | 39 | 5 | 7 | 9 | .342 | .491 | .374 |
| June | 3-1 | 3.90 | 120 | 34 | 1 | 11 | 8 | .283 | .333 | .343 |
| July | 2-3 | 9.11 | 117 | 39 | 4 | 12 | 10 | .333 | .521 | .395 |
| August | 0-1 | 5.40 | 21 | 5 | 0 | 2 | 5 | .238 | .238 | .304 |
| Sept./Oct. | 3-1 | 4.08 | 65 | 16 | 3 | 12 | 3 | .246 | .415 | .372 |
| Leading Off Inn. | | | 146 | 43 | 2 | 9 | 8 | .295 | .370 | .344 |
| Runners On | | | 245 | 72 | 11 | 36 | 20 | .294 | .465 | .375 |
| Runners/Scor. Pos. | | | 127 | 33 | 8 | 18 | 15 | .260 | .512 | .336 |
| Runners On/2 Out | | | 102 | 30 | 4 | 17 | 7 | .294 | .431 | .395 |
| Scor. Pos./2 Out | | | 62 | 17 | 3 | 9 | 6 | .274 | .452 | .366 |
| Late Inning Pressure | | | 34 | 15 | 3 | 1 | 1 | .441 | .765 | .457 |
| Leading Off | | | 11 | 4 | 2 | 1 | 0 | .364 | .909 | .417 |
| Runners On | | | 9 | 4 | 0 | 0 | 0 | .444 | .444 | .444 |
| Runners/Scor. Pos. | | | 3 | 1 | 0 | 0 | 0 | .333 | .333 | .333 |
| First 9 Batters | | | 240 | 72 | 7 | 27 | 26 | .300 | .417 | .372 |
| Second 9 Batters | | | 187 | 54 | 7 | 16 | 16 | .289 | .444 | .341 |
| All Batters Thereafter | | | 152 | 49 | 3 | 15 | 9 | .322 | .441 | .379 |

Loves to face: Brian Downing (0-for-12)
Hates to face: Mel Hall (.714, 5-for-7, 1 HR)
Ground outs-to-air outs ratio: 1.19 last season, 1.24 for career. . . . Additional statistics: 15 double-play ground outs in 131 opportunities, 16 doubles, 4 triples in 142.1 innings last season. . . . Allowed 19 first-inning runs in 25 starts. . . . Batting support: 3.88 runs per start. . . . Had a 1.86 ERA in his 10 victories as a starter, 10.65 in his losses. . . . Averaged 5.11 innings per start, tied for the lowest in majors (minimum: 20 GS). . . . First Brewers pitcher with more walks than strikeouts in 25 or more starts since Jaime Cocanower (1984). . . . Fly-ball hitters batted .341 against him, ground-ballers hit for a .269 average. . . . Career record of 8–1 in . . . the month *after* August.

## Scott Bailes

Throws Left

| Cleveland Indians | W–L | ERA | AB | H | HR | BB | SO | BA | SA | OBA |
|---|---|---|---|---|---|---|---|---|---|---|
| Season | 5-9 | 4.28 | 431 | 116 | 7 | 29 | 47 | .269 | .383 | .316 |
| vs. Left-Handers | | | 125 | 29 | 1 | 5 | 14 | .232 | .280 | .271 |
| vs. Right-Handers | | | 306 | 87 | 6 | 24 | 33 | .284 | .425 | .334 |
| Home | 5-2 | 4.09 | 228 | 56 | 5 | 9 | 26 | .246 | .342 | .274 |
| Road | 0-7 | 4.50 | 203 | 60 | 2 | 20 | 21 | .296 | .429 | .361 |
| Grass | 5-6 | 4.13 | 368 | 98 | 7 | 23 | 42 | .266 | .386 | .312 |
| Artificial Turf | 0-3 | 5.17 | 63 | 18 | 0 | 6 | 5 | .286 | .365 | .343 |
| April | 1-1 | 3.71 | 63 | 18 | 0 | 10 | 8 | .286 | .381 | .378 |
| May | 0-1 | 4.00 | 34 | 9 | 0 | 3 | 4 | .265 | .412 | .342 |
| June | 2-1 | 2.64 | 111 | 25 | 3 | 4 | 10 | .225 | .351 | .252 |
| July | 1-3 | 6.27 | 130 | 36 | 4 | 7 | 12 | .277 | .408 | .321 |
| August | 0-2 | 7.30 | 51 | 19 | 0 | 2 | 5 | .373 | .471 | .382 |
| Sept./Oct. | 1-1 | 0.77 | 42 | 9 | 0 | 3 | 8 | .214 | .262 | .261 |
| Leading Off Inn. | | | 105 | 37 | 2 | 6 | 10 | .352 | .495 | .393 |
| Runners On | | | 196 | 53 | 3 | 17 | 23 | .270 | .403 | .324 |
| Runners/Scor. Pos. | | | 115 | 32 | 2 | 13 | 14 | .278 | .417 | .343 |
| Runners On/2 Out | | | 73 | 22 | 2 | 6 | 10 | .301 | .507 | .354 |
| Scor. Pos./2 Out | | | 51 | 16 | 1 | 5 | 6 | .314 | .490 | .375 |
| Late Inning Pressure | | | 70 | 18 | 1 | 4 | 7 | .257 | .343 | .297 |
| Leading Off | | | 20 | 6 | 0 | 1 | 3 | .300 | .400 | .333 |
| Runners On | | | 25 | 6 | 0 | 2 | 2 | .240 | .280 | .296 |
| Runners/Scor. Pos. | | | 14 | 3 | 0 | 2 | 1 | .214 | .286 | .313 |
| First 9 Batters | | | 225 | 62 | 4 | 12 | 28 | .276 | .387 | .318 |
| Second 9 Batters | | | 117 | 30 | 1 | 12 | 10 | .256 | .359 | .318 |
| All Batters Thereafter | | | 89 | 24 | 2 | 5 | 9 | .270 | .404 | .309 |

Loves to face: Cal Ripken (0-for-17)
Hates to face: Pete Incaviglia (.615, 8-for-13, 3 HR)
Ground outs-to-air outs ratio: 1.28 last season, 1.15 for career. . . . Additional statistics: 17 double-play ground outs in 100 opportunities, 24 doubles, 2 triples in 113.2 innings last season. . . . Only pitcher to start and relieve in at least 10 games in each of last four seasons. Only pitcher with a five-year streak since 1970: Bob Shirley (1978–82). . . . Among 41 pitchers with streaks of five seasons: Dizzy Dean and Lefty Grove. All-time record of eight years is shared by Red Ames, Guy Bush, Larry French, and Sherry Smith. . . . With addition of Langston to already deep rotation, Bailes's streak is likely to end in Angels' bullpen. . . . Just as well. Career breakdown: 17–27, 5.04 ERA as a starter; 14–14, 3.95 ERA in relief.

## Jeff Ballard

Throws Left

| Baltimore Orioles | W–L | ERA | AB | H | HR | BB | SO | BA | SA | OBA |
|---|---|---|---|---|---|---|---|---|---|---|
| Season | 18-8 | 3.43 | 836 | 240 | 16 | 57 | 62 | .287 | .403 | .334 |
| vs. Left-Handers | | | 139 | 39 | 4 | 10 | 22 | .281 | .403 | .331 |
| vs. Right-Handers | | | 697 | 201 | 12 | 47 | 40 | .288 | .403 | .334 |
| Home | 9-4 | 3.19 | 427 | 122 | 5 | 28 | 32 | .286 | .384 | .330 |
| Road | 9-4 | 3.67 | 409 | 118 | 11 | 29 | 30 | .289 | .423 | .338 |
| Grass | 16-7 | 3.56 | 688 | 200 | 13 | 51 | 53 | .291 | .401 | .340 |
| Artificial Turf | 2-1 | 2.82 | 148 | 40 | 3 | 6 | 9 | .270 | .412 | .303 |
| April | 5-0 | 1.46 | 133 | 33 | 2 | 6 | 9 | .248 | .323 | .281 |
| May | 3-1 | 2.86 | 107 | 28 | 2 | 6 | 6 | .262 | .383 | .298 |
| June | 1-2 | 7.32 | 91 | 37 | 1 | 14 | 6 | .407 | .505 | .495 |
| July | 2-2 | 3.72 | 151 | 38 | 3 | 7 | 9 | .252 | .358 | .281 |
| August | 4-1 | 3.89 | 176 | 55 | 5 | 7 | 12 | .313 | .466 | .342 |
| Sept./Oct. | 3-2 | 3.02 | 178 | 49 | 3 | 17 | 20 | .275 | .399 | .338 |
| Leading Off Inn. | | | 217 | 70 | 2 | 10 | 13 | .323 | .396 | .358 |
| Runners On | | | 339 | 93 | 11 | 36 | 33 | .274 | .428 | .341 |
| Runners/Scor. Pos. | | | 172 | 41 | 4 | 29 | 25 | .238 | .349 | .343 |
| Runners On/2 Out | | | 130 | 33 | 4 | 23 | 13 | .254 | .408 | .366 |
| Scor. Pos./2 Out | | | 76 | 16 | 0 | 20 | 9 | .211 | .250 | .375 |
| Late Inning Pressure | | | 61 | 12 | 0 | 3 | 5 | .197 | .197 | .234 |
| Leading Off | | | 21 | 5 | 0 | 1 | 2 | .238 | .238 | .273 |
| Runners On | | | 14 | 3 | 0 | 2 | 2 | .214 | .214 | .313 |
| Runners/Scor. Pos. | | | 7 | 1 | 0 | 2 | 2 | .143 | .143 | .333 |
| First 9 Batters | | | 288 | 92 | 3 | 17 | 24 | .319 | .417 | .358 |
| Second 9 Batters | | | 273 | 78 | 9 | 20 | 15 | .286 | .458 | .333 |
| All Batters Thereafter | | | 275 | 70 | 4 | 20 | 23 | .255 | .335 | .309 |

Loves to face: Mike Gallego (0-for-12)
Hates to face: Henry Cotto (.474, 9-for-19, 1 HR)
Ground outs-to-air outs ratio: 1.14 last season, 1.11 for career. . . . Additional statistics: 25 double-play ground outs in 169 opportunities, 41 doubles, 4 triples in 215.1 innings last season. . . . Allowed 16 first-inning runs in 35 starts. . . . Hasn't allowed a first-inning home run in his last 47 starts. . . . Batting support: 5.66 runs per start. . . . Complete-game shutout without a walk or strikeout on Aug. 21 was first of its kind since Roger Clemens did it in 1987. . . . Struck out only 2.6 batters per nine innings, but became only pitcher ever to fan Don Mattingly three times in one game. . . . Only pitchers to face more batters in LIPS without allowing an extra-base hit: Bud Black, 1988 (80) and Ray Searage, 1984 (69).

## Scott Bankhead

Throws Right

| Seattle Mariners | W–L | ERA | AB | H | HR | BB | SO | BA | SA | OBA |
|---|---|---|---|---|---|---|---|---|---|---|
| Season | 14-6 | 3.34 | 784 | 187 | 19 | 63 | 140 | .239 | .376 | .295 |
| vs. Left-Handers | | | 417 | 96 | 13 | 33 | 73 | .230 | .381 | .284 |
| vs. Right-Handers | | | 367 | 91 | 6 | 30 | 67 | .248 | .371 | .308 |
| Home | 7-3 | 3.40 | 394 | 96 | 10 | 26 | 67 | .244 | .388 | .288 |
| Road | 7-3 | 3.28 | 390 | 91 | 9 | 37 | 73 | .233 | .364 | .302 |
| Grass | 5-2 | 3.61 | 292 | 73 | 8 | 25 | 54 | .250 | .401 | .312 |
| Artificial Turf | 9-4 | 3.18 | 492 | 114 | 11 | 38 | 86 | .232 | .362 | .285 |
| April | 1-2 | 3.82 | 148 | 41 | 5 | 9 | 25 | .277 | .439 | .316 |
| May | 1-2 | 5.73 | 84 | 24 | 3 | 8 | 17 | .286 | .488 | .347 |
| June | 4-0 | 1.05 | 147 | 23 | 1 | 11 | 24 | .156 | .218 | .214 |
| July | 4-0 | 3.66 | 146 | 32 | 6 | 5 | 22 | .219 | .411 | .248 |
| August | 1-2 | 4.60 | 117 | 35 | 2 | 15 | 22 | .299 | .410 | .378 |
| Sept./Oct. | 3-0 | 2.75 | 142 | 32 | 2 | 15 | 30 | .225 | .345 | .297 |
| Leading Off Inn. | | | 200 | 42 | 3 | 18 | 31 | .210 | .310 | .275 |
| Runners On | | | 293 | 75 | 10 | 28 | 61 | .256 | .430 | .317 |
| Runners/Scor. Pos. | | | 156 | 37 | 4 | 21 | 35 | .237 | .391 | .317 |
| Runners On/2 Out | | | 121 | 30 | 5 | 10 | 31 | .248 | .438 | .305 |
| Scor. Pos./2 Out | | | 77 | 16 | 3 | 10 | 19 | .208 | .403 | .299 |
| Late Inning Pressure | | | 40 | 10 | 1 | 7 | 10 | .250 | .350 | .362 |
| Leading Off | | | 11 | 2 | 0 | 2 | 2 | .182 | .182 | .308 |
| Runners On | | | 15 | 4 | 0 | 2 | 4 | .267 | .333 | .353 |
| Runners/Scor. Pos. | | | 6 | 2 | 0 | 2 | 2 | .333 | .333 | .500 |
| First 9 Batters | | | 267 | 55 | 6 | 23 | 58 | .206 | .348 | .270 |
| Second 9 Batters | | | 270 | 78 | 8 | 21 | 43 | .289 | .459 | .341 |
| All Batters Thereafter | | | 247 | 54 | 5 | 19 | 39 | .219 | .316 | .271 |

Loves to face: Mickey Tettleton (0-for-12)
Hates to face: George Bell (.481, 13-for-27, 5 HR)
Ground outs-to-air outs ratio: 0.69 last season, 0.70 for career. . . . Additional statistics: 15 double-play ground outs in 152 opportunities, 31 doubles, 10 triples in 210.1 innings last season. . . . Allowed 10 first-inning runs in 33 starts. . . . Batting support: 4.52 runs per start. . . . Only Seattle pitcher to throw a shutout at the Kingdome. . . . Winning percentage was 5th highest in A.L. (minimum: 10 wins). . . . Compare 1989 seasons of Bankhead and Dave Stewart. Same winning percentage. ERAs within two points. Bankhead had advantage in hits and strikeouts per nine innings, Stewart had slightly better control. . . . If he reaches the seventh inning, he's home free. Opponents batted .174 (16-for-92) over final three frames. . . . Has completed seven of 96 career starts.

## Floyd Bannister

Throws Left

| Kansas City Royals | W–L | ERA | AB | H | HR | BB | SO | BA | SA | OBA |
|---|---|---|---|---|---|---|---|---|---|---|
| Season | 4-1 | 4.66 | 300 | 87 | 8 | 18 | 35 | .290 | .430 | .330 |
| vs. Left-Handers | | | 48 | 17 | 1 | 4 | 6 | .354 | .500 | .404 |
| vs. Right-Handers | | | 252 | 70 | 7 | 14 | 29 | .278 | .417 | .316 |
| Home | 2-1 | 4.60 | 182 | 51 | 2 | 12 | 22 | .280 | .379 | .327 |
| Road | 2-0 | 4.75 | 118 | 36 | 6 | 6 | 13 | .305 | .508 | .336 |
| Grass | 1-0 | 3.45 | 57 | 16 | 2 | 5 | 7 | .281 | .386 | .333 |
| Artificial Turf | 3-1 | 4.98 | 243 | 71 | 6 | 13 | 28 | .292 | .440 | .329 |
| April | 3-0 | 4.67 | 134 | 36 | 2 | 10 | 13 | .269 | .410 | .317 |
| May | 1-1 | 4.99 | 127 | 41 | 6 | 6 | 15 | .323 | .488 | .356 |
| June | 0-0 | 3.60 | 39 | 10 | 0 | 2 | 7 | .256 | .308 | .293 |
| July | | | 0 | 0 | 0 | 0 | 0 | — | — | — |
| August | | | 0 | 0 | 0 | 0 | 0 | — | — | — |
| Sept./Oct. | | | 0 | 0 | 0 | 0 | 0 | — | — | — |
| Leading Off Inn. | | | 78 | 21 | 2 | 6 | 11 | .269 | .397 | .321 |
| Runners On | | | 114 | 33 | 2 | 8 | 13 | .289 | .421 | .336 |
| Runners/Scor. Pos. | | | 63 | 18 | 1 | 6 | 8 | .286 | .429 | .338 |
| Runners On/2 Out | | | 49 | 14 | 1 | 2 | 7 | .286 | .490 | .314 |
| Scor. Pos./2 Out | | | 33 | 9 | 0 | 2 | 4 | .273 | .394 | .314 |
| Late Inning Pressure | | | 14 | 5 | 0 | 2 | 0 | .357 | .571 | .412 |
| Leading Off | | | 6 | 2 | 0 | 0 | 0 | .333 | .667 | .333 |
| Runners On | | | 2 | 1 | 0 | 1 | 0 | .500 | .500 | .500 |
| Runners/Scor. Pos. | | | 1 | 1 | 0 | 1 | 0 | 1.000 | 1.000 | .667 |
| First 9 Batters | | | 123 | 34 | 3 | 2 | 13 | .276 | .407 | .288 |
| Second 9 Batters | | | 107 | 33 | 3 | 9 | 16 | .308 | .467 | .364 |
| All Batters Thereafter | | | 70 | 20 | 2 | 7 | 6 | .286 | .414 | .346 |

Loves to face: Mike Greenwell (.077, 1-for-13)
Hates to face: Gary Gaetti (.425, 17-for-40, 7 HR)
Ground outs-to-air outs ratio: 0.90 last season, 0.89 for career. . . . Additional statistics: 8 double-play ground outs in 58 opportunities, 14 doubles, 2 triples in 75.1 innings last season. . . . Allowed 7 first-inning runs in 14 starts. . . . Batting support: 4.79 runs per start. . . . Royals had an 11–3 record in his starts, 7–2 in his no-decisions. . . . Opponents' overall batting average was the highest of his career. . . . One of five pitchers active in 1989 with at least 100 career wins, but a losing record nonetheless. Others: Bob Knepper, Jim Clancy, Shane Rawley, and Danny Darwin. . . . Only Jack Morris, Dave Stieb, and Frank Tanana started more A.L. games than Bannister (294) during the 1980s.

## Jose Bautista

Throws Right

| Baltimore Orioles | W–L | ERA | AB | H | HR | BB | SO | BA | SA | OBA |
|---|---|---|---|---|---|---|---|---|---|---|
| Season | 3-4 | 5.31 | 307 | 84 | 17 | 15 | 30 | .274 | .492 | .309 |
| vs. Left-Handers | | | 157 | 44 | 6 | 6 | 13 | .280 | .471 | .307 |
| vs. Right-Handers | | | 150 | 40 | 11 | 9 | 17 | .267 | .513 | .311 |
| Home | 2-3 | 5.36 | 191 | 51 | 10 | 7 | 16 | .267 | .461 | .293 |
| Road | 1-1 | 5.22 | 116 | 33 | 7 | 8 | 14 | .284 | .543 | .333 |
| Grass | 3-3 | 4.82 | 275 | 73 | 14 | 13 | 22 | .265 | .473 | .298 |
| Artificial Turf | 0-1 | 10.29 | 32 | 11 | 3 | 2 | 8 | .344 | .656 | .400 |
| April | 2-2 | 5.10 | 114 | 30 | 6 | 9 | 8 | .263 | .465 | .320 |
| May | 0-2 | 4.94 | 92 | 26 | 5 | 2 | 8 | .283 | .478 | .298 |
| June | 1-0 | 6.35 | 69 | 19 | 5 | 3 | 9 | .275 | .551 | .306 |
| July | | | 0 | 0 | 0 | 0 | 0 | — | — | — |
| August | | | 0 | 0 | 0 | 0 | 0 | — | — | — |
| Sept./Oct. | 0-0 | 4.91 | 32 | 9 | 1 | 1 | 5 | .281 | .500 | .303 |
| Leading Off Inn. | | | 76 | 8 | 2 | 3 | 4 | .105 | .211 | .139 |
| Runners On | | | 102 | 37 | 11 | 4 | 13 | .363 | .745 | .383 |
| Runners/Scor. Pos. | | | 49 | 16 | 2 | 4 | 6 | .327 | .531 | .370 |
| Runners On/2 Out | | | 49 | 16 | 3 | 1 | 4 | .327 | .551 | .340 |
| Scor. Pos./2 Out | | | 25 | 8 | 1 | 1 | 2 | .320 | .520 | .346 |
| Late Inning Pressure | | | 15 | 3 | 2 | 1 | 1 | .200 | .667 | .250 |
| Leading Off | | | 4 | 0 | 0 | 1 | 0 | .000 | .000 | .200 |
| Runners On | | | 4 | 1 | 1 | 0 | 0 | .250 | 1.000 | .250 |
| Runners/Scor. Pos. | | | 3 | 0 | 0 | 0 | 0 | .000 | .000 | .000 |
| First 9 Batters | | | 120 | 33 | 4 | 6 | 18 | .275 | .433 | .313 |
| Second 9 Batters | | | 111 | 32 | 8 | 6 | 7 | .288 | .541 | .325 |
| All Batters Thereafter | | | 76 | 19 | 5 | 3 | 5 | .250 | .513 | .278 |

Loves to face: Dave Henderson (0-for-8)
Hates to face: Mike Greenwell (.533, 8-for-15, 3 HR)
Ground outs-to-air outs ratio: 0.91 last season, 0.83 for career. . . . Additional statistics: 7 double-play ground outs in 41 opportunities, 8 doubles, 4 triples in 78.0 innings last season. . . . Allowed 6 first-inning runs in 10 starts. . . . Batting support: 3.50 runs per start. . . . Career record of 8–10 before the All-Star break, 1–9 after the break. . . . Average of one home run every 19 at-bats was the worst in majors. . . . Opponents' on-base average leading off innings was the lowest in majors. . . . Career strikeout rates: one per 8.2 batters on first pass through order; one per 10.6 on second pass; one per 12.4 thereafter. . . . Teammate of Dwight Gooden at Kingsport in 1982: Bautista, 0–4, 8.92; Doc, 5–4, 2.47.

## Juan Berenguer

Throws Right

| Minnesota Twins | W–L | ERA | AB | H | HR | BB | SO | BA | SA | OBA |
|---|---|---|---|---|---|---|---|---|---|---|
| Season | 9-3 | 3.48 | 391 | 96 | 11 | 47 | 93 | .246 | .376 | .326 |
| vs. Left-Handers | | | 164 | 54 | 7 | 23 | 33 | .329 | .524 | .407 |
| vs. Right-Handers | | | 227 | 42 | 4 | 24 | 60 | .185 | .269 | .266 |
| Home | 8-2 | 3.36 | 255 | 58 | 8 | 26 | 72 | .227 | .361 | .297 |
| Road | 1-1 | 3.72 | 136 | 38 | 3 | 21 | 21 | .279 | .404 | .377 |
| Grass | 0-0 | 4.30 | 110 | 31 | 2 | 18 | 18 | .282 | .409 | .388 |
| Artificial Turf | 9-3 | 3.17 | 281 | 65 | 9 | 29 | 75 | .231 | .363 | .301 |
| April | 0-0 | 2.35 | 54 | 9 | 3 | 7 | 11 | .167 | .370 | .274 |
| May | 2-2 | 4.66 | 71 | 16 | 2 | 8 | 17 | .225 | .366 | .293 |
| June | 2-1 | 3.65 | 90 | 25 | 3 | 13 | 22 | .278 | .422 | .371 |
| July | 2-0 | 1.76 | 51 | 10 | 1 | 7 | 12 | .196 | .314 | .293 |
| August | 2-0 | 6.59 | 57 | 20 | 0 | 6 | 13 | .351 | .421 | .406 |
| Sept./Oct. | 1-0 | 2.04 | 68 | 16 | 2 | 6 | 18 | .235 | .338 | .297 |
| Leading Off Inn. | | | 86 | 24 | 0 | 10 | 19 | .279 | .349 | .354 |
| Runners On | | | 186 | 41 | 5 | 22 | 40 | .220 | .349 | .299 |
| Runners/Scor. Pos. | | | 108 | 26 | 2 | 15 | 22 | .241 | .352 | .320 |
| Runners On/2 Out | | | 82 | 15 | 0 | 14 | 19 | .183 | .220 | .302 |
| Scor. Pos./2 Out | | | 55 | 9 | 0 | 11 | 12 | .164 | .200 | .303 |
| Late Inning Pressure | | | 159 | 34 | 6 | 16 | 47 | .214 | .340 | .284 |
| Leading Off | | | 39 | 7 | 0 | 4 | 10 | .179 | .205 | .256 |
| Runners On | | | 60 | 13 | 3 | 6 | 16 | .217 | .383 | .284 |
| Runners/Scor. Pos. | | | 29 | 7 | 1 | 4 | 8 | .241 | .379 | .324 |
| First 9 Batters | | | 324 | 82 | 8 | 42 | 75 | .253 | .370 | .337 |
| Second 9 Batters | | | 65 | 14 | 3 | 5 | 16 | .215 | .415 | .278 |
| All Batters Thereafter | | | 2 | 0 | 0 | 0 | 2 | .000 | .000 | .000 |

Loves to face: Dave Henderson (.045, 1-for-22, 9 SO)
Hates to face: Rickey Henderson (.458, 11-for-24)
Ground outs-to-air outs ratio: 0.69 last season, 0.62 for career. . . . Additional statistics: 8 double-play ground outs in 92 opportunities, 18 doubles, 0 triples in 106.0 innings last season. . . . Inherited 56 runners, stranded 40 (71%). . . . Winning percentage over the last three seasons (.738, 25–8) is highest in majors (minimum: 30 decisions). Career record is now above .500 for first time. . . . Career breakdown: 26–35, 6.61 SO per nine innings as a starter; 29–14, 8.53 in relief. . . . Breakdown of right- and left-handed batters for 1989 is exaggeration of career-long trend. Career marks: .254 by LHB, .210 by RHB. . . . Berenguer's middle name is Bautista. Bautista's is Joaquin. Andujar doesn't have one. . . . Figures.

## Bud Black

Throws Left

| Cleveland Indians | W–L | ERA | AB | H | HR | BB | SO | BA | SA | OBA |
|---|---|---|---|---|---|---|---|---|---|---|
| Season | 12-11 | 3.36 | 844 | 213 | 14 | 52 | 88 | .252 | .363 | .295 |
| vs. Left-Handers | | | 120 | 19 | 2 | 9 | 10 | .158 | .233 | .215 |
| vs. Right-Handers | | | 724 | 194 | 12 | 43 | 78 | .268 | .384 | .308 |
| Home | 5-9 | 4.06 | 441 | 118 | 10 | 29 | 44 | .268 | .404 | .311 |
| Road | 7-2 | 2.61 | 403 | 95 | 4 | 23 | 44 | .236 | .318 | .277 |
| Grass | 10-10 | 3.50 | 647 | 162 | 10 | 42 | 67 | .250 | .363 | .295 |
| Artificial Turf | 2-1 | 2.88 | 197 | 51 | 4 | 10 | 21 | .259 | .360 | .293 |
| April | 1-4 | 5.40 | 121 | 37 | 2 | 7 | 6 | .306 | .438 | .344 |
| May | 3-2 | 2.87 | 138 | 32 | 3 | 12 | 16 | .232 | .333 | .296 |
| June | 2-1 | 2.92 | 141 | 35 | 3 | 6 | 12 | .248 | .390 | .277 |
| July | 2-1 | 4.46 | 158 | 44 | 5 | 10 | 25 | .278 | .430 | .320 |
| August | 1-3 | 4.66 | 116 | 33 | 0 | 6 | 9 | .284 | .371 | .317 |
| Sept./Oct. | 3-0 | 1.12 | 170 | 32 | 1 | 11 | 20 | .188 | .241 | .236 |
| Leading Off Inn. | | | 225 | 56 | 2 | 12 | 19 | .249 | .329 | .287 |
| Runners On | | | 316 | 80 | 5 | 26 | 41 | .253 | .351 | .305 |
| Runners/Scor. Pos. | | | 176 | 40 | 4 | 12 | 27 | .227 | .330 | .269 |
| Runners On/2 Out | | | 124 | 25 | 3 | 15 | 18 | .202 | .315 | .288 |
| Scor. Pos./2 Out | | | 77 | 15 | 2 | 7 | 14 | .195 | .312 | .262 |
| Late Inning Pressure | | | 108 | 29 | 2 | 6 | 14 | .269 | .407 | .302 |
| Leading Off | | | 32 | 7 | 0 | 3 | 3 | .219 | .250 | .286 |
| Runners On | | | 34 | 9 | 0 | 2 | 6 | .265 | .294 | .289 |
| Runners/Scor. Pos. | | | 19 | 5 | 0 | 1 | 5 | .263 | .316 | .273 |
| First 9 Batters | | | 279 | 56 | 3 | 15 | 37 | .201 | .301 | .240 |
| Second 9 Batters | | | 265 | 69 | 4 | 21 | 28 | .260 | .358 | .316 |
| All Batters Thereafter | | | 300 | 88 | 7 | 16 | 23 | .293 | .423 | .327 |

Loves to face: Wally Joyner (.056, 1-for-18)
Hates to face: Gene Larkin (.643, 9-for-14, 1 HR)
Ground outs-to-air outs ratio: 1.14 last season, 1.09 for career. . . . Additional statistics: 19 double-play ground outs in 150 opportunities, 37 doubles, 7 triples in 222.1 innings last season. . . . Allowed 13 first-inning runs in 32 starts. . . . Batting support: 3.81 runs per start. . . . Three shutouts in his last 20 starts, compared to three in previous 147. . . . Completed six games, after an 0-for-33 starts streak dating to 1986. . . . Allowed only one home run in 77 innings over his last 11 starts. . . . Career ERA: 3.85 as a starter, 2.98 in relief. . . . Career record of 29–40 on grass fields, 41–31 on artificial surfaces. . . . Opponents' career BA: .235 on first pass through order, .252 on second pass, .277 after that.

## Bert Blyleven

Throws Right

| California Angels | W–L | ERA | AB | H | HR | BB | SO | BA | SA | OBA |
|---|---|---|---|---|---|---|---|---|---|---|
| Season | 17-5 | 2.73 | 907 | 225 | 14 | 44 | 131 | .248 | .336 | .287 |
| vs. Left-Handers | | | 485 | 122 | 4 | 24 | 73 | .252 | .318 | .290 |
| vs. Right-Handers | | | 422 | 103 | 10 | 20 | 58 | .244 | .358 | .283 |
| Home | 8-1 | 2.64 | 446 | 106 | 11 | 20 | 68 | .238 | .336 | .270 |
| Road | 9-4 | 2.81 | 461 | 119 | 3 | 24 | 63 | .258 | .336 | .303 |
| Grass | 12-5 | 3.38 | 707 | 187 | 13 | 35 | 97 | .264 | .368 | .301 |
| Artificial Turf | 5-0 | 0.63 | 200 | 38 | 1 | 9 | 34 | .190 | .225 | .238 |
| April | 3-1 | 2.41 | 137 | 31 | 4 | 7 | 19 | .226 | .350 | .269 |
| May | 2-1 | 2.31 | 136 | 39 | 2 | 6 | 15 | .287 | .397 | .315 |
| June | 2-0 | 2.17 | 140 | 32 | 1 | 6 | 25 | .229 | .300 | .265 |
| July | 3-0 | 2.82 | 168 | 42 | 2 | 5 | 25 | .250 | .321 | .273 |
| August | 4-1 | 3.25 | 163 | 38 | 4 | 11 | 27 | .233 | .325 | .286 |
| Sept./Oct. | 3-2 | 3.19 | 163 | 43 | 1 | 9 | 20 | .264 | .331 | .313 |
| Leading Off Inn. | | | 237 | 67 | 3 | 6 | 23 | .283 | .371 | .309 |
| Runners On | | | 351 | 77 | 4 | 26 | 52 | .219 | .296 | .272 |
| Runners/Scor. Pos. | | | 188 | 40 | 2 | 16 | 32 | .213 | .271 | .265 |
| Runners On/2 Out | | | 144 | 25 | 1 | 17 | 26 | .174 | .257 | .270 |
| Scor. Pos./2 Out | | | 87 | 16 | 1 | 11 | 16 | .184 | .264 | .276 |
| Late Inning Pressure | | | 92 | 23 | 1 | 6 | 17 | .250 | .315 | .296 |
| Leading Off | | | 25 | 7 | 1 | 0 | 2 | .280 | .400 | .280 |
| Runners On | | | 34 | 5 | 0 | 5 | 8 | .147 | .235 | .256 |
| Runners/Scor. Pos. | | | 18 | 4 | 0 | 4 | 5 | .222 | .333 | .364 |
| First 9 Batters | | | 273 | 74 | 8 | 14 | 36 | .271 | .403 | .308 |
| Second 9 Batters | | | 279 | 61 | 0 | 11 | 38 | .219 | .258 | .254 |
| All Batters Thereafter | | | 355 | 90 | 6 | 19 | 57 | .254 | .346 | .296 |

Loves to face: Gary Gaetti (.107, 3-for-28)
Hates to face: Ron Kittle (.359, 14-for-39, 9 HR)
Ground outs-to-air outs ratio: 1.18 last season, 1.21 for career. . . . Additional statistics: 25 double-play ground outs in 170 opportunities, 30 doubles, 4 triples in 241.0 innings last season. . . . Allowed 17 first-inning runs in 33 starts. . . . Batting support: 4.82 runs per start. . . . Had an ERA of 1.64 with Schroeder catching, 3.58 with Parrish. . . . Had a career-low winning percentage (.370) in 1988, his 19th season in the majors, then posted career high last season. . . . Has allowed 398 HR, eighth most in major league history: Robin Roberts (505), Ferguson Jenkins (484), Phil Niekro (482), Don Sutton (472), Warren Spahn (434), Steve Carlton (414), and Gaylord Perry (399).

## Mike Boddicker

Throws Right

| Boston Red Sox | W–L | ERA | AB | H | HR | BB | SO | BA | SA | OBA |
|---|---|---|---|---|---|---|---|---|---|---|
| Season | 15-11 | 4.00 | 813 | 217 | 19 | 71 | 145 | .267 | .400 | .330 |
| vs. Left-Handers | | | 444 | 124 | 12 | 37 | 58 | .279 | .421 | .333 |
| vs. Right-Handers | | | 369 | 93 | 7 | 34 | 87 | .252 | .374 | .325 |
| Home | 7-8 | 4.89 | 417 | 127 | 9 | 29 | 75 | .305 | .448 | .354 |
| Road | 8-3 | 3.15 | 396 | 90 | 10 | 42 | 70 | .227 | .348 | .305 |
| Grass | 11-9 | 4.17 | 662 | 181 | 15 | 58 | 124 | .273 | .405 | .337 |
| Artificial Turf | 4-2 | 3.29 | 151 | 36 | 4 | 13 | 21 | .238 | .377 | .296 |
| April | 1-2 | 7.89 | 87 | 27 | 1 | 14 | 18 | .310 | .425 | .411 |
| May | 2-2 | 3.83 | 152 | 36 | 1 | 14 | 27 | .237 | .322 | .304 |
| June | 2-3 | 5.26 | 156 | 50 | 6 | 10 | 22 | .321 | .500 | .361 |
| July | 4-0 | 1.10 | 117 | 25 | 0 | 12 | 17 | .214 | .239 | .292 |
| August | 3-2 | 2.86 | 166 | 41 | 6 | 7 | 32 | .247 | .404 | .277 |
| Sept./Oct. | 3-2 | 4.50 | 135 | 38 | 5 | 14 | 29 | .281 | .489 | .357 |
| Leading Off Inn. | | | 208 | 60 | 7 | 17 | 32 | .288 | .486 | .348 |
| Runners On | | | 336 | 87 | 5 | 36 | 59 | .259 | .354 | .331 |
| Runners/Scor. Pos. | | | 183 | 39 | 1 | 23 | 34 | .213 | .273 | .300 |
| Runners On/2 Out | | | 134 | 36 | 2 | 15 | 29 | .269 | .343 | .347 |
| Scor. Pos./2 Out | | | 82 | 16 | 0 | 11 | 19 | .195 | .207 | .298 |
| Late Inning Pressure | | | 65 | 11 | 2 | 3 | 10 | .169 | .292 | .229 |
| Leading Off | | | 21 | 3 | 1 | 0 | 3 | .143 | .333 | .143 |
| Runners On | | | 12 | 3 | 0 | 2 | 1 | .250 | .333 | .357 |
| Runners/Scor. Pos. | | | 6 | 0 | 0 | 1 | 1 | .000 | .000 | .143 |
| First 9 Batters | | | 268 | 65 | 7 | 26 | 57 | .243 | .369 | .315 |
| Second 9 Batters | | | 264 | 74 | 6 | 28 | 49 | .280 | .420 | .350 |
| All Batters Thereafter | | | 281 | 78 | 6 | 17 | 39 | .278 | .409 | .325 |

Loves to face: Gary Pettis (.036, 1-for-28, 9 SO)
Hates to face: Matt Nokes (.600, 12-for-20, 2 HR)
Ground outs-to-air outs ratio: 1.21 last season, 1.37 for career. . . . Additional statistics: 19 double-play ground outs in 171 opportunities, 43 doubles, 4 triples in 211.2 innings last season. . . . Allowed 18 first-inning runs in 34 starts. . . . Batting support: 4.71 runs per start. . . . Most hit batters over last two seasons: Steib (26), Boddicker (24), Blyleven (24). . . . Boddicker didn't hit a batter in his first 325 career innings. Then someone whispered in his ear, and he's averaged one per 24 innings since. . . . Best record of any Red Sox starter (22–14) since arriving in July 1988. . . . Longest tenure (seven full seasons) among active pitchers with at least 10 wins as a rookie, and in every season thereafter.

## Chris Bosio

Throws Right

| Milwaukee Brewers | W–L | ERA | AB | H | HR | BB | SO | BA | SA | OBA |
|---|---|---|---|---|---|---|---|---|---|---|
| Season | 15-10 | 2.95 | 905 | 225 | 16 | 48 | 173 | .249 | .336 | .289 |
| vs. Left-Handers | | | 458 | 113 | 8 | 28 | 73 | .247 | .325 | .294 |
| vs. Right-Handers | | | 447 | 112 | 8 | 20 | 100 | .251 | .347 | .285 |
| Home | 9-3 | 2.06 | 489 | 120 | 6 | 22 | 98 | .245 | .315 | .284 |
| Road | 6-7 | 4.01 | 416 | 105 | 10 | 26 | 75 | .252 | .361 | .295 |
| Grass | 14-7 | 2.59 | 786 | 194 | 14 | 38 | 148 | .247 | .331 | .285 |
| Artificial Turf | 1-3 | 5.46 | 119 | 31 | 2 | 10 | 25 | .261 | .370 | .318 |
| April | 4-0 | 1.37 | 143 | 26 | 2 | 7 | 25 | .182 | .259 | .235 |
| May | 2-3 | 4.10 | 158 | 50 | 5 | 4 | 30 | .316 | .456 | .337 |
| June | 1-2 | 3.15 | 174 | 43 | 1 | 10 | 32 | .247 | .299 | .290 |
| July | 5-1 | 2.53 | 157 | 38 | 3 | 14 | 35 | .242 | .331 | .304 |
| August | 2-3 | 2.40 | 171 | 39 | 2 | 9 | 28 | .228 | .304 | .264 |
| Sept./Oct. | 1-1 | 5.11 | 102 | 29 | 3 | 4 | 23 | .284 | .382 | .312 |
| Leading Off Inn. | | | 232 | 52 | 1 | 11 | 42 | .224 | .280 | .262 |
| Runners On | | | 354 | 92 | 9 | 23 | 70 | .260 | .381 | .310 |
| Runners/Scor. Pos. | | | 184 | 44 | 4 | 17 | 45 | .239 | .342 | .300 |
| Runners On/2 Out | | | 138 | 24 | 3 | 12 | 31 | .174 | .290 | .250 |
| Scor. Pos./2 Out | | | 82 | 11 | 2 | 11 | 23 | .134 | .256 | .237 |
| Late Inning Pressure | | | 78 | 19 | 1 | 5 | 12 | .244 | .295 | .289 |
| Leading Off | | | 22 | 4 | 0 | 1 | 3 | .182 | .182 | .217 |
| Runners On | | | 29 | 6 | 0 | 2 | 5 | .207 | .241 | .258 |
| Runners/Scor. Pos. | | | 13 | 2 | 0 | 1 | 2 | .154 | .231 | .214 |
| First 9 Batters | | | 276 | 78 | 2 | 14 | 61 | .283 | .341 | .319 |
| Second 9 Batters | | | 271 | 61 | 7 | 14 | 53 | .225 | .336 | .266 |
| All Batters Thereafter | | | 358 | 86 | 7 | 20 | 59 | .240 | .332 | .284 |

Loves to face: Willie Wilson (.053, 1-for-19)
Hates to face: Greg Walker (.556, 10-for-18, 2 HR)
Ground outs-to-air outs ratio: 1.21 last season, 1.31 for career. . . . Additional statistics: 14 double-play ground outs in 192 opportunities, 25 doubles, 3 triples in 234.2 innings last season. . . . Allowed 9 first-inning runs in 33 starts. . . . Batting support: 5.24 runs per start. . . . Career record of 10–2 in April, 23–35 in other months. . . . Career ratio of strikeouts to walks is 5th best among active pitchers (minimum: 500 IP), behind Saberhagen, Clemens, Gooden, and Swindell. . . . Opponents' average has decreased in each season in the majors: .293, .276, .268, .249. . . . Decline in ERA has been steeper: 7.01, 5.24, 3.36, 2.95. . . . Most wins by a Brewers right-hander since Pete Vuckovich won 18 in 1982.

## Kevin Brown

Throws Right

| Texas Rangers | W–L | ERA | AB | H | HR | BB | SO | BA | SA | OBA |
|---|---|---|---|---|---|---|---|---|---|---|
| Season | 12-9 | 3.35 | 715 | 167 | 10 | 70 | 104 | .234 | .312 | .303 |
| vs. Left-Handers | | | 351 | 79 | 5 | 35 | 44 | .225 | .291 | .294 |
| vs. Right-Handers | | | 364 | 88 | 5 | 35 | 60 | .242 | .332 | .312 |
| Home | 6-3 | 3.25 | 291 | 66 | 3 | 38 | 47 | .227 | .285 | .317 |
| Road | 6-6 | 3.42 | 424 | 101 | 7 | 32 | 57 | .238 | .330 | .293 |
| Grass | 11-7 | 3.19 | 600 | 140 | 7 | 57 | 88 | .233 | .298 | .301 |
| Artificial Turf | 1-2 | 4.15 | 115 | 27 | 3 | 13 | 16 | .235 | .383 | .313 |
| April | 1-1 | 4.70 | 91 | 20 | 2 | 15 | 14 | .220 | .341 | .324 |
| May | 3-0 | 1.88 | 133 | 25 | 0 | 15 | 17 | .188 | .218 | .268 |
| June | 3-3 | 2.68 | 173 | 37 | 4 | 11 | 22 | .214 | .295 | .263 |
| July | 2-2 | 3.11 | 139 | 30 | 2 | 11 | 20 | .216 | .295 | .276 |
| August | 2-2 | 4.10 | 148 | 45 | 2 | 14 | 22 | .304 | .399 | .362 |
| Sept./Oct. | 1-1 | 8.22 | 31 | 10 | 0 | 4 | 9 | .323 | .387 | .432 |
| Leading Off Inn. | | | 183 | 41 | 2 | 17 | 28 | .224 | .273 | .294 |
| Runners On | | | 295 | 70 | 4 | 25 | 43 | .237 | .319 | .298 |
| Runners/Scor. Pos. | | | 146 | 37 | 2 | 16 | 27 | .253 | .322 | .320 |
| Runners On/2 Out | | | 130 | 31 | 2 | 8 | 20 | .238 | .315 | .288 |
| Scor. Pos./2 Out | | | 72 | 20 | 2 | 6 | 15 | .278 | .389 | .333 |
| Late Inning Pressure | | | 73 | 15 | 2 | 9 | 9 | .205 | .315 | .293 |
| Leading Off | | | 22 | 3 | 0 | 1 | 4 | .136 | .136 | .174 |
| Runners On | | | 26 | 5 | 1 | 4 | 2 | .192 | .346 | .300 |
| Runners/Scor. Pos. | | | 11 | 3 | 1 | 3 | 0 | .273 | .545 | .429 |
| First 9 Batters | | | 219 | 53 | 2 | 26 | 40 | .242 | .301 | .329 |
| Second 9 Batters | | | 218 | 47 | 2 | 17 | 26 | .216 | .275 | .269 |
| All Batters Thereafter | | | 278 | 67 | 6 | 27 | 38 | .241 | .349 | .308 |

Loves to face: Steve Sax (0-for-12)
Hates to face: Lance Johnson (.833, 5-for-6)
Ground outs-to-air outs ratio: 2.60 last season, 2.50 for career. . . . Additional statistics: 22 double-play ground outs in 143 opportunities, 24 doubles, 1 triple in 191.0 innings last season. . . . Allowed 19 first-inning runs in 28 starts. . . . Batting support: 4.21 runs per start. . . . Limited top 10 hitters in A.L. to .070 batting average (3-for-43), lowest in league: Puckett, 2-for-6; Lansford, 1-for-7; Boggs, 0-for-5; Greenwell, 0-for-6; Baines, 0-for-7; Sax, 0-for-12. (Didn't face others). . . . Among A.L. rookies, only Bob Milacki (36) and Jim Abbott (29) started more games than Brown (28), who led in complete games (7). . . . Tied team record for wins by a rookie, set in 1986 by Edwin Correa.

## Todd Burns

Throws Right

| Oakland As | W–L | ERA | AB | H | HR | BB | SO | BA | SA | OBA |
|---|---|---|---|---|---|---|---|---|---|---|
| Season | 6-5 | 2.24 | 337 | 66 | 3 | 28 | 49 | .196 | .264 | .259 |
| vs. Left-Handers | | | 134 | 23 | 0 | 14 | 15 | .172 | .231 | .250 |
| vs. Right-Handers | | | 203 | 43 | 3 | 14 | 34 | .212 | .286 | .265 |
| Home | 4-2 | 2.59 | 169 | 33 | 1 | 13 | 23 | .195 | .260 | .251 |
| Road | 2-3 | 1.89 | 168 | 33 | 2 | 15 | 26 | .196 | .268 | .266 |
| Grass | 5-3 | 2.26 | 285 | 59 | 1 | 21 | 41 | .207 | .260 | .263 |
| Artificial Turf | 1-2 | 2.16 | 52 | 7 | 2 | 7 | 8 | .135 | .288 | .237 |
| April | 1-0 | 2.12 | 58 | 10 | 0 | 3 | 7 | .172 | .207 | .213 |
| May | 3-0 | 1.48 | 83 | 16 | 0 | 4 | 9 | .193 | .229 | .230 |
| June | 0-2 | 1.84 | 52 | 9 | 1 | 2 | 14 | .173 | .231 | .204 |
| July | 2-0 | 3.94 | 55 | 11 | 1 | 4 | 8 | .200 | .345 | .250 |
| August | 0-0 | 2.70 | 36 | 8 | 0 | 9 | 6 | .222 | .306 | .391 |
| Sept./Oct. | 0-3 | 1.88 | 53 | 12 | 1 | 6 | 5 | .226 | .302 | .305 |
| Leading Off Inn. | | | 87 | 22 | 0 | 4 | 13 | .253 | .299 | .293 |
| Runners On | | | 142 | 27 | 1 | 15 | 21 | .190 | .246 | .266 |
| Runners/Scor. Pos. | | | 76 | 14 | 0 | 14 | 12 | .184 | .197 | .308 |
| Runners On/2 Out | | | 52 | 7 | 0 | 3 | 7 | .135 | .154 | .182 |
| Scor. Pos./2 Out | | | 32 | 5 | 0 | 3 | 4 | .156 | .156 | .229 |
| Late Inning Pressure | | | 120 | 24 | 2 | 16 | 19 | .200 | .283 | .299 |
| Leading Off | | | 35 | 7 | 0 | 3 | 5 | .200 | .229 | .282 |
| Runners On | | | 43 | 9 | 1 | 8 | 5 | .209 | .302 | .333 |
| Runners/Scor. Pos. | | | 21 | 5 | 0 | 7 | 3 | .238 | .238 | .429 |
| First 9 Batters | | | 271 | 54 | 3 | 24 | 40 | .199 | .273 | .266 |
| Second 9 Batters | | | 58 | 10 | 0 | 3 | 8 | .172 | .224 | .213 |
| All Batters Thereafter | | | 8 | 2 | 0 | 1 | 1 | .250 | .250 | .333 |

Loves to face: Jack Howell (0-for-10)
Hates to face: Wally Joyner (.500, 4-for-8, 2 HR)
Ground outs-to-air outs ratio: 0.98 last season, 0.84 for career. . . . Additional statistics: 10 double-play ground outs (all vs. right-handers) in 83 opportunities, 10 doubles, 2 triples in 96.1 innings last season. . . . Inherited 40 runners, stranded 32 (80%), 3d-highest average in A.L. (minimum: 40 runners). . . . Held left-handed batters to two hits in 24 at-bats with runners in scoring position. . . . Averaged 6.9 batters faced per relief appearance. Averages of his bullpenmates: Nelson 6.7, Honeycutt 4.8, Eckersley 4.0. . . . Only 12 percent of batters faced in 1988 were in Late-Inning Pressure Situations, compared to 38 percent last season. . . . Career record of 9–2, 2.07 ERA at home; 5–5, 3.56 on the road.

## Greg Cadaret

Throws Left

| As/Yankees | W–L | ERA | AB | H | HR | BB | SO | BA | SA | OBA |
|---|---|---|---|---|---|---|---|---|---|---|
| Season | 5-5 | 4.05 | 464 | 130 | 7 | 57 | 80 | .280 | .379 | .358 |
| vs. Left-Handers | | | 123 | 31 | 1 | 12 | 22 | .252 | .325 | .319 |
| vs. Right-Handers | | | 341 | 99 | 6 | 45 | 58 | .290 | .399 | .372 |
| Home | 4-2 | 4.41 | 243 | 64 | 4 | 29 | 43 | .263 | .350 | .345 |
| Road | 1-3 | 3.65 | 221 | 66 | 3 | 28 | 37 | .299 | .412 | .372 |
| Grass | 5-4 | 4.15 | 391 | 106 | 6 | 46 | 68 | .271 | .373 | .347 |
| Artificial Turf | 0-1 | 3.50 | 73 | 24 | 1 | 11 | 12 | .329 | .411 | .417 |
| April | 0-0 | 3.86 | 31 | 6 | 0 | 7 | 5 | .194 | .194 | .325 |
| May | 0-0 | 1.80 | 37 | 9 | 0 | 6 | 6 | .243 | .270 | .349 |
| June | 1-0 | 2.57 | 53 | 12 | 0 | 8 | 8 | .226 | .264 | .328 |
| July | 1-2 | 4.88 | 94 | 30 | 2 | 9 | 14 | .319 | .489 | .368 |
| August | 2-2 | 4.42 | 156 | 44 | 3 | 16 | 28 | .282 | .378 | .356 |
| Sept./Oct. | 1-1 | 4.50 | 93 | 29 | 2 | 11 | 19 | .312 | .441 | .385 |
| Leading Off Inn. | | | 105 | 29 | 2 | 11 | 12 | .276 | .410 | .345 |
| Runners On | | | 222 | 74 | 3 | 33 | 41 | .333 | .432 | .414 |
| Runners/Scor. Pos. | | | 134 | 44 | 3 | 22 | 26 | .328 | .448 | .414 |
| Runners On/2 Out | | | 93 | 33 | 2 | 17 | 17 | .355 | .473 | .459 |
| Scor. Pos./2 Out | | | 65 | 21 | 2 | 15 | 11 | .323 | .446 | .457 |
| Late Inning Pressure | | | 54 | 21 | 0 | 9 | 7 | .389 | .519 | .462 |
| Leading Off | | | 13 | 5 | 0 | 1 | 0 | .385 | .615 | .429 |
| Runners On | | | 28 | 13 | 0 | 6 | 3 | .464 | .571 | .528 |
| Runners/Scor. Pos. | | | 16 | 10 | 0 | 4 | 0 | .625 | .813 | .636 |
| First 9 Batters | | | 235 | 62 | 3 | 41 | 37 | .264 | .357 | .371 |
| Second 9 Batters | | | 116 | 27 | 1 | 10 | 22 | .233 | .302 | .289 |
| All Batters Thereafter | | | 113 | 41 | 3 | 6 | 21 | .363 | .504 | .400 |

Loves to face: Wade Boggs (.091, 1-for-11)
Hates to face: Gary Gaetti (.800, 4-for-5)
Ground outs-to-air outs ratio: 1.16 last season, 0.97 for career. . . . Additional statistics: 14 double-play ground outs in 122 opportunities, 25 doubles, 0 triples in 120.0 innings last season. . . . Allowed 6 first-inning runs in 13 starts. . . . Batting support: 4.08 runs per start. . . . Made 13 starts for Yankees after working exclusively in relief for Oakland (113 games). Career breakdown: 4–5, 4.02 ERA as a starter; 12–4, 3.64 in relief. . . . Opponents' career BA: .232 with bases empty, .287 with runners on base. Left-handers: .227 (one HR per 98.3 AB); right-handers: .275 (one HR per 48.5 AB). . . . Has never allowed a triple. . . . Has walked 5 of 37 career batters faced with the bases loaded.

## Tom Candiotti

Throws Right

| Cleveland Indians | W–L | ERA | AB | H | HR | BB | SO | BA | SA | OBA |
|---|---|---|---|---|---|---|---|---|---|---|
| Season | 13-10 | 3.10 | 778 | 188 | 10 | 55 | 124 | .242 | .319 | .294 |
| vs. Left-Handers | | | 395 | 97 | 5 | 34 | 58 | .246 | .327 | .306 |
| vs. Right-Handers | | | 383 | 91 | 5 | 21 | 66 | .238 | .311 | .280 |
| Home | 7-3 | 2.95 | 388 | 99 | 3 | 24 | 54 | .255 | .317 | .301 |
| Road | 6-7 | 3.25 | 390 | 89 | 7 | 31 | 70 | .228 | .321 | .286 |
| Grass | 11-9 | 3.12 | 679 | 167 | 8 | 50 | 114 | .246 | .320 | .300 |
| Artificial Turf | 2-1 | 2.96 | 99 | 21 | 2 | 5 | 10 | .212 | .313 | .248 |
| April | 2-1 | 4.00 | 104 | 27 | 4 | 10 | 21 | .260 | .433 | .325 |
| May | 4-1 | 2.35 | 169 | 39 | 1 | 13 | 25 | .231 | .272 | .283 |
| June | 1-4 | 5.34 | 121 | 37 | 1 | 10 | 17 | .306 | .380 | .364 |
| July | 2-0 | 1.13 | 81 | 11 | 0 | 4 | 10 | .136 | .173 | .176 |
| August | 3-0 | 1.87 | 159 | 33 | 2 | 9 | 27 | .208 | .258 | .262 |
| Sept./Oct. | 1-4 | 4.33 | 144 | 41 | 2 | 9 | 24 | .285 | .389 | .325 |
| Leading Off Inn. | | | 208 | 45 | 2 | 6 | 41 | .216 | .279 | .238 |
| Runners On | | | 282 | 73 | 4 | 30 | 35 | .259 | .351 | .330 |
| Runners/Scor. Pos. | | | 160 | 40 | 2 | 22 | 21 | .250 | .369 | .337 |
| Runners On/2 Out | | | 129 | 30 | 1 | 15 | 17 | .233 | .295 | .317 |
| Scor. Pos./2 Out | | | 83 | 20 | 1 | 12 | 12 | .241 | .337 | .344 |
| Late Inning Pressure | | | 84 | 22 | 0 | 10 | 5 | .262 | .298 | .337 |
| Leading Off | | | 24 | 6 | 0 | 0 | 1 | .250 | .250 | .250 |
| Runners On | | | 35 | 9 | 0 | 6 | 3 | .257 | .343 | .357 |
| Runners/Scor. Pos. | | | 17 | 4 | 0 | 3 | 2 | .235 | .412 | .333 |
| First 9 Batters | | | 249 | 58 | 3 | 18 | 47 | .233 | .313 | .289 |
| Second 9 Batters | | | 246 | 56 | 4 | 13 | 45 | .228 | .313 | .271 |
| All Batters Thereafter | | | 283 | 74 | 3 | 24 | 32 | .261 | .329 | .317 |

Loves to face: Tim Laudner (.077, 1-for-13)
Hates to face: George Bell (.552, 16-for-29, 2 HR)
Ground outs-to-air outs ratio: 1.39 last season, 1.28 for career. . . . Additional statistics: 11 double-play ground outs in 123 opportunities, 22 doubles, 4 triples in 206.0 innings last season. . . . Allowed 15 first-inning runs in 31 starts. . . . Batting support: 3.29 runs per start, 2d lowest among A.L. pitchers with at least 15 starts. . . . First Indians pitcher since Sam McDowell (1967–71) to make at least 30 starts for 200 or more innings in four consecutive seasons. . . . Opponents have hit better in day games than at night in each of his four seasons with Cleveland. . . . Like most knuckleballers, better after the All-Star break (32–26, 3.40 ERA) than before (24–28, 4.02). . . . Career record of 16–4 (2.31) in August.

## Chuck Cary

Throws Left

| New York Yankees | W–L | ERA | AB | H | HR | BB | SO | BA | SA | OBA |
|---|---|---|---|---|---|---|---|---|---|---|
| Season | 4-4 | 3.26 | 373 | 78 | 13 | 29 | 79 | .209 | .381 | .266 |
| vs. Left-Handers | | | 67 | 13 | 2 | 4 | 13 | .194 | .343 | .239 |
| vs. Right-Handers | | | 306 | 65 | 11 | 25 | 66 | .212 | .389 | .271 |
| Home | 3-2 | 3.26 | 233 | 52 | 7 | 17 | 45 | .223 | .382 | .276 |
| Road | 1-2 | 3.26 | 140 | 26 | 6 | 12 | 34 | .186 | .379 | .248 |
| Grass | 4-4 | 3.06 | 349 | 70 | 12 | 26 | 78 | .201 | .364 | .255 |
| Artificial Turf | 0-0 | 6.75 | 24 | 8 | 1 | 3 | 1 | .333 | .625 | .407 |
| April | | | 0 | 0 | 0 | 0 | 0 | — | — | — |
| May | 0-0 | 1.64 | 36 | 4 | 1 | 6 | 13 | .111 | .194 | .238 |
| June | 0-0 | 3.77 | 58 | 12 | 2 | 2 | 9 | .207 | .362 | .233 |
| July | 1-0 | 1.82 | 85 | 15 | 1 | 9 | 16 | .176 | .282 | .255 |
| August | 2-3 | 5.21 | 155 | 41 | 9 | 7 | 27 | .265 | .529 | .296 |
| Sept./Oct. | 1-1 | 0.79 | 39 | 6 | 0 | 5 | 14 | .154 | .205 | .244 |
| Leading Off Inn. | | | 96 | 18 | 2 | 4 | 18 | .188 | .333 | .220 |
| Runners On | | | 130 | 29 | 7 | 15 | 22 | .223 | .431 | .301 |
| Runners/Scor. Pos. | | | 80 | 20 | 6 | 15 | 14 | .250 | .538 | .365 |
| Runners On/2 Out | | | 54 | 8 | 1 | 8 | 13 | .148 | .241 | .258 |
| Scor. Pos./2 Out | | | 33 | 5 | 1 | 8 | 7 | .152 | .273 | .317 |
| Late Inning Pressure | | | 40 | 8 | 0 | 5 | 10 | .200 | .250 | .289 |
| Leading Off | | | 12 | 2 | 0 | 2 | 4 | .167 | .250 | .286 |
| Runners On | | | 11 | 3 | 0 | 2 | 3 | .273 | .273 | .385 |
| Runners/Scor. Pos. | | | 5 | 2 | 0 | 2 | 1 | .400 | .400 | .571 |
| First 9 Batters | | | 155 | 31 | 6 | 12 | 39 | .200 | .381 | .256 |
| Second 9 Batters | | | 118 | 23 | 6 | 8 | 23 | .195 | .415 | .246 |
| All Batters Thereafter | | | 100 | 24 | 1 | 9 | 17 | .240 | .340 | .303 |

Loves to face: Orioles' outfielders (see below)
Hates to face: Chili Davis (.600, 3-for-5, 1 HR)
Bradley (11), Devereaux (11), and Jefferson (7) are hitless in 29 at-bats. . . . Ground outs-to-air outs ratio: 0.59 last season, 0.66 for career. . . . Additional statistics: 3 double-play ground outs in 47 opportunities, 21 doubles, 2 triples in 99.1 innings last season. . . . Allowed 7 first-inning runs in 11 starts. . . . Batting support: 4.27 runs per start. . . . Exclusively a reliever in 58 games for Detroit and Atlanta (1984–88). Made 11 starts in 22 appearances for Yankees last year. . . . Only complete games came in back-to-back victories. . . . Has faced 133 batters in LIP Situations without allowing a home run. . . . Opposing right-handers have hit one HR per 27 at-bats; left-handers, one per 55 AB.

## John Cerutti

Throws Left

| Toronto Blue Jays | W–L | ERA | AB | H | HR | BB | SO | BA | SA | OBA |
|---|---|---|---|---|---|---|---|---|---|---|
| Season | 11-11 | 3.07 | 785 | 214 | 19 | 53 | 69 | .273 | .403 | .322 |
| vs. Left-Handers | | | 126 | 28 | 3 | 11 | 15 | .222 | .341 | .290 |
| vs. Right-Handers | | | 659 | 186 | 16 | 42 | 54 | .282 | .414 | .328 |
| Home | 5-5 | 2.63 | 393 | 106 | 9 | 26 | 40 | .270 | .394 | .315 |
| Road | 6-6 | 3.51 | 392 | 108 | 10 | 27 | 29 | .276 | .411 | .328 |
| Grass | 5-4 | 3.13 | 292 | 75 | 7 | 22 | 25 | .257 | .384 | .311 |
| Artificial Turf | 6-7 | 3.03 | 493 | 139 | 12 | 31 | 44 | .282 | .414 | .328 |
| April | 0-1 | 1.41 | 107 | 22 | 1 | 9 | 8 | .206 | .262 | .267 |
| May | 1-2 | 4.75 | 119 | 36 | 4 | 6 | 10 | .303 | .471 | .333 |
| June | 2-1 | 1.94 | 167 | 49 | 2 | 12 | 12 | .293 | .365 | .339 |
| July | 4-1 | 2.78 | 122 | 36 | 2 | 9 | 10 | .295 | .402 | .351 |
| August | 2-3 | 3.86 | 144 | 38 | 7 | 11 | 15 | .264 | .472 | .325 |
| Sept./Oct. | 2-3 | 3.98 | 126 | 33 | 3 | 6 | 14 | .262 | .429 | .301 |
| Leading Off Inn. | | | 208 | 48 | 4 | 10 | 17 | .231 | .341 | .266 |
| Runners On | | | 289 | 76 | 6 | 22 | 20 | .263 | .398 | .319 |
| Runners/Scor. Pos. | | | 145 | 38 | 4 | 11 | 10 | .262 | .428 | .317 |
| Runners On/2 Out | | | 118 | 25 | 1 | 16 | 14 | .212 | .271 | .311 |
| Scor. Pos./2 Out | | | 70 | 15 | 1 | 7 | 10 | .214 | .300 | .295 |
| Late Inning Pressure | | | 88 | 26 | 2 | 9 | 13 | .295 | .386 | .361 |
| Leading Off | | | 27 | 7 | 0 | 2 | 3 | .259 | .259 | .310 |
| Runners On | | | 28 | 5 | 0 | 3 | 7 | .179 | .179 | .258 |
| Runners/Scor. Pos. | | | 5 | 0 | 0 | 1 | 1 | .000 | .000 | .167 |
| First 9 Batters | | | 269 | 64 | 8 | 18 | 25 | .238 | .368 | .296 |
| Second 9 Batters | | | 249 | 76 | 7 | 16 | 17 | .305 | .450 | .347 |
| All Batters Thereafter | | | 267 | 74 | 4 | 19 | 27 | .277 | .393 | .324 |

Loves to face: Greg Walker (0-for-13)
Hates to face: Gary Gaetti (.467, 7-for-15, 4 HR)
Ground outs-to-air outs ratio: 1.18 last season, 0.96 for career. . . . Additional statistics: 22 double-play ground outs in 139 opportunities, 33 doubles, 6 triples in 205.1 innings last season. . . . Allowed 9 first-inning runs in 31 starts. . . . Batting support: 4.55 runs per start. . . . Opponents stole only 12 bases in 26 attempts (46%), compared to 56-for-79 (71%) against Toronto's other starters. . . . Career breakdown: 32–24, 3.90 ERA as a starter; 5–4, 2.87 in relief. . . . Career record of 13–13 in Canada, 24–15 in the States. . . . Opponents' career BA is .237 in day games, .280 at night. Difference of 43 points is largest over the last 10 years. But his record is far better at night (25–16) than in day games (12–12).

## Roger Clemens

Throws Right

| Boston Red Sox | W–L | ERA | AB | H | HR | BB | SO | BA | SA | OBA |
|---|---|---|---|---|---|---|---|---|---|---|
| Season | 17-11 | 3.13 | 929 | 215 | 20 | 93 | 230 | .231 | .338 | .305 |
| vs. Left-Handers | | | 503 | 122 | 7 | 57 | 110 | .243 | .332 | .320 |
| vs. Right-Handers | | | 426 | 93 | 13 | 36 | 120 | .218 | .345 | .287 |
| Home | 9-3 | 2.90 | 399 | 99 | 9 | 33 | 107 | .248 | .363 | .310 |
| Road | 8-8 | 3.29 | 530 | 116 | 11 | 60 | 123 | .219 | .319 | .302 |
| Grass | 14-11 | 3.49 | 790 | 190 | 19 | 82 | 200 | .241 | .356 | .316 |
| Artificial Turf | 3-0 | 1.29 | 139 | 25 | 1 | 11 | 30 | .180 | .237 | .242 |
| April | 3-1 | 1.96 | 164 | 33 | 4 | 13 | 40 | .201 | .299 | .263 |
| May | 2-3 | 3.83 | 157 | 35 | 4 | 15 | 38 | .223 | .350 | .299 |
| June | 3-2 | 3.57 | 138 | 36 | 3 | 12 | 33 | .261 | .370 | .320 |
| July | 3-2 | 3.65 | 151 | 35 | 4 | 24 | 39 | .232 | .364 | .341 |
| August | 3-1 | 3.66 | 151 | 34 | 2 | 16 | 36 | .225 | .305 | .304 |
| Sept./Oct. | 3-2 | 2.35 | 168 | 42 | 3 | 13 | 44 | .250 | .345 | .308 |
| Leading Off Inn. | | | 242 | 54 | 6 | 20 | 54 | .223 | .318 | .285 |
| Runners On | | | 339 | 79 | 3 | 48 | 79 | .233 | .327 | .331 |
| Runners/Scor. Pos. | | | 183 | 41 | 2 | 28 | 48 | .224 | .333 | .329 |
| Runners On/2 Out | | | 150 | 39 | 1 | 25 | 36 | .260 | .360 | .376 |
| Scor. Pos./2 Out | | | 96 | 24 | 1 | 17 | 23 | .250 | .354 | .374 |
| Late Inning Pressure | | | 111 | 28 | 5 | 12 | 28 | .252 | .423 | .331 |
| Leading Off | | | 30 | 10 | 2 | 5 | 4 | .333 | .567 | .429 |
| Runners On | | | 36 | 7 | 1 | 7 | 12 | .194 | .306 | .326 |
| Runners/Scor. Pos. | | | 21 | 2 | 0 | 5 | 10 | .095 | .095 | .269 |
| First 9 Batters | | | 274 | 66 | 8 | 27 | 75 | .241 | .380 | .313 |
| Second 9 Batters | | | 267 | 56 | 2 | 31 | 67 | .210 | .255 | .298 |
| All Batters Thereafter | | | 388 | 93 | 10 | 35 | 88 | .240 | .366 | .305 |

Loves to face: Ron Kittle (0-for-14, 10 SO)
Hates to face: Steve Sax (.600, 9-for-15, 1 HR)
Ground outs-to-air outs ratio: 1.26 last season, 0.97 for career. . . . Additional statistics: 23 double-play ground outs in 175 opportunities, 31 doubles, 4 triples in 253.1 innings last season. . . . Allowed 22 first-inning runs in 35 starts. . . . Batting support: 4.54 runs per start. . . . Opposing base runners stole 19 bases, were caught 17 times (most in A.L.). . . . He and Gooden are only pitchers with winning records in each of last six seasons. . . . Red Sox record for consecutive winning seasons is seven, held by El Tiante (1972–78). Others with six: Babe Ruth (1914–19), Lefty Grove (1935–40), Ike Delock (1953–59), and Bob Stanley (1977–82). . . . Career record of 18–4 (2.24 ERA) on artificial turf; 77–41 (3.21) on grass fields.

## Chuck Crim

Throws Right

| Milwaukee Brewers | W–L | ERA | AB | H | HR | BB | SO | BA | SA | OBA |
|---|---|---|---|---|---|---|---|---|---|---|
| Season | 9-7 | 2.83 | 440 | 114 | 7 | 36 | 59 | .259 | .355 | .314 |
| vs. Left-Handers | | | 166 | 45 | 3 | 18 | 21 | .271 | .367 | .344 |
| vs. Right-Handers | | | 274 | 69 | 4 | 18 | 38 | .252 | .347 | .295 |
| Home | 4-3 | 2.60 | 234 | 56 | 1 | 15 | 27 | .239 | .303 | .283 |
| Road | 5-4 | 3.12 | 206 | 58 | 6 | 21 | 32 | .282 | .413 | .348 |
| Grass | 7-6 | 2.56 | 372 | 92 | 5 | 30 | 45 | .247 | .333 | .301 |
| Artificial Turf | 2-1 | 4.60 | 68 | 22 | 2 | 6 | 14 | .324 | .471 | .387 |
| April | 1-2 | 4.26 | 51 | 14 | 0 | 7 | 4 | .275 | .314 | .362 |
| May | 3-0 | 2.75 | 75 | 22 | 1 | 1 | 13 | .293 | .400 | .295 |
| June | 3-3 | 3.65 | 93 | 23 | 2 | 7 | 10 | .247 | .387 | .307 |
| July | 0-0 | 1.65 | 57 | 12 | 0 | 5 | 8 | .211 | .281 | .274 |
| August | 1-0 | 2.70 | 74 | 22 | 2 | 7 | 11 | .297 | .378 | .349 |
| Sept./Oct. | 1-2 | 2.22 | 90 | 21 | 2 | 9 | 13 | .233 | .333 | .304 |
| Leading Off Inn. | | | 96 | 28 | 4 | 3 | 9 | .292 | .479 | .313 |
| Runners On | | | 224 | 59 | 3 | 24 | 32 | .263 | .353 | .329 |
| Runners/Scor. Pos. | | | 132 | 31 | 1 | 22 | 21 | .235 | .326 | .335 |
| Runners On/2 Out | | | 92 | 23 | 2 | 10 | 10 | .250 | .391 | .324 |
| Scor. Pos./2 Out | | | 65 | 15 | 0 | 9 | 8 | .231 | .323 | .324 |
| Late Inning Pressure | | | 220 | 52 | 4 | 23 | 28 | .236 | .336 | .306 |
| Leading Off | | | 55 | 12 | 2 | 1 | 5 | .218 | .345 | .232 |
| Runners On | | | 96 | 25 | 2 | 16 | 13 | .260 | .375 | .353 |
| Runners/Scor. Pos. | | | 56 | 12 | 1 | 15 | 9 | .214 | .321 | .360 |
| First 9 Batters | | | 374 | 101 | 4 | 29 | 49 | .270 | .348 | .321 |
| Second 9 Batters | | | 66 | 13 | 3 | 7 | 10 | .197 | .394 | .274 |
| All Batters Thereafter | | | 0 | 0 | 0 | 0 | 0 | — | — | — |

Loves to face: Cory Snyder (.091, 1-for-11, 4 SO)
Hates to face: Alan Trammell (.667, 8-for-12)
Ground outs-to-air outs ratio: 1.82 last season, 1.47 for career. . . . Additional statistics: 20 double-play ground outs in 118 opportunities, 11 doubles, 5 triples in 117.2 innings last season. . . . Inherited 51 runners, stranded 22 (43%), lowest rate in A.L. (minimum: 20 runners). . . . Tied with Cubs' Mitch Williams for most relief appearances (76), and leads A.L. with 199 appearances over last three seasons. . . . First pitcher to lead A.L. in appearances in consecutive seasons since Rollie Fingers (1974–75). . . . Led Brewers with six "save setups." (See Rick Honeycutt comments for definition.) . . .Only one of his 9 wins came after he'd blown an inherited lead.

## Storm Davis

Throws Right

| Oakland As | W–L | ERA | AB | H | HR | BB | SO | BA | SA | OBA |
|---|---|---|---|---|---|---|---|---|---|---|
| Season | 19-7 | 4.36 | 649 | 187 | 19 | 68 | 91 | .288 | .435 | .355 |
| vs. Left-Handers | | | 314 | 83 | 10 | 45 | 48 | .264 | .414 | .353 |
| vs. Right-Handers | | | 335 | 104 | 9 | 23 | 43 | .310 | .454 | .356 |
| Home | 9-3 | 4.70 | 318 | 90 | 10 | 32 | 46 | .283 | .421 | .349 |
| Road | 10-4 | 4.03 | 331 | 97 | 9 | 36 | 45 | .293 | .447 | .360 |
| Grass | 17-7 | 4.42 | 585 | 169 | 18 | 61 | 80 | .289 | .434 | .356 |
| Artificial Turf | 2-0 | 3.78 | 64 | 18 | 1 | 7 | 11 | .281 | .438 | .347 |
| April | 2-2 | 5.87 | 96 | 33 | 3 | 13 | 13 | .344 | .510 | .422 |
| May | 1-1 | 6.59 | 56 | 20 | 3 | 9 | 7 | .357 | .571 | .439 |
| June | 3-0 | 4.43 | 74 | 18 | 2 | 9 | 14 | .243 | .351 | .325 |
| July | 3-2 | 6.68 | 120 | 36 | 5 | 11 | 18 | .300 | .525 | .356 |
| August | 6-1 | 2.36 | 174 | 44 | 4 | 13 | 20 | .253 | .368 | .312 |
| Sept./Oct. | 4-1 | 3.03 | 129 | 36 | 2 | 13 | 19 | .279 | .372 | .338 |
| Leading Off Inn. | | | 165 | 61 | 7 | 14 | 16 | .370 | .576 | .422 |
| Runners On | | | 297 | 80 | 6 | 28 | 46 | .269 | .364 | .327 |
| Runners/Scor. Pos. | | | 160 | 43 | 3 | 21 | 27 | .269 | .375 | .344 |
| Runners On/2 Out | | | 100 | 20 | 1 | 12 | 19 | .200 | .260 | .292 |
| Scor. Pos./2 Out | | | 65 | 14 | 0 | 11 | 14 | .215 | .262 | .338 |
| Late Inning Pressure | | | 36 | 10 | 2 | 2 | 7 | .278 | .472 | .325 |
| Leading Off | | | 10 | 3 | 0 | 1 | 2 | .300 | .300 | .417 |
| Runners On | | | 13 | 2 | 1 | 0 | 2 | .154 | .385 | .143 |
| Runners/Scor. Pos. | | | 5 | 1 | 1 | 0 | 0 | .200 | .800 | .167 |
| First 9 Batters | | | 249 | 75 | 6 | 23 | 29 | .301 | .434 | .360 |
| Second 9 Batters | | | 229 | 69 | 7 | 29 | 35 | .301 | .476 | .379 |
| All Batters Thereafter | | | 171 | 43 | 6 | 16 | 27 | .251 | .380 | .314 |

Loves to face: Randy Bush (.086, 3-for-35)
Hates to face: Robin Yount (.360, 18-for-50, 1 HR)
Ground outs-to-air outs ratio: 1.01 last season, 1.10 for career. . . . Additional statistics: 24 double-play ground outs in 175 opportunities, 30 doubles, 4 triples in 169.1 innings last season. . . . Allowed 21 first-inning runs in 31 starts. . . . Batting support: 5.61 runs per start. . . . A.L. pitchers with comparable ERA (within a quarter-run) had combined record of 97–145 (.401). . . . Opponents stole only eight bases in 18 attempts. . . . Opposing leadoff batters hit .370, highest in last 15 years (min.: 100 BFP). . . . Career record of 39–36 before All-Star break, 53–26 after. . . . In first Series start (1983), fanned first three batters: Morgan, Rose, Schmidt. Probably thought, "Three Hall of Famers." Now, who knows?

## John Dopson

Throws Right

| Boston Red Sox | W–L | ERA | AB | H | HR | BB | SO | BA | SA | OBA |
|---|---|---|---|---|---|---|---|---|---|---|
| Season | 12-8 | 3.99 | 647 | 166 | 14 | 69 | 95 | .257 | .365 | .328 |
| vs. Left-Handers | | | 316 | 78 | 5 | 33 | 41 | .247 | .323 | .315 |
| vs. Right-Handers | | | 331 | 88 | 9 | 36 | 54 | .266 | .405 | .341 |
| Home | 6-5 | 4.07 | 392 | 99 | 8 | 50 | 61 | .253 | .355 | .337 |
| Road | 6-3 | 3.86 | 255 | 67 | 6 | 19 | 34 | .263 | .380 | .314 |
| Grass | 10-6 | 4.23 | 530 | 138 | 13 | 61 | 77 | .260 | .375 | .337 |
| Artificial Turf | 2-2 | 2.90 | 117 | 28 | 1 | 8 | 18 | .239 | .316 | .288 |
| April | 2-1 | 2.45 | 104 | 20 | 1 | 9 | 22 | .192 | .260 | .252 |
| May | 3-2 | 4.59 | 131 | 39 | 4 | 12 | 18 | .298 | .450 | .357 |
| June | 3-2 | 5.23 | 120 | 33 | 3 | 17 | 17 | .275 | .417 | .367 |
| July | 1-0 | 3.76 | 104 | 29 | 1 | 14 | 13 | .279 | .327 | .370 |
| August | 0-1 | 6.00 | 36 | 12 | 0 | 9 | 4 | .333 | .361 | .467 |
| Sept./Oct. | 3-2 | 3.35 | 152 | 33 | 5 | 8 | 21 | .217 | .349 | .255 |
| Leading Off Inn. | | | 162 | 40 | 3 | 21 | 22 | .247 | .327 | .333 |
| Runners On | | | 285 | 72 | 6 | 24 | 34 | .253 | .368 | .309 |
| Runners/Scor. Pos. | | | 169 | 43 | 3 | 14 | 21 | .254 | .373 | .305 |
| Runners On/2 Out | | | 108 | 23 | 2 | 9 | 18 | .213 | .287 | .280 |
| Scor. Pos./2 Out | | | 77 | 13 | 1 | 7 | 12 | .169 | .221 | .238 |
| Late Inning Pressure | | | 44 | 11 | 1 | 1 | 5 | .250 | .341 | .261 |
| Leading Off | | | 15 | 5 | 1 | 0 | 0 | .333 | .533 | .333 |
| Runners On | | | 14 | 2 | 0 | 0 | 3 | .143 | .214 | .133 |
| Runners/Scor. Pos. | | | 5 | 1 | 0 | 0 | 1 | .200 | .400 | .167 |
| First 9 Batters | | | 233 | 55 | 2 | 25 | 34 | .236 | .279 | .308 |
| Second 9 Batters | | | 222 | 65 | 6 | 24 | 32 | .293 | .446 | .362 |
| All Batters Thereafter | | | 192 | 46 | 6 | 20 | 29 | .240 | .375 | .315 |

Loves to face: Steve Sax (.095, 2-for-21)
Hates to face: Gary Pettis (.625, 5-for-8)
Ground outs-to-air outs ratio: 2.07 last season, 1.93 for career. . . . Additional statistics: 19 double-play ground outs in 139 opportunities, 22 doubles, 3 triples in 169.1 innings last season. . . . Allowed 10 first-inning runs in 28 starts. Walked more batters (11) than he struck out (9) during the first inning. . . . Batting support: 4.64 runs per start. . . . Led the A.L. with 15 balks. No other pitcher had more than eight. . . . Career record of 11–9 on grass fields, 4–12 on artificial surfaces. . . . Career batting average is .221 by opposing ground-ball hitters, .283 by fly-ballers. . . . Opponents' career average is .225 during his first pass through the batting order, .260 his second time through, .275 after that.

## Richard Dotson

Throws Right

| Yankees/White Sox | W–L | ERA | AB | H | HR | BB | SO | BA | SA | OBA |
|---|---|---|---|---|---|---|---|---|---|---|
| Season | 5-12 | 4.46 | 615 | 181 | 16 | 58 | 69 | .294 | .457 | .354 |
| vs. Left-Handers | | | 313 | 91 | 9 | 26 | 31 | .291 | .479 | .342 |
| vs. Right-Handers | | | 302 | 90 | 7 | 32 | 38 | .298 | .434 | .366 |
| Home | 3-7 | 4.54 | 307 | 92 | 8 | 31 | 41 | .300 | .453 | .363 |
| Road | 2-5 | 4.38 | 308 | 89 | 8 | 27 | 28 | .289 | .461 | .345 |
| Grass | 5-9 | 4.42 | 544 | 159 | 13 | 48 | 57 | .292 | .447 | .349 |
| Artificial Turf | 0-3 | 4.76 | 71 | 22 | 3 | 10 | 12 | .310 | .535 | .390 |
| April | 0-0 | 12.00 | 17 | 7 | 2 | 1 | 3 | .412 | .941 | .444 |
| May | 2-2 | 4.85 | 121 | 38 | 3 | 8 | 9 | .314 | .479 | .351 |
| June | 0-3 | 5.68 | 80 | 24 | 3 | 8 | 2 | .300 | .500 | .371 |
| July | 1-1 | 4.67 | 108 | 26 | 2 | 17 | 12 | .241 | .370 | .339 |
| August | 1-2 | 4.37 | 143 | 46 | 3 | 14 | 16 | .322 | .483 | .382 |
| Sept./Oct. | 1-4 | 2.87 | 146 | 40 | 3 | 10 | 27 | .274 | .397 | .321 |
| Leading Off Inn. | | | 149 | 41 | 4 | 12 | 18 | .275 | .443 | .329 |
| Runners On | | | 281 | 77 | 6 | 28 | 30 | .274 | .413 | .338 |
| Runners/Scor. Pos. | | | 153 | 40 | 1 | 14 | 16 | .261 | .379 | .320 |
| Runners On/2 Out | | | 117 | 24 | 2 | 14 | 15 | .205 | .308 | .290 |
| Scor. Pos./2 Out | | | 69 | 15 | 0 | 9 | 7 | .217 | .304 | .308 |
| Late Inning Pressure | | | 44 | 8 | 0 | 5 | 5 | .182 | .205 | .265 |
| Leading Off | | | 13 | 1 | 0 | 2 | 2 | .077 | .077 | .200 |
| Runners On | | | 13 | 3 | 0 | 2 | 0 | .231 | .231 | .333 |
| Runners/Scor. Pos. | | | 7 | 2 | 0 | 1 | 0 | .286 | .286 | .375 |
| First 9 Batters | | | 226 | 61 | 7 | 20 | 27 | .270 | .438 | .332 |
| Second 9 Batters | | | 195 | 62 | 6 | 20 | 16 | .318 | .518 | .376 |
| All Batters Thereafter | | | 194 | 58 | 3 | 18 | 26 | .299 | .418 | .357 |

Loves to face: Scott Fletcher (.091, 2-for-22)
Hates to face: Julio Franco (.462, 18-for-39, 1 HR))
Ground outs-to-air outs ratio: 0.95 last season, 1.27 for career. . . . Additional statistics: 13 double-play ground outs in 133 opportunities, 32 doubles, 10 triples in 151.1 innings last season. . . . Allowed 7 first-inning runs in 26 starts, but only two in 17 starts after joining Sox. . . . Batting support: 4.23 runs per start. . . . Batting average of opposing left-handers was the highest of his career, but right-handers hit .295 or better in three of last four seasons. . . . Opponents have hit better on artificial turf than on grass fields for five consecutive seasons. During that time: 36–42, 4.45 ERA on plastic; 5–12, 6.59 on grass. . . . Has made at least 25 starts in each of the last four seasons, despite a 4.78 ERA.

## Mike Dunne

Throws Right

| Seattle Mariners | W–L | ERA | AB | H | HR | BB | SO | BA | SA | OBA |
|---|---|---|---|---|---|---|---|---|---|---|
| Season | 2-9 | 5.27 | 339 | 104 | 7 | 37 | 38 | .307 | .437 | .373 |
| vs. Left-Handers | | | 183 | 61 | 3 | 19 | 12 | .333 | .470 | .390 |
| vs. Right-Handers | | | 156 | 43 | 4 | 18 | 26 | .276 | .397 | .354 |
| Home | 2-4 | 3.76 | 209 | 60 | 6 | 12 | 24 | .287 | .435 | .326 |
| Road | 0-5 | 7.71 | 130 | 44 | 1 | 25 | 14 | .338 | .438 | .440 |
| Grass | 0-4 | 7.77 | 90 | 31 | 1 | 16 | 12 | .344 | .456 | .440 |
| Artificial Turf | 2-5 | 4.41 | 249 | 73 | 6 | 21 | 26 | .293 | .430 | .347 |
| April | 0-1 | 10.13 | 24 | 10 | 1 | 1 | 2 | .417 | .667 | .440 |
| May | 1-2 | 5.48 | 88 | 28 | 2 | 15 | 8 | .318 | .455 | .413 |
| June | | | 0 | 0 | 0 | 0 | 0 | — | — | — |
| July | 0-2 | 5.71 | 65 | 17 | 1 | 6 | 6 | .262 | .338 | .329 |
| August | 1-3 | 3.43 | 153 | 45 | 3 | 10 | 21 | .294 | .425 | .335 |
| Sept./Oct. | 0-1 | 22.50 | 9 | 4 | 0 | 5 | 1 | .444 | .556 | .643 |
| Leading Off Inn. | | | 85 | 30 | 3 | 9 | 10 | .353 | .494 | .415 |
| Runners On | | | 155 | 45 | 2 | 16 | 14 | .290 | .406 | .354 |
| Runners/Scor. Pos. | | | 89 | 25 | 1 | 11 | 11 | .281 | .404 | .349 |
| Runners On/2 Out | | | 59 | 13 | 0 | 3 | 8 | .220 | .305 | .258 |
| Scor. Pos./2 Out | | | 38 | 8 | 0 | 2 | 6 | .211 | .316 | .250 |
| Late Inning Pressure | | | 17 | 4 | 0 | 2 | 1 | .235 | .235 | .300 |
| Leading Off | | | 7 | 1 | 0 | 1 | 1 | .143 | .143 | .250 |
| Runners On | | | 2 | 1 | 0 | 0 | 0 | .500 | .500 | .333 |
| Runners/Scor. Pos. | | | 0 | 0 | 0 | 0 | 0 | — | — | .000 |
| First 9 Batters | | | 117 | 37 | 3 | 15 | 12 | .316 | .427 | .394 |
| Second 9 Batters | | | 116 | 35 | 2 | 11 | 10 | .302 | .448 | .369 |
| All Batters Thereafter | | | 106 | 32 | 2 | 11 | 16 | .302 | .434 | .355 |

Loves to face: Jeff Reed (.091, 1-for-11)
Hates to face: Rob Thompson (.500, 7-for-14, 1 HR)
Ground outs-to-air outs ratio: 1.25 last season, 1.46 for career. . . . Additional statistics: 11 double-play ground outs in 84 opportunities, 17 doubles, 3 triples in 85.1 innings last season. . . . Allowed 18 first-inning runs in 15 starts. . . . Batting support: 3.73 runs per start. . . . Opposing fly-ball hitters batted .353, raising career BA to .299. That's 71 points higher than ground-ball hitters, largest margin of the last 10 years. . . . Career breakdown: .286 (129 BB, 55 SO) by opposing left-handers, .238 (73 BB, 129 SO) by right-handers. . . . Six pitchers from 1984 U.S. Olympic team have reached majors. Only Dunne has a career ERA below 4.00 (3.97). Composite statistics: 152–157, 4.44.

## Mike Dyer
Throws Right

| Minnesota Twins | W-L | ERA | AB | H | HR | BB | SO | BA | SA | OBA |
|---|---|---|---|---|---|---|---|---|---|---|
| Season | 4-7 | 4.82 | 271 | 74 | 2 | 37 | 37 | .273 | .362 | .362 |
| vs. Left-Handers | | | 139 | 38 | 2 | 24 | 16 | .273 | .396 | .386 |
| vs. Right-Handers | | | 132 | 36 | 0 | 13 | 21 | .273 | .326 | .336 |
| Home | 2-3 | 7.09 | 112 | 38 | 0 | 12 | 22 | .339 | .429 | .408 |
| Road | 2-4 | 3.45 | 159 | 36 | 2 | 25 | 15 | .226 | .314 | .332 |
| Grass | 2-2 | 2.08 | 122 | 24 | 1 | 19 | 13 | .197 | .254 | .310 |
| Artificial Turf | 2-5 | 7.43 | 149 | 50 | 1 | 18 | 24 | .336 | .450 | .406 |
| April | | | 0 | 0 | 0 | 0 | 0 | — | — | — |
| May | | | 0 | 0 | 0 | 0 | 0 | — | — | — |
| June | 0-1 | 27.00 | 11 | 6 | 0 | 3 | 1 | .545 | .636 | .643 |
| July | 1-1 | 4.82 | 71 | 19 | 1 | 13 | 4 | .268 | .380 | .376 |
| August | 2-1 | 2.17 | 105 | 23 | 1 | 8 | 20 | .219 | .324 | .287 |
| Sept./Oct. | 1-4 | 6.33 | 84 | 26 | 0 | 13 | 12 | .310 | .357 | .398 |
| Leading Off Inn. | | | 65 | 19 | 2 | 9 | 8 | .292 | .431 | .378 |
| Runners On | | | 131 | 35 | 0 | 20 | 19 | .267 | .344 | .364 |
| Runners/Scor. Pos. | | | 73 | 20 | 0 | 12 | 8 | .274 | .342 | .375 |
| Runners On/2 Out | | | 52 | 11 | 0 | 10 | 7 | .212 | .288 | .339 |
| Scor. Pos./2 Out | | | 33 | 7 | 0 | 4 | 4 | .212 | .242 | .297 |
| Late Inning Pressure | | | 16 | 5 | 0 | 0 | 4 | .313 | .375 | .353 |
| Leading Off | | | 4 | 1 | 0 | 0 | 0 | .250 | .250 | .250 |
| Runners On | | | 9 | 2 | 0 | 0 | 3 | .222 | .333 | .222 |
| Runners/Scor. Pos. | | | 3 | 1 | 0 | 0 | 1 | .333 | .667 | .333 |
| First 9 Batters | | | 114 | 29 | 2 | 18 | 17 | .254 | .351 | .358 |
| Second 9 Batters | | | 85 | 31 | 0 | 15 | 11 | .365 | .482 | .461 |
| All Batters Thereafter | | | 72 | 14 | 0 | 4 | 9 | .194 | .236 | .237 |

Loves to face: Scott Bradley (0-for-5, 2 SO)
Hates to face: Bobby Rose (3-for-3, 1 3B)
Ground outs-to-air outs ratio: 0.86 last season, his first in majors. . . . Additional statistics: 4 double-play ground outs in 65 opportunities, 14 doubles, 2 triples in 71.0 innings last season. . . . Allowed 10 first-inning runs in 12 starts. . . . Batting support: 3.67 runs per start. . . . Opposing ground-ball hitters batted .232, fly-ballers .318. . . . Anyone out there want to feel old? Dyer was born on September 8, 1966. The Yankees beat the Red Sox, temporarily escaping the A.L. basement, where they'd eventually finish for the first time since 1912. Jim Kaat won his 23d game, en route to a 25–13 season. And Tony Oliva passed Frank Robinson in the A.L. batting race. Robinson went on to capture the Triple Crown.

## Dennis Eckersley
Throws Right

| Oakland As | W-L | ERA | AB | H | HR | BB | SO | BA | SA | OBA |
|---|---|---|---|---|---|---|---|---|---|---|
| Season | 4-0 | 1.56 | 198 | 32 | 5 | 3 | 55 | .162 | .258 | .175 |
| vs. Left-Handers | | | 97 | 20 | 1 | 1 | 21 | .206 | .258 | .218 |
| vs. Right-Handers | | | 101 | 12 | 4 | 2 | 34 | .119 | .257 | .133 |
| Home | 2-0 | 2.01 | 108 | 19 | 3 | 2 | 30 | .176 | .287 | .186 |
| Road | 2-0 | 1.03 | 90 | 13 | 2 | 1 | 25 | .144 | .222 | .161 |
| Grass | 4-0 | 1.81 | 171 | 29 | 5 | 3 | 50 | .170 | .281 | .184 |
| Artificial Turf | 0-0 | 0.00 | 27 | 3 | 0 | 0 | 5 | .111 | .111 | .111 |
| April | 1-0 | 0.00 | 39 | 6 | 0 | 1 | 13 | .154 | .154 | .171 |
| May | 0-0 | 3.68 | 27 | 6 | 2 | 1 | 7 | .222 | .481 | .241 |
| June | | | 0 | 0 | 0 | 0 | 0 | — | — | — |
| July | 0-0 | 1.00 | 28 | 2 | 1 | 0 | 11 | .071 | .179 | .071 |
| August | 0-0 | 0.00 | 47 | 9 | 0 | 1 | 13 | .191 | .191 | .224 |
| Sept./Oct. | 3-0 | 3.24 | 57 | 9 | 2 | 0 | 11 | .158 | .316 | .153 |
| Leading Off Inn. | | | 45 | 9 | 1 | 0 | 14 | .200 | .311 | .217 |
| Runners On | | | 67 | 13 | 3 | 1 | 16 | .194 | .343 | .194 |
| Runners/Scor. Pos. | | | 32 | 5 | 1 | 1 | 6 | .156 | .281 | .162 |
| Runners On/2 Out | | | 33 | 6 | 1 | 0 | 6 | .182 | .303 | .182 |
| Scor. Pos./2 Out | | | 17 | 2 | 0 | 0 | 3 | .118 | .176 | .118 |
| Late Inning Pressure | | | 131 | 17 | 5 | 2 | 43 | .130 | .260 | .140 |
| Leading Off | | | 28 | 2 | 1 | 0 | 11 | .071 | .214 | .071 |
| Runners On | | | 38 | 9 | 3 | 0 | 10 | .237 | .500 | .220 |
| Runners/Scor. Pos. | | | 21 | 3 | 1 | 0 | 6 | .143 | .333 | .125 |
| First 9 Batters | | | 198 | 32 | 5 | 3 | 55 | .162 | .258 | .175 |
| Second 9 Batters | | | 0 | 0 | 0 | 0 | 0 | — | — | — |
| All Batters Thereafter | | | 0 | 0 | 0 | 0 | 0 | — | — | — |

Loves to face: Frank White (.085, 4-for-47)
Hates to face: Kent Hrbek (.429, 9-for-21, 2 HR)
Ground outs-to-air outs ratio: 0.70 last season, 0.71 for career. . . . Additional statistics: 2 double-play ground outs in 26 opportunities, 4 doubles, 0 triples in 57.2 innings last season. . . . Allowed three walks in those 57.2 innings, lowest rate in major league history among pitchers with 50+ innings. Previous record: 8 BB in 141.1 IP by Hal ("Skinny") Brown with Houston in 1963. . . . Opposing right-handed batters hit .119, lowest in majors over past 15 years (minimum: 100 AB). . . . Entered a game with runners in scoring position only 11 times in 51 appearances. Inherited 24 runners, stranded 15 (63%). . . . Has walked the leadoff batters in only 2 of 212 innings he's started over the last three seasons.

## Steve Farr
Throws Right

| Kansas City Royals | W-L | ERA | AB | H | HR | BB | SO | BA | SA | OBA |
|---|---|---|---|---|---|---|---|---|---|---|
| Season | 2-5 | 4.12 | 253 | 75 | 5 | 22 | 56 | .296 | .431 | .351 |
| vs. Left-Handers | | | 125 | 35 | 0 | 10 | 24 | .280 | .352 | .333 |
| vs. Right-Handers | | | 128 | 40 | 5 | 12 | 32 | .313 | .508 | .368 |
| Home | 2-1 | 3.00 | 139 | 35 | 0 | 6 | 35 | .252 | .345 | .281 |
| Road | 0-4 | 5.60 | 114 | 40 | 5 | 16 | 21 | .351 | .535 | .429 |
| Grass | 0-2 | 4.12 | 80 | 25 | 3 | 10 | 15 | .313 | .475 | .387 |
| Artificial Turf | 2-3 | 4.12 | 173 | 50 | 2 | 12 | 41 | .289 | .410 | .333 |
| April | 0-1 | 1.04 | 31 | 6 | 0 | 3 | 8 | .194 | .226 | .257 |
| May | 0-1 | 2.45 | 44 | 13 | 1 | 3 | 5 | .295 | .409 | .340 |
| June | 0-1 | 5.68 | 49 | 15 | 2 | 5 | 14 | .306 | .551 | .364 |
| July | 1-1 | 6.23 | 40 | 13 | 1 | 3 | 9 | .325 | .475 | .372 |
| August | 0-1 | 9.00 | 29 | 11 | 0 | 6 | 6 | .379 | .448 | .486 |
| Sept./Oct. | 1-0 | 2.35 | 60 | 17 | 1 | 2 | 14 | .283 | .417 | .313 |
| Leading Off Inn. | | | 59 | 14 | 0 | 4 | 13 | .237 | .305 | .286 |
| Runners On | | | 112 | 32 | 3 | 15 | 26 | .286 | .393 | .362 |
| Runners/Scor. Pos. | | | 69 | 18 | 2 | 9 | 17 | .261 | .362 | .333 |
| Runners On/2 Out | | | 50 | 12 | 0 | 5 | 15 | .240 | .260 | .309 |
| Scor. Pos./2 Out | | | 31 | 9 | 0 | 4 | 8 | .290 | .290 | .371 |
| Late Inning Pressure | | | 109 | 31 | 4 | 8 | 27 | .284 | .459 | .331 |
| Leading Off | | | 25 | 3 | 0 | 3 | 8 | .120 | .160 | .214 |
| Runners On | | | 40 | 13 | 3 | 3 | 9 | .325 | .575 | .364 |
| Runners/Scor. Pos. | | | 20 | 7 | 2 | 2 | 7 | .350 | .650 | .391 |
| First 9 Batters | | | 222 | 66 | 4 | 20 | 50 | .297 | .419 | .355 |
| Second 9 Batters | | | 20 | 6 | 0 | 1 | 2 | .300 | .400 | .318 |
| All Batters Thereafter | | | 11 | 3 | 1 | 1 | 4 | .273 | .727 | .333 |

Loves to face: Carlton Fisk (.125, 2-for-16, 1 HR)
Hates to face: Bill Schroeder (.714, 5-for-7, 3 2B, 2 HR)
Ground outs-to-air outs ratio: 1.11 last season, 1.11 for career. . . . Additional statistics: 6 double-play ground outs in 56 opportunities, 15 doubles, 2 triples in 63.1 innings last season. . . . A pampered reliever: Was brought in to start an inning in 41 of 49 relief appearances. Inherited only 11 base runners, stranded seven. . . . Has not allowed a home run to a left-handed batter since Eddie Murray and Fred McGriff homered against him within a span six days in April 1988. . . . Career record of 6–10 (4.38 ERA) on grass fields, 18–8 (3.05) on artificial turf. . . . Opponents have hit for a lower average with runners on base than with the bases empty in each of the last five seasons.

## John Farrell
Throws Right

| Cleveland Indians | W-L | ERA | AB | H | HR | BB | SO | BA | SA | OBA |
|---|---|---|---|---|---|---|---|---|---|---|
| Season | 9-14 | 3.63 | 803 | 196 | 14 | 71 | 132 | .244 | .341 | .309 |
| vs. Left-Handers | | | 420 | 98 | 6 | 41 | 59 | .233 | .333 | .304 |
| vs. Right-Handers | | | 383 | 98 | 8 | 30 | 73 | .256 | .350 | .315 |
| Home | 5-6 | 3.21 | 424 | 100 | 5 | 38 | 68 | .236 | .304 | .304 |
| Road | 4-8 | 4.10 | 379 | 96 | 9 | 33 | 64 | .253 | .383 | .314 |
| Grass | 6-12 | 4.00 | 612 | 154 | 11 | 57 | 110 | .252 | .348 | .320 |
| Artificial Turf | 3-2 | 2.49 | 191 | 42 | 3 | 14 | 22 | .220 | .319 | .272 |
| April | 1-1 | 3.86 | 69 | 15 | 0 | 10 | 9 | .217 | .232 | .313 |
| May | 2-4 | 4.89 | 143 | 32 | 3 | 10 | 23 | .224 | .357 | .277 |
| June | 1-3 | 4.11 | 138 | 37 | 2 | 12 | 17 | .268 | .333 | .333 |
| July | 2-2 | 3.72 | 145 | 40 | 2 | 16 | 21 | .276 | .372 | .348 |
| August | 2-3 | 3.24 | 161 | 37 | 5 | 13 | 34 | .230 | .342 | .295 |
| Sept./Oct. | 1-1 | 2.15 | 147 | 35 | 2 | 10 | 28 | .238 | .354 | .289 |
| Leading Off Inn. | | | 204 | 51 | 5 | 12 | 26 | .250 | .402 | .301 |
| Runners On | | | 327 | 91 | 4 | 32 | 58 | .278 | .358 | .342 |
| Runners/Scor. Pos. | | | 194 | 48 | 2 | 19 | 39 | .247 | .320 | .309 |
| Runners On/2 Out | | | 137 | 30 | 0 | 20 | 32 | .219 | .241 | .323 |
| Scor. Pos./2 Out | | | 85 | 15 | 0 | 12 | 23 | .176 | .200 | .278 |
| Late Inning Pressure | | | 74 | 19 | 3 | 8 | 12 | .257 | .405 | .329 |
| Leading Off | | | 19 | 4 | 2 | 3 | 2 | .211 | .526 | .318 |
| Runners On | | | 22 | 9 | 0 | 2 | 3 | .409 | .500 | .458 |
| Runners/Scor. Pos. | | | 14 | 5 | 0 | 2 | 2 | .357 | .429 | .438 |
| First 9 Batters | | | 249 | 60 | 4 | 21 | 47 | .241 | .361 | .305 |
| Second 9 Batters | | | 248 | 62 | 5 | 17 | 35 | .250 | .355 | .305 |
| All Batters Thereafter | | | 306 | 74 | 5 | 33 | 50 | .242 | .314 | .315 |

Loves to face: Danny Tartabull (.071, 1-for-14, 5 SO)
Hates to face: Dave Bergman (.467, 7-for-15)
Ground outs-to-air outs ratio: 0.91 last season, 0.88 for career. . . . Additional statistics: 5 double-play ground outs in 144 opportunities, 2d-lowest rate in A.L. (min.: 75 opp.), 28 doubles, 4 triples in 208.0 innings last season. . . . Allowed 14 first-inning runs in 31 starts. . . . Batting support: 3.68 runs per start. . . . Opponents stole 20 bases in 23 attempts, highest rate on team. . . . Faced 34 consecutive batters without allowing a hit. . . . Had walked at least one batter in each of his previous 53 starts before ending season with back-to-back games in which he did not walk a batter. . . . Was 1–8 in day games. Career records: 7–10 (4.71 ERA) in the day, 21–15 (3.54 ERA) at night.

## Tom Filer

| Milwaukee Brewers | W–L | ERA | AB | H | HR | BB | SO | BA | SA | OBA |
|---|---|---|---|---|---|---|---|---|---|---|
| | | | | | | | | | | Throws Right |
| Season | 7-3 | 3.61 | 273 | 74 | 6 | 23 | 20 | .271 | .385 | .337 |
| vs. Left-Handers | | | 144 | 33 | 3 | 15 | 10 | .229 | .340 | .315 |
| vs. Right-Handers | | | 129 | 41 | 3 | 8 | 10 | .318 | .434 | .362 |
| Home | 3-1 | 3.79 | 78 | 27 | 2 | 6 | 7 | .346 | .449 | .393 |
| Road | 4-2 | 3.54 | 195 | 47 | 4 | 17 | 13 | .241 | .359 | .315 |
| Grass | 6-2 | 3.52 | 235 | 66 | 5 | 18 | 16 | .281 | .387 | .337 |
| Artificial Turf | 1-1 | 4.09 | 38 | 8 | 1 | 5 | 4 | .211 | .368 | .333 |
| April | | | 0 | 0 | 0 | 0 | 0 | — | — | — |
| May | | | 0 | 0 | 0 | 0 | 0 | — | — | — |
| June | | | 0 | 0 | 0 | 0 | 0 | — | — | — |
| July | 2-1 | 2.84 | 66 | 13 | 2 | 9 | 6 | .197 | .318 | .303 |
| August | 3-1 | 3.26 | 112 | 32 | 1 | 8 | 9 | .286 | .375 | .344 |
| Sept./Oct. | 2-1 | 4.70 | 95 | 29 | 3 | 6 | 5 | .305 | .442 | .353 |
| Leading Off Inn. | | | 71 | 20 | 1 | 7 | 4 | .282 | .394 | .346 |
| Runners On | | | 111 | 30 | 5 | 7 | 6 | .270 | .423 | .325 |
| Runners/Scor. Pos. | | | 58 | 16 | 3 | 2 | 3 | .276 | .448 | .311 |
| Runners On/2 Out | | | 45 | 12 | 2 | 5 | 5 | .267 | .400 | .340 |
| Scor. Pos./2 Out | | | 26 | 5 | 0 | 1 | 3 | .192 | .192 | .222 |
| Late Inning Pressure | | | 6 | 2 | 0 | 1 | 1 | .333 | .500 | .429 |
| Leading Off | | | 2 | 0 | 0 | 0 | 0 | .000 | .000 | .000 |
| Runners On | | | 1 | 1 | 0 | 1 | 0 | 1.000 | 2.000 | 1.000 |
| Runners/Scor. Pos. | | | 0 | 0 | 0 | 1 | 0 | — | — | 1.000 |
| First 9 Batters | | | 104 | 25 | 4 | 10 | 9 | .240 | .375 | .319 |
| Second 9 Batters | | | 98 | 28 | 0 | 7 | 9 | .286 | .367 | .340 |
| All Batters Thereafter | | | 71 | 21 | 2 | 6 | 2 | .296 | .423 | .359 |

Loves to face: Cal Ripken (0-for-12)
Hates to face: Rick Cerone (4-for-4)
Ground outs-to-air outs ratio: 1.62 last season, 1.46 for career. . . . Additional statistics: 13 double-play ground outs in 49 opportunities, highest rate in majors (min.: 10 GIDP), 7 doubles, 3 triples in 72.1 innings last season. . . . Allowed 8 first-inning runs in 13 starts. . . . Batting support: 5.54 runs per start. . . . Opponents' career batting average is .296 (one HR per 28 AB) with runners on base, .255 (one HR per 54 AB) with bases empty. . . . Has completed only two of 46 career starts. . . . Has faced 19 batters with bases loaded, allowing no walks, one hit (a single), and three runs. . . . He's older than you think: Played for 1982 Cubs, whose other rookies included Ryne Sandberg, Scott Fletcher, Mel Hall, Pat Tabler.

## Chuck Finley

| California Angels | W–L | ERA | AB | H | HR | BB | SO | BA | SA | OBA |
|---|---|---|---|---|---|---|---|---|---|---|
| | | | | | | | | | | Throws Left |
| Season | 16-9 | 2.57 | 733 | 171 | 13 | 82 | 156 | .233 | .334 | .311 |
| vs. Left-Handers | | | 99 | 17 | 0 | 10 | 15 | .172 | .192 | .252 |
| vs. Right-Handers | | | 634 | 154 | 13 | 72 | 141 | .243 | .356 | .320 |
| Home | 8-7 | 2.20 | 420 | 102 | 8 | 34 | 94 | .243 | .355 | .300 |
| Road | 8-2 | 3.01 | 313 | 69 | 5 | 48 | 62 | .220 | .307 | .325 |
| Grass | 13-9 | 2.57 | 646 | 152 | 12 | 72 | 146 | .235 | .337 | .313 |
| Artificial Turf | 3-0 | 2.55 | 87 | 19 | 1 | 10 | 10 | .218 | .310 | .296 |
| April | 3-2 | 2.43 | 115 | 34 | 2 | 12 | 16 | .296 | .391 | .364 |
| May | 4-0 | 1.37 | 139 | 28 | 0 | 13 | 27 | .201 | .237 | .270 |
| June | 2-4 | 3.09 | 178 | 42 | 4 | 11 | 43 | .236 | .348 | .277 |
| July | 3-1 | 2.77 | 142 | 30 | 2 | 16 | 34 | .211 | .317 | .291 |
| August | 2-1 | 3.27 | 81 | 18 | 3 | 10 | 22 | .222 | .383 | .308 |
| Sept./Oct. | 2-1 | 2.74 | 78 | 19 | 2 | 20 | 14 | .244 | .372 | .404 |
| Leading Off Inn. | | | 199 | 46 | 2 | 11 | 40 | .231 | .312 | .271 |
| Runners On | | | 292 | 66 | 6 | 29 | 63 | .226 | .336 | .298 |
| Runners/Scor. Pos. | | | 142 | 26 | 0 | 20 | 38 | .183 | .218 | .279 |
| Runners On/2 Out | | | 130 | 28 | 2 | 12 | 30 | .215 | .308 | .287 |
| Scor. Pos./2 Out | | | 69 | 12 | 0 | 9 | 20 | .174 | .188 | .269 |
| Late Inning Pressure | | | 78 | 20 | 3 | 10 | 14 | .256 | .462 | .341 |
| Leading Off | | | 22 | 7 | 2 | 3 | 3 | .318 | .591 | .400 |
| Runners On | | | 30 | 8 | 1 | 2 | 6 | .267 | .533 | .313 |
| Runners/Scor. Pos. | | | 18 | 2 | 0 | 1 | 5 | .111 | .222 | .158 |
| First 9 Batters | | | 230 | 54 | 6 | 22 | 50 | .235 | .352 | .300 |
| Second 9 Batters | | | 210 | 52 | 3 | 31 | 52 | .248 | .343 | .347 |
| All Batters Thereafter | | | 293 | 65 | 4 | 29 | 54 | .222 | .314 | .292 |

Loves to face: Bob Melvin (0-for-7, 6 SO)
Hates to face: Chet Lemon (.700, 7-for-10, 2 HR)
Ground outs-to-air outs ratio: 0.97 last season, 1.08 for career. . . . Additional statistics: 14 double-play ground outs in 139 opportunities, 31 doubles, 2 triples in 199.2 innings last season. . . . Allowed 10 first-inning runs in 29 starts. Has started 63 games in his career, but has never allowed a first-innning home run. . . . Batting support: 3.83 runs per start. . . . Led A.L. in ERA during May. . . . Opposing left-handed batters were 1-for-37 with runners on base and 0-for-18 with runners in scoring position. . . . Career average of one home run allowed per 252 opposing left-handers is lowest over last 15 years (minimum: 400 BFP). Only lefties to homer against him: Fred Lynn (1987) and George Brett (1988).

## Mike Flanagan

| Toronto Blue Jays | W–L | ERA | AB | H | HR | BB | SO | BA | SA | OBA |
|---|---|---|---|---|---|---|---|---|---|---|
| | | | | | | | | | | Throws Left |
| Season | 8-10 | 3.93 | 658 | 186 | 10 | 47 | 47 | .283 | .406 | .331 |
| vs. Left-Handers | | | 97 | 20 | 0 | 9 | 11 | .206 | .237 | .279 |
| vs. Right-Handers | | | 561 | 166 | 10 | 38 | 36 | .296 | .435 | .341 |
| Home | 5-4 | 3.51 | 325 | 90 | 7 | 18 | 28 | .277 | .418 | .316 |
| Road | 3-6 | 4.34 | 333 | 96 | 3 | 29 | 19 | .288 | .393 | .346 |
| Grass | 1-3 | 5.44 | 198 | 60 | 3 | 17 | 13 | .303 | .424 | .357 |
| Artificial Turf | 7-7 | 3.32 | 460 | 126 | 7 | 30 | 34 | .274 | .398 | .320 |
| April | 1-1 | 2.67 | 118 | 32 | 1 | 11 | 10 | .271 | .381 | .326 |
| May | 2-4 | 6.31 | 108 | 35 | 0 | 5 | 10 | .324 | .417 | .351 |
| June | 1-1 | 2.25 | 86 | 18 | 0 | 8 | 7 | .209 | .291 | .271 |
| July | 2-1 | 4.25 | 145 | 42 | 4 | 8 | 7 | .290 | .421 | .335 |
| August | 2-1 | 3.42 | 103 | 33 | 1 | 2 | 7 | .320 | .456 | .336 |
| Sept./Oct. | 0-2 | 4.85 | 98 | 26 | 4 | 13 | 6 | .265 | .449 | .360 |
| Leading Off Inn. | | | 173 | 55 | 3 | 9 | 8 | .318 | .486 | .352 |
| Runners On | | | 280 | 83 | 3 | 14 | 22 | .296 | .396 | .326 |
| Runners/Scor. Pos. | | | 138 | 47 | 2 | 11 | 12 | .341 | .457 | .373 |
| Runners On/2 Out | | | 108 | 30 | 1 | 5 | 9 | .278 | .361 | .310 |
| Scor. Pos./2 Out | | | 59 | 22 | 1 | 5 | 6 | .373 | .508 | .422 |
| Late Inning Pressure | | | 45 | 9 | 0 | 5 | 8 | .200 | .222 | .280 |
| Leading Off | | | 12 | 2 | 0 | 4 | 2 | .167 | .167 | .375 |
| Runners On | | | 12 | 6 | 0 | 0 | 2 | .500 | .583 | .500 |
| Runners/Scor. Pos. | | | 4 | 3 | 0 | 0 | 0 | .750 | 1.000 | .750 |
| First 9 Batters | | | 253 | 78 | 2 | 9 | 16 | .308 | .423 | .332 |
| Second 9 Batters | | | 219 | 63 | 6 | 22 | 13 | .288 | .461 | .357 |
| All Batters Thereafter | | | 186 | 45 | 2 | 16 | 18 | .242 | .317 | .299 |

Loves to face: Pete O'Brien (.154, 4-for-26)
Hates to face: Robin Yount (.436, 34-for-78, 4 HR)
Ground outs-to-air outs ratio: 1.36 last season, 1.29 for career. . . . Additional statistics: 23 double-play ground outs in 137 opportunities, 39 doubles, 6 triples in 171.2 innings last season. . . . Allowed 18 first-inning runs in 30 starts. Hasn't allowed a first-inning home run in last 34 starts. . . . Batting support: 4.40 runs per start. . . . Averaged 2.46 strikeouts per nine innings, lowest rate in majors (minimum: 15 GS). . . . Walked as many batters as he fanned for the first time in his career. . . . Record of 0–4 vs. the Twins marked the first time that a team defeated him four times in a season. . . . Had winning records in every season from 1977 through 1983. At or below .500 in all six seasons since that streak ended.

## Willie Fraser

| California Angels | W–L | ERA | AB | H | HR | BB | SO | BA | SA | OBA |
|---|---|---|---|---|---|---|---|---|---|---|
| | | | | | | | | | | Throws Right |
| Season | 4-7 | 3.24 | 340 | 80 | 6 | 23 | 46 | .235 | .341 | .291 |
| vs. Left-Handers | | | 138 | 34 | 4 | 10 | 15 | .246 | .406 | .303 |
| vs. Right-Handers | | | 202 | 46 | 2 | 13 | 31 | .228 | .297 | .283 |
| Home | 3-2 | 1.98 | 185 | 43 | 4 | 10 | 29 | .232 | .346 | .284 |
| Road | 1-5 | 4.75 | 155 | 37 | 2 | 13 | 17 | .239 | .335 | .300 |
| Grass | 4-6 | 3.00 | 309 | 69 | 6 | 21 | 41 | .223 | .327 | .281 |
| Artificial Turf | 0-1 | 5.87 | 31 | 11 | 0 | 2 | 5 | .355 | .484 | .394 |
| April | 0-1 | 4.91 | 39 | 10 | 1 | 3 | 4 | .256 | .410 | .341 |
| May | 1-2 | 3.27 | 36 | 6 | 1 | 5 | 6 | .167 | .333 | .295 |
| June | 0-1 | 2.45 | 60 | 18 | 1 | 2 | 5 | .300 | .417 | .323 |
| July | 2-1 | 2.25 | 74 | 18 | 2 | 3 | 10 | .243 | .351 | .269 |
| August | 0-1 | 4.40 | 54 | 13 | 0 | 6 | 4 | .241 | .278 | .328 |
| Sept./Oct. | 1-1 | 3.05 | 77 | 15 | 1 | 4 | 17 | .195 | .286 | .232 |
| Leading Off Inn. | | | 81 | 19 | 0 | 2 | 11 | .235 | .284 | .253 |
| Runners On | | | 142 | 40 | 2 | 11 | 22 | .282 | .408 | .340 |
| Runners/Scor. Pos. | | | 75 | 22 | 2 | 10 | 12 | .293 | .440 | .378 |
| Runners On/2 Out | | | 71 | 22 | 2 | 3 | 9 | .310 | .521 | .364 |
| Scor. Pos./2 Out | | | 41 | 10 | 2 | 3 | 6 | .244 | .488 | .326 |
| Late Inning Pressure | | | 137 | 34 | 3 | 12 | 18 | .248 | .380 | .309 |
| Leading Off | | | 34 | 7 | 0 | 2 | 5 | .206 | .265 | .250 |
| Runners On | | | 56 | 18 | 1 | 5 | 11 | .321 | .482 | .365 |
| Runners/Scor. Pos. | | | 28 | 9 | 1 | 5 | 5 | .321 | .500 | .400 |
| First 9 Batters | | | 278 | 64 | 3 | 16 | 43 | .230 | .306 | .280 |
| Second 9 Batters | | | 61 | 16 | 3 | 7 | 3 | .262 | .508 | .343 |
| All Batters Thereafter | | | 1 | 0 | 0 | 0 | 0 | .000 | .000 | .000 |

Loves to face: Steve Balboni (0-for-14)
Hates to face: Greg Gagne (.429, 3-for-7, 3 HR)
Ground outs-to-air outs ratio: 0.96 last season, 0.81 for career. . . . Additional statistics: 4 double-play ground outs in 63 opportunities, 16 doubles, 1 triple in 91.2 innings last season. . . . Inherited 39 runners, stranded 25 (64%). . . . Pitched exclusively as a reliever in 44 games, after 56 starts in 71 appearances over two previous seasons. . . . Batting average was .199 by opposing ground-ball hitters, .272 by fly-ballers. . . . Allowed one home run per 23 at-bats in 1988, only one per 57 at-bats last season. . . . Also sliced 34 percent from his rate of walks. . . . Opponents' career breakdown: .241 with bases empty, .267 with runners on base, .272 with runners in scoring position.

## Wes Gardner

Boston Red Sox — Throws Right

| | W–L | ERA | AB | H | HR | BB | SO | BA | SA | OBA |
|---|---|---|---|---|---|---|---|---|---|---|
| Season | 3-7 | 5.97 | 338 | 97 | 10 | 47 | 81 | .287 | .447 | .372 |
| vs. Left-Handers | | | 147 | 46 | 2 | 30 | 33 | .313 | .429 | .425 |
| vs. Right-Handers | | | 191 | 51 | 8 | 17 | 48 | .267 | .461 | .327 |
| Home | 2-2 | 4.33 | 132 | 30 | 2 | 19 | 34 | .227 | .341 | .322 |
| Road | 1-5 | 7.11 | 206 | 67 | 8 | 28 | 47 | .325 | .515 | .403 |
| Grass | 3-7 | 5.67 | 309 | 88 | 9 | 40 | 74 | .285 | .443 | .364 |
| Artificial Turf | 0-0 | 9.45 | 29 | 9 | 1 | 7 | 7 | .310 | .483 | .444 |
| April | 1-1 | 6.56 | 91 | 27 | 2 | 11 | 20 | .297 | .440 | .365 |
| May | 0-3 | 9.00 | 34 | 12 | 1 | 8 | 5 | .353 | .618 | .476 |
| June | 1-0 | 3.86 | 32 | 5 | 0 | 8 | 13 | .156 | .156 | .325 |
| July | 0-2 | 6.60 | 58 | 17 | 3 | 10 | 15 | .293 | .552 | .406 |
| August | 1-1 | 5.17 | 123 | 36 | 4 | 10 | 28 | .293 | .431 | .341 |
| Sept./Oct. | | | 0 | 0 | 0 | 0 | 0 | — | — | — |
| Leading Off Inn. | | | 83 | 21 | 0 | 11 | 18 | .253 | .277 | .340 |
| Runners On | | | 142 | 48 | 7 | 22 | 31 | .338 | .592 | .420 |
| Runners/Scor. Pos. | | | 85 | 29 | 5 | 15 | 20 | .341 | .600 | .423 |
| Runners On/2 Out | | | 55 | 18 | 2 | 13 | 14 | .327 | .564 | .456 |
| Scor. Pos./2 Out | | | 37 | 13 | 2 | 10 | 9 | .351 | .649 | .489 |
| Late Inning Pressure | | | 28 | 6 | 0 | 8 | 5 | .214 | .286 | .389 |
| Leading Off | | | 8 | 1 | 0 | 1 | 0 | .125 | .125 | .222 |
| Runners On | | | 14 | 3 | 0 | 3 | 4 | .214 | .286 | .353 |
| Runners/Scor. Pos. | | | 11 | 2 | 0 | 3 | 3 | .182 | .273 | .357 |
| First 9 Batters | | | 162 | 43 | 5 | 22 | 39 | .265 | .407 | .349 |
| Second 9 Batters | | | 110 | 35 | 3 | 15 | 27 | .318 | .509 | .394 |
| All Batters Thereafter | | | 66 | 19 | 2 | 10 | 15 | .288 | .439 | .390 |

Loves to face: Kent Hrbek (0-for-11)
Hates to face: Alvin Davis (.556, 5-for-9, 2 HR)
Ground outs-to-air outs ratio: 0.98 last season, 0.85 for career. . . . Additional statistics: 7 double-play ground outs in 69 opportunities, 18 doubles, 3 triples in 86.0 innings last season. . . . Allowed 22 first-inning runs in 16 starts. . . . Batting support: 5.25 runs per start. . . . Averaged 4.56 innings per start, lowest rate in majors (minimum: 15 GS). . . . Matched Mike Smithson's ERA of 1988, the highest by a Red Sox pitcher since Willard Nixon's 6.04 in 1950. ERA was the highest in majors last year (minimum: 15 GS). . . . Boston had a 6–1 record in his no-decision starts. . . . Batting average was .251 by opposing ground-ball hitters, .327 by fly-ballers. . . . Career record of 0–5 with a 6.75 ERA in May.

## Paul Gibson

Detroit Tigers — Throws Left

| | W–L | ERA | AB | H | HR | BB | SO | BA | SA | OBA |
|---|---|---|---|---|---|---|---|---|---|---|
| Season | 4-8 | 4.64 | 498 | 129 | 11 | 57 | 77 | .259 | .388 | .339 |
| vs. Left-Handers | | | 117 | 31 | 4 | 14 | 13 | .265 | .410 | .341 |
| vs. Right-Handers | | | 381 | 98 | 7 | 43 | 64 | .257 | .381 | .339 |
| Home | 2-3 | 3.49 | 252 | 56 | 3 | 29 | 40 | .222 | .310 | .308 |
| Road | 2-5 | 5.92 | 246 | 73 | 8 | 28 | 37 | .297 | .467 | .371 |
| Grass | 4-7 | 4.15 | 428 | 108 | 10 | 43 | 61 | .252 | .376 | .325 |
| Artificial Turf | 0-1 | 7.94 | 70 | 21 | 1 | 14 | 16 | .300 | .457 | .419 |
| April | 1-1 | 3.86 | 51 | 14 | 1 | 8 | 8 | .275 | .412 | .367 |
| May | 1-2 | 5.81 | 104 | 33 | 1 | 15 | 17 | .317 | .413 | .416 |
| June | 0-1 | 4.94 | 86 | 19 | 1 | 10 | 11 | .221 | .326 | .302 |
| July | 0-1 | 3.32 | 151 | 33 | 5 | 14 | 20 | .219 | .344 | .285 |
| August | 1-3 | 3.48 | 78 | 21 | 2 | 4 | 14 | .269 | .436 | .314 |
| Sept./Oct. | 1-0 | 12.15 | 28 | 9 | 1 | 6 | 7 | .321 | .536 | .441 |
| Leading Off Inn. | | | 118 | 35 | 2 | 13 | 21 | .297 | .424 | .371 |
| Runners On | | | 224 | 56 | 6 | 31 | 36 | .250 | .384 | .347 |
| Runners/Scor. Pos. | | | 133 | 37 | 4 | 27 | 20 | .278 | .436 | .392 |
| Runners On/2 Out | | | 87 | 17 | 4 | 19 | 12 | .195 | .379 | .352 |
| Scor. Pos./2 Out | | | 54 | 11 | 3 | 18 | 6 | .204 | .407 | .403 |
| Late Inning Pressure | | | 87 | 22 | 2 | 11 | 19 | .253 | .368 | .343 |
| Leading Off | | | 22 | 7 | 0 | 4 | 6 | .318 | .318 | .423 |
| Runners On | | | 40 | 9 | 2 | 5 | 6 | .225 | .450 | .326 |
| Runners/Scor. Pos. | | | 20 | 8 | 1 | 5 | 2 | .400 | .700 | .520 |
| First 9 Batters | | | 256 | 63 | 4 | 31 | 45 | .246 | .363 | .331 |
| Second 9 Batters | | | 151 | 41 | 4 | 12 | 23 | .272 | .397 | .333 |
| All Batters Thereafter | | | 91 | 25 | 3 | 14 | 9 | .275 | .440 | .370 |

Loves to face: Jose Canseco (0-for-5, 4 SO)
Hates to face: Jim Gantner (.500, 8-for-16)
Ground outs-to-air outs ratio: 0.77 last season, 0.82 for career. . . . Additional statistics: 7 double-play ground outs in 111 opportunities, 27 doubles, 2 triples in 132.0 innings last season. . . . Allowed 6 first-inning runs in 13 starts. . . . Batting support: 3.23 runs per start. . . . Record of 1–5 (4.66 ERA) as a starter, 3–3 (4.61 ERA) in 32 relief appearances. . . . Started only 13 games, but his streak of seven consecutive starts without a decision was longest in majors. . . . Opposing ground-ball hitters hit more home runs (6) than flyballers (5). . . . Career record of 4–3 (3.03 ERA) at Tiger Stadium, 4–7 (5.01) on the road. . . . Career total of 71 relief appearances, most among active pitchers without a save.

## Tom Gordon

Kansas City Royals — Throws Right

| | W–L | ERA | AB | H | HR | BB | SO | BA | SA | OBA |
|---|---|---|---|---|---|---|---|---|---|---|
| Season | 17-9 | 3.64 | 582 | 122 | 10 | 86 | 153 | .210 | .306 | .311 |
| vs. Left-Handers | | | 307 | 67 | 4 | 48 | 66 | .218 | .306 | .322 |
| vs. Right-Handers | | | 275 | 55 | 6 | 38 | 87 | .200 | .305 | .297 |
| Home | 11-5 | 3.38 | 348 | 75 | 5 | 44 | 86 | .216 | .299 | .303 |
| Road | 6-4 | 4.06 | 234 | 47 | 5 | 42 | 67 | .201 | .316 | .321 |
| Grass | 3-4 | 5.44 | 160 | 39 | 4 | 31 | 40 | .244 | .369 | .365 |
| Artificial Turf | 14-5 | 3.03 | 422 | 83 | 6 | 55 | 113 | .197 | .282 | .289 |
| April | 4-0 | 2.66 | 82 | 15 | 2 | 12 | 28 | .183 | .305 | .287 |
| May | 1-2 | 2.50 | 51 | 4 | 2 | 11 | 17 | .078 | .196 | .234 |
| June | 4-0 | 3.52 | 54 | 11 | 0 | 11 | 22 | .204 | .241 | .338 |
| July | 2-2 | 3.77 | 122 | 30 | 1 | 13 | 28 | .246 | .320 | .324 |
| August | 5-1 | 2.20 | 153 | 25 | 2 | 17 | 41 | .163 | .268 | .246 |
| Sept./Oct. | 1-4 | 7.20 | 120 | 37 | 3 | 22 | 17 | .308 | .417 | .413 |
| Leading Off Inn. | | | 142 | 25 | 4 | 17 | 38 | .176 | .331 | .264 |
| Runners On | | | 241 | 66 | 4 | 43 | 55 | .274 | .382 | .381 |
| Runners/Scor. Pos. | | | 146 | 42 | 3 | 26 | 35 | .288 | .432 | .390 |
| Runners On/2 Out | | | 95 | 24 | 2 | 15 | 28 | .253 | .389 | .355 |
| Scor. Pos./2 Out | | | 65 | 16 | 2 | 10 | 19 | .246 | .431 | .347 |
| Late Inning Pressure | | | 170 | 32 | 2 | 26 | 57 | .188 | .282 | .296 |
| Leading Off | | | 40 | 6 | 2 | 6 | 12 | .150 | .350 | .261 |
| Runners On | | | 68 | 17 | 0 | 14 | 22 | .250 | .338 | .378 |
| Runners/Scor. Pos. | | | 48 | 11 | 0 | 12 | 13 | .229 | .333 | .383 |
| First 9 Batters | | | 309 | 67 | 3 | 53 | 97 | .217 | .298 | .329 |
| Second 9 Batters | | | 147 | 23 | 2 | 12 | 29 | .156 | .224 | .219 |
| All Batters Thereafter | | | 126 | 32 | 5 | 21 | 27 | .254 | .421 | .365 |

Loves to face: Jack Howell (0-for-8, 4 SO)
Hates to face: Ozzie Guillen (.800, 4-for-5)
Ground outs-to-air outs ratio: 1.46 last season, 1.35 for career. . . . Additional statistics: 20 double-play ground outs in 139 opportunities, 18 doubles, 4 triples in 163.0 innings last season. . . . Allowed 15 first-inning runs in 16 starts. . . . Didn't allow a home run before fifth inning of any start. . . . Batting support: 3.63 runs per start. . . . Led rookie pitchers in wins and strikeouts. . . . Blew leads in five of his 10 relief wins. (When Roy Face went 18–1 as a reliever in 1959, 8 of his 18 wins were thusly tainted.) . . .Only four pitchers listed under 5-foot-10 who played in the 1960s or later won more than 50 games in their careers: Bobby Shantz, Face, Fredie Norman, Tom Phoebus.

## Cecilio Guante

Texas Rangers — Throws Right

| | W–L | ERA | AB | H | HR | BB | SO | BA | SA | OBA |
|---|---|---|---|---|---|---|---|---|---|---|
| Season | 6-6 | 3.91 | 265 | 66 | 7 | 36 | 69 | .249 | .385 | .343 |
| vs. Left-Handers | | | 86 | 22 | 5 | 21 | 15 | .256 | .488 | .414 |
| vs. Right-Handers | | | 179 | 44 | 2 | 15 | 54 | .246 | .335 | .303 |
| Home | 5-3 | 2.95 | 149 | 35 | 4 | 14 | 40 | .235 | .376 | .304 |
| Road | 1-3 | 5.22 | 116 | 31 | 3 | 22 | 29 | .267 | .397 | .390 |
| Grass | 5-5 | 4.13 | 237 | 62 | 6 | 34 | 58 | .262 | .401 | .358 |
| Artificial Turf | 1-1 | 2.25 | 28 | 4 | 1 | 2 | 11 | .143 | .250 | .200 |
| April | 2-1 | 2.45 | 53 | 9 | 2 | 4 | 16 | .170 | .340 | .254 |
| May | 1-1 | 4.40 | 58 | 15 | 2 | 11 | 20 | .259 | .379 | .386 |
| June | 1-1 | 4.20 | 61 | 19 | 0 | 9 | 12 | .311 | .344 | .403 |
| July | 1-1 | 3.21 | 50 | 11 | 2 | 9 | 14 | .220 | .480 | .328 |
| August | 0-1 | 6.75 | 21 | 5 | 1 | 2 | 2 | .238 | .429 | .304 |
| Sept./Oct. | 1-1 | 4.76 | 22 | 7 | 0 | 1 | 5 | .318 | .364 | .333 |
| Leading Off Inn. | | | 59 | 17 | 5 | 3 | 12 | .288 | .576 | .333 |
| Runners On | | | 132 | 35 | 2 | 24 | 32 | .265 | .356 | .369 |
| Runners/Scor. Pos. | | | 96 | 19 | 1 | 20 | 28 | .198 | .250 | .325 |
| Runners On/2 Out | | | 64 | 12 | 0 | 8 | 20 | .188 | .234 | .278 |
| Scor. Pos./2 Out | | | 50 | 7 | 0 | 7 | 18 | .140 | .160 | .246 |
| Late Inning Pressure | | | 116 | 28 | 2 | 14 | 28 | .241 | .336 | .333 |
| Leading Off | | | 30 | 10 | 2 | 1 | 7 | .333 | .567 | .375 |
| Runners On | | | 53 | 12 | 0 | 11 | 10 | .226 | .283 | .348 |
| Runners/Scor. Pos. | | | 36 | 5 | 0 | 8 | 8 | .139 | .167 | .283 |
| First 9 Batters | | | 241 | 62 | 6 | 32 | 65 | .257 | .386 | .346 |
| Second 9 Batters | | | 24 | 4 | 1 | 4 | 4 | .167 | .375 | .310 |
| All Batters Thereafter | | | 0 | 0 | 0 | 0 | 0 | — | — | — |

Loves to face: Darnell Coles (0-for-8)
Hates to face: Brian Downing (.800, 4-for-5, 2 HR)
Ground outs-to-air outs ratio: 0.54 last season, 0.63 for career. . . . Additional statistics: 2 double-play ground outs in 61 opportunities, 13 doubles, 1 triple in 69.0 innings last season. . . . Opponents stole 11 bases in 12 attempts. . . . Entered in the eighth inning or later in only three of his 50 appearances. . . . Inherited 63 runners, stranded 49 (78%), 3d-lowest rate in A.L. (minimum: 50 runners). . . . Set up man for some pretty good relievers (Tekulve and Righetti), but until last season, never for a league leader in saves. . . . Opponents' BA with runners in scoring position in LIP Situations has been below .200 in five of last seven seasons, and never higher than .215. Career mark: .148.

## Mark Gubicza

Throws Right

| Kansas City Royals | W–L | ERA | AB | H | HR | BB | SO | BA | SA | OBA |
|---|---|---|---|---|---|---|---|---|---|---|
| Season | 15-11 | 3.04 | 973 | 252 | 10 | 63 | 173 | .259 | .343 | .305 |
| vs. Left-Handers | | | 513 | 126 | 4 | 38 | 82 | .246 | .320 | .299 |
| vs. Right-Handers | | | 460 | 126 | 6 | 25 | 91 | .274 | .370 | .312 |
| Home | 8-6 | 3.17 | 544 | 141 | 3 | 41 | 90 | .259 | .333 | .315 |
| Road | 7-5 | 2.87 | 429 | 111 | 7 | 22 | 83 | .259 | .357 | .293 |
| Grass | 4-4 | 2.67 | 320 | 81 | 5 | 11 | 67 | .253 | .344 | .278 |
| Artificial Turf | 11-7 | 3.22 | 653 | 171 | 5 | 52 | 106 | .262 | .343 | .318 |
| April | 1-2 | 3.09 | 183 | 52 | 0 | 13 | 21 | .284 | .333 | .332 |
| May | 3-2 | 2.42 | 173 | 37 | 0 | 10 | 27 | .214 | .254 | .258 |
| June | 4-1 | 2.34 | 194 | 51 | 3 | 9 | 36 | .263 | .345 | .294 |
| July | 1-3 | 4.25 | 166 | 47 | 3 | 12 | 32 | .283 | .410 | .330 |
| August | 4-2 | 2.42 | 167 | 40 | 1 | 15 | 38 | .240 | .329 | .306 |
| Sept./Oct. | 2-1 | 4.70 | 90 | 25 | 3 | 4 | 19 | .278 | .433 | .316 |
| Leading Off Inn. | | | 252 | 74 | 3 | 7 | 36 | .294 | .397 | .315 |
| Runners On | | | 394 | 98 | 5 | 35 | 71 | .249 | .338 | .309 |
| Runners/Scor. Pos. | | | 229 | 51 | 2 | 23 | 49 | .223 | .301 | .290 |
| Runners On/2 Out | | | 165 | 35 | 2 | 18 | 28 | .212 | .291 | .297 |
| Scor. Pos./2 Out | | | 100 | 19 | 1 | 15 | 20 | .190 | .260 | .302 |
| Late Inning Pressure | | | 135 | 31 | 0 | 6 | 21 | .230 | .296 | .262 |
| Leading Off | | | 38 | 11 | 0 | 0 | 5 | .289 | .342 | .289 |
| Runners On | | | 51 | 10 | 0 | 5 | 7 | .196 | .275 | .268 |
| Runners/Scor. Pos. | | | 33 | 6 | 0 | 5 | 5 | .182 | .273 | .289 |
| First 9 Batters | | | 294 | 69 | 4 | 23 | 56 | .235 | .330 | .297 |
| Second 9 Batters | | | 278 | 80 | 3 | 19 | 47 | .288 | .378 | .333 |
| All Batters Thereafter | | | 401 | 103 | 3 | 21 | 70 | .257 | .329 | .291 |

Loves to face: Dick Schofield (0-for-25)
Hates to face: Fred McGriff (.474, 9-for-19, 4 HR)
Ground outs-to-air outs ratio: 2.04 last season, 1.64 for career. . . . Additional statistics: 20 double-play ground outs in 175 opportunities, 42 doubles, 5 triples in 255.0 innings last season. . . . Allowed 9 first-inning runs in 36 starts. . . . Batting support: 4.36 runs per start. . . . Fewest home runs vs. an A.L. pitcher with at least 250 innings since Tommy John in 1979 (9 HR in 276 IP). . . . Pitched 25 scoreless innings vs. the Athletics last season, and enters 1990 with a shutout streak of 34 innings against them. (Remember Larry Jaster and the Dodgers?) . . . Has a 3–0 record vs. the Mariners in each of the last two seasons. . . . Career record is 5–12 in April (his only losing month), 79–55 after that.

## Lee Guetterman

Throws Left

| New York Yankees | W–L | ERA | AB | H | HR | BB | SO | BA | SA | OBA |
|---|---|---|---|---|---|---|---|---|---|---|
| Season | 5-5 | 2.45 | 380 | 98 | 6 | 26 | 51 | .258 | .337 | .304 |
| vs. Left-Handers | | | 106 | 25 | 1 | 8 | 18 | .236 | .283 | .289 |
| vs. Right-Handers | | | 274 | 73 | 5 | 18 | 33 | .266 | .358 | .310 |
| Home | 3-1 | 2.30 | 214 | 56 | 3 | 11 | 27 | .262 | .336 | .296 |
| Road | 2-4 | 2.64 | 166 | 42 | 3 | 15 | 24 | .253 | .337 | .313 |
| Grass | 4-5 | 2.55 | 338 | 90 | 5 | 25 | 43 | .266 | .346 | .315 |
| Artificial Turf | 1-0 | 1.59 | 42 | 8 | 1 | 1 | 8 | .190 | .262 | .209 |
| April | 0-0 | 0.00 | 49 | 12 | 0 | 3 | 6 | .245 | .245 | .283 |
| May | 0-0 | 2.08 | 72 | 13 | 1 | 5 | 12 | .181 | .250 | .231 |
| June | 1-1 | 4.15 | 59 | 23 | 0 | 2 | 6 | .390 | .441 | .410 |
| July | 2-4 | 6.48 | 71 | 23 | 2 | 9 | 7 | .324 | .437 | .400 |
| August | 1-0 | 1.31 | 73 | 15 | 1 | 3 | 12 | .205 | .301 | .237 |
| Sept./Oct. | 1-0 | 1.10 | 56 | 12 | 2 | 4 | 8 | .214 | .339 | .267 |
| Leading Off Inn. | | | 79 | 24 | 2 | 1 | 14 | .304 | .405 | .313 |
| Runners On | | | 192 | 50 | 3 | 17 | 25 | .260 | .349 | .318 |
| Runners/Scor. Pos. | | | 112 | 27 | 2 | 15 | 17 | .241 | .339 | .326 |
| Runners On/2 Out | | | 79 | 21 | 2 | 5 | 8 | .266 | .405 | .310 |
| Scor. Pos./2 Out | | | 48 | 9 | 1 | 5 | 6 | .188 | .313 | .264 |
| Late Inning Pressure | | | 186 | 49 | 4 | 11 | 24 | .263 | .349 | .305 |
| Leading Off | | | 42 | 15 | 2 | 1 | 6 | .357 | .524 | .372 |
| Runners On | | | 91 | 24 | 2 | 7 | 13 | .264 | .352 | .316 |
| Runners/Scor. Pos. | | | 53 | 13 | 2 | 6 | 8 | .245 | .377 | .322 |
| First 9 Batters | | | 351 | 92 | 5 | 23 | 48 | .262 | .333 | .306 |
| Second 9 Batters | | | 29 | 6 | 1 | 3 | 3 | .207 | .379 | .281 |
| All Batters Thereafter | | | 0 | 0 | 0 | 0 | 0 | — | — | — |

Loves to face: Darnell Coles (0-for-8)
Hates to face: Pete Incaviglia (.636, 7-for-11)
Ground outs-to-air outs ratio: 1.74 last season, 1.61 for career. . . . Additional statistics: 18 double-play ground outs in 92 opportunities, 5th-highest rate in majors (min.: 10 GIDP), 12 doubles, 0 triples in 103.0 innings last season. . . . Inherited 70 runners, stranded 50 (71%). . . . Streak of 30.2 innings without an earned run was the longest to start a season since Harry Brecheen's 32-inning start in 1948. Guetterman's was the longest ever by a reliever to start a season. . . . Gap of 30 points between left-handed and right-handed opponents' BAs was narrowest in past three seasons. Career marks: LHB, .256; RHB, .303. . . . Had 13 saves in 70 appearances, after making 66 relief appearances without a save in four previous seasons.

## Erik Hanson

Throws Right

| Seattle Mariners | W–L | ERA | AB | H | HR | BB | SO | BA | SA | OBA |
|---|---|---|---|---|---|---|---|---|---|---|
| Season | 9-5 | 3.18 | 423 | 103 | 7 | 32 | 75 | .243 | .336 | .304 |
| vs. Left-Handers | | | 226 | 48 | 2 | 16 | 38 | .212 | .283 | .267 |
| vs. Right-Handers | | | 197 | 55 | 5 | 16 | 37 | .279 | .396 | .344 |
| Home | 5-2 | 3.57 | 222 | 61 | 3 | 17 | 36 | .275 | .365 | .328 |
| Road | 4-3 | 2.77 | 201 | 42 | 4 | 15 | 39 | .209 | .303 | .277 |
| Grass | 3-3 | 2.98 | 175 | 39 | 3 | 14 | 33 | .223 | .314 | .295 |
| Artificial Turf | 6-2 | 3.32 | 248 | 64 | 4 | 18 | 42 | .258 | .351 | .310 |
| April | 2-2 | 2.23 | 119 | 27 | 1 | 9 | 25 | .227 | .294 | .285 |
| May | 2-2 | 5.53 | 105 | 28 | 3 | 14 | 15 | .267 | .410 | .358 |
| June | | | 0 | 0 | 0 | 0 | 0 | — | — | — |
| July | | | 0 | 0 | 0 | 0 | 0 | — | — | — |
| August | 1-0 | 3.12 | 29 | 4 | 1 | 1 | 5 | .138 | .241 | .194 |
| Sept./Oct. | 4-1 | 2.42 | 170 | 44 | 2 | 8 | 30 | .259 | .335 | .300 |
| Leading Off Inn. | | | 109 | 17 | 0 | 8 | 19 | .156 | .174 | .220 |
| Runners On | | | 156 | 44 | 2 | 16 | 26 | .282 | .397 | .351 |
| Runners/Scor. Pos. | | | 83 | 19 | 1 | 10 | 17 | .229 | .301 | .316 |
| Runners On/2 Out | | | 62 | 12 | 1 | 4 | 10 | .194 | .306 | .254 |
| Scor. Pos./2 Out | | | 39 | 6 | 1 | 2 | 6 | .154 | .282 | .214 |
| Late Inning Pressure | | | 38 | 8 | 0 | 4 | 10 | .211 | .237 | .286 |
| Leading Off | | | 9 | 2 | 0 | 2 | 0 | .222 | .222 | .364 |
| Runners On | | | 12 | 2 | 0 | 2 | 4 | .167 | .167 | .286 |
| Runners/Scor. Pos. | | | 9 | 0 | 0 | 1 | 3 | .000 | .000 | .100 |
| First 9 Batters | | | 138 | 34 | 2 | 9 | 27 | .246 | .333 | .309 |
| Second 9 Batters | | | 143 | 39 | 1 | 8 | 18 | .273 | .336 | .316 |
| All Batters Thereafter | | | 142 | 30 | 4 | 15 | 30 | .211 | .338 | .287 |

Loves to face: Rob Deer (0-for-10, 5 SO)
Hates to face: Ellis Burks (6-for-6, 2 HR)
Ground outs-to-air outs ratio: 1.39 last season, 1.31 for career. . . . Additional statistics: 11 double-play ground outs in 91 opportunities, 16 doubles, 1 triple in 113.1 innings last season. . . . Allowed 10 first-inning runs in 17 starts. . . . Batting support: 4.18 runs per start. . . . Lowest ERA by a Mariners rookie with 100+ innings since Enrique Romo posted a 2.84 mark in 1977, the *team's* rookie season. By comparison, Mark Langston had a 3.40 ERA as a rookie; Rick Honeycutt, 4.89; Mike Moore, 5.36. . . . Right-handers batted 67 points higher than left-handers, largest difference in majors. . . . Difference of 66 points between opponents' BA at home and on road was 3d largest in A.L.

## Pete Harnisch

Throws Right

| Baltimore Orioles | W–L | ERA | AB | H | HR | BB | SO | BA | SA | OBA |
|---|---|---|---|---|---|---|---|---|---|---|
| Season | 5-9 | 4.62 | 390 | 97 | 10 | 64 | 70 | .249 | .385 | .358 |
| vs. Left-Handers | | | 183 | 47 | 3 | 36 | 33 | .257 | .377 | .390 |
| vs. Right-Handers | | | 207 | 50 | 7 | 28 | 37 | .242 | .391 | .328 |
| Home | 3-1 | 3.41 | 127 | 29 | 2 | 19 | 22 | .228 | .331 | .329 |
| Road | 2-8 | 5.22 | 263 | 68 | 8 | 45 | 48 | .259 | .411 | .371 |
| Grass | 5-7 | 4.30 | 338 | 83 | 10 | 56 | 65 | .246 | .396 | .355 |
| Artificial Turf | 0-2 | 6.75 | 52 | 14 | 0 | 8 | 5 | .269 | .308 | .375 |
| April | 0-1 | 3.27 | 40 | 9 | 1 | 10 | 7 | .225 | .300 | .377 |
| May | | | 0 | 0 | 0 | 0 | 0 | — | — | — |
| June | | | 0 | 0 | 0 | 0 | 0 | — | — | — |
| July | 1-3 | 7.43 | 94 | 27 | 4 | 14 | 11 | .287 | .468 | .389 |
| August | 2-4 | 3.48 | 192 | 47 | 4 | 25 | 36 | .245 | .385 | .332 |
| Sept./Oct. | 2-1 | 5.09 | 64 | 14 | 1 | 15 | 16 | .219 | .313 | .370 |
| Leading Off Inn. | | | 100 | 26 | 3 | 13 | 13 | .260 | .420 | .351 |
| Runners On | | | 173 | 44 | 3 | 30 | 34 | .254 | .376 | .362 |
| Runners/Scor. Pos. | | | 94 | 18 | 1 | 22 | 23 | .191 | .266 | .331 |
| Runners On/2 Out | | | 73 | 15 | 0 | 14 | 18 | .205 | .233 | .333 |
| Scor. Pos./2 Out | | | 48 | 5 | 0 | 9 | 14 | .104 | .125 | .246 |
| Late Inning Pressure | | | 31 | 9 | 1 | 6 | 2 | .290 | .484 | .405 |
| Leading Off | | | 10 | 3 | 0 | 2 | 1 | .300 | .300 | .417 |
| Runners On | | | 10 | 6 | 1 | 2 | 0 | .600 | 1.200 | .667 |
| Runners/Scor. Pos. | | | 4 | 2 | 0 | 2 | 0 | .500 | 1.000 | .667 |
| First 9 Batters | | | 127 | 31 | 4 | 22 | 32 | .244 | .370 | .364 |
| Second 9 Batters | | | 122 | 30 | 1 | 17 | 19 | .246 | .328 | .340 |
| All Batters Thereafter | | | 141 | 36 | 5 | 25 | 19 | .255 | .447 | .367 |

Loves to face: Dwight Evans (0-for-10)
Hates to face: Wade Boggs (.500, 5-for-10, 4 2B)
Ground outs-to-air outs ratio: 0.69 last season, 0.69 for career. . . . Additional statistics: 9 double-play ground outs in 90 opportunities, 21 doubles, 1 triple in 103.1 innings last season. . . . Allowed 5 first-inning runs in 17 starts. . . . Batting support: 3.47 runs per start. . . . Opposing base runners stole 14 bases, the most against any pitcher in either league not to catch a thief. . . . Had much higher ERA with Tettleton catching (6.25) than with Melvin (3.35), in an equal number of innings. . . . Averaged 5.57 walks per nine innings, highest rate in majors (minimum: 15 GS). . . . Rookies with comparable figures: Steve Dunning (1970), Steve Stone (1971), Dick Ruthven (1973), Jim Clancy (1977), and Shane Rawley (1978).

## Bryan Harvey

| California Angels | W–L | ERA | AB | H | HR | BB | SO | BA | SA | OBA |
|---|---|---|---|---|---|---|---|---|---|---|
| Season | 3-3 | 3.44 | 197 | 36 | 6 | 41 | 78 | .183 | .299 | .321 |
| vs. Left-Handers | | | 100 | 16 | 3 | 21 | 35 | .160 | .280 | .303 |
| vs. Right-Handers | | | 97 | 20 | 3 | 20 | 43 | .206 | .320 | .339 |
| Home | 2-0 | 2.56 | 116 | 22 | 4 | 17 | 44 | .190 | .310 | .293 |
| Road | 1-3 | 4.63 | 81 | 14 | 2 | 24 | 34 | .173 | .284 | .355 |
| Grass | 2-2 | 3.40 | 180 | 32 | 4 | 38 | 71 | .178 | .272 | .318 |
| Artificial Turf | 1-1 | 3.86 | 17 | 4 | 2 | 3 | 7 | .235 | .588 | .350 |
| April | 0-0 | 0.00 | 26 | 3 | 0 | 3 | 10 | .115 | .154 | .200 |
| May | 1-1 | 8.59 | 31 | 10 | 3 | 8 | 9 | .323 | .677 | .462 |
| June | 0-0 | 2.79 | 35 | 7 | 0 | 10 | 15 | .200 | .229 | .370 |
| July | 2-2 | 3.97 | 44 | 9 | 2 | 8 | 14 | .205 | .364 | .327 |
| August | 0-0 | 0.00 | 26 | 0 | 0 | 6 | 18 | .000 | .000 | .188 |
| Sept./Oct. | 0-0 | 5.79 | 35 | 7 | 1 | 6 | 12 | .200 | .286 | .317 |
| Leading Off Inn. | | | 39 | 7 | 2 | 3 | 16 | .179 | .333 | .238 |
| Runners On | | | 104 | 19 | 2 | 28 | 43 | .183 | .269 | .351 |
| Runners/Scor. Pos. | | | 68 | 10 | 2 | 25 | 30 | .147 | .250 | .368 |
| Runners On/2 Out | | | 53 | 6 | 0 | 11 | 27 | .113 | .132 | .266 |
| Scor. Pos./2 Out | | | 38 | 1 | 0 | 9 | 22 | .026 | .026 | .213 |
| Late Inning Pressure | | | 127 | 25 | 4 | 30 | 47 | .197 | .307 | .350 |
| Leading Off | | | 23 | 5 | 1 | 2 | 7 | .217 | .348 | .280 |
| Runners On | | | 74 | 13 | 2 | 23 | 29 | .176 | .270 | .371 |
| Runners/Scor. Pos. | | | 52 | 9 | 2 | 21 | 22 | .173 | .308 | .411 |
| First 9 Batters | | | 197 | 36 | 6 | 41 | 78 | .183 | .299 | .321 |
| Second 9 Batters | | | 0 | 0 | 0 | 0 | 0 | — | — | — |
| All Batters Thereafter | | | 0 | 0 | 0 | 0 | 0 | — | — | — |

Throws Right

Loves to face: Cal Ripken (0-for-5, 3 SO)
Hates to face: Paul Molitor (4-for-4, 2 2B)
Ground outs-to-air outs ratio: 0.58 last season, 0.60 for career. . . . Additional statistics: 0 double-play ground outs in 53 opportunities (2d-highest total in majors among pitchers without a GIDP) 5 doubles, 0 triples in 55.0 innings last season. . . . Inherited 40 runners, stranded 31 (78%). . . . Led A.L. relievers in strikeouts (12.76) and walks (6.71) per nine innings (minimum: 30 games). Latter was highest in either league. . . . Streak of 40 consecutive batters faced without allowing a hit was 4th longest in A.L. during 1980s. . . . Opponents' career average is .201 on grass fields, lowest among active A.L. pitchers (minimum: 500 BFP). ERA is almost a run per game higher on artificial turf (3.38) than on grass (2.49).

## Andy Hawkins

| New York Yankees | W–L | ERA | AB | H | HR | BB | SO | BA | SA | OBA |
|---|---|---|---|---|---|---|---|---|---|---|
| Season | 15-15 | 4.80 | 820 | 238 | 23 | 76 | 98 | .290 | .460 | .354 |
| vs. Left-Handers | | | 436 | 141 | 14 | 53 | 34 | .323 | .534 | .397 |
| vs. Right-Handers | | | 384 | 97 | 9 | 23 | 64 | .253 | .375 | .302 |
| Home | 9-10 | 4.54 | 506 | 153 | 17 | 42 | 59 | .302 | .486 | .360 |
| Road | 6-5 | 5.18 | 314 | 85 | 6 | 34 | 39 | .271 | .417 | .344 |
| Grass | 11-14 | 4.53 | 696 | 201 | 19 | 67 | 87 | .289 | .447 | .354 |
| Artificial Turf | 4-1 | 6.15 | 124 | 37 | 4 | 9 | 11 | .298 | .532 | .350 |
| April | 3-2 | 4.86 | 123 | 32 | 4 | 18 | 11 | .260 | .415 | .355 |
| May | 2-4 | 7.64 | 151 | 56 | 4 | 14 | 16 | .371 | .596 | .432 |
| June | 4-2 | 2.95 | 154 | 42 | 3 | 11 | 13 | .273 | .429 | .321 |
| July | 3-2 | 2.39 | 134 | 28 | 3 | 10 | 24 | .209 | .336 | .264 |
| August | 1-3 | 6.82 | 127 | 40 | 7 | 5 | 15 | .315 | .559 | .351 |
| Sept./Oct. | 2-2 | 4.78 | 131 | 40 | 2 | 18 | 19 | .305 | .412 | .389 |
| Leading Off Inn. | | | 206 | 52 | 9 | 16 | 17 | .252 | .485 | .313 |
| Runners On | | | 326 | 105 | 7 | 37 | 38 | .322 | .466 | .395 |
| Runners/Scor. Pos. | | | 191 | 67 | 4 | 24 | 16 | .351 | .487 | .428 |
| Runners On/2 Out | | | 133 | 45 | 2 | 16 | 18 | .338 | .474 | .409 |
| Scor. Pos./2 Out | | | 78 | 30 | 1 | 10 | 7 | .385 | .513 | .455 |
| Late Inning Pressure | | | 53 | 26 | 3 | 7 | 0 | .491 | .849 | .550 |
| Leading Off | | | 17 | 6 | 1 | 1 | 0 | .353 | .765 | .389 |
| Runners On | | | 16 | 8 | 1 | 5 | 0 | .500 | .875 | .619 |
| Runners/Scor. Pos. | | | 9 | 5 | 1 | 3 | 0 | .556 | 1.000 | .667 |
| First 9 Batters | | | 277 | 74 | 6 | 25 | 51 | .267 | .419 | .334 |
| Second 9 Batters | | | 273 | 76 | 6 | 18 | 27 | .278 | .407 | .327 |
| All Batters Thereafter | | | 270 | 88 | 11 | 33 | 20 | .326 | .556 | .399 |

Throws Right

Loves to face: Mookie Wilson (.045, 1-for-22, 8 SO)
Hates to face: Ron Hassey (5-for-5, 2 2B)
Ground outs-to-air outs ratio: 0.83 last season, 0.96 for career. . . . Additional statistics: 25 double-play ground outs in 153 opportunities, 56 doubles, 7 triples in 208.1 innings last season. . . . Allowed 18 first-inning runs in 34 starts. . . . Batting support: 4.21 runs per start. . . . Opponents stole only 8 bases in 19 attempts, lowest rate on team. . . . Needs a new catcher: Had Don Slaught as a batterymate for 87 percent of his work. Bob Geren caught 40 percent of time for other pitchers, but only 4.1 innings with Hawkins. . . . Not a candidate for winter league MVP. His career records by month: April, 15–8 (.652); May, 16–15 (.516); June, 11–12 (.478); July, 12–13 (.480); August, 12–14 (.462); September, 7–11 (.389).

## Tom Henke

| Toronto Blue Jays | W–L | ERA | AB | H | HR | BB | SO | BA | SA | OBA |
|---|---|---|---|---|---|---|---|---|---|---|
| Season | 8-3 | 1.92 | 322 | 66 | 5 | 25 | 116 | .205 | .314 | .264 |
| vs. Left-Handers | | | 149 | 29 | 3 | 16 | 46 | .195 | .315 | .272 |
| vs. Right-Handers | | | 173 | 37 | 2 | 9 | 70 | .214 | .312 | .257 |
| Home | 6-0 | 2.48 | 130 | 26 | 3 | 11 | 54 | .200 | .331 | .266 |
| Road | 2-3 | 1.54 | 192 | 40 | 2 | 14 | 62 | .208 | .302 | .263 |
| Grass | 2-3 | 1.39 | 165 | 33 | 2 | 11 | 57 | .200 | .285 | .251 |
| Artificial Turf | 6-0 | 2.47 | 157 | 33 | 3 | 14 | 59 | .210 | .344 | .277 |
| April | 1-3 | 9.00 | 24 | 9 | 1 | 6 | 5 | .375 | .792 | .500 |
| May | 2-0 | 3.65 | 42 | 7 | 2 | 7 | 13 | .167 | .357 | .294 |
| June | 3-0 | 1.17 | 53 | 9 | 0 | 5 | 15 | .170 | .170 | .241 |
| July | 0-0 | 0.55 | 60 | 11 | 1 | 2 | 26 | .183 | .283 | .210 |
| August | 0-0 | 1.33 | 77 | 18 | 1 | 3 | 32 | .234 | .338 | .272 |
| Sept./Oct. | 2-0 | 0.96 | 66 | 12 | 0 | 2 | 25 | .182 | .227 | .200 |
| Leading Off Inn. | | | 75 | 17 | 1 | 3 | 29 | .227 | .307 | .256 |
| Runners On | | | 141 | 27 | 4 | 18 | 48 | .191 | .348 | .282 |
| Runners/Scor. Pos. | | | 85 | 20 | 4 | 15 | 27 | .235 | .471 | .340 |
| Runners On/2 Out | | | 67 | 10 | 2 | 7 | 26 | .149 | .269 | .240 |
| Scor. Pos./2 Out | | | 42 | 6 | 2 | 7 | 14 | .143 | .310 | .265 |
| Late Inning Pressure | | | 184 | 36 | 4 | 14 | 75 | .196 | .315 | .254 |
| Leading Off | | | 42 | 6 | 1 | 3 | 20 | .143 | .262 | .200 |
| Runners On | | | 72 | 17 | 3 | 9 | 27 | .236 | .431 | .321 |
| Runners/Scor. Pos. | | | 42 | 13 | 3 | 9 | 13 | .310 | .619 | .415 |
| First 9 Batters | | | 307 | 64 | 5 | 22 | 110 | .208 | .319 | .263 |
| Second 9 Batters | | | 15 | 2 | 0 | 3 | 6 | .133 | .200 | .278 |
| All Batters Thereafter | | | 0 | 0 | 0 | 0 | 0 | — | — | — |

Throws Right

Loves to face: Lou Whitaker (0-for-22)
Hates to face: Don Mattingly (.438, 7-for-16, 2 HR)
Ground outs-to-air outs ratio: 0.85 last season, 0.72 for career. . . . Additional statistics: 3 double-play ground outs in 59 opportunities, 16 doubles, 2 triples in 89.0 innings last season. . . . Inherited 42 runners, stranded 26 (62%). Stranded 21 of 30 (70%) after managerial change. (See Toronto essay for more.) . . .Opposing ground-ball hitters batted .286, compared to .131 for fly-ball hitters. Difference was largest in majors. . . . Opponents have hit for a higher average with runners in scoring position than in other at-bats in each of his five seasons with the Jays. . . . All-time leaders, strikeouts per nine innings (minimum: 500 SO): Henke, 10.6; Radatz, 9.7; Duren, 9.6; Ryan, 9.5; Koufax, 9.3.

## Mike Henneman

| Detroit Tigers | W–L | ERA | AB | H | HR | BB | SO | BA | SA | OBA |
|---|---|---|---|---|---|---|---|---|---|---|
| Season | 11-4 | 3.70 | 335 | 84 | 4 | 51 | 69 | .251 | .337 | .355 |
| vs. Left-Handers | | | 154 | 41 | 1 | 28 | 24 | .266 | .364 | .379 |
| vs. Right-Handers | | | 181 | 43 | 3 | 23 | 45 | .238 | .315 | .335 |
| Home | 8-0 | 3.65 | 181 | 40 | 1 | 25 | 46 | .221 | .304 | .327 |
| Road | 3-4 | 3.76 | 154 | 44 | 3 | 26 | 23 | .286 | .377 | .388 |
| Grass | 10-3 | 3.45 | 284 | 69 | 3 | 41 | 64 | .243 | .327 | .346 |
| Artificial Turf | 1-1 | 5.02 | 51 | 15 | 1 | 10 | 5 | .294 | .392 | .403 |
| April | 0-0 | 6.14 | 25 | 4 | 0 | 4 | 7 | .160 | .240 | .290 |
| May | 3-1 | 4.91 | 40 | 10 | 1 | 4 | 4 | .250 | .350 | .318 |
| June | 2-0 | 1.74 | 75 | 18 | 2 | 12 | 19 | .240 | .373 | .352 |
| July | 2-3 | 7.23 | 70 | 20 | 1 | 16 | 18 | .286 | .400 | .420 |
| August | 2-0 | 1.72 | 63 | 15 | 0 | 9 | 12 | .238 | .302 | .342 |
| Sept./Oct. | 2-0 | 2.16 | 62 | 17 | 0 | 6 | 9 | .274 | .290 | .343 |
| Leading Off Inn. | | | 78 | 20 | 1 | 8 | 17 | .256 | .346 | .326 |
| Runners On | | | 155 | 43 | 1 | 31 | 30 | .277 | .355 | .401 |
| Runners/Scor. Pos. | | | 89 | 23 | 0 | 26 | 21 | .258 | .326 | .415 |
| Runners On/2 Out | | | 77 | 23 | 0 | 14 | 17 | .299 | .351 | .413 |
| Scor. Pos./2 Out | | | 49 | 13 | 0 | 10 | 13 | .265 | .306 | .390 |
| Late Inning Pressure | | | 214 | 55 | 3 | 37 | 42 | .257 | .346 | .371 |
| Leading Off | | | 53 | 17 | 1 | 6 | 9 | .321 | .453 | .390 |
| Runners On | | | 95 | 27 | 0 | 22 | 16 | .284 | .326 | .421 |
| Runners/Scor. Pos. | | | 56 | 13 | 0 | 19 | 11 | .232 | .268 | .416 |
| First 9 Batters | | | 314 | 75 | 3 | 46 | 65 | .239 | .312 | .343 |
| Second 9 Batters | | | 21 | 9 | 1 | 5 | 4 | .429 | .714 | .519 |
| All Batters Thereafter | | | 0 | 0 | 0 | 0 | 0 | — | — | — |

Throws Right

Loves to face: Fred McGriff (0-for-13, 4 SO)
Hates to face: Mel Hall (.417, 5-for-12, 1 HR)
Ground outs-to-air outs ratio: 1.34 last season, 1.31 for career. . . . Additional statistics: 10 double-play ground outs in 82 opportunities, 13 doubles, 2 triples in 90.0 innings last season. . . . Inherited 38 runners, stranded 28 (74%). . . . Only Tigers pitcher with a winning record in 1989. Other A.L. teams of 1980s with only one pitcher above .500: 1980 Mariners (Dave Heaverlo), 1988 Rangers (Jeff Russell). . . . Led A.L. relievers with 11 wins, none after having blown leads. . . . Career winning percentage of .704 (31–13), second to Dwight Gooden (.719) among active pitchers (minimum: 30 wins). . . . Second pitcher ever to win at least nine relief games in rookie season, and in each of the next two seasons. The first: Dick Radatz.

## Willie Hernandez

Throws Left

| Detroit Tigers | W–L | ERA | AB | H | HR | BB | SO | BA | SA | OBA |
|---|---|---|---|---|---|---|---|---|---|---|
| Season | 2-2 | 5.74 | 123 | 36 | 4 | 16 | 30 | .293 | .455 | .379 |
| vs. Left-Handers | | | 40 | 8 | 1 | 4 | 10 | .200 | .275 | .289 |
| vs. Right-Handers | | | 83 | 28 | 3 | 12 | 20 | .337 | .542 | .421 |
| Home | 2-2 | 8.00 | 72 | 22 | 4 | 12 | 19 | .306 | .542 | .412 |
| Road | 0-0 | 2.70 | 51 | 14 | 0 | 4 | 11 | .275 | .333 | .327 |
| Grass | 2-2 | 5.40 | 111 | 31 | 4 | 14 | 27 | .279 | .450 | .365 |
| Artificial Turf | 0-0 | 9.00 | 12 | 5 | 0 | 2 | 3 | .417 | .500 | .500 |
| April | 0-0 | 4.70 | 27 | 5 | 1 | 1 | 6 | .185 | .370 | .241 |
| May | 2-1 | 5.56 | 46 | 14 | 1 | 9 | 12 | .304 | .435 | .418 |
| June | 0-0 | 7.20 | 22 | 9 | 0 | 2 | 4 | .409 | .545 | .458 |
| July | 0-1 | 11.57 | 12 | 5 | 1 | 2 | 1 | .417 | .667 | .500 |
| August | 0-0 | 3.60 | 16 | 3 | 1 | 2 | 7 | .188 | .375 | .278 |
| Sept./Oct. | | | 0 | 0 | 0 | 0 | 0 | — | — | — |
| Leading Off Inn. | | | 21 | 4 | 0 | 0 | 6 | .190 | .238 | .227 |
| Runners On | | | 70 | 23 | 4 | 12 | 16 | .329 | .571 | .427 |
| Runners/Scor. Pos. | | | 42 | 16 | 3 | 7 | 8 | .381 | .690 | .469 |
| Runners On/2 Out | | | 34 | 9 | 2 | 4 | 6 | .265 | .441 | .342 |
| Scor. Pos./2 Out | | | 20 | 5 | 1 | 2 | 4 | .250 | .400 | .318 |
| Late Inning Pressure | | | 66 | 19 | 1 | 9 | 21 | .288 | .394 | .373 |
| Leading Off | | | 12 | 2 | 0 | 0 | 5 | .167 | .167 | .167 |
| Runners On | | | 36 | 11 | 1 | 7 | 11 | .306 | .472 | .419 |
| Runners/Scor. Pos. | | | 17 | 7 | 1 | 5 | 5 | .412 | .706 | .545 |
| First 9 Batters | | | 123 | 36 | 4 | 16 | 30 | .293 | .455 | .379 |
| Second 9 Batters | | | 0 | 0 | 0 | 0 | 0 | — | — | — |
| All Batters Thereafter | | | 0 | 0 | 0 | 0 | 0 | — | — | — |

Loves to face: Pete O'Brien (0-for-19)
Hates to face: Pat Tabler (.357, 5-for-14, 3 HR)
Ground outs-to-air outs ratio: 0.88 last season, 1.07 for career. . . . Additional statistics: 2 double-play ground outs in 35 opportunities, 8 doubles, 0 triples in 31.1 innings last season. . . . Inherited 31 runners, stranded 19 (61%). . . . Walked 4.3 batters per nine innings over last two seasons, compared to 2.9 per nine innings over first 11 seasons. . . . Over the past four seasons, opposing ground-ball hitters have out-hit fly-ballers by a .290 to .221 margin. . . . Walked leadoff batters in only three of 155 innings in LIPS over last five seasons. . . . Beneficiary of first major league save: a younger (27), slimmer (225) Rick Reuschel. . . . Last manager to write his name on a starting lineup card: Lee Elia, on May 7, 1983.

## Greg Hibbard

Throws Left

| Chicago White Sox | W–L | ERA | AB | H | HR | BB | SO | BA | SA | OBA |
|---|---|---|---|---|---|---|---|---|---|---|
| Season | 6-7 | 3.21 | 529 | 142 | 5 | 41 | 55 | .268 | .365 | .321 |
| vs. Left-Handers | | | 70 | 22 | 0 | 9 | 11 | .314 | .400 | .390 |
| vs. Right-Handers | | | 459 | 120 | 5 | 32 | 44 | .261 | .359 | .310 |
| Home | 4-3 | 2.86 | 259 | 64 | 2 | 24 | 27 | .247 | .320 | .315 |
| Road | 2-4 | 3.57 | 270 | 78 | 3 | 17 | 28 | .289 | .407 | .328 |
| Grass | 6-6 | 3.01 | 428 | 110 | 4 | 35 | 48 | .257 | .353 | .315 |
| Artificial Turf | 0-1 | 4.18 | 101 | 32 | 1 | 6 | 7 | .317 | .416 | .349 |
| April | | | 0 | 0 | 0 | 0 | 0 | — | — | — |
| May | 0-0 | 3.00 | 22 | 4 | 1 | 2 | 3 | .182 | .455 | .250 |
| June | 0-2 | 3.03 | 118 | 33 | 1 | 7 | 10 | .280 | .398 | .317 |
| July | 2-0 | 3.42 | 104 | 26 | 1 | 11 | 15 | .250 | .346 | .328 |
| August | 2-3 | 3.08 | 138 | 38 | 1 | 9 | 14 | .275 | .348 | .315 |
| Sept./Oct. | 2-2 | 3.38 | 147 | 41 | 1 | 12 | 13 | .279 | .354 | .335 |
| Leading Off Inn. | | | 141 | 33 | 1 | 7 | 14 | .234 | .326 | .270 |
| Runners On | | | 229 | 59 | 3 | 18 | 25 | .258 | .371 | .307 |
| Runners/Scor. Pos. | | | 127 | 31 | 0 | 8 | 13 | .244 | .339 | .281 |
| Runners On/2 Out | | | 93 | 21 | 2 | 9 | 8 | .226 | .387 | .294 |
| Scor. Pos./2 Out | | | 60 | 9 | 0 | 6 | 4 | .150 | .233 | .227 |
| Late Inning Pressure | | | 34 | 10 | 0 | 2 | 4 | .294 | .324 | .351 |
| Leading Off | | | 10 | 3 | 0 | 1 | 3 | .300 | .400 | .364 |
| Runners On | | | 13 | 3 | 0 | 0 | 0 | .231 | .231 | .231 |
| Runners/Scor. Pos. | | | 2 | 0 | 0 | 0 | 0 | .000 | .000 | .000 |
| First 9 Batters | | | 186 | 45 | 1 | 16 | 16 | .242 | .301 | .304 |
| Second 9 Batters | | | 178 | 48 | 2 | 17 | 17 | .270 | .393 | .328 |
| All Batters Thereafter | | | 165 | 49 | 2 | 8 | 22 | .297 | .406 | .333 |

Loves to face: Darnell Coles (0-for-6)
Hates to face: Greg Gagne (.800, 4-for-5, 3 2B)
Ground outs-to-air outs ratio: 1.46 last season, his first in majors. . . . Additional statistics: 16 double-play ground outs in 103 opportunities, 26 doubles, 5 triples in 137.1 innings last season. . . . Allowed 4 first-inning runs in 23 starts. Didn't allow a first-inning home run. . . . Batting support: 4.61 runs per start. . . . Lowest home-run ratio among the 14 rookies with at least 100 innings (one HR per 27 innings). . . . Lowest ERA by a White Sox rookie since Britt Burns posted a 2.84 mark in 1980 (minimum: 100 IP). . . . Recent rookie with most similar statistics: Chuck Crim, 1987: 6–8, 3.67 ERA, 39 walks, 56 strikeouts in 130 innings. (Unlike Hibbard, Crim worked almost exclusively in relief.)

## Ted Higuera

Throws Left

| Milwaukee Brewers | W–L | ERA | AB | H | HR | BB | SO | BA | SA | OBA |
|---|---|---|---|---|---|---|---|---|---|---|
| Season | 9-6 | 3.46 | 504 | 125 | 9 | 48 | 91 | .248 | .345 | .316 |
| vs. Left-Handers | | | 93 | 20 | 2 | 4 | 14 | .215 | .323 | .245 |
| vs. Right-Handers | | | 411 | 105 | 7 | 44 | 77 | .255 | .350 | .330 |
| Home | 7-3 | 2.94 | 299 | 65 | 6 | 29 | 60 | .217 | .328 | .289 |
| Road | 2-3 | 4.27 | 205 | 60 | 3 | 19 | 31 | .293 | .371 | .354 |
| Grass | 9-5 | 3.24 | 422 | 102 | 8 | 37 | 79 | .242 | .336 | .305 |
| Artificial Turf | 0-1 | 4.64 | 82 | 23 | 1 | 11 | 12 | .280 | .390 | .367 |
| April | | | 0 | 0 | 0 | 0 | 0 | — | — | — |
| May | 0-2 | 6.62 | 63 | 17 | 1 | 12 | 9 | .270 | .349 | .390 |
| June | 2-0 | 1.89 | 139 | 28 | 1 | 15 | 30 | .201 | .252 | .277 |
| July | 4-2 | 3.00 | 155 | 39 | 3 | 10 | 28 | .252 | .348 | .299 |
| August | 3-1 | 3.18 | 130 | 34 | 4 | 11 | 20 | .262 | .400 | .326 |
| Sept./Oct. | 0-1 | 12.27 | 17 | 7 | 0 | 0 | 4 | .412 | .647 | .389 |
| Leading Off Inn. | | | 131 | 36 | 4 | 12 | 20 | .275 | .405 | .336 |
| Runners On | | | 206 | 56 | 3 | 20 | 28 | .272 | .359 | .335 |
| Runners/Scor. Pos. | | | 114 | 26 | 0 | 14 | 20 | .228 | .281 | .306 |
| Runners On/2 Out | | | 86 | 28 | 2 | 10 | 8 | .326 | .453 | .402 |
| Scor. Pos./2 Out | | | 58 | 15 | 0 | 8 | 8 | .259 | .293 | .348 |
| Late Inning Pressure | | | 31 | 7 | 0 | 1 | 5 | .226 | .258 | .250 |
| Leading Off | | | 10 | 4 | 0 | 0 | 1 | .400 | .400 | .400 |
| Runners On | | | 8 | 2 | 0 | 1 | 0 | .250 | .375 | .333 |
| Runners/Scor. Pos. | | | 4 | 2 | 0 | 1 | 0 | .500 | .750 | .600 |
| First 9 Batters | | | 174 | 38 | 3 | 22 | 36 | .218 | .322 | .306 |
| Second 9 Batters | | | 182 | 42 | 1 | 11 | 33 | .231 | .302 | .276 |
| All Batters Thereafter | | | 148 | 45 | 5 | 15 | 22 | .304 | .426 | .373 |

Loves to face: Gary Pettis (0-for-22, 7 SO)
Hates to face: Mark McGwire (.462, 6-for-13, 2 HR)
Ground outs-to-air outs ratio: 0.70 last season, 0.78 for career. . . . Additional statistics: 10 double-play ground outs in 104 opportunities, 20 doubles, 1 triple in 135.1 innings last season. . . . Allowed 6 first-inning runs in 22 starts. Hasn't allowed a first-inning home run in his last 44 starts. . . . Batting support: 4.18 runs per start. . . . Career record of 32–27 (3.68 ERA) before the All-Star break, 46–17 (2.86) after the break. . . . Bad news: Winning percentage has decreased in every season since his rookie year. . . . Good news: Only pitcher with five straight seasons of .600 or better, with at least 15 decisions in each. Longest streak in major league history: 12, Christy Mathewson (1903–14).

## Shawn Hillegas

Throws Right

| Chicago White Sox | W–L | ERA | AB | H | HR | BB | SO | BA | SA | OBA |
|---|---|---|---|---|---|---|---|---|---|---|
| Season | 7-11 | 4.74 | 473 | 132 | 12 | 51 | 76 | .279 | .429 | .352 |
| vs. Left-Handers | | | 227 | 71 | 4 | 30 | 27 | .313 | .449 | .395 |
| vs. Right-Handers | | | 246 | 61 | 8 | 21 | 49 | .248 | .411 | .310 |
| Home | 6-5 | 4.62 | 236 | 63 | 5 | 25 | 38 | .267 | .407 | .337 |
| Road | 1-6 | 4.85 | 237 | 69 | 7 | 26 | 38 | .291 | .451 | .366 |
| Grass | 7-8 | 4.44 | 383 | 103 | 8 | 38 | 60 | .269 | .407 | .336 |
| Artificial Turf | 0-3 | 6.04 | 90 | 29 | 4 | 13 | 16 | .322 | .522 | .413 |
| April | 0-3 | 5.04 | 99 | 26 | 3 | 14 | 12 | .263 | .444 | .354 |
| May | 1-3 | 7.39 | 133 | 43 | 5 | 16 | 19 | .323 | .526 | .401 |
| June | 2-1 | 3.00 | 68 | 17 | 1 | 7 | 9 | .250 | .338 | .320 |
| July | 3-2 | 3.31 | 62 | 14 | 1 | 5 | 14 | .226 | .355 | .294 |
| August | 0-1 | 2.19 | 49 | 16 | 1 | 6 | 10 | .327 | .449 | .393 |
| Sept./Oct. | 1-1 | 4.41 | 62 | 16 | 1 | 3 | 12 | .258 | .355 | .292 |
| Leading Off Inn. | | | 111 | 29 | 5 | 10 | 17 | .261 | .450 | .322 |
| Runners On | | | 215 | 61 | 6 | 26 | 41 | .284 | .433 | .363 |
| Runners/Scor. Pos. | | | 132 | 37 | 4 | 19 | 28 | .280 | .432 | .366 |
| Runners On/2 Out | | | 97 | 26 | 2 | 15 | 21 | .268 | .381 | .372 |
| Scor. Pos./2 Out | | | 68 | 17 | 0 | 13 | 16 | .250 | .279 | .370 |
| Late Inning Pressure | | | 119 | 34 | 2 | 15 | 16 | .286 | .395 | .368 |
| Leading Off | | | 25 | 6 | 2 | 5 | 3 | .240 | .480 | .367 |
| Runners On | | | 61 | 16 | 0 | 6 | 9 | .262 | .311 | .324 |
| Runners/Scor. Pos. | | | 37 | 9 | 0 | 4 | 4 | .243 | .297 | .310 |
| First 9 Batters | | | 280 | 75 | 8 | 34 | 52 | .268 | .436 | .347 |
| Second 9 Batters | | | 118 | 31 | 1 | 8 | 18 | .263 | .364 | .320 |
| All Batters Thereafter | | | 75 | 26 | 3 | 9 | 6 | .347 | .507 | .417 |

Loves to face: Ken Griffey, Sr. (0-for-10)
Hates to face: Ken Griffey, Jr. (3-for-3, 1 HR)
Ground outs-to-air outs ratio: 0.73 last season, 0.77 for career. . . . Additional statistics: 7 double-play ground outs in 95 opportunities, 25 doubles, 5 triples in 119.2 innings last season. . . . Allowed 18 first-inning runs in 13 starts. . . . Batting support: 4.31 runs per start. . . . Record of 2–7 (6.00 ERA) as a starter, 5–4 (3.19 ERA, three saves) in 37 relief appearances. . . . Inherited 37 runners, stranded 24 (65%). . . . Had a 2.78 ERA in 55 innings with Fisk behind the plate, 7.11 ERA in 50.1 innings with Ron Karkovice. . . . Opponents' career batting averages: .235 (one HR per 51 at-bats) on first two passes through batting order; .325 (one HR per 24 AB) thereafter.

## Brian Holman

Throws Right

| Seattle Mariners | W-L | ERA | AB | H | HR | BB | SO | BA | SA | OBA |
|---|---|---|---|---|---|---|---|---|---|---|
| Season | 8-10 | 3.44 | 613 | 160 | 9 | 62 | 82 | .261 | .367 | .333 |
| vs. Left-Handers | | | 292 | 75 | 4 | 37 | 30 | .257 | .366 | .344 |
| vs. Right-Handers | | | 321 | 85 | 5 | 25 | 52 | .265 | .368 | .323 |
| Home | 3-4 | 3.88 | 260 | 71 | 6 | 25 | 34 | .273 | .412 | .341 |
| Road | 5-6 | 3.12 | 353 | 89 | 3 | 37 | 48 | .252 | .334 | .327 |
| Grass | 4-4 | 3.47 | 242 | 64 | 3 | 24 | 39 | .264 | .372 | .333 |
| Artificial Turf | 4-6 | 3.42 | 371 | 96 | 6 | 38 | 43 | .259 | .364 | .333 |
| April | | | 0 | 0 | 0 | 0 | 0 | — | — | — |
| May | 0-1 | 6.75 | 33 | 11 | 0 | 6 | 4 | .333 | .333 | .436 |
| June | 2-1 | 3.63 | 132 | 35 | 1 | 15 | 12 | .265 | .348 | .340 |
| July | 2-1 | 2.75 | 133 | 33 | 3 | 16 | 23 | .248 | .368 | .329 |
| August | 1-5 | 3.60 | 178 | 48 | 1 | 16 | 28 | .270 | .393 | .347 |
| Sept./Oct. | 3-2 | 3.00 | 137 | 33 | 4 | 9 | 15 | .241 | .358 | .286 |
| Leading Off Inn. | | | 151 | 46 | 5 | 17 | 17 | .305 | .430 | .375 |
| Runners On | | | 260 | 67 | 3 | 31 | 31 | .258 | .358 | .344 |
| Runners/Scor. Pos. | | | 148 | 29 | 0 | 25 | 22 | .196 | .270 | .318 |
| Runners On/2 Out | | | 102 | 18 | 0 | 15 | 13 | .176 | .245 | .288 |
| Scor. Pos./2 Out | | | 64 | 9 | 0 | 12 | 10 | .141 | .250 | .286 |
| Late Inning Pressure | | | 61 | 15 | 1 | 9 | 7 | .246 | .328 | .352 |
| Leading Off | | | 18 | 5 | 0 | 1 | 1 | .278 | .278 | .316 |
| Runners On | | | 17 | 5 | 1 | 6 | 2 | .294 | .529 | .478 |
| Runners/Scor. Pos. | | | 7 | 2 | 0 | 3 | 1 | .286 | .429 | .500 |
| First 9 Batters | | | 183 | 51 | 4 | 20 | 33 | .279 | .399 | .351 |
| Second 9 Batters | | | 176 | 44 | 2 | 20 | 17 | .250 | .335 | .332 |
| All Batters Thereafter | | | 254 | 65 | 3 | 22 | 32 | .256 | .366 | .321 |

Loves to face: Steve Sax (.067, 1-for-15)
Hates to face: Kevin Seitzer (.467, 7-for-15)
Ground outs-to-air outs ratio: 1.30 last season, 1.10 for career. . . . Additional statistics: 18 double-play ground outs in 138 opportunities, 24 doubles, 7 triples in 159.2 innings last season. . . . Allowed 9 first-inning runs in 22 starts. . . . Batting support: 4.05 runs per start. . . . Averaged 7.17 innings per start, 6th-highest rate in A.L., behind a general manager's wish list of starters: Ryan (7.48), Saberhagen (7.43), Viola (7.32), Blyleven (7.30), and Clemens (7.24) (minimum: 15 GS). . . . Walked more left-handed batters (72) than he struck out (68) over two seasons. Totals vs. right-handers: 39 BB, 95 SO. . . . His bat is best kept in mothballs: Struck out 20 times in 41 plate appearances before being traded to A.L.

## Brian Holton

Throws Right

| Baltimore Orioles | W-L | ERA | AB | H | HR | BB | SO | BA | SA | OBA |
|---|---|---|---|---|---|---|---|---|---|---|
| Season | 5-7 | 4.02 | 467 | 140 | 11 | 39 | 51 | .300 | .433 | .352 |
| vs. Left-Handers | | | 230 | 71 | 7 | 18 | 13 | .309 | .452 | .359 |
| vs. Right-Handers | | | 237 | 69 | 4 | 21 | 38 | .291 | .414 | .345 |
| Home | 3-4 | 3.53 | 272 | 84 | 8 | 20 | 28 | .309 | .445 | .356 |
| Road | 2-3 | 4.68 | 195 | 56 | 3 | 19 | 23 | .287 | .415 | .346 |
| Grass | 5-5 | 3.61 | 410 | 120 | 10 | 30 | 48 | .293 | .427 | .339 |
| Artificial Turf | 0-2 | 7.07 | 57 | 20 | 1 | 9 | 3 | .351 | .474 | .433 |
| April | 1-3 | 5.30 | 71 | 22 | 1 | 5 | 5 | .310 | .437 | .359 |
| May | 1-1 | 1.77 | 82 | 24 | 1 | 5 | 11 | .293 | .354 | .333 |
| June | 0-1 | 3.95 | 110 | 33 | 2 | 5 | 8 | .300 | .418 | .325 |
| July | 2-1 | 5.63 | 102 | 31 | 4 | 18 | 14 | .304 | .471 | .408 |
| August | 0-0 | 4.24 | 68 | 21 | 2 | 5 | 8 | .309 | .471 | .347 |
| Sept./Oct. | 1-1 | 2.00 | 34 | 9 | 1 | 1 | 5 | .265 | .471 | .286 |
| Leading Off Inn. | | | 111 | 33 | 2 | 6 | 11 | .297 | .432 | .339 |
| Runners On | | | 220 | 58 | 5 | 18 | 24 | .264 | .373 | .313 |
| Runners/Scor. Pos. | | | 129 | 39 | 4 | 16 | 11 | .302 | .457 | .367 |
| Runners On/2 Out | | | 96 | 21 | 2 | 11 | 12 | .219 | .323 | .299 |
| Scor. Pos./2 Out | | | 60 | 13 | 1 | 10 | 6 | .217 | .317 | .329 |
| Late Inning Pressure | | | 47 | 18 | 2 | 5 | 4 | .383 | .638 | .442 |
| Leading Off | | | 12 | 3 | 1 | 2 | 2 | .250 | .667 | .357 |
| Runners On | | | 16 | 5 | 1 | 2 | 1 | .313 | .563 | .389 |
| Runners/Scor. Pos. | | | 11 | 2 | 1 | 2 | 1 | .182 | .545 | .308 |
| First 9 Batters | | | 281 | 79 | 7 | 20 | 31 | .281 | .427 | .328 |
| Second 9 Batters | | | 140 | 43 | 3 | 16 | 16 | .307 | .421 | .373 |
| All Batters Thereafter | | | 46 | 18 | 1 | 3 | 4 | .391 | .500 | .429 |

Loves to face: Gene Larkin (0-for-6)
Hates to face: Dion James (.800, 4-for-5, 1 3B, 1 HR)
Ground outs-to-air outs ratio: 1.09 last season, 1.24 for career. . . . Additional statistics: 11 double-play ground outs in 92 opportunities, 25 doubles, 2 triples in 116.1 innings last season. . . . Allowed 3 first-inning runs in 12 starts. . . . Batting support: 4.67 runs per start. . . . Inherited 30 runners, stranded 14 (47%), 2d-lowest average in A.L. (minimum: 25 runners). . . . Orioles won all six of his no-decision starts. . . . Opponents have hit for lower averages with runners on base than with bases empty in each of last four seasons. Difference of 68 points in '89 was 2d largest in majors. . . . Walked more left-handed batters (64) than he struck out (51) over five seasons. Totals vs. right-handers: 40 BB, 132 SO.

## Rick Honeycutt

Throws Left

| Oakland As | W-L | ERA | AB | H | HR | BB | SO | BA | SA | OBA |
|---|---|---|---|---|---|---|---|---|---|---|
| Season | 2-2 | 2.35 | 271 | 56 | 5 | 26 | 52 | .207 | .277 | .277 |
| vs. Left-Handers | | | 90 | 14 | 1 | 10 | 16 | .156 | .200 | .248 |
| vs. Right-Handers | | | 181 | 42 | 4 | 16 | 36 | .232 | .315 | .291 |
| Home | 0-2 | 2.85 | 149 | 34 | 2 | 11 | 30 | .228 | .275 | .282 |
| Road | 2-0 | 1.77 | 122 | 22 | 3 | 15 | 22 | .180 | .279 | .270 |
| Grass | 1-2 | 2.26 | 243 | 51 | 4 | 22 | 47 | .210 | .272 | .276 |
| Artificial Turf | 1-0 | 3.00 | 28 | 5 | 1 | 4 | 5 | .179 | .321 | .281 |
| April | 0-0 | 2.40 | 49 | 7 | 2 | 5 | 14 | .143 | .286 | .236 |
| May | 1-0 | 2.19 | 43 | 8 | 0 | 6 | 9 | .186 | .209 | .286 |
| June | 0-0 | 1.32 | 46 | 7 | 0 | 1 | 8 | .152 | .152 | .167 |
| July | 0-1 | 3.46 | 47 | 13 | 0 | 8 | 11 | .277 | .298 | .375 |
| August | 1-1 | 3.38 | 39 | 9 | 1 | 2 | 7 | .231 | .308 | .268 |
| Sept./Oct. | 0-0 | 1.50 | 47 | 12 | 2 | 4 | 3 | .255 | .404 | .314 |
| Leading Off Inn. | | | 61 | 14 | 2 | 2 | 12 | .230 | .328 | .254 |
| Runners On | | | 123 | 24 | 2 | 15 | 23 | .195 | .276 | .279 |
| Runners/Scor. Pos. | | | 56 | 15 | 1 | 11 | 11 | .268 | .321 | .377 |
| Runners On/2 Out | | | 54 | 10 | 0 | 7 | 13 | .185 | .222 | .279 |
| Scor. Pos./2 Out | | | 28 | 7 | 0 | 5 | 7 | .250 | .250 | .364 |
| Late Inning Pressure | | | 157 | 33 | 1 | 20 | 29 | .210 | .242 | .296 |
| Leading Off | | | 36 | 5 | 1 | 1 | 4 | .139 | .222 | .162 |
| Runners On | | | 66 | 15 | 0 | 12 | 14 | .227 | .258 | .338 |
| Runners/Scor. Pos. | | | 32 | 9 | 0 | 8 | 7 | .281 | .281 | .405 |
| First 9 Batters | | | 257 | 52 | 5 | 22 | 49 | .202 | .272 | .267 |
| Second 9 Batters | | | 14 | 4 | 0 | 4 | 3 | .286 | .357 | .421 |
| All Batters Thereafter | | | 0 | 0 | 0 | 0 | 0 | — | — | — |

Loves to face: Brad Komminsk (0-for-17)
Hates to face: Chili Davis (.435, 10-for-23, 4 HR)
Ground outs-to-air outs ratio: 1.73 last season, 1.90 for career. . . . Additional statistics: 10 double-play ground outs in 62 opportunities, 4 doubles, 0 triples in 76.2 innings last season. . . . Led majors with 12 "save setups" (at least one inning in relief, without a decision, immediately preceding a pitcher who earns a save). A.L. runners-up: Greg Minton, 11; Rob Murphy, Kenny Rogers, and Mark Williamson, 7. . . . Allowed two extra-base hits to left-handers, both in April. . . . Had a hand in nine multipitcher shutouts, tying Ken Dayley for major league lead. That broke previous record of eight, set by Bob Lee of the Angels in 1964. . . . Has defeated every major league club except the Orioles and the Dodgers.

## Charlie Hough

Throws Right

| Texas Rangers | W-L | ERA | AB | H | HR | BB | SO | BA | SA | OBA |
|---|---|---|---|---|---|---|---|---|---|---|
| Season | 10-13 | 4.35 | 685 | 168 | 28 | 95 | 94 | .245 | .415 | .340 |
| vs. Left-Handers | | | 336 | 80 | 9 | 44 | 41 | .238 | .366 | .327 |
| vs. Right-Handers | | | 349 | 88 | 19 | 51 | 53 | .252 | .461 | .351 |
| Home | 5-6 | 4.88 | 306 | 83 | 12 | 34 | 44 | .271 | .428 | .343 |
| Road | 5-7 | 3.94 | 379 | 85 | 16 | 61 | 50 | .224 | .404 | .337 |
| Grass | 9-9 | 4.69 | 531 | 132 | 24 | 76 | 77 | .249 | .422 | .344 |
| Artificial Turf | 1-4 | 3.21 | 154 | 36 | 4 | 19 | 17 | .234 | .390 | .326 |
| April | 2-2 | 4.88 | 121 | 30 | 5 | 16 | 15 | .248 | .446 | .343 |
| May | 1-3 | 7.29 | 88 | 30 | 1 | 19 | 15 | .341 | .432 | .459 |
| June | 2-3 | 3.67 | 151 | 35 | 9 | 13 | 19 | .232 | .437 | .299 |
| July | 0-3 | 5.79 | 91 | 24 | 5 | 13 | 19 | .264 | .473 | .358 |
| August | 4-1 | 2.25 | 123 | 20 | 3 | 21 | 14 | .163 | .260 | .283 |
| Sept./Oct. | 1-1 | 4.08 | 111 | 29 | 5 | 13 | 12 | .261 | .459 | .336 |
| Leading Off Inn. | | | 174 | 41 | 5 | 20 | 18 | .236 | .402 | .318 |
| Runners On | | | 271 | 69 | 10 | 42 | 37 | .255 | .406 | .356 |
| Runners/Scor. Pos. | | | 158 | 30 | 1 | 37 | 29 | .190 | .228 | .340 |
| Runners On/2 Out | | | 109 | 21 | 3 | 21 | 14 | .193 | .294 | .328 |
| Scor. Pos./2 Out | | | 72 | 10 | 1 | 19 | 10 | .139 | .194 | .319 |
| Late Inning Pressure | | | 66 | 18 | 6 | 7 | 6 | .273 | .621 | .351 |
| Leading Off | | | 19 | 4 | 0 | 3 | 2 | .211 | .368 | .318 |
| Runners On | | | 17 | 5 | 2 | 0 | 1 | .294 | .765 | .333 |
| Runners/Scor. Pos. | | | 5 | 0 | 0 | 0 | 0 | .000 | .000 | .167 |
| First 9 Batters | | | 227 | 54 | 5 | 35 | 41 | .238 | .339 | .342 |
| Second 9 Batters | | | 216 | 57 | 13 | 23 | 28 | .264 | .509 | .340 |
| All Batters Thereafter | | | 242 | 57 | 10 | 37 | 25 | .236 | .401 | .337 |

Loves to face: Jack Howell (.048, 1-for-21)
Hates to face: Tom Brookens (.393, 11-for-28, 2 HR)
Ground outs-to-air outs ratio: 0.88 last season, 1.04 since 1975. . . . Additional statistics: 10 double-play ground outs in 128 opportunities, 28 doubles, 2 triples in 182.0 innings last season. . . . Allowed 16 first-inning runs in 30 starts. . . . Batting support: 3.97 runs per start. . . . Became oldest pitcher in A.L. history to pitch an opening-day shutout (41 years, 3 months). Oldest in N.L.: Rip Sewell, 1949 (41 years, 11 months). . . . That was his only shutout in 104 starts (including 28 complete games) over last three seasons. . . . Walked more batters than he struck out for first time since breaking in with 17 innings for Dodgers in 1970. . . . Allowed one home run per 6.5 innings pitched, worst rate in majors (minimum: 15 GS).

## Mike Jackson

Throws Right

| Seattle Mariners | W–L | ERA | AB | H | HR | BB | SO | BA | SA | OBA |
|---|---|---|---|---|---|---|---|---|---|---|
| Season | 4-6 | 3.17 | 363 | 81 | 8 | 54 | 94 | .223 | .339 | .332 |
| vs. Left-Handers | | | 158 | 35 | 5 | 29 | 32 | .222 | .367 | .344 |
| vs. Right-Handers | | | 205 | 46 | 3 | 25 | 62 | .224 | .317 | .322 |
| Home | 2-2 | 3.50 | 207 | 51 | 7 | 26 | 56 | .246 | .401 | .339 |
| Road | 2-4 | 2.78 | 156 | 30 | 1 | 28 | 38 | .192 | .256 | .323 |
| Grass | 2-3 | 2.52 | 125 | 27 | 1 | 20 | 27 | .216 | .296 | .333 |
| Artificial Turf | 2-3 | 3.53 | 238 | 54 | 7 | 34 | 67 | .227 | .361 | .331 |
| April | 0-0 | 5.27 | 52 | 17 | 0 | 8 | 9 | .327 | .385 | .426 |
| May | 2-0 | 2.60 | 67 | 15 | 2 | 5 | 13 | .224 | .358 | .278 |
| June | 0-2 | 4.79 | 74 | 15 | 3 | 15 | 23 | .203 | .365 | .348 |
| July | 1-3 | 1.84 | 53 | 12 | 0 | 8 | 14 | .226 | .283 | .339 |
| August | 1-0 | 2.45 | 50 | 8 | 2 | 10 | 17 | .160 | .300 | .323 |
| Sept./Oct. | 0-1 | 1.96 | 67 | 14 | 1 | 8 | 18 | .209 | .328 | .289 |
| Leading Off Inn. | | | 80 | 21 | 5 | 4 | 17 | .263 | .500 | .306 |
| Runners On | | | 169 | 41 | 2 | 36 | 45 | .243 | .337 | .384 |
| Runners/Scor. Pos. | | | 129 | 33 | 1 | 25 | 34 | .256 | .333 | .380 |
| Runners On/2 Out | | | 85 | 19 | 1 | 22 | 21 | .224 | .341 | .383 |
| Scor. Pos./2 Out | | | 68 | 16 | 0 | 17 | 20 | .235 | .324 | .388 |
| Late Inning Pressure | | | 192 | 40 | 3 | 37 | 43 | .208 | .313 | .343 |
| Leading Off | | | 47 | 13 | 1 | 3 | 6 | .277 | .404 | .320 |
| Runners On | | | 85 | 18 | 1 | 24 | 20 | .212 | .329 | .398 |
| Runners/Scor. Pos. | | | 66 | 13 | 1 | 16 | 15 | .197 | .303 | .365 |
| First 9 Batters | | | 336 | 77 | 7 | 50 | 86 | .229 | .345 | .336 |
| Second 9 Batters | | | 27 | 4 | 1 | 4 | 8 | .148 | .259 | .281 |
| All Batters Thereafter | | | 0 | 0 | 0 | 0 | 0 | — | — | — |

Loves to face: Rob Deer (0-for-7, 5 SO)
Hates to face: Rafael Palmeiro (.667, 4-for-6, 1 HR)
Ground outs-to-air outs ratio: 0.74 last season, 0.70 for career.... Additional statistics: 7 double-play ground outs in 75 opportunities, 18 doubles, 0 triples in 99.1 innings last season.... Inherited 65 runners, stranded 45 (69%).... Career average of .190 by opposing right-handers is 2d-lowest among active pitchers (minimum: 600 BFP).... During two seasons with Mariners, has allowed 14 home runs in Kingdome, only four outside it.... Among 540 pitchers who've allowed 25 or more HR over last 15 years, Jackson is one of three who's allowed more to ground-ball hitters (19) than to fly-ballers (17). Others: Lance McCullers and Danny Cox.... Finished only 68 of 184 relief appearances. Other times, was told to beat it.

## Mike Jeffcoat

Throws Left

| Texas Rangers | W–L | ERA | AB | H | HR | BB | SO | BA | SA | OBA |
|---|---|---|---|---|---|---|---|---|---|---|
| Season | 9-6 | 3.58 | 514 | 139 | 7 | 33 | 64 | .270 | .395 | .317 |
| vs. Left-Handers | | | 99 | 26 | 1 | 5 | 14 | .263 | .384 | .295 |
| vs. Right-Handers | | | 415 | 113 | 6 | 28 | 50 | .272 | .398 | .322 |
| Home | 5-1 | 3.60 | 236 | 66 | 4 | 16 | 29 | .280 | .398 | .331 |
| Road | 4-5 | 3.57 | 278 | 73 | 3 | 17 | 35 | .263 | .392 | .304 |
| Grass | 7-5 | 3.76 | 411 | 114 | 7 | 29 | 52 | .277 | .404 | .329 |
| Artificial Turf | 2-1 | 2.93 | 103 | 25 | 0 | 4 | 12 | .243 | .359 | .266 |
| April | | | 0 | 0 | 0 | 0 | 0 | — | — | — |
| May | | | 0 | 0 | 0 | 0 | 0 | — | — | — |
| June | 4-1 | 2.75 | 153 | 40 | 1 | 10 | 20 | .261 | .373 | .303 |
| July | 1-2 | 8.47 | 73 | 25 | 0 | 7 | 8 | .342 | .438 | .412 |
| August | 2-2 | 3.16 | 141 | 36 | 3 | 9 | 20 | .255 | .397 | .303 |
| Sept./Oct. | 2-1 | 2.65 | 147 | 38 | 3 | 7 | 16 | .259 | .395 | .292 |
| Leading Off Inn. | | | 135 | 41 | 0 | 6 | 17 | .304 | .415 | .343 |
| Runners On | | | 220 | 55 | 5 | 15 | 25 | .250 | .391 | .298 |
| Runners/Scor. Pos. | | | 110 | 32 | 2 | 10 | 10 | .291 | .427 | .336 |
| Runners On/2 Out | | | 88 | 21 | 2 | 6 | 12 | .239 | .352 | .295 |
| Scor. Pos./2 Out | | | 47 | 12 | 2 | 5 | 7 | .255 | .404 | .327 |
| Late Inning Pressure | | | 35 | 15 | 1 | 1 | 4 | .429 | .600 | .444 |
| Leading Off | | | 13 | 4 | 0 | 0 | 1 | .308 | .385 | .308 |
| Runners On | | | 10 | 7 | 1 | 0 | 0 | .700 | 1.000 | .700 |
| Runners/Scor. Pos. | | | 6 | 4 | 0 | 0 | 0 | .667 | .667 | .667 |
| First 9 Batters | | | 183 | 52 | 2 | 11 | 19 | .284 | .383 | .332 |
| Second 9 Batters | | | 167 | 38 | 1 | 11 | 22 | .228 | .335 | .280 |
| All Batters Thereafter | | | 164 | 49 | 4 | 11 | 23 | .299 | .470 | .337 |

Loves to face: Rich Gedman (0-for-6, 3 SO)
Hates to face: Wally Joyner (.455, 5-for-11)
Ground outs-to-air outs ratio: 1.21 last season, 1.15 for career.... Additional statistics: 11 double-play ground outs in 104 opportunities, 29 doubles, 7 triples in 130.2 innings last season.... Allowed 14 first-inning runs in 22 starts.... Batting support: 4.86 runs per start.... Pitched exclusively as a starter. Previous career totals: eight starts, 101 relief appearances.... Career breakdown: 10–11, 4.68 ERA as a starter; 5–5, 3.12 in relief.... Has started 41 innings in Late-Inning Pressure Situations without walking a leadoff batter.... Career record is 1–6 in day games, 14–10 at night. But ERA is more than a run per game higher at night (4.32 to 3.16).... Go figure.

## Dave Johnson

Throws Right

| Baltimore Orioles | W–L | ERA | AB | H | HR | BB | SO | BA | SA | OBA |
|---|---|---|---|---|---|---|---|---|---|---|
| Season | 4-7 | 4.23 | 340 | 90 | 11 | 28 | 26 | .265 | .424 | .325 |
| vs. Left-Handers | | | 155 | 47 | 4 | 19 | 10 | .303 | .465 | .375 |
| vs. Right-Handers | | | 185 | 43 | 7 | 9 | 16 | .232 | .389 | .281 |
| Home | 3-3 | 3.79 | 209 | 57 | 5 | 15 | 18 | .273 | .416 | .328 |
| Road | 1-4 | 4.93 | 131 | 33 | 6 | 13 | 8 | .252 | .435 | .322 |
| Grass | 4-7 | 4.37 | 317 | 88 | 11 | 25 | 26 | .278 | .445 | .335 |
| Artificial Turf | 0-0 | 2.57 | 23 | 2 | 0 | 3 | 0 | .087 | .130 | .192 |
| April | | | 0 | 0 | 0 | 0 | 0 | — | — | — |
| May | | | 0 | 0 | 0 | 0 | 0 | — | — | — |
| June | | | 0 | 0 | 0 | 0 | 0 | — | — | — |
| July | | | 0 | 0 | 0 | 0 | 0 | — | — | — |
| August | 4-3 | 3.86 | 177 | 47 | 6 | 13 | 16 | .266 | .418 | .321 |
| Sept./Oct. | 0-4 | 4.64 | 163 | 43 | 5 | 15 | 10 | .264 | .429 | .330 |
| Leading Off Inn. | | | 85 | 20 | 3 | 8 | 5 | .235 | .388 | .316 |
| Runners On | | | 127 | 31 | 3 | 15 | 11 | .244 | .362 | .327 |
| Runners/Scor. Pos. | | | 72 | 15 | 2 | 8 | 9 | .208 | .319 | .294 |
| Runners On/2 Out | | | 48 | 8 | 1 | 5 | 4 | .167 | .250 | .273 |
| Scor. Pos./2 Out | | | 31 | 4 | 1 | 4 | 4 | .129 | .226 | .270 |
| Late Inning Pressure | | | 30 | 5 | 0 | 3 | 1 | .167 | .200 | .242 |
| Leading Off | | | 8 | 1 | 0 | 2 | 1 | .125 | .125 | .300 |
| Runners On | | | 8 | 0 | 0 | 0 | 1 | .000 | .000 | .000 |
| Runners/Scor. Pos. | | | 0 | 0 | 0 | 0 | 0 | — | — | — |
| First 9 Batters | | | 113 | 28 | 6 | 6 | 13 | .248 | .487 | .306 |
| Second 9 Batters | | | 104 | 37 | 4 | 12 | 10 | .356 | .548 | .415 |
| All Batters Thereafter | | | 123 | 25 | 1 | 10 | 3 | .203 | .260 | .263 |

Loves to face: Tony Fernandez (0-for-5, 2 SO)
Hates to face: Cory Snyder (.833, 5-for-6)
Ground outs-to-air outs ratio: 0.63 last season, 0.70 for career.... Additional statistics: 6 double-play ground outs in 71 opportunities, 17 doubles, 2 triples in 89.1 innings last season.... Allowed 10 first-inning runs in 14 starts.... Batting support: 3.00 runs per start.... Oldest rookie starting pitcher in majors last season. Turned 30 during World Series hiatus, as did veterans Kevin McReynolds and George Bell.... Won four of first six starts (including three complete games); was 0-for-8 thereafter (five losses, three no-decisions).... Namesake made Orioles' final out of 1969 World Series. This Dave Johnson was hard-luck loser when Toronto eliminated Baltimore on next-to-last day of season.

## Randy Johnson

Throws Left

| Seattle Mariners | W–L | ERA | AB | H | HR | BB | SO | BA | SA | OBA |
|---|---|---|---|---|---|---|---|---|---|---|
| Season | 7-9 | 4.40 | 483 | 118 | 11 | 70 | 104 | .244 | .373 | .338 |
| vs. Left-Handers | | | 59 | 10 | 1 | 6 | 11 | .169 | .271 | .254 |
| vs. Right-Handers | | | 424 | 108 | 10 | 64 | 93 | .255 | .387 | .349 |
| Home | 2-5 | 5.56 | 193 | 47 | 5 | 31 | 47 | .244 | .389 | .346 |
| Road | 5-4 | 3.55 | 290 | 71 | 6 | 39 | 57 | .245 | .362 | .332 |
| Grass | 5-3 | 3.31 | 254 | 59 | 6 | 33 | 51 | .232 | .354 | .321 |
| Artificial Turf | 2-6 | 5.57 | 229 | 59 | 5 | 37 | 53 | .258 | .393 | .356 |
| April | | | 0 | 0 | 0 | 0 | 0 | — | — | — |
| May | 1-0 | 3.00 | 22 | 6 | 0 | 3 | 6 | .273 | .318 | .360 |
| June | 2-0 | 4.12 | 67 | 17 | 0 | 15 | 15 | .254 | .284 | .375 |
| July | 2-2 | 2.91 | 153 | 34 | 3 | 22 | 31 | .222 | .333 | .315 |
| August | 1-3 | 5.82 | 133 | 34 | 5 | 21 | 23 | .256 | .421 | .361 |
| Sept./Oct. | 1-4 | 5.46 | 108 | 27 | 3 | 9 | 29 | .250 | .435 | .311 |
| Leading Off Inn. | | | 120 | 32 | 1 | 20 | 28 | .267 | .342 | .371 |
| Runners On | | | 197 | 50 | 5 | 30 | 39 | .254 | .386 | .347 |
| Runners/Scor. Pos. | | | 134 | 37 | 3 | 20 | 27 | .276 | .403 | .358 |
| Runners On/2 Out | | | 83 | 20 | 2 | 11 | 15 | .241 | .386 | .330 |
| Scor. Pos./2 Out | | | 61 | 18 | 2 | 10 | 11 | .295 | .475 | .394 |
| Late Inning Pressure | | | 38 | 10 | 1 | 2 | 12 | .263 | .368 | .293 |
| Leading Off | | | 13 | 4 | 0 | 1 | 6 | .308 | .308 | .357 |
| Runners On | | | 7 | 0 | 0 | 1 | 2 | .000 | .000 | .111 |
| Runners/Scor. Pos. | | | 5 | 0 | 0 | 1 | 2 | .000 | .000 | .143 |
| First 9 Batters | | | 169 | 42 | 5 | 22 | 35 | .249 | .408 | .335 |
| Second 9 Batters | | | 151 | 37 | 3 | 27 | 33 | .245 | .344 | .361 |
| All Batters Thereafter | | | 163 | 39 | 3 | 21 | 36 | .239 | .362 | .319 |

Loves to face: Rafael Palmeiro (0-for-7)
Hates to face: Chili Davis (.571, 4-for-7, 1 HR)
Ground outs-to-air outs ratio: 1.04 last season, 1.09 for career.... Additional statistics: 9 double-play ground outs in 98 opportunities, 25 doubles, 2 triples in 131.0 innings last season.... Allowed 14 first-inning runs in 22 starts.... Batting support: 4.05 runs per start.... One of three pitchers to allow more than 30 stolen bases: Mike Scott (39), Nolan Ryan (36), Johnson (32; 24 with Seattle, eight with Montreal).... Walked leadoff batters in 28 of 171 innings (two-league totals). Only pitchers with higher averages over past 15 years: Dan Warthen (once), Bobby Witt (twice), and Ryan (thrice).... Career average of one walk per 8.0 batters faced. But he's faced 23 batters with bases loaded without walking in a run.

## Doug Jones

Throws Right

| Cleveland Indians | W–L | ERA | AB | H | HR | BB | SO | BA | SA | OBA |
|---|---|---|---|---|---|---|---|---|---|---|
| Season | 7-10 | 2.34 | 303 | 76 | 4 | 13 | 65 | .251 | .337 | .279 |
| vs. Left-Handers | | | 160 | 39 | 4 | 9 | 27 | .244 | .369 | .281 |
| vs. Right-Handers | | | 143 | 37 | 0 | 4 | 38 | .259 | .301 | .276 |
| Home | 6-4 | 2.15 | 167 | 40 | 3 | 5 | 31 | .240 | .341 | .257 |
| Road | 1-6 | 2.60 | 136 | 36 | 1 | 8 | 34 | .265 | .331 | .304 |
| Grass | 6-6 | 2.00 | 248 | 59 | 3 | 9 | 56 | .238 | .319 | .261 |
| Artificial Turf | 1-4 | 4.05 | 55 | 17 | 1 | 4 | 9 | .309 | .418 | .355 |
| April | 1-1 | 1.93 | 37 | 11 | 1 | 2 | 8 | .297 | .459 | .333 |
| May | 1-1 | 2.25 | 41 | 9 | 1 | 1 | 8 | .220 | .341 | .227 |
| June | 0-1 | 1.50 | 44 | 12 | 0 | 1 | 7 | .273 | .318 | .277 |
| July | 2-2 | 3.00 | 68 | 16 | 2 | 3 | 12 | .235 | .338 | .274 |
| August | 2-2 | 3.29 | 53 | 15 | 0 | 2 | 13 | .283 | .358 | .304 |
| Sept./Oct. | 1-3 | 1.72 | 60 | 13 | 0 | 4 | 17 | .217 | .250 | .266 |
| Leading Off Inn. | | | 60 | 19 | 0 | 2 | 15 | .317 | .417 | .339 |
| Runners On | | | 159 | 36 | 3 | 6 | 28 | .226 | .314 | .250 |
| Runners/Scor. Pos. | | | 94 | 22 | 3 | 5 | 18 | .234 | .372 | .264 |
| Runners On/2 Out | | | 78 | 15 | 1 | 2 | 12 | .192 | .231 | .213 |
| Scor. Pos./2 Out | | | 46 | 9 | 1 | 1 | 7 | .196 | .261 | .213 |
| Late Inning Pressure | | | 246 | 65 | 4 | 10 | 51 | .264 | .366 | .291 |
| Leading Off | | | 50 | 16 | 0 | 2 | 12 | .320 | .420 | .346 |
| Runners On | | | 125 | 30 | 3 | 4 | 20 | .240 | .352 | .261 |
| Runners/Scor. Pos. | | | 74 | 19 | 3 | 4 | 14 | .257 | .432 | .289 |
| First 9 Batters | | | 289 | 75 | 4 | 12 | 62 | .260 | .349 | .286 |
| Second 9 Batters | | | 14 | 1 | 0 | 1 | 3 | .071 | .071 | .133 |
| All Batters Thereafter | | | 0 | 0 | 0 | 0 | 0 | — | — | — |

Loves to face: Dan Pasqua (.091, 1-for-11)
Hates to face: Kent Hrbek (.444, 4-for-9, 2 HR)
Ground outs-to-air outs ratio: 1.32 last season, 1.45 for career. . . . Additional statistics: 5 double-play ground outs in 66 opportunities, 14 doubles, 0 triples in 80.2 innings last season. . . . Inherited 40 runners, stranded 31 (78%). . . . Shared A.L. lead for relief losses with Duane Ward. . . . Had the lowest ERA of any pitcher in majors with a losing record (minimum: 15 decisions). . . . Hasn't surrendered a home run to a right-handed batter since July 24, 1987 (to Larry Parrish). . . . Career average of one home run per 149 batters faced in Late-Inning Pressure Situations is best among active pitchers (minimum: 400 BFP). . . . But opponents' batting average has been higher in LIPS than otherwise in each of his five seasons.

## Jimmy Key

Throws Left

| Toronto Blue Jays | W–L | ERA | AB | H | HR | BB | SO | BA | SA | OBA |
|---|---|---|---|---|---|---|---|---|---|---|
| Season | 13-14 | 3.88 | 838 | 226 | 18 | 27 | 118 | .270 | .415 | .292 |
| vs. Left-Handers | | | 150 | 34 | 2 | 4 | 30 | .227 | .327 | .245 |
| vs. Right-Handers | | | 688 | 192 | 16 | 23 | 88 | .279 | .435 | .302 |
| Home | 7-8 | 3.81 | 463 | 124 | 8 | 17 | 64 | .268 | .415 | .294 |
| Road | 6-6 | 3.95 | 375 | 102 | 10 | 10 | 54 | .272 | .416 | .289 |
| Grass | 5-5 | 3.76 | 324 | 86 | 9 | 9 | 45 | .265 | .404 | .283 |
| Artificial Turf | 8-9 | 3.94 | 514 | 140 | 9 | 18 | 73 | .272 | .422 | .298 |
| April | 2-2 | 3.24 | 156 | 37 | 1 | 4 | 28 | .237 | .333 | .255 |
| May | 4-1 | 2.98 | 185 | 45 | 3 | 3 | 18 | .243 | .368 | .259 |
| June | 1-4 | 4.54 | 144 | 40 | 6 | 7 | 17 | .278 | .472 | .308 |
| July | 0-5 | 6.10 | 132 | 45 | 5 | 5 | 13 | .341 | .545 | .357 |
| August | 3-1 | 1.78 | 83 | 14 | 0 | 6 | 13 | .169 | .241 | .231 |
| Sept./Oct. | 3-1 | 4.78 | 138 | 45 | 3 | 2 | 29 | .326 | .493 | .336 |
| Leading Off Inn. | | | 219 | 61 | 6 | 5 | 32 | .279 | .466 | .295 |
| Runners On | | | 310 | 88 | 7 | 14 | 37 | .284 | .432 | .308 |
| Runners/Scor. Pos. | | | 175 | 49 | 4 | 10 | 24 | .280 | .423 | .308 |
| Runners On/2 Out | | | 133 | 36 | 4 | 5 | 21 | .271 | .429 | .302 |
| Scor. Pos./2 Out | | | 83 | 24 | 3 | 4 | 13 | .289 | .482 | .330 |
| Late Inning Pressure | | | 82 | 19 | 1 | 1 | 6 | .232 | .293 | .235 |
| Leading Off | | | 24 | 6 | 1 | 0 | 1 | .250 | .458 | .250 |
| Runners On | | | 19 | 8 | 0 | 1 | 2 | .421 | .421 | .409 |
| Runners/Scor. Pos. | | | 10 | 4 | 0 | 1 | 1 | .400 | .400 | .385 |
| First 9 Batters | | | 284 | 68 | 3 | 6 | 44 | .239 | .349 | .257 |
| Second 9 Batters | | | 278 | 81 | 7 | 10 | 42 | .291 | .464 | .316 |
| All Batters Thereafter | | | 276 | 77 | 8 | 11 | 32 | .279 | .435 | .302 |

Loves to face: Gary Pettis (.133, 4-for-30, 11 SO)
Hates to face: Rickey Henderson (.382, 21-for-55, 4 HR)
Ground outs-to-air outs ratio: 1.02 last season, 1.29 for career. . . . Additional statistics: 16 double-play ground outs in 129 opportunities, 54 doubles, 7 triples in 216.0 innings last season. . . . Allowed 10 first-inning runs in 33 starts. . . . Batting support: 4.00 runs per start. . . . Average of 1.13 walks per nine innings was lowest in majors. . . . Didn't walk a leadoff batter until June 25, when he passed Mike Gallego, the 124th leadoff hitter he'd faced. . . . Led A.L. in losses during month of June. . . . Opposing ground-ball hitters have out-hit fly-ball hitters in each of his six seasons. Difference of 51 points between career averages (.277 and .226, respectively) is 2d largest over the last 10 years.

## Eric King

Throws Right

| Chicago White Sox | W–L | ERA | AB | H | HR | BB | SO | BA | SA | OBA |
|---|---|---|---|---|---|---|---|---|---|---|
| Season | 9-10 | 3.39 | 591 | 144 | 13 | 64 | 72 | .244 | .342 | .320 |
| vs. Left-Handers | | | 308 | 71 | 11 | 35 | 41 | .231 | .373 | .312 |
| vs. Right-Handers | | | 283 | 73 | 2 | 29 | 31 | .258 | .307 | .328 |
| Home | 6-7 | 3.20 | 364 | 87 | 5 | 46 | 45 | .239 | .316 | .327 |
| Road | 3-3 | 3.69 | 227 | 57 | 8 | 18 | 27 | .251 | .383 | .308 |
| Grass | 8-9 | 3.27 | 521 | 126 | 7 | 64 | 62 | .242 | .311 | .327 |
| Artificial Turf | 1-1 | 4.26 | 70 | 18 | 6 | 0 | 10 | .257 | .571 | .264 |
| April | 1-3 | 2.78 | 125 | 30 | 3 | 11 | 19 | .240 | .360 | .307 |
| May | 3-3 | 3.82 | 135 | 29 | 3 | 27 | 23 | .215 | .304 | .350 |
| June | 0-2 | 9.00 | 42 | 12 | 2 | 9 | 2 | .286 | .452 | .412 |
| July | 0-0 | 2.77 | 50 | 13 | 0 | 3 | 4 | .260 | .320 | .296 |
| August | 2-0 | 3.76 | 99 | 27 | 5 | 4 | 9 | .273 | .465 | .305 |
| Sept./Oct. | 3-2 | 1.96 | 140 | 33 | 0 | 10 | 15 | .236 | .250 | .287 |
| Leading Off Inn. | | | 149 | 36 | 6 | 20 | 24 | .242 | .416 | .335 |
| Runners On | | | 238 | 59 | 2 | 26 | 29 | .248 | .298 | .320 |
| Runners/Scor. Pos. | | | 126 | 30 | 2 | 14 | 18 | .238 | .302 | .306 |
| Runners On/2 Out | | | 95 | 25 | 2 | 11 | 18 | .263 | .347 | .340 |
| Scor. Pos./2 Out | | | 60 | 14 | 2 | 8 | 10 | .233 | .333 | .324 |
| Late Inning Pressure | | | 57 | 14 | 1 | 6 | 6 | .246 | .351 | .313 |
| Leading Off | | | 18 | 6 | 1 | 2 | 4 | .333 | .667 | .400 |
| Runners On | | | 18 | 4 | 0 | 4 | 2 | .222 | .222 | .348 |
| Runners/Scor. Pos. | | | 9 | 1 | 0 | 1 | 2 | .111 | .111 | .182 |
| First 9 Batters | | | 197 | 46 | 3 | 23 | 32 | .234 | .320 | .314 |
| Second 9 Batters | | | 201 | 48 | 4 | 18 | 26 | .239 | .318 | .311 |
| All Batters Thereafter | | | 193 | 50 | 6 | 23 | 14 | .259 | .389 | .335 |

Loves to face: Harold Reynolds (0-for-19)
Hates to face: Jesse Barfield (.385, 5-for-13, 2 HR)
Ground outs-to-air outs ratio: 1.64 last season, 1.23 for career. . . . Additional statistics: 25 double-play ground outs in 128 opportunities, 13 doubles, 3 triples in 159.1 innings last season. . . . Allowed 17 first-inning runs in 25 starts. . . . Batting support: 4.80 runs per start. . . . Used exclusively as a starter, after three years of mostly relief work. Career figures: 20–17, 3.84 ERA as a starter; 10–7, 3.69 in relief. . . . Led the White Sox with 6.37 innings per start. . . . Allowed five home runs in the stadium named for him (more than any other Mariners opponent). . . . Career records: 14–18 before All-Star break, 16–6 after. . . . Career record of 6–1 vs. Baltimore. No more than three wins against any other team.

## Mark Knudson

Throws Right

| Milwaukee Brewers | W–L | ERA | AB | H | HR | BB | SO | BA | SA | OBA |
|---|---|---|---|---|---|---|---|---|---|---|
| Season | 8-5 | 3.35 | 464 | 110 | 15 | 29 | 47 | .237 | .377 | .286 |
| vs. Left-Handers | | | 201 | 48 | 5 | 12 | 17 | .239 | .373 | .285 |
| vs. Right-Handers | | | 263 | 62 | 10 | 17 | 30 | .236 | .380 | .286 |
| Home | 3-3 | 2.41 | 213 | 54 | 3 | 13 | 22 | .254 | .347 | .303 |
| Road | 5-2 | 4.12 | 251 | 56 | 12 | 16 | 25 | .223 | .402 | .271 |
| Grass | 7-4 | 3.25 | 399 | 97 | 13 | 25 | 42 | .243 | .388 | .293 |
| Artificial Turf | 1-1 | 3.93 | 65 | 13 | 2 | 4 | 5 | .200 | .308 | .243 |
| April | 1-0 | 1.38 | 47 | 10 | 0 | 4 | 1 | .213 | .234 | .288 |
| May | 0-1 | 3.86 | 91 | 27 | 3 | 8 | 12 | .297 | .473 | .360 |
| June | 1-2 | 7.36 | 75 | 25 | 4 | 3 | 9 | .333 | .560 | .354 |
| July | 0-0 | 2.00 | 30 | 5 | 1 | 2 | 4 | .167 | .267 | .219 |
| August | 3-1 | 3.45 | 110 | 27 | 5 | 7 | 12 | .245 | .427 | .291 |
| Sept./Oct. | 3-1 | 1.72 | 111 | 16 | 2 | 5 | 9 | .144 | .216 | .188 |
| Leading Off Inn. | | | 117 | 26 | 3 | 8 | 10 | .222 | .342 | .272 |
| Runners On | | | 179 | 41 | 7 | 12 | 19 | .229 | .385 | .276 |
| Runners/Scor. Pos. | | | 86 | 24 | 6 | 7 | 9 | .279 | .523 | .330 |
| Runners On/2 Out | | | 75 | 18 | 4 | 10 | 10 | .240 | .480 | .329 |
| Scor. Pos./2 Out | | | 41 | 12 | 3 | 7 | 5 | .293 | .585 | .396 |
| Late Inning Pressure | | | 77 | 25 | 2 | 3 | 9 | .325 | .455 | .354 |
| Leading Off | | | 20 | 4 | 1 | 2 | 1 | .200 | .400 | .273 |
| Runners On | | | 29 | 12 | 1 | 1 | 3 | .414 | .552 | .419 |
| Runners/Scor. Pos. | | | 13 | 8 | 1 | 1 | 1 | .615 | .923 | .600 |
| First 9 Batters | | | 262 | 60 | 8 | 21 | 29 | .229 | .359 | .291 |
| Second 9 Batters | | | 142 | 36 | 6 | 7 | 16 | .254 | .444 | .287 |
| All Batters Thereafter | | | 60 | 14 | 1 | 1 | 2 | .233 | .300 | .258 |

Loves to face: Brian Downing (0-for-9)
Hates to face: Chili Davis (.625, 5-for-8, 1 HR)
Ground outs-to-air outs ratio: 1.13 last season, 0.96 for career. . . . Additional statistics: 14 double-play ground outs in 86 opportunities, 14 doubles, 3 triples in 123.2 innings last season. . . . Inherited 23 runners, stranded 12 (52%). . . . Opponents stole only five bases in 11 attempts. . . . Record of 6–1 (2.23 ERA) in seven starts, 2–4 (3.97 ERA, kno saves) in 33 relief appearances. Career breakdown: 9–12, 4.61 ERA as a starter; 4–5, 3.97 in relief. . . . Opponents' career batting average is .315 with two outs and runners in scoring position. . . . Career average of 2.24 walks per knine innings. . . . Knever had a winning record in scraps of four previous seasons in majors.

## Bill Krueger

Throws Left

| Milwaukee Brewers | W–L | ERA | AB | H | HR | BB | SO | BA | SA | OBA |
|---|---|---|---|---|---|---|---|---|---|---|
| Season | 3-2 | 3.84 | 364 | 96 | 9 | 33 | 72 | .264 | .376 | .324 |
| vs. Left-Handers | | | 94 | 21 | 0 | 10 | 25 | .223 | .245 | .298 |
| vs. Right-Handers | | | 270 | 75 | 9 | 23 | 47 | .278 | .422 | .333 |
| Home | 2-2 | 3.61 | 184 | 48 | 2 | 15 | 43 | .261 | .342 | .315 |
| Road | 1-0 | 4.08 | 180 | 48 | 7 | 18 | 29 | .267 | .411 | .333 |
| Grass | 2-2 | 4.17 | 307 | 85 | 6 | 29 | 62 | .277 | .371 | .338 |
| Artificial Turf | 1-0 | 2.25 | 57 | 11 | 3 | 4 | 10 | .193 | .404 | .246 |
| April | 0-0 | 0.00 | 12 | 3 | 0 | 0 | 3 | .250 | .250 | .250 |
| May | 1-0 | 4.76 | 71 | 23 | 2 | 8 | 12 | .324 | .479 | .392 |
| June | 2-2 | 5.18 | 104 | 33 | 4 | 12 | 14 | .317 | .481 | .385 |
| July | 0-0 | 1.25 | 77 | 15 | 1 | 6 | 16 | .195 | .247 | .253 |
| August | 0-0 | 1.04 | 51 | 4 | 1 | 3 | 14 | .078 | .137 | .130 |
| Sept./Oct. | 0-0 | 10.80 | 49 | 18 | 1 | 4 | 13 | .367 | .490 | .415 |
| Leading Off Inn. | | | 79 | 26 | 3 | 8 | 13 | .329 | .506 | .391 |
| Runners On | | | 171 | 47 | 3 | 17 | 36 | .275 | .374 | .339 |
| Runners/Scor. Pos. | | | 106 | 26 | 2 | 13 | 30 | .245 | .330 | .325 |
| Runners On/2 Out | | | 73 | 19 | 1 | 7 | 14 | .260 | .315 | .325 |
| Scor. Pos./2 Out | | | 49 | 11 | 1 | 5 | 12 | .224 | .286 | .296 |
| Late Inning Pressure | | | 42 | 10 | 0 | 3 | 7 | .238 | .262 | .289 |
| Leading Off | | | 11 | 1 | 0 | 1 | 2 | .091 | .091 | .167 |
| Runners On | | | 11 | 5 | 0 | 1 | 2 | .455 | .545 | .500 |
| Runners/Scor. Pos. | | | 6 | 2 | 0 | 1 | 2 | .333 | .333 | .429 |
| First 9 Batters | | | 223 | 59 | 5 | 16 | 51 | .265 | .359 | .313 |
| Second 9 Batters | | | 107 | 28 | 2 | 14 | 17 | .262 | .393 | .347 |
| All Batters Thereafter | | | 34 | 9 | 2 | 3 | 4 | .265 | .441 | .324 |

Loves to face: Rick Cerone (0-for-10)
Hates to face: Greg Gagne (.533, 8-for-15, 3 2B, 1 HR)
Ground outs-to-air outs ratio: 0.98 last season, 1.13 for career. . . . Additional statistics: 6 double-play ground outs in 75 opportunities, 10 doubles, 2 triples in 93.2 innings last season. . . . Inherited 31 runners, stranded 13 (58%). . . . Record of 2–2 (5.25 ERA) in five starts, 1–0 (3.36 ERA, three saves) in 29 relief appearances. Career ERA: 4.47 as a starter, 3.40 in relief. . . . Career record of 14–10 in day games, 16–23 at night. . . . Opponents have hit better with runners on base than with bases empty in each of seven seasons in majors. . . . Hasn't allowed a home run to a left-hander since May 1986, when Ernie Whitt and Lloyd Moseby homered in consecutive innings. . . . That was six teams ago: two major and four minor league.

## Dennis Lamp

Throws Right

| Boston Red Sox | W–L | ERA | AB | H | HR | BB | SO | BA | SA | OBA |
|---|---|---|---|---|---|---|---|---|---|---|
| Season | 4-2 | 2.32 | 408 | 96 | 4 | 27 | 61 | .235 | .297 | .280 |
| vs. Left-Handers | | | 180 | 52 | 2 | 18 | 16 | .289 | .350 | .352 |
| vs. Right-Handers | | | 228 | 44 | 2 | 9 | 45 | .193 | .254 | .220 |
| Home | 3-1 | 2.93 | 266 | 63 | 4 | 13 | 34 | .237 | .312 | .270 |
| Road | 1-1 | 1.16 | 142 | 33 | 0 | 14 | 27 | .232 | .268 | .297 |
| Grass | 4-2 | 2.31 | 378 | 86 | 4 | 24 | 56 | .228 | .286 | .270 |
| Artificial Turf | 0-0 | 2.57 | 30 | 10 | 0 | 3 | 5 | .333 | .433 | .394 |
| April | 0-0 | 2.16 | 32 | 8 | 0 | 3 | 6 | .250 | .250 | .314 |
| May | 0-0 | 3.18 | 65 | 20 | 1 | 5 | 9 | .308 | .415 | .352 |
| June | 0-1 | 4.29 | 79 | 21 | 1 | 9 | 9 | .266 | .329 | .337 |
| July | 1-0 | 2.70 | 47 | 10 | 0 | 2 | 4 | .213 | .234 | .235 |
| August | 2-0 | 1.24 | 103 | 24 | 1 | 1 | 17 | .233 | .301 | .238 |
| Sept./Oct. | 1-1 | 1.14 | 82 | 13 | 1 | 7 | 16 | .159 | .220 | .225 |
| Leading Off Inn. | | | 93 | 19 | 1 | 7 | 13 | .204 | .258 | .260 |
| Runners On | | | 167 | 44 | 2 | 14 | 18 | .263 | .311 | .312 |
| Runners/Scor. Pos. | | | 115 | 27 | 1 | 12 | 15 | .235 | .270 | .295 |
| Runners On/2 Out | | | 70 | 11 | 0 | 6 | 9 | .157 | .157 | .224 |
| Scor. Pos./2 Out | | | 52 | 8 | 0 | 4 | 8 | .154 | .154 | .214 |
| Late Inning Pressure | | | 62 | 18 | 1 | 4 | 6 | .290 | .371 | .328 |
| Leading Off | | | 17 | 7 | 0 | 1 | 1 | .412 | .471 | .444 |
| Runners On | | | 25 | 9 | 1 | 2 | 2 | .360 | .520 | .393 |
| Runners/Scor. Pos. | | | 20 | 6 | 1 | 2 | 2 | .300 | .450 | .348 |
| First 9 Batters | | | 305 | 65 | 2 | 20 | 46 | .213 | .249 | .258 |
| Second 9 Batters | | | 95 | 29 | 2 | 7 | 15 | .305 | .442 | .353 |
| All Batters Thereafter | | | 8 | 2 | 0 | 0 | 0 | .250 | .375 | .250 |

Loves to face: Lance Parrish (.128, 5-for-39, 1 HR, 16 SO)
Hates to face: Carney Lansford (.455, 10-for-22, 1 HR)
Ground outs-to-air outs ratio: 1.97 last season, 2.29 for career. . . . Additional statistics: 12 double-play ground outs in 76 opportunities, 11 doubles, 1 triple in 112.1 innings last season. . . . Has appeared in 88 games, all in relief, in his two seasons with Boston, after starting at least one game in each of the previous 10 seasons. . . . One of three major league relievers to average more than 10 batters per appearance (minimum: 20 games). . . . Opposing base runners stole 23 bases in 28 attempts. . . . Career record of 11–0 vs. the Tigers is the best mark of any active pitcher against any club. . . . Opposing left-handers have out-hit right-handers by at least 40 points in five of the last seven seasons.

## Dave LaPoint

Throws Left

| New York Yankees | W–L | ERA | AB | H | HR | BB | SO | BA | SA | OBA |
|---|---|---|---|---|---|---|---|---|---|---|
| Season | 6-9 | 5.62 | 470 | 146 | 12 | 45 | 51 | .311 | .481 | .370 |
| vs. Left-Handers | | | 86 | 28 | 4 | 8 | 6 | .326 | .535 | .389 |
| vs. Right-Handers | | | 384 | 118 | 8 | 37 | 45 | .307 | .469 | .366 |
| Home | 3-3 | 4.60 | 192 | 55 | 5 | 20 | 21 | .286 | .427 | .355 |
| Road | 3-6 | 6.35 | 278 | 91 | 7 | 25 | 30 | .327 | .518 | .381 |
| Grass | 5-7 | 5.52 | 377 | 118 | 12 | 35 | 40 | .313 | .491 | .371 |
| Artificial Turf | 1-2 | 6.04 | 93 | 28 | 0 | 10 | 11 | .301 | .441 | .369 |
| April | 3-1 | 4.60 | 119 | 31 | 4 | 10 | 16 | .261 | .437 | .323 |
| May | 2-2 | 5.97 | 124 | 36 | 5 | 19 | 14 | .290 | .484 | .382 |
| June | 1-3 | 5.77 | 149 | 53 | 0 | 9 | 10 | .356 | .470 | .391 |
| July | 0-3 | 6.19 | 67 | 22 | 3 | 6 | 10 | .328 | .567 | .378 |
| August | 0-0 | 7.71 | 11 | 4 | 0 | 1 | 1 | .364 | .545 | .417 |
| Sept./Oct. | | | 0 | 0 | 0 | 0 | 0 | — | — | — |
| Leading Off Inn. | | | 109 | 33 | 5 | 15 | 10 | .303 | .541 | .387 |
| Runners On | | | 211 | 71 | 2 | 21 | 20 | .336 | .464 | .395 |
| Runners/Scor. Pos. | | | 108 | 35 | 1 | 14 | 10 | .324 | .444 | .398 |
| Runners On/2 Out | | | 84 | 26 | 1 | 13 | 9 | .310 | .405 | .402 |
| Scor. Pos./2 Out | | | 56 | 13 | 0 | 9 | 6 | .232 | .268 | .338 |
| Late Inning Pressure | | | 20 | 10 | 0 | 2 | 4 | .500 | .600 | .565 |
| Leading Off | | | 7 | 4 | 0 | 0 | 1 | .571 | .571 | .571 |
| Runners On | | | 8 | 4 | 0 | 2 | 1 | .500 | .625 | .636 |
| Runners/Scor. Pos. | | | 3 | 1 | 0 | 0 | 1 | .333 | .333 | .500 |
| First 9 Batters | | | 157 | 46 | 4 | 18 | 18 | .293 | .452 | .365 |
| Second 9 Batters | | | 161 | 45 | 4 | 12 | 22 | .280 | .422 | .328 |
| All Batters Thereafter | | | 152 | 55 | 4 | 15 | 11 | .362 | .572 | .420 |

Loves to face: Mark McGwire (.067, 1-for-15)
Hates to face: Ruben Sierra (.435, 10-for-23, 1 HR)
Ground outs-to-air outs ratio: 0.95 last season, 1.27 for career. . . . Additional statistics: 12 double-play ground outs in 110 opportunities, 38 doubles, 3 triples in 113.2 innings last season. . . . Allowed 16 first-inning runs in 20 starts. Hasn't allowed a first-inning home run in any of his last 39 starts. . . . Batting support: 4.30 runs per start. . . . Allowed 11.6 hits per nine innings, highest by a Yankees pitcher since 1932, when Herb Pennock allowed 11.8 per nine. . . . Only two other players in major league history played in both the American and National Leagues in each of three consecutive seasons, as LaPoint did from 1986 through 1988: Sal Maglie (four years, 1955–58) and Dal Maxvill (1972–74).

## Terry Leach

Throws Right

| Kansas City Royals | W–L | ERA | AB | H | HR | BB | SO | BA | SA | OBA |
|---|---|---|---|---|---|---|---|---|---|---|
| Season | 5-6 | 4.15 | 281 | 78 | 4 | 36 | 34 | .278 | .381 | .357 |
| vs. Left-Handers | | | 137 | 42 | 2 | 21 | 10 | .307 | .423 | .391 |
| vs. Right-Handers | | | 144 | 36 | 2 | 15 | 24 | .250 | .340 | .323 |
| Home | 3-0 | 2.70 | 147 | 37 | 2 | 14 | 17 | .252 | .374 | .311 |
| Road | 2-6 | 5.88 | 134 | 41 | 2 | 22 | 17 | .306 | .388 | .405 |
| Grass | 1-6 | 6.67 | 119 | 37 | 2 | 21 | 16 | .311 | .403 | .415 |
| Artificial Turf | 4-0 | 2.45 | 162 | 41 | 2 | 15 | 18 | .253 | .364 | .311 |
| April | | | 0 | 0 | 0 | 0 | 0 | — | — | — |
| May | | | 0 | 0 | 0 | 0 | 0 | — | — | — |
| June | 1-2 | 4.70 | 57 | 18 | 0 | 8 | 1 | .316 | .404 | .403 |
| July | 1-1 | 4.63 | 90 | 25 | 3 | 10 | 14 | .278 | .444 | .347 |
| August | 3-0 | 0.00 | 61 | 9 | 0 | 5 | 8 | .148 | .164 | .209 |
| Sept./Oct. | 0-3 | 7.41 | 73 | 26 | 1 | 13 | 11 | .356 | .466 | .448 |
| Leading Off Inn. | | | 62 | 15 | 1 | 10 | 12 | .242 | .306 | .356 |
| Runners On | | | 136 | 43 | 2 | 19 | 11 | .316 | .426 | .390 |
| Runners/Scor. Pos. | | | 89 | 30 | 1 | 15 | 9 | .337 | .449 | .417 |
| Runners On/2 Out | | | 55 | 14 | 1 | 10 | 4 | .255 | .345 | .369 |
| Scor. Pos./2 Out | | | 40 | 11 | 1 | 9 | 3 | .275 | .375 | .408 |
| Late Inning Pressure | | | 31 | 3 | 0 | 9 | 7 | .097 | .129 | .317 |
| Leading Off | | | 8 | 0 | 0 | 3 | 3 | .000 | .000 | .333 |
| Runners On | | | 13 | 3 | 0 | 4 | 0 | .231 | .308 | .412 |
| Runners/Scor. Pos. | | | 7 | 1 | 0 | 4 | 0 | .143 | .143 | .455 |
| First 9 Batters | | | 178 | 47 | 1 | 28 | 23 | .264 | .343 | .359 |
| Second 9 Batters | | | 84 | 23 | 2 | 7 | 8 | .274 | .393 | .333 |
| All Batters Thereafter | | | 19 | 8 | 1 | 1 | 3 | .421 | .684 | .450 |

Loves to face: Steve Sax (.105, 2-for-19, 5 SO)
Hates to face: Fred Manrique (.667, 6-for-9)
Ground outs-to-air outs ratio: 1.15 last season, 1.53 for career. . . . Additional statistics: 6 double-play ground outs in 67 opportunities, 13 doubles, 2 triples in 73.2 innings last season. . . . Inherited 20 runners, stranded only nine (45%), 2d-lowest average in A.L. (minimum: 20 runners). . . . Opponents' batting average in LIP Situations (both leagues combined) was lowest in majors. . . . Allowed seven hits in 15 at-bats with the bases loaded. Career average: .349 (15-for-43). . . . Career records: 15–2 on artificial surfaces, 14–13 on grass fields; 5–11 in day games, 24–4 at night. Undefeated in 13 decisions in night games on artificial turf. . . . Career averages: ground-ball hitters, .234; fly-ballers, .281.

## Charlie Leibrandt

Throws Left

| Kansas City Royals | W–L | ERA | AB | H | HR | BB | SO | BA | SA | OBA |
|---|---|---|---|---|---|---|---|---|---|---|
| Season | 5-11 | 5.14 | 644 | 196 | 13 | 54 | 73 | .304 | .439 | .358 |
| vs. Left-Handers | | | 130 | 44 | 0 | 5 | 7 | .338 | .431 | .365 |
| vs. Right-Handers | | | 514 | 152 | 13 | 49 | 66 | .296 | .442 | .356 |
| Home | 3-3 | 3.71 | 269 | 80 | 3 | 21 | 22 | .297 | .401 | .349 |
| Road | 2-8 | 6.19 | 375 | 116 | 10 | 33 | 51 | .309 | .467 | .364 |
| Grass | 2-7 | 6.94 | 288 | 91 | 9 | 26 | 43 | .316 | .500 | .369 |
| Artificial Turf | 3-4 | 3.76 | 356 | 105 | 4 | 28 | 30 | .295 | .390 | .349 |
| April | 2-2 | 2.72 | 157 | 38 | 2 | 13 | 15 | .242 | .306 | .300 |
| May | 1-3 | 5.19 | 141 | 43 | 3 | 11 | 12 | .305 | .461 | .357 |
| June | 2-3 | 3.25 | 169 | 43 | 3 | 10 | 23 | .254 | .367 | .298 |
| July | 0-2 | 13.50 | 76 | 36 | 3 | 11 | 4 | .474 | .750 | .528 |
| August | 0-0 | 9.26 | 52 | 22 | 1 | 5 | 9 | .423 | .577 | .474 |
| Sept./Oct. | 0-1 | 6.00 | 49 | 14 | 1 | 4 | 10 | .286 | .429 | .340 |
| Leading Off Inn. | | | 159 | 44 | 3 | 11 | 22 | .277 | .415 | .327 |
| Runners On | | | 292 | 91 | 6 | 22 | 28 | .312 | .452 | .355 |
| Runners/Scor. Pos. | | | 166 | 43 | 1 | 16 | 16 | .259 | .367 | .317 |
| Runners On/2 Out | | | 111 | 27 | 3 | 11 | 11 | .243 | .351 | .311 |
| Scor. Pos./2 Out | | | 70 | 14 | 0 | 8 | 7 | .200 | .229 | .282 |
| Late Inning Pressure | | | 48 | 13 | 0 | 9 | 3 | .271 | .313 | .386 |
| Leading Off | | | 11 | 2 | 0 | 2 | 1 | .182 | .182 | .308 |
| Runners On | | | 23 | 5 | 0 | 6 | 1 | .217 | .261 | .379 |
| Runners/Scor. Pos. | | | 16 | 3 | 0 | 4 | 0 | .188 | .250 | .350 |
| First 9 Batters | | | 249 | 72 | 7 | 25 | 35 | .289 | .454 | .354 |
| Second 9 Batters | | | 201 | 74 | 3 | 12 | 17 | .368 | .512 | .400 |
| All Batters Thereafter | | | 194 | 50 | 3 | 17 | 21 | .258 | .345 | .321 |

Loves to face: Mike Pagliarulo (.118, 2-for-17, 6 SO)
Hates to face: Kirk Gibson (.500, 6-for-12, 1 HR)
Ground outs-to-air outs ratio: 0.96 last season, 1.18 for career.... Additional statistics: 15 double-play ground outs in 138 opportunities, 36 doubles, 6 triples in 161.0 innings last season.... Allowed 18 first-inning runs in 27 starts.... Batting support: 4.85 runs per start.... Hasn't allowed a home run to a left-hander since July 15, 1988 (Wade Boggs).... Career records: 32–35 on grass fields, 60–43 on artificial turf. ... Opponents have had a lower average with runners in scoring position than in other at-bats in each of the last seven seasons, matching Dave Stewart for the longest streak over the last 15 years.... One of the 10 best one-for-one trades of the 1980s: Leibrandt from Reds to Royals for Bob Tufts.

## Bill Long

Throws Right

| Chicago White Sox | W–L | ERA | AB | H | HR | BB | SO | BA | SA | OBA |
|---|---|---|---|---|---|---|---|---|---|---|
| Season | 5-5 | 3.92 | 381 | 101 | 8 | 37 | 51 | .265 | .407 | .332 |
| vs. Left-Handers | | | 176 | 47 | 4 | 16 | 20 | .267 | .432 | .327 |
| vs. Right-Handers | | | 205 | 54 | 4 | 21 | 31 | .263 | .385 | .336 |
| Home | 2-2 | 4.17 | 159 | 43 | 4 | 12 | 19 | .270 | .434 | .322 |
| Road | 3-3 | 3.75 | 222 | 58 | 4 | 25 | 32 | .261 | .387 | .339 |
| Grass | 4-4 | 3.81 | 291 | 80 | 7 | 29 | 36 | .275 | .419 | .343 |
| Artificial Turf | 1-1 | 4.30 | 90 | 21 | 1 | 8 | 15 | .233 | .367 | .293 |
| April | 1-3 | 8.31 | 96 | 32 | 1 | 9 | 13 | .333 | .438 | .402 |
| May | 1-2 | 3.86 | 80 | 20 | 4 | 6 | 7 | .250 | .525 | .302 |
| June | 1-0 | 2.45 | 42 | 11 | 1 | 2 | 4 | .262 | .333 | .311 |
| July | 1-0 | 2.70 | 24 | 7 | 0 | 8 | 0 | .292 | .458 | .471 |
| August | 1-0 | 3.38 | 64 | 16 | 1 | 4 | 10 | .250 | .375 | .290 |
| Sept./Oct. | 0-0 | 1.21 | 75 | 15 | 1 | 8 | 17 | .200 | .293 | .264 |
| Leading Off Inn. | | | 86 | 19 | 1 | 6 | 14 | .221 | .384 | .287 |
| Runners On | | | 182 | 46 | 5 | 22 | 19 | .253 | .379 | .324 |
| Runners/Scor. Pos. | | | 117 | 29 | 3 | 17 | 14 | .248 | .376 | .329 |
| Runners On/2 Out | | | 81 | 20 | 1 | 10 | 12 | .247 | .358 | .330 |
| Scor. Pos./2 Out | | | 58 | 11 | 0 | 7 | 11 | .190 | .259 | .277 |
| Late Inning Pressure | | | 29 | 4 | 1 | 6 | 4 | .138 | .345 | .286 |
| Leading Off | | | 10 | 0 | 0 | 1 | 1 | .000 | .000 | .091 |
| Runners On | | | 6 | 0 | 0 | 3 | 0 | .000 | .000 | .333 |
| Runners/Scor. Pos. | | | 4 | 0 | 0 | 2 | 0 | .000 | .000 | .333 |
| First 9 Batters | | | 195 | 51 | 3 | 22 | 26 | .262 | .369 | .333 |
| Second 9 Batters | | | 128 | 33 | 4 | 7 | 21 | .258 | .453 | .307 |
| All Batters Thereafter | | | 58 | 17 | 1 | 8 | 4 | .293 | .431 | .379 |

Loves to face: Claudell Washington (.083, 1-for-12)
Hates to face: Wade Boggs (.625, 10-for-16)
Ground outs-to-air outs ratio: 1.07 last season, 1.15 for career.... Additional statistics: 7 double-play ground outs in 82 opportunities, 20 doubles, 5 triples in 98.2 innings last season.... Record of 3–5 (5.44 ERA) in eight starts, 2–0 (2.75 ERA, one save) in 22 relief appearances.... He averaged 10.86 batters faced per relief appearance, highest average in majors (minimum: 20 games).... Inherited at least one runner in 18 of his 22 relief appearances. Stranded only 19 of 31 runners (61%).... A leap-day baby, born February 29, 1960, making him the first player ever to win 20 games before his eighth birthday. Take that, Doc Gooden!...The most prominent of baseball's eight leap-day babies: Al Rosen.

## Kirk McCaskill

Throws Right

| California Angels | W–L | ERA | AB | H | HR | BB | SO | BA | SA | OBA |
|---|---|---|---|---|---|---|---|---|---|---|
| Season | 15-10 | 2.93 | 795 | 202 | 16 | 59 | 107 | .254 | .357 | .307 |
| vs. Left-Handers | | | 401 | 101 | 10 | 26 | 52 | .252 | .369 | .297 |
| vs. Right-Handers | | | 394 | 101 | 6 | 33 | 55 | .256 | .345 | .316 |
| Home | 10-4 | 3.12 | 427 | 105 | 12 | 28 | 61 | .246 | .382 | .295 |
| Road | 5-6 | 2.71 | 368 | 97 | 4 | 31 | 46 | .264 | .329 | .319 |
| Grass | 13-9 | 2.93 | 689 | 172 | 14 | 51 | 96 | .250 | .356 | .303 |
| Artificial Turf | 2-1 | 2.89 | 106 | 30 | 2 | 8 | 11 | .283 | .368 | .333 |
| April | 4-1 | 0.74 | 126 | 21 | 0 | 10 | 15 | .167 | .183 | .228 |
| May | 2-0 | 2.23 | 140 | 37 | 1 | 10 | 18 | .264 | .336 | .313 |
| June | 2-3 | 7.71 | 99 | 34 | 8 | 8 | 16 | .343 | .646 | .389 |
| July | 2-2 | 3.38 | 114 | 32 | 2 | 11 | 10 | .281 | .351 | .341 |
| August | 4-2 | 2.34 | 162 | 42 | 1 | 6 | 22 | .259 | .321 | .290 |
| Sept./Oct. | 1-2 | 3.02 | 154 | 36 | 4 | 14 | 26 | .234 | .377 | .302 |
| Leading Off Inn. | | | 207 | 58 | 4 | 14 | 28 | .280 | .396 | .329 |
| Runners On | | | 319 | 75 | 5 | 27 | 41 | .235 | .301 | .291 |
| Runners/Scor. Pos. | | | 172 | 38 | 3 | 15 | 31 | .221 | .291 | .277 |
| Runners On/2 Out | | | 119 | 25 | 1 | 10 | 20 | .210 | .261 | .271 |
| Scor. Pos./2 Out | | | 70 | 12 | 1 | 6 | 16 | .171 | .243 | .237 |
| Late Inning Pressure | | | 70 | 13 | 2 | 5 | 8 | .186 | .314 | .240 |
| Leading Off | | | 23 | 3 | 1 | 1 | 3 | .130 | .261 | .167 |
| Runners On | | | 15 | 3 | 0 | 2 | 1 | .200 | .200 | .294 |
| Runners/Scor. Pos. | | | 7 | 2 | 0 | 2 | 0 | .286 | .286 | .444 |
| First 9 Batters | | | 266 | 76 | 6 | 18 | 43 | .286 | .383 | .331 |
| Second 9 Batters | | | 259 | 66 | 4 | 19 | 34 | .255 | .344 | .308 |
| All Batters Thereafter | | | 270 | 60 | 6 | 22 | 30 | .222 | .344 | .281 |

Loves to face: Scott Fletcher (.043, 1-for-23)
Hates to face: Tony Fernandez (.514, 18-for-35, 3 HR)
Ground outs-to-air outs ratio: 1.13 last season, 1.07 for career.... Additional statistics: 32 double-play ground outs (most in majors) in 169 opportunities, 26 doubles, 4 triples in 212.0 innings last season.... Allowed 19 first-inning runs in 32 starts. ERA of 5.34 in the first was his highest in any inning.... Batting support: 3.72 runs per start.... Interesting pattern: Has decreased his ERA by 1.25 or more and increased his innings by at least 50 for two consecutive seasons. The only other starter of the past 30 years to do that from a base of 50+ innings: Doyle Alexander (1983–84).... Grew up dreaming of a hat trick against the Canadians. Allowed three HR in 1.2 innings vs. Toronto in June. Joke of the gods.

## Bob McClure

Throws Left

| California Angels | W–L | ERA | AB | H | HR | BB | SO | BA | SA | OBA |
|---|---|---|---|---|---|---|---|---|---|---|
| Season | 6-1 | 1.55 | 184 | 39 | 2 | 15 | 36 | .212 | .283 | .270 |
| vs. Left-Handers | | | 65 | 10 | 1 | 8 | 11 | .154 | .215 | .237 |
| vs. Right-Handers | | | 119 | 29 | 1 | 7 | 25 | .244 | .319 | .289 |
| Home | 4-0 | 1.88 | 88 | 21 | 1 | 4 | 14 | .239 | .307 | .274 |
| Road | 2-1 | 1.27 | 96 | 18 | 1 | 11 | 22 | .188 | .260 | .266 |
| Grass | 5-0 | 1.64 | 158 | 37 | 2 | 14 | 30 | .234 | .310 | .294 |
| Artificial Turf | 1-1 | 1.08 | 26 | 2 | 0 | 1 | 6 | .077 | .115 | .111 |
| April | 1-0 | 1.13 | 30 | 6 | 1 | 0 | 4 | .200 | .300 | .226 |
| May | 1-0 | 0.00 | 12 | 1 | 0 | 1 | 2 | .083 | .167 | .154 |
| June | 0-0 | 3.24 | 28 | 7 | 0 | 3 | 6 | .250 | .286 | .313 |
| July | 1-1 | 3.00 | 23 | 6 | 1 | 2 | 6 | .261 | .435 | .320 |
| August | 1-0 | 0.77 | 38 | 7 | 0 | 1 | 7 | .184 | .211 | .195 |
| Sept./Oct. | 2-0 | 1.26 | 53 | 12 | 0 | 8 | 11 | .226 | .283 | .323 |
| Leading Off Inn. | | | 42 | 9 | 0 | 1 | 5 | .214 | .262 | .233 |
| Runners On | | | 88 | 16 | 2 | 11 | 19 | .182 | .295 | .262 |
| Runners/Scor. Pos. | | | 46 | 10 | 1 | 7 | 8 | .217 | .304 | .298 |
| Runners On/2 Out | | | 44 | 8 | 1 | 6 | 9 | .182 | .250 | .280 |
| Scor. Pos./2 Out | | | 28 | 6 | 1 | 3 | 5 | .214 | .321 | .290 |
| Late Inning Pressure | | | 94 | 17 | 1 | 7 | 16 | .181 | .245 | .233 |
| Leading Off | | | 24 | 4 | 0 | 1 | 2 | .167 | .208 | .200 |
| Runners On | | | 36 | 6 | 1 | 6 | 6 | .167 | .278 | .273 |
| Runners/Scor. Pos. | | | 22 | 3 | 0 | 5 | 1 | .136 | .136 | .276 |
| First 9 Batters | | | 173 | 36 | 2 | 14 | 35 | .208 | .283 | .266 |
| Second 9 Batters | | | 11 | 3 | 0 | 1 | 1 | .273 | .273 | .333 |
| All Batters Thereafter | | | 0 | 0 | 0 | 0 | 0 | — | — | — |

Loves to face: Kent Hrbek (0-for-12)
Hates to face: Chet Lemon (.556, 10-for-18)
Ground outs-to-air outs ratio: 1.05 last season, 0.81 for career.... Additional statistics: 5 double-play ground outs in 38 opportunities, 5 doubles, 1 triple in 52.1 innings last season.... Lowest ERA since he debuted in the majors with 15 scoreless innings for the 1975 Kansas City Royals.... Called on to face a single batter 13 times, most in the majors. Summmoned to protect a lead in only one of his last 13 appearances. . . Stranded 43 of 50 inherited runners (86%), highest mark in A.L. (minimum: 50 runners).... Opposing left-handed batters have hit below .200 in seven of 15 seasons.... Opponents have hit for a higher average in home games than road games in each of last five seasons.

## Lance McCullers

Throws Right

| New York Yankees | W–L | ERA | AB | H | HR | BB | SO | BA | SA | OBA |
|---|---|---|---|---|---|---|---|---|---|---|
| Season | 4-3 | 4.57 | 325 | 83 | 9 | 37 | 82 | .255 | .418 | .332 |
| vs. Left-Handers | | | 143 | 36 | 3 | 23 | 28 | .252 | .392 | .357 |
| vs. Right-Handers | | | 182 | 47 | 6 | 14 | 54 | .258 | .440 | .312 |
| Home | 2-1 | 5.13 | 199 | 51 | 6 | 22 | 53 | .256 | .417 | .333 |
| Road | 2-2 | 3.66 | 126 | 32 | 3 | 15 | 29 | .254 | .421 | .331 |
| Grass | 3-3 | 4.81 | 277 | 69 | 7 | 33 | 72 | .249 | .404 | .330 |
| Artificial Turf | 1-0 | 3.09 | 48 | 14 | 2 | 4 | 10 | .292 | .500 | .346 |
| April | 0-0 | 2.45 | 40 | 9 | 2 | 7 | 14 | .225 | .400 | .327 |
| May | 1-1 | 3.75 | 46 | 12 | 1 | 5 | 11 | .261 | .413 | .340 |
| June | 2-1 | 6.27 | 75 | 21 | 1 | 7 | 15 | .280 | .413 | .345 |
| July | 0-1 | 9.00 | 41 | 11 | 3 | 7 | 10 | .268 | .561 | .388 |
| August | 1-0 | 2.49 | 79 | 18 | 1 | 8 | 22 | .228 | .354 | .295 |
| Sept./Oct. | 0-0 | 4.35 | 44 | 12 | 1 | 3 | 10 | .273 | .432 | .319 |
| Leading Off Inn. | | | 67 | 17 | 0 | 8 | 17 | .254 | .343 | .342 |
| Runners On | | | 152 | 43 | 7 | 21 | 38 | .283 | .480 | .367 |
| Runners/Scor. Pos. | | | 106 | 31 | 5 | 14 | 26 | .292 | .453 | .370 |
| Runners On/2 Out | | | 70 | 16 | 2 | 9 | 16 | .229 | .329 | .316 |
| Scor. Pos./2 Out | | | 55 | 13 | 2 | 5 | 12 | .236 | .364 | .300 |
| Late Inning Pressure | | | 104 | 26 | 3 | 14 | 33 | .250 | .404 | .347 |
| Leading Off | | | 23 | 6 | 0 | 3 | 9 | .261 | .348 | .370 |
| Runners On | | | 48 | 14 | 3 | 8 | 13 | .292 | .542 | .397 |
| Runners/Scor. Pos. | | | 37 | 10 | 2 | 6 | 9 | .270 | .459 | .378 |
| First 9 Batters | | | 258 | 64 | 5 | 31 | 74 | .248 | .388 | .330 |
| Second 9 Batters | | | 58 | 17 | 4 | 6 | 8 | .293 | .569 | .359 |
| All Batters Thereafter | | | 9 | 2 | 0 | 0 | 0 | .222 | .333 | .222 |

Loves to face: Danny Heep (0-for-10)
Hates to face: Dave Parker (.500, 6-for-12)
Ground outs-to-air outs ratio: 0.58 last season, 0.86 for career. . . . Additional statistics: 0 double-play ground outs in 71 opportunities, most opportunities without a GIDP of any major league pitcher, 20 doubles, 3 triples in 84.2 innings last season. . . . Opponents stole 11 bases in 12 attempts. . . . Opponents have hit .188 (13-for-69, one HR) with the bases loaded. But McCullers has walked eight of 84 batters he's faced in those situations. . . . Career averages are .246 by opposing ground-ball hitters, .209 by fly-ballers—a margin far greater than that between left-handed batters (.232) and right-handers (.223). . . . Has allowed more HR to ground-ballers (23) than fly-ballers (20). (See Mike Jackson for related note.)

## Bob Milacki

Throws Right

| Baltimore Orioles | W–L | ERA | AB | H | HR | BB | SO | BA | SA | OBA |
|---|---|---|---|---|---|---|---|---|---|---|
| Season | 14-12 | 3.74 | 919 | 233 | 21 | 88 | 113 | .254 | .373 | .318 |
| vs. Left-Handers | | | 466 | 118 | 10 | 47 | 57 | .253 | .371 | .322 |
| vs. Right-Handers | | | 453 | 115 | 11 | 41 | 56 | .254 | .375 | .315 |
| Home | 7-7 | 3.53 | 481 | 120 | 9 | 52 | 62 | .249 | .349 | .320 |
| Road | 7-5 | 3.98 | 438 | 113 | 12 | 36 | 51 | .258 | .400 | .316 |
| Grass | 12-11 | 3.31 | 765 | 184 | 17 | 75 | 97 | .241 | .345 | .306 |
| Artificial Turf | 2-1 | 6.19 | 154 | 49 | 4 | 13 | 16 | .318 | .513 | .379 |
| April | 1-1 | 4.20 | 112 | 28 | 1 | 11 | 9 | .250 | .321 | .323 |
| May | 1-4 | 3.92 | 160 | 41 | 2 | 21 | 19 | .256 | .338 | .343 |
| June | 2-3 | 4.66 | 149 | 43 | 5 | 12 | 23 | .289 | .430 | .333 |
| July | 1-1 | 4.20 | 124 | 36 | 6 | 9 | 15 | .290 | .540 | .343 |
| August | 4-2 | 3.42 | 172 | 33 | 4 | 12 | 27 | .192 | .308 | .243 |
| Sept./Oct. | 5-1 | 2.70 | 202 | 52 | 3 | 23 | 20 | .257 | .342 | .332 |
| Leading Off Inn. | | | 237 | 57 | 6 | 23 | 32 | .241 | .371 | .310 |
| Runners On | | | 364 | 95 | 9 | 31 | 40 | .261 | .385 | .314 |
| Runners/Scor. Pos. | | | 183 | 46 | 5 | 20 | 23 | .251 | .388 | .316 |
| Runners On/2 Out | | | 147 | 33 | 4 | 22 | 16 | .224 | .333 | .325 |
| Scor. Pos./2 Out | | | 82 | 16 | 3 | 16 | 12 | .195 | .317 | .327 |
| Late Inning Pressure | | | 100 | 20 | 1 | 15 | 8 | .200 | .280 | .310 |
| Leading Off | | | 31 | 3 | 1 | 5 | 4 | .097 | .226 | .222 |
| Runners On | | | 31 | 6 | 0 | 3 | 2 | .194 | .258 | .265 |
| Runners/Scor. Pos. | | | 15 | 1 | 0 | 3 | 1 | .067 | .067 | .222 |
| First 9 Batters | | | 294 | 74 | 7 | 30 | 40 | .252 | .378 | .320 |
| Second 9 Batters | | | 285 | 73 | 7 | 24 | 36 | .256 | .379 | .313 |
| All Batters Thereafter | | | 340 | 86 | 7 | 34 | 37 | .253 | .365 | .321 |

Loves to face: Alan Trammell (.056, 1-for-18)
Hates to face: Paul Molitor (.556, 5-for-9)
Ground outs-to-air outs ratio: 1.04 last season, 1.10 for career. . . . Additional statistics: 29 double-play ground outs (2d most in A.L.) in 169 opportunities, 35 doubles, 6 triples in 243.0 innings last season. . . . Allowed 21 first-inning runs in 36 starts. . . . Batting support: 3.94 runs per start. . . . Only A.L. rookie pitcher to start 30 or more games, and one of three in majors with two shutouts. Others: Jim Abbott and Ramon Martinez. . . . Allowed two or more HR in seven games, most in A.L. . . . Career record of 7–1 in September. . . Opponents' career BA: .228 on grass, .318 on synthetics. . . . Opponents have only one hit in 18 career at-bats with runners in scoring position in Late-Inning Pressure Situations.

## Greg Minton

Throws Right

| California Angels | W–L | ERA | AB | H | HR | BB | SO | BA | SA | OBA |
|---|---|---|---|---|---|---|---|---|---|---|
| Season | 4-3 | 2.20 | 331 | 76 | 4 | 37 | 42 | .230 | .299 | .310 |
| vs. Left-Handers | | | 147 | 31 | 0 | 15 | 22 | .211 | .272 | .282 |
| vs. Right-Handers | | | 184 | 45 | 4 | 22 | 20 | .245 | .321 | .332 |
| Home | 4-2 | 1.97 | 190 | 46 | 3 | 16 | 27 | .242 | .321 | .308 |
| Road | 0-1 | 2.50 | 141 | 30 | 1 | 21 | 15 | .213 | .270 | .313 |
| Grass | 4-2 | 1.79 | 297 | 68 | 3 | 32 | 40 | .229 | .290 | .308 |
| Artificial Turf | 0-1 | 5.59 | 34 | 8 | 1 | 5 | 2 | .235 | .382 | .325 |
| April | 1-0 | 1.69 | 62 | 17 | 0 | 3 | 10 | .274 | .306 | .308 |
| May | 0-0 | 0.57 | 51 | 8 | 0 | 11 | 6 | .157 | .176 | .302 |
| June | 0-2 | 3.65 | 49 | 14 | 1 | 6 | 4 | .286 | .388 | .375 |
| July | 0-0 | 5.68 | 49 | 12 | 0 | 5 | 4 | .245 | .367 | .315 |
| August | 1-1 | 2.30 | 61 | 15 | 3 | 2 | 11 | .246 | .393 | .270 |
| Sept./Oct. | 2-0 | 0.51 | 59 | 10 | 0 | 10 | 7 | .169 | .169 | .300 |
| Leading Off Inn. | | | 73 | 11 | 0 | 4 | 9 | .151 | .151 | .195 |
| Runners On | | | 162 | 45 | 1 | 19 | 20 | .278 | .340 | .359 |
| Runners/Scor. Pos. | | | 103 | 24 | 0 | 13 | 17 | .233 | .291 | .322 |
| Runners On/2 Out | | | 59 | 12 | 0 | 13 | 7 | .203 | .220 | .347 |
| Scor. Pos./2 Out | | | 42 | 5 | 0 | 9 | 6 | .119 | .119 | .275 |
| Late Inning Pressure | | | 159 | 27 | 3 | 25 | 20 | .170 | .245 | .285 |
| Leading Off | | | 41 | 4 | 0 | 3 | 5 | .098 | .098 | .159 |
| Runners On | | | 63 | 13 | 0 | 13 | 7 | .206 | .254 | .346 |
| Runners/Scor. Pos. | | | 36 | 3 | 0 | 11 | 7 | .083 | .139 | .292 |
| First 9 Batters | | | 309 | 69 | 4 | 35 | 37 | .223 | .294 | .305 |
| Second 9 Batters | | | 22 | 7 | 0 | 2 | 5 | .318 | .364 | .375 |
| All Batters Thereafter | | | 0 | 0 | 0 | 0 | 0 | — | — | — |

Loves to face: Carlton Fisk (.091, 1-for-11, 5 SO)
Hates to face: Dave Parker (.522, 12-for-23, 5 2B)
Ground outs-to-air outs ratio: 2.03 last season, 2.37 for career. . . . Additional statistics: 11 double-play ground outs in 86 opportunities, 7 doubles, 2 triples in 90.0 innings last season. . . . He and Nolan Ryan are the only two pitchers to have an ERA of under 4.00 in every season since 1979. . . . Leads active pitchers, and ranks sixth on all-time list, with 130 intentional walks. Top five: Kent Tekulve (179), Gaylord Perry (164), Gene Garber (155), Steve Carlton (150), Lindy McDaniel (136). . . . Career average of one home run allowed per 26.6 innings is best among active pitchers (minimum: 1000 innings). . . . Opponents' batting average in Late-Inning Pressure Situations was the lowest of his 15-year career.

## Jeff Montgomery

Throws Right

| Kansas City Royals | W–L | ERA | AB | H | HR | BB | SO | BA | SA | OBA |
|---|---|---|---|---|---|---|---|---|---|---|
| Season | 7-3 | 1.37 | 334 | 66 | 3 | 25 | 94 | .198 | .251 | .257 |
| vs. Left-Handers | | | 152 | 32 | 2 | 11 | 30 | .211 | .270 | .264 |
| vs. Right-Handers | | | 182 | 34 | 1 | 14 | 64 | .187 | .236 | .251 |
| Home | 6-3 | 1.32 | 168 | 31 | 1 | 12 | 48 | .185 | .226 | .242 |
| Road | 1-0 | 1.42 | 166 | 35 | 2 | 13 | 46 | .211 | .277 | .272 |
| Grass | 1-0 | 1.09 | 121 | 24 | 1 | 9 | 32 | .198 | .240 | .260 |
| Artificial Turf | 6-3 | 1.53 | 213 | 42 | 2 | 16 | 62 | .197 | .258 | .255 |
| April | 2-1 | 3.27 | 40 | 8 | 1 | 4 | 7 | .200 | .350 | .267 |
| May | 4-0 | 0.96 | 68 | 12 | 1 | 0 | 18 | .176 | .235 | .176 |
| June | 0-0 | 1.04 | 63 | 13 | 0 | 9 | 22 | .206 | .222 | .306 |
| July | 1-1 | 0.86 | 72 | 15 | 0 | 4 | 22 | .208 | .208 | .250 |
| August | 0-0 | 1.29 | 53 | 9 | 1 | 2 | 19 | .170 | .283 | .214 |
| Sept./Oct. | 0-1 | 1.80 | 38 | 9 | 0 | 6 | 6 | .237 | .263 | .356 |
| Leading Off Inn. | | | 77 | 19 | 1 | 6 | 19 | .247 | .299 | .301 |
| Runners On | | | 152 | 25 | 1 | 10 | 43 | .164 | .217 | .220 |
| Runners/Scor. Pos. | | | 80 | 13 | 1 | 8 | 24 | .163 | .238 | .236 |
| Runners On/2 Out | | | 73 | 17 | 1 | 7 | 20 | .233 | .301 | .300 |
| Scor. Pos./2 Out | | | 44 | 9 | 1 | 6 | 14 | .205 | .295 | .300 |
| Late Inning Pressure | | | 189 | 40 | 2 | 12 | 59 | .212 | .280 | .261 |
| Leading Off | | | 44 | 12 | 1 | 2 | 10 | .273 | .364 | .304 |
| Runners On | | | 82 | 14 | 1 | 7 | 25 | .171 | .268 | .233 |
| Runners/Scor. Pos. | | | 44 | 8 | 1 | 6 | 14 | .182 | .318 | .275 |
| First 9 Batters | | | 316 | 64 | 3 | 25 | 91 | .203 | .259 | .265 |
| Second 9 Batters | | | 18 | 2 | 0 | 0 | 3 | .111 | .111 | .111 |
| All Batters Thereafter | | | 0 | 0 | 0 | 0 | 0 | — | — | — |

Loves to face: Jesse Barfield (0-for-7)
Hates to face: Jose Canseco (3-for-3, 1 2B, 1 HR)
Ground outs-to-air outs ratio: 1.21 last season, 1.19 for career. . . . Additional statistics: 5 double-play ground outs in 65 opportunities, 7 doubles, 1 triple in 92.0 innings last season. . . . Shared league lead for wins during May. . . . All seven wins were before the All-Star break; 16 of 18 saves were after the break. Collected those 16 saves in 18 opportunities. . . . Average of 3.29 extra-base hits allowed per 100 at-bats was best in A.L. Particularly impressive since Royals Stadium has increased the extra-base hits more than any park in the majors over the last five years. . . . Career batting average of .194 by opposing ground-ball hitters, .247 by fly-ballers.

## Mike Moore

Throws Right

| Oakland As | W–L | ERA | AB | H | HR | BB | SO | BA | SA | OBA |
|---|---|---|---|---|---|---|---|---|---|---|
| Season | 19-11 | 2.61 | 880 | 193 | 14 | 83 | 172 | .219 | .307 | .286 |
| vs. Left-Handers | | | 426 | 93 | 3 | 46 | 85 | .218 | .277 | .296 |
| vs. Right-Handers | | | 454 | 100 | 11 | 37 | 87 | .220 | .335 | .277 |
| Home | 10-4 | 2.02 | 440 | 89 | 5 | 48 | 91 | .202 | .270 | .280 |
| Road | 9-7 | 3.23 | 440 | 104 | 9 | 35 | 81 | .236 | .343 | .293 |
| Grass | 18-7 | 2.27 | 717 | 151 | 9 | 62 | 143 | .211 | .283 | .273 |
| Artificial Turf | 1-4 | 4.19 | 163 | 42 | 5 | 21 | 29 | .258 | .411 | .342 |
| April | 3-1 | 1.91 | 113 | 19 | 1 | 16 | 28 | .168 | .212 | .277 |
| May | 3-2 | 1.96 | 147 | 27 | 3 | 19 | 26 | .184 | .272 | .280 |
| June | 3-2 | 2.74 | 154 | 33 | 3 | 12 | 25 | .214 | .325 | .269 |
| July | 5-0 | 2.30 | 162 | 41 | 1 | 8 | 41 | .253 | .302 | .285 |
| August | 2-3 | 3.51 | 158 | 44 | 4 | 10 | 29 | .278 | .405 | .318 |
| Sept./Oct. | 3-3 | 3.10 | 146 | 29 | 2 | 18 | .23 | .199 | .295 | .287 |
| Leading Off Inn. | | | 231 | 41 | 4 | 18 | 49 | .177 | .264 | .240 |
| Runners On | | | 326 | 76 | 7 | 36 | 65 | .233 | .337 | .306 |
| Runners/Scor. Pos. | | | 164 | 38 | 5 | 19 | 33 | .232 | .372 | .302 |
| Runners On/2 Out | | | 144 | 37 | 1 | 18 | 30 | .257 | .313 | .344 |
| Scor. Pos./2 Out | | | 85 | 20 | 1 | 10 | 17 | .235 | .329 | .316 |
| Late Inning Pressure | | | 79 | 18 | 1 | 7 | 16 | .228 | .367 | .287 |
| Leading Off | | | 24 | 6 | 0 | 0 | 5 | .250 | .417 | .250 |
| Runners On | | | 22 | 7 | 0 | 5 | 4 | .318 | .455 | .429 |
| Runners/Scor. Pos. | | | 19 | 5 | 0 | 2 | 4 | .263 | .421 | .318 |
| First 9 Batters | | | 284 | 57 | 4 | 26 | 64 | .201 | .292 | .265 |
| Second 9 Batters | | | 281 | 59 | 4 | 30 | 51 | .210 | .278 | .288 |
| All Batters Thereafter | | | 315 | 77 | 6 | 27 | 57 | .244 | .346 | .304 |

Loves to face: Paul Molitor (.118, 4-for-34)
Hates to face: Rob Deer (.423, 11-for-26, 4 HR)
Ground outs-to-air outs ratio: 1.01 last season, 1.24 for career.... Additional statistics: 18 double-play ground outs in 153 opportunities, 29 doubles, 3 triples in 241.2 innings last season.... Allowed 7 first-inning runs in 35 starts. Hasn't allowed a first-inning HR in last 40 starts.... Batting support: 3.97 runs per start.... One of two A.L. pitchers in top 10 in wins, SO, and ERA last year. The other: Bret Saberhagen.... Had 66–96 record through 1988. Only one pitcher in history with a previous record as poor as that (in 150+ decisions) rebounded with a season as good: Red Ruffing was 70–115 through 1931, then 18–7 in 1932.... Opponents stole only eight bases in 18 attempts, lowest rate in A.L. (minimum: 15 att.).

## Jack Morris

Throws Right

| Detroit Tigers | W–L | ERA | AB | H | HR | BB | SO | BA | SA | OBA |
|---|---|---|---|---|---|---|---|---|---|---|
| Season | 6-14 | 4.86 | 669 | 189 | 23 | 59 | 115 | .283 | .450 | .339 |
| vs. Left-Handers | | | 307 | 91 | 11 | 33 | 55 | .296 | .479 | .358 |
| vs. Right-Handers | | | 362 | 98 | 12 | 26 | 60 | .271 | .425 | .322 |
| Home | 4-6 | 4.75 | 337 | 96 | 15 | 30 | 55 | .285 | .469 | .341 |
| Road | 2-8 | 4.98 | 332 | 93 | 8 | 29 | 60 | .280 | .431 | .338 |
| Grass | 6-12 | 4.40 | 593 | 159 | 21 | 51 | 102 | .268 | .432 | .325 |
| Artificial Turf | 0-2 | 9.00 | 76 | 30 | 2 | 8 | 13 | .395 | .592 | .443 |
| April | 0-5 | 4.45 | 116 | 35 | 3 | 15 | 26 | .302 | .457 | .382 |
| May | 2-2 | 5.40 | 128 | 39 | 6 | 9 | 22 | .305 | .523 | .348 |
| June | | | 0 | 0 | 0 | 0 | 0 | — | — | — |
| July | 0-1 | 5.02 | 58 | 16 | 0 | 4 | 9 | .276 | .310 | .323 |
| August | 1-3 | 5.20 | 178 | 46 | 6 | 16 | 26 | .258 | .427 | .320 |
| Sept./Oct. | 3-3 | 4.41 | 189 | 53 | 8 | 15 | 32 | .280 | .460 | .330 |
| Leading Off Inn. | | | 168 | 51 | 11 | 9 | 29 | .304 | .571 | .339 |
| Runners On | | | 277 | 83 | 3 | 26 | 46 | .300 | .401 | .356 |
| Runners/Scor. Pos. | | | 168 | 52 | 1 | 20 | 37 | .310 | .387 | .376 |
| Runners On/2 Out | | | 113 | 30 | 2 | 11 | 18 | .265 | .363 | .336 |
| Scor. Pos./2 Out | | | 70 | 22 | 1 | 8 | 15 | .314 | .386 | .392 |
| Late Inning Pressure | | | 99 | 25 | 2 | 7 | 20 | .253 | .354 | .299 |
| Leading Off | | | 25 | 10 | 1 | 2 | 3 | .400 | .560 | .444 |
| Runners On | | | 40 | 9 | 1 | 3 | 7 | .225 | .350 | .273 |
| Runners/Scor. Pos. | | | 23 | 6 | 1 | 1 | 4 | .261 | .435 | .280 |
| First 9 Batters | | | 197 | 47 | 8 | 17 | 38 | .239 | .421 | .301 |
| Second 9 Batters | | | 191 | 59 | 10 | 17 | 28 | .309 | .545 | .362 |
| All Batters Thereafter | | | 281 | 83 | 5 | 25 | 49 | .295 | .406 | .350 |

Loves to face: Ken Phelps (.032, 1-for-31, 13 SO)
Hates to face: George Brett (.367, 22-for-60, 3 HR)
Ground outs-to-air outs ratio: 1.12 last season, 1.13 for career.... Additional statistics: 15 double-play ground outs in 122 opportunities, 33 doubles, 5 triples in 170.1 innings last season.... Allowed 8 first-inning runs in 24 starts. Hasn't allowed a first-inning home run in last 53 starts.... Batting support: 3.50 runs per start.... Started 360 games since last relief appearance, A.L. mark for consecutive starts. Major league mark: 544, Steve Carlton.... Won 162 games during 1980s, 22 more than runner-up Dave Stieb, largest gap since Hal Newhouser won 37 more than Dizzy Trout during 1940s. Since then: 1970s, Carlton 192, Palmer 182; 1960s, Marichal 197, Gibson 184; 1950s, Spahn 202, Roberts 191.

## Jamie Moyer

Throws Left

| Texas Rangers | W–L | ERA | AB | H | HR | BB | SO | BA | SA | OBA |
|---|---|---|---|---|---|---|---|---|---|---|
| Season | 4-9 | 4.86 | 297 | 84 | 10 | 33 | 44 | .283 | .438 | .354 |
| vs. Left-Handers | | | 42 | 9 | 1 | 8 | 6 | .214 | .310 | .365 |
| vs. Right-Handers | | | 255 | 75 | 9 | 25 | 38 | .294 | .459 | .352 |
| Home | 3-4 | 4.34 | 179 | 46 | 6 | 15 | 33 | .257 | .402 | .310 |
| Road | 1-5 | 5.72 | 118 | 38 | 4 | 18 | 11 | .322 | .492 | .417 |
| Grass | 4-8 | 4.73 | 273 | 75 | 9 | 31 | 43 | .275 | .425 | .348 |
| Artificial Turf | 0-1 | 6.35 | 24 | 9 | 1 | 2 | 1 | .375 | .583 | .423 |
| April | 3-0 | 2.28 | 99 | 21 | 3 | 12 | 23 | .212 | .333 | .307 |
| May | 0-5 | 6.66 | 104 | 32 | 2 | 14 | 14 | .308 | .433 | .383 |
| June | | | 0 | 0 | 0 | 0 | 0 | — | — | — |
| July | | | 0 | 0 | 0 | 0 | 0 | — | — | — |
| August | | | 0 | 0 | 0 | 0 | 0 | — | — | — |
| Sept./Oct. | 1-4 | 5.96 | 94 | 31 | 5 | 7 | 7 | .330 | .553 | .373 |
| Leading Off Inn. | | | 75 | 21 | 1 | 10 | 10 | .280 | .347 | .365 |
| Runners On | | | 123 | 37 | 4 | 14 | 17 | .301 | .472 | .371 |
| Runners/Scor. Pos. | | | 62 | 18 | 2 | 11 | 11 | .290 | .452 | .377 |
| Runners On/2 Out | | | 44 | 13 | 0 | 4 | 8 | .295 | .364 | .354 |
| Scor. Pos./2 Out | | | 28 | 8 | 0 | 3 | 6 | .286 | .393 | .355 |
| Late Inning Pressure | | | 17 | 6 | 1 | 4 | 3 | .353 | .588 | .476 |
| Leading Off | | | 4 | 3 | 0 | 3 | 0 | .750 | 1.000 | .857 |
| Runners On | | | 7 | 2 | 1 | 1 | 1 | .286 | .714 | .375 |
| Runners/Scor. Pos. | | | 4 | 1 | 0 | 1 | 1 | .250 | .250 | .400 |
| First 9 Batters | | | 123 | 31 | 6 | 10 | 18 | .252 | .455 | .311 |
| Second 9 Batters | | | 95 | 30 | 1 | 15 | 14 | .316 | .432 | .404 |
| All Batters Thereafter | | | 79 | 23 | 3 | 8 | 12 | .291 | .418 | .356 |

Loves to face: Gerald Perry (.143, 2-for-14, 3 SO)
Hates to face: Mookie Wilson (.522, 12-for-23, 1 HR)
Ground outs-to-air outs ratio: 1.07 last season, 1.44 for career.... Additional statistics: 10 double-play ground outs in 72 opportunities, 14 doubles, 1 triple in 76.0 innings last season.... Average of 5.07 innings pitched per start was 3d-lowest in A.L. (minimum: 15 GS).... Winning percentage has dropped at least 50 points in each of three seasons since he posted a .636 mark (7–4) as a rookie in 1986.... Bad news: The streak might not be over. Scott McGregor and Sheldon Jones actually had *five-year* streaks.... Good news: Ralph Terry (1965), George Stone (1973), Catfish Hunter (1978), Jerry Reuss (1985), and Storm Davis (1988) are some recent examples of pitchers who bounced back from three-year streaks.

## Rob Murphy

Throws Left

| Boston Red Sox | W–L | ERA | AB | H | HR | BB | SO | BA | SA | OBA |
|---|---|---|---|---|---|---|---|---|---|---|
| Season | 5-7 | 2.74 | 386 | 97 | 7 | 41 | 107 | .251 | .363 | .323 |
| vs. Left-Handers | | | 114 | 29 | 2 | 4 | 25 | .254 | .386 | .280 |
| vs. Right-Handers | | | 272 | 68 | 5 | 37 | 82 | .250 | .353 | .339 |
| Home | 2-2 | 3.26 | 175 | 44 | 5 | 20 | 52 | .251 | .411 | .330 |
| Road | 3-5 | 2.33 | 211 | 53 | 2 | 21 | 55 | .251 | .322 | .316 |
| Grass | 4-5 | 2.78 | 330 | 81 | 7 | 33 | 95 | .245 | .370 | .313 |
| Artificial Turf | 1-2 | 2.51 | 56 | 16 | 0 | 8 | 12 | .286 | .321 | .375 |
| April | 0-2 | 3.95 | 54 | 16 | 2 | 8 | 15 | .296 | .481 | .381 |
| May | 0-0 | 0.64 | 47 | 9 | 0 | 9 | 14 | .191 | .255 | .316 |
| June | 0-1 | 2.95 | 68 | 17 | 1 | 2 | 15 | .250 | .338 | .278 |
| July | 1-2 | 1.61 | 82 | 19 | 1 | 4 | 28 | .232 | .305 | .267 |
| August | 3-1 | 3.71 | 62 | 16 | 1 | 12 | 19 | .258 | .355 | .378 |
| Sept./Oct. | 1-1 | 3.66 | 73 | 20 | 2 | 6 | 16 | .274 | .438 | .329 |
| Leading Off Inn. | | | 81 | 17 | 1 | 7 | 21 | .210 | .321 | .273 |
| Runners On | | | 197 | 49 | 4 | 25 | 65 | .249 | .355 | .332 |
| Runners/Scor. Pos. | | | 129 | 35 | 3 | 19 | 46 | .271 | .388 | .362 |
| Runners On/2 Out | | | 83 | 18 | 1 | 14 | 33 | .217 | .313 | .330 |
| Scor. Pos./2 Out | | | 56 | 14 | 1 | 11 | 25 | .250 | .375 | .373 |
| Late Inning Pressure | | | 169 | 49 | 3 | 21 | 50 | .290 | .385 | .368 |
| Leading Off | | | 37 | 9 | 1 | 4 | 12 | .243 | .378 | .317 |
| Runners On | | | 83 | 26 | 2 | 13 | 27 | .313 | .422 | .406 |
| Runners/Scor. Pos. | | | 53 | 19 | 2 | 10 | 18 | .358 | .509 | .460 |
| First 9 Batters | | | 365 | 90 | 7 | 40 | 100 | .247 | .362 | .320 |
| Second 9 Batters | | | 21 | 7 | 0 | 1 | 7 | .333 | .381 | .364 |
| All Batters Thereafter | | | 0 | 0 | 0 | 0 | 0 | — | — | — |

Loves to face: Chet Lemon (0-for-5, 3 SO)
Hates to face: Randy Milligan (3-for-3, 1 HR, 3 BB)
Ground outs-to-air outs ratio: 1.16 last season, 1.22 for career.... Additional statistics: 12 double-play ground outs in 98 opportunities, 20 doubles, 1 triple in 105.0 innings last season.... Inherited 66 runners, stranded 46 (70%).... Has started career with 273 errorless games. All-time record for pitchers at start of career: 286, by Rawly Eastwick.... Last season, Ken Dayley reached 285. Then in his next game, he made a wild pick-off throw for first error of career. Blame it on the witches of Eastwick.... First Red Sox reliever to strike out 100 batters since Mark Clear in 1982 (109). By comparison, Dick Radatz fanned 181 in 1984.... Career record of 5–10 before the All-Star break, 14–8 after.

## Jaime Navarro

Throws Right

| Milwaukee Brewers | W–L | ERA | AB | H | HR | BB | SO | BA | SA | OBA |
|---|---|---|---|---|---|---|---|---|---|---|
| Season | 7-8 | 3.12 | 430 | 119 | 6 | 32 | 56 | .277 | .370 | .327 |
| vs. Left-Handers | | | 194 | 53 | 2 | 16 | 26 | .273 | .356 | .327 |
| vs. Right-Handers | | | 236 | 66 | 4 | 16 | 30 | .280 | .381 | .327 |
| Home | 6-4 | 2.82 | 254 | 67 | 2 | 17 | 33 | .264 | .335 | .308 |
| Road | 1-4 | 3.59 | 176 | 52 | 4 | 15 | 23 | .295 | .420 | .354 |
| Grass | 6-8 | 3.05 | 401 | 109 | 4 | 32 | 49 | .272 | .349 | .326 |
| Artificial Turf | 1-0 | 4.26 | 29 | 10 | 2 | 0 | 7 | .345 | .655 | .345 |
| April | | | 0 | 0 | 0 | 0 | 0 | — | — | — |
| May | | | 0 | 0 | 0 | 0 | 0 | — | — | — |
| June | 1-0 | 2.21 | 85 | 26 | 0 | 4 | 13 | .306 | .329 | .337 |
| July | 1-3 | 3.54 | 83 | 26 | 0 | 8 | 10 | .313 | .373 | .370 |
| August | 2-3 | 4.03 | 109 | 25 | 2 | 8 | 14 | .229 | .321 | .286 |
| Sept./Oct. | 3-2 | 2.70 | 153 | 42 | 4 | 12 | 19 | .275 | .425 | .327 |
| Leading Off Inn. | | | 108 | 28 | 2 | 8 | 12 | .259 | .380 | .310 |
| Runners On | | | 182 | 54 | 3 | 12 | 27 | .297 | .379 | .340 |
| Runners/Scor. Pos. | | | 96 | 27 | 0 | 9 | 17 | .281 | .313 | .343 |
| Runners On/2 Out | | | 78 | 25 | 2 | 8 | 9 | .321 | .410 | .384 |
| Scor. Pos./2 Out | | | 51 | 11 | 0 | 5 | 7 | .216 | .235 | .286 |
| Late Inning Pressure | | | 39 | 17 | 1 | 0 | 7 | .436 | .590 | .436 |
| Leading Off | | | 11 | 6 | 1 | 0 | 0 | .545 | .909 | .545 |
| Runners On | | | 16 | 9 | 0 | 0 | 3 | .563 | .625 | .563 |
| Runners/Scor. Pos. | | | 10 | 4 | 0 | 0 | 2 | .400 | .500 | .400 |
| First 9 Batters | | | 149 | 37 | 1 | 8 | 23 | .248 | .315 | .285 |
| Second 9 Batters | | | 139 | 36 | 3 | 13 | 15 | .259 | .353 | .322 |
| All Batters Thereafter | | | 142 | 46 | 2 | 11 | 18 | .324 | .444 | .374 |

Loves to face: Fred Manrique (0-for-7)
Hates to face: Jeffrey Leonard (.667, 4-for-6, 1 HR)
Ground outs-to-air outs ratio: 1.14 last season, his first in majors. . . . Additional statistics: 10 double-play ground outs in 87 opportunities, 16 doubles, 3 triples in 109.2 innings last season. . . . Allowed 6 first-inning runs in 17 starts. . . . Batting support: 3.29 runs per start, 3d-lowest in A.L. (minimum: 15 GS). . . . Completed only one of 17 starts. . . . Had the lowest ERA of any rookie with at least 100 innings. . . . Had an ERA of 2.20 in 32.2 innings with Charlie O'Brien catching, 3.51 ERA in 77 innings with B. J. Surhoff. . . . Rookies with such good control are supposed to allow more home runs. Last A.L. rookie starter with rates as low as Navarro's (2.62 BB, 0.49 HR per nine innings) was Mark Fidrych in 1976.

## Gene Nelson

Throws Right

| Oakland As | W–L | ERA | AB | H | HR | BB | SO | BA | SA | OBA |
|---|---|---|---|---|---|---|---|---|---|---|
| Season | 3-5 | 3.26 | 296 | 60 | 5 | 30 | 70 | .203 | .294 | .277 |
| vs. Left-Handers | | | 112 | 28 | 3 | 14 | 19 | .250 | .384 | .331 |
| vs. Right-Handers | | | 184 | 32 | 2 | 16 | 51 | .174 | .239 | .244 |
| Home | 3-2 | 3.18 | 145 | 27 | 3 | 11 | 39 | .186 | .276 | .247 |
| Road | 0-3 | 3.35 | 151 | 33 | 2 | 19 | 31 | .219 | .311 | .305 |
| Grass | 3-4 | 2.69 | 265 | 50 | 4 | 25 | 66 | .189 | .279 | .258 |
| Artificial Turf | 0-1 | 9.95 | 31 | 10 | 1 | 5 | 4 | .323 | .419 | .432 |
| April | 1-0 | 0.00 | 21 | 2 | 0 | 1 | 8 | .095 | .095 | .136 |
| May | 0-1 | 3.75 | 43 | 10 | 1 | 3 | 5 | .233 | .419 | .306 |
| June | 1-2 | 3.60 | 76 | 17 | 0 | 13 | 14 | .224 | .250 | .333 |
| July | 0-2 | 7.20 | 61 | 15 | 3 | 5 | 15 | .246 | .443 | .303 |
| August | 0-0 | 2.45 | 43 | 9 | 1 | 3 | 13 | .209 | .302 | .261 |
| Sept./Oct. | 1-0 | 0.57 | 52 | 7 | 0 | 5 | 15 | .135 | .154 | .203 |
| Leading Off Inn. | | | 72 | 13 | 1 | 4 | 18 | .181 | .250 | .234 |
| Runners On | | | 126 | 24 | 1 | 20 | 27 | .190 | .246 | .293 |
| Runners/Scor. Pos. | | | 73 | 13 | 0 | 16 | 17 | .178 | .233 | .312 |
| Runners On/2 Out | | | 63 | 12 | 1 | 16 | 12 | .190 | .254 | .354 |
| Scor. Pos./2 Out | | | 41 | 6 | 0 | 13 | 8 | .146 | .171 | .352 |
| Late Inning Pressure | | | 111 | 26 | 2 | 9 | 21 | .234 | .315 | .298 |
| Leading Off | | | 33 | 9 | 1 | 0 | 5 | .273 | .424 | .294 |
| Runners On | | | 41 | 7 | 0 | 5 | 6 | .171 | .171 | .261 |
| Runners/Scor. Pos. | | | 28 | 4 | 0 | 3 | 6 | .143 | .143 | .226 |
| First 9 Batters | | | 255 | 50 | 3 | 24 | 65 | .196 | .275 | .267 |
| Second 9 Batters | | | 40 | 10 | 2 | 4 | 5 | .250 | .425 | .318 |
| All Batters Thereafter | | | 1 | 0 | 0 | 2 | 0 | .000 | .000 | .667 |

Loves to face: Brook Jacoby (.148, 4-for-27, 7 SO)
Hates to face: George Brett (.417, 10-for-24, 5 HR)
Ground outs-to-air outs ratio: 0.78 last season, 1.11 for career. . . . Additional statistics: 5 double-play ground outs in 57 opportunities, 6 doubles, 3 triples in 80.0 innings last season. . . . Opponents' batting average was the lowest of his career. . . . Batting average of opposing right-handers has decreased in each of the last five seasons: .274, .267, .259, .239, .225, .174. . . . Opponents have hit better on artificial turf than on grass fields in each of the last five seasons. . . . Debuted for Yankees in 1981, the last time they reached postseason. But Nelson and five teammates have pitched in postseason games for other clubs: Tommy John, Rick Reuschel, Rich Gossage, Tom Underwood, and George Frazier.

## Rod Nichols

Throws Right

| Cleveland Indians | W–L | ERA | AB | H | HR | BB | SO | BA | SA | OBA |
|---|---|---|---|---|---|---|---|---|---|---|
| Season | 4-6 | 4.40 | 284 | 81 | 9 | 24 | 42 | .285 | .430 | .343 |
| vs. Left-Handers | | | 127 | 41 | 5 | 12 | 20 | .323 | .488 | .386 |
| vs. Right-Handers | | | 157 | 40 | 4 | 12 | 22 | .255 | .382 | .308 |
| Home | 2-2 | 3.22 | 170 | 41 | 3 | 12 | 31 | .241 | .329 | .292 |
| Road | 2-4 | 6.33 | 114 | 40 | 6 | 12 | 11 | .351 | .579 | .417 |
| Grass | 4-6 | 4.40 | 284 | 81 | 9 | 24 | 42 | .285 | .430 | .343 |
| Artificial Turf | | | 0 | 0 | 0 | 0 | 0 | — | — | — |
| April | | | 0 | 0 | 0 | 0 | 0 | — | — | — |
| May | | | 0 | 0 | 0 | 0 | 0 | — | — | — |
| June | | | 0 | 0 | 0 | 0 | 0 | — | — | — |
| July | 1-1 | 4.00 | 37 | 10 | 1 | 1 | 7 | .270 | .351 | .289 |
| August | 2-2 | 5.13 | 134 | 42 | 5 | 15 | 10 | .313 | .478 | .384 |
| Sept./Oct. | 1-3 | 3.68 | 113 | 29 | 3 | 8 | 25 | .257 | .398 | .309 |
| Leading Off Inn. | | | 73 | 23 | 3 | 4 | 9 | .315 | .493 | .359 |
| Runners On | | | 118 | 33 | 4 | 13 | 19 | .280 | .449 | .346 |
| Runners/Scor. Pos. | | | 53 | 18 | 2 | 8 | 12 | .340 | .528 | .413 |
| Runners On/2 Out | | | 47 | 11 | 1 | 6 | 10 | .234 | .362 | .321 |
| Scor. Pos./2 Out | | | 23 | 8 | 1 | 2 | 5 | .348 | .565 | .400 |
| Late Inning Pressure | | | 29 | 7 | 2 | 2 | 5 | .241 | .448 | .290 |
| Leading Off | | | 9 | 2 | 0 | 0 | 2 | .222 | .222 | .222 |
| Runners On | | | 9 | 2 | 0 | 1 | 2 | .222 | .222 | .300 |
| Runners/Scor. Pos. | | | 2 | 2 | 0 | 1 | 0 | 1.000 | 1.000 | 1.000 |
| First 9 Batters | | | 118 | 29 | 2 | 9 | 20 | .246 | .339 | .297 |
| Second 9 Batters | | | 91 | 28 | 3 | 11 | 11 | .308 | .484 | .388 |
| All Batters Thereafter | | | 75 | 24 | 4 | 4 | 11 | .320 | .507 | .358 |

Loves to face: George Bell (.100, 1-for-10)
Hates to face: Danny Heep (.625, 5-for-8, 1 HR)
Ground outs-to-air outs ratio: 0.73 last season, 0.70 for career. . . . Additional statistics: 5 double-play ground outs in 63 opportunities, 12 doubles, 1 triple in 71.2 innings last season. . . . Allowed 7 first-inning runs in 11 starts. . . . Batting support: 3.64 runs per start. . . . Didn't complete any of his 11 starts. Reached the ninth inning only once. . . . Pitched 15 games, all on grass fields. . . . Opponents' batting average in road games was highest in A.L. . . . Opponents' career average is .255 at Cleveland Stadium, .318 on the road. . . . Career record of 5–4 vs. Eastern Division clubs, 0–9 vs. the West. . . . Opposing leadoff batters hit even better in 1988 (.318).

## Gregg Olson

Throws Right

| Baltimore Orioles | W–L | ERA | AB | H | HR | BB | SO | BA | SA | OBA |
|---|---|---|---|---|---|---|---|---|---|---|
| Season | 5-2 | 1.69 | 304 | 57 | 1 | 46 | 90 | .188 | .247 | .295 |
| vs. Left-Handers | | | 141 | 19 | 0 | 20 | 39 | .135 | .149 | .247 |
| vs. Right-Handers | | | 163 | 38 | 1 | 26 | 51 | .233 | .331 | .337 |
| Home | 3-0 | 0.77 | 162 | 25 | 0 | 25 | 58 | .154 | .204 | .271 |
| Road | 2-2 | 2.82 | 142 | 32 | 1 | 21 | 32 | .225 | .296 | .323 |
| Grass | 4-1 | 1.18 | 239 | 37 | 1 | 35 | 76 | .155 | .218 | .264 |
| Artificial Turf | 1-1 | 3.86 | 65 | 20 | 0 | 11 | 14 | .308 | .354 | .408 |
| April | 2-0 | 3.18 | 62 | 14 | 1 | 10 | 13 | .226 | .339 | .329 |
| May | 1-0 | 1.20 | 51 | 7 | 0 | 8 | 19 | .137 | .176 | .254 |
| June | 0-0 | 0.77 | 43 | 7 | 0 | 3 | 13 | .163 | .209 | .217 |
| July | 0-2 | 4.30 | 58 | 17 | 0 | 15 | 16 | .293 | .362 | .438 |
| August | 0-0 | 0.00 | 40 | 4 | 0 | 5 | 13 | .100 | .150 | .217 |
| Sept./Oct. | 2-0 | 0.00 | 50 | 8 | 0 | 5 | 16 | .160 | .180 | .236 |
| Leading Off Inn. | | | 56 | 8 | 1 | 10 | 21 | .143 | .214 | .273 |
| Runners On | | | 165 | 27 | 0 | 31 | 48 | .164 | .200 | .298 |
| Runners/Scor. Pos. | | | 111 | 18 | 0 | 25 | 33 | .162 | .189 | .319 |
| Runners On/2 Out | | | 79 | 10 | 0 | 16 | 25 | .127 | .152 | .274 |
| Scor. Pos./2 Out | | | 62 | 7 | 0 | 16 | 22 | .113 | .129 | .295 |
| Late Inning Pressure | | | 176 | 35 | 0 | 33 | 50 | .199 | .256 | .329 |
| Leading Off | | | 34 | 6 | 0 | 5 | 11 | .176 | .206 | .282 |
| Runners On | | | 99 | 17 | 0 | 24 | 30 | .172 | .212 | .339 |
| Runners/Scor. Pos. | | | 64 | 12 | 0 | 20 | 20 | .188 | .219 | .388 |
| First 9 Batters | | | 289 | 55 | 1 | 41 | 85 | .190 | .249 | .293 |
| Second 9 Batters | | | 15 | 2 | 0 | 5 | 5 | .133 | .200 | .333 |
| All Batters Thereafter | | | 0 | 0 | 0 | 0 | 0 | — | — | — |

Loves to face: Manny Lee (0-for-4, 3 SO)
Hates to face: Jody Reed (.500, 2-for-4, 2 BB)
Ground outs-to-air outs ratio: 1.05 last season, 0.94 for career. . . . Additional statistics: 4 double-play ground outs in 76 opportunities, 15 doubles, 0 triples in 85.0 innings last season. . . . Inherited 44 runners, stranded 34 (77%). . . . Led major league rookies in ERA, hits per nine innings (6.04), strikeouts per nine (9.53), and innings per home run (85.0) (minimum: 50 IP). . . . Opposing base runners stole 15 bases in 16 attempts. . . . Batting average by opposing left-handers was lowest in A.L. in last 15 years. . . . Likewise, his average by opposing ground-ball hitters: .158; fly-ballers hit .215. . . . Has faced 236 batters with runners on base in his career, hasn't allowed a home run.

## Jesse Orosco

Throws Left

| Cleveland Indians | W–L | ERA | AB | H | HR | BB | SO | BA | SA | OBA |
|---|---|---|---|---|---|---|---|---|---|---|
| Season | 3-4 | 2.08 | 273 | 54 | 7 | 26 | 79 | .198 | .333 | .270 |
| vs. Left-Handers | | | 87 | 12 | 0 | 8 | 30 | .138 | .184 | .211 |
| vs. Right-Handers | | | 186 | 42 | 7 | 18 | 49 | .226 | .403 | .297 |
| Home | 2-2 | 1.69 | 147 | 28 | 3 | 16 | 43 | .190 | .313 | .277 |
| Road | 1-2 | 2.55 | 126 | 26 | 4 | 10 | 36 | .206 | .357 | .261 |
| Grass | 3-3 | 1.76 | 230 | 42 | 6 | 23 | 69 | .183 | .322 | .261 |
| Artificial Turf | 0-1 | 3.97 | 43 | 12 | 1 | 3 | 10 | .279 | .395 | .319 |
| April | 0-0 | 0.00 | 14 | 3 | 0 | 3 | 2 | .214 | .286 | .353 |
| May | 0-0 | 1.46 | 41 | 7 | 1 | 4 | 9 | .171 | .317 | .239 |
| June | 0-1 | 3.97 | 43 | 11 | 0 | 3 | 15 | .256 | .349 | .319 |
| July | 1-1 | 1.62 | 62 | 12 | 1 | 4 | 14 | .194 | .306 | .242 |
| August | 0-2 | 2.70 | 58 | 11 | 4 | 5 | 19 | .190 | .431 | .246 |
| Sept./Oct. | 2-0 | 1.56 | 55 | 10 | 1 | 7 | 20 | .182 | .273 | .286 |
| Leading Off Inn. | | | 61 | 18 | 4 | 6 | 14 | .295 | .525 | .368 |
| Runners On | | | 122 | 19 | 1 | 10 | 37 | .156 | .246 | .215 |
| Runners/Scor. Pos. | | | 68 | 10 | 0 | 8 | 24 | .147 | .206 | .228 |
| Runners On/2 Out | | | 60 | 7 | 0 | 6 | 22 | .117 | .167 | .197 |
| Scor. Pos./2 Out | | | 36 | 3 | 0 | 5 | 15 | .083 | .139 | .195 |
| Late Inning Pressure | | | 184 | 38 | 5 | 12 | 56 | .207 | .337 | .260 |
| Leading Off | | | 42 | 14 | 2 | 2 | 13 | .333 | .524 | .378 |
| Runners On | | | 78 | 11 | 1 | 6 | 24 | .141 | .218 | .198 |
| Runners/Scor. Pos. | | | 42 | 5 | 0 | 5 | 14 | .119 | .143 | .204 |
| First 9 Batters | | | 268 | 52 | 7 | 24 | 78 | .194 | .325 | .263 |
| Second 9 Batters | | | 5 | 2 | 0 | 2 | 1 | .400 | .800 | .571 |
| All Batters Thereafter | | | 0 | 0 | 0 | 0 | 0 | — | — | — |

Loves to face: Dave Parker (.125, 2-for-16, 7 SO)
Hates to face: Jeffrey Leonard (.357, 5-for-14, 2 HR)
Ground outs-to-air outs ratio: 0.77 last season, 0.88 for career. . . . Additional statistics: 5 double-play ground outs in 56 opportunities, 12 doubles, 2 triples in 78.0 innings last season. . . . Opponents' career BA of .193 on artificial turf is lowest over last 15 years (minimum: 500 PA). That despite marks of .270 or higher in each of last three seasons (after seven years below .200). . . . Career records: 40–39, 2.85 ERA on grass; 12–11, 1.79 on artificial turf. . . . Opponents have hit better with bases empty than with runners on in each of last nine seasons. Over last 15 years, no one else had even a six-year streak. . . . Opponents have hit below .200 with runners in scoring position in seven of last nine years.

## Donn Pall

Throws Right

| Chicago White Sox | W–L | ERA | AB | H | HR | BB | SO | BA | SA | OBA |
|---|---|---|---|---|---|---|---|---|---|---|
| Season | 4-5 | 3.31 | 333 | 90 | 9 | 19 | 58 | .270 | .411 | .323 |
| vs. Left-Handers | | | 157 | 40 | 4 | 10 | 28 | .255 | .389 | .306 |
| vs. Right-Handers | | | 176 | 50 | 5 | 9 | 30 | .284 | .432 | .339 |
| Home | 1-2 | 3.38 | 142 | 37 | 2 | 9 | 29 | .261 | .394 | .314 |
| Road | 3-3 | 3.26 | 191 | 53 | 7 | 10 | 29 | .277 | .424 | .330 |
| Grass | 4-3 | 3.30 | 291 | 78 | 7 | 18 | 56 | .268 | .405 | .317 |
| Artificial Turf | 0-2 | 3.38 | 42 | 12 | 2 | 1 | 2 | .286 | .452 | .362 |
| April | 1-0 | 2.61 | 83 | 21 | 2 | 4 | 16 | .253 | .361 | .303 |
| May | 0-1 | 6.52 | 39 | 11 | 1 | 2 | 10 | .282 | .462 | .317 |
| June | 1-0 | 1.98 | 48 | 11 | 1 | 5 | 6 | .229 | .292 | .333 |
| July | 1-1 | 0.93 | 65 | 13 | 0 | 2 | 11 | .200 | .262 | .224 |
| August | 1-3 | 5.17 | 65 | 23 | 4 | 3 | 9 | .354 | .615 | .408 |
| Sept./Oct. | 0-0 | 5.63 | 33 | 11 | 1 | 3 | 6 | .333 | .545 | .378 |
| Leading Off Inn. | | | 66 | 21 | 4 | 5 | 7 | .318 | .561 | .384 |
| Runners On | | | 185 | 49 | 3 | 8 | 32 | .265 | .368 | .299 |
| Runners/Scor. Pos. | | | 108 | 27 | 1 | 7 | 24 | .250 | .306 | .291 |
| Runners On/2 Out | | | 85 | 28 | 2 | 5 | 13 | .329 | .471 | .374 |
| Scor. Pos./2 Out | | | 56 | 16 | 1 | 4 | 12 | .286 | .375 | .333 |
| Late Inning Pressure | | | 169 | 50 | 5 | 11 | 25 | .296 | .444 | .349 |
| Leading Off | | | 38 | 12 | 2 | 3 | 4 | .316 | .500 | .381 |
| Runners On | | | 82 | 25 | 1 | 4 | 10 | .305 | .390 | .337 |
| Runners/Scor. Pos. | | | 44 | 14 | 0 | 4 | 7 | .318 | .318 | .360 |
| First 9 Batters | | | 298 | 79 | 8 | 18 | 54 | .265 | .406 | .322 |
| Second 9 Batters | | | 35 | 11 | 1 | 1 | 4 | .314 | .457 | .333 |
| All Batters Thereafter | | | 0 | 0 | 0 | 0 | 0 | — | — | — |

Loves to face: Tony Phillips (0-for-6)
Hates to face: George Brett (4-for-4, 2 2B)
Ground outs-to-air outs ratio: 1.84 last season, 1.89 for career. . . . Additional statistics: 12 double-play ground outs in 79 opportunities, 18 doubles, 1 triple in 87.0 innings last season. . . . Average of 1.97 walks per nine innings was lowest among A.L. rookies (minimum: 50 IP). . . . Ranked second among A.L. rookies with six saves. . . . Lost four of last seven games he entered with the score tied. . . . Stranded only 24 of 47 inherited base runners (51%), 3d-lowest mark in A.L. (minimum: 25 runners). . . . Career average of .255 by opposing ground-ball hitters, .314 by fly-ballers. . . . Lost his best shot at endorsement for a national product when Pall Mall cigarettes went south.

## Clay Parker

Throws Right

| New York Yankees | W–L | ERA | AB | H | HR | BB | SO | BA | SA | OBA |
|---|---|---|---|---|---|---|---|---|---|---|
| Season | 4-5 | 3.68 | 466 | 123 | 12 | 31 | 53 | .264 | .391 | .311 |
| vs. Left-Handers | | | 217 | 61 | 4 | 16 | 26 | .281 | .401 | .330 |
| vs. Right-Handers | | | 249 | 62 | 8 | 15 | 27 | .249 | .382 | .295 |
| Home | 2-2 | 3.83 | 218 | 58 | 8 | 20 | 26 | .266 | .427 | .328 |
| Road | 2-3 | 3.53 | 248 | 65 | 4 | 11 | 27 | .262 | .359 | .296 |
| Grass | 3-4 | 3.86 | 412 | 113 | 11 | 29 | 42 | .274 | .405 | .324 |
| Artificial Turf | 1-1 | 2.40 | 54 | 10 | 1 | 2 | 11 | .185 | .278 | .214 |
| April | | | 0 | 0 | 0 | 0 | 0 | — | — | — |
| May | 2-1 | 3.22 | 81 | 17 | 3 | 4 | 18 | .210 | .383 | .247 |
| June | 0-0 | 2.25 | 46 | 10 | 2 | 2 | 3 | .217 | .391 | .265 |
| July | 1-0 | 5.50 | 142 | 45 | 5 | 14 | 15 | .317 | .486 | .377 |
| August | 0-3 | 3.25 | 108 | 29 | 0 | 7 | 11 | .269 | .296 | .313 |
| Sept./Oct. | 1-1 | 2.66 | 89 | 22 | 2 | 4 | 6 | .247 | .360 | .280 |
| Leading Off Inn. | | | 120 | 32 | 4 | 5 | 9 | .267 | .392 | .302 |
| Runners On | | | 176 | 49 | 2 | 16 | 19 | .278 | .369 | .338 |
| Runners/Scor. Pos. | | | 109 | 29 | 1 | 11 | 14 | .266 | .358 | .328 |
| Runners On/2 Out | | | 73 | 18 | 1 | 4 | 12 | .247 | .342 | .286 |
| Scor. Pos./2 Out | | | 47 | 10 | 1 | 3 | 8 | .213 | .319 | .260 |
| Late Inning Pressure | | | 25 | 7 | 1 | 2 | 1 | .280 | .440 | .333 |
| Leading Off | | | 8 | 1 | 0 | 1 | 1 | .125 | .125 | .222 |
| Runners On | | | 7 | 1 | 0 | 0 | 0 | .143 | .143 | .143 |
| Runners/Scor. Pos. | | | 6 | 1 | 0 | 0 | 0 | .167 | .167 | .167 |
| First 9 Batters | | | 175 | 42 | 0 | 15 | 19 | .240 | .286 | .298 |
| Second 9 Batters | | | 157 | 42 | 5 | 10 | 18 | .268 | .427 | .320 |
| All Batters Thereafter | | | 134 | 39 | 7 | 6 | 16 | .291 | .485 | .319 |

Loves to face: Terry Steinbach (0-for-9)
Hates to face: Carney Lansford (.545, 6-for-11, 3 2B)
Ground outs-to-air outs ratio: 1.83 last season, 1.76 for career. . . . Additional statistics: 13 double-play ground outs in 86 opportunities, 17 doubles, 3 triples in 120.0 innings last season. . . . Allowed 7 first-inning runs in 17 starts. Opponents batted .324 during first inning, but he didn't allow a first-inning home run. . . . Batting support: 4.00 runs per start. . . . Yankees had a 7–1 record in his first eight starts, but were 2–7 in his last nine. . . . The only home runs he allowed over his last 52.2 innings were hit an inning apart by Jose Canseco and Dave Henderson. . . . Yanks have had three "Clays" in their history, totalling 12 wins among them: Ken (6), Parker (4), and Christiansen (2).

## Melido Perez

Throws Right

| Chicago White Sox | W–L | ERA | AB | H | HR | BB | SO | BA | SA | OBA |
|---|---|---|---|---|---|---|---|---|---|---|
| Season | 11-14 | 5.01 | 708 | 187 | 23 | 90 | 141 | .264 | .432 | .348 |
| vs. Left-Handers | | | 371 | 98 | 12 | 48 | 68 | .264 | .445 | .352 |
| vs. Right-Handers | | | 337 | 89 | 11 | 42 | 73 | .264 | .418 | .344 |
| Home | 4-6 | 5.06 | 304 | 84 | 8 | 35 | 60 | .276 | .428 | .350 |
| Road | 7-8 | 4.97 | 404 | 103 | 15 | 55 | 81 | .255 | .436 | .346 |
| Grass | 9-13 | 5.10 | 568 | 149 | 15 | 73 | 117 | .262 | .419 | .348 |
| Artificial Turf | 2-1 | 4.63 | 140 | 38 | 8 | 17 | 24 | .271 | .486 | .348 |
| April | 1-3 | 6.46 | 96 | 34 | 2 | 10 | 19 | .354 | .531 | .417 |
| May | 2-2 | 5.79 | 118 | 34 | 4 | 16 | 20 | .288 | .458 | .373 |
| June | 2-4 | 5.88 | 128 | 33 | 5 | 16 | 24 | .258 | .453 | .345 |
| July | 2-2 | 4.15 | 94 | 21 | 3 | 15 | 12 | .223 | .383 | .330 |
| August | 0-2 | 4.71 | 140 | 36 | 5 | 17 | 30 | .257 | .414 | .335 |
| Sept./Oct. | 4-1 | 3.53 | 132 | 29 | 4 | 16 | 36 | .220 | .371 | .304 |
| Leading Off Inn. | | | 176 | 42 | 6 | 22 | 37 | .239 | .403 | .323 |
| Runners On | | | 304 | 87 | 10 | 35 | 59 | .286 | .461 | .359 |
| Runners/Scor. Pos. | | | 182 | 45 | 7 | 23 | 39 | .247 | .418 | .332 |
| Runners On/2 Out | | | 129 | 37 | 3 | 18 | 32 | .287 | .434 | .378 |
| Scor. Pos./2 Out | | | 83 | 19 | 3 | 12 | 23 | .229 | .386 | .333 |
| Late Inning Pressure | | | 49 | 14 | 1 | 3 | 12 | .286 | .408 | .327 |
| Leading Off | | | 16 | 5 | 1 | 0 | 4 | .313 | .563 | .313 |
| Runners On | | | 14 | 3 | 0 | 2 | 4 | .214 | .214 | .313 |
| Runners/Scor. Pos. | | | 8 | 2 | 0 | 2 | 3 | .250 | .250 | .400 |
| First 9 Batters | | | 240 | 68 | 3 | 31 | 48 | .283 | .379 | .367 |
| Second 9 Batters | | | 244 | 50 | 8 | 28 | 54 | .205 | .361 | .288 |
| All Batters Thereafter | | | 224 | 69 | 12 | 31 | 39 | .308 | .567 | .391 |

Loves to face: Dan Gladden (.111, 2-for-18, 7 SO)
Hates to face: Kirby Puckett (.609, 14-for-23, 1 HR)
Ground outs-to-air outs ratio: 0.76 last season, 0.80 for career. . . . Additional statistics: 10 double-play ground outs in 125 opportunities, 32 doubles, 9 triples in 183.1 innings last season. . . . Allowed 22 first-inning runs in 31 starts. . . . Batting support: 4.06 runs per start. . . . League's top 10 hitters batted .465 against him (33-for-71). . . . Opponents stole 18 bases in 30 attempts, lowest percentage on team. . . . Career record of 11–5 in day games, 13–20 at night. Last season, opponents batted 62 points higher in day games (.302) than at night (.241), largest difference in A.L. . . . Different pitcher has led Sox in wins in each of last seven years: Hoyt, Seaver, Burns, Cowley, Bannister, Reuss, and Perez.

## Dan Plesac

Throws Left

| Milwaukee Brewers | W–L | ERA | AB | H | HR | BB | SO | BA | SA | OBA |
|---|---|---|---|---|---|---|---|---|---|---|
| Season | 3-4 | 2.35 | 221 | 47 | 6 | 17 | 52 | .213 | .326 | .264 |
| vs. Left-Handers | | | 49 | 11 | 1 | 1 | 11 | .224 | .306 | .231 |
| vs. Right-Handers | | | 172 | 36 | 5 | 16 | 41 | .209 | .331 | .274 |
| Home | 2-1 | 1.89 | 117 | 24 | 3 | 4 | 28 | .205 | .308 | .228 |
| Road | 1-3 | 2.89 | 104 | 23 | 3 | 13 | 24 | .221 | .346 | .303 |
| Grass | 3-3 | 2.44 | 182 | 38 | 5 | 12 | 46 | .209 | .319 | .253 |
| Artificial Turf | 0-1 | 1.86 | 39 | 9 | 1 | 5 | 6 | .231 | .359 | .318 |
| April | 1-1 | 3.00 | 33 | 7 | 1 | 4 | 13 | .212 | .333 | .289 |
| May | 1-1 | 2.51 | 51 | 11 | 2 | 3 | 16 | .216 | .373 | .250 |
| June | 0-1 | 1.54 | 40 | 9 | 2 | 3 | 6 | .225 | .400 | .279 |
| July | 0-0 | 4.26 | 27 | 10 | 0 | 2 | 2 | .370 | .444 | .414 |
| August | 1-0 | 1.29 | 51 | 8 | 0 | 2 | 8 | .157 | .176 | .185 |
| Sept./Oct. | 0-1 | 3.00 | 19 | 2 | 1 | 3 | 7 | .105 | .263 | .227 |
| Leading Off Inn. | | | 42 | 12 | 1 | 4 | 8 | .286 | .357 | .348 |
| Runners On | | | 117 | 24 | 3 | 6 | 23 | .205 | .299 | .236 |
| Runners/Scor. Pos. | | | 68 | 16 | 2 | 3 | 8 | .235 | .338 | .253 |
| Runners On/2 Out | | | 55 | 10 | 1 | 1 | 11 | .182 | .255 | .196 |
| Scor. Pos./2 Out | | | 37 | 9 | 1 | 0 | 5 | .243 | .351 | .243 |
| Late Inning Pressure | | | 142 | 27 | 6 | 17 | 31 | .190 | .352 | .272 |
| Leading Off | | | 27 | 6 | 1 | 4 | 6 | .222 | .333 | .323 |
| Runners On | | | 74 | 13 | 3 | 6 | 13 | .176 | .311 | .229 |
| Runners/Scor. Pos. | | | 43 | 9 | 2 | 3 | 6 | .209 | .349 | .245 |
| First 9 Batters | | | 213 | 46 | 6 | 16 | 50 | .216 | .333 | .266 |
| Second 9 Batters | | | 8 | 1 | 0 | 1 | 2 | .125 | .125 | .222 |
| All Batters Thereafter | | | 0 | 0 | 0 | 0 | 0 | — | — | — |

Loves to face: Brook Jacoby (0-for-9, 4 SO)
Hates to face: Cory Snyder (.571, 4-for-7, 2 HR)
Ground outs-to-air outs ratio: 0.87 last season, 0.83 for career. . . . Additional statistics: 5 double-play ground outs in 63 opportunities, 7 doubles, 0 triples in 61.1 innings last season. . . . Inherited 42 runners, stranded 30 (71%). . . . All-time team leader in saves, after increasing his total for a third straight season: 14 as a rookie in 1986, then 23, 30, and 33. . . . ERA has steadily decreased during that time: 2.97, 2.61, 2.41, 2.35. . . . Strikeouts per nine innings have decreased over the last three seasons: 10.10, 8.94, 7.63. . . . Has been removed from only three of his 102 appearances over the last two seasons. . . . Has allowed 21 career home runs, 15 with runners on base.

## Eric Plunk

Throws Right

| As/Yankees | W–L | ERA | AB | H | HR | BB | SO | BA | SA | OBA |
|---|---|---|---|---|---|---|---|---|---|---|
| Season | 8-6 | 3.28 | 373 | 82 | 10 | 64 | 85 | .220 | .346 | .333 |
| vs. Left-Handers | | | 166 | 37 | 6 | 35 | 45 | .223 | .380 | .353 |
| vs. Right-Handers | | | 207 | 45 | 4 | 29 | 40 | .217 | .319 | .315 |
| Home | 4-2 | 2.32 | 185 | 40 | 4 | 29 | 42 | .216 | .330 | .326 |
| Road | 4-4 | 4.17 | 188 | 42 | 6 | 35 | 43 | .223 | .362 | .339 |
| Grass | 6-6 | 3.34 | 330 | 74 | 9 | 55 | 75 | .224 | .358 | .334 |
| Artificial Turf | 2-0 | 2.84 | 43 | 8 | 1 | 9 | 10 | .186 | .256 | .321 |
| April | 1-0 | 1.69 | 38 | 7 | 1 | 7 | 12 | .184 | .289 | .326 |
| May | 0-1 | 2.79 | 32 | 4 | 0 | 3 | 6 | .125 | .156 | .200 |
| June | 1-0 | 1.23 | 49 | 9 | 0 | 6 | 12 | .184 | .306 | .263 |
| July | 2-0 | 3.26 | 72 | 21 | 2 | 13 | 16 | .292 | .417 | .400 |
| August | 1-3 | 5.68 | 74 | 18 | 4 | 13 | 11 | .243 | .446 | .356 |
| Sept./Oct. | 3-2 | 3.48 | 108 | 23 | 3 | 22 | 28 | .213 | .324 | .341 |
| Leading Off Inn. | | | 86 | 20 | 3 | 15 | 18 | .233 | .407 | .347 |
| Runners On | | | 170 | 36 | 4 | 25 | 42 | .212 | .329 | .310 |
| Runners/Scor. Pos. | | | 91 | 21 | 3 | 20 | 24 | .231 | .374 | .362 |
| Runners On/2 Out | | | 75 | 14 | 0 | 14 | 23 | .187 | .213 | .322 |
| Scor. Pos./2 Out | | | 42 | 4 | 0 | 11 | 16 | .095 | .095 | .296 |
| Late Inning Pressure | | | 86 | 21 | 3 | 14 | 17 | .244 | .395 | .347 |
| Leading Off | | | 25 | 6 | 1 | 4 | 7 | .240 | .440 | .345 |
| Runners On | | | 32 | 7 | 1 | 4 | 5 | .219 | .375 | .297 |
| Runners/Scor. Pos. | | | 13 | 4 | 1 | 3 | 2 | .308 | .538 | .412 |
| First 9 Batters | | | 244 | 56 | 6 | 45 | 61 | .230 | .361 | .348 |
| Second 9 Batters | | | 78 | 16 | 4 | 13 | 15 | .205 | .385 | .319 |
| All Batters Thereafter | | | 51 | 10 | 0 | 6 | 9 | .196 | .216 | .276 |

Loves to face: Cal Ripken (.063, 1-for-16)
Hates to face: Carlton Fisk (.400, 4-for-10, 2 HR)
Ground outs-to-air outs ratio: 0.71 last season, 0.86 for career. . . . Additional statistics: 10 double-play ground outs in 76 opportunities, 8 doubles, 1 triple in 104.1 innings last season. . . . Record of 4–3 (4.07 ERA) in seven starts, 4–3 (2.74 ERA, one save) in 43 relief appearances. Career figures: 9–13, 5.08 ERA as a starter; 14–8, 3.40 in relief. . . . Faced 15 batters with bases loaded, walked four. Career figures: .429 BA (15-for-35), 4 HR, 7 BB. . . . Opponents' career average of .196 in day games is lowest over the last 15 years (minimum: 250 BFP). . . . Opponents' career average is .178 with two outs and runners in scoring position. . . . Opposing right-handed batters have never hit better than .228.

## Joe Price

Throws Left

| Boston Red Sox | W–L | ERA | AB | H | HR | BB | SO | BA | SA | OBA |
|---|---|---|---|---|---|---|---|---|---|---|
| Season | 2-5 | 4.35 | 271 | 71 | 8 | 30 | 52 | .262 | .399 | .332 |
| vs. Left-Handers | | | 82 | 22 | 0 | 4 | 19 | .268 | .341 | .295 |
| vs. Right-Handers | | | 189 | 49 | 8 | 26 | 33 | .259 | .423 | .347 |
| Home | 1-3 | 3.41 | 136 | 35 | 4 | 14 | 33 | .257 | .382 | .325 |
| Road | 1-2 | 5.25 | 135 | 36 | 4 | 16 | 19 | .267 | .415 | .340 |
| Grass | 2-5 | 4.46 | 264 | 70 | 8 | 30 | 49 | .265 | .402 | .337 |
| Artificial Turf | 0-0 | 0.00 | 7 | 1 | 0 | 0 | 3 | .143 | .286 | .143 |
| April | | | 0 | 0 | 0 | 0 | 0 | — | — | — |
| May | 0-0 | 1.13 | 54 | 10 | 1 | 7 | 6 | .185 | .315 | .274 |
| June | 1-3 | 7.17 | 88 | 27 | 4 | 8 | 9 | .307 | .500 | .361 |
| July | 0-2 | 3.86 | 30 | 9 | 1 | 5 | 8 | .300 | .467 | .400 |
| August | 1-0 | 3.60 | 77 | 20 | 2 | 7 | 25 | .260 | .351 | .318 |
| Sept./Oct. | 0-0 | 6.00 | 22 | 5 | 0 | 3 | 4 | .227 | .273 | .320 |
| Leading Off Inn. | | | 55 | 16 | 4 | 9 | 11 | .291 | .564 | .391 |
| Runners On | | | 141 | 36 | 4 | 13 | 27 | .255 | .397 | .312 |
| Runners/Scor. Pos. | | | 67 | 16 | 0 | 7 | 13 | .239 | .284 | .299 |
| Runners On/2 Out | | | 59 | 15 | 2 | 7 | 16 | .254 | .424 | .333 |
| Scor. Pos./2 Out | | | 30 | 5 | 0 | 3 | 8 | .167 | .200 | .242 |
| Late Inning Pressure | | | 40 | 11 | 2 | 4 | 11 | .275 | .450 | .341 |
| Leading Off | | | 11 | 5 | 1 | 2 | 4 | .455 | .818 | .538 |
| Runners On | | | 17 | 4 | 1 | 1 | 4 | .235 | .412 | .278 |
| Runners/Scor. Pos. | | | 8 | 1 | 0 | 1 | 3 | .125 | .125 | .222 |
| First 9 Batters | | | 181 | 44 | 4 | 21 | 40 | .243 | .354 | .319 |
| Second 9 Batters | | | 68 | 19 | 2 | 4 | 8 | .279 | .426 | .315 |
| All Batters Thereafter | | | 22 | 8 | 2 | 5 | 4 | .364 | .682 | .481 |

Loves to face: Brad Komminsk (0-for-10, 4 SO)
Hates to face: Claudell Washington (.600, 6-for-10, 3 2B)
Ground outs-to-air outs ratio: 0.76 last season, 0.69 for career. . . . Additional statistics: 5 double-play ground outs in 71 opportunities, 9 doubles, 2 triples in 70.1 innings last season. . . . Combined-leagues record of 2–3 (6.00 ERA) in six starts, 1–3 (3.81 ERA, no saves) in 32 relief appearances. . . . Opponents batted .229 in day games, .308 at night. Difference of 79 points was the 3d largest in majors. . . . Red Sox lost 22 of the first 23 games in which he appeared. . . . Allowed a triple and home run to first two left-handed batters he faced (Gwynn and Wynne, April 4), but didn't allow a hit longer than a double to a left-hander after that. . . . Has won fewer than four games in every season since 1985.

## Shane Rawley

Throws Left

| Minnesota Twins | W–L | ERA | AB | H | HR | BB | SO | BA | SA | OBA |
|---|---|---|---|---|---|---|---|---|---|---|
| Season | 5-12 | 5.21 | 569 | 167 | 19 | 60 | 68 | .293 | .467 | .359 |
| vs. Left-Handers | | | 116 | 42 | 4 | 6 | 10 | .362 | .543 | .393 |
| vs. Right-Handers | | | 453 | 125 | 15 | 54 | 58 | .276 | .448 | .350 |
| Home | 2-7 | 6.18 | 309 | 95 | 10 | 35 | 41 | .307 | .479 | .376 |
| Road | 3-5 | 4.07 | 260 | 72 | 9 | 25 | 27 | .277 | .454 | .338 |
| Grass | 3-5 | 4.39 | 213 | 61 | 9 | 23 | 22 | .286 | .484 | .354 |
| Artificial Turf | 2-7 | 5.69 | 356 | 106 | 10 | 37 | 46 | .298 | .458 | .361 |
| April | 1-3 | 4.33 | 103 | 25 | 3 | 14 | 14 | .243 | .417 | .333 |
| May | 2-1 | 4.04 | 141 | 40 | 5 | 9 | 16 | .284 | .461 | .322 |
| June | 1-2 | 3.80 | 91 | 24 | 2 | 9 | 7 | .264 | .374 | .327 |
| July | 0-2 | 5.93 | 110 | 36 | 3 | 10 | 11 | .327 | .527 | .383 |
| August | 1-4 | 8.26 | 113 | 38 | 6 | 18 | 19 | .336 | .549 | .424 |
| Sept./Oct. | 0-0 | 3.00 | 11 | 4 | 0 | 0 | 1 | .364 | .364 | .364 |
| Leading Off Inn. | | | 135 | 43 | 5 | 17 | 16 | .319 | .526 | .395 |
| Runners On | | | 257 | 73 | 8 | 22 | 33 | .284 | .416 | .336 |
| Runners/Scor. Pos. | | | 144 | 44 | 4 | 13 | 18 | .306 | .424 | .354 |
| Runners On/2 Out | | | 96 | 24 | 3 | 6 | 14 | .250 | .365 | .294 |
| Scor. Pos./2 Out | | | 56 | 14 | 1 | 5 | 8 | .250 | .304 | .311 |
| Late Inning Pressure | | | 47 | 19 | 0 | 4 | 1 | .404 | .532 | .442 |
| Leading Off | | | 13 | 6 | 0 | 1 | 0 | .462 | .615 | .500 |
| Runners On | | | 21 | 8 | 0 | 2 | 0 | .381 | .429 | .417 |
| Runners/Scor. Pos. | | | 13 | 7 | 0 | 2 | 0 | .538 | .615 | .563 |
| First 9 Batters | | | 206 | 60 | 7 | 28 | 25 | .291 | .451 | .374 |
| Second 9 Batters | | | 193 | 53 | 9 | 20 | 33 | .275 | .456 | .341 |
| All Batters Thereafter | | | 170 | 54 | 3 | 12 | 10 | .318 | .500 | .359 |

Loves to face: Candy Maldonado (.100, 3-for-30)
Hates to face: Frank White (.484, 15-for-31)
Ground outs-to-air outs ratio: 0.84 last season, 1.16 for career. . . . Additional statistics: 17 double-play ground outs in 136 opportunities, 28 doubles, 7 triples in 145.0 innings last season. . . . Allowed 18 first-inning runs in 25 starts. . . . Batting support: 3.88 runs per start. . . . Compiled 13–28 mark over last two years, after three consecutive years above the .600 mark. There have been 295 other instances of pitchers with three consecutive seasons of 15 or more decisions above .600. *Only one had a lower percentage over his next two seasons than Rawley did:* Whitlow Wyatt (year by year, from 1941: 22–10, 19–7, 14–5, 2–6, 0–7). . . . Now for the *really* bad news: Rawley had only one winning record in eight seasons in A.L.

## Jeff Reardon

Throws Right

| Minnesota Twins | W–L | ERA | AB | H | HR | BB | SO | BA | SA | OBA |
|---|---|---|---|---|---|---|---|---|---|---|
| Season | 5-4 | 4.07 | 276 | 68 | 8 | 12 | 46 | .246 | .384 | .280 |
| vs. Left-Handers | | | 129 | 32 | 5 | 6 | 18 | .248 | .434 | .286 |
| vs. Right-Handers | | | 147 | 36 | 3 | 6 | 28 | .245 | .340 | .276 |
| Home | 4-2 | 4.12 | 150 | 36 | 4 | 8 | 23 | .240 | .373 | .275 |
| Road | 1-2 | 4.01 | 126 | 32 | 4 | 4 | 23 | .254 | .397 | .287 |
| Grass | 1-1 | 3.95 | 102 | 24 | 4 | 3 | 17 | .235 | .392 | .273 |
| Artificial Turf | 4-3 | 4.14 | 174 | 44 | 4 | 9 | 29 | .253 | .379 | .285 |
| April | 0-1 | 4.66 | 36 | 8 | 1 | 1 | 4 | .222 | .306 | .263 |
| May | 0-1 | 5.91 | 44 | 12 | 2 | 1 | 6 | .273 | .500 | .283 |
| June | 2-0 | 2.81 | 56 | 10 | 1 | 3 | 12 | .179 | .286 | .233 |
| July | 1-0 | 4.09 | 44 | 14 | 1 | 1 | 9 | .318 | .477 | .340 |
| August | 2-1 | 3.38 | 71 | 18 | 1 | 3 | 12 | .254 | .338 | .276 |
| Sept./Oct. | 0-1 | 5.14 | 25 | 6 | 2 | 3 | 3 | .240 | .480 | .310 |
| Leading Off Inn. | | | 53 | 7 | 1 | 3 | 10 | .132 | .245 | .193 |
| Runners On | | | 136 | 37 | 5 | 5 | 17 | .272 | .441 | .293 |
| Runners/Scor. Pos. | | | 82 | 21 | 3 | 5 | 9 | .256 | .415 | .290 |
| Runners On/2 Out | | | 69 | 17 | 2 | 2 | 9 | .246 | .420 | .268 |
| Scor. Pos./2 Out | | | 42 | 9 | 1 | 2 | 7 | .214 | .357 | .250 |
| Late Inning Pressure | | | 170 | 39 | 5 | 10 | 26 | .229 | .359 | .276 |
| Leading Off | | | 30 | 4 | 1 | 2 | 5 | .133 | .333 | .212 |
| Runners On | | | 91 | 22 | 2 | 4 | 11 | .242 | .352 | .265 |
| Runners/Scor. Pos. | | | 59 | 15 | 2 | 4 | 6 | .254 | .390 | .288 |
| First 9 Batters | | | 271 | 68 | 8 | 12 | 45 | .251 | .391 | .285 |
| Second 9 Batters | | | 5 | 0 | 0 | 0 | 1 | .000 | .000 | .000 |
| All Batters Thereafter | | | 0 | 0 | 0 | 0 | 0 | — | — | — |

Loves to face: Jeffrey Leonard (.111, 2-for-18, 8 SO)
Hates to face: Thad Bosley (.667, 4-for-6, 3 HR)
Ground outs-to-air outs ratio: 0.44 last season, 0.54 for career. . . . Additional statistics: 2 double-play ground outs in 52 opportunities, 14 doubles, 0 triples in 73.0 innings last season. . . . Inherited 47 runners, stranded 33 (70%). . . . Walked only 1.48 batters per nine innings. Previous career average was 3.18. . . . Strikeouts per nine innings, year by year since 1987: 9.30, 6.90, 5.67. . . . Hasn't allowed a triple since 1986. . . . Career average of .245 by opposing left-handers, .212 by right-handers. . . . Only four relievers in baseball history have appeared in more games without ever starting one: Kent Tekulve (1050), Sparky Lyle (899), Dan Quisenberry (669), Bruce Sutter (661), Reardon (647).

## Jerry Reed

Throws Right

| Seattle Mariners | W–L | ERA | AB | H | HR | BB | SO | BA | SA | OBA |
|---|---|---|---|---|---|---|---|---|---|---|
| Season | 7-7 | 3.19 | 379 | 89 | 10 | 43 | 50 | .235 | .377 | .313 |
| vs. Left-Handers | | | 148 | 38 | 4 | 22 | 14 | .257 | .399 | .355 |
| vs. Right-Handers | | | 231 | 51 | 6 | 21 | 36 | .221 | .364 | .285 |
| Home | 6-4 | 2.75 | 193 | 44 | 3 | 19 | 30 | .228 | .337 | .296 |
| Road | 1-3 | 3.65 | 186 | 45 | 7 | 24 | 20 | .242 | .419 | .330 |
| Grass | 1-2 | 4.54 | 140 | 35 | 7 | 18 | 12 | .250 | .471 | .338 |
| Artificial Turf | 6-5 | 2.39 | 239 | 54 | 3 | 25 | 38 | .226 | .322 | .298 |
| April | 2-2 | 3.57 | 72 | 19 | 2 | 8 | 14 | .264 | .417 | .338 |
| May | 1-1 | 3.72 | 72 | 16 | 2 | 8 | 9 | .222 | .389 | .296 |
| June | 0-2 | 1.74 | 73 | 13 | 0 | 9 | 14 | .178 | .233 | .277 |
| July | 0-0 | 3.77 | 51 | 12 | 2 | 6 | 1 | .235 | .373 | .316 |
| August | 2-1 | 2.95 | 64 | 13 | 1 | 8 | 6 | .203 | .328 | .288 |
| Sept./Oct. | 2-1 | 3.97 | 47 | 16 | 3 | 4 | 6 | .340 | .596 | .392 |
| Leading Off Inn. | | | 86 | 24 | 3 | 5 | 12 | .279 | .453 | .326 |
| Runners On | | | 168 | 40 | 5 | 31 | 23 | .238 | .375 | .353 |
| Runners/Scor. Pos. | | | 117 | 22 | 3 | 25 | 20 | .188 | .291 | .326 |
| Runners On/2 Out | | | 70 | 11 | 0 | 19 | 13 | .157 | .186 | .337 |
| Scor. Pos./2 Out | | | 54 | 5 | 0 | 15 | 12 | .093 | .093 | .290 |
| Late Inning Pressure | | | 97 | 32 | 2 | 19 | 14 | .330 | .495 | .440 |
| Leading Off | | | 25 | 11 | 1 | 3 | 4 | .440 | .680 | .500 |
| Runners On | | | 54 | 15 | 1 | 14 | 7 | .278 | .426 | .426 |
| Runners/Scor. Pos. | | | 39 | 10 | 1 | 12 | 6 | .256 | .410 | .431 |
| First 9 Batters | | | 305 | 73 | 5 | 36 | 38 | .239 | .348 | .318 |
| Second 9 Batters | | | 69 | 16 | 5 | 7 | 11 | .232 | .536 | .312 |
| All Batters Thereafter | | | 5 | 0 | 0 | 0 | 1 | .000 | .000 | .000 |

Loves to face: Dave Henderson (0-for-11, 4 SO)
Hates to face: Don Mattingly (.571, 4-for-7, 1 2B, 2 HR)
Ground outs-to-air outs ratio: 0.99 last season, 1.12 for career. . . . Additional statistics: 6 double-play ground outs in 74 opportunities, 20 doubles, 2 triples in 101.2 innings last season. . . . Opponents' batting average was career low. . . . Career averages: .290 by opposing left-handers, .230 by right-handers. . . . Allowed more home runs on the road than in the Kingdome in three of his four seasons with Seattle. . . . ERA has been between 3.00 and 4.00 in each of last four seasons, compared to prior career mark of 4.77. . . . Hasn't played for a team with a winning record since traded from 1982 Phillies. (Spent two-and-a-half years in Cleveland before joining Seattle in 1986.)

## Jerry Reuss

Throws Left

| White Sox/Brewers | W–L | ERA | AB | H | HR | BB | SO | BA | SA | OBA |
|---|---|---|---|---|---|---|---|---|---|---|
| Season | 9-9 | 5.13 | 570 | 171 | 19 | 34 | 40 | .300 | .446 | .340 |
| vs. Left-Handers | | | 101 | 32 | 6 | 3 | 6 | .317 | .535 | .349 |
| vs. Right-Handers | | | 469 | 139 | 13 | 31 | 34 | .296 | .426 | .339 |
| Home | 4-5 | 4.38 | 301 | 85 | 8 | 14 | 22 | .282 | .392 | .315 |
| Road | 5-4 | 6.02 | 269 | 86 | 11 | 20 | 18 | .320 | .506 | .369 |
| Grass | 7-9 | 4.81 | 519 | 153 | 16 | 29 | 37 | .295 | .432 | .332 |
| Artificial Turf | 2-0 | 8.74 | 51 | 18 | 3 | 5 | 3 | .353 | .588 | .421 |
| April | 2-2 | 6.49 | 106 | 30 | 3 | 7 | 8 | .283 | .425 | .325 |
| May | 1-0 | 7.48 | 98 | 37 | 5 | 5 | 5 | .378 | .622 | .400 |
| June | 4-2 | 3.58 | 133 | 39 | 1 | 8 | 8 | .293 | .361 | .333 |
| July | 1-1 | 3.46 | 101 | 29 | 3 | 1 | 6 | .287 | .396 | .305 |
| August | 0-2 | 3.95 | 53 | 12 | 4 | 5 | 7 | .226 | .491 | .293 |
| Sept./Oct. | 1-2 | 6.30 | 79 | 24 | 3 | 8 | 6 | .304 | .430 | .375 |
| Leading Off Inn. | | | 135 | 35 | 4 | 11 | 8 | .259 | .393 | .320 |
| Runners On | | | 239 | 87 | 7 | 14 | 18 | .364 | .519 | .392 |
| Runners/Scor. Pos. | | | 134 | 48 | 4 | 9 | 9 | .358 | .515 | .387 |
| Runners On/2 Out | | | 93 | 25 | 2 | 7 | 9 | .269 | .376 | .320 |
| Scor. Pos./2 Out | | | 58 | 15 | 2 | 6 | 5 | .259 | .414 | .328 |
| Late Inning Pressure | | | 11 | 5 | 1 | 1 | 0 | .455 | .818 | .462 |
| Leading Off | | | 3 | 1 | 0 | 0 | 0 | .333 | .333 | .333 |
| Runners On | | | 3 | 2 | 0 | 1 | 0 | .667 | 1.000 | .600 |
| Runners/Scor. Pos. | | | 2 | 1 | 0 | 1 | 0 | .500 | .500 | .500 |
| First 9 Batters | | | 229 | 71 | 7 | 13 | 16 | .310 | .463 | .348 |
| Second 9 Batters | | | 200 | 63 | 5 | 12 | 11 | .315 | .435 | .353 |
| All Batters Thereafter | | | 141 | 37 | 7 | 9 | 13 | .262 | .433 | .309 |

Loves to face: Bob Boone (.148, 9-for-61, 0 XBH)
Hates to face: Alan Trammell (.692, 9-for-13, 1 HR)
Ground outs-to-air outs ratio: 1.15 last season, 1.83 since 1975. . . . Additional statistics: 13 double-play ground outs in 124 opportunities, 21 doubles, 1 triple in 140.1 innings last season. . . . Allowed 22 first-inning runs in 26 starts. . . . Batting support: 4.42 runs per start. . . . Along with Carlton Fisk, comprised the oldest opening-day battery in major league history. Combined age: over 81 years. Previous oldest: 79 years, Johnny Niggeling and Rick Ferrell (1944 Senators). . . . Has defeated every major league club except the Red Sox. . . . Allowed the ninth grand slam of his career in 1980, tying the all-time record. Since 1981, faced 83 batters with bases loaded without allowing a home run.

## Dave Righetti

Throws Left

| New York Yankees | W–L | ERA | AB | H | HR | BB | SO | BA | SA | OBA |
|---|---|---|---|---|---|---|---|---|---|---|
| Season | 2-6 | 3.00 | 264 | 73 | 3 | 26 | 51 | .277 | .364 | .341 |
| vs. Left-Handers | | | 62 | 17 | 1 | 7 | 12 | .274 | .355 | .343 |
| vs. Right-Handers | | | 202 | 56 | 2 | 19 | 39 | .277 | .366 | .341 |
| Home | 0-1 | 3.16 | 127 | 37 | 0 | 8 | 21 | .291 | .362 | .338 |
| Road | 2-5 | 2.87 | 137 | 36 | 3 | 18 | 30 | .263 | .365 | .344 |
| Grass | 2-6 | 3.12 | 228 | 65 | 3 | 21 | 42 | .285 | .377 | .345 |
| Artificial Turf | 0-0 | 2.38 | 36 | 8 | 0 | 5 | 9 | .222 | .278 | .317 |
| April | 0-1 | 5.73 | 45 | 16 | 0 | 5 | 10 | .356 | .378 | .431 |
| May | 1-0 | 0.00 | 31 | 5 | 0 | 1 | 9 | .161 | .161 | .176 |
| June | 1-1 | 1.53 | 69 | 19 | 1 | 6 | 11 | .275 | .362 | .333 |
| July | 0-1 | 4.05 | 25 | 7 | 1 | 3 | 4 | .280 | .480 | .357 |
| August | 0-2 | 4.86 | 65 | 19 | 0 | 9 | 9 | .292 | .415 | .378 |
| Sept./Oct. | 0-1 | 1.17 | 29 | 7 | 1 | 2 | 8 | .241 | .345 | .290 |
| Leading Off Inn. | | | 53 | 12 | 2 | 4 | 14 | .226 | .434 | .293 |
| Runners On | | | 139 | 37 | 1 | 16 | 26 | .266 | .345 | .338 |
| Runners/Scor. Pos. | | | 83 | 23 | 0 | 14 | 12 | .277 | .349 | .374 |
| Runners On/2 Out | | | 69 | 21 | 1 | 7 | 16 | .304 | .420 | .368 |
| Scor. Pos./2 Out | | | 42 | 13 | 0 | 7 | 8 | .310 | .381 | .408 |
| Late Inning Pressure | | | 163 | 44 | 3 | 22 | 32 | .270 | .387 | .353 |
| Leading Off | | | 34 | 10 | 2 | 4 | 8 | .294 | .588 | .368 |
| Runners On | | | 87 | 23 | 1 | 12 | 16 | .264 | .356 | .347 |
| Runners/Scor. Pos. | | | 54 | 13 | 0 | 11 | 9 | .241 | .296 | .358 |
| First 9 Batters | | | 254 | 68 | 2 | 25 | 48 | .268 | .346 | .333 |
| Second 9 Batters | | | 10 | 5 | 1 | 1 | 3 | .500 | .800 | .545 |
| All Batters Thereafter | | | 0 | 0 | 0 | 0 | 0 | — | — | — |

Loves to face: Jack Howell (0-for-10, 9 SO)
Hates to face: Lou Whitaker (.433, 13-for-30, 1 HR)
Ground outs-to-air outs ratio: 1.11 last season, 1.04 for career. . . . Additional statistics: 7 double-play ground outs in 65 opportunities, 12 doubles, 1 triple in 69.0 innings last season. . . . Stranded 25 of 31 inherited runners (81%), 5th-highest average in A.L. (minimum: 25 runners). . . . Career records: 11–17 in September, 1–3 in October (his only months with losing records). . . . Opponents have batted over .300 with bases loaded in each of last six seasons. . . . Over last four seasons, opposing left-handers have out-hit right-handers by 36 points (.281 to .245). . . . Needs 30 appearances to pass Whitey Ford as all-time team leader. Top five: Ford (498), Righetti (469), Ruffing (426), Lyle (420), Shawkey (415).

## Kevin Ritz

Throws Right

| Detroit Tigers | W-L | ERA | AB | H | HR | BB | SO | BA | SA | OBA |
|---|---|---|---|---|---|---|---|---|---|---|
| Season | 4-6 | 4.38 | 283 | 75 | 2 | 44 | 56 | .265 | .353 | .360 |
| vs. Left-Handers | | | 139 | 37 | 2 | 26 | 26 | .266 | .388 | .381 |
| vs. Right-Handers | | | 144 | 38 | 0 | 18 | 30 | .264 | .319 | .339 |
| Home | 4-2 | 4.10 | 145 | 41 | 1 | 21 | 28 | .283 | .359 | .373 |
| Road | 0-4 | 4.66 | 138 | 34 | 1 | 23 | 28 | .246 | .348 | .348 |
| Grass | 4-5 | 4.70 | 256 | 70 | 2 | 40 | 49 | .273 | .363 | .368 |
| Artificial Turf | 0-1 | 1.29 | 27 | 5 | 0 | 4 | 7 | .185 | .259 | .290 |
| April | | | 0 | 0 | 0 | 0 | 0 | — | — | — |
| May | | | 0 | 0 | 0 | 0 | 0 | — | — | — |
| June | | | 0 | 0 | 0 | 0 | 0 | — | — | — |
| July | 1-1 | 4.58 | 69 | 18 | 1 | 15 | 9 | .261 | .348 | .400 |
| August | 2-2 | 4.24 | 126 | 28 | 0 | 18 | 27 | .222 | .302 | .315 |
| Sept./Oct. | 1-3 | 4.43 | 88 | 29 | 1 | 11 | 20 | .330 | .432 | .392 |
| Leading Off Inn. | | | 67 | 14 | 1 | 11 | 14 | .209 | .299 | .321 |
| Runners On | | | 125 | 37 | 0 | 24 | 30 | .296 | .360 | .400 |
| Runners/Scor. Pos. | | | 77 | 22 | 0 | 19 | 22 | .286 | .338 | .412 |
| Runners On/2 Out | | | 51 | 13 | 0 | 14 | 15 | .255 | .314 | .424 |
| Scor. Pos./2 Out | | | 36 | 11 | 0 | 11 | 10 | .306 | .389 | .479 |
| Late Inning Pressure | | | 27 | 3 | 0 | 2 | 4 | .111 | .148 | .172 |
| Leading Off | | | 8 | 1 | 0 | 0 | 2 | .125 | .125 | .125 |
| Runners On | | | 5 | 1 | 0 | 1 | 1 | .200 | .400 | .333 |
| Runners/Scor. Pos. | | | 2 | 0 | 0 | 1 | 0 | .000 | .000 | .333 |
| First 9 Batters | | | 91 | 24 | 1 | 14 | 20 | .264 | .374 | .361 |
| Second 9 Batters | | | 95 | 27 | 1 | 12 | 18 | .284 | .358 | .361 |
| All Batters Thereafter | | | 97 | 24 | 0 | 18 | 18 | .247 | .330 | .359 |

Loves to face: Bo Jackson (0-for-7, 5 SO)
Hates to face: Rafael Palmeiro (.500, 3-for-6, 2 3B)
Ground outs-to-air outs ratio: 1.42 last season, 1.42 for career. . . . Additional statistics: 4 double-play ground outs in 64 opportunities, 13 doubles, 3 triples in 74.0 innings last season. . . . Allowed 8 first-inning runs in 12 starts. . . . Batting support: 3.83 runs per start. . . . One home run per 37 innings was best among A.L. starters (50 IP). Allowed a home run in his first and last games, but none in between. . . . Was the losing pitcher in five of his last six starts. . . . Has never had a winning record at any level of professional ball. Career minor league record: 27–36. . . . Didn't allow a triple or home run to the 179 ground-ball hitters he faced. Fly-ballers out-slugged ground-ballers by .405 to .312.

## Jeff M. Robinson

Throws Right

| Detroit Tigers | W-L | ERA | AB | H | HR | BB | SO | BA | SA | OBA |
|---|---|---|---|---|---|---|---|---|---|---|
| Season | 4-5 | 4.73 | 294 | 76 | 10 | 46 | 40 | .259 | .418 | .358 |
| vs. Left-Handers | | | 147 | 39 | 6 | 28 | 17 | .265 | .463 | .382 |
| vs. Right-Handers | | | 147 | 37 | 4 | 18 | 23 | .252 | .374 | .331 |
| Home | 4-2 | 2.76 | 165 | 38 | 3 | 25 | 22 | .230 | .358 | .326 |
| Road | 0-3 | 7.52 | 129 | 38 | 7 | 21 | 18 | .295 | .496 | .397 |
| Grass | 4-3 | 3.53 | 243 | 57 | 5 | 40 | 35 | .235 | .350 | .339 |
| Artificial Turf | 0-2 | 11.57 | 51 | 19 | 5 | 6 | 5 | .373 | .745 | .448 |
| April | 1-1 | 4.29 | 79 | 19 | 2 | 9 | 16 | .241 | .367 | .318 |
| May | 0-0 | 4.70 | 28 | 6 | 0 | 7 | 2 | .214 | .250 | .361 |
| June | 0-0 | 0.00 | 4 | 2 | 0 | 3 | 1 | .500 | .500 | .714 |
| July | 0-1 | 1.93 | 20 | 7 | 1 | 1 | 2 | .350 | .550 | .364 |
| August | 2-2 | 5.25 | 134 | 35 | 6 | 21 | 14 | .261 | .455 | .363 |
| Sept./Oct. | 1-1 | 6.14 | 29 | 7 | 1 | 5 | 5 | .241 | .448 | .353 |
| Leading Off Inn. | | | 72 | 25 | 5 | 12 | 8 | .347 | .625 | .440 |
| Runners On | | | 136 | 35 | 4 | 18 | 15 | .257 | .397 | .342 |
| Runners/Scor. Pos. | | | 73 | 20 | 3 | 8 | 9 | .274 | .438 | .341 |
| Runners On/2 Out | | | 54 | 12 | 1 | 6 | 6 | .222 | .333 | .311 |
| Scor. Pos./2 Out | | | 31 | 8 | 1 | 5 | 4 | .258 | .355 | .378 |
| Late Inning Pressure | | | 3 | 0 | 0 | 0 | 2 | .000 | .000 | .000 |
| Leading Off | | | 1 | 0 | 0 | 0 | 0 | .000 | .000 | .000 |
| Runners On | | | 0 | 0 | 0 | 0 | 0 | — | — | — |
| Runners/Scor. Pos. | | | 0 | 0 | 0 | 0 | 0 | — | — | — |
| First 9 Batters | | | 111 | 26 | 5 | 22 | 17 | .234 | .423 | .358 |
| Second 9 Batters | | | 97 | 27 | 3 | 14 | 10 | .278 | .423 | .366 |
| All Batters Thereafter | | | 86 | 23 | 2 | 10 | 13 | .267 | .407 | .347 |

Loves to face: Kevin Seitzer (.077, 1-for-13)
Hates to face: Fred McGriff (.545, 6-for-11, 3 HR)
Ground outs-to-air outs ratio: 0.99 last season, 1.01 for career. . . . Additional statistics: 7 double-play ground outs in 75 opportunities, 15 doubles, 1 triple in 78.0 innings last season. . . . Allowed 9 first-inning runs in 16 starts. . . . Batting support: 5.88 runs per start, highest in majors (minimum: 15 GS). . . . Average of 4.88 innings pitched per start was 3d lowest in majors. . . . Phillies-Padres game last May 20 featured battle of two Greg Harrises. This season, Tigers and Yankees could provide matchup of Jeff Robinsons. . . . Has completed nine of 60 career starts, four of them for shutouts. . . . Opponents' career average is .199 (19 HR) at Tiger Stadium, .270 (26 HR) on the road.

## Kenny Rogers

Throws Left

| Texas Rangers | W-L | ERA | AB | H | HR | BB | SO | BA | SA | OBA |
|---|---|---|---|---|---|---|---|---|---|---|
| Season | 3-4 | 2.93 | 259 | 60 | 2 | 42 | 63 | .232 | .301 | .344 |
| vs. Left-Handers | | | 83 | 14 | 0 | 13 | 22 | .169 | .217 | .303 |
| vs. Right-Handers | | | 176 | 46 | 2 | 29 | 41 | .261 | .341 | .364 |
| Home | 3-3 | 3.33 | 162 | 39 | 1 | 26 | 34 | .241 | .315 | .351 |
| Road | 0-1 | 2.28 | 97 | 21 | 1 | 16 | 29 | .216 | .278 | .333 |
| Grass | 3-3 | 3.14 | 225 | 53 | 1 | 38 | 54 | .236 | .298 | .352 |
| Artificial Turf | 0-1 | 1.69 | 34 | 7 | 1 | 4 | 9 | .206 | .324 | .289 |
| April | 1-0 | 1.04 | 30 | 7 | 0 | 6 | 8 | .233 | .233 | .378 |
| May | 1-0 | 2.20 | 59 | 11 | 0 | 13 | 17 | .186 | .237 | .338 |
| June | 0-0 | 4.35 | 40 | 13 | 1 | 7 | 7 | .325 | .475 | .417 |
| July | 0-0 | 3.86 | 42 | 10 | 0 | 4 | 14 | .238 | .286 | .319 |
| August | 0-2 | 3.60 | 48 | 10 | 0 | 7 | 13 | .208 | .229 | .316 |
| Sept./Oct. | 1-2 | 2.31 | 40 | 9 | 1 | 5 | 4 | .225 | .375 | .311 |
| Leading Off Inn. | | | 44 | 8 | 1 | 11 | 10 | .182 | .273 | .357 |
| Runners On | | | 152 | 40 | 1 | 21 | 35 | .263 | .349 | .358 |
| Runners/Scor. Pos. | | | 95 | 24 | 1 | 15 | 22 | .253 | .347 | .362 |
| Runners On/2 Out | | | 61 | 12 | 0 | 11 | 17 | .197 | .230 | .329 |
| Scor. Pos./2 Out | | | 42 | 10 | 0 | 8 | 11 | .238 | .286 | .373 |
| Late Inning Pressure | | | 120 | 24 | 1 | 16 | 28 | .200 | .250 | .300 |
| Leading Off | | | 21 | 3 | 0 | 6 | 4 | .143 | .143 | .357 |
| Runners On | | | 67 | 16 | 1 | 6 | 14 | .239 | .328 | .303 |
| Runners/Scor. Pos. | | | 38 | 8 | 1 | 5 | 7 | .211 | .342 | .304 |
| First 9 Batters | | | 256 | 59 | 2 | 39 | 62 | .230 | .297 | .338 |
| Second 9 Batters | | | 3 | 1 | 0 | 3 | 1 | .333 | .667 | .667 |
| All Batters Thereafter | | | 0 | 0 | 0 | 0 | 0 | — | — | — |

Loves to face: Lance Johnson (0-for-5, 2 SO)
Hates to face: Wade Boggs (.750, 3-for-4)
Ground outs-to-air outs ratio: 0.99 last season, his first in majors . . . . Additional statistics: 6 double-play ground outs in 80 opportunities, 12 doubles, 0 triples in 73.2 innings last season. . . . Inherited 72 runners (highest total in majors), stranded 51 (71%). . . . His namesake "knows when to hold 'em." This Kenny Rogers knows *how* to hold 'em. Opponents stole only three bases in nine attempts. . . . Opposing ground-ball hitters batted .295, compared to .169 by fly-ballers. . . . Made 73 appearances. Rookie record: 80, set by Mitch Williams in 1986. . . . Had never before appeared in more than 39 games at any level of pro ball. . . . Only three A.L. rookies had more than one save: Gregg Olson (27), Donn Pall (6), Rogers (2).

## Steve Rosenberg

Throws Left

| Chicago White Sox | W-L | ERA | AB | H | HR | BB | SO | BA | SA | OBA |
|---|---|---|---|---|---|---|---|---|---|---|
| Season | 4-13 | 4.94 | 541 | 148 | 14 | 58 | 77 | .274 | .438 | .340 |
| vs. Left-Handers | | | 100 | 28 | 1 | 11 | 15 | .280 | .390 | .354 |
| vs. Right-Handers | | | 441 | 120 | 13 | 47 | 62 | .272 | .449 | .337 |
| Home | 2-7 | 4.73 | 273 | 78 | 7 | 26 | 41 | .286 | .451 | .344 |
| Road | 2-6 | 5.15 | 268 | 70 | 7 | 32 | 36 | .261 | .425 | .336 |
| Grass | 4-12 | 4.78 | 468 | 130 | 13 | 46 | 68 | .278 | .447 | .338 |
| Artificial Turf | 0-1 | 5.95 | 73 | 18 | 1 | 12 | 9 | .247 | .384 | .349 |
| April | 0-0 | 2.91 | 76 | 16 | 1 | 8 | 13 | .211 | .303 | .291 |
| May | 1-2 | 5.60 | 63 | 15 | 0 | 12 | 8 | .238 | .349 | .351 |
| June | 1-3 | 5.93 | 117 | 39 | 4 | 7 | 18 | .333 | .556 | .368 |
| July | 1-2 | 4.60 | 114 | 29 | 3 | 12 | 14 | .254 | .404 | .318 |
| August | 1-3 | 5.03 | 132 | 35 | 5 | 14 | 16 | .265 | .455 | .333 |
| Sept./Oct. | 0-3 | 6.30 | 39 | 14 | 1 | 5 | 8 | .359 | .538 | .422 |
| Leading Off Inn. | | | 137 | 44 | 5 | 15 | 18 | .321 | .496 | .392 |
| Runners On | | | 241 | 68 | 4 | 18 | 29 | .282 | .436 | .321 |
| Runners/Scor. Pos. | | | 140 | 41 | 3 | 13 | 23 | .293 | .450 | .333 |
| Runners On/2 Out | | | 101 | 31 | 2 | 12 | 16 | .307 | .465 | .381 |
| Scor. Pos./2 Out | | | 69 | 22 | 2 | 10 | 12 | .319 | .522 | .405 |
| Late Inning Pressure | | | 60 | 15 | 2 | 10 | 9 | .250 | .367 | .357 |
| Leading Off | | | 20 | 5 | 0 | 2 | 2 | .250 | .250 | .318 |
| Runners On | | | 21 | 5 | 1 | 2 | 1 | .238 | .429 | .304 |
| Runners/Scor. Pos. | | | 8 | 0 | 0 | 1 | 1 | .000 | .000 | .111 |
| First 9 Batters | | | 260 | 68 | 7 | 30 | 32 | .262 | .423 | .331 |
| Second 9 Batters | | | 176 | 53 | 5 | 16 | 29 | .301 | .494 | .357 |
| All Batters Thereafter | | | 105 | 27 | 2 | 12 | 16 | .257 | .381 | .333 |

Loves to face: Don Mattingly (0-for-11)
Hates to face: Jerry Browne (.667, 6-for-9)
Ground outs-to-air outs ratio: 0.72 last season, 0.71 for career. . . . Additional statistics: 14 double-play ground outs in 99 opportunities, 35 doubles, 6 triples in 142.0 innings last season. . . . Allowed 10 first-inning runs in 21 starts. . . . Batting support: 3.38 runs per start, 5th lowest in A.L. (minimum: 15 GS). . . . Record of 3–11 (5.45 ERA) as a starter, 1–2 (3.38 ERA, no saves) in 17 relief appearances. . . . Only two of 19 career home runs have been hit by left-handers (Dave Parker and George Brett). . . . Opponents' career breakdown: .292 at Comiskey Park, .276 on other grass fields, .239 on artificial surfaces. . . . Lowest career winning percentage (4–14, .222) of any active pitcher with at least 10 decisions.

## Jeff Russell

Throws Right

| Texas Rangers | W–L | ERA | AB | H | HR | BB | SO | BA | SA | OBA |
|---|---|---|---|---|---|---|---|---|---|---|
| Season | 6-4 | 1.98 | 247 | 45 | 4 | 24 | 77 | .182 | .279 | .260 |
| vs. Left-Handers | | | 112 | 23 | 0 | 12 | 33 | .205 | .241 | .289 |
| vs. Right-Handers | | | 135 | 22 | 4 | 12 | 44 | .163 | .311 | .235 |
| Home | 2-1 | 1.64 | 121 | 17 | 2 | 8 | 46 | .140 | .231 | .209 |
| Road | 4-3 | 2.36 | 126 | 28 | 2 | 16 | 31 | .222 | .325 | .308 |
| Grass | 6-3 | 1.83 | 211 | 33 | 4 | 23 | 70 | .156 | .256 | .246 |
| Artificial Turf | 0-1 | 3.12 | 36 | 12 | 0 | 1 | 7 | .333 | .417 | .351 |
| April | 2-0 | 0.73 | 41 | 7 | 1 | 1 | 11 | .171 | .244 | .190 |
| May | 1-1 | 2.08 | 47 | 10 | 0 | 3 | 13 | .213 | .255 | .255 |
| June | 0-1 | 3.86 | 26 | 4 | 0 | 3 | 12 | .154 | .269 | .267 |
| July | 2-0 | 0.77 | 36 | 6 | 1 | 3 | 10 | .167 | .306 | .244 |
| August | 0-2 | 3.52 | 55 | 11 | 1 | 11 | 17 | .200 | .327 | .343 |
| Sept./Oct. | 1-0 | 1.35 | 42 | 7 | 1 | 3 | 14 | .167 | .262 | .217 |
| Leading Off Inn. | | | 41 | 3 | 0 | 3 | 13 | .073 | .073 | .156 |
| Runners On | | | 126 | 28 | 3 | 16 | 34 | .222 | .365 | .308 |
| Runners/Scor. Pos. | | | 85 | 20 | 0 | 11 | 27 | .235 | .341 | .320 |
| Runners On/2 Out | | | 60 | 10 | 1 | 8 | 21 | .167 | .250 | .275 |
| Scor. Pos./2 Out | | | 43 | 7 | 0 | 6 | 15 | .163 | .209 | .280 |
| Late Inning Pressure | | | 167 | 36 | 4 | 18 | 49 | .216 | .341 | .298 |
| Leading Off | | | 26 | 3 | 0 | 2 | 8 | .115 | .115 | .207 |
| Runners On | | | 92 | 23 | 3 | 12 | 20 | .250 | .424 | .333 |
| Runners/Scor. Pos. | | | 59 | 17 | 0 | 8 | 15 | .288 | .407 | .366 |
| First 9 Batters | | | 243 | 44 | 4 | 24 | 76 | .181 | .280 | .260 |
| Second 9 Batters | | | 4 | 1 | 0 | 0 | 1 | .250 | .250 | .250 |
| All Batters Thereafter | | | 0 | 0 | 0 | 0 | 0 | — | — | — |

Loves to face: Carlton Fisk (0-for-10, 4 SO)
Hates to face: Ellis Burks (.538, 7-for-13, 2 HR)
Ground outs-to-air outs ratio: 2.16 last season, 1.21 for career.... Additional statistics: 13 double-play ground outs in 57 opportunities, 3d-highest rate in majors (min.: 10 GIDP), 10 doubles, 1 triple in 72.2 innings last season.... Earned seven saves against Chicago, most by any A.L. pitcher against any club.... One of four relievers (minimum: 20 games) to average less than four batters faced per game. The other three don't have player comments in the 1990 *Analyst*, so here's the list: Keith Comstock (3.58), Ray Searage (3.70), Kevin Hickey (3.90), and Russell (3.91).... Opponents' career average in Late-Inning Pressure Situations (.212) is 57 points lower than in other at-bats (.269).

## Nolan Ryan

Throws Right

| Texas Rangers | W–L | ERA | AB | H | HR | BB | SO | BA | SA | OBA |
|---|---|---|---|---|---|---|---|---|---|---|
| Season | 16-10 | 3.20 | 867 | 162 | 17 | 98 | 301 | .187 | .283 | .275 |
| vs. Left-Handers | | | 446 | 79 | 8 | 51 | 144 | .177 | .262 | .261 |
| vs. Right-Handers | | | 421 | 83 | 9 | 47 | 157 | .197 | .304 | .289 |
| Home | 9-6 | 3.68 | 517 | 104 | 11 | 59 | 172 | .201 | .306 | .291 |
| Road | 7-4 | 2.52 | 350 | 58 | 6 | 39 | 129 | .166 | .249 | .251 |
| Grass | 12-10 | 3.52 | 726 | 144 | 17 | 84 | 246 | .198 | .307 | .288 |
| Artificial Turf | 4-0 | 1.70 | 141 | 18 | 0 | 14 | 55 | .128 | .156 | .208 |
| April | 3-1 | 2.06 | 120 | 19 | 0 | 18 | 49 | .158 | .192 | .277 |
| May | 2-2 | 4.95 | 137 | 34 | 7 | 15 | 40 | .248 | .416 | .320 |
| June | 4-1 | 2.53 | 161 | 26 | 6 | 12 | 47 | .161 | .298 | .223 |
| July | 3-2 | 3.60 | 132 | 25 | 1 | 11 | 54 | .189 | .280 | .260 |
| August | 2-3 | 2.93 | 142 | 23 | 1 | 20 | 53 | .162 | .225 | .273 |
| Sept./Oct. | 2-1 | 3.28 | 175 | 35 | 2 | 22 | 58 | .200 | .274 | .296 |
| Leading Off Inn. | | | 224 | 38 | 4 | 23 | 80 | .170 | .272 | .259 |
| Runners On | | | 307 | 80 | 6 | 39 | 97 | .261 | .355 | .345 |
| Runners/Scor. Pos. | | | 203 | 48 | 4 | 26 | 66 | .236 | .335 | .319 |
| Runners On/2 Out | | | 137 | 28 | 2 | 17 | 41 | .204 | .277 | .297 |
| Scor. Pos./2 Out | | | 95 | 17 | 2 | 12 | 28 | .179 | .263 | .278 |
| Late Inning Pressure | | | 109 | 23 | 2 | 9 | 42 | .211 | .321 | .277 |
| Leading Off | | | 32 | 8 | 1 | 1 | 9 | .250 | .469 | .294 |
| Runners On | | | 32 | 9 | 1 | 5 | 12 | .281 | .406 | .378 |
| Runners/Scor. Pos. | | | 21 | 6 | 1 | 4 | 10 | .286 | .476 | .400 |
| First 9 Batters | | | 251 | 43 | 7 | 29 | 96 | .171 | .283 | .263 |
| Second 9 Batters | | | 247 | 38 | 4 | 31 | 85 | .154 | .227 | .260 |
| All Batters Thereafter | | | 369 | 81 | 6 | 38 | 120 | .220 | .320 | .293 |

Loves to face: Joe Orsulak (.056, 1-for-18)
Hates to face: Larry Sheets (.556, 5-for-9, 1 HR)
Ground outs-to-air outs ratio: 0.77 last season, 1.06 since 1975.... Additional statistics: 4 double-play ground outs in 131 opportunities, lowest rate in A.L. (min.: 75 opp.), 28 doubles, 2 triples in 239.1 innings last season.... Allowed 15 first-inning runs in 32 starts.... Batting support: 4.34 runs per start.... Opponents stole 36 bases, highest total in A.L.... Had separate streaks of 30 and 38 consecutive batters faced without allowing a hit last season.... He and Charlie Hough became second pair of 40-year-old pitchers in last 55 years to start a doubleheader for same club. Last to do it: Tommy John and Joe Niekro (1986 Yankees), Sad Sam Jones and Red Faber (1933 White Sox).

## Bret Saberhagen

Throws Right

| Kansas City Royals | W–L | ERA | AB | H | HR | BB | SO | BA | SA | OBA |
|---|---|---|---|---|---|---|---|---|---|---|
| Season | 23-6 | 2.16 | 961 | 209 | 13 | 43 | 193 | .217 | .317 | .251 |
| vs. Left-Handers | | | 524 | 102 | 8 | 29 | 125 | .195 | .290 | .236 |
| vs. Right-Handers | | | 437 | 107 | 5 | 14 | 68 | .245 | .350 | .270 |
| Home | 11-1 | 1.71 | 472 | 98 | 3 | 15 | 102 | .208 | .288 | .234 |
| Road | 12-5 | 2.61 | 489 | 111 | 10 | 28 | 91 | .227 | .346 | .267 |
| Grass | 10-4 | 2.17 | 413 | 91 | 8 | 23 | 79 | .220 | .339 | .260 |
| Artificial Turf | 13-2 | 2.16 | 548 | 118 | 5 | 20 | 114 | .215 | .301 | .244 |
| April | 2-2 | 3.35 | 163 | 44 | 1 | 7 | 24 | .270 | .380 | .304 |
| May | 3-2 | 2.23 | 161 | 34 | 3 | 8 | 31 | .211 | .323 | .247 |
| June | 2-0 | 2.33 | 97 | 19 | 1 | 5 | 22 | .196 | .278 | .231 |
| July | 3-1 | 3.25 | 141 | 37 | 1 | 9 | 32 | .262 | .362 | .305 |
| August | 7-0 | 1.58 | 203 | 42 | 5 | 5 | 36 | .207 | .310 | .225 |
| Sept./Oct. | 6-1 | 0.98 | 196 | 33 | 2 | 9 | 48 | .168 | .255 | .208 |
| Leading Off Inn. | | | 258 | 63 | 4 | 6 | 53 | .244 | .368 | .264 |
| Runners On | | | 336 | 70 | 4 | 24 | 65 | .208 | .304 | .259 |
| Runners/Scor. Pos. | | | 183 | 41 | 2 | 17 | 40 | .224 | .311 | .285 |
| Runners On/2 Out | | | 140 | 24 | 4 | 15 | 31 | .171 | .307 | .256 |
| Scor. Pos./2 Out | | | 78 | 17 | 2 | 10 | 17 | .218 | .346 | .315 |
| Late Inning Pressure | | | 135 | 30 | 4 | 9 | 16 | .222 | .356 | .274 |
| Leading Off | | | 35 | 9 | 0 | 2 | 6 | .257 | .343 | .316 |
| Runners On | | | 50 | 9 | 2 | 5 | 4 | .180 | .320 | .250 |
| Runners/Scor. Pos. | | | 27 | 5 | 0 | 4 | 3 | .185 | .222 | .281 |
| First 9 Batters | | | 304 | 73 | 1 | 14 | 66 | .240 | .322 | .272 |
| Second 9 Batters | | | 290 | 61 | 4 | 9 | 70 | .210 | .314 | .234 |
| All Batters Thereafter | | | 367 | 75 | 8 | 20 | 57 | .204 | .316 | .247 |

Loves to face: Devon White (.100, 3-for-30, 9 SO)
Hates to face: Wade Boggs (.514, 18-for-35, 1 HR)
Ground outs-to-air outs ratio: 0.92 last season, 1.11 for career.... Additional statistics: 12 double-play ground outs in 137 opportunities, 45 doubles, 6 triples in 262.1 innings last season.... Allowed 16 first-inning runs in 35 starts. Hasn't allowed a first-inning home run in his last 45 starts.... Batting support: 4.57 runs per start.... Had an ERA of 2.95 in his five losses. Royals had a 6–1 record in his no-decision starts.... First pitcher to lead A.L. in both ERA and innings pitched since Dean Chance in 1964.... Career record of 16–18 (3.84 ERA) in day games, 76–43 (3.06) at night.... Opposing fly-ball hitters have hit better than ground-ballers in each of the last five seasons.

## Dave Schmidt

Throws Right

| Baltimore Orioles | W–L | ERA | AB | H | HR | BB | SO | BA | SA | OBA |
|---|---|---|---|---|---|---|---|---|---|---|
| Season | 10-13 | 5.69 | 632 | 196 | 24 | 36 | 46 | .310 | .481 | .346 |
| vs. Left-Handers | | | 310 | 94 | 12 | 15 | 28 | .303 | .471 | .332 |
| vs. Right-Handers | | | 322 | 102 | 12 | 21 | 18 | .317 | .491 | .358 |
| Home | 3-3 | 6.67 | 239 | 81 | 11 | 10 | 19 | .339 | .536 | .361 |
| Road | 7-10 | 5.13 | 393 | 115 | 13 | 26 | 27 | .293 | .448 | .336 |
| Grass | 9-10 | 5.56 | 538 | 164 | 22 | 31 | 39 | .305 | .489 | .341 |
| Artificial Turf | 1-3 | 6.45 | 94 | 32 | 2 | 5 | 7 | .340 | .436 | .373 |
| April | 1-3 | 6.23 | 143 | 44 | 6 | 9 | 15 | .308 | .490 | .344 |
| May | 3-1 | 3.45 | 104 | 23 | 2 | 5 | 11 | .221 | .346 | .255 |
| June | 3-3 | 5.24 | 141 | 46 | 8 | 5 | 6 | .326 | .560 | .349 |
| July | 1-4 | 6.00 | 136 | 47 | 2 | 11 | 5 | .346 | .441 | .392 |
| August | 2-1 | 5.03 | 76 | 22 | 3 | 4 | 8 | .289 | .461 | .333 |
| Sept./Oct. | 0-1 | 15.63 | 32 | 14 | 3 | 2 | 1 | .438 | .750 | .457 |
| Leading Off Inn. | | | 154 | 52 | 10 | 12 | 11 | .338 | .584 | .386 |
| Runners On | | | 266 | 87 | 9 | 19 | 22 | .327 | .477 | .365 |
| Runners/Scor. Pos. | | | 166 | 53 | 7 | 15 | 14 | .319 | .494 | .362 |
| Runners On/2 Out | | | 102 | 27 | 2 | 11 | 5 | .265 | .353 | .336 |
| Scor. Pos./2 Out | | | 75 | 19 | 1 | 11 | 5 | .253 | .320 | .349 |
| Late Inning Pressure | | | 35 | 6 | 1 | 3 | 2 | .171 | .286 | .237 |
| Leading Off | | | 9 | 1 | 0 | 3 | 0 | .111 | .222 | .333 |
| Runners On | | | 9 | 2 | 0 | 0 | 1 | .222 | .222 | .222 |
| Runners/Scor. Pos. | | | 8 | 2 | 0 | 0 | 1 | .250 | .250 | .250 |
| First 9 Batters | | | 295 | 81 | 13 | 12 | 25 | .275 | .451 | .303 |
| Second 9 Batters | | | 198 | 64 | 2 | 12 | 16 | .323 | .409 | .362 |
| All Batters Thereafter | | | 139 | 51 | 9 | 12 | 5 | .367 | .647 | .409 |

Loves to face: Mike Pagliarulo (.118, 2-for-17)
Hates to face: Fred Lynn (.500, 5-for-10, 2 HR)
Ground outs-to-air outs ratio: 1.04 last season, 1.34 for career.... Additional statistics: 8 double-play ground outs in 128 opportunities, 32 doubles, 2 triples in 156.2 innings last season.... Allowed 23 first-inning runs in 26 starts.... Batting support: 4.31 runs per start.... Only A.L. pitcher to lose 10 or more games on the road.... Career breakdown: 21–28, 4.67 ERA as a starter; 30–23, 3.12 ERA in relief.... Career record of 30–22 before the All-Star break, 21–28 after the break.... Has faced a career total of 71 batters with the bases loaded but has never allowed a grand slam.... Walked 19 leadoff batters over last two seasons (one per 15 batters), compared to 12 in his first seven years (one per 43 batters).

## Mike Schooler

Throws Right

| Seattle Mariners | W–L | ERA | AB | H | HR | BB | SO | BA | SA | OBA |
|---|---|---|---|---|---|---|---|---|---|---|
| Season | 1-7 | 2.81 | 304 | 81 | 2 | 19 | 69 | .266 | .342 | .313 |
| vs. Left-Handers | | | 140 | 40 | 1 | 11 | 27 | .286 | .386 | .340 |
| vs. Right-Handers | | | 164 | 41 | 1 | 8 | 42 | .250 | .305 | .289 |
| Home | 1-4 | 3.32 | 172 | 40 | 0 | 11 | 37 | .279 | .360 | .321 |
| Road | 0-3 | 2.14 | 132 | 33 | 2 | 8 | 32 | .250 | .318 | .303 |
| Grass | 0-1 | 1.65 | 102 | 24 | 2 | 6 | 24 | .235 | .304 | .284 |
| Artificial Turf | 1-6 | 3.44 | 202 | 57 | 0 | 13 | 45 | .282 | .361 | .327 |
| April | 0-0 | 2.89 | 38 | 11 | 0 | 3 | 9 | .289 | .421 | .357 |
| May | 0-0 | 1.15 | 58 | 15 | 0 | 2 | 9 | .259 | .345 | .283 |
| June | 1-2 | 1.23 | 59 | 15 | 0 | 8 | 18 | .254 | .288 | .353 |
| July | 0-0 | 3.00 | 49 | 14 | 1 | 1 | 9 | .286 | .347 | .300 |
| August | 0-3 | 3.46 | 48 | 10 | 1 | 3 | 12 | .208 | .354 | .255 |
| Sept./Oct. | 0-2 | 5.84 | 52 | 16 | 0 | 2 | 12 | .308 | .327 | .327 |
| Leading Off Inn. | | | 61 | 20 | 1 | 2 | 12 | .328 | .443 | .349 |
| Runners On | | | 172 | 45 | 0 | 13 | 38 | .262 | .314 | .316 |
| Runners/Scor. Pos. | | | 108 | 30 | 0 | 7 | 25 | .278 | .333 | .319 |
| Runners On/2 Out | | | 77 | 20 | 0 | 6 | 15 | .260 | .299 | .313 |
| Scor. Pos./2 Out | | | 53 | 13 | 0 | 5 | 12 | .245 | .264 | .310 |
| Late Inning Pressure | | | 227 | 60 | 2 | 13 | 59 | .264 | .339 | .306 |
| Leading Off | | | 44 | 14 | 1 | 1 | 10 | .318 | .432 | .333 |
| Runners On | | | 128 | 35 | 0 | 9 | 33 | .273 | .320 | .324 |
| Runners/Scor. Pos. | | | 84 | 23 | 0 | 5 | 20 | .274 | .321 | .311 |
| First 9 Batters | | | 302 | 79 | 2 | 17 | 69 | .262 | .338 | .304 |
| Second 9 Batters | | | 2 | 2 | 0 | 2 | 0 | 1.000 | 1.000 | 1.000 |
| All Batters Thereafter | | | 0 | 0 | 0 | 0 | 0 | — | — | — |

Loves to face: Rickey Henderson (0-for-5)
Hates to face: Harold Baines (.800, 4-for-5, 1 HR)
Ground outs-to-air outs ratio: 1.18 last season, 1.08 for career. . . . Additional statistics: 3 double-play ground outs in 79 opportunities, 3d-lowest rate of any pitcher in the A.L. (min.: 75 opp.), 13 doubles, 2 triples in 77.0 innings last season. . . . Led the majors with 10 saves in May. . . . Inherited 41 runners, stranded 24 (59%), lowest percentage among the 12 A.L. pitchers with 25 or more saves. . . . Career ERA is 0.62 ERA (2–0 record) in day games, 3.83 (4–15) at night. . . . Has finished 93 of 107 career appearances, the highest percentage (87%) of any active pitcher (minimum: 100 relief appearances). . . . Opponents' career average is .278 in Late-Inning Pressure Situations, .203 in other at-bats.

## Lee Smith

Throws Right

| Boston Red Sox | W–L | ERA | AB | H | HR | BB | SO | BA | SA | OBA |
|---|---|---|---|---|---|---|---|---|---|---|
| Season | 6-1 | 3.57 | 253 | 53 | 6 | 33 | 96 | .209 | .304 | .299 |
| vs. Left-Handers | | | 121 | 27 | 5 | 17 | 46 | .223 | .364 | .317 |
| vs. Right-Handers | | | 132 | 26 | 1 | 16 | 50 | .197 | .250 | .282 |
| Home | 6-0 | 4.06 | 138 | 28 | 4 | 19 | 57 | .203 | .326 | .297 |
| Road | 0-1 | 3.00 | 115 | 25 | 2 | 14 | 39 | .217 | .278 | .300 |
| Grass | 6-0 | 3.12 | 211 | 40 | 4 | 27 | 86 | .190 | .275 | .279 |
| Artificial Turf | 0-1 | 6.30 | 42 | 13 | 2 | 6 | 10 | .310 | .452 | .396 |
| April | 1-1 | 7.71 | 28 | 9 | 0 | 4 | 10 | .321 | .357 | .406 |
| May | 3-0 | 4.70 | 33 | 10 | 1 | 3 | 10 | .303 | .424 | .361 |
| June | 0-0 | 5.68 | 44 | 10 | 2 | 5 | 14 | .227 | .386 | .306 |
| July | 1-0 | 1.93 | 48 | 7 | 2 | 7 | 15 | .146 | .271 | .255 |
| August | 0-0 | 2.03 | 45 | 7 | 0 | 7 | 20 | .156 | .200 | .264 |
| Sept./Oct. | 1-0 | 2.25 | 55 | 10 | 1 | 7 | 27 | .182 | .255 | .270 |
| Leading Off Inn. | | | 52 | 13 | 1 | 6 | 15 | .250 | .308 | .328 |
| Runners On | | | 129 | 30 | 2 | 20 | 46 | .233 | .318 | .331 |
| Runners/Scor. Pos. | | | 82 | 18 | 1 | 13 | 29 | .220 | .317 | .320 |
| Runners On/2 Out | | | 51 | 6 | 1 | 8 | 21 | .118 | .176 | .237 |
| Scor. Pos./2 Out | | | 35 | 3 | 0 | 7 | 17 | .086 | .086 | .238 |
| Late Inning Pressure | | | 135 | 30 | 3 | 15 | 55 | .222 | .304 | .298 |
| Leading Off | | | 26 | 9 | 1 | 2 | 8 | .346 | .462 | .393 |
| Runners On | | | 76 | 15 | 0 | 10 | 28 | .197 | .211 | .287 |
| Runners/Scor. Pos. | | | 51 | 8 | 0 | 9 | 20 | .157 | .176 | .279 |
| First 9 Batters | | | 252 | 53 | 6 | 33 | 95 | .210 | .306 | .300 |
| Second 9 Batters | | | 1 | 0 | 0 | 0 | 1 | .000 | .000 | .000 |
| All Batters Thereafter | | | 0 | 0 | 0 | 0 | 0 | — | — | — |

Loves to face: Terry Francona (.100, 1-for-10)
Hates to face: Kirby Puckett (.833, 5-for-6, 1 HR)
Ground outs-to-air outs ratio: 0.68 last season, 1.14 for career. . . . Additional statistics: 6 double-play ground outs in 67 opportunities, 6 doubles, 0 triples in 70.2 innings last season. . . . One of two pitchers to appear in at least 60 games in each of last eight seasons. The other: new penmate, Jeff Reardon. . . . Reardon (264) and Smith (234) ranked first and third, respectively, in saves during the 1980s, sandwiching Dan Quisenberry (239). . . . Only 53 percent of batters faced last season were in Late-Inning Pressure Situations, his lowest percentage since 1982. . . . Innings pitched haven't increased from one year to next for seven consecutive seasons, one short of all-time longest streak (Billy Pierce, 1957–64).

## Roy Smith

Throws Right

| Minnesota Twins | W–L | ERA | AB | H | HR | BB | SO | BA | SA | OBA |
|---|---|---|---|---|---|---|---|---|---|---|
| Season | 10-6 | 3.92 | 668 | 180 | 22 | 51 | 92 | .269 | .422 | .325 |
| vs. Left-Handers | | | 314 | 85 | 5 | 27 | 51 | .271 | .382 | .333 |
| vs. Right-Handers | | | 354 | 95 | 17 | 24 | 41 | .268 | .458 | .317 |
| Home | 5-1 | 4.22 | 331 | 89 | 8 | 30 | 44 | .269 | .402 | .336 |
| Road | 5-5 | 3.62 | 337 | 91 | 14 | 21 | 48 | .270 | .442 | .313 |
| Grass | 4-3 | 3.66 | 247 | 69 | 10 | 15 | 30 | .279 | .445 | .321 |
| Artificial Turf | 6-3 | 4.07 | 421 | 111 | 12 | 36 | 62 | .264 | .409 | .327 |
| April | 2-1 | 3.75 | 90 | 21 | 5 | 5 | 14 | .233 | .478 | .274 |
| May | 2-1 | 3.49 | 114 | 33 | 5 | 6 | 14 | .289 | .474 | .325 |
| June | 0-1 | 5.59 | 119 | 37 | 3 | 11 | 5 | .311 | .471 | .368 |
| July | 2-1 | 3.10 | 107 | 26 | 4 | 11 | 17 | .243 | .374 | .322 |
| August | 4-0 | 3.48 | 159 | 45 | 2 | 11 | 23 | .283 | .371 | .337 |
| Sept./Oct. | 0-2 | 4.35 | 79 | 18 | 3 | 7 | 19 | .228 | .380 | .291 |
| Leading Off Inn. | | | 167 | 48 | 8 | 11 | 22 | .287 | .521 | .335 |
| Runners On | | | 282 | 73 | 9 | 21 | 41 | .259 | .418 | .309 |
| Runners/Scor. Pos. | | | 156 | 42 | 2 | 14 | 22 | .269 | .397 | .328 |
| Runners On/2 Out | | | 113 | 25 | 3 | 10 | 16 | .221 | .354 | .290 |
| Scor. Pos./2 Out | | | 65 | 14 | 0 | 9 | 8 | .215 | .292 | .320 |
| Late Inning Pressure | | | 48 | 8 | 0 | 6 | 7 | .167 | .188 | .259 |
| Leading Off | | | 15 | 3 | 0 | 1 | 1 | .200 | .267 | .250 |
| Runners On | | | 16 | 3 | 0 | 2 | 4 | .188 | .188 | .278 |
| Runners/Scor. Pos. | | | 10 | 1 | 0 | 1 | 2 | .100 | .100 | .182 |
| First 9 Batters | | | 254 | 63 | 6 | 19 | 42 | .248 | .366 | .304 |
| Second 9 Batters | | | 221 | 68 | 9 | 17 | 32 | .308 | .471 | .361 |
| All Batters Thereafter | | | 193 | 49 | 7 | 15 | 18 | .254 | .440 | .310 |

Loves to face: Bo Jackson (0-for-10, 5 SO)
Hates to face: Danny Tartabull (.556, 5-for-9, 3 HR)
Ground outs-to-air outs ratio: 0.69 last season, 0.59 for career. . . . Additional statistics: 10 double-play ground outs in 129 opportunities, 30 doubles, 3 triples in 172.1 innings last season. . . . Allowed 13 first-inning runs in 26 starts. . . . Batting support: 5.73 runs per start, 2d highest in A.L. (minimum: 15 GS). . . . Twins had a record of 8–2 in his no-decision starts. . . . Opponents batted .200 in day games, .304 at night. Difference of 104 points was 2d largest in majors. . . . Has fielded his last 39 chances without incident, after committing three errors in his first 13 chances in the majors. . . . First three years: 6–11, 5.04 ERA. Last three years: 14–6, 3.79 ERA.

## Mike Smithson

Throws Right

| Boston Red Sox | W–L | ERA | AB | H | HR | BB | SO | BA | SA | OBA |
|---|---|---|---|---|---|---|---|---|---|---|
| Season | 7-14 | 4.95 | 573 | 170 | 21 | 35 | 61 | .297 | .468 | .343 |
| vs. Left-Handers | | | 289 | 90 | 13 | 19 | 32 | .311 | .519 | .358 |
| vs. Right-Handers | | | 284 | 80 | 8 | 16 | 29 | .282 | .415 | .328 |
| Home | 5-6 | 4.88 | 317 | 100 | 9 | 19 | 37 | .315 | .470 | .359 |
| Road | 2-8 | 5.04 | 256 | 70 | 12 | 16 | 24 | .273 | .465 | .323 |
| Grass | 7-12 | 5.02 | 526 | 159 | 18 | 35 | 56 | .302 | .470 | .351 |
| Artificial Turf | 0-2 | 4.26 | 47 | 11 | 3 | 0 | 5 | .234 | .447 | .245 |
| April | 0-2 | 6.86 | 78 | 26 | 3 | 6 | 8 | .333 | .590 | .375 |
| May | 2-2 | 3.54 | 113 | 37 | 3 | 4 | 18 | .327 | .460 | .355 |
| June | 2-2 | 5.18 | 126 | 33 | 3 | 15 | 19 | .262 | .381 | .345 |
| July | 1-3 | 3.72 | 74 | 18 | 3 | 4 | 5 | .243 | .405 | .282 |
| August | 2-3 | 4.40 | 128 | 40 | 4 | 5 | 9 | .313 | .461 | .343 |
| Sept./Oct. | 0-2 | 7.62 | 54 | 16 | 5 | 1 | 2 | .296 | .611 | .345 |
| Leading Off Inn. | | | 140 | 47 | 5 | 6 | 11 | .336 | .536 | .367 |
| Runners On | | | 248 | 71 | 9 | 20 | 24 | .286 | .440 | .343 |
| Runners/Scor. Pos. | | | 134 | 43 | 7 | 13 | 12 | .321 | .507 | .379 |
| Runners On/2 Out | | | 103 | 25 | 0 | 10 | 14 | .243 | .291 | .322 |
| Scor. Pos./2 Out | | | 58 | 16 | 0 | 7 | 7 | .276 | .310 | .373 |
| Late Inning Pressure | | | 46 | 18 | 4 | 3 | 6 | .391 | .717 | .420 |
| Leading Off | | | 12 | 3 | 1 | 0 | 3 | .250 | .500 | .250 |
| Runners On | | | 16 | 7 | 0 | 3 | 1 | .438 | .563 | .500 |
| Runners/Scor. Pos. | | | 11 | 5 | 0 | 3 | 1 | .455 | .455 | .533 |
| First 9 Batters | | | 277 | 82 | 13 | 15 | 25 | .296 | .505 | .342 |
| Second 9 Batters | | | 175 | 53 | 4 | 11 | 20 | .303 | .434 | .347 |
| All Batters Thereafter | | | 121 | 35 | 4 | 9 | 16 | .289 | .430 | .338 |

Loves to face: Ivan Calderon (.040, 1-for-25)
Hates to face: George Brett (.553, 21-for-38, 2 HR)
Ground outs-to-air outs ratio: 0.83 last season, 1.12 for career. . . . Additional statistics: 9 double-play ground outs in 126 opportunities, 29 doubles, 3 triples in 143.2 innings last season. . . . Allowed 9 first-inning runs in 19 starts. . . . Batting support: 4.89 runs per start. . . . When he's good, he's very, very good: ERA of 0.60 in his six victories as a starter. . . . Most innings of any A.L. pitcher who did not throw a wild pitch. . . . Career breakdowns: 14–9 in April, 62–77 in other months; 46–31 in home games, 30–55 in road games; 18–29 in day games, 58–57 at night. . . . Completed 39 of 147 starts (27%) over the first five years of his career, but only two of 57 starts (4%) since then.

## Bob Stanley

Throws Right

| Boston Red Sox | W–L | ERA | AB | H | HR | BB | SO | BA | SA | OBA |
|---|---|---|---|---|---|---|---|---|---|---|
| Season | 5-2 | 4.88 | 318 | 102 | 4 | 26 | 32 | .321 | .425 | .366 |
| vs. Left-Handers | | | 141 | 49 | 2 | 16 | 9 | .348 | .489 | .415 |
| vs. Right-Handers | | | 177 | 53 | 2 | 10 | 23 | .299 | .373 | .326 |
| Home | 3-0 | 4.32 | 163 | 50 | 3 | 13 | 18 | .307 | .423 | .356 |
| Road | 2-2 | 5.50 | 155 | 52 | 1 | 13 | 14 | .335 | .426 | .378 |
| Grass | 5-2 | 4.98 | 276 | 86 | 4 | 24 | 30 | .312 | .417 | .364 |
| Artificial Turf | 0-0 | 4.22 | 42 | 16 | 0 | 2 | 2 | .381 | .476 | .383 |
| April | 1-1 | 5.82 | 64 | 18 | 0 | 7 | 5 | .281 | .344 | .342 |
| May | 1-0 | 2.55 | 67 | 18 | 1 | 2 | 6 | .269 | .343 | .296 |
| June | 0-1 | 6.75 | 78 | 29 | 2 | 9 | 8 | .372 | .526 | .432 |
| July | 1-0 | 7.50 | 26 | 10 | 1 | 1 | 4 | .385 | .577 | .393 |
| August | 2-0 | 2.75 | 76 | 23 | 0 | 5 | 9 | .303 | .395 | .341 |
| Sept./Oct. | 0-0 | 16.20 | 7 | 4 | 0 | 2 | 0 | .571 | .571 | .600 |
| Leading Off Inn. | | | 65 | 20 | 1 | 5 | 7 | .308 | .446 | .366 |
| Runners On | | | 169 | 61 | 2 | 16 | 17 | .361 | .462 | .401 |
| Runners/Scor. Pos. | | | 116 | 40 | 1 | 13 | 16 | .345 | .431 | .390 |
| Runners On/2 Out | | | 73 | 25 | 1 | 7 | 5 | .342 | .438 | .400 |
| Scor. Pos./2 Out | | | 52 | 19 | 1 | 7 | 5 | .365 | .481 | .441 |
| Late Inning Pressure | | | 94 | 28 | 2 | 10 | 8 | .298 | .426 | .368 |
| Leading Off | | | 21 | 7 | 1 | 1 | 0 | .333 | .571 | .391 |
| Runners On | | | 47 | 15 | 1 | 7 | 6 | .319 | .426 | .400 |
| Runners/Scor. Pos. | | | 30 | 10 | 1 | 7 | 6 | .333 | .467 | .447 |
| First 9 Batters | | | 264 | 83 | 3 | 23 | 26 | .314 | .394 | .363 |
| Second 9 Batters | | | 53 | 19 | 1 | 3 | 6 | .358 | .585 | .393 |
| All Batters Thereafter | | | 1 | 0 | 0 | 0 | 0 | .000 | .000 | .000 |

Loves to face: Dave Collins (.043, 1-for-23)
Hates to face: Fred McGriff (.538, 7-for-13, 1 HR)
Ground outs-to-air outs ratio: 2.10 last season, 2.18 for career. . . . Additional statistics: 13 double-play ground outs in 86 opportunities, 19 doubles, 1 triple in 79.1 innings last season. . . . Baseball's version of mandatory retirement: The highest opponents' batting averages in the majors last season belonged to Tommy John (.336) and Stanley. . . . Last two losses boosted him into 2d place in Red Sox history, 15 behind Cy Young (112). . . . Ends career with a team-record total of 637 games, 272 more than runner-up Ellis Kinder. . . . Steamer's total was also 80 higher than that of Boston Braves leader, Kid Nichols. . . . Face it. When it comes to pitching, Stanley—not "May Day" Malone—was Mr. Baseball in Boston.

## Dave Stewart

Throws Right

| Oakland As | W–L | ERA | AB | H | HR | BB | SO | BA | SA | OBA |
|---|---|---|---|---|---|---|---|---|---|---|
| Season | 21-9 | 3.32 | 986 | 260 | 23 | 69 | 155 | .264 | .395 | .313 |
| vs. Left-Handers | | | 522 | 138 | 12 | 42 | 58 | .264 | .387 | .315 |
| vs. Right-Handers | | | 464 | 122 | 11 | 27 | 97 | .263 | .403 | .310 |
| Home | 11-4 | 2.77 | 499 | 120 | 11 | 35 | 80 | .240 | .357 | .297 |
| Road | 10-5 | 3.91 | 487 | 140 | 12 | 34 | 75 | .287 | .433 | .330 |
| Grass | 17-7 | 3.19 | 833 | 216 | 18 | 56 | 134 | .259 | .378 | .308 |
| Artificial Turf | 4-2 | 3.98 | 153 | 44 | 5 | 13 | 21 | .288 | .484 | .339 |
| April | 5-0 | 2.79 | 161 | 40 | 1 | 14 | 20 | .248 | .317 | .313 |
| May | 4-2 | 4.04 | 168 | 50 | 4 | 12 | 19 | .298 | .435 | .342 |
| June | 3-2 | 3.72 | 145 | 38 | 1 | 11 | 21 | .262 | .372 | .314 |
| July | 3-2 | 3.53 | 165 | 44 | 9 | 10 | 37 | .267 | .461 | .313 |
| August | 3-2 | 3.30 | 179 | 51 | 5 | 8 | 34 | .285 | .413 | .311 |
| Sept./Oct. | 3-1 | 2.60 | 168 | 37 | 3 | 14 | 24 | .220 | .363 | .284 |
| Leading Off Inn. | | | 255 | 70 | 8 | 13 | 42 | .275 | .439 | .312 |
| Runners On | | | 408 | 99 | 7 | 36 | 69 | .243 | .353 | .303 |
| Runners/Scor. Pos. | | | 234 | 52 | 2 | 25 | 39 | .222 | .312 | .292 |
| Runners On/2 Out | | | 176 | 44 | 4 | 15 | 26 | .250 | .375 | .320 |
| Scor. Pos./2 Out | | | 114 | 29 | 1 | 12 | 15 | .254 | .360 | .331 |
| Late Inning Pressure | | | 96 | 28 | 0 | 7 | 12 | .292 | .375 | .340 |
| Leading Off | | | 28 | 10 | 0 | 2 | 4 | .357 | .464 | .400 |
| Runners On | | | 36 | 11 | 0 | 3 | 3 | .306 | .389 | .359 |
| Runners/Scor. Pos. | | | 21 | 5 | 0 | 1 | 1 | .238 | .333 | .273 |
| First 9 Batters | | | 293 | 75 | 7 | 22 | 49 | .256 | .382 | .313 |
| Second 9 Batters | | | 296 | 71 | 7 | 21 | 51 | .240 | .375 | .291 |
| All Batters Thereafter | | | 397 | 114 | 9 | 26 | 55 | .287 | .418 | .329 |

Loves to face: Steve Lyons (.045, 1-for-22)
Hates to face: Danny Tartabull (.538, 7-for-13, 1 HR)
Ground outs-to-air outs ratio: 0.79 last season, 0.85 for career. . . . Additional statistics: 19 double-play ground outs in 189 opportunities, 52 doubles, 4 triples in 257.2 innings last season. . . . Allowed 13 first-inning runs in 36 starts. . . . Batting support: 4.31 runs per start. . . . First pitcher to win two games in L.C.S. and two more in World Series in same year. . . . Best winning percentage (71–39, .645) since A's moved to Oakland (minimum: 100 decisions). . . . First pitcher to win 20 games without a shutout since 1973, when Ron Bryant and Luis Tiant did it. . . . Three pitchers had *four* consecutive 20-win seasons without a Cy Young Award: Juan Marichal (1963–66), Dave McNally (1968–71), and Wilbur Wood (1971–74).

## Dave Stieb

Throws Right

| Toronto Blue Jays | W–L | ERA | AB | H | HR | BB | SO | BA | SA | OBA |
|---|---|---|---|---|---|---|---|---|---|---|
| Season | 17-8 | 3.35 | 748 | 164 | 12 | 76 | 101 | .219 | .316 | .301 |
| vs. Left-Handers | | | 387 | 96 | 7 | 38 | 46 | .248 | .346 | .319 |
| vs. Right-Handers | | | 361 | 68 | 5 | 38 | 55 | .188 | .283 | .283 |
| Home | 7-4 | 3.34 | 340 | 72 | 5 | 36 | 52 | .212 | .312 | .297 |
| Road | 10-4 | 3.36 | 408 | 92 | 7 | 40 | 49 | .225 | .319 | .305 |
| Grass | 10-2 | 2.46 | 322 | 66 | 6 | 33 | 42 | .205 | .292 | .291 |
| Artificial Turf | 7-6 | 4.06 | 426 | 98 | 6 | 43 | 59 | .230 | .333 | .309 |
| April | 2-0 | 4.50 | 111 | 23 | 0 | 12 | 18 | .207 | .252 | .282 |
| May | 1-3 | 6.29 | 135 | 40 | 1 | 10 | 13 | .296 | .422 | .358 |
| June | 4-1 | 2.70 | 109 | 25 | 3 | 16 | 8 | .229 | .339 | .339 |
| July | 3-2 | 2.83 | 121 | 24 | 3 | 15 | 15 | .198 | .306 | .297 |
| August | 4-2 | 2.14 | 144 | 24 | 2 | 14 | 29 | .167 | .257 | .250 |
| Sept./Oct. | 3-0 | 2.04 | 128 | 28 | 3 | 9 | 18 | .219 | .313 | .286 |
| Leading Off Inn. | | | 187 | 36 | 2 | 24 | 27 | .193 | .257 | .298 |
| Runners On | | | 311 | 81 | 4 | 22 | 33 | .260 | .354 | .317 |
| Runners/Scor. Pos. | | | 166 | 45 | 3 | 14 | 17 | .271 | .380 | .326 |
| Runners On/2 Out | | | 122 | 25 | 1 | 7 | 18 | .205 | .254 | .265 |
| Scor. Pos./2 Out | | | 74 | 16 | 1 | 4 | 9 | .216 | .270 | .256 |
| Late Inning Pressure | | | 36 | 6 | 0 | 4 | 6 | .167 | .194 | .268 |
| Leading Off | | | 10 | 1 | 0 | 2 | 2 | .100 | .100 | .250 |
| Runners On | | | 11 | 3 | 0 | 0 | 0 | .273 | .273 | .273 |
| Runners/Scor. Pos. | | | 4 | 2 | 0 | 0 | 0 | .500 | .500 | .500 |
| First 9 Batters | | | 258 | 56 | 3 | 30 | 37 | .217 | .302 | .311 |
| Second 9 Batters | | | 244 | 58 | 7 | 27 | 31 | .238 | .377 | .321 |
| All Batters Thereafter | | | 246 | 50 | 2 | 19 | 33 | .203 | .268 | .270 |

Loves to face: Rob Deer (.050, 1-for-20, 7 SO)
Hates to face: Jack Howell (.524, 11-for-21, 3 HR)
Ground outs-to-air outs ratio: 1.18 last season, 1.15 for career. . . . Additional statistics: 18 double-play ground outs in 156 opportunities, 30 doubles, 3 triples in 206.2 innings last season. . . . Allowed 17 first-inning runs in 33 starts. . . . Batting support: 5.18 runs per start. . . . Only pitcher with at least one shutout in every season of the 1980s. His 11-year streak is still a decade short of Walter Johnson's record of 21 years (his entire career). . . . Lost three no-hitters with two outs in the ninth within a year's time (Sept. 24 and Sept. 30, 1988; and Aug. 4, 1989). Did anyone else besides Bill Burns (1908, 1909) lose more than two in his career? . . . Led majors in hit batsmen for fifth time, one shy of Howard Ehmke's record.

## Todd Stottlemyre

Throws Right

| Toronto Blue Jays | W–L | ERA | AB | H | HR | BB | SO | BA | SA | OBA |
|---|---|---|---|---|---|---|---|---|---|---|
| Season | 7-7 | 3.88 | 486 | 137 | 11 | 44 | 63 | .282 | .424 | .343 |
| vs. Left-Handers | | | 223 | 70 | 7 | 17 | 18 | .314 | .480 | .362 |
| vs. Right-Handers | | | 263 | 67 | 4 | 27 | 45 | .255 | .376 | .328 |
| Home | 4-3 | 3.53 | 298 | 84 | 6 | 27 | 41 | .282 | .423 | .345 |
| Road | 3-4 | 4.44 | 188 | 53 | 5 | 17 | 22 | .282 | .426 | .340 |
| Grass | 2-2 | 4.20 | 117 | 31 | 5 | 12 | 16 | .265 | .470 | .336 |
| Artificial Turf | 5-5 | 3.78 | 369 | 106 | 6 | 32 | 47 | .287 | .409 | .345 |
| April | 0-3 | 5.06 | 87 | 28 | 2 | 13 | 13 | .322 | .460 | .410 |
| May | 0-0 | 9.00 | 20 | 7 | 0 | 1 | 1 | .350 | .450 | .391 |
| June | | | 0 | 0 | 0 | 0 | 0 | — | — | — |
| July | 2-1 | 3.60 | 90 | 25 | 2 | 9 | 14 | .278 | .444 | .340 |
| August | 3-1 | 2.79 | 145 | 38 | 3 | 12 | 18 | .262 | .414 | .325 |
| Sept./Oct. | 2-2 | 3.82 | 144 | 39 | 4 | 9 | 17 | .271 | .396 | .314 |
| Leading Off Inn. | | | 121 | 42 | 3 | 9 | 13 | .347 | .504 | .392 |
| Runners On | | | 219 | 50 | 4 | 16 | 30 | .228 | .329 | .282 |
| Runners/Scor. Pos. | | | 119 | 22 | 0 | 14 | 19 | .185 | .235 | .273 |
| Runners On/2 Out | | | 92 | 18 | 3 | 7 | 15 | .196 | .304 | .260 |
| Scor. Pos./2 Out | | | 57 | 9 | 0 | 6 | 11 | .158 | .175 | .250 |
| Late Inning Pressure | | | 53 | 17 | 0 | 8 | 5 | .321 | .415 | .410 |
| Leading Off | | | 16 | 8 | 0 | 0 | 1 | .500 | .625 | .500 |
| Runners On | | | 20 | 6 | 0 | 8 | 3 | .300 | .400 | .500 |
| Runners/Scor. Pos. | | | 15 | 4 | 0 | 8 | 3 | .267 | .400 | .522 |
| First 9 Batters | | | 181 | 45 | 6 | 25 | 24 | .249 | .376 | .340 |
| Second 9 Batters | | | 162 | 52 | 3 | 15 | 25 | .321 | .481 | .383 |
| All Batters Thereafter | | | 143 | 40 | 2 | 4 | 14 | .280 | .420 | .300 |

Loves to face: Pete Incaviglia (0-for-10, 6 SO)
Hates to face: Matt Nokes (.667, 6-for-9, 2 2B, 1 HR)
Ground outs-to-air outs ratio: 1.03 last season, 0.96 for career. . . . Additional statistics: 11 double-play ground outs in 95 opportunities, 28 doubles, 4 triples in 127.2 innings last season. . . . Allowed 11 first-inning runs in 18 starts. . . . Batting support: 3.33 runs per start, 4th-lowest among A.L. pitchers with at least 15 starts. . . . Blue Jays were 5–0 in his no-decision starts. . . . ERA was over one run per game higher with Ernie Whitt behind the plate (4.53) than with Pat Borders (3.41). . . . Opponents batted 98 points lower with runners on base than with the bases empty, largest difference in majors. . . . Career average of .340 by opposing left-handed batters, .228 by right-handers.

## Bill Swift

Throws Right

| Seattle Mariners | W–L | ERA | AB | H | HR | BB | SO | BA | SA | OBA |
|---|---|---|---|---|---|---|---|---|---|---|
| Season | 7-3 | 4.43 | 504 | 140 | 7 | 38 | 45 | .278 | .371 | .329 |
| vs. Left-Handers | | | 231 | 73 | 3 | 19 | 16 | .316 | .411 | .368 |
| vs. Right-Handers | | | 273 | 67 | 4 | 19 | 29 | .245 | .337 | .296 |
| Home | 3-2 | 4.93 | 292 | 86 | 4 | 21 | 23 | .295 | .390 | .340 |
| Road | 4-1 | 3.79 | 212 | 54 | 3 | 17 | 22 | .255 | .344 | .315 |
| Grass | 3-1 | 3.50 | 159 | 42 | 2 | 14 | 17 | .264 | .358 | .330 |
| Artificial Turf | 4-2 | 4.90 | 345 | 98 | 5 | 24 | 28 | .284 | .377 | .329 |
| April | 0-0 | 0.00 | 9 | 2 | 0 | 0 | 1 | .222 | .333 | .222 |
| May | 2-0 | 4.91 | 132 | 41 | 1 | 14 | 17 | .311 | .379 | .376 |
| June | 2-2 | 7.22 | 115 | 37 | 4 | 12 | 6 | .322 | .478 | .386 |
| July | 2-1 | 3.80 | 81 | 26 | 1 | 3 | 7 | .321 | .432 | .353 |
| August | 0-0 | 3.00 | 56 | 13 | 0 | 4 | 6 | .232 | .268 | .279 |
| Sept./Oct. | 1-0 | 2.76 | 111 | 21 | 1 | 5 | 8 | .189 | .261 | .224 |
| Leading Off Inn. | | | 121 | 34 | 0 | 7 | 18 | .281 | .314 | .320 |
| Runners On | | | 233 | 71 | 5 | 18 | 17 | .305 | .438 | .350 |
| Runners/Scor. Pos. | | | 128 | 35 | 2 | 13 | 12 | .273 | .375 | .333 |
| Runners On/2 Out | | | 85 | 26 | 0 | 13 | 10 | .306 | .376 | .398 |
| Scor. Pos./2 Out | | | 58 | 18 | 0 | 10 | 7 | .310 | .397 | .412 |
| Late Inning Pressure | | | 48 | 8 | 0 | 5 | 3 | .167 | .208 | .245 |
| Leading Off | | | 13 | 1 | 0 | 0 | 2 | .077 | .077 | .077 |
| Runners On | | | 15 | 3 | 0 | 2 | 0 | .200 | .267 | .294 |
| Runners/Scor. Pos. | | | 8 | 1 | 0 | 2 | 0 | .125 | .125 | .300 |
| First 9 Batters | | | 267 | 66 | 1 | 20 | 29 | .247 | .315 | .301 |
| Second 9 Batters | | | 158 | 47 | 4 | 12 | 9 | .297 | .405 | .345 |
| All Batters Thereafter | | | 79 | 27 | 2 | 6 | 7 | .342 | .494 | .391 |

Loves to face: Rickey Henderson (.053, 1-for-19)
Hates to face: Rich Gedman (.750, 9-for-12)
Ground outs-to-air outs ratio: 3.96 last season (highest in A.L. during 1980s among pitchers facing 500+ batters), 2.74 for career. . . . Additional statistics: 26 double-play ground outs (3d most in A.L.) in 130 opportunities, 20 doubles, 3 triples in 130.0 innings last season. . . . Allowed 4 first-inning runs in 16 starts. Hasn't allowed a first-inning home run in his last 24 starts. . . . Batting support: 5.56 runs per start. . . . Career breakdown: 17–33, 5.34 ERA as a starter; 6–1, 2.64 ERA in relief. . . . Opposing left-handed batters have hit above .300 in each of his four seasons. . . . Career averages: .327 by left-handers, .256 by right-handers. Difference of 71 points is largest over the past 10 years.

## Greg Swindell

Throws Left

| Cleveland Indians | W–L | ERA | AB | H | HR | BB | SO | BA | SA | OBA |
|---|---|---|---|---|---|---|---|---|---|---|
| Season | 13-6 | 3.37 | 690 | 170 | 16 | 51 | 129 | .246 | .368 | .297 |
| vs. Left-Handers | | | 109 | 24 | 1 | 7 | 15 | .220 | .284 | .265 |
| vs. Right-Handers | | | 581 | 146 | 15 | 44 | 114 | .251 | .384 | .303 |
| Home | 6-4 | 3.34 | 347 | 84 | 6 | 28 | 68 | .242 | .323 | .296 |
| Road | 7-2 | 3.40 | 343 | 86 | 10 | 23 | 61 | .251 | .414 | .298 |
| Grass | 12-5 | 3.46 | 627 | 158 | 13 | 44 | 119 | .252 | .367 | .299 |
| Artificial Turf | 1-1 | 2.55 | 63 | 12 | 3 | 7 | 10 | .190 | .381 | .271 |
| April | 2-0 | 2.50 | 134 | 30 | 2 | 7 | 29 | .224 | .328 | .262 |
| May | 3-1 | 2.66 | 162 | 35 | 3 | 10 | 29 | .216 | .333 | .260 |
| June | 5-1 | 3.09 | 177 | 51 | 4 | 11 | 28 | .288 | .412 | .328 |
| July | 3-1 | 2.30 | 96 | 19 | 2 | 10 | 22 | .198 | .292 | .274 |
| August | 0-1 | 81.00 | 6 | 4 | 0 | 2 | 0 | .667 | .833 | .750 |
| Sept./Oct. | 0-2 | 5.16 | 115 | 31 | 5 | 11 | 21 | .270 | .435 | .328 |
| Leading Off Inn. | | | 184 | 43 | 6 | 8 | 36 | .234 | .397 | .266 |
| Runners On | | | 251 | 62 | 4 | 23 | 46 | .247 | .347 | .306 |
| Runners/Scor. Pos. | | | 128 | 28 | 1 | 13 | 29 | .219 | .281 | .283 |
| Runners On/2 Out | | | 108 | 26 | 2 | 9 | 16 | .241 | .361 | .299 |
| Scor. Pos./2 Out | | | 61 | 14 | 0 | 5 | 11 | .230 | .279 | .288 |
| Late Inning Pressure | | | 74 | 16 | 0 | 4 | 16 | .216 | .257 | .256 |
| Leading Off | | | 20 | 3 | 0 | 2 | 4 | .150 | .200 | .227 |
| Runners On | | | 25 | 4 | 0 | 2 | 4 | .160 | .200 | .222 |
| Runners/Scor. Pos. | | | 13 | 2 | 0 | 1 | 2 | .154 | .231 | .214 |
| First 9 Batters | | | 226 | 52 | 5 | 20 | 43 | .230 | .332 | .290 |
| Second 9 Batters | | | 223 | 53 | 6 | 17 | 47 | .238 | .372 | .292 |
| All Batters Thereafter | | | 241 | 65 | 5 | 14 | 39 | .270 | .398 | .307 |

Loves to face: Pete Incaviglia (0-for-18, 12 SO)
Hates to face: Alan Trammell (.500, 7-for-14, 1 HR)
Ground outs-to-air outs ratio: 0.72 last season, 0.76 for career. . . . Additional statistics: 10 double-play ground outs in 124 opportunities, 26 doubles, 5 triples in 184.1 innings last season. . . . Allowed 19 first-inning runs in 28 starts. . . . Batting support: 4.00 runs per start. . . . ERA of 1.73 in wins, 11.41 in losses. . . . Youngest opening-day starting pitcher in majors last season. Of 14 A.L. opening-day starters, only Clemens, Stewart, and Swindell led their teams in wins. . . . Opponents stole 18 bases in 31 attempts, lowest rate on team. . . . Career record of 36–22 (3.44 ERA) on grass fields, 3–8 (5.21 ERA) on artificial surfaces. . . . Opponents' career BA: .225 on first pass through lineup, .268 thereafter.

## Frank Tanana

Throws Left

| Detroit Tigers | W–L | ERA | AB | H | HR | BB | SO | BA | SA | OBA |
|---|---|---|---|---|---|---|---|---|---|---|
| Season | 10-14 | 3.58 | 856 | 227 | 21 | 74 | 147 | .265 | .380 | .326 |
| vs. Left-Handers | | | 125 | 38 | 2 | 13 | 17 | .304 | .400 | .374 |
| vs. Right-Handers | | | 731 | 189 | 19 | 61 | 130 | .259 | .376 | .318 |
| Home | 4-6 | 3.48 | 449 | 109 | 13 | 38 | 88 | .243 | .363 | .302 |
| Road | 6-8 | 3.70 | 407 | 118 | 8 | 36 | 59 | .290 | .398 | .352 |
| Grass | 10-11 | 3.59 | 769 | 204 | 21 | 62 | 133 | .265 | .386 | .321 |
| Artificial Turf | 0-3 | 3.52 | 87 | 23 | 0 | 12 | 14 | .264 | .322 | .368 |
| April | 2-3 | 3.82 | 132 | 36 | 2 | 10 | 17 | .273 | .371 | .322 |
| May | 3-1 | 3.53 | 160 | 38 | 4 | 15 | 28 | .238 | .338 | .302 |
| June | 2-3 | 3.83 | 168 | 47 | 4 | 15 | 34 | .280 | .405 | .346 |
| July | 0-2 | 2.89 | 104 | 29 | 2 | 8 | 13 | .279 | .346 | .333 |
| August | 2-3 | 3.82 | 148 | 38 | 4 | 12 | 26 | .257 | .405 | .315 |
| Sept./Oct. | 1-2 | 3.41 | 144 | 39 | 5 | 14 | 29 | .271 | .403 | .340 |
| Leading Off Inn. | | | 221 | 58 | 3 | 9 | 41 | .262 | .348 | .291 |
| Runners On | | | 352 | 89 | 10 | 38 | 56 | .253 | .369 | .319 |
| Runners/Scor. Pos. | | | 172 | 49 | 3 | 25 | 23 | .285 | .384 | .361 |
| Runners On/2 Out | | | 162 | 41 | 9 | 23 | 26 | .253 | .444 | .346 |
| Scor. Pos./2 Out | | | 86 | 25 | 3 | 16 | 9 | .291 | .442 | .402 |
| Late Inning Pressure | | | 109 | 28 | 4 | 9 | 25 | .257 | .422 | .325 |
| Leading Off | | | 32 | 9 | 1 | 0 | 11 | .281 | .406 | .281 |
| Runners On | | | 33 | 5 | 1 | 5 | 4 | .152 | .273 | .282 |
| Runners/Scor. Pos. | | | 17 | 3 | 0 | 5 | 2 | .176 | .235 | .391 |
| First 9 Batters | | | 259 | 78 | 7 | 26 | 46 | .301 | .413 | .359 |
| Second 9 Batters | | | 264 | 76 | 6 | 20 | 39 | .288 | .405 | .344 |
| All Batters Thereafter | | | 333 | 73 | 8 | 28 | 62 | .219 | .333 | .285 |

Loves to face: Stan Javier (.095, 2-for-21)
Hates to face: Mickey Tettleton (.391, 9-for-23, 2 2B, 3 HR)
Ground outs-to-air outs ratio: 1.17 last season, 1.00 for career. . . . Additional statistics: 20 double-play ground outs in 166 opportunities, 33 doubles, 1 triple in 223.2 innings last season. . . . Allowed 31 first-inning runs (most in the A.L.) in 33 starts. . . . Batting support: 3.67 runs per start. . . . Strikeout total was his highest since 1977, when he topped the 200 mark for the third and last time. . . . Has been active for 17 seasons, most of any active A.L. pitcher who never played in the N.L. Bob Forsch is Tanana's N.L. counterpart (16 years). . . . Career record of 8–21 vs. the Royals, 0–12 at Royals Stadium. . . . Led A.L. in losses for the 1980s (122), four fewer than the major league leader, Jim Clancy.

## Walt Terrell

Throws Right

| New York Yankees | W–L | ERA | AB | H | HR | BB | SO | BA | SA | OBA |
|---|---|---|---|---|---|---|---|---|---|---|
| Season | 6-5 | 5.20 | 332 | 102 | 9 | 24 | 30 | .307 | .470 | .356 |
| vs. Left-Handers | | | 171 | 57 | 8 | 17 | 13 | .333 | .556 | .392 |
| vs. Right-Handers | | | 161 | 45 | 1 | 7 | 17 | .280 | .379 | .316 |
| Home | 2-3 | 6.32 | 131 | 43 | 6 | 11 | 12 | .328 | .542 | .378 |
| Road | 4-2 | 4.53 | 201 | 59 | 3 | 13 | 18 | .294 | .423 | .341 |
| Grass | 4-4 | 5.49 | 251 | 78 | 7 | 19 | 22 | .311 | .466 | .361 |
| Artificial Turf | 2-1 | 4.35 | 81 | 24 | 2 | 5 | 8 | .296 | .481 | .337 |
| April | | | 0 | 0 | 0 | 0 | 0 | — | — | — |
| May | | | 0 | 0 | 0 | 0 | 0 | — | — | — |
| June | | | 0 | 0 | 0 | 0 | 0 | — | — | — |
| July | 0-0 | 11.57 | 24 | 11 | 0 | 3 | 2 | .458 | .542 | .519 |
| August | 2-4 | 5.92 | 152 | 48 | 6 | 13 | 13 | .316 | .526 | .367 |
| Sept./Oct. | 4-1 | 3.79 | 156 | 43 | 3 | 8 | 15 | .276 | .404 | .317 |
| Leading Off Inn. | | | 81 | 21 | 4 | 6 | 5 | .259 | .519 | .326 |
| Runners On | | | 154 | 45 | 3 | 7 | 16 | .292 | .390 | .319 |
| Runners/Scor. Pos. | | | 72 | 24 | 1 | 4 | 8 | .333 | .431 | .359 |
| Runners On/2 Out | | | 60 | 19 | 1 | 4 | 4 | .317 | .433 | .359 |
| Scor. Pos./2 Out | | | 32 | 11 | 0 | 3 | 3 | .344 | .438 | .400 |
| Late Inning Pressure | | | 15 | 7 | 3 | 1 | 0 | .467 | 1.200 | .500 |
| Leading Off | | | 5 | 1 | 1 | 0 | 0 | .200 | .800 | .200 |
| Runners On | | | 3 | 3 | 2 | 0 | 0 | 1.000 | 3.000 | 1.000 |
| Runners/Scor. Pos. | | | 2 | 2 | 1 | 0 | 0 | 1.000 | 2.500 | 1.000 |
| First 9 Batters | | | 106 | 22 | 0 | 10 | 9 | .208 | .264 | .274 |
| Second 9 Batters | | | 108 | 40 | 3 | 7 | 7 | .370 | .556 | .410 |
| All Batters Thereafter | | | 118 | 40 | 6 | 7 | 14 | .339 | .576 | .381 |

Loves to face: Oddibe McDowell (.074, 2-for-27)
Hates to face: Todd Benzinger (.455, 5-for-11, 4 HR)
Ground outs-to-air outs ratio: 2.21 last season, 1.40 for career. . . . Additional statistics: 14 double-play ground outs in 75 opportunities, 21 doubles, 3 triples in 83.0 innings last season. . . . Allowed 5 first-inning runs in 13 starts. . . . Batting support: 5.23 runs per start. . . . Only pitcher in majors to lose six games in June. Goodbye, S.D., hello, N.Y. . . . Career record of 47–35 in home games, 37–54 on the road. . . . Pitched in Three Rivers Stadium only twice, but both were complete-game victories without allowing an earned run. . . . Has pitched 200 or more innings in each of the past six seasons, but never with an ERA below 3.50. His composite record during that time: 76–78, 4.07 ERA

## Bobby Thigpen

Throws Right

| Chicago White Sox | W–L | ERA | AB | H | HR | BB | SO | BA | SA | OBA |
|---|---|---|---|---|---|---|---|---|---|---|
| Season | 2-6 | 3.76 | 285 | 62 | 10 | 40 | 47 | .218 | .368 | .311 |
| vs. Left-Handers | | | 136 | 26 | 5 | 25 | 18 | .191 | .338 | .311 |
| vs. Right-Handers | | | 149 | 36 | 5 | 15 | 29 | .242 | .396 | .311 |
| Home | 1-2 | 3.60 | 146 | 32 | 4 | 21 | 24 | .219 | .370 | .312 |
| Road | 1-4 | 3.92 | 139 | 30 | 6 | 19 | 23 | .216 | .367 | .311 |
| Grass | 1-4 | 3.22 | 240 | 50 | 7 | 36 | 42 | .208 | .346 | .307 |
| Artificial Turf | 1-2 | 6.75 | 45 | 12 | 3 | 4 | 5 | .267 | .489 | .333 |
| April | 0-0 | 0.84 | 38 | 9 | 1 | 7 | 6 | .237 | .368 | .356 |
| May | 0-2 | 7.07 | 60 | 20 | 5 | 7 | 10 | .333 | .617 | .397 |
| June | 0-1 | 3.95 | 47 | 7 | 2 | 4 | 9 | .149 | .277 | .226 |
| July | 1-1 | 3.57 | 61 | 10 | 2 | 9 | 9 | .164 | .311 | .268 |
| August | 1-1 | 2.70 | 48 | 12 | 0 | 4 | 8 | .250 | .354 | .296 |
| Sept./Oct. | 0-1 | 3.72 | 31 | 4 | 0 | 9 | 5 | .129 | .161 | .325 |
| Leading Off Inn. | | | 52 | 10 | 0 | 12 | 9 | .192 | .250 | .344 |
| Runners On | | | 162 | 33 | 7 | 13 | 24 | .204 | .377 | .256 |
| Runners/Scor. Pos. | | | 82 | 21 | 5 | 9 | 13 | .256 | .500 | .313 |
| Runners On/2 Out | | | 74 | 11 | 2 | 8 | 9 | .149 | .270 | .232 |
| Scor. Pos./2 Out | | | 39 | 7 | 2 | 7 | 5 | .179 | .385 | .304 |
| Late Inning Pressure | | | 186 | 40 | 7 | 26 | 33 | .215 | .360 | .312 |
| Leading Off | | | 35 | 9 | 0 | 8 | 6 | .257 | .343 | .395 |
| Runners On | | | 105 | 22 | 6 | 10 | 16 | .210 | .410 | .274 |
| Runners/Scor. Pos. | | | 51 | 14 | 4 | 8 | 10 | .275 | .529 | .361 |
| First 9 Batters | | | 279 | 61 | 10 | 39 | 47 | .219 | .373 | .312 |
| Second 9 Batters | | | 6 | 1 | 0 | 1 | 0 | .167 | .167 | .286 |
| All Batters Thereafter | | | 0 | 0 | 0 | 0 | 0 | — | — | — |

Loves to face: B. J. Surhoff (0-for-9, 7 ground outs)
Hates to face: Randy Bush (.800, 4-for-5, 1 HR)
Ground outs-to-air outs ratio: 0.84 last season, 0.86 for career.... Additional statistics: 4 double-play ground outs in 75 opportunities, 11 doubles, 1 triple in 79.0 innings last season.... Inherited 34 runners, stranded 21 (62%).... Earned 34 saves, and *really* earned 18 of them by pitching more than an inning, highest total in A.L. ... Batting average by opposing left-handers dropped 124 points from 1988. Right-handers have hit between .230 and .242 in each of his four seasons.... Career record of 11–8 at Comiskey Park, 5–11 elsewhere.... ERA has increased, winning percentage decreased in each of last three seasons. Recent four-year streaks: Dave Rozema (1983–86) and Frank Tanana (1977–80).

## Mark Thurmond

Throws Left

| Baltimore Orioles | W–L | ERA | AB | H | HR | BB | SO | BA | SA | OBA |
|---|---|---|---|---|---|---|---|---|---|---|
| Season | 2-4 | 3.90 | 354 | 102 | 6 | 17 | 34 | .288 | .407 | .322 |
| vs. Left-Handers | | | 109 | 31 | 1 | 5 | 11 | .284 | .422 | .316 |
| vs. Right-Handers | | | 245 | 71 | 5 | 12 | 23 | .290 | .400 | .324 |
| Home | 2-3 | 3.83 | 181 | 53 | 4 | 10 | 22 | .293 | .431 | .330 |
| Road | 0-1 | 3.97 | 173 | 49 | 2 | 7 | 12 | .283 | .382 | .313 |
| Grass | 2-4 | 3.98 | 296 | 88 | 6 | 14 | 30 | .297 | .429 | .330 |
| Artificial Turf | 0-0 | 3.52 | 58 | 14 | 0 | 3 | 4 | .241 | .293 | .279 |
| April | 0-1 | 3.44 | 65 | 15 | 2 | 1 | 2 | .231 | .338 | .242 |
| May | 1-0 | 2.70 | 27 | 10 | 0 | 2 | 2 | .370 | .407 | .414 |
| June | 1-0 | 4.05 | 79 | 22 | 2 | 6 | 10 | .278 | .392 | .329 |
| July | 0-2 | 3.32 | 87 | 27 | 2 | 3 | 11 | .310 | .414 | .330 |
| August | 0-1 | 4.08 | 71 | 18 | 0 | 4 | 8 | .254 | .408 | .303 |
| Sept./Oct. | 0-0 | 7.94 | 25 | 10 | 0 | 1 | 1 | .400 | .600 | .423 |
| Leading Off Inn. | | | 79 | 24 | 4 | 4 | 8 | .304 | .532 | .337 |
| Runners On | | | 167 | 50 | 1 | 11 | 17 | .299 | .371 | .344 |
| Runners/Scor. Pos. | | | 101 | 31 | 0 | 10 | 11 | .307 | .386 | .372 |
| Runners On/2 Out | | | 62 | 18 | 1 | 7 | 10 | .290 | .435 | .362 |
| Scor. Pos./2 Out | | | 41 | 16 | 0 | 7 | 7 | .390 | .537 | .479 |
| Late Inning Pressure | | | 39 | 15 | 2 | 4 | 0 | .385 | .615 | .442 |
| Leading Off | | | 11 | 6 | 1 | 2 | 0 | .545 | .909 | .615 |
| Runners On | | | 16 | 6 | 1 | 1 | 0 | .375 | .625 | .412 |
| Runners/Scor. Pos. | | | 5 | 2 | 0 | 1 | 0 | .400 | .400 | .500 |
| First 9 Batters | | | 291 | 88 | 6 | 16 | 27 | .302 | .430 | .340 |
| Second 9 Batters | | | 58 | 13 | 0 | 1 | 7 | .224 | .310 | .237 |
| All Batters Thereafter | | | 5 | 1 | 0 | 0 | 0 | .200 | .200 | .200 |

Loves to face: Mike Heath (.091, 1-for-11, 1 HR)
Hates to face: Rob Deer (.636, 7-for-11, 1 HR)
Ground outs-to-air outs ratio: 1.69 last season, 1.36 for career.... Additional statistics: 16 double-play ground outs in 85 opportunities, 18 doubles, 3 triples in 90.0 innings last season.... Opposing right-handers outslugged left-handers by at least 100 points in each of four previous seasons.... Opposing fly-ball hitters have hit better than ground-ballers in each of last five seasons. Career BA: .297 and .260, respectively.... Career record of 3–11 in April, 35–32 in other months.... Faced 43 batters in LIP Situations without a strikeout. Andy Hawkins was 0-for-61. (Jerry Augustine was 0-for-80 in '80). ... Had 21–11 record, 2.85 ERA in first two seasons; losing records in each of five seasons since then (4.23 ERA).

## Duane Ward

Throws Right

| Toronto Blue Jays | W–L | ERA | AB | H | HR | BB | SO | BA | SA | OBA |
|---|---|---|---|---|---|---|---|---|---|---|
| Season | 4-10 | 3.77 | 408 | 94 | 4 | 58 | 122 | .230 | .304 | .326 |
| vs. Left-Handers | | | 172 | 45 | 2 | 35 | 46 | .262 | .360 | .383 |
| vs. Right-Handers | | | 236 | 49 | 2 | 23 | 76 | .208 | .263 | .280 |
| Home | 2-6 | 3.81 | 191 | 46 | 2 | 27 | 57 | .241 | .314 | .326 |
| Road | 2-4 | 3.73 | 217 | 48 | 2 | 31 | 65 | .221 | .295 | .326 |
| Grass | 2-3 | 3.21 | 168 | 35 | 1 | 24 | 53 | .208 | .262 | .317 |
| Artificial Turf | 2-7 | 4.16 | 240 | 59 | 3 | 34 | 69 | .246 | .333 | .332 |
| April | 1-3 | 4.41 | 62 | 15 | 0 | 11 | 17 | .242 | .258 | .351 |
| May | 0-3 | 1.77 | 70 | 13 | 0 | 12 | 21 | .186 | .243 | .301 |
| June | 3-1 | 4.07 | 81 | 18 | 0 | 13 | 27 | .222 | .272 | .333 |
| July | 0-1 | 2.18 | 77 | 18 | 1 | 4 | 24 | .234 | .325 | .272 |
| August | 0-1 | 6.28 | 52 | 18 | 1 | 8 | 13 | .346 | .462 | .413 |
| Sept./Oct. | 0-1 | 4.82 | 66 | 12 | 2 | 10 | 20 | .182 | .303 | .304 |
| Leading Off Inn. | | | 85 | 22 | 0 | 15 | 22 | .259 | .353 | .370 |
| Runners On | | | 214 | 49 | 3 | 34 | 56 | .229 | .290 | .331 |
| Runners/Scor. Pos. | | | 139 | 33 | 2 | 25 | 39 | .237 | .302 | .343 |
| Runners On/2 Out | | | 88 | 18 | 0 | 14 | 25 | .205 | .216 | .320 |
| Scor. Pos./2 Out | | | 58 | 9 | 0 | 11 | 18 | .155 | .172 | .300 |
| Late Inning Pressure | | | 249 | 59 | 4 | 39 | 74 | .237 | .329 | .342 |
| Leading Off | | | 52 | 16 | 0 | 13 | 8 | .308 | .423 | .446 |
| Runners On | | | 132 | 33 | 3 | 21 | 34 | .250 | .333 | .352 |
| Runners/Scor. Pos. | | | 85 | 26 | 2 | 17 | 21 | .306 | .400 | .407 |
| First 9 Batters | | | 365 | 82 | 4 | 51 | 110 | .225 | .299 | .319 |
| Second 9 Batters | | | 43 | 12 | 0 | 7 | 12 | .279 | .349 | .385 |
| All Batters Thereafter | | | 0 | 0 | 0 | 0 | 0 | — | — | — |

Loves to face: Tony Phillips (0-for-8)
Hates to face: Rickey Henderson (.500, 6-for-12)
Ground outs-to-air outs ratio: 2.11 last season, 2.12 for career.... Additional statistics: 9 double-play ground outs in 120 opportunities, 14 doubles, 2 triples in 114.2 innings last season.... Inherited 65 runners, stranded 43 (66%).... Threw 13 wild pitches, most of any reliever in the majors.... Faced 31 batters with bases loaded, most in the majors.... Two of the four home runs he allowed were grand slams.... Career average of one home run per 161 right-handed batters faced is lowest among active pitchers (minimum: 600 PA).... Has walked 23 of 127 leadoff batters in Late-Inning Pressure Situations (18.1%). Over the last 15 years, only Mark Clear had a higher average (18.7%).

## Gary Wayne

Throws Left

| Minnesota Twins | W–L | ERA | AB | H | HR | BB | SO | BA | SA | OBA |
|---|---|---|---|---|---|---|---|---|---|---|
| Season | 3-4 | 3.30 | 259 | 55 | 4 | 36 | 41 | .212 | .332 | .309 |
| vs. Left-Handers | | | 83 | 16 | 2 | 9 | 17 | .193 | .301 | .280 |
| vs. Right-Handers | | | 176 | 39 | 2 | 27 | 24 | .222 | .347 | .322 |
| Home | 2-0 | 2.16 | 146 | 27 | 1 | 23 | 28 | .185 | .281 | .292 |
| Road | 1-4 | 4.91 | 113 | 28 | 3 | 13 | 13 | .248 | .398 | .331 |
| Grass | 1-3 | 4.55 | 104 | 25 | 3 | 12 | 13 | .240 | .394 | .325 |
| Artificial Turf | 2-1 | 2.49 | 155 | 30 | 1 | 24 | 28 | .194 | .290 | .298 |
| April | 0-0 | 7.45 | 41 | 14 | 3 | 11 | 7 | .341 | .634 | .491 |
| May | 0-0 | 2.50 | 65 | 11 | 0 | 3 | 6 | .169 | .246 | .203 |
| June | 3-0 | 1.47 | 58 | 8 | 0 | 11 | 16 | .138 | .241 | .275 |
| July | 0-2 | 5.56 | 43 | 10 | 1 | 4 | 7 | .233 | .372 | .292 |
| August | 0-2 | 2.08 | 33 | 8 | 0 | 5 | 3 | .242 | .273 | .342 |
| Sept./Oct. | 0-0 | 1.80 | 19 | 4 | 0 | 2 | 2 | .211 | .263 | .286 |
| Leading Off Inn. | | | 57 | 16 | 1 | 11 | 6 | .281 | .491 | .397 |
| Runners On | | | 134 | 28 | 3 | 17 | 22 | .209 | .328 | .299 |
| Runners/Scor. Pos. | | | 87 | 20 | 2 | 14 | 18 | .230 | .368 | .337 |
| Runners On/2 Out | | | 55 | 11 | 2 | 7 | 9 | .200 | .345 | .302 |
| Scor. Pos./2 Out | | | 38 | 9 | 2 | 7 | 7 | .237 | .447 | .370 |
| Late Inning Pressure | | | 82 | 16 | 0 | 13 | 14 | .195 | .232 | .305 |
| Leading Off | | | 19 | 4 | 0 | 6 | 2 | .211 | .263 | .400 |
| Runners On | | | 42 | 10 | 0 | 5 | 6 | .238 | .286 | .319 |
| Runners/Scor. Pos. | | | 21 | 8 | 0 | 4 | 4 | .381 | .429 | .480 |
| First 9 Batters | | | 237 | 47 | 3 | 36 | 40 | .198 | .308 | .304 |
| Second 9 Batters | | | 22 | 8 | 1 | 0 | 1 | .364 | .591 | .364 |
| All Batters Thereafter | | | 0 | 0 | 0 | 0 | 0 | — | — | — |

Loves to face: Ken Griffey, Jr. (0-for-4, 2 SO)
Hates to face: Brian Downing (2-for-2, 2 2B)
Ground outs-to-air outs ratio: 1.03 last season, his first in majors. ... Additional statistics: 8 double-play ground outs in 63 opportunities, 17 doubles, 1 triple in 71.0 innings last season.... Batting average of .240 by opposing ground-ball hitters, .188 by fly-ballers; .271 in day games, .190 at night.... Inherited 54 runners, stranded 39 (72%).... Was called into bases-loaded situations in five of his first 11 appearances in majors.... Entered a game with the Twins leading by three runs or less in only 7 of his first 49 appearances, but 7 times in his last 11.... Made 60 appearances, highest total by a Twins rookie since Rick Lysander (61) and Len Whitehouse (60) in 1983.

## Bob Welch

Throws Right

| Oakland As | W–L | ERA | AB | H | HR | BB | SO | BA | SA | OBA |
|---|---|---|---|---|---|---|---|---|---|---|
| Season | 17-8 | 3.00 | 792 | 191 | 13 | 78 | 137 | .241 | .357 | .313 |
| vs. Left-Handers | | | 418 | 88 | 3 | 51 | 67 | .211 | .304 | .300 |
| vs. Right-Handers | | | 374 | 103 | 10 | 27 | 70 | .275 | .417 | .327 |
| Home | 10-2 | 2.77 | 403 | 95 | 5 | 29 | 76 | .236 | .337 | .289 |
| Road | 7-6 | 3.25 | 389 | 96 | 8 | 49 | 61 | .247 | .378 | .336 |
| Grass | 15-6 | 2.96 | 639 | 151 | 9 | 65 | 116 | .236 | .343 | .310 |
| Artificial Turf | 2-2 | 3.20 | 153 | 40 | 4 | 13 | 21 | .261 | .418 | .324 |
| April | 3-2 | 2.31 | 128 | 23 | 2 | 15 | 24 | .180 | .297 | .264 |
| May | 3-2 | 4.05 | 153 | 36 | 5 | 20 | 25 | .235 | .405 | .331 |
| June | 3-0 | 0.78 | 85 | 22 | 1 | 7 | 13 | .259 | .329 | .315 |
| July | 2-1 | 3.82 | 119 | 31 | 1 | 11 | 20 | .261 | .370 | .331 |
| August | 4-2 | 2.32 | 158 | 41 | 1 | 13 | 35 | .259 | .361 | .314 |
| Sept./Oct. | 2-1 | 3.99 | 149 | 38 | 3 | 12 | 20 | .255 | .362 | .317 |
| Leading Off Inn. | | | 205 | 45 | 3 | 12 | 35 | .220 | .317 | .269 |
| Runners On | | | 321 | 71 | 6 | 39 | 68 | .221 | .336 | .310 |
| Runners/Scor. Pos. | | | 191 | 43 | 4 | 26 | 43 | .225 | .340 | .318 |
| Runners On/2 Out | | | 141 | 28 | 3 | 22 | 30 | .199 | .319 | .311 |
| Scor. Pos./2 Out | | | 93 | 21 | 3 | 13 | 20 | .226 | .376 | .327 |
| Late Inning Pressure | | | 58 | 17 | 3 | 8 | 9 | .293 | .500 | .379 |
| Leading Off | | | 17 | 6 | 1 | 3 | 3 | .353 | .647 | .450 |
| Runners On | | | 22 | 5 | 1 | 4 | 2 | .227 | .364 | .346 |
| Runners/Scor. Pos. | | | 14 | 4 | 0 | 3 | 0 | .286 | .286 | .412 |
| First 9 Batters | | | 269 | 59 | 2 | 18 | 48 | .219 | .286 | .280 |
| Second 9 Batters | | | 262 | 69 | 6 | 29 | 47 | .263 | .405 | .336 |
| All Batters Thereafter | | | 261 | 63 | 5 | 31 | 42 | .241 | .383 | .322 |

Loves to face: Wade Boggs (0-for-12 [2-for-2 in 1988 L.C.S.])
Hates to face: Kirby Puckett (.550, 11-for-20)
Ground outs-to-air outs ratio: 1.05 last season, 0.92 for career.... Additional statistics: 17 double-play ground outs in 139 opportunities, 41 doubles, 6 triples in 209.2 innings last season.... Allowed 11 first-inning runs in 33 starts.... Batting support: 4.58 runs per start.... Past two seasons: 30–10, 2.80 ERA with Hassey catching; 4–7, 6.09 with Steinbach.... Only pitcher with 15+ wins and fewer than 10 losses in each of last three seasons. Dwight Gooden holds the all-time major league record: five straight seasons (1984–88).... Has averaged less than three innings in six postseason starts. Career rate of walks per nine innings (5.9) is highest in postseason history (minimum 25 IP).

## David Wells

Throws Left

| Toronto Blue Jays | W–L | ERA | AB | H | HR | BB | SO | BA | SA | OBA |
|---|---|---|---|---|---|---|---|---|---|---|
| Season | 7-4 | 2.40 | 319 | 66 | 5 | 28 | 78 | .207 | .298 | .269 |
| vs. Left-Handers | | | 78 | 18 | 1 | 7 | 12 | .231 | .346 | .294 |
| vs. Right-Handers | | | 241 | 48 | 4 | 21 | 66 | .199 | .282 | .261 |
| Home | 5-2 | 2.40 | 184 | 39 | 3 | 18 | 42 | .212 | .288 | .282 |
| Road | 2-2 | 2.39 | 135 | 27 | 2 | 10 | 36 | .200 | .311 | .252 |
| Grass | 2-0 | 1.97 | 116 | 23 | 1 | 9 | 31 | .198 | .284 | .254 |
| Artificial Turf | 5-4 | 2.65 | 203 | 43 | 4 | 19 | 47 | .212 | .305 | .278 |
| April | 1-1 | 4.00 | 69 | 16 | 1 | 6 | 17 | .232 | .348 | .293 |
| May | 1-1 | 1.32 | 46 | 6 | 0 | 6 | 16 | .130 | .152 | .226 |
| June | 0-1 | 2.70 | 75 | 19 | 2 | 4 | 18 | .253 | .347 | .291 |
| July | 3-1 | 2.51 | 52 | 9 | 1 | 3 | 14 | .173 | .250 | .214 |
| August | 1-0 | 2.00 | 33 | 7 | 1 | 5 | 6 | .212 | .424 | .316 |
| Sept./Oct. | 1-0 | 0.79 | 44 | 9 | 0 | 4 | 7 | .205 | .250 | .271 |
| Leading Off Inn. | | | 74 | 13 | 2 | 8 | 20 | .176 | .284 | .256 |
| Runners On | | | 138 | 27 | 1 | 14 | 29 | .196 | .275 | .266 |
| Runners/Scor. Pos. | | | 85 | 17 | 0 | 11 | 19 | .200 | .247 | .286 |
| Runners On/2 Out | | | 64 | 14 | 1 | 6 | 15 | .219 | .359 | .286 |
| Scor. Pos./2 Out | | | 43 | 8 | 0 | 5 | 9 | .186 | .233 | .271 |
| Late Inning Pressure | | | 164 | 40 | 4 | 18 | 39 | .244 | .354 | .315 |
| Leading Off | | | 38 | 6 | 1 | 6 | 9 | .158 | .263 | .273 |
| Runners On | | | 71 | 16 | 1 | 10 | 15 | .225 | .296 | .313 |
| Runners/Scor. Pos. | | | 39 | 10 | 0 | 8 | 7 | .256 | .308 | .367 |
| First 9 Batters | | | 259 | 54 | 4 | 24 | 62 | .208 | .301 | .274 |
| Second 9 Batters | | | 57 | 10 | 1 | 4 | 16 | .175 | .246 | .230 |
| All Batters Thereafter | | | 3 | 2 | 0 | 0 | 0 | .667 | 1.000 | .667 |

Loves to face: Wade Boggs (.111, 1-for-9, 3 SO)
Hates to face: Chili Davis (.500, 5-for-10, 2 HR)
Brad Wellman also hits well against Wells, with four hits in four career at-bats.... Ground outs-to-air outs ratio: 1.09 last season, 1.28 for career.... Additional statistics: 6 double-play ground outs in 56 opportunities, 10 doubles, 2 triples in 86.1 innings last season. ... Inherited 40 runners, stranded 28 (70%).... Only one of 16 career home runs allowed has been hit by a left-handed batter (Ken Griffey, Jr.).... Opponents have career average of one home run per 29 at-bats in Late-Inning Pressure Situations, one per 66 otherwise.... What number comes next in this pattern: 11.4, 9.1, 6.9? Significance: those are Wells's year-by-year figures for hits allowed per nine innings.... Answer: 4.8.

## Frank Williams

Throws Right

| Detroit Tigers | W–L | ERA | AB | H | HR | BB | SO | BA | SA | OBA |
|---|---|---|---|---|---|---|---|---|---|---|
| Season | 3-3 | 3.64 | 276 | 70 | 5 | 46 | 33 | .254 | .348 | .362 |
| vs. Left-Handers | | | 123 | 32 | 3 | 27 | 12 | .260 | .382 | .392 |
| vs. Right-Handers | | | 153 | 38 | 2 | 19 | 21 | .248 | .320 | .335 |
| Home | 1-1 | 4.25 | 136 | 33 | 4 | 25 | 15 | .243 | .346 | .366 |
| Road | 2-2 | 3.03 | 140 | 37 | 1 | 21 | 18 | .264 | .350 | .358 |
| Grass | 2-3 | 3.39 | 234 | 57 | 4 | 36 | 32 | .244 | .321 | .345 |
| Artificial Turf | 1-0 | 5.06 | 42 | 13 | 1 | 10 | 1 | .310 | .500 | .444 |
| April | 1-2 | 4.32 | 60 | 10 | 2 | 13 | 11 | .167 | .283 | .324 |
| May | 1-0 | 2.57 | 77 | 19 | 1 | 15 | 7 | .247 | .325 | .376 |
| June | 1-1 | 1.50 | 70 | 19 | 0 | 9 | 9 | .271 | .314 | .354 |
| July | 0-0 | 6.75 | 16 | 5 | 0 | 5 | 2 | .313 | .313 | .435 |
| August | 0-0 | 3.00 | 27 | 10 | 0 | 1 | 2 | .370 | .519 | .367 |
| Sept./Oct. | 0-0 | 10.50 | 26 | 7 | 2 | 3 | 2 | .269 | .500 | .367 |
| Leading Off Inn. | | | 57 | 13 | 0 | 7 | 6 | .228 | .263 | .323 |
| Runners On | | | 152 | 36 | 3 | 30 | 17 | .237 | .329 | .362 |
| Runners/Scor. Pos. | | | 94 | 19 | 2 | 22 | 12 | .202 | .298 | .352 |
| Runners On/2 Out | | | 68 | 14 | 0 | 14 | 8 | .206 | .235 | .341 |
| Scor. Pos./2 Out | | | 50 | 6 | 0 | 13 | 6 | .120 | .140 | .302 |
| Late Inning Pressure | | | 74 | 20 | 2 | 16 | 12 | .270 | .405 | .407 |
| Leading Off | | | 18 | 2 | 0 | 2 | 4 | .111 | .222 | .200 |
| Runners On | | | 34 | 11 | 1 | 11 | 5 | .324 | .441 | .500 |
| Runners/Scor. Pos. | | | 21 | 5 | 0 | 10 | 4 | .238 | .286 | .500 |
| First 9 Batters | | | 239 | 58 | 4 | 40 | 27 | .243 | .335 | .353 |
| Second 9 Batters | | | 37 | 12 | 1 | 6 | 6 | .324 | .432 | .419 |
| All Batters Thereafter | | | 0 | 0 | 0 | 0 | 0 | — | — | — |

Loves to face: Rick Schu (0-for-7)
Hates to face: Dave Parker (.429, 6-for-14, 1 HR)
Ground outs-to-air outs ratio: 1.36 last season, 1.63 for career.... Additional statistics: 6 double-play ground outs in 84 opportunities, 9 doubles, 1 triple in 71.2 innings last season. ... Inherited 39 runners, stranded 26 (67%).... Highest ratio of walks to strikeouts by a Tigers pitcher with as many innings since Joe Sparma in 1969. ... Has handled 335 batters with runners on base in LIP Situations with care: 50 BB, two HR. That walk rate is fifth highest over last six years; the HR rate is fourth lowest (min.: 300 BFP).... Career average of .277 by opposing left-handed batters, .215 by right-handers.... One of five active pitchers with 100+ chances and a career fielding percentage below .900. His mark: .896.

## Mark Williamson

Throws Right

| Baltimore Orioles | W–L | ERA | AB | H | HR | BB | SO | BA | SA | OBA |
|---|---|---|---|---|---|---|---|---|---|---|
| Season | 10-5 | 2.93 | 403 | 105 | 4 | 30 | 55 | .261 | .345 | .313 |
| vs. Left-Handers | | | 177 | 46 | 0 | 10 | 24 | .260 | .305 | .296 |
| vs. Right-Handers | | | 226 | 59 | 4 | 20 | 31 | .261 | .376 | .325 |
| Home | 7-2 | 2.61 | 216 | 53 | 1 | 17 | 34 | .245 | .315 | .304 |
| Road | 3-3 | 3.33 | 187 | 52 | 3 | 13 | 21 | .278 | .380 | .323 |
| Grass | 9-2 | 3.22 | 341 | 91 | 4 | 25 | 49 | .267 | .364 | .319 |
| Artificial Turf | 1-3 | 1.50 | 62 | 14 | 0 | 5 | 6 | .226 | .242 | .279 |
| April | 0-1 | 5.79 | 56 | 16 | 1 | 3 | 7 | .286 | .411 | .322 |
| May | 3-1 | 1.64 | 76 | 15 | 1 | 4 | 11 | .197 | .316 | .247 |
| June | 2-0 | 2.55 | 67 | 19 | 1 | 2 | 7 | .284 | .388 | .304 |
| July | 2-1 | 3.10 | 77 | 21 | 0 | 10 | 7 | .273 | .325 | .352 |
| August | 2-0 | 3.38 | 53 | 18 | 1 | 6 | 9 | .340 | .415 | .400 |
| Sept./Oct. | 1-2 | 2.25 | 74 | 16 | 0 | 5 | 14 | .216 | .257 | .272 |
| Leading Off Inn. | | | 88 | 22 | 0 | 1 | 12 | .250 | .318 | .258 |
| Runners On | | | 193 | 56 | 4 | 25 | 34 | .290 | .409 | .369 |
| Runners/Scor. Pos. | | | 119 | 36 | 2 | 19 | 25 | .303 | .412 | .394 |
| Runners On/2 Out | | | 86 | 26 | 2 | 10 | 14 | .302 | .407 | .375 |
| Scor. Pos./2 Out | | | 58 | 18 | 1 | 8 | 10 | .310 | .397 | .394 |
| Late Inning Pressure | | | 214 | 61 | 2 | 22 | 29 | .285 | .383 | .354 |
| Leading Off | | | 47 | 13 | 0 | 1 | 7 | .277 | .362 | .292 |
| Runners On | | | 104 | 35 | 2 | 17 | 17 | .337 | .462 | .427 |
| Runners/Scor. Pos. | | | 73 | 24 | 1 | 14 | 15 | .329 | .438 | .433 |
| First 9 Batters | | | 371 | 100 | 4 | 25 | 49 | .270 | .361 | .317 |
| Second 9 Batters | | | 32 | 5 | 0 | 5 | 6 | .156 | .156 | .270 |
| All Batters Thereafter | | | 0 | 0 | 0 | 0 | 0 | — | — | — |

Loves to face: Gary Ward (0-for-11, 4 SO)
Hates to face: Mark McGwire (.429, 6-for-14, 2 2B, 2 HR)
Ground outs-to-air outs ratio: 1.07 last season, 1.24 for career.... Additional statistics: 12 double-play ground outs in 100 opportunities, 18 doubles, 2 triples in 107.1 innings last season.... Used solely as a reliever for first time in three seasons. Career figures: 1–7, 4.46 ERA as a starter; 22–15, 3.84 in relief.... Career on-base average of .251 by opposing leadoff batters is lowest over last 15 years (minimum: 250 BFP).... One walk per 22 leadoff batters faced, one per 12 at other times. ... Career record of 9–13 before All-Star break, 14–9 after break.... Opponents' career average in LIP Situations (.306) is 65 points higher than otherwise (.240), largest difference over the last 10 years.

## Frank Wills

Throws Right

| Toronto Blue Jays | W–L | ERA | AB | H | HR | BB | SO | BA | SA | OBA |
|---|---|---|---|---|---|---|---|---|---|---|
| Season | 3-1 | 3.66 | 269 | 65 | 4 | 30 | 41 | .242 | .353 | .319 |
| vs. Left-Handers | | | 94 | 25 | 1 | 19 | 4 | .266 | .372 | .389 |
| vs. Right-Handers | | | 175 | 40 | 3 | 11 | 37 | .229 | .343 | .277 |
| Home | 2-1 | 1.93 | 136 | 29 | 2 | 13 | 18 | .213 | .309 | .282 |
| Road | 1-0 | 5.56 | 133 | 36 | 2 | 17 | 23 | .271 | .398 | .355 |
| Grass | 1-0 | 6.75 | 112 | 31 | 2 | 17 | 20 | .277 | .429 | .374 |
| Artificial Turf | 2-1 | 1.66 | 157 | 34 | 2 | 13 | 21 | .217 | .299 | .276 |
| April | | | 0 | 0 | 0 | 0 | 0 | — | — | — |
| May | 0-0 | 1.42 | 49 | 12 | 0 | 4 | 11 | .245 | .327 | .302 |
| June | 0-1 | 7.59 | 83 | 22 | 3 | 16 | 8 | .265 | .434 | .380 |
| July | 0-0 | 1.93 | 33 | 9 | 0 | 2 | 4 | .273 | .303 | .314 |
| August | 1-0 | 3.95 | 54 | 13 | 1 | 4 | 11 | .241 | .370 | .293 |
| Sept./Oct. | 2-0 | 0.63 | 50 | 9 | 0 | 4 | 7 | .180 | .260 | .255 |
| Leading Off Inn. | | | 60 | 16 | 1 | 5 | 11 | .267 | .383 | .333 |
| Runners On | | | 127 | 31 | 2 | 21 | 19 | .244 | .354 | .349 |
| Runners/Scor. Pos. | | | 83 | 20 | 2 | 16 | 15 | .241 | .410 | .360 |
| Runners On/2 Out | | | 48 | 10 | 1 | 7 | 6 | .208 | .313 | .309 |
| Scor. Pos./2 Out | | | 33 | 8 | 1 | 6 | 5 | .242 | .394 | .359 |
| Late Inning Pressure | | | 39 | 9 | 0 | 3 | 8 | .231 | .282 | .302 |
| Leading Off | | | 9 | 4 | 0 | 0 | 1 | .444 | .556 | .500 |
| Runners On | | | 20 | 3 | 0 | 3 | 4 | .150 | .150 | .261 |
| Runners/Scor. Pos. | | | 12 | 1 | 0 | 3 | 3 | .083 | .083 | .267 |
| First 9 Batters | | | 167 | 43 | 2 | 17 | 24 | .257 | .377 | .328 |
| Second 9 Batters | | | 78 | 18 | 1 | 9 | 11 | .231 | .321 | .310 |
| All Batters Thereafter | | | 24 | 4 | 1 | 4 | 6 | .167 | .292 | .286 |

Loves to face: Brook Jacoby (.077, 1-for-13)
Hates to face: Willie Wilson (.500, 4-for-8, 2 3B)
Ground outs-to-air outs ratio: 1.11 last season, 1.02 for career. . . . Additional statistics: 2 double-play ground outs in 70 opportunities, 10 doubles, 4 triples in 71.1 innings last season. . . . Average of 10.85 batters faced per relief appearance was 2d highest in majors (minimum: 20 games). Entered 11 of those 20 games in the fifth inning or earlier. . . . Inherited 24 runners, stranded only 13 (54%). . . . Ratio of 5.5 walks per strikeout vs. left-handed batters equals the worst in the A.L. over the past 15 years (min.: 100 BFP). Rich Thompson of the Indians posted same figures in 1985. . . . Prior to last season, opponents had hit 24 points higher on grass fields (.280) than on artificial turf (.256).

## Bobby Witt

Throws Right

| Texas Rangers | W–L | ERA | AB | H | HR | BB | SO | BA | SA | OBA |
|---|---|---|---|---|---|---|---|---|---|---|
| Season | 12-13 | 5.14 | 733 | 182 | 14 | 114 | 166 | .248 | .355 | .348 |
| vs. Left-Handers | | | 349 | 87 | 10 | 66 | 82 | .249 | .387 | .364 |
| vs. Right-Handers | | | 384 | 95 | 4 | 48 | 84 | .247 | .326 | .332 |
| Home | 5-7 | 4.74 | 334 | 79 | 7 | 50 | 76 | .237 | .329 | .334 |
| Road | 7-6 | 5.49 | 399 | 103 | 7 | 64 | 90 | .258 | .376 | .359 |
| Grass | 11-10 | 4.95 | 635 | 155 | 11 | 99 | 148 | .244 | .348 | .345 |
| Artificial Turf | 1-3 | 6.39 | 98 | 27 | 3 | 15 | 18 | .276 | .398 | .365 |
| April | 3-0 | 4.50 | 90 | 23 | 3 | 13 | 19 | .256 | .389 | .352 |
| May | 1-5 | 7.34 | 152 | 47 | 2 | 23 | 29 | .309 | .428 | .397 |
| June | 1-3 | 6.20 | 98 | 31 | 2 | 16 | 17 | .316 | .459 | .405 |
| July | 4-1 | 3.11 | 159 | 24 | 2 | 23 | 39 | .151 | .208 | .258 |
| August | 1-3 | 5.92 | 144 | 35 | 4 | 25 | 37 | .243 | .361 | .351 |
| Sept./Oct. | 2-1 | 3.86 | 90 | 22 | 1 | 14 | 25 | .244 | .333 | .346 |
| Leading Off Inn. | | | 173 | 42 | 4 | 35 | 46 | .243 | .353 | .370 |
| Runners On | | | 332 | 96 | 5 | 50 | 62 | .289 | .410 | .378 |
| Runners/Scor. Pos. | | | 204 | 59 | 4 | 28 | 40 | .289 | .417 | .365 |
| Runners On/2 Out | | | 146 | 47 | 3 | 17 | 25 | .322 | .459 | .396 |
| Scor. Pos./2 Out | | | 101 | 32 | 2 | 11 | 16 | .317 | .446 | .384 |
| Late Inning Pressure | | | 49 | 10 | 0 | 9 | 15 | .204 | .204 | .328 |
| Leading Off | | | 15 | 4 | 0 | 3 | 4 | .267 | .267 | .389 |
| Runners On | | | 18 | 5 | 0 | 2 | 4 | .278 | .278 | .350 |
| Runners/Scor. Pos. | | | 11 | 3 | 0 | 2 | 2 | .273 | .273 | .385 |
| First 9 Batters | | | 240 | 63 | 4 | 34 | 62 | .263 | .375 | .351 |
| Second 9 Batters | | | 210 | 52 | 6 | 38 | 46 | .248 | .357 | .365 |
| All Batters Thereafter | | | 283 | 67 | 4 | 42 | 58 | .237 | .336 | .331 |

Loves to face: Gary Gaetti (0-for-14, 5 SO)
Hates to face: Larry Sheets (.417, 5-for-12, 2 HR)
Ground outs-to-air outs ratio: 0.95 last season, 0.96 for career. . . . Additional statistics: 13 double-play ground outs in 175 opportunities, 26 doubles, 5 triples in 194.1 innings last season. . . . Allowed 20 first-inning runs in 31 starts. Hasn't allowed a first-inning home run in last 50 starts. . . . Batting support: 4.65 runs per start. . . . Opponents stole 30 bases (2d most in A.L. to Nolan Ryan [36]) in 34 attempts. . . . Witt and Langston have walked 100 batters in each of last four seasons, longest streaks since Ryan set record with nine in a row (1971–79). . . . Most career walks per nine innings: Tommy Byrne, 6.86; Witt, 6.69; Herb Score, 6.01; Lou Kretlow, 5.99; Mickey McDermott, 5.74 (minimum: 500 IP).

## Mike Witt

Throws Right

| California Angels | W–L | ERA | AB | H | HR | BB | SO | BA | SA | OBA |
|---|---|---|---|---|---|---|---|---|---|---|
| Season | 9-15 | 4.54 | 864 | 252 | 26 | 48 | 123 | .292 | .433 | .326 |
| vs. Left-Handers | | | 434 | 128 | 12 | 24 | 54 | .295 | .424 | .326 |
| vs. Right-Handers | | | 430 | 124 | 14 | 24 | 69 | .288 | .442 | .325 |
| Home | 5-7 | 4.85 | 420 | 119 | 18 | 20 | 53 | .283 | .464 | .313 |
| Road | 4-8 | 4.25 | 444 | 133 | 8 | 28 | 70 | .300 | .403 | .338 |
| Grass | 8-13 | 4.61 | 726 | 208 | 24 | 40 | 103 | .287 | .439 | .320 |
| Artificial Turf | 1-2 | 4.15 | 138 | 44 | 2 | 8 | 20 | .319 | .399 | .356 |
| April | 2-3 | 4.43 | 165 | 50 | 6 | 8 | 21 | .303 | .461 | .326 |
| May | 1-2 | 4.41 | 139 | 41 | 6 | 8 | 12 | .295 | .475 | .331 |
| June | 3-2 | 3.93 | 127 | 33 | 5 | 9 | 13 | .260 | .409 | .312 |
| July | 1-1 | 4.31 | 158 | 45 | 2 | 8 | 27 | .285 | .380 | .318 |
| August | 1-3 | 5.12 | 125 | 37 | 3 | 8 | 22 | .296 | .432 | .333 |
| Sept./Oct. | 1-4 | 5.11 | 150 | 46 | 4 | 7 | 28 | .307 | .440 | .335 |
| Leading Off Inn. | | | 226 | 68 | 9 | 7 | 29 | .301 | .482 | .322 |
| Runners On | | | 336 | 108 | 9 | 18 | 51 | .321 | .449 | .347 |
| Runners/Scor. Pos. | | | 174 | 54 | 5 | 11 | 35 | .310 | .443 | .332 |
| Runners On/2 Out | | | 145 | 43 | 4 | 9 | 27 | .297 | .414 | .342 |
| Scor. Pos./2 Out | | | 83 | 23 | 3 | 4 | 22 | .277 | .434 | .318 |
| Late Inning Pressure | | | 75 | 26 | 1 | 3 | 14 | .347 | .413 | .372 |
| Leading Off | | | 22 | 9 | 1 | 0 | 5 | .409 | .591 | .409 |
| Runners On | | | 30 | 12 | 0 | 3 | 5 | .400 | .433 | .455 |
| Runners/Scor. Pos. | | | 16 | 7 | 0 | 2 | 3 | .438 | .500 | .500 |
| First 9 Batters | | | 271 | 69 | 6 | 16 | 48 | .255 | .358 | .293 |
| Second 9 Batters | | | 273 | 82 | 10 | 18 | 31 | .300 | .480 | .341 |
| All Batters Thereafter | | | 320 | 101 | 10 | 14 | 44 | .316 | .456 | .341 |

Loves to face: Ivan Calderon (.080, 2-for-25)
Hates to face: Carney Lansford (.390, 23-for-59, 2 HR)
Ground outs-to-air outs ratio: 1.33 last season, 1.39 for career. . . . Additional statistics: 17 double-play ground outs in 154 opportunities, 42 doubles, 1 triple in 220.0 innings last season. . . . Allowed 13 first-inning runs in 33 starts. . . . Batting support: 4.18 runs per start. . . . Career record of 12–27 during September, 97–77 otherwise. . . . Starts 1990 tied with Dave LaRoche for lead in games by an Angels pitcher (304). . . . Could overtake Nolan Ryan as team's all-time leader in starts. Ryan, 288; Witt, 276. . . . ERA has increased, winning percentage decreased in each of last three seasons while pitching 200 innings in each. Christy Mathewson once did that, his ERA rising to 2.12, his winning percentage falling to .657.

## Rich Yett

Throws Right

| Cleveland Indians | W–L | ERA | AB | H | HR | BB | SO | BA | SA | OBA |
|---|---|---|---|---|---|---|---|---|---|---|
| Season | 5-6 | 5.00 | 392 | 111 | 10 | 47 | 47 | .283 | .431 | .360 |
| vs. Left-Handers | | | 197 | 59 | 7 | 26 | 21 | .299 | .467 | .381 |
| vs. Right-Handers | | | 195 | 52 | 3 | 21 | 26 | .267 | .395 | .339 |
| Home | 2-3 | 5.10 | 195 | 61 | 6 | 23 | 32 | .313 | .477 | .380 |
| Road | 3-3 | 4.91 | 197 | 50 | 4 | 24 | 15 | .254 | .386 | .341 |
| Grass | 5-6 | 4.80 | 354 | 100 | 10 | 42 | 45 | .282 | .432 | .358 |
| Artificial Turf | 0-0 | 7.00 | 38 | 11 | 0 | 5 | 2 | .289 | .421 | .386 |
| April | 1-2 | 6.86 | 83 | 25 | 2 | 8 | 12 | .301 | .494 | .363 |
| May | 3-1 | 3.82 | 126 | 30 | 2 | 16 | 16 | .238 | .373 | .322 |
| June | 0-2 | 5.56 | 42 | 11 | 1 | 5 | 2 | .262 | .357 | .354 |
| July | 1-1 | 4.50 | 59 | 18 | 1 | 11 | 7 | .305 | .390 | .423 |
| August | 0-0 | 3.21 | 50 | 15 | 2 | 1 | 6 | .300 | .440 | .302 |
| Sept./Oct. | 0-0 | 9.00 | 32 | 12 | 2 | 6 | 4 | .375 | .656 | .474 |
| Leading Off Inn. | | | 94 | 27 | 4 | 9 | 9 | .287 | .489 | .350 |
| Runners On | | | 184 | 51 | 2 | 24 | 26 | .277 | .397 | .358 |
| Runners/Scor. Pos. | | | 106 | 30 | 2 | 16 | 16 | .283 | .425 | .373 |
| Runners On/2 Out | | | 83 | 25 | 2 | 10 | 11 | .301 | .422 | .376 |
| Scor. Pos./2 Out | | | 56 | 16 | 2 | 5 | 9 | .286 | .446 | .344 |
| Late Inning Pressure | | | 29 | 8 | 1 | 2 | 4 | .276 | .414 | .323 |
| Leading Off | | | 8 | 2 | 0 | 1 | 1 | .250 | .250 | .333 |
| Runners On | | | 12 | 3 | 1 | 1 | 2 | .250 | .500 | .308 |
| Runners/Scor. Pos. | | | 8 | 2 | 1 | 1 | 2 | .250 | .625 | .333 |
| First 9 Batters | | | 198 | 52 | 4 | 28 | 31 | .263 | .394 | .358 |
| Second 9 Batters | | | 124 | 43 | 5 | 13 | 11 | .347 | .524 | .403 |
| All Batters Thereafter | | | 70 | 16 | 1 | 6 | 5 | .229 | .371 | .289 |

Loves to face: Devon White (.067, 1-for-15)
Hates to face: Alan Trammell (.529, 9-for-17, 1 HR)
Ground outs-to-air outs ratio: 0.96 last season, 0.93 for career. . . . Additional statistics: 6 double-play ground outs in 81 opportunities, 20 doubles, 4 triples in 99.0 innings last season. . . . Allowed 7 first-inning runs in 12 starts. . . . Batting support: 4.83 runs per start. . . . Inherited 23 runners, stranded 15 (65%). . . . From the Choose Your Poison Dept.: Has been used as both a starter and reliever in each of four seasons with Indians. Career records: 16–16, 4.71 ERA as a starter; 6–8, 5.47 in relief. . . . Has completed only one of his last 36 starts. . . . Opponents' career batting averages: .236 during his first pass through the order, .310 after that. . . . Career record of 13–8 at home, 9–16 on the road.

## Curt Young

Throws Left

| Oakland As | W–L | ERA | AB | H | HR | BB | SO | BA | SA | OBA |
|---|---|---|---|---|---|---|---|---|---|---|
| Season | 5-9 | 3.73 | 444 | 117 | 10 | 47 | 55 | .264 | .399 | .338 |
| vs. Left-Handers | | | 80 | 17 | 0 | 6 | 7 | .213 | .250 | .276 |
| vs. Right-Handers | | | 364 | 100 | 10 | 41 | 48 | .275 | .431 | .351 |
| Home | 3-4 | 4.05 | 234 | 63 | 5 | 21 | 31 | .269 | .380 | .332 |
| Road | 2-5 | 3.35 | 210 | 54 | 5 | 26 | 24 | .257 | .419 | .345 |
| Grass | 5-6 | 3.47 | 377 | 95 | 7 | 40 | 47 | .252 | .374 | .329 |
| Artificial Turf | 0-3 | 5.40 | 67 | 22 | 3 | 7 | 8 | .328 | .537 | .392 |
| April | 1-3 | 5.27 | 112 | 32 | 7 | 13 | 15 | .286 | .536 | .360 |
| May | 1-1 | 3.60 | 62 | 18 | 2 | 7 | 8 | .290 | .452 | .362 |
| June | 0-4 | 7.71 | 81 | 24 | 0 | 9 | 9 | .296 | .370 | .374 |
| July | 0-0 | 2.38 | 39 | 9 | 0 | 3 | 4 | .231 | .256 | .302 |
| August | 2-1 | 1.57 | 91 | 23 | 1 | 7 | 13 | .253 | .374 | .306 |
| Sept./Oct. | 1-0 | 0.57 | 59 | 11 | 0 | 8 | 6 | .186 | .254 | .294 |
| Leading Off Inn. | | | 112 | 18 | 1 | 8 | 16 | .161 | .250 | .217 |
| Runners On | | | 183 | 52 | 3 | 20 | 16 | .284 | .388 | .361 |
| Runners/Scor. Pos. | | | 110 | 29 | 1 | 14 | 11 | .264 | .345 | .352 |
| Runners On/2 Out | | | 81 | 21 | 1 | 11 | 7 | .259 | .358 | .348 |
| Scor. Pos./2 Out | | | 53 | 13 | 0 | 7 | 5 | .245 | .321 | .333 |
| Late Inning Pressure | | | 28 | 7 | 1 | 5 | 1 | .250 | .393 | .364 |
| Leading Off | | | 8 | 1 | 0 | 0 | 0 | .125 | .250 | .125 |
| Runners On | | | 9 | 3 | 1 | 2 | 0 | .333 | .667 | .455 |
| Runners/Scor. Pos. | | | 4 | 1 | 0 | 2 | 0 | .250 | .250 | .500 |
| First 9 Batters | | | 182 | 44 | 3 | 21 | 29 | .242 | .352 | .327 |
| Second 9 Batters | | | 151 | 36 | 2 | 12 | 16 | .238 | .351 | .299 |
| All Batters Thereafter | | | 111 | 37 | 5 | 14 | 10 | .333 | .541 | .408 |

Loves to face: Carlton Fisk (.077, 2-for-26)
Hates to face: George Bell (.500, 11-for-22, 1 HR)
Ground outs-to-air outs ratio: 0.91 last season, 0.84 for career. . . . Additional statistics: 11 double-play ground outs in 77 opportunities, 26 doubles, 2 triples in 111.0 innings last season. . . . Allowed 13 first-inning runs in 20 starts. . . . Batting support: 3.60 runs per start. . . . Had a 2.48 ERA in 65.1 innings with Steinbach catching, 5.64 ERA in 44.2 innings with Ron Hassey. . . . Career record of 25–28 before the All-Star break, 26–14 thereafter. . . . Opponents have hit better with runners in scoring position than otherwise in each of the last five seasons. . . . Opposing left-handed batters have hit below .220 in four of last five seasons. . . . Has faced 669 left-handed batters in his career, has never allowed a triple.

## Baltimore Orioles

| | W–L | ERA | AB | H | HR | BB | SO | BA | SA | OBA |
|---|---|---|---|---|---|---|---|---|---|---|
| Season | 87-75 | 4.00 | 5583 | 1518 | 134 | 486 | 676 | .272 | .399 | .331 |
| vs. Left-Handers | | | 2363 | 635 | 52 | 217 | 287 | .269 | .390 | .331 |
| vs. Right-Handers | | | 3220 | 883 | 82 | 269 | 389 | .274 | .405 | .331 |
| Home | 47-34 | 3.87 | 2877 | 789 | 65 | 242 | 369 | .274 | .394 | .331 |
| Road | 40-41 | 4.14 | 2706 | 729 | 69 | 244 | 307 | .269 | .404 | .331 |
| Grass | 77-61 | 3.88 | 4741 | 1282 | 119 | 410 | 589 | .270 | .399 | .329 |
| Artificial Turf | 10-14 | 4.69 | 842 | 236 | 15 | 76 | 87 | .280 | .397 | .343 |
| April | 12-12 | 4.17 | 824 | 218 | 22 | 65 | 79 | .265 | .391 | .319 |
| May | 14-10 | 3.03 | 813 | 206 | 13 | 62 | 113 | .253 | .349 | .306 |
| June | 17-11 | 4.41 | 992 | 294 | 26 | 68 | 119 | .296 | .427 | .341 |
| July | 11-16 | 4.68 | 944 | 272 | 26 | 107 | 105 | .288 | .425 | .360 |
| August | 18-13 | 3.67 | 1059 | 273 | 25 | 87 | 142 | .258 | .394 | .317 |
| Sept./Oct. | 15-13 | 4.02 | 951 | 255 | 22 | 97 | 118 | .268 | .399 | .337 |
| Leading Off Inn. | | | 1340 | 352 | 35 | 103 | 160 | .263 | .392 | .319 |
| Runners On | | | 2418 | 662 | 65 | 254 | 313 | .274 | .404 | .340 |
| Runners/Scor. Pos. | | | 1368 | 362 | 31 | 194 | 202 | .265 | .382 | .349 |
| Runners On/2 Out | | | 1010 | 244 | 22 | 137 | 138 | .242 | .347 | .334 |
| Scor. Pos./2 Out | | | 643 | 146 | 9 | 116 | 101 | .227 | .308 | .347 |
| Late Inning Pressure | | | 854 | 211 | 14 | 115 | 122 | .247 | .354 | .339 |
| Leading Off | | | 210 | 46 | 3 | 28 | 34 | .219 | .310 | .311 |
| Runners On | | | 364 | 94 | 8 | 63 | 62 | .258 | .379 | .370 |
| Runners/Scor. Pos. | | | 229 | 55 | 3 | 52 | 47 | .240 | .332 | .381 |
| First 9 Batters | | | 2925 | 779 | 64 | 243 | 427 | .266 | .386 | .324 |
| Second 9 Batters | | | 1448 | 416 | 36 | 127 | 144 | .287 | .419 | .343 |
| All Batters Thereafter | | | 1210 | 323 | 34 | 116 | 105 | .267 | .406 | .331 |

Starting pitchers: 61–58, 4.20 ERA
Relief pitchers: 26–17, 3.61 ERA
Ground outs-to-air outs ratio: 1.04, 3d lowest in A.L. . . . Allowed the fewest unearned runs (42) in majors. . . . Opponents' batting average was 33 points higher than that of the Texas Rangers, but Texas allowed 38 more runs than the Orioles. . . . Have not won a 1–0 game since July 19, 1986, when Rick Dempsey's home run against the Twins supported a 6-hitter by Mike Flanagan and Don Aase. . . . Average time of game last season (3:01) was the longest in majors. (They were the only club to average over three hours per game). . . . Rookie pitchers combined for 569.2 innings pitched. Distant runner-up was Atlanta, with 401 innings. Next-highest A.L. total: 287.2 innings, White Sox.

## Boston Red Sox

| | W–L | ERA | AB | H | HR | BB | SO | BA | SA | OBA |
|---|---|---|---|---|---|---|---|---|---|---|
| Season | 83-79 | 4.01 | 5555 | 1448 | 131 | 548 | 1054 | .261 | .383 | .328 |
| vs. Left-Handers | | | 2624 | 709 | 57 | 273 | 437 | .270 | .387 | .338 |
| vs. Right-Handers | | | 2931 | 739 | 74 | 275 | 617 | .252 | .378 | .318 |
| Home | 46-35 | 4.12 | 2847 | 766 | 70 | 270 | 556 | .269 | .399 | .333 |
| Road | 37-44 | 3.89 | 2708 | 682 | 61 | 278 | 498 | .252 | .365 | .322 |
| Grass | 71-66 | 4.08 | 4715 | 1238 | 116 | 465 | 920 | .263 | .388 | .330 |
| Artificial Turf | 12-13 | 3.59 | 840 | 210 | 15 | 83 | 134 | .250 | .354 | .317 |
| April | 10-12 | 4.69 | 787 | 209 | 17 | 83 | 153 | .266 | .390 | .334 |
| May | 14-12 | 3.60 | 880 | 233 | 18 | 80 | 153 | .265 | .386 | .328 |
| June | 12-15 | 5.03 | 943 | 265 | 26 | 99 | 160 | .281 | .414 | .349 |
| July | 14-12 | 3.35 | 860 | 212 | 20 | 98 | 169 | .247 | .357 | .325 |
| August | 18-15 | 3.76 | 1137 | 296 | 23 | 103 | 229 | .260 | .366 | .321 |
| Sept./Oct. | 15-13 | 3.74 | 948 | 233 | 27 | 85 | 190 | .246 | .385 | .311 |
| Leading Off Inn. | | | 1332 | 343 | 34 | 127 | 223 | .258 | .384 | .325 |
| Runners On | | | 2413 | 660 | 54 | 269 | 438 | .274 | .395 | .343 |
| Runners/Scor. Pos. | | | 1399 | 376 | 27 | 178 | 268 | .269 | .379 | .344 |
| Runners On/2 Out | | | 991 | 247 | 15 | 127 | 212 | .249 | .347 | .339 |
| Scor. Pos./2 Out | | | 636 | 149 | 7 | 96 | 140 | .234 | .314 | .339 |
| Late Inning Pressure | | | 862 | 228 | 24 | 90 | 195 | .265 | .387 | .335 |
| Leading Off | | | 218 | 63 | 10 | 18 | 37 | .289 | .463 | .346 |
| Runners On | | | 360 | 98 | 6 | 53 | 92 | .272 | .367 | .361 |
| Runners/Scor. Pos. | | | 226 | 56 | 4 | 46 | 68 | .248 | .332 | .368 |
| First 9 Batters | | | 2872 | 717 | 64 | 297 | 596 | .250 | .361 | .320 |
| Second 9 Batters | | | 1480 | 416 | 33 | 144 | 255 | .281 | .411 | .346 |
| All Batters Thereafter | | | 1203 | 315 | 34 | 107 | 203 | .262 | .397 | .325 |

Starting pitchers: 57–58, 4.29 ERA
Relief pitchers: 26–21, 3.46 ERA
Ground outs-to-air outs ratio: 1.23, 2d highest in A.L. . . . Opponents stole 161 bases, the most of any A.L. club. . . . Royals and Brewers both stole 24 bases against the Sox, the most by any A.L. club against another. . . . Rookie pitchers (Hetzel and Rochford) combined for a 6.29 ERA, highest of any staff in the majors for second consecutive season. . . . No left-handed pitcher won or lost any game in Boston's season series against either Oakland or Seattle. The only other series in majors of which that was true: Texas vs. Milwaukee. . . . Haven't used a position player as a pitcher since 1952, when outfielder George Schmees pitched in relief.

## California Angels

| | W–L | ERA | AB | H | HR | BB | SO | BA | SA | OBA |
|---|---|---|---|---|---|---|---|---|---|---|
| Season | 91-71 | 3.28 | 5470 | 1384 | 113 | 465 | 897 | .253 | .360 | .312 |
| vs. Left-Handers | | | 2184 | 562 | 44 | 171 | 323 | .257 | .366 | .310 |
| vs. Right-Handers | | | 3286 | 822 | 69 | 294 | 574 | .250 | .355 | .314 |
| Home | 52-29 | 3.14 | 2845 | 709 | 75 | 205 | 474 | .249 | .372 | .301 |
| Road | 39-42 | 3.43 | 2625 | 675 | 38 | 260 | 423 | .257 | .346 | .324 |
| Grass | 76-59 | 3.32 | 4604 | 1164 | 99 | 394 | 766 | .253 | .363 | .312 |
| Artificial Turf | 15-12 | 3.06 | 866 | 220 | 14 | 71 | 131 | .254 | .343 | .312 |
| April | 15-10 | 2.69 | 831 | 210 | 17 | 61 | 118 | .253 | .353 | .304 |
| May | 18-7 | 2.68 | 829 | 203 | 16 | 83 | 120 | .245 | .346 | .313 |
| June | 12-14 | 3.63 | 888 | 227 | 26 | 69 | 149 | .256 | .385 | .311 |
| July | 18-10 | 3.38 | 965 | 250 | 15 | 68 | 164 | .259 | .352 | .308 |
| August | 15-14 | 3.52 | 957 | 241 | 18 | 84 | 177 | .252 | .355 | .312 |
| Sept./Oct. | 13-16 | 3.65 | 1000 | 253 | 21 | 100 | 169 | .253 | .366 | .324 |
| Leading Off Inn. | | | 1384 | 365 | 25 | 69 | 194 | .264 | .370 | .302 |
| Runners On | | | 2277 | 571 | 41 | 225 | 393 | .251 | .347 | .316 |
| Runners/Scor. Pos. | | | 1238 | 288 | 20 | 156 | 252 | .233 | .316 | .310 |
| Runners On/2 Out | | | 963 | 219 | 14 | 102 | 190 | .227 | .315 | .307 |
| Scor. Pos./2 Out | | | 584 | 115 | 11 | 67 | 137 | .197 | .286 | .284 |
| Late Inning Pressure | | | 940 | 214 | 18 | 115 | 172 | .228 | .326 | .312 |
| Leading Off | | | 243 | 55 | 6 | 15 | 33 | .226 | .333 | .271 |
| Runners On | | | 387 | 91 | 5 | 70 | 82 | .235 | .328 | .351 |
| Runners/Scor. Pos. | | | 231 | 47 | 3 | 59 | 55 | .203 | .290 | .358 |
| First 9 Batters | | | 2524 | 627 | 59 | 225 | 456 | .248 | .357 | .310 |
| Second 9 Batters | | | 1453 | 364 | 24 | 128 | 221 | .251 | .350 | .314 |
| All Batters Thereafter | | | 1493 | 393 | 30 | 112 | 220 | .263 | .374 | .315 |

Starting pitchers: 70–55, 3.42 ERA
Relief pitchers: 21–16, 2.89 ERA
Ground outs-to-air outs ratio: 1.24, highest in A.L. . . . First A.L. team during the era of the DH with three pitchers with ERA below 3.00 in 162 or more innings (Blyleven, Finley, and McCaskill). . . . Led the league with 32 complete games, the lowest figure ever to lead the American League. . . . Tied Oakland for the A.L. lead in shutouts with 20. No A.L. club had recorded that many since the 1972 Athletics. . . . Used only seven starting pitchers, the fewest of any team in the majors. And their average of 6.65 inning per start led the A.L. . . . Had a 38–1 record in home games in which they led after six innings, but in the same situation on the road they were 32–9.

## Chicago White Sox

| | W–L | ERA | AB | H | HR | BB | SO | BA | SA | OBA |
|---|---|---|---|---|---|---|---|---|---|---|
| Season | 69-92 | 4.23 | 5477 | 1472 | 144 | 539 | 778 | .269 | .410 | .335 |
| vs. Left-Handers | | | 2135 | 579 | 60 | 243 | 302 | .271 | .422 | .347 |
| vs. Right-Handers | | | 3342 | 893 | 84 | 296 | 476 | .267 | .402 | .327 |
| Home | 35-45 | 3.95 | 2761 | 728 | 58 | 267 | 392 | .264 | .388 | .329 |
| Road | 34-47 | 4.52 | 2716 | 744 | 86 | 272 | 386 | .274 | .433 | .341 |
| Grass | 61-76 | 4.10 | 4659 | 1237 | 112 | 460 | 674 | .266 | .399 | .332 |
| Artificial Turf | 8-16 | 4.98 | 818 | 235 | 32 | 79 | 104 | .287 | .474 | .353 |
| April | 8-16 | 4.68 | 832 | 228 | 20 | 82 | 124 | .274 | .419 | .343 |
| May | 10-17 | 5.72 | 947 | 270 | 39 | 120 | 125 | .285 | .478 | .365 |
| June | 12-17 | 4.55 | 1004 | 282 | 26 | 88 | 126 | .281 | .415 | .342 |
| July | 14-11 | 3.53 | 809 | 193 | 17 | 83 | 103 | .239 | .363 | .310 |
| August | 12-16 | 3.86 | 956 | 265 | 28 | 78 | 134 | .277 | .432 | .331 |
| Sept./Oct. | 13-15 | 3.04 | 929 | 234 | 14 | 88 | 166 | .252 | .346 | .315 |
| Leading Off Inn. | | | 1290 | 338 | 42 | 130 | 186 | .262 | .426 | .333 |
| Runners On | | | 2532 | 685 | 55 | 229 | 353 | .271 | .397 | .327 |
| Runners/Scor. Pos. | | | 1462 | 387 | 33 | 151 | 225 | .265 | .391 | .324 |
| Runners On/2 Out | | | 1068 | 271 | 24 | 128 | 177 | .254 | .381 | .336 |
| Scor. Pos./2 Out | | | 689 | 156 | 14 | 99 | 123 | .226 | .340 | .325 |
| Late Inning Pressure | | | 933 | 242 | 28 | 100 | 136 | .259 | .400 | .334 |
| Leading Off | | | 233 | 59 | 8 | 27 | 36 | .253 | .403 | .333 |
| Runners On | | | 413 | 106 | 12 | 40 | 53 | .257 | .383 | .319 |
| Runners/Scor. Pos. | | | 221 | 58 | 6 | 29 | 36 | .262 | .367 | .336 |
| First 9 Batters | | | 2875 | 748 | 74 | 303 | 439 | .260 | .395 | .332 |
| Second 9 Batters | | | 1501 | 408 | 35 | 122 | 205 | .272 | .416 | .328 |
| All Batters Thereafter | | | 1101 | 316 | 35 | 114 | 134 | .287 | .442 | .354 |

Starting pitchers: 45–68, 4.54 ERA
Relief pitchers: 24–24, 3.73 ERA
Ground outs-to-air outs ratio: 1.08. . . . Set an American League record for fewest complete games (9) in a season. Starters registered only five complete-game victories all year. . . . Average of 5.65 innings per start was the lowest in the A.L. . . . White Sox' pitchers hit Mariners' batters with pitches 10 times, the most by any one club against another in the A.L. last season. . . . Team leader in innings pitched has had fewer than 200 innings only five times in history, but three times in the last four seasons. . . . No Chisox pitcher has started an All-Star game since Early Wynn in 1959. Only nonexpansion team that hasn't had one since then is the Cubs, whose last All-Star starting pitcher was Claude Passeau in 1946.

## Cleveland Indians

| | W-L | ERA | AB | H | HR | BB | SO | BA | SA | OBA |
|---|---|---|---|---|---|---|---|---|---|---|
| Season | 73-89 | 3.65 | 5545 | 1423 | 107 | 452 | 844 | .257 | .371 | .313 |
| vs. Left-Handers | | | 1997 | 494 | 39 | 184 | 276 | .247 | .354 | .311 |
| vs. Right-Handers | | | 3548 | 929 | 68 | 268 | 568 | .262 | .380 | .314 |
| Home | 41-40 | 3.47 | 2875 | 736 | 51 | 224 | 443 | .256 | .357 | .309 |
| Road | 32-49 | 3.84 | 2670 | 687 | 56 | 228 | 401 | .257 | .386 | .317 |
| Grass | 64-74 | 3.69 | 4737 | 1223 | 92 | 393 | 746 | .258 | .373 | .316 |
| Artificial Turf | 9-15 | 3.42 | 808 | 200 | 15 | 59 | 98 | .248 | .360 | .297 |
| April | 9-13 | 4.21 | 761 | 211 | 16 | 72 | 111 | .277 | .418 | .340 |
| May | 16-13 | 3.04 | 946 | 216 | 17 | 79 | 138 | .228 | .341 | .287 |
| June | 11-15 | 3.63 | 876 | 238 | 18 | 56 | 116 | .272 | .382 | .317 |
| July | 15-12 | 3.60 | 937 | 231 | 19 | 73 | 135 | .247 | .353 | .302 |
| August | 12-17 | 4.11 | 987 | 270 | 19 | 76 | 146 | .274 | .386 | .326 |
| Sept./Oct. | 10-19 | 3.45 | 1038 | 257 | 18 | 96 | 198 | .248 | .355 | .310 |
| Leading Off Inn. | | | 1373 | 356 | 31 | 79 | 200 | .259 | .388 | .302 |
| Runners On | | | 2338 | 615 | 38 | 223 | 359 | .263 | .373 | .323 |
| Runners/Scor. Pos. | | | 1337 | 341 | 22 | 148 | 234 | .255 | .365 | .321 |
| Runners On/2 Out | | | 1015 | 242 | 15 | 111 | 171 | .238 | .337 | .315 |
| Scor. Pos./2 Out | | | 643 | 153 | 10 | 72 | 122 | .238 | .341 | .316 |
| Late Inning Pressure | | | 1049 | 266 | 23 | 80 | 195 | .254 | .373 | .306 |
| Leading Off | | | 265 | 68 | 5 | 15 | 50 | .257 | .358 | .299 |
| Runners On | | | 433 | 105 | 7 | 38 | 78 | .242 | .346 | .299 |
| Runners/Scor. Pos. | | | 243 | 62 | 5 | 32 | 52 | .255 | .379 | .332 |
| First 9 Batters | | | 2675 | 660 | 51 | 222 | 464 | .247 | .365 | .305 |
| Second 9 Batters | | | 1476 | 392 | 29 | 121 | 207 | .266 | .381 | .322 |
| All Batters Thereafter | | | 1394 | 371 | 27 | 109 | 173 | .266 | .372 | .318 |

Starting pitchers: 58–59, 3.79 ERA
Relief pitchers: 15–30, 3.32 ERA
Ground outs-to-air outs ratio: 1.05. . . . Staff hasn't thrown consecutive shutouts since July 1984. . . . Tribe relievers ranked fourth in the A.L. in ERA, but had the lowest winning percentage of any bullpen in the league (.333). . . . Fewest games started by rookies last season: Oakland (1), Cleveland and Houston (3). . . . Angels-Indians season series produced nine games decided by a one-run margin, the most of any A.L. matchup last season. . . . Shut out the Yankees three times at Cleveland Stadium. . . . Allowed the fewest walks of any A.L. club for the first time since 1954. . . . Only club in the majors to have a losing record (7–9) in games in which their pitchers did not walk a batter.

## Detroit Tigers

| | W-L | ERA | AB | H | HR | BB | SO | BA | SA | OBA |
|---|---|---|---|---|---|---|---|---|---|---|
| Season | 59-103 | 4.53 | 5522 | 1514 | 150 | 652 | 831 | .274 | .415 | .352 |
| vs. Left-Handers | | | 2221 | 625 | 61 | 277 | 281 | .281 | .430 | .361 |
| vs. Right-Handers | | | 3301 | 889 | 89 | 375 | 550 | .269 | .404 | .346 |
| Home | 38-43 | 4.18 | 2813 | 724 | 77 | 340 | 452 | .257 | .395 | .338 |
| Road | 21-60 | 4.92 | 2709 | 790 | 73 | 312 | 379 | .292 | .434 | .366 |
| Grass | 55-82 | 4.36 | 4675 | 1256 | 129 | 539 | 728 | .269 | .407 | .345 |
| Artificial Turf | 4-21 | 5.55 | 847 | 258 | 21 | 113 | 103 | .305 | .457 | .389 |
| April | 8-14 | 4.10 | 704 | 180 | 18 | 77 | 109 | .256 | .396 | .331 |
| May | 14-14 | 4.30 | 929 | 246 | 19 | 112 | 135 | .265 | .386 | .345 |
| June | 8-18 | 4.51 | 915 | 264 | 24 | 104 | 131 | .289 | .431 | .361 |
| July | 6-21 | 5.57 | 968 | 281 | 31 | 129 | 127 | .290 | .434 | .376 |
| August | 11-22 | 4.14 | 1117 | 292 | 34 | 120 | 179 | .261 | .419 | .334 |
| Sept./Oct. | 12-14 | 4.56 | 889 | 251 | 24 | 110 | 150 | .282 | .415 | .361 |
| Leading Off Inn. | | | 1299 | 364 | 40 | 124 | 189 | .280 | .435 | .347 |
| Runners On | | | 2512 | 696 | 63 | 345 | 387 | .277 | .412 | .361 |
| Runners/Scor. Pos. | | | 1433 | 395 | 34 | 257 | 244 | .276 | .407 | .376 |
| Runners On/2 Out | | | 1061 | 265 | 30 | 166 | 172 | .250 | .378 | .356 |
| Scor. Pos./2 Out | | | 668 | 166 | 16 | 135 | 113 | .249 | .359 | .379 |
| Late Inning Pressure | | | 940 | 250 | 23 | 130 | 175 | .266 | .390 | .358 |
| Leading Off | | | 243 | 73 | 6 | 21 | 45 | .300 | .428 | .356 |
| Runners On | | | 390 | 97 | 9 | 74 | 65 | .249 | .374 | .373 |
| Runners/Scor. Pos. | | | 204 | 53 | 4 | 62 | 36 | .260 | .382 | .431 |
| First 9 Batters | | | 2601 | 696 | 67 | 361 | 434 | .268 | .404 | .358 |
| Second 9 Batters | | | 1494 | 438 | 43 | 152 | 197 | .293 | .438 | .360 |
| All Batters Thereafter | | | 1427 | 380 | 40 | 139 | 200 | .266 | .409 | .331 |

Starting pitchers: 35–81, 4.55 ERA
Relief pitchers: 24–22, 4.51 ERA
Ground outs-to-air outs ratio: 1.10. . . . Decline of 179 percentage points from 1988 (88–74) to 1989 (59–103) was the largest single-season decrease in the A.L. since the Philadelphia A's slid from 81–73 (.526) in 1949 to 52–102 (.338) a year later. . . . Jack Morris was only the second pitcher of this century to start for the same team on opening day in every year of a decade. The other: Robin Roberts, for Phillies during 1950s. . . . Allowed 97 unearned runs, highest total in majors. . . . Only team in either league with a losing record even in games in which their starters went all the way. . . . Have not used a batter as a pitcher since 1931, when utility infielder Mark Koenig took the mound.

## Kansas City Royals

| | W-L | ERA | AB | H | HR | BB | SO | BA | SA | OBA |
|---|---|---|---|---|---|---|---|---|---|---|
| Season | 92-70 | 3.55 | 5508 | 1415 | 86 | 455 | 978 | .257 | .360 | .314 |
| vs. Left-Handers | | | 2430 | 604 | 33 | 221 | 401 | .249 | .344 | .310 |
| vs. Right-Handers | | | 3078 | 811 | 53 | 234 | 577 | .263 | .373 | .317 |
| Home | 55-26 | 3.15 | 2786 | 690 | 26 | 202 | 499 | .248 | .336 | .301 |
| Road | 37-44 | 3.96 | 2722 | 725 | 60 | 253 | 479 | .266 | .384 | .328 |
| Grass | 25-37 | 3.96 | 2075 | 551 | 42 | 193 | 375 | .266 | .380 | .327 |
| Artificial Turf | 67-33 | 3.30 | 3433 | 864 | 44 | 262 | 603 | .252 | .348 | .306 |
| April | 16-8 | 3.21 | 838 | 211 | 8 | 70 | 121 | .252 | .339 | .309 |
| May | 14-13 | 3.47 | 883 | 219 | 16 | 59 | 144 | .248 | .349 | .296 |
| June | 14-12 | 3.50 | 900 | 235 | 16 | 76 | 169 | .261 | .360 | .317 |
| July | 13-14 | 4.46 | 943 | 266 | 14 | 82 | 168 | .282 | .401 | .338 |
| August | 21-8 | 2.94 | 959 | 231 | 16 | 71 | 191 | .241 | .345 | .295 |
| Sept./Oct. | 14-15 | 3.70 | 985 | 253 | 16 | 97 | 185 | .257 | .363 | .327 |
| Leading Off Inn. | | | 1355 | 354 | 21 | 96 | 245 | .261 | .367 | .313 |
| Runners On | | | 2346 | 623 | 38 | 225 | 390 | .266 | .372 | .328 |
| Runners/Scor. Pos. | | | 1369 | 347 | 19 | 158 | 253 | .253 | .359 | .325 |
| Runners On/2 Out | | | 966 | 228 | 17 | 104 | 179 | .236 | .336 | .313 |
| Scor. Pos./2 Out | | | 618 | 144 | 9 | 81 | 117 | .233 | .324 | .324 |
| Late Inning Pressure | | | 979 | 219 | 13 | 98 | 213 | .224 | .314 | .296 |
| Leading Off | | | 243 | 52 | 3 | 23 | 53 | .214 | .296 | .287 |
| Runners On | | | 390 | 86 | 6 | 54 | 73 | .221 | .321 | .313 |
| Runners/Scor. Pos. | | | 230 | 49 | 3 | 45 | 47 | .213 | .313 | .337 |
| First 9 Batters | | | 2680 | 687 | 35 | 258 | 547 | .256 | .351 | .323 |
| Second 9 Batters | | | 1453 | 390 | 20 | 98 | 221 | .268 | .375 | .314 |
| All Batters Thereafter | | | 1375 | 338 | 31 | 99 | 210 | .246 | .361 | .297 |

Starting pitchers: 63–53, 3.75 ERA
Relief pitchers: 29–17, 3.06 ERA
Ground outs-to-air outs ratio: 1.18. . . . Allowed the fewest home runs of any A.L. club for the fifth consecutive season, longest streak since the Orioles allowed the fewest from 1956 through 1961. . . . Didn't allow a home run to either the Rangers or the Tigers at Royals Stadium. . . . Haven't allowed an extra-inning home run since May 13, 1987 (Larry Sheets off Steve Farr). . . . Opponents stole only 79 bases, fewest of any A.L. club. . . . First team in A.L. history with two pitchers with 18 or more saves in the same season. (Farr and Montgomery both had exactly 18.). . . . Had a record of 13–1 in games in which their pitchers didn't walk a batter.

## Milwaukee Brewers

| | W-L | ERA | AB | H | HR | BB | SO | BA | SA | OBA |
|---|---|---|---|---|---|---|---|---|---|---|
| Season | 81-81 | 3.80 | 5529 | 1463 | 129 | 457 | 812 | .265 | .379 | .321 |
| vs. Left-Handers | | | 2287 | 593 | 50 | 187 | 315 | .259 | .371 | .316 |
| vs. Right-Handers | | | 3242 | 870 | 79 | 270 | 497 | .268 | .386 | .325 |
| Home | 45-36 | 3.37 | 2859 | 753 | 54 | 215 | 448 | .263 | .364 | .315 |
| Road | 36-45 | 4.26 | 2670 | 710 | 75 | 242 | 364 | .266 | .396 | .328 |
| Grass | 69-68 | 3.66 | 4698 | 1240 | 107 | 375 | 687 | .264 | .374 | .318 |
| Artificial Turf | 12-13 | 4.54 | 831 | 223 | 22 | 82 | 125 | .268 | .408 | .339 |
| April | 10-12 | 3.52 | 747 | 190 | 14 | 68 | 109 | .254 | .359 | .316 |
| May | 12-16 | 4.77 | 987 | 293 | 28 | 77 | 145 | .297 | .437 | .348 |
| June | 15-14 | 3.90 | 1028 | 283 | 26 | 82 | 153 | .275 | .389 | .329 |
| July | 14-12 | 3.51 | 851 | 220 | 14 | 78 | 134 | .259 | .354 | .322 |
| August | 16-15 | 3.16 | 1025 | 243 | 25 | 78 | 153 | .237 | .348 | .292 |
| Sept./Oct. | 14-12 | 3.90 | 891 | 234 | 22 | 74 | 118 | .263 | .383 | .321 |
| Leading Off Inn. | | | 1337 | 356 | 29 | 96 | 169 | .266 | .384 | .317 |
| Runners On | | | 2405 | 659 | 65 | 233 | 350 | .274 | .397 | .335 |
| Runners/Scor. Pos. | | | 1348 | 342 | 36 | 160 | 224 | .254 | .378 | .325 |
| Runners On/2 Out | | | 996 | 251 | 28 | 116 | 143 | .252 | .377 | .332 |
| Scor. Pos./2 Out | | | 643 | 146 | 15 | 83 | 100 | .227 | .339 | .315 |
| Late Inning Pressure | | | 797 | 213 | 21 | 72 | 116 | .267 | .388 | .326 |
| Leading Off | | | 202 | 50 | 7 | 14 | 25 | .248 | .376 | .296 |
| Runners On | | | 331 | 97 | 9 | 40 | 46 | .293 | .417 | .360 |
| Runners/Scor. Pos. | | | 184 | 50 | 5 | 35 | 29 | .272 | .402 | .371 |
| First 9 Batters | | | 2779 | 719 | 58 | 239 | 452 | .259 | .361 | .318 |
| Second 9 Batters | | | 1558 | 406 | 44 | 128 | 220 | .261 | .397 | .317 |
| All Batters Thereafter | | | 1192 | 338 | 27 | 90 | 140 | .284 | .398 | .336 |

Starting pitchers: 60–63, 3.96 ERA
Relief pitchers: 21–18, 3.47 ERA
Ground outs-to-air outs ratio: 1.18. . . . Staff hasn't thrown consecutive shutouts since April 1984, the longest streak of any A.L. club. . . . Allowed only 184 doubles and 345 extra-base hits, both league-low figures. . . . Had a record of 73–1 in games in which they led after eight innings, tying them with the Rangers for the best record in the majors. Have won 156 consecutive home games (since April 17, 1986) in which they led after eight innings. . . . All-time record against the Angels is 130–131. . . . Royals-Brewers season series was the only one in the A.L. to produce as many as five extra-inning games. . . . Only team in the majors to open the last season with back-to-back complete games. Last team to do that was the 1986 Dodgers, who opened the season with three complete games.

## Minnesota Twins

| | W–L | ERA | AB | H | HR | BB | SO | BA | SA | OBA |
|---|---|---|---|---|---|---|---|---|---|---|
| Season | 80-82 | 4.28 | 5548 | 1495 | 139 | 500 | 851 | .269 | .408 | .332 |
| vs. Left-Handers | | | 1862 | 530 | 45 | 179 | 262 | .285 | .428 | .350 |
| vs. Right-Handers | | | 3686 | 965 | 94 | 321 | 589 | .262 | .398 | .322 |
| Home | 45-36 | 4.70 | 2875 | 782 | 69 | 268 | 484 | .272 | .411 | .336 |
| Road | 35-46 | 3.84 | 2673 | 713 | 70 | 232 | 367 | .267 | .404 | .327 |
| Grass | 28-34 | 3.88 | 2052 | 552 | 59 | 193 | 270 | .269 | .412 | .334 |
| Artificial Turf | 52-48 | 4.52 | 3496 | 943 | 80 | 307 | 581 | .270 | .405 | .330 |
| April | 10-12 | 4.37 | 746 | 198 | 27 | 72 | 107 | .265 | .438 | .334 |
| May | 13-15 | 4.37 | 980 | 262 | 27 | 70 | 149 | .267 | .415 | .315 |
| June | 17-12 | 4.26 | 1000 | 273 | 19 | 102 | 133 | .273 | .396 | .341 |
| July | 11-14 | 4.25 | 824 | 214 | 27 | 80 | 132 | .260 | .426 | .330 |
| August | 17-12 | 4.30 | 997 | 279 | 20 | 91 | 163 | .280 | .405 | .341 |
| Sept./Oct. | 12-17 | 4.17 | 1001 | 269 | 19 | 85 | 167 | .269 | .378 | .328 |
| Leading Off Inn. | | | 1314 | 370 | 36 | 114 | 188 | .282 | .439 | .341 |
| Runners On | | | 2501 | 667 | 60 | 232 | 383 | .267 | .403 | .329 |
| Runners/Scor. Pos. | | | 1449 | 395 | 30 | 157 | 230 | .273 | .405 | .339 |
| Runners On/2 Out | | | 1054 | 254 | 24 | 102 | 159 | .241 | .363 | .312 |
| Scor. Pos./2 Out | | | 662 | 159 | 15 | 80 | 102 | .240 | .363 | .328 |
| Late Inning Pressure | | | 870 | 221 | 17 | 73 | 154 | .254 | .352 | .313 |
| Leading Off | | | 208 | 50 | 3 | 18 | 27 | .240 | .346 | .307 |
| Runners On | | | 383 | 99 | 8 | 36 | 70 | .258 | .347 | .319 |
| Runners/Scor. Pos. | | | 225 | 62 | 5 | 26 | 39 | .276 | .369 | .345 |
| First 9 Batters | | | 2804 | 748 | 70 | 291 | 472 | .267 | .400 | .338 |
| Second 9 Batters | | | 1462 | 424 | 41 | 120 | 225 | .290 | .439 | .345 |
| All Batters Thereafter | | | 1282 | 323 | 28 | 89 | 154 | .252 | .390 | .302 |

Starting pitchers: 57–65, 4.23 ERA
Relief pitchers: 23–17, 4.39 ERA
Ground outs-to-air outs ratio: 0.94, lowest in A.L. . . . Twins pitchers didn't intentionally walk a batter until their 58th game of the season. They didn't intentionally walk a batter in a road game until August 2. . . . Highest home-game ERA in the majors, despite their winning record (45–36) at the Metrodome. . . . Were undefeated (5–0) in extra-inning games at the Metrodome last season. . . . Allowed 18 ninth-inning home runs, most in the majors, but were one of three A.L. clubs that didn't give up one homer in extra innings last season. . . . Ten opposing batters hit two or more home runs in a game against them last season, highest total in the majors.

## New York Yankees

| | W–L | ERA | AB | H | HR | BB | SO | BA | SA | OBA |
|---|---|---|---|---|---|---|---|---|---|---|
| Season | 74-87 | 4.50 | 5518 | 1550 | 150 | 521 | 787 | .281 | .428 | .344 |
| vs. Left-Handers | | | 1975 | 585 | 62 | 216 | 241 | .296 | .463 | .365 |
| vs. Right-Handers | | | 3543 | 965 | 88 | 305 | 546 | .272 | .408 | .332 |
| Home | 41-40 | 4.54 | 2888 | 819 | 88 | 260 | 431 | .284 | .436 | .345 |
| Road | 33-47 | 4.46 | 2630 | 731 | 62 | 261 | 356 | .278 | .418 | .344 |
| Grass | 59-78 | 4.55 | 4728 | 1331 | 133 | 452 | 679 | .282 | .429 | .346 |
| Artificial Turf | 15-9 | 4.22 | 790 | 219 | 17 | 69 | 108 | .277 | .423 | .335 |
| April | 12-12 | 4.31 | 813 | 218 | 22 | 87 | 130 | .268 | .392 | .342 |
| May | 11-15 | 5.00 | 883 | 252 | 25 | 80 | 122 | .285 | .443 | .348 |
| June | 15-12 | 4.21 | 968 | 279 | 21 | 74 | 100 | .288 | .425 | .342 |
| July | 11-16 | 5.03 | 918 | 272 | 30 | 98 | 135 | .296 | .463 | .363 |
| August | 10-21 | 4.67 | 1071 | 298 | 33 | 88 | 160 | .278 | .444 | .335 |
| Sept./Oct. | 15-11 | 3.76 | 865 | 231 | 19 | 94 | 140 | .267 | .392 | .338 |
| Leading Off Inn. | | | 1309 | 354 | 41 | 101 | 161 | .270 | .439 | .327 |
| Runners On | | | 2422 | 727 | 65 | 268 | 345 | .300 | .441 | .368 |
| Runners/Scor. Pos. | | | 1398 | 429 | 38 | 191 | 199 | .307 | .447 | .386 |
| Runners On/2 Out | | | 1005 | 283 | 24 | 118 | 158 | .282 | .410 | .358 |
| Scor. Pos./2 Out | | | 639 | 171 | 13 | 89 | 101 | .268 | .383 | .359 |
| Late Inning Pressure | | | 861 | 254 | 24 | 95 | 141 | .295 | .438 | .366 |
| Leading Off | | | 217 | 65 | 7 | 19 | 37 | .300 | .484 | .359 |
| Runners On | | | 373 | 118 | 11 | 54 | 58 | .316 | .453 | .403 |
| Runners/Scor. Pos. | | | 229 | 72 | 8 | 42 | 32 | .314 | .459 | .420 |
| First 9 Batters | | | 2725 | 734 | 59 | 277 | 459 | .269 | .396 | .337 |
| Second 9 Batters | | | 1509 | 408 | 51 | 124 | 179 | .270 | .431 | .330 |
| All Batters Thereafter | | | 1284 | 408 | 40 | 120 | 149 | .318 | .490 | .377 |

Starting pitchers: 55–69, 4.87 ERA
Relief pitchers: 19–18, 3.80 ERA
Ground outs-to-air outs ratio: 1.16. . . . Outscored the Tigers 17–8 in season-ending series to avoid having the league's worst ERA for the first time in franchise history. . . . Used 16 starting pitchers, the most of any team in the majors since the 1983 A's. . . . Were the only undefeated club in either league (34–0) in home games in which they led after seven innings. . . . Opponents scored four or more runs in an inning 44 times, highest total in majors. . . . Different leaders in wins in six consecutive seasons for first time in team history. Since 1984: Joe Niekro, Guidry, Rasmussen, Rhoden, Candelaria, and Hawkins. . . . Failed to win consecutive games in August, first time in club history that they failed to win two straight games in a month in which they played at least 15 games.

## Oakland A's

| | W–L | ERA | AB | H | HR | BB | SO | BA | SA | OBA |
|---|---|---|---|---|---|---|---|---|---|---|
| Season | 99-63 | 3.09 | 5395 | 1287 | 103 | 510 | 930 | .239 | .348 | .305 |
| vs. Left-Handers | | | 2418 | 547 | 35 | 258 | 376 | .226 | .321 | .301 |
| vs. Right-Handers | | | 2977 | 740 | 68 | 252 | 554 | .249 | .370 | .309 |
| Home | 54-27 | 3.06 | 2741 | 639 | 51 | 243 | 498 | .233 | .332 | .297 |
| Road | 45-36 | 3.12 | 2654 | 648 | 52 | 267 | 432 | .244 | .364 | .314 |
| Grass | 87-49 | 3.02 | 4551 | 1075 | 81 | 417 | 809 | .236 | .339 | .301 |
| Artificial Turf | 12-14 | 3.45 | 844 | 212 | 22 | 93 | 121 | .251 | .397 | .327 |
| April | 18-8 | 2.90 | 846 | 185 | 17 | 95 | 159 | .219 | .323 | .299 |
| May | 16-10 | 3.19 | 861 | 205 | 20 | 92 | 131 | .238 | .360 | .314 |
| June | 13-14 | 3.23 | 902 | 215 | 10 | 89 | 139 | .238 | .324 | .306 |
| July | 16-10 | 3.92 | 886 | 223 | 23 | 79 | 177 | .252 | .381 | .314 |
| August | 18-11 | 2.52 | 973 | 248 | 17 | 68 | 181 | .255 | .361 | .305 |
| Sept./Oct. | 18-10 | 2.83 | 927 | 211 | 16 | 87 | 143 | .228 | .337 | .294 |
| Leading Off Inn. | | | 1351 | 326 | 30 | 92 | 232 | .241 | .360 | .294 |
| Runners On | | | 2264 | 530 | 38 | 250 | 394 | .234 | .333 | .309 |
| Runners/Scor. Pos. | | | 1256 | 289 | 17 | 175 | 231 | .230 | .320 | .318 |
| Runners On/2 Out | | | 965 | 213 | 13 | 129 | 172 | .221 | .305 | .317 |
| Scor. Pos./2 Out | | | 610 | 136 | 5 | 92 | 111 | .223 | .300 | .329 |
| Late Inning Pressure | | | 933 | 205 | 18 | 91 | 184 | .220 | .320 | .289 |
| Leading Off | | | 249 | 54 | 4 | 11 | 48 | .217 | .329 | .259 |
| Runners On | | | 337 | 81 | 8 | 47 | 58 | .240 | .356 | .326 |
| Runners/Scor. Pos. | | | 194 | 45 | 2 | 31 | 35 | .232 | .309 | .325 |
| First 9 Batters | | | 2700 | 601 | 43 | 247 | 508 | .223 | .316 | .290 |
| Second 9 Batters | | | 1412 | 346 | 29 | 143 | 227 | .245 | .366 | .315 |
| All Batters Thereafter | | | 1283 | 340 | 31 | 120 | 195 | .265 | .395 | .327 |

Starting pitchers: 82–46, 3.34 ERA
Relief pitchers: 17–17, 2.63 ERA
Ground outs-to-air outs ratio: 0.99, 2d lowest in A.L. . . . Didn't commit a balk after June 18. Went from a major league record 76 balks in 1988 to the lowest total in the majors last season (6). . . . First club to lead the A.L. in ERA in consecutive seasons since the Orioles led from 1969 through 1973. . . . Only three of 20 shutouts were complete games. . . . Both starters and relievers led the A.L. in ERA. . . . Were undefeated (37–0) in road games in which they led after six innings. No other A.L. club had fewer than three losses in those situations. . . . Rookies combined for only 45 innings pitched, lowest rookie total by any major league staff. . . . First team with four pitchers with 17 or more wins since the 1971 Orioles had four 20-game winners

## Seattle Mariners

| | W–L | ERA | AB | H | HR | BB | SO | BA | SA | OBA |
|---|---|---|---|---|---|---|---|---|---|---|
| Season | 73-89 | 4.00 | 5480 | 1422 | 114 | 560 | 897 | .259 | .383 | .330 |
| vs. Left-Handers | | | 2348 | 616 | 50 | 249 | 312 | .262 | .388 | .334 |
| vs. Right-Handers | | | 3132 | 806 | 64 | 311 | 585 | .257 | .380 | .327 |
| Home | 40-41 | 4.22 | 2854 | 762 | 67 | 274 | 473 | .267 | .403 | .332 |
| Road | 33-48 | 3.77 | 2626 | 660 | 47 | 286 | 424 | .251 | .363 | .328 |
| Grass | 27-35 | 3.79 | 1996 | 509 | 41 | 213 | 329 | .255 | .377 | .331 |
| Artificial Turf | 46-54 | 4.12 | 3484 | 913 | 73 | 347 | 568 | .262 | .387 | .330 |
| April | 11-15 | 4.42 | 881 | 233 | 22 | 83 | 154 | .264 | .406 | .331 |
| May | 14-13 | 4.42 | 912 | 253 | 16 | 99 | 138 | .277 | .393 | .349 |
| June | 12-14 | 3.98 | 881 | 223 | 14 | 112 | 140 | .253 | .356 | .337 |
| July | 13-12 | 3.65 | 847 | 218 | 21 | 78 | 130 | .257 | .381 | .322 |
| August | 9-20 | 3.89 | 985 | 250 | 21 | 102 | 167 | .254 | .387 | .330 |
| Sept./Oct. | 14-15 | 3.67 | 974 | 245 | 20 | 86 | 168 | .252 | .377 | .312 |
| Leading Off Inn. | | | 1316 | 349 | 28 | 124 | 215 | .265 | .383 | .330 |
| Runners On | | | 2405 | 667 | 52 | 283 | 377 | .277 | .409 | .353 |
| Runners/Scor. Pos. | | | 1438 | 380 | 27 | 204 | 253 | .264 | .385 | .352 |
| Runners On/2 Out | | | 974 | 234 | 15 | 127 | 170 | .240 | .350 | .330 |
| Scor. Pos./2 Out | | | 656 | 149 | 11 | 99 | 130 | .227 | .341 | .331 |
| Late Inning Pressure | | | 977 | 250 | 16 | 128 | 196 | .256 | .355 | .343 |
| Leading Off | | | 243 | 67 | 5 | 19 | 42 | .276 | .383 | .328 |
| Runners On | | | 428 | 115 | 6 | 78 | 89 | .269 | .371 | .382 |
| Runners/Scor. Pos. | | | 276 | 70 | 5 | 57 | 58 | .254 | .362 | .376 |
| First 9 Batters | | | 2866 | 733 | 60 | 310 | 511 | .256 | .378 | .332 |
| Second 9 Batters | | | 1426 | 392 | 33 | 139 | 194 | .275 | .411 | .341 |
| All Batters Thereafter | | | 1188 | 297 | 21 | 111 | 192 | .250 | .364 | .313 |

Starting pitchers: 53–60, 4.19 ERA
Relief pitchers: 20–29, 3.63 ERA
Ground outs-to-air outs ratio: 1.16. . . . Lost six games in which they led after eight innings, the most losses of any A.L. club. . . . Had the lowest average age in the A.L. for both batters (27.1 years old) and pitchers (26.7) last season. That's been done only three times over the last 22 years. Both other teams were on verge of major turnarounds: the 1968 A's and the 1983 Twins. . . . Made 330 pitching changes, most in A.L. . . . Allowed only 114 home runs last season. Team's previous low total for a full season was 138 in 1984. . . . Only major league club that has never been involved in a no-hit game. . . . Yearly ERA since 1985: 4.68, 4.65, 4.49, 4.15, 4.00. . . . Last season's ERA was actually under four runs per game (3.9993).

## Texas Rangers

| | W-L | ERA | AB | H | HR | BB | SO | BA | SA | OBA |
|---|---|---|---|---|---|---|---|---|---|---|
| Season | 83-79 | 3.91 | 5361 | 1279 | 119 | 654 | 1112 | .239 | .355 | .324 |
| vs. Left-Handers | | | 2165 | 484 | 48 | 292 | 441 | .224 | .333 | .318 |
| vs. Right-Handers | | | 3196 | 795 | 71 | 362 | 671 | .249 | .369 | .328 |
| Home | 45-36 | 3.96 | 2761 | 666 | 63 | 326 | 593 | .241 | .354 | .325 |
| Road | 38-43 | 3.85 | 2600 | 613 | 56 | 328 | 519 | .236 | .355 | .323 |
| Grass | 72-65 | 4.00 | 4582 | 1102 | 105 | 573 | 954 | .241 | .357 | .328 |
| Artificial Turf | 11-14 | 3.39 | 779 | 177 | 14 | 81 | 158 | .227 | .343 | .300 |
| April | 17-5 | 3.09 | 729 | 153 | 17 | 98 | 170 | .210 | .320 | .312 |
| May | 10-17 | 5.19 | 918 | 250 | 21 | 145 | 191 | .272 | .393 | .370 |
| June | 16-13 | 3.42 | 947 | 224 | 25 | 90 | 174 | .237 | .360 | .305 |
| July | 13-12 | 4.24 | 826 | 189 | 17 | 97 | 189 | .229 | .347 | .313 |
| August | 12-16 | 3.74 | 893 | 202 | 15 | 117 | 187 | .226 | .327 | .317 |
| Sept./Oct. | 15-16 | 3.75 | 1048 | 261 | 24 | 107 | 201 | .249 | .369 | .322 |
| Leading Off Inn. | | | 1277 | 301 | 29 | 148 | 267 | .236 | .359 | .321 |
| Runners On | | | 2339 | 622 | 49 | 305 | 434 | .266 | .383 | .350 |
| Runners/Scor. Pos. | | | 1398 | 364 | 23 | 218 | 296 | .260 | .356 | .354 |
| Runners On/2 Out | | | 1001 | 242 | 16 | 129 | 204 | .242 | .329 | .333 |
| Scor. Pos./2 Out | | | 665 | 156 | 11 | 100 | 145 | .235 | .320 | .337 |
| Late Inning Pressure | | | 852 | 207 | 20 | 104 | 201 | .243 | .362 | .331 |
| Leading Off | | | 211 | 53 | 3 | 22 | 44 | .251 | .355 | .333 |
| Runners On | | | 371 | 99 | 11 | 49 | 72 | .267 | .410 | .353 |
| Runners/Scor. Pos. | | | 222 | 57 | 4 | 39 | 51 | .257 | .365 | .368 |
| First 9 Batters | | | 2621 | 629 | 56 | 333 | 590 | .240 | .351 | .329 |
| Second 9 Batters | | | 1309 | 303 | 30 | 157 | 245 | .231 | .351 | .319 |
| All Batters Thereafter | | | 1431 | 347 | 33 | 164 | 277 | .242 | .363 | .319 |

Starting pitchers: 63–63, 4.07 ERA
Relief pitchers: 20–16, 3.54 ERA
Ground outs-to-air outs ratio: 1.16. . . . Led their league in passed balls for the sixth consecutive season, tying record set by the Atlanta Braves from 1974 through 1979. . . . Threw 65 wild pitches and were charged with 42 passed balls. That total of 107 was highest in majors. The Orioles (38 WP, 8 PB) and the Brewers (35 WP, 11 PB) had the fewest. . . . League-leading total of walks (654) was exactly the same as in 1988. First club to lead the A.L. in walks for four consecutive seasons since the Indians from 1957 through 1960. . . . Didn't allow a home run to the Angels at Arlington Stadium. . . . Had a 4–0 record in games in which their pitchers didn't walk a batter, but had the fewest such games in A.L.

## Toronto Blue Jays

| | W-L | ERA | AB | H | HR | BB | SO | BA | SA | OBA |
|---|---|---|---|---|---|---|---|---|---|---|
| Season | 89-73 | 3.58 | 5513 | 1408 | 99 | 478 | 849 | .255 | .373 | .317 |
| vs. Left-Handers | | | 1716 | 446 | 29 | 199 | 251 | .260 | .371 | .337 |
| vs. Right-Handers | | | 3797 | 962 | 70 | 279 | 598 | .253 | .374 | .307 |
| Home | 46-35 | 3.34 | 2796 | 697 | 50 | 234 | 441 | .249 | .367 | .309 |
| Road | 43-38 | 3.84 | 2717 | 711 | 49 | 244 | 408 | .262 | .379 | .325 |
| Grass | 38-25 | 3.63 | 2137 | 538 | 42 | 199 | 349 | .252 | .368 | .318 |
| Artificial Turf | 51-48 | 3.56 | 3376 | 870 | 57 | 279 | 500 | .258 | .376 | .316 |
| April | 9-16 | 3.92 | 813 | 204 | 7 | 87 | 127 | .251 | .344 | .321 |
| May | 11-15 | 4.34 | 883 | 236 | 12 | 72 | 127 | .267 | .384 | .323 |
| June | 17-10 | 3.64 | 944 | 241 | 18 | 108 | 126 | .255 | .359 | .331 |
| July | 15-12 | 3.60 | 912 | 244 | 24 | 64 | 134 | .268 | .404 | .318 |
| August | 20-9 | 2.75 | 959 | 232 | 18 | 76 | 159 | .242 | .371 | .302 |
| Sept./Oct. | 17-11 | 3.40 | 1002 | 251 | 20 | 71 | 176 | .250 | .373 | .306 |
| Leading Off Inn. | | | 1353 | 354 | 26 | 113 | 200 | .262 | .393 | .321 |
| Runners On | | | 2371 | 615 | 39 | 216 | 332 | .259 | .370 | .320 |
| Runners/Scor. Pos. | | | 1350 | 356 | 25 | 152 | 213 | .264 | .384 | .331 |
| Runners On/2 Out | | | 963 | 214 | 16 | 86 | 168 | .222 | .313 | .292 |
| Scor. Pos./2 Out | | | 605 | 135 | 11 | 64 | 110 | .223 | .321 | .303 |
| Late Inning Pressure | | | 1064 | 253 | 17 | 114 | 256 | .238 | .331 | .313 |
| Leading Off | | | 263 | 63 | 3 | 33 | 53 | .240 | .338 | .327 |
| Runners On | | | 437 | 109 | 8 | 60 | 103 | .249 | .339 | .337 |
| Runners/Scor. Pos. | | | 240 | 67 | 5 | 52 | 56 | .279 | .388 | .394 |
| First 9 Batters | | | 2792 | 690 | 47 | 261 | 518 | .247 | .357 | .314 |
| Second 9 Batters | | | 1504 | 408 | 33 | 134 | 195 | .271 | .412 | .334 |
| All Batters Thereafter | | | 1217 | 310 | 19 | 83 | 136 | .255 | .362 | .302 |

Starting pitchers: 60–52, 3.65 ERA
Relief pitchers: 29–21, 3.46 ERA
Ground outs-to-air outs ratio: 1.18, 3d highest in A.L. . . . Had best record in A.L. (10–2) in games in which their starter pitched a complete game. . . . Didn't walk an opposing batter in 19 games, most in the majors. Blue Jays had a 15–4 record in those games. . . . Only major league club that has never had a pitcher who struck out 200 batters in a season. Team record of 198 was set in 1984 by Dave Stieb. . . . Only team from A.L. East to play above .500 against the West last season. . . . Won 12 of their last 13 extra-inning contests. . . . Rookie pitchers combined for a record of 8–3, highest winning percentage in majors (.727).

## American League

| | W-L | ERA | AB | H | HR | BB | SO | BA | SA | OBA |
|---|---|---|---|---|---|---|---|---|---|---|
| Season | 1133-1133 | 3.88 | 77004 | 20078 | 1718 | 7277 | 12296 | .261 | .384 | .326 |
| vs. Left-Handers | | | 30725 | 8009 | 665 | 3166 | 4505 | .261 | .382 | .330 |
| vs. Right-Handers | | | 46279 | 12069 | 1053 | 4111 | 7791 | .261 | .385 | .323 |
| Home | 630-503 | 3.79 | 39578 | 10260 | 864 | 3570 | 6553 | .259 | .380 | .322 |
| Road | 503-630 | 3.99 | 37426 | 9818 | 854 | 3707 | 5743 | .262 | .388 | .330 |
| Grass | 809-809 | 3.86 | 54950 | 14298 | 1277 | 5276 | 8875 | .260 | .383 | .326 |
| Artificial Turf | 324-324 | 3.95 | 22054 | 5780 | 441 | 2001 | 3421 | .262 | .385 | .325 |
| April | 165-165 | 3.86 | 11152 | 2848 | 244 | 1100 | 1771 | .255 | .378 | .324 |
| May | 187-187 | 4.09 | 12651 | 3344 | 287 | 1230 | 1931 | .264 | .391 | .330 |
| June | 191-191 | 3.99 | 13188 | 3543 | 295 | 1217 | 1935 | .269 | .388 | .331 |
| July | 184-184 | 4.06 | 12490 | 3285 | 298 | 1214 | 2002 | .263 | .389 | .330 |
| August | 209-209 | 3.65 | 14075 | 3620 | 312 | 1239 | 2368 | .257 | .382 | .319 |
| Sept./Oct. | 197-197 | 3.68 | 13448 | 3438 | 282 | 1277 | 2289 | .256 | .374 | .322 |
| Leading Off Inn. | | | 18630 | 4882 | 447 | 1516 | 2829 | .262 | .394 | .321 |
| Runners On | | | 33543 | 8999 | 722 | 3557 | 5248 | .268 | .389 | .336 |
| Runners/Scor. Pos. | | | 19243 | 5051 | 382 | 2499 | 3324 | .262 | .378 | .340 |
| Runners On/2 Out | | | 14032 | 3407 | 273 | 1682 | 2413 | .243 | .350 | .327 |
| Scor. Pos./2 Out | | | 8961 | 2081 | 157 | 1273 | 1652 | .232 | .332 | .331 |
| Late Inning Pressure | | | 12911 | 3233 | 276 | 1405 | 2456 | .250 | .362 | .325 |
| Leading Off | | | 3248 | 818 | 73 | 283 | 564 | .252 | .371 | .315 |
| Runners On | | | 5397 | 1395 | 114 | 756 | 1001 | .258 | .370 | .347 |
| Runners/Scor. Pos. | | | 3154 | 803 | 62 | 607 | 641 | .255 | .360 | .368 |
| First 9 Batters | | | 38439 | 9768 | 807 | 3867 | 6873 | .254 | .370 | .324 |
| Second 9 Batters | | | 20485 | 5511 | 481 | 1837 | 2935 | .269 | .401 | .331 |
| All Batters Thereafter | | | 18080 | 4799 | 430 | 1573 | 2488 | .265 | .393 | .324 |

# National League

## Don Aase

Throws Right

| New York Mets | W–L | ERA | AB | H | HR | BB | SO | BA | SA | OBA |
|---|---|---|---|---|---|---|---|---|---|---|
| Season | 1-5 | 3.94 | 229 | 56 | 5 | 26 | 34 | .245 | .380 | .320 |
| vs. Left-Handers | | | 114 | 31 | 1 | 15 | 15 | .272 | .395 | .354 |
| vs. Right-Handers | | | 115 | 25 | 4 | 11 | 19 | .217 | .365 | .287 |
| Home | 1-2 | 4.06 | 110 | 22 | 1 | 16 | 16 | .200 | .291 | .297 |
| Road | 0-3 | 3.81 | 119 | 34 | 4 | 10 | 18 | .286 | .462 | .344 |
| Grass | 1-3 | 4.11 | 174 | 42 | 3 | 20 | 23 | .241 | .356 | .318 |
| Artificial Turf | 0-2 | 3.38 | 55 | 14 | 2 | 6 | 11 | .255 | .455 | .328 |
| April | 0-1 | 1.93 | 38 | 10 | 0 | 1 | 7 | .263 | .316 | .282 |
| May | 0-0 | 1.86 | 30 | 6 | 1 | 5 | 2 | .200 | .300 | .289 |
| June | 1-1 | 3.29 | 57 | 14 | 0 | 7 | 11 | .246 | .368 | .338 |
| July | 0-1 | 6.97 | 38 | 8 | 1 | 6 | 4 | .211 | .395 | .318 |
| August | 0-1 | 4.38 | 51 | 15 | 1 | 5 | 7 | .294 | .392 | .357 |
| Sept./Oct. | 0-1 | 6.75 | 15 | 3 | 2 | 2 | 3 | .200 | .667 | .294 |
| Leading Off Inn. | | | 53 | 10 | 2 | 6 | 6 | .189 | .415 | .271 |
| Runners On | | | 99 | 24 | 2 | 12 | 21 | .242 | .343 | .322 |
| Runners/Scor. Pos. | | | 63 | 14 | 2 | 9 | 15 | .222 | .333 | .316 |
| Runners On/2 Out | | | 52 | 12 | 2 | 7 | 11 | .231 | .423 | .322 |
| Scor. Pos./2 Out | | | 31 | 6 | 2 | 4 | 7 | .194 | .419 | .286 |
| Late Inning Pressure | | | 108 | 26 | 3 | 15 | 15 | .241 | .361 | .331 |
| Leading Off | | | 28 | 6 | 1 | 4 | 2 | .214 | .393 | .313 |
| Runners On | | | 41 | 10 | 1 | 6 | 8 | .244 | .317 | .333 |
| Runners/Scor. Pos. | | | 26 | 7 | 1 | 3 | 5 | .269 | .385 | .333 |
| First 9 Batters | | | 219 | 51 | 4 | 25 | 34 | .233 | .352 | .310 |
| Second 9 Batters | | | 10 | 5 | 1 | 1 | 0 | .500 | 1.000 | .545 |
| All Batters Thereafter | | | 0 | 0 | 0 | 0 | 0 | — | — | — |

Loves to face: Tom Brunansky (0-for-13)
Hates to face: Eddie Murray (.393, 11-for-28, 2 HR)
Ground outs-to-air outs ratio: 0.69 last season (N.L. avg.: 1.12), 0.93 for career.... Additional statistics: 3 double-play ground outs in 34 opportunities (N.L. avg.: one per 10.4 chances), 14 doubles, 1 triple in 59.1 innings last season.... Ground-ball hitters batted .280 against him, fly-ballers .217.... Signed his own walking papers by allowing 9th-inning HRs to both Willie Randolph (while trying to protect a one-run lead) and Dickie Thon (in a tie game) over last six weeks of season.... Opposing batters have hit below .200 leading off innings in four of the last six seasons.... Began major league career with 69 consecutive starts. Has now made 319 relief appearances since his last start (1980).

## Jim Acker

Throws Right

| Atlanta Braves | W–L | ERA | AB | H | HR | BB | SO | BA | SA | OBA |
|---|---|---|---|---|---|---|---|---|---|---|
| Season | 0-6 | 2.67 | 354 | 84 | 5 | 20 | 68 | .237 | .331 | .278 |
| vs. Left-Handers | | | 183 | 52 | 3 | 14 | 19 | .284 | .383 | .333 |
| vs. Right-Handers | | | 171 | 32 | 2 | 6 | 49 | .187 | .275 | .217 |
| Home | 0-3 | 2.76 | 166 | 37 | 3 | 10 | 31 | .223 | .331 | .270 |
| Road | 0-3 | 2.60 | 188 | 47 | 2 | 10 | 37 | .250 | .330 | .285 |
| Grass | 0-4 | 2.88 | 247 | 58 | 5 | 17 | 43 | .235 | .340 | .285 |
| Artificial Turf | 0-2 | 2.17 | 107 | 26 | 0 | 3 | 25 | .243 | .308 | .261 |
| April | 0-1 | 4.58 | 68 | 21 | 1 | 6 | 11 | .309 | .441 | .355 |
| May | 0-1 | 1.96 | 62 | 12 | 0 | 2 | 7 | .194 | .242 | .215 |
| June | 0-1 | 2.31 | 82 | 17 | 1 | 6 | 16 | .207 | .280 | .261 |
| July | 0-1 | 1.74 | 75 | 15 | 2 | 3 | 19 | .200 | .293 | .231 |
| August | 0-2 | 3.06 | 67 | 19 | 1 | 3 | 15 | .284 | .403 | .324 |
| Sept./Oct. | | | 0 | 0 | 0 | 0 | 0 | — | — | — |
| Leading Off Inn. | | | 86 | 24 | 3 | 1 | 15 | .279 | .477 | .287 |
| Runners On | | | 150 | 35 | 1 | 13 | 28 | .233 | .293 | .289 |
| Runners/Scor. Pos. | | | 99 | 20 | 1 | 12 | 19 | .202 | .273 | .281 |
| Runners On/2 Out | | | 68 | 15 | 1 | 9 | 15 | .221 | .279 | .312 |
| Scor. Pos./2 Out | | | 48 | 10 | 1 | 8 | 9 | .208 | .271 | .321 |
| Late Inning Pressure | | | 135 | 36 | 1 | 8 | 29 | .267 | .348 | .306 |
| Leading Off | | | 35 | 8 | 0 | 1 | 6 | .229 | .257 | .250 |
| Runners On | | | 54 | 18 | 0 | 5 | 12 | .333 | .426 | .383 |
| Runners/Scor. Pos. | | | 32 | 10 | 0 | 4 | 7 | .313 | .406 | .378 |
| First 9 Batters | | | 338 | 80 | 4 | 18 | 64 | .237 | .325 | .275 |
| Second 9 Batters | | | 16 | 4 | 1 | 2 | 4 | .250 | .438 | .333 |
| All Batters Thereafter | | | 0 | 0 | 0 | 0 | 0 | — | — | — |

Loves to face: Willie Wilson (.077, 1-for-13)
Hates to face: Robin Yount (.556, 5-for-9)
Ground outs-to-air outs ratio: 1.75 last season, 1.91 for career.... Additional statistics: 7 double-play ground outs in 59 opportunities, 14 doubles, 2 triples in 97.2 innings last season.... Opposing base runners stole only five bases in 12 attempts while with Braves, one-for-three after trade to Toronto.... Lost his last 13 decisions in an Atlanta uniform.... Opponents' batting average (.237 combined-leagues mark) was lowest of his career.... Career records of 1–6 in both April and May, 24–26 in other months.... Blue Jays' answer to Expos' mascot Youppi. Toronto has gone on to postseason play in each of the last two seasons he finished in a Blue Jays' uniform (1989 and 1985).

## Juan Agosto

Throws Left

| Houston Astros | W–L | ERA | AB | H | HR | BB | SO | BA | SA | OBA |
|---|---|---|---|---|---|---|---|---|---|---|
| Season | 4-5 | 2.93 | 316 | 81 | 3 | 32 | 46 | .256 | .329 | .323 |
| vs. Left-Handers | | | 109 | 24 | 0 | 10 | 23 | .220 | .266 | .276 |
| vs. Right-Handers | | | 207 | 57 | 3 | 22 | 23 | .275 | .362 | .348 |
| Home | 3-2 | 2.66 | 173 | 46 | 0 | 16 | 34 | .266 | .306 | .333 |
| Road | 1-3 | 3.23 | 143 | 35 | 3 | 16 | 12 | .245 | .357 | .311 |
| Grass | 1-1 | 2.29 | 70 | 15 | 0 | 9 | 7 | .214 | .214 | .296 |
| Artificial Turf | 3-4 | 3.13 | 246 | 66 | 3 | 23 | 39 | .268 | .362 | .331 |
| April | 0-0 | 4.66 | 42 | 14 | 0 | 8 | 6 | .333 | .405 | .442 |
| May | 1-1 | 2.77 | 51 | 14 | 1 | 2 | 8 | .275 | .431 | .302 |
| June | 1-2 | 2.70 | 65 | 17 | 0 | 9 | 11 | .262 | .277 | .347 |
| July | 0-1 | 3.55 | 49 | 12 | 2 | 5 | 6 | .245 | .429 | .321 |
| August | 1-1 | 3.50 | 67 | 19 | 0 | 5 | 12 | .284 | .313 | .324 |
| Sept./Oct. | 1-0 | 0.69 | 42 | 5 | 0 | 3 | 3 | .119 | .119 | .174 |
| Leading Off Inn. | | | 78 | 24 | 1 | 3 | 14 | .308 | .385 | .333 |
| Runners On | | | 156 | 37 | 2 | 21 | 25 | .237 | .308 | .321 |
| Runners/Scor. Pos. | | | 105 | 23 | 0 | 21 | 17 | .219 | .257 | .338 |
| Runners On/2 Out | | | 64 | 10 | 0 | 14 | 11 | .156 | .203 | .316 |
| Scor. Pos./2 Out | | | 45 | 6 | 0 | 14 | 7 | .133 | .200 | .350 |
| Late Inning Pressure | | | 113 | 31 | 1 | 11 | 19 | .274 | .327 | .328 |
| Leading Off | | | 35 | 13 | 0 | 1 | 7 | .371 | .429 | .389 |
| Runners On | | | 45 | 13 | 1 | 9 | 10 | .289 | .378 | .379 |
| Runners/Scor. Pos. | | | 28 | 7 | 0 | 9 | 7 | .250 | .286 | .390 |
| First 9 Batters | | | 292 | 73 | 3 | 29 | 41 | .250 | .329 | .317 |
| Second 9 Batters | | | 24 | 8 | 0 | 3 | 5 | .333 | .333 | .393 |
| All Batters Thereafter | | | 0 | 0 | 0 | 0 | 0 | — | — | — |

Loves to face: Barry Bonds (0-for-12)
Hates to face: Spike Owen (.625, 5-for-8, 2 2B, 1 HR)
Ground outs-to-air outs ratio: 1.62 last season, 2.43 for career.... Additional statistics: 7 double-play ground outs in 65 opportunities, 10 doubles, 2 triples in 83.0 innings last season.... Opponents stole 11 bases, highest total against any N.L. pitcher who didn't catch a thief.... Career record of 15–7 (2.99 ERA) in home games, 9–11 (4.03 ERA) on the road.... Career average of .206 (4 HR) by opposing left-handed batters, .296 (15 HR) by right-handers.... Leads N.L. pitchers with 146 appearances over the last two seasons.... One of four N.L. pitchers with ERA below 3.00 in each of last three seasons. Others: Tim Belcher, Ken Dayley, and teammate Dave Smith, whose streak began in 1984.

## Larry Andersen

Throws Right

| Houston Astros | W–L | ERA | AB | H | HR | BB | SO | BA | SA | OBA |
|---|---|---|---|---|---|---|---|---|---|---|
| Season | 4-4 | 1.54 | 318 | 63 | 2 | 24 | 85 | .198 | .245 | .251 |
| vs. Left-Handers | | | 161 | 40 | 2 | 14 | 33 | .248 | .304 | .303 |
| vs. Right-Handers | | | 157 | 23 | 0 | 10 | 52 | .146 | .185 | .195 |
| Home | 2-3 | 1.22 | 188 | 38 | 2 | 13 | 57 | .202 | .282 | .250 |
| Road | 2-1 | 2.00 | 130 | 25 | 0 | 11 | 28 | .192 | .192 | .252 |
| Grass | 1-0 | 3.00 | 78 | 17 | 0 | 8 | 17 | .218 | .218 | .287 |
| Artificial Turf | 3-4 | 1.08 | 240 | 46 | 2 | 16 | 68 | .192 | .254 | .238 |
| April | 0-0 | 0.00 | 52 | 6 | 0 | 3 | 6 | .115 | .135 | .164 |
| May | 1-1 | 0.71 | 43 | 7 | 0 | 2 | 13 | .163 | .163 | .191 |
| June | 0-0 | 0.52 | 61 | 11 | 0 | 4 | 20 | .180 | .213 | .231 |
| July | 1-2 | 2.87 | 62 | 18 | 0 | 4 | 11 | .290 | .355 | .324 |
| August | 1-1 | 4.41 | 65 | 16 | 2 | 8 | 22 | .246 | .369 | .324 |
| Sept./Oct. | 1-0 | 0.00 | 35 | 5 | 0 | 3 | 13 | .143 | .143 | .211 |
| Leading Off Inn. | | | 73 | 13 | 1 | 5 | 24 | .178 | .247 | .231 |
| Runners On | | | 137 | 28 | 0 | 12 | 31 | .204 | .219 | .260 |
| Runners/Scor. Pos. | | | 83 | 12 | 0 | 9 | 18 | .145 | .157 | .216 |
| Runners On/2 Out | | | 64 | 9 | 0 | 8 | 16 | .141 | .156 | .236 |
| Scor. Pos./2 Out | | | 44 | 4 | 0 | 7 | 11 | .091 | .091 | .216 |
| Late Inning Pressure | | | 162 | 33 | 1 | 19 | 37 | .204 | .253 | .284 |
| Leading Off | | | 37 | 5 | 0 | 4 | 11 | .135 | .135 | .220 |
| Runners On | | | 71 | 17 | 0 | 9 | 13 | .239 | .254 | .317 |
| Runners/Scor. Pos. | | | 44 | 7 | 0 | 7 | 10 | .159 | .182 | .264 |
| First 9 Batters | | | 300 | 59 | 2 | 24 | 81 | .197 | .247 | .252 |
| Second 9 Batters | | | 18 | 4 | 0 | 0 | 4 | .222 | .222 | .222 |
| All Batters Thereafter | | | 0 | 0 | 0 | 0 | 0 | — | — | — |

Loves to face: Benito Santiago (.083, 1-for-12)
Hates to face: Ozzie Smith (.538, 7-for-13, 8 BB)
Ground outs-to-air outs ratio: 1.23 last season, 1.27 for career.... Additional statistics: 4 double-play ground outs in 68 opportunities, 5 doubles, 2 triples in 87.2 innings last season.... Was summoned from the bullpen to start an inning in 12 of his last 15 appearances.... Hasn't allowed a home run in his last 38 appearances *outside* the Astrodome. He'll pick up the streak at 61.1 innings this season.... Both ERA and opponents' batting average were career lows.... Career average of .278 by opposing left-handed batters, .238 by right-handers.... Has only one start among his 469 career appearances. Who is the only manager to write his name on a starting lineup card? Answer: Rene Lachemann (1982 Mariners).

## Paul Assenmacher

Throws Left

| Braves/Cubs | W–L | ERA | AB | H | HR | BB | SO | BA | SA | OBA |
|---|---|---|---|---|---|---|---|---|---|---|
| Season | 3-4 | 3.99 | 290 | 74 | 3 | 28 | 79 | .255 | .338 | .320 |
| vs. Left-Handers | | | 85 | 21 | 0 | 7 | 30 | .247 | .271 | .304 |
| vs. Right-Handers | | | 205 | 53 | 3 | 21 | 49 | .259 | .366 | .326 |
| Home | 3-3 | 3.86 | 161 | 40 | 1 | 12 | 45 | .248 | .323 | .301 |
| Road | 0-1 | 4.15 | 129 | 34 | 2 | 16 | 34 | .264 | .357 | .342 |
| Grass | 3-3 | 3.67 | 217 | 52 | 2 | 14 | 64 | .240 | .318 | .286 |
| Artificial Turf | 0-1 | 4.87 | 73 | 22 | 1 | 14 | 15 | .301 | .397 | .409 |
| April | 0-1 | 0.93 | 35 | 7 | 1 | 3 | 9 | .200 | .314 | .256 |
| May | 0-0 | 2.08 | 51 | 12 | 0 | 2 | 13 | .235 | .294 | .264 |
| June | 0-1 | 13.03 | 42 | 16 | 1 | 6 | 12 | .381 | .548 | .469 |
| July | 1-1 | 2.04 | 62 | 13 | 0 | 2 | 20 | .210 | .258 | .231 |
| August | 1-0 | 0.79 | 43 | 8 | 0 | 3 | 13 | .186 | .209 | .239 |
| Sept./Oct. | 1-1 | 6.46 | 57 | 18 | 1 | 12 | 12 | .316 | .421 | .429 |
| Leading Off Inn. | | | 66 | 21 | 2 | 4 | 13 | .318 | .500 | .357 |
| Runners On | | | 142 | 34 | 1 | 20 | 43 | .239 | .310 | .331 |
| Runners/Scor. Pos. | | | 91 | 23 | 1 | 17 | 32 | .253 | .341 | .366 |
| Runners On/2 Out | | | 58 | 10 | 1 | 5 | 24 | .172 | .241 | .238 |
| Scor. Pos./2 Out | | | 38 | 7 | 1 | 5 | 16 | .184 | .263 | .279 |
| Late Inning Pressure | | | 155 | 50 | 2 | 14 | 33 | .323 | .432 | .378 |
| Leading Off | | | 39 | 15 | 1 | 3 | 7 | .385 | .590 | .429 |
| Runners On | | | 77 | 22 | 1 | 9 | 17 | .286 | .377 | .360 |
| Runners/Scor. Pos. | | | 51 | 15 | 1 | 8 | 13 | .294 | .412 | .387 |
| First 9 Batters | | | 276 | 69 | 2 | 27 | 74 | .250 | .326 | .316 |
| Second 9 Batters | | | 14 | 5 | 1 | 1 | 5 | .357 | .571 | .400 |
| All Batters Thereafter | | | 0 | 0 | 0 | 0 | 0 | — | — | — |

Loves to face: Darryl Strawberry (.063, 1-for-16, 5 SO)
Hates to face: Dave Magadan (.857, 6-for-7)
Ground outs-to-air outs ratio: 1.15 last season, 1.30 for career. . . . Additional statistics: 6 double-play ground outs in 79 opportunities, 15 doubles, 0 triples in 76.2 innings last season. . . . Has played 240 games, most of any active N.L. pitcher who has never committed an error. All 240 games, incidentally, were in relief. . . . Faced 35 consecutive batters with runners on base without allowing a hit, tied for the longest streak in the majors last season. . . . Opponents batted 145 points higher in Late-Inning Pressure Situations than in other at-bats, largest difference in the majors (minimum: 75 AB each). . . . Made 63 appearances without a save last season. See comments on Norm Charlton for more.

## Steve Bedrosian

Throws Right

| Phillies/Giants | W–L | ERA | AB | H | HR | BB | SO | BA | SA | OBA |
|---|---|---|---|---|---|---|---|---|---|---|
| Season | 3-7 | 2.87 | 297 | 56 | 12 | 39 | 58 | .189 | .330 | .282 |
| vs. Left-Handers | | | 164 | 33 | 8 | 27 | 32 | .201 | .372 | .314 |
| vs. Right-Handers | | | 133 | 23 | 4 | 12 | 26 | .173 | .278 | .238 |
| Home | 2-2 | 1.96 | 158 | 27 | 7 | 20 | 37 | .171 | .323 | .267 |
| Road | 1-5 | 3.96 | 139 | 29 | 5 | 19 | 21 | .209 | .338 | .298 |
| Grass | 1-3 | 2.09 | 160 | 25 | 3 | 19 | 32 | .156 | .213 | .243 |
| Artificial Turf | 2-4 | 3.86 | 137 | 31 | 9 | 20 | 26 | .226 | .467 | .325 |
| April | 1-2 | 4.22 | 37 | 8 | 3 | 3 | 7 | .216 | .514 | .268 |
| May | 1-0 | 1.29 | 47 | 8 | 2 | 9 | 13 | .170 | .319 | .304 |
| June | 0-2 | 4.02 | 52 | 9 | 3 | 7 | 8 | .173 | .385 | .279 |
| July | 0-1 | 5.27 | 53 | 13 | 2 | 7 | 10 | .245 | .358 | .328 |
| August | 0-1 | 1.35 | 49 | 9 | 0 | 7 | 8 | .184 | .184 | .286 |
| Sept./Oct. | 1-1 | 1.56 | 59 | 9 | 2 | 6 | 12 | .153 | .271 | .227 |
| Leading Off Inn. | | | 66 | 9 | 0 | 7 | 10 | .136 | .152 | .219 |
| Runners On | | | 127 | 25 | 7 | 20 | 24 | .197 | .386 | .298 |
| Runners/Scor. Pos. | | | 79 | 18 | 7 | 18 | 18 | .228 | .519 | .356 |
| Runners On/2 Out | | | 55 | 6 | 3 | 10 | 10 | .109 | .273 | .246 |
| Scor. Pos./2 Out | | | 37 | 6 | 3 | 10 | 9 | .162 | .405 | .340 |
| Late Inning Pressure | | | 187 | 37 | 9 | 30 | 43 | .198 | .374 | .306 |
| Leading Off | | | 39 | 8 | 0 | 4 | 7 | .205 | .231 | .279 |
| Runners On | | | 89 | 15 | 6 | 18 | 17 | .169 | .404 | .297 |
| Runners/Scor. Pos. | | | 58 | 13 | 6 | 17 | 15 | .224 | .569 | .380 |
| First 9 Batters | | | 285 | 53 | 10 | 39 | 55 | .186 | .312 | .283 |
| Second 9 Batters | | | 12 | 3 | 2 | 0 | 3 | .250 | .750 | .250 |
| All Batters Thereafter | | | 0 | 0 | 0 | 0 | 0 | — | — | — |

Loves to face: Mike Fitzgerald (0-for-17)
Hates to face: Nick Esasky (.500, 8-for-16, 1 HR)
Ground outs-to-air outs ratio: 0.53 last season, 0.79 for career. . . . Additional statistics: 5 double-play ground outs in 56 opportunities, 6 doubles, 0 triples in 84.2 innings last season. . . . Allowed 12 home runs, most of any reliever in majors. . . . Saved six games in nine opportunities for Phillies, 17-of-22 for Giants. . . . Greg Minton's club record of 30 saves in a season could be in jeopardy in 1990. . . . Opponents have a career average of .199 with runners in scoring position. . . . World Series appearance leaves Mark Davis and Mike Scott as only N.L. Cy Young Award winners since 1978 never to have pitched in the Fall Classic. . . . Career record of 9–2 vs. St. Louis, 47–59 vs. other teams.

## Tim Belcher

Throws Right

| Los Angeles Dodgers | W–L | ERA | AB | H | HR | BB | SO | BA | SA | OBA |
|---|---|---|---|---|---|---|---|---|---|---|
| Season | 15-12 | 2.82 | 838 | 182 | 20 | 80 | 200 | .217 | .322 | .289 |
| vs. Left-Handers | | | 473 | 103 | 7 | 51 | 104 | .218 | .292 | .298 |
| vs. Right-Handers | | | 365 | 79 | 13 | 29 | 96 | .216 | .362 | .278 |
| Home | 10-4 | 2.10 | 442 | 88 | 10 | 28 | 117 | .199 | .294 | .249 |
| Road | 5-8 | 3.66 | 396 | 94 | 10 | 52 | 83 | .237 | .354 | .330 |
| Grass | 12-6 | 2.27 | 570 | 119 | 14 | 45 | 141 | .209 | .311 | .267 |
| Artificial Turf | 3-6 | 4.04 | 268 | 63 | 6 | 35 | 59 | .235 | .347 | .332 |
| April | 2-2 | 2.54 | 143 | 31 | 2 | 12 | 30 | .217 | .322 | .277 |
| May | 2-2 | 3.38 | 134 | 27 | 4 | 11 | 33 | .201 | .291 | .267 |
| June | 0-4 | 4.05 | 123 | 30 | 2 | 14 | 30 | .244 | .317 | .324 |
| July | 4-1 | 2.66 | 153 | 36 | 3 | 14 | 41 | .235 | .353 | .304 |
| August | 2-3 | 3.38 | 121 | 30 | 5 | 15 | 27 | .248 | .388 | .341 |
| Sept./Oct. | 5-0 | 1.51 | 164 | 28 | 4 | 14 | 39 | .171 | .274 | .236 |
| Leading Off Inn. | | | 218 | 45 | 4 | 17 | 34 | .206 | .280 | .264 |
| Runners On | | | 312 | 60 | 7 | 39 | 86 | .192 | .295 | .287 |
| Runners/Scor. Pos. | | | 180 | 34 | 4 | 24 | 49 | .189 | .300 | .283 |
| Runners On/2 Out | | | 133 | 22 | 2 | 17 | 37 | .165 | .271 | .260 |
| Scor. Pos./2 Out | | | 93 | 15 | 1 | 14 | 27 | .161 | .280 | .271 |
| Late Inning Pressure | | | 132 | 25 | 2 | 11 | 27 | .189 | .265 | .255 |
| Leading Off | | | 36 | 6 | 0 | 3 | 4 | .167 | .194 | .231 |
| Runners On | | | 41 | 6 | 1 | 6 | 13 | .146 | .244 | .250 |
| Runners/Scor. Pos. | | | 25 | 4 | 0 | 5 | 7 | .160 | .200 | .290 |
| First 9 Batters | | | 298 | 62 | 8 | 33 | 102 | .208 | .336 | .296 |
| Second 9 Batters | | | 251 | 62 | 7 | 26 | 44 | .247 | .359 | .322 |
| All Batters Thereafter | | | 289 | 58 | 5 | 21 | 54 | .201 | .277 | .252 |

Loves to face: Ken Caminiti (.063, 1-for-16)
Hates to face: Andre Dawson (.412, 7-for-17, 2 HR)
Ground outs-to-air outs ratio: 0.72 last season, 0.75 for career. . . . Additional statistics: 9 double-play ground outs in 169 opportunities, 24 doubles, 2 triples in 230.0 innings last season. . . . Allowed 10 first-inning runs in 30 starts. . . . Batting support: 3.57 runs per start. . . . Tied Bruce Hurst for league lead in complete games with 10, lowest total ever to lead either league. . . . Started his first 15 games and his last 15 games, making nine relief appearances in between. . . . In 1988, became first N.L. rookie with at least 4 saves and 4 complete games since Lew Burdette in 1952. . . . Career record of 10–12 (3.54 ERA) before the All-Star break, 21–8 (2.25) after the break (including 11–4, 1.60 after Sept. 1).

## Mike Bielecki

Throws Right

| Chicago Cubs | W–L | ERA | AB | H | HR | BB | SO | BA | SA | OBA |
|---|---|---|---|---|---|---|---|---|---|---|
| Season | 18-7 | 3.14 | 789 | 187 | 16 | 81 | 147 | .237 | .362 | .307 |
| vs. Left-Handers | | | 420 | 106 | 10 | 55 | 70 | .252 | .398 | .338 |
| vs. Right-Handers | | | 369 | 81 | 6 | 26 | 77 | .220 | .322 | .270 |
| Home | 9-3 | 2.83 | 412 | 90 | 10 | 48 | 86 | .218 | .340 | .299 |
| Road | 9-4 | 3.49 | 377 | 97 | 6 | 33 | 61 | .257 | .387 | .316 |
| Grass | 12-5 | 2.95 | 556 | 125 | 11 | 63 | 109 | .225 | .342 | .303 |
| Artificial Turf | 6-2 | 3.62 | 233 | 62 | 5 | 18 | 38 | .266 | .412 | .317 |
| April | 1-1 | 1.83 | 75 | 14 | 1 | 7 | 19 | .187 | .280 | .256 |
| May | 3-1 | 1.51 | 129 | 30 | 1 | 10 | 22 | .233 | .310 | .288 |
| June | 2-2 | 4.15 | 148 | 36 | 5 | 16 | 29 | .243 | .405 | .315 |
| July | 4-1 | 3.23 | 143 | 33 | 1 | 16 | 26 | .231 | .301 | .306 |
| August | 4-0 | 4.06 | 165 | 39 | 7 | 19 | 31 | .236 | .436 | .314 |
| Sept./Oct. | 4-2 | 3.12 | 129 | 35 | 1 | 13 | 20 | .271 | .388 | .338 |
| Leading Off Inn. | | | 203 | 49 | 7 | 18 | 35 | .241 | .389 | .303 |
| Runners On | | | 301 | 68 | 4 | 42 | 62 | .226 | .326 | .318 |
| Runners/Scor. Pos. | | | 161 | 38 | 2 | 27 | 34 | .236 | .311 | .340 |
| Runners On/2 Out | | | 130 | 33 | 2 | 16 | 35 | .254 | .362 | .336 |
| Scor. Pos./2 Out | | | 80 | 18 | 1 | 12 | 19 | .225 | .313 | .326 |
| Late Inning Pressure | | | 49 | 12 | 2 | 6 | 13 | .245 | .388 | .327 |
| Leading Off | | | 16 | 2 | 0 | 0 | 3 | .125 | .125 | .125 |
| Runners On | | | 10 | 3 | 1 | 3 | 2 | .300 | .700 | .462 |
| Runners/Scor. Pos. | | | 5 | 1 | 1 | 1 | 1 | .200 | .800 | .333 |
| First 9 Batters | | | 258 | 55 | 5 | 31 | 59 | .213 | .333 | .297 |
| Second 9 Batters | | | 266 | 71 | 5 | 27 | 40 | .267 | .391 | .332 |
| All Batters Thereafter | | | 265 | 61 | 6 | 23 | 48 | .230 | .362 | .292 |

Loves to face: Barry Bonds (.053, 1-for-19)
Hates to face: Jay Bell (.833, 5-for-6)
Ground outs-to-air outs ratio: 1.01 last season, 1.13 for career. . . . Additional statistics: 18 double-play ground outs in 151 opportunities, 41 doubles, 5 triples in 212.1 innings last season. . . . Allowed 14 first-inning runs in 33 starts. . . . Batting support: 4.48 runs per start. . . . Streak of 35 hitless opponents' at-bats was longest in N.L. . . . Opponents stole only five bases in 12 tries. . . . Lost consecutive starts only once last season. . . . Three of his four complete games were shutouts. No shutouts in 47 starts prior to '89. . . . Turnaround was due mainly to new-found success vs. right-handers (prior career BA: .261). . . . Hitless in 45 career AB vs. southpaws. One hit in 80 regular-season AB on grass fields.

## Tim Birtsas

Throws Left

| Cincinnati Reds | W–L | ERA | AB | H | HR | BB | SO | BA | SA | OBA |
|---|---|---|---|---|---|---|---|---|---|---|
| Season | 2-2 | 3.75 | 261 | 68 | 5 | 27 | 57 | .261 | .391 | .330 |
| vs. Left-Handers | | | 81 | 16 | 2 | 4 | 18 | .198 | .346 | .233 |
| vs. Right-Handers | | | 180 | 52 | 3 | 23 | 39 | .289 | .411 | .370 |
| Home | 2-1 | 4.40 | 179 | 49 | 5 | 16 | 40 | .274 | .430 | .335 |
| Road | 0-1 | 2.38 | 82 | 19 | 0 | 11 | 17 | .232 | .305 | .319 |
| Grass | 0-1 | 3.12 | 62 | 14 | 0 | 8 | 12 | .226 | .323 | .310 |
| Artificial Turf | 2-1 | 3.96 | 199 | 54 | 5 | 19 | 45 | .271 | .412 | .336 |
| April | 2-0 | 5.40 | 23 | 5 | 1 | 3 | 6 | .217 | .435 | .333 |
| May | 0-0 | 1.02 | 57 | 8 | 1 | 3 | 12 | .140 | .211 | .194 |
| June | 0-2 | 6.75 | 49 | 14 | 0 | 4 | 6 | .286 | .367 | .340 |
| July | 0-0 | 4.35 | 46 | 16 | 0 | 7 | 9 | .348 | .478 | .436 |
| August | 0-0 | 3.77 | 56 | 19 | 2 | 5 | 12 | .339 | .536 | .375 |
| Sept./Oct. | 0-0 | 3.12 | 30 | 6 | 1 | 5 | 12 | .200 | .333 | .306 |
| Leading Off Inn. | | | 58 | 13 | 2 | 6 | 15 | .224 | .414 | .297 |
| Runners On | | | 119 | 33 | 2 | 15 | 23 | .277 | .437 | .343 |
| Runners/Scor. Pos. | | | 64 | 16 | 0 | 13 | 18 | .250 | .344 | .349 |
| Runners On/2 Out | | | 56 | 13 | 1 | 7 | 15 | .232 | .357 | .317 |
| Scor. Pos./2 Out | | | 34 | 8 | 0 | 6 | 12 | .235 | .324 | .350 |
| Late Inning Pressure | | | 24 | 8 | 0 | 7 | 4 | .333 | .417 | .485 |
| Leading Off | | | 8 | 2 | 0 | 1 | 3 | .250 | .375 | .333 |
| Runners On | | | 9 | 3 | 0 | 5 | 1 | .333 | .444 | .533 |
| Runners/Scor. Pos. | | | 5 | 1 | 0 | 4 | 0 | .200 | .200 | .500 |
| First 9 Batters | | | 228 | 62 | 5 | 19 | 49 | .272 | .412 | .327 |
| Second 9 Batters | | | 33 | 6 | 0 | 8 | 8 | .182 | .242 | .349 |
| All Batters Thereafter | | | 0 | 0 | 0 | 0 | 0 | — | — | — |

Loves to face: Kirk Gibson (.133, 2-for-15, 5 SO)
Hates to face: Dale Murphy (.400, 2-for-5, 2 HR, 2 BB)
Ground outs-to-air outs ratio: 0.92 last season, 0.85 for career. . . . Additional statistics: 5 double-play ground outs in 51 opportunities, 13 doubles, 3 triples in 69.2 innings last season. . . . Entered 28 of his 41 relief appearances with the Reds trailing by at least three runs. Was summoned to hold leads twice, of six and seven runs. . . . Inherited 23 runners, stranded 10 (43%), lowest average in N.L. (minimum: 20 runners). . . . Has lost only five games in his N.L. career, but three of those losses have been at the hands of the Padres. . . . Pitched 141.1 innings as a rookie for Oakland in 1985, only 136.0 in majors since then. . . . Walked 5.79 batters per nine innings as a rookie, 3.64 thereafter.

## Joe Boever

Throws Right

| Atlanta Braves | W–L | ERA | AB | H | HR | BB | SO | BA | SA | OBA |
|---|---|---|---|---|---|---|---|---|---|---|
| Season | 4-11 | 3.94 | 309 | 78 | 6 | 34 | 68 | .252 | .356 | .328 |
| vs. Left-Handers | | | 179 | 45 | 1 | 22 | 36 | .251 | .307 | .333 |
| vs. Right-Handers | | | 130 | 33 | 5 | 12 | 32 | .254 | .423 | .322 |
| Home | 4-6 | 3.53 | 192 | 45 | 2 | 18 | 42 | .234 | .313 | .303 |
| Road | 0-5 | 4.60 | 117 | 33 | 4 | 16 | 26 | .282 | .427 | .368 |
| Grass | 4-8 | 3.26 | 247 | 60 | 3 | 24 | 56 | .243 | .332 | .313 |
| Artificial Turf | 0-3 | 6.75 | 62 | 18 | 3 | 10 | 12 | .290 | .452 | .389 |
| April | 1-1 | 3.86 | 53 | 12 | 0 | 5 | 13 | .226 | .245 | .293 |
| May | 1-1 | 1.72 | 56 | 12 | 0 | 4 | 11 | .214 | .339 | .267 |
| June | 0-0 | 6.30 | 41 | 11 | 0 | 7 | 12 | .268 | .317 | .388 |
| July | 2-1 | 0.48 | 61 | 6 | 0 | 5 | 13 | .098 | .115 | .167 |
| August | 0-3 | 6.91 | 55 | 21 | 3 | 8 | 9 | .382 | .582 | .460 |
| Sept./Oct. | 0-5 | 7.45 | 43 | 16 | 3 | 5 | 10 | .372 | .605 | .438 |
| Leading Off Inn. | | | 70 | 17 | 3 | 7 | 15 | .243 | .457 | .312 |
| Runners On | | | 149 | 34 | 2 | 16 | 33 | .228 | .302 | .307 |
| Runners/Scor. Pos. | | | 83 | 21 | 1 | 14 | 19 | .253 | .349 | .367 |
| Runners On/2 Out | | | 71 | 16 | 1 | 9 | 12 | .225 | .338 | .321 |
| Scor. Pos./2 Out | | | 44 | 12 | 1 | 8 | 9 | .273 | .455 | .396 |
| Late Inning Pressure | | | 209 | 55 | 5 | 26 | 49 | .263 | .378 | .345 |
| Leading Off | | | 50 | 13 | 3 | 4 | 11 | .260 | .540 | .315 |
| Runners On | | | 99 | 25 | 2 | 12 | 20 | .253 | .343 | .333 |
| Runners/Scor. Pos. | | | 58 | 15 | 1 | 11 | 11 | .259 | .362 | .377 |
| First 9 Batters | | | 297 | 76 | 6 | 33 | 67 | .256 | .364 | .330 |
| Second 9 Batters | | | 12 | 2 | 0 | 1 | 1 | .167 | .167 | .286 |
| All Batters Thereafter | | | 0 | 0 | 0 | 0 | 0 | — | — | — |

Loves to face: Kevin Bass (0-for-7)
Hates to face: Tony Gywnn (.750, 6-for-8)
Ground outs-to-air outs ratio: 1.02 last season, 0.84 for career. . . . Additional statistics: 6 double-play ground outs in 66 opportunities, 10 doubles, 2 triples in 82.1 innings last season. . . . Inherited 23 runners, stranded 19 (83%), 3d-highest rate in N.L. (minimum: 20 runners). . . . Led major league relievers in losses (11). . . . Blew each of his last five save opportunities after going 21-for-28. Teammate Mike Stanton was 7-for-8 down the stretch. . . . Career record of 1–8 in September. . . . Opposing ground-ball hitters had higher BA than fly-ball hitters in each of his five seasons. Career BA: .301 by ground-ballers, .215 by fly-ballers. . . . No balks in major league career. (He was in minors during April 1988, Month of the Balk.)

## Jeff Brantley

Throws Right

| San Francisco Giants | W–L | ERA | AB | H | HR | BB | SO | BA | SA | OBA |
|---|---|---|---|---|---|---|---|---|---|---|
| Season | 7-1 | 4.07 | 373 | 101 | 10 | 37 | 69 | .271 | .394 | .337 |
| vs. Left-Handers | | | 192 | 58 | 4 | 20 | 26 | .302 | .422 | .364 |
| vs. Right-Handers | | | 181 | 43 | 6 | 17 | 43 | .238 | .365 | .308 |
| Home | 4-1 | 3.60 | 174 | 47 | 3 | 16 | 37 | .270 | .374 | .333 |
| Road | 3-0 | 4.47 | 199 | 54 | 7 | 21 | 32 | .271 | .412 | .341 |
| Grass | 4-1 | 3.95 | 263 | 73 | 6 | 26 | 51 | .278 | .392 | .342 |
| Artificial Turf | 3-0 | 4.34 | 110 | 28 | 4 | 11 | 18 | .255 | .400 | .325 |
| April | 0-0 | 4.32 | 59 | 15 | 0 | 11 | 10 | .254 | .322 | .380 |
| May | 0-0 | 1.42 | 47 | 9 | 0 | 7 | 9 | .191 | .213 | .296 |
| June | 1-0 | 6.00 | 62 | 20 | 5 | 3 | 8 | .323 | .597 | .348 |
| July | 5-0 | 4.12 | 74 | 21 | 3 | 4 | 13 | .284 | .473 | .316 |
| August | 1-1 | 3.43 | 77 | 18 | 1 | 10 | 19 | .234 | .299 | .326 |
| Sept./Oct. | 0-0 | 5.11 | 54 | 18 | 1 | 2 | 10 | .333 | .426 | .357 |
| Leading Off Inn. | | | 81 | 20 | 3 | 8 | 20 | .247 | .395 | .322 |
| Runners On | | | 173 | 48 | 5 | 20 | 28 | .277 | .405 | .350 |
| Runners/Scor. Pos. | | | 96 | 29 | 3 | 14 | 18 | .302 | .417 | .381 |
| Runners On/2 Out | | | 76 | 23 | 2 | 10 | 9 | .303 | .408 | .384 |
| Scor. Pos./2 Out | | | 45 | 14 | 2 | 8 | 5 | .311 | .444 | .415 |
| Late Inning Pressure | | | 112 | 29 | 2 | 9 | 22 | .259 | .375 | .320 |
| Leading Off | | | 28 | 5 | 0 | 2 | 7 | .179 | .214 | .258 |
| Runners On | | | 46 | 12 | 1 | 6 | 9 | .261 | .348 | .346 |
| Runners/Scor. Pos. | | | 27 | 6 | 0 | 5 | 7 | .222 | .222 | .344 |
| First 9 Batters | | | 316 | 84 | 8 | 30 | 60 | .266 | .383 | .330 |
| Second 9 Batters | | | 53 | 15 | 2 | 6 | 9 | .283 | .453 | .356 |
| All Batters Thereafter | | | 4 | 2 | 0 | 1 | 0 | .500 | .500 | .600 |

Loves to face: Mike Marshall (0-for-7, 3 SO)
Hates to face: Paul O'Neill (3-for-3, 2 HR, 2 BB)
Ground outs-to-air outs ratio: 1.40 last season, 1.53 for career. . . . Additional statistics: 10 double-play ground outs in 83 opportunities, 14 doubles, 1 triple in 97.1 innings last season. . . . Opponents stole 11 bases in 13 attempts. Rafael Belliard was 0-for-2, non-Belliards were 11-for-11. . . . Led N.L. rookie pitchers with 59 appearances, fifth-highest total ever by a Giants rookie. Record: 71, set by Hoyt Wilhelm (1952), tied by Elias Sosa (1973). . . . Lost his only start, had a 7–0 record in relief. . . . Shared N.L. lead for wins in July with victories in five consecutive appearances. . . . Opponents' career breakdown: .264 with bases empty; .280 with runners on base; .295 with runners in scoring position.

## Tom Browning

Throws Left

| Cincinnati Reds | W–L | ERA | AB | H | HR | BB | SO | BA | SA | OBA |
|---|---|---|---|---|---|---|---|---|---|---|
| Season | 15-12 | 3.39 | 946 | 241 | 31 | 64 | 118 | .255 | .408 | .302 |
| vs. Left-Handers | | | 132 | 35 | 6 | 13 | 24 | .265 | .424 | .327 |
| vs. Right-Handers | | | 814 | 206 | 25 | 51 | 94 | .253 | .405 | .298 |
| Home | 7-8 | 4.14 | 491 | 138 | 19 | 32 | 52 | .281 | .452 | .326 |
| Road | 8-4 | 2.62 | 455 | 103 | 12 | 32 | 66 | .226 | .360 | .277 |
| Grass | 4-2 | 2.88 | 275 | 64 | 6 | 19 | 41 | .233 | .345 | .279 |
| Artificial Turf | 11-10 | 3.61 | 671 | 177 | 25 | 45 | 77 | .264 | .434 | .312 |
| April | 3-1 | 2.83 | 151 | 35 | 4 | 9 | 17 | .232 | .384 | .272 |
| May | 1-4 | 5.63 | 141 | 46 | 9 | 15 | 14 | .326 | .603 | .389 |
| June | 2-1 | 2.05 | 168 | 37 | 2 | 12 | 26 | .220 | .298 | .275 |
| July | 2-4 | 4.20 | 156 | 40 | 6 | 6 | 21 | .256 | .404 | .282 |
| August | 6-0 | 1.70 | 193 | 39 | 5 | 11 | 25 | .202 | .316 | .245 |
| Sept./Oct. | 1-2 | 5.50 | 137 | 44 | 5 | 11 | 15 | .321 | .504 | .377 |
| Leading Off Inn. | | | 248 | 68 | 14 | 12 | 28 | .274 | .492 | .313 |
| Runners On | | | 344 | 90 | 8 | 27 | 44 | .262 | .404 | .310 |
| Runners/Scor. Pos. | | | 171 | 44 | 2 | 22 | 17 | .257 | .351 | .332 |
| Runners On/2 Out | | | 147 | 32 | 1 | 12 | 19 | .218 | .313 | .277 |
| Scor. Pos./2 Out | | | 77 | 15 | 1 | 12 | 9 | .195 | .273 | .303 |
| Late Inning Pressure | | | 65 | 10 | 0 | 5 | 7 | .154 | .200 | .225 |
| Leading Off | | | 21 | 4 | 0 | 2 | 2 | .190 | .286 | .261 |
| Runners On | | | 19 | 4 | 0 | 2 | 2 | .211 | .263 | .286 |
| Runners/Scor. Pos. | | | 13 | 3 | 0 | 2 | 2 | .231 | .231 | .333 |
| First 9 Batters | | | 299 | 64 | 9 | 23 | 56 | .214 | .338 | .271 |
| Second 9 Batters | | | 309 | 92 | 15 | 19 | 31 | .298 | .515 | .338 |
| All Batters Thereafter | | | 338 | 85 | 7 | 22 | 31 | .251 | .373 | .298 |

Loves to face: Howard Johnson (.042, 1-for-24)
Hates to face: Glenn Davis (.360, 18-for-50, 5 2B, 6 HR)
Ground outs-to-air outs ratio: 0.60 last season, 0.65 for career. . . . Additional statistics: 18 double-play ground outs in 161 opportunities, 46 doubles, 3 triples in 249.2 innings last season. . . . Allowed 7 first-inning runs in 37 starts. . . . Batting support: 4.30 runs per start. . . . Allowed most HR in N.L. in each of last two seasons. Last pitcher to lead for three straight seasons: Ferguson Jenkins (1971–73). . . . Retired 25 consecutive leadoff batters, longest streak by a Reds pitcher during 1980s. . . . Opponents batted .203 in first inning, .263 thereafter. . . . Led majors with 181 starts over last five seasons. . . . Opponents' career average is .205 in Late-Inning Pressure Situations, .254 in other at-bats.

## Tim Burke

Throws Right

| Montreal Expos | W–L | ERA | AB | H | HR | BB | SO | BA | SA | OBA |
|---|---|---|---|---|---|---|---|---|---|---|
| Season | 9-3 | 2.55 | 302 | 68 | 6 | 22 | 54 | .225 | .325 | .274 |
| vs. Left-Handers | | | 159 | 38 | 5 | 12 | 23 | .239 | .371 | .287 |
| vs. Right-Handers | | | 143 | 30 | 1 | 10 | 31 | .210 | .273 | .258 |
| Home | 7-0 | 2.35 | 170 | 39 | 5 | 11 | 34 | .229 | .341 | .273 |
| Road | 2-3 | 2.79 | 132 | 29 | 1 | 11 | 20 | .220 | .303 | .274 |
| Grass | 1-2 | 1.96 | 60 | 13 | 0 | 5 | 11 | .217 | .267 | .273 |
| Artificial Turf | 8-1 | 2.71 | 242 | 55 | 6 | 17 | 43 | .227 | .339 | .274 |
| April | 1-1 | 4.26 | 47 | 12 | 1 | 8 | 10 | .255 | .362 | .357 |
| May | 3-0 | 2.81 | 59 | 18 | 1 | 3 | 10 | .305 | .424 | .328 |
| June | 1-0 | 1.02 | 61 | 12 | 1 | 2 | 11 | .197 | .311 | .215 |
| July | 0-0 | 2.35 | 57 | 12 | 1 | 2 | 8 | .211 | .281 | .237 |
| August | 2-1 | 1.80 | 51 | 9 | 1 | 3 | 8 | .176 | .255 | .222 |
| Sept./Oct. | 2-1 | 4.50 | 27 | 5 | 1 | 4 | 7 | .185 | .296 | .290 |
| Leading Off Inn. | | | 70 | 16 | 3 | 1 | 7 | .229 | .400 | .239 |
| Runners On | | | 131 | 30 | 1 | 14 | 29 | .229 | .305 | .293 |
| Runners/Scor. Pos. | | | 81 | 21 | 1 | 12 | 18 | .259 | .333 | .337 |
| Runners On/2 Out | | | 62 | 16 | 0 | 5 | 13 | .258 | .339 | .313 |
| Scor. Pos./2 Out | | | 42 | 14 | 0 | 4 | 10 | .333 | .405 | .391 |
| Late Inning Pressure | | | 207 | 45 | 3 | 13 | 34 | .217 | .300 | .262 |
| Leading Off | | | 46 | 11 | 3 | 0 | 6 | .239 | .478 | .239 |
| Runners On | | | 89 | 18 | 0 | 11 | 19 | .202 | .247 | .287 |
| Runners/Scor. Pos. | | | 59 | 12 | 0 | 11 | 14 | .203 | .220 | .324 |
| First 9 Batters | | | 299 | 68 | 6 | 22 | 53 | .227 | .328 | .276 |
| Second 9 Batters | | | 3 | 0 | 0 | 0 | 1 | .000 | .000 | .000 |
| All Batters Thereafter | | | 0 | 0 | 0 | 0 | 0 | — | — | — |

Loves to face: Garry Templeton (0-for-11)
Hates to face: Bobby Bonilla (.800, 4-for-5, 2 HR)
Ground outs-to-air outs ratio: 1.35 last season, 1.51 for career.... Additional statistics: 6 double-play ground outs in 65 opportunities, 10 doubles, 1 triple in 84.2 innings last season.... Has walked only one of 71 leadoff batters in each of last two seasons, and has faced 129 consecutive leadoff batters in LIP Situations without a walk.... Opponents have a lower average in LIPS than in other at-bats in each of the last six seasons. Shares longest current streak with Johns Franco and Candelaria.... Career average of .199 by opposing right-handed batters, .264 by lefties.... Career record of 6–6 in day games, 31–13 at night.... Career ERA of 2.48, lowest among active pitchers with 300 IP.

## Don Carman

Throws Left

| Philadelphia Phillies | W–L | ERA | AB | H | HR | BB | SO | BA | SA | OBA |
|---|---|---|---|---|---|---|---|---|---|---|
| Season | 5-15 | 5.24 | 584 | 152 | 21 | 86 | 81 | .260 | .442 | .355 |
| vs. Left-Handers | | | 108 | 24 | 6 | 9 | 14 | .222 | .435 | .294 |
| vs. Right-Handers | | | 476 | 128 | 15 | 77 | 67 | .269 | .443 | .369 |
| Home | 4-5 | 4.26 | 289 | 72 | 10 | 47 | 39 | .249 | .443 | .354 |
| Road | 1-10 | 6.26 | 295 | 80 | 11 | 39 | 42 | .271 | .441 | .357 |
| Grass | 1-7 | 8.33 | 170 | 53 | 9 | 23 | 24 | .312 | .529 | .393 |
| Artificial Turf | 4-8 | 4.12 | 414 | 99 | 12 | 63 | 57 | .239 | .406 | .340 |
| April | 1-3 | 4.45 | 115 | 32 | 9 | 11 | 13 | .278 | .557 | .339 |
| May | 0-5 | 6.31 | 138 | 35 | 4 | 21 | 18 | .254 | .413 | .354 |
| June | 1-2 | 3.26 | 71 | 14 | 0 | 12 | 6 | .197 | .310 | .321 |
| July | 1-1 | 4.96 | 68 | 20 | 3 | 6 | 11 | .294 | .471 | .351 |
| August | 1-4 | 5.91 | 121 | 32 | 4 | 23 | 16 | .264 | .455 | .384 |
| Sept./Oct. | 1-0 | 5.60 | 71 | 19 | 1 | 13 | 17 | .268 | .394 | .372 |
| Leading Off Inn. | | | 142 | 32 | 8 | 14 | 26 | .225 | .458 | .304 |
| Runners On | | | 241 | 62 | 5 | 51 | 31 | .257 | .382 | .380 |
| Runners/Scor. Pos. | | | 140 | 37 | 2 | 34 | 19 | .264 | .386 | .397 |
| Runners On/2 Out | | | 110 | 20 | 3 | 18 | 18 | .182 | .327 | .297 |
| Scor. Pos./2 Out | | | 67 | 11 | 1 | 14 | 11 | .164 | .269 | .309 |
| Late Inning Pressure | | | 79 | 16 | 1 | 14 | 8 | .203 | .304 | .337 |
| Leading Off | | | 22 | 2 | 1 | 2 | 2 | .091 | .273 | .200 |
| Runners On | | | 32 | 8 | 0 | 6 | 3 | .250 | .313 | .368 |
| Runners/Scor. Pos. | | | 16 | 4 | 0 | 4 | 2 | .250 | .313 | .400 |
| First 9 Batters | | | 283 | 72 | 6 | 49 | 37 | .254 | .406 | .366 |
| Second 9 Batters | | | 166 | 45 | 9 | 19 | 25 | .271 | .494 | .340 |
| All Batters Thereafter | | | 135 | 35 | 6 | 18 | 19 | .259 | .452 | .351 |

Loves to face: Otis Nixon (0-for-11)
Hates to face: Jose Lind (.533, 8-for-15, 1 HR)
Ground outs-to-air outs ratio: 0.67 last season, 0.58 for career.... Additional statistics: 6 double-play ground outs in 122 opportunities (lowest rate on Phils' staff), 35 doubles, 4 triples in 149.1 innings last season.... Allowed 11 first-inning runs in 20 starts.... Batting support: 3.35 runs per start.... Winning percentage year by year since 1985: .692, .667, .542, .417, .250. One more step down and he could join Gus Weyhing, Chick Fraser, Doc White, Three Finger Brown, Eppa Rixey, Jack Harshman, and Mickey Lolich as only pitchers to decline in five consecutive seasons of 15 or more decisions.... Career records: 29–20 at home, 18–30 on road; 17–26 before All-Star break, 30–24 thereafter.

## Cris Carpenter

Throws Right

| St. Louis Cardinals | W–L | ERA | AB | H | HR | BB | SO | BA | SA | OBA |
|---|---|---|---|---|---|---|---|---|---|---|
| Season | 4-4 | 3.18 | 267 | 70 | 4 | 26 | 35 | .262 | .393 | .328 |
| vs. Left-Handers | | | 137 | 38 | 1 | 17 | 14 | .277 | .372 | .357 |
| vs. Right-Handers | | | 130 | 32 | 3 | 9 | 21 | .246 | .415 | .297 |
| Home | 1-3 | 4.42 | 150 | 42 | 2 | 16 | 18 | .280 | .420 | .349 |
| Road | 3-1 | 1.72 | 117 | 28 | 2 | 10 | 17 | .239 | .359 | .300 |
| Grass | 2-0 | 2.12 | 61 | 13 | 2 | 6 | 11 | .213 | .344 | .279 |
| Artificial Turf | 2-4 | 3.53 | 206 | 57 | 2 | 20 | 24 | .277 | .408 | .342 |
| April | 1-1 | 1.59 | 66 | 16 | 0 | 3 | 3 | .242 | .333 | .282 |
| May | 0-3 | 3.44 | 75 | 20 | 1 | 9 | 12 | .267 | .400 | .337 |
| June | 1-0 | 6.43 | 56 | 16 | 2 | 12 | 8 | .286 | .500 | .420 |
| July | | | 0 | 0 | 0 | 0 | 0 | — | — | — |
| August | | | 0 | 0 | 0 | 0 | 0 | — | — | — |
| Sept./Oct. | 2-0 | 1.93 | 70 | 18 | 1 | 2 | 12 | .257 | .357 | .274 |
| Leading Off Inn. | | | 65 | 16 | 0 | 5 | 10 | .246 | .338 | .300 |
| Runners On | | | 115 | 30 | 3 | 15 | 11 | .261 | .443 | .346 |
| Runners/Scor. Pos. | | | 76 | 19 | 1 | 13 | 9 | .250 | .421 | .351 |
| Runners On/2 Out | | | 54 | 13 | 1 | 6 | 3 | .241 | .389 | .317 |
| Scor. Pos./2 Out | | | 37 | 9 | 0 | 5 | 3 | .243 | .378 | .333 |
| Late Inning Pressure | | | 66 | 15 | 0 | 10 | 9 | .227 | .333 | .316 |
| Leading Off | | | 20 | 3 | 0 | 1 | 2 | .150 | .250 | .190 |
| Runners On | | | 18 | 4 | 0 | 7 | 2 | .222 | .389 | .393 |
| Runners/Scor. Pos. | | | 13 | 4 | 0 | 7 | 2 | .308 | .538 | .478 |
| First 9 Batters | | | 188 | 47 | 2 | 21 | 29 | .250 | .388 | .324 |
| Second 9 Batters | | | 55 | 15 | 2 | 2 | 5 | .273 | .418 | .293 |
| All Batters Thereafter | | | 24 | 8 | 0 | 3 | 1 | .333 | .375 | .429 |

Loves to face: Von Hayes (.111, 1-for-9, 3 SO)
Hates to face: Darryl Strawberry (2-for-2, 2 HR)
Ground outs-to-air outs ratio: 0.87 last season, 0.91 for career.... Additional statistics: 2 double-play ground outs in 49 opportunities (worst rate on Cardinals' staff), 15 doubles, 4 triples in 68.0 innings last season.... Entered while the Cardinals held a lead in only one of his last 19 relief appearances. Faced only 10 batters while protecting leads of three runs or fewer in 7th inning or later.... Allowed 10 of 17 inherited runners to score.... Opponents have a career average of .260 in his first pass through the batting order, .294 in his second time through, and .305 after that.... Career average of .309 by opposing left-handers, .246 by right-handers; .307 at Busch Stadium, .248 on the road.

## Norm Charlton

Throws Left

| Cincinnati Reds | W–L | ERA | AB | H | HR | BB | SO | BA | SA | OBA |
|---|---|---|---|---|---|---|---|---|---|---|
| Season | 8-3 | 2.93 | 340 | 67 | 5 | 40 | 98 | .197 | .288 | .284 |
| vs. Left-Handers | | | 81 | 12 | 0 | 11 | 27 | .148 | .173 | .258 |
| vs. Right-Handers | | | 259 | 55 | 5 | 29 | 71 | .212 | .324 | .292 |
| Home | 2-1 | 2.93 | 164 | 27 | 3 | 20 | 45 | .165 | .268 | .259 |
| Road | 6-2 | 2.92 | 176 | 40 | 2 | 20 | 53 | .227 | .307 | .307 |
| Grass | 6-2 | 2.29 | 120 | 23 | 2 | 12 | 36 | .192 | .292 | .263 |
| Artificial Turf | 2-1 | 3.30 | 220 | 44 | 3 | 28 | 62 | .200 | .286 | .295 |
| April | 1-0 | 1.86 | 33 | 5 | 0 | 4 | 6 | .152 | .212 | .237 |
| May | 1-0 | 2.77 | 44 | 7 | 0 | 5 | 11 | .159 | .182 | .275 |
| June | 1-0 | 4.42 | 64 | 12 | 1 | 9 | 14 | .188 | .297 | .288 |
| July | 1-1 | 3.63 | 64 | 17 | 1 | 7 | 13 | .266 | .406 | .333 |
| August | 2-0 | 3.21 | 50 | 9 | 3 | 8 | 20 | .180 | .400 | .293 |
| Sept./Oct. | 2-2 | 1.57 | 85 | 17 | 0 | 7 | 34 | .200 | .212 | .261 |
| Leading Off Inn. | | | 86 | 23 | 1 | 12 | 26 | .267 | .372 | .364 |
| Runners On | | | 138 | 30 | 3 | 13 | 34 | .217 | .312 | .286 |
| Runners/Scor. Pos. | | | 75 | 15 | 2 | 11 | 21 | .200 | .307 | .295 |
| Runners On/2 Out | | | 61 | 11 | 2 | 5 | 18 | .180 | .295 | .242 |
| Scor. Pos./2 Out | | | 42 | 6 | 1 | 4 | 14 | .143 | .214 | .217 |
| Late Inning Pressure | | | 190 | 35 | 1 | 23 | 55 | .184 | .253 | .273 |
| Leading Off | | | 52 | 14 | 0 | 8 | 15 | .269 | .365 | .377 |
| Runners On | | | 73 | 12 | 1 | 7 | 16 | .164 | .219 | .232 |
| Runners/Scor. Pos. | | | 40 | 6 | 1 | 6 | 11 | .150 | .225 | .250 |
| First 9 Batters | | | 318 | 64 | 5 | 39 | 87 | .201 | .292 | .291 |
| Second 9 Batters | | | 22 | 3 | 0 | 1 | 11 | .136 | .227 | .174 |
| All Batters Thereafter | | | 0 | 0 | 0 | 0 | 0 | — | — | — |

Loves to face: Kevin Bass (0-for-9)
Hates to face: Jose Lind (.400, 4-for-10)
Ground outs-to-air outs ratio: 1.65 last season, 1.25 for career.... Additional statistics: 2 double-play ground outs in 73 opportunities, 10 doubles, 3 triples in 95.1 innings last season.... Fanned nine consecutive right-handed batters, 3d-longest streak of the last 15 years.... Set record for relief appearances in a season without a save (69). Previous record: 60, by Ed Vande Berg (1986) and Jeff Dedmon (1985). Frank DiPino (68) and Paul Assenmacher (63) also topped 60 mark in 1989.... Honorable mention to Jim Dickson, who made 68 saveless appearances for the Athletics in 1965, four years before saves gained "official" status.... See Ricky Horton comments for a related "achievement."

## Jim Clancy

Throws Right

| Houston Astros | W–L | ERA | AB | H | HR | BB | SO | BA | SA | OBA |
|---|---|---|---|---|---|---|---|---|---|---|
| Season | 7-14 | 5.08 | 576 | 155 | 13 | 66 | 91 | .269 | .422 | .342 |
| vs. Left-Handers | | | 313 | 91 | 10 | 45 | 49 | .291 | .460 | .377 |
| vs. Right-Handers | | | 263 | 64 | 3 | 21 | 42 | .243 | .376 | .298 |
| Home | 4-5 | 5.66 | 252 | 72 | 5 | 24 | 38 | .286 | .456 | .345 |
| Road | 3-9 | 4.66 | 324 | 83 | 8 | 42 | 53 | .256 | .395 | .340 |
| Grass | 2-6 | 3.20 | 214 | 46 | 6 | 20 | 34 | .215 | .341 | .280 |
| Artificial Turf | 5-8 | 6.34 | 362 | 109 | 7 | 46 | 57 | .301 | .470 | .378 |
| April | 1-1 | 2.66 | 87 | 16 | 2 | 8 | 19 | .184 | .310 | .250 |
| May | 1-3 | 6.75 | 118 | 38 | 2 | 14 | 20 | .322 | .492 | .394 |
| June | 3-1 | 1.45 | 109 | 23 | 1 | 12 | 16 | .211 | .321 | .289 |
| July | 0-3 | 7.71 | 88 | 28 | 3 | 10 | 13 | .318 | .511 | .384 |
| August | 1-3 | 7.62 | 111 | 34 | 2 | 12 | 16 | .306 | .459 | .368 |
| Sept./Oct. | 1-3 | 5.19 | 63 | 16 | 3 | 10 | 7 | .254 | .429 | .356 |
| Leading Off Inn. | | | 139 | 41 | 3 | 16 | 23 | .295 | .432 | .368 |
| Runners On | | | 255 | 74 | 5 | 37 | 38 | .290 | .451 | .375 |
| Runners/Scor. Pos. | | | 150 | 49 | 3 | 34 | 27 | .327 | .520 | .441 |
| Runners On/2 Out | | | 87 | 17 | 2 | 20 | 16 | .195 | .322 | .346 |
| Scor. Pos./2 Out | | | 55 | 11 | 1 | 18 | 11 | .200 | .345 | .397 |
| Late Inning Pressure | | | 46 | 8 | 2 | 4 | 6 | .174 | .304 | .240 |
| Leading Off | | | 13 | 2 | 1 | 2 | 2 | .154 | .385 | .267 |
| Runners On | | | 11 | 3 | 0 | 1 | 2 | .273 | .273 | .333 |
| Runners/Scor. Pos. | | | 7 | 0 | 0 | 1 | 1 | .000 | .000 | .125 |
| First 9 Batters | | | 237 | 58 | 5 | 30 | 45 | .245 | .397 | .327 |
| Second 9 Batters | | | 179 | 61 | 4 | 20 | 21 | .341 | .531 | .407 |
| All Batters Thereafter | | | 160 | 36 | 4 | 16 | 25 | .225 | .338 | .292 |

Loves to face: Benito Santiago (0-for-13)
Hates to face: Tom Foley (5-for-5, 2 2B, 1 HR)
Ground outs-to-air outs ratio: 1.07 last season, 1.05 for career. . . . Additional statistics: 13 double-play ground outs in 113 opportunities, 37 doubles, 6 triples in 147.0 innings last season. . . . Allowed 19 first-inning runs in 26 starts. . . . Batting support: 3.23 runs per start. . . . Led N.L. in ERA during June. . . . Opponents stole 14 bases in 16 attempts. . . . Had a 7–7 record in night games, 0–7 in day games. . . . Astros lost 15 of the last 18 games in which he appeared (including five in relief). . . . Completed only one of his 26 starts. . . . Averaged more than four walks per nine innings for the first time since 1981. . . . Had only one balk in 2206 innings in A.L., three in his first N.L. season.

## Marty Clary

Throws Right

| Atlanta Braves | W–L | ERA | AB | H | HR | BB | SO | BA | SA | OBA |
|---|---|---|---|---|---|---|---|---|---|---|
| Season | 4-3 | 3.15 | 412 | 103 | 6 | 31 | 30 | .250 | .352 | .302 |
| vs. Left-Handers | | | 255 | 61 | 3 | 20 | 17 | .239 | .333 | .293 |
| vs. Right-Handers | | | 157 | 42 | 3 | 11 | 13 | .268 | .382 | .316 |
| Home | 3-1 | 3.27 | 217 | 57 | 1 | 16 | 13 | .263 | .346 | .311 |
| Road | 1-2 | 3.02 | 195 | 46 | 5 | 15 | 17 | .236 | .359 | .292 |
| Grass | 3-3 | 3.51 | 330 | 90 | 4 | 25 | 24 | .273 | .373 | .323 |
| Artificial Turf | 1-0 | 1.88 | 82 | 13 | 2 | 6 | 6 | .159 | .268 | .216 |
| April | | | 0 | 0 | 0 | 0 | 0 | — | — | — |
| May | | | 0 | 0 | 0 | 0 | 0 | — | — | — |
| June | 1-0 | 2.79 | 32 | 5 | 2 | 2 | 1 | .156 | .375 | .206 |
| July | 2-1 | 4.76 | 113 | 32 | 1 | 8 | 8 | .283 | .381 | .331 |
| August | 1-1 | 1.21 | 161 | 34 | 1 | 8 | 15 | .211 | .280 | .249 |
| Sept./Oct. | 0-1 | 4.85 | 106 | 32 | 2 | 13 | 6 | .302 | .425 | .375 |
| Leading Off Inn. | | | 105 | 25 | 0 | 7 | 6 | .238 | .333 | .286 |
| Runners On | | | 169 | 43 | 4 | 10 | 10 | .254 | .361 | .295 |
| Runners/Scor. Pos. | | | 100 | 17 | 2 | 7 | 7 | .170 | .260 | .225 |
| Runners On/2 Out | | | 70 | 15 | 1 | 2 | 3 | .214 | .271 | .247 |
| Scor. Pos./2 Out | | | 48 | 5 | 1 | 1 | 3 | .104 | .188 | .140 |
| Late Inning Pressure | | | 36 | 9 | 0 | 6 | 2 | .250 | .306 | .349 |
| Leading Off | | | 11 | 3 | 0 | 2 | 1 | .273 | .364 | .385 |
| Runners On | | | 12 | 4 | 0 | 1 | 1 | .333 | .417 | .357 |
| Runners/Scor. Pos. | | | 5 | 1 | 0 | 1 | 1 | .200 | .200 | .286 |
| First 9 Batters | | | 142 | 35 | 3 | 13 | 11 | .246 | .352 | .312 |
| Second 9 Batters | | | 141 | 33 | 3 | 10 | 12 | .234 | .355 | .285 |
| All Batters Thereafter | | | 129 | 35 | 0 | 8 | 7 | .271 | .349 | .309 |

Loves to face: Todd Benzinger (.091, 1-for-11, 1 HR)
Hates to face: Kevin Mitchell (.462, 6-for-13, 2 HR)
Ground outs-to-air outs ratio: 1.12 last season, 1.14 for career. . . . Additional statistics: 8 double-play ground outs in 78 opportunities, 22 doubles, 1 triple in 108.2 innings last season. . . . Allowed 15 first-inning runs in 17 starts. . . . Batting support: 3.65 runs per start. . . . Struck out 2.48 batters per nine innings, lowest rate in N.L. . . . Led majors in ERA during August. . . . Won three of first four starts, only one of 13 thereafter. . . . Opponents stole only five bases in 15 attempts (.333), lowest average in N.L. (minimum: 15 attempts). . . . Braves had a 2–8 record in his no-decision starts. . . . A potential spokesman for Greyhound. He pitched 989 innings in his minor league career.

## David Cone

Throws Right

| New York Mets | W–L | ERA | AB | H | HR | BB | SO | BA | SA | OBA |
|---|---|---|---|---|---|---|---|---|---|---|
| Season | 14-8 | 3.52 | 822 | 183 | 20 | 74 | 190 | .223 | .359 | .289 |
| vs. Left-Handers | | | 449 | 105 | 9 | 47 | 73 | .234 | .379 | .309 |
| vs. Right-Handers | | | 373 | 78 | 11 | 27 | 117 | .209 | .335 | .263 |
| Home | 8-2 | 2.61 | 416 | 84 | 12 | 33 | 112 | .202 | .325 | .264 |
| Road | 6-6 | 4.50 | 406 | 99 | 8 | 41 | 78 | .244 | .394 | .313 |
| Grass | 9-5 | 3.26 | 544 | 115 | 15 | 46 | 138 | .211 | .338 | .276 |
| Artificial Turf | 5-3 | 4.05 | 278 | 68 | 5 | 28 | 52 | .245 | .399 | .313 |
| April | 2-2 | 3.74 | 127 | 31 | 2 | 13 | 21 | .244 | .362 | .313 |
| May | 1-2 | 3.21 | 120 | 27 | 3 | 13 | 37 | .225 | .350 | .301 |
| June | 1-1 | 6.66 | 98 | 26 | 3 | 11 | 17 | .265 | .531 | .345 |
| July | 4-0 | 2.89 | 159 | 32 | 5 | 14 | 36 | .201 | .321 | .269 |
| August | 4-1 | 2.56 | 166 | 33 | 4 | 12 | 39 | .199 | .319 | .253 |
| Sept./Oct. | 2-2 | 3.49 | 152 | 34 | 3 | 11 | 40 | .224 | .336 | .280 |
| Leading Off Inn. | | | 214 | 45 | 3 | 12 | 44 | .210 | .299 | .256 |
| Runners On | | | 306 | 72 | 8 | 34 | 69 | .235 | .382 | .312 |
| Runners/Scor. Pos. | | | 178 | 42 | 4 | 27 | 48 | .236 | .399 | .336 |
| Runners On/2 Out | | | 131 | 28 | 2 | 22 | 32 | .214 | .298 | .331 |
| Scor. Pos./2 Out | | | 82 | 18 | 1 | 17 | 26 | .220 | .305 | .360 |
| Late Inning Pressure | | | 90 | 23 | 1 | 7 | 23 | .256 | .311 | .306 |
| Leading Off | | | 26 | 5 | 0 | 0 | 8 | .192 | .192 | .192 |
| Runners On | | | 31 | 7 | 0 | 4 | 8 | .226 | .226 | .306 |
| Runners/Scor. Pos. | | | 16 | 3 | 0 | 3 | 5 | .188 | .188 | .300 |
| First 9 Batters | | | 276 | 62 | 6 | 21 | 64 | .225 | .355 | .281 |
| Second 9 Batters | | | 255 | 56 | 8 | 22 | 70 | .220 | .380 | .281 |
| All Batters Thereafter | | | 291 | 65 | 6 | 31 | 56 | .223 | .344 | .303 |

Loves to face: Barry Larkin (.071, 1-for-14)
Hates to face: Milt Thompson (.571, 12-for-21, 1 HR, 5 BB)
Ground outs-to-air outs ratio: 0.77 last season, 0.84 for career. . . . Additional statistics: 6 double-play ground outs in 118 opportunities, 30 doubles, 11 triples in 219.2 innings last season. . . . Allowed 19 first-inning runs in 33 starts. . . . Batting support: 4.55 runs per start. . . . Led N.L. pitchers with 18 hits. . . . Had 4.50 ERA over first three innings of his starts, 2.79 thereafter. . . . Eight-game winning streak was longest on Mets. . . . Career average of .250 by opposing left-handers, .198 by right-handers. . . . Career record of 21–6 at Shea Stadium, 18–11 on road. . . . Record of 34–11 (.756) represents best winning percentage in majors over last two seasons (minimum: 20 wins).

## Dennis Cook

Throws Left

| Giants/Phillies | W–L | ERA | AB | H | HR | BB | SO | BA | SA | OBA |
|---|---|---|---|---|---|---|---|---|---|---|
| Season | 7-8 | 3.72 | 452 | 110 | 18 | 38 | 67 | .243 | .425 | .304 |
| vs. Left-Handers | | | 63 | 13 | 4 | 8 | 12 | .206 | .429 | .311 |
| vs. Right-Handers | | | 389 | 97 | 14 | 30 | 55 | .249 | .424 | .302 |
| Home | 5-3 | 2.54 | 252 | 48 | 9 | 25 | 40 | .190 | .345 | .269 |
| Road | 2-5 | 5.40 | 200 | 62 | 9 | 13 | 27 | .310 | .525 | .349 |
| Grass | 1-3 | 4.79 | 84 | 26 | 4 | 5 | 10 | .310 | .548 | .348 |
| Artificial Turf | 6-5 | 3.50 | 368 | 84 | 14 | 33 | 57 | .228 | .397 | .294 |
| April | | | 0 | 0 | 0 | 0 | 0 | — | — | — |
| May | | | 0 | 0 | 0 | 0 | 0 | — | — | — |
| June | 3-0 | 1.80 | 103 | 20 | 2 | 10 | 18 | .194 | .311 | .263 |
| July | 2-3 | 3.86 | 150 | 38 | 9 | 11 | 24 | .253 | .493 | .302 |
| August | 0-3 | 6.08 | 97 | 30 | 6 | 11 | 10 | .309 | .577 | .391 |
| Sept./Oct. | 2-2 | 3.58 | 102 | 22 | 1 | 6 | 15 | .216 | .294 | .259 |
| Leading Off Inn. | | | 116 | 29 | 3 | 8 | 17 | .250 | .397 | .310 |
| Runners On | | | 149 | 42 | 7 | 19 | 21 | .282 | .490 | .359 |
| Runners/Scor. Pos. | | | 91 | 27 | 4 | 10 | 13 | .297 | .505 | .359 |
| Runners On/2 Out | | | 57 | 11 | 2 | 10 | 10 | .193 | .333 | .313 |
| Scor. Pos./2 Out | | | 38 | 9 | 2 | 7 | 5 | .237 | .447 | .356 |
| Late Inning Pressure | | | 35 | 6 | 1 | 4 | 6 | .171 | .257 | .256 |
| Leading Off | | | 10 | 1 | 0 | 2 | 1 | .100 | .100 | .250 |
| Runners On | | | 5 | 1 | 0 | 1 | 0 | .200 | .200 | .333 |
| Runners/Scor. Pos. | | | 4 | 1 | 0 | 0 | 0 | .250 | .250 | .250 |
| First 9 Batters | | | 180 | 37 | 6 | 15 | 32 | .206 | .367 | .267 |
| Second 9 Batters | | | 145 | 36 | 5 | 9 | 17 | .248 | .434 | .295 |
| All Batters Thereafter | | | 127 | 37 | 7 | 14 | 18 | .291 | .496 | .364 |

Loves to face: Jeff Blauser (.125, 1-for-8)
Hates to face: Lonnie Smith (.667, 6-for-9, 3 HR)
Ground outs-to-air outs ratio: 0.71 last season, 0.68 for career. . . . Additional statistics: 6 double-play ground outs in 69 opportunities, 22 doubles, 3 triples in 121.0 innings last season. . . . Allowed 6 first-inning runs in 18 starts. . . . Batting support: 4.06 runs per start. . . . Allowed one home run per 6.7 innings pitched, worst rate in N.L. . . . June ERA was 2d lowest in the N.L. . . . Allowed hits to seven consecutive right-handed batters, longest streak by a Phillies pitcher since Randy Lerch in 1979. . . . Turned 27 right after season ended. Over past 50 years, only one rookie that old has accumulated 150 career wins: Allie Reynolds. Dazzy Vance, a 31-year-old rookie in 1922, won 197 games.

## Ron Darling

Throws Right

| New York Mets | W–L | ERA | AB | H | HR | BB | SO | BA | SA | OBA |
|---|---|---|---|---|---|---|---|---|---|---|
| Season | 14-14 | 3.52 | 829 | 214 | 19 | 70 | 153 | .258 | .385 | .314 |
| vs. Left-Handers | | | 481 | 136 | 9 | 41 | 79 | .283 | .407 | .338 |
| vs. Right-Handers | | | 348 | 78 | 10 | 29 | 74 | .224 | .353 | .281 |
| Home | 8-6 | 3.04 | 453 | 113 | 11 | 30 | 80 | .249 | .373 | .296 |
| Road | 6-8 | 4.13 | 376 | 101 | 8 | 40 | 73 | .269 | .399 | .334 |
| Grass | 10-9 | 3.20 | 608 | 153 | 16 | 42 | 118 | .252 | .387 | .299 |
| Artificial Turf | 4-5 | 4.42 | 221 | 61 | 3 | 28 | 35 | .276 | .380 | .352 |
| April | 1-3 | 5.96 | 101 | 28 | 4 | 15 | 12 | .277 | .446 | .371 |
| May | 2-1 | 2.67 | 126 | 31 | 3 | 10 | 35 | .246 | .389 | .304 |
| June | 3-1 | 4.19 | 145 | 35 | 4 | 13 | 27 | .241 | .386 | .301 |
| July | 2-4 | 3.95 | 157 | 46 | 2 | 15 | 24 | .293 | .382 | .345 |
| August | 4-1 | 2.33 | 147 | 37 | 4 | 5 | 26 | .252 | .415 | .277 |
| Sept./Oct. | 2-4 | 2.72 | 153 | 37 | 2 | 12 | 29 | .242 | .314 | .295 |
| Leading Off Inn. | | | 216 | 48 | 2 | 8 | 38 | .222 | .306 | .253 |
| Runners On | | | 322 | 90 | 9 | 36 | 66 | .280 | .419 | .341 |
| Runners/Scor. Pos. | | | 201 | 50 | 5 | 29 | 50 | .249 | .368 | .328 |
| Runners On/2 Out | | | 133 | 31 | 6 | 21 | 32 | .233 | .429 | .342 |
| Scor. Pos./2 Out | | | 99 | 20 | 4 | 16 | 27 | .202 | .384 | .319 |
| Late Inning Pressure | | | 71 | 17 | 2 | 2 | 10 | .239 | .366 | .267 |
| Leading Off | | | 22 | 7 | 0 | 0 | 3 | .318 | .409 | .348 |
| Runners On | | | 21 | 5 | 1 | 1 | 3 | .238 | .381 | .261 |
| Runners/Scor. Pos. | | | 12 | 2 | 1 | 1 | 3 | .167 | .417 | .214 |
| First 9 Batters | | | 258 | 60 | 6 | 31 | 48 | .233 | .364 | .308 |
| Second 9 Batters | | | 260 | 72 | 3 | 20 | 50 | .277 | .369 | .330 |
| All Batters Thereafter | | | 311 | 82 | 10 | 19 | 55 | .264 | .415 | .305 |

Loves to face: Mark Grace (.083, 1-for-12)
Hates to face: Tony Gwynn (.500, 24-for-48)
Ground outs-to-air outs ratio: 0.89 last season, 1.06 for career. . . . Additional statistics: 10 double-play ground outs in 147 opportunities, 40 doubles, 4 triples in 217.1 innings last season. . . . Allowed 18 first-inning runs in 33 starts. . . . Batting support: 3.91 runs per start. . . . Didn't walk a batter after the 7th inning (faced 62 batters). . . . Only N.L. pitcher to toss 200 innings in each of the last six seasons. . . . Did those critical of his many no-decisions in the past notice 28 decisions in 33 starts last season, including one in each of his last 19? And by the way, does that make him a better or worse pitcher? . . . Career record of 52–23 (2.88 ERA) at Shea Stadium, 35–32 (3.95) elsewhere.

## Danny Darwin

Throws Right

| Houston Astros | W–L | ERA | AB | H | HR | BB | SO | BA | SA | OBA |
|---|---|---|---|---|---|---|---|---|---|---|
| Season | 11-4 | 2.36 | 434 | 92 | 8 | 33 | 104 | .212 | .302 | .268 |
| vs. Left-Handers | | | 240 | 59 | 3 | 17 | 45 | .246 | .329 | .295 |
| vs. Right-Handers | | | 194 | 33 | 5 | 16 | 59 | .170 | .268 | .236 |
| Home | 7-0 | 1.98 | 249 | 45 | 1 | 21 | 61 | .181 | .221 | .248 |
| Road | 4-4 | 2.92 | 185 | 47 | 7 | 12 | 43 | .254 | .411 | .295 |
| Grass | 2-2 | 2.40 | 113 | 27 | 5 | 4 | 28 | .239 | .398 | .265 |
| Artificial Turf | 9-2 | 2.35 | 321 | 65 | 3 | 29 | 76 | .202 | .268 | .269 |
| April | 2-1 | 1.85 | 85 | 17 | 0 | 8 | 20 | .200 | .212 | .266 |
| May | 2-0 | 2.61 | 76 | 19 | 2 | 11 | 14 | .250 | .382 | .352 |
| June | 3-1 | 2.84 | 72 | 18 | 1 | 4 | 21 | .250 | .361 | .299 |
| July | 3-0 | 1.52 | 84 | 18 | 0 | 4 | 24 | .214 | .226 | .247 |
| August | 1-1 | 2.89 | 64 | 10 | 3 | 3 | 16 | .156 | .297 | .194 |
| Sept./Oct. | 0-1 | 2.87 | 53 | 10 | 2 | 3 | 9 | .189 | .377 | .220 |
| Leading Off Inn. | | | 99 | 22 | 1 | 6 | 25 | .222 | .273 | .267 |
| Runners On | | | 193 | 41 | 3 | 17 | 49 | .212 | .290 | .270 |
| Runners/Scor. Pos. | | | 117 | 28 | 1 | 14 | 32 | .239 | .308 | .309 |
| Runners On/2 Out | | | 86 | 17 | 1 | 7 | 25 | .198 | .291 | .258 |
| Scor. Pos./2 Out | | | 58 | 13 | 0 | 5 | 18 | .224 | .310 | .286 |
| Late Inning Pressure | | | 270 | 55 | 5 | 21 | 62 | .204 | .285 | .260 |
| Leading Off | | | 67 | 14 | 1 | 5 | 19 | .209 | .284 | .264 |
| Runners On | | | 106 | 21 | 2 | 9 | 24 | .198 | .255 | .252 |
| Runners/Scor. Pos. | | | 56 | 13 | 0 | 8 | 15 | .232 | .232 | .309 |
| First 9 Batters | | | 404 | 83 | 6 | 28 | 101 | .205 | .280 | .256 |
| Second 9 Batters | | | 30 | 9 | 2 | 5 | 3 | .300 | .600 | .417 |
| All Batters Thereafter | | | 0 | 0 | 0 | 0 | 0 | — | — | — |

Loves to face: R. J. Reynolds (0-for-15, 7 SO)
Hates to face: Kal Daniels (.526, 10-for-19, 3 HR)
Ground outs-to-air outs ratio: 0.43 last season, 0.85 for career. . . . Additional statistics: 4 double-play ground outs in 94 opportunities, 9 doubles, 3 triples in 122.0 innings last season. . . . Nine of his 11 relief wins were legit, blowing leads to pick up a victory only twice. . . . One of two pitchers to win at least eight games in each season during the 1980s. The other: Nolan Ryan. . . . One of five active pitchers with 100 career victories and a losing record. Others: Bob Knepper, Jim Clancy, Floyd Bannister, Shane Rawley. . . . Opponents' average has been higher with runners on base than with the bases empty in each of his 12 seasons in the majors. Career breakdown: .274 with runners on, .229 with bases empty.

## Mark Davis

Throws Left

| San Diego Padres | W–L | ERA | AB | H | HR | BB | SO | BA | SA | OBA |
|---|---|---|---|---|---|---|---|---|---|---|
| Season | 4-3 | 1.85 | 330 | 66 | 6 | 31 | 92 | .200 | .294 | .270 |
| vs. Left-Handers | | | 46 | 11 | 2 | 4 | 11 | .239 | .457 | .321 |
| vs. Right-Handers | | | 284 | 55 | 4 | 27 | 81 | .194 | .268 | .261 |
| Home | 2-0 | 1.17 | 164 | 29 | 2 | 16 | 48 | .177 | .244 | .253 |
| Road | 2-3 | 2.51 | 166 | 37 | 4 | 15 | 44 | .223 | .343 | .286 |
| Grass | 3-1 | 1.57 | 248 | 50 | 5 | 18 | 70 | .202 | .298 | .259 |
| Artificial Turf | 1-2 | 2.66 | 82 | 16 | 1 | 13 | 22 | .195 | .280 | .299 |
| April | 0-0 | 2.08 | 61 | 13 | 3 | 5 | 17 | .213 | .426 | .284 |
| May | 2-0 | 2.13 | 50 | 15 | 0 | 6 | 15 | .300 | .320 | .375 |
| June | 0-3 | 4.50 | 43 | 9 | 2 | 6 | 15 | .209 | .419 | .294 |
| July | 0-0 | 0.00 | 30 | 3 | 0 | 5 | 9 | .100 | .133 | .222 |
| August | 1-0 | 1.86 | 71 | 13 | 1 | 4 | 16 | .183 | .282 | .234 |
| Sept./Oct. | 1-0 | 0.86 | 75 | 13 | 0 | 5 | 20 | .173 | .173 | .225 |
| Leading Off Inn. | | | 58 | 16 | 3 | 7 | 14 | .276 | .448 | .364 |
| Runners On | | | 190 | 33 | 3 | 20 | 58 | .174 | .263 | .248 |
| Runners/Scor. Pos. | | | 106 | 13 | 1 | 18 | 39 | .123 | .189 | .242 |
| Runners On/2 Out | | | 88 | 16 | 1 | 12 | 27 | .182 | .250 | .280 |
| Scor. Pos./2 Out | | | 53 | 5 | 0 | 12 | 19 | .094 | .094 | .262 |
| Late Inning Pressure | | | 233 | 44 | 5 | 18 | 64 | .189 | .283 | .250 |
| Leading Off | | | 38 | 9 | 2 | 3 | 8 | .237 | .395 | .310 |
| Runners On | | | 138 | 23 | 3 | 11 | 43 | .167 | .268 | .224 |
| Runners/Scor. Pos. | | | 76 | 8 | 1 | 11 | 30 | .105 | .171 | .211 |
| First 9 Batters | | | 312 | 63 | 6 | 29 | 90 | .202 | .301 | .271 |
| Second 9 Batters | | | 18 | 3 | 0 | 2 | 2 | .167 | .167 | .250 |
| All Batters Thereafter | | | 0 | 0 | 0 | 0 | 0 | — | — | — |

Loves to face: Brad Komminsk (.182, 2-for-11)
Hates to face: Keith Hernandez (.324, 11-for-34, 1 HR, 5 BB)
Ground outs-to-air outs ratio: 1.25 last season, 1.02 for career. . . . Additional statistics: 12 double-play ground outs in 88 opportunities, 9 doubles, 2 triples in 92.2 innings last season. . . . Saved 25 games in his last 26 opportunities. . . . Ended the season with a streak of 101 opponents faced without an extra-base hit. Ended 1988 with 158 BFP without an XBH. . . . Opponents' batting average with runners on base, year by year since 1984: .298, .278, .250, .247, .207, .174. . . . Opponents' BA with runners in scoring position was the lowest over the last 15 years (minimum: 125 BFP). . . . Career winning percentage (.381) is 2d lowest among active pitchers with 100 decisions. Lowest: Mike Morgan (.347).

## Ken Dayley

Throws Left

| St. Louis Cardinals | W–L | ERA | AB | H | HR | BB | SO | BA | SA | OBA |
|---|---|---|---|---|---|---|---|---|---|---|
| Season | 4-3 | 2.87 | 276 | 63 | 3 | 30 | 40 | .228 | .333 | .303 |
| vs. Left-Handers | | | 101 | 19 | 1 | 8 | 15 | .188 | .287 | .248 |
| vs. Right-Handers | | | 175 | 44 | 2 | 22 | 25 | .251 | .360 | .333 |
| Home | 2-1 | 3.65 | 142 | 37 | 1 | 14 | 21 | .261 | .380 | .327 |
| Road | 2-2 | 2.11 | 134 | 26 | 2 | 16 | 19 | .194 | .284 | .278 |
| Grass | 1-2 | 1.40 | 67 | 13 | 0 | 9 | 6 | .194 | .239 | .286 |
| Artificial Turf | 3-1 | 3.38 | 209 | 50 | 3 | 21 | 34 | .239 | .364 | .309 |
| April | 0-0 | 3.24 | 33 | 9 | 1 | 4 | 3 | .273 | .515 | .351 |
| May | 3-1 | 2.25 | 61 | 18 | 0 | 4 | 7 | .295 | .377 | .338 |
| June | 0-0 | 4.61 | 55 | 14 | 1 | 2 | 10 | .255 | .327 | .281 |
| July | 0-0 | 0.71 | 41 | 2 | 0 | 4 | 6 | .049 | .049 | .133 |
| August | 0-0 | 0.82 | 39 | 8 | 1 | 3 | 6 | .205 | .359 | .256 |
| Sept./Oct. | 1-2 | 5.27 | 47 | 12 | 0 | 13 | 8 | .255 | .383 | .417 |
| Leading Off Inn. | | | 56 | 9 | 0 | 6 | 11 | .161 | .196 | .242 |
| Runners On | | | 138 | 30 | 1 | 17 | 20 | .217 | .304 | .301 |
| Runners/Scor. Pos. | | | 74 | 17 | 1 | 14 | 13 | .230 | .338 | .348 |
| Runners On/2 Out | | | 61 | 12 | 0 | 8 | 11 | .197 | .246 | .290 |
| Scor. Pos./2 Out | | | 38 | 7 | 0 | 7 | 8 | .184 | .263 | .311 |
| Late Inning Pressure | | | 185 | 43 | 3 | 24 | 24 | .232 | .351 | .319 |
| Leading Off | | | 39 | 6 | 0 | 4 | 6 | .154 | .205 | .233 |
| Runners On | | | 88 | 19 | 1 | 15 | 11 | .216 | .307 | .327 |
| Runners/Scor. Pos. | | | 50 | 12 | 1 | 13 | 7 | .240 | .380 | .391 |
| First 9 Batters | | | 267 | 60 | 3 | 30 | 39 | .225 | .333 | .302 |
| Second 9 Batters | | | 9 | 3 | 0 | 0 | 1 | .333 | .333 | .333 |
| All Batters Thereafter | | | 0 | 0 | 0 | 0 | 0 | — | — | — |

Loves to face: Andres Galarraga (.125, 1-for-8, 1 HR, 6 SO)
Hates to face: Darrell Evans (.529, 9-for-17)
Ground outs-to-air outs ratio: 0.86 last season, 1.07 for career. . . . Additional statistics: 5 double-play ground outs in 68 opportunities, 14 doubles, 3 triples in 75.1 innings last season. . . . Inherited 60 runners, stranded 50 (83%), 2d-highest rate in N.L. . . . Leading contender to replace injured Worrell as closer. Led all committee members with 123 batters faced in 8th inning or later while protecting leads of three runs or fewer. . . . Opponents were 0-for-14 with the bases loaded, driving in only one run . . . . Committed his first error on July 18, in the 286th game of his career. . . . Home run by Von Hayes last April is the only one allowed to a left-handed batter in regular season since 1985.

## Jose DeLeon

Throws Right

| St. Louis Cardinals | W–L | ERA | AB | H | HR | BB | SO | BA | SA | OBA |
|---|---|---|---|---|---|---|---|---|---|---|
| Season | 16-12 | 3.05 | 878 | 173 | 16 | 80 | 201 | .197 | .309 | .268 |
| vs. Left-Handers | | | 509 | 119 | 10 | 57 | 86 | .234 | .360 | .312 |
| vs. Right-Handers | | | 369 | 54 | 6 | 23 | 115 | .146 | .238 | .204 |
| Home | 8-6 | 2.55 | 477 | 88 | 8 | 39 | 99 | .184 | .287 | .248 |
| Road | 8-6 | 3.67 | 401 | 85 | 8 | 41 | 102 | .212 | .334 | .291 |
| Grass | 4-4 | 2.65 | 244 | 51 | 4 | 24 | 61 | .209 | .307 | .285 |
| Artificial Turf | 12-8 | 3.21 | 634 | 122 | 12 | 56 | 140 | .192 | .309 | .261 |
| April | 4-1 | 1.96 | 142 | 20 | 5 | 11 | 30 | .141 | .268 | .203 |
| May | 2-2 | 3.63 | 167 | 44 | 2 | 16 | 40 | .263 | .359 | .326 |
| June | 2-4 | 4.84 | 130 | 30 | 1 | 16 | 32 | .231 | .346 | .327 |
| July | 3-2 | 2.45 | 134 | 25 | 1 | 13 | 33 | .187 | .276 | .262 |
| August | 3-2 | 2.94 | 172 | 30 | 3 | 8 | 39 | .174 | .279 | .220 |
| Sept./Oct. | 2-1 | 2.63 | 133 | 24 | 4 | 16 | 27 | .180 | .323 | .268 |
| Leading Off Inn. | | | 227 | 39 | 4 | 28 | 48 | .172 | .260 | .263 |
| Runners On | | | 311 | 77 | 6 | 26 | 74 | .248 | .386 | .307 |
| Runners/Scor. Pos. | | | 173 | 42 | 2 | 20 | 38 | .243 | .387 | .323 |
| Runners On/2 Out | | | 125 | 27 | 4 | 9 | 31 | .216 | .392 | .274 |
| Scor. Pos./2 Out | | | 75 | 16 | 2 | 7 | 19 | .213 | .400 | .289 |
| Late Inning Pressure | | | 97 | 11 | 1 | 12 | 23 | .113 | .165 | .211 |
| Leading Off | | | 29 | 3 | 0 | 3 | 7 | .103 | .138 | .188 |
| Runners On | | | 24 | 3 | 1 | 5 | 5 | .125 | .250 | .276 |
| Runners/Scor. Pos. | | | 12 | 1 | 0 | 4 | 4 | .083 | .083 | .313 |
| First 9 Batters | | | 293 | 63 | 6 | 25 | 73 | .215 | .348 | .280 |
| Second 9 Batters | | | 290 | 59 | 4 | 21 | 66 | .203 | .314 | .264 |
| All Batters Thereafter | | | 295 | 51 | 6 | 34 | 62 | .173 | .264 | .259 |

Loves to face: Andres Galarraga (0-for-14, 6 SO)
Hates to face: Ricky Jordan (.500, 7-for-14, 2 2B, 2 HR)
Ground outs-to-air outs ratio: 0.74 last season, 0.80 for career. . . . Additional statistics: 12 double-play ground outs in 145 opportunities, 36 doubles, 7 triples in 244.2 innings last season. . . . Allowed 15 first-inning runs in 36 starts. Opponents batted .233 in first two innings, .182 after that. . . . Batting support: 3.33 runs per start. . . . Lowest strikeout total to lead N.L. since Jack Sanford in 1957 (188). Last Cardinals pitcher to lead N.L.: Bob Gibson (1968). . . . Career average of 10.05 runners per nine innings is lowest among active pitchers (minimum: 300 IP). . . . Opponents' base stealers were 13-for-25 (.520), lowest rate vs. St. Louis starters. . . . Completed three of first six starts, two of 30 thereafter.

## Jim Deshaies

Throws Left

| Houston Astros | W–L | ERA | AB | H | HR | BB | SO | BA | SA | OBA |
|---|---|---|---|---|---|---|---|---|---|---|
| Season | 15-10 | 2.91 | 829 | 180 | 15 | 79 | 153 | .217 | .331 | .287 |
| vs. Left-Handers | | | 120 | 31 | 0 | 21 | 20 | .258 | .317 | .361 |
| vs. Right-Handers | | | 709 | 149 | 15 | 58 | 133 | .210 | .333 | .273 |
| Home | 8-4 | 3.13 | 431 | 95 | 9 | 42 | 89 | .220 | .332 | .288 |
| Road | 7-6 | 2.67 | 398 | 85 | 6 | 37 | 64 | .214 | .329 | .285 |
| Grass | 3-4 | 2.37 | 224 | 46 | 4 | 19 | 38 | .205 | .326 | .270 |
| Artificial Turf | 12-6 | 3.11 | 605 | 134 | 11 | 60 | 115 | .221 | .332 | .293 |
| April | 2-2 | 3.00 | 120 | 28 | 3 | 8 | 24 | .233 | .408 | .287 |
| May | 3-1 | 2.91 | 157 | 35 | 1 | 18 | 18 | .223 | .325 | .303 |
| June | 3-0 | 3.58 | 142 | 37 | 3 | 19 | 28 | .261 | .387 | .339 |
| July | 2-1 | 2.16 | 118 | 22 | 3 | 12 | 27 | .186 | .305 | .265 |
| August | 1-3 | 3.66 | 125 | 29 | 2 | 12 | 25 | .232 | .312 | .309 |
| Sept./Oct. | 4-3 | 2.33 | 167 | 29 | 3 | 10 | 31 | .174 | .263 | .220 |
| Leading Off Inn. | | | 212 | 44 | 7 | 19 | 35 | .208 | .354 | .279 |
| Runners On | | | 321 | 73 | 4 | 34 | 71 | .227 | .336 | .299 |
| Runners/Scor. Pos. | | | 181 | 38 | 3 | 24 | 50 | .210 | .315 | .299 |
| Runners On/2 Out | | | 144 | 31 | 1 | 15 | 39 | .215 | .306 | .289 |
| Scor. Pos./2 Out | | | 94 | 21 | 1 | 10 | 27 | .223 | .298 | .298 |
| Late Inning Pressure | | | 72 | 13 | 2 | 5 | 10 | .181 | .278 | .234 |
| Leading Off | | | 21 | 4 | 1 | 1 | 2 | .190 | .333 | .227 |
| Runners On | | | 19 | 2 | 0 | 2 | 5 | .105 | .105 | .190 |
| Runners/Scor. Pos. | | | 9 | 0 | 0 | 1 | 2 | .000 | .000 | .100 |
| First 9 Batters | | | 268 | 53 | 7 | 28 | 62 | .198 | .328 | .276 |
| Second 9 Batters | | | 271 | 59 | 3 | 26 | 50 | .218 | .339 | .289 |
| All Batters Thereafter | | | 290 | 68 | 5 | 25 | 41 | .234 | .324 | .295 |

Loves to face: Howard Johnson (0-for-16, 8 SO)
Hates to face: Jeff Blauser (.455, 10-for-22, 2 HR)
Ground outs-to-air outs ratio: 0.71 last season, 0.63 for career. . . . Additional statistics: 12 double-play ground outs in 148 opportunities, 37 doubles, 6 triples in 225.2 innings last season. . . . Allowed 12 first-inning runs in 34 starts. . . . Batting support: 4.15 runs per start. . . . Yielded the last of Mike Schmidt's 548 home runs. . . . Last opposing left-hander to hit a HR: Kal Daniels (Sept. 1988). . . . Has faced 45 batters with bases loaded, never allowed an extra-base hit. . . . Traded by Yankees in Sept. 1985. Despite spotting pinstripes a month, Deshaies has 20 more wins since then (49) than any Yankees pitcher. New York's leaders: Tommy John (29), Rick Rhoden (28), Dennis Rasmussen (27).

## Rob Dibble

Throws Right

| Cincinnati Reds | W–L | ERA | AB | H | HR | BB | SO | BA | SA | OBA |
|---|---|---|---|---|---|---|---|---|---|---|
| Season | 10-5 | 2.09 | 352 | 62 | 4 | 39 | 141 | .176 | .250 | .261 |
| vs. Left-Handers | | | 172 | 32 | 1 | 25 | 72 | .186 | .256 | .286 |
| vs. Right-Handers | | | 180 | 30 | 3 | 14 | 69 | .167 | .244 | .236 |
| Home | 4-2 | 1.00 | 159 | 24 | 1 | 21 | 63 | .151 | .201 | .251 |
| Road | 6-3 | 3.00 | 193 | 38 | 3 | 18 | 78 | .197 | .290 | .270 |
| Grass | 3-2 | 3.67 | 123 | 26 | 3 | 12 | 49 | .211 | .333 | .288 |
| Artificial Turf | 7-3 | 1.25 | 229 | 36 | 1 | 27 | 92 | .157 | .205 | .247 |
| April | 3-0 | 3.45 | 60 | 13 | 0 | 8 | 18 | .217 | .250 | .314 |
| May | 1-1 | 1.59 | 60 | 9 | 1 | 6 | 30 | .150 | .217 | .227 |
| June | 2-2 | 1.64 | 75 | 11 | 2 | 8 | 36 | .147 | .280 | .226 |
| July | 0-0 | 4.15 | 32 | 7 | 1 | 4 | 9 | .219 | .406 | .316 |
| August | 2-1 | 1.37 | 69 | 11 | 0 | 7 | 33 | .159 | .203 | .247 |
| Sept./Oct. | 2-1 | 1.69 | 56 | 11 | 0 | 6 | 15 | .196 | .214 | .270 |
| Leading Off Inn. | | | 77 | 16 | 1 | 2 | 30 | .208 | .312 | .238 |
| Runners On | | | 174 | 29 | 2 | 23 | 65 | .167 | .230 | .262 |
| Runners/Scor. Pos. | | | 134 | 22 | 1 | 20 | 53 | .164 | .216 | .266 |
| Runners On/2 Out | | | 80 | 9 | 1 | 11 | 30 | .113 | .163 | .228 |
| Scor. Pos./2 Out | | | 62 | 7 | 0 | 10 | 26 | .113 | .129 | .236 |
| Late Inning Pressure | | | 234 | 43 | 3 | 32 | 92 | .184 | .261 | .286 |
| Leading Off | | | 52 | 12 | 1 | 2 | 23 | .231 | .365 | .273 |
| Runners On | | | 117 | 20 | 1 | 19 | 42 | .171 | .231 | .285 |
| Runners/Scor. Pos. | | | 86 | 14 | 0 | 18 | 35 | .163 | .198 | .305 |
| First 9 Batters | | | 348 | 60 | 4 | 37 | 141 | .172 | .244 | .255 |
| Second 9 Batters | | | 4 | 2 | 0 | 2 | 0 | .500 | .750 | .667 |
| All Batters Thereafter | | | 0 | 0 | 0 | 0 | 0 | — | — | — |

Loves to face: Tom Brunansky (0-for-7, 3 SO)
Hates to face: Garry Templeton (.556, 5-for-9, 4 SO)
Ground outs-to-air outs ratio: 0.87 last season, 0.88 for career. . . . Additional statistics: 3 double-play ground outs in 66 opportunities, 14 doubles, 0 triples in 99.0 innings last season. . . . Struck out 12.8 batters per nine innings, highest average ever among pitchers with 100 or more strikeouts. . . . Led N.L. with eight save "set-ups", one more than Craig Lefferts. (See Rick Honeycutt comments.) . . .Opponents were 18-for-19 stealing second base. . . . Opposing fly-ball hitters batted .151, lowest in N.L. (minimum: 150 PA). . . . Entered four bases-loaded situations, stranded all 12 runners. . . . Has faced 28 batters with bases loaded, allowed three hits, one walk. . . . Opponents' career BA with two outs and runners in scoring position is .108 (10-for-93).

## Frank DiPino

Throws Left

| St. Louis Cardinals | W–L | ERA | AB | H | HR | BB | SO | BA | SA | OBA |
|---|---|---|---|---|---|---|---|---|---|---|
| Season | 9-0 | 2.45 | 321 | 73 | 6 | 20 | 44 | .227 | .349 | .269 |
| vs. Left-Handers | | | 129 | 27 | 0 | 6 | 20 | .209 | .248 | .241 |
| vs. Right-Handers | | | 192 | 46 | 6 | 14 | 24 | .240 | .417 | .287 |
| Home | 4-0 | 1.58 | 164 | 33 | 2 | 13 | 25 | .201 | .299 | .256 |
| Road | 5-0 | 3.38 | 157 | 40 | 4 | 7 | 19 | .255 | .401 | .283 |
| Grass | 3-0 | 2.25 | 72 | 14 | 2 | 1 | 8 | .194 | .333 | .205 |
| Artificial Turf | 6-0 | 2.50 | 249 | 59 | 4 | 19 | 36 | .237 | .353 | .286 |
| April | 0-0 | 1.64 | 36 | 3 | 1 | 1 | 5 | .083 | .222 | .108 |
| May | 2-0 | 2.55 | 62 | 12 | 2 | 4 | 4 | .194 | .339 | .242 |
| June | 2-0 | 4.61 | 48 | 14 | 1 | 4 | 6 | .292 | .458 | .321 |
| July | 1-0 | 2.13 | 48 | 12 | 2 | 3 | 7 | .250 | .396 | .294 |
| August | 1-0 | 3.18 | 44 | 10 | 0 | 3 | 7 | .227 | .295 | .277 |
| Sept./Oct. | 3-0 | 1.23 | 83 | 22 | 0 | 5 | 15 | .265 | .349 | .303 |
| Leading Off Inn. | | | 74 | 17 | 2 | 2 | 7 | .230 | .365 | .250 |
| Runners On | | | 139 | 31 | 3 | 12 | 21 | .223 | .367 | .276 |
| Runners/Scor. Pos. | | | 88 | 20 | 2 | 12 | 13 | .227 | .375 | .305 |
| Runners On/2 Out | | | 58 | 7 | 1 | 6 | 12 | .121 | .172 | .203 |
| Scor. Pos./2 Out | | | 41 | 5 | 1 | 6 | 7 | .122 | .195 | .234 |
| Late Inning Pressure | | | 95 | 25 | 2 | 6 | 17 | .263 | .379 | .301 |
| Leading Off | | | 23 | 6 | 1 | 1 | 4 | .261 | .391 | .292 |
| Runners On | | | 40 | 10 | 1 | 3 | 8 | .250 | .375 | .289 |
| Runners/Scor. Pos. | | | 25 | 5 | 0 | 3 | 6 | .200 | .200 | .267 |
| First 9 Batters | | | 299 | 70 | 6 | 19 | 42 | .234 | .365 | .276 |
| Second 9 Batters | | | 22 | 3 | 0 | 1 | 2 | .136 | .136 | .174 |
| All Batters Thereafter | | | 0 | 0 | 0 | 0 | 0 | — | — | — |

Loves to face: Tony Gwynn (.063, 1-for-16)
Hates to face: Glenn Wilson (.667, 8-for-12, 2 HR, 3 BB)
Ground outs-to-air outs ratio: 2.35 last season, 1.29 for career. . . . Additional statistics: 11 double-play ground outs in 67 opportunities, 13 doubles, 4 triples in 88.1 innings last season. . . . Career record stood at 18–35 before he ripped off 11 straight wins, a streak that he carries into the 1990s. Credit Rule 10.19(a) with four of those wins, games in which DiPino assumed leads from starters who failed to complete five innings. . . . Held opponents hitless in 14 at-bats with bases loaded, increasing to 104 his career total of batters faced with bags full. He's never allowed a grand slam. . . . Has pitched between 70 and 90 innings in each of the last seven seasons, an all-time "record" streak.

## Kelly Downs

Throws Right

| San Francisco Giants | W–L | ERA | AB | H | HR | BB | SO | BA | SA | OBA |
|---|---|---|---|---|---|---|---|---|---|---|
| Season | 4-8 | 4.79 | 314 | 82 | 7 | 26 | 49 | .261 | .411 | .316 |
| vs. Left-Handers | | | 178 | 54 | 4 | 14 | 20 | .303 | .478 | .349 |
| vs. Right-Handers | | | 136 | 28 | 3 | 12 | 29 | .206 | .324 | .273 |
| Home | 3-2 | 5.09 | 153 | 39 | 5 | 15 | 20 | .255 | .425 | .320 |
| Road | 1-6 | 4.50 | 161 | 43 | 2 | 11 | 29 | .267 | .398 | .312 |
| Grass | 4-5 | 4.57 | 230 | 61 | 6 | 21 | 32 | .265 | .417 | .324 |
| Artificial Turf | 0-3 | 5.40 | 84 | 21 | 1 | 5 | 17 | .250 | .393 | .292 |
| April | 2-3 | 5.14 | 105 | 33 | 1 | 11 | 18 | .314 | .419 | .375 |
| May | | | 1 | 0 | 0 | 2 | 0 | .000 | .000 | .667 |
| June | | | 0 | 0 | 0 | 0 | 0 | — | — | — |
| July | | | 0 | 0 | 0 | 0 | 0 | — | — | — |
| August | 1-2 | 2.92 | 88 | 18 | 2 | 9 | 12 | .205 | .352 | .276 |
| Sept./Oct. | 1-3 | 5.70 | 120 | 31 | 4 | 4 | 19 | .258 | .450 | .282 |
| Leading Off Inn. | | | 79 | 23 | 2 | 8 | 7 | .291 | .405 | .364 |
| Runners On | | | 128 | 37 | 3 | 12 | 20 | .289 | .461 | .340 |
| Runners/Scor. Pos. | | | 64 | 22 | 1 | 11 | 12 | .344 | .516 | .418 |
| Runners On/2 Out | | | 51 | 13 | 2 | 5 | 10 | .255 | .471 | .321 |
| Scor. Pos./2 Out | | | 30 | 10 | 1 | 5 | 7 | .333 | .533 | .429 |
| Late Inning Pressure | | | 33 | 6 | 1 | 2 | 4 | .182 | .333 | .229 |
| Leading Off | | | 11 | 4 | 1 | 1 | 0 | .364 | .727 | .417 |
| Runners On | | | 9 | 2 | 0 | 0 | 2 | .222 | .333 | .222 |
| Runners/Scor. Pos. | | | 1 | 1 | 0 | 0 | 0 | 1.000 | 1.000 | 1.000 |
| First 9 Batters | | | 131 | 37 | 3 | 15 | 28 | .282 | .427 | .358 |
| Second 9 Batters | | | 110 | 26 | 2 | 5 | 9 | .236 | .382 | .267 |
| All Batters Thereafter | | | 73 | 19 | 2 | 6 | 12 | .260 | .425 | .309 |

Loves to face: John Kruk (.125, 3-for-24, 7 SO)
Hates to face: Chris Sabo (.714, 5-for-7, 3 2B, 1 HR)
Ground outs-to-air outs ratio: 1.08 last season, 1.30 for career. . . . Additional statistics: 7 double-play ground outs in 64 opportunities, 22 doubles, 2 triples in 82.2 innings last season. . . . Allowed 10 first-inning runs in 15 starts. Had a 6.37 ERA over the first three innings, 2.48 thereafter. . . . Batting support: 3.07 runs per start. . . . Didn't complete any of 15 starts, and reached the ninth inning only once. . . . Allowed only one stolen base during regular season (in five attempts). Rickey Henderson matched that total in the postseason. . . . Left-handed batters hit .406 against him with runners in scoring position. . . . Opponents' career average is .229 at Candlestick, .259 on the road.

## Doug Drabek

Throws Right

| Pittsburgh Pirates | W–L | ERA | AB | H | HR | BB | SO | BA | SA | OBA |
|---|---|---|---|---|---|---|---|---|---|---|
| Season | 14-12 | 2.80 | 902 | 215 | 21 | 69 | 123 | .238 | .350 | .293 |
| vs. Left-Handers | | | 492 | 123 | 7 | 45 | 52 | .250 | .339 | .311 |
| vs. Right-Handers | | | 410 | 92 | 14 | 24 | 71 | .224 | .363 | .270 |
| Home | 8-5 | 1.85 | 482 | 98 | 13 | 33 | 74 | .203 | .307 | .254 |
| Road | 6-7 | 3.99 | 420 | 117 | 8 | 36 | 49 | .279 | .400 | .335 |
| Grass | 4-7 | 5.11 | 294 | 87 | 7 | 27 | 34 | .296 | .442 | .356 |
| Artificial Turf | 10-5 | 1.80 | 608 | 128 | 14 | 42 | 89 | .211 | .306 | .261 |
| April | 1-2 | 1.98 | 127 | 25 | 1 | 11 | 13 | .197 | .244 | .261 |
| May | 2-3 | 2.20 | 151 | 38 | 2 | 17 | 20 | .252 | .351 | .322 |
| June | 2-0 | 2.55 | 126 | 27 | 6 | 12 | 21 | .214 | .389 | .283 |
| July | 3-2 | 4.91 | 157 | 44 | 6 | 13 | 20 | .280 | .459 | .339 |
| August | 3-3 | 2.68 | 182 | 41 | 5 | 11 | 28 | .225 | .335 | .268 |
| Sept./Oct. | 3-2 | 2.41 | 159 | 40 | 1 | 5 | 21 | .252 | .314 | .277 |
| Leading Off Inn. | | | 239 | 63 | 7 | 11 | 36 | .264 | .402 | .296 |
| Runners On | | | 329 | 84 | 8 | 31 | 34 | .255 | .374 | .319 |
| Runners/Scor. Pos. | | | 202 | 46 | 5 | 20 | 24 | .228 | .361 | .297 |
| Runners On/2 Out | | | 147 | 39 | 4 | 19 | 16 | .265 | .388 | .353 |
| Scor. Pos./2 Out | | | 102 | 23 | 3 | 13 | 12 | .225 | .363 | .319 |
| Late Inning Pressure | | | 146 | 31 | 2 | 14 | 19 | .212 | .281 | .280 |
| Leading Off | | | 42 | 12 | 2 | 3 | 2 | .286 | .452 | .333 |
| Runners On | | | 48 | 12 | 0 | 5 | 7 | .250 | .292 | .315 |
| Runners/Scor. Pos. | | | 28 | 6 | 0 | 5 | 5 | .214 | .286 | .324 |
| First 9 Batters | | | 281 | 63 | 6 | 25 | 35 | .224 | .335 | .289 |
| Second 9 Batters | | | 274 | 65 | 8 | 15 | 43 | .237 | .350 | .277 |
| All Batters Thereafter | | | 347 | 87 | 7 | 29 | 45 | .251 | .363 | .307 |

Loves to face: Ricky Jordan (0-for-10, 4 SO)
Hates to face: Jack Clark (.417, 5-for-12, 2 HR, 4 BB)
Ground outs-to-air outs ratio: 1.00 last season, 0.97 for career. . . . Additional statistics: 13 double-play ground outs in 134 opportunities, 30 doubles, 4 triples in 244.1 innings last season. . . . Allowed 9 first-inning runs in 34 starts. . . . Batting support: 2.91 runs per start, 4th-lowest in majors (minimum: 15 starts). . . . Home-game ERA ranked 3d in majors, behind Scott Garrelts and Bret Saberhagen. . . . Three of last four starts were complete-game shutouts, good for a 2–1–1 record thanks to a scoreless tie with the St. Louis Blues—make that Cardinals. . . . Opponents' career average is .223 in first two passes through batting order, .283 thereafter. . . . ERA year by year: 4.10, 3.88, 3.08, 2.80.

## Sid Fernandez

Throws Left

| New York Mets | W–L | ERA | AB | H | HR | BB | SO | BA | SA | OBA |
|---|---|---|---|---|---|---|---|---|---|---|
| Season | 14-5 | 2.83 | 794 | 157 | 21 | 75 | 198 | .198 | .334 | .271 |
| vs. Left-Handers | | | 117 | 23 | 2 | 9 | 30 | .197 | .299 | .258 |
| vs. Right-Handers | | | 677 | 134 | 19 | 66 | 168 | .198 | .340 | .273 |
| Home | 7-2 | 2.78 | 473 | 96 | 11 | 45 | 121 | .203 | .332 | .276 |
| Road | 7-3 | 2.91 | 321 | 61 | 10 | 30 | 77 | .190 | .336 | .263 |
| Grass | 8-4 | 2.96 | 581 | 122 | 17 | 55 | 153 | .210 | .353 | .281 |
| Artificial Turf | 6-1 | 2.51 | 213 | 35 | 4 | 20 | 45 | .164 | .282 | .243 |
| April | 3-0 | 2.19 | 87 | 15 | 0 | 12 | 14 | .172 | .218 | .277 |
| May | 1-2 | 4.22 | 126 | 31 | 5 | 14 | 29 | .246 | .437 | .321 |
| June | 1-0 | 2.83 | 104 | 19 | 3 | 14 | 29 | .183 | .375 | .277 |
| July | 3-1 | 2.50 | 141 | 26 | 4 | 9 | 37 | .184 | .298 | .248 |
| August | 2-0 | 2.37 | 174 | 37 | 7 | 15 | 41 | .213 | .374 | .274 |
| Sept./Oct. | 4-2 | 3.00 | 162 | 29 | 2 | 11 | 48 | .179 | .278 | .239 |
| Leading Off Inn. | | | 215 | 32 | 4 | 10 | 62 | .149 | .223 | .190 |
| Runners On | | | 270 | 62 | 10 | 25 | 45 | .230 | .404 | .296 |
| Runners/Scor. Pos. | | | 117 | 30 | 5 | 15 | 24 | .256 | .462 | .341 |
| Runners On/2 Out | | | 132 | 28 | 2 | 13 | 22 | .212 | .333 | .288 |
| Scor. Pos./2 Out | | | 63 | 15 | 1 | 9 | 12 | .238 | .397 | .342 |
| Late Inning Pressure | | | 66 | 19 | 3 | 2 | 17 | .288 | .500 | .314 |
| Leading Off | | | 20 | 7 | 2 | 0 | 4 | .350 | .700 | .350 |
| Runners On | | | 16 | 3 | 0 | 2 | 3 | .188 | .250 | .300 |
| Runners/Scor. Pos. | | | 7 | 0 | 0 | 2 | 1 | .000 | .000 | .273 |
| First 9 Batters | | | 276 | 45 | 8 | 27 | 82 | .163 | .283 | .242 |
| Second 9 Batters | | | 261 | 47 | 1 | 25 | 66 | .180 | .245 | .256 |
| All Batters Thereafter | | | 257 | 65 | 12 | 23 | 50 | .253 | .479 | .317 |

Loves to face: Otis Nixon (0-for-10, 9 SO)
Hates to face: Jeff Hamilton (.462, 6-for-13, 1 HR)
Ground outs-to-air outs ratio: 0.36 last season, 0.46 for career, lowest of any pitcher over the last 15 years (minimum: 1000 BFP). . . . Additional statistics: 8 double-play ground outs in 124 opportunities, 31 doubles, 7 triples in 219.1 innings last season. . . . Allowed 16 first-inning runs in 32 starts. . . . Batting support: 4.69 runs per start. . . . Held opponents to a .164 average on first pass through batting order, lowest mark in majors (minimum: 150 BFP). . . . Completed nine of 146 career starts (6 percent) before going distance in six of his last 17. . . . First time opposing batters topped .200 mark at Shea Stadium since 1984. . . . Career record of 42–20 (.677) vs. N.L. West clubs, 27–25 (.519) vs. N.L. East.

## Bob Forsch

Throws Right

| Houston Astros | W–L | ERA | AB | H | HR | BB | SO | BA | SA | OBA |
|---|---|---|---|---|---|---|---|---|---|---|
| Season | 4-5 | 5.32 | 439 | 133 | 10 | 46 | 40 | .303 | .435 | .367 |
| vs. Left-Handers | | | 253 | 77 | 6 | 32 | 19 | .304 | .447 | .379 |
| vs. Right-Handers | | | 186 | 56 | 4 | 14 | 21 | .301 | .419 | .350 |
| Home | 2-1 | 4.92 | 226 | 66 | 5 | 30 | 23 | .292 | .407 | .375 |
| Road | 2-4 | 5.75 | 213 | 67 | 5 | 16 | 17 | .315 | .465 | .359 |
| Grass | 1-3 | 7.17 | 86 | 27 | 1 | 9 | 6 | .314 | .442 | .371 |
| Artificial Turf | 3-2 | 4.86 | 353 | 106 | 9 | 37 | 34 | .300 | .433 | .366 |
| April | 1-1 | 4.85 | 53 | 15 | 1 | 4 | 4 | .283 | .453 | .333 |
| May | 0-0 | 3.18 | 63 | 15 | 1 | 11 | 4 | .238 | .333 | .360 |
| June | 0-1 | 4.30 | 115 | 34 | 3 | 13 | 9 | .296 | .417 | .359 |
| July | 2-1 | 4.37 | 88 | 24 | 1 | 12 | 10 | .273 | .318 | .360 |
| August | 1-1 | 9.30 | 91 | 35 | 3 | 3 | 10 | .385 | .593 | .400 |
| Sept./Oct. | 0-1 | 7.50 | 29 | 10 | 1 | 3 | 3 | .345 | .552 | .406 |
| Leading Off Inn. | | | 102 | 29 | 3 | 9 | 6 | .284 | .480 | .348 |
| Runners On | | | 216 | 66 | 7 | 22 | 21 | .306 | .458 | .364 |
| Runners/Scor. Pos. | | | 122 | 41 | 4 | 18 | 11 | .336 | .492 | .410 |
| Runners On/2 Out | | | 88 | 25 | 4 | 12 | 6 | .284 | .477 | .370 |
| Scor. Pos./2 Out | | | 58 | 17 | 3 | 11 | 5 | .293 | .500 | .406 |
| Late Inning Pressure | | | 41 | 8 | 1 | 2 | 5 | .195 | .317 | .233 |
| Leading Off | | | 9 | 2 | 0 | 1 | 0 | .222 | .222 | .300 |
| Runners On | | | 18 | 3 | 1 | 1 | 3 | .167 | .389 | .211 |
| Runners/Scor. Pos. | | | 8 | 2 | 1 | 1 | 0 | .250 | .625 | .333 |
| First 9 Batters | | | 239 | 77 | 5 | 27 | 22 | .322 | .456 | .392 |
| Second 9 Batters | | | 125 | 36 | 1 | 10 | 11 | .288 | .384 | .333 |
| All Batters Thereafter | | | 75 | 20 | 4 | 9 | 7 | .267 | .453 | .345 |

Loves to face: Steve Jeltz (.042, 1-for-24)
Hates to face: Darryl Strawberry (.458, 11-for-24, 5 HR)
Ground outs-to-air outs ratio: 1.33 last season, 1.42 for career. . . . Additional statistics: 8 double-play ground outs in 105 opportunities, 22 doubles, 3 triples in 108.1 innings last season. . . . Allowed 15 first-inning runs in 15 starts. . . . Batting support: 4.13 runs per start. . . . Made 22 relief appearances, but never entered with Houston leading. . . . First of 16 seasons in which he walked more batters than he struck out. . . . Made M.L. debut on July 7, 1975, three days before manager Art Howe. . . . Allowed hits to nine consecutive batters on August 3, matching Erskine Mayer's N.L. mark that had stood alone since 1913. . . . Has lost five straight to the Giants since last beating them in 1980.

## John Franco

Throws Left

| Cincinnati Reds | W–L | ERA | AB | H | HR | BB | SO | BA | SA | OBA |
|---|---|---|---|---|---|---|---|---|---|---|
| Season | 4-8 | 3.12 | 299 | 77 | 3 | 36 | 60 | .258 | .311 | .334 |
| vs. Left-Handers | | | 50 | 10 | 0 | 3 | 10 | .200 | .240 | .245 |
| vs. Right-Handers | | | 249 | 67 | 3 | 33 | 50 | .269 | .325 | .351 |
| Home | 4 4 | 3.92 | 152 | 39 | 1 | 19 | 30 | .257 | .296 | .333 |
| Road | 0-4 | 2.29 | 147 | 38 | 2 | 17 | 30 | .259 | .327 | .335 |
| Grass | 0-1 | 1.07 | 92 | 20 | 0 | 10 | 20 | .217 | .250 | .294 |
| Artificial Turf | 4-7 | 4.07 | 207 | 57 | 3 | 26 | 40 | .275 | .338 | .352 |
| April | 0-0 | 2.13 | 40 | 4 | 0 | 4 | 7 | .100 | .125 | .178 |
| May | 1-0 | 0.64 | 52 | 11 | 0 | 5 | 11 | .212 | .231 | .281 |
| June | 1-1 | 1.74 | 37 | 12 | 0 | 7 | 7 | .324 | .324 | .432 |
| July | 0-3 | 5.28 | 60 | 19 | 3 | 4 | 10 | .317 | .500 | .359 |
| August | 1-2 | 1.98 | 54 | 16 | 0 | 8 | 13 | .296 | .352 | .387 |
| Sept./Oct. | 1-2 | 6.14 | 56 | 15 | 0 | 8 | 12 | .268 | .268 | .348 |
| Leading Off Inn. | | | 70 | 14 | 0 | 5 | 11 | .200 | .214 | .253 |
| Runners On | | | 142 | 39 | 3 | 21 | 34 | .275 | .373 | .361 |
| Runners/Scor. Pos. | | | 74 | 21 | 2 | 15 | 18 | .284 | .405 | .391 |
| Runners On/2 Out | | | 64 | 15 | 0 | 11 | 18 | .234 | .250 | .347 |
| Scor. Pos./2 Out | | | 39 | 11 | 0 | 7 | 10 | .282 | .308 | .391 |
| Late Inning Pressure | | | 225 | 54 | 2 | 28 | 47 | .240 | .284 | .320 |
| Leading Off | | | 55 | 9 | 0 | 3 | 11 | .164 | .164 | .207 |
| Runners On | | | 99 | 27 | 2 | 16 | 23 | .273 | .364 | .364 |
| Runners/Scor. Pos. | | | 46 | 11 | 1 | 13 | 12 | .239 | .326 | .387 |
| First 9 Batters | | | 283 | 73 | 2 | 34 | 57 | .258 | .304 | .334 |
| Second 9 Batters | | | 16 | 4 | 1 | 2 | 3 | .250 | .438 | .333 |
| All Batters Thereafter | | | 0 | 0 | 0 | 0 | 0 | — | — | — |

Loves to face: Von Hayes (.111, 2-for-18, 5 SO)
Hates to face: Bob Dernier (.538, 7-for-13, 1 HR)
Ground outs-to-air outs ratio: 1.90 last season, 1.87 for career. . . . Additional statistics: 8 double-play ground outs in 78 opportunities, 7 doubles, 0 triples in 80.2 innings last season. . . . Blew six of his last 15 save opportunities after converting 23 of his first 25. . . . Career ERA of 2.49, lowest among active pitchers (min.: 500 IP). . . . Leaves Reds with 393 relief appearances, 4th most in team history. The leaders: Pedro Borbon (524), Clay Carroll (471), and Tom Hume (409). . . . The Mets acquired Franco because he's more effective than Randy Myers against right-handers? Don't these guys consult their *Analysts?* Right-handers have a career .221 average vs. Myers, .248 vs. Franco.

## Scott Garrelts

Throws Right

| San Francisco Giants | W–L | ERA | AB | H | HR | BB | SO | BA | SA | OBA |
|---|---|---|---|---|---|---|---|---|---|---|
| Season | 14-5 | 2.28 | 704 | 149 | 11 | 46 | 119 | .212 | .313 | .258 |
| vs. Left-Handers | | | 377 | 89 | 6 | 34 | 53 | .236 | .353 | .296 |
| vs. Right-Handers | | | 327 | 60 | 5 | 12 | 66 | .183 | .266 | .211 |
| Home | 10-2 | 1.57 | 377 | 74 | 5 | 29 | 72 | .196 | .204 | .250 |
| Road | 4-3 | 3.19 | 327 | 75 | 6 | 17 | 47 | .229 | .346 | .267 |
| Grass | 13-4 | 2.15 | 588 | 124 | 10 | 41 | 104 | .211 | .311 | .259 |
| Artificial Turf | 1-1 | 2.97 | 116 | 25 | 1 | 5 | 15 | .216 | .319 | .248 |
| April | 2-1 | 3.25 | 106 | 28 | 0 | 10 | 12 | .264 | .340 | .328 |
| May | 1-0 | 1.90 | 164 | 32 | 1 | 16 | 35 | .195 | .250 | .264 |
| June | 3-2 | 3.55 | 128 | 33 | 4 | 6 | 22 | .258 | .391 | .291 |
| July | 2-0 | 0.44 | 76 | 13 | 2 | 3 | 11 | .171 | .289 | .200 |
| August | 2-0 | 2.41 | 66 | 10 | 1 | 5 | 11 | .152 | .273 | .211 |
| Sept./Oct. | 4-2 | 1.96 | 164 | 33 | 3 | 6 | 28 | .201 | .323 | .224 |
| Leading Off Inn. | | | 189 | 39 | 3 | 10 | 27 | .206 | .296 | .246 |
| Runners On | | | 250 | 56 | 6 | 17 | 48 | .224 | .360 | .266 |
| Runners/Scor. Pos. | | | 142 | 27 | 3 | 9 | 29 | .190 | .303 | .228 |
| Runners On/2 Out | | | 107 | 18 | 4 | 8 | 23 | .168 | .318 | .226 |
| Scor. Pos./2 Out | | | 65 | 9 | 2 | 6 | 13 | .138 | .246 | .211 |
| Late Inning Pressure | | | 56 | 13 | 0 | 3 | 9 | .232 | .339 | .271 |
| Leading Off | | | 18 | 4 | 0 | 0 | 1 | .222 | .333 | .222 |
| Runners On | | | 15 | 4 | 0 | 1 | 4 | .267 | .333 | .313 |
| Runners/Scor. Pos. | | | 9 | 3 | 0 | 0 | 3 | .333 | .333 | .333 |
| First 9 Batters | | | 244 | 55 | 3 | 15 | 46 | .225 | .316 | .268 |
| Second 9 Batters | | | 231 | 42 | 3 | 17 | 40 | .182 | .255 | .235 |
| All Batters Thereafter | | | 229 | 52 | 5 | 14 | 33 | .227 | .367 | .269 |

Loves to face: Tom Herr (.056, 1-for-18, 5 SO)
Hates to face: Mark Grace (.700, 7-for-10, 1 HR)
Ground outs-to-air outs ratio: 1.00 last season, 1.23 for career. . . . Additional statistics: 9 double-play ground outs in 109 opportunities, 28 doubles, 5 triples in 193.1 innings last season. . . . Allowed 17 first-inning runs in 29 starts; opponents batted .271 in first inning, .200 thereafter. . . . Batting support: 4.59 runs per start. . . . Allowed 9.1 base runners per nine innings, lowest rate in N.L. . . . First N.L. pitcher to lead league in ERA and winning percentage since John Candelaria in 1977. Last Giants pitcher to do that: Johnny Antonelli (1954). . . . Had a 3.24 ERA in 58.1 innings with Kirt Manwaring catching, 1.89 in 119.0 innings with Terry Kennedy. . . . Career record of 32–16 in day games, 24–25 at night.

## Tom Glavine

Throws Left

| Atlanta Braves | W–L | ERA | AB | H | HR | BB | SO | BA | SA | OBA |
|---|---|---|---|---|---|---|---|---|---|---|
| Season | 14-8 | 3.68 | 709 | 172 | 20 | 40 | 90 | .243 | .371 | .283 |
| vs. Left-Handers | | | 108 | 22 | 0 | 6 | 26 | .204 | .269 | .252 |
| vs. Right-Handers | | | 601 | 150 | 20 | 34 | 64 | .250 | .389 | .289 |
| Home | 6-4 | 3.72 | 361 | 86 | 13 | 21 | 39 | .238 | .388 | .282 |
| Road | 8-4 | 3.63 | 348 | 86 | 7 | 19 | 51 | .247 | .353 | .285 |
| Grass | 11-5 | 3.15 | 523 | 122 | 16 | 25 | 63 | .233 | .363 | .270 |
| Artificial Turf | 3-3 | 5.18 | 186 | 50 | 4 | 15 | 27 | .269 | .392 | .320 |
| April | 3-0 | 2.37 | 141 | 33 | 3 | 8 | 12 | .234 | .326 | .278 |
| May | 2-1 | 2.63 | 91 | 19 | 1 | 3 | 12 | .209 | .319 | .234 |
| June | 3-3 | 5.19 | 139 | 41 | 6 | 6 | 19 | .295 | .460 | .324 |
| July | 1-2 | 3.73 | 121 | 28 | 5 | 8 | 23 | .231 | .421 | .277 |
| August | 3-2 | 4.26 | 143 | 35 | 4 | 9 | 16 | .245 | .364 | .292 |
| Sept./Oct. | 2-0 | 3.60 | 74 | 16 | 1 | 6 | 8 | .216 | .284 | .272 |
| Leading Off Inn. | | | 189 | 47 | 5 | 4 | 23 | .249 | .386 | .272 |
| Runners On | | | 242 | 63 | 9 | 24 | 28 | .260 | .409 | .322 |
| Runners/Scor. Pos. | | | 119 | 30 | 4 | 22 | 16 | .252 | .420 | .359 |
| Runners On/2 Out | | | 105 | 21 | 3 | 14 | 13 | .200 | .305 | .294 |
| Scor. Pos./2 Out | | | 53 | 11 | 3 | 14 | 7 | .208 | .415 | .373 |
| Late Inning Pressure | | | 59 | 11 | 3 | 3 | 2 | .186 | .339 | .226 |
| Leading Off | | | 15 | 1 | 0 | 2 | 1 | .067 | .067 | .176 |
| Runners On | | | 18 | 5 | 3 | 1 | 1 | .278 | .778 | .316 |
| Runners/Scor. Pos. | | | 6 | 2 | 1 | 1 | 0 | .333 | .833 | .429 |
| First 9 Batters | | | 240 | 60 | 3 | 7 | 37 | .250 | .338 | .272 |
| Second 9 Batters | | | 222 | 56 | 7 | 19 | 31 | .252 | .396 | .313 |
| All Batters Thereafter | | | 247 | 56 | 10 | 14 | 22 | .227 | .381 | .267 |

Loves to face: Mark Parent (.067, 1-for-15)
Hates to face: Pedro Guerrero (.474, 9-for-19, 2 HR)
Ground outs-to-air outs ratio: 1.30 last season, 1.24 for career. . . . Additional statistics: 14 double-play ground outs in 116 opportunities, 25 doubles, 3 triples in 186.0 innings last season. . . . Allowed 17 first-inning runs in 29 starts. Opposing batters hit better in first inning (.299) than in any other. . . . Batting support: 5.24 runs per start, highest in N.L. (minimum: 15 starts). . . . Allowed 12 stolen bases in 23 attempts. . . . Four of his six complete games were shutouts, but completed only one of his last 18 starts. . . . Had an ERA of 1.29 in his victories, 9.25 in his losses. . . . Ratio of strikeouts to walks: 0.6 in 1987, 1.3 in 1988, 2.3 last season. . . . Has allowed 37 career home runs, only three to left-handers.

## Dwight Gooden

Throws Right

| New York Mets | W–L | ERA | AB | H | HR | BB | SO | BA | SA | OBA |
|---|---|---|---|---|---|---|---|---|---|---|
| Season | 9-4 | 2.89 | 441 | 93 | 9 | 47 | 101 | .211 | .313 | .288 |
| vs. Left-Handers | | | 232 | 42 | 3 | 29 | 57 | .181 | .259 | .270 |
| vs. Right-Handers | | | 209 | 51 | 6 | 18 | 44 | .244 | .373 | .309 |
| Home | 6-1 | 2.33 | 242 | 46 | 3 | 33 | 65 | .190 | .252 | .288 |
| Road | 3-3 | 3.59 | 199 | 47 | 6 | 14 | 36 | .236 | .387 | .288 |
| Grass | 8-2 | 2.66 | 352 | 75 | 5 | 42 | 79 | .213 | .295 | .298 |
| Artificial Turf | 1-2 | 3.80 | 89 | 18 | 4 | 5 | 22 | .202 | .382 | .245 |
| April | 4-0 | 2.41 | 135 | 22 | 3 | 16 | 33 | .163 | .259 | .257 |
| May | 2-2 | 2.36 | 155 | 36 | 1 | 16 | 33 | .232 | .271 | .301 |
| June | 3-1 | 4.20 | 116 | 27 | 3 | 13 | 28 | .233 | .379 | .315 |
| July | 0-1 | 9.00 | 10 | 3 | 2 | 0 | 1 | .300 | .900 | .300 |
| August | | | 0 | 0 | 0 | 0 | 0 | — | — | — |
| Sept./Oct. | 0-0 | 1.29 | 25 | 5 | 0 | 2 | 6 | .200 | .320 | .250 |
| Leading Off Inn. | | | 114 | 19 | 3 | 8 | 29 | .167 | .281 | .221 |
| Runners On | | | 176 | 35 | 2 | 22 | 45 | .199 | .267 | .287 |
| Runners/Scor. Pos. | | | 116 | 23 | 2 | 19 | 32 | .198 | .293 | .309 |
| Runners On/2 Out | | | 76 | 11 | 2 | 10 | 19 | .145 | .224 | .244 |
| Scor. Pos./2 Out | | | 54 | 8 | 2 | 8 | 13 | .148 | .259 | .258 |
| Late Inning Pressure | | | 47 | 10 | 1 | 5 | 12 | .213 | .298 | .283 |
| Leading Off | | | 14 | 4 | 0 | 0 | 5 | .286 | .357 | .286 |
| Runners On | | | 19 | 4 | 0 | 1 | 3 | .211 | .211 | .238 |
| Runners/Scor. Pos. | | | 9 | 2 | 0 | 1 | 1 | .222 | .222 | .273 |
| First 9 Batters | | | 149 | 26 | 2 | 19 | 37 | .174 | .262 | .266 |
| Second 9 Batters | | | 141 | 39 | 5 | 12 | 29 | .277 | .440 | .338 |
| All Batters Thereafter | | | 151 | 28 | 2 | 16 | 35 | .185 | .245 | .265 |

Loves to face: Nick Esasky (0-for-10, 5 SO)
Hates to face: Doug Drabek (.667, 4-for-6, 2 2B)
Ground outs-to-air outs ratio: 1.29 last season, 1.26 for career. . . . Additional statistics: 5 double-play ground outs in 70 opportunities, 16 doubles, 1 triple in 118.1 innings last season. . . . Allowed 7 first-inning runs in 17 starts. . . . Batting support: 3.59 runs per start. . . . Faced 130 consecutive batters without an extra-base hit, longest streak in N.L. . . . Opposing pitchers were 0-for-32. . . . First player since Kid Nichols (1890–95) to pitch five games above .500 in each of first six seasons. Jack Stivetts and Bob Caruthers also did it. And three more were plus-five or better in non-debut rookie years and for five seasons thereafter: John Clarkson, Vic Raschi, and Ron Guidry.

## Rich Gossage

San Francisco Giants — Throws Right

| San Francisco Giants | W–L | ERA | AB | H | HR | BB | SO | BA | SA | OBA |
|---|---|---|---|---|---|---|---|---|---|---|
| Season | 2-1 | 2.68 | 151 | 32 | 2 | 27 | 24 | .212 | .298 | .328 |
| vs. Left-Handers | | | 79 | 17 | 0 | 15 | 11 | .215 | .278 | .337 |
| vs. Right-Handers | | | 72 | 15 | 2 | 12 | 13 | .208 | .319 | .318 |
| Home | 1-1 | 0.63 | 49 | 11 | 1 | 7 | 10 | .224 | .306 | .321 |
| Road | 1-0 | 3.68 | 102 | 21 | 1 | 20 | 14 | .206 | .294 | .331 |
| Grass | 2-1 | 2.39 | 91 | 19 | 2 | 20 | 16 | .209 | .286 | .351 |
| Artificial Turf | 0-0 | 3.12 | 60 | 13 | 0 | 7 | 8 | .217 | .317 | .290 |
| April | 0-0 | 0.93 | 27 | 3 | 0 | 5 | 3 | .111 | .185 | .242 |
| May | 0-0 | 0.00 | 19 | 5 | 0 | 4 | 2 | .263 | .368 | .391 |
| June | 2-1 | 3.38 | 45 | 10 | 1 | 7 | 11 | .222 | .289 | .321 |
| July | 0-0 | 3.60 | 55 | 12 | 1 | 9 | 8 | .218 | .327 | .328 |
| August | 0-0 | 13.50 | 5 | 2 | 0 | 2 | 0 | .400 | .400 | .571 |
| Sept./Oct. | | | 0 | 0 | 0 | 0 | 0 | — | — | — |
| Leading Off Inn. | | | 33 | 5 | 0 | 7 | 5 | .152 | .182 | .300 |
| Runners On | | | 72 | 18 | 2 | 11 | 11 | .250 | .375 | .341 |
| Runners/Scor. Pos. | | | 39 | 11 | 1 | 9 | 4 | .282 | .385 | .400 |
| Runners On/2 Out | | | 30 | 6 | 1 | 6 | 5 | .200 | .300 | .333 |
| Scor. Pos./2 Out | | | 19 | 4 | 1 | 5 | 2 | .211 | .368 | .375 |
| Late Inning Pressure | | | 42 | 7 | 1 | 9 | 10 | .167 | .286 | .314 |
| Leading Off | | | 12 | 1 | 0 | 0 | 3 | .083 | .083 | .083 |
| Runners On | | | 13 | 1 | 1 | 5 | 3 | .077 | .308 | .333 |
| Runners/Scor. Pos. | | | 5 | 0 | 0 | 3 | 0 | .000 | .000 | .375 |
| First 9 Batters | | | 145 | 31 | 2 | 26 | 23 | .214 | .303 | .329 |
| Second 9 Batters | | | 6 | 1 | 0 | 1 | 1 | .167 | .167 | .286 |
| All Batters Thereafter | | | 0 | 0 | 0 | 0 | 0 | — | — | — |

Loves to face: Harry and the Hendersons (see below)
Hates to face: Keith Moreland (.429, 6-for-14, 1 HR)
Spilman: 0-for-1, 1 SO; Rickey: 0-for-9, 9 SO; Dave: 0-for-6, 5 SO. . . . Ground outs-to-air outs ratio: 1.15 last season, 0.85 for career. . . . Additional statistics: 4 double-play ground outs in 37 opportunities, 7 doubles, 0 triples in 43.2 innings last season. . . . Faced only 61 batters in Late-Inning Pressure Situations, his lowest total of the past 15 years, including 1976, when he started 29 games for the White Sox. Faced only 10 while protecting leads of three runs or fewer in 9th inning or overtime. . . . Has pitched in 853 games, the most of any player active at the end of last season. Within range: Phil Niekro (10th place, 864 games), Don McMahon (874), Jim Kaat (898), Sparky Lyle (899), and Cy Young (906).

## Mark Grant

San Diego Padres — Throws Right

| San Diego Padres | W–L | ERA | AB | H | HR | BB | SO | BA | SA | OBA |
|---|---|---|---|---|---|---|---|---|---|---|
| Season | 8-2 | 3.33 | 424 | 105 | 11 | 32 | 69 | .248 | .380 | .304 |
| vs. Left-Handers | | | 199 | 49 | 4 | 18 | 28 | .246 | .347 | .307 |
| vs. Right-Handers | | | 225 | 56 | 7 | 14 | 41 | .249 | .409 | .300 |
| Home | 3-1 | 4.33 | 197 | 50 | 9 | 16 | 32 | .254 | .442 | .316 |
| Road | 5-1 | 2.45 | 227 | 55 | 2 | 16 | 37 | .242 | .326 | .293 |
| Grass | 5-1 | 4.09 | 299 | 78 | 10 | 22 | 47 | .261 | .421 | .317 |
| Artificial Turf | 3-1 | 1.54 | 125 | 27 | 1 | 10 | 22 | .216 | .280 | .272 |
| April | 0-0 | 2.70 | 49 | 12 | 1 | 3 | 11 | .245 | .347 | .315 |
| May | 1-1 | 1.93 | 47 | 8 | 0 | 5 | 8 | .170 | .234 | .259 |
| June | 1-0 | 3.86 | 58 | 15 | 2 | 5 | 8 | .259 | .379 | .317 |
| July | 2-0 | 2.21 | 73 | 19 | 2 | 5 | 6 | .260 | .411 | .308 |
| August | 2-1 | 2.51 | 100 | 22 | 2 | 6 | 15 | .220 | .330 | .264 |
| Sept./Oct. | 2-0 | 6.08 | 97 | 29 | 4 | 8 | 21 | .299 | .495 | .349 |
| Leading Off Inn. | | | 103 | 28 | 4 | 5 | 19 | .272 | .408 | .312 |
| Runners On | | | 176 | 45 | 5 | 16 | 26 | .256 | .415 | .318 |
| Runners/Scor. Pos. | | | 97 | 20 | 4 | 14 | 16 | .206 | .392 | .307 |
| Runners On/2 Out | | | 70 | 19 | 3 | 6 | 14 | .271 | .443 | .329 |
| Scor. Pos./2 Out | | | 44 | 9 | 3 | 6 | 10 | .205 | .409 | .300 |
| Late Inning Pressure | | | 105 | 26 | 3 | 9 | 16 | .248 | .362 | .313 |
| Leading Off | | | 32 | 8 | 1 | 1 | 7 | .250 | .344 | .294 |
| Runners On | | | 29 | 9 | 2 | 6 | 3 | .310 | .552 | .429 |
| Runners/Scor. Pos. | | | 14 | 3 | 1 | 6 | 3 | .214 | .500 | .450 |
| First 9 Batters | | | 328 | 83 | 10 | 24 | 52 | .253 | .393 | .308 |
| Second 9 Batters | | | 85 | 21 | 1 | 7 | 15 | .247 | .365 | .304 |
| All Batters Thereafter | | | 11 | 1 | 0 | 1 | 2 | .091 | .091 | .167 |

Loves to face: Rafael Ramirez (0-for-10)
Hates to face: Eric and Glenn Davis (see below)
Eric (.500, 8-for-16, 4 HR); Glenn (.571, 4-for-7, 2 HR). . . . Ground outs-to-air outs ratio: 1.44 last season, 1.28 for career. . . . Additional statistics: 14 double-play ground outs in 90 opportunities, 19 doubles, 2 triples in 116.1 innings last season. . . . Faced 9.32 batters per relief appearance, highest average in N.L. (minimum: 20 games). . . . Opponents' BA with runners in scoring position has declined throughout his career: .386, .273, .247, .222, .206. . . . Among active players with at least 100 PAs, only Don Carman (.047) and Andy McGaffigan (.048) have lower BAs than Grant (.051). . . . Footnote to history: Was among extras in 1987 swap that included future Cy Young–winner Mark Davis and future MVP Kevin Mitchell.

## Kevin Gross

Montreal Expos — Throws Right

| Montreal Expos | W–L | ERA | AB | H | HR | BB | SO | BA | SA | OBA |
|---|---|---|---|---|---|---|---|---|---|---|
| Season | 11-12 | 4.38 | 760 | 188 | 20 | 88 | 158 | .247 | .388 | .329 |
| vs. Left-Handers | | | 415 | 100 | 10 | 57 | 79 | .241 | .378 | .337 |
| vs. Right-Handers | | | 345 | 88 | 10 | 31 | 79 | .255 | .400 | .319 |
| Home | 6-4 | 4.29 | 356 | 90 | 6 | 40 | 73 | .253 | .379 | .331 |
| Road | 5-8 | 4.46 | 404 | 98 | 14 | 48 | 85 | .243 | .396 | .327 |
| Grass | 3-4 | 3.25 | 232 | 54 | 6 | 26 | 43 | .233 | .336 | .318 |
| Artificial Turf | 8-8 | 4.90 | 528 | 134 | 14 | 62 | 115 | .254 | .411 | .334 |
| April | 3-2 | 4.06 | 123 | 35 | 4 | 12 | 23 | .285 | .480 | .353 |
| May | 2-1 | 3.68 | 167 | 41 | 4 | 11 | 37 | .246 | .383 | .294 |
| June | 2-4 | 5.95 | 147 | 34 | 4 | 21 | 26 | .231 | .395 | .335 |
| July | 1-1 | 3.38 | 92 | 21 | 1 | 16 | 22 | .228 | .348 | .343 |
| August | 2-1 | 4.19 | 138 | 31 | 5 | 17 | 32 | .225 | .348 | .310 |
| Sept./Oct. | 1-3 | 4.81 | 93 | 26 | 2 | 11 | 18 | .280 | .366 | .362 |
| Leading Off Inn. | | | 193 | 56 | 3 | 17 | 36 | .290 | .399 | .351 |
| Runners On | | | 318 | 77 | 9 | 48 | 69 | .242 | .409 | .342 |
| Runners/Scor. Pos. | | | 204 | 46 | 6 | 35 | 51 | .225 | .402 | .335 |
| Runners On/2 Out | | | 129 | 29 | 4 | 25 | 25 | .225 | .372 | .351 |
| Scor. Pos./2 Out | | | 93 | 18 | 3 | 21 | 19 | .194 | .344 | .342 |
| Late Inning Pressure | | | 47 | 14 | 1 | 2 | 10 | .298 | .362 | .340 |
| Leading Off | | | 13 | 3 | 1 | 1 | 1 | .231 | .462 | .286 |
| Runners On | | | 18 | 6 | 0 | 1 | 5 | .333 | .333 | .368 |
| Runners/Scor. Pos. | | | 8 | 3 | 0 | 1 | 1 | .375 | .375 | .444 |
| First 9 Batters | | | 233 | 54 | 5 | 37 | 48 | .232 | .352 | .336 |
| Second 9 Batters | | | 246 | 67 | 9 | 24 | 58 | .272 | .451 | .344 |
| All Batters Thereafter | | | 281 | 67 | 6 | 27 | 52 | .238 | .363 | .310 |

Loves to face: Luis Quinones (0-for-9)
Hates to face: Eric Davis (.455, 10-for-22, 3 HR, 5 BB)
Ground outs-to-air outs ratio: 1.01 last season, 0.98 for career. . . . Additional statistics: 5 double-play ground outs in 137 opportunities, 3d-lowest rate of any pitcher in the N.L. (min.: 75 opp.), 33 doubles, 7 triples in 201.1 innings last season. . . . Allowed 26 first-inning runs in 31 starts. . . . Batting support: 3.58 runs per start. . . . ERA of 1.31 in his 11 wins, 9.28 in 12 losses. . . . Allowed eight consecutive batters to reach base on July 4 vs. Braves, 2d-longest streak in N.L. . . . Hasn't won consecutive starts since July 1988. . . . Career record of 18–11 in June, 53–67 in other months. . . . One of 14 pitchers with 30 or more starts in each of the past five seasons; has the lowest winning percentage among them during that time (.468, 59–67).

## Atlee Hammaker

San Francisco Giants — Throws Left

| San Francisco Giants | W–L | ERA | AB | H | HR | BB | SO | BA | SA | OBA |
|---|---|---|---|---|---|---|---|---|---|---|
| Season | 6-6 | 3.76 | 288 | 78 | 5 | 23 | 30 | .271 | .354 | .323 |
| vs. Left-Handers | | | 65 | 18 | 0 | 7 | 5 | .277 | .292 | .351 |
| vs. Right-Handers | | | 223 | 60 | 5 | 16 | 25 | .269 | .372 | .314 |
| Home | 3-1 | 2.55 | 125 | 27 | 2 | 11 | 18 | .216 | .288 | .277 |
| Road | 3-5 | 4.79 | 163 | 51 | 3 | 12 | 12 | .313 | .405 | .358 |
| Grass | 5-4 | 2.66 | 222 | 54 | 4 | 19 | 26 | .243 | .324 | .300 |
| Artificial Turf | 1-2 | 8.04 | 66 | 24 | 1 | 4 | 4 | .364 | .455 | .397 |
| April | 1-2 | 3.86 | 69 | 20 | 0 | 7 | 6 | .290 | .319 | .342 |
| May | 3-1 | 2.18 | 68 | 9 | 2 | 5 | 9 | .132 | .235 | .200 |
| June | 2-1 | 4.34 | 76 | 23 | 0 | 4 | 6 | .303 | .342 | .338 |
| July | 0-2 | 5.27 | 56 | 21 | 3 | 5 | 5 | .375 | .589 | .426 |
| August | 0-0 | 9.00 | 7 | 2 | 0 | 2 | 1 | .286 | .286 | .444 |
| Sept./Oct. | 0-0 | 0.00 | 12 | 3 | 0 | 0 | 3 | .250 | .250 | .250 |
| Leading Off Inn. | | | 74 | 23 | 3 | 3 | 7 | .311 | .459 | .346 |
| Runners On | | | 116 | 30 | 2 | 16 | 6 | .259 | .336 | .338 |
| Runners/Scor. Pos. | | | 55 | 16 | 1 | 11 | 2 | .291 | .382 | .386 |
| Runners On/2 Out | | | 48 | 12 | 1 | 7 | 1 | .250 | .333 | .345 |
| Scor. Pos./2 Out | | | 28 | 4 | 0 | 6 | 1 | .143 | .143 | .294 |
| Late Inning Pressure | | | 68 | 17 | 0 | 7 | 4 | .250 | .265 | .316 |
| Leading Off | | | 19 | 6 | 0 | 1 | 1 | .316 | .316 | .350 |
| Runners On | | | 27 | 5 | 0 | 4 | 1 | .185 | .185 | .281 |
| Runners/Scor. Pos. | | | 9 | 2 | 0 | 4 | 0 | .222 | .222 | .429 |
| First 9 Batters | | | 183 | 49 | 4 | 15 | 19 | .268 | .350 | .317 |
| Second 9 Batters | | | 71 | 16 | 0 | 7 | 8 | .225 | .282 | .295 |
| All Batters Thereafter | | | 34 | 13 | 1 | 1 | 3 | .382 | .529 | .417 |

Loves to face: Von Hayes (.100, 2-for-20, 6 SO)
Hates to face: Dale Murphy (.450, 18-for-40, 5 HR)
Ground outs-to-air outs ratio: 1.64 last season, 1.45 for career. . . . Additional statistics: 13 double-play ground outs in 71 opportunities, highest rate of any N.L. pitcher (min.: 10 GIDPs), 9 doubles, 0 triples in 76.2 innings last season. . . . Faced 69 batters between strikeouts (April 15–May 16), 2d longest streak in N.L. . . . Had a 2.76 ERA in 42.1 innings with Kirt Manwaring as his partner, 5.13 ERA in 33.1 innings with Terry Kennedy. . . . Has faced 295 left-handed batters over last three seasons, allowed them only 15 RBI. . . . Allowed six hits in 10 at-bats with the bases loaded. Career mark: .309 (17-for-55). . . . Career record of 34–16 (2.96 ERA) at Candlestick, 21–41 (4.15 ERA) elsewhere.

## Greg A. Harris

Throws Right

| Philadelphia Phillies | W–L | ERA | AB | H | HR | BB | SO | BA | SA | OBA |
|---|---|---|---|---|---|---|---|---|---|---|
| Season | 2-2 | 3.58 | 274 | 64 | 7 | 43 | 51 | .234 | .369 | .340 |
| vs. Left-Handers | | | 121 | 23 | 1 | 25 | 20 | .190 | .281 | .329 |
| vs. Right-Handers | | | 153 | 41 | 6 | 18 | 31 | .268 | .438 | .349 |
| Home | 1-1 | 5.01 | 157 | 42 | 4 | 26 | 29 | .268 | .420 | .371 |
| Road | 1-1 | 1.85 | 117 | 22 | 3 | 17 | 22 | .188 | .299 | .296 |
| Grass | 0-0 | 2.70 | 44 | 7 | 1 | 7 | 10 | .159 | .273 | .275 |
| Artificial Turf | 2-2 | 3.77 | 230 | 57 | 6 | 36 | 41 | .248 | .387 | .352 |
| April | 1-0 | 2.60 | 58 | 8 | 3 | 7 | 14 | .138 | .310 | .227 |
| May | 0-0 | 4.24 | 64 | 18 | 1 | 10 | 9 | .281 | .391 | .378 |
| June | 0-1 | 3.10 | 74 | 18 | 0 | 16 | 11 | .243 | .351 | .378 |
| July | 1-1 | 4.35 | 78 | 20 | 3 | 10 | 17 | .256 | .410 | .352 |
| August | | | 0 | 0 | 0 | 0 | 0 | — | — | — |
| Sept./Oct. | | | 0 | 0 | 0 | 0 | 0 | — | — | — |
| Leading Off Inn. | | | 61 | 12 | 2 | 10 | 13 | .197 | .426 | .319 |
| Runners On | | | 134 | 33 | 2 | 19 | 24 | .246 | .328 | .340 |
| Runners/Scor. Pos. | | | 78 | 21 | 2 | 18 | 17 | .269 | .372 | .404 |
| Runners On/2 Out | | | 52 | 12 | 1 | 12 | 7 | .231 | .365 | .375 |
| Scor. Pos./2 Out | | | 31 | 8 | 1 | 12 | 5 | .258 | .387 | .465 |
| Late Inning Pressure | | | 42 | 15 | 1 | 7 | 4 | .357 | .500 | .460 |
| Leading Off | | | 10 | 2 | 1 | 2 | 1 | .200 | .600 | .385 |
| Runners On | | | 18 | 10 | 0 | 3 | 3 | .556 | .611 | .619 |
| Runners/Scor. Pos. | | | 13 | 8 | 0 | 3 | 2 | .615 | .692 | .688 |
| First 9 Batters | | | 244 | 57 | 6 | 40 | 45 | .234 | .365 | .344 |
| Second 9 Batters | | | 30 | 7 | 1 | 3 | 6 | .233 | .400 | .303 |
| All Batters Thereafter | | | 0 | 0 | 0 | 0 | 0 | — | — | — |

Loves to face: Mookie Wilson (.083, 1-for-12)
Hates to face: Gary Gaetti (.667, 8-for-12, 1 HR)
Ground outs-to-air outs ratio: 1.15 last season, 1.28 for career.... Additional statistics: 4 double-play ground outs in 63 opportunities, 12 doubles, 2 triples in 75.1 innings last season.... Led N.L. relievers with 10 wild pitches.... Allowed hits to six consecutive batters in Late-Inning Pressure Situations, longest streak in majors. Opponents batted 84 points higher in LIPS (.293) than otherwise (.208), 5th-largest difference (minimum: 75 AB each).... Called on to protect leads in only two of his last 36 appearances with Phillies.... Earned 20 saves for Texas in 1986, only two in last three seasons.... Has pitched for seven clubs in nine-year career, including Boston, where he finished 1989.

## Greg W. Harris

Throws Right

| San Diego Padres | W–L | ERA | AB | H | HR | BB | SO | BA | SA | OBA |
|---|---|---|---|---|---|---|---|---|---|---|
| Season | 8-9 | 2.60 | 493 | 106 | 8 | 52 | 106 | .215 | .298 | .291 |
| vs. Left-Handers | | | 281 | 55 | 2 | 30 | 54 | .196 | .253 | .276 |
| vs. Right-Handers | | | 212 | 51 | 6 | 22 | 52 | .241 | .358 | .312 |
| Home | 6-4 | 2.36 | 224 | 47 | 4 | 30 | 53 | .210 | .313 | .301 |
| Road | 2-5 | 2.80 | 269 | 59 | 4 | 22 | 53 | .219 | .286 | .283 |
| Grass | 7-6 | 2.00 | 363 | 74 | 5 | 40 | 79 | .204 | .289 | .281 |
| Artificial Turf | 1-3 | 4.25 | 130 | 32 | 3 | 12 | 27 | .246 | .323 | .319 |
| April | 0-0 | 0.00 | 16 | 3 | 0 | 1 | 5 | .188 | .188 | .235 |
| May | 1-2 | 1.80 | 69 | 11 | 3 | 6 | 20 | .159 | .304 | .237 |
| June | 2-1 | 2.75 | 70 | 15 | 0 | 10 | 20 | .214 | .257 | .309 |
| July | 0-3 | 4.37 | 86 | 22 | 3 | 8 | 17 | .256 | .442 | .316 |
| August | 3-1 | 3.31 | 132 | 30 | 2 | 12 | 24 | .227 | .295 | .292 |
| Sept./Oct. | 2-2 | 1.38 | 120 | 25 | 0 | 15 | 20 | .208 | .233 | .301 |
| Leading Off Inn. | | | 128 | 19 | 0 | 5 | 33 | .148 | .195 | .180 |
| Runners On | | | 173 | 43 | 2 | 33 | 34 | .249 | .324 | .365 |
| Runners/Scor. Pos. | | | 98 | 22 | 1 | 23 | 24 | .224 | .286 | .366 |
| Runners On/2 Out | | | 83 | 20 | 0 | 24 | 18 | .241 | .277 | .411 |
| Scor. Pos./2 Out | | | 55 | 9 | 0 | 15 | 17 | .164 | .182 | .343 |
| Late Inning Pressure | | | 201 | 43 | 2 | 22 | 43 | .214 | .264 | .296 |
| Leading Off | | | 55 | 7 | 0 | 3 | 16 | .127 | .164 | .172 |
| Runners On | | | 63 | 18 | 0 | 13 | 9 | .286 | .286 | .403 |
| Runners/Scor. Pos. | | | 38 | 11 | 0 | 8 | 4 | .289 | .289 | .404 |
| First 9 Batters | | | 326 | 62 | 7 | 31 | 75 | .190 | .288 | .263 |
| Second 9 Batters | | | 106 | 28 | 0 | 9 | 16 | .264 | .302 | .322 |
| All Batters Thereafter | | | 61 | 16 | 1 | 12 | 15 | .262 | .344 | .384 |

Loves to face: Gerald Young (.077, 1-for-13)
Hates to face: Glenn Wilson (.750, 3-for-4, 2 HR)
Ground outs-to-air outs ratio: 1.26 last season, 1.16 for career.... Additional statistics: 10 double-play ground outs in 76 opportunities, 13 doubles, 2 triples in 135.0 innings last season.... Opponents had only two hits in 25 at-bats during the first innings of his eight starts.... Shared N.L. lead for wins among rookies with Derek Lilliquist, ranked second to Mike Stanton with six saves.... N.L. rookies in double figures in both categories: Joe Black, Hoyt Wilhelm, Dave Jolly, Dick Farrell, Sammy Ellis, Elias Sosa, and Butch Metzger.... Opponents' on-base average leading off innings was the 2d lowest of the past 15 years (minimum: 100 BFP). The lowest belongs to Greg *A.* Harris (.175 in 1985).

## Neal Heaton

Throws Left

| Pittsburgh Pirates | W–L | ERA | AB | H | HR | BB | SO | BA | SA | OBA |
|---|---|---|---|---|---|---|---|---|---|---|
| Season | 6-7 | 3.05 | 544 | 127 | 12 | 55 | 67 | .233 | .360 | .309 |
| vs. Left-Handers | | | 114 | 15 | 0 | 7 | 17 | .132 | .158 | .194 |
| vs. Right-Handers | | | 430 | 112 | 12 | 48 | 50 | .260 | .414 | .339 |
| Home | 2-4 | 2.52 | 275 | 66 | 4 | 31 | 31 | .240 | .338 | .323 |
| Road | 4-3 | 3.61 | 269 | 61 | 8 | 24 | 36 | .227 | .383 | .295 |
| Grass | 0-3 | 4.40 | 105 | 24 | 3 | 8 | 9 | .229 | .390 | .302 |
| Artificial Turf | 6-4 | 2.73 | 439 | 103 | 9 | 47 | 58 | .235 | .353 | .311 |
| April | 0-2 | 2.73 | 96 | 21 | 2 | 11 | 8 | .219 | .313 | .299 |
| May | 1-4 | 5.35 | 140 | 39 | 6 | 8 | 8 | .279 | .486 | .331 |
| June | 0-0 | 5.40 | 52 | 15 | 1 | 11 | 7 | .288 | .365 | .413 |
| July | 1-1 | 2.45 | 81 | 20 | 1 | 13 | 8 | .247 | .383 | .361 |
| August | 1-0 | 0.61 | 48 | 6 | 1 | 5 | 10 | .125 | .208 | .208 |
| Sept./Oct. | 3-0 | 1.51 | 127 | 26 | 1 | 7 | 26 | .205 | .299 | .248 |
| Leading Off Inn. | | | 139 | 37 | 6 | 9 | 12 | .266 | .446 | .311 |
| Runners On | | | 230 | 56 | 3 | 30 | 36 | .243 | .348 | .330 |
| Runners/Scor. Pos. | | | 153 | 33 | 2 | 24 | 25 | .216 | .314 | .320 |
| Runners On/2 Out | | | 102 | 21 | 2 | 18 | 19 | .206 | .304 | .325 |
| Scor. Pos./2 Out | | | 78 | 15 | 1 | 17 | 15 | .192 | .269 | .337 |
| Late Inning Pressure | | | 67 | 15 | 1 | 9 | 8 | .224 | .313 | .316 |
| Leading Off | | | 20 | 5 | 0 | 1 | 1 | .250 | .300 | .286 |
| Runners On | | | 23 | 5 | 0 | 5 | 4 | .217 | .217 | .357 |
| Runners/Scor. Pos. | | | 15 | 4 | 0 | 5 | 2 | .267 | .267 | .450 |
| First 9 Batters | | | 266 | 47 | 2 | 33 | 39 | .177 | .244 | .277 |
| Second 9 Batters | | | 166 | 42 | 4 | 10 | 19 | .253 | .373 | .300 |
| All Batters Thereafter | | | 112 | 38 | 6 | 12 | 9 | .339 | .616 | .400 |

Loves to face: Ken Griffey, Sr. (0-for-16)
Hates to face: Kevin Bass (.471, 8-for-17, 3 2B, 3 HR)
Ground outs-to-air outs ratio: 0.99 last season, 0.95 for career.... Additional statistics: 9 double-play ground outs in 102 opportunities, 25 doubles, 4 triples in 147.1 innings last season.... Allowed 3 first-inning runs in 18 starts. ERA increased in every inning from first (1.00) through sixth (7.20).... Batting support: 3.67 runs per start.... Batting average by opposing left-handers was lowest in majors over past 15 years (minimum: 125 BFP). Faced 54 consecutive *left*-handed batters without allowing a hit (July 15–Aug. 15), longest streak of last 15 years.... ERA by catcher: LaValliere, 1.41 (38.1 innings); Bilardello, 1.71 (26.1); Ortiz, 3.58 (65.1); others, 8.36 (17.1).

## Orel Hershiser

Throws Right

| Los Angeles Dodgers | W–L | ERA | AB | H | HR | BB | SO | BA | SA | OBA |
|---|---|---|---|---|---|---|---|---|---|---|
| Season | 15-15 | 2.31 | 942 | 226 | 9 | 77 | 178 | .240 | .316 | .298 |
| vs. Left-Handers | | | 519 | 134 | 5 | 50 | 81 | .258 | .339 | .323 |
| vs. Right-Handers | | | 423 | 92 | 4 | 27 | 97 | .217 | .288 | .265 |
| Home | 9-8 | 2.71 | 467 | 115 | 6 | 33 | 70 | .246 | .325 | .297 |
| Road | 6-7 | 1.93 | 475 | 111 | 3 | 44 | 108 | .234 | .307 | .298 |
| Grass | 11-14 | 2.63 | 725 | 180 | 8 | 58 | 131 | .248 | .332 | .305 |
| Artificial Turf | 4-1 | 1.31 | 217 | 46 | 1 | 19 | 47 | .212 | .263 | .274 |
| April | 3-2 | 1.96 | 131 | 29 | 0 | 12 | 29 | .221 | .267 | .283 |
| May | 4-2 | 3.06 | 170 | 35 | 2 | 12 | 30 | .206 | .288 | .263 |
| June | 2-3 | 2.09 | 160 | 43 | 4 | 11 | 32 | .269 | .375 | .316 |
| July | 3-1 | 2.20 | 153 | 33 | 0 | 12 | 24 | .216 | .268 | .271 |
| August | 2-2 | 2.15 | 163 | 40 | 2 | 12 | 32 | .245 | .325 | .297 |
| Sept./Oct. | 1-5 | 2.30 | 165 | 46 | 1 | 18 | 31 | .279 | .364 | .351 |
| Leading Off Inn. | | | 242 | 67 | 3 | 15 | 39 | .277 | .368 | .322 |
| Runners On | | | 392 | 89 | 4 | 41 | 83 | .227 | .309 | .299 |
| Runners/Scor. Pos. | | | 219 | 37 | 3 | 31 | 62 | .169 | .256 | .271 |
| Runners On/2 Out | | | 164 | 34 | 2 | 19 | 40 | .207 | .274 | .290 |
| Scor. Pos./2 Out | | | 103 | 14 | 2 | 16 | 33 | .136 | .214 | .252 |
| Late Inning Pressure | | | 137 | 30 | 1 | 21 | 25 | .219 | .299 | .323 |
| Leading Off | | | 37 | 8 | 1 | 4 | 7 | .216 | .351 | .293 |
| Runners On | | | 57 | 11 | 0 | 9 | 9 | .193 | .263 | .304 |
| Runners/Scor. Pos. | | | 27 | 4 | 0 | 8 | 5 | .148 | .222 | .342 |
| First 9 Batters | | | 283 | 81 | 3 | 20 | 55 | .286 | .364 | .333 |
| Second 9 Batters | | | 282 | 63 | 2 | 19 | 57 | .223 | .284 | .272 |
| All Batters Thereafter | | | 377 | 82 | 4 | 38 | 66 | .218 | .305 | .290 |

Loves to face: Albert Hall (.095, 2-for-21)
Hates to face: R. J. Reynolds (.410, 16-for-39, 7 BB)
Ground outs-to-air outs ratio: 1.99 last season, 2.13 for career.... Additional statistics: 29 double-play ground outs (most in N.L.) in 193 opportunities, 41 doubles, 2 triples in 256.2 innings last season.... Allowed 14 first-inning runs in 33 starts. Opponents batted .295 in the first inning, .233 thereafter.... Batting support: 3.30 runs per start.... First pitcher since Phil Niekro to lead N.L. in innings for three straight seasons. Last to lead for at least four in a row: Robin Roberts (1951–55).... Had a 2.70 ERA in 203 innings with Scioscia behind the plate, 0.82 ERA in 43.2 innings with Dempsey.... Opponents' career average is .178 (18-for-101, two HR) with the bases loaded.

## Ken Hill

Throws Right

| St. Louis Cardinals | W–L | ERA | AB | H | HR | BB | SO | BA | SA | OBA |
|---|---|---|---|---|---|---|---|---|---|---|
| Season | 7-15 | 3.80 | 739 | 186 | 9 | 99 | 112 | .252 | .346 | .342 |
| vs. Left-Handers | | | 395 | 107 | 3 | 63 | 53 | .271 | .359 | .372 |
| vs. Right-Handers | | | 344 | 79 | 6 | 36 | 59 | .230 | .331 | .306 |
| Home | 2-5 | 3.80 | 364 | 90 | 3 | 47 | 49 | .247 | .327 | .337 |
| Road | 5-10 | 3.79 | 375 | 96 | 6 | 52 | 63 | .256 | .365 | .347 |
| Grass | 2-4 | 3.16 | 192 | 46 | 3 | 23 | 30 | .240 | .339 | .323 |
| Artificial Turf | 5-11 | 4.03 | 547 | 140 | 6 | 76 | 82 | .256 | .349 | .349 |
| April | 1-1 | 2.05 | 75 | 15 | 0 | 7 | 9 | .200 | .280 | .277 |
| May | 1-3 | 2.55 | 155 | 38 | 1 | 19 | 33 | .245 | .323 | .330 |
| June | 2-0 | 3.98 | 121 | 32 | 2 | 22 | 17 | .264 | .364 | .379 |
| July | 2-3 | 3.68 | 138 | 36 | 0 | 15 | 15 | .261 | .326 | .333 |
| August | 1-3 | 6.29 | 98 | 27 | 2 | 17 | 15 | .276 | .388 | .385 |
| Sept./Oct. | 0-5 | 4.54 | 152 | 38 | 4 | 19 | 23 | .250 | .382 | .333 |
| Leading Off Inn. | | | 173 | 47 | 3 | 32 | 19 | .272 | .393 | .391 |
| Runners On | | | 336 | 85 | 4 | 47 | 54 | .253 | .354 | .344 |
| Runners/Scor. Pos. | | | 187 | 47 | 3 | 40 | 33 | .251 | .369 | .378 |
| Runners On/2 Out | | | 144 | 36 | 1 | 26 | 28 | .250 | .354 | .365 |
| Scor. Pos./2 Out | | | 94 | 23 | 1 | 21 | 18 | .245 | .372 | .383 |
| Late Inning Pressure | | | 47 | 19 | 1 | 5 | 7 | .404 | .489 | .472 |
| Leading Off | | | 12 | 6 | 0 | 2 | 1 | .500 | .500 | .600 |
| Runners On | | | 24 | 9 | 1 | 3 | 3 | .375 | .542 | .444 |
| Runners/Scor. Pos. | | | 16 | 5 | 1 | 2 | 3 | .313 | .563 | .389 |
| First 9 Batters | | | 257 | 57 | 4 | 36 | 40 | .222 | .331 | .319 |
| Second 9 Batters | | | 250 | 61 | 3 | 30 | 42 | .244 | .360 | .324 |
| All Batters Thereafter | | | 232 | 68 | 2 | 33 | 30 | .293 | .349 | .387 |

Loves to face: Mike Marshall (.083, 1-for-12)
Hates to face: Tim Raines (.818, 9-for-11, 6 BB)
Ground outs-to-air outs ratio: 1.65 last season, 1.65 for career. . . . Additional statistics: 13 double-play ground outs in 168 opportunities, 27 doubles, 8 triples in 196.2 innings last season. . . . Allowed 23 first-inning runs in 33 starts for a 6.00 ERA (his highest of any inning). . . . Batting support: 3.82 runs per start. . . . Shared N.L. lead in losses with Don Carman and Orel Hershiser. Last Cardinals pitcher (and last Phillies pitcher) to do so was Steve Carlton. Last rookie: Steve Arlin, who lost 19 for 1971 Padres. . . . Led N.L. rookies in games started (33). . . . Only pitcher in majors to walk five consecutive batters (Did it over two games.) . . . Ended season with 1–9 record (4.88 ERA) over last 13 starts.

## Ricky Horton

Throws Left

| Dodgers/Cardinals | W–L | ERA | AB | H | HR | BB | SO | BA | SA | OBA |
|---|---|---|---|---|---|---|---|---|---|---|
| Season | 0-3 | 4.85 | 279 | 85 | 3 | 21 | 26 | .305 | .412 | .357 |
| vs. Left-Handers | | | 70 | 24 | 0 | 6 | 6 | .343 | .429 | .405 |
| vs. Right-Handers | | | 209 | 61 | 3 | 15 | 20 | .292 | .407 | .341 |
| Home | 0-2 | 4.62 | 147 | 44 | 1 | 11 | 17 | .299 | .381 | .350 |
| Road | 0-1 | 5.09 | 132 | 41 | 2 | 10 | 9 | .311 | .447 | .365 |
| Grass | 0-1 | 3.82 | 128 | 40 | 2 | 7 | 12 | .313 | .422 | .360 |
| Artificial Turf | 0-2 | 5.72 | 151 | 45 | 1 | 14 | 14 | .298 | .404 | .355 |
| April | 0-0 | 4.70 | 28 | 8 | 0 | 1 | 2 | .286 | .429 | .300 |
| May | 0-0 | 3.60 | 41 | 15 | 1 | 1 | 5 | .366 | .512 | .372 |
| June | 0-0 | 1.80 | 13 | 2 | 0 | 5 | 3 | .154 | .154 | .421 |
| July | 0-0 | 13.50 | 20 | 10 | 0 | 4 | 2 | .500 | .700 | .583 |
| August | 0-1 | 4.25 | 113 | 30 | 1 | 7 | 7 | .265 | .372 | .317 |
| Sept./Oct. | 0-2 | 5.63 | 64 | 20 | 1 | 3 | 7 | .313 | .375 | .348 |
| Leading Off Inn. | | | 65 | 16 | 2 | 6 | 6 | .246 | .354 | .310 |
| Runners On | | | 130 | 41 | 0 | 14 | 12 | .315 | .408 | .388 |
| Runners/Scor. Pos. | | | 83 | 26 | 0 | 9 | 8 | .313 | .422 | .371 |
| Runners On/2 Out | | | 48 | 14 | 0 | 7 | 6 | .292 | .354 | .404 |
| Scor. Pos./2 Out | | | 33 | 10 | 0 | 4 | 4 | .303 | .364 | .378 |
| Late Inning Pressure | | | 37 | 15 | 0 | 7 | 4 | .405 | .541 | .489 |
| Leading Off | | | 8 | 2 | 0 | 3 | 1 | .250 | .250 | .455 |
| Runners On | | | 21 | 10 | 0 | 4 | 1 | .476 | .667 | .538 |
| Runners/Scor. Pos. | | | 16 | 9 | 0 | 3 | 0 | .563 | .813 | .600 |
| First 9 Batters | | | 167 | 48 | 2 | 14 | 20 | .287 | .413 | .344 |
| Second 9 Batters | | | 78 | 23 | 1 | 5 | 3 | .295 | .385 | .333 |
| All Batters Thereafter | | | 34 | 14 | 0 | 2 | 3 | .412 | .471 | .474 |

Loves to face: Carmelo Martinez (.077, 1-for-13)
Hates to face: Glenn Davis (.500, 6-for-12, 3 2B, 2 HR)
Ground outs-to-air outs ratio: 1.46 last season, 1.45 for career. . . . Additional statistics: 11 double-play ground outs in 74 opportunities, 15 doubles, 3 triples in 72.1 innings last season. . . . Opponents batted .138 in first innings of eight starts, with no extra-base hits in 29 at-bats. . . . Made 34 appearances without a win or a save. Highest season totals for such ignominy: Arnold Earley, Bos. (57, 1965); Dave Tomlin, S.D. (49, 1976); Pete Burnside, Balt.-Wash. (44, 1963); Lee Guetterman, Sea. (41, 1986). Record for pitchers without a loss as well: Don Aase, Balt. (35, 1988). . . . Career BA: .239 by ground-ball hitters, .299 by fly-ballers. . . . Never allowed more than two HRs to left-handers in same season.

## Jay Howell

Throws Right

| Los Angeles Dodgers | W–L | ERA | AB | H | HR | BB | SO | BA | SA | OBA |
|---|---|---|---|---|---|---|---|---|---|---|
| Season | 5-3 | 1.58 | 284 | 60 | 3 | 22 | 55 | .211 | .289 | .266 |
| vs. Left-Handers | | | 159 | 33 | 1 | 17 | 32 | .208 | .270 | .282 |
| vs. Right-Handers | | | 125 | 27 | 2 | 5 | 23 | .216 | .312 | .244 |
| Home | 4-3 | 1.16 | 162 | 30 | 1 | 14 | 35 | .185 | .265 | .247 |
| Road | 1-0 | 2.18 | 122 | 30 | 2 | 8 | 20 | .246 | .320 | .292 |
| Grass | 5-3 | 1.71 | 227 | 47 | 2 | 20 | 48 | .207 | .286 | .269 |
| Artificial Turf | 0-0 | 1.10 | 57 | 13 | 1 | 2 | 7 | .228 | .298 | .254 |
| April | 1-2 | 1.17 | 53 | 14 | 0 | 8 | 8 | .264 | .283 | .355 |
| May | 1-1 | 0.73 | 43 | 8 | 0 | 4 | 5 | .186 | .233 | .250 |
| June | 0-0 | 0.51 | 64 | 11 | 1 | 1 | 17 | .172 | .234 | .185 |
| July | 0-0 | 1.04 | 29 | 4 | 0 | 2 | 8 | .138 | .172 | .194 |
| August | 1-0 | 0.63 | 50 | 11 | 0 | 1 | 10 | .220 | .260 | .235 |
| Sept./Oct. | 2-0 | 6.35 | 45 | 12 | 2 | 6 | 7 | .267 | .533 | .353 |
| Leading Off Inn. | | | 68 | 15 | 1 | 4 | 9 | .221 | .309 | .264 |
| Runners On | | | 117 | 22 | 1 | 13 | 32 | .188 | .248 | .265 |
| Runners/Scor. Pos. | | | 71 | 14 | 1 | 11 | 21 | .197 | .268 | .298 |
| Runners On/2 Out | | | 56 | 9 | 0 | 6 | 19 | .161 | .196 | .242 |
| Scor. Pos./2 Out | | | 37 | 7 | 0 | 6 | 12 | .189 | .243 | .302 |
| Late Inning Pressure | | | 228 | 47 | 2 | 18 | 39 | .206 | .272 | .262 |
| Leading Off | | | 56 | 12 | 0 | 3 | 7 | .214 | .250 | .254 |
| Runners On | | | 92 | 16 | 1 | 10 | 23 | .174 | .239 | .250 |
| Runners/Scor. Pos. | | | 55 | 10 | 1 | 9 | 14 | .182 | .273 | .288 |
| First 9 Batters | | | 271 | 57 | 3 | 22 | 54 | .210 | .292 | .268 |
| Second 9 Batters | | | 13 | 3 | 0 | 0 | 1 | .231 | .231 | .231 |
| All Batters Thereafter | | | 0 | 0 | 0 | 0 | 0 | — | — | — |

Loves to face: Darren Daulton (0-for-4, 4 SO)
Hates to face: Paul O'Neill (.800, 4-for-5, 1 2B, 1 3B, 1 HR)
Ground outs-to-air outs ratio: 0.72 last season, 1.06 for career. . . . Additional statistics: 9 double-play ground outs in 55 opportunities, 11 doubles, 1 triple in 79.2 innings last season. . . . Saved 28 games in 32 opportunities, 2d-highest percentage (.875) in N.L. (minimum: 10 saves). Converted 17 consecutive opportunities from June 5 through September 4. . . . Set a club record for saves on the only major league team never to have a player save 30 or more games in a season. . . . Opponents batting average is .201 in two seasons with the Dodgers, .267 in eight previous seasons. . . . Home, sweet home, wherever it is: five-team career record of 26–13 in home games, 11–23 on the road.

## Ken Howell

Throws Right

| Philadelphia Phillies | W–L | ERA | AB | H | HR | BB | SO | BA | SA | OBA |
|---|---|---|---|---|---|---|---|---|---|---|
| Season | 12-12 | 3.44 | 722 | 155 | 11 | 86 | 164 | .215 | .313 | .297 |
| vs. Left-Handers | | | 413 | 97 | 6 | 55 | 77 | .235 | .341 | .321 |
| vs. Right-Handers | | | 309 | 58 | 5 | 31 | 87 | .188 | .275 | .264 |
| Home | 4-5 | 3.19 | 360 | 85 | 7 | 39 | 84 | .236 | .342 | .309 |
| Road | 8-7 | 3.69 | 362 | 70 | 4 | 47 | 80 | .193 | .285 | .285 |
| Grass | 4-4 | 5.26 | 182 | 37 | 2 | 23 | 37 | .203 | .302 | .292 |
| Artificial Turf | 8-8 | 2.86 | 540 | 118 | 9 | 63 | 127 | .219 | .317 | .298 |
| April | 2-1 | 6.04 | 92 | 22 | 3 | 11 | 18 | .239 | .424 | .314 |
| May | 3-2 | 2.93 | 102 | 19 | 0 | 16 | 23 | .186 | .255 | .308 |
| June | 1-2 | 4.37 | 126 | 32 | 3 | 18 | 33 | .254 | .405 | .340 |
| July | 2-2 | 1.87 | 119 | 24 | 0 | 12 | 26 | .202 | .252 | .273 |
| August | 3-2 | 3.18 | 138 | 23 | 2 | 16 | 31 | .167 | .225 | .250 |
| Sept./Oct. | 1-3 | 2.95 | 145 | 35 | 3 | 13 | 33 | .241 | .338 | .302 |
| Leading Off Inn. | | | 185 | 44 | 3 | 24 | 39 | .238 | .357 | .329 |
| Runners On | | | 288 | 65 | 7 | 33 | 59 | .226 | .358 | .297 |
| Runners/Scor. Pos. | | | 147 | 36 | 3 | 27 | 28 | .245 | .388 | .344 |
| Runners On/2 Out | | | 115 | 19 | 4 | 13 | 25 | .165 | .313 | .250 |
| Scor. Pos./2 Out | | | 67 | 11 | 1 | 12 | 15 | .164 | .269 | .291 |
| Late Inning Pressure | | | 64 | 18 | 0 | 7 | 18 | .281 | .313 | .352 |
| Leading Off | | | 18 | 5 | 0 | 2 | 4 | .278 | .333 | .350 |
| Runners On | | | 23 | 8 | 0 | 4 | 4 | .348 | .391 | .444 |
| Runners/Scor. Pos. | | | 11 | 3 | 0 | 3 | 2 | .273 | .364 | .429 |
| First 9 Batters | | | 266 | 56 | 2 | 22 | 64 | .211 | .297 | .274 |
| Second 9 Batters | | | 245 | 52 | 7 | 33 | 58 | .212 | .347 | .301 |
| All Batters Thereafter | | | 211 | 47 | 2 | 31 | 42 | .223 | .294 | .318 |

Loves to face: Rafael Ramirez (0-for-12)
Hates to face: Bobby Bonilla (.636, 7-for-11, 1 HR)
Ground outs-to-air outs ratio: 1.50 last season, 1.32 for career. . . . Additional statistics: 17 double-play ground outs in 142 opportunities, 30 doubles, 4 triples in 204.0 innings last season. . . . Allowed 17 first-inning runs in 32 starts. . . . Batting support: 4.06 runs per start. . . . Streak of 35 consecutive hitless batters with runners on base was tied for longest in majors. . . . Shutout vs. Cubs was his first and only complete game in 36 career starts. . . . Career average of 8.51 strikeouts per nine innings is virtually the same as Roger Clemens's. . . . Opponents' BA with runners in scoring position has been higher than in other at-bats in each of his six seasons. Career marks: .270 vs. .220.

## Bruce Hurst

Throws Left

| San Diego Padres | W–L | ERA | AB | H | HR | BB | SO | BA | SA | OBA |
|---|---|---|---|---|---|---|---|---|---|---|
| Season | 15-11 | 2.69 | 903 | 214 | 16 | 66 | 179 | .237 | .339 | .288 |
| vs. Left-Handers | | | 144 | 43 | 2 | 13 | 20 | .299 | .424 | .357 |
| vs. Right-Handers | | | 759 | 171 | 14 | 53 | 159 | .225 | .323 | .275 |
| Home | 9-6 | 2.58 | 505 | 114 | 9 | 38 | 109 | .226 | .325 | .278 |
| Road | 6-5 | 2.83 | 398 | 100 | 7 | 28 | 70 | .251 | .357 | .300 |
| Grass | 13-8 | 2.65 | 734 | 171 | 14 | 55 | 146 | .233 | .335 | .285 |
| Artificial Turf | 2-3 | 2.86 | 169 | 43 | 2 | 11 | 33 | .254 | .355 | .300 |
| April | 3-1 | 3.55 | 140 | 28 | 5 | 6 | 31 | .200 | .350 | .233 |
| May | 2-2 | 3.00 | 158 | 35 | 4 | 13 | 32 | .222 | .329 | .281 |
| June | 1-2 | 2.31 | 154 | 43 | 2 | 6 | 31 | .279 | .351 | .306 |
| July | 3-3 | 3.13 | 165 | 47 | 2 | 14 | 32 | .285 | .400 | .337 |
| August | 3-1 | 2.91 | 127 | 32 | 2 | 11 | 18 | .252 | .378 | .312 |
| Sept./Oct. | 3-2 | 1.38 | 159 | 29 | 1 | 16 | 35 | .182 | .233 | .256 |
| Leading Off Inn. | | | 230 | 55 | 5 | 18 | 50 | .239 | .352 | .294 |
| Runners On | | | 343 | 81 | 4 | 33 | 57 | .236 | .321 | .301 |
| Runners/Scor. Pos. | | | 186 | 47 | 1 | 26 | 32 | .253 | .312 | .340 |
| Runners On/2 Out | | | 159 | 40 | 2 | 20 | 25 | .252 | .340 | .335 |
| Scor. Pos./2 Out | | | 101 | 26 | 0 | 16 | 16 | .257 | .297 | .359 |
| Late Inning Pressure | | | 124 | 26 | 3 | 6 | 22 | .210 | .306 | .246 |
| Leading Off | | | 35 | 8 | 1 | 1 | 5 | .229 | .343 | .250 |
| Runners On | | | 32 | 5 | 0 | 3 | 8 | .156 | .156 | .229 |
| Runners/Scor. Pos. | | | 16 | 2 | 0 | 2 | 5 | .125 | .125 | .222 |
| First 9 Batters | | | 269 | 60 | 2 | 20 | 66 | .223 | .279 | .276 |
| Second 9 Batters | | | 259 | 68 | 7 | 22 | 49 | .263 | .398 | .319 |
| All Batters Thereafter | | | 375 | 86 | 7 | 24 | 64 | .229 | .341 | .275 |

Loves to face: Jeff Hamilton (0-for-14, 5 SO)
Hates to face: Willie Randolph (.407, 33-for-81, 1 HR)
Ground outs-to-air outs ratio: 1.16 last season, 1.13 for career.... Additional statistics: 13 double-play ground outs in 158 opportunities, 40 doubles, 2 triples in 244.2 innings last season.... Allowed 8 first-inning runs in 33 starts. (Hasn't allowed a first-inning homer in his last 39 starts.) Allowed only one run in 30 innings pitched during the eighth inning or later.... Batting support: 3.73 runs per start.... Faced 37 consecutive batters without allowing a hit, longest streak in N.L.... Had a 1.91 ERA in 75.1 innings with Mark Parent catching, 3.20 in 160.1 IP with Santiago.... Had an ERA of 1.29 in seven no-decision starts.... Led N.L. pitchers in fielding percentage with 50 errorless chances.

## Danny Jackson

Throws Left

| Cincinnati Reds | W–L | ERA | AB | H | HR | BB | SO | BA | SA | OBA |
|---|---|---|---|---|---|---|---|---|---|---|
| Season | 6-11 | 5.60 | 451 | 122 | 10 | 57 | 70 | .271 | .395 | .351 |
| vs. Left-Handers | | | 67 | 18 | 1 | 7 | 21 | .269 | .373 | .333 |
| vs. Right-Handers | | | 384 | 104 | 9 | 50 | 49 | .271 | .398 | .354 |
| Home | 3-5 | 5.10 | 235 | 62 | 4 | 30 | 37 | .264 | .370 | .345 |
| Road | 3-6 | 6.14 | 216 | 60 | 6 | 27 | 33 | .278 | .421 | .358 |
| Grass | 2-4 | 5.31 | 157 | 42 | 3 | 21 | 29 | .268 | .382 | .350 |
| Artificial Turf | 4-7 | 5.76 | 294 | 80 | 7 | 36 | 41 | .272 | .401 | .351 |
| April | 1-5 | 6.88 | 140 | 42 | 6 | 15 | 17 | .300 | .493 | .368 |
| May | 2-3 | 5.45 | 131 | 30 | 0 | 16 | 24 | .229 | .298 | .311 |
| June | 2-1 | 5.64 | 92 | 29 | 1 | 13 | 18 | .315 | .402 | .396 |
| July | 1-2 | 4.01 | 88 | 21 | 3 | 13 | 11 | .239 | .375 | .337 |
| August | | | 0 | 0 | 0 | 0 | 0 | — | — | — |
| Sept./Oct. | | | 0 | 0 | 0 | 0 | 0 | — | — | — |
| Leading Off Inn. | | | 109 | 26 | 0 | 12 | 18 | .239 | .275 | .314 |
| Runners On | | | 199 | 62 | 7 | 32 | 32 | .312 | .477 | .403 |
| Runners/Scor. Pos. | | | 125 | 39 | 5 | 21 | 20 | .312 | .496 | .404 |
| Runners On/2 Out | | | 79 | 22 | 4 | 16 | 16 | .278 | .506 | .400 |
| Scor. Pos./2 Out | | | 57 | 15 | 4 | 13 | 11 | .263 | .561 | .400 |
| Late Inning Pressure | | | 23 | 4 | 1 | 3 | 3 | .174 | .348 | .269 |
| Leading Off | | | 7 | 1 | 0 | 1 | 2 | .143 | .143 | .250 |
| Runners On | | | 5 | 0 | 0 | 2 | 0 | .000 | .000 | .286 |
| Runners/Scor. Pos. | | | 3 | 0 | 0 | 2 | 0 | .000 | .000 | .400 |
| First 9 Batters | | | 157 | 38 | 3 | 20 | 30 | .242 | .363 | .328 |
| Second 9 Batters | | | 153 | 45 | 3 | 19 | 20 | .294 | .444 | .368 |
| All Batters Thereafter | | | 141 | 39 | 4 | 18 | 20 | .277 | .376 | .358 |

Loves to face: Gary Redus (0-for-17)
Hates to face: Darrin Jackson (.667, 6-for-9, 1 HR)
Ground outs-to-air outs ratio: 1.87 last season, 1.70 for career.... Additional statistics: 9 double-play ground outs in 107 opportunities, 22 doubles, 2 triples in 115.2 innings last season.... Allowed 20 first-inning runs in 20 starts.... Batting support: 3.55 runs per start.... Highest ERA of any N.L. starter (minimum: 15 GS).... Led N.L. in losses during April.... Career mark of 33–40 (4.10 ERA) before the All-Star break, 33–28 (3.18) in the second half.... Opponents' average with runners on base has been higher than with the bases empty in each of the last six seasons.... Struck out in 10 consecutive plate appearances, longest streak of the 1980s, and two short of Koufax's all-time record.

## Paul Kilgus

Throws Left

| Chicago Cubs | W–L | ERA | AB | H | HR | BB | SO | BA | SA | OBA |
|---|---|---|---|---|---|---|---|---|---|---|
| Season | 6-10 | 4.39 | 579 | 164 | 9 | 49 | 61 | .283 | .408 | .342 |
| vs. Left-Handers | | | 107 | 27 | 3 | 12 | 11 | .252 | .411 | .344 |
| vs. Right-Handers | | | 472 | 137 | 6 | 37 | 50 | .290 | .407 | .342 |
| Home | 3-4 | 3.68 | 335 | 89 | 7 | 23 | 35 | .266 | .403 | .318 |
| Road | 3-6 | 5.40 | 244 | 75 | 2 | 26 | 26 | .307 | .414 | .375 |
| Grass | 4-7 | 3.76 | 478 | 129 | 8 | 38 | 52 | .270 | .397 | .327 |
| Artificial Turf | 2-3 | 7.61 | 101 | 35 | 1 | 11 | 9 | .347 | .455 | .412 |
| April | 2-2 | 2.93 | 120 | 31 | 2 | 8 | 10 | .258 | .350 | .308 |
| May | 2-3 | 4.25 | 144 | 41 | 1 | 14 | 14 | .285 | .389 | .348 |
| June | 1-3 | 8.57 | 88 | 28 | 1 | 9 | 4 | .318 | .455 | .388 |
| July | 1-2 | 3.08 | 99 | 26 | 1 | 6 | 16 | .263 | .384 | .302 |
| August | 0-0 | 21.60 | 10 | 6 | 1 | 2 | 0 | .600 | 1.200 | .692 |
| Sept./Oct. | 0-0 | 3.30 | 118 | 32 | 3 | 10 | 17 | .271 | .407 | .333 |
| Leading Off Inn. | | | 147 | 40 | 3 | 7 | 16 | .272 | .395 | .314 |
| Runners On | | | 253 | 79 | 5 | 25 | 27 | .312 | .478 | .373 |
| Runners/Scor. Pos. | | | 135 | 41 | 3 | 18 | 17 | .304 | .481 | .380 |
| Runners On/2 Out | | | 95 | 23 | 2 | 15 | 11 | .242 | .368 | .345 |
| Scor. Pos./2 Out | | | 58 | 15 | 2 | 12 | 8 | .259 | .431 | .386 |
| Late Inning Pressure | | | 46 | 16 | 0 | 6 | 6 | .348 | .370 | .423 |
| Leading Off | | | 15 | 5 | 0 | 1 | 4 | .333 | .333 | .375 |
| Runners On | | | 17 | 5 | 0 | 3 | 0 | .294 | .353 | .400 |
| Runners/Scor. Pos. | | | 6 | 1 | 0 | 3 | 0 | .167 | .167 | .444 |
| First 9 Batters | | | 245 | 70 | 3 | 21 | 29 | .286 | .392 | .347 |
| Second 9 Batters | | | 189 | 47 | 2 | 11 | 19 | .249 | .333 | .291 |
| All Batters Thereafter | | | 145 | 47 | 4 | 17 | 13 | .324 | .531 | .399 |

Loves to face: Steve Balboni (.118, 2-for-17, 1 HR)
Hates to face: Mark McGwire (.625, 5-for-8, 2 2B, 2 HR)
Ground outs-to-air outs ratio: 1.41 last season, 1.36 for career.... Additional statistics: 16 double-play ground outs in 125 opportunities, 31 doubles, 7 triples in 145.2 innings last season.... Allowed 22 first-inning runs in 23 starts.... Batting support: 4.13 runs per start.... Had an ERA of 4.72 as a starter, 2.49 (no decisions, two saves) in 12 relief appearances.... Was the winning pitcher in only one of his last 11 starts. Recorded saves in his first two games as a reliever, but none after that.... Career record of 0–5 in September.... Opponents' career breakdown: .249 with bases empty, .281 with runners on base, .293 with runners in scoring position, .400 (10-for-25, one HR) with the bases loaded.

## Bob Kipper

Throws Left

| Pittsburgh Pirates | W–L | ERA | AB | H | HR | BB | SO | BA | SA | OBA |
|---|---|---|---|---|---|---|---|---|---|---|
| Season | 3-4 | 2.93 | 293 | 55 | 5 | 33 | 58 | .188 | .321 | .267 |
| vs. Left-Handers | | | 94 | 16 | 0 | 11 | 20 | .170 | .277 | .257 |
| vs. Right-Handers | | | 199 | 39 | 5 | 22 | 38 | .196 | .342 | .272 |
| Home | 2-0 | 1.85 | 139 | 23 | 2 | 13 | 29 | .165 | .230 | .237 |
| Road | 1-4 | 3.89 | 154 | 32 | 3 | 20 | 29 | .208 | .403 | .294 |
| Grass | 1-1 | 2.43 | 99 | 16 | 2 | 12 | 20 | .162 | .333 | .246 |
| Artificial Turf | 2-3 | 3.21 | 194 | 39 | 3 | 21 | 38 | .201 | .314 | .279 |
| April | 0-0 | 2.77 | 48 | 8 | 0 | 6 | 10 | .167 | .250 | .259 |
| May | 0-1 | 2.12 | 60 | 13 | 0 | 10 | 14 | .217 | .283 | .324 |
| June | 1-2 | 2.63 | 84 | 15 | 2 | 7 | 18 | .179 | .345 | .242 |
| July | 2-1 | 5.65 | 52 | 13 | 1 | 7 | 6 | .250 | .385 | .328 |
| August | | | 0 | 0 | 0 | 0 | 0 | — | — | — |
| Sept./Oct. | 0-0 | 1.84 | 49 | 6 | 2 | 3 | 10 | .122 | .327 | .173 |
| Leading Off Inn. | | | 67 | 11 | 1 | 9 | 10 | .164 | .299 | .263 |
| Runners On | | | 117 | 27 | 2 | 16 | 27 | .231 | .359 | .316 |
| Runners/Scor. Pos. | | | 69 | 15 | 1 | 13 | 16 | .217 | .333 | .329 |
| Runners On/2 Out | | | 57 | 15 | 0 | 10 | 15 | .263 | .298 | .373 |
| Scor. Pos./2 Out | | | 37 | 8 | 0 | 8 | 10 | .216 | .270 | .356 |
| Late Inning Pressure | | | 152 | 24 | 2 | 17 | 26 | .158 | .263 | .243 |
| Leading Off | | | 38 | 5 | 1 | 3 | 7 | .132 | .237 | .195 |
| Runners On | | | 53 | 10 | 1 | 8 | 10 | .189 | .302 | .295 |
| Runners/Scor. Pos. | | | 28 | 5 | 0 | 8 | 5 | .179 | .286 | .361 |
| First 9 Batters | | | 254 | 45 | 4 | 30 | 46 | .177 | .291 | .262 |
| Second 9 Batters | | | 36 | 10 | 1 | 3 | 12 | .278 | .556 | .325 |
| All Batters Thereafter | | | 3 | 0 | 0 | 0 | 0 | .000 | .000 | .000 |

Loves to face: Andre Dawson (0-for-12)
Hates to face: John Kruk (.538, 7-for-13, 3 2B, 1 3B)
Ground outs-to-air outs ratio: 0.60 last season, 0.70 for career.... Additional statistics: 2 double-play ground outs in 39 opportunities, 12 doubles, 6 triples in 83.0 innings last season.... Opponents stole eight bases in eight attempts.... Opponents' career average is .197 (one HR per 76 AB) in Late-Inning Pressure Situations, .261 (one HR per 22 AB) in other at-bats.... Opponents have hit for a higher average in night games than in day games in each of his five years in the majors. Career record: 7–10, 4.04 ERA in day games; 10–20, 4.71 ERA in night games.... Career average of one home run allowed per 6.79 innings is the highest rate among active pitchers (minumum: 400 IP).

## Bob Knepper

Astros/Giants — Throws Left

| Astros/Giants | W–L | ERA | AB | H | HR | BB | SO | BA | SA | OBA |
|---|---|---|---|---|---|---|---|---|---|---|
| Season | 7-12 | 5.13 | 649 | 190 | 16 | 75 | 64 | .293 | .433 | .366 |
| vs. Left-Handers | | | 100 | 30 | 3 | 9 | 16 | .300 | .470 | .364 |
| vs. Right-Handers | | | 549 | 160 | 13 | 66 | 48 | .291 | .426 | .366 |
| Home | 0-7 | 6.56 | 293 | 99 | 8 | 29 | 26 | .338 | .481 | .396 |
| Road | 7-5 | 4.04 | 356 | 91 | 8 | 46 | 38 | .256 | .393 | .341 |
| Grass | 3-5 | 4.11 | 277 | 75 | 8 | 32 | 20 | .271 | .433 | .345 |
| Artificial Turf | 4-7 | 5.92 | 372 | 115 | 8 | 43 | 44 | .309 | .433 | .381 |
| April | 1-4 | 5.54 | 102 | 31 | 2 | 13 | 11 | .304 | .402 | .379 |
| May | 2-2 | 4.04 | 131 | 36 | 3 | 21 | 8 | .275 | .389 | .379 |
| June | 0-3 | 5.66 | 139 | 39 | 4 | 19 | 19 | .281 | .424 | .366 |
| July | 1-1 | 11.02 | 73 | 29 | 3 | 7 | 7 | .397 | .644 | .450 |
| August | 2-1 | 2.03 | 119 | 29 | 2 | 6 | 8 | .244 | .336 | .283 |
| Sept./Oct. | 1-1 | 5.57 | 85 | 26 | 2 | 9 | 11 | .306 | .506 | .365 |
| Leading Off Inn. | | | 154 | 37 | 2 | 17 | 16 | .240 | .338 | .316 |
| Runners On | | | 298 | 91 | 9 | 34 | 29 | .305 | .473 | .374 |
| Runners/Scor. Pos. | | | 170 | 50 | 3 | 25 | 19 | .294 | .400 | .376 |
| Runners On/2 Out | | | 130 | 29 | 1 | 23 | 13 | .223 | .323 | .344 |
| Scor. Pos./2 Out | | | 81 | 18 | 1 | 18 | 10 | .222 | .333 | .370 |
| Late Inning Pressure | | | 9 | 5 | 1 | 2 | 0 | .556 | 1.000 | .636 |
| Leading Off | | | 3 | 2 | 0 | 1 | 0 | .667 | .667 | .750 |
| Runners On | | | 5 | 2 | 1 | 0 | 0 | .400 | 1.000 | .400 |
| Runners/Scor. Pos. | | | 3 | 0 | 0 | 0 | 0 | .000 | .000 | .000 |
| First 9 Batters | | | 255 | 68 | 8 | 28 | 28 | .267 | .408 | .334 |
| Second 9 Batters | | | 212 | 60 | 3 | 27 | 17 | .283 | .406 | .366 |
| All Batters Thereafter | | | 182 | 62 | 5 | 20 | 19 | .341 | .500 | .409 |

Loves to face: Eddie Murray (.091, 1-for-11)
Hates to face: Dale Murphy (.384, 33-for-86, 7 HR, 30 BB)
Ground outs-to-air outs ratio: 1.43 last season, 1.34 for career. . . . Additional statistics: 14 double-play ground outs in 137 opportunities, 29 doubles, 7 triples in 165.0 innings last season. . . . Allowed 15 first-inning runs in 26 starts. . . . Batting support: 3.88 runs per start. . . . Joined Giants in August, but wasn't on postseason roster, nor on 40-man winter roster. . . . Most career decisions (295 [143–152]) among active pitchers with losing records. Eighteen pitchers with losing records reached 300 mark, including Rudy May, Tom Zachary, Bob Friend, Bobo Newsom, and leader Jack Powell (501). . . . First batter faced in majors: Pete Rose. Two of next three were Hall of Famers Joe Morgan and Johnny Bench.

## Randy Kramer

Pittsburgh Pirates — Throws Right

| Pittsburgh Pirates | W–L | ERA | AB | H | HR | BB | SO | BA | SA | OBA |
|---|---|---|---|---|---|---|---|---|---|---|
| Season | 5-9 | 3.96 | 401 | 90 | 10 | 61 | 52 | .224 | .352 | .334 |
| vs. Left-Handers | | | 220 | 50 | 6 | 39 | 22 | .227 | .373 | .344 |
| vs. Right-Handers | | | 181 | 40 | 4 | 22 | 30 | .221 | .326 | .322 |
| Home | 2-4 | 4.66 | 187 | 48 | 8 | 24 | 25 | .257 | .417 | .352 |
| Road | 3-5 | 3.43 | 214 | 42 | 2 | 37 | 27 | .196 | .294 | .319 |
| Grass | 2-2 | 2.70 | 91 | 19 | 2 | 15 | 10 | .209 | .330 | .318 |
| Artificial Turf | 3-7 | 4.36 | 310 | 71 | 8 | 46 | 42 | .229 | .358 | .339 |
| April | 0-0 | 3.38 | 21 | 5 | 0 | 6 | 5 | .238 | .238 | .407 |
| May | 1-1 | 1.25 | 76 | 12 | 2 | 6 | 8 | .158 | .276 | .238 |
| June | 1-3 | 6.75 | 87 | 25 | 1 | 15 | 7 | .287 | .425 | .390 |
| July | 2-2 | 4.34 | 110 | 26 | 5 | 13 | 12 | .236 | .445 | .320 |
| August | 1-1 | 2.20 | 51 | 9 | 0 | 10 | 6 | .176 | .176 | .323 |
| Sept./Oct. | 0-2 | 4.96 | 56 | 13 | 2 | 11 | 14 | .232 | .357 | .371 |
| Leading Off Inn. | | | 94 | 19 | 2 | 19 | 14 | .202 | .277 | .342 |
| Runners On | | | 186 | 48 | 5 | 23 | 21 | .258 | .382 | .346 |
| Runners/Scor. Pos. | | | 112 | 26 | 3 | 18 | 13 | .232 | .366 | .338 |
| Runners On/2 Out | | | 75 | 18 | 1 | 11 | 10 | .240 | .333 | .352 |
| Scor. Pos./2 Out | | | 52 | 9 | 0 | 9 | 6 | .173 | .212 | .317 |
| Late Inning Pressure | | | 90 | 24 | 2 | 11 | 15 | .267 | .367 | .365 |
| Leading Off | | | 24 | 6 | 0 | 2 | 6 | .250 | .250 | .333 |
| Runners On | | | 41 | 13 | 2 | 4 | 5 | .317 | .488 | .391 |
| Runners/Scor. Pos. | | | 24 | 8 | 1 | 4 | 3 | .333 | .500 | .429 |
| First 9 Batters | | | 212 | 44 | 3 | 34 | 31 | .208 | .292 | .324 |
| Second 9 Batters | | | 118 | 28 | 4 | 16 | 15 | .237 | .398 | .338 |
| All Batters Thereafter | | | 71 | 18 | 3 | 11 | 6 | .254 | .451 | .357 |

Loves to face: Andre Dawson (.111, 1-for-9, 4 SO)
Hates to face: Kevin Mitchell (.500, 4-for-8, 2 HR)
Ground outs-to-air outs ratio: 1.10 last season, 1.10 for career. . . . Additional statistics: 10 double-play ground outs in 95 opportunities, 15 doubles, 3 triples in 111.1 innings last season. . . . Allowed 8 first-inning runs in 15 starts. . . . Batting support: 3.80 runs per start. . . . Edged Don August for highest ratio of walks to strikeouts vs. left-handers in majors (minimum: 250 BFP). . . . One of four N.L. pitchers to toss one-hitters. Others: Bruce Hurst, Mike Scott, and Jose DeLeon. . . . One of 11 active pitchers with at least 100 career innings pitched and more walks than strikeouts. . . . Opponents' career average is .257 at Three Rivers, .211 on the road. . . . Career minor league record: 38–52.

## Mike LaCoss

San Francisco Giants — Throws Right

| San Francisco Giants | W–L | ERA | AB | H | HR | BB | SO | BA | SA | OBA |
|---|---|---|---|---|---|---|---|---|---|---|
| Season | 10-10 | 3.17 | 560 | 143 | 3 | 65 | 78 | .255 | .316 | .336 |
| vs. Left-Handers | | | 305 | 81 | 3 | 42 | 39 | .266 | .331 | .361 |
| vs. Right-Handers | | | 255 | 62 | 0 | 23 | 39 | .243 | .298 | .307 |
| Home | 6-4 | 2.90 | 257 | 70 | 2 | 29 | 32 | .272 | .327 | .348 |
| Road | 4-6 | 3.40 | 303 | 73 | 1 | 36 | 46 | .241 | .307 | .327 |
| Grass | 9-5 | 2.76 | 402 | 103 | 2 | 43 | 59 | .256 | .313 | .329 |
| Artificial Turf | 1-5 | 4.22 | 158 | 40 | 1 | 22 | 19 | .253 | .323 | .354 |
| April | 1-1 | 3.14 | 49 | 8 | 1 | 11 | 9 | .163 | .245 | .311 |
| May | 1-2 | 1.31 | 72 | 17 | 1 | 9 | 6 | .236 | .292 | .325 |
| June | 1-2 | 2.79 | 71 | 16 | 0 | 12 | 9 | .225 | .282 | .349 |
| July | 2-2 | 4.73 | 126 | 37 | 0 | 7 | 25 | .294 | .357 | .338 |
| August | 2-2 | 3.09 | 120 | 31 | 0 | 17 | 12 | .258 | .308 | .353 |
| Sept./Oct. | 3-1 | 3.13 | 122 | 34 | 1 | 9 | 17 | .279 | .344 | .328 |
| Leading Off Inn. | | | 139 | 33 | 1 | 13 | 19 | .237 | .302 | .303 |
| Runners On | | | 254 | 67 | 2 | 30 | 31 | .264 | .331 | .345 |
| Runners/Scor. Pos. | | | 143 | 33 | 2 | 25 | 19 | .231 | .329 | .343 |
| Runners On/2 Out | | | 103 | 16 | 0 | 14 | 17 | .155 | .194 | .275 |
| Scor. Pos./2 Out | | | 67 | 10 | 0 | 12 | 12 | .149 | .179 | .288 |
| Late Inning Pressure | | | 100 | 25 | 2 | 20 | 13 | .250 | .340 | .374 |
| Leading Off | | | 26 | 7 | 1 | 2 | 2 | .269 | .385 | .321 |
| Runners On | | | 41 | 12 | 1 | 15 | 7 | .293 | .415 | .466 |
| Runners/Scor. Pos. | | | 27 | 7 | 1 | 14 | 5 | .259 | .444 | .488 |
| First 9 Batters | | | 285 | 66 | 2 | 43 | 42 | .232 | .284 | .335 |
| Second 9 Batters | | | 165 | 47 | 1 | 10 | 26 | .285 | .358 | .331 |
| All Batters Thereafter | | | 110 | 30 | 0 | 12 | 10 | .273 | .336 | .347 |

Loves to face: R.J. Reynolds (.063, 1-for-16)
Hates to face: Ryne Sandberg (.432, 16-for-37, 3 HR)
Ground outs-to-air outs ratio: 1.57 last season, 1.87 for career. . . . Additional statistics: 14 double-play ground outs in 142 opportunities, 25 doubles, 0 triples in 150.1 innings last season. . . . Allowed 9 first-inning runs in 18 starts. . . . Batting support: 5.06 runs per start, 3d-highest in N.L. (minimum: 15 starts). . . . Led majors with an average of one home run allowed per 50 innings (minimum: 150 innings). . . . Record of 7–5 (3.86 ERA) as a starter, 3–5 (1.70, 6 saves) in 27 relief appearances. Used exclusively in relief until the Giants acquired Bedrosian, then started in 18 of his last 19 appearances. . . . Has never struck out more than 86 batters in a season. . . . Last man to pitch to Mike Schmidt.

## Bill Landrum

Pittsburgh Pirates — Throws Right

| Pittsburgh Pirates | W–L | ERA | AB | H | HR | BB | SO | BA | SA | OBA |
|---|---|---|---|---|---|---|---|---|---|---|
| Season | 2-3 | 1.67 | 292 | 60 | 2 | 28 | 51 | .205 | .264 | .273 |
| vs. Left-Handers | | | 159 | 28 | 0 | 14 | 19 | .176 | .214 | .241 |
| vs. Right-Handers | | | 133 | 32 | 2 | 14 | 32 | .241 | .323 | .311 |
| Home | 1-2 | 2.75 | 128 | 29 | 0 | 15 | 20 | .227 | .281 | .306 |
| Road | 1-1 | 0.80 | 164 | 31 | 2 | 13 | 31 | .189 | .250 | .247 |
| Grass | 1-0 | 0.76 | 80 | 9 | 1 | 5 | 16 | .113 | .188 | .163 |
| Artificial Turf | 1-3 | 2.04 | 212 | 51 | 1 | 23 | 35 | .241 | .292 | .314 |
| April | 0-0 | 0.00 | 20 | 4 | 0 | 5 | 5 | .200 | .200 | .346 |
| May | 1-1 | 1.13 | 29 | 5 | 0 | 4 | 6 | .172 | .172 | .273 |
| June | 1-0 | 0.00 | 79 | 14 | 0 | 4 | 14 | .177 | .203 | .217 |
| July | 0-0 | 1.29 | 45 | 5 | 0 | 6 | 10 | .111 | .178 | .216 |
| August | 0-1 | 2.37 | 71 | 17 | 1 | 5 | 12 | .239 | .324 | .286 |
| Sept./Oct. | 0-1 | 5.40 | 48 | 15 | 1 | 4 | 4 | .313 | .438 | .365 |
| Leading Off Inn. | | | 69 | 14 | 0 | 3 | 12 | .203 | .232 | .236 |
| Runners On | | | 126 | 28 | 2 | 18 | 22 | .222 | .302 | .315 |
| Runners/Scor. Pos. | | | 79 | 19 | 0 | 17 | 16 | .241 | .291 | .367 |
| Runners On/2 Out | | | 58 | 11 | 1 | 12 | 13 | .190 | .276 | .329 |
| Scor. Pos./2 Out | | | 39 | 7 | 0 | 12 | 9 | .179 | .231 | .373 |
| Late Inning Pressure | | | 180 | 30 | 0 | 20 | 30 | .167 | .200 | .249 |
| Leading Off | | | 43 | 9 | 0 | 2 | 5 | .209 | .233 | .244 |
| Runners On | | | 77 | 10 | 0 | 14 | 14 | .130 | .143 | .261 |
| Runners/Scor. Pos. | | | 49 | 7 | 0 | 13 | 10 | .143 | .163 | .317 |
| First 9 Batters | | | 277 | 57 | 2 | 26 | 47 | .206 | .267 | .272 |
| Second 9 Batters | | | 15 | 3 | 0 | 2 | 4 | .200 | .200 | .294 |
| All Batters Thereafter | | | 0 | 0 | 0 | 0 | 0 | — | — | — |

Loves to face: Kevin Bass (0-for-9)
Hates to face: Kevin McReynolds (.636, 7-for-11)
Ground outs-to-air outs ratio: 0.92 last season, 1.20 for career. . . . Additional statistics: 6 double-play ground outs in 58 opportunities, 11 doubles, 0 triples in 81.0 innings last season. . . . Saves and opportunities by month: April, 0-for-0; May, 1-for-3; June, 8-for-9 (led league in saves); July, 6-for-6; August, 5-for-7; September, 6-for-7. . . . Faced 121 consecutive batters without allowing an extra-base hit, longest streak by an N.L. reliever. . . . Opponents' career BA: .185 in Late-Inning Pressure Situations (no HR in 248 AB), .320 in other at-bats. . . . Career ERA prior to last season was 5.16 in 90.2 innings. . . . This late bloomer is older than Willie McGee, Dave Righetti, Dan Petry, and new teammate Don Slaught.

## Mark Langston

Throws Left

| Montreal Expos | W–L | ERA | AB | H | HR | BB | SO | BA | SA | OBA |
|---|---|---|---|---|---|---|---|---|---|---|
| Season | 12-9 | 2.39 | 634 | 138 | 13 | 93 | 175 | .218 | .320 | .316 |
| vs. Left-Handers | | | 81 | 15 | 1 | 11 | 24 | .185 | .247 | .283 |
| vs. Right-Handers | | | 553 | 123 | 12 | 82 | 151 | .222 | .331 | .321 |
| Home | 6-3 | 2.62 | 291 | 66 | 7 | 39 | 76 | .227 | .337 | .317 |
| Road | 6-6 | 2.21 | 343 | 72 | 6 | 54 | 99 | .210 | .306 | .315 |
| Grass | 3-4 | 2.61 | 179 | 38 | 3 | 33 | 58 | .212 | .318 | .332 |
| Artificial Turf | 9-5 | 2.30 | 455 | 100 | 10 | 60 | 117 | .220 | .321 | .309 |
| April | | | 0 | 0 | 0 | 0 | 0 | — | — | — |
| May | 1-0 | 1.13 | 28 | 4 | 0 | 3 | 12 | .143 | .179 | .226 |
| June | 3-2 | 2.76 | 166 | 40 | 4 | 25 | 40 | .241 | .355 | .339 |
| July | 5-1 | 1.47 | 175 | 32 | 2 | 22 | 55 | .183 | .240 | .273 |
| August | 1-2 | 3.93 | 121 | 30 | 4 | 20 | 27 | .248 | .397 | .352 |
| Sept./Oct. | 2-4 | 2.04 | 144 | 32 | 3 | 23 | 41 | .222 | .340 | .327 |
| Leading Off Inn. | | | 162 | 39 | 6 | 17 | 38 | .241 | .407 | .313 |
| Runners On | | | 271 | 56 | 4 | 38 | 82 | .207 | .284 | .300 |
| Runners/Scor. Pos. | | | 150 | 30 | 2 | 24 | 52 | .200 | .280 | .303 |
| Runners On/2 Out | | | 117 | 18 | 2 | 26 | 41 | .154 | .239 | .308 |
| Scor. Pos./2 Out | | | 78 | 12 | 1 | 16 | 31 | .154 | .231 | .298 |
| Late Inning Pressure | | | 90 | 20 | 2 | 19 | 22 | .222 | .333 | .355 |
| Leading Off | | | 23 | 8 | 2 | 4 | 4 | .348 | .739 | .444 |
| Runners On | | | 42 | 7 | 0 | 9 | 12 | .167 | .167 | .308 |
| Runners/Scor. Pos. | | | 25 | 3 | 0 | 4 | 7 | .120 | .120 | .233 |
| First 9 Batters | | | 183 | 42 | 7 | 26 | 55 | .230 | .383 | .325 |
| Second 9 Batters | | | 189 | 41 | 3 | 22 | 53 | .217 | .307 | .294 |
| All Batters Thereafter | | | 262 | 55 | 3 | 45 | 67 | .210 | .286 | .325 |

Loves to face: Bo Jackson (.091, 1-for-11, 1 HR, 9 SO)
Hates to face: Brook Jacoby (.382, 13-for-34, 4 HR)
Ground outs-to-air outs ratio: 1.04 last season, 1.05 for career. . . . Additional statistics: 11 double-play ground outs in 133 opportunities, 24 doubles, 1 triple in 176.2 innings last season. . . . Allowed 11 first-inning runs in 24 starts. . . . Batting support: 3.58 runs per start. . . . Led N.L. in strikeouts per nine innings (8.92). . . . Combined-leagues batting average by opposing left-handers (.142) was 4th lowest of last 15 years (minimum: 125 BFP). . . . Didn't allow a left-hander to drive in a run in 73.1 innings with Seattle prior to joining Expos. . . . He and Bobby Witt have four consecutive 100-walk seasons, longest streaks since Nolan Ryan set major league mark with nine in a row (1971–79).

## Tim Leary

Throws Right

| Dodgers/Reds | W–L | ERA | AB | H | HR | BB | SO | BA | SA | OBA |
|---|---|---|---|---|---|---|---|---|---|---|
| Season | 8-14 | 3.52 | 786 | 205 | 17 | 68 | 123 | .261 | .383 | .321 |
| vs. Left-Handers | | | 406 | 122 | 12 | 38 | 53 | .300 | .453 | .360 |
| vs. Right-Handers | | | 380 | 83 | 5 | 30 | 70 | .218 | .308 | .278 |
| Home | 4-8 | 3.43 | 447 | 114 | 11 | 39 | 77 | .255 | .369 | .316 |
| Road | 4-6 | 3.64 | 339 | 91 | 6 | 29 | 46 | .268 | .401 | .327 |
| Grass | 5-4 | 3.07 | 346 | 87 | 8 | 32 | 52 | .251 | .370 | .313 |
| Artificial Turf | 3-10 | 3.89 | 440 | 118 | 9 | 36 | 71 | .268 | .393 | .327 |
| April | 2-2 | 3.82 | 122 | 27 | 2 | 9 | 19 | .221 | .336 | .271 |
| May | 1-2 | 2.55 | 134 | 35 | 2 | 14 | 21 | .261 | .351 | .336 |
| June | 3-1 | 3.03 | 130 | 33 | 5 | 7 | 10 | .254 | .400 | .293 |
| July | 1-3 | 3.62 | 101 | 26 | 1 | 10 | 20 | .257 | .337 | .324 |
| August | 1-4 | 5.71 | 143 | 44 | 3 | 17 | 21 | .308 | .455 | .389 |
| Sept./Oct. | 0-2 | 2.63 | 156 | 40 | 4 | 11 | 32 | .256 | .397 | .302 |
| Leading Off Inn. | | | 199 | 54 | 5 | 13 | 25 | .271 | .372 | .319 |
| Runners On | | | 324 | 79 | 6 | 40 | 56 | .244 | .383 | .324 |
| Runners/Scor. Pos. | | | 170 | 34 | 2 | 33 | 39 | .200 | .324 | .321 |
| Runners On/2 Out | | | 132 | 28 | 2 | 21 | 23 | .212 | .333 | .329 |
| Scor. Pos./2 Out | | | 86 | 16 | 0 | 17 | 18 | .186 | .279 | .327 |
| Late Inning Pressure | | | 82 | 24 | 1 | 8 | 23 | .293 | .415 | .359 |
| Leading Off | | | 21 | 6 | 0 | 2 | 7 | .286 | .333 | .348 |
| Runners On | | | 35 | 11 | 1 | 5 | 8 | .314 | .514 | .405 |
| Runners/Scor. Pos. | | | 17 | 4 | 0 | 5 | 5 | .235 | .235 | .417 |
| First 9 Batters | | | 271 | 58 | 4 | 18 | 38 | .214 | .299 | .265 |
| Second 9 Batters | | | 253 | 71 | 5 | 20 | 36 | .281 | .411 | .333 |
| All Batters Thereafter | | | 262 | 76 | 8 | 30 | 49 | .290 | .443 | .364 |

Loves to face: Candy Maldonado (0-for-17, 5 SO)
Hates to face: Wade Boggs (.438, 7-for-16)
Ground outs-to-air outs ratio: 1.12 last season, 1.25 for career. . . . Additional statistics: 20 double-play ground outs in 166 opportunities, 29 doubles, 8 triples in 207.0 innings last season. . . . Allowed 12 first-inning runs in 31 starts. . . . Batting support: 2.81 runs per start, 2d lowest in majors (minimum: 15 starts). Allowed three runs or fewer in five of his 13 losses. . . . John Candelaria's 16 career wins for Yankees and his 13 in a season (1988) are the most by an ex-Mets pitcher after moving from Queens to the Bronx. . . . Strikeouts fell from 180 in 1988, walks increased from 56. First pitcher to gain *that* many BBs (12) while losing *that* many SOs (57) since Steve Carlton in 1973 (plus-26, minus-87).

## Craig Lefferts

Throws Left

| San Francisco Giants | W–L | ERA | AB | H | HR | BB | SO | BA | SA | OBA |
|---|---|---|---|---|---|---|---|---|---|---|
| Season | 2-4 | 2.69 | 399 | 93 | 11 | 22 | 71 | .233 | .376 | .272 |
| vs. Left-Handers | | | 85 | 17 | 2 | 3 | 15 | .200 | .282 | .227 |
| vs. Right-Handers | | | 314 | 76 | 9 | 19 | 56 | .242 | .401 | .284 |
| Home | 0-2 | 2.28 | 199 | 43 | 5 | 5 | 40 | .216 | .327 | .237 |
| Road | 2-2 | 3.14 | 200 | 50 | 6 | 17 | 31 | .250 | .425 | .306 |
| Grass | 1-3 | 2.61 | 293 | 68 | 8 | 13 | 60 | .232 | .362 | .265 |
| Artificial Turf | 1-1 | 2.93 | 106 | 25 | 3 | 9 | 11 | .236 | .415 | .291 |
| April | 1-0 | 0.51 | 61 | 10 | 1 | 2 | 13 | .164 | .279 | .190 |
| May | 0-3 | 2.11 | 81 | 20 | 1 | 5 | 14 | .247 | .321 | .287 |
| June | 1-0 | 4.60 | 57 | 16 | 1 | 2 | 5 | .281 | .404 | .306 |
| July | 0-0 | 2.00 | 65 | 13 | 2 | 6 | 18 | .200 | .338 | .264 |
| August | 0-1 | 4.05 | 82 | 21 | 3 | 5 | 12 | .256 | .451 | .299 |
| Sept./Oct. | 0-0 | 3.14 | 53 | 13 | 3 | 2 | 9 | .245 | .472 | .273 |
| Leading Off Inn. | | | 93 | 24 | 0 | 3 | 22 | .258 | .301 | .281 |
| Runners On | | | 185 | 37 | 7 | 11 | 30 | .200 | .357 | .244 |
| Runners/Scor. Pos. | | | 118 | 19 | 5 | 9 | 22 | .161 | .322 | .220 |
| Runners On/2 Out | | | 76 | 9 | 2 | 5 | 17 | .118 | .237 | .173 |
| Scor. Pos./2 Out | | | 56 | 5 | 2 | 4 | 14 | .089 | .214 | .150 |
| Late Inning Pressure | | | 227 | 53 | 3 | 14 | 38 | .233 | .348 | .279 |
| Leading Off | | | 56 | 14 | 0 | 1 | 12 | .250 | .286 | .263 |
| Runners On | | | 102 | 18 | 2 | 8 | 15 | .176 | .284 | .239 |
| Runners/Scor. Pos. | | | 65 | 9 | 2 | 6 | 10 | .138 | .246 | .216 |
| First 9 Batters | | | 374 | 87 | 9 | 21 | 68 | .233 | .369 | .273 |
| Second 9 Batters | | | 25 | 6 | 2 | 1 | 3 | .240 | .480 | .269 |
| All Batters Thereafter | | | 0 | 0 | 0 | 0 | 0 | — | — | — |

Loves to face: Ozzie Smith (.091, 2-for-22)
Hates to face: Tim Raines (.550, 11-for-20, 1 HR)
Ground outs-to-air outs ratio: 0.95 last season, 0.84 for career. . . . Additional statistics: 9 double-play ground outs in 88 opportunities, 18 doubles, 3 triples in 107.0 innings last season. . . . Had 14 saves in 18 opportunities before Bedrosian arrived at the 'Stick in June. Didn't enter a game to protect a 9th-inning lead after that, although he did manage six more saves. . . . Allowed only one hit in 19 at-bats with runners in scoring position and Giants leading by a run. . . . Left-handed batters went 2-for-26 with runners in scoring position. . . . Career records: 0–14 in May, 32–25 in other months; 28–21 on grass fields, 4–18 on artificial turf. . . . Other career records: 8–0 vs. Dodgers, 0–7 vs. Mets.

## Derek Lilliquist

Throws Left

| Atlanta Braves | W–L | ERA | AB | H | HR | BB | SO | BA | SA | OBA |
|---|---|---|---|---|---|---|---|---|---|---|
| Season | 8-10 | 3.97 | 671 | 202 | 16 | 34 | 79 | .301 | .435 | .335 |
| vs. Left-Handers | | | 102 | 27 | 3 | 3 | 19 | .265 | .412 | .292 |
| vs. Right-Handers | | | 569 | 175 | 13 | 31 | 60 | .308 | .439 | .343 |
| Home | 5-5 | 3.32 | 400 | 122 | 8 | 17 | 43 | .305 | .415 | .335 |
| Road | 3-5 | 4.90 | 271 | 80 | 8 | 17 | 36 | .295 | .465 | .336 |
| Grass | 6-8 | 3.80 | 559 | 165 | 13 | 28 | 64 | .295 | .429 | .329 |
| Artificial Turf | 2-2 | 4.85 | 112 | 37 | 3 | 6 | 15 | .330 | .464 | .364 |
| April | 1-2 | 4.09 | 92 | 25 | 4 | 6 | 13 | .272 | .446 | .316 |
| May | 2-1 | 1.36 | 125 | 29 | 1 | 5 | 8 | .232 | .304 | .260 |
| June | 2-1 | 4.60 | 124 | 41 | 1 | 6 | 15 | .331 | .427 | .362 |
| July | 1-2 | 6.04 | 105 | 37 | 5 | 8 | 12 | .352 | .543 | .400 |
| August | 1-2 | 5.87 | 99 | 38 | 2 | 7 | 10 | .384 | .545 | .425 |
| Sept./Oct. | 1-2 | 3.00 | 126 | 32 | 3 | 2 | 21 | .254 | .389 | .269 |
| Leading Off Inn. | | | 168 | 41 | 4 | 7 | 25 | .244 | .381 | .278 |
| Runners On | | | 261 | 91 | 6 | 17 | 26 | .349 | .471 | .387 |
| Runners/Scor. Pos. | | | 145 | 47 | 3 | 10 | 16 | .324 | .448 | .365 |
| Runners On/2 Out | | | 120 | 42 | 1 | 8 | 15 | .350 | .408 | .391 |
| Scor. Pos./2 Out | | | 73 | 24 | 0 | 6 | 10 | .329 | .356 | .380 |
| Late Inning Pressure | | | 33 | 14 | 1 | 1 | 4 | .424 | .576 | .429 |
| Leading Off | | | 9 | 5 | 0 | 0 | 2 | .556 | .667 | .556 |
| Runners On | | | 15 | 6 | 0 | 0 | 2 | .400 | .400 | .375 |
| Runners/Scor. Pos. | | | 6 | 3 | 0 | 0 | 2 | .500 | .500 | .429 |
| First 9 Batters | | | 261 | 86 | 5 | 9 | 36 | .330 | .464 | .351 |
| Second 9 Batters | | | 244 | 65 | 6 | 17 | 30 | .266 | .410 | .317 |
| All Batters Thereafter | | | 166 | 51 | 5 | 8 | 13 | .307 | .428 | .339 |

Loves to face: Vince Coleman (0-for-9)
Hates to face: Todd Benzinger (.727, 8-for-11)
Ground outs-to-air outs ratio: 0.78 last season, his first in majors. . . . Additional statistics: 13 double-play ground outs in 109 opportunities, 36 doubles, 3 triples in 165.2 innings last season. . . . Allowed 15 first-inning runs in 30 starts. . . . Batting support: 3.50 runs per start. . . . Average of 1.85 walks per nine innings was 2d lowest in N.L. . . . First N.L. rookie since Jim Turner of 1937 Boston Braves to walk fewer than two batters per nine innings in 30 starts or more. Two A.L. rookies have done it since: Fritz Peterson (1966) and Bill Wegman (1986). . . . Tied with Greg Harris of Padres for most wins by an N.L. rookie. . . . Only other Atlanta Braves rookie to lead the team in starts: Craig McMurtry (1983).

## Greg Maddux

Chicago Cubs — Throws Right

| Chicago Cubs | W–L | ERA | AB | H | HR | BB | SO | BA | SA | OBA |
|---|---|---|---|---|---|---|---|---|---|---|
| Season | 19-12 | 2.95 | 890 | 222 | 13 | 82 | 135 | .249 | .343 | .315 |
| vs. Left-Handers | | | 495 | 138 | 4 | 56 | 65 | .279 | .366 | .356 |
| vs. Right-Handers | | | 395 | 84 | 9 | 26 | 70 | .213 | .314 | .262 |
| Home | 10-5 | 3.03 | 420 | 102 | 6 | 36 | 68 | .243 | .324 | .302 |
| Road | 9-7 | 2.87 | 470 | 120 | 7 | 46 | 67 | .255 | .360 | .326 |
| Grass | 14-8 | 3.01 | 624 | 152 | 10 | 60 | 91 | .244 | .337 | .312 |
| Artificial Turf | 5-4 | 2.79 | 266 | 70 | 3 | 22 | 44 | .263 | .357 | .323 |
| April | 1-3 | 4.20 | 120 | 34 | 3 | 9 | 17 | .283 | .375 | .333 |
| May | 3-2 | 2.27 | 162 | 34 | 2 | 16 | 21 | .210 | .296 | .285 |
| June | 2-2 | 2.51 | 114 | 23 | 0 | 16 | 16 | .202 | .263 | .298 |
| July | 5-1 | 3.10 | 152 | 42 | 1 | 18 | 22 | .276 | .362 | .355 |
| August | 4-2 | 2.45 | 187 | 43 | 4 | 18 | 34 | .230 | .321 | .306 |
| Sept./Oct. | 4-2 | 3.57 | 155 | 46 | 3 | 5 | 25 | .297 | .432 | .317 |
| Leading Off Inn. | | | 231 | 66 | 3 | 15 | 32 | .286 | .372 | .335 |
| Runners On | | | 387 | 96 | 6 | 37 | 54 | .248 | .357 | .313 |
| Runners/Scor. Pos. | | | 202 | 45 | 0 | 29 | 36 | .223 | .287 | .318 |
| Runners On/2 Out | | | 153 | 33 | 1 | 23 | 24 | .216 | .281 | .322 |
| Scor. Pos./2 Out | | | 93 | 18 | 0 | 20 | 21 | .194 | .226 | .342 |
| Late Inning Pressure | | | 70 | 13 | 0 | 7 | 13 | .186 | .200 | .260 |
| Leading Off | | | 23 | 6 | 0 | 2 | 5 | .261 | .304 | .320 |
| Runners On | | | 19 | 3 | 0 | 3 | 2 | .158 | .158 | .273 |
| Runners/Scor. Pos. | | | 12 | 2 | 0 | 2 | 2 | .167 | .167 | .286 |
| First 9 Batters | | | 287 | 66 | 3 | 18 | 49 | .230 | .331 | .281 |
| Second 9 Batters | | | 276 | 59 | 4 | 30 | 44 | .214 | .297 | .292 |
| All Batters Thereafter | | | 327 | 97 | 6 | 34 | 42 | .297 | .391 | .363 |

Loves to face: Rob Thompson (.143, 3-for-21, 7 SO)
Hates to face: Sid Bream (.588, 10-for-17, 1 HR)
Ground outs-to-air outs ratio: 1.81 last season, 1.89 for career. . . . Additional statistics: 17 double-play ground outs in 203 opportunities, 36 doubles, 4 triples in 238.1 innings last season. . . . Allowed 9 first-inning runs in 35 starts. . . . Batting support: 4.46 runs per start. . . . Went 18–8 in 1988, with figures almost identical to last season's totals for innings (249), hits (230) home runs (13), walks (82), and strikeouts (135). . . . Opponents stole only two bases in nine attempts after July 18, 11 of 23 for the season. . . . Cubs' early clinching cost him a shot at 20 wins. Would have started season finale if the game had any meaning. . . . Career record of 24–26 in day games, 21–12 at night.

## Joe Magrane

St. Louis Cardinals — Throws Left

| St. Louis Cardinals | W–L | ERA | AB | H | HR | BB | SO | BA | SA | OBA |
|---|---|---|---|---|---|---|---|---|---|---|
| Season | 18-9 | 2.91 | 871 | 219 | 5 | 72 | 127 | .251 | .336 | .310 |
| vs. Left-Handers | | | 128 | 30 | 0 | 15 | 24 | .234 | .289 | .319 |
| vs. Right-Handers | | | 743 | 189 | 5 | 57 | 103 | .254 | .345 | .309 |
| Home | 9-5 | 3.09 | 445 | 116 | 2 | 39 | 58 | .261 | .348 | .323 |
| Road | 9-4 | 2.73 | 426 | 103 | 3 | 33 | 69 | .242 | .324 | .297 |
| Grass | 4-1 | 2.81 | 182 | 45 | 1 | 11 | 34 | .247 | .308 | .292 |
| Artificial Turf | 14-8 | 2.94 | 689 | 174 | 4 | 61 | 93 | .253 | .344 | .315 |
| April | 2-2 | 8.27 | 84 | 30 | 0 | 6 | 14 | .357 | .429 | .404 |
| May | 1-1 | 1.74 | 109 | 23 | 0 | 12 | 18 | .211 | .248 | .287 |
| June | 4-3 | 2.45 | 167 | 38 | 1 | 16 | 24 | .228 | .329 | .296 |
| July | 5-1 | 2.25 | 176 | 39 | 1 | 14 | 27 | .222 | .318 | .281 |
| August | 6-0 | 2.08 | 183 | 36 | 2 | 10 | 24 | .197 | .295 | .242 |
| Sept./Oct. | 0-2 | 3.57 | 152 | 53 | 1 | 14 | 20 | .349 | .428 | .402 |
| Leading Off Inn. | | | 227 | 50 | 0 | 13 | 34 | .220 | .286 | .269 |
| Runners On | | | 336 | 89 | 2 | 41 | 52 | .265 | .345 | .339 |
| Runners/Scor. Pos. | | | 203 | 54 | 0 | 27 | 37 | .266 | .335 | .343 |
| Runners On/2 Out | | | 146 | 34 | 0 | 18 | 26 | .233 | .308 | .317 |
| Scor. Pos./2 Out | | | 97 | 22 | 0 | 14 | 20 | .227 | .309 | .324 |
| Late Inning Pressure | | | 89 | 17 | 0 | 5 | 13 | .191 | .213 | .242 |
| Leading Off | | | 26 | 5 | 0 | 2 | 3 | .192 | .192 | .276 |
| Runners On | | | 24 | 5 | 0 | 2 | 5 | .208 | .250 | .269 |
| Runners/Scor. Pos. | | | 7 | 2 | 0 | 1 | 2 | .286 | .429 | .375 |
| First 9 Batters | | | 273 | 73 | 3 | 21 | 47 | .267 | .381 | .321 |
| Second 9 Batters | | | 254 | 60 | 0 | 26 | 34 | .236 | .307 | .306 |
| All Batters Thereafter | | | 344 | 86 | 2 | 25 | 46 | .250 | .323 | .305 |

Loves to face: Len Dykstra (.053, 1-for-19)
Hates to face: Lloyd McClendon (.583, 7-for-12)
Ground outs-to-air outs ratio: 1.71 last season, 1.95 for career. . . . Additional statistics: 24 double-play ground outs (2d most in N.L.) in 165 opportunities, 43 doubles, 8 triples in 234.2 innings last season. . . . Allowed 13 first-inning runs in 33 starts. . . . Batting support: 4.52 runs per start. . . . Matchup of Magrane and Gooden featured the two youngest opening-day pitchers in majors. . . . Pinch ran for Vince Coleman on May 6. . . . Won seven consecutive starts to reach 18 victories, winless in six after that. . . . Allowed one home run per 46.9 innings, best rate in N.L. . . . One of three active pitchers with 75+ starts and an ERA below 3.00: Gooden, 2.64; Hershiser, 2.69; Magrane, 2.89.

## Rick Mahler

Cincinnati Reds — Throws Right

| Cincinnati Reds | W–L | ERA | AB | H | HR | BB | SO | BA | SA | OBA |
|---|---|---|---|---|---|---|---|---|---|---|
| Season | 9-13 | 3.83 | 859 | 242 | 15 | 51 | 102 | .282 | .407 | .328 |
| vs. Left-Handers | | | 488 | 149 | 8 | 25 | 48 | .305 | .451 | .344 |
| vs. Right-Handers | | | 371 | 93 | 7 | 26 | 54 | .251 | .350 | .307 |
| Home | 6-6 | 4.43 | 480 | 146 | 10 | 32 | 54 | .304 | .444 | .353 |
| Road | 3-7 | 3.13 | 379 | 96 | 5 | 19 | 48 | .253 | .361 | .295 |
| Grass | 1-4 | 3.93 | 192 | 53 | 3 | 8 | 22 | .276 | .411 | .305 |
| Artificial Turf | 8-9 | 3.80 | 667 | 189 | 12 | 43 | 80 | .283 | .406 | .334 |
| April | 2-3 | 1.83 | 128 | 31 | 1 | 11 | 12 | .242 | .289 | .310 |
| May | 4-2 | 3.80 | 189 | 54 | 2 | 11 | 22 | .286 | .392 | .330 |
| June | 2-3 | 4.10 | 184 | 54 | 6 | 10 | 28 | .293 | .484 | .327 |
| July | 1-2 | 3.40 | 156 | 36 | 1 | 5 | 22 | .231 | .321 | .264 |
| August | 0-3 | 5.50 | 146 | 50 | 4 | 10 | 10 | .342 | .514 | .392 |
| Sept./Oct. | 0-0 | 5.14 | 56 | 17 | 1 | 4 | 8 | .304 | .446 | .365 |
| Leading Off Inn. | | | 217 | 60 | 5 | 6 | 25 | .276 | .438 | .302 |
| Runners On | | | 345 | 100 | 8 | 30 | 42 | .290 | .420 | .352 |
| Runners/Scor. Pos. | | | 194 | 60 | 5 | 27 | 29 | .309 | .433 | .398 |
| Runners On/2 Out | | | 159 | 46 | 3 | 19 | 22 | .289 | .403 | .372 |
| Scor. Pos./2 Out | | | 95 | 30 | 3 | 18 | 16 | .316 | .432 | .430 |
| Late Inning Pressure | | | 49 | 13 | 1 | 4 | 10 | .265 | .449 | .321 |
| Leading Off | | | 17 | 6 | 0 | 0 | 4 | .353 | .412 | .353 |
| Runners On | | | 12 | 3 | 1 | 3 | 2 | .250 | .667 | .400 |
| Runners/Scor. Pos. | | | 7 | 2 | 1 | 3 | 2 | .286 | .857 | .500 |
| First 9 Batters | | | 312 | 100 | 8 | 13 | 38 | .321 | .481 | .352 |
| Second 9 Batters | | | 258 | 73 | 3 | 20 | 36 | .283 | .391 | .340 |
| All Batters Thereafter | | | 289 | 69 | 4 | 18 | 28 | .239 | .343 | .289 |

Loves to face: Jose Oquendo (.120, 3-for-25)
Hates to face: Darrell Evans (.438, 7-for-16, 3 HR)
Ground outs-to-air outs ratio: 1.46 last season, 1.56 for career. . . . Additional statistics: 14 double-play ground outs in 145 opportunities, 49 doubles, 7 triples in 220.2 innings last season. . . . Allowed 31 first-inning runs in 31 starts. Opponents batted .388 during the first inning, .258 thereafter. . . . Batting support: 4.00 runs per start. . . . Allowed most hits in N.L. for fourth time (all within last five years). N.L. record: five, by Robin Roberts. . . . Opponents' BA with runners on base was higher than with the bases empty in each of last six seasons. . . . Second consecutive losing season despite ERA below 4.00 and more than 200 innings in each. The last three-year streak: Tommy John (1969–71).

## Dennis Martinez

Montreal Expos — Throws Right

| Montreal Expos | W–L | ERA | AB | H | HR | BB | SO | BA | SA | OBA |
|---|---|---|---|---|---|---|---|---|---|---|
| Season | 16-7 | 3.18 | 884 | 227 | 21 | 49 | 142 | .257 | .390 | .300 |
| vs. Left-Handers | | | 492 | 140 | 12 | 33 | 74 | .285 | .429 | .330 |
| vs. Right-Handers | | | 392 | 87 | 9 | 16 | 68 | .222 | .342 | .263 |
| Home | 7-4 | 2.79 | 438 | 107 | 11 | 22 | 79 | .244 | .374 | .284 |
| Road | 9-3 | 3.58 | 446 | 120 | 10 | 27 | 63 | .269 | .406 | .316 |
| Grass | 5-1 | 3.00 | 207 | 56 | 4 | 11 | 40 | .271 | .386 | .312 |
| Artificial Turf | 11-6 | 3.24 | 677 | 171 | 17 | 38 | 102 | .253 | .391 | .297 |
| April | 1-1 | 3.44 | 146 | 41 | 2 | 6 | 20 | .281 | .418 | .314 |
| May | 3-0 | 2.28 | 162 | 37 | 3 | 11 | 24 | .228 | .352 | .277 |
| June | 4-0 | 2.18 | 175 | 42 | 3 | 8 | 20 | .240 | .314 | .281 |
| July | 4-0 | 4.88 | 122 | 40 | 4 | 11 | 20 | .328 | .484 | .383 |
| August | 3-3 | 2.47 | 160 | 36 | 6 | 5 | 39 | .225 | .381 | .254 |
| Sept./Oct. | 1-3 | 4.83 | 119 | 31 | 3 | 8 | 19 | .261 | .437 | .318 |
| Leading Off Inn. | | | 232 | 66 | 10 | 7 | 31 | .284 | .474 | .305 |
| Runners On | | | 333 | 80 | 7 | 23 | 53 | .240 | .360 | .296 |
| Runners/Scor. Pos. | | | 188 | 38 | 4 | 18 | 36 | .202 | .309 | .276 |
| Runners On/2 Out | | | 148 | 37 | 2 | 13 | 29 | .250 | .378 | .315 |
| Scor. Pos./2 Out | | | 96 | 18 | 2 | 11 | 21 | .188 | .292 | .278 |
| Late Inning Pressure | | | 101 | 23 | 2 | 2 | 17 | .228 | .337 | .243 |
| Leading Off | | | 29 | 9 | 2 | 0 | 3 | .310 | .552 | .310 |
| Runners On | | | 30 | 6 | 0 | 2 | 2 | .200 | .200 | .250 |
| Runners/Scor. Pos. | | | 18 | 2 | 0 | 2 | 2 | .111 | .111 | .200 |
| First 9 Batters | | | 279 | 66 | 6 | 15 | 49 | .237 | .366 | .282 |
| Second 9 Batters | | | 277 | 67 | 7 | 13 | 46 | .242 | .375 | .275 |
| All Batters Thereafter | | | 328 | 94 | 8 | 21 | 47 | .287 | .424 | .337 |

Loves to face: Garry Templeton (.056, 1-for-18)
Hates to face: Paul O'Neill (.563, 9-for-16, 2 HR)
Ground outs-to-air outs ratio: 1.41 last season, 1.17 for career. . . . Additional statistics: 21 double-play ground outs (3d most in N.L.) in 143 opportunities, 37 doubles, 9 triples in 232.0 innings last season. . . . Allowed 19 first-inning runs in 33 starts. . . . Batting support: 4.45 runs per start. . . . First time since 1980 that opposing left-handers outhit right-handers. . . . Streak of 31 consecutive hitless batters faced with runners in scoring position was longest in N.L. Opponents' average with RISP was the lowest of his career. . . . Among active pitchers with at least 150 career victories, only John Candelaria (.609) and Jack Morris (.581) have higher winning percentages than Martinez (.554).

## Ramon Martinez

Throws Right

| Los Angeles Dodgers | W–L | ERA | AB | H | HR | BB | SO | BA | SA | OBA |
|---|---|---|---|---|---|---|---|---|---|---|
| Season | 6-4 | 3.19 | 360 | 79 | 11 | 41 | 89 | .219 | .347 | .308 |
| vs. Left-Handers | | | 203 | 50 | 6 | 27 | 44 | .246 | .369 | .343 |
| vs. Right-Handers | | | 157 | 29 | 5 | 14 | 45 | .185 | .318 | .260 |
| Home | 3-3 | 2.17 | 176 | 32 | 4 | 22 | 50 | .182 | .278 | .284 |
| Road | 3-1 | 4.22 | 184 | 47 | 7 | 19 | 39 | .255 | .413 | .332 |
| Grass | 5-4 | 2.62 | 273 | 57 | 6 | 30 | 70 | .209 | .308 | .296 |
| Artificial Turf | 1-0 | 5.09 | 87 | 22 | 5 | 11 | 19 | .253 | .471 | .343 |
| April | | | 0 | 0 | 0 | 0 | 0 | — | — | — |
| May | | | 0 | 0 | 0 | 0 | 0 | — | — | — |
| June | 1-0 | 0.00 | 31 | 6 | 0 | 1 | 9 | .194 | .194 | .219 |
| July | 1-0 | 5.82 | 62 | 15 | 4 | 11 | 15 | .242 | .500 | .373 |
| August | 1-3 | 3.79 | 133 | 30 | 6 | 16 | 28 | .226 | .398 | .318 |
| Sept./Oct. | 3-1 | 2.19 | 134 | 28 | 1 | 13 | 37 | .209 | .261 | .284 |
| Leading Off Inn. | | | 88 | 26 | 4 | 14 | 25 | .295 | .489 | .398 |
| Runners On | | | 145 | 33 | 4 | 13 | 24 | .228 | .338 | .304 |
| Runners/Scor. Pos. | | | 70 | 15 | 1 | 8 | 8 | .214 | .271 | .321 |
| Runners On/2 Out | | | 62 | 15 | 1 | 6 | 7 | .242 | .323 | .329 |
| Scor. Pos./2 Out | | | 35 | 5 | 0 | 5 | 2 | .143 | .143 | .286 |
| Late Inning Pressure | | | 27 | 8 | 0 | 4 | 7 | .296 | .296 | .387 |
| Leading Off | | | 8 | 3 | 0 | 1 | 3 | .375 | .375 | .444 |
| Runners On | | | 11 | 2 | 0 | 1 | 1 | .182 | .182 | .250 |
| Runners/Scor. Pos. | | | 4 | 1 | 0 | 0 | 0 | .250 | .250 | .250 |
| First 9 Batters | | | 122 | 22 | 5 | 8 | 38 | .180 | .352 | .248 |
| Second 9 Batters | | | 118 | 23 | 3 | 14 | 27 | .195 | .305 | .291 |
| All Batters Thereafter | | | 120 | 34 | 3 | 19 | 24 | .283 | .383 | .381 |

Loves to face: Brett Butler (.071, 1-for-14)
Hates to face: Will Clark (.455, 5-for-11, 1 HR)
Ground outs-to-air outs ratio: 0.97 last season, 0.97 for career. . . . Additional statistics: 5 double-play ground outs in 77 opportunities, 11 doubles, 1 triple in 98.2 innings last season. . . . Allowed 8 first-inning runs in 15 starts. . . . Opponents batted .189 through the first four innings, .264 thereafter. . . . Batting support: 4.93 runs per start, more than a run per game more than Dodgers scored for any other starter. . . . Only N.L. rookie to throw two shutouts. . . . Youngest N.L. pitcher to start a game. . . . Opponents stole only six bases in 14 attempts. . . . Allowed 10 homers in first eight starts, only one in seven thereafter. . . . Lower ERA in four losses (3.42) than in five no-decisions (5.06).

## Roger McDowell

Throws Right

| Mets/Phillies | W–L | ERA | AB | H | HR | BB | SO | BA | SA | OBA |
|---|---|---|---|---|---|---|---|---|---|---|
| Season | 4-8 | 1.96 | 339 | 79 | 3 | 38 | 47 | .233 | .304 | .315 |
| vs. Left-Handers | | | 185 | 49 | 3 | 26 | 17 | .265 | .351 | .358 |
| vs. Right-Handers | | | 154 | 30 | 0 | 12 | 30 | .195 | .247 | .260 |
| Home | 4-5 | 1.38 | 141 | 29 | 1 | 14 | 23 | .206 | .291 | .285 |
| Road | 0-3 | 2.38 | 198 | 50 | 2 | 24 | 24 | .253 | .313 | .336 |
| Grass | 1-4 | 1.79 | 148 | 35 | 1 | 14 | 20 | .236 | .304 | .305 |
| Artificial Turf | 3-4 | 2.09 | 191 | 44 | 2 | 24 | 27 | .230 | .304 | .323 |
| April | 0-0 | 0.96 | 33 | 6 | 0 | 1 | 5 | .182 | .242 | .206 |
| May | 1-4 | 5.27 | 59 | 19 | 1 | 7 | 6 | .322 | .458 | .388 |
| June | 0-1 | 2.16 | 58 | 13 | 0 | 10 | 7 | .224 | .224 | .357 |
| July | 1-0 | 0.00 | 66 | 13 | 0 | 6 | 5 | .197 | .212 | .264 |
| August | 1-1 | 2.25 | 60 | 15 | 2 | 8 | 14 | .250 | .417 | .348 |
| Sept./Oct. | 1-2 | 1.50 | 63 | 13 | 0 | 6 | 10 | .206 | .254 | .275 |
| Leading Off Inn. | | | 69 | 15 | 0 | 8 | 12 | .217 | .275 | .308 |
| Runners On | | | 172 | 38 | 2 | 24 | 27 | .221 | .291 | .322 |
| Runners/Scor. Pos. | | | 116 | 23 | 2 | 20 | 22 | .198 | .293 | .324 |
| Runners On/2 Out | | | 73 | 18 | 2 | 8 | 15 | .247 | .356 | .329 |
| Scor. Pos./2 Out | | | 52 | 10 | 2 | 7 | 12 | .192 | .346 | .300 |
| Late Inning Pressure | | | 197 | 44 | 2 | 25 | 25 | .223 | .279 | .314 |
| Leading Off | | | 41 | 7 | 0 | 5 | 6 | .171 | .195 | .261 |
| Runners On | | | 98 | 21 | 1 | 16 | 15 | .214 | .265 | .330 |
| Runners/Scor. Pos. | | | 60 | 9 | 1 | 13 | 14 | .150 | .217 | .311 |
| First 9 Batters | | | 319 | 73 | 2 | 34 | 45 | .229 | .295 | .308 |
| Second 9 Batters | | | 20 | 6 | 1 | 4 | 2 | .300 | .450 | .417 |
| All Batters Thereafter | | | 0 | 0 | 0 | 0 | 0 | — | — | — |

Loves to face: Juan Samuel (.111, 2-for-18)
Hates to face: Glenn Wilson (.563, 9-for-16, 1 HR)
Ground outs-to-air outs ratio: 3.09 last season, 3.07 for career, highest of past 15 years (minimum: 1000 BFP). . . . Additional statistics: 13 double-play ground outs in 89 opportunities, 13 doubles, 1 triple in 92.0 innings last season. . . . Hadn't been summoned to protect a lead in 10 appearances with Mets prior to his showcase against the Phillies two days before trade. . . . Had an ERA of 10.05 during 1989 spring training, 3.31 in 25 regular-season games for the Mets, 1.11 in 44 games for the Phillies. . . . Opposing ground-ball hitters batted .189, fly-ballers hit .280. . . . Career record of 7–0 in April. . . . Wasn't Tug McGraw supposed to be washed up when the Phillies snatched him from Mets in 1975?

## Andy McGaffigan

Throws Right

| Montreal Expos | W–L | ERA | AB | H | HR | BB | SO | BA | SA | OBA |
|---|---|---|---|---|---|---|---|---|---|---|
| Season | 3-5 | 4.68 | 290 | 85 | 3 | 30 | 40 | .293 | .393 | .361 |
| vs. Left-Handers | | | 140 | 32 | 0 | 22 | 19 | .229 | .321 | .331 |
| vs. Right-Handers | | | 150 | 53 | 3 | 8 | 21 | .353 | .460 | .390 |
| Home | 3-2 | 4.66 | 135 | 36 | 0 | 18 | 16 | .267 | .326 | .353 |
| Road | 0-3 | 4.70 | 155 | 49 | 3 | 12 | 24 | .316 | .452 | .368 |
| Grass | 0-0 | 5.09 | 73 | 22 | 3 | 3 | 16 | .301 | .479 | .346 |
| Artificial Turf | 3-5 | 4.55 | 217 | 63 | 0 | 27 | 24 | .290 | .364 | .365 |
| April | 1-1 | 4.15 | 46 | 12 | 0 | 9 | 7 | .261 | .348 | .368 |
| May | 0-1 | 5.27 | 53 | 16 | 1 | 7 | 5 | .302 | .396 | .371 |
| June | 0-1 | 2.16 | 60 | 12 | 0 | 5 | 6 | .200 | .250 | .273 |
| July | 2-1 | 2.51 | 52 | 14 | 0 | 6 | 10 | .269 | .288 | .345 |
| August | 0-1 | 6.75 | 36 | 13 | 1 | 1 | 6 | .361 | .500 | .378 |
| Sept./Oct. | 0-0 | 10.61 | 43 | 18 | 1 | 2 | 6 | .419 | .674 | .468 |
| Leading Off Inn. | | | 61 | 17 | 0 | 9 | 2 | .279 | .311 | .371 |
| Runners On | | | 151 | 47 | 2 | 13 | 25 | .311 | .430 | .361 |
| Runners/Scor. Pos. | | | 94 | 30 | 0 | 8 | 17 | .319 | .404 | .364 |
| Runners On/2 Out | | | 70 | 20 | 1 | 10 | 15 | .286 | .414 | .375 |
| Scor. Pos./2 Out | | | 46 | 13 | 0 | 5 | 10 | .283 | .348 | .353 |
| Late Inning Pressure | | | 134 | 36 | 1 | 16 | 17 | .269 | .336 | .346 |
| Leading Off | | | 31 | 8 | 0 | 8 | 0 | .258 | .290 | .410 |
| Runners On | | | 64 | 18 | 1 | 5 | 10 | .281 | .375 | .324 |
| Runners/Scor. Pos. | | | 40 | 11 | 0 | 4 | 7 | .275 | .325 | .326 |
| First 9 Batters | | | 281 | 83 | 2 | 29 | 37 | .295 | .388 | .361 |
| Second 9 Batters | | | 9 | 2 | 1 | 1 | 3 | .222 | .556 | .364 |
| All Batters Thereafter | | | 0 | 0 | 0 | 0 | 0 | — | — | — |

Loves to face: Dave Magadan (0-for-11)
Hates to face: Ozzie Smith (.458, 11-for-24)
Ground outs-to-air outs ratio: 1.12 last season, 1.17 for career. . . . Additional statistics: 5 double-play ground outs in 67 opportunities, 14 doubles, 3 triples in 75.0 innings last season. . . . Became the sixth reliever to win a season opener for the Expos. Others: Woodie Fryman (1981), Elias ("Baseball Analyst") Sosa (1979), Jackie Brown (1977), Chuck Taylor (1974), and Don Shaw (1969). . . . Struck out 4.80 batters per nine innings, compared to previous career average of 6.94. . . . Career record of 8–15 on grass fields, 26–15 on artificial surfaces. . . . Career record of 8–1 during September and October. . . . Opponents' career batting averages: .218 by ground-ball hitters, .267 by fly-ballers.

## Larry McWilliams

Throws Left

| Philadelphia Phillies | W–L | ERA | AB | H | HR | BB | SO | BA | SA | OBA |
|---|---|---|---|---|---|---|---|---|---|---|
| Season | 2-11 | 4.10 | 465 | 123 | 3 | 49 | 54 | .265 | .342 | .337 |
| vs. Left-Handers | | | 83 | 15 | 1 | 11 | 13 | .181 | .253 | .277 |
| vs. Right-Handers | | | 382 | 108 | 2 | 38 | 41 | .283 | .361 | .350 |
| Home | 1-7 | 4.09 | 276 | 70 | 0 | 31 | 35 | .254 | .304 | .331 |
| Road | 1-4 | 4.11 | 189 | 53 | 3 | 18 | 19 | .280 | .397 | .346 |
| Grass | 1-2 | 3.16 | 109 | 28 | 2 | 11 | 15 | .257 | .376 | .333 |
| Artificial Turf | 1-9 | 4.43 | 356 | 95 | 1 | 38 | 39 | .267 | .331 | .338 |
| April | 1-1 | 1.86 | 69 | 13 | 0 | 10 | 9 | .188 | .203 | .291 |
| May | 1-4 | 3.77 | 115 | 32 | 1 | 11 | 10 | .278 | .383 | .349 |
| June | 0-3 | 3.64 | 114 | 30 | 0 | 12 | 10 | .263 | .316 | .328 |
| July | 0-2 | 4.15 | 92 | 25 | 1 | 8 | 13 | .272 | .370 | .337 |
| August | 0-1 | 7.58 | 75 | 23 | 1 | 8 | 12 | .307 | .413 | .376 |
| Sept./Oct. | | | 0 | 0 | 0 | 0 | 0 | — | — | — |
| Leading Off Inn. | | | 118 | 27 | 1 | 8 | 13 | .229 | .288 | .283 |
| Runners On | | | 201 | 61 | 2 | 27 | 22 | .303 | .418 | .382 |
| Runners/Scor. Pos. | | | 108 | 32 | 0 | 17 | 14 | .296 | .398 | .380 |
| Runners On/2 Out | | | 87 | 25 | 1 | 12 | 8 | .287 | .425 | .374 |
| Scor. Pos./2 Out | | | 53 | 16 | 0 | 6 | 6 | .302 | .415 | .373 |
| Late Inning Pressure | | | 59 | 13 | 0 | 9 | 10 | .220 | .237 | .324 |
| Leading Off | | | 15 | 4 | 0 | 3 | 1 | .267 | .333 | .389 |
| Runners On | | | 27 | 5 | 0 | 3 | 6 | .185 | .185 | .267 |
| Runners/Scor. Pos. | | | 13 | 1 | 0 | 1 | 4 | .077 | .077 | .143 |
| First 9 Batters | | | 239 | 70 | 1 | 27 | 32 | .293 | .368 | .372 |
| Second 9 Batters | | | 127 | 21 | 1 | 11 | 12 | .165 | .228 | .236 |
| All Batters Thereafter | | | 99 | 32 | 1 | 11 | 10 | .323 | .424 | .381 |

Loves to face: Greg Brock (0-for-10)
Hates to face: Rick Schu (.524, 11-for-21, 1 HR)
Ground outs-to-air outs ratio: 1.06 last season, 1.17 for career. . . . Additional statistics: 7 double-play ground outs in 109 opportunities, 23 doubles, 2 triples in 120.2 innings last season. . . . Allowed 20 first-inning runs in 16 starts. . . . Batting support: 3.81 runs per start. . . . Record of 4–12 (3.54 ERA) as a starter, 0–1 (6.09, no saves) in 27 relief appearances. . . . Was summoned to protect a lead of five runs or fewer only once in his 40 appearances with Philadelphia. . . . Opponents stole only six bases in 13 attempts. . . . Has a 13–34 record over the last four seasons (.382). Among pitchers with at least 30 decisions since 1986, only Jim Acker has a lower winning percentage (11–32, .256).

## Mike Morgan

Throws Right

| Los Angeles Dodgers | W–L | ERA | AB | H | HR | BB | SO | BA | SA | OBA |
|---|---|---|---|---|---|---|---|---|---|---|
| Season | 8-11 | 2.53 | 555 | 130 | 6 | 33 | 72 | .234 | .319 | .277 |
| vs. Left-Handers | | | 299 | 76 | 5 | 24 | 41 | .254 | .355 | .310 |
| vs. Right-Handers | | | 256 | 54 | 1 | 9 | 31 | .211 | .277 | .236 |
| Home | 4-6 | 2.27 | 311 | 67 | 5 | 17 | 39 | .215 | .302 | .259 |
| Road | 4-5 | 2.89 | 244 | 63 | 1 | 16 | 33 | .258 | .340 | .299 |
| Grass | 6-7 | 2.03 | 441 | 96 | 6 | 23 | 60 | .218 | .297 | .257 |
| Artificial Turf | 2-4 | 4.76 | 114 | 34 | 0 | 10 | 12 | .298 | .404 | .349 |
| April | 2-1 | 1.08 | 83 | 14 | 1 | 2 | 10 | .169 | .217 | .186 |
| May | 2-1 | 1.27 | 120 | 25 | 1 | 9 | 31 | .208 | .267 | .269 |
| June | 1-5 | 2.43 | 158 | 41 | 2 | 5 | 15 | .259 | .361 | .280 |
| July | 2-4 | 5.65 | 112 | 35 | 2 | 13 | 7 | .313 | .446 | .380 |
| August | 0-0 | 2.76 | 58 | 12 | 0 | 3 | 4 | .207 | .259 | .242 |
| Sept./Oct. | 1-0 | 1.35 | 24 | 3 | 0 | 1 | 5 | .125 | .208 | .160 |
| Leading Off Inn. | | | 146 | 35 | 2 | 6 | 15 | .240 | .315 | .270 |
| Runners On | | | 208 | 49 | 2 | 17 | 28 | .236 | .327 | .292 |
| Runners/Scor. Pos. | | | 113 | 26 | 1 | 16 | 20 | .230 | .319 | .316 |
| Runners On/2 Out | | | 83 | 19 | 2 | 11 | 15 | .229 | .349 | .333 |
| Scor. Pos./2 Out | | | 52 | 12 | 1 | 10 | 9 | .231 | .327 | .365 |
| Late Inning Pressure | | | 100 | 16 | 1 | 4 | 12 | .160 | .230 | .190 |
| Leading Off | | | 28 | 8 | 1 | 1 | 2 | .286 | .429 | .310 |
| Runners On | | | 35 | 4 | 0 | 2 | 2 | .114 | .143 | .158 |
| Runners/Scor. Pos. | | | 20 | 3 | 0 | 2 | 2 | .150 | .200 | .217 |
| First 9 Batters | | | 265 | 54 | 1 | 16 | 37 | .204 | .253 | .246 |
| Second 9 Batters | | | 155 | 42 | 4 | 11 | 24 | .271 | .426 | .323 |
| All Batters Thereafter | | | 135 | 34 | 1 | 6 | 11 | .252 | .326 | .283 |

Loves to face: Lonnie Smith (.150, 3-for-20)
Hates to face: Mark Grace (.500, 5-for-10)
Ground outs-to-air outs ratio: 2.11 last season, 1.67 for career.... Additional statistics: 17 double-play ground outs in 100 opportunities, 21 doubles, 4 triples in 152.2 innings last season.... Allowed 8 first-inning runs in 19 starts.... Batting support: 2.53 runs per start, lowest in majors (minimum: 15 starts).... Record of 6–11 (2.74 ERA) as a starter, 2–0 (1.72, no saves) in 21 relief appearances. Last 17 appearances were all in relief.... Shaved 46 percent from his previous career average of 3.59 walks per nine innings. Had a 103-batter walkless streak.... Lowest career winning percentage (.347, 42–79) among active pitchers with 100 decisions. All-time low: Jim Hughey, .266 (29–80).

## Terry Mulholland

Throws Left

| Giants/Phillies | W–L | ERA | AB | H | HR | BB | SO | BA | SA | OBA |
|---|---|---|---|---|---|---|---|---|---|---|
| Season | 4-7 | 4.92 | 465 | 137 | 8 | 36 | 66 | .295 | .409 | .350 |
| vs. Left-Handers | | | 85 | 18 | 0 | 5 | 19 | .212 | .282 | .253 |
| vs. Right-Handers | | | 380 | 119 | 8 | 31 | 47 | .313 | .437 | .371 |
| Home | 2-3 | 3.94 | 225 | 54 | 5 | 21 | 26 | .240 | .360 | .310 |
| Road | 2-4 | 5.95 | 240 | 83 | 3 | 15 | 40 | .346 | .454 | .388 |
| Grass | 1-3 | 6.23 | 152 | 52 | 2 | 11 | 26 | .342 | .447 | .388 |
| Artificial Turf | 3-4 | 4.35 | 313 | 85 | 6 | 25 | 40 | .272 | .390 | .331 |
| April | | | 0 | 0 | 0 | 0 | 0 | — | — | — |
| May | 0-0 | 2.25 | 16 | 3 | 0 | 2 | 2 | .188 | .188 | .278 |
| June | 1-2 | 6.20 | 99 | 31 | 2 | 9 | 17 | .313 | .465 | .376 |
| July | 0-3 | 3.83 | 152 | 39 | 3 | 12 | 19 | .257 | .375 | .313 |
| August | 3-1 | 3.23 | 121 | 33 | 1 | 6 | 20 | .273 | .331 | .318 |
| Sept./Oct. | 0-1 | 9.56 | 77 | 31 | 2 | 7 | 8 | .403 | .571 | .452 |
| Leading Off Inn. | | | 115 | 35 | 1 | 5 | 17 | .304 | .365 | .344 |
| Runners On | | | 211 | 59 | 5 | 22 | 33 | .280 | .441 | .352 |
| Runners/Scor. Pos. | | | 109 | 34 | 1 | 14 | 15 | .312 | .440 | .392 |
| Runners On/2 Out | | | 89 | 25 | 2 | 10 | 18 | .281 | .404 | .360 |
| Scor. Pos./2 Out | | | 58 | 18 | 1 | 7 | 9 | .310 | .379 | .385 |
| Late Inning Pressure | | | 39 | 12 | 0 | 3 | 3 | .308 | .333 | .357 |
| Leading Off | | | 11 | 5 | 0 | 0 | 0 | .455 | .455 | .455 |
| Runners On | | | 16 | 4 | 0 | 3 | 2 | .250 | .250 | .368 |
| Runners/Scor. Pos. | | | 6 | 2 | 0 | 1 | 0 | .333 | .333 | .429 |
| First 9 Batters | | | 182 | 51 | 2 | 13 | 31 | .280 | .363 | .335 |
| Second 9 Batters | | | 146 | 42 | 3 | 14 | 22 | .288 | .418 | .348 |
| All Batters Thereafter | | | 137 | 44 | 3 | 9 | 13 | .321 | .460 | .372 |

Loves to face: Todd Benzinger (0-for-7)
Hates to face: Ryne Sandberg (.385, 5-for-13, 2 HR)
Ground outs-to-air outs ratio: 1.40 last season, 1.47 for career.... Additional statistics: 11 double-play ground outs in 109 opportunities, 29 doubles, 0 triples in 115.1 innings last season.... Allowed 8 first-inning runs in 18 starts.... Batting support: 3.28 runs per start.... His only shutout of the season came against his former mates, the Giants.... First home run he allowed in majors was hit by Graig Nettles, but he hasn't surrendered one to a left-handed batter since then. Career averages: .232 (one HR) by left-handers, .292 (13 HR) by right-handers.... Allowed 18 hits in 37 at-bats in LIP situations prior to 1989.... Has one hit in 57 career at-bats (.018) vs. right-handed pitchers.

## Randy Myers

Throws Left

| New York Mets | W–L | ERA | AB | H | HR | BB | SO | BA | SA | OBA |
|---|---|---|---|---|---|---|---|---|---|---|
| Season | 7-4 | 2.35 | 301 | 62 | 4 | 40 | 88 | .206 | .309 | .297 |
| vs. Left-Handers | | | 73 | 12 | 2 | 8 | 28 | .164 | .315 | .244 |
| vs. Right-Handers | | | 228 | 50 | 2 | 32 | 60 | .219 | .307 | .314 |
| Home | 4-0 | 2.02 | 172 | 33 | 0 | 22 | 49 | .192 | .238 | .282 |
| Road | 3-4 | 2.80 | 129 | 29 | 4 | 18 | 39 | .225 | .403 | .318 |
| Grass | 5-1 | 2.43 | 210 | 40 | 2 | 27 | 58 | .190 | .276 | .282 |
| Artificial Turf | 2-3 | 2.16 | 91 | 22 | 2 | 13 | 30 | .242 | .385 | .333 |
| April | 1-1 | 1.46 | 42 | 7 | 0 | 5 | 18 | .167 | .167 | .250 |
| May | 4-0 | 0.56 | 54 | 8 | 0 | 5 | 17 | .148 | .167 | .220 |
| June | 1-2 | 2.29 | 74 | 20 | 2 | 11 | 16 | .270 | .392 | .365 |
| July | 0-0 | 2.70 | 36 | 7 | 1 | 5 | 8 | .194 | .389 | .286 |
| August | 0-1 | 2.63 | 48 | 10 | 1 | 7 | 11 | .208 | .375 | .309 |
| Sept./Oct. | 1-0 | 4.97 | 47 | 10 | 0 | 7 | 18 | .213 | .340 | .315 |
| Leading Off Inn. | | | 62 | 14 | 1 | 7 | 21 | .226 | .355 | .304 |
| Runners On | | | 161 | 34 | 3 | 22 | 43 | .211 | .342 | .303 |
| Runners/Scor. Pos. | | | 102 | 17 | 2 | 16 | 27 | .167 | .314 | .275 |
| Runners On/2 Out | | | 85 | 18 | 2 | 12 | 18 | .212 | .365 | .309 |
| Scor. Pos./2 Out | | | 61 | 10 | 1 | 9 | 12 | .164 | .311 | .271 |
| Late Inning Pressure | | | 234 | 45 | 4 | 35 | 67 | .192 | .303 | .296 |
| Leading Off | | | 50 | 11 | 1 | 5 | 18 | .220 | .380 | .291 |
| Runners On | | | 120 | 23 | 3 | 21 | 31 | .192 | .342 | .310 |
| Runners/Scor. Pos. | | | 74 | 12 | 2 | 15 | 17 | .162 | .338 | .300 |
| First 9 Batters | | | 289 | 58 | 4 | 40 | 87 | .201 | .308 | .296 |
| Second 9 Batters | | | 12 | 4 | 0 | 0 | 1 | .333 | .333 | .333 |
| All Batters Thereafter | | | 0 | 0 | 0 | 0 | 0 | — | — | — |

Loves to face: Andy Van Slyke (.095, 2-for-21, 10 SO)
Hates to face: Mark Grace (.800, 4-for-5, 2 3B, 1 HR)
Ground outs-to-air outs ratio: 0.55 last season, 0.66 for career.... Additional statistics: 2 double-play ground outs in 71 opportunities, 9 doubles, 5 triples in 84.1 innings last season.... Opponents' career average of .171 at Shea Stadium is the lowest home-game average over the last 15 years (minimum: 500 BFP). Career records: 11–1 at Shea, 6–12 elsewhere.... Saved 24 games in 31 opportunities.... Stranded the first 18 runners he inherited; finished the season 44-for-54 (81%). Incidentally, Franco, who entered only 12 of his 60 games in mid-inning, wasn't bad either: 13-for-17 (76%).... Opponents' batting average in Late-Inning Pressure Situations has been under .200 in each of his five seasons.

## Bob Ojeda

Throws Left

| New York Mets | W–L | ERA | AB | H | HR | BB | SO | BA | SA | OBA |
|---|---|---|---|---|---|---|---|---|---|---|
| Season | 13-11 | 3.47 | 731 | 179 | 16 | 78 | 95 | .245 | .360 | .317 |
| vs. Left-Handers | | | 161 | 38 | 5 | 21 | 29 | .236 | .379 | .324 |
| vs. Right-Handers | | | 570 | 141 | 11 | 57 | 66 | .247 | .354 | .314 |
| Home | 6-4 | 2.95 | 326 | 77 | 7 | 31 | 52 | .236 | .353 | .301 |
| Road | 7-7 | 3.88 | 405 | 102 | 9 | 47 | 43 | .252 | .365 | .329 |
| Grass | 9-7 | 3.25 | 531 | 129 | 13 | 50 | 75 | .243 | .367 | .307 |
| Artificial Turf | 4-4 | 4.02 | 200 | 50 | 3 | 28 | 20 | .250 | .340 | .341 |
| April | 0-3 | 6.38 | 78 | 30 | 2 | 9 | 10 | .385 | .526 | .433 |
| May | 2-2 | 1.88 | 154 | 29 | 3 | 16 | 23 | .188 | .286 | .266 |
| June | 3-2 | 3.41 | 128 | 33 | 3 | 16 | 17 | .258 | .391 | .340 |
| July | 1-2 | 5.72 | 114 | 32 | 2 | 18 | 15 | .281 | .368 | .381 |
| August | 4-0 | 2.65 | 132 | 31 | 1 | 12 | 12 | .235 | .333 | .297 |
| Sept./Oct. | 3-2 | 2.91 | 125 | 24 | 5 | 7 | 18 | .192 | .336 | .235 |
| Leading Off Inn. | | | 181 | 44 | 6 | 20 | 20 | .243 | .392 | .322 |
| Runners On | | | 304 | 74 | 5 | 37 | 40 | .243 | .342 | .321 |
| Runners/Scor. Pos. | | | 165 | 42 | 2 | 28 | 30 | .255 | .327 | .350 |
| Runners On/2 Out | | | 127 | 25 | 1 | 20 | 21 | .197 | .252 | .306 |
| Scor. Pos./2 Out | | | 79 | 16 | 0 | 16 | 17 | .203 | .241 | .337 |
| Late Inning Pressure | | | 39 | 9 | 1 | 5 | 5 | .231 | .333 | .318 |
| Leading Off | | | 11 | 2 | 0 | 1 | 3 | .182 | .182 | .250 |
| Runners On | | | 14 | 5 | 1 | 1 | 0 | .357 | .643 | .400 |
| Runners/Scor. Pos. | | | 5 | 2 | 0 | 0 | 0 | .400 | .400 | .400 |
| First 9 Batters | | | 248 | 67 | 6 | 21 | 34 | .270 | .399 | .326 |
| Second 9 Batters | | | 239 | 56 | 6 | 27 | 38 | .234 | .360 | .311 |
| All Batters Thereafter | | | 244 | 56 | 4 | 30 | 23 | .230 | .320 | .313 |

Loves to face: Von Hayes (.103, 3-for-29)
Hates to face: Ryne Sandberg (.478, 11-for-23, 3 HR)
Ground outs-to-air outs ratio: 1.20 last season, 1.04 for career.... Additional statistics: 14 double-play ground outs in 147 opportunities, 32 doubles, 2 triples in 192.0 innings last season.... Allowed 21 first-inning runs in 31 starts.... Batting support: 4.16 runs per start.... ERA of 1.65 in his 13 victories, 7.47 in his 11 losses. N.L. averages: 1.82 and 6.16, respectively, for starting pitchers of decision.... Ratio of strikeouts to walks fell from 3.18 over three previous seasons to 1.22.... Never before allowed more than two home runs to left-handed batters in one season.... The Fenway factor? Four years with Mets: 44–34, 3.02 ERA; four full seasons with Red Sox: 37–36, 4.21 ERA.

## Jeff Parrett

Throws Right

| Philadelphia Phillies | W-L | ERA | AB | H | HR | BB | SO | BA | SA | OBA |
|---|---|---|---|---|---|---|---|---|---|---|
| Season | 12-6 | 2.98 | 388 | 90 | 6 | 44 | 98 | .232 | .361 | .307 |
| vs. Left-Handers | | | 202 | 44 | 0 | 27 | 48 | .218 | .292 | .309 |
| vs. Right-Handers | | | 186 | 46 | 6 | 17 | 50 | .247 | .435 | .304 |
| Home | 7-0 | 2.22 | 172 | 34 | 2 | 22 | 35 | .198 | .308 | .283 |
| Road | 5-6 | 3.63 | 216 | 56 | 4 | 22 | 63 | .259 | .403 | .326 |
| Grass | 3-2 | 1.99 | 116 | 27 | 1 | 8 | 34 | .233 | .336 | .282 |
| Artificial Turf | 9-4 | 3.41 | 272 | 63 | 5 | 36 | 64 | .232 | .371 | .316 |
| April | 1-1 | 2.16 | 60 | 16 | 1 | 9 | 12 | .267 | .383 | .352 |
| May | 0-1 | 3.38 | 17 | 3 | 0 | 3 | 1 | .176 | .294 | .300 |
| June | 3-0 | 3.86 | 93 | 22 | 1 | 7 | 18 | .237 | .398 | .287 |
| July | 4-1 | 0.89 | 73 | 11 | 1 | 8 | 19 | .151 | .205 | .235 |
| August | 3-1 | 1.16 | 82 | 14 | 1 | 5 | 27 | .171 | .280 | .216 |
| Sept./Oct. | 1-2 | 8.16 | 63 | 24 | 2 | 12 | 21 | .381 | .587 | .474 |
| Leading Off Inn. | | | 89 | 19 | 3 | 10 | 23 | .213 | .393 | .293 |
| Runners On | | | 163 | 40 | 3 | 28 | 42 | .245 | .368 | .347 |
| Runners/Scor. Pos. | | | 112 | 31 | 1 | 24 | 32 | .277 | .384 | .390 |
| Runners On/2 Out | | | 77 | 21 | 2 | 15 | 22 | .273 | .429 | .391 |
| Scor. Pos./2 Out | | | 56 | 14 | 1 | 13 | 17 | .250 | .375 | .391 |
| Late Inning Pressure | | | 242 | 51 | 4 | 35 | 67 | .211 | .326 | .306 |
| Leading Off | | | 58 | 11 | 2 | 8 | 16 | .190 | .345 | .288 |
| Runners On | | | 93 | 20 | 2 | 22 | 25 | .215 | .323 | .353 |
| Runners/Scor. Pos. | | | 61 | 16 | 1 | 20 | 20 | .262 | .361 | .424 |
| First 9 Batters | | | 368 | 85 | 6 | 43 | 91 | .231 | .361 | .308 |
| Second 9 Batters | | | 20 | 5 | 0 | 1 | 7 | .250 | .350 | .286 |
| All Batters Thereafter | | | 0 | 0 | 0 | 0 | 0 | — | — | — |

Loves to face: Howard Johnson (0-for-11, 4 SO)
Hates to face: Kevin McReynolds (.533, 8-for-15, 3 HR)
Ground outs-to-air outs ratio: 0.80 last season, 0.87 for career.... Additional statistics: 7 double-play ground outs in 69 opportunities, 28 doubles, 2 triples in 105.2 innings last season.... Led major league relievers with 12 wins. Only two of those were games in which he blew a lead.... Career record of 9–0 at Veterans Stadium.... Sixth player in major league history to win 12 or more relief games in consecutive seasons. Others: Dill Campbell, Mike Marshall, Lindy McDaniel, Dick Radatz, and Phil Regan.... Won two games against the Cubs, holding them to only two hits in 37 at-bats over 12.1 scoreless innings.... Has faced 1171 batters in his career, but has hit only one of them with a pitch.

## Alejandro Pena

Throws Right

| Los Angeles Dodgers | W-L | ERA | AB | H | HR | BB | SO | BA | SA | OBA |
|---|---|---|---|---|---|---|---|---|---|---|
| Season | 4-3 | 2.13 | 282 | 62 | 6 | 18 | 75 | .220 | .323 | .271 |
| vs. Left-Handers | | | 151 | 35 | 4 | 10 | 40 | .232 | .338 | .280 |
| vs. Right-Handers | | | 131 | 27 | 2 | 8 | 35 | .206 | .305 | .261 |
| Home | 1-0 | 2.80 | 137 | 34 | 3 | 7 | 39 | .248 | .343 | .285 |
| Road | 3-3 | 1.55 | 145 | 28 | 3 | 11 | 36 | .193 | .303 | .258 |
| Grass | 4-1 | 2.42 | 197 | 45 | 5 | 10 | 52 | .228 | .330 | .269 |
| Artificial Turf | 0-2 | 1.50 | 85 | 17 | 1 | 8 | 23 | .200 | .306 | .274 |
| April | 1-0 | 2.76 | 61 | 14 | 3 | 5 | 15 | .230 | .410 | .299 |
| May | 1-1 | 6.14 | 33 | 12 | 2 | 1 | 5 | .364 | .606 | .382 |
| June | 0-1 | 1.15 | 56 | 12 | 0 | 7 | 15 | .214 | .268 | .297 |
| July | 0-0 | 0.00 | 27 | 4 | 0 | 3 | 4 | .148 | .185 | .258 |
| August | 1-0 | 2.20 | 61 | 13 | 1 | 1 | 19 | .213 | .295 | .226 |
| Sept./Oct. | 1-1 | 1.42 | 44 | 7 | 0 | 1 | 17 | .159 | .182 | .178 |
| Leading Off Inn. | | | 68 | 14 | 2 | 6 | 18 | .206 | .338 | .280 |
| Runners On | | | 114 | 25 | 0 | 7 | 29 | .219 | .272 | .268 |
| Runners/Scor. Pos. | | | 58 | 12 | 0 | 6 | 15 | .207 | .259 | .288 |
| Runners On/2 Out | | | 52 | 13 | 0 | 2 | 15 | .250 | .308 | .291 |
| Scor. Pos./2 Out | | | 32 | 8 | 0 | 2 | 10 | .250 | .344 | .314 |
| Late Inning Pressure | | | 182 | 46 | 5 | 12 | 44 | .253 | .390 | .305 |
| Leading Off | | | 44 | 12 | 2 | 3 | 10 | .273 | .455 | .333 |
| Runners On | | | 75 | 20 | 0 | 6 | 17 | .267 | .347 | .325 |
| Runners/Scor. Pos. | | | 40 | 10 | 0 | 6 | 10 | .250 | .325 | .354 |
| First 9 Batters | | | 265 | 61 | 6 | 18 | 68 | .230 | .340 | .283 |
| Second 9 Batters | | | 17 | 1 | 0 | 0 | 7 | .059 | .059 | .059 |
| All Batters Thereafter | | | 0 | 0 | 0 | 0 | 0 | — | — | — |

Loves to face: Terry Kennedy (.045, 1-for-22, 1 HR)
Hates to face: Brett Butler (.421, 8-for-19, 1 HR)
Ground outs-to-air outs ratio: 0.68 last season, 1.05 for career.... Additional statistics: 4 double-play ground outs in 59 opportunities, 9 doubles, 1 triple in 76.0 innings last season.... Average of 8.88 strikeouts per nine innings last season was the highest of his career.... Opponents batted 93 points higher in Late-Inning Pressure Situations than in other at-bats, 2d largest difference in N.L. (minimum. 75 AB each).... Career total of 364 batters faced with runners on base in LIPS, but only one home run allowed. His Mets predecessor, Don Aase, has surrendered 15 such homers (to 689 batters).... Among active pitchers with 750 career innings, only Gooden, Hershiser, Quisenberry, and Gossage have lower ERAs.

## Pascual Perez

Throws Right

| Montreal Expos | W-L | ERA | AB | H | HR | BB | SO | BA | SA | OBA |
|---|---|---|---|---|---|---|---|---|---|---|
| Season | 9-13 | 3.31 | 751 | 178 | 15 | 45 | 152 | .237 | .360 | .282 |
| vs. Left-Handers | | | 414 | 98 | 9 | 30 | 78 | .237 | .362 | .290 |
| vs. Right-Handers | | | 337 | 80 | 6 | 15 | 74 | .237 | .356 | .273 |
| Home | 6-9 | 2.80 | 463 | 100 | 9 | 24 | 105 | .216 | .343 | .258 |
| Road | 3-4 | 4.19 | 288 | 78 | 6 | 21 | 47 | .271 | .385 | .321 |
| Grass | 1-2 | 5.74 | 108 | 33 | 4 | 10 | 16 | .306 | .491 | .367 |
| Artificial Turf | 8-11 | 2.94 | 643 | 145 | 11 | 35 | 136 | .226 | .337 | .268 |
| April | 0-2 | 3.48 | 120 | 28 | 1 | 6 | 23 | .233 | .300 | .271 |
| May | 1-5 | 6.83 | 121 | 41 | 4 | 12 | 19 | .339 | .545 | .400 |
| June | 3-1 | 2.03 | 112 | 22 | 1 | 5 | 29 | .196 | .304 | .237 |
| July | 1-2 | 3.25 | 134 | 27 | 3 | 6 | 29 | .201 | .313 | .239 |
| August | 2-2 | 2.27 | 161 | 37 | 5 | 11 | 32 | .230 | .373 | .279 |
| Sept./Oct. | 2-1 | 2.60 | 103 | 23 | 1 | 5 | 20 | .223 | .311 | .259 |
| Leading Off Inn. | | | 197 | 51 | 5 | 4 | 41 | .259 | .391 | .277 |
| Runners On | | | 285 | 69 | 6 | 28 | 51 | .242 | .375 | .308 |
| Runners/Scor. Pos. | | | 170 | 39 | 3 | 24 | 35 | .229 | .371 | .322 |
| Runners On/2 Out | | | 123 | 26 | 2 | 19 | 23 | .211 | .333 | .317 |
| Scor. Pos./2 Out | | | 86 | 19 | 1 | 17 | 16 | .221 | .349 | .350 |
| Late Inning Pressure | | | 72 | 27 | 1 | 8 | 8 | .375 | .542 | .439 |
| Leading Off | | | 16 | 7 | 0 | 2 | 0 | .438 | .500 | .526 |
| Runners On | | | 40 | 15 | 1 | 6 | 4 | .375 | .575 | .447 |
| Runners/Scor. Pos. | | | 22 | 8 | 0 | 6 | 3 | .364 | .545 | .483 |
| First 9 Batters | | | 261 | 51 | 3 | 12 | 68 | .195 | .284 | .237 |
| Second 9 Batters | | | 231 | 53 | 4 | 19 | 40 | .229 | .351 | .287 |
| All Batters Thereafter | | | 259 | 74 | 8 | 14 | 44 | .286 | .444 | .324 |

Loves to face: Lance Parrish (0-for-11, 5 SO)
Hates to face: Chris James (.417, 5-for-12, 2 HR)
Ground outs-to-air outs ratio: 1.92 last season, 1.74 for career.... Additional statistics: 13 double-play ground outs in 119 opportunities, 29 doubles, 9 triples in 198.1 innings last season.... Allowed 8 first-inning runs in 28 starts. ERA of 2.54 over first six innings, 7.22 thereafter.... Opponents have batted under .200 in his first pass through batting order in each of last three seasons.... Batting support: 3.75 runs per start.... Highest ratio of strikeouts to walks of any N.L. starter (3.38). Fanned 26 batters between walks, longest streak in the majors.... Only player to lose more games in his home ballpark: new teammate Andy Hawkins.... What happens if he repeats his 0–7 start this season?

## Jeff Pico

Throws Right

| Chicago Cubs | W-L | ERA | AB | H | HR | BB | SO | BA | SA | OBA |
|---|---|---|---|---|---|---|---|---|---|---|
| Season | 3-1 | 3.77 | 356 | 99 | 8 | 31 | 38 | .278 | .404 | .334 |
| vs. Left-Handers | | | 163 | 51 | 5 | 18 | 11 | .313 | .491 | .381 |
| vs. Right-Handers | | | 193 | 48 | 3 | 13 | 27 | .249 | .332 | .293 |
| Home | 1-1 | 3.94 | 185 | 46 | 5 | 18 | 22 | .249 | .378 | .314 |
| Road | 2-0 | 3.59 | 171 | 53 | 3 | 13 | 16 | .310 | .433 | .357 |
| Grass | 2-1 | 3.84 | 253 | 66 | 6 | 22 | 30 | .261 | .395 | .318 |
| Artificial Turf | 1-0 | 3.60 | 103 | 33 | 2 | 9 | 8 | .320 | .427 | .375 |
| April | 0-0 | 4.00 | 34 | 9 | 1 | 3 | 4 | .265 | .412 | .324 |
| May | 2-0 | 2.25 | 74 | 15 | 1 | 8 | 9 | .203 | .284 | .280 |
| June | 0-0 | 5.54 | 57 | 20 | 2 | 2 | 7 | .351 | .526 | .373 |
| July | 0-1 | 2.93 | 60 | 15 | 0 | 9 | 7 | .250 | .333 | .348 |
| August | 0-0 | 10.03 | 49 | 18 | 3 | 8 | 1 | .367 | .612 | .448 |
| Sept./Oct. | 1-0 | 1.25 | 82 | 22 | 1 | 1 | 10 | .268 | .354 | .274 |
| Leading Off Inn. | | | 80 | 19 | 1 | 3 | 9 | .238 | .313 | .265 |
| Runners On | | | 164 | 51 | 5 | 19 | 15 | .311 | .488 | .378 |
| Runners/Scor. Pos. | | | 100 | 27 | 3 | 17 | 12 | .270 | .440 | .370 |
| Runners On/2 Out | | | 87 | 32 | 3 | 12 | 6 | .368 | .563 | .444 |
| Scor. Pos./2 Out | | | 56 | 17 | 2 | 10 | 4 | .304 | .518 | .409 |
| Late Inning Pressure | | | 69 | 14 | 1 | 7 | 9 | .203 | .304 | .276 |
| Leading Off | | | 17 | 1 | 0 | 0 | 1 | .059 | .059 | .059 |
| Runners On | | | 23 | 5 | 0 | 5 | 3 | .217 | .348 | .357 |
| Runners/Scor. Pos. | | | 17 | 2 | 0 | 5 | 3 | .118 | .176 | .318 |
| First 9 Batters | | | 260 | 73 | 5 | 24 | 29 | .281 | .404 | .340 |
| Second 9 Batters | | | 66 | 19 | 2 | 4 | 8 | .288 | .439 | .329 |
| All Batters Thereafter | | | 30 | 7 | 1 | 3 | 1 | .233 | .333 | .294 |

Loves to face: Barry Larkin (.083, 1-for-12)
Hates to face: Andy Van Slyke (.625, 5-for-8, 2 HR)
Ground outs-to-air outs ratio: 1.25 last season, 1.34 for career.... Additional statistics: 6 double-play ground outs in 63 opportunities, 17 doubles, 2 triples in 90.2 innings last season.... Had a 1–1 record (5.74 ERA) in five starts, 2–0 (2.95, two saves) in 48 relief appearances.... Opponents stole only one base in six attempts, including 0-for-4 with Berryhill catching.... Opponents' career breakdowns: .237 with bases empty, .299 with runners on, .300 with runners in scoring position; .303 (nine HR) by left-handers, .225 (five HR) by right-handers.... Has pitched 26.1 innings against Atlanta without allowing an earned run. Starts 1990 with a streak of 23.1 consecutive shutout innings vs. Braves.

## Mark Portugal

Throws Right

| Houston Astros | W–L | ERA | AB | H | HR | BB | SO | BA | SA | OBA |
|---|---|---|---|---|---|---|---|---|---|---|
| Season | 7-1 | 2.75 | 392 | 91 | 7 | 37 | 86 | .232 | .329 | .301 |
| vs. Left-Handers | | | 209 | 46 | 3 | 23 | 41 | .220 | .321 | .297 |
| vs. Right-Handers | | | 183 | 45 | 4 | 14 | 45 | .246 | .339 | .305 |
| Home | 4-1 | 3.12 | 189 | 46 | 6 | 17 | 43 | .243 | .381 | .304 |
| Road | 3-0 | 2.41 | 203 | 45 | 1 | 20 | 43 | .222 | .281 | .298 |
| Grass | 2-0 | 2.06 | 125 | 28 | 1 | 11 | 28 | .224 | .280 | .297 |
| Artificial Turf | 5-1 | 3.08 | 267 | 63 | 6 | 26 | 58 | .236 | .352 | .303 |
| April | | | 0 | 0 | 0 | 0 | 0 | — | — | — |
| May | | | 0 | 0 | 0 | 0 | 0 | — | — | — |
| June | 0-1 | 8.53 | 26 | 10 | 2 | 2 | 4 | .385 | .692 | .429 |
| July | 2-0 | 1.66 | 79 | 16 | 1 | 8 | 19 | .203 | .291 | .276 |
| August | 1-0 | 3.22 | 134 | 34 | 2 | 12 | 29 | .254 | .336 | .322 |
| Sept./Oct. | 4-0 | 2.06 | 153 | 31 | 2 | 15 | 34 | .203 | .281 | .274 |
| Leading Off Inn. | | | 103 | 25 | 2 | 9 | 23 | .243 | .350 | .310 |
| Runners On | | | 154 | 33 | 3 | 13 | 34 | .214 | .318 | .278 |
| Runners/Scor. Pos. | | | 83 | 14 | 0 | 8 | 17 | .169 | .205 | .239 |
| Runners On/2 Out | | | 68 | 15 | 0 | 7 | 12 | .221 | .265 | .293 |
| Scor. Pos./2 Out | | | 45 | 8 | 0 | 4 | 9 | .178 | .200 | .245 |
| Late Inning Pressure | | | 34 | 8 | 0 | 1 | 7 | .235 | .265 | .257 |
| Leading Off | | | 12 | 6 | 0 | 0 | 4 | .500 | .583 | .500 |
| Runners On | | | 10 | 0 | 0 | 0 | 1 | .000 | .000 | .000 |
| Runners/Scor. Pos. | | | 7 | 0 | 0 | 0 | 1 | .000 | .000 | .000 |
| First 9 Batters | | | 149 | 32 | 2 | 9 | 36 | .215 | .282 | .264 |
| Second 9 Batters | | | 117 | 28 | 4 | 17 | 26 | .239 | .410 | .333 |
| All Batters Thereafter | | | 126 | 31 | 1 | 11 | 24 | .246 | .310 | .312 |

Loves to face: Matt Williams (.083, 1-for-12)
Hates to face: Ron Gant (3-for-3, 1 HR)
Ground outs-to-air outs ratio: 1.42 last season, 1.28 for career. . . . Additional statistics: 6 double-play ground outs in 74 opportunities, 15 doubles, 1 triple in 108.0 innings last season. . . . Allowed 5 first-inning runs in 15 starts. . . . Batting support: 4.27 runs per start. . . . Seven-game winning streak was longest by a Houston pitcher. Career record prior to streak: 11–20. . . . Career record of 3–13 (6.25 ERA) before All-Star break, 15–7 (3.09 ERA) after. . . . Opponents' batting average with runners in scoring position has been lower than in other at-bats in each of five seasons. Career averages: .211 with RISP, .299 otherwise. . . . Right-handers have outhit left-handers .288 to .245.

## Ted Power

Throws Right

| St. Louis Cardinals | W–L | ERA | AB | H | HR | BB | SO | BA | SA | OBA |
|---|---|---|---|---|---|---|---|---|---|---|
| Season | 7-7 | 3.71 | 377 | 96 | 7 | 21 | 43 | .255 | .385 | .294 |
| vs. Left-Handers | | | 207 | 58 | 3 | 14 | 23 | .280 | .396 | .324 |
| vs. Right-Handers | | | 170 | 38 | 4 | 7 | 20 | .224 | .371 | .256 |
| Home | 3-2 | 2.95 | 154 | 40 | 2 | 7 | 16 | .260 | .351 | .290 |
| Road | 4-5 | 4.24 | 223 | 56 | 5 | 14 | 27 | .251 | .408 | .296 |
| Grass | 2-3 | 5.27 | 108 | 27 | 5 | 8 | 13 | .250 | .444 | .308 |
| Artificial Turf | 5-4 | 3.10 | 269 | 69 | 2 | 13 | 30 | .257 | .361 | .288 |
| April | | | 0 | 0 | 0 | 0 | 0 | — | — | — |
| May | 0-1 | 4.70 | 29 | 8 | 0 | 6 | 2 | .276 | .276 | .400 |
| June | 0-1 | 7.00 | 40 | 14 | 0 | 2 | 4 | .350 | .550 | .372 |
| July | 3-2 | 4.56 | 92 | 22 | 3 | 2 | 10 | .239 | .402 | .263 |
| August | 2-2 | 2.61 | 155 | 35 | 2 | 10 | 19 | .226 | .323 | .269 |
| Sept./Oct. | 2-1 | 2.93 | 61 | 17 | 2 | 1 | 8 | .279 | .459 | .290 |
| Leading Off Inn. | | | 97 | 28 | 0 | 3 | 8 | .289 | .402 | .310 |
| Runners On | | | 158 | 41 | 5 | 11 | 18 | .259 | .418 | .306 |
| Runners/Scor. Pos. | | | 97 | 28 | 3 | 7 | 13 | .289 | .454 | .327 |
| Runners On/2 Out | | | 65 | 13 | 2 | 4 | 7 | .200 | .338 | .246 |
| Scor. Pos./2 Out | | | 42 | 8 | 1 | 3 | 6 | .190 | .310 | .244 |
| Late Inning Pressure | | | 22 | 8 | 0 | 1 | 2 | .364 | .500 | .375 |
| Leading Off | | | 6 | 1 | 0 | 0 | 0 | .167 | .500 | .167 |
| Runners On | | | 7 | 4 | 0 | 1 | 0 | .571 | .714 | .556 |
| Runners/Scor. Pos. | | | 3 | 2 | 0 | 1 | 0 | .667 | 1.000 | .600 |
| First 9 Batters | | | 157 | 35 | 1 | 10 | 25 | .223 | .293 | .274 |
| Second 9 Batters | | | 128 | 34 | 4 | 6 | 12 | .266 | .445 | .296 |
| All Batters Thereafter | | | 92 | 27 | 2 | 5 | 6 | .293 | .457 | .323 |

Loves to face: Benito Santiago (.077, 1-for-13)
Hates to face: John Kruk (.625, 10-for-16)
Ground outs-to-air outs ratio: 0.93 last season, 0.86 for career. . . . Additional statistics: 5 double-play ground outs in 69 opportunities, 20 doubles, 4 triples in 97.0 innings last season. . . . Allowed 5 first-inning runs in 15 starts. . . . Batting support: 4.13 runs per start. . . . Had a 5–7 record (4.07 ERA) as a starter, 2–0 (1.38) in eight relief appearances. . . . One save in 66 relief appearances since saving 27 games for the 1985 Reds. . . . Snapped streak of increasing ERA that began in 1985: 2.70, 3.70, 4.50, 5.91. No pitcher ever climbed from the twos to the sixes, one step at a time, in five seasons. A couple dozen others went from two to five, including Steve Rogers, Andy Messersmith, and Mike Torrez.

## Dan Quisenberry

Throws Right

| St. Louis Cardinals | W–L | ERA | AB | H | HR | BB | SO | BA | SA | OBA |
|---|---|---|---|---|---|---|---|---|---|---|
| Season | 3-1 | 2.64 | 299 | 78 | 2 | 14 | 37 | .261 | .351 | .293 |
| vs. Left-Handers | | | 143 | 34 | 2 | 12 | 17 | .238 | .336 | .297 |
| vs. Right-Handers | | | 156 | 44 | 0 | 2 | 20 | .282 | .365 | .289 |
| Home | 3-0 | 4.30 | 151 | 44 | 2 | 5 | 17 | .291 | .437 | .314 |
| Road | 0-1 | 1.11 | 148 | 34 | 0 | 9 | 20 | .230 | .264 | .272 |
| Grass | 0-1 | 1.57 | 86 | 24 | 0 | 8 | 15 | .279 | .291 | .337 |
| Artificial Turf | 3-0 | 3.09 | 213 | 54 | 2 | 6 | 22 | .254 | .376 | .274 |
| April | 1-0 | 5.63 | 34 | 12 | 0 | 1 | 3 | .353 | .500 | .371 |
| May | 0-1 | 1.62 | 61 | 15 | 0 | 5 | 11 | .246 | .262 | .303 |
| June | 1-0 | 1.15 | 57 | 10 | 0 | 2 | 8 | .175 | .211 | .203 |
| July | 0-0 | 2.70 | 48 | 11 | 1 | 1 | 7 | .229 | .333 | .245 |
| August | 1-0 | 3.00 | 48 | 16 | 0 | 3 | 4 | .333 | .458 | .365 |
| Sept./Oct. | 0-0 | 3.55 | 51 | 14 | 1 | 2 | 4 | .275 | .431 | .302 |
| Leading Off Inn. | | | 76 | 16 | 0 | 1 | 9 | .211 | .263 | .221 |
| Runners On | | | 117 | 34 | 1 | 11 | 10 | .291 | .385 | .349 |
| Runners/Scor. Pos. | | | 81 | 25 | 1 | 10 | 8 | .309 | .420 | .380 |
| Runners On/2 Out | | | 53 | 14 | 1 | 5 | 6 | .264 | .358 | .328 |
| Scor. Pos./2 Out | | | 36 | 9 | 1 | 5 | 5 | .250 | .333 | .341 |
| Late Inning Pressure | | | 90 | 26 | 0 | 5 | 11 | .289 | .367 | .326 |
| Leading Off | | | 26 | 6 | 0 | 0 | 3 | .231 | .269 | .231 |
| Runners On | | | 31 | 10 | 0 | 5 | 4 | .323 | .452 | .417 |
| Runners/Scor. Pos. | | | 20 | 8 | 0 | 5 | 4 | .400 | .550 | .520 |
| First 9 Batters | | | 285 | 74 | 1 | 13 | 35 | .260 | .344 | .291 |
| Second 9 Batters | | | 14 | 4 | 1 | 1 | 2 | .286 | .500 | .333 |
| All Batters Thereafter | | | 0 | 0 | 0 | 0 | 0 | — | — | — |

Loves to face: John Shelby (0-for-11)
Hates to face: Tim Wallach (.833, 5-for-6, 1 HR)
Ground outs-to-air outs ratio: 2.16 last season, 2.32 for career. . . . Additional statistics: 8 double-play ground outs in 42 opportunities, 15 doubles, 3 triples in 78.1 innings last season. . . . Opponents stole 15 bases in 17 attempts. . . . Allowed two HRs, both to top sluggers: Will Clark and Sid Fernandez. . . . Opposing left-handers outhit right-handers in each of 10 previous seasons, with marks above .300 in each of the past four. . . . Nine of 14 walks, including his only two to right-handers, were intentional. . . . Career average of 1.38 walks per nine innings is the lowest among all pitchers whose careers began in the 20th century (minimum: 1000 IP).

## Dennis Rasmussen

Throws Left

| San Diego Padres | W–L | ERA | AB | H | HR | BB | SO | BA | SA | OBA |
|---|---|---|---|---|---|---|---|---|---|---|
| Season | 10-10 | 4.26 | 704 | 190 | 18 | 72 | 87 | .270 | .403 | .335 |
| vs. Left-Handers | | | 133 | 33 | 4 | 13 | 17 | .248 | .391 | .311 |
| vs. Right-Handers | | | 571 | 157 | 14 | 59 | 70 | .275 | .406 | .341 |
| Home | 5-4 | 3.42 | 280 | 69 | 10 | 29 | 45 | .246 | .393 | .314 |
| Road | 5-6 | 4.86 | 424 | 121 | 8 | 43 | 42 | .285 | .410 | .349 |
| Grass | 7-10 | 4.10 | 544 | 145 | 16 | 56 | 70 | .267 | .410 | .330 |
| Artificial Turf | 3-0 | 4.83 | 160 | 45 | 2 | 16 | 17 | .281 | .381 | .356 |
| April | 1-4 | 7.20 | 109 | 39 | 5 | 7 | 11 | .358 | .569 | .395 |
| May | 1-1 | 3.25 | 131 | 33 | 4 | 17 | 12 | .252 | .374 | .336 |
| June | 1-0 | 2.88 | 132 | 34 | 3 | 12 | 18 | .258 | .371 | .315 |
| July | 1-2 | 5.92 | 96 | 27 | 2 | 11 | 14 | .281 | .458 | .364 |
| August | 4-2 | 3.05 | 155 | 33 | 2 | 18 | 19 | .213 | .290 | .290 |
| Sept./Oct. | 2-1 | 5.49 | 81 | 24 | 2 | 7 | 13 | .296 | .432 | .344 |
| Leading Off Inn. | | | 180 | 58 | 2 | 17 | 17 | .322 | .456 | .387 |
| Runners On | | | 303 | 89 | 11 | 32 | 36 | .294 | .446 | .352 |
| Runners/Scor. Pos. | | | 149 | 42 | 3 | 23 | 23 | .282 | .389 | .359 |
| Runners On/2 Out | | | 117 | 30 | 0 | 17 | 16 | .256 | .299 | .351 |
| Scor. Pos./2 Out | | | 72 | 21 | 0 | 16 | 13 | .292 | .333 | .420 |
| Late Inning Pressure | | | 36 | 9 | 1 | 9 | 4 | .250 | .361 | .400 |
| Leading Off | | | 11 | 5 | 1 | 3 | 1 | .455 | .818 | .571 |
| Runners On | | | 14 | 2 | 0 | 2 | 1 | .143 | .143 | .250 |
| Runners/Scor. Pos. | | | 4 | 1 | 0 | 1 | 1 | .250 | .250 | .400 |
| First 9 Batters | | | 264 | 76 | 11 | 21 | 42 | .288 | .458 | .336 |
| Second 9 Batters | | | 238 | 56 | 3 | 21 | 26 | .235 | .340 | .296 |
| All Batters Thereafter | | | 202 | 58 | 4 | 30 | 19 | .287 | .406 | .380 |

Loves to face: Willie McGee (.071, 1-for-14)
Hates to face: Pedro Guerrero (.750, 9-for-12)
Ground outs-to-air outs ratio: 1.03 last season, 0.77 for career. . . . Additional statistics: 19 double-play ground outs in 166 opportunities, 30 doubles, 5 triples in 183.2 innings last season. . . . Allowed 32 runs and nine HR in first inning, both most in majors, in 33 starts. ERA was 8.72 in first frame, when opponents batted .366. . . . Batting support: 3.91 runs per start. . . . Allowed hits to eight consecutive right-handers, 2d-longest streak of 1980s. . . . Led majors with 13 starts without a decision. . . . Has lost last six decisions on artificial turf, after going 22–4 on plastic. . . . Career records: 18–18 in day games, 51–27 at night. . . . Has defeated every major league team except Pittsburgh and the Yankees.

## Rick Reuschel

Throws Right

| San Francisco Giants | W-L | ERA | AB | H | HR | BB | SO | BA | SA | OBA |
|---|---|---|---|---|---|---|---|---|---|---|
| Season | 17-8 | 2.94 | 790 | 195 | 18 | 54 | 111 | .247 | .380 | .294 |
| vs. Left-Handers | | | 445 | 116 | 5 | 32 | 42 | .261 | .364 | .309 |
| vs. Right-Handers | | | 345 | 79 | 13 | 22 | 69 | .229 | .400 | .275 |
| Home | 8-5 | 2.79 | 415 | 102 | 10 | 26 | 66 | .246 | .395 | .290 |
| Road | 9-3 | 3.10 | 375 | 93 | 8 | 28 | 45 | .248 | .363 | .299 |
| Grass | 12-6 | 3.34 | 566 | 145 | 16 | 40 | 84 | .256 | .408 | .305 |
| Artificial Turf | 5-2 | 1.94 | 224 | 50 | 2 | 14 | 27 | .223 | .308 | .268 |
| April | 3-2 | 3.68 | 137 | 35 | 5 | 16 | 23 | .255 | .423 | .333 |
| May | 6-0 | 0.84 | 157 | 35 | 0 | 7 | 22 | .223 | .287 | .255 |
| June | 3-0 | 2.03 | 167 | 39 | 2 | 8 | 21 | .234 | .293 | .267 |
| July | 1-3 | 3.90 | 119 | 35 | 2 | 9 | 14 | .294 | .454 | .344 |
| August | 2-1 | 5.02 | 60 | 18 | 0 | 3 | 2 | .300 | .450 | .328 |
| Sept./Oct. | 2-2 | 4.05 | 150 | 33 | 9 | 11 | 29 | .220 | .447 | .273 |
| Leading Off Inn. | | | 208 | 54 | 6 | 8 | 27 | .260 | .438 | .287 |
| Runners On | | | 298 | 78 | 5 | 20 | 46 | .262 | .376 | .304 |
| Runners/Scor. Pos. | | | 160 | 37 | 3 | 12 | 26 | .231 | .369 | .278 |
| Runners On/2 Out | | | 127 | 25 | 1 | 13 | 19 | .197 | .268 | .277 |
| Scor. Pos./2 Out | | | 78 | 13 | 1 | 9 | 11 | .167 | .269 | .261 |
| Late Inning Pressure | | | 86 | 20 | 0 | 4 | 10 | .233 | .302 | .267 |
| Leading Off | | | 23 | 5 | 0 | 0 | 4 | .217 | .348 | .217 |
| Runners On | | | 31 | 7 | 0 | 3 | 4 | .226 | .258 | .294 |
| Runners/Scor. Pos. | | | 23 | 5 | 0 | 2 | 2 | .217 | .261 | .280 |
| First 9 Batters | | | 264 | 69 | 6 | 12 | 36 | .261 | .402 | .287 |
| Second 9 Batters | | | 262 | 63 | 11 | 22 | 44 | .240 | .416 | .302 |
| All Batters Thereafter | | | 264 | 63 | 1 | 20 | 31 | .239 | .322 | .294 |

Loves to face: Eric Davis (.050, 1-for-20)
Hates to face: Tim Raines (.429, 27-for-63)
Ground outs-to-air outs ratio: 1.14 last season, 1.83 for career.... Additional statistics: 10 double-play ground outs in 139 opportunities, 37 doubles, 7 triples in 208.1 innings last season.... Allowed 12 first-inning runs in 32 starts. Opponents batted .282 in first two innings, .231 thereafter.... Batting support: 4.19 runs per start.... Led the majors in wins and ERA in May. Has won his last eight decisions during that month.... From the Jinx Dept.: No N.L. All-Star Game starter has won 20 or more games in that season since Randy Jones in 1976.... Hasn't allowed back-to-back home runs in regular season since 1980, but Bo Jackson and Wade Boggs did it in the first inning inning of All-Star Game.

## Jose Rijo

Throws Right

| Cincinnati Reds | W-L | ERA | AB | H | HR | BB | SO | BA | SA | OBA |
|---|---|---|---|---|---|---|---|---|---|---|
| Season | 7-6 | 2.84 | 405 | 101 | 6 | 48 | 86 | .249 | .338 | .328 |
| vs. Left-Handers | | | 242 | 66 | 5 | 40 | 47 | .273 | .384 | .372 |
| vs. Right-Handers | | | 163 | 35 | 1 | 8 | 39 | .215 | .270 | .256 |
| Home | 2-2 | 3.16 | 157 | 40 | 1 | 22 | 45 | .255 | .338 | .344 |
| Road | 5-4 | 2.63 | 248 | 61 | 5 | 26 | 41 | .246 | .339 | .317 |
| Grass | 2-3 | 3.44 | 138 | 39 | 4 | 17 | 25 | .283 | .391 | .361 |
| Artificial Turf | 5-3 | 2.54 | 267 | 62 | 2 | 31 | 61 | .232 | .311 | .310 |
| April | 1-0 | 0.87 | 111 | 24 | 0 | 15 | 24 | .216 | .288 | .307 |
| May | 4-1 | 3.35 | 135 | 30 | 3 | 14 | 35 | .222 | .326 | .292 |
| June | 2-4 | 4.33 | 135 | 43 | 3 | 14 | 20 | .319 | .415 | .384 |
| July | 0-1 | 1.29 | 24 | 4 | 0 | 5 | 7 | .167 | .208 | .310 |
| August | | | 0 | 0 | 0 | 0 | 0 | — | — | — |
| Sept./Oct. | | | 0 | 0 | 0 | 0 | 0 | — | — | — |
| Leading Off Inn. | | | 101 | 28 | 3 | 12 | 13 | .277 | .406 | .354 |
| Runners On | | | 172 | 39 | 1 | 20 | 44 | .227 | .262 | .305 |
| Runners/Scor. Pos. | | | 105 | 25 | 1 | 16 | 35 | .238 | .286 | .323 |
| Runners On/2 Out | | | 73 | 14 | 0 | 10 | 24 | .192 | .219 | .289 |
| Scor. Pos./2 Out | | | 47 | 9 | 0 | 8 | 17 | .191 | .213 | .309 |
| Late Inning Pressure | | | 24 | 9 | 0 | 4 | 7 | .375 | .458 | .464 |
| Leading Off | | | 5 | 2 | 0 | 2 | 2 | .400 | .400 | .571 |
| Runners On | | | 15 | 5 | 0 | 1 | 4 | .333 | .333 | .375 |
| Runners/Scor. Pos. | | | 10 | 3 | 0 | 1 | 3 | .300 | .300 | .364 |
| First 9 Batters | | | 147 | 31 | 3 | 18 | 42 | .211 | .340 | .302 |
| Second 9 Batters | | | 137 | 34 | 2 | 20 | 24 | .248 | .328 | .338 |
| All Batters Thereafter | | | 121 | 36 | 1 | 10 | 20 | .298 | .347 | .348 |

Loves to face: Glenn Davis (.083, 1-for-12)
Hates to face: Eddie Murray (.412, 7-for-17, 1 HR, 8 BB)
Ground outs-to-air outs ratio: 1.37 last season, 1.18 for career.... Additional statistics: 10 double-play ground outs in 80 opportunities, 16 doubles, 1 triple in 111.0 innings last season.... Allowed 7 first-inning runs in 19 starts.... Batting support: 3.53 runs per start.... Led N.L. in ERA at end of April. Reds won each of the first nine games he started.... ERA of 1.32 in his six starts without a decision. Reds won five of those games.... Record of 19–30, 4.75 ERA in four seasons in A.L., 20–14, 2.57 in two N.L. seasons.... Career average of 8.01 strikeouts per nine innings ranks third among active N.L. pitchers behind Sid Fernandez and Dwight Gooden (minimum: 600 IP).

## Rick Rhoden

Throws Right

| Houston Astros | W-L | ERA | AB | H | HR | BB | SO | BA | SA | OBA |
|---|---|---|---|---|---|---|---|---|---|---|
| Season | 2-6 | 4.28 | 374 | 108 | 7 | 41 | 41 | .289 | .414 | .361 |
| vs. Left-Handers | | | 221 | 60 | 4 | 23 | 18 | .271 | .403 | .344 |
| vs. Right-Handers | | | 153 | 48 | 3 | 18 | 23 | .314 | .431 | .385 |
| Home | 1-6 | 4.42 | 220 | 64 | 4 | 22 | 23 | .291 | .405 | .359 |
| Road | 1-0 | 4.08 | 154 | 44 | 3 | 19 | 18 | .286 | .429 | .364 |
| Grass | 0-0 | 5.28 | 61 | 19 | 1 | 10 | 4 | .311 | .426 | .408 |
| Artificial Turf | 2-6 | 4.09 | 313 | 89 | 6 | 31 | 37 | .284 | .412 | .351 |
| April | 0-2 | 4.45 | 119 | 34 | 2 | 10 | 12 | .286 | .395 | .348 |
| May | 0-0 | 1.80 | 19 | 5 | 0 | 2 | 2 | .263 | .316 | .333 |
| June | | | 0 | 0 | 0 | 0 | 0 | — | — | — |
| July | 0-1 | 3.18 | 22 | 6 | 0 | 2 | 1 | .273 | .273 | .333 |
| August | 1-2 | 3.69 | 124 | 38 | 4 | 15 | 13 | .306 | .468 | .381 |
| Sept./Oct. | 1-1 | 5.63 | 90 | 25 | 1 | 12 | 13 | .278 | .422 | .362 |
| Leading Off Inn. | | | 92 | 24 | 1 | 9 | 5 | .261 | .370 | .327 |
| Runners On | | | 158 | 47 | 4 | 24 | 19 | .297 | .437 | .390 |
| Runners/Scor. Pos. | | | 99 | 28 | 2 | 22 | 15 | .283 | .424 | .413 |
| Runners On/2 Out | | | 73 | 23 | 1 | 16 | 12 | .315 | .452 | .444 |
| Scor. Pos./2 Out | | | 53 | 16 | 1 | 15 | 9 | .302 | .472 | .464 |
| Late Inning Pressure | | | 18 | 6 | 1 | 1 | 1 | .333 | .500 | .368 |
| Leading Off | | | 6 | 1 | 0 | 0 | 1 | .167 | .167 | .167 |
| Runners On | | | 4 | 3 | 1 | 0 | 0 | .750 | 1.500 | .750 |
| Runners/Scor. Pos. | | | 2 | 1 | 1 | 0 | 0 | .500 | 2.000 | .500 |
| First 9 Batters | | | 155 | 41 | 1 | 10 | 26 | .265 | .348 | .317 |
| Second 9 Batters | | | 120 | 41 | 3 | 16 | 8 | .342 | .492 | .414 |
| All Batters Thereafter | | | 99 | 26 | 3 | 15 | 7 | .263 | .424 | .360 |

Loves to face: Kevin Bass (.133, 2-for-15)
Hates to face: Rob Thompson (.857, 6-for-7, 1 2B, 2 3B)
Ground outs-to-air outs ratio: 1.12 last season, 1.32 for career. Opposing ground-ball hitters batted .249 through 1986, .293 since then, coinciding with decline in G/A ratio from 1.35 to 1.17 over last three seasons.... Additional statistics: 5 double-play ground outs in 68 opportunities, 22 doubles, 2 triples in 96.2 innings last season.... Allowed 12 first-inning runs in 17 starts.... Batting support: 3.29 runs per start.... Opponents stole 18 bases in 21 attempts.... Opponents' batting average with runners on base was highest of career.... Never reached eighth inning in any of his 17 starts.... Two relief appearances were his first since saving a game for John Candelaria in April 1983.

## Don Robinson

Throws Right

| San Francisco Giants | W-L | ERA | AB | H | HR | BB | SO | BA | SA | OBA |
|---|---|---|---|---|---|---|---|---|---|---|
| Season | 12-11 | 3.43 | 743 | 184 | 22 | 37 | 96 | .248 | .396 | .283 |
| vs. Left-Handers | | | 434 | 113 | 13 | 25 | 50 | .260 | .412 | .301 |
| vs. Right-Handers | | | 309 | 71 | 9 | 12 | 46 | .230 | .372 | .258 |
| Home | 9-4 | 2.10 | 432 | 96 | 13 | 17 | 64 | .222 | .359 | .252 |
| Road | 3-7 | 5.49 | 311 | 88 | 9 | 20 | 32 | .283 | .447 | .326 |
| Grass | 10-7 | 2.49 | 556 | 129 | 15 | 25 | 73 | .232 | .363 | .265 |
| Artificial Turf | 2-4 | 6.55 | 187 | 55 | 7 | 12 | 23 | .294 | .492 | .337 |
| April | 1-2 | 4.03 | 116 | 33 | 4 | 10 | 13 | .284 | .448 | .339 |
| May | 2-2 | 2.63 | 148 | 36 | 4 | 8 | 21 | .243 | .412 | .285 |
| June | 4-1 | 2.31 | 144 | 31 | 3 | 8 | 18 | .215 | .333 | .255 |
| July | 2-2 | 5.24 | 138 | 41 | 3 | 6 | 21 | .297 | .435 | .329 |
| August | 2-2 | 3.27 | 117 | 23 | 4 | 4 | 14 | .197 | .333 | .221 |
| Sept./Oct. | 1-2 | 3.48 | 80 | 20 | 4 | 1 | 9 | .250 | .425 | .259 |
| Leading Off Inn. | | | 194 | 49 | 7 | 10 | 21 | .253 | .423 | .289 |
| Runners On | | | 255 | 61 | 6 | 16 | 32 | .239 | .361 | .284 |
| Runners/Scor. Pos. | | | 147 | 32 | 2 | 12 | 24 | .218 | .327 | .277 |
| Runners On/2 Out | | | 112 | 25 | 3 | 9 | 14 | .223 | .366 | .281 |
| Scor. Pos./2 Out | | | 69 | 15 | 1 | 6 | 11 | .217 | .333 | .280 |
| Late Inning Pressure | | | 63 | 12 | 1 | 3 | 9 | .190 | .270 | .224 |
| Leading Off | | | 17 | 1 | 0 | 0 | 3 | .059 | .118 | .059 |
| Runners On | | | 15 | 5 | 1 | 2 | 2 | .333 | .533 | .389 |
| Runners/Scor. Pos. | | | 7 | 1 | 0 | 2 | 1 | .143 | .143 | .300 |
| First 9 Batters | | | 273 | 70 | 9 | 13 | 35 | .256 | .436 | .290 |
| Second 9 Batters | | | 248 | 62 | 7 | 14 | 37 | .250 | .379 | .291 |
| All Batters Thereafter | | | 222 | 52 | 6 | 10 | 24 | .234 | .365 | .267 |

Loves to face: Ken Caminiti (.083, 2-for-24, 7 SO)
Hates to face: Darryl Strawberry (.500, 12-for-24, 2 HR)
Ground outs-to-air outs ratio: 0.76 last season, 0.86 for career.... Additional statistics: 11 double-play ground outs in 102 opportunities, 36 doubles, 4 triples in 197.0 innings last season.... Allowed 21 first-inning runs in 32 starts.... Batting support: 4.31 runs per start.... Rate of 1.69 walks per nine innings was lowest among N.L. starters. Faced 122 consecutive batters without a walk, longest streak in majors. ... Eighth pitcher with three HR in a season during 1980s. Others: Tim Lollar (twice), Bob Forsch, Rick Rhoden, Walt Terrell, Eric Show, Fernando Valenzuela, and Jim Gott. ... Waited 10 years for return to Series, then lost Game 4, allowing Mike Moore's double that ended 0-for-70 streak by A.L. pitchers.

## Jeff D. Robinson

Throws Right

| Pittsburgh Pirates | W–L | ERA | AB | H | HR | BB | SO | BA | SA | OBA |
|---|---|---|---|---|---|---|---|---|---|---|
| Season | 7-13 | 4.58 | 569 | 161 | 14 | 59 | 95 | .283 | .427 | .347 |
| vs. Left-Handers | | | 302 | 78 | 5 | 33 | 40 | .258 | .384 | .328 |
| vs. Right-Handers | | | 267 | 83 | 9 | 26 | 55 | .311 | .476 | .369 |
| Home | 3-6 | 4.16 | 250 | 65 | 8 | 27 | 44 | .260 | .424 | .331 |
| Road | 4-7 | 4.92 | 319 | 96 | 6 | 32 | 51 | .301 | .429 | .360 |
| Grass | 2-2 | 1.96 | 140 | 36 | 1 | 8 | 24 | .257 | .336 | .298 |
| Artificial Turf | 5-11 | 5.50 | 429 | 125 | 13 | 51 | 71 | .291 | .457 | .363 |
| April | 2-3 | 4.40 | 57 | 18 | 2 | 6 | 7 | .316 | .596 | .375 |
| May | 0-2 | 6.35 | 50 | 14 | 1 | 5 | 10 | .280 | .380 | .345 |
| June | 2-1 | 6.57 | 98 | 26 | 3 | 13 | 22 | .265 | .429 | .351 |
| July | 1-3 | 2.33 | 106 | 25 | 2 | 11 | 18 | .236 | .330 | .311 |
| August | 1-2 | 4.50 | 142 | 42 | 4 | 12 | 18 | .296 | .465 | .346 |
| Sept./Oct. | 1-2 | 4.50 | 116 | 36 | 2 | 12 | 20 | .310 | .405 | .366 |
| Leading Off Inn. | | | 138 | 41 | 4 | 6 | 22 | .297 | .486 | .326 |
| Runners On | | | 249 | 68 | 6 | 41 | 43 | .273 | .390 | .367 |
| Runners/Scor. Pos. | | | 183 | 48 | 5 | 34 | 36 | .262 | .393 | .366 |
| Runners On/2 Out | | | 118 | 37 | 3 | 23 | 19 | .314 | .424 | .426 |
| Scor. Pos./2 Out | | | 89 | 27 | 2 | 19 | 16 | .303 | .416 | .426 |
| Late Inning Pressure | | | 135 | 36 | 4 | 17 | 24 | .267 | .452 | .346 |
| Leading Off | | | 33 | 8 | 1 | 2 | 8 | .242 | .455 | .286 |
| Runners On | | | 55 | 15 | 1 | 13 | 10 | .273 | .382 | .406 |
| Runners/Scor. Pos. | | | 46 | 11 | 1 | 10 | 9 | .239 | .370 | .368 |
| First 9 Batters | | | 304 | 80 | 7 | 33 | 55 | .263 | .405 | .334 |
| Second 9 Batters | | | 167 | 51 | 3 | 18 | 31 | .305 | .419 | .369 |
| All Batters Thereafter | | | 98 | 30 | 4 | 8 | 9 | .306 | .510 | .352 |

Loves to face: Chris James (0-for-10)
Hates to face: Keith Hernandez (.455, 5-for-11)
Ground outs-to-air outs ratio: 1.80 last season, 1.67 for career. . . . Additional statistics: 6 double-play ground outs in 84 opportunities, 26 doubles, 7 triples in 141.1 innings last season. . . . Allowed 6 first-inning runs in 19 starts. . . . Record of 5–7 (3.53 ERA) in 19 starts, 2–6 (7.32, four saves) in 31 relief appearances. . . . Batting support: 4.58 runs per start. . . . Highest ERA and most hits (11.67) and base runners (16.93) per nine innings of any reliever in the majors (minimum: 30 games). . . . Pirates won six of his seven no-decision starts. . . . Opponents' career BA prior to 1989: .275 by left-handers, .229 by right-handers. . . . Has thrown 25 wild pitches in 266 innings over past two seasons.

## Ron Robinson

Throws Right

| Cincinnati Reds | W–L | ERA | AB | H | HR | BB | SO | BA | SA | OBA |
|---|---|---|---|---|---|---|---|---|---|---|
| Season | 5-3 | 3.35 | 317 | 80 | 8 | 28 | 36 | .252 | .385 | .316 |
| vs. Left-Handers | | | 175 | 48 | 3 | 16 | 12 | .274 | .383 | .339 |
| vs. Right-Handers | | | 142 | 32 | 5 | 12 | 24 | .225 | .387 | .288 |
| Home | 2-1 | 3.04 | 100 | 28 | 3 | 9 | 9 | .280 | .430 | .351 |
| Road | 3-2 | 3.49 | 217 | 52 | 5 | 19 | 27 | .240 | .364 | .300 |
| Grass | 2-1 | 3.58 | 122 | 28 | 2 | 12 | 13 | .230 | .344 | .296 |
| Artificial Turf | 3-2 | 3.20 | 195 | 52 | 6 | 16 | 23 | .267 | .410 | .329 |
| April | | | 0 | 0 | 0 | 0 | 0 | — | — | — |
| May | | | 0 | 0 | 0 | 0 | 0 | — | — | — |
| June | | | 0 | 0 | 0 | 0 | 0 | — | — | — |
| July | 0-1 | 2.12 | 62 | 14 | 1 | 6 | 9 | .226 | .306 | .294 |
| August | 3-0 | 3.12 | 129 | 34 | 4 | 15 | 13 | .264 | .434 | .342 |
| Sept./Oct. | 2-2 | 4.26 | 126 | 32 | 3 | 7 | 14 | .254 | .373 | .299 |
| Leading Off Inn. | | | 79 | 18 | 4 | 7 | 8 | .228 | .494 | .299 |
| Runners On | | | 123 | 31 | 1 | 14 | 16 | .252 | .309 | .326 |
| Runners/Scor. Pos. | | | 68 | 17 | 1 | 10 | 6 | .250 | .324 | .342 |
| Runners On/2 Out | | | 56 | 15 | 0 | 6 | 6 | .268 | .304 | .339 |
| Scor. Pos./2 Out | | | 32 | 8 | 0 | 4 | 3 | .250 | .281 | .333 |
| Late Inning Pressure | | | 9 | 3 | 0 | 0 | 1 | .333 | .333 | .333 |
| Leading Off | | | 2 | 1 | 0 | 0 | 0 | .500 | .500 | .500 |
| Runners On | | | 4 | 0 | 0 | 0 | 1 | .000 | .000 | .000 |
| Runners/Scor. Pos. | | | 0 | 0 | 0 | 0 | 0 | — | — | — |
| First 9 Batters | | | 122 | 27 | 1 | 10 | 17 | .221 | .303 | .280 |
| Second 9 Batters | | | 120 | 29 | 3 | 12 | 15 | .242 | .358 | .316 |
| All Batters Thereafter | | | 75 | 24 | 4 | 6 | 4 | .320 | .560 | .373 |

Loves to face: Andres Galarraga (0-for-14, 5 SO)
Hates to face: Will Clark (.625, 10-for-16, 1 HR)
Ground outs-to-air outs ratio: 1.18 last season, 1.00 for career. . . . Additional statistics: 4 double-play ground outs in 58 opportunities, 12 doubles, 3 triples in 83.1 innings last season. . . . Allowed 6 first-inning runs in 15 starts. . . . Batting support: 5.13 runs per start, 2d-highest in the N.L. last season (minimum: 15 starts). . . . Opponents stole only two bases in seven attempts. . . . Had a lower ERA in his seven no-decision starts (2.63) than he had in his five wins (3.04). . . . Opposing left-handers outhit right-handers by 49 points, his lowest margin of the past five years. Career breakdown: .293 by left-handers, .223 by right-handers. . . . Has completed only one of his 66 career starts. No shutouts.

## Bruce Ruffin

Throws Left

| Philadelphia Phillies | W–L | ERA | AB | H | HR | BB | SO | BA | SA | OBA |
|---|---|---|---|---|---|---|---|---|---|---|
| Season | 6-10 | 4.44 | 505 | 152 | 10 | 62 | 70 | .301 | .432 | .377 |
| vs. Left-Handers | | | 64 | 18 | 1 | 17 | 8 | .281 | .438 | .427 |
| vs. Right-Handers | | | 441 | 134 | 9 | 45 | 62 | .304 | .431 | .368 |
| Home | 4-7 | 4.90 | 306 | 97 | 9 | 36 | 48 | .317 | .467 | .388 |
| Road | 2-3 | 3.75 | 199 | 55 | 1 | 26 | 22 | .276 | .377 | .360 |
| Grass | 2-0 | 1.66 | 81 | 19 | 1 | 8 | 12 | .235 | .309 | .303 |
| Artificial Turf | 4-10 | 5.02 | 424 | 133 | 9 | 54 | 58 | .314 | .455 | .390 |
| April | 0-2 | 12.15 | 30 | 15 | 0 | 4 | 4 | .500 | .700 | .543 |
| May | | | 0 | 0 | 0 | 0 | 0 | — | — | — |
| June | 0-1 | 7.52 | 86 | 30 | 0 | 13 | 7 | .349 | .477 | .434 |
| July | 3-1 | 3.31 | 129 | 31 | 2 | 22 | 17 | .240 | .333 | .351 |
| August | 1-4 | 4.11 | 135 | 38 | 5 | 13 | 23 | .281 | .452 | .345 |
| Sept./Oct. | 2-2 | 2.32 | 125 | 38 | 3 | 10 | 19 | .304 | .416 | .356 |
| Leading Off Inn. | | | 113 | 39 | 4 | 18 | 14 | .345 | .540 | .435 |
| Runners On | | | 251 | 74 | 2 | 33 | 29 | .295 | .398 | .375 |
| Runners/Scor. Pos. | | | 144 | 43 | 2 | 23 | 15 | .299 | .431 | .393 |
| Runners On/2 Out | | | 111 | 35 | 1 | 17 | 15 | .315 | .414 | .406 |
| Scor. Pos./2 Out | | | 74 | 22 | 1 | 12 | 10 | .297 | .419 | .395 |
| Late Inning Pressure | | | 21 | 4 | 0 | 1 | 1 | .190 | .238 | .227 |
| Leading Off | | | 6 | 1 | 0 | 0 | 1 | .167 | .333 | .167 |
| Runners On | | | 7 | 1 | 0 | 1 | 0 | .143 | .143 | .250 |
| Runners/Scor. Pos. | | | 3 | 1 | 0 | 1 | 0 | .333 | .333 | .500 |
| First 9 Batters | | | 179 | 57 | 4 | 25 | 32 | .318 | .469 | .402 |
| Second 9 Batters | | | 163 | 50 | 4 | 21 | 18 | .307 | .454 | .384 |
| All Batters Thereafter | | | 163 | 45 | 2 | 16 | 20 | .276 | .368 | .341 |

Loves to face: Barry Bonds (.200, 3-for-15)
Hates to face: Tim Wallach (.500, 9-for-18, 2 HR)
Ground outs-to-air outs ratio: 2.63 last season, 2.48 for career. . . . Additional statistics: 13 double-play ground outs in 116 opportunities, 28 doubles, 4 triples in 125.2 innings last season. . . . Allowed 27 first-inning runs in 23 starts. . . . Batting support: 4.17 runs per start. . . . Allowed 15.33 base runners per nine innings, most in majors. . . . Career record of 12–6 in July, 20–32 in other months. . . . ERA is virtually the same, but career record is much better at Veterans Stadium (20–17, 3.95 ERA) than on the road (12–21, 3.93 ERA.). . . . Fly-ball hitters have hit at least 40 points higher than ground-ballers in each of his four seasons. Career breakdown: .250 by ground-ballers, .318 by fly-ballers.

## Scott Sanderson

Throws Right

| Chicago Cubs | W–L | ERA | AB | H | HR | BB | SO | BA | SA | OBA |
|---|---|---|---|---|---|---|---|---|---|---|
| Season | 11-9 | 3.94 | 566 | 155 | 16 | 31 | 86 | .274 | .413 | .312 |
| vs. Left-Handers | | | 341 | 100 | 8 | 21 | 45 | .293 | .422 | .335 |
| vs. Right-Handers | | | 225 | 55 | 8 | 10 | 41 | .244 | .400 | .277 |
| Home | 6-3 | 3.75 | 271 | 77 | 8 | 14 | 42 | .284 | .435 | .322 |
| Road | 5-6 | 4.11 | 295 | 78 | 8 | 17 | 44 | .264 | .393 | .304 |
| Grass | 8-5 | 3.87 | 376 | 110 | 9 | 17 | 58 | .293 | .428 | .325 |
| Artificial Turf | 3-4 | 4.06 | 190 | 45 | 7 | 14 | 28 | .237 | .384 | .288 |
| April | 2-2 | 4.50 | 101 | 23 | 4 | 3 | 17 | .228 | .406 | .248 |
| May | 3-1 | 4.03 | 84 | 22 | 1 | 2 | 15 | .262 | .345 | .284 |
| June | 2-3 | 2.77 | 142 | 33 | 2 | 12 | 19 | .232 | .345 | .290 |
| July | 2-0 | 6.11 | 75 | 28 | 3 | 1 | 5 | .373 | .560 | .390 |
| August | 0-2 | 4.76 | 112 | 33 | 6 | 7 | 20 | .295 | .491 | .336 |
| Sept./Oct. | 2-1 | 1.38 | 52 | 16 | 0 | 6 | 10 | .308 | .346 | .379 |
| Leading Off Inn. | | | 149 | 46 | 2 | 4 | 21 | .309 | .389 | .327 |
| Runners On | | | 219 | 66 | 6 | 18 | 34 | .301 | .461 | .350 |
| Runners/Scor. Pos. | | | 124 | 34 | 4 | 15 | 21 | .274 | .435 | .345 |
| Runners On/2 Out | | | 86 | 19 | 2 | 6 | 16 | .221 | .337 | .272 |
| Scor. Pos./2 Out | | | 54 | 9 | 1 | 4 | 11 | .167 | .241 | .224 |
| Late Inning Pressure | | | 52 | 15 | 1 | 8 | 9 | .288 | .423 | .383 |
| Leading Off | | | 15 | 8 | 1 | 1 | 3 | .533 | .800 | .563 |
| Runners On | | | 22 | 5 | 0 | 6 | 3 | .227 | .364 | .393 |
| Runners/Scor. Pos. | | | 10 | 1 | 0 | 6 | 3 | .100 | .200 | .438 |
| First 9 Batters | | | 272 | 74 | 6 | 12 | 49 | .272 | .386 | .301 |
| Second 9 Batters | | | 192 | 54 | 7 | 7 | 21 | .281 | .458 | .310 |
| All Batters Thereafter | | | 102 | 27 | 3 | 12 | 16 | .265 | .402 | .345 |

Loves to face: Gerald Perry (.115, 3-for-26)
Hates to face: Keith Hernandez (.350, 21-for-60, 2 HR, 7 BB)
Ground outs-to-air outs ratio: 0.65 last season, 0.81 for career. . . . Additional statistics: 9 double-play ground outs in 107 opportunities, 29 doubles, 1 triple in 146.1 innings last season. . . . Allowed 10 first-inning runs in 23 starts. . . . Batting support: 4.04 runs per start. . . . Had a 10–7 record (4.06 ERA) as a starter, 1–2 (3.38, no saves) in 14 relief appearances. . . . Hadn't pitched more than 11 games in relief in any previous season. Career totals: 252 starts, 57 relief games. . . . Won four consecutive starts for the first time since 1982. . . . Opponents' batting average with two outs and runners in scoring position has been under .200 in four of last five seasons. Career mark is .199 in those situations.

## Calvin Schiraldi

Throws Right

| Cubs/Padres | W–L | ERA | AB | H | HR | BB | SO | BA | SA | OBA |
|---|---|---|---|---|---|---|---|---|---|---|
| Season | 6-7 | 3.51 | 361 | 72 | 8 | 63 | 71 | .199 | .310 | .319 |
| vs. Left-Handers | | | 201 | 41 | 3 | 40 | 30 | .204 | .294 | .337 |
| vs. Right-Handers | | | 160 | 31 | 5 | 23 | 41 | .194 | .331 | .293 |
| Home | 3-4 | 3.91 | 198 | 45 | 5 | 27 | 40 | .227 | .354 | .319 |
| Road | 3-3 | 3.06 | 163 | 27 | 3 | 36 | 31 | .166 | .258 | .318 |
| Grass | 4-5 | 4.02 | 264 | 56 | 7 | 45 | 58 | .212 | .333 | .328 |
| Artificial Turf | 2-2 | 2.22 | 97 | 16 | 1 | 18 | 13 | .165 | .247 | .293 |
| April | 1-1 | 4.70 | 55 | 11 | 3 | 9 | 8 | .200 | .382 | .308 |
| May | 0-1 | 1.50 | 62 | 11 | 1 | 6 | 16 | .177 | .242 | .246 |
| June | 1-2 | 6.50 | 70 | 19 | 1 | 17 | 12 | .271 | .386 | .420 |
| July | 1-0 | 3.29 | 48 | 7 | 1 | 11 | 12 | .146 | .250 | .305 |
| August | 0-2 | 2.63 | 52 | 12 | 1 | 7 | 6 | .231 | .385 | .322 |
| Sept./Oct. | 3-1 | 2.53 | 74 | 12 | 1 | 13 | 17 | .162 | .230 | .287 |
| Leading Off Inn. | | | 88 | 17 | 1 | 14 | 17 | .193 | .284 | .304 |
| Runners On | | | 161 | 33 | 6 | 29 | 25 | .205 | .354 | .326 |
| Runners/Scor. Pos. | | | 89 | 15 | 1 | 17 | 14 | .169 | .258 | .303 |
| Runners On/2 Out | | | 70 | 11 | 2 | 19 | 9 | .157 | .286 | .344 |
| Scor. Pos./2 Out | | | 46 | 7 | 1 | 12 | 5 | .152 | .283 | .339 |
| Late Inning Pressure | | | 149 | 32 | 5 | 27 | 31 | .215 | .376 | .335 |
| Leading Off | | | 37 | 10 | 1 | 10 | 7 | .270 | .405 | .426 |
| Runners On | | | 64 | 14 | 4 | 13 | 11 | .219 | .469 | .351 |
| Runners/Scor. Pos. | | | 36 | 8 | 0 | 7 | 6 | .222 | .333 | .349 |
| First 9 Batters | | | 298 | 60 | 6 | 50 | 61 | .201 | .312 | .316 |
| Second 9 Batters | | | 51 | 9 | 2 | 10 | 10 | .176 | .294 | .311 |
| All Batters Thereafter | | | 12 | 3 | 0 | 3 | 0 | .250 | .333 | .400 |

Loves to face: Darryl Strawberry (0-for-13, 5 SO)
Hates to face: Bobby Bonilla (.500, 7-for-14, 2 HR)
Ground outs-to-air outs ratio: 0.71 last season, 0.78 for career. . . . Additional statistics: 4 double-play ground outs in 76 opportunities, 16 doubles, 0 triples in 100.0 innings last season. . . . Had a record of 3–0 (2.33 ERA) in four starts, 3–7 (3.79, 4 saves) in 55 relief appearances. . . . Didn't earn a save after May 23. . . . Third time in past four years that he didn't allow a triple. . . . Same number of walks in 1988 and 1989, strikeouts cut nearly in half, from 140 to 71. . . . Strikeouts per nine innings, year by year starting with 1986: 9.71, 10.00, 7.58, 6.39. . . . Has completed only two of 39 career starts. . . . Opponents' career average is .218 in Late-Inning Pressure Situations, .253 in other at-bats.

## Mike Scott

Throws Right

| Houston Astros | W–L | ERA | AB | H | HR | BB | SO | BA | SA | OBA |
|---|---|---|---|---|---|---|---|---|---|---|
| Season | 20-10 | 3.10 | 848 | 180 | 23 | 62 | 172 | .212 | .344 | .267 |
| vs. Left-Handers | | | 482 | 119 | 14 | 36 | 70 | .247 | .392 | .298 |
| vs. Right-Handers | | | 366 | 61 | 9 | 26 | 102 | .167 | .281 | .227 |
| Home | 12-6 | 3.03 | 502 | 107 | 11 | 40 | 100 | .213 | .339 | .274 |
| Road | 8-4 | 3.21 | 346 | 73 | 12 | 22 | 72 | .211 | .353 | .257 |
| Grass | 6-4 | 3.32 | 291 | 59 | 12 | 18 | 61 | .203 | .368 | .248 |
| Artificial Turf | 14-6 | 2.99 | 557 | 121 | 11 | 44 | 111 | .217 | .332 | .277 |
| April | 4-1 | 2.79 | 158 | 32 | 5 | 10 | 38 | .203 | .335 | .249 |
| May | 3-2 | 2.39 | 138 | 27 | 2 | 7 | 27 | .196 | .268 | .233 |
| June | 6-1 | 2.20 | 177 | 37 | 4 | 15 | 26 | .209 | .322 | .271 |
| July | 4-1 | 2.45 | 127 | 26 | 3 | 8 | 34 | .205 | .331 | .268 |
| August | 1-2 | 5.74 | 122 | 34 | 5 | 11 | 25 | .279 | .475 | .338 |
| Sept./Oct. | 2-3 | 3.75 | 126 | 24 | 4 | 11 | 22 | .190 | .357 | .252 |
| Leading Off Inn. | | | 217 | 49 | 6 | 13 | 47 | .226 | .355 | .273 |
| Runners On | | | 309 | 67 | 7 | 31 | 59 | .217 | .359 | .289 |
| Runners/Scor. Pos. | | | 198 | 35 | 2 | 26 | 48 | .177 | .288 | .271 |
| Runners On/2 Out | | | 132 | 29 | 5 | 21 | 26 | .220 | .424 | .331 |
| Scor. Pos./2 Out | | | 92 | 17 | 2 | 17 | 22 | .185 | .348 | .318 |
| Late Inning Pressure | | | 65 | 12 | 1 | 14 | 15 | .185 | .277 | .329 |
| Leading Off | | | 17 | 5 | 1 | 3 | 3 | .294 | .529 | .400 |
| Runners On | | | 27 | 3 | 0 | 8 | 5 | .111 | .111 | .314 |
| Runners/Scor. Pos. | | | 18 | 1 | 0 | 8 | 4 | .056 | .056 | .346 |
| First 9 Batters | | | 267 | 57 | 8 | 19 | 68 | .213 | .352 | .266 |
| Second 9 Batters | | | 266 | 63 | 9 | 14 | 49 | .237 | .387 | .273 |
| All Batters Thereafter | | | 315 | 60 | 6 | 29 | 55 | .190 | .302 | .263 |

Loves to face: Andy Van Slyke (.029, 1-for-35, 10 SO)
Hates to face: Willie McGee (.567, 17-for-30)
Ground outs-to-air outs ratio: 0.83 last season, 1.12 for career. . . . Additional statistics: 10 double-play ground outs in 115 opportunities, 31 doubles, 6 triples in 229.0 innings last season. . . . Allowed 23 first-inning runs in 32 starts. Opponents batted .270 in the first inning, .202 thereafter. . . . Batting support: 4.69 runs per start. . . . Had five wins vs. Dodgers, the most by any pitcher against any club. . . . Opponents stole 39 bases in 41 attempts (including 36 in a row). . . . Career mark of 67–43 before the All-Star break, 48–50 in the second half. . . . Joins Ryan (260) and Seaver (113) as pitchers with more than 100 wins for other teams after leaving Mets. Scott has 101. After that: Koosman, 82; Terrell, 65.

## Scott Scudder

Throws Right

| Cincinnati Reds | W–L | ERA | AB | H | HR | BB | SO | BA | SA | OBA |
|---|---|---|---|---|---|---|---|---|---|---|
| Season | 4-9 | 4.49 | 380 | 91 | 14 | 61 | 66 | .239 | .403 | .345 |
| vs. Left-Handers | | | 197 | 44 | 4 | 29 | 30 | .223 | .340 | .322 |
| vs. Right-Handers | | | 183 | 47 | 10 | 32 | 36 | .257 | .470 | .369 |
| Home | 2-4 | 4.95 | 165 | 40 | 8 | 25 | 30 | .242 | .436 | .339 |
| Road | 2-5 | 4.13 | 215 | 51 | 6 | 36 | 36 | .237 | .377 | .349 |
| Grass | 2-4 | 4.62 | 148 | 34 | 3 | 29 | 25 | .230 | .351 | .360 |
| Artificial Turf | 2-5 | 4.40 | 232 | 57 | 11 | 32 | 41 | .246 | .435 | .335 |
| April | | | 0 | 0 | 0 | 0 | 0 | — | — | — |
| May | | | 0 | 0 | 0 | 0 | 0 | — | — | — |
| June | 2-1 | 2.70 | 86 | 16 | 1 | 16 | 14 | .186 | .256 | .314 |
| July | 0-2 | 6.32 | 61 | 20 | 2 | 8 | 11 | .328 | .508 | .394 |
| August | 1-2 | 3.98 | 115 | 24 | 6 | 21 | 19 | .209 | .426 | .331 |
| Sept./Oct. | 1-4 | 5.46 | 118 | 31 | 5 | 16 | 22 | .263 | .432 | .356 |
| Leading Off Inn. | | | 97 | 19 | 1 | 9 | 14 | .196 | .268 | .264 |
| Runners On | | | 163 | 41 | 8 | 27 | 27 | .252 | .454 | .358 |
| Runners/Scor. Pos. | | | 86 | 22 | 4 | 20 | 14 | .256 | .442 | .389 |
| Runners On/2 Out | | | 73 | 15 | 2 | 16 | 13 | .205 | .329 | .348 |
| Scor. Pos./2 Out | | | 41 | 10 | 2 | 13 | 7 | .244 | .439 | .426 |
| Late Inning Pressure | | | 27 | 6 | 1 | 2 | 4 | .222 | .370 | .276 |
| Leading Off | | | 9 | 1 | 0 | 0 | 1 | .111 | .111 | .111 |
| Runners On | | | 6 | 2 | 0 | 0 | 1 | .333 | .333 | .333 |
| Runners/Scor. Pos. | | | 1 | 0 | 0 | 0 | 0 | .000 | .000 | .000 |
| First 9 Batters | | | 162 | 35 | 6 | 26 | 33 | .216 | .377 | .323 |
| Second 9 Batters | | | 120 | 28 | 3 | 23 | 21 | .233 | .392 | .359 |
| All Batters Thereafter | | | 98 | 28 | 5 | 12 | 12 | .286 | .459 | .364 |

Loves to face: Tommy Gregg (.083, 1-for-12)
Hates to face: Howard Johnson (3-for-3, 3 2B, 1 BB)
Ground outs-to-air outs ratio: 0.70 last season, his first in majors. . . . Additional statistics: 2 double-play ground outs in 79 opportunities, lowest rate in majors (min.: 75 opp.), 16 doubles, 2 triples in 100.1 innings last season. . . . Allowed 12 first-inning runs in 17 starts. . . . Batting support: 3.71 runs per start. . . . Allowed 5.47 walks per nine innings, highest rate in N.L. (minimum: 50 IP). . . . Walked 10 batters between strikeouts, tied for longest streak in N.L. . . . Opponents stole 15 bases in 16 attempts. Will Clark was caught. . . . ERA was 1.44 in four wins as a starter, 7.19 in nine losses. . . . Opponents batted .284 in day games (1–6, 7.00 ERA), .213 at night (3–3, 3.08 ERA).

## Eric Show

Throws Right

| San Diego Padres | W–L | ERA | AB | H | HR | BB | SO | BA | SA | OBA |
|---|---|---|---|---|---|---|---|---|---|---|
| Season | 8-6 | 4.23 | 412 | 113 | 9 | 39 | 66 | .274 | .434 | .336 |
| vs. Left-Handers | | | 234 | 63 | 4 | 27 | 43 | .269 | .427 | .345 |
| vs. Right-Handers | | | 178 | 50 | 5 | 12 | 23 | .281 | .444 | .325 |
| Home | 4-3 | 4.37 | 216 | 62 | 6 | 21 | 37 | .287 | .477 | .347 |
| Road | 4-3 | 4.09 | 196 | 51 | 3 | 18 | 29 | .260 | .388 | .324 |
| Grass | 5-4 | 4.54 | 262 | 73 | 7 | 26 | 43 | .279 | .462 | .341 |
| Artificial Turf | 3-2 | 3.69 | 150 | 40 | 2 | 13 | 23 | .267 | .387 | .327 |
| April | 4-2 | 3.79 | 160 | 42 | 2 | 12 | 28 | .263 | .394 | .316 |
| May | 2-3 | 4.31 | 118 | 31 | 2 | 17 | 16 | .263 | .415 | .355 |
| June | 2-1 | 4.67 | 134 | 40 | 5 | 10 | 22 | .299 | .500 | .342 |
| July | | | 0 | 0 | 0 | 0 | 0 | — | — | — |
| August | | | 0 | 0 | 0 | 0 | 0 | — | — | — |
| Sept./Oct. | | | 0 | 0 | 0 | 0 | 0 | — | — | — |
| Leading Off Inn. | | | 101 | 23 | 0 | 10 | 17 | .228 | .347 | .304 |
| Runners On | | | 164 | 49 | 7 | 20 | 31 | .299 | .500 | .368 |
| Runners/Scor. Pos. | | | 94 | 28 | 6 | 16 | 18 | .298 | .574 | .388 |
| Runners On/2 Out | | | 81 | 26 | 4 | 8 | 17 | .321 | .531 | .389 |
| Scor. Pos./2 Out | | | 51 | 15 | 3 | 7 | 10 | .294 | .529 | .390 |
| Late Inning Pressure | | | 54 | 12 | 0 | 8 | 6 | .222 | .241 | .323 |
| Leading Off | | | 16 | 0 | 0 | 2 | 4 | .000 | .000 | .111 |
| Runners On | | | 15 | 6 | 0 | 3 | 1 | .400 | .467 | .500 |
| Runners/Scor. Pos. | | | 7 | 2 | 0 | 2 | 1 | .286 | .429 | .444 |
| First 9 Batters | | | 128 | 33 | 1 | 13 | 19 | .258 | .383 | .324 |
| Second 9 Batters | | | 121 | 38 | 3 | 11 | 21 | .314 | .529 | .372 |
| All Batters Thereafter | | | 163 | 42 | 5 | 15 | 26 | .258 | .405 | .318 |

Loves to face: Shawon Dunston (.067, 1-for-15, 7 SO)
Hates to face: Dickie Thon (.391, 9-for-23, 3 HR)
Ground outs-to-air outs ratio: 0.98 last season, 0.98 for career. . . . Additional statistics: 6 double-play ground outs in 64 opportunities, 31 doubles, 4 triples in 106.1 innings last season. . . . Allowed 11 first-inning runs in 16 starts. . . . Batting support: 4.13 runs per start. . . . Completed only one of his 16 starts, after completing 13 of 32 in 1988. . . . Opponents' batting average was highest of his career. . . . Had a 6.35 ERA in 28.1 innings with Mark Parent catching, 3.46 in 78 innings with Santiago. . . . Opponents' career batting average of .145 (12-for-83) with the bases loaded was 2d lowest over the last 15 years (minimum 50 BFP). . . . Led N.L. pitchers with a .235 batting average (minimum 25 AB).

## John Smiley

Pittsburgh Pirates — Throws Left

| Pittsburgh Pirates | W–L | ERA | AB | H | HR | BB | SO | BA | SA | OBA |
|---|---|---|---|---|---|---|---|---|---|---|
| Season | 12-8 | 2.81 | 770 | 174 | 22 | 49 | 123 | .226 | .349 | .273 |
| vs. Left-Handers | | | 103 | 25 | 1 | 6 | 15 | .243 | .320 | .291 |
| vs. Right-Handers | | | 667 | 149 | 21 | 43 | 108 | .223 | .354 | .271 |
| Home | 8-4 | 2.64 | 410 | 91 | 14 | 27 | 68 | .222 | .361 | .271 |
| Road | 4-4 | 2.99 | 360 | 83 | 8 | 22 | 55 | .231 | .336 | .276 |
| Grass | 4-2 | 2.35 | 211 | 42 | 6 | 14 | 30 | .199 | .308 | .252 |
| Artificial Turf | 8-6 | 2.98 | 559 | 132 | 16 | 35 | 93 | .236 | .365 | .281 |
| April | 2-1 | 1.96 | 138 | 31 | 1 | 8 | 22 | .225 | .290 | .270 |
| May | 3-1 | 3.86 | 144 | 35 | 7 | 8 | 26 | .243 | .424 | .283 |
| June | 2-0 | 3.48 | 129 | 31 | 3 | 11 | 25 | .240 | .380 | .296 |
| July | 2-4 | 2.13 | 186 | 35 | 6 | 13 | 26 | .188 | .306 | .248 |
| August | 1-1 | 1.23 | 103 | 23 | 1 | 5 | 14 | .223 | .291 | .252 |
| Sept./Oct. | 2-1 | 5.60 | 70 | 19 | 4 | 4 | 10 | .271 | .457 | .320 |
| Leading Off Inn. | | | 200 | 40 | 6 | 10 | 37 | .200 | .330 | .242 |
| Runners On | | | 279 | 59 | 9 | 19 | 41 | .211 | .341 | .261 |
| Runners/Scor. Pos. | | | 146 | 33 | 5 | 14 | 26 | .226 | .356 | .290 |
| Runners On/2 Out | | | 130 | 27 | 3 | 9 | 18 | .208 | .300 | .270 |
| Scor. Pos./2 Out | | | 81 | 18 | 1 | 6 | 13 | .222 | .284 | .292 |
| Late Inning Pressure | | | 93 | 21 | 5 | 7 | 20 | .226 | .441 | .284 |
| Leading Off | | | 25 | 6 | 1 | 3 | 4 | .240 | .400 | .321 |
| Runners On | | | 30 | 6 | 1 | 2 | 8 | .200 | .367 | .242 |
| Runners/Scor. Pos. | | | 16 | 2 | 0 | 1 | 6 | .125 | .188 | .167 |
| First 9 Batters | | | 232 | 51 | 8 | 16 | 41 | .220 | .358 | .271 |
| Second 9 Batters | | | 238 | 45 | 3 | 11 | 39 | .189 | .244 | .227 |
| All Batters Thereafter | | | 300 | 78 | 11 | 22 | 43 | .260 | .427 | .311 |

Loves to face: Howard Johnson (.083, 2-for-24, 10 SO)
Hates to face: Andre Dawson (.565, 13-for-23, 4 HR)
Ground outs-to-air outs ratio: 0.62 last season, 0.87 for career.... Additional statistics: 12 double-play ground outs in 121 opportunities, 29 doubles, 0 triples in 205.1 innings last season.... Allowed 15 first-inning runs in 28 starts.... Batting support: 3.82 runs per start.... ERA of 2.52 through first seven innings, 5.08 after that. ... Opposing left-handers had hit below .200 in each of his three previous seasons.... Career record of 19–9 before the All-Star break (including 6–0 in June), 12–15 after the break.... Smiley and Drabek both have winning records in consecutive seasons of 200 or more innings. Last Pirates pitcher with three in a row: Jerry Reuss (1974–76). Last with four: Bob Veale (1964–67).

## Bryn Smith

Montreal Expos — Throws Right

| Montreal Expos | W–L | ERA | AB | H | HR | BB | SO | BA | SA | OBA |
|---|---|---|---|---|---|---|---|---|---|---|
| Season | 10-11 | 2.84 | 794 | 177 | 16 | 54 | 129 | .223 | .335 | .274 |
| vs. Left-Handers | | | 446 | 96 | 6 | 28 | 64 | .215 | .305 | .265 |
| vs. Right-Handers | | | 348 | 81 | 10 | 26 | 65 | .233 | .374 | .286 |
| Home | 5-5 | 2.73 | 466 | 105 | 10 | 34 | 81 | .225 | .333 | .282 |
| Road | 5-6 | 2.99 | 328 | 72 | 6 | 20 | 48 | .220 | .338 | .263 |
| Grass | 2-5 | 3.10 | 213 | 48 | 3 | 13 | 32 | .225 | .319 | .270 |
| Artificial Turf | 8-6 | 2.74 | 581 | 129 | 13 | 41 | 97 | .222 | .341 | .276 |
| April | 2-0 | 2.55 | 94 | 19 | 2 | 9 | 10 | .202 | .351 | .272 |
| May | 3-1 | 1.64 | 159 | 30 | 0 | 9 | 23 | .189 | .245 | .231 |
| June | 2-2 | 2.61 | 137 | 29 | 5 | 6 | 25 | .212 | .343 | .248 |
| July | 2-1 | 1.96 | 144 | 28 | 2 | 12 | 32 | .194 | .271 | .259 |
| August | 1-4 | 4.59 | 127 | 34 | 3 | 5 | 19 | .268 | .378 | .293 |
| Sept./Oct. | 0-3 | 4.19 | 133 | 37 | 4 | 13 | 20 | .278 | .451 | .349 |
| Leading Off Inn. | | | 210 | 48 | 4 | 10 | 36 | .229 | .324 | .267 |
| Runners On | | | 291 | 68 | 6 | 21 | 49 | .234 | .388 | .283 |
| Runners/Scor. Pos. | | | 153 | 30 | 4 | 16 | 27 | .196 | .386 | .264 |
| Runners On/2 Out | | | 125 | 26 | 1 | 13 | 26 | .208 | .336 | .283 |
| Scor. Pos./2 Out | | | 78 | 13 | 1 | 11 | 17 | .167 | .308 | .270 |
| Late Inning Pressure | | | 62 | 17 | 2 | 2 | 12 | .274 | .387 | .308 |
| Leading Off | | | 18 | 6 | 1 | 1 | 3 | .333 | .500 | .368 |
| Runners On | | | 19 | 4 | 0 | 1 | 2 | .211 | .263 | .286 |
| Runners/Scor. Pos. | | | 10 | 0 | 0 | 1 | 2 | .000 | .000 | .091 |
| First 9 Batters | | | 266 | 56 | 7 | 25 | 46 | .211 | .320 | .279 |
| Second 9 Batters | | | 269 | 61 | 4 | 13 | 44 | .227 | .338 | .267 |
| All Batters Thereafter | | | 259 | 60 | 5 | 16 | 39 | .232 | .347 | .277 |

Loves to face: Ron Gant (0-for-15, 6 SO)
Hates to face: Franklin Stubbs (.471, 8-for-17, 4 HR)
Ground outs-to-air outs ratio: 1.52 last season, 1.70 for career.... Additional statistics: 20 double-play ground outs in 133 opportunities, 27 doubles, 7 triples in 215.2 innings last season.... Allowed 15 first-inning runs in 32 starts.... Batting support: 4.38 runs per start.... Lowest ERA in majors among pitchers with losing records (minimum: 162 innings).... Opposing batters have hit better on grass fields than on artificial turf in each of last seven seasons, longest current streak. Career records: 20–29 on grass, 60–42 on turf.... Career statistics at Busch Stadium: 13 games, 7–2 record, 2.58 ERA.... Has been within two games of .500 mark in each of four seasons since going 18–5 in 1985.

## Dave Smith

Houston Astros — Throws Right

| Houston Astros | W–L | ERA | AB | H | HR | BB | SO | BA | SA | OBA |
|---|---|---|---|---|---|---|---|---|---|---|
| Season | 3-4 | 2.64 | 210 | 49 | 1 | 19 | 31 | .233 | .295 | .299 |
| vs. Left-Handers | | | 118 | 28 | 1 | 10 | 17 | .237 | .322 | .302 |
| vs. Right-Handers | | | 92 | 21 | 0 | 9 | 14 | .228 | .261 | .294 |
| Home | 3-1 | 3.81 | 103 | 24 | 1 | 8 | 15 | .233 | .330 | .295 |
| Road | 0-3 | 1.52 | 107 | 25 | 0 | 11 | 16 | .234 | .262 | .303 |
| Grass | 0-3 | 2.25 | 59 | 16 | 0 | 8 | 11 | .271 | .322 | .353 |
| Artificial Turf | 3-1 | 2.79 | 151 | 33 | 1 | 11 | 20 | .219 | .285 | .276 |
| April | 0-2 | 5.59 | 39 | 10 | 0 | 5 | 6 | .256 | .308 | .341 |
| May | 0-0 | 0.90 | 32 | 4 | 0 | 3 | 3 | .125 | .156 | .200 |
| June | 1-0 | 0.90 | 36 | 8 | 0 | 0 | 8 | .222 | .278 | .222 |
| July | 0-0 | 2.79 | 40 | 11 | 1 | 1 | 7 | .275 | .375 | .293 |
| August | 2-2 | 4.91 | 38 | 13 | 0 | 9 | 5 | .342 | .421 | .458 |
| Sept./Oct. | 0-0 | 0.00 | 25 | 3 | 0 | 1 | 2 | .120 | .160 | .185 |
| Leading Off Inn. | | | 51 | 13 | 0 | 5 | 8 | .255 | .255 | .321 |
| Runners On | | | 92 | 21 | 1 | 11 | 12 | .228 | .315 | .308 |
| Runners/Scor. Pos. | | | 58 | 14 | 1 | 9 | 8 | .241 | .328 | .338 |
| Runners On/2 Out | | | 40 | 7 | 0 | 1 | 7 | .175 | .225 | .195 |
| Scor. Pos./2 Out | | | 26 | 5 | 0 | 1 | 4 | .192 | .269 | .222 |
| Late Inning Pressure | | | 154 | 31 | 1 | 14 | 27 | .201 | .279 | .271 |
| Leading Off | | | 40 | 9 | 0 | 3 | 7 | .225 | .225 | .279 |
| Runners On | | | 58 | 11 | 1 | 9 | 9 | .190 | .310 | .294 |
| Runners/Scor. Pos. | | | 38 | 8 | 1 | 8 | 5 | .211 | .342 | .340 |
| First 9 Batters | | | 210 | 49 | 1 | 19 | 31 | .233 | .295 | .299 |
| Second 9 Batters | | | 0 | 0 | 0 | 0 | 0 | — | — | — |
| All Batters Thereafter | | | 0 | 0 | 0 | 0 | 0 | — | — | — |

Loves to face: Von Hayes (O-for 11)
Hates to face: Andre Dawson (.444, 8-for-18, 2 HR)
Ground outs-to-air outs ratio: 1.62 last season, 1.46 for career.... Additional statistics: 5 double-play ground outs in 45 opportunities, 6 doubles, 2 triples in 58.0 innings last season.... Saved 25 games in 29 opportunities, 3d-highest percentage (.862) in N.L. (minimum: 10 saves).... Entered only six of his 52 appearances in mid-inning. Inherited only eight runners, stranded five.... Career average of one home run per 29.3 innings is lowest among active pitchers (minimum: 100 IP).... Had winning records in each of his first six seasons, losing records in each of his last four.... Enters the 1990s with a streak of 218 consecutive errorless games. N.L. record: 364, Lee Smith.

## Pete Smith

Atlanta Braves — Throws Right

| Atlanta Braves | W–L | ERA | AB | H | HR | BB | SO | BA | SA | OBA |
|---|---|---|---|---|---|---|---|---|---|---|
| Season | 5-14 | 4.75 | 547 | 144 | 13 | 57 | 115 | .263 | .378 | .330 |
| vs. Left-Handers | | | 321 | 82 | 7 | 45 | 50 | .255 | .355 | .346 |
| vs. Right-Handers | | | 226 | 62 | 6 | 12 | 65 | .274 | .412 | .306 |
| Home | 2-7 | 4.48 | 276 | 74 | 7 | 32 | 52 | .268 | .384 | .342 |
| Road | 3-7 | 5.04 | 271 | 70 | 6 | 25 | 63 | .258 | .373 | .318 |
| Grass | 4-10 | 3.83 | 416 | 103 | 12 | 38 | 95 | .248 | .373 | .309 |
| Artificial Turf | 1-4 | 7.96 | 131 | 41 | 1 | 19 | 20 | .313 | .397 | .392 |
| April | 0-3 | 4.44 | 109 | 30 | 3 | 7 | 31 | .275 | .413 | .319 |
| May | 1-4 | 4.96 | 120 | 30 | 2 | 19 | 27 | .250 | .350 | .350 |
| June | 1-1 | 3.86 | 50 | 13 | 0 | 6 | 9 | .260 | .260 | .333 |
| July | 0-3 | 5.81 | 105 | 31 | 3 | 11 | 18 | .295 | .419 | .359 |
| August | 2-2 | 3.95 | 103 | 23 | 2 | 11 | 14 | .223 | .330 | .293 |
| Sept./Oct. | 1-1 | 5.28 | 60 | 17 | 3 | 3 | 16 | .283 | .483 | .317 |
| Leading Off Inn. | | | 140 | 30 | 3 | 12 | 33 | .214 | .314 | .276 |
| Runners On | | | 207 | 63 | 5 | 28 | 37 | .304 | .435 | .379 |
| Runners/Scor. Pos. | | | 123 | 36 | 2 | 17 | 22 | .293 | .423 | .366 |
| Runners On/2 Out | | | 90 | 27 | 2 | 11 | 17 | .300 | .433 | .376 |
| Scor. Pos./2 Out | | | 55 | 17 | 1 | 6 | 9 | .309 | .455 | .377 |
| Late Inning Pressure | | | 21 | 5 | 0 | 3 | 4 | .238 | .286 | .333 |
| Leading Off | | | 5 | 2 | 0 | 3 | 1 | .400 | .400 | .625 |
| Runners On | | | 9 | 2 | 0 | 0 | 2 | .222 | .333 | .222 |
| Runners/Scor. Pos. | | | 6 | 1 | 0 | 0 | 2 | .167 | .333 | .167 |
| First 9 Batters | | | 222 | 51 | 2 | 21 | 53 | .230 | .306 | .293 |
| Second 9 Batters | | | 198 | 51 | 4 | 17 | 44 | .258 | .348 | .313 |
| All Batters Thereafter | | | 127 | 42 | 7 | 19 | 18 | .331 | .551 | .418 |

Loves to face: Pedro Guerrero (.118, 2-for-17)
Hates to face: Mike Marshall (.667, 8-for-12, 1 HR)
Ground outs-to-air outs ratio: 1.17 last season, 0.92 for career.... Additional statistics: 11 double-play ground outs in 91 opportunities, 20 doubles, 2 triples in 142.0 innings last season.... Allowed 12 first-inning runs in 27 starts.... Batting support: 3.07 runs per start.... Struck out eight consecutive right-handers, 2d-longest streak in majors.... Career winning percentage of .295 (13–31) is lowest among active pitchers (minimum: 25 decisions).... First pitcher with winning percentage of .318 (his 1988 mark) or lower in consecutive seasons of 25+ starts since Bob Knepper (1982–83). Among 14 others: Roger Craig, Red Ruffing, Warren Spahn.... Career record of 1–8 on artificial turf.

## Zane Smith

Throws Left

| Braves/Expos | W–L | ERA | AB | H | HR | BB | SO | BA | SA | OBA |
|---|---|---|---|---|---|---|---|---|---|---|
| Season | 1-13 | 3.49 | 559 | 141 | 7 | 52 | 93 | .252 | .345 | .317 |
| vs. Left-Handers | | | 137 | 19 | 1 | 10 | 41 | .139 | .190 | .196 |
| vs. Right-Handers | | | 422 | 122 | 6 | 42 | 52 | .289 | .396 | .355 |
| Home | 1-5 | 2.81 | 294 | 67 | 3 | 19 | 56 | .228 | .293 | .276 |
| Road | 0-8 | 4.24 | 265 | 74 | 4 | 33 | 37 | .279 | .404 | .359 |
| Grass | 1-9 | 3.56 | 348 | 86 | 4 | 27 | 55 | .247 | .342 | .301 |
| Artificial Turf | 0-4 | 3.38 | 211 | 55 | 3 | 25 | 38 | .261 | .351 | .342 |
| April | 0-3 | 5.13 | 100 | 25 | 2 | 8 | 13 | .250 | .390 | .313 |
| May | 1-4 | 4.50 | 142 | 40 | 2 | 11 | 25 | .282 | .380 | .333 |
| June | 0-5 | 3.93 | 140 | 37 | 1 | 14 | 20 | .264 | .343 | .325 |
| July | 0-1 | 0.57 | 51 | 7 | 0 | 10 | 12 | .137 | .176 | .279 |
| August | 0-0 | 2.16 | 63 | 16 | 1 | 6 | 9 | .254 | .349 | .329 |
| Sept./Oct. | 0-0 | 1.72 | 63 | 16 | 1 | 3 | 14 | .254 | .333 | .288 |
| Leading Off Inn. | | | 136 | 39 | 1 | 12 | 17 | .287 | .382 | .345 |
| Runners On | | | 251 | 60 | 5 | 32 | 41 | .239 | .351 | .324 |
| Runners/Scor. Pos. | | | 139 | 41 | 3 | 21 | 18 | .295 | .432 | .376 |
| Runners On/2 Out | | | 109 | 28 | 3 | 14 | 19 | .257 | .394 | .347 |
| Scor. Pos./2 Out | | | 69 | 21 | 2 | 10 | 12 | .304 | .478 | .392 |
| Late Inning Pressure | | | 149 | 37 | 2 | 17 | 31 | .248 | .336 | .329 |
| Leading Off | | | 37 | 10 | 0 | 4 | 8 | .270 | .351 | .341 |
| Runners On | | | 63 | 17 | 2 | 10 | 12 | .270 | .397 | .378 |
| Runners/Scor. Pos. | | | 32 | 10 | 2 | 9 | 6 | .313 | .531 | .463 |
| First 9 Batters | | | 304 | 69 | 3 | 33 | 58 | .227 | .296 | .305 |
| Second 9 Batters | | | 141 | 36 | 3 | 9 | 20 | .255 | .390 | .301 |
| All Batters Thereafter | | | 114 | 36 | 1 | 10 | 15 | .316 | .421 | .367 |

Loves to face: John Kruk (0-for-11, 5 SO)
Hates to face: Terry Pendleton (.500, 17-for-34)
Ground outs-to-air outs ratio: 2.25 last season, 2.02 for career. . . . Additional statistics: 13 double-play ground outs in 130 opportunities, 21 doubles, 5 triples in 147.0 innings last season. . . . Allowed 7 first-inning runs in 17 starts. . . . Batting support: 2.94 runs per start. . . . Faced 37 consecutive batters without allowing a hit, longest streak in N.L. Streak of 35 hitless batters faced in LIP Situations was longest in majors. . . . Batting average by opposing left-handers was 3d lowest of last 15 years (minimum: 125 BFP). . . . Career averages: .219 by left-handers, .276 by right-handers. Has allowed only three HR to left-handers: Greg Brock (1984), Barry Bonds (1987), and Darryl Strawberry (1989).

## John Smoltz

Throws Right

| Atlanta Braves | W–L | ERA | AB | H | HR | BB | SO | BA | SA | OBA |
|---|---|---|---|---|---|---|---|---|---|---|
| Season | 12-11 | 2.94 | 756 | 160 | 15 | 72 | 168 | .212 | .319 | .280 |
| vs. Left-Handers | | | 454 | 97 | 6 | 47 | 82 | .214 | .317 | .289 |
| vs. Right-Handers | | | 302 | 63 | 9 | 25 | 86 | .209 | .321 | .266 |
| Home | 6-4 | 2.63 | 349 | 66 | 12 | 33 | 83 | .189 | .324 | .258 |
| Road | 6-7 | 3.23 | 407 | 94 | 3 | 39 | 85 | .231 | .314 | .298 |
| Grass | 8-6 | 2.96 | 475 | 98 | 15 | 44 | 107 | .206 | .339 | .272 |
| Artificial Turf | 4-5 | 2.91 | 281 | 62 | 0 | 28 | 61 | .221 | .285 | .292 |
| April | 3-2 | 3.06 | 119 | 26 | 3 | 16 | 26 | .218 | .387 | .307 |
| May | 4-1 | 1.84 | 170 | 30 | 2 | 12 | 36 | .176 | .253 | .232 |
| June | 2-3 | 2.10 | 131 | 31 | 2 | 11 | 35 | .237 | .321 | .296 |
| July | 2-2 | 2.06 | 163 | 29 | 4 | 11 | 35 | .178 | .301 | .227 |
| August | 1-3 | 6.34 | 151 | 42 | 2 | 19 | 27 | .278 | .351 | .360 |
| Sept./Oct. | 0-0 | 1.50 | 22 | 2 | 2 | 3 | 9 | .091 | .364 | .200 |
| Leading Off Inn. | | | 195 | 43 | 2 | 18 | 42 | .221 | .292 | .290 |
| Runners On | | | 300 | 72 | 7 | 25 | 62 | .240 | .357 | .294 |
| Runners/Scor. Pos. | | | 165 | 32 | 2 | 22 | 44 | .194 | .273 | .282 |
| Runners On/2 Out | | | 115 | 22 | 3 | 13 | 29 | .191 | .296 | .273 |
| Scor. Pos./2 Out | | | 74 | 10 | 0 | 13 | 22 | .135 | .135 | .264 |
| Late Inning Pressure | | | 118 | 19 | 1 | 10 | 22 | .161 | .229 | .231 |
| Leading Off | | | 33 | 7 | 0 | 3 | 8 | .212 | .212 | .297 |
| Runners On | | | 39 | 9 | 1 | 2 | 6 | .231 | .333 | .262 |
| Runners/Scor. Pos. | | | 15 | 3 | 0 | 2 | 3 | .200 | .200 | .278 |
| First 9 Batters | | | 233 | 58 | 6 | 21 | 66 | .249 | .369 | .311 |
| Second 9 Batters | | | 226 | 47 | 6 | 21 | 51 | .208 | .327 | .271 |
| All Batters Thereafter | | | 297 | 55 | 3 | 30 | 51 | .185 | .273 | .261 |

Loves to face: Darren Daulton (0-for-15)
Hates to face: Eric Davis (.625, 5-for-8, 3 HR)
Ground outs-to-air outs ratio: 0.76 last season, 0.72 for career. . . . Additional statistics: 13 double-play ground outs in 149 opportunities, 30 doubles, 3 triples in 208.0 innings last season. . . . Allowed 13 first-inning runs in 29 starts. . . . Batting support: 3.24 runs per start. . . . Was 11–6 at All-Star break, 1–5 during second half. . . . Allowed 10.1 base runners per nine innings, compared to 15.3 in 1988, when his ERA was 5.48. . . . Career record of 6–0 in day games, 8–18 at night. . . . Has allowed 18 home runs at Atlanta Stadium, only seven (one per 20 innings) elsewhere. . . . Opposing fly-ball hitters have outslugged ground-ball hitters by 101 points. Career slugging averages: .410 and .309, respectively.

## Rick Sutcliffe

Throws Right

| Chicago Cubs | W–L | ERA | AB | H | HR | BB | SO | BA | SA | OBA |
|---|---|---|---|---|---|---|---|---|---|---|
| Season | 16-11 | 3.66 | 842 | 202 | 18 | 69 | 153 | .240 | .354 | .296 |
| vs. Left-Handers | | | 503 | 123 | 11 | 46 | 88 | .245 | .362 | .305 |
| vs. Right-Handers | | | 339 | 79 | 7 | 23 | 65 | .233 | .342 | .283 |
| Home | 5-7 | 4.80 | 377 | 98 | 9 | 30 | 75 | .260 | .390 | .311 |
| Road | 11-4 | 2.78 | 465 | 104 | 9 | 39 | 78 | .224 | .325 | .284 |
| Grass | 7-10 | 4.58 | 529 | 135 | 14 | 42 | 98 | .255 | .384 | .307 |
| Artificial Turf | 9-1 | 2.22 | 313 | 67 | 4 | 27 | 55 | .214 | .304 | .276 |
| April | 4-1 | 3.76 | 141 | 30 | 3 | 10 | 34 | .213 | .340 | .261 |
| May | 2-2 | 3.11 | 134 | 27 | 3 | 10 | 18 | .201 | .269 | .255 |
| June | 3-2 | 3.63 | 127 | 33 | 1 | 9 | 22 | .260 | .370 | .304 |
| July | 2-4 | 3.22 | 163 | 36 | 3 | 13 | 28 | .221 | .294 | .275 |
| August | 2-2 | 4.43 | 147 | 38 | 6 | 15 | 28 | .259 | .429 | .323 |
| Sept./Oct. | 3-0 | 3.82 | 130 | 38 | 2 | 12 | 23 | .292 | .431 | .359 |
| Leading Off Inn. | | | 229 | 60 | 9 | 11 | 30 | .262 | .432 | .296 |
| Runners On | | | 309 | 75 | 6 | 34 | 63 | .243 | .353 | .311 |
| Runners/Scor. Pos. | | | 167 | 37 | 3 | 28 | 40 | .222 | .335 | .317 |
| Runners On/2 Out | | | 129 | 26 | 4 | 21 | 34 | .202 | .326 | .318 |
| Scor. Pos./2 Out | | | 79 | 16 | 2 | 18 | 23 | .203 | .329 | .351 |
| Late Inning Pressure | | | 59 | 19 | 2 | 2 | 14 | .322 | .458 | .339 |
| Leading Off | | | 16 | 9 | 0 | 1 | 1 | .563 | .688 | .588 |
| Runners On | | | 26 | 8 | 2 | 1 | 6 | .308 | .538 | .321 |
| Runners/Scor. Pos. | | | 14 | 3 | 1 | 1 | 4 | .214 | .429 | .250 |
| First 9 Batters | | | 273 | 63 | 6 | 28 | 52 | .231 | .359 | .298 |
| Second 9 Batters | | | 272 | 68 | 6 | 18 | 51 | .250 | .368 | .296 |
| All Batters Thereafter | | | 297 | 71 | 6 | 23 | 50 | .239 | .337 | .294 |

Loves to face: Mariano Duncan (0-for-11, 4 SO)
Hates to face: Von Hayes (.456, 26-for-57, 8 2B, 5 HR, 9 BB)
Ground outs-to-air outs ratio: 1.36 last season, 0.97 for career. . . . Additional statistics: 12 double-play ground outs in 150 opportunities, 32 doubles, 5 triples in 229.0 innings last season. . . . Allowed 17 first-inning runs in 34 starts. . . . Batting support: 4.41 runs per start. . . . Walked 10 times, the most among N.L. pitchers, and was the only pitcher to steal two bases. . . . Only N.L. pitcher to reach double figures in road wins. . . . Opponents stole 25 bases in 32 attempts, highest percentage on team. . . . ERA according to batterymate: Berryhill 2.96; Girardi 3.89; Wrona 5.08. . . . 14th Dodgers expatriate to win 100 or more games for other teams after leaving. For complete list, see Doyle Alexander comments.

## Kent Tekulve

Throws Right

| Cincinnati Reds | W–L | ERA | AB | H | HR | BB | SO | BA | SA | OBA |
|---|---|---|---|---|---|---|---|---|---|---|
| Season | 0-3 | 5.02 | 206 | 56 | 5 | 23 | 31 | .272 | .398 | .342 |
| vs. Left-Handers | | | 105 | 38 | 4 | 15 | 7 | .362 | .543 | .442 |
| vs. Right-Handers | | | 101 | 18 | 1 | 8 | 24 | .178 | .248 | .234 |
| Home | 0-2 | 5.76 | 118 | 34 | 3 | 16 | 16 | .288 | .415 | .370 |
| Road | 0-1 | 4.03 | 88 | 22 | 2 | 7 | 15 | .250 | .375 | .302 |
| Grass | 0-0 | 3.12 | 65 | 14 | 2 | 6 | 9 | .215 | .354 | .282 |
| Artificial Turf | 0-3 | 5.97 | 141 | 42 | 3 | 17 | 22 | .298 | .418 | .369 |
| April | 0-0 | 2.57 | 52 | 11 | 0 | 8 | 9 | .212 | .231 | .317 |
| May | 0-1 | 4.80 | 61 | 20 | 0 | 5 | 12 | .328 | .393 | .368 |
| June | 0-0 | 7.50 | 51 | 15 | 4 | 4 | 4 | .294 | .588 | .345 |
| July | 0-2 | 5.73 | 42 | 10 | 1 | 6 | 6 | .238 | .381 | .333 |
| August | | | 0 | 0 | 0 | 0 | 0 | — | — | — |
| Sept./Oct. | | | 0 | 0 | 0 | 0 | 0 | — | — | — |
| Leading Off Inn. | | | 43 | 10 | 1 | 4 | 5 | .233 | .349 | .298 |
| Runners On | | | 99 | 33 | 3 | 12 | 16 | .333 | .465 | .398 |
| Runners/Scor. Pos. | | | 67 | 21 | 3 | 12 | 13 | .313 | .493 | .407 |
| Runners On/2 Out | | | 47 | 17 | 2 | 5 | 7 | .362 | .553 | .423 |
| Scor. Pos./2 Out | | | 30 | 10 | 2 | 5 | 5 | .333 | .600 | .429 |
| Late Inning Pressure | | | 54 | 19 | 0 | 5 | 9 | .352 | .389 | .407 |
| Leading Off | | | 12 | 3 | 0 | 1 | 0 | .250 | .250 | .308 |
| Runners On | | | 30 | 13 | 0 | 3 | 5 | .433 | .467 | .485 |
| Runners/Scor. Pos. | | | 25 | 10 | 0 | 3 | 4 | .400 | .440 | .464 |
| First 9 Batters | | | 193 | 52 | 5 | 22 | 29 | .269 | .399 | .341 |
| Second 9 Batters | | | 13 | 4 | 0 | 1 | 2 | .308 | .385 | .357 |
| All Batters Thereafter | | | 0 | 0 | 0 | 0 | 0 | — | — | — |

Loves to face: Bo Diaz (.080, 2-for-25)
Hates to face: Keith Hernandez (.474, 9-for-19, 1 HR, 7 BB)
Ground outs-to-air outs ratio: 2.31 last season, 2.23 since 1975. . . . Additional statistics: 4 double-play ground outs in 37 opportunities, 11 doubles, 0 triples in 52.0 innings last season. . . . Could have emulated his deposed manager, and hung around for singular purpose of breaking Hoyt Wilhelm's record of 1070 games on the mound. Instead, he retired gracefully, 20 games short. We applaud Tekulve for choosing not to manipulate the record book. . . . Here's one that hasn't appeared in any book until now: Tekulve holds all-time major league record for issuing intentional walks (179). . . . Never started a game in the majors. . . . Had only 10 hits, none for extra bases, and scored eight runs in his 16-year career.

## Scott Terry

Throws Right

| St. Louis Cardinals | W–L | ERA | AB | H | HR | BB | SO | BA | SA | OBA |
|---|---|---|---|---|---|---|---|---|---|---|
| Season | 8-10 | 3.57 | 561 | 142 | 14 | 43 | 69 | .253 | .405 | .308 |
| vs. Left-Handers | | | 280 | 73 | 6 | 30 | 34 | .261 | .400 | .331 |
| vs. Right-Handers | | | 281 | 69 | 8 | 13 | 35 | .246 | .409 | .283 |
| Home | 6-4 | 3.08 | 327 | 76 | 7 | 16 | 43 | .232 | .379 | .271 |
| Road | 2-6 | 4.28 | 234 | 66 | 7 | 27 | 26 | .282 | .440 | .356 |
| Grass | 2-5 | 4.84 | 135 | 39 | 4 | 17 | 17 | .289 | .430 | .370 |
| Artificial Turf | 6-5 | 3.18 | 426 | 103 | 10 | 26 | 52 | .242 | .397 | .287 |
| April | 3-1 | 1.80 | 126 | 27 | 1 | 4 | 12 | .214 | .317 | .248 |
| May | 1-3 | 4.18 | 92 | 25 | 2 | 11 | 10 | .272 | .380 | .346 |
| June | 2-3 | 5.40 | 137 | 41 | 6 | 13 | 14 | .299 | .533 | .358 |
| July | 1-2 | 3.86 | 92 | 21 | 2 | 6 | 14 | .228 | .337 | .283 |
| August | 1-1 | 2.45 | 63 | 13 | 1 | 6 | 7 | .206 | .333 | .275 |
| Sept./Oct. | 0-0 | 3.55 | 51 | 15 | 2 | 3 | 12 | .294 | .529 | .327 |
| Leading Off Inn. | | | 141 | 41 | 1 | 10 | 21 | .291 | .418 | .346 |
| Runners On | | | 226 | 58 | 8 | 19 | 28 | .257 | .425 | .312 |
| Runners/Scor. Pos. | | | 134 | 32 | 4 | 16 | 13 | .239 | .366 | .312 |
| Runners On/2 Out | | | 94 | 18 | 1 | 12 | 12 | .191 | .277 | .290 |
| Scor. Pos./2 Out | | | 65 | 12 | 1 | 11 | 7 | .185 | .262 | .303 |
| Late Inning Pressure | | | 57 | 14 | 1 | 3 | 10 | .246 | .351 | .295 |
| Leading Off | | | 15 | 5 | 0 | 0 | 1 | .333 | .400 | .375 |
| Runners On | | | 23 | 7 | 1 | 1 | 4 | .304 | .478 | .333 |
| Runners/Scor. Pos. | | | 12 | 4 | 0 | 1 | 1 | .333 | .333 | .385 |
| First 9 Batters | | | 226 | 54 | 5 | 18 | 35 | .239 | .389 | .294 |
| Second 9 Batters | | | 187 | 41 | 5 | 11 | 21 | .219 | .358 | .266 |
| All Batters Thereafter | | | 148 | 47 | 4 | 14 | 13 | .318 | .486 | .378 |

Loves to face: Ricky Jordan (.083, 1-for-12)
Hates to face: Von Hayes (.462, 6-for-13, 2 HR)
Ground outs-to-air outs ratio: 2.25 last season, 2.03 for career. . . . Additional statistics: 9 double-play ground outs in 89 opportunities, 31 doubles, 6 triples in 148.2 innings last season. . . . Allowed 8 first-inning runs in 24 starts. . . . Batting support: 3.83 runs per start. . . . Completed only one of his 24 starts. . . . Career records at .500 level in both day and night games, but 5.40 night-game ERA is almost double his day-game figure (2.96). . . . Record of 5–11 from April through June, 13–7 from July on. . . . Opponents' career batting average is .289 with runners on base, .237 with bases empty. . . . Hit 21 home runs in three minor league seasons as a full-time outfielder before transition to the mound.

## Fernando Valenzuela

Throws Left

| Los Angeles Dodgers | W–L | ERA | AB | H | HR | BB | SO | BA | SA | OBA |
|---|---|---|---|---|---|---|---|---|---|---|
| Season | 10-13 | 3.43 | 738 | 185 | 11 | 98 | 116 | .251 | .351 | .337 |
| vs. Left-Handers | | | 125 | 32 | 1 | 13 | 21 | .256 | .352 | .324 |
| vs. Right-Handers | | | 613 | 153 | 10 | 85 | 95 | .250 | .351 | .340 |
| Home | 4-6 | 3.26 | 372 | 93 | 5 | 50 | 56 | .250 | .331 | .336 |
| Road | 6-7 | 3.61 | 366 | 92 | 6 | 48 | 60 | .251 | .372 | .339 |
| Grass | 6-9 | 3.57 | 515 | 128 | 9 | 71 | 83 | .249 | .348 | .338 |
| Artificial Turf | 4-4 | 3.12 | 223 | 57 | 2 | 27 | 33 | .256 | .359 | .336 |
| April | 0-2 | 3.58 | 105 | 28 | 1 | 15 | 17 | .267 | .371 | .358 |
| May | 0-2 | 6.27 | 69 | 17 | 2 | 13 | 12 | .246 | .377 | .357 |
| June | 4-2 | 3.07 | 158 | 41 | 2 | 17 | 20 | .259 | .348 | .331 |
| July | 1-4 | 3.86 | 122 | 32 | 1 | 17 | 13 | .262 | .385 | .352 |
| August | 4-2 | 2.14 | 159 | 38 | 3 | 15 | 26 | .239 | .340 | .305 |
| Sept./Oct. | 1-1 | 3.38 | 125 | 29 | 2 | 21 | 28 | .232 | .304 | .340 |
| Leading Off Inn. | | | 187 | 46 | 1 | 14 | 32 | .246 | .321 | .302 |
| Runners On | | | 312 | 82 | 5 | 53 | 44 | .263 | .369 | .363 |
| Runners/Scor. Pos. | | | 196 | 47 | 4 | 36 | 34 | .240 | .357 | .347 |
| Runners On/2 Out | | | 146 | 42 | 2 | 27 | 22 | .288 | .384 | .399 |
| Scor. Pos./2 Out | | | 104 | 27 | 1 | 21 | 17 | .260 | .356 | .384 |
| Late Inning Pressure | | | 50 | 18 | 1 | 4 | 6 | .360 | .500 | .407 |
| Leading Off | | | 13 | 5 | 0 | 1 | 3 | .385 | .538 | .429 |
| Runners On | | | 23 | 7 | 0 | 2 | 2 | .304 | .348 | .360 |
| Runners/Scor. Pos. | | | 15 | 5 | 0 | 2 | 2 | .333 | .400 | .412 |
| First 9 Batters | | | 239 | 56 | 5 | 32 | 43 | .234 | .347 | .324 |
| Second 9 Batters | | | 235 | 57 | 3 | 36 | 39 | .243 | .328 | .343 |
| All Batters Thereafter | | | 264 | 72 | 3 | 30 | 34 | .273 | .375 | .344 |

Loves to face: Steve Jeltz (0-for-15)
Hates to face: Randy Ready (.400, 10-for-25, 2 HR)
Ground outs-to-air outs ratio: 0.83 last season, 1.28 for career. . . . Additional statistics: 9 double-play ground outs in 151 opportunities, 41 doubles, 0 triples in 196.2 innings last season. . . . Allowed 18 first-inning runs in 31 starts. . . . Batting support: 3.65 runs per start. . . . Allowed three or fewer earned runs in nine of 13 losses. Lower ERA in eight no-decision starts (2.55) than in 10 wins (2.75). . . . ERA of 2.24 with Dempsey catching, 4.01 with Scioscia. . . . Opponents stole only 15 bases in 30 attempts. . . . Broke a streak of 27 starts without a complete game with three in 14 starts after All-Star break. . . . Five shutouts in first seven major league starts, none in last 68.

## Frank Viola

Throws Left

| New York Mets | W–L | ERA | AB | H | HR | BB | SO | BA | SA | OBA |
|---|---|---|---|---|---|---|---|---|---|---|
| Season | 5-5 | 3.38 | 318 | 75 | 5 | 27 | 73 | .236 | .318 | .296 |
| vs. Left-Handers | | | 54 | 13 | 0 | 2 | 9 | .241 | .259 | .268 |
| vs. Right-Handers | | | 264 | 62 | 5 | 25 | 64 | .235 | .330 | .301 |
| Home | 2-3 | 4.78 | 128 | 37 | 3 | 10 | 30 | .289 | .406 | .338 |
| Road | 3-2 | 2.53 | 190 | 38 | 2 | 17 | 43 | .200 | .258 | .268 |
| Grass | 3-5 | 4.73 | 206 | 54 | 5 | 19 | 46 | .262 | .369 | .323 |
| Artificial Turf | 2-0 | 1.13 | 112 | 21 | 0 | 8 | 27 | .188 | .223 | .246 |
| April | | | 0 | 0 | 0 | 0 | 0 | — | — | — |
| May | | | 0 | 0 | 0 | 0 | 0 | — | — | — |
| June | | | 0 | 0 | 0 | 0 | 0 | — | — | — |
| July | | | 0 | 0 | 0 | 0 | 0 | — | — | — |
| August | 2-3 | 2.66 | 160 | 35 | 1 | 12 | 36 | .219 | .281 | .272 |
| Sept./Oct. | 3-2 | 4.14 | 158 | 40 | 4 | 15 | 37 | .253 | .354 | .320 |
| Leading Off Inn. | | | 77 | 23 | 0 | 9 | 13 | .299 | .325 | .372 |
| Runners On | | | 137 | 33 | 4 | 14 | 35 | .241 | .372 | .312 |
| Runners/Scor. Pos. | | | 70 | 19 | 3 | 10 | 22 | .271 | .457 | .354 |
| Runners On/2 Out | | | 51 | 11 | 2 | 6 | 14 | .216 | .373 | .298 |
| Scor. Pos./2 Out | | | 30 | 5 | 1 | 6 | 11 | .167 | .267 | .306 |
| Late Inning Pressure | | | 31 | 2 | 0 | 1 | 9 | .065 | .065 | .121 |
| Leading Off | | | 10 | 2 | 0 | 0 | 2 | .200 | .200 | .200 |
| Runners On | | | 7 | 0 | 0 | 1 | 2 | .000 | .000 | .222 |
| Runners/Scor. Pos. | | | 4 | 0 | 0 | 1 | 1 | .000 | .000 | .200 |
| First 9 Batters | | | 97 | 21 | 0 | 7 | 28 | .216 | .268 | .267 |
| Second 9 Batters | | | 98 | 29 | 2 | 7 | 20 | .296 | .408 | .340 |
| All Batters Thereafter | | | 123 | 25 | 3 | 13 | 25 | .203 | .285 | .285 |

Loves to face: Glenn Wilson (0-for-12)
Hates to face: Willie Randolph (.372, 16-for-43, 2 HR, 10 BB)
Ground outs-to-air outs ratio: 1.06 last season, 0.83 for career. . . . Additional statistics: 6 double-play ground outs in 76 opportunities, 7 doubles, 2 triples in 85.1 innings last season. . . . Allowed 4 first-inning runs in 12 starts. . . . Batting support: 4.08 runs per start. . . . Opponents were 0-for-21 from 8th inning on after he joined the Mets. . . . Has allowed six career grand slams, including one in each league last season. . . . Opposing ground-ball hitters have outhit fly-ballers in each of last five seasons. . . . First pitcher since Steve Carlton (1971–80) and Phil Niekro (1974–80) to start at least 34 games in seven consecutive seasons. All-time record: 14 years, Cy Young (1891–1904).

## Bob Walk

Throws Right

| Pittsburgh Pirates | W–L | ERA | AB | H | HR | BB | SO | BA | SA | OBA |
|---|---|---|---|---|---|---|---|---|---|---|
| Season | 13-10 | 4.41 | 768 | 208 | 15 | 65 | 83 | .271 | .391 | .330 |
| vs. Left-Handers | | | 431 | 123 | 9 | 38 | 34 | .285 | .406 | .343 |
| vs. Right-Handers | | | 337 | 85 | 6 | 27 | 49 | .252 | .371 | .313 |
| Home | 7-4 | 3.28 | 355 | 98 | 5 | 26 | 39 | .276 | .377 | .328 |
| Road | 6-6 | 5.38 | 413 | 110 | 10 | 39 | 44 | .266 | .402 | .332 |
| Grass | 2-4 | 6.46 | 190 | 58 | 4 | 17 | 22 | .305 | .411 | .364 |
| Artificial Turf | 11-6 | 3.78 | 578 | 150 | 11 | 48 | 61 | .260 | .384 | .319 |
| April | 2-2 | 3.98 | 159 | 41 | 1 | 12 | 15 | .258 | .340 | .308 |
| May | 3-1 | 2.70 | 131 | 29 | 1 | 10 | 8 | .221 | .305 | .282 |
| June | 2-1 | 6.86 | 91 | 28 | 5 | 9 | 15 | .308 | .527 | .376 |
| July | 1-3 | 5.52 | 119 | 38 | 3 | 15 | 12 | .319 | .454 | .401 |
| August | 3-2 | 4.46 | 164 | 44 | 4 | 13 | 14 | .268 | .390 | .322 |
| Sept./Oct. | 2-1 | 4.15 | 104 | 28 | 1 | 6 | 19 | .269 | .385 | .309 |
| Leading Off Inn. | | | 194 | 43 | 3 | 13 | 19 | .222 | .304 | .271 |
| Runners On | | | 308 | 95 | 8 | 27 | 37 | .308 | .468 | .366 |
| Runners/Scor. Pos. | | | 180 | 57 | 5 | 20 | 25 | .317 | .489 | .387 |
| Runners On/2 Out | | | 139 | 38 | 2 | 14 | 19 | .273 | .417 | .348 |
| Scor. Pos./2 Out | | | 94 | 25 | 1 | 10 | 14 | .266 | .404 | .349 |
| Late Inning Pressure | | | 59 | 17 | 2 | 6 | 1 | .288 | .475 | .364 |
| Leading Off | | | 16 | 5 | 1 | 3 | 0 | .313 | .625 | .421 |
| Runners On | | | 23 | 5 | 1 | 1 | 1 | .217 | .391 | .250 |
| Runners/Scor. Pos. | | | 10 | 2 | 0 | 1 | 0 | .200 | .200 | .273 |
| First 9 Batters | | | 264 | 66 | 4 | 23 | 40 | .250 | .352 | .315 |
| Second 9 Batters | | | 233 | 61 | 4 | 23 | 29 | .262 | .361 | .328 |
| All Batters Thereafter | | | 271 | 81 | 7 | 19 | 14 | .299 | .454 | .347 |

Loves to face: Ken Griffey, Sr. (0-for-16)
Hates to face: Lonnie Smith (.692, 9-for-13, 2 HR)
Ground outs-to-air outs ratio: 1.20 last season, 1.27 for career. . . . Additional statistics: 11 double-play ground outs in 131 opportunities, 37 doubles, 5 triples in 196.0 innings last season. . . . Allowed 20 first-inning runs in 31 starts. Opponents batted .313 in first, .262 thereafter. . . . Batting support: 4.90 runs per start. . . . His only complete games of season came in consecutive starts (Apr. 30 and May 5). Had completed exactly one game in each of four previous seasons, and all were shutouts. . . . Faced same number of left-handed hitters as in 1988, when he allowed them only two home runs. . . . Largest one-season ERA increase in majors among pitchers at least with 30 starts in both 1988 and 1989 (from 2.71 to 4.41).

## John Wetteland

Throws Right

| Los Angeles Dodgers | W–L | ERA | AB | H | HR | BB | SO | BA | SA | OBA |
|---|---|---|---|---|---|---|---|---|---|---|
| Season | 5-8 | 3.77 | 371 | 81 | 8 | 34 | 96 | .218 | .329 | .283 |
| vs. Left-Handers | | | 193 | 41 | 3 | 15 | 45 | .212 | .295 | .269 |
| vs. Right-Handers | | | 178 | 40 | 5 | 19 | 51 | .225 | .365 | .296 |
| Home | 4-3 | 3.45 | 171 | 39 | 4 | 12 | 45 | .228 | .345 | .279 |
| Road | 1-5 | 4.04 | 200 | 42 | 4 | 22 | 51 | .210 | .315 | .286 |
| Grass | 4-7 | 3.89 | 286 | 65 | 5 | 27 | 70 | .227 | .329 | .292 |
| Artificial Turf | 1-1 | 3.38 | 85 | 16 | 3 | 7 | 26 | .188 | .329 | .250 |
| April | | | 0 | 0 | 0 | 0 | 0 | — | — | — |
| May | 0-0 | 0.00 | 2 | 0 | 0 | 1 | 1 | .000 | .000 | .333 |
| June | 1-0 | 2.16 | 89 | 15 | 1 | 5 | 28 | .169 | .236 | .213 |
| July | 1-3 | 3.13 | 82 | 18 | 0 | 9 | 21 | .220 | .280 | .293 |
| August | 2-3 | 3.10 | 101 | 20 | 1 | 10 | 24 | .198 | .287 | .268 |
| Sept./Oct. | 1-2 | 6.93 | 97 | 28 | 6 | 9 | 22 | .289 | .505 | .349 |
| Leading Off Inn. | | | 95 | 27 | 3 | 12 | 24 | .284 | .442 | .364 |
| Runners On | | | 155 | 36 | 4 | 11 | 38 | .232 | .361 | .280 |
| Runners/Scor. Pos. | | | 84 | 22 | 4 | 10 | 23 | .262 | .476 | .333 |
| Runners On/2 Out | | | 59 | 15 | 2 | 6 | 16 | .254 | .407 | .323 |
| Scor. Pos./2 Out | | | 39 | 9 | 2 | 6 | 13 | .231 | .436 | .333 |
| Late Inning Pressure | | | 76 | 17 | 0 | 6 | 19 | .224 | .289 | .280 |
| Leading Off | | | 20 | 5 | 0 | 1 | 5 | .250 | .400 | .286 |
| Runners On | | | 34 | 6 | 0 | 3 | 8 | .176 | .206 | .243 |
| Runners/Scor. Pos. | | | 25 | 3 | 0 | 3 | 7 | .120 | .120 | .214 |
| First 9 Batters | | | 203 | 37 | 2 | 16 | 60 | .182 | .251 | .240 |
| Second 9 Batters | | | 117 | 30 | 4 | 10 | 24 | .256 | .419 | .315 |
| All Batters Thereafter | | | 51 | 14 | 2 | 8 | 12 | .275 | .431 | .373 |

Loves to face: Marvell Wynne (0-for-8)
Hates to face: Craig Biggio (.500, 3-for-6, 2 HR, 3 SO)
Ground outs-to-air outs ratio: 0.70 last season, his first in majors. . . . Additional statistics: 9 double-play ground outs in 73 opportunities, 15 doubles, 1 triple in 102.2 innings last season. . . . Allowed 5 first-inning runs in 12 starts. . . . Batting support: 3.67 runs per start. . . . Record of 2–6 (4.97 ERA) as a starter, 3–2 (1.83, one save) in 19 relief appearances. . . . Entered only two of his relief appearances in mid-inning. . . . Averaged 8.416 strikeouts per nine innings, 2d-highest by a Dodgers rookie since the move from Brooklyn (minimum: 100 innings). Number one: Valenzuela, 8.423 (1981). . . . Threw 16 wild pitches, despite an average of less than three walks per nine innings (2.98).

## Ed Whitson

Throws Right

| San Diego Padres | W–L | ERA | AB | H | HR | BB | SO | BA | SA | OBA |
|---|---|---|---|---|---|---|---|---|---|---|
| Season | 16-11 | 2.66 | 841 | 198 | 22 | 48 | 117 | .235 | .360 | .278 |
| vs. Left-Handers | | | 497 | 130 | 16 | 33 | 57 | .262 | .408 | .305 |
| vs. Right-Handers | | | 344 | 68 | 6 | 15 | 60 | .198 | .291 | .238 |
| Home | 9-6 | 2.98 | 457 | 107 | 18 | 26 | 64 | .234 | .383 | .279 |
| Road | 7-5 | 2.27 | 384 | 91 | 4 | 22 | 53 | .237 | .333 | .277 |
| Grass | 10-11 | 3.05 | 641 | 155 | 22 | 38 | 89 | .242 | .387 | .287 |
| Artificial Turf | 6-0 | 1.46 | 200 | 43 | 0 | 10 | 28 | .215 | .275 | .251 |
| April | 3-2 | 2.72 | 131 | 30 | 5 | 12 | 20 | .229 | .374 | .306 |
| May | 5-0 | 1.91 | 174 | 44 | 6 | 5 | 16 | .253 | .374 | .276 |
| June | 2-3 | 3.27 | 121 | 26 | 5 | 9 | 15 | .215 | .397 | .267 |
| July | 4-2 | 3.46 | 147 | 37 | 1 | 8 | 24 | .252 | .340 | .287 |
| August | 1-3 | 2.32 | 157 | 34 | 3 | 9 | 25 | .217 | .325 | .257 |
| Sept./Oct. | 1-1 | 2.48 | 111 | 27 | 2 | 5 | 17 | .243 | .360 | .277 |
| Leading Off Inn. | | | 225 | 55 | 7 | 6 | 26 | .244 | .387 | .270 |
| Runners On | | | 301 | 66 | 6 | 26 | 47 | .219 | .326 | .275 |
| Runners/Scor. Pos. | | | 147 | 34 | 2 | 19 | 25 | .231 | .327 | .305 |
| Runners On/2 Out | | | 137 | 34 | 5 | 16 | 23 | .248 | .409 | .327 |
| Scor. Pos./2 Out | | | 76 | 17 | 1 | 11 | 15 | .224 | .316 | .322 |
| Late Inning Pressure | | | 85 | 18 | 1 | 3 | 15 | .212 | .294 | .239 |
| Leading Off | | | 26 | 5 | 0 | 0 | 6 | .192 | .192 | .192 |
| Runners On | | | 23 | 3 | 0 | 2 | 3 | .130 | .217 | .200 |
| Runners/Scor. Pos. | | | 8 | 1 | 0 | 1 | 2 | .125 | .250 | .222 |
| First 9 Batters | | | 260 | 69 | 11 | 19 | 46 | .265 | .438 | .319 |
| Second 9 Batters | | | 265 | 63 | 4 | 14 | 32 | .238 | .336 | .277 |
| All Batters Thereafter | | | 316 | 66 | 7 | 15 | 39 | .209 | .316 | .244 |

Loves to face: Kirk Gibson (0-for-12)
Hates to face: Mackey Sasser (.692, 9-for-13, 1 HR)
Ground outs-to-air outs ratio: 1.15 last season, 1.02 for career. . . . Additional statistics: 16 double-play ground outs in 133 opportunities, 35 doubles, 2 triples in 227.0 innings last season. . . . Allowed 21 first-inning runs in 33 starts. Eight first-inning HR were 2d most in majors. . . . Batting support: 3.94 runs per start. . . . Retired 30 consecutive leadoff batters (June 16–July 14), 2d-longest streak in majors over last 15 years. . . . Lowest career batting average (.122) of any active N.L. pitcher (minimum: 400 AB). No extra-base hits in first 314 at-bats, eight in last 171 (all doubles). . . . Largest one-season ERA decrease among N.L. pitchers with at least 30 starts in both 1988 and 1989 (from 3.77 to 2.66).

## Mitch Williams

Throws Left

| Chicago Cubs | W–L | ERA | AB | H | HR | BB | SO | BA | SA | OBA |
|---|---|---|---|---|---|---|---|---|---|---|
| Season | 4-4 | 2.76 | 298 | 71 | 6 | 52 | 67 | .238 | .342 | .361 |
| vs. Left-Handers | | | 71 | 18 | 0 | 10 | 26 | .254 | .296 | .345 |
| vs. Right-Handers | | | 227 | 53 | 6 | 42 | 41 | .233 | .357 | .366 |
| Home | 3-2 | 3.65 | 143 | 40 | 4 | 25 | 34 | .280 | .413 | .399 |
| Road | 1-2 | 2.01 | 155 | 31 | 2 | 27 | 33 | .200 | .277 | .326 |
| Grass | 3-4 | 3.14 | 212 | 52 | 5 | 38 | 46 | .245 | .363 | .370 |
| Artificial Turf | 1-0 | 1.85 | 86 | 19 | 1 | 14 | 21 | .221 | .291 | .340 |
| April | 0-1 | 2.25 | 47 | 15 | 1 | 7 | 13 | .319 | .404 | .407 |
| May | 0-1 | 2.03 | 46 | 10 | 1 | 15 | 14 | .217 | .304 | .418 |
| June | 1-0 | 2.20 | 57 | 11 | 1 | 6 | 12 | .193 | .298 | .288 |
| July | 0-0 | 0.00 | 44 | 7 | 0 | 6 | 6 | .159 | .205 | .260 |
| August | 3-0 | 3.50 | 68 | 16 | 1 | 11 | 16 | .235 | .338 | .354 |
| Sept./Oct. | 0-2 | 8.64 | 36 | 12 | 2 | 7 | 6 | .333 | .556 | .455 |
| Leading Off Inn. | | | 58 | 14 | 1 | 4 | 12 | .241 | .310 | .290 |
| Runners On | | | 168 | 37 | 3 | 35 | 46 | .220 | .315 | .358 |
| Runners/Scor. Pos. | | | 109 | 23 | 2 | 20 | 32 | .211 | .284 | .331 |
| Runners On/2 Out | | | 83 | 17 | 0 | 16 | 21 | .205 | .265 | .347 |
| Scor. Pos./2 Out | | | 60 | 12 | 0 | 11 | 17 | .200 | .233 | .333 |
| Late Inning Pressure | | | 206 | 42 | 5 | 34 | 48 | .204 | .311 | .320 |
| Leading Off | | | 38 | 6 | 0 | 3 | 9 | .158 | .158 | .220 |
| Runners On | | | 117 | 20 | 3 | 21 | 32 | .171 | .282 | .294 |
| Runners/Scor. Pos. | | | 73 | 13 | 2 | 11 | 21 | .178 | .288 | .281 |
| First 9 Batters | | | 294 | 71 | 6 | 51 | 64 | .241 | .347 | .364 |
| Second 9 Batters | | | 4 | 0 | 0 | 1 | 3 | .000 | .000 | .167 |
| All Batters Thereafter | | | 0 | 0 | 0 | 0 | 0 | — | — | — |

Loves to face: Kirk Gibson (.143, 1-for-7, 6 SO)
Hates to face: Kevin Bass (.500, 2-for-4, 2 HR)
Ground outs-to-air outs ratio: 0.62 last season, 0.71 for career. . . . Additional statistics: 3 double-play ground outs in 93 opportunities, 2d-lowest rate in N.L. (min.: 75 opp.), 11 doubles, 1 triple in 81.2 innings last season. . . . Third Cubs pitcher to lead N.L. in appearances during the 1980s. Others: Bill Campbell (1983) and Dick Tidrow (1980). Only one pitcher over the last 15 years has led the N.L. in consecutive seasons: Kent Tekulve. . . . Saved 36 games, but had the opportunity to save 17 more. Had only five saves in his last nine chances. . . . Lowest career fielding percentage (.859) of any active pitcher with at least 300 games. . . . Career average of .241 by ground-ball hitters, .181 by fly-ballers.

## Steve Wilson

Throws Left

| Chicago Cubs | W–L | ERA | AB | H | HR | BB | SO | BA | SA | OBA |
|---|---|---|---|---|---|---|---|---|---|---|
| Season | 6-4 | 4.20 | 323 | 83 | 6 | 31 | 65 | .257 | .393 | .320 |
| vs. Left-Handers | | | 91 | 24 | 1 | 9 | 16 | .264 | .396 | .330 |
| vs. Right-Handers | | | 232 | 59 | 5 | 22 | 49 | .254 | .392 | .317 |
| Home | 3-3 | 4.43 | 160 | 42 | 5 | 14 | 35 | .263 | .413 | .318 |
| Road | 3-1 | 3.98 | 163 | 41 | 1 | 17 | 30 | .252 | .374 | .322 |
| Grass | 4-4 | 4.30 | 221 | 57 | 6 | 20 | 48 | .258 | .398 | .317 |
| Artificial Turf | 2-0 | 4.00 | 102 | 26 | 0 | 11 | 17 | .255 | .382 | .327 |
| April | 1-0 | 4.91 | 28 | 7 | 0 | 2 | 3 | .250 | .393 | .300 |
| May | 1-0 | 0.00 | 20 | 2 | 0 | 3 | 4 | .100 | .100 | .217 |
| June | 1-0 | 3.27 | 82 | 20 | 1 | 5 | 13 | .244 | .366 | .281 |
| July | 0-0 | 3.27 | 47 | 15 | 1 | 2 | 8 | .319 | .489 | .347 |
| August | 2-2 | 4.19 | 68 | 17 | 1 | 10 | 16 | .250 | .368 | .346 |
| Sept./Oct. | 1-2 | 6.98 | 78 | 22 | 3 | 9 | 21 | .282 | .462 | .356 |
| Leading Off Inn. | | | 83 | 22 | 2 | 4 | 22 | .265 | .398 | .299 |
| Runners On | | | 140 | 33 | 1 | 15 | 22 | .236 | .343 | .302 |
| Runners/Scor. Pos. | | | 84 | 20 | 1 | 9 | 11 | .238 | .357 | .299 |
| Runners On/2 Out | | | 65 | 17 | 0 | 8 | 10 | .262 | .385 | .342 |
| Scor. Pos./2 Out | | | 45 | 11 | 0 | 4 | 6 | .244 | .356 | .306 |
| Late Inning Pressure | | | 74 | 22 | 1 | 12 | 14 | .297 | .419 | .386 |
| Leading Off | | | 20 | 5 | 0 | 2 | 5 | .250 | .250 | .318 |
| Runners On | | | 27 | 8 | 0 | 7 | 3 | .296 | .407 | .417 |
| Runners/Scor. Pos. | | | 16 | 4 | 0 | 5 | 2 | .250 | .375 | .391 |
| First 9 Batters | | | 238 | 54 | 3 | 26 | 50 | .227 | .332 | .303 |
| Second 9 Batters | | | 67 | 22 | 3 | 4 | 14 | .328 | .552 | .356 |
| All Batters Thereafter | | | 18 | 7 | 0 | 1 | 1 | .389 | .611 | .421 |

Loves to face: Jose Oquendo (.143, 1-for-7, 3 SO)
Hates to face: Terry Pendleton (.444, 4-for-9)
Ground outs-to-air outs ratio: 0.76 last season, 0.80 for career. . . . Additional statistics: 3 double-play ground outs in 67 opportunities, 14 doubles, 6 triples in 85.2 innings last season. . . . Record of 3–2 (5.08 ERA) in eight starts, 3–2 (3.63, 2 saves) in 45 relief appearances. . . . Entered seven bases-loaded situations, stranded 18 of those 21 runners. . . . Spectacular season totals: inherited 51 runners, stranded 43 (84%). . . . Only opposing left-hander to hit a HR was Darryl Strawberry. . . . Career average of .289 by opposing ground-ball hitters, .234 by fly-ballers. Slugging averages: .443 and .353, respectively. . . . Fred MacMurray Fan Club will be interested to know Wilson's middle name is Douglas.

## Todd Worrell

Throws Right

| St. Louis Cardinals | W–L | ERA | AB | H | HR | BB | SO | BA | SA | OBA |
|---|---|---|---|---|---|---|---|---|---|---|
| Season | 3-5 | 2.96 | 189 | 42 | 4 | 26 | 41 | .222 | .365 | .315 |
| vs. Left-Handers | | | 88 | 22 | 3 | 14 | 21 | .250 | .455 | .350 |
| vs. Right-Handers | | | 101 | 20 | 1 | 12 | 20 | .198 | .287 | .283 |
| Home | 3-4 | 3.08 | 97 | 21 | 1 | 13 | 22 | .216 | .351 | .306 |
| Road | 0-1 | 2.84 | 92 | 21 | 3 | 13 | 19 | .228 | .380 | .324 |
| Grass | 0-0 | 1.88 | 52 | 11 | 2 | 6 | 12 | .212 | .365 | .293 |
| Artificial Turf | 3-5 | 3.38 | 137 | 31 | 2 | 20 | 29 | .226 | .365 | .323 |
| April | 0-1 | 1.35 | 45 | 8 | 2 | 4 | 9 | .178 | .333 | .245 |
| May | 0-0 | 1.69 | 19 | 3 | 1 | 4 | 4 | .158 | .368 | .304 |
| June | 1-1 | 0.96 | 35 | 10 | 0 | 7 | 4 | .286 | .371 | .405 |
| July | 0-0 | 0.96 | 32 | 4 | 0 | 1 | 13 | .125 | .156 | .152 |
| August | 1-3 | 8.53 | 52 | 16 | 1 | 10 | 10 | .308 | .519 | .413 |
| Sept./Oct. | 1-0 | 0.00 | 6 | 1 | 0 | 0 | 1 | .167 | .333 | .167 |
| Leading Off Inn. | | | 37 | 7 | 2 | 1 | 7 | .189 | .432 | .211 |
| Runners On | | | 95 | 21 | 2 | 19 | 17 | .221 | .358 | .348 |
| Runners/Scor. Pos. | | | 70 | 14 | 1 | 17 | 15 | .200 | .329 | .352 |
| Runners On/2 Out | | | 43 | 6 | 0 | 7 | 11 | .140 | .186 | .260 |
| Scor. Pos./2 Out | | | 33 | 4 | 0 | 7 | 10 | .121 | .152 | .275 |
| Late Inning Pressure | | | 130 | 29 | 2 | 23 | 27 | .223 | .354 | .338 |
| Leading Off | | | 26 | 3 | 1 | 1 | 6 | .115 | .269 | .148 |
| Runners On | | | 64 | 15 | 1 | 18 | 10 | .234 | .375 | .398 |
| Runners/Scor. Pos. | | | 46 | 10 | 1 | 16 | 8 | .217 | .413 | .413 |
| First 9 Batters | | | 185 | 41 | 4 | 26 | 41 | .222 | .368 | .316 |
| Second 9 Batters | | | 4 | 1 | 0 | 0 | 0 | .250 | .250 | .250 |
| All Batters Thereafter | | | 0 | 0 | 0 | 0 | 0 | — | — | — |

Loves to face: Hubie Brooks (.095, 2-for-21)
Hates to face: Howard Johnson (.556, 5-for-9, 4 HR, 6 BB)
Ground outs-to-air outs ratio: 1.09 last season, 0.83 for career.... Additional statistics: 3 double-play ground outs in 43 opportunities, 13 doubles, 1 triple in 51.2 innings last season.... Recorded 20 saves in 26 opportunities.... Inherited 30 runners, stranded 22 (73%).... Has finished 218 of 281 career appearances (78%), highest rate of any active reliever who has pitched predominantly in the National League.... Opponents' career average of .186 with two outs and runners on base is lowest of the last 15 years (minimum: 250 BFP).... Has faced 55 batters with bases loaded, most among active N.L. pitchers who've never walked one in that situation.... Innings pitched, year by year since 1986: 103.2, 94.2, 90.0, 51.2.

## Atlanta Braves

| | W-L | ERA | AB | H | HR | BB | SO | BA | SA | OBA |
|---|---|---|---|---|---|---|---|---|---|---|
| Season | 63-97 | 3.70 | 5470 | 1370 | 114 | 468 | 966 | .250 | .366 | .309 |
| vs. Left-Handers | | | 2254 | 547 | 34 | 246 | 381 | .243 | .342 | .317 |
| vs. Right-Handers | | | 3216 | 823 | 80 | 222 | 585 | .256 | .383 | .303 |
| Home | 33-46 | 3.45 | 2828 | 688 | 61 | 229 | 487 | .243 | .356 | .301 |
| Road | 30-51 | 3.97 | 2642 | 682 | 53 | 239 | 479 | .258 | .377 | .318 |
| Grass | 46-72 | 3.49 | 4077 | 1007 | 90 | 325 | 718 | .247 | .364 | .303 |
| Artificial Turf | 17-25 | 4.32 | 1393 | 363 | 24 | 143 | 248 | .261 | .371 | .328 |
| April | 10-15 | 3.82 | 839 | 216 | 19 | 72 | 153 | .257 | .384 | .314 |
| May | 12-14 | 2.81 | 909 | 204 | 9 | 73 | 156 | .224 | .310 | .282 |
| June | 10-17 | 4.02 | 903 | 241 | 18 | 79 | 167 | .267 | .375 | .326 |
| July | 11-16 | 3.43 | 937 | 222 | 21 | 70 | 178 | .237 | .353 | .289 |
| August | 10-18 | 4.25 | 946 | 254 | 20 | 80 | 138 | .268 | .381 | .326 |
| Sept./Oct. | 10-17 | 3.90 | 936 | 233 | 27 | 94 | 174 | .249 | .393 | .318 |
| Leading Off Inn. | | | 1351 | 342 | 29 | 95 | 220 | .253 | .380 | .305 |
| Runners On | | | 2264 | 601 | 51 | 234 | 388 | .265 | .385 | .330 |
| Runners/Scor. Pos. | | | 1336 | 335 | 23 | 176 | 260 | .251 | .365 | .331 |
| Runners On/2 Out | | | 972 | 237 | 17 | 109 | 183 | .244 | .342 | .321 |
| Scor. Pos./2 Out | | | 624 | 147 | 11 | 90 | 132 | .236 | .338 | .334 |
| Late Inning Pressure | | | 1074 | 276 | 20 | 104 | 231 | .257 | .362 | .321 |
| Leading Off | | | 271 | 79 | 6 | 28 | 50 | .292 | .413 | .360 |
| Runners On | | | 458 | 127 | 9 | 48 | 99 | .277 | .393 | .341 |
| Runners/Scor. Pos. | | | 266 | 70 | 3 | 41 | 67 | .263 | .365 | .353 |
| First 9 Batters | | | 2953 | 745 | 52 | 256 | 605 | .252 | .359 | .311 |
| Second 9 Batters | | | 1371 | 331 | 32 | 116 | 229 | .241 | .364 | .301 |
| All Batters Thereafter | | | 1146 | 294 | 30 | 96 | 132 | .257 | .387 | .313 |

Starting pitchers: 47–62, 3.81 ERA
Relief pitchers: 16–35, 3.51 ERA
Ground outs-to-air outs ratio: 1.11. . . . Lost 18 games in which they led after six innings, 15 of them at home. But didn't lose a home game in which they led after eight innings (31–0). . . . Lost their last nine extra-inning contests. . . . Pitchers hit only 16 batters, fewest in N.L., after leading league in each of the two previous seasons. . . . Braves pitchers also walked the fewest batters in the league, for first time since 1962. . . . Bullpen lost 35 games, most of any team in majors. . . . Haven't pitched consecutive shutouts since 1982, the longest streak of any major league club. . . . At the plate, pitchers struck out only 89 times, by far the fewest of any N.L. club. Pittsburgh pitchers whiffed 109 times, the 2d fewest.

## Chicago Cubs

| | W-L | ERA | AB | H | HR | BB | SO | BA | SA | OBA |
|---|---|---|---|---|---|---|---|---|---|---|
| Season | 93-69 | 3.43 | 5483 | 1369 | 106 | 532 | 918 | .250 | .364 | .317 |
| vs. Left-Handers | | | 2561 | 665 | 45 | 279 | 406 | .260 | .375 | .333 |
| vs. Right-Handers | | | 2922 | 704 | 61 | 253 | 512 | .241 | .355 | .302 |
| Home | 48-33 | 3.54 | 2806 | 708 | 64 | 259 | 506 | .252 | .375 | .316 |
| Road | 45-36 | 3.31 | 2677 | 661 | 42 | 273 | 412 | .247 | .353 | .317 |
| Grass | 63-51 | 3.50 | 3871 | 966 | 80 | 372 | 663 | .250 | .367 | .316 |
| Artificial Turf | 30-18 | 3.26 | 1612 | 403 | 26 | 160 | 255 | .250 | .357 | .318 |
| April | 12-11 | 3.54 | 764 | 182 | 19 | 67 | 136 | .238 | .360 | .299 |
| May | 16-11 | 2.51 | 889 | 197 | 11 | 86 | 135 | .222 | .299 | .292 |
| June | 13-15 | 3.88 | 957 | 237 | 15 | 100 | 145 | .248 | .365 | .319 |
| July | 18-9 | 2.99 | 888 | 219 | 11 | 83 | 142 | .247 | .340 | .311 |
| August | 16-12 | 4.03 | 1001 | 260 | 34 | 109 | 185 | .260 | .416 | .334 |
| Sept./Oct. | 18-11 | 3.55 | 984 | 274 | 16 | 87 | 175 | .278 | .395 | .338 |
| Leading Off Inn. | | | 1370 | 360 | 32 | 89 | 212 | .263 | .382 | .310 |
| Runners On | | | 2331 | 592 | 44 | 284 | 400 | .254 | .373 | .332 |
| Runners/Scor. Pos. | | | 1314 | 314 | 21 | 202 | 255 | .239 | .346 | .333 |
| Runners On/2 Out | | | 1004 | 237 | 18 | 149 | 191 | .236 | .345 | .338 |
| Scor. Pos./2 Out | | | 645 | 138 | 11 | 114 | 135 | .214 | .318 | .335 |
| Late Inning Pressure | | | 987 | 236 | 20 | 128 | 199 | .239 | .347 | .326 |
| Leading Off | | | 244 | 61 | 2 | 24 | 47 | .250 | .316 | .317 |
| Runners On | | | 419 | 92 | 11 | 74 | 82 | .220 | .346 | .333 |
| Runners/Scor. Pos. | | | 247 | 49 | 5 | 49 | 57 | .198 | .304 | .325 |
| First 9 Batters | | | 2852 | 687 | 48 | 302 | 522 | .241 | .349 | .315 |
| Second 9 Batters | | | 1445 | 364 | 32 | 115 | 225 | .252 | .373 | .306 |
| All Batters Thereafter | | | 1186 | 318 | 26 | 115 | 171 | .268 | .391 | .333 |

Starting pitchers: 73–51, 3.67 ERA
Relief pitchers: 20–18, 2.92 ERA
Ground outs-to-air outs ratio: 1.11. . . . Most wins by a starting staff of any N.L. club. . . . Cubs led the N.L. in saves for the first time in franchise history. Until last season, they were the only N.L. club never to lead the league. . . . Used only eight starting pitchers, matching the Astros and the Dodgers for the fewest of any N.L. club. . . . Cubs had an 8–0 record in games in which their pitchers didn't walk a batter. . . . Cardinals stole 18 bases in 21 attempts against them, but the Giants stole only 3 in 12 tries. . . . Lost first game of N.L.C.S. by an 11–3 count, the 2d most runs ever given up in a Champioship Series opener. Cubs won 1985 opener by a 13–0 score over the Padres.

## Cincinnati Reds

| | W-L | ERA | AB | H | HR | BB | SO | BA | SA | OBA |
|---|---|---|---|---|---|---|---|---|---|---|
| Season | 75-87 | 3.73 | 5540 | 1404 | 125 | 559 | 981 | .253 | .376 | .323 |
| vs. Left-Handers | | | 2144 | 575 | 42 | 234 | 362 | .268 | .391 | .341 |
| vs. Right-Handers | | | 3396 | 829 | 83 | 325 | 619 | .244 | .367 | .312 |
| Home | 38-43 | 4.07 | 2858 | 753 | 71 | 293 | 495 | .263 | .395 | .333 |
| Road | 37-44 | 3.38 | 2682 | 651 | 54 | 266 | 486 | .243 | .357 | .312 |
| Grass | 22-26 | 3.57 | 1622 | 395 | 32 | 167 | 302 | .244 | .359 | .314 |
| Artificial Turf | 53-61 | 3.80 | 3918 | 1009 | 93 | 392 | 679 | .258 | .383 | .327 |
| April | 13-9 | 3.07 | 738 | 170 | 12 | 77 | 116 | .230 | .332 | .304 |
| May | 14-13 | 3.75 | 918 | 223 | 17 | 94 | 176 | .243 | .354 | .314 |
| June | 14-15 | 3.86 | 961 | 253 | 20 | 100 | 174 | .263 | .380 | .331 |
| July | 7-19 | 4.03 | 899 | 237 | 21 | 81 | 149 | .264 | .393 | .325 |
| August | 16-13 | 3.59 | 1012 | 261 | 31 | 113 | 175 | .258 | .414 | .335 |
| Sept./Oct. | 11-18 | 3.96 | 1012 | 260 | 24 | 94 | 191 | .257 | .374 | .322 |
| Leading Off Inn. | | | 1358 | 336 | 37 | 105 | 216 | .247 | .386 | .305 |
| Runners On | | | 2336 | 618 | 55 | 275 | 427 | .265 | .391 | .339 |
| Runners/Scor. Pos. | | | 1335 | 346 | 29 | 217 | 275 | .259 | .372 | .354 |
| Runners On/2 Out | | | 1040 | 246 | 22 | 141 | 214 | .237 | .350 | .331 |
| Scor. Pos./2 Out | | | 650 | 150 | 15 | 117 | 145 | .231 | .340 | .350 |
| Late Inning Pressure | | | 983 | 222 | 12 | 122 | 250 | .226 | .312 | .313 |
| Leading Off | | | 254 | 58 | 1 | 22 | 67 | .228 | .295 | .295 |
| Runners On | | | 418 | 99 | 8 | 63 | 101 | .237 | .340 | .333 |
| Runners/Scor. Pos. | | | 252 | 54 | 4 | 54 | 72 | .214 | .290 | .346 |
| First 9 Batters | | | 2928 | 696 | 59 | 309 | 635 | .238 | .349 | .311 |
| Second 9 Batters | | | 1387 | 376 | 36 | 144 | 203 | .271 | .412 | .341 |
| All Batters Thereafter | | | 1225 | 332 | 30 | 106 | 143 | .271 | .401 | .331 |

Starting pitchers: 50–65, 3.88 ERA
Relief pitchers: 25–22 3.46 ERA
Ground outs-to-air outs ratio: 1.08. . . . Defense chipped in with only 108 double plays. Since 1935, when the Pirates failed to break the century mark, only one N.L. club turned fewer double plays: the 1963 Houston Colt .45s. . . . Defense did, however, pull off its first triple play since 1967. Gap of 21 seasons was the longest in club history. . . . Pitchers issued 105 intentional passes, most since Jerry Coleman's 1980 San Diego Padres. . . . As batters, Reds pitchers had the highest on-base average in N.L. (.212). . . . Back-to-back shutouts of the Dodgers in L.A. by Jose Rijo and Tom Browning (June 9–10) were the only consecutive complete games by Reds' starters last season. . . . Didn't have a complete-game victory after August 22.

## Houston Astros

| | W-L | ERA | AB | H | HR | BB | SO | BA | SA | OBA |
|---|---|---|---|---|---|---|---|---|---|---|
| Season | 86-76 | 3.64 | 5579 | 1379 | 105 | 551 | 965 | .247 | .361 | .315 |
| vs. Left-Handers | | | 2459 | 647 | 46 | 257 | 380 | .263 | .381 | .331 |
| vs. Right-Handers | | | 3120 | 732 | 59 | 294 | 585 | .235 | .346 | .303 |
| Home | 47-35 | 3.58 | 2900 | 714 | 50 | 278 | 538 | .246 | .354 | .313 |
| Road | 39-41 | 3.71 | 2679 | 665 | 55 | 273 | 427 | .248 | .369 | .317 |
| Grass | 21-27 | 3.41 | 1563 | 366 | 37 | 154 | 267 | .234 | .353 | .302 |
| Artificial Turf | 65-49 | 3.74 | 4016 | 1013 | 68 | 397 | 698 | .252 | .365 | .320 |
| April | 11-14 | 3.49 | 867 | 206 | 15 | 81 | 148 | .238 | .345 | .304 |
| May | 16-10 | 3.13 | 907 | 216 | 13 | 96 | 131 | .238 | .343 | .313 |
| June | 18-10 | 3.02 | 992 | 246 | 18 | 104 | 175 | .248 | .357 | .318 |
| July | 15-11 | 3.99 | 900 | 241 | 18 | 80 | 169 | .268 | .389 | .330 |
| August | 11-17 | 4.81 | 984 | 272 | 24 | 94 | 178 | .276 | .407 | .339 |
| Sept./Oct. | 15-14 | 3.46 | 929 | 198 | 17 | 96 | 164 | .213 | .325 | .286 |
| Leading Off Inn. | | | 1359 | 327 | 27 | 120 | 237 | .241 | .351 | .305 |
| Runners On | | | 2398 | 622 | 45 | 276 | 409 | .259 | .381 | .334 |
| Runners/Scor. Pos. | | | 1449 | 364 | 19 | 229 | 276 | .251 | .358 | .349 |
| Runners On/2 Out | | | 1009 | 223 | 16 | 149 | 191 | .221 | .336 | .325 |
| Scor. Pos./2 Out | | | 678 | 143 | 10 | 127 | 139 | .211 | .327 | .340 |
| Late Inning Pressure | | | 1063 | 221 | 16 | 103 | 207 | .208 | .284 | .278 |
| Leading Off | | | 279 | 66 | 4 | 25 | 59 | .237 | .305 | .299 |
| Runners On | | | 410 | 85 | 7 | 49 | 79 | .207 | .278 | .290 |
| Runners/Scor. Pos. | | | 238 | 43 | 3 | 44 | 50 | .181 | .235 | .304 |
| First 9 Batters | | | 2987 | 715 | 46 | 289 | 589 | .239 | .339 | .307 |
| Second 9 Batters | | | 1367 | 369 | 31 | 136 | 201 | .270 | .413 | .335 |
| All Batters Thereafter | | | 1225 | 295 | 28 | 126 | 175 | .241 | .358 | .313 |

Starting pitchers: 57–55, 3.91 ERA
Relief pitchers: 29–21 3.16 ERA
Ground outs-to-air outs ratio: 1.03, 2d lowest in N.L. . . . Opponents' batting average in Late-Inning Pressure Situations was 3d lowest in N.L. over the last 15 years. . . . Opponents' mark with runners in scoring position in LIPS was best in N.L. during that time. Major league low was .171 by 1988 Tigers. . . . Finally, with two outs and runners on base in LIPS, Astros opponents had lowest mark in majors since 1975. . . . Won eight of nine games (June 2–10), despite allowing as many runs as they scored. (Eight one-run wins, one eight-run loss). . . . Won 20 of their first 64 games by a single run. Only three other teams this century had as many one-run wins over their first 64 games (1966 Indians, 1978 Giants, 1984 Royals). None had more.

## Los Angeles Dodgers

| | W–L | ERA | AB | H | HR | BB | SO | BA | SA | OBA |
|---|---|---|---|---|---|---|---|---|---|---|
| Season | 77-83 | 2.95 | 5390 | 1278 | 95 | 504 | 1052 | .237 | .339 | .304 |
| vs. Left-Handers | | | 2581 | 630 | 41 | 263 | 484 | .244 | .339 | .315 |
| vs. Right-Handers | | | 2809 | 648 | 54 | 241 | 568 | .231 | .339 | .293 |
| Home | 44-37 | 2.61 | 2744 | 625 | 46 | 232 | 539 | .228 | .316 | .289 |
| Road | 33-46 | 3.30 | 2646 | 653 | 49 | 272 | 513 | .247 | .362 | .318 |
| Grass | 61-57 | 2.81 | 3961 | 932 | 70 | 350 | 783 | .235 | .332 | .298 |
| Artificial Turf | 16-26 | 3.31 | 1429 | 346 | 25 | 154 | 269 | .242 | .357 | .318 |
| April | 11-13 | 2.53 | 806 | 187 | 10 | 71 | 149 | .232 | .325 | .292 |
| May | 14-11 | 2.95 | 827 | 194 | 14 | 78 | 163 | .235 | .328 | .303 |
| June | 12-17 | 2.50 | 1039 | 250 | 18 | 78 | 191 | .241 | .330 | .295 |
| July | 12-16 | 3.75 | 903 | 225 | 13 | 102 | 160 | .249 | .363 | .327 |
| August | 13-14 | 2.85 | 928 | 216 | 22 | 84 | 185 | .233 | .344 | .299 |
| Sept./Oct. | 15-12 | 3.14 | 887 | 206 | 18 | 91 | 204 | .232 | .340 | .304 |
| Leading Off Inn. | | | 1362 | 348 | 24 | 99 | 233 | .256 | .353 | .308 |
| Runners On | | | 2200 | 519 | 36 | 259 | 437 | .236 | .340 | .316 |
| Runners/Scor. Pos. | | | 1256 | 279 | 24 | 197 | 285 | .222 | .338 | .324 |
| Runners On/2 Out | | | 947 | 215 | 14 | 123 | 202 | .227 | .321 | .321 |
| Scor. Pos./2 Out | | | 624 | 130 | 10 | 102 | 147 | .208 | .316 | .324 |
| Late Inning Pressure | | | 1160 | 274 | 16 | 112 | 227 | .236 | .332 | .303 |
| Leading Off | | | 301 | 77 | 5 | 22 | 51 | .256 | .369 | .309 |
| Runners On | | | 467 | 106 | 3 | 61 | 96 | .227 | .302 | .313 |
| Runners/Scor. Pos. | | | 277 | 64 | 1 | 54 | 63 | .231 | .307 | .350 |
| First 9 Batters | | | 2629 | 607 | 47 | 237 | 580 | .231 | .335 | .296 |
| Second 9 Batters | | | 1376 | 336 | 27 | 130 | 244 | .244 | .352 | .312 |
| All Batters Thereafter | | | 1385 | 335 | 21 | 137 | 228 | .242 | .332 | .309 |

Starting pitchers: 58–65, 3.02 ERA
Relief pitchers: 19–18 2.75 ERA
Ground outs-to-air outs ratio: 1.10. . . . First club since 1972 Cleveland Indians with a losing record despite an ERA below 3.00. Last N.L. teams: the Dodgers, the Pirates, and the Mets in 1968. . . . Had league's lowest ERA both at home and on the road; both before and after the All-Star break; for both starters and relievers. . . . Led N.L. in shutouts for 6th time during 1980s, and 10th time in last 20 years. . . . Opponents' batting average with runners on base was lowest in N.L. since 1986, when both division winners had lower marks: Houston, .226; New York, .230. . . . Opponents batted .400 with two outs and bases loaded (20-for-50). . . . At the plate, Dodgers' pitchers drew only eight walks last season, the fewest of any N.L. staff.

## Montreal Expos

| | W–L | ERA | AB | H | HR | BB | SO | BA | SA | OBA |
|---|---|---|---|---|---|---|---|---|---|---|
| Season | 81-81 | 3.48 | 5482 | 1344 | 120 | 519 | 1059 | .245 | .367 | .312 |
| vs. Left-Handers | | | 2552 | 619 | 52 | 250 | 445 | .243 | .363 | .312 |
| vs. Right-Handers | | | 2930 | 725 | 68 | 269 | 614 | .247 | .370 | .312 |
| Home | 44-37 | 3.22 | 2827 | 676 | 60 | 248 | 572 | .239 | .356 | .302 |
| Road | 37-44 | 3.75 | 2655 | 668 | 60 | 271 | 487 | .252 | .379 | .322 |
| Grass | 17-25 | 3.84 | 1351 | 346 | 33 | 135 | 271 | .256 | .383 | .328 |
| Artificial Turf | 64-56 | 3.36 | 4131 | 998 | 87 | 384 | 788 | .242 | .361 | .307 |
| April | 13-11 | 3.86 | 800 | 205 | 14 | 86 | 129 | .256 | .376 | .327 |
| May | 14-14 | 4.18 | 965 | 250 | 17 | 93 | 180 | .259 | .379 | .324 |
| June | 17-10 | 2.85 | 913 | 206 | 20 | 83 | 163 | .226 | .341 | .294 |
| July | 17-9 | 2.73 | 882 | 200 | 13 | 90 | 201 | .227 | .313 | .299 |
| August | 11-17 | 3.45 | 977 | 239 | 32 | 75 | 193 | .245 | .384 | .300 |
| Sept./Oct. | 9-20 | 3.81 | 945 | 244 | 24 | 92 | 193 | .258 | .403 | .328 |
| Leading Off Inn. | | | 1374 | 365 | 41 | 94 | 236 | .266 | .408 | .315 |
| Runners On | | | 2267 | 557 | 45 | 262 | 450 | .246 | .371 | .322 |
| Runners/Scor. Pos. | | | 1324 | 316 | 28 | 193 | 296 | .239 | .374 | .328 |
| Runners On/2 Out | | | 992 | 230 | 17 | 160 | 213 | .232 | .349 | .340 |
| Scor. Pos./2 Out | | | 665 | 143 | 13 | 124 | 154 | .215 | .334 | .339 |
| Late Inning Pressure | | | 1079 | 293 | 24 | 110 | 190 | .272 | .388 | .340 |
| Leading Off | | | 272 | 86 | 14 | 27 | 31 | .316 | .522 | .380 |
| Runners On | | | 458 | 123 | 6 | 64 | 83 | .269 | .362 | .355 |
| Runners/Scor. Pos. | | | 263 | 68 | 4 | 52 | 52 | .259 | .357 | .370 |
| First 9 Batters | | | 2645 | 635 | 55 | 265 | 521 | .240 | .352 | .309 |
| Second 9 Batters | | | 1359 | 337 | 32 | 118 | 272 | .248 | .384 | .311 |
| All Batters Thereafter | | | 1478 | 372 | 33 | 136 | 266 | .252 | .376 | .317 |

Starting pitchers: 58–60, 3.44 ERA
Relief pitchers: 23–21, 3.60 ERA
Ground outs-to-air outs ratio: 1.33, highest in majors. . . . Only team in the majors to throw shutouts in three consecutive games. . . . Starters led the major leagues with an average of 6.70 innings pitched per start. . . . Won 19 of 20 games in which their starter pitched a complete game. Only complete-game loss was by Dennis Martinez during the final week. . . . Expos pitchers hit Mets batters with 10 pitches, highest total by one club against another. . . . Only N.L. club without a home run hit by a pitcher in either of the last two seasons. Last was hit on April 28, 1987, by Floyd Youmans. . . . Different pitcher has led team in strikeouts in each of the last seven seasons: Rogers, Lea, Smith, Youmans, Sebra, Perez, Langston.

## New York Mets

| | W–L | ERA | AB | H | HR | BB | SO | BA | SA | OBA |
|---|---|---|---|---|---|---|---|---|---|---|
| Season | 87-75 | 3.29 | 5443 | 1260 | 115 | 532 | 1108 | .231 | .348 | .301 |
| vs. Left-Handers | | | 2097 | 507 | 37 | 220 | 390 | .242 | .359 | .314 |
| vs. Right-Handers | | | 3346 | 753 | 78 | 312 | 718 | .225 | .342 | .292 |
| Home | 51-30 | 2.92 | 2767 | 607 | 56 | 257 | 615 | .219 | .326 | .287 |
| Road | 36-45 | 3.68 | 2676 | 653 | 59 | 275 | 493 | .244 | .371 | .315 |
| Grass | 63-51 | 3.35 | 3878 | 900 | 91 | 362 | 816 | .232 | .352 | .298 |
| Artificial Turf | 24-24 | 3.16 | 1565 | 360 | 24 | 170 | 292 | .230 | .340 | .306 |
| April | 12-10 | 3.18 | 725 | 165 | 11 | 77 | 136 | .228 | .320 | .303 |
| May | 13-14 | 2.54 | 912 | 205 | 17 | 91 | 211 | .225 | .326 | .294 |
| June | 15-11 | 3.73 | 896 | 215 | 19 | 107 | 174 | .240 | .383 | .324 |
| July | 13-15 | 4.47 | 922 | 229 | 27 | 94 | 169 | .248 | .380 | .319 |
| August | 19-10 | 2.73 | 980 | 226 | 21 | 85 | 183 | .231 | .355 | .291 |
| Sept./Oct. | 15-15 | 3.16 | 1008 | 220 | 20 | 78 | 235 | .218 | .323 | .276 |
| Leading Off Inn. | | | 1358 | 278 | 23 | 98 | 277 | .205 | .301 | .262 |
| Runners On | | | 2206 | 539 | 52 | 254 | 445 | .244 | .370 | .320 |
| Runners/Scor. Pos. | | | 1271 | 300 | 28 | 193 | 301 | .236 | .363 | .330 |
| Runners On/2 Out | | | 991 | 219 | 24 | 141 | 208 | .221 | .343 | .321 |
| Scor. Pos./2 Out | | | 635 | 131 | 14 | 107 | 151 | .206 | .324 | .324 |
| Late Inning Pressure | | | 1005 | 235 | 18 | 104 | 226 | .234 | .331 | .307 |
| Leading Off | | | 262 | 59 | 5 | 14 | 66 | .225 | .340 | .270 |
| Runners On | | | 402 | 97 | 7 | 55 | 86 | .241 | .336 | .331 |
| Runners/Scor. Pos. | | | 233 | 50 | 4 | 42 | 53 | .215 | .313 | .330 |
| First 9 Batters | | | 2653 | 587 | 45 | 275 | 575 | .221 | .323 | .295 |
| Second 9 Batters | | | 1401 | 349 | 32 | 124 | 289 | .249 | .376 | .311 |
| All Batters Thereafter | | | 1389 | 324 | 38 | 133 | 244 | .233 | .368 | .302 |

Starting pitchers: 69–50, 3.43 ERA
Relief pitchers: 18–25, 2.96 ERA
Ground outs-to-air outs ratio: 0.88, lowest in majors. . . . Opponents' on-base average leading off innings was lowest in majors since the 1975 Dodgers (.262). . . . Issued the fewest intentional walks (45) in the N.L., as they had in three of four previous seasons. . . . Relievers allowed 19 home runs, or one per 21 innings, best rate in majors. . . . Only team in the majors that did not get a victory from a rookie pitcher. . . . Mets pitchers had the highest batting average (.163) and scored the most runs (27) of any N.L. staff. . . . Only major league team that's never used a position player as a pitcher. Dave Kingman pitched for the Giants, but never for the Mets.

## Phila. Phillies

| | W–L | ERA | AB | H | HR | BB | SO | BA | SA | OBA |
|---|---|---|---|---|---|---|---|---|---|---|
| Season | 67-95 | 4.04 | 5445 | 1408 | 127 | 613 | 899 | .259 | .393 | .335 |
| vs. Left-Handers | | | 1909 | 476 | 39 | 256 | 295 | .249 | .381 | .339 |
| vs. Right-Handers | | | 3536 | 932 | 88 | 357 | 604 | .264 | .400 | .332 |
| Home | 38-42 | 3.97 | 2793 | 714 | 67 | 319 | 464 | .256 | .394 | .334 |
| Road | 29-53 | 4.12 | 2652 | 694 | 60 | 294 | 435 | .262 | .393 | .336 |
| Grass | 14-28 | 4.50 | 1358 | 363 | 33 | 138 | 234 | .267 | .404 | .336 |
| Artificial Turf | 53-67 | 3.89 | 4087 | 1045 | 94 | 475 | 665 | .256 | .390 | .334 |
| April | 11-12 | 3.91 | 732 | 180 | 23 | 90 | 110 | .246 | .388 | .327 |
| May | 7-19 | 4.66 | 854 | 231 | 19 | 104 | 142 | .270 | .420 | .354 |
| June | 9-17 | 4.63 | 906 | 242 | 19 | 119 | 128 | .267 | .415 | .353 |
| July | 15-14 | 3.00 | 991 | 235 | 22 | 97 | 162 | .237 | .350 | .307 |
| August | 12-17 | 4.28 | 965 | 245 | 27 | 101 | 178 | .254 | .398 | .328 |
| Sept./Oct. | 13-16 | 3.90 | 997 | 275 | 17 | 102 | 179 | .276 | .392 | .341 |
| Leading Off Inn. | | | 1295 | 315 | 30 | 131 | 215 | .243 | .385 | .317 |
| Runners On | | | 2359 | 633 | 49 | 337 | 387 | .268 | .397 | .358 |
| Runners/Scor. Pos. | | | 1419 | 385 | 27 | 255 | 251 | .271 | .400 | .377 |
| Runners On/2 Out | | | 1023 | 256 | 23 | 149 | 182 | .250 | .381 | .348 |
| Scor. Pos./2 Out | | | 687 | 170 | 14 | 121 | 129 | .247 | .371 | .363 |
| Late Inning Pressure | | | 889 | 204 | 16 | 115 | 163 | .229 | .331 | .320 |
| Leading Off | | | 221 | 42 | 4 | 24 | 33 | .190 | .303 | .275 |
| Runners On | | | 343 | 85 | 8 | 68 | 66 | .248 | .347 | .369 |
| Runners/Scor. Pos. | | | 208 | 53 | 6 | 54 | 50 | .255 | .380 | .402 |
| First 9 Batters | | | 2983 | 749 | 55 | 341 | 541 | .251 | .375 | .330 |
| Second 9 Batters | | | 1413 | 372 | 48 | 146 | 210 | .263 | .426 | .331 |
| All Batters Thereafter | | | 1049 | 287 | 24 | 126 | 148 | .274 | .400 | .353 |

Starting pitchers: 44–75, 4.23 ERA
Relief pitchers: 23–20, 3.77 ERA
Ground outs-to-air outs ratio: 1.23. . . . Had N.L.'s best record in home games in which they led after six innings (25–1). . . . Tied N.L. record for most wild pitches (91 by the 1970 Astors), but their catchers had fewest passed balls (6) in the majors. Pitchers shut out catchers, 47–0, in road games. . . . Ranked seventh in N.L. in fielding percentage, but allowed the most unearned runs (91). . . . Record of 7–3 in games in which their starter pitched a complete game was worst in N.L. League winning percentage: .885. . . . Opponents' batting average leading off innings in Late-Inning Pressure Situations was lowest in N.L. over last 15 years. . . . Lowest batting average (.097) and fewest RBI (9) of any N.L. staff.

## Pittsburgh Pirates

| | W-L | ERA | AB | H | HR | BB | SO | BA | SA | OBA |
|---|---|---|---|---|---|---|---|---|---|---|
| Season | 74-88 | 3.64 | 5627 | 1394 | 121 | 539 | 827 | .248 | .368 | .314 |
| vs. Left-Handers | | | 2357 | 582 | 33 | 269 | 284 | .247 | .348 | .324 |
| vs. Right-Handers | | | 3270 | 812 | 88 | 270 | 543 | .248 | .382 | .308 |
| Home | 39-42 | 3.10 | 2873 | 680 | 62 | 263 | 435 | .237 | .348 | .302 |
| Road | 35-46 | 4.22 | 2754 | 714 | 59 | 276 | 392 | .259 | .389 | .327 |
| Grass | 18-24 | 4.04 | 1407 | 361 | 31 | 130 | 193 | .257 | .382 | .320 |
| Artificial Turf | 56-64 | 3.51 | 4220 | 1033 | 90 | 409 | 634 | .245 | .363 | .313 |
| April | 10-14 | 3.61 | 818 | 202 | 9 | 88 | 99 | .247 | .345 | .320 |
| May | 11-14 | 3.16 | 865 | 204 | 19 | 79 | 114 | .236 | .358 | .303 |
| June | 12-13 | 4.42 | 888 | 227 | 24 | 109 | 146 | .256 | .400 | .336 |
| July | 12-18 | 3.75 | 1010 | 247 | 29 | 101 | 146 | .245 | .389 | .317 |
| August | 13-15 | 3.32 | 988 | 243 | 21 | 86 | 140 | .246 | .356 | .304 |
| Sept./Oct. | 16-14 | 3.63 | 1058 | 271 | 19 | 76 | 182 | .256 | .357 | .307 |
| Leading Off Inn. | | | 1386 | 332 | 34 | 105 | 198 | .240 | .366 | .295 |
| Runners On | | | 2333 | 622 | 56 | 273 | 332 | .267 | .395 | .341 |
| Runners/Scor. Pos. | | | 1463 | 379 | 35 | 220 | 229 | .259 | .392 | .351 |
| Runners On/2 Out | | | 1038 | 267 | 19 | 153 | 160 | .257 | .362 | .356 |
| Scor. Pos./2 Out | | | 726 | 176 | 10 | 130 | 117 | .242 | .336 | .363 |
| Late Inning Pressure | | | 1195 | 272 | 23 | 129 | 201 | .228 | .344 | .304 |
| Leading Off | | | 311 | 74 | 7 | 28 | 49 | .238 | .363 | .305 |
| Runners On | | | 461 | 111 | 9 | 67 | 78 | .241 | .351 | .334 |
| Runners/Scor. Pos. | | | 296 | 68 | 5 | 61 | 54 | .230 | .345 | .354 |
| First 9 Batters | | | 2903 | 680 | 47 | 313 | 468 | .234 | .337 | .310 |
| Second 9 Batters | | | 1445 | 366 | 32 | 118 | 226 | .253 | .366 | .311 |
| All Batters Thereafter | | | 1279 | 348 | 42 | 108 | 133 | .272 | .440 | .328 |

Starting pitchers: 55–63, 3.71 ERA
Relief pitchers: 19–25, 3.49 ERA
Ground outs-to-air outs ratio: 1.03, 3d lowest in N.L. . . . Used 20 different pitchers out of the bullpen, most in the majors. Also had major league–high total of eight pitchers with saves. . . . Pirates'opponents stole 190 bases. To put that in perspective, it was 25 more than any team's baserunners stole. . . . Haven't pitched consecutive shutouts since September 1984. . . . Pirates pitchers had the most RBI (27) of any staff in the league. . . . Had the N.L.'s lowest ERA vs. Houston (2.53) and San Francisco (3.14), but the highest against Philadelphia (5.42). . . . Season series against the Astros and the Mets produced five extra-inning games apiece. Only one other 1989 matchup produced as many (Royals vs. Brewers).

## San Diego Padres

| | W–L | ERA | AB | H | HR | BB | SO | BA | SA | OBA |
|---|---|---|---|---|---|---|---|---|---|---|
| Season | 89-73 | 3.38 | 5465 | 1359 | 133 | 481 | 933 | .249 | .376 | .310 |
| vs. Left-Handers | | | 2163 | 548 | 52 | 217 | 331 | .253 | .381 | .322 |
| vs. Right-Handers | | | 3302 | 811 | 81 | 264 | 602 | .246 | .373 | .302 |
| Home | 46 35 | 3.43 | 2755 | 676 | 82 | 257 | 496 | .245 | .384 | .310 |
| Road | 43-38 | 3.32 | 2710 | 683 | 51 | 224 | 437 | .252 | .368 | .309 |
| Grass | 66-54 | 3.41 | 4108 | 1024 | 116 | 366 | 710 | .249 | .385 | .310 |
| Artificial Turf | 23-19 | 3.28 | 1357 | 335 | 17 | 115 | 223 | .247 | .349 | .307 |
| April | 14-12 | 3.62 | 876 | 221 | 25 | 64 | 151 | .252 | .398 | .308 |
| May | 15-13 | 2.80 | 937 | 228 | 21 | 88 | 143 | .243 | .358 | .310 |
| June | 10-16 | 3.80 | 922 | 247 | 26 | 73 | 151 | .268 | .408 | .319 |
| July | 12-13 | 3.82 | 823 | 222 | 20 | 77 | 132 | .270 | .413 | .332 |
| August | 18-11 | 3.38 | 954 | 220 | 26 | 85 | 159 | .231 | .364 | .293 |
| Sept./Oct. | 20-8 | 2.96 | 953 | 221 | 15 | 94 | 197 | .232 | .324 | .300 |
| Leading Off Inn. | | | 1346 | 335 | 29 | 104 | 221 | .249 | .372 | .308 |
| Runners On | | | 2244 | 577 | 56 | 237 | 373 | .257 | .388 | .323 |
| Runners/Scor. Pos. | | | 1208 | 301 | 29 | 184 | 226 | .249 | .377 | .339 |
| Runners On/2 Out | | | 989 | 255 | 22 | 128 | 178 | .258 | .375 | .343 |
| Scor. Pos./2 Out | | | 613 | 145 | 12 | 105 | 121 | .237 | .341 | .349 |
| Late Inning Pressure | | | 1019 | 228 | 26 | 89 | 194 | .224 | .330 | .290 |
| Leading Off | | | 260 | 54 | 8 | 18 | 54 | .208 | .315 | .267 |
| Runners On | | | 377 | 87 | 9 | 47 | 76 | .231 | .337 | .313 |
| Runners/Scor. Pos. | | | 193 | 36 | 3 | 38 | 48 | .187 | .264 | .315 |
| First 9 Batters | | | 2609 | 637 | 73 | 243 | 506 | .244 | .378 | .309 |
| Second 9 Batters | | | 1434 | 358 | 25 | 120 | 223 | .250 | .368 | .307 |
| All Batters Thereafter | | | 1422 | 364 | 35 | 118 | 204 | .256 | .382 | .312 |

Starting pitchers: 68–60, 3.46 ERA
Relief pitchers: 21–13, 3.19 ERA
Ground outs-to-air outs ratio: 1.24, 3d highest in N.L. . . . Opponents stole only 68 bases, fewest of any team in majors. . . . Only major league team not to allow a grand slam home run. Opposing batters hit .162 was bases loaded, 2d-lowest mark in N.L. over last 15 years. . . . Padres led majors in sacrifice bunts, despite the fact that their pitchers contributed fewer than those of any other N.L. team (31). . . . Pitchers struck out 170 times, by far the most of any staff. . . . Used only 11 different pitchers out of the bullpen, fewest of any N.L. club. . . . Relievers averaged 6.99 batters faced per appearance, most in the league. . . . Allowed 22 home runs to the Braves, the most of any club against any other club.

## St. Louis Cardinals

| | W-L | ERA | AB | H | HR | BB | SO | BA | SA | OBA |
|---|---|---|---|---|---|---|---|---|---|---|
| Season | 86-76 | 3.36 | 5468 | 1330 | 84 | 482 | 844 | .243 | .358 | .306 |
| vs. Left-Handers | | | 2396 | 613 | 33 | 264 | 341 | .256 | .365 | .330 |
| vs. Right-Handers | | | 3072 | 717 | 51 | 218 | 503 | .233 | .353 | .286 |
| Home | 46-35 | 3.26 | 2835 | 682 | 36 | 242 | 414 | .241 | .352 | .302 |
| Road | 40-41 | 3.47 | 2633 | 648 | 48 | 240 | 430 | .246 | .365 | .310 |
| Grass | 20-22 | 3.34 | 1367 | 338 | 27 | 119 | 232 | .247 | .357 | .309 |
| Artificial Turf | 66-54 | 3.37 | 4101 | 992 | 57 | 363 | 612 | .242 | .359 | .304 |
| April | 13-9 | 3.07 | 737 | 172 | 12 | 54 | 102 | .233 | .360 | .289 |
| May | 10-16 | 3.16 | 917 | 233 | 10 | 95 | 157 | .254 | .341 | .323 |
| June | 15-12 | 4.01 | 906 | 232 | 15 | 99 | 136 | .256 | .391 | .329 |
| July | 16-10 | 2.80 | 830 | 176 | 11 | 60 | 141 | .212 | .307 | .268 |
| August | 18-13 | 3.44 | 1020 | 234 | 15 | 81 | 144 | .229 | .345 | .289 |
| Sept./Oct. | 14-16 | 3.59 | 1058 | 283 | 21 | 93 | 164 | .267 | .397 | .327 |
| Leading Off Inn. | | | 1345 | 317 | 19 | 112 | 200 | .236 | .346 | .298 |
| Runners On | | | 2249 | 581 | 40 | 248 | 341 | .258 | .384 | .330 |
| Runners/Scor. Pos. | | | 1350 | 351 | 22 | 200 | 218 | .260 | .386 | .348 |
| Runners On/2 Out | | | 950 | 207 | 14 | 120 | 161 | .218 | .327 | .309 |
| Scor. Pos./2 Out | | | 634 | 133 | 10 | 101 | 114 | .210 | .320 | .320 |
| Late Inning Pressure | | | 1024 | 242 | 15 | 109 | 166 | .236 | .343 | .309 |
| Leading Off | | | 264 | 54 | 5 | 18 | 39 | .205 | .311 | .263 |
| Runners On | | | 395 | 100 | 7 | 66 | 63 | .253 | .372 | .353 |
| Runners/Scor. Pos. | | | 237 | 63 | 4 | 59 | 47 | .266 | .405 | .400 |
| First 9 Batters | | | 2891 | 691 | 45 | 252 | 483 | .239 | .363 | .300 |
| Second 9 Batters | | | 1376 | 328 | 21 | 107 | 198 | .238 | .351 | .294 |
| All Batters Thereafter | | | 1201 | 311 | 18 | 123 | 163 | .259 | .356 | .332 |

Starting pitchers: 57–60, 3.46 ERA
Relief pitchers: 29–16 3.16 ERA
Ground outs-to-air outs ratio: 1.27, 2d highest in N.L. . . . Cardinals pitchers collected 43 sacrifice bunts last season, tied with the Cubs and Dodgers for the most of any staff. They grounded into only one double play (Jose DeLeon). . . . Cardinals relievers averaged 5.13 batters faced per appearance, fewest of any club in the majors. Whitey changed pitchers 358 times, most of any manager. . . . Allowed 67 first inning runs, the fewest in the majors. . . . Allowed only two home runs to Dodgers' batters last season, the fewest hit by any N.L. club against any other. . . . Cardinals-Giants series was the only one in the N.L. in which every games was decided by more than one run.

## San Francisco Giants

| | W–L | ERA | AB | H | HR | BB | SO | BA | SA | OBA |
|---|---|---|---|---|---|---|---|---|---|---|
| Season | 92-70 | 3.30 | 5425 | 1320 | 120 | 471 | 802 | .243 | .365 | .304 |
| vs. Left-Handers | | | 2535 | 652 | 47 | 248 | 314 | .257 | .372 | .323 |
| vs. Right-Handers | | | 2890 | 668 | 73 | 223 | 488 | .231 | .358 | .287 |
| Home | 53-28 | 2.72 | 2736 | 640 | 61 | 222 | 430 | .234 | .351 | .291 |
| Road | 39-42 | 3.92 | 2689 | 680 | 59 | 249 | 372 | .253 | .379 | .316 |
| Grass | 73-47 | 3.04 | 4021 | 965 | 90 | 343 | 610 | .240 | .357 | .299 |
| Artificial Turf | 19-23 | 4.10 | 1404 | 355 | 30 | 128 | 192 | .253 | .386 | .317 |
| April | 12-12 | 3.64 | 796 | 203 | 16 | 89 | 120 | .255 | .376 | .328 |
| May | 17-10 | 1.99 | 893 | 193 | 12 | 79 | 134 | .216 | .302 | .280 |
| June | 18-10 | 3.33 | 937 | 239 | 19 | 71 | 125 | .255 | .364 | .308 |
| July | 14-12 | 3.96 | 882 | 236 | 22 | 76 | 144 | .268 | .402 | .326 |
| August | 14-14 | 3.38 | 933 | 214 | 21 | 94 | 115 | .229 | .355 | .302 |
| Sept./Oct. | 17-12 | 3.60 | 984 | 235 | 30 | 62 | 164 | .239 | .388 | .283 |
| Leading Off Inn. | | | 1355 | 336 | 30 | 101 | 191 | .248 | .367 | .302 |
| Runners On | | | 2206 | 541 | 55 | 216 | 322 | .245 | .375 | .310 |
| Runners/Scor. Pos. | | | 1231 | 296 | 35 | 156 | 198 | .240 | .384 | .318 |
| Runners On/2 Out | | | 944 | 195 | 24 | 106 | 153 | .207 | .327 | .289 |
| Scor. Pos./2 Out | | | 588 | 116 | 17 | 81 | 102 | .197 | .321 | .297 |
| Late Inning Pressure | | | 968 | 221 | 14 | 99 | 152 | .228 | .325 | .299 |
| Leading Off | | | 253 | 60 | 2 | 12 | 39 | .237 | .304 | .274 |
| Runners On | | | 380 | 79 | 9 | 60 | 61 | .208 | .316 | .311 |
| Runners/Scor. Pos. | | | 220 | 43 | 5 | 50 | 38 | .195 | .286 | .336 |
| First 9 Batters | | | 2927 | 700 | 66 | 288 | 468 | .239 | .358 | .307 |
| Second 9 Batters | | | 1426 | 348 | 34 | 106 | 201 | .244 | .371 | .297 |
| All Batters Thereafter | | | 1072 | 272 | 20 | 77 | 133 | .254 | .373 | .304 |

Starting pitchers: 68–49, 3.42 ERA
Relief pitchers: 24–21, 3.08 ERA
Ground outs-to-air outs ratio: 1.09. . . . Although Giants' starters ranked second in the N.L. with a 3.42 ERA, they ranked eleventh in innings pitched per start (5.89). . . . Starters lost fewer games than any N.L. club. . . . Only N.L. team that had more wild pitches thrown by their bullpen than by their starters. . . . Opponents' batting average with two outs and runners on base was lowest in N.L. since 1986. Ditto with two outs and runners in scoring position. . . . Rookies combined for a 11–7 record, best winning percentage (.611) of any N.L. club. Others with winning records: Cubs (7–5) and Padres (14–12). . . . World Series ERA of 8.21 was the 2d highest in history, behind the 1932 Cubs (9.26), who were swept by the Yankees.

## National League

| | W–L | ERA | AB | H | HR | BB | SO | BA | SA | OBA |
|---|---|---|---|---|---|---|---|---|---|---|
| Season | 973-973 | 3.49 | 65817 | 16215 | 1365 | 6251 | 11354 | .246 | .365 | .312 |
| vs. Left-Handers | | | 28008 | 7061 | 501 | 3003 | 4413 | .252 | .366 | .325 |
| vs. Right-Handers | | | 37809 | 9154 | 864 | 3248 | 6941 | .242 | .365 | .303 |
| Home | 527-443 | 3.32 | 33722 | 8163 | 716 | 3099 | 5991 | .242 | .359 | .307 |
| Road | 443-527 | 3.68 | 32095 | 8052 | 649 | 3152 | 5363 | .251 | .372 | .318 |
| Grass | 484-484 | 3.40 | 32584 | 7963 | 730 | 2961 | 5799 | .244 | .363 | .308 |
| Artificial Turf | 489-489 | 3.59 | 33233 | 8252 | 635 | 3290 | 5555 | .248 | .367 | .317 |
| April | 142-142 | 3.45 | 9498 | 2309 | 185 | 916 | 1549 | .243 | .360 | .310 |
| May | 160-160 | 3.13 | 10793 | 2578 | 179 | 1056 | 1842 | .239 | .343 | .308 |
| June | 164-164 | 3.64 | 11220 | 2835 | 231 | 1122 | 1875 | .253 | .375 | .321 |
| July | 162-162 | 3.56 | 10867 | 2689 | 228 | 1011 | 1893 | .247 | .366 | .313 |
| August | 171-171 | 3.62 | 11688 | 2884 | 294 | 1087 | 1973 | .247 | .377 | .312 |
| Sept./Oct. | 174-174 | 3.56 | 11751 | 2920 | 248 | 1059 | 2222 | .248 | .368 | .311 |
| Leading Off Inn. | | | 16259 | 3991 | 355 | 1253 | 2656 | .245 | .366 | .302 |
| Runners On | | | 27393 | 7002 | 584 | 3155 | 4711 | .256 | .379 | .330 |
| Runners/Scor. Pos. | | | 15956 | 3966 | 320 | 2422 | 3070 | .249 | .372 | .341 |
| Runners On/2 Out | | | 11899 | 2787 | 230 | 1628 | 2236 | .234 | .347 | .329 |
| Scor. Pos./2 Out | | | 7769 | 1722 | 147 | 1319 | 1586 | .222 | .333 | .337 |
| Late Inning Pressure | | | 12446 | 2924 | 220 | 1324 | 2406 | .235 | .336 | .309 |
| Leading Off | | | 3192 | 770 | 63 | 262 | 585 | .241 | .348 | .302 |
| Runners On | | | 4988 | 1191 | 93 | 722 | 970 | .239 | .340 | .331 |
| Runners/Scor. Pos. | | | 2930 | 661 | 47 | 598 | 651 | .226 | .322 | .349 |
| First 9 Batters | | | 33960 | 8129 | 638 | 3370 | 6493 | .239 | .352 | .309 |
| Second 9 Batters | | | 16800 | 4234 | 382 | 1480 | 2721 | .252 | .380 | .313 |
| All Batters Thereafter | | | 15057 | 3852 | 345 | 1401 | 2140 | .256 | .380 | .320 |

# V
# Rankings Section

# *Rankings Section*

The Rankings Section consists of a series of lists ranking players in a wide variety of batting and pitching categories. Players are ranked in 24 batting categories and 24 pitching categories ranging from the simple (batting average, for example) to the more esoteric (like percentage of runners driven in from third base with less than two out). Listed are the players ranking in the top 20 and bottom 20 in each league.

The exact number of plate appearances required to qualify for ranking in each category varies. The number of eligible players for each ranking is determined by the number of players in each league who had 200 or more plate appearances, or who faced 200 or more batters. In the American League, the 171 players and 155 pitchers with the most plate appearances or batters faced in a given category are eligible for ranking; in the National League, the top 132 batters and 123 pitchers are eligible. (If there is a tie for the final position, all tied players are included.) In some categories, a large number of players tied for last place (as, for example, in Home Run Percentage vs. Left-Handed Pitchers). In such cases, a line indicating "42 players tied with 0.00" is used in place of the Bottom 20 list.

The material in this section is generally based on the categories used in the Batter and Pitcher Sections. If any of the breakdowns are unfamiliar, detailed descriptions can be found in the introductions to the Batter and Pitcher Sections.

## Batting Average vs. Left-Handed Pitchers

### American League

| Top 20 | | | Bottom 20 | | |
|---|---|---|---|---|---|
| 1. Carney Lansford | OAK | .389 | 173. Brady Anderson | BAL | .129 |
| 2. Alvaro Espinoza | NY | .383 | 172. Jack Howell | CAL | .140 |
| 3. Steve Sax | NY | .381 | 171. Mel Hall | NY | .159 |
| 4. Roberto Kelly | NY | .372 | 170. Bob Brenly | TOR | .165 |
| 5. Gene Larkin | MIN | .365 | 169. Brad Komminsk | CLE | .169 |
| 6. Pat Tabler | KC | .350 | 168. Mike Macfarlane | KC | .172 |
| 7. Kevin Romine | BOS | .346 | 167. Fred Lynn | DET | .175 |
| 7. Sammy Sosa | CHI | .346 | 166. Gus Polidor | MIL | .176 |
| 7. Mookie Wilson | TOR | .346 | 165. Bill Schroeder | CAL | .182 |
| 10. Ruben Sierra | TEX | .341 | 164. Lou Whitaker | DET | .188 |
| 11. Robin Yount | MIL | .341 | 163. Lloyd Moseby | TOR | .196 |
| 12. Don Mattingly | NY | .338 | 162. Omar Vizquel | SEA | .196 |
| 13. Jim Eisenreich | KC | .336 | 161. Dave Bergman | DET | .200 |
| 14. Greg Brock | MIL | .333 | 160. Junior Felix | TOR | .202 |
| 15. Ivan Calderon | CHI | .332 | 159. Joe Orsulak | BAL | .202 |
| 16. Jim Presley | SEA | .328 | 158. Glenn Hoffman | CAL | .207 |
| 17. Kelly Gruber | TOR | .325 | 157. Russ Morman | CHI | .208 |
| 18. Carlton Fisk | CHI | .325 | 156. Pete Incaviglia | TEX | .209 |
| 19. Paul Molitor | MIL | .325 | 155. Stan Jefferson | BAL | .210 |
| 20. Harold Reynolds | SEA | .324 | 154. Ken Griffey Jr. | SEA | .212 |

### National League

| Top 20 | | | Bottom 20 | | |
|---|---|---|---|---|---|
| 1. Andres Galarraga | MTL | .385 | 132. Ron Gant | ATL | .114 |
| 2. Domingo Ramos | CHI | .373 | 131. John Russell | ATL | .118 |
| 3. Barry Larkin | CIN | .372 | 130. Kirk Gibson | LA | .126 |
| 4. Joe Oliver | CIN | .346 | 129. Willie McGee | STL | .156 |
| 5. Damon Berryhill | CHI | .340 | 128. Mookie Wilson | NY | .164 |
| 6. Lloyd McClendon | CHI | .339 | 127. Gary Carter | NY | .167 |
| 7. Shawon Dunston | CHI | .338 | 126. John Shelby | LA | .168 |
| 8. Gerald Perry | ATL | .337 | 125. Rick Dempsey | LA | .171 |
| 9. Ricky Jordan | PHI | .333 | 124. Ron Oester | CIN | .175 |
| 10. Bip Roberts | SD | .325 | 123. Paul O'Neill | CIN | .178 |
| 11. Glenn Wilson | HOU | .322 | 122. Lenny Harris | LA | .191 |
| 12. Lonnie Smith | ATL | .321 | 121. Kal Daniels | LA | .193 |
| 13. Will Clark | SF | .321 | 120. Jeff King | PIT | .196 |
| 14. Mickey Hatcher | LA | .321 | 119. Bob Dernier | PHI | .197 |
| 15. Jerome Walton | CHI | .320 | 118. Jeff Treadway | ATL | .198 |
| 16. Garry Templeton | SD | .317 | 117. Jody Davis | ATL | .204 |
| 17. Pedro Guerrero | STL | .317 | 116. Kirt Manwaring | SF | .205 |
| 18. Ken Caminiti | HOU | .315 | 115. John Cangelosi | PIT | .207 |
| 19. Ryne Sandberg | CHI | .314 | 114. Andres Thomas | ATL | .208 |
| 20. Mitch Webster | CHI | .311 | 113. Dave Anderson | LA | .209 |

## Batting Average vs. Right-Handed Pitchers

### American League

| Top 20 | | | Bottom 20 | | |
|---|---|---|---|---|---|
| 1. Kirby Puckett | MIN | .354 | 171. Chad Kreuter | TEX | .130 |
| 2. Wade Boggs | BOS | .348 | 170. Rick Schu | DET | .161 |
| 3. Brian Harper | MIN | .335 | 169. Bob Melvin | BAL | .165 |
| 4. Harold Baines | TEX | .330 | 168. Mike Brumley | DET | .181 |
| 5. Julio Franco | TEX | .328 | 167. Kenny Williams | DET | .186 |
| 6. Mike Greenwell | BOS | .327 | 166. Mike Pagliarulo | NY | .189 |
| 7. Lance Johnson | CHI | .320 | 165. Rob Deer | MIL | .193 |
| 8. George Brett | KC | .317 | 164. Pat Tabler | KC | .196 |
| 9. Carney Lansford | OAK | .316 | 163. Bill Buckner | KC | .196 |
| 10. Jim Dwyer | MIN | .315 | 162. Cory Snyder | CLE | .197 |
| 11. Geno Petralli | TEX | .314 | 161. Jim Presley | SEA | .197 |
| 12. Paul Molitor | MIL | .312 | 160. Rich Gedman | BOS | .202 |
| 13. Dion James | CLE | .312 | 159. Jim Traber | BAL | .202 |
| 14. Ellis Burks | BOS | .312 | 158. Tim Laudner | MIN | .203 |
| 15. Robin Yount | MIL | .309 | 157. Dick Schofield | CAL | .206 |
| 16. Danny Heep | BOS | .308 | 156. Kent Anderson | CAL | .208 |
| 17. Joe Orsulak | BAL | .307 | 155. Andy Allanson | CLE | .210 |
| 18. Ron Kittle | CHI | .307 | 154. Joey Belle | CLE | .213 |
| 19. Randy Milligan | BAL | .306 | 153. Gene Larkin | MIN | .214 |
| 20. Johnny Ray | CAL | .304 | 152. Chet Lemon | DET | .215 |

### National League

| Top 20 | | | Bottom 20 | | |
|---|---|---|---|---|---|
| 1. Tony Gwynn | SD | .351 | 132. Jody Davis | ATL | .145 |
| 2. Oddibe McDowell | ATL | .344 | 131. Matt Williams | SF | .176 |
| 3. Will Clark | SF | .340 | 130. Carmelo Martinez | SD | .181 |
| 4. Mark Grace | CHI | .336 | 129. Rey Quinones | PIT | .191 |
| 5. Dwight Smith | CHI | .331 | 128. John Shelby | LA | .191 |
| 6. Paul O'Neill | CIN | .330 | 127. Darrell Evans | ATL | .192 |
| 7. Barry Larkin | CIN | .324 | 126. Darren Daulton | PHI | .194 |
| 8. Mike LaValliere | PIT | .321 | 125. Gerald Perry | ATL | .198 |
| 9. Roberto Alomar | SD | .313 | 124. Keith Hernandez | NY | .199 |
| 10. Kevin Bass | HOU | .313 | 123. Andres Galarraga | MTL | .201 |
| 11. John Kruk | PHI | .313 | 121. Craig Reynolds | HOU | .204 |
| 12. Lonnie Smith | ATL | .312 | 121. Ron Gant | ATL | .204 |
| 13. Bobby Bonilla | PIT | .311 | 120. Billy Hatcher | PIT | .205 |
| 14. Jose Oquendo | STL | .309 | 119. Mike Pagliarulo | SD | .205 |
| 15. Pedro Guerrero | STL | .307 | 118. Rob Thompson | SF | .207 |
| 16. Milt Thompson | STL | .304 | 117. Domingo Ramos | CHI | .208 |
| 17. Mackey Sasser | NY | .304 | 116. Vance Law | CHI | .212 |
| 18. Jeff Treadway | ATL | .300 | 115. Curt Ford | PHI | .213 |
| 19. Eric Davis | CIN | .297 | 114. Andres Thomas | ATL | .215 |
| 20. Ken Oberkfell | SF | .296 | 113. Bill Doran | HOU | .215 |

## Slugging Average vs. Left-Handed Pitchers

### American League

| Top 20 | | | Bottom 20 | | |
|---|---|---|---|---|---|
| 1. Jose Canseco | OAK | .700 | 173. Fred Lynn | DET | .190 |
| 2. Ruben Sierra | TEX | .600 | 172. Mike Macfarlane | KC | .203 |
| 3. Robin Yount | MIL | .587 | 171. Mel Hall | NY | .217 |
| 4. Danny Tartabull | KC | .568 | 170. Gus Polidor | MIL | .224 |
| 5. Ron Kittle | CHI | .564 | 169. Bob Brenly | TOR | .228 |
| 6. Carmen Castillo | MIN | .561 | 168. Oddibe McDowell | CLE | .229 |
| 7. Mickey Tettleton | BAL | .532 | 167. Russ Morman | CHI | .229 |
| 8. Don Mattingly | NY | .532 | 166. Dave Bergman | DET | .233 |
| 9. Phil Bradley | BAL | .531 | 165. Jack Howell | CAL | .235 |
| 10. Alvin Davis | SEA | .526 | 164. Brady Anderson | BAL | .243 |
| 11. George Bell | TOR | .517 | 163. Tom Lawless | TOR | .250 |
| 12. Greg Gagne | MIN | .515 | 162. Steve Lyons | CHI | .255 |
| 13. Carlton Fisk | CHI | .508 | 161. Joe Orsulak | BAL | .262 |
| 14. Jeff Kunkel | TEX | .507 | 160. Omar Vizquel | SEA | .265 |
| 15. Steve Balboni | NY | .505 | 159. Lloyd Moseby | TOR | .268 |
| 16. Carney Lansford | OAK | .503 | 158. Glenn Hoffman | CAL | .276 |
| 17. Kelly Gruber | TOR | .500 | 157. Felix Fermin | CLE | .277 |
| 18. Jeffrey Leonard | SEA | .497 | 156. Walt Weiss | OAK | .281 |
| 19. Roberto Kelly | NY | .497 | 155. Kent Anderson | CAL | .290 |
| 20. Ivan Calderon | CHI | .495 | 154. Ozzie Guillen | CHI | .292 |

### National League

| Top 20 | | | Bottom 20 | | |
|---|---|---|---|---|---|
| 1. Kevin Mitchell | SF | .725 | 132. John Russell | ATL | .162 |
| 2. Andres Galarraga | MTL | .672 | 131. Ron Oester | CIN | .175 |
| 3. Matt Williams | SF | .644 | 130. Ron Gant | ATL | .203 |
| 4. Glenn Davis | HOU | .616 | 129. Jeff Treadway | ATL | .208 |
| 5. Andre Dawson | CHI | .579 | 128. John Shelby | LA | .208 |
| 6. Lonnie Smith | ATL | .564 | 127. Dave Anderson | LA | .209 |
| 7. Gary Redus | PIT | .558 | 126. Lenny Harris | LA | .221 |
| 8. Lloyd McClendon | CHI | .554 | 125. Mookie Wilson | NY | .221 |
| 9. Glenn Wilson | HOU | .517 | 124. Kirt Manwaring | SF | .235 |
| 10. Ryne Sandberg | CHI | .517 | 123. Rick Dempsey | LA | .239 |
| 11. Mark Carreon | NY | .513 | 122. Bo Diaz | CIN | .241 |
| 12. Bip Roberts | SD | .513 | 121. Bob Dernier | PHI | .250 |
| 13. Will Clark | SF | .512 | 120. Jose Uribe | SF | .253 |
| 14. Kevin McReynolds | NY | .508 | 119. Kirk Gibson | LA | .263 |
| 15. Rob Thompson | SF | .505 | 118. Donell Nixon | SF | .265 |
| 16. Pedro Guerrero | STL | .505 | 117. Gerald Young | HOU | .265 |
| 17. Tim Wallach | MTL | .500 | 116. John Cangelosi | PIT | .268 |
| 18. Shawon Dunston | CHI | .489 | 114. Willie McGee | STL | .273 |
| 19. Luis Salazar | CHI | .488 | 114. Gary Carter | NY | .273 |
| 20. Barry Larkin | CIN | .488 | 113. Otis Nixon | MTL | .273 |

## *Slugging Average vs. Right-Handed Pitchers*

### *American League*

| Top 20 | | | Bottom 20 | | |
|---|---|---|---|---|---|
| 1. Fred McGriff | TOR | .602 | 171. Bob Melvin | BAL | .173 |
| 2. Ron Kittle | CHI | .553 | 170. Chad Kreuter | TEX | .195 |
| 3. Kent Hrbek | MIN | .538 | 169. Rick Schu | DET | .226 |
| 4. Jay Buhner | SEA | .528 | 168. Mike Brumley | DET | .229 |
| 5. Ruben Sierra | TEX | .515 | 167. Pat Tabler | KC | .235 |
| 6. Randy Milligan | BAL | .510 | 166. Bill Buckner | KC | .248 |
| 7. Lou Whitaker | DET | .508 | 165. Kent Anderson | CAL | .253 |
| 8. Nick Esasky | BOS | .505 | 164. Felix Fermin | CLE | .254 |
| 9. Mike Greenwell | BOS | .503 | 163. Omar Vizquel | SEA | .260 |
| 10. Harold Baines | TEX | .501 | 162. Ed Romero | MIL | .263 |
| 11. Wade Boggs | BOS | .499 | 161. Wally Backman | MIN | .269 |
| 12. Jose Canseco | OAK | .497 | 160. Andy Allanson | CLE | .271 |
| 13. Joe Carter | CLE | .497 | 159. Kenny Williams | DET | .271 |
| 14. Mickey Tettleton | BAL | .496 | 158. Doug Strange | DET | .273 |
| 15. Bo Jackson | KC | .496 | 157. Rich Gedman | BOS | .274 |
| 16. George Brett | KC | .493 | 156. Jim Traber | BAL | .282 |
| 17. Ellis Burks | BOS | .492 | 155. Joel Skinner | CLE | .285 |
| 18. Kirby Puckett | MIN | .491 | 154. Scott Fletcher | CHI | .285 |
| 19. Robin Yount | MIL | .483 | 153. Chet Lemon | DET | .287 |
| 20. Alvin Davis | SEA | .483 | 152. Alvaro Espinoza | NY | .287 |

### *National League*

| Top 20 | | | Bottom 20 | | |
|---|---|---|---|---|---|
| 1. Howard Johnson | NY | .607 | 132. Jody Davis | ATL | .217 |
| 2. Kevin Mitchell | SF | .594 | 131. Junior Ortiz | PIT | .241 |
| 3. Oddibe McDowell | ATL | .578 | 130. John Shelby | LA | .241 |
| 4. Eric Davis | CIN | .572 | 129. Gerald Perry | ATL | .253 |
| 5. Will Clark | SF | .566 | 128. Rey Quinones | PIT | .257 |
| 6. Bobby Bonilla | PIT | .547 | 127. Craig Reynolds | HOU | .260 |
| 7. Paul O'Neill | CIN | .525 | 126. Barry Lyons | NY | .265 |
| 8. Lonnie Smith | ATL | .517 | 125. Curt Ford | PHI | .268 |
| 9. Dwight Smith | CHI | .500 | 124. Jose Lind | PIT | .274 |
| 10. Von Hayes | PHI | .497 | 123. Tim Flannery | SD | .279 |
| 11. Ryne Sandberg | CHI | .488 | 122. Gerald Young | HOU | .280 |
| 12. Darryl Strawberry | NY | .483 | 121. Billy Hatcher | PIT | .281 |
| 13. John Kruk | PHI | .480 | 120. Damon Berryhill | CHI | .283 |
| 14. Mark Grace | CHI | .473 | 119. Domingo Ramos | CHI | .283 |
| 15. Jack Clark | SD | .467 | 118. Mariano Duncan | CIN | .289 |
| 16. Tony Gwynn | SD | .463 | 117. Alfredo Griffin | LA | .292 |
| 17. Pedro Guerrero | STL | .460 | 116. Jose Uribe | SF | .294 |
| 18. Glenn Davis | HOU | .451 | 115. Jeff Reed | CIN | .305 |
| 19. Eddie Murray | LA | .440 | 114. Darren Daulton | PHI | .306 |
| 20. Kal Daniels | LA | .439 | 113. Juan Samuel | NY | .307 |

## *Home Run Percentage vs. Left-Handed Pitchers*

### *American League*

| Top 20 | | | Bottom 20 |
|---|---|---|---|
| 1. Jose Canseco | OAK | 14.00 | 40 players tied with .000 |
| 2. Ron Kittle | CHI | 7.27 | |
| 3. Mickey Tettleton | BAL | 7.19 | |
| 4. Steve Balboni | NY | 6.70 | |
| 5. Danny Tartabull | KC | 6.40 | |
| 6. Nick Esasky | BOS | 6.40 | |
| 7. Cory Snyder | CLE | 6.10 | |
| 8. Bill Schroeder | CAL | 6.06 | |
| 9. Rob Deer | MIL | 5.97 | |
| 10. Luis Medina | CLE | 5.71 | |
| 11. Kent Hrbek | MIN | 5.50 | |
| 12. Bo Jackson | KC | 5.47 | |
| 13. Joey Belle | CLE | 5.17 | |
| 14. Carmen Castillo | MIN | 5.16 | |
| 15. Jeffrey Leonard | SEA | 5.10 | |
| 16. George Bell | TOR | 5.06 | |
| 17. Jesse Barfield | NY | 5.00 | |
| 18. Tony Armas | CAL | 4.90 | |
| 19. Ruben Sierra | TEX | 4.88 | |
| 20. Lance Parrish | CAL | 4.86 | |

### *National League*

| Top 20 | | | Bottom 20 |
|---|---|---|---|
| 1. Kevin Mitchell | SF | 11.11 | 21 players tied with .000 |
| 2. Matt Williams | SF | 10.34 | |
| 3. Glenn Davis | HOU | 9.59 | |
| 4. Andre Dawson | CHI | 7.02 | |
| 5. Mark Carreon | NY | 6.58 | |
| 6. Eric Davis | CIN | 6.41 | |
| 7. Luis Quinones | CIN | 6.34 | |
| 8. Andres Galarraga | MTL | 6.32 | |
| 9. Mike Marshall | LA | 5.38 | |
| 10. Kevin McReynolds | NY | 5.29 | |
| 11. Darryl Strawberry | NY | 5.06 | |
| 12. Tom Brunansky | STL | 5.00 | |
| 12. Tim Wallach | MTL | 5.00 | |
| 14. Lloyd McClendon | CHI | 4.96 | |
| 15. Rex Hudler | MTL | 4.39 | |
| 16. Lonnie Smith | ATL | 4.24 | |
| 17. Kirk Gibson | LA | 4.21 | |
| 18. Chris James | SD | 4.17 | |
| 19. Ryne Sandberg | CHI | 4.07 | |
| 20. Luis Salazar | CHI | 4.00 | |

## *Home Run Percentage vs. Right-Handed Pitchers*

### *American League*

| Top 20 | | | Bottom 20 | | |
|---|---|---|---|---|---|
| 1. Fred McGriff | TOR | 8.56 | 158. Kent Anderson | CAL | 0.00 |
| 2. Mark McGwire | OAK | 7.54 | 158. Mike Brumley | DET | 0.00 |
| 3. Kent Hrbek | MIN | 7.14 | 158. Alvaro Espinoza | NY | 0.00 |
| 4. Bo Jackson | KC | 6.46 | 158. Cecil Espy | TEX | 0.00 |
| 5. Lou Whitaker | DET | 6.39 | 158. Felix Fermin | CLE | 0.00 |
| 6. Ron Kittle | CHI | 6.14 | 158. Jim Gantner | MIL | 0.00 |
| 7. Mickey Tettleton | BAL | 5.88 | 158. Stan Javier | OAK | 0.00 |
| 8. Joe Carter | CLE | 5.81 | 158. Lance Johnson | CHI | 0.00 |
| 9. Jose Canseco | OAK | 5.65 | 158. Bob Melvin | BAL | 0.00 |
| 10. Mel Hall | NY | 5.48 | 158. Al Newman | MIN | 0.00 |
| 11. Rob Deer | MIL | 5.42 | 158. Harold Reynolds | SEA | 0.00 |
| 12. Jack Howell | CAL | 5.33 | 158. Ed Romero | MIL | 0.00 |
| 13. Brad Komminsk | CLE | 5.26 | 158. Pat Tabler | KC | 0.00 |
| 14. Bob Geren | NY | 5.07 | 158. Omar Vizquel | SEA | 0.00 |
| 15. Pete Incaviglia | TEX | 4.92 | 157. Kevin Seitzer | KC | 0.24 |
| 16. Jay Buhner | SEA | 4.86 | 156. Carney Lansford | OAK | 0.25 |
| 17. Nick Esasky | BOS | 4.85 | 155. Dave Gallagher | CHI | 0.25 |
| 18. Dan Pasqua | CHI | 4.71 | 154. Ozzie Guillen | CHI | 0.26 |
| 19. Ruben Sierra | TEX | 4.43 | 153. Scott Fletcher | CHI | 0.26 |
| 20. Dwight Evans | BOS | 4.38 | 152. Bob Boone | KC | 0.32 |

### *National League*

| Top 20 | | | Bottom 20 | | |
|---|---|---|---|---|---|
| 1. Eric Davis | CIN | 7.84 | 124. Vince Coleman | STL | 0.00 |
| 2. Howard Johnson | NY | 7.69 | 124. Tim Flannery | SD | 0.00 |
| 3. Kevin Mitchell | SF | 7.53 | 124. Alfredo Griffin | LA | 0.00 |
| 4. Darryl Strawberry | NY | 6.71 | 124. Barry Lyons | NY | 0.00 |
| 5. Jack Clark | SD | 6.67 | 124. Junior Ortiz | PIT | 0.00 |
| 6. Dwayne Murphy | PHI | 5.76 | 124. Terry Puhl | HOU | 0.00 |
| 7. Von Hayes | PHI | 5.42 | 124. Domingo Ramos | CHI | 0.00 |
| 8. Ryne Sandberg | CHI | 5.30 | 124. Bip Roberts | SD | 0.00 |
| 9. Glenn Davis | HOU | 4.60 | 124. Gerald Young | HOU | 0.00 |
| 10. Darrell Evans | ATL | 4.43 | 123. Jose Lind | PIT | 0.26 |
| 11. Ron Gant | ATL | 4.42 | 122. Willie Randolph | LA | 0.28 |
| 12. Lonnie Smith | ATL | 4.42 | 121. Ozzie Smith | STL | 0.29 |
| 13. Matt Williams | SF | 4.39 | 120. Tom Herr | PHI | 0.30 |
| 14. Lloyd McClendon | CHI | 4.35 | 119. Jose Oquendo | STL | 0.31 |
| 15. Andre Dawson | CHI | 4.30 | 118. Jose Uribe | SF | 0.33 |
| 16. Eddie Murray | LA | 4.17 | 117. Ron Oester | CIN | 0.41 |
| 17. Benito Santiago | SD | 4.06 | 116. John Shelby | LA | 0.45 |
| 18. Bobby Bonilla | PIT | 4.05 | 115. Jay Bell | PIT | 0.61 |
| 19. Will Clark | SF | 4.02 | 114. Gerald Perry | ATL | 0.62 |
| 20. Paul O'Neill | CIN | 3.99 | 113. Mariano Duncan | CIN | 0.63 |

## *Batting Average, Day Games*

### *American League*

#### *Top 20*

|  |  |  |  |
|---|---|---|---|
| 1. | Harold Baines | TEX | .429 |
| 2. | Dion James | CLE | .385 |
| 3. | Alvin Davis | SEA | .370 |
| 4. | Brian Harper | MIN | .367 |
| 5. | Jay Buhner | SEA | .367 |
| 6. | Kirby Puckett | MIN | .365 |
| 7. | Carney Lansford | OAK | .359 |
| 8. | Carmen Castillo | MIN | .353 |
| 9. | Luis Polonia | NY | .351 |
| 10. | Paul Molitor | MIL | .351 |
| 11. | Robin Yount | MIL | .349 |
| 12. | Larry Sheets | BAL | .345 |
| 13. | Johnny Ray | CAL | .344 |
| 14. | Don Mattingly | NY | .342 |
| 15. | Wade Boggs | BOS | .335 |
| 16. | Jim Eisenreich | KC | .328 |
| 17. | Pat Sheridan | DET | .327 |
| 18. | Mike Greenwell | BOS | .327 |
| 19. | Bob Geren | NY | .324 |
| 20. | Greg Briley | SEA | .324 |

#### *Bottom 20*

|  |  |  |  |
|---|---|---|---|
| 174. | Billy Ripken | BAL | .117 |
| 173. | Rene Gonzales | BAL | .132 |
| 172. | Jim Presley | SEA | .143 |
| 171. | Mike Felder | MIL | .151 |
| 170. | Kenny Williams | DET | .174 |
| 169. | Cory Snyder | CLE | .174 |
| 168. | Gus Polidor | MIL | .175 |
| 167. | Jack Howell | CAL | .176 |
| 166. | Glenn Hubbard | OAK | .180 |
| 165. | Tim Laudner | MIN | .183 |
| 164. | Randy Kutcher | BOS | .183 |
| 163. | Pat Borders | TOR | .184 |
| 162. | Andy Allanson | CLE | .184 |
| 161. | Don Slaught | NY | .186 |
| 160. | Oddibe McDowell | CLE | .191 |
| 159. | Ron Hassey | OAK | .193 |
| 157. | Gary Ward | DET | .193 |
| 157. | Steve Balboni | NY | .193 |
| 156. | Mike Pagliarulo | NY | .194 |
| 155. | Walt Weiss | OAK | .196 |

### *National League*

#### *Top 20*

|  |  |  |  |
|---|---|---|---|
| 1. | Rolando Roomes | CIN | .402 |
| 2. | Tony Gwynn | SD | .371 |
| 3. | Bip Roberts | SD | .353 |
| 4. | Will Clark | SF | .351 |
| 5. | Dwight Smith | CHI | .339 |
| 6. | Pedro Guerrero | STL | .333 |
| 6. | Mickey Hatcher | LA | .333 |
| 8. | Ozzie Smith | STL | .328 |
| 9. | Jerome Walton | CHI | .327 |
| 10. | R.J. Reynolds | PIT | .326 |
| 11. | Terry Puhl | HOU | .323 |
| 12. | Lloyd McClendon | CHI | .321 |
| 13. | Ryne Sandberg | CHI | .319 |
| 14. | Tom Herr | PHI | .318 |
| 14. | Lonnie Smith | ATL | .318 |
| 16. | Mark Grace | CHI | .318 |
| 17. | Jeff Blauser | ATL | .316 |
| 17. | Charlie Hayes | PHI | .316 |
| 19. | Kevin Bass | HOU | .311 |
| 20. | Nelson Santovenia | MTL | .309 |

#### *Bottom 20*

|  |  |  |  |
|---|---|---|---|
| 132. | Ron Gant | ATL | .109 |
| 131. | Doug Dascenzo | CHI | .150 |
| 130. | Mark Parent | SD | .165 |
| 129. | Candy Maldonado | SF | .171 |
| 128. | John Shelby | LA | .173 |
| 127. | Rey Quinones | PIT | .178 |
| 126. | Mookie Wilson | NY | .182 |
| 125. | Kal Daniels | LA | .192 |
| 124. | Bill Doran | HOU | .194 |
| 123. | Jose Uribe | SF | .200 |
| 122. | Juan Samuel | NY | .201 |
| 121. | Terry Kennedy | SF | .201 |
| 120. | Darren Daulton | PHI | .202 |
| 119. | Jose Lind | PIT | .205 |
| 118. | Lenny Harris | LA | .205 |
| 117. | Len Dykstra | PHI | .208 |
| 116. | Andres Thomas | ATL | .209 |
| 115. | Chris Sabo | CIN | .211 |
| 114. | Curtis Wilkerson | CHI | .215 |
| 113. | Pat Sheridan | SF | .215 |

## *Batting Average, Night Games*

### *American League*

#### *Top 20*

|  |  |  |  |
|---|---|---|---|
| 1. | Steve Sax | NY | .341 |
| 2. | Carlos Martinez | CHI | .335 |
| 3. | Wade Boggs | BOS | .328 |
| 4. | Kirby Puckett | MIN | .327 |
| 5. | Jim Dwyer | MIN | .325 |
| 6. | Julio Franco | TEX | .324 |
| 7. | Dwight Evans | BOS | .324 |
| 8. | Carney Lansford | OAK | .323 |
| 9. | George Bell | TOR | .321 |
| 10. | Ruben Sierra | TEX | .321 |
| 11. | Roberto Kelly | NY | .316 |
| 12. | Dan Gladden | MIN | .315 |
| 13. | Ron Kittle | CHI | .311 |
| 14. | Brian Harper | MIN | .308 |
| 15. | Mookie Wilson | TOR | .308 |
| 16. | Harold Reynolds | SEA | .307 |
| 17. | Kelly Gruber | TOR | .305 |
| 18. | Robin Yount | MIL | .303 |
| 19. | Jerry Browne | CLE | .301 |
| 20. | Joe Orsulak | BAL | .300 |

#### *Bottom 20*

|  |  |  |  |
|---|---|---|---|
| 171. | Chad Kreuter | TEX | .157 |
| 170. | Jim Sundberg | TEX | .168 |
| 169. | Greg Walker | CHI | .184 |
| 168. | Mike Brumley | DET | .191 |
| 167. | Jim Traber | BAL | .194 |
| 166. | Mike Pagliarulo | NY | .199 |
| 165. | Brady Anderson | BAL | .203 |
| 164. | Rob Deer | MIL | .205 |
| 163. | Dick Schofield | CAL | .205 |
| 162. | Mark McGwire | OAK | .208 |
| 161. | Doug Strange | DET | .212 |
| 160. | Joey Belle | CLE | .212 |
| 159. | Carmen Castillo | MIN | .213 |
| 158. | Rich Gedman | BOS | .219 |
| 157. | Omar Vizquel | SEA | .219 |
| 156. | Larry Sheets | BAL | .220 |
| 155. | Lloyd Moseby | TOR | .220 |
| 154. | Kent Anderson | CAL | .221 |
| 153. | Rick Schu | DET | .222 |
| 152. | Dan Pasqua | CHI | .222 |

### *National League*

#### *Top 20*

|  |  |  |  |
|---|---|---|---|
| 1. | Barry Larkin | CIN | .366 |
| 2. | Mike LaValliere | PIT | .349 |
| 3. | Will Clark | SF | .322 |
| 4. | Tony Gwynn | SD | .322 |
| 5. | Lonnie Smith | ATL | .315 |
| 6. | Jose Oquendo | STL | .313 |
| 7. | Milt Thompson | STL | .309 |
| 8. | Mark Grace | CHI | .309 |
| 9. | Dwight Smith | CHI | .306 |
| 10. | Ernest Riles | SF | .305 |
| 11. | John Kruk | PHI | .305 |
| 12. | Oddibe McDowell | ATL | .302 |
| 13. | Brett Butler | SF | .300 |
| 14. | Pedro Guerrero | STL | .300 |
| 15. | Luis Salazar | CHI | .297 |
| 16. | Paul O'Neill | CIN | .296 |
| 17. | Kevin Bass | HOU | .295 |
| 18. | Eric Davis | CIN | .295 |
| 19. | Kevin Mitchell | SF | .293 |
| 20. | Glenn Davis | HOU | .293 |

#### *Bottom 20*

|  |  |  |  |
|---|---|---|---|
| 132. | Jody Davis | ATL | .167 |
| 131. | Bob Dernier | PHI | .176 |
| 130. | Craig Reynolds | HOU | .177 |
| 129. | Kirt Manwaring | SF | .179 |
| 128. | Matt Williams | SF | .181 |
| 127. | John Shelby | LA | .187 |
| 126. | Rolando Roomes | CIN | .192 |
| 125. | Bruce Benedict | ATL | .195 |
| 124. | Darrell Evans | ATL | .197 |
| 123. | Jeff King | PIT | .197 |
| 122. | Ron Gant | ATL | .199 |
| 121. | Otis Nixon | MTL | .200 |
| 120. | Darren Daulton | PHI | .201 |
| 119. | Jeff Reed | CIN | .202 |
| 118. | Darryl Strawberry | NY | .208 |
| 117. | Kirk Gibson | LA | .208 |
| 116. | Junior Ortiz | PIT | .212 |
| 115. | Dwayne Murphy | PHI | .212 |
| 114. | Spike Owen | MTL | .214 |
| 113. | Andres Thomas | ATL | .214 |

## *Batting Average, Grass Surfaces*

### *American League*

#### *Top 20*

|  |  |  |  |
|---|---|---|---|
| 1. | Wade Boggs | BOS | .346 |
| 2. | Julio Franco | TEX | .338 |
| 3. | Carney Lansford | OAK | .333 |
| 4. | Geno Petralli | TEX | .316 |
| 4. | Steve Sax | NY | .316 |
| 6. | Mike Greenwell | BOS | .315 |
| 7. | Manny Lee | TOR | .314 |
| 8. | Robin Yount | MIL | .314 |
| 9. | Ron Kittle | CHI | .313 |
| 10. | Jerry Browne | CLE | .311 |
| 11. | Paul Molitor | MIL | .310 |
| 12. | Dan Gladden | MIN | .309 |
| 13. | Ruben Sierra | TEX | .308 |
| 14. | Danny Heep | BOS | .306 |
| 15. | Luis Polonia | NY | .306 |
| 16. | Harold Baines | TEX | .303 |
| 17. | Lance Johnson | CHI | .302 |
| 18. | Brian Harper | MIN | .301 |
| 19. | George Bell | TOR | .300 |
| 20. | Jose Canseco | OAK | .299 |

#### *Bottom 20*

|  |  |  |  |
|---|---|---|---|
| 171. | Chad Kreuter | TEX | .148 |
| 170. | Jim Sundberg | TEX | .157 |
| 169. | Mike Pagliarulo | NY | .185 |
| 168. | Gus Polidor | MIL | .196 |
| 167. | Dave Valle | SEA | .200 |
| 166. | Doug Strange | DET | .201 |
| 165. | Brady Anderson | BAL | .204 |
| 164. | Greg Walker | CHI | .208 |
| 163. | Kenny Williams | DET | .210 |
| 162. | Oddibe McDowell | CLE | .213 |
| 161. | Rene Gonzales | BAL | .213 |
| 160. | Joey Belle | CLE | .213 |
| 159. | Mike Brumley | DET | .214 |
| 158. | Jim Presley | SEA | .216 |
| 157. | Omar Vizquel | SEA | .217 |
| 156. | Bob Melvin | BAL | .217 |
| 155. | Andy Allanson | CLE | .219 |
| 154. | Rick Schu | DET | .219 |
| 153. | Rob Deer | MIL | .220 |
| 152. | Rich Gedman | BOS | .222 |

### *National League*

#### *Top 20*

|  |  |  |  |
|---|---|---|---|
| 1. | Pedro Guerrero | STL | .364 |
| 2. | Dwight Smith | CHI | .354 |
| 3. | Will Clark | SF | .339 |
| 4. | Mark Grace | CHI | .333 |
| 5. | Oddibe McDowell | ATL | .327 |
| 6. | Tony Gwynn | SD | .325 |
| 7. | Dave Martinez | MTL | .324 |
| 8. | Lonnie Smith | ATL | .321 |
| 9. | Mackey Sasser | NY | .317 |
| 10. | Barry Larkin | CIN | .317 |
| 11. | Jose Oquendo | STL | .309 |
| 12. | Dave Magadan | NY | .305 |
| 13. | Jerome Walton | CHI | .302 |
| 14. | Bip Roberts | SD | .302 |
| 15. | Roberto Alomar | SD | .300 |
| 16. | Glenn Wilson | HOU | .298 |
| 17. | Von Hayes | PHI | .297 |
| 18. | Kevin Mitchell | SF | .297 |
| 19. | Mickey Hatcher | LA | .296 |
| 20. | Donell Nixon | SF | .293 |

#### *Bottom 20*

|  |  |  |  |
|---|---|---|---|
| 132. | John Russell | ATL | .153 |
| 131. | Jody Davis | ATL | .158 |
| 130. | Jeff Reed | CIN | .159 |
| 129. | Shawn Abner | SD | .160 |
| 128. | Doug Dascenzo | CHI | .165 |
| 127. | Ron Gant | ATL | .165 |
| 126. | Spike Owen | MTL | .167 |
| 125. | Bill Doran | HOU | .174 |
| 124. | Glenn Davis | HOU | .174 |
| 123. | Rick Dempsey | LA | .178 |
| 122. | Mike Fitzgerald | MTL | .181 |
| 121. | Mike Pagliarulo | SD | .185 |
| 120. | Gary Carter | NY | .188 |
| 119. | Bruce Benedict | ATL | .189 |
| 118. | Mookie Wilson | NY | .192 |
| 117. | Andy Van Slyke | PIT | .194 |
| 116. | John Shelby | LA | .196 |
| 115. | Darrell Evans | ATL | .197 |
| 114. | Tom Brunansky | STL | .201 |
| 113. | Matt Williams | SF | .206 |

## Batting Average, Artificial Surfaces

### American League

| Top 20 | | | Bottom 20 | | |
|---|---|---|---|---|---|
| 1. Kevin Romine | BOS | .400 | 171. Mario Diaz | SEA | .075 |
| 2. Dion James | CLE | .377 | 170. Bill Schroeder | CAL | .111 |
| 3. Joe Orsulak | BAL | .373 | 169. Mike Brumley | DET | .136 |
| 4. Kirby Puckett | MIN | .372 | 168. Cory Snyder | CLE | .138 |
| 5. Wally Joyner | CAL | .365 | 166. Jim Traber | BAL | .146 |
| 6. Roberto Kelly | NY | .358 | 166. Bill Pecota | KC | .146 |
| 7. Tony Armas | CAL | .357 | 165. Mickey Brantley | SEA | .146 |
| 8. Ellis Burks | BOS | .354 | 164. Rich Gedman | BOS | .154 |
| 9. Carney Lansford | OAK | .349 | 163. Rob Deer | MIL | .167 |
| 10. Dave Bergman | DET | .344 | 162. Jose Canseco | OAK | .170 |
| 11. Paul Molitor | MIL | .343 | 161. Lee Mazzilli | TOR | .170 |
| 12. Harold Baines | TEX | .342 | 160. Charlie O'Brien | MIL | .171 |
| 13. Brian Harper | MIN | .341 | 159. Dave Henderson | OAK | .172 |
| 14. Carlos Martinez | CHI | .338 | 158. Pete Incaviglia | TEX | .174 |
| 15. Don Mattingly | NY | .337 | 157. Matt Nokes | DET | .178 |
| 16. Rafael Palmeiro | TEX | .337 | 156. Cecil Espy | TEX | .182 |
| 17. Robin Yount | MIL | .337 | 155. Mark McGwire | OAK | .184 |
| 18. Alvin Davis | SEA | .333 | 154. Chip Hale | MIN | .185 |
| 19. Fred Manrique | TEX | .329 | 153. Bob Brenly | TOR | .189 |
| 20. John Moses | MIN | .328 | 152. Kenny Williams | DET | .190 |

### National League

| Top 20 | | | Bottom 20 | | |
|---|---|---|---|---|---|
| 1. Tony Gwynn | SD | .366 | 132. Jeff Richardson | CIN | .146 |
| 2. Barry Larkin | CIN | .353 | 131. Bob Dernier | PHI | .171 |
| 3. Mike LaValliere | PIT | .326 | 130. Gerald Perry | ATL | .173 |
| 4. Will Clark | SF | .319 | 129. Rob Thompson | SF | .173 |
| 5. John Kruk | PHI | .316 | 128. Jeff King | PIT | .184 |
| 6. Kevin Bass | HOU | .314 | 127. Bo Diaz | CIN | .193 |
| 7. Glenn Davis | HOU | .310 | 126. Marvell Wynne | CHI | .196 |
| 8. Jeff Treadway | ATL | .309 | 125. Darren Daulton | PHI | .197 |
| 9. Lloyd McClendon | CHI | .305 | 124. Rafael Belliard | PIT | .204 |
| 10. Ernest Riles | SF | .304 | 123. Gregg Jefferies | NY | .207 |
| 11. Tom Herr | PHI | .303 | 122. Mike Marshall | LA | .208 |
| 12. Jose Gonzalez | LA | .300 | 121. Darryl Strawberry | NY | .209 |
| 13. Paul O'Neill | CIN | .299 | 120. Mike Aldrete | MTL | .210 |
| 14. Lonnie Smith | ATL | .299 | 119. Dale Murphy | ATL | .210 |
| 15. Bip Roberts | SD | .298 | 118. Mike Schmidt | PHI | .213 |
| 16. Tim Wallach | MTL | .296 | 117. Rey Quinones | PIT | .215 |
| 17. Jeff Blauser | ATL | .295 | 116. Otis Nixon | MTL | .216 |
| 18. Eric Davis | CIN | .294 | 115. Andres Thomas | ATL | .219 |
| 19. Milt Thompson | STL | .292 | 114. Benito Santiago | SD | .219 |
| 20. Bobby Bonilla | PIT | .292 | 113. John Cangelosi | PIT | .222 |

## Batting Average, Home Games

### American League

| Top 20 | | | Bottom 20 | | |
|---|---|---|---|---|---|
| 1. Kirby Puckett | MIN | .390 | 171. Greg Walker | CHI | .165 |
| 2. Wade Boggs | BOS | .377 | 170. Mike Felder | MIL | .180 |
| 3. Luis Polonia | NY | .372 | 169. Lloyd Moseby | TOR | .180 |
| 4. Alvin Davis | SEA | .365 | 168. Jim Traber | BAL | .191 |
| 5. Julio Franco | TEX | .356 | 167. Rick Schu | DET | .192 |
| 6. Carlton Fisk | CHI | .343 | 166. Geno Petralli | TEX | .193 |
| 7. Don Mattingly | NY | .334 | 165. Walt Weiss | OAK | .200 |
| 8. Jerry Browne | CLE | .332 | 164. Rob Deer | MIL | .201 |
| 9. Paul Molitor | MIL | .328 | 163. Kenny Williams | DET | .202 |
| 10. Mike Greenwell | BOS | .325 | 162. Dick Schofield | CAL | .203 |
| 11. Steve Sax | NY | .324 | 161. Mike Pagliarulo | NY | .204 |
| 12. Ellis Burks | BOS | .319 | 159. Cory Snyder | CLE | .207 |
| 13. Ruben Sierra | TEX | .317 | 159. Greg Briley | SEA | .207 |
| 14. Roberto Kelly | NY | .317 | 158. Mike Brumley | DET | .208 |
| 15. Bob Boone | KC | .317 | 157. Andy Allanson | CLE | .208 |
| 16. Fred Manrique | TEX | .316 | 156. Doug Strange | DET | .208 |
| 17. Bob Geren | NY | .311 | 155. Kent Anderson | CAL | .209 |
| 18. Kevin Seitzer | KC | .311 | 154. Dion James | CLE | .210 |
| 19. Mickey Tettleton | BAL | .310 | 153. Glenn Braggs | MIL | .211 |
| 20. John Moses | MIN | .309 | 152. Rick Leach | TEX | .214 |

### National League

| Top 20 | | | Bottom 20 | | |
|---|---|---|---|---|---|
| 1. Mike LaValliere | PIT | .378 | 132. Jody Davis | ATL | .143 |
| 2. Dwight Smith | CHI | .363 | 131. Darren Daulton | PHI | .163 |
| 3. Lonnie Smith | ATL | .358 | 129. Rey Quinones | PIT | .165 |
| 4. Barry Larkin | CIN | .353 | 129. Bob Dernier | PHI | .165 |
| 5. Mark Grace | CHI | .337 | 128. Carmelo Martinez | SD | .165 |
| 6. Roberto Alomar | SD | .329 | 127. Ron Gant | ATL | .178 |
| 7. Tony Gwynn | SD | .326 | 126. John Shelby | LA | .183 |
| 8. Will Clark | SF | .325 | 125. Jeff King | PIT | .185 |
| 9. Tim Wallach | MTL | .318 | 124. Mookie Wilson | NY | .192 |
| 10. Glenn Davis | HOU | .317 | 123. Andres Thomas | ATL | .195 |
| 11. Oddibe McDowell | ATL | .316 | 122. Craig Reynolds | HOU | .196 |
| 12. Paul O'Neill | CIN | .316 | 121. Candy Maldonado | SF | .199 |
| 13. John Kruk | PHI | .313 | 120. Bruce Benedict | ATL | .202 |
| 14. Damon Berryhill | CHI | .311 | 119. Barry Bonds | PIT | .204 |
| 14. Bobby Bonilla | PIT | .311 | 118. Dave Martinez | MTL | .208 |
| 16. Shawon Dunston | CHI | .307 | 117. Otis Nixon | MTL | .212 |
| 17. Dave Magadan | NY | .306 | 116. Andy Van Slyke | PIT | .213 |
| 18. Willie Randolph | LA | .305 | 115. Tim Teufel | NY | .215 |
| 19. Brett Butler | SF | .304 | 114. Matt Williams | SF | .215 |
| 20. Jerome Walton | CHI | .303 | 113. Tom Foley | MTL | .217 |

## Batting Average, Road Games

### American League

| Top 20 | | | Bottom 20 | | |
|---|---|---|---|---|---|
| 1. Geno Petralli | TEX | .406 | 171. Rick Cerone | BOS | .177 |
| 2. Dion James | CLE | .397 | 170. Mike Brumley | DET | .189 |
| 3. Carney Lansford | OAK | .360 | 169. Brady Anderson | BAL | .191 |
| 4. Mookie Wilson | TOR | .351 | 168. Mike Pagliarulo | NY | .191 |
| 5. Brian Harper | MIN | .343 | 166. Oddibe McDowell | CLE | .203 |
| 6. Robin Yount | MIL | .328 | 166. Rich Gedman | BOS | .203 |
| 7. Rick Leach | TEX | .328 | 165. Joey Belle | CLE | .204 |
| 8. Jim Dwyer | MIN | .324 | 164. Mickey Tettleton | BAL | .207 |
| 9. Ron Kittle | CHI | .323 | 163. Kenny Williams | DET | .209 |
| 10. Harold Baines | TEX | .322 | 162. Jim Presley | SEA | .209 |
| 11. Ivan Calderon | CHI | .318 | 161. Daryl Boston | CHI | .212 |
| 12. Carlos Martinez | CHI | .318 | 160. Omar Vizquel | SEA | .212 |
| 13. Johnny Ray | CAL | .313 | 159. Wally Backman | MIN | .215 |
| 14. Eddie Williams | CHI | .311 | 158. Luis Rivera | BOS | .219 |
| 15. Greg Briley | SEA | .309 | 157. Rob Deer | MIL | .220 |
| 16. Danny Heep | BOS | .309 | 156. Doug Strange | DET | .220 |
| 17. Steve Sax | NY | .306 | 155. Dave Henderson | OAK | .221 |
| 18. Dan Gladden | MIN | .305 | 154. Jack Howell | CAL | .221 |
| 19. Steve Lyons | CHI | .305 | 153. Pete Incaviglia | TEX | .222 |
| 20. Paul Molitor | MIL | .304 | 150. Dave Valle | SEA | .222 |
| | | | 150. Jim Rice | BOS | .222 |
| | | | 150. Cory Snyder | CLE | .222 |

### National League

| Top 20 | | | Bottom 20 | | |
|---|---|---|---|---|---|
| 1. Tony Gwynn | SD | .345 | 132. John Cangelosi | PIT | .171 |
| 2. Will Clark | SF | .341 | 131. Ron Gant | ATL | .176 |
| 3. Dave Martinez | MTL | .339 | 130. Rick Dempsey | LA | .177 |
| 4. Pedro Guerrero | STL | .332 | 129. Bob Dernier | PHI | .178 |
| 5. Barry Larkin | CIN | .331 | 128. Darrell Evans | ATL | .182 |
| 6. Luis Salazar | CHI | .309 | 127. John Shelby | LA | .182 |
| 7. Mickey Hatcher | LA | .306 | 126. Darryl Strawberry | NY | .183 |
| 8. Kevin Bass | HOU | .303 | 125. Junior Ortiz | PIT | .186 |
| 9. Ernest Riles | SF | .302 | 124. Bill Doran | HOU | .187 |
| 10. Tim Raines | MTL | .301 | 123. Mike Schmidt | PHI | .188 |
| 11. Bip Roberts | SD | .300 | 122. Matt Williams | SF | .189 |
| 12. Ricky Jordan | PHI | .296 | 121. Jody Davis | ATL | .190 |
| 13. Tim Teufel | NY | .295 | 120. Mike Fitzgerald | MTL | .195 |
| 14. Ozzie Smith | STL | .294 | 119. Spike Owen | MTL | .199 |
| 15. Jeff Treadway | ATL | .293 | 118. Dale Murphy | ATL | .201 |
| 16. Oddibe McDowell | ATL | .292 | 117. Kirt Manwaring | SF | .202 |
| 17. Terry Puhl | HOU | .291 | 116. Kirk Gibson | LA | .203 |
| 18. Jeff Blauser | ATL | .291 | 115. Jeff Reed | CIN | .204 |
| 19. Jose Gonzalez | LA | .291 | 114. Tommy Gregg | ATL | .206 |
| 20. Dwight Smith | CHI | .290 | 112. Jeff King | PIT | .208 |
| | | | 112. Keith Hernandez | NY | .208 |

## Slugging Average, Home Games

### American League

| Top 20 | | | Bottom 20 | | |
|---|---|---|---|---|---|
| 1. Ruben Sierra | TEX | .621 | 171. Jim Traber | BAL | .227 |
| 2. Alvin Davis | SEA | .614 | 170. Mike Felder | MIL | .230 |
| 3. Mickey Tettleton | BAL | .611 | 169. Geno Petralli | TEX | .239 |
| 4. Kent Hrbek | MIN | .597 | 168. Bob Melvin | BAL | .247 |
| 5. Don Mattingly | NY | .577 | 167. Andy Allanson | CLE | .248 |
| 6. Julio Franco | TEX | .554 | 166. Steve Finley | BAL | .254 |
| 7. Kirby Puckett | MIN | .552 | 165. Kent Anderson | CAL | .255 |
| 8. Fred McGriff | TOR | .549 | 164. Felix Fermin | CLE | .255 |
| 9. Wade Boggs | BOS | .547 | 163. Doug Strange | DET | .260 |
| 10. Nick Esasky | BOS | .541 | 162. Dion James | CLE | .261 |
| 11. Jose Canseco | OAK | .538 | 161. Joel Skinner | CLE | .266 |
| 12. Robin Yount | MIL | .533 | 160. Dick Schofield | CAL | .273 |
| 13. Jay Buhner | SEA | .529 | 159. Steve Lyons | CHI | .275 |
| 14. Lou Whitaker | DET | .519 | 158. Billy Ripken | BAL | .275 |
| 15. Carlton Fisk | CHI | .500 | 157. Rick Leach | TEX | .282 |
| 16. Claudell Washington | CAL | .495 | 156. Walt Weiss | OAK | .283 |
| 17. Jeff Kunkel | TEX | .490 | 155. Terry Francona | MIL | .289 |
| 18. Jim Eisenreich | KC | .482 | 154. Stan Javier | OAK | .290 |
| 19. Ellis Burks | BOS | .480 | 153. Lloyd Moseby | TOR | .293 |
| 20. Pete Incaviglia | TEX | .480 | 152. Wally Backman | MIN | .293 |

### National League

| Top 20 | | | Bottom 20 | | |
|---|---|---|---|---|---|
| 1. Kevin Mitchell | SF | .663 | 132. Jody Davis | ATL | .200 |
| 2. Lonnie Smith | ATL | .597 | 131. Craig Reynolds | HOU | .206 |
| 3. Howard Johnson | NY | .572 | 130. Bob Dernier | PHI | .206 |
| 4. Bobby Bonilla | PIT | .551 | 129. Bruce Benedict | ATL | .213 |
| 5. Glenn Davis | HOU | .551 | 128. John Shelby | LA | .215 |
| 6. Darryl Strawberry | NY | .549 | 127. Carmelo Martinez | SD | .248 |
| 7. Lloyd McClendon | CHI | .549 | 125. Kirt Manwaring | SF | .250 |
| 8. Paul O'Neill | CIN | .545 | 125. Darren Daulton | PHI | .250 |
| 9. Eric Davis | CIN | .544 | 124. Tim Teufel | NY | .252 |
| 10. Dwight Smith | CHI | .541 | 123. Rey Quinones | PIT | .258 |
| 11. Will Clark | SF | .516 | 122. Dave Martinez | MTL | .264 |
| 12. Matt Williams | SF | .514 | 121. Mookie Wilson | NY | .267 |
| 13. Ryne Sandberg | CHI | .505 | 120. Candy Maldonado | SF | .269 |
| 14. Mark Grace | CHI | .504 | 119. Otis Nixon | MTL | .273 |
| 15. John Kruk | PHI | .500 | 118. Jose Lind | PIT | .277 |
| 16. Mike LaValliere | PIT | .490 | 117. Jose Uribe | SF | .285 |
| 17. Mike Marshall | LA | .480 | 116. Andres Thomas | ATL | .287 |
| 18. Tim Wallach | MTL | .479 | 115. Junior Ortiz | PIT | .291 |
| 19. Von Hayes | PHI | .479 | 114. Gerald Young | HOU | .292 |
| 20. Gregg Jefferies | NY | .464 | 113. Billy Hatcher | PIT | .299 |

## Slugging Average, Road Games

### American League

| Top 20 | | | Bottom 20 | | |
|---|---|---|---|---|---|
| 1. Geno Petralli | TEX | .563 | 171. Mike Brumley | DET | .216 |
| 2. Bo Jackson | KC | .554 | 170. Omar Vizquel | SEA | .227 |
| 3. Jose Canseco | OAK | .545 | 169. Doug Strange | DET | .260 |
| 4. Ron Kittle | CHI | .535 | 168. Felix Fermin | CLE | .265 |
| 5. Dion James | CLE | .532 | 167. Oddibe McDowell | CLE | .266 |
| 6. Carmen Castillo | MIN | .514 | 166. Rick Cerone | BOS | .270 |
| 7. Chili Davis | CAL | .514 | 165. Gary Pettis | DET | .271 |
| 8. Mark McGwire | OAK | .508 | 164. Mike Pagliarulo | NY | .273 |
| 9. Greg Briley | SEA | .504 | 163. Kent Anderson | CAL | .274 |
| 10. Ivan Calderon | CHI | .500 | 162. Wally Backman | MIN | .275 |
| 10. Fred McGriff | TOR | .500 | 161. Bob Boone | KC | .277 |
| 12. Dwight Evans | BOS | .493 | 160. Pat Tabler | KC | .278 |
| 13. Robin Yount | MIL | .490 | 159. Luis Rivera | BOS | .281 |
| 14. Steve Balboni | NY | .486 | 158. Rich Gedman | BOS | .287 |
| 15. Harold Baines | TEX | .484 | 157. Daryl Boston | CHI | .288 |
| 16. Joe Carter | CLE | .475 | 156. Brady Anderson | BAL | .290 |
| 17. Joe Orsulak | BAL | .474 | 155. Marty Barrett | BOS | .296 |
| 18. George Brett | KC | .474 | 154. Mike Gallego | OAK | .296 |
| 19. Ruben Sierra | TEX | .468 | 153. Cecil Espy | TEX | .297 |
| 20. Dan Gladden | MIN | .464 | 152. Ed Romero | MIL | .298 |

### National League

| Top 20 | | | Bottom 20 | | |
|---|---|---|---|---|---|
| 1. Kevin Mitchell | SF | .611 | 132. John Cangelosi | PIT | .207 |
| 2. Andre Dawson | CHI | .576 | 131. Bob Dernier | PHI | .222 |
| 3. Will Clark | SF | .572 | 130. Junior Ortiz | PIT | .239 |
| 4. Howard Johnson | NY | .546 | 129. John Shelby | LA | .245 |
| 5. Pedro Guerrero | STL | .543 | 128. Otis Nixon | MTL | .246 |
| 6. Eric Davis | CIN | .539 | 127. Kirt Manwaring | SF | .250 |
| 7. Barry Bonds | PIT | .503 | 126. Ron Oester | CIN | .255 |
| 8. Dave Martinez | MTL | .497 | 125. Gerald Young | HOU | .259 |
| 9. Oddibe McDowell | ATL | .493 | 124. Spike Owen | MTL | .267 |
| 10. Ryne Sandberg | CHI | .488 | 123. Jose Uribe | SF | .276 |
| 11. Jack Clark | SD | .480 | 122. Jody Davis | ATL | .278 |
| 12. Gary Redus | PIT | .479 | 121. Steve Jeltz | PHI | .278 |
| 13. Lonnie Smith | ATL | .477 | 120. Jeff Reed | CIN | .280 |
| 14. Ken Griffey | CIN | .474 | 119. Lenny Harris | LA | .282 |
| 15. Tom Brunansky | STL | .461 | 118. Nelson Santovenia | MTL | .284 |
| 16. Kevin Bass | HOU | .455 | 117. Damon Berryhill | CHI | .285 |
| 17. Kevin McReynolds | NY | .454 | 116. Bill Doran | HOU | .288 |
| 18. Eddie Murray | LA | .454 | 115. Gerald Perry | ATL | .290 |
| 19. Dwight Smith | CHI | .452 | 113. Keith Hernandez | NY | .300 |
| 20. Luis Quinones | CIN | .447 | 113. Tommy Gregg | ATL | .300 |

## Batting Average with Runners On Base

### American League

| Top 20 | | | Bottom 20 | | |
|---|---|---|---|---|---|
| 1. Fred Manrique | TEX | .368 | 172. Mike Brumley | DET | .177 |
| 2. Wade Boggs | BOS | .351 | 171. Rick Schu | DET | .177 |
| 3. Julio Franco | TEX | .345 | 170. Oddibe McDowell | CLE | .194 |
| 4. Scott Bradley | SEA | .345 | 169. Felix Fermin | CLE | .197 |
| 5. Danny Heep | BOS | .344 | 168. Dick Schofield | CAL | .198 |
| 6. Kirby Puckett | MIN | .343 | 167. Mickey Tettleton | BAL | .200 |
| 7. Ron Kittle | CHI | .338 | 165. Kenny Williams | DET | .202 |
| 8. Paul Molitor | MIL | .337 | 165. Rich Gedman | BOS | .202 |
| 9. Carlton Fisk | CHI | .333 | 164. Andy Allanson | CLE | .204 |
| 9. Dion James | CLE | .333 | 163. Cecil Espy | TEX | .206 |
| 11. Robin Yount | MIL | .330 | 162. Greg Walker | CHI | .216 |
| 12. Ruben Sierra | TEX | .329 | 161. Greg Gagne | MIN | .217 |
| 13. Alvin Davis | SEA | .327 | 160. Rick Leach | TEX | .218 |
| 14. Jim Eisenreich | KC | .326 | 159. Rance Mulliniks | TOR | .219 |
| 15. Alvaro Espinoza | NY | .325 | 158. Ron Hassey | OAK | .223 |
| 16. Henry Cotto | SEA | .325 | 157. Steve Finley | BAL | .223 |
| 17. Jose Canseco | OAK | .322 | 156. Eddie Williams | CHI | .225 |
| 18. Carney Lansford | OAK | .321 | 155. Jesse Barfield | NY | .226 |
| 19. Harold Reynolds | SEA | .320 | 154. Jim Rice | BOS | .226 |
| 20. Don Mattingly | NY | .319 | 153. Cory Snyder | CLE | .227 |

### National League

| Top 20 | | | Bottom 20 | | |
|---|---|---|---|---|---|
| 1. Lonnie Smith | ATL | .407 | 132. Jeff King | PIT | .134 |
| 2. Barry Larkin | CIN | .359 | 131. Ron Gant | ATL | .137 |
| 3. Pedro Guerrero | STL | .356 | 130. Jody Davis | ATL | .148 |
| 4. Will Clark | SF | .355 | 129. Matt Williams | SF | .172 |
| 5. Mark Grace | CHI | .349 | 128. John Shelby | LA | .176 |
| 6. Kevin Bass | HOU | .341 | 127. Carmelo Martinez | SD | .179 |
| 7. Bip Roberts | SD | .340 | 126. Mookie Wilson | NY | .182 |
| 8. Milt Thompson | STL | .337 | 125. Dwayne Murphy | PHI | .184 |
| 9. Oddibe McDowell | ATL | .330 | 124. Kal Daniels | LA | .191 |
| 10. Tony Gwynn | SD | .327 | 123. Rick Dempsey | LA | .200 |
| 11. Paul O'Neill | CIN | .323 | 122. Kirk Gibson | LA | .207 |
| 12. Dwight Smith | CHI | .321 | 121. Mike Schmidt | PHI | .207 |
| 13. Dickie Thon | PHI | .316 | 119. Vince Coleman | STL | .208 |
| 14. Mariano Duncan | CIN | .314 | 119. Todd Benzinger | CIN | .208 |
| 15. Jerome Walton | CHI | .314 | 118. Vance Law | CHI | .209 |
| 16. Howard Johnson | NY | .313 | 117. Otis Nixon | MTL | .211 |
| 17. Mackey Sasser | NY | .309 | 116. Randy Ready | PHI | .215 |
| 18. Luis Salazar | CHI | .308 | 115. Craig Reynolds | HOU | .217 |
| 19. Dave Magadan | NY | .307 | 114. Ken Griffey | CIN | .220 |
| 20. Tim Raines | MTL | .306 | 113. Andres Thomas | ATL | .220 |

## *Batting Average in Pressure Situations*

### *American League*

#### *Top 20*

|  |  |  |  |
|---|---|---|---|
| 1. | Mike Greenwell | BOS | .413 |
| 2. | Carmen Castillo | MIN | .412 |
| 3. | Ron Kittle | CHI | .393 |
| 4. | Kirby Puckett | MIN | .390 |
| 5. | Danny Tartabull | KC | .373 |
| 6. | Steve Finley | BAL | .367 |
| 7. | George Bell | TOR | .349 |
| 8. | Randy Milligan | BAL | .348 |
| 9. | Brady Anderson | BAL | .346 |
| 10. | Marty Barrett | BOS | .345 |
| 10. | Bob Boone | KC | .345 |
| 12. | Steve Sax | NY | .345 |
| 13. | Luis Polonia | NY | .344 |
| 14. | Dick Schofield | CAL | .344 |
| 15. | Andy Allanson | CLE | .341 |
| 16. | Dan Gladden | MIN | .333 |
| 16. | Fred Manrique | TEX | .333 |
| 18. | Kelly Gruber | TOR | .329 |
| 19. | Brian Downing | CAL | .325 |
| 20. | Harold Reynolds | SEA | .324 |
| 20. | Kevin Seitzer | KC | .324 |
| 20. | Bill Spiers | MIL | .324 |

#### *Bottom 20*

|  |  |  |  |
|---|---|---|---|
| 172. | Greg Walker | CHI | .061 |
| 171. | Kenny Williams | DET | .109 |
| 170. | Mike Gallego | OAK | .118 |
| 169. | Walt Weiss | OAK | .121 |
| 166. | Brad Komminsk | CLE | .125 |
| 166. | Dave Valle | SEA | .125 |
| 166. | Ron Karkovice | CHI | .125 |
| 165. | Jesse Barfield | NY | .141 |
| 164. | Mike Felder | MIL | .143 |
| 163. | Junior Felix | TOR | .148 |
| 162. | Oddibe McDowell | CLE | .148 |
| 161. | Joe Carter | CLE | .149 |
| 160. | Cory Snyder | CLE | .151 |
| 159. | Craig Worthington | BAL | .155 |
| 158. | Pete Incaviglia | TEX | .156 |
| 157. | Greg Brock | MIL | .159 |
| 155. | Mike Brumley | DET | .172 |
| 155. | Mike Macfarlane | KC | .172 |
| 154. | Rick Cerone | BOS | .178 |
| 153. | Rick Schu | DET | .179 |

### *National League*

#### *Top 20*

|  |  |  |  |
|---|---|---|---|
| 1. | Mark Grace | CHI | .375 |
| 2. | Ozzie Smith | STL | .351 |
| 3. | Hubie Brooks | MTL | .350 |
| 4. | Ken Oberkfell | SF | .349 |
| 5. | John Kruk | PHI | .343 |
| 6. | Craig Biggio | HOU | .342 |
| 7. | Roberto Alomar | SD | .338 |
| 7. | Tony Gwynn | SD | .338 |
| 7. | Glenn Wilson | HOU | .338 |
| 10. | Ernest Riles | SF | .333 |
| 10. | Luis Salazar | CHI | .333 |
| 12. | Barry Larkin | CIN | .327 |
| 13. | Herm Winningham | CIN | .326 |
| 14. | Jose Gonzalez | LA | .321 |
| 15. | Paul O'Neill | CIN | .320 |
| 16. | Rolando Roomes | CIN | .318 |
| 17. | Jose Oquendo | STL | .314 |
| 18. | Pedro Guerrero | STL | .312 |
| 19. | Shawon Dunston | CHI | .310 |
| 20. | Gary Redus | PIT | .309 |

#### *Bottom 20*

|  |  |  |  |
|---|---|---|---|
| 132. | Jody Davis | ATL | .100 |
| 131. | Ron Gant | ATL | .119 |
| 130. | Gerald Perry | ATL | .132 |
| 129. | Darren Daulton | PHI | .133 |
| 128. | Kirk Gibson | LA | .136 |
| 127. | Chris Sabo | CIN | .139 |
| 126. | Rey Quinones | PIT | .140 |
| 125. | Carmelo Martinez | SD | .143 |
| 124. | John Shelby | LA | .149 |
| 122. | Jeff Reed | CIN | .150 |
| 122. | Andy Van Slyke | PIT | .150 |
| 121. | Todd Benzinger | CIN | .159 |
| 120. | Darryl Strawberry | NY | .160 |
| 118. | Mike Aldrete | MTL | .162 |
| 118. | Domingo Ramos | CHI | .162 |
| 116. | Vance Law | CHI | .167 |
| 116. | Mike Davis | LA | .167 |
| 115. | Tony Pena | STL | .175 |
| 114. | Eddie Murray | LA | .179 |
| 113. | Kal Daniels | LA | .182 |

## *Home Run Percentage in Pressure Situations*

### *American League*

#### *Top 20*

|  |  |  |  |
|---|---|---|---|
| 1. | Kent Hrbek | MIN | 10.42 |
| 2. | Gary Gaetti | MIN | 8.45 |
| 3. | Rob Deer | MIL | 8.06 |
| 4. | Steve Balboni | NY | 7.50 |
| 5. | Lou Whitaker | DET | 7.23 |
| 6. | Danny Tartabull | KC | 6.78 |
| 7. | Ken Griffey Jr. | SEA | 6.67 |
| 8. | Tony Armas | CAL | 6.45 |
| 8. | Jay Buhner | SEA | 6.45 |
| 10. | Nick Esasky | BOS | 6.41 |
| 11. | Brad Komminsk | CLE | 6.25 |
| 12. | Tim Laudner | MIN | 6.06 |
| 13. | Jeffrey Leonard | SEA | 6.02 |
| 14. | Ellis Burks | BOS | 5.97 |
| 15. | Carmen Castillo | MIN | 5.88 |
| 15. | Bob Geren | NY | 5.88 |
| 17. | Alvin Davis | SEA | 5.56 |
| 18. | Bo Jackson | KC | 5.48 |
| 19. | Jim Presley | SEA | 5.36 |
| 20. | Ken Phelps | OAK | 5.26 |

#### *Bottom 20*

66 players tied with .000

### *National League*

#### *Top 20*

|  |  |  |  |
|---|---|---|---|
| 1. | Eric Davis | CIN | 8.54 |
| 2. | Glenn Davis | HOU | 7.00 |
| 3. | Mark Grace | CHI | 6.25 |
| 4. | Will Clark | SF | 6.17 |
| 4. | Darryl Strawberry | NY | 6.17 |
| 6. | Jack Clark | SD | 6.15 |
| 7. | John Kruk | PHI | 5.71 |
| 8. | Kevin Mitchell | SF | 5.48 |
| 9. | Howard Johnson | NY | 5.33 |
| 10. | Kevin McReynolds | NY | 5.32 |
| 11. | Tom Brunansky | STL | 4.82 |
| 12. | Rick Dempsey | LA | 4.76 |
| 12. | Von Hayes | PHI | 4.76 |
| 14. | Eddie Murray | LA | 4.46 |
| 15. | Lonnie Smith | ATL | 4.41 |
| 16. | Rob Thompson | SF | 4.23 |
| 17. | Craig Biggio | HOU | 4.11 |
| 18. | Kevin Bass | HOU | 4.08 |
| 18. | Andre Dawson | CHI | 4.08 |
| 20. | Glenn Wilson | HOU | 3.75 |

#### *Bottom 20*

52 players tied with .000

## *% of Runners Driven in from Scoring Position, Pressure Situations*

### *American League*

#### *Top 20*

|  |  |  |  |
|---|---|---|---|
| 1. | Joey Belle | CLE | .889 |
| 2. | Robin Yount | MIL | .542 |
| 3. | Mike Greenwell | BOS | .538 |
| 3. | Don Mattingly | NY | .538 |
| 5. | Randy Milligan | BAL | .500 |
| 5. | Danny Tartabull | KC | .500 |
| 7. | Mark McGwire | OAK | .476 |
| 8. | Bob Boone | KC | .462 |
| 8. | Joe Orsulak | BAL | .462 |
| 8. | Kirby Puckett | MIN | .462 |
| 11. | Pat Borders | TOR | .455 |
| 12. | Carmen Castillo | MIN | .444 |
| 12. | Brian Harper | MIN | .444 |
| 14. | George Bell | TOR | .419 |
| 15. | Rick Cerone | BOS | .417 |
| 15. | Steve Finley | BAL | .417 |
| 15. | Danny Heep | BOS | .417 |
| 15. | Nelson Liriano | TOR | .417 |
| 19. | Julio Franco | TEX | .400 |
| 19. | Jim Gantner | MIL | .400 |
| 19. | Mel Hall | NY | .400 |
| 19. | Ruben Sierra | TEX | .400 |

#### *Bottom 20*

|  |  |  |  |
|---|---|---|---|
| 165. | Andy Allanson | CLE | .000 |
| 165. | Kent Anderson | CAL | .000 |
| 165. | Mike Brumley | DET | .000 |
| 165. | Steve Buechele | TEX | .000 |
| 165. | Ron Karkovice | CHI | .000 |
| 165. | Fred Lynn | DET | .000 |
| 165. | Jim Rice | BOS | .000 |
| 165. | Rick Schu | DET | .000 |
| 164. | Bo Jackson | KC | .048 |
| 163. | Lance Parrish | CAL | .056 |
| 162. | Chili Davis | CAL | .067 |
| 160. | Mookie Wilson | TOR | .071 |
| 160. | Kenny Williams | DET | .071 |
| 158. | Oddibe McDowell | CLE | .077 |
| 158. | Rance Mulliniks | TOR | .077 |
| 156. | Kevin Romine | BOS | .083 |
| 156. | John Moses | MIN | .083 |
| 155. | Dave Gallagher | CHI | .091 |
| 151. | Mike Gallego | OAK | .111 |
| 151. | Doug Strange | DET | .111 |
| 151. | Phil Bradley | BAL | .111 |
| 151. | Randy Bush | MIN | .111 |

### *National League*

#### *Top 20*

|  |  |  |  |
|---|---|---|---|
| 1. | Kevin Mitchell | SF | .583 |
| 2. | Dave Magadan | NY | .571 |
| 2. | Lonnie Smith | ATL | .571 |
| 4. | Glenn Wilson | HOU | .500 |
| 5. | Pedro Guerrero | STL | .486 |
| 6. | Dale Murphy | ATL | .481 |
| 7. | Jay Bell | PIT | .462 |
| 8. | Rafael Ramirez | HOU | .452 |
| 9. | Wallace Johnson | MTL | .444 |
| 10. | Hubie Brooks | MTL | .409 |
| 10. | Will Clark | SF | .409 |
| 10. | Tony Gwynn | SD | .409 |
| 13. | Damaso Garcia | MTL | .400 |
| 13. | Rolando Roomes | CIN | .400 |
| 15. | Kevin Bass | HOU | .389 |
| 16. | Jerome Walton | CHI | .385 |
| 17. | Dickie Thon | PHI | .368 |
| 18. | Alex Trevino | HOU | .364 |
| 19. | Mookie Wilson | NY | .357 |
| 20. | Eric Davis | CIN | .346 |

#### *Bottom 20*

|  |  |  |  |
|---|---|---|---|
| 131. | Lenny Harris | LA | .000 |
| 131. | Gerald Perry | ATL | .000 |
| 131. | John Shelby | LA | .000 |
| 130. | Garry Templeton | SD | .056 |
| 129. | Steve Jeltz | PHI | .063 |
| 128. | John Cangelosi | PIT | .071 |
| 127. | Kal Daniels | LA | .083 |
| 126. | Jose Uribe | SF | .091 |
| 124. | Tim Teufel | NY | .100 |
| 124. | Matt Williams | SF | .100 |
| 121. | Mike Scioscia | LA | .111 |
| 121. | Darrell Evans | ATL | .111 |
| 121. | Tony Pena | STL | .111 |
| 120. | Darryl Strawberry | NY | .115 |
| 119. | Alfredo Griffin | LA | .118 |
| 118. | Andres Thomas | ATL | .120 |
| 116. | Jody Davis | ATL | .125 |
| 116. | Rey Quinones | PIT | .125 |
| 114. | Andy Van Slyke | PIT | .130 |
| 114. | Vince Coleman | STL | .130 |

## On Base Average Leading Off the Inning

### American League

| Top 20 | | | Bottom 20 | | |
|---|---|---|---|---|---|
| 1. Jim Dwyer | MIN | .500 | 171. Jim Traber | BAL | .169 |
| 2. Alvin Davis | SEA | .451 | 170. Mel Hall | NY | .207 |
| 3. Ellis Burks | BOS | .443 | 169. Ozzie Guillen | CHI | .207 |
| 4. Rick Leach | TEX | .435 | 168. Rene Gonzales | BAL | .229 |
| 5. Mookie Wilson | TOR | .435 | 167. Mike Pagliarulo | NY | .230 |
| 6. Randy Milligan | BAL | .434 | 165. Cory Snyder | CLE | .231 |
| 7. George Brett | KC | .419 | 165. Henry Cotto | SEA | .231 |
| 8. Rickey Henderson | OAK | .409 | 164. Alvaro Espinoza | NY | .233 |
| 9. Ron Kittle | CHI | .408 | 163. Mike Brumley | DET | .236 |
| 10. Don Slaught | NY | .408 | 162. Rick Cerone | BOS | .238 |
| 11. Dwight Evans | BOS | .406 | 161. B.j. Surhoff | MIL | .240 |
| 12. Fred McGriff | TOR | .403 | 160. Scott Bradley | SEA | .240 |
| 13. Wade Boggs | BOS | .402 | 159. Dave Clark | CLE | .241 |
| 14. Robin Yount | MIL | .394 | 158. Bob Melvin | BAL | .243 |
| 15. Pat Borders | TOR | .391 | 156. Alan Trammell | DET | .250 |
| 16. Jody Reed | BOS | .390 | 156. Tony Armas | CAL | .250 |
| 17. Pete O'Brien | CLE | .387 | 155. Kent Anderson | CAL | .255 |
| 18. Phil Bradley | BAL | .385 | 154. Fred Manrique | TEX | .257 |
| 19. Carney Lansford | OAK | .385 | 153. Terry Francona | MIL | .259 |
| 20. Walt Weiss | OAK | .383 | 152. Kenny Williams | DET | .259 |

### National League

| Top 20 | | | Bottom 20 | | |
|---|---|---|---|---|---|
| 1. John Kruk | PHI | .455 | 132. Rey Quinones | PIT | .185 |
| 2. Randy Ready | PHI | .435 | 131. Tommy Gregg | ATL | .186 |
| 3. Mark Grace | CHI | .430 | 130. Kirt Manwaring | SF | .204 |
| 4. Gary Redus | PIT | .427 | 129. Keith Miller | NY | .212 |
| 5. Tony Gwynn | SD | .419 | 128. Doug Dascenzo | CHI | .218 |
| 6. Bobby Bonilla | PIT | .417 | 127. Barry Lyons | NY | .224 |
| 7. Lloyd McClendon | CHI | .413 | 126. John Shelby | LA | .226 |
| 8. Bip Roberts | SD | .412 | 125. Nelson Santovenia | MTL | .227 |
| 9. Mike Marshall | LA | .409 | 124. Kevin Elster | NY | .228 |
| 10. Kal Daniels | LA | .408 | 123. Dale Murphy | ATL | .231 |
| 11. Dwight Smith | CHI | .400 | 121. Kirk Gibson | LA | .232 |
| 12. Will Clark | SF | .395 | 121. Andre Dawson | CHI | .232 |
| 13. Ernest Riles | SF | .392 | 120. Jose Uribe | SF | .236 |
| 14. Terry Pendleton | STL | .383 | 119. Bob Dernier | PHI | .239 |
| 15. Willie Randolph | LA | .382 | 118. Curt Ford | PHI | .240 |
| 16. Howard Johnson | NY | .380 | 117. Jay Bell | PIT | .241 |
| 17. Jack Clark | SD | .379 | 116. Andres Thomas | ATL | .242 |
| 18. Oddibe McDowell | ATL | .378 | 115. Glenn Wilson | HOU | .243 |
| 19. Jerome Walton | CHI | .377 | 114. Rex Hudler | MTL | .245 |
| 20. Von Hayes | PHI | .377 | 113. Jeff Reed | CIN | .246 |

## Batting Average with Runners in Scoring Position

### American League

| Top 20 | | | Bottom 20 | | |
|---|---|---|---|---|---|
| 1. Julio Franco | TEX | .407 | 172. Eddie Williams | CHI | .122 |
| 2. Charlie O'Brien | MIL | .385 | 171. Rich Gedman | BOS | .130 |
| 3. Fred Manrique | TEX | .384 | 170. Mike Brumley | DET | .133 |
| 4. Alvin Davis | SEA | .362 | 169. Andy Allanson | CLE | .163 |
| 5. Jose Canseco | OAK | .359 | 168. Rick Schu | DET | .167 |
| 6. Robin Yount | MIL | .355 | 167. Omar Vizquel | SEA | .178 |
| 7. Carlton Fisk | CHI | .352 | 166. Oddibe McDowell | CLE | .182 |
| 8. Bob Boone | KC | .350 | 165. Felix Fermin | CLE | .183 |
| 9. George Bell | TOR | .343 | 164. Gary Ward | DET | .187 |
| 10. Joey Belle | CLE | .339 | 163. Jesse Barfield | NY | .190 |
| 11. Rick Cerone | BOS | .338 | 162. Mickey Tettleton | BAL | .190 |
| 12. Ruben Sierra | TEX | .337 | 160. Gary Pettis | DET | .190 |
| 13. Danny Heep | BOS | .337 | 160. Dave Clark | CLE | .190 |
| 14. Wade Boggs | BOS | .336 | 159. Rick Leach | TEX | .191 |
| 15. Don Mattingly | NY | .331 | 158. Jack Howell | CAL | .195 |
| 16. Paul Molitor | MIL | .331 | 157. Rance Mulliniks | TOR | .195 |
| 17. Brian Harper | MIN | .330 | 156. Brady Anderson | BAL | .200 |
| 18. Kirby Puckett | MIN | .330 | 154. Greg Gagne | MIN | .205 |
| 19. John Moses | MIN | .328 | 154. Keith Moreland | BAL | .205 |
| 20. Dwight Evans | BOS | .323 | 153. Danny Tartabull | KC | .207 |

### National League

| Top 20 | | | Bottom 20 | | |
|---|---|---|---|---|---|
| 1. Lonnie Smith | ATL | .414 | 132. Ron Gant | ATL | .145 |
| 2. Pedro Guerrero | STL | .405 | 131. Matt Williams | SF | .150 |
| 3. Will Clark | SF | .389 | 130. Craig Reynolds | HOU | .152 |
| 4. Jay Bell | PIT | .358 | 129. Mookie Wilson | NY | .156 |
| 5. Dickie Thon | PHI | .356 | 128. Rob Thompson | SF | .173 |
| 6. Domingo Ramos | CHI | .354 | 127. John Shelby | LA | .175 |
| 7. Jerome Walton | CHI | .348 | 126. Randy Ready | PHI | .179 |
| 8. Tim Raines | MTL | .330 | 125. Keith Hernandez | NY | .183 |
| 9. Damon Berryhill | CHI | .326 | 124. Jeff King | PIT | .184 |
| 10. Kevin Bass | HOU | .324 | 123. Kirk Gibson | LA | .185 |
| 11. Jeff Blauser | ATL | .321 | 122. Carmelo Martinez | SD | .187 |
| 12. Eric Davis | CIN | .318 | 120. Jody Davis | ATL | .191 |
| 12. Tony Gwynn | SD | .318 | 120. Herm Winningham | CIN | .191 |
| 14. Milt Thompson | STL | .318 | 119. Vance Law | CHI | .197 |
| 15. Glenn Wilson | HOU | .314 | 118. Todd Benzinger | CIN | .199 |
| 16. Paul O'Neill | CIN | .312 | 115. Lenny Harris | LA | .200 |
| 17. Mark Grace | CHI | .311 | 115. Dwayne Murphy | PHI | .200 |
| 18. Ron Oester | CIN | .310 | 115. Vince Coleman | STL | .200 |
| 19. Dave Martinez | MTL | .309 | 114. Candy Maldonado | SF | .202 |
| 20. Howard Johnson | NY | .305 | 113. Len Dykstra | PHI | .203 |

## Batting Average with Runners in Scoring Position and Two Outs

### American League

| Top 20 | | | Bottom 20 | | |
|---|---|---|---|---|---|
| 1. Alvin Davis | SEA | .390 | 173. Oddibe McDowell | CLE | .045 |
| 2. Danny Heep | BOS | .386 | 172. Mike Brumley | DET | .080 |
| 3. Fred Manrique | TEX | .372 | 171. Brad Wellman | KC | .083 |
| 4. Rick Cerone | BOS | .368 | 169. Daryl Boston | CHI | .087 |
| 5. George Bell | TOR | .366 | 169. Eddie Williams | CHI | .087 |
| 6. Alvaro Espinoza | NY | .352 | 167. Rick Schu | DET | .091 |
| 7. Kirby Puckett | MIN | .345 | 167. Carmen Castillo | MIN | .091 |
| 8. Randy Milligan | BAL | .344 | 166. Dave Clark | CLE | .100 |
| 9. Julio Franco | TEX | .343 | 165. Danny Tartabull | KC | .105 |
| 10. Luis Polonia | NY | .340 | 164. Jerry Browne | CLE | .109 |
| 11. Bob Melvin | BAL | .333 | 163. Felix Fermin | CLE | .111 |
| 11. Charlie O'Brien | MIL | .333 | 162. Walt Weiss | OAK | .115 |
| 11. Geno Petralli | TEX | .333 | 161. Mickey Tettleton | BAL | .122 |
| 14. Kevin Romine | BOS | .324 | 160. Andy Allanson | CLE | .130 |
| 15. Nelson Liriano | TOR | .321 | 158. Gary Ward | DET | .133 |
| 16. Harold Baines | TEX | .321 | 158. Glenn Braggs | MIL | .133 |
| 17. Jay Buhner | SEA | .318 | 157. Tony Fernandez | TOR | .138 |
| 17. Lou Whitaker | DET | .318 | 156. Junior Felix | TOR | .140 |
| 19. Ruben Sierra | TEX | .314 | 155. Ken Phelps | OAK | .143 |
| 20. Jeff Kunkel | TEX | .308 | 154. Greg Walker | CHI | .148 |

### National League

| Top 20 | | | Bottom 20 | | |
|---|---|---|---|---|---|
| 1. Will Clark | SF | .435 | 132. Ron Gant | ATL | .086 |
| 2. Pedro Guerrero | STL | .424 | 130. Kal Daniels | LA | .100 |
| 3. Dave Martinez | MTL | .400 | 130. Tim Teufel | NY | .100 |
| 3. Lonnie Smith | ATL | .400 | 128. Tony Gwynn | SD | .111 |
| 5. Dwight Smith | CHI | .394 | 128. Tommy Gregg | ATL | .111 |
| 6. Eric Davis | CIN | .390 | 127. Charlie Hayes | PHI | .114 |
| 7. Milt Thompson | STL | .365 | 126. John Shelby | LA | .121 |
| 8. Domingo Ramos | CHI | .348 | 125. Rick Dempsey | LA | .130 |
| 9. Jerome Walton | CHI | .339 | 123. Barry Bonds | PIT | .133 |
| 10. Ken Caminiti | HOU | .333 | 123. Todd Benzinger | CIN | .133 |
| 10. Von Hayes | PHI | .333 | 122. Matt Williams | SF | .137 |
| 10. Barry Larkin | CIN | .333 | 121. Rey Quinones | PIT | .143 |
| 10. Gary Redus | PIT | .333 | 120. Andres Galarraga | MTL | .148 |
| 14. Mark Grace | CHI | .323 | 119. Lloyd McClendon | CHI | .156 |
| 15. Paul O'Neill | CIN | .321 | 118. Tony Pena | STL | .157 |
| 16. Andre Dawson | CHI | .320 | 117. Luis Salazar | CHI | .158 |
| 17. Lenny Harris | LA | .314 | 116. Rob Thompson | SF | .159 |
| 18. Jay Bell | PIT | .310 | 114. Junior Ortiz | PIT | .160 |
| 19. Ron Oester | CIN | .304 | 114. Kirk Gibson | LA | .160 |
| 20. Bip Roberts | SD | .303 | 113. Randy Ready | PHI | .162 |

## *Batting Average with Runners On Base and Two Outs*

### *American League*

#### *Top 20*

|  |  |  |  |
|---|---|---|---|
| 1. | Rick Cerone | BOS | .389 |
| 2. | Danny Heep | BOS | .375 |
| 3. | Fred Manrique | TEX | .366 |
| 4. | Jose Canseco | OAK | .364 |
| 5. | Geno Petralli | TEX | .351 |
| 6. | Kirby Puckett | MIN | .349 |
| 7. | Jeff Kunkel | TEX | .348 |
| 8. | Kevin Romine | BOS | .327 |
| 9. | Julio Franco | TEX | .322 |
| 10. | Harold Baines | TEX | .321 |
| 11. | Henry Cotto | SEA | .317 |
| 12. | George Bell | TOR | .316 |
| 13. | Carney Lansford | OAK | .314 |
| 14. | Alvin Davis | SEA | .313 |
| 15. | Bob Melvin | BAL | .311 |
| 16. | Jim Dwyer | MIN | .311 |
| 17. | Nelson Liriano | TOR | .311 |
| 18. | Ruben Sierra | TEX | .310 |
| 19. | Tony Armas | CAL | .310 |
| 20. | Kelly Gruber | TOR | .309 |

#### *Bottom 20*

|  |  |  |  |
|---|---|---|---|
| 172. | Rick Schu | DET | .109 |
| 171. | Brad Wellman | KC | .135 |
| 169. | Mickey Tettleton | BAL | .139 |
| 169. | Mike Brumley | DET | .139 |
| 168. | Tony Fernandez | TOR | .143 |
| 167. | Larry Sheets | BAL | .148 |
| 166. | Kent Hrbek | MIN | .149 |
| 165. | Andy Allanson | CLE | .151 |
| 164. | Danny Tartabull | KC | .154 |
| 163. | Stan Javier | OAK | .155 |
| 162. | Junior Felix | TOR | .162 |
| 161. | Darnell Coles | SEA | .165 |
| 160. | Rick Leach | TEX | .167 |
| 159. | Felix Fermin | CLE | .174 |
| 158. | Steve Buechele | TEX | .176 |
| 157. | Marty Barrett | BOS | .178 |
| 156. | Pat Borders | TOR | .179 |
| 155. | Jerry Browne | CLE | .182 |
| 154. | Carmen Castillo | MIN | .185 |
| 153. | Frank White | KC | .188 |

### *National League*

#### *Top 20*

|  |  |  |  |
|---|---|---|---|
| 1. | Lonnie Smith | ATL | .429 |
| 2. | Dwight Smith | CHI | .407 |
| 3. | Will Clark | SF | .405 |
| 4. | Barry Larkin | CIN | .400 |
| 5. | Pedro Guerrero | STL | .367 |
| 6. | Milt Thompson | STL | .365 |
| 7. | Paul O'Neill | CIN | .356 |
| 8. | Bip Roberts | SD | .341 |
| 9. | Mark Grace | CHI | .337 |
| 10. | Jay Bell | PIT | .333 |
| 10. | Ron Oester | CIN | .333 |
| 12. | Brett Butler | SF | .321 |
| 13. | Eric Davis | CIN | .315 |
| 14. | Domingo Ramos | CHI | .314 |
| 15. | Gary Redus | PIT | .313 |
| 16. | Dave Martinez | MTL | .310 |
| 17. | Jerome Walton | CHI | .310 |
| 18. | Von Hayes | PHI | .310 |
| 19. | Terry Pendleton | STL | .306 |
| 20. | Steve Jeltz | PHI | .302 |

#### *Bottom 20*

|  |  |  |  |
|---|---|---|---|
| 132. | Kal Daniels | LA | .091 |
| 131. | Ron Gant | ATL | .104 |
| 130. | Matt Williams | SF | .123 |
| 129. | Jeff King | PIT | .128 |
| 128. | Lloyd McClendon | CHI | .130 |
| 126. | Ken Griffey | CIN | .143 |
| 126. | Rick Dempsey | LA | .143 |
| 125. | Jose Uribe | SF | .149 |
| 124. | John Shelby | LA | .156 |
| 123. | Junior Ortiz | PIT | .159 |
| 122. | Otis Nixon | MTL | .160 |
| 121. | Darryl Strawberry | NY | .162 |
| 120. | Rey Quinones | PIT | .163 |
| 119. | Carmelo Martinez | SD | .164 |
| 118. | Vince Coleman | STL | .169 |
| 117. | Dwayne Murphy | PHI | .170 |
| 116. | Chris Sabo | CIN | .171 |
| 115. | Todd Benzinger | CIN | .172 |
| 114. | Luis Salazar | CHI | .176 |
| 113. | Tim Teufel | NY | .179 |

## *% of Runners Driven in from Scoring Position*

### *American League*

#### *Top 20*

|  |  |  |  |
|---|---|---|---|
| 1. | Jose Canseco | OAK | .423 |
| 2. | Rick Cerone | BOS | .384 |
| 3. | Julio Franco | TEX | .384 |
| 4. | Robin Yount | MIL | .380 |
| 5. | Ruben Sierra | TEX | .378 |
| 6. | Fred Manrique | TEX | .375 |
| 7. | Johnny Ray | CAL | .374 |
| 8. | George Bell | TOR | .373 |
| 9. | Charlie O'Brien | MIL | .371 |
| 10. | Don Mattingly | NY | .370 |
| 11. | Dan Pasqua | CHI | .368 |
| 12. | Alvin Davis | SEA | .361 |
| 13. | Kent Hrbek | MIN | .354 |
| 14. | George Brett | KC | .352 |
| 15. | John Moses | MIN | .351 |
| 16. | B.j. Surhoff | MIL | .344 |
| 17. | Dwight Evans | BOS | .340 |
| 18. | Tracy Jones | DET | .339 |
| 19. | Scott Bradley | SEA | .337 |
| 20. | Joe Orsulak | BAL | .336 |

#### *Bottom 20*

|  |  |  |  |
|---|---|---|---|
| 171. | Andy Allanson | CLE | .124 |
| 170. | Mike Brumley | DET | .130 |
| 169. | Rich Gedman | BOS | .139 |
| 168. | Rick Schu | DET | .147 |
| 167. | Gary Pettis | DET | .149 |
| 166. | Mike Pagliarulo | NY | .154 |
| 165. | Felix Fermin | CLE | .159 |
| 164. | Omar Vizquel | SEA | .165 |
| 163. | Jack Howell | CAL | .169 |
| 162. | Brady Anderson | BAL | .182 |
| 161. | Jim Presley | SEA | .191 |
| 159. | Kent Anderson | CAL | .194 |
| 159. | Kenny Williams | DET | .194 |
| 158. | Luis Rivera | BOS | .198 |
| 157. | Jesse Barfield | NY | .199 |
| 154. | Gary Ward | DET | .200 |
| 154. | Walt Weiss | OAK | .200 |
| 154. | Mike Felder | MIL | .200 |
| 153. | Jody Reed | BOS | .206 |
| 152. | Mookie Wilson | TOR | .209 |

### *National League*

#### *Top 20*

|  |  |  |  |
|---|---|---|---|
| 1. | Pedro Guerrero | STL | .447 |
| 2. | Lonnie Smith | ATL | .420 |
| 3. | Will Clark | SF | .392 |
| 4. | Jerome Walton | CHI | .351 |
| 5. | Mark Grace | CHI | .348 |
| 6. | Tony Gwynn | SD | .346 |
| 7. | Eric Davis | CIN | .345 |
| 8. | Barry Larkin | CIN | .341 |
| 9. | Jeff Blauser | ATL | .333 |
| 9. | Mike LaValliere | PIT | .333 |
| 9. | Tim Raines | MTL | .333 |
| 12. | Kevin Bass | HOU | .330 |
| 13. | Howard Johnson | NY | .327 |
| 14. | Lloyd McClendon | CHI | .325 |
| 15. | Dwight Smith | CHI | .324 |
| 16. | Charlie Hayes | PHI | .323 |
| 17. | Paul O'Neill | CIN | .323 |
| 18. | Milt Thompson | STL | .318 |
| 19. | Glenn Wilson | HOU | .318 |
| 20. | Kevin Mitchell | SF | .314 |

#### *Bottom 20*

|  |  |  |  |
|---|---|---|---|
| 132. | John Shelby | LA | .127 |
| 131. | Gerald Perry | ATL | .148 |
| 130. | Herm Winningham | CIN | .161 |
| 129. | Rob Thompson | SF | .167 |
| 128. | Tim Teufel | NY | .169 |
| 127. | Ron Gant | ATL | .171 |
| 126. | Vince Coleman | STL | .177 |
| 125. | Bob Dernier | PHI | .183 |
| 124. | Keith Hernandez | NY | .185 |
| 123. | Mookie Wilson | NY | .185 |
| 122. | Ron Oester | CIN | .194 |
| 121. | Randy Ready | PHI | .198 |
| 119. | Matt Williams | SF | .200 |
| 119. | Kirk Gibson | LA | .200 |
| 118. | Alfredo Griffin | LA | .203 |
| 117. | Mitch Webster | CHI | .205 |
| 116. | Jeff Reed | CIN | .207 |
| 115. | Luis Salazar | CHI | .209 |
| 114. | Mike Scioscia | LA | .210 |
| 113. | Lenny Harris | LA | .210 |

## *% of Runners Driven in from Third with Less than Two Out*

### *American League*

#### *Top 20*

|  |  |  |  |
|---|---|---|---|
| 1. | Rick Leach | TEX | .923 |
| 2. | Tony Fernandez | TOR | .900 |
| 3. | Robin Yount | MIL | .848 |
| 4. | Al Newman | MIN | .842 |
| 5. | Carlton Fisk | CHI | .818 |
| 6. | Brian Harper | MIN | .810 |
| 7. | Daryl Boston | CHI | .800 |
| 7. | Tracy Jones | DET | .800 |
| 7. | Joey Meyer | MIL | .800 |
| 7. | Tony Phillips | OAK | .800 |
| 11. | Rafael Palmeiro | TEX | .786 |
| 12. | Jose Canseco | OAK | .773 |
| 13. | Kent Hrbek | MIN | .750 |
| 13. | Stan Jefferson | BAL | .750 |
| 13. | Manny Lee | TOR | .750 |
| 13. | Oddibe McDowell | CLE | .750 |
| 13. | Ken Phelps | OAK | .750 |
| 18. | Paul Molitor | MIL | .739 |
| 19. | Jim Gantner | MIL | .733 |
| 20. | Jerry Browne | CLE | .731 |

#### *Bottom 20*

|  |  |  |  |
|---|---|---|---|
| 173. | Gary Pettis | DET | .083 |
| 172. | Bill Schroeder | CAL | .182 |
| 169. | Sammy Sosa | CHI | .300 |
| 169. | Matt Winters | KC | .300 |
| 169. | Tom Brookens | NY | .300 |
| 168. | Mike Pagliarulo | NY | .308 |
| 167. | Jack Howell | CAL | .313 |
| 163. | Lloyd Moseby | TOR | .333 |
| 163. | Mike Brumley | DET | .333 |
| 163. | Rob Deer | MIL | .333 |
| 163. | Jeff Kunkel | TEX | .333 |
| 162. | Omar Vizquel | SEA | .350 |
| 161. | Rich Gedman | BOS | .357 |
| 158. | Eddie Williams | CHI | .364 |
| 158. | Steve Buechele | TEX | .364 |
| 158. | Bob Melvin | BAL | .364 |
| 156. | Cecil Espy | TEX | .375 |
| 156. | Cory Snyder | CLE | .375 |
| 155. | Jim Presley | SEA | .381 |
| 154. | Lance Parrish | CAL | .385 |

### *National League*

#### *Top 20*

|  |  |  |  |
|---|---|---|---|
| 1. | Shawn Abner | SD | .875 |
| 2. | Charlie Hayes | PHI | .864 |
| 3. | Doug Dascenzo | CHI | .800 |
| 4. | Dave Magadan | NY | .786 |
| 5. | Rey Quinones | PIT | .778 |
| 6. | Terry Kennedy | SF | .769 |
| 7. | Mark Grace | CHI | .765 |
| 8. | Barry Larkin | CIN | .762 |
| 8. | Jeff Treadway | ATL | .762 |
| 10. | Mark Parent | SD | .750 |
| 10. | Domingo Ramos | CHI | .750 |
| 10. | Luis Salazar | CHI | .750 |
| 13. | Ken Oberkfell | SF | .727 |
| 13. | Nelson Santovenia | MTL | .727 |
| 15. | Jeff Blauser | ATL | .706 |
| 16. | Tony Gwynn | SD | .705 |
| 17. | Steve Jeltz | PHI | .700 |
| 17. | Tim Raines | MTL | .700 |
| 19. | Damaso Garcia | MTL | .692 |
| 20. | Ricky Jordan | PHI | .688 |
| 20. | Mike Schmidt | PHI | .688 |

#### *Bottom 20*

|  |  |  |  |
|---|---|---|---|
| 147. | Lenny Harris | LA | .125 |
| 147. | Pat Sheridan | SF | .125 |
| 144. | Benny Distefano | PIT | .222 |
| 144. | Gerald Perry | ATL | .222 |
| 144. | Jody Davis | ATL | .222 |
| 143. | Dave Collins | CIN | .250 |
| 142. | Mitch Webster | CHI | .286 |
| 141. | Carmelo Martinez | SD | .345 |
| 140. | Ron Oester | CIN | .357 |
| 136. | Gary Carter | NY | .375 |
| 136. | Joe Girardi | CHI | .375 |
| 136. | Keith Hernandez | NY | .375 |
| 136. | Steve Lake | PHI | .375 |
| 135. | Spike Owen | MTL | .389 |
| 130. | John Shelby | LA | .400 |
| 130. | Otis Nixon | MTL | .400 |
| 130. | Rolando Roomes | CIN | .400 |
| 130. | Bob Dernier | PHI | .400 |
| 130. | Jose Gonzalez | LA | .400 |
| 129. | Vince Coleman | STL | .409 |

## *Opponents' Batting Average*

### *American League*

#### *Top 20*

|  |  |  |  |
|---|---|---|---|
| 1. | Jeff Russell | TEX | .182 |
| 2. | Nolan Ryan | TEX | .187 |
| 3. | Gregg Olson | BAL | .188 |
| 4. | Todd Burns | OAK | .196 |
| 5. | Jeff Montgomery | KC | .198 |
| 6. | Jesse Orosco | CLE | .198 |
| 7. | Gene Nelson | OAK | .203 |
| 8. | Tom Henke | TOR | .205 |
| 9. | Rick Honeycutt | OAK | .207 |
| 10. | David Wells | TOR | .207 |
| 11. | Chuck Cary | NY | .209 |
| 12. | Lee Smith | BOS | .209 |
| 13. | Tom Gordon | KC | .210 |
| 14. | Gary Wayne | MIN | .212 |
| 15. | Bret Saberhagen | KC | .217 |
| 16. | Bobby Thigpen | CHI | .218 |
| 17. | Dave Stieb | TOR | .219 |
| 18. | Mike Moore | OAK | .219 |
| 19. | Eric Plunk | NY | .220 |
| 20. | Mark Langston | SEA | .221 |

#### *Bottom 20*

|  |  |  |  |
|---|---|---|---|
| 134. | Tommy John | NY | .336 |
| 133. | Bob Stanley | BOS | .321 |
| 132. | Dave LaPoint | NY | .311 |
| 131. | Dave Schmidt | BAL | .310 |
| 130. | Walt Terrell | NY | .307 |
| 129. | Mike Dunne | SEA | .307 |
| 128. | Charlie Leibrandt | KC | .304 |
| 127. | Don August | MIL | .302 |
| 126. | Jerry Reuss | MIL | .300 |
| 125. | Brian Holton | BAL | .300 |
| 124. | Mike Smithson | BOS | .297 |
| 123. | Steve Farr | KC | .296 |
| 122. | Richard Dotson | CHI | .294 |
| 121. | Shane Rawley | MIN | .293 |
| 120. | Mark Guthrie | MIN | .292 |
| 119. | Mike Witt | CAL | .292 |
| 118. | Andy Hawkins | NY | .290 |
| 117. | Floyd Bannister | KC | .290 |
| 116. | Charles Hudson | DET | .288 |
| 114. | Mark Thurmond | BAL | .288 |
| 114. | Storm Davis | OAK | .288 |

### *National League*

#### *Top 20*

|  |  |  |  |
|---|---|---|---|
| 1. | Rob Dibble | CIN | .176 |
| 2. | Bob Kipper | PIT | .188 |
| 3. | Steve Bedrosian | SF | .189 |
| 4. | Jose DeLeon | STL | .197 |
| 5. | Norm Charlton | CIN | .197 |
| 6. | Sid Fernandez | NY | .198 |
| 7. | Larry Andersen | HOU | .198 |
| 8. | Calvin Schiraldi | SD | .199 |
| 9. | Mark Davis | SD | .200 |
| 10. | Bill Landrum | PIT | .205 |
| 11. | Randy Myers | NY | .206 |
| 12. | Dwight Gooden | NY | .211 |
| 13. | Jay Howell | LA | .211 |
| 14. | Doug Bair | PIT | .211 |
| 15. | John Smoltz | ATL | .212 |
| 16. | Scott Garrelts | SF | .212 |
| 17. | Danny Darwin | HOU | .212 |
| 18. | Mike Scott | HOU | .212 |
| 19. | Andrew Benes | SD | .213 |
| 20. | John Costello | STL | .213 |

#### *Bottom 20*

|  |  |  |  |
|---|---|---|---|
| 116. | Ricky Horton | STL | .305 |
| 115. | Bob Forsch | HOU | .303 |
| 114. | Derek Lilliquist | ATL | .301 |
| 113. | Bruce Ruffin | PHI | .301 |
| 112. | Bob Sebra | CIN | .295 |
| 111. | Terry Mulholland | PHI | .295 |
| 110. | Andy McGaffigan | MTL | .293 |
| 109. | Bob Knepper | SF | .293 |
| 108. | Rick Rhoden | HOU | .289 |
| 107. | Dan Schatzeder | HOU | .287 |
| 106. | Tim Crews | LA | .284 |
| 105. | Paul Kilgus | CHI | .283 |
| 104. | Jeff Robinson | PIT | .283 |
| 103. | Rick Mahler | CIN | .282 |
| 102. | Jeff Pico | CHI | .278 |
| 101. | Walt Terrell | SD | .277 |
| 100. | Mark Eichhorn | ATL | .275 |
| 99. | Eric Show | SD | .274 |
| 98. | Scott Sanderson | CHI | .274 |
| 96. | Bob Walk | PIT | .271 |
| 96. | Atlee Hammaker | SF | .271 |

## *Opponents' Slugging Average*

### *American League*

#### *Top 20*

|  |  |  |  |
|---|---|---|---|
| 1. | Gregg Olson | BAL | .247 |
| 2. | Jeff Montgomery | KC | .251 |
| 3. | Todd Burns | OAK | .264 |
| 4. | Rick Honeycutt | OAK | .277 |
| 5. | Jeff Russell | TEX | .279 |
| 6. | Nolan Ryan | TEX | .283 |
| 7. | Gene Nelson | OAK | .294 |
| 8. | Dennis Lamp | BOS | .297 |
| 9. | David Wells | TOR | .298 |
| 10. | Greg Minton | CAL | .299 |
| 11. | Kenny Rogers | TEX | .301 |
| 12. | Duane Ward | TOR | .304 |
| 13. | Lee Smith | BOS | .304 |
| 14. | Tom Gordon | KC | .306 |
| 15. | Mike Moore | OAK | .307 |
| 16. | Kevin Brown | TEX | .312 |
| 17. | Tom Henke | TOR | .314 |
| 18. | Dave Stieb | TOR | .316 |
| 19. | Bret Saberhagen | KC | .317 |
| 20. | Tom Candiotti | CLE | .319 |

#### *Bottom 20*

|  |  |  |  |
|---|---|---|---|
| 134. | Charles Hudson | DET | .504 |
| 133. | Jose Bautista | BAL | .492 |
| 132. | Dave Schmidt | BAL | .481 |
| 131. | Dave LaPoint | NY | .481 |
| 130. | Walt Terrell | NY | .470 |
| 129. | Mike Smithson | BOS | .468 |
| 128. | Shane Rawley | MIN | .467 |
| 127. | Ken Patterson | CHI | .462 |
| 126. | Andy Hawkins | NY | .460 |
| 125. | Dale Mohorcic | NY | .458 |
| 124. | Richard Dotson | CHI | .457 |
| 123. | Jack Morris | DET | .450 |
| 122. | Wes Gardner | BOS | .447 |
| 121. | Jerry Reuss | MIL | .446 |
| 120. | Tommy John | NY | .444 |
| 119. | Mark Guthrie | MIN | .442 |
| 118. | Charlie Leibrandt | KC | .439 |
| 117. | Bryan Clutterbuck | MIL | .439 |
| 116. | Steve Rosenberg | CHI | .438 |
| 115. | Jamie Moyer | TEX | .438 |

### *National League*

#### *Top 20*

|  |  |  |  |
|---|---|---|---|
| 1. | Larry Andersen | HOU | .245 |
| 2. | Rob Dibble | CIN | .250 |
| 3. | Bill Landrum | PIT | .264 |
| 4. | Les Lancaster | CHI | .287 |
| 5. | Norm Charlton | CIN | .288 |
| 6. | Jay Howell | LA | .289 |
| 7. | Mark Davis | SD | .294 |
| 8. | Rick Aguilera | NY | .298 |
| 9. | Greg Harris | SD | .298 |
| 10. | Doug Bair | PIT | .301 |
| 11. | Danny Darwin | HOU | .302 |
| 12. | Roger McDowell | PHI | .304 |
| 13. | Jose DeLeon | STL | .309 |
| 14. | Randy Myers | NY | .309 |
| 15. | Calvin Schiraldi | SD | .310 |
| 16. | John Franco | CIN | .311 |
| 17. | Scott Garrelts | SF | .313 |
| 18. | Dwight Gooden | NY | .313 |
| 19. | Ken Howell | PHI | .313 |
| 20. | Mike LaCoss | SF | .316 |

#### *Bottom 20*

|  |  |  |  |
|---|---|---|---|
| 116. | Bob Sebra | CIN | .486 |
| 115. | Tim Crews | LA | .461 |
| 114. | Don Carman | PHI | .442 |
| 113. | Derek Lilliquist | ATL | .435 |
| 112. | Bob Forsch | HOU | .435 |
| 111. | Eric Show | SD | .434 |
| 110. | Bob Knepper | SF | .433 |
| 109. | Bruce Ruffin | PHI | .432 |
| 108. | Walt Terrell | SD | .430 |
| 107. | Jeff Robinson | PIT | .427 |
| 106. | Dennis Cook | PHI | .425 |
| 105. | Jim Clancy | HOU | .422 |
| 104. | Rick Rhoden | HOU | .414 |
| 103. | Scott Sanderson | CHI | .413 |
| 102. | Ricky Horton | STL | .412 |
| 101. | Kelly Downs | SF | .411 |
| 100. | Terry Mulholland | PHI | .409 |
| 99. | Dan Schatzeder | HOU | .408 |
| 98. | Tom Browning | CIN | .408 |
| 97. | Mark Eichhorn | ATL | .408 |

## *Opponents' Home Run Percentage*

### *American League*

#### *Top 20*

|  |  |  |  |
|---|---|---|---|
| 1. | Gregg Olson | BAL | 0.33 |
| 2. | Mike Schooler | SEA | 0.66 |
| 3. | Kevin Ritz | DET | 0.71 |
| 4. | Mike Dyer | MIN | 0.74 |
| 5. | Kenny Rogers | TEX | 0.77 |
| 6. | Todd Burns | OAK | 0.89 |
| 7. | Jeff Montgomery | KC | 0.90 |
| 8. | Greg Hibbard | CHI | 0.95 |
| 9. | Dennis Lamp | BOS | 0.98 |
| 9. | Duane Ward | TOR | 0.98 |
| 11. | Mark Williamson | BAL | 0.99 |
| 12. | Mark Gubicza | KC | 1.03 |
| 13. | Luis Aquino | KC | 1.10 |
| 14. | Mark Langston | SEA | 1.11 |
| 15. | Dave Righetti | NY | 1.14 |
| 16. | Mike Henneman | DET | 1.19 |
| 17. | Greg Minton | CAL | 1.21 |
| 18. | Bob Stanley | BOS | 1.26 |
| 19. | Tom Candiotti | CLE | 1.29 |
| 20. | Doug Jones | CLE | 1.32 |

#### *Bottom 20*

|  |  |  |  |
|---|---|---|---|
| 134. | Jose Bautista | BAL | 5.54 |
| 133. | Charles Hudson | DET | 5.38 |
| 132. | Ken Patterson | CHI | 4.42 |
| 131. | Charlie Hough | TEX | 4.09 |
| 130. | Bryan Clutterbuck | MIL | 4.06 |
| 129. | Dave Schmidt | BAL | 3.80 |
| 128. | Mike Smithson | BOS | 3.66 |
| 127. | Dale Mohorcic | NY | 3.52 |
| 126. | Bobby Thigpen | CHI | 3.51 |
| 125. | Chuck Cary | NY | 3.49 |
| 124. | Jack Morris | DET | 3.44 |
| 123. | Jeff Robinson | DET | 3.40 |
| 122. | Jamie Moyer | TEX | 3.37 |
| 121. | Shane Rawley | MIN | 3.34 |
| 120. | Jerry Reuss | MIL | 3.33 |
| 119. | Roy Smith | MIN | 3.29 |
| 118. | Melido Perez | CHI | 3.25 |
| 117. | Dave Johnson | BAL | 3.24 |
| 116. | Mark Knudson | MIL | 3.23 |
| 115. | Doyle Alexander | DET | 3.20 |

### *National League*

#### *Top 20*

|  |  |  |  |
|---|---|---|---|
| 1. | Mike LaCoss | SF | 0.54 |
| 2. | Joe Magrane | STL | 0.57 |
| 3. | Larry Andersen | HOU | 0.63 |
| 4. | Larry McWilliams | PHI | 0.65 |
| 5. | Dan Quisenberry | STL | 0.67 |
| 6. | Bill Landrum | PIT | 0.68 |
| 7. | Les Lancaster | CHI | 0.75 |
| 8. | Roger McDowell | PHI | 0.88 |
| 9. | Dan Schatzeder | HOU | 0.90 |
| 10. | Juan Agosto | HOU | 0.95 |
| 11. | Orel Hershiser | LA | 0.96 |
| 12. | John Franco | CIN | 1.00 |
| 13. | Paul Assenmacher | CHI | 1.03 |
| 13. | Andy McGaffigan | MTL | 1.03 |
| 15. | Jay Howell | LA | 1.06 |
| 16. | Ricky Horton | STL | 1.08 |
| 17. | Mike Morgan | LA | 1.08 |
| 18. | Ken Dayley | STL | 1.09 |
| 19. | Rob Dibble | CIN | 1.14 |
| 20. | Rick Aguilera | NY | 1.18 |

#### *Bottom 20*

|  |  |  |  |
|---|---|---|---|
| 116. | Steve Bedrosian | SF | 4.04 |
| 115. | Dennis Cook | PHI | 3.98 |
| 114. | Scott Scudder | CIN | 3.68 |
| 113. | Bob Sebra | CIN | 3.64 |
| 112. | Don Carman | PHI | 3.60 |
| 111. | Tom Browning | CIN | 3.28 |
| 110. | Ramon Martinez | LA | 3.06 |
| 109. | Don Robinson | SF | 2.96 |
| 108. | Andrew Benes | SD | 2.92 |
| 107. | Walt Terrell | SD | 2.89 |
| 106. | Tim Crews | LA | 2.88 |
| 105. | John Smiley | PIT | 2.86 |
| 104. | Scott Sanderson | CHI | 2.83 |
| 103. | Tom Glavine | ATL | 2.82 |
| 102. | Craig Lefferts | SF | 2.76 |
| 101. | Mike Scott | HOU | 2.71 |
| 100. | Jeff Brantley | SF | 2.68 |
| 99. | Sid Fernandez | NY | 2.64 |
| 98. | Kevin Gross | MTL | 2.63 |
| 97. | Ed Whitson | SD | 2.62 |

## *Opponents' Extra Base Hits per 100 At Bats*

### *American League*

| Top 20 | | | Bottom 20 | | |
|---|---|---|---|---|---|
| 1. Jeff Montgomery | KC | 3.29 | 134. Dave LaPoint | NY | 11.28 |
| 2. Rick Honeycutt | OAK | 3.32 | 133. Andy Hawkins | NY | 10.49 |
| 3. Dennis Lamp | BOS | 3.92 | 132. Steve Rosenberg | CHI | 10.17 |
| 4. Greg Minton | CAL | 3.93 | 131. Ken Patterson | CHI | 10.04 |
| 5. Todd Burns | OAK | 4.45 | 130. Charles Hudson | DET | 10.00 |
| 6. Tony Fossas | MIL | 4.48 | 129. Walt Terrell | NY | 9.94 |
| 7. Tom Candiotti | CLE | 4.63 | 128. Lance McCullers | NY | 9.85 |
| 8. Gene Nelson | OAK | 4.73 | 127. Chuck Cary | NY | 9.65 |
| 9. Lee Guetterman | NY | 4.74 | 126. Shane Rawley | MIN | 9.49 |
| 10. Lee Smith | BOS | 4.74 | 125. Jose Bautista | BAL | 9.45 |
| 11. Chris Bosio | MIL | 4.86 | 124. Richard Dotson | CHI | 9.43 |
| 12. Kevin Brown | TEX | 4.90 | 123. Jimmy Key | TOR | 9.43 |
| 13. Duane Ward | TOR | 4.90 | 122. Rick Aguilera | MIN | 9.31 |
| 14. Eric King | CHI | 4.91 | 121. Dale Mohorcic | NY | 9.25 |
| 15. Luis Aquino | KC | 5.13 | 120. Mike Smithson | BOS | 9.25 |
| 16. Chuck Crim | MIL | 5.23 | 119. Dave Schmidt | BAL | 9.18 |
| 16. Mike Moore | OAK | 5.23 | 118. Wes Gardner | BOS | 9.17 |
| 18. Gregg Olson | BAL | 5.26 | 117. Jack Morris | DET | 9.12 |
| 19. Bert Blyleven | CAL | 5.29 | 116. Melido Perez | CHI | 9.04 |
| 20. David Wells | TOR | 5.33 | 115. Shawn Hillegas | CHI | 8.88 |

### *National League*

| Top 20 | | | Bottom 20 | | |
|---|---|---|---|---|---|
| 1. Larry Andersen | HOU | 2.83 | 116. Eric Show | SD | 10.68 |
| 2. John Franco | CIN | 3.34 | 115. Bob Sebra | CIN | 10.45 |
| 3. Les Lancaster | CHI | 3.77 | 114. Tim Crews | LA | 10.29 |
| 4. Rick Aguilera | NY | 4.31 | 113. Don Carman | PHI | 10.27 |
| 5. Frank Viola | NY | 4.40 | 112. Kelly Downs | SF | 9.87 |
| 6. Bill Landrum | PIT | 4.45 | 111. Jim Clancy | HOU | 9.72 |
| 7. Danny Darwin | HOU | 4.61 | 110. Dennis Cook | PHI | 9.51 |
| 8. Greg Harris | SD | 4.67 | 109. Jeff Parrett | PHI | 9.28 |
| 9. Juan Agosto | HOU | 4.75 | 108. Scott Terry | STL | 9.09 |
| 10. Atlee Hammaker | SF | 4.86 | 107. Dan Schatzeder | HOU | 8.97 |
| 11. Mike LaCoss | SF | 5.00 | 106. Don Aase | NY | 8.73 |
| 12. Roger McDowell | PHI | 5.01 | 105. Cris Carpenter | STL | 8.61 |
| 13. Rob Dibble | CIN | 5.11 | 104. Tom Browning | CIN | 8.46 |
| 14. Mark Davis | SD | 5.15 | 103. John Costello | STL | 8.44 |
| 15. Jay Howell | LA | 5.28 | 102. Scott Scudder | CIN | 8.42 |
| 16. Norm Charlton | CIN | 5.29 | 101. Don Robinson | SF | 8.34 |
| 17. Tim Belcher | LA | 5.49 | 100. Bruce Ruffin | PHI | 8.32 |
| 18. Orel Hershiser | LA | 5.52 | 99. Rick Rhoden | HOU | 8.29 |
| 19. Mike Morgan | LA | 5.59 | 98. Rick Mahler | CIN | 8.27 |
| 20. Tim Burke | MTL | 5.63 | 97. Jeff Robinson | PIT | 8.26 |

## *Opponents' Batting Average, Left-Handed Batters*

### *American League*

| Top 20 | | | Bottom 20 | | |
|---|---|---|---|---|---|
| 1. Gregg Olson | BAL | .135 | 135. Shane Rawley | MIN | .362 |
| 2. Jesse Orosco | CLE | .138 | 134. Mike Schwabe | DET | .362 |
| 3. Rick Honeycutt | OAK | .156 | 133. Bill Wegman | MIL | .360 |
| 4. Bud Black | CLE | .158 | 132. Dan Petry | CAL | .352 |
| 5. Bryan Harvey | CAL | .160 | 131. Bob Stanley | BOS | .348 |
| 6. Kenny Rogers | TEX | .169 | 130. Charlie Leibrandt | KC | .338 |
| 7. Todd Burns | OAK | .172 | 128. Walt Terrell | NY | .333 |
| 8. Chuck Finley | CAL | .172 | 128. Mike Dunne | SEA | .333 |
| 9. Nolan Ryan | TEX | .177 | 127. Juan Berenguer | MIN | .329 |
| 10. Tony Fossas | MIL | .183 | 126. Dave LaPoint | NY | .326 |
| 11. Bobby Thigpen | CHI | .191 | 125. Jim Abbott | CAL | .325 |
| 12. Gary Wayne | MIN | .193 | 124. Andy Hawkins | NY | .323 |
| 13. Tom Henke | TOR | .195 | 123. Rod Nichols | CLE | .323 |
| 14. Bret Saberhagen | KC | .195 | 122. Dale Mohorcic | NY | .320 |
| 15. Jeff Russell | TEX | .205 | 121. Jerry Reuss | MIL | .317 |
| 16. Dennis Eckersley | OAK | .206 | 120. Bill Swift | SEA | .316 |
| 16. Mike Flanagan | TOR | .206 | 119. Todd Stottlemyre | TOR | .314 |
| 18. Jeff Montgomery | KC | .211 | 118. Wes Gardner | BOS | .313 |
| 18. Bob Welch | OAK | .211 | 117. Shawn Hillegas | CHI | .313 |
| 20. Greg Minton | CAL | .211 | 116. Mike Smithson | BOS | .311 |

### *National League*

| Top 20 | | | Bottom 20 | | |
|---|---|---|---|---|---|
| 1. Neal Heaton | PIT | .132 | 116. Kent Tekulve | CIN | .362 |
| 2. Zane Smith | MTL | .139 | 115. Todd Frohwirth | PHI | .350 |
| 3. Norm Charlton | CIN | .148 | 114. Mark Eichhorn | ATL | .350 |
| 4. Bob Kipper | PIT | .170 | 113. Bob Sebra | CIN | .345 |
| 5. Bill Landrum | PIT | .176 | 112. Jeff Pico | CHI | .313 |
| 6. Larry McWilliams | PHI | .181 | 111. Floyd Youmans | PHI | .311 |
| 7. Dwight Gooden | NY | .181 | 110. Rick Reed | PIT | .307 |
| 8. Mark Langston | MTL | .185 | 109. Rick Mahler | CIN | .305 |
| 9. Rob Dibble | CIN | .186 | 108. Bob Forsch | HOU | .304 |
| 10. Ken Dayley | STL | .188 | 107. Kelly Downs | SF | .303 |
| 11. Greg Harris | PHI | .190 | 106. Jeff Brantley | SF | .302 |
| 12. Doug Bair | PIT | .193 | 105. Tim Leary | CIN | .300 |
| 13. Greg Harris | SD | .196 | 104. Bob Knepper | SF | .300 |
| 14. Sid Fernandez | NY | .197 | 103. Bruce Hurst | SD | .299 |
| 15. Tim Birtsas | CIN | .198 | 102. Scott Sanderson | CHI | .293 |
| 16. Craig Lefferts | SF | .200 | 101. Walt Terrell | SD | .291 |
| 17. Steve Bedrosian | SF | .201 | 100. Jim Clancy | HOU | .291 |
| 18. Les Lancaster | CHI | .203 | 99. Dan Schatzeder | HOU | .288 |
| 19. Tom Glavine | ATL | .204 | 98. Bob Walk | PIT | .285 |
| 20. Calvin Schiraldi | SD | .204 | 97. Dennis Martinez | MTL | .285 |

## *Opponents' Batting Average, Right-Handed Batters*

### *American League*

| Top 20 | | | Bottom 20 | | |
|---|---|---|---|---|---|
| 1. Jeff Russell | TEX | .163 | 134. Dave West | MIN | .319 |
| 2. Gene Nelson | OAK | .174 | 133. Tommy John | NY | .318 |
| 3. Juan Berenguer | MIN | .185 | 132. Dave Schmidt | BAL | .317 |
| 4. Jeff Montgomery | KC | .187 | 131. Storm Davis | OAK | .310 |
| 5. Dave Stieb | TOR | .188 | 130. Dave LaPoint | NY | .307 |
| 6. Dennis Lamp | BOS | .193 | 129. Don August | MIL | .304 |
| 7. Lee Smith | BOS | .197 | 128. Bob Stanley | BOS | .299 |
| 8. Nolan Ryan | TEX | .197 | 127. Richard Dotson | CHI | .298 |
| 9. David Wells | TOR | .199 | 126. Tony Fossas | MIL | .298 |
| 10. Tom Gordon | KC | .200 | 125. Jerry Reuss | MIL | .296 |
| 11. Duane Ward | TOR | .208 | 124. Mike Flanagan | TOR | .296 |
| 12. Dan Plesac | MIL | .209 | 123. Charlie Leibrandt | KC | .296 |
| 13. Todd Burns | OAK | .212 | 121. Jamie Moyer | TEX | .294 |
| 14. Chuck Cary | NY | .212 | 121. Gary Mielke | TEX | .294 |
| 15. Tom Henke | TOR | .214 | 120. Mark Guthrie | MIN | .291 |
| 16. Rick Aguilera | MIN | .216 | 119. Brian Holton | BAL | .291 |
| 17. Eric Plunk | NY | .217 | 118. Greg Cadaret | NY | .290 |
| 18. Roger Clemens | BOS | .218 | 117. Mark Thurmond | BAL | .290 |
| 19. Mike Moore | OAK | .220 | 116. Jeff Ballard | BAL | .288 |
| 20. Jerry Reed | SEA | .221 | 115. Mike Witt | CAL | .288 |

### *National League*

| Top 20 | | | Bottom 20 | | |
|---|---|---|---|---|---|
| 1. Jose DeLeon | STL | .146 | 116. Andy McGaffigan | MTL | .353 |
| 2. Larry Andersen | HOU | .146 | 115. Tim Crews | LA | .316 |
| 3. Todd Frohwirth | PHI | .159 | 114. Rick Rhoden | HOU | .314 |
| 4. Rob Dibble | CIN | .167 | 113. Terry Mulholland | PHI | .313 |
| 4. Mike Scott | HOU | .167 | 112. Jeff Robinson | PIT | .311 |
| 6. Danny Darwin | HOU | .170 | 111. Derek Lilliquist | ATL | .308 |
| 7. Steve Bedrosian | SF | .173 | 110. Bruce Ruffin | PHI | .304 |
| 8. Scott Garrelts | SF | .183 | 109. Bob Forsch | HOU | .301 |
| 9. Ramon Martinez | LA | .185 | 108. Ricky Horton | STL | .292 |
| 10. Jim Acker | ATL | .187 | 107. Bob Knepper | SF | .291 |
| 11. Ken Howell | PHI | .188 | 106. Paul Kilgus | CHI | .290 |
| 12. Mark Davis | SD | .194 | 105. Zane Smith | MTL | .289 |
| 13. Calvin Schiraldi | SD | .194 | 104. Joe Hesketh | MTL | .289 |
| 14. Roger McDowell | PHI | .195 | 103. Tim Birtsas | CIN | .289 |
| 15. Bob Kipper | PIT | .196 | 102. Dan Schatzeder | HOU | .287 |
| 16. Ed Whitson | SD | .198 | 101. Larry McWilliams | PHI | .283 |
| 17. Sid Fernandez | NY | .198 | 100. Dan Quisenberry | STL | .282 |
| 18. Trevor Wilson | SF | .204 | 99. Eric Show | SD | .281 |
| 19. John Costello | STL | .204 | 98. Juan Agosto | HOU | .275 |
| 20. Mark Eichhorn | ATL | .205 | 97. Dennis Rasmussen | SD | .275 |

## Opponents' Slugging Average, Left-Handed Batters

### American League

#### Top 20

|  |  |  |  |
|---|---|---|---|
| 1. | Gregg Olson | BAL | .149 |
| 2. | Jesse Orosco | CLE | .184 |
| 3. | Chuck Finley | CAL | .192 |
| 4. | Rick Honeycutt | OAK | .200 |
| 5. | Kenny Rogers | TEX | .217 |
| 6. | Tony Fossas | MIL | .220 |
| 7. | Todd Burns | OAK | .231 |
| 8. | Bud Black | CLE | .233 |
| 9. | Mike Flanagan | TOR | .237 |
| 10. | Jeff Russell | TEX | .241 |
| 11. | Bill Krueger | MIL | .245 |
| 12. | Dennis Eckersley | OAK | .258 |
| 13. | Nolan Ryan | TEX | .262 |
| 14. | Jeff Montgomery | KC | .270 |
| 15. | Greg Minton | CAL | .272 |
| 16. | Mike Moore | OAK | .277 |
| 17. | Scott Bailes | CLE | .280 |
| 17. | Bryan Harvey | CAL | .280 |
| 19. | Lee Guetterman | NY | .283 |
| 20. | Erik Hanson | SEA | .283 |

#### Bottom 20

|  |  |  |  |
|---|---|---|---|
| 135. | Mike Schwabe | DET | .619 |
| 134. | Dan Petry | CAL | .602 |
| 133. | Bill Wegman | MIL | .588 |
| 132. | Walt Terrell | NY | .556 |
| 131. | Shane Rawley | MIN | .543 |
| 130. | Dave LaPoint | NY | .535 |
| 129. | Jerry Reuss | MIL | .535 |
| 128. | Andy Hawkins | NY | .534 |
| 127. | Juan Berenguer | MIN | .524 |
| 126. | Dale Mohorcic | NY | .520 |
| 125. | Mike Smithson | BOS | .519 |
| 124. | Bryan Clutterbuck | MIL | .503 |
| 123. | Bob Stanley | BOS | .489 |
| 122. | Cecilio Guante | TEX | .488 |
| 121. | Rod Nichols | CLE | .488 |
| 120. | Todd Stottlemyre | TOR | .480 |
| 119. | Richard Dotson | CHI | .479 |
| 118. | Jack Morris | DET | .479 |
| 117. | Frank Viola | MIN | .475 |
| 116. | Francisc Oliveras | MIN | .472 |

### National League

#### Top 20

|  |  |  |  |
|---|---|---|---|
| 1. | Neal Heaton | PIT | .158 |
| 2. | Norm Charlton | CIN | .173 |
| 3. | Zane Smith | MTL | .190 |
| 4. | Bill Landrum | PIT | .214 |
| 5. | Mark Langston | MTL | .247 |
| 6. | Frank DiPino | STL | .248 |
| 7. | Les Lancaster | CHI | .248 |
| 8. | Doug Bair | PIT | .252 |
| 9. | Greg Harris | SD | .253 |
| 10. | Larry McWilliams | PHI | .253 |
| 11. | Rob Dibble | CIN | .256 |
| 12. | Dwight Gooden | NY | .259 |
| 13. | Juan Agosto | HOU | .266 |
| 14. | Tom Glavine | ATL | .269 |
| 15. | Jay Howell | LA | .270 |
| 16. | Paul Assenmacher | CHI | .271 |
| 17. | Bob Kipper | PIT | .277 |
| 18. | Rich Gossage | SF | .278 |
| 19. | Greg Harris | PHI | .281 |
| 20. | Craig Lefferts | SF | .282 |
| 20. | Terry Mulholland | PHI | .282 |

#### Bottom 20

|  |  |  |  |
|---|---|---|---|
| 116. | Bob Sebra | CIN | .555 |
| 115. | Kent Tekulve | CIN | .543 |
| 114. | Todd Frohwirth | PHI | .530 |
| 113. | Mark Eichhorn | ATL | .504 |
| 112. | Jeff Pico | CHI | .491 |
| 111. | Floyd Youmans | PHI | .489 |
| 110. | Kelly Downs | SF | .478 |
| 109. | Bob Knepper | SF | .470 |
| 108. | Jim Clancy | HOU | .460 |
| 107. | Todd Worrell | STL | .455 |
| 106. | Tim Leary | CIN | .453 |
| 105. | Rick Mahler | CIN | .451 |
| 104. | Bob Forsch | HOU | .447 |
| 103. | Rick Reed | PIT | .436 |
| 102. | Don Carman | PHI | .435 |
| 101. | Dennis Martinez | MTL | .429 |
| 100. | Eric Show | SD | .427 |
| 99. | Tom Browning | CIN | .424 |
| 98. | Bruce Hurst | SD | .424 |
| 97. | Scott Sanderson | CHI | .422 |

## Opponents' Slugging Average, Right-Handed Batters

### American League

#### Top 20

|  |  |  |  |
|---|---|---|---|
| 1. | Jeff Montgomery | KC | .236 |
| 2. | Gene Nelson | OAK | .239 |
| 3. | Lee Smith | BOS | .250 |
| 4. | Dennis Lamp | BOS | .254 |
| 5. | Duane Ward | TOR | .263 |
| 6. | Juan Berenguer | MIN | .269 |
| 7. | David Wells | TOR | .282 |
| 8. | Dave Stieb | TOR | .283 |
| 9. | Todd Burns | OAK | .286 |
| 10. | Willie Fraser | CAL | .297 |
| 11. | Doug Jones | CLE | .301 |
| 12. | Nolan Ryan | TEX | .304 |
| 13. | Mike Schooler | SEA | .305 |
| 14. | Tom Gordon | KC | .305 |
| 15. | Eric King | CHI | .307 |
| 16. | Tom Candiotti | CLE | .311 |
| 17. | Jeff Russell | TEX | .311 |
| 18. | Tom Henke | TOR | .312 |
| 19. | Mike Henneman | DET | .315 |
| 19. | Rick Honeycutt | OAK | .315 |

#### Bottom 20

|  |  |  |  |
|---|---|---|---|
| 134. | Jose Bautista | BAL | .513 |
| 133. | Dave West | MIN | .496 |
| 132. | John Candelaria | NY | .494 |
| 131. | Dave Schmidt | BAL | .491 |
| 130. | Dave LaPoint | NY | .469 |
| 129. | Don August | MIL | .462 |
| 128. | Charlie Hough | TEX | .461 |
| 127. | Wes Gardner | BOS | .461 |
| 126. | Jamie Moyer | TEX | .459 |
| 125. | Roy Smith | MIN | .458 |
| 124. | Storm Davis | OAK | .454 |
| 123. | Tom McCarthy | CHI | .450 |
| 122. | Steve Rosenberg | CHI | .449 |
| 121. | Shane Rawley | MIN | .448 |
| 120. | Ken Patterson | CHI | .443 |
| 119. | Mike Witt | CAL | .442 |
| 118. | Charlie Leibrandt | KC | .442 |
| 117. | Lance McCullers | NY | .440 |
| 116. | Mike Flanagan | TOR | .435 |
| 115. | Jimmy Key | TOR | .435 |

### National League

#### Top 20

|  |  |  |  |
|---|---|---|---|
| 1. | Larry Andersen | HOU | .185 |
| 2. | Todd Frohwirth | PHI | .212 |
| 3. | Jose DeLeon | STL | .238 |
| 4. | Rob Dibble | CIN | .244 |
| 5. | Roger McDowell | PHI | .247 |
| 6. | Scott Garrelts | SF | .266 |
| 7. | Mark Davis | SD | .268 |
| 8. | Danny Darwin | HOU | .268 |
| 9. | Jose Rijo | CIN | .270 |
| 10. | Tim Burke | MTL | .273 |
| 11. | Jim Acker | ATL | .275 |
| 12. | Ken Howell | PHI | .275 |
| 13. | Mike Morgan | LA | .277 |
| 14. | Steve Bedrosian | SF | .278 |
| 15. | Mike Scott | HOU | .281 |
| 16. | Orel Hershiser | LA | .288 |
| 17. | Ed Whitson | SD | .291 |
| 18. | Trevor Wilson | SF | .296 |
| 19. | Mike LaCoss | SF | .298 |
| 20. | Rick Aguilera | NY | .303 |

#### Bottom 20

|  |  |  |  |
|---|---|---|---|
| 116. | Tim Crews | LA | .519 |
| 115. | Jeff Robinson | PIT | .476 |
| 114. | Scott Scudder | CIN | .470 |
| 113. | Walt Terrell | SD | .463 |
| 112. | Andy McGaffigan | MTL | .460 |
| 111. | Dan Schatzeder | HOU | .448 |
| 110. | Eric Show | SD | .444 |
| 109. | Don Carman | PHI | .443 |
| 108. | Derek Lilliquist | ATL | .439 |
| 107. | Greg Harris | PHI | .438 |
| 106. | Terry Mulholland | PHI | .437 |
| 105. | Jeff Parrett | PHI | .435 |
| 104. | Rick Rhoden | HOU | .431 |
| 103. | Bruce Ruffin | PHI | .431 |
| 102. | Bob Knepper | SF | .426 |
| 101. | Dennis Cook | PHI | .424 |
| 100. | Joe Boever | ATL | .423 |
| 99. | Bob Forsch | HOU | .419 |
| 98. | Frank DiPino | STL | .417 |
| 97. | Cris Carpenter | STL | .415 |

## Opponents' Home Run Percentage, Left-Handed Batters

### American League

#### Top 20

|  |  |  |  |
|---|---|---|---|
| 1. | Todd Burns | OAK | 0.00 |
| 1. | Steve Farr | KC | 0.00 |
| 1. | Chuck Finley | CAL | 0.00 |
| 1. | Mike Flanagan | TOR | 0.00 |
| 1. | Bill Krueger | MIL | 0.00 |
| 1. | Charlie Leibrandt | KC | 0.00 |
| 1. | Greg Minton | CAL | 0.00 |
| 1. | Gregg Olson | BAL | 0.00 |
| 1. | Jesse Orosco | CLE | 0.00 |
| 1. | Kenny Rogers | TEX | 0.00 |
| 1. | Jeff Russell | TEX | 0.00 |
| 1. | Mark Williamson | BAL | 0.00 |
| 13. | Mike Henneman | DET | 0.65 |
| 14. | Mike Moore | OAK | 0.70 |
| 15. | Mike Schooler | SEA | 0.71 |
| 16. | Bob Welch | OAK | 0.72 |
| 17. | Mark Gubicza | KC | 0.78 |
| 18. | Scott Bailes | CLE | 0.80 |
| 19. | Greg Cadaret | NY | 0.81 |
| 20. | Bert Blyleven | CAL | 0.82 |

#### Bottom 20

|  |  |  |  |
|---|---|---|---|
| 135. | Dan Petry | CAL | 6.82 |
| 134. | Bryan Clutterbuck | MIL | 6.29 |
| 133. | Jerry Reuss | MIL | 5.94 |
| 132. | Cecilio Guante | TEX | 5.81 |
| 131. | Mike Schwabe | DET | 5.71 |
| 130. | Francisc Oliveras | MIN | 5.66 |
| 129. | Walt Terrell | NY | 4.68 |
| 128. | Dave LaPoint | NY | 4.65 |
| 127. | Jimmy Jones | NY | 4.55 |
| 126. | Mike Smithson | BOS | 4.50 |
| 125. | Charles Hudson | DET | 4.44 |
| 124. | Bill Wegman | MIL | 4.39 |
| 123. | Juan Berenguer | MIN | 4.27 |
| 122. | Lee Smith | BOS | 4.13 |
| 121. | Jeff Robinson | DET | 4.08 |
| 120. | Dale Mohorcic | NY | 4.00 |
| 119. | Rod Nichols | CLE | 3.94 |
| 118. | Jeff Reardon | MIN | 3.88 |
| 117. | Dave Schmidt | BAL | 3.87 |
| 116. | Jose Bautista | BAL | 3.82 |

### National League

#### Top 20

|  |  |  |  |
|---|---|---|---|
| 1. | Juan Agosto | HOU | 0.00 |
| 1. | Paul Assenmacher | CHI | 0.00 |
| 1. | Norm Charlton | CIN | 0.00 |
| 1. | Jim Deshaies | HOU | 0.00 |
| 1. | Frank DiPino | STL | 0.00 |
| 1. | Tom Glavine | ATL | 0.00 |
| 1. | Rich Gossage | SF | 0.00 |
| 1. | Neal Heaton | PIT | 0.00 |
| 1. | Bob Kipper | PIT | 0.00 |
| 1. | Les Lancaster | CHI | 0.00 |
| 1. | Bill Landrum | PIT | 0.00 |
| 1. | Joe Magrane | STL | 0.00 |
| 1. | Andy McGaffigan | MTL | 0.00 |
| 1. | Terry Mulholland | PHI | 0.00 |
| 1. | Jeff Parrett | PHI | 0.00 |
| 1. | Dan Schatzeder | HOU | 0.00 |
| 17. | Joe Boever | ATL | 0.56 |
| 18. | Rob Dibble | CIN | 0.58 |
| 19. | Jay Howell | LA | 0.63 |
| 20. | Greg Harris | SD | 0.71 |

#### Bottom 20

|  |  |  |  |
|---|---|---|---|
| 116. | Don Carman | PHI | 5.56 |
| 115. | Steve Bedrosian | SF | 4.88 |
| 114. | Tom Browning | CIN | 4.55 |
| 113. | Kent Tekulve | CIN | 3.81 |
| 112. | Bob Sebra | CIN | 3.64 |
| 111. | Mike Krukow | SF | 3.49 |
| 110. | Todd Worrell | STL | 3.41 |
| 109. | Floyd Youmans | PHI | 3.33 |
| 108. | Ed Whitson | SD | 3.22 |
| 107. | Jim Clancy | HOU | 3.19 |
| 106. | Tim Burke | MTL | 3.14 |
| 105. | Bob Ojeda | NY | 3.11 |
| 104. | Jeff Pico | CHI | 3.07 |
| 103. | Andrew Benes | SD | 3.05 |
| 102. | Dennis Rasmussen | SD | 3.01 |
| 100. | Todd Frohwirth | PHI | 3.00 |
| 100. | Bob Knepper | SF | 3.00 |
| 99. | Don Robinson | SF | 3.00 |
| 97. | Ramon Martinez | LA | 2.96 |
| 97. | Tim Leary | CIN | 2.96 |

## Opponents' Home Run Percentage, Right-Handed Batters

### American League

#### Top 20

|  |  |  |  |
|---|---|---|---|
| 1. | Mike Dyer | MIN | 0.00 |
| 1. | Doug Jones | CLE | 0.00 |
| 1. | Kevin Ritz | DET | 0.00 |
| 4. | Jeff Montgomery | KC | 0.55 |
| 5. | Mike Schooler | SEA | 0.61 |
| 6. | Gregg Olson | BAL | 0.61 |
| 7. | Walt Terrell | NY | 0.62 |
| 8. | Eric King | CHI | 0.71 |
| 9. | Lee Smith | BOS | 0.76 |
| 10. | Duane Ward | TOR | 0.85 |
| 11. | Dennis Lamp | BOS | 0.88 |
| 12. | Willie Fraser | CAL | 0.99 |
| 12. | Dave Righetti | NY | 0.99 |
| 14. | Luis Aquino | KC | 1.02 |
| 15. | Bobby Witt | TEX | 1.04 |
| 16. | Gene Nelson | OAK | 1.09 |
| 17. | Greg Hibbard | CHI | 1.09 |
| 18. | Cecilio Guante | TEX | 1.12 |
| 19. | Bob Stanley | BOS | 1.13 |
| 20. | Kenny Rogers | TEX | 1.14 |
| 20. | Gary Wayne | MIN | 1.14 |

#### Bottom 20

|  |  |  |  |
|---|---|---|---|
| 134. | Jose Bautista | BAL | 7.33 |
| 133. | Charlie Hough | TEX | 5.44 |
| 132. | John Candelaria | NY | 5.13 |
| 131. | Roy Smith | MIN | 4.80 |
| 130. | Tom McCarthy | CHI | 4.64 |
| 129. | Joe Price | BOS | 4.23 |
| 128. | Wes Gardner | BOS | 4.19 |
| 127. | Don August | MIL | 3.85 |
| 126. | Mark Knudson | MIL | 3.80 |
| 124. | Ken Patterson | CHI | 3.78 |
| 124. | Dave Johnson | BAL | 3.78 |
| 123. | Jesse Orosco | CLE | 3.76 |
| 122. | Dave Schmidt | BAL | 3.73 |
| 121. | Dave West | MIN | 3.70 |
| 120. | Doyle Alexander | DET | 3.63 |
| 119. | Chuck Cary | NY | 3.59 |
| 118. | Jamie Moyer | TEX | 3.53 |
| 117. | Pete Harnisch | BAL | 3.38 |
| 116. | Bobby Thigpen | CHI | 3.36 |
| 115. | Bill Krueger | MIL | 3.33 |

### National League

#### Top 20

|  |  |  |  |
|---|---|---|---|
| 1. | Larry Andersen | HOU | 0.00 |
| 1. | Mike LaCoss | SF | 0.00 |
| 1. | Roger McDowell | PHI | 0.00 |
| 1. | Dan Quisenberry | STL | 0.00 |
| 5. | Mike Morgan | LA | 0.39 |
| 6. | Larry McWilliams | PHI | 0.52 |
| 7. | Jose Rijo | CIN | 0.61 |
| 8. | Joe Magrane | STL | 0.67 |
| 9. | Tim Burke | MTL | 0.70 |
| 10. | Todd Frohwirth | PHI | 0.76 |
| 11. | Randy Myers | NY | 0.88 |
| 12. | Orel Hershiser | LA | 0.95 |
| 13. | Jim Clancy | HOU | 1.14 |
| 14. | Ken Dayley | STL | 1.14 |
| 15. | Jim Acker | ATL | 1.17 |
| 16. | John Franco | CIN | 1.20 |
| 17. | Paul Kilgus | CHI | 1.27 |
| 18. | Tim Leary | CIN | 1.32 |
| 19. | Dan Schatzeder | HOU | 1.40 |
| 20. | Mark Davis | SD | 1.41 |

#### Bottom 20

|  |  |  |  |
|---|---|---|---|
| 116. | Scott Scudder | CIN | 5.46 |
| 115. | Greg Harris | PHI | 3.92 |
| 114. | Joe Boever | ATL | 3.85 |
| 113. | Rick Reuschel | SF | 3.77 |
| 112. | Tim Crews | LA | 3.76 |
| 111. | Walt Terrell | SD | 3.75 |
| 110. | Dennis Cook | PHI | 3.60 |
| 109. | Tim Belcher | LA | 3.56 |
| 108. | Scott Sanderson | CHI | 3.56 |
| 107. | Ron Robinson | CIN | 3.52 |
| 106. | Doug Drabek | PIT | 3.41 |
| 105. | Jeff Robinson | PIT | 3.37 |
| 104. | Tom Glavine | ATL | 3.33 |
| 103. | Jeff Brantley | SF | 3.31 |
| 102. | Jeff Parrett | PHI | 3.23 |
| 101. | Ramon Martinez | LA | 3.18 |
| 100. | Don Carman | PHI | 3.15 |
| 99. | John Smiley | PIT | 3.15 |
| 97. | Calvin Schiraldi | SD | 3.13 |
| 97. | Frank DiPino | STL | 3.13 |

## Opponents' Batting Average, Day Games

### American League

#### Top 20

|  |  |  |  |
|---|---|---|---|
| 1. | Nolan Ryan | TEX | .104 |
| 2. | Dan Plesac | MIL | .146 |
| 3. | Todd Burns | OAK | .164 |
| 4. | Eric Plunk | NY | .182 |
| 5. | David Wells | TOR | .184 |
| 6. | Dennis Eckersley | OAK | .188 |
| 7. | Gene Nelson | OAK | .189 |
| 8. | Doug Jones | CLE | .190 |
| 9. | Lee Smith | BOS | .192 |
| 10. | Chuck Cary | NY | .194 |
| 11. | Joe Price | BOS | .197 |
| 12. | Greg Swindell | CLE | .197 |
| 13. | Roy Smith | MIN | .200 |
| 14. | Frank Wills | TOR | .206 |
| 15. | Bobby Thigpen | CHI | .207 |
| 16. | Luis Aquino | KC | .209 |
| 16. | Jamie Moyer | TEX | .209 |
| 18. | Randy Johnson | SEA | .209 |
| 19. | Mike Moore | OAK | .211 |
| 20. | Chris Bosio | MIL | .212 |

#### Bottom 20

|  |  |  |  |
|---|---|---|---|
| 134. | Bill Wegman | MIL | .394 |
| 133. | Jimmy Jones | NY | .362 |
| 132. | Tommy John | NY | .358 |
| 131. | Charlie Leibrandt | KC | .335 |
| 130. | Walt Terrell | NY | .331 |
| 129. | Bob Stanley | BOS | .330 |
| 128. | Shawn Hillegas | CHI | .325 |
| 127. | Jack Morris | DET | .323 |
| 126. | Todd Stottlemyre | TOR | .321 |
| 125. | Brian Holton | BAL | .318 |
| 124. | Greg Cadaret | NY | .315 |
| 123. | Bobby Witt | TEX | .311 |
| 122. | Mike Boddicker | BOS | .310 |
| 121. | Mark Williamson | BAL | .308 |
| 120. | Mike Flanagan | TOR | .306 |
| 119. | Wes Gardner | BOS | .304 |
| 118. | Storm Davis | OAK | .304 |
| 117. | Keith Atherton | CLE | .303 |
| 116. | Melido Perez | CHI | .302 |
| 115. | Dave Schmidt | BAL | .301 |

### National League

#### Top 20

|  |  |  |  |
|---|---|---|---|
| 1. | Rob Dibble | CIN | .148 |
| 2. | Tim Burke | MTL | .149 |
| 3. | Steve Bedrosian | SF | .153 |
| 4. | Pete Smith | ATL | .172 |
| 5. | Alejandro Pena | LA | .177 |
| 6. | Kevin Gross | MTL | .189 |
| 7. | Rick Aguilera | NY | .190 |
| 8. | Norm Charlton | CIN | .195 |
| 9. | Mark Portugal | HOU | .200 |
| 10. | John Smoltz | ATL | .200 |
| 11. | Randy Myers | NY | .202 |
| 12. | Bryn Smith | MTL | .203 |
| 13. | Jim Deshaies | HOU | .204 |
| 14. | Randy Kramer | PIT | .204 |
| 15. | Bob Kipper | PIT | .205 |
| 16. | Calvin Schiraldi | SD | .206 |
| 17. | Marty Clary | ATL | .208 |
| 18. | Greg Harris | SD | .209 |
| 19. | Jay Howell | LA | .210 |
| 20. | Pascual Perez | MTL | .213 |

#### Bottom 20

|  |  |  |  |
|---|---|---|---|
| 117. | Dave Leiper | SD | .403 |
| 116. | Pat Combs | PHI | .352 |
| 115. | Terry Mulholland | PHI | .350 |
| 114. | Tom Glavine | ATL | .345 |
| 113. | Bruce Ruffin | PHI | .322 |
| 112. | Ron Robinson | CIN | .319 |
| 111. | Joe Magrane | STL | .315 |
| 110. | Bob Forsch | HOU | .312 |
| 109. | Roger McDowell | PHI | .312 |
| 108. | Danny Jackson | CIN | .311 |
| 107. | Ken Howell | PHI | .310 |
| 105. | Kent Tekulve | CIN | .308 |
| 105. | Todd Frohwirth | PHI | .308 |
| 104. | Scott Terry | STL | .307 |
| 103. | Dan Schatzeder | HOU | .307 |
| 102. | Derek Lilliquist | ATL | .306 |
| 101. | Frank Viola | NY | .303 |
| 100. | Bob Sebra | CIN | .303 |
| 99. | Doug Drabek | PIT | .301 |
| 98. | Dennis Rasmussen | SD | .299 |

## Opponents' Batting Average, Night Games

### American League

#### Top 20

|  |  |  |  |
|---|---|---|---|
| 1. | Jeff Russell | TEX | .163 |
| 2. | Gregg Olson | BAL | .175 |
| 3. | Tom Henke | TOR | .184 |
| 4. | Jeff Montgomery | KC | .190 |
| 5. | Gary Wayne | MIN | .190 |
| 6. | Rick Honeycutt | OAK | .194 |
| 7. | Bryan Harvey | CAL | .196 |
| 8. | Tom Gordon | KC | .196 |
| 9. | Dave Stieb | TOR | .197 |
| 10. | Jesse Orosco | CLE | .197 |
| 11. | Nolan Ryan | TEX | .198 |
| 12. | Gene Nelson | OAK | .211 |
| 13. | Duane Ward | TOR | .212 |
| 14. | Bret Saberhagen | KC | .212 |
| 15. | Mark Langston | SEA | .213 |
| 16. | Drew Hall | TEX | .214 |
| 17. | Chuck Cary | NY | .215 |
| 18. | David Wells | TOR | .216 |
| 19. | Todd Burns | OAK | .218 |
| 20. | Mike Jackson | SEA | .219 |

#### Bottom 20

|  |  |  |  |
|---|---|---|---|
| 134. | Jerry Reuss | MIL | .333 |
| 133. | Mike Witt | CAL | .319 |
| 132. | Bob Stanley | BOS | .317 |
| 131. | Dave LaPoint | NY | .315 |
| 130. | Shane Rawley | MIN | .314 |
| 129. | Dave Schmidt | BAL | .311 |
| 128. | Mike Smithson | BOS | .307 |
| 127. | Don August | MIL | .307 |
| 126. | Steve Farr | KC | .306 |
| 125. | Rich Yett | CLE | .305 |
| 124. | Jamie Moyer | TEX | .304 |
| 123. | Richard Dotson | CHI | .304 |
| 122. | Roy Smith | MIN | .304 |
| 121. | Mike Dunne | SEA | .303 |
| 120. | Andy Hawkins | NY | .303 |
| 119. | Dave West | MIN | .303 |
| 118. | Mark Thurmond | BAL | .298 |
| 117. | Brian Holton | BAL | .294 |
| 116. | Walt Terrell | NY | .293 |
| 115. | Charlie Leibrandt | KC | .292 |

### National League

#### Top 20

|  |  |  |  |
|---|---|---|---|
| 1. | Larry Andersen | HOU | .168 |
| 2. | Bob Kipper | PIT | .169 |
| 3. | Jose DeLeon | STL | .174 |
| 4. | Mark Davis | SD | .188 |
| 5. | Rob Dibble | CIN | .189 |
| 6. | Sid Fernandez | NY | .189 |
| 7. | Bill Landrum | PIT | .190 |
| 8. | Mike Scott | HOU | .191 |
| 9. | Calvin Schiraldi | SD | .192 |
| 10. | Roger McDowell | PHI | .196 |
| 11. | John Wetteland | LA | .197 |
| 12. | Mike Bielecki | CHI | .197 |
| 13. | Norm Charlton | CIN | .198 |
| 14. | Dwight Gooden | NY | .199 |
| 15. | Ken Howell | PHI | .199 |
| 16. | Tim Belcher | LA | .200 |
| 17. | Ramon Martinez | LA | .201 |
| 18. | Scott Garrelts | SF | .202 |
| 19. | Mitch Williams | CHI | .203 |
| 20. | Steve Bedrosian | SF | .203 |

#### Bottom 20

|  |  |  |  |
|---|---|---|---|
| 116. | Ricky Horton | STL | .316 |
| 115. | Tim Crews | LA | .310 |
| 114. | Bob Knepper | SF | .309 |
| 113. | Andy McGaffigan | MTL | .306 |
| 112. | Jeff Pico | CHI | .306 |
| 111. | Scott Sanderson | CHI | .305 |
| 110. | Paul Kilgus | CHI | .302 |
| 109. | Derek Lilliquist | ATL | .299 |
| 108. | Rick Rhoden | HOU | .299 |
| 107. | Bob Forsch | HOU | .299 |
| 106. | Rick Reed | PIT | .297 |
| 105. | Atlee Hammaker | SF | .297 |
| 104. | Bruce Ruffin | PHI | .296 |
| 103. | Bob Sebra | CIN | .292 |
| 102. | Jeff Robinson | PIT | .284 |
| 101. | Walt Terrell | SD | .284 |
| 100. | Pete Smith | ATL | .283 |
| 99. | Bob Walk | PIT | .281 |
| 98. | Rick Mahler | CIN | .279 |
| 97. | Kelly Downs | SF | .277 |

## Opponents' Batting Average, Grass Surfaces

### American League

| Top 20 | | | Bottom 20 | | |
|---|---|---|---|---|---|
| 1. Gregg Olson | BAL | .155 | 135. Tommy John | NY | .350 |
| 2. Jeff Russell | TEX | .156 | 134. Bill Wegman | MIL | .340 |
| 3. Dennis Eckersley | OAK | .170 | 133. Brad Havens | DET | .324 |
| 4. Bryan Harvey | CAL | .178 | 132. Mike Schwabe | DET | .320 |
| 5. Jesse Orosco | CLE | .183 | 131. Charlie Leibrandt | KC | .316 |
| 6. Gene Nelson | OAK | .189 | 130. Dave LaPoint | NY | .313 |
| 7. Lee Smith | BOS | .190 | 129. Bob Stanley | BOS | .312 |
| 8. Nolan Ryan | TEX | .198 | 128. Walt Terrell | NY | .311 |
| 9. Tom Henke | TOR | .200 | 127. Don August | MIL | .310 |
| 10. Chuck Cary | NY | .201 | 126. Mike Birkbeck | MIL | .306 |
| 11. Dave Stieb | TOR | .205 | 125. Dave Schmidt | BAL | .305 |
| 12. Todd Burns | OAK | .207 | 124. Mike Flanagan | TOR | .303 |
| 13. Bobby Thigpen | CHI | .208 | 123. Mike Smithson | BOS | .302 |
| 13. Duane Ward | TOR | .208 | 122. Dale Mohorcic | NY | .298 |
| 15. Dan Plesac | MIL | .209 | 121. Mark Thurmond | BAL | .297 |
| 16. Rick Honeycutt | OAK | .210 | 120. Eric Hetzel | BOS | .295 |
| 17. Mike Moore | OAK | .211 | 119. Jerry Reuss | MIL | .295 |
| 18. Drew Hall | TEX | .213 | 118. Jay Tibbs | BAL | .293 |
| 19. Bret Saberhagen | KC | .220 | 117. Jimmy Jones | NY | .293 |
| 20. Kevin Hickey | BAL | .222 | 116. Brian Holton | BAL | .293 |

### National League

| Top 20 | | | Bottom 20 | | |
|---|---|---|---|---|---|
| 1. Bill Landrum | PIT | .113 | 116. Don Schulze | SD | .352 |
| 2. Steve Bedrosian | SF | .156 | 115. Terry Mulholland | PHI | .342 |
| 3. Bob Kipper | PIT | .162 | 114. Dave Leiper | SD | .330 |
| 4. Randy Myers | NY | .190 | 113. Bob Forsch | HOU | .314 |
| 5. Norm Charlton | CIN | .192 | 112. Ricky Horton | STL | .313 |
| 6. Trevor Wilson | SF | .196 | 111. Don Carman | PHI | .312 |
| 7. John Smiley | PIT | .199 | 110. Dennis Cook | PHI | .310 |
| 8. Gary Eave | ATL | .200 | 109. Pascual Perez | MTL | .306 |
| 8. Pat Perry | CHI | .200 | 108. Bob Walk | PIT | .305 |
| 10. Mark Davis | SD | .202 | 107. Randy O'Neal | PHI | .302 |
| 11. Mike Scott | HOU | .203 | 106. Doug Drabek | PIT | .296 |
| 12. Rick Aguilera | NY | .203 | 105. Derek Lilliquist | ATL | .295 |
| 13. Ken Howell | PHI | .203 | 104. Scott Sanderson | CHI | .293 |
| 14. Greg Harris | SD | .204 | 103. Scott Terry | STL | .289 |
| 15. Jim Deshaies | HOU | .205 | 102. Jose Rijo | CIN | .283 |
| 16. John Smoltz | ATL | .206 | 101. Tim Crews | LA | .282 |
| 17. Jay Howell | LA | .207 | 100. Dan Quisenberry | STL | .279 |
| 18. Tim Belcher | LA | .209 | 99. Eric Show | SD | .279 |
| 19. Rich Gossage | SF | .209 | 98. Jeff Brantley | SF | .278 |
| 19. Randy Kramer | PIT | .209 | 97. Mark Eichhorn | ATL | .277 |
| 19. Ramon Martinez | LA | .209 | | | |

## Opponents' Batting Average, Artificial Surfaces

### American League

| Top 20 | | | Bottom 20 | | |
|---|---|---|---|---|---|
| 1. Nolan Ryan | TEX | .128 | 134. Jack Morris | DET | .395 |
| 2. Todd Burns | OAK | .135 | 133. Steve Shields | MIN | .391 |
| 3. Jim Acker | TOR | .175 | 132. Jeff Robinson | DET | .373 |
| 4. Roger Clemens | BOS | .180 | 131. Keith Comstock | SEA | .354 |
| 5. Clay Parker | NY | .185 | 130. Jerry Reuss | MIL | .353 |
| 6. Eric Plunk | NY | .186 | 128. Brian Holton | BAL | .351 |
| 7. Bert Blyleven | CAL | .190 | 128. Mike Campbell | SEA | .351 |
| 8. Greg Swindell | CLE | .190 | 127. Dave Schmidt | BAL | .340 |
| 9. Bill Krueger | MIL | .193 | 126. Mike Dyer | MIN | .336 |
| 10. Gary Wayne | MIN | .194 | 125. Greg Cadaret | NY | .329 |
| 11. Tom Gordon | KC | .197 | 124. Curt Young | OAK | .328 |
| 12. Jeff Montgomery | KC | .197 | 123. Tom Niedenfuer | SEA | .325 |
| 13. Mark Knudson | MIL | .200 | 122. Chuck Crim | MIL | .324 |
| 14. Tom Henke | TOR | .210 | 121. Shawn Hillegas | CHI | .322 |
| 15. David Wells | TOR | .212 | 120. Mike Birkbeck | MIL | .320 |
| 16. Tom Candiotti | CLE | .212 | 119. Mike Witt | CAL | .319 |
| 17. Brian Dubois | DET | .213 | 118. Bob Milacki | BAL | .318 |
| 18. Bret Saberhagen | KC | .215 | 117. Greg Hibbard | CHI | .317 |
| 19. Frank Wills | TOR | .217 | 116. Gene Harris | SEA | .314 |
| 20. Steve Crawford | KC | .218 | 115. Francisc Oliveras | MIN | .310 |

### National League

| Top 20 | | | Bottom 20 | | |
|---|---|---|---|---|---|
| 1. Rob Dibble | CIN | .157 | 116. Mike Maddux | PHI | .359 |
| 2. Sid Fernandez | NY | .164 | 115. Don Heinkel | STL | .355 |
| 3. Calvin Schiraldi | SD | .165 | 114. Paul Kilgus | CHI | .347 |
| 4. John Costello | STL | .171 | 113. Derek Lilliquist | ATL | .330 |
| 5. Frank Viola | NY | .188 | 112. Walt Terrell | SD | .324 |
| 6. Larry Andersen | HOU | .192 | 111. Jeff Pico | CHI | .320 |
| 7. Jose DeLeon | STL | .192 | 110. Bruce Ruffin | PHI | .314 |
| 8. Doug Bair | PIT | .193 | 109. Pete Smith | ATL | .313 |
| 9. Mark Davis | SD | .195 | 108. Bob Knepper | SF | .309 |
| 10. Norm Charlton | CIN | .200 | 107. Jim Clancy | HOU | .301 |
| 10. Alejandro Pena | LA | .200 | 106. Bob Forsch | HOU | .300 |
| 10. Bob Tewksbury | STL | .200 | 105. Mike Morgan | LA | .298 |
| 13. Bob Kipper | PIT | .201 | 104. Ricky Horton | STL | .298 |
| 14. Danny Darwin | HOU | .202 | 103. Kent Tekulve | CIN | .298 |
| 15. Doug Drabek | PIT | .211 | 102. Don Robinson | SF | .294 |
| 16. Orel Hershiser | LA | .212 | 101. Jeff Robinson | PIT | .291 |
| 17. Rick Sutcliffe | CHI | .214 | 99. Andy McGaffigan | MTL | .290 |
| 18. Ed Whitson | SD | .215 | 99. Joe Hesketh | MTL | .290 |
| 19. Scott Garrelts | SF | .216 | 98. Rick Reed | PIT | .289 |
| 20. Mark Grant | SD | .216 | 97. Rick Rhoden | HOU | .284 |

## Opponents' Batting Average, Home Games

### American League

| Top 20 | | | Bottom 20 | | |
|---|---|---|---|---|---|
| 1. Gregg Olson | BAL | .154 | 134. Dale Mohorcic | NY | .347 |
| 2. Jeff Montgomery | KC | .185 | 133. Don August | MIL | .340 |
| 3. Gary Wayne | MIN | .185 | 132. Dave Schmidt | BAL | .339 |
| 4. Gene Nelson | OAK | .186 | 131. Walt Terrell | NY | .328 |
| 5. Bryan Harvey | CAL | .190 | 130. Allan Anderson | MIN | .317 |
| 6. Jesse Orosco | CLE | .190 | 129. Mike Smithson | BOS | .315 |
| 7. Todd Burns | OAK | .195 | 128. Rich Yett | CLE | .313 |
| 8. Tom Henke | TOR | .200 | 127. Brian Holton | BAL | .309 |
| 9. Nolan Ryan | TEX | .201 | 126. Shane Rawley | MIN | .307 |
| 10. Mike Moore | OAK | .202 | 125. Bob Stanley | BOS | .307 |
| 11. Lee Smith | BOS | .203 | 124. Mike Boddicker | BOS | .305 |
| 12. Bret Saberhagen | KC | .208 | 123. Andy Hawkins | NY | .302 |
| 13. Dave Stieb | TOR | .212 | 122. Richard Dotson | CHI | .300 |
| 14. David Wells | TOR | .212 | 121. Charlie Leibrandt | KC | .297 |
| 15. Frank Wills | TOR | .213 | 120. Jay Tibbs | BAL | .296 |
| 16. Tom Gordon | KC | .216 | 119. Eric Hetzel | BOS | .295 |
| 17. Eric Plunk | NY | .216 | 118. Bill Swift | SEA | .295 |
| 18. Ted Higuera | MIL | .217 | 117. Jim Abbott | CAL | .294 |
| 19. Bobby Thigpen | CHI | .219 | 116. Mark Thurmond | BAL | .293 |
| 20. Drew Hall | TEX | .220 | 115. Dave Righetti | NY | .291 |

### National League

| Top 20 | | | Bottom 20 | | |
|---|---|---|---|---|---|
| 1. Rob Dibble | CIN | .151 | 116. Bob Knepper | SF | .338 |
| 2. Norm Charlton | CIN | .165 | 115. Joe Hesketh | MTL | .333 |
| 3. Bob Kipper | PIT | .165 | 114. Bruce Ruffin | PHI | .317 |
| 4. Steve Bedrosian | SF | .171 | 113. Derek Lilliquist | ATL | .305 |
| 5. Rick Aguilera | NY | .173 | 112. Rick Mahler | CIN | .304 |
| 6. Mark Davis | SD | .177 | 111. Ricky Horton | STL | .299 |
| 7. Doug Bair | PIT | .179 | 110. Bob Forsch | HOU | .292 |
| 8. Danny Darwin | HOU | .181 | 109. Mark Eichhorn | ATL | .292 |
| 9. Ramon Martinez | LA | .182 | 108. Dan Quisenberry | STL | .291 |
| 10. Jose DeLeon | STL | .184 | 107. Rick Rhoden | HOU | .291 |
| 11. Jay Howell | LA | .185 | 106. Frank Viola | NY | .289 |
| 12. John Smoltz | ATL | .189 | 105. Kent Tekulve | CIN | .288 |
| 13. Dwight Gooden | NY | .190 | 104. Eric Show | SD | .287 |
| 14. Dennis Cook | PHI | .190 | 103. Jim Clancy | HOU | .286 |
| 15. Randy Myers | NY | .192 | 102. Scott Sanderson | CHI | .284 |
| 16. Scott Garrelts | SF | .196 | 101. Les Lancaster | CHI | .283 |
| 17. Jeff Parrett | PHI | .198 | 100. Tom Browning | CIN | .281 |
| 18. Tim Belcher | LA | .199 | 99. Cris Carpenter | STL | .280 |
| 19. Don Aase | NY | .200 | 98. Mitch Williams | CHI | .280 |
| 20. Frank DiPino | STL | .201 | 97. Tim Crews | LA | .277 |

## Opponents' Batting Average, Road Games

### American League

| Top 20 | | | Bottom 20 | | |
|---|---|---|---|---|---|
| 1. Nolan Ryan | TEX | .166 | 133. Rod Nichols | CLE | .351 |
| 2. Mark Langston | SEA | .175 | 133. Steve Farr | KC | .351 |
| 3. Rick Honeycutt | OAK | .180 | 132. Mike Dunne | SEA | .338 |
| 4. Chuck Cary | NY | .186 | 131. Bob Stanley | BOS | .335 |
| 5. Mike Jackson | SEA | .192 | 130. Dave LaPoint | NY | .327 |
| 6. Todd Burns | OAK | .196 | 129. Wes Gardner | BOS | .325 |
| 7. David Wells | TOR | .200 | 128. Tommy John | NY | .325 |
| 8. Tom Gordon | KC | .201 | 127. Jamie Moyer | TEX | .322 |
| 9. Jesse Orosco | CLE | .206 | 126. Jerry Reuss | MIL | .320 |
| 10. Tom Henke | TOR | .208 | 125. Tom McCarthy | CHI | .310 |
| 11. Erik Hanson | SEA | .209 | 124. Charlie Leibrandt | KC | .309 |
| 12. Jeff Montgomery | KC | .211 | 123. Terry Leach | KC | .306 |
| 13. Oil Can Boyd | BOS | .213 | 122. Doyle Alexander | DET | .305 |
| 13. Greg Minton | CAL | .213 | 121. Floyd Bannister | KC | .305 |
| 15. Bobby Thigpen | CHI | .216 | 120. Mike Witt | CAL | .300 |
| 16. Lee Smith | BOS | .217 | 119. Charles Hudson | DET | .299 |
| 17. Gene Nelson | OAK | .219 | 118. Greg Cadaret | NY | .299 |
| 18. Roger Clemens | BOS | .219 | 117. Paul Gibson | DET | .297 |
| 19. Chuck Finley | CAL | .220 | 116. Scott Bailes | CLE | .296 |
| 20. Dan Plesac | MIL | .221 | 115. Jaime Navarro | MIL | .295 |

### National League

| Top 20 | | | Bottom 20 | | |
|---|---|---|---|---|---|
| 1. Les Lancaster | CHI | .158 | 116. Bob Sebra | CIN | .359 |
| 2. Calvin Schiraldi | SD | .166 | 115. Terry Mulholland | PHI | .346 |
| 3. Greg Harris | PHI | .188 | 114. Dan Schatzeder | HOU | .324 |
| 4. Bill Landrum | PIT | .189 | 113. Andy McGaffigan | MTL | .316 |
| 5. Sid Fernandez | NY | .190 | 112. Bob Forsch | HOU | .315 |
| 6. Larry Andersen | HOU | .192 | 111. Atlee Hammaker | SF | .313 |
| 7. Alejandro Pena | LA | .193 | 110. Ricky Horton | STL | .311 |
| 8. Ken Howell | PHI | .193 | 109. Dennis Cook | PHI | .310 |
| 9. Ken Dayley | STL | .194 | 108. Jeff Pico | CHI | .310 |
| 10. Randy Kramer | PIT | .196 | 107. Paul Kilgus | CHI | .307 |
| 11. Rob Dibble | CIN | .197 | 106. Jeff Robinson | PIT | .301 |
| 12. Jose Alvarez | ATL | .198 | 105. Derek Lilliquist | ATL | .295 |
| 13. Frank Viola | NY | .200 | 104. Tim Crews | LA | .290 |
| 13. Mitch Williams | CHI | .200 | 103. Rick Aguilera | NY | .289 |
| 15. Rich Gossage | SF | .206 | 101. Rick Rhoden | HOU | .286 |
| 16. Bob Kipper | PIT | .208 | 101. Don Aase | NY | .286 |
| 17. Steve Bedrosian | SF | .209 | 100. Dennis Rasmussen | SD | .285 |
| 18. Mark Langston | MTL | .210 | 99. Walt Terrell | SD | .285 |
| 19. John Wetteland | LA | .210 | 98. Don Robinson | SF | .283 |
| 20. Mike Scott | HOU | .211 | 96. Scott Terry | STL | .282 |
| | | | 96. Joe Boever | ATL | .282 |

## Opponents' Batting Average with Runners On Base

### American League

| Top 20 | | | Bottom 20 | | |
|---|---|---|---|---|---|
| 1. Jesse Orosco | CLE | .156 | 134. Jerry Reuss | MIL | .364 |
| 2. Gregg Olson | BAL | .164 | 133. Bob Stanley | BOS | .361 |
| 3. Jeff Montgomery | KC | .164 | 132. Wes Gardner | BOS | .338 |
| 4. Bryan Harvey | CAL | .183 | 131. Dave LaPoint | NY | .336 |
| 5. Todd Burns | OAK | .190 | 130. Greg Cadaret | NY | .333 |
| 6. Gene Nelson | OAK | .190 | 129. Tommy John | NY | .330 |
| 7. Tom Henke | TOR | .191 | 128. Dave Schmidt | BAL | .327 |
| 8. Rick Honeycutt | OAK | .195 | 127. Andy Hawkins | NY | .322 |
| 9. David Wells | TOR | .196 | 126. Mike Witt | CAL | .321 |
| 10. Bobby Thigpen | CHI | .204 | 125. Charles Hudson | DET | .321 |
| 11. Dan Plesac | MIL | .205 | 124. Terry Leach | KC | .316 |
| 12. Bret Saberhagen | KC | .208 | 123. Charlie Leibrandt | KC | .312 |
| 13. Gary Wayne | MIN | .209 | 122. Bill Swift | SEA | .305 |
| 14. Eric Plunk | NY | .212 | 121. Gary Mielke | TEX | .303 |
| 15. Edwin Nunez | DET | .219 | 120. Jamie Moyer | TEX | .301 |
| 16. Bert Blyleven | CAL | .219 | 119. Jack Morris | DET | .300 |
| 17. Juan Berenguer | MIN | .220 | 118. Mark Thurmond | BAL | .299 |
| 18. Bob Welch | OAK | .221 | 117. Dale Mohorcic | NY | .299 |
| 19. Jeff Russell | TEX | .222 | 116. Jaime Navarro | MIL | .297 |
| 20. Chuck Cary | NY | .223 | 115. Mike Flanagan | TOR | .296 |

### National League

| Top 20 | | | Bottom 20 | | |
|---|---|---|---|---|---|
| 1. Rob Dibble | CIN | .167 | 116. Derek Lilliquist | ATL | .349 |
| 2. Mark Davis | SD | .174 | 114. Kent Tekulve | CIN | .333 |
| 3. Jay Howell | LA | .188 | 114. Dan Schatzeder | HOU | .333 |
| 4. Tim Belcher | LA | .192 | 113. Ricky Horton | STL | .315 |
| 5. Steve Bedrosian | SF | .197 | 112. Paul Kilgus | CHI | .312 |
| 6. Dwight Gooden | NY | .199 | 111. Danny Jackson | CIN | .312 |
| 7. Craig Lefferts | SF | .200 | 110. Andy McGaffigan | MTL | .311 |
| 8. Doug Bair | PIT | .202 | 109. Jeff Pico | CHI | .311 |
| 9. Larry Andersen | HOU | .204 | 108. Bob Walk | PIT | .308 |
| 10. Calvin Schiraldi | SD | .205 | 107. Mark Eichhorn | ATL | .306 |
| 11. Mark Langston | MTL | .207 | 106. Bob Forsch | HOU | .306 |
| 12. Les Lancaster | CHI | .208 | 105. Bob Knepper | SF | .305 |
| 13. Randy Myers | NY | .211 | 104. Walt Terrell | SD | .305 |
| 14. John Smiley | PIT | .211 | 103. Pete Smith | ATL | .304 |
| 15. Danny Darwin | HOU | .212 | 102. Larry McWilliams | PHI | .303 |
| 16. Mark Portugal | HOU | .214 | 101. Scott Sanderson | CHI | .301 |
| 17. Mike Scott | HOU | .217 | 100. Eric Show | SD | .299 |
| 18. Norm Charlton | CIN | .217 | 99. Rick Rhoden | HOU | .297 |
| 18. Ken Dayley | STL | .217 | 98. Tim Crews | LA | .296 |
| 20. Ed Whitson | SD | .219 | 97. Bruce Ruffin | PHI | .295 |

## Opponents' Batting Average with Bases Empty

### American League

| Top 20 | | | Bottom 20 | | |
|---|---|---|---|---|---|
| 1. Dennis Eckersley | OAK | .145 | 135. Tommy John | NY | .340 |
| 2. Nolan Ryan | TEX | .146 | 134. Brian Holton | BAL | .332 |
| 3. Tom Gordon | KC | .164 | 133. Todd Stottlemyre | TOR | .326 |
| 4. Greg Minton | CAL | .183 | 132. Mike Dunne | SEA | .321 |
| 5. Lee Smith | BOS | .185 | 131. Mark Guthrie | MIN | .320 |
| 6. Dave Stieb | TOR | .190 | 130. Walt Terrell | NY | .320 |
| 7. Drew Hall | TEX | .192 | 129. Richard Dotson | CHI | .311 |
| 8. Todd Burns | OAK | .200 | 128. Don August | MIL | .308 |
| 9. Chuck Cary | NY | .202 | 127. Tom McCarthy | CHI | .306 |
| 10. Willie Fraser | CAL | .202 | 126. Steve Farr | KC | .305 |
| 11. Mike Jackson | SEA | .206 | 125. Mike Smithson | BOS | .305 |
| 12. Mike Moore | OAK | .211 | 124. Storm Davis | OAK | .304 |
| 13. Gene Nelson | OAK | .212 | 123. Shane Rawley | MIN | .301 |
| 14. Mark Langston | SEA | .213 | 122. Charlie Leibrandt | KC | .298 |
| 15. Bobby Witt | TEX | .214 | 121. Dave Schmidt | BAL | .298 |
| 16. Tom Henke | TOR | .215 | 120. Jeff Ballard | BAL | .296 |
| 16. David Wells | TOR | .215 | 118. Francisc Oliveras | MIN | .290 |
| 18. Dennis Lamp | BOS | .216 | 118. Floyd Bannister | KC | .290 |
| 19. Gregg Olson | BAL | .216 | 117. Dave LaPoint | NY | .290 |
| 20. Gary Wayne | MIN | .216 | 116. Rod Nichols | CLE | .289 |

### National League

| Top 20 | | | Bottom 20 | | |
|---|---|---|---|---|---|
| 1. Bob Kipper | PIT | .159 | 116. Bob Sebra | CIN | .331 |
| 2. Jose DeLeon | STL | .169 | 114. Bruce Ruffin | PHI | .307 |
| 3. Andrew Benes | SD | .170 | 114. Terry Mulholland | PHI | .307 |
| 4. Sid Fernandez | NY | .181 | 113. Bob Forsch | HOU | .300 |
| 5. Steve Bedrosian | SF | .182 | 112. Ricky Horton | STL | .295 |
| 6. Norm Charlton | CIN | .183 | 111. Jeff Robinson | PIT | .291 |
| 7. Rob Dibble | CIN | .185 | 110. Rick Rhoden | HOU | .282 |
| 8. John Costello | STL | .190 | 109. Bob Knepper | SF | .282 |
| 9. Bill Landrum | PIT | .193 | 108. Atlee Hammaker | SF | .279 |
| 10. John Smoltz | ATL | .193 | 107. Rick Mahler | CIN | .276 |
| 11. Larry Andersen | HOU | .193 | 105. Joe Boever | ATL | .275 |
| 12. Calvin Schiraldi | SD | .195 | 105. Juan Agosto | HOU | .275 |
| 13. Randy Kramer | PIT | .195 | 104. Tim Crews | LA | .274 |
| 14. Greg Harris | SD | .197 | 103. Andy McGaffigan | MTL | .273 |
| 15. Randy Myers | NY | .200 | 102. Steve Wilson | CHI | .273 |
| 16. Rick Aguilera | NY | .203 | 101. Tim Leary | CIN | .273 |
| 17. Scott Garrelts | SF | .205 | 100. Derek Lilliquist | ATL | .271 |
| 18. Ken Howell | PHI | .207 | 99. Paul Assenmacher | CHI | .270 |
| 19. John Wetteland | LA | .208 | 98. Dennis Martinez | MTL | .267 |
| 20. Mike Scott | HOU | .210 | 97. Jose Rijo | CIN | .266 |

## Opponents' Home Run Percentage with Runners On Base

### American League

#### Top 20

|  |  |  |  |
|---|---|---|---|
| 1. | Mike Dyer | MIN | 0.00 |
| 1. | Gregg Olson | BAL | 0.00 |
| 1. | Kevin Ritz | DET | 0.00 |
| 1. | Mike Schooler | SEA | 0.00 |
| 5. | Mark Thurmond | BAL | 0.60 |
| 6. | Greg Minton | CAL | 0.62 |
| 7. | Mike Henneman | DET | 0.65 |
| 8. | Jeff Montgomery | KC | 0.66 |
| 8. | Kenny Rogers | TEX | 0.66 |
| 10. | Todd Burns | OAK | 0.70 |
| 11. | Dave Righetti | NY | 0.72 |
| 12. | David Wells | TOR | 0.72 |
| 13. | Gene Nelson | OAK | 0.79 |
| 14. | Tom McCarthy | CHI | 0.81 |
| 15. | Jesse Orosco | CLE | 0.82 |
| 16. | Eric King | CHI | 0.84 |
| 17. | Roger Clemens | BOS | 0.88 |
| 18. | Dave LaPoint | NY | 0.95 |
| 19. | Mike Flanagan | TOR | 1.07 |
| 20. | Jack Morris | DET | 1.08 |

#### Bottom 20

|  |  |  |  |
|---|---|---|---|
| 134. | Charles Hudson | DET | 5.50 |
| 133. | Chuck Cary | NY | 5.38 |
| 132. | Ken Patterson | CHI | 5.36 |
| 131. | Dale Mohorcic | NY | 5.13 |
| 130. | Wes Gardner | BOS | 4.93 |
| 129. | Lance McCullers | NY | 4.61 |
| 128. | Tom Filer | MIL | 4.50 |
| 127. | Don August | MIL | 4.49 |
| 126. | Bobby Thigpen | CHI | 4.32 |
| 125. | Mark Knudson | MIL | 3.91 |
| 124. | Charlie Hough | TEX | 3.69 |
| 123. | Jeff Reardon | MIN | 3.68 |
| 122. | Mike Smithson | BOS | 3.63 |
| 121. | Scott Bankhead | SEA | 3.41 |
| 120. | Rod Nichols | CLE | 3.39 |
| 119. | Dave Schmidt | BAL | 3.38 |
| 118. | Melido Perez | CHI | 3.29 |
| 117. | Jamie Moyer | TEX | 3.25 |
| 116. | Jeff Ballard | BAL | 3.24 |
| 115. | Roy Smith | MIN | 3.19 |

### National League

#### Top 20

|  |  |  |  |
|---|---|---|---|
| 1. | Larry Andersen | HOU | 0.00 |
| 1. | Ricky Horton | STL | 0.00 |
| 1. | Les Lancaster | CHI | 0.00 |
| 1. | Alejandro Pena | LA | 0.00 |
| 5. | Jose Rijo | CIN | 0.58 |
| 6. | Joe Magrane | STL | 0.60 |
| 7. | Jim Acker | ATL | 0.67 |
| 8. | Paul Assenmacher | CHI | 0.70 |
| 9. | Steve Wilson | CHI | 0.71 |
| 10. | Ken Dayley | STL | 0.72 |
| 11. | Tim Burke | MTL | 0.76 |
| 12. | Mike LaCoss | SF | 0.79 |
| 13. | Bruce Ruffin | PHI | 0.80 |
| 14. | Ron Robinson | CIN | 0.81 |
| 15. | Dan Schatzeder | HOU | 0.83 |
| 16. | Jay Howell | LA | 0.85 |
| 16. | Dan Quisenberry | STL | 0.85 |
| 18. | Doug Bair | PIT | 0.92 |
| 19. | Mike Morgan | LA | 0.96 |
| 20. | Larry McWilliams | PHI | 1.00 |

#### Bottom 20

|  |  |  |  |
|---|---|---|---|
| 116. | Steve Bedrosian | SF | 5.51 |
| 115. | Mark Eichhorn | ATL | 4.96 |
| 114. | Scott Scudder | CIN | 4.91 |
| 113. | Dennis Cook | PHI | 4.70 |
| 112. | Eric Show | SD | 4.27 |
| 111. | Craig Lefferts | SF | 3.78 |
| 110. | Calvin Schiraldi | SD | 3.73 |
| 109. | Tom Glavine | ATL | 3.72 |
| 107. | Sid Fernandez | NY | 3.70 |
| 107. | Tim Crews | LA | 3.70 |
| 106. | Dennis Rasmussen | SD | 3.63 |
| 105. | Scott Terry | STL | 3.54 |
| 104. | Danny Jackson | CIN | 3.52 |
| 103. | Bob Forsch | HOU | 3.24 |
| 102. | John Smiley | PIT | 3.23 |
| 101. | Ted Power | STL | 3.16 |
| 100. | Walt Terrell | SD | 3.16 |
| 99. | Jeff Pico | CHI | 3.05 |
| 98. | Kent Tekulve | CIN | 3.03 |
| 97. | Bob Knepper | SF | 3.02 |

## Opponents' Home Run Percentage Bases Empty

### American League

#### Top 20

|  |  |  |  |
|---|---|---|---|
| 1. | Mark Williamson | BAL | 0.00 |
| 2. | Duane Ward | TOR | 0.52 |
| 3. | Tom Henke | TOR | 0.55 |
| 4. | Tom Filer | MIL | 0.62 |
| 5. | Mark Langston | SEA | 0.63 |
| 6. | Greg Hibbard | CHI | 0.67 |
| 7. | Mike Jeffcoat | TEX | 0.68 |
| 8. | Luis Aquino | KC | 0.68 |
| 9. | Doug Jones | CLE | 0.69 |
| 10. | Gregg Olson | BAL | 0.72 |
| 11. | Bill Swift | SEA | 0.74 |
| 12. | Gary Wayne | MIN | 0.80 |
| 13. | Dennis Lamp | BOS | 0.83 |
| 14. | Mark Gubicza | KC | 0.86 |
| 15. | Jeff Ballard | BAL | 1.01 |
| 16. | Todd Burns | OAK | 1.03 |
| 17. | Jeff Montgomery | KC | 1.10 |
| 18. | Lance McCullers | NY | 1.16 |
| 19. | Tom Candiotti | CLE | 1.21 |
| 19. | Jaime Navarro | MIL | 1.21 |

#### Bottom 20

|  |  |  |  |
|---|---|---|---|
| 135. | Charles Hudson | DET | 5.30 |
| 134. | Tom McCarthy | CHI | 5.22 |
| 133. | Jack Morris | DET | 5.10 |
| 132. | Charlie Hough | TEX | 4.35 |
| 131. | Dave Schmidt | BAL | 4.10 |
| 130. | Donn Pall | CHI | 4.05 |
| 129. | Francisc Oliveras | MIN | 4.03 |
| 128. | Jesse Orosco | CLE | 3.97 |
| 127. | Dave LaPoint | NY | 3.86 |
| 126. | Rich Yett | CLE | 3.85 |
| 125. | Doyle Alexander | DET | 3.80 |
| 124. | Jeff Robinson | DET | 3.80 |
| 123. | Cecilio Guante | TEX | 3.76 |
| 122. | Dave Johnson | BAL | 3.76 |
| 121. | Storm Davis | OAK | 3.69 |
| 120. | Mike Smithson | BOS | 3.69 |
| 119. | Bryan Clutterbuck | MIL | 3.68 |
| 118. | Ken Patterson | CHI | 3.65 |
| 117. | Jerry Reuss | MIL | 3.63 |
| 116. | Shane Rawley | MIN | 3.53 |

### National League

#### Top 20

|  |  |  |  |
|---|---|---|---|
| 1. | Mark Eichhorn | ATL | 0.00 |
| 1. | John Franco | CIN | 0.00 |
| 1. | Bill Landrum | PIT | 0.00 |
| 4. | Mike LaCoss | SF | 0.33 |
| 5. | Larry McWilliams | PHI | 0.38 |
| 6. | Dan Quisenberry | STL | 0.55 |
| 7. | Frank Viola | NY | 0.55 |
| 8. | Joe Magrane | STL | 0.56 |
| 9. | Roger McDowell | PHI | 0.60 |
| 10. | Juan Agosto | HOU | 0.63 |
| 11. | Zane Smith | MTL | 0.65 |
| 12. | Rick Aguilera | NY | 0.65 |
| 13. | Cris Carpenter | STL | 0.66 |
| 14. | Randy Myers | NY | 0.71 |
| 15. | Andy McGaffigan | MTL | 0.72 |
| 16. | Eric Show | SD | 0.81 |
| 17. | Marty Clary | ATL | 0.82 |
| 18. | Orel Hershiser | LA | 0.91 |
| 19. | Ted Power | STL | 0.91 |
| 20. | Ken Howell | PHI | 0.92 |

#### Bottom 20

|  |  |  |  |
|---|---|---|---|
| 116. | Bob Sebra | CIN | 5.08 |
| 115. | Don Carman | PHI | 4.66 |
| 114. | Tom Browning | CIN | 3.82 |
| 113. | Dennis Cook | PHI | 3.63 |
| 112. | Ron Robinson | CIN | 3.61 |
| 110. | Alejandro Pena | LA | 3.57 |
| 110. | Greg Harris | PHI | 3.57 |
| 109. | Don Robinson | SF | 3.28 |
| 108. | Ramon Martinez | LA | 3.26 |
| 107. | Bruce Ruffin | PHI | 3.15 |
| 106. | Mike Scott | HOU | 2.97 |
| 105. | Ed Whitson | SD | 2.96 |
| 104. | Steve Bedrosian | SF | 2.94 |
| 103. | Tim Burke | MTL | 2.92 |
| 102. | Scott Sanderson | CHI | 2.88 |
| 101. | Neal Heaton | PIT | 2.87 |
| 100. | Andrew Benes | SD | 2.84 |
| 99. | Scott Scudder | CIN | 2.76 |
| 98. | Steve Wilson | CHI | 2.73 |
| 97. | Walt Terrell | SD | 2.72 |

## Opponents' On Base Average Leading Off the Inning

### American League

#### Top 20

|  |  |  |  |
|---|---|---|---|
| 1. | Jose Bautista | BAL | .139 |
| 2. | Jeff Reardon | MIN | .193 |
| 3. | Greg Minton | CAL | .195 |
| 4. | Curt Young | OAK | .217 |
| 5. | Chuck Cary | NY | .220 |
| 6. | Erik Hanson | SEA | .220 |
| 7. | Gene Nelson | OAK | .234 |
| 8. | Tom Candiotti | CLE | .238 |
| 9. | Mike Moore | OAK | .240 |
| 10. | Tom McCarthy | CHI | .241 |
| 11. | Willie Fraser | CAL | .253 |
| 12. | Rick Honeycutt | OAK | .254 |
| 13. | David Wells | TOR | .256 |
| 14. | Tom Henke | TOR | .256 |
| 15. | Bryan Clutterbuck | MIL | .257 |
| 16. | Mark Williamson | BAL | .258 |
| 17. | Nolan Ryan | TEX | .259 |
| 18. | Dennis Lamp | BOS | .260 |
| 19. | Chris Bosio | MIL | .262 |
| 20. | Tom Gordon | KC | .264 |
| 20. | Bret Saberhagen | KC | .264 |

#### Bottom 20

|  |  |  |  |
|---|---|---|---|
| 135. | Charles Hudson | DET | .457 |
| 134. | Jeff Robinson | DET | .440 |
| 133. | Storm Davis | OAK | .422 |
| 132. | Mike Dunne | SEA | .415 |
| 131. | Tommy John | NY | .412 |
| 130. | Francisc Oliveras | MIN | .400 |
| 129. | Gary Wayne | MIN | .397 |
| 128. | Shane Rawley | MIN | .395 |
| 127. | Scott Bailes | CLE | .393 |
| 126. | Todd Stottlemyre | TOR | .392 |
| 125. | Steve Rosenberg | CHI | .392 |
| 124. | Bill Krueger | MIL | .391 |
| 123. | Joe Price | BOS | .391 |
| 122. | Dave LaPoint | NY | .387 |
| 121. | Dave Schmidt | BAL | .386 |
| 120. | Donn Pall | CHI | .384 |
| 119. | Mike Dyer | MIN | .378 |
| 118. | Brian Holman | SEA | .375 |
| 117. | Mark Guthrie | MIN | .373 |
| 116. | Randy Johnson | SEA | .371 |

### National League

#### Top 20

|  |  |  |  |
|---|---|---|---|
| 1. | Todd Frohwirth | PHI | .161 |
| 2. | Greg Harris | SD | .180 |
| 3. | Sid Fernandez | NY | .190 |
| 4. | Rick Aguilera | NY | .212 |
| 5. | Doug Bair | PIT | .217 |
| 5. | John Costello | STL | .217 |
| 7. | Steve Bedrosian | SF | .219 |
| 8. | Dan Quisenberry | STL | .221 |
| 9. | Dwight Gooden | NY | .221 |
| 10. | Larry Andersen | HOU | .231 |
| 11. | Bill Landrum | PIT | .236 |
| 12. | Rob Dibble | CIN | .238 |
| 13. | Tim Burke | MTL | .239 |
| 14. | John Smiley | PIT | .242 |
| 15. | Ken Dayley | STL | .242 |
| 16. | Scott Garrelts | SF | .246 |
| 17. | Frank DiPino | STL | .250 |
| 18. | Ron Darling | NY | .253 |
| 18. | John Franco | CIN | .253 |
| 20. | David Cone | NY | .256 |

#### Bottom 20

|  |  |  |  |
|---|---|---|---|
| 117. | Bruce Ruffin | PHI | .435 |
| 116. | Ramon Martinez | LA | .398 |
| 115. | Ken Hill | STL | .391 |
| 114. | Dennis Rasmussen | SD | .387 |
| 113. | Frank Viola | NY | .372 |
| 112. | Andy McGaffigan | MTL | .371 |
| 111. | Jim Clancy | HOU | .368 |
| 110. | John Wetteland | LA | .364 |
| 107. | Mark Davis | SD | .364 |
| 107. | Kelly Downs | SF | .364 |
| 107. | Norm Charlton | CIN | .364 |
| 106. | Bob Sebra | CIN | .362 |
| 105. | Paul Assenmacher | CHI | .357 |
| 104. | Jose Rijo | CIN | .354 |
| 103. | Kevin Gross | MTL | .351 |
| 102. | Bob Forsch | HOU | .348 |
| 101. | Scott Terry | STL | .346 |
| 100. | Atlee Hammaker | SF | .346 |
| 99. | Zane Smith | MTL | .345 |
| 97. | Terry Mulholland | PHI | .344 |
| 97. | Mark Eichhorn | ATL | .344 |

## Opponents' Batting Average with Runners in Scoring Position

### American League

#### Top 20

|  |  |  |  |
|---|---|---|---|
| 1. | Bryan Harvey | CAL | .147 |
| 1. | Jesse Orosco | CLE | .147 |
| 3. | Gregg Olson | BAL | .162 |
| 4. | Jeff Montgomery | KC | .163 |
| 5. | Gene Nelson | OAK | .178 |
| 6. | Chuck Finley | CAL | .183 |
| 7. | Todd Burns | OAK | .184 |
| 8. | Todd Stottlemyre | TOR | .185 |
| 9. | Jerry Reed | SEA | .188 |
| 10. | Charlie Hough | TEX | .190 |
| 11. | Pete Harnisch | BAL | .191 |
| 12. | Brian Holman | SEA | .196 |
| 13. | Cecilio Guante | TEX | .198 |
| 14. | David Wells | TOR | .200 |
| 15. | Frank Williams | DET | .202 |
| 16. | Dave Johnson | BAL | .208 |
| 17. | Bert Blyleven | CAL | .213 |
| 18. | Mike Boddicker | BOS | .213 |
| 19. | Greg Swindell | CLE | .219 |
| 20. | Lee Smith | BOS | .220 |

#### Bottom 20

|  |  |  |  |
|---|---|---|---|
| 135. | Jerry Reuss | MIL | .358 |
| 134. | Andy Hawkins | NY | .351 |
| 133. | Gary Mielke | TEX | .347 |
| 132. | Bob Stanley | BOS | .345 |
| 131. | Wes Gardner | BOS | .341 |
| 130. | Mike Flanagan | TOR | .341 |
| 129. | Tommy John | NY | .339 |
| 128. | Terry Leach | KC | .337 |
| 127. | Walt Terrell | NY | .333 |
| 126. | Greg Cadaret | NY | .328 |
| 125. | Dave LaPoint | NY | .324 |
| 124. | Mike Smithson | BOS | .321 |
| 123. | Dave Schmidt | BAL | .319 |
| 122. | Mike Witt | CAL | .310 |
| 121. | Jack Morris | DET | .310 |
| 120. | Mark Thurmond | BAL | .307 |
| 119. | Shane Rawley | MIN | .306 |
| 118. | Mark Williamson | BAL | .303 |
| 117. | Brian Holton | BAL | .302 |
| 116. | Mike Schwabe | DET | .297 |

### National League

#### Top 20

|  |  |  |  |
|---|---|---|---|
| 1. | Mark Davis | SD | .123 |
| 2. | Larry Andersen | HOU | .145 |
| 3. | Craig Lefferts | SF | .161 |
| 4. | Les Lancaster | CHI | .162 |
| 5. | Rob Dibble | CIN | .164 |
| 6. | Randy Myers | NY | .167 |
| 7. | Calvin Schiraldi | SD | .169 |
| 8. | Mark Portugal | HOU | .169 |
| 9. | Orel Hershiser | LA | .169 |
| 10. | Marty Clary | ATL | .170 |
| 11. | Mike Scott | HOU | .177 |
| 12. | Doug Bair | PIT | .182 |
| 13. | Tim Belcher | LA | .189 |
| 14. | Scott Garrelts | SF | .190 |
| 15. | John Smoltz | ATL | .194 |
| 16. | Bryn Smith | MTL | .196 |
| 17. | Jay Howell | LA | .197 |
| 18. | Dwight Gooden | NY | .198 |
| 18. | Roger McDowell | PHI | .198 |
| 20. | Norm Charlton | CIN | .200 |
| 20. | Mark Langston | MTL | .200 |
| 20. | Tim Leary | CIN | .200 |

#### Bottom 20

|  |  |  |  |
|---|---|---|---|
| 116. | Kelly Downs | SF | .344 |
| 115. | Dan Schatzeder | HOU | .341 |
| 114. | Bob Forsch | HOU | .336 |
| 113. | Walt Terrell | SD | .333 |
| 112. | Jim Clancy | HOU | .327 |
| 111. | Derek Lilliquist | ATL | .324 |
| 110. | Andy McGaffigan | MTL | .319 |
| 109. | Tim Crews | LA | .319 |
| 108. | Bob Walk | PIT | .317 |
| 107. | Kent Tekulve | CIN | .313 |
| 106. | Ricky Horton | STL | .313 |
| 105. | Danny Jackson | CIN | .312 |
| 104. | Terry Mulholland | PHI | .312 |
| 103. | Rick Mahler | CIN | .309 |
| 102. | Dan Quisenberry | STL | .309 |
| 101. | Paul Kilgus | CHI | .304 |
| 100. | Todd Frohwirth | PHI | .303 |
| 99. | Jeff Brantley | SF | .302 |
| 98. | Bruce Ruffin | PHI | .299 |
| 97. | Eric Show | SD | .298 |

## Opponents' Batting Average in Pressure Situations

### American League

#### Top 20

|  |  |  |  |
|---|---|---|---|
| 1. | Terry Leach | KC | .097 |
| 2. | Dennis Eckersley | OAK | .130 |
| 3. | Bill Long | CHI | .138 |
| 4. | Steve Crawford | KC | .160 |
| 5. | Roy Smith | MIN | .167 |
| 5. | Dave Stieb | TOR | .167 |
| 5. | Bill Swift | SEA | .167 |
| 8. | Mike Boddicker | BOS | .169 |
| 9. | Greg Minton | CAL | .170 |
| 10. | Dave Schmidt | BAL | .171 |
| 11. | Mark Langston | SEA | .176 |
| 12. | Bob McClure | CAL | .181 |
| 13. | Richard Dotson | CHI | .182 |
| 14. | Kirk McCaskill | CAL | .186 |
| 15. | Tom Gordon | KC | .188 |
| 16. | Dan Plesac | MIL | .190 |
| 17. | James Corsi | OAK | .195 |
| 17. | Gary Wayne | MIN | .195 |
| 19. | Tom Henke | TOR | .196 |
| 20. | Jim Acker | TOR | .197 |
| 20. | Jeff Ballard | BAL | .197 |

#### Bottom 20

|  |  |  |  |
|---|---|---|---|
| 134. | Tommy John | NY | .500 |
| 133. | Andy Hawkins | NY | .491 |
| 132. | Don August | MIL | .441 |
| 131. | Jaime Navarro | MIL | .436 |
| 130. | Mike Jeffcoat | TEX | .429 |
| 129. | Shane Rawley | MIN | .404 |
| 128. | Mike Smithson | BOS | .391 |
| 127. | Greg Cadaret | NY | .389 |
| 126. | Mark Thurmond | BAL | .385 |
| 125. | Brian Holton | BAL | .383 |
| 124. | Keith Comstock | SEA | .359 |
| 123. | Gary Mielke | TEX | .357 |
| 122. | Tom Niedenfuer | SEA | .351 |
| 121. | Mike Witt | CAL | .347 |
| 120. | Charles Hudson | DET | .345 |
| 119. | Jerry Reed | SEA | .330 |
| 118. | Jim Abbott | CAL | .326 |
| 117. | Mark Knudson | MIL | .325 |
| 116. | Todd Stottlemyre | TOR | .321 |
| 115. | Ken Patterson | CHI | .303 |

### National League

#### Top 20

|  |  |  |  |
|---|---|---|---|
| 1. | Jose DeLeon | STL | .113 |
| 2. | Dan Schatzeder | HOU | .143 |
| 3. | Tom Browning | CIN | .154 |
| 4. | Bob Kipper | PIT | .158 |
| 5. | Mike Morgan | LA | .160 |
| 6. | John Smoltz | ATL | .161 |
| 7. | Rich Gossage | SF | .167 |
| 7. | Bill Landrum | PIT | .167 |
| 9. | Dennis Cook | PHI | .171 |
| 10. | Jim Clancy | HOU | .174 |
| 11. | Jim Deshaies | HOU | .181 |
| 12. | Kelly Downs | SF | .182 |
| 13. | Rob Dibble | CIN | .184 |
| 14. | Norm Charlton | CIN | .184 |
| 15. | Mike Scott | HOU | .185 |
| 16. | Greg Maddux | CHI | .186 |
| 17. | Tom Glavine | ATL | .186 |
| 18. | Mark Davis | SD | .189 |
| 19. | Tim Belcher | LA | .189 |
| 20. | Don Robinson | SF | .190 |

#### Bottom 20

|  |  |  |  |
|---|---|---|---|
| 117. | Gene Harris | MTL | .478 |
| 116. | Derek Lilliquist | ATL | .424 |
| 115. | Ricky Horton | STL | .405 |
| 114. | Ken Hill | STL | .404 |
| 113. | Pascual Perez | MTL | .375 |
| 112. | Fernando Valenzuela | LA | .360 |
| 111. | Greg Harris | PHI | .357 |
| 110. | Kent Tekulve | CIN | .352 |
| 109. | Paul Kilgus | CHI | .348 |
| 108. | Paul Assenmacher | CHI | .323 |
| 107. | Rick Sutcliffe | CHI | .322 |
| 106. | Joe Hesketh | MTL | .321 |
| 105. | John Candelaria | MTL | .317 |
| 104. | Terry Mulholland | PHI | .308 |
| 103. | Jeff Musselman | NY | .306 |
| 102. | Tim Crews | LA | .301 |
| 101. | Jose Alvarez | ATL | .298 |
| 100. | Kevin Gross | MTL | .298 |
| 99. | Steve Wilson | CHI | .297 |
| 97. | Tim Leary | CIN | .293 |
| 97. | Dwayne Henry | ATL | .293 |

## Strikeout Percentage in Pressure Situations

### American League

#### Top 20

|  |  |  |  |
|---|---|---|---|
| 1. | Tom Henke | TOR | 36.76 |
| 2. | Lee Smith | BOS | 35.95 |
| 3. | Nolan Ryan | TEX | 35.00 |
| 4. | Dennis Eckersley | OAK | 31.62 |
| 5. | Bryan Harvey | CAL | 29.01 |
| 6. | Jeff Montgomery | KC | 28.92 |
| 7. | Tom Gordon | KC | 28.50 |
| 8. | Randy Johnson | SEA | 27.91 |
| 9. | Willie Hernandez | DET | 27.63 |
| 10. | Jesse Orosco | CLE | 26.92 |
| 11. | Lance McCullers | NY | 26.83 |
| 12. | Juan Berenguer | MIN | 26.11 |
| 13. | Rob Murphy | BOS | 25.64 |
| 14. | Jeff Russell | TEX | 25.52 |
| 15. | Bobby Witt | TEX | 25.00 |
| 16. | Joe Price | BOS | 24.44 |
| 17. | Mike Schooler | SEA | 24.28 |
| 18. | Duane Ward | TOR | 23.72 |
| 19. | Gregg Olson | BAL | 23.36 |
| 20. | Steve Farr | KC | 22.88 |

#### Bottom 20

|  |  |  |  |
|---|---|---|---|
| 133. | Mark Thurmond | BAL | 0.00 |
| 133. | Andy Hawkins | NY | 0.00 |
| 132. | Shane Rawley | MIN | 1.89 |
| 131. | Don August | MIL | 2.86 |
| 130. | Tom McCarthy | CHI | 3.70 |
| 129. | Doyle Alexander | DET | 4.00 |
| 128. | Dave Schmidt | BAL | 5.13 |
| 127. | Charlie Leibrandt | KC | 5.17 |
| 126. | Tom Candiotti | CLE | 5.21 |
| 125. | Pete Harnisch | BAL | 5.26 |
| 124. | Bill Swift | SEA | 5.45 |
| 123. | Bob Milacki | BAL | 6.78 |
| 122. | Jimmy Key | TOR | 6.98 |
| 121. | Jeff Ballard | BAL | 7.35 |
| 119. | Bob Stanley | BOS | 7.41 |
| 119. | Brian Holton | BAL | 7.41 |
| 118. | Dale Mohorcic | NY | 7.69 |
| 117. | Todd Stottlemyre | TOR | 8.06 |
| 116. | Charlie Hough | TEX | 8.11 |
| 115. | Tom Niedenfuer | SEA | 8.33 |

### National League

#### Top 20

|  |  |  |  |
|---|---|---|---|
| 1. | Rob Dibble | CIN | 33.82 |
| 2. | Mike Stanton | ATL | 32.88 |
| 3. | Jose Alvarez | ATL | 29.51 |
| 4. | Rick Aguilera | NY | 28.29 |
| 5. | Dwayne Henry | ATL | 27.08 |
| 6. | Mark Davis | SD | 24.71 |
| 7. | Norm Charlton | CIN | 24.66 |
| 8. | Ken Howell | PHI | 24.66 |
| 9. | Sid Fernandez | NY | 24.29 |
| 10. | Randy Myers | NY | 24.28 |
| 11. | Tim Leary | CIN | 24.21 |
| 12. | Mike Bielecki | CHI | 23.64 |
| 13. | David Cone | NY | 23.47 |
| 14. | Jeff Parrett | PHI | 23.34 |
| 15. | Dwight Gooden | NY | 22.64 |
| 16. | John Wetteland | LA | 22.62 |
| 17. | Doug Bair | PIT | 22.60 |
| 18. | John Candelaria | MTL | 22.22 |
| 19. | Alejandro Pena | LA | 22.11 |
| 20. | Jose DeLeon | STL | 20.91 |

#### Bottom 20

|  |  |  |  |
|---|---|---|---|
| 117. | Bob Walk | PIT | 1.49 |
| 116. | Tom Glavine | ATL | 3.17 |
| 115. | Marty Clary | ATL | 4.55 |
| 114. | Atlee Hammaker | SF | 5.19 |
| 113. | Gene Harris | MTL | 5.56 |
| 112. | Dave Leiper | SD | 6.25 |
| 111. | Terry Mulholland | PHI | 6.67 |
| 110. | Greg Harris | PHI | 8.00 |
| 109. | Ricky Horton | STL | 8.16 |
| 106. | Dennis Rasmussen | SD | 8.33 |
| 106. | Rick Thompson | MTL | 8.33 |
| 106. | Don Carman | PHI | 8.33 |
| 105. | Jeff Musselman | NY | 9.09 |
| 104. | Eric Show | SD | 9.52 |
| 103. | Pascual Perez | MTL | 9.64 |
| 102. | Tom Browning | CIN | 9.72 |
| 101. | Neal Heaton | PIT | 10.00 |
| 100. | Todd Frohwirth | PHI | 10.13 |
| 99. | Pat Clements | SD | 10.20 |
| 98. | Mike LaCoss | SF | 10.40 |

# VI
# Player Tendencies

# *Player Tendencies*

This isn't *X*-rated stuff. After all, we are a family publication. But if, after studying the statistics in other sections of this book, you wondered just which players had demonstrated the most pronounced differences in performance in day and night games, vs. left- and right-handers, or in several other category breakdowns, the Player Tendencies section will answer your questions.

We've examined eight different pairs of categories for batters and nine for pitchers. For each pair, we've ranked the players according to the differences in their batting averages (or, for pitchers, the averages of opposing batters). For example, we noted each player's difference in batting average with runners on base as opposed to bases-empty situations. The 25 with the largest differences in both directions are listed. And we've looked at the question not only for last season, but for the past five years as well, adding some additional perspective.

Incidentally, the additional pair of categories we've included for pitchers illuminates an area that's never before been addressed in a comprehensive fashion: how a pitcher's performance varies from his first time through the batting order to subsequent passes. Take a look at page 381 to find out who thrives on those second and third at-bats, and whose performance deteriorates most noticeably.

For each pair of categories, we've established a minimum number of at-bats needed to qualify. A player had to qualify on both sides (for instance, in both home and road games) in order to be ranked.

In most cases, those minimums are the same: for batters, 100 at-bats to qualify for last season, 300 to qualify for the last five years. Pitchers qualify if opposing batters accumulated 150 at-bats last season, or 400 over the last five years. The exceptions are for late-inning pressure situations (50 AB last season, 150 over the last five for batters, 75 and 250, respectively, for pitchers); runners in scoring position (75 and 150 for batters, 100 and 250 for pitchers); and first time through the batting order (200 and 300).

# Late-Inning Pressure Situations

## LAST SEASON

### BETTER UNDER PRESSURE

| | LATE-INNING PRESSURE | | | OTHER AT BATS | | | |
|---|---|---|---|---|---|---|---|
| PLAYER | AB | H | AVG | AB | H | AVG | DIFF |
| Mike Pagliarulo | 59 | 18 | .305 | 312 | 55 | .176 | .129 |
| Danny Tartabull | 59 | 22 | .373 | 382 | 96 | .251 | .122 |
| Mike Greenwell | 75 | 31 | .413 | 503 | 147 | .292 | .121 |
| Marty Barrett | 55 | 19 | .345 | 281 | 67 | .238 | .107 |
| Craig Biggio | 73 | 25 | .342 | 370 | 89 | .241 | .102 |
| Hubie Brooks | 80 | 28 | .350 | 462 | 117 | .253 | .097 |
| Ozzie Smith | 74 | 26 | .351 | 519 | 136 | .262 | .089 |
| Glenn Wilson | 80 | 27 | .338 | 352 | 88 | .250 | .088 |
| Alan Trammell | 67 | 21 | .313 | 382 | 88 | .230 | .083 |
| Bob Boone | 55 | 19 | .345 | 350 | 92 | .263 | .083 |
| Benito Santiago | 66 | 20 | .303 | 396 | 89 | .225 | .078 |
| Jack Howell | 72 | 21 | .292 | 402 | 87 | .216 | .075 |
| Ozzie Guillen | 102 | 32 | .314 | 495 | 119 | .240 | .073 |
| Al Newman | 67 | 21 | .313 | 379 | 92 | .243 | .071 |
| Dale Murphy | 94 | 27 | .287 | 480 | 104 | .217 | .071 |
| Mark Grace | 64 | 24 | .375 | 446 | 136 | .305 | .070 |
| Ernest Riles | 51 | 17 | .333 | 251 | 67 | .267 | .066 |
| Jose Gonzalez | 53 | 17 | .321 | 208 | 53 | .255 | .066 |
| Cecil Espy | 61 | 19 | .311 | 414 | 103 | .249 | .063 |
| Luis Salazar | 57 | 19 | .333 | 269 | 73 | .271 | .062 |
| George Bell | 86 | 30 | .349 | 527 | 152 | .288 | .060 |
| Rafael Ramirez | 88 | 26 | .295 | 449 | 106 | .236 | .059 |
| Kirby Puckett | 77 | 30 | .390 | 558 | 185 | .332 | .058 |
| Nelson Santovenia | 54 | 16 | .296 | 250 | 60 | .240 | .056 |
| Jim Gantner | 53 | 17 | .321 | 356 | 95 | .267 | .054 |

### BETTER IN OTHER AT BATS

| | LATE-INNING PRESSURE | | | OTHER AT BATS | | | |
|---|---|---|---|---|---|---|---|
| PLAYER | AB | H | AVG | AB | H | AVG | DIFF |
| Junior Felix | 61 | 9 | .148 | 354 | 98 | .277 | .129 |
| Wade Boggs | 94 | 22 | .234 | 527 | 183 | .347 | .113 |
| Joe Carter | 94 | 14 | .149 | 557 | 144 | .259 | .110 |
| Jesse Barfield | 71 | 10 | .141 | 450 | 112 | .249 | .108 |
| Craig Worthington | 71 | 11 | .155 | 426 | 112 | .263 | .108 |
| Phil Bradley | 60 | 11 | .183 | 485 | 140 | .289 | .105 |
| Andy Van Slyke | 80 | 12 | .150 | 396 | 101 | .255 | .105 |
| Keith Moreland | 68 | 13 | .191 | 357 | 105 | .294 | .103 |
| Todd Benzinger | 88 | 14 | .159 | 540 | 140 | .259 | .100 |
| Dave Bergman | 60 | 11 | .183 | 325 | 92 | .283 | .100 |
| Tony Pena | 63 | 11 | .175 | 361 | 99 | .274 | .100 |
| Jim Eisenreich | 58 | 12 | .207 | 417 | 127 | .305 | .098 |
| Alvin Davis | 72 | 16 | .222 | 426 | 136 | .319 | .097 |
| Ernie Whitt | 55 | 10 | .182 | 330 | 91 | .276 | .094 |
| Ivan Calderon | 101 | 21 | .208 | 521 | 157 | .301 | .093 |
| Pete Incaviglia | 64 | 10 | .156 | 389 | 97 | .249 | .093 |
| Greg Gagne | 52 | 10 | .192 | 408 | 115 | .282 | .090 |
| Jody Davis | 50 | 5 | .100 | 181 | 34 | .188 | .088 |
| Eddie Murray | 112 | 20 | .179 | 482 | 127 | .263 | .085 |
| Bobby Bonilla | 109 | 23 | .211 | 507 | 150 | .296 | .085 |
| Dave Martinez | 59 | 12 | .203 | 302 | 87 | .288 | .085 |
| Rickey Henderson | 65 | 13 | .200 | 476 | 135 | .284 | .084 |
| Carney Lansford | 61 | 16 | .262 | 490 | 169 | .345 | .083 |
| Darren Daulton | 60 | 8 | .133 | 308 | 66 | .214 | .081 |
| Jerome Walton | 54 | 12 | .222 | 421 | 127 | .302 | .079 |

## LAST 5 YEARS

### BETTER UNDER PRESSURE

| | LATE-INNING PRESSURE | | | OTHER AT BATS | | | |
|---|---|---|---|---|---|---|---|
| PLAYER | AB | H | AVG | AB | H | AVG | DIFF |
| Curtis Wilkerson | 171 | 60 | .351 | 1061 | 259 | .244 | .107 |
| Cecil Cooper | 188 | 64 | .340 | 1235 | 323 | .262 | .079 |
| Jim Sundberg | 191 | 54 | .283 | 1036 | 223 | .215 | .067 |
| Andy Allanson | 155 | 47 | .303 | 1049 | 249 | .237 | .066 |
| Dave Anderson | 174 | 49 | .282 | 953 | 213 | .224 | .058 |
| Thad Bosley | 173 | 56 | .324 | 403 | 109 | .270 | .053 |
| Mariano Duncan | 203 | 57 | .281 | 1285 | 293 | .228 | .053 |
| Luis Aguayo | 158 | 43 | .272 | 683 | 150 | .220 | .053 |
| Steve Sax | 425 | 145 | .341 | 2589 | 752 | .290 | .051 |
| Benito Santiago | 258 | 79 | .306 | 1304 | 334 | .256 | .050 |
| Milt Thompson | 295 | 97 | .329 | 1636 | 459 | .281 | .048 |
| Phil Garner | 172 | 50 | .291 | 855 | 208 | .243 | .047 |
| Wallace Johnson | 173 | 53 | .306 | 247 | 64 | .259 | .047 |
| Jerry Browne | 181 | 58 | .320 | 1109 | 303 | .273 | .047 |
| Tony Fernandez | 419 | 140 | .334 | 2631 | 755 | .287 | .047 |
| Alan Trammell | 350 | 115 | .329 | 2341 | 659 | .282 | .047 |
| Darrell Evans | 328 | 90 | .274 | 1896 | 433 | .228 | .046 |
| Gene Larkin | 170 | 52 | .306 | 1014 | 264 | .260 | .046 |
| Chris Brown | 259 | 79 | .305 | 1180 | 307 | .260 | .045 |
| Bill Madlock | 190 | 59 | .311 | 1089 | 290 | .266 | .044 |
| Billy Hatcher | 306 | 92 | .301 | 1851 | 476 | .257 | .043 |
| Tim Raines | 422 | 146 | .346 | 2209 | 671 | .304 | .042 |
| Tom Brookens | 218 | 61 | .280 | 1601 | 382 | .239 | .041 |
| Dale Sveum | 206 | 58 | .282 | 1113 | 268 | .241 | .041 |
| Don Slaught | 255 | 75 | .294 | 1311 | 336 | .256 | .038 |

### BETTER IN OTHER AT BATS

| | LATE-INNING PRESSURE | | | OTHER AT BATS | | | |
|---|---|---|---|---|---|---|---|
| PLAYER | AB | H | AVG | AB | H | AVG | DIFF |
| Roy Smalley | 169 | 31 | .183 | 987 | 267 | .271 | .087 |
| Danny Heep | 191 | 39 | .204 | 842 | 240 | .285 | .081 |
| Rick Dempsey | 175 | 27 | .154 | 973 | 227 | .233 | .079 |
| Tony Armas | 215 | 42 | .195 | 1246 | 340 | .273 | .078 |
| Carney Lansford | 350 | 80 | .229 | 2303 | 699 | .304 | .075 |
| Dave Magadan | 159 | 37 | .233 | 739 | 226 | .306 | .073 |
| Reggie Jackson | 180 | 32 | .178 | 1035 | 259 | .250 | .072 |
| Mike Heath | 278 | 54 | .194 | 1331 | 354 | .266 | .072 |
| Greg Brock | 261 | 51 | .195 | 1771 | 470 | .265 | .070 |
| Lonnie Smith | 263 | 58 | .221 | 1552 | 449 | .289 | .069 |
| Rick Cerone | 187 | 36 | .193 | 1155 | 293 | .254 | .061 |
| Tim Hulett | 172 | 33 | .192 | 1080 | 272 | .252 | .060 |
| Darryl Strawberry | 363 | 77 | .212 | 2056 | 559 | .272 | .060 |
| Jody Davis | 316 | 58 | .184 | 1610 | 390 | .242 | .059 |
| Ted Simmons | 228 | 50 | .219 | 711 | 196 | .276 | .056 |
| Daryl Boston | 198 | 39 | .197 | 1069 | 270 | .253 | .056 |
| Tim Flannery | 239 | 52 | .218 | 1089 | 297 | .273 | .055 |
| Mike Aldrete | 194 | 45 | .232 | 904 | 259 | .287 | .055 |
| Lance Parrish | 343 | 69 | .201 | 1856 | 473 | .255 | .054 |
| Randy Ready | 214 | 49 | .229 | 984 | 277 | .282 | .053 |
| Jim Morrison | 245 | 51 | .208 | 1167 | 304 | .260 | .052 |
| Wade Boggs | 370 | 115 | .311 | 2619 | 951 | .363 | .052 |
| Todd Benzinger | 176 | 37 | .210 | 1080 | 282 | .261 | .051 |
| Tony Phillips | 247 | 51 | .206 | 1397 | 359 | .257 | .051 |
| Bobby Bonilla | 359 | 85 | .237 | 1733 | 497 | .287 | .050 |

# *Runners On Base*

## *LAST SEASON*

### *BETTER WITH RUNNERS ON*

| | RUNNERS ON | | | BASES EMPTY | | | |
|---|---|---|---|---|---|---|---|
| PLAYER | AB | H | AVG | AB | H | AVG | DIFF |
| Lonnie Smith | 189 | 77 | .407 | 293 | 75 | .256 | .151 |
| Fred Manrique | 155 | 57 | .368 | 223 | 54 | .242 | .126 |
| Bob Melvin | 122 | 38 | .311 | 156 | 29 | .186 | .126 |
| Scott Bradley | 113 | 39 | .345 | 157 | 35 | .223 | .122 |
| Darrell Evans | 116 | 32 | .276 | 160 | 25 | .156 | .120 |
| Jose Canseco | 118 | 38 | .322 | 109 | 23 | .211 | .111 |
| Craig Worthington | 220 | 68 | .309 | 277 | 55 | .199 | .111 |
| Gerald Young | 180 | 54 | .300 | 353 | 70 | .198 | .102 |
| Henry Cotto | 117 | 38 | .325 | 178 | 40 | .225 | .100 |
| Ron Oester | 125 | 38 | .304 | 180 | 37 | .206 | .098 |
| Danny Heep | 163 | 56 | .344 | 157 | 40 | .255 | .089 |
| Rick Cerone | 150 | 43 | .287 | 146 | 29 | .199 | .088 |
| Milt Thompson | 249 | 84 | .337 | 296 | 74 | .250 | .087 |
| Paul O'Neill | 195 | 63 | .323 | 233 | 55 | .236 | .087 |
| Bill Doran | 203 | 55 | .271 | 304 | 56 | .184 | .087 |
| Dan Pasqua | 112 | 33 | .295 | 134 | 28 | .209 | .086 |
| Pedro Guerrero | 267 | 95 | .356 | 303 | 82 | .271 | .085 |
| Kurt Stillwell | 201 | 62 | .308 | 262 | 59 | .225 | .083 |
| Mike Pagliarulo | 155 | 38 | .245 | 216 | 35 | .162 | .083 |
| Steve Jeltz | 106 | 31 | .292 | 157 | 33 | .210 | .082 |
| Jay Bell | 108 | 33 | .306 | 163 | 37 | .227 | .079 |
| Carlton Fisk | 183 | 61 | .333 | 192 | 49 | .255 | .078 |
| Al Newman | 166 | 50 | .301 | 280 | 63 | .225 | .076 |
| Dickie Thon | 174 | 55 | .316 | 261 | 63 | .241 | .075 |
| Darren Daulton | 156 | 38 | .244 | 212 | 36 | .170 | .074 |

### *BETTER WITH BASES EMPTY*

| | RUNNERS ON | | | BASES EMPTY | | | |
|---|---|---|---|---|---|---|---|
| PLAYER | AB | H | AVG | AB | H | AVG | DIFF |
| Mickey Tettleton | 170 | 34 | .200 | 241 | 72 | .299 | .099 |
| Greg Gagne | 203 | 44 | .217 | 257 | 81 | .315 | .098 |
| Rick Leach | 101 | 22 | .218 | 138 | 43 | .312 | .094 |
| Carmelo Martinez | 145 | 26 | .179 | 122 | 33 | .270 | .091 |
| Randy Ready | 107 | 23 | .215 | 147 | 44 | .299 | .084 |
| Cecil Espy | 175 | 36 | .206 | 300 | 86 | .287 | .081 |
| Mickey Hatcher | 106 | 27 | .255 | 118 | 39 | .331 | .076 |
| Kent Hrbek | 184 | 43 | .234 | 191 | 59 | .309 | .075 |
| Ken Griffey | 100 | 22 | .220 | 136 | 40 | .294 | .074 |
| Jim Dwyer | 112 | 31 | .277 | 123 | 43 | .350 | .073 |
| Rick Schu | 124 | 22 | .177 | 142 | 35 | .246 | .069 |
| Felix Fermin | 183 | 36 | .197 | 301 | 79 | .262 | .066 |
| Vince Coleman | 168 | 35 | .208 | 395 | 108 | .273 | .065 |
| Todd Benzinger | 264 | 55 | .208 | 364 | 99 | .272 | .064 |
| Danny Tartabull | 197 | 46 | .234 | 244 | 72 | .295 | .062 |
| Mookie Wilson | 188 | 40 | .213 | 299 | 82 | .274 | .061 |
| Terry Steinbach | 189 | 45 | .238 | 265 | 79 | .298 | .060 |
| Matt Williams | 134 | 23 | .172 | 158 | 36 | .228 | .056 |
| Mike Heath | 160 | 37 | .231 | 236 | 67 | .284 | .053 |
| Vance Law | 191 | 40 | .209 | 217 | 56 | .258 | .049 |
| Andy Allanson | 137 | 28 | .204 | 186 | 47 | .253 | .048 |
| Mike A. Marshall | 179 | 42 | .235 | 198 | 56 | .283 | .048 |
| Greg Briley | 175 | 42 | .240 | 219 | 63 | .288 | .048 |
| Ryne Sandberg | 244 | 64 | .262 | 362 | 112 | .309 | .047 |
| Garry Templeton | 202 | 46 | .228 | 304 | 83 | .273 | .045 |

## *LAST 5 YEARS*

### *BETTER WITH RUNNERS ON*

| | RUNNERS ON | | | BASES EMPTY | | | |
|---|---|---|---|---|---|---|---|
| PLAYER | AB | H | AVG | AB | H | AVG | DIFF |
| Danny Heep | 474 | 150 | .316 | 559 | 129 | .231 | .086 |
| Jim Traber | 372 | 101 | .272 | 426 | 80 | .188 | .084 |
| Cliff Johnson | 312 | 94 | .301 | 393 | 86 | .219 | .082 |
| Dave Valle | 465 | 133 | .286 | 588 | 121 | .206 | .080 |
| John Russell | 359 | 93 | .259 | 442 | 80 | .181 | .078 |
| Kurt Stillwell | 646 | 191 | .296 | 950 | 211 | .222 | .074 |
| Bob Melvin | 490 | 129 | .263 | 657 | 129 | .196 | .067 |
| Tim Flannery | 501 | 152 | .303 | 827 | 197 | .238 | .065 |
| Dave Parker | 1343 | 412 | .307 | 1448 | 352 | .243 | .064 |
| Greg Brock | 959 | 278 | .290 | 1073 | 243 | .226 | .063 |
| Cecil Cooper | 679 | 207 | .305 | 744 | 180 | .242 | .063 |
| Jim Eisenreich | 336 | 101 | .301 | 446 | 107 | .240 | .061 |
| Kelly Gruber | 677 | 203 | .300 | 934 | 224 | .240 | .060 |
| Bill Buckner | 1090 | 332 | .305 | 1142 | 280 | .245 | .059 |
| Ruppert Jones | 404 | 108 | .267 | 570 | 119 | .209 | .059 |
| Jose Canseco | 1011 | 304 | .301 | 1152 | 279 | .242 | .059 |
| Hal McRae | 320 | 92 | .287 | 310 | 71 | .229 | .058 |
| Bruce Bochte | 356 | 110 | .309 | 475 | 119 | .251 | .058 |
| Kevin Elster | 386 | 99 | .256 | 518 | 103 | .199 | .058 |
| Gerald Young | 423 | 127 | .300 | 960 | 233 | .243 | .058 |
| Manny Trillo | 408 | 117 | .287 | 612 | 141 | .230 | .056 |
| Pat Tabler | 1048 | 337 | .322 | 1216 | 324 | .266 | .055 |
| Al Newman | 468 | 123 | .263 | 759 | 158 | .208 | .055 |
| Rick Leach | 396 | 124 | .313 | 518 | 134 | .259 | .054 |
| Larry Parrish | 819 | 232 | .283 | 954 | 219 | .230 | .054 |

### *BETTER WITH BASES EMPTY*

| | RUNNERS ON | | | BASES EMPTY | | | |
|---|---|---|---|---|---|---|---|
| PLAYER | AB | H | AVG | AB | H | AVG | DIFF |
| Matt Williams | 303 | 49 | .162 | 390 | 88 | .226 | .064 |
| Ken Griffey | 801 | 202 | .252 | 1005 | 306 | .304 | .052 |
| Joe Orsulak | 546 | 135 | .247 | 1021 | 304 | .298 | .050 |
| Jim Dwyer | 446 | 109 | .244 | 517 | 152 | .294 | .050 |
| Todd Benzinger | 568 | 130 | .229 | 688 | 189 | .275 | .046 |
| Dave Concepcion | 575 | 137 | .238 | 772 | 213 | .276 | .038 |
| Gorman Thomas | 409 | 76 | .186 | 390 | 87 | .223 | .037 |
| Mookie Wilson | 710 | 183 | .258 | 1258 | 369 | .293 | .036 |
| Rafael Palmeiro | 627 | 168 | .268 | 806 | 243 | .301 | .034 |
| Benito Santiago | 722 | 178 | .247 | 840 | 235 | .280 | .033 |
| Fred McGriff | 606 | 152 | .251 | 781 | 221 | .283 | .032 |
| Ivan Calderon | 831 | 214 | .258 | 971 | 280 | .288 | .031 |
| Terry Harper | 408 | 99 | .243 | 479 | 131 | .273 | .031 |
| Jim Gantner | 899 | 226 | .251 | 1334 | 376 | .282 | .030 |
| Mickey Tettleton | 573 | 127 | .222 | 754 | 190 | .252 | .030 |
| Phil Garner | 444 | 104 | .234 | 583 | 154 | .264 | .030 |
| Gary Redus | 587 | 136 | .232 | 1086 | 284 | .262 | .030 |
| Greg Gagne | 908 | 213 | .235 | 1215 | 321 | .264 | .030 |
| Larry Herndon | 488 | 118 | .242 | 636 | 172 | .270 | .029 |
| Daryl Boston | 490 | 111 | .227 | 777 | 198 | .255 | .028 |
| Steve Garvey | 625 | 157 | .251 | 662 | 185 | .279 | .028 |
| Kal Daniels | 450 | 128 | .284 | 765 | 239 | .312 | .028 |
| Chris James | 675 | 163 | .241 | 777 | 209 | .269 | .028 |
| Geno Petralli | 433 | 117 | .270 | 541 | 161 | .298 | .027 |
| Bob Horner | 587 | 149 | .254 | 619 | 174 | .281 | .027 |

# *Runners In Scoring Position*

## *LAST SEASON*

### *BETTER WITH RUNNERS IN SCORING POSITION*

| | SCORING POSITION | | | OTHER AT BATS | | | |
|---|---|---|---|---|---|---|---|
| PLAYER | AB | H | AVG | AB | H | AVG | DIFF |
| Pedro Guerrero | 168 | 68 | .405 | 402 | 109 | .271 | .134 |
| Lonnie Smith | 99 | 41 | .414 | 383 | 111 | .290 | .124 |
| Julio Franco | 140 | 57 | .407 | 408 | 116 | .284 | .123 |
| Fred Manrique | 86 | 33 | .384 | 292 | 78 | .267 | .117 |
| Dickie Thon | 104 | 37 | .356 | 331 | 81 | .245 | .111 |
| Bob Boone | 100 | 35 | .350 | 305 | 76 | .249 | .101 |
| Damon Berryhill | 92 | 30 | .326 | 242 | 56 | .231 | .095 |
| Craig Worthington | 135 | 42 | .311 | 362 | 81 | .224 | .087 |
| Bill Doran | 120 | 34 | .283 | 387 | 77 | .199 | .084 |
| Tracy Jones | 76 | 22 | .289 | 179 | 37 | .207 | .083 |
| Carlton Fisk | 105 | 37 | .352 | 270 | 73 | .270 | .082 |
| Alvin Davis | 127 | 46 | .362 | 371 | 106 | .286 | .076 |
| Dale Murphy | 152 | 43 | .283 | 422 | 88 | .209 | .074 |
| Will Clark | 144 | 56 | .389 | 444 | 140 | .315 | .074 |
| Bob Melvin | 75 | 22 | .293 | 203 | 45 | .222 | .072 |
| Gerald Young | 107 | 31 | .290 | 426 | 93 | .218 | .071 |
| Pete Incaviglia | 129 | 37 | .287 | 324 | 70 | .216 | .071 |
| Chet Lemon | 104 | 30 | .288 | 310 | 68 | .219 | .069 |
| Jerome Walton | 92 | 32 | .348 | 383 | 107 | .279 | .068 |
| Chili Davis | 150 | 48 | .320 | 410 | 104 | .254 | .066 |
| Glenn Wilson | 118 | 37 | .314 | 314 | 78 | .248 | .065 |
| George Bell | 169 | 58 | .343 | 444 | 124 | .279 | .064 |
| Jeff Blauser | 78 | 25 | .321 | 378 | 98 | .259 | .061 |
| Nelson Liriano | 121 | 37 | .306 | 297 | 73 | .246 | .060 |
| Kevin Elster | 116 | 32 | .276 | 342 | 74 | .216 | .059 |

### *BETTER IN OTHER AT BATS*

| | SCORING POSITION | | | OTHER AT BATS | | | |
|---|---|---|---|---|---|---|---|
| PLAYER | AB | H | AVG | AB | H | AVG | DIFF |
| John Kruk | 98 | 22 | .224 | 259 | 85 | .328 | .104 |
| Keith Moreland | 112 | 23 | .205 | 313 | 95 | .304 | .098 |
| Carlos Martinez | 96 | 22 | .229 | 254 | 83 | .327 | .098 |
| Andy Allanson | 80 | 13 | .162 | 243 | 62 | .255 | .093 |
| Gary Ward | 75 | 14 | .187 | 217 | 60 | .276 | .090 |
| Mickey Tettleton | 100 | 19 | .190 | 311 | 87 | .280 | .090 |
| Rob Thompson | 127 | 22 | .173 | 420 | 110 | .262 | .089 |
| Greg Gagne | 112 | 23 | .205 | 348 | 102 | .293 | .088 |
| Ryne Sandberg | 130 | 29 | .223 | 476 | 147 | .309 | .086 |
| Danny Tartabull | 116 | 24 | .207 | 325 | 94 | .289 | .082 |
| Gary Pettis | 84 | 16 | .190 | 360 | 98 | .272 | .082 |
| Dan Gladden | 105 | 25 | .238 | 356 | 111 | .312 | .074 |
| Matt Williams | 80 | 12 | .150 | 212 | 47 | .222 | .072 |
| Dion James | 95 | 22 | .232 | 320 | 97 | .303 | .072 |
| Felix Fermin | 109 | 20 | .183 | 375 | 95 | .253 | .070 |
| Mookie Wilson | 121 | 24 | .198 | 366 | 98 | .268 | .069 |
| Vince Coleman | 115 | 23 | .200 | 448 | 120 | .268 | .068 |
| Carney Lansford | 133 | 38 | .286 | 418 | 147 | .352 | .066 |
| Brook Jacoby | 109 | 24 | .220 | 410 | 117 | .285 | .065 |
| Cecil Espy | 106 | 22 | .208 | 369 | 100 | .271 | .063 |
| Todd Benzinger | 166 | 33 | .199 | 462 | 121 | .262 | .063 |
| Rance Mulliniks | 82 | 16 | .195 | 191 | 49 | .257 | .061 |
| Mike Scioscia | 98 | 20 | .204 | 310 | 82 | .265 | .060 |
| Jesse Barfield | 137 | 26 | .190 | 384 | 96 | .250 | .060 |
| Jody Reed | 131 | 32 | .244 | 393 | 119 | .303 | .059 |

## *LAST 5 YEARS*

### *BETTER WITH RUNNERS IN SCORING POSITION*

| | SCORING POSITION | | | OTHER AT BATS | | | |
|---|---|---|---|---|---|---|---|
| PLAYER | AB | H | AVG | AB | H | AVG | DIFF |
| Toby Harrah | 151 | 50 | .331 | 534 | 120 | .225 | .106 |
| Rudy Law | 159 | 54 | .340 | 538 | 127 | .236 | .104 |
| Dave Valle | 283 | 85 | .300 | 770 | 169 | .219 | .081 |
| Fred Manrique | 234 | 75 | .321 | 817 | 201 | .246 | .074 |
| Larry Parrish | 450 | 139 | .309 | 1323 | 312 | .236 | .073 |
| Joel Youngblood | 200 | 61 | .305 | 546 | 127 | .233 | .072 |
| Cliff Johnson | 186 | 57 | .306 | 519 | 123 | .237 | .069 |
| Gerald Young | 259 | 82 | .317 | 1124 | 278 | .247 | .069 |
| Hal McRae | 184 | 56 | .304 | 446 | 107 | .240 | .064 |
| Jose Cruz | 379 | 121 | .319 | 1089 | 279 | .256 | .063 |
| Mark McGwire | 416 | 127 | .305 | 1234 | 300 | .243 | .062 |
| Garth Iorg | 247 | 75 | .304 | 678 | 165 | .243 | .060 |
| Craig Worthington | 152 | 43 | .283 | 426 | 95 | .223 | .060 |
| Jay Bell | 152 | 43 | .283 | 469 | 105 | .224 | .059 |
| Pete Rose | 154 | 45 | .292 | 488 | 114 | .234 | .059 |
| Dave Winfield | 662 | 215 | .325 | 1670 | 445 | .266 | .058 |
| Curt Ford | 215 | 62 | .288 | 509 | 118 | .232 | .057 |
| Cecil Cooper | 377 | 118 | .313 | 1046 | 269 | .257 | .056 |
| Andre Thornton | 259 | 68 | .263 | 688 | 143 | .208 | .055 |
| Jose Canseco | 594 | 183 | .308 | 1569 | 400 | .255 | .053 |
| Dale Sveum | 335 | 96 | .287 | 984 | 230 | .234 | .053 |
| Kurt Stillwell | 381 | 111 | .291 | 1215 | 291 | .240 | .052 |
| Jerry Royster | 158 | 47 | .297 | 646 | 159 | .246 | .051 |
| Paul Molitor | 529 | 186 | .352 | 2173 | 656 | .302 | .050 |
| Argenis Salazar | 151 | 40 | .265 | 524 | 113 | .216 | .049 |

### *BETTER IN OTHER AT BATS*

| | SCORING POSITION | | | OTHER AT BATS | | | |
|---|---|---|---|---|---|---|---|
| PLAYER | AB | H | AVG | AB | H | AVG | DIFF |
| Ken Landreaux | 231 | 45 | .195 | 716 | 195 | .272 | .078 |
| Rick Schu | 297 | 58 | .195 | 1059 | 276 | .261 | .065 |
| Ken Griffey | 494 | 117 | .237 | 1312 | 391 | .298 | .061 |
| Dan Driessen | 169 | 34 | .201 | 424 | 110 | .259 | .058 |
| Mickey Tettleton | 328 | 64 | .195 | 999 | 253 | .253 | .058 |
| Alex Trevino | 228 | 47 | .206 | 599 | 158 | .264 | .058 |
| Jeff Stone | 153 | 32 | .209 | 597 | 158 | .265 | .056 |
| Joe Orsulak | 312 | 74 | .237 | 1255 | 365 | .291 | .054 |
| Rickey Henderson | 532 | 131 | .246 | 2076 | 622 | .300 | .053 |
| Barry Bonds | 400 | 85 | .213 | 1682 | 447 | .266 | .053 |
| Fred McGriff | 328 | 75 | .229 | 1059 | 298 | .281 | .053 |
| Benito Santiago | 412 | 93 | .226 | 1150 | 320 | .278 | .053 |
| Matt Williams | 188 | 30 | .160 | 505 | 107 | .212 | .052 |
| Gorman Thomas | 238 | 40 | .168 | 561 | 123 | .219 | .051 |
| Mark Salas | 256 | 57 | .223 | 795 | 217 | .273 | .050 |
| Dave Lopes | 158 | 38 | .241 | 415 | 120 | .289 | .049 |
| Leon Durham | 371 | 85 | .229 | 1236 | 343 | .278 | .048 |
| Ron Hassey | 344 | 81 | .235 | 1000 | 283 | .283 | .048 |
| Todd Benzinger | 365 | 81 | .222 | 891 | 238 | .267 | .045 |
| Phil Bradley | 700 | 181 | .259 | 2184 | 654 | .299 | .041 |
| Rafael Palmeiro | 358 | 92 | .257 | 1075 | 319 | .297 | .040 |
| Kent Hrbek | 643 | 163 | .253 | 1862 | 546 | .293 | .040 |
| Brook Jacoby | 652 | 160 | .245 | 2148 | 610 | .284 | .039 |
| Carmelo Castillo | 258 | 60 | .233 | 745 | 201 | .270 | .037 |
| Luis Rivera | 232 | 47 | .203 | 660 | 158 | .239 | .037 |

# Vs. Left- and Right-Handers

## LAST SEASON

### BETTER VS. LEFT-HANDERS

| PLAYER | VS. LEFT-HANDERS AB | H | AVG | VS. RIGHT-HANDERS AB | H | AVG | DIFF |
|---|---|---|---|---|---|---|---|
| Andres Galarraga | 174 | 67 | .385 | 398 | 80 | .201 | .184 |
| Pat Tabler | 160 | 56 | .350 | 230 | 45 | .196 | .154 |
| Gene Larkin | 156 | 57 | .365 | 290 | 62 | .214 | .152 |
| Alvaro Espinoza | 162 | 62 | .383 | 341 | 80 | .235 | .148 |
| Bob Melvin | 151 | 46 | .305 | 127 | 21 | .165 | .139 |
| Gerald Perry | 104 | 35 | .337 | 162 | 32 | .198 | .139 |
| Jim Presley | 116 | 38 | .328 | 274 | 54 | .197 | .131 |
| Kevin Romine | 104 | 36 | .346 | 170 | 39 | .229 | .117 |
| Tracy Jones | 101 | 30 | .297 | 154 | 29 | .188 | .109 |
| Roberto Kelly | 145 | 54 | .372 | 296 | 79 | .267 | .106 |
| Lloyd McClendon | 121 | 41 | .339 | 138 | 33 | .239 | .100 |
| Rick Schu | 142 | 37 | .261 | 124 | 20 | .161 | .099 |
| Rob Thompson | 194 | 59 | .304 | 353 | 73 | .207 | .097 |
| Steve Sax | 202 | 77 | .381 | 449 | 128 | .285 | .096 |
| Mike Heath | 161 | 51 | .317 | 235 | 53 | .226 | .091 |
| Carmelo Martinez | 118 | 32 | .271 | 149 | 27 | .181 | .090 |
| Garry Templeton | 145 | 46 | .317 | 361 | 83 | .230 | .087 |
| Vance Law | 111 | 33 | .297 | 297 | 63 | .212 | .085 |
| Shawon Dunston | 139 | 47 | .338 | 332 | 84 | .253 | .085 |
| Ken Caminiti | 165 | 52 | .315 | 420 | 97 | .231 | .084 |
| Glenn Wilson | 143 | 46 | .322 | 289 | 69 | .239 | .083 |
| Ricky Jordan | 201 | 67 | .333 | 322 | 82 | .255 | .079 |
| Jose Gonzalez | 134 | 41 | .306 | 127 | 29 | .228 | .078 |
| Glenn Braggs | 142 | 43 | .303 | 372 | 84 | .226 | .077 |
| Chris James | 168 | 49 | .292 | 314 | 68 | .217 | .075 |

### BETTER VS. RIGHT-HANDERS

| PLAYER | VS. LEFT-HANDERS AB | H | AVG | VS. RIGHT-HANDERS AB | H | AVG | DIFF |
|---|---|---|---|---|---|---|---|
| Paul O'Neill | 152 | 27 | .178 | 276 | 91 | .330 | .152 |
| Jack Howell | 136 | 19 | .140 | 338 | 89 | .263 | .124 |
| Jeff Treadway | 106 | 21 | .198 | 367 | 110 | .300 | .102 |
| George Brett | 167 | 37 | .222 | 290 | 92 | .317 | .096 |
| Lou Whitaker | 149 | 28 | .188 | 360 | 100 | .278 | .090 |
| Bobby Bonilla | 221 | 50 | .226 | 395 | 123 | .311 | .085 |
| Junior Felix | 129 | 26 | .202 | 286 | 81 | .283 | .082 |
| Randy Milligan | 169 | 38 | .225 | 196 | 60 | .306 | .081 |
| Mark Grace | 159 | 42 | .264 | 351 | 118 | .336 | .072 |
| Ken Griffey Jr. | 118 | 25 | .212 | 337 | 95 | .282 | .070 |
| Harold Baines | 156 | 41 | .263 | 349 | 115 | .330 | .067 |
| Oddibe McDowell | 170 | 38 | .224 | 349 | 100 | .287 | .063 |
| Eddie Murray | 210 | 44 | .210 | 384 | 103 | .268 | .059 |
| Jeff Hamilton | 210 | 44 | .210 | 338 | 90 | .266 | .057 |
| Roberto Alomar | 195 | 50 | .256 | 428 | 134 | .313 | .057 |
| Mike Greenwell | 202 | 55 | .272 | 376 | 123 | .327 | .055 |
| Wade Boggs | 210 | 62 | .295 | 411 | 143 | .348 | .053 |
| Kirby Puckett | 191 | 58 | .304 | 444 | 157 | .354 | .050 |
| Eric Davis | 156 | 39 | .250 | 306 | 91 | .297 | .047 |
| Tony Gwynn | 200 | 61 | .305 | 404 | 142 | .351 | .046 |
| Dave Parker | 127 | 29 | .228 | 426 | 117 | .275 | .046 |
| John Kruk | 101 | 27 | .267 | 256 | 80 | .313 | .045 |
| Tony Armas | 102 | 24 | .235 | 100 | 28 | .280 | .045 |
| Johnny Ray | 195 | 51 | .262 | 335 | 102 | .304 | .043 |
| Jose Oquendo | 229 | 61 | .266 | 327 | 101 | .309 | .042 |

## LAST 5 YEARS

### BETTER VS. LEFT-HANDERS

| PLAYER | VS. LEFT-HANDERS AB | H | AVG | VS. RIGHT-HANDERS AB | H | AVG | DIFF |
|---|---|---|---|---|---|---|---|
| Tracy Jones | 444 | 148 | .333 | 480 | 111 | .231 | .102 |
| Bob Melvin | 477 | 135 | .283 | 670 | 123 | .184 | .099 |
| Gene Larkin | 383 | 125 | .326 | 801 | 191 | .238 | .088 |
| Bob Dernier | 633 | 183 | .289 | 712 | 152 | .213 | .076 |
| Tony Phillips | 530 | 157 | .296 | 1114 | 253 | .227 | .069 |
| Rob Thompson | 645 | 197 | .305 | 1348 | 320 | .237 | .068 |
| Pat Tabler | 775 | 259 | .334 | 1489 | 402 | .270 | .064 |
| Mariano Duncan | 545 | 150 | .275 | 943 | 200 | .212 | .063 |
| Barry Larkin | 447 | 149 | .333 | 1064 | 288 | .271 | .063 |
| Mike Schmidt | 593 | 189 | .319 | 1568 | 403 | .257 | .062 |
| Jim Presley | 785 | 232 | .296 | 1910 | 447 | .234 | .062 |
| Manny Lee | 350 | 106 | .303 | 570 | 138 | .242 | .061 |
| Juan Beniquez | 471 | 152 | .323 | 596 | 157 | .263 | .059 |
| Andres Galarraga | 673 | 217 | .322 | 1455 | 383 | .263 | .059 |
| Bob Horner | 395 | 121 | .306 | 811 | 202 | .249 | .057 |
| Dave Valle | 426 | 117 | .275 | 627 | 137 | .219 | .056 |
| Tim Laudner | 524 | 137 | .261 | 735 | 151 | .205 | .056 |
| Rick Dempsey | 576 | 143 | .248 | 572 | 111 | .194 | .054 |
| Tony Pena | 798 | 233 | .292 | 1571 | 375 | .239 | .053 |
| Spike Owen | 574 | 162 | .282 | 1437 | 330 | .230 | .053 |
| Hubie Brooks | 711 | 224 | .315 | 1760 | 465 | .264 | .051 |
| Mike Gallego | 330 | 88 | .267 | 542 | 117 | .216 | .051 |
| Mike Heath | 797 | 222 | .279 | 812 | 186 | .229 | .049 |
| Larry Herndon | 678 | 188 | .277 | 446 | 102 | .229 | .049 |
| Mickey Hatcher | 670 | 208 | .310 | 793 | 208 | .262 | .048 |

### BETTER VS. RIGHT-HANDERS

| PLAYER | VS. LEFT-HANDERS AB | H | AVG | VS. RIGHT-HANDERS AB | H | AVG | DIFF |
|---|---|---|---|---|---|---|---|
| Wally Backman | 310 | 54 | .174 | 1490 | 445 | .299 | .124 |
| Kal Daniels | 300 | 68 | .227 | 915 | 299 | .327 | .100 |
| Andy Van Slyke | 765 | 162 | .212 | 1704 | 508 | .298 | .086 |
| Jack Howell | 429 | 77 | .179 | 1282 | 336 | .262 | .083 |
| Von Hayes | 829 | 184 | .222 | 1814 | 546 | .301 | .079 |
| Lou Whitaker | 775 | 167 | .215 | 1934 | 559 | .289 | .074 |
| Ernest Riles | 391 | 85 | .217 | 1473 | 418 | .284 | .066 |
| Ron Oester | 433 | 95 | .219 | 1308 | 372 | .284 | .065 |
| Mickey Brantley | 364 | 80 | .220 | 774 | 215 | .278 | .058 |
| John Kruk | 415 | 105 | .253 | 1045 | 319 | .305 | .052 |
| Dwayne Murphy | 355 | 71 | .200 | 1016 | 255 | .251 | .051 |
| Fred Lynn | 546 | 121 | .222 | 1439 | 392 | .272 | .051 |
| Milt Thompson | 378 | 94 | .249 | 1553 | 462 | .297 | .049 |
| Sid Bream | 512 | 119 | .232 | 1172 | 327 | .279 | .047 |
| Mark Grace | 306 | 84 | .275 | 690 | 220 | .319 | .044 |
| Ed Romero | 302 | 63 | .209 | 674 | 170 | .252 | .044 |
| Mike Easler | 315 | 78 | .248 | 1020 | 297 | .291 | .044 |
| Darryl Strawberry | 967 | 229 | .237 | 1452 | 407 | .280 | .043 |
| Len Dykstra | 460 | 108 | .235 | 1578 | 439 | .278 | .043 |
| Stan Javier | 300 | 62 | .207 | 672 | 168 | .250 | .043 |
| Larry Sheets | 341 | 79 | .232 | 1550 | 425 | .274 | .043 |
| Fred McGriff | 386 | 92 | .238 | 1001 | 281 | .281 | .042 |
| Johnny Ray | 1035 | 274 | .265 | 1869 | 573 | .307 | .042 |
| Kent Hrbek | 730 | 185 | .253 | 1775 | 524 | .295 | .042 |
| Wally Joyner | 811 | 212 | .261 | 1536 | 464 | .302 | .041 |

# Vs. Ground- and Fly-Ballers

## LAST SEASON

### BETTER VS. GROUND-BALLERS

| PLAYER | VS. GROUND-BALLERS AB | H | AVG | VS. FLY-BALLERS AB | H | AVG | DIFF |
|---|---|---|---|---|---|---|---|
| Luis Rivera | 158 | 52 | .329 | 165 | 31 | .188 | .141 |
| Jody Davis | 113 | 27 | .239 | 118 | 12 | .102 | .137 |
| Dick Schofield | 115 | 36 | .313 | 187 | 33 | .176 | .137 |
| Alfredo Griffin | 272 | 84 | .309 | 234 | 41 | .175 | .134 |
| Mitch Webster | 145 | 46 | .317 | 127 | 24 | .189 | .128 |
| Bo Jackson | 232 | 75 | .323 | 283 | 57 | .201 | .122 |
| Nelson Santovenia | 160 | 49 | .306 | 144 | 27 | .188 | .119 |
| Charlie Hayes | 145 | 46 | .317 | 159 | 32 | .201 | .116 |
| Ron Oester | 171 | 50 | .292 | 134 | 25 | .187 | .106 |
| Howard Johnson | 304 | 102 | .336 | 267 | 62 | .232 | .103 |
| Scott Bradley | 125 | 41 | .328 | 145 | 33 | .228 | .100 |
| Marty Barrett | 155 | 48 | .310 | 181 | 38 | .210 | .100 |
| Kurt Stillwell | 220 | 69 | .314 | 243 | 52 | .214 | .100 |
| Terry Kennedy | 164 | 48 | .293 | 191 | 37 | .194 | .099 |
| Wally Joyner | 229 | 78 | .341 | 364 | 89 | .245 | .096 |
| Brady Anderson | 115 | 30 | .261 | 151 | 25 | .166 | .095 |
| Dwight Smith | 198 | 72 | .364 | 145 | 39 | .269 | .095 |
| Darren Daulton | 166 | 42 | .253 | 202 | 32 | .158 | .095 |
| Lou Whitaker | 247 | 74 | .300 | 262 | 54 | .206 | .093 |
| Mookie Wilson | 246 | 73 | .297 | 241 | 49 | .203 | .093 |
| Pete Incaviglia | 208 | 59 | .284 | 245 | 48 | .196 | .088 |
| Jeff Blauser | 201 | 64 | .318 | 255 | 59 | .231 | .087 |
| Dan Pasqua | 128 | 37 | .289 | 118 | 24 | .203 | .086 |
| Milt Thompson | 267 | 89 | .333 | 278 | 69 | .248 | .085 |
| Candy Maldonado | 174 | 45 | .259 | 171 | 30 | .175 | .083 |

### BETTER VS. FLY-BALLERS

| PLAYER | VS. GROUND-BALLERS AB | H | AVG | VS. FLY-BALLERS AB | H | AVG | DIFF |
|---|---|---|---|---|---|---|---|
| Jose Canseco | 110 | 23 | .209 | 117 | 38 | .325 | .116 |
| John Moses | 106 | 23 | .217 | 136 | 45 | .331 | .114 |
| Barry Lyons | 123 | 25 | .203 | 112 | 33 | .295 | .091 |
| Jim Presley | 229 | 46 | .201 | 161 | 46 | .286 | .085 |
| Carlton Fisk | 173 | 43 | .249 | 202 | 67 | .332 | .083 |
| Roberto Kelly | 216 | 56 | .259 | 225 | 77 | .342 | .083 |
| Manny Lee | 143 | 31 | .217 | 157 | 47 | .299 | .083 |
| Rick Leach | 113 | 26 | .230 | 126 | 39 | .310 | .079 |
| Matt Williams | 136 | 22 | .162 | 156 | 37 | .237 | .075 |
| Steve Jeltz | 110 | 22 | .200 | 153 | 42 | .275 | .075 |
| Jerome Walton | 247 | 64 | .259 | 228 | 75 | .329 | .070 |
| Garry Templeton | 233 | 51 | .219 | 273 | 78 | .286 | .067 |
| Henry Cotto | 158 | 37 | .234 | 137 | 41 | .299 | .065 |
| Kelly Gruber | 236 | 60 | .254 | 309 | 98 | .317 | .063 |
| Claudell Washington | 166 | 39 | .235 | 252 | 75 | .298 | .063 |
| Jim Dwyer | 110 | 31 | .282 | 125 | 43 | .344 | .062 |
| Danny Heep | 153 | 41 | .268 | 167 | 55 | .329 | .061 |
| Lenny Harris | 178 | 37 | .208 | 157 | 42 | .268 | .060 |
| Dave Clark | 117 | 24 | .205 | 136 | 36 | .265 | .060 |
| Steve Buechele | 213 | 43 | .202 | 273 | 71 | .260 | .058 |
| Greg Brock | 171 | 40 | .234 | 202 | 59 | .292 | .058 |
| Walt Weiss | 126 | 26 | .206 | 110 | 29 | .264 | .057 |
| Mel Hall | 177 | 41 | .232 | 184 | 53 | .288 | .056 |
| Carlos Martinez | 159 | 43 | .270 | 191 | 62 | .325 | .054 |
| Scott Fletcher | 234 | 52 | .222 | 312 | 86 | .276 | .053 |

## LAST 5 YEARS

### BETTER VS. GROUND-BALLERS

| PLAYER | VS. GROUND-BALLERS AB | H | AVG | VS. FLY-BALLERS AB | H | AVG | DIFF |
|---|---|---|---|---|---|---|---|
| Bo Jackson | 615 | 183 | .298 | 817 | 167 | .204 | .093 |
| Mike Felder | 408 | 117 | .287 | 488 | 98 | .201 | .086 |
| Jeff Blauser | 331 | 100 | .302 | 357 | 79 | .221 | .081 |
| Jerry Browne | 527 | 172 | .326 | 763 | 189 | .248 | .079 |
| Luis Rivera | 473 | 126 | .266 | 419 | 79 | .189 | .078 |
| Roy Smalley | 488 | 147 | .301 | 668 | 151 | .226 | .075 |
| Franklin Stubbs | 615 | 164 | .267 | 545 | 107 | .196 | .070 |
| Donnie Hill | 540 | 163 | .302 | 823 | 191 | .232 | .070 |
| Jeff Reed | 496 | 127 | .256 | 438 | 82 | .187 | .069 |
| Stan Jefferson | 376 | 94 | .250 | 320 | 58 | .181 | .069 |
| Darren Daulton | 446 | 106 | .238 | 436 | 75 | .172 | .066 |
| Ed Romero | 425 | 117 | .275 | 551 | 116 | .211 | .065 |
| Brian Harper | 307 | 102 | .332 | 349 | 94 | .269 | .063 |
| Rich Gedman | 733 | 210 | .286 | 937 | 211 | .225 | .061 |
| Eddie Milner | 577 | 163 | .282 | 565 | 125 | .221 | .061 |
| Gary Redus | 879 | 246 | .280 | 794 | 174 | .219 | .061 |
| Mark Salas | 429 | 127 | .296 | 622 | 147 | .236 | .060 |
| Chris Sabo | 451 | 133 | .295 | 391 | 92 | .235 | .060 |
| Mark McGwire | 760 | 221 | .291 | 890 | 206 | .231 | .059 |
| Andy Allanson | 531 | 148 | .279 | 673 | 148 | .220 | .059 |
| Jim Traber | 381 | 98 | .257 | 417 | 83 | .199 | .058 |
| Larry Parrish | 725 | 209 | .288 | 1048 | 242 | .231 | .057 |
| Gary Carter | 1095 | 303 | .277 | 1081 | 239 | .221 | .056 |
| Steve Lombardozzi | 538 | 142 | .264 | 725 | 152 | .210 | .054 |
| Cecil Espy | 344 | 97 | .282 | 486 | 111 | .228 | .054 |

### BETTER VS. FLY-BALLERS

| PLAYER | VS. GROUND-BALLERS AB | H | AVG | VS. FLY-BALLERS AB | H | AVG | DIFF |
|---|---|---|---|---|---|---|---|
| Walt Weiss | 351 | 69 | .197 | 363 | 111 | .306 | .109 |
| Curt Ford | 382 | 83 | .217 | 342 | 97 | .284 | .066 |
| Manny Lee | 361 | 82 | .227 | 559 | 162 | .290 | .063 |
| Dion James | 699 | 179 | .256 | 645 | 204 | .316 | .060 |
| Alan Wiggins | 429 | 95 | .221 | 451 | 123 | .273 | .051 |
| Mike Aldrete | 573 | 145 | .253 | 525 | 159 | .303 | .050 |
| Billy Ripken | 464 | 98 | .211 | 600 | 156 | .260 | .049 |
| Dave Magadan | 415 | 111 | .267 | 483 | 152 | .315 | .047 |
| Mike Heath | 671 | 153 | .228 | 938 | 255 | .272 | .044 |
| Spike Owen | 834 | 183 | .219 | 1177 | 309 | .263 | .043 |
| Phil Garner | 553 | 128 | .231 | 474 | 130 | .274 | .043 |
| Wayne Tolleson | 533 | 122 | .229 | 813 | 220 | .271 | .042 |
| Rudy Law | 308 | 73 | .237 | 389 | 108 | .278 | .041 |
| Herm Winningham | 702 | 153 | .218 | 596 | 154 | .258 | .040 |
| Otis Nixon | 405 | 86 | .212 | 398 | 100 | .251 | .039 |
| John Kruk | 737 | 200 | .271 | 723 | 224 | .310 | .038 |
| Jay Bell | 306 | 67 | .219 | 315 | 81 | .257 | .038 |
| Rick Leach | 368 | 96 | .261 | 546 | 162 | .297 | .036 |
| Ron Hassey | 642 | 162 | .252 | 702 | 202 | .288 | .035 |
| George Hendrick | 338 | 75 | .222 | 531 | 136 | .256 | .034 |
| Jerry Mumphrey | 585 | 161 | .275 | 543 | 168 | .309 | .034 |
| Gary Matthews | 424 | 98 | .231 | 405 | 107 | .264 | .033 |
| Ellis Burks | 651 | 176 | .270 | 846 | 256 | .303 | .032 |
| Dave Bergman | 499 | 121 | .242 | 617 | 169 | .274 | .031 |
| Tim Teufel | 739 | 182 | .246 | 765 | 212 | .277 | .031 |

# Home and Road Games

## LAST SEASON

### BETTER IN HOME GAMES

| PLAYER | HOME GAMES AB | H | AVG | ROAD GAMES AB | H | AVG | DIFF |
|---|---|---|---|---|---|---|---|
| Luis Polonia | 199 | 74 | .372 | 234 | 56 | .239 | .133 |
| Rick Cerone | 155 | 47 | .303 | 141 | 25 | .177 | .126 |
| Alvin Davis | 249 | 91 | .365 | 249 | 61 | .245 | .120 |
| Kirby Puckett | 328 | 128 | .390 | 307 | 87 | .283 | .107 |
| Mickey Tettleton | 203 | 63 | .310 | 208 | 43 | .207 | .104 |
| Glenn Davis | 287 | 91 | .317 | 294 | 65 | .221 | .096 |
| Damon Berryhill | 148 | 46 | .311 | 186 | 40 | .215 | .096 |
| Carlton Fisk | 172 | 59 | .343 | 203 | 51 | .251 | .092 |
| Wade Boggs | 300 | 113 | .377 | 321 | 92 | .287 | .090 |
| Darryl Strawberry | 224 | 61 | .272 | 252 | 46 | .183 | .090 |
| Mike R. Fitzgerald | 141 | 40 | .284 | 149 | 29 | .195 | .089 |
| Paul O'Neill | 231 | 73 | .316 | 197 | 45 | .228 | .088 |
| Tommy Gregg | 116 | 34 | .293 | 160 | 33 | .206 | .087 |
| Nelson Santovenia | 142 | 42 | .296 | 162 | 34 | .210 | .086 |
| Bob Boone | 199 | 63 | .317 | 206 | 48 | .233 | .084 |
| Tim Wallach | 286 | 91 | .318 | 287 | 68 | .237 | .081 |
| Lonnie Smith | 226 | 81 | .358 | 256 | 71 | .277 | .081 |
| Gerald Perry | 142 | 41 | .289 | 124 | 26 | .210 | .079 |
| Julio Franco | 267 | 95 | .356 | 281 | 78 | .278 | .078 |
| Daryl Boston | 114 | 33 | .289 | 104 | 22 | .212 | .078 |
| Luis Rivera | 163 | 48 | .294 | 160 | 35 | .219 | .076 |
| Spike Owen | 201 | 55 | .274 | 236 | 47 | .199 | .074 |
| Dwight Smith | 157 | 57 | .363 | 186 | 54 | .290 | .073 |
| Jerry Browne | 316 | 105 | .332 | 282 | 74 | .262 | .070 |
| Steve Jeltz | 130 | 36 | .277 | 133 | 28 | .211 | .066 |

### BETTER IN ROAD GAMES

| PLAYER | HOME GAMES AB | H | AVG | ROAD GAMES AB | H | AVG | DIFF |
|---|---|---|---|---|---|---|---|
| Dave Martinez | 178 | 37 | .208 | 183 | 62 | .339 | .131 |
| Dion James | 200 | 44 | .220 | 215 | 75 | .349 | .129 |
| Rick Leach | 117 | 25 | .214 | 122 | 40 | .328 | .114 |
| Mike Felder | 139 | 25 | .180 | 176 | 51 | .290 | .110 |
| Carmelo Martinez | 121 | 20 | .165 | 146 | 39 | .267 | .102 |
| Greg Briley | 164 | 34 | .207 | 230 | 71 | .309 | .101 |
| Steve Lyons | 207 | 45 | .217 | 236 | 72 | .305 | .088 |
| Rey Quinones | 116 | 18 | .155 | 128 | 31 | .242 | .087 |
| Barry Bonds | 280 | 57 | .204 | 300 | 87 | .290 | .086 |
| Tim Teufel | 107 | 23 | .215 | 112 | 33 | .295 | .080 |
| Glenn Braggs | 275 | 58 | .211 | 239 | 69 | .289 | .078 |
| Lloyd Moseby | 222 | 40 | .180 | 280 | 71 | .254 | .073 |
| Darren Daulton | 172 | 28 | .163 | 196 | 46 | .235 | .072 |
| Ivan Calderon | 286 | 71 | .248 | 336 | 107 | .318 | .070 |
| Walt Weiss | 120 | 24 | .200 | 116 | 31 | .267 | .067 |
| Kurt Stillwell | 217 | 49 | .226 | 246 | 72 | .293 | .067 |
| Steve Finley | 114 | 25 | .219 | 103 | 29 | .282 | .062 |
| Tony Pena | 201 | 46 | .229 | 223 | 64 | .287 | .058 |
| Mookie Wilson | 247 | 55 | .223 | 240 | 67 | .279 | .056 |
| Ernest Riles | 130 | 32 | .246 | 172 | 52 | .302 | .056 |
| Ernie Whitt | 184 | 43 | .234 | 201 | 58 | .289 | .055 |
| Chris Sabo | 158 | 37 | .234 | 146 | 42 | .288 | .053 |
| Charlie Hayes | 156 | 36 | .231 | 148 | 42 | .284 | .053 |
| Fred Lynn | 173 | 37 | .214 | 180 | 48 | .267 | .053 |
| Jose Gonzalez | 113 | 27 | .239 | 148 | 43 | .291 | .052 |

## LAST 5 YEARS

### BETTER IN HOME GAMES

| PLAYER | HOME GAMES AB | H | AVG | ROAD GAMES AB | H | AVG | DIFF |
|---|---|---|---|---|---|---|---|
| Lee Mazzilli | 306 | 88 | .288 | 328 | 63 | .192 | .096 |
| Nelson Santovenia | 306 | 87 | .284 | 308 | 62 | .201 | .083 |
| Carmelo Castillo | 468 | 142 | .303 | 535 | 119 | .222 | .081 |
| Damon Berryhill | 339 | 99 | .292 | 332 | 72 | .217 | .075 |
| Jerry Browne | 704 | 220 | .313 | 586 | 141 | .241 | .072 |
| Dave Magadan | 455 | 148 | .325 | 443 | 115 | .260 | .066 |
| Wade Boggs | 1455 | 567 | .390 | 1534 | 499 | .325 | .064 |
| Gregg Jefferies | 308 | 93 | .302 | 315 | 76 | .241 | .061 |
| Kirby Puckett | 1658 | 593 | .358 | 1629 | 485 | .298 | .060 |
| Bo Jackson | 700 | 192 | .274 | 732 | 158 | .216 | .058 |
| Glenn Davis | 1311 | 385 | .294 | 1333 | 315 | .236 | .057 |
| Gary Roenicke | 305 | 79 | .259 | 321 | 65 | .202 | .057 |
| Gary Ward | 973 | 291 | .299 | 1052 | 256 | .243 | .056 |
| Charlie Moore | 330 | 88 | .267 | 361 | 77 | .213 | .053 |
| Todd Benzinger | 616 | 173 | .281 | 640 | 146 | .228 | .053 |
| Jim Rice | 1111 | 348 | .313 | 1151 | 300 | .261 | .053 |
| Leon Durham | 843 | 245 | .291 | 764 | 183 | .240 | .051 |
| Cecil Espy | 401 | 111 | .277 | 429 | 97 | .226 | .051 |
| Junior Ortiz | 344 | 101 | .294 | 378 | 92 | .243 | .050 |
| Kevin Seitzer | 938 | 309 | .329 | 955 | 267 | .280 | .050 |
| Andre Thornton | 486 | 120 | .247 | 461 | 91 | .197 | .050 |
| Ozzie Virgil | 755 | 202 | .268 | 790 | 173 | .219 | .049 |
| Curt Ford | 324 | 89 | .275 | 400 | 91 | .228 | .047 |
| Mike Schmidt | 1032 | 308 | .298 | 1129 | 284 | .252 | .047 |
| Gary Matthews | 374 | 102 | .273 | 455 | 103 | .226 | .046 |

### BETTER IN ROAD GAMES

| PLAYER | HOME GAMES AB | H | AVG | ROAD GAMES AB | H | AVG | DIFF |
|---|---|---|---|---|---|---|---|
| Candy Maldonado | 930 | 209 | .225 | 974 | 272 | .279 | .055 |
| Dave Collins | 571 | 131 | .229 | 592 | 168 | .284 | .054 |
| John Moses | 641 | 153 | .239 | 658 | 190 | .289 | .050 |
| Alex Trevino | 428 | 96 | .224 | 399 | 109 | .273 | .049 |
| Geno Petralli | 437 | 113 | .259 | 537 | 165 | .307 | .049 |
| Dickie Thon | 623 | 146 | .234 | 665 | 186 | .280 | .045 |
| Dave Martinez | 675 | 163 | .241 | 700 | 199 | .284 | .043 |
| Jim Sundberg | 593 | 121 | .204 | 634 | 156 | .246 | .042 |
| Rafael Santana | 916 | 204 | .223 | 926 | 245 | .265 | .042 |
| Gorman Thomas | 389 | 71 | .183 | 410 | 92 | .224 | .042 |
| Mike C. Brown | 315 | 77 | .244 | 336 | 96 | .286 | .041 |
| Rick Leach | 486 | 128 | .263 | 428 | 130 | .304 | .040 |
| Joel Skinner | 453 | 92 | .203 | 474 | 113 | .238 | .035 |
| Butch Wynegar | 328 | 66 | .201 | 322 | 76 | .236 | .035 |
| Cory Snyder | 978 | 225 | .230 | 1015 | 268 | .264 | .034 |
| Walt Weiss | 345 | 81 | .235 | 369 | 99 | .268 | .034 |
| Jim Dwyer | 433 | 110 | .254 | 530 | 151 | .285 | .031 |
| Wally Joyner | 1177 | 321 | .273 | 1170 | 355 | .303 | .031 |
| Terry Kennedy | 1041 | 246 | .236 | 1055 | 280 | .265 | .029 |
| Bobby Meacham | 434 | 93 | .214 | 526 | 128 | .243 | .029 |
| Rafael Belliard | 457 | 93 | .204 | 515 | 119 | .231 | .028 |
| Ernie Whitt | 978 | 240 | .245 | 1058 | 288 | .272 | .027 |
| Devon White | 865 | 209 | .242 | 923 | 246 | .267 | .025 |
| Jeff Reed | 450 | 95 | .211 | 484 | 114 | .236 | .024 |
| Bobby Bonilla | 1005 | 267 | .266 | 1087 | 315 | .290 | .024 |

# Grass and Artificial Surfaces

## LAST SEASON

### BETTER ON GRASS SURFACES

| | GRASS FIELDS | | | ARTIFICIAL TURF | | | |
|---|---|---|---|---|---|---|---|
| PLAYER | AB | H | AVG | AB | H | AVG | DIFF |
| Manny Lee | 140 | 44 | .314 | 160 | 34 | .213 | .102 |
| Wade Boggs | 518 | 179 | .346 | 103 | 26 | .252 | .093 |
| Rob Thompson | 414 | 109 | .263 | 133 | 23 | .173 | .090 |
| Dwight Smith | 226 | 80 | .354 | 117 | 31 | .265 | .089 |
| Pedro Guerrero | 151 | 55 | .364 | 419 | 122 | .291 | .073 |
| Gregg Jefferies | 363 | 101 | .278 | 145 | 30 | .207 | .071 |
| Dave Martinez | 108 | 35 | .324 | 253 | 64 | .253 | .071 |
| Mike A. Marshall | 276 | 77 | .279 | 101 | 21 | .208 | .071 |
| Mark Grace | 369 | 123 | .333 | 141 | 37 | .262 | .071 |
| Marvell Wynne | 230 | 61 | .265 | 112 | 22 | .196 | .069 |
| Lloyd Moseby | 216 | 56 | .259 | 286 | 55 | .192 | .067 |
| Rance Mulliniks | 124 | 34 | .274 | 149 | 31 | .208 | .066 |
| Dave Magadan | 262 | 80 | .305 | 112 | 27 | .241 | .064 |
| Pat Borders | 103 | 30 | .291 | 138 | 32 | .232 | .059 |
| Frank White | 158 | 46 | .291 | 260 | 61 | .235 | .057 |
| Von Hayes | 148 | 44 | .297 | 392 | 96 | .245 | .052 |
| Tony Fernandez | 237 | 68 | .287 | 336 | 79 | .235 | .052 |
| Gene Larkin | 163 | 48 | .294 | 283 | 71 | .251 | .044 |
| Junior Felix | 177 | 50 | .282 | 238 | 57 | .239 | .043 |
| Glenn Wilson | 104 | 31 | .298 | 328 | 84 | .256 | .042 |
| Ivan Calderon | 519 | 152 | .293 | 103 | 26 | .252 | .040 |
| Nelson Liriano | 176 | 50 | .284 | 242 | 60 | .248 | .036 |
| Bo Jackson | 213 | 59 | .277 | 302 | 73 | .242 | .035 |
| Ernie Whitt | 159 | 45 | .283 | 226 | 56 | .248 | .035 |
| Henry Cotto | 105 | 30 | .286 | 190 | 48 | .253 | .033 |

### BETTER ON ARTIFICIAL TURF

| | GRASS FIELDS | | | ARTIFICIAL TURF | | | |
|---|---|---|---|---|---|---|---|
| PLAYER | AB | H | AVG | AB | H | AVG | DIFF |
| Glenn Davis | 178 | 31 | .174 | 403 | 125 | .310 | .136 |
| John Moses | 117 | 27 | .231 | 125 | 41 | .328 | .097 |
| Spike Owen | 126 | 21 | .167 | 311 | 81 | .260 | .094 |
| Kirby Puckett | 234 | 66 | .282 | 401 | 149 | .372 | .090 |
| Paul O'Neill | 114 | 24 | .211 | 314 | 94 | .299 | .089 |
| Alvin Davis | 180 | 46 | .256 | 318 | 106 | .333 | .078 |
| Tim Wallach | 151 | 34 | .225 | 422 | 125 | .296 | .071 |
| Tom Herr | 138 | 33 | .239 | 423 | 128 | .303 | .063 |
| Dave Valle | 130 | 26 | .200 | 186 | 49 | .263 | .063 |
| Bill Doran | 144 | 25 | .174 | 363 | 86 | .237 | .063 |
| Fred McGriff | 217 | 50 | .230 | 334 | 98 | .293 | .063 |
| Andy Van Slyke | 124 | 24 | .194 | 352 | 89 | .253 | .059 |
| Kevin Seitzer | 224 | 55 | .246 | 373 | 113 | .303 | .057 |
| Bob Boone | 155 | 37 | .239 | 250 | 74 | .296 | .057 |
| Wally Backman | 107 | 21 | .196 | 192 | 48 | .250 | .054 |
| Tom Brunansky | 154 | 31 | .201 | 402 | 102 | .254 | .052 |
| Kent Hrbek | 134 | 32 | .239 | 241 | 70 | .290 | .052 |
| Vance Law | 262 | 57 | .218 | 146 | 39 | .267 | .050 |
| Mike Scioscia | 292 | 69 | .236 | 116 | 33 | .284 | .048 |
| Greg Gagne | 192 | 47 | .245 | 268 | 78 | .291 | .046 |
| Vince Coleman | 154 | 34 | .221 | 409 | 109 | .267 | .046 |
| Jeff Treadway | 337 | 89 | .264 | 136 | 42 | .309 | .045 |
| John Kruk | 132 | 36 | .273 | 225 | 71 | .316 | .043 |
| Jim Eisenreich | 205 | 55 | .268 | 270 | 81 | .311 | .043 |
| Danny Tartabull | 150 | 36 | .240 | 291 | 82 | .282 | .042 |

## LAST 5 YEARS

### BETTER ON GRASS SURFACES

| | GRASS FIELDS | | | ARTIFICIAL TURF | | | |
|---|---|---|---|---|---|---|---|
| PLAYER | AB | H | AVG | AB | H | AVG | DIFF |
| Rafael Belliard | 307 | 81 | .264 | 665 | 131 | .197 | .067 |
| Julio Franco | 2451 | 771 | .315 | 440 | 112 | .255 | .060 |
| Manny Lee | 376 | 112 | .298 | 544 | 132 | .243 | .055 |
| Pat Tabler | 1642 | 504 | .307 | 622 | 157 | .252 | .055 |
| Kirk Gibson | 1861 | 529 | .284 | 443 | 102 | .230 | .054 |
| Leon Durham | 1099 | 310 | .282 | 508 | 118 | .232 | .050 |
| Keith Moreland | 1956 | 566 | .289 | 716 | 172 | .240 | .049 |
| Jim Rice | 1901 | 559 | .294 | 361 | 89 | .247 | .048 |
| Paul Molitor | 2291 | 730 | .319 | 411 | 112 | .273 | .046 |
| Henry Cotto | 508 | 141 | .278 | 458 | 106 | .231 | .046 |
| Claudell Washington | 1496 | 432 | .289 | 359 | 88 | .245 | .044 |
| Kevin Mitchell | 1355 | 387 | .286 | 485 | 119 | .245 | .040 |
| Bob Dernier | 804 | 213 | .265 | 541 | 122 | .226 | .039 |
| Ken Oberkfell | 1463 | 416 | .284 | 592 | 145 | .245 | .039 |
| Randy Ready | 781 | 223 | .286 | 417 | 103 | .247 | .039 |
| Denny Walling | 386 | 119 | .308 | 979 | 265 | .271 | .038 |
| Von Hayes | 714 | 216 | .303 | 1929 | 514 | .266 | .036 |
| Mike R. Fitzgerald | 316 | 85 | .269 | 920 | 215 | .234 | .035 |
| Gorman Thomas | 350 | 78 | .223 | 449 | 85 | .189 | .034 |
| Nick Esasky | 921 | 255 | .277 | 1123 | 274 | .244 | .033 |
| Dale Murphy | 2169 | 590 | .272 | 793 | 190 | .240 | .032 |
| Alex Trevino | 454 | 119 | .262 | 373 | 86 | .231 | .032 |
| Lance Parrish | 1317 | 341 | .259 | 882 | 201 | .228 | .031 |
| Will Clark | 1567 | 488 | .311 | 533 | 150 | .281 | .030 |
| Chris Brown | 1105 | 304 | .275 | 334 | 82 | .246 | .030 |

### BETTER ON ARTIFICIAL TURF

| | GRASS FIELDS | | | ARTIFICIAL TURF | | | |
|---|---|---|---|---|---|---|---|
| PLAYER | AB | H | AVG | AB | H | AVG | DIFF |
| Tracy Jones | 394 | 93 | .236 | 530 | 166 | .313 | .077 |
| Glenn Davis | 801 | 169 | .211 | 1843 | 531 | .288 | .077 |
| Jose Cruz | 481 | 109 | .227 | 987 | 291 | .295 | .068 |
| Rick Leach | 430 | 106 | .247 | 484 | 152 | .314 | .068 |
| Rick Schu | 702 | 153 | .218 | 654 | 181 | .277 | .059 |
| Mickey Hatcher | 801 | 207 | .258 | 662 | 209 | .316 | .057 |
| John Cangelosi | 472 | 103 | .218 | 428 | 115 | .269 | .050 |
| Jim Sundberg | 643 | 130 | .202 | 584 | 147 | .252 | .050 |
| Rafael Palmeiro | 1068 | 293 | .274 | 365 | 118 | .323 | .049 |
| Kevin Seitzer | 711 | 196 | .276 | 1182 | 380 | .321 | .046 |
| Alan Ashby | 360 | 83 | .231 | 818 | 226 | .276 | .046 |
| Wally Joyner | 1995 | 561 | .281 | 352 | 115 | .327 | .046 |
| Tony Pena | 613 | 138 | .225 | 1756 | 470 | .268 | .043 |
| Mark Salas | 590 | 143 | .242 | 461 | 131 | .284 | .042 |
| Kirby Puckett | 1241 | 375 | .302 | 2046 | 703 | .344 | .041 |
| Bo Jackson | 564 | 124 | .220 | 868 | 226 | .260 | .041 |
| John Kruk | 941 | 260 | .276 | 519 | 164 | .316 | .040 |
| Kevin McReynolds | 2044 | 533 | .261 | 767 | 230 | .300 | .039 |
| Domingo Ramos | 304 | 66 | .217 | 306 | 78 | .255 | .038 |
| Jose Lind | 330 | 75 | .227 | 1002 | 265 | .264 | .037 |
| Terry Kennedy | 1631 | 396 | .243 | 465 | 130 | .280 | .037 |
| Dick Schofield | 1869 | 435 | .233 | 335 | 90 | .269 | .036 |
| Tim Teufel | 882 | 218 | .247 | 622 | 176 | .283 | .036 |
| Cal Ripken | 2629 | 689 | .262 | 485 | 144 | .297 | .035 |
| Lou Whitaker | 2275 | 597 | .262 | 434 | 129 | .297 | .035 |

# Day and Night Games

## LAST SEASON

### BETTER IN DAY GAMES

| PLAYER | DAY GAMES AB | H | AVG | NIGHT GAMES AB | H | AVG | DIFF |
|---|---|---|---|---|---|---|---|
| Rolando Roomes | 107 | 43 | .402 | 208 | 40 | .192 | .210 |
| Harold Baines | 119 | 51 | .429 | 386 | 105 | .272 | .157 |
| Dion James | 132 | 48 | .364 | 283 | 71 | .251 | .113 |
| Alvin Davis | 135 | 50 | .370 | 363 | 102 | .281 | .089 |
| R.J. Reynolds | 132 | 43 | .326 | 231 | 55 | .238 | .088 |
| Ozzie Smith | 180 | 59 | .328 | 413 | 103 | .249 | .078 |
| Greg Briley | 105 | 34 | .324 | 289 | 71 | .246 | .078 |
| Lloyd McClendon | 140 | 45 | .321 | 119 | 29 | .244 | .078 |
| Luis Polonia | 148 | 52 | .351 | 285 | 78 | .274 | .078 |
| Pat Sheridan | 117 | 31 | .265 | 164 | 31 | .189 | .076 |
| Bip Roberts | 102 | 36 | .353 | 227 | 63 | .278 | .075 |
| Johnny Ray | 128 | 44 | .344 | 402 | 109 | .271 | .073 |
| Jerome Walton | 251 | 82 | .327 | 224 | 57 | .254 | .072 |
| Spike Owen | 119 | 34 | .286 | 318 | 68 | .214 | .072 |
| Rafael Ramirez | 176 | 51 | .290 | 361 | 81 | .224 | .065 |
| Ryne Sandberg | 323 | 103 | .319 | 283 | 73 | .258 | .061 |
| Pat Tabler | 102 | 31 | .304 | 288 | 70 | .243 | .061 |
| Gene Larkin | 143 | 44 | .308 | 303 | 75 | .248 | .060 |
| Mark McGwire | 187 | 50 | .267 | 303 | 63 | .208 | .059 |
| Terry Pendleton | 190 | 58 | .305 | 423 | 104 | .246 | .059 |
| Alan Trammell | 145 | 41 | .283 | 304 | 68 | .224 | .059 |
| Brian Harper | 109 | 40 | .367 | 276 | 85 | .308 | .059 |
| Jeff Reed | 104 | 27 | .260 | 183 | 37 | .202 | .057 |
| Al Newman | 133 | 39 | .293 | 313 | 74 | .236 | .057 |
| Don Mattingly | 184 | 63 | .342 | 447 | 128 | .286 | .056 |

### BETTER IN NIGHT GAMES

| PLAYER | DAY GAMES AB | H | AVG | NIGHT GAMES AB | H | AVG | DIFF |
|---|---|---|---|---|---|---|---|
| Jim Presley | 105 | 15 | .143 | 285 | 77 | .270 | .127 |
| Dwight Evans | 187 | 40 | .214 | 333 | 108 | .324 | .110 |
| Steve Sax | 187 | 47 | .251 | 464 | 158 | .341 | .089 |
| Stan Javier | 144 | 29 | .201 | 166 | 48 | .289 | .088 |
| Ruben Sierra | 113 | 27 | .239 | 521 | 167 | .321 | .082 |
| Glenn Davis | 181 | 39 | .215 | 400 | 117 | .292 | .077 |
| George Bell | 192 | 47 | .245 | 421 | 135 | .321 | .076 |
| Candy Maldonado | 129 | 22 | .171 | 216 | 53 | .245 | .075 |
| Ernest Riles | 112 | 26 | .232 | 190 | 58 | .305 | .073 |
| Barry Larkin | 109 | 32 | .294 | 216 | 79 | .366 | .072 |
| Andy Allanson | 103 | 19 | .184 | 220 | 56 | .255 | .070 |
| Glenn Braggs | 169 | 34 | .201 | 345 | 93 | .270 | .068 |
| Jose Oquendo | 179 | 44 | .246 | 377 | 118 | .313 | .067 |
| George Brett | 100 | 23 | .230 | 357 | 106 | .297 | .067 |
| Dan Gladden | 137 | 34 | .248 | 324 | 102 | .315 | .067 |
| Jack Howell | 102 | 18 | .176 | 372 | 90 | .242 | .065 |
| Terry Kennedy | 139 | 28 | .201 | 216 | 57 | .264 | .062 |
| Paul O'Neill | 141 | 33 | .234 | 287 | 85 | .296 | .062 |
| Ron Hassey | 109 | 21 | .193 | 159 | 40 | .252 | .059 |
| Brian Downing | 138 | 33 | .239 | 406 | 121 | .298 | .059 |
| Milt Thompson | 183 | 46 | .251 | 362 | 112 | .309 | .058 |
| Cory Snyder | 149 | 26 | .174 | 340 | 79 | .232 | .058 |
| Roberto Kelly | 121 | 32 | .264 | 320 | 101 | .316 | .051 |
| Jesse Barfield | 150 | 30 | .200 | 371 | 92 | .248 | .048 |
| Mookie Wilson | 168 | 37 | .220 | 319 | 85 | .266 | .046 |

## LAST 5 YEARS

### BETTER IN DAY GAMES

| PLAYER | DAY GAMES AB | H | AVG | NIGHT GAMES AB | H | AVG | DIFF |
|---|---|---|---|---|---|---|---|
| Randy Ready | 362 | 120 | .331 | 836 | 206 | .246 | .085 |
| Tim Hulett | 331 | 99 | .299 | 921 | 206 | .224 | .075 |
| Mark McGwire | 626 | 185 | .296 | 1024 | 242 | .236 | .059 |
| Dan Pasqua | 447 | 126 | .282 | 967 | 218 | .225 | .056 |
| Mickey Hatcher | 446 | 144 | .323 | 1017 | 272 | .267 | .055 |
| Gene Larkin | 364 | 111 | .305 | 820 | 205 | .250 | .055 |
| Gerald Young | 389 | 116 | .298 | 994 | 244 | .245 | .053 |
| Pat Sheridan | 543 | 150 | .276 | 948 | 212 | .224 | .053 |
| Mike R. Fitzgerald | 418 | 116 | .278 | 818 | 184 | .225 | .053 |
| Al Newman | 422 | 111 | .263 | 805 | 170 | .211 | .052 |
| Darrell Evans | 718 | 194 | .270 | 1506 | 329 | .218 | .052 |
| Leon Durham | 1047 | 297 | .284 | 560 | 131 | .234 | .050 |
| Andre Dawson | 1347 | 407 | .302 | 1306 | 331 | .253 | .049 |
| Dave Bergman | 387 | 112 | .289 | 729 | 178 | .244 | .045 |
| Dave Kingman | 448 | 113 | .252 | 705 | 146 | .207 | .045 |
| Carney Lansford | 1024 | 328 | .320 | 1629 | 451 | .277 | .043 |
| Randy Bush | 495 | 143 | .289 | 1174 | 289 | .246 | .043 |
| Ron Cey | 533 | 138 | .259 | 327 | 71 | .217 | .042 |
| Ken Griffey | 575 | 178 | .310 | 1231 | 330 | .268 | .041 |
| Bruce Benedict | 314 | 74 | .236 | 545 | 106 | .194 | .041 |
| Terry Steinbach | 456 | 137 | .300 | 755 | 196 | .260 | .041 |
| Donnie Hill | 479 | 137 | .286 | 884 | 217 | .245 | .041 |
| Terry Pendleton | 936 | 265 | .283 | 1788 | 435 | .243 | .040 |
| Jim Morrison | 446 | 124 | .278 | 966 | 231 | .239 | .039 |
| Steve Jeltz | 428 | 103 | .241 | 1142 | 233 | .204 | .037 |

### BETTER IN NIGHT GAMES

| PLAYER | DAY GAMES AB | H | AVG | NIGHT GAMES AB | H | AVG | DIFF |
|---|---|---|---|---|---|---|---|
| Ron Oester | 565 | 130 | .230 | 1176 | 337 | .287 | .056 |
| Cory Snyder | 611 | 128 | .209 | 1382 | 365 | .264 | .055 |
| Paul O'Neill | 362 | 82 | .227 | 725 | 203 | .280 | .053 |
| Bob Melvin | 411 | 80 | .195 | 736 | 178 | .242 | .047 |
| Buddy Bell | 652 | 147 | .225 | 1403 | 380 | .271 | .045 |
| Dale Sveum | 424 | 92 | .217 | 895 | 234 | .261 | .044 |
| Scott Bradley | 327 | 78 | .239 | 889 | 251 | .282 | .044 |
| Gary Ward | 537 | 130 | .242 | 1488 | 417 | .280 | .038 |
| Kelly Gruber | 546 | 131 | .240 | 1065 | 296 | .278 | .038 |
| Jim Sundberg | 357 | 71 | .199 | 870 | 206 | .237 | .038 |
| Steve Garvey | 440 | 106 | .241 | 847 | 236 | .279 | .038 |
| Manny Lee | 303 | 73 | .241 | 617 | 171 | .277 | .036 |
| Glenn Davis | 783 | 188 | .240 | 1861 | 512 | .275 | .035 |
| Rafael Santana | 595 | 131 | .220 | 1247 | 318 | .255 | .035 |
| Ron Kittle | 366 | 81 | .221 | 942 | 241 | .256 | .035 |
| Garth Iorg | 324 | 77 | .238 | 601 | 163 | .271 | .034 |
| Lance Parrish | 577 | 128 | .222 | 1622 | 414 | .255 | .033 |
| Darnell Coles | 498 | 115 | .231 | 1291 | 336 | .260 | .029 |
| Rick Schu | 390 | 88 | .226 | 966 | 246 | .255 | .029 |
| Sid Bream | 495 | 121 | .244 | 1189 | 325 | .273 | .029 |
| Jim Presley | 663 | 153 | .231 | 2032 | 526 | .259 | .028 |
| Brook Jacoby | 909 | 233 | .256 | 1891 | 537 | .284 | .028 |
| Tony Bernazard | 520 | 134 | .258 | 1049 | 299 | .285 | .027 |
| Greg Gagne | 628 | 146 | .232 | 1495 | 388 | .260 | .027 |
| Fred McGriff | 462 | 116 | .251 | 925 | 257 | .278 | .027 |

# *Late-Inning Pressure Situations*

## *LAST SEASON*

### *BETTER IN OTHER AT BATS*

| | LATE-INNING PRESSURE | | | OTHER AT BATS | | | |
|---|---|---|---|---|---|---|---|
| PLAYER | AB | H | AVG | AB | H | AVG | DIFF |
| Paul Assenmacher | 155 | 50 | .323 | 135 | 24 | .178 | .145 |
| Jerry Reed | 97 | 32 | .330 | 282 | 57 | .202 | .128 |
| Mark Knudson | 77 | 25 | .325 | 387 | 85 | .220 | .105 |
| Jeff Russell | 167 | 36 | .216 | 80 | 9 | .112 | .103 |
| Alejandro Pena | 182 | 46 | .253 | 100 | 16 | .160 | .093 |
| Greg A. Harris | 82 | 24 | .293 | 293 | 61 | .208 | .084 |
| David Wells | 164 | 40 | .244 | 155 | 26 | .168 | .076 |
| Rob Murphy | 169 | 49 | .290 | 217 | 48 | .221 | .069 |
| Mike Witt | 75 | 26 | .347 | 789 | 226 | .286 | .060 |
| Randy Kramer | 90 | 24 | .267 | 311 | 66 | .212 | .054 |
| Joe Hesketh | 84 | 27 | .321 | 101 | 27 | .267 | .054 |
| Mark Williamson | 214 | 61 | .285 | 189 | 44 | .233 | .052 |
| Donn Pall | 169 | 50 | .296 | 164 | 40 | .244 | .052 |
| Frank DiPino | 95 | 25 | .263 | 226 | 48 | .212 | .051 |
| Gene Nelson | 111 | 26 | .234 | 185 | 34 | .184 | .050 |
| Les Lancaster | 150 | 37 | .247 | 115 | 23 | .200 | .047 |
| Dan Quisenberry | 90 | 26 | .289 | 209 | 52 | .249 | .040 |
| David Cone | 90 | 23 | .256 | 732 | 160 | .219 | .037 |
| Tim Leary | 82 | 24 | .293 | 704 | 181 | .257 | .036 |
| Joe Boever | 209 | 55 | .263 | 100 | 23 | .230 | .033 |
| Jeff Montgomery | 189 | 40 | .212 | 145 | 26 | .179 | .032 |
| Eric Plunk | 86 | 21 | .244 | 287 | 61 | .213 | .032 |
| Dave Stewart | 96 | 28 | .292 | 890 | 232 | .261 | .031 |
| John Costello | 119 | 27 | .227 | 106 | 21 | .198 | .029 |
| Juan Agosto | 113 | 31 | .274 | 203 | 50 | .246 | .028 |

### *BETTER UNDER PRESSURE*

| | LATE-INNING PRESSURE | | | OTHER AT BATS | | | |
|---|---|---|---|---|---|---|---|
| PLAYER | AB | H | AVG | AB | H | AVG | DIFF |
| Greg Minton | 159 | 27 | .170 | 172 | 49 | .285 | .115 |
| Mitch Williams | 206 | 42 | .204 | 92 | 29 | .315 | .111 |
| Bill Landrum | 180 | 30 | .167 | 112 | 30 | .268 | .101 |
| Jose DeLeon | 97 | 11 | .113 | 781 | 162 | .207 | .094 |
| Mike Morgan | 100 | 16 | .160 | 455 | 114 | .251 | .091 |
| Frank Viola | 133 | 23 | .173 | 853 | 223 | .261 | .088 |
| Joe Magrane | 89 | 17 | .191 | 782 | 202 | .258 | .067 |
| Don Carman | 79 | 16 | .203 | 505 | 136 | .269 | .067 |
| Bob McClure | 94 | 17 | .181 | 90 | 22 | .244 | .064 |
| Dan Plesac | 142 | 27 | .190 | 79 | 20 | .253 | .063 |
| Bob Kipper | 152 | 24 | .158 | 141 | 31 | .220 | .062 |
| Bob Milacki | 100 | 20 | .200 | 819 | 213 | .260 | .060 |
| John Smoltz | 118 | 19 | .161 | 638 | 141 | .221 | .060 |
| Kenny Rogers | 120 | 24 | .200 | 139 | 36 | .259 | .059 |
| Jeff Parrett | 242 | 51 | .211 | 146 | 39 | .267 | .056 |
| Juan Berenguer | 159 | 34 | .214 | 232 | 62 | .267 | .053 |
| Mark Eichhorn | 103 | 25 | .243 | 152 | 45 | .296 | .053 |
| Chuck Crim | 220 | 52 | .236 | 220 | 62 | .282 | .045 |
| Andy McGaffigan | 134 | 36 | .269 | 156 | 49 | .314 | .045 |
| Jeff Reardon | 170 | 39 | .229 | 106 | 29 | .274 | .044 |
| Jimmy Key | 82 | 19 | .232 | 756 | 207 | .274 | .042 |
| Mark Davis | 233 | 44 | .189 | 97 | 22 | .227 | .038 |
| Jack Morris | 99 | 25 | .253 | 570 | 164 | .288 | .035 |
| Mark Gubicza | 135 | 31 | .230 | 838 | 221 | .264 | .034 |
| Tim Belcher | 132 | 23 | .189 | 706 | 157 | .222 | .033 |

## *LAST 5 YEARS*

### *BETTER IN OTHER AT BATS*

| | LATE-INNING PRESSURE | | | OTHER AT BATS | | | |
|---|---|---|---|---|---|---|---|
| PLAYER | AB | H | AVG | AB | H | AVG | DIFF |
| Jim Clancy | 214 | 75 | .350 | 3357 | 840 | .250 | .100 |
| Rich Bordi | 252 | 80 | .317 | 700 | 168 | .240 | .077 |
| Mark Williamson | 494 | 151 | .306 | 836 | 201 | .240 | .065 |
| Andy Hawkins | 297 | 97 | .327 | 3455 | 915 | .265 | .062 |
| Oil Can Boyd | 278 | 90 | .324 | 2486 | 656 | .264 | .060 |
| Ken Dayley | 796 | 206 | .259 | 303 | 64 | .211 | .048 |
| George Frazier | 350 | 108 | .309 | 545 | 143 | .262 | .046 |
| Pat Clements | 377 | 112 | .297 | 670 | 169 | .252 | .045 |
| Tim Stoddard | 356 | 100 | .281 | 870 | 207 | .238 | .043 |
| Jim Acker | 643 | 186 | .289 | 1314 | 325 | .247 | .042 |
| Barry Jones | 364 | 98 | .269 | 349 | 80 | .229 | .040 |
| Doug Sisk | 438 | 137 | .313 | 794 | 218 | .275 | .038 |
| Dan Plesac | 683 | 163 | .239 | 368 | 74 | .201 | .038 |
| Dave LaPoint | 225 | 69 | .307 | 2763 | 744 | .269 | .037 |
| Sid Fernandez | 246 | 58 | .236 | 3137 | 625 | .199 | .037 |
| Lee Smith | 1099 | 266 | .242 | 479 | 99 | .207 | .035 |
| DeWayne Buice | 338 | 84 | .249 | 286 | 61 | .213 | .035 |
| Joe Hesketh | 354 | 97 | .274 | 1087 | 260 | .239 | .035 |
| Bob Ojeda | 323 | 88 | .272 | 2701 | 645 | .239 | .034 |
| Frank DiPino | 631 | 172 | .273 | 924 | 221 | .239 | .033 |
| Tom Niedenfuer | 745 | 203 | .272 | 590 | 142 | .241 | .032 |
| Dale Mohorcic | 518 | 149 | .288 | 674 | 173 | .257 | .031 |
| Jesse Orosco | 940 | 220 | .234 | 407 | 83 | .204 | .030 |
| Storm Davis | 213 | 64 | .300 | 2847 | 770 | .270 | .030 |
| Steve Farr | 530 | 145 | .274 | 923 | 225 | .244 | .030 |

### *BETTER UNDER PRESSURE*

| | LATE-INNING PRESSURE | | | OTHER AT BATS | | | |
|---|---|---|---|---|---|---|---|
| PLAYER | AB | H | AVG | AB | H | AVG | DIFF |
| Bill Landrum | 248 | 46 | .185 | 388 | 124 | .320 | .134 |
| Doug Bair | 247 | 42 | .170 | 467 | 133 | .285 | .115 |
| Jay Baller | 217 | 51 | .235 | 311 | 97 | .312 | .077 |
| Dickie Noles | 200 | 45 | .225 | 732 | 212 | .290 | .065 |
| Bob Kipper | 305 | 60 | .197 | 1214 | 317 | .261 | .064 |
| Randy Myers | 513 | 94 | .183 | 345 | 85 | .246 | .063 |
| Dave Leiper | 216 | 47 | .218 | 469 | 131 | .279 | .062 |
| Charlie Kerfeld | 234 | 49 | .209 | 373 | 100 | .268 | .059 |
| Jeff Russell | 405 | 88 | .217 | 1503 | 408 | .271 | .054 |
| Tom Browning | 333 | 67 | .201 | 4142 | 1047 | .253 | .052 |
| Dan Petry | 265 | 55 | .208 | 2318 | 597 | .258 | .050 |
| John Franco | 1196 | 266 | .222 | 441 | 120 | .272 | .050 |
| Ron Davis | 251 | 66 | .263 | 449 | 140 | .312 | .049 |
| Dan Schatzeder | 313 | 75 | .240 | 1074 | 309 | .288 | .048 |
| Norm Charlton | 209 | 40 | .191 | 365 | 87 | .238 | .047 |
| Tim Crews | 244 | 61 | .250 | 388 | 115 | .296 | .046 |
| Mark Davis | 1019 | 202 | .198 | 859 | 209 | .243 | .045 |
| Mike Morgan | 246 | 58 | .236 | 2289 | 641 | .280 | .044 |
| Tom Henke | 879 | 165 | .188 | 496 | 115 | .232 | .044 |
| Mark Thurmond | 254 | 65 | .256 | 1652 | 494 | .299 | .043 |
| Stu Cliburn | 240 | 54 | .225 | 433 | 116 | .268 | .043 |
| Dennis Eckersley | 583 | 121 | .208 | 1739 | 433 | .249 | .041 |
| John Candelaria | 311 | 69 | .222 | 1854 | 486 | .262 | .040 |
| Cecilio Guante | 638 | 133 | .208 | 776 | 191 | .246 | .038 |
| Greg Maddux | 270 | 62 | .230 | 2309 | 615 | .266 | .037 |

# Runners On Base

## LAST SEASON

### BETTER WITH BASES EMPTY

| PLAYER | RUNNERS ON AB | H | AVG | BASES EMPTY AB | H | AVG | DIFF |
|---|---|---|---|---|---|---|---|
| Nolan Ryan | 307 | 80 | .261 | 560 | 82 | .146 | .114 |
| Jerry Reuss | 239 | 87 | .364 | 331 | 84 | .254 | .110 |
| Tom Gordon | 241 | 66 | .274 | 341 | 56 | .164 | .110 |
| Greg Cadaret | 222 | 74 | .333 | 242 | 56 | .231 | .102 |
| Greg Minton | 162 | 45 | .278 | 169 | 31 | .183 | .094 |
| Terry Leach | 162 | 51 | .315 | 197 | 46 | .234 | .081 |
| Jose DeLeon | 311 | 77 | .248 | 567 | 96 | .169 | .078 |
| Derek Lilliquist | 261 | 91 | .349 | 410 | 111 | .271 | .078 |
| Bobby Witt | 332 | 96 | .289 | 401 | 86 | .214 | .075 |
| Danny Jackson | 199 | 62 | .312 | 252 | 60 | .238 | .073 |
| Dave Stieb | 311 | 81 | .260 | 437 | 83 | .190 | .071 |
| Pete Smith | 207 | 63 | .304 | 340 | 81 | .238 | .066 |
| Bob Walk | 308 | 95 | .308 | 460 | 113 | .246 | .063 |
| Randy Kramer | 186 | 48 | .258 | 215 | 42 | .195 | .063 |
| Erik Hanson | 156 | 44 | .282 | 267 | 59 | .221 | .061 |
| Jeff Pico | 164 | 51 | .311 | 192 | 48 | .250 | .061 |
| John Farrell | 327 | 91 | .278 | 476 | 105 | .221 | .058 |
| Mark Williamson | 193 | 56 | .290 | 210 | 49 | .233 | .057 |
| Larry McWilliams | 251 | 74 | .295 | 336 | 80 | .238 | .057 |
| Andy Hawkins | 326 | 105 | .322 | 494 | 133 | .269 | .053 |
| Lance McCullers | 152 | 43 | .283 | 173 | 40 | .231 | .052 |
| Greg W. Harris | 173 | 43 | .249 | 320 | 63 | .197 | .052 |
| Paul Kilgus | 253 | 79 | .312 | 326 | 85 | .261 | .052 |
| Bill Swift | 233 | 71 | .305 | 271 | 69 | .255 | .050 |
| Mike Henneman | 155 | 43 | .277 | 180 | 41 | .228 | .050 |

### BETTER WITH RUNNERS ON

| PLAYER | RUNNERS ON AB | H | AVG | BASES EMPTY AB | H | AVG | DIFF |
|---|---|---|---|---|---|---|---|
| Todd Stottlemyre | 219 | 50 | .228 | 267 | 87 | .326 | .098 |
| Brian Holton | 220 | 58 | .264 | 247 | 82 | .332 | .068 |
| Craig Lefferts | 185 | 37 | .200 | 214 | 56 | .262 | .062 |
| Jeff Montgomery | 152 | 25 | .164 | 182 | 41 | .225 | .061 |
| Juan Berenguer | 186 | 41 | .220 | 205 | 55 | .268 | .048 |
| Bert Blyleven | 351 | 77 | .219 | 556 | 148 | .266 | .047 |
| Tim Belcher | 312 | 60 | .192 | 526 | 122 | .232 | .040 |
| Jose Rijo | 172 | 39 | .227 | 233 | 62 | .266 | .039 |
| Juan Agosto | 156 | 37 | .237 | 160 | 44 | .275 | .038 |
| Richard Dotson | 281 | 77 | .274 | 334 | 104 | .311 | .037 |
| Dave Stewart | 408 | 99 | .243 | 578 | 161 | .279 | .036 |
| Mike Jeffcoat | 220 | 55 | .250 | 294 | 84 | .286 | .036 |
| Storm Davis | 297 | 80 | .269 | 352 | 107 | .304 | .035 |
| Bob Welch | 321 | 71 | .221 | 471 | 120 | .255 | .034 |
| Kirk McCaskill | 319 | 75 | .235 | 476 | 127 | .267 | .032 |
| Mark Portugal | 154 | 33 | .214 | 238 | 58 | .244 | .029 |
| Tim Leary | 324 | 79 | .244 | 462 | 126 | .273 | .029 |
| Terry Mulholland | 211 | 59 | .280 | 254 | 78 | .307 | .027 |
| Dennis Martinez | 333 | 80 | .240 | 551 | 147 | .267 | .027 |
| Mike Dunne | 192 | 57 | .297 | 211 | 68 | .322 | .025 |
| Ed Whitson | 301 | 66 | .219 | 540 | 132 | .244 | .025 |
| Roger McDowell | 172 | 38 | .221 | 167 | 41 | .246 | .025 |
| Zane Smith | 251 | 60 | .239 | 308 | 81 | .263 | .024 |
| Bill Long | 182 | 46 | .253 | 199 | 55 | .276 | .024 |
| Jim Abbott | 303 | 79 | .261 | 391 | 111 | .284 | .023 |

## LAST 5 YEARS

### BETTER WITH BASES EMPTY

| PLAYER | RUNNERS ON AB | H | AVG | BASES EMPTY AB | H | AVG | DIFF |
|---|---|---|---|---|---|---|---|
| Jimmy Jones | 616 | 194 | .315 | 899 | 218 | .242 | .072 |
| Mark Williamson | 595 | 181 | .304 | 735 | 171 | .233 | .072 |
| Dickie Noles | 437 | 135 | .309 | 495 | 122 | .246 | .062 |
| Doug Sisk | 638 | 203 | .318 | 594 | 152 | .256 | .062 |
| Steve Shields | 411 | 140 | .341 | 463 | 129 | .279 | .062 |
| Bob Shirley | 437 | 130 | .297 | 533 | 127 | .238 | .059 |
| Greg Cadaret | 428 | 123 | .287 | 449 | 104 | .232 | .056 |
| Willie Hernandez | 600 | 160 | .267 | 692 | 148 | .214 | .053 |
| Scott Terry | 558 | 161 | .289 | 754 | 179 | .237 | .051 |
| Jay Tibbs | 1129 | 341 | .302 | 1577 | 397 | .252 | .050 |
| Pete Smith | 541 | 157 | .290 | 865 | 209 | .242 | .049 |
| Jim Gott | 554 | 153 | .276 | 684 | 157 | .230 | .047 |
| Bob Kipper | 607 | 167 | .275 | 912 | 210 | .230 | .045 |
| Dave Stieb | 1628 | 426 | .262 | 2324 | 504 | .217 | .045 |
| Edwin Nunez | 455 | 134 | .295 | 520 | 130 | .250 | .045 |
| Dennis Lamp | 766 | 228 | .298 | 888 | 225 | .253 | .044 |
| Charles Hudson | 1041 | 296 | .284 | 1500 | 362 | .241 | .043 |
| Jeff M. Robinson | 550 | 142 | .258 | 863 | 187 | .217 | .041 |
| Frank DiPino | 736 | 202 | .274 | 819 | 191 | .233 | .041 |
| John Butcher | 555 | 183 | .330 | 776 | 224 | .289 | .041 |
| Don Aase | 531 | 141 | .266 | 520 | 117 | .225 | .041 |
| John Smoltz | 413 | 105 | .254 | 603 | 129 | .214 | .040 |
| Ray Burris | 440 | 135 | .307 | 645 | 172 | .267 | .040 |
| Jeff Sellers | 581 | 178 | .306 | 697 | 186 | .267 | .040 |
| Jeff Russell | 871 | 245 | .281 | 1037 | 251 | .242 | .039 |

### BETTER WITH RUNNERS ON

| PLAYER | RUNNERS ON AB | H | AVG | BASES EMPTY AB | H | AVG | DIFF |
|---|---|---|---|---|---|---|---|
| Brian Holton | 567 | 140 | .247 | 641 | 193 | .301 | .054 |
| Jesse Orosco | 694 | 139 | .200 | 653 | 164 | .251 | .051 |
| Mark Portugal | 566 | 136 | .240 | 734 | 209 | .285 | .044 |
| Tom Hume | 453 | 104 | .230 | 509 | 139 | .273 | .044 |
| Ed Vande Berg | 540 | 151 | .280 | 443 | 143 | .323 | .043 |
| Todd Worrell | 672 | 139 | .207 | 649 | 161 | .248 | .041 |
| Randy Myers | 432 | 82 | .190 | 426 | 97 | .228 | .038 |
| Jeff Ballard | 712 | 195 | .274 | 1015 | 312 | .307 | .034 |
| Steve Farr | 713 | 170 | .238 | 740 | 200 | .270 | .032 |
| Gene Garber | 547 | 140 | .256 | 571 | 163 | .285 | .030 |
| Bobby Thigpen | 585 | 136 | .232 | 515 | 134 | .260 | .028 |
| Vida Blue | 459 | 103 | .224 | 593 | 149 | .251 | .027 |
| Shane Rawley | 1548 | 406 | .262 | 2054 | 585 | .285 | .023 |
| Chuck Crim | 621 | 153 | .246 | 703 | 189 | .269 | .022 |
| Chris Codiroli | 593 | 149 | .251 | 782 | 214 | .274 | .022 |
| John Cerutti | 950 | 238 | .251 | 1466 | 400 | .273 | .022 |
| Tom Candiotti | 1352 | 324 | .240 | 1978 | 516 | .261 | .021 |
| Tommy John | 995 | 292 | .293 | 1336 | 418 | .313 | .019 |
| Steve Ontiveros | 636 | 147 | .231 | 811 | 202 | .249 | .018 |
| Gene Nelson | 976 | 230 | .236 | 1203 | 305 | .254 | .018 |
| Neal Heaton | 1324 | 345 | .261 | 1912 | 532 | .278 | .018 |
| Jim Deshaies | 1045 | 228 | .218 | 1656 | 390 | .236 | .017 |
| Mike Birkbeck | 420 | 122 | .290 | 531 | 163 | .307 | .016 |
| Kent Tekulve | 767 | 189 | .246 | 849 | 223 | .263 | .016 |
| Joe Cowley | 488 | 108 | .221 | 750 | 178 | .237 | .016 |

# *Runners In Scoring Position*

## *LAST SEASON*

### *BETTER IN OTHER AT BATS*

| | SCORING POSITION | | | OTHER AT BATS | | | |
|---|---|---|---|---|---|---|---|
| PLAYER | AB | H | AVG | AB | H | AVG | DIFF |
| Tom Gordon | 146 | 42 | .288 | 436 | 80 | .183 | .104 |
| Andy Hawkins | 191 | 67 | .351 | 629 | 171 | .272 | .079 |
| Jim Clancy | 150 | 49 | .327 | 426 | 106 | .249 | .078 |
| Jerry Reuss | 134 | 48 | .358 | 436 | 123 | .282 | .076 |
| Mike Flanagan | 138 | 47 | .341 | 520 | 139 | .267 | .073 |
| Terry Leach | 106 | 34 | .321 | 253 | 63 | .249 | .072 |
| Sid Fernandez | 117 | 30 | .256 | 677 | 127 | .188 | .069 |
| Greg Cadaret | 134 | 44 | .328 | 330 | 86 | .261 | .068 |
| Dave Stieb | 166 | 45 | .271 | 582 | 119 | .204 | .067 |
| Nolan Ryan | 203 | 48 | .236 | 664 | 114 | .172 | .065 |
| Jeff Parrett | 112 | 31 | .277 | 276 | 59 | .214 | .063 |
| Bob Walk | 180 | 57 | .317 | 588 | 151 | .257 | .060 |
| Mark Williamson | 119 | 36 | .303 | 284 | 69 | .243 | .060 |
| Danny Jackson | 125 | 39 | .312 | 326 | 83 | .255 | .057 |
| Jose DeLeon | 173 | 42 | .243 | 705 | 131 | .186 | .057 |
| Zane Smith | 139 | 41 | .295 | 420 | 100 | .238 | .057 |
| Bobby Witt | 204 | 59 | .289 | 529 | 123 | .233 | .057 |
| Randy D. Johnson | 170 | 49 | .288 | 423 | 98 | .232 | .057 |
| Walt Terrell | 171 | 57 | .333 | 645 | 179 | .278 | .056 |
| Greg A. Harris | 101 | 27 | .267 | 274 | 58 | .212 | .056 |
| Lance McCullers | 106 | 31 | .292 | 219 | 52 | .237 | .055 |
| Mike Jackson | 129 | 33 | .256 | 234 | 48 | .205 | .051 |
| Bob Forsch | 122 | 41 | .336 | 317 | 92 | .290 | .046 |
| Pete Smith | 123 | 36 | .293 | 424 | 108 | .255 | .038 |
| Ken Howell | 147 | 36 | .245 | 575 | 119 | .207 | .038 |

### *BETTER WITH RUNNERS IN SCORING POSITION*

| | SCORING POSITION | | | OTHER AT BATS | | | |
|---|---|---|---|---|---|---|---|
| PLAYER | AB | H | AVG | AB | H | AVG | DIFF |
| Todd Stottlemyre | 119 | 22 | .185 | 367 | 115 | .313 | .128 |
| Mark Davis | 106 | 13 | .123 | 224 | 53 | .237 | .114 |
| Marty Clary | 100 | 17 | .170 | 312 | 86 | .276 | .106 |
| Craig Lefferts | 118 | 19 | .161 | 281 | 74 | .263 | .102 |
| Orel Hershiser | 219 | 37 | .169 | 723 | 189 | .261 | .092 |
| Tim Leary | 170 | 34 | .200 | 616 | 171 | .278 | .078 |
| Charlie Hough | 158 | 30 | .190 | 527 | 138 | .262 | .072 |
| Brian Holman | 190 | 40 | .211 | 549 | 154 | .281 | .070 |
| Mike Boddicker | 183 | 39 | .213 | 630 | 178 | .283 | .069 |
| Dennis Martinez | 188 | 38 | .202 | 696 | 189 | .272 | .069 |
| Jerry Reed | 117 | 22 | .188 | 262 | 67 | .256 | .068 |
| Chuck Finley | 142 | 26 | .183 | 591 | 145 | .245 | .062 |
| Jeff Ballard | 172 | 41 | .238 | 664 | 199 | .300 | .061 |
| Charlie Leibrandt | 166 | 43 | .259 | 478 | 153 | .320 | .061 |
| Randy Myers | 102 | 17 | .167 | 199 | 45 | .226 | .059 |
| Doyle Alexander | 196 | 46 | .235 | 680 | 199 | .293 | .058 |
| Jim Abbott | 173 | 40 | .231 | 521 | 150 | .288 | .057 |
| Juan Agosto | 105 | 23 | .219 | 211 | 58 | .275 | .056 |
| Dave Stewart | 234 | 52 | .222 | 752 | 208 | .277 | .054 |
| Don August | 127 | 33 | .260 | 452 | 142 | .314 | .054 |
| Roger McDowell | 116 | 23 | .198 | 223 | 56 | .251 | .053 |
| Mark Gubicza | 229 | 51 | .223 | 744 | 201 | .270 | .047 |
| Mike Scott | 198 | 35 | .177 | 650 | 145 | .223 | .046 |
| Bert Blyleven | 188 | 40 | .213 | 719 | 185 | .257 | .045 |
| Richard Dotson | 153 | 40 | .261 | 462 | 141 | .305 | .044 |

## *LAST 5 YEARS*

### *BETTER IN OTHER AT BATS*

| | SCORING POSITION | | | OTHER AT BATS | | | |
|---|---|---|---|---|---|---|---|
| PLAYER | AB | H | AVG | AB | H | AVG | DIFF |
| Jimmy Jones | 348 | 114 | .328 | 1167 | 298 | .255 | .072 |
| Brad Havens | 263 | 84 | .319 | 598 | 153 | .256 | .064 |
| Don Aase | 329 | 95 | .289 | 722 | 163 | .226 | .063 |
| Pat Clements | 287 | 90 | .314 | 760 | 191 | .251 | .062 |
| Ken Howell | 404 | 109 | .270 | 1249 | 268 | .215 | .055 |
| Mark Williamson | 376 | 114 | .303 | 954 | 238 | .249 | .054 |
| Jeff M. Robinson | 287 | 78 | .272 | 1126 | 251 | .223 | .049 |
| Dickie Noles | 281 | 87 | .310 | 651 | 170 | .261 | .048 |
| Charlie Puleo | 275 | 78 | .284 | 780 | 184 | .236 | .048 |
| Steve Shields | 264 | 90 | .341 | 610 | 179 | .293 | .047 |
| Greg Cadaret | 260 | 75 | .288 | 617 | 152 | .246 | .042 |
| Jim Clancy | 756 | 218 | .288 | 2815 | 697 | .248 | .041 |
| Bill Wegman | 547 | 167 | .305 | 2159 | 572 | .265 | .040 |
| Dennis Lamp | 500 | 151 | .302 | 1154 | 302 | .262 | .040 |
| John Smiley | 414 | 109 | .263 | 1444 | 323 | .224 | .040 |
| Willie Hernandez | 352 | 94 | .267 | 940 | 214 | .228 | .039 |
| Paul Kilgus | 372 | 109 | .293 | 1339 | 340 | .254 | .039 |
| Joe Price | 262 | 73 | .279 | 831 | 200 | .241 | .038 |
| Frank DiPino | 451 | 126 | .279 | 1104 | 267 | .242 | .038 |
| Jeff Sellers | 320 | 100 | .313 | 958 | 264 | .276 | .037 |
| Rick Honeycutt | 517 | 146 | .282 | 1815 | 447 | .246 | .036 |
| Jeff Russell | 541 | 154 | .285 | 1367 | 342 | .250 | .034 |
| Scott Bailes | 463 | 140 | .302 | 1463 | 393 | .269 | .034 |
| Dan Plesac | 322 | 80 | .248 | 729 | 157 | .215 | .033 |
| John Butcher | 336 | 111 | .330 | 995 | 296 | .297 | .033 |

### *BETTER WITH RUNNERS IN SCORING POSITION*

| | SCORING POSITION | | | OTHER AT BATS | | | |
|---|---|---|---|---|---|---|---|
| PLAYER | AB | H | AVG | AB | H | AVG | DIFF |
| Mark Portugal | 313 | 66 | .211 | 987 | 279 | .283 | .072 |
| Jesse Orosco | 425 | 75 | .176 | 922 | 228 | .247 | .071 |
| Kent Tekulve | 516 | 110 | .213 | 1100 | 302 | .275 | .061 |
| Brian Holman | 280 | 61 | .218 | 841 | 234 | .278 | .060 |
| Randy Myers | 259 | 45 | .174 | 599 | 134 | .224 | .050 |
| Mike Henneman | 286 | 58 | .203 | 742 | 184 | .248 | .045 |
| Don August | 251 | 60 | .239 | 887 | 252 | .284 | .045 |
| Steve Bedrosian | 563 | 116 | .206 | 1479 | 371 | .251 | .045 |
| John Denny | 369 | 90 | .244 | 1182 | 341 | .288 | .045 |
| Brian Holton | 352 | 86 | .244 | 856 | 247 | .289 | .044 |
| Fred Toliver | 258 | 65 | .252 | 662 | 196 | .296 | .044 |
| George Frazier | 287 | 72 | .251 | 608 | 179 | .294 | .044 |
| Todd Worrell | 448 | 89 | .199 | 873 | 211 | .242 | .043 |
| Shane Rawley | 865 | 211 | .244 | 2737 | 780 | .285 | .041 |
| Ed Vande Berg | 338 | 92 | .272 | 645 | 202 | .313 | .041 |
| Mike Krukow | 650 | 138 | .212 | 2262 | 572 | .253 | .041 |
| Mark Grant | 347 | 80 | .231 | 1103 | 298 | .270 | .040 |
| Jim Deshaies | 585 | 116 | .198 | 2116 | 502 | .237 | .039 |
| Tommy John | 567 | 156 | .275 | 1764 | 554 | .314 | .039 |
| Randy O'Neal | 338 | 81 | .240 | 1099 | 306 | .278 | .039 |
| John Cerutti | 525 | 123 | .234 | 1891 | 515 | .272 | .038 |
| Bob Sebra | 384 | 94 | .245 | 985 | 278 | .282 | .037 |
| Charlie Leibrandt | 989 | 235 | .238 | 3297 | 901 | .273 | .036 |
| Frank Wills | 282 | 66 | .234 | 701 | 189 | .270 | .036 |
| Chuck Crim | 361 | 84 | .233 | 963 | 258 | .268 | .035 |

# Vs. Left- and Right-Handers

## LAST SEASON

### BETTER VS. RIGHT-HANDERS

| PLAYER | VS. LEFT-HANDERS AB | H | AVG | VS. RIGHT-HANDERS AB | H | AVG | DIFF |
|---|---|---|---|---|---|---|---|
| Juan Berenguer | 164 | 54 | .329 | 227 | 42 | .185 | .144 |
| Larry Andersen | 161 | 40 | .248 | 157 | 23 | .146 | .102 |
| Dennis Lamp | 180 | 52 | .289 | 228 | 44 | .193 | .096 |
| Jim Acker | 221 | 63 | .285 | 235 | 45 | .191 | .094 |
| Jose DeLeon | 509 | 119 | .234 | 369 | 54 | .146 | .087 |
| Tim Leary | 406 | 122 | .300 | 380 | 83 | .218 | .082 |
| Mike Scott | 482 | 119 | .247 | 366 | 61 | .167 | .080 |
| Danny Darwin | 240 | 59 | .246 | 194 | 33 | .170 | .076 |
| Dave W. Johnson | 155 | 47 | .303 | 185 | 43 | .232 | .071 |
| Andy Hawkins | 436 | 141 | .323 | 384 | 97 | .253 | .071 |
| Bill Swift | 231 | 73 | .316 | 273 | 67 | .245 | .071 |
| Roger McDowell | 185 | 49 | .265 | 154 | 30 | .195 | .070 |
| Terry Leach | 173 | 53 | .306 | 186 | 44 | .237 | .070 |
| Mike Dunne | 204 | 70 | .343 | 199 | 55 | .276 | .067 |
| Greg Maddux | 495 | 138 | .279 | 395 | 84 | .213 | .066 |
| Shawn Hillegas | 227 | 71 | .313 | 246 | 61 | .248 | .065 |
| Jeff Brantley | 192 | 58 | .302 | 181 | 43 | .238 | .065 |
| Jeff Pico | 163 | 51 | .313 | 193 | 48 | .249 | .064 |
| Ed Whitson | 497 | 130 | .262 | 344 | 68 | .198 | .064 |
| Dennis Martinez | 492 | 140 | .285 | 392 | 87 | .222 | .063 |
| Ramon Martinez | 203 | 50 | .246 | 157 | 29 | .185 | .062 |
| Dave Stieb | 387 | 96 | .248 | 361 | 68 | .188 | .060 |
| Todd Stottlemyre | 223 | 70 | .314 | 263 | 67 | .255 | .059 |
| Ron Darling | 481 | 136 | .283 | 348 | 78 | .224 | .059 |
| Jose Rijo | 242 | 66 | .273 | 163 | 35 | .215 | .058 |

### BETTER VS. LEFT-HANDERS

| PLAYER | VS. LEFT-HANDERS AB | H | AVG | VS. RIGHT-HANDERS AB | H | AVG | DIFF |
|---|---|---|---|---|---|---|---|
| Erik Hanson | 226 | 48 | .212 | 197 | 55 | .279 | .067 |
| Greg A. Harris | 177 | 34 | .192 | 198 | 51 | .258 | .065 |
| Bob Welch | 418 | 88 | .211 | 374 | 103 | .275 | .065 |
| Dwight Gooden | 232 | 42 | .181 | 209 | 51 | .244 | .063 |
| Jeff D. Robinson | 302 | 78 | .258 | 267 | 83 | .311 | .053 |
| Jimmy Key | 150 | 34 | .227 | 688 | 192 | .279 | .052 |
| Bret Saberhagen | 524 | 102 | .195 | 437 | 107 | .245 | .050 |
| Storm Davis | 314 | 83 | .264 | 335 | 104 | .310 | .046 |
| Greg W. Harris | 281 | 55 | .196 | 212 | 51 | .241 | .045 |
| Rick Rhoden | 221 | 60 | .271 | 153 | 48 | .314 | .042 |
| Scott Scudder | 197 | 44 | .223 | 183 | 47 | .257 | .033 |
| Jeff Parrett | 202 | 44 | .218 | 186 | 46 | .247 | .029 |
| Donn Pall | 157 | 40 | .255 | 176 | 50 | .284 | .029 |
| Marty Clary | 255 | 61 | .239 | 157 | 42 | .268 | .028 |
| Mark Gubicza | 513 | 126 | .246 | 460 | 126 | .274 | .028 |
| Eric King | 308 | 71 | .231 | 283 | 73 | .258 | .027 |
| Mark Portugal | 209 | 46 | .220 | 183 | 45 | .246 | .026 |
| John Farrell | 420 | 98 | .233 | 383 | 98 | .256 | .023 |
| Nolan Ryan | 446 | 79 | .177 | 421 | 83 | .197 | .020 |
| John Dopson | 316 | 78 | .247 | 331 | 88 | .266 | .019 |
| Pete Smith | 321 | 82 | .255 | 226 | 62 | .274 | .019 |
| Scott Bankhead | 417 | 96 | .230 | 367 | 91 | .248 | .018 |
| Bryn Smith | 446 | 96 | .215 | 348 | 81 | .233 | .018 |
| Kevin Brown | 351 | 79 | .225 | 364 | 88 | .242 | .017 |
| Kevin Gross | 415 | 100 | .241 | 345 | 88 | .255 | .014 |

## LAST 5 YEARS

### BETTER VS. RIGHT-HANDERS

| PLAYER | VS. LEFT-HANDERS AB | H | AVG | VS. RIGHT-HANDERS AB | H | AVG | DIFF |
|---|---|---|---|---|---|---|---|
| Todd Stottlemyre | 420 | 143 | .340 | 451 | 103 | .228 | .112 |
| Dickie Noles | 475 | 151 | .318 | 457 | 106 | .232 | .086 |
| Rich Bordi | 411 | 126 | .307 | 541 | 122 | .226 | .081 |
| Mark Eichhorn | 674 | 190 | .282 | 860 | 174 | .202 | .080 |
| Don Schulze | 497 | 169 | .340 | 460 | 121 | .263 | .077 |
| Juan Berenguer | 908 | 251 | .276 | 895 | 179 | .200 | .076 |
| Ron Robinson | 1021 | 304 | .298 | 1032 | 229 | .222 | .076 |
| Steve Shields | 419 | 145 | .346 | 455 | 124 | .273 | .074 |
| Bill Swift | 1078 | 353 | .327 | 1035 | 265 | .256 | .071 |
| Tim Burke | 867 | 229 | .264 | 885 | 176 | .199 | .065 |
| Jose DeLeon | 1790 | 448 | .250 | 1628 | 304 | .187 | .064 |
| Mike Jackson | 531 | 134 | .252 | 636 | 121 | .190 | .062 |
| Andy Hawkins | 1904 | 569 | .299 | 1848 | 443 | .240 | .059 |
| Dale Mohorcic | 504 | 153 | .304 | 688 | 169 | .246 | .058 |
| Jerry Reed | 608 | 172 | .283 | 813 | 183 | .225 | .058 |
| Brian Fisher | 1024 | 298 | .291 | 1060 | 251 | .237 | .054 |
| Steve Crawford | 518 | 165 | .319 | 551 | 146 | .265 | .054 |
| Jim Acker | 1000 | 287 | .287 | 957 | 224 | .234 | .053 |
| Dennis Eckersley | 1154 | 306 | .265 | 1168 | 248 | .212 | .053 |
| David Cone | 1120 | 280 | .250 | 996 | 197 | .198 | .052 |
| Kent Tekulve | 746 | 211 | .283 | 870 | 201 | .231 | .052 |
| Jeff Russell | 934 | 267 | .286 | 974 | 229 | .235 | .051 |
| Charlie Puleo | 530 | 145 | .274 | 525 | 117 | .223 | .051 |
| Tom Hume | 459 | 128 | .279 | 503 | 115 | .229 | .050 |
| Ed Lynch | 792 | 235 | .297 | 768 | 190 | .247 | .049 |

### BETTER VS. LEFT-HANDERS

| PLAYER | VS. LEFT-HANDERS AB | H | AVG | VS. RIGHT-HANDERS AB | H | AVG | DIFF |
|---|---|---|---|---|---|---|---|
| Donnie Moore | 477 | 105 | .220 | 418 | 122 | .292 | .072 |
| Mike Birkbeck | 464 | 125 | .269 | 487 | 160 | .329 | .059 |
| Rick Honeycutt | 477 | 99 | .208 | 1855 | 494 | .266 | .059 |
| Mark Langston | 656 | 124 | .189 | 3614 | 894 | .247 | .058 |
| Zane Smith | 522 | 115 | .220 | 2795 | 774 | .277 | .057 |
| Scott McGregor | 412 | 101 | .245 | 1604 | 480 | .299 | .054 |
| Mark Thurmond | 468 | 120 | .256 | 1438 | 439 | .305 | .049 |
| Bud Black | 619 | 135 | .218 | 2261 | 602 | .266 | .048 |
| Frank DiPino | 505 | 112 | .222 | 1050 | 281 | .268 | .046 |
| Bruce Ruffin | 402 | 99 | .246 | 1992 | 578 | .290 | .044 |
| Mark Portugal | 689 | 169 | .245 | 611 | 176 | .288 | .043 |
| Curt Young | 518 | 116 | .224 | 2221 | 590 | .266 | .042 |
| Ray Burris | 549 | 145 | .264 | 536 | 162 | .302 | .038 |
| Neal Heaton | 632 | 152 | .241 | 2604 | 725 | .278 | .038 |
| John Cerutti | 519 | 122 | .235 | 1897 | 516 | .272 | .037 |
| Gene Garber | 546 | 138 | .253 | 572 | 165 | .288 | .036 |
| Mark Davis | 443 | 86 | .194 | 1435 | 325 | .226 | .032 |
| Tommy John | 431 | 120 | .278 | 1900 | 590 | .311 | .032 |
| Bret Saberhagen | 2435 | 570 | .234 | 2000 | 532 | .266 | .032 |
| Craig Lefferts | 473 | 103 | .218 | 1322 | 329 | .249 | .031 |
| Greg A. Harris | 1014 | 222 | .219 | 1109 | 277 | .250 | .031 |
| Don Sutton | 1390 | 335 | .241 | 1357 | 368 | .271 | .030 |
| Mike Flanagan | 490 | 123 | .251 | 2545 | 711 | .279 | .028 |
| Edwin Correa | 547 | 126 | .230 | 522 | 135 | .259 | .028 |
| Jimmy Key | 729 | 163 | .224 | 3229 | 810 | .251 | .027 |

# Vs. Ground- and Fly-Ballers

## LAST SEASON

### BETTER VS. FLY-BALLERS

| PLAYER | VS. GROUND-BALLERS AB | H | AVG | VS. FLY-BALLERS AB | H | AVG | DIFF |
|---|---|---|---|---|---|---|---|
| Tom Henke | 154 | 44 | .286 | 168 | 22 | .131 | .155 |
| Joe Boever | 157 | 46 | .293 | 152 | 32 | .211 | .082 |
| Scott Garrelts | 317 | 80 | .252 | 387 | 69 | .178 | .074 |
| Don August | 267 | 91 | .341 | 312 | 84 | .269 | .072 |
| John Smiley | 332 | 88 | .265 | 438 | 86 | .196 | .069 |
| Paul Gibson | 262 | 76 | .290 | 236 | 53 | .225 | .066 |
| Mike Henneman | 170 | 48 | .282 | 165 | 36 | .218 | .064 |
| Ted Higuera | 238 | 67 | .282 | 266 | 58 | .218 | .063 |
| Rick Rhoden | 160 | 52 | .325 | 214 | 56 | .262 | .063 |
| Andy Hawkins | 417 | 134 | .321 | 403 | 104 | .258 | .063 |
| Bob Ojeda | 349 | 97 | .278 | 382 | 82 | .215 | .063 |
| Jose DeLeon | 430 | 98 | .228 | 448 | 75 | .167 | .060 |
| Norm Charlton | 157 | 36 | .229 | 183 | 31 | .169 | .060 |
| Roy Smith | 333 | 99 | .297 | 335 | 81 | .242 | .056 |
| Jim Deshaies | 399 | 98 | .246 | 430 | 82 | .191 | .055 |
| Chuck Crim | 216 | 62 | .287 | 224 | 52 | .232 | .055 |
| Bud Black | 399 | 112 | .281 | 445 | 101 | .227 | .054 |
| Rob Dibble | 168 | 34 | .202 | 184 | 28 | .152 | .050 |
| Joe Price | 152 | 45 | .296 | 170 | 42 | .247 | .049 |
| Bobby Witt | 371 | 101 | .272 | 362 | 81 | .224 | .048 |
| Steve Rosenberg | 265 | 79 | .298 | 276 | 69 | .250 | .048 |
| Sid Fernandez | 398 | 88 | .221 | 396 | 69 | .174 | .047 |
| Mike Jackson | 206 | 50 | .243 | 157 | 31 | .197 | .045 |
| Richard Dotson | 283 | 90 | .318 | 332 | 91 | .274 | .044 |
| Todd Stottlemyre | 252 | 76 | .302 | 234 | 61 | .261 | .041 |

### BETTER VS. GROUND-BALLERS

| PLAYER | VS. GROUND-BALLERS AB | H | AVG | VS. FLY-BALLERS AB | H | AVG | DIFF |
|---|---|---|---|---|---|---|---|
| Roger McDowell | 175 | 33 | .189 | 164 | 46 | .280 | .092 |
| Frank DiPino | 164 | 30 | .183 | 157 | 43 | .274 | .091 |
| Jeff D. Robinson | 317 | 77 | .243 | 252 | 84 | .333 | .090 |
| Bruce Ruffin | 286 | 75 | .262 | 219 | 77 | .352 | .089 |
| Mike Dunne | 202 | 54 | .267 | 201 | 71 | .353 | .086 |
| Wes Gardner | 179 | 45 | .251 | 159 | 52 | .327 | .076 |
| Terry Leach | 191 | 45 | .236 | 168 | 52 | .310 | .074 |
| Willie Fraser | 171 | 34 | .199 | 169 | 46 | .272 | .073 |
| Mark Thurmond | 174 | 44 | .253 | 180 | 58 | .322 | .069 |
| Mike Morgan | 251 | 50 | .199 | 304 | 80 | .263 | .064 |
| Jeff Parrett | 168 | 33 | .196 | 220 | 57 | .259 | .063 |
| Ed Whitson | 382 | 78 | .204 | 459 | 120 | .261 | .057 |
| Jeff Brantley | 189 | 46 | .243 | 184 | 55 | .299 | .056 |
| Dennis Martinez | 466 | 109 | .234 | 418 | 118 | .282 | .048 |
| Kevin Gross | 344 | 76 | .221 | 416 | 112 | .269 | .048 |
| Paul Kilgus | 271 | 70 | .258 | 308 | 94 | .305 | .047 |
| Greg Swindell | 355 | 80 | .225 | 335 | 90 | .269 | .043 |
| Rick Mahler | 402 | 104 | .259 | 457 | 138 | .302 | .043 |
| Dennis Rasmussen | 305 | 75 | .246 | 399 | 115 | .288 | .042 |
| Randy Kramer | 206 | 42 | .204 | 195 | 48 | .246 | .042 |
| Fernando Valenzuela | 361 | 83 | .230 | 377 | 102 | .271 | .041 |
| Bryn Smith | 426 | 87 | .204 | 368 | 90 | .245 | .040 |
| Kevin Brown | 317 | 67 | .211 | 398 | 100 | .251 | .040 |
| Tom Candiotti | 408 | 91 | .223 | 370 | 97 | .262 | .039 |
| Ken Hill | 362 | 84 | .232 | 377 | 102 | .271 | .039 |

## LAST 5 YEARS

### BETTER VS. FLY-BALLERS

| PLAYER | VS. GROUND-BALLERS AB | H | AVG | VS. FLY-BALLERS AB | H | AVG | DIFF |
|---|---|---|---|---|---|---|---|
| Mitch Williams | 457 | 110 | .241 | 779 | 141 | .181 | .060 |
| Willie Hernandez | 556 | 151 | .272 | 736 | 157 | .213 | .058 |
| Ken Schrom | 844 | 264 | .313 | 1181 | 302 | .256 | .057 |
| Don August | 443 | 135 | .305 | 695 | 177 | .255 | .050 |
| Ray Burris | 497 | 154 | .310 | 588 | 153 | .260 | .050 |
| Jimmy Key | 1740 | 476 | .274 | 2218 | 497 | .224 | .049 |
| Rich Gossage | 539 | 148 | .275 | 564 | 128 | .227 | .048 |
| Joe Niekro | 927 | 266 | .287 | 1051 | 255 | .243 | .044 |
| Tom Niedenfuer | 680 | 190 | .279 | 655 | 155 | .237 | .043 |
| Calvin Schiraldi | 701 | 187 | .267 | 915 | 205 | .224 | .043 |
| John Butcher | 569 | 186 | .327 | 762 | 221 | .290 | .037 |
| Lance McCullers | 854 | 210 | .246 | 879 | 184 | .209 | .037 |
| Scott Bailes | 827 | 246 | .297 | 1099 | 287 | .261 | .036 |
| Shawn Hillegas | 492 | 135 | .274 | 558 | 133 | .238 | .036 |
| Jose DeLeon | 1589 | 380 | .239 | 1829 | 372 | .203 | .036 |
| John Farrell | 818 | 226 | .276 | 1055 | 254 | .241 | .036 |
| Dickie Noles | 438 | 129 | .295 | 494 | 128 | .259 | .035 |
| Tom Henke | 561 | 126 | .225 | 814 | 154 | .189 | .035 |
| Frank Viola | 2039 | 559 | .274 | 2801 | 672 | .240 | .034 |
| Doyle Alexander | 1981 | 571 | .288 | 2496 | 635 | .254 | .034 |
| Tim Stoddard | 560 | 150 | .268 | 666 | 157 | .236 | .032 |
| Mike Jackson | 571 | 134 | .235 | 596 | 121 | .203 | .032 |
| Don Aase | 412 | 109 | .265 | 639 | 149 | .233 | .031 |
| Mike Mason | 641 | 195 | .304 | 879 | 240 | .273 | .031 |
| Juan Berenguer | 815 | 208 | .255 | 988 | 222 | .225 | .031 |

### BETTER VS. GROUND-BALLERS

| PLAYER | VS. GROUND-BALLERS AB | H | AVG | VS. FLY-BALLERS AB | H | AVG | DIFF |
|---|---|---|---|---|---|---|---|
| Ray Fontenot | 485 | 115 | .237 | 406 | 146 | .360 | .122 |
| Mike Dunne | 830 | 189 | .228 | 809 | 242 | .299 | .071 |
| Bruce Ruffin | 1229 | 307 | .250 | 1165 | 370 | .318 | .068 |
| Andy McGaffigan | 926 | 194 | .210 | 1025 | 279 | .272 | .063 |
| John Dopson | 665 | 147 | .221 | 686 | 194 | .283 | .062 |
| Jesse Orosco | 665 | 130 | .195 | 682 | 173 | .254 | .058 |
| Ricky Horton | 872 | 205 | .235 | 1024 | 299 | .292 | .057 |
| Pat Clements | 480 | 115 | .240 | 567 | 166 | .293 | .053 |
| Mike LaCoss | 1301 | 301 | .231 | 1241 | 353 | .284 | .053 |
| Jimmy Jones | 750 | 184 | .245 | 765 | 228 | .298 | .053 |
| Dale Mohorcic | 503 | 121 | .241 | 689 | 201 | .292 | .051 |
| Terry Leach | 716 | 169 | .236 | 731 | 209 | .286 | .050 |
| Mark Thurmond | 928 | 250 | .269 | 978 | 309 | .316 | .047 |
| Bobby Thigpen | 440 | 97 | .220 | 660 | 173 | .262 | .042 |
| Frank Williams | 685 | 155 | .226 | 656 | 175 | .267 | .040 |
| Jeff Sellers | 535 | 140 | .262 | 743 | 224 | .301 | .040 |
| Wes Gardner | 559 | 133 | .238 | 723 | 200 | .277 | .039 |
| Bill Gullickson | 1236 | 305 | .247 | 1209 | 345 | .285 | .039 |
| Fred Toliver | 408 | 107 | .262 | 512 | 154 | .301 | .039 |
| Dan Quisenberry | 685 | 182 | .266 | 902 | 274 | .304 | .038 |
| David Palmer | 1281 | 307 | .240 | 1172 | 325 | .277 | .038 |
| Tom Hume | 485 | 114 | .235 | 477 | 129 | .270 | .035 |
| Floyd Youmans | 1007 | 203 | .202 | 953 | 225 | .236 | .035 |
| Joe Johnson | 590 | 158 | .268 | 693 | 209 | .302 | .034 |
| Roger McDowell | 954 | 212 | .222 | 1004 | 257 | .256 | .034 |

# Home and Road Games

## LAST SEASON

### BETTER IN ROAD GAMES

| PLAYER | HOME GAMES AB | H | AVG | ROAD GAMES AB | H | AVG | DIFF |
|---|---|---|---|---|---|---|---|
| Bob Knepper | 293 | 99 | .338 | 356 | 91 | .256 | .082 |
| Mike Boddicker | 417 | 127 | .305 | 396 | 90 | .227 | .077 |
| Greg A. Harris | 190 | 50 | .263 | 185 | 35 | .189 | .074 |
| Allan Anderson | 300 | 95 | .317 | 477 | 119 | .249 | .067 |
| Erik Hanson | 222 | 61 | .275 | 201 | 42 | .209 | .066 |
| Calvin Schiraldi | 198 | 45 | .227 | 163 | 27 | .166 | .062 |
| Randy Kramer | 187 | 48 | .257 | 214 | 42 | .196 | .060 |
| Rich Yett | 195 | 61 | .313 | 197 | 50 | .254 | .059 |
| Don August | 212 | 72 | .340 | 367 | 103 | .281 | .059 |
| Tom Browning | 491 | 138 | .281 | 455 | 103 | .226 | .055 |
| Mike Jackson | 207 | 51 | .246 | 156 | 30 | .192 | .054 |
| Rick Mahler | 480 | 146 | .304 | 379 | 96 | .253 | .051 |
| Charlie Hough | 306 | 83 | .271 | 379 | 85 | .224 | .047 |
| Dave J. Schmidt | 239 | 81 | .339 | 393 | 115 | .293 | .046 |
| Ken Howell | 360 | 85 | .236 | 362 | 70 | .193 | .043 |
| Mike Smithson | 317 | 100 | .315 | 256 | 70 | .273 | .042 |
| Bruce Ruffin | 306 | 97 | .317 | 199 | 55 | .276 | .041 |
| Mark Langston | 425 | 102 | .240 | 480 | 96 | .200 | .040 |
| Bill Swift | 292 | 86 | .295 | 212 | 54 | .255 | .040 |
| Jim Abbott | 344 | 101 | .294 | 350 | 89 | .254 | .039 |
| Rick Sutcliffe | 377 | 98 | .260 | 465 | 104 | .224 | .036 |
| Nolan Ryan | 517 | 104 | .201 | 350 | 58 | .166 | .035 |
| Bud Black | 441 | 118 | .268 | 403 | 95 | .236 | .032 |
| Andy Hawkins | 506 | 153 | .302 | 314 | 85 | .271 | .032 |
| Mike LaCoss | 257 | 70 | .272 | 303 | 73 | .241 | .031 |

### BETTER IN HOME GAMES

| PLAYER | HOME GAMES AB | H | AVG | ROAD GAMES AB | H | AVG | DIFF |
|---|---|---|---|---|---|---|---|
| Dennis Cook | 252 | 48 | .190 | 200 | 62 | .310 | .120 |
| Terry Mulholland | 225 | 54 | .240 | 240 | 83 | .346 | .106 |
| Ted Higuera | 299 | 65 | .217 | 205 | 60 | .293 | .075 |
| Doug Drabek | 482 | 98 | .203 | 420 | 117 | .279 | .075 |
| Paul Gibson | 252 | 56 | .222 | 246 | 73 | .297 | .075 |
| Ramon Martinez | 176 | 32 | .182 | 184 | 47 | .255 | .074 |
| Danny Darwin | 249 | 45 | .181 | 185 | 47 | .254 | .073 |
| Mike Dunne | 253 | 72 | .285 | 150 | 53 | .353 | .069 |
| Mike Henneman | 181 | 40 | .221 | 154 | 44 | .286 | .065 |
| Norm Charlton | 164 | 27 | .165 | 176 | 40 | .227 | .063 |
| Jeff Parrett | 172 | 34 | .198 | 216 | 56 | .259 | .062 |
| Jeff Pico | 185 | 46 | .249 | 171 | 53 | .310 | .061 |
| Don Robinson | 432 | 96 | .222 | 311 | 88 | .283 | .061 |
| Rick Aguilera | 265 | 55 | .208 | 280 | 75 | .268 | .060 |
| Jim Acker | 225 | 47 | .209 | 231 | 61 | .264 | .055 |
| Pascual Perez | 463 | 100 | .216 | 288 | 78 | .271 | .055 |
| Frank DiPino | 164 | 33 | .201 | 157 | 40 | .255 | .054 |
| Zane Smith | 294 | 67 | .228 | 265 | 74 | .279 | .051 |
| Scott Bailes | 228 | 56 | .246 | 203 | 60 | .296 | .050 |
| Scott Terry | 327 | 76 | .232 | 234 | 66 | .282 | .050 |
| Doyle Alexander | 457 | 117 | .256 | 419 | 128 | .305 | .049 |
| Terry Leach | 175 | 43 | .246 | 184 | 54 | .293 | .048 |
| Frank Tanana | 449 | 109 | .243 | 407 | 118 | .290 | .047 |
| Dave Stewart | 499 | 120 | .240 | 487 | 140 | .287 | .047 |
| Dwight Gooden | 242 | 46 | .190 | 199 | 47 | .236 | .046 |

## LAST 5 YEARS

### BETTER IN ROAD GAMES

| PLAYER | HOME GAMES AB | H | AVG | ROAD GAMES AB | H | AVG | DIFF |
|---|---|---|---|---|---|---|---|
| Mark Knudson | 543 | 174 | .320 | 546 | 132 | .242 | .079 |
| Pat Perry | 449 | 115 | .256 | 480 | 91 | .190 | .067 |
| Brian Fisher | 1093 | 316 | .289 | 991 | 233 | .235 | .054 |
| Mark Portugal | 619 | 181 | .292 | 681 | 164 | .241 | .052 |
| Doug Jones | 569 | 155 | .272 | 481 | 109 | .227 | .046 |
| Allan Anderson | 917 | 276 | .301 | 1009 | 263 | .261 | .040 |
| Bob McClure | 589 | 160 | .272 | 531 | 123 | .232 | .040 |
| Mitch Williams | 634 | 141 | .222 | 602 | 110 | .183 | .040 |
| Joe Hesketh | 734 | 196 | .267 | 707 | 161 | .228 | .039 |
| Jeff Dedmon | 613 | 166 | .271 | 538 | 125 | .232 | .038 |
| Todd Stottlemyre | 461 | 138 | .299 | 410 | 108 | .263 | .036 |
| Fred Toliver | 461 | 139 | .302 | 459 | 122 | .266 | .036 |
| Calvin Schiraldi | 757 | 198 | .262 | 859 | 194 | .226 | .036 |
| Ken Dayley | 567 | 149 | .263 | 532 | 121 | .227 | .035 |
| John Butcher | 586 | 190 | .324 | 745 | 217 | .291 | .033 |
| Brad Havens | 443 | 129 | .291 | 418 | 108 | .258 | .033 |
| Gene Garber | 625 | 178 | .285 | 493 | 125 | .254 | .031 |
| Tom Seaver | 711 | 193 | .271 | 873 | 210 | .241 | .031 |
| Oil Can Boyd | 1452 | 411 | .283 | 1312 | 335 | .255 | .028 |
| Bill Long | 805 | 235 | .292 | 968 | 257 | .265 | .026 |
| Ken Dixon | 1019 | 272 | .267 | 806 | 194 | .241 | .026 |
| Les Lancaster | 618 | 167 | .270 | 488 | 120 | .246 | .024 |
| Kent Tekulve | 860 | 229 | .266 | 756 | 183 | .242 | .024 |
| Juan Nieves | 793 | 222 | .280 | 1114 | 285 | .256 | .024 |
| Steve Crawford | 497 | 151 | .304 | 572 | 160 | .280 | .024 |

### BETTER IN HOME GAMES

| PLAYER | HOME GAMES AB | H | AVG | ROAD GAMES AB | H | AVG | DIFF |
|---|---|---|---|---|---|---|---|
| Jeff M. Robinson | 739 | 147 | .199 | 674 | 182 | .270 | .071 |
| Jeff Parrett | 505 | 97 | .192 | 499 | 131 | .263 | .070 |
| Randy Myers | 446 | 79 | .177 | 412 | 100 | .243 | .066 |
| Jim Gott | 604 | 131 | .217 | 634 | 179 | .282 | .065 |
| Frank DiPino | 761 | 169 | .222 | 794 | 224 | .282 | .060 |
| Paul Gibson | 443 | 99 | .223 | 401 | 113 | .282 | .058 |
| Mike Henneman | 507 | 105 | .207 | 521 | 137 | .263 | .056 |
| Atlee Hammaker | 1157 | 262 | .226 | 971 | 272 | .280 | .054 |
| Walt Terrell | 2030 | 479 | .236 | 2181 | 630 | .289 | .053 |
| Bob Sebra | 687 | 169 | .246 | 682 | 203 | .298 | .052 |
| Dan Schatzeder | 753 | 191 | .254 | 634 | 193 | .304 | .051 |
| Matt Young | 925 | 241 | .261 | 692 | 213 | .308 | .047 |
| Mark Thurmond | 973 | 263 | .270 | 933 | 296 | .317 | .047 |
| Chris Codiroli | 645 | 155 | .240 | 730 | 208 | .285 | .045 |
| Don Aase | 580 | 131 | .226 | 471 | 127 | .270 | .044 |
| Dave Righetti | 872 | 200 | .229 | 876 | 238 | .272 | .042 |
| Vida Blue | 629 | 140 | .223 | 423 | 112 | .265 | .042 |
| George Frazier | 440 | 114 | .259 | 455 | 137 | .301 | .042 |
| Wes Gardner | 637 | 152 | .239 | 645 | 181 | .281 | .042 |
| Keith Atherton | 762 | 178 | .234 | 746 | 205 | .275 | .041 |
| Sid Fernandez | 1771 | 324 | .183 | 1612 | 359 | .223 | .040 |
| Pat Clements | 545 | 136 | .250 | 502 | 145 | .289 | .039 |
| Willie Hernandez | 653 | 143 | .219 | 639 | 165 | .258 | .039 |
| John Smiley | 924 | 197 | .213 | 934 | 235 | .252 | .038 |
| Roger McDowell | 950 | 209 | .220 | 1008 | 260 | .258 | .038 |

# Grass and Artificial Surfaces

## LAST SEASON

### BETTER ON ARTIFICIAL TURF

| PLAYER | GRASS FIELDS AB | H | AVG | ARTIFICIAL TURF AB | H | AVG | DIFF |
|---|---|---|---|---|---|---|---|
| Doug Drabek | 294 | 87 | .296 | 608 | 128 | .211 | .085 |
| Terry Leach | 176 | 55 | .313 | 183 | 42 | .230 | .083 |
| Bert Blyleven | 707 | 187 | .264 | 200 | 38 | .190 | .074 |
| Don Carman | 170 | 53 | .312 | 414 | 99 | .239 | .073 |
| Terry Mulholland | 152 | 52 | .342 | 313 | 85 | .272 | .071 |
| Scott Sanderson | 376 | 110 | .293 | 190 | 45 | .237 | .056 |
| Tom Gordon | 160 | 39 | .244 | 422 | 83 | .197 | .047 |
| Bob Walk | 190 | 58 | .305 | 578 | 150 | .260 | .046 |
| Sid Fernandez | 581 | 122 | .210 | 213 | 35 | .164 | .046 |
| Rick Sutcliffe | 529 | 135 | .255 | 313 | 67 | .214 | .041 |
| Orel Hershiser | 725 | 180 | .248 | 217 | 46 | .212 | .036 |
| Mike Boddicker | 662 | 181 | .273 | 151 | 36 | .238 | .035 |
| Rick Reuschel | 566 | 145 | .256 | 224 | 50 | .223 | .033 |
| John Farrell | 612 | 154 | .252 | 191 | 42 | .220 | .032 |
| Jim Acker | 286 | 71 | .248 | 170 | 37 | .218 | .031 |
| Frank Viola | 471 | 125 | .265 | 515 | 121 | .235 | .030 |
| Mike Flanagan | 198 | 60 | .303 | 460 | 126 | .274 | .029 |
| Ed Whitson | 641 | 155 | .242 | 200 | 43 | .215 | .027 |
| Charlie Leibrandt | 288 | 91 | .316 | 356 | 105 | .295 | .021 |
| Scott Bankhead | 292 | 73 | .250 | 492 | 114 | .232 | .018 |
| Dennis Martinez | 207 | 56 | .271 | 677 | 171 | .253 | .018 |
| Jose DeLeon | 244 | 51 | .209 | 634 | 122 | .192 | .017 |
| Roy Smith | 247 | 69 | .279 | 421 | 111 | .264 | .016 |
| Charlie Hough | 531 | 132 | .249 | 154 | 36 | .234 | .015 |
| Brian Holman | 281 | 76 | .270 | 458 | 118 | .258 | .013 |

### BETTER ON GRASS SURFACES

| PLAYER | GRASS FIELDS AB | H | AVG | ARTIFICIAL TURF AB | H | AVG | DIFF |
|---|---|---|---|---|---|---|---|
| Jim Clancy | 214 | 46 | .215 | 362 | 109 | .301 | .086 |
| Bob Milacki | 765 | 184 | .241 | 154 | 49 | .318 | .078 |
| Don Robinson | 556 | 129 | .232 | 187 | 55 | .294 | .062 |
| Mike Moore | 717 | 151 | .211 | 163 | 42 | .258 | .047 |
| Mike Bielecki | 556 | 125 | .225 | 233 | 62 | .266 | .041 |
| Rick Aguilera | 287 | 63 | .220 | 258 | 67 | .260 | .040 |
| Allan Anderson | 373 | 95 | .255 | 404 | 119 | .295 | .040 |
| Bob Knepper | 277 | 75 | .271 | 372 | 115 | .309 | .038 |
| Walt Terrell | 559 | 155 | .277 | 257 | 81 | .315 | .038 |
| Duane Ward | 168 | 35 | .208 | 240 | 59 | .246 | .038 |
| John Smiley | 211 | 42 | .199 | 559 | 132 | .236 | .037 |
| Tom Glavine | 523 | 122 | .233 | 186 | 50 | .269 | .036 |
| Doyle Alexander | 694 | 189 | .272 | 182 | 56 | .308 | .035 |
| Erik Hanson | 175 | 39 | .223 | 248 | 64 | .258 | .035 |
| David Cone | 544 | 115 | .211 | 278 | 68 | .245 | .033 |
| Tom Browning | 275 | 64 | .233 | 671 | 177 | .264 | .031 |
| Randy D. Johnson | 271 | 63 | .232 | 322 | 84 | .261 | .028 |
| Dave Stewart | 833 | 216 | .259 | 153 | 44 | .288 | .028 |
| Tim Belcher | 570 | 119 | .209 | 268 | 63 | .235 | .026 |
| Bob Welch | 639 | 151 | .236 | 153 | 40 | .261 | .025 |
| John Cerutti | 292 | 75 | .257 | 493 | 139 | .282 | .025 |
| Dave Stieb | 322 | 66 | .205 | 426 | 98 | .230 | .025 |
| Ron Darling | 608 | 153 | .252 | 221 | 61 | .276 | .024 |
| Bruce Hurst | 734 | 171 | .233 | 169 | 43 | .254 | .021 |
| Kevin Gross | 232 | 54 | .233 | 528 | 134 | .254 | .021 |

## LAST 5 YEARS

### BETTER ON ARTIFICIAL TURF

| PLAYER | GRASS FIELDS AB | H | AVG | ARTIFICIAL TURF AB | H | AVG | DIFF |
|---|---|---|---|---|---|---|---|
| Terry Leach | 888 | 252 | .284 | 559 | 126 | .225 | .058 |
| Pascual Perez | 579 | 157 | .271 | 1488 | 321 | .216 | .055 |
| Ken Schrom | 1389 | 411 | .296 | 636 | 155 | .244 | .052 |
| Dan Quisenberry | 582 | 183 | .314 | 1005 | 273 | .272 | .043 |
| Frank Wills | 447 | 125 | .280 | 536 | 130 | .243 | .037 |
| Larry Andersen | 450 | 125 | .278 | 1142 | 276 | .242 | .036 |
| Joe Johnson | 769 | 231 | .300 | 514 | 136 | .265 | .036 |
| Matt Young | 609 | 184 | .302 | 1008 | 270 | .268 | .034 |
| Dennis Martinez | 1311 | 367 | .280 | 2130 | 525 | .246 | .033 |
| Roger Clemens | 3620 | 820 | .227 | 630 | 122 | .194 | .033 |
| Kevin Gross | 1061 | 294 | .277 | 3038 | 742 | .244 | .033 |
| Edwin Nunez | 488 | 140 | .287 | 487 | 124 | .255 | .032 |
| Roy Smith | 594 | 173 | .291 | 586 | 153 | .261 | .030 |
| Bob Kipper | 482 | 129 | .268 | 1037 | 248 | .239 | .028 |
| Doug Drabek | 1048 | 273 | .260 | 1835 | 427 | .233 | .028 |
| Jay Tibbs | 1118 | 323 | .289 | 1588 | 415 | .261 | .028 |
| Bryn Smith | 1183 | 309 | .261 | 2499 | 586 | .234 | .027 |
| Floyd Youmans | 496 | 118 | .238 | 1464 | 310 | .212 | .026 |
| Don Carman | 752 | 199 | .265 | 2184 | 523 | .239 | .025 |
| Nolan Ryan | 1638 | 366 | .223 | 2308 | 460 | .199 | .024 |
| Bob Forsch | 781 | 225 | .288 | 2246 | 593 | .264 | .024 |
| Juan Berenguer | 866 | 217 | .251 | 937 | 213 | .227 | .023 |
| Mike Scott | 1212 | 275 | .227 | 3148 | 642 | .204 | .023 |
| Mark Eichhorn | 652 | 163 | .250 | 882 | 201 | .228 | .022 |
| Cecilio Guante | 814 | 194 | .238 | 600 | 130 | .217 | .022 |

### BETTER ON GRASS SURFACES

| PLAYER | GRASS FIELDS AB | H | AVG | ARTIFICIAL TURF AB | H | AVG | DIFF |
|---|---|---|---|---|---|---|---|
| Richard Dotson | 2606 | 690 | .265 | 470 | 149 | .317 | .052 |
| Mike Morgan | 1193 | 297 | .249 | 1342 | 402 | .300 | .051 |
| Curt Young | 2328 | 583 | .250 | 411 | 123 | .299 | .049 |
| Walt Terrell | 3443 | 877 | .255 | 768 | 232 | .302 | .047 |
| Don Sutton | 2211 | 546 | .247 | 536 | 157 | .293 | .046 |
| Rick Honeycutt | 1836 | 450 | .245 | 496 | 143 | .288 | .043 |
| Frank Williams | 696 | 157 | .226 | 645 | 173 | .268 | .043 |
| John Candelaria | 1592 | 391 | .246 | 573 | 164 | .286 | .041 |
| Tim Burke | 490 | 99 | .202 | 1262 | 306 | .242 | .040 |
| Craig Lefferts | 1317 | 304 | .231 | 478 | 128 | .268 | .037 |
| Mike LaCoss | 1798 | 444 | .247 | 744 | 210 | .282 | .035 |
| Brian Fisher | 880 | 214 | .243 | 1204 | 335 | .278 | .035 |
| Greg Mathews | 451 | 103 | .228 | 1073 | 281 | .262 | .034 |
| Mark Portugal | 513 | 126 | .246 | 787 | 219 | .278 | .033 |
| Rick Aguilera | 1333 | 331 | .248 | 767 | 215 | .280 | .032 |
| Frank Tanana | 3549 | 922 | .260 | 515 | 150 | .291 | .031 |
| John Denny | 427 | 109 | .255 | 1124 | 322 | .286 | .031 |
| David Cone | 1408 | 303 | .215 | 708 | 174 | .246 | .031 |
| Jerry Reuss | 2241 | 630 | .281 | 636 | 196 | .308 | .027 |
| Greg A. Harris | 1395 | 315 | .226 | 728 | 184 | .253 | .027 |
| Mike Bielecki | 938 | 224 | .239 | 960 | 255 | .266 | .027 |
| Kelly Downs | 1477 | 351 | .238 | 508 | 134 | .264 | .026 |
| Bret Saberhagen | 1718 | 400 | .233 | 2717 | 702 | .258 | .026 |
| Allan Anderson | 782 | 207 | .265 | 1144 | 332 | .290 | .026 |
| Dave Dravecky | 1622 | 395 | .244 | 684 | 181 | .265 | .021 |

# Day and Night Games

## LAST SEASON

### BETTER IN NIGHT GAMES

| PLAYER | DAY GAMES AB | H | AVG | NIGHT GAMES AB | H | AVG | DIFF |
|---|---|---|---|---|---|---|---|
| Joe Magrane | 289 | 91 | .315 | 582 | 128 | .220 | .095 |
| Doug Drabek | 219 | 66 | .301 | 683 | 149 | .218 | .083 |
| Bob Ojeda | 356 | 102 | .287 | 375 | 77 | .205 | .081 |
| Danny Jackson | 219 | 68 | .311 | 232 | 54 | .233 | .078 |
| Mike Bielecki | 470 | 124 | .264 | 319 | 63 | .197 | .066 |
| Melido Perez | 268 | 81 | .302 | 440 | 106 | .241 | .061 |
| Neal Heaton | 159 | 44 | .277 | 385 | 83 | .216 | .061 |
| Mike Boddicker | 229 | 71 | .310 | 584 | 146 | .250 | .060 |
| Tim Belcher | 247 | 64 | .259 | 591 | 118 | .200 | .059 |
| John Farrell | 272 | 77 | .283 | 531 | 119 | .224 | .059 |
| Jose DeLeon | 354 | 82 | .232 | 524 | 91 | .174 | .058 |
| Todd Stottlemyre | 159 | 51 | .321 | 327 | 86 | .263 | .058 |
| Dave Stieb | 291 | 74 | .254 | 457 | 90 | .197 | .057 |
| Mike Scott | 324 | 80 | .247 | 524 | 100 | .191 | .056 |
| Jack Morris | 158 | 51 | .323 | 511 | 138 | .270 | .053 |
| Bud Black | 235 | 67 | .285 | 609 | 146 | .240 | .045 |
| Charlie Leibrandt | 185 | 62 | .335 | 459 | 134 | .292 | .043 |
| Dennis Rasmussen | 187 | 56 | .299 | 517 | 134 | .259 | .040 |
| Mike Flanagan | 170 | 52 | .306 | 488 | 134 | .275 | .031 |
| Scott Garrelts | 210 | 49 | .233 | 494 | 100 | .202 | .031 |
| Dwight Gooden | 170 | 39 | .229 | 271 | 54 | .199 | .030 |
| Storm Davis | 303 | 92 | .304 | 346 | 95 | .275 | .029 |
| Mark Grant | 158 | 42 | .266 | 266 | 63 | .237 | .029 |
| Sid Fernandez | 244 | 53 | .217 | 550 | 104 | .189 | .028 |
| John Smiley | 284 | 69 | .243 | 486 | 105 | .216 | .027 |

### BETTER IN DAY GAMES

| PLAYER | DAY GAMES AB | H | AVG | NIGHT GAMES AB | H | AVG | DIFF |
|---|---|---|---|---|---|---|---|
| Jerry Reuss | 167 | 37 | .222 | 403 | 134 | .333 | .111 |
| Roy Smith | 220 | 44 | .200 | 448 | 136 | .304 | .104 |
| Joe Price | 153 | 35 | .229 | 169 | 52 | .308 | .079 |
| Greg Swindell | 198 | 39 | .197 | 492 | 131 | .266 | .069 |
| Bob Knepper | 163 | 40 | .245 | 486 | 150 | .309 | .063 |
| Mike Witt | 378 | 97 | .257 | 486 | 155 | .319 | .062 |
| Scott Sanderson | 294 | 72 | .245 | 272 | 83 | .305 | .060 |
| Chris Bosio | 358 | 76 | .212 | 547 | 149 | .272 | .060 |
| Jeff Pico | 176 | 44 | .250 | 180 | 55 | .306 | .056 |
| Shane Rawley | 228 | 60 | .263 | 341 | 107 | .314 | .051 |
| Rich Yett | 169 | 43 | .254 | 223 | 68 | .305 | .050 |
| Bob Walk | 185 | 44 | .238 | 583 | 164 | .281 | .043 |
| Tim Leary | 279 | 65 | .233 | 507 | 140 | .276 | .043 |
| John Cerutti | 289 | 71 | .246 | 496 | 143 | .288 | .043 |
| Rick Aguilera | 214 | 46 | .215 | 331 | 84 | .254 | .039 |
| Richard Dotson | 154 | 41 | .266 | 461 | 140 | .304 | .037 |
| Paul Kilgus | 304 | 81 | .266 | 275 | 83 | .302 | .035 |
| Randy Kramer | 162 | 33 | .204 | 239 | 57 | .238 | .035 |
| Bryn Smith | 301 | 61 | .203 | 493 | 116 | .235 | .033 |
| Dennis Lamp | 188 | 41 | .218 | 220 | 55 | .250 | .032 |
| Pascual Perez | 164 | 35 | .213 | 587 | 143 | .244 | .030 |
| Dave Stewart | 417 | 103 | .247 | 569 | 157 | .276 | .029 |
| Mike Smithson | 225 | 63 | .280 | 348 | 107 | .307 | .027 |
| Rick Reuschel | 306 | 71 | .232 | 484 | 124 | .256 | .024 |
| Craig Lefferts | 168 | 37 | .220 | 231 | 56 | .242 | .022 |

## LAST 5 YEARS

### BETTER IN NIGHT GAMES

| PLAYER | DAY GAMES AB | H | AVG | NIGHT GAMES AB | H | AVG | DIFF |
|---|---|---|---|---|---|---|---|
| Joe Magrane | 642 | 182 | .283 | 1481 | 327 | .221 | .063 |
| Scott Terry | 441 | 131 | .297 | 871 | 209 | .240 | .057 |
| Dave Stieb | 1347 | 364 | .270 | 2605 | 566 | .217 | .053 |
| Juan Berenguer | 600 | 163 | .272 | 1203 | 267 | .222 | .050 |
| Shane Rawley | 1114 | 343 | .308 | 2488 | 648 | .260 | .047 |
| John Smiley | 587 | 155 | .264 | 1271 | 277 | .218 | .046 |
| Jesse Orosco | 421 | 106 | .252 | 926 | 197 | .213 | .039 |
| Steve Farr | 444 | 125 | .282 | 1009 | 245 | .243 | .039 |
| Calvin Schiraldi | 746 | 196 | .263 | 870 | 196 | .225 | .037 |
| Eric King | 459 | 121 | .264 | 1333 | 302 | .227 | .037 |
| Melido Perez | 459 | 131 | .285 | 1046 | 260 | .249 | .037 |
| Ken Dixon | 522 | 147 | .282 | 1303 | 319 | .245 | .037 |
| Jeff Dedmon | 428 | 118 | .276 | 723 | 173 | .239 | .036 |
| Chuck Crim | 450 | 127 | .282 | 874 | 215 | .246 | .036 |
| Joe Hesketh | 525 | 142 | .270 | 916 | 215 | .235 | .036 |
| Mark Eichhorn | 566 | 147 | .260 | 968 | 217 | .224 | .036 |
| Storm Davis | 981 | 291 | .297 | 2079 | 543 | .261 | .035 |
| Tom Candiotti | 1202 | 329 | .274 | 2128 | 511 | .240 | .034 |
| Jeff Sellers | 515 | 157 | .305 | 763 | 207 | .271 | .034 |
| Mike Bielecki | 844 | 228 | .270 | 1054 | 251 | .238 | .032 |
| Tom Henke | 435 | 98 | .225 | 940 | 182 | .194 | .032 |
| Jeff D. Robinson | 707 | 189 | .267 | 1193 | 282 | .236 | .031 |
| Dwight Gooden | 1411 | 346 | .245 | 2542 | 546 | .215 | .030 |
| Tim Belcher | 505 | 121 | .240 | 1117 | 234 | .209 | .030 |
| Dennis Rasmussen | 1083 | 292 | .270 | 2244 | 538 | .240 | .030 |

### BETTER IN DAY GAMES

| PLAYER | DAY GAMES AB | H | AVG | NIGHT GAMES AB | H | AVG | DIFF |
|---|---|---|---|---|---|---|---|
| David Palmer | 699 | 155 | .222 | 1754 | 477 | .272 | .050 |
| Eric Plunk | 501 | 98 | .196 | 942 | 228 | .242 | .046 |
| Steve Ontiveros | 473 | 100 | .211 | 974 | 249 | .256 | .044 |
| John Cerutti | 874 | 207 | .237 | 1542 | 431 | .280 | .043 |
| Craig Lefferts | 650 | 139 | .214 | 1145 | 293 | .256 | .042 |
| Ron Guidry | 789 | 179 | .227 | 1620 | 434 | .268 | .041 |
| Bob Kipper | 481 | 106 | .220 | 1038 | 271 | .261 | .041 |
| Charles Hudson | 886 | 206 | .233 | 1655 | 452 | .273 | .041 |
| John Candelaria | 592 | 135 | .228 | 1573 | 420 | .267 | .039 |
| Dave J. Schmidt | 531 | 130 | .245 | 1765 | 498 | .282 | .037 |
| Jeff Reardon | 500 | 106 | .212 | 1011 | 251 | .248 | .036 |
| Floyd Bannister | 600 | 137 | .228 | 2743 | 721 | .263 | .035 |
| Ricky Horton | 529 | 128 | .242 | 1367 | 376 | .275 | .033 |
| Atlee Hammaker | 1033 | 242 | .234 | 1095 | 292 | .267 | .032 |
| Vida Blue | 585 | 132 | .226 | 467 | 120 | .257 | .031 |
| Joe Price | 436 | 101 | .232 | 657 | 172 | .262 | .030 |
| Dave Righetti | 531 | 122 | .230 | 1217 | 316 | .260 | .030 |
| Rick Aguilera | 754 | 183 | .243 | 1346 | 363 | .270 | .027 |
| Joe Cowley | 448 | 96 | .214 | 790 | 190 | .241 | .026 |
| Gene Nelson | 693 | 158 | .228 | 1486 | 377 | .254 | .026 |
| Scott McGregor | 573 | 155 | .271 | 1443 | 426 | .295 | .025 |
| Paul Kilgus | 549 | 135 | .246 | 1162 | 314 | .270 | .024 |
| Kelly Downs | 754 | 173 | .229 | 1231 | 312 | .253 | .024 |
| Tim Burke | 630 | 136 | .216 | 1122 | 269 | .240 | .024 |
| Andy Hawkins | 1249 | 317 | .254 | 2503 | 695 | .278 | .024 |

# First Time Through Batting Order

## LAST SEASON

### BETTER FIRST TIME THROUGH

| PLAYER | FIRST TIME THROUGH AB | H | AVG | OTHER AT BATS AB | H | AVG | DIFF |
|---|---|---|---|---|---|---|---|
| Neal Heaton | 267 | 47 | .176 | 277 | 80 | .289 | .113 |
| Walt Terrell | 260 | 61 | .235 | 556 | 175 | .315 | .080 |
| Bud Black | 280 | 57 | .204 | 564 | 156 | .277 | .073 |
| Tim Leary | 272 | 58 | .213 | 514 | 147 | .286 | .073 |
| Dave J. Schmidt | 295 | 81 | .275 | 337 | 115 | .341 | .067 |
| Pascual Perez | 261 | 51 | .195 | 490 | 127 | .259 | .064 |
| Bill Swift | 269 | 67 | .249 | 235 | 73 | .311 | .062 |
| Tom Browning | 300 | 64 | .213 | 646 | 177 | .274 | .061 |
| Pete Smith | 223 | 51 | .229 | 324 | 93 | .287 | .058 |
| Mike Morgan | 265 | 54 | .204 | 290 | 76 | .262 | .058 |
| Zane Smith | 305 | 69 | .226 | 254 | 72 | .283 | .057 |
| Mike Witt | 271 | 69 | .255 | 593 | 183 | .309 | .054 |
| Sid Fernandez | 276 | 45 | .163 | 518 | 112 | .216 | .053 |
| John Cerutti | 269 | 64 | .238 | 516 | 150 | .291 | .053 |
| Scott Bankhead | 267 | 55 | .206 | 517 | 132 | .255 | .049 |
| Mike LaCoss | 285 | 66 | .232 | 275 | 77 | .280 | .048 |
| Jimmy Key | 285 | 68 | .239 | 553 | 158 | .286 | .047 |
| Ken Hill | 257 | 57 | .222 | 482 | 129 | .268 | .046 |
| Jeff D. Robinson | 305 | 80 | .262 | 264 | 81 | .307 | .045 |
| Jim Clancy | 238 | 58 | .244 | 338 | 97 | .287 | .043 |
| Bob Knepper | 255 | 68 | .267 | 394 | 122 | .310 | .043 |
| Richard Dotson | 226 | 61 | .270 | 389 | 120 | .308 | .039 |
| Mike Boddicker | 269 | 65 | .242 | 544 | 152 | .279 | .038 |
| Doyle Alexander | 264 | 67 | .254 | 612 | 178 | .291 | .037 |
| Bob Welch | 272 | 59 | .217 | 520 | 132 | .254 | .037 |

### BETTER ON LATER AT BATS

| PLAYER | FIRST TIME THROUGH AB | H | AVG | OTHER AT BATS AB | H | AVG | DIFF |
|---|---|---|---|---|---|---|---|
| Allan Anderson | 269 | 88 | .327 | 508 | 126 | .248 | .079 |
| Orel Hershiser | 283 | 81 | .286 | 659 | 145 | .220 | .066 |
| Rick Mahler | 312 | 100 | .321 | 547 | 142 | .260 | .061 |
| Larry McWilliams | 290 | 85 | .293 | 297 | 69 | .232 | .061 |
| John Smoltz | 234 | 58 | .248 | 522 | 102 | .195 | .052 |
| Frank Tanana | 260 | 78 | .300 | 596 | 149 | .250 | .050 |
| Jeff Ballard | 288 | 92 | .319 | 548 | 148 | .270 | .049 |
| Kirk McCaskill | 266 | 76 | .286 | 529 | 126 | .238 | .048 |
| Derek Lilliquist | 261 | 86 | .330 | 410 | 116 | .283 | .047 |
| Chris Bosio | 278 | 78 | .281 | 627 | 147 | .234 | .046 |
| Bob Forsch | 239 | 77 | .322 | 200 | 56 | .280 | .042 |
| Mike Flanagan | 253 | 78 | .308 | 405 | 108 | .267 | .042 |
| Ed Whitson | 263 | 69 | .262 | 578 | 129 | .223 | .039 |
| Bob Ojeda | 248 | 67 | .270 | 483 | 112 | .232 | .038 |
| Mark Langston | 264 | 64 | .242 | 641 | 134 | .209 | .033 |
| Bert Blyleven | 273 | 74 | .271 | 634 | 151 | .238 | .033 |
| Bret Saberhagen | 305 | 73 | .239 | 656 | 136 | .207 | .032 |
| Dennis Rasmussen | 266 | 77 | .289 | 438 | 113 | .258 | .031 |
| Jose DeLeon | 293 | 63 | .215 | 585 | 110 | .188 | .027 |
| Melido Perez | 242 | 68 | .281 | 466 | 119 | .255 | .026 |
| Joe Magrane | 273 | 73 | .267 | 598 | 146 | .244 | .023 |
| Rick Aguilera | 323 | 80 | .248 | 222 | 50 | .225 | .022 |
| Rick Reuschel | 264 | 69 | .261 | 526 | 126 | .240 | .022 |
| Storm Davis | 249 | 75 | .301 | 400 | 112 | .280 | .021 |
| Bobby Witt | 240 | 63 | .262 | 493 | 119 | .241 | .021 |

## LAST 5 YEARS

### BETTER FIRST TIME THROUGH

| PLAYER | FIRST TIME THROUGH AB | H | AVG | OTHER AT BATS AB | H | AVG | DIFF |
|---|---|---|---|---|---|---|---|
| Jimmy Jones | 569 | 127 | .223 | 946 | 285 | .301 | .078 |
| Rick Honeycutt | 1232 | 269 | .218 | 1100 | 324 | .295 | .076 |
| Rich Yett | 805 | 190 | .236 | 800 | 248 | .310 | .074 |
| Ray Fontenot | 524 | 138 | .263 | 367 | 123 | .335 | .072 |
| Bob Kipper | 846 | 184 | .217 | 673 | 193 | .287 | .069 |
| Dickie Noles | 620 | 157 | .253 | 312 | 100 | .321 | .067 |
| Steve Carlton | 628 | 151 | .240 | 1043 | 314 | .301 | .061 |
| Les Straker | 362 | 83 | .229 | 533 | 153 | .287 | .058 |
| Jose Guzman | 808 | 176 | .218 | 1558 | 426 | .273 | .056 |
| David Palmer | 898 | 201 | .224 | 1555 | 431 | .277 | .053 |
| Tim Conroy | 314 | 78 | .248 | 380 | 114 | .300 | .052 |
| Bill Swift | 942 | 250 | .265 | 1171 | 368 | .314 | .049 |
| Greg A. Harris | 1642 | 368 | .224 | 481 | 131 | .272 | .048 |
| Dennis Eckersley | 1266 | 275 | .217 | 1056 | 279 | .264 | .047 |
| Bill Wegman | 939 | 228 | .243 | 1767 | 511 | .289 | .046 |
| Jerry Reed | 1061 | 253 | .238 | 360 | 102 | .283 | .045 |
| Fred Toliver | 423 | 110 | .260 | 497 | 151 | .304 | .044 |
| Steve Trout | 842 | 226 | .268 | 1130 | 352 | .312 | .043 |
| Greg Swindell | 701 | 158 | .225 | 1548 | 415 | .268 | .043 |
| Tim Belcher | 622 | 120 | .193 | 1000 | 235 | .235 | .042 |
| Mike Morgan | 961 | 240 | .250 | 1574 | 459 | .292 | .042 |
| Steve Bedrosian | 1519 | 346 | .228 | 523 | 141 | .270 | .042 |
| John Dopson | 479 | 108 | .225 | 872 | 233 | .267 | .042 |
| Frank Viola | 1485 | 335 | .226 | 3355 | 896 | .267 | .041 |
| Walt Terrell | 1302 | 306 | .235 | 2909 | 803 | .276 | .041 |

### BETTER ON LATER AT BATS

| PLAYER | FIRST TIME THROUGH AB | H | AVG | OTHER AT BATS AB | H | AVG | DIFF |
|---|---|---|---|---|---|---|---|
| Jeff Pico | 467 | 131 | .281 | 317 | 76 | .240 | .041 |
| Bob Shirley | 561 | 158 | .282 | 409 | 99 | .242 | .040 |
| Jeff Ballard | 612 | 192 | .314 | 1115 | 315 | .283 | .031 |
| Mike Jeffcoat | 330 | 100 | .303 | 381 | 104 | .273 | .030 |
| Luis Aquino | 331 | 96 | .290 | 377 | 99 | .263 | .027 |
| Danny Cox | 897 | 249 | .278 | 1911 | 479 | .251 | .027 |
| Tim Lollar | 382 | 105 | .275 | 346 | 86 | .249 | .026 |
| Kirk McCaskill | 1071 | 290 | .271 | 2221 | 547 | .246 | .024 |
| Les Lancaster | 657 | 177 | .269 | 449 | 110 | .245 | .024 |
| John Smoltz | 327 | 80 | .245 | 689 | 154 | .224 | .021 |
| Allan Anderson | 699 | 205 | .293 | 1227 | 334 | .272 | .021 |
| Phil Niekro | 737 | 211 | .286 | 1493 | 396 | .265 | .021 |
| Eric King | 868 | 214 | .247 | 924 | 209 | .226 | .020 |
| Joe Hesketh | 848 | 217 | .256 | 593 | 140 | .236 | .020 |
| Chuck Finley | 819 | 217 | .265 | 1165 | 287 | .246 | .019 |
| Dan Petry | 939 | 248 | .264 | 1644 | 404 | .246 | .018 |
| Chris Bosio | 947 | 261 | .276 | 1485 | 382 | .257 | .018 |
| Tim Birtsas | 639 | 162 | .254 | 394 | 93 | .236 | .017 |
| Ray Burris | 440 | 129 | .293 | 645 | 178 | .276 | .017 |
| John Candelaria | 972 | 258 | .265 | 1193 | 297 | .249 | .016 |
| Scott McGregor | 730 | 218 | .299 | 1286 | 363 | .282 | .016 |
| John Farrell | 571 | 152 | .266 | 1302 | 328 | .252 | .014 |
| Don Robinson | 1450 | 363 | .250 | 990 | 234 | .236 | .014 |
| Mark Williamson | 951 | 255 | .268 | 379 | 97 | .256 | .012 |
| Bob Sebra | 563 | 157 | .279 | 806 | 215 | .267 | .012 |

# VII
# Single Season and Career Leaders

# *Single Season and Career Leaders*

The Single Season and Career Leaders section lists, for a variety of batting and pitching categories, the top 25 performers since we began *The Player Analysis* in 1975.

When we began our analysis of play-by-play data from every game, we had a dual purpose: we recognized the value of the information for immediate use, and we knew we were accumulating and building a valuable resource for future study as well. This section gives us a chance to take stock of the results from our unparalleled files—files representing more than a million and a half plate appearances.

The leader categories for this section were chosen both for significance and for general interest (however quirky). The single season bests listed here provide an important context for evaluating the performances throughout this book. The career lists do considerably more; they provide the definitive look at situational statistics since 1975.

Minimum qualifiers for most batting categories are expressed in hits rather than in the equivalent number of plate appearances. As a general rule, the number of hits is one third the number of at bats of the qualifying range, if you're more comfortable thinking about it in those terms.

In dealing with last season's statistics in the Ranking Section of this book, we used a more inclusive level for rankings qualification: the equivalent of 200 plate appearances. The levels used here are more stringent, corresponding more to everyday play than part-time or "semiregular" status.

In the pitching categories, it should not be too surprising that relievers dominate. They allow consistently lower batting averages than starters for a variety of reasons, not only in traditional statistics but in these situational statistics as well. We have tried to set qualifying levels that are meaningful for both starters and relievers; the levels are the equivalent of about one and a half seasons as a full-time starter, or three as a primary reliever.

Bear in mind that *The Player Analysis* began in 1975. For the vast majority of active players, this poses no obstacle to calling these "career" statistics. In some cases, the missing information is very minor (67 at bats out of Jim Rice's career; a little under 500 from George Brett's); in the case of a Pete Rose or Tony Perez, obviously, a larger chunk is missing. We'd love to be able to fill in the gaps; we'd also love to know how Lou Gehrig hit with runners in scoring position in late-inning pressure. Maybe someday . . .

## CAREER BATTING AVERAGE VS. LEFT-HANDED PITCHERS

*Min. 150 Hits*

|  |  |
|---|---|
| Kirby Puckett | .339 |
| Andres Galarraga | .322 |
| Julio Franco | .319 |
| Bob Watson | .318 |
| Tony Gwynn | .316 |
| Pat Tabler | .316 |
| Wade Boggs | .314 |
| Jim Rice | .313 |
| Don Mattingly | .313 |
| Paul Molitor | .311 |
| Rod Carew | .310 |
| Rickey Henderson | .309 |
| Pedro Guerrero | .309 |
| Ron LeFlore | .309 |
| Ellis Valentine | .307 |
| John Castino | .307 |
| Hubie Brooks | .307 |
| Hal McRae | .305 |
| Rob Thompson | .305 |
| Bill Madlock | .305 |
| Gary Matthews | .305 |
| Dwight Evans | .305 |
| Wayne Nordhagen | .304 |
| Dave Cash | .304 |
| Kevin Seitzer | .303 |

## CAREER SLUGGING AVERAGE VS. LEFT-HANDED PITCHERS

*Min. 200 Total Bases*

|  |  |
|---|---|
| Mike Schmidt | .573 |
| Jose Canseco | .572 |
| Eric Davis | .566 |
| Ellis Valentine | .562 |
| Pete Incaviglia | .549 |
| Kevin Mitchell | .547 |
| Andres Galarraga | .544 |
| Dave Winfield | .540 |
| Mark McGwire | .534 |
| Johnny Bench | .531 |
| Jack Clark | .530 |
| George Foster | .530 |
| Dwight Evans | .528 |
| George Bell | .525 |
| Jim Rice | .524 |
| Ron Cey | .523 |
| Danny Tartabull | .523 |
| Cliff Johnson | .518 |
| Dave Kingman | .518 |
| Bill Robinson | .513 |
| Andre Dawson | .512 |
| Hal McRae | .511 |
| Cory Snyder | .511 |
| Dale Murphy | .510 |
| Rob Deer | .510 |

## CAREER HOME RUN PCT. VS. LEFT-HANDED PITCHERS

*Min. 20 Home Runs*

|  |  |
|---|---|
| Eric Davis | 7.85 |
| Dave Kingman | 7.58 |
| Mark McGwire | 7.16 |
| Rob Deer | 6.75 |
| Mike Schmidt | 6.74 |
| Jose Canseco | 6.62 |
| Ron Kittle | 6.58 |
| Ron Cey | 6.56 |
| Pete Incaviglia | 6.49 |
| Cecil Fielder | 6.39 |
| Glenn Davis | 6.15 |
| Gorman Thomas | 6.12 |
| Mike Diaz | 6.10 |
| Bill Schroeder | 6.07 |
| Ellis Valentine | 6.07 |
| Kevin Mitchell | 6.07 |
| Johnny Bench | 6.03 |
| George Foster | 5.93 |
| Gene Tenace | 5.90 |
| John Wockenfuss | 5.85 |
| Darryl Strawberry | 5.76 |
| Cory Snyder | 5.76 |
| Steve Balboni | 5.72 |
| Bo Jackson | 5.71 |
| Dave Winfield | 5.63 |

## CAREER STRIKEOUT PCT. VS. LEFT-HANDED PITCHERS

*Min. 500 PA*

|  |  |
|---|---|
| Ted Sizemore | 2.90 |
| Dave Cash | 3.05 |
| Tim Foli | 3.08 |
| Marty Barrett | 3.18 |
| Bob Bailor | 3.41 |
| Manny Sanguillen | 3.48 |
| Felix Millan | 3.49 |
| Barry Larkin | 3.79 |
| Doug Flynn | 4.69 |
| Rennie Stennett | 4.72 |
| Rich Dauer | 4.96 |
| Mickey Hatcher | 4.96 |
| Bob Boone | 4.99 |
| Bucky Dent | 5.09 |
| Pete Rose | 5.21 |
| Don Kessinger | 5.30 |
| Bill Russell | 5.34 |
| Mario Guerrero | 5.46 |
| Rob Andrews | 5.48 |
| Jerry Terrell | 5.54 |
| Steve Nicosia | 5.71 |
| Bill Buckner | 5.80 |
| Willie Randolph | 5.81 |
| Bruce Benedict | 5.93 |
| Eric Soderholm | 6.03 |

## CAREER BATTING AVERAGE VS. RIGHT-HANDED PITCHERS

*Min. 250 Hits*

|  |  |
|---|---|
| Wade Boggs | .370 |
| Tony Gwynn | .341 |
| Rod Carew | .341 |
| Don Mattingly | .329 |
| George Brett | .327 |
| Mike Greenwell | .327 |
| Kal Daniels | .327 |
| Al Oliver | .326 |
| Lyman Bostock | .325 |
| Kirby Puckett | .317 |
| Pedro Guerrero | .307 |
| Mike Easler | .307 |
| Thurman Munson | .306 |
| Will Clark | .306 |
| Bake McBride | .306 |
| Cecil Cooper | .305 |
| John Kruk | .305 |
| Mickey Rivers | .305 |
| Kevin Seitzer | .305 |
| Johnny Ray | .303 |
| Jerry Mumphrey | .303 |
| Jose Cruz | .303 |
| Tim Raines | .303 |
| Bill Madlock | .302 |
| Wally Joyner | .302 |

## CAREER SLUGGING AVERAGE VS. RIGHT-HANDED PITCHERS

*Min. 300 Total Bases*

|  |  |
|---|---|
| Fred McGriff | .591 |
| Kal Daniels | .570 |
| Darryl Strawberry | .556 |
| Mike Greenwell | .550 |
| Will Clark | .547 |
| George Brett | .544 |
| Reggie Smith | .539 |
| Don Mattingly | .532 |
| Willie Stargell | .532 |
| Kent Hrbek | .527 |
| Mike Schmidt | .523 |
| Fred Lynn | .522 |
| Ken Phelps | .516 |
| Mark McGwire | .512 |
| Eric Davis | .512 |
| Wade Boggs | .509 |
| Alvin Davis | .504 |
| Reggie Jackson | .503 |
| Kirk Gibson | .503 |
| Pedro Guerrero | .502 |
| Eddie Murray | .502 |
| Oscar Gamble | .498 |
| Leon Durham | .497 |
| Bob Horner | .497 |
| Cecil Cooper | .496 |

## CAREER HOME RUN PCT. VS. RIGHT-HANDED PITCHERS

*Min. 40 Home Runs*

|  |  |
|---|---|
| Fred McGriff | 7.89 |
| Ken Phelps | 7.52 |
| Mark McGwire | 7.06 |
| Ron Kittle | 6.81 |
| Darryl Strawberry | 6.77 |
| Mike Schmidt | 6.66 |
| Dave Kingman | 6.35 |
| Willie Stargell | 6.19 |
| Eric Davis | 6.14 |
| Reggie Jackson | 6.10 |
| Reggie Smith | 5.99 |
| Dan Pasqua | 5.90 |
| Bob Horner | 5.87 |
| Gorman Thomas | 5.80 |
| Steve Balboni | 5.78 |
| Oscar Gamble | 5.67 |
| Bo Jackson | 5.64 |
| Jose Canseco | 5.63 |
| Will Clark | 5.44 |
| Rob Deer | 5.40 |
| Kent Hrbek | 5.38 |
| Kal Daniels | 5.36 |
| Tony Armas | 5.33 |
| Graig Nettles | 5.32 |
| Jason Thompson | 5.29 |

## CAREER STRIKEOUT PCT. VS. RIGHT-HANDED PITCHERS

*Min. 750 PA*

|  |  |
|---|---|
| Felix Millan | 3.29 |
| Bill Buckner | 3.98 |
| Dave Cash | 4.30 |
| Tony Gwynn | 4.68 |
| Scott Bradley | 4.87 |
| Johnny Ray | 4.95 |
| Don Mattingly | 4.99 |
| Larry Bowa | 5.04 |
| Jack Brohamer | 5.17 |
| Mike Squires | 5.17 |
| Greg Gross | 5.22 |
| Ken Oberkfell | 5.23 |
| Wade Boggs | 5.30 |
| Rich Dauer | 5.31 |
| Ozzie Smith | 5.34 |
| Mike Scioscia | 5.36 |
| Al Oliver | 5.37 |
| Rusty Staub | 5.40 |
| Mark Grace | 5.64 |
| Tom Poquette | 5.72 |
| Pete Rose | 5.83 |
| Dan Meyer | 5.95 |
| George Brett | 5.95 |
| Bob Bailor | 5.98 |
| Duane Kuiper | 5.99 |

## SINGLE-SEASON BATTING AVERAGE VS. LEFT-HANDED PITCHERS

*Min. 40 Hits*

|  |  |
|---|---|
| Rennie Stennett, 1977 | .435 |
| Sixto Lezcano, 1979 | .411 |
| Kirby Puckett, 1988 | .398 |
| Tim Raines, 1987 | .396 |
| Steve Henderson, 1979 | .395 |
| Mike Vail, 1979 | .395 |
| Ken Griffey, 1976 | .393 |
| Gerald Young, 1987 | .390 |
| Carney Lansford, 1989 | .389 |
| Bill Buckner, 1978 | .389 |
| Paul Molitor, 1979 | .387 |
| Brian Downing, 1979 | .386 |
| Andres Galarraga, 1989 | .385 |
| Chet Lemon, 1984 | .384 |
| Julio Franco, 1988 | .383 |
| Alvaro Espinoza, 1989 | .383 |
| Keith Moreland, 1983 | .382 |
| Buddy Bell, 1977 | .382 |
| Steve Sax, 1989 | .381 |
| Rico Carty, 1975 | .381 |
| Don Baylor, 1975 | .380 |
| Jack Clark, 1980 | .380 |
| Jeffrey Leonard, 1984 | .380 |
| Jose Cardenal, 1975 | .379 |
| Ray Knight, 1986 | .379 |

## SINGLE-SEASON BATTING AVERAGE VS. RIGHT-HANDED PITCHERS

*Min. 75 Hits*

|  |  |
|---|---|
| George Brett, 1980 | .437 |
| Wade Boggs, 1983 | .398 |
| Rod Carew, 1977 | .398 |
| Wade Boggs, 1988 | .381 |
| Rod Carew, 1975 | .379 |
| Wade Boggs, 1985 | .377 |
| Wade Boggs, 1987 | .377 |
| Tony Gwynn, 1987 | .376 |
| Tony Gwynn, 1984 | .371 |
| Oscar Gamble, 1979 | .370 |
| Kal Daniels, 1987 | .370 |
| Cecil Cooper, 1980 | .365 |
| Fred Lynn, 1979 | .364 |
| Paul Molitor, 1987 | .363 |
| Willie Wilson, 1982 | .360 |
| Wade Boggs, 1986 | .359 |
| Rod Carew, 1983 | .358 |
| Bill Madlock, 1975 | .357 |
| Mike Easler, 1980 | .357 |
| Wade Boggs, 1982 | .356 |
| Wade Boggs, 1984 | .356 |
| Willie McGee, 1985 | .356 |
| Rod Carew, 1982 | .355 |
| Kirby Puckett, 1989 | .354 |
| Al Oliver, 1979 | .353 |

## SINGLE-SEASON BATTING AVERAGE IN HOME GAMES

*Min. 75 Hits*

|  |  |
|---|---|
| Wade Boggs, 1985 | .418 |
| Wade Boggs, 1987 | .411 |
| Kirby Puckett, 1988 | .406 |
| Rod Carew, 1977 | .401 |
| Juan Beniquez, 1984 | .399 |
| Wade Boggs, 1983 | .397 |
| Paul Molitor, 1987 | .394 |
| George Brett, 1980 | .391 |
| Kirby Puckett, 1989 | .390 |
| Tony Gwynn, 1987 | .390 |
| Rod Carew, 1975 | .387 |
| Fred Lynn, 1979 | .386 |
| Al Oliver, 1980 | .385 |
| Wade Boggs, 1988 | .382 |
| Hal McRae, 1976 | .382 |
| Miguel Dilone, 1980 | .378 |
| Wade Boggs, 1989 | .377 |
| Tony Gwynn, 1984 | .376 |
| Dion James, 1987 | .376 |
| Mike Easler, 1984 | .375 |
| George Brett, 1979 | .373 |
| Bill Buckner, 1977 | .372 |
| Jim Rice, 1979 | .369 |
| Fred Lynn, 1975 | .368 |
| George Brett, 1985 | .368 |

## SINGLE-SEASON BATTING AVERAGE IN ROAD GAMES

*Min. 75 Hits*

|  |  |
|---|---|
| George Brett, 1980 | .388 |
| Cecil Cooper, 1980 | .386 |
| Rod Carew, 1977 | .374 |
| Johnny Ray, 1984 | .370 |
| Rod Carew, 1983 | .369 |
| Don Mattingly, 1986 | .367 |
| Don Mattingly, 1984 | .364 |
| Kirby Puckett, 1987 | .362 |
| Carney Lansford, 1989 | .360 |
| Brian Downing, 1979 | .360 |
| Bob Watson, 1975 | .358 |
| Mickey Rivers, 1977 | .358 |
| Bill Madlock, 1975 | .357 |
| Wade Boggs, 1986 | .356 |
| Ken Singleton, 1977 | .354 |
| Ben Oglivie, 1980 | .353 |
| Willie McGee, 1985 | .353 |
| Pedro Guerrero, 1987 | .352 |
| Tony Gwynn, 1987 | .352 |
| Steve Sax, 1986 | .352 |
| Wade Boggs, 1988 | .351 |
| Keith Hernandez, 1979 | .350 |
| Dion James, 1989 | .349 |
| Dave Winfield, 1984 | .349 |
| Enos Cabell, 1984 | .348 |

## CAREER HOME RUN PCT. IN HOME GAMES

*Min. 25 Home Runs*

|  |  |
|---|---|
| Ken Phelps | 7.92 |
| Bob Horner | 7.47 |
| Mike Schmidt | 6.66 |
| Ron Kittle | 6.55 |
| Dave Kingman | 6.52 |
| Fred McGriff | 6.49 |
| Eric Davis | 6.39 |
| Oscar Gamble | 6.31 |
| Willie Stargell | 6.26 |
| Greg Luzinski | 6.25 |
| Darryl Strawberry | 6.17 |
| Rob Deer | 6.12 |
| Dale Murphy | 5.98 |
| Gorman Thomas | 5.87 |
| Reggie Jackson | 5.80 |
| Mark McGwire | 5.74 |
| George Foster | 5.71 |
| Pete Incaviglia | 5.60 |
| Jose Canseco | 5.60 |
| Rick Monday | 5.48 |
| Dan Pasqua | 5.48 |
| Matt Nokes | 5.46 |
| Gary Alexander | 5.46 |
| Jesse Barfield | 5.42 |
| Ruben Sierra | 5.39 |

## CAREER HOME RUN PCT. IN ROAD GAMES

*Min. 25 Home Runs*

|  |  |
|---|---|
| Mark McGwire | 8.36 |
| Eric Davis | 6.97 |
| Dave Kingman | 6.90 |
| Ron Kittle | 6.87 |
| Mike Schmidt | 6.69 |
| Darryl Strawberry | 6.60 |
| Steve Balboni | 6.51 |
| Fred McGriff | 6.49 |
| Jose Canseco | 6.21 |
| Bo Jackson | 6.15 |
| Ken Phelps | 6.12 |
| Gorman Thomas | 5.93 |
| Bill Schroeder | 5.84 |
| Kevin Mitchell | 5.78 |
| Glenn Davis | 5.61 |
| Reggie Jackson | 5.51 |
| Rob Deer | 5.49 |
| Pedro Guerrero | 5.43 |
| Cory Snyder | 5.42 |
| Jack Clark | 5.41 |
| Willie Stargell | 5.35 |
| Howard Johnson | 5.33 |
| Willie Aikens | 5.29 |
| Tom Brunansky | 5.28 |
| Tony Armas | 5.11 |

## CAREER BATTING AVERAGE IN HOME GAMES

*Min. 200 Hits*

|  |  |
|---|---|
| Wade Boggs | .383 |
| Kirby Puckett | .353 |
| Tony Gwynn | .338 |
| Rod Carew | .334 |
| George Brett | .332 |
| Mike Greenwell | .330 |
| Kevin Seitzer | .329 |
| Al Oliver | .326 |
| Don Mattingly | .324 |
| Jim Rice | .320 |
| Julio Franco | .319 |
| Lyman Bostock | .318 |
| Will Clark | .316 |
| Paul Molitor | .313 |
| Jerry Browne | .313 |
| Thurman Munson | .311 |
| Ellis Burks | .310 |
| Pat Tabler | .310 |
| Dave Parker | .309 |
| Kent Hrbek | .308 |
| Mike Easler | .308 |
| Lonnie Smith | .307 |
| Lou Brock | .306 |
| Milt Thompson | .306 |
| Hal McRae | .306 |

## CAREER BATTING AVERAGE IN ROAD GAMES

*Min. 200 Hits*

|  |  |
|---|---|
| Rod Carew | .328 |
| Tony Gwynn | .326 |
| Don Mattingly | .323 |
| Wade Boggs | .322 |
| Pedro Guerrero | .312 |
| Mike Greenwell | .309 |
| Mickey Rivers | .308 |
| Lyman Bostock | .305 |
| Bob Watson | .305 |
| Wally Joyner | .303 |
| Manny Sanguillen | .303 |
| Cecil Cooper | .301 |
| Tim Raines | .301 |
| Bill Madlock | .301 |
| Thurman Munson | .297 |
| Gene Richards | .297 |
| Dave Winfield | .297 |
| Ken Singleton | .296 |
| Tony Fernandez | .295 |
| Keith Hernandez | .295 |
| Ken Griffey | .295 |
| Johnny Ray | .294 |
| George Brett | .294 |
| Glenn Adams | .293 |
| Kirby Puckett | .293 |

### CAREER BATTING AVERAGE VS. GROUND-BALL PITCHERS

*Min. 200 Hits*

|  |  |
|---|---|
| Wade Boggs | .359 |
| Don Mattingly | .334 |
| Tony Gwynn | .333 |
| Mike Greenwell | .331 |
| Kirby Puckett | .324 |
| Kal Daniels | .323 |
| George Brett | .322 |
| Al Oliver | .321 |
| Rod Carew | .317 |
| Lonnie Smith | .317 |
| Lyman Bostock | .317 |
| Reggie Smith | .315 |
| Cecil Cooper | .314 |
| Pedro Guerrero | .312 |
| Hal McRae | .311 |
| Bob Watson | .309 |
| Ron LeFlore | .309 |
| Jim Rice | .307 |
| Lee Lacy | .307 |
| Keith Hernandez | .305 |
| Tim Raines | .305 |
| Robin Yount | .304 |
| Kevin Seitzer | .304 |
| Bill Madlock | .304 |
| Mickey Rivers | .303 |

### CAREER SLUGGING AVERAGE VS. GROUND-BALL PITCHERS

*Min. 300 Total Bases*

|  |  |
|---|---|
| Fred McGriff | .561 |
| Mike Schmidt | .547 |
| Reggie Smith | .539 |
| Ken Phelps | .533 |
| Mark McGwire | .533 |
| Bo Jackson | .527 |
| Eric Davis | .525 |
| Don Mattingly | .520 |
| Mike Greenwell | .514 |
| Pete Incaviglia | .513 |
| Kal Daniels | .513 |
| George Brett | .511 |
| Willie Stargell | .511 |
| Fred Lynn | .506 |
| Bobby Bonds | .504 |
| Kent Hrbek | .504 |
| Cecil Cooper | .500 |
| Reggie Jackson | .498 |
| Kevin Mitchell | .496 |
| Bob Horner | .496 |
| Jim Rice | .495 |
| Jose Canseco | .493 |
| Darryl Strawberry | .492 |
| Greg Luzinski | .491 |
| Larry Hisle | .489 |

### SINGLE-SEASON BATTING AVERAGE VS. GROUND-BALL PITCHERS

*Min. 60 Hits*

|  |  |
|---|---|
| Wade Boggs, 1985 | .394 |
| Hal McRae, 1976 | .391 |
| Hubie Brooks, 1986 | .390 |
| Keith Hernandez, 1979 | .389 |
| Rod Carew, 1975 | .386 |
| Wade Boggs, 1983 | .383 |
| Al Oliver, 1978 | .382 |
| Ron LeFlore, 1976 | .381 |
| Don Mattingly, 1986 | .379 |
| Wade Boggs, 1987 | .378 |
| Mike Hargrove, 1977 | .376 |
| George Brett, 1985 | .376 |
| George Brett, 1980 | .372 |
| Robin Yount, 1987 | .371 |
| Don Mattingly, 1984 | .369 |
| Tony Gwynn, 1984 | .369 |
| Cecil Cooper, 1982 | .369 |
| Mickey Rivers, 1976 | .365 |
| Cecil Cooper, 1980 | .365 |
| Bill Madlock, 1975 | .365 |
| Bill Madlock, 1976 | .365 |
| Bill Buckner, 1980 | .364 |
| Dwight Smith, 1989 | .364 |
| Warren Cromartie, 1981 | .361 |
| Brian Downing, 1979 | .361 |

### SINGLE-SEASON SLUGGING AVERAGE VS. GROUND-BALL PITCHERS

*Min. 100 Total Bases*

|  |  |
|---|---|
| Mike Schmidt, 1981 | .739 |
| Mark McGwire, 1987 | .690 |
| George Bell, 1987 | .672 |
| Brian Downing, 1983 | .647 |
| Mike Greenwell, 1987 | .647 |
| Howard Johnson, 1989 | .641 |
| Dave Kingman, 1979 | .634 |
| George Brett, 1985 | .633 |
| Mike Schmidt, 1977 | .629 |
| Cecil Cooper, 1982 | .627 |
| Hubie Brooks, 1986 | .622 |
| Greg Luzinski, 1977 | .622 |
| Andres Galarraga, 1988 | .621 |
| Reggie Jackson, 1977 | .618 |
| Dwight Evans, 1987 | .616 |
| Ben Oglivie, 1980 | .615 |
| Frank White, 1986 | .613 |
| Dave Winfield, 1982 | .608 |
| Don Mattingly, 1986 | .608 |
| George Brett, 1983 | .607 |
| Ken Phelps, 1987 | .606 |
| Richie Zisk, 1977 | .605 |
| Kevin Mitchell, 1989 | .605 |
| Dave Parker, 1978 | .605 |
| Bobby Bonds, 1975 | .605 |

### CAREER BATTING AVERAGE VS. FLY-BALL PITCHERS

*Min. 200 Hits*

|  |  |
|---|---|
| Wade Boggs | .347 |
| Rod Carew | .342 |
| Tony Gwynn | .331 |
| Kirby Puckett | .323 |
| Dion James | .315 |
| Thurman Munson | .315 |
| Don Mattingly | .315 |
| Will Clark | .315 |
| Mike Greenwell | .310 |
| John Kruk | .310 |
| Jose Morales | .307 |
| Lyman Bostock | .307 |
| George Brett | .306 |
| Kevin Seitzer | .305 |
| Pete Rose | .305 |
| Manny Sanguillen | .303 |
| Bill Madlock | .303 |
| Pedro Guerrero | .303 |
| Paul Molitor | .303 |
| Ellis Burks | .303 |
| Rico Carty | .302 |
| Mike Easler | .301 |
| Bake McBride | .301 |
| Julio Franco | .300 |
| Rafael Palmeiro | .300 |

### CAREER SLUGGING AVERAGE VS. FLY-BALL PITCHERS

*Min. 300 Total Bases*

|  |  |
|---|---|
| Will Clark | .594 |
| Darryl Strawberry | .550 |
| Eric Davis | .537 |
| Danny Tartabull | .529 |
| Kevin Mitchell | .523 |
| Mike Schmidt | .522 |
| Don Mattingly | .521 |
| Pedro Guerrero | .521 |
| Willie Stargell | .514 |
| George Foster | .514 |
| Andre Dawson | .513 |
| George Brett | .511 |
| George Bell | .510 |
| Jose Canseco | .510 |
| Jim Rice | .510 |
| Ellis Burks | .509 |
| Jack Clark | .509 |
| Fred McGriff | .509 |
| Dale Murphy | .508 |
| Dave Winfield | .507 |
| Mike Greenwell | .507 |
| Mark McGwire | .507 |
| Matt Nokes | .503 |
| Bob Horner | .502 |
| Bill Robinson | .501 |

### SINGLE-SEASON BATTING AVERAGE VS. FLY-BALL PITCHERS

*Min. 60 Hits*

|  |  |
|---|---|
| Rod Carew, 1977 | .424 |
| George Brett, 1980 | .405 |
| Tony Gwynn, 1987 | .401 |
| Willie McGee, 1985 | .375 |
| Rod Carew, 1979 | .375 |
| Wade Boggs, 1988 | .372 |
| Tony Gwynn, 1986 | .368 |
| Von Joshua, 1975 | .368 |
| Wade Boggs, 1982 | .367 |
| Paul Molitor, 1987 | .365 |
| Wade Boggs, 1986 | .364 |
| Rennie Stennett, 1977 | .364 |
| Manny Sanguillen, 1975 | .364 |
| Dion James, 1987 | .363 |
| Ted Simmons, 1975 | .363 |
| Mike Easler, 1980 | .363 |
| Kirby Puckett, 1988 | .362 |
| Pedro Guerrero, 1987 | .359 |
| Larry Biittner, 1975 | .357 |
| Will Clark, 1989 | .356 |
| Ken Griffey, 1976 | .355 |
| George Brett, 1976 | .353 |
| Andre Dawson, 1982 | .352 |
| Ron Hassey, 1986 | .351 |
| Rico Carty, 1975 | .351 |

### SINGLE-SEASON SLUGGING AVERAGE VS. FLY-BALL PITCHERS

*Min. 100 Total Bases*

|  |  |
|---|---|
| George Foster, 1977 | .749 |
| Will Clark, 1987 | .726 |
| George Brett, 1980 | .715 |
| Jack Clark, 1987 | .712 |
| Fred Lynn, 1979 | .690 |
| Darryl Strawberry, 1985 | .686 |
| Mike Schmidt, 1980 | .675 |
| Mike Easler, 1980 | .672 |
| Willie Stargell, 1978 | .670 |
| Chris James, 1987 | .665 |
| Kevin Mitchell, 1989 | .664 |
| Rod Carew, 1977 | .661 |
| Mike Schmidt, 1987 | .653 |
| Don Money, 1982 | .645 |
| Larry Parrish, 1979 | .637 |
| Tony Armas, 1985 | .636 |
| Cecil Cooper, 1975 | .635 |
| Andre Dawson, 1987 | .635 |
| Pedro Guerrero, 1987 | .634 |
| Pedro Guerrero, 1982 | .633 |
| Kal Daniels, 1987 | .632 |
| Dale Murphy, 1987 | .632 |
| Larry Hisle, 1978 | .628 |
| Jim Rice, 1979 | .628 |
| Rickey Henderson, 1987 | .627 |

### CAREER BATTING AVERAGE WITH RUNNERS ON BASE

*Min. 200 Hits*

|  |  |
|---|---|
| Wade Boggs | .357 |
| Rod Carew | .348 |
| Tony Gwynn | .343 |
| Kirby Puckett | .332 |
| Lyman Bostock | .326 |
| Mike Greenwell | .325 |
| Don Mattingly | .324 |
| George Brett | .323 |
| Thurman Munson | .321 |
| Pete Rose | .319 |
| Pedro Guerrero | .318 |
| Dave Parker | .318 |
| Milt Thompson | .318 |
| Al Oliver | .316 |
| Cecil Cooper | .315 |
| Keith Hernandez | .315 |
| Bill Madlock | .313 |
| Pat Tabler | .313 |
| Tim Raines | .312 |
| Will Clark | .310 |
| Bill Buckner | .308 |
| Mike Easler | .307 |
| Kevin Seitzer | .307 |
| Manny Sanguillen | .307 |
| Robin Yount | .307 |

### SINGLE-SEASON BATTING AVERAGE WITH RUNNERS ON BASE

*Min. 75 Hits*

|  |  |
|---|---|
| Rod Carew, 1977 | .422 |
| Lonnie Smith, 1989 | .407 |
| Tony Gwynn, 1984 | .406 |
| George Brett, 1980 | .400 |
| Garry Templeton, 1979 | .388 |
| Wade Boggs, 1985 | .387 |
| Fred Lynn, 1979 | .387 |
| Keith Hernandez, 1979 | .383 |
| Dave Parker, 1978 | .383 |
| Tony Gwynn, 1988 | .382 |
| Wade Boggs, 1986 | .379 |
| Garry Templeton, 1977 | .378 |
| Rod Carew, 1975 | .377 |
| Robin Yount, 1987 | .376 |
| Mickey Rivers, 1977 | .373 |
| Bill Madlock, 1975 | .370 |
| Manny Sanguillen, 1975 | .370 |
| Bill Madlock, 1976 | .368 |
| Hal McRae, 1976 | .368 |
| George Brett, 1985 | .367 |
| Hal McRae, 1982 | .366 |
| Pete Rose, 1975 | .366 |
| Fred Lynn, 1975 | .365 |
| Ken Griffey, 1976 | .362 |
| Cecil Cooper, 1980 | .362 |

### CAREER BATTING AVERAGE WITH RUNNERS IN SCORING POSITION

*Min. 100 Hits*

|  |  |
|---|---|
| Wade Boggs | .354 |
| Rod Carew | .345 |
| Tony Gwynn | .333 |
| Thurman Munson | .329 |
| Pat Tabler | .324 |
| Lyman Bostock | .324 |
| Kirby Puckett | .323 |
| Pete Rose | .323 |
| Al Oliver | .323 |
| Don Mattingly | .322 |
| George Brett | .319 |
| Broderick Perkins | .318 |
| Rennie Stennett | .315 |
| Cecil Cooper | .315 |
| Lou Piniella | .314 |
| Will Clark | .314 |
| Bill Madlock | .314 |
| Dane Iorg | .313 |
| Lamar Johnson | .312 |
| Mike Greenwell | .312 |
| Julio Franco | .310 |
| Paul Molitor | .310 |
| Tim Raines | .310 |
| Jim Rice | .310 |
| Robin Yount | .310 |

### SINGLE-SEASON BATTING AVERAGE WITH RUNNERS IN SCORING POSITION

*Min. 50 Hits*

|  |  |
|---|---|
| George Brett, 1980 | .466 |
| Cecil Cooper, 1980 | .421 |
| Tony Gwynn, 1984 | .418 |
| Bill Madlock, 1976 | .414 |
| Ken Griffey, 1976 | .412 |
| Pete Rose, 1975 | .412 |
| Julio Franco, 1989 | .407 |
| Don Mattingly, 1984 | .405 |
| Pedro Guerrero, 1989 | .405 |
| Fred Lynn, 1975 | .400 |
| Mickey Rivers, 1977 | .400 |
| Kent Hrbek, 1982 | .398 |
| Wade Boggs, 1985 | .392 |
| Robin Yount, 1982 | .392 |
| Joe Morgan, 1976 | .391 |
| Willie McGee, 1985 | .391 |
| Will Clark, 1989 | .389 |
| Hal McRae, 1982 | .383 |
| Pat Tabler, 1987 | .383 |
| Rod Carew, 1977 | .382 |
| Bake McBride, 1980 | .380 |
| Bill Robinson, 1977 | .380 |
| Garry Templeton, 1977 | .379 |
| Thurman Munson, 1975 | .376 |
| Rod Carew, 1978 | .375 |

### CAREER BATTING AVERAGE WITH 2 OUTS AND RUNNERS ON BASE

*Min. 75 Hits*

|  |  |
|---|---|
| Wade Boggs | .332 |
| Milt Thompson | .331 |
| Kirby Puckett | .330 |
| Larry Hisle | .321 |
| Thurman Munson | .320 |
| John Kruk | .317 |
| Eric Davis | .315 |
| Al Oliver | .311 |
| Larry Biittner | .307 |
| Cecil Cooper | .305 |
| Tony Gwynn | .304 |
| Jose Cardenal | .304 |
| Will Clark | .303 |
| Rico Carty | .303 |
| Bill Madlock | .302 |
| Rod Carew | .301 |
| Gene Richards | .301 |
| Lyman Bostock | .301 |
| Pedro Guerrero | .299 |
| Dave Parker | .298 |
| Don Mattingly | .298 |
| Pete Rose | .298 |
| Jose Canseco | .297 |
| Oscar Gamble | .297 |
| Alvin Davis | .296 |

### SINGLE-SEASON BATTING AVERAGE WITH 2 OUTS AND RUNNERS ON BASE

*Min. 30 Hits*

|  |  |
|---|---|
| Barry Bonnell, 1977 | .437 |
| Lee Lacy, 1984 | .432 |
| Lonnie Smith, 1989 | .429 |
| Al Oliver, 1980 | .424 |
| Bruce Bochte, 1982 | .418 |
| Dave Parker, 1986 | .412 |
| Pat Tabler, 1987 | .407 |
| Will Clark, 1989 | .405 |
| Ted Simmons, 1983 | .404 |
| Sixto Lezcano, 1979 | .402 |
| Garry Templeton, 1979 | .400 |
| Ray Knight, 1986 | .400 |
| Rod Carew, 1977 | .398 |
| Harold Baines, 1985 | .391 |
| Greg Gross, 1975 | .390 |
| Lee Mazzilli, 1979 | .390 |
| Larry Parrish, 1979 | .388 |
| Rod Carew, 1975 | .388 |
| Joe Rudi, 1976 | .386 |
| Frank Taveras, 1978 | .386 |
| Rennie Stennett, 1975 | .383 |
| Larry Hisle, 1978 | .379 |
| Steve Garvey, 1979 | .377 |
| Rod Carew, 1978 | .376 |
| Garry Templeton, 1977 | .376 |

### CAREER BATTING AVERAGE WITH 2 OUTS & RUNNERS IN SCORING POSITION

*Min. 50 Hits*

|  |  |
|---|---|
| Larry Hisle | .332 |
| Wade Boggs | .328 |
| Thurman Munson | .325 |
| John Kruk | .321 |
| Al Oliver | .320 |
| Eric Davis | .319 |
| Kirby Puckett | .317 |
| Milt Thompson | .315 |
| Will Clark | .313 |
| Lamar Johnson | .307 |
| Lyman Bostock | .304 |
| Pedro Guerrero | .304 |
| Gene Richards | .303 |
| Pete Rose | .303 |
| Lou Piniella | .303 |
| Tony Fernandez | .302 |
| John Castino | .302 |
| Dane Iorg | .302 |
| Terry Harper | .302 |
| Bill Madlock | .302 |
| Chris Brown | .302 |
| Jose Morales | .301 |
| Kevin Mitchell | .300 |
| Dale Sveum | .299 |
| Rod Carew | .299 |

### SINGLE-SEASON BATTING AVERAGE WITH 2 OUTS & RUNNERS IN SCORING POSITION

*Min. 20 Hits*

|  |  |
|---|---|
| Kent Hrbek, 1982 | .466 |
| Bruce Bochte, 1982 | .457 |
| Al Oliver, 1980 | .446 |
| Rod Carew, 1975 | .440 |
| Pat Tabler, 1987 | .440 |
| Ted Simmons, 1983 | .437 |
| Will Clark, 1989 | .435 |
| George Foster, 1981 | .426 |
| Chris Speier, 1978 | .426 |
| Pedro Guerrero, 1989 | .424 |
| Dave Parker, 1986 | .419 |
| Steve Sax, 1988 | .419 |
| Rod Carew, 1978 | .414 |
| Cecil Cooper, 1980 | .414 |
| Rod Carew, 1977 | .412 |
| Lee Mazzilli, 1978 | .412 |
| Joe Rudi, 1976 | .410 |
| Lyman Bostock, 1978 | .407 |
| Dave Winfield, 1979 | .407 |
| Mike Ivie, 1979 | .404 |
| Tony Fernandez, 1986 | .404 |
| Larry Hisle, 1978 | .403 |
| Lee Lacy, 1984 | .400 |
| Paul Molitor, 1986 | .400 |
| Rusty Staub, 1976 | .397 |

### CAREER BATTING AVERAGE IN LATE-INNING PRESSURE SITUATIONS

*Min. 50 Hits*

|  |  |
|---|---|
| Tony Gwynn | .344 |
| Tim Raines | .343 |
| Mike Greenwell | .335 |
| Kirby Puckett | .331 |
| Tony Fernandez | .325 |
| Milt Thompson | .325 |
| Wade Boggs | .322 |
| Steve Sax | .321 |
| Jerry Browne | .320 |
| Joe Lefebvre | .320 |
| George Brett | .318 |
| Cecil Cooper | .318 |
| Barry Larkin | .316 |
| Ken Griffey | .313 |
| Ron LeFlore | .312 |
| Tom Paciorek | .309 |
| Thurman Munson | .309 |
| Mickey Rivers | .309 |
| Jose Cardenal | .309 |
| Rickey Henderson | .309 |
| Mike Ivie | .308 |
| Ed Romero | .308 |
| Benito Santiago | .306 |
| George Bell | .306 |
| Gene Larkin | .306 |

### SINGLE-SEASON BATTING AVERAGE IN LATE-INNING PRESSURE SITUATIONS

*Min. 25 Hits*

|  |  |
|---|---|
| Manny Trillo, 1981 | .466 |
| Bill Madlock, 1975 | .464 |
| Mickey Rivers, 1977 | .439 |
| Wade Boggs, 1986 | .433 |
| George Brett, 1976 | .433 |
| Alan Trammell, 1987 | .431 |
| Steve Kemp, 1979 | .429 |
| Ken Griffey, 1975 | .423 |
| Tom Paciorek, 1976 | .419 |
| Mike Easler, 1984 | .416 |
| Mike Greenwell, 1989 | .413 |
| Scot Thompson, 1979 | .413 |
| Cecil Cooper, 1982 | .412 |
| Lloyd Moseby, 1983 | .410 |
| Luis Salazar, 1981 | .408 |
| Bill Buckner, 1984 | .403 |
| Chris Chambliss, 1981 | .403 |
| Alan Trammell, 1988 | .403 |
| Rick Manning, 1983 | .402 |
| Ken Griffey, 1986 | .402 |
| Cal Ripken, 1984 | .398 |
| Bill Buckner, 1978 | .397 |
| Will Clark, 1986 | .397 |
| Wade Boggs, 1985 | .395 |
| Tim Raines, 1987 | .394 |

### CAREER HOME RUN PCT. IN LATE-INNING PRESSURE SITUATIONS

*Min. 10 Home Runs*

|  |  |
|---|---|
| Gary Alexander | 7.80 |
| Ken Phelps | 7.69 |
| Steve Balboni | 7.18 |
| Dave Kingman | 6.90 |
| Mark McGwire | 6.84 |
| Craig Kusick | 6.78 |
| Eric Davis | 6.33 |
| Tony Armas | 6.03 |
| Andre Thornton | 6.01 |
| Eddie Murray | 5.90 |
| Darryl Strawberry | 5.64 |
| Mike Schmidt | 5.60 |
| Oscar Gamble | 5.57 |
| Reggie Smith | 5.56 |
| Graig Nettles | 5.51 |
| Bernie Carbo | 5.41 |
| Howard Johnson | 5.37 |
| Cory Snyder | 5.35 |
| Richie Zisk | 5.32 |
| Rob Deer | 5.28 |
| Dan Pasqua | 5.26 |
| Willie Stargell | 5.25 |
| Cliff Johnson | 5.24 |
| Reggie Jackson | 5.19 |
| Pat Putnam | 5.14 |

### CAREER BATTING AVG. IN LATE-INNING PRESSURE SITUATIONS WITH RUNNERS IN SCORING POSITION

*Min. 25 Hits*

|  |  |
|---|---|
| Eric Soderholm | .429 |
| Kevin Seitzer | .415 |
| Jose Canseco | .414 |
| Don Mattingly | .373 |
| Steve Lyons | .373 |
| Tim Raines | .370 |
| Will Clark | .361 |
| Willie Montanez | .355 |
| Luis Salazar | .353 |
| Eddie Murray | .352 |
| Lee May | .352 |
| Pete Rose | .346 |
| Dickie Thon | .345 |
| Oscar Gamble | .343 |
| George Bell | .342 |
| Thurman Munson | .341 |
| Tony Gwynn | .341 |
| Milt Thompson | .338 |
| Pedro Guerrero | .338 |
| Bruce Bochte | .337 |
| Mike Ivie | .333 |
| Reggie Smith | .333 |
| Dave Chalk | .333 |
| Garth Iorg | .333 |
| Wade Boggs | .331 |

### CAREER BATTING AVERAGE IN LATE-INNING PRESSURE SITUATIONS WITH RUNNERS ON BASE

*Min. 25 Hits*

|  |  |
|---|---|
| Mike Ivie | .370 |
| Tim Raines | .366 |
| Gene Larkin | .364 |
| Kevin Seitzer | .353 |
| Tony Gwynn | .350 |
| Dale Sveum | .348 |
| Eric Soderholm | .348 |
| Wade Boggs | .344 |
| Garth Iorg | .342 |
| Manny Mota | .342 |
| Bill Buckner | .339 |
| John Kruk | .337 |
| Thad Bosley | .336 |
| Jose Cardenal | .335 |
| Alan Trammell | .335 |
| Eddie Murray | .334 |
| Reggie Smith | .333 |
| Dave Rader | .333 |
| Herm Winningham | .333 |
| Pete Rose | .332 |
| Thurman Munson | .331 |
| U.L. Washington | .329 |
| Joe Torre | .329 |
| Jose Canseco | .328 |
| Will Clark | .328 |

### SINGLE-SEASON BATTING AVERAGE IN LATE-INNING PRESSURE SITUATIONS WITH RUNNERS ON BASE

*Min. 10 Hits*

|  |  |
|---|---|
| Rance Mulliniks, 1984 | .684 |
| Eddie Murray, 1985 | .567 |
| Bill Buckner, 1984 | .563 |
| Rey Quinones, 1987 | .538 |
| Rowland Office, 1975 | .536 |
| Rusty Staub, 1981 | .536 |
| Jack Clark, 1984 | .526 |
| Ron Oester, 1981 | .524 |
| Carmelo Castillo, 1989 | .524 |
| Pedro Guerrero, 1980 | .520 |
| Manny Trillo, 1981 | .520 |
| Carl Yastrzemski, 1975 | .500 |
| Ken Griffey, 1975 | .500 |
| Bernie Carbo, 1976 | .500 |
| Mickey Rivers, 1977 | .500 |
| Ken Singleton, 1977 | .500 |
| Pete Rose, 1977 | .500 |
| Barry Foote, 1979 | .500 |
| Glenn Adams, 1979 | .500 |
| Dan Ford, 1983 | .500 |
| Rob Deer, 1987 | .500 |
| Paul Molitor, 1987 | .500 |
| Milt Thompson, 1988 | .500 |
| Al Newman, 1989 | .500 |
| Rick Manning, 1983 | .486 |

### CAREER BATTING AVERAGE IN LATE-INNING PRESSURE SITUATIONS WITH 2 OUTS AND RUNNERS ON BASE

*Min. 15 Hits*

|  |  |
|---|---|
| Garth Iorg | .446 |
| Eric Soderholm | .429 |
| Benito Santiago | .417 |
| Tim Raines | .414 |
| Marty Perez | .405 |
| Milt Thompson | .388 |
| Mike Ivie | .387 |
| Dave Rader | .383 |
| Jose Canseco | .367 |
| Thurman Munson | .365 |
| Wade Boggs | .363 |
| Oscar Gamble | .355 |
| Hubie Brooks | .352 |
| Steve Henderson | .352 |
| Will Clark | .345 |
| Glenn Adams | .345 |
| Alan Trammell | .344 |
| H. Pat Kelly | .344 |
| Ed Ott | .343 |
| Manny Sanguillen | .341 |
| U.L. Washington | .338 |
| Tony Gwynn | .333 |
| Dave Revering | .333 |
| Rico Carty | .333 |
| Donnie Hill | .333 |

### CAREER BATTING AVG. IN LATE-INNING PRESSURE SITUATIONS WITH 2 OUTS AND RUNNERS IN SCORING POSITION

*Min. 10 Hits*

|  |  |
|---|---|
| Gene Larkin | .478 |
| Benito Santiago | .452 |
| Eric Soderholm | .444 |
| Garth Iorg | .441 |
| Wallace Johnson | .435 |
| Marty Perez | .435 |
| John Kruk | .417 |
| Jim Norris | .417 |
| Rusty Staub | .405 |
| Jose Canseco | .400 |
| Cesar Geronimo | .391 |
| Thurman Munson | .387 |
| Oscar Gamble | .381 |
| Vance Law | .380 |
| Don Mattingly | .379 |
| Willie Horton | .373 |
| Tim Raines | .372 |
| Pete Rose | .372 |
| Scott Bradley | .370 |
| Ernest Riles | .370 |
| Milt Thompson | .370 |
| Will Clark | .367 |
| Gary Pettis | .366 |
| Jose Cruz | .355 |
| Lee May | .352 |

## HIGHEST CAREER RATIO OF GROUND OUTS TO AIR OUTS

*Min. 1,000 PA*

|  |  |
|---|---|
| Milt Thompson | 2.48 |
| Wally Backman | 2.46 |
| Willie McGee | 2.21 |
| Steve Jeltz | 2.20 |
| Juan Bonilla | 2.10 |
| Rick Reuschel | 2.06 |
| Gary Pettis | 2.06 |
| Steve Henderson | 2.04 |
| Rafael Belliard | 2.03 |
| Duane Kuiper | 2.02 |
| Billy North | 2.02 |
| Bob Forsch | 2.01 |
| Steve Sax | 2.00 |
| Steve Carlton | 1.99 |
| Junior Ortiz | 1.95 |
| Joel Skinner | 1.94 |
| Gene Richards | 1.91 |
| Rod Carew | 1.89 |
| Alan Wiggins | 1.84 |
| Ron LeFlore | 1.82 |
| Miguel Dilone | 1.82 |
| Tony Gwynn | 1.79 |
| Jackie Gutierrez | 1.79 |
| Pete Rose | 1.79 |
| Jerry Mumphrey | 1.76 |

## LOWEST CAREER RATIO OF GROUND OUTS TO AIR OUTS

*Min. 1,000 PA*

|  |  |
|---|---|
| Howard Johnson | 0.61 |
| Mark McGwire | 0.62 |
| Rob Deer | 0.62 |
| Gene Tenace | 0.63 |
| Joe Carter | 0.65 |
| Ken Phelps | 0.65 |
| Joe Morgan | 0.65 |
| Andre Thornton | 0.65 |
| Jim Dwyer | 0.66 |
| Franklin Stubbs | 0.66 |
| Darrell Evans | 0.66 |
| Gary Redus | 0.67 |
| Don Baylor | 0.67 |
| Steve Balboni | 0.68 |
| Tom Brunansky | 0.69 |
| Mark Salas | 0.69 |
| Richie Hebner | 0.70 |
| Ron Kittle | 0.70 |
| Buck Martinez | 0.71 |
| Mike Schmidt | 0.71 |
| Dave Revering | 0.72 |
| Bobby Murcer | 0.73 |
| Jerry White | 0.74 |
| Tim Hulett | 0.74 |
| Dave Kingman | 0.75 |

## CAREER BATTING AVERAGE IN DAY GAMES

*Min. 100 Hits*

|  |  |
|---|---|
| Rod Carew | .347 |
| Wade Boggs | .344 |
| Don Mattingly | .332 |
| Tony Gwynn | .329 |
| Randy Ready | .326 |
| Mike Greenwell | .326 |
| Kevin Seitzer | .326 |
| Will Clark | .322 |
| George Brett | .318 |
| Paul Molitor | .318 |
| Willie McGee | .317 |
| Kirby Puckett | .317 |
| Bake McBride | .316 |
| Al Oliver | .315 |
| Carney Lansford | .313 |
| Lyman Bostock | .313 |
| Tim Raines | .313 |
| Ken Griffey | .312 |
| Jerry Grote | .312 |
| Wayne Krenchicki | .312 |
| Thurman Munson | .311 |
| Jose Morales | .311 |
| Reggie Smith | .310 |
| Gene Richards | .309 |
| Steve Kemp | .307 |

## CAREER BATTING AVERAGE IN NIGHT GAMES

*Min. 100 Hits*

|  |  |
|---|---|
| Wade Boggs | .356 |
| Tony Gwynn | .333 |
| Kirby Puckett | .326 |
| Rod Carew | .324 |
| Don Mattingly | .319 |
| Mike Greenwell | .316 |
| Pedro Guerrero | .313 |
| George Brett | .311 |
| Lyman Bostock | .310 |
| Mickey Rivers | .309 |
| Al Oliver | .306 |
| Mark Grace | .305 |
| Kal Daniels | .305 |
| Cecil Cooper | .304 |
| Manny Sanguillen | .303 |
| Bill Madlock | .302 |
| Julio Franco | .301 |
| Mike Easler | .301 |
| Rick Peters | .301 |
| Jim Rice | .300 |
| Thurman Munson | .300 |
| George Bell | .298 |
| Roberto Kelly | .298 |
| Pete Rose | .298 |
| Tim Raines | .298 |

## CAREER BATTING AVERAGE ON GRASS SURFACES

*Min. 150 Hits*

|  |  |
|---|---|
| Wade Boggs | .356 |
| Tony Gwynn | .332 |
| Rod Carew | .331 |
| Don Mattingly | .320 |
| Mike Greenwell | .318 |
| Al Oliver | .318 |
| Mark Grace | .313 |
| Lyman Bostock | .313 |
| Pedro Guerrero | .312 |
| Will Clark | .311 |
| Julio Franco | .306 |
| Thurman Munson | .306 |
| Bob Watson | .305 |
| Keith Hernandez | .305 |
| Dave Magadan | .304 |
| Jim Rice | .303 |
| Bill Madlock | .303 |
| Paul Molitor | .302 |
| Steve Garvey | .301 |
| Cecil Cooper | .301 |
| Jose Cardenal | .300 |
| Reggie Smith | .300 |
| Tim Raines | .300 |
| Kirby Puckett | .300 |
| Pat Tabler | .299 |

## CAREER BATTING AVERAGE ON ARTIFICIAL TURF

*Min. 150 Hits*

|  |  |
|---|---|
| Don Mattingly | .341 |
| Kirby Puckett | .338 |
| Rod Carew | .333 |
| Tony Gwynn | .332 |
| Wade Boggs | .332 |
| George Brett | .330 |
| Kevin Seitzer | .321 |
| John Kruk | .316 |
| Al Bumbry | .314 |
| Tracy Jones | .313 |
| Mickey Rivers | .312 |
| Von Joshua | .311 |
| Alan Trammell | .309 |
| Kal Daniels | .308 |
| Lee Lacy | .308 |
| Rick Leach | .307 |
| Mickey Hatcher | .306 |
| Mike Easler | .306 |
| Jim Gantner | .305 |
| Bill Madlock | .304 |
| Tim Raines | .304 |
| Chris Chambliss | .303 |
| Ken Griffey | .303 |
| Robin Yount | .303 |
| Cal Ripken | .303 |

## SINGLE-SEASON BATTING AVERAGE ON GRASS SURFACES

*Min. 60 Hits*

|  |  |
|---|---|
| George Brett, 1980 | .396 |
| Rod Carew, 1977 | .393 |
| Paul Molitor, 1987 | .376 |
| Tony Gwynn, 1987 | .374 |
| Pete Rose, 1979 | .373 |
| Ray Knight, 1983 | .370 |
| Wade Boggs, 1987 | .369 |
| Ken Griffey, 1976 | .368 |
| Rod Carew, 1975 | .367 |
| Keith Hernandez, 1979 | .366 |
| Gary Gaetti, 1986 | .364 |
| Wade Boggs, 1983 | .364 |
| Wade Boggs, 1985 | .363 |
| Wade Boggs, 1988 | .363 |
| Cecil Cooper, 1980 | .363 |
| Oscar Gamble, 1979 | .362 |
| Pat Sheridan, 1984 | .358 |
| Dan Gladden, 1984 | .357 |
| Dwight Smith, 1989 | .354 |
| Wade Boggs, 1982 | .354 |
| Wade Boggs, 1986 | .352 |
| Juan Beniquez, 1984 | .352 |
| Alan Trammell, 1987 | .352 |
| Bill Buckner, 1978 | .351 |
| Fred Lynn, 1979 | .350 |

## SINGLE-SEASON BATTING AVERAGE ON ARTIFICIAL TURF

*Min. 60 Hits*

|  |  |
|---|---|
| Bill Madlock, 1975 | .398 |
| Steve Sax, 1986 | .387 |
| George Brett, 1980 | .386 |
| Hal McRae, 1976 | .382 |
| Kirby Puckett, 1989 | .372 |
| Kirby Puckett, 1988 | .370 |
| George Brett, 1979 | .369 |
| George Brett, 1976 | .367 |
| Keith Hernandez, 1985 | .364 |
| George Brett, 1978 | .357 |
| Lee Lacy, 1980 | .356 |
| Willie McGee, 1985 | .356 |
| George Brett, 1981 | .356 |
| Greg Gross, 1983 | .356 |
| Pete Rose, 1976 | .354 |
| Bake McBride, 1976 | .354 |
| Barry Larkin, 1989 | .353 |
| George Brett, 1975 | .352 |
| Bill Madlock, 1981 | .352 |
| Kirby Puckett, 1986 | .352 |
| George Brett, 1985 | .352 |
| Mike Easler, 1980 | .349 |
| Kent Hrbek, 1984 | .349 |
| Willie Wilson, 1982 | .349 |
| Pete Rose, 1981 | .348 |

### CAREER ON-BASE AVERAGE LEADING OFF INNINGS

*Min. 200 PA*

|  |  |
|---|---|
| Wade Boggs | .441 |
| Fred McGriff | .414 |
| Mark Grace | .410 |
| Kal Daniels | .409 |
| Tony Gwynn | .401 |
| Rickey Henderson | .397 |
| Rod Carew | .392 |
| Willie Randolph | .385 |
| Pepe Mangual | .384 |
| Mike Hargrove | .382 |
| Tony Solaita | .382 |
| Alvin Davis | .380 |
| John Kruk | .379 |
| Mike Schmidt | .378 |
| Tim Raines | .378 |
| Bob Stinson | .377 |
| Greg Gross | .377 |
| Mike Greenwell | .377 |
| Jerome Walton | .377 |
| Bobby Grich | .377 |
| Jack Clark | .376 |
| Jody Reed | .375 |
| Gene Tenace | .375 |
| Otto Velez | .375 |
| Phil Bradley | .374 |

### SINGLE-SEASON ON-BASE AVERAGE LEADING OFF INNINGS

*Min. 100 PA*

|  |  |
|---|---|
| Rod Carew, 1982 | .523 |
| Andre Thornton, 1975 | .519 |
| Carlton Fisk, 1977 | .504 |
| Wade Boggs, 1983 | .494 |
| Toby Harrah, 1981 | .491 |
| Wade Boggs, 1988 | .476 |
| Joe Morgan, 1975 | .470 |
| Ozzie Smith, 1987 | .469 |
| Wade Boggs, 1985 | .468 |
| Ken Griffey, 1977 | .466 |
| Phil Bradley, 1987 | .463 |
| Kirby Puckett, 1987 | .462 |
| Fred McGriff, 1988 | .460 |
| Willie Randolph, 1980 | .457 |
| Wade Boggs, 1987 | .457 |
| Hal McRae, 1977 | .456 |
| Kirby Puckett, 1988 | .453 |
| Mike Hargrove, 1977 | .453 |
| Mitchell Page, 1977 | .452 |
| Cal Ripken, 1984 | .452 |
| Alvin Davis, 1989 | .451 |
| Kal Daniels, 1987 | .450 |
| Willie Randolph, 1985 | .448 |
| Jose Cruz, 1979 | .448 |
| Richie Zisk, 1981 | .447 |

### CAREER WALK PCT. LEADING OFF INNINGS

*Min. 25 Walks*

|  |  |
|---|---|
| Jim Wynn | 19.71 |
| Gene Tenace | 15.78 |
| Joe Morgan | 15.34 |
| Bernie Carbo | 15.05 |
| Fred McGriff | 14.85 |
| Pepe Mangual | 14.76 |
| Otto Velez | 14.55 |
| Glenn Borgmann | 14.35 |
| Jerry Hairston | 14.15 |
| Rickey Henderson | 14.09 |
| Dwayne Murphy | 14.03 |
| Tommy Hutton | 14.00 |
| Steve Jeltz | 13.86 |
| Joe Ferguson | 13.84 |
| Ken Phelps | 13.75 |
| Mike Hargrove | 13.67 |
| Willie Randolph | 13.65 |
| Billy North | 13.62 |
| Bud Harrelson | 13.56 |
| Lee Mazzilli | 13.46 |
| Jack Clark | 13.40 |
| Merv Rettenmund | 13.27 |
| Toby Harrah | 13.17 |
| Tony Solaita | 13.16 |
| Rick Peters | 13.13 |

### SINGLE-SEASON WALK PCT. LEADING OFF INNINGS

*Min. 15 Walks*

|  |  |
|---|---|
| John Cangelosi, 1987 | 24.77 |
| Jim Wynn, 1975 | 23.85 |
| Jack Clark, 1987 | 23.39 |
| Dwayne Murphy, 1987 | 23.08 |
| Lee Mazzilli, 1982 | 22.97 |
| Lee Mazzilli, 1983 | 22.50 |
| Joe Morgan, 1975 | 22.00 |
| Gene Tenace, 1977 | 21.43 |
| Dwayne Murphy, 1981 | 21.43 |
| Andre Thornton, 1975 | 21.30 |
| Carlton Fisk, 1977 | 21.17 |
| Bernie Carbo, 1975 | 21.05 |
| Jerry Hairston, 1984 | 20.55 |
| Mike Scioscia, 1985 | 20.54 |
| Jack Clark, 1989 | 20.45 |
| Gary Matthews, 1984 | 19.82 |
| Toby Harrah, 1981 | 19.81 |
| Steve Kemp, 1981 | 19.74 |
| Toby Harrah, 1985 | 19.71 |
| Johnny Briggs, 1975 | 19.15 |
| Gene Tenace, 1979 | 19.05 |
| Mike Hargrove, 1977 | 18.95 |
| Willie Randolph, 1980 | 18.78 |
| Darrell Porter, 1975 | 18.75 |
| Willie Randolph, 1981 | 18.75 |

### CAREER BATTING AVERAGE WITH BASES LOADED

*Min. 15 Hits*

|  |  |
|---|---|
| Pat Tabler | .507 |
| Rudy Law | .469 |
| Miguel Dilone | .436 |
| Biff Pocoroba | .435 |
| Rick Bosetti | .429 |
| Lou Brock | .423 |
| Ken Singleton | .417 |
| Ellis Valentine | .417 |
| Bill Madlock | .411 |
| Rico Carty | .404 |
| Denny Walling | .404 |
| Lee May | .402 |
| Eddie Murray | .401 |
| Jay Johnstone | .400 |
| Tony Gwynn | .400 |
| Oscar Gamble | .392 |
| Larry Hisle | .389 |
| Rod Carew | .388 |
| Alan Trammell | .385 |
| Eric Davis | .385 |
| Dale Berra | .383 |
| Richie Zisk | .382 |
| Mel Hall | .379 |
| Johnny Grubb | .379 |
| Larry Sheets | .375 |

### CAREER RBI RATIO (PER PA) WITH BASES LOADED

*Min. 30 RBI*

|  |  |
|---|---|
| Darryl Motley | 1.13 |
| John Milner | 1.10 |
| Eddie Murray | 1.07 |
| Biff Pocoroba | 1.06 |
| Terry Crowley | 1.05 |
| Mike Cubbage | 1.04 |
| Pat Tabler | 1.04 |
| Dane Iorg | 1.03 |
| Rico Carty | 1.00 |
| Lee Stanton | 1.00 |
| Roy Howell | 0.99 |
| Oscar Gamble | 0.99 |
| Jose Cruz | 0.98 |
| H. Pat Kelly | 0.98 |
| Dale Berra | 0.98 |
| Ellis Burks | 0.98 |
| Steve Garvey | 0.98 |
| Joe Rudi | 0.98 |
| George Bell | 0.97 |
| Greg Walker | 0.97 |
| Todd Benzinger | 0.96 |
| John Wockenfuss | 0.96 |
| Cory Snyder | 0.96 |
| Wally Joyner | 0.96 |
| Rod Carew | 0.96 |

### CAREER WALK PCT. WITH BASES LOADED

*Min. 10 Walks*

|  |  |
|---|---|
| Mickey Tettleton | 21.28 |
| Oscar Gamble | 17.65 |
| Mike Hargrove | 17.48 |
| Sixto Lezcano | 17.12 |
| Gene Tenace | 16.09 |
| Gary Roenicke | 15.91 |
| Pete Rose | 15.57 |
| Leon Durham | 15.49 |
| Darrell Porter | 15.32 |
| Joe Morgan | 14.55 |
| Terry Puhl | 13.41 |
| Dwight Evans | 13.33 |
| Alvin Davis | 13.25 |
| Jeff Burroughs | 12.90 |
| Dave Winfield | 12.77 |
| Ken Oberkfell | 12.63 |
| Jack Clark | 12.42 |
| Dan Driessen | 12.40 |
| Carl Yastrzemski | 12.15 |
| Rickey Henderson | 11.86 |
| Bobby Murcer | 11.58 |
| Ken Singleton | 11.48 |
| Darrell Evans | 11.36 |
| Butch Wynegar | 10.94 |
| Dave Lopes | 10.91 |

### CAREER STRIKEOUT PCT. WITH BASES LOADED

*Min. 50 PA*

|  |  |
|---|---|
| Rico Carty | 1.43 |
| Jim Spencer | 1.89 |
| Biff Pocoroba | 1.92 |
| Craig Reynolds | 1.98 |
| Jerry Morales | 2.02 |
| Ozzie Smith | 2.78 |
| Dave Cash | 3.03 |
| Brett Butler | 3.37 |
| Dave Bergman | 3.45 |
| Bruce Benedict | 3.53 |
| Bill Buckner | 3.61 |
| Lyman Bostock | 3.92 |
| Jose Cardenal | 4.00 |
| Ellis Valentine | 4.00 |
| Doug Flynn | 4.08 |
| Pete O'Brien | 4.17 |
| Rich Dauer | 4.35 |
| Bill Madlock | 4.46 |
| Lenny Randle | 4.62 |
| Frank Taveras | 4.62 |
| Jose Cruz | 4.72 |
| Larry Bowa | 4.81 |
| Mike Scioscia | 4.82 |
| Rafael Ramirez | 5.04 |
| Ozzie Guillen | 5.08 |

## CAREER PCT. OF RUNS BATTED IN FROM SCORING POSITION

*Min. 100 RBI*

|  |  |
|---|---|
| Don Mattingly | .366 |
| Thurman Munson | .352 |
| Dane Iorg | .352 |
| Broderick Perkins | .349 |
| George Brett | .349 |
| Al Oliver | .349 |
| Rusty Staub | .349 |
| Cecil Cooper | .347 |
| Rod Carew | .346 |
| Wade Boggs | .344 |
| Pedro Guerrero | .343 |
| Wally Joyner | .341 |
| Lou Piniella | .341 |
| Ted Simmons | .340 |
| Rico Carty | .340 |
| Dave Winfield | .340 |
| Mike Hargrove | .340 |
| Larry Hisle | .338 |
| Kent Hrbek | .338 |
| Keith Hernandez | .336 |
| Bill Madlock | .335 |
| Hal McRae | .335 |
| Lyman Bostock | .334 |
| Dave Parker | .333 |
| Bill Buckner | .332 |

## SINGLE-SEASON PCT. OF RUNS BATTED IN FROM SCORING POSITION

*Min. 50 RBI*

|  |  |
|---|---|
| George Brett, 1980 | .507 |
| Bill Buckner, 1981 | .476 |
| Cecil Cooper, 1980 | .470 |
| Bill Madlock, 1976 | .448 |
| Pedro Guerrero, 1989 | .447 |
| Dave Parker, 1976 | .430 |
| Eddie Murray, 1985 | .428 |
| Bill Buckner, 1978 | .427 |
| Richie Hebner, 1980 | .422 |
| Lonnie Smith, 1989 | .420 |
| Cecil Cooper, 1976 | .420 |
| Bake McBride, 1980 | .419 |
| Buddy Bell, 1984 | .418 |
| Larry Parrish, 1986 | .415 |
| John Milner, 1976 | .412 |
| Harold Baines, 1987 | .412 |
| Rod Carew, 1977 | .411 |
| Tony Gwynn, 1988 | .410 |
| Ted Simmons, 1983 | .410 |
| Tom Herr, 1985 | .409 |
| Rod Carew, 1975 | .408 |
| Joe Morgan, 1978 | .408 |
| Joe Morgan, 1976 | .408 |
| Pat Tabler, 1985 | .407 |
| Kent Hrbek, 1984 | .405 |

## CAREER PCT. OF RUNS BATTED IN FROM SCORING POSITION IN LATE-INNING PRESSURE SITUATIONS

*Min. 20 RBI*

|  |  |
|---|---|
| Eric Soderholm | .427 |
| Jose Canseco | .404 |
| Jim Essian | .403 |
| Pedro Guerrero | .401 |
| Jim Norris | .392 |
| Don Mattingly | .390 |
| Eddie Murray | .388 |
| Pete LaCock | .379 |
| Lenn Sakata | .377 |
| Gene Larkin | .375 |
| Kevin Seitzer | .372 |
| Mike Hargrove | .369 |
| Eddie Milner | .367 |
| Rico Carty | .364 |
| Ernest Riles | .362 |
| Bill Melton | .361 |
| Tony Gwynn | .358 |
| Rusty Staub | .357 |
| Reggie Smith | .354 |
| Ellis Valentine | .352 |
| Oscar Gamble | .349 |
| Garth Iorg | .346 |
| Wally Joyner | .346 |
| Ken Singleton | .345 |
| Tommy Hutton | .344 |

## SINGLE-SEASON RBI OPPORTUNITIES FROM SCORING POSITION

|  |  |
|---|---|
| Tony Perez, 1975 | 268 |
| Willie McGee, 1987 | 260 |
| Don Baylor, 1979 | 257 |
| Jim Rice, 1986 | 250 |
| Tim Wallach, 1987 | 247 |
| Johnny Bench, 1975 | 246 |
| George Foster, 1976 | 245 |
| Julio Franco, 1985 | 244 |
| George Foster, 1977 | 243 |
| Bill Buckner, 1986 | 242 |
| Keith Moreland, 1985 | 238 |
| Jerry Morales, 1975 | 236 |
| Bob Watson, 1976 | 236 |
| Lance Parrish, 1983 | 235 |
| Ruben Sierra, 1987 | 233 |
| Tom Herr, 1985 | 232 |
| Joe Carter, 1987 | 232 |
| Greg Luzinski, 1975 | 230 |
| Thurman Munson, 1976 | 229 |
| Cecil Cooper, 1983 | 229 |
| Mike Greenwell, 1988 | 229 |
| Jim Rice, 1975 | 228 |
| Jim Rice, 1984 | 228 |
| Willie Montanez, 1975 | 227 |
| Steve Garvey, 1978 | 227 |

## CAREER PCT. OF RUNS BATTED IN FROM 3D BASE WITH LESS THAN 2 OUTS

*Min. 40 RBI*

|  |  |
|---|---|
| Broderick Perkins | .753 |
| Rico Carty | .722 |
| Ed Kranepool | .720 |
| Tony Solaita | .719 |
| Mark Grace | .719 |
| Rod Carew | .719 |
| Tony Gwynn | .707 |
| Wade Boggs | .705 |
| Don Mattingly | .701 |
| Jerry Hairston | .699 |
| Manny Sanguillen | .695 |
| Al Oliver | .692 |
| Wally Joyner | .690 |
| Mike Hargrove | .689 |
| Rick Leach | .689 |
| George Brett | .687 |
| Rusty Staub | .686 |
| Wayne Krenchicki | .682 |
| Bill Madlock | .680 |
| Mel Hall | .679 |
| Pete Rose | .677 |
| Dave Winfield | .677 |
| Pat Tabler | .676 |
| Hal McRae | .675 |
| Toby Harrah | .674 |

## SINGLE-SEASON PCT. OF RUNS BATTED IN FROM 3D BASE WITH LESS THAN 2 OUTS

*Min. 15 RBI*

|  |  |
|---|---|
| Ben Oglivie, 1986 | .913 |
| Rod Carew, 1983 | .900 |
| Toby Harrah, 1981 | .889 |
| Bill Madlock, 1986 | .880 |
| Elliott Maddox, 1978 | .875 |
| Rickey Henderson, 1988 | .870 |
| Bill Madlock, 1976 | .868 |
| Tony Fernandez, 1989 | .867 |
| Charlie Hayes, 1989 | .864 |
| Dave Revering, 1979 | .857 |
| Kevin McReynolds, 1984 | .852 |
| Robin Yount, 1989 | .848 |
| Al Oliver, 1983 | .846 |
| Jerry Mumphrey, 1985 | .846 |
| Sid Bream, 1986 | .846 |
| Paul Molitor, 1978 | .842 |
| Dave Bergman, 1984 | .842 |
| Tom Foley, 1988 | .842 |
| Al Newman, 1989 | .842 |
| Pat Tabler, 1985 | .840 |
| George Brett, 1980 | .838 |
| Richie Hebner, 1976 | .833 |
| Rich Dauer, 1978 | .833 |
| Denny Walling, 1978 | .833 |
| Brian Downing, 1982 | .833 |

## CAREER PCT. OF RUNS BATTED IN FROM 1ST BASE

*Min. 30 RBI*

|  |  |
|---|---|
| Willie Stargell | .110 |
| Eric Davis | .107 |
| Mark McGwire | .100 |
| Darryl Strawberry | .099 |
| Jose Canseco | .098 |
| Glenn Davis | .097 |
| Mike Schmidt | .096 |
| Paul O'Neill | .095 |
| Alvin Davis | .095 |
| Greg Luzinski | .092 |
| Larry Hisle | .091 |
| Will Clark | .091 |
| Dave Kingman | .091 |
| Danny Tartabull | .089 |
| Hal McRae | .089 |
| Dave Parker | .088 |
| Ken Phelps | .088 |
| Steve Balboni | .087 |
| Reggie Jackson | .087 |
| Oscar Gamble | .086 |
| Bill Robinson | .086 |
| Ron Kittle | .085 |
| Dale Murphy | .084 |
| Nick Esasky | .083 |
| George Brett | .083 |

## SINGLE-SEASON RUNS BATTED IN FROM 1ST BASE

|  |  |
|---|---|
| Hal McRae, 1982 | 36 |
| George Foster, 1977 | 31 |
| Jim Rice, 1978 | 29 |
| Don Mattingly, 1985 | 29 |
| Greg Luzinski, 1977 | 28 |
| Alvin Davis, 1984 | 28 |
| Keith Hernandez, 1979 | 27 |
| Joe Carter, 1986 | 26 |
| Jim Rice, 1983 | 25 |
| Kevin Mitchell, 1989 | 25 |
| Fred Lynn, 1979 | 24 |
| Steve Garvey, 1979 | 24 |
| Dave Kingman, 1984 | 24 |
| Jose Canseco, 1986 | 24 |
| Mike Greenwell, 1988 | 24 |
| Jeff Burroughs, 1977 | 23 |
| Ron Cey, 1977 | 23 |
| Jim Rice, 1979 | 23 |
| Tony Armas, 1980 | 23 |
| Tony Perez, 1980 | 23 |
| Mike Schmidt, 1983 | 23 |
| Eddie Murray, 1985 | 23 |
| Darryl Strawberry, 1987 | 23 |
| Fred Lynn, 1975 | 22 |
| Johnny Bench, 1975 | 22 |

## CAREER OPP. BATTING AVERAGE VS. LEFT-HANDED BATTERS

*Min. 400 PA*

|  |  |
|---|---|
| Jesse Orosco | .184 |
| Mark Langston | .188 |
| Mitch Williams | .191 |
| John Franco | .201 |
| Pat Underwood | .201 |
| Bob Lacey | .201 |
| Dave Dravecky | .203 |
| Mark Davis | .204 |
| Atlee Hammaker | .205 |
| Juan Agosto | .206 |
| Rod Scurry | .206 |
| Nolan Ryan | .206 |
| Sid Fernandez | .206 |
| John Candelaria | .207 |
| Willie Hernandez | .210 |
| Bill Scherrer | .210 |
| Frank DiPino | .212 |
| Bob McClure | .215 |
| Al Holland | .215 |
| Mike Norris | .216 |
| John Fulgham | .216 |
| Craig Lefferts | .217 |
| Joe Sambito | .218 |
| Dwight Gooden | .218 |
| Larry Gura | .218 |

## CAREER OPP. HOME RUN PCT. VS. LEFT-HANDED BATTERS

*Min. 400 PA*

|  |  |
|---|---|
| Chuck Finley | 0.45 |
| Mickey Lolich | 0.46 |
| Doug Sisk | 0.47 |
| Bert Roberge | 0.51 |
| Paul Mirabella | 0.55 |
| Zane Smith | 0.56 |
| Dave Smith | 0.58 |
| Jim Crawford | 0.64 |
| Bruce Berenyi | 0.69 |
| Joe Sambito | 0.69 |
| Ken Hill | 0.72 |
| Juan Agosto | 0.73 |
| John Franco | 0.78 |
| Jeff Lahti | 0.80 |
| Greg Minton | 0.80 |
| Ricky Horton | 0.82 |
| Gary Lavelle | 0.82 |
| Jesse Orosco | 0.86 |
| Steve Trout | 0.94 |
| Pedro Borbon | 0.94 |
| Andy Hassler | 0.95 |
| Danny Jackson | 0.96 |
| Bob Shirley | 0.99 |
| Jay Howell | 0.99 |
| Dwight Gooden | 0.99 |

## CAREER OPP. WALK PCT. VS. LEFT-HANDED BATTERS

*Min. 400 PA*

|  |  |
|---|---|
| Steve Howe | 3.06 |
| Gary Nolan | 3.23 |
| Scott McGregor | 4.16 |
| Dick Bosman | 4.75 |
| Curt Young | 4.78 |
| Tom Burgmeier | 4.80 |
| Jim Kaat | 5.13 |
| Jon Matlack | 5.14 |
| Ted Higuera | 5.14 |
| John Tudor | 5.34 |
| Dave Tomlin | 5.37 |
| Will McEnaney | 5.42 |
| Dan Quisenberry | 5.42 |
| Jose Bautista | 5.52 |
| Oil Can Boyd | 5.55 |
| John Candelaria | 5.59 |
| Randy Jones | 5.63 |
| Jimmy Key | 5.65 |
| Frank Viola | 5.65 |
| Bob Knepper | 5.66 |
| Charlie Leibrandt | 5.67 |
| Pedro Borbon | 5.69 |
| Ron Guidry | 5.72 |
| Frank Tanana | 5.72 |
| Bret Saberhagen | 5.78 |

## CAREER OPP. STRIKEOUT PCT. VS. LEFT-HANDED BATTERS

*Min. 100 Strikeouts*

|  |  |
|---|---|
| Rob Dibble | 32.69 |
| Tom Henke | 28.22 |
| Sid Fernandez | 26.66 |
| Mitch Williams | 26.55 |
| Mark Davis | 25.45 |
| Nolan Ryan | 24.97 |
| Jesse Orosco | 24.65 |
| Mark Langston | 24.31 |
| John Candelaria | 24.19 |
| John Tudor | 23.42 |
| Al Holland | 23.35 |
| Joe Sambito | 23.22 |
| Dave Righetti | 22.94 |
| Zane Smith | 22.61 |
| Rod Scurry | 22.12 |
| Matt Young | 21.90 |
| Ted Higuera | 21.65 |
| Tippy Martinez | 21.48 |
| Lee Smith | 21.35 |
| Steve Carlton | 21.31 |
| Todd Worrell | 21.22 |
| Gary Lavelle | 21.08 |
| Dave Dravecky | 21.03 |
| Frank DiPino | 20.94 |
| Bill Caudill | 20.84 |

## CAREER OPP. BATTING AVERAGE VS. RIGHT-HANDED BATTERS

*Min. 600 PA*

|  |  |
|---|---|
| Jose DeLeon | .184 |
| J.R. Richard | .190 |
| Mike Jackson | .190 |
| David Cone | .198 |
| Tim Burke | .199 |
| Floyd Youmans | .201 |
| Mark Littell | .202 |
| Rich Gossage | .203 |
| Luis DeLeon | .204 |
| Pat Perry | .204 |
| Sid Fernandez | .204 |
| Tom Henke | .205 |
| Victor Cruz | .206 |
| Mario Soto | .207 |
| Scott Garrelts | .208 |
| Mitch Williams | .208 |
| Andy Messersmith | .209 |
| Mark Eichhorn | .209 |
| Orel Hershiser | .210 |
| Juan Berenguer | .210 |
| Nolan Ryan | .211 |
| Jeff Reardon | .212 |
| Roger Clemens | .212 |
| Skip Lockwood | .213 |
| Dan Warthen | .213 |

## CAREER OPP. HOME RUN PCT. VS. RIGHT-HANDED BATTERS

*Min. 600 PA*

|  |  |
|---|---|
| Mark Fidrych | 0.63 |
| Rick Lysander | 0.70 |
| Duane Ward | 0.74 |
| Steve Howe | 0.80 |
| Randy Niemann | 0.93 |
| Joe Magrane | 0.95 |
| Doug Sisk | 0.95 |
| J.R. Richard | 0.98 |
| Dave Heaverlo | 1.00 |
| Kent Tekulve | 1.02 |
| Brian Holman | 1.07 |
| Dave Frost | 1.09 |
| Mike Barlow | 1.14 |
| Greg Minton | 1.19 |
| Roger McDowell | 1.20 |
| Dave Smith | 1.22 |
| Pablo Torrealba | 1.24 |
| Ed Farmer | 1.24 |
| Bill Swift | 1.26 |
| Mark Littell | 1.26 |
| Terry Forster | 1.27 |
| Jim Kern | 1.28 |
| Dan Quisenberry | 1.28 |
| Dale Murray | 1.31 |
| Dave Tomlin | 1.34 |

## CAREER OPP. WALK PCT. VS. RIGHT-HANDED BATTERS

*Min. 600 PA*

|  |  |
|---|---|
| Dan Quisenberry | 2.16 |
| LaMarr Hoyt | 3.49 |
| Gary Nolan | 3.51 |
| Bret Saberhagen | 3.61 |
| Bob Stanley | 4.24 |
| Lary Sorensen | 4.43 |
| Ferguson Jenkins | 4.52 |
| Dick Bosman | 4.65 |
| Jim Barr | 4.73 |
| Luis DeLeon | 4.77 |
| Larry Andersen | 4.84 |
| Fernando Arroyo | 4.84 |
| Dennis Leonard | 4.95 |
| Tom Hausman | 4.96 |
| Bill Gullickson | 5.03 |
| Roger Erickson | 5.08 |
| Derek Lilliquist | 5.08 |
| Rick Reuschel | 5.09 |
| Scott Sanderson | 5.09 |
| Moose Haas | 5.10 |
| Rick Wise | 5.12 |
| Tim Burke | 5.15 |
| Tim Leary | 5.15 |
| Ed Lynch | 5.19 |
| Mike Caldwell | 5.19 |

## CAREER OPP. STRIKEOUT PCT. VS. RIGHT-HANDED BATTERS

*Min. 150 Strikeouts*

|  |  |
|---|---|
| Tom Henke | 29.68 |
| Ken Howell | 27.55 |
| David Cone | 27.12 |
| Jose DeLeon | 27.10 |
| Lee Smith | 26.97 |
| Roger Clemens | 26.52 |
| Calvin Schiraldi | 26.15 |
| J.R. Richard | 26.06 |
| Mike Jackson | 25.76 |
| Nolan Ryan | 25.15 |
| Dwight Gooden | 25.11 |
| Skip Lockwood | 24.68 |
| Randy Myers | 24.59 |
| Cecilio Guante | 24.55 |
| Victor Cruz | 24.38 |
| Jeff Reardon | 24.38 |
| Mark Huismann | 24.23 |
| Mark Clear | 24.14 |
| Bobby Witt | 24.05 |
| Lance McCullers | 23.43 |
| Dan Plesac | 23.20 |
| Rich Gossage | 23.11 |
| Luis DeLeon | 22.96 |
| Mark Littell | 22.95 |
| Mark Eichhorn | 22.82 |

## SINGLE-SEASON OPP. BATTING AVERAGE VS. LEFT-HANDED BATTERS

*Min. 125 PA*

|  |  |
|---|---|
| Neal Heaton, 1989 | .132 |
| Gregg Olson, 1989 | .135 |
| Zane Smith, 1989 | .139 |
| Mark Langston, 1989 | .142 |
| Bill Dawley, 1983 | .142 |
| Bob Lacey, 1977 | .146 |
| Mitch Williams, 1987 | .146 |
| Bryan Harvey, 1988 | .147 |
| Mark Clear, 1984 | .147 |
| Dave Smith, 1984 | .152 |
| Nolan Ryan, 1981 | .153 |
| Lance McCullers, 1988 | .153 |
| Ron Guidry, 1978 | .156 |
| Bob Shirley, 1978 | .156 |
| Larry McWilliams, 1983 | .156 |
| Matt Young, 1983 | .158 |
| Gary Lavelle, 1984 | .158 |
| Bill Scherrer, 1983 | .158 |
| Bud Black, 1989 | .158 |
| Rich Wortham, 1979 | .159 |
| Larry Gura, 1983 | .159 |
| John Smiley, 1988 | .159 |
| Tom Burgmeier, 1980 | .159 |
| Mike Caldwell, 1978 | .160 |
| Sid Monge, 1979 | .161 |

## SINGLE-SEASON OPP. BATTING AVERAGE VS. RIGHT-HANDED BATTERS

*Min. 175 PA*

|  |  |
|---|---|
| J.R. Richard, 1980 | .124 |
| Mark Eichhorn, 1986 | .135 |
| Dave LaRoche, 1976 | .139 |
| Rich Gossage, 1977 | .140 |
| Jose DeLeon, 1989 | .146 |
| Mario Soto, 1980 | .147 |
| Lance McCullers, 1986 | .154 |
| Hank Webb, 1975 | .156 |
| Mike Scott, 1986 | .156 |
| Mark Clear, 1979 | .157 |
| Don Carman, 1985 | .161 |
| Jim Kern, 1979 | .161 |
| Jeff Reardon, 1984 | .161 |
| Aurelio Lopez, 1983 | .162 |
| Tom Niedenfuer, 1983 | .162 |
| Luis DeLeon, 1982 | .163 |
| Sid Monge, 1978 | .164 |
| Frank Williams, 1985 | .164 |
| David Cone, 1988 | .165 |
| Frank Williams, 1984 | .166 |
| Tim Burke, 1985 | .166 |
| Cecilio Guante, 1985 | .166 |
| Mike Scott, 1989 | .167 |
| Rob Dibble, 1989 | .167 |
| Jose DeLeon, 1984 | .168 |

## CAREER OPP. BATTING AVERAGE IN HOME GAMES

*Min. 500 PA*

|  |  |
|---|---|
| Randy Myers | .177 |
| Sid Fernandez | .187 |
| Jeff Parrett | .192 |
| Nolan Ryan | .197 |
| J.R. Richard | .197 |
| Jeff M. Robinson | .199 |
| Mike Jackson | .205 |
| Scott Garrelts | .205 |
| Dwight Gooden | .206 |
| Tom Henke | .207 |
| Mike Henneman | .207 |
| David Cone | .209 |
| Jose DeLeon | .210 |
| Bert Roberge | .212 |
| John Smiley | .213 |
| Lance McCullers | .215 |
| Mike Armstrong | .215 |
| John Smoltz | .215 |
| Joe Cowley | .215 |
| Mario Soto | .216 |
| Tim Belcher | .216 |
| Todd Worrell | .216 |
| Skip Lockwood | .217 |
| Bobby Witt | .218 |
| Al Holland | .218 |

## CAREER OPP. BATTING AVERAGE IN ROAD GAMES

*Min. 500 PA*

|  |  |
|---|---|
| Mitch Williams | .183 |
| Pat Perry | .190 |
| Mark Littell | .203 |
| John Fulgham | .208 |
| Jesse Orosco | .211 |
| Floyd Youmans | .216 |
| Bruce Sutter | .219 |
| Rich Gossage | .219 |
| Nolan Ryan | .221 |
| Steve Bedrosian | .222 |
| Tim Belcher | .222 |
| Rob Murphy | .222 |
| John Martin | .222 |
| Lee Smith | .223 |
| J.R. Richard | .223 |
| Tom Henke | .223 |
| Sid Fernandez | .224 |
| Dan Warthen | .224 |
| Roger Clemens | .224 |
| Mario Soto | .224 |
| Jose DeLeon | .225 |
| Dan Plesac | .226 |
| Andy Messersmith | .226 |
| Calvin Schiraldi | .226 |
| Tim Burke | .227 |

## CAREER OPP. BATTING AVERAGE ON GRASS SURFACES

*Min. 500 PA*

|  |  |
|---|---|
| Randy Myers | .186 |
| J.R. Richard | .195 |
| Danny Frisella | .199 |
| Sid Fernandez | .199 |
| Bryan Harvey | .201 |
| Tim Burke | .202 |
| Mitch Williams | .206 |
| Chuck Cary | .209 |
| Mark Littell | .211 |
| Nolan Ryan | .211 |
| Dan Warthen | .213 |
| David Cone | .215 |
| Dwight Gooden | .219 |
| Scott Garrelts | .219 |
| Tom Henke | .219 |
| Tim Belcher | .219 |
| Rod Scurry | .221 |
| Andy Messersmith | .221 |
| Rich Gossage | .222 |
| Dan Plesac | .222 |
| Bill Laxton | .222 |
| Jeff M. Robinson | .223 |
| DeWayne Buice | .223 |
| Joe Cowley | .223 |
| Brent Strom | .223 |

## CAREER OPP. BATTING AVERAGE ON ARTIFICIAL TURF

*Min. 500 PA*

|  |  |
|---|---|
| Jesse Orosco | .193 |
| Mike Norris | .194 |
| Roger Clemens | .201 |
| Craig McMurtry | .202 |
| Tom Gordon | .203 |
| Nolan Ryan | .205 |
| Mike Jackson | .206 |
| Jose DeLeon | .209 |
| Tom Henke | .211 |
| Mark Littell | .212 |
| Floyd Youmans | .212 |
| Rich Gossage | .213 |
| Jeff Parrett | .215 |
| J.R. Richard | .215 |
| Pat Perry | .215 |
| Sid Fernandez | .216 |
| Jim Kern | .216 |
| Tim Belcher | .217 |
| Mark Clear | .218 |
| Todd Worrell | .218 |
| Mario Soto | .219 |
| Rob Murphy | .219 |
| Al Holland | .220 |
| Scott Garrelts | .221 |
| Frank LaCorte | .222 |

## CAREER OPP. BATTING AVERAGE IN DAY GAMES

*Min. 250 PA*

|  |  |
|---|---|
| Eric Plunk | .196 |
| Nolan Ryan | .200 |
| Sid Fernandez | .205 |
| Scott Garrelts | .211 |
| Steve Ontiveros | .211 |
| Mark Littell | .214 |
| Joe Cowley | .214 |
| Roger Clemens | .215 |
| Mario Soto | .216 |
| Tim Burke | .216 |
| Al Hrabosky | .216 |
| Craig Lefferts | .216 |
| Steve Bedrosian | .217 |
| Bob James | .218 |
| Bob Kipper | .220 |
| Andy Messersmith | .221 |
| Rollie Fingers | .222 |
| Steve Busby | .222 |
| Bruce Berenyi | .223 |
| Rich Gossage | .224 |
| Rod Scurry | .224 |
| Tim Lollar | .225 |
| Dave Smith | .225 |
| J.R. Richard | .226 |
| Ted Higuera | .227 |

## CAREER OPP. BATTING AVERAGE IN NIGHT GAMES

*Min. 250 PA*

|  |  |
|---|---|
| Mitch Williams | .191 |
| Tom Gordon | .203 |
| Sid Fernandez | .204 |
| J.R. Richard | .205 |
| Randy Myers | .206 |
| Dwight Gooden | .207 |
| Jesse Orosco | .209 |
| Tom Henke | .209 |
| Tim Belcher | .209 |
| Jose DeLeon | .210 |
| Mark Littell | .210 |
| Nolan Ryan | .211 |
| Floyd Youmans | .213 |
| Pat Perry | .215 |
| Jeff Lahti | .215 |
| Rich Gossage | .217 |
| Mike Norris | .218 |
| John Smiley | .218 |
| Mike Jackson | .219 |
| David Cone | .221 |
| Joe Magrane | .221 |
| Chuck Cary | .221 |
| Luis DeLeon | .222 |
| Al Holland | .222 |
| Mario Soto | .222 |

### CAREER OPP. BATTING AVERAGE VS. GROUND-BALL HITTERS

*Min.: 500 PA*

|  |  |
|---|---|
| Jesse Orosco | .197 |
| Floyd Youmans | .202 |
| Sid Fernandez | .206 |
| J.R. Richard | .206 |
| Nolan Ryan | .208 |
| Doug Corbett | .209 |
| David Cone | .213 |
| Tim Belcher | .214 |
| Dwight Gooden | .215 |
| Pat Perry | .215 |
| Rod Scurry | .216 |
| Clay Carroll | .216 |
| Jeff Lahti | .218 |
| Andy McGaffigan | .218 |
| Scott Garrelts | .220 |
| Larry Demery | .220 |
| Bobby Thigpen | .220 |
| John Dopson | .221 |
| Jeff Parrett | .222 |
| John Smoltz | .222 |
| Orel Hershiser | .222 |
| Roger McDowell | .222 |
| Andy Messersmith | .222 |
| Mark Littell | .223 |
| Tim Burke | .225 |

### SINGLE-SEASON OPP. BATTING AVERAGE VS. GROUND-BALL HITTERS

*Min.: 150 PA*

|  |  |
|---|---|
| Jesse Orosco, 1983 | .144 |
| Floyd Youmans, 1986 | .156 |
| Gregg Olson, 1989 | .158 |
| Juan Nieves, 1988 | .160 |
| Tom Henke, 1986 | .160 |
| Tippy Martinez, 1983 | .165 |
| Jeff Lahti, 1984 | .165 |
| Andy McGaffigan, 1986 | .165 |
| Aurelio Lopez, 1978 | .165 |
| Sid Fernandez, 1985 | .166 |
| Mike Scott, 1988 | .166 |
| Bill Caudill, 1982 | .168 |
| Mike Madden, 1983 | .170 |
| Andy McGaffigan, 1988 | .170 |
| Tom Griffin, 1980 | .171 |
| Nolan Ryan, 1976 | .171 |
| Joe Sambito, 1980 | .172 |
| Don Carman, 1985 | .173 |
| Rich Gossage, 1977 | .173 |
| Charlie Hough, 1978 | .173 |
| David Palmer, 1982 | .174 |
| Bruce Sutter, 1977 | .176 |
| Dave LaRoche, 1976 | .178 |
| John Dopson, 1988 | .178 |
| Dave Stieb, 1988 | .179 |

### CAREER OPP. BATTING AVERAGE VS. FLY-BALL HITTERS

*Min.: 500 PA*

|  |  |
|---|---|
| Mitch Williams | .181 |
| Randy Myers | .196 |
| Tom Henke | .199 |
| Mark Littell | .201 |
| Jose DeLeon | .203 |
| Mike Jackson | .203 |
| Sid Fernandez | .203 |
| Nolan Ryan | .209 |
| Lance McCullers | .209 |
| Mario Soto | .210 |
| J.R. Richard | .213 |
| Rich Gossage | .214 |
| Jeff A. Jones | .216 |
| Bobby Witt | .216 |
| Dan Plesac | .216 |
| Buddy Schultz | .217 |
| Steve Bedrosian | .218 |
| Al Holland | .218 |
| Todd Worrell | .218 |
| Tom Niedenfuer | .218 |
| Dan Warthen | .218 |
| Scott Garrelts | .219 |
| Juan Berenguer | .219 |
| Jeff Reardon | .220 |
| Cecilio Guante | .220 |

### SINGLE-SEASON OPP. BATTING AVERAGE VS. FLY-BALL HITTERS

*Min.: 150 PA*

|  |  |
|---|---|
| Grant Jackson, 1976 | .129 |
| Tom Henke, 1989 | .131 |
| Tom Niedenfuer, 1983 | .133 |
| Mitch Williams, 1987 | .144 |
| Tom Hausman, 1979 | .147 |
| Rogelio Moret, 1977 | .147 |
| Mark Littell, 1976 | .149 |
| J.R. Richard, 1980 | .152 |
| Bob Stoddard, 1982 | .152 |
| Rob Dibble, 1989 | .152 |
| Tom Henke, 1987 | .154 |
| Bob Kipper, 1989 | .154 |
| John D'Acquisto, 1978 | .160 |
| Steve Ontiveros, 1985 | .161 |
| Ron Reed, 1976 | .162 |
| Lee Smith, 1983 | .162 |
| Sid Monge, 1979 | .163 |
| Jose Rijo, 1988 | .164 |
| Steve Bedrosian, 1989 | .164 |
| Ron Davis, 1981 | .164 |
| Bruce Sutter, 1981 | .167 |
| Cecilio Guante, 1985 | .167 |
| Rich Gossage, 1977 | .167 |
| Jose DeLeon, 1989 | .167 |
| Ed Vande Berg, 1982 | .168 |

### CAREER OPP. BATTING AVERAGE ON FIRST PASS THROUGH BATTING ORDER

*Min.: 500 PA*

|  |  |
|---|---|
| Rob Dibble | .184 |
| Sid Fernandez | .184 |
| Tim Belcher | .193 |
| Floyd Youmans | .194 |
| J.R. Richard | .194 |
| Dwight Gooden | .198 |
| Nolan Ryan | .204 |
| Mitch Williams | .204 |
| Jose DeLeon | .205 |
| Mark Littell | .205 |
| Bryan Harvey | .205 |
| Randy Myers | .210 |
| Roger Clemens | .210 |
| Mario Soto | .211 |
| Mike Jackson | .211 |
| Rod Scurry | .212 |
| Dan Warthen | .213 |
| Jesse Orosco | .213 |
| Ted Higuera | .214 |
| Rich Gossage | .214 |
| Jeff Calhoun | .215 |
| Tom Henke | .215 |
| Scott Garrelts | .217 |
| Steve Bedrosian | .217 |
| Eric Plunk | .217 |

### SINGLE-SEASON OPP. BATTING AVERAGE ON FIRST PASS THROUGH BATTING ORDER

*Min.: 150 PA*

|  |  |
|---|---|
| Rich Gossage, 1981 | .133 |
| Sid Fernandez, 1985 | .134 |
| Danny Darwin, 1979 | .137 |
| Nolan Ryan, 1983 | .143 |
| Nolan Ryan, 1986 | .147 |
| Atlee Hammaker, 1983 | .149 |
| Scott Bankhead, 1988 | .149 |
| J.R. Richard, 1980 | .156 |
| Rob Murphy, 1986 | .156 |
| Kevin Saucier, 1981 | .156 |
| Jose Guzman, 1988 | .158 |
| Dave LaRoche, 1976 | .158 |
| Rich Gossage, 1977 | .160 |
| Frank Viola, 1987 | .161 |
| Roger Clemens, 1986 | .161 |
| Juan Berenguer, 1983 | .161 |
| John D'Acquisto, 1978 | .161 |
| Dennis Eckersley, 1989 | .162 |
| Sid Fernandez, 1989 | .163 |
| Dennis Eckersley, 1975 | .164 |
| Bill Gullickson, 1981 | .165 |
| Jose DeLeon, 1986 | .167 |
| Tom Browning, 1988 | .168 |
| Bruce Sutter, 1979 | .168 |
| Dave Dravecky, 1982 | .168 |

### CAREER OPP. STRIKEOUT PCT. ON FIRST PASS THROUGH BATTING ORDER

*Min.: 100 SO*

|  |  |
|---|---|
| Rob Dibble | 31.75 |
| Tom Henke | 29.39 |
| Tim Belcher | 28.69 |
| Tom Gordon | 27.65 |
| Roger Clemens | 27.55 |
| Randy Myers | 27.39 |
| Sid Fernandez | 27.12 |
| J.R. Richard | 26.92 |
| Bryan Harvey | 26.35 |
| Nolan Ryan | 25.91 |
| Bobby Witt | 25.56 |
| Lee Smith | 24.63 |
| Floyd Youmans | 24.19 |
| Mark Langston | 24.18 |
| Dwight Gooden | 24.11 |
| Dan Plesac | 24.09 |
| Ken Howell | 24.07 |
| Jose DeLeon | 23.87 |
| Jose Rijo | 23.84 |
| Mark Davis | 23.60 |
| Eric Plunk | 23.24 |
| Bill Caudill | 23.14 |
| Mike Schooler | 23.06 |
| Ken Dixon | 23.04 |
| Calvin Schiraldi | 22.83 |

### SINGLE-SEASON OPP. STRIKEOUT PCT. ON FIRST PASS THROUGH BATTING ORDER

*Min.: 30 SO*

|  |  |
|---|---|
| Tom Henke, 1987 | 36.47 |
| Rob Dibble, 1989 | 35.61 |
| Andy Benes, 1989 | 34.44 |
| J.R. Richard, 1980 | 34.44 |
| Nolan Ryan, 1989 | 33.33 |
| Skip Lockwood, 1975 | 33.13 |
| Frank Tanana, 1975 | 33.11 |
| Lee Smith, 1989 | 32.87 |
| Tom Henke, 1989 | 32.74 |
| Tom Henke, 1986 | 32.64 |
| Bruce Sutter, 1977 | 32.53 |
| J.R. Richard, 1979 | 32.46 |
| Bruce Hurst, 1986 | 32.44 |
| Dwight Gooden, 1984 | 32.26 |
| Jose DeLeon, 1983 | 31.85 |
| Bryan Harvey, 1989 | 31.84 |
| Bill Caudill, 1979 | 31.51 |
| J.R. Richard, 1978 | 31.48 |
| Mario Soto, 1982 | 31.43 |
| Nolan Ryan, 1987 | 31.05 |
| Joe Price, 1987 | 31.03 |
| Bobby Witt, 1987 | 31.00 |
| Len Barker, 1977 | 31.00 |
| Roger Clemens, 1986 | 30.74 |
| Bill Caudill, 1982 | 30.70 |

### CAREER OPP. BATTING AVERAGE IN LATE-INNING PRESSURE SITUATIONS

*Min. 400 PA*

|  |  |
|---|---|
| Randy Myers | .183 |
| Tom Henke | .196 |
| Mark Davis | .198 |
| Nolan Ryan | .199 |
| Mitch Williams | .206 |
| J.R. Richard | .209 |
| Cecilio Guante | .209 |
| Jeff Russell | .212 |
| Mark Littell | .214 |
| Mike Boddicker | .217 |
| Mario Soto | .218 |
| Calvin Schiraldi | .218 |
| Mike Jackson | .218 |
| Steve Bedrosian | .220 |
| Rich Gossage | .221 |
| Eric Plunk | .221 |
| Sid Monge | .221 |
| Jesse Orosco | .222 |
| Don Stanhouse | .222 |
| John Candelaria | .223 |
| Scott Garrelts | .223 |
| Don Carman | .223 |
| Jeff Parrett | .223 |
| Skip Lockwood | .224 |
| Frank LaCorte | .224 |

### SINGLE-SEASON OPP. BATTING AVERAGE IN LATE-INNING PRESSURE SITUATIONS

*Min. 150 PA*

|  |  |
|---|---|
| Dave LaRoche, 1976 | .142 |
| Tom Niedenfuer, 1983 | .146 |
| Don Carman, 1985 | .157 |
| Bob Kipper, 1989 | .158 |
| Tom Seaver, 1976 | .163 |
| Ron Davis, 1981 | .166 |
| Fernando Valenzuela, 1985 | .167 |
| Bill Landrum, 1989 | .167 |
| Dennis Eckersley, 1977 | .168 |
| Bill Dawley, 1983 | .169 |
| Rich Gossage, 1977 | .169 |
| Greg Minton, 1989 | .170 |
| Tom Henke, 1986 | .171 |
| Randy Myers, 1988 | .171 |
| Aurelio Lopez, 1979 | .173 |
| Tom Henke, 1987 | .174 |
| Nolan Ryan, 1976 | .174 |
| Bill Caudill, 1982 | .175 |
| Manny Sarmiento, 1978 | .176 |
| Willie Hernandez, 1984 | .176 |
| Ed Farmer, 1979 | .177 |
| Jay Howell, 1988 | .177 |
| Skip Lockwood, 1976 | .179 |
| Roger Clemens, 1988 | .179 |
| J.R. Richard, 1976 | .179 |

### CAREER OPP. HOME RUN PCT. IN LATE-INNING PRESSURE SITUATIONS

*Min. 400 PA*

|  |  |
|---|---|
| Steve Comer | 0.61 |
| Jim Todd | 0.71 |
| Jeff Lahti | 0.73 |
| Doug Jones | 0.75 |
| Dave A. Roberts | 0.75 |
| Joe Hesketh | 0.81 |
| Doug Sisk | 0.84 |
| Don Stanhouse | 0.84 |
| Fernando Valenzuela | 0.87 |
| Bill Gullickson | 0.87 |
| Dale Murray | 0.96 |
| Randy Jones | 0.98 |
| Zane Smith | 0.98 |
| Clay Carroll | 1.00 |
| Steve Howe | 1.00 |
| Jay Howell | 1.02 |
| Dave Giusti | 1.04 |
| Juan Agosto | 1.06 |
| Pat Clements | 1.06 |
| Tommy John | 1.07 |
| Frank Williams | 1.09 |
| Ken Dayley | 1.09 |
| Darold Knowles | 1.09 |
| Chris Bosio | 1.10 |
| Don Carman | 1.11 |

### CAREER OPP. STRIKEOUT PCT. IN LATE-INNING PRESSURE SITUATIONS

*Min. 100 Strikeouts*

|  |  |
|---|---|
| Rob Dibble | 32.05 |
| Tom Henke | 31.31 |
| Bryan Harvey | 26.51 |
| Randy Myers | 25.88 |
| Nolan Ryan | 25.27 |
| Ken Howell | 24.75 |
| Mark Davis | 24.61 |
| Lee Smith | 24.08 |
| Scott Garrelts | 23.63 |
| Dwight Gooden | 23.61 |
| Roger Clemens | 23.43 |
| Calvin Schiraldi | 23.28 |
| Bill Caudill | 22.94 |
| Mark Clear | 22.77 |
| Duane Ward | 22.64 |
| Skip Lockwood | 22.56 |
| Mark Eichhorn | 22.33 |
| Mark Littell | 22.26 |
| Rich Gossage | 22.08 |
| Mitch Williams | 21.82 |
| Rob Murphy | 21.57 |
| Rod Scurry | 21.56 |
| John Hiller | 21.46 |
| Dan Plesac | 21.42 |
| Jesse Orosco | 21.20 |

### CAREER OPP. BATTING AVERAGE IN LATE-INNING PRESSURE SITUATIONS WITH RUNNERS ON BASE

*Min. 150 PA*

|  |  |
|---|---|
| Kevin Saucier | .160 |
| Randy Myers | .167 |
| Rob Dibble | .174 |
| Dave Tobik | .177 |
| Bryan Harvey | .178 |
| Cecilio Guante | .186 |
| Steve McCatty | .197 |
| Steve Bedrosian | .202 |
| Ron Darling | .202 |
| Dave Dravecky | .203 |
| Jesse Orosco | .204 |
| Roger Clemens | .204 |
| Jeff Montgomery | .207 |
| Sid Monge | .209 |
| Todd Worrell | .210 |
| Eric Plunk | .210 |
| Danny Frisella | .210 |
| Jack Morris | .210 |
| Dock Ellis | .211 |
| Randy Lerch | .211 |
| Kevin Hickey | .212 |
| Nolan Ryan | .212 |
| Mitch Williams | .213 |
| Bill Greif | .213 |
| Bret Saberhagen | .213 |

### SINGLE-SEASON OPP. BATTING AVERAGE IN LATE-INNING PRESSURE SITUATIONS WITH RUNNERS ON BASE

*Min. 60 PA*

|  |  |
|---|---|
| Frank Tanana, 1976 | .116 |
| Joe Sambito, 1981 | .121 |
| Randy Myers, 1988 | .126 |
| Jim Kern, 1976 | .128 |
| Dave LaRoche, 1976 | .128 |
| Bill Greif, 1976 | .130 |
| Dave Tobik, 1979 | .130 |
| Bill Landrum, 1989 | .130 |
| Bud Black, 1986 | .132 |
| Joaquin Andujar, 1978 | .133 |
| Nolan Ryan, 1978 | .134 |
| Steve Bedrosian, 1982 | .136 |
| Kevin Saucier, 1981 | .140 |
| Tim Burke, 1987 | .141 |
| Jesse Orosco, 1989 | .141 |
| Mike Torrez, 1975 | .143 |
| George Frazier, 1982 | .143 |
| Tug McGraw, 1980 | .146 |
| Andy Hassler, 1980 | .148 |
| Dave Dravecky, 1984 | .148 |
| George Frazier, 1983 | .149 |
| Tom Niedenfuer, 1983 | .150 |
| Jeff Reardon, 1981 | .151 |
| Jesse Orosco, 1983 | .152 |
| Jose Rijo, 1988 | .152 |

### CAREER OPP. HOME RUN PCT. IN LATE-INNING PRESSURE SITUATIONS WITH RUNNERS ON BASE

*Min. 150 PA*

|  |  |
|---|---|
| Bill Lee | 0.00 |
| Steve Comer | 0.00 |
| Joe Hesketh | 0.00 |
| Chris Bosio | 0.00 |
| Charlie Williams | 0.00 |
| Mark L. Lee | 0.00 |
| Ken Kravec | 0.00 |
| Kevin Saucier | 0.00 |
| Alejandro Pena | 0.32 |
| Dave Tomlin | 0.41 |
| Greg Minton | 0.43 |
| Steve Howe | 0.43 |
| Dwight Gooden | 0.44 |
| Dave A. Roberts | 0.45 |
| Vern Ruhle | 0.47 |
| Dave J. Schmidt | 0.53 |
| Bill Gullickson | 0.53 |
| Bob Ojeda | 0.54 |
| Fernando Valenzuela | 0.61 |
| Pete Vuckovich | 0.62 |
| Andy McGaffigan | 0.68 |
| Oil Can Boyd | 0.69 |
| Roy Thomas | 0.69 |
| Randy Lerch | 0.70 |
| Bill Bonham | 0.73 |

### CAREER OPP. STRIKEOUT PCT. IN LATE-INNING PRESSURE SITUATIONS WITH RUNNERS ON BASE

*Min. 40 Strikeouts*

|  |  |
|---|---|
| Rob Dibble | 30.06 |
| Tom Henke | 27.94 |
| Bryan Harvey | 27.32 |
| Randy Myers | 24.75 |
| Roger Clemens | 24.34 |
| Mark Clear | 24.06 |
| Bill Caudill | 23.28 |
| Nolan Ryan | 23.28 |
| Dwight Gooden | 23.26 |
| Calvin Schiraldi | 22.94 |
| Scott Garrelts | 22.85 |
| Mitch Williams | 22.76 |
| Lee Smith | 22.70 |
| Mark Davis | 21.70 |
| Ken Howell | 21.56 |
| Skip Lockwood | 21.50 |
| Mike Schooler | 21.30 |
| Duane Ward | 21.20 |
| Mark Littell | 21.19 |
| Matt Young | 20.97 |
| Alejandro Pena | 20.88 |
| Cecilio Guante | 20.43 |
| Lance McCullers | 20.30 |
| Rod Scurry | 20.09 |
| John Hiller | 20.00 |

### CAREER OPP. BATTING AVERAGE WITH RUNNERS ON BASE

*Min. 500 PA*

|  |  |
|---|---|
| Randy Myers | .190 |
| Jesse Orosco | .200 |
| Todd Worrell | .207 |
| Mitch Williams | .209 |
| Sid Fernandez | .215 |
| Tim Belcher | .217 |
| Mike Jackson | .218 |
| Dwight Gooden | .220 |
| Rod Scurry | .222 |
| Jim Deshaies | .222 |
| Tom Henke | .222 |
| Bill Caudill | .223 |
| Mark Clear | .223 |
| Craig Lefferts | .223 |
| J.R. Richard | .224 |
| Jeff Reardon | .225 |
| Mark Littell | .225 |
| Eric Plunk | .226 |
| Nolan Ryan | .226 |
| Orel Hershiser | .226 |
| Lance McCullers | .227 |
| Lee Smith | .227 |
| Mario Soto | .228 |
| Victor Cruz | .228 |
| Bruce Sutter | .228 |

### SINGLE-SEASON OPP. BATTING AVERAGE WITH RUNNERS ON BASE

*Min. 175 PA*

|  |  |
|---|---|
| John D'Acquisto, 1978 | .155 |
| Gene Garber, 1978 | .160 |
| Gregg Olson, 1989 | .164 |
| Jesse Orosco, 1984 | .167 |
| Rob Dibble, 1989 | .167 |
| Bill Caudill, 1980 | .173 |
| Mark Davis, 1989 | .174 |
| Jesse Orosco, 1983 | .175 |
| Jeff M. Robinson, 1988 | .175 |
| Jose DeLeon, 1986 | .175 |
| Rich Gossage, 1977 | .175 |
| Willie Hernandez, 1984 | .176 |
| Al Holland, 1983 | .177 |
| Charlie Hough, 1976 | .177 |
| Lee Smith, 1983 | .178 |
| Mike Jackson, 1988 | .179 |
| Jim Deshaies, 1986 | .180 |
| Dwight Gooden, 1985 | .180 |
| Mitch Williams, 1987 | .180 |
| Doug Bair, 1978 | .181 |
| Mike Scott, 1986 | .181 |
| Tippy Martinez, 1983 | .181 |
| Sid Monge, 1979 | .182 |
| Bruce Sutter, 1977 | .182 |
| Jesse Orosco, 1986 | .183 |

### CAREER OPP. BATTING AVERAGE WITH RUNNERS IN SCORING POSITION

*Min. 300 PA*

|  |  |
|---|---|
| Randy Myers | .174 |
| Jesse Orosco | .188 |
| Mitch Williams | .193 |
| Todd Worrell | .199 |
| Cecilio Guante | .199 |
| Steve Bedrosian | .199 |
| Bob Apodaca | .199 |
| Jim Deshaies | .203 |
| Mike Henneman | .203 |
| Craig Lefferts | .204 |
| Sid Fernandez | .205 |
| Steve Busby | .206 |
| Orel Hershiser | .208 |
| Floyd Youmans | .208 |
| Dwight Gooden | .208 |
| Lee Smith | .209 |
| Tim Burke | .209 |
| Mark Portugal | .211 |
| Jeff Lahti | .212 |
| David Cone | .213 |
| Stan Thomas | .213 |
| Joe Cowley | .214 |
| Rich Gossage | .215 |
| Mike Jackson | .216 |
| Nolan Ryan | .217 |

### SINGLE-SEASON OPP. BATTING AVERAGE WITH RUNNERS IN SCORING POSITION

*Min. 125 PA*

|  |  |
|---|---|
| Mark Davis, 1989 | .123 |
| Jim Deshaies, 1986 | .140 |
| Rich Gossage, 1978 | .143 |
| Dwight Gooden, 1985 | .144 |
| Eric Show, 1986 | .145 |
| Tim Burke, 1985 | .147 |
| Joe Cowley, 1985 | .148 |
| Tom Hilgendorf, 1975 | .149 |
| John Candelaria, 1977 | .149 |
| Cecilio Guante, 1983 | .151 |
| Lance McCullers, 1988 | .153 |
| Don Sutton, 1980 | .153 |
| Gene Garber, 1982 | .156 |
| Bob Lacey, 1977 | .157 |
| Sid Fernandez, 1988 | .157 |
| Tom Hausman, 1975 | .159 |
| Rich Gossage, 1977 | .159 |
| Mike Scott, 1986 | .159 |
| Steve McCatty, 1981 | .161 |
| Joe Magrane, 1988 | .161 |
| Jeff D. Robinson, 1987 | .161 |
| Craig Lefferts, 1989 | .161 |
| Gregg Olson, 1989 | .162 |
| Mitch Williams, 1987 | .162 |
| Tom Seaver, 1981 | .163 |

### CAREER OPP. BATTING AVERAGE WITH 2 OUTS AND RUNNERS ON BASE

*Min. 250 PA*

|  |  |
|---|---|
| Todd Worrell | .186 |
| Bill Caudill | .186 |
| Jesse Orosco | .188 |
| Victor Cruz | .190 |
| Dwight Gooden | .190 |
| Pete Ladd | .190 |
| Bobby Thigpen | .191 |
| Craig Lefferts | .191 |
| Dave Smith | .193 |
| Cecilio Guante | .195 |
| Pat Dobson | .196 |
| Mitch Williams | .197 |
| Scott Garrelts | .198 |
| Tim Belcher | .198 |
| Calvin Schiraldi | .199 |
| Sid Fernandez | .200 |
| Lance McCullers | .202 |
| Eric King | .202 |
| Bruce Sutter | .202 |
| Rob Murphy | .202 |
| J.R. Richard | .202 |
| Rollie Fingers | .204 |
| Ron Darling | .204 |
| Mike Jackson | .204 |
| Ed Glynn | .205 |

### SINGLE-SEASON OPP. BATTING AVERAGE WITH 2 OUTS AND RUNNERS ON BASE

*Min. 100 PA*

|  |  |
|---|---|
| Bill Caudill, 1980 | .103 |
| Mike Scott, 1986 | .109 |
| Pat Dobson, 1976 | .115 |
| Jerry Ujdur, 1982 | .122 |
| Joe Magrane, 1988 | .133 |
| Jeff M. Robinson, 1988 | .133 |
| Eric Show, 1986 | .138 |
| Jose Rijo, 1988 | .141 |
| John Tudor, 1984 | .143 |
| Ed Whitson, 1984 | .143 |
| Ron Darling, 1986 | .143 |
| Jose DeLeon, 1985 | .144 |
| Bob Forsch, 1978 | .147 |
| Lance McCullers, 1986 | .148 |
| Eduardo Rodriguez, 1976 | .149 |
| Sparky Lyle, 1978 | .149 |
| Dan Warthen, 1975 | .149 |
| Bill Campbell, 1977 | .149 |
| Ron Darling, 1988 | .150 |
| Frank Tanana, 1977 | .150 |
| Fred Norman, 1978 | .152 |
| Scott Garrelts, 1985 | .152 |
| Tom Seaver, 1981 | .153 |
| Scott Sanderson, 1980 | .154 |
| Luis Tiant, 1978 | .155 |

### CAREER OPP. BATTING AVERAGE WITH 2 OUTS AND RUNNERS IN SCORING POSITION

*Min. 150 PA*

|  |  |
|---|---|
| Bob Apodaca | .165 |
| Cecilio Guante | .167 |
| Todd Worrell | .167 |
| Craig Lefferts | .169 |
| Victor Cruz | .175 |
| Lee Smith | .175 |
| Jesse Orosco | .176 |
| Eric Plunk | .178 |
| Duane Ward | .180 |
| Pete Ladd | .181 |
| Terry Leach | .182 |
| Doug Jones | .182 |
| Eric King | .182 |
| Mitch Williams | .183 |
| Randy Myers | .184 |
| J.R. Richard | .185 |
| Dwight Gooden | .186 |
| Steve Busby | .186 |
| Scott Garrelts | .186 |
| Dave Smith | .188 |
| Tippy Martinez | .189 |
| Floyd Youmans | .191 |
| Bill Caudill | .192 |
| Dave Stewart | .193 |
| Rob Murphy | .194 |

### SINGLE-SEASON OPP. BATTING AVERAGE WITH 2 OUTS AND RUNNERS IN SCORING POSITION

*Min. 75 PA*

|  |  |
|---|---|
| Jack Morris, 1987 | .082 |
| Joe Magrane, 1988 | .097 |
| Dan Warthen, 1975 | .100 |
| John Tudor, 1984 | .110 |
| Bobby Witt, 1987 | .111 |
| Luis Tiant, 1978 | .113 |
| Gregg Olson, 1989 | .113 |
| Bill Gullickson, 1982 | .118 |
| Mike Scott, 1986 | .119 |
| Rich Gossage, 1978 | .119 |
| Ed Whitson, 1984 | .119 |
| Mike Krukow, 1986 | .123 |
| Brian Fisher, 1987 | .125 |
| Doug Corbett, 1980 | .127 |
| Ron Darling, 1986 | .129 |
| Mark Langston, 1988 | .129 |
| Frank Tanana, 1977 | .130 |
| Fred Norman, 1978 | .130 |
| Dwight Gooden, 1985 | .133 |
| Pat Dobson, 1976 | .133 |
| Chris Bosio, 1989 | .134 |
| Tim Burke, 1985 | .134 |
| John Smoltz, 1989 | .135 |
| Frank Tanana, 1976 | .135 |
| Bill Campbell, 1977 | .136 |

### SINGLE-SEASON DOUBLES ALLOWED

|  | |
|---|---|
| Dennis Leonard, 1978 | 62 |
| Bruce Hurst, 1984 | 60 |
| Rick Sutcliffe, 1983 | 58 |
| Dennis Eckersley, 1986 | 58 |
| Jim Barr, 1977 | 57 |
| Jim Clancy, 1983 | 57 |
| Bill Gullickson, 1983 | 56 |
| Shane Rawley, 1987 | 56 |
| Andy Hawkins, 1989 | 56 |
| Scott McGregor, 1983 | 55 |
| John Montefusco, 1975 | 54 |
| Dennis Leonard, 1980 | 54 |
| Steve Rogers, 1983 | 54 |
| Doyle Alexander, 1986 | 54 |
| Mike Moore, 1987 | 54 |
| Jimmy Key, 1989 | 54 |
| Wilbur Wood, 1975 | 53 |
| Mike Torrez, 1983 | 53 |
| Ron Guidry, 1983 | 53 |
| Doyle Alexander, 1984 | 53 |
| Bob Knepper, 1985 | 53 |
| Charlie Leibrandt, 1986 | 53 |
| Ron Reed, 1975 | 52 |
| Larry Christenson, 1977 | 52 |
| Steve Carlton, 1977 | 52 |

### SINGLE-SEASON TRIPLES ALLOWED

|  | |
|---|---|
| Larry Christenson, 1976 | 17 |
| Paul Thormodsgard, 1977 | 16 |
| Bret Saberhagen, 1988 | 16 |
| Jim Barr, 1975 | 14 |
| Jim Kaat, 1977 | 14 |
| Jim Barr, 1977 | 14 |
| Dave Goltz, 1977 | 14 |
| Craig Swan, 1979 | 14 |
| Randy Jones, 1979 | 14 |
| Rick Sutcliffe, 1984 | 14 |
| Ray Burris, 1976 | 13 |
| Rick Reuschel, 1976 | 13 |
| Luis Tiant, 1979 | 13 |
| Dick Ruthven, 1980 | 13 |
| Steve Carlton, 1980 | 13 |
| Rich Gale, 1982 | 13 |
| Tommy John, 1982 | 13 |
| Mike Smithson, 1983 | 13 |
| John Montefusco, 1975 | 12 |
| Jim Kaat, 1976 | 12 |
| Ken Holtzman, 1976 | 12 |
| Ray Burris, 1978 | 12 |
| Roger Erickson, 1979 | 12 |
| Bob Forsch, 1979 | 12 |
| Doc Medich, 1980 | 12 |

### SINGLE-SEASON EXTRA-BASE HITS ALLOWED

|  | |
|---|---|
| Bert Blyleven, 1986 | 100 |
| Phil Niekro, 1979 | 97 |
| Dennis Leonard, 1978 | 94 |
| Dennis Leonard, 1980 | 92 |
| Rick Sutcliffe, 1983 | 92 |
| Bert Blyleven, 1987 | 92 |
| LaMarr Hoyt, 1984 | 91 |
| Mike Witt, 1987 | 91 |
| Doyle Alexander, 1988 | 91 |
| Jerry Garvin, 1977 | 90 |
| Mike Moore, 1987 | 90 |
| Wilbur Wood, 1975 | 89 |
| Jim Barr, 1977 | 89 |
| Dan Petry, 1983 | 89 |
| Mark Langston, 1986 | 89 |
| Jim Clancy, 1983 | 88 |
| Bill Gullickson, 1987 | 88 |
| Ferguson Jenkins, 1979 | 87 |
| Frank Viola, 1986 | 87 |
| Willie Fraser, 1988 | 87 |
| Luis Tiant, 1975 | 86 |
| Ferguson Jenkins, 1975 | 86 |
| Scott McGregor, 1983 | 86 |
| Bruce Hurst, 1984 | 86 |
| Charlie Hough, 1984 | 86 |

### CAREER OPP. EXTRA-BASE HIT PCT. (PER 100 AB)

*Min. 1,000 PA*

|  | |
|---|---|
| Steve Howe | 4.04 |
| John Franco | 4.47 |
| Doug Jones | 4.70 |
| Roger McDowell | 4.75 |
| Doug Sisk | 4.84 |
| Greg Minton | 4.92 |
| Mark Fidrych | 5.13 |
| Bobby Thigpen | 5.18 |
| Tim Belcher | 5.24 |
| Gary Lavelle | 5.24 |
| Alejandro Pena | 5.25 |
| J.R. Richard | 5.28 |
| Dwight Gooden | 5.35 |
| Jim Kern | 5.35 |
| Scott Garrelts | 5.38 |
| Mark Littell | 5.40 |
| Dave Smith | 5.41 |
| Orel Hershiser | 5.42 |
| Nolan Ryan | 5.47 |
| Jesse Orosco | 5.54 |
| Ernie Camacho | 5.55 |
| Dave Righetti | 5.55 |
| Clay Carroll | 5.56 |
| Frank Williams | 5.61 |
| Rich Gossage | 5.61 |

### HIGHEST CAREER RATIO OF GROUND OUTS TO AIR OUTS

*Min. 1,000 PA*

|  | |
|---|---|
| Roger McDowell | 3.07 |
| Doug Corbett | 2.96 |
| Doug Sisk | 2.81 |
| Bill Swift | 2.74 |
| Tommy John | 2.55 |
| Ray Fontenot | 2.53 |
| Bruce Ruffin | 2.48 |
| Juan Agosto | 2.43 |
| Jeff Dedmon | 2.42 |
| Jim Todd | 2.39 |
| Greg Minton | 2.37 |
| Jaime Cocanower | 2.34 |
| Dan Quisenberry | 2.32 |
| Dennis Lamp | 2.29 |
| Kent Tekulve | 2.23 |
| John Denny | 2.21 |
| Bob Stanley | 2.18 |
| Bill Castro | 2.17 |
| Gene Garber | 2.17 |
| Randy Jones | 2.13 |
| Orel Hershiser | 2.13 |
| Duane Ward | 2.12 |
| Jim Winn | 2.11 |
| Steve Trout | 2.09 |
| Terry Forster | 2.06 |

### LOWEST CAREER RATIO OF GROUND OUTS TO AIR OUTS

*Min. 1,000 PA*

|  | |
|---|---|
| Sid Fernandez | 0.46 |
| Jeff Reardon | 0.54 |
| Mike Armstrong | 0.55 |
| Tom Niedenfuer | 0.55 |
| Keith Atherton | 0.56 |
| Don Carman | 0.58 |
| Victor Cruz | 0.59 |
| Roy Smith | 0.59 |
| Pete Ladd | 0.60 |
| Bill Caudill | 0.60 |
| Dave LaRoche | 0.61 |
| Chris Knapp | 0.62 |
| Juan Berenguer | 0.62 |
| Jim Deshaies | 0.63 |
| Cecilio Guante | 0.63 |
| Al Hrabosky | 0.63 |
| Tom Browning | 0.65 |
| Al Holland | 0.65 |
| Skip Lockwood | 0.66 |
| Aurelio Lopez | 0.67 |
| Tim Conroy | 0.67 |
| Luis Tiant | 0.67 |
| John Henry Johnson | 0.68 |
| Joe Price | 0.69 |
| Catfish Hunter | 0.69 |

### CAREER GROUND OUT PCT. (PER 100 PA)

*Min. 1,000 PA*

|  | |
|---|---|
| Roger McDowell | 43.1 |
| Dan Quisenberry | 42.5 |
| Randy Jones | 41.3 |
| Tommy John | 41.3 |
| Doug Sisk | 40.4 |
| Bill Castro | 40.0 |
| Doug Corbett | 39.9 |
| Bill Swift | 39.8 |
| Ray Fontenot | 39.2 |
| Greg Minton | 39.2 |
| Jim Todd | 38.6 |
| Dennis Lamp | 38.6 |
| Kent Tekulve | 38.5 |
| Bob Stanley | 38.4 |
| Juan Agosto | 38.4 |
| Paul Hartzell | 38.2 |
| Fernando Arroyo | 38.0 |
| Rob Dressler | 37.8 |
| Clay Carroll | 37.5 |
| Jaime Cocanower | 37.4 |
| Bruce Ruffin | 37.3 |
| Rick Matula | 37.3 |
| Jeff Dedmon | 37.2 |
| Scott Terry | 37.2 |
| Dave Rozema | 37.2 |

### CAREER AIR OUT PCT. (PER 100 PA)

*Min. 1,000 PA*

|  | |
|---|---|
| Gary Nolan | 36.0 |
| Catfish Hunter | 35.8 |
| Tom Browning | 35.4 |
| Keith Atherton | 35.3 |
| John Martin | 35.2 |
| Roy Smith | 34.8 |
| Mike Armstrong | 34.8 |
| Luis Tiant | 34.3 |
| Manny Sarmiento | 34.2 |
| Scott McGregor | 34.1 |
| Don Carman | 34.1 |
| Jeff Reardon | 34.0 |
| Tom Niedenfuer | 34.0 |
| Sid Fernandez | 34.0 |
| Larry Gura | 33.6 |
| Jim Deshaies | 33.4 |
| Jose Bautista | 33.4 |
| Chris Knapp | 33.3 |
| Pete Ladd | 33.3 |
| Grant Jackson | 33.2 |
| Steve McCatty | 33.1 |
| Brian Kingman | 32.9 |
| Craig Swan | 32.9 |
| Al Hrabosky | 32.8 |
| Ken Schrom | 32.8 |

### CAREER OPP. ON-BASE AVERAGE LEADING OFF INNINGS

*Min. 250 PA*

|  |  |
|---|---|
| Mark Williamson | .251 |
| Mike Armstrong | .252 |
| Dan Quisenberry | .252 |
| Tom Henke | .257 |
| John Martin | .261 |
| Brad Havens | .262 |
| Dave Tobik | .262 |
| Jose Bautista | .264 |
| Rich Gossage | .264 |
| Steve Howe | .266 |
| Tug McGraw | .269 |
| John Smiley | .269 |
| Rob Murphy | .270 |
| Gary Nolan | .272 |
| Darold Knowles | .273 |
| Sid Fernandez | .273 |
| Greg Swindell | .276 |
| Jeff Reardon | .276 |
| David Cone | .276 |
| Tim Belcher | .278 |
| Tom Niedenfuer | .278 |
| Gene Garber | .279 |
| Frank Tanana | .279 |
| Pete Filson | .279 |
| Marty Pattin | .279 |

### SINGLE-SEASON OPP. ON-BASE AVERAGE LEADING OFF INNINGS

*Min. 100 PA*

|  |  |
|---|---|
| Greg A. Harris, 1985 | .175 |
| Greg W. Harris, 1989 | .180 |
| Dan Quisenberry, 1984 | .188 |
| Sid Fernandez, 1989 | .190 |
| Vern Ruhle, 1983 | .191 |
| Randy Martz, 1981 | .202 |
| Jeff D. Robinson, 1988 | .211 |
| Jeff D. Robinson, 1986 | .212 |
| Joe Price, 1983 | .212 |
| Dan Quisenberry, 1983 | .215 |
| Curt Young, 1989 | .217 |
| Dave J. Schmidt, 1982 | .217 |
| John Tudor, 1985 | .217 |
| Rich Gossage, 1978 | .219 |
| Mike Armstrong, 1982 | .220 |
| Chuck Cary, 1989 | .220 |
| Erik Hanson, 1989 | .220 |
| Dan Schatzeder, 1984 | .221 |
| Don Sutton, 1975 | .221 |
| Dwight Gooden, 1989 | .221 |
| Dennis Eckersley, 1977 | .223 |
| Pat Underwood, 1982 | .223 |
| Ken Forsch, 1979 | .223 |
| Bob Forsch, 1977 | .224 |
| Marty Pattin, 1976 | .224 |

### CAREER OPP. WALK PCT. LEADING OFF INNINGS

*Min. 250 PA*

|  |  |
|---|---|
| Dan Quisenberry | 2.29 |
| Gene Garber | 2.48 |
| Gary Nolan | 2.49 |
| Brian Holton | 3.00 |
| Kevin Kobel | 3.02 |
| Tom Glavine | 3.52 |
| Ron Reed | 3.54 |
| Atlee Hammaker | 3.54 |
| Mark Fidrych | 3.55 |
| Steve Howe | 3.58 |
| Gary Lucas | 3.78 |
| Dave J. Schmidt | 3.84 |
| Gary Ross | 3.88 |
| Bret Saberhagen | 3.90 |
| Pedro Borbon | 3.95 |
| Dave Rozema | 4.04 |
| Jim Barr | 4.05 |
| Tommy John | 4.06 |
| Rick Reuschel | 4.13 |
| Dennis Eckersley | 4.15 |
| Roger Erickson | 4.16 |
| Jimmy Key | 4.17 |
| Scott Sanderson | 4.24 |
| LaMarr Hoyt | 4.25 |
| Ferguson Jenkins | 4.27 |

### SINGLE-SEASON OPP. WALK PCT. LEADING OFF INNINGS

*Min. 100 PA*

|  |  |
|---|---|
| Gene Garber, 1982 | 0.00 |
| Dan Quisenberry, 1983 | 0.00 |
| Dan Quisenberry, 1985 | 0.00 |
| Rick Langford, 1982 | 0.41 |
| John Candelaria, 1988 | 0.62 |
| Jim Barr, 1982 | 0.78 |
| Tom Hausman, 1980 | 0.82 |
| Bob Forsch, 1980 | 0.89 |
| Dave J. Schmidt, 1982 | 0.94 |
| Dennis Eckersley, 1987 | 0.94 |
| Dennis Martinez, 1986 | 0.95 |
| Jeff D. Robinson, 1986 | 0.96 |
| Ron Reed, 1978 | 1.00 |
| Mike Smithson, 1983 | 1.29 |
| Gaylord Perry, 1981 | 1.29 |
| Bryn Smith, 1987 | 1.29 |
| Ferguson Jenkins, 1976 | 1.38 |
| Glenn Abbott, 1983 | 1.45 |
| Roger Clemens, 1984 | 1.45 |
| Neal Heaton, 1987 | 1.48 |
| Ron Guidry, 1981 | 1.49 |
| Bob Shirley, 1980 | 1.50 |
| Rick Rhoden, 1983 | 1.60 |
| Atlee Hammaker, 1982 | 1.62 |
| Gary Nolan, 1976 | 1.64 |

### CAREER OPP. BATTING AVERAGE WITH BASES LOADED

*Min. 50 PA*

|  |  |
|---|---|
| Jesse Orosco | .143 |
| Eric Show | .145 |
| Ed Figueroa | .147 |
| Doug Rau | .152 |
| Dave LaRoche | .159 |
| Charlie Lea | .159 |
| Don Carman | .162 |
| Dave Lemanczyk | .167 |
| Greg Maddux | .174 |
| Ken Schrom | .175 |
| Orel Hershiser | .178 |
| Tom House | .179 |
| Jeff Dedmon | .182 |
| Tippy Martinez | .183 |
| Duane Ward | .184 |
| Bruce Berenyi | .185 |
| Ed Halicki | .185 |
| Mitch Williams | .186 |
| Mike Dunne | .186 |
| Butch Metzger | .188 |
| Tom Griffin | .188 |
| Cecilio Guante | .188 |
| Lance McCullers | .188 |
| Craig Swan | .189 |
| Mike Smithson | .189 |

### CAREER MOST BATTERS FACED WITH BASES LOADED WITHOUT ALLOWING A GRAND-SLAM HOME RUN

|  |  |
|---|---|
| Joaquin Andujar | 158 |
| Jim Kern | 148 |
| Mike Krukow | 148 |
| Pat Zachry | 128 |
| Juan Berenguer | 108 |
| Jim Palmer | 105 |
| Frank DiPino | 104 |
| Gene Nelson | 103 |
| Joe Price | 100 |
| Eric Show | 96 |
| Al Hrabosky | 96 |
| Andy Hassler | 93 |
| Jesse Jefferson | 91 |
| Mike Boddicker | 89 |
| Bruce Berenyi | 84 |
| Ed Figueroa | 82 |
| Dwight Gooden | 80 |
| Doug Corbett | 80 |
| Roy Thomas | 75 |
| Don Hood | 74 |
| Rawly Eastwick | 73 |
| Mike T. Stanton | 73 |
| Steve Crawford | 71 |
| Roger Erickson | 71 |
| Dave J. Schmidt | 71 |

### CAREER OPP. WALK PCT. WITH BASES LOADED

*Min. 50 PA*

|  |  |
|---|---|
| Steve Crawford | 0.00 |
| Todd Worrell | 0.00 |
| Dave Heaverlo | 0.81 |
| Vern Ruhle | 1.01 |
| Steve McCatty | 1.10 |
| Craig Lefferts | 1.11 |
| Ed Vande Berg | 1.20 |
| Ed Lynch | 1.39 |
| Dave Tobik | 1.43 |
| Jim Gott | 1.52 |
| Dennis Eckersley | 1.55 |
| Mike G. Marshall | 1.64 |
| Bill Swift | 1.69 |
| Fred Breining | 1.72 |
| Jay Tibbs | 1.72 |
| John Butcher | 1.75 |
| Dave Dravecky | 1.79 |
| Larry Christenson | 1.79 |
| Ferguson Jenkins | 1.82 |
| Odell Jones | 1.82 |
| Mike Garman | 1.82 |
| Jim Umbarger | 1.82 |
| Butch Metzger | 1.82 |
| Mike Parrott | 1.89 |
| Will McEnaney | 1.89 |

### CAREER OPP. STRIKEOUT PCT. WITH BASES LOADED

*Min. 15 Strikeouts*

|  |  |
|---|---|
| Tim Birtsas | 38.30 |
| Paul Assenmacher | 37.93 |
| Kirk McCaskill | 31.91 |
| Bobby Witt | 29.73 |
| Tom Henke | 28.99 |
| John Hiller | 28.13 |
| Bruce Berenyi | 27.38 |
| Nolan Ryan | 27.18 |
| Sid Fernandez | 26.98 |
| Mark Littell | 26.51 |
| Mitch Williams | 26.04 |
| Dave LaRoche | 25.20 |
| Bill Caudill | 25.00 |
| Lance McCullers | 25.00 |
| Andy McGaffigan | 25.00 |
| Dave Smith | 24.39 |
| Jose Rijo | 24.36 |
| Roger Clemens | 24.19 |
| Al Holland | 24.14 |
| Steve Carlton | 24.11 |
| Ron Guidry | 23.76 |
| Cecilio Guante | 23.75 |
| Sammy Stewart | 23.61 |
| Mario Soto | 23.53 |
| Greg A. Harris | 22.88 |

# VIII
# Batter-Pitcher Matchups

# *Batter-Pitcher Matchups*

The Batter-Pitcher Matchup section lists, for the selected players, their performances against every pitcher or batter they have faced for at least five at bats in their careers. These statistics include all regular season appearances since the beginning of their careers.

Earl Weaver used to keep them on index cards. Dave Johnson maintains his on a PC. But until the past few years the public was largely unaware of the importance many managers place on specific matchup statistics in setting a lineup. The figures do not even out over the long run, and the differences can be massive. In this section, we expand the "Loves to Face" and "Hates to Face" matchups listed in the Batter and Pitcher Sections to take a look at the career performances of some of the most extraordinary players in the game.

Now you can see in detail just how few pitchers really give Kevin Mitchell trouble. Or if anyone really owns Mark Langston yet. Here, at last, are the answers.

# Tony Gwynn

| Pitcher | AB | H | 2B | 3B | HR | BB | SO | BA | SA | OBA |
|---|---|---|---|---|---|---|---|---|---|---|
| Jim Acker | 13 | 3 | 0 | 0 | 0 | 2 | 1 | .231 | .231 | .333 |
| Juan Agosto | 10 | 4 | 0 | 0 | 0 | 1 | 1 | .400 | .400 | .455 |
| Rick Aguilera | 9 | 1 | 0 | 0 | 0 | 2 | 0 | .111 | .111 | .273 |
| Doyle Alexander | 17 | 8 | 1 | 0 | 2 | 1 | 1 | .471 | .882 | .500 |
| Neil Allen | 11 | 3 | 0 | 0 | 0 | 1 | 1 | .273 | .273 | .333 |
| Larry Andersen | 20 | 5 | 0 | 0 | 1 | 2 | 4 | .250 | .400 | .318 |
| Joaquin Andujar | 27 | 9 | 2 | 0 | 0 | 4 | 0 | .333 | .407 | .419 |
| Jack Armstrong | 8 | 3 | 1 | 0 | 2 | 0 | 0 | .375 | 1.250 | .375 |
| Paul Assenmacher | 13 | 4 | 0 | 0 | 0 | 1 | 0 | .308 | .308 | .357 |
| Len Barker | 6 | 3 | 0 | 1 | 0 | 1 | 0 | .500 | .833 | .571 |
| Steve Bedrosian | 31 | 8 | 1 | 0 | 0 | 2 | 3 | .258 | .290 | .303 |
| Tim Belcher | 20 | 4 | 1 | 0 | 0 | 6 | 0 | .200 | .250 | .385 |
| Bruce Berenyi | 21 | 6 | 0 | 0 | 1 | 4 | 4 | .286 | .429 | .400 |
| Mike Bielecki | 22 | 7 | 3 | 0 | 0 | 4 | 3 | .318 | .455 | .423 |
| Tim Birtsas | 5 | 0 | 0 | 0 | 0 | 1 | 1 | .000 | .000 | .167 |
| Vida Blue | 15 | 6 | 1 | 0 | 1 | 4 | 1 | .400 | .667 | .526 |
| Randy Bockus | 7 | 1 | 0 | 1 | 0 | 0 | 0 | .143 | .429 | .143 |
| Joe Boever | 8 | 6 | 1 | 0 | 0 | 0 | 0 | .750 | .875 | .750 |
| Jeff Brantley | 5 | 4 | 0 | 0 | 0 | 0 | 0 | .800 | .800 | .800 |
| Fred Breining | 6 | 1 | 1 | 0 | 0 | 0 | 1 | .167 | .333 | .167 |
| Tom Brennan | 5 | 2 | 1 | 0 | 0 | 0 | 0 | .400 | .600 | .400 |
| Tom Browning | 65 | 26 | 1 | 0 | 3 | 5 | 4 | .400 | .554 | .437 |
| Tim Burke | 12 | 6 | 0 | 0 | 0 | 1 | 2 | .500 | .500 | .538 |
| Marty Bystrom | 5 | 1 | 0 | 0 | 0 | 2 | 1 | .200 | .200 | .429 |
| Jeff Calhoun | 8 | 1 | 1 | 0 | 0 | 0 | 0 | .125 | .250 | .125 |
| Rick Camp | 20 | 7 | 1 | 0 | 0 | 3 | 0 | .350 | .400 | .435 |
| Bill Campbell | 5 | 1 | 0 | 0 | 1 | 0 | 0 | .200 | .800 | .200 |
| John Candelaria | 11 | 3 | 0 | 0 | 0 | 0 | 1 | .273 | .273 | .273 |
| Steve Carlton | 21 | 5 | 1 | 0 | 0 | 1 | 1 | .238 | .286 | .273 |
| Don Carman | 28 | 13 | 4 | 0 | 0 | 3 | 1 | .464 | .607 | .516 |
| Norm Charlton | 5 | 2 | 0 | 0 | 0 | 0 | 0 | .400 | .400 | .400 |
| Jim Clancy | 13 | 5 | 0 | 0 | 0 | 2 | 0 | .385 | .385 | .467 |
| Marty Clary | 7 | 4 | 0 | 0 | 0 | 0 | 0 | .571 | .571 | .571 |
| David Cone | 13 | 6 | 2 | 0 | 0 | 0 | 2 | .462 | .615 | .462 |
| Tim Conroy | 8 | 3 | 1 | 0 | 0 | 1 | 0 | .375 | .500 | .400 |
| Danny Cox | 22 | 6 | 0 | 0 | 2 | 0 | 1 | .273 | .545 | .273 |
| Tim Crews | 6 | 4 | 0 | 0 | 0 | 3 | 0 | .667 | .667 | .778 |
| Ron Darling | 48 | 24 | 4 | 2 | 0 | 1 | 5 | .500 | .667 | .500 |
| Danny Darwin | 22 | 8 | 3 | 0 | 0 | 1 | 1 | .364 | .500 | .391 |
| Mark Davis | 23 | 10 | 0 | 0 | 0 | 5 | 4 | .435 | .435 | .536 |
| Bill Dawley | 7 | 5 | 1 | 1 | 0 | 1 | 0 | .714 | 1.143 | .667 |
| Ken Dayley | 17 | 7 | 1 | 0 | 0 | 2 | 3 | .412 | .471 | .474 |
| Jeff Dedmon | 12 | 3 | 1 | 0 | 0 | 1 | 0 | .250 | .333 | .308 |
| Jose DeLeon | 31 | 7 | 1 | 0 | 0 | 3 | 2 | .226 | .258 | .278 |
| John Denny | 35 | 15 | 4 | 0 | 1 | 3 | 2 | .429 | .629 | .474 |
| Jim Deshaies | 33 | 11 | 1 | 0 | 0 | 3 | 2 | .333 | .364 | .389 |
| Carlos Diaz | 11 | 4 | 1 | 0 | 0 | 0 | 0 | .364 | .455 | .364 |
| Rob Dibble | 5 | 0 | 0 | 0 | 0 | 2 | 3 | .000 | .000 | .286 |
| Frank DiPino | 16 | 1 | 0 | 0 | 0 | 1 | 1 | .063 | .063 | .111 |
| Kelly Downs | 15 | 3 | 0 | 0 | 0 | 2 | 2 | .200 | .200 | .294 |
| Doug Drabek | 16 | 7 | 3 | 1 | 0 | 1 | 1 | .438 | .750 | .471 |
| Dave Dravecky | 9 | 3 | 0 | 0 | 0 | 0 | 1 | .333 | .333 | .333 |
| Mike Dunne | 5 | 2 | 0 | 0 | 0 | 1 | 0 | .400 | .400 | .500 |
| Dennis Eckersley | 12 | 4 | 2 | 0 | 0 | 0 | 1 | .333 | .500 | .333 |
| Pete Falcone | 13 | 5 | 1 | 0 | 0 | 1 | 0 | .385 | .462 | .429 |
| Sid Fernandez | 37 | 11 | 1 | 0 | 1 | 1 | 2 | .297 | .405 | .316 |
| Brian Fisher | 16 | 5 | 2 | 0 | 1 | 4 | 1 | .313 | .625 | .429 |
| Ray Fontenot | 7 | 1 | 1 | 0 | 0 | 0 | 1 | .143 | .286 | .143 |
| Bob Forsch | 27 | 11 | 1 | 0 | 0 | 3 | 0 | .407 | .444 | .467 |
| Terry Forster | 9 | 1 | 0 | 0 | 0 | 3 | 0 | .111 | .111 | .333 |
| John Franco | 36 | 10 | 2 | 0 | 0 | 0 | 1 | .278 | .333 | .270 |
| Brent Gaff | 10 | 3 | 0 | 0 | 0 | 1 | 0 | .300 | .300 | .364 |
| Rich Gale | 5 | 3 | 0 | 0 | 0 | 0 | 0 | .600 | .600 | .600 |
| Gene Garber | 17 | 5 | 2 | 0 | 0 | 1 | 0 | .294 | .412 | .333 |
| Scott Garrelts | 40 | 10 | 3 | 1 | 1 | 1 | 2 | .250 | .450 | .268 |
| Tom Glavine | 31 | 8 | 0 | 0 | 0 | 3 | 1 | .258 | .258 | .324 |
| Dwight Gooden | 37 | 8 | 0 | 1 | 0 | 5 | 4 | .216 | .270 | .310 |
| Jim Gott | 14 | 8 | 1 | 0 | 0 | 1 | 2 | .571 | .643 | .600 |
| Kevin Gross | 28 | 9 | 4 | 0 | 0 | 4 | 2 | .321 | .464 | .406 |
| Cecilio Guante | 7 | 2 | 0 | 1 | 0 | 1 | 2 | .286 | .571 | .375 |
| Bill Gullickson | 30 | 11 | 0 | 0 | 0 | 2 | 1 | .367 | .367 | .406 |
| Atlee Hammaker | 31 | 9 | 0 | 1 | 0 | 1 | 1 | .290 | .355 | .313 |
| Jeff Heathcock | 8 | 1 | 0 | 0 | 0 | 0 | 0 | .125 | .125 | .125 |
| Neal Heaton | 22 | 8 | 0 | 0 | 0 | 0 | 2 | .364 | .364 | .364 |
| Orel Hershiser | 58 | 16 | 5 | 0 | 0 | 3 | 0 | .276 | .362 | .306 |
| Joe Hesketh | 16 | 3 | 0 | 0 | 0 | 4 | 2 | .188 | .188 | .381 |
| Ken Hill | 8 | 1 | 0 | 0 | 0 | 0 | 1 | .125 | .125 | .125 |
| Guy Hoffman | 14 | 6 | 0 | 0 | 0 | 5 | 1 | .429 | .429 | .579 |
| Al Holland | 8 | 2 | 0 | 1 | 0 | 2 | 2 | .250 | .500 | .400 |
| Brian Holton | 9 | 4 | 1 | 0 | 0 | 4 | 0 | .444 | .556 | .615 |
| Rick Honeycutt | 41 | 11 | 1 | 1 | 0 | 2 | 2 | .268 | .341 | .302 |
| Burt Hooton | 14 | 5 | 1 | 0 | 0 | 1 | 0 | .357 | .429 | .400 |
| Ricky Horton | 24 | 9 | 1 | 0 | 0 | 1 | 0 | .375 | .417 | .400 |
| Ken Howell | 14 | 5 | 0 | 0 | 0 | 4 | 3 | .357 | .357 | .500 |
| Charles Hudson | 23 | 10 | 1 | 2 | 0 | 1 | 2 | .435 | .652 | .458 |
| Tom Hume | 12 | 6 | 3 | 0 | 1 | 2 | 0 | .500 | 1.000 | .571 |
| Danny Jackson | 21 | 8 | 1 | 0 | 0 | 2 | 1 | .381 | .429 | .435 |
| Joe Johnson | 10 | 5 | 0 | 0 | 0 | 2 | 0 | .500 | .500 | .583 |
| Kurt Kepshire | 9 | 1 | 0 | 0 | 0 | 0 | 0 | .111 | .111 | .111 |
| Charlie Kerfeld | 7 | 3 | 0 | 0 | 0 | 0 | 0 | .429 | .429 | .429 |
| Paul Kilgus | 10 | 1 | 0 | 1 | 0 | 2 | 0 | .100 | .300 | .250 |
| Bob Kipper | 18 | 8 | 1 | 1 | 0 | 0 | 0 | .444 | .611 | .444 |
| Bob Knepper | 66 | 24 | 3 | 1 | 1 | 7 | 2 | .364 | .485 | .425 |
| Mark Knudson | 5 | 1 | 0 | 0 | 0 | 1 | 0 | .200 | .200 | .333 |
| Jerry Koosman | 9 | 3 | 0 | 0 | 0 | 2 | 1 | .333 | .333 | .455 |
| Randy Kramer | 5 | 0 | 0 | 0 | 0 | 0 | 0 | .000 | .000 | .000 |
| Mike Krukow | 49 | 18 | 4 | 0 | 2 | 5 | 3 | .367 | .571 | .418 |
| Mike LaCoss | 44 | 15 | 0 | 0 | 0 | 4 | 4 | .341 | .341 | .396 |
| Bill Landrum | 5 | 1 | 0 | 1 | 0 | 1 | 0 | .200 | .600 | .333 |
| Dave LaPoint | 23 | 9 | 2 | 0 | 0 | 0 | 1 | .391 | .478 | .391 |
| Bill Laskey | 34 | 14 | 4 | 0 | 2 | 0 | 2 | .412 | .706 | .412 |
| Gary Lavelle | 10 | 4 | 0 | 0 | 0 | 1 | 2 | .400 | .400 | .455 |
| Charlie Lea | 14 | 4 | 0 | 0 | 0 | 2 | 0 | .286 | .286 | .375 |
| Tim Leary | 27 | 9 | 2 | 1 | 0 | 2 | 0 | .333 | .481 | .379 |
| Craig Lefferts | 15 | 5 | 0 | 0 | 0 | 0 | 2 | .333 | .333 | .333 |
| Derek Lilliquist | 9 | 2 | 0 | 0 | 0 | 0 | 0 | .222 | .222 | .222 |
| Gary Lucas | 6 | 3 | 1 | 0 | 0 | 0 | 0 | .500 | .667 | .500 |
| Ed Lynch | 19 | 6 | 0 | 0 | 1 | 1 | 0 | .316 | .474 | .350 |
| Mike Madden | 15 | 4 | 0 | 0 | 0 | 0 | 5 | .267 | .267 | .267 |
| Greg Maddux | 12 | 5 | 0 | 0 | 0 | 3 | 0 | .417 | .417 | .533 |
| Mike Maddux | 12 | 1 | 1 | 0 | 0 | 1 | 0 | .083 | .167 | .154 |
| Joe Magrane | 25 | 6 | 0 | 1 | 0 | 1 | 3 | .240 | .320 | .269 |
| Rick Mahler | 74 | 29 | 7 | 2 | 1 | 1 | 0 | .392 | .581 | .395 |
| Dennis Martinez | 12 | 3 | 1 | 0 | 0 | 0 | 1 | .250 | .333 | .250 |
| Roger Mason | 11 | 5 | 0 | 1 | 1 | 0 | 2 | .455 | .909 | .455 |
| Greg Mathews | 13 | 2 | 0 | 0 | 0 | 1 | 0 | .154 | .154 | .214 |
| Bob McClure | 6 | 1 | 0 | 0 | 0 | 0 | 0 | .167 | .167 | .167 |
| Roger McDowell | 15 | 3 | 0 | 0 | 0 | 2 | 2 | .200 | .200 | .294 |
| Andy McGaffigan | 21 | 8 | 2 | 0 | 0 | 5 | 2 | .381 | .476 | .500 |
| Craig McMurtry | 24 | 11 | 0 | 0 | 0 | 2 | 0 | .458 | .458 | .481 |
| Larry McWilliams | 30 | 13 | 1 | 1 | 1 | 3 | 1 | .433 | .633 | .500 |
| Greg Minton | 13 | 5 | 1 | 0 | 0 | 7 | 0 | .385 | .462 | .600 |
| John Mitchell | 6 | 3 | 0 | 0 | 0 | 1 | 0 | .500 | .500 | .571 |
| Jamie Moyer | 18 | 7 | 0 | 0 | 1 | 3 | 1 | .389 | .556 | .455 |
| Terry Mulholland | 6 | 2 | 0 | 1 | 0 | 2 | 0 | .333 | .667 | .500 |
| Rob Murphy | 17 | 3 | 0 | 0 | 0 | 2 | 0 | .176 | .176 | .263 |
| Randy Myers | 7 | 1 | 0 | 1 | 0 | 2 | 2 | .143 | .429 | .333 |
| Tom Niedenfuer | 12 | 5 | 1 | 1 | 0 | 0 | 1 | .417 | .667 | .417 |
| Joe Niekro | 32 | 9 | 1 | 1 | 0 | 0 | 3 | .281 | .375 | .281 |
| Phil Niekro | 15 | 3 | 0 | 0 | 0 | 1 | 1 | .200 | .200 | .235 |
| Dickie Noles | 6 | 1 | 0 | 1 | 0 | 2 | 0 | .167 | .500 | .375 |
| Bob Ojeda | 15 | 5 | 0 | 0 | 0 | 1 | 2 | .333 | .333 | .375 |
| Ed Olwine | 8 | 2 | 0 | 0 | 1 | 1 | 0 | .250 | .625 | .333 |
| Randy O'Neal | 6 | 4 | 1 | 2 | 0 | 0 | 0 | .667 | 1.500 | .667 |
| Jesse Orosco | 18 | 6 | 0 | 0 | 1 | 2 | 0 | .333 | .500 | .400 |
| Bob Owchinko | 6 | 2 | 0 | 0 | 0 | 1 | 0 | .333 | .333 | .429 |
| David Palmer | 25 | 10 | 2 | 1 | 1 | 2 | 1 | .400 | .680 | .414 |
| Jeff Parrett | 11 | 5 | 0 | 0 | 0 | 2 | 1 | .455 | .455 | .538 |
| Frank Pastore | 13 | 2 | 0 | 0 | 0 | 1 | 0 | .154 | .154 | .214 |
| Alejandro Pena | 26 | 10 | 2 | 0 | 0 | 1 | 1 | .385 | .462 | .429 |
| Pascual Perez | 46 | 18 | 1 | 2 | 0 | 2 | 4 | .391 | .500 | .417 |
| Pat Perry | 11 | 7 | 1 | 1 | 0 | 0 | 0 | .636 | .909 | .636 |
| Mark Portugal | 6 | 3 | 0 | 0 | 0 | 0 | 1 | .500 | .500 | .500 |
| Dennis Powell | 5 | 0 | 0 | 0 | 0 | 1 | 0 | .000 | .000 | .167 |
| Ted Power | 31 | 13 | 2 | 1 | 1 | 5 | 2 | .419 | .645 | .500 |
| Joe Price | 20 | 6 | 0 | 1 | 0 | 4 | 1 | .300 | .400 | .417 |
| Charlie Puleo | 32 | 10 | 0 | 0 | 1 | 1 | 0 | .313 | .406 | .333 |
| Shane Rawley | 22 | 4 | 0 | 0 | 0 | 1 | 1 | .182 | .182 | .217 |
| Jeff Reardon | 6 | 1 | 0 | 0 | 0 | 1 | 0 | .167 | .167 | .286 |
| Rick Reuschel | 49 | 16 | 2 | 0 | 1 | 1 | 1 | .327 | .429 | .340 |

# Tony Gwynn continued

| Pitcher | AB | H | 2B | 3B | HR | BB | SO | BA | SA | OBA |
|---|---|---|---|---|---|---|---|---|---|---|
| Jerry Reuss | 15 | 4 | 1 | 0 | 0 | 0 | 0 | .267 | .333 | .313 |
| Rick Rhoden | 34 | 9 | 2 | 0 | 0 | 2 | 0 | .265 | .324 | .306 |
| Jose Rijo | 13 | 3 | 0 | 0 | 0 | 2 | 3 | .231 | .231 | .333 |
| Don Robinson | 27 | 6 | 0 | 0 | 0 | 0 | 1 | .222 | .222 | .214 |
| Jeff D. Robinson | 27 | 13 | 2 | 2 | 0 | 2 | 0 | .481 | .704 | .517 |
| Ron Robinson | 21 | 5 | 1 | 0 | 0 | 1 | 0 | .238 | .286 | .273 |
| Steve Rogers | 21 | 7 | 0 | 0 | 0 | 1 | 0 | .333 | .333 | .364 |
| Dave Rucker | 10 | 2 | 0 | 0 | 0 | 1 | 0 | .200 | .200 | .273 |
| Bruce Ruffin | 16 | 3 | 0 | 0 | 0 | 3 | 0 | .188 | .188 | .316 |
| Vern Ruhle | 9 | 4 | 0 | 0 | 1 | 3 | 0 | .444 | .778 | .583 |
| Jeff Russell | 14 | 7 | 1 | 0 | 0 | 1 | 0 | .500 | .571 | .533 |
| Dick Ruthven | 15 | 4 | 0 | 0 | 0 | 0 | 0 | .267 | .267 | .267 |
| Nolan Ryan | 63 | 19 | 0 | 1 | 0 | 3 | 9 | .302 | .333 | .328 |
| Scott Sanderson | 29 | 11 | 1 | 0 | 0 | 2 | 1 | .379 | .414 | .419 |
| Dan Schatzeder | 15 | 1 | 0 | 0 | 0 | 1 | 1 | .067 | .067 | .125 |
| Bill Scherrer | 9 | 3 | 1 | 0 | 0 | 0 | 1 | .333 | .444 | .333 |
| Calvin Schiraldi | 12 | 5 | 1 | 1 | 1 | 0 | 0 | .417 | .917 | .417 |
| Mike Scott | 75 | 27 | 4 | 1 | 0 | 9 | 3 | .360 | .440 | .424 |
| Rod Scurry | 8 | 1 | 0 | 0 | 0 | 3 | 1 | .125 | .125 | .364 |
| Tom Seaver | 14 | 3 | 0 | 0 | 0 | 0 | 1 | .214 | .214 | .214 |
| Bob Sebra | 9 | 3 | 1 | 0 | 0 | 0 | 0 | .333 | .444 | .300 |
| Bob Shirley | 7 | 1 | 0 | 0 | 0 | 0 | 2 | .143 | .143 | .143 |
| Doug Sisk | 5 | 2 | 0 | 0 | 0 | 2 | 0 | .400 | .400 | .571 |
| John Smiley | 19 | 3 | 0 | 0 | 0 | 2 | 6 | .158 | .158 | .238 |
| Bryn Smith | 44 | 16 | 1 | 1 | 1 | 0 | 1 | .364 | .500 | .364 |
| Dave Smith | 12 | 7 | 0 | 0 | 0 | 1 | 0 | .583 | .583 | .615 |
| Lee Smith | 10 | 4 | 0 | 0 | 0 | 2 | 1 | .400 | .400 | .500 |
| Pete Smith | 23 | 9 | 1 | 1 | 1 | 2 | 0 | .391 | .652 | .440 |
| Zane Smith | 35 | 12 | 3 | 0 | 0 | 4 | 3 | .343 | .429 | .410 |

| Pitcher | AB | H | 2B | 3B | HR | BB | SO | BA | SA | OBA |
|---|---|---|---|---|---|---|---|---|---|---|
| John Smoltz | 20 | 8 | 1 | 0 | 1 | 1 | 1 | .400 | .600 | .429 |
| Lary Sorensen | 5 | 1 | 1 | 0 | 0 | 1 | 1 | .200 | .400 | .333 |
| Mario Soto | 33 | 7 | 2 | 0 | 1 | 4 | 3 | .212 | .364 | .297 |
| John Stuper | 6 | 1 | 0 | 0 | 0 | 1 | 0 | .167 | .167 | .286 |
| Rick Sutcliffe | 43 | 15 | 5 | 0 | 0 | 3 | 2 | .349 | .465 | .391 |
| Bruce Sutter | 10 | 3 | 0 | 0 | 0 | 0 | 0 | .300 | .300 | .300 |
| Don Sutton | 12 | 2 | 1 | 0 | 0 | 3 | 1 | .167 | .250 | .333 |
| Craig Swan | 7 | 3 | 2 | 0 | 0 | 0 | 0 | .429 | .714 | .429 |
| Kent Tekulve | 10 | 3 | 0 | 1 | 0 | 2 | 0 | .300 | .500 | .417 |
| Walt Terrell | 10 | 5 | 1 | 0 | 0 | 1 | 0 | .500 | .600 | .545 |
| Scott Terry | 9 | 2 | 0 | 0 | 0 | 0 | 0 | .222 | .222 | .222 |
| Jay Tibbs | 25 | 10 | 2 | 0 | 1 | 3 | 0 | .400 | .600 | .464 |
| Steve Trout | 29 | 11 | 2 | 0 | 0 | 2 | 0 | .379 | .448 | .455 |
| John Tudor | 38 | 15 | 3 | 0 | 2 | 1 | 6 | .395 | .632 | .425 |
| Lee Tunnell | 9 | 4 | 0 | 0 | 0 | 1 | 0 | .444 | .444 | .500 |
| Fernando Valenzuela | 67 | 21 | 3 | 0 | 1 | 3 | 5 | .313 | .403 | .343 |
| Dave Von Ohlen | 5 | 2 | 1 | 0 | 0 | 0 | 0 | .400 | .600 | .400 |
| Bob Walk | 37 | 14 | 2 | 1 | 0 | 2 | 1 | .378 | .486 | .410 |
| Bob Welch | 48 | 14 | 2 | 0 | 0 | 2 | 4 | .292 | .333 | .320 |
| Chris Welsh | 8 | 4 | 3 | 0 | 0 | 0 | 0 | .500 | .875 | .500 |
| John Wetteland | 6 | 1 | 0 | 0 | 0 | 0 | 1 | .167 | .167 | .167 |
| Frank Williams | 13 | 4 | 0 | 0 | 0 | 1 | 1 | .308 | .308 | .357 |
| Carl Willis | 5 | 3 | 0 | 0 | 0 | 0 | 0 | .600 | .600 | .600 |
| Steve Wilson | 5 | 2 | 0 | 0 | 0 | 0 | 0 | .400 | .400 | .400 |
| Trevor Wilson | 7 | 3 | 0 | 0 | 0 | 0 | 0 | .429 | .429 | .429 |
| Todd Worrell | 5 | 2 | 1 | 0 | 0 | 2 | 1 | .400 | .600 | .571 |
| Floyd Youmans | 20 | 5 | 1 | 0 | 0 | 2 | 0 | .250 | .300 | .318 |
| Pat Zachry | 5 | 1 | 0 | 0 | 0 | 1 | 0 | .200 | .200 | .333 |

# Howard Johnson

| Pitcher | AB | H | 2B | 3B | HR | BB | SO | BA | SA | OBA |
|---|---|---|---|---|---|---|---|---|---|---|
| Jim Acker | 15 | 8 | 2 | 0 | 4 | 1 | 1 | .533 | 1.467 | .563 |
| Doyle Alexander | 6 | 0 | 0 | 0 | 0 | 2 | 2 | .000 | .000 | .333 |
| Larry Andersen | 8 | 1 | 0 | 0 | 0 | 3 | 4 | .125 | .125 | .333 |
| Bud Anderson | 5 | 1 | 0 | 0 | 0 | 1 | 0 | .200 | .200 | .333 |
| Joaquin Andujar | 19 | 6 | 1 | 0 | 0 | 1 | 1 | .316 | .368 | .333 |
| Jack Armstrong | 6 | 3 | 1 | 0 | 1 | 0 | 1 | .500 | 1.167 | .500 |
| Paul Assenmacher | 7 | 2 | 1 | 0 | 1 | 0 | 4 | .286 | .857 | .286 |
| Jay Baller | 5 | 0 | 0 | 0 | 0 | 3 | 1 | .000 | .000 | .375 |
| Len Barker | 12 | 2 | 0 | 0 | 0 | 0 | 3 | .167 | .167 | .167 |
| Jim Beattie | 6 | 2 | 0 | 0 | 0 | 0 | 1 | .333 | .333 | .333 |
| Steve Bedrosian | 14 | 4 | 0 | 0 | 2 | 1 | 3 | .286 | .714 | .333 |
| Mike Bielecki | 24 | 6 | 2 | 0 | 2 | 1 | 5 | .250 | .583 | .269 |
| Bert Blyleven | 8 | 1 | 1 | 0 | 0 | 2 | 1 | .125 | .250 | .300 |
| Mike Boddicker | 6 | 3 | 1 | 0 | 0 | 0 | 0 | .500 | .667 | .500 |
| Greg Booker | 5 | 2 | 0 | 0 | 1 | 1 | 1 | .400 | 1.000 | .500 |
| Derek Botelho | 5 | 1 | 0 | 0 | 0 | 0 | 0 | .200 | .200 | .200 |
| Oil Can Boyd | 6 | 1 | 0 | 0 | 0 | 0 | 1 | .167 | .167 | .167 |
| Tom Brennan | 8 | 4 | 0 | 0 | 0 | 0 | 0 | .500 | .500 | .500 |
| Tom Browning | 24 | 1 | 0 | 0 | 0 | 1 | 6 | .042 | .042 | .077 |
| Tim Burke | 18 | 4 | 1 | 0 | 1 | 2 | 4 | .222 | .444 | .300 |
| Ernie Camacho | 5 | 0 | 0 | 0 | 0 | 0 | 1 | .000 | .000 | .000 |
| Don Carman | 34 | 5 | 0 | 0 | 1 | 5 | 9 | .147 | .235 | .256 |
| Jim Clancy | 14 | 4 | 0 | 0 | 1 | 2 | 1 | .286 | .500 | .375 |
| Pat Clements | 8 | 1 | 0 | 0 | 0 | 0 | 2 | .125 | .125 | .125 |
| Danny Cox | 24 | 5 | 1 | 0 | 3 | 1 | 3 | .208 | .625 | .269 |
| Tim Crews | 8 | 2 | 0 | 0 | 0 | 1 | 1 | .250 | .250 | .333 |
| Danny Darwin | 24 | 10 | 1 | 0 | 3 | 4 | 5 | .417 | .833 | .483 |
| Mark Davis | 11 | 5 | 0 | 0 | 2 | 2 | 4 | .455 | 1.000 | .538 |
| Ron Davis | 8 | 0 | 0 | 0 | 0 | 0 | 1 | .000 | .000 | .111 |
| Storm Davis | 10 | 4 | 2 | 0 | 1 | 1 | 1 | .400 | .900 | .455 |
| Bill Dawley | 9 | 4 | 1 | 0 | 1 | 1 | 0 | .444 | .889 | .500 |
| Ken Dayley | 10 | 3 | 0 | 0 | 0 | 5 | 4 | .300 | .300 | .563 |
| Jose DeLeon | 32 | 5 | 1 | 0 | 0 | 4 | 10 | .156 | .188 | .270 |
| John Denny | 13 | 2 | 0 | 0 | 0 | 1 | 6 | .154 | .154 | .214 |
| Jim Deshaies | 16 | 0 | 0 | 0 | 0 | 0 | 8 | .000 | .000 | .000 |
| Frank DiPino | 14 | 6 | 0 | 0 | 3 | 2 | 2 | .429 | 1.071 | .529 |
| John Dopson | 6 | 2 | 0 | 0 | 0 | 0 | 2 | .333 | .333 | .333 |
| Richard Dotson | 8 | 2 | 0 | 0 | 0 | 1 | 0 | .250 | .250 | .333 |
| Kelly Downs | 10 | 1 | 0 | 0 | 0 | 3 | 1 | .100 | .100 | .308 |
| Doug Drabek | 26 | 5 | 1 | 0 | 2 | 4 | 4 | .192 | .462 | .300 |

| Pitcher | AB | H | 2B | 3B | HR | BB | SO | BA | SA | OBA |
|---|---|---|---|---|---|---|---|---|---|---|
| Mike Dunne | 11 | 2 | 2 | 0 | 0 | 2 | 2 | .182 | .364 | .308 |
| Dennis Eckersley | 9 | 3 | 2 | 0 | 0 | 1 | 1 | .333 | .556 | .400 |
| Brian Fisher | 8 | 4 | 0 | 0 | 2 | 4 | 0 | .500 | 1.250 | .667 |
| Bob Forsch | 15 | 7 | 0 | 0 | 2 | 0 | 3 | .467 | .867 | .467 |
| Ken Forsch | 6 | 3 | 0 | 0 | 1 | 0 | 0 | .500 | 1.000 | .500 |
| John Franco | 15 | 3 | 1 | 0 | 0 | 1 | 5 | .200 | .267 | .250 |
| George Frazier | 6 | 2 | 0 | 0 | 1 | 1 | 1 | .333 | .833 | .429 |
| Marvin Freeman | 6 | 1 | 0 | 0 | 0 | 2 | 1 | .167 | .167 | .375 |
| Gene Garber | 10 | 2 | 1 | 0 | 0 | 0 | 3 | .200 | .300 | .200 |
| Scott Garrelts | 20 | 7 | 1 | 1 | 0 | 1 | 2 | .350 | .500 | .381 |
| Tom Glavine | 10 | 1 | 1 | 0 | 0 | 0 | 0 | .100 | .200 | .100 |
| Rich Gossage | 6 | 3 | 0 | 0 | 0 | 1 | 0 | .500 | .500 | .500 |
| Jim Gott | 15 | 4 | 1 | 0 | 1 | 2 | 2 | .267 | .533 | .353 |
| Mark Grant | 6 | 1 | 0 | 0 | 0 | 2 | 2 | .167 | .167 | .375 |
| Kevin Gross | 45 | 17 | 3 | 0 | 3 | 11 | 13 | .378 | .644 | .500 |
| Cecilio Guante | 6 | 3 | 1 | 0 | 1 | 0 | 1 | .500 | 1.167 | .500 |
| Bill Gullickson | 15 | 1 | 0 | 0 | 1 | 5 | 1 | .067 | .267 | .300 |
| Moose Haas | 6 | 3 | 0 | 0 | 0 | 0 | 1 | .500 | .500 | .500 |
| Drew Hall | 9 | 3 | 0 | 0 | 1 | 0 | 2 | .333 | .667 | .333 |
| Atlee Hammaker | 14 | 5 | 0 | 0 | 1 | 0 | 1 | .357 | .571 | .357 |
| Greg A. Harris | 5 | 1 | 0 | 1 | 0 | 2 | 2 | .200 | .600 | .429 |
| Andy Hawkins | 5 | 2 | 0 | 0 | 0 | 2 | 2 | .400 | .400 | .571 |
| Neal Heaton | 13 | 4 | 2 | 0 | 1 | 5 | 4 | .308 | .692 | .474 |
| Orel Hershiser | 37 | 7 | 1 | 0 | 1 | 2 | 12 | .189 | .297 | .231 |
| Joe Hesketh | 5 | 1 | 0 | 0 | 0 | 1 | 1 | .200 | .200 | .286 |
| Ken Hill | 5 | 1 | 0 | 0 | 0 | 0 | 1 | .200 | .200 | .200 |
| Guy Hoffman | 9 | 1 | 0 | 0 | 1 | 0 | 1 | .111 | .444 | .111 |
| Ricky Horton | 20 | 9 | 0 | 0 | 0 | 1 | 3 | .450 | .450 | .476 |
| Charlie Hough | 6 | 1 | 0 | 0 | 0 | 0 | 0 | .167 | .167 | .167 |
| Jay Howell | 5 | 0 | 0 | 0 | 0 | 1 | 0 | .000 | .000 | .167 |
| Ken Howell | 15 | 2 | 0 | 0 | 1 | 2 | 6 | .133 | .333 | .235 |
| LaMarr Hoyt | 23 | 5 | 0 | 0 | 0 | 1 | 3 | .217 | .217 | .240 |
| Charles Hudson | 6 | 3 | 1 | 0 | 0 | 1 | 0 | .500 | .667 | .571 |
| Bruce Hurst | 19 | 8 | 2 | 0 | 2 | 0 | 1 | .421 | .842 | .421 |
| Danny Jackson | 13 | 3 | 1 | 0 | 0 | 2 | 1 | .231 | .308 | .333 |
| Roy Lee Jackson | 6 | 2 | 0 | 1 | 0 | 0 | 1 | .333 | .667 | .333 |
| Tommy John | 6 | 0 | 0 | 0 | 0 | 0 | 0 | .000 | .000 | .000 |
| Joe Johnson | 5 | 2 | 1 | 0 | 0 | 0 | 1 | .400 | .600 | .400 |
| Jimmy Jones | 11 | 3 | 0 | 0 | 0 | 1 | 1 | .273 | .273 | .333 |
| Mike Jones | 6 | 0 | 0 | 0 | 0 | 0 | 2 | .000 | .000 | .000 |

# Howard Johnson continued

| Pitcher | AB | H | 2B | 3B | HR | BB | SO | BA | SA | OBA |
|---|---|---|---|---|---|---|---|---|---|---|
| Paul Kilgus | 8 | 1 | 0 | 0 | 0 | 2 | 2 | .125 | .125 | .300 |
| Bob Kipper | 16 | 3 | 0 | 0 | 1 | 3 | 4 | .188 | .375 | .316 |
| Bob Knepper | 25 | 9 | 0 | 0 | 3 | 3 | 3 | .360 | .720 | .429 |
| Randy Kramer | 5 | 1 | 0 | 0 | 0 | 1 | 1 | .200 | .200 | .333 |
| Mike Krukow | 24 | 5 | 1 | 0 | 2 | 4 | 5 | .208 | .500 | .321 |
| Mike LaCoss | 15 | 5 | 1 | 0 | 2 | 2 | 2 | .333 | .800 | .412 |
| Dennis Lamp | 8 | 1 | 0 | 0 | 0 | 1 | 0 | .125 | .125 | .222 |
| Les Lancaster | 19 | 7 | 2 | 0 | 1 | 1 | 2 | .368 | .632 | .400 |
| Mark Langston | 18 | 2 | 1 | 0 | 0 | 3 | 9 | .111 | .167 | .238 |
| Jack Lazorko | 6 | 1 | 0 | 0 | 0 | 0 | 1 | .167 | .167 | .167 |
| Luis Leal | 6 | 2 | 1 | 0 | 0 | 1 | 3 | .333 | .500 | .429 |
| Tim Leary | 9 | 2 | 0 | 0 | 0 | 2 | 2 | .222 | .222 | .364 |
| Craig Lefferts | 9 | 4 | 2 | 0 | 0 | 4 | 4 | .444 | .667 | .615 |
| Dennis Leonard | 7 | 2 | 0 | 0 | 0 | 1 | 1 | .286 | .286 | .375 |
| Derek Lilliquist | 5 | 1 | 1 | 0 | 0 | 0 | 0 | .200 | .400 | .200 |
| Ed Lynch | 8 | 2 | 0 | 0 | 1 | 1 | 2 | .250 | .625 | .333 |
| Rick Lysander | 5 | 0 | 0 | 0 | 0 | 0 | 1 | .000 | .000 | .000 |
| Greg Maddux | 26 | 9 | 4 | 0 | 2 | 6 | 3 | .346 | .731 | .469 |
| Mike Maddux | 7 | 1 | 1 | 0 | 0 | 0 | 2 | .143 | .286 | .143 |
| Joe Magrane | 12 | 4 | 0 | 0 | 0 | 3 | 3 | .333 | .333 | .467 |
| Rick Mahler | 27 | 8 | 1 | 0 | 1 | 3 | 4 | .296 | .444 | .367 |
| Dennis Martinez | 41 | 13 | 3 | 0 | 3 | 2 | 9 | .317 | .610 | .349 |
| Ramon Martinez | 5 | 2 | 0 | 0 | 1 | 2 | 1 | .400 | 1.000 | .571 |
| Mike Mason | 8 | 3 | 0 | 0 | 0 | 1 | 1 | .375 | .375 | .444 |
| Greg Mathews | 15 | 4 | 2 | 0 | 0 | 2 | 4 | .267 | .400 | .353 |
| Lance McCullers | 8 | 2 | 1 | 0 | 0 | 1 | 0 | .250 | .375 | .333 |
| Andy McGaffigan | 18 | 3 | 1 | 0 | 0 | 0 | 3 | .167 | .222 | .158 |
| Larry McWilliams | 22 | 6 | 1 | 0 | 0 | 3 | 2 | .273 | .318 | .346 |
| Doc Medich | 6 | 2 | 0 | 0 | 0 | 0 | 1 | .333 | .333 | .333 |
| Mike Moore | 9 | 2 | 0 | 0 | 0 | 1 | 3 | .222 | .222 | .300 |
| Mike Morgan | 9 | 2 | 1 | 1 | 0 | 0 | 2 | .222 | .556 | .200 |
| Jamie Moyer | 10 | 1 | 0 | 0 | 0 | 0 | 5 | .100 | .100 | .100 |
| Joe Niekro | 11 | 2 | 0 | 0 | 0 | 0 | 0 | .182 | .182 | .182 |
| Mike Norris | 7 | 2 | 0 | 0 | 0 | 0 | 2 | .286 | .286 | .286 |
| Randy O'Neal | 8 | 3 | 0 | 0 | 0 | 0 | 3 | .375 | .375 | .375 |
| David Palmer | 14 | 2 | 0 | 0 | 0 | 0 | 5 | .143 | .143 | .143 |
| Jim Palmer | 6 | 1 | 0 | 0 | 0 | 0 | 2 | .167 | .167 | .167 |
| Jeff Parrett | 11 | 0 | 0 | 0 | 0 | 0 | 4 | .000 | .000 | .000 |
| Bob Patterson | 8 | 2 | 0 | 0 | 0 | 2 | 3 | .250 | .250 | .400 |
| Alejandro Pena | 10 | 2 | 0 | 0 | 0 | 0 | 3 | .200 | .200 | .200 |
| Pascual Perez | 23 | 8 | 1 | 0 | 2 | 3 | 8 | .348 | .652 | .407 |
| Gaylord Perry | 5 | 3 | 0 | 0 | 0 | 1 | 1 | .600 | .600 | .667 |
| Pat Perry | 13 | 6 | 1 | 0 | 4 | 2 | 1 | .462 | 1.462 | .533 |
| Jeff Pico | 13 | 4 | 1 | 0 | 1 | 1 | 1 | .308 | .615 | .357 |
| Ted Power | 13 | 4 | 0 | 0 | 3 | 2 | 5 | .308 | 1.000 | .400 |
| Joe Price | 5 | 2 | 0 | 0 | 1 | 1 | 1 | .400 | 1.000 | .500 |
| Charlie Puleo | 10 | 1 | 0 | 0 | 0 | 1 | 2 | .100 | .100 | .182 |
| Dan Quisenberry | 11 | 3 | 0 | 0 | 0 | 0 | 0 | .273 | .273 | .250 |
| Chuck Rainey | 6 | 1 | 0 | 0 | 1 | 0 | 0 | .167 | .667 | .167 |
| Dennis Rasmussen | 14 | 4 | 1 | 0 | 0 | 4 | 3 | .286 | .357 | .444 |
| Shane Rawley | 17 | 5 | 1 | 0 | 0 | 5 | 4 | .294 | .353 | .455 |
| Rick Reuschel | 27 | 8 | 2 | 0 | 2 | 1 | 4 | .296 | .593 | .321 |
| Rick Rhoden | 8 | 1 | 0 | 0 | 0 | 1 | 1 | .125 | .125 | .222 |
| Jose Rijo | 13 | 2 | 1 | 0 | 1 | 1 | 5 | .154 | .462 | .214 |
| Don Robinson | 21 | 3 | 0 | 0 | 0 | 2 | 4 | .143 | .143 | .217 |
| Jeff D. Robinson | 20 | 3 | 0 | 0 | 2 | 1 | 6 | .150 | .450 | .190 |
| Ron Robinson | 12 | 5 | 2 | 0 | 1 | 1 | 2 | .417 | .833 | .462 |
| Dave Rucker | 8 | 1 | 0 | 0 | 0 | 0 | 1 | .125 | .125 | .125 |
| Bruce Ruffin | 20 | 7 | 0 | 0 | 2 | 6 | 3 | .350 | .650 | .500 |
| Nolan Ryan | 16 | 6 | 2 | 0 | 0 | 6 | 4 | .375 | .500 | .545 |
| Bret Saberhagen | 5 | 0 | 0 | 0 | 0 | 0 | 1 | .000 | .000 | .000 |
| Scott Sanderson | 21 | 7 | 4 | 0 | 2 | 2 | 3 | .333 | .810 | .391 |
| Dan Schatzeder | 7 | 1 | 0 | 0 | 0 | 1 | 3 | .143 | .143 | .250 |
| Calvin Schiraldi | 11 | 2 | 0 | 1 | 0 | 2 | 4 | .182 | .364 | .308 |
| Mike Scott | 22 | 4 | 0 | 0 | 1 | 1 | 7 | .182 | .318 | .208 |
| Eric Show | 30 | 9 | 4 | 0 | 0 | 7 | 8 | .300 | .433 | .432 |
| John Smiley | 24 | 2 | 0 | 0 | 0 | 0 | 10 | .083 | .083 | .083 |
| Bryn Smith | 39 | 10 | 1 | 0 | 2 | 2 | 6 | .256 | .436 | .293 |
| Dave Smith | 11 | 4 | 0 | 0 | 0 | 2 | 2 | .364 | .364 | .462 |
| Pete Smith | 11 | 4 | 1 | 0 | 0 | 3 | 4 | .364 | .455 | .500 |
| Zane Smith | 18 | 2 | 1 | 0 | 0 | 4 | 3 | .111 | .167 | .273 |
| John Smoltz | 6 | 1 | 1 | 0 | 0 | 0 | 2 | .167 | .333 | .167 |
| Mario Soto | 24 | 3 | 1 | 0 | 0 | 1 | 7 | .125 | .167 | .160 |
| Dan Spillner | 8 | 1 | 0 | 0 | 1 | 0 | 2 | .125 | .500 | .125 |
| Randy St.Claire | 8 | 2 | 0 | 0 | 2 | 1 | 4 | .250 | 1.000 | .333 |
| Bob Stanley | 6 | 0 | 0 | 0 | 0 | 3 | 2 | .000 | .000 | .333 |
| Dave Stewart | 5 | 2 | 0 | 0 | 1 | 2 | 1 | .400 | 1.000 | .571 |
| Sammy Stewart | 7 | 4 | 0 | 0 | 0 | 0 | 1 | .571 | .571 | .571 |
| Dave Stieb | 5 | 1 | 0 | 0 | 1 | 0 | 1 | .200 | .800 | .200 |
| Bob Stoddard | 8 | 2 | 1 | 0 | 0 | 0 | 0 | .250 | .375 | .250 |
| Rick Sutcliffe | 40 | 10 | 3 | 1 | 2 | 4 | 10 | .250 | .525 | .318 |
| Bruce Sutter | 5 | 1 | 0 | 0 | 0 | 1 | 1 | .200 | .200 | .333 |
| Don Sutton | 11 | 6 | 1 | 0 | 1 | 1 | 4 | .545 | .909 | .583 |
| Frank Tanana | 6 | 3 | 0 | 0 | 1 | 0 | 2 | .500 | 1.000 | .500 |
| Kent Tekulve | 12 | 2 | 0 | 0 | 2 | 4 | 0 | .167 | .667 | .375 |
| Scott Terry | 12 | 3 | 1 | 0 | 0 | 1 | 4 | .250 | .333 | .308 |
| Jay Tibbs | 11 | 2 | 1 | 0 | 0 | 1 | 1 | .182 | .273 | .250 |
| Mike Torrez | 6 | 2 | 2 | 0 | 0 | 0 | 1 | .333 | .667 | .333 |
| John Tudor | 17 | 3 | 0 | 0 | 0 | 3 | 4 | .176 | .176 | .286 |
| Lee Tunnell | 8 | 4 | 1 | 0 | 0 | 0 | 2 | .500 | .625 | .500 |
| Fernando Valenzuela | 19 | 6 | 1 | 1 | 1 | 5 | 4 | .316 | .632 | .480 |
| Frank Viola | 7 | 1 | 1 | 0 | 0 | 0 | 3 | .143 | .286 | .143 |
| Bob Walk | 14 | 2 | 0 | 0 | 0 | 1 | 5 | .143 | .143 | .200 |
| Bob Welch | 15 | 2 | 0 | 0 | 0 | 1 | 5 | .133 | .133 | .188 |
| John Wetteland | 5 | 1 | 1 | 0 | 0 | 0 | 1 | .200 | .400 | .200 |
| Ed Whitson | 23 | 7 | 3 | 0 | 2 | 1 | 6 | .304 | .696 | .333 |
| Al Williams | 12 | 5 | 1 | 0 | 0 | 0 | 1 | .417 | .500 | .417 |
| Mike Witt | 12 | 3 | 0 | 0 | 1 | 1 | 3 | .250 | .500 | .308 |
| Todd Worrell | 9 | 5 | 0 | 0 | 4 | 6 | 1 | .556 | 1.889 | .733 |
| Floyd Youmans | 12 | 3 | 0 | 0 | 2 | 4 | 1 | .250 | .750 | .438 |

# Kevin Mitchell

| Pitcher | AB | H | 2B | 3B | HR | BB | SO | BA | SA | OBA |
|---|---|---|---|---|---|---|---|---|---|---|
| Juan Agosto | 5 | 2 | 0 | 0 | 0 | 1 | 0 | .400 | .400 | .500 |
| Rick Aguilera | 8 | 2 | 0 | 0 | 0 | 0 | 0 | .250 | .250 | .250 |
| Jose Alvarez | 12 | 6 | 1 | 0 | 1 | 0 | 2 | .500 | .833 | .500 |
| Larry Andersen | 9 | 2 | 0 | 0 | 1 | 1 | 3 | .222 | .556 | .300 |
| Paul Assenmacher | 6 | 0 | 0 | 0 | 0 | 3 | 2 | .000 | .000 | .333 |
| Steve Bedrosian | 5 | 3 | 0 | 0 | 1 | 1 | 2 | .600 | 1.200 | .667 |
| Tim Belcher | 9 | 1 | 0 | 0 | 0 | 4 | 2 | .111 | .111 | .385 |
| Tom Browning | 49 | 11 | 1 | 1 | 3 | 2 | 7 | .224 | .469 | .255 |
| Tim Burke | 11 | 4 | 0 | 0 | 0 | 0 | 2 | .364 | .364 | .364 |
| Don Carman | 14 | 2 | 1 | 0 | 0 | 2 | 3 | .143 | .214 | .250 |
| Norm Charlton | 6 | 2 | 0 | 0 | 1 | 0 | 3 | .333 | .833 | .333 |
| Rocky Childress | 6 | 3 | 0 | 0 | 0 | 0 | 2 | .500 | .500 | .500 |
| Jim Clancy | 8 | 2 | 1 | 0 | 1 | 1 | 0 | .250 | .750 | .333 |
| Marty Clary | 13 | 6 | 0 | 0 | 2 | 0 | 1 | .462 | .923 | .462 |
| Pat Clements | 5 | 2 | 0 | 0 | 1 | 0 | 0 | .400 | 1.000 | .400 |
| Kevin Coffman | 6 | 2 | 0 | 0 | 0 | 0 | 1 | .333 | .333 | .333 |
| David Cone | 15 | 3 | 0 | 0 | 1 | 0 | 5 | .200 | .400 | .200 |
| Tim Conroy | 5 | 1 | 0 | 0 | 1 | 1 | 2 | .200 | .800 | .333 |
| Danny Cox | 9 | 1 | 1 | 0 | 0 | 2 | 3 | .111 | .222 | .273 |
| Tim Crews | 9 | 4 | 0 | 0 | 1 | 0 | 1 | .444 | .778 | .444 |
| Ron Darling | 24 | 5 | 0 | 0 | 2 | 3 | 3 | .208 | .458 | .296 |
| Danny Darwin | 16 | 4 | 0 | 0 | 1 | 2 | 4 | .250 | .438 | .333 |
| Mark Davis | 17 | 5 | 1 | 0 | 0 | 1 | 3 | .294 | .353 | .333 |
| Ken Dayley | 6 | 1 | 1 | 0 | 0 | 0 | 3 | .167 | .333 | .167 |
| Jose DeLeon | 12 | 4 | 0 | 0 | 1 | 1 | 3 | .333 | .583 | .385 |
| Jim Deshaies | 12 | 3 | 0 | 0 | 1 | 6 | 0 | .250 | .500 | .500 |
| Rob Dibble | 8 | 1 | 0 | 0 | 1 | 0 | 5 | .125 | .500 | .125 |
| Frank DiPino | 8 | 3 | 0 | 0 | 1 | 1 | 1 | .375 | .750 | .444 |
| Kelly Downs | 6 | 1 | 1 | 0 | 0 | 2 | 2 | .167 | .333 | .375 |
| Doug Drabek | 13 | 5 | 0 | 1 | 2 | 0 | 1 | .385 | 1.000 | .429 |
| Mike Dunne | 14 | 4 | 0 | 0 | 2 | 0 | 0 | .286 | .714 | .267 |
| Dennis Eckersley | 6 | 3 | 2 | 0 | 0 | 0 | 1 | .500 | .833 | .500 |
| Sid Fernandez | 12 | 4 | 1 | 0 | 2 | 1 | 3 | .333 | .917 | .385 |
| Brian Fisher | 8 | 2 | 0 | 0 | 0 | 0 | 0 | .250 | .250 | .250 |
| Bob Forsch | 11 | 4 | 0 | 1 | 2 | 1 | 0 | .364 | 1.091 | .417 |
| John Franco | 9 | 3 | 0 | 0 | 0 | 2 | 2 | .333 | .333 | .455 |

# Kevin Mitchell continued

| Pitcher | AB | H | 2B | 3B | HR | BB | SO | BA | SA | OBA |
|---|---|---|---|---|---|---|---|---|---|---|
| Marvin Freeman | 5 | 0 | 0 | 0 | 0 | 1 | 1 | .000 | .000 | .167 |
| Tom Glavine | 14 | 6 | 1 | 0 | 2 | 2 | 4 | .429 | .929 | .500 |
| Dwight Gooden | 9 | 2 | 1 | 0 | 0 | 3 | 3 | .222 | .333 | .385 |
| Jim Gott | 8 | 0 | 0 | 0 | 0 | 1 | 2 | .000 | .000 | .111 |
| Mark Grant | 14 | 5 | 1 | 0 | 2 | 2 | 4 | .357 | .857 | .438 |
| Kevin Gross | 22 | 2 | 1 | 0 | 0 | 2 | 6 | .091 | .136 | .192 |
| Bill Gullickson | 11 | 3 | 0 | 0 | 2 | 0 | 1 | .273 | .818 | .273 |
| Greg W. Harris | 6 | 3 | 2 | 0 | 0 | 0 | 0 | .500 | .833 | .429 |
| Andy Hawkins | 5 | 0 | 0 | 0 | 0 | 2 | 3 | .000 | .000 | .286 |
| Jeff Heathcock | 7 | 4 | 0 | 0 | 0 | 1 | 0 | .571 | .571 | .625 |
| Neal Heaton | 5 | 1 | 0 | 0 | 0 | 3 | 0 | .200 | .200 | .500 |
| Orel Hershiser | 41 | 11 | 2 | 0 | 1 | 3 | 14 | .268 | .390 | .318 |
| Joe Hesketh | 9 | 5 | 1 | 0 | 1 | 1 | 0 | .556 | 1.000 | .600 |
| Shawn Hillegas | 5 | 2 | 0 | 1 | 0 | 1 | 0 | .400 | .800 | .500 |
| Guy Hoffman | 8 | 0 | 0 | 0 | 0 | 0 | 1 | .000 | .000 | .000 |
| Brian Holman | 7 | 2 | 0 | 0 | 0 | 1 | 1 | .286 | .286 | .375 |
| Brian Holton | 8 | 1 | 0 | 0 | 0 | 0 | 2 | .125 | .125 | .125 |
| Rick Honeycutt | 12 | 6 | 2 | 0 | 2 | 0 | 0 | .500 | 1.167 | .500 |
| Ricky Horton | 13 | 4 | 2 | 0 | 0 | 2 | 0 | .308 | .462 | .400 |
| Jay Howell | 9 | 3 | 0 | 0 | 1 | 0 | 2 | .333 | .667 | .333 |
| Ken Howell | 11 | 2 | 2 | 0 | 0 | 2 | 2 | .182 | .364 | .308 |
| Bruce Hurst | 6 | 3 | 0 | 0 | 2 | 4 | 0 | .500 | 1.500 | .700 |
| Danny Jackson | 22 | 6 | 2 | 0 | 2 | 1 | 4 | .273 | .636 | .304 |
| German Jimenez | 5 | 2 | 0 | 0 | 0 | 0 | 0 | .400 | .400 | .400 |
| Barry Jones | 6 | 0 | 0 | 0 | 0 | 0 | 1 | .000 | .000 | .000 |
| Jimmy Jones | 6 | 3 | 0 | 0 | 1 | 0 | 0 | .500 | 1.000 | .500 |
| Bob Kipper | 15 | 4 | 3 | 0 | 0 | 4 | 4 | .267 | .467 | .421 |
| Bob Knepper | 23 | 5 | 2 | 0 | 1 | 0 | 1 | .217 | .435 | .217 |
| Randy Kramer | 8 | 4 | 0 | 0 | 2 | 0 | 2 | .500 | 1.250 | .500 |
| Mike Krukow | 5 | 1 | 0 | 0 | 0 | 0 | 0 | .200 | .200 | .200 |
| Les Lancaster | 12 | 4 | 1 | 0 | 2 | 2 | 2 | .333 | .917 | .429 |
| Bill Landrum | 6 | 3 | 1 | 1 | 0 | 0 | 0 | .500 | 1.000 | .500 |
| Mark Langston | 5 | 2 | 0 | 0 | 1 | 0 | 1 | .400 | 1.000 | .400 |
| Terry Leach | 5 | 3 | 0 | 0 | 0 | 1 | 0 | .600 | .600 | .667 |
| Tim Leary | 19 | 6 | 2 | 0 | 2 | 2 | 2 | .316 | .737 | .348 |
| Derek Lilliquist | 8 | 2 | 0 | 0 | 0 | 2 | 0 | .250 | .250 | .455 |
| Ed Lynch | 6 | 0 | 0 | 0 | 0 | 1 | 2 | .000 | .000 | .143 |
| Greg Maddux | 20 | 6 | 4 | 0 | 1 | 1 | 3 | .300 | .650 | .333 |
| Alex Madrid | 5 | 1 | 0 | 0 | 0 | 1 | 0 | .200 | .200 | .333 |
| Joe Magrane | 16 | 3 | 2 | 0 | 0 | 0 | 3 | .188 | .313 | .188 |
| Rick Mahler | 28 | 12 | 1 | 0 | 3 | 4 | 3 | .429 | .786 | .485 |
| Dennis Martinez | 13 | 2 | 0 | 0 | 1 | 2 | 2 | .154 | .385 | .267 |
| Ramon Martinez | 11 | 1 | 1 | 0 | 0 | 3 | 3 | .091 | .182 | .286 |
| Roger Mason | 6 | 2 | 0 | 0 | 0 | 0 | 2 | .333 | .333 | .333 |
| Greg Mathews | 15 | 4 | 3 | 0 | 1 | 1 | 2 | .267 | .667 | .313 |
| Bob McClure | 5 | 1 | 0 | 0 | 0 | 0 | 1 | .200 | .200 | .200 |
| Lance McCullers | 9 | 2 | 1 | 0 | 0 | 0 | 3 | .222 | .333 | .222 |
| Roger McDowell | 8 | 3 | 0 | 0 | 0 | 0 | 1 | .375 | .375 | .444 |
| Andy McGaffigan | 9 | 3 | 1 | 0 | 0 | 0 | 0 | .333 | .444 | .333 |
| Larry McWilliams | 14 | 6 | 3 | 0 | 1 | 1 | 2 | .429 | .857 | .500 |
| John Mitchell | 6 | 1 | 0 | 0 | 0 | 0 | 3 | .167 | .167 | .167 |
| Jamie Moyer | 15 | 3 | 1 | 0 | 1 | 1 | 3 | .200 | .467 | .250 |
| Terry Mulholland | 8 | 1 | 0 | 0 | 0 | 1 | 2 | .125 | .125 | .222 |
| Rob Murphy | 7 | 2 | 0 | 0 | 0 | 0 | 3 | .286 | .286 | .286 |
| Randy Myers | 7 | 1 | 1 | 0 | 0 | 1 | 4 | .143 | .286 | .250 |
| Bob Ojeda | 14 | 4 | 1 | 0 | 1 | 2 | 1 | .286 | .571 | .353 |
| Randy O'Neal | 7 | 1 | 0 | 0 | 0 | 0 | 0 | .143 | .143 | .143 |
| Jesse Orosco | 5 | 1 | 1 | 0 | 0 | 0 | 3 | .200 | .400 | .200 |
| David Palmer | 10 | 1 | 0 | 0 | 0 | 0 | 3 | .100 | .100 | .100 |
| Jeff Parrett | 8 | 3 | 2 | 0 | 1 | 0 | 1 | .375 | 1.000 | .375 |
| Bob Patterson | 5 | 2 | 0 | 0 | 0 | 1 | 0 | .400 | .400 | .500 |
| Alejandro Pena | 7 | 0 | 0 | 0 | 0 | 2 | 4 | .000 | .000 | .222 |
| Pascual Perez | 12 | 2 | 0 | 0 | 0 | 2 | 3 | .167 | .167 | .333 |
| Pat Perry | 8 | 3 | 1 | 0 | 1 | 0 | 2 | .375 | .875 | .333 |
| Mark Portugal | 12 | 4 | 0 | 0 | 0 | 1 | 6 | .333 | .333 | .385 |
| Ted Power | 13 | 3 | 1 | 0 | 1 | 0 | 2 | .231 | .538 | .286 |
| Charlie Puleo | 11 | 5 | 3 | 0 | 0 | 1 | 1 | .455 | .727 | .462 |
| Dennis Rasmussen | 24 | 7 | 1 | 1 | 0 | 4 | 2 | .292 | .417 | .393 |
| Shane Rawley | 15 | 4 | 1 | 0 | 0 | 1 | 3 | .267 | .333 | .313 |
| Rick Reuschel | 7 | 0 | 0 | 0 | 0 | 0 | 1 | .000 | .000 | .000 |
| Jose Rijo | 10 | 2 | 0 | 0 | 0 | 0 | 4 | .200 | .200 | .200 |
| Don Robinson | 6 | 0 | 0 | 0 | 0 | 0 | 2 | .000 | .000 | .000 |
| Jeff D. Robinson | 13 | 5 | 1 | 0 | 1 | 1 | 3 | .385 | .692 | .429 |
| Ron Robinson | 16 | 4 | 1 | 0 | 2 | 3 | 6 | .250 | .688 | .368 |
| Bruce Ruffin | 23 | 6 | 2 | 1 | 0 | 1 | 1 | .261 | .435 | .292 |
| Nolan Ryan | 12 | 2 | 0 | 0 | 1 | 2 | 3 | .167 | .417 | .286 |
| Scott Sanderson | 15 | 5 | 1 | 0 | 1 | 1 | 6 | .333 | .600 | .375 |
| Dan Schatzeder | 6 | 1 | 0 | 0 | 0 | 2 | 2 | .167 | .167 | .375 |
| Calvin Schiraldi | 5 | 1 | 0 | 0 | 0 | 1 | 2 | .200 | .200 | .333 |
| Mike Scott | 28 | 7 | 1 | 0 | 1 | 5 | 9 | .250 | .393 | .364 |
| Bob Sebra | 5 | 1 | 0 | 1 | 0 | 0 | 1 | .200 | .600 | .200 |
| Eric Show | 22 | 8 | 1 | 0 | 2 | 2 | 1 | .364 | .682 | .417 |
| John Smiley | 25 | 5 | 0 | 0 | 3 | 4 | 2 | .200 | .560 | .310 |
| Bryn Smith | 22 | 5 | 1 | 2 | 0 | 2 | 6 | .227 | .455 | .292 |
| Dave Smith | 5 | 0 | 0 | 0 | 0 | 0 | 1 | .000 | .000 | .000 |
| Lee Smith | 6 | 1 | 0 | 0 | 0 | 0 | 4 | .167 | .167 | .167 |
| Pete Smith | 15 | 2 | 1 | 1 | 0 | 1 | 3 | .133 | .333 | .188 |
| Zane Smith | 14 | 4 | 1 | 0 | 2 | 0 | 2 | .286 | .786 | .286 |
| John Smoltz | 13 | 4 | 2 | 0 | 2 | 2 | 3 | .308 | .923 | .400 |
| Rick Sutcliffe | 26 | 5 | 0 | 0 | 1 | 2 | 2 | .192 | .308 | .250 |
| Kent Tekulve | 12 | 2 | 0 | 1 | 0 | 0 | 2 | .167 | .333 | .154 |
| Walt Terrell | 6 | 0 | 0 | 0 | 0 | 0 | 3 | .000 | .000 | .000 |
| Scott Terry | 6 | 3 | 2 | 1 | 0 | 1 | 0 | .500 | 1.167 | .500 |
| Mark Thurmond | 5 | 4 | 0 | 0 | 0 | 0 | 1 | .800 | .800 | .800 |
| Steve Trout | 9 | 1 | 0 | 0 | 0 | 1 | 0 | .111 | .111 | .200 |
| John Tudor | 14 | 9 | 1 | 0 | 2 | 3 | 1 | .643 | 1.143 | .706 |
| Fernando Valenzuela | 42 | 12 | 2 | 1 | 4 | 5 | 6 | .286 | .667 | .347 |
| Frank Viola | 5 | 2 | 0 | 0 | 1 | 2 | 2 | .400 | 1.000 | .571 |
| Bob Walk | 17 | 7 | 0 | 0 | 1 | 1 | 1 | .412 | .588 | .474 |
| Gene Walter | 5 | 1 | 1 | 0 | 0 | 1 | 0 | .200 | .400 | .333 |
| Bob Welch | 21 | 5 | 1 | 0 | 0 | 1 | 4 | .238 | .286 | .273 |
| John Wetteland | 5 | 3 | 0 | 0 | 0 | 1 | 0 | .600 | .600 | .667 |
| Ed Whitson | 14 | 3 | 1 | 0 | 0 | 2 | 4 | .214 | .286 | .333 |
| Frank Williams | 9 | 3 | 1 | 0 | 1 | 0 | 4 | .333 | .778 | .333 |
| Todd Worrell | 13 | 5 | 0 | 0 | 1 | 1 | 3 | .385 | .615 | .429 |
| Floyd Youmans | 18 | 4 | 0 | 1 | 0 | 3 | 4 | .222 | .333 | .333 |

# Robin Yount

| Pitcher | AB | H | 2B | 3B | HR | BB | SO | BA | SA | OBA |
|---|---|---|---|---|---|---|---|---|---|---|
| Don Aase | 29 | 9 | 3 | 0 | 0 | 2 | 3 | .310 | .414 | .344 |
| Glenn Abbott | 43 | 16 | 1 | 1 | 4 | 0 | 3 | .372 | .721 | .372 |
| Jim Acker | 9 | 5 | 0 | 0 | 0 | 2 | 2 | .556 | .556 | .636 |
| Darrel Akerfelds | 5 | 1 | 0 | 0 | 0 | 2 | 0 | .200 | .200 | .429 |
| Doyle Alexander | 70 | 24 | 6 | 2 | 1 | 7 | 8 | .343 | .529 | .403 |
| Brian Allard | 8 | 3 | 0 | 0 | 2 | 0 | 0 | .375 | 1.125 | .375 |
| Neil Allen | 5 | 3 | 1 | 0 | 1 | 1 | 0 | .600 | 1.400 | .667 |
| Allan Anderson | 12 | 2 | 0 | 0 | 0 | 2 | 2 | .167 | .167 | .286 |
| Joaquin Andujar | 10 | 2 | 0 | 0 | 1 | 2 | 2 | .200 | .500 | .333 |
| Luis Aponte | 7 | 2 | 0 | 0 | 0 | 2 | 0 | .286 | .286 | .444 |
| Mike Armstrong | 7 | 1 | 1 | 0 | 0 | 0 | 0 | .143 | .286 | .143 |
| Tony Arnold | 5 | 1 | 0 | 0 | 0 | 1 | 0 | .200 | .200 | .333 |
| Brad Arnsberg | 6 | 2 | 1 | 0 | 0 | 0 | 1 | .333 | .500 | .333 |
| Fernando Arroyo | 14 | 2 | 0 | 0 | 0 | 2 | 2 | .143 | .143 | .250 |
| Keith Atherton | 14 | 5 | 1 | 1 | 0 | 1 | 3 | .357 | .571 | .400 |
| Mike Bacsik | 5 | 0 | 0 | 0 | 0 | 0 | 1 | .000 | .000 | .000 |
| Stan Bahnsen | 21 | 6 | 2 | 0 | 1 | 1 | 1 | .286 | .524 | .318 |
| Scott Bailes | 23 | 8 | 0 | 1 | 2 | 3 | 1 | .348 | .696 | .423 |
| Doug Bair | 9 | 3 | 0 | 0 | 1 | 1 | 0 | .333 | .667 | .400 |
| Steve Baker | 5 | 1 | 1 | 0 | 0 | 2 | 0 | .200 | .400 | .429 |
| Jeff Ballard | 13 | 4 | 2 | 0 | 0 | 0 | 0 | .308 | .462 | .308 |
| Eddie Bane | 5 | 3 | 1 | 0 | 0 | 0 | 0 | .600 | .800 | .600 |
| Scott Bankhead | 11 | 6 | 2 | 0 | 0 | 1 | 1 | .545 | .727 | .583 |
| Floyd Bannister | 61 | 21 | 3 | 0 | 4 | 5 | 9 | .344 | .590 | .394 |
| Ray Bare | 21 | 7 | 2 | 0 | 0 | 3 | 3 | .333 | .429 | .400 |
| Len Barker | 33 | 9 | 4 | 2 | 0 | 1 | 4 | .273 | .515 | .294 |
| Mike Barlow | 5 | 3 | 0 | 1 | 0 | 2 | 0 | .600 | 1.000 | .714 |
| Salome Barojas | 14 | 3 | 1 | 0 | 0 | 0 | 1 | .214 | .286 | .188 |
| Jim Barr | 8 | 3 | 1 | 0 | 0 | 0 | 1 | .375 | .500 | .375 |
| Francisco Barrios | 22 | 4 | 0 | 2 | 0 | 0 | 5 | .182 | .364 | .182 |

# Robin Yount *continued*

| Pitcher | AB | H | 2B | 3B | HR | BB | SO | BA | SA | OBA |
|---|---|---|---|---|---|---|---|---|---|---|
| Ross Baumgarten | 12 | 2 | 0 | 0 | 0 | 1 | 2 | .167 | .167 | .231 |
| Jose Bautista | 8 | 2 | 0 | 0 | 0 | 0 | 1 | .250 | .250 | .250 |
| Dave Beard | 12 | 5 | 2 | 0 | 1 | 0 | 1 | .417 | .833 | .417 |
| Jim Beattie | 32 | 6 | 1 | 0 | 0 | 2 | 8 | .188 | .219 | .235 |
| Joe Beckwith | 6 | 2 | 0 | 0 | 0 | 0 | 0 | .333 | .333 | .333 |
| Eric Bell | 6 | 2 | 1 | 0 | 0 | 0 | 0 | .333 | .500 | .333 |
| Juan Berenguer | 34 | 10 | 1 | 1 | 1 | 5 | 8 | .294 | .471 | .390 |
| Karl Best | 5 | 2 | 0 | 0 | 0 | 0 | 1 | .400 | .400 | .400 |
| Jim Bibby | 46 | 15 | 3 | 1 | 0 | 1 | 6 | .326 | .435 | .340 |
| Jack Billingham | 9 | 4 | 0 | 1 | 0 | 1 | 1 | .444 | .667 | .500 |
| Doug Bird | 19 | 10 | 3 | 0 | 0 | 1 | 1 | .526 | .684 | .524 |
| Tim Birtsas | 8 | 3 | 1 | 0 | 0 | 0 | 1 | .375 | .500 | .375 |
| Bud Black | 29 | 10 | 3 | 1 | 0 | 6 | 4 | .345 | .517 | .457 |
| Vida Blue | 35 | 12 | 6 | 0 | 1 | 6 | 1 | .343 | .600 | .429 |
| Bert Blyleven | 96 | 18 | 6 | 1 | 1 | 3 | 4 | .188 | .302 | .212 |
| Mike Boddicker | 52 | 12 | 1 | 2 | 3 | 5 | 9 | .231 | .500 | .298 |
| Mark Bomback | 5 | 3 | 0 | 0 | 0 | 1 | 0 | .600 | .600 | .667 |
| Rich Bordi | 5 | 0 | 0 | 0 | 0 | 0 | 0 | .000 | .000 | .000 |
| Dick Bosman | 19 | 6 | 1 | 1 | 0 | 0 | 1 | .316 | .474 | .316 |
| Oil Can Boyd | 28 | 8 | 2 | 0 | 0 | 3 | 1 | .286 | .357 | .355 |
| Ken Brett | 17 | 3 | 0 | 0 | 0 | 1 | 1 | .176 | .176 | .222 |
| Nelson Briles | 19 | 9 | 0 | 0 | 1 | 1 | 1 | .474 | .632 | .500 |
| Pete Broberg | 8 | 2 | 1 | 0 | 0 | 0 | 0 | .250 | .375 | .250 |
| Jackie Brown | 26 | 9 | 2 | 0 | 0 | 2 | 2 | .346 | .423 | .393 |
| Mike G. Brown | 14 | 5 | 2 | 1 | 1 | 4 | 2 | .357 | .857 | .500 |
| DeWayne Buice | 6 | 1 | 0 | 0 | 0 | 1 | 1 | .167 | .167 | .286 |
| Tom Burgmeier | 19 | 6 | 0 | 0 | 0 | 0 | 2 | .316 | .316 | .316 |
| Britt Burns | 28 | 8 | 4 | 0 | 1 | 4 | 1 | .286 | .536 | .375 |
| Todd Burns | 8 | 2 | 0 | 0 | 0 | 0 | 1 | .250 | .250 | .250 |
| Ray Burris | 13 | 5 | 0 | 0 | 1 | 0 | 1 | .385 | .615 | .385 |
| Steve Busby | 19 | 6 | 2 | 0 | 0 | 0 | 1 | .316 | .421 | .316 |
| Tom Buskey | 18 | 2 | 0 | 1 | 0 | 0 | 3 | .111 | .222 | .111 |
| John Butcher | 20 | 6 | 2 | 0 | 1 | 0 | 2 | .300 | .550 | .300 |
| Jeff Byrd | 5 | 2 | 0 | 0 | 0 | 2 | 1 | .400 | .400 | .571 |
| Greg Cadaret | 7 | 3 | 0 | 0 | 0 | 2 | 0 | .429 | .429 | .556 |
| Bill Campbell | 19 | 5 | 2 | 0 | 0 | 2 | 4 | .263 | .368 | .333 |
| Mike Campbell | 10 | 5 | 3 | 0 | 0 | 0 | 2 | .500 | .800 | .455 |
| John Candelaria | 13 | 4 | 0 | 0 | 1 | 0 | 2 | .308 | .538 | .308 |
| Tom Candiotti | 26 | 9 | 0 | 0 | 0 | 3 | 4 | .346 | .346 | .414 |
| Steve Carlton | 10 | 1 | 0 | 0 | 0 | 1 | 2 | .100 | .100 | .182 |
| Bobby Castillo | 10 | 0 | 0 | 0 | 0 | 0 | 0 | .000 | .000 | .000 |
| Bill Castro | 5 | 1 | 0 | 0 | 1 | 0 | 1 | .200 | .800 | .167 |
| Bill Caudill | 8 | 4 | 1 | 0 | 0 | 0 | 1 | .500 | .625 | .500 |
| John Cerutti | 23 | 9 | 1 | 0 | 2 | 0 | 0 | .391 | .696 | .391 |
| Jim Clancy | 75 | 21 | 2 | 2 | 2 | 9 | 9 | .280 | .440 | .353 |
| Bryan Clark | 14 | 5 | 1 | 0 | 0 | 5 | 1 | .357 | .429 | .526 |
| Ken Clay | 8 | 3 | 1 | 0 | 0 | 2 | 0 | .375 | .500 | .500 |
| Mark Clear | 14 | 1 | 1 | 0 | 0 | 1 | 5 | .071 | .143 | .125 |
| Roger Clemens | 48 | 11 | 1 | 0 | 2 | 1 | 10 | .229 | .375 | .245 |
| Reggie Cleveland | 31 | 9 | 2 | 0 | 0 | 2 | 5 | .290 | .355 | .333 |
| Stu Cliburn | 5 | 0 | 0 | 0 | 0 | 0 | 3 | .000 | .000 | .000 |
| David Clyde | 12 | 4 | 0 | 2 | 0 | 1 | 2 | .333 | .667 | .385 |
| Chris Codiroli | 25 | 6 | 1 | 0 | 1 | 2 | 0 | .240 | .400 | .286 |
| Jim Colborn | 7 | 2 | 0 | 0 | 0 | 0 | 0 | .286 | .286 | .286 |
| Joe Coleman | 31 | 5 | 2 | 0 | 0 | 2 | 4 | .161 | .226 | .235 |
| Steve Comer | 23 | 4 | 1 | 0 | 0 | 3 | 0 | .174 | .217 | .250 |
| Tim Conroy | 7 | 3 | 1 | 0 | 1 | 3 | 1 | .429 | 1.000 | .600 |
| Doug Corbett | 19 | 5 | 1 | 0 | 1 | 0 | 4 | .263 | .474 | .250 |
| Ray Corbin | 6 | 1 | 0 | 0 | 0 | 1 | 1 | .167 | .167 | .286 |
| Edwin Correa | 10 | 3 | 0 | 0 | 0 | 1 | 2 | .300 | .300 | .364 |
| Jim Crawford | 9 | 4 | 0 | 0 | 0 | 1 | 0 | .444 | .444 | .500 |
| Steve Crawford | 10 | 3 | 0 | 0 | 1 | 1 | 2 | .300 | .600 | .364 |
| Victor Cruz | 8 | 1 | 1 | 0 | 0 | 2 | 2 | .125 | .250 | .273 |
| Mike Cuellar | 20 | 5 | 0 | 0 | 0 | 0 | 2 | .250 | .250 | .238 |
| John Curtis | 7 | 2 | 0 | 0 | 1 | 0 | 0 | .286 | .714 | .286 |
| Danny Darwin | 23 | 10 | 2 | 0 | 0 | 1 | 2 | .435 | .522 | .458 |
| Joel Davis | 18 | 6 | 0 | 0 | 1 | 3 | 0 | .333 | .500 | .409 |
| Ron Davis | 18 | 5 | 1 | 1 | 0 | 0 | 4 | .278 | .444 | .278 |
| Storm Davis | 50 | 18 | 4 | 1 | 1 | 0 | 6 | .360 | .540 | .353 |
| Joe Decker | 19 | 6 | 0 | 0 | 0 | 3 | 2 | .316 | .316 | .409 |
| Jose DeLeon | 10 | 3 | 0 | 0 | 1 | 1 | 2 | .300 | .600 | .364 |
| John Denny | 10 | 3 | 1 | 0 | 1 | 0 | 1 | .300 | .700 | .300 |
| Adrian Devine | 5 | 2 | 0 | 0 | 0 | 1 | 0 | .400 | .400 | .500 |
| Ken Dixon | 14 | 6 | 1 | 0 | 1 | 1 | 0 | .429 | .714 | .467 |
| Pat Dobson | 33 | 10 | 2 | 0 | 0 | 0 | 6 | .303 | .364 | .303 |
| John Dopson | 8 | 3 | 1 | 0 | 1 | 0 | 1 | .375 | .875 | .375 |
| Richard Dotson | 57 | 17 | 1 | 1 | 1 | 9 | 4 | .298 | .404 | .394 |
| Dick Drago | 17 | 7 | 2 | 0 | 1 | 1 | 0 | .412 | .706 | .421 |
| Rob Dressler | 12 | 4 | 1 | 0 | 0 | 2 | 1 | .333 | .417 | .429 |
| Jamie Easterly | 6 | 4 | 0 | 0 | 1 | 2 | 1 | .667 | 1.167 | .750 |
| Dennis Eckersley | 77 | 18 | 3 | 1 | 1 | 3 | 16 | .234 | .338 | .259 |
| Juan Eichelberger | 6 | 2 | 1 | 0 | 0 | 0 | 0 | .333 | .500 | .333 |
| Mark Eichhorn | 13 | 5 | 1 | 0 | 0 | 0 | 0 | .385 | .462 | .385 |
| Dave Eiland | 6 | 1 | 0 | 0 | 0 | 0 | 0 | .167 | .167 | .167 |
| Dock Ellis | 20 | 5 | 0 | 0 | 1 | 0 | 0 | .250 | .400 | .250 |
| Roger Erickson | 33 | 4 | 1 | 1 | 0 | 1 | 4 | .121 | .212 | .143 |
| Ed Farmer | 8 | 4 | 0 | 0 | 0 | 0 | 2 | .500 | .500 | .500 |
| Steve Farr | 11 | 6 | 0 | 0 | 0 | 3 | 2 | .545 | .545 | .643 |
| John Farrell | 19 | 6 | 0 | 0 | 0 | 3 | 1 | .316 | .316 | .409 |
| Terry Felton | 5 | 2 | 0 | 1 | 0 | 0 | 1 | .400 | .800 | .400 |
| Mark Fidrych | 16 | 4 | 1 | 0 | 0 | 1 | 2 | .250 | .313 | .294 |
| Ed Figueroa | 51 | 9 | 1 | 0 | 0 | 0 | 4 | .176 | .196 | .176 |
| Pete Filson | 12 | 4 | 0 | 0 | 1 | 1 | 1 | .333 | .583 | .385 |
| Rollie Fingers | 9 | 4 | 0 | 1 | 1 | 0 | 1 | .444 | 1.000 | .444 |
| Chuck Finley | 21 | 4 | 2 | 0 | 0 | 2 | 7 | .190 | .286 | .261 |
| Brian Fisher | 7 | 2 | 0 | 0 | 0 | 1 | 0 | .286 | .286 | .375 |
| Al Fitzmorris | 26 | 8 | 1 | 0 | 0 | 0 | 2 | .308 | .346 | .308 |
| Mike Flanagan | 78 | 34 | 8 | 2 | 4 | 3 | 6 | .436 | .744 | .446 |
| Ray Fontenot | 12 | 6 | 1 | 0 | 0 | 2 | 2 | .500 | .583 | .571 |
| Dave Ford | 6 | 2 | 0 | 0 | 0 | 1 | 0 | .333 | .333 | .429 |
| Ken Forsch | 11 | 2 | 0 | 0 | 0 | 1 | 1 | .182 | .182 | .250 |
| Terry Forster | 9 | 1 | 0 | 0 | 0 | 0 | 4 | .111 | .111 | .111 |
| Steve Foucault | 17 | 3 | 1 | 0 | 0 | 0 | 2 | .176 | .235 | .176 |
| Willie Fraser | 15 | 3 | 1 | 0 | 0 | 0 | 3 | .200 | .267 | .200 |
| George Frazier | 22 | 7 | 1 | 0 | 0 | 2 | 2 | .318 | .364 | .375 |
| Dave Frost | 8 | 2 | 2 | 0 | 0 | 1 | 0 | .250 | .500 | .300 |
| Woody Fryman | 6 | 0 | 0 | 0 | 0 | 0 | 1 | .000 | .000 | .000 |
| Rich Gale | 23 | 7 | 2 | 0 | 0 | 0 | 2 | .304 | .391 | .304 |
| Wes Gardner | 9 | 2 | 0 | 1 | 0 | 1 | 1 | .222 | .444 | .300 |
| Wayne Garland | 49 | 13 | 3 | 0 | 1 | 3 | 2 | .265 | .388 | .308 |
| Jerry Garvin | 20 | 11 | 2 | 1 | 1 | 2 | 0 | .550 | .900 | .591 |
| Dave Geisel | 11 | 1 | 0 | 0 | 0 | 0 | 3 | .091 | .091 | .091 |
| Paul Gibson | 14 | 4 | 2 | 0 | 0 | 2 | 1 | .286 | .429 | .375 |
| Jerry Don Gleaton | 7 | 3 | 1 | 0 | 1 | 2 | 1 | .429 | 1.000 | .556 |
| Ed Glynn | 7 | 0 | 0 | 0 | 0 | 0 | 1 | .000 | .000 | .000 |
| Dave Goltz | 56 | 15 | 4 | 0 | 1 | 6 | 5 | .268 | .393 | .333 |
| Don Gordon | 9 | 5 | 0 | 0 | 0 | 0 | 0 | .556 | .556 | .556 |
| Tom Gordon | 6 | 3 | 0 | 0 | 0 | 1 | 1 | .500 | .500 | .571 |
| Rich Gossage | 30 | 6 | 2 | 0 | 0 | 3 | 6 | .200 | .267 | .273 |
| Jim Gott | 13 | 1 | 0 | 0 | 0 | 0 | 2 | .077 | .077 | .077 |
| Steve Grilli | 7 | 2 | 0 | 0 | 0 | 0 | 1 | .286 | .286 | .286 |
| Ross Grimsley | 23 | 5 | 1 | 0 | 2 | 0 | 5 | .217 | .522 | .217 |
| Cecilio Guante | 5 | 1 | 0 | 0 | 0 | 0 | 0 | .200 | .200 | .200 |
| Mark Gubicza | 35 | 13 | 2 | 0 | 0 | 2 | 2 | .371 | .429 | .410 |
| Lee Guetterman | 8 | 4 | 0 | 0 | 1 | 1 | 1 | .500 | .875 | .556 |
| Ron Guidry | 70 | 18 | 5 | 1 | 2 | 0 | 11 | .257 | .443 | .254 |
| Don Gullett | 13 | 4 | 1 | 0 | 0 | 3 | 2 | .308 | .385 | .438 |
| Bill Gullickson | 7 | 2 | 0 | 0 | 0 | 0 | 2 | .286 | .286 | .286 |
| Larry Gura | 75 | 24 | 4 | 2 | 6 | 3 | 5 | .320 | .667 | .346 |
| Jose Guzman | 24 | 10 | 1 | 1 | 2 | 3 | 4 | .417 | .792 | .500 |
| Moose Haas | 5 | 2 | 1 | 0 | 0 | 0 | 1 | .400 | .600 | .400 |
| John Habyan | 6 | 1 | 0 | 0 | 0 | 0 | 0 | .167 | .167 | .167 |
| Ed Halicki | 9 | 4 | 2 | 0 | 0 | 0 | 1 | .444 | .667 | .444 |
| Dave Hamilton | 12 | 3 | 0 | 0 | 0 | 0 | 3 | .250 | .250 | .250 |
| Bill Hands | 5 | 1 | 0 | 0 | 0 | 0 | 0 | .200 | .200 | .200 |
| Erik Hanson | 14 | 2 | 1 | 0 | 1 | 0 | 1 | .143 | .429 | .143 |
| Steve Hargan | 15 | 6 | 1 | 0 | 0 | 0 | 3 | .400 | .467 | .400 |
| Greg A. Harris | 20 | 8 | 1 | 0 | 0 | 0 | 5 | .400 | .450 | .400 |
| Roric Harrison | 10 | 1 | 0 | 0 | 0 | 2 | 1 | .100 | .100 | .250 |
| Paul Hartzell | 35 | 8 | 1 | 0 | 0 | 1 | 2 | .229 | .257 | .250 |
| Andy Hassler | 29 | 11 | 0 | 0 | 1 | 1 | 3 | .379 | .483 | .400 |
| Brad Havens | 22 | 11 | 1 | 1 | 1 | 3 | 0 | .500 | .773 | .560 |
| Andy Hawkins | 8 | 5 | 1 | 0 | 0 | 3 | 1 | .625 | .750 | .727 |
| Neal Heaton | 29 | 10 | 1 | 2 | 0 | 4 | 2 | .345 | .517 | .400 |
| Dave Heaverlo | 9 | 4 | 1 | 0 | 0 | 0 | 0 | .444 | .556 | .444 |
| Tom Henke | 11 | 5 | 0 | 0 | 0 | 1 | 4 | .455 | .455 | .500 |
| Mike Henneman | 7 | 3 | 0 | 0 | 0 | 2 | 2 | .429 | .429 | .556 |
| Willie Hernandez | 9 | 2 | 0 | 0 | 0 | 3 | 2 | .222 | .222 | .417 |
| Shawn Hillegas | 8 | 3 | 1 | 0 | 0 | 0 | 0 | .375 | .500 | .444 |
| John Hiller | 26 | 6 | 0 | 0 | 0 | 0 | 6 | .231 | .231 | .231 |

# Robin Yount continued

| Pitcher | AB | H | 2B | 3B | HR | BB | SO | BA | SA | OBA |
|---|---|---|---|---|---|---|---|---|---|---|
| Ed Hodge | 7 | 4 | 0 | 1 | 1 | 1 | 1 | .571 | 1.286 | .625 |
| Ken Holtzman | 31 | 7 | 1 | 0 | 0 | 4 | 3 | .226 | .258 | .314 |
| Rick Honeycutt | 30 | 7 | 0 | 0 | 0 | 4 | 3 | .233 | .233 | .324 |
| Don Hood | 27 | 3 | 0 | 0 | 0 | 2 | 3 | .111 | .111 | .167 |
| Charlie Hough | 45 | 15 | 4 | 0 | 1 | 4 | 3 | .333 | .489 | .388 |
| Tom House | 8 | 4 | 2 | 0 | 0 | 1 | 0 | .500 | .750 | .556 |
| Fred Howard | 5 | 1 | 1 | 0 | 0 | 0 | 0 | .200 | .400 | .200 |
| Jay Howell | 12 | 7 | 1 | 0 | 1 | 1 | 1 | .583 | .917 | .615 |
| LaMarr Hoyt | 37 | 14 | 2 | 0 | 3 | 0 | 1 | .378 | .676 | .378 |
| Charles Hudson | 13 | 6 | 0 | 1 | 1 | 0 | 2 | .462 | .846 | .462 |
| Jim Hughes | 15 | 6 | 1 | 0 | 1 | 0 | 2 | .400 | .667 | .400 |
| Mark Huismann | 8 | 1 | 0 | 0 | 0 | 1 | 0 | .125 | .125 | .182 |
| Catfish Hunter | 42 | 12 | 3 | 2 | 1 | 1 | 5 | .286 | .524 | .295 |
| Bruce Hurst | 39 | 7 | 2 | 1 | 0 | 5 | 5 | .179 | .282 | .273 |
| Danny Jackson | 19 | 5 | 1 | 0 | 0 | 4 | 4 | .263 | .316 | .391 |
| Mike Jackson | 6 | 4 | 1 | 0 | 1 | 2 | 0 | .667 | 1.333 | .750 |
| Roy Lee Jackson | 10 | 3 | 1 | 0 | 0 | 0 | 1 | .300 | .400 | .300 |
| Mike Jeffcoat | 7 | 3 | 1 | 0 | 0 | 0 | 1 | .429 | .571 | .500 |
| Jesse Jefferson | 30 | 8 | 2 | 0 | 3 | 2 | 3 | .267 | .633 | .313 |
| Ferguson Jenkins | 50 | 13 | 1 | 0 | 1 | 3 | 6 | .260 | .340 | .302 |
| Tommy John | 75 | 23 | 5 | 1 | 1 | 6 | 0 | .307 | .440 | .366 |
| Bart Johnson | 18 | 7 | 2 | 0 | 0 | 0 | 2 | .389 | .500 | .389 |
| Dave W. Johnson | 5 | 0 | 0 | 0 | 0 | 0 | 1 | .000 | .000 | .167 |
| Jerry Johnson | 5 | 3 | 0 | 0 | 0 | 1 | 0 | .600 | .600 | .667 |
| Joe Johnson | 8 | 4 | 1 | 0 | 1 | 0 | 0 | .500 | 1.000 | .500 |
| John Henry Johnson | 8 | 2 | 0 | 0 | 0 | 1 | 0 | .250 | .250 | .333 |
| Randy D. Johnson | 5 | 2 | 2 | 0 | 0 | 1 | 1 | .400 | .800 | .500 |
| Tom Johnson | 5 | 0 | 0 | 0 | 0 | 0 | 0 | .000 | .000 | .000 |
| Doug Jones | 5 | 2 | 1 | 0 | 0 | 1 | 0 | .400 | .600 | .375 |
| Jimmy Jones | 6 | 3 | 0 | 0 | 1 | 1 | 1 | .500 | 1.000 | .571 |
| Odell Jones | 5 | 1 | 0 | 0 | 1 | 0 | 2 | .200 | .800 | .200 |
| Rick Jones | 6 | 1 | 1 | 0 | 0 | 0 | 1 | .167 | .333 | .167 |
| Jim Kaat | 17 | 4 | 0 | 0 | 0 | 0 | 1 | .235 | .235 | .235 |
| Matt Keough | 37 | 13 | 3 | 0 | 0 | 3 | 4 | .351 | .432 | .400 |
| Jim Kern | 15 | 2 | 0 | 0 | 0 | 4 | 6 | .133 | .133 | .300 |
| Jimmy Key | 26 | 8 | 2 | 0 | 0 | 2 | 3 | .308 | .385 | .345 |
| Paul Kilgus | 6 | 1 | 1 | 0 | 0 | 2 | 0 | .167 | .333 | .375 |
| Eric King | 7 | 1 | 0 | 0 | 0 | 3 | 1 | .143 | .143 | .400 |
| Don Kirkwood | 14 | 6 | 2 | 0 | 0 | 1 | 1 | .429 | .571 | .467 |
| Bruce Kison | 11 | 1 | 0 | 0 | 0 | 2 | 2 | .091 | .091 | .231 |
| Chris Knapp | 10 | 4 | 1 | 0 | 0 | 0 | 2 | .400 | .500 | .455 |
| Jerry Koosman | 24 | 8 | 1 | 1 | 1 | 4 | 6 | .333 | .583 | .429 |
| Ken Kravec | 14 | 2 | 0 | 0 | 0 | 2 | 2 | .143 | .143 | .250 |
| Rick Kreuger | 8 | 1 | 0 | 0 | 0 | 0 | 0 | .125 | .125 | .125 |
| Bill Krueger | 19 | 4 | 0 | 0 | 0 | 0 | 2 | .211 | .211 | .190 |
| Jack Kucek | 5 | 1 | 0 | 0 | 1 | 2 | 0 | .200 | .800 | .375 |
| Bob Lacey | 14 | 2 | 0 | 0 | 0 | 0 | 3 | .143 | .143 | .143 |
| Lerrin LaGrow | 9 | 2 | 0 | 0 | 0 | 1 | 1 | .222 | .222 | .300 |
| Dennis Lamp | 24 | 5 | 2 | 0 | 0 | 2 | 5 | .208 | .292 | .269 |
| Rick Langford | 35 | 9 | 1 | 0 | 2 | 1 | 2 | .257 | .457 | .278 |
| Mark Langston | 39 | 5 | 1 | 2 | 0 | 3 | 10 | .128 | .256 | .190 |
| Dave LaPoint | 13 | 2 | 0 | 0 | 0 | 1 | 1 | .154 | .154 | .214 |
| Dave LaRoche | 14 | 3 | 1 | 0 | 0 | 3 | 0 | .214 | .286 | .353 |
| Jack Lazorko | 8 | 1 | 0 | 0 | 0 | 0 | 0 | .125 | .125 | .125 |
| Charlie Lea | 7 | 4 | 1 | 0 | 0 | 0 | 0 | .571 | .714 | .571 |
| Luis Leal | 26 | 11 | 2 | 0 | 2 | 0 | 1 | .423 | .731 | .407 |
| Bill Lee | 30 | 11 | 2 | 1 | 0 | 3 | 2 | .367 | .500 | .412 |
| Charlie Leibrandt | 39 | 8 | 3 | 0 | 0 | 3 | 4 | .205 | .282 | .262 |
| Dave Leiper | 5 | 2 | 0 | 0 | 0 | 0 | 1 | .400 | .400 | .400 |
| John Leister | 6 | 3 | 0 | 0 | 1 | 0 | 0 | .500 | 1.000 | .500 |
| Al Leiter | 5 | 0 | 0 | 0 | 0 | 1 | 3 | .000 | .000 | .167 |
| Dave Lemanczyk | 38 | 20 | 1 | 0 | 0 | 2 | 2 | .526 | .553 | .550 |
| Dennis Leonard | 59 | 11 | 2 | 1 | 1 | 4 | 8 | .186 | .305 | .239 |
| Paul Lindblad | 8 | 2 | 0 | 0 | 0 | 1 | 0 | .250 | .250 | .333 |
| Skip Lockwood | 5 | 3 | 1 | 0 | 0 | 0 | 0 | .600 | .800 | .600 |
| Mickey Lolich | 12 | 5 | 0 | 1 | 0 | 2 | 0 | .417 | .583 | .467 |
| Bill Long | 18 | 7 | 1 | 2 | 0 | 2 | 0 | .389 | .667 | .429 |
| Aurelio Lopez | 26 | 7 | 2 | 0 | 2 | 5 | 5 | .269 | .577 | .364 |
| Mike Loynd | 6 | 1 | 0 | 0 | 0 | 1 | 1 | .167 | .167 | .286 |
| Sparky Lyle | 15 | 2 | 0 | 0 | 0 | 1 | 1 | .133 | .133 | .188 |
| Rick Lysander | 7 | 2 | 0 | 0 | 0 | 1 | 1 | .286 | .286 | .375 |
| Mike G. Marshall | 12 | 6 | 1 | 0 | 0 | 1 | 2 | .500 | .583 | .538 |
| Renie Martin | 5 | 1 | 0 | 0 | 1 | 1 | 0 | .200 | .800 | .333 |
| Alfredo Martinez | 5 | 2 | 0 | 0 | 0 | 0 | 0 | .400 | .400 | .400 |
| Dennis Martinez | 48 | 18 | 2 | 0 | 1 | 1 | 3 | .375 | .479 | .392 |
| Tippy Martinez | 12 | 6 | 1 | 1 | 0 | 1 | 1 | .500 | .750 | .538 |
| Mike Mason | 19 | 5 | 1 | 0 | 0 | 1 | 2 | .263 | .316 | .300 |
| Jon Matlack | 24 | 7 | 3 | 0 | 0 | 0 | 1 | .292 | .417 | .280 |
| Rudy May | 52 | 16 | 1 | 0 | 1 | 5 | 6 | .308 | .385 | .362 |
| Tom McCarthy | 5 | 3 | 1 | 0 | 1 | 0 | 0 | .600 | 1.400 | .600 |
| Kirk McCaskill | 25 | 7 | 0 | 0 | 1 | 2 | 4 | .280 | .400 | .357 |
| Steve McCatty | 38 | 11 | 1 | 1 | 2 | 2 | 5 | .289 | .526 | .325 |
| Lindy McDaniel | 6 | 1 | 0 | 0 | 0 | 0 | 1 | .167 | .167 | .167 |
| Scott McGregor | 68 | 16 | 4 | 1 | 1 | 8 | 7 | .235 | .368 | .316 |
| Byron McLaughlin | 15 | 7 | 2 | 0 | 2 | 1 | 2 | .467 | 1.000 | .500 |
| Joey McLaughlin | 11 | 3 | 0 | 0 | 0 | 0 | 2 | .273 | .273 | .273 |
| Dave McNally | 7 | 2 | 1 | 0 | 0 | 0 | 0 | .286 | .429 | .286 |
| Doc Medich | 55 | 19 | 3 | 3 | 0 | 1 | 6 | .345 | .509 | .351 |
| Bob Milacki | 10 | 1 | 0 | 0 | 0 | 1 | 1 | .100 | .100 | .182 |
| Dyar Miller | 19 | 4 | 0 | 0 | 0 | 0 | 3 | .211 | .211 | .200 |
| Craig Minetto | 6 | 0 | 0 | 0 | 0 | 0 | 0 | .000 | .000 | .000 |
| Steve Mingori | 5 | 3 | 0 | 0 | 0 | 0 | 0 | .600 | .600 | .600 |
| Greg Minton | 9 | 2 | 1 | 0 | 0 | 0 | 0 | .222 | .333 | .222 |
| Paul Mirabella | 12 | 3 | 1 | 0 | 0 | 0 | 1 | .250 | .333 | .250 |
| Paul Mitchell | 14 | 3 | 0 | 0 | 1 | 0 | 0 | .214 | .429 | .200 |
| Dale Mohorcic | 9 | 3 | 1 | 0 | 0 | 0 | 0 | .333 | .444 | .333 |
| Sid Monge | 17 | 1 | 0 | 0 | 0 | 0 | 2 | .059 | .059 | .059 |
| John Montague | 12 | 4 | 2 | 0 | 1 | 1 | 0 | .333 | .750 | .385 |
| Jeff Montgomery | 5 | 1 | 0 | 0 | 0 | 0 | 4 | .200 | .200 | .200 |
| Balor Moore | 5 | 1 | 0 | 0 | 0 | 0 | 0 | .200 | .200 | .200 |
| Donnie Moore | 5 | 1 | 0 | 0 | 0 | 3 | 0 | .200 | .200 | .500 |
| Mike Moore | 62 | 16 | 1 | 0 | 2 | 8 | 7 | .258 | .371 | .338 |
| Rogelio Moret | 14 | 2 | 1 | 0 | 1 | 0 | 1 | .143 | .429 | .143 |
| Mike Morgan | 40 | 15 | 1 | 1 | 0 | 3 | 4 | .375 | .450 | .432 |
| Jack Morris | 93 | 25 | 1 | 1 | 4 | 8 | 15 | .269 | .430 | .327 |
| Tom Murphy | 16 | 7 | 1 | 1 | 1 | 0 | 1 | .438 | .813 | .438 |
| Dale Murray | 5 | 1 | 0 | 0 | 0 | 1 | 1 | .200 | .200 | .333 |
| Jeff Musselman | 7 | 2 | 0 | 1 | 0 | 3 | 1 | .286 | .571 | .500 |
| Gene Nelson | 30 | 7 | 3 | 1 | 1 | 5 | 4 | .233 | .500 | .343 |
| Joe Niekro | 11 | 3 | 0 | 2 | 0 | 0 | 0 | .273 | .636 | .273 |
| Phil Niekro | 22 | 8 | 4 | 0 | 1 | 1 | 4 | .364 | .682 | .417 |
| Al Nipper | 17 | 5 | 1 | 0 | 0 | 0 | 4 | .294 | .353 | .294 |
| Dickie Noles | 10 | 1 | 0 | 0 | 0 | 1 | 1 | .100 | .100 | .182 |
| Mike Norris | 27 | 9 | 0 | 0 | 1 | 2 | 2 | .333 | .444 | .400 |
| Edwin Nunez | 9 | 3 | 0 | 0 | 0 | 1 | 2 | .333 | .333 | .400 |
| Jose Nunez | 8 | 4 | 0 | 1 | 1 | 0 | 0 | .500 | 1.125 | .500 |
| Jack O'Connor | 11 | 3 | 0 | 0 | 1 | 2 | 0 | .273 | .545 | .385 |
| Bob Ojeda | 23 | 4 | 1 | 0 | 0 | 3 | 2 | .174 | .217 | .259 |
| Randy O'Neal | 9 | 3 | 0 | 0 | 0 | 3 | 2 | .333 | .333 | .500 |
| Steve Ontiveros | 11 | 5 | 1 | 0 | 0 | 0 | 1 | .455 | .545 | .455 |
| Danny Osborn | 5 | 0 | 0 | 0 | 0 | 0 | 1 | .000 | .000 | .000 |
| Claude Osteen | 7 | 3 | 1 | 0 | 0 | 1 | 0 | .429 | .571 | .500 |
| Bob Owchinko | 15 | 6 | 5 | 1 | 0 | 1 | 1 | .400 | .867 | .438 |
| Dave Pagan | 5 | 0 | 0 | 0 | 0 | 2 | 1 | .000 | .000 | .286 |
| Jim Palmer | 75 | 20 | 6 | 0 | 3 | 3 | 11 | .267 | .467 | .300 |
| Clay Parker | 9 | 1 | 0 | 0 | 0 | 1 | 1 | .111 | .111 | .200 |
| Mike Parrott | 26 | 9 | 0 | 0 | 0 | 0 | 3 | .346 | .346 | .346 |
| Marty Pattin | 30 | 7 | 1 | 0 | 0 | 2 | 3 | .233 | .267 | .281 |
| Mike Paxton | 21 | 7 | 1 | 0 | 1 | 2 | 1 | .333 | .524 | .391 |
| Oswaldo Peraza | 8 | 1 | 1 | 0 | 0 | 0 | 3 | .125 | .250 | .125 |
| Melido Perez | 12 | 5 | 2 | 1 | 2 | 0 | 3 | .417 | 1.250 | .417 |
| Gaylord Perry | 45 | 15 | 4 | 0 | 3 | 1 | 5 | .333 | .622 | .348 |
| Jim Perry | 13 | 1 | 0 | 0 | 0 | 0 | 2 | .077 | .077 | .077 |
| Fritz Peterson | 14 | 8 | 1 | 0 | 1 | 0 | 0 | .571 | .857 | .571 |
| Dan Petry | 72 | 21 | 7 | 0 | 1 | 4 | 6 | .292 | .431 | .329 |
| Eric Plunk | 11 | 1 | 0 | 0 | 0 | 1 | 5 | .091 | .091 | .231 |
| Dick Pole | 21 | 5 | 1 | 0 | 0 | 0 | 1 | .238 | .286 | .238 |
| Mark Portugal | 6 | 2 | 0 | 0 | 1 | 1 | 0 | .333 | .833 | .429 |
| Mike Proly | 13 | 5 | 2 | 1 | 1 | 0 | 1 | .385 | .923 | .385 |
| Dan Quisenberry | 21 | 9 | 1 | 1 | 1 | 2 | 4 | .429 | .714 | .478 |
| Chuck Rainey | 19 | 7 | 0 | 0 | 3 | 3 | 0 | .368 | .842 | .455 |
| Dave Rajsich | 5 | 2 | 0 | 0 | 0 | 0 | 1 | .400 | .400 | .400 |
| Dennis Rasmussen | 17 | 4 | 0 | 0 | 0 | 2 | 3 | .235 | .235 | .300 |
| Shane Rawley | 24 | 8 | 1 | 2 | 0 | 4 | 2 | .333 | .542 | .448 |
| Jeff Reardon | 6 | 1 | 0 | 0 | 0 | 0 | 2 | .167 | .167 | .167 |
| Pete Redfern | 24 | 5 | 1 | 0 | 1 | 3 | 1 | .208 | .375 | .296 |
| Jerry Reed | 21 | 7 | 1 | 1 | 0 | 2 | 1 | .333 | .476 | .391 |
| Steve Renko | 32 | 8 | 2 | 1 | 0 | 1 | 6 | .250 | .375 | .273 |
| Paul Reuschel | 9 | 3 | 0 | 0 | 0 | 0 | 0 | .333 | .333 | .333 |
| Jerry Reuss | 24 | 11 | 2 | 1 | 1 | 3 | 2 | .458 | .750 | .519 |

# Robin Yount *continued*

| Pitcher | AB | H | 2B | 3B | HR | BB | SO | BA | SA | OBA |
|---|---|---|---|---|---|---|---|---|---|---|
| Bob Reynolds | 5 | 2 | 0 | 0 | 0 | 0 | 0 | .400 | .400 | .400 |
| Rick Rhoden | 9 | 4 | 1 | 0 | 1 | 1 | 2 | .444 | .889 | .500 |
| Dave Righetti | 35 | 9 | 2 | 0 | 1 | 5 | 8 | .257 | .400 | .350 |
| Jose Rijo | 12 | 3 | 0 | 0 | 0 | 1 | 6 | .250 | .250 | .308 |
| Allen Ripley | 7 | 1 | 0 | 0 | 0 | 0 | 1 | .143 | .143 | .143 |
| Dave A. Roberts | 23 | 5 | 2 | 0 | 0 | 1 | 0 | .217 | .304 | .240 |
| Jeff M. Robinson | 7 | 2 | 0 | 0 | 1 | 1 | 0 | .286 | .714 | .375 |
| Ron Romanick | 23 | 7 | 1 | 0 | 1 | 5 | 1 | .304 | .478 | .429 |
| Gary Ross | 13 | 2 | 0 | 0 | 0 | 0 | 2 | .154 | .154 | .154 |
| Dave Rozema | 47 | 11 | 1 | 1 | 1 | 0 | 6 | .234 | .362 | .234 |
| Vern Ruhle | 29 | 8 | 2 | 1 | 0 | 3 | 2 | .276 | .414 | .344 |
| Jeff Russell | 19 | 4 | 0 | 0 | 1 | 0 | 2 | .211 | .368 | .211 |
| Nolan Ryan | 46 | 8 | 1 | 0 | 0 | 8 | 10 | .174 | .196 | .309 |
| Bret Saberhagen | 37 | 15 | 4 | 1 | 1 | 1 | 5 | .405 | .649 | .436 |
| Luis Sanchez | 10 | 4 | 0 | 0 | 0 | 0 | 0 | .400 | .400 | .400 |
| Randy Scarbery | 5 | 1 | 1 | 0 | 0 | 0 | 1 | .200 | .400 | .200 |
| Dan Schatzeder | 10 | 3 | 0 | 0 | 0 | 1 | 0 | .300 | .300 | .364 |
| Calvin Schiraldi | 6 | 2 | 1 | 0 | 0 | 0 | 1 | .333 | .500 | .333 |
| Dave J. Schmidt | 31 | 7 | 2 | 0 | 0 | 2 | 1 | .226 | .290 | .273 |
| Ken Schrom | 24 | 5 | 0 | 0 | 1 | 5 | 4 | .208 | .333 | .333 |
| Don Schulze | 5 | 4 | 0 | 0 | 0 | 0 | 0 | .800 | .800 | .800 |
| Tom Seaver | 20 | 7 | 1 | 0 | 2 | 3 | 1 | .350 | .700 | .417 |
| Diego Segui | 10 | 1 | 0 | 0 | 0 | 1 | 4 | .100 | .100 | .182 |
| Jeff Sellers | 18 | 7 | 2 | 0 | 1 | 6 | 1 | .389 | .667 | .542 |
| Gary Serum | 21 | 5 | 2 | 0 | 0 | 0 | 1 | .238 | .333 | .238 |
| Bob Shirley | 15 | 3 | 0 | 1 | 1 | 4 | 4 | .200 | .533 | .368 |
| Bill Singer | 22 | 4 | 1 | 0 | 0 | 3 | 3 | .182 | .227 | .280 |
| Jim Slaton | 21 | 4 | 1 | 0 | 0 | 1 | 2 | .190 | .238 | .217 |
| Roy Smith | 13 | 4 | 1 | 0 | 0 | 2 | 4 | .308 | .385 | .400 |
| Mike Smithson | 51 | 12 | 1 | 0 | 1 | 6 | 5 | .235 | .314 | .316 |
| Lary Sorensen | 26 | 14 | 1 | 2 | 2 | 3 | 1 | .538 | .962 | .586 |
| Dan Spillner | 41 | 15 | 4 | 0 | 2 | 0 | 5 | .366 | .610 | .366 |
| Paul Splittorff | 52 | 18 | 4 | 1 | 1 | 3 | 4 | .346 | .519 | .382 |
| Don Stanhouse | 5 | 3 | 0 | 0 | 1 | 2 | 1 | .600 | 1.200 | .714 |
| Bob Stanley | 55 | 17 | 3 | 0 | 0 | 2 | 3 | .309 | .364 | .333 |
| Mike T. Stanton | 14 | 3 | 1 | 0 | 0 | 0 | 4 | .214 | .286 | .200 |
| Dave Stewart | 43 | 13 | 5 | 0 | 1 | 6 | 5 | .302 | .488 | .388 |
| Sammy Stewart | 29 | 4 | 1 | 0 | 1 | 2 | 4 | .138 | .276 | .194 |
| Dave Stieb | 78 | 27 | 3 | 2 | 3 | 11 | 10 | .346 | .551 | .418 |
| Bob Stoddard | 10 | 3 | 0 | 0 | 1 | 3 | 0 | .300 | .600 | .462 |
| Tim Stoddard | 25 | 8 | 0 | 0 | 0 | 0 | 4 | .320 | .320 | .346 |
| Steve Stone | 46 | 12 | 3 | 1 | 1 | 2 | 3 | .261 | .435 | .286 |
| Mel Stottlemyre | 6 | 3 | 0 | 0 | 0 | 0 | 0 | .500 | .500 | .500 |
| Todd Stottlemyre | 5 | 2 | 1 | 0 | 0 | 3 | 1 | .400 | .600 | .625 |
| Rick Sutcliffe | 23 | 5 | 1 | 0 | 0 | 2 | 5 | .217 | .261 | .280 |
| Don Sutton | 22 | 5 | 1 | 0 | 1 | 0 | 2 | .227 | .409 | .227 |
| Bill Swift | 19 | 7 | 2 | 1 | 0 | 1 | 0 | .368 | .579 | .400 |
| Greg Swindell | 18 | 4 | 1 | 0 | 1 | 0 | 2 | .222 | .444 | .222 |
| Bob Sykes | 6 | 0 | 0 | 0 | 0 | 0 | 3 | .000 | .000 | .000 |
| Frank Tanana | 104 | 31 | 6 | 0 | 2 | 12 | 9 | .298 | .413 | .381 |
| Walt Terrell | 35 | 6 | 3 | 0 | 0 | 3 | 4 | .171 | .257 | .237 |

| Pitcher | AB | H | 2B | 3B | HR | BB | SO | BA | SA | OBA |
|---|---|---|---|---|---|---|---|---|---|---|
| Bobby Thigpen | 12 | 2 | 0 | 0 | 0 | 1 | 0 | .167 | .167 | .231 |
| Roy Thomas | 6 | 3 | 0 | 0 | 0 | 1 | 0 | .500 | .500 | .625 |
| Stan Thomas | 6 | 1 | 0 | 0 | 0 | 0 | 1 | .167 | .167 | .167 |
| Paul Thormodsgard | 13 | 1 | 0 | 0 | 0 | 0 | 0 | .077 | .077 | .077 |
| Mark Thurmond | 10 | 2 | 1 | 0 | 0 | 0 | 1 | .200 | .300 | .200 |
| Luis Tiant | 42 | 18 | 1 | 1 | 1 | 2 | 5 | .429 | .571 | .455 |
| Dick Tidrow | 27 | 6 | 1 | 1 | 1 | 4 | 6 | .222 | .444 | .303 |
| Dave Tobik | 14 | 3 | 0 | 0 | 0 | 1 | 1 | .214 | .214 | .267 |
| Jackson Todd | 10 | 3 | 2 | 0 | 0 | 2 | 1 | .300 | .500 | .417 |
| Jim Todd | 17 | 2 | 0 | 0 | 0 | 0 | 0 | .118 | .118 | .118 |
| Fred Toliver | 5 | 2 | 0 | 0 | 0 | 0 | 1 | .400 | .400 | .400 |
| Mike Torrez | 76 | 25 | 3 | 3 | 1 | 6 | 5 | .329 | .487 | .378 |
| Steve Trout | 14 | 5 | 0 | 1 | 1 | 0 | 2 | .357 | .714 | .357 |
| Mike Trujillo | 6 | 1 | 0 | 0 | 0 | 0 | 0 | .167 | .167 | .167 |
| John Tudor | 11 | 1 | 1 | 0 | 0 | 2 | 1 | .091 | .182 | .214 |
| Jerry Ujdur | 15 | 6 | 1 | 2 | 0 | 1 | 0 | .400 | .733 | .438 |
| Jim Umbarger | 13 | 3 | 0 | 0 | 0 | 0 | 2 | .231 | .231 | .231 |
| Pat Underwood | 7 | 4 | 1 | 0 | 0 | 2 | 0 | .571 | .714 | .667 |
| Tom Underwood | 40 | 10 | 2 | 1 | 0 | 1 | 6 | .250 | .350 | .268 |
| Ed Vande Berg | 11 | 6 | 1 | 0 | 0 | 0 | 1 | .545 | .636 | .545 |
| John Verhoeven | 11 | 3 | 1 | 0 | 1 | 0 | 3 | .273 | .636 | .273 |
| Frank Viola | 50 | 16 | 3 | 0 | 2 | 6 | 2 | .320 | .500 | .393 |
| Pete Vuckovich | 8 | 3 | 0 | 0 | 0 | 0 | 0 | .375 | .375 | .375 |
| Tom Waddell | 8 | 0 | 0 | 0 | 0 | 0 | 0 | .000 | .000 | .000 |
| Rick Waits | 24 | 4 | 1 | 0 | 0 | 1 | 3 | .167 | .208 | .200 |
| Duane Ward | 12 | 6 | 1 | 0 | 0 | 1 | 1 | .500 | .583 | .538 |
| Gary Wayne | 5 | 0 | 0 | 0 | 0 | 0 | 0 | .000 | .000 | .000 |
| Bob Welch | 19 | 4 | 2 | 0 | 0 | 2 | 2 | .211 | .316 | .286 |
| Gary Wheelock | 6 | 0 | 0 | 0 | 0 | 0 | 0 | .000 | .000 | .000 |
| Ed Whitson | 12 | 3 | 2 | 0 | 0 | 1 | 1 | .250 | .417 | .308 |
| Milt Wilcox | 53 | 13 | 0 | 0 | 0 | 5 | 3 | .245 | .302 | .322 |
| Eric Wilkins | 5 | 2 | 0 | 0 | 0 | 1 | 1 | .400 | .400 | .500 |
| Al Williams | 23 | 7 | 1 | 0 | 2 | 2 | 0 | .304 | .609 | .360 |
| Mitch Williams | 6 | 2 | 0 | 0 | 0 | 3 | 2 | .333 | .333 | .500 |
| Mark Williamson | 8 | 2 | 1 | 0 | 0 | 1 | 0 | .250 | .375 | .333 |
| Mike Willis | 9 | 2 | 1 | 0 | 0 | 1 | 1 | .222 | .333 | .300 |
| Jim Willoughby | 16 | 3 | 1 | 0 | 0 | 0 | 2 | .188 | .250 | .188 |
| Frank Wills | 13 | 3 | 0 | 0 | 1 | 0 | 1 | .231 | .462 | .214 |
| Rick Wise | 46 | 13 | 4 | 0 | 0 | 0 | 8 | .283 | .370 | .283 |
| Bobby Witt | 36 | 9 | 3 | 0 | 0 | 10 | 13 | .250 | .333 | .413 |
| Mike Witt | 65 | 18 | 3 | 1 | 1 | 13 | 10 | .277 | .400 | .392 |
| Ed Wojna | 5 | 0 | 0 | 0 | 0 | 0 | 0 | .000 | .000 | .000 |
| Wilbur Wood | 34 | 6 | 1 | 0 | 0 | 2 | 5 | .176 | .206 | .222 |
| Dick Woodson | 5 | 1 | 0 | 0 | 0 | 0 | 1 | .200 | .200 | .200 |
| Rich Wortham | 5 | 1 | 0 | 0 | 1 | 1 | 0 | .200 | .800 | .333 |
| Jim C. Wright | 6 | 2 | 1 | 0 | 0 | 0 | 1 | .333 | .500 | .333 |
| Rich Yett | 14 | 7 | 1 | 1 | 0 | 2 | 2 | .500 | .714 | .529 |
| Curt Young | 17 | 3 | 0 | 0 | 0 | 5 | 3 | .176 | .176 | .333 |
| Kip Young | 7 | 2 | 0 | 0 | 0 | 0 | 0 | .286 | .286 | .286 |
| Matt Young | 19 | 5 | 1 | 0 | 0 | 6 | 2 | .263 | .316 | .440 |
| Geoff Zahn | 15 | 8 | 2 | 0 | 1 | 3 | 0 | .533 | .867 | .611 |

# Mark Davis

| Batter | AB | H | 2B | 3B | HR | BB | SO | BA | SA | OBA |
|---|---|---|---|---|---|---|---|---|---|---|
| Luis Aguayo | 7 | 3 | 0 | 0 | 0 | 1 | 1 | .429 | .429 | .500 |
| Mike Aldrete | 5 | 2 | 1 | 0 | 0 | 0 | 3 | .400 | .600 | .400 |
| Bill Almon | 7 | 0 | 0 | 0 | 0 | 1 | 4 | .000 | .000 | .125 |
| Dave Anderson | 14 | 0 | 0 | 0 | 0 | 3 | 5 | .000 | .000 | .176 |
| Alan Ashby | 13 | 3 | 1 | 0 | 0 | 3 | 2 | .231 | .308 | .353 |
| Wally Backman | 5 | 0 | 0 | 0 | 0 | 2 | 1 | .000 | .000 | .286 |
| Mark Bailey | 13 | 3 | 2 | 0 | 0 | 4 | 4 | .231 | .385 | .444 |
| Bob Bailor | 5 | 3 | 0 | 0 | 0 | 0 | 0 | .600 | .600 | .600 |
| Dusty Baker | 5 | 2 | 1 | 0 | 0 | 0 | 0 | .400 | .600 | .400 |
| Kevin Bass | 26 | 11 | 3 | 0 | 1 | 1 | 3 | .423 | .654 | .444 |
| Buddy Bell | 7 | 1 | 1 | 0 | 0 | 2 | 1 | .143 | .286 | .333 |
| Johnny Bench | 6 | 1 | 0 | 0 | 0 | 0 | 0 | .167 | .167 | .167 |
| Bruce Benedict | 20 | 6 | 0 | 1 | 1 | 5 | 0 | .300 | .550 | .423 |
| Todd Benzinger | 6 | 1 | 0 | 0 | 0 | 0 | 1 | .167 | .167 | .167 |
| Dale Berra | 10 | 4 | 1 | 0 | 1 | 1 | 1 | .400 | .800 | .455 |
| Kurt Bevacqua | 11 | 4 | 1 | 0 | 1 | 2 | 1 | .364 | .727 | .462 |
| Dann Bilardello | 5 | 1 | 0 | 0 | 1 | 2 | 1 | .200 | .800 | .429 |

| Batter | AB | H | 2B | 3B | HR | BB | SO | BA | SA | OBA |
|---|---|---|---|---|---|---|---|---|---|---|
| Jeff Blauser | 6 | 1 | 0 | 0 | 0 | 0 | 1 | .167 | .167 | .167 |
| Bruce Bochy | 7 | 2 | 0 | 0 | 1 | 0 | 2 | .286 | .714 | .286 |
| Barry Bonds | 5 | 1 | 1 | 0 | 0 | 0 | 4 | .200 | .400 | .200 |
| Bobby Bonilla | 8 | 2 | 0 | 0 | 0 | 2 | 1 | .250 | .250 | .400 |
| Juan Bonilla | 5 | 1 | 0 | 0 | 0 | 0 | 0 | .200 | .200 | .200 |
| Larry Bowa | 16 | 7 | 2 | 0 | 0 | 1 | 4 | .438 | .563 | .471 |
| Sid Bream | 10 | 4 | 1 | 0 | 2 | 1 | 0 | .400 | 1.100 | .455 |
| Greg Brock | 9 | 2 | 1 | 0 | 1 | 1 | 3 | .222 | .667 | .300 |
| Hubie Brooks | 23 | 6 | 1 | 0 | 0 | 1 | 1 | .261 | .304 | .292 |
| Bobby Brown | 9 | 2 | 0 | 0 | 0 | 0 | 1 | .222 | .222 | .222 |
| Bill Buckner | 8 | 1 | 0 | 0 | 0 | 0 | 0 | .125 | .125 | .125 |
| Brett Butler | 10 | 3 | 1 | 0 | 0 | 5 | 4 | .300 | .400 | .533 |
| Enos Cabell | 16 | 6 | 0 | 0 | 1 | 0 | 1 | .375 | .563 | .444 |
| Ken Caminiti | 9 | 1 | 0 | 0 | 0 | 0 | 3 | .111 | .111 | .111 |
| Steve Carlton | 6 | 1 | 0 | 0 | 0 | 0 | 2 | .167 | .167 | .167 |
| Gary Carter | 15 | 3 | 1 | 0 | 1 | 4 | 3 | .200 | .467 | .368 |
| Cesar Cedeno | 8 | 3 | 1 | 0 | 1 | 2 | 0 | .375 | .875 | .500 |

# Mark Davis continued

| Batter | AB | H | 2B | 3B | HR | BB | SO | BA | SA | OBA |
|---|---|---|---|---|---|---|---|---|---|---|
| Ron Cey | 15 | 2 | 0 | 0 | 2 | 3 | 4 | .133 | .533 | .364 |
| Chris Chambliss | 6 | 1 | 1 | 0 | 0 | 0 | 1 | .167 | .333 | .167 |
| Kelvin Chapman | 11 | 6 | 1 | 0 | 1 | 0 | 2 | .545 | .909 | .545 |
| Jack Clark | 6 | 3 | 1 | 0 | 0 | 0 | 1 | .500 | .667 | .500 |
| Will Clark | 14 | 7 | 2 | 1 | 1 | 0 | 3 | .500 | 1.000 | .500 |
| Vince Coleman | 15 | 3 | 0 | 0 | 0 | 0 | 6 | .200 | .200 | .200 |
| Dave Collins | 8 | 1 | 0 | 0 | 0 | 1 | 0 | .125 | .125 | .222 |
| Dave Concepcion | 19 | 5 | 0 | 0 | 0 | 2 | 1 | .263 | .263 | .318 |
| Jose Cruz | 27 | 10 | 0 | 1 | 1 | 2 | 5 | .370 | .556 | .400 |
| Kal Daniels | 13 | 0 | 0 | 0 | 0 | 2 | 4 | .000 | .000 | .133 |
| Eric Davis | 25 | 4 | 0 | 0 | 1 | 2 | 11 | .160 | .280 | .222 |
| Glenn Davis | 21 | 4 | 0 | 0 | 3 | 3 | 7 | .190 | .619 | .292 |
| Jody Davis | 27 | 9 | 3 | 0 | 1 | 2 | 3 | .333 | .556 | .367 |
| Andre Dawson | 21 | 5 | 1 | 0 | 0 | 2 | 4 | .238 | .286 | .333 |
| Ivan DeJesus | 13 | 2 | 0 | 0 | 0 | 0 | 2 | .154 | .154 | .154 |
| Rick Dempsey | 7 | 0 | 0 | 0 | 0 | 1 | 2 | .000 | .000 | .125 |
| Bob Dernier | 24 | 6 | 1 | 1 | 0 | 2 | 2 | .250 | .375 | .308 |
| Bo Diaz | 16 | 3 | 1 | 0 | 0 | 0 | 3 | .188 | .250 | .235 |
| Bill Doran | 38 | 12 | 2 | 1 | 0 | 5 | 5 | .316 | .421 | .386 |
| Dan Driessen | 5 | 1 | 0 | 0 | 0 | 0 | 1 | .200 | .200 | .200 |
| Mariano Duncan | 18 | 2 | 1 | 0 | 0 | 1 | 6 | .111 | .167 | .158 |
| Shawon Dunston | 8 | 2 | 1 | 0 | 0 | 0 | 5 | .250 | .375 | .250 |
| Leon Durham | 23 | 6 | 1 | 0 | 1 | 3 | 7 | .261 | .435 | .346 |
| Len Dykstra | 7 | 3 | 1 | 0 | 0 | 1 | 0 | .429 | .571 | .500 |
| Mike Easler | 5 | 0 | 0 | 0 | 0 | 1 | 2 | .000 | .000 | .167 |
| Nick Esasky | 23 | 4 | 0 | 0 | 0 | 3 | 4 | .174 | .174 | .269 |
| Mike R. Fitzgerald | 18 | 4 | 0 | 0 | 1 | 0 | 4 | .222 | .389 | .222 |
| Tim Flannery | 9 | 2 | 0 | 1 | 0 | 0 | 2 | .222 | .444 | .222 |
| Doug Flynn | 7 | 2 | 1 | 0 | 0 | 0 | 1 | .286 | .429 | .286 |
| George Foster | 16 | 4 | 0 | 0 | 1 | 1 | 3 | .250 | .438 | .294 |
| Andres Galarraga | 7 | 0 | 0 | 0 | 0 | 1 | 4 | .000 | .000 | .125 |
| Ron Gant | 7 | 1 | 0 | 0 | 0 | 1 | 3 | .143 | .143 | .250 |
| Ron Gardenhire | 10 | 0 | 0 | 0 | 0 | 0 | 2 | .000 | .000 | .000 |
| Phil Garner | 25 | 9 | 1 | 0 | 2 | 2 | 4 | .360 | .640 | .393 |
| Steve Garvey | 24 | 8 | 2 | 0 | 1 | 1 | 6 | .333 | .542 | .360 |
| Kirk Gibson | 12 | 2 | 0 | 0 | 0 | 0 | 3 | .167 | .167 | .167 |
| David Green | 5 | 2 | 0 | 0 | 1 | 1 | 0 | .400 | 1.000 | .500 |
| Ken Griffey | 13 | 4 | 0 | 0 | 0 | 2 | 0 | .308 | .308 | .400 |
| Alfredo Griffin | 10 | 1 | 0 | 0 | 0 | 1 | 3 | .100 | .100 | .182 |
| Greg Gross | 5 | 0 | 0 | 0 | 0 | 0 | 1 | .000 | .000 | .000 |
| Pedro Guerrero | 21 | 5 | 1 | 1 | 0 | 1 | 2 | .238 | .381 | .273 |
| Tony Gwynn | 23 | 10 | 0 | 0 | 0 | 5 | 4 | .435 | .435 | .536 |
| Albert Hall | 10 | 1 | 0 | 0 | 0 | 0 | 2 | .100 | .100 | .100 |
| Jeff Hamilton | 13 | 1 | 0 | 0 | 0 | 0 | 5 | .077 | .077 | .077 |
| Brian Harper | 8 | 2 | 0 | 0 | 2 | 0 | 3 | .250 | 1.000 | .250 |
| Terry Harper | 8 | 0 | 0 | 0 | 0 | 1 | 4 | .000 | .000 | .111 |
| Billy Hatcher | 16 | 3 | 0 | 0 | 0 | 1 | 4 | .188 | .188 | .235 |
| Mickey Hatcher | 9 | 3 | 0 | 0 | 0 | 3 | 1 | .333 | .333 | .462 |
| Von Hayes | 17 | 6 | 0 | 1 | 2 | 2 | 3 | .353 | .824 | .421 |
| George Hendrick | 9 | 0 | 0 | 0 | 0 | 1 | 1 | .000 | .000 | .100 |
| Keith Hernandez | 34 | 11 | 0 | 0 | 1 | 5 | 8 | .324 | .412 | .400 |
| Tom Herr | 14 | 3 | 0 | 0 | 0 | 3 | 1 | .214 | .214 | .353 |
| Bob Horner | 8 | 4 | 1 | 0 | 1 | 3 | 1 | .500 | 1.000 | .636 |
| Glenn Hubbard | 22 | 3 | 0 | 0 | 1 | 3 | 7 | .136 | .273 | .240 |
| Rex Hudler | 5 | 0 | 0 | 0 | 0 | 0 | 2 | .000 | .000 | .000 |
| Chris James | 6 | 2 | 0 | 0 | 1 | 0 | 0 | .333 | .833 | .333 |
| Dion James | 6 | 2 | 0 | 0 | 0 | 1 | 0 | .333 | .333 | .429 |
| Steve Jeltz | 9 | 3 | 0 | 0 | 0 | 1 | 0 | .333 | .333 | .400 |
| Howard Johnson | 11 | 5 | 0 | 0 | 2 | 2 | 4 | .455 | 1.000 | .538 |
| Randy G. Johnson | 10 | 6 | 1 | 0 | 0 | 0 | 1 | .600 | .700 | .600 |
| Tracy Jones | 12 | 6 | 1 | 0 | 0 | 2 | 1 | .500 | .583 | .571 |
| Terry Kennedy | 21 | 1 | 1 | 0 | 0 | 1 | 12 | .048 | .095 | .087 |
| Alan Knicely | 9 | 1 | 0 | 0 | 0 | 0 | 5 | .111 | .111 | .111 |
| Ray Knight | 11 | 1 | 0 | 0 | 0 | 2 | 2 | .091 | .091 | .214 |
| Brad Komminsk | 11 | 2 | 1 | 0 | 0 | 1 | 3 | .182 | .273 | .250 |
| Lee Lacy | 18 | 6 | 1 | 1 | 1 | 0 | 2 | .333 | .667 | .333 |
| Steve Lake | 6 | 3 | 2 | 0 | 1 | 0 | 1 | .500 | 1.333 | .429 |
| Rafael Landestoy | 5 | 0 | 0 | 0 | 0 | 1 | 0 | .000 | .000 | .167 |
| Ken Landreaux | 14 | 2 | 1 | 0 | 1 | 1 | 2 | .143 | .429 | .200 |
| Tito Landrum | 11 | 3 | 1 | 0 | 0 | 0 | 2 | .273 | .364 | .250 |
| Barry Larkin | 13 | 6 | 1 | 0 | 0 | 0 | 1 | .462 | .538 | .462 |
| Vance Law | 8 | 1 | 0 | 0 | 0 | 1 | 1 | .125 | .125 | .222 |
| Tom Lawless | 5 | 2 | 0 | 0 | 0 | 1 | 0 | .400 | .400 | .500 |
| Sixto Lezcano | 10 | 4 | 1 | 0 | 0 | 1 | 2 | .400 | .500 | .500 |
| Tim Lollar | 5 | 1 | 0 | 0 | 0 | 0 | 2 | .200 | .200 | .200 |
| Dave Lopes | 6 | 0 | 0 | 0 | 0 | 3 | 0 | .000 | .000 | .333 |
| Garry Maddox | 6 | 1 | 0 | 0 | 0 | 0 | 2 | .167 | .167 | .167 |
| Bill Madlock | 18 | 9 | 2 | 0 | 3 | 4 | 2 | .500 | 1.111 | .591 |
| Dave Magadan | 5 | 0 | 0 | 0 | 0 | 1 | 1 | .000 | .000 | .286 |
| Rick Mahler | 5 | 1 | 0 | 0 | 0 | 1 | 1 | .200 | .200 | .333 |
| Candy Maldonado | 28 | 7 | 2 | 0 | 2 | 3 | 10 | .250 | .536 | .323 |
| Mike A. Marshall | 31 | 11 | 3 | 0 | 2 | 1 | 10 | .355 | .645 | .400 |
| Carmelo Martinez | 16 | 7 | 1 | 0 | 1 | 4 | 2 | .438 | .688 | .550 |
| Dave Martinez | 5 | 0 | 0 | 0 | 0 | 0 | 3 | .000 | .000 | .000 |
| Gary Matthews | 14 | 6 | 0 | 0 | 1 | 4 | 1 | .429 | .643 | .526 |
| Len Matuszek | 8 | 0 | 0 | 0 | 0 | 0 | 2 | .000 | .000 | .000 |
| Lee Mazzilli | 9 | 2 | 1 | 0 | 0 | 0 | 0 | .222 | .333 | .222 |
| Lloyd McClendon | 6 | 1 | 0 | 0 | 0 | 0 | 2 | .167 | .167 | .167 |
| Willie McGee | 15 | 6 | 1 | 0 | 2 | 2 | 4 | .400 | .867 | .471 |
| Kevin McReynolds | 30 | 3 | 0 | 0 | 0 | 2 | 7 | .100 | .100 | .156 |
| Eddie Milner | 8 | 2 | 0 | 1 | 0 | 1 | 0 | .250 | .500 | .333 |
| Kevin Mitchell | 17 | 5 | 1 | 0 | 0 | 1 | 3 | .294 | .353 | .333 |
| Keith Moreland | 26 | 9 | 4 | 0 | 1 | 0 | 3 | .346 | .615 | .346 |
| Omar Moreno | 7 | 1 | 0 | 0 | 0 | 1 | 4 | .143 | .143 | .250 |
| Jim Morrison | 22 | 8 | 0 | 0 | 2 | 1 | 2 | .364 | .636 | .391 |
| Jerry Mumphrey | 14 | 4 | 2 | 0 | 0 | 1 | 3 | .286 | .429 | .333 |
| Dale Murphy | 35 | 11 | 0 | 0 | 4 | 6 | 6 | .314 | .657 | .405 |
| Eddie Murray | 5 | 0 | 0 | 0 | 0 | 1 | 4 | .000 | .000 | .167 |
| Graig Nettles | 12 | 0 | 0 | 0 | 0 | 0 | 4 | .000 | .000 | .000 |
| Ken Oberkfell | 16 | 3 | 0 | 0 | 0 | 3 | 3 | .188 | .188 | .316 |
| Ron Oester | 18 | 2 | 1 | 0 | 0 | 1 | 6 | .111 | .167 | .158 |
| Al Oliver | 9 | 2 | 0 | 0 | 0 | 0 | 2 | .222 | .222 | .222 |
| Paul O'Neill | 6 | 0 | 0 | 0 | 0 | 0 | 2 | .000 | .000 | .000 |
| Jose Oquendo | 12 | 3 | 0 | 0 | 0 | 2 | 2 | .250 | .250 | .357 |
| Junior Ortiz | 12 | 4 | 2 | 0 | 0 | 0 | 1 | .333 | .500 | .333 |
| Rafael Palmeiro | 5 | 1 | 0 | 0 | 0 | 1 | 0 | .200 | .200 | .333 |
| Jim Pankovits | 11 | 3 | 0 | 0 | 1 | 0 | 4 | .273 | .545 | .273 |
| Dave Parker | 28 | 4 | 1 | 0 | 0 | 1 | 10 | .143 | .179 | .226 |
| Lance Parrish | 6 | 0 | 0 | 0 | 0 | 1 | 2 | .000 | .000 | .143 |
| Bert Pena | 6 | 1 | 0 | 0 | 0 | 0 | 1 | .167 | .167 | .167 |
| Tony Pena | 26 | 8 | 1 | 0 | 2 | 0 | 4 | .308 | .577 | .296 |
| Terry Pendleton | 19 | 5 | 1 | 0 | 0 | 1 | 3 | .263 | .316 | .300 |
| Tony Perez | 10 | 1 | 0 | 0 | 0 | 2 | 2 | .100 | .100 | .250 |
| Gerald Perry | 12 | 2 | 1 | 0 | 0 | 2 | 1 | .167 | .250 | .333 |
| Terry Puhl | 12 | 1 | 1 | 0 | 0 | 0 | 5 | .083 | .167 | .083 |
| Luis Quinones | 7 | 2 | 0 | 0 | 0 | 0 | 2 | .286 | .286 | .286 |
| Tim Raines | 19 | 3 | 0 | 0 | 0 | 3 | 4 | .158 | .158 | .273 |
| Rafael Ramirez | 27 | 4 | 1 | 0 | 0 | 2 | 3 | .148 | .185 | .207 |
| Mike J. Ramsey | 6 | 1 | 0 | 0 | 0 | 0 | 0 | .167 | .167 | .167 |
| Johnny Ray | 17 | 5 | 2 | 0 | 0 | 3 | 0 | .294 | .412 | .429 |
| Randy Ready | 7 | 2 | 1 | 0 | 0 | 2 | 3 | .286 | .429 | .444 |
| Gary Redus | 14 | 5 | 2 | 0 | 0 | 5 | 4 | .357 | .500 | .526 |
| Craig Reynolds | 13 | 0 | 0 | 0 | 0 | 0 | 2 | .000 | .000 | .000 |
| R.J. Reynolds | 12 | 2 | 0 | 0 | 0 | 0 | 4 | .167 | .167 | .167 |
| German Rivera | 9 | 3 | 0 | 0 | 0 | 2 | 3 | .333 | .333 | .455 |
| Bill Robinson | 5 | 2 | 1 | 0 | 0 | 1 | 1 | .400 | .600 | .500 |
| Ron Roenicke | 5 | 3 | 2 | 0 | 0 | 0 | 1 | .600 | 1.000 | .600 |
| Pete Rose | 5 | 1 | 0 | 0 | 0 | 0 | 0 | .200 | .200 | .200 |
| Jerry Royster | 16 | 2 | 1 | 0 | 0 | 3 | 3 | .125 | .188 | .250 |
| Bill Russell | 13 | 2 | 0 | 0 | 0 | 0 | 1 | .154 | .154 | .133 |
| John Russell | 6 | 0 | 0 | 0 | 0 | 2 | 4 | .000 | .000 | .250 |
| Luis Salazar | 16 | 6 | 0 | 0 | 0 | 0 | 5 | .375 | .375 | .375 |
| Juan Samuel | 20 | 6 | 1 | 2 | 0 | 3 | 8 | .300 | .550 | .391 |
| Ryne Sandberg | 29 | 11 | 1 | 1 | 0 | 3 | 2 | .379 | .483 | .438 |
| Rafael Santana | 6 | 3 | 0 | 1 | 0 | 0 | 0 | .500 | .833 | .500 |
| Steve Sax | 26 | 5 | 0 | 0 | 1 | 6 | 5 | .192 | .308 | .344 |
| Mike Schmidt | 12 | 2 | 0 | 0 | 1 | 5 | 4 | .167 | .417 | .412 |
| Rick Schu | 7 | 3 | 0 | 0 | 1 | 2 | 3 | .429 | .857 | .556 |
| Mike Scioscia | 23 | 6 | 1 | 0 | 0 | 0 | 3 | .261 | .304 | .261 |
| Mike Scott | 7 | 0 | 0 | 0 | 0 | 0 | 3 | .000 | .000 | .000 |
| Tony Scott | 10 | 2 | 1 | 0 | 0 | 1 | 3 | .200 | .300 | .250 |
| John Shelby | 8 | 3 | 0 | 0 | 0 | 1 | 2 | .375 | .375 | .444 |
| Ted Simmons | 5 | 1 | 0 | 0 | 0 | 0 | 1 | .200 | .200 | .200 |
| Lonnie Smith | 13 | 2 | 0 | 0 | 0 | 3 | 3 | .154 | .154 | .313 |
| Ozzie Smith | 16 | 6 | 0 | 0 | 1 | 1 | 2 | .375 | .563 | .412 |
| Chris Speier | 10 | 2 | 0 | 0 | 0 | 2 | 4 | .200 | .200 | .333 |
| Kurt Stillwell | 9 | 3 | 0 | 0 | 0 | 1 | 1 | .333 | .333 | .400 |
| Darryl Strawberry | 27 | 3 | 0 | 0 | 2 | 3 | 12 | .111 | .333 | .200 |
| Franklin Stubbs | 7 | 1 | 0 | 0 | 0 | 0 | 4 | .143 | .143 | .143 |
| Garry Templeton | 30 | 5 | 0 | 0 | 0 | 2 | 8 | .167 | .167 | .242 |

## Mark Davis continued

| Batter | AB | H | 2B | 3B | HR | BB | SO | BA | SA | OBA |
|---|---|---|---|---|---|---|---|---|---|---|
| Gene Tenace | 7 | 2 | 0 | 0 | 2 | 1 | 1 | .286 | 1.143 | .375 |
| Tim Teufel | 7 | 0 | 0 | 0 | 0 | 2 | 2 | .000 | .000 | .222 |
| Andres Thomas | 14 | 4 | 0 | 0 | 1 | 0 | 3 | .286 | .500 | .286 |
| Jason Thompson | 10 | 3 | 0 | 0 | 0 | 1 | 2 | .300 | .300 | .364 |
| Milt Thompson | 8 | 2 | 0 | 0 | 0 | 0 | 3 | .250 | .250 | .250 |
| Rob Thompson | 5 | 1 | 0 | 0 | 0 | 1 | 4 | .200 | .200 | .333 |
| Dickie Thon | 16 | 6 | 0 | 1 | 1 | 4 | 4 | .375 | .688 | .500 |
| Alex Trevino | 7 | 1 | 0 | 0 | 0 | 1 | 1 | .143 | .143 | .222 |
| Manny Trillo | 7 | 1 | 0 | 0 | 0 | 2 | 3 | .143 | .143 | .333 |
| Jose Uribe | 7 | 2 | 1 | 0 | 0 | 0 | 2 | .286 | .429 | .286 |
| Fernando Valenzuela | 5 | 0 | 0 | 0 | 0 | 0 | 2 | .000 | .000 | .000 |
| Andy Van Slyke | 10 | 4 | 1 | 0 | 1 | 0 | 3 | .400 | .800 | .364 |
| Ozzie Virgil | 17 | 6 | 0 | 0 | 0 | 3 | 5 | .353 | .353 | .476 |
| Tim Wallach | 18 | 1 | 0 | 0 | 0 | 1 | 8 | .056 | .056 | .105 |
| Denny Walling | 11 | 1 | 0 | 0 | 0 | 0 | 3 | .091 | .091 | .091 |
| Claudell Washington | 12 | 5 | 2 | 0 | 0 | 2 | 3 | .417 | .583 | .500 |
| Bob Watson | 10 | 3 | 1 | 0 | 1 | 2 | 1 | .300 | .700 | .417 |
| Mitch Webster | 9 | 2 | 0 | 0 | 0 | 1 | 3 | .222 | .222 | .300 |
| Alan Wiggins | 14 | 4 | 1 | 0 | 0 | 0 | 1 | .286 | .357 | .286 |
| Glenn Wilson | 16 | 3 | 2 | 0 | 0 | 0 | 2 | .188 | .313 | .188 |
| Mookie Wilson | 24 | 6 | 0 | 1 | 0 | 3 | 5 | .250 | .333 | .333 |
| Jim Wohlford | 7 | 2 | 0 | 0 | 0 | 0 | 3 | .286 | .286 | .286 |
| Gary Woods | 8 | 4 | 0 | 0 | 1 | 1 | 0 | .500 | .875 | .556 |
| Tracy Woodson | 8 | 1 | 0 | 0 | 0 | 0 | 1 | .125 | .125 | .125 |
| Marvell Wynne | 12 | 1 | 0 | 0 | 0 | 1 | 3 | .083 | .083 | .154 |
| Steve Yeager | 10 | 0 | 0 | 0 | 0 | 0 | 1 | .000 | .000 | .000 |
| Gerald Young | 7 | 2 | 0 | 0 | 0 | 2 | 0 | .286 | .286 | .444 |
| Joel Youngblood | 6 | 2 | 0 | 0 | 0 | 1 | 2 | .333 | .333 | .429 |

## Dennis Eckersley

| Batter | AB | H | 2B | 3B | HR | BB | SO | BA | SA | OBA |
|---|---|---|---|---|---|---|---|---|---|---|
| Hank Aaron | 12 | 3 | 1 | 0 | 0 | 0 | 3 | .250 | .333 | .250 |
| Glenn Adams | 21 | 5 | 1 | 1 | 0 | 3 | 2 | .238 | .381 | .333 |
| Luis Aguayo | 5 | 3 | 0 | 0 | 1 | 0 | 1 | .600 | 1.200 | .600 |
| Willie Aikens | 24 | 5 | 1 | 0 | 1 | 0 | 5 | .208 | .375 | .200 |
| Danny Ainge | 5 | 2 | 0 | 0 | 0 | 1 | 0 | .400 | .400 | .500 |
| Gary Alexander | 17 | 3 | 0 | 0 | 0 | 1 | 7 | .176 | .176 | .222 |
| Jamie Allen | 6 | 0 | 0 | 0 | 0 | 0 | 2 | .000 | .000 | .000 |
| Bill Almon | 6 | 2 | 0 | 0 | 0 | 0 | 2 | .333 | .333 | .333 |
| Sandy Alomar, Sr. | 7 | 2 | 0 | 0 | 1 | 1 | 3 | .286 | .714 | .375 |
| Dave Anderson | 9 | 2 | 0 | 0 | 0 | 0 | 2 | .222 | .222 | .222 |
| Tony Armas | 27 | 5 | 1 | 0 | 2 | 1 | 12 | .185 | .444 | .214 |
| Alan Ashby | 25 | 7 | 0 | 1 | 1 | 2 | 6 | .280 | .480 | .333 |
| Wally Backman | 17 | 3 | 0 | 0 | 0 | 1 | 3 | .176 | .176 | .222 |
| Mark Bailey | 10 | 6 | 1 | 0 | 0 | 1 | 1 | .600 | .700 | .636 |
| Bob Bailor | 32 | 3 | 0 | 0 | 0 | 1 | 6 | .094 | .094 | .118 |
| Harold Baines | 25 | 8 | 3 | 0 | 1 | 2 | 3 | .320 | .560 | .370 |
| Steve Balboni | 15 | 3 | 0 | 0 | 2 | 0 | 7 | .200 | .600 | .200 |
| Billy Baldwin | 11 | 2 | 1 | 0 | 0 | 0 | 2 | .182 | .273 | .182 |
| Sal Bando | 36 | 6 | 2 | 0 | 2 | 5 | 6 | .167 | .389 | .268 |
| Alan Bannister | 19 | 2 | 0 | 0 | 1 | 4 | 2 | .105 | .263 | .250 |
| Jesse Barfield | 13 | 2 | 1 | 1 | 0 | 0 | 4 | .154 | .385 | .154 |
| Marty Barrett | 14 | 3 | 0 | 0 | 0 | 0 | 1 | .214 | .214 | .214 |
| Kevin Bass | 11 | 3 | 1 | 0 | 0 | 0 | 0 | .273 | .364 | .273 |
| Don Baylor | 63 | 14 | 3 | 1 | 0 | 1 | 13 | .222 | .302 | .265 |
| Mark Belanger | 27 | 3 | 1 | 0 | 0 | 6 | 13 | .111 | .148 | .273 |
| Buddy Bell | 68 | 23 | 6 | 0 | 3 | 6 | 4 | .338 | .559 | .387 |
| George Bell | 13 | 2 | 0 | 0 | 2 | 0 | 4 | .154 | .615 | .154 |
| Rafael Belliard | 7 | 3 | 1 | 0 | 0 | 1 | 0 | .429 | .571 | .500 |
| Juan Beniquez | 29 | 8 | 1 | 0 | 1 | 3 | 6 | .276 | .414 | .333 |
| Dave Bergman | 6 | 1 | 0 | 0 | 0 | 0 | 3 | .167 | .167 | .167 |
| Tony Bernazard | 28 | 12 | 2 | 1 | 1 | 0 | 2 | .429 | .679 | .429 |
| Dale Berra | 6 | 2 | 0 | 0 | 0 | 1 | 1 | .333 | .333 | .375 |
| Kurt Bevacqua | 8 | 2 | 0 | 0 | 0 | 0 | 1 | .250 | .250 | .250 |
| Paul Blair | 7 | 0 | 0 | 0 | 0 | 1 | 4 | .000 | .000 | .222 |
| Larvell Blanks | 12 | 2 | 1 | 0 | 0 | 0 | 1 | .167 | .250 | .167 |
| Bruce Bochte | 39 | 13 | 2 | 0 | 1 | 2 | 5 | .333 | .462 | .341 |
| Wade Boggs | 13 | 4 | 2 | 0 | 0 | 0 | 1 | .308 | .462 | .286 |
| Barry Bonds | 6 | 2 | 1 | 0 | 0 | 1 | 0 | .333 | .500 | .429 |
| Bobby Bonds | 32 | 9 | 2 | 0 | 1 | 5 | 9 | .281 | .438 | .378 |
| Barry Bonnell | 18 | 4 | 0 | 1 | 0 | 1 | 2 | .222 | .333 | .263 |
| Bob Boone | 10 | 1 | 0 | 0 | 0 | 0 | 4 | .100 | .100 | .100 |
| Glenn Borgmann | 5 | 2 | 1 | 0 | 0 | 0 | 2 | .400 | .600 | .400 |
| Rick Bosetti | 23 | 5 | 1 | 0 | 0 | 0 | 4 | .217 | .261 | .217 |
| Thad Bosley | 7 | 2 | 0 | 0 | 0 | 0 | 3 | .286 | .286 | .250 |
| Lyman Bostock | 25 | 7 | 0 | 1 | 0 | 1 | 1 | .280 | .360 | .308 |
| Phil Bradley | 6 | 2 | 0 | 0 | 0 | 0 | 1 | .333 | .333 | .333 |
| Scott Bradley | 5 | 2 | 0 | 0 | 0 | 1 | 0 | .400 | .400 | .500 |
| Steve Braun | 23 | 2 | 0 | 0 | 0 | 6 | 5 | .087 | .087 | .267 |
| Sid Bream | 11 | 4 | 1 | 0 | 2 | 1 | 0 | .364 | 1.000 | .385 |
| Bob Brenly | 18 | 4 | 0 | 0 | 1 | 0 | 3 | .222 | .389 | .222 |
| George Brett | 48 | 15 | 2 | 1 | 2 | 4 | 5 | .313 | .521 | .365 |
| Dan Briggs | 8 | 1 | 0 | 1 | 0 | 0 | 1 | .125 | .375 | .125 |
| Greg Brock | 11 | 3 | 0 | 0 | 1 | 1 | 2 | .273 | .545 | .308 |
| Tom Brookens | 12 | 2 | 0 | 0 | 0 | 1 | 2 | .167 | .167 | .231 |
| Hubie Brooks | 16 | 4 | 0 | 0 | 0 | 0 | 3 | .250 | .250 | .250 |
| Bobby Brown | 25 | 6 | 1 | 0 | 0 | 0 | 2 | .240 | .280 | .240 |
| Chris Brown | 16 | 5 | 0 | 0 | 0 | 0 | 5 | .313 | .313 | .313 |
| Darrell Brown | 8 | 2 | 0 | 0 | 0 | 0 | 0 | .250 | .250 | .250 |
| Tom Browning | 5 | 1 | 0 | 0 | 0 | 0 | 2 | .200 | .200 | .200 |
| Tom Brunansky | 21 | 8 | 2 | 0 | 2 | 0 | 3 | .381 | .762 | .381 |
| Steve Brye | 10 | 2 | 1 | 0 | 0 | 1 | 3 | .200 | .300 | .273 |
| Bill Buckner | 8 | 3 | 0 | 0 | 0 | 0 | 0 | .375 | .375 | .375 |
| Al Bumbry | 69 | 19 | 4 | 1 | 1 | 4 | 11 | .275 | .406 | .324 |
| Ellis Burks | 11 | 1 | 1 | 0 | 0 | 0 | 4 | .091 | .182 | .091 |
| Rick Burleson | 40 | 11 | 5 | 1 | 0 | 3 | 7 | .275 | .450 | .341 |
| Jeff Burroughs | 17 | 2 | 0 | 0 | 1 | 1 | 5 | .118 | .294 | .167 |
| Randy Bush | 14 | 5 | 1 | 0 | 0 | 1 | 1 | .357 | .429 | .400 |
| Sal Butera | 11 | 2 | 1 | 0 | 0 | 0 | 2 | .182 | .273 | .182 |
| Brett Butler | 10 | 3 | 2 | 0 | 0 | 1 | 2 | .300 | .500 | .364 |
| Enos Cabell | 24 | 4 | 1 | 0 | 0 | 0 | 4 | .167 | .208 | .167 |
| Bert Campaneris | 42 | 7 | 0 | 0 | 1 | 1 | 13 | .167 | .238 | .186 |
| Bernie Carbo | 20 | 8 | 3 | 0 | 1 | 2 | 3 | .400 | .700 | .455 |
| Rod Carew | 56 | 18 | 8 | 0 | 2 | 2 | 5 | .321 | .571 | .350 |
| Gary Carter | 29 | 7 | 3 | 0 | 2 | 3 | 5 | .241 | .552 | .303 |
| Joe Carter | 9 | 2 | 0 | 0 | 0 | 0 | 1 | .222 | .222 | .222 |
| Rico Carty | 9 | 3 | 0 | 0 | 0 | 1 | 2 | .333 | .333 | .400 |
| John Castino | 28 | 8 | 1 | 0 | 0 | 1 | 7 | .286 | .321 | .310 |
| Rick Cerone | 23 | 6 | 1 | 0 | 1 | 2 | 4 | .261 | .435 | .320 |
| Dave Chalk | 21 | 1 | 0 | 0 | 0 | 5 | 5 | .048 | .048 | .222 |
| Chris Chambliss | 45 | 18 | 4 | 1 | 2 | 2 | 7 | .400 | .667 | .438 |
| Harry Chappas | 6 | 1 | 0 | 0 | 0 | 0 | 1 | .167 | .167 | .167 |
| Joe Charboneau | 8 | 0 | 0 | 0 | 0 | 0 | 2 | .000 | .000 | .000 |
| Rich Chiles | 12 | 3 | 1 | 0 | 0 | 0 | 0 | .250 | .333 | .250 |
| Jack Clark | 12 | 1 | 0 | 0 | 0 | 1 | 5 | .083 | .083 | .154 |
| Rich Coggins | 6 | 2 | 1 | 0 | 0 | 1 | 0 | .333 | .500 | .429 |
| Vince Coleman | 13 | 4 | 1 | 0 | 0 | 2 | 1 | .308 | .385 | .400 |
| Darnell Coles | 6 | 2 | 0 | 0 | 1 | 0 | 1 | .333 | .833 | .333 |
| Dave Collins | 31 | 8 | 2 | 0 | 1 | 2 | 7 | .258 | .419 | .303 |
| Dave Concepcion | 14 | 4 | 1 | 0 | 0 | 2 | 5 | .286 | .357 | .375 |
| Cecil Cooper | 68 | 23 | 6 | 1 | 5 | 5 | 8 | .338 | .676 | .373 |
| Tim Corcoran | 21 | 11 | 1 | 1 | 0 | 1 | 3 | .524 | .667 | .545 |
| Al Cowens | 36 | 10 | 2 | 1 | 1 | 7 | 3 | .278 | .472 | .395 |
| Jeff Cox | 5 | 0 | 0 | 0 | 0 | 0 | 2 | .000 | .000 | .000 |
| Larry Cox | 7 | 0 | 0 | 0 | 0 | 0 | 3 | .000 | .000 | .000 |
| Ted Cox | 10 | 1 | 0 | 0 | 1 | 2 | 2 | .100 | .400 | .250 |
| Terry Crowley | 6 | 2 | 0 | 0 | 1 | 1 | 0 | .333 | .833 | .429 |
| Jose Cruz | 14 | 1 | 1 | 0 | 0 | 0 | 2 | .071 | .143 | .071 |
| Julio Cruz | 33 | 10 | 2 | 0 | 0 | 2 | 6 | .303 | .364 | .333 |
| Todd Cruz | 16 | 3 | 0 | 1 | 0 | 0 | 5 | .188 | .313 | .188 |
| Mike Cubbage | 21 | 5 | 0 | 2 | 2 | 4 | 1 | .238 | .714 | .360 |
| Rich Dauer | 31 | 10 | 3 | 0 | 1 | 1 | 2 | .323 | .516 | .344 |
| Alvin Davis | 6 | 2 | 0 | 0 | 1 | 2 | 1 | .333 | .833 | .500 |
| Chili Davis | 24 | 6 | 0 | 0 | 1 | 1 | 6 | .250 | .375 | .280 |
| Dick Davis | 10 | 3 | 2 | 0 | 0 | 0 | 1 | .300 | .500 | .300 |
| Glenn Davis | 7 | 2 | 0 | 0 | 0 | 0 | 1 | .286 | .286 | .286 |
| Mike Davis | 8 | 2 | 1 | 0 | 0 | 0 | 2 | .250 | .375 | .250 |
| Tommy Davis | 13 | 5 | 0 | 0 | 1 | 0 | 1 | .385 | .615 | .385 |
| Andre Dawson | 38 | 6 | 2 | 1 | 1 | 0 | 4 | .158 | .342 | .154 |

# Dennis Eckersley continued

| Batter | AB | H | 2B | 3B | HR | BB | SO | BA | SA | OBA |
|---|---|---|---|---|---|---|---|---|---|---|
| Doug DeCinces | 44 | 5 | 2 | 0 | 0 | 0 | 9 | .114 | .159 | .114 |
| Rob Deer | 7 | 1 | 0 | 0 | 0 | 0 | 4 | .143 | .143 | .143 |
| Ivan DeJesus | 10 | 1 | 0 | 0 | 0 | 1 | 3 | .100 | .100 | .182 |
| Rick Dempsey | 31 | 7 | 1 | 0 | 1 | 2 | 10 | .226 | .355 | .265 |
| Bucky Dent | 33 | 7 | 0 | 0 | 2 | 7 | 5 | .212 | .394 | .350 |
| Bo Diaz | 13 | 4 | 0 | 0 | 0 | 0 | 0 | .308 | .308 | .308 |
| Steve Dillard | 8 | 2 | 1 | 0 | 0 | 1 | 1 | .250 | .375 | .333 |
| Miguel Dilone | 22 | 8 | 1 | 0 | 1 | 2 | 1 | .364 | .545 | .417 |
| John Doherty | 6 | 1 | 0 | 0 | 0 | 1 | 0 | .167 | .167 | .286 |
| Bill Doran | 19 | 5 | 0 | 1 | 1 | 1 | 2 | .263 | .526 | .300 |
| Brian Downing | 44 | 8 | 2 | 0 | 2 | 5 | 5 | .182 | .364 | .265 |
| Brian Doyle | 7 | 1 | 0 | 0 | 0 | 0 | 0 | .143 | .143 | .143 |
| Denny Doyle | 20 | 3 | 0 | 0 | 0 | 2 | 3 | .150 | .150 | .227 |
| Dan Driessen | 20 | 4 | 1 | 0 | 1 | 2 | 1 | .200 | .400 | .261 |
| Keith Drumright | 6 | 1 | 0 | 0 | 0 | 0 | 0 | .167 | .167 | .167 |
| Mariano Duncan | 10 | 1 | 1 | 0 | 0 | 1 | 3 | .100 | .200 | .182 |
| Jim Dwyer | 18 | 6 | 0 | 0 | 2 | 0 | 2 | .333 | .667 | .333 |
| Jerry Dybzinski | 7 | 3 | 1 | 0 | 0 | 0 | 1 | .429 | .571 | .500 |
| Len Dykstra | 15 | 5 | 2 | 0 | 0 | 0 | 1 | .333 | .467 | .333 |
| Dave Edler | 7 | 1 | 0 | 0 | 0 | 0 | 1 | .143 | .143 | .143 |
| Mike Edwards | 7 | 0 | 0 | 0 | 0 | 0 | 1 | .000 | .000 | .000 |
| Johnny Ellis | 12 | 2 | 0 | 0 | 0 | 0 | 5 | .167 | .167 | .167 |
| Dave Engle | 9 | 4 | 1 | 0 | 0 | 2 | 2 | .444 | .556 | .545 |
| Nick Esasky | 14 | 2 | 0 | 0 | 0 | 1 | 6 | .143 | .143 | .200 |
| Jim Essian | 14 | 3 | 1 | 0 | 0 | 1 | 4 | .214 | .286 | .267 |
| Darrell Evans | 5 | 0 | 0 | 0 | 0 | 1 | 1 | .000 | .000 | .167 |
| Dwight Evans | 23 | 7 | 1 | 0 | 4 | 6 | 8 | .304 | .870 | .448 |
| Sam Ewing | 12 | 3 | 0 | 0 | 1 | 0 | 1 | .250 | .500 | .250 |
| Ron Fairly | 12 | 2 | 0 | 0 | 0 | 2 | 1 | .167 | .167 | .286 |
| Mike Fischlin | 5 | 3 | 0 | 0 | 0 | 2 | 0 | .600 | .600 | .714 |
| Carlton Fisk | 43 | 13 | 4 | 1 | 2 | 3 | 7 | .302 | .581 | .375 |
| Mike R. Fitzgerald | 5 | 2 | 0 | 0 | 0 | 1 | 0 | .400 | .400 | .500 |
| Tim Flannery | 11 | 0 | 0 | 0 | 0 | 2 | 1 | .000 | .000 | .154 |
| Scott Fletcher | 10 | 2 | 0 | 0 | 0 | 0 | 3 | .200 | .200 | .273 |
| Doug Flynn | 21 | 3 | 0 | 0 | 0 | 0 | 2 | .143 | .143 | .143 |
| Tom Foley | 19 | 6 | 3 | 0 | 0 | 0 | 1 | .316 | .474 | .316 |
| Tim Foli | 7 | 2 | 0 | 0 | 0 | 0 | 0 | .286 | .286 | .286 |
| Dan Ford | 43 | 12 | 4 | 0 | 1 | 1 | 12 | .279 | .442 | .304 |
| Bob Forsch | 6 | 1 | 1 | 0 | 0 | 0 | 0 | .167 | .333 | .167 |
| George Foster | 7 | 2 | 1 | 0 | 0 | 0 | 2 | .286 | .429 | .250 |
| Julio Franco | 13 | 5 | 2 | 0 | 0 | 0 | 0 | .385 | .538 | .385 |
| Terry Francona | 11 | 2 | 2 | 0 | 0 | 0 | 0 | .182 | .364 | .182 |
| Bill Freehan | 12 | 3 | 1 | 0 | 0 | 2 | 5 | .250 | .333 | .400 |
| Doug Frobel | 10 | 0 | 0 | 0 | 0 | 2 | 2 | .000 | .000 | .167 |
| Gary Gaetti | 22 | 3 | 1 | 0 | 0 | 2 | 6 | .136 | .182 | .231 |
| Oscar Gamble | 30 | 6 | 2 | 0 | 1 | 3 | 4 | .200 | .367 | .265 |
| Jim Gantner | 32 | 8 | 3 | 0 | 0 | 0 | 1 | .250 | .344 | .242 |
| Damaso Garcia | 27 | 8 | 0 | 0 | 0 | 2 | 3 | .296 | .296 | .345 |
| Kiko Garcia | 11 | 4 | 0 | 0 | 1 | 0 | 4 | .364 | .636 | .364 |
| Pedro Garcia | 13 | 4 | 2 | 0 | 0 | 0 | 4 | .308 | .462 | .308 |
| Phil Garner | 16 | 4 | 1 | 0 | 0 | 0 | 4 | .250 | .313 | .250 |
| Ralph Garr | 24 | 9 | 0 | 1 | 0 | 1 | 2 | .375 | .458 | .400 |
| Steve Garvey | 12 | 2 | 1 | 0 | 0 | 0 | 0 | .167 | .250 | .167 |
| Rich Gedman | 5 | 0 | 0 | 0 | 0 | 0 | 1 | .000 | .000 | .000 |
| Cesar Geronimo | 5 | 1 | 0 | 0 | 0 | 0 | 1 | .200 | .200 | .200 |
| Kirk Gibson | 30 | 7 | 1 | 2 | 1 | 6 | 1 | .233 | .500 | .378 |
| Dan Gladden | 18 | 3 | 0 | 0 | 0 | 0 | 7 | .167 | .167 | .167 |
| Luis Gomez | 12 | 4 | 1 | 0 | 0 | 1 | 2 | .333 | .417 | .385 |
| Danny Goodwin | 11 | 0 | 0 | 0 | 0 | 1 | 3 | .000 | .000 | .083 |
| Dan Graham | 6 | 1 | 0 | 0 | 0 | 0 | 1 | .167 | .167 | .167 |
| Gary Gray | 7 | 1 | 0 | 0 | 0 | 0 | 1 | .143 | .143 | .143 |
| David Green | 9 | 1 | 1 | 0 | 0 | 0 | 3 | .111 | .222 | .100 |
| Mike Greenwell | 9 | 2 | 0 | 0 | 0 | 0 | 0 | .222 | .222 | .300 |
| Bobby Grich | 56 | 11 | 2 | 0 | 0 | 7 | 18 | .196 | .232 | .297 |
| Tom Grieve | 12 | 1 | 1 | 0 | 0 | 1 | 3 | .083 | .167 | .154 |
| Ken Griffey | 14 | 7 | 3 | 0 | 1 | 0 | 2 | .500 | .929 | .500 |
| Alfredo Griffin | 30 | 6 | 0 | 1 | 1 | 1 | 1 | .200 | .367 | .250 |
| Greg Gross | 10 | 3 | 2 | 0 | 0 | 0 | 0 | .300 | .500 | .300 |
| Wayne Gross | 33 | 8 | 1 | 0 | 3 | 8 | 3 | .242 | .545 | .395 |
| Johnny Grubb | 44 | 19 | 4 | 1 | 2 | 7 | 2 | .432 | .705 | .509 |
| Kelly Gruber | 6 | 0 | 0 | 0 | 0 | 0 | 1 | .000 | .000 | .000 |
| Mario Guerrero | 15 | 4 | 1 | 0 | 1 | 0 | 2 | .267 | .533 | .250 |
| Pedro Guerrero | 9 | 0 | 0 | 0 | 0 | 0 | 2 | .000 | .000 | .000 |
| Ozzie Guillen | 7 | 2 | 0 | 0 | 0 | 0 | 0 | .286 | .286 | .286 |
| Brad Gulden | 8 | 3 | 1 | 1 | 0 | 0 | 0 | .375 | .750 | .375 |

| Batter | AB | H | 2B | 3B | HR | BB | SO | BA | SA | OBA |
|---|---|---|---|---|---|---|---|---|---|---|
| Glenn Gulliver | 5 | 1 | 1 | 0 | 0 | 1 | 0 | .200 | .400 | .333 |
| Tony Gwynn | 12 | 4 | 2 | 0 | 0 | 0 | 1 | .333 | .500 | .333 |
| Jerry Hairston | 6 | 2 | 1 | 0 | 0 | 0 | 0 | .333 | .500 | .333 |
| John Hale | 7 | 1 | 0 | 0 | 0 | 2 | 2 | .143 | .143 | .333 |
| Mel Hall | 7 | 1 | 0 | 0 | 1 | 0 | 1 | .143 | .571 | .143 |
| Larry Haney | 10 | 0 | 0 | 0 | 0 | 0 | 5 | .000 | .000 | .000 |
| Mike Hargrove | 77 | 26 | 1 | 0 | 3 | 10 | 5 | .338 | .468 | .414 |
| Larry Harlow | 14 | 4 | 1 | 0 | 1 | 1 | 1 | .286 | .571 | .333 |
| Toby Harrah | 69 | 16 | 3 | 0 | 2 | 6 | 12 | .232 | .362 | .289 |
| Ron Hassey | 30 | 10 | 3 | 0 | 0 | 2 | 0 | .333 | .433 | .364 |
| Mickey Hatcher | 11 | 4 | 0 | 0 | 0 | 0 | 0 | .364 | .364 | .364 |
| Von Hayes | 40 | 13 | 1 | 0 | 2 | 5 | 7 | .325 | .500 | .391 |
| Mike Heath | 17 | 3 | 1 | 0 | 0 | 0 | 4 | .176 | .235 | .222 |
| Richie Hebner | 13 | 5 | 0 | 0 | 2 | 1 | 2 | .385 | .846 | .429 |
| Danny Heep | 8 | 3 | 0 | 0 | 0 | 1 | 0 | .375 | .375 | .444 |
| Mike Hegan | 15 | 5 | 0 | 0 | 1 | 0 | 5 | .333 | .533 | .333 |
| Dave Henderson | 9 | 1 | 0 | 0 | 0 | 0 | 3 | .111 | .111 | .111 |
| Ken Henderson | 8 | 2 | 0 | 0 | 0 | 0 | 4 | .250 | .250 | .250 |
| Rickey Henderson | 39 | 5 | 1 | 0 | 0 | 6 | 11 | .128 | .154 | .244 |
| Steve Henderson | 6 | 2 | 0 | 0 | 0 | 0 | 2 | .333 | .333 | .333 |
| Elrod Hendricks | 14 | 1 | 0 | 0 | 0 | 2 | 4 | .071 | .071 | .176 |
| Keith Hernandez | 12 | 2 | 0 | 0 | 0 | 2 | 2 | .167 | .167 | .286 |
| Larry Herndon | 21 | 4 | 2 | 1 | 0 | 0 | 2 | .190 | .381 | .182 |
| Tom Herr | 20 | 5 | 0 | 0 | 0 | 0 | 4 | .250 | .250 | .238 |
| Larry Hisle | 22 | 5 | 3 | 0 | 1 | 1 | 4 | .227 | .500 | .250 |
| Butch Hobson | 28 | 4 | 1 | 0 | 1 | 1 | 11 | .143 | .286 | .172 |
| Bob Horner | 9 | 5 | 1 | 0 | 1 | 0 | 0 | .556 | 1.000 | .556 |
| Willie Horton | 45 | 7 | 0 | 0 | 2 | 0 | 16 | .156 | .289 | .156 |
| Dave Hostetler | 10 | 4 | 0 | 0 | 1 | 0 | 1 | .400 | .700 | .400 |
| Roy Howell | 49 | 15 | 1 | 0 | 1 | 0 | 8 | .306 | .388 | .314 |
| LaMarr Hoyt | 6 | 2 | 0 | 0 | 0 | 0 | 1 | .333 | .333 | .333 |
| Kent Hrbek | 21 | 9 | 4 | 0 | 2 | 3 | 3 | .429 | .905 | .500 |
| Glenn Hubbard | 13 | 2 | 1 | 0 | 0 | 1 | 2 | .154 | .231 | .214 |
| Charles Hudson | 10 | 1 | 1 | 0 | 0 | 0 | 4 | .100 | .200 | .100 |
| Clint Hurdle | 14 | 3 | 2 | 0 | 1 | 2 | 2 | .214 | .571 | .333 |
| Reggie Jackson | 78 | 17 | 1 | 0 | 5 | 7 | 18 | .218 | .423 | .282 |
| Ron Jackson | 19 | 4 | 1 | 0 | 1 | 1 | 6 | .211 | .421 | .304 |
| Brook Jacoby | 13 | 3 | 0 | 0 | 1 | 1 | 5 | .231 | .462 | .286 |
| Steve Jeltz | 10 | 0 | 0 | 0 | 0 | 1 | 2 | .000 | .000 | .091 |
| Cliff Johnson | 14 | 3 | 0 | 0 | 1 | 0 | 3 | .214 | .429 | .214 |
| Howard Johnson | 9 | 3 | 2 | 0 | 0 | 1 | 1 | .333 | .556 | .400 |
| Lamar Johnson | 13 | 0 | 0 | 0 | 0 | 1 | 3 | .000 | .000 | .071 |
| Randy S. Johnson | 11 | 5 | 0 | 0 | 0 | 0 | 0 | .455 | .455 | .455 |
| Tim Johnson | 13 | 0 | 0 | 0 | 0 | 0 | 2 | .000 | .000 | .000 |
| Jay Johnstone | 5 | 1 | 0 | 0 | 1 | 0 | 2 | .200 | .800 | .200 |
| Ruppert Jones | 25 | 6 | 3 | 0 | 1 | 8 | 6 | .240 | .480 | .424 |
| Von Joshua | 21 | 4 | 0 | 0 | 0 | 0 | 5 | .190 | .190 | .190 |
| H. Pat Kelly | 23 | 8 | 1 | 0 | 0 | 4 | 8 | .348 | .391 | .444 |
| Steve Kemp | 39 | 16 | 6 | 0 | 3 | 4 | 2 | .410 | .795 | .455 |
| Terry Kennedy | 14 | 2 | 0 | 0 | 0 | 0 | 4 | .143 | .143 | .143 |
| Don Kessinger | 8 | 1 | 0 | 0 | 0 | 1 | 1 | .125 | .125 | .222 |
| Bruce Kimm | 5 | 0 | 0 | 0 | 0 | 0 | 1 | .000 | .000 | .000 |
| Mike Kingery | 8 | 3 | 1 | 0 | 0 | 0 | 2 | .375 | .500 | .375 |
| Ron Kittle | 11 | 3 | 1 | 0 | 0 | 0 | 4 | .273 | .364 | .273 |
| Bob Knepper | 7 | 1 | 0 | 0 | 0 | 0 | 1 | .143 | .143 | .143 |
| Alan Knicely | 7 | 2 | 0 | 0 | 2 | 0 | 3 | .286 | 1.143 | .286 |
| Ray Knight | 11 | 2 | 0 | 0 | 0 | 1 | 5 | .182 | .182 | .308 |
| John Knox | 12 | 3 | 0 | 0 | 0 | 3 | 2 | .250 | .250 | .400 |
| Wayne Krenchicki | 19 | 9 | 2 | 0 | 0 | 2 | 1 | .474 | .579 | .524 |
| Duane Kuiper | 39 | 16 | 2 | 0 | 0 | 5 | 1 | .410 | .462 | .467 |
| Randy Kutcher | 8 | 1 | 0 | 0 | 0 | 0 | 1 | .125 | .125 | .125 |
| Pete LaCock | 18 | 4 | 1 | 0 | 0 | 2 | 0 | .222 | .278 | .300 |
| Lee Lacy | 5 | 2 | 0 | 0 | 1 | 0 | 2 | .400 | 1.000 | .400 |
| Mike Laga | 6 | 1 | 1 | 0 | 0 | 0 | 3 | .167 | .333 | .167 |
| Joe Lahoud | 6 | 2 | 0 | 0 | 0 | 3 | 2 | .333 | .333 | .556 |
| Ken Landreaux | 35 | 6 | 2 | 0 | 1 | 2 | 2 | .171 | .314 | .216 |
| Carney Lansford | 24 | 5 | 1 | 0 | 0 | 2 | 3 | .208 | .250 | .269 |
| Gene Larkin | 9 | 3 | 2 | 0 | 0 | 0 | 0 | .333 | .556 | .333 |
| Tim Laudner | 6 | 0 | 0 | 0 | 0 | 0 | 3 | .000 | .000 | .000 |
| Rudy Law | 11 | 6 | 0 | 0 | 0 | 0 | 0 | .545 | .545 | .545 |
| Vance Law | 27 | 5 | 0 | 1 | 0 | 0 | 8 | .185 | .259 | .185 |
| Tom Lawless | 6 | 0 | 0 | 0 | 0 | 1 | 1 | .000 | .000 | .143 |
| Rick Leach | 22 | 5 | 3 | 0 | 0 | 0 | 1 | .227 | .364 | .227 |
| Joe Lefebvre | 13 | 4 | 0 | 0 | 2 | 0 | 3 | .308 | .769 | .357 |
| Ron LeFlore | 46 | 16 | 3 | 0 | 0 | 0 | 13 | .348 | .413 | .348 |

# Dennis Eckersley continued

| Batter | AB | H | 2B | 3B | HR | BB | SO | BA | SA | OBA |
|---|---|---|---|---|---|---|---|---|---|---|
| Johnnie LeMaster | 6 | 2 | 0 | 0 | 0 | 0 | 0 | .333 | .333 | .333 |
| Chet Lemon | 53 | 12 | 1 | 0 | 3 | 2 | 8 | .226 | .415 | .281 |
| Jeffrey Leonard | 26 | 4 | 2 | 0 | 1 | 1 | 12 | .154 | .346 | .185 |
| Sixto Lezcano | 41 | 10 | 2 | 0 | 3 | 2 | 7 | .244 | .512 | .279 |
| Nelson Liriano | 5 | 1 | 0 | 0 | 0 | 0 | 1 | .200 | .200 | .200 |
| Steve Lombardozzi | 5 | 1 | 0 | 0 | 0 | 0 | 3 | .200 | .200 | .200 |
| Carlos Lopez | 6 | 1 | 1 | 0 | 0 | 0 | 0 | .167 | .333 | .167 |
| John Lowenstein | 23 | 5 | 0 | 0 | 0 | 1 | 4 | .217 | .217 | .250 |
| Greg Luzinski | 10 | 2 | 1 | 0 | 0 | 0 | 5 | .200 | .300 | .200 |
| Fred Lynn | 42 | 9 | 2 | 0 | 2 | 1 | 8 | .214 | .405 | .227 |
| Steve Lyons | 6 | 2 | 0 | 0 | 0 | 0 | 1 | .333 | .333 | .333 |
| Garry Maddox | 6 | 1 | 0 | 0 | 0 | 0 | 1 | .167 | .167 | .167 |
| Bill Madlock | 12 | 5 | 3 | 0 | 0 | 0 | 0 | .417 | .667 | .417 |
| Phil Mankowski | 21 | 5 | 1 | 0 | 2 | 1 | 5 | .238 | .571 | .273 |
| Rick Manning | 44 | 16 | 3 | 0 | 0 | 5 | 4 | .364 | .432 | .420 |
| Fred Manrique | 6 | 0 | 0 | 0 | 0 | 0 | 1 | .000 | .000 | .000 |
| Mike A. Marshall | 15 | 3 | 0 | 0 | 2 | 0 | 4 | .200 | .600 | .200 |
| Carmelo Martinez | 6 | 2 | 0 | 0 | 0 | 0 | 2 | .333 | .333 | .333 |
| Jim Mason | 6 | 2 | 1 | 0 | 0 | 2 | 1 | .333 | .500 | .500 |
| Don Mattingly | 14 | 4 | 1 | 0 | 0 | 1 | 0 | .286 | .357 | .333 |
| Len Matuszek | 17 | 3 | 0 | 0 | 0 | 1 | 3 | .176 | .176 | .222 |
| Carlos May | 11 | 3 | 0 | 0 | 0 | 2 | 1 | .273 | .273 | .385 |
| Dave May | 5 | 1 | 1 | 0 | 0 | 1 | 1 | .200 | .400 | .333 |
| Lee May | 43 | 11 | 3 | 0 | 0 | 2 | 10 | .256 | .326 | .304 |
| Milt May | 20 | 3 | 1 | 0 | 1 | 0 | 2 | .150 | .350 | .150 |
| John Mayberry | 53 | 13 | 1 | 0 | 4 | 4 | 8 | .245 | .491 | .298 |
| Lee Mazzilli | 22 | 3 | 0 | 0 | 0 | 0 | 1 | .136 | .136 | .136 |
| Willie McGee | 26 | 9 | 2 | 0 | 0 | 0 | 3 | .346 | .423 | .346 |
| Fred McGriff | 7 | 1 | 1 | 0 | 0 | 1 | 4 | .143 | .286 | .250 |
| Dave McKay | 28 | 7 | 0 | 0 | 1 | 0 | 4 | .250 | .357 | .250 |
| Mark McLemore | 5 | 2 | 0 | 0 | 0 | 0 | 1 | .400 | .400 | .400 |
| Hal McRae | 61 | 18 | 4 | 2 | 3 | 0 | 9 | .295 | .574 | .295 |
| Kevin McReynolds | 10 | 4 | 2 | 0 | 0 | 1 | 1 | .400 | .600 | .455 |
| Bill Melton | 11 | 1 | 0 | 0 | 0 | 0 | 5 | .091 | .091 | .167 |
| Mario Mendoza | 13 | 1 | 0 | 0 | 0 | 1 | 2 | .077 | .077 | .133 |
| Dan Meyer | 56 | 14 | 4 | 1 | 1 | 1 | 3 | .250 | .411 | .263 |
| Larry Milbourne | 19 | 9 | 2 | 0 | 0 | 0 | 0 | .474 | .579 | .474 |
| Rick Miller | 27 | 8 | 1 | 0 | 0 | 4 | 4 | .296 | .333 | .387 |
| Eddie Milner | 23 | 7 | 0 | 0 | 2 | 1 | 0 | .304 | .565 | .333 |
| Bobby Van Mitchell | 11 | 4 | 0 | 0 | 0 | 2 | 1 | .364 | .364 | .462 |
| Kevin Mitchell | 6 | 3 | 2 | 0 | 0 | 0 | 1 | .500 | .833 | .500 |
| Bob Molinaro | 14 | 1 | 1 | 0 | 0 | 2 | 2 | .071 | .143 | .188 |
| Paul Molitor | 34 | 8 | 2 | 1 | 3 | 0 | 10 | .235 | .618 | .235 |
| Don Money | 39 | 3 | 0 | 0 | 0 | 5 | 11 | .077 | .077 | .200 |
| Bob Montgomery | 5 | 0 | 0 | 0 | 0 | 0 | 1 | .000 | .000 | .000 |
| Charlie Moore | 40 | 13 | 1 | 0 | 0 | 1 | 6 | .325 | .350 | .341 |
| Omar Moreno | 13 | 4 | 1 | 2 | 0 | 0 | 2 | .308 | .692 | .308 |
| Jim Morrison | 33 | 6 | 0 | 0 | 2 | 0 | 7 | .182 | .364 | .176 |
| Lloyd Moseby | 28 | 8 | 2 | 0 | 2 | 0 | 5 | .286 | .571 | .286 |
| John Moses | 11 | 2 | 0 | 0 | 0 | 0 | 1 | .182 | .182 | .182 |
| Rance Mulliniks | 26 | 6 | 2 | 0 | 2 | 2 | 2 | .231 | .538 | .310 |
| Jerry Mumphrey | 16 | 6 | 0 | 0 | 1 | 1 | 0 | .375 | .563 | .412 |
| Thurman Munson | 38 | 6 | 1 | 0 | 0 | 1 | 9 | .158 | .184 | .200 |
| Bobby Murcer | 16 | 4 | 1 | 0 | 1 | 0 | 1 | .250 | .500 | .250 |
| Dale Murphy | 17 | 4 | 1 | 0 | 1 | 0 | 3 | .235 | .471 | .235 |
| Dwayne Murphy | 34 | 5 | 0 | 0 | 1 | 3 | 6 | .147 | .235 | .216 |
| Eddie Murray | 44 | 15 | 2 | 0 | 3 | 1 | 6 | .341 | .591 | .356 |
| Larry Murray | 8 | 3 | 1 | 0 | 0 | 0 | 2 | .375 | .500 | .375 |
| Tony Muser | 10 | 1 | 0 | 0 | 0 | 1 | 5 | .100 | .100 | .182 |
| Bill Nahorodny | 5 | 1 | 0 | 0 | 0 | 0 | 0 | .200 | .200 | .167 |
| Ricky Nelson | 7 | 2 | 1 | 0 | 1 | 0 | 1 | .286 | .857 | .286 |
| Graig Nettles | 71 | 17 | 2 | 0 | 6 | 6 | 17 | .239 | .521 | .299 |
| Al Newman | 7 | 0 | 0 | 0 | 0 | 0 | 3 | .000 | .000 | .000 |
| Jeff Newman | 22 | 6 | 1 | 0 | 1 | 1 | 6 | .273 | .455 | .304 |
| Tom Nieto | 10 | 0 | 0 | 0 | 0 | 1 | 5 | .000 | .000 | .231 |
| Matt Nokes | 7 | 1 | 0 | 0 | 0 | 0 | 1 | .143 | .143 | .143 |
| Joe Nolan | 11 | 2 | 1 | 0 | 0 | 1 | 2 | .182 | .273 | .231 |
| Wayne Nordhagen | 11 | 3 | 1 | 0 | 0 | 0 | 3 | .273 | .364 | .273 |
| Nelson Norman | 10 | 1 | 0 | 0 | 0 | 1 | 4 | .100 | .100 | .182 |
| Jim Norris | 25 | 7 | 2 | 0 | 2 | 1 | 1 | .280 | .600 | .308 |
| Billy North | 13 | 5 | 0 | 0 | 0 | 3 | 1 | .385 | .385 | .500 |
| Jim Northrup | 5 | 3 | 1 | 0 | 0 | 2 | 0 | .600 | .800 | .750 |
| Willie Norwood | 7 | 2 | 0 | 0 | 1 | 0 | 1 | .286 | .714 | .286 |
| Nyls Nyman | 7 | 0 | 0 | 0 | 0 | 0 | 1 | .000 | .000 | .000 |
| Ken Oberkfell | 14 | 7 | 0 | 0 | 0 | 1 | 0 | .500 | .500 | .533 |

| Batter | AB | H | 2B | 3B | HR | BB | SO | BA | SA | OBA |
|---|---|---|---|---|---|---|---|---|---|---|
| Pete O'Brien | 19 | 4 | 0 | 0 | 2 | 1 | 2 | .211 | .526 | .250 |
| Ron Oester | 13 | 2 | 0 | 0 | 0 | 0 | 0 | .154 | .154 | .154 |
| Ben Oglivie | 67 | 17 | 3 | 0 | 6 | 2 | 7 | .254 | .567 | .275 |
| Tony Oliva | 8 | 1 | 0 | 0 | 0 | 1 | 0 | .125 | .125 | .222 |
| Al Oliver | 41 | 8 | 1 | 0 | 1 | 3 | 1 | .195 | .293 | .250 |
| Joe Orsulak | 9 | 5 | 1 | 0 | 0 | 1 | 0 | .556 | .667 | .600 |
| Jorge Orta | 50 | 25 | 2 | 2 | 3 | 4 | 1 | .500 | .800 | .527 |
| Amos Otis | 35 | 10 | 3 | 0 | 1 | 2 | 12 | .286 | .457 | .324 |
| Ed Ott | 6 | 1 | 1 | 0 | 0 | 1 | 1 | .167 | .333 | .286 |
| Spike Owen | 13 | 3 | 0 | 0 | 0 | 0 | 0 | .231 | .231 | .231 |
| Tom Paciorek | 15 | 4 | 1 | 0 | 0 | 1 | 5 | .267 | .333 | .313 |
| Mitchell Page | 37 | 10 | 1 | 1 | 2 | 2 | 6 | .270 | .514 | .300 |
| Mike Pagliarulo | 7 | 2 | 1 | 0 | 0 | 1 | 1 | .286 | .429 | .375 |
| David Palmer | 5 | 4 | 1 | 0 | 0 | 0 | 1 | .800 | 1.000 | .800 |
| Dave Parker | 23 | 8 | 3 | 0 | 2 | 0 | 1 | .348 | .739 | .348 |
| Lance Parrish | 41 | 11 | 1 | 0 | 3 | 1 | 15 | .268 | .512 | .286 |
| Larry Parrish | 18 | 4 | 1 | 1 | 1 | 1 | 3 | .222 | .556 | .263 |
| Dan Pasqua | 7 | 1 | 0 | 0 | 0 | 0 | 4 | .143 | .143 | .143 |
| Fred Patek | 23 | 4 | 2 | 0 | 0 | 2 | 8 | .174 | .261 | .240 |
| Tony Pena | 19 | 5 | 0 | 0 | 0 | 2 | 3 | .263 | .263 | .364 |
| Terry Pendleton | 14 | 2 | 0 | 0 | 0 | 0 | 3 | .143 | .143 | .143 |
| Jack Perconte | 7 | 1 | 0 | 0 | 0 | 0 | 0 | .143 | .143 | .143 |
| Marty Perez | 11 | 1 | 0 | 0 | 0 | 0 | 3 | .091 | .091 | .091 |
| Gerald Perry | 11 | 2 | 1 | 0 | 0 | 0 | 1 | .182 | .273 | .182 |
| Rick Peters | 8 | 1 | 0 | 0 | 0 | 0 | 1 | .125 | .125 | .125 |
| Gary Pettis | 8 | 2 | 0 | 0 | 0 | 0 | 3 | .250 | .250 | .250 |
| Ken Phelps | 7 | 2 | 0 | 0 | 1 | 2 | 1 | .286 | .714 | .444 |
| Tony Phillips | 7 | 1 | 0 | 0 | 0 | 0 | 1 | .143 | .143 | .143 |
| Rob Picciolo | 12 | 1 | 1 | 0 | 0 | 0 | 1 | .083 | .167 | .083 |
| Jack Pierce | 9 | 2 | 1 | 0 | 0 | 2 | 3 | .222 | .333 | .364 |
| Lou Piniella | 20 | 4 | 1 | 0 | 1 | 1 | 3 | .200 | .400 | .238 |
| Tom Poquette | 29 | 8 | 1 | 1 | 0 | 0 | 2 | .276 | .379 | .276 |
| Darrell Porter | 53 | 14 | 2 | 0 | 2 | 2 | 8 | .264 | .415 | .291 |
| Hosken Powell | 35 | 7 | 1 | 1 | 0 | 2 | 1 | .200 | .286 | .243 |
| Jim Presley | 8 | 1 | 0 | 0 | 0 | 0 | 5 | .125 | .125 | .125 |
| Greg Pryor | 9 | 1 | 0 | 0 | 0 | 1 | 1 | .111 | .111 | .200 |
| Kirby Puckett | 5 | 0 | 0 | 0 | 0 | 0 | 1 | .000 | .000 | .000 |
| Terry Puhl | 14 | 5 | 0 | 0 | 0 | 1 | 0 | .357 | .357 | .400 |
| Pat Putnam | 42 | 14 | 4 | 0 | 0 | 0 | 5 | .333 | .429 | .349 |
| Rey Quinones | 7 | 0 | 0 | 0 | 0 | 1 | 1 | .000 | .000 | .125 |
| Jamie Quirk | 12 | 2 | 1 | 0 | 0 | 2 | 4 | .167 | .250 | .286 |
| Doug Rader | 8 | 1 | 0 | 0 | 0 | 1 | 3 | .125 | .125 | .273 |
| Tim Raines | 43 | 15 | 3 | 1 | 0 | 3 | 4 | .349 | .465 | .391 |
| Rafael Ramirez | 11 | 5 | 2 | 0 | 1 | 0 | 0 | .455 | .909 | .455 |
| Bob Randall | 14 | 2 | 0 | 0 | 0 | 0 | 3 | .143 | .143 | .143 |
| Lenny Randle | 14 | 2 | 0 | 0 | 0 | 2 | 2 | .143 | .143 | .250 |
| Willie Randolph | 55 | 11 | 3 | 1 | 2 | 6 | 6 | .200 | .400 | .279 |
| Johnny Ray | 20 | 6 | 1 | 0 | 1 | 1 | 1 | .300 | .500 | .318 |
| Gary Redus | 12 | 3 | 1 | 0 | 0 | 0 | 5 | .250 | .333 | .250 |
| Jerry Remy | 14 | 1 | 0 | 0 | 0 | 0 | 3 | .071 | .071 | .071 |
| Dave Revering | 27 | 8 | 3 | 1 | 2 | 0 | 2 | .296 | .704 | .296 |
| Craig Reynolds | 33 | 6 | 1 | 0 | 0 | 1 | 1 | .182 | .212 | .206 |
| Harold Reynolds | 8 | 3 | 1 | 0 | 0 | 0 | 1 | .375 | .500 | .375 |
| R.J. Reynolds | 10 | 1 | 0 | 0 | 1 | 1 | 4 | .100 | .400 | .182 |
| Rick Rhoden | 6 | 2 | 0 | 0 | 0 | 0 | 1 | .333 | .333 | .333 |
| Jim Rice | 37 | 9 | 0 | 1 | 1 | 0 | 15 | .243 | .378 | .243 |
| Mike Richardt | 10 | 2 | 0 | 1 | 0 | 0 | 1 | .200 | .400 | .200 |
| Cal Ripken | 20 | 4 | 0 | 0 | 2 | 1 | 9 | .200 | .500 | .238 |
| Mickey Rivers | 61 | 22 | 1 | 0 | 0 | 0 | 3 | .361 | .377 | .361 |
| Leon Roberts | 26 | 9 | 1 | 2 | 0 | 2 | 2 | .346 | .538 | .393 |
| Andre Robertson | 8 | 3 | 1 | 0 | 0 | 0 | 0 | .375 | .500 | .375 |
| Brooks Robinson | 9 | 1 | 0 | 0 | 0 | 1 | 3 | .111 | .111 | .200 |
| Bruce Robinson | 5 | 1 | 0 | 0 | 0 | 0 | 1 | .200 | .200 | .200 |
| Aurelio Rodriguez | 32 | 5 | 1 | 0 | 2 | 3 | 8 | .156 | .375 | .229 |
| Ellie Rodriguez | 5 | 3 | 0 | 0 | 0 | 1 | 0 | .600 | .600 | .667 |
| Gary Roenicke | 7 | 1 | 1 | 0 | 0 | 0 | 5 | .143 | .286 | .143 |
| Cookie Rojas | 8 | 3 | 0 | 0 | 0 | 1 | 0 | .375 | .375 | .444 |
| Ed Romero | 5 | 3 | 0 | 0 | 0 | 0 | 1 | .600 | .600 | .600 |
| Pete Rose | 18 | 4 | 1 | 0 | 0 | 2 | 4 | .222 | .278 | .333 |
| Joe Rudi | 39 | 10 | 1 | 0 | 4 | 5 | 7 | .256 | .590 | .341 |
| John Russell | 7 | 3 | 1 | 0 | 0 | 0 | 3 | .429 | .571 | .429 |
| Lenn Sakata | 10 | 3 | 0 | 0 | 0 | 0 | 2 | .300 | .300 | .300 |
| Billy Sample | 24 | 8 | 2 | 0 | 2 | 2 | 5 | .333 | .667 | .357 |
| Juan Samuel | 33 | 8 | 3 | 0 | 1 | 2 | 10 | .242 | .424 | .278 |
| Manny Sanguillen | 5 | 2 | 0 | 0 | 1 | 0 | 1 | .400 | 1.000 | .500 |

## Dennis Eckersley *continued*

| Batter | AB | H | 2B | 3B | HR | BB | SO | BA | SA | OBA |
|---|---|---|---|---|---|---|---|---|---|---|
| Rafael Santana | 10 | 2 | 0 | 0 | 0 | 0 | 2 | .200 | .200 | .200 |
| Steve Sax | 21 | 5 | 0 | 0 | 0 | 0 | 1 | .238 | .238 | .238 |
| Mike Schmidt | 35 | 9 | 1 | 0 | 0 | 0 | 13 | .257 | .286 | .257 |
| Dick Schofield | 8 | 2 | 0 | 0 | 0 | 0 | 3 | .250 | .250 | .250 |
| Bill Schroeder | 6 | 2 | 1 | 0 | 0 | 0 | 1 | .333 | .500 | .333 |
| Rick Schu | 6 | 2 | 0 | 0 | 0 | 0 | 2 | .333 | .333 | .333 |
| Mike Scioscia | 13 | 6 | 2 | 0 | 0 | 2 | 0 | .462 | .615 | .533 |
| Daryl Sconiers | 6 | 2 | 0 | 0 | 0 | 0 | 0 | .333 | .333 | .333 |
| George Scott | 30 | 8 | 1 | 1 | 0 | 2 | 11 | .267 | .367 | .313 |
| John Scott | 8 | 2 | 1 | 0 | 0 | 1 | 5 | .250 | .375 | .333 |
| Rodney Scott | 7 | 0 | 0 | 0 | 0 | 0 | 1 | .000 | .000 | .000 |
| Kevin Seitzer | 7 | 3 | 0 | 0 | 0 | 0 | 0 | .429 | .429 | .429 |
| Bill Sharp | 10 | 6 | 1 | 0 | 0 | 1 | 1 | .600 | .700 | .636 |
| Pat Sheridan | 11 | 5 | 2 | 0 | 0 | 0 | 2 | .455 | .636 | .455 |
| Ruben Sierra | 5 | 1 | 0 | 0 | 0 | 0 | 0 | .200 | .200 | .200 |
| Ted Simmons | 20 | 2 | 2 | 0 | 0 | 1 | 2 | .100 | .200 | .182 |
| Joe Simpson | 14 | 1 | 0 | 0 | 0 | 0 | 1 | .071 | .071 | .071 |
| Ken Singleton | 60 | 25 | 3 | 0 | 3 | 11 | 6 | .417 | .617 | .507 |
| Don Slaught | 5 | 1 | 0 | 0 | 0 | 0 | 2 | .200 | .200 | .167 |
| Roy Smalley | 50 | 12 | 2 | 0 | 1 | 5 | 9 | .240 | .340 | .298 |
| Billy E. Smith | 20 | 7 | 1 | 0 | 1 | 3 | 3 | .350 | .550 | .435 |
| Lonnie Smith | 7 | 0 | 0 | 0 | 0 | 0 | 3 | .000 | .000 | .000 |
| Ozzie Smith | 18 | 7 | 3 | 1 | 0 | 3 | 0 | .389 | .667 | .476 |
| Cory Snyder | 9 | 1 | 0 | 0 | 0 | 0 | 4 | .111 | .111 | .111 |
| Eric Soderholm | 14 | 3 | 0 | 0 | 1 | 1 | 4 | .214 | .429 | .267 |
| Rick Sofield | 7 | 0 | 0 | 0 | 0 | 0 | 1 | .000 | .000 | .000 |
| Tony Solaita | 6 | 2 | 0 | 0 | 2 | 2 | 2 | .333 | 1.333 | .500 |
| Jim Spencer | 46 | 12 | 0 | 1 | 3 | 1 | 8 | .261 | .500 | .277 |
| Harry Spilman | 10 | 1 | 0 | 0 | 1 | 0 | 0 | .100 | .400 | .100 |
| Mike Squires | 31 | 8 | 2 | 0 | 1 | 2 | 0 | .258 | .419 | .294 |
| Fred Stanley | 19 | 6 | 0 | 0 | 0 | 1 | 3 | .316 | .316 | .350 |
| Lee Stanton | 24 | 2 | 0 | 0 | 0 | 2 | 7 | .083 | .083 | .185 |
| Rusty Staub | 38 | 12 | 1 | 0 | 1 | 1 | 2 | .316 | .421 | .333 |
| Bill Stein | 23 | 2 | 1 | 0 | 0 | 0 | 1 | .087 | .130 | .087 |
| Mike Stenhouse | 6 | 2 | 1 | 0 | 0 | 0 | 0 | .333 | .500 | .333 |
| Bob Stinson | 23 | 7 | 1 | 0 | 0 | 4 | 0 | .304 | .348 | .407 |
| Jeff Stone | 14 | 4 | 0 | 0 | 0 | 0 | 2 | .286 | .286 | .286 |
| Darryl Strawberry | 13 | 2 | 1 | 0 | 0 | 0 | 3 | .154 | .231 | .154 |
| Franklin Stubbs | 14 | 2 | 0 | 0 | 1 | 0 | 5 | .143 | .357 | .143 |
| Champ Summers | 14 | 5 | 0 | 0 | 1 | 2 | 2 | .357 | .571 | .471 |
| Jim Sundberg | 60 | 14 | 1 | 0 | 2 | 6 | 14 | .233 | .350 | .309 |
| B.J. Surhoff | 7 | 3 | 1 | 0 | 0 | 0 | 1 | .429 | .571 | .429 |
| Rick Sweet | 10 | 4 | 0 | 0 | 0 | 0 | 0 | .400 | .400 | .400 |
| Jerry Tabb | 6 | 2 | 0 | 0 | 2 | 0 | 1 | .333 | 1.333 | .333 |
| Pat Tabler | 10 | 1 | 0 | 0 | 0 | 1 | 3 | .100 | .100 | .182 |
| Danny Tartabull | 7 | 3 | 2 | 0 | 0 | 0 | 2 | .429 | .714 | .429 |
| Garry Templeton | 8 | 3 | 1 | 0 | 1 | 0 | 1 | .375 | .875 | .375 |
| Gene Tenace | 6 | 0 | 0 | 0 | 0 | 2 | 1 | .000 | .000 | .333 |
| Jerry Terrell | 10 | 1 | 0 | 0 | 0 | 0 | 3 | .100 | .100 | .100 |
| Dan Thomas | 5 | 2 | 0 | 0 | 1 | 0 | 2 | .400 | 1.000 | .500 |
| Derrel Thomas | 8 | 4 | 0 | 0 | 0 | 0 | 0 | .500 | .500 | .500 |
| Gorman Thomas | 49 | 8 | 0 | 0 | 2 | 4 | 13 | .163 | .286 | .226 |
| Gary Thomasson | 14 | 4 | 1 | 0 | 1 | 1 | 1 | .286 | .571 | .333 |
| Danny Thompson | 6 | 0 | 0 | 0 | 0 | 0 | 2 | .000 | .000 | .000 |
| Jason Thompson | 61 | 17 | 4 | 0 | 3 | 5 | 8 | .279 | .492 | .333 |
| Rob Thompson | 9 | 3 | 1 | 0 | 0 | 0 | 3 | .333 | .444 | .333 |
| Dickie Thon | 8 | 2 | 0 | 0 | 0 | 0 | 3 | .250 | .250 | .250 |
| Andre Thornton | 50 | 12 | 5 | 0 | 1 | 3 | 9 | .240 | .400 | .283 |

| Batter | AB | H | 2B | 3B | HR | BB | SO | BA | SA | OBA |
|---|---|---|---|---|---|---|---|---|---|---|
| Jay Tibbs | 5 | 1 | 0 | 0 | 0 | 0 | 2 | .200 | .200 | .200 |
| Wayne Tolleson | 9 | 3 | 2 | 0 | 0 | 0 | 2 | .333 | .556 | .364 |
| Rusty Torres | 6 | 2 | 0 | 0 | 1 | 4 | 1 | .333 | .833 | .600 |
| Cesar Tovar | 8 | 0 | 0 | 0 | 0 | 0 | 1 | .000 | .000 | .000 |
| Alan Trammell | 54 | 15 | 6 | 1 | 0 | 3 | 9 | .278 | .426 | .316 |
| Alex Trevino | 6 | 0 | 0 | 0 | 0 | 0 | 1 | .000 | .000 | .000 |
| Manny Trillo | 14 | 1 | 0 | 0 | 0 | 0 | 2 | .071 | .071 | .071 |
| Jim Tyrone | 5 | 1 | 0 | 0 | 0 | 1 | 1 | .200 | .200 | .333 |
| Willie Upshaw | 33 | 10 | 3 | 0 | 1 | 3 | 4 | .303 | .485 | .351 |
| Jose Uribe | 13 | 3 | 0 | 0 | 0 | 0 | 0 | .231 | .231 | .231 |
| Dave Valle | 5 | 0 | 0 | 0 | 0 | 0 | 1 | .000 | .000 | .000 |
| Andy Van Slyke | 20 | 7 | 2 | 1 | 1 | 3 | 3 | .350 | .700 | .435 |
| Otto Velez | 6 | 0 | 0 | 0 | 0 | 1 | 5 | .000 | .000 | .143 |
| Max Venable | 6 | 2 | 0 | 0 | 0 | 0 | 1 | .333 | .333 | .429 |
| Tom Veryzer | 35 | 7 | 0 | 0 | 0 | 4 | 5 | .200 | .200 | .282 |
| Ozzie Virgil | 33 | 11 | 2 | 0 | 2 | 1 | 6 | .333 | .576 | .371 |
| George Vukovich | 12 | 2 | 1 | 0 | 0 | 1 | 1 | .167 | .250 | .231 |
| Mark Wagner | 12 | 2 | 0 | 0 | 0 | 1 | 6 | .167 | .167 | .231 |
| Greg Walker | 10 | 1 | 0 | 0 | 1 | 1 | 2 | .100 | .400 | .182 |
| Tim Wallach | 34 | 12 | 2 | 0 | 1 | 2 | 4 | .353 | .500 | .405 |
| Denny Walling | 13 | 2 | 0 | 0 | 0 | 1 | 1 | .154 | .154 | .200 |
| Joe Wallis | 7 | 2 | 0 | 0 | 0 | 0 | 1 | .286 | .286 | .286 |
| Gary Ward | 20 | 2 | 0 | 0 | 0 | 0 | 8 | .100 | .100 | .100 |
| Claudell Washington | 51 | 17 | 3 | 0 | 0 | 1 | 6 | .333 | .392 | .346 |
| Ron Washington | 11 | 3 | 1 | 0 | 0 | 2 | 4 | .273 | .364 | .357 |
| U.L. Washington | 22 | 9 | 0 | 0 | 0 | 1 | 6 | .409 | .409 | .435 |
| John Wathan | 16 | 6 | 1 | 0 | 0 | 0 | 3 | .375 | .438 | .375 |
| Bob Watson | 10 | 3 | 0 | 0 | 0 | 0 | 2 | .300 | .300 | .364 |
| Mitch Webster | 14 | 4 | 1 | 1 | 0 | 1 | 1 | .286 | .500 | .333 |
| Bob Welch | 5 | 0 | 0 | 0 | 0 | 0 | 2 | .000 | .000 | .000 |
| Lou Whitaker | 41 | 10 | 2 | 0 | 2 | 5 | 4 | .244 | .439 | .326 |
| Devon White | 5 | 3 | 0 | 0 | 0 | 0 | 0 | .600 | .600 | .600 |
| Frank White | 47 | 4 | 1 | 0 | 0 | 2 | 13 | .085 | .106 | .120 |
| Roy White | 31 | 9 | 1 | 0 | 2 | 6 | 3 | .290 | .516 | .405 |
| Terry Whitfield | 10 | 5 | 1 | 0 | 0 | 0 | 3 | .500 | .600 | .500 |
| Ernie Whitt | 28 | 6 | 1 | 0 | 1 | 2 | 6 | .214 | .357 | .267 |
| Rob Wilfong | 20 | 3 | 0 | 0 | 0 | 2 | 0 | .150 | .150 | .227 |
| Curtis Wilkerson | 5 | 0 | 0 | 0 | 0 | 0 | 1 | .000 | .000 | .000 |
| Billy Williams | 14 | 3 | 0 | 0 | 1 | 0 | 1 | .214 | .429 | .214 |
| Kenny Williams | 5 | 2 | 0 | 0 | 0 | 0 | 2 | .400 | .400 | .400 |
| Bump Wills | 40 | 15 | 2 | 0 | 0 | 3 | 5 | .375 | .425 | .432 |
| Glenn Wilson | 31 | 6 | 0 | 1 | 0 | 0 | 9 | .194 | .258 | .194 |
| Mookie Wilson | 8 | 2 | 1 | 0 | 0 | 0 | 2 | .250 | .375 | .250 |
| Willie Wilson | 30 | 9 | 1 | 0 | 0 | 2 | 2 | .300 | .333 | .364 |
| Dave Winfield | 24 | 7 | 3 | 0 | 0 | 1 | 3 | .292 | .417 | .320 |
| Herm Winningham | 12 | 2 | 0 | 0 | 1 | 1 | 3 | .167 | .417 | .231 |
| John Wockenfuss | 19 | 3 | 0 | 0 | 2 | 1 | 3 | .158 | .474 | .200 |
| Jim Wohlford | 7 | 1 | 0 | 0 | 0 | 1 | 2 | .143 | .143 | .250 |
| Al Woods | 27 | 5 | 0 | 0 | 2 | 2 | 2 | .185 | .407 | .233 |
| George Wright | 25 | 6 | 2 | 0 | 0 | 1 | 2 | .240 | .320 | .269 |
| Butch Wynegar | 39 | 11 | 2 | 0 | 0 | 3 | 5 | .282 | .333 | .333 |
| Jim Wynn | 7 | 0 | 0 | 0 | 0 | 0 | 5 | .000 | .000 | .000 |
| Marvell Wynne | 13 | 3 | 2 | 0 | 0 | 0 | 0 | .231 | .385 | .231 |
| Carl Yastrzemski | 26 | 7 | 2 | 0 | 0 | 1 | 3 | .269 | .346 | .321 |
| Ned Yost | 6 | 1 | 0 | 0 | 0 | 0 | 2 | .167 | .167 | .167 |
| Robin Yount | 77 | 18 | 3 | 1 | 1 | 3 | 16 | .234 | .338 | .259 |
| Richie Zisk | 33 | 9 | 2 | 1 | 1 | 2 | 7 | .273 | .485 | .306 |

## Mark Langston

| Batter | AB | H | 2B | 3B | HR | BB | SO | BA | SA | OBA |
|---|---|---|---|---|---|---|---|---|---|---|
| Andy Allanson | 17 | 3 | 0 | 0 | 0 | 2 | 3 | .176 | .176 | .263 |
| Brady Anderson | 9 | 1 | 0 | 1 | 0 | 1 | 2 | .111 | .333 | .200 |
| Tony Armas | 24 | 7 | 1 | 0 | 2 | 4 | 6 | .292 | .583 | .393 |
| Benny Ayala | 8 | 1 | 1 | 0 | 0 | 1 | 0 | .125 | .250 | .222 |
| Harold Baines | 36 | 5 | 0 | 0 | 1 | 0 | 12 | .139 | .222 | .139 |
| Dusty Baker | 16 | 5 | 2 | 0 | 0 | 4 | 1 | .313 | .438 | .450 |
| Steve Balboni | 21 | 5 | 2 | 0 | 1 | 7 | 12 | .238 | .476 | .414 |
| Chris Bando | 10 | 2 | 0 | 0 | 0 | 0 | 4 | .200 | .200 | .200 |
| Jesse Barfield | 33 | 8 | 1 | 1 | 3 | 4 | 15 | .242 | .606 | .324 |
| Marty Barrett | 37 | 11 | 0 | 0 | 0 | 6 | 4 | .297 | .297 | .395 |
| Don Baylor | 43 | 9 | 1 | 0 | 2 | 4 | 11 | .209 | .372 | .333 |

| Batter | AB | H | 2B | 3B | HR | BB | SO | BA | SA | OBA |
|---|---|---|---|---|---|---|---|---|---|---|
| Billy Beane | 8 | 5 | 1 | 0 | 0 | 0 | 2 | .625 | .750 | .625 |
| Buddy Bell | 5 | 4 | 1 | 0 | 0 | 3 | 1 | .800 | 1.000 | .875 |
| George Bell | 39 | 10 | 1 | 0 | 4 | 3 | 12 | .256 | .590 | .310 |
| Jay Bell | 17 | 3 | 1 | 0 | 0 | 2 | 3 | .176 | .235 | .263 |
| Juan Beniquez | 25 | 8 | 1 | 0 | 0 | 2 | 4 | .320 | .360 | .357 |
| Todd Benzinger | 16 | 7 | 1 | 0 | 1 | 2 | 4 | .438 | .688 | .500 |
| Tony Bernazard | 12 | 1 | 1 | 0 | 0 | 2 | 2 | .083 | .167 | .200 |
| Dante Bichette | 7 | 3 | 2 | 0 | 0 | 0 | 2 | .429 | .714 | .429 |
| Wade Boggs | 31 | 7 | 0 | 0 | 1 | 13 | 3 | .226 | .323 | .455 |
| Barry Bonds | 5 | 0 | 0 | 0 | 0 | 1 | 0 | .000 | .000 | .167 |
| Bobby Bonilla | 14 | 2 | 1 | 0 | 0 | 3 | 6 | .143 | .214 | .294 |

# Mark Langston continued

| Batter | AB | H | 2B | 3B | HR | BB | SO | BA | SA | OBA |
|---|---|---|---|---|---|---|---|---|---|---|
| Bob Boone | 25 | 7 | 1 | 0 | 0 | 4 | 1 | .280 | .320 | .367 |
| Pat Borders | 7 | 1 | 0 | 0 | 0 | 0 | 4 | .143 | .143 | .143 |
| Phil Bradley | 5 | 1 | 0 | 1 | 0 | 2 | 1 | .200 | .600 | .429 |
| Glenn Braggs | 13 | 4 | 1 | 0 | 1 | 5 | 3 | .308 | .615 | .500 |
| George Brett | 28 | 5 | 1 | 0 | 1 | 4 | 4 | .179 | .321 | .281 |
| Greg Brock | 8 | 2 | 0 | 0 | 1 | 0 | 0 | .250 | .625 | .250 |
| Tom Brookens | 32 | 12 | 2 | 0 | 0 | 4 | 4 | .375 | .438 | .444 |
| Mark Brouhard | 10 | 3 | 1 | 0 | 1 | 0 | 3 | .300 | .700 | .300 |
| Bob Brower | 20 | 3 | 1 | 0 | 0 | 4 | 6 | .150 | .200 | .292 |
| Darrell Brown | 6 | 1 | 0 | 0 | 0 | 0 | 0 | .167 | .167 | .167 |
| Marty Brown | 6 | 0 | 0 | 0 | 0 | 1 | 4 | .000 | .000 | .143 |
| Mike C. Brown | 7 | 1 | 0 | 0 | 0 | 0 | 1 | .143 | .143 | .143 |
| Jerry Browne | 7 | 0 | 0 | 0 | 0 | 3 | 1 | .000 | .000 | .273 |
| Tom Brunansky | 30 | 4 | 1 | 0 | 2 | 3 | 8 | .133 | .367 | .206 |
| Bill Buckner | 21 | 3 | 1 | 0 | 0 | 3 | 6 | .143 | .190 | .240 |
| Steve Buechele | 21 | 3 | 1 | 0 | 0 | 4 | 5 | .143 | .190 | .280 |
| Ellis Burks | 15 | 5 | 3 | 0 | 0 | 1 | 5 | .333 | .533 | .412 |
| Rick Burleson | 15 | 3 | 2 | 1 | 0 | 1 | 0 | .200 | .467 | .250 |
| Jeff Burroughs | 13 | 4 | 0 | 0 | 0 | 2 | 3 | .308 | .308 | .400 |
| Sal Butera | 6 | 3 | 0 | 0 | 0 | 0 | 1 | .500 | .500 | .500 |
| Brett Butler | 30 | 7 | 1 | 0 | 0 | 5 | 10 | .233 | .267 | .361 |
| Ivan Calderon | 17 | 4 | 1 | 1 | 1 | 4 | 8 | .235 | .588 | .381 |
| John Cangelosi | 12 | 3 | 0 | 0 | 0 | 3 | 3 | .250 | .250 | .400 |
| Jose Canseco | 22 | 5 | 0 | 0 | 2 | 3 | 8 | .227 | .500 | .296 |
| Mark Carreon | 8 | 4 | 1 | 0 | 0 | 3 | 1 | .500 | .625 | .636 |
| Gary Carter | 6 | 3 | 0 | 0 | 0 | 0 | 2 | .500 | .500 | .500 |
| Joe Carter | 40 | 12 | 1 | 2 | 3 | 4 | 13 | .300 | .650 | .364 |
| Carmelo Castillo | 31 | 8 | 1 | 0 | 2 | 2 | 11 | .258 | .484 | .303 |
| Juan Castillo | 8 | 4 | 1 | 0 | 0 | 0 | 1 | .500 | .625 | .500 |
| Marty Castillo | 5 | 0 | 0 | 0 | 0 | 1 | 3 | .000 | .000 | .167 |
| Rick Cerone | 18 | 1 | 1 | 0 | 0 | 2 | 6 | .056 | .111 | .150 |
| Jack Clark | 5 | 1 | 0 | 0 | 0 | 1 | 2 | .200 | .200 | .333 |
| Vince Coleman | 8 | 2 | 1 | 0 | 0 | 0 | 1 | .250 | .375 | .250 |
| Darnell Coles | 19 | 4 | 1 | 0 | 2 | 5 | 2 | .211 | .579 | .375 |
| Dave Collins | 14 | 2 | 0 | 0 | 0 | 1 | 1 | .143 | .143 | .200 |
| Onix Concepcion | 5 | 0 | 0 | 0 | 0 | 4 | 0 | .000 | .000 | .444 |
| Cecil Cooper | 12 | 4 | 0 | 0 | 0 | 1 | 2 | .333 | .333 | .385 |
| Julio Cruz | 10 | 4 | 1 | 0 | 0 | 3 | 3 | .400 | .500 | .538 |
| Todd Cruz | 5 | 2 | 0 | 0 | 0 | 0 | 2 | .400 | .400 | .400 |
| Mark Davidson | 17 | 4 | 1 | 0 | 0 | 2 | 7 | .235 | .294 | .316 |
| Chili Davis | 16 | 3 | 1 | 0 | 1 | 1 | 4 | .188 | .438 | .235 |
| Eric Davis | 8 | 3 | 0 | 0 | 1 | 0 | 3 | .375 | .750 | .375 |
| Mike Davis | 20 | 5 | 1 | 0 | 2 | 1 | 7 | .250 | .600 | .286 |
| Andre Dawson | 8 | 3 | 1 | 0 | 1 | 2 | 1 | .375 | .875 | .500 |
| Brian Dayett | 7 | 2 | 1 | 0 | 0 | 1 | 0 | .286 | .429 | .375 |
| Doug DeCinces | 31 | 9 | 4 | 0 | 1 | 11 | 4 | .290 | .516 | .465 |
| Rob Deer | 18 | 4 | 1 | 0 | 0 | 3 | 5 | .222 | .278 | .333 |
| Rick Dempsey | 14 | 4 | 0 | 0 | 2 | 5 | 5 | .286 | .714 | .474 |
| Mike Devereaux | 7 | 2 | 1 | 0 | 0 | 0 | 0 | .286 | .429 | .286 |
| Brian Downing | 47 | 14 | 3 | 0 | 2 | 10 | 13 | .298 | .489 | .431 |
| Shawon Dunston | 5 | 4 | 0 | 1 | 0 | 0 | 0 | .800 | 1.200 | .800 |
| Len Dykstra | 5 | 1 | 1 | 0 | 0 | 2 | 0 | .200 | .400 | .429 |
| Mike Easler | 10 | 0 | 0 | 0 | 0 | 1 | 5 | .000 | .000 | .091 |
| Kevin Elster | 12 | 2 | 0 | 0 | 0 | 0 | 3 | .167 | .167 | .154 |
| Dave Engle | 8 | 1 | 0 | 1 | 0 | 1 | 3 | .125 | .375 | .222 |
| Darrell Evans | 14 | 2 | 0 | 0 | 0 | 2 | 7 | .143 | .143 | .250 |
| Dwight Evans | 37 | 12 | 3 | 0 | 3 | 6 | 9 | .324 | .649 | .419 |
| Mike Felder | 5 | 1 | 0 | 0 | 0 | 0 | 0 | .200 | .200 | .200 |
| Tony Fernandez | 29 | 7 | 3 | 0 | 0 | 7 | 4 | .241 | .345 | .368 |
| Cecil Fielder | 15 | 4 | 2 | 0 | 2 | 4 | 7 | .267 | .800 | .421 |
| Carlton Fisk | 33 | 12 | 1 | 0 | 4 | 2 | 2 | .364 | .758 | .400 |
| Scott Fletcher | 28 | 4 | 1 | 0 | 0 | 7 | 4 | .143 | .179 | .314 |
| Julio Franco | 36 | 12 | 1 | 1 | 2 | 6 | 6 | .333 | .583 | .419 |
| Gary Gaetti | 32 | 4 | 3 | 1 | 0 | 1 | 6 | .125 | .281 | .152 |
| Greg Gagne | 15 | 3 | 1 | 0 | 0 | 2 | 9 | .200 | .267 | .294 |
| Mike Gallego | 10 | 1 | 0 | 0 | 0 | 2 | 5 | .100 | .100 | .250 |
| Jim Gantner | 23 | 8 | 1 | 0 | 0 | 0 | 3 | .348 | .391 | .375 |
| Barbaro Garbey | 19 | 2 | 0 | 0 | 0 | 1 | 4 | .105 | .105 | .150 |
| Damaso Garcia | 25 | 8 | 3 | 1 | 0 | 2 | 2 | .320 | .520 | .393 |
| Rich Gedman | 5 | 0 | 0 | 0 | 0 | 1 | 2 | .000 | .000 | .143 |
| Ken Gerhart | 18 | 4 | 1 | 0 | 1 | 2 | 6 | .222 | .444 | .300 |
| Kirk Gibson | 16 | 2 | 1 | 0 | 0 | 2 | 7 | .125 | .188 | .222 |
| Dan Gladden | 23 | 6 | 1 | 1 | 1 | 1 | 2 | .261 | .522 | .292 |
| Rene Gonzales | 13 | 4 | 0 | 0 | 0 | 2 | 3 | .308 | .308 | .400 |
| Mike Greenwell | 10 | 4 | 1 | 0 | 0 | 1 | 1 | .400 | .500 | .455 |

| Batter | AB | H | 2B | 3B | HR | BB | SO | BA | SA | OBA |
|---|---|---|---|---|---|---|---|---|---|---|
| Bobby Grich | 24 | 6 | 2 | 0 | 1 | 5 | 5 | .250 | .458 | .400 |
| Alfredo Griffin | 34 | 10 | 1 | 0 | 0 | 4 | 3 | .294 | .324 | .368 |
| Kelly Gruber | 17 | 1 | 0 | 0 | 0 | 0 | 8 | .059 | .059 | .059 |
| Pedro Guerrero | 6 | 1 | 0 | 0 | 0 | 2 | 2 | .167 | .167 | .375 |
| Ozzie Guillen | 10 | 4 | 1 | 0 | 0 | 0 | 1 | .400 | .500 | .400 |
| Jackie Gutierrez | 7 | 1 | 0 | 0 | 0 | 0 | 0 | .143 | .143 | .143 |
| Jerry Hairston | 13 | 3 | 0 | 0 | 1 | 4 | 4 | .231 | .462 | .412 |
| Jeff Hamilton | 7 | 1 | 0 | 0 | 0 | 0 | 0 | .143 | .143 | .143 |
| Brian Harper | 8 | 0 | 0 | 0 | 0 | 2 | 0 | .000 | .000 | .200 |
| Toby Harrah | 12 | 3 | 1 | 0 | 0 | 8 | 0 | .250 | .333 | .550 |
| Billy Hatcher | 6 | 3 | 0 | 0 | 0 | 1 | 2 | .500 | .500 | .571 |
| Mickey Hatcher | 12 | 6 | 2 | 0 | 1 | 2 | 0 | .500 | .917 | .533 |
| Charlie Hayes | 7 | 1 | 0 | 0 | 0 | 0 | 2 | .143 | .143 | .143 |
| Von Hayes | 9 | 2 | 0 | 0 | 1 | 1 | 4 | .222 | .556 | .300 |
| Mike Heath | 45 | 15 | 4 | 1 | 3 | 4 | 6 | .333 | .667 | .388 |
| Dave Henderson | 20 | 6 | 3 | 0 | 1 | 0 | 5 | .300 | .600 | .333 |
| Rickey Henderson | 28 | 8 | 1 | 0 | 2 | 6 | 4 | .286 | .536 | .412 |
| Steve Henderson | 7 | 4 | 1 | 0 | 0 | 2 | 0 | .571 | .714 | .667 |
| George Hendrick | 33 | 17 | 1 | 0 | 4 | 3 | 5 | .515 | .909 | .556 |
| Larry Herndon | 40 | 9 | 4 | 0 | 1 | 4 | 9 | .225 | .400 | .295 |
| Tom Herr | 13 | 6 | 1 | 0 | 0 | 1 | 2 | .462 | .538 | .500 |
| Donnie Hill | 33 | 5 | 0 | 0 | 1 | 0 | 5 | .152 | .242 | .147 |
| Glenn Hoffman | 5 | 1 | 0 | 0 | 0 | 0 | 0 | .200 | .200 | .333 |
| Jack Howell | 19 | 3 | 1 | 0 | 1 | 0 | 12 | .158 | .368 | .158 |
| Kent Hrbek | 16 | 3 | 0 | 0 | 0 | 1 | 5 | .188 | .188 | .235 |
| Tim Hulett | 12 | 4 | 1 | 0 | 0 | 0 | 2 | .333 | .417 | .308 |
| Pete Incaviglia | 9 | 1 | 1 | 0 | 0 | 2 | 7 | .111 | .222 | .273 |
| Garth Iorg | 22 | 6 | 2 | 1 | 0 | 1 | 5 | .273 | .455 | .304 |
| Bo Jackson | 11 | 1 | 0 | 0 | 1 | 0 | 9 | .091 | .364 | .091 |
| Brook Jacoby | 34 | 13 | 1 | 0 | 4 | 2 | 6 | .382 | .765 | .417 |
| Stan Javier | 12 | 2 | 0 | 0 | 0 | 0 | 5 | .167 | .167 | .167 |
| Gregg Jefferies | 6 | 2 | 1 | 0 | 1 | 1 | 0 | .333 | 1.000 | .429 |
| Cliff Johnson | 11 | 4 | 0 | 0 | 1 | 1 | 2 | .364 | .636 | .417 |
| Howard Johnson | 18 | 2 | 1 | 0 | 0 | 3 | 9 | .111 | .167 | .238 |
| Lynn Jones | 12 | 1 | 0 | 0 | 0 | 1 | 1 | .083 | .083 | .154 |
| Ricky Jordan | 10 | 3 | 0 | 0 | 1 | 0 | 1 | .300 | .600 | .300 |
| Wally Joyner | 23 | 3 | 0 | 0 | 1 | 1 | 4 | .130 | .261 | .167 |
| Pat Keedy | 7 | 2 | 0 | 0 | 1 | 0 | 3 | .286 | .714 | .286 |
| Terry Kennedy | 9 | 2 | 0 | 0 | 1 | 1 | 3 | .222 | .556 | .300 |
| Steve Kiefer | 7 | 1 | 0 | 1 | 0 | 0 | 3 | .143 | .429 | .143 |
| Jeff King | 7 | 0 | 0 | 0 | 0 | 1 | 2 | .000 | .000 | .125 |
| Dave Kingman | 27 | 9 | 1 | 0 | 4 | 4 | 3 | .333 | .815 | .419 |
| Ron Kittle | 31 | 9 | 2 | 0 | 3 | 3 | 11 | .290 | .645 | .371 |
| Ray Knight | 22 | 5 | 1 | 0 | 0 | 2 | 6 | .227 | .273 | .292 |
| Chad Kreuter | 5 | 1 | 1 | 0 | 0 | 2 | 2 | .200 | .400 | .429 |
| Jeff Kunkel | 7 | 2 | 0 | 0 | 1 | 1 | 3 | .286 | .714 | .375 |
| Rusty Kuntz | 6 | 2 | 0 | 0 | 0 | 1 | 1 | .333 | .333 | .429 |
| Lee Lacy | 24 | 5 | 2 | 0 | 0 | 1 | 5 | .208 | .292 | .231 |
| Steve Lake | 6 | 1 | 0 | 0 | 0 | 1 | 0 | .167 | .167 | .286 |
| Carney Lansford | 40 | 13 | 2 | 1 | 0 | 8 | 8 | .325 | .425 | .438 |
| Gene Larkin | 11 | 4 | 0 | 0 | 0 | 2 | 1 | .364 | .364 | .462 |
| Tim Laudner | 19 | 4 | 0 | 0 | 2 | 3 | 6 | .211 | .526 | .348 |
| Vance Law | 15 | 4 | 2 | 0 | 0 | 2 | 3 | .267 | .400 | .353 |
| Manny Lee | 6 | 1 | 0 | 0 | 0 | 0 | 0 | .167 | .167 | .167 |
| Chet Lemon | 24 | 7 | 3 | 0 | 1 | 11 | 4 | .292 | .542 | .514 |
| Jeffrey Leonard | 6 | 1 | 1 | 0 | 0 | 0 | 0 | .167 | .333 | .167 |
| Jose Lind | 10 | 3 | 1 | 0 | 0 | 0 | 1 | .300 | .400 | .300 |
| Steve Lombardozzi | 14 | 4 | 1 | 0 | 1 | 4 | 6 | .286 | .571 | .444 |
| Greg Luzinski | 6 | 1 | 0 | 0 | 0 | 1 | 3 | .167 | .167 | .286 |
| Fred Lynn | 16 | 4 | 2 | 1 | 0 | 4 | 4 | .250 | .500 | .381 |
| Steve Lyons | 7 | 0 | 0 | 0 | 0 | 0 | 2 | .000 | .000 | .000 |
| Mike Macfarlane | 6 | 1 | 0 | 0 | 0 | 1 | 2 | .167 | .167 | .286 |
| Bill Madlock | 5 | 1 | 0 | 0 | 0 | 1 | 2 | .200 | .200 | .429 |
| Rick Mahler | 5 | 0 | 0 | 0 | 0 | 0 | 1 | .000 | .000 | .000 |
| Rick Manning | 6 | 0 | 0 | 0 | 0 | 1 | 2 | .000 | .000 | .143 |
| Fred Manrique | 17 | 6 | 0 | 0 | 0 | 1 | 4 | .353 | .353 | .389 |
| Mike A. Marshall | 5 | 1 | 1 | 0 | 0 | 1 | 2 | .200 | .400 | .333 |
| Buck Martinez | 14 | 3 | 0 | 0 | 1 | 4 | 2 | .214 | .429 | .389 |
| Vic Mata | 6 | 4 | 0 | 0 | 0 | 0 | 1 | .667 | .667 | .667 |
| Don Mattingly | 38 | 11 | 4 | 1 | 2 | 3 | 1 | .289 | .605 | .341 |
| Lloyd McClendon | 8 | 3 | 0 | 0 | 0 | 2 | 0 | .375 | .375 | .500 |
| Oddibe McDowell | 6 | 0 | 0 | 0 | 0 | 2 | 3 | .000 | .000 | .250 |
| Fred McGriff | 6 | 1 | 0 | 0 | 0 | 0 | 2 | .167 | .167 | .167 |
| Mark McGwire | 19 | 5 | 1 | 0 | 1 | 2 | 6 | .263 | .474 | .318 |
| Mark McLemore | 19 | 6 | 0 | 0 | 1 | 2 | 4 | .316 | .474 | .381 |

## Mark Langston continued

| Batter | AB | H | 2B | 3B | HR | BB | SO | BA | SA | OBA |
|---|---|---|---|---|---|---|---|---|---|---|
| Hal McRae | 18 | 2 | 1 | 0 | 0 | 4 | 5 | .111 | .167 | .273 |
| Kevin McReynolds | 8 | 4 | 0 | 0 | 1 | 1 | 1 | .500 | .875 | .556 |
| Bobby Meacham | 14 | 3 | 1 | 0 | 0 | 3 | 2 | .214 | .286 | .333 |
| Joey Meyer | 5 | 2 | 1 | 0 | 0 | 0 | 1 | .400 | .600 | .400 |
| Darrell Miller | 16 | 1 | 1 | 0 | 0 | 2 | 5 | .063 | .125 | .158 |
| Keith A. Miller | 12 | 1 | 1 | 0 | 0 | 0 | 3 | .083 | .167 | .083 |
| Randy Milligan | 7 | 0 | 0 | 0 | 0 | 0 | 3 | .000 | .000 | .000 |
| Kevin Mitchell | 5 | 2 | 0 | 0 | 1 | 0 | 1 | .400 | 1.000 | .400 |
| Paul Molitor | 21 | 7 | 3 | 0 | 1 | 8 | 5 | .333 | .619 | .517 |
| Russ Morman | 7 | 2 | 0 | 0 | 1 | 1 | 3 | .286 | .714 | .375 |
| Lloyd Moseby | 39 | 10 | 2 | 1 | 1 | 3 | 12 | .256 | .436 | .341 |
| Darryl Motley | 14 | 4 | 0 | 1 | 0 | 1 | 2 | .286 | .429 | .333 |
| Dwayne Murphy | 25 | 4 | 1 | 0 | 1 | 9 | 6 | .160 | .320 | .382 |
| Eddie Murray | 46 | 14 | 5 | 1 | 1 | 8 | 5 | .304 | .522 | .407 |
| Al Newman | 5 | 2 | 0 | 1 | 0 | 2 | 0 | .400 | .800 | .571 |
| Jeff Newman | 5 | 0 | 0 | 0 | 0 | 1 | 3 | .000 | .000 | .167 |
| Reid Nichols | 11 | 2 | 0 | 0 | 0 | 1 | 1 | .182 | .182 | .250 |
| Tom Nieto | 8 | 1 | 1 | 0 | 0 | 1 | 3 | .125 | .250 | .222 |
| Otis Nixon | 10 | 2 | 2 | 0 | 0 | 2 | 3 | .200 | .400 | .333 |
| Charlie O'Brien | 6 | 1 | 0 | 0 | 0 | 0 | 2 | .167 | .167 | .167 |
| Pete O'Brien | 26 | 7 | 0 | 0 | 1 | 2 | 7 | .269 | .385 | .321 |
| Joe Oliver | 5 | 2 | 0 | 0 | 0 | 1 | 2 | .400 | .400 | .429 |
| Paul O'Neill | 5 | 2 | 0 | 0 | 0 | 1 | 1 | .400 | .400 | .500 |
| Jose Oquendo | 7 | 1 | 1 | 0 | 0 | 1 | 1 | .143 | .286 | .250 |
| Joe Orsulak | 5 | 0 | 0 | 0 | 0 | 1 | 1 | .000 | .000 | .167 |
| Junior Ortiz | 7 | 4 | 0 | 0 | 0 | 0 | 1 | .571 | .571 | .571 |
| Spike Owen | 10 | 5 | 0 | 0 | 1 | 0 | 1 | .500 | .800 | .500 |
| Jim Paciorek | 7 | 1 | 0 | 0 | 0 | 0 | 2 | .143 | .143 | .143 |
| Tom Paciorek | 17 | 4 | 1 | 0 | 1 | 0 | 6 | .235 | .471 | .235 |
| Dave Parker | 9 | 2 | 0 | 0 | 0 | 1 | 4 | .222 | .222 | .300 |
| Lance Parrish | 17 | 2 | 0 | 0 | 0 | 5 | 12 | .118 | .118 | .318 |
| Larry Parrish | 26 | 4 | 0 | 0 | 0 | 4 | 17 | .154 | .154 | .258 |
| Dan Pasqua | 18 | 4 | 1 | 0 | 1 | 1 | 6 | .222 | .444 | .263 |
| Bill Pecota | 11 | 3 | 1 | 0 | 1 | 1 | 4 | .273 | .636 | .333 |
| Tony Pena | 6 | 2 | 0 | 0 | 0 | 0 | 0 | .333 | .333 | .333 |
| Terry Pendleton | 7 | 2 | 0 | 0 | 0 | 1 | 0 | .286 | .286 | .375 |
| Gary Pettis | 38 | 9 | 0 | 1 | 0 | 5 | 10 | .237 | .289 | .326 |
| Tony Phillips | 32 | 8 | 3 | 0 | 0 | 9 | 6 | .250 | .344 | .429 |
| Rob Picciolo | 5 | 3 | 1 | 0 | 0 | 0 | 1 | .600 | .800 | .600 |
| Gus Polidor | 12 | 3 | 0 | 0 | 0 | 0 | 2 | .250 | .250 | .250 |
| Greg Pryor | 10 | 2 | 0 | 0 | 0 | 0 | 2 | .200 | .200 | .200 |
| Kirby Puckett | 28 | 10 | 0 | 1 | 1 | 1 | 4 | .357 | .536 | .379 |
| Luis Quinones | 7 | 1 | 0 | 0 | 0 | 1 | 2 | .143 | .143 | .250 |
| Rey Quinones | 6 | 0 | 0 | 0 | 0 | 2 | 1 | .000 | .000 | .250 |
| Domingo Ramos | 8 | 3 | 1 | 0 | 0 | 2 | 1 | .375 | .500 | .500 |
| Willie Randolph | 39 | 10 | 2 | 1 | 1 | 13 | 4 | .256 | .436 | .442 |
| Johnny Ray | 5 | 3 | 0 | 0 | 0 | 2 | 0 | .600 | .600 | .714 |
| Floyd Rayford | 16 | 3 | 1 | 0 | 2 | 0 | 5 | .188 | .625 | .188 |
| Randy Ready | 10 | 2 | 0 | 0 | 0 | 0 | 2 | .200 | .200 | .200 |
| Gary Redus | 20 | 4 | 2 | 0 | 0 | 3 | 5 | .200 | .300 | .304 |
| Jim Rice | 27 | 4 | 1 | 0 | 1 | 5 | 7 | .148 | .296 | .281 |
| Ernest Riles | 9 | 1 | 1 | 0 | 0 | 1 | 3 | .111 | .222 | .200 |
| Billy Ripken | 18 | 6 | 2 | 0 | 0 | 3 | 1 | .333 | .444 | .409 |
| Cal Ripken | 50 | 18 | 2 | 0 | 1 | 4 | 6 | .360 | .460 | .407 |
| Andre Robertson | 10 | 4 | 1 | 0 | 1 | 0 | 2 | .400 | .800 | .400 |
| Billy Jo Robidoux | 7 | 0 | 0 | 0 | 0 | 1 | 4 | .000 | .000 | .125 |
| Gary Roenicke | 15 | 4 | 0 | 0 | 0 | 0 | 4 | .267 | .267 | .267 |
| Ed Romero | 11 | 2 | 0 | 0 | 0 | 3 | 1 | .182 | .182 | .357 |
| Kevin Romine | 7 | 1 | 0 | 0 | 0 | 1 | 0 | .143 | .143 | .250 |
| Rolando Roomes | 6 | 0 | 0 | 0 | 0 | 1 | 4 | .000 | .000 | .143 |
| Jerry Royster | 6 | 2 | 1 | 0 | 0 | 1 | 0 | .333 | .500 | .375 |
| Argenis Salazar | 6 | 2 | 1 | 1 | 0 | 0 | 2 | .333 | .833 | .333 |

| Batter | AB | H | 2B | 3B | HR | BB | SO | BA | SA | OBA |
|---|---|---|---|---|---|---|---|---|---|---|
| Luis Salazar | 17 | 4 | 1 | 0 | 1 | 2 | 7 | .235 | .471 | .316 |
| Billy Sample | 14 | 3 | 0 | 0 | 1 | 0 | 1 | .214 | .429 | .214 |
| Juan Samuel | 16 | 1 | 0 | 0 | 0 | 3 | 5 | .063 | .063 | .211 |
| Ryne Sandberg | 8 | 0 | 0 | 0 | 0 | 3 | 3 | .000 | .000 | .273 |
| Dick Schofield | 32 | 4 | 0 | 0 | 0 | 6 | 8 | .125 | .125 | .263 |
| Bill Schroeder | 29 | 6 | 0 | 0 | 2 | 0 | 12 | .207 | .414 | .233 |
| Kevin Seitzer | 18 | 8 | 0 | 1 | 0 | 4 | 3 | .444 | .556 | .545 |
| Larry Sheets | 13 | 2 | 0 | 0 | 0 | 2 | 6 | .154 | .154 | .313 |
| Gary Sheffield | 8 | 4 | 1 | 0 | 1 | 0 | 1 | .500 | 1.000 | .500 |
| John Shelby | 21 | 7 | 1 | 1 | 2 | 1 | 2 | .333 | .762 | .364 |
| Pat Sheridan | 6 | 1 | 1 | 0 | 0 | 1 | 2 | .167 | .333 | .286 |
| Ruben Sierra | 21 | 4 | 0 | 0 | 2 | 1 | 1 | .190 | .476 | .217 |
| Ted Simmons | 7 | 1 | 0 | 0 | 0 | 0 | 0 | .143 | .143 | .143 |
| Joel Skinner | 12 | 1 | 1 | 0 | 0 | 2 | 5 | .083 | .167 | .214 |
| Don Slaught | 19 | 3 | 1 | 0 | 0 | 3 | 6 | .158 | .211 | .273 |
| Roy Smalley | 5 | 2 | 0 | 0 | 0 | 0 | 0 | .400 | .400 | .400 |
| Lonnie Smith | 16 | 5 | 1 | 0 | 1 | 8 | 5 | .313 | .563 | .542 |
| Ozzie Smith | 6 | 1 | 1 | 0 | 0 | 2 | 0 | .167 | .333 | .375 |
| Cory Snyder | 28 | 4 | 1 | 0 | 0 | 1 | 16 | .143 | .179 | .172 |
| Pete Stanicek | 10 | 3 | 2 | 0 | 0 | 2 | 2 | .300 | .500 | .417 |
| Mike Stanley | 16 | 2 | 0 | 0 | 0 | 2 | 6 | .125 | .125 | .222 |
| Dave Stegman | 6 | 2 | 0 | 0 | 0 | 0 | 1 | .333 | .333 | .333 |
| Terry Steinbach | 16 | 4 | 2 | 1 | 0 | 3 | 4 | .250 | .500 | .368 |
| Kurt Stillwell | 9 | 3 | 1 | 0 | 0 | 0 | 2 | .333 | .444 | .333 |
| Marc Sullivan | 10 | 2 | 0 | 0 | 2 | 0 | 2 | .200 | .800 | .200 |
| Jim Sundberg | 16 | 2 | 0 | 0 | 0 | 1 | 6 | .125 | .125 | .176 |
| Dale Sveum | 12 | 5 | 1 | 0 | 0 | 2 | 3 | .417 | .500 | .438 |
| Pat Tabler | 34 | 11 | 1 | 0 | 0 | 2 | 4 | .324 | .353 | .378 |
| Danny Tartabull | 14 | 6 | 3 | 0 | 0 | 5 | 2 | .429 | .643 | .579 |
| Mickey Tettleton | 29 | 5 | 0 | 0 | 0 | 1 | 10 | .172 | .172 | .200 |
| Tim Teufel | 15 | 2 | 0 | 0 | 0 | 8 | 5 | .133 | .133 | .435 |
| Milt Thompson | 6 | 0 | 0 | 0 | 0 | 1 | 2 | .000 | .000 | .143 |
| Rob Thompson | 5 | 2 | 0 | 0 | 0 | 1 | 0 | .400 | .400 | .500 |
| Dickie Thon | 8 | 0 | 0 | 0 | 0 | 0 | 5 | .000 | .000 | .000 |
| Andre Thornton | 16 | 6 | 1 | 0 | 0 | 1 | 3 | .375 | .438 | .412 |
| Gary Thurman | 11 | 2 | 0 | 0 | 0 | 2 | 6 | .182 | .182 | .308 |
| Wayne Tolleson | 17 | 2 | 0 | 0 | 0 | 2 | 6 | .118 | .118 | .200 |
| Alan Trammell | 43 | 16 | 4 | 0 | 2 | 3 | 6 | .372 | .605 | .413 |
| Willie Upshaw | 26 | 6 | 1 | 0 | 0 | 5 | 8 | .231 | .269 | .355 |
| Mark Wagner | 5 | 1 | 1 | 0 | 0 | 0 | 0 | .200 | .400 | .200 |
| Jim Walewander | 7 | 2 | 0 | 0 | 0 | 0 | 0 | .286 | .286 | .286 |
| Greg Walker | 17 | 4 | 0 | 0 | 0 | 0 | 3 | .235 | .235 | .235 |
| Jerome Walton | 10 | 3 | 0 | 0 | 0 | 1 | 4 | .300 | .300 | .364 |
| Gary Ward | 18 | 5 | 1 | 0 | 1 | 2 | 4 | .278 | .500 | .350 |
| Ron Washington | 8 | 1 | 0 | 0 | 0 | 0 | 1 | .125 | .125 | .125 |
| John Wathan | 6 | 1 | 0 | 0 | 0 | 0 | 1 | .167 | .167 | .167 |
| Walt Weiss | 7 | 1 | 0 | 0 | 0 | 1 | 1 | .143 | .143 | .250 |
| Lou Whitaker | 17 | 3 | 0 | 0 | 0 | 3 | 6 | .176 | .176 | .300 |
| Devon White | 25 | 2 | 0 | 0 | 0 | 0 | 6 | .080 | .080 | .080 |
| Frank White | 35 | 10 | 0 | 0 | 1 | 1 | 5 | .286 | .371 | .306 |
| Alan Wiggins | 8 | 2 | 0 | 0 | 0 | 2 | 1 | .250 | .250 | .455 |
| Curtis Wilkerson | 7 | 2 | 0 | 0 | 0 | 2 | 1 | .286 | .286 | .444 |
| Kenny Williams | 22 | 4 | 2 | 0 | 1 | 2 | 8 | .182 | .409 | .250 |
| Matt Williams | 5 | 2 | 1 | 0 | 1 | 0 | 3 | .400 | 1.200 | .400 |
| Glenn Wilson | 7 | 4 | 3 | 0 | 0 | 1 | 0 | .571 | 1.000 | .625 |
| Willie Wilson | 42 | 7 | 1 | 2 | 1 | 3 | 11 | .167 | .357 | .239 |
| Dave Winfield | 34 | 7 | 0 | 1 | 1 | 6 | 9 | .206 | .353 | .325 |
| Craig Worthington | 5 | 1 | 0 | 0 | 0 | 1 | 2 | .200 | .200 | .333 |
| Butch Wynegar | 17 | 2 | 0 | 0 | 0 | 7 | 3 | .118 | .118 | .375 |
| Mike Young | 18 | 4 | 1 | 0 | 0 | 2 | 6 | .222 | .278 | .333 |
| Robin Yount | 39 | 5 | 1 | 2 | 0 | 3 | 10 | .128 | .256 | .190 |

## Bret Saberhagen

| Batter | AB | H | 2B | 3B | HR | BB | SO | BA | SA | OBA |
|---|---|---|---|---|---|---|---|---|---|---|
| Luis Aguayo | 5 | 2 | 0 | 0 | 0 | 0 | 0 | .400 | .400 | .333 |
| Andy Allanson | 23 | 4 | 0 | 0 | 0 | 0 | 2 | .174 | .174 | .174 |
| Brady Anderson | 12 | 3 | 0 | 0 | 0 | 0 | 3 | .250 | .250 | .250 |
| Tony Armas | 18 | 3 | 0 | 0 | 1 | 1 | 9 | .167 | .333 | .200 |
| Wally Backman | 5 | 0 | 0 | 0 | 0 | 0 | 2 | .000 | .000 | .000 |
| Harold Baines | 41 | 7 | 1 | 0 | 1 | 2 | 12 | .171 | .268 | .205 |
| Chris Bando | 10 | 0 | 0 | 0 | 0 | 0 | 2 | .000 | .000 | .000 |

| Batter | AB | H | 2B | 3B | HR | BB | SO | BA | SA | OBA |
|---|---|---|---|---|---|---|---|---|---|---|
| Jesse Barfield | 33 | 13 | 4 | 0 | 2 | 1 | 6 | .394 | .697 | .400 |
| Marty Barrett | 24 | 4 | 1 | 0 | 0 | 1 | 3 | .167 | .208 | .200 |
| Don Baylor | 25 | 7 | 0 | 1 | 0 | 0 | 1 | .280 | .360 | .308 |
| Buddy Bell | 15 | 3 | 2 | 0 | 0 | 1 | 0 | .200 | .333 | .250 |
| George Bell | 37 | 13 | 4 | 0 | 4 | 1 | 1 | .351 | .784 | .359 |
| Juan Beniquez | 14 | 6 | 0 | 0 | 0 | 1 | 0 | .429 | .429 | .467 |
| Todd Benzinger | 5 | 0 | 0 | 0 | 0 | 0 | 3 | .000 | .000 | .000 |

# Bret Saberhagen continued

| Batter | AB | H | 2B | 3B | HR | BB | SO | BA | SA | OBA |
|---|---|---|---|---|---|---|---|---|---|---|
| Dave Bergman | 40 | 9 | 0 | 1 | 0 | 3 | 9 | .225 | .275 | .279 |
| Tony Bernazard | 33 | 10 | 2 | 0 | 1 | 0 | 3 | .303 | .455 | .303 |
| Lance Blankenship | 6 | 1 | 0 | 1 | 0 | 0 | 0 | .167 | .500 | .167 |
| Bruce Bochte | 18 | 2 | 0 | 0 | 1 | 2 | 7 | .111 | .278 | .200 |
| Wade Boggs | 35 | 18 | 3 | 1 | 1 | 4 | 3 | .514 | .743 | .564 |
| Bob Boone | 23 | 4 | 0 | 0 | 0 | 0 | 0 | .174 | .174 | .174 |
| Daryl Boston | 15 | 3 | 1 | 0 | 0 | 1 | 4 | .200 | .267 | .250 |
| Phil Bradley | 41 | 10 | 4 | 0 | 0 | 1 | 8 | .244 | .341 | .262 |
| Scott Bradley | 20 | 3 | 0 | 0 | 0 | 1 | 0 | .150 | .150 | .190 |
| Glenn Braggs | 20 | 8 | 2 | 0 | 1 | 0 | 5 | .400 | .650 | .400 |
| Mickey Brantley | 13 | 1 | 0 | 0 | 1 | 0 | 0 | .077 | .308 | .077 |
| Greg Brock | 13 | 2 | 1 | 0 | 0 | 1 | 3 | .154 | .231 | .214 |
| Tom Brookens | 20 | 6 | 2 | 1 | 0 | 1 | 2 | .300 | .500 | .333 |
| Bob Brower | 5 | 1 | 1 | 0 | 0 | 0 | 0 | .200 | .400 | .200 |
| Jerry Browne | 24 | 6 | 2 | 0 | 0 | 1 | 4 | .250 | .333 | .280 |
| Mike Brumley | 6 | 0 | 0 | 0 | 0 | 0 | 2 | .000 | .000 | .000 |
| Tom Brunansky | 24 | 9 | 0 | 0 | 0 | 2 | 4 | .375 | .375 | .423 |
| Bill Buckner | 20 | 7 | 2 | 1 | 1 | 0 | 1 | .350 | .700 | .350 |
| Steve Buechele | 20 | 10 | 2 | 0 | 1 | 0 | 3 | .500 | .750 | .500 |
| Ellis Burks | 14 | 4 | 0 | 1 | 1 | 0 | 3 | .286 | .643 | .286 |
| Randy Bush | 38 | 11 | 2 | 1 | 2 | 4 | 3 | .289 | .553 | .372 |
| Brett Butler | 31 | 6 | 1 | 1 | 0 | 3 | 4 | .194 | .290 | .265 |
| Ivan Calderon | 14 | 4 | 1 | 0 | 0 | 0 | 4 | .286 | .357 | .267 |
| John Cangelosi | 7 | 0 | 0 | 0 | 0 | 0 | 0 | .000 | .000 | .000 |
| Jose Canseco | 41 | 9 | 0 | 0 | 1 | 2 | 9 | .220 | .293 | .256 |
| Rod Carew | 15 | 3 | 0 | 0 | 0 | 0 | 1 | .200 | .200 | .188 |
| Joe Carter | 51 | 19 | 5 | 0 | 3 | 0 | 7 | .373 | .647 | .373 |
| Juan Castillo | 6 | 1 | 1 | 0 | 0 | 0 | 1 | .167 | .333 | .167 |
| Rick Cerone | 5 | 1 | 0 | 0 | 0 | 1 | 0 | .200 | .200 | .333 |
| Darnell Coles | 15 | 3 | 0 | 0 | 0 | 1 | 3 | .200 | .200 | .294 |
| Dave Collins | 19 | 2 | 0 | 0 | 0 | 2 | 4 | .105 | .105 | .190 |
| Cecil Cooper | 6 | 2 | 1 | 0 | 0 | 0 | 1 | .333 | .500 | .333 |
| Henry Cotto | 5 | 1 | 0 | 0 | 0 | 0 | 0 | .200 | .200 | .167 |
| Rich Dauer | 5 | 1 | 1 | 0 | 0 | 1 | 0 | .200 | .400 | .333 |
| Alvin Davis | 31 | 10 | 2 | 0 | 1 | 6 | 3 | .323 | .484 | .436 |
| Chili Davis | 13 | 6 | 0 | 0 | 0 | 3 | 3 | .462 | .462 | .563 |
| Mike Davis | 33 | 8 | 2 | 0 | 1 | 1 | 8 | .242 | .394 | .265 |
| Doug DeCinces | 20 | 3 | 1 | 0 | 1 | 2 | 4 | .150 | .350 | .227 |
| Rob Deer | 22 | 3 | 0 | 0 | 0 | 0 | 8 | .136 | .136 | .174 |
| Rick Dempsey | 15 | 3 | 0 | 0 | 0 | 0 | 2 | .200 | .200 | .200 |
| Brian Downing | 26 | 7 | 0 | 0 | 2 | 2 | 2 | .269 | .500 | .310 |
| Jim Dwyer | 15 | 4 | 0 | 0 | 0 | 1 | 5 | .267 | .267 | .313 |
| Mike Easler | 12 | 6 | 0 | 0 | 1 | 1 | 2 | .500 | .750 | .538 |
| Jim Eppard | 5 | 1 | 0 | 0 | 0 | 0 | 1 | .200 | .200 | .200 |
| Alvaro Espinoza | 6 | 2 | 0 | 0 | 0 | 0 | 0 | .333 | .333 | .333 |
| Cecil Espy | 10 | 2 | 0 | 1 | 0 | 0 | 4 | .200 | .400 | .200 |
| Darrell Evans | 41 | 9 | 1 | 1 | 1 | 8 | 5 | .220 | .366 | .347 |
| Dwight Evans | 28 | 10 | 4 | 1 | 1 | 2 | 2 | .357 | .679 | .387 |
| Felix Fermin | 12 | 3 | 1 | 0 | 0 | 0 | 2 | .250 | .333 | .250 |
| Tony Fernandez | 33 | 5 | 0 | 0 | 0 | 2 | 8 | .152 | .152 | .200 |
| Carlton Fisk | 35 | 11 | 2 | 0 | 3 | 1 | 4 | .314 | .629 | .308 |
| Scott Fletcher | 33 | 11 | 0 | 1 | 0 | 1 | 2 | .333 | .394 | .333 |
| Julio Franco | 49 | 17 | 2 | 0 | 2 | 1 | 1 | .347 | .510 | .360 |
| Terry Francona | 10 | 2 | 0 | 0 | 0 | 1 | 1 | .200 | .200 | .273 |
| Gary Gaetti | 30 | 5 | 1 | 0 | 0 | 1 | 2 | .167 | .200 | .194 |
| Greg Gagne | 29 | 4 | 1 | 0 | 0 | 2 | 3 | .138 | .172 | .194 |
| Dave Gallagher | 18 | 5 | 2 | 0 | 0 | 0 | 2 | .278 | .389 | .278 |
| Mike Gallego | 13 | 4 | 0 | 0 | 0 | 0 | 3 | .308 | .308 | .308 |
| Oscar Gamble | 5 | 1 | 0 | 0 | 1 | 1 | 1 | .200 | .800 | .333 |
| Jim Gantner | 32 | 11 | 2 | 0 | 0 | 2 | 4 | .344 | .406 | .382 |
| Damaso Garcia | 9 | 4 | 1 | 0 | 0 | 0 | 0 | .444 | .556 | .444 |
| Rich Gedman | 22 | 8 | 1 | 0 | 1 | 0 | 2 | .364 | .545 | .364 |
| Craig Gerber | 8 | 6 | 0 | 1 | 0 | 1 | 0 | .750 | 1.000 | .778 |
| Kirk Gibson | 32 | 4 | 0 | 0 | 0 | 2 | 16 | .125 | .125 | .176 |
| Dan Gladden | 30 | 11 | 3 | 2 | 1 | 0 | 4 | .367 | .700 | .355 |
| Rene Gonzales | 5 | 0 | 0 | 0 | 0 | 0 | 1 | .000 | .000 | .167 |
| Mike Greenwell | 16 | 5 | 0 | 0 | 1 | 3 | 2 | .313 | .500 | .400 |
| Bobby Grich | 17 | 3 | 0 | 0 | 1 | 3 | 5 | .176 | .353 | .300 |
| Ken Griffey | 18 | 8 | 3 | 0 | 0 | 1 | 1 | .444 | .611 | .474 |
| Alfredo Griffin | 36 | 10 | 0 | 1 | 0 | 1 | 5 | .278 | .333 | .289 |
| Wayne Gross | 7 | 1 | 0 | 0 | 1 | 1 | 3 | .143 | .571 | .250 |
| Johnny Grubb | 14 | 3 | 1 | 0 | 0 | 2 | 2 | .214 | .286 | .313 |
| Kelly Gruber | 17 | 6 | 0 | 0 | 0 | 0 | 3 | .353 | .353 | .353 |
| Ozzie Guillen | 27 | 8 | 1 | 0 | 0 | 1 | 6 | .296 | .333 | .321 |
| Jerry Hairston | 12 | 2 | 0 | 1 | 0 | 0 | 2 | .167 | .333 | .167 |

| Batter | AB | H | 2B | 3B | HR | BB | SO | BA | SA | OBA |
|---|---|---|---|---|---|---|---|---|---|---|
| Mel Hall | 42 | 10 | 3 | 0 | 1 | 0 | 9 | .238 | .381 | .238 |
| Darryl Hamilton | 6 | 3 | 0 | 0 | 1 | 0 | 2 | .500 | 1.000 | .500 |
| Mike Hargrove | 6 | 2 | 0 | 0 | 0 | 0 | 1 | .333 | .333 | .333 |
| Toby Harrah | 6 | 2 | 1 | 1 | 0 | 0 | 0 | .333 | .833 | .333 |
| Ron Hassey | 13 | 0 | 0 | 0 | 0 | 1 | 5 | .000 | .000 | .071 |
| Mickey Hatcher | 7 | 2 | 0 | 0 | 0 | 0 | 1 | .286 | .286 | .286 |
| Mike Heath | 20 | 4 | 1 | 0 | 0 | 2 | 4 | .200 | .250 | .261 |
| Dave Henderson | 31 | 5 | 2 | 0 | 0 | 1 | 8 | .161 | .226 | .188 |
| Rickey Henderson | 39 | 15 | 2 | 0 | 0 | 3 | 6 | .385 | .436 | .429 |
| Steve Henderson | 5 | 1 | 1 | 0 | 0 | 0 | 0 | .200 | .400 | .200 |
| Larry Herndon | 10 | 1 | 1 | 0 | 0 | 0 | 0 | .100 | .200 | .100 |
| Tom Herr | 11 | 2 | 0 | 0 | 0 | 2 | 1 | .182 | .182 | .308 |
| Donnie Hill | 17 | 6 | 0 | 0 | 0 | 0 | 1 | .353 | .353 | .353 |
| Sam Horn | 6 | 2 | 0 | 0 | 1 | 0 | 3 | .333 | .833 | .333 |
| Paul Householder | 9 | 2 | 0 | 0 | 0 | 0 | 2 | .222 | .222 | .222 |
| Jack Howell | 30 | 5 | 3 | 1 | 0 | 1 | 8 | .167 | .333 | .194 |
| Kent Hrbek | 34 | 10 | 1 | 0 | 1 | 3 | 9 | .294 | .412 | .342 |
| Glenn Hubbard | 6 | 1 | 0 | 0 | 0 | 0 | 2 | .167 | .167 | .167 |
| Tim Hulett | 13 | 3 | 1 | 1 | 1 | 0 | 2 | .231 | .692 | .231 |
| Pete Incaviglia | 15 | 3 | 0 | 0 | 0 | 1 | 7 | .200 | .200 | .250 |
| Reggie Jackson | 31 | 2 | 1 | 0 | 1 | 2 | 9 | .065 | .194 | .121 |
| Brook Jacoby | 44 | 7 | 0 | 0 | 0 | 3 | 14 | .159 | .159 | .213 |
| Dion James | 8 | 0 | 0 | 0 | 0 | 0 | 1 | .000 | .000 | .000 |
| Stan Javier | 10 | 2 | 0 | 0 | 0 | 1 | 1 | .200 | .200 | .250 |
| Cliff Johnson | 9 | 2 | 0 | 0 | 0 | 0 | 1 | .222 | .222 | .222 |
| Howard Johnson | 5 | 0 | 0 | 0 | 0 | 0 | 1 | .000 | .000 | .000 |
| Lance Johnson | 10 | 2 | 0 | 0 | 0 | 1 | 2 | .200 | .200 | .273 |
| Ruppert Jones | 25 | 5 | 2 | 0 | 2 | 1 | 5 | .200 | .520 | .231 |
| Wally Joyner | 27 | 7 | 2 | 0 | 0 | 2 | 2 | .259 | .333 | .323 |
| Roberto Kelly | 6 | 1 | 1 | 0 | 0 | 0 | 1 | .167 | .333 | .167 |
| Terry Kennedy | 16 | 5 | 0 | 0 | 1 | 1 | 3 | .313 | .500 | .353 |
| Mike Kingery | 13 | 1 | 0 | 0 | 0 | 2 | 3 | .077 | .077 | .200 |
| Dave Kingman | 22 | 6 | 1 | 0 | 1 | 0 | 6 | .273 | .455 | .273 |
| Ron Kittle | 7 | 1 | 0 | 0 | 0 | 0 | 3 | .143 | .143 | .143 |
| Ray Knight | 7 | 1 | 0 | 0 | 0 | 0 | 1 | .143 | .143 | .143 |
| Lee Lacy | 10 | 2 | 0 | 0 | 0 | 1 | 0 | .200 | .200 | .273 |
| Carney Lansford | 49 | 9 | 2 | 0 | 0 | 1 | 2 | .184 | .224 | .196 |
| Gene Larkin | 21 | 5 | 1 | 0 | 0 | 0 | 3 | .238 | .286 | .227 |
| Tim Laudner | 21 | 5 | 0 | 0 | 1 | 0 | 2 | .238 | .381 | .238 |
| Rudy Law | 12 | 4 | 0 | 0 | 0 | 0 | 2 | .333 | .333 | .333 |
| Rick Leach | 16 | 3 | 0 | 0 | 0 | 1 | 2 | .188 | .188 | .235 |
| Manny Lee | 15 | 2 | 0 | 0 | 0 | 1 | 7 | .133 | .133 | .188 |
| Chet Lemon | 48 | 7 | 3 | 0 | 0 | 1 | 11 | .146 | .208 | .180 |
| Jeffrey Leonard | 11 | 2 | 0 | 0 | 0 | 0 | 2 | .182 | .182 | .182 |
| Nelson Liriano | 12 | 2 | 1 | 0 | 0 | 0 | 2 | .167 | .250 | .167 |
| Bryan Little | 5 | 3 | 0 | 0 | 0 | 2 | 0 | .600 | .600 | .714 |
| Steve Lombardozzi | 18 | 5 | 0 | 0 | 0 | 1 | 2 | .278 | .278 | .316 |
| Fred Lynn | 41 | 7 | 1 | 0 | 3 | 2 | 8 | .171 | .415 | .209 |
| Steve Lyons | 19 | 6 | 2 | 0 | 0 | 1 | 4 | .316 | .421 | .333 |
| Rick Manning | 6 | 1 | 0 | 0 | 0 | 1 | 1 | .167 | .167 | .286 |
| Fred Manrique | 14 | 4 | 0 | 0 | 0 | 0 | 1 | .286 | .286 | .267 |
| Carlos Martinez | 6 | 2 | 1 | 0 | 0 | 0 | 0 | .333 | .500 | .333 |
| Don Mattingly | 40 | 12 | 5 | 0 | 0 | 0 | 1 | .300 | .425 | .293 |
| Oddibe McDowell | 35 | 6 | 2 | 1 | 0 | 4 | 8 | .171 | .286 | .250 |
| Fred McGriff | 25 | 10 | 2 | 1 | 1 | 2 | 8 | .400 | .680 | .444 |
| Mark McGwire | 29 | 10 | 4 | 1 | 0 | 3 | 2 | .345 | .552 | .406 |
| Bobby Meacham | 15 | 2 | 0 | 1 | 1 | 0 | 4 | .133 | .467 | .133 |
| Joey Meyer | 7 | 1 | 1 | 0 | 0 | 0 | 1 | .143 | .286 | .143 |
| Paul Molitor | 34 | 7 | 0 | 2 | 0 | 2 | 2 | .206 | .324 | .250 |
| Charlie Moore | 11 | 2 | 0 | 0 | 0 | 1 | 2 | .182 | .182 | .250 |
| Jim Morrison | 6 | 1 | 0 | 0 | 1 | 0 | 2 | .167 | .667 | .167 |
| Lloyd Moseby | 30 | 9 | 1 | 0 | 0 | 4 | 3 | .300 | .333 | .382 |
| John Moses | 16 | 3 | 0 | 1 | 0 | 0 | 4 | .188 | .313 | .188 |
| Rance Mulliniks | 36 | 11 | 3 | 0 | 0 | 1 | 10 | .306 | .389 | .324 |
| Dwayne Murphy | 24 | 8 | 1 | 0 | 1 | 4 | 3 | .333 | .500 | .429 |
| Eddie Murray | 29 | 8 | 2 | 0 | 1 | 3 | 3 | .276 | .448 | .344 |
| Jerry Narron | 5 | 3 | 0 | 1 | 0 | 0 | 0 | .600 | 1.000 | .667 |
| Al Newman | 9 | 4 | 0 | 0 | 0 | 1 | 0 | .444 | .444 | .500 |
| Donell Nixon | 5 | 2 | 1 | 0 | 1 | 0 | 1 | .400 | 1.200 | .400 |
| Matt Nokes | 23 | 3 | 1 | 0 | 0 | 0 | 5 | .130 | .174 | .130 |
| Charlie O'Brien | 6 | 0 | 0 | 0 | 0 | 0 | 0 | .000 | .000 | .000 |
| Pete O'Brien | 44 | 12 | 0 | 0 | 2 | 3 | 3 | .273 | .409 | .319 |
| Ben Oglivie | 8 | 1 | 0 | 0 | 0 | 0 | 1 | .125 | .125 | .125 |
| Tom O'Malley | 5 | 0 | 0 | 0 | 0 | 1 | 0 | .000 | .000 | .167 |
| Joe Orsulak | 20 | 5 | 2 | 0 | 0 | 0 | 1 | .250 | .350 | .250 |

# Bret Saberhagen continued

| Batter | AB | H | 2B | 3B | HR | BB | SO | BA | SA | OBA |
|---|---|---|---|---|---|---|---|---|---|---|
| Spike Owen | 17 | 5 | 0 | 1 | 0 | 1 | 2 | .294 | .412 | .333 |
| Tom Paciorek | 5 | 2 | 0 | 0 | 0 | 1 | 1 | .400 | .400 | .500 |
| Mike Pagliarulo | 28 | 7 | 1 | 0 | 4 | 3 | 6 | .250 | .714 | .323 |
| Rafael Palmeiro | 9 | 5 | 0 | 1 | 0 | 2 | 1 | .556 | .778 | .636 |
| Dave Parker | 21 | 2 | 0 | 0 | 0 | 1 | 10 | .095 | .095 | .136 |
| Lance Parrish | 36 | 5 | 1 | 0 | 1 | 2 | 8 | .139 | .250 | .184 |
| Larry Parrish | 21 | 7 | 1 | 0 | 0 | 0 | 7 | .333 | .381 | .333 |
| Dan Pasqua | 24 | 7 | 3 | 1 | 3 | 1 | 9 | .292 | .875 | .320 |
| Jack Perconte | 16 | 3 | 0 | 0 | 0 | 0 | 2 | .188 | .188 | .188 |
| Geno Petralli | 18 | 5 | 1 | 0 | 0 | 1 | 5 | .278 | .333 | .316 |
| Gary Pettis | 42 | 11 | 2 | 1 | 0 | 4 | 12 | .262 | .357 | .326 |
| Ken Phelps | 27 | 8 | 2 | 0 | 2 | 9 | 5 | .296 | .593 | .459 |
| Tony Phillips | 29 | 5 | 1 | 0 | 0 | 4 | 13 | .172 | .207 | .273 |
| Chris Pittaro | 6 | 1 | 0 | 0 | 0 | 0 | 0 | .167 | .167 | .167 |
| Luis Polonia | 23 | 4 | 1 | 1 | 0 | 1 | 4 | .174 | .304 | .208 |
| Jim Presley | 27 | 9 | 3 | 0 | 0 | 2 | 5 | .333 | .444 | .379 |
| Kirby Puckett | 46 | 18 | 2 | 1 | 1 | 0 | 3 | .391 | .543 | .404 |
| Rey Quinones | 15 | 3 | 1 | 1 | 0 | 1 | 1 | .200 | .400 | .294 |
| Willie Randolph | 21 | 5 | 0 | 0 | 0 | 1 | 1 | .238 | .238 | .273 |
| Johnny Ray | 21 | 7 | 4 | 0 | 0 | 1 | 1 | .333 | .524 | .364 |
| Floyd Rayford | 6 | 1 | 0 | 0 | 0 | 0 | 1 | .167 | .167 | .167 |
| Jody Reed | 8 | 4 | 1 | 0 | 0 | 2 | 2 | .500 | .625 | .600 |
| Harold Reynolds | 23 | 4 | 0 | 0 | 0 | 0 | 1 | .174 | .174 | .174 |
| Jim Rice | 32 | 8 | 1 | 0 | 0 | 0 | 5 | .250 | .281 | .273 |
| Ernest Riles | 23 | 6 | 1 | 0 | 0 | 1 | 4 | .261 | .304 | .292 |
| Billy Ripken | 17 | 2 | 1 | 0 | 0 | 0 | 1 | .118 | .176 | .118 |
| Cal Ripken | 43 | 14 | 1 | 0 | 5 | 2 | 1 | .326 | .698 | .356 |
| Billy Jo Robidoux | 7 | 0 | 0 | 0 | 0 | 0 | 1 | .000 | .000 | .000 |
| Ed Romero | 14 | 2 | 1 | 0 | 0 | 0 | 1 | .143 | .214 | .143 |
| Mark Ryal | 5 | 1 | 0 | 0 | 0 | 0 | 3 | .200 | .200 | .200 |
| Mark Salas | 12 | 3 | 1 | 0 | 0 | 1 | 4 | .250 | .333 | .286 |
| Billy Sample | 8 | 3 | 0 | 0 | 0 | 1 | 0 | .375 | .375 | .444 |
| Steve Sax | 8 | 2 | 1 | 0 | 0 | 0 | 1 | .250 | .375 | .250 |
| Dick Schofield | 28 | 6 | 1 | 1 | 0 | 1 | 7 | .214 | .321 | .241 |
| Bill Schroeder | 6 | 1 | 0 | 0 | 0 | 0 | 2 | .167 | .167 | .167 |
| Rick Schu | 5 | 1 | 0 | 0 | 0 | 0 | 1 | .200 | .200 | .200 |
| Daryl Sconiers | 13 | 2 | 0 | 0 | 1 | 1 | 4 | .154 | .385 | .214 |
| Donnie Scott | 8 | 1 | 0 | 0 | 0 | 2 | 3 | .125 | .125 | .300 |
| Larry Sheets | 34 | 6 | 0 | 0 | 1 | 1 | 7 | .176 | .265 | .200 |
| Gary Sheffield | 8 | 2 | 0 | 0 | 0 | 0 | 0 | .250 | .250 | .250 |
| Pat Sheridan | 20 | 5 | 0 | 1 | 1 | 1 | 6 | .250 | .500 | .286 |
| Ruben Sierra | 26 | 6 | 2 | 0 | 1 | 2 | 3 | .231 | .423 | .286 |
| Ted Simmons | 5 | 0 | 0 | 0 | 0 | 0 | 2 | .000 | .000 | .000 |

| Batter | AB | H | 2B | 3B | HR | BB | SO | BA | SA | OBA |
|---|---|---|---|---|---|---|---|---|---|---|
| Joel Skinner | 6 | 1 | 0 | 0 | 0 | 0 | 2 | .167 | .167 | .167 |
| Don Slaught | 9 | 2 | 1 | 0 | 0 | 0 | 0 | .222 | .333 | .222 |
| Roy Smalley | 19 | 7 | 1 | 0 | 2 | 0 | 4 | .368 | .737 | .368 |
| Cory Snyder | 33 | 8 | 1 | 1 | 2 | 2 | 9 | .242 | .515 | .286 |
| Mike Stanley | 11 | 2 | 0 | 0 | 0 | 0 | 1 | .182 | .182 | .182 |
| Terry Steinbach | 20 | 5 | 1 | 0 | 0 | 1 | 2 | .250 | .300 | .348 |
| Jeff Stone | 9 | 0 | 0 | 0 | 0 | 0 | 4 | .000 | .000 | .000 |
| Doug Strange | 6 | 2 | 0 | 0 | 1 | 0 | 0 | .333 | .833 | .333 |
| B.J. Surhoff | 27 | 3 | 0 | 0 | 0 | 0 | 1 | .111 | .111 | .111 |
| Dale Sveum | 26 | 4 | 0 | 1 | 0 | 0 | 7 | .154 | .231 | .154 |
| Pat Tabler | 20 | 6 | 1 | 0 | 0 | 0 | 4 | .300 | .350 | .333 |
| Danny Tartabull | 6 | 2 | 0 | 0 | 0 | 0 | 1 | .333 | .333 | .333 |
| Mickey Tettleton | 18 | 2 | 0 | 1 | 0 | 0 | 8 | .111 | .222 | .111 |
| Tim Teufel | 7 | 4 | 2 | 0 | 0 | 0 | 0 | .571 | .857 | .571 |
| Gorman Thomas | 11 | 4 | 1 | 0 | 0 | 0 | 3 | .364 | .455 | .364 |
| Andre Thornton | 17 | 5 | 1 | 0 | 1 | 0 | 2 | .294 | .529 | .294 |
| Wayne Tolleson | 15 | 4 | 0 | 0 | 0 | 4 | 4 | .267 | .267 | .421 |
| Jim Traber | 13 | 4 | 0 | 0 | 2 | 0 | 0 | .308 | .769 | .308 |
| Alan Trammell | 48 | 17 | 2 | 1 | 0 | 1 | 8 | .354 | .438 | .360 |
| Willie Upshaw | 23 | 5 | 1 | 1 | 1 | 1 | 4 | .217 | .478 | .250 |
| George Vukovich | 10 | 2 | 0 | 0 | 0 | 0 | 4 | .200 | .200 | .200 |
| Greg Walker | 31 | 12 | 2 | 0 | 2 | 3 | 5 | .387 | .645 | .441 |
| Gary Ward | 27 | 5 | 0 | 0 | 0 | 1 | 3 | .185 | .185 | .214 |
| Claudell Washington | 13 | 2 | 1 | 0 | 0 | 1 | 2 | .154 | .231 | .214 |
| Ron Washington | 5 | 1 | 0 | 1 | 0 | 0 | 2 | .200 | .600 | .200 |
| Walt Weiss | 15 | 6 | 0 | 0 | 0 | 1 | 5 | .400 | .400 | .412 |
| Lou Whitaker | 65 | 22 | 5 | 0 | 2 | 1 | 5 | .338 | .508 | .348 |
| Devon White | 30 | 3 | 2 | 0 | 0 | 0 | 9 | .100 | .167 | .100 |
| Ernie Whitt | 39 | 11 | 1 | 2 | 3 | 1 | 4 | .282 | .641 | .300 |
| Alan Wiggins | 15 | 3 | 0 | 0 | 0 | 0 | 2 | .200 | .200 | .200 |
| Rob Wilfong | 5 | 1 | 0 | 0 | 0 | 0 | 2 | .200 | .200 | .200 |
| Curtis Wilkerson | 20 | 3 | 0 | 0 | 0 | 2 | 4 | .150 | .150 | .227 |
| Jerry Willard | 8 | 4 | 0 | 0 | 0 | 0 | 1 | .500 | .500 | .500 |
| Kenny Williams | 6 | 2 | 0 | 0 | 0 | 0 | 0 | .333 | .333 | .333 |
| Glenn Wilson | 6 | 1 | 1 | 0 | 0 | 0 | 2 | .167 | .333 | .167 |
| Dave Winfield | 28 | 5 | 0 | 1 | 0 | 3 | 3 | .179 | .250 | .258 |
| Craig Worthington | 8 | 1 | 0 | 0 | 0 | 0 | 1 | .125 | .125 | .125 |
| George Wright | 7 | 1 | 1 | 0 | 0 | 0 | 4 | .143 | .286 | .143 |
| Butch Wynegar | 9 | 1 | 0 | 0 | 0 | 0 | 2 | .111 | .111 | .111 |
| Mike Young | 18 | 5 | 0 | 0 | 2 | 0 | 6 | .278 | .611 | .278 |
| Robin Yount | 37 | 15 | 4 | 1 | 1 | 1 | 5 | .405 | .649 | .436 |
| Paul Zuvella | 6 | 3 | 0 | 0 | 0 | 0 | 0 | .500 | .500 | .500 |

# IX
# Ballparks

# *Ballparks*

The Ballparks section lists, for all 26 ballparks in use in the major leagues, a variety of statistics about the games played there over the past several years.

A ballpark's effect on performance has been a popular topic in recent years. Analysis that used to be limited to, "Gee, Fenway's a tough place for a lefty to pitch," has gotten increasingly sophisticated. Even the simplest conversation about an off-season trade now gets into such factors as the dimensions of a park, whether it has natural or artificial turf, the size of its foul territory, and how far it is above sea level. Our own analysis has led us to note in past editions those ballparks that promote doubles (like Fenway) or double plays (like Anaheim Stadium). This section takes a systematic look at the general effects of a given park.

The characteristics of each stadium are illustrated by a box containing basic statistics for the games played there, as contrasted with that home team's games on the road. The totals listed are the complete statistics *for both teams* in those games. Totals and percentage differences are listed for the 1989 season, and for the five-year period from 1985 through 1989. (The differences, in many cases, don't reflect the change between the actual raw totals printed, but rather between related averages. For instance, we print the number of runs scored in home and road games, but compute the difference between the average number of runs *per game*. Since the statistics represent performance by the same set of players, the differences can be attributed to the peculiarities of the park. The significance or causes of these differences are "why" questions and are open to debate; the questions we're answering here are "what" and "how many."

Following the pages of ballpark data are tables that rank the stadiums according to their effects on various elements of play. To illustrate, let's say that you find that the Oakland Coliseum reduced scoring by 12.2 percent over the past five seasons. You won't have to flip through the pages to check the corresponding figures for the 25 other stadiums to see where the Coliseum ranks. Just check the table at the end of the Ballparks section that ranks the 26 stadiums by their effect on scoring.

In addition to scoring, we've also included tables that rank the 26 parks by seven other categories. The fields with synthetic playing surfaces are indicated, giving you a quick read on what kind of impact plastic grass has on the category in question. For instance, if you check the table ranking the stadiums by their effect on stolen-base percentage, you'll see that the carpet has a nearly universal impact on base stealing.

## *Baltimore Memorial Stadium*

| | 1989 SEASON Home Games | Road Games | Pct. Diff. | 1985 – 1989 Home Games | Road Games | Pct. Diff. |
|---|---|---|---|---|---|---|
| G | 81 | 81 | 0.0 | 403 | 405 | – 0.5 |
| AB | 5531 | 5492 | 0.7 | 27553 | 27568 | – 0.1 |
| 1B | 1075 | 999 | 6.8 | 5014 | 5022 | – 0.1 |
| 2B | 240 | 249 | – 4.3 | 1179 | 1258 | – 6.2 |
| 3B | 24 | 37 | – 35.6 | 88 | 196 | – 55.1 |
| HR | 126 | 137 | – 8.7 | 887 | 823 | 7.8 |
| R | 685 | 709 | – 3.4 | 3630 | 3762 | – 3.0 |
| BA | .265 | .259 | 2.3 | .260 | .265 | – 1.7 |
| SLG | .385 | .393 | – 1.9 | .406 | .414 | – 2.0 |
| XB% | .197 | .223 | – 11.4 | .202 | .225 | – 10.2 |
| E | 111 | 106 | 4.7 | 574 | 591 | – 2.4 |
| SHO | 12 | 10 | 20.0 | 46 | 44 | 5.1 |

## *Boston Fenway Park*

| | 1989 SEASON Home Games | Road Games | Pct. Diff. | 1985 – 1989 Home Games | Road Games | Pct. Diff. |
|---|---|---|---|---|---|---|
| G | 81 | 81 | 0.0 | 404 | 406 | – 0.5 |
| AB | 5614 | 5607 | 0.1 | 27901 | 27885 | 0.1 |
| 1B | 1101 | 1062 | 3.5 | 5392 | 5187 | 3.9 |
| 2B | 323 | 241 | 33.9 | 1607 | 1246 | 28.9 |
| 3B | 28 | 25 | 11.9 | 153 | 142 | 7.7 |
| HR | 122 | 117 | 4.1 | 701 | 772 | – 9.2 |
| R | 793 | 716 | 10.8 | 3939 | 3749 | 5.6 |
| BA | .280 | .258 | 8.8 | .281 | .263 | 6.8 |
| SLG | .413 | .372 | 11.0 | .425 | .401 | 6.0 |
| XB% | .242 | .200 | 20.7 | .246 | .211 | 16.6 |
| E | 147 | 131 | 12.2 | 621 | 630 | – 0.9 |
| SHO | 12 | 6 | 100.0 | 51 | 44 | 16.5 |

## *California Anaheim Stadium*

| | 1989 SEASON Home Games | Road Games | Pct. Diff. | 1985 – 1989 Home Games | Road Games | Pct. Diff. |
|---|---|---|---|---|---|---|
| G | 81 | 81 | 0.0 | 404 | 406 | – 0.5 |
| AB | 5530 | 5485 | 0.8 | 27384 | 27833 | – 1.6 |
| 1B | 1010 | 1070 | – 6.4 | 4892 | 5114 | – 2.8 |
| 2B | 201 | 208 | – 4.2 | 1074 | 1277 | – 14.5 |
| 3B | 30 | 29 | 2.6 | 123 | 189 | – 33.9 |
| HR | 148 | 110 | 33.5 | 821 | 724 | 15.3 |
| R | 602 | 645 | – 6.7 | 3492 | 3718 | – 5.6 |
| BA | .251 | .258 | – 2.8 | .252 | .262 | – 3.8 |
| SLG | .379 | .367 | 3.2 | .390 | .400 | – 2.4 |
| XB% | .186 | .181 | 2.7 | .197 | .223 | – 11.8 |
| E | 90 | 126 | – 28.6 | 600 | 629 | – 4.1 |
| SHO | 18 | 14 | 28.6 | 55 | 51 | 8.4 |

## *Chicago Comiskey Park*

| | 1989 SEASON Home Games | Road Games | Pct. Diff. | 1985 – 1989 Home Games | Road Games | Pct. Diff. |
|---|---|---|---|---|---|---|
| G | 80 | 81 | – 1.2 | 404 | 405 | – 0.2 |
| AB | 5363 | 5618 | – 4.5 | 27283 | 27551 | – 1.0 |
| 1B | 1032 | 1103 | – 2.0 | 4932 | 4918 | 1.3 |
| 2B | 218 | 289 | – 21.0 | 1191 | 1243 | – 3.2 |
| 3B | 56 | 29 | 102.3 | 242 | 148 | 65.1 |
| HR | 94 | 144 | – 31.6 | 646 | 795 | – 17.9 |
| R | 666 | 777 | – 13.2 | 3554 | 3570 | – 0.2 |
| BA | .261 | .279 | – 6.3 | .257 | .258 | – 0.3 |
| SLG | .375 | .417 | – 10.1 | .389 | .400 | – 2.7 |
| XB% | .210 | .224 | – 6.2 | .225 | .220 | 2.1 |
| E | 137 | 129 | 7.5 | 626 | 661 | – 5.1 |
| SHO | 8 | 5 | 62.0 | 38 | 43 | – 11.4 |

## *Cleveland*
## *Cleveland Stadium*

| | 1989 SEASON | | | 1985 – 1989 | | |
|---|---|---|---|---|---|---|
| | Home Games | Road Games | Pct. Diff. | Home Games | Road Games | Pct. Diff. |
| G | 81 | 81 | 0.0 | 405 | 406 | -0.2 |
| AB | 5570 | 5438 | 2.4 | 27982 | 27745 | 0.9 |
| 1B | 1046 | 963 | 6.0 | 5432 | 5120 | 5.2 |
| 2B | 225 | 230 | -4.5 | 1230 | 1311 | -7.0 |
| 3B | 29 | 36 | -21.4 | 159 | 174 | -9.4 |
| HR | 107 | 127 | -17.7 | 721 | 783 | -8.7 |
| R | 651 | 607 | 7.2 | 3832 | 3784 | 1.5 |
| BA | .253 | .249 | 1.3 | .270 | .266 | 1.2 |
| SLG | .361 | .375 | -3.7 | .402 | .411 | -2.1 |
| XB% | .195 | .216 | -9.7 | .204 | .225 | -9.4 |
| E | 113 | 101 | 11.9 | 671 | 655 | 2.7 |
| SHO | 10 | 14 | -28.6 | 48 | 43 | 11.9 |

## *Detroit*
## *Tiger Stadium*

| | 1989 SEASON | | | 1985 – 1989 | | |
|---|---|---|---|---|---|---|
| | Home Games | Road Games | Pct. Diff. | Home Games | Road Games | Pct. Diff. |
| G | 81 | 81 | 0.0 | 405 | 404 | 0.2 |
| AB | 5448 | 5506 | -1.1 | 27371 | 27766 | -1.4 |
| 1B | 947 | 1102 | -13.2 | 4613 | 5046 | -7.3 |
| 2B | 222 | 235 | -4.5 | 1085 | 1299 | -15.3 |
| 3B | 33 | 24 | 39.0 | 144 | 185 | -21.0 |
| HR | 151 | 115 | 32.7 | 916 | 772 | 20.4 |
| R | 710 | 723 | -1.8 | 3588 | 3766 | -5.0 |
| BA | .248 | .268 | -7.4 | .247 | .263 | -6.1 |
| SLG | .384 | .382 | 0.6 | .397 | .407 | -2.2 |
| XB% | .212 | .190 | 11.5 | .210 | .227 | -7.4 |
| E | 140 | 131 | 6.9 | 642 | 603 | 6.2 |
| SHO | 9 | 10 | -10.0 | 51 | 34 | 49.6 |

## *Kansas City*
## *Royals Stadium*

| | 1989 SEASON | | | 1985 – 1989 | | |
|---|---|---|---|---|---|---|
| | Home Games | Road Games | Pct. Diff. | Home Games | Road Games | Pct. Diff. |
| G | 81 | 81 | 0.0 | 405 | 404 | 0.2 |
| AB | 5413 | 5570 | -2.8 | 27638 | 27355 | 1.0 |
| 1B | 1032 | 1079 | -1.6 | 5035 | 4963 | 0.4 |
| 2B | 241 | 230 | 7.8 | 1390 | 1137 | 21.0 |
| 3B | 44 | 30 | 50.9 | 274 | 157 | 72.7 |
| HR | 64 | 123 | -46.5 | 502 | 719 | -30.9 |
| R | 623 | 702 | -11.3 | 3369 | 3367 | -0.2 |
| BA | .255 | .262 | -2.8 | .261 | .255 | 2.2 |
| SLG | .351 | .381 | -7.7 | .385 | .387 | -0.5 |
| XB% | .216 | .194 | 11.4 | .248 | .207 | 20.1 |
| E | 104 | 116 | -10.3 | 588 | 596 | -1.6 |
| SHO | 15 | 16 | -6.3 | 61 | 62 | -1.9 |

## *Milwaukee*
## *County Stadium*

| | 1989 SEASON | | | 1985 – 1989 | | |
|---|---|---|---|---|---|---|
| | Home Games | Road Games | Pct. Diff. | Home Games | Road Games | Pct. Diff. |
| G | 81 | 81 | 0.0 | 403 | 405 | -0.5 |
| AB | 5532 | 5470 | 1.1 | 27778 | 27649 | 0.5 |
| 1B | 1067 | 1073 | -1.7 | 5286 | 5151 | 2.1 |
| 2B | 207 | 212 | -3.5 | 1237 | 1199 | 2.7 |
| 3B | 27 | 37 | -27.8 | 175 | 156 | 11.7 |
| HR | 123 | 132 | -7.9 | 677 | 709 | -5.0 |
| R | 665 | 721 | -7.8 | 3686 | 3570 | 3.8 |
| BA | .257 | .266 | -3.2 | .265 | .261 | 1.7 |
| SLG | .371 | .390 | -4.9 | .396 | .393 | 0.8 |
| XB% | .180 | .188 | -4.5 | .211 | .208 | 1.2 |
| E | 156 | 117 | 33.3 | 706 | 625 | 13.5 |
| SHO | 11 | 8 | 37.5 | 43 | 42 | 2.9 |

## *Minnesota Metrodome*

| | 1989 SEASON Home Games | Road Games | Pct. Diff. | 1985 – 1989 Home Games | Road Games | Pct. Diff. |
|---|---|---|---|---|---|---|
| G | 81 | 81 | 0.0 | 408 | 402 | 1.5 |
| AB | 5624 | 5505 | 2.2 | 28156 | 27047 | 4.1 |
| 1B | 1097 | 1051 | 2.2 | 5122 | 4948 | – 0.6 |
| 2B | 308 | 259 | 16.4 | 1513 | 1252 | 16.1 |
| 3B | 32 | 34 | – 7.9 | 190 | 150 | 21.7 |
| HR | 128 | 128 | – 2.1 | 858 | 802 | 2.8 |
| R | 791 | 687 | 15.1 | 3971 | 3597 | 8.8 |
| BA | .278 | .267 | 4.1 | .273 | .264 | 3.2 |
| SLG | .413 | .397 | 4.1 | .432 | .411 | 5.1 |
| XB% | .237 | .218 | 8.5 | .250 | .221 | 13.0 |
| E | 106 | 119 | – 10.9 | 570 | 572 | – 1.8 |
| SHO | 4 | 11 | – 63.6 | 30 | 52 | – 43.2 |

## *New York Yankee Stadium*

| | 1989 SEASON Home Games | Road Games | Pct. Diff. | 1985 – 1989 Home Games | Road Games | Pct. Diff. |
|---|---|---|---|---|---|---|
| G | 81 | 80 | 1.2 | 402 | 405 | – 0.7 |
| AB | 5594 | 5382 | 3.9 | 27418 | 27919 | – 1.8 |
| 1B | 1143 | 1018 | 8.0 | 5131 | 5100 | 2.4 |
| 2B | 273 | 250 | 5.1 | 1225 | 1343 | – 7.1 |
| 3B | 21 | 35 | – 42.3 | 119 | 151 | – 19.8 |
| HR | 152 | 128 | 14.2 | 838 | 818 | 4.3 |
| R | 792 | 698 | 12.1 | 3741 | 3849 | – 2.1 |
| BA | .284 | .266 | 6.8 | .267 | .265 | 0.5 |
| SLG | .422 | .397 | 6.3 | .412 | .412 | – 0.1 |
| XB% | .205 | .219 | – 6.5 | .208 | .227 | – 8.4 |
| E | 126 | 118 | 5.5 | 612 | 604 | 2.1 |
| SHO | 9 | 10 | – 11.1 | 41 | 42 | – 1.7 |

## *Oakland Oakland-Alameda County Coliseum*

| | 1989 SEASON Home Games | Road Games | Pct. Diff. | 1985 – 1989 Home Games | Road Games | Pct. Diff. |
|---|---|---|---|---|---|---|
| G | 81 | 81 | 0.0 | 405 | 405 | 0.0 |
| AB | 5364 | 5447 | – 1.5 | 27255 | 27849 | – 2.1 |
| 1B | 1008 | 968 | 5.7 | 4865 | 4969 | 0.0 |
| 2B | 192 | 248 | – 21.4 | 1064 | 1325 | – 17.9 |
| 3B | 21 | 34 | – 37.3 | 117 | 182 | – 34.3 |
| HR | 116 | 114 | 3.3 | 686 | 847 | – 17.2 |
| R | 654 | 634 | 3.2 | 3431 | 3907 | – 12.2 |
| BA | .249 | .250 | – 0.5 | .247 | .263 | – 6.1 |
| SLG | .358 | .371 | – 3.6 | .370 | .415 | – 10.8 |
| XB% | .174 | .226 | – 22.7 | .195 | .233 | – 16.1 |
| E | 140 | 132 | 6.1 | 664 | 661 | 0.5 |
| SHO | 12 | 13 | – 7.7 | 51 | 31 | 64.5 |

## *Seattle Kingdome*

| | 1989 SEASON Home Games | Road Games | Pct. Diff. | 1985 – 1989 Home Games | Road Games | Pct. Diff. |
|---|---|---|---|---|---|---|
| G | 81 | 81 | 0.0 | 408 | 401 | 1.7 |
| AB | 5568 | 5424 | 2.7 | 27979 | 27039 | 3.5 |
| 1B | 1031 | 998 | 0.6 | 4918 | 4981 | – 4.6 |
| 2B | 274 | 218 | 22.4 | 1392 | 1270 | 5.9 |
| 3B | 35 | 35 | – 2.6 | 187 | 169 | 6.9 |
| HR | 135 | 113 | 16.4 | 897 | 657 | 31.9 |
| R | 739 | 683 | 8.2 | 3895 | 3586 | 6.8 |
| BA | .265 | .251 | 5.3 | .264 | .262 | 1.0 |
| SLG | .399 | .367 | 8.8 | .424 | .394 | 7.5 |
| XB% | .231 | .202 | 14.0 | .243 | .224 | 8.4 |
| E | 129 | 138 | – 6.5 | 631 | 635 | – 2.3 |
| SHO | 6 | 13 | – 53.8 | 44 | 53 | – 18.4 |

## *Texas*
## *Arlington Stadium*

| | 1989 SEASON | | | 1985 – 1989 | | |
|---|---|---|---|---|---|---|
| | Home Games | Road Games | Pct. Diff. | Home Games | Road Games | Pct. Diff. |
| G | 81 | 81 | 0.0 | 404 | 404 | 0.0 |
| AB | 5404 | 5415 | – 0.2 | 27320 | 27251 | 0.3 |
| 1B | 972 | 952 | 2.3 | 4992 | 4697 | 6.0 |
| 2B | 217 | 260 | – 16.4 | 1157 | 1262 | – 8.6 |
| 3B | 33 | 37 | – 10.6 | 155 | 170 | – 9.1 |
| HR | 138 | 103 | 34.3 | 793 | 713 | 10.9 |
| R | 723 | 686 | 5.4 | 3779 | 3590 | 5.3 |
| BA | .252 | .250 | 0.8 | .260 | .251 | 3.5 |
| SLG | .381 | .368 | 3.3 | .401 | .388 | 3.1 |
| XB% | .205 | .238 | – 14.0 | .208 | .234 | – 10.9 |
| E | 127 | 138 | – 8.0 | 631 | 624 | 1.1 |
| SHO | 8 | 7 | 14.3 | 29 | 41 | – 29.3 |

## *Toronto*
## *Skydome*

| | 1989 SEASON | | | 1985 – 1989 | | |
|---|---|---|---|---|---|---|
| | Home Games | Road Games | Pct. Diff. | Home Games | Road Games | Pct. Diff. |
| G | 55 | 81 | – 32.1 | 55 | 81 | – 32.1 |
| AB | 3713 | 5645 | – 34.2 | 3713 | 5645 | – 34.2 |
| 1B | 627 | 1061 | – 10.2 | 627 | 1061 | – 10.2 |
| 2B | 176 | 275 | – 2.7 | 176 | 275 | – 2.7 |
| 3B | 31 | 35 | 34.7 | 31 | 35 | 34.7 |
| HR | 84 | 127 | 0.6 | 84 | 127 | 0.6 |
| R | 411 | 744 | – 18.6 | 411 | 744 | – 18.6 |
| BA | .247 | .265 | – 6.8 | .247 | .265 | – 6.8 |
| SLG | .379 | .394 | – 3.7 | .379 | .394 | – 3.7 |
| XB% | .248 | .226 | 9.8 | .248 | .226 | 9.8 |
| E | 75 | 140 | – 21.1 | 75 | 140 | – 21.1 |
| SHO | 8 | 8 | 47.3 | 8 | 8 | 47.3 |

## *Atlanta*
## *Atlanta-Fulton County Stadium*

| | 1989 SEASON | | | 1985 – 1989 | | |
|---|---|---|---|---|---|---|
| | Home Games | Road Games | Pct. Diff. | Home Games | Road Games | Pct. Diff. |
| G | 79 | 82 | – 3.7 | 401 | 404 | – 0.7 |
| AB | 5526 | 5407 | 2.2 | 27820 | 26949 | 3.2 |
| 1B | 980 | 940 | 2.0 | 5242 | 4836 | 5.0 |
| 2B | 224 | 219 | 0.1 | 1255 | 1156 | 5.2 |
| 3B | 22 | 24 | – 10.3 | 136 | 142 | – 7.2 |
| HR | 116 | 126 | – 9.9 | 691 | 585 | 14.4 |
| R | 643 | 621 | 7.5 | 3658 | 3225 | 14.3 |
| BA | .243 | .242 | 0.3 | .263 | .249 | 5.6 |
| SLG | .354 | .361 | – 2.0 | .393 | .368 | 6.7 |
| XB% | .201 | .205 | – 2.3 | .210 | .212 | – 0.9 |
| E | 148 | 127 | 21.0 | 727 | 671 | 9.2 |
| SHO | 12 | 10 | 24.6 | 38 | 58 | – 34.0 |

## *Chicago*
## *Wrigley Field*

| | 1989 SEASON | | | 1985 – 1989 | | |
|---|---|---|---|---|---|---|
| | Home Games | Road Games | Pct. Diff. | Home Games | Road Games | Pct. Diff. |
| G | 81 | 81 | 0.0 | 404 | 404 | 0.0 |
| AB | 5504 | 5492 | 0.2 | 28107 | 27383 | 2.6 |
| 1B | 1052 | 968 | 8.4 | 5365 | 4895 | 6.8 |
| 2B | 227 | 252 | – 10.1 | 1237 | 1321 | – 8.8 |
| 3B | 38 | 40 | – 5.2 | 197 | 180 | 6.6 |
| HR | 125 | 105 | 18.8 | 828 | 602 | 34.0 |
| R | 715 | 610 | 17.2 | 3819 | 3257 | 17.3 |
| BA | .262 | .249 | 5.4 | .271 | .256 | 6.2 |
| SLG | .385 | .366 | 5.1 | .418 | .383 | 9.1 |
| XB% | .201 | .232 | – 13.2 | .211 | .235 | – 10.1 |
| E | 165 | 114 | 44.7 | 735 | 589 | 24.8 |
| SHO | 11 | 11 | 0.0 | 43 | 52 | – 17.3 |

## *Cincinnati*
## *Riverfront Stadium*

| | 1989 SEASON | | | 1985 – 1989 | | |
|---|---|---|---|---|---|---|
| | Home Games | Road Games | Pct. Diff. | Home Games | Road Games | Pct. Diff. |
| G | 81 | 81 | 0.0 | 404 | 405 | – 0.2 |
| AB | 5544 | 5516 | 0.5 | 27617 | 27295 | 1.2 |
| 1B | 1006 | 958 | 4.5 | 4922 | 4809 | 1.2 |
| 2B | 271 | 222 | 21.5 | 1376 | 1132 | 20.1 |
| 3B | 26 | 30 | – 13.8 | 168 | 146 | 13.7 |
| HR | 130 | 123 | 5.2 | 738 | 645 | 13.1 |
| R | 689 | 634 | 8.7 | 3590 | 3297 | 9.2 |
| BA | .258 | .242 | 7.0 | .261 | .247 | 5.8 |
| SLG | .387 | .360 | 7.6 | .403 | .370 | 9.0 |
| XB% | .228 | .208 | 9.4 | .239 | .210 | 13.7 |
| E | 125 | 122 | 2.5 | 598 | 688 | – 12.9 |
| SHO | 10 | 14 | – 28.6 | 42 | 64 | – 34.2 |

## *Houston*
## *Astrodome*

| | 1989 SEASON | | | 1985 – 1989 | | |
|---|---|---|---|---|---|---|
| | Home Games | Road Games | Pct. Diff. | Home Games | Road Games | Pct. Diff. |
| G | 82 | 80 | 2.5 | 406 | 404 | 0.5 |
| AB | 5653 | 5442 | 3.9 | 27494 | 27401 | 0.3 |
| 1B | 1005 | 942 | 2.7 | 4928 | 4727 | 3.9 |
| 2B | 258 | 217 | 14.5 | 1181 | 1202 | – 2.1 |
| 3B | 38 | 33 | 10.9 | 165 | 194 | – 15.2 |
| HR | 92 | 110 | – 19.5 | 471 | 694 | – 32.4 |
| R | 684 | 632 | 5.6 | 3148 | 3362 | – 6.8 |
| BA | .246 | .239 | 3.0 | .245 | .249 | – 1.4 |
| SLG | .354 | .352 | 0.7 | .352 | .383 | – 8.1 |
| XB% | .228 | .210 | 8.5 | .215 | .228 | – 5.9 |
| E | 140 | 145 | – 5.8 | 643 | 695 | – 7.9 |
| SHO | 7 | 15 | – 54.5 | 66 | 50 | 31.3 |

## Los Angeles
## Dodger Stadium

| | 1989 SEASON | | | 1985 – 1989 | | |
|---|---|---|---|---|---|---|
| | Home Games | Road Games | Pct. Diff. | Home Games | Road Games | Pct. Diff. |
| G | 81 | 79 | 2.5 | 405 | 403 | 0.5 |
| AB | 5403 | 5452 | – 0.9 | 27263 | 27540 | – 1.0 |
| 1B | 963 | 945 | 2.8 | 5102 | 4818 | 7.0 |
| 2B | 200 | 261 | – 22.7 | 975 | 1310 | – 24.8 |
| 3B | 20 | 18 | 12.1 | 90 | 154 | – 41.0 |
| HR | 83 | 101 | – 17.1 | 482 | 616 | – 21.0 |
| R | 497 | 593 | – 18.3 | 2880 | 3270 | – 12.4 |
| BA | .234 | .243 | – 3.6 | .244 | .250 | – 2.6 |
| SLG | .325 | .353 | – 8.0 | .339 | .376 | – 9.8 |
| XB% | .186 | .228 | – 18.4 | .173 | .233 | – 25.9 |
| E | 113 | 128 | – 13.9 | 711 | 739 | – 4.3 |
| SHO | 21 | 15 | 36.5 | 86 | 63 | 35.8 |

## Montreal
## Olympic Stadium

| | 1989 SEASON | | | 1985 – 1989 | | |
|---|---|---|---|---|---|---|
| | Home Games | Road Games | Pct. Diff. | Home Games | Road Games | Pct. Diff. |
| G | 81 | 81 | 0.0 | 404 | 405 | – 0.2 |
| AB | 5538 | 5426 | 2.1 | 27430 | 27584 | – 0.6 |
| 1B | 968 | 950 | – 0.2 | 4746 | 4913 | – 2.9 |
| 2B | 257 | 228 | 10.4 | 1316 | 1203 | 10.0 |
| 3B | 32 | 42 | – 25.4 | 218 | 185 | 18.5 |
| HR | 115 | 105 | 7.3 | 550 | 610 | – 9.3 |
| R | 645 | 617 | 4.5 | 3293 | 3244 | 1.8 |
| BA | .248 | .244 | 1.5 | .249 | .251 | – 0.6 |
| SLG | .368 | .360 | 2.3 | .373 | .374 | – 0.2 |
| XB% | .230 | .221 | 3.9 | .244 | .220 | 10.9 |
| E | 139 | 140 | – 0.7 | 664 | 657 | 1.3 |
| SHO | 10 | 18 | – 44.4 | 55 | 62 | – 11.1 |

## New York
## Shea Stadium

| | 1989 SEASON | | | 1985 – 1989 | | |
|---|---|---|---|---|---|---|
| | Home Games | Road Games | Pct. Diff. | Home Games | Road Games | Pct. Diff. |
| G | 81 | 81 | 0.0 | 404 | 404 | 0.0 |
| AB | 5416 | 5516 | – 1.8 | 27042 | 27914 | – 3.1 |
| 1B | 884 | 910 | – 1.1 | 4683 | 4927 | – 1.9 |
| 2B | 222 | 275 | – 17.8 | 1123 | 1305 | – 11.2 |
| 3B | 27 | 31 | – 11.3 | 130 | 171 | – 21.5 |
| HR | 134 | 128 | 6.6 | 631 | 684 | – 4.8 |
| R | 608 | 670 | – 9.3 | 3109 | 3549 | – 12.4 |
| BA | .234 | .244 | – 4.0 | .243 | .254 | – 4.3 |
| SLG | .359 | .374 | – 4.1 | .364 | .386 | – 5.8 |
| XB% | .220 | .252 | – 12.7 | .211 | .231 | – 8.4 |
| E | 143 | 133 | 7.5 | 664 | 682 | – 2.6 |
| SHO | 10 | 11 | – 9.1 | 60 | 46 | 30.4 |

## Philadelphia
## Veterans Stadium

| | 1989 SEASON | | | 1985 – 1989 | | |
|---|---|---|---|---|---|---|
| | Home Games | Road Games | Pct. Diff. | Home Games | Road Games | Pct. Diff. |
| G | 81 | 82 | – 1.2 | 404 | 406 | – 0.5 |
| AB | 5437 | 5455 | – 0.3 | 27439 | 27352 | 0.3 |
| 1B | 935 | 975 | – 3.8 | 4756 | 4918 | – 3.6 |
| 2B | 261 | 244 | 7.3 | 1366 | 1159 | 17.5 |
| 3B | 40 | 27 | 48.6 | 230 | 163 | 40.7 |
| HR | 128 | 122 | 5.3 | 676 | 674 | – 0.0 |
| R | 697 | 667 | 5.8 | 3588 | 3350 | 7.6 |
| BA | .251 | .251 | 0.0 | .256 | .253 | 1.3 |
| SLG | .384 | .373 | 3.1 | .397 | .381 | 4.1 |
| XB% | .244 | .217 | 12.0 | .251 | .212 | 18.6 |
| E | 119 | 137 | – 12.1 | 634 | 667 | – 4.5 |
| SHO | 16 | 10 | 62.0 | 53 | 47 | 13.3 |

## Pittsburgh
## Three Rivers Stadium

| | 1989 SEASON Home Games | Road Games | Pct. Diff. | 1985 – 1989 Home Games | Road Games | Pct. Diff. |
|---|---|---|---|---|---|---|
| G | 81 | 83 | – 2.4 | 404 | 405 | – 0.2 |
| AB | 5551 | 5615 | – 1.1 | 27430 | 27353 | 0.3 |
| 1B | 939 | 979 | – 3.0 | 4718 | 4881 | – 3.6 |
| 2B | 242 | 264 | – 7.3 | 1340 | 1252 | 6.7 |
| 3B | 34 | 54 | – 36.3 | 197 | 201 | – 2.3 |
| HR | 107 | 109 | – 0.7 | 584 | 581 | 0.2 |
| R | 609 | 708 | – 11.9 | 3349 | 3341 | 0.5 |
| BA | .238 | .250 | – 4.9 | .249 | .253 | – 1.4 |
| SLG | .352 | .375 | – 6.2 | .376 | .377 | – 0.2 |
| XB% | .227 | .245 | – 7.3 | .246 | .229 | 7.1 |
| E | 141 | 158 | – 8.6 | 672 | 644 | 4.6 |
| SHO | 12 | 7 | 75.7 | 51 | 52 | – 1.7 |

## St. Louis
## Busch Stadium

| | 1989 SEASON Home Games | Road Games | Pct. Diff. | 1985 – 1989 Home Games | Road Games | Pct. Diff. |
|---|---|---|---|---|---|---|
| G | 83 | 81 | 2.5 | 407 | 404 | 0.7 |
| AB | 5510 | 5450 | 1.1 | 27456 | 27383 | 0.3 |
| 1B | 953 | 1006 | – 6.3 | 4977 | 4974 | – 0.2 |
| 2B | 285 | 245 | 15.1 | 1342 | 1213 | 10.3 |
| 3B | 67 | 35 | 89.3 | 252 | 186 | 35.1 |
| HR | 63 | 94 | – 33.7 | 398 | 522 | – 24.0 |
| R | 627 | 613 | – 0.2 | 3222 | 3251 | – 1.6 |
| BA | .248 | .253 | – 1.9 | .254 | .252 | 0.8 |
| SLG | .359 | .363 | – 1.1 | .365 | .367 | – 0.6 |
| XB% | .270 | .218 | 23.9 | .243 | .220 | 10.5 |
| E | 99 | 121 | – 20.2 | 637 | 660 | – 4.2 |
| SHO | 10 | 17 | – 42.6 | 50 | 63 | – 21.2 |

## San Diego
## San Diego/Jack Murphy Stadium

| | 1989 SEASON Home Games | Road Games | Pct. Diff. | 1985 – 1989 Home Games | Road Games | Pct. Diff. |
|---|---|---|---|---|---|---|
| G | 81 | 81 | 0.0 | 405 | 404 | 0.2 |
| AB | 5347 | 5540 | – 3.5 | 27010 | 27498 | – 1.8 |
| 1B | 936 | 1014 | – 4.4 | 4774 | 5192 | – 6.4 |
| 2B | 216 | 239 | – 6.4 | 1055 | 1239 | – 13.3 |
| 3B | 26 | 35 | – 23.0 | 160 | 160 | 1.8 |
| HR | 148 | 105 | 46.0 | 716 | 553 | 31.8 |
| R | 636 | 632 | 0.6 | 3203 | 3324 | – 3.9 |
| BA | .248 | .251 | – 1.4 | .248 | .260 | – 4.4 |
| SLG | .381 | .364 | 4.7 | .379 | .377 | 0.5 |
| XB% | .205 | .213 | – 3.4 | .203 | .212 | – 4.4 |
| E | 143 | 168 | – 14.9 | 662 | 674 | – 2.0 |
| SHO | 15 | 6 | 150.0 | 54 | 53 | 1.6 |

## San Francisco
## Candlestick Park

| | 1989 SEASON Home Games | Road Games | Pct. Diff. | 1985 – 1989 Home Games | Road Games | Pct. Diff. |
|---|---|---|---|---|---|---|
| G | 81 | 81 | 0.0 | 405 | 405 | 0.0 |
| AB | 5388 | 5506 | – 2.1 | 27096 | 27552 | – 1.7 |
| 1B | 915 | 949 | – 1.5 | 4584 | 4907 | – 5.0 |
| 2B | 240 | 237 | 3.5 | 1143 | 1217 | – 4.5 |
| 3B | 41 | 42 | – 0.2 | 142 | 203 | – 28.9 |
| HR | 124 | 137 | – 7.5 | 650 | 649 | 1.8 |
| R | 623 | 676 | – 7.8 | 3102 | 3491 | – 11.1 |
| BA | .245 | .248 | – 1.2 | .241 | .253 | – 5.0 |
| SLG | .374 | .381 | – 1.9 | .365 | .383 | – 4.6 |
| XB% | .235 | .227 | 3.4 | .219 | .224 | – 2.4 |
| E | 135 | 117 | 15.4 | 698 | 679 | 2.8 |
| SHO | 11 | 11 | 0.0 | 60 | 48 | 25.0 |

## Ranked by Effect on Runs

| | 1989 SEASON | | | 1985 – 1989 | | |
|---|---|---|---|---|---|---|
| | Home Games | Road Games | Pct. Diff. | Home Games | Road Games | Pct. Diff. |
| Wrigley Field | 715 | 610 | 17.2 | 3819 | 3257 | 17.3 |
| Atlanta Stadium | 643 | 621 | 7.5 | 3658 | 3225 | 14.3 |
| *Riverfront Stadium | 689 | 634 | 8.7 | 3590 | 3297 | 9.2 |
| *Metrodome | 791 | 687 | 15.1 | 3971 | 3597 | 8.8 |
| *Veterans Stadium | 697 | 667 | 5.8 | 3588 | 3350 | 7.6 |
| *Kingdome | 739 | 683 | 8.2 | 3895 | 3586 | 6.8 |
| Fenway Park | 793 | 716 | 10.8 | 3939 | 3749 | 5.6 |
| Arlington Stadium | 723 | 686 | 5.4 | 3779 | 3590 | 5.3 |
| County Stadium | 665 | 721 | – 7.8 | 3686 | 3570 | 3.8 |
| *Olympic Stadium | 645 | 617 | 4.5 | 3293 | 3244 | 1.8 |
| Cleveland Stadium | 651 | 607 | 7.2 | 3832 | 3784 | 1.5 |
| *Three Rivers Stadium | 609 | 708 | – 11.9 | 3349 | 3341 | 0.5 |
| *Royals Stadium | 623 | 702 | – 11.3 | 3369 | 3367 | – 0.2 |
| Comiskey Park | 666 | 777 | – 13.2 | 3554 | 3570 | – 0.2 |
| *Busch Stadium | 627 | 613 | – 0.2 | 3222 | 3251 | – 1.6 |
| *Exhibition Stadium | 638 | 744 | – 14.2 | 3561 | 3653 | – 2.0 |
| Yankee Stadium | 792 | 698 | 12.1 | 3741 | 3849 | – 2.1 |
| Memorial Stadium | 685 | 709 | – 3.4 | 3630 | 3762 | – 3.0 |
| San Diego Stadium | 636 | 632 | 0.6 | 3203 | 3324 | – 3.9 |
| Tiger Stadium | 710 | 723 | – 1.8 | 3588 | 3766 | – 5.0 |
| Anaheim Stadium | 602 | 645 | – 6.7 | 3492 | 3718 | – 5.6 |
| *Astrodome | 684 | 632 | 5.6 | 3148 | 3362 | – 6.8 |
| Candlestick Park | 623 | 676 | – 7.8 | 3102 | 3491 | – 11.1 |
| Oakland Coliseum | 654 | 634 | 3.2 | 3431 | 3907 | – 12.2 |
| Dodger Stadium | 497 | 593 | – 18.3 | 2880 | 3270 | – 12.4 |
| Shea Stadium | 608 | 670 | – 9.3 | 3109 | 3549 | – 12.4 |

## Ranked by Effect on Home Runs

| | 1989 SEASON | | | 1985 – 1989 | | |
|---|---|---|---|---|---|---|
| | Home Games | Road Games | Pct. Diff. | Home Games | Road Games | Pct. Diff. |
| Wrigley Field | 125 | 105 | 18.8 | 828 | 602 | 34.0 |
| *Kingdome | 135 | 113 | 16.4 | 897 | 657 | 31.9 |
| San Diego Stadium | 148 | 105 | 46.0 | 716 | 553 | 31.8 |
| Tiger Stadium | 151 | 115 | 32.7 | 916 | 772 | 20.4 |
| Anaheim Stadium | 148 | 110 | 33.5 | 821 | 724 | 15.3 |
| Atlanta Stadium | 116 | 126 | – 9.9 | 691 | 585 | 14.4 |
| *Riverfront Stadium | 130 | 123 | 5.2 | 738 | 645 | 13.1 |
| Arlington Stadium | 138 | 103 | 34.3 | 793 | 713 | 10.9 |
| Memorial Stadium | 126 | 137 | – 8.7 | 887 | 823 | 7.8 |
| Yankee Stadium | 152 | 128 | 14.2 | 838 | 818 | 4.3 |
| *Metrodome | 128 | 128 | – 2.1 | 858 | 802 | 2.8 |
| Candlestick Park | 124 | 137 | – 7.5 | 650 | 649 | 1.8 |
| *Exhibition Stadium | 114 | 127 | – 7.0 | 778 | 787 | 0.9 |
| *Three Rivers Stadium | 107 | 109 | – 0.7 | 584 | 581 | 0.2 |
| *Veterans Stadium | 128 | 122 | 5.3 | 676 | 674 | – 0.0 |
| Shea Stadium | 134 | 128 | 6.6 | 631 | 684 | – 4.8 |
| County Stadium | 123 | 132 | – 7.9 | 677 | 709 | – 5.0 |
| Cleveland Stadium | 107 | 127 | – 17.7 | 721 | 783 | – 8.7 |
| Fenway Park | 122 | 117 | 4.1 | 701 | 772 | – 9.2 |
| *Olympic Stadium | 115 | 105 | 7.3 | 550 | 610 | – 9.3 |
| Oakland Coliseum | 116 | 114 | 3.3 | 686 | 847 | – 17.2 |
| Comiskey Park | 94 | 144 | – 31.6 | 646 | 795 | – 17.9 |
| Dodger Stadium | 83 | 101 | – 17.1 | 482 | 616 | – 21.0 |
| *Busch Stadium | 63 | 94 | – 33.7 | 398 | 522 | – 24.0 |
| *Royals Stadium | 64 | 123 | – 46.5 | 502 | 719 | – 30.9 |
| *Astrodome | 92 | 110 | – 19.5 | 471 | 694 | – 32.4 |

*Playing surface is artificial turf.

## *Ranked by Effect on Batting Average*

| | 1989 SEASON | | | 1985 – 1989 | | |
|---|---|---|---|---|---|---|
| | Home Games | Road Games | Pct. Diff. | Home Games | Road Games | Pct. Diff. |
| Fenway Park | .280 | .258 | 8.8 | .281 | .263 | 6.8 |
| Wrigley Field | .262 | .249 | 5.4 | .271 | .256 | 6.2 |
| *Riverfront Stadium | .258 | .242 | 7.0 | .261 | .247 | 5.8 |
| Atlanta Stadium | .243 | .242 | 0.3 | .263 | .249 | 5.6 |
| Arlington Stadium | .252 | .250 | 0.8 | .260 | .251 | 3.5 |
| *Metrodome | .278 | .267 | 4.1 | .273 | .264 | 3.2 |
| *Royals Stadium | .255 | .262 | – 2.8 | .261 | .255 | 2.2 |
| County Stadium | .257 | .266 | – 3.2 | .265 | .261 | 1.7 |
| *Veterans Stadium | .251 | .251 | 0.0 | .256 | .253 | 1.3 |
| Cleveland Stadium | .253 | .249 | 1.3 | .270 | .266 | 1.2 |
| *Kingdome | .265 | .251 | 5.3 | .264 | .262 | 1.0 |
| *Busch Stadium | .248 | .253 | – 1.9 | .254 | .252 | 0.8 |
| Yankee Stadium | .284 | .266 | 6.8 | .267 | .265 | 0.5 |
| Comiskey Park | .261 | .279 | – 6.3 | .257 | .258 | – 0.3 |
| *Olympic Stadium | .248 | .244 | 1.5 | .249 | .251 | – 0.6 |
| *Three Rivers Stadium | .238 | .250 | – 4.9 | .249 | .253 | – 1.4 |
| *Astrodome | .246 | .239 | 3.0 | .245 | .249 | – 1.4 |
| Memorial Stadium | .265 | .259 | 2.3 | .260 | .265 | – 1.7 |
| *Exhibition Stadium | .249 | .265 | – 6.0 | .257 | .262 | – 2.1 |
| Dodger Stadium | .234 | .243 | – 3.6 | .244 | .250 | – 2.6 |
| Anaheim Stadium | .251 | .258 | – 2.8 | .252 | .262 | – 3.8 |
| Shea Stadium | .234 | .244 | – 4.0 | .243 | .254 | – 4.3 |
| San Diego Stadium | .248 | .251 | – 1.4 | .248 | .260 | – 4.4 |
| Candlestick Park | .245 | .248 | – 1.2 | .241 | .253 | – 5.0 |
| Oakland Coliseum | .249 | .250 | – 0.5 | .247 | .263 | – 6.1 |
| Tiger Stadium | .248 | .268 | – 7.4 | .247 | .263 | – 6.1 |

## *Ranked by Effect on Slugging Percentage*

| | 1989 SEASON | | | 1985 – 1989 | | |
|---|---|---|---|---|---|---|
| | Home Games | Road Games | Pct. Diff. | Home Games | Road Games | Pct. Diff. |
| Wrigley Field | .385 | .366 | 5.1 | .418 | .383 | 9.1 |
| *Riverfront Stadium | .387 | .360 | 7.6 | .403 | .370 | 9.0 |
| *Kingdome | .399 | .367 | 8.8 | .424 | .394 | 7.5 |
| Atlanta Stadium | .354 | .361 | – 2.0 | .393 | .368 | 6.7 |
| Fenway Park | .413 | .372 | 11.0 | .425 | .401 | 6.0 |
| *Metrodome | .413 | .397 | 4.1 | .432 | .411 | 5.1 |
| *Veterans Stadium | .384 | .373 | 3.1 | .397 | .381 | 4.1 |
| Arlington Stadium | .381 | .368 | 3.3 | .401 | .388 | 3.1 |
| County Stadium | .371 | .390 | – 4.9 | .396 | .393 | 0.8 |
| *Exhibition Stadium | .377 | .394 | – 4.4 | .407 | .405 | 0.6 |
| San Diego Stadium | .381 | .364 | 4.7 | .379 | .377 | 0.5 |
| Yankee Stadium | .422 | .397 | 6.3 | .412 | .412 | – 0.1 |
| *Three Rivers Stadium | .352 | .375 | – 6.2 | .376 | .377 | – 0.2 |
| *Olympic Stadium | .368 | .360 | 2.3 | .373 | .374 | – 0.2 |
| *Royals Stadium | .351 | .381 | – 7.7 | .385 | .387 | – 0.5 |
| *Busch Stadium | .359 | .363 | – 1.1 | .365 | .367 | – 0.6 |
| Memorial Stadium | .385 | .393 | – 1.9 | .406 | .414 | – 2.0 |
| Cleveland Stadium | .361 | .375 | – 3.7 | .402 | .411 | – 2.1 |
| Tiger Stadium | .384 | .382 | 0.6 | .397 | .407 | – 2.2 |
| Anaheim Stadium | .379 | .367 | 3.2 | .390 | .400 | – 2.4 |
| Comiskey Park | .375 | .417 | – 10.1 | .389 | .400 | – 2.7 |
| Candlestick Park | .374 | .381 | – 1.9 | .365 | .383 | – 4.6 |
| Shea Stadium | .359 | .374 | – 4.1 | .364 | .386 | – 5.8 |
| *Astrodome | .354 | .352 | 0.7 | .352 | .383 | – 8.1 |
| Dodger Stadium | .325 | .353 | – 8.0 | .339 | .376 | – 9.8 |
| Oakland Coliseum | .358 | .371 | – 3.6 | .370 | .415 | – 10.8 |

*Playing surface is artificial turf.

# Ranked by Effect on Extra-Base Hit Percentage

| | 1989 SEASON | | | 1985 – 1989 | | |
|---|---|---|---|---|---|---|
| | Home Games | Road Games | Pct. Diff. | Home Games | Road Games | Pct. Diff. |
| *Royals Stadium | .216 | .194 | 11.4 | .248 | .207 | 20.1 |
| *Veterans Stadium | .244 | .217 | 12.0 | .251 | .212 | 18.6 |
| Fenway Park | .242 | .200 | 20.7 | .246 | .211 | 16.6 |
| *Riverfront Stadium | .228 | .208 | 9.4 | .239 | .210 | 13.7 |
| *Exhibition Stadium | .247 | .226 | 9.1 | .252 | .223 | 13.3 |
| *Metrodome | .237 | .218 | 8.5 | .250 | .221 | 13.0 |
| *Olympic Stadium | .230 | .221 | 3.9 | .244 | .220 | 10.9 |
| *Busch Stadium | .270 | .218 | 23.9 | .243 | .220 | 10.5 |
| *Kingdome | .231 | .202 | 14.0 | .243 | .224 | 8.4 |
| *Three Rivers Stadium | .227 | .245 | – 7.3 | .246 | .229 | 7.1 |
| Comiskey Park | .210 | .224 | – 6.2 | .225 | .220 | 2.1 |
| County Stadium | .180 | .188 | – 4.5 | .211 | .208 | 1.2 |
| Atlanta Stadium | .201 | .205 | – 2.3 | .210 | .212 | – 0.9 |
| Candlestick Park | .235 | .227 | 3.4 | .219 | .224 | – 2.4 |
| San Diego Stadium | .205 | .213 | – 3.4 | .203 | .212 | – 4.4 |
| *Astrodome | .228 | .210 | 8.5 | .215 | .228 | – 5.9 |
| Tiger Stadium | .212 | .190 | 11.5 | .210 | .227 | – 7.4 |
| Yankee Stadium | .205 | .219 | – 6.5 | .208 | .227 | – 8.4 |
| Shea Stadium | .220 | .252 | – 12.7 | .211 | .231 | – 8.4 |
| Cleveland Stadium | .195 | .216 | – 9.7 | .204 | .225 | – 9.4 |
| Wrigley Field | .201 | .232 | – 13.2 | .211 | .235 | – 10.1 |
| Memorial Stadium | .197 | .223 | – 11.4 | .202 | .225 | – 10.2 |
| Arlington Stadium | .205 | .238 | – 14.0 | .208 | .234 | – 10.9 |
| Anaheim Stadium | .186 | .181 | 2.7 | .197 | .223 | – 11.8 |
| Oakland Coliseum | .174 | .226 | – 22.7 | .195 | .233 | – 16.1 |
| Dodger Stadium | .186 | .228 | – 18.4 | .173 | .233 | – 25.9 |

# Ranked by Effect on Strikeout Percentage

| | 1989 SEASON | | | 1985 – 1989 | | |
|---|---|---|---|---|---|---|
| | Home Games | Road Games | Pct. Diff. | Home Games | Road Games | Pct. Diff. |
| San Diego Stadium | .163 | .156 | 4.0 | .155 | .139 | 11.3 |
| Shea Stadium | .174 | .160 | 8.9 | .167 | .157 | 6.1 |
| Oakland Coliseum | .152 | .142 | 6.7 | .155 | .147 | 5.5 |
| *Metrodome | .128 | .129 | – 0.9 | .144 | .138 | 4.6 |
| Memorial Stadium | .130 | .134 | – 2.4 | .141 | .136 | 3.3 |
| Tiger Stadium | .143 | .135 | 6.0 | .147 | .142 | 3.2 |
| *Olympic Stadium | .170 | .157 | 8.2 | .161 | .156 | 3.2 |
| *Astrodome | .150 | .142 | 5.8 | .159 | .154 | 3.1 |
| County Stadium | .141 | .121 | 16.5 | .146 | .143 | 2.0 |
| Wrigley Field | .151 | .148 | 1.8 | .153 | .150 | 1.8 |
| Arlington Stadium | .175 | .167 | 4.9 | .164 | .162 | 1.3 |
| Anaheim Stadium | .154 | .159 | – 2.9 | .144 | .143 | 1.1 |
| Candlestick Park | .153 | .154 | – 0.5 | .163 | .161 | 1.1 |
| *Exhibition Stadium | .139 | .148 | – 6.0 | .148 | .147 | 0.8 |
| Yankee Stadium | .132 | .132 | 0.3 | .141 | .140 | 0.8 |
| Fenway Park | .141 | .144 | – 2.3 | .143 | .142 | 0.8 |
| *Kingdome | .140 | .141 | – 0.5 | .148 | .149 | – 0.7 |
| *Three Rivers Stadium | .136 | .141 | – 3.1 | .144 | .146 | – 1.4 |
| *Veterans Stadium | .148 | .148 | 0.3 | .155 | .157 | – 1.6 |
| Comiskey Park | .129 | .140 | – 8.0 | .142 | .144 | – 1.6 |
| Dodger Stadium | .161 | .158 | 1.8 | .158 | .161 | – 1.8 |
| Cleveland Stadium | .143 | .148 | – 3.6 | .133 | .141 | – 5.5 |
| *Riverfront Stadium | .155 | .168 | – 7.6 | .147 | .156 | – 5.8 |
| *Busch Stadium | .131 | .146 | – 10.5 | .134 | .143 | – 6.7 |
| Atlanta Stadium | .154 | .168 | – 8.2 | .136 | .148 | – 8.4 |
| *Royals Stadium | .150 | .157 | – 4.4 | .139 | .161 | – 14.0 |

*Playing surface is artificial turf.

## Ranked by Effect on Stolen Base Percentage

| | 1989 SEASON | | | 1985 – 1989 | | |
|---|---|---|---|---|---|---|
| | Home Games | Road Games | Pct. Diff. | Home Games | Road Games | Pct. Diff. |
| *Astrodome | .820 | .688 | 19.2 | .776 | .713 | 8.8 |
| *Metrodome | .675 | .704 | – 4.1 | .703 | .647 | 8.6 |
| *Exhibition Stadium | .730 | .665 | 9.8 | .709 | .659 | 7.5 |
| *Royals Stadium | .669 | .697 | – 4.0 | .707 | .662 | 6.8 |
| *Olympic Stadium | .716 | .684 | 4.8 | .738 | .721 | 2.4 |
| *Busch Stadium | .721 | .733 | – 1.6 | .746 | .729 | 2.3 |
| *Kingdome | .632 | .667 | – 5.2 | .663 | .648 | 2.2 |
| *Veterans Stadium | .658 | .646 | 2.0 | .723 | .709 | 2.0 |
| Oakland Coliseum | .710 | .699 | 1.5 | .692 | .683 | 1.4 |
| *Riverfront Stadium | .679 | .649 | 4.6 | .707 | .703 | 0.7 |
| Comiskey Park | .626 | .682 | – 8.2 | .675 | .672 | 0.4 |
| Memorial Stadium | .701 | .673 | 4.2 | .685 | .683 | 0.3 |
| San Diego Stadium | .630 | .661 | – 4.8 | .664 | .664 | – 0.0 |
| Tiger Stadium | .676 | .655 | 3.3 | .673 | .673 | – 0.1 |
| County Stadium | .716 | .725 | – 1.2 | .684 | .685 | – 0.2 |
| Dodger Stadium | .579 | .599 | – 3.2 | .652 | .658 | – 0.9 |
| *Three Rivers Stadium | .751 | .716 | 5.0 | .668 | .675 | – 1.0 |
| Cleveland Stadium | .731 | .593 | 23.2 | .680 | .695 | – 2.2 |
| Candlestick Park | .581 | .677 | – 14.1 | .622 | .641 | – 3.1 |
| Anaheim Stadium | .674 | .745 | – 9.5 | .639 | .661 | – 3.3 |
| Wrigley Field | .646 | .678 | – 4.7 | .663 | .687 | – 3.6 |
| Arlington Stadium | .698 | .716 | – 2.5 | .685 | .711 | – 3.6 |
| Atlanta Stadium | .536 | .643 | – 16.6 | .635 | .673 | – 5.7 |
| Shea Stadium | .726 | .755 | – 3.8 | .709 | .756 | – 6.2 |
| Yankee Stadium | .648 | .674 | – 3.8 | .678 | .739 | – 8.2 |
| Fenway Park | .689 | .711 | – 3.1 | .611 | .676 | – 9.5 |

## Ranked by Effect on Errors

| | 1989 SEASON | | | 1985 – 1989 | | |
|---|---|---|---|---|---|---|
| | Home Games | Road Games | Pct. Diff. | Home Games | Road Games | Pct. Diff. |
| Wrigley Field | 165 | 114 | 44.7 | 735 | 589 | 24.8 |
| County Stadium | 156 | 117 | 33.3 | 706 | 625 | 13.5 |
| Atlanta Stadium | 148 | 127 | 21.0 | 727 | 671 | 9.2 |
| Tiger Stadium | 140 | 131 | 6.9 | 642 | 603 | 6.2 |
| *Three Rivers Stadium | 141 | 158 | – 8.6 | 672 | 644 | 4.6 |
| Candlestick Park | 135 | 117 | 15.4 | 698 | 679 | 2.8 |
| Cleveland Stadium | 113 | 101 | 11.9 | 671 | 655 | 2.7 |
| Yankee Stadium | 126 | 118 | 5.5 | 612 | 604 | 2.1 |
| *Olympic Stadium | 139 | 140 | – 0.7 | 664 | 657 | 1.3 |
| Arlington Stadium | 127 | 138 | – 8.0 | 631 | 624 | 1.1 |
| Oakland Coliseum | 140 | 132 | 6.1 | 664 | 661 | 0.5 |
| Fenway Park | 147 | 131 | 12.2 | 621 | 630 | – 0.9 |
| *Royals Stadium | 104 | 116 | – 10.3 | 588 | 596 | – 1.6 |
| *Metrodome | 106 | 119 | – 10.9 | 570 | 572 | – 1.8 |
| San Diego Stadium | 143 | 168 | – 14.9 | 662 | 674 | – 2.0 |
| *Kingdome | 129 | 138 | – 6.5 | 631 | 635 | – 2.3 |
| Memorial Stadium | 111 | 106 | 4.7 | 574 | 591 | – 2.4 |
| Shea Stadium | 143 | 133 | 7.5 | 664 | 682 | – 2.6 |
| Anaheim Stadium | 90 | 126 | – 28.6 | 600 | 629 | – 4.1 |
| *Busch Stadium | 99 | 121 | – 20.2 | 637 | 660 | – 4.2 |
| Dodger Stadium | 113 | 128 | – 13.9 | 711 | 739 | – 4.3 |
| *Veterans Stadium | 119 | 137 | – 12.1 | 634 | 667 | – 4.5 |
| Comiskey Park | 137 | 129 | 7.5 | 626 | 661 | – 5.1 |
| *Exhibition Stadium | 116 | 140 | – 17.1 | 585 | 635 | – 7.4 |
| *Astrodome | 140 | 145 | – 5.8 | 643 | 695 | – 7.9 |
| *Riverfront Stadium | 125 | 122 | 2.5 | 598 | 688 | – 12.9 |

*Playing surface is artificial turf.